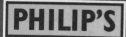

PHILIP'S

C000173740

STREE

Kent

First published 2005 by

Philip's, a division of
Octopus Publishing Group Ltd
2-4 Heron Quays, London E14 4JP

First edition 2005
First impression 2005

ISBN-10   0-540-08751-3 (pocket)
ISBN-13   978-0-540-08751-8 (pocket)

© Philip's 2005

Ordnance Survey®

This product includes mapping data licensed from
Ordnance Survey® with the permission of the
Controller of Her Majesty's Stationery Office.
© Crown copyright 2005. All rights reserved.
Licence number 100011710.

Printed and bound in Spain
by Cayfosa-Quebecor

Contents

III **Key to map symbols**

IV **Key to map pages**

VI **Route planning**

X **Administrative and Postcode boundaries**

1 **Street maps** at 2⅔ inches to 1 mile

381 **Index** of towns and villages

384 **Index** of streets, hospitals, industrial estates, railway stations, schools, shopping centres and universities and places of interest

Digital Data

The exceptionally high-quality mapping found in this atlas is available as digital data in TIFF format, which is easily convertible to other bitmapped (raster) image formats.

The index is also available in digital form as a standard database table. It contains all the details found in the printed index together with the National Grid reference for the map square in which each entry is named.

For further information and to discuss your requirements, please contact Philip's on 020 7644 6932 or james.mann@philips-maps.co.uk

PHILIP'S MAPS
the Gold Standard for serious driving

◆ Philip's street atlases cover every county in England and Wales, plus much of Scotland.

◆ All our atlases use the same style of mapping, with the same colours and symbols, so you can move with confidence from one atlas to the next

◆ Widely used by the emergency services, transport companies and local authorities.

◆ Created from the most up-to-date and detailed information available from Ordnance Survey

◆ Based on the National Grid

For national mapping, choose **Philip's Navigator Britain** – the most detailed road atlas available of England, Wales and Scotland. Hailed by Auto Express as 'the ultimate road atlas', this is the only one-volume atlas to show every road and lane in Britain.

Street atlases currently available

England
Bedfordshire
Berkshire
Birmingham and West Midlands
Bristol and Bath
Buckinghamshire
Cambridgeshire
Cheshire
Cornwall
Cumbria
Derbyshire
Devon
Dorset
County Durham and Teesside
Essex
North Essex
South Essex
Gloucestershire
North Hampshire
South Hampshire
Herefordshire Monmouthshire
Hertfordshire
Isle of Wight
Kent
East Kent
West Kent
Lancashire
Leicestershire and Rutland
Lincolnshire
London
Greater Manchester
Merseyside
Norfolk
Northamptonshire
Northumberland
Nottinghamshire
Oxfordshire
Shropshire
Somerset

All England and Wales coverage

Staffordshire
Suffolk
Surrey
East Sussex
West Sussex
Tyne and Wear
Warwickshire
Birmingham and West Midlands
Wiltshire and Swindon
Worcestershire
East Yorkshire Northern Lincolnshire
North Yorkshire
South Yorkshire
West Yorkshire

Wales
Anglesey, Conwy and Gwynedd
Cardiff, Swansea and The Valleys
Carmarthenshire, Pembrokeshire and Swansea
Ceredigion and South Gwynedd
Denbighshire, Flintshire, Wrexham
Herefordshire Monmouthshire
Powys

Scotland
Aberdeenshire
Ayrshire
Edinburgh and East Central Scotland
Fife and Tayside
Glasgow and West Central Scotland
Inverness and Moray

How to order

Philip's maps and atlases are available from bookshops, motorway services and petrol stations. You can order direct from the publisher by phoning **01903 828503** or online at **www.philips-maps.co.uk**
For bulk orders only, phone 020 7644 6940

Key to map symbols

III

Symbol	Description
(22a)	**Motorway** with junction number
	Primary route – dual/single carriageway
	A road – dual/single carriageway
	B road – dual/single carriageway
	Minor road – dual/single carriageway
	Other minor road – dual/single carriageway
	Road under construction
	Tunnel, covered road
	Rural track, private road or narrow road in urban area
	Gate or obstruction to traffic (restrictions may not apply at all times or to all vehicles)
	Path, bridleway, byway open to all traffic, road used as a public path
	Pedestrianised area
DY7	**Postcode boundaries**
	County and unitary authority boundaries
	Railway, tunnel, railway under construction
	Tramway, tramway under construction
	Miniature railway
Walsall	**Railway station**
	Private railway station
	Docklands Light Railway station
	Tram stop, tram stop under construction
	Bus, coach station

Symbol	Description
◆	**Ambulance station**
◆	**Coastguard station**
◆	**Fire station**
◆	**Police station**
✚	**Accident and Emergency entrance to hospital**
H	**Hospital**
✝	**Place of worship**
i	**Information Centre** (open all year)
🛒	**Shopping Centre**
P P&R	**Parking, Park and Ride**
PO	**Post Office**
Å	**Camping site**
⊕	**Caravan site**
►	**Golf course**
✕	**Picnic site**
Prim Sch	**Important buildings, schools, colleges, universities and hospitals**
	Built up area
	Woods
River Medway	**Water name**
	River, weir, stream
	Canal, lock, tunnel
	Water
	Tidal water
Church	**Non-Roman antiquity**
ROMAN FORT	**Roman antiquity**
87	**Adjoining page indicators and overlap bands**
24	

Abbr	Full	Abbr	Full	Abbr	Full
Acad	Academy	Inst	Institute	Recn Gd	Recreation Ground
Allot Gdns	Allotments	Ct	Law Court		
Cemy	Cemetery	L Ctr	Leisure Centre	Resr	Reservoir
C Ctr	Civic Centre	LC	Level Crossing	Ret Pk	Retail Park
CH	Club House	Liby	Library	Sch	School
Coll	College	Mkt	Market	Sh Ctr	Shopping Centre
Crem	Crematorium	Meml	Memorial	TH	Town Hall/House
Ent	Enterprise	Mon	Monument	Trad Est	Trading Estate
Ex H	Exhibition Hall	Mus	Museum	Univ	University
Ind Est	Industrial Estate	Obsy	Observatory	W Twr	Water Tower
IRB Sta	Inshore Rescue Boat Station	Pal	Royal Palace	Wks	Works
		PH	Public House	YH	Youth Hostel

■ The small numbers around the edges of the maps identify the 1 kilometre National Grid lines

■ The dark grey border on the inside edge of some pages indicates that the mapping does not continue onto the adjacent page

The scale of the maps on the pages numbered in blue is 4.2 cm to 1 km • 2⅔ inches to 1 mile • 1: 23810

0	¼	½	¾	1 mile
0	250m 500m	750m 1 kilometre		

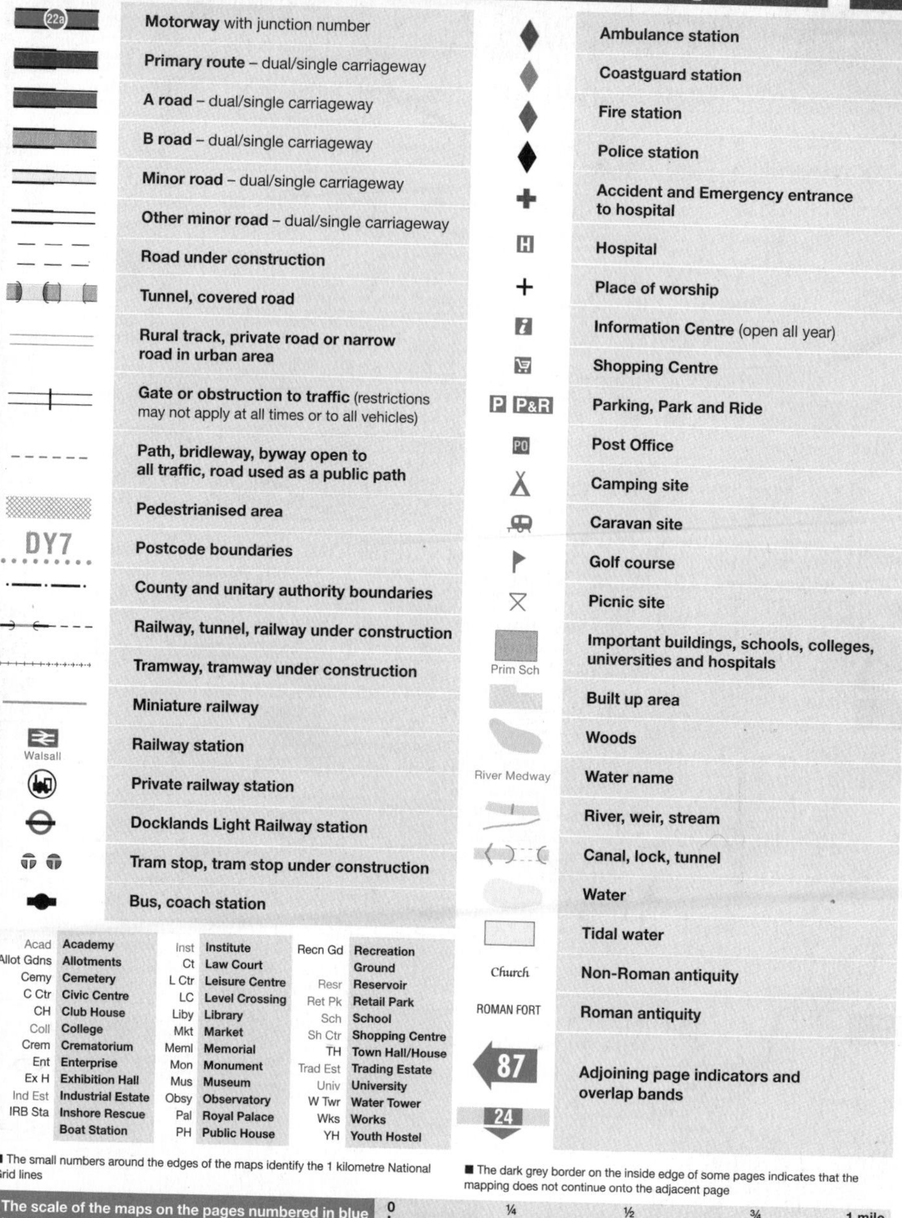

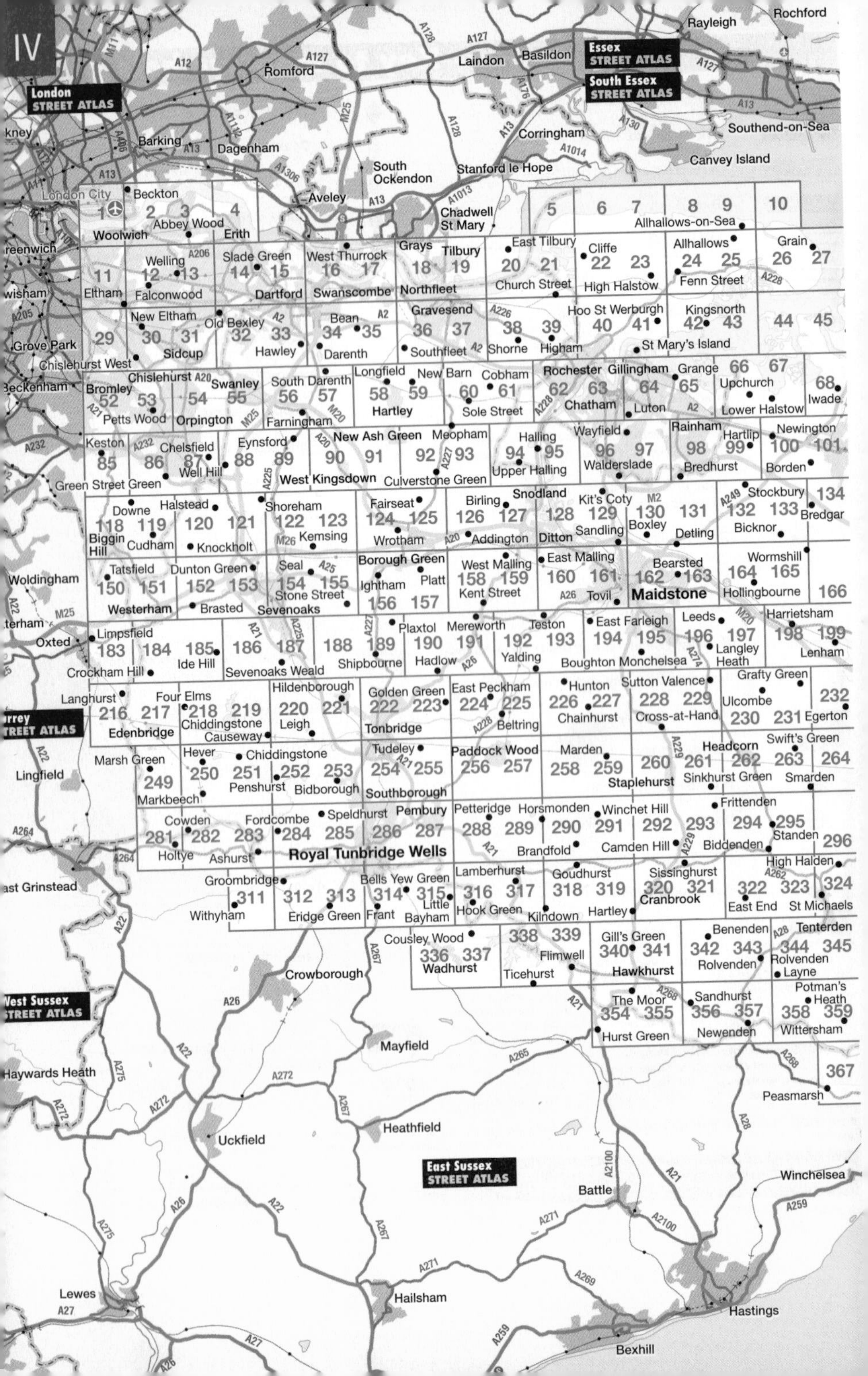

London STREET ATLAS

Essex STREET ATLAS
South Essex STREET ATLAS

Rayleigh   Rochford

Romford   Laindon   Basildon

Barking   Dagenham   Corringham   Southend-on-Sea

hney   South Ockendon   Stanford le Hope   Canvey Island

London City   Beckton   Aveley   Chadwell St Mary

Woolwich   Abbey Wood   Erith

reenwich

wisham

Grove Park

Chislehurst West

Beckenham

Bromley

| 2 | 3 | 4 | | 5 | 6 | 7 | 8 | 9 | 10 |

Welling   Slade Green   West Thurrock   Grays   Tilbury   East Tilbury   Cliffe   Allhallows-on-Sea   Allhallows   Grain

| 11 | 12 | 13 | 14 | 15 | 16 | 17 | 18 | 19 | 20 | 21 | 22 | 23 | 24 | 25 | 26 | 27 |

Eltham   Falconwood   Dartford   Swanscombe   Northfleet   Church Street   High Halstow   Fenn Street   Kingsnorth

New Eltham   Old Bexley   Bean   Gravesend   Hoo St Werburgh

| 29 | 30 | 31 | 32 | 33 | 34 | 35 | 36 | 37 | 38 | 39 | 40 | 41 | 42 | 43 | 44 | 45 |

Sidcup   Hawley   Darenth   Southfleet   Shorne   Higham   St Mary's Island

Chislehurst   Swanley   South Darenth   Longfield   New Barn   Cobham   Rochester   Gillingham   Grange   Upchurch   Iwade

| 52 | 53 | 54 | 55 | 56 | 57 | 58 | 59 | 60 | 61 | 62 | 63 | 64 | 65 | 66 | 67 | 68 |

Petts Wood   Orpington   Farningham   Sole Street   Chatham   Luton   Lower Halstow

Keston   Chelsfield   Eynsford   New Ash Green   Meopham   Halling   Wayfield   Rainham   Hartlip   Newington

| 85 | 86 | 87 | 88 | 89 | 90 | 91 | 92 | 93 | 94 | 95 | 96 | 97 | 98 | 99 | 100 | 101 |

Well Hill   West Kingsdown   Culverstone Green   Upper Halling   Walderslade   Bredhurst   Borden

Green Street Green   Downe   Halstead   Shoreham   Fairseat   Birling   Snodland   Kit's Coty   Stockbury

| 118 | 119 | 120 | 121 | 122 | 123 | 124 | 125 | 126 | 127 | 128 | 129 | 130 | 131 | 132 | 133 | 134 |

Biggin Hill   Cudham   Knockholt   Kemsing   Wrotham   Addington   Ditton   Sandling   Boxley   Detling   Bicknor   Bredgar

Tatsfield   Dunton Green   Seal   Borough Green   West Malling   Bearsted   Wormshill

| 150 | 151 | 152 | 153 | 154 | 155 | 156 | 157 | 158 | 159 | 160 | 161 | 162 | 163 | 164 | 165 | 166 |

Westerham   Brasted   Stone Street   Ightham   Platt   Kent Street   Tovil   Hollingbourne

Woldingham   Sevenoaks   Maidstone

Oxted   Limpsfield   Plaxtol   Mereworth   Teston   East Farleigh   Leeds   Harrietsham

| 183 | 184 | 185 | 186 | 187 | 188 | 189 | 190 | 191 | 192 | 193 | 194 | 195 | 196 | 197 | 198 | 199 |

terham   Crockham Hill   Ide Hill   Sevenoaks Weald   Shipbourne   Hadlow   Yalding   Boughton Monchelsea   Langley Heath   Lenham

Langhurst   Four Elms   Hildenborough   Golden Green   East Peckham   Hunton   Sutton Valence   Grafty Green

| 216 | 217 | 218 | 219 | 220 | 221 | 222 | 223 | 224 | 225 | 226 | 227 | 228 | 229 | 230 | 231 | 232 |

Edenbridge   Chiddingstone Causeway   Leigh   Tonbridge   Beltring   Chainhurst   Cross-at-Hand   Ulcombe   Egerton

Marsh Green   Hever   Chiddingstone   Tudeley   Paddock Wood   Marden   Headcorn   Swift's Green

| 249 | 250 | 251 | 252 | 253 | 254 | 255 | 256 | 257 | 258 | 259 | 260 | 261 | 262 | 263 | 264 |

Markbeech   Penshurst   Bidborough   Southborough   Staplehurst   Sinkhurst Green   Smarden

Cowden   Fordcombe   Speldhurst   Pembury   Petteridge   Horsmonden   Winchet Hill   Frittenden

| 281 | 282 | 283 | 284 | 285 | 286 | 287 | 288 | 289 | 290 | 291 | 292 | 293 | 294 | 295 | 296 |

Holtye   Ashurst   Royal Tunbridge Wells   Brandfold   Camden Hill   Biddenden   Standen

ast Grinstead

Lingfield

Groombridge   Bells Yew Green   Lamberhurst   Goudhurst   Sissinghurst   High Halden

| 311 | 312 | 313 | 314 | 315 | 316 | 317 | 318 | 319 | 320 | 321 | 322 | 323 | 324 |

Withyham   Eridge Green   Frant   Little Bayham   Hook Green   Kilndown   Hartley   Cranbrook   East End   St Michaels

rrey TREET ATLAS

West Sussex STREET ATLAS

Cousley Wood   Benenden   Tenterden

| 336 | 337 | 338 | 339 | 340 | 341 | 342 | 343 | 344 | 345 |

Wadhurst   Flimwell   Gill's Green   Rolvenden   Rolvenden Layne

Crowborough   Ticehurst   Hawkhurst

The Moor   Sandhurst   Potman's Heath

| 354 | 355 | 356 | 357 | 358 | 359 |

Hurst Green   Newenden   Wittersham

Mayfield

Haywards Heath

East Sussex STREET ATLAS

Uckfield

| 367 |

Peasmarsh

Heathfield

Winchelsea

Battle

Lewes

Hailsham

Hastings

Bexhill

Key to map pages

28
Sheerness
Minster 46 47 Rushenden Eastchurch 48 49 Warden Leysdown-on-Sea
Westgate-on-Sea 50 51 Margate Kingsgate
A249 69 Isle of Sheppey 70 71 72 73 Kemsley
74 75 Whitstable A2990 Herne Bay 76 77 Broomfield
Reculver 78 79 St Nicholas at Wade Birchington 80 A28 81 Kent International
St Peter's 82 83 Manston A254 84 Broadstairs
Sittingbourne 102 103 Teynham 104 105 Oare Seasalter 106 107 Graveney Yorkletts South Street 108 A290 109 Calcott 110 Herne Common 111 Hersden A28 Sarre 112 113 Upstreet Minster Monkton 114 115 Ramsgate 116 117 A256
135 Lynsted A2 136 M2 137 Painter's Forstal Faversham 138 139 Boughton Street Hernhill 140 141 Upper Harbledown Blean 142 Sturry 143 Fordwich Stodmarsh 144 145 Wickhambreaux Preston 146 147 A257 Ash 148 149 Great Stonar Sandwich
Doddington Eastling Sheldwich A251 Selling Throwley 167 168 169 170 171 Old Wives Lees 172 173 A28 Chartham Canterbury 174 175 Nackington Littlebourne 176 177 Bridge Staple 178 179 Goodnestone 180 181 Worth Eastry 182
Warren Street 200 201 A20 A252 Challock 202 203 Molash A252 Chilham 204 205 Godmersham Garlinge Green 206 207 Petham Lower Hardres 208 209 Kingston Aylesham 210 211 Woolage Village Betteshanger 212 A256 213 Elvington A258 Deal 214 215 Great Mongeham
233 Charing 234 235 Westwell 236 A251 Bilting 237 Wye Crundale Waltham 238 239 Bossingham 240 241 Stelling Minnis Barham 242 243 Denton A2 Eythorne 244 245 Shepherdswell Ringwould 246 247 West Langdon Kingsdown 248
Pluckley 265 Chambers' Green Hothfield 266 267 A28 268 Naccolt 269 Ashford Brook 270 Hastingleigh 271 272 Lymbridge Green North Elham 273 Elham 274 Selsted 275 A260 Alkham 276 Whitfield 277 Kearsney West Cliffe 278 279 A256 St Margaret's at Cliffe 280
Bethersden 297 Daniel's Water 298 299 Stubb's Cross Willesborough 300 301 Mersham Kingsnorth M20 Brabourne Lees 302 303 Sellindge Lyminge 304 305 Postling Hawkinge Paddlesworth 306 307 A20 Farthingloe 308 309 Capel-le-Ferne Dover 310
325 Bromley Green 326 327 Woodchurch Bliby 328 329 Bilsington Aldington 330 331 Lympne Westenhanger 332 333 A259 Hythe Folkestone 334 335 Sandgate
Brook Street 346 347 Appledore Heath Hamstreet Warehorne 348 349 350 351 Newchurch Palmarsh 352 353 Burmarsh
Appledore 360 361 The Stocks Snargate 362 363 Brenzett Ivychurch 364 Dymchurch 365 366 St Mary's Bay
Brookland 368 369 Iden A259 370 371 Old Romney 372 373 New Romney Greatstone-on-Sea
Rye 374 375 Camber Lydd 376 Lade 377 Lydd-on-Sea
378 379 380 Dungeness

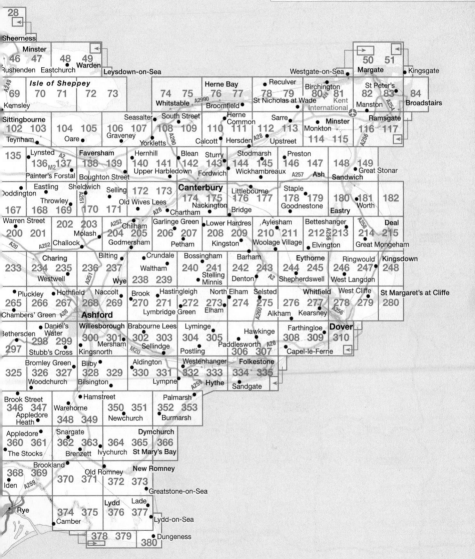

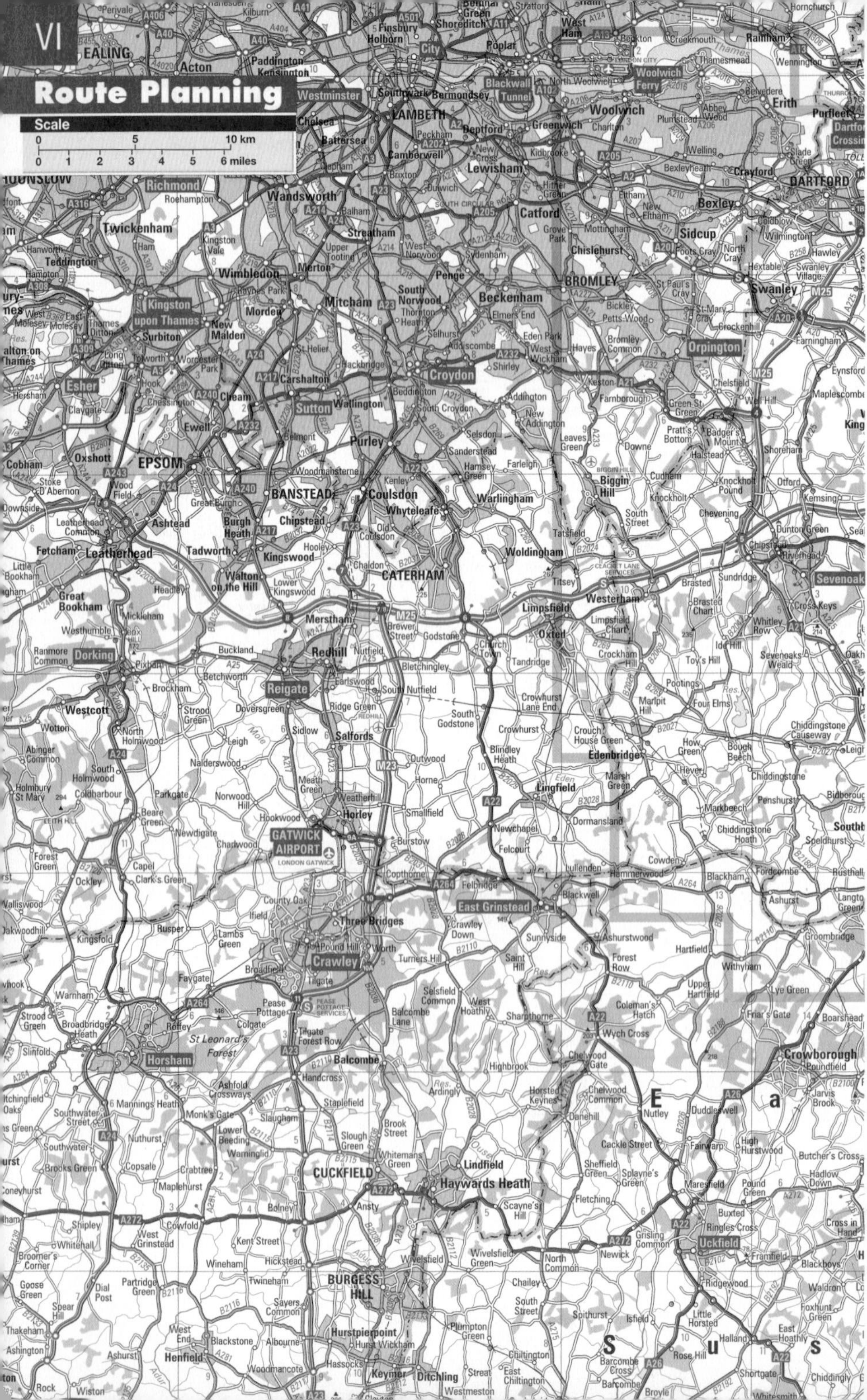
VI
Route Planning
Scale
0
5
10 km
0
1
2
3
4
5
6 miles
EALING
Acton
Paddington
Holborn
Finsbury
Shoreditch
City
Poplar
West Ham
Beckton
Creekmouth
Rainham
Hornchurch
Wennington
Westminster
Southwark
Bermondsey
Blackwall Tunnel
Thamesmead
Woolwich Ferry
North Woolwich
Woolwich
Erith
Purfleet
LAMBETH
Chelsea
Battersea
Camberwell
Peckham
Deptford
Greenwich
Charlton
Plumstead
Abbey Wood
Belvedere
Welling
Bexleyheath
Crayford
DARTFORD
Lewisham
Kidbrooke
HOUNSLOW
Richmond
Roehampton
Wandsworth
Clapham
Brixton
Dulwich
Catford
Eltham
Bexley
Twickenham
Balham
Streatham
Sydenham
Mottingham
Sidcup
Wilmington
Hanworth
Teddington
Hampton
Kingston Vale
Wimbledon
Merton
Upper Tooting
West Norwood
Penge
Chislehurst
BROMLEY
Foots Cray
North Cray
Hextable
Swanley
Hawley
Kingston upon Thames
Surbiton
New Malden
Morden
Mitcham
South Norwood
Thornton Heath
Beckenham
Elmers End
Bickley
Petts Wood
St Paul's Cray
St Mary Cray
Crockenhill
Farningham
Walton on Thames
Esher
Tolworth
Worcester Park
St Helier
Hackbridge
Selhurst
Addiscombe
Eden Park
West Wickham
Shirley
Hayes
Bromley Common
Orpington
Eynsford
Croydon
Hersham
Claygate
Hook
Chessington
Cheam
Carshalton
Sutton
Wallington
Beddington
South Croydon
Addington
New Addington
Keston
Farnborough
Chelsfield
Green St Green
Well Hill
Maplescombe
Cobham
Oxshott
EPSOM
Ewell
Belmont
Purley
Selsdon
Sanderstead
Leaves Green
Downe
Pratt's Bottom
Badger's Mount
Halstead
Shoreham
Stoke D'Abernon
Woodmansterne
Kenley
Hamsey Green
Farleigh
Biggin Hill
Cudham
Knockholt
Knockholt Pound
Otford
Kemsing
Leatherhead
Ashtead
BANSTEAD
Coulsdon
Whyteleafe
Warlingham
Fetcham
Great Bookham
Tadworth
Burgh Heath
Chipstead
Kingswood
Walton on the Hill
Old Coulsdon
Chaldon
CATERHAM
Woldingham
Tatsfield
South Street
Chevening
Dunton Green
Chipstead
Riverhead
Sevenoaks
Titsey
Westerham
Brasted
Sundridge
Mickleham
Westhumble
Headley
Lower Kingswood
Merstham
Brewer Street
Godstone
Limpsfield
Oxted
Limpsfield Chart
Brasted Chart
Whitley Row
Cross Keys
Ranmore Common
Dorking
Buckland
Redhill
Nutfield
Bletchingley
Church Town
Tandridge
Crockham Hill
Toy's Hill
Ide Hill
Sevenoaks Weald
Westcott
Pixham
Brockham
Betchworth
Reigate
Earlswood
South Nutfield
Doversgreen
Strood Green
Ridge Green
South Godstone
Crowhurst Lane End
Crowhurst
Pootings
Four Elms
Marlpit Hill
Crouch House Green
Edenbridge
How Green
Bough Beech
Chiddingstone Causeway
Leigh
Wotton
Abinger Common
North Holmwood
South Holmwood
Holmbury St Mary
Coldharbour
Leith Hill
Sidlow
Salfords
Outwood
Horne
Blindley Heath
Lingfield
Hever
Chiddingstone
Penshurst
Marsh Green
Nalderswood
Parkgate
Norwood Hill
Meath Green
Weatherhill
Horley
Smallfield
Dormansland
Markbeech
Chiddingstone Hoath
Beare Green
Newdigate
Hookwood
Charlwood
GATWICK AIRPORT
London Gatwick
Burstow
Newchapel
Felcourt
Forest Green
Capel
Ockley
Clark's Green
Copthorne
Felbridge
Lullenden
Hammerwood
Cowden
Blackham
Fordcombe
Rusthall
Walliswood
Oakwoodhill
Kingsfold
Rusper
Ifield
County Oak
Three Bridges
Crawley Down
East Grinstead
Blackwell
Sunnyside
Ashurst
Langton Green
Lambs Green
Crawley
Pound Hill
Worth
Turners Hill
Saint Hill
Ashurstwood
Forest Row
Hartfield
Withyham
Groombridge
Faygate
Broadfield
Tilgate
Pease Pottage
Selsfield Common
West Hoathly
Upper Hartfield
Lye Green
Warnham
Strood Green
Broadbridge Heath
Roffey
Colgate
Balcombe Lane
Sharpthorne
Coleman's Hatch
Friar's Gate
Boarshead
Slinfold
Horsham
St Leonard's Forest
Tilgate Forest Row
Balcombe
Wych Cross
Chelwood Gate
Crowborough
Poundfield
Highbrook
Handcross
Ashfold Crossways
Ardingly
Horsted Keynes
Chelwood Common
Nutley
Duddleswell
Jarvis Brook
Itchingfield
Mannings Heath
Monk's Gate
Staplefield
Danehill
Southwater Street
Lower Beeding
Slaugham
Brook Street
Slough Green
Cackle Street
High Hurstwood
Fairwarp
Butcher's Cross
Nuthurst
Southwater
Warninglid
Whitemans Green
Lindfield
Sheffield Green
Splayne's Green
Brooks Green
Copsale
Crabtree
CUCKFIELD
Haywards Heath
Fletching
Maresfield
Pound Green
Hadlow Down
Coneyhurst
Maplehurst
Ansty
Scayne's Hill
Bolney
Buxted
Ringles Cross
Cross in Hand
Shipley
Cowfold
Whitehall
West Grinstead
Kent Street
Piltdown
Gisling Common
Newick
Uckfield
Framfield
Broomer's Corner
Wineham
Hickstead
Wivelsfield
Wivelsfield Green
North Common
Blackboys
Goose Green
Dial Post
Partridge Green
Twineham
BURGESS HILL
Chailey
Ridgewood
Waldron
Spear Hill
Sayers Common
South Street
Foxhunt Green
Thakeham
West End
Blackstone
Albourne
Hurstpierpoint
Hurst Wickham
Plumpton Green
Spithurst
Isfield
Little Horsted
East Hoathly
Ashington
Ashurst
Henfield
Chiltington
Halland
Rose Hill
Woodmancote
Hassocks
Keymer
Ditchling
Streat
East Chiltington
Barcombe Cross
Barcombe
Shortgate
Chiddingly
Rock
Wiston
Westmeston
Broyle
Whitesmith
E a s t
S u s s

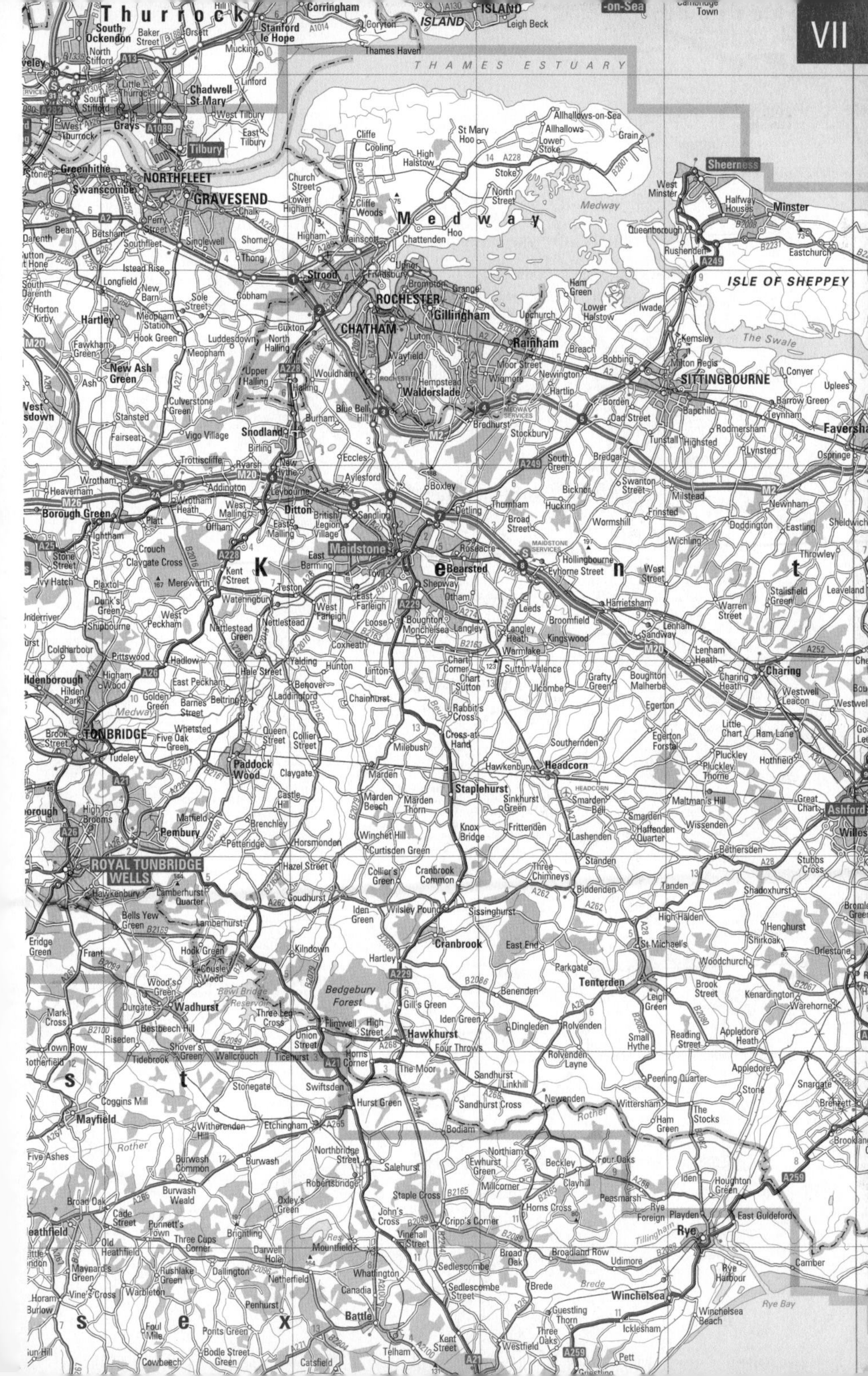

Thurrock
South Ockendon
Baker Street
Orsett
Stanford le Hope
Corringham
Coryton
ISLAND
Leigh Beck
-on-Sea
Town
Thames Haven
Mucking
Linford
North Stifford
Little Thurrock
South Stifford
Chadwell St Mary
West Tilbury
East Tilbury
Grays
West Thurrock
Tilbury
THAMES ESTUARY
Allhallows-on-Sea
Allhallows
Grain
Lower Stoke
St Mary Hoo
Cliffe
Cooling
High Halstow
Stoke
North Street
Sheerness
West Minster
Halfway Houses
Minster
Queenborough
Rushenden
Eastchurch
ISLE OF SHEPPEY
Medway
Greenhithe
Swanscombe
NORTHFLEET
GRAVESEND
Chalk
Church Street
Lower Higham
Cliffe Woods
Higham
Wainscott
Chattenden
Hoo
Medway
Darenth
Bean
Betsham
Perry Street
Southfleet
Singlewell
Shorne
Thong
Istead Rise
Longfield
New Barn
South Darenth
Horton Kirby
Hartley
Meopham Station
Sole Street
Cobham
Strood
Frindsbury
Upnor
Brompton
Grange
ROCHESTER
Gillingham
CHATHAM
Ham Green
Lower Halstow
Iwade
Upchurch
Rainham
Kemsley
The Swale
Milton Regis
Conyer
Uplees
SITTINGBOURNE
Fawkham Green
Hook Green
Luddesdown
Cuxton
North Halling
Meopham
New Ash Green
Ash
Upper Halling
Halling
Wouldham
Luton
Wayfield
Hempstead
Walderslade
Wigmore
Moor Street
Newington
Breach
Bobbing
Hartlip
Borden
Oad Street
Bapchild
Barrow Green
Teynham
Faversham
West Kingsdown
Culverstone Green
Stansted
Fairseat
Vigo Village
Snodland
Birling
Burham
Blue Bell Hill
Bredhurst
MEDWAY SERVICES
Stockbury
Tunstall
Highsted
Rodmersham
Lynsted
Ospringe
Trottiscliffe
Ryarsh
New Hythe
Eccles
Aylesford
Boxley
South Green
Bredgar
Wrotham
Heaverham
Addington
Leybourne
Swanton Street
Bicknor
Milstead
Borough Green
Wrotham Heath
West Malling
Ditton
British Legion Village
Sandling
Detling
Thurnham
Hucking
Wormshill
Frinsted
Newnham
Doddington
Eastling
Sheldwich
Platt
Offham
East Malling
Broad Street
MAIDSTONE SERVICES
Wichling
Ightham
Stone Street
Crouch
Claygate Cross
Kent Street
East Barming
Maidstone
Roseacre
Hollingbourne
Bearsted
Eyhorne Street
West Street
Throwley
Ivy Hatch
Plaxtol
Mereworth
Teston
Tovil
Shepway
Leaveland
Stalisfield Green
Dunk's Green
Wateringbury
East Farleigh
Otham
Leeds
Harrietsham
Warren Street
Underriver
Shipbourne
West Peckham
Nettlestead
West Farleigh
Loose
Boughton Monchelsea
Langley
Broomfield
Lenham
Nettlestead Green
Coxheath
Langley Heath
Kingswood
Sandway
Lenham Heath
Coldharbour
Pittswood
Hadlow
Hale Street
Yalding
Hunton
Linton
Chart Corner
Warmlake
Chart Sutton
Sutton Valence
Grafty Green
Boughton Malherbe
Charing
Charing Heath
Westwell
Westwell Leacon
Hildenborough
Hilden Park
Higham Wood
East Peckham
Golden Green
Barnes Street
Beltring
Benover
Laddingford
Chainhurst
Ulcombe
Rabbit's Cross
Egerton
Medway
Tonbridge
Brook Street
Five Oak Green
Whetsted
Queen Street
Collier Street
Cross-at-Hand
Milebush
Egerton Forstal
Little Chart
Ram Lane
Southernden
Tudeley
Paddock Wood
Claygate
Marden
Hawkenbury
Headcorn
Pluckley
Pluckley Thorne
Hothfield
Staplehurst
Sinkhurst Green
HEADCORN
Smarden Bell
Smarden
Maltman's Hill
Great Chart
Ashford
Willesborough
Southborough
High Brooms
Matfield
Pembury
Castle Hill
Brenchley
Marden Beech
Marden Thorn
Knox Bridge
Frittenden
Lashenden
Haffenden Quarter
Wissenden
Pettridge
Horsmonden
Winchet Hill
Curtisden Green
Bethersden
Stubbs Cross
ROYAL TUNBRIDGE WELLS
Hazel Street
Collier's Green
Cranbrook Common
Three Chimneys
Standen
Tanden
Shadoxhurst
Hawkenbury
Lamberhurst Quarter
Goudhurst
Iden Green
Wilsley Pound
Sissinghurst
Biddenden
High Halden
Bromley Green
Henghurst
Bells Yew Green
Lamberhurst
Eridge Green
Frant
Hook Green
Kilndown
Hartley
Cranbrook
East End
St Michael's
Shirkoak
Orlestone
Woodchurch
Cousley Wood
Wood's Green
Bewl Bridge Reservoir
Bedgebury Forest
Parkgate
Tenterden
Leigh Green
Brook Street
Kenardington
Warehorne
Benenden
Mark Cross
Durgates
Wadhurst
Three Leg Cross
Gill's Green
Iden Green
Dingleden
Rolvenden
Small Hythe
Reading Street
Appledore Heath
Bestbeech Hill
Flimwell
High Street
Hawkhurst
Riseden
Town Row
Tidebrook
Shover's Green
Wallcrouch
Union Street
Ticehurst
Four Throws
Rolvenden Layne
Appledore
Rotherfield
Horns Corner
The Moor
Peening Quarter
Stonegate
Swiftsden
Sandhurst
Linkhill
Snargate
Stone
Coggins Mill
Hurst Green
Sandhurst Cross
Newenden
Wittersham
The Stocks
Brenzett
Mayfield
Witherenden Hill
Etchingham
Bodiam
Rother
Ham Green
Brookland
Five Ashes
Rother
Burwash Common
Burwash
Northbridge Street
Salehurst
Northiam
Ewhurst Green
Beckley
Four Oaks
Iden
Houghton Green
Robertsbridge
Millcorner
Clayhill
Burwash Weald
Broad Oak
Oxley's Green
Staple Cross
Peasmarsh
Rye Foreign
Playden
East Guldeford
Cade Street
Punnett's Town
Brightling
John's Cross
Cripp's Corner
Horns Cross
Heathfield
Three Cups Corner
Vinehall Street
Tillingham
Rye
Old Heathfield
Darwell Hole
Mountfield
Broad Oak
Broadland Row
Udimore
Camber
Maynard's Green
Rushlake Green
Dallington
Netherfield
Sedlescombe
Rye Harbour
Vine's Cross
Warbleton
Whatlington
Sedlescombe Street
Brede
Brede
Horam
Burlow
Canadia
Winchelsea
Penhurst
Rye Bay
Guestling Thorn
Winchelsea Beach
Foul Mile
Battle
Three Oaks
Icklesham
Ponts Green
Kent Street
Westfield
Bodle Street Green
Telham
Cowbeech
Catsfield
Pett
Guestling
K e n t
s s e x

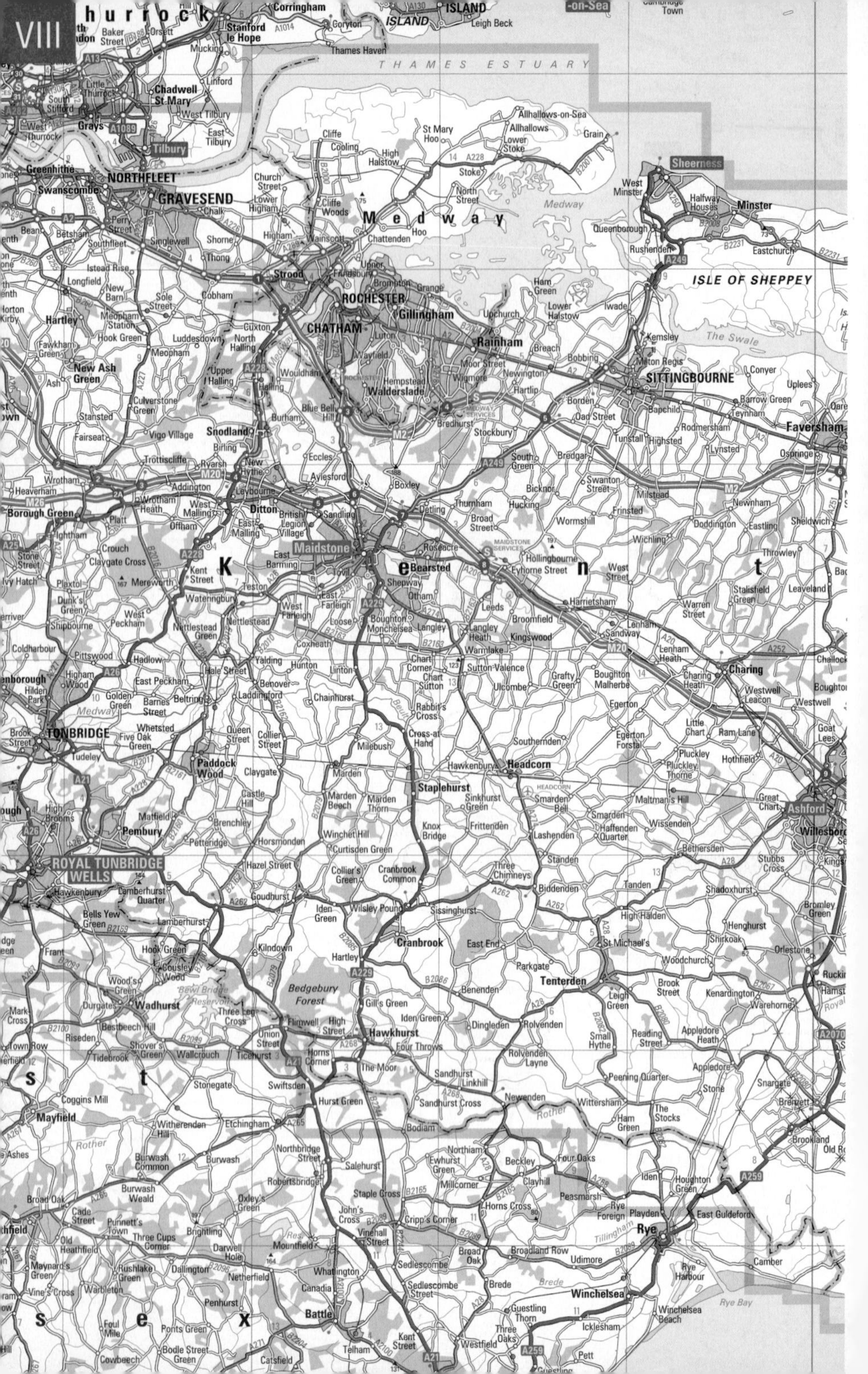
Thurrock
Corringham
ISLAND
Stanford le Hope
Orsett
Baker Street
Mucking
Coryton
Thames Haven
Leigh Beck
THAMES ESTUARY
Linford
Chadwell St Mary
Little Thurrock
South Stifford
Grays
West Thurrock
West Tilbury
East Tilbury
Tilbury
Greenhithe
Swanscombe
NORTHFLEET
GRAVESEND
Perry Street
Chalk
Bean
Betsham
Southfleet
Singlewell
Shorne
Thong
Istead Rise
Longfield
New Barn
Sole Street
Cobham
Hartley
Meopham Station
Hook Green
Luddesdown
Meopham
Fawkham Green
New Ash Green
Ash
Culverstone Green
Stansted
Fairseat
Vigo Village
Trottiscliffe
Wrotham
Heaverham
Borough Green
Wrotham Heath
Platt
Ightham
Stone Street
Crouch
Claygate Cross
Plaxtol
Dunk's Green
Shipbourne
Coldharbour
Pittswood
Hadlow
Higham Wood
Hilden Park
Golden Green
Barnes Street
East Peckham
Beltring
Medway
TONBRIDGE
Brook Street
Five Oak Green
Whetsted
Tudeley
High Brooms
Pembury
Matfield
ROYAL TUNBRIDGE WELLS
Hawkenbury
Lamberhurst Quarter
Bells Yew Green
Lamberhurst
Frant
Hook Green
Cousley Wood
Wood's Green
Wadhurst
Bewl Bridge Reservoir
Durgates
Mark Cross
Bestbeech Hill
Riseden
Town Row
Tidebrook
Shover's Green
Wallcrouch
Ticehurst
Three Leg Cross
Stonegate
Coggins Mill
Mayfield
Witherenden Hill
Etchingham
Rother
Burwash Common
Burwash
Burwash Weald
Broad Oak
Cade Street
Punnett's Town
Three Cups Corner
Old Heathfield
Heathfield
Maynard's Green
Rushlake Green
Dallington
Vine's Cross
Warbleton
Foul Mile
Ponts Green
Cowbeech
Bodle Street Green
Penhurst
Brightling
Darwell Hole
Netherfield
Mountfield
Oxley's Green
Cliffe
Cooling
High Halstow
St Mary Hoo
Allhallows-on-Sea
Allhallows
Lower Stoke
Stoke
Grain
North Street
Church Street
Lower Higham
Cliffe Woods
Higham
Wainscott
Chattenden
Hoo
Medway
Strood
Frindsbury
Upnor
ROCHESTER
Brompton
Gillingham
CHATHAM
Cuxton
North Halling
Upper Halling
Halling
Wouldham
Luton
Wayfield
Hempstead
Walderslade
Blue Bell Hill
Burham
Snodland
Birling
Ryarsh
Addington
New Hythe
Leybourne
West Malling
Ditton
Offham
East Malling
Mereworth
Kent Street
Eccles
Aylesford
British Legion Village
Sandling
Boxley
Maidstone
East Barming
Teston
Wateringbury
Nettlestead
Nettlestead Green
West Peckham
Hale Street
Yalding
West Farleigh
East Farleigh
Loose
Coxheath
Hunton
Linton
Benover
Laddingford
Collier Street
Queen Street
Paddock Wood
Claygate
Castle Hill
Brenchley
Petteridge
Horsmonden
Hazel Street
Goudhurst
Kilndown
Bedgebury Forest
Flimwell
High Street
Union Street
Horns Corner
Swiftsden
Hurst Green
Northbridge Street
Robertsbridge
Salehurst
Staple Cross
John's Cross
Vinehall Street
Whatlington
Sedlescombe
Sedlescombe Street
Canadia
Battle
Telham
Kent Street
Catsfield
Upchurch
Ham Green
Lower Halstow
Iwade
Rainham
Moor Street
Wigmore
Bredhurst
Hartlip
Newington
Breach
Bobbing
Stockbury
South Green
Detling
Thurnham
Bearsted
Roseacre
Otham
Shepway
Langley
Boughton Monchelsea
Langley Heath
Warmlake
Chart Corner
Chart Sutton
Sutton Valence
Chainhurst
Rabbit's Cross
Cross-at-Hand
Milebush
Marden
Marden Beech
Marden Thorn
Staplehurst
Winchet Hill
Curtisden Green
Collier's Green
Cranbrook Common
Knox Bridge
Frittenden
Sinkhurst Green
Iden Green
Wilsley Pound
Sissinghurst
Cranbrook
Hartley
Benenden
Gill's Green
Iden Green
Hawkhurst
Four Throws
The Moor
Sandhurst
Sandhurst Cross
Bodiam
Northiam
Ewhurst Green
Millcorner
Cripp's Corner
Broad Oak
Brede
Westfield
Three Oaks
Guestling Thorn
Icklesham
Pett
Winchelsea
Winchelsea Beach
Rye Bay
Rye
Rye Harbour
Camber
Udimore
Broadland Row
Playden
Rye Foreign
Peasmarsh
Beckley
Four Oaks
Clayhill
Horns Cross
Iden
Houghton Green
East Guldeford
Newenden
Wittersham
Ham Green
The Stocks
Rolvenden
Rolvenden Layne
Dingleden
Tenterden
Leigh Green
Small Hythe
Reading Street
Peening Quarter
Appledore
Appledore Heath
Stone
Snargate
Brenzett
Brookland
Old Romney
Kenardington
Warehorne
Brook Street
Woodchurch
Shirkoak
Henghurst
Orlestone
Ruckinge
St Michael's
High Halden
Biddenden
Three Chimneys
East End
Parkgate
Headcorn
Smarden
Smarden Bell
Haffenden Quarter
Lashenden
Standen
Tanden
Bethersden
Wissenden
Shadoxhurst
Bromley Green
Stubbs Cross
Ashford
Willesborough
Great Chart
Maltman's Hill
Pluckley
Pluckley Thorne
Hothfield
Little Chart
Ram Lane
Southernden
Hawkenbury
Egerton Forstal
Egerton
Charing Heath
Charing
Westwell Leacon
Westwell
Lenham Heath
Lenham
Sandway
Harrietsham
Boughton Malherbe
Grafty Green
Ulcombe
Kingswood
Broomfield
Leeds
Eyhorne Street
Hollingbourne
Broad Street
Hucking
Bicknor
Wormshill
Bredgar
Swanton Street
Milstead
Frinsted
Wichling
Warren Street
Stalisfield Green
Leaveland
Throwley
Eastling
Doddington
Newnham
Sheldwich
Challock
Borden
Oad Street
Tunstall
Highsted
Bapchild
Rodmersham
Lynsted
Teynham
Conyer
Barrow Green
Uplees
Ospringe
Faversham
SITTINGBOURNE
Milton Regis
Kemsley
The Swale
ISLE OF SHEPPEY
Sheerness
West Minster
Halfway Houses
Minster
Queenborough
Rushenden
Eastchurch
Kent
Sussex
Medway

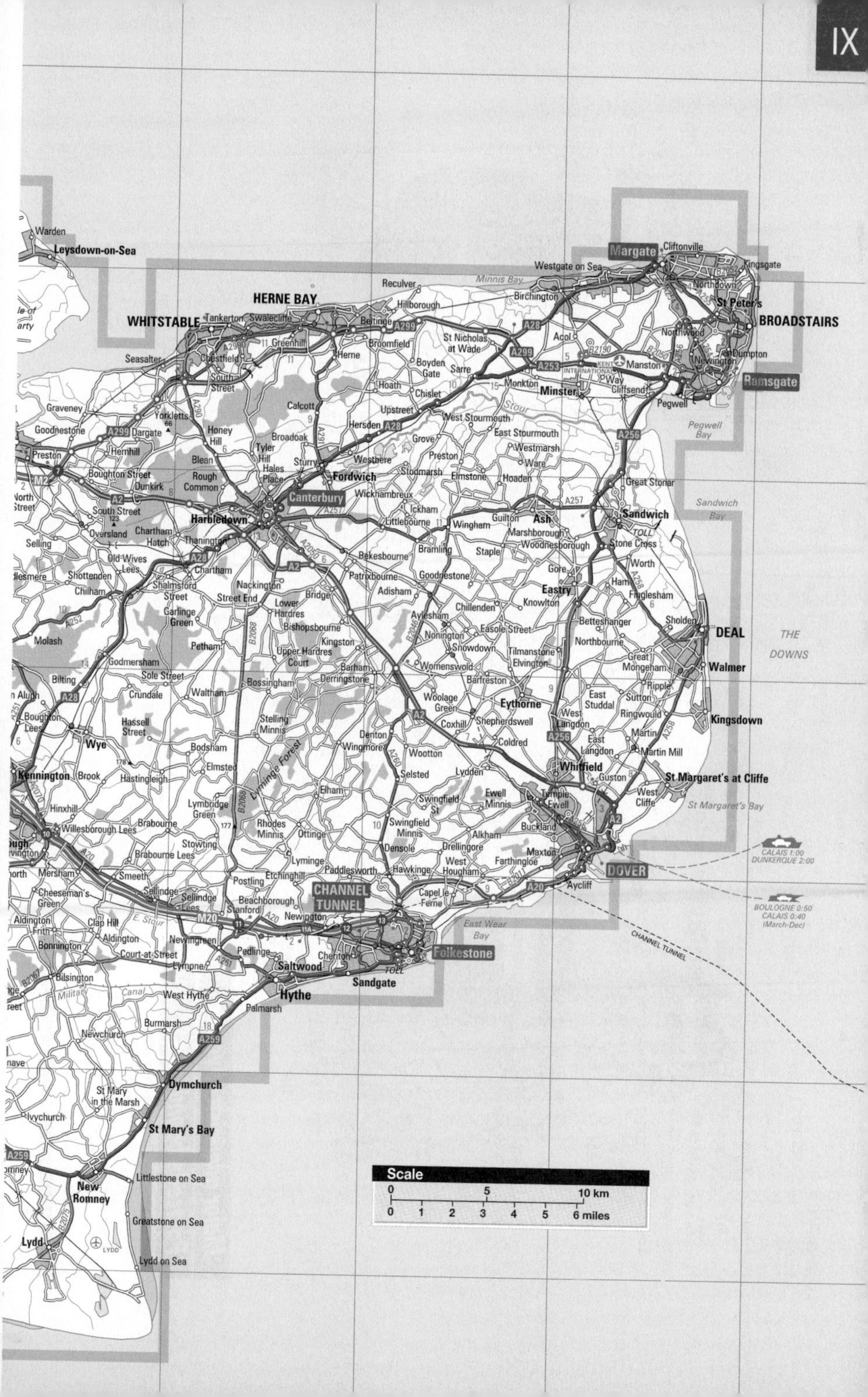

Warden
Leysdown-on-Sea
Isle of ... arty

WHITSTABLE
HERNE BAY
Tankerton
Swalecliffe
Chestfield
Seasalter
South Street
Graveney
Goodnestone
Hernhill
Dunkirk
Preston
Boughton Street
North Street
South Street
Selling
Oversland
Old Wives Lees
Chartham Hatch
Shottenden
Chilham
Molash
Bilting
Boughton Lees
Godmersham
Crundale
Sole Street
Waltham
Wye
Hassell Street
Bodsham
Kennington
Brook
Hastingleigh
Hinxhill
Willesborough Lees
Lymbridge Green
Brabourne
Stowting
Mersham
Brabourne Lees
Smeeth
Cheeseman's Green
Sellindge
Sellinge Lees
Stanford
Clap Hill
Aldington
Bonnington
Court-at-Street
Aldington Frith
Newingreen
Lympne
Bilsington
West Hythe
Palmarsh
Newchurch
Burmarsh
St Mary in the Marsh
Ivychurch
Dymchurch
St Mary's Bay
New Romney
Littlestone on Sea
Greatstone on Sea
Lydd
Lydd on Sea

Reculver
Hillborough
Beltinge
Herne
Broomfield
Hoath
Calcott
Honey Hill
Broadoak
Tyler Hill
Sturry
Blean
Rough Common
Hales Place
Harbledown
CANTERBURY
Fordwich
Wickhambreux
Ickham
Littlebourne
Bekesbourne
Bramling
Patrixbourne
Adisham
Goodnestone
Nackington
Lower Hardres
Bridge
Garlinge Green
Kingston
Bishopsbourne
Upper Hardres Court
Petham
Barham
Derringstone
Bossingham
Stelling Minnis
Denton
Wootton
Wingmore
Elmsted
Lyminge
Rhodes Minnis
Ottinge
Etchinghill
Postling
Beachborough
Paddlesworth
Hawkinge
Capel le Ferne
CHANNEL TUNNEL
Newington
Cheriton
Saltwood
Sandgate
HYTHE
FOLKESTONE

St Nicholas at Wade
Chislet
Sarre
Monkton
Minster
Upstreet
West Stourmouth
East Stourmouth
Grove
Preston
Westmarsh
Hersden
Stodmarsh
Elmstone
Hoaden
Westbere
Wingham
Marshborough
Woodnesborough
Staple
Ash
Guilton
Stone Cross
Worth
Gore
Eastry
Knowlton
Chillenden
Ham
Eythorne
Knowlton
Easole Street
Aylesham
Nonington
Snowdown
Tilmanstone
Elvington
Womenswold
Barfreston
Woolage Green
Coxhill
Shepherdswell
Coldred
Eythorne
East Studdal
Ripple
West Langdon
East Langdon
Ringwould
Martin
Martin Mill
Whitfield
Guston
Temple Ewell
Ewell Minnis
Maxton
Buckland
Aycliff
DOVER
Swingfield St
Swingfield Minnis
Alkham
Densole
Drellingore
West Hougham
Farthingloe
Selsted
Lydden
Elham
River
Capel le Ferne
East Wear Bay

Westgate on Sea
MARGATE
Cliftonville
Kingsgate
Northdown
St Peter's
BROADSTAIRS
Acol
Manston
Dumpton
Ramsgate
Cliffsend
Pegwell
Minnis Bay
Birchington
Birchington
Monkton
Great Stonar
Sandwich
Betteshanger
Sholden
DEAL
Walmer
Northbourne
Great Mongeham
Sutton
Kingsdown
St Margaret's at Cliffe
West Cliffe
St Margaret's Bay

Pegwell Bay
Sandwich Bay
THE DOWNS

CALAIS 1:00
DUNKERQUE 2:00
BOULOGNE 0:50
CALAIS 0:40
(March-Dec)
CHANNEL TUNNEL

Scale
0 ... 5 ... 10 km
0 1 2 3 4 5 6 miles

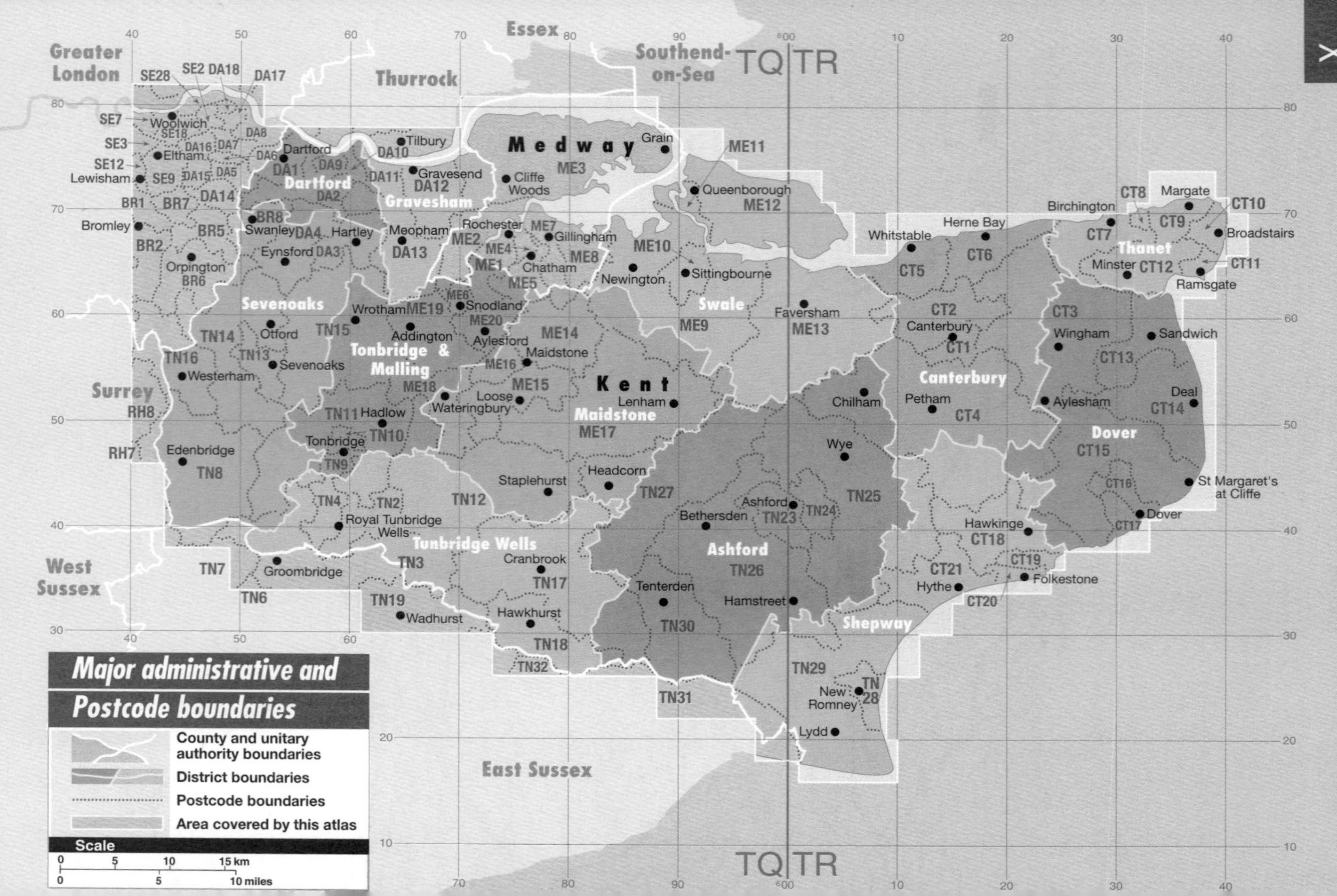

Major administrative and Postcode boundaries

	County and unitary authority boundaries
	District boundaries
	Postcode boundaries
	Area covered by this atlas

Scale

0   5   10   15 km
0   5   10 miles

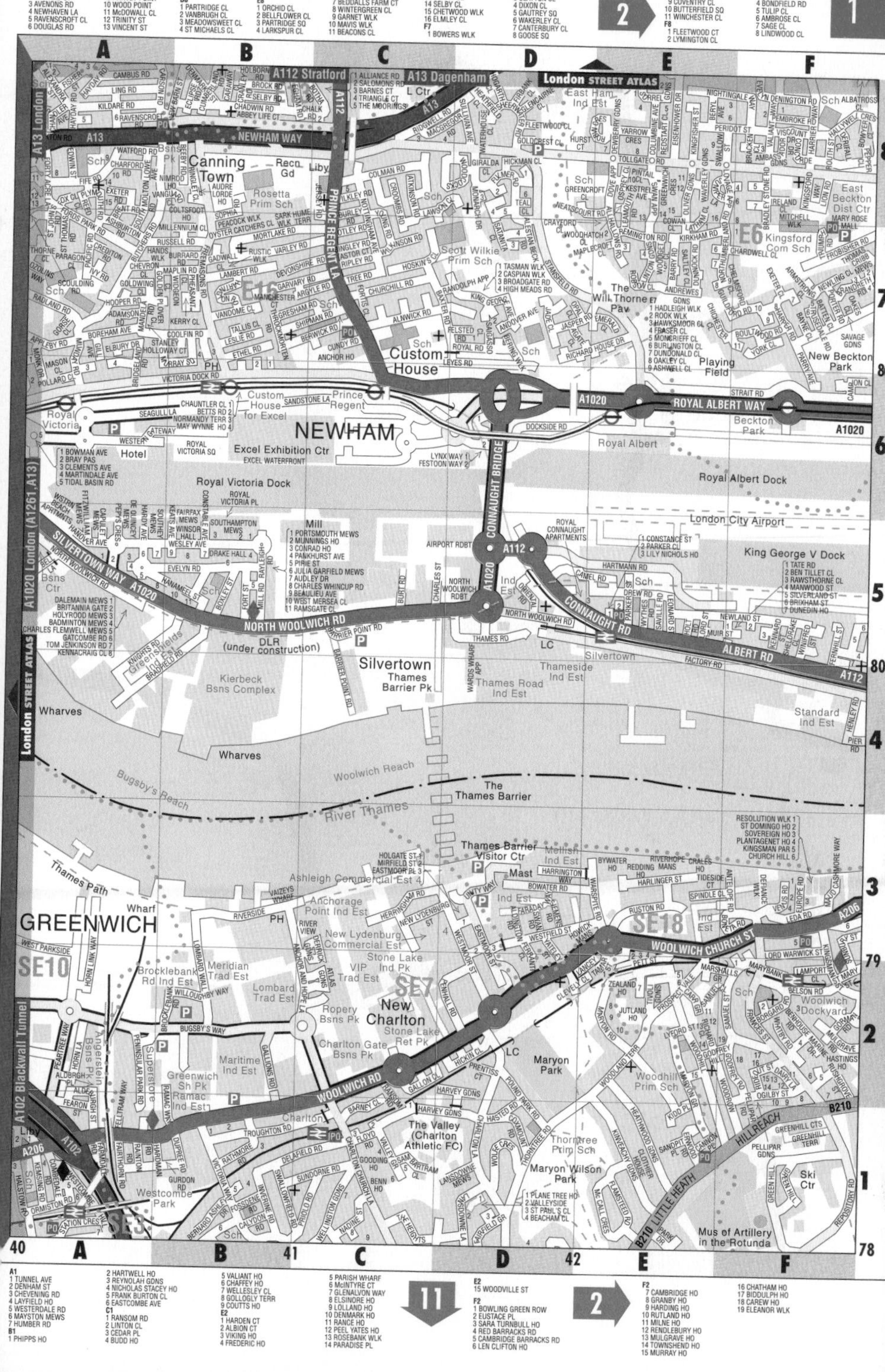

A8
1 ODEON CT
2 EDWARD CT
3 AVENONS RD
4 NEWHAVEN LA
5 RAVENSCROFT CL
6 DOUGLAS RD
7 BOTHWELL CL
8 FERRIER POINT
9 HARVEY POINT
10 WOOD POINT
11 McDOWALL CL
12 TRINITY ST
13 VINCENT ST
14 PATTINSON POINT
15 CLINCH CT
D8
1 PARTRIDGE CL
2 VANBRUGH CL
3 MEADOWSWEET CL
4 ST MICHAELS CL
5 LONG MARK RD
6 CONGREVE WLK
E8
1 ORCHID CL
2 BELLFLOWER CL
3 PARTRIDGE SQ
4 LARKSPUR CL
5 LOBELIA CL
6 STONECHAT SQ
7 BEDDALLS FARM CT
8 WINTERGREEN CL
9 GARNET WLK
10 MAVIS WLK
11 BEACONS CL
12 ABBESS CL
13 DENNY CL
14 SELBY CL
15 CHETWOOD WLK
16 ELMLEY CL
F7
1 BOWERS WLK
2 BARTON CL
3 CLAYTON CL
4 DIXON CL
5 GAUTREY SQ
6 WAKERLEY CL
7 CANTERBURY CL
8 GOOSE SQ
2
F7
9 COVENTRY CL
10 BUTTERFIELD SQ
11 WINCHESTER CL
F8
1 FLEETWOOD CT
2 LYMINGTON CL
3 HOLYHEAD CL
4 BONDFIELD RD
5 TULIP CL
6 AMBROSE CL
7 SAGE CL
8 LINDWOOD CL
1
A
B
C
D
E
F
A112 Stratford
A13 Dagenham
London STREET ATLAS
A13 London
NEWHAM WAY
Canning Town
Reco Gd
Rosetta Prim Sch
PRINCE REGENT LA
Scott Wilkie Prim Sch
East Ham Ind Est
East Beckton Dist Ctr
Kingsford Com Sch
E6
E16
The Will Thorne Pav
Custom House
Playing Field
New Beckton Park
8
7
6
5
4
3
2
1
80
79
78
ROYAL ALBERT WAY
A1020
Royal Victoria
Custom House for Excel
Prince Regent
NEWHAM
Excel Exhibition Ctr
EXCEL WATERFRONT
Royal Albert
Beckton Park
Royal Victoria Dock
Royal Albert Dock
London City Airport
CONNAUGHT BRIDGE
King George V Dock
SILVERTOWN WAY
A1020 London (A1261,A13)
NORTH WOOLWICH RD
DLR (under construction)
CONNAUGHT RD
ALBERT RD
Silvertown
Silvertown Thames Barrier Pk
Thameside Ind Est
Thames Road Ind Est
Kierbeck Bsns Complex
Wharves
Standard Ind Est
Bugsby's Reach
Woolwich Reach
The Thames Barrier
River Thames
Thames Barrier Visitor Ctr
Thames Path
Ashleigh Commercial Est
Anchorage Point Ind Est
GREENWICH
SE10
SE18
SE7
SE3
WOOLWICH CHURCH ST
New Lydenburg Commercial Est
Stone Lake Ind Pk
VIP Trad Est
Meridian Trad Est
Brocklebank Rd Ind Est
Lombard Trad Est
Ropery Bsns Pk
New Charlton
Stone Lake Ret Pk
Charlton Gate Bsns Pk
Maritime Ind Est
Greenwich Sh Pk
Ramac Ind Est
Angerstein Bsns Pk
WOOLWICH RD
Charlton
The Valley (Charlton Athletic FC)
Maryon Park
Woodhill Prim Sch
Thorntree Prim Sch
Maryon Wilson Park
Woolwich Dockyard
HILLREACH
B210
LITTLE HEATH
Ski Ctr
Mus of Artillery in the Rotunda
Westcombe Park
A102 Blackwall Tunnel
A206
40
41
42
A1
1 TUNNEL AVE
2 DENHAM ST
3 CHEVENING RD
4 LAYFIELD HO
5 WESTERDALE RD
6 MAYSTON MEWS
7 HUMBER RD
B1
1 PHIPPS HO
2 HARTWELL HO
3 REYNOLAH GDNS
4 NICHOLAS STACEY HO
5 FRANK BURTON CL
6 EASTCOMBE AVE
C1
1 RANSOM RD
2 LINTON CL
3 CEDAR PL
4 BUDD HO
5 VALIANT HO
6 CHAFFEY HO
7 WELLESLEY CL
8 GOLLOGLY TERR
9 COUTTS HO
E2
1 HARDEN CT
2 ALBION CT
3 VIKING HO
4 FREDERIC HO
5 PARISH WHARF
6 McINTYRE CT
7 GLENALVON WAY
8 ELSINORE HO
9 LOLLAND HO
10 DENMARK HO
11 RANCE HO
12 PEEL YATES HO
13 ROSEBANK WLK
14 PARADISE PL
11
E2
15 WOODVILLE ST
F2
1 BOWLING GREEN ROW
2 EUSTACE PL
3 SARA TURNBULL HO
4 RED BARRACKS RD
5 CAMBRIDGE BARRACKS RD
6 LEN CLIFTON HO
2
F2
7 CAMBRIDGE HO
8 GRANBY HO
9 HARDING HO
10 RUTLAND HO
11 MILNE HO
12 RENDLEBURY HO
13 MULGRAVE HO
14 TOWNSHEND HO
15 MURRAY HO
16 CHATHAM HO
17 BIDDULPH HO
18 CAREW HO
19 ELEANOR HO

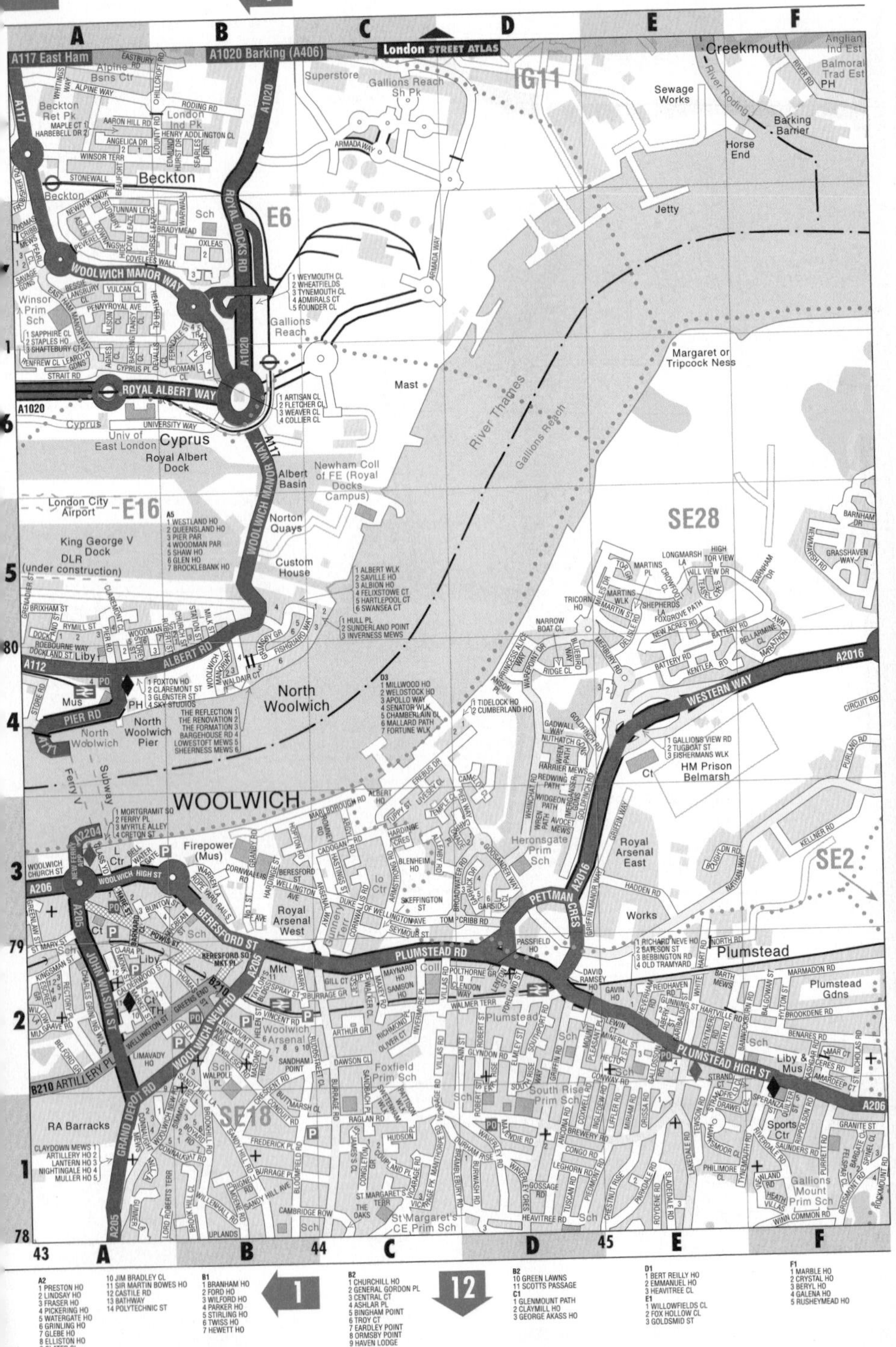

London STREET ATLAS

A2
1 PRESTON HO
2 LINDSAY HO
3 FRASER HO
4 PICKERING HO
5 WATERGATE HO
6 GRINLING HO
7 GLEBE HO
8 ELLISTON HO
9 SLATER CL
10 JIM BRADLEY CL
11 SIR MARTIN BOWES HO
12 CASTILE RD
13 BATHWAY
14 POLYTECHNIC ST

B1
1 BRANHAM HO
2 FORD HO
3 WILFORD HO
4 PARKER HO
5 STIRLING HO
6 TWISS HO
7 HEWETT HO

B2
2 CHURCHILL HO
3 GENERAL GORDON PL
3 CENTRAL CT
4 ASHLAR PL
5 BINGHAM POINT
6 TROY CT
7 EARDLEY POINT
8 ORMSBY POINT
9 HAVEN LODGE

B2
10 GREEN LAWNS
11 SCOTTS PASSAGE
C1
1 GLENMOUNT PATH
2 CLAYMILL HO
3 GEORGE AKASS HO

D1
1 BERT REILLY HO
2 EMMANUEL HO
3 HEAVITREE CL
E1
1 WILLOWFIELDS CL
2 FOX HOLLOW CL
3 GOLDSMID ST

F1
1 MARBLE HO
2 CRYSTAL HO
3 BERYL HO
4 GALENA HO
5 RUSHEYMEAD HO

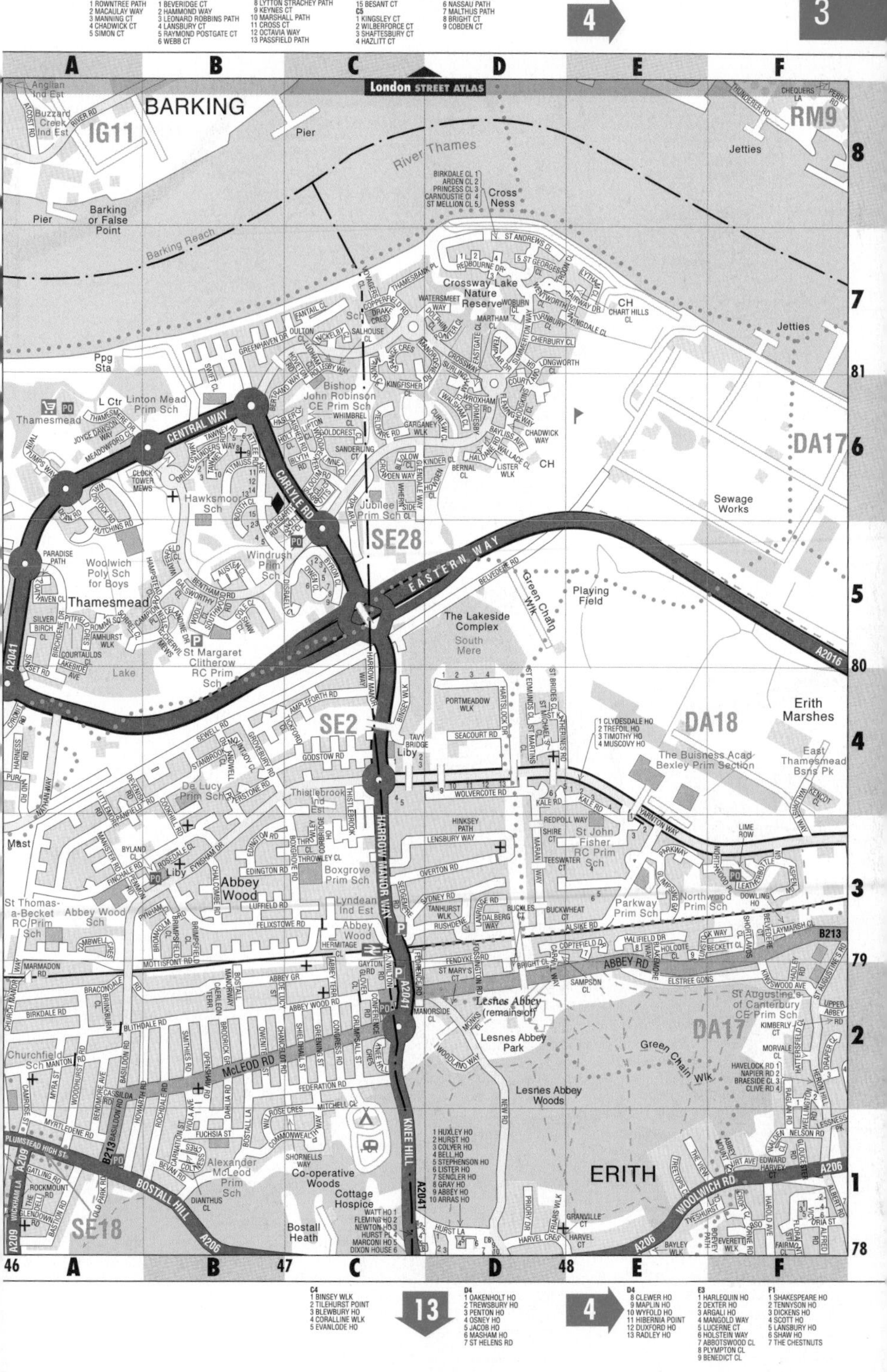

London STREET ATLAS

4 →

BARKING

IG11

RM9

River Thames

DA17

SE28

SE2

Thamesmead

Abbey Wood

DA18

Erith Marshes

DA17

ERITH

SE18

4 →

A13 Dagenham, London

RAINHAM

RM9

RM13

DA18

DA17

DA8

Belvedere

ERITH

Lessness Heath

A2016 EASTERN WAY

A206 WOOLWICH RD

River Thames

Erith Reach

Rainham Marshes

Wennington Marshes

Coldharbour Point

E1
1 CARRACK HO
2 SALFORD CL
3 BOSWORTH HO
4 BEXLEY RD
5 BLYTH HO
6 CUTTER HO
7 FRANCIS CT
8 WINDRUSH CT
9 TRITON LODGE
10 VICTORY LODGE
11 SCHOONER HO
12 DRAKE POINT
13 CORRAL HTS
14 CHICHESTER WHARF
15 PLEASANT VIEW

A1
1 STEVANNE CT
2 TOLCAIRN CT
3 CHALFONT CT
4 ALONSO HO
5 ARIEL CT
6 MIRANDA HO
7 PROSPERO HO
8 SMARDEN CL
9 BERKHAMPSTEAD RD
10 CAMDEN CT
11 THE CHESTNUTS
12 LESSNESS RD
13 HARTFORD WLK
14 WINCHESTER CT
15 BRAMLEY CT
16 RIVERVIEW CT
17 RUSSET CT
18 THE LAURELS

A2
1 BRUSHWOOD LODGE
2 STICKLAND RD
3 BLETCHINGTON CT
4 VENMEAD CT
5 MITRE CT
6 CHAPELSITE CT

A3
1 CRESSINGHAM CT
2 TELFORD HO
3 KELVIN HO
4 JENNER HO
5 MARY MACARTHUR HO
6 LENNOX HO
7 KEIR HARDY HO
8 MONARCH RD
9 ELIZABETH GARRETT ANDERSON HO

A3
10 WILLIAM SMITH HO
11 BADEN POWELL HO
12 BOYLE HO
13 BAIRD HO
14 MARY SLESSOR HO

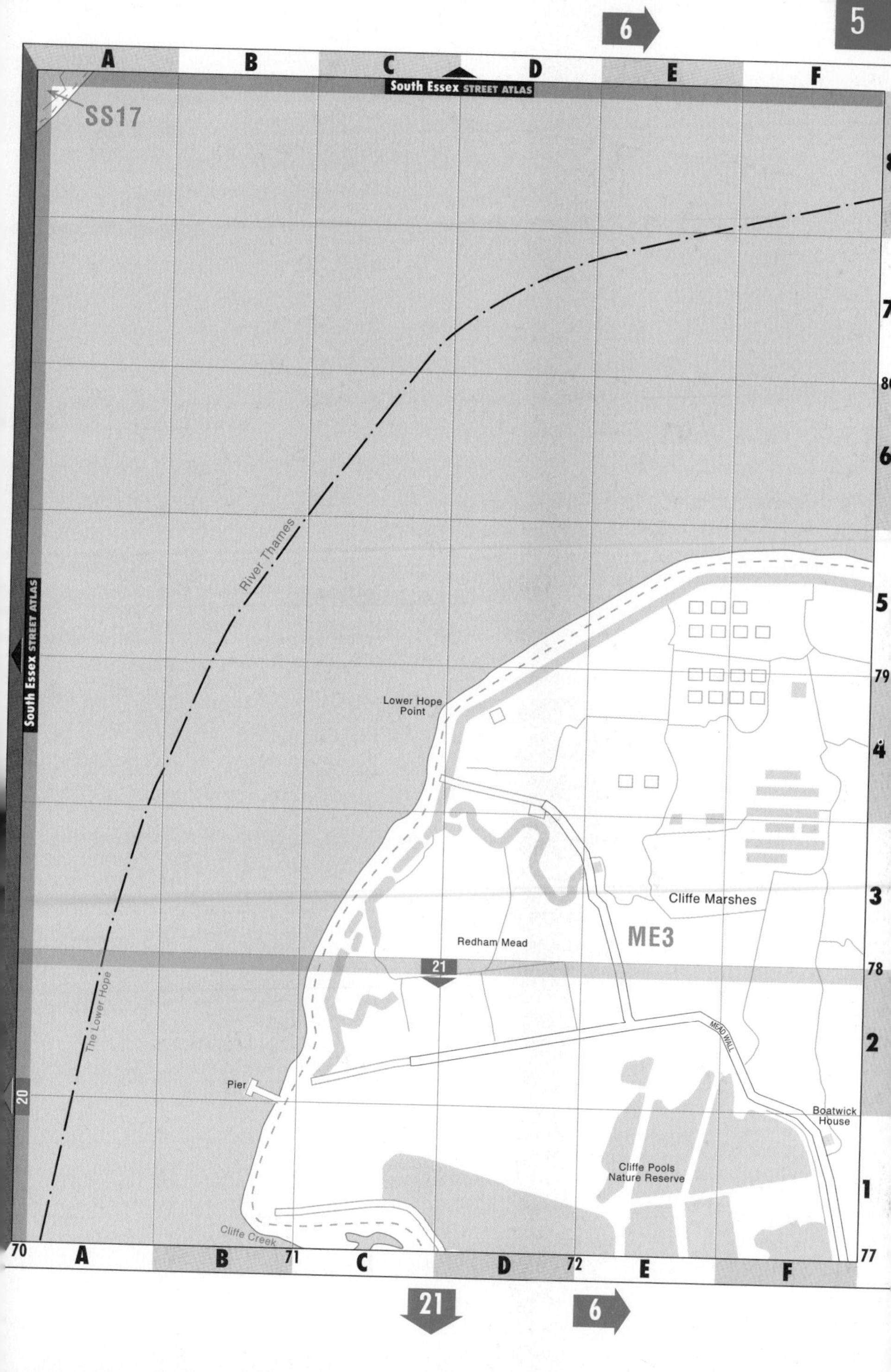

SS17

River Thames

The Lower Hope

Lower Hope
Point

Redham Mead

Cliffe Marshes

ME3

Pier

MEAD WALL

Boatwick
House

Cliffe Pools
Nature Reserve

Cliffe Creek

A B C D E F

South Essex STREET ATLAS

River Thames

Sheep
Wash

Cliffe Fleet

Sheepfold

Cliffe Marshes   ME3

22

Ryestreet
Common

Ham Wall

Farthing Wall

COMMON WALL

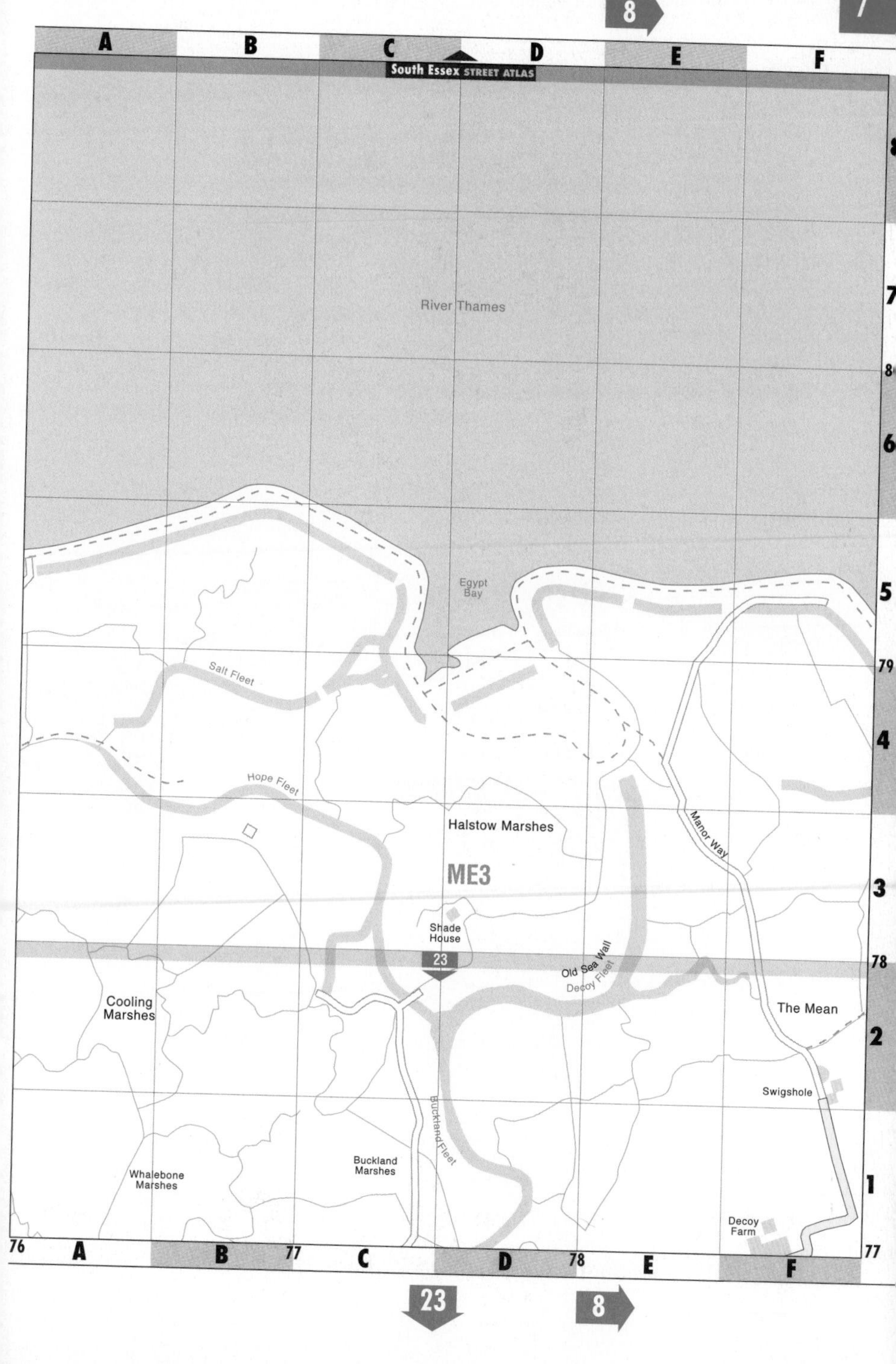

8

South Essex STREET ATLAS

A B C D E F

River Thames

Egypt
Bay

Salt Fleet

Hope Fleet

Halstow Marshes

ME3

Shade
House

23

Old Sea Wall
Decoy Fleet

Manor Way

The Mean

Cooling
Marshes

Swigshole

Buckland Fleet

Buckland
Marshes

Whalebone
Marshes

Decoy
Farm

A　　B　　C　　D　　E　　F

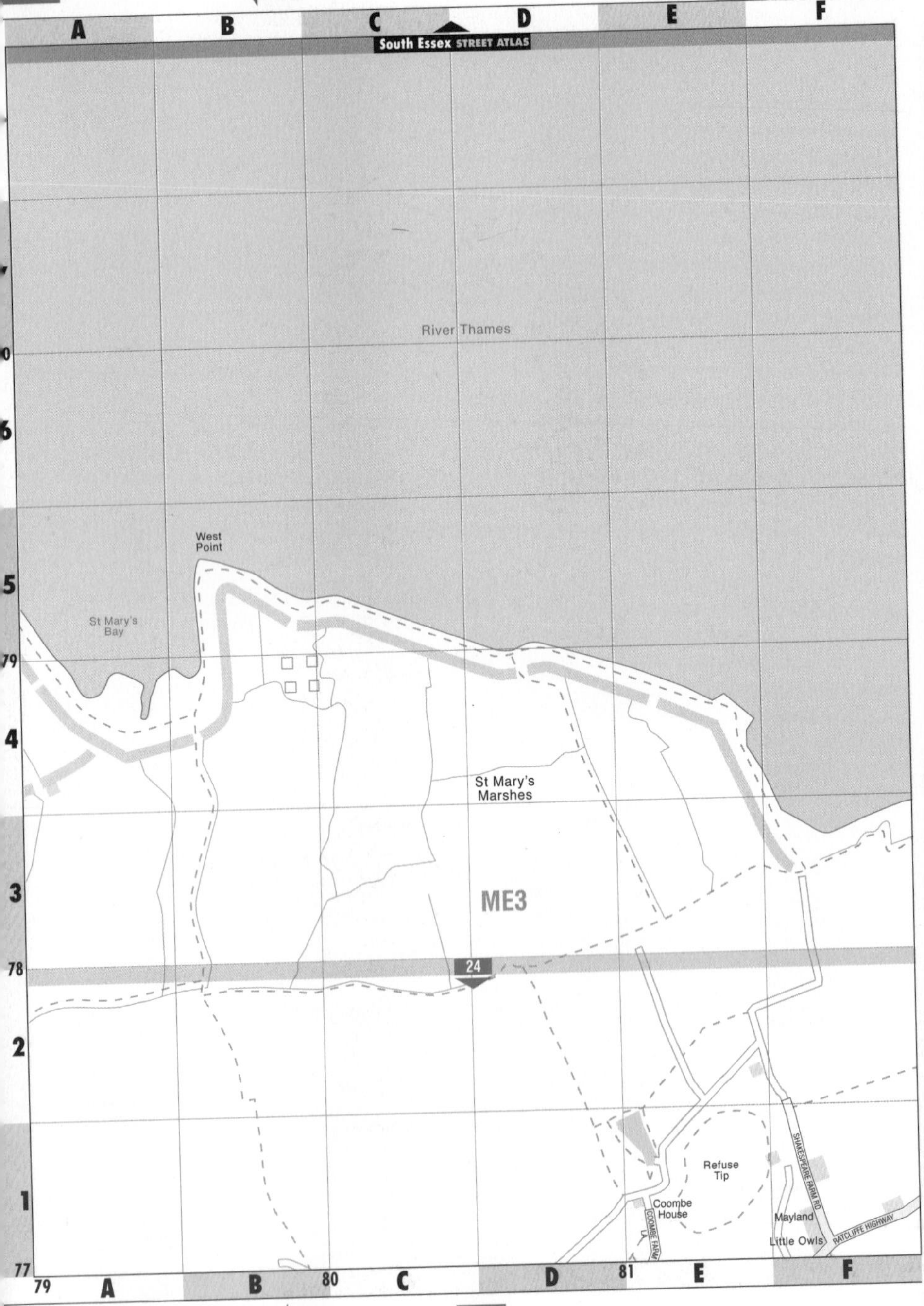

River Thames

West
Point

St Mary's
Bay

79

St Mary's
Marshes

ME3

24

78

Refuse
Tip

Coombe
House

Mayland

Little Owls

RATCLIFFE HIGHWAY

COOMBE HAVEN

SHAKESPEARE FARM RD

77

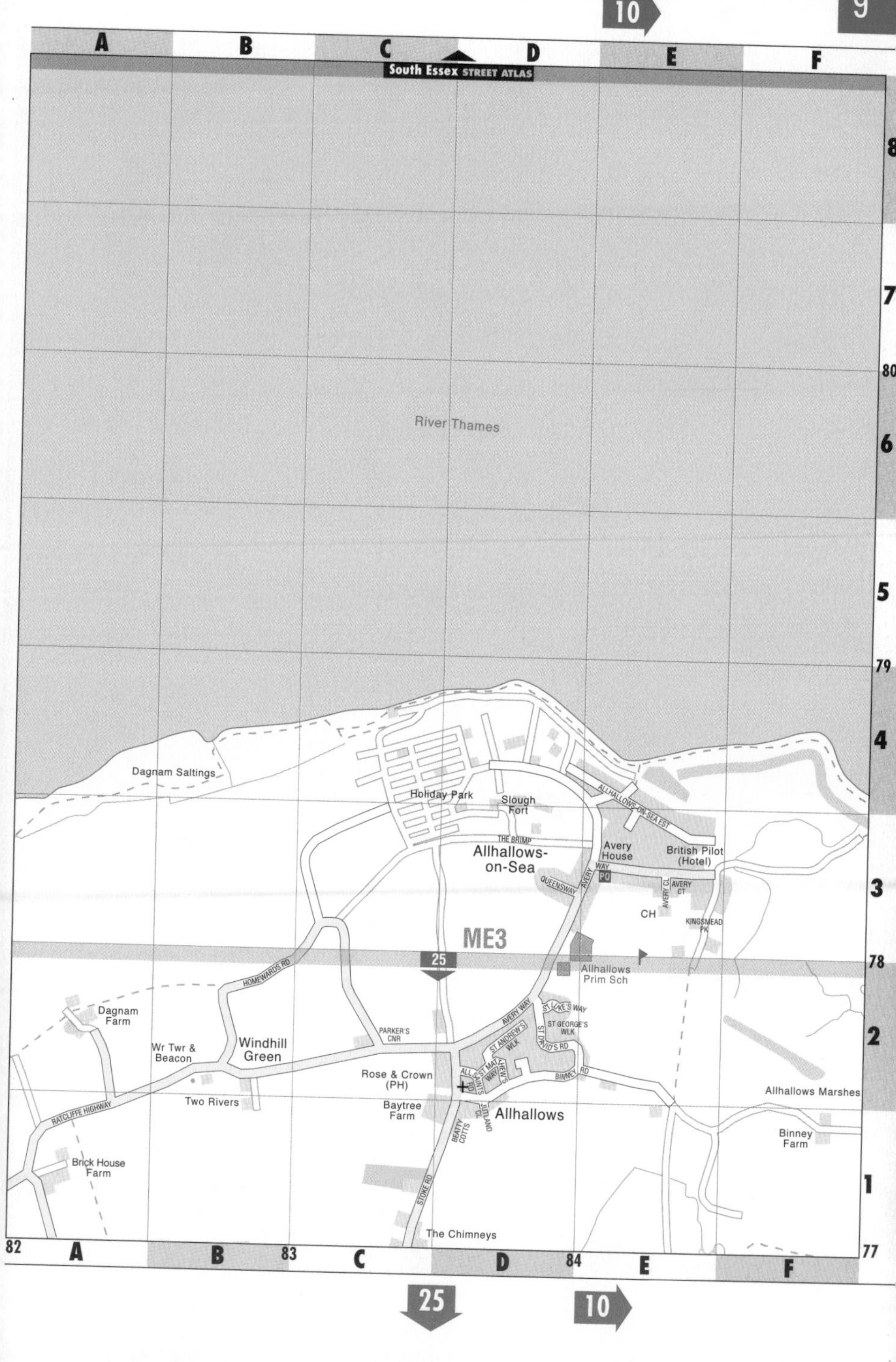

South Essex STREET ATLAS

River Thames

Dagnam Saltings

Holiday Park

Slough Fort

THE BRUMP

Allhallows-on-Sea

Avery House

British Pilot (Hotel)

ALLHALLOWS-ON-SEA EST

QUEENSWAY

AVERY WAY

AVERY CL

AVERY CT

CH

KINGSMEAD PK

ME3

25

Allhallows Prim Sch

HOMEWARDS RD

Dagnam Farm

Wr Twr & Beacon

Windhill Green

PARKER'S CNR

AVERY WAY

ST ANDREW WLK

ST GEORGE'S WAY

ST GEORGE'S WLK

ST TID'S RD

Allhallows Marshes

Rose & Crown (PH)

ST ANDREW WLK

ALL SAINTS WLK

ST MARY'S WLK

BINNEY RD

Two Rivers

RATCLIFFE HIGHWAY

Baytree Farm

Allhallows

BINNEY CLOSE

AVETLAND

Binney Farm

Brick House Farm

STONE RD

BINNEY COTTS

The Chimneys

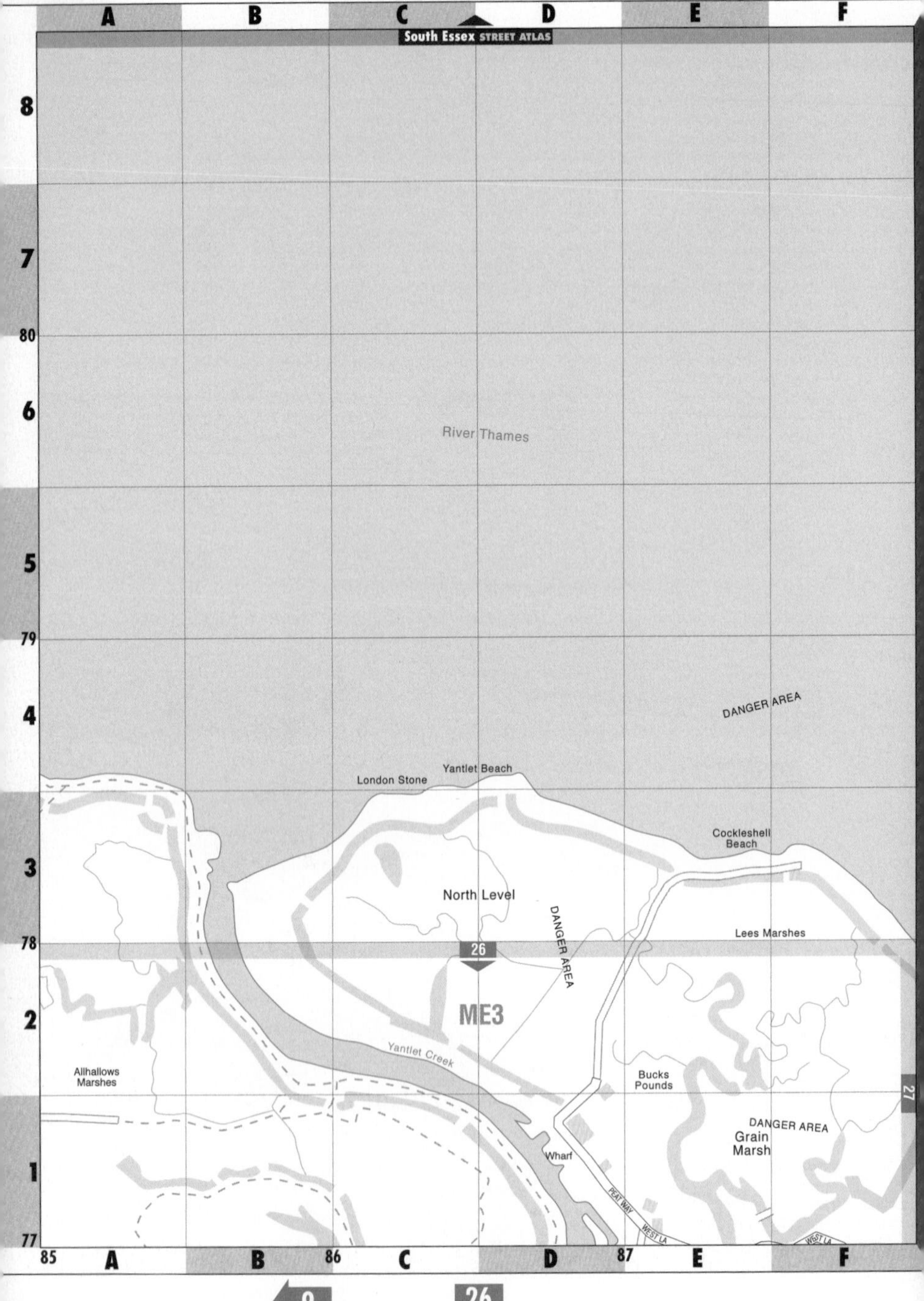

South Essex STREET ATLAS

River Thames

DANGER AREA

Yantlet Beach
London Stone

Cockleshell
Beach

North Level

DANGER AREA

Lees Marshes

26

ME3

Yantlet Creek

Allhallows
Marshes

Bucks
Pounds

DANGER AREA
Grain
Marsh

Wharf

27

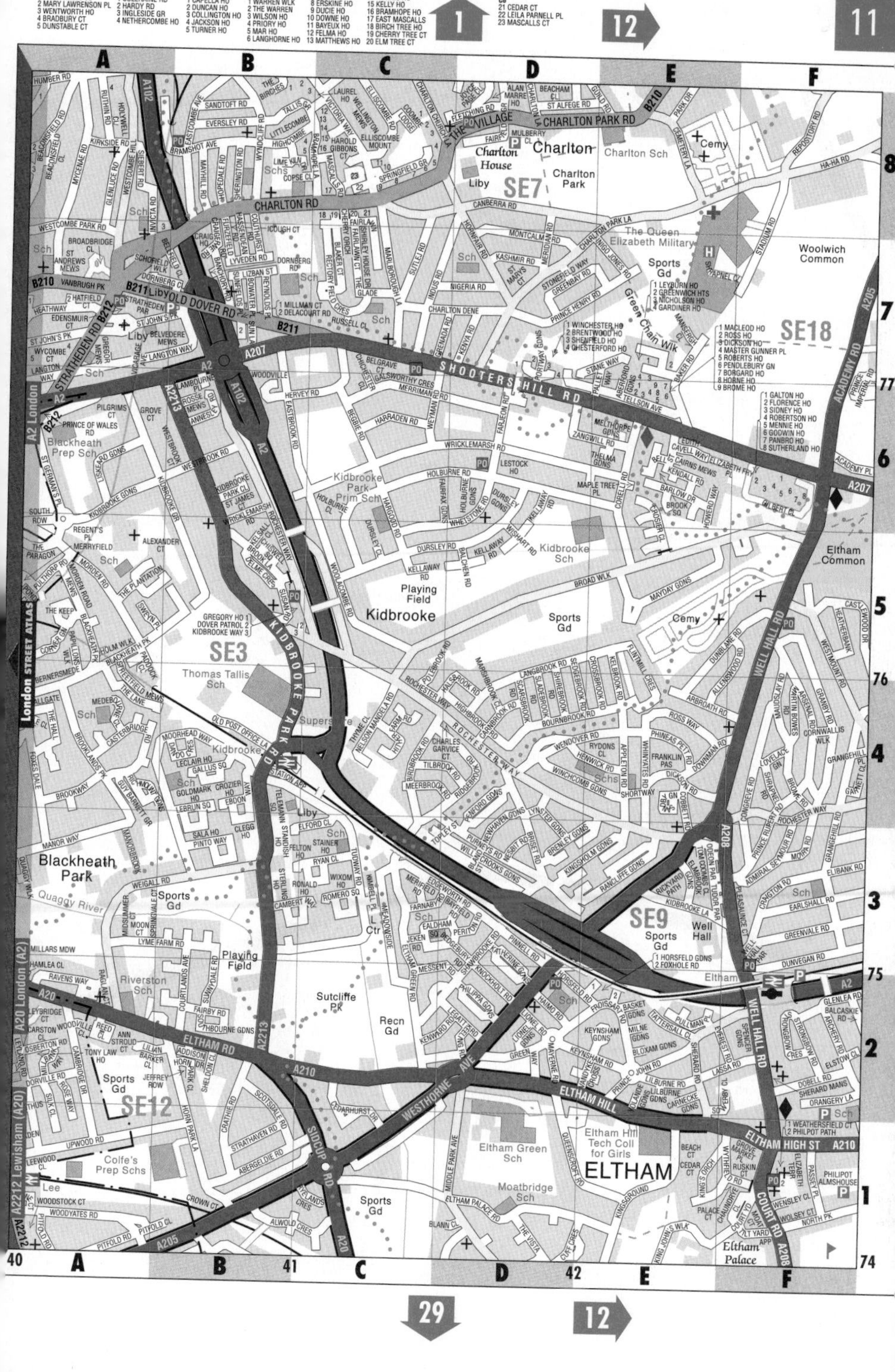

A7
1 MANDEVILLE CL
2 MARY LAWRENSON PL
3 WENTWORTH HO
4 BRADBURY CT
5 DUNSTABLE CT
A8
1 COLERAINE RD
2 HARDY RD
3 INGLESIDE GR
4 NETHERCOMBE HO
B8
1 CAPELLA HO
2 DUNCAN HO
3 COLLINGTON HO
4 JACKSON HO
5 TURNER HO
C8
1 WARREN WLK
2 THE WARREN
3 WILSON HO
4 PRIORY HO
5 MAR HO
6 LANGHORNE HO
7 GAMES HO
8 ERSKINE HO
9 DUCIE HO
10 DOWNE HO
11 BAYEUX HO
12 FELMA HO
13 MATTHEWS HO
14 NORRIS HO
15 KELLY HO
16 BRAMHOPE HO
17 EAST MASCALLS
18 BIRCH TREE HO
19 CHERRY TREE CT
20 ELM TREE CT
C8
21 CEDAR CT
22 LEILA PARNELL PL
23 MASCALLS CT
1
12
11
A
B
C
D
E
F
Charlton
Charlton House
Charlton Park
Charlton Sch
SE7
CHARLTON RD
CHARLTON PARK RD
THE VILLAGE
OLD DOVER RD
SHOOTERS HILL RD
The Queen Elizabeth Military
Woolwich Common
SE18
Green Chain Wlk
Kidbrooke
Playing Field
Kidbrooke Sch
Sports Gd
Cemy
Eltham Common
SE3
Thomas Tallis Sch
KIDBROOKE PARK RD
ROCHESTER WAY
WELL HALL RD
Blackheath Park
Blackheath Prep Sch
Quaggy River
Playing Field
Riverston Sch
ELTHAM RD
SE12
Sutcliffe Pk
Recn Gd
SE9
Well Hall
Eltham
ELTHAM HILL
ELTHAM HIGH ST
Eltham Green Sch
Eltham Hill Tech Coll for Girls
ELTHAM
Moatbridge Sch
Colfe's Prep Schs
Lee
Eltham Palace
London STREET ATLAS
8
7
77
6
5
76
4
3
75
2
1
74
40
41
42
29
12

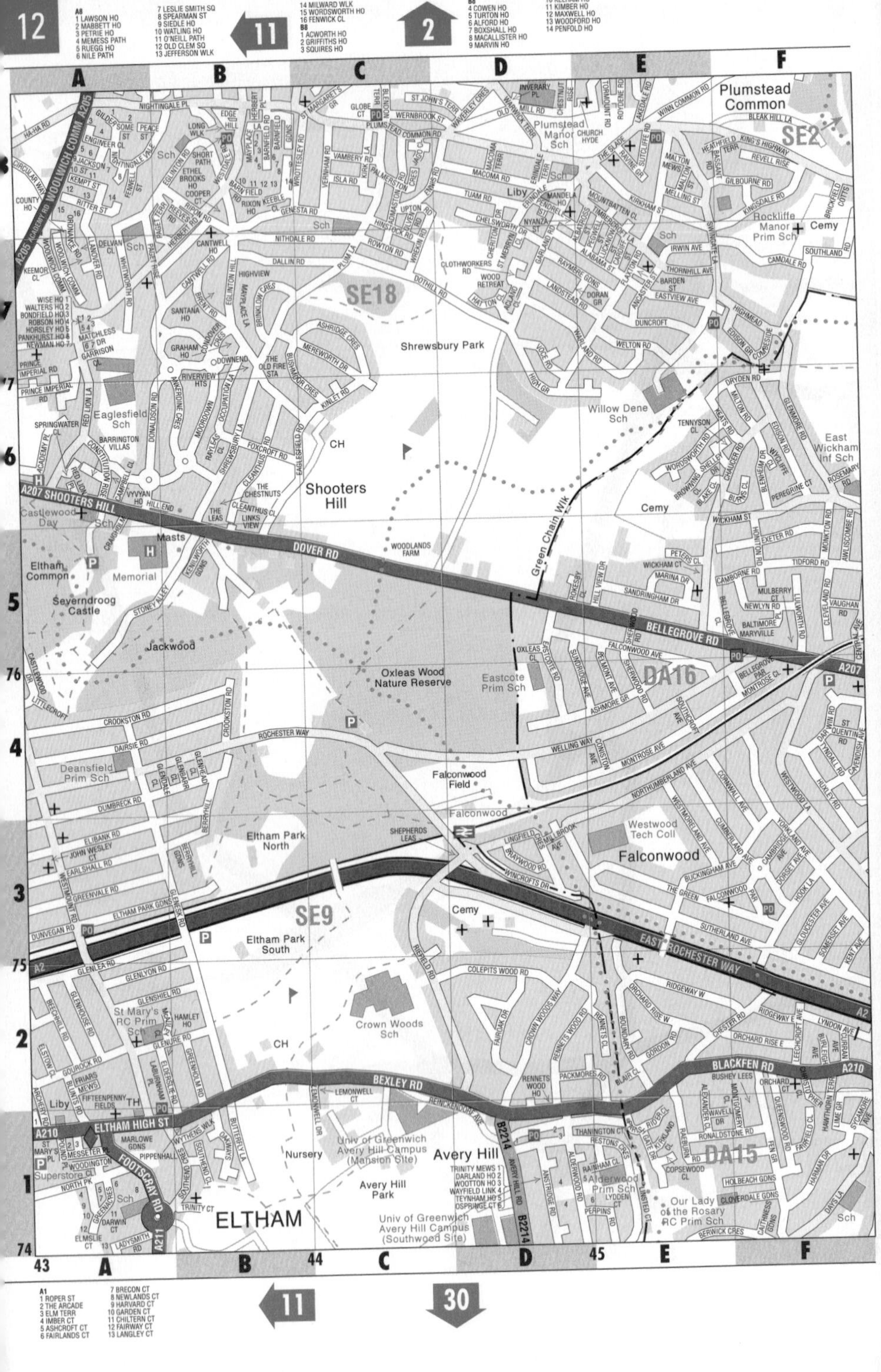

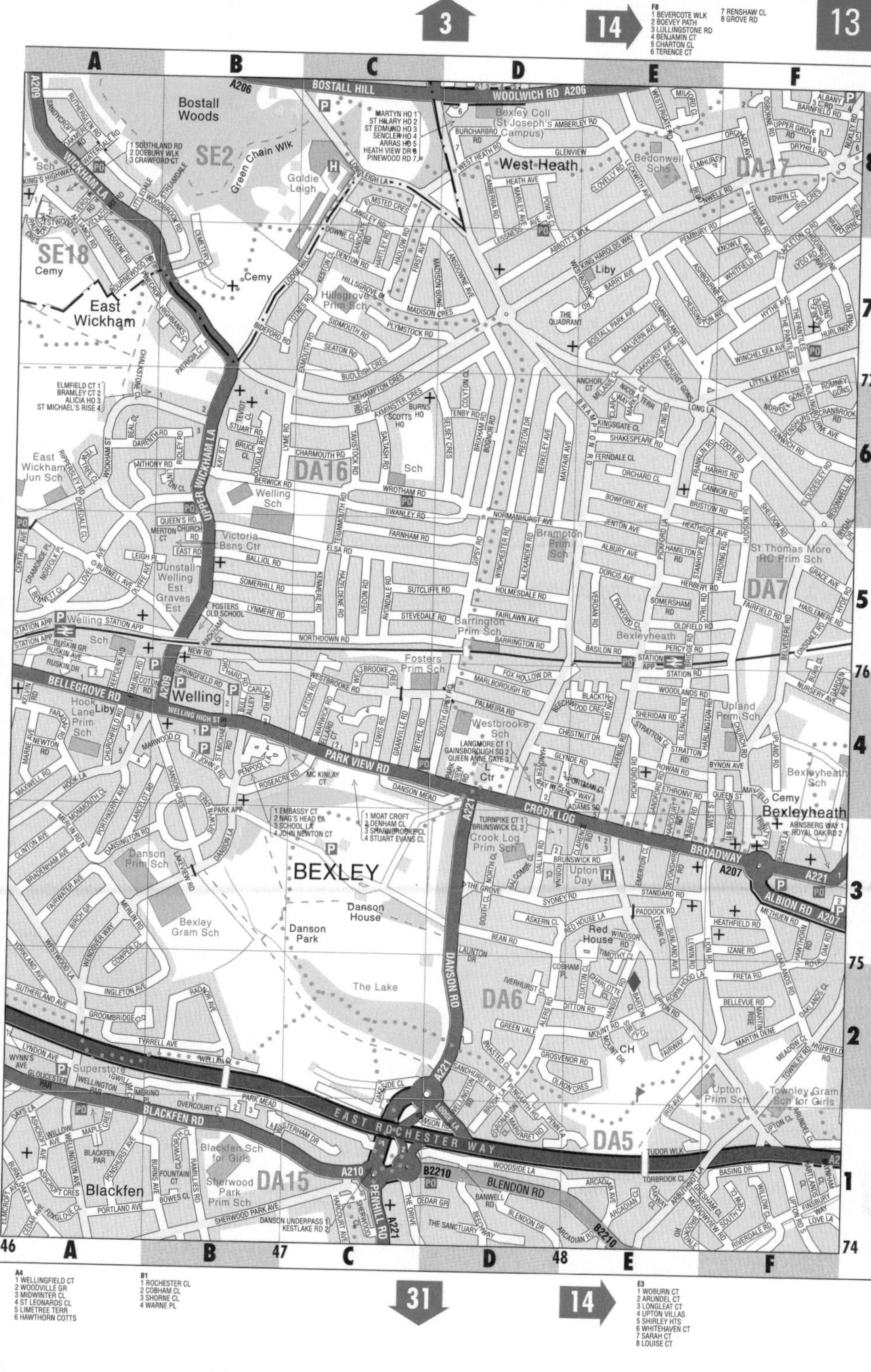
3
14
F8
1 BEVERCOTE WLK
2 BOEVEY PATH
3 LULLINGSTONE RD
4 BENJAMIN CT
5 CHARTON CL
6 TERENCE CT
7 RENSHAW CL
8 GROVE RD
A
B
C
D
E
F
Bostall Woods
SE2
Green Chain Wlk
BOSTALL HILL
WOOLWICH RD A206
Bexley Coll (St Joseph's Campus)
West Heath
Bedonwell Schs
DA17
Goldie Leigh
SE18
East Wickham
1 SOUTHLAND RD
2 DOEBURY WLK
3 CRAWFORD CT
MARTYN HO 1
ST HILARY HO 2
ST EDMUND HO 3
SENCLER HO 4
ARRAS HO 5
HEATH VIEW DR 6
PINEWOOD RD 7
ELMFIELD CT 1
BRAMLEY CT 2
ALICIA HO 3
ST MICHAEL'S RISE 4
WICKHAM LA
UPPER WICKHAM LA
Hillsgrove Prim Sch
East Wickham Jun Sch
DA16
Welling Sch
Victoria Bsns Ctr
Dunstall Welling Est
Graves Est
Brampton Prim Sch
St Thomas More RC Prim Sch
DA7
Barrington Prim Sch
Bexleyheath
Welling
Hook Lane Prim Sch
Fosters Prim Sch
Westbrooke Sch
Upland Prim Sch
BELLEGROVE RD
WELLING HIGH ST
PARK VIEW RD
CROOK LOG
BROADWAY
ALBION RD A207
Bexleyheath Sch
Cemy
LANGMORE CT 1
GAINSBOROUGH SQ 2
QUEEN ANNE GATE 3
1 EMBASSY CT
2 NAG'S HEAD LA
3 SCHOOL LA
4 JOHN NEWTON CT
1 MOAT CROFT
2 DENHAM CL
3 SHARNBROOKE CL
4 STUART EVANS CL
TURNPIKE CT 1
BRUNSWICK CL 2
ARNSBERG WAY 1
ROYAL OAK RD 2
Crook Log Prim Sch
BEXLEY
Danson Prim Sch
Bexley Gram Sch
Danson House
Danson Park
The Lake
Upton Day
Red House
DA6
DANSON RD
Superstore
EAST ROCHESTER WAY
BLACKFEN RD
Blackfen Sch for Girls
Sherwood Park Prim Sch
DA15
Blackfen
DA5
Upton Prim Sch
Townley Gram Sch for Girls
BLENDON RD
DANSON UNDERPASS 1
KESTLAKE RD 2
PENHILL RD
46
47
48
74
75
76
77
1
2
3
4
5
6
7
8
A4
1 WELLINGFIELD CT
2 WOODVILLE GR
3 MIDWINTER CL
4 ST LEONARDS CL
5 LIMETREE TERR
6 HAWTHORN COTTS
B1
1 ROCHESTER CL
2 COBHAM CL
3 SHORNE CL
4 WARNE PL
31
14
E3
1 WOBURN CT
2 ARUNDEL CT
3 LONGLEAT CT
4 UPTON VILLAS
5 SHIRLEY HTS
6 WHITEHAVEN CT
7 SARAH CT
8 LOUISE CT

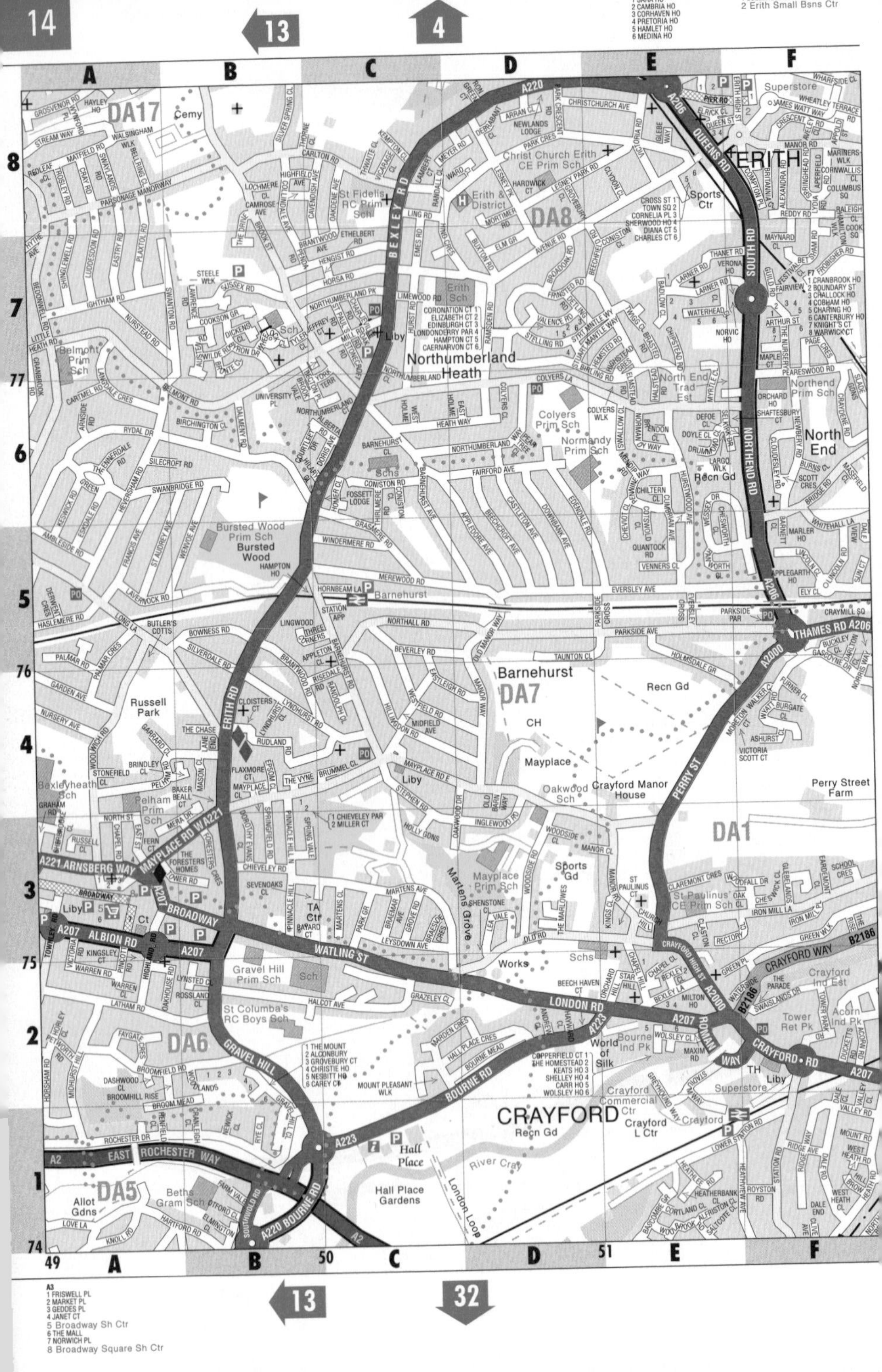
14
13
4
E7
1 SARA HO
2 CAMBRIA HO
3 CORHAVEN HO
4 PRETORIA HO
5 HAMLET HO
6 MEDINA HO
F8
1 COLEBROOK ST
2 Erith Small Bsns Ctr
A
B
C
D
E
F
DA17
DA8
DA7
DA6
DA5
DA1
ERITH
Northumberland Heath
Barnehurst
North End
CRAYFORD
Russell Park
Bursted Wood
Mayplace
Crayford Manor House
Perry Street Farm
Hall Place
Hall Place Gardens
River Cray
London Loop
Martens Grove
World of Silk
Crayford Commercial Ctr
Crayford L Ctr
Tower Ret Pk
Acorn Ind Pk
Crayford Ind Est
Bourne Ind Pk
Superstore
Erith & District
Christ Church Erith CE Prim Sch
St Fidelis RC Prim Sch
Erith Sch
Belmont Prim Sch
Bursted Wood Prim Sch
Colyers Prim Sch
Normandy Prim Sch
Northend Prim Sch
Bexleyheath Sch
Pelham Prim Sch
Mayplace Prim Sch
Oakwood Sch
St Paulinus' CE Prim Sch
Gravel Hill Prim Sch
St Columba's RC Boys Sch
Beths Gram Sch
Allot Gdns
Sports Ctr
Sports Gd
Recn Gd
BEXLEY RD
ERITH RD
GRAVEL HILL
BOURNE RD
WATLING ST
LONDON RD
PERRY ST
NORTHEND RD
SOUTH RD
QUEENS RD
THAMES RD
CRAYFORD RD
CRAYFORD WAY
EAST ROCHESTER WAY
BROADWAY
ALBION RD
MAYPLACE RD W
A221 ARNSBERG WAY
A220
A206
A2000
A207
A223
A2
B2186
8
7
77
6
5
76
4
3
75
2
1
74
49
50
51
1 THE MOUNT
2 ALCONBURY
3 GROVEBURY CT
4 CHRISTIE HO
5 NESBITT HO
6 CAREY CT
COPPERFIELD CT 1
THE HOMESTEAD 2
KEATS HO 3
SHELLEY HO 4
CARR HO 5
WOLSLEY HO 6
CORONATION CT 1
ELIZABETH CT 2
EDINBURGH CT 3
LONDONDERRY PAR 4
HAMPTON CT 5
CAERNARVON CT 6
CROSS ST 1
TOWN SQ 2
CORNELIA PL 3
SHERWOOD HO 4
DIANA CT 5
CHARLES CT 6
F7
1 CRANBROOK HO
2 BOUNDARY ST
3 CHALLOCK HO
4 COBHAM HO
5 CHARING HO
6 CANTERBURY HO
7 KNIGHT'S CT
8 WARWICK CT
1 CHIEVELEY PAR
2 MILLER CT
13
32
A3
1 FRISWELL PL
2 MARKET PL
3 GEDDES PL
4 JANET CT
5 Broadway Sh Ctr
6 THE MALL
7 NORWICH PL
8 Broadway Square Sh Ctr

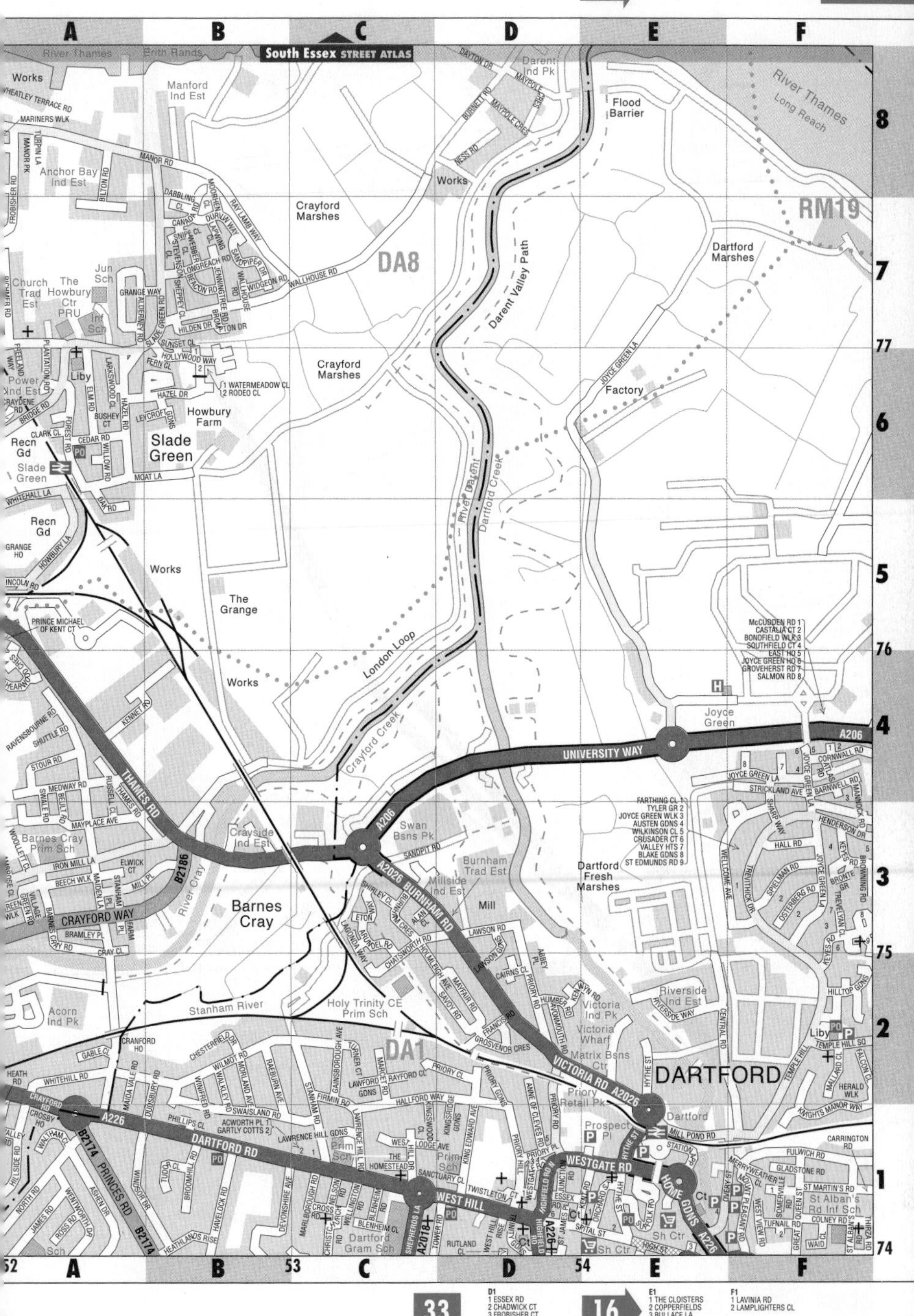

South Essex STREET ATLAS

D1
1 ESSEX RD
2 CHADWICK CT
3 FROBISHER CT
4 CLEVES VIEW
5 PRIORY CT
6 WESTGATE HO

E1
1 THE CLOISTERS
2 COPPERFIELDS
3 BULLACE LA
4 CHURCH VIEW

F1
1 LAVINIA RD
2 LAMPLIGHTERS CL

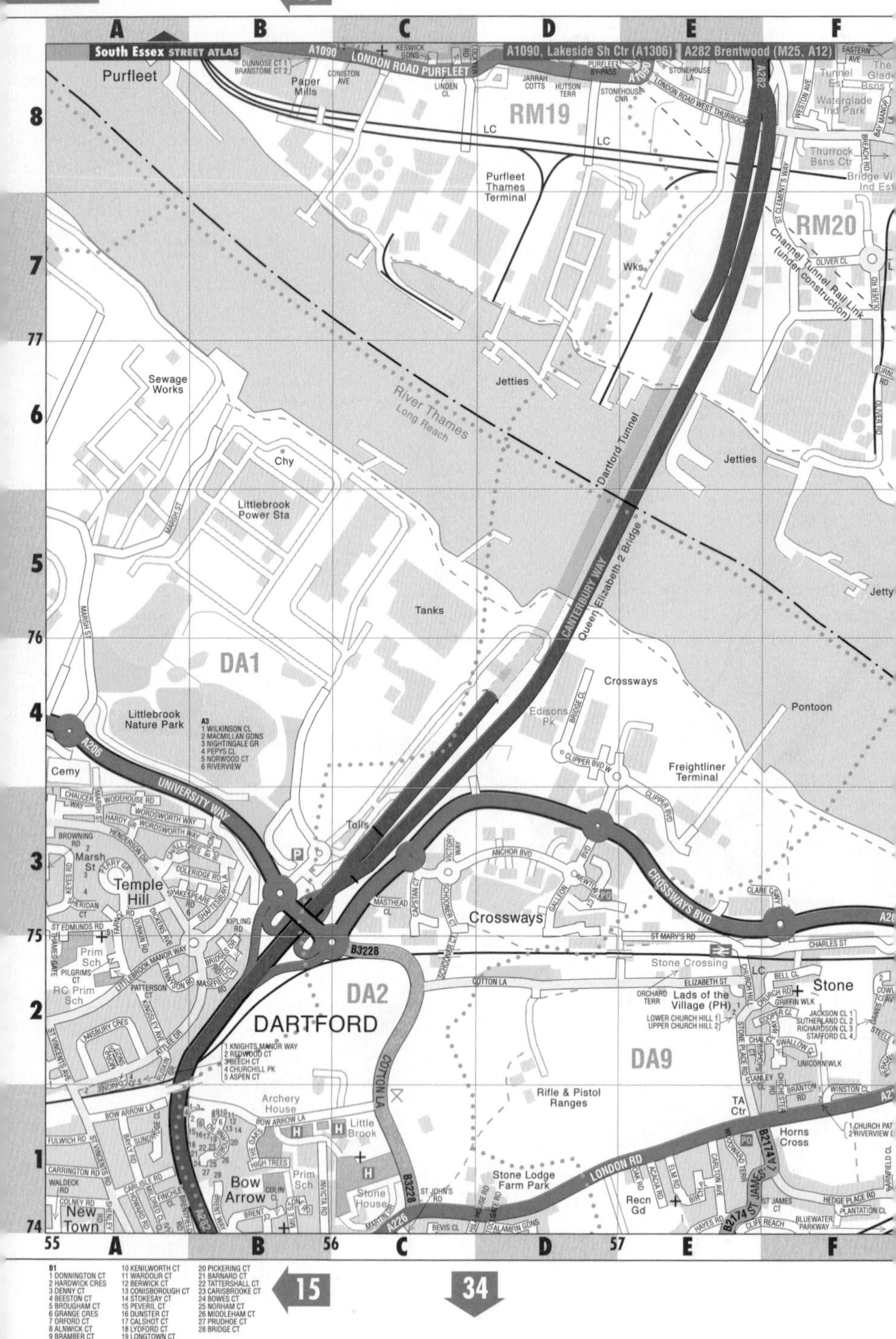

South Essex STREET ATLAS

Purfleet

A1090 LONDON ROAD PURFLEET

A1090, Lakeside Sh Ctr (A1306)

A282 Brentwood (M25, A12)

RM19

RM20

Jetties

River Thames Long Reach

Dartford Tunnel

Jetties

Sewage Works

Chy

Littlebrook Power Sta

Queen Elizabeth 2 Bridge

Canterbury Way

Jetty

Tanks

DA1

Crossways

Pontoon

Littlebrook Nature Park

A3
1 WILKINSON CL
2 MACMILLAN GDNS
3 NIGHTINGALE GR
4 PEPYS CL
5 NORWOOD CT
6 RIVERVIEW

Edisons Pk

Freightliner Terminal

Cemy

A206

UNIVERSITY WAY

Tolls

Temple Hill

Crossways

CROSSWAYS BVD

A226

Prim Sch

RC Prim Sch

DA2

DARTFORD

Stone Crossing

Stone

Lads of the Village (PH)

DA9

B1 KNIGHTS MANOR WAY
2 REDWOOD CT
3 CHURCHILL PK
4 ASPEN CT

Rifle & Pistol Ranges

Archery House

Bow Arrow

Little Brook

Stone House

Prim Sch

Stone Lodge Farm Park

LONDON RD

Horns Cross

Recn Gd

New Town

Bluewater Parkway

A B C D E F

A126, Dagenham (A13)
South Essex STREET ATLAS

HILLTOP RD
Recn Gd
CHARLOTTE PL
FIFTH AVE
HILLCREST AVE
MOTHERWELL WAY
FIRST AVE
SECOND AVE
FOURTH AVE
THIRD AVE
ROOKERY CT
PARK AVE
Sch
THE ROOKERY
ST CLEMENT'S AVE
JUBILEE RD
CREDO WAY
CHAPEL
SANDY LA
WEST THURROCK WAY
A126
PO
LONDON ROAD WEST THURROCK
ESSEX RD
TUNNEL COTTS
SCHOOLFIELD RD
Queenbridge Ind Pk
FOX MANOR WAY
FLINT ST
ELM TERR
West Thurrock
Lyndale Est
MANOR RD
STONENESS RD
MAGNET RD
SOUTH VIEW RD
SOUTHVIEW HTS
Europa Pk
ANGLE RD
OAKLEY CL
PARSONAGE RD
PORTER CL
HAYES CL
HEDLEY AVE
ST CLEMENT'S RD
Factory
OLIVER RD
RM20
MOORE AVE
LONDON RD
THE CHASE
FOXTON RD
PO
CHARLTON ST
EAST ST
DEVONSHIRE RD
GUMLEY RD
Acorn Trad Ctr
LCs
1 BANISTER HO
2 MILL LA
3 PALMERSTON RD
Wks
WOULDHAM RD
HASTINGS CL
WORTHING CL
ASKEWS FARM LA
GRAYLANDS
ROSEBERY RD
CASTLE RD
BELMONT RD
PARKER RD
MEESON'S LA
GROVELANDS WAY
ST CLEMENTS CT
A126
FLORENCE CL
BROMLEY
ENSIGN HO
EAGLE HO
BELL HO
WHARF RD
ARGENT ST
GLADYS DACE
SMITH ST
BEXHILL DR
JOSLING CL
ST LEONARDS
POLEGATE COTTS
The Wharf (PH)
RM17
8
7
77
West Thurrock Marshes
WATSON CL
BURNLEY RD
6
Mast
River Thames
St Clement's or Fiddler's Reach
Broadness Salt Marsh
5
DA11
Stone Ness
76
4
Swanscombe Marshes
Sewage Works
Green Manor Way
Botany Marshes
Channel Tunnel Rail Link (under construction)
DA10

A2
1 JACKSON CL
2 CHAMBERS CL
3 BULLIVANT CL
4 ARGLES CL
5 BORLAND CL
6 CUTTY SARK CT
7 RICHARDSON CL

ELIZA COOK CL 1
SYLVAN MEWS 2
MERIEL WK 3
MONK'S WELL 4
WORCESTER CL 5
LUCAS CRES 6
COLLEGE PL 7
PRIORESS CRES 8
LIVERYMAN WLK 9

CHANDLERS MEWS
LIGHTERMANS WAY
FROBISHER WAY
PIER RD
BRIDGE VIEW
THE BOULEVARD
PARK CLIFF RD
SARA CRES
HIGH ST
CREST VIEW 1
MARINERS CT 2
CHARLES ST
Superstore
B255
STATION RD
QUAY LA
FIDDLERS CL
ARETHUSA PL
SKIPPERS CL
THE AVENUE
WATERMANS WAY
INGRESS GDNS
CAPABILITY WAY
1 COULTER HO
2 THAMESVIEW
3 COLLINGWOOD HO
4 NELSON HO
Lower Rd
3
Northfleet Ind Est
MANOR WAY
PILGRIMS RD
CROSSWAYS BVD
A206
CHARLES ST
WOODLAND WAY
EAGLES RD
ADMIRALS WLK
SMUGGLERS
BEATON CL
MARITIME CL
B255
THE DELL
PARK AVE
BERE CL
HYNDFORD CRES
CALFORD CL
LOVERS LA
Swanscombe Bsns Ctr
Kent Kraft Ind Est
75
KING EDWARD RD
SALTS CL
COWLEY AVE
STEELE AVE
LOW CL
KING EDWARD RD
CASTLE ST
HILLCREST
STATION RD
RIVERVIEW RD
BOWER RD
IVY
Greenhithe for Bluewater
LONDON RD
Liby
PO
PARK TERR
Knockhall Com Prim Sch
ALEXANDER RD
WAKEFIELD RD
DIAL CL
NEWTON HO
INGRESS GDNS
CRAYLANDS SQ
GALLEY HILL RD A226
B259
ALL SAINTS CL
Galley Hill Trad Est
Swanscombe
2
WHITBY CL
RUFFETT CL
SWAN ST
PROVIDENCE ST
A206
Greenhithe
DA9
BREAKNECK HILL
EYNSFORD RD
ABBEY RD
KNOCKHALL RD
KNOCKHALL CHASE
HALE COTTS
THE FLATS
DAVIDSON HO
SWANSCOMBE
CASPIAN WAY
PENTSTEMON DR
PACIFIC CL
ATLANTIC CL
BROOMFIELD RD
RADBURN PL
Recn Gd
ORCHARD RD
ALMA RD
HIGH ST
GROVE
PO
P
THE PARADE
IVY VILLAS
B255
KINGFISHER DR
SANDPIPER CL
SANDERLING
COBHAM TERR
BEAN RD
RESERVOIR CL
THE CRESCENT
LANE AVE
AUSTEN CL
Knockhall
JUBILEE CL
CRAYLANDS LA
KINGSDALE CT
MILTON RD
CHAPEL CT
LEWIS RD
SWEYNE RD
GASSON RD
STANLEY RD
Liby
1 HARMER CT
2 HERBERT RD
3 WARDONA CT
HOPE RD
HARMER ST
ALBERT RD
CHURCH RD
STANHOPE RD
DEIDRE CHAPMAN HO 1
MAYFIELD 2
WALLACE GDNS 3
WRIGHT CL 4
MADDEN CL
AMES RD
PORT AVE
STARBOARD AVE
MOUNTS RD
VALLEY VIEW
VALE
SPRING
WESTERN
HASTED CL
ROSS CL
WHITES CL
PILGRIMS VIEW
GILBERT CL
CHILDS CRES
MILTON ST
TREBBLE RD
MOORE RD
BROAD RD
PARK RD
P
Cemy
EGLINTON RD
CASTLE RD
VERNON RD
SUN RD
1
ELMHURST 1
WHARNECLIFFE HO 2
LORRAINE CT 3
HOMEMEAD 4
Stone Castle
VALLEY GDNS
KEMSLEY CL
ALKERDEN LA
1 BEVANS CL
2 JOHNSONS WAY
MANOR RD
ALAMEIN RD
BODLE AVE
GUNN RD
SWANSCOMBE ST
B259
HEDGE PLACE RD
BLUEWATER PARKWAY
B255
74

58 A B 59 C D 60 E F

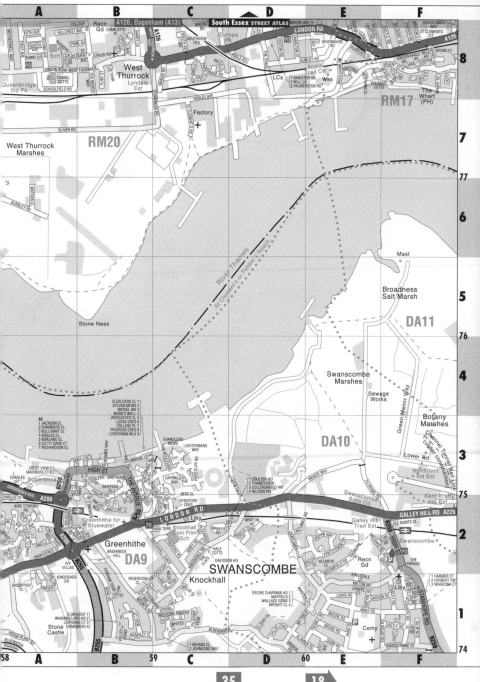

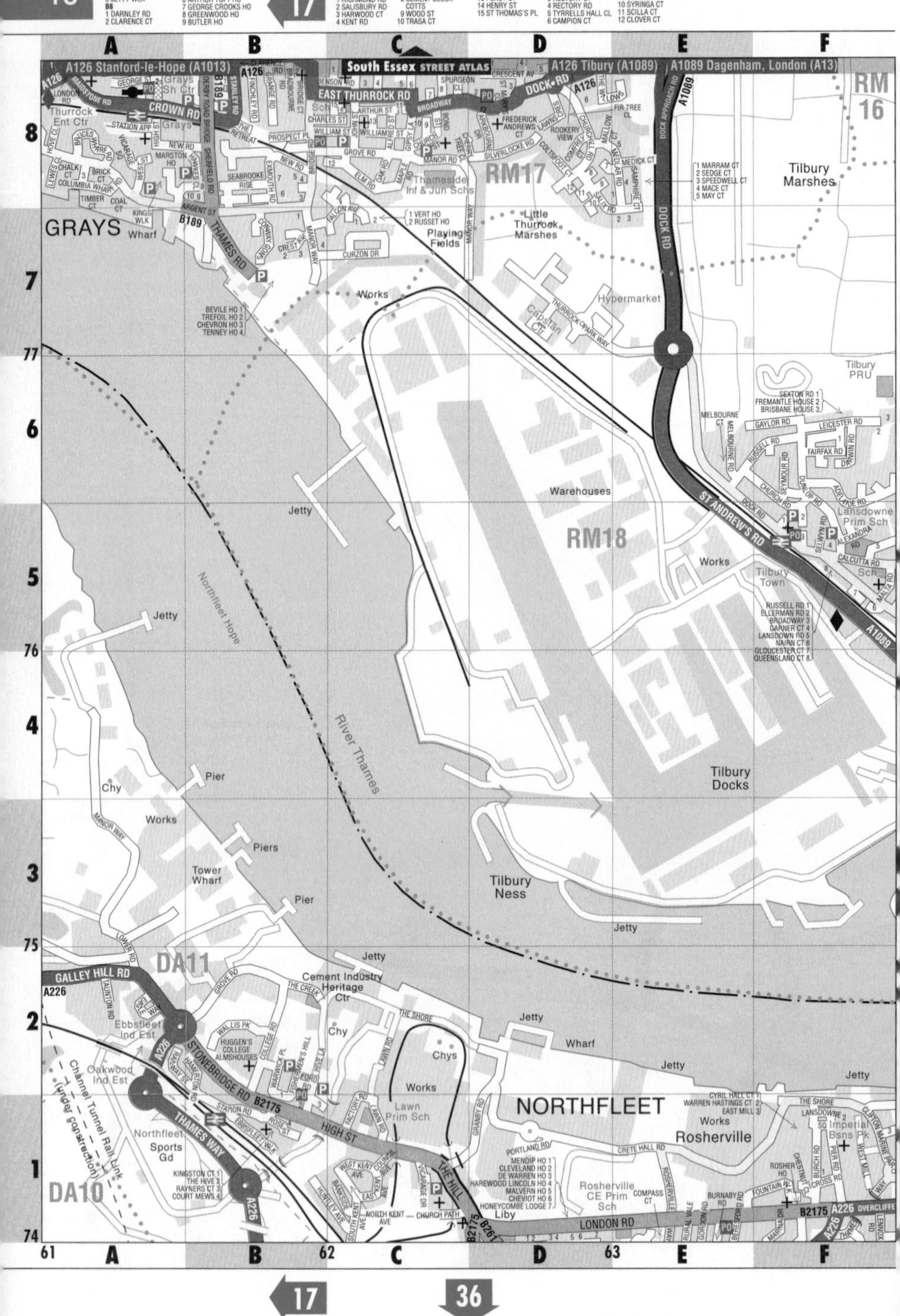

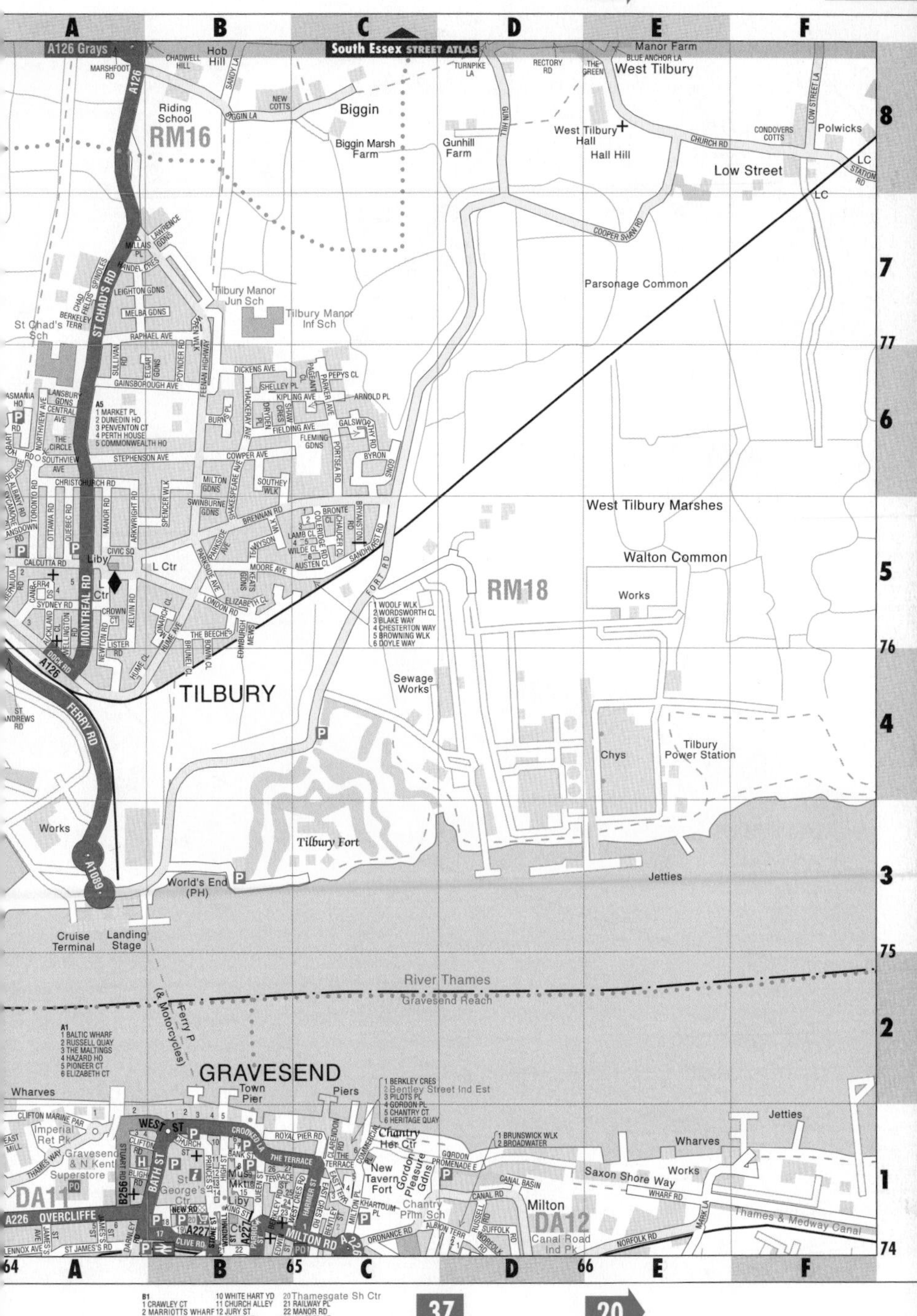

South Essex STREET ATLAS

A126 Grays

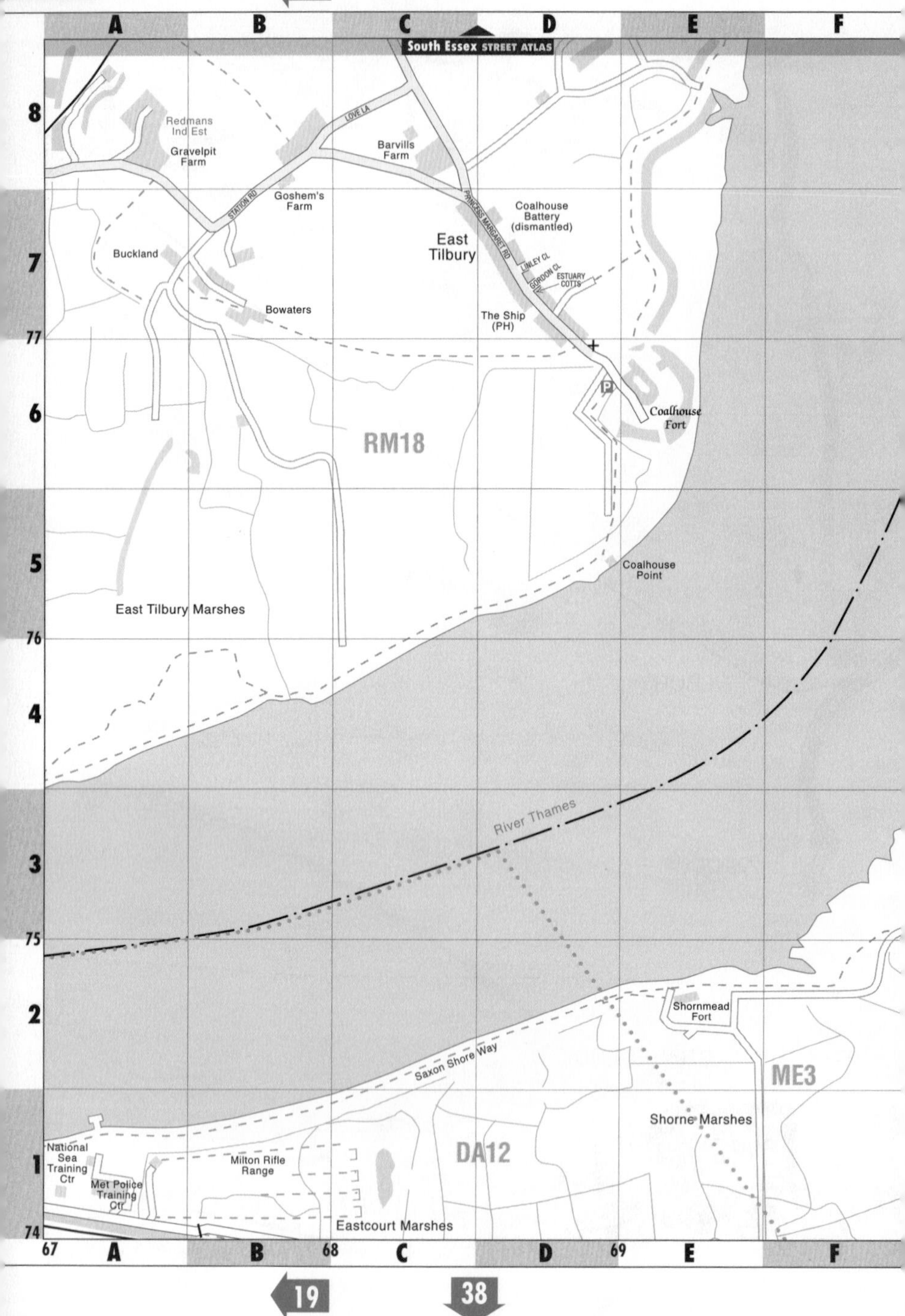

South Essex STREET ATLAS

A   **B**   **C**   **D**   **E**   **F**

8

Redmans
Ind Est

Gravelpit
Farm

Goshem's
Farm

LOVE LA

Barvills
Farm

Coalhouse
Battery
(dismantled)

7

Buckland

East
Tilbury

STATION RD

PRINCESS MARGARET RD

DAILEY CL

GORDON CL

ESTUARY
COTTS

Bowaters

77

The Ship
(PH)

P

6

RM18

Coalhouse
Fort

5

East Tilbury Marshes

Coalhouse
Point

76

4

River Thames

3

75

2

Shornmead
Fort

Saxon Shore Way

ME3

Shorne Marshes

1

National
Sea
Training
Ctr

Met Police
Training
Ctr

Milton Rifle
Range

DA12

Eastcourt Marshes

74

67   **A**   **B**   68   **C**   **D**   69   **E**   **F**

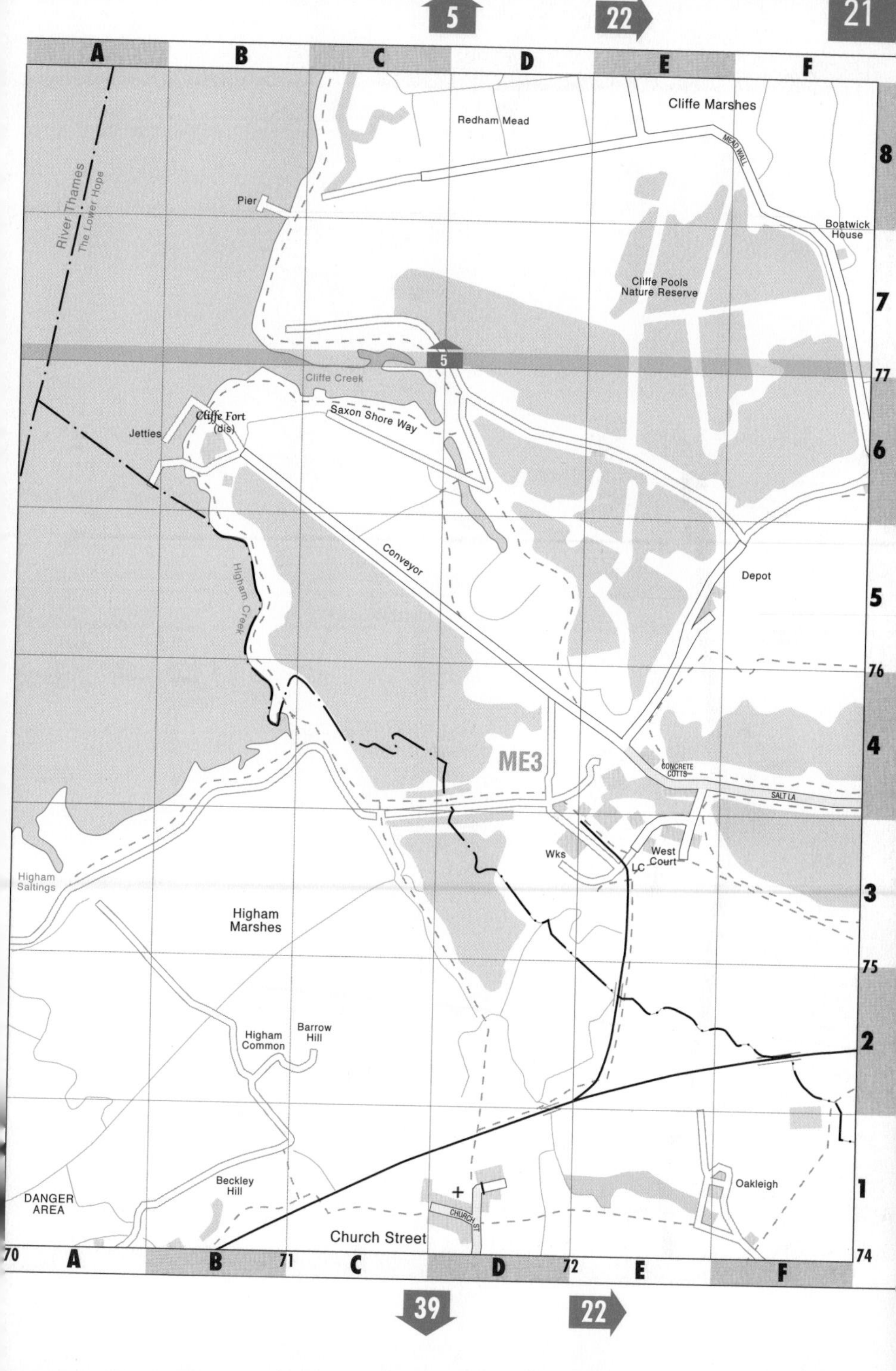

Cliffe Marshes

Redham Mead

Pier

Cliffe Creek

Cliffe Fort
(dis)

Jetties

Saxon Shore Way

Cliffe Pools
Nature Reserve

Boatwick
House

River Thames
The Lower Hope

Higham Creek

Conveyor

Depot

ME3

CONCRETE
COTTS

SALT LA.

Wks

West
Court

LC

Higham
Saltings

Higham
Marshes

Higham
Common

Barrow
Hill

Beckley
Hill

DANGER
AREA

Oakleigh

CHURCH ST

Church Street

21
6

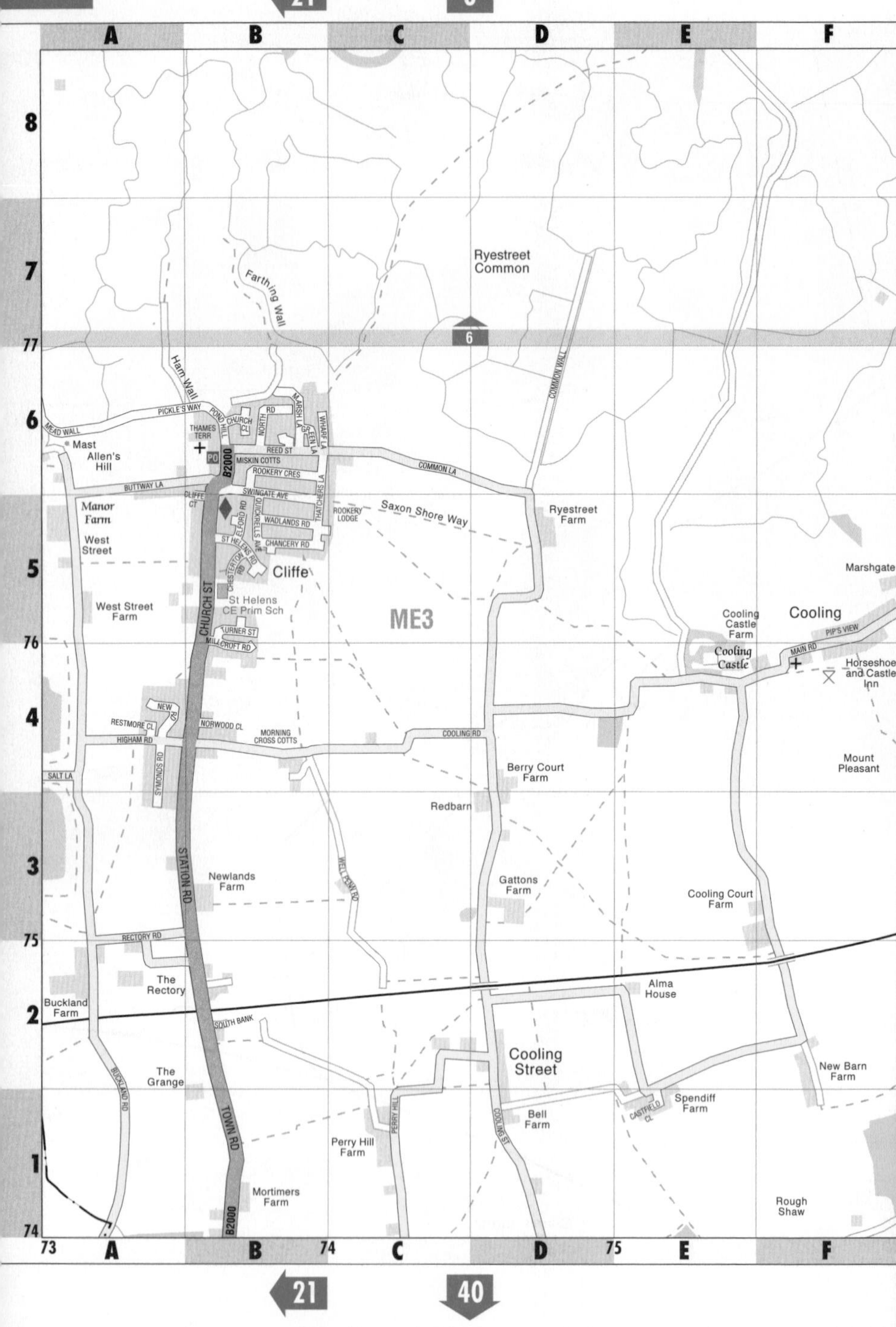
Ryestreet Common
Farthing Wall
Ham Wall
6
COMMON WALL
PICKLE'S WAY
MEAD WALL
Mast
Allen's Hill
THAMES TERR
POND HILL
CHURCH CL
NORTH RD
MARSH LA
GREEN LA
WHARF LA
REED ST
MISKIN COTTS
ROOKERY CRES
B2000
BUTTWAY LA
CLIFFE CT
SWINGATE AVE
THATCHERS LA
WADLANDS RD
CHANCERY RD
ROOKERY LODGE
Saxon Shore Way
COMMON LA
Ryestreet Farm
Manor Farm
West Street
Cliffe
ST HELENS RD
CHESTERTON RD
St Helens CE Prim Sch
ME3
West Street Farm
CHURCH ST
TURNER ST
MILLCROFT RD
NEW RD
RESTMORE CL
NORWOOD CL
HIGHAM RD
MORNING CROSS COTTS
COOLING RD
SALT LA
SYMONDS RD
Marshgate
Cooling
Cooling Castle Farm
Cooling Castle
PIP'S VIEW
MAIN RD
Horseshoe and Castle Inn
Mount Pleasant
Berry Court Farm
Redbarn
Newlands Farm
STATION RD
WELL PENN RD
Gattons Farm
Cooling Court Farm
RECTORY RD
The Rectory
Alma House
Buckland Farm
SOUTH BANK
Cooling Street
New Barn Farm
The Grange
BUCKLAND RD
TOWN RD
PERRY HILL
COOLING ST
Bell Farm
CASTFIELD CL
Spendiff Farm
Perry Hill Farm
Mortimers Farm
Rough Shaw
A B C D E F
8 7 77 6 5 76 4 3 75 2 1 74
73 74 75

21
40

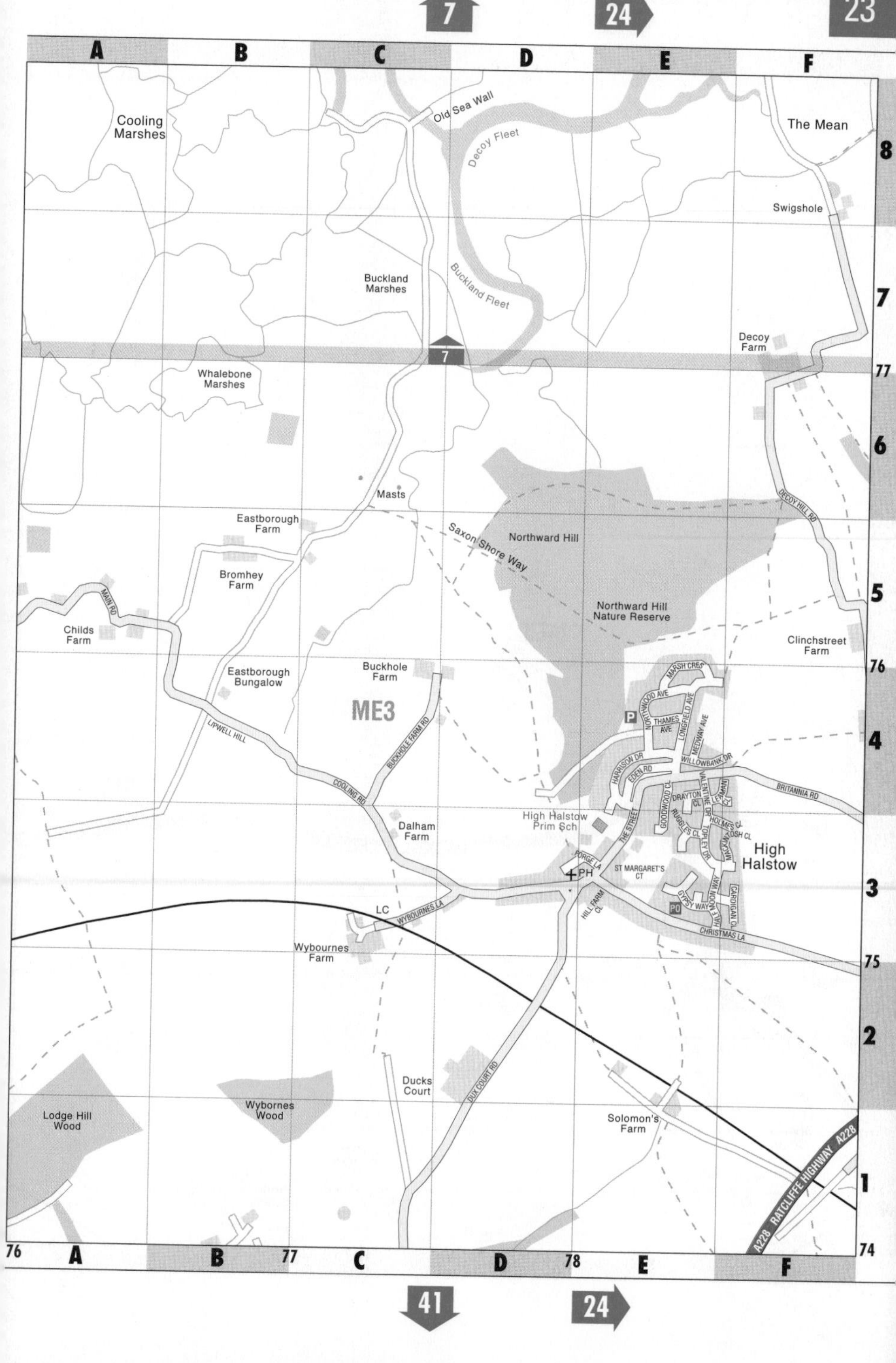
7
24
A
B
C
D
E
F
Cooling Marshes
Old Sea Wall
Decoy Fleet
The Mean
8
Swigshole
Buckland Marshes
Buckland Fleet
7
Decoy Farm
77
Whalebone Marshes
6
Masts
Eastborough Farm
Saxon Shore Way
Northward Hill
DECOY HILL RD
Bromhey Farm
MAIN RD
5
Northward Hill Nature Reserve
Childs Farm
Clinchstreet Farm
76
Buckhole Farm
Eastborough Bungalow
MARSH CRES
NORTHWOOD AVE
LONGFIELD AVE
ME3
THAMES AVE
MEDWAY AVE
BUCKHOLE FARM RD
LIPWELL HILL
4
WILLOWBANK DR
HARRISON DR
EDEN RD
COOLING RD
DRAYTON CL
BRITANNIA RD
GOODWOOD CL
VALENTINE DR
High Halstow Prim Sch
Dalham Farm
RUGGLES CL
TOPLEY DR
HOLMES CL
MACKINTOSH CL
High Halstow
THE STREET
FORGE LA
PH
ST MARGARET'S CT
3
HILL FARM CL
GYPSY WAY
HALF MOON WAY
CARDIGAN CL
LC
WYBOURNES LA
PO
CHRISTMAS LA
Wybournes Farm
75
2
Ducks Court
DUX COURT RD
Lodge Hill Wood
Wybornes Wood
Solomon's Farm
A228
RATCLIFFE HIGHWAY
1
76
A
B
77
C
D
78
E
F
74
41
24

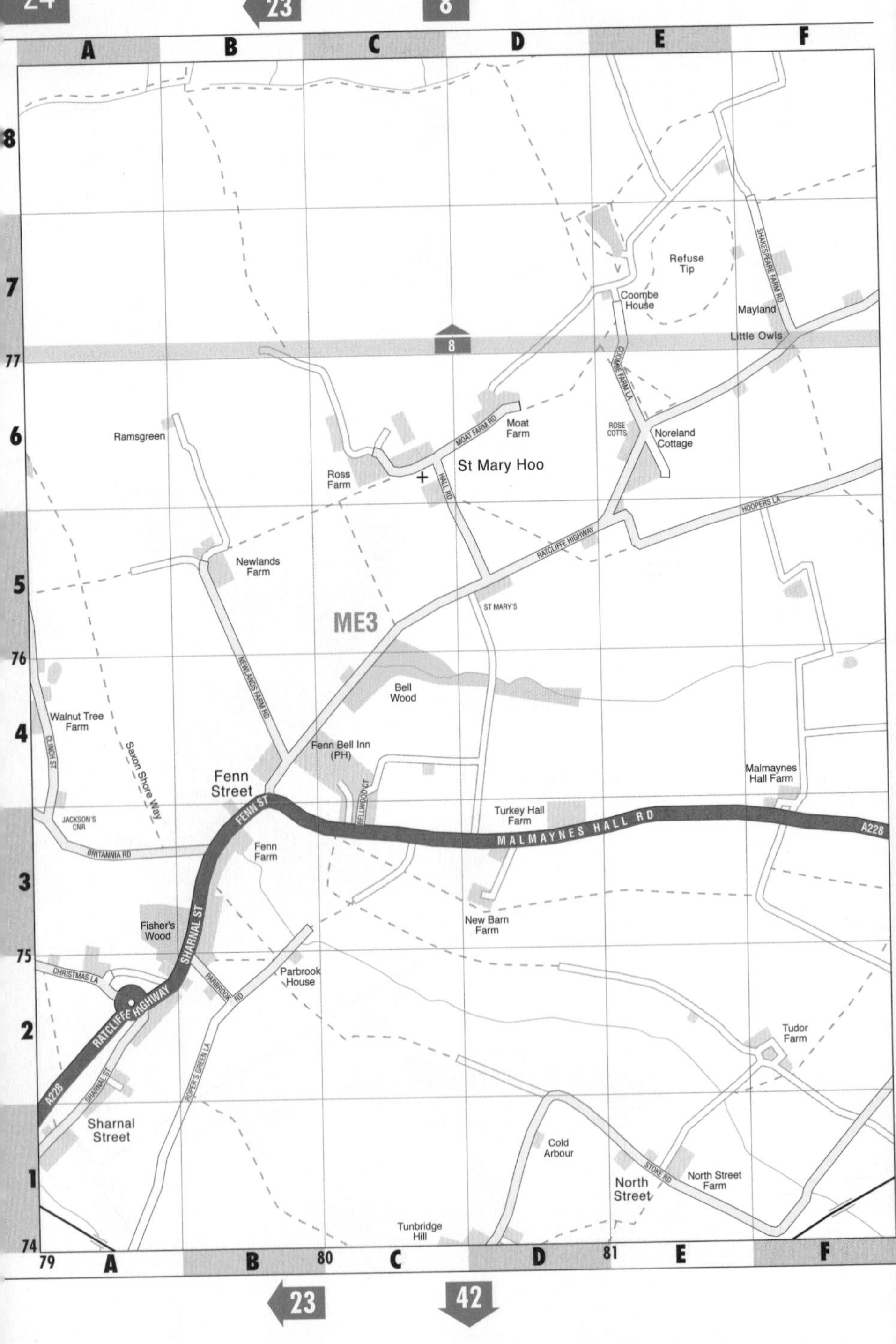
23
8
A
B
C
D
E
F
Refuse Tip
Coombe House
Mayland
Little Owls
SHAKESPEARE FARM RD
COOMBE FARM LA
Ramsgreen
MOAT FARM RD
Moat Farm
ROSE COTTS
Noreland Cottage
St Mary Hoo
Ross Farm
HALL RD
HOOPERS LA
RATCLIFFE HIGHWAY
Newlands Farm
ST MARY'S
ME3
NEWLANDS FARM RD
Bell Wood
Walnut Tree Farm
CLINCH ST
Saxon Shore Way
Fenn Bell Inn (PH)
Fenn Street
BELLWOOD CT
Malmaynes Hall Farm
Turkey Hall Farm
FENN ST
MALMAYNES HALL RD
A228
JACKSON'S CNR
BRITANNIA RD
Fenn Farm
SHARNAL ST
New Barn Farm
Fisher's Wood
CHRISTMAS LA
PARBROOK RD
Parbrook House
RATCLIFFE HIGHWAY
Tudor Farm
ROPER'S GREEN LA
SHARNAL ST
Sharnal Street
Cold Arbour
STOKE RD
North Street Farm
North Street
Tunbridge Hill
8
7
77
6
5
76
4
3
75
2
1
74
79
80
81

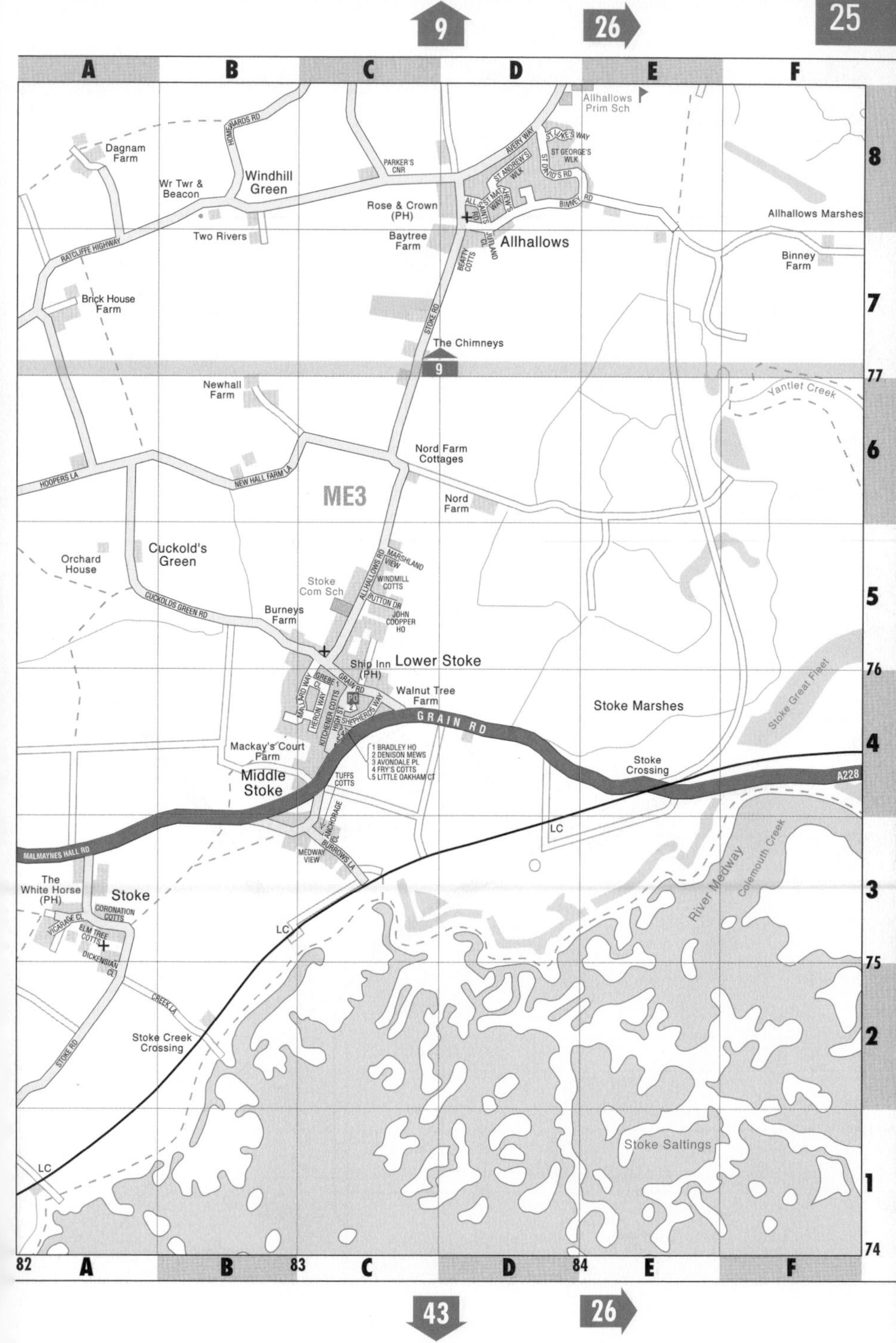
9
26
A
B
C
D
E
F
Allhallows Prim Sch
HOMEWARDS RD
Dagnam Farm
Wr Twr & Beacon
Windhill Green
PARKER'S CNR
AVERY WAY
ST LUKE'S WAY
ST GEORGE'S WLK
ST ANDREW'S WLK
ST DAVID'S RD
Rose & Crown (PH)
BINNEY RD
Allhallows Marshes
Two Rivers
Baytree Farm
Allhallows
JUTLAND CL
BEATTY COTTS
RATCLIFFE HIGHWAY
Binney Farm
Brick House Farm
STOKE RD
The Chimneys
Newhall Farm
Yantlet Creek
Nord Farm Cottages
HOOPERS LA
NEW HALL FARM LA
ME3
Nord Farm
Orchard House
Cuckold's Green
MARSHLAND VIEW
ALLHALLOWS RD
WINDMILL COTTS
Stoke Com Sch
BUTTON DR
JOHN COOPPER HO
CUCKOLDS GREEN RD
Burneys Farm
Ship Inn (PH)
Lower Stoke
Walnut Tree Farm
GRAIN RD
Stoke Marshes
Stoke Great Fleet
MALLARD WAY
GREBE CL
HERON WAY
KITCHENER COTTS
HIGH ST
SHEPHERDS WAY
Mackay's Court Farm
1 BRADLEY HO
2 DENISON MEWS
3 AVONDALE PL
4 FRY'S COTTS
5 LITTLE OAKHAM CT
Stoke Crossing
Middle Stoke
TUFFS COTTS
A228
ANCHORAGE CL
LC
MALMAYNES HALL RD
BURROWS LA
MEDWAY VIEW
River Medway
Colemouth Creek
The White Horse (PH)
Stoke
CORONATION COTTS
VICARAGE CL
ELM TREE COTTS
DICKENSIAN CL
CREEK LA
Stoke Creek Crossing
STOKE RD
Stoke Saltings
8
7
77
6
5
76
4
3
75
2
1
74
82
83
84
43
26

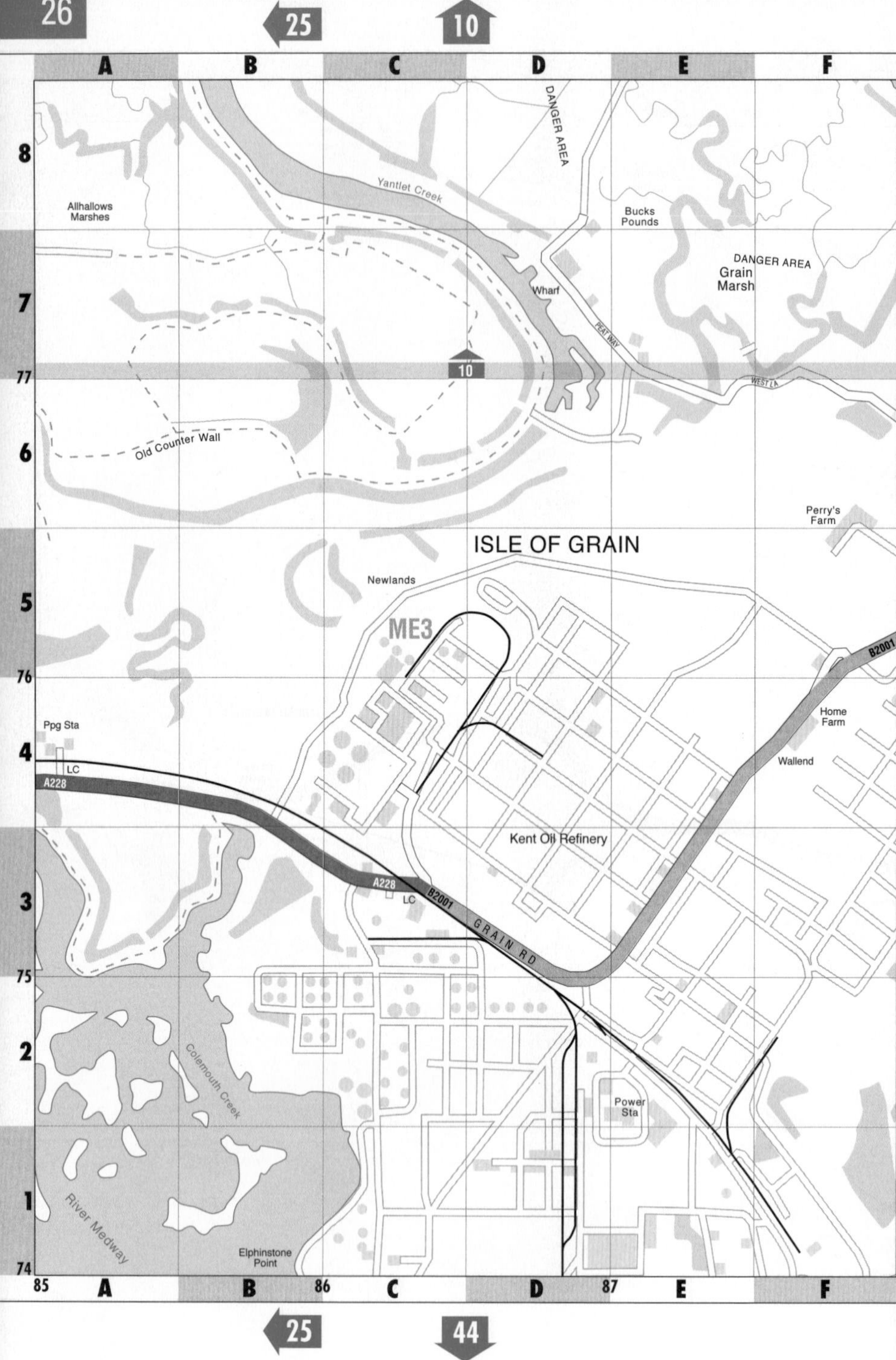

25
10

A B C D E F

8

Yantlet Creek

DANGER AREA

Allhallows
Marshes

Bucks
Pounds

DANGER AREA
Grain
Marsh

7

Wharf

PEN WAY

WEST LA

77

10

6

Old Counter Wall

Perry's
Farm

ISLE OF GRAIN

Newlands

5

ME3

B2001

76

Home
Farm

Ppg Sta

Wallend

4

LC

A228

Kent Oil Refinery

3

A228

LC

B2001

GRAIN RD

75

2

Colemouth Creek

Power
Sta

1

River Medway

Elphinstone
Point

74

85 **A** 86 **B** **C** 87 **D** **E** **F**

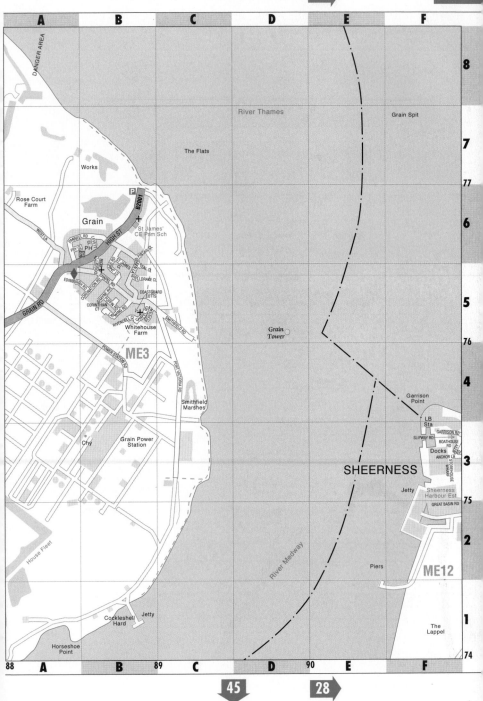

DANGER AREA

River Thames

Grain Spit

The Flats

Works

Rose Court
Farm

Grain

St James'
CE Prim Sch

SMBELL RD
FRY CL
PH
PO

HIGH ST

WEST LA

EDINBURGH RD

GRAIN RD

CHAPEL RD

JAMES
TEAL CL

SHELLDRAKE CL

COASTGUARD
COTTS

CORINTHIAN

COCKLESHELL RD

RIVENDELL CL

SMITHFIELD RD

ME3

POWER STATION RD

PORT VICTORIA RD

Whitehouse
Farm

Grain
Tower

Garrison
Point

Smithfield
Marshes

Chy

Grain Power
Station

LB
Sta

GARRISON RD

SLIPWAY RD

BOATHOUSE
RD

Docks

ANCHOR LA

STOREHOUSE
WHARF

SHEERNESS

Jetty

Sheerness
Harbour Est.

GREAT BASIN RD

House Fleet

River Medway

Piers

ME12

Cockleshell
Hard

Jetty

Horseshoe
Point

The
Lappel

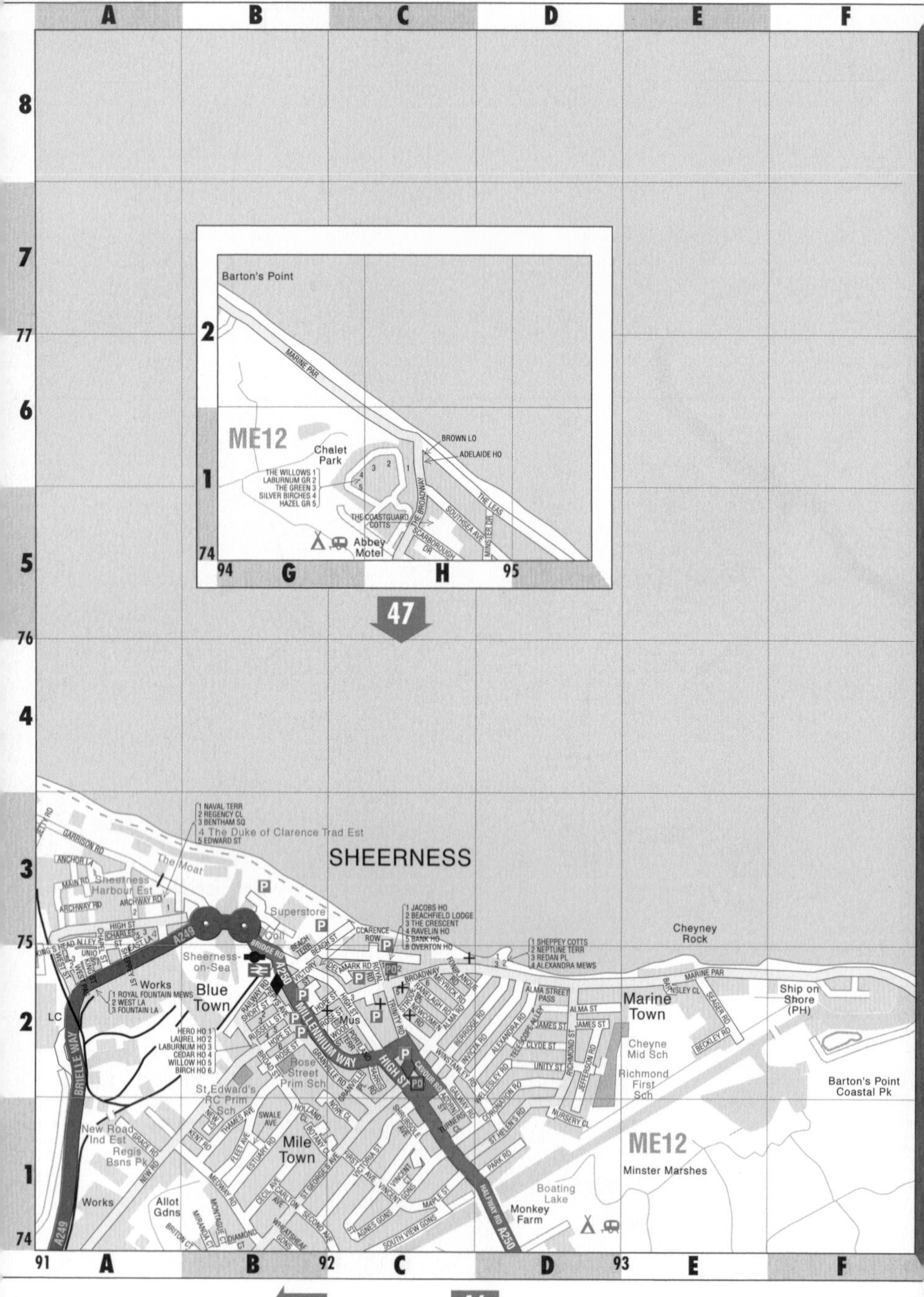

SHEERNESS

ME12

Barton's Point

Chalet Park

THE WILLOWS 1
LABURNUM GR 2
THE GREEN 3
SILVER BIRCHES 4
HAZEL GR 5

THE COASTGUARD COTTS

Abbey Motel

BROWN LO
ADELAIDE HO

47

1 NAVAL TERR
2 REGENCY CL
3 BENTHAM SQ
4 The Duke of Clarence Trad Est
5 EDWARD ST

Sheerness Harbour Est

The Moat

Superstore

Sheerness-on-Sea

Blue Town

1 ROYAL FOUNTAIN MEWS
2 WEST LA
3 FOUNTAIN LA

HERO HO 1
LAUREL HO 2
LABURNUM HO 3
CEDAR HO 4
WILLOW HO 5
BIRCH HO 6

Works

St Edward's RC Prim Sch

Rose Street Prim Sch

New Road Ind Est Regis Bsns Pk

Mile Town

Allot Gdns

1 JACOBS HO
2 BEACHFIELD LODGE
3 THE CRESCENT
4 RAVELIN HO
5 BANK HO
6 OVERTON HO

CLARENCE ROW

1 SHEPPEY COTTS
2 NEPTUNE TERR
3 REDAN PL
4 ALEXANDRA MEWS

Cheyney Rock

Marine Town

Cheyne Mid Sch

Richmond First Sch

Ship on Shore (PH)

Barton's Point Coastal Pk

ME12

Minster Marshes

Boating Lake

Monkey Farm

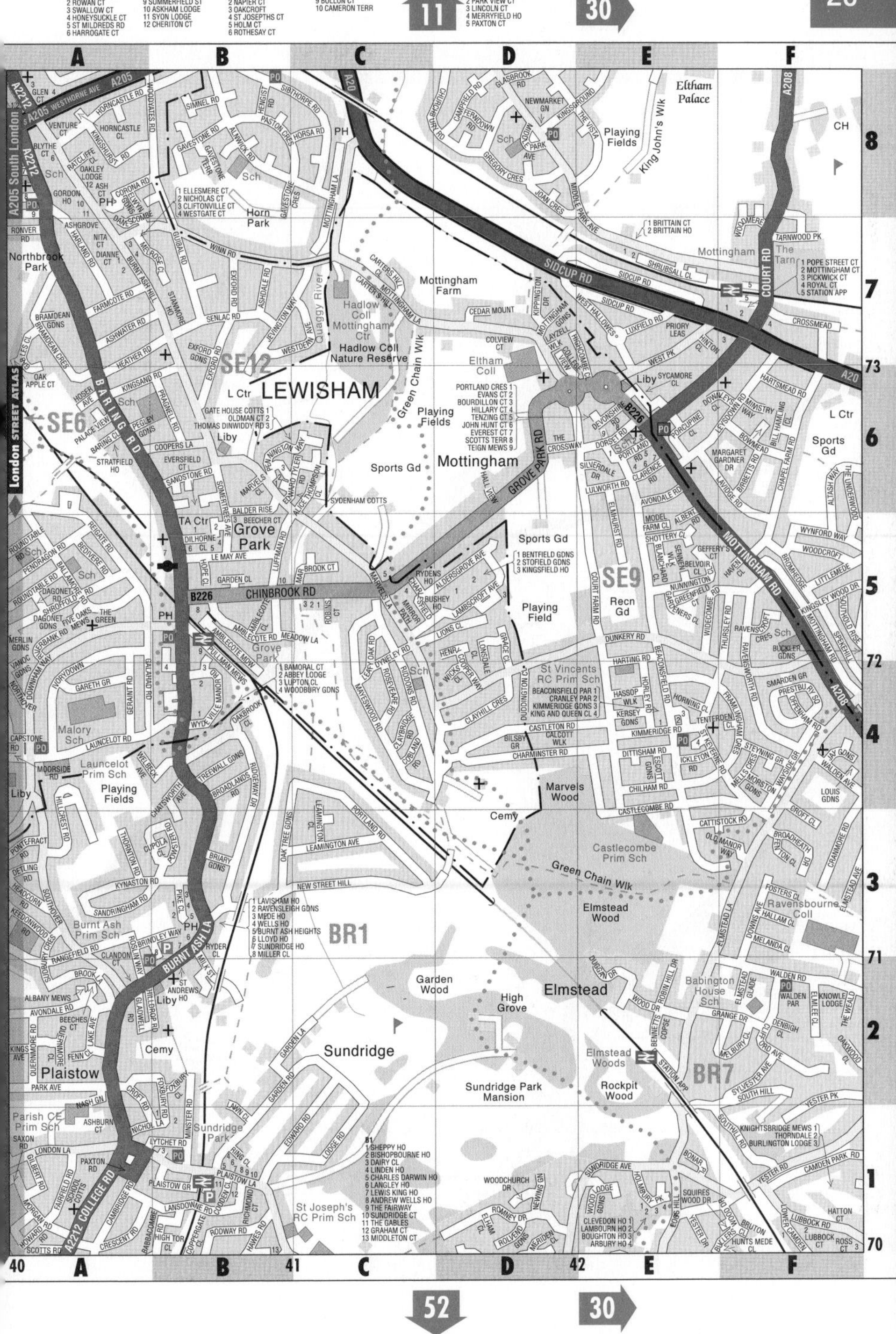

29
12

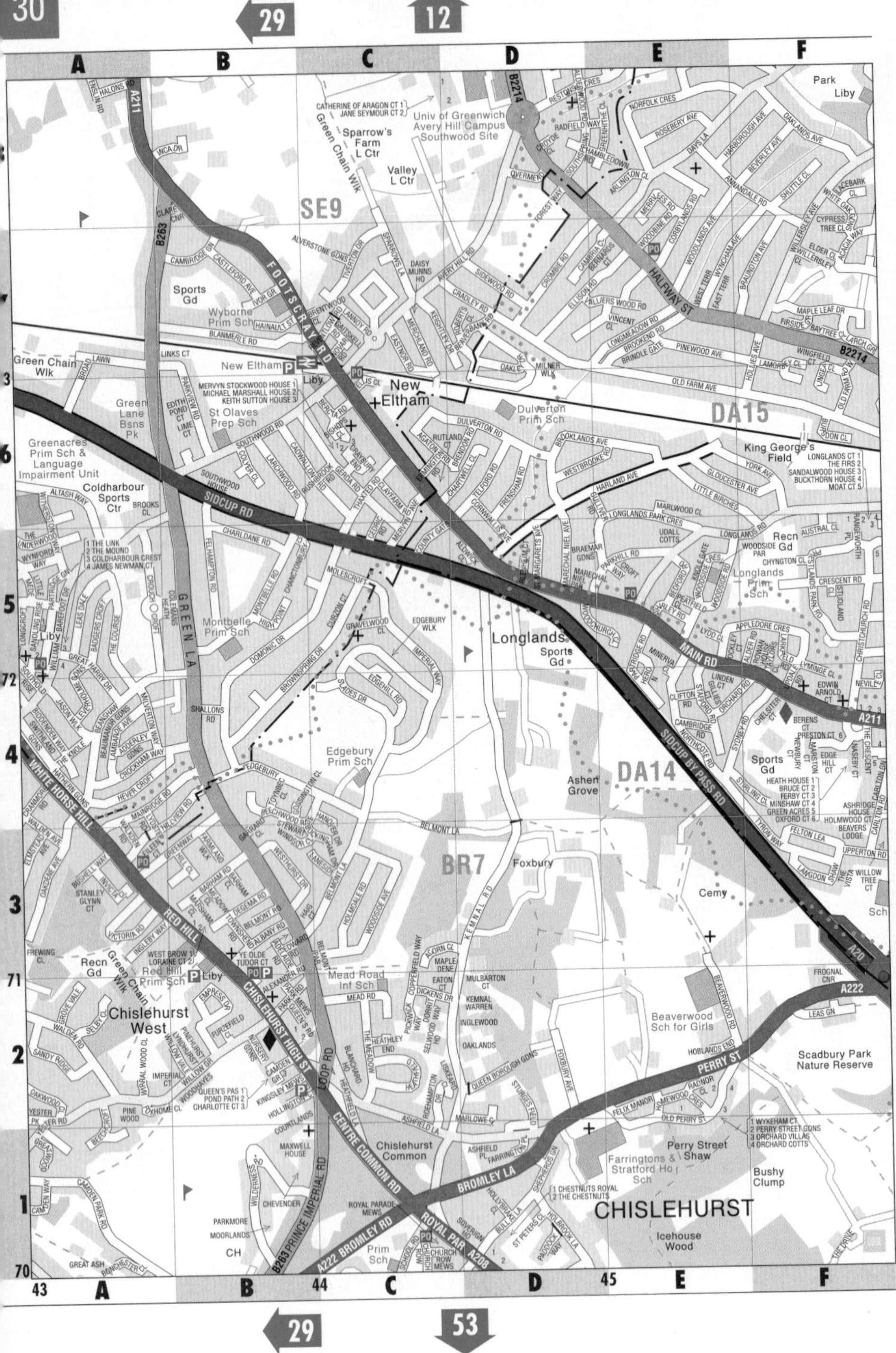
A
B
C
D
E
F
SE9
DA15
DA14
BR7
A211
B263
B2214
A20
A222
A208
FOOTSCRAY RD
SIDCUP RD
GREEN LA
HALFWAY ST
MAIN RD
SIDCUP BY PASS RD
WHITE HORSE HILL
RED HILL
CHISLEHURST HIGH ST
CENTRE COMMON RD
PRINCE IMPERIAL RD
BROMLEY LA
PERRY ST
A222 BROMLEY RD
ROYAL PAR
KEMNAL RD
LOOP RD
Univ of Greenwich
Avery Hill Campus
Southwood Site
Sparrow's
Farm
L Ctr
Valley
L Ctr
Green Chain Wlk
Sports
Gd
Wyborne
Prim Sch
New Eltham
Liby
New
Eltham
Green
Lane
Bsns
Pk
St Olaves
Prep Sch
Greenacres
Prim Sch &
Language
Impairment Unit
Coldharbour
Sports
Ctr
Dulverton
Prim Sch
King George's
Field
Recn
Gd
Longlands
Prim
Sch
Montbelle
Prim Sch
Longlands
Sports
Gd
Edgebury
Prim Sch
Ashen
Grove
Foxbury
Cemy
Mead Road
Inf Sch
Red Hill
Prim Sch
Chislehurst
West
Beaverwood
Sch for Girls
Scadbury Park
Nature Reserve
Chislehurst
Common
Perry Street
Shaw
Farringtons &
Stratford Ho
Sch
Bushy
Clump
CHISLEHURST
Icehouse
Wood
Prim
Sch
CH
Park
Liby
43
44
45
70
71
72

29
53

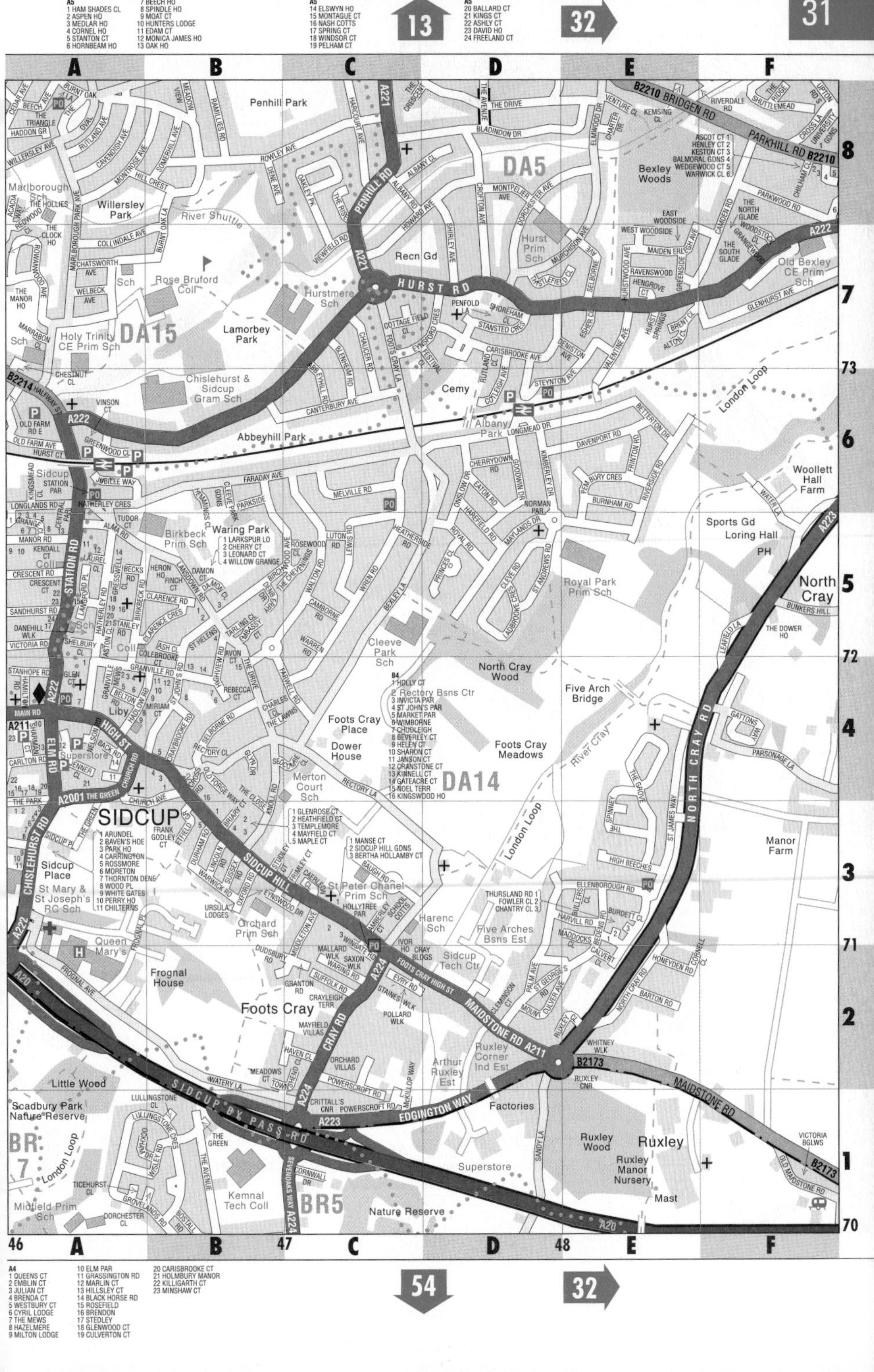

31
A5
1 HAM SHADES CL
2 ASPEN HO
3 MEDLAR HO
4 CORNEL HO
5 STANTON CT
6 HORNBEAM HO
7 BEECH HO
8 SPINDLE HO
9 MOAT CT
10 HUNTERS LODGE
11 EDAM CT
12 MONICA JAMES HO
13 OAK HO
A5
14 ELSWYN HO
15 MONTAGUE CT
16 NASH COTTS
17 SPRING CT
18 WINDSOR CT
19 PELHAM CT
13
A5
20 BALLARD CT
21 KINGS CT
22 ASHLY CT
23 DAVID HO
24 FREELAND CT
32
A
B
C
D
E
F
8
7
73
6
5
72
4
3
71
2
1
70
46
47
48
Penhill Park
DA5
Bexley Woods
Willersley Park
River Shuttle
Rose Bruford Coll
Hurstmere Sch
Recn Gd
Hurst Prim Sch
Old Bexley CE Prim Sch
HURST RD
DA15
Lamorbey Park
Holy Trinity CE Prim Sch
Chislehurst & Sidcup Gram Sch
Cemy
Albany Park
Abbeyhill Park
London Loop
Sidcup
Woollett Hall Farm
Waring Park
1 LARKSPUR LO
2 CHERRY CT
3 LEONARD CT
4 WILLOW GRANGE
Birkbeck Prim Sch
Sports Gd
Loring Hall
PH
Royal Park Prim Sch
North Cray
Cleeve Park Sch
North Cray Wood
B4
1 HOLLY CT
2 Rectory Bsns Ctr
3 INVICTA PAR
4 ST JOHN'S PAR
5 MARKET PAR
6 WIMBORNE
7 CHUDLEIGH
8 BEVERLEY CT
9 HELEN CT
10 SHARON CT
11 JANSON CT
12 CRANSTONE CT
13 KINNELL CT
14 GATEACRE CT
15 NOEL TERR
16 KINGSWOOD HO
Five Arch Bridge
Foots Cray Place
Dower House
Foots Cray Meadows
River Cray
DA14
Merton Court Sch
SIDCUP
1 GLENROSE CT
2 HEATHFIELD CT
3 TEMPLEMORE
4 MAYFIELD CT
5 MAPLE CT
1 MANSE CT
2 SIDCUP HILL GDNS
3 BERTHA HOLLAMBY CT
1 ARUNDEL
2 RAVEN'S HOE
3 PARK HO
4 CARRINGTON
5 ROSSMORE
6 MORETON
7 THORNTON DENE
8 WOOD PL
9 WHITE GATES
10 PERRY HO
11 CHILTERNS
Sidcup Place
St Mary & St Joseph's RC Sch
St Peter Chanel Prim Sch
Manor Farm
NORTH CRAY RD
THURSLAND RD 1
FOWLER CL 2
CHANTRY CL 3
Orchard Prim Sch
Harenc Sch
Five Arches Bsns Est
Queen Mary's
Frognal House
Sidcup Tech Ctr
Foots Cray
MAIDSTONE RD A211
Arthur Ruxley Est
Ruxley Corner Ind Est
Little Wood
Scadbury Park Nature Reserve
SIDCUP BY PASS RD
EDGINGTON WAY
Factories
MAIDSTONE RD
BR7
London Loop
Kemnal Tech Coll
BR5
Superstore
Ruxley Wood
Ruxley
Ruxley Manor Nursery
Mast
Nature Reserve
Midfield Prim Sch
VICTORIA BGLWS
A4
1 QUEENS CT
2 EMBLIN CT
3 JULIAN CT
4 BRENDA CT
5 WESTBURY CT
6 CYRIL LODGE
7 THE MEWS
8 HAZELMERE
9 MILTON LODGE
10 ELM PAR
11 GRASSINGTON RD
12 MARLIN CT
13 HILLSLEY CT
14 BLACK HORSE RD
15 ROSEFIELD
16 BRENDON
17 STEDLEY
18 GLENWOOD CT
19 CULVERTON CT
20 CARISBROOKE CT
21 HOLMBURY MANOR
22 KILLIGARTH CT
23 MINSHAW CT
54
32

31
14

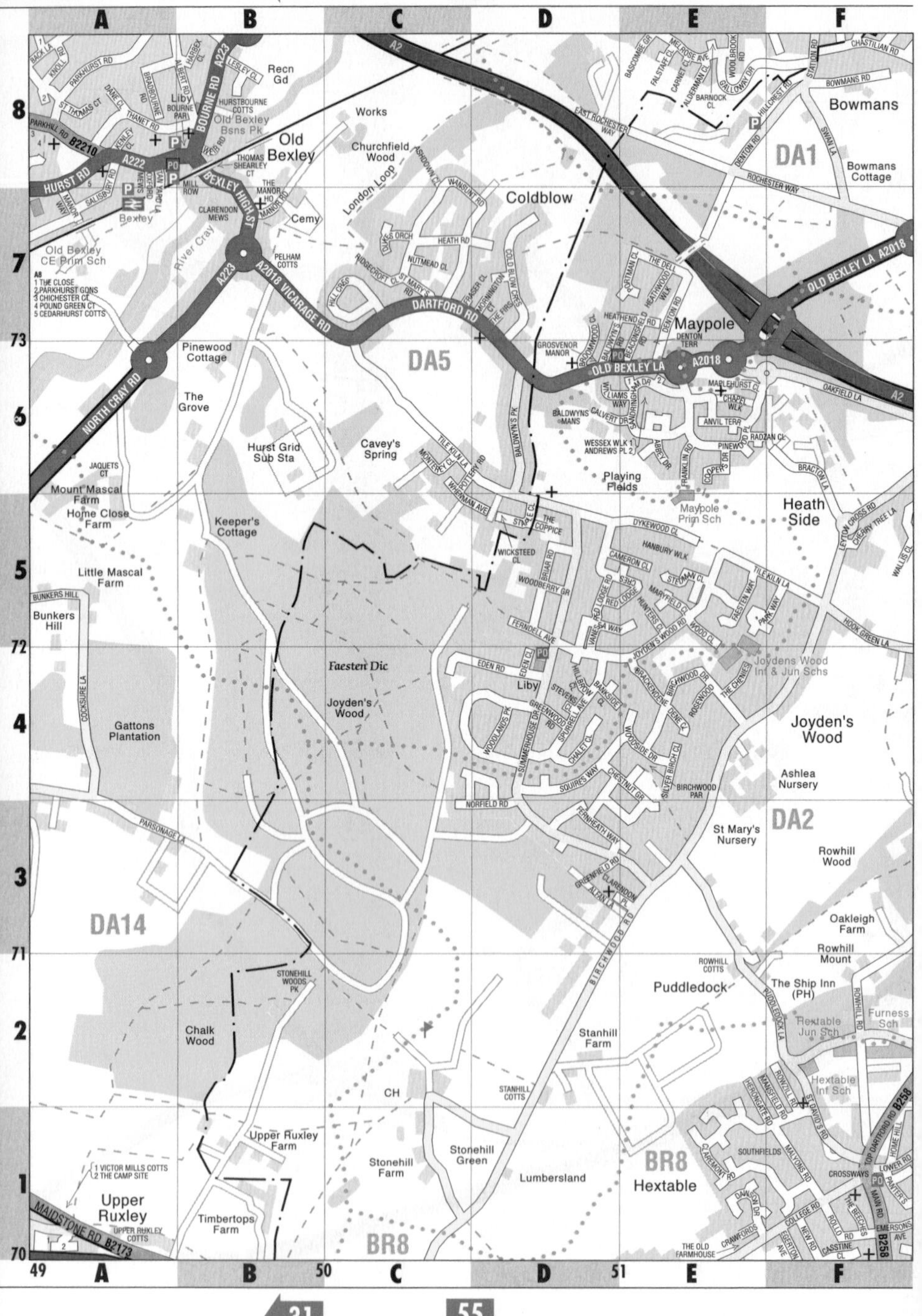
A
B
C
D
E
F
8
7
73
6
5
72
4
3
71
2
1
70
49
50
51
Recn Gd
Works
Old Bexley
Churchfield Wood
London Loop
Coldblow
Bowmans
DA1
Bowmans Cottage
Old Bexley Bsns Pk
Liby
Bexley
Cemy
River Cray
Old Bexley CE Prim Sch
Maypole
DA5
Pinewood Cottage
The Grove
Hurst Grid Sub Sta
Cavey's Spring
Playing Fields
Maypole Prim Sch
Heath Side
Mount Mascal Farm
Home Close Farm
Keeper's Cottage
Little Mascal Farm
Bunkers Hill
Faesten Dic
Joyden's Wood
Joydens Wood Inf & Jun Schs
Gattons Plantation
Ashlea Nursery
St Mary's Nursery
DA2
Rowhill Wood
DA14
Oakleigh Farm
Rowhill Mount
Puddledock
The Ship Inn (PH)
Chalk Wood
Stanhill Farm
Hextable Jun Sch
Furness Sch
Hextable Inf Sch
CH
Upper Ruxley Farm
Stonehill Green
Stonehill Farm
Lumbersland
BR8
Hextable
Upper Ruxley
Timbertops Farm
A2
A223
A222
A2018
B2210
B2173
B258
HURST RD
BOURNE RD
BEXLEY HIGH ST
A2018 VICARAGE RD
DARTFORD RD
NORTH CRAY RD
OLD BEXLEY LA
ROCHESTER WAY
EAST ROCHESTER WAY
PARSONAGE LA
COCKSURE LA
BIRCHWOOD RD
PUDDLEDOCK LA
MAIDSTONE RD
TILE KILN LA
HOOK GREEN LA
SQUIRES WAY
NORFIELD RD
EDEN RD
A8
1 THE CLOSE
2 PARKHURST GDNS
3 CHICHESTER CT
4 POUND GREEN CT
5 CEDARHURST COTTS
WESSEX WLK 1
ANDREWS PL 2
1 VICTOR MILLS COTTS
2 THE CAMP SITE

31
55

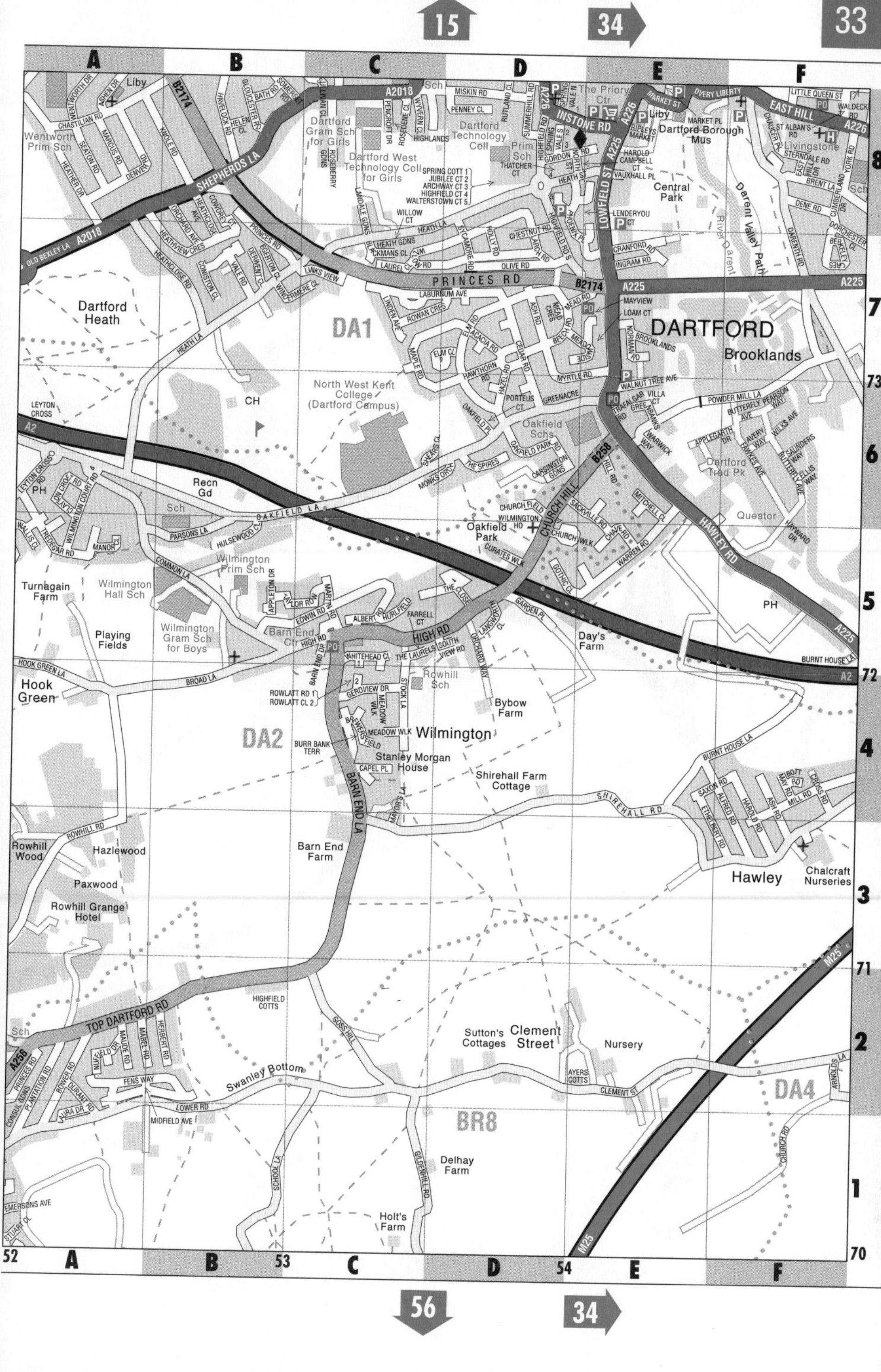
15
34
A
B
C
D
E
F
8
7
73
6
5
72
4
3
71
2
1
70
52
53
54
DARTFORD
Dartford Heath
DA1
DA2
DA4
BR8
Wentworth Prim Sch
Dartford Gram Sch for Girls
Dartford West Technology Coll for Girls
Dartford Technology Coll
Dartford Borough Mus
Central Park
Brooklands
North West Kent College (Dartford Campus)
Oakfield Schs
Dartford Trad Pk
Oakfield Park
Wilmington Prim Sch
Wilmington Hall Sch
Wilmington Gram Sch for Boys
Turnagain Farm
Playing Fields
Hook Green
Recn Gd
Day's Farm
Bybow Farm
Wilmington
Stanley Morgan House
Shirehall Farm Cottage
Barn End Farm
Rowhill Wood
Hazlewood
Paxwood
Rowhill Grange Hotel
Hawley
Chalcraft Nurseries
Sutton's Cottages
Clement Street
Nursery
Delhay Farm
Holt's Farm
Swanley Bottom
Questor
Darent Valley Path
River Darent
The Priory Ctr
Livingstone
Rowhill Sch
A2018
A226
A225
A2
A258
B2174
B258
M25
SHEPHERDS LA
PRINCES RD
LOWFIELD ST
INSTONE RD
EAST HILL
HAWLEY RD
HIGH RD
CHURCH HILL
BARN END LA
TOP DARTFORD RD
OAKFIELD LA
SHIREHALL RD
BURNT HOUSE LA
CLEMENT ST
GOSS HILL
SCHOOL LA
GILDENHILL RD
CHURCH RD
BROAD LA
HOOK GREEN LA
ROWHILL RD
LOWER RD
FENS WAY
MIDFIELD AVE
HEATH LA
COMMON LA
OLD BEXLEY LA

33 16

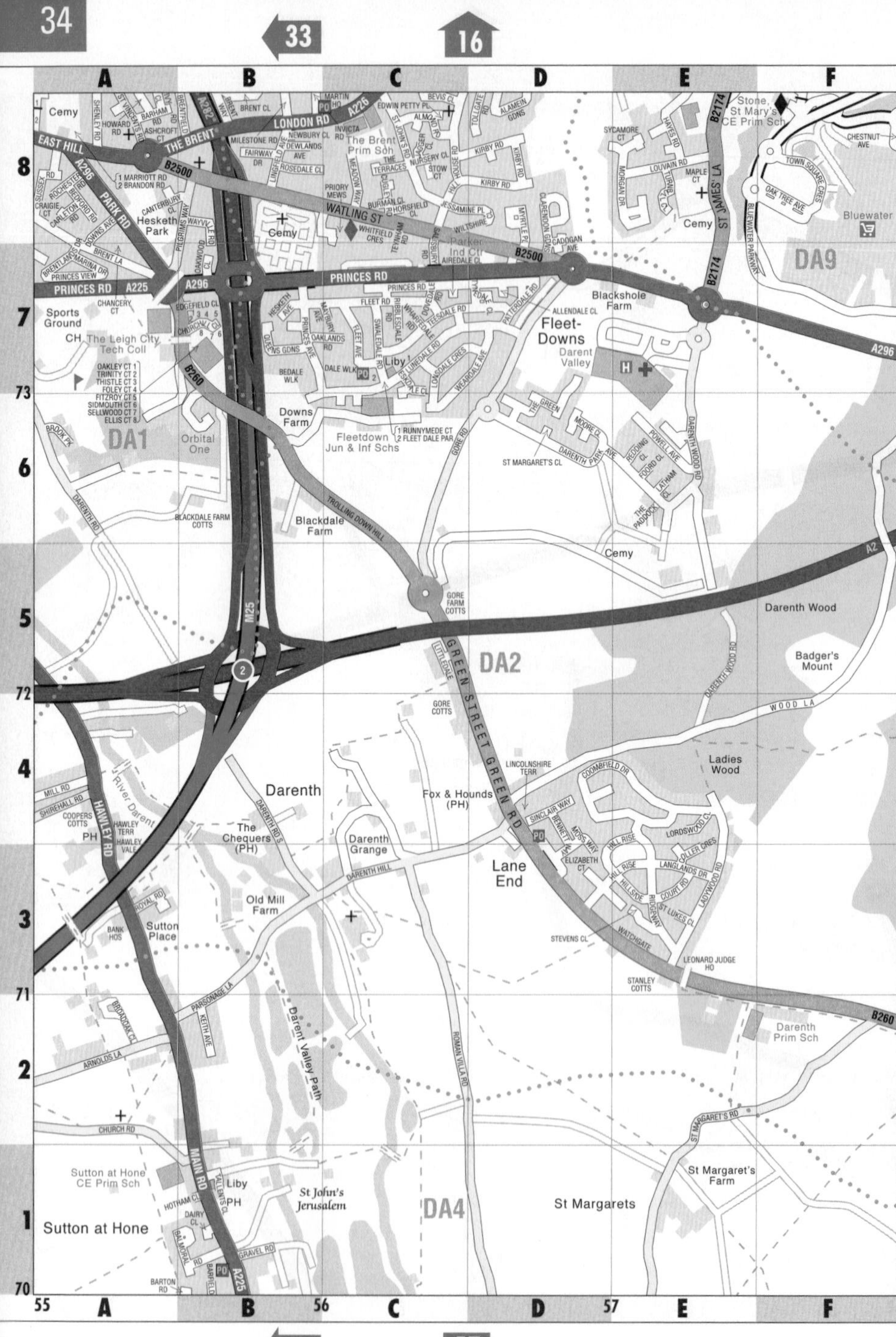

A B C D E F

8

Cemy

EAST HILL

Hesketh Park

THE BRENT

LONDON RD

Milestone Dr

FAIRWAY DR

ROSEDALE CL

The Brent Prim Sch

Priory Mews

Cemy

WATLING ST

WHITFIELD CRES

Stone, St Mary's CE Prim Sch

CHESTNUT AVE

TOWN SQUARE CRES

OAK TREE AVE

Bluewater

DA9

7

Sports Ground

CH The Leigh City Tech Coll

PRINCES RD A225 A296

PRINCES RD

PRINCES RD

Fleet Downs

Darent Valley

Blackshole Farm

B2500

B2774

A296

73

OAKLEY CT 1
TRINITY CT 2
THISTLE CT 3
FOLEY CT 4
FITZROY CT 5
SIDMOUTH CT 6
SELLWOOD CT 7
ELLIS CT 8

DA1

BEDALE WLK

DALE WLK

Liby

Downs Farm

Orbital One

St Margaret's Cl

6

BLACKDALE FARM COTTS

Blackdale Farm

Fleetdown Jun & Inf Schs

1 RUNNYMEDE CT
2 FLEET DALE PAR

THE PADDOCK

Cemy

5

M25

TROLLING DOWN HILL

GORE FARM COTTS

Darenth Wood

A2

DA2

72

GREEN STREET GREEN RD

GORE COTTS

WOOD LA

Badger's Mount

4

MILL RD

SHIREHALL RD

COOPERS COTTS

River Darent

HAWLEY TERR

HAWLEY VALLEY

Darenth

The Chequers (PH)

Fox & Hounds (PH)

LINCOLNSHIRE TERR

COOMBFIELD DR

Ladies Wood

LORDSWOOD

3

PH

HAWLEY RD

BANK HO

Sutton Place

Old Mill Farm

Darenth Grange

DARENTH HILL

Lane End

ELIZABETH

STEVENS CL

WATCHGATE

LEONARD JUDGE HO

71

ARNOLDS LA

BROADWATER CL

PARSONAGE LA

KEITH AVE

Darent Valley Path

ROMAN VILLA RD

STANLEY COTTS

ST MARGARET'S RD

Darenth Prim Sch

B260

2

CHURCH RD

Sutton at Hone CE Prim Sch

Sutton at Hone

MAIN RD

Liby

PH

DAIRY

HOTHAM CL

St John's Jerusalem

DA4

St Margarets

St Margaret's Farm

1

70

BARTON RD

GRAVEL HILL

A225

55 A B 56 C D 57 E F

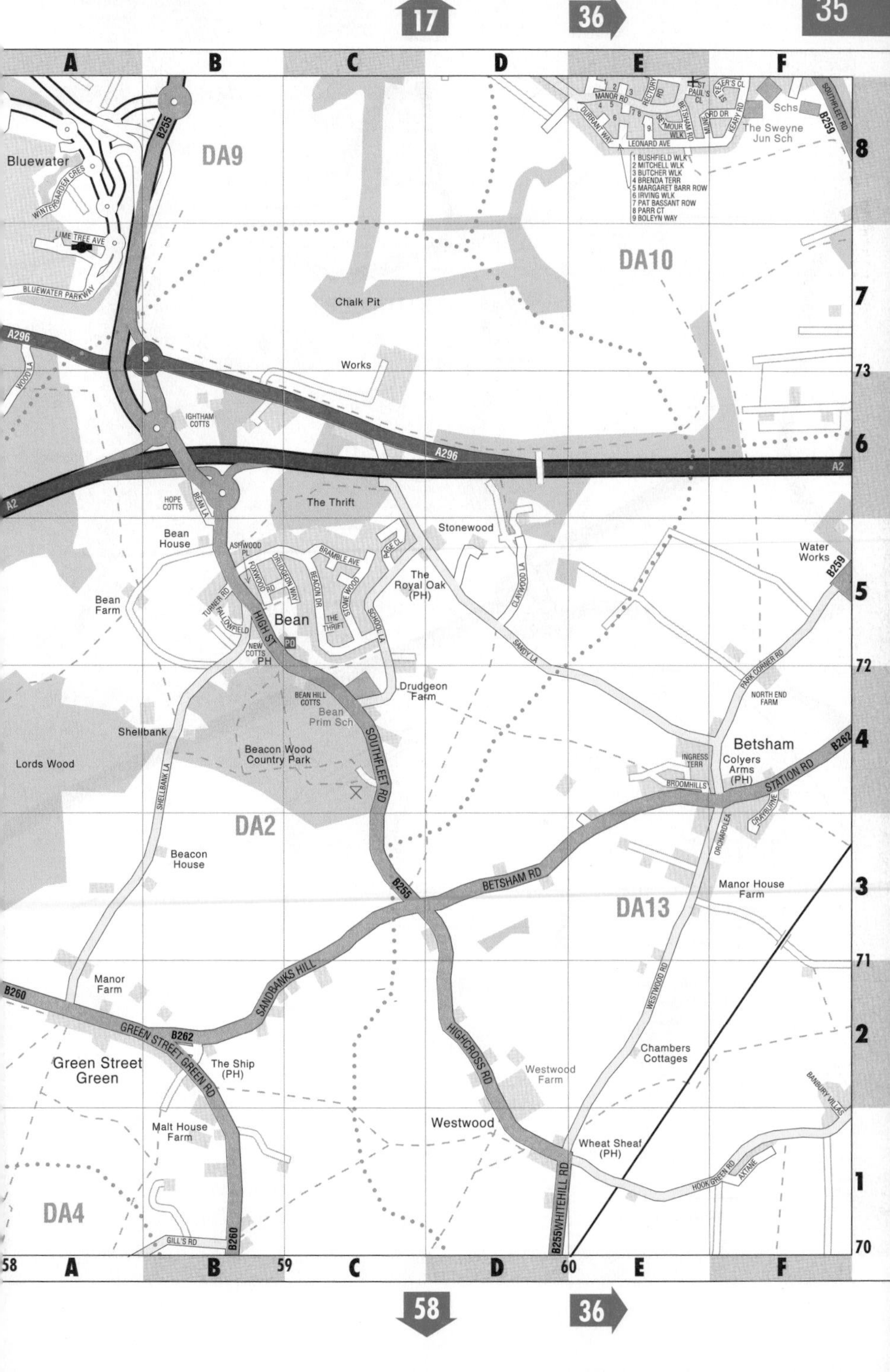

17
36
A
B
C
D
E
F
Bluewater
WINTERGARDEN CRES
LIME TREE AVE
BLUEWATER PARKWAY
DA9
B255
MANOR RD
RECTORY RD
ST PAUL'S CL
ST PETER'S CL
DURRANT WAY
BETSHAM RD
SEYMOUR WLK
MUNFORD DR
KEARY RD
LEONARD AVE
Schs
The Sweyne Jun Sch
SOUTHFLEET RD
B259
1 BUSHFIELD WLK
2 MITCHELL WLK
3 BUTCHER WLK
4 BRENDA TERR
5 MARGARET BARR ROW
6 IRVING WLK
7 PAT BASSANT ROW
8 PARR CT
9 BOLEYN WAY
8
DA10
Chalk Pit
7
A296
Works
WOOD LA
73
IGHTHAM COTTS
A296
6
A2
A2
HOPE COTTS
BEAN LA
The Thrift
Stonewood
Bean House
ASHWOOD PL
FOXWOOD RD
DRUDGEON WAY
BRAMBLE AVE
BEACON DR
STONE WOOD
PAGE CL
The Royal Oak (PH)
CLAYWOOD LA
Water Works
B259
5
Bean Farm
TURNER RD
FALLOWFIELD
HIGH ST
Bean
THE THRIFT
SCHOOL LA
SANDY LA
NEW COTTS
PH
PO
72
PARK CORNER RD
NORTH END FARM
BEAN HILL COTTS
Bean Prim Sch
Drudgeon Farm
SOUTHFLEET RD
Shellbank
Betsham
Lords Wood
Beacon Wood Country Park
INGRESS TERR
Colyers Arms (PH)
4
B262
STATION RD
BROOMHILLS
SHELLBANK LA
DA2
CRAYBURNE
ORCHARDLEA
Beacon House
BETSHAM RD
Manor House Farm
3
B255
DA13
71
WESTWOOD RD
Manor Farm
SANDBANKS HILL
B260
GREEN STREET GREEN RD
B262
2
HIGHCROSS RD
Chambers Cottages
Green Street Green
The Ship (PH)
Westwood Farm
BANBURY VILLAS
Westwood
Malt House Farm
Wheat Sheaf (PH)
WHITEHILL RD
HOOK GREEN RD
AXTANE
1
DA4
GILL'S RD
B260
B255
70
58
A
B
59
C
D
60
E
F
58
36

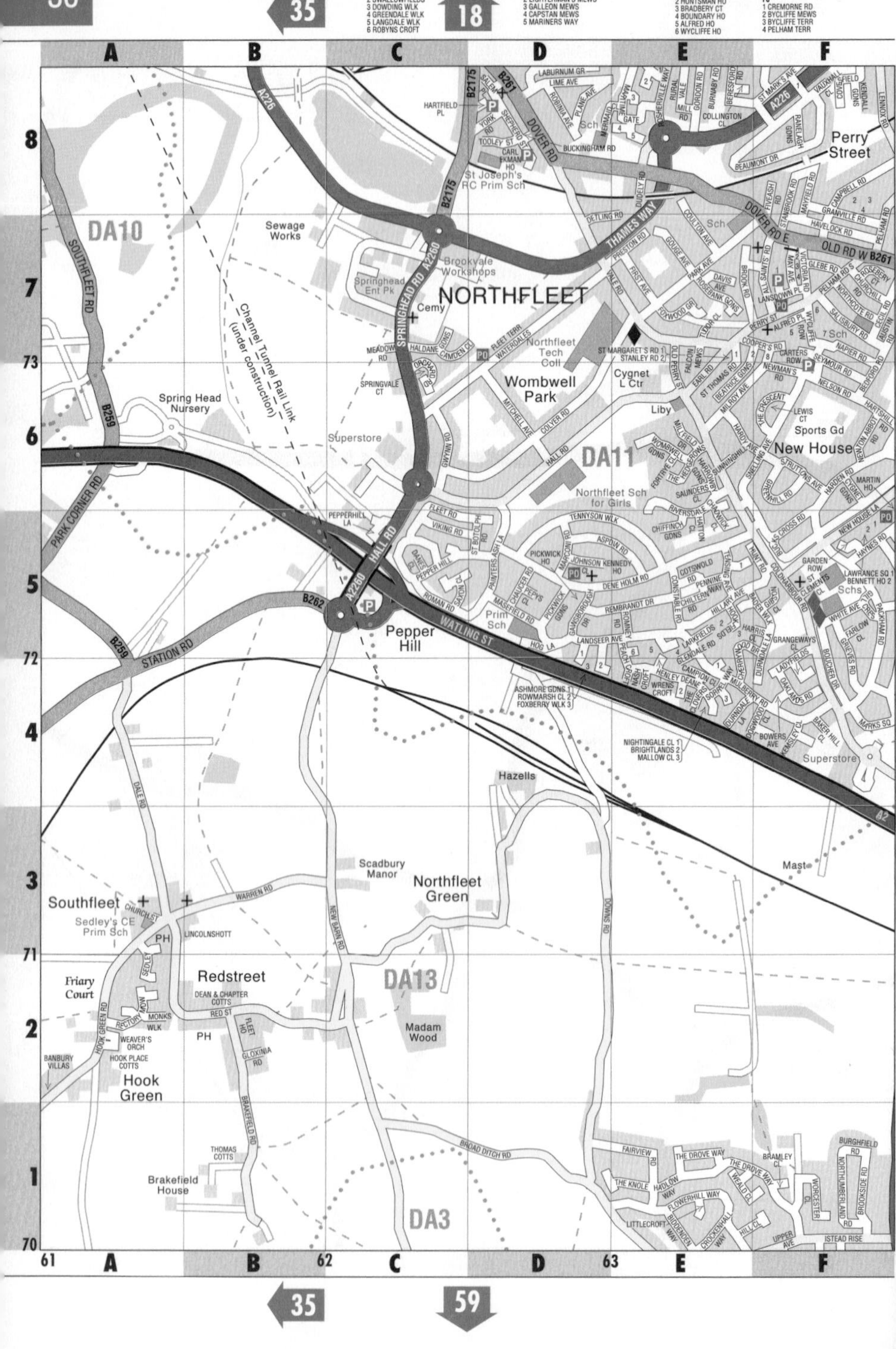

B8
1 CLAREMONT PL
2 LYDIA COTTS
3 VICTORIA AVE
4 WILLIAM HO
5 PETER ST
6 HOME MEAD CL

B8
7 HOMEMEAD
8 GRAVESHAM CT
9 PRESENTATION HO
10 ST ANDREW'S RD
11 FAIRWAYS CT

C8
1 WATERLOO ST
2 CHRIST CHURCH CRES
3 CHRIST CHURCH RD
4 Milton Rd Bsns Pk
5 CUMBERLAND VILLAS

19

D8
1 BRUNSWICK WLK
2 Canal Road Ind Pk
3 ELLERSLIE CT

38

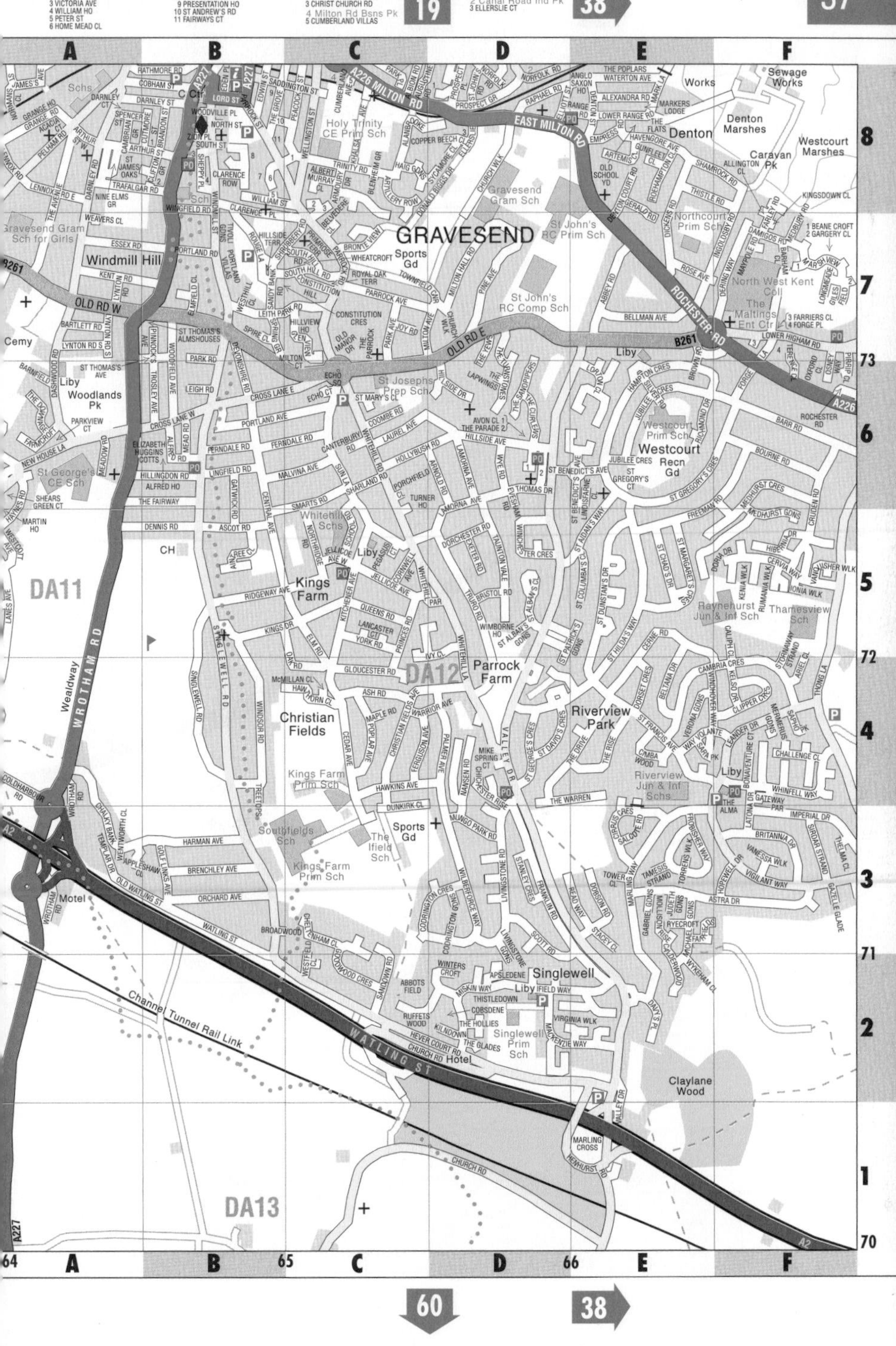

60

38

37
20

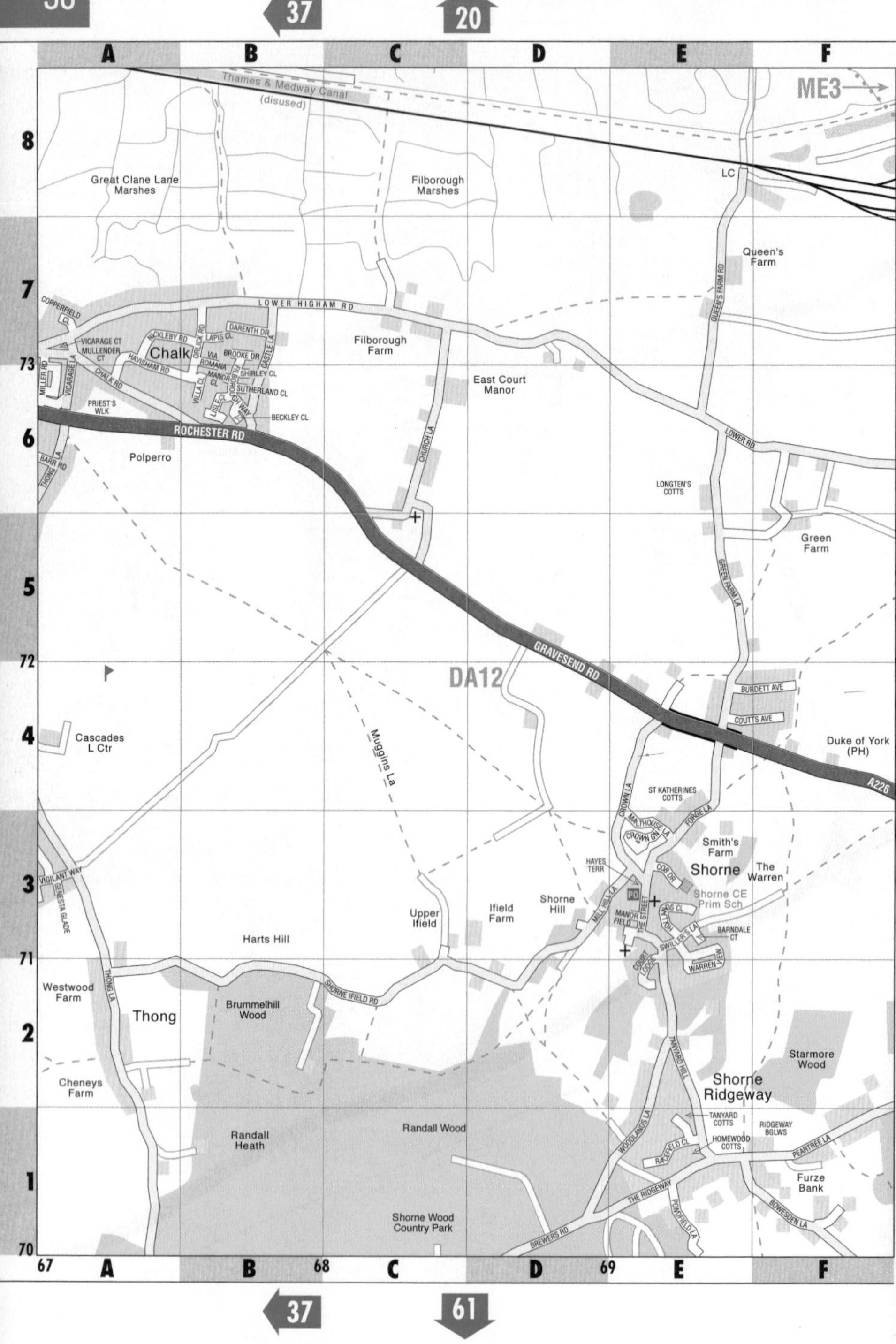
A
B
C
D
E
F
8
7
73
6
5
72
4
3
71
2
1
70
67
68
69
Thames & Medway Canal
(disused)
ME3
LC
Great Clane Lane
Marshes
Filborough
Marshes
Queen's
Farm
QUEEN'S FARM RD
LOWER HIGHAM RD
COPPERFIELD
CL
VICARAGE CT
MULLENDER
CT
NICKLEBY RD
ORLICK RD
LAPIS CL
DARENTH DR
Chalk
VIA
ROMANA
BROOKE DR
CASTLE LA
HAVISHAM RD
MANOR
CL
FILBOROUGH WAY
SHIRLEY CL
SUTHERLAND CL
VILLA CL
LISLE CL
BECKLEY CL
MILLER RD
VICARAGE LA
CHALK RD
PRIEST'S
WLK
ROCHESTER RD
Polperro
BARR RD
THONG LA
Filborough
Farm
East Court
Manor
CHURCH LA
LOWER RD
LONGTEN'S
COTTS
Green
Farm
GREEN FARM LA
GRAVESEND RD
DA12
BURDETT AVE
COUTTS AVE
Duke of York
(PH)
A226
Cascades
L Ctr
Muggins La
ST KATHERINES
COTTS
CROWN LA
MALTHOUSE LA
CROWN GN
FORGE LA
Smith's
Farm
HAYES
TERR
COB DR
Shorne
The
Warren
PO
Shorne CE
Prim Sch
MILL HILL LA
MANOR
FIELD
THE STREET
HOLLANDS CL
BARNDALE
CT
SWILLER'S LA
COURT
LODGE
WARREN VIEW
VIGILANT WAY
GENESTA GLADE
Upper
Ifield
Ifield
Farm
Shorne
Hill
Harts Hill
Westwood
Farm
THONG LA
Thong
SHORNE IFIELD RD
Brummelhill
Wood
Cheneys
Farm
TANYARD HILL
Starmore
Wood
Shorne
Ridgeway
TANYARD
COTTS
RIDGEWAY
BGLWS
HOMEWOOD
COTTS
WOODLANDS LA
RAYFIELD CL
PEARTREE LA
Furze
Bank
Randall
Heath
Randall Wood
THE RIDGEWAY
POMFIELD LA
BOWESDEN LA
BREWERS RD
Shorne Wood
Country Park

37
61

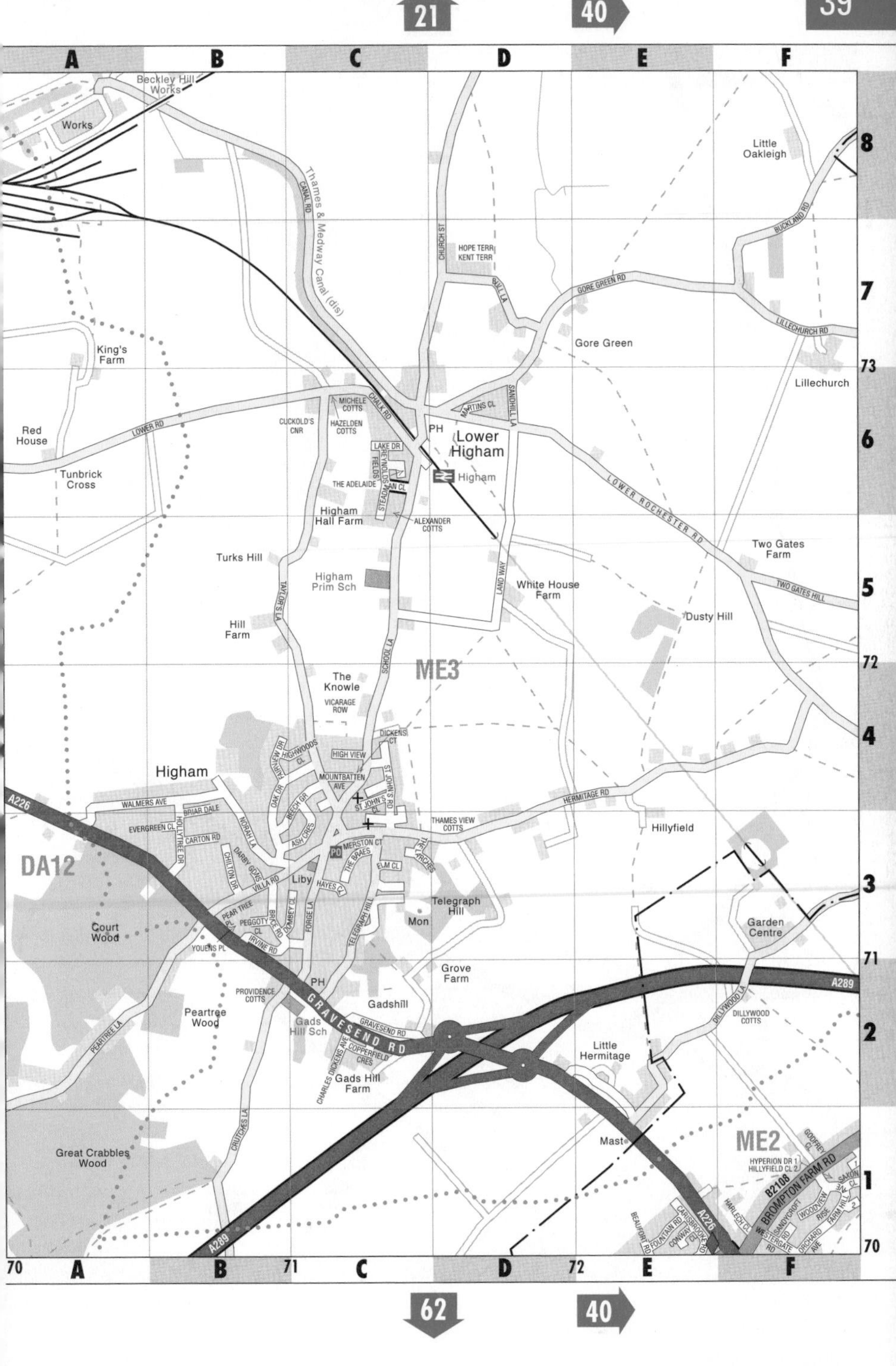
21
40
A
B
C
D
E
F
Beckley Hill Works
Works
Thames & Medway Canal (dis)
CANAL RD
CHURCH ST
HOPE TERR
KENT TERR
BULL LA
GORE GREEN RD
Gore Green
Little Oakleigh
BUCKLAND RD
LILLECHURCH RD
Lillechurch
King's Farm
Red House
LOWER RD
Tunbrick Cross
CUCKOLD'S CNR
MICHELE COTTS
HAZELDEN COTTS
CHALK RD
PH
MARTINS CL
SANDHILL LA
Lower Higham
Higham
LAKE DR
REYNOLDS FIELDS
THE ADELAIDE
STEADMAN CL
LOWER ROCHESTER RD
Higham Hall Farm
ALEXANDER COTTS
Two Gates Farm
TWO GATES HILL
Turks Hill
Higham Prim Sch
TAYLOR'S LA
LAND WAY
White House Farm
Dusty Hill
Hill Farm
SCHOOL LA
ME3
The Knowle
VICARAGE ROW
DICKENS CT
HIGHWOODS CL
FAIRVIEW DR
HIGH VIEW
Higham
MOUNTBATTEN AVE
ST JOHN'S RD
ST JOHN'S CL
OAK DR
BEECH GR
HERMITAGE RD
A226
WALMERS AVE
BRIAR DALE
NORAH LA
EVERGREEN CL
THAMES VIEW COTTS
Hillyfield
HOLLYTREE DR
CARTON RD
ASH CRES
MERSTON CT
THE LARCHES
DA12
CHILTON DR
DARBY GDNS
THE BRAES
ELM CL
VILLA RD
Liby
HAYES CL
Telegraph Hill
PEAR TREE PL
BRICE RD
DOMBEY CL
FORGE LA
TELEGRAPH HILL
Garden Centre
PEGGOTY CL
Mon
Court Wood
IRVINE RD
YOUENS PL
Grove Farm
A289
PH
PROVIDENCE COTTS
Gadshill
GRAVESEND RD
DILLYWOOD LA
DILLYWOOD COTTS
Peartree Wood
Gads Hill Sch
GRAVESEND RD
PEARTREE LA
CHARLES DICKENS AVE
COPPERFIELD CRES
Little Hermitage
Gads Hill Farm
CRUTCHES LA
Mast
ME2
GODFREY CL
Great Crabbles Wood
HYPERION DR 1
HILLYFIELD CL 2
BROMPTON FARM RD
B2108
SAXON
HARLECH CL
SANDYCROFT RD
WOODVIEW RISE
FARM HILL AVE
BEAUFORT RD
FOUNTAIN RD
CARISBROOKE RD
CONWAY CL
A226
WESTERGATE RD
ORCHARD AVE
A289
8
7
73
6
5
72
4
3
71
2
1
70
70
71
72
62
40

39
22

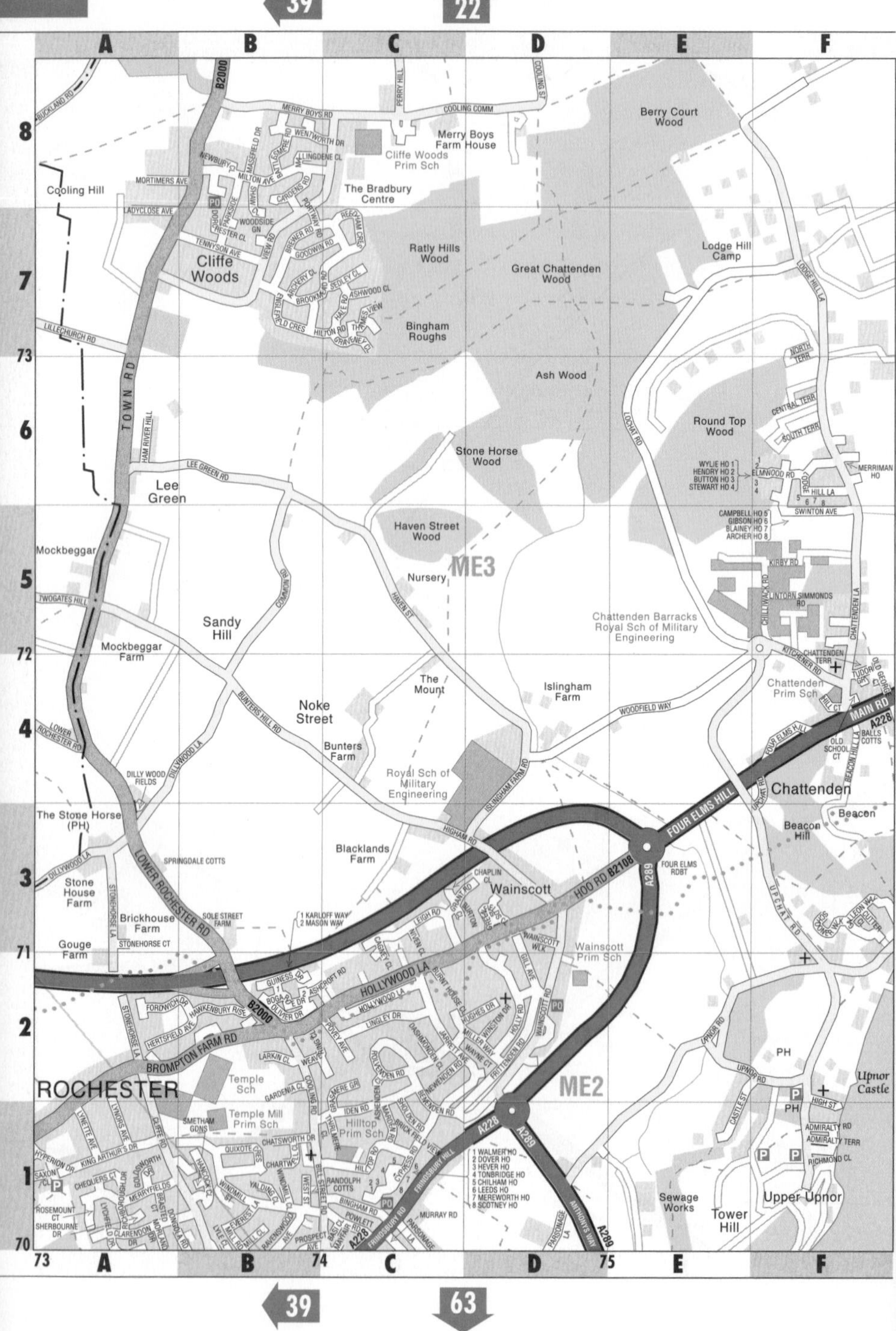
Cooling Hill
Cliffe Woods
Cliffe Woods Prim Sch
The Bradbury Centre
Merry Boys Farm House
Berry Court Wood
Ratly Hills Wood
Great Chattenden Wood
Lodge Hill Camp
Bingham Roughs
Ash Wood
Round Top Wood
Stone Horse Wood
Lee Green
Haven Street Wood
Mockbeggar
ME3
Nursery
Sandy Hill
Mockbeggar Farm
Chattenden Barracks Royal Sch of Military Engineering
The Mount
Islingham Farm
Noke Street
Chattenden Prim Sch
Bunters Farm
Royal Sch of Military Engineering
Chattenden
The Stone Horse (PH)
Beacon Hill
Blacklands Farm
Wainscott
Stone House Farm
Brickhouse Farm
Gouge Farm
Wainscott Prim Sch
ROCHESTER
Temple Sch
Temple Mill Prim Sch
Hilltop Prim Sch
ME2
Upnor Castle
Sewage Works
Tower Hill
Upper Upnor
TOWN RD
LOWER ROCHESTER RD
HOLLYWOOD LA
BROMPTON FARM RD
FOUR ELMS HILL
HOO RD B2108
A289
A228
B2000
MAIN RD

A   B   C   D   E   F

8
7
73
6
5
72
4

3
71
2
1
70

Depot

Deangate Ridge Sports Gd

Deangate Wood

Deangate

CH

Angel Farm

Chattenden Farm

Mill Farm

Caravan Site

Mast

The Windmill (PH)

STREET FARM COTTS

Sundown

Stonebridge

ME3

Hoo St Werburgh

Hoo St Werburgh Prim Sch

The Hundred of Hoo Comp Sch

JENNIFER CT

KINGSNORTH CL

1 NURSERY GDNS
2 BUTT HAW CL

Broad Street

MAIN RD

ST WERBURGH

Lby

ABBOTS COURT RD

HAIG VILLAS

MAIN RD

ARMYTAGE CL 1
EVEREST MEWS 2

WHITE HOUSE CL

CHURCH DISM CL

A228

HOO COMM BROADWOOD

ELM AVE

Cockham Farm

Saxon Shore Way

Hoo Lodge

VICARAGE LA

ME2

Saxon Shore Way

Cockham Wood

Gull Down Plantation

Hoo Marina Park

Works

P

Lower Upnor

Pier

GALLEON WAY

OAK CL

WILLOW AVE
HAZEL AVE
DAMSON DR

CYPRESS AVE 1
CLOVER RD 2

Hoo Marina

Upnor Reach

Pier

River Medway

ME4

EGRET CL 1
PARTRIDGE DR 2

St Mary's Island CE Prim Sch

MEADOWSWEET VIEW

WOODRUSH PL

THE PINNACLES

Finsborough Ness

ME3

Hoo Salt Marsh

Marina

REDSHANK

THE CRESCENT

STONES ROBT

HAVEN WAY 1
THE WHIMBRELS 2
WILLOWHERB CL 3
DEWBERRY CL 4

St Mary's Island

Short Reach

RIVERSIDE EAST RD

Hoo Ness

ME7

PADDOCK HEAD RD

41
24

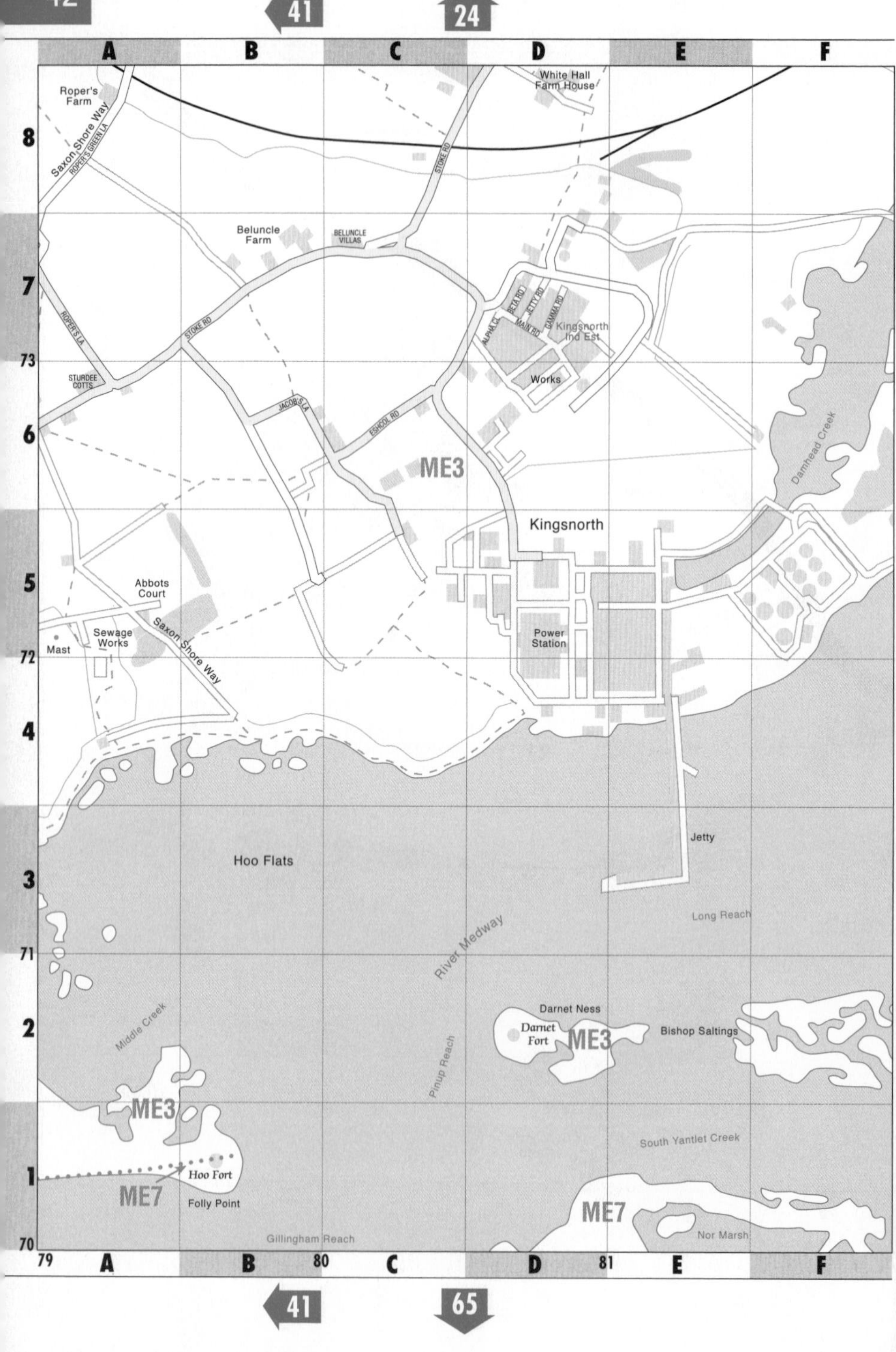
A
B
C
D
E
F
8
7
73
6
5
72
4
3
71
2
1
70
79
80
81
Roper's Farm
Saxon Shore Way
ROPER'S GREEN LA
STOKE RD
White Hall Farm House
Beluncle Farm
BELUNCLE VILLAS
ROPER'S LA
STURDEE COTTS
ALPHA CL
BETA RD
JETTY RD
GAMMA RD
MAIN RD
Kingsnorth Ind Est
Works
JACOB'S LA
ESCOL RD
ME3
Damhead Creek
Kingsnorth
Abbots Court
Sewage Works
Mast
Saxon Shore Way
Power Station
Jetty
Hoo Flats
Long Reach
River Medway
Darnet Ness
Darnet Fort
ME3
Bishop Saltings
Middle Creek
Pinup Reach
ME3
South Yantlet Creek
Hoo Fort
ME7
Folly Point
ME7
Nor Marsh
Gillingham Reach

41
65

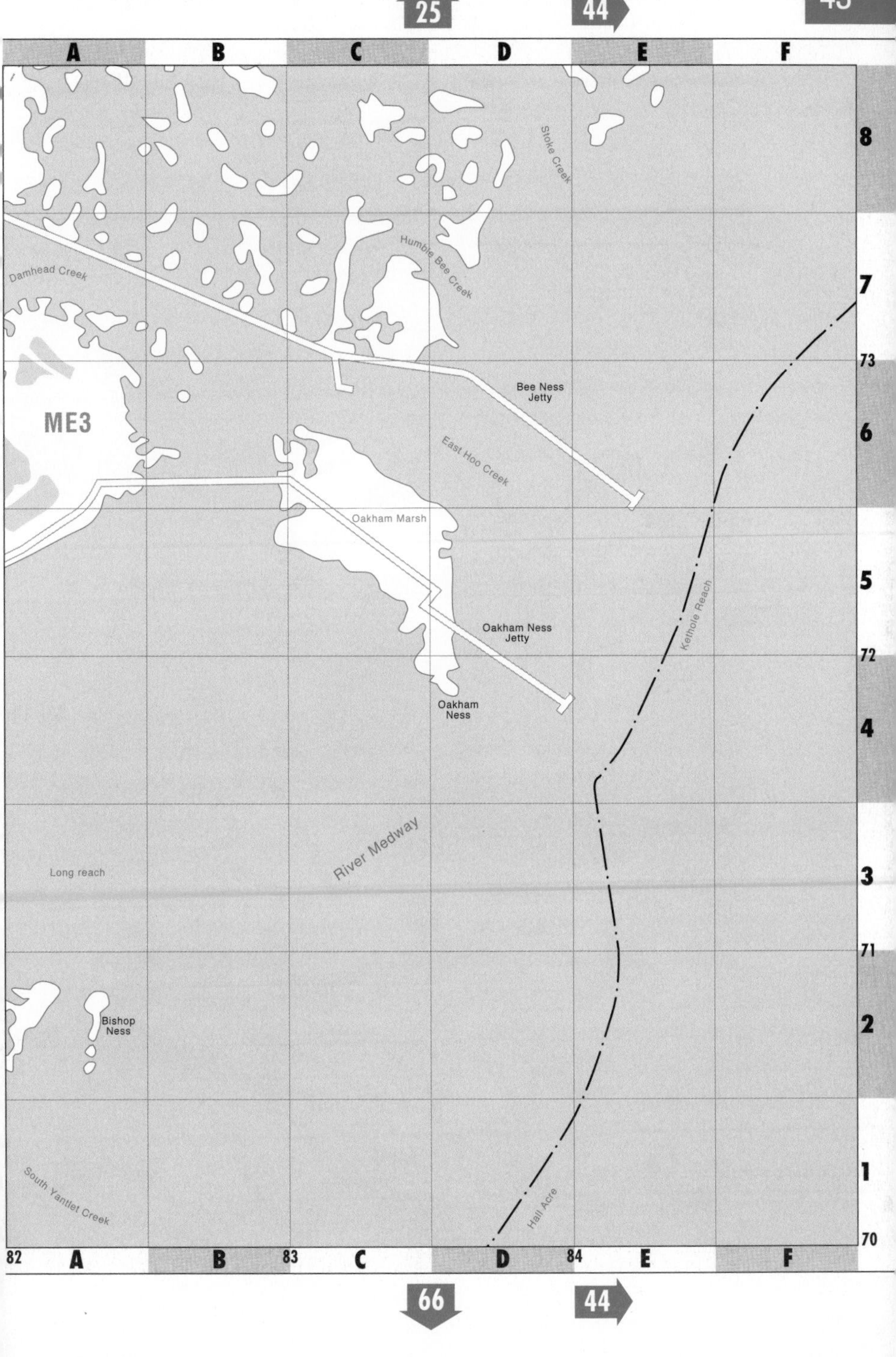

A   B   C   D   E   F

8

Stoke Creek

7

Damhead Creek

Humbig Bee Creek

73

Bee Ness
Jetty

ME3

6

East Hoo Creek

Oakham Marsh

5

72

Oakham Ness
Jetty

Kethole Reach

Oakham
Ness

4

River Medway

Long reach

3

71

Bishop
Ness

2

1

South Yantlet Creek

Hall Acre

70

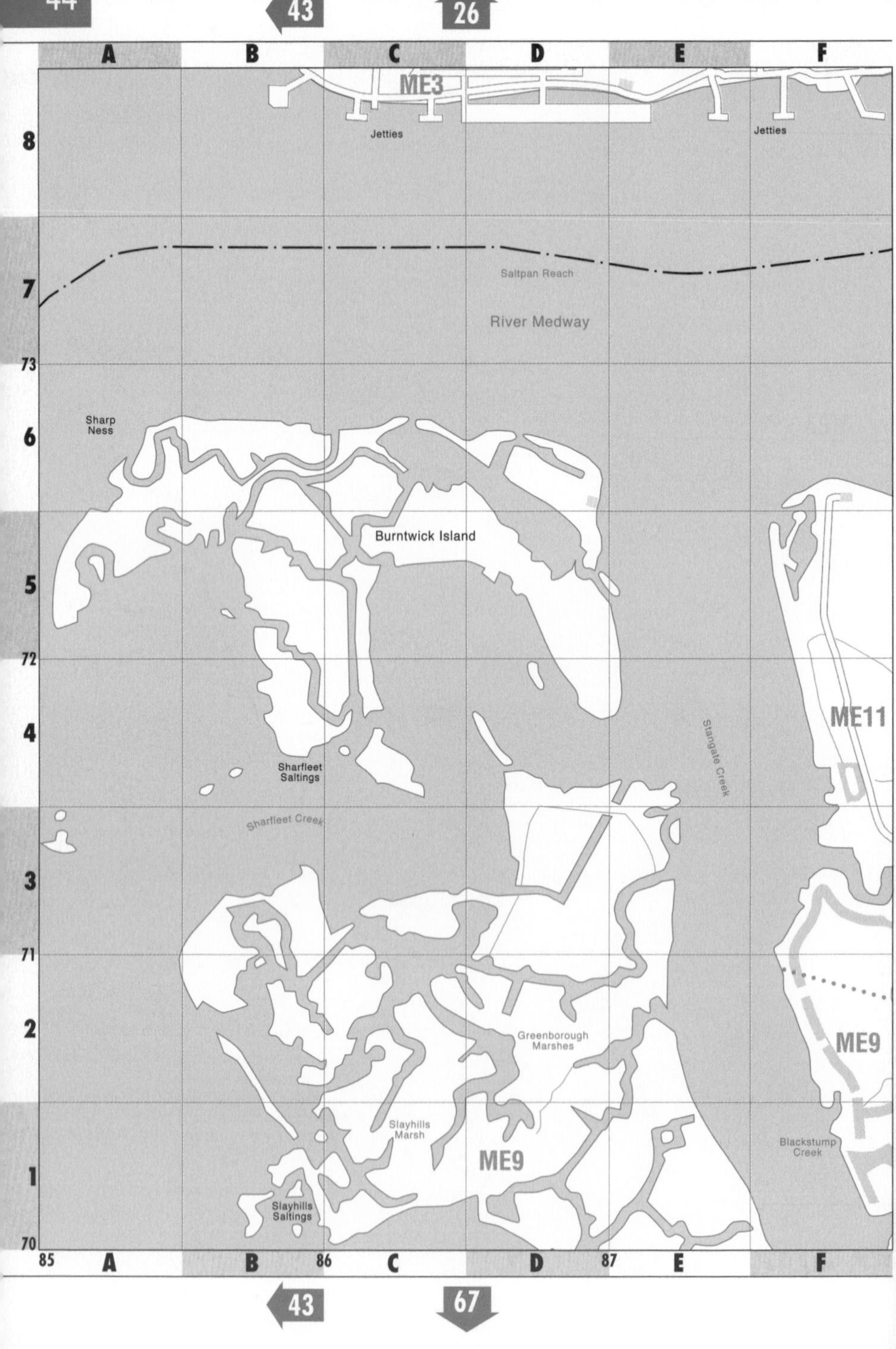

43
26

ME3

Jetties

Jetties

Saltpan Reach

River Medway

Sharp
Ness

Burntwick Island

Sharfleet
Saltings

ME11

Sharfleet Creek

Stangate Creek

Greenborough
Marshes

ME9

Slayhills
Marsh

Blackstump
Creek

ME9

Slayhills
Saltings

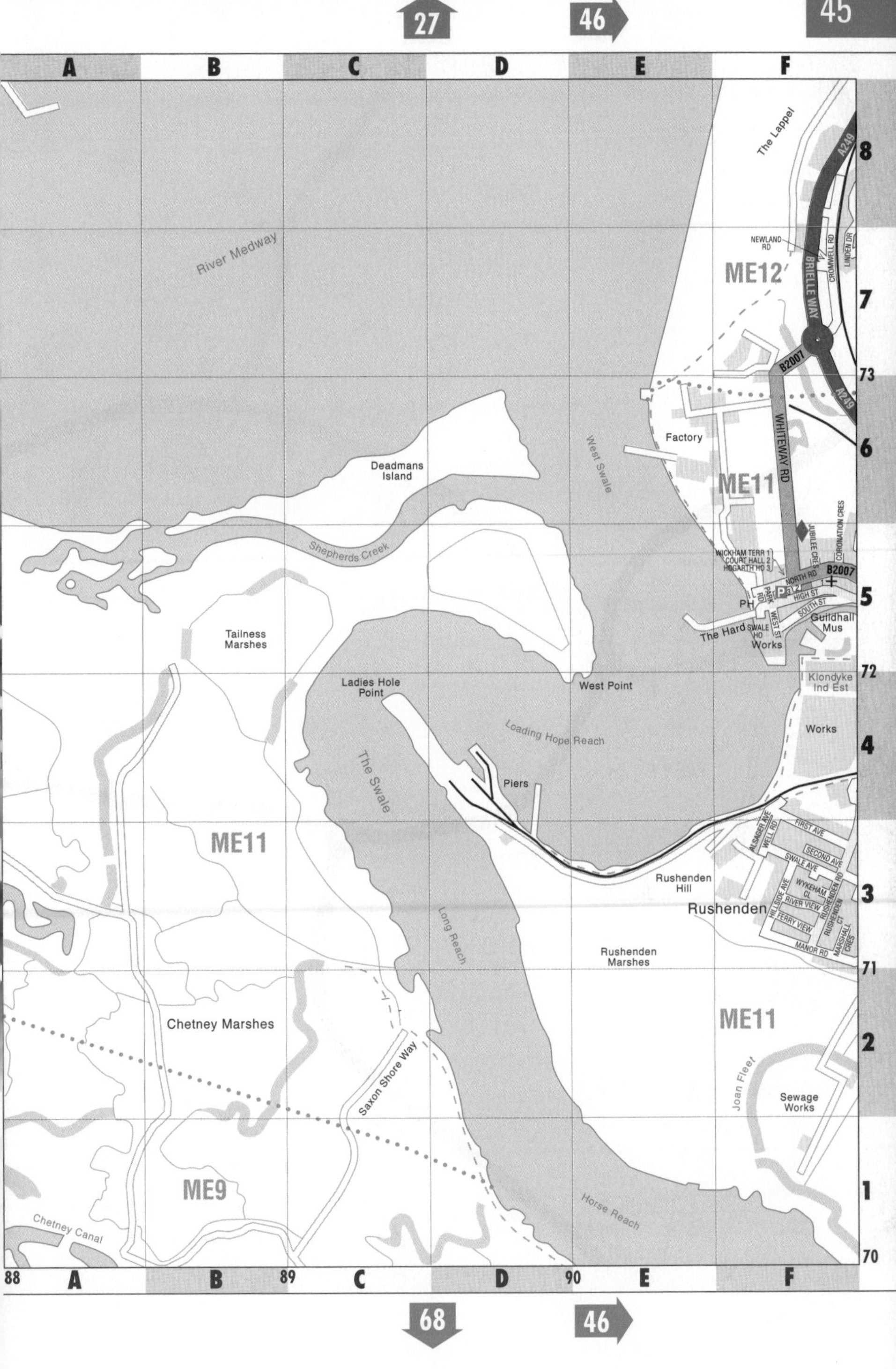

A B C D E F

The Lappel

A249

8

NEWLAND RD

ME12

BRIELLE WAY

UNION RD

REGENT RD

B2007

7

73

A249

WHITEWAY RD

Factory

6

ME11

CORONATION CRES

JUBILEE DRI

River Medway

5

B2007

WICKHAM TERR 1
COURT HALL 2
HOGARTH HO 3

NORTH RD

HIGH ST

SOUTH ST

WEST ST

PH

The Hard

SWALE
HO

Works

Guildhall
Mus

Deadmans
Island

Shepherds Creek

West Swale

Klondyke
Ind Est

72

Works

Tailness
Marshes

Ladies Hole
Point

West Point

4

The Swale

Loading Hope Reach

Piers

ME11

Rushenden
Hill

RUSHENDEN RD

WELL RD

FIRST AVE

SECOND AVE

SWALE AVE

WYKEHAM
CL

RIVER VIEW

FERRY VIEW

MARSHALL
CRES

MANOR RD

Rushenden

3

Long Reach

Rushenden
Marshes

71

Chetney Marshes

Saxon Shore Way

ME11

Joan Fleet

2

Sewage
Works

ME9

Horse Reach

1

Chetney Canal

70

88
89
90

45
28

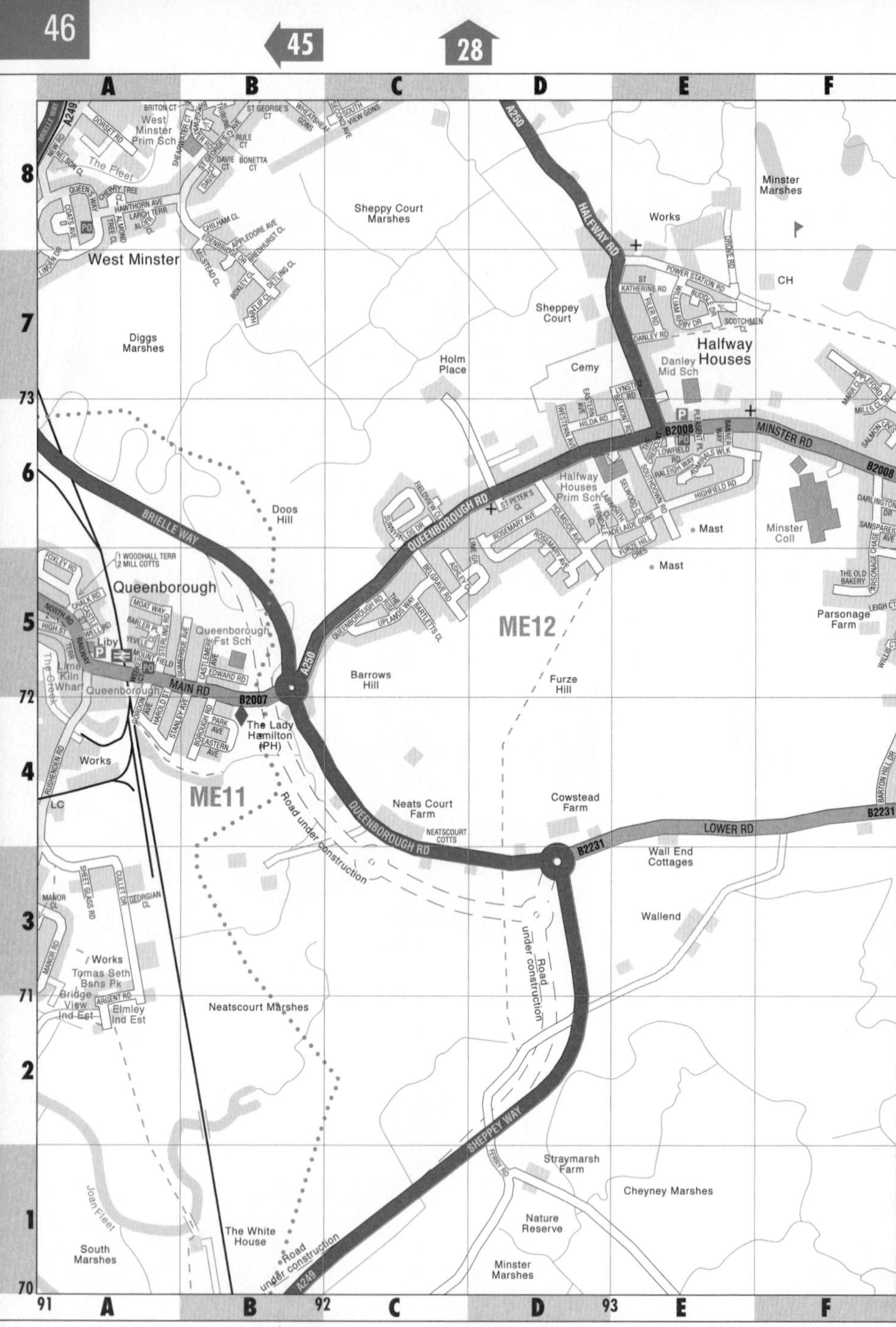
West Minster
West Minster Prim Sch
The Fleet
Sheppy Court Marshes
Minster Marshes
Works
Halfway Houses
Danley Mid Sch
Sheppey Court
Cemy
Holm Place
Diggs Marshes
Doos Hill
Halfway Houses Prim Sch
Minster Coll
Queenborough
Queenborough Fst Sch
Parsonage Farm
ME12
Barrows Hill
Furze Hill
The Lady Hamilton (PH)
ME11
Works
Neats Court Farm
Cowstead Farm
Wall End Cottages
Wallend
Tomas Seth Bsns Pk
Bridge View Ind Est
Elmley Ind Est
Neatscourt Marshes
Straymarsh Farm
Cheyney Marshes
Nature Reserve
The White House
South Marshes
Minster Marshes
BRIELLE WAY
QUEENBOROUGH RD
MAIN RD
MINSTER RD
LOWER RD
HALFWAY RD
SHEPPEY WAY
Road under construction

45
69

A B C D E F

8
7
73
6
5
72
4
3
71
2
1
70

Ripney Hill Farm
Elliott Park Sch
Minster
Merryman's Hill
Sheppey
Minster-in-Sheppey Prim Sch
Minster Abbey
Mus
Liby
Royal Oak Point
Seacliff
Round Hill
East End Farm
Caravan Pk
Mill Hill
Sports Gd
St George's CE Mid Sch
British Queen (PH)
Tadwell Farm
The Mount
Sheppey Community
Rape Hill
Thistle Hill
Scocles Farm
Scocles Cotts
Boarers Farm
Woottons Farm
ME12
Brambledown
Shardens Farm
Shrubsoles Hill
Brambledown Spring
Marshlands Farm
Piggery
Elm Tree Inn (PH)
Primrose Cottage
Flatcreek Head
South Lees
Poors
New Hook Farm
Southlees Marshes
Newhook Marshes
Old Hook Farm

B2008 MINSTER RD
HIGH ST
BACK LA
CHAPEL ST
CHEQUERS RD
B2008 EASTCHURCH RD
B2231 LOWER RD
FORTY ACRES HILL
LOWER RD
B2231
Greyhound Rd
ELMLEY RD
WINDMILL QUAY RD
OLD HOOK RD
SCOCLES RD
ELM LA
NELSON AVE
DRAKE AVE
THISTLE HILL WAY
THE LEAS
SOUTHSEA AVE
SEASIDE AVE
SCARBOROUGH DR
MINSTER DR
AUGUSTINE RD
SEXBURGA DR
CLOVELLY DR
THE GLEN
WOODLAND DR
GLENDALE RD
WARDS HILL RD
RODMER CL
ALSTON CL
HOWARD CL
SEATHORPE AVE
LYNMOUTH DR
WESTCLIFF DR
LOVE LA
KINGS RD
PRINCES AVE
IMPERIAL AVE
STANLEY AVE
BALDWIN RD
CHURCHILL RD
THE BROADWAY
WAVERLEY AVE
HILLSIDE RD
SCRAPSGATE RD
MARINA DR
JOHNSON WAY
KENT AVE
THE ROWANS
QUEENBOROUGH DR
ABBEYVIEW DR
SHURLAND AVE
SAXON AVE
GLENWOOD DR
ORCHARD GR
BELLEVUE RD
WAYBORNES CHASE
NORWOOD RISE
HIGHVIEW RD
BRECON CHASE
CHURCH TERR
CARDINAL CL
VICARAGE RD
QUEENS RD
FALCON GDNS
UNION RD
WATERLOO HILL
ABBEY CL
CHIDDINGFOLD CL
PETFIELD CL
PRINCE CHARLES AVE
TAMS GDNS
ECHO WLK
BOUNDARY CL
CLIFF GDNS
WINDMILL RISE
OAK LA
OAK AVE
PIGTAIL CNR
DANEDALE AVE
BELL FARM LA
PLOUGH RD
SHEPPEY TERR
MARIAN AVE
EDWINA AVE
STILES CL
APPLEFORD DR
SALMON CRES
ST MARY'S ROW
MALLARD CT
NOREEN AVE
MAGPIE CT
SUNNYSIDE AVE
SILVERDALE AVE
CROIDENE CT
PORTER CL
THE MAPLES
TRAFALGAR PAR
WORCESTER CL
NEW RD
BRAMSTON RD
COPLAND AVE
GEORGE PARRIS CT
HARPS AVE
BLATCHER CL
FLEETWOOD CL
LAPWING CL
HERON DR
HOPSONS PL
DARLINGTON DR
SANSPAREIL AVE
SUMMERVILLE AVE
DREADNOUGHT AVE
NAUTILUS DR
NAUTILUS CL
PARISH RD
SANDERS CT
HILLTOP RD
HOLYROOD DR
LOVELL RD
BRASIER CT
ALLEN CT
WAIN CT
BARTON HILL DR
PLOVER RD
MILLER CT
1 ALASEUN TERR
2 MURTHWAITE CT
3 MENZIES CT
4 TURMINE CT
BUCKTHORNE HO
BUCKTHORNE RD
BELL CT
FLOWER AVE
ORCHID CL
HAREBELL CL
THISTLE HILL WAY
PENNY CRESS RD

94 A B 95 C D 96 E F

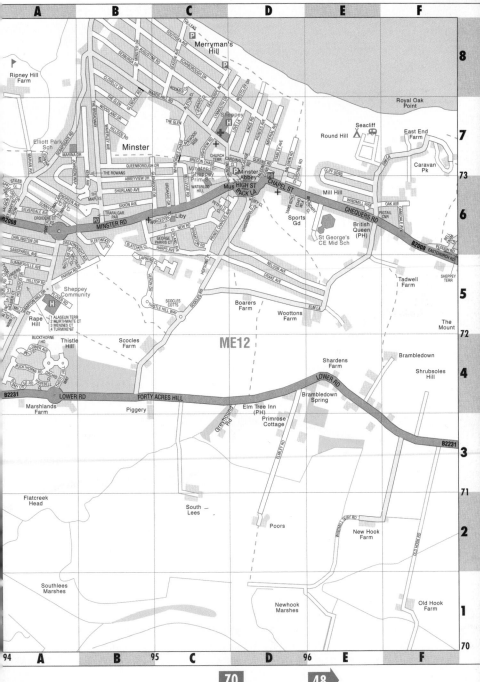

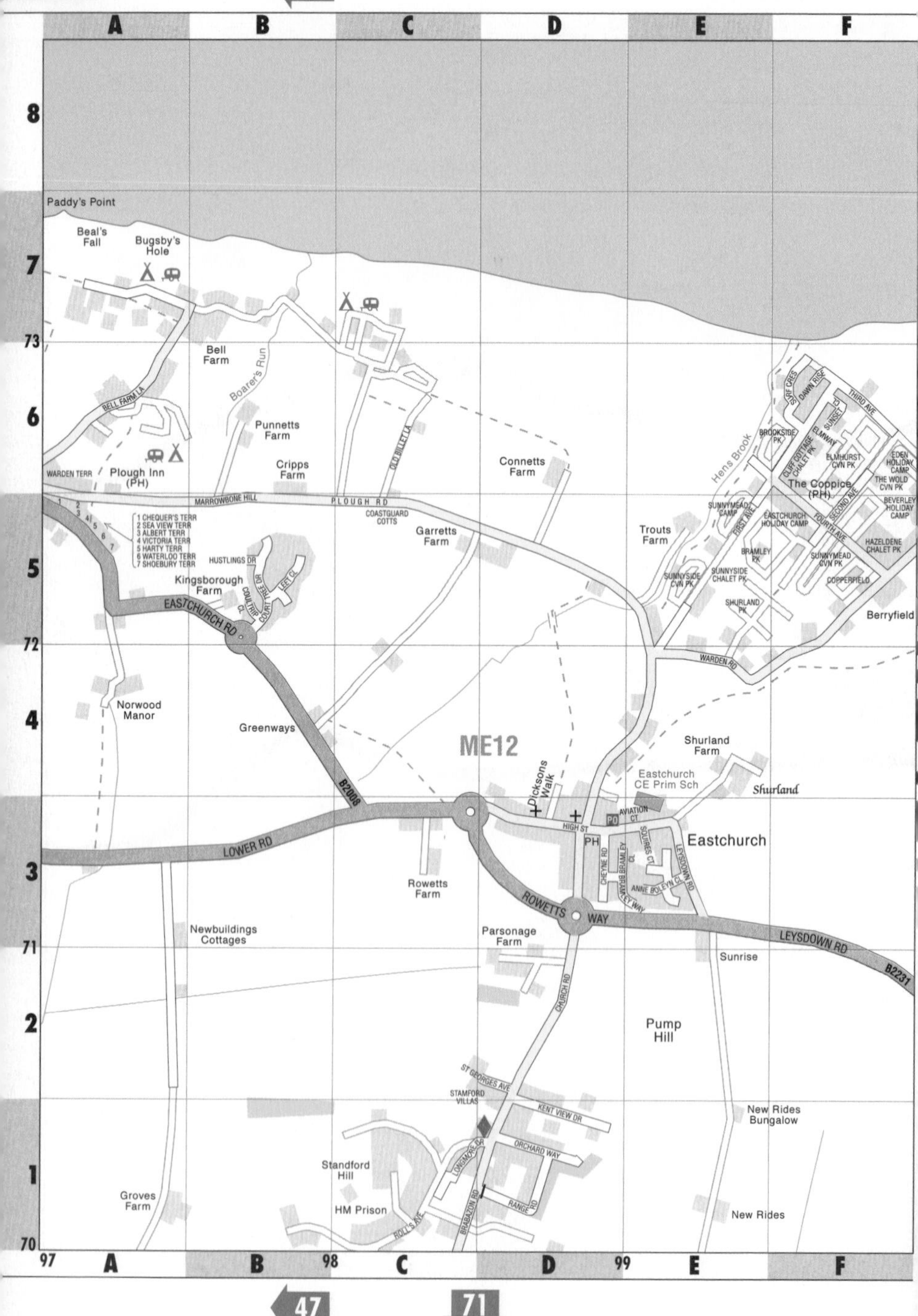

47

A   **B**   **C**   **D**   **E**   **F**

8

Paddy's Point

Beal's
Fall
Bugsby's
Hole

7

73

Bell
Farm

Boarer's Run

Punnetts
Farm

6

BELL FARM LA

Cripps
Farm

Connetts
Farm

WARDEN TERR

Plough Inn
(PH)

MARROWBONE HILL

PLOUGH RD

OLD MILL LA

COASTGUARD
COTTS

Garretts
Farm

Trouts
Farm

Hens Brook

BROOKSIDE
PK

SEA VIEW CRES

ELMHAY

THIRD AVE

EDEN
HOLIDAY
CAMP

CLIFF GARDENS

OAST OWN PK

ELMHURST
PK

THE WOLD
CVN PK

The Coppice
(PH)

BEVERLEY
HOLIDAY
CAMP

EASTCHURCH
HOLIDAY CAMP

SUNNYMEAD
CAMP

SECOND AVE

FIRST AVE

HAZELDENE
CHALET PK

COPPERFIELD

5

1 CHEQUER'S TERR
2 SEA VIEW TERR
3 ALBERT TERR
4 VICTORIA TERR
5 HARTY TERR
6 WATERLOO TERR
7 SHOEBURY TERR

HUSTLINGS DR

ORCHARD LEE CL

Kingsborough
Farm

BRAMLEY
PK

SUNNYSIDE
CVN PK

BUNNYSIDE
CHALET PK

SUNNYMEAD
CVN PK

Berryfield

SHURLAND
PK

72

EASTCHURCH RD

B2008

WARDEN RD

4

Norwood
Manor

Greenways

ME12

Dicksons Walk

Shurland
Farm

Eastchurch
CE Prim Sch

Shurland

B2008

LOWER RD

HIGH ST

AVIATION
CT.

PH

Eastchurch

3

Rowetts
Farm

ROWETTS WAY

CHEYNE RD

BRAMLEY WAY

ANNIE POLLY CLH

SOUTHS CT

LEYSDOWN RD

B2231

71

Newbuildings
Cottages

Parsonage
Farm

Sunrise

CHURCH RD

2

Pump
Hill

New Rides
Bungalow

ST GEORGES AVE

STAMFORD
VILLAS

KENT VIEW DR

ORCHARD WAY

1

Groves
Farm

Standford
Hill

HM Prison

LONSDALE DR

BORSTAL RD

RANGE RD

BULL'S RD

New Rides

70

97   **A**   **B**   98   **C**   **D**   99   **E**   **F**

47
71

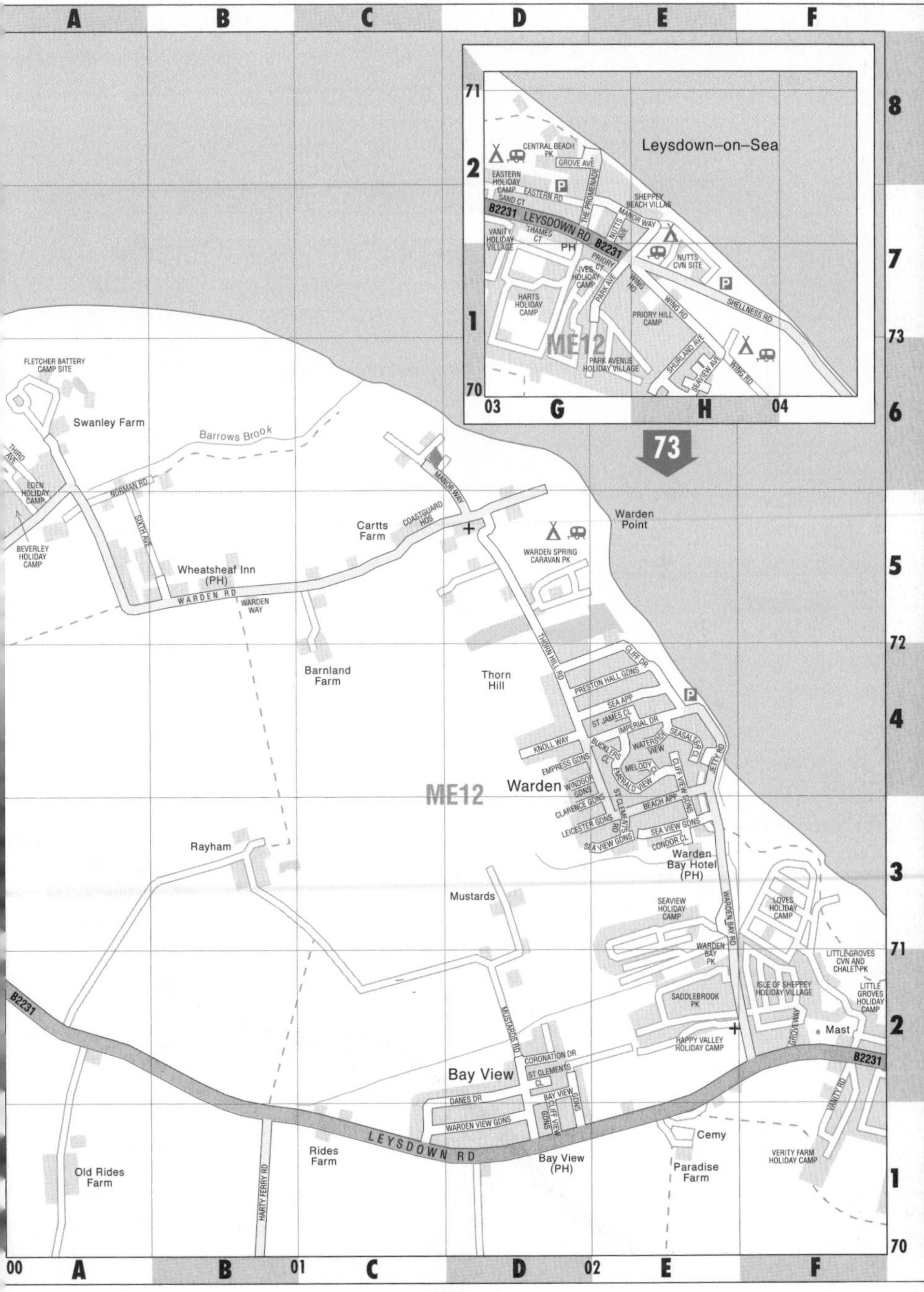

A B C D E F

Leysdown–on–Sea

71
2
1
70

CENTRAL BEACH PK
GROVE AVE
EASTERN HOLIDAY CAMP
EASTERN RD
SAND CT
B2231 LEYSDOWN RD
VANITY HOLIDAY VILLAGE
THAMES CT
PH
HARTS HOLIDAY CAMP
PRIORY CT
LVEL HOLIDAY CAMP
PARK AVENUE HOLIDAY VILLAGE
THE PROMENADE
SHEPPEY BEACH VILLAG
MARSH WAY
B2231
NUTTS CVN SITE
WING RD
SHELLNESS RD
PRIORY HILL CAMP
SOUTHLANDS AVE
WING RD

ME12

03 G H 04

8
7
73
6

FLETCHER BATTERY CAMP SITE
Swanley Farm
Barrows Brook

EDEN HOLIDAY CAMP
THIRD AVE
NORMAN RD
BAYES AVE
BEVERLEY HOLIDAY CAMP
Wheatsheaf Inn (PH)
WARDEN RD
WARDEN WAY

MANOR WAY
COASTGUARD HSS
Cartts Farm

Warden Point

WARDEN SPRING CARAVAN PK

5
72
4

Barnland Farm

Thorn Hill

THORN HILL RD
PRESTON HALL GDNS
SEA APP
ST JAMES CL
IMPERIAL DR
WATERSIDE VIEW
KNOLL WAY
EMPRESS GDNS
WINDSOR GDNS
MELODY
CLARENCE GDNS
LEICESTER GDNS
SEA VIEW GDNS
CLARE DR
EASA APP
BEACH APP
SEA VIEW GDNS
CONDOR CL

ME12

Warden

Warden Bay Hotel (PH)

Rayham

Mustards

SEAVIEW HOLIDAY CAMP
WARDEN BAY PK
SADDLEBROOK PK
HAPPY VALLEY HOLIDAY CAMP
ISLE OF SHEPPEY HOLIDAY VILLAGE
WARDEN BAY RD

LOVES HOLIDAY CAMP
LITTLE GROVES CVN AND CHALET PK
LITTLE GROVES HOLIDAY CAMP

3
71
2

B2231

GROVE WAY
Mast
B2231

Bay View

CORONATION DR
ST CLEMENTS
DANES DR
WARDEN VIEW GDNS
BAY VIEW
BAY VIEW CL
HARTY FERRY RD
MUSTARDS ROAD

Old Rides Farm

Rides Farm

LEYSDOWN RD

Bay View (PH)

Cemy
Paradise Farm

VERITY FARM HOLIDAY CAMP
TRINITY RD

1
70

00 A B 01 C D 02 E F

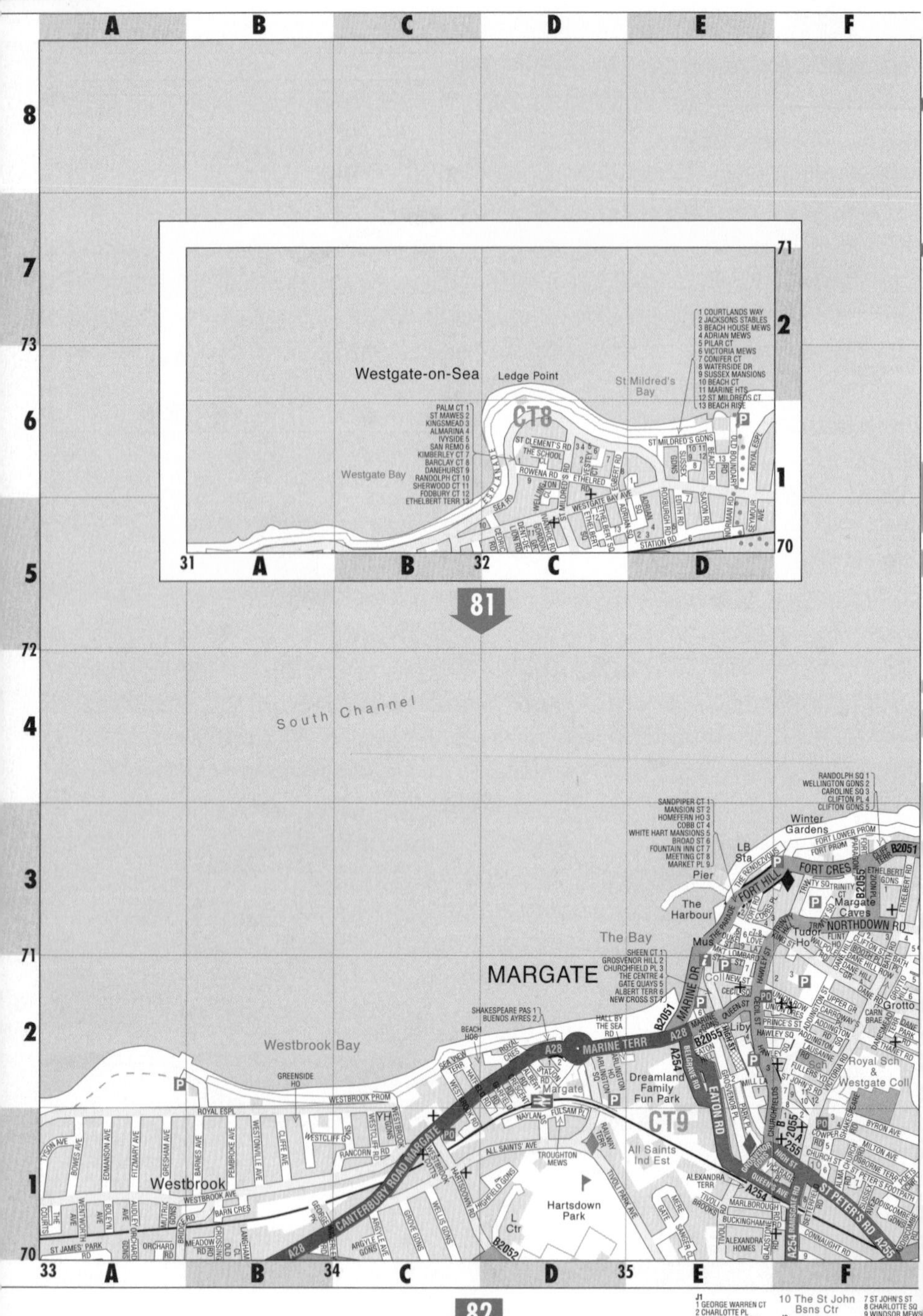

Westgate-on-Sea

Ledge Point

St Mildred's Bay

CT8

1 COURTLANDS WAY
2 JACKSONS STABLES
3 BEACH HOUSE MEWS
4 ADRIAN MEWS
5 PILAR CT
6 VICTORIA MEWS
7 CONIFER CT
8 WATERSIDE DR
9 SUSSEX MANSIONS
10 BEACH CT
11 MARINE HTS
12 ST MILDREDS CT
13 BEACH RISE

PALM CT 1
ST MAWES 2
KINGSMEAD 3
ALMARINA 4
IVYSIDE 5
SAN REMO 6
KIMBERLEY CT 7
BARCLAY CT 8
DANEHURST 9
RANDOLPH CT 10
SHERWOOD CT 11
FODBURY CT 12
ETHELBERT TERR 13

Westgate Bay

ST CLEMENT'S RD
THE SCHOOL
ROWENA RD
ST MILDRED'S GDNS

81

South Channel

RANDOLPH SQ 1
WELLINGTON GDNS 2
CAROLINE SQ 3
CLIFTON PL 4
CLIFTON GDNS 5

SANDPIPER CT 1
MANSION ST 2
HOMEFERN HO 3
COBB CT 4
WHITE HART MANSIONS 5
BROAD ST 6
FOUNTAIN INN CT 7
MEETING CT 8
MARKET PL 9

Winter Gardens

LB Sta

FORT LOWER PROM
FORT PROM
FORT CRES
B2051
NORTHDOWN RD

Pier

The Harbour

Margate

Tudor Ho

Grotto

MARGATE

SHEEN CT 1
GROSVENOR HILL 2
CHURCHFIELD PL 3
THE CENTRE 4
GATE QUAYS 5
ALBERT TERR 6
NEW CROSS ST 7

The Bay

Coll

Royal Sch & Westgate Coll

SHAKESPEARE PAS 1
BUENOS AYRES 2

Westbrook Bay

BEACH HO

HALL BY THE SEA RD

MARINE TERR

A28

Dreamland Family Fun Park

EATON RD

CT9

GREENSIDE HO

WESTBROOK PROM

Margate

NAYLAND

All Saints Ind Est

ST PETER'S RD

Westbrook

CANTERBURY RD MARGATE

ALL SAINTS AVE

TROUGHTON MEWS

ALEXANDRA TERR

BYRON AVE

Westbrook Bay

ROYAL ESPL
CLIFF AVE
WESTCLIFF

Hartsdown Park

L Ctr

B2052

ALEXANDRA HOMES

CONNAUGHT RD

ST JAMES' PARK

ORCHARD

MEADOW

APSLEY

WELLS

82

J1
1 GEORGE WARREN CT
2 CHARLOTTE PL
3 SPARROW CASTLE
4 MILTON SQ
5 ARNOLD RD
6 OXFORD ST
7 HOMESTEAD CL
8 VICARAGE CRES
9 CONNAUGHT GDNS

10 The St John
Bsns Ctr

J2
1 PUMP LA
2 COLLEGE SQ
3 COLLEGE WLK
4 ANCHOR HILL
5 GROTTO RD
6 GROTTO GDNS

7 ST JOHN'S ST
8 CHARLOTTE SQ
9 WINDSOR MEWS
10 PRINCES GATE
11 LAUSANNE TERR
12 VENTNOR LA

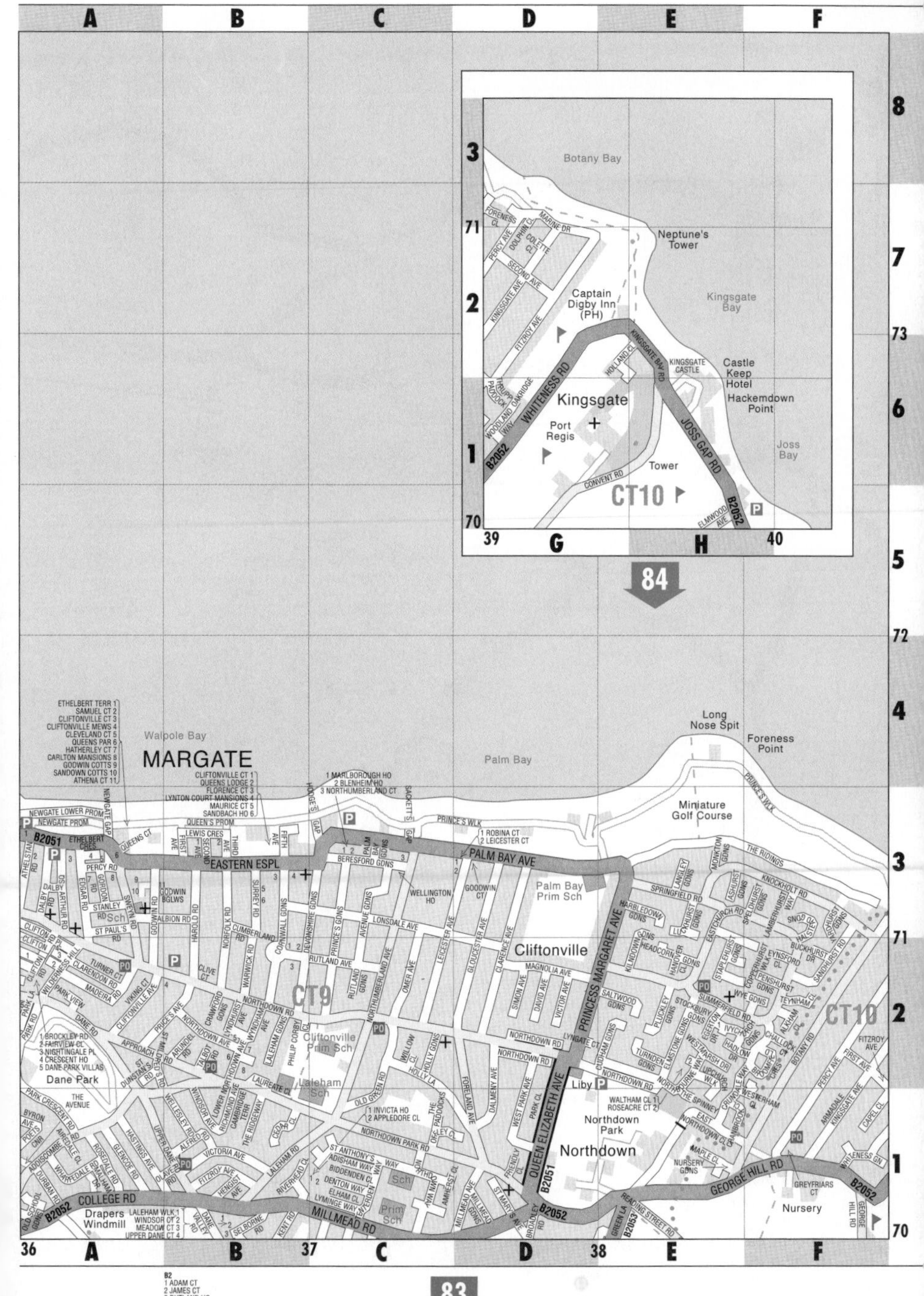

B8
1 HANSOM TERR
2 DAINTON CL
3 ST TIMOTHY'S MEWS
4 NORTH CT
5 PALACE CT
6 SUMMERFIELD
7 ANDRINGHAM LODGE
8 PARK PLACE
9 KENDALL LODGE
10 WINSTON CT
11 VOGUE CT
12 THE LAURELS

29

C5
1 SHERIDAN LODGE
2 LANGLEY GDNS
3 GAINSBOROUGH CT
4 GERRARD HO

C7
1 RUXLEY CT
2 WESTLAND LODGE
3 EASTLAND CT
4 DAIRSIE CT
5 NORTHLANDS
6 BEECHFIELD COTTS
7 THE OASIS
8 CROMARTY CT
9 STANTON CT
10 SILVERSTONE CT
11 SOUTH VIEW CT

E6
1 WINDSOR CT
2 BICKLEY CT
3 BANSTEAD CT
4 NEWTON CT
5 HOLMDENE CT
6 CHELSEA CT

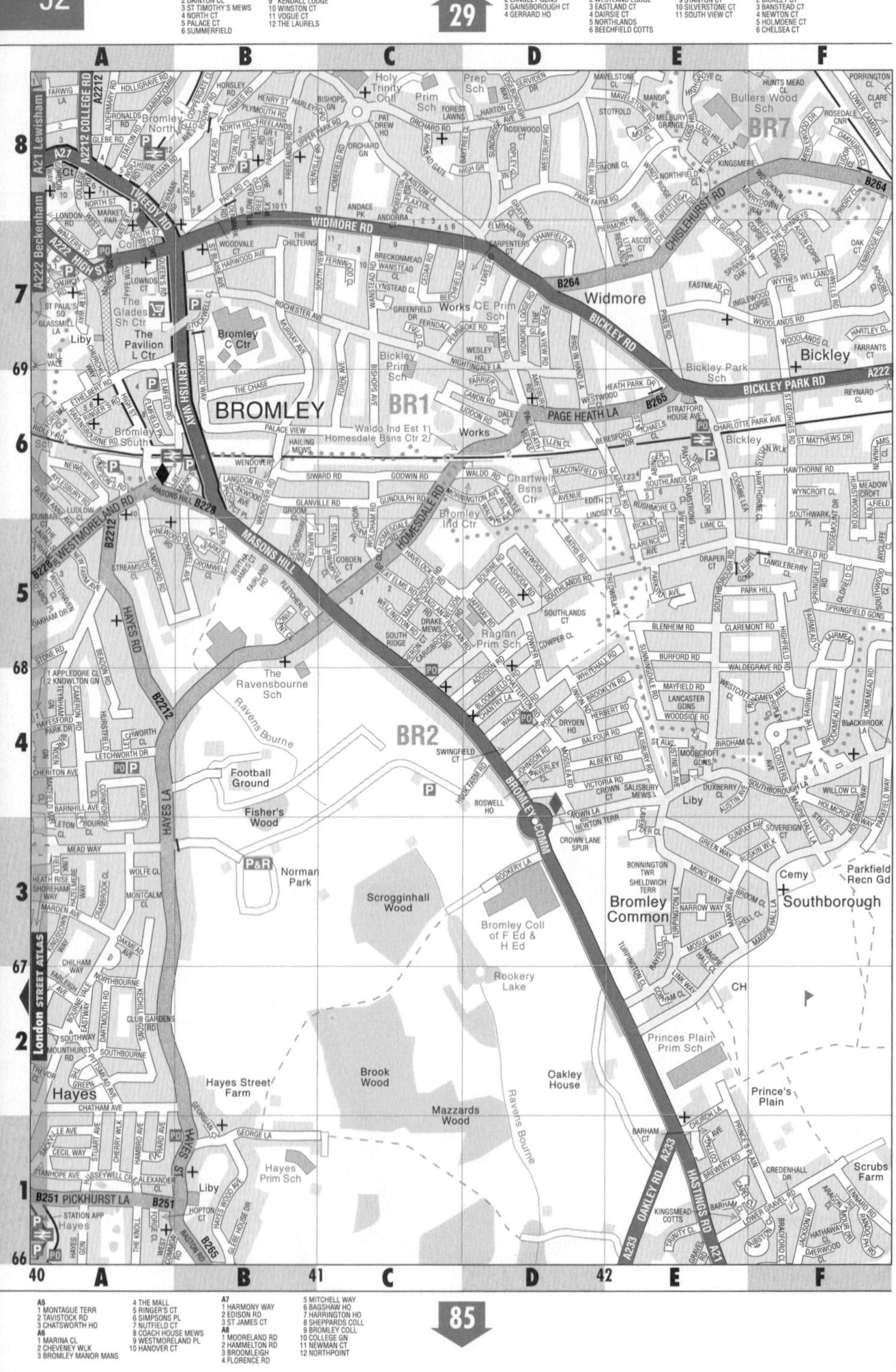

40 A B 41 C D 42 E F

A5
1 MONTAGUE TERR
2 TAVISTOCK RD
3 CHATSWORTH HO

A6
1 MARINA CL
2 CHEVENEY WLK
3 BROMLEY MANOR MANS
4 THE MALL
5 RINGER'S CT
6 SIMPSONS PL
7 NUTFIELD CT
8 COACH HOUSE MEWS
9 WESTMORELAND PL
10 HANOVER CT

A7
1 HARMONY WAY
2 EDISON RD
3 ST JAMES CT

A8
1 MOORELAND RD
2 HAMMELTON RD
3 BROOMLEIGH
4 FLORENCE RD
5 MITCHELL WAY
6 BAGSHAW HO
7 HARRINGTON HO
8 SHEPPARDS COLL
9 BROMLEY COLL
10 COLLEGE GN
11 NEWMAN CT
12 NORTHPOINT

85

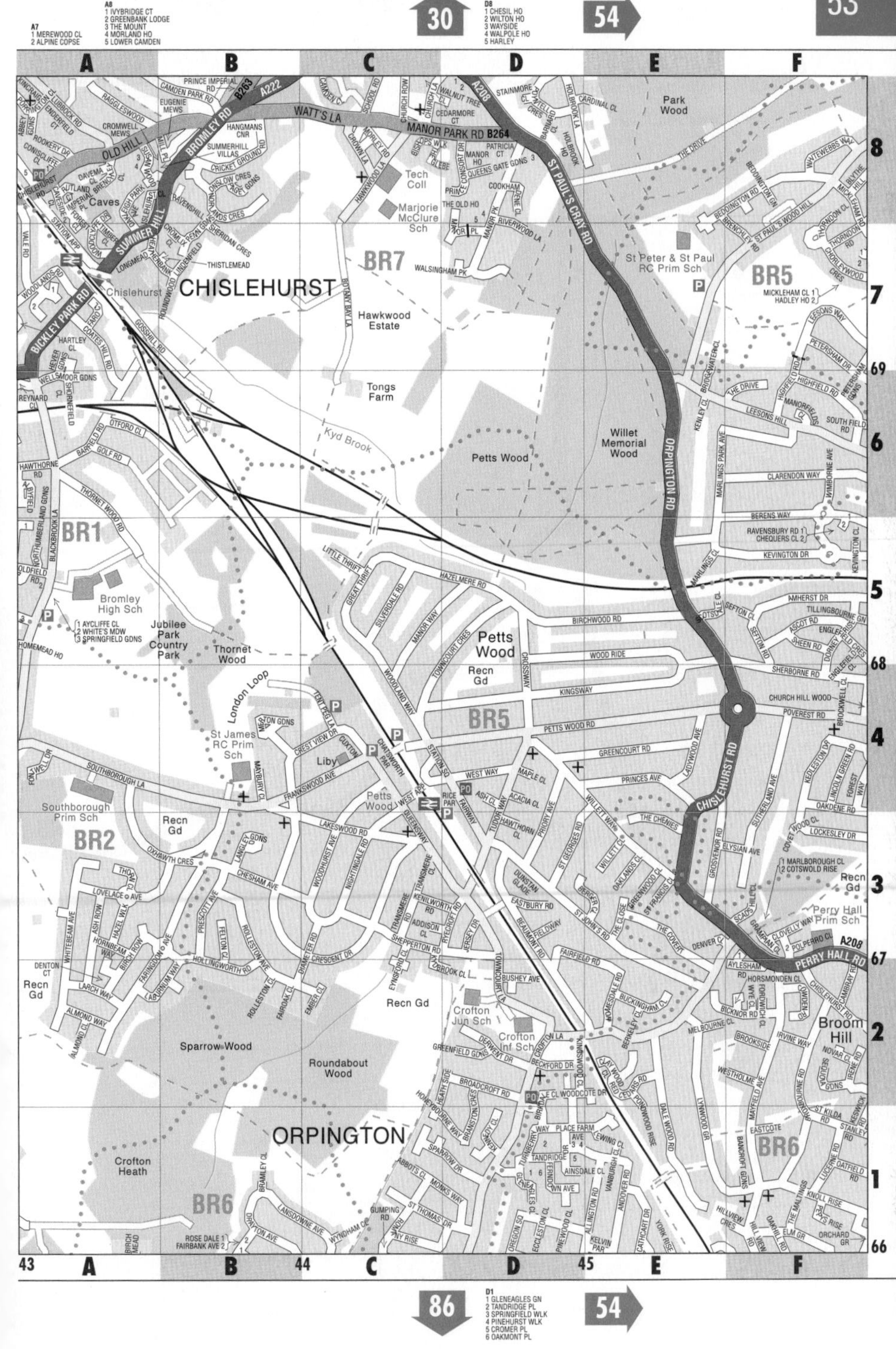

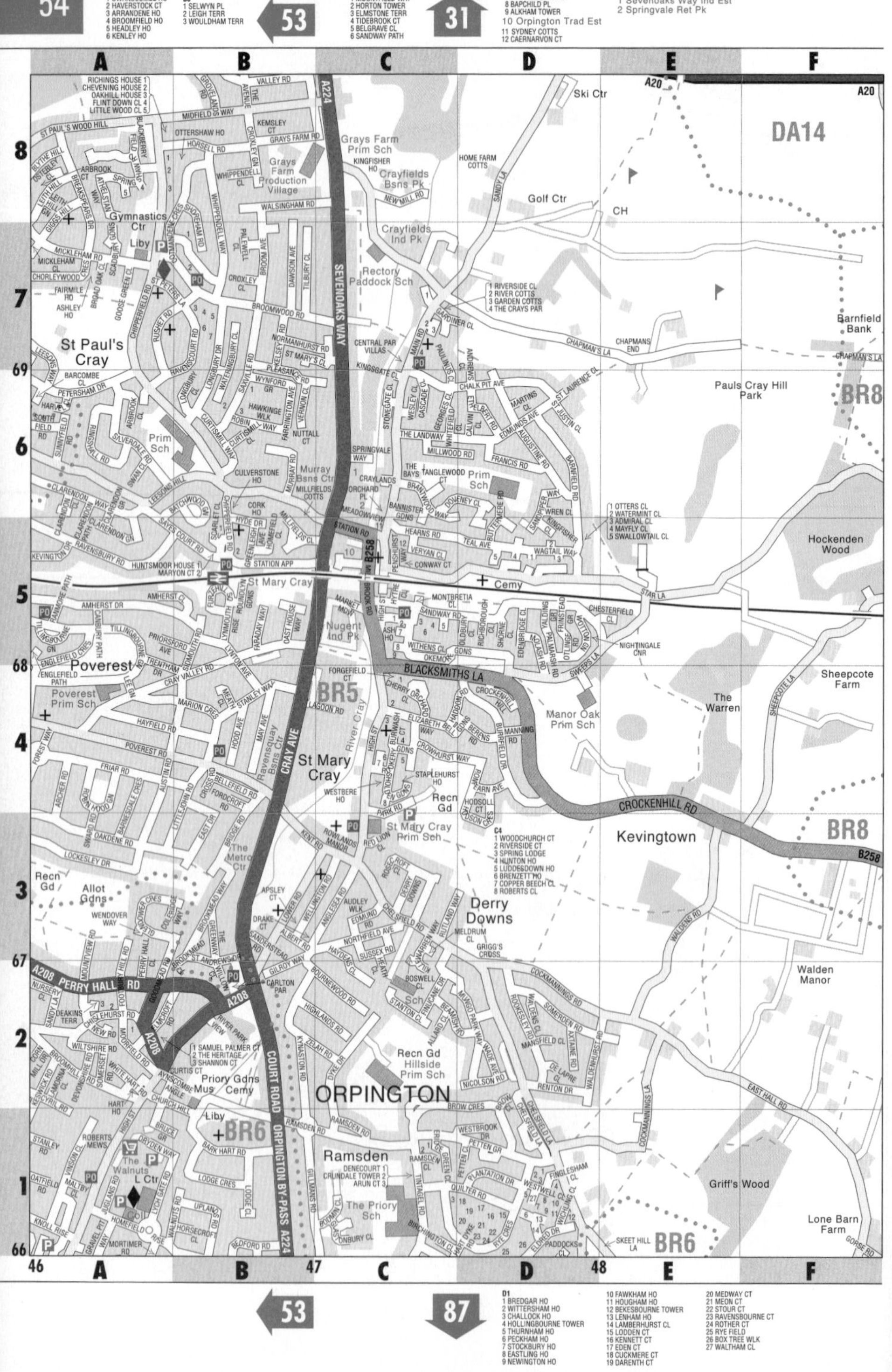
B7
1 SWANSCOMBE HO
2 HAVERSTOCK CT
3 ARRANDENE HO
4 BROOMFIELD HO
5 HEADLEY HO
6 KENLEY HO
7 LADYWELL HO
B6
1 SELWYN PL
2 LEIGH TERR
3 WOULDHAM TERR
53
C5
1 MOUNTFIELD WAY
2 HORTON TOWER
3 ELMSTONE TERR
4 TIDEBROOK CT
5 BELGRAVE CL
6 SANDWAY PATH
31
C5
7 HARBLEDOWN PL
8 BAPCHILD PL
9 ALKHAM TOWER
10 Orpington Trad Est
11 SYDNEY COTTS
12 CAERNARVON CT
C6
1 Sevenoaks Way Ind Est
2 Springvale Ret Pk
A
B
C
D
E
F
8
7
69
6
5
68
4
3
67
2
1
66
46
47
48
A20
DA14
Ski Ctr
Grays Farm Prim Sch
Grays Farm Production Village
Crayfields Bsns Pk
Crayfields Ind Pk
Rectory Paddock Sch
Golf Ctr
CH
Gymnastics Ctr
Liby
St Paul's Cray
SEVENOAKS WAY
A224
Barnfield Bank
Pauls Cray Hill Park
BR8
Prim Sch
Murray Bsns Ctr
Hockenden Wood
St Mary Cray
Cemy
Poverest
Poverest Prim Sch
Nugent Ind Pk
BR5
BLACKSMITHS LA
Manor Oak Prim Sch
The Warren
Sheepcote Farm
St Mary Cray
Ravensquay Bsns Ctr
CRAY AVE
River Cray
CROCKENHILL RD
Kevingtown
B258
St Mary Cray Prim Sch
Recn Gd
The Metro Ctr
Allot Gdns
Derry Downs
Walden Manor
A208
PERRY HALL RD
COURT ROAD
ORPINGTON BY-PASS A224
Priory Gdns
Mus
Cemy
Recn Gd
Hillside Prim Sch
ORPINGTON
BR6
Ramsden
The Walnuts
L Ctr
Coll
The Priory Sch
Griff's Wood
Lone Barn Farm
EAST HALL RD
C4
1 WOODCHURCH CT
2 RIVERSIDE CT
3 SPRING LODGE
4 HUNTON HO
5 LUDDESDOWN HO
6 BRENZETT HO
7 COPPER BEECH CL
8 ROBERTS CL
53
87
D1
1 BREDGAR HO
2 WITTERSHAM HO
3 CHALLOCK HO
4 HOLLINGBOURNE TOWER
5 THURNHAM HO
6 PECKHAM HO
7 STOCKBURY HO
8 EASTLING HO
9 NEWINGTON HO
10 FAWKHAM HO
11 HOUGHAM HO
12 BEKESBOURNE TOWER
13 LENHAM HO
14 LAMBERHURST CL
15 LODDEN CT
16 KENNETT CT
17 EDEN CT
18 CUCKMERE CT
19 DARENTH CT
20 MEDWAY CT
21 MEON CT
22 STOUR CT
23 RAVENSBOURNE CT
24 ROTHER CT
25 RYE FIELD
26 BOX TREE WLK
27 WALTHAM CL

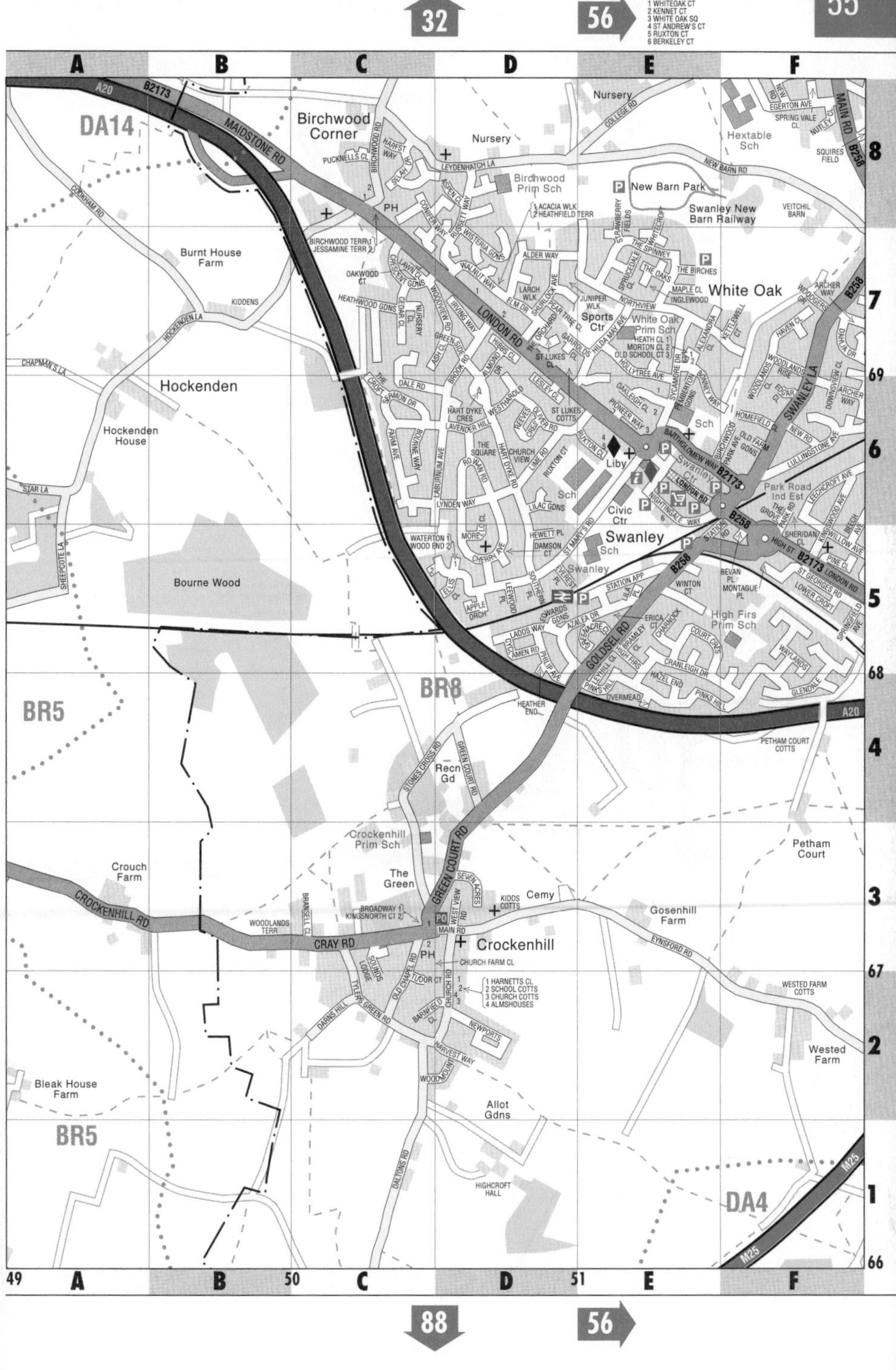
32
56
E6
1 WHITEOAK CT
2 KENNET CT
3 WHITE OAK SQ
4 ST ANDREW'S CT
5 RUXTON CT
6 BERKELEY CT
A
B
C
D
E
F
DA14
A20
B2173
MAIDSTONE RD
Birchwood Corner
Nursery
COLLEGE RD
Hextable Sch
EGERTON AVE
SPRING VALE CL
NUTLEY CL
MAIN RD
B258
SQUIRES FIELD
PUCKNELLS CL
BIRCHWOOD RD
HARFST WAY
LEYDENHATCH LA
Birchwood Prim Sch
New Barn Park
NEW BARN RD
Swanley New Barn Railway
VEITCHIL BARN
COOKHAM RD
PH
1 ACACIA WLK
2 HEATHFIELD TERR
ASPEN CL
CONIFER WAY
RUSSETT WAY
WISTERIA GDNS
BIRCHWOOD TERR 1
JESSAMINE TERR 2
Burnt House Farm
KIDDENS
OAKWOOD CT
ALDER WAY
THE SPINNEY
THE OAKS
THE BIRCHES
MAPLE CL
INGLEWOOD
White Oak
ARCHER WAY
HEATHWOOD GDNS
WALNUT WAY
ELM DR
LARCH WLK
JUNIPER WLK
NORTHVIEW
HOCKENDEN LA
LONDON RD
Sports Ctr
White Oak Prim Sch
HEATH CL 1
MORTON CL 2
OLD SCHOOL CT 3
HAVEN CL
WOODLANDS RISE
SWANLEY LA
CHAPMAN'S LA
Hockenden
DALE RD
BROOK RD
ST LUKES CL
LESLEY CL
HOLLYTREE AVE
DOWNSVIEW CL
Hockenden House
HART DYKE CRES
LAVENDER HILL
ST LUKES COTTS
OAKLEIGH CL
PIONEER WAY
Sch
HOMEFIELD CL
NEW RD
OLD FARM GDNS
LULLINGSTONE AVE
FARM AVE
BOURNE WAY
THE SQUARE
CHURCH VIEW
RUXTON CL
Liby
BARTHOLOMEW WAY
B2173
Swanley Ctr
Park Road Ind Est
LECHCROFT AVE
STAR LA
LYNDEN WAY
LILAC GDNS
NIGHTINGALE WAY
Civic Ctr
THE GROVE
SHERIDAN CL
WILLOW AVE
PINE CL
HIGH ST
Swanley
Sch
WATERTON 1
WOOD END 2
CHERRY AVE
HEWETT PL
DAMSON CT
ST MARY'S RD
STATION RD
SHEEPCOTE LA
Bourne Wood
STATION APP
WINTON CT
BEVAN PL
MONTAGUE PL
ST GEORGES RD
LOWER CROFT
APPLE ORCH
LEEWOOD PL
SOUTHERN PL
High Firs Prim Sch
LADDS WAY
AZALEA DR
GOLDSEL RD
ERICA CT
CHARNOCK
COURT CRES
WAYLANDS
SPRINGFIELD AVE
BR8
BR5
CRANLEIGH DR
HAZEL END
PINKS HILL
OVERMEAD
GLENDALE
HEATHER END
PETHAM COURT COTTS
STONES CROSS RD
GREEN COURT RD
Recn Gd
Petham Court
Crockenhill Prim Sch
Crouch Farm
The Green
SEVEN ACRES
KIDDS COTTS
Cemy
Gosenhill Farm
CROCKENHILL RD
BRANSELL CL
WOODLANDS TERR
BROADWAY 1
KINGSNORTH CT 2
PO
WEST VIEW RD
MAIN RD
CRAY RD
Crockenhill
EYNSFORD RD
SOUNDS LODGE
CHURCH FARM CL
TUDOR CT
OLD CHAPEL RD
CHURCH RD
1 HARNETTS CL
2 SCHOOL COTTS
3 CHURCH COTTS
4 ALMSHOUSES
WESTED FARM COTTS
DARNS HILL
TYLERS GREEN RD
BARNFIELD CL
NEWPORTS
HARVEST WAY
Wested Farm
Bleak House Farm
WOOD MOUNT
Allot Gdns
DALTONS RD
HIGHCROFT HALL
DA4
M25
8
7
69
6
5
68
4
3
67
2
1
66
49
50
51
88
56

55
33

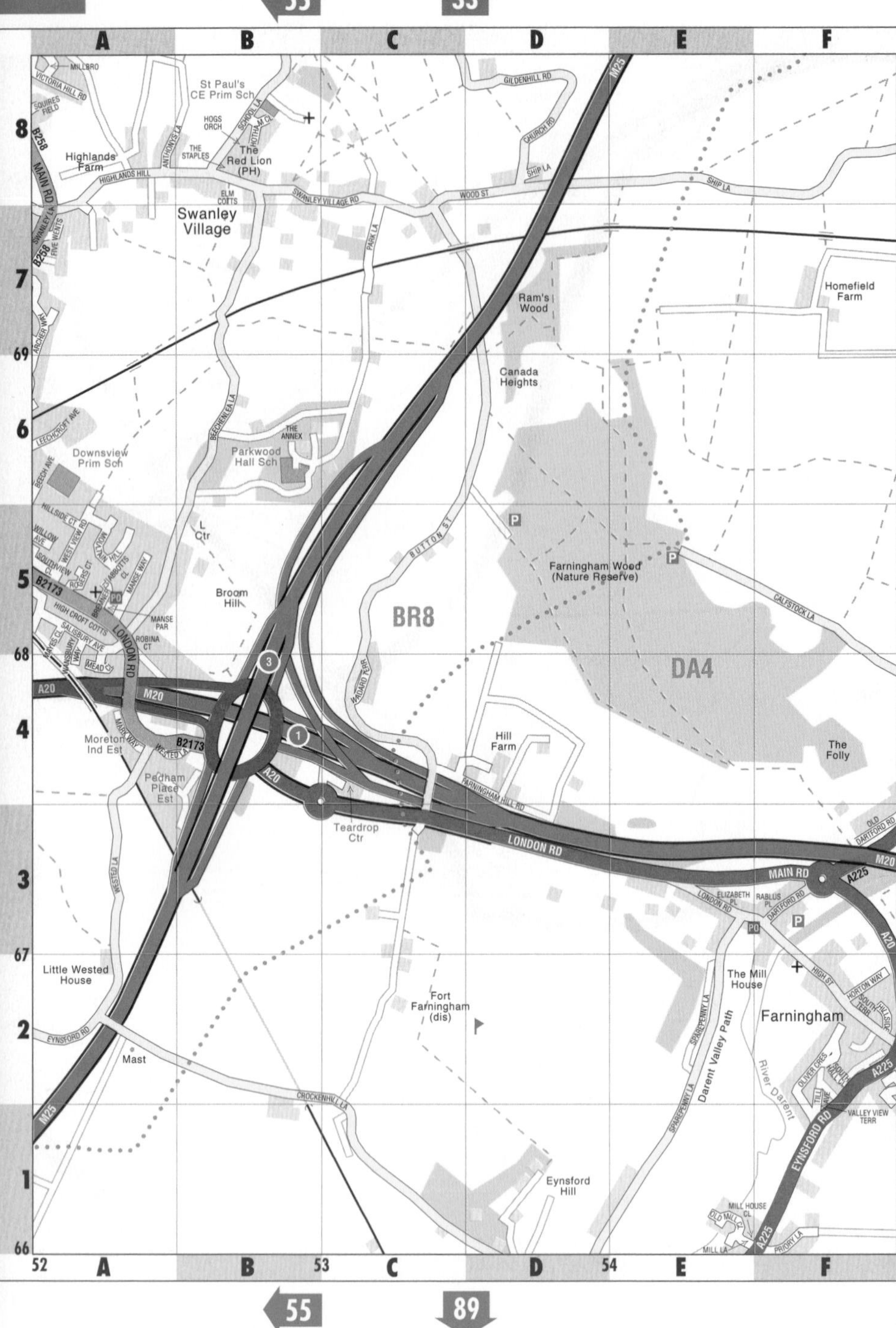
A
B
C
D
E
F
8
7
69
6
5
68
4
3
67
2
1
66
52
53
54
St Paul's CE Prim Sch
Highlands Farm
The Red Lion (PH)
Swanley Village
Ram's Wood
Homefield Farm
Canada Heights
Downsview Prim Sch
Parkwood Hall Sch
L Ctr
Broom Hill
BR8
Farningham Wood (Nature Reserve)
DA4
Hill Farm
The Folly
Moreton Ind Est
Pedham Place Est
Teardrop Ctr
Little Wested House
Fort Farningham (dis)
The Mill House
Farningham
Mast
Eynsford Hill
Darent Valley Path
River Darent
M25
M20
A20
A225
B258
B2173
MAIN RD
LONDON RD
SHIP LA
WOOD ST
SWANLEY VILLAGE RD
HIGHLANDS HILL
GILDENHILL RD
CHURCH RD
PARK LA
BEECHENLEA LA
BUTTON ST
CALFSTOCK LA
FARNINGHAM HILL RD
WESTED LA
EYNSFORD RD
CROCKENHILL LA
SPAREPENNY LA
HIGH ST
EYNSFORD RD
MILL LA
PRIORY LA

55
89

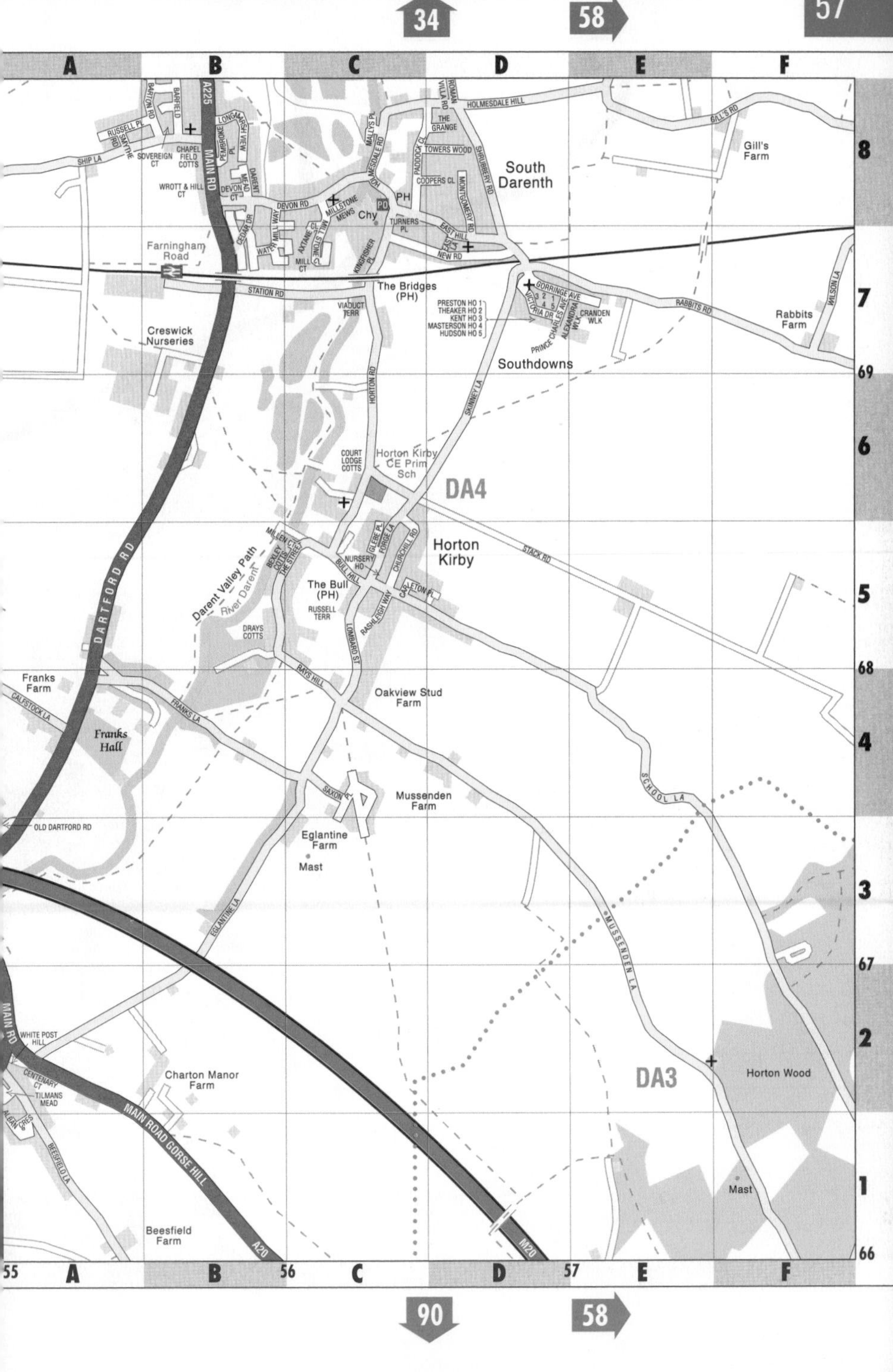
34
58
A
B
C
D
E
F
South Darenth
Farningham Road
The Bridges (PH)
Creswick Nurseries
Southdowns
Gill's Farm
Rabbits Farm
Horton Kirby CE Prim Sch
DA4
Horton Kirby
The Bull (PH)
Darent Valley Path
River Darent
Franks Farm
Franks Hall
Oakview Stud Farm
Mussenden Farm
Eglantine Farm
Mast
Charton Manor Farm
Beesfield Farm
DA3
Horton Wood
DARTFORD RD
MAIN RD
A225
HOLMESDALE HILL
GILL'S RD
STATION RD
RABBITS RD
STACK RD
SCHOOL LA
MUSSENDEN LA
RAYS HILL
FRANKS LA
CALFSTOCK LA
OLD DARTFORD RD
EGLANTINE LA
MAIN ROAD GORSE HILL
BEESFIELD LA
HORTON RD
SKINNEY LA
SHRUBBERY RD
ROMAN VILLA RD
WILSON LA
PRESTON HO 1
THEAKER HO 2
KENT HO 3
MASTERSON HO 4
HUDSON HO 5
M20
A20
8
7
69
6
5
68
4
3
67
2
1
66
55
56
57
90
58

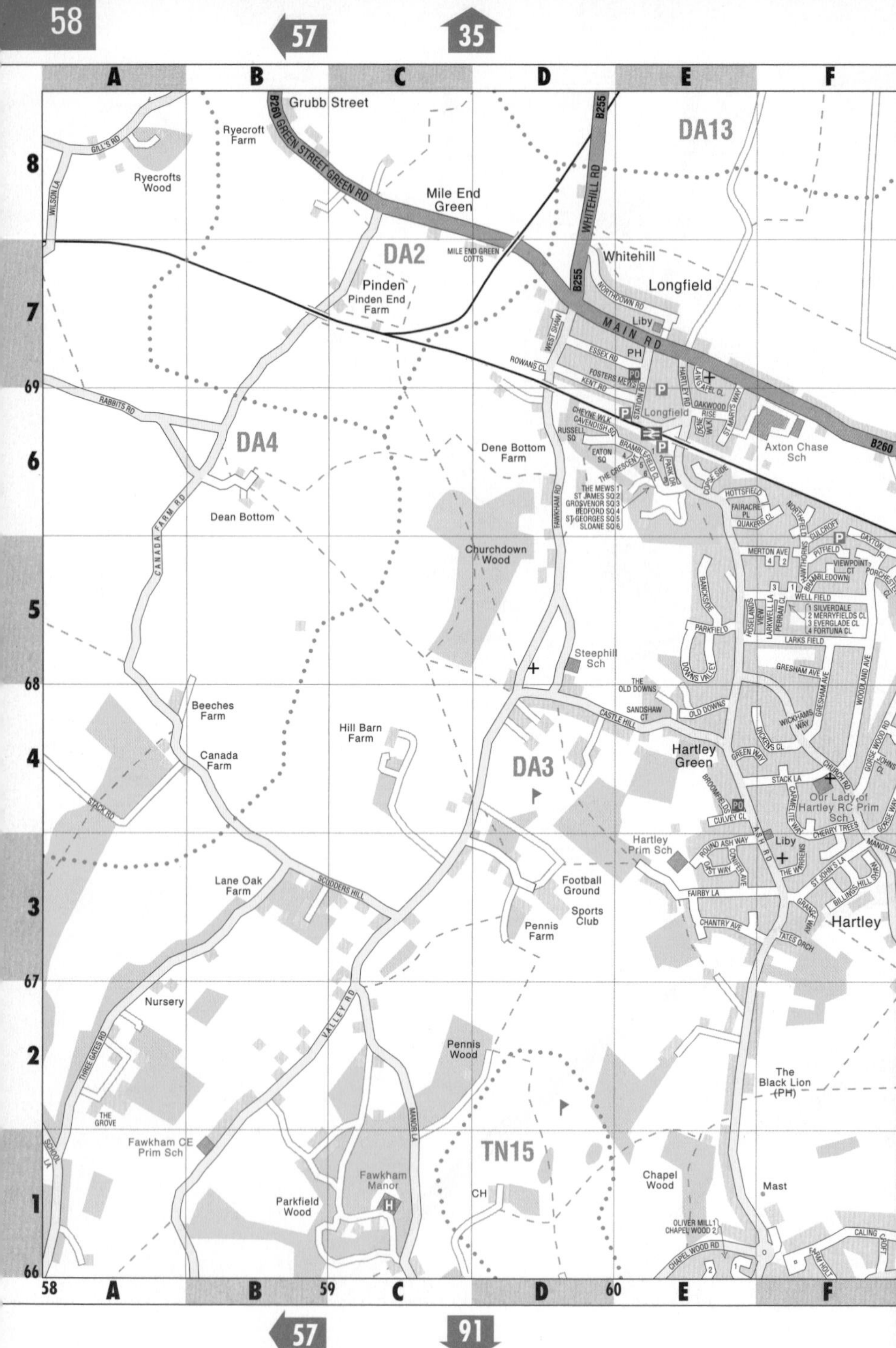

57
35

8

Gill's Rd

Grubb Street

Ryecroft Farm

Ryecrofts Wood

B260 GREEN STREET GREEN RD

WILSON LA

Mile End Green

DA13

B255

WHITEHILL RD

7

DA2

Pinden

Pinden End Farm

MILE END GREEN COTTS

NORTHDOWN RD

B255

Whitehill

Longfield

WEST HILL

ESSEX RD

MAIN RD

Liby

69

RABBITS RD

ROWANS CL

KENT RD

FOSTERS MDW

PH

Longfield

P

Axton Chase Sch

B260

DA4

CHEYNE WLK

CAVENDISH CL

RUSSELL SQ

EATON SQ

P

OAKWOOD RISE

HARTLEY RD

THE DRIVE

6

Dene Bottom Farm

THINKSHAM RD

THE MEWS 1
ST. JAMES 1
GROSVENOR SQ 3
BEDFORD SQ 4
ST.GEORGES SQ 5
SLOANE SQ 6

BRAXBY FIELDS

HOTTSFIELD

FAIRACRES
PL
QUAKERS

Dean Bottom

Churchdown Wood

CANADA FARM RD

MERTON AVE

VIEWPOINT

SMILEDOWN

WELL FIELD

1 SILVERDALE
2 MERRYFIELDS CL
3 EVERGLADE CL
4 FORTUNA CL

PITFIELD

SATTON

GRESHAM AVE

WICKHAM WAY

WOODLAND AVE

5

Steephill Sch

PARKFIELD

LARKS FIELD

GRESHAM AVE

GRESHAM AVE

68

Beeches Farm

THE OLD DOWNS

SANDSHAW CT

OLD DOWNS

CASTLE HILL

DOWNS VW

DOWNS VALLEY

Canada Farm

Hill Barn Farm

DA3

Hartley Green

GREEN HVVT

DICKENS CL

BROMHOLM CT

STACK LA

STACK RD

CAMILTE LANE

PH

Our Lady of Hartley RC Prim Sch

4

Lane Oak Farm

Hartley Prim Sch

CULVEY CL

YOUNG ASH WAY

ASH WAY

Liby

CHERRY TREES

THE VW

ST. JOHN LA

MANOR DR

3

SCUDDERS HILL

Pennis Farm

Football Ground

Sports Club

FAIRBY LA

CHANTRY AVE

GRANGE RD

BILLINGS HILL

TATES ORCH

Hartley

67

Nursery

VALLEY RD

Pennis Wood

The Black Lion (PH)

THREE GATES RD

2

THE GROVE

MANOR LA

Fawkham CE Prim Sch

Parkfield Wood

Fawkham Manor

H

TN15

CH

Chapel Wood

Mast

CALING CRST

1

OLIVER MILL 1
CHAPEL WOOD 2

CHAPEL WOOD RD

2

66

57
91

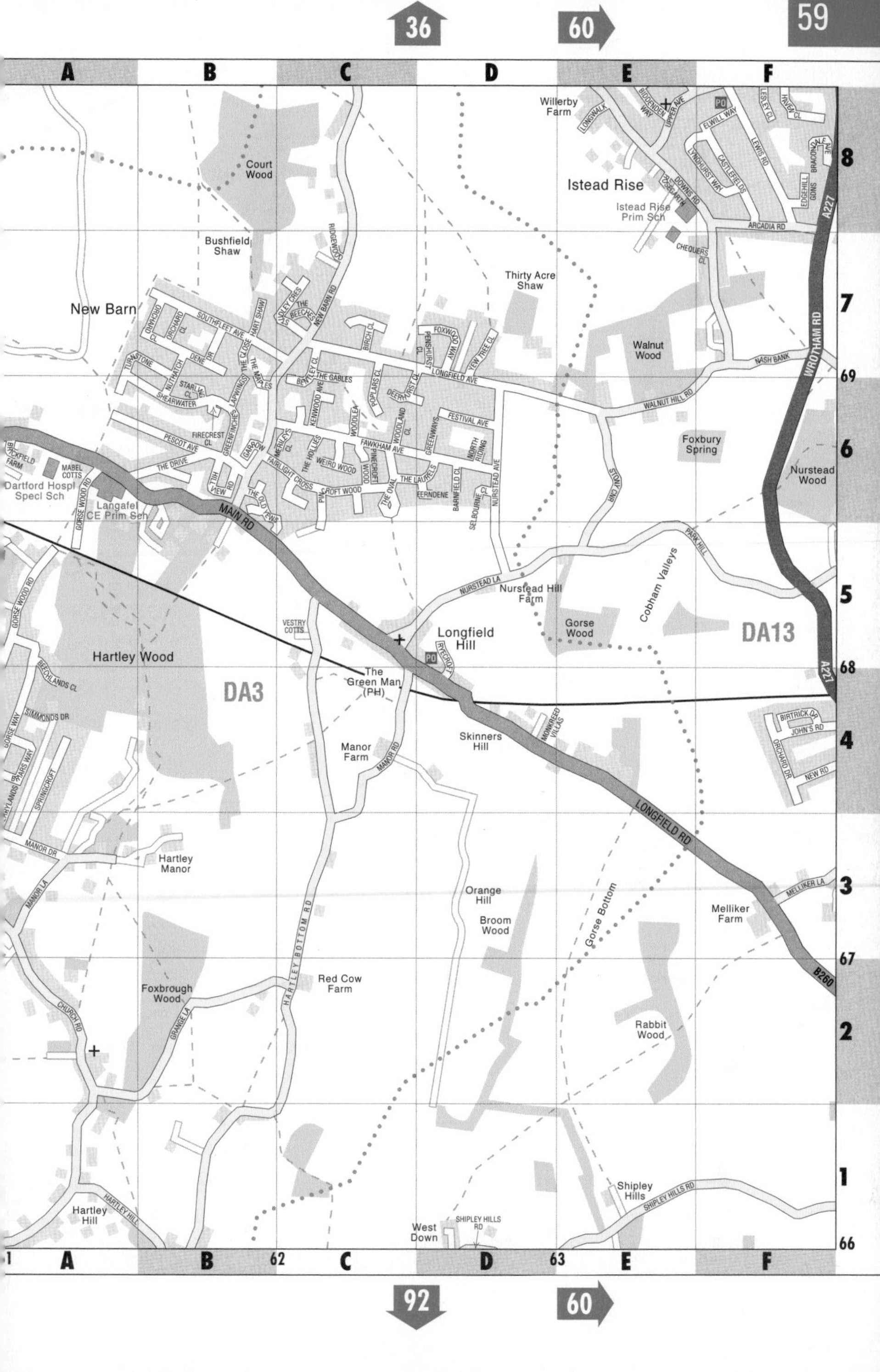
36
60
Court Wood
Bushfield Shaw
New Barn
Istead Rise
Istead Rise Prim Sch
Willerby Farm
Thirty Acre Shaw
Walnut Wood
Foxbury Spring
Nurstead Wood
Dartford Hospl Specl Sch
Langafel CE Prim Sch
Hartley Wood
DA3
Nurstead Hill Farm
Longfield Hill
Gorse Wood
Cobham Valleys
DA13
The Green Man (PH)
Manor Farm
Skinners Hill
Hartley Manor
Orange Hill
Broom Wood
Gorse Bottom
Melliker Farm
Red Cow Farm
Foxbrough Wood
Rabbit Wood
Shipley Hills
Hartley Hill
West Down
MAIN RD
LONGFIELD RD
WROTHAM RD
A227
B260
NURSTEAD LA
WALNUT HILL RD
NASH BANK
HARTLEY BOTTOM RD
MANOR RD
SHIPLEY HILLS RD
92
60

59
37

| | A | B | C | D | E | F |

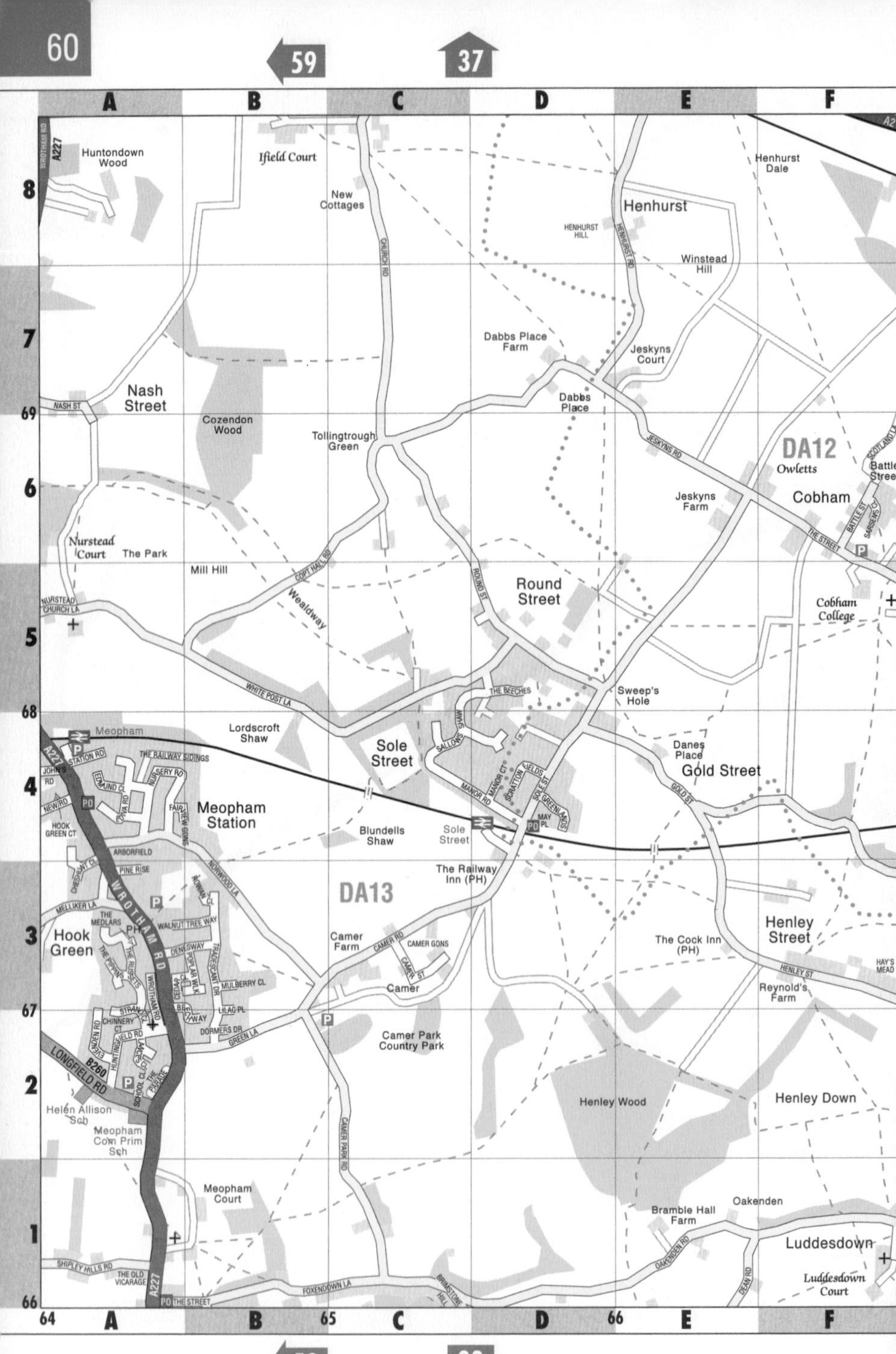

8

A227
HURSTEAD RD
Huntondown Wood
Ifield Court
New Cottages
Henhurst
Henhurst Dale
A2
HENHURST HILL
Winstead Hill

7

Dabbs Place Farm
Jeskyns Court

69
NASH ST
Nash Street
Cozendon Wood
Tollingtrough Green
Dabbs Place
JESKYNS RD
DA12
Owletts
Battle Street
BATTLE ST

6
Nurstead Court
The Park
Mill Hill
Jeskyns Farm
Cobham
THE STREET
Cobham College
SCOTLAND LA

Wealdway
OPT HALL RD
Round Street
ROUND ST

5
NURSTEAD CHURCH LA
WHITE POST LA
THE BEECHES
Sweep's Hole
Danes Place

68
Meopham
STATION RD
JOHN'S RD
Lordscroft Shaw
Sole Street
SATION
MANOR RD
Gold Street
GOLD ST

4
A227
NEW RD
Meopham Station
ARBORFIELD
Blundells Shaw
Sole Street
MAY PL
Henley Street

HOOK GREEN CT
PINE RISE
The Railway Inn (PH)

3
MELLIKER LA
WROTHAM RD
THE MEDLARS
WALNUT TREE WAY
Hook Green
DA13
Camer Farm
CAMER RD
CAMER GDNS
The Cock Inn (PH)
Henley Street
HENLEY ST
HAY'S MEAD
Reynold's Farm
Camer

67
CHINNERY
MULBERRY CL
LILAC PL
Camer Park Country Park
DORMERS DR
GREEN LA

2
B260
LONGFIELD RD
Helen Allison Sch
Meopham Com Prim Sch
Henley Wood
Henley Down

1
Meopham Court
Bramble Hall Farm
Oakenden
Luddesdown
SHIPLEY HILLS RD
THE OLD VICARAGE
A227
PO THE STREET
FOXENDOWN LA
BRIMSTONE HILL
OAKENDEN RD
DEAN RD
Luddesdown Court

66

| 64 | A | B | 65 | C | D | 66 | E | F |

59
93

38
62

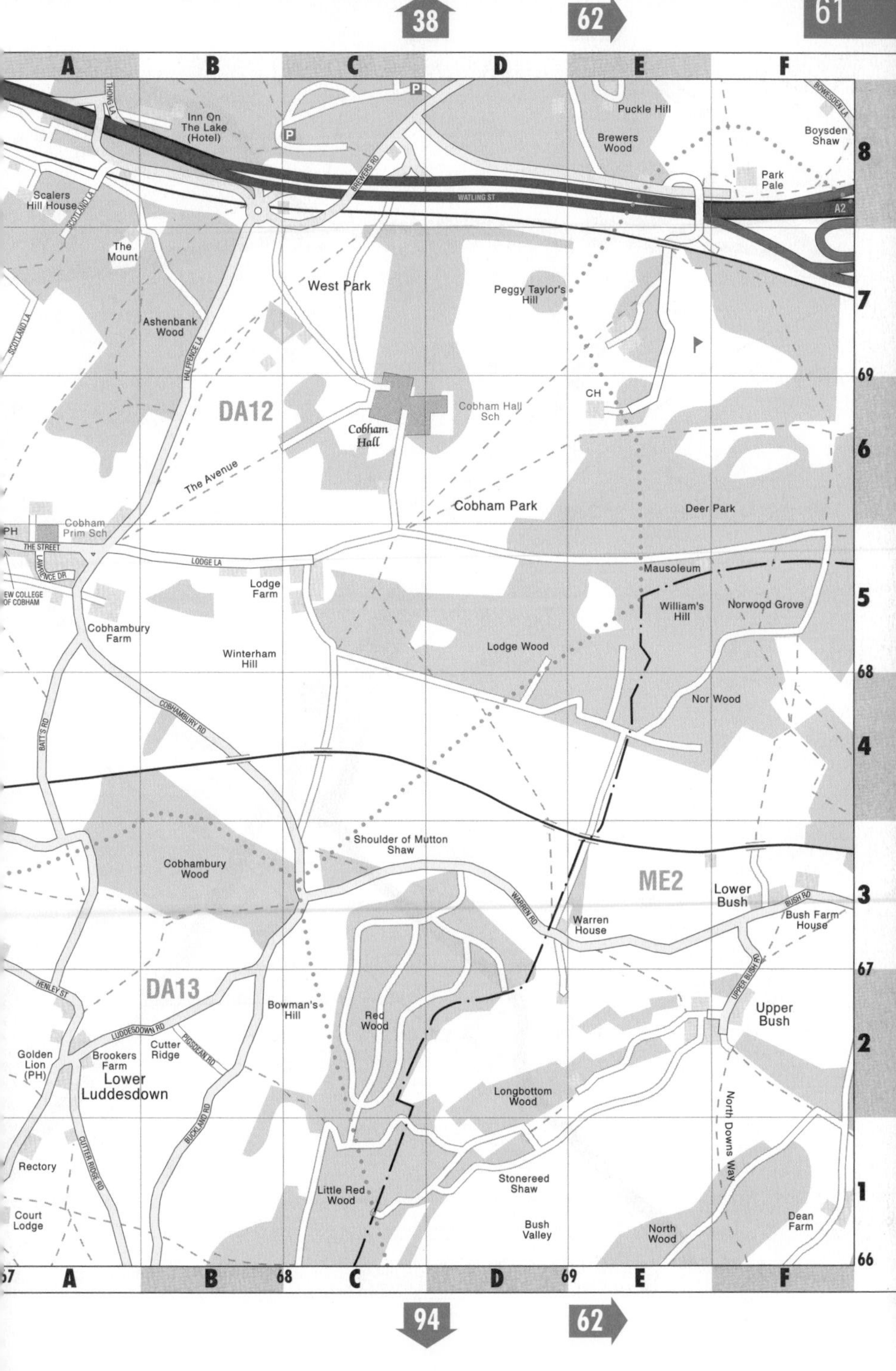
Inn On
The Lake
(Hotel)
Puckle Hill
Brewers
Wood
Boysden
Shaw
Park
Pale
Scalers
Hill House
WATLING ST
A2
The
Mount
West Park
Peggy Taylor's
Hill
Ashenbank
Wood
DA12
CH
Cobham Hall
Sch
Cobham
Hall
The Avenue
Cobham Park
Deer Park
Cobham
Prim Sch
PH
THE STREET
LODGE LA
Mausoleum
Lodge
Farm
William's
Hill
Norwood Grove
Cobhambury
Farm
Winterham
Hill
Lodge Wood
Nor Wood
COBHAMBURY RD
BAIT'S RD
Shoulder of Mutton
Shaw
Cobhambury
Wood
ME2
Lower
Bush
BUSH RD
Bush Farm
House
WARREN RD
Warren
House
DA13
HENLEY ST
Bowman's
Hill
Red
Wood
UPPER BUSH RD
Upper
Bush
LUDDESDOWN RD
Golden
Lion
(PH)
Brookers
Farm
Cutter
Ridge
PIGSDEAN RD
Lower
Luddesdown
Longbottom
Wood
North Downs Way
BUCKLAND RD
CUTTER RIDGE RD
Rectory
Little Red
Wood
Stonereed
Shaw
Court
Lodge
Bush
Valley
North
Wood
Dean
Farm
A
B
C
D
E
F
8
7
69
6
5
68
4
3
67
2
1
66
67
68
69

94
62

61
39

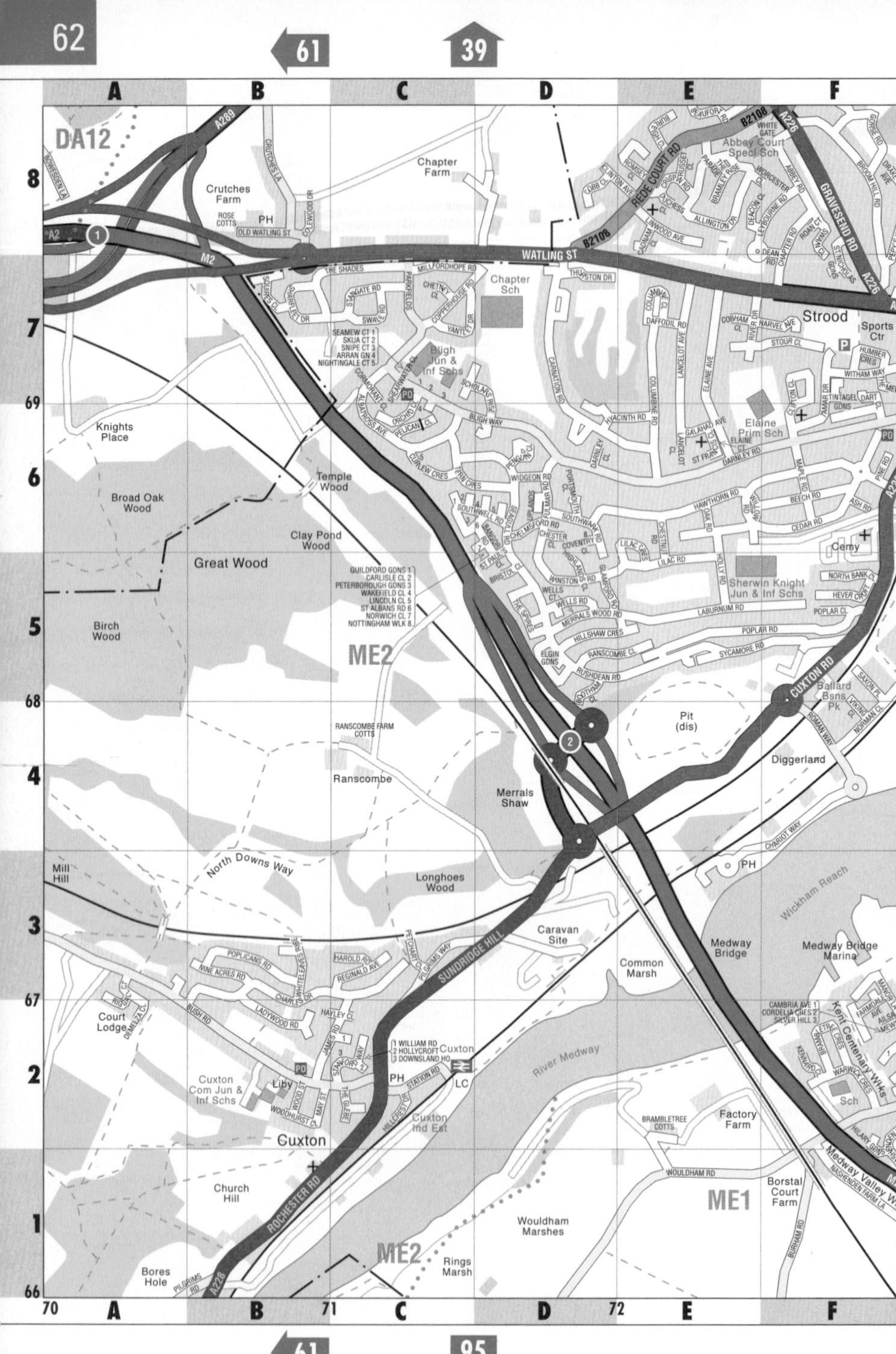
A
B
C
D
E
F
8
7
69
6
5
68
4
3
67
2
1
66
70
71
72
DA12
A289
A2
M2
A226
B2108
A228
WATLING ST
REDE COURT RD
GRAVESEND RD
CUXTON RD
SUNDRIDGE HILL
ROCHESTER RD
Crutches Farm
Chapter Farm
Abbey Court Specl Sch
Chapter Sch
Bligh Jun & Inf Schs
Elaine Prim Sch
Sherwin Knight Jun & Inf Schs
Strood
Sports Ctr
Cemy
Knights Place
Temple Wood
Broad Oak Wood
Clay Pond Wood
Great Wood
Birch Wood
ME2
Ballard Bsns Pk
Pit (dis)
Diggerland
Ranscombe
Merrals Shaw
Mill Hill
North Downs Way
Longhoes Wood
Caravan Site
Common Marsh
Medway Bridge
Medway Bridge Marina
Wickham Reach
River Medway
Court Lodge
Cuxton Com Jun & Inf Schs
Liby
Cuxton
Cuxton Ind Est
Church Hill
Factory Farm
Borstal Court Farm
ME1
Wouldham Marshes
Rings Marsh
Bores Hole
Kent Centenary Wks
Sch
SEAMEW CT 1
SKUA CT 2
SNIPE CT 3
ARRAN GN 4
NIGHTINGALE CT 5
GUILDFORD GDNS 1
CARLISLE CL 2
PETERBOROUGH GDNS 3
WAKEFIELD CL 4
LINCOLN CL 5
ST ALBANS RD 6
NORWICH CL 7
NOTTINGHAM WLK 8
1 WILLIAM RD
2 HOLLYCROFT
3 DOWNSLAND HO
CAMBRIA AVE 1
CORDELIA CRES 2
SILVER HILL 3
RANSCOMBE FARM COTTS
BRAMBLETREE COTTS
WOULDHAM RD
BURHAM RD
NASHENDEN FARM LA
Medway Valley Wk
POPLICANS RD
NINE ACRES RD
WHITEWALLS RD
HAROLD RD
REGINALD AVE
CHARLES DR
LADYWOOD RD
BUSH RD
HAYLEY CL
JAMES RD
STAFFORD
WOOD ST
MAY ST
THE GLEBE
WOODHURST CL
STATION RD
HILLCREST RD
PILGRIMS WAY
PILGRIMS RD
BLIGH WAY
CARNATION RD
COLUMBINE RD
LANCELOT AVE
ELAINE AVE
DARNLEY RD
HAWTHORN RD
BEECH RD
CEDAR RD
LILAC RD
LABURNUM RD
POPLAR RD
SYCAMORE RD
RUSHDEAN RD
RANSCOMBE CL
HILLSHAW CRES
MERRALS WOOD RD
WELLS RD
WIDGEON RD
MAPLE RD
HOLLY RD
NORTH BANK CL
HEVER CROFT
POPLAR CL
HYACINTH RD
DAFFODIL RD
COBHAM CL
HARVEL AVE
STOUR CL
HUMBER CRES
WITHAM WAY
ALLINGTON DR
LINWOOD AVE
ROMAN WAY
CHARIOT WAY
ROSE COTTS
OLD WATLING ST
COLEWOOD DR
THE SHADES
MILLFORDHOPE RD
PARKFIELDS
CHETNEY CL
COPPERHOUSE RD
YANTLET DR
STANGATE RD
PH
PO
LC

61
95

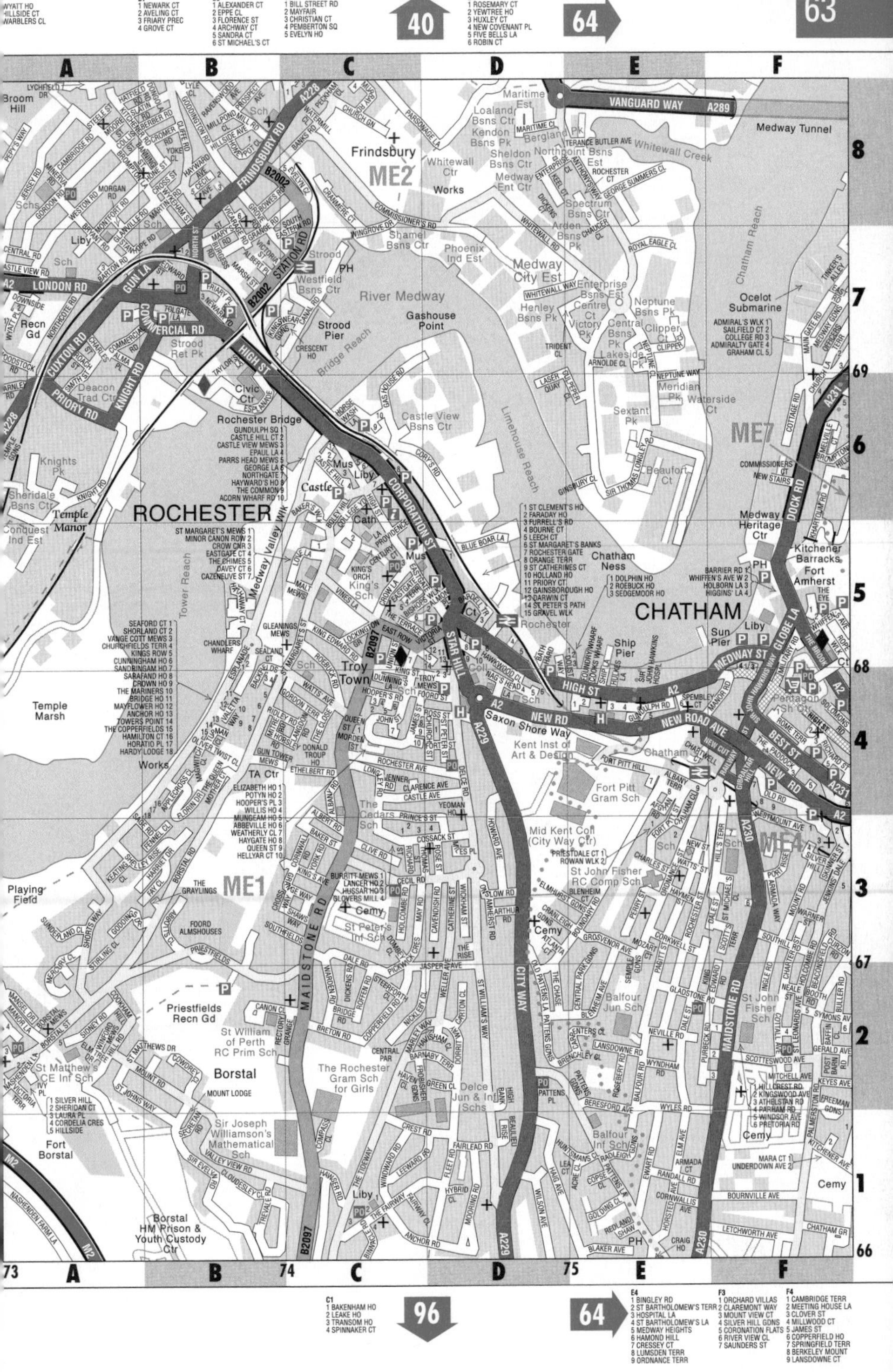

WYATT HO
HILLSIDE CT
WARBLERS CL
B7
1 NEWARK CT
2 AVELING CT
3 FRIARY PREC
4 GROVE CT
B8
1 ALEXANDER CT
2 EPPE CL
3 FLORENCE ST
4 ARCHWAY CT
5 SANDRA CT
6 ST MICHAEL'S CT
C8
1 BILL STREET RD
2 MAYFAIR
3 CHRISTIAN CT
4 PEMBERTON SQ
5 EVELYN HO
40
D4
1 ROSEMARY CT
2 YEWTREE HO
3 HUXLEY CT
4 NEW COVENANT PL
5 FIVE BELLS LA
6 ROBIN CT
64
A
B
C
D
E
F
8
7
69
6
5
68
4
3
67
2
1
66
73
74
75
Broom Hill
Frindsbury
ME2
Maritime Est
VANGUARD WAY
A289
Medway Tunnel
Whitewall Creek
Whitewall Ctr
Works
Medway City Est
River Medway
Gashouse Point
Strood Pier
Bridge Reach
Strood
Westfield Bsns Ctr
LONDON RD
A2
FRINDSBURY RD
A228
B2002
STATION RD
HIGH ST
CUXTON RD
PRIORY RD
KNIGHT RD
COMMERCIAL RD
Recn Gd
Strood Ret Pk
Deacon Trad Ctr
Civic Ctr
Rochester Bridge
Knights Pk
Sheridale Bsns Ctr
Temple Manor
Conquest Ind Est
ROCHESTER
Castle
Cath
Mus
Liby
CORPORATION ST
Castle View Bsns Ctr
Limehouse Reach
Chatham Reach
Ocelot Submarine
ME7
Medway Heritage Ctr
Kitchener Barracks
Fort Amherst
DOCK RD
CHATHAM
Chatham Ness
Sun Pier
Ship Pier
MEDWAY ST
HIGH ST
NEW RD
NEW ROAD AVE
Pentagon Sh Ctr
Chatham
Troy Town
STAR HILL
Rochester
Tower Reach
Medway Valley Wlk
Temple Marsh
Works
TA Ctr
ME1
Playing Field
The Cedars Sch
Saxon Shore Way
Kent Inst of Art & Design
Fort Pitt Gram Sch
Mid Kent Coll (City Way Ctr)
St John Fisher RC Comp Sch
ME4
MAIDSTONE RD
A229
CITY WAY
A230
B2097
Cemy
St Peter's Inf Sch
Priestfields Recn Gd
St William of Perth RC Prim Sch
Borstal
St Matthew's CE Inf Sch
The Rochester Gram Sch for Girls
Delce Jun & Inf Schs
Balfour Jun Sch
Balfour Inf Sch
St John Fisher Sch
Sir Joseph Williamson's Mathematical Sch
Fort Borstal
Borstal HM Prison & Youth Custody Ctr
M2
Liby
Cemy

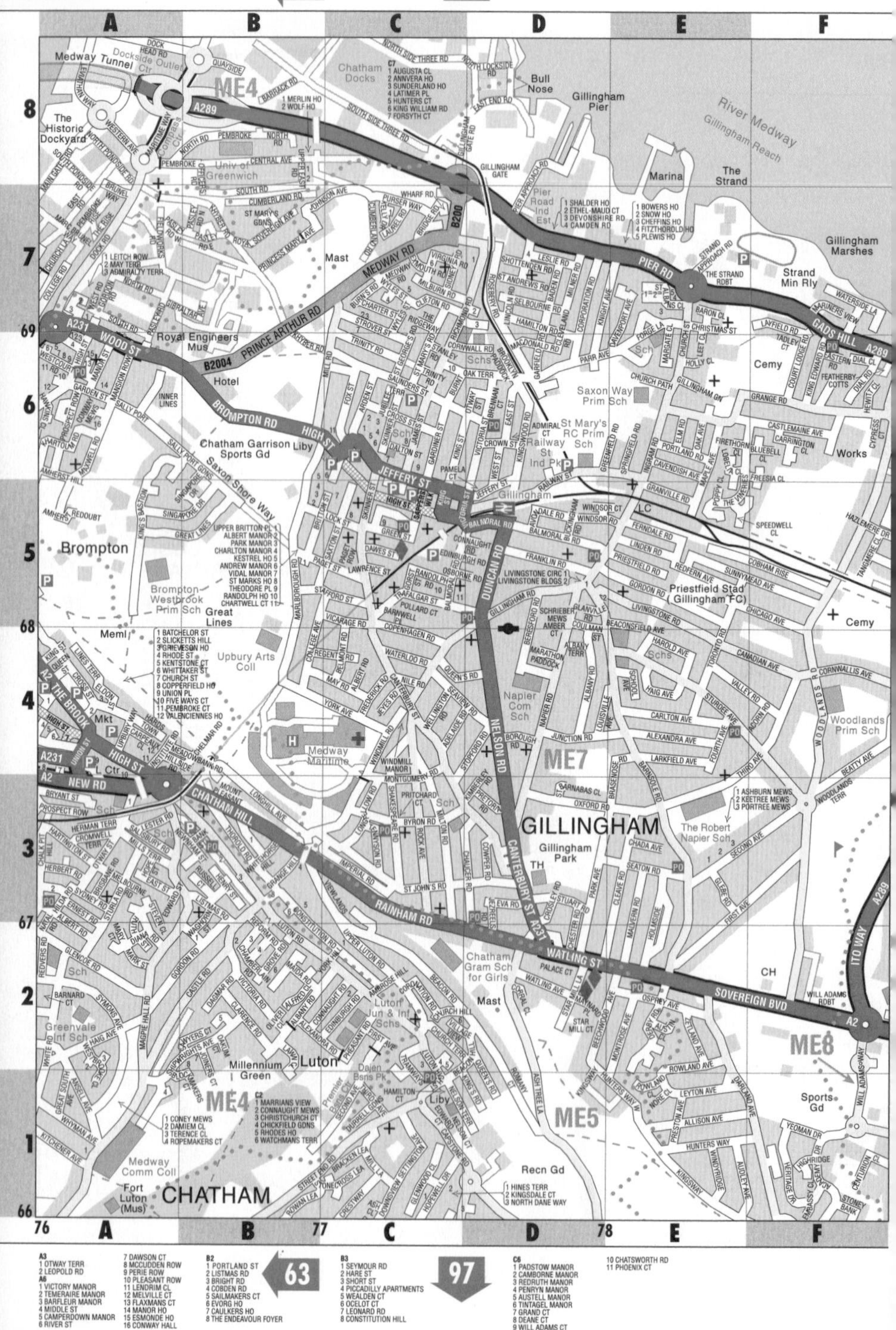

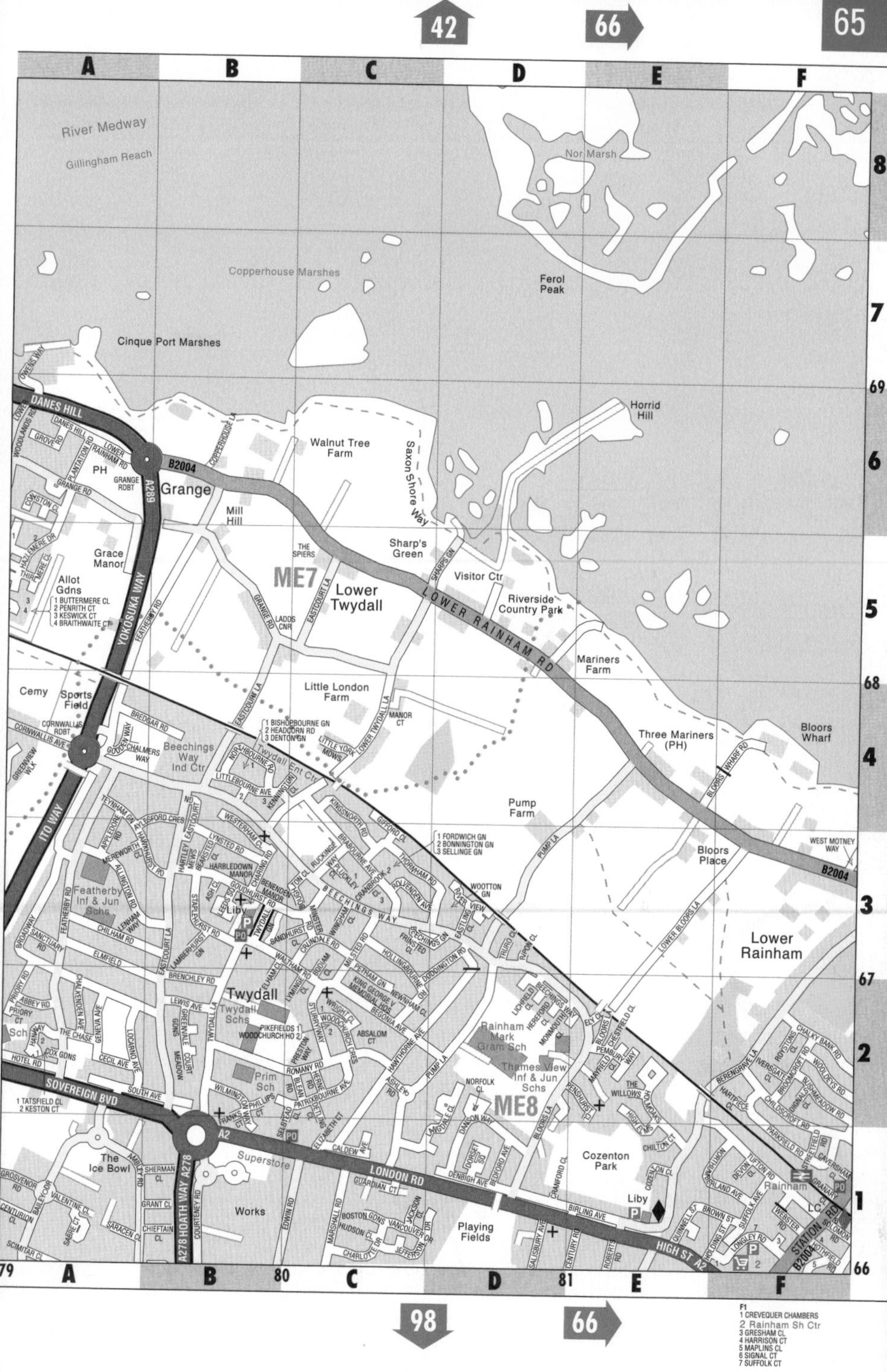

42   66

98   66

River Medway
Gillingham Reach

Nor Marsh

Copperhouse Marshes

Ferol Peak

Cinque Port Marshes

Horrid Hill

DANES HILL

Walnut Tree Farm

B2004   A289   Grange

Mill Hill

Grace Manor

THE SPIERS

Sharp's Green

Visitor Ctr

ME7   Lower Twydall

Riverside Country Park

Allot Gdns
1 BUTTERMERE CL
2 PENRITH CT
3 KESWICK CT
4 BRAITHWAITE CL

LADOS CNR

LOWER RAINHAM RD

Mariners Farm

Cemy

Sports Field

Little London Farm

MANOR CT

1 BISHOPBOURNE GN
2 HEADCORN RD
3 DENTON GN

Bloors Wharf

Three Mariners (PH)

Beechings Way Ind Ctr

Pump Farm

Bloors Place

1 FORDWICH GN
2 BONNINGTON GN
3 SELLINGE GN

WOOTTON GN

WEST MOTNEY WAY

B2004

Featherby Inf & Jun Schs

Liby
P

Lower Rainham

Twydall

Twydall Schs

Pikefields
WOODCHURCH HO

ABSALOM CT

Rainham Mark Gram Sch

Thames View Inf & Jun Schs

Prim Sch

ME8

The Willows

1 TATSFIELD CL
2 KESTON CT

NORFOLK CL

Cozenton Park

Liby
P

Rainham

SOVEREIGN BVD

A2

The Ice Bowl

Superstore

LONDON RD

GUARDIAN CT

HIGH ST A2

STATION RD

Works

Playing Fields

BIRLING AVE

F1
1 CREVEQUER CHAMBERS
2 Rainham Sh Ctr
3 GRESHAM CL
4 HARRISON CT
5 MAPLINS CL
6 SIGNAL CT
7 SUFFOLK CT

65 43

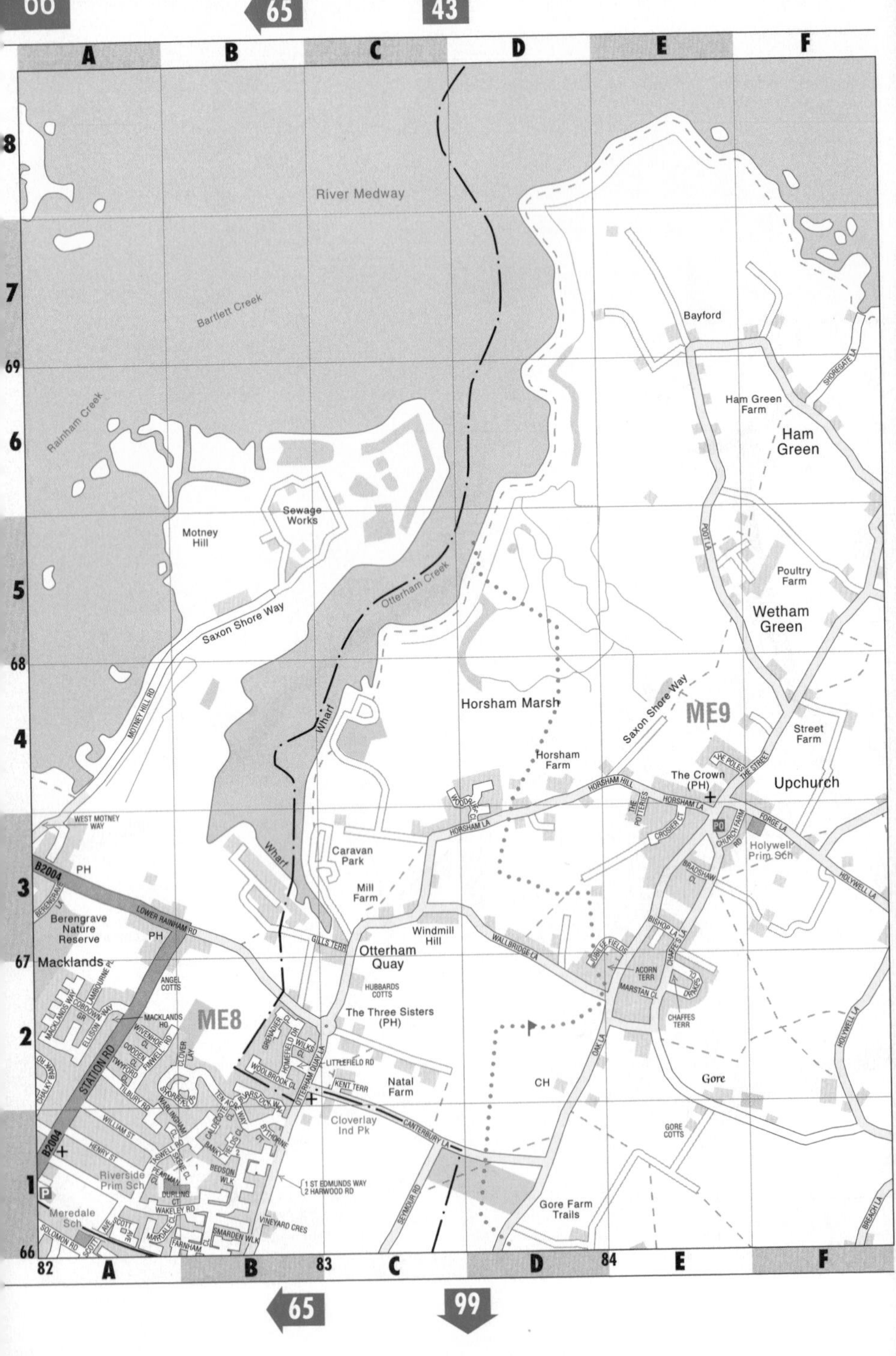
A
B
C
D
E
F
8
7
69
6
5
68
4
3
67
2
1
66
82
83
84
River Medway
Bartlett Creek
Rainham Creek
Otterham Creek
Motney Hill
Sewage Works
Saxon Shore Way
MOTNEY HILL RD
WEST MOTNEY WAY
B2004
PH
BERENGRAVE LA
Berengrave Nature Reserve
LOWER RAINHAM RD
Macklands
ANGEL COTTS
MACKLANDS HO
ME8
STATION RD
Wharf
Caravan Park
Mill Farm
Windmill Hill
GILLS TERR
Otterham Quay
HUBBARDS COTTS
The Three Sisters (PH)
LITTLEFIELD RD
KENT TERR
Natal Farm
Cloverlay Ind Pk
CANTERBURY LA
SEYMOUR RD
Riverside Prim Sch
Meredale Sch
Horsham Marsh
Horsham Farm
HORSHAM LA
HORSHAM HILL
WALLBRIDGE LA
CH
OAK LA
Gore Farm Trails
Bayford
Ham Green Farm
Ham Green
SHOREGATE LA
POOT LA
Poultry Farm
Wetham Green
ME9
Street Farm
The Crown (PH)
Upchurch
FORGE LA
Holywell Prim Sch
HOLYWELL LA
CHURCH FARM RD
BRADSHAW CL
BISHOP LA
CHAFFES LA
ACORN TERR
MARSTAN CL
CHAFFES TERR
JUBILEE FIELDS
CROSIER CT
THE POTTERIES
THE STREET
THE POLES
Gore
GORE COTTS
BREACH LA
1 ST EDMUNDS WAY
2 HARWOOD RD

65 99

44
68

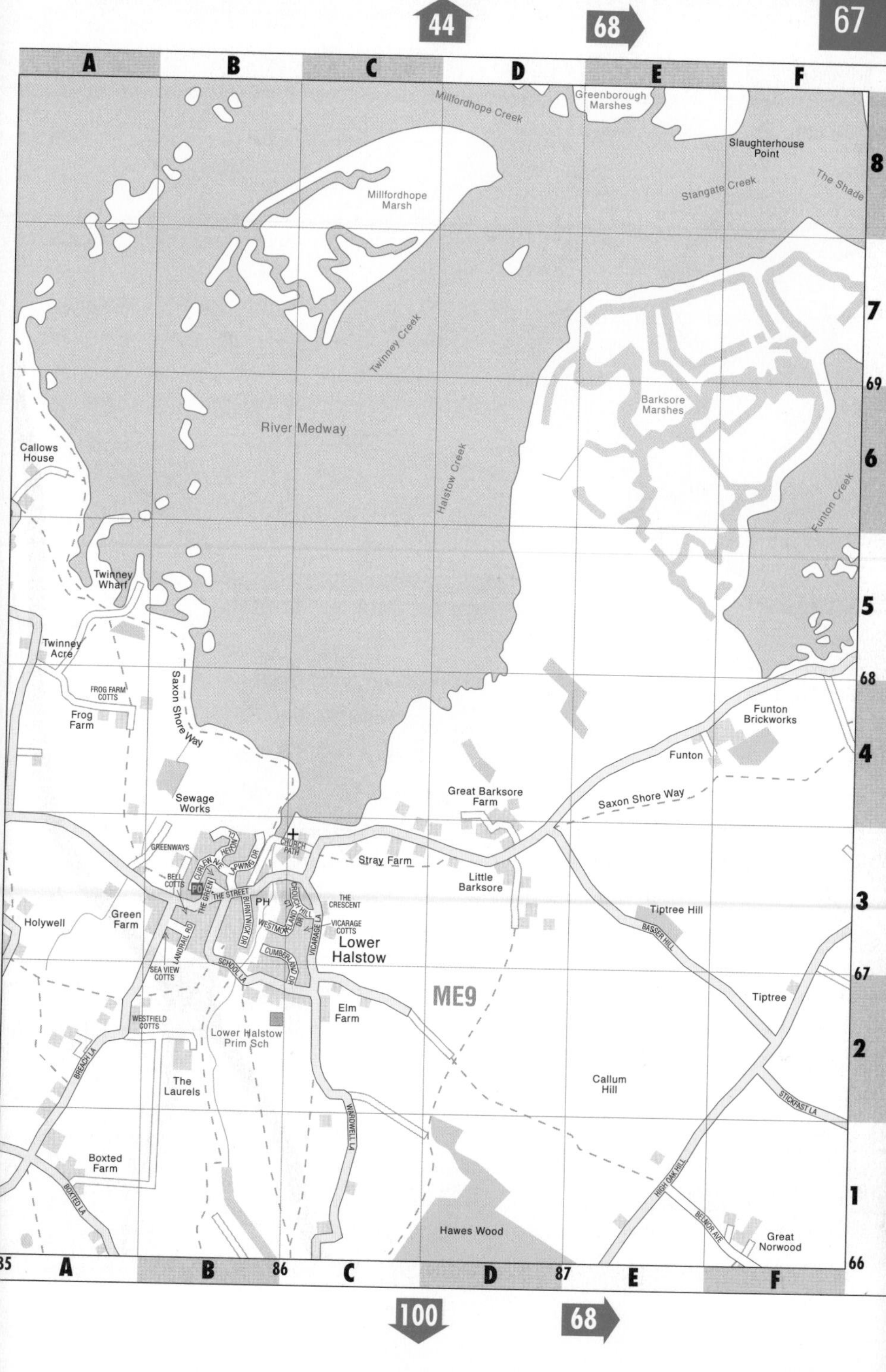
A
B
C
D
E
F
Millfordhope Creek
Greenborough Marshes
Slaughterhouse Point
Stangate Creek
The Shade
Millfordhope Marsh
8
Twinney Creek
7
69
River Medway
Barksore Marshes
Halstow Creek
Callows House
6
Funton Creek
Twinney Wharf
5
Twinney Acre
FROG FARM COTTS
Frog Farm
Saxon Shore Way
68
Funton Brickworks
Funton
4
Sewage Works
Great Barksore Farm
Saxon Shore Way
GREENWAYS
CHURCH PATH
Stray Farm
LAPWING DR
CURLEW AVE
BELL COTTS
PO
THE GREEN
THE STREET
Little Barksore
PH
CROUCH HILL CT
THE CRESCENT
3
Holywell
Green Farm
BURNTWICK DR
Tiptree Hill
BASSER HILL
LANDRAIL RD
WESTMORELAND DR
VICARAGE COTTS
VICARAGE LA
Lower Halstow
CUMBERLAND DR
SEA VIEW COTTS
SCHOOL LA
67
ME9
Tiptree
Elm Farm
WESTFIELD COTTS
Lower Halstow Prim Sch
2
BREACH LA
The Laurels
Callum Hill
STICKFAST LA
WARDWELL LA
Boxted Farm
1
BOXTED LA
HIGH OAK HILL
BELNOR AVE
Hawes Wood
Great Norwood
85
86
87
66

100
68

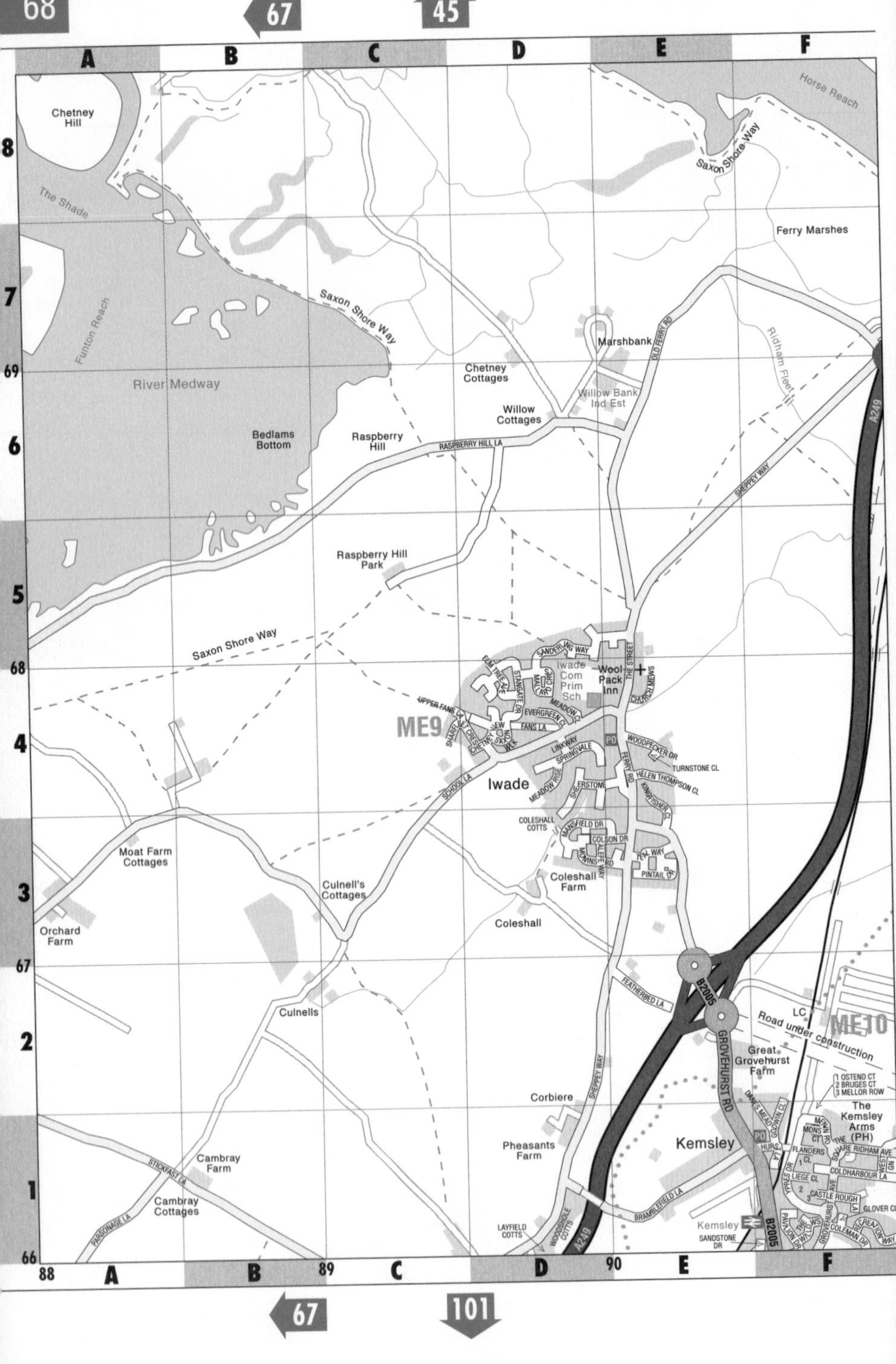
67
45
A
B
C
D
E
F
Chetney Hill
Horse Reach
Saxon Shore Way
The Shade
Ferry Marshes
Funton Reach
Saxon Shore Way
Marshbank
OLD FERRY RD
Ridham Fleet
River Medway
Chetney Cottages
Willow Bank Ind Est
A249
Willow Cottages
Bedlams Bottom
Raspberry Hill
RASPBERRY HILL LA
SHEPPEY WAY
Raspberry Hill Park
Saxon Shore Way
SANDERLING WAY
Iwade Com Prim Sch
Wool Pack Inn
THE STREET
CHURCH MEWS
ELM TREE AVE
STANGATE DR
UPPER FANS LA
EVERGREEN CL
MEADOW CL
FANS LA
ME9
PO
WOODPECKER DR
TURNSTONE CL
LINKWAY
SPRINGVALE
FERRY RD
HELEN THOMPSON CL
SCHOOL LA
Iwade
MEADOW RISE
KINGFISHER CL
COLESHALL COTTS
MANSFIELD DR
COLSON DR
TEAL WAY
PINTAIL DR
Moat Farm Cottages
Coleshall Farm
Culnell's Cottages
Orchard Farm
Coleshall
B2005
FEATHERBED LA
Culnells
LC
ME10
Road under construction
GROVEHURST RD
Great Grovehurst Farm
1 OSTEND CT
2 BRUGES CT
3 MELLOR ROW
SHEPPEY WAY
Corbiere
The Kemsley Arms (PH)
Pheasants Farm
Kemsley
FLANDERS
SQUARE
RIDHAM AVE
Cambray Farm
STICKFAST LA
COLDHARBOUR LA
LIEGE CL
CASTLE ROUGH
Cambray Cottages
BRAMBLEFIELD LA
GLOVER CL
PARSONAGE LA
LAYFIELD COTTS
WOODSHOLE COTTS
Kemsley
SANDSTONE DR
COLEMAN DR
B2005
8
7
69
6
5
68
4
3
67
2
1
66
88
89
90
67
101

46
70

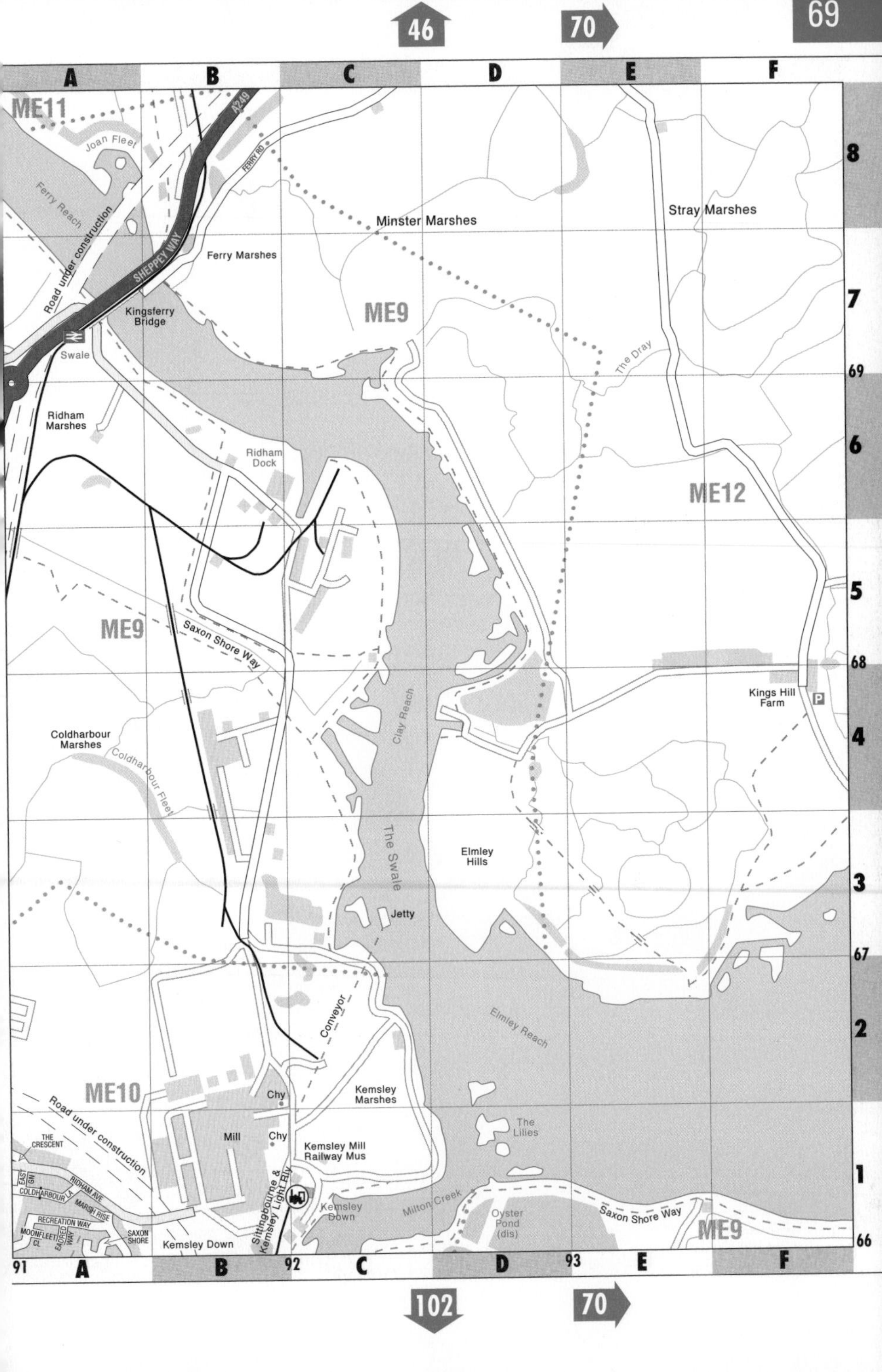
A
B
C
D
E
F
ME11
Joan Fleet
A249
FERRY RD
Ferry Reach
Road under construction
SHEPPEY WAY
Minster Marshes
Stray Marshes
Ferry Marshes
Kingsferry Bridge
ME9
Swale
The Dray
Ridham Marshes
Ridham Dock
ME12
ME9
Saxon Shore Way
Kings Hill Farm
Coldharbour Marshes
Coldharbour Fleet
Clay Reach
The Swale
Elmley Hills
Jetty
Conveyor
Elmley Reach
ME10
Chy
Kemsley Marshes
Road under construction
THE CRESCENT
Mill
Chy
Kemsley Mill Railway Mus
The Lilies
Sittingbourne & Kemsley Light Rly
EAST GN
RIDHAM AVE
COLDHARBOUR LA
MARSH RISE
RECREATION WAY
MOONFLEET CL
EADRED WAY
SAXON SHORE
Kemsley Down
Kemsley Down
Milton Creek
Oyster Pond (dis)
Saxon Shore Way
ME9
8
7
69
6
5
68
4
3
67
2
1
66
91
92
93

102
70

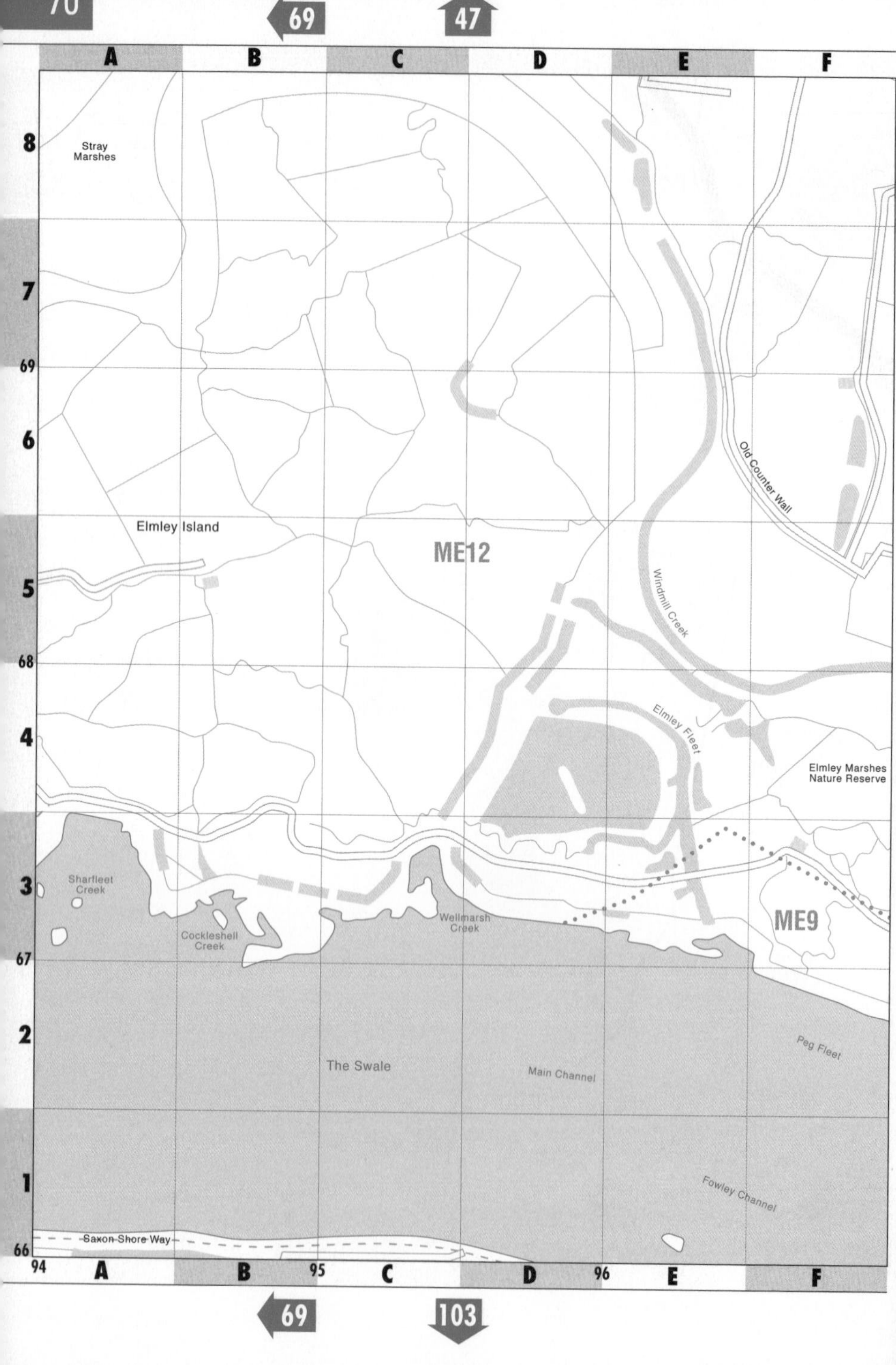

Stray
Marshes

Elmley Island

ME12

Old Counter Wall

Windmill Creek

Elmley Fleet

Elmley Marshes
Nature Reserve

Sharfleet
Creek

Cockleshell
Creek

Wellmarsh
Creek

ME9

Peg Fleet

The Swale

Main Channel

Fowley Channel

Saxon Shore Way

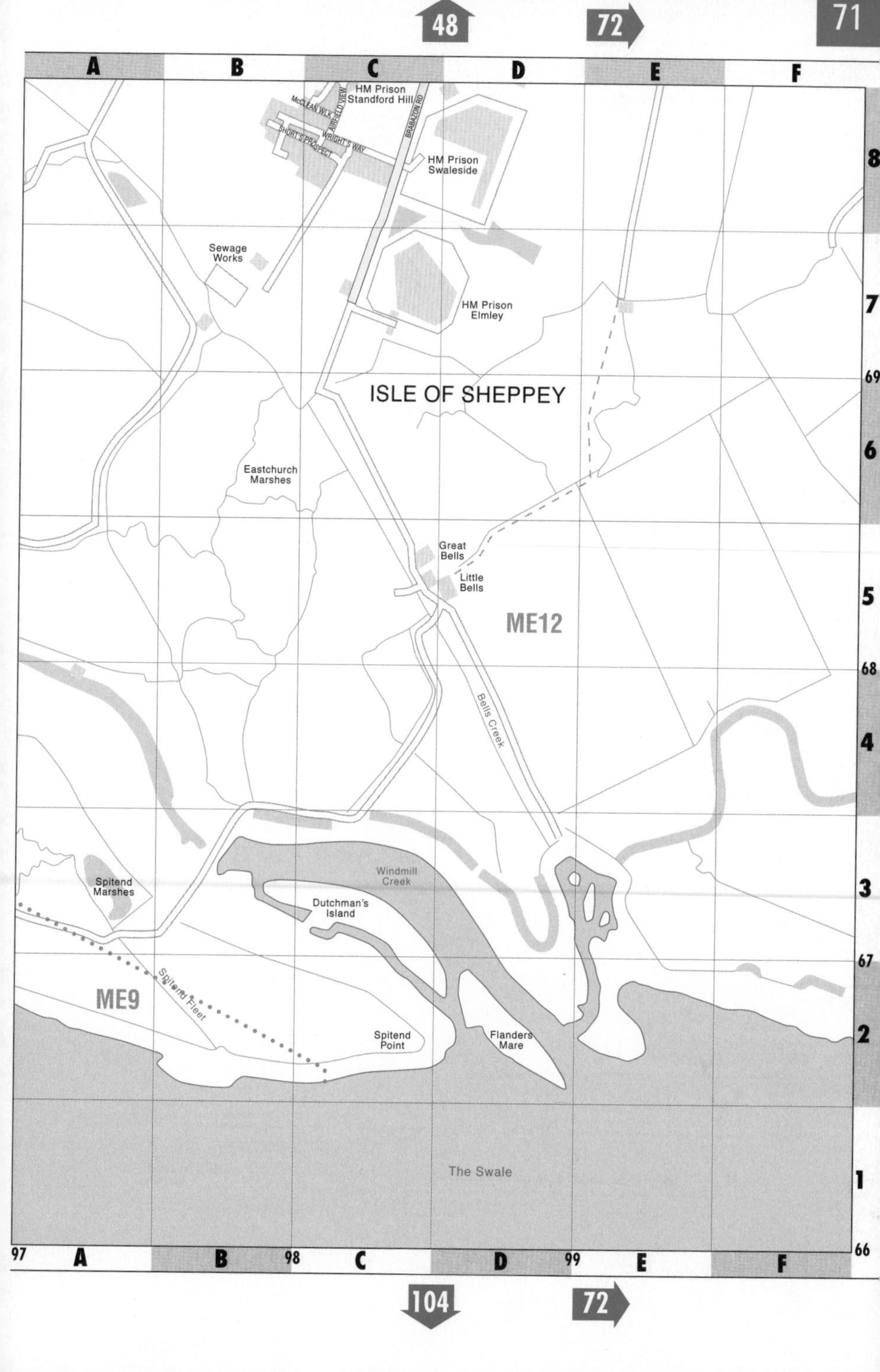

A B C D E F

8
7
69
6
5
68
4
3
67
2
1
66

HM Prison
Standford Hill

McLEAN WLK
WRIGHT'S WAY
SHORT'S PROSPECT
BRABAZON RD

HM Prison
Swaleside

Sewage
Works

HM Prison
Elmley

ISLE OF SHEPPEY

Eastchurch
Marshes

Great
Bells

Little
Bells

ME12

Bells Creek

Spitend
Marshes

Windmill
Creek

Dutchman's
Island

ME9

Spitend Fleet

Spitend
Point

Flanders
Mare

The Swale

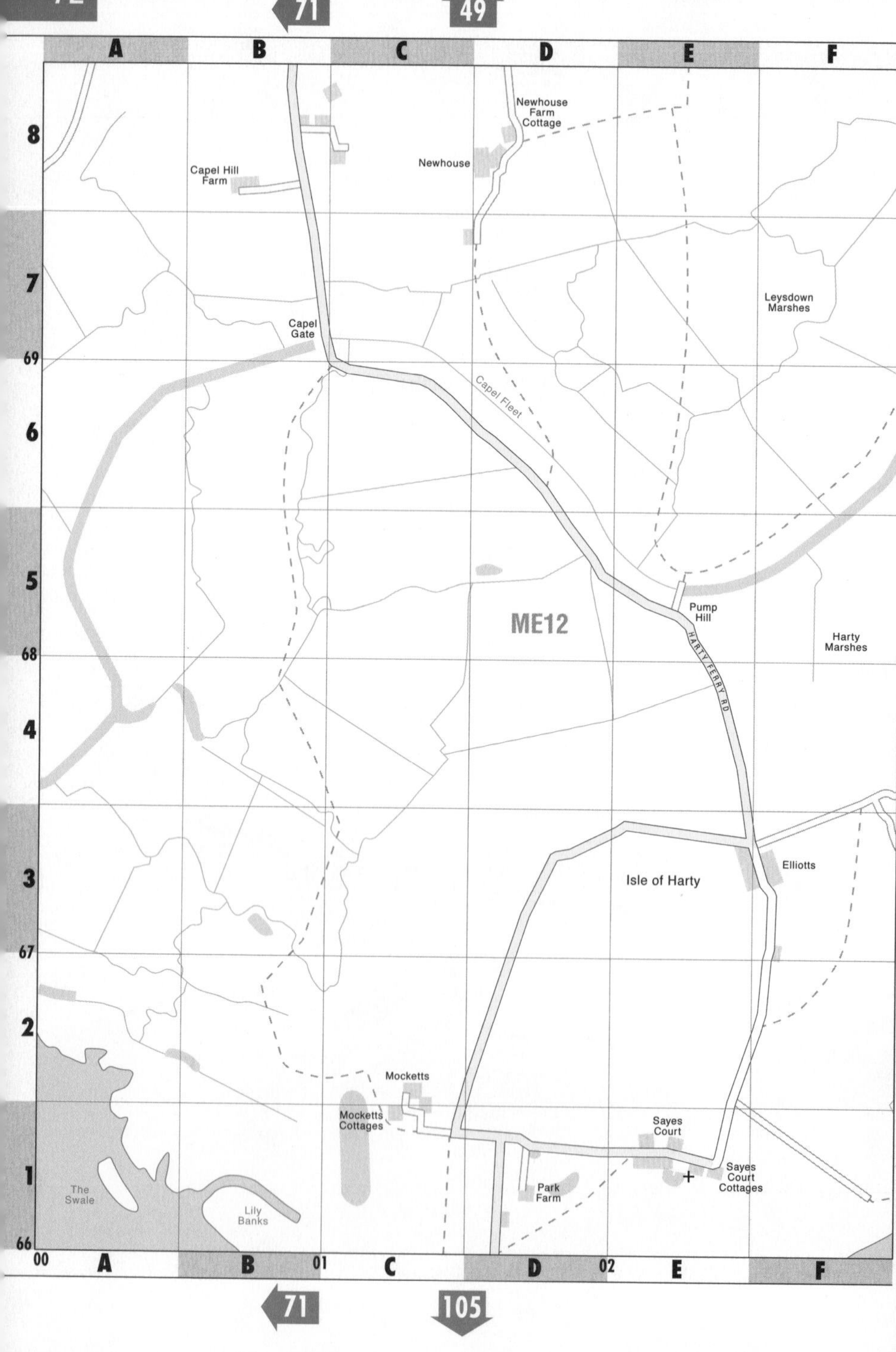

A   B   C   D   E   F

8

Newhouse
Farm
Cottage

Capel Hill
Farm

Newhouse

7

Leysdown
Marshes

Capel
Gate

69

Capel Fleet

6

5

Pump
Hill

ME12

68

Harty
Marshes

HARTY FERRY RD

4

3

Isle of Harty

Elliotts

67

2

Mocketts

The
Swale

Mocketts
Cottages

Sayes
Court

Sayes
Court
Cottages

1

Park
Farm

Lily
Banks

66

00   A   B   01   C   D   02   E   F

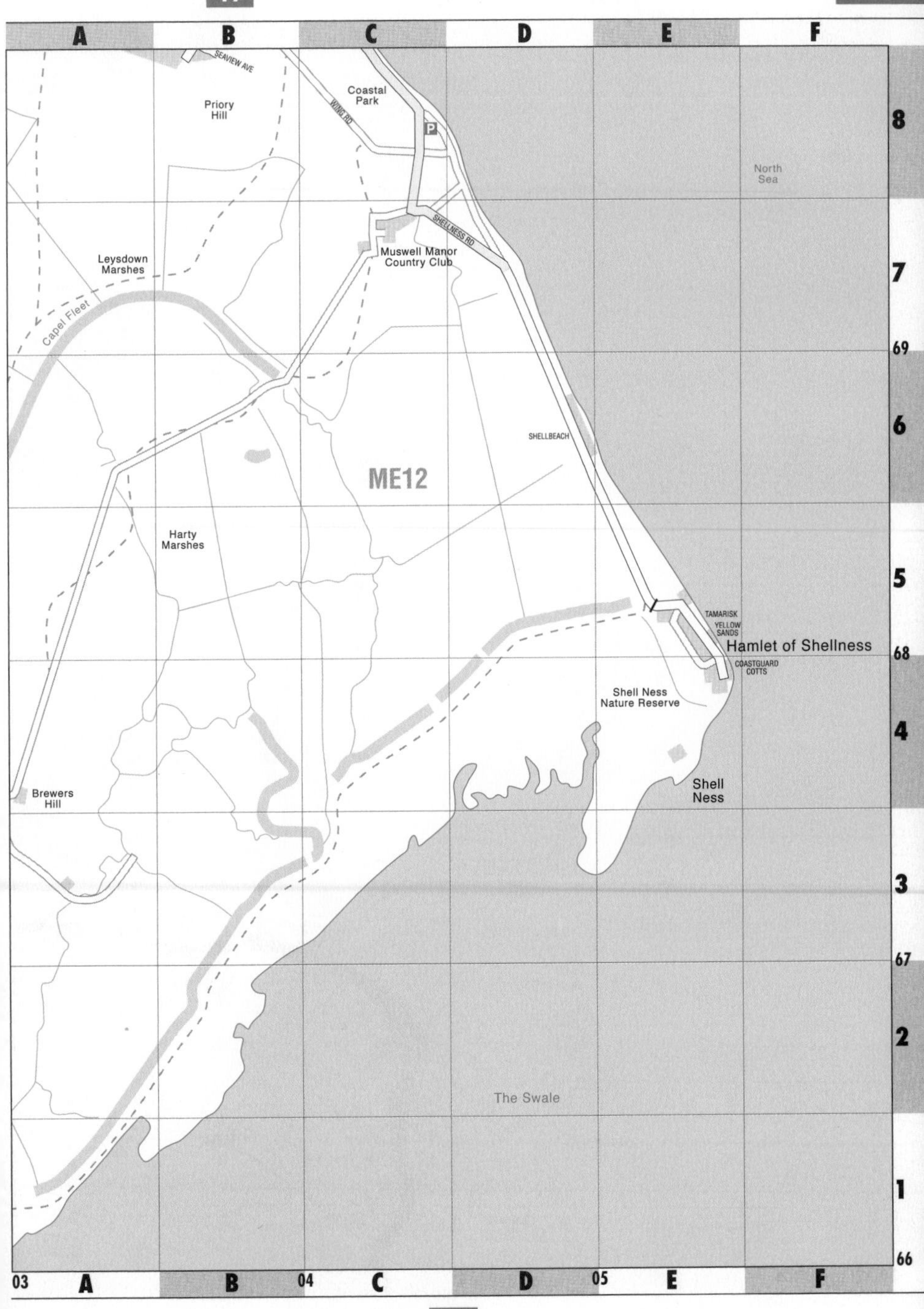

A   B   C   D   E   F

8

North
Sea

SEAVIEW AVE

Priory
Hill

Coastal
Park

7

Leysdown
Marshes

Muswell Manor
Country Club

69

Capel Fleet

6

ME12

SHELLBEACH

Harty
Marshes

5

TAMARISK
YELLOW
SANDS

Hamlet of Shellness

68

COASTGUARD
COTTS

Shell Ness
Nature Reserve

4

Shell
Ness

Brewers
Hill

3

67

The Swale

2

1

66

03   A   B   04   C   D   05   E   F

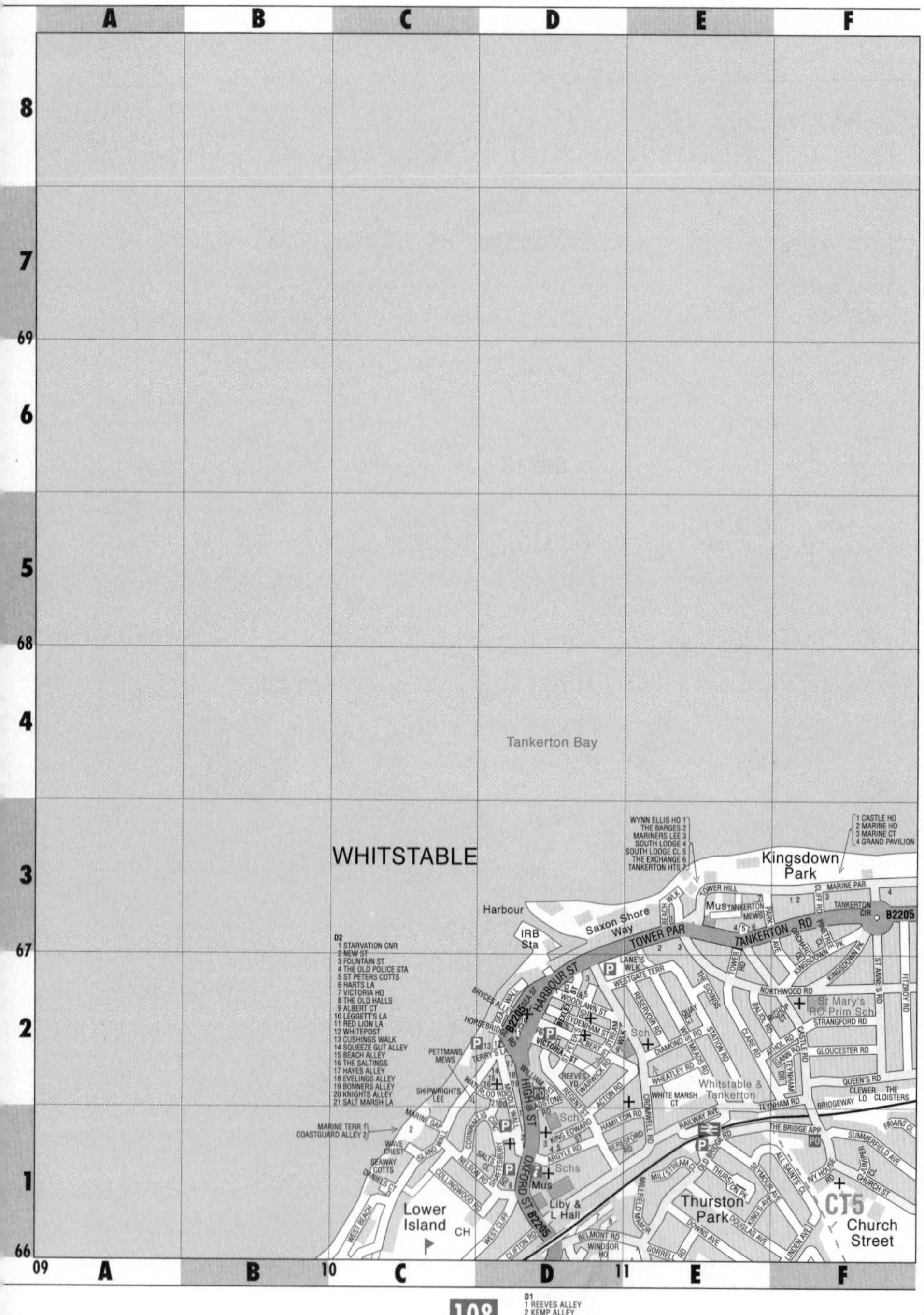

WHITSTABLE

Tankerton Bay

Kingsdown
Park

Harbour

WYNN ELLIS HO 1
THE BARGES 2
MARINERS LEE 3
SOUTH LODGE 4
SOUTH LODGE CL 5
THE EXCHANGE 6
TANKERTON HTS 7

1 CASTLE HO
2 MARINE HO
3 MARINE CT
4 GRAND PAVILION

D2
1 STARVATION CNR
2 NEW ST
3 FOUNTAIN ST
4 THE OLD POLICE STA
5 ST PETERS COTTS
6 HARTS LA
7 VICTORIA HO
8 THE OLD HALLS
9 ALBERT CT
10 LEGGETT'S LA
11 RED LION LA
12 WHITEPOST
13 CUSHINGS WALK
14 SQUEEZE GUT ALLEY
15 BEACH ALLEY
16 THE SALTINGS
17 HAYES ALLEY
18 EVELINGS ALLEY
19 BONNERS ALLEY
20 KNIGHTS ALLEY
21 SALT MARSH LA

MARINE TERR 1
COASTGUARD ALLEY 2

Lower
Island

Thurston
Park

CT5
Church
Street

108

D1
1 REEVES ALLEY
2 KEMP ALLEY
3 SKINNER'S ALLEY
4 OYSTER MEWS
5 OXFORD CL
6 OXFORD MANS
7 THE OLD COAL YD
8 BELMONT YD

	A	B	C	D	E	F
8						
7						
6						
5						
4						
3						
2						
1						

76

A	B	C	D	E	F

8
7
69
6
5
68
4
3
67
2
1
66

Long Rock
Saxon Shore Way
SEAVIEW CVN & CHALET PK
COASTGUARD COTTS
MORRIS AVE
AUSTIN AVE
HUMBER AVE
SUNBEAM AVE
CROSSLEY AVE
CRESTA CL
RILEY AVE
1 LINCOLN CL
2 DELMAR CL
3 SWAKELEY WLK
1 JUBILEE CT
2 KESTREL CT
3 ABBEY CT
4 ROBIN CT
5 TUDOR CT
6 ROYAL CT
Sewage Works
CT5
KITE FARM
PLOUGH LA
Swalecliffe
Tankerton
PRIEST & SOW CNR
MARINE CRES
LANE CT
BROOK RD
MARINE PAR
B2205
PRIEST WLK
PRINCESS RD
PRINCESS CL
TANKERTON CT
TANKERTON RD
SEAFIELD RD
HERNE BAY RD
BROOK RD
Cvn Pk
TASSELL'S WLK
ROCK WLK
SWALECLIFFE COURT DR
CHURCH WAY
ST AUGUSTINE'S CRES
COWPER RD
EDGAR PL
ST JOHN'S RD
RUSSELL DR
WOODMAN AVE
COLEWOOD RD
TYLER WAY
WHITSTABLE RD
B2205
St Augustines Bsns Pk
ESTUARY WAY
BENNELLS AVE
ST SWITHIN'S RD
BRIDGEFIELD CT
BRIDGEFIELD RD
BUCKINGHAM RD
KEMP RD
BURNAN RD
BURNAN CT
EMMERSON GDNS
RECTORY GDNS
GOODWIN AVE
LONGFIELD CT
LONGFIELD CL
A2990
BADDLESMERE RD
GRAYSTONE RD
MANOR RD
WYNN RD
LISA CT
PIER AVE
ELLIS RD
NORTHWOOD RD
NEWTON RD
SOUTHWOOD RD
Swalecliffe Com Prim Sch
ELM WOOD W
ELM WOOD E
Liby
Whitstable & Tankerton
PALACE CL
SWALECLIFFE RD
SUMMER CT
Chestfield & Swalecliffe
Bodkin Farm
Purchas Wood
QUEENS RD
THANET WAY
REEVES WAY
CH
Superstore
LAVENDER CL
MAYDOWNS RD
PLANTATION RD
ALMOND CL
SADDLERS MEWS
May Downs
OAKWOOD DR
HAM SHADES LA
NACHOL CL
FOXGROVE RD
John Wilson Bsns Pk
CHAUCER AVE
FLETCHER RD
MARLOW CL
HIGHGATE RD
PRIMROSE WAY
SHARE AND COULTER RD
CHURCHWOOD DR
KENDAL MDW
FRIARS CL
ENTICOTT CL
THE HEATH
HARVEY DR
GREEN LEAS
LONGACRE
NURSERY CL
BECKET CL
CLOVER RISE
HILLSIDE RD
RIDGEWAY
FERN CL
CHESTFIELD RD
THE LEAS
FAIRLAWN
BEECHCROFT
WOODCOTE
THE RIDINGS
LODGE FIELD RD
Chestfield
CT6
Ash Plantation
BRIDEWELL PK
RICHMOND RD
Highgate Lodge
LAXTON WAY
South Tankerton
BARTLETT DR
ELLISON CL
YOEMAN'S AVE
POLO WAY
THE LEAS
Woodcroft
CHURCH ST
A2990
GRASMERE RD
THE RUSSETS
CHARNWOOD
MOLEHILL RD

2 A	B	13 C	D	14 E	F

109
76

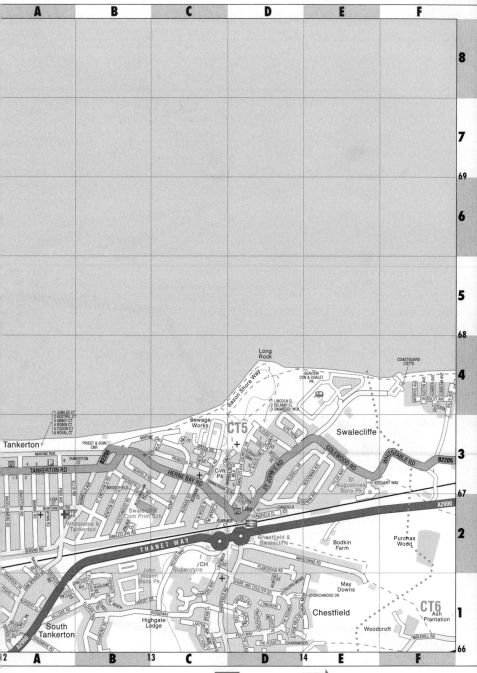

75

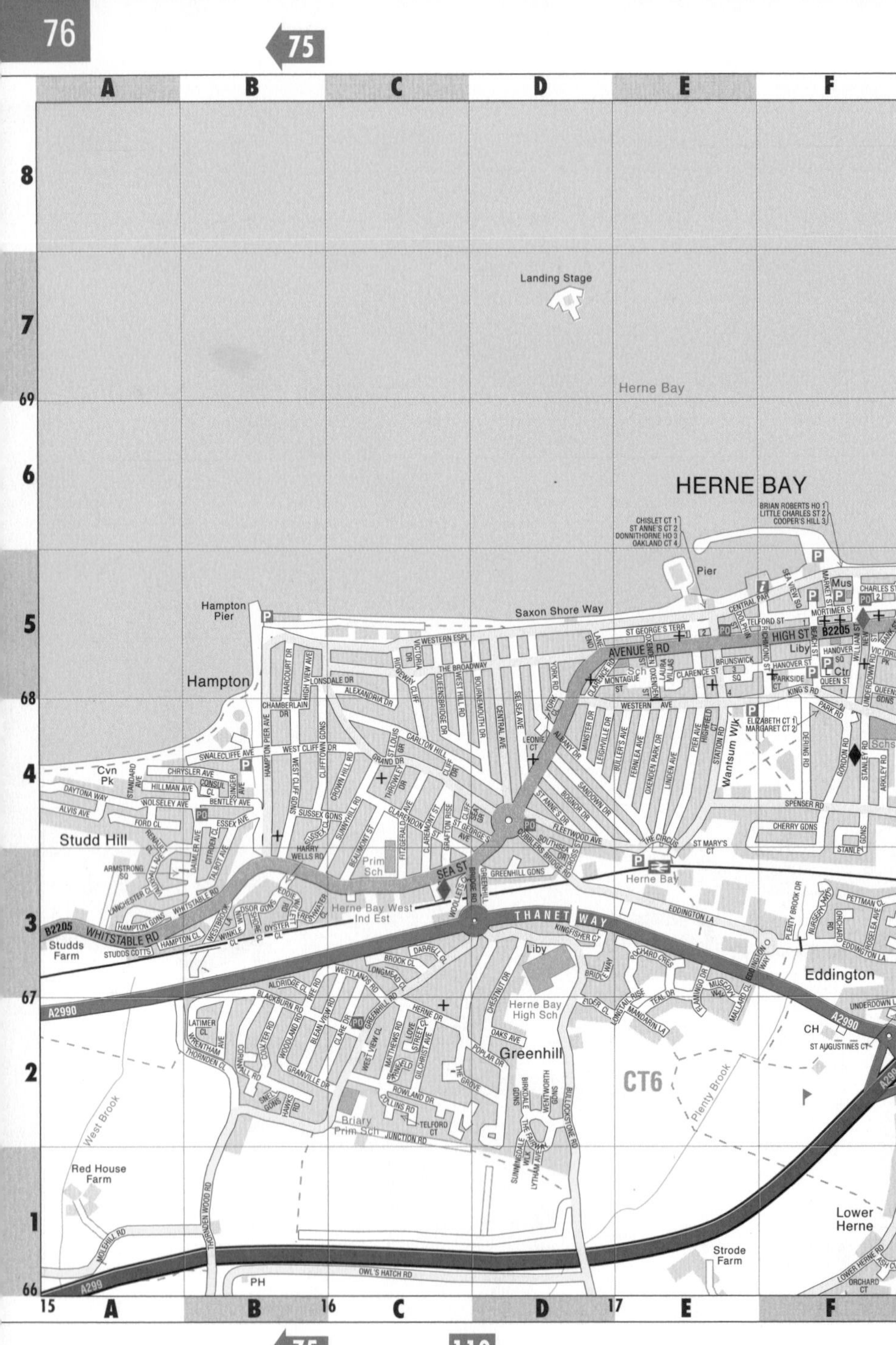

HERNE BAY
Herne Bay
Landing Stage
Pier
Hampton Pier
Hampton
Saxon Shore Way
Studd Hill
Cvn Pk
Studds Farm
Herne Bay West Ind Est
THANET WAY
A2990
A299
B2205
WHITSTABLE RD
SEA ST
HIGH ST
AVENUE RD
Greenhill
Herne Bay High Sch
Briary Prim Sch
Eddington
CT6
Plenty Brook
West Brook
Red House Farm
Strode Farm
Lower Herne
Wantsum Wlk
THE CIRCUS

75

110

A B C D E F

8
7
69
6

1 PROSPECT HILL
2 CHAPEL ST
3 CAVENDISH CT
4 HERTFORD HO

Wantsum Wlk
Beltinge Cliff
EAST CLIFF PAR
Saxon Shore Way
The Downs
CHARLES ST
NORTH ST
EAST ST
CANTERBURY RD
HIGH ST
BEACON WLK
BELLE VUE RD
HILL TOP RD
BEACON HILL
ALMA RD
THE LEES
ASHBEE GDNS
KNOWLER WAY
BURLINGTON DR
HAZLEMERE DR
LISMORE RD
CONYNGHAM RD
RECULVER RD
BELTINGE RD
RECULVER DR
FRESHLANDS
OCEAN VIEW
GLENBERVIE DR
GAINSBOROUGH DR
GARTH CL
SEAVILLE DR
PINE WLK
THE PADDOCKS
WANTSUM CL
PRIEST FIELDS
FAIRFAX DR
HILLBOROUGH DR
BISHOPSTONE DR
RECULVER CL
BISHOPSTONE LA
MANOR RD
HAVEN DR
MANOR CL
Bishopstone
5
SANDERLING RD
KINGSTON CL
ROSEBERY AVE
ROWLAND CRES
RICHMOND DR
PLOVER CL
CORMORANT WAY
KESTREL CL
KEAT FARM CL
KITTIWAKE CL
FULMAR WAY
PETREL CL
PUFFIN RD
68
Works
Hillborough Bsns Pk
Elm Court Farm
Sweech Bridge
Maystreet Bridge
MAY ST
SWEECHBRIDGE RD
Sewage Works
Mast
MAYSTREET CROSS
VICTORIA PK
SOUTH RD
FENOULHET WAY
CAVENDISH RD
BEACON RD
HILLBOROUGH RD
SALISBURY RD
THURLOW AVE
SYCAMORE CL
QUEENS AVE
REGENTS WLK
DOWNS PK
TYNDALE PK
HADLEIGH GDNS
DENCE CL
DENCE PK
BEACON AVE
SEA VIEW RD
LANDON RD
ASHBURN GDNS
GLEN AVE
ROSE GDNS
CLIFF AVE
HILARY CL
THE HORSHAMS
GLENBROOK CL
TERMINUS DR
HOLMSCROFT RD
LANCASTER GDNS
COVENTRY GDNS
OSBORNE GDNS
WILLOW TREE CL
MAXTED CT
ORCHARD PK
THORNHURST
CHURCHILL AVE
CLEMENTINE CL
WINSTON GDNS
Beltinge
CECIL PK
CECIL CT
REYNOLDS CL
Queen Victoria Meml
REEDS CL
MICKLEBURGH HILL
KING EDWARD AVE
KING EDWARD CT
GRANGE RD
HIGHFIELDS VIEW
MALVERN PK
HIGHFIELDS AVE
CHARTWELL AVE
GOSFIELD RD
Sch
QUEEN'S CT
ST ANDREWS CL
4
DOUGLAS RD
OAKDALE RD
IVANHOE RD
HERNE AVE
MICKLEBURGH AVE
HERNEVILLE GDNS
BURTON FIELDS
MEADOW CL
LAWRENCE GDNS
CHURCH VIEW
ACRES CL
MARITIME AVE
ARDOLLA RD
BHUTAN RD
SPENSER RD
COLLARD CL
THUNDERSLAND RD
FAIROAKS
ASH TREES
ELIZABETH WAY
COURTLANDS
ELLIOT CT
AMOS CL
SELBEY CL
CORNWALLIS AVE
CAMPBELL CL
CORSICAN WLK
SHAPLAND CL
MAYFIELD RD
BOGSHOLE LA
ST CLEMENT'S CT
PARSONAGE RD
Blacksole Farm
CT6
3
MILL LA
MARGATE RD
WALCOT PL
Herne Bay Court
CANTERBURY RD
B2205
PRIORY LA
BOWES LA
PO
THANET WAY
A299
67
SWALE CL
HILLCROFT RD
EASTGATE CL
RAVENSBOURNE AVE
DARENTH CL
GREEN ACRES
LIMES CL
PIGEON LA
THE DOWNINGS
UPPER FREE DOWN
HILLBROW AVE
PEARTREE RD
HELDING CL
ELLIS WAY
PARTRIDGE CL
CURLEW CL
GOLDFINCH CL
KINGSFIELD RD
PINTAIL WAY
WILLOW FARM WAY
HOOPERS LA
BOGSHOLE LA
BRAMLEY GDNS
SPICERS FIELD
MARGATE RD
HEART IN HAND RD
Cemy
SONDES CL
WINDMILL CL
MILL COURT CL
MILL LA
HUNTERS FORSTAL RD
BRAMBLEFIELDS CL
ROCKINGHAM PL
PLOUGH CT
WLK
THE MEADOWS
BARLEY CL
MERRYWOOD GR
SILVERDALE DR
2
Heart in Hand
HEART IN HAND CNR
A291
WINDMILL RD
Windmill
MOUNT VIEW RD
EPPING CL
LAKE DR
HAWE FARM WAY
DEAN CROFT
HALFORD CL
BOWLAND CL
ARDEN RD
SHERWOOD CL
GORSE LA
HUNTERS CHASE
CHALFONT DR
LADYFIELDS
MAGNOLIA RISE
POND COTTS
STRODE PARK RD
CHARNWOOD RD
STRANGFORD PL
ASHDOWN CL
BROOMFIELD RD
Broomfield
RADNOR CL
MILL VIEW RD
Hunters Forstal
Oxenden House Farm
WOODROW CHASE
SEYMOUR CL
Claver House
OXENDEN CNR
1
BLENHEIM CL
LOWER HERNE RD
ORCHARD ROW
RUSKINS VIEW
BENSTEDE CL
SCHOOL LA
STREETFIELD
Hawe Farm
FORD HILL
CT3
Strode Park
66

18 A B 19 C D 20 E F

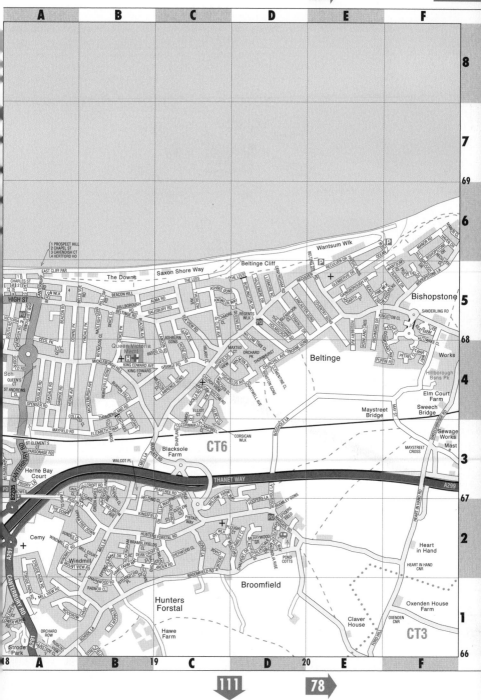

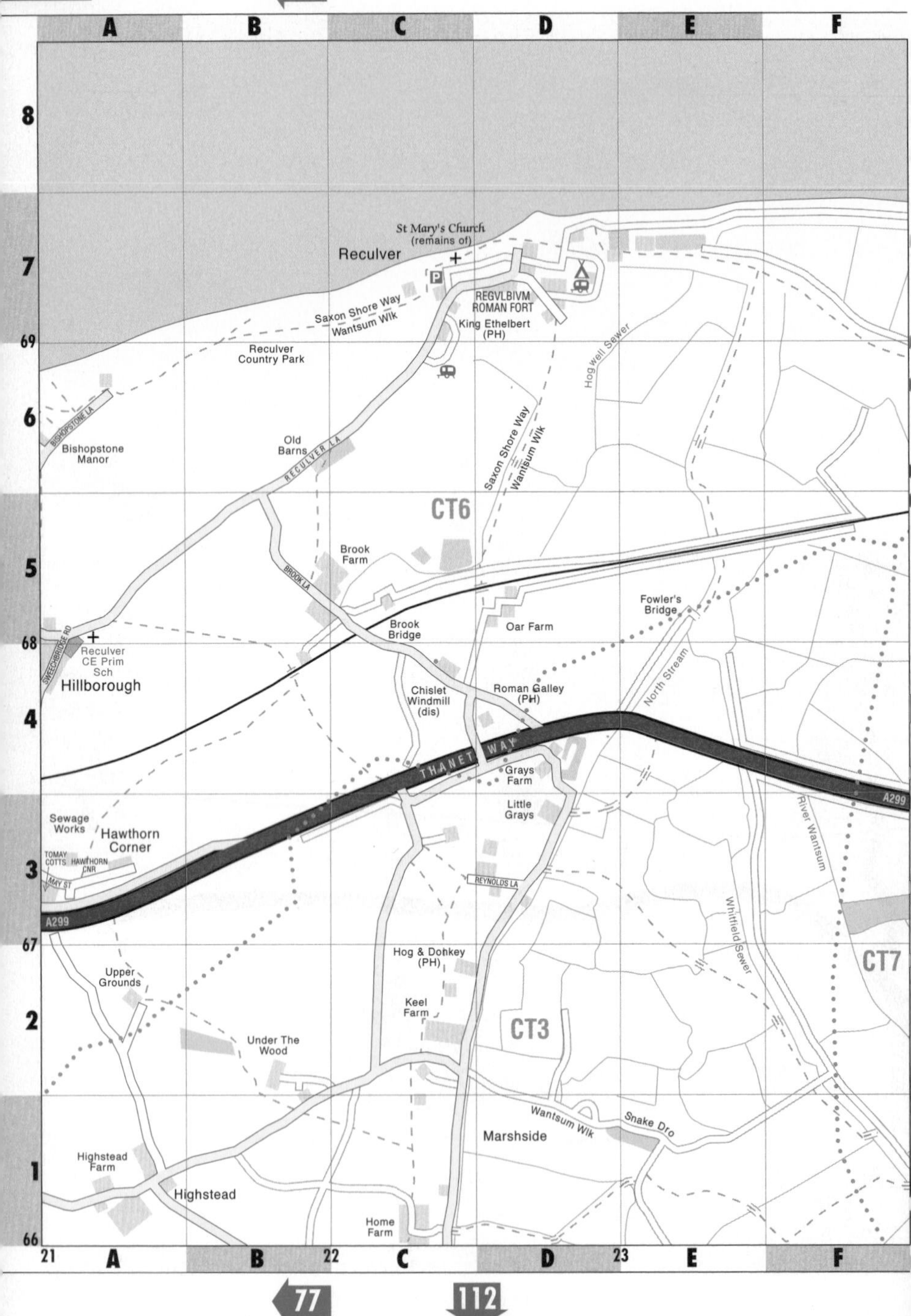

8

7   St Mary's Church
     (remains of)
Reculver
                    REGVLBIVM
                    ROMAN FORT
69   Saxon Shore Way   King Ethelbert
     Wantsum Wlk   (PH)
     Reculver
     Country Park   Hog well Sewer
6
     Bishopstone
     Manor   Old   Saxon Shore Way
                     Barns   Wantsum Wlk
                              RECULVER LA
                                        CT6
                     Brook
5   Farm
             BROOK LA
68   Brook   Oar Farm   Fowler's
     Reculver   Bridge   Bridge
     CE Prim
     Sch   North Stream
Hillborough   Chislet   Roman Galley
4   Windmill   (PH)
                     (dis)
                              THANET WAY   A299
                                        Grays
                                        Farm
                                        Little
     Sewage   Grays
     Works   Hawthorn
3   TOMAY   Corner
     COTTS HAWTHORN
     TAMY ST CNR   REYNOLDS LA
     A299
67   River Wantsum
     Upper   Hog & Donkey
     Grounds   (PH)   CT7
2   Keel
                               Farm
             Under The   CT3   Whitfield Sewer
             Wood
                                              Wantsum Wlk   Snake Dro
1   Highstead   Marshside
     Farm
          Highstead
                     Home
66   Farm
     21   A   B   22   C   D   23   E   F

80

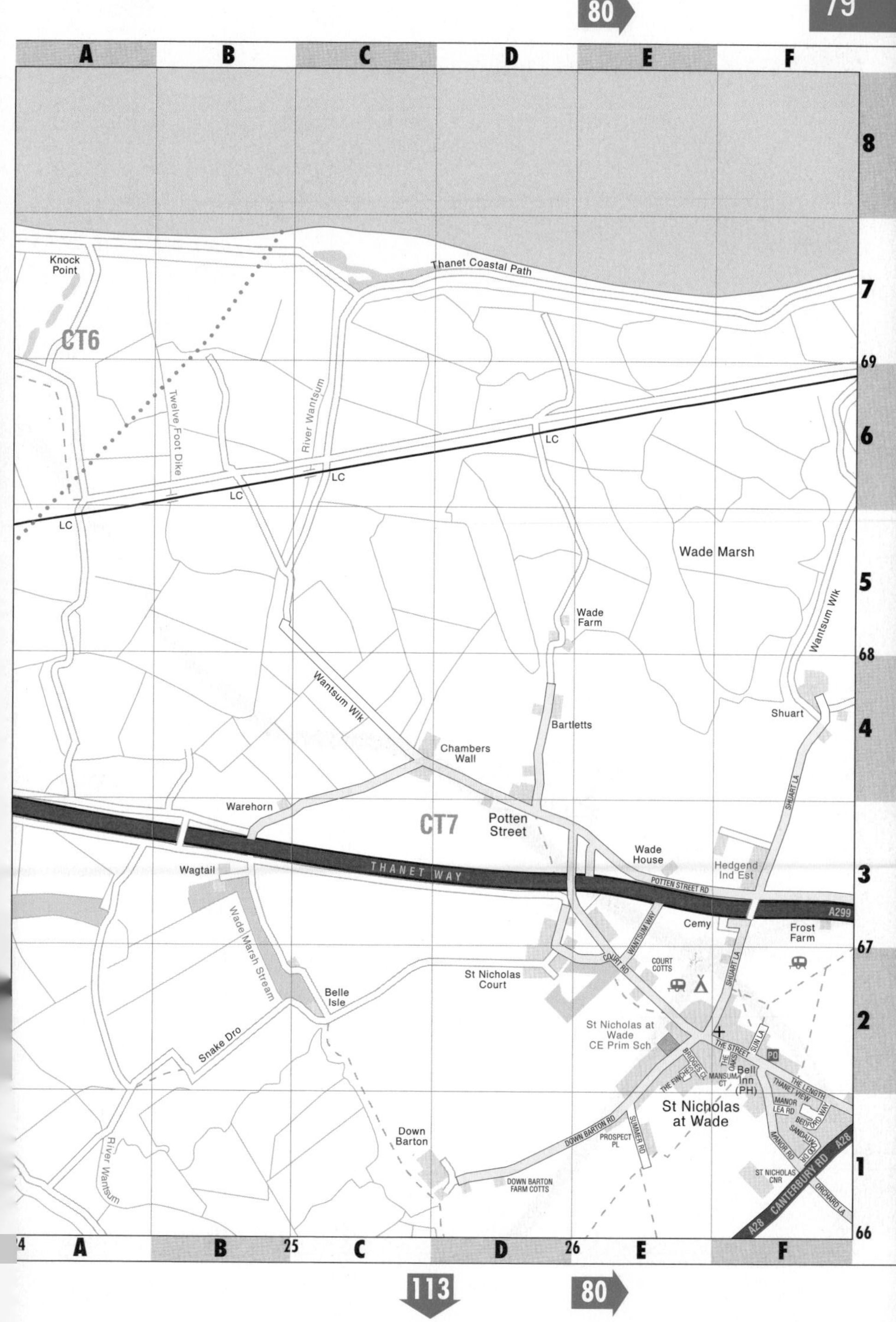
A
B
C
D
E
F
8
7
69
6
5
68
4
3
67
2
1
66
24
25
26
Knock Point
CT6
Thanet Coastal Path
Twelve Foot Dike
River Wantsum
LC
LC
LC
LC
Wade Marsh
Wade Farm
Wantsum Wlk
Wantsum Wlk
Shuart
Bartletts
Chambers Wall
Warehorn
CT7
Potten Street
Wade House
Hedgend Ind Est
SHUART LA
Wagtail
THANET WAY
POTTEN STREET RD
A299
Cemy
Frost Farm
Wade Marsh Stream
WANTSUM WAY
COURT RD
COURT COTTS
St Nicholas Court
SHUART LA
Belle Isle
St Nicholas at Wade CE Prim Sch
THE STREET
SUN LA
PO
Snake Dro
BRIDGES CL
THE OAKS
THE FINCHES
MANSUMA CT
Bell Inn (PH)
THE LENGTH
THANET VIEW
MANOR LEA RD
BEDFORD WAY
St Nicholas at Wade
SANDALWOOD DR
Down Barton
DOWN BARTON RD
SUMMER RD
PROSPECT PL
MANOR RD
A28
CANTERBURY RD
River Wantsum
DOWN BARTON FARM COTTS
ST NICHOLAS CNR
ORCHARD LA
A28

113
80

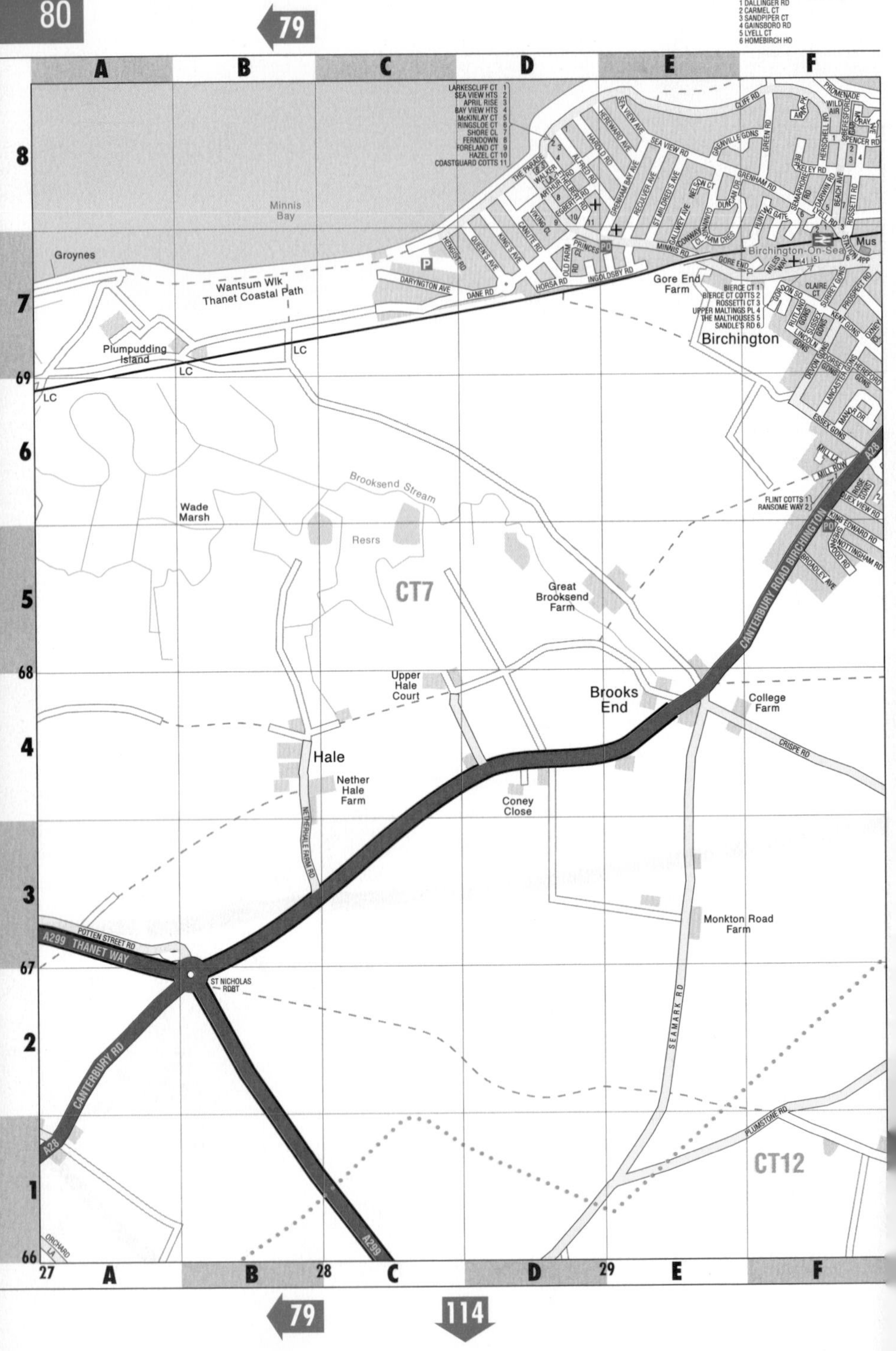

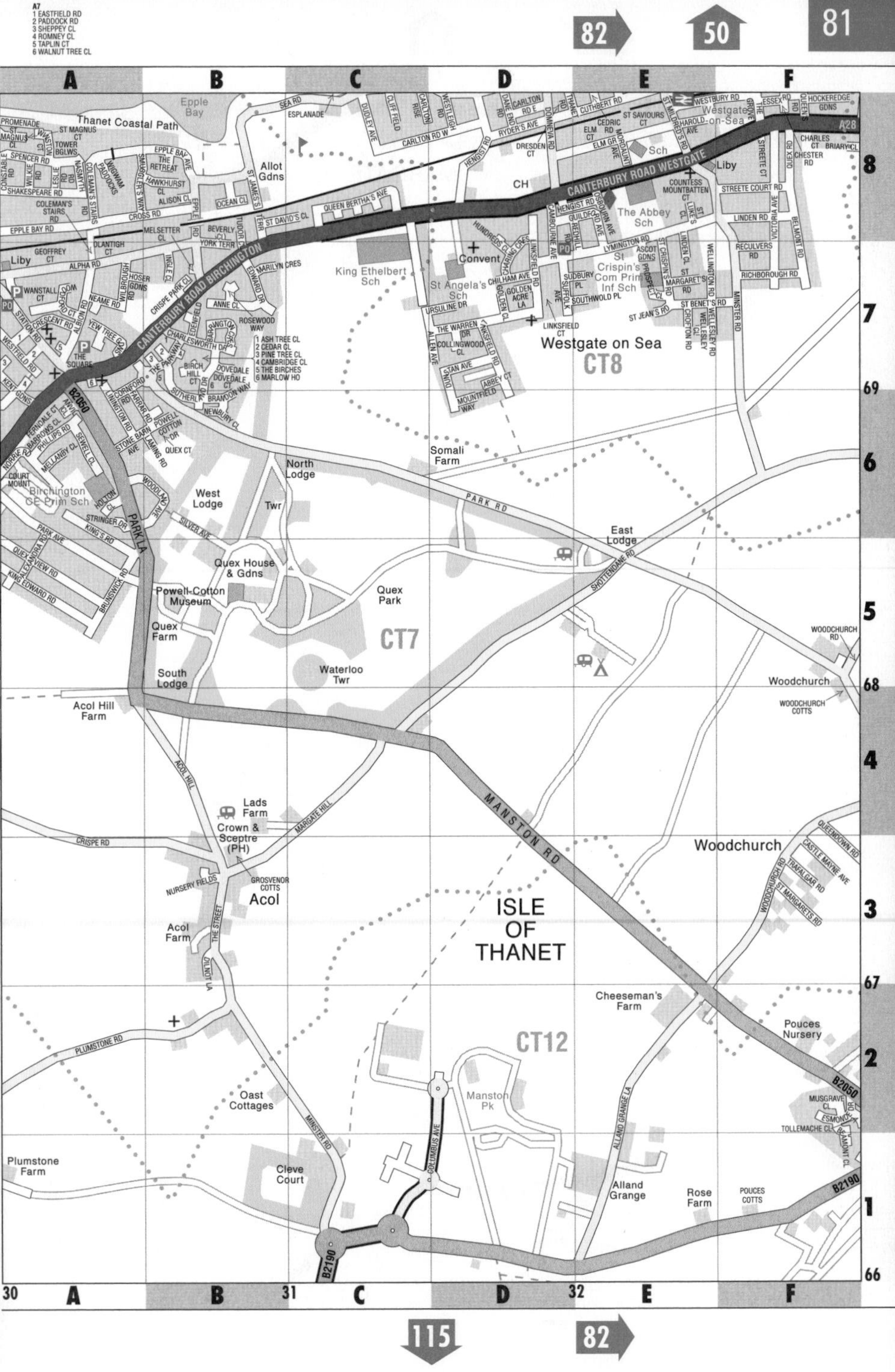

81
50

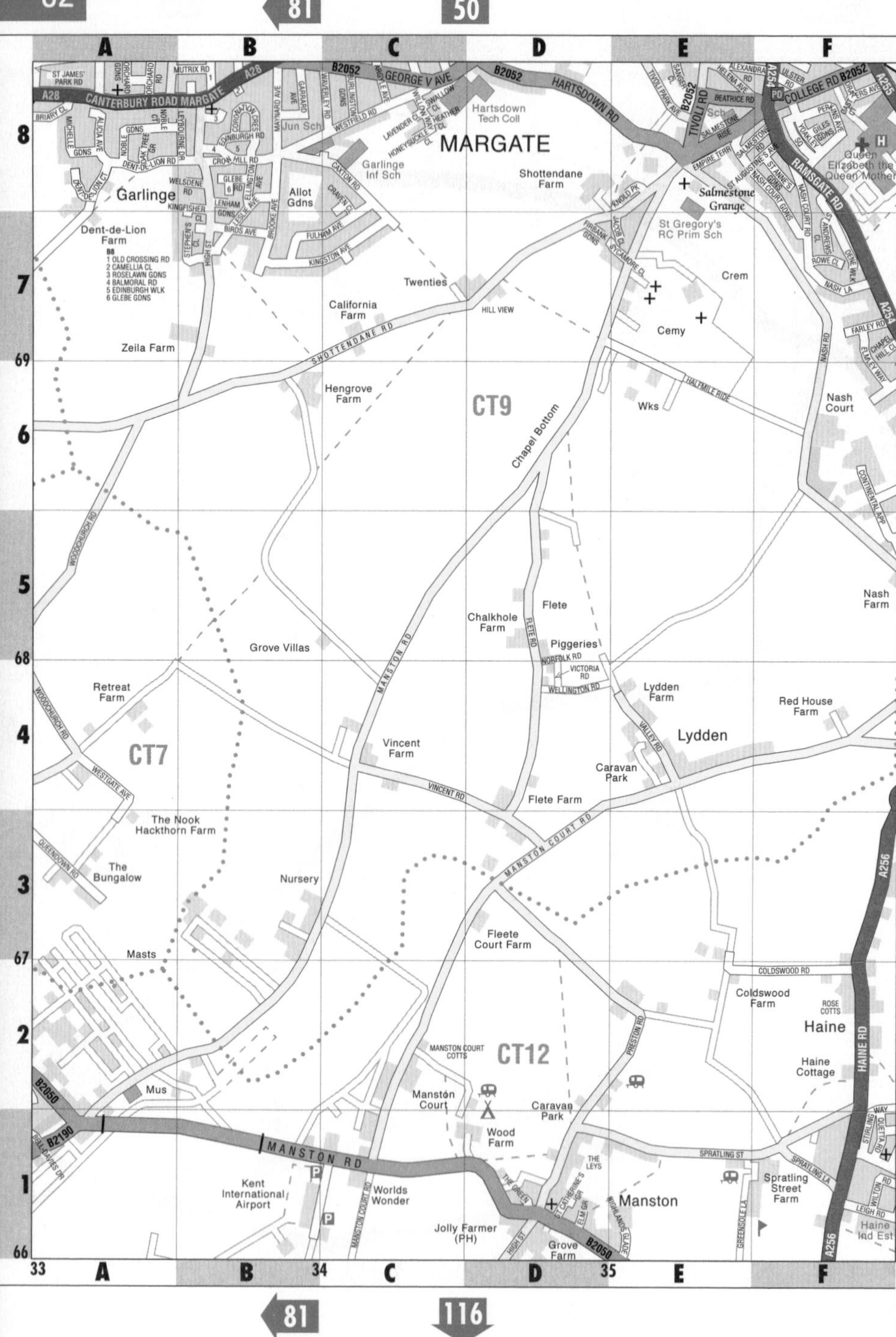
MARGATE
Garlinge
Dent-de-Lion Farm
B8
1 OLD CROSSING RD
2 CAMELLIA CL
3 ROSELAWN GDNS
4 BALMORAL RD
5 EDINBURGH WLK
6 GLEBE GDNS
CANTERBURY ROAD MARGATE
GEORGE V AVE
HARTSDOWN RD
Hartsdown Tech Coll
Jun Sch
Garlinge Inf Sch
Allot Gdns
Shottendane Farm
Salmestone Grange
St Gregory's RC Prim Sch
Crem
Cemy
Queen Elizabeth the Queen Mother
COLLEGE RD
RAMSGATE RD
TIVOLI RD
Twenties
California Farm
HILL VIEW
SHOTTENDANE RD
Zeila Farm
Hengrove Farm
CT9
Chapel Bottom
HALFMILE RIDE
Wks
Nash Court
NASH RD
WOODCHURCH RD
Flete
Chalkhole Farm
FLETE RD
Piggeries
Nash Farm
Grove Villas
Retreat Farm
Lydden Farm
Red House Farm
Lydden
CT7
Vincent Farm
MANSTON RD
VINCENT RD
Caravan Park
Flete Farm
The Nook Hackthorn Farm
MANSTON COURT RD
The Bungalow
Nursery
Fleete Court Farm
Masts
COLDSWOOD RD
Coldswood Farm
Haine
HAINE RD
CT12
MANSTON COURT COTTS
PRESTON RD
Haine Cottage
Mus
Manston Court
Caravan Park
Wood Farm
SPRATLING ST
SPRATLING LA
Kent International Airport
Worlds Wonder
Manston
Spratling Street Farm
Jolly Farmer (PH)
Grove Farm
Haine Ind Est
A28
B2052
A254
A255
A256
B2050
B2190
A
B
C
D
E
F
8
7
6
5
4
3
2
1
69
68
67
66
33
34
35

81
116

51
84

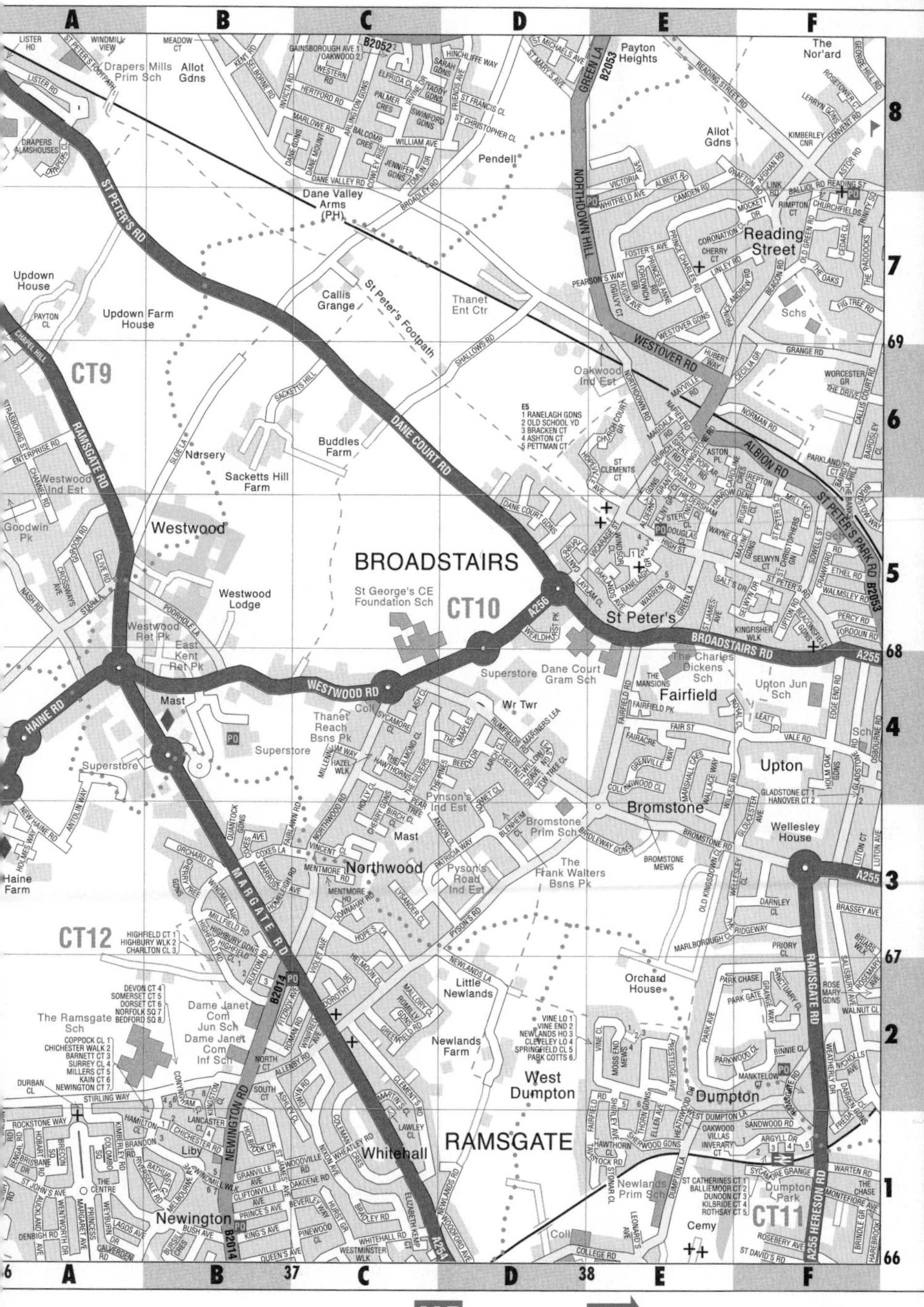
BROADSTAIRS
RAMSGATE
CT9
CT10
CT11
CT12
Reading Street
St Peter's
Westwood
Northwood
Upton
Bromstone
Fairfield
Dumpton
West Dumpton
Newington
Whitehall
Pendell
Payton Heights
The Nor'ard
Updown House
Updown Farm House
Callis Grange
Buddles Farm
Sacketts Hill Farm
Westwood Lodge
Little Newlands
Newlands Farm
Orchard House
Wellesley House
Haine Farm
Drapers Mills Prim Sch
St George's CE Foundation Sch
Dane Court Gram Sch
The Charles Dickens Sch
Upton Jun Sch
Bromstone Prim Sch
The Ramsgate Sch
Dane Janet Com Jun Sch
Dame Janet Com Inf Sch
Newlands Prim Sch
Dane Valley Arms (PH)
Thanet Ent Ctr
Oakwood Ind Est
Westwood Ind Est
Westwood Ret Pk
East Kent Ret Pk
Thanet Reach Bsns Pk
Pynson's Ind Est
Pyson's Road Ind Est
The Frank Walters Bsns Pk
Goodwin Pk
Dumpton Park
ST PETER'S RD
DANE COURT RD
WESTWOOD RD
BROADSTAIRS RD
RAMSGATE RD
MARGATE RD
NEWINGTON RD
HAINE RD
NORTHDOWN HILL
WESTOVER RD
ALBION RD
ST PETER'S PARK RD
A255 HERESON RD
A255
A256
A254
B2014
B2052
B2053
St Peter's Footpath
E5
1 RANELAGH GDNS
2 OLD SCHOOL YD
3 BRACKEN CT
4 ASHTON CT
5 PETTMAN CT
A B C D E F
8 7 6 5 4 3 2 1
69 68 67 66
37 38

117
84

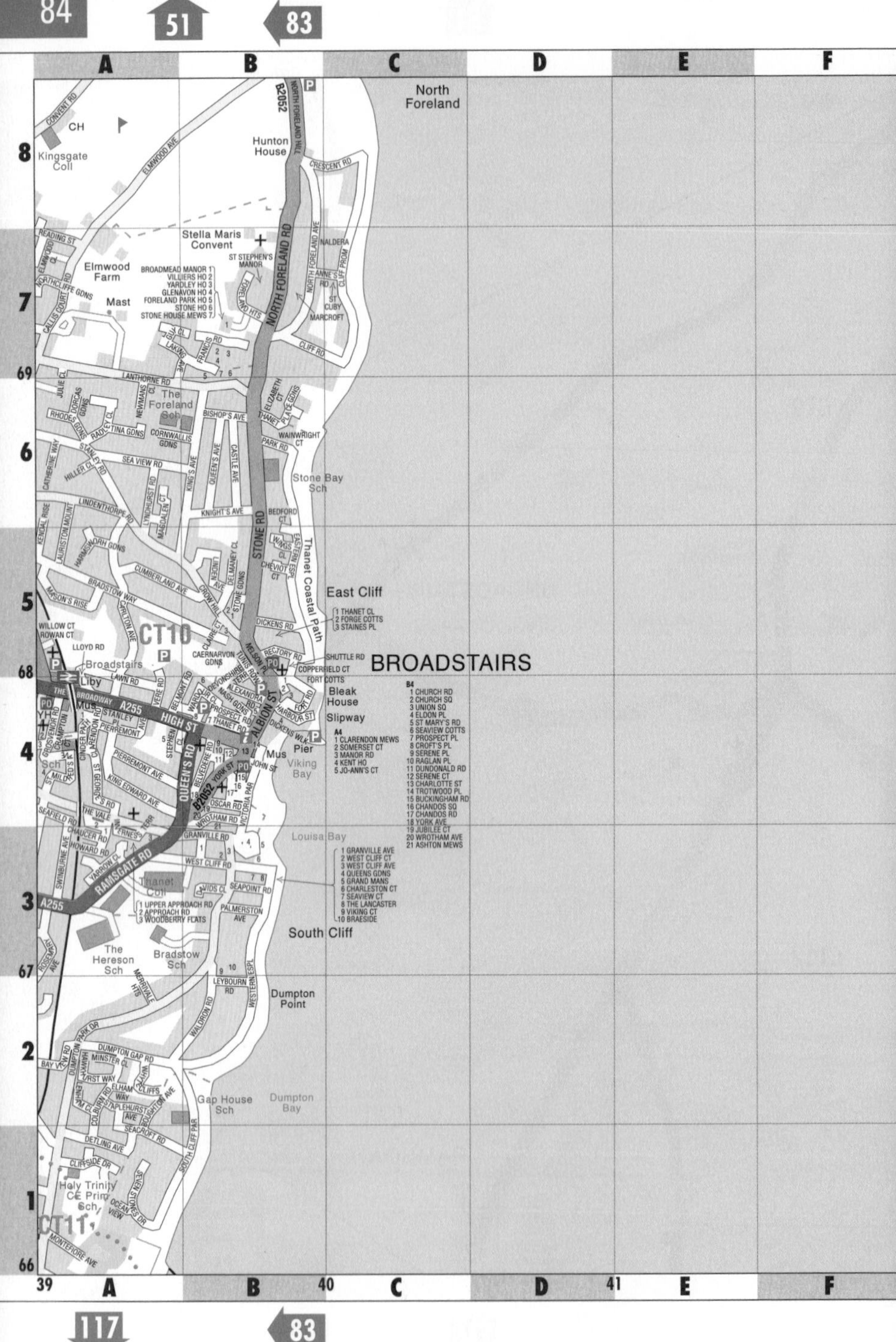

North
Foreland

CH
Kingsgate
Coll

Hunton
House

CRESCENT RD

Stella Maris
Convent

St STEPHEN'S
MANOR

NALDERA

Elmwood
Farm

BROADMEAD MANOR 1
VILLIERS HO 2
YARDLEY HO 3
GLENAVON HO 4
FORELAND PARK HO 5
STONE HO 6
STONE HOUSE MEWS 7

St ANNE'S S

Mast

St
CUB

MARCROFT

CLIFF RD

The
Foreland
Sch

BISHOP'S AVE

WAINWRIGHT

PARK RD

CORNWALLIS
GDNS

SEA VIEW RD

Stone Bay
Sch

LINDENTHORPE RD

BEDFORD

KNIGHT'S AVE

CHEVIOT
RD

East Cliff

DICKENS RD

BRADSTOW WAY

1 THANET CL
2 FORGE COTTS
3 STAINES PL

WILLOW CT
ROWAN CT
LLOYD RD

RECTORY RD

SHUTTLE RD

Broadstairs
Liby

CAERNARVON
GDNS

COPPERFIELD CT

BROADSTAIRS

FORT COTTS

Bleak
House

Slipway

84
1 CHURCH RD
2 CHURCH SQ
3 UNION SQ
4 ELDON PL
5 St MARY'S RD
6 SEAVIEW COTTS
7 PROSPECT PL
8 CROFT'S PL
9 SERENE PL
10 RAGLAN PL
11 DUNDONALD RD
12 SERENE CT
13 CHARLOTTE ST
14 TROTWOOD PL
15 BUCKINGHAM RD
16 CHANDOS SQ
17 CHANDOS RD
18 YORK AVE
19 JUBILEE CT
20 WROTHAM AVE
21 ASHTON MEWS

HIGH ST

A255

Broadway

Mus

STANLEY

Pierpoint

A4
1 CLARENDON MEWS
2 SOMERSET CT
3 MANOR RD
4 KENT HO
5 JO-ANN'S CT

Mus

Pier

Viking
Bay

JOHN ST

QUEEN'S RD

PIERREMONT AVE

KING EDWARD AVE

OSCAR RD

GRANVILLE AVE

Louisa Bay

1 GRANVILLE AVE
2 WEST CLIFF CT
3 WEST CLIFF AVE
4 QUEENS GDNS
6 GRAND MANS
6 CHARLESTON CT
7 SEAVIEW CT
8 THE LANCASTER
9 VIKING CT
10 BRAESIDE

WEST CLIFF RD

Thanet
Coll

SEAPOINT RD

1 UPPER APPROACH RD
2 APPROACH RD
3 WOODBERRY FLATS

RAMSGATE RD

A255

PALMERSTON
AVE

South Cliff

The
Hereson
Sch

Bradstow
Sch

LEYBOURN
RD

Dumpton
Point

DUMPTON GAP RD

MINSTER
DR

FIRST WAY

ELHAM
CLIFFS
WAY

STAPLEHURST AVE

Gap House
Sch

Dumpton
Bay

SEACROFT RD

DETLING AVE

CLIFFSEND DR

Holy Trinity
CE Prim
Sch

CT11

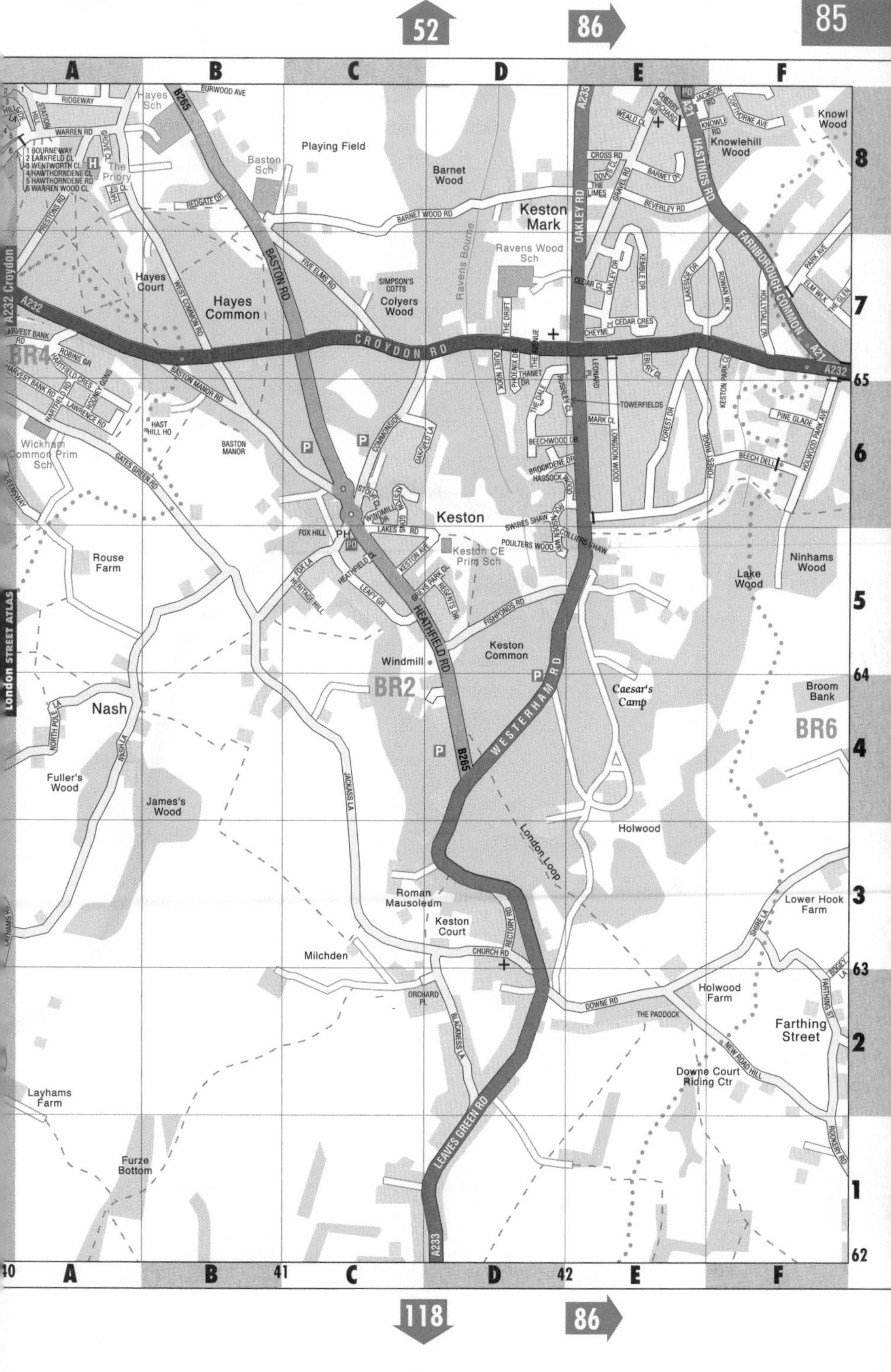
52
86
A
B
C
D
E
F
RIDGEWAY
BURWOOD AVE
Hayes Sch
B265
WARREN RD
1 BOURNE WAY
2 LARKFIELD CL
3 WENTWORTH CL
4 HAWTHORNDENE CL
5 HAWTHORNDENE RD
6 WARREN WOOD CL
The Priory
PRESTONS RD
Baston Sch
Playing Field
REDGATE DR
BARNET WOOD RD
Barnet Wood
Keston Mark
Ravens Wood Sch
Ravens Bourne
A232 Croydon
A232
Hayes Court
Hayes Common
WEST COMMON RD
BASTON RD
FIVE ELMS RD
SIMPSON'S COTTS
Colyers Wood
CROYDON RD
THE DRIFT
THE AVENUE
OAKLEY RD
A233
CROSS RD
DOVES CL
THE LIMES
GRAVEL RD
BARNET DR
BEVERLEY RD
CEDAR CL
OAKLEY DR
KEMBLE DR
CEDAR CRES
CHEYNE CL
WEALD CL
CHERRY ORCHARD RD
PO
A21
JACKSON RD
COPTHORNE AVE
KNOWLE RD
Knowlehill Wood
Knowl Wood
HASTINGS RD
FARNBOROUGH COMMON
LAKESIDE DR
ROWAN WLK
HOLLYDALE DR
PARK AVE
ELM WLK
THE GLEN
BR4
HARVEST BANK RD
ROBINS GR
HARTFIELD CRES
RODNEY GDNS
HARTFIELD RD
LAWRENCE RD
BASTON MANOR RD
HAST HILL HO
BASTON MANOR
Wickham Common Prim Sch
GATES GREEN RD
QUEENSWAY
COMMONSIDE
OAKFIELD LA
QUIET NOOK
PHOENIX DR
THANET DR
THE DALE
RUSHLEY CL
LEONARD PL
TOWERFIELDS
MARK CL
BEECHWOOD DR
BROCKDENE DR
HASSOCK WOOD
LONGDON WOOD
FOREST DR
FOREST RIDGE
EBURY CL
KESTON PARK CL
PINE GLADE
HOLWOOD PARK AVE
BEECH DELL
65
8
7
6
5
4
3
2
1
64
63
62
STOUR CL
WINDMILL DR
KESTON GDNS
Keston
LAKES RD
FOX HILL
PH
FOX LA
HERITAGE HILL
HEATHFIELD CL
KESTON AVE
Keston CE Prim Sch
SWIRES SHAW
ROUNDS WAY
POULTERS WOOD
COLLIERS SHAW
LEAFY GR
GREYS PARK CL
REGENTS DR
Rouse Farm
Ninhams Wood
Lake Wood
FISHPONDS RD
HEATHFIELD RD
Keston Common
Windmill
WESTERHAM RD
Caesar's Camp
BR2
Broom Bank
BR6
Nash
NORTH POLE LA
NASH LA
Fuller's Wood
James's Wood
JACKASS LA
London Loop
Holwood
Roman Mausoleum
Keston Court
RECTORY RD
Lower Hook Farm
SHIRE LA
Milchden
CHURCH RD
ORCHARD PL
DOWNE RD
THE PADDOCK
Holwood Farm
FARTHING ST
Farthing Street
NEW ROAD HILL
BLACKNESS LA
Downe Court Riding Ctr
LAYHAMS RD
Layhams Farm
LEAVES GREEN RD
Furze Bottom
ROOKERY RD
40
41
42
118
86
London STREET ATLAS

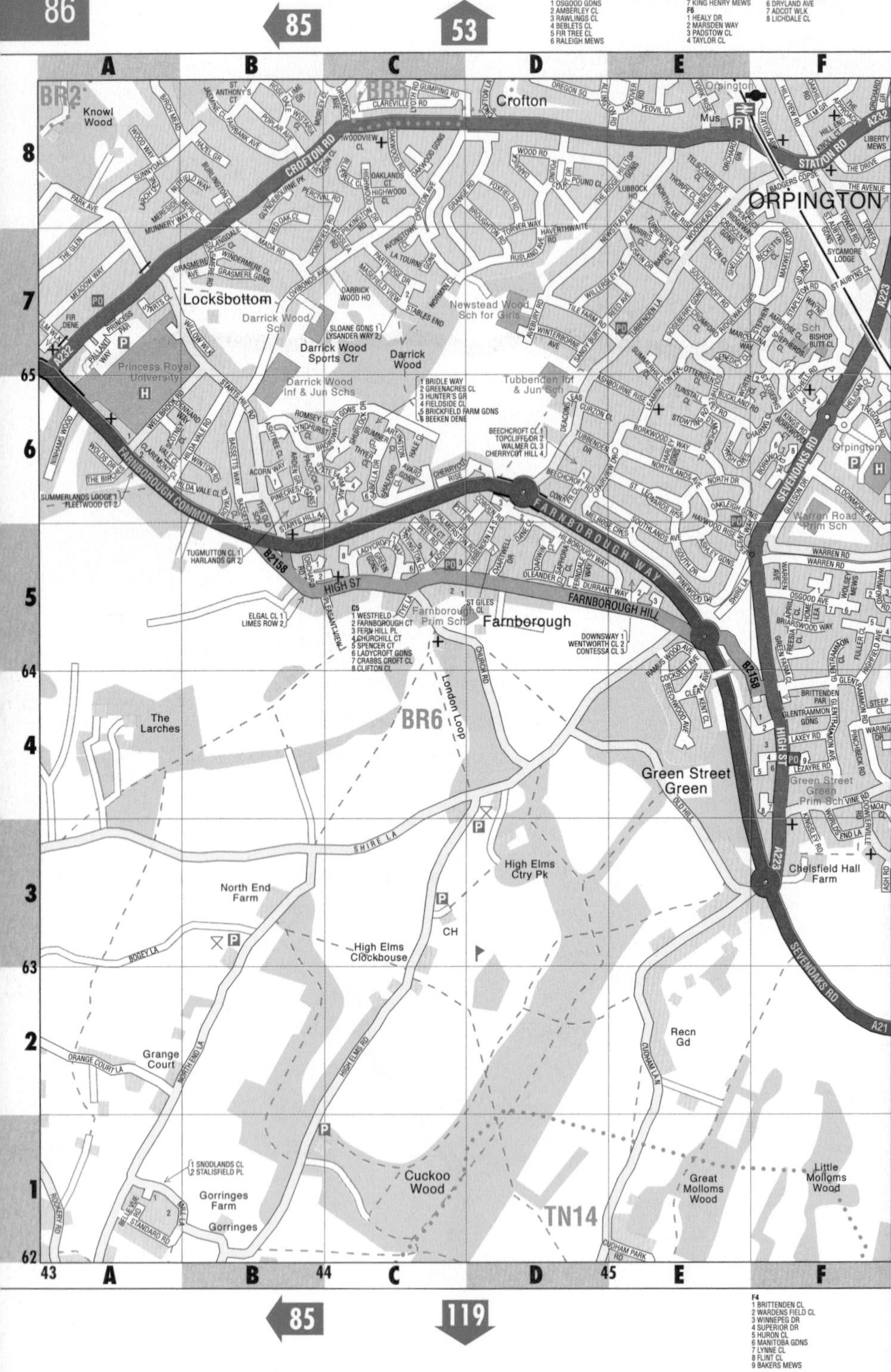

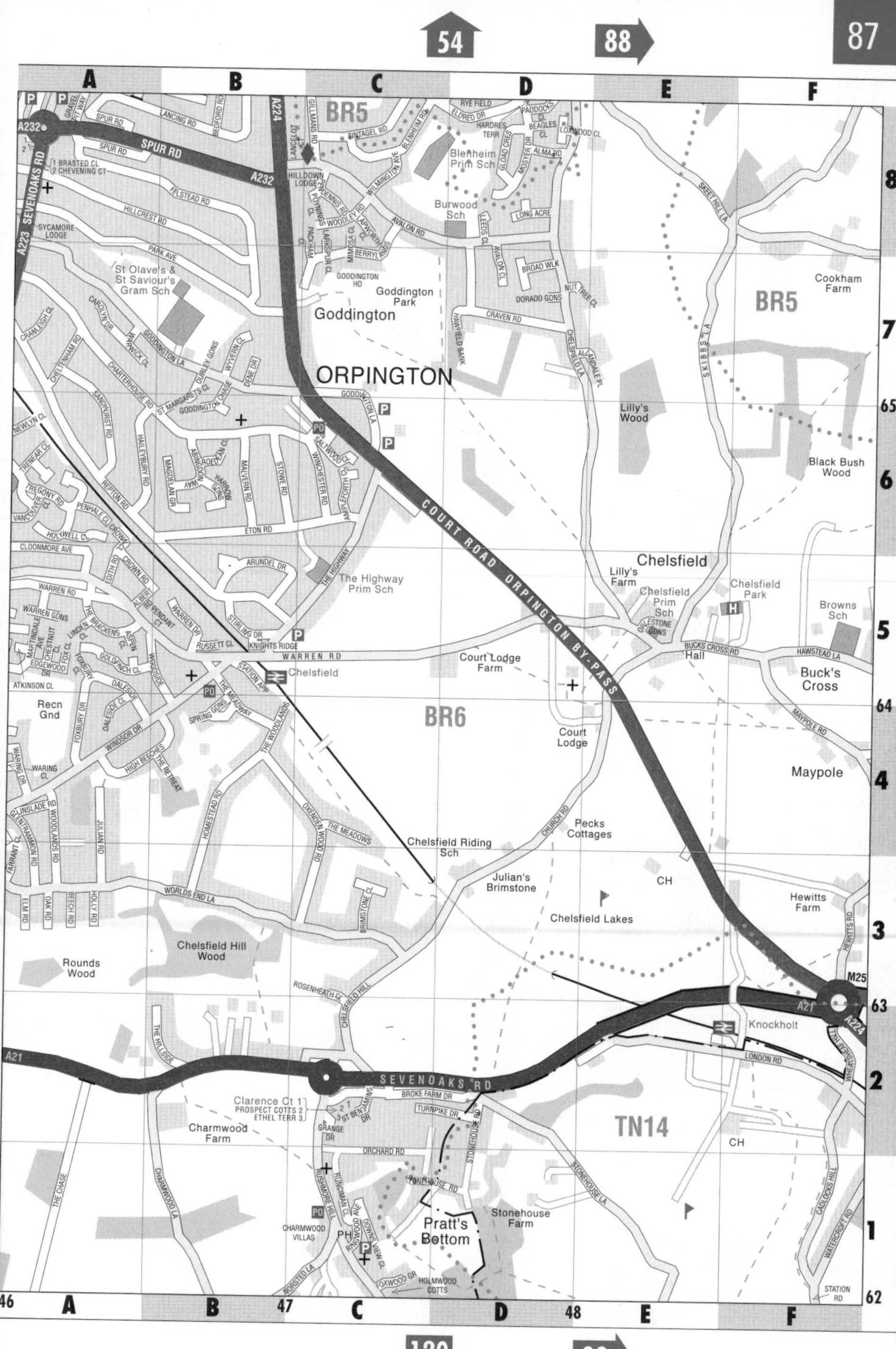

A   B   C   D   E   F

BR5

8

SPUR RD
A232
A232
A223
SEVENOAKS RD
A224

BR5
Cookham Farm

Blenheim Prim Sch
Burwood Sch
LONG ACRE
BROAD WLK

St Olave's & St Saviour's Gram Sch

Goddington
Goddington Ho
Goddington Park

7

65

Black Bush Wood

6

ORPINGTON

COURT ROAD ORPINGTON BY-PASS

Chelsfield
Lilly's Wood
Lilly's Farm
Chelsfield Prim Sch
Chelsfield Park
Browns Sch

The Highway Prim Sch

Chelsfield

Court Lodge Farm

BR6

Court Lodge

Bucks Cross Rd
Hall
Buck's Cross

Maypole

5

64

4

Chelsfield Riding Sch

Pecks Cottages
Julian's Brimstone
Chelsfield Lakes

CH

Hewitts Farm

3

63

Rounds Wood

Chelsfield Hill Wood

WORLDS END LA

ROSENHEATH CL

A21

Knockholt
LONDON RD
A21
A224
M25

M25

2

SEVENOAKS RD
BROKE FARM DR
TURNPIKE DR

TN14

CH

Charmwood Farm
Clarence Ct 1
PROSPECT COTTS 2
ETHEL TERR 3
GRANGE DR
ORCHARD RD
Pratt's Bottom
Stonehouse Farm

1

CHARMWOOD VILLAS
PH
P
HOLMWOOD COTTS

STATION RD

62

46   A   B   47   C   D   48   E   F

87
55

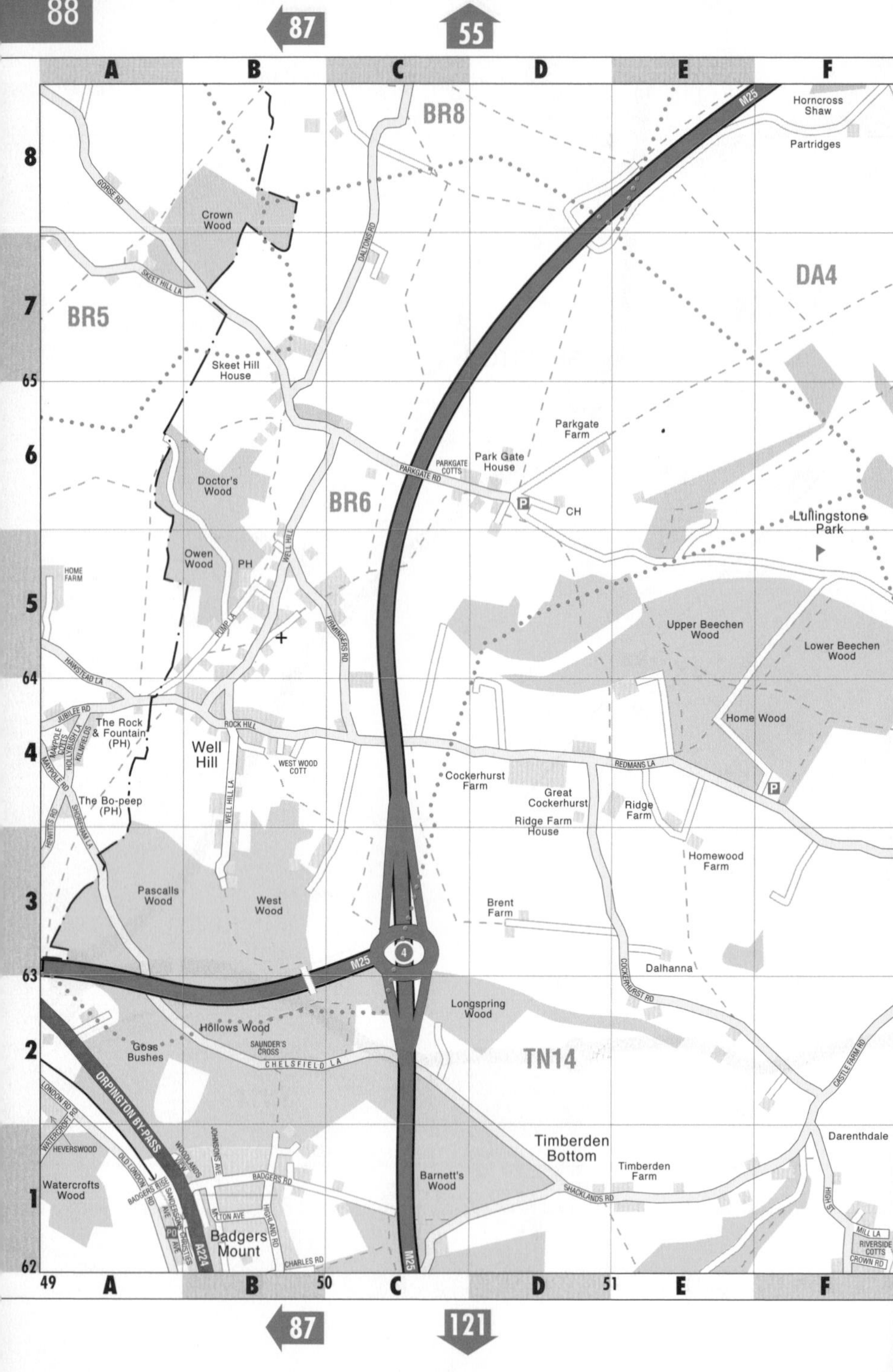
A
B
C
D
E
F
BR8
Horncross Shaw
Partridges
M25
GORSE RD
Crown Wood
DALTONS RD
DA4
SKEET HILL LA
BR5
Skeet Hill House
Parkgate Farm
PARKGATE COTTS
Park Gate House
PARKGATE RD
Doctor's Wood
BR6
CH
Lullingstone Park
Owen Wood
PH
WELL HILL
HOME FARM
PUMP LA
FIRMINGERS RD
Upper Beechen Wood
Lower Beechen Wood
HAWSTEAD LA
JUBILEE RD
The Rock & Fountain (PH)
ROCK HILL
Home Wood
MAYPOLE COTTS
HOLLYBUSH LA
KILNFIELDS
Well Hill
WEST WOOD COTT
REDMANS LA
MAYPOLE RD
Cockerhurst Farm
Great Cockerhurst
Ridge Farm
The Bo-peep (PH)
WELL HILL LA
Ridge Farm House
HEWITTS RD
SHOREHAM LA
Homewood Farm
Pascalls Wood
West Wood
Brent Farm
4
M25
Dalhanna
COCKERHURST RD
Longspring Wood
Hollows Wood
Goss Bushes
SAUNDER'S CROSS
TN14
CHELSFIELD LA
CASTLE FARM RD
ORPINGTON BY-PASS
LONDON RD
WATERCROFT RD
HEVERSWOOD
OLD LONDON RD
WOODLANDS VIEW
JOHNSONS AVE
Timberden Bottom
Darenthdale
Timberden Farm
Watercrofts Wood
BADGERS RISE
SANDERSONS AVE
BADGERS RD
Barnett's Wood
SHACKLANDS RD
HIGH ST
MILTON AVE
HIGHLAND RD
PO
CHRISTIES AVE
A224
Badgers Mount
CHARLES RD
M25
MILL LA
RIVERSIDE COTTS
CROWN RD
8
7
65
6
5
64
4
3
63
2
1
62
49
50
51

87
121

56
90

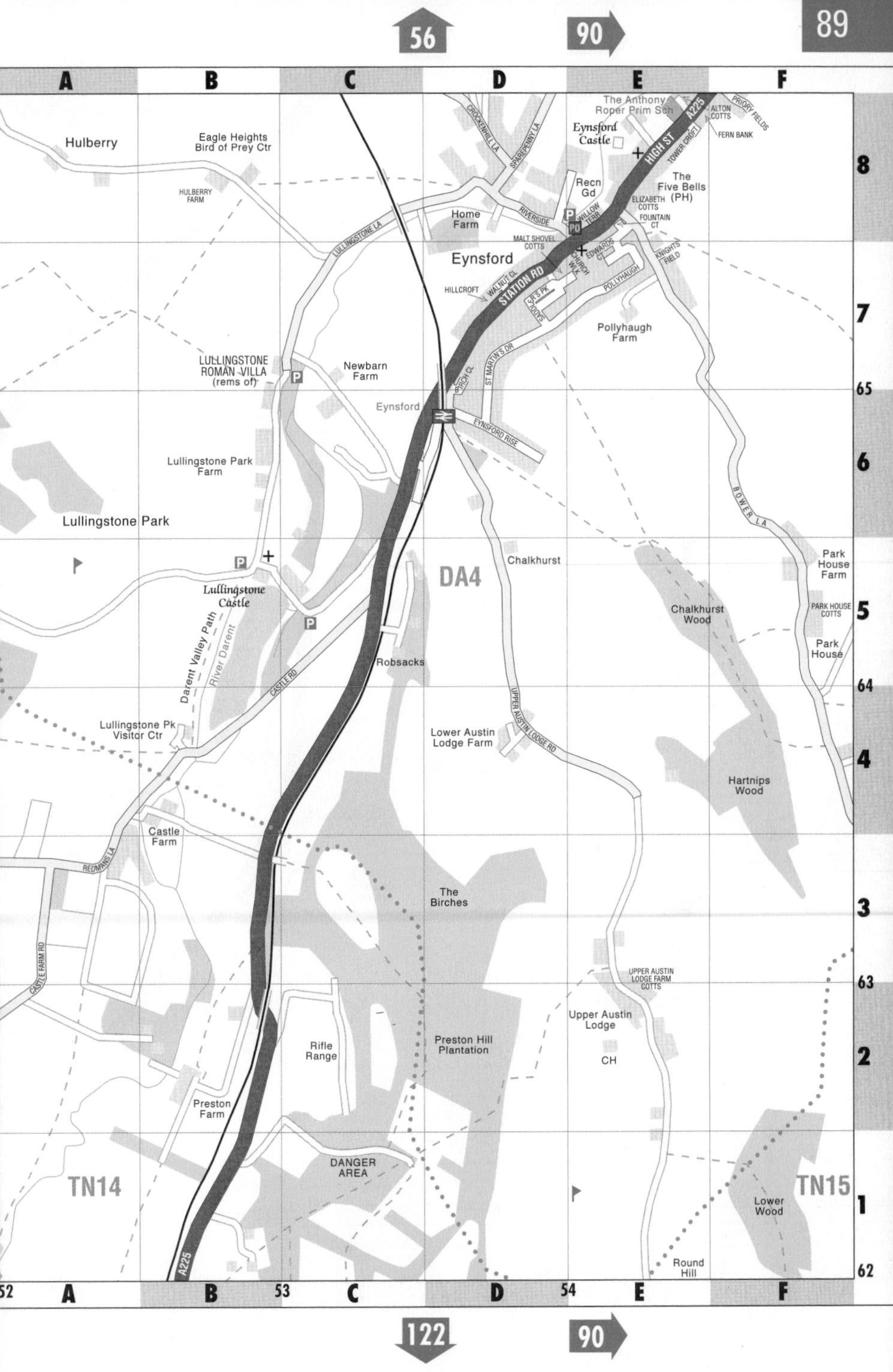
A
B
C
D
E
F
Hulberry
Eagle Heights
Bird of Prey Ctr
HULBERRY
FARM
The Anthony
Roper Prim Sch
Eynsford
Castle
A225
HIGH ST
ALTON
COTTS
PRIORY FIELDS
FERN BANK
TOWER CROFT
CROCKENHILL LA
SPAREPENNY LA
The
Five Bells
(PH)
Recn
Gd
ELIZABETH
COTTS
FOUNTAIN
CT
WILLOW
TERR
Home
Farm
RIVERSIDE
MALT SHOVEL
COTTS
LULLINGSTONE LA
Eynsford
KNIGHTS
FIELD
EDWARDS
CT
CHURCH
WK
POLLYHAUGH
HILLCROFT
WALNUT CL
STATION RD
SADDLER'S PK
Pollyhaugh
Farm
ST MARTIN'S DR
BIRCH CL
LULLINGSTONE
ROMAN VILLA
(rems of)
Newbarn
Farm
Eynsford
EYNSFORD RISE
Lullingstone Park
Farm
Lullingstone Park
BOWER LA
Chalkhurst
Park
House
Farm
DA4
Lullingstone
Castle
Chalkhurst
Wood
PARK HOUSE
COTTS
Darent Valley Path
River Darent
Robsacks
Park
House
CASTLE RD
UPPER AUSTIN LODGE RD
Lullingstone Pk
Visitor Ctr
Lower Austin
Lodge Farm
Hartnips
Wood
Castle
Farm
REDMANS LA
The
Birches
CASTLE FARM RD
UPPER AUSTIN
LODGE FARM
COTTS
Upper Austin
Lodge
Rifle
Range
Preston Hill
Plantation
CH
Preston
Farm
DANGER
AREA
TN14
TN15
Lower
Wood
Round
Hill
8
7
65
6
5
64
4
3
63
2
1
62
52
53
54

122
90

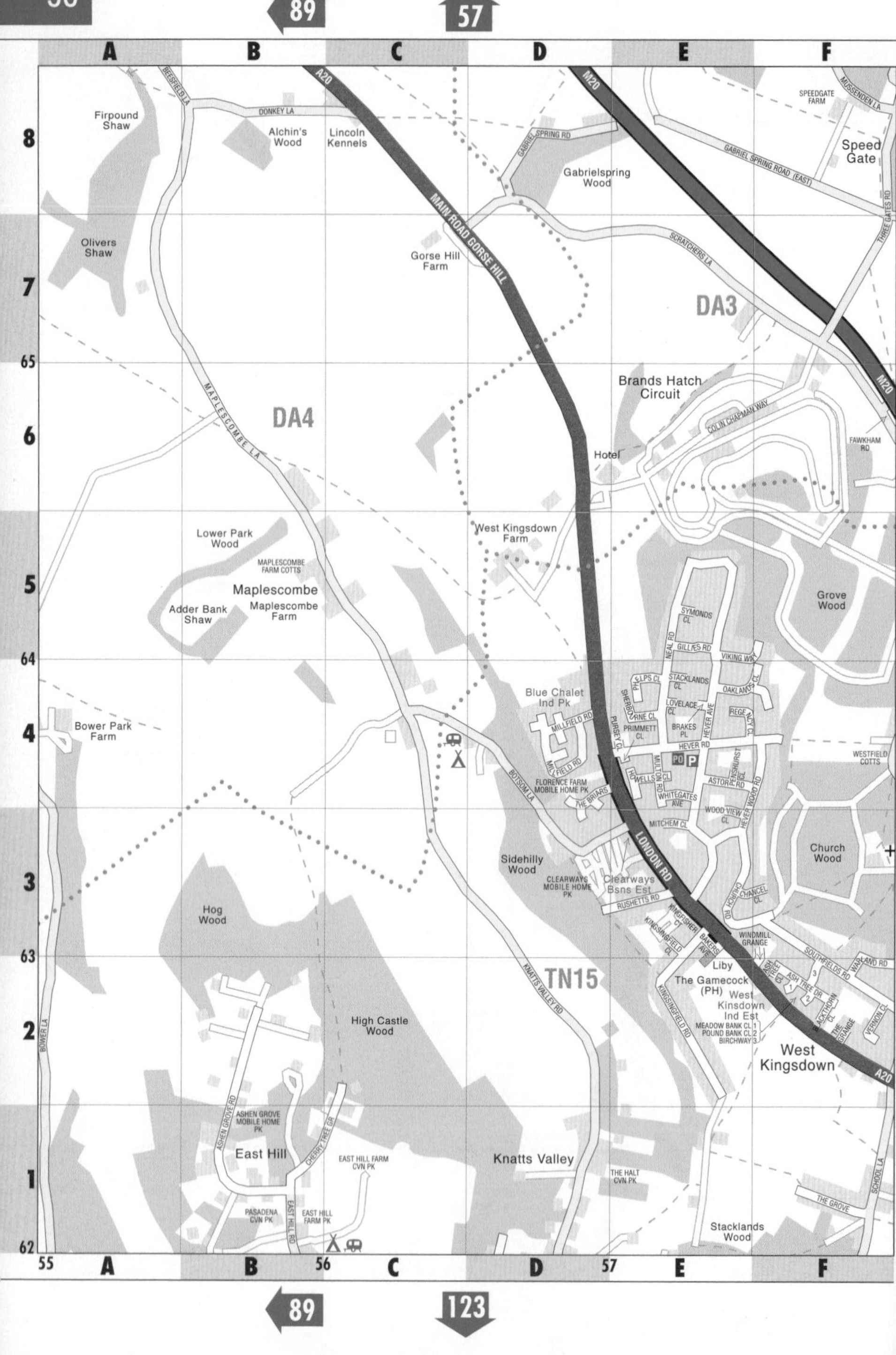
89
57
A B C D E F
8
7
65
6
5
64
4
3
63
2
1
62
55 A B 56 C D 57 E F
Firpound Shaw
Alchin's Wood
Lincoln Kennels
DONKEY LA
BEESFIELD LA
A20
M20
GABRIEL SPRING RD
Gabrielspring Wood
SPEEDGATE FARM
MUSSENDEN LA
Speed Gate
GABRIEL SPRING ROAD (EAST)
THREE GATES RD
Olivers Shaw
Gorse Hill Farm
MAIN ROAD GORSE HILL
SCRATCHERS LA
DA3
Brands Hatch Circuit
COLIN CHAPMAN WAY
MAPLESCOMBE LA
DA4
Hotel
FAWKHAM RD
Lower Park Wood
West Kingsdown Farm
MAPLESCOMBE FARM COTTS
Maplescombe
Adder Bank Shaw
Maplescombe Farm
Grove Wood
SYMONDS CL
NEAL RD
GILLIES RD
VIKING WAY
STACKLANDS CL
OAKLANDS CL
Blue Chalet Ind Pk
LOVELACE CL
BRAKES PL
HEVER AVE
REGENCY CL
PRIMMETT CL
PURSEY CL
MILLFIELD RD
Bower Park Farm
HEVER RD
WESTFIELD COTTS
PO
P
MILTON RD
PENSHURST CL
HOWELLS CL
ASTOR RD
BOTSOM LA
FLORENCE FARM MOBILE HOME PK
THE BRIARS
WHITEGATES AVE
WOOD VIEW CL
HEVER WOOD RD
MITCHEM CL
Church Wood
LONDON RD
Sidehilly Wood
CLEARWAYS MOBILE HOME PK
Clearways Bsns Est
CHURCH RD
CHANCEL CL
RUSHETTS RD
Hog Wood
KINGFISHER CT
KINGSINGFIELD CL
BAKERS AVE
WINDMILL GRANGE
SOUTHFIELDS RD
WARLAND RD
Liby
ASH TREE CL
ASH TREE DR
TN15
The Gamecock (PH)
West Kinsdown Ind Est
KNATTS VALLEY RD
KINGSINGFIELD RD
BLACKTHORN CL
THE GRANGE
VERNON CL
High Castle Wood
MEADOW BANK CL 1
POUND BANK CL 2
BIRCHWAY 3
West Kingsdown
BOWER LA
ASHEN GROVE RD
ASHEN GROVE MOBILE HOME PK
CHERRY TREE GR
East Hill
EAST HILL FARM CVN PK
Knatts Valley
THE HALT CVN PK
SCHOOL LA
THE GROVE
PASADENA CVN PK
EAST HILL RD
EAST HILL FARM PK
Stacklands Wood
89
123

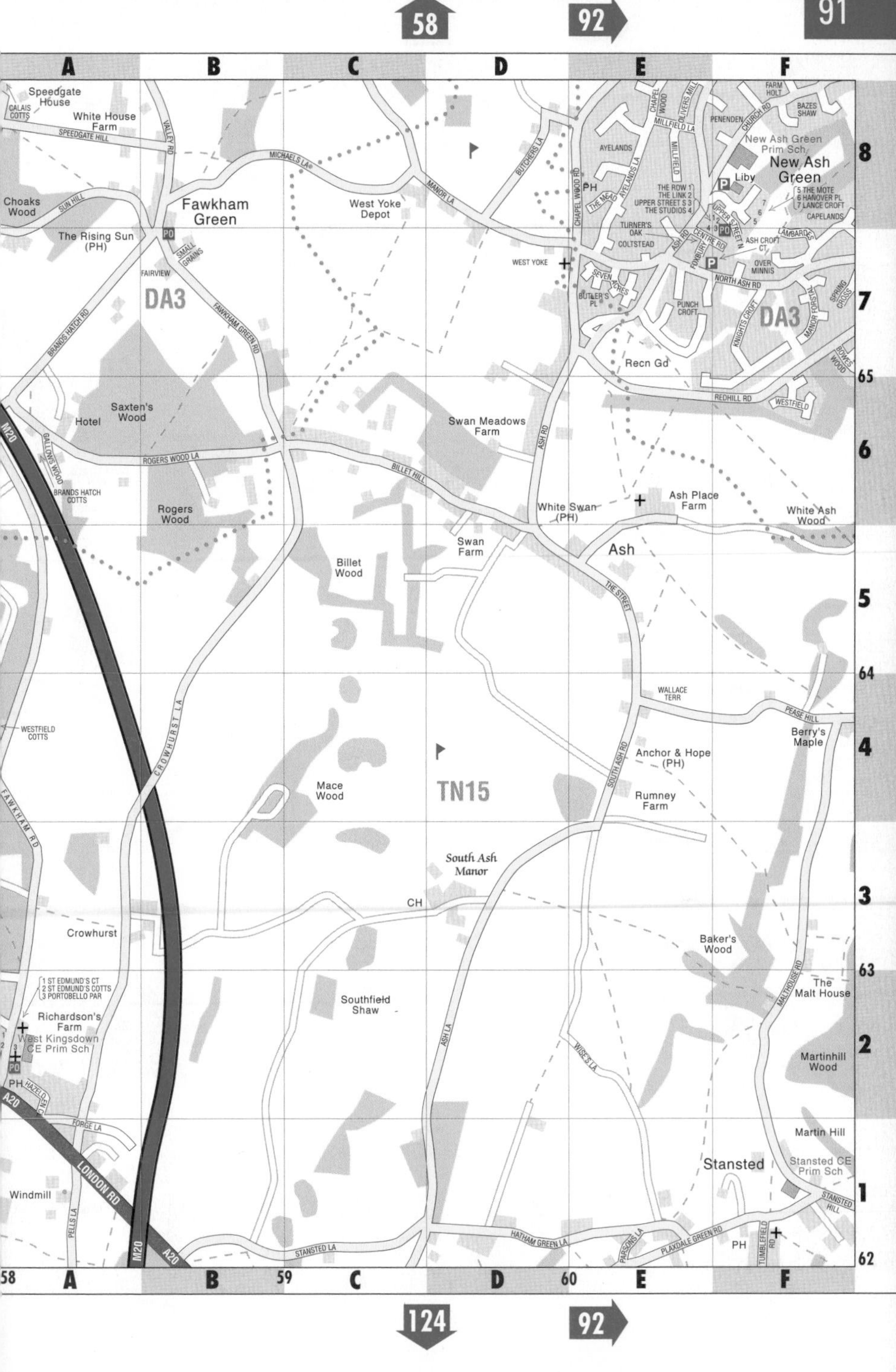
A B C D E F
8 7 65 6 5 64 4 3 63 2 1 62
Speedgate House
CALAIS COTTS
White House Farm
SPEEDGATE HILL
VALLEY RD
MICHAELS LA
Choaks Wood
SUN HILL
Fawkham Green
The Rising Sun (PH)
PO
SMALL GRAINS
FAIRVIEW
DA3
West Yoke Depot
MANOR LA
BUTCHERS LA
CHAPEL WOOD RD
PH
THE MEAD
AYELANDS LA
AYELANDS
MILLFIELD LA
MILLFIELD
CHAPEL WOOD
OLIVERS MILL
FARM HOLT
PENENDEN
CHURCH RD
BAZES SHAW
New Ash Green Prim Sch
New Ash Green
Liby
THE ROW 1
THE LINK 2
UPPER STREET S 3
THE STUDIOS 4
5 THE MOTE
6 HANOVER PL
7 LANCE CROFT
CAPELANDS
TURNER'S OAK
COLTSTEAD
ASH RD
CENTRE RD
UPPER STREET N
LAMBARDES
ASH CROFT CT
OVER MINNIS
FOXBURY
NORTH ASH RD
WEST YOKE
SEVEN ACRES
BUTLER'S PL
PUNCH CROFT
KNIGHTS CROFT
MANOR FORSTAL
SPRING CROSS
BOWES WOOD
Recn Gd
REDHILL RD
WESTFIELD
BRANDS HATCH RD
FAWKHAM GREEN RD
Saxten's Wood
Hotel
M20
GALLOWS WOOD
ROGERS WOOD LA
BRANDS HATCH COTTS
Rogers Wood
Swan Meadows Farm
ASH RD
BILLET HILL
White Swan (PH)
Ash Place Farm
White Ash Wood
Swan Farm
Ash
Billet Wood
THE STREET
WALLACE TERR
PEASE HILL
Berry's Maple
WESTFIELD COTTS
CROWHURST LA
Anchor & Hope (PH)
SOUTH ASH RD
Mace Wood
TN15
Rumney Farm
FAWKHAM RD
South Ash Manor
CH
Crowhurst
Baker's Wood
MALTHOUSE RD
The Malt House
1 ST EDMUND'S CT
2 ST EDMUND'S COTTS
3 PORTOBELLO PAR
Southfield Shaw
Richardson's Farm
West Kingsdown CE Prim Sch
ASH LA
WISE'S LA
Martinhill Wood
PH
HAZEL END
A20
FORGE LA
Martin Hill
LONDON RD
Stansted
Stansted CE Prim Sch
Windmill
PELLS LA
STANSTED HILL
HATHAM GREEN LA
PARSONS LA
PLAXDALE GREEN RD
TUMBLEFIELD RD
PH
STANSTED LA
58 59 60

91
59

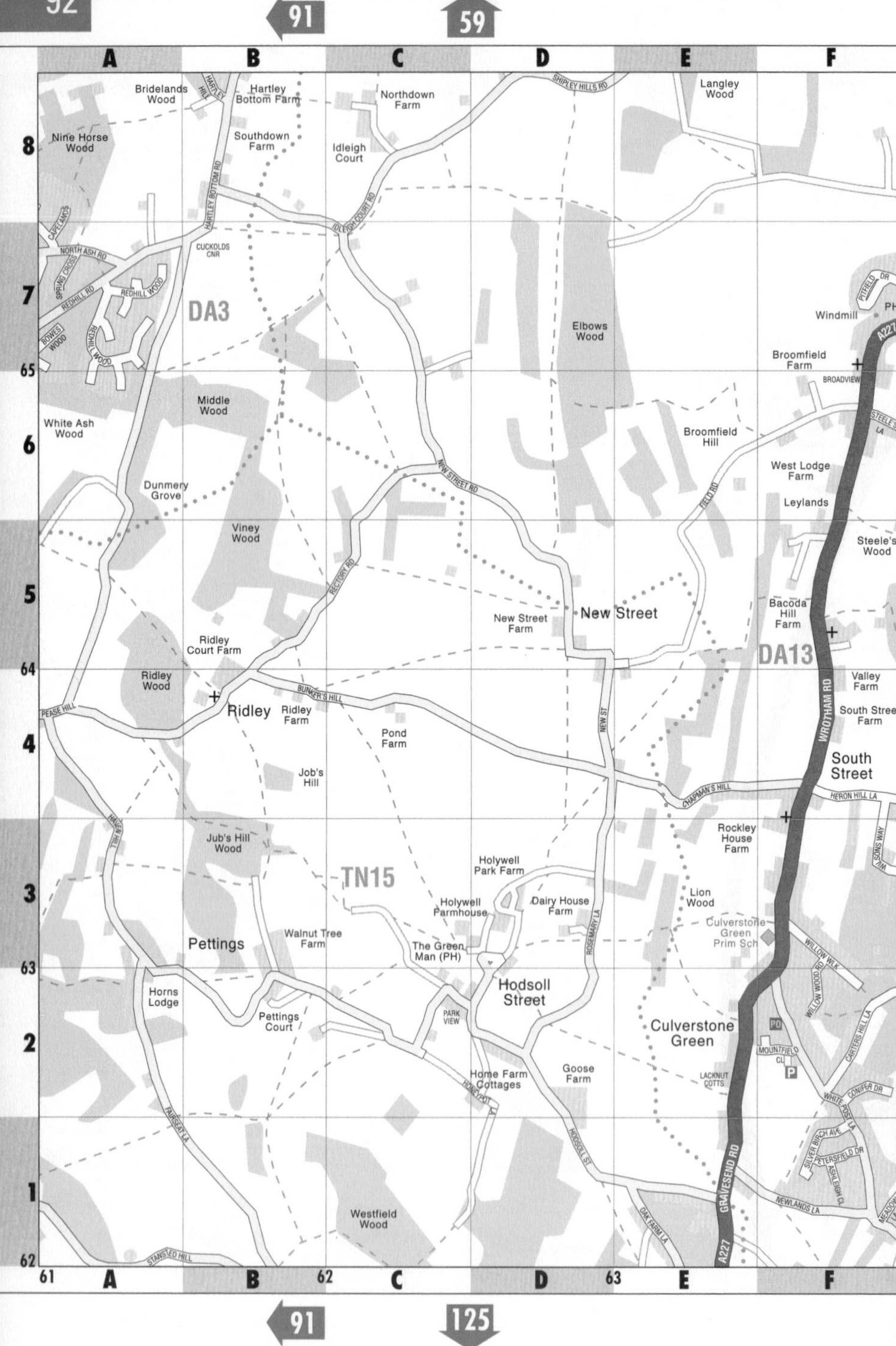
A
B
C
D
E
F
8
7
65
6
5
64
4
3
63
2
1
62
61
62
63
Bridelands Wood
Hartley Bottom Farm
Northdown Farm
Shipley Hills Rd
Langley Wood
Nine Horse Wood
Southdown Farm
Idleigh Court
Hartley Bottom Rd
Idleigh Court Rd
Cuckolds Cnr
North Ash Rd
Spring Cross
Redhill Rd
Redhill Wood
Bowes Wood
DA3
Elbows Wood
Windmill
PH
Pitfield Dr
A227
Broomfield Farm
Broadview
Middle Wood
White Ash Wood
Broomfield Hill
Steele's La
West Lodge Farm
New Street Rd
Dunmery Grove
Field Rd
Leylands
Viney Wood
Steele's Wood
Rectory Rd
Bacoda Hill Farm
New Street
New Street Farm
Ridley Court Farm
DA13
Ridley Wood
Valley Farm
Pease Hill
Bunker's Hill
Ridley
Ridley Farm
South Street Farm
Pond Farm
New St
Wrotham Rd
South Street
Job's Hill
Chapman's Hill
Heron Hill La
Rockley House Farm
Jub's Hill Wood
Holywell Park Farm
TN15
Lion Wood
Holywell Farmhouse
Dairy House Farm
Culverstone Green Prim Sch
Walnut Tree Farm
Pettings
The Green Man (PH)
Rosemary La
Willow Wlk
Willow Wood Rd
Horns Lodge
Hodsoll Street
Park View
Pettings Court
Culverstone Green
Mountfield Cl
P
Carters Hill La
Home Farm Cottages
Goose Farm
Lacknut Cotts
Honeypot La
White Post La
Conifer Dr
Fairseat La
Hodsoll St
Silver Birch Ave
Petersfield Dr
Ashleigh Cl
Gravesend Rd
Newlands La
Westfield Wood
Oak Farm La
Meadow La
Stansted Hill

91
125

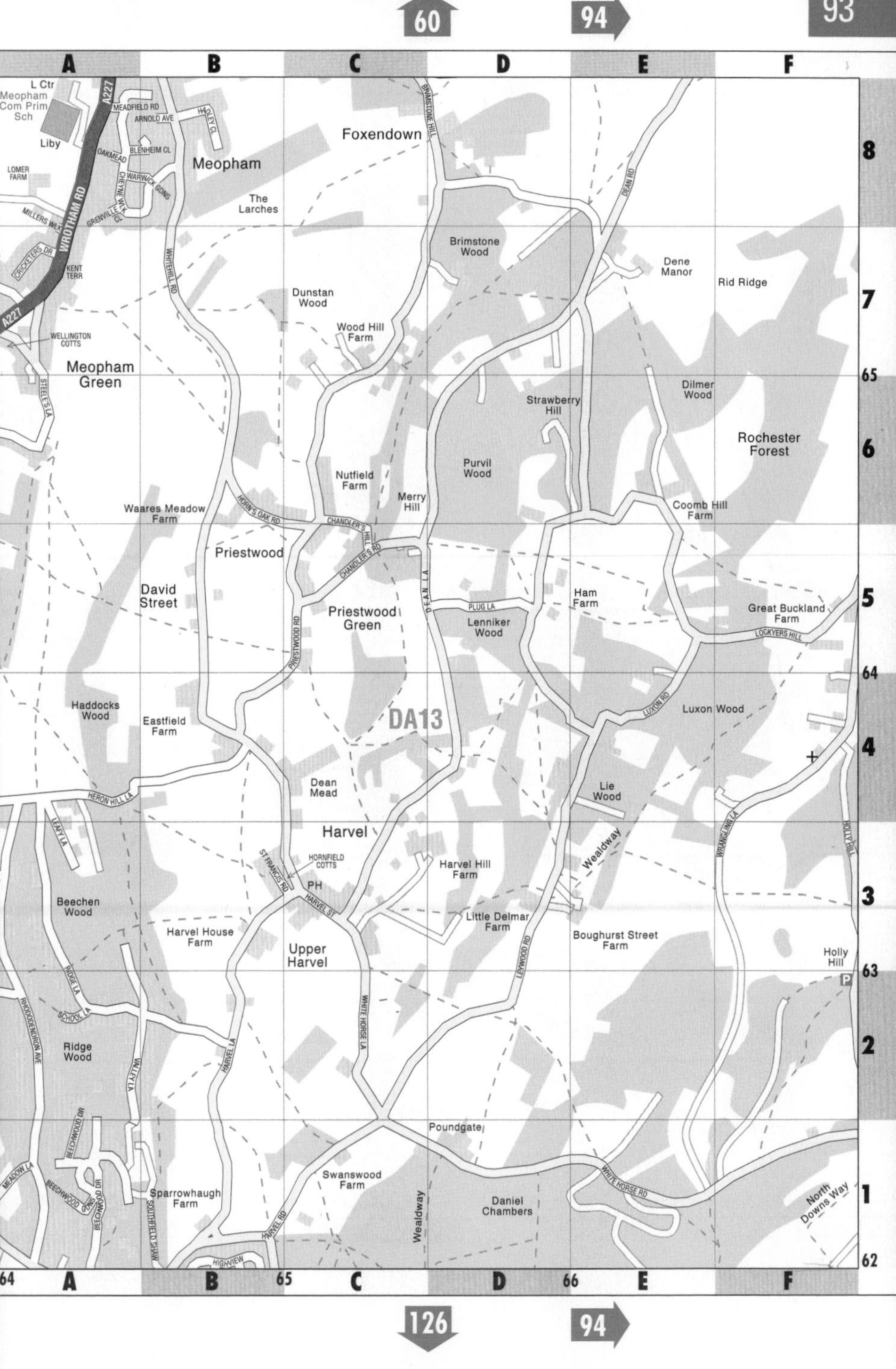
A
B
C
D
E
F
L Ctr
Meopham Com Prim Sch
Liby
A227
MEADFIELD RD
ARNOLD AVE
HADLEY CL
BLENHEIM CL
OAKMEAD
WARWICK GDNS
CHEYNE WLK
GRENVILLE CL
LOMER FARM
WROTHAM RD
MILLERS WLK
CRICKETERS DR
KENT TERR
WELLINGTON COTTS
STEELE'S LA
Meopham
Meopham Green
The Larches
Foxendown
BRIMSTONE HILL
DEAN RD
Brimstone Wood
Dene Manor
Rid Ridge
Dunstan Wood
Wood Hill Farm
WHITEHILL RD
Dilmer Wood
Strawberry Hill
Rochester Forest
Purvil Wood
Nutfield Farm
Merry Hill
Coomb Hill Farm
Waares Meadow Farm
HORN'S OAK RD
CHANDLER'S HILL
CHANDLER'S RD
Priestwood
David Street
Ham Farm
PLUG LA
DEAN LA
Priestwood Green
Lenniker Wood
Great Buckland Farm
LOCKYERS HILL
PRIESTWOOD RD
Haddocks Wood
Eastfield Farm
DA13
LUXON RD
Luxon Wood
Dean Mead
Lie Wood
HERON HILL LA
LEAFY LA
Harvel
HORNFIELD COTTS
ST FRANCIS RD
PH
HARVEL ST
Harvel Hill Farm
Wealdway
WRANGLING LA
HOLLY HILL
Beechen Wood
Harvel House Farm
Upper Harvel
Little Delmar Farm
LEYWOOD RD
Boughurst Street Farm
Holly Hill
RIDGE LA
SCHOOL LA
RHODODENDRON AVE
Ridge Wood
VALLEY LA
HARVEL LA
WHITE HORSE LA
Poundgate
BEECHWOOD DR
MEADOW LA
BEECHWOOD GDNS
Sparrowhaugh Farm
SOUTHFIELD SHAW
Swanswood Farm
Wealdway
Daniel Chambers
WHITE HORSE RD
North Downs Way
HARVEL RD
HIGHVIEW
8
7
6
5
4
3
2
1
65
64
63
62
64
65
66

93
61

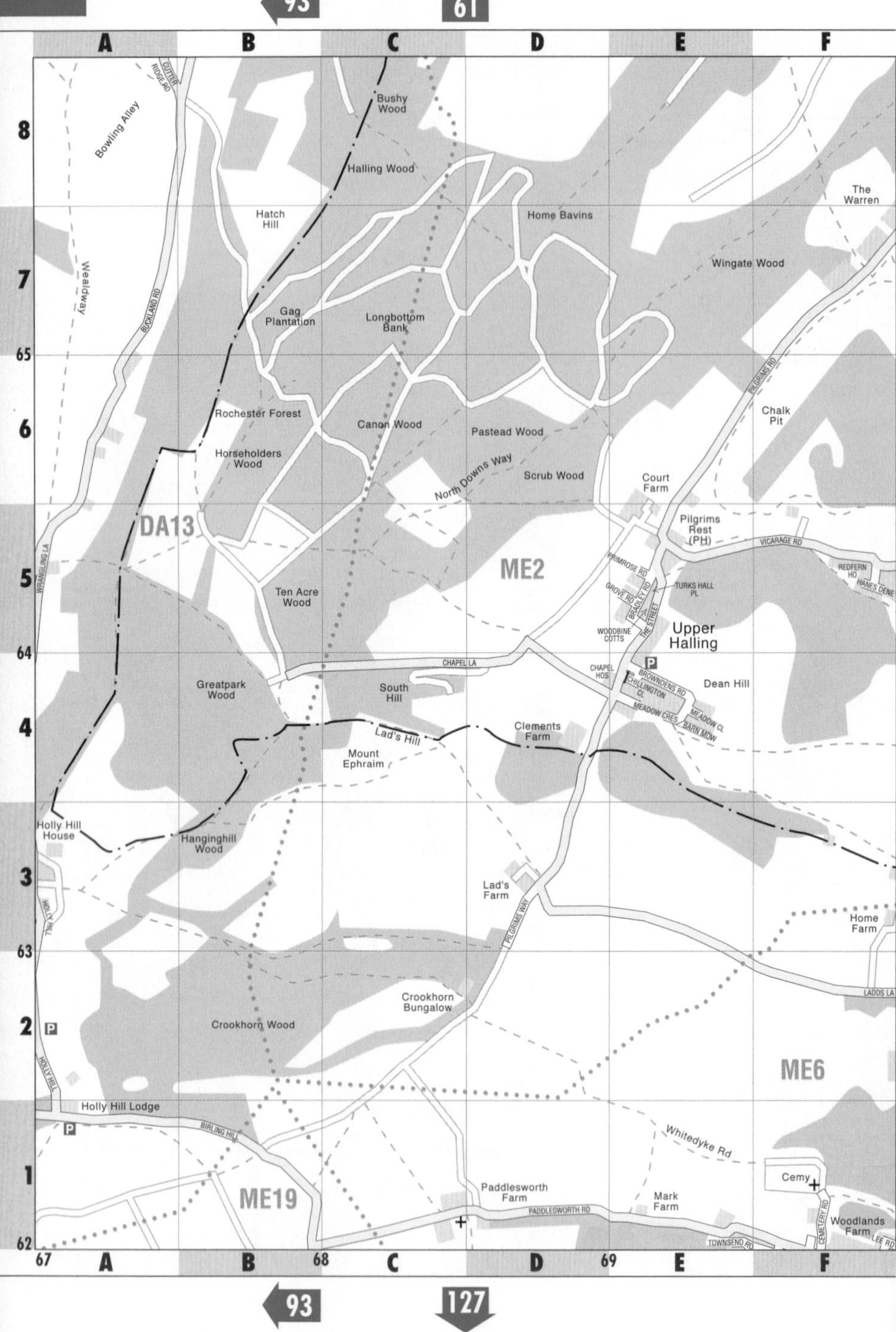
A
B
C
D
E
F
8
7
65
6
5
64
4
3
63
2
1
62
67
68
69
CUTTER RIDGE RD
Bowling Alley
Bushy Wood
Halling Wood
Hatch Hill
Home Bavins
The Warren
Wingate Wood
Wealdway
BUCKLAND RD
Gag Plantation
Longbottom Bank
PILGRIMS RD
Rochester Forest
Canon Wood
Pastead Wood
Chalk Pit
Horseholders Wood
North Downs Way
Scrub Wood
Court Farm
DA13
Pilgrims Rest (PH)
VICARAGE RD
WRANGLING LA
PRIMROSE RD
ME2
REDFERN HO
HANES DENE
GROVE RD
BRADLEY RD
TURKS HALL PL
Ten Acre Wood
THE STREET
WOODBINE COTTS
Upper Halling
P
CHAPEL LA
CHAPEL HOS
BROWNDENS RD
CHILLINGTON CL
Dean Hill
Greatpark Wood
South Hill
MEADOW CRES
MEADOW CL
BARN MDW
Clements Farm
Lad's Hill
Mount Ephraim
Holly Hill House
Hanginghill Wood
Lad's Farm
HOLLY HILL
PILGRIMS WAY
Home Farm
LADDS LA
Crookhorn Bungalow
Crookhorn Wood
P
ME6
Holly Hill Lodge
P
BIRLING HILL
Whitedyke Rd
Cemy
ME19
Paddlesworth Farm
Mark Farm
PADDLESWORTH RD
CEMETERY RD
Woodlands Farm
TOWNSEND RD
LEE RD

93
127

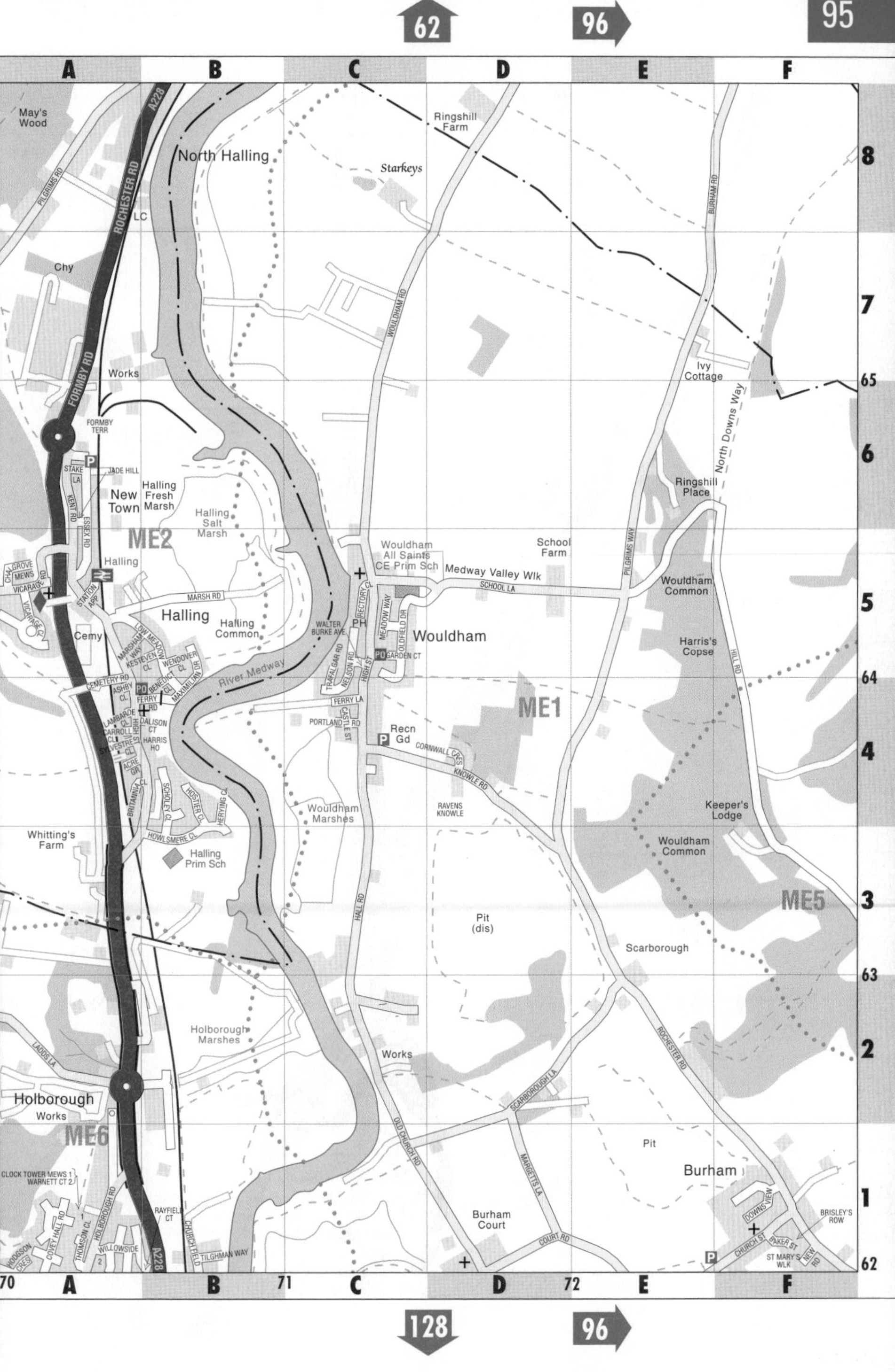
A
B
C
D
E
F
8
7
65
6
5
64
4
3
63
2
1
62
70
71
72
May's Wood
PILGRIMS RD
A228
ROCHESTER RD
LC
North Halling
Ringshill Farm
Starkeys
BURHAM RD
Chy
WOULDHAM RD
Works
FORMBY RD
FORMBY TERR
Ivy Cottage
North Downs Way
STAKE LA
JADE HILL
KENT RD
ESSEX RD
New Town
Halling Fresh Marsh
Halling Salt Marsh
ME2
Ringshill Place
School Farm
Wouldham All Saints CE Prim Sch
Medway Valley Wlk
SCHOOL LA
PILGRIMS WAY
Wouldham Common
Halling
CHALGROVE MEWS
VICARAGE RD
VICARAGE CL
STATION APP
MARSH RD
Halling Common
Cemy
WALTER BURKE AVE
RECTORY CL
PH
MEADOW WAY
OLDFIELD DR
Wouldham
GARDEN CT
Harris's Copse
HILL RD
MARSHAM WAY
DW MEADOW
KESTEVEN CL
WENDOVER CL
MAXIMILIAN DR
CEMETERY RD
ASHBY CL
BENEDICT CL
FERRY RD
River Medway
TRAFALGAR RD
NELSON RD
HIGH ST
FERRY LA
ME1
LAMBARDE CL
CARROLL CL
SYLVESTRE CL
ACRE GR
DALISON CT
HARRIS HO
PORTLAND RD
CASTLE ST
Recn Gd
CORNWALL CRES
KNOWLE RD
BRITANNIA CL
SCHOLEY CL
HOSTIER CL
HERYING CL
Wouldham Marshes
RAVENS KNOWLE
Keeper's Lodge
Whitting's Farm
HOWLSMERE CL
Halling Prim Sch
Wouldham Common
ME5
HALL RD
Pit (dis)
Scarborough
Holborough Marshes
ROCHESTER RD
LADDS LA
Works
Holborough
Works
SCARBOROUGH LA
ME6
OLD CHURCH RD
MARGETTS LA
Pit
Burham
CLOCK TOWER MEWS 1
WARNETT CT 2
HOLBOROUGH RD
COVEY HALL RD
THOMSON CL
RAYFIELD CT
CHURCHFIELD
Burham Court
DOWNS VIEW
BRISLEY'S ROW
HODGSON CRES
WILLOWSIDE
TILGHMAN WAY
COURT RD
CHURCH ST
BAKER ST
ST MARY'S WLK
NEW RD

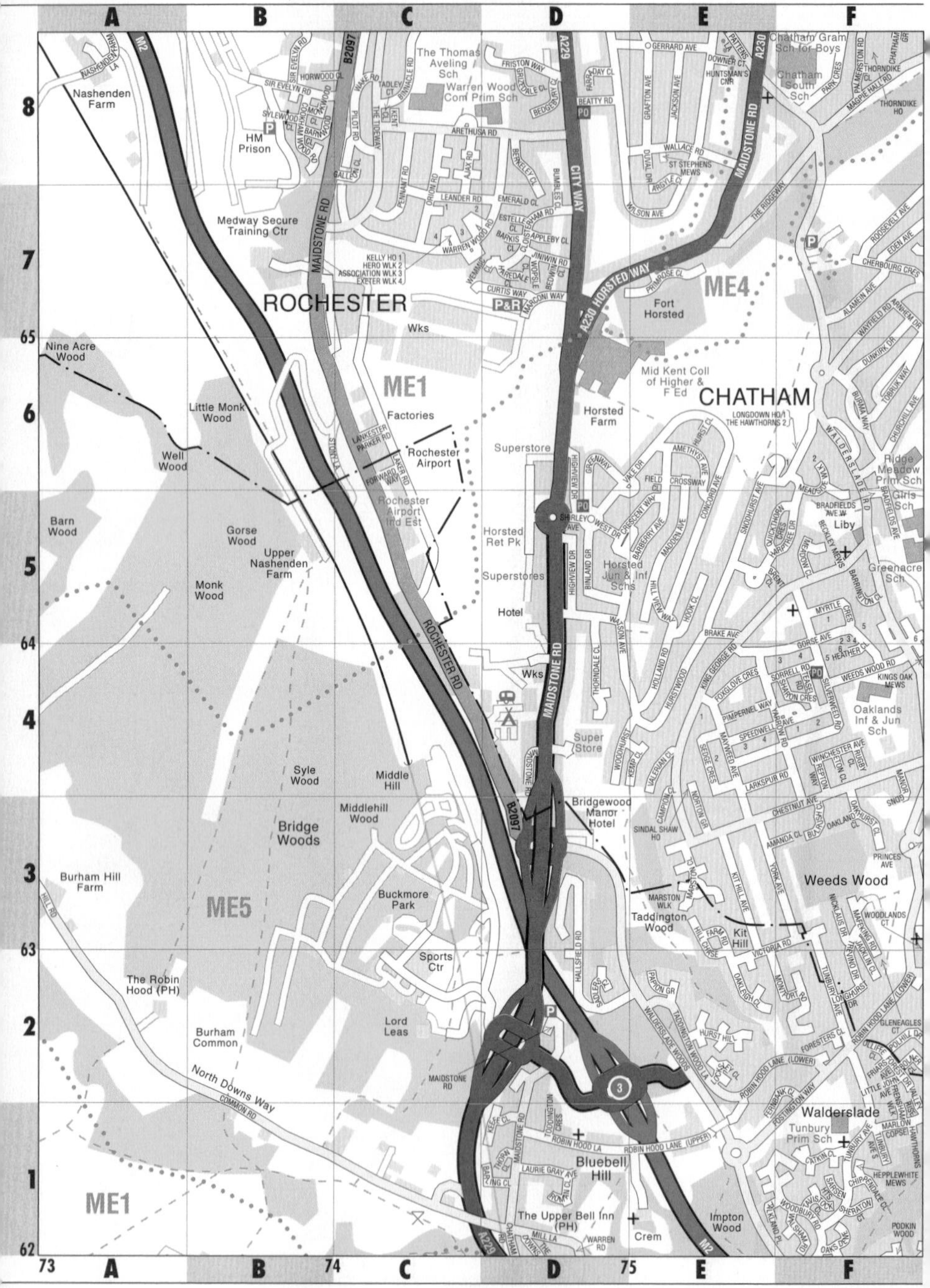

95 63

A B C D E F

8

Nashenden Farm

MAGSON LA

M2

SIR EVELYN RD

HORWOOD RD

TADLEY RD

The Thomas Aveling Sch

FRISTON WAY

Warren Wood Com Prim Sch

A229

O GERRARD AVE

Chatham Gram Sch for Boys

A230

Chatham South Sch

THORNDIKE

THORNDIKE HO

HM Prison

PILOT RD

ARETHUSA RD

DAY CL

BEATTY RD

HUNTSMAN'S CRR

GRAY NLTON AVE

JACKSON AVE

WALLACE RD

St STEPHENS MEWS

THE ROSEDENE

WOODFIELD RD

LOCH SQ

CHERBURG CRES

ALAMEIN AVE

Medway Secure Training Ctr

CITY WAY

EMERALD CL

LEANDER RD

BRUMBEL CL

WILSON AVE

MAIDSTONE RD

HATFIELD RD

7

MAIDSTONE RD

KELLY HO 1
HERD WLK 2
ASSOCIATION WLK 3
EXETER WLK 4

WARREN WOOD

CURTIS WAY

P&R

A230 HORSTED WAY

Fort Horsted

A230

ME4

ROCHESTER

Wks

65

Nine Acre Wood

Mid Kent Coll of Higher & F Ed

LONGDOWN HO 1
THE HAWTHORNS 2

CHATHAM

6

Little Monk Wood

ME1

Factories

Horsted Farm

Ridge Meadow Prim Sch

Girls Sch

Liby

Well Wood

LANKESTER PARKER RD

Rochester Airport

Superstore

Greenacre Sch

5

Barn Wood

Gorse Wood

Upper Nashenden Farm

Rochester Airport Rd Est

Horsted Ret Pk

CROSSWAY

FIELD VW

BRADFIELDS AVE W

KINGS OAK MEWS

Monk Wood

Superstores

Horsted Jun & Inf Sch

WEEDS WOOD RD

64

Hotel

Oaklands Inf & Jun Sch

ROCHESTER RD

Wks

R2097

Super Store

4

Syle Wood

Middle Hill

Bridgewood Manor Hotel

SINDAL SHAW HO

PRINCES AVE

3

Burham Hill Farm

Bridge Woods

Middlehill Wood

ME5

Buckmore Park

MARSTON WLK

Taddington Wood

Kit Hill

Weeds Wood

WOODLANDS CT

63

The Robin Hood (PH)

Sports Ctr

HALFSIDE RD

2

Burham Common

Lord Leas

P

GLENEAGLES CT

MARLOW COPSE

North Downs Way

COMMON RD

MAIDSTONE RD

3

ROBIN HOOD LANE (LOWER)

Walderslade

Tunbury Prim Sch

PEPPLEWHITE RD

1

ME1

ROBIN HOOD LA

LAURIE GRAY AVE

ROBIN HOOD LANE (UPPER)

Bluebell Hill

Impton Wood

PODKIN WOOD

62

A229

The Upper Bell Inn (PH)

WARREN RD

Crem

M2

73 A B 74 C D 75 E F

E4
1 LAVENDER CL
2 ASPEN WAY
3 HONEYSUCKLE CL
4 GENTIAN CL

F4
1 MALLOW WAY
2 JASMINE CL
3 HAREBELL CL
4 ROSEMARY CL
5 LINDEN HO
6 OAK HO

F5
1 SAFFRON WAY
2 WILLOW HO
3 PINE HO
4 ROWAN HO
5 HAWTHORN HO
6 BLEAKWOOD RD

64
98

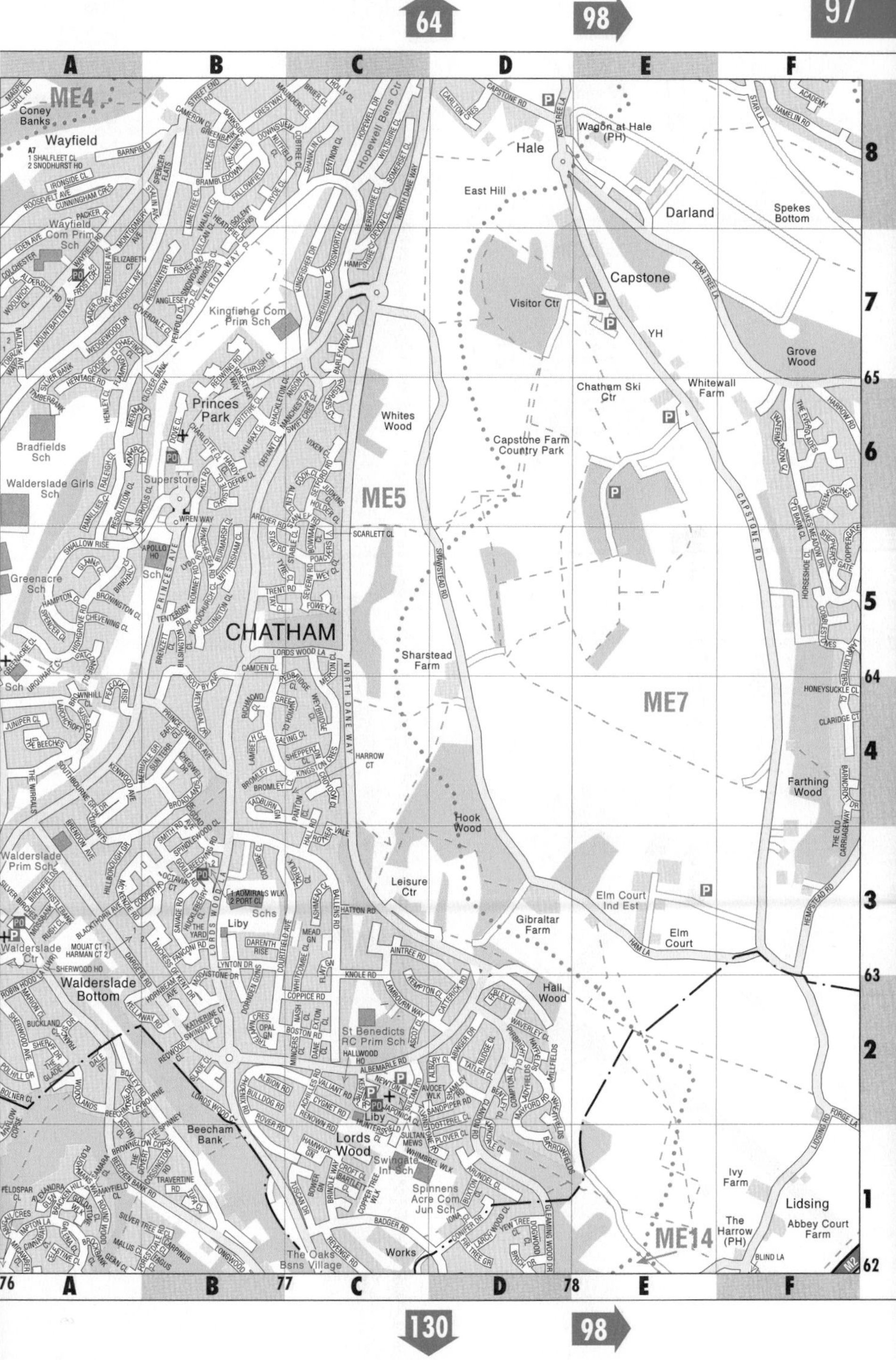
A
B
C
D
E
F
ME4
Coney Banks
Wayfield
Wayfield Com Prim Sch
Kingfisher Com Prim Sch
Princes Park
Bradfields Sch
Walderslade Girls Sch
Superstore
Greenacre Sch
CHATHAM
ME5
Whites Wood
Sharstead Farm
Hook Wood
Leisure Ctr
Gibraltar Farm
Hall Wood
Hale
Wagon at Hale (PH)
East Hill
Darland
Spekes Bottom
Capstone
Visitor Ctr
YH
Grove Wood
Chatham Ski Ctr
Whitewall Farm
Capstone Farm Country Park
ME7
Farthing Wood
Elm Court Ind Est
Elm Court
Walderslade Prim Sch
Walderslade Ctr
Walderslade Bottom
Liby
Schs
St Benedicts RC Prim Sch
Beecham Bank
Lords Wood
Swingate Inf Sch
Spinnens Acre Com Jun Sch
The Oaks Bsns Village
Works
Ivy Farm
Lidsing
The Harrow (PH)
Abbey Court Farm
ME14
CAPSTONE RD
NORTH DANE WAY
SHARSTEAD RD
PRINCES AVE
LORDS WOOD LA
HAM LA
8
7
65
6
5
64
4
3
63
2
1
62
76
77
78

130
98

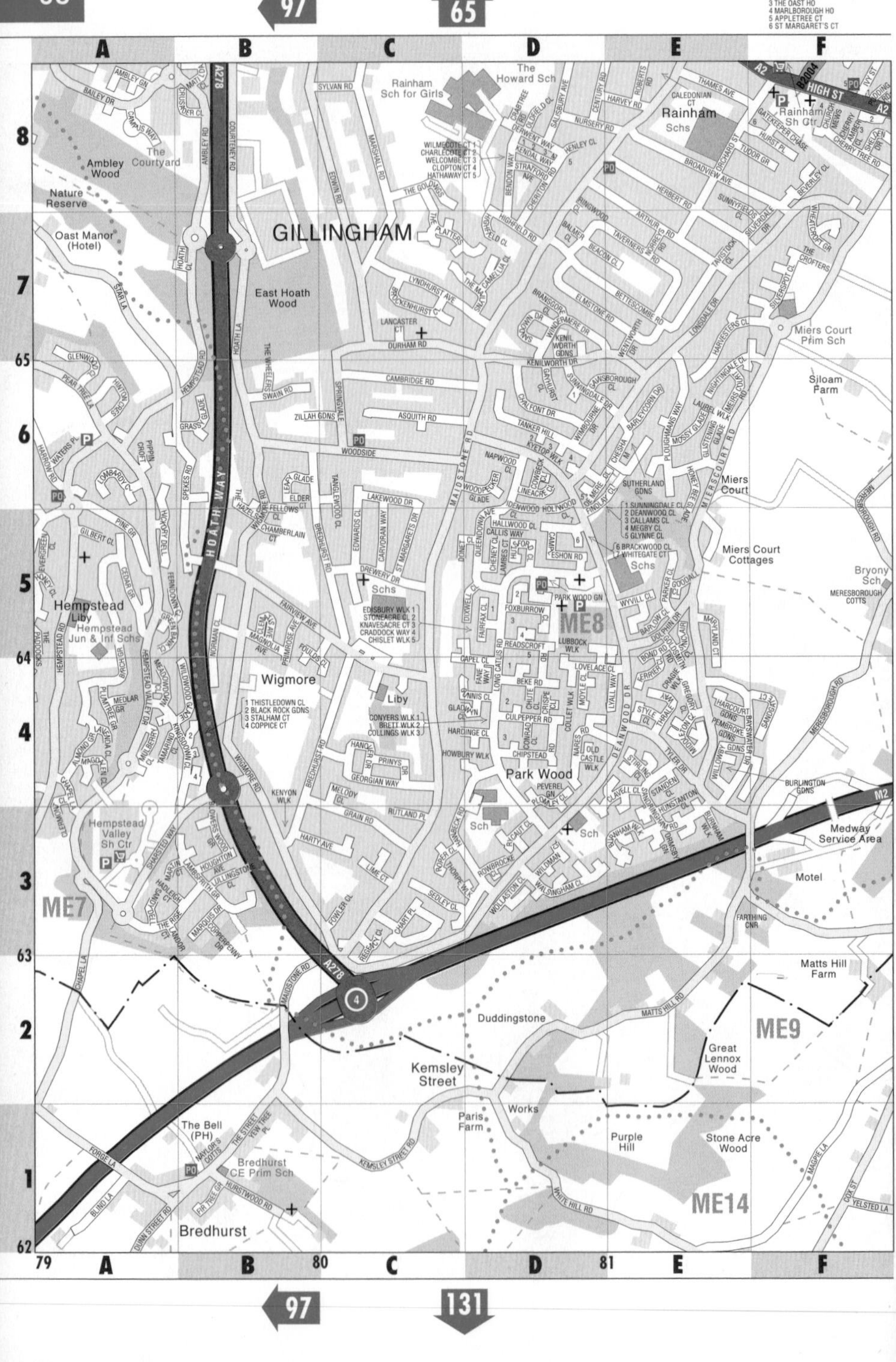
97
65
F8
1 SUNSHINE CT
2 STRATFORD LA
3 THE OAST HO
4 MARLBOROUGH HO
5 APPLETREE CT
6 ST MARGARET'S CT
A
B
C
D
E
F
8
7
65
6
5
64
4
3
63
2
1
62
79
80
81
A278
HOATH WAY
M2
A2
B2004
HIGH ST
GILLINGHAM
Rainham Sch for Girls
The Howard Sch
Rainham Schs
Rainham Sh Ctr
Ambley Wood
The Courtyard
Nature Reserve
Oast Manor (Hotel)
East Hoath Wood
Miers Court Prim Sch
Siloam Farm
Miers Court
Miers Court Cottages
Bryony Sch
MERESBOROUGH COTTS
Hempstead Liby
Hempstead Jun & Inf Schs
Wigmore
Liby
Schs
ME8
ME7
ME9
ME14
Park Wood
Sch
Hempstead Valley Sh Ctr
Medway Service Area
Motel
FARTHING CNR
Matts Hill Farm
Duddingstone
Kemsley Street
Great Lennox Wood
Works
Paris Farm
Purple Hill
Stone Acre Wood
The Bell (PH)
Bredhurst CE Prim Sch
Bredhurst
WILMECOTE CT 1
CHARLECOTE CT 2
WELCOMBE CT 3
CLOPTON CT 4
HATHAWAY CT 5
1 SUNNINGDALE CL
2 DEANWOOD CL
3 CALLAMS CL
4 MEGBY CL
5 GLYNNE CL
6 BRACKWOOD CL
7 WHITEGATE CT
EDISBURY WLK 1
STONEACRE CL 2
KNAVESACRE CT 3
CRADDOCK WAY 4
CHISLET WLK 5
1 THISTLEDOWN CL
2 BLACK ROCK GDNS
3 STALHAM CT
4 COPPICE CT
CONYERS WLK 1
BRETT WLK 2
COLLINGS WLK 3
BURLINGTON GDNS
SYLVAN RD
MARSHALL RD
EDWIN RD
DURHAM RD
CAMBRIDGE RD
ASQUITH RD
ZILLAH GDNS
WOODSIDE
SPRINGVALE
MAIDSTONE RD
KENILWORTH DR
CHALFONT DR
TANKER HILL
NAPWOOD CL
HOLLYWOOD
FAIRVIEW AVE
DREWERY DR
LAKEWOOD DR
BREDHURST RD
WIGMORE RD
HEMPSTEAD RD
PEAR TREE LA
HARROW RD
GILBERT CL
CEDAR GR
PINE GR
SHARSTED WAY
MATTS HILL RD
KEMSLEY STREET RD
WHITE HILL RD
FORGE LA
BLIND LA
DUNN STREET RD
HURSTWOOD RD
FIR TREE GR
CHAPEL LA
MAGPIE LA
COX ST
YELSTED LA
HARTY AVE
GRAIN RD
RUTLAND PL
SEDLEY CL
FOWLER CL
LIME CT
CHART PL
REGENCY CL
DEANWOOD DR
MIERSCOURT RD
MERESBOROUGH RD
MARYLAND CT
PARKER CL
BARLOW CL
BOND RD
TYLER DR
HUNSTANTON CL
BURNHAM WLK
WALSINGHAM CL
WOLLASTON CL
ROWBROCKE CL
LONG CATLIS RD
READSCROFT
LUBBOCK WLK
PARK WOOD GN
FOXBURROW CL
PEVEREL GN
PLOMLEY CL
OLD CASTLE WLK
CHIPSTEAD RD
CULPEPPER RD
HARDINGE CL
HOWBURY WLK
BEKE RD
CAPEL CL
LOVELACE CL
THAMES AVE
HARVEY RD
NURSERY RD
BROADVIEW AVE
HERBERT RD
ARTHUR RD
TAVERNERS RD
BEACON CL
BETTESCOMBE RD
ELMSTONE RD
LONGSDALE DR
HARVESTERS CL
SILVERSPOT CL
THE CROFTERS
WHEATCROFT GR
BEVERLEY CL
HURST PL
TUDOR GR
ORCHARD ST
GATEKEEPER CHASE
CHERRY TREE RD
MAIDSTONE RD
THE STREET
YEW TREE PL
NAYLOR'S COTTS

66
100

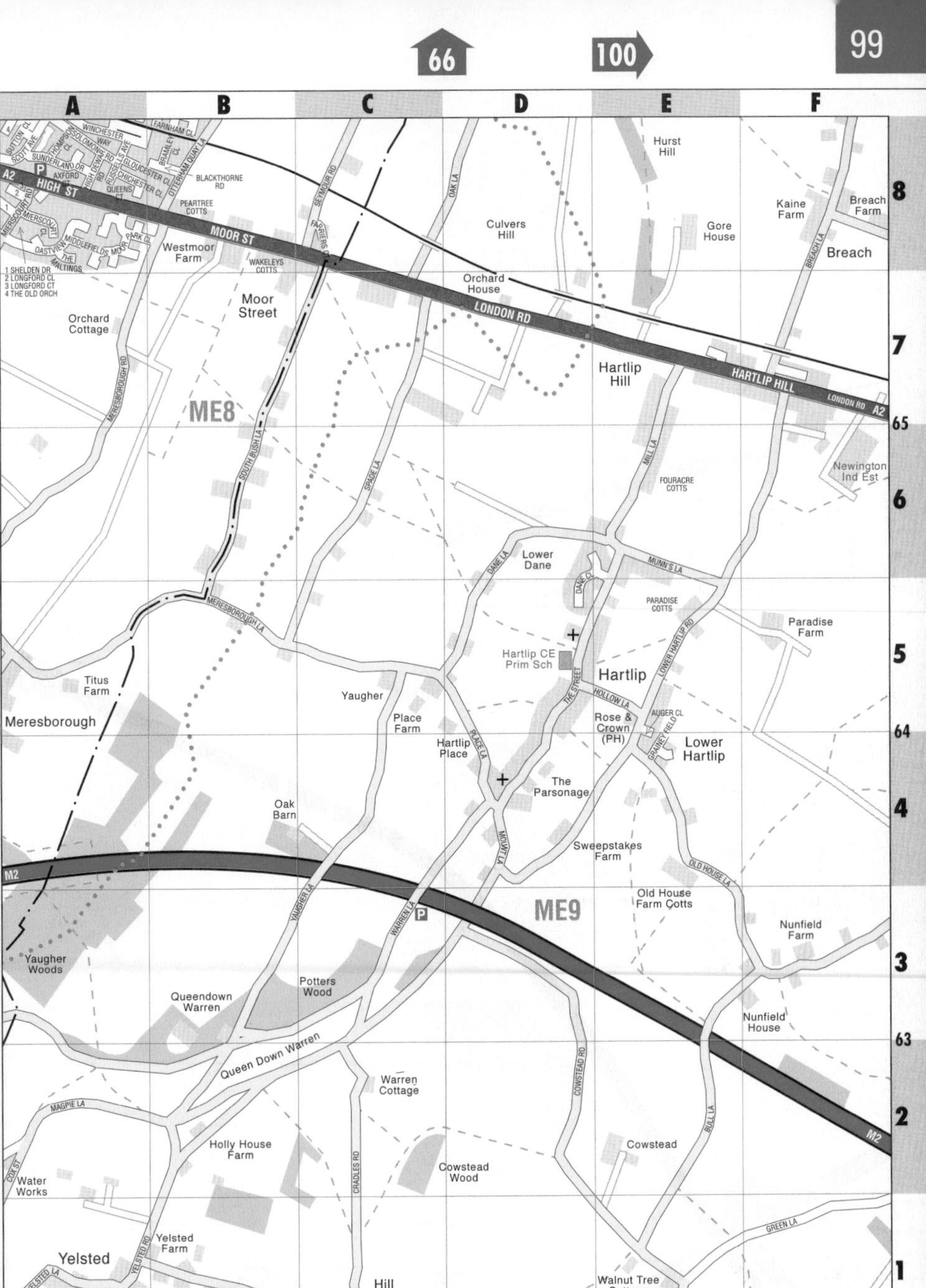
A
B
C
D
E
F
8
7
6
5
4
3
2
1
65
64
63
62
82
83
84
A2
HIGH ST
MOOR ST
LONDON RD
HARTLIP HILL
M2
ME8
ME9
WINCHESTER WAY
FARNHAM CL
SUTTON CL
SCOTT AVE
THOMPSON CL
SOLOMON RD
SUNDERLAND DR
AXFORD
HIGH DEWAR RD
RUSSELLS AVE
BRAMLEY CL
GLOUCESTER CL
CHICHESTER CL
QUEENS CT
OTTERHAM QUAY LA
BLACKTHORNE RD
PEARTREE COTTS
MIERSCOURT RD
MIERSCOURT CL
MIDDLEFIELDS
OASTVIEW
THE MALTINGS
MOOR PARK CL
1 SHELDEN DR
2 LONGFORD CL
3 LONGFORD CT
4 THE OLD ORCH
Westmoor Farm
WAKELEYS COTTS
Moor Street
Orchard Cottage
SEYMOUR RD
FARRIERS CT
OAK LA
Culvers Hill
Orchard House
Hurst Hill
Gore House
Kaine Farm
Breach Farm
Breach
BREACH LA
Hartlip Hill
LONDON RD
Newington Ind Est
MERESBOROUGH RD
SOUTH BUSH LA
SPADE LA
MILL LA
FOURACRE COTTS
Lower Dane
DANE LA
DANE CL
MUNN'S LA
PARADISE COTTS
Paradise Farm
MERESBOROUGH LA
Hartlip CE Prim Sch
Hartlip
LOWER HARTLIP RD
Titus Farm
Meresborough
Yaugher
Place Farm
Hartlip Place
PLACE LA
THE STREET
HOLLOW LA
Rose & Crown (PH)
AUGER CL
GRAINEY FIELD
Lower Hartlip
The Parsonage
Oak Barn
MOUNT LA
Sweepstakes Farm
OLD HOUSE LA
Old House Farm Cotts
YAUGHER LA
WARREN LA
Nunfield Farm
Yaugher Woods
Queendown Warren
Potters Wood
Nunfield House
Queen Down Warren
Warren Cottage
COWSTEAD RD
MAGPIE LA
Holly House Farm
Cowstead Wood
Cowstead
BULL LA
COX ST
Water Works
CRADLES RD
GREEN LA
Yelsted Farm
YELSTED RD
Yelsted
YELSTED LA
Hill Green
Walnut Tree Cottage
Yelsted Court Farm
PLUM TREE RD
WEST WOOD RD
HILL GREEN RD
BULL LANE COTTS
Nettlestead

132
100

99
67

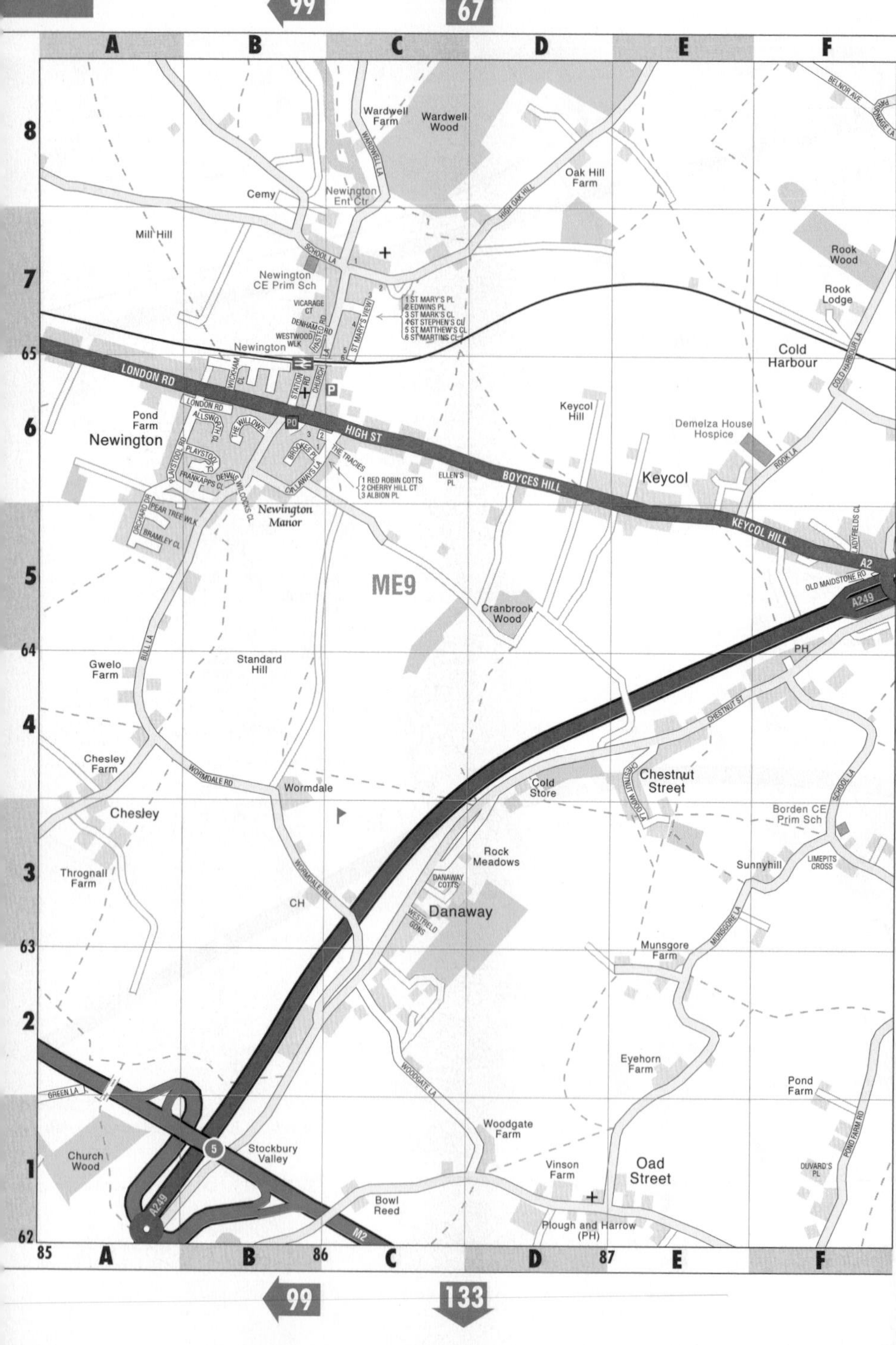
A
B
C
D
E
F
8
7
65
6
5
64
4
3
63
2
1
62
85
86
87
Wardwell Farm
Wardwell Wood
WARDWELL LA
HIGH OAK HILL
Oak Hill Farm
BELNOR AVE
PARSONAGE LA
Cemy
Newington Ent Ctr
Mill Hill
SCHOOL LA
Newington CE Prim Sch
VICARAGE CT
DENHAM
HASTED RD
WESTWOOD WLK
ST MARY'S VIEW
1 ST MARY'S PL
2 EDWINS PL
3 ST MARK'S CL
4 ST STEPHEN'S CL
5 ST MATTHEW'S CL
6 ST MARTINS CL
Rook Wood
Rook Lodge
Cold Harbour
COLD HARBOUR LA
Newington
LONDON RD
WICKHAM CL
STATION RD
CHURCH LA
P
PO
LONDON RD
ALLSWORTH CL
THE WILLOWS
PLAYSTOOL RD
PLAYSTOOL CL
FRANKAPPS CL
DENNIS WILCOCKS CL
BROOKES PL
CALLAWAYS LA
THE TRACIES
1 RED ROBIN COTTS
2 CHERRY HILL CT
3 ALBION PL
HIGH ST
Pond Farm
Newington
ORCHARD DR
PEAR TREE WLK
BRAMLEY CL
Newington Manor
ELLEN'S PL
BOYCES HILL
Keycol Hill
Keycol
Demelza House Hospice
ROOK LA
KEYCOL HILL
LADYFIELDS CL
A2
OLD MAIDSTONE RD
A249
ME9
Cranbrook Wood
BULL LA
Gwelo Farm
Standard Hill
PH
CHESTNUT ST
Chesley Farm
WORMDALE RD
Wormdale
Cold Store
CHESTNUT WOOD LA
Chestnut Street
SCHOOL LA
Borden CE Prim Sch
Chesley
Rock Meadows
Sunnyhill
LIMEPITS CROSS
Thrognall Farm
WORMDALE HILL
DANAWAY COTTS
CH
Danaway
WESTFIELD GDNS
MUNSGORE LA
Munsgore Farm
Eyehorn Farm
Pond Farm
GREEN LA
WOODGATE LA
Woodgate Farm
POND FARM RD
Church Wood
5
Stockbury Valley
Vinson Farm
Oad Street
DUVARD'S PL
A249
Bowl Reed
Plough and Harrow (PH)
M2

99
133

68
102

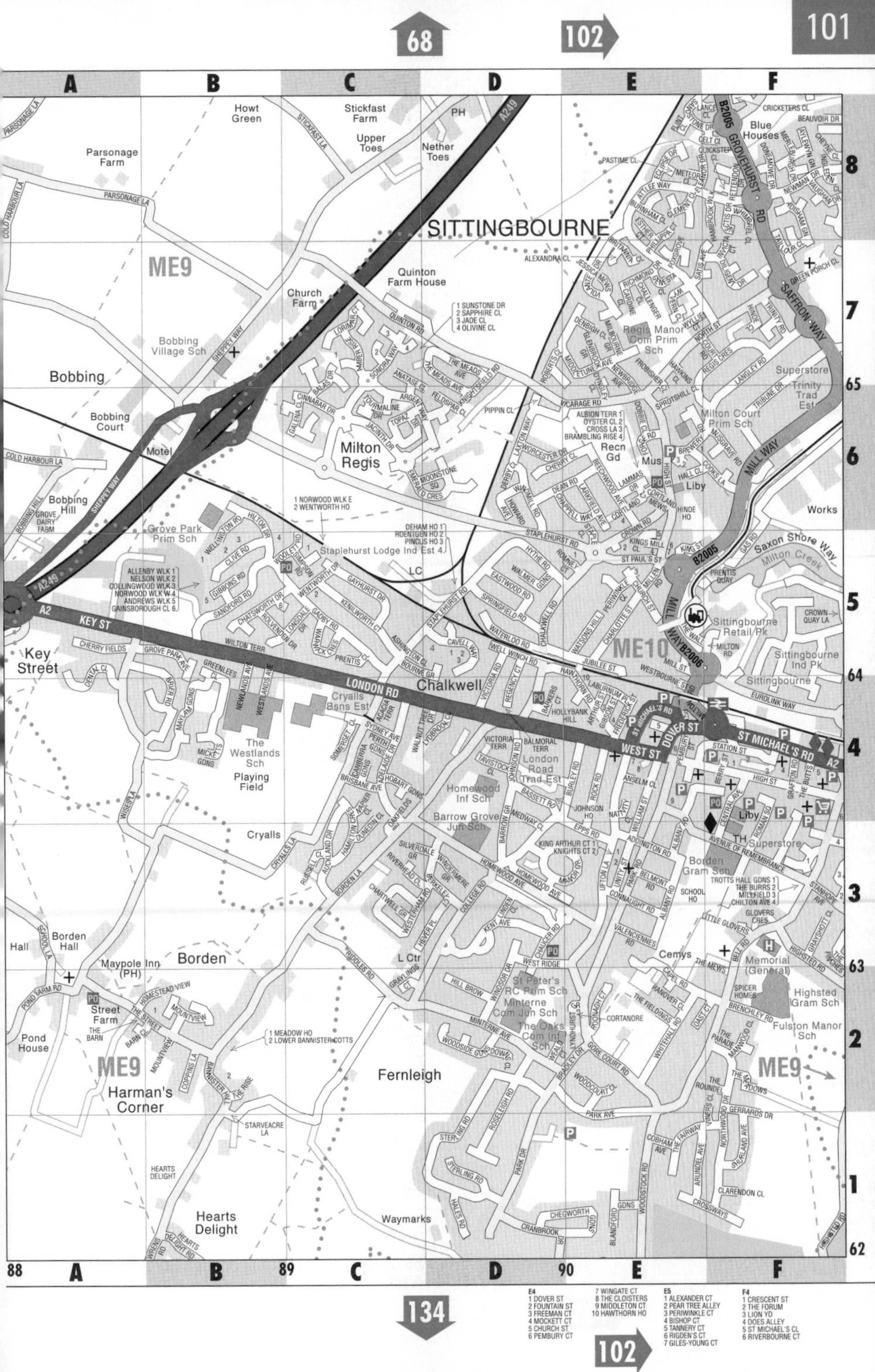
A
B
C
D
E
F
8
7
65
6
5
64
4
3
63
2
1
62
88
89
90
Howt Green
Stickfast Farm
Upper Toes
Nether Toes
PH
Parsonage Farm
PARSONAGE LA
PARSONAGE LA
COLD HARBOUR LA
STICKFAST LA
A249
SITTINGBOURNE
ME9
Church Farm
Quinton Farm House
1 SUNSTONE DR
2 SAPPHIRE CL
3 JADE CL
4 OLIVINE CL
QUINTON RD
Bobbing Village Sch
SHEPPEY WAY
Bobbing
Bobbing Court
Motel
COLD HARBOUR LA
Milton Regis
THE MEADS AVE
KNIGHTSFIELD RD
FELDSPAR CL
ANATASE CL
SONORA WAY
CINNABAR DR
GALENA CL
TOURMALINE DR
TOPAZ DR
JACINTH DR
EMERALD CRES
MOONSTONE SQ
PIPPIN CL
Bobbing Hill
GROVE DAIRY FARM
BOBBING HILL
SHEPPEY WAY
Grove Park Prim Sch
HILTON DR
WELLINGTON RD
CLIVE RD
GIBBONS RD
SANDFORD RD
1 NORWOOD WLK E
2 WENTWORTH HO
DEHAM HO 1
ROENTGEN HO 2
PINCUS HO 3
Staplehurst Lodge Ind Est 4
LC
ALLENBY WLK 1
NELSON WLK 2
COLLINGWOOD WLK 3
NORWOOD WLK W 4
ANDREWS WLK 5
GAINSBOROUGH CL 6
CHATSWORTH DR
ROLVENDEN DR
LONSDALE DR
GADBY RD
WARWICK CRES
PRENTIS CL
KENILWORTH CT
GAYHURST DR
WENTWORTH DR
WOOLLETT RD
SIMPSON RD
STAPLEHURST RD
ASHINGTON CL
BOURNE GR
CAVELL WAY
A2
KEY ST
Key Street
CHERRY FIELDS
GROVE PARK AVE
WILTON TERR
GREENLEES CL
DENTAL CL
BRIER RD
MAYLAM GDNS
MICKETTS GDNS
NEWLANDS AVE
WESTLANDS AVE
The Westlands Sch
Playing Field
Cryalls Bsns Est
LONDON RD
Chalkwell
SYDNEY AVE
ACACIA TERR
PERTH GDNS
CANBERRA GDNS
ADELAIDE DR
BRISBANE AVE
HOBART GDNS
OAKFIELDS
SOMERSET CL
WALNUT TREE DR
LYDBROOK CL
VICTORIA RD
REGENCY CT
WISES LA
Cryalls
CRYALLS LA
RUSSELL CL
AUCKLAND DR
HAMILTON CRES
NAPIER CL
DUNEDIN CL
BORDEN LA
SILVERDALE GR
WINDERMERE
RIVERHEAD CL
BERKELEY CT
CHARTWELL GR
WESTERHAM RD
HEVER PL
COLLEGE RD
KENT AVE
HOMEWOOD AVE
Homewood Inf Sch
Barrow Grove Jun Sch
BARROW GR
MEDWAY CL
TAVISTOCK CL
JOHNSON RD
VICTORIA TERR
BALMORAL TERR
London Road Trad Est
BASSETT RD
L Ctr
RIDDLES RD
GRAYLINGS
Hall
SCHOOL LA
Borden Hall
Borden
Maypole Inn (PH)
POND FARM RD
Street Farm
THE BARN
Pond House
HOMESTEAD VIEW
MOUNTVIEW
THE STREET
BARN CL
ME9
Harman's Corner
COPPINS LA
BANNISTER HILL
THE RISE
1 MEADOW HO
2 LOWER BANNISTER COTTS
STARVEACRE LA
HEARTS DELIGHT
Hearts Delight
HEARTS DELIGHT RD
Fernleigh
Waymarks
STERLING RD
ROSELEIGH RD
HALES RD
PARK DR
CHEGWORTH
CRANBROOK DR
BLANDFORD GDNS
WOODSTOCK RD
HILL BROW
WINDSOR DR
WEST RIDGE
CHAUCER RD
St Peter's RC Prim Sch
Minterne Com Jun Sch
The Oaks Com Inf Sch
MINTERNE AVE
WOODSIDE GDNS
LYNDHURST GR
ROONAGH CT
CORTANORE
BRADLEY DR
GORE COURT RD
WOODCOURT CL
PARK AVE
Blue Houses
B2005
GROVEHURST RD
CRICKETERS CL
BEAUVOIR DR
PASTIME CL
METEOR CL
EARLE WAY
BURNHAM CL
ESTHER CT
PHILIPPA CT
CLEMENT CL
ALEXANDRA CL
BRITANNIA CL
JESSICA MEWS
VOLANTE DR
RICHMOND DR
CARDINE CL
CHALLENGER CL
Regis Manor Com Prim Sch
DENBIGH CL
GLENBROOK GR
MILBOURNE GR
ETUNE AVE
NEWBRIDGE AVE
FROBISHER CL
ROBERTS CL
VICARAGE RD
ALBION TERR 1
OYSTER CL 2
CROSS LA 3
BRAMBLING RISE 4
Recn Gd
Mus
Liby
HIGH ST
LAMMAS
CORTLAND MEWS
HINDE HO
WORCESTER DR
CHERRY CL
LAXTON WAY
DERBY CL
HOWARD AVE
DEAN RD
ARKFIELD AVE
CHAPPELL WAY
BEECHWOOD AVE
STAPLEHURST RD
CROWN RD
KINGS MILL CL
ST PAUL'S ST
HYTHE RD
WALMER GDNS
EASTWOOD RD
SPRINGFIELD RD
WATERLOO RD
WELL WINCH RD
CHALKWELL RD
WATSONS HILL
CHARLOTTE ST
PERIWINKLE CL
CHURCH ST
ME10
JUBILEE ST
HAWTHORN RD
LABURNUM PL
BARKERS CT
HOLLYBANK HILL
ARTHUR ST
GIBSON ST
FREDERICK ST
ST MICHAEL'S RD
DOVER ST
WEST ST
PEMBURY ST
BURLEY RD
ROCK RD
ANSELM CL
JOHNSON HO
NATIVITY CL
WILLIAM ST
EPPS RD
KING ARTHUR CT 1
KNIGHTS CT 2
MANOR GR
ADDINGTON RD
UFTON LA
UNITY ST
PARK RD
BELMONT RD
CONNAUGHT RD
ALBANY RD
VALENCIENNES RD
Borden Gram Sch
SCHOOL HO
AVENUE OF REMEMBRANCE
TRUTTS HALL GDNS 1
THE BURRS 2
MILLFIELD 3
CHILTON AVE 4
GLOVERS CRES
LITTLE GLOVERS
Cemys
THE MEWS
BELL RD
CAPEL RD
HANOVER CL
THE FIELDINGS
WHITEHALL RD
OAST CT
Memorial (General)
SPICER HOMES
Highsted Gram Sch
BRENCHLEY RD
THE PARADE
MANWOOD CL
Fulston Manor Sch
ME9
THE ROUNDEL
THE MEADOWS
NORTHWOOD DR
GERRARDS DR
VINERS CL
COBHAM AVE
THE FAIRWAY
ARUNDEL AVE
SHORLAND AVE
CLARENDON CL
CROSSWAYS
STATION ST
HIGH ST
ST MICHAEL'S RD
A2
BERRY ST
CENTRAL AVE
Liby
ROMAN SQ
GRAFTON RD
THE BUTTS
TH
Superstore
STANHOPE AVE
GRAYSHOTT CL
HIGHSTED RD
THE FINCHES
SAFFRON WAY
GREEN PORCH CL
TRINITY RD
NORTH ST
WYLLIE CT
HINDE CT
REGIS CRES
LANGLEY RD
Superstore
Trinity Trad Est
TRIBUNE DR
Milton Court Prim Sch
MUSGRAVE RD
BREWERY RD
HALL CL
COOKS LA
MILL WAY
Works
HAWKINS CL
SPROTSHILL CL
B2005
KING ST
GAS RD
Saxon Shore Way
Milton Creek
PRENTIS QUAY
MILL WAY
B2006
THE WALL
Sittingbourne Retail Pk
MILTON RD
CROWN QUAY LA
Sittingbourne Ind Pk
Sittingbourne
EUROLINK WAY
MILL ST
WESTBOURNE ST
DOMETRE WAY
NEWMAN DR
VAUGHAN DR
ADISHAM GN
TAILLOUR CL
E4
1 DOVER ST
2 FOUNTAIN ST
3 FREEMAN CT
4 MOCKETT CT
5 CHURCH ST
6 PEMBURY CT
7 WINGATE CT
8 THE CLOISTERS
9 MIDDLETON CT
10 HAWTHORN HO
E5
1 ALEXANDER CT
2 PEAR TREE ALLEY
3 PERIWINKLE CT
4 BISHOP CT
5 TANNERY CT
6 RIGDEN'S CT
7 GILES-YOUNG CT
F4
1 CRESCENT ST
2 THE FORUM
3 LION YD
4 DOES ALLEY
5 ST MICHAEL'S CL
6 RIVERBOURNE CT

134
102

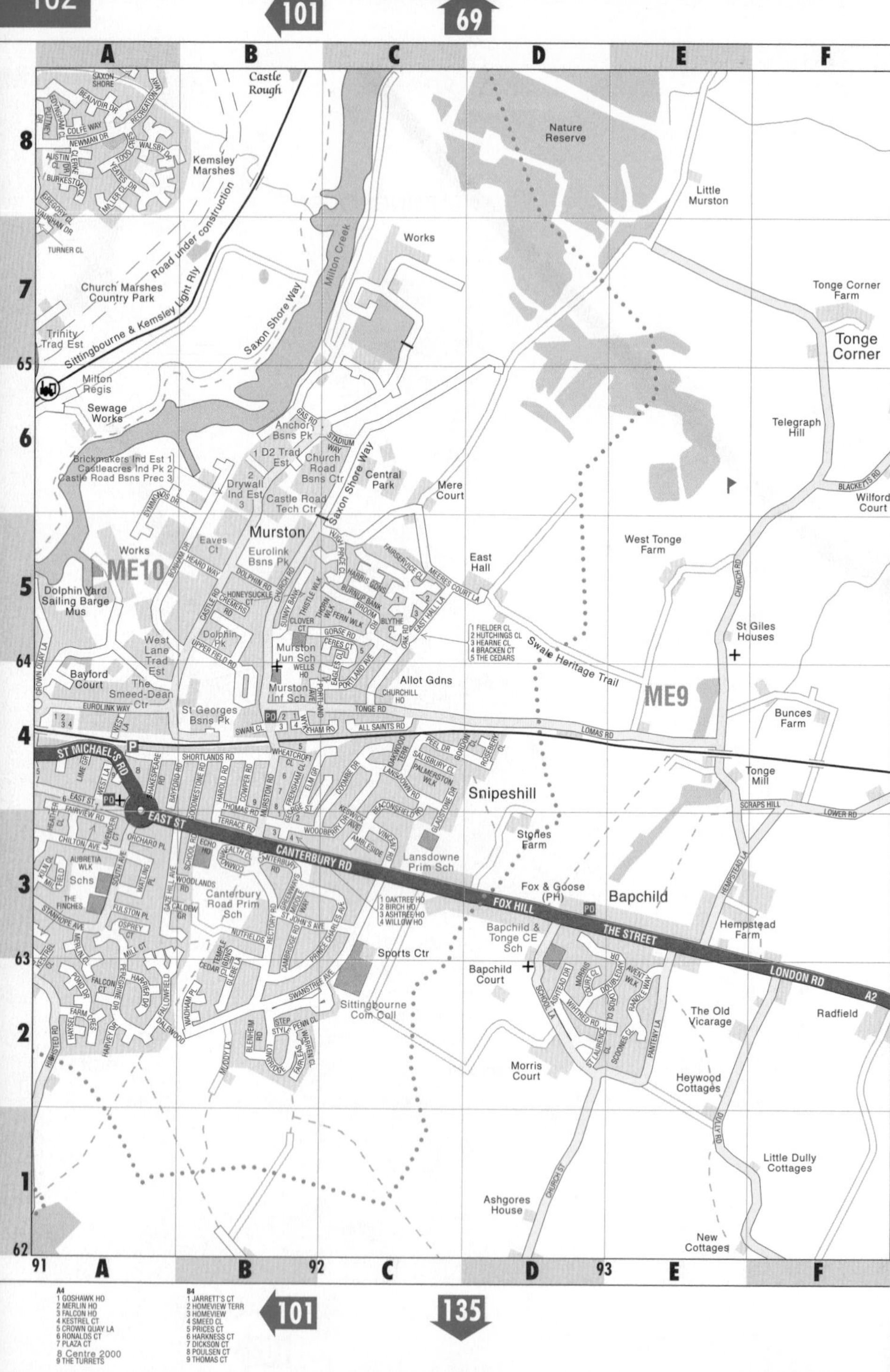

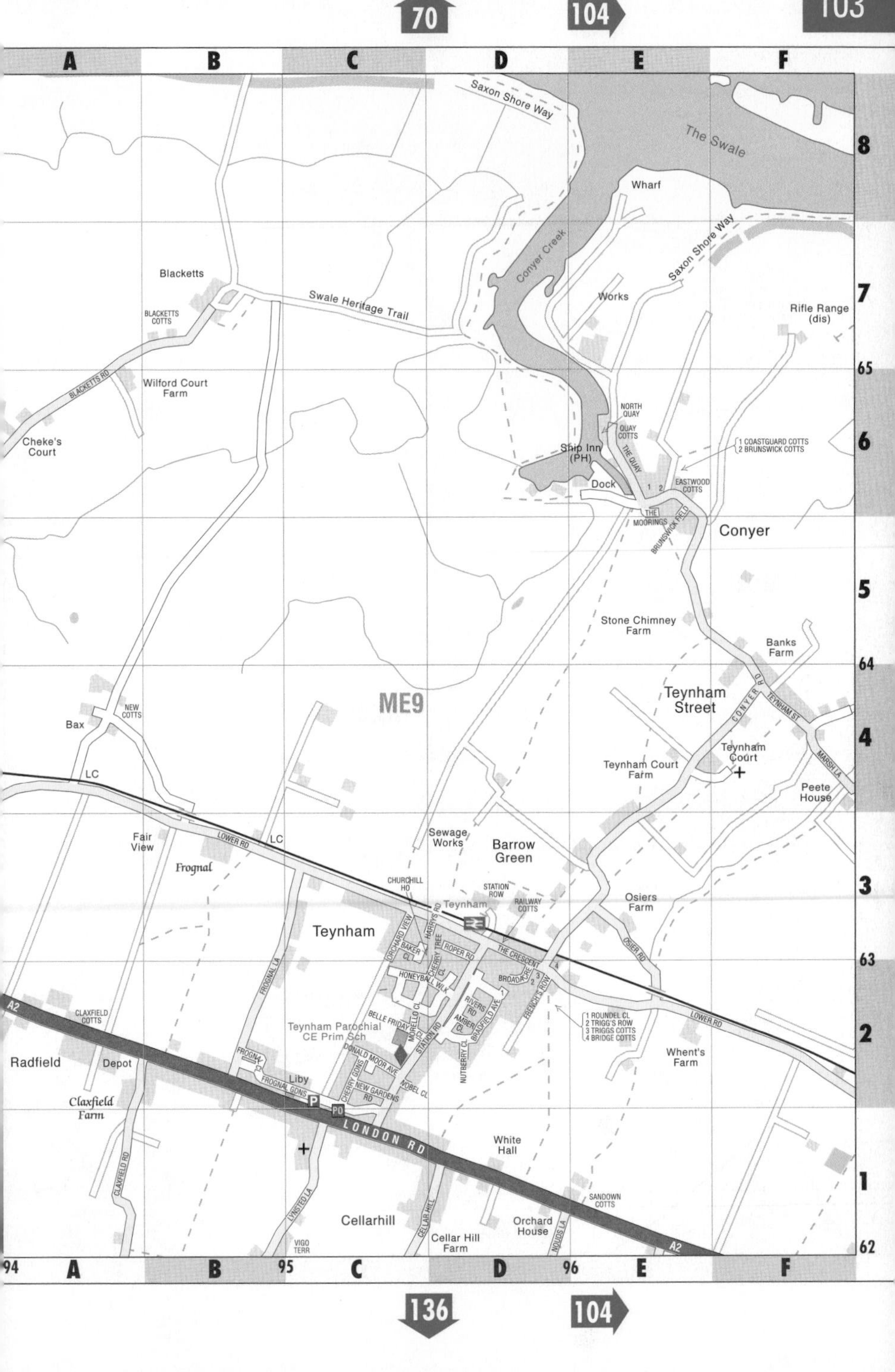

70
104

A B C D E F

Saxon Shore Way

The Swale

8

Wharf

Conyer Creek

Blacketts

Swale Heritage Trail

Works

Rifle Range
(dis)

7

BLACKETTS
COTTS

BLACKETTS RD

65

Wilford Court
Farm

NORTH
QUAY

1 COASTGUARD COTTS
2 BRUNSWICK COTTS

6

Cheke's
Court

QUAY
COTTS

THE QUAY

Ship Inn
(PH)

EASTWOOD
COTTS

Dock

1 2

THE
MOORINGS

Conyer

5

BRUNSWICK RD

Stone Chimney
Farm

Banks
Farm

64

NEW
COTTS

ME9

Teynham
Street

CONYER

TEYNHAM ST

4

Bax

MARSHLA

Teynham
Court

LC

Teynham Court
Farm

Peete
House

Fair
View

LOWER RD

LC

Sewage
Works

Barrow
Green

Osiers
Farm

3

Frognal

CHURCHILL
HO

STATION
ROW

OSIER RD

FROGNAL LA

Teynham

RAILWAY
COTTS

63

Teynham

THE CRESCENT

A2

CLAXFIELD
COTTS

HONEYBALL LA

ROPER RD

BROAD A

FRENCH'S AV

1 ROUNDEL CL
2 TRIGG'S ROW
3 TRIGGS COTTS
4 BRIDGE COTTS

LOWER RD

2

Radfield

Depot

Teynham Parochial
CE Prim Sch

BELLE FRIDAY CL

NUTBERRY CL

Whent's
Farm

Claxfield
Farm

Liby

NEW GARDENS

FOREL CL

CLAXFIELD RD

P PO

CHERRY TREE RD

VIGO

LONDON RD

White
Hall

SANDOWN
COTTS

1

Cellarhill

CELLAR HILL

MOORS LA

Orchard
House

A2

VIGO
TERR

Cellar Hill
Farm

62

94   A   B   95   C   D   96   E   F

136
104

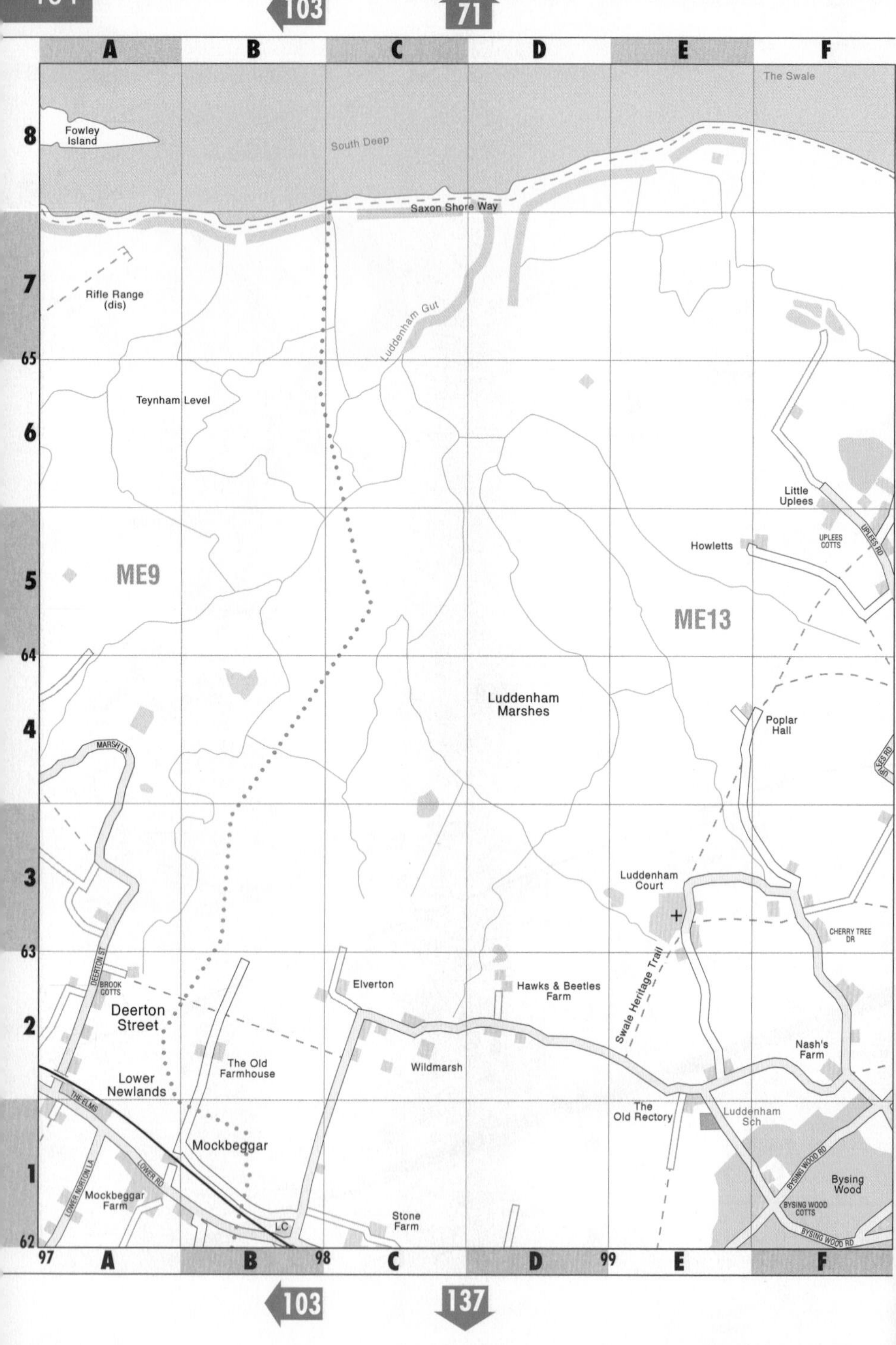

103
71

The Swale

8 Fowley Island

South Deep

Saxon Shore Way

7 Rifle Range (dis)

65

Teynham Level

Luddenham Gut

6

Little Uplees

UPLEES COTTS

UPLEES RD

5 ME9

Howletts

ME13

64

4 Luddenham Marshes

Poplar Hall

MARSH LA

SCR RD

3 Luddenham Court

CHERRY TREE DR

63

DEERTON RD

BROOK COTTS

2 Deerton Street

Elverton

Hawks & Beetles Farm

Swale Heritage Trail

Nash's Farm

The Old Farmhouse

Wildmarsh

THE ELMS

Lower Newlands

The Old Rectory

Luddenham Sch

BYSING WOOD RD

LOWER RD

Mockbeggar

1

LOWER & DEERTON LA

Mockbeggar Farm

LC

Stone Farm

Bysing Wood

BYSING WOOD COTTS

BYSING WOOD RD

62

97 **A** 98 **C** **D** 99 **E** **F**

103
137

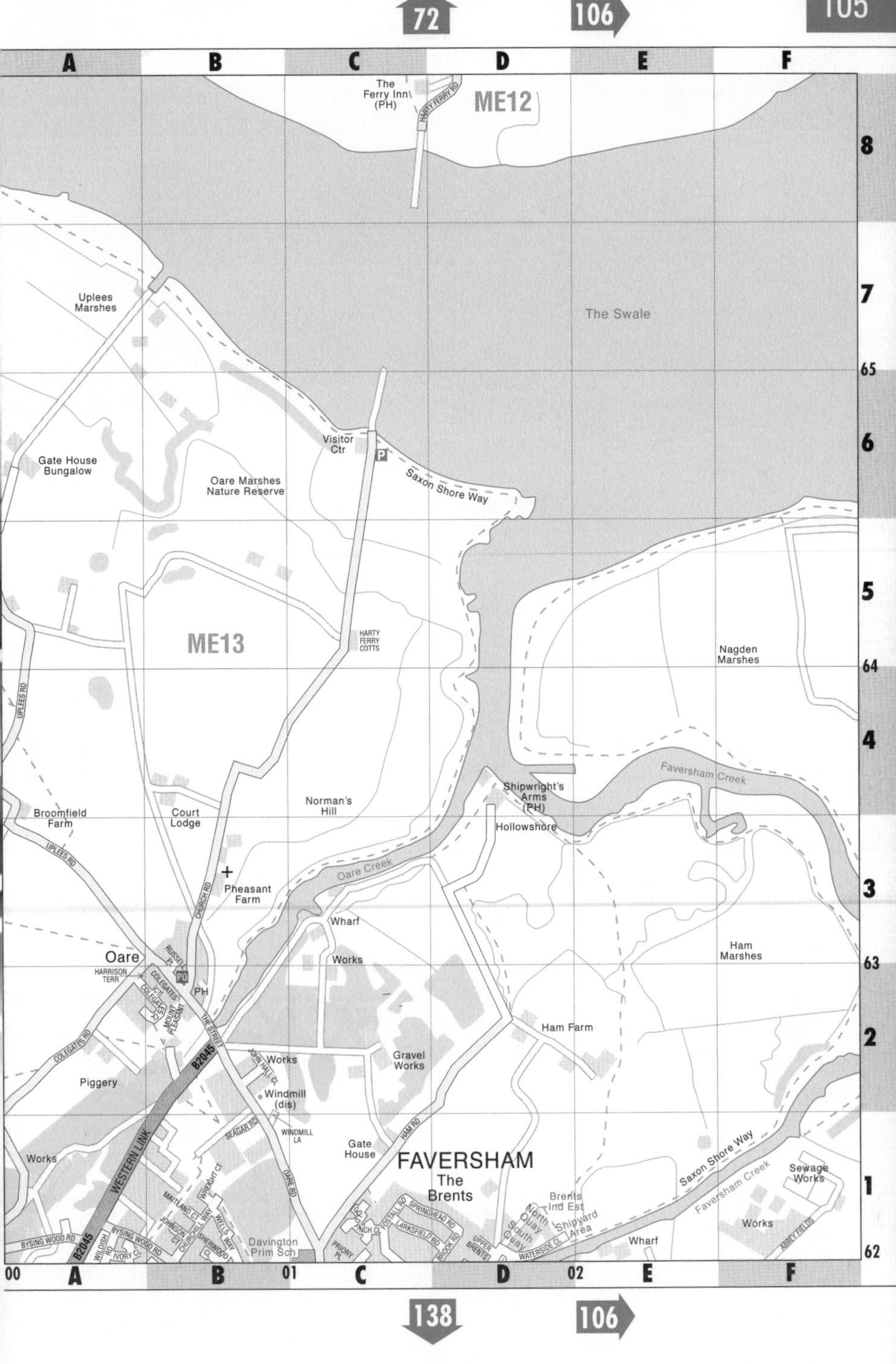
72
106
A
B
C
D
E
F
8
7
6
5
4
3
2
1
65
64
63
62
00
01
02
The Ferry Inn (PH)
HARTY FERRY RD
ME12
The Swale
Uplees Marshes
Gate House Bungalow
Oare Marshes Nature Reserve
Visitor Ctr
Saxon Shore Way
ME13
HARTY FERRY COTTS
Nagden Marshes
UPLEES RD
Faversham Creek
Shipwright's Arms (PH)
Hollowshore
Broomfield Farm
Court Lodge
Norman's Hill
Oare Creek
Pheasant Farm
CHURCH RD
Wharf
Works
Ham Marshes
Oare
RUSSELL PL
HARRISON TERR
COLEGATES CL
COLEGATES CT
MOUNT PLEASANT
PH
THE STREET
Ham Farm
COLEGATES RD
B2045
JOHN HALL CL
Works
Gravel Works
Piggery
Windmill (dis)
SEAGAR RD
WINDMILL LA
WESTERN LINK
Works
Gate House
HAM RD
FAVERSHAM
The Brents
Saxon Shore Way
Sewage Works
WRIGHT CT
OARE RD
MAITLAND CT
JOHNSON CT
CHURCHILL WAY
WELLS WAY
SHERWOOD CL
BYSING WOOD RD
WILDISH RD
IVORY CL
Davington Prim Sch
PRIORY PL
SPRINGHEAD RD
FOSTALL RD
LARKSFIELD RD
BROOK RD
UPPER BRENTS
North Quay
South Quay
Brents Ind Est
Shipyard Area
WATERSIDE CL
Faversham Creek
Works
Wharf
ABBEY FIELDS
138
106

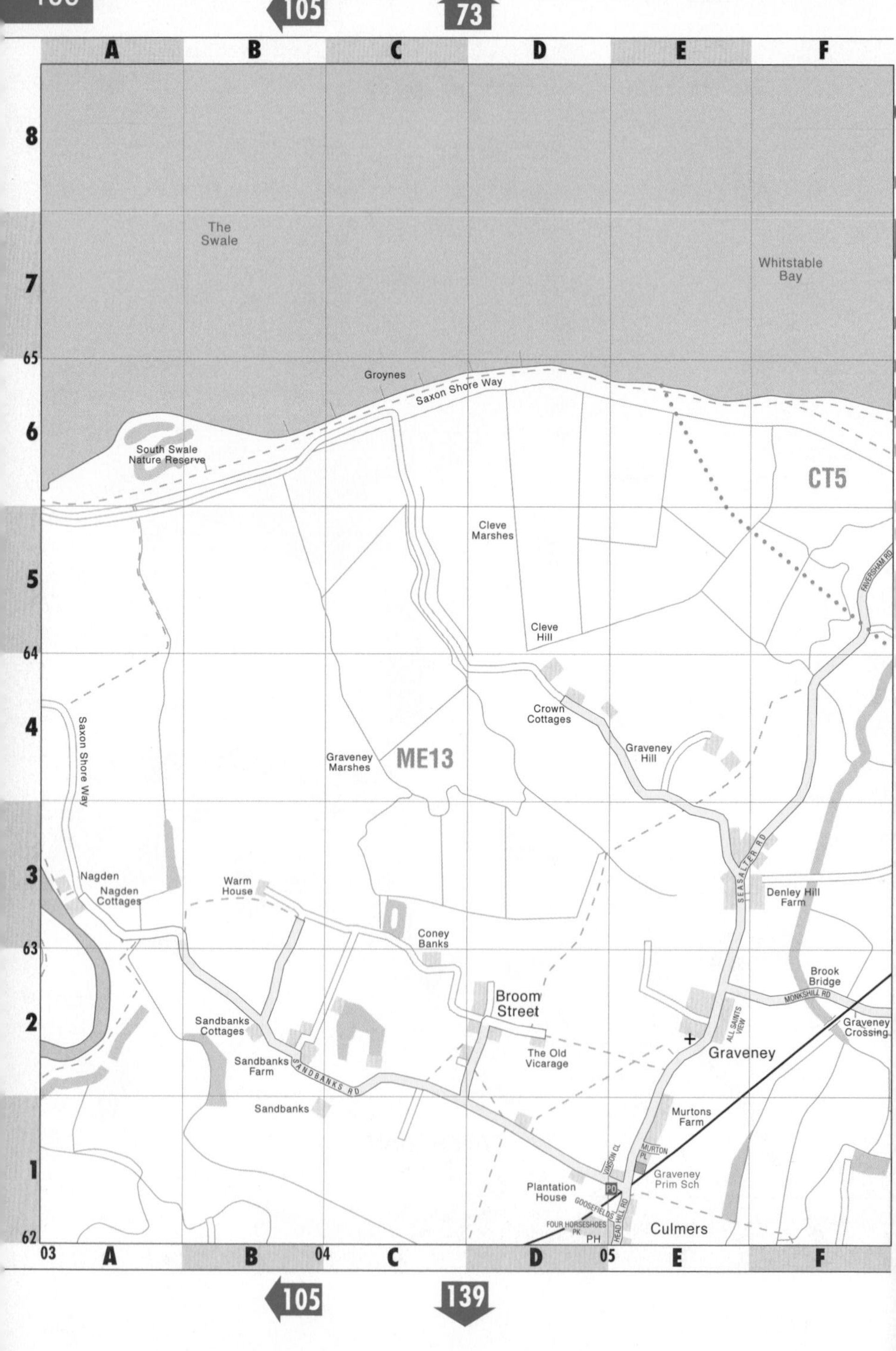

105
73

The Swale

Whitstable Bay

Groynes

Saxon Shore Way

South Swale Nature Reserve

CT5

Cleve Marshes

Cleve Hill

Crown Cottages

Graveney Hill

Graveney Marshes

ME13

Saxon Shore Way

Denley Hill Farm

Nagden

Nagden Cottages

Warm House

Coney Banks

Brook Bridge

MORKSHILL RD

SEASALTER RD

ALL SAINTS VIEW

Broom Street

Sandbanks Cottages

Sandbanks Farm

SANDBANKS RD

The Old Vicarage

Graveney

Graveney Crossing

Sandbanks

Murtons Farm

MURTON PL

Plantation House

GOODSFIELDS

VICARAGE CL

HEAD HILL RD

Graveney Prim Sch

FOUR HORSESHOES PH

Culmers

105
139

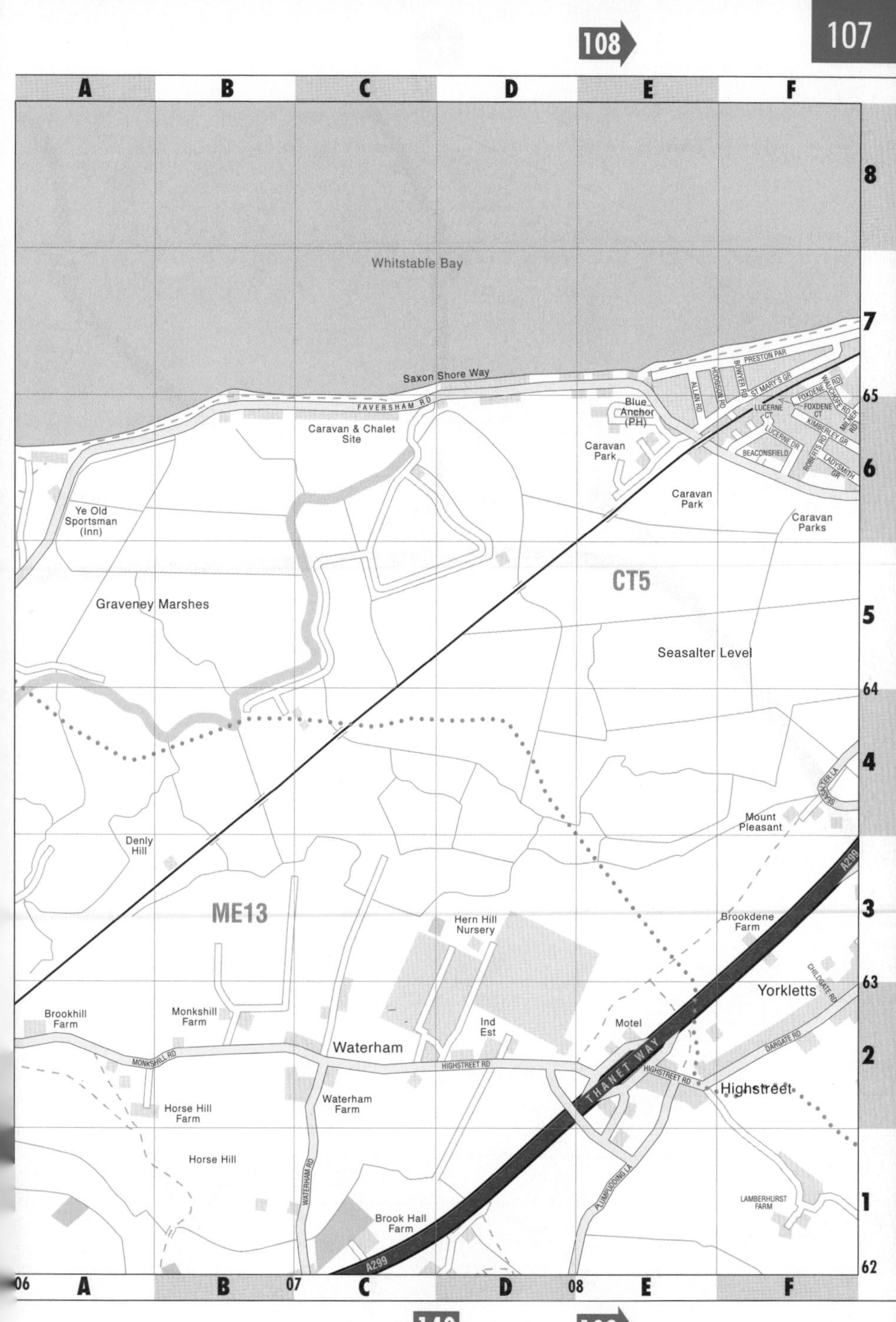

Whitstable Bay

Saxon Shore Way

FAVERSHAM RD

PRESTON PAR

ST MARY'S GR

ALLAN RD

BORSTAL RD

HORSHAM RD

LUCERNE CT

FOXDENE RD

FOXDENE CT

WHEATLEY RD

KIMBERLEY GR

Blue Anchor (PH)

LUCERNE DR

Caravan Park

BEACONSFIELD

ROMNEY RD

LADYSMITH

Caravan Park

Caravan Parks

Ye Old Sportsman (Inn)

CT5

Graveney Marshes

Seasalter Level

64

Denly Hill

Mount Pleasant

CASTERBELA

ME13

Hern Hill Nursery

Brookdene Farm

A299

Yorkletts

CHILDCATE RD

63

Brookhill Farm

Monkshill Farm

Ind Est

Motel

THANET WAY

DARGATE RD

Waterham

HIGHSTREET RD

HIGHSTREET RD

Highstreet

MONKSHILL RD

Horse Hill Farm

Waterham Farm

WATERHAM RD

PLUMPUDDING LA

LAMBERHURST FARM

Horse Hill

Brook Hall Farm

A299

62

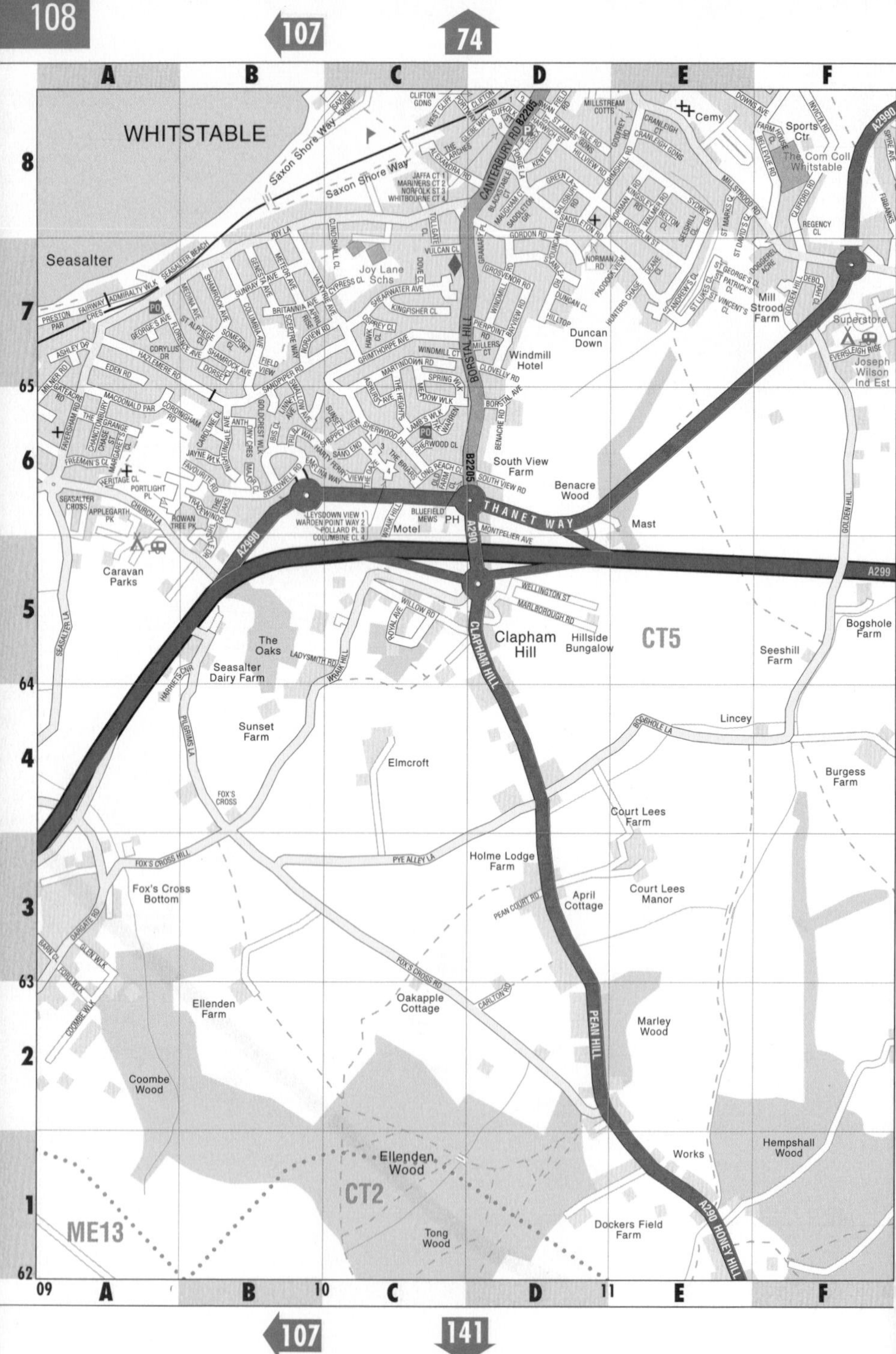

WHITSTABLE

Seasalter

Saxon Shore Way
Saxon Shore Way

CLIFTON GDNS

MILLSTREAM COTTS

Cemy

Sports Ctr

The Com Coll Whitstable

A290

Joy Lane Schs

VULCAN CL

Duncan Down

Windmill Hotel

REGENCY CL

Mill Strood Farm

Superstore

Joseph Wilson Ind Est

Caravan Parks

BLUEFIELD MEWS PH

Motel

THANET WAY

South View Farm

South View Rd

Benacre Wood

Mast

A299

MONTPELIER AVE

A290

WELLINGTON ST

MARLBOROUGH RD

Clapham Hill

Hillside Bungalow

CT5

Seeshill Farm

Bogshole Farm

The Oaks

LADYSMITH HILL

Seasalter Dairy Farm

CLAPHAM HILL

Lincey

Burgess Farm

Sunset Farm

Elmcroft

FOX'S CROSS

BOGSHOLE LA

Court Lees Farm

FOX'S CROSS HILL

PYE ALLEY LA

Holme Lodge Farm

April Cottage

Court Lees Manor

Fox's Cross Bottom

PEAN COURT RD

FOX'S CROSS RD

Oakapple Cottage

CARLTON RD

PEAN HILL

Marley Wood

Ellenden Farm

Coombe Wood

Ellenden Wood

CT2

ME13

Tong Wood

Works

Hempshall Wood

Dockers Field Farm

A299 HONEY HILL

75
110

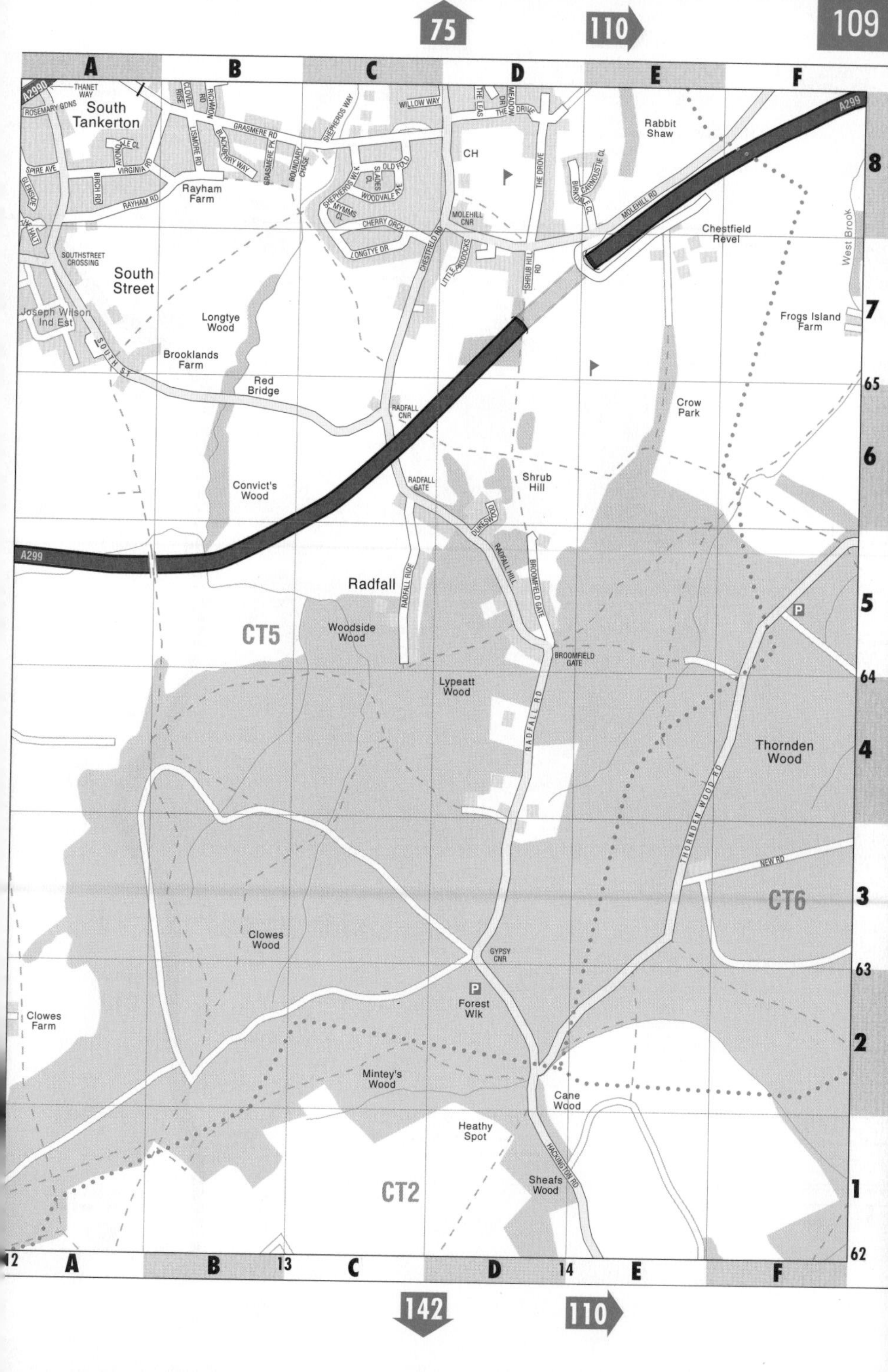
A
B
C
D
E
F
8
7
65
6
5
64
4
3
63
2
1
62
12
13
14
A2990
THANET WAY
South Tankerton
ROSEMARY GDNS
SPIRE AVE
GLENSIDE
BIRCH RD
VIRGINIA RD
AVONDALE CL
RAYHAM RD
Rayham Farm
CLOVER RISE
RICHMOND RD
LISMORE RD
BLACKBERRY WAY
GRASMERE RD
GRASMERE PK
BOUNDARY CHASE
SHEPHERDS WAY
WILLOW WAY
THE LEAS
MEADOW DR
THE DRIVE
THE DROVE
CH
SHEPHERDS WLK
SLADES CL
OLD FOLD
WOODVALE AVE
MYMMS CL
CHERRY ORCH
LONGTYE DR
CHESTFIELD RD
LITTLE PADDOCKS
MOLEHILL CNR
SHRUB HILL RD
CARNOUSTIE CL
BIRKDALE CL
MOLEHILL RD
Rabbit Shaw
A299
Chestfield Revel
West Brook
Frogs Island Farm
THE HALT
SOUTHSTREET CROSSING
South Street
Joseph Wilson Ind Est
SOUTH ST
Longtye Wood
Brooklands Farm
Red Bridge
RADFALL CNR
Crow Park
Convict's Wood
RADFALL GATE
Shrub Hill
DUKESWOOD
A299
Radfall
RADFALL RIDE
RADFALL HILL
BROOMFIELD GATE
CT5
Woodside Wood
BROOMFIELD GATE
P
Lypeatt Wood
RADFALL RD
Thornden Wood
THORNDEN WOOD RD
NEW RD
CT6
Clowes Wood
GYPSY CNR
P
Forest Wlk
Clowes Farm
Mintey's Wood
Cane Wood
Heathy Spot
HACKINGTON RD
Sheafs Wood
CT2

142
110

109
76

A B C D E F

A299

Prospect Farm
OWL'S RD

West End

Knowel Hill

Home Farm

LOWER HERNE RD

Bullockstone Farm

Bullockstone

Plenty Brook

Ruckinge Farm

THORNDEN WOOD RD

BULLOCKSTONE RD

CASTLE ROAD RD

A291

8

Bleanbottom Shaw

Round Wood

Grove Farm

SWALLOW CT

DOVE CL

ANEMONE WAY

ROBIN RD

FALCON

First & Last (PH)

NIGHTINGALE RD

7

65

Herne Common

West Brook

Warren Farm

Banker's Wood

CT6

BRAGGS LA

Nursery

BUSHEYFIELDS RD

6

Knockhimdown Hill

Bleangate

Hoath Wood

CANTERBURY RD

5

Cripps Wood

West Blean Wood

NEW ROAD COTTS

64

NEW RD

Wildwood Wealden Forest Park

Saw Mill

West Blean House

Boarded House Farm

HICKS FORSTAL RD

4

Blaxland Farm

Belce Wood

Farthings Wood

Woodlands Farm

3

63

Greenacres

CT2

Punch Tavern (PH)

CT3

Cole Wood

Calcott

2

Brambles Farm

HERNE BAY RD

Cadehill Wood

Little Mayton

MAYTON LA

Vale Farm

BARN LA

Nursery

Nursery

CT2

1

62

Aspley Lodge

A291

15 A B 16 C D 17 E F

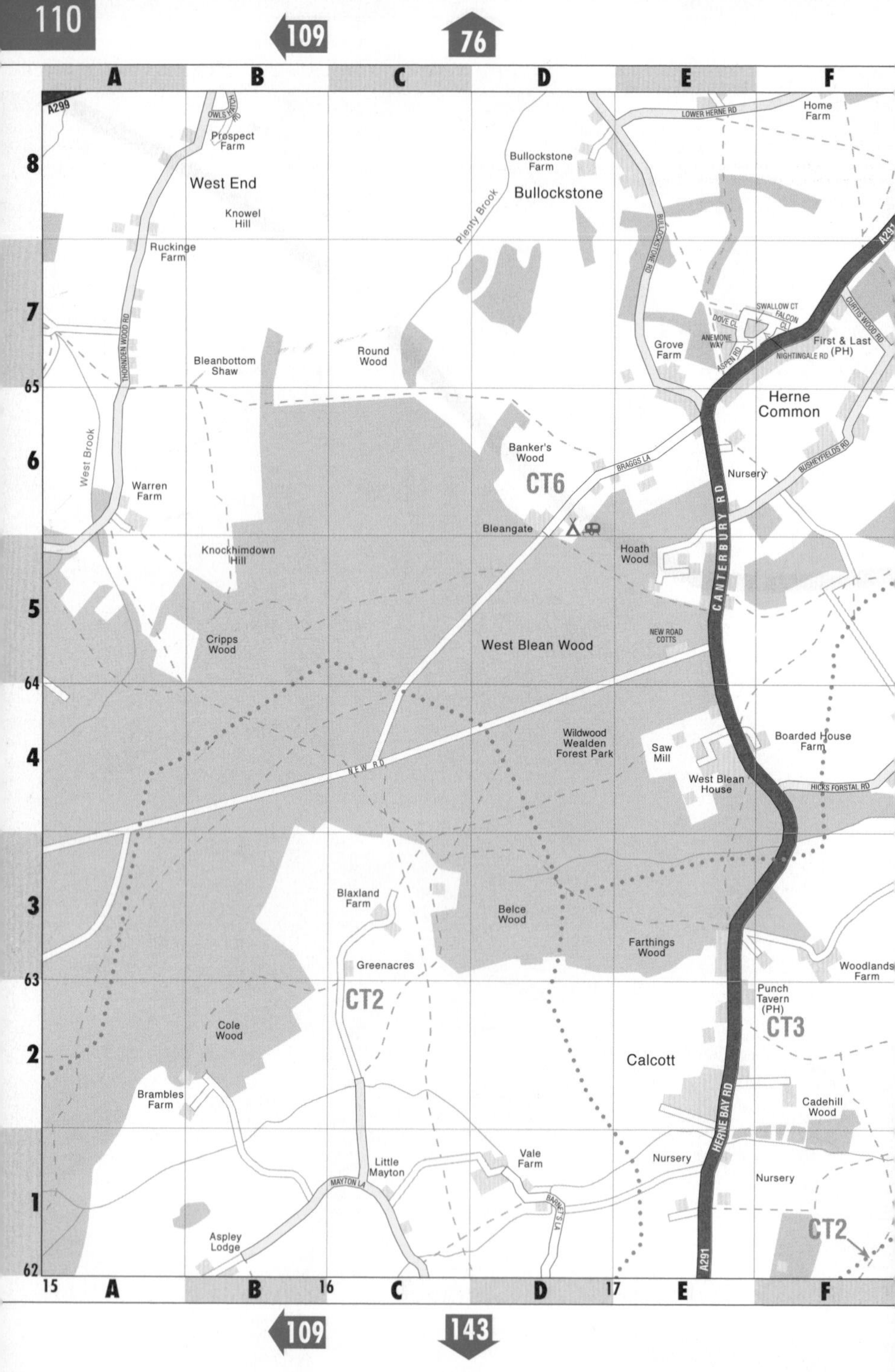

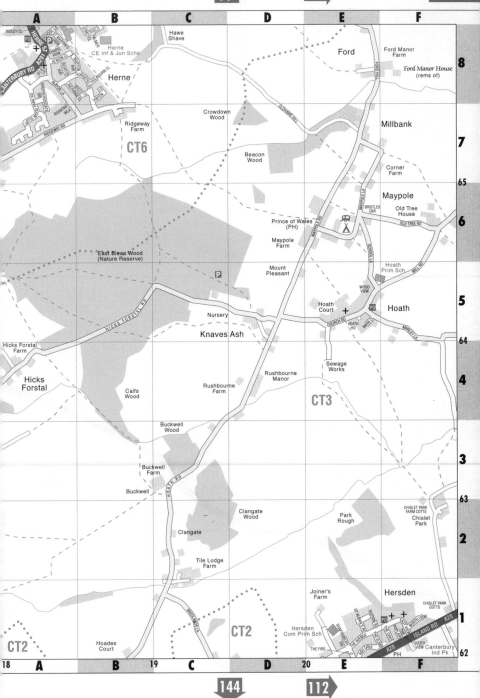

8

RIDLEY CL

Herne
CE Inf & Jun Schs

Hawe
Shave

Ford

Ford Manor
Farm

Ford Manor House
(rems of)

Herne

Crowdown
Wood

Millbank

Ridgeway
Farm

CT6

Corner
Farm

7

65

Beacon
Wood

Maypole

6

Prince of Wales
(PH)

Old Tree
House

Maypole
Farm

BRISTLES
CNR

Old Tree Rd

East Blean Wood
(Nature Reserve)

Mount
Pleasant

Hoath
Prim Sch

P

WOOD
VIEW

5

Nursery

Hoath
Court

Knaves Ash

CHURCH RD

HEATH
HO

Hoath

64

Hicks Forstal
Farm

Rushbourne
Manor

Sewage
Works

MARLEY LA

Hicks
Forstal

Calfs
Wood

Rushbourne
Farm

CT3

4

Buckwell
Wood

3

63

Buckwell
Farm

Clangate
Wood

Park
Rough

CHISLET PARK
FARM COTTS

Chislet
Park

Buckwell

Clangate

2

Tile Lodge
Farm

Joiner's
Farm

Hersden

CHISLET PARK
COTTS

CT2

CT2

Hersden
Com Prim Sch

ISLAND RD

A28

1

62

Hoades
Court

THE FIRS

PH

SOUTH
VIEW

Canterbury
Ind Pk

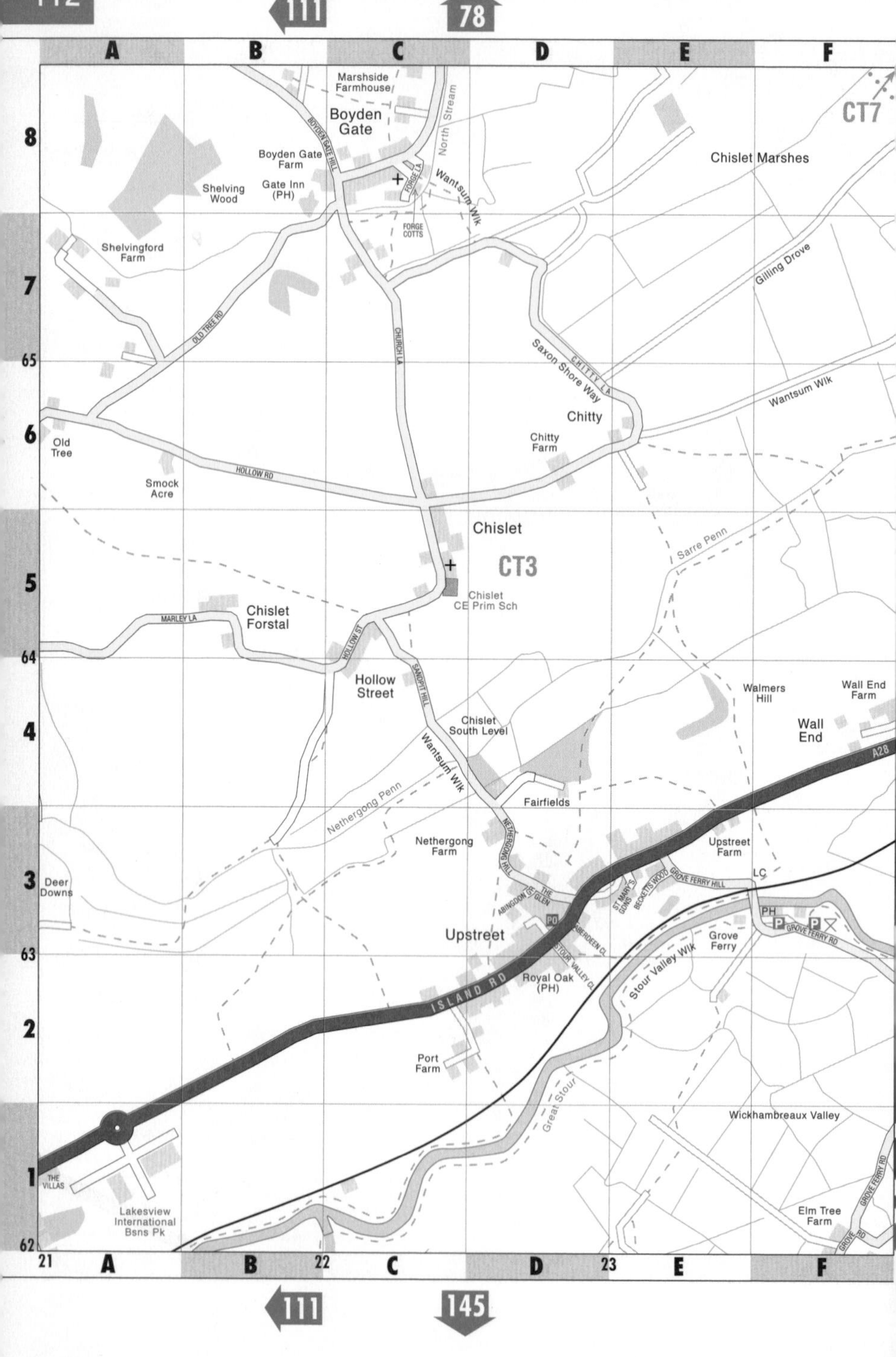

CT7

8 Boyden Gate
Marshside Farmhouse
North Stream
Chislet Marshes

Boyden Gate Farm
Gate Inn (PH)
Shelving Wood
Wantsum Wlk
FORGE COTTS

7 Shelvingford Farm
Gilling Drove
OLD TREE RD
CHURCH LA

65 Saxon Shore Way
CHITTY LA
Wantsum Wlk

6 Old Tree
HOLLOW RD
Chitty
Chitty Farm

Smock Acre

Chislet
CT3
Sarre Penn

5 MARLEY LA
Chislet CE Prim Sch
Chislet Forstal

64 Hollow Street
HOLLOW ST
Walmers Hill
Wall End Farm

4 Chislet South Level
Wall End
A28

Fairfields
Wantsum Wlk
NETHERGONG PENN

3 Deer Downs
Nethergong Farm
Upstreet Farm
LC
ST MARY'S GRO
BEKESBOURNE
GROVE FERRY HILL
PH
P P

THE GLEN
ABINGDON DR
PO
BEKESBOURNE CL
Grove Ferry
GROVE FERRY RD

63 Upstreet
ISLAND RD
Royal Oak (PH)
Stour Valley Wlk

2 Port Farm
Great Stour
Wickhambreaux Valley

1 THE VILLAS
Lakesview International Bsns Pk
Elm Tree Farm
GROVE FERRY RD

62

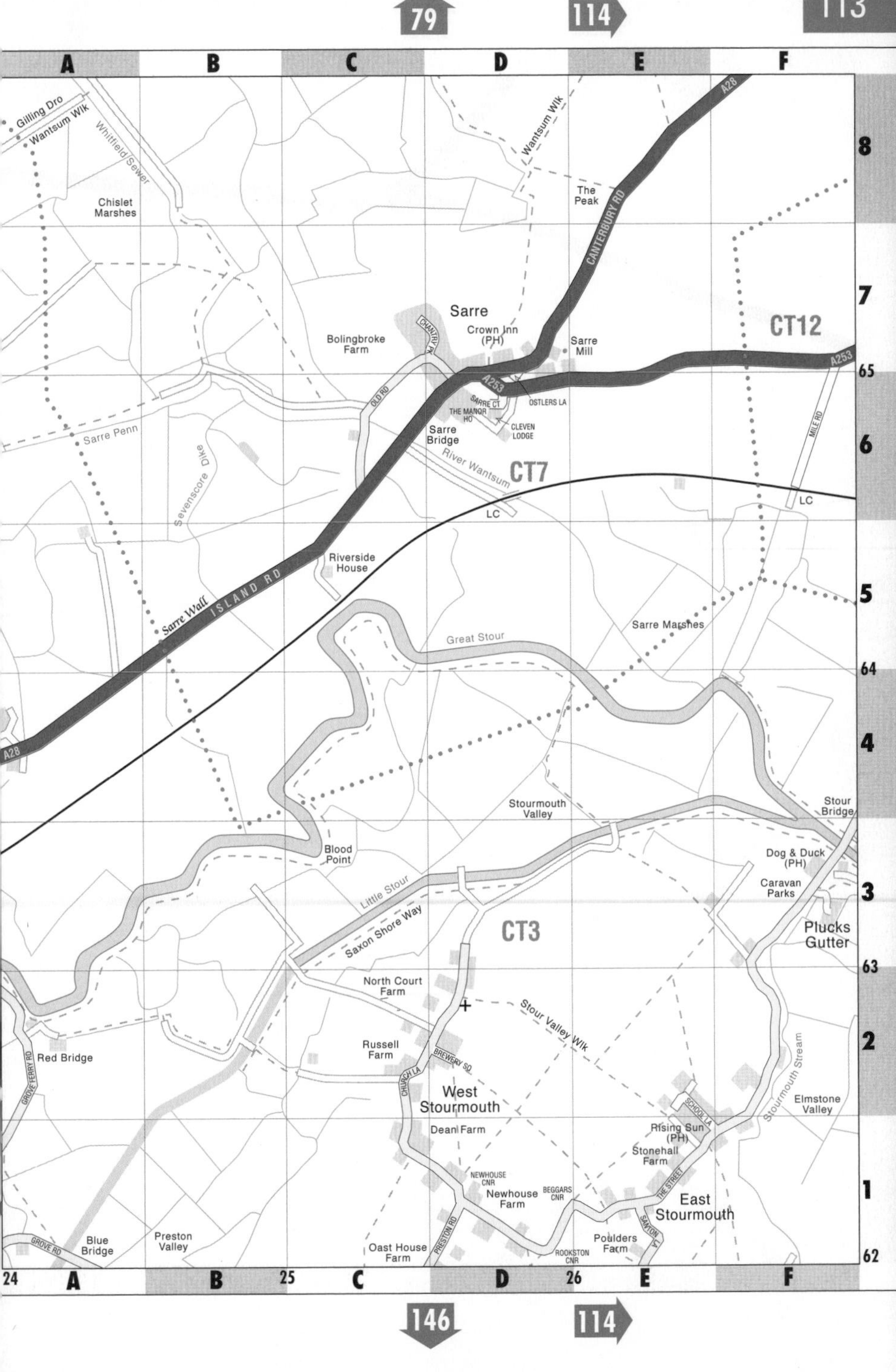
79
114
Gilling Dro
Wantsum Wlk
Whitfield Sewer
Chislet Marshes
Wantsum Wlk
A28
The Peak
CANTERBURY RD
Sarre
CHANTRY PK
Bolingbroke Farm
Crown Inn (PH)
Sarre Mill
CT12
A253
OLD RD
SARRE CT
THE MANOR HO
OSTLERS LA
CLEVEN LODGE
Sarre Bridge
MILE RD
Sarre Penn
Sevenscore Dike
River Wantsum
CT7
LC
Riverside House
Sarre Wall
ISLAND RD
Sarre Marshes
Great Stour
Stourmouth Valley
Stour Bridge
Blood Point
Dog & Duck (PH)
Caravan Parks
Little Stour
Saxon Shore Way
CT3
Plucks Gutter
North Court Farm
Stour Valley Wlk
Russell Farm
GROVE FERRY RD
Red Bridge
BREWERY SQ
CHURCH LA
West Stourmouth
Stourmouth Stream
Elmstone Valley
SCHOOL LA
Dean Farm
Rising Sun (PH)
Stonehall Farm
NEWHOUSE CNR
Newhouse Farm
BEGGARS CNR
THE STREET
East Stourmouth
SANTON LA
Poulders Farm
GROVE RD
Blue Bridge
Preston Valley
Oast House Farm
PRESTON RD
ROOKSTON CNR
A B C D E F
8 7 65 6 5 64 4 3 63 2 1 62
24 25 26
146
114

113
80

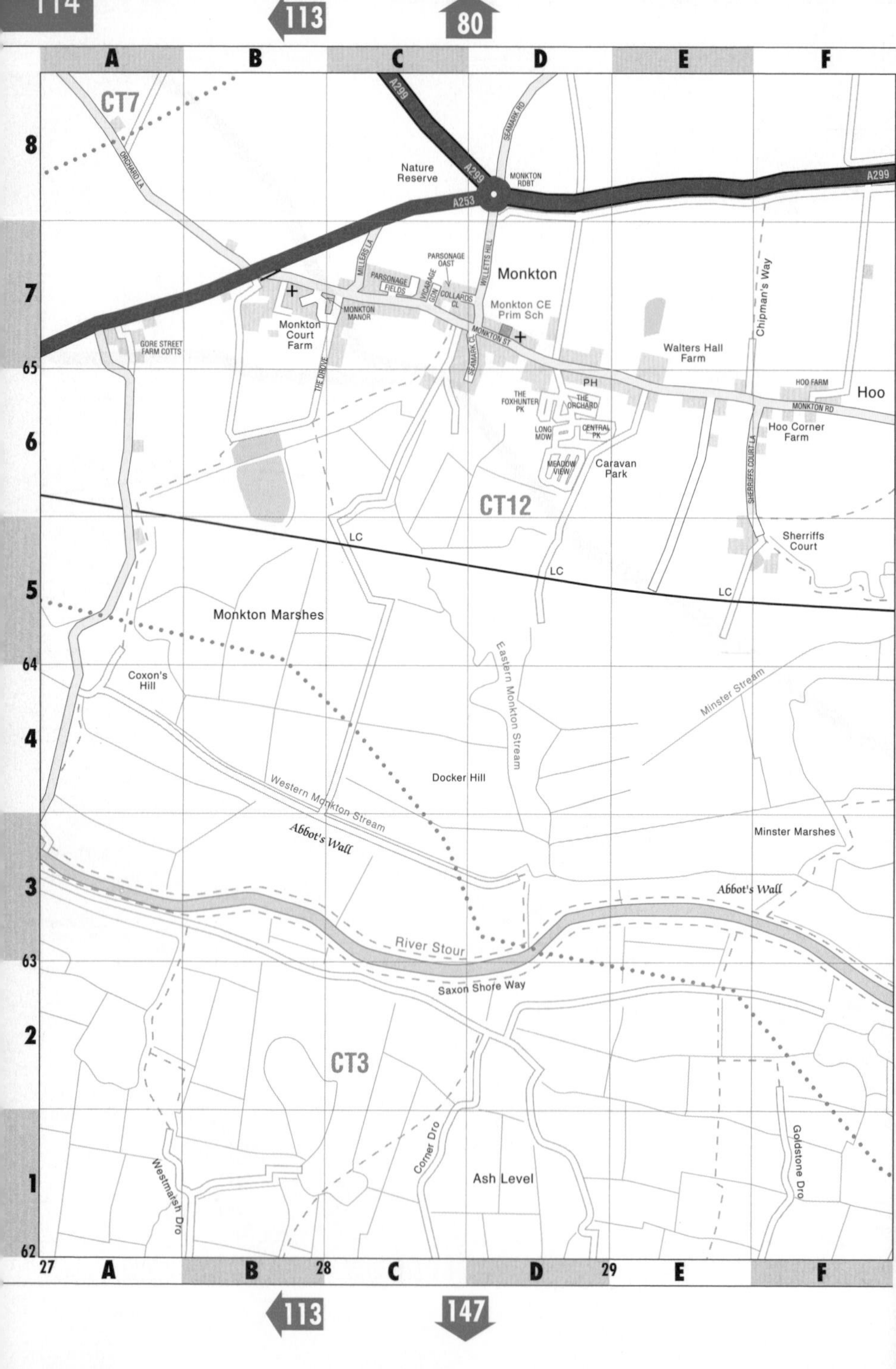
CT7
ORCHARD LA
A299
SEAMARK RD
Nature Reserve
MONKTON RDBT
A253
MILLERS LA
PARSONAGE OAST
WILLETTS HILL
Monkton
PARSONAGE FIELDS
VICARAGE GDN
COLLARDS CL
MONKTON MANOR
Monkton Court Farm
Monkton CE Prim Sch
GORE STREET FARM COTTS
MONKTON ST
SEAMARK CL
THE DROVE
Chipman's Way
Walters Hall Farm
PH
THE FOXHUNTER PK
THE ORCHARD
LONG MDW
CENTRAL PK
MEADOW VIEW
Caravan Park
HOO FARM
Hoo
MONKTON RD
Hoo Corner Farm
SHERRIFFS COURT LA
CT12
LC
Sherriffs Court
Monkton Marshes
Coxon's Hill
Eastern Monkton Stream
Minster Stream
Docker Hill
Western Monkton Stream
Abbot's Wall
Minster Marshes
River Stour
Saxon Shore Way
CT3
Corner Dro
Ash Level
Goldstone Dro
Westmarsh Dro
A B C D E F
8 7 65 6 5 64 4 3 63 2 1 62
27 28 29

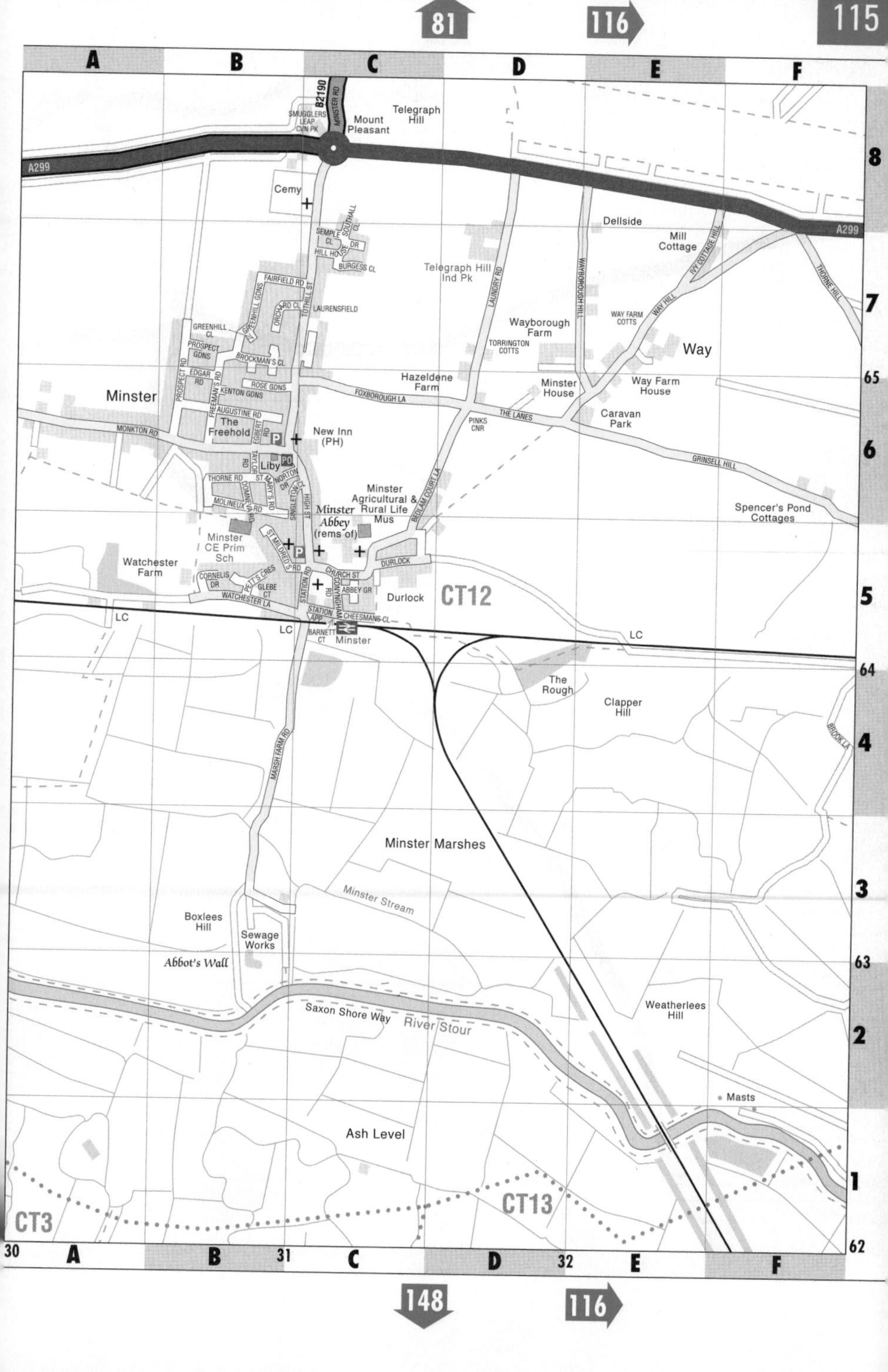
81
116
A
B
C
D
E
F
8
7
65
6
5
64
4
3
63
2
1
62
30
31
32
A299
B2190
MINSTER RD
SMUGGLERS LEAP CVN PK
Mount Pleasant
Telegraph Hill
Cemy
SEMPLE CL
SOUTHALL CL
DR
HILL HOUSE
BURGESS CL
FAIRFIELD RD
TOTHILL ST
GREENHILL GDNS
ORCHARD CL
LAURENSFIELD
GREENHILL CL
GREENHILL RD
PROSPECT GDNS
BROCKMAN'S CL
PROSPECT RD
EDGAR RD
FREEMAN'S RD
ROSE GDNS
KENTON GDNS
AUGUSTINE RD
Minster
The Freehold
EGBERT RD
MONKTON RD
New Inn (PH)
Liby
PO
TAYLOR RD
THORNE RD
ST MARY'S RD
NORTON DR
SINGLETON CL
HIGH ST
DOMNEVA RD
MOLINEUX RD
Minster Abbey (rems of)
Minster Agricultural & Rural Life Mus
Minster CE Prim Sch
ST MILDRED'S RD
Watchester Farm
CORNELIS DR
PETT'S CRES
GLEBE CT
STATION RD
CHURCH ST
CONYNGHAM RD
ABBEY GR
DURLOCK
Durlock
CT12
WATCHESTER LA
STATION APP
CHEESMANS CL
LC
BARNETT CT
Minster
Telegraph Hill Ind Pk
LAUNDRY RD
Wayborough Farm
TORRINGTON COTTS
Hazeldene Farm
FOXBOROUGH LA
PINKS CNR
BEDLAM COURT LA
THE LANES
Minster House
WAYBOROUGH HILL
Dellside
Mill Cottage
IVY COTTAGE HILL
WAY HILL
WAY FARM COTTS
Way
Way Farm House
Caravan Park
GRINSELL HILL
THORNE HILL
Spencer's Pond Cottages
The Rough
Clapper Hill
BROOK LA
MARSH FARM RD
Minster Marshes
Minster Stream
Boxlees Hill
Sewage Works
Abbot's Wall
Saxon Shore Way
River Stour
Weatherlees Hill
Masts
Ash Level
CT3
CT13
148
116

115
82

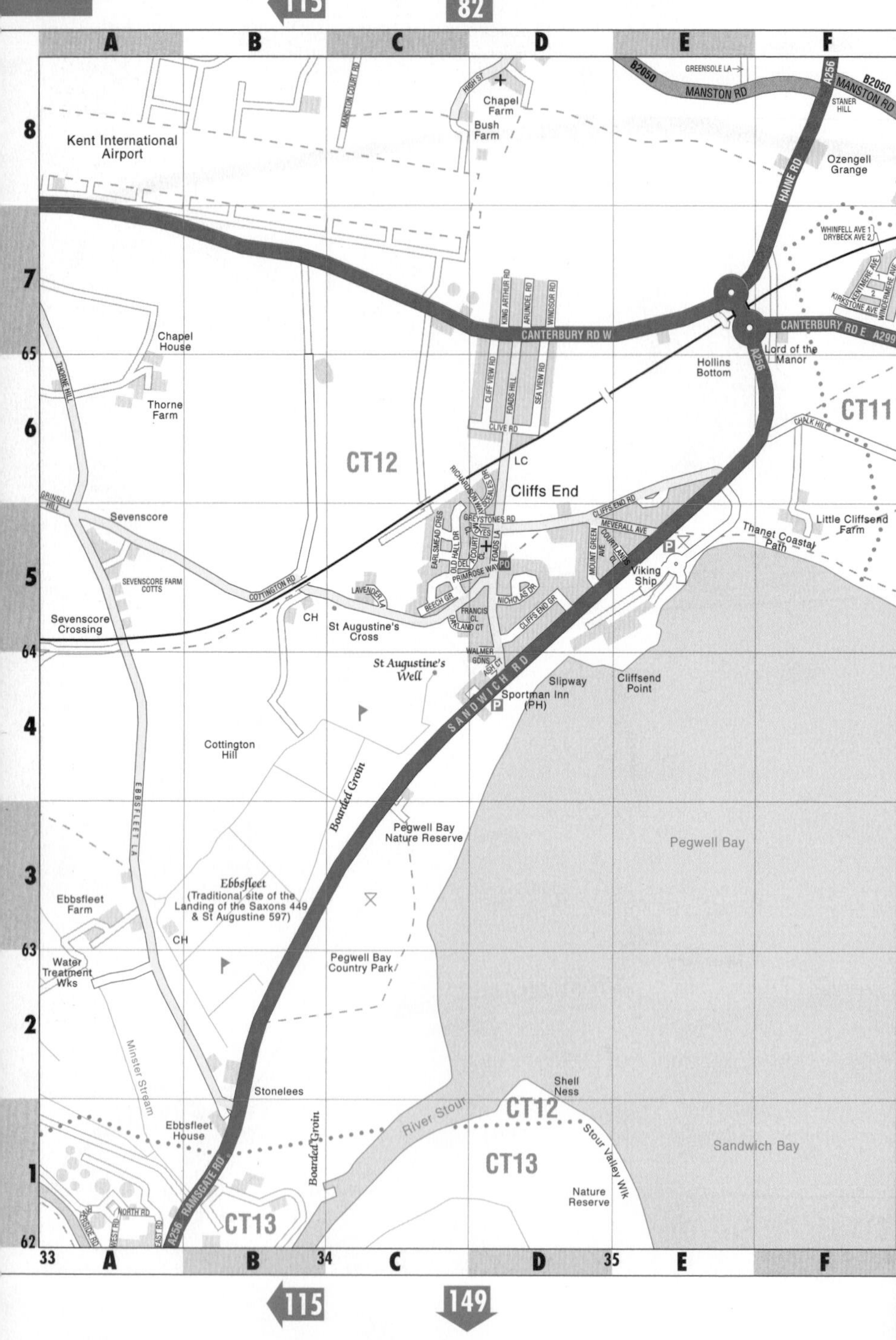
A
B
C
D
E
F
8
7
65
6
5
64
4
3
63
2
1
62
33
34
35
Kent International Airport
Chapel Farm
Bush Farm
HIGH ST
MANSTON COURT RD
B2050
GREENSOLE LA
MANSTON RD
A256
STANER HILL
Ozengell Grange
HAINE RD
WHINFELL AVE 1
DRYBECK AVE 2
KENTMERE AVE
WINDERMERE AVE
KIRKSTONE AVE
CANTERBURY RD E
A299
CANTERBURY RD W
KING ARTHUR RD
ARUNDEL RD
WINDSOR RD
CLIFF VIEW RD
FOADS HILL
SEA VIEW RD
CLIVE RD
Chapel House
THORNE HILL
Thorne Farm
Lord of the Manor
Hollins Bottom
CT11
CHALK HILL
CT12
LC
Cliffs End
RICHARDSON WAY
BEALES DR
GREYSTONES RD
CLIFFS END RD
MEVERALL AVE
EARLSMEAD CRES
OLD HALL DR
DEL CL
ACOURT CL
HAYES
FOADS LA
PD
PRIMROSE WAY
MOUNT GREEN AVE
COURTLANDS CL
Thanet Coastal Path
Little Cliffsend Farm
Viking Ship
GRINSELL HILL
Sevenscore
SEVENSCORE FARM COTTS
COTTINGTON RD
LAVENDER LA
BEECH GR
NICHOLAS DR
FRANCIS CL
OAKLAND CT
CLIFFS END GR
Sevenscore Crossing
CH
St Augustine's Cross
WALMER GDNS
ASH CT
St Augustine's Well
SANDWICH RD
Slipway
Sportman Inn (PH)
Cliffsend Point
Cottington Hill
EBBSFLEET LA
Boarded Groin
Pegwell Bay Nature Reserve
Pegwell Bay
Ebbsfleet
(Traditional site of the Landing of the Saxons 449 & St Augustine 597)
Ebbsfleet Farm
CH
Water Treatment Wks
Pegwell Bay Country Park
Minster Stream
Stonelees
Shell Ness
River Stour
CT12
Ebbsfleet House
Boarded Groin
Stour Valley Wlk
Sandwich Bay
CT13
Nature Reserve
RAMSGATE RD
A256
NORTH RD
WEST RD
EAST RD
CT13

115
149

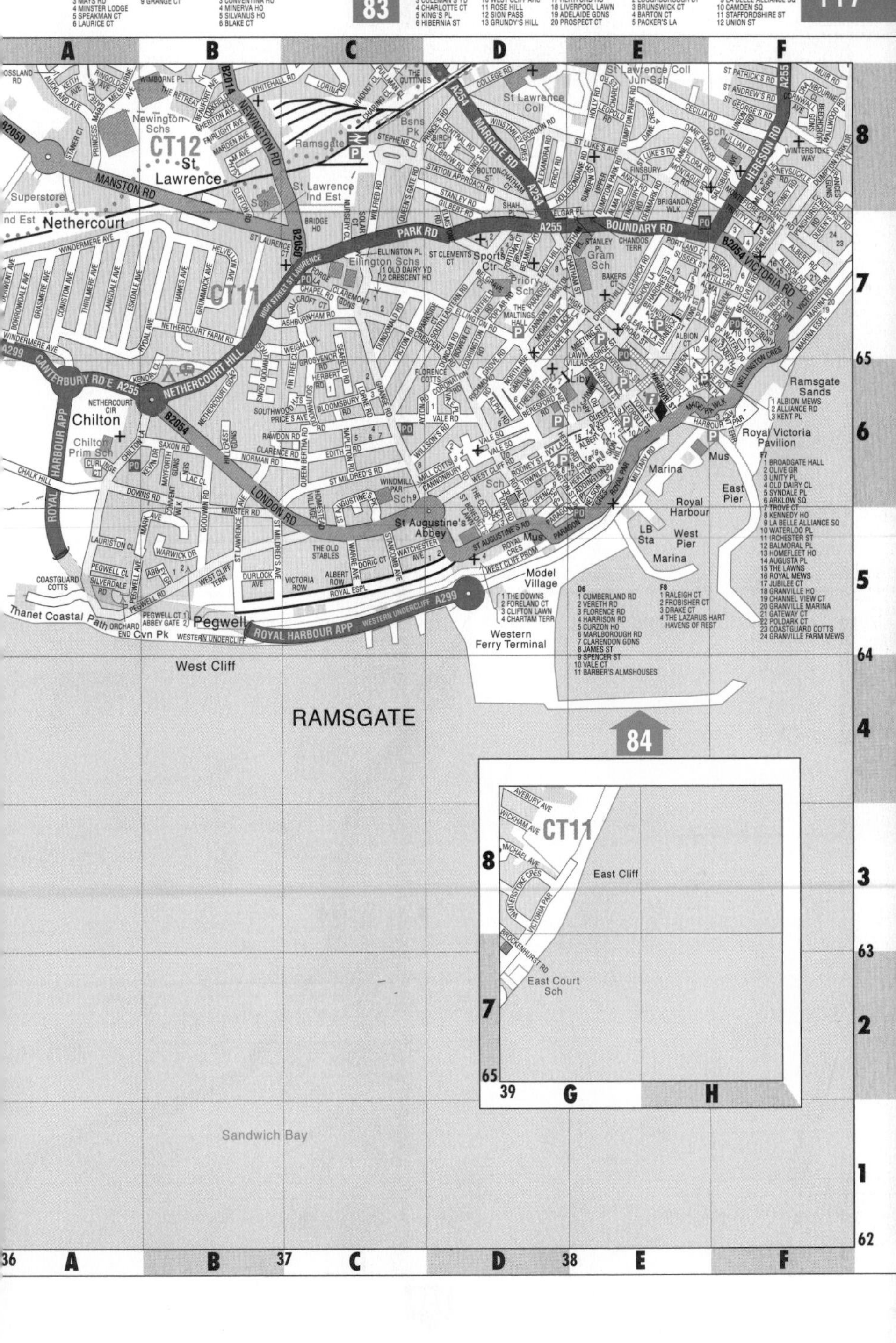
C6
1 KING EDWARD RD
2 TARYES HO
3 MAYS RD
4 MINSTER LODGE
5 SPEAKMAN CT
6 LAURICE CT
7 NAPLETON CT
8 THE SAVOY
9 GRANGE CT
D7
1 CHURCHILL CT
2 BELMONT CT
3 CONVENTINA HO
4 MINERVA HO
5 SILVANUS HO
6 BLAKE CT
7 COLLINGWOOD CT
8 EAGLE COTTS
83
E6
1 GUILDFORD LAWN
2 CAVENDISH PL
3 COLEMAN'S YD
4 CHARLOTTE CT
5 KING'S PL
6 HIBERNIA ST
7 ALBION HILL
8 ALBERT CT
9 PRINCE'S ST
10 WEST CLIFF ARC
11 ROSE HILL
12 SION PASS
13 GRUNDY'S HILL
14 ST MICHAEL'S ALLEY
15 CORNHILL
16 HARBOUR TWRS
17 HERTFORD HO
18 LIVERPOOL LAWN
19 ADELAIDE GDNS
20 PROSPECT CT
21 PROSPECT TERR
E7
1 PEMBROKE CT
2 LOUGHBOROUGH CT
3 BRUNSWICK CT
4 BARTON CT
5 PACKER'S LA
6 DOVE CT
7 DALTON CT
8 NEWCASTLE HILL
9 LA BELLE ALLIANCE SQ
10 CAMDEN SQ
11 STAFFORDSHIRE ST
12 UNION ST
A
B
C
D
E
F
8
7
65
6
5
64
4
3
63
2
1
62
36
37
38
CT12
St Lawrence
Newington Schs
Ramsgate
St Lawrence Ind Est
Superstore
Nethercourt
CT11
St Lawrence Coll
St Lawrence Coll Jun Sch
Bsns Pk
Ellington Schs
1 OLD DAIRY YD
2 CRESCENT HO
Sports Ctr
Priory Sch
Gram Sch
Liby
Chilton
Chilton Prim Sch
St Augustine's Abbey
THE OLD STABLES
Pegwell
Thanet Coastal Path
ORCHARD END Cvn Pk
PEGWELL CT 1
ABBEY GATE 2
West Cliff
Model Village
1 THE DOWNS
2 FORELAND CT
3 CLIFTON LAWN
4 CHARTAM TERR
Western Ferry Terminal
Marina
Royal Harbour
LB Sta
West Pier
East Pier
Mus
Ramsgate Sands
1 ALBION MEWS
2 ALLIANCE RD
3 KENT PL
Royal Victoria Pavilion
F7
1 BROADGATE HALL
2 OLIVE GR
3 UNITY PL
4 OLD DAIRY CL
5 SYNDALE PL
6 ARKLOW SQ
7 TROVE CT
8 KENNEDY HO
9 LA BELLE ALLIANCE SQ
10 WATERLOO PL
11 IRCHESTER ST
12 BALMORAL PL
13 HOMEFLEET HO
14 AUGUSTA PL
15 THE LAWNS
16 ROYAL MEWS
17 JUBILEE CT
18 GRANVILLE HO
19 CHANNEL VIEW CT
20 GRANVILLE MARINA
21 GATEWAY CT
22 POLDARK CT
23 COASTGUARD COTTS
24 GRANVILLE FARM MEWS
D6
1 CUMBERLAND RD
2 VERETH RD
3 FLORENCE RD
4 HARRISON RD
5 CURZON HO
6 MARLBOROUGH RD
7 CLARENDON GDNS
8 JAMES ST
9 SPENCER ST
10 VALE CT
11 BARBER'S ALMSHOUSES
F8
1 RALEIGH CT
2 FROBISHER CT
3 DRAKE CT
4 THE LAZARUS HART HAVENS OF REST
RAMSGATE
84
CT11
East Cliff
East Court Sch
8
7
65
39
G
H
Sandwich Bay

85

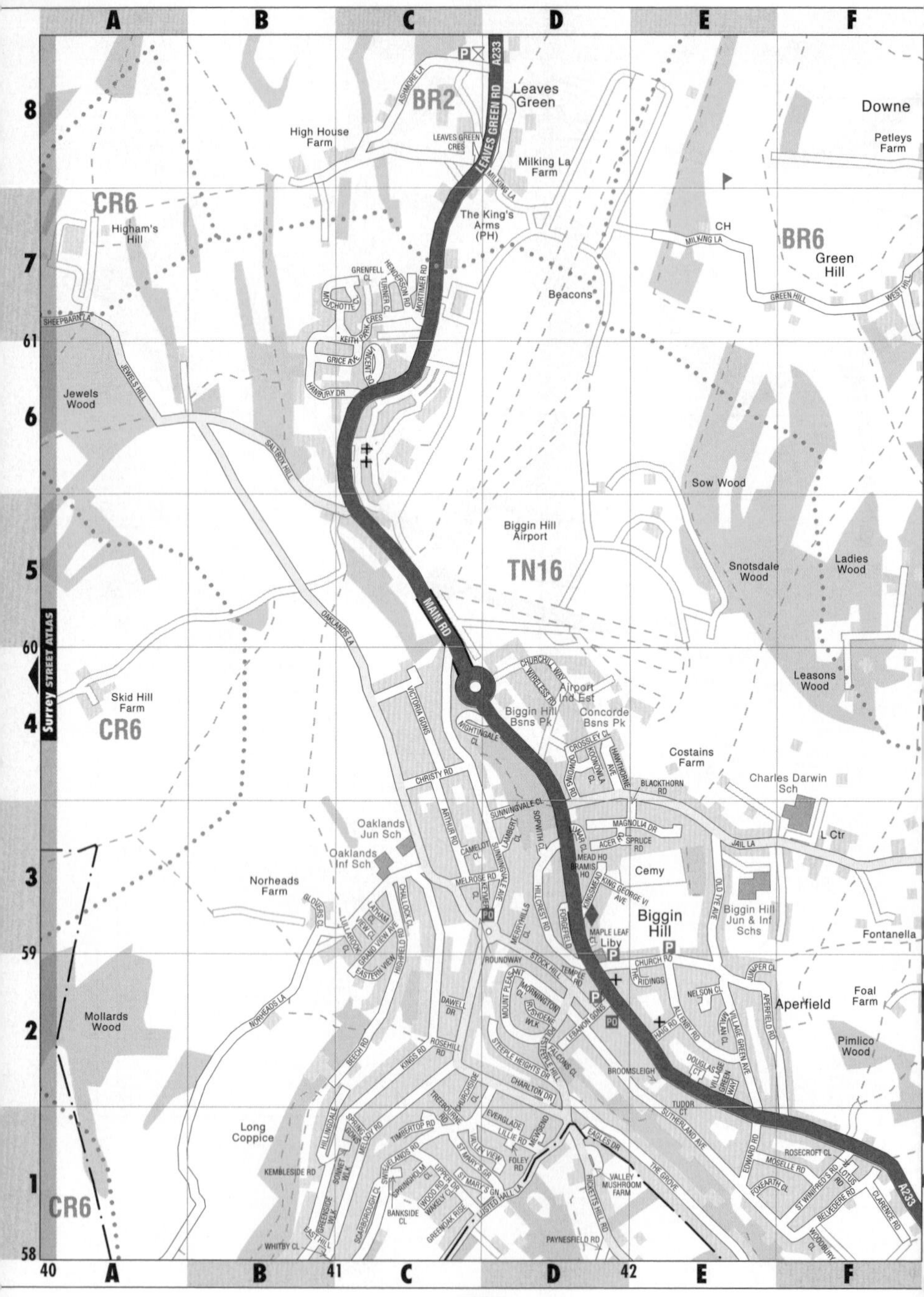
A
B
C
D
E
F
8
7
61
6
5
60
4
3
59
2
1
58
40
41
42
CR6
BR2
BR6
TN16
Leaves Green
Downe
Petleys Farm
High House Farm
Milking La Farm
The King's Arms (PH)
Higham's Hill
Green Hill
Beacons
Jewels Wood
Sow Wood
Biggin Hill Airport
Snotsdale Wood
Ladies Wood
Skid Hill Farm
Leasons Wood
Airport Ind Est
Biggin Hill Bsns Pk
Concorde Bsns Pk
Costains Farm
Charles Darwin Sch
Oaklands Jun Sch
Oaklands Inf Sch
L Ctr
Norheads Farm
Cemy
Biggin Hill
Biggin Hill Jun & Inf Schs
Fontanella
Liby
Aperfield
Foal Farm
Mollards Wood
Pimlico Wood
Long Coppice
VALLEY MUSHROOM FARM
LEAVES GREEN RD
MAIN RD
A233
Surrey STREET ATLAS

150

86
120

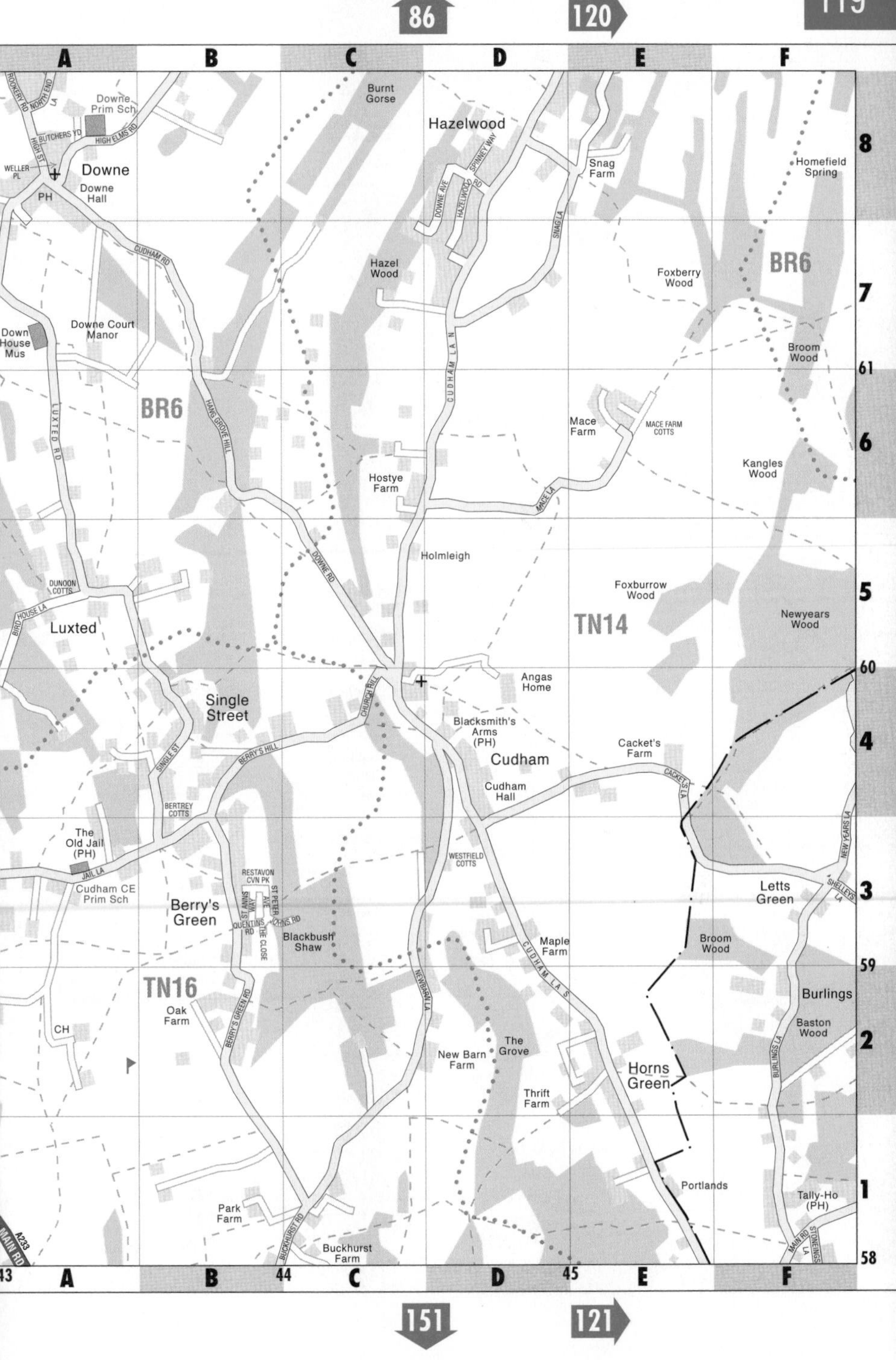
A
B
C
D
E
F
Downe Prim Sch
Downe
Downe Hall
PH
HIGH ELMS RD
BUTCHERS YD
HIGH ST
ROCKERY RD
NORTH END LA
WELLER PL
Burnt Gorse
Hazelwood
SPINNEY WAY
DOWNE AVE
HAZELWOOD RD
Snag Farm
SNAG LA
Homefield Spring
Hazel Wood
Foxberry Wood
BR6
CUDHAM RD
Down House Mus
Downe Court Manor
CUDHAM LA N
Broom Wood
BR6
LUXTED RD
HANG GROVE HILL
Mace Farm
MACE FARM COTTS
Kangles Wood
Hostye Farm
MACE LA
Holmleigh
DOWNE RD
DUNOON COTTS
Foxburrow Wood
BIRD HOUSE LA
Luxted
TN14
Newyears Wood
Angas Home
CHURCH HILL
Single Street
Blacksmith's Arms (PH)
Cacket's Farm
BERRY'S HILL
Cudham
SINGLE ST
Cudham Hall
CACKET'S LA
BERTREY COTTS
The Old Jail (PH)
WESTFIELD COTTS
NEW YEARS LA
JAIL LA
RESTAVON CVN PK
Letts Green
SHELLEYS LA
Cudham CE Prim Sch
Berry's Green
ST ANNS WAY
ST PETER AVE
JOHNS RD
QUENTINS RD
THE CLOSE
Blackbush Shaw
Maple Farm
Broom Wood
TN16
CUDHAM LA S
Burlings
Oak Farm
BERRY'S GREEN RD
NEWBARN LA
Baston Wood
CH
The Grove
New Barn Farm
Horns Green
BURLINGS LA
Thrift Farm
Portlands
Tally-Ho (PH)
Park Farm
A233 MAIN RD
BUCKHURST RD
Buckhurst Farm
MAIN RD
STONEINGS LA
8
7
61
6
5
60
4
3
59
2
1
58
43
44
45

151
121

8

Charm Wood
LAMBARDES CL
Pratts Bottom Prim Sch
HOOKWOOD COTTS
Hook Wood
Pratt's Grove
Bighday Wood

7

Norsted Manor
Fairtrough Farm
BR6
Lower Brooms Wood

The Old Rectory
YEW TREE COTTS
CLAIGS LA
Village House
Halstead Com Prim Sch
PH

61

High Wood
Nurseries

6

The Washneys
Perry Wood
Rushmore Hill Farm
Warren Court Farm
Park Farm
Halstead

5

Hayman's Wood
Piece Wood
Curry Farm

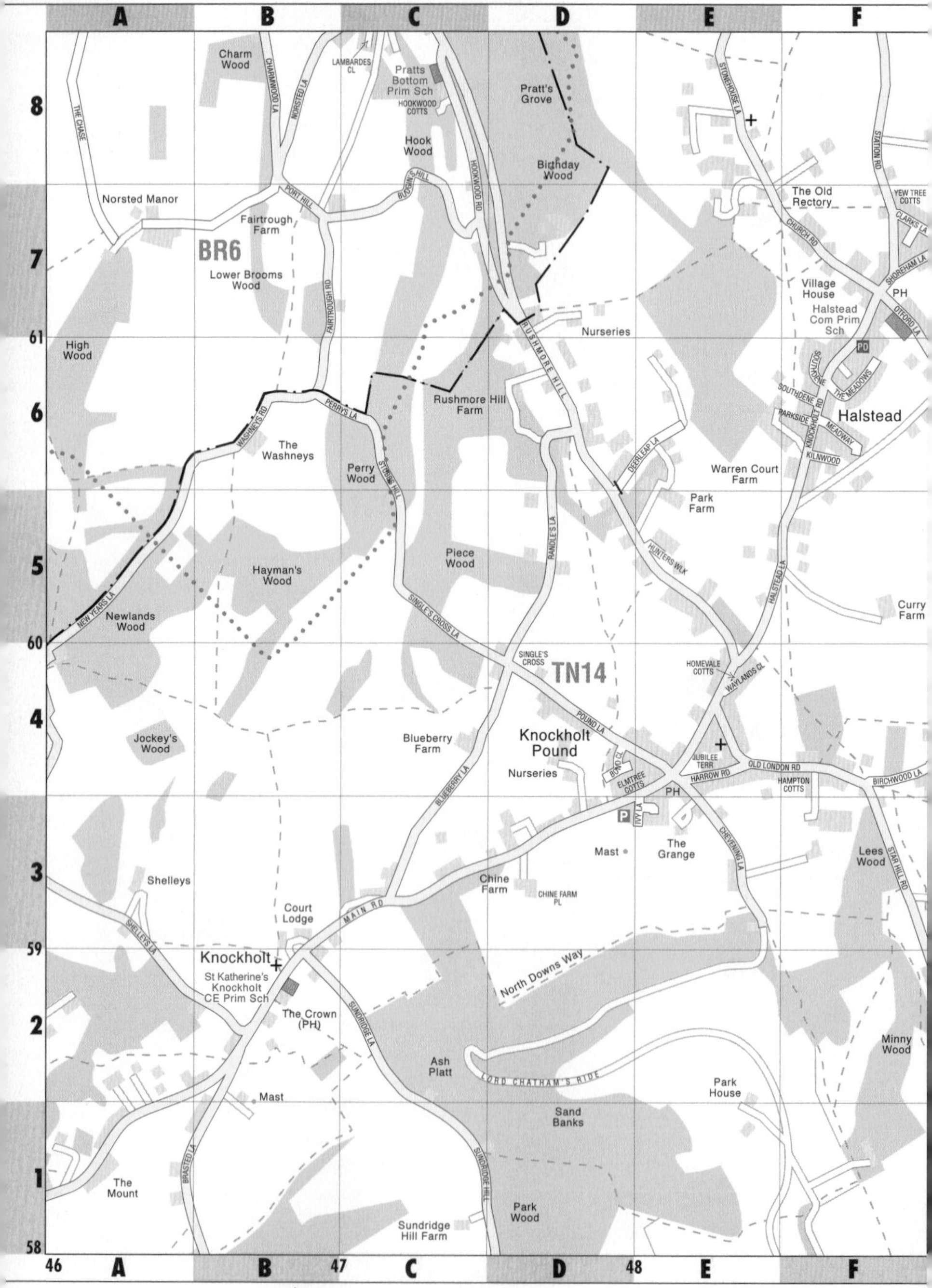

60

Newlands Wood
SINGLE'S CROSS LA
SINGLE'S CROSS
TN14
HOMEVALE COTTS

4

Jockey's Wood
Blueberry Farm
Knockholt Pound
Nurseries
JUBILEE TERR
HAMPTON COTTS
OLD LONDON RD
BIRCHWOOD LA

3

Shelleys
Chine Farm
CHINE FARM PL
Mast
The Grange
Lees Wood

Court Lodge
MAIN RD

59

Knockholt
St Katherine's Knockholt CE Prim Sch

2

The Crown (PH)
Ash Platt
Minny Wood
Park House

Mast
Sand Banks

1

The Mount
Park Wood

58

Sundridge Hill Farm

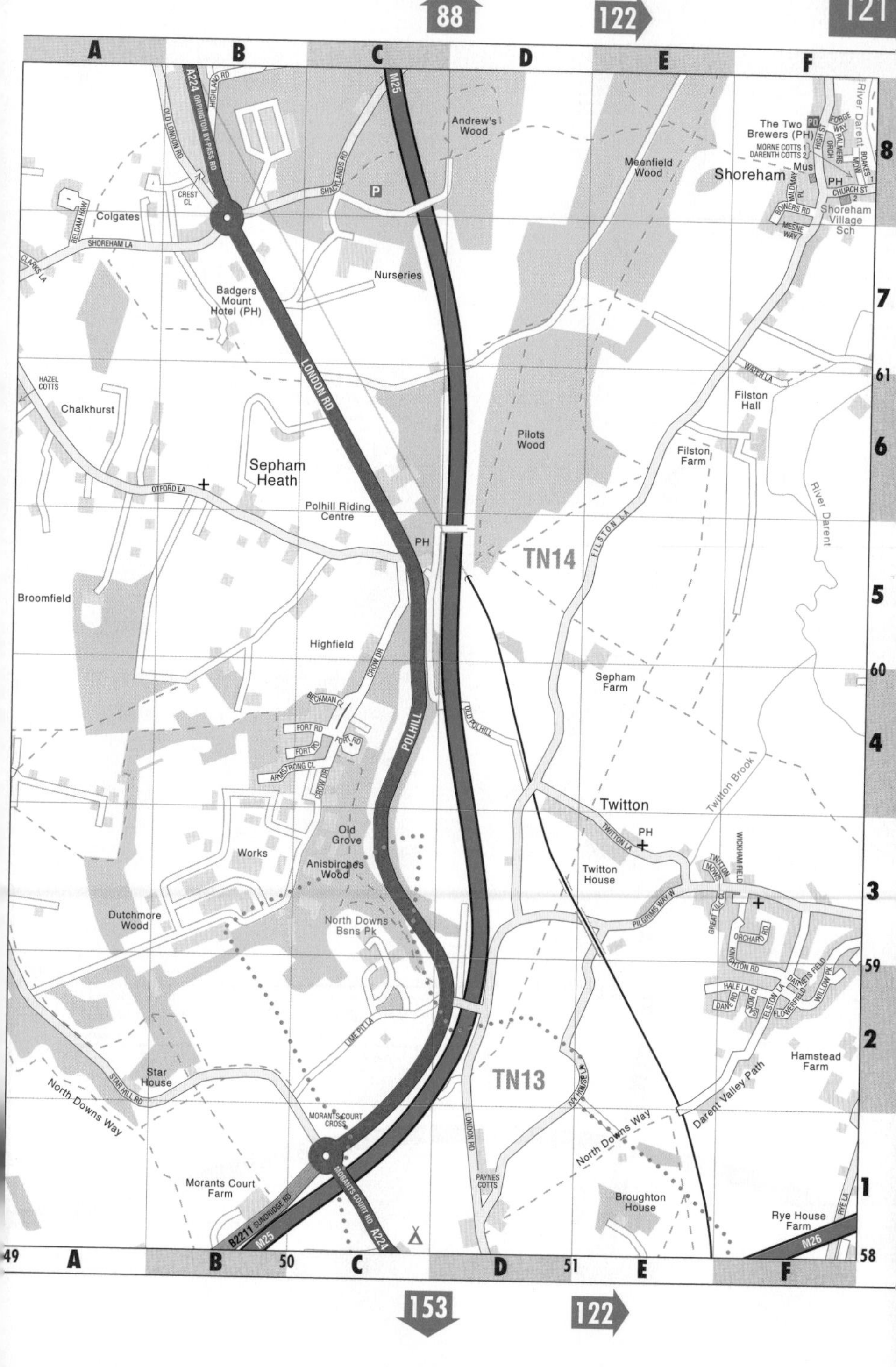

88
122
153
122

A B C D E F

Andrew's Wood

The Two Brewers (PH)
MORNE COTTS
DARENTH COTTS 2
Shoreham
Mus
PH
Shoreham Village Sch

Meenfield Wood

APPINGTON ST PASS RD
OLD LONDON RD
CREST CL
Colgates
SHOREHAM LA
CLARKS LA

Badgers Mount Hotel (PH)

Nurseries

HAZEL COTTS
Chalkhurst

Sepham Heath

LONDON RD

OTFORD LA

Polhill Riding Centre

PH

Pilots Wood

TN14

Filston Hall
Filston Farm

River Darent

Broomfield

Highfield

BECKMAN RD
FORT RD
FORT RD
PINES RD
ARMSTRONG
CROWN DR
COURT DR

POLHILL

OLD POLHILL

Sepham Farm

Twitton Brook

Works

Old Grove

Anisbirches Wood

Twitton
PH
Twitton House

WICKHAMFIELD
TWITTON MANOR
GREAT FIELD

ORCHARD RD
PILGRIMS WAY W
KNIGHTON RD

Dutchmore Wood

North Downs Bsns Pk

HALE LA CL
DAN
TESTILL
FLOWERFIELD
FELLOW PK

LIME PIT LA

Star House

North Downs Way

OAK HILL RD
FACE HILL RD

Morants Court Cross

TN13

LONDON RD

PAYNES COTTS

North Downs Way

Hamstead Farm

Darent Valley Path

Morants Court Farm

B2211
SUNDRIDGE RD
M25
MORANTS COURT RD
A224

Broughton House

Rye House Farm

M26

49 A B 50 C D 51 E F 58

61 7
6
5
60 4
3
59 2
1

121
89

	A	B	C	D	E	F

8

Chapel Alley Cotts
CHURCH COTTS
CHURCH ST
PH
SHOREHAM RD
Shoreham
STATION RD
CH
River Darent

Dunstall Priory

Dunstall Woods

Austin Spring

DA4

Romney Street Farm

7

White Hill

TACKENDEN LA

Dunstall Farm

Rose Cottage Farm

61

Home Farm

Whitehill Farm

Doctor's Wood

MAGPIE BOTTOM

Eastdown

6

Warren Farm

Highfield

SHOREHAM RD

Sevenacre Stubs

5

Darent Valley Path

Mast

Greenhill Wood

Paine's Farm

The Mount

ROW DOW LA

Great Wood

TN15

60

Lower Barn

TN14

GREENHILL RD

HILLYDEAL RD

BIRCHIN CROSS RD

KIPPINGTON LA

4

Hillydeal Wood

COOMBE RD

North Downs Way

Otford Mount

Otford Court (St Michael's Sch)

Rowdow Wood

Shore Hill

3

The Horns (PH)
Liby
HIGH ST
Otford Prim Sch
Otford

Russell House Sch

Park Farm

LEONARD AVE

STATION RD

STATION APP

Otford

PILGRIMS WAY

ST MICHAELS DR

CHALKWAYS

Kemsing Down Nature Reserve

PILGRIMS WAY

Otford

SEVENOAKS RD

59

PILGRIMS WAY W

WICKHAM

Shinecroft

THE CHARNE

Bishop's Palace (remains of)

BUBBLESTONE RD

THE BUTTS

BECKET WAY

BELL'S LA

TUDOR DR

HIGHFIELD RD

SHOREHILL CT

COPPERFIELDS ORCH

2

Oxenhill Shaw

THE PARADE 1
BARCLAY FIELD 2
NORMAN

NIGHTINGALE RD

DYNES RD

EDGAR RD

GREYSTONES

WEST END

Liby

COPPERFIELDS

SPRING HEAD RD

Kemsing

1

M26

OTFORD RD

A225

OLD POUND RD

Ladds House

Childsbridge House

M26

58

| 52 | A | B | 53 | C | D | 54 | E | F |

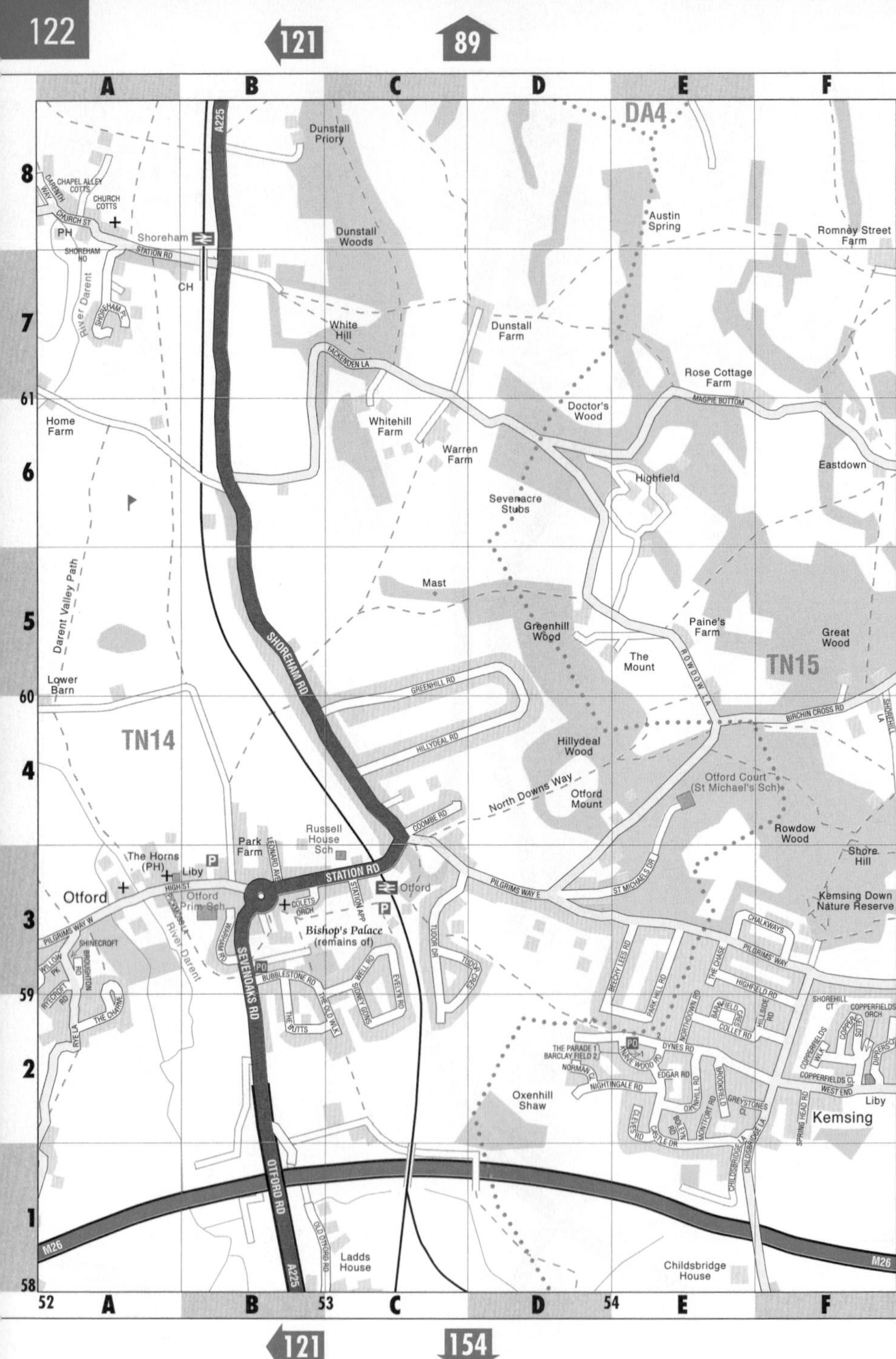

121
154

90
124

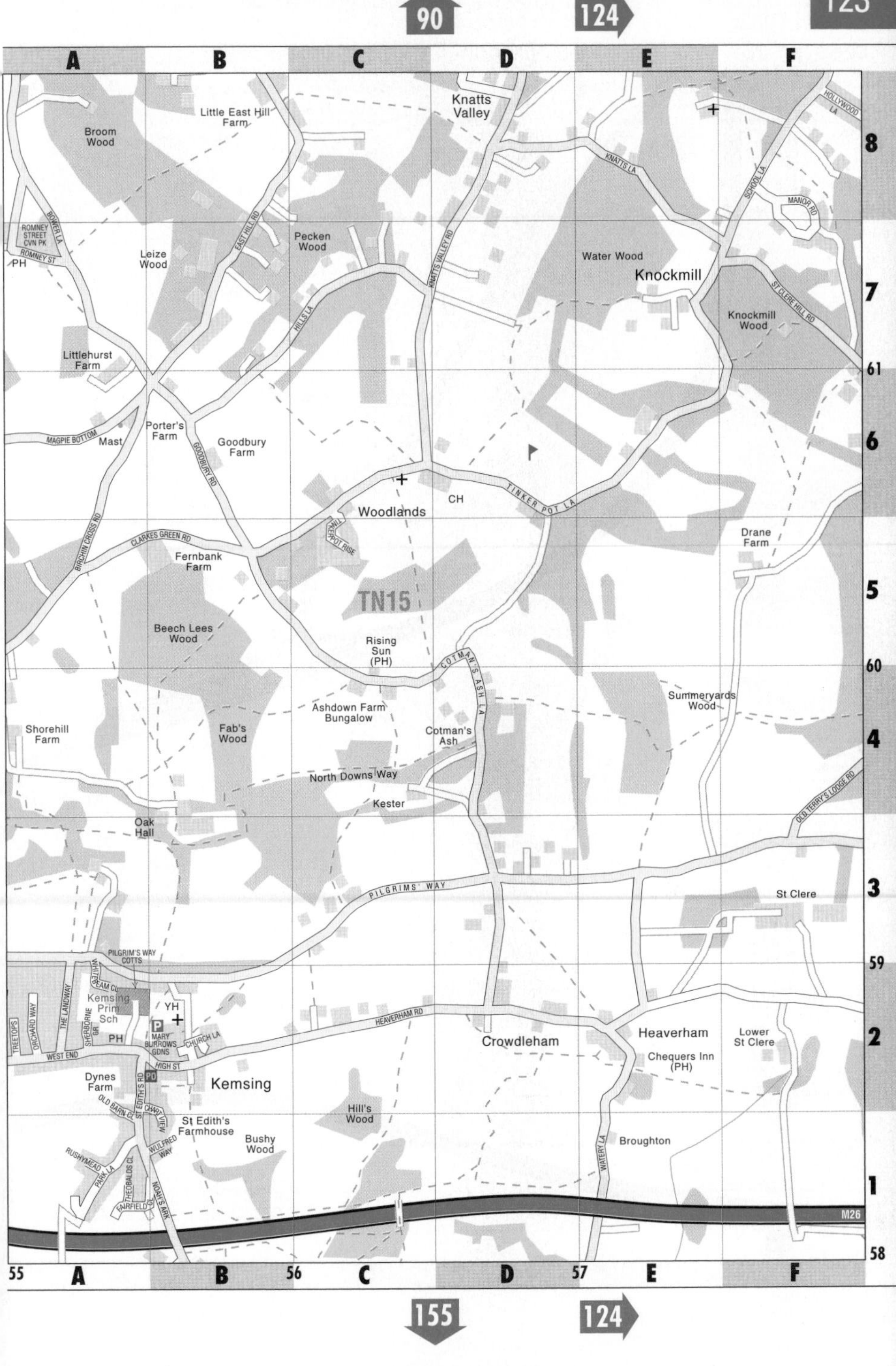
A B C D E F
8 7 6 5 4 3 2 1
61 60 59 58
55 56 57
Broom Wood
Little East Hill Farm
Knatts Valley
Pecken Wood
Leize Wood
Romney Street CVN PK
Romney St
PH
Bower La
East Hill Rd
Hills La
Knatts Valley Rd
Knatts La
School La
Manor Rd
Hollywood La
Water Wood
Knockmill
Knockmill Wood
St Clere Hill Rd
Littlehurst Farm
Magpie Bottom
Mast
Porter's Farm
Goodbury Farm
Goodbury Rd
Woodlands
CH
Tinker Pot La
Tinker Pot Rise
Clarkes Green Rd
Birchin Cross Rd
Fernbank Farm
Drane Farm
TN15
Beech Lees Wood
Rising Sun (PH)
Cotman's Ash La
Summeryards Wood
Ashdown Farm Bungalow
Shorehill Farm
Fab's Wood
Cotman's Ash
North Downs Way
Kester
Old Terry's Lodge Rd
Oak Hall
Pilgrims' Way
St Clere
Pilgrim's Way Cotts
Whitebeam Cl
Kemsing Prim Sch
YH
Heaverham Rd
Treetops
Orchard Way
The Landway
Sherborne Gr
PH
Mary Burrows Gdns
Church La
West End
High St
Crowdleham
Heaverham
Lower St Clere
Chequers Inn (PH)
Dynes Farm
PO
Kemsing
Old Barn Cl
St Edith's Rd
Chart View
St Edith's Farmhouse
Bushy Wood
Hill's Wood
Wulfred Way
Rushymead
Park La
Theobalds Cl
Fairfield Cl
Noah's Ark
Watery La
Broughton
M26

155
124

123
91

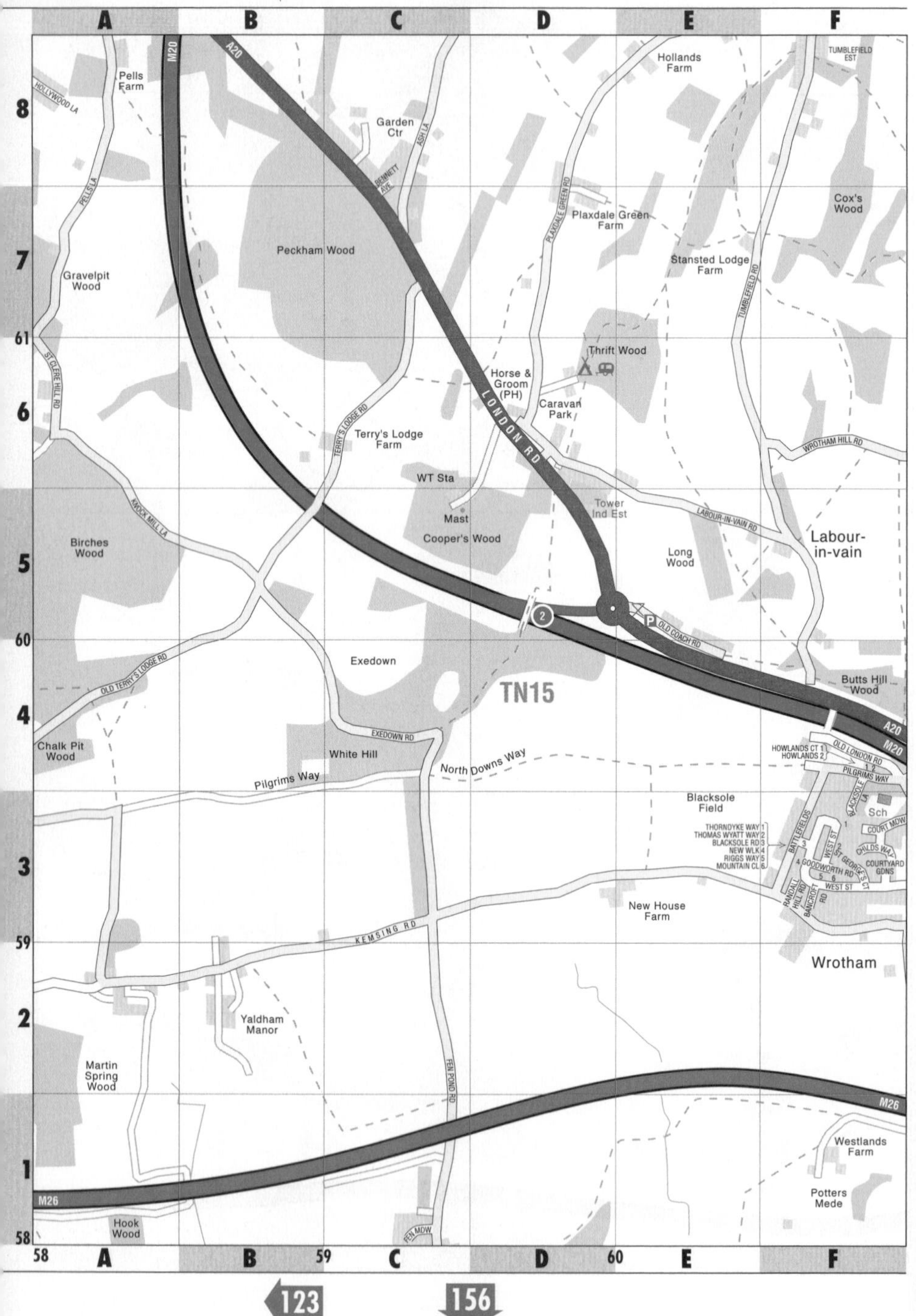
A
B
C
D
E
F
8
7
61
6
5
60
4
3
59
2
1
58
Pells Farm
HOLLYWOOD LA
M20
A20
Garden Ctr
ASH LA
BENNETT AVE
Hollands Farm
TUMBLEFIELD EST
PELLS LA
PLAXDALE GREEN RD
Plaxdale Green Farm
Cox's Wood
Peckham Wood
Stansted Lodge Farm
Gravelpit Wood
TUMBLEFIELD RD
Thrift Wood
ST CLERE HILL RD
Horse & Groom (PH)
LONDON RD
Caravan Park
TERRY'S LODGE RD
Terry's Lodge Farm
WROTHAM HILL RD
WT Sta
Mast
Tower Ind Est
LABOUR-IN-VAIN RD
KNOCK MILL LA
Birches Wood
Cooper's Wood
Long Wood
Labour-in-vain
2
P
OLD COACH RD
Exedown
OLD TERRY'S LODGE RD
TN15
Butts Hill Wood
A20
M20
Chalk Pit Wood
EXEDOWN RD
White Hill
HOWLANDS CT 1
HOWLANDS 2
OLD LONDON RD
North Downs Way
Pilgrims Way
PILGRIMS WAY
Blacksole Field
BLACKSOLE LA
Sch
COURT MDW
THORNDYKE WAY 1
THOMAS WYATT WAY 2
BLACKSOLE RD 3
NEW WLK 4
RIGGS WAY 5
MOUNTAIN CL 6
BATTLEFIELDS
WEST ST
ST GEORGE'S CT
CHILDS WAY
COURTYARD GDNS
GOODWORTH RD
RANDALL HILL RD
BANCROFT RD
New House Farm
KEMSING RD
Wrotham
Yaldham Manor
Martin Spring Wood
FEN POND RD
M26
Westlands Farm
Potters Mede
Hook Wood
FEN MDW
58
59
60

123
156

92
126

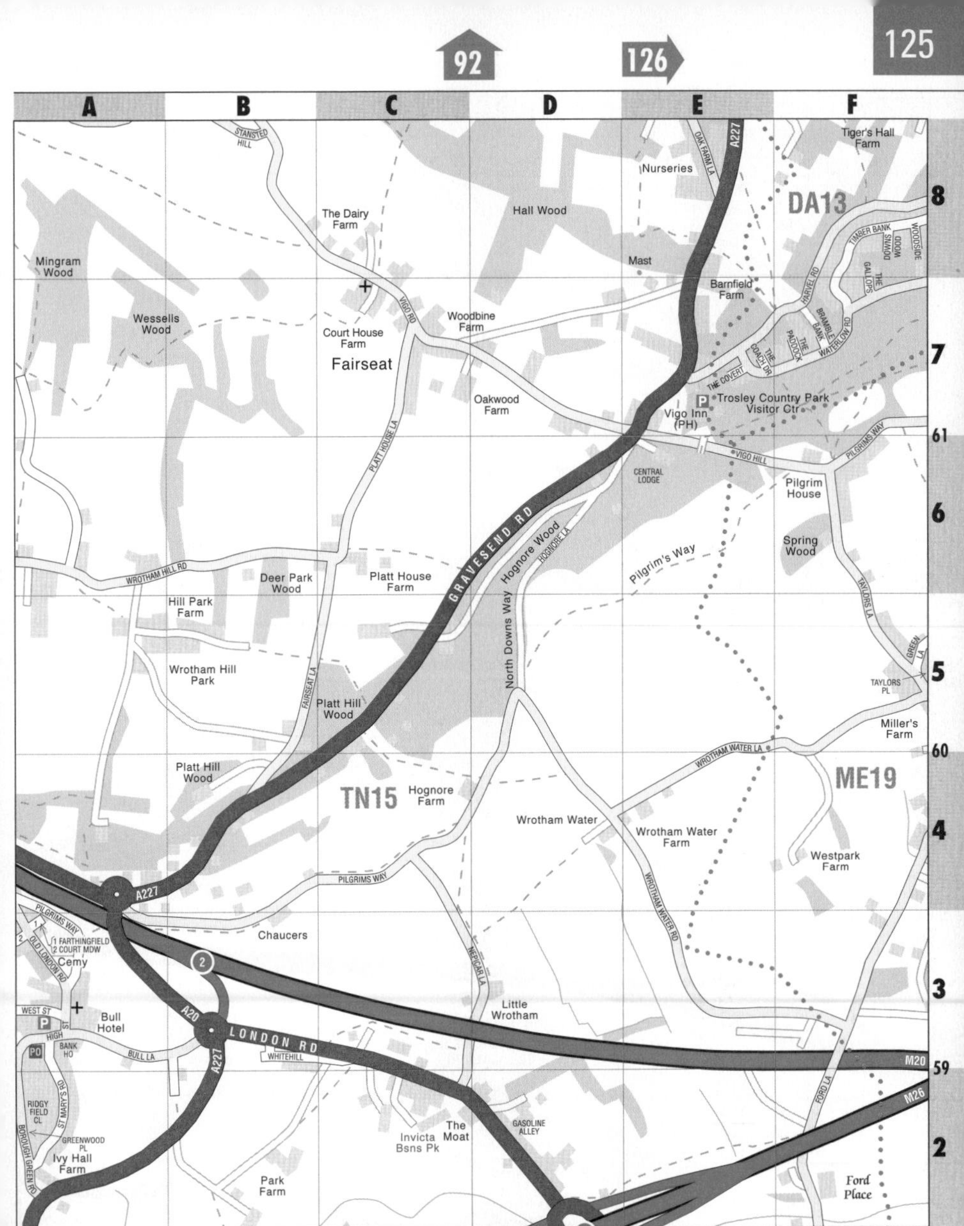
A
B
C
D
E
F
Tiger's Hall Farm
Nurseries
DA13
The Dairy Farm
Hall Wood
Mingram Wood
Mast
Barnfield Farm
Wessells Wood
Court House Farm
Woodbine Farm
Fairseat
Oakwood Farm
Trosley Country Park Visitor Ctr
Vigo Inn (PH)
VIGO HILL
CENTRAL LODGE
Pilgrim House
GRAVESEND RD
Hognore Wood
Pilgrim's Way
Spring Wood
WROTHAM HILL RD
Deer Park Wood
Platt House Farm
Hill Park Farm
North Downs Way
Wrotham Hill Park
Platt Hill Wood
TAYLORS PL
Miller's Farm
WROTHAM WATER LA
Platt Hill Wood
TN15
Hognore Farm
ME19
Wrotham Water
Wrotham Water Farm
Westpark Farm
PILGRIMS WAY
A227
Chaucers
1 FARTHINGFIELD
2 COURT MDW
Cemy
Bull Hotel
LONDON RD
WHITEHILL
Little Wrotham
M20
M26
The Moat
GASOLINE ALLEY
Invicta Bsns Pk
Ivy Hall Farm
Park Farm
Ford Place
Park Wood
Wealdway
Wrotham Sch
Nepicar House
Hotel
Wrotham Heath Place
DUNKLEY VILLAS
Firemanshaw Wood
Royal Oak (PH)
FORGE COTTS
Nepicar Farm
LONDON RD
A20
A25
SANDY LA
BOROUGH GREEN RD
8
7
61
6
5
60
4
3
59
2
1
58
61
62
63

157
126

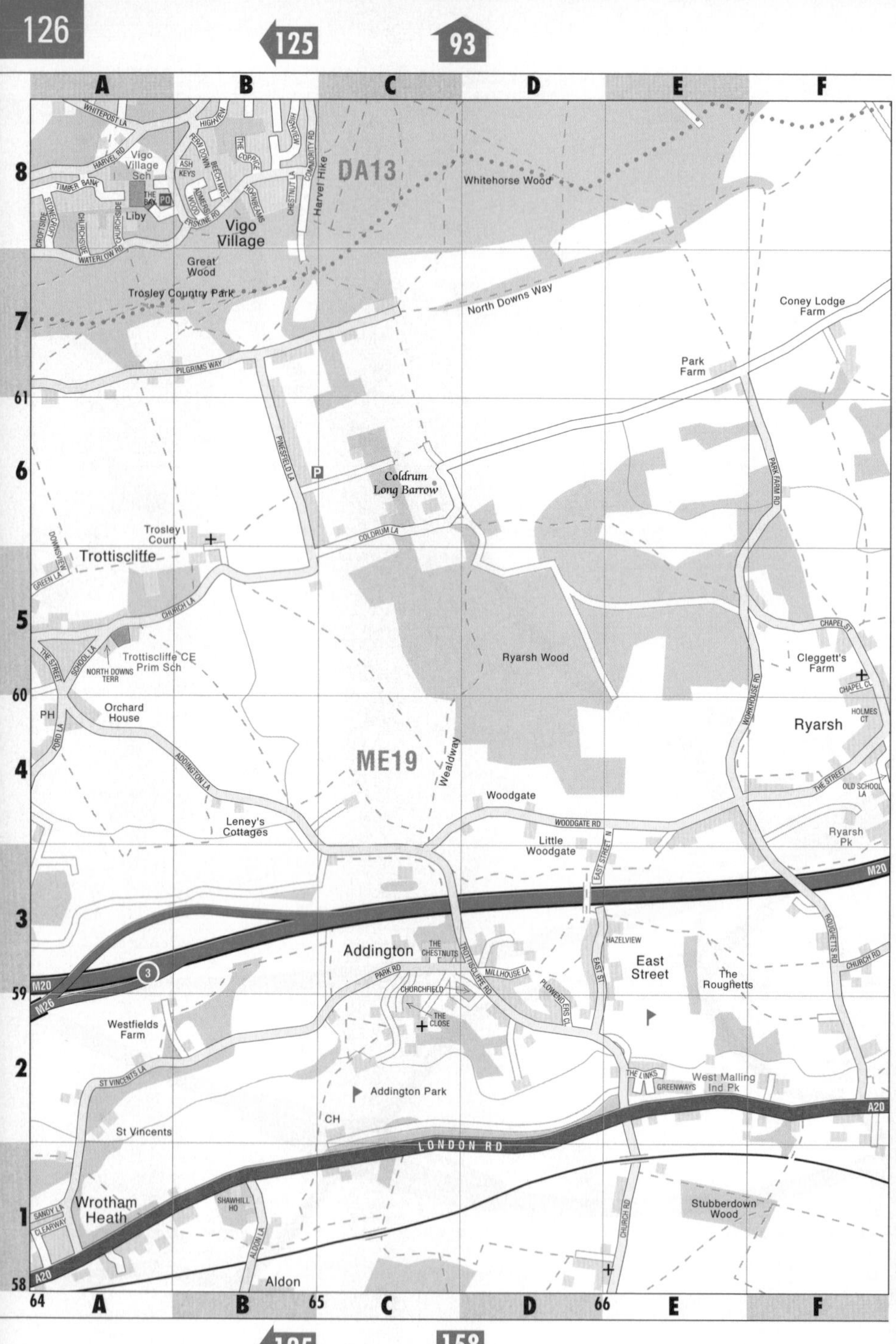
A
B
C
D
E
F
8
7
61
6
5
60
4
3
59
2
1
58
64
65
66
DA13
ME19
Vigo Village
Vigo Village Sch
Liby
PO
Great Wood
Trosley Country Park
Harvel Hike
Whitehorse Wood
North Downs Way
Coney Lodge Farm
Park Farm
PILGRIMS WAY
PINESFIELD LA
Coldrum Long Barrow
COLDRUM LA
Trosley Court
Trottiscliffe
CHURCH LA
Trottiscliffe CE Prim Sch
NORTH DOWNS TERR
Orchard House
PH
ADDINGTON LA
Ryarsh Wood
Wealdway
PARK FARM RD
WORKHOUSE RD
CHAPEL ST
Cleggett's Farm
CHAPEL CL
HOLMES CT
Ryarsh
THE STREET
OLD SCHOOL LA
Ryarsh Pk
Woodgate
WOODGATE RD
Little Woodgate
EAST STREET N
Leney's Cottages
M20
M26
Addington
THE CHESTNUTS
PARK RD
TROTTISCLIFFE RD
MILLHOUSE LA
CHURCHFIELD
THE CLOSE
HAZELVIEW
EAST ST
East Street
The Roughetts
ROUGHETTS RD
CHURCH RD
PLOWENDERS CL
Westfields Farm
ST VINCENTS LA
Addington Park
CH
THE LINKS
GREENWAYS
West Malling Ind Pk
A20
St Vincents
LONDON RD
Wrotham Heath
SANDY LA
CLEARWAY
SHAWHILL HO
ALDON LA
Aldon
Stubberdown Wood

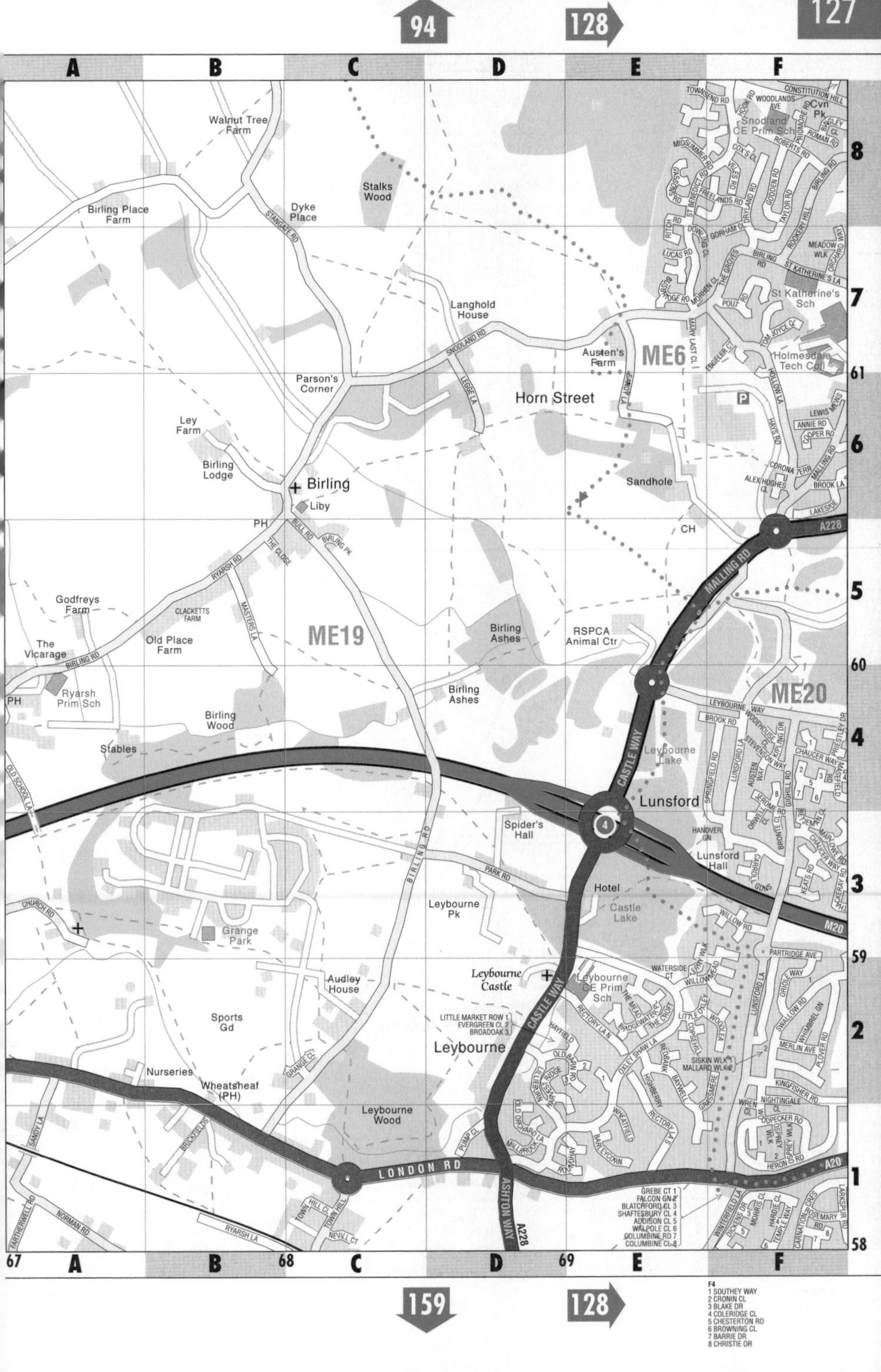
94
128
A
B
C
D
E
F
Walnut Tree Farm
Birling Place Farm
Dyke Place
STANGATE RD
Stalks Wood
Langhold House
SNODLAND RD
LEGGE LA
Parson's Corner
Austen's Farm
Horn Street
ME6
Ley Farm
Birling Lodge
Birling
Liby
PH
BULL RD
BIRLING PK
THE CLOSE
RYARSH RD
Sandhole
CH
A228
MALLING RD
Godfreys Farm
CLACKETTS FARM
MASTERS LA
ME19
Birling Ashes
RSPCA Animal Ctr
The Vicarage
BIRLING RD
Old Place Farm
Ryarsh Prim Sch
PH
Birling Wood
Birling Ashes
ME20
Stables
OLD SCHOOL LA
CASTLE WAY
Leybourne Lake
Lunsford
Spider's Hall
Lunsford Hall
PARK RD
BIRLING RD
Hotel
Castle Lake
M20
CHURCH RD
Grange Park
Leybourne Pk
Leybourne Castle
Leybourne CE Prim Sch
Audley House
Sports Gd
LITTLE MARKET ROW 1
EVERGREEN CL 2
BROADOAK 3
Leybourne
Nurseries
Wheatsheaf (PH)
GRANGE CL
Leybourne Wood
BRICKFIELDS
SANDY LA
LONDON RD
PUMP CL
ASHTON WAY
A228
A20
TOWN HILL
TOWN HILL CL
NEVILL CT
RYARSH LA
NORMAN RD
FARTHERWELL RD
GREBE CT 1
FALCON GN 2
BLATCHFORD CL 3
SHAFTESBURY CL 4
ADDISON CL 5
WALPOLE CL 6
COLUMBINE RD 7
COLUMBINE CL 8
SISKIN WLK 1
MALLARD WLK 2
TOWNSEND RD
WOODLANDS AVE
CONSTITUTION HILL
Cvn Pk
Snodland CE Prim Sch
ROMAN RD
ROBERTS RD
COX'S CL
MIDSUMMER RD
FREELANDS RD
GODDEN RD
TAYLOR RD
BIRLING RD
ROOKERY HILL
GORHAM CL
LUCAS RD
ST KATHERINE'S LA
St Katherine's Sch
POUT RD
TOM JOYCE CL
MARY LAST CL
Holmesdale Tech Coll
HOLLOW LA
HAYS RD
LEWIS MEWS
ANNIE RD
COOPER RD
CORONA TERR
MALLING RD
ALEX HUGHES CL
BROOK LA
LAKESIDE
LEYBOURNE WAY
BROOK RD
SPRINGFIELD RD
LUNSFORD LA
CHAUCER WAY
PRIESTLEY DR
HANOVER GN
CARROLL GDNS
KEATS RD
WILLOW RD
PARTRIDGE AVE
ORIOLE WAY
SWALLOW RD
WHIMBREL GN
MERLIN AVE
PLOVER RD
KINGFISHER RD
NIGHTINGALE CL
WOODPECKER RD
HERONS RD
LARKSPUR RD
ROSEMARY RD
CARNATION CRES
TEMPLE WAY
HARDIE CL
MORRIS CL
DICKENS DR
WINTERFIELD LA
RECTORY LA N
RECTORY LA S
HIGHBERRY
BAYWELL
OXLEY SHAW LA
OLD BARN RD
HAYFIELD
WHEATFIELD
BARLEYCORN
OLD ORCHARD LA
MILLBROOK
67
68
69
58
59
60
61
1
2
3
4
5
6
7
8
159
128
F4
1 SOUTHEY WAY
2 CRONIN CL
3 BLAKE DR
4 COLERIDGE CL
5 CHESTERTON RD
6 BROWNING CL
7 BARRIE DR
8 CHRISTIE DR

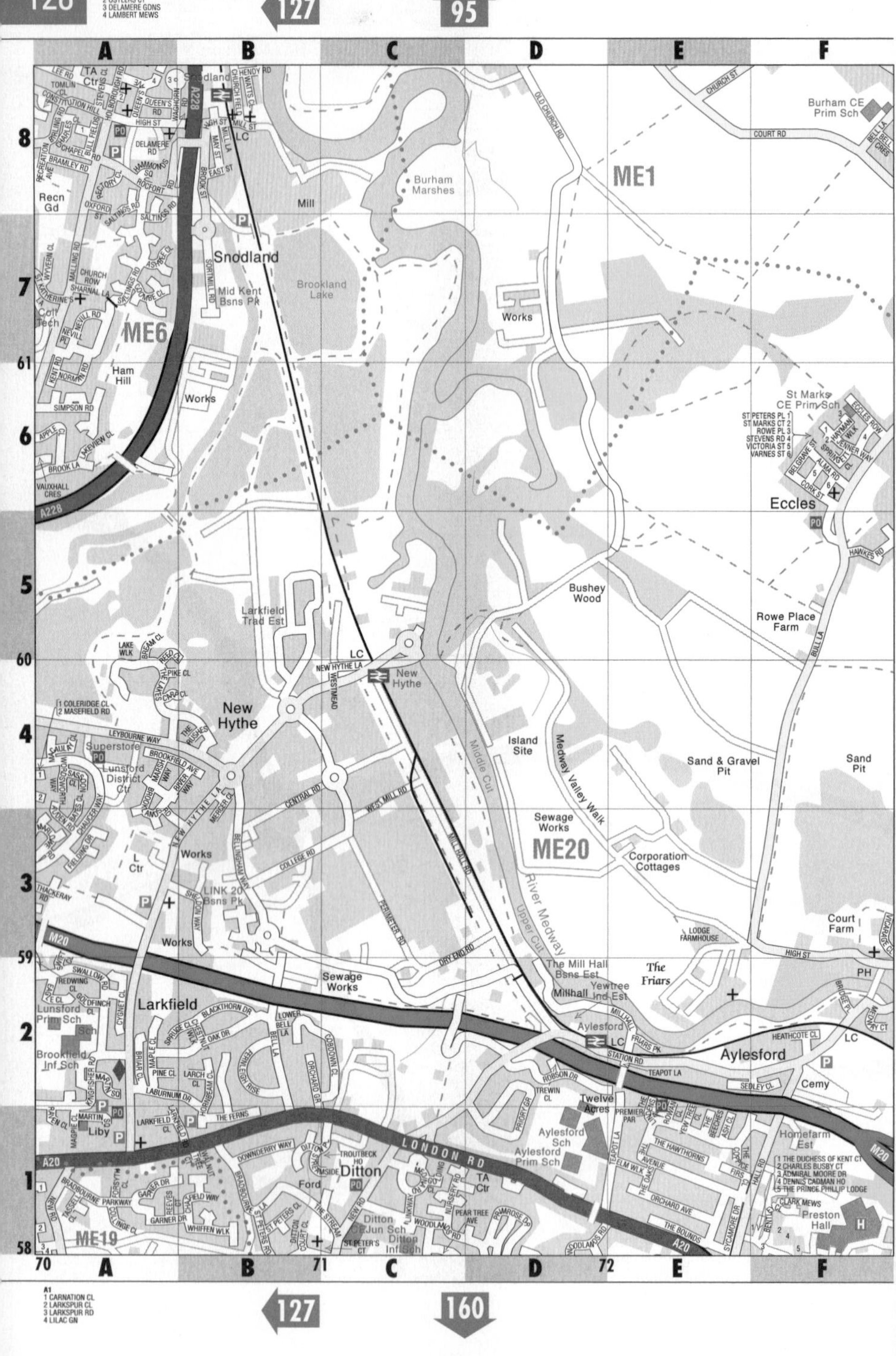

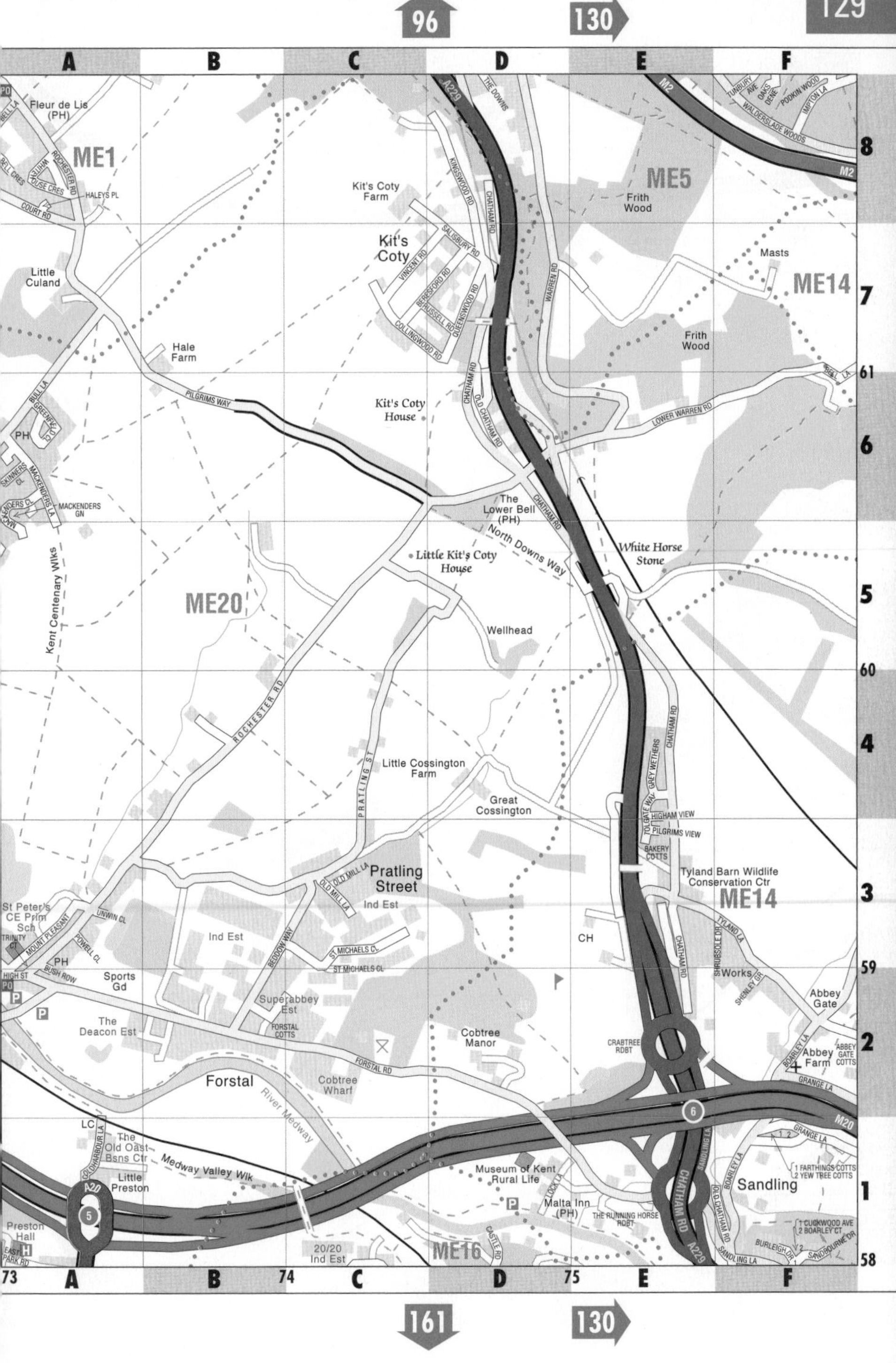
96
130
A B C D E F
8 7 61 6 5 60 4 3 59 2 1 58
73 74 75
ME1
ME5
ME14
ME20
ME16
Fleur de Lis (PH)
Kit's Coty Farm
Kit's Coty
Frith Wood
Masts
Little Culand
Hale Farm
Kit's Coty House
The Lower Bell (PH)
North Downs Way
White Horse Stone
Little Kit's Coty House
Wellhead
Kent Centenary Wlks
Little Cossington Farm
Great Cossington
Pratling Street
Ind Est
Tyland Barn Wildlife Conservation Ctr
St Peter's CE Prim Sch
Sports Gd
Superabbey Est
The Deacon Est
Cobtree Manor
Cobtree Wharf
Forstal
River Medway
Abbey Gate
Abbey Farm
Works
CH
CRABTREE RDBT
Museum of Kent Rural Life
Malta Inn (PH)
THE RUNNING HORSE RDBT
Sandling
The Old Oast Bsns Ctr
Little Preston
Preston Hall
Medway Valley Wlk
20/20 Ind Est
PILGRIMS WAY
ROCHESTER RD
PRATLING ST
CHATHAM RD
OLD CHATHAM RD
LOWER WARREN RD
WARREN RD
FORSTAL RD
BEDDOW WAY
M2
M20
A229
A20
161
130

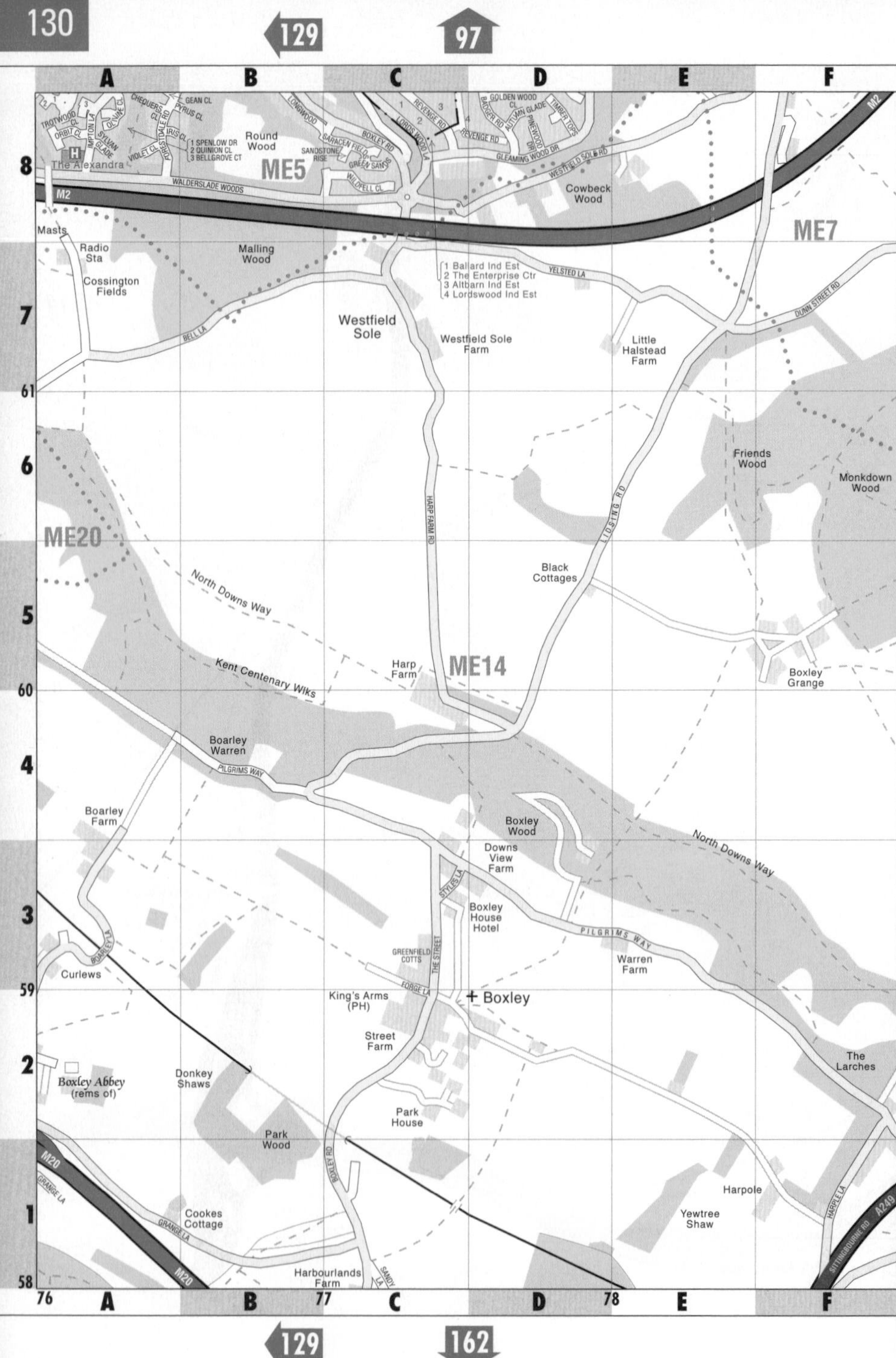

129
97

8

H
The Alexandra

TROYWOOD
ORBIT CL

GEAN CL
CYRUS CL

CHEQUERS LA
VIOLET CL

CAUSTON
JUSS

SPENLOW DR
QUINION CL
BELLGROVE CT

LONGWOOD
SANDSTONE
RISE

BOXLEY RD

CORPUS WAY LA

REVENGE RD

GOLDEN WOOD
CL
AUTUMN GLADE

GLEAMING WOOD DR

WESTFIELD SOLE RD

LIMEFIELD

Round
Wood

ME5

GARDEN FIELD

WELL HELL CL

WALDERSLADE WOODS

Cowbeck
Wood

M2

ME7

M2

Masts

Radio
Sta

Cossington
Fields

Malling
Wood

BELL LA

Westfield
Sole

YELSTED LA

1 Ballard Ind Est
2 The Enterprise Ctr
3 Altbarn Ind Est
4 Lordswood Ind Est

Westfield Sole
Farm

Little
Halstead
Farm

DUNN STREET RD

7

61

ME20

6

HARP FARM RD

TILSDEN RD

Friends
Wood

Monkdown
Wood

5

North Downs Way

Kent Centenary Wlks

Harp
Farm

ME14

Black
Cottages

Boxley
Grange

60

4

Boarley
Warren

PILGRIMS WAY

Boarley
Farm

Boxley
Wood

Downs
View
Farm

North Downs Way

PILGRIMS WAY

3

Curlews

BOXLEY RD

GREENFIELD
COTTS

THE STREET

BELL LA

FORGE LA

Boxley
House
Hotel

Warren
Farm

59

King's Arms
(PH)

+ Boxley

The
Larches

2

Boxley Abbey
(rems of)

Donkey
Shaws

Street
Farm

Park
House

Park
Wood

BOXLEY RD

SANDLING

M20

GRANGE LA

Cookes
Cottage

GRANGE LA

Harpole

Yewtree
Shaw

HARPLE LA

SITTINGBOURNE RD

A249

A249

1

58

Harbourlands
Farm

76   **A**   **B**   **77**   **C**   **D**   **78**   **E**   **F**

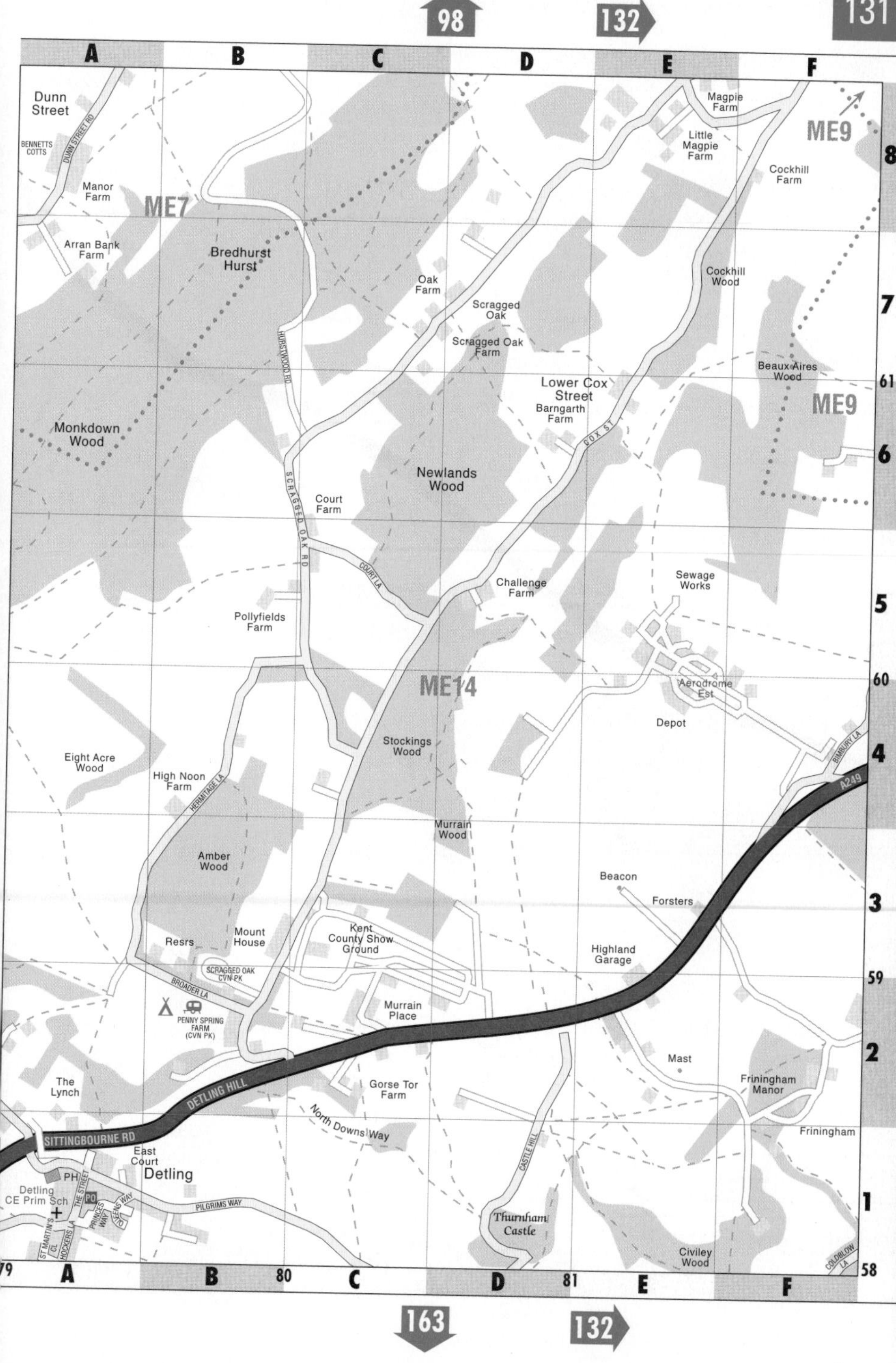
98
132
A
B
C
D
E
F
Dunn Street
BENNETTS COTTS
DUNN STREET RD
Manor Farm
ME7
Arran Bank Farm
Bredhurst Hurst
Monkdown Wood
Magpie Farm
Little Magpie Farm
ME9
Cockhill Farm
Cockhill Wood
Oak Farm
Scragged Oak
Scragged Oak Farm
HURSTWOOD RD
Lower Cox Street
Barngarth Farm
Beaux Aires Wood
ME9
COX ST
Newlands Wood
Court Farm
SCRAGGED OAK RD
COURT LA
Challenge Farm
Sewage Works
Pollyfields Farm
ME14
Aerodrome Est
Depot
Eight Acre Wood
High Noon Farm
HERMITAGE LA
Stockings Wood
BIMBURY LA
A249
Murrain Wood
Amber Wood
Beacon
Forsters
Kent County Show Ground
Resrs
Mount House
Highland Garage
SCRAGGED OAK CVN PK
BROADER LA
PENNY SPRING FARM (CVN PK)
Murrain Place
Mast
The Lynch
DETLING HILL
Gorse Tor Farm
Friningham Manor
North Downs Way
Friningham
SITTINGBOURNE RD
East Court
Detling
PH
THE STREET
PO
PRINCES WAY
QUEENS WAY
PILGRIMS WAY
CASTLE HILL
Detling CE Prim Sch
ST MARTIN'S CL
HOCKERS LA
Thurnham Castle
Civiley Wood
COLDBLOW LA
8
7
61
6
5
60
4
3
59
2
1
58
79
80
81
163
132

A B C D E F

8

Plum Tree Farm

Stockbury

Church Farm

Parsonage Farm

West Wood

South Street

7

Four Oaks

Appsmoor Farm

SOUTH STREET RD

The Squirrels (PH)

Hillside Farm

Beaux Aires House

61

Hove Cottage

Steppes Hill Farm

Steps Hill Wood (Nature Reserve)

Maple House

CHALK RD

STEPS HILL RD

Squirrels Farm

6

Beaux Aires Farm

Hall Wood

Keepers Cottage

5

Longreach Wood

ME9

Squirrel Wood

Bimbury Cottages

60

Ballingdane

4

A249

Rumsted Court

Yetnor Farm

Longton Wood

RUMSTEAD LA

RUMSTEAD RD

OLD FORGE LA

3

ME14

Appsfield

Old Forge Farm

Cam Hill Farm

59

Friningham Farm

Little Budds Farm

Long Wood

2

South Leas Farm

Pond Farm

ME17

COLDBLOW LA

Hucking

1

Wireless Transmitting Station

CHURCH RD

Coldblow

58

Stanhope Farm

Hook and Hatobet Inn (PH)

RAGGED OAK RD

BROAD STREET HILL

82 A 83 B C 83 D 84 E F

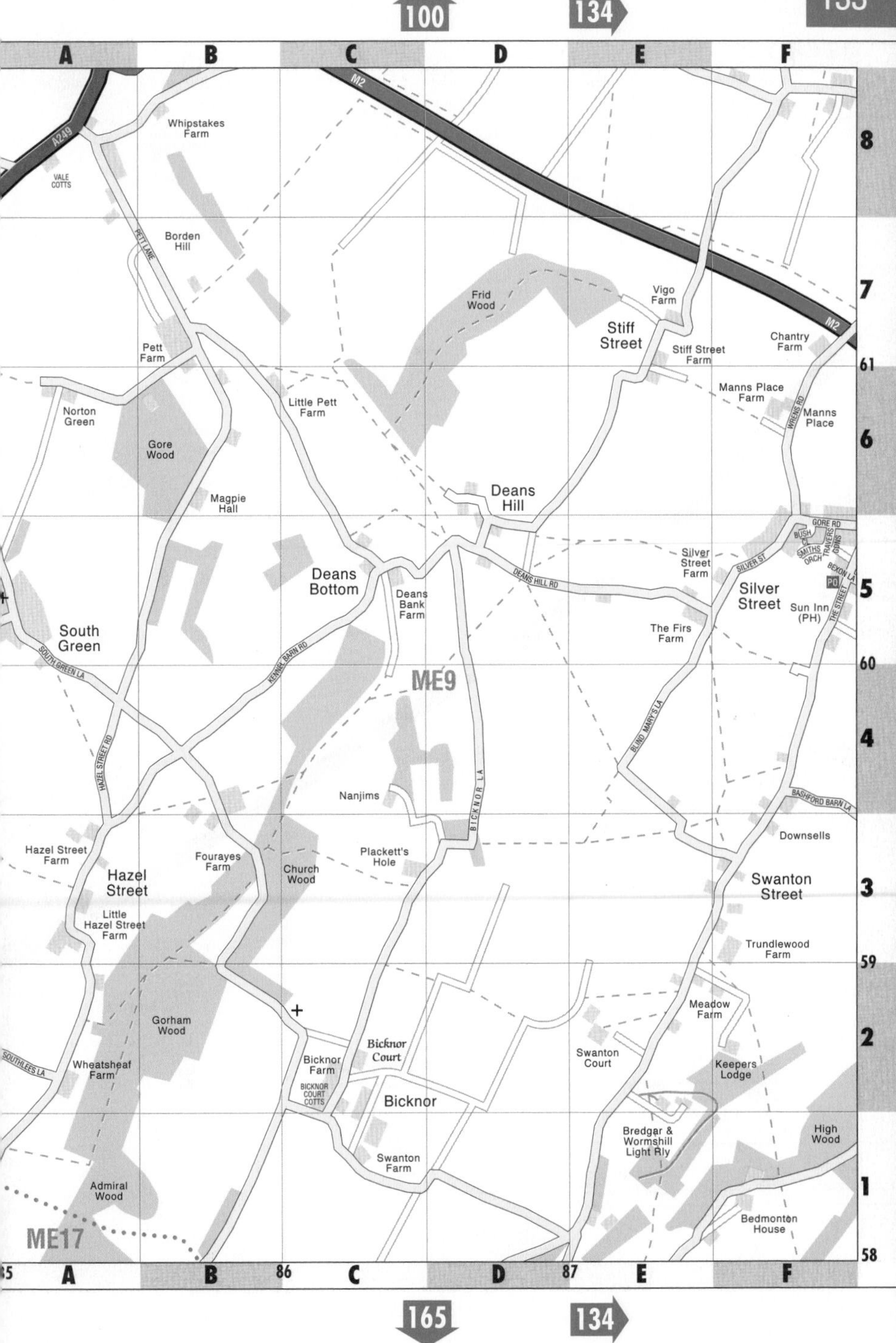

A B C D E F

8

VALE
COTTS

Whipstakes
Farm

M2

Borden
Hill

7

Frid
Wood

Vigo
Farm

Stiff
Street

M2

61

Pett
Farm

Little Pett
Farm

Stiff Street
Farm

Chantry
Farm

Manns Place
Farm

MARNS RD

Manns
Place

Norton
Green

6

Gore
Wood

Magpie
Hall

Deans
Hill

GORE RD

BUSH
SMITHS
FARM
ORCH

THE ORCHS

5

SILVER ST

Silver
Street
Farm

SILVER ST

Silver
Street

RIXON LA

THE STREET

P.O

Deans
Bottom

DEANS HILL RD

Deans
Bank
Farm

Sun Inn
(PH)

SOUTH GREEN LA

South
Green

ME9

The Firs
Farm

60

BICKNOR LA

HAZEL STREET RD

4

BLIND MARYS LA

Nanjims

BASHFORD BARN LA

Downsells

Hazel Street
Farm

Fourayes
Farm

Plackett's
Hole

Swanton
Street

3

Church
Wood

Hazel
Street

Little
Hazel Street
Farm

Trundlewood
Farm

59

Gorham
Wood

Meadow
Farm

2

SOUTHLEES LA

Wheatsheaf
Farm

Bicknor
Farm

Bicknor
Court

Swanton
Court

Keepers
Lodge

BICKNOR
COURT
COTTS

Bicknor

Bredger &
Wormshill
Light Rly

High
Wood

1

Admiral
Wood

Swanton
Farm

ME17

Bedmonton
House

58

85

A

B

86

C

D

87

E

F

133 101

A B C D E F

8

7

61

6

5

60

4

59

3

2

1

58

SUTTON BARON RD
WRENS CT
HEARTS DELIGHT RD
Tunstall House
Tunstall CE Prim Sch
TUNSTALL RD
Cedar House
POND COTTS
CROMER RD
ME10

Wren's Farm House

Wrens Cottages

SCHOOL VIEW

Tunstall

Mast

Highsted Wood

Highsted Farm House

Highsted

Grove End Farm

GREENLA RD

DOVES CROFT

Grove End

RUINS BARN RD

Woodstock

Mast

GORDON COTTS

White House

Oakwood Cottages

Oakwood Farm

Sports Gd

Broadoak Ent Village

Cromer's Wood

M2

PRIMROSE GR
BERRY CL
THE BAKERY
Bredgar

MELLAN CL
GORE RD

Gibbens Farm

Bredgar CE Prim Sch

Oakwood Orchard

Kent Science Pk

BROADOAK RD

Woodstock Cottage Farm

Mast

ME9

PARSONAGE COTTS

Parsonage Farm

Broadoak

BEXON LA

Broadoak Farm

Rawling Street Farm

Red Lion (PH)

BASHFORD BARN LA

Bexon

DANES HILL LA

Bexon Manor Farm

Lion Farm

Bexon Manor Cottages

Milstead Wood

RAWLING ST

M2

MINTCHING WOOD LA

BOTTOM POND RD

HOPA HILL

ROBESHAW

Milstead

Manor Farm House

BEDGROW LA

Trundle Wood

Bottom Pond Farm

Bottom Pond

FRINSTED RD

MANOR RD

High Wood

Woodmans

Norwood Farm

Stock Wood

Milstead Manor Farm

Milstead & Frinsted CE Prim Sch

102
136

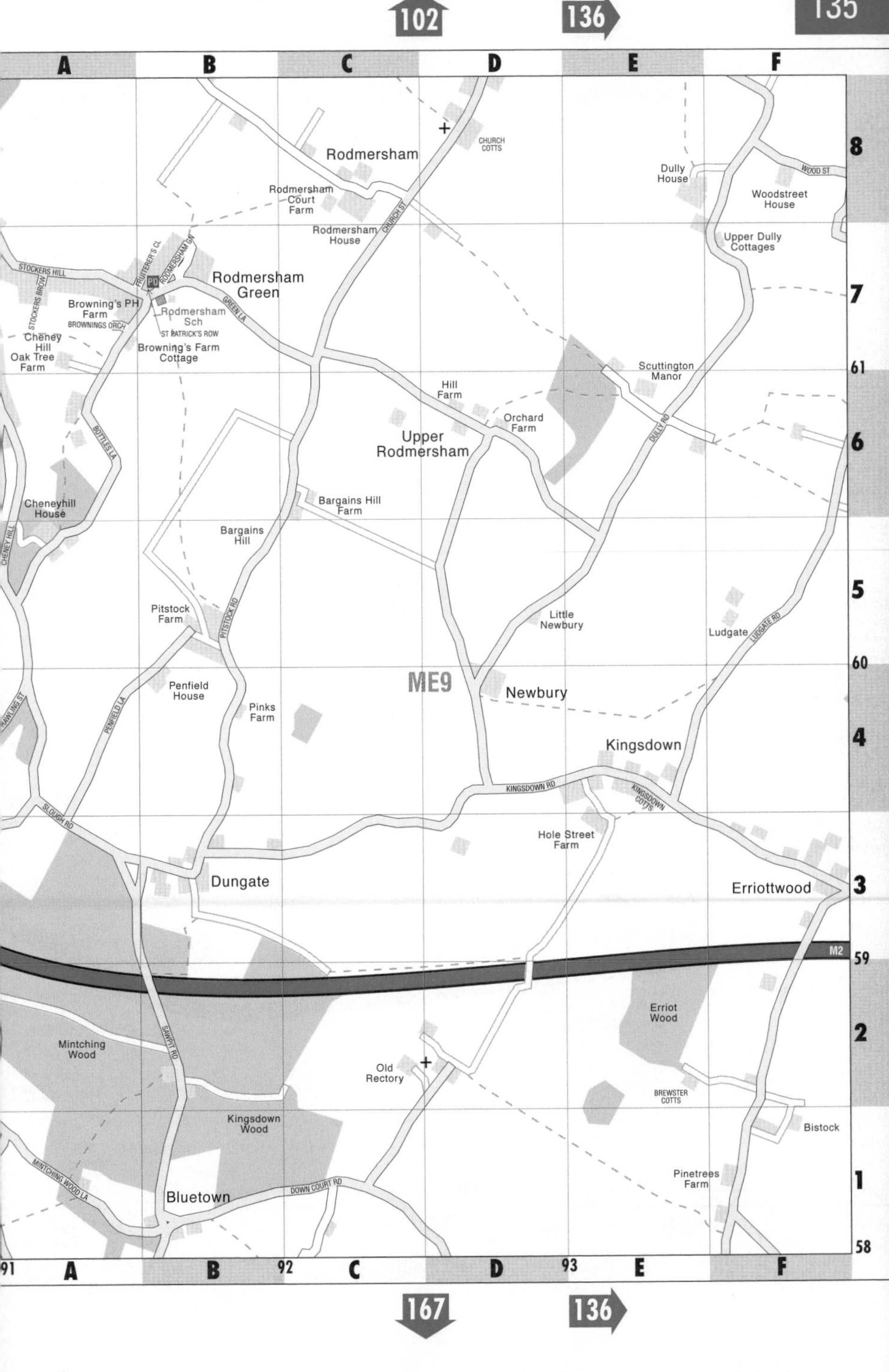
A
B
C
D
E
F
Rodmersham
CHURCH COTTS
Dully House
WOOD ST
Woodstreet House
Rodmersham Court Farm
Rodmersham House
CHURCH ST
Upper Dully Cottages
STOCKERS HILL
FRUITERER'S CL
RODMERSHAM GN
PO
Rodmersham Green
STOCKERS BROW
Browning's PH Farm
BROWNINGS ORCH
Rodmersham Sch
GREEN LA
ST PATRICK'S ROW
Cheney Hill
Oak Tree Farm
Browning's Farm Cottage
Scuttington Manor
Hill Farm
Orchard Farm
Upper Rodmersham
DULLY RD
BOTTLES LA
Cheneyhill House
Bargains Hill Farm
Bargains Hill
CHENEY HILL
Pitstock Farm
PITSTOCK RD
Little Newbury
Ludgate
LUDGATE RD
ME9
Penfield House
Newbury
Pinks Farm
PENFIELD LA
HAWLING ST
Kingsdown
KINGSDOWN RD
KINGSDOWN COTTS
SLOUGH RD
Hole Street Farm
Dungate
Erriottwood
M2
Erriot Wood
Mintching Wood
SAWPIT RD
Old Rectory
BREWSTER COTTS
Kingsdown Wood
Bistock
MINTCHING WOOD LA
Pinetrees Farm
Bluetown
DOWN COURT RD
8
7
61
6
5
60
4
3
59
2
1
58
91
92
93

167
136

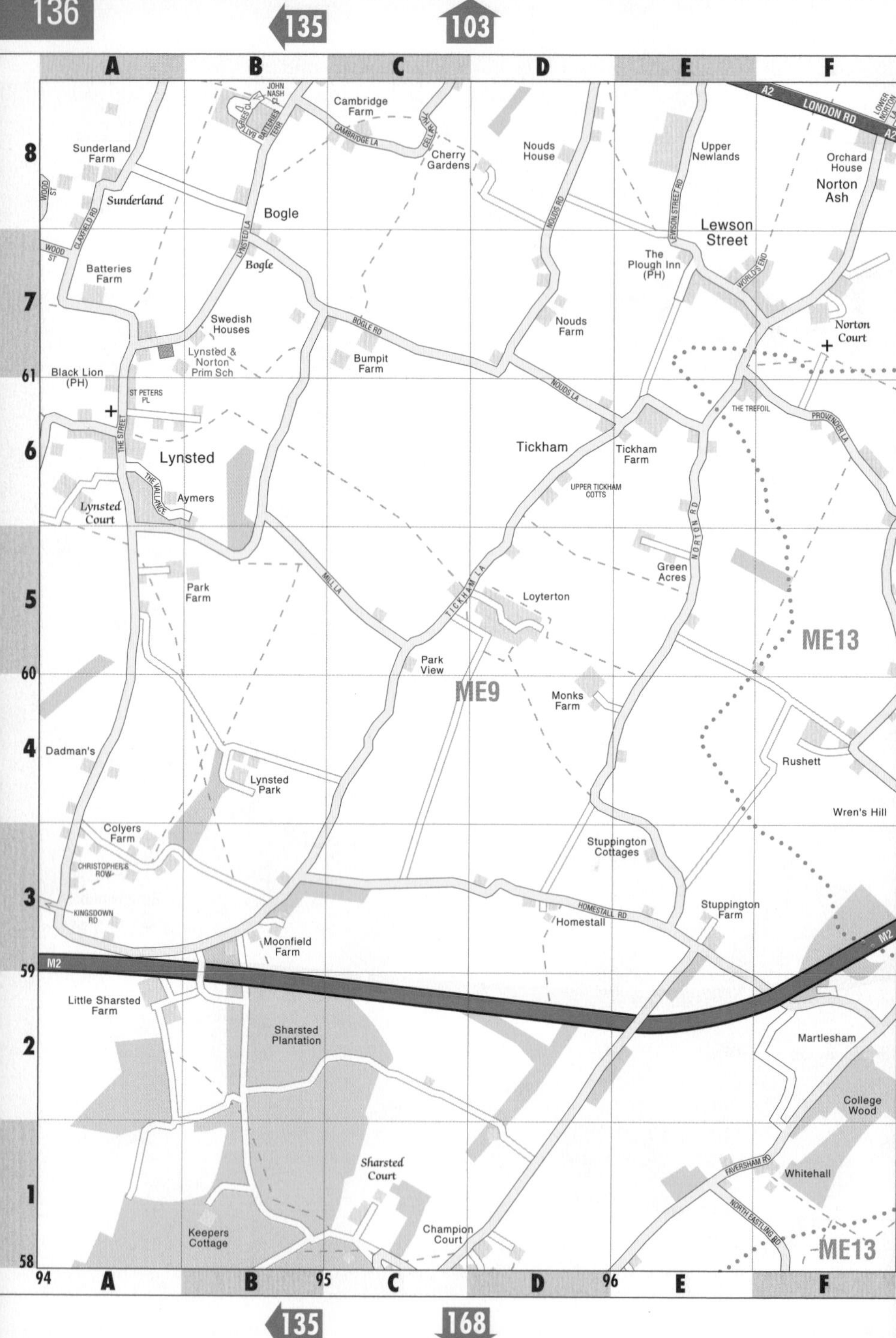

A B C D E F

A2 LONDON RD A2

8

Sunderland
Farm

Sunderland

JOHN NASH
CLOSE

Cambridge
Farm

Cherry
Gardens

CAMBRIDGE LA

Nouds
House

Upper
Newlands

Orchard
House

Norton
Ash

Bogle

Lewson
Street

7

Batteries
Farm

Bogle

BOGLE RD

The
Plough Inn
(PH)

Norton
Court

Swedish
Houses

Nouds
Farm

61

Lynsted &
Norton
Prim Sch

Black Lion
(PH)

St Peters
Pl

Bumpit
Farm

NOUDS LA

THE TREFOIL

PROVENDER LA

6

THE STREET

Lynsted

Tickham

Tickham
Farm

Aymers

THE WALLANDS

UPPER TICKHAM
COTTS

NORTON RD

Lynsted
Court

5

Park
Farm

MILL LA

TICKHAM LA

Loyterton

Green
Acres

ME13

60

Park
View

ME9

Monks
Farm

4

Dadman's

Lynsted
Park

Rushett

Wren's Hill

3

Colyers
Farm

CHRISTOPHERS
ROW

Stuppington
Cottages

Stuppington
Farm

KINGSDOWN
RD

Moonfield
Farm

HOMESTALL RD

Homestall

M2

59

M2

Little Sharsted
Farm

Martlesham

2

Sharsted
Plantation

College
Wood

FAVERSHAM RD

1

Sharsted
Court

Whitehall

Keepers
Cottage

Champion
Court

NORTH EASTLING RD

ME13

58

94 A 95 B C 96 D E F

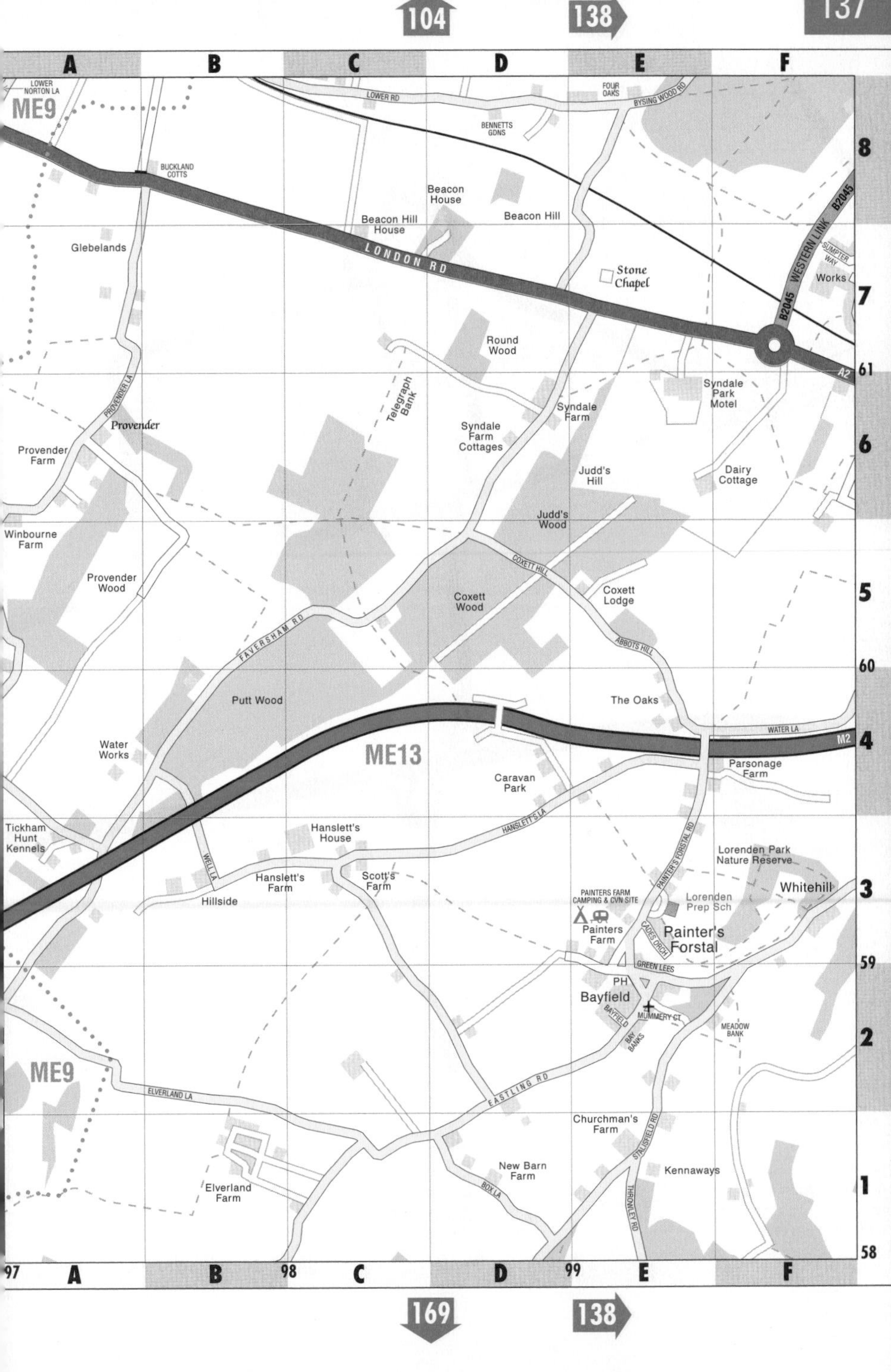
104
138
LOWER NORTON LA
ME9
LOWER RD
FOUR OAKS
BYSING WOOD RD
BENNETTS GDNS
BUCKLAND COTTS
Beacon House
Beacon Hill House
Beacon Hill
LONDON RD
Glebelands
Stone Chapel
B2045
WESTERN LINK
SUMPTER WAY
Works
Round Wood
A2
PROVENDER LA
Telegraph Bank
Syndale Park Motel
Syndale Farm
Provender
Syndale Farm Cottages
Provender Farm
Judd's Hill
Dairy Cottage
Judd's Wood
Winbourne Farm
COXETT HILL
Provender Wood
Coxett Wood
Coxett Lodge
FAVERSHAM RD
ABBOTS HILL
Putt Wood
The Oaks
WATER LA
Water Works
ME13
M2
Parsonage Farm
Caravan Park
Tickham Hunt Kennels
HANSLETT'S LA
Hanslett's House
PAINTER'S FORSTAL RD
Lorenden Park Nature Reserve
WELL LA
Hanslett's Farm
Scott's Farm
Whitehill
Hillside
PAINTERS FARM CAMPING & CVN SITE
Lorenden Prep Sch
Painters Farm
CADES ORCH
Painter's Forstal
GREEN LEES
PH
Bayfield
BAYFIELD
MUMMERY CT
MEADOW BANK
BAY BANKS
ME9
ELVERLAND LA
EASTLING RD
Churchman's Farm
STALISFIELD RD
New Barn Farm
Kennaways
BOX LA
Elverland Farm
THRONLEY RD
169
138

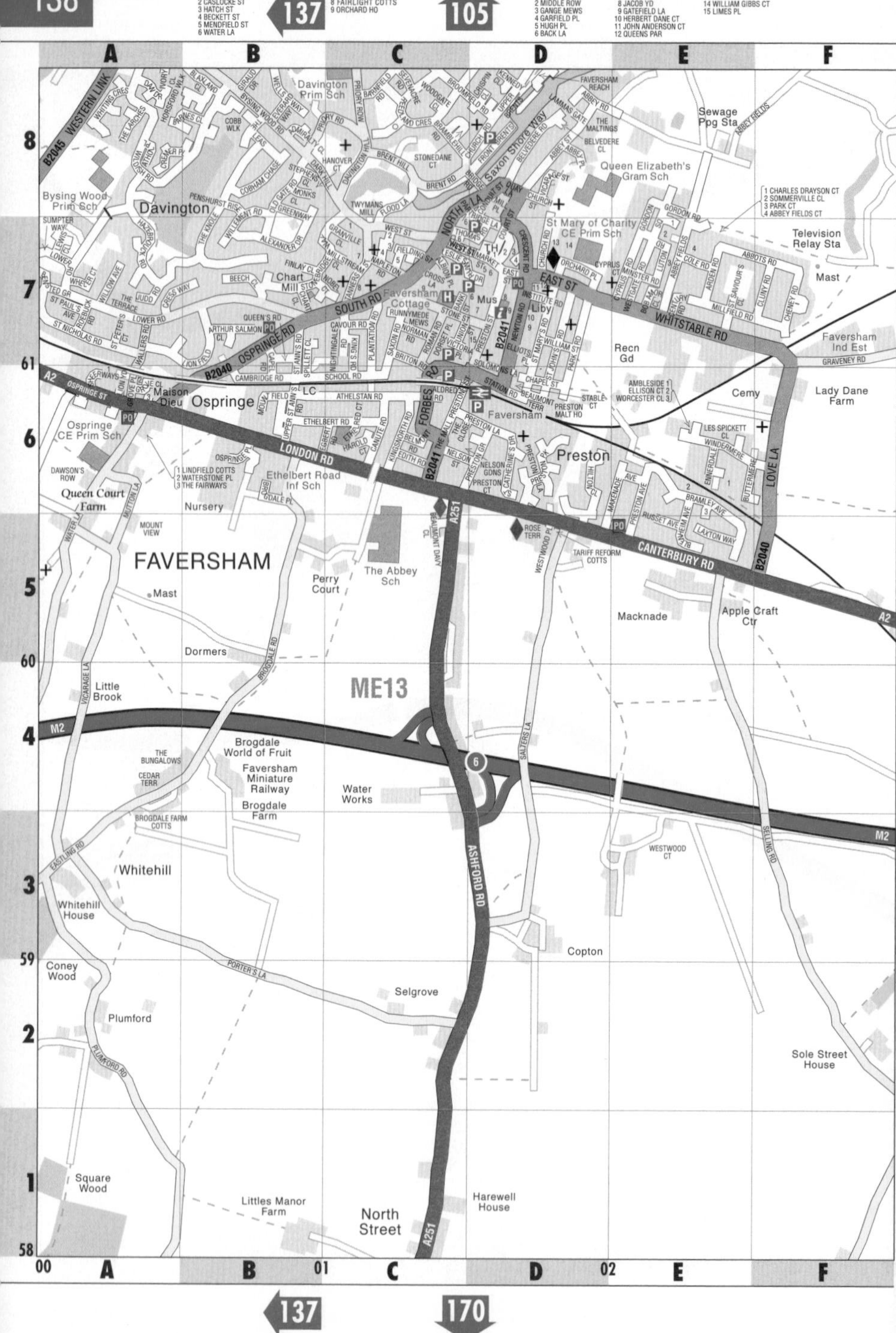

106
140

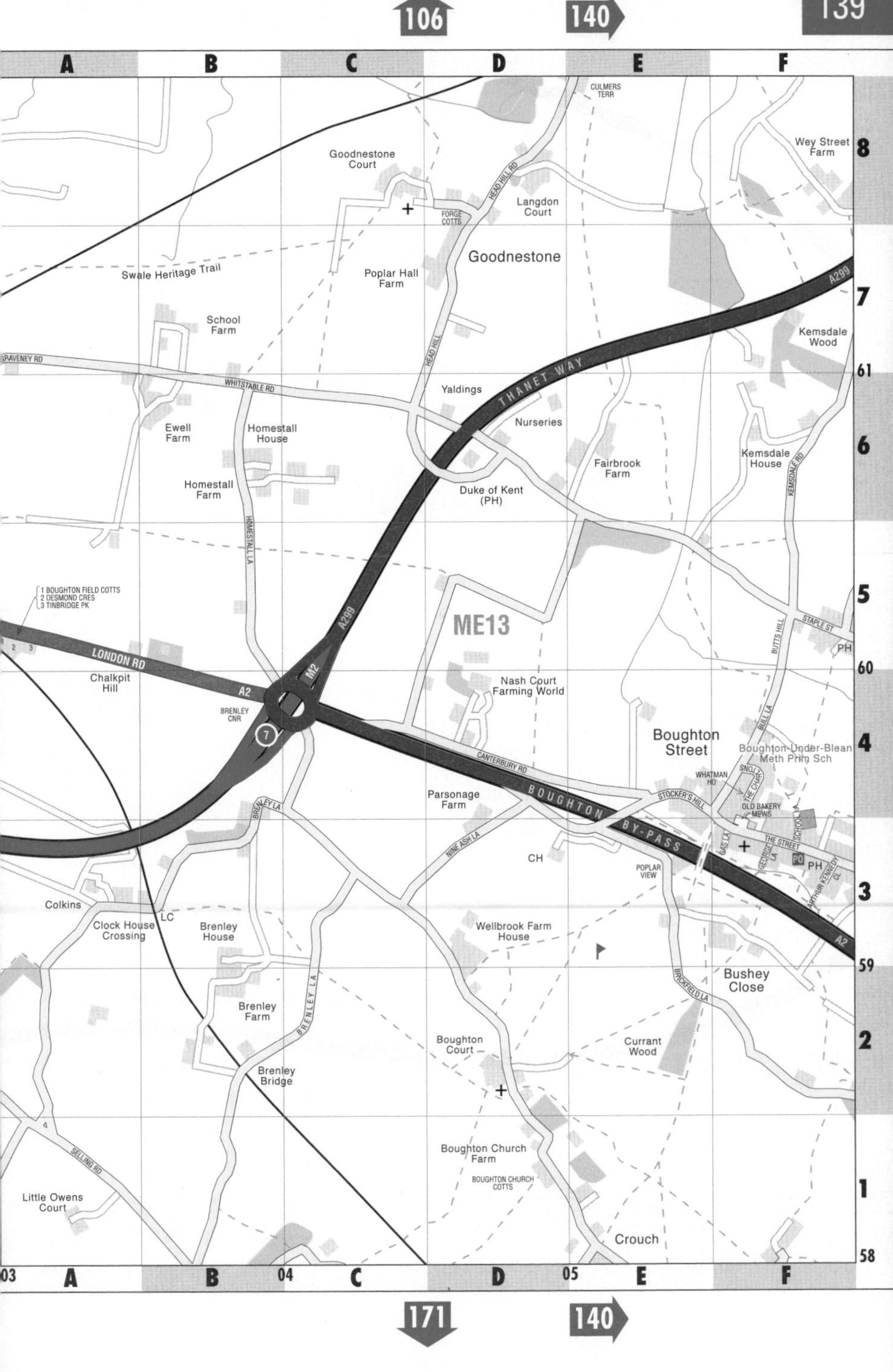
A
B
C
D
E
F
8
7
61
6
5
60
4
3
59
2
1
58
03
04
05
CULMERS TERR
Wey Street Farm
Goodnestone Court
HEAD HILL RD
Langdon Court
FORGE COTTS
Goodnestone
Swale Heritage Trail
Poplar Hall Farm
A299
School Farm
Kemsdale Wood
GRAVENEY RD
HEAD HILL
WHITSTABLE RD
Yaldings
THANET WAY
Nurseries
Ewell Farm
Homestall House
Kemsdale House
Fairbrook Farm
KEMSDALE RD
Homestall Farm
Duke of Kent (PH)
HOMESTALL LA
1 BOUGHTON FIELD COTTS
2 DESMOND CRES
3 TINBRIDGE PK
ME13
STAPLE ST
BUTTS HILL
PH
LONDON RD
M2
Chalkpit Hill
Nash Court Farming World
A2
BRENLEY CNR
7
BULL LA
Boughton Street
Boughton-Under-Blean Meth Prim Sch
CANTERBURY RD
WHATMAN HO
SNOLL
THE CHAR
Parsonage Farm
BOUGHTON BY-PASS
STOCKER'S HILL
OLD BAKERY MEWS
BRENLEY LA
SCHOOL LA
GAS LA
THE STREET
NINE ASH LA
CH
GEORGE LA
PO
PH
POPLAR VIEW
ARTHUR KENNEDY CL
Colkins
LC
Clock House Crossing
Brenley House
Wellbrook Farm House
Bushey Close
BRACKFIELD LA
Brenley Farm
Boughton Court
Currant Wood
Brenley Bridge
Boughton Church Farm
SELLING RD
BOUGHTON CHURCH COTTS
Little Owens Court
Crouch

171
140

139
107

| | A | B | C | D | E | F |

8

Wey Street Farm

Lavender Farm

A299

THANET WAY

Dargate House

Dargate Farm

OAST COTTS

PLUMPUDDING LA

The Dove (PH)

Dargate

Belvedere Farm

DARGATE RD

Fostall

Beesborough Farm

BUTLER'S HILL

Dargate Common

7

Summer Lees

GODFREY'S GRAVE

WOODLANDS

Hernhill CE Prim Sch

61

Bradbourne Cottages

A299

FOSTALL RD

SWALE VIEW

Hernhill

PH

MANOR COTTS

Blean Wood

Acorn Cottage

6

Church Farm

CROCKHAM LA

OLD PARK RD

Crockham Wood

Twr

Holly Hill

CHURCH HILL

Slutshole

Crockham Farm

Holly Hill Farm

CT2

5

Staplestreet

Mount Ephraim Wood

Firtree Cottages

HOLLY HILL RD

CROW RD

60

Mount Ephraim

STAPLESTREET RD

THREAD LA

Courtenay Farm

COURTENAY RD

Bossenden Wood

4

ME13

Thread Wood

DAWES RD

Bossenden Farm

Clay Pits Wood

GEORGE LA

3

1 CHESTNUT CT
2 GROVE COURT FARM

Boughton Street

THE STREET

ST PAUL'S

STAPLE ST

STONE ST

FERNLEIGH

High Wood

ST PAUL'S GDNS

Dunkirk Village Sch

Mast

Dunkirk

Hospital Wood

LEACH HO

CANTERBURY RD

COURTENAY RD

59

A2

Horselees

Boughton Hill

WOODSIDE COTTS

Red Lion (PH)

LONDON RD

2

BROUGHTON BY-PASS

A2

Hickmans Green

BRICKFIELD LA

DUNKIRK RD

Poundfall Wood

Brotherhood Woods

1

Hurst Wood

Arnolds Wood

Forester's Lodge Farm

Fishpond Wood

Iron Hill

58

| 06 | A | | B | 07 | C | | D | 08 | E | | F |

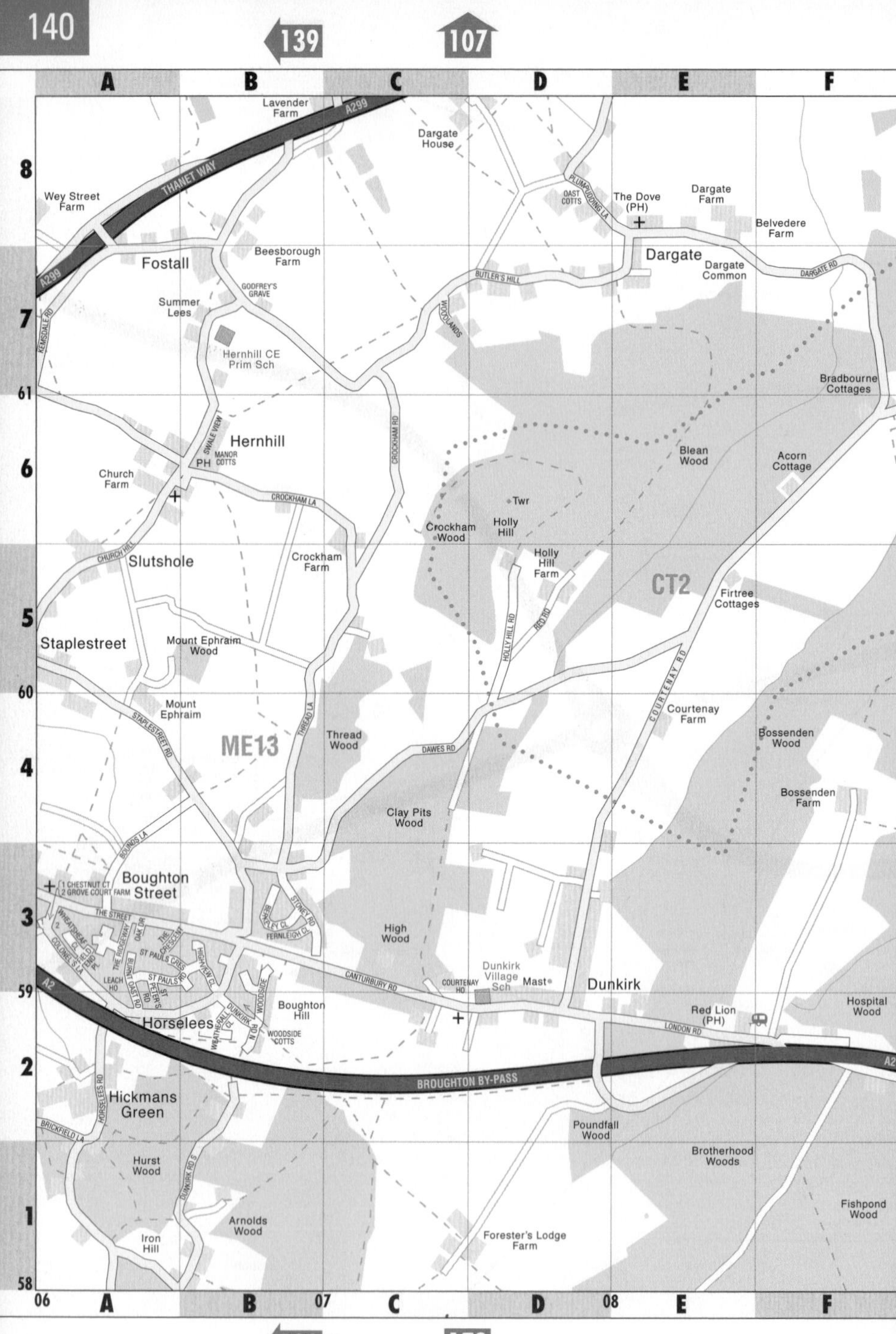

139
172

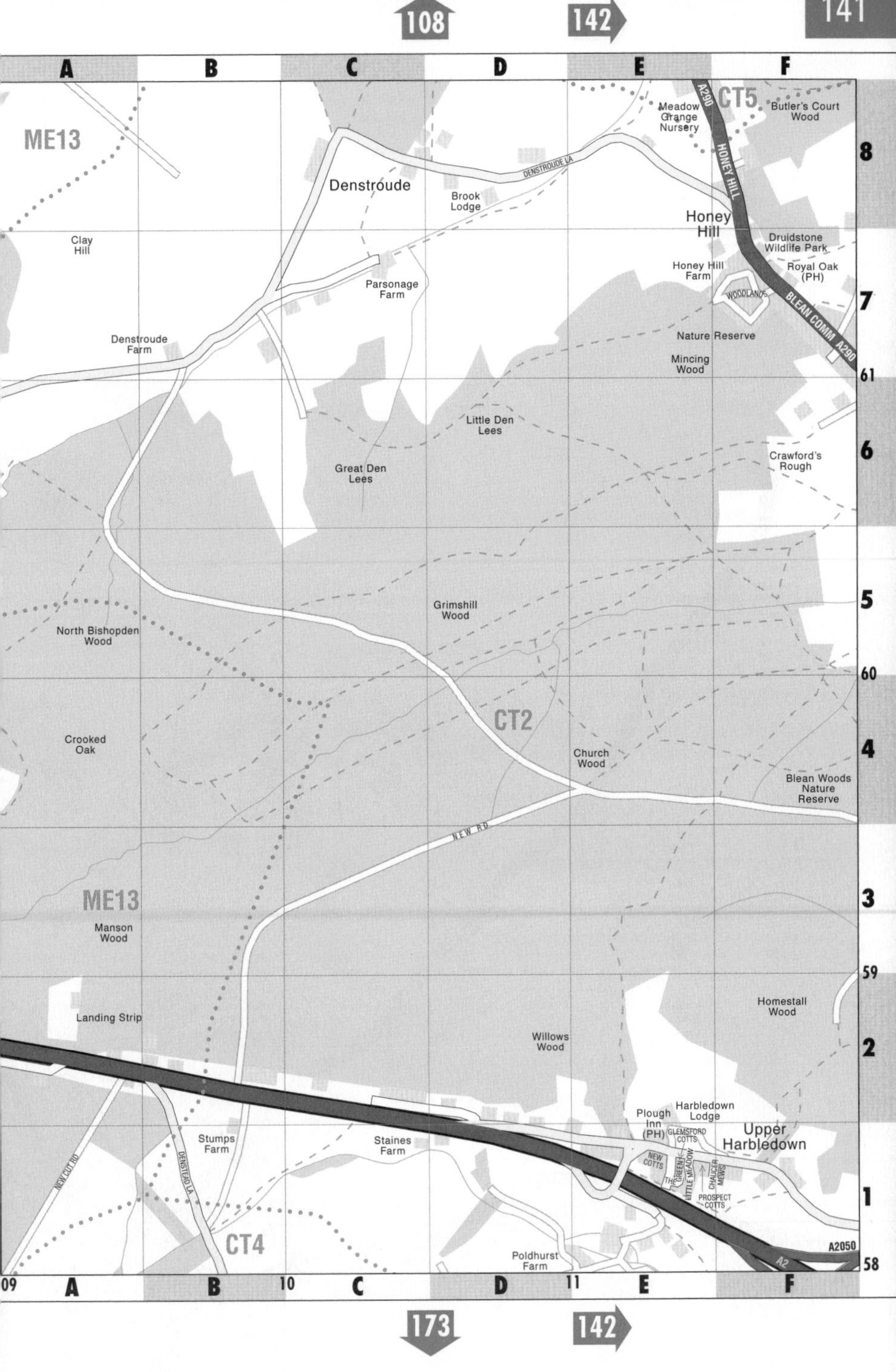

ME13

Denstroude

Clay
Hill

Brook
Lodge

Meadow
Grange
Nursery

CT5

Butler's Court
Wood

DENSTROUDE LA

HONEY HILL

Honey
Hill

Parsonage
Farm

Druidstone
Wildlife Park

Royal Oak
(PH)

Honey Hill
Farm

WOODLANDS

BLEAN COMM A290

Denstroude
Farm

Nature Reserve

Mincing
Wood

Little Den
Lees

Crawford's
Rough

Great Den
Lees

Grimshill
Wood

North Bishopden
Wood

CT2

Crooked
Oak

Church
Wood

Blean Woods
Nature
Reserve

NEW RD

ME13

Manson
Wood

Homestall
Wood

Landing Strip

Willows
Wood

Harbledown
Lodge

Plough
Inn
(PH)

GLEMSFORD
COTTS

Upper
Harbledown

NEW CUT RD

DENSTROUDE LA

Stumps
Farm

Staines
Farm

NEW
COTTS

GREEN
CT

LITTLE MEADOW

A290

CHURCH
MEWS

PROSPECT
COTTS

CT4

Poldhurst
Farm

A2

A2050

09   10   11

A   B   C   D   E   F

8
7
61
6
5
60
4
3
59
2
1
58

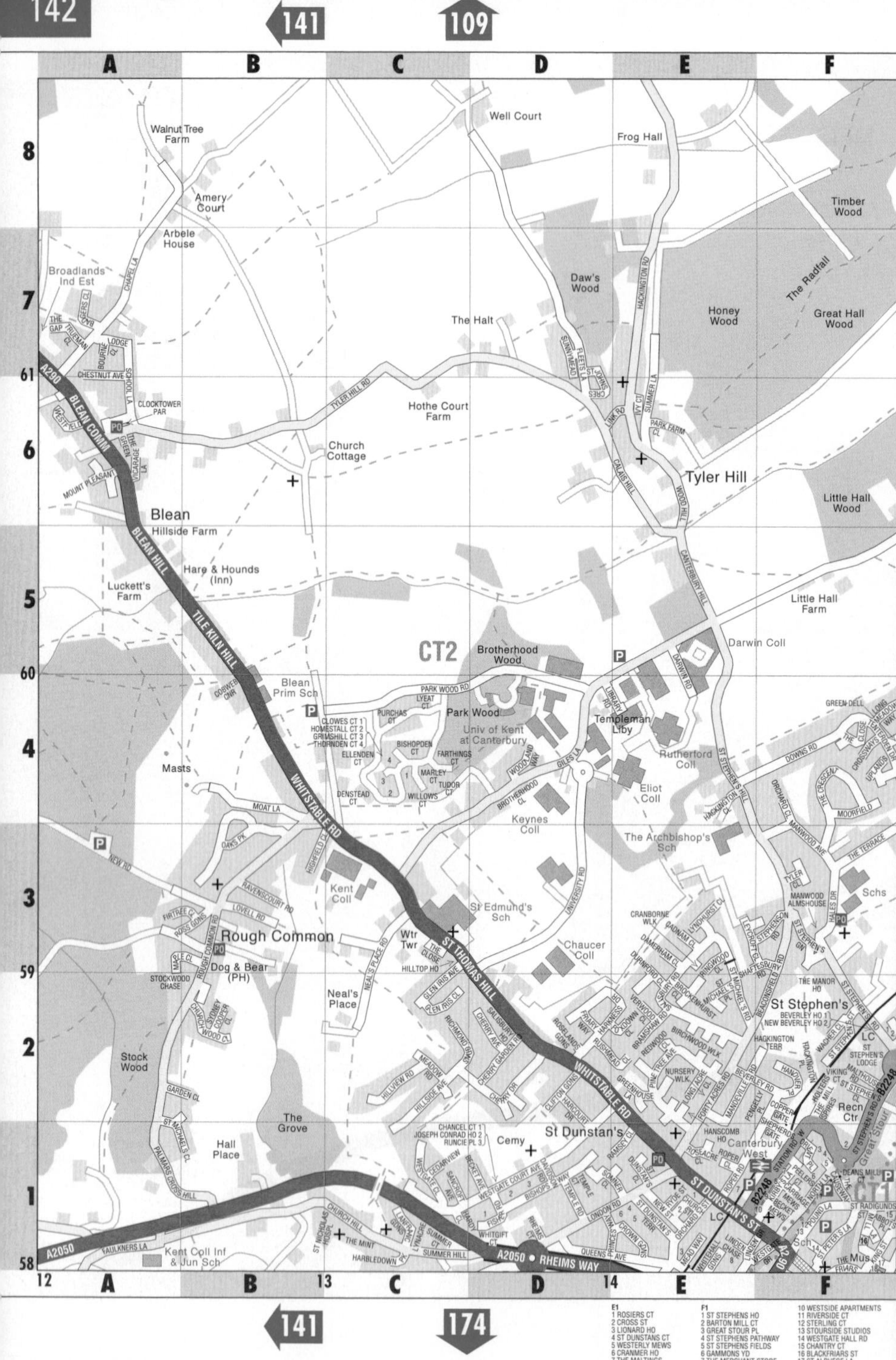

141
109

E1
1 ROSIERS CT
2 CROSS ST
3 LIONARD HO
4 ST DUNSTANS CT
5 WESTERLY MEWS
6 CRAMMER HO
7 THE MALTINGS
8 WESTGATE CT

F1
1 ST STEPHENS HO
2 BARTON MILL CT
3 GREAT STOUR PL
4 ST STEPHENS PATHWAY
5 ST STEPHENS FIELDS
6 GAMMONS YD
7 THE MERCHANT STORE
8 KIRBY'S HEIGHTS
9 TEMPLAR CT

10 WESTSIDE APARTMENTS
11 RIVERSIDE CT
12 STERLING CT
13 STOURSIDE STUDIOS
14 WESTGATE HALL RD
15 CHANTRY CT
16 BLACKFRIARS ST
17 ST ALPHEGE LA
18 THE CLOISTERS

141
174

A   B   C   D   E   F

8   7   61   6   5   60   4   3   59   2   1   58

Mayton Farm
Brookside
Langton Lodge
Nook Farm
Golden Lion (PH)
Foxhill House
Kemberland Wood
CT3
Sweech Farm
Broad Oak
Little Hall Wood
GOOSE FARM
Alcroft Grange
Barton Wood
BLUEBELL WOODS MOBILE HOME PK
Den Grove Wood
Sturry
CT2
DENGROVE CVN SITE
THE COPPICE
Shelford Farm
Brickhouse Wood
Broad Oak Lodge Farm
Sturry
Lib
Broadoak Crossing
Junior King's Sch
CHAFY CRES
FRANKLYN HO
Barton Down
Great Stour
WATER MDWS
MILL RD
George & Dragon Hotel
BROOKLANDS CL
1 HALSTEAD CL
2 FRENCHAM CL
Cvn Pk
Sewage Works
Maybrook Ind Est
P&R
Folly Farm
LC
Abbotsbury Hts
Hales Place
Vauxhall Lakes (Nature Reserve)
City Bsns Pk
Recn Gd
1 TENNYSON PL
2 TENNYSON PL
Chequers Wood
EAST ST
PARKSIDE PL
Stour Valley Wlk
Old Park Ct
Parkside Com Prim Sch
CT1
Mills
TA Ctr
Jesus Hospl
Cold Harbour
Old Park Farm
ALBUHERA SQ
Scotland Hills
Northgate
Sch
St Elisabeth
CANTERBURY
DVROVERNVM
CAMBRAI CT
BURMA CRES
Chaucer Wood Ct
Crown & City Cts
The Conduit Ho
SANGRO PL
SEVASTOPOL
Canterbury Christ Church Univ Coll (The Mount)
King's Sch
COLLEGE RD

A1
1 CLYDE ST
2 ALMA PL
3 NOTLEY TERR
4 UNION PL
5 LANFRANC HO
6 ST JOHN'S HOSPL
7 KINGS MEWS
8 HIGH ST
9 ST GREGORY'S
10 DRAGOON HO
11 ARTILLERY ST
12 ARTILLERY GDNS
13 ARTILLERY HO
14 DEAN CT
15 THE FORRENS
16 THE PRECINCTS
17 PALACE ST
18 COBDEN PL
19 HOMESPIRE HO
20 KNOTT'S LA
21 CHURCH LA
22 VICTORIA YD
B1
1 KNOWLTON WLK
2 JESSICA MEWS
3 PYOTT MEWS
4 PAYTON MEWS
5 PLUMPTON WLK
6 MANNOCK HO
7 THE RIDINGS
8 CRADDOCK DR
B2
1 METCALFE MEWS
2 GREEN CLOTH MEWS
3 GORE MEWS
4 ARRAN MEWS
5 MARY GREEN WLK
6 CALCRAFT MEWS
7 KEYWORTH MEWS
8 ANNE GREEN WLK
9 GILLON MEWS
10 HALLETT WLK
11 PETCHELL MEWS
12 REMSTON MEWS
13 WEMYSS CT
14 WEMYSS HO
15 ANZIO HO
16 CASSINO HO
17 MALTA HO

143
111

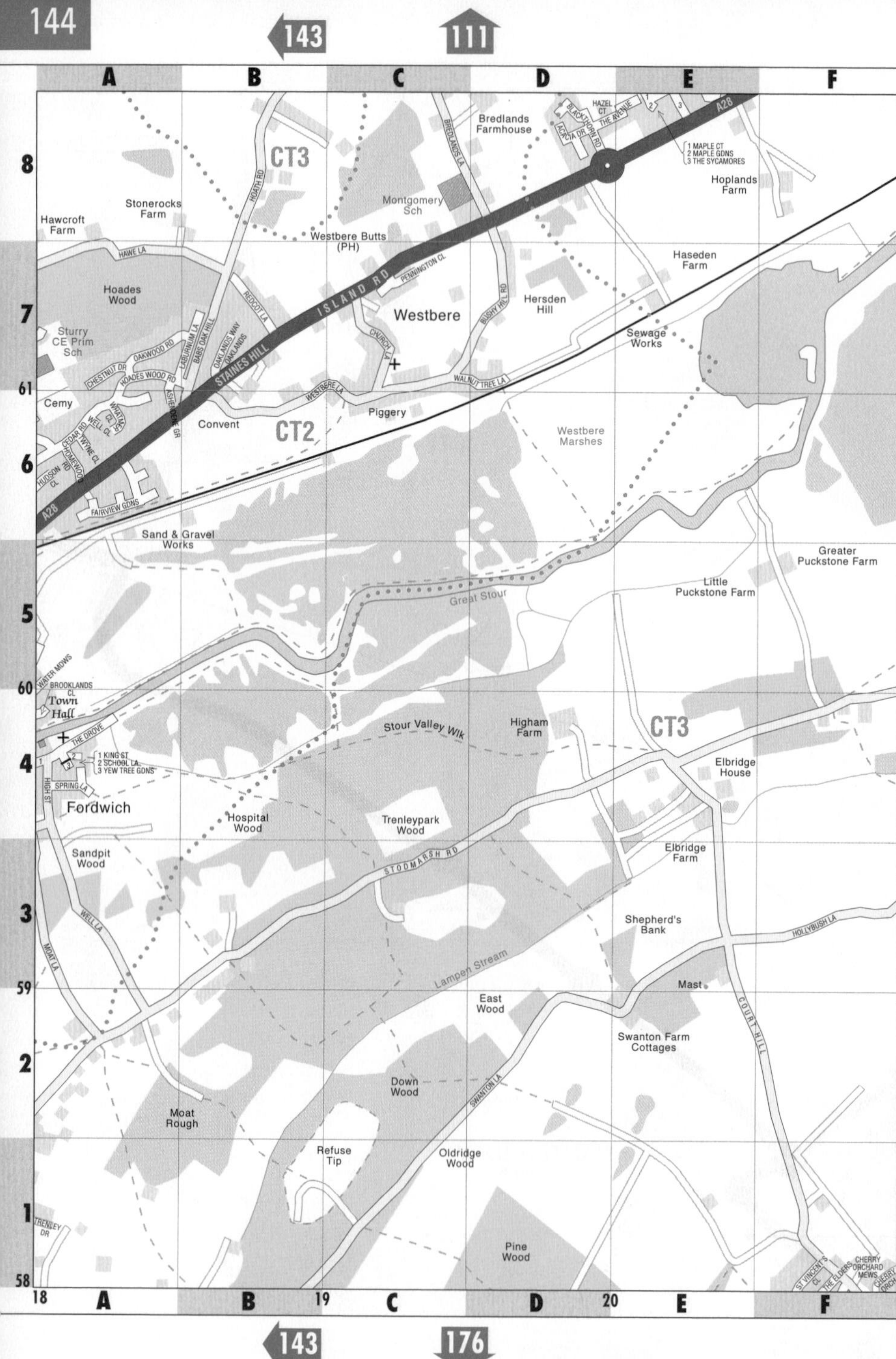
A
B
C
D
E
F
8
7
61
6
5
60
4
3
59
2
1
58
18
19
20
CT3
CT2
A28
Hawcroft Farm
Stonerocks Farm
Montgomery Sch
Westbere Butts (PH)
Bredlands Farmhouse
Hoplands Farm
1 MAPLE CT
2 MAPLE GDNS
3 THE SYCAMORES
HAZEL CT
THE AVENUE
BLACKTHORN RD
ACACIA DR
BREDLANDS LA
HOATH RD
HAWE LA
Hoades Wood
Sturry CE Prim Sch
Haseden Farm
Westbere
Hersden Hill
Sewage Works
ISLAND RD
STAINES HILL
PENNINGTON CL
REDCOT LA
CHURCH LA
BUSHY HILL RD
WALNUT TREE LA
WESTBERE LA
Cemy
Convent
Piggery
Westbere Marshes
CHESTNUT DR
OAKWOOD RD
HOADES WOOD RD
LABURNUM LA
BABS OAK HILL
OAKLANDS WAY
OAKLANDS
ASHENDEN GR
CEDAR RD
WELL CL
WHATMER CL
TWYNE CL
HOMEWOOD RD
HUDSON CL
FAIRVIEW GDNS
Sand & Gravel Works
Greater Puckstone Farm
Little Puckstone Farm
Great Stour
WATER MDWS
BROOKLANDS CL
Town Hall
THE DROVE
Stour Valley Wlk
Higham Farm
Elbridge House
1 KING ST
2 SCHOOL LA
3 YEW TREE GDNS
SPRING LA
HIGH ST
Fordwich
Hospital Wood
Trenleypark Wood
Elbridge Farm
Sandpit Wood
STODMARSH RD
WELL LA
Shepherd's Bank
HOLLYBUSH LA
MOAT LA
Lampen Stream
Mast
East Wood
COURT HILL
Swanton Farm Cottages
Down Wood
SWANTON LA
Moat Rough
Refuse Tip
Oldridge Wood
TRENLEY DR
Pine Wood
ST VINCENT'S CL
THE ELDERS
CHERRY ORCHARD MEWS
CHERRY ORCH

143
176

112
146

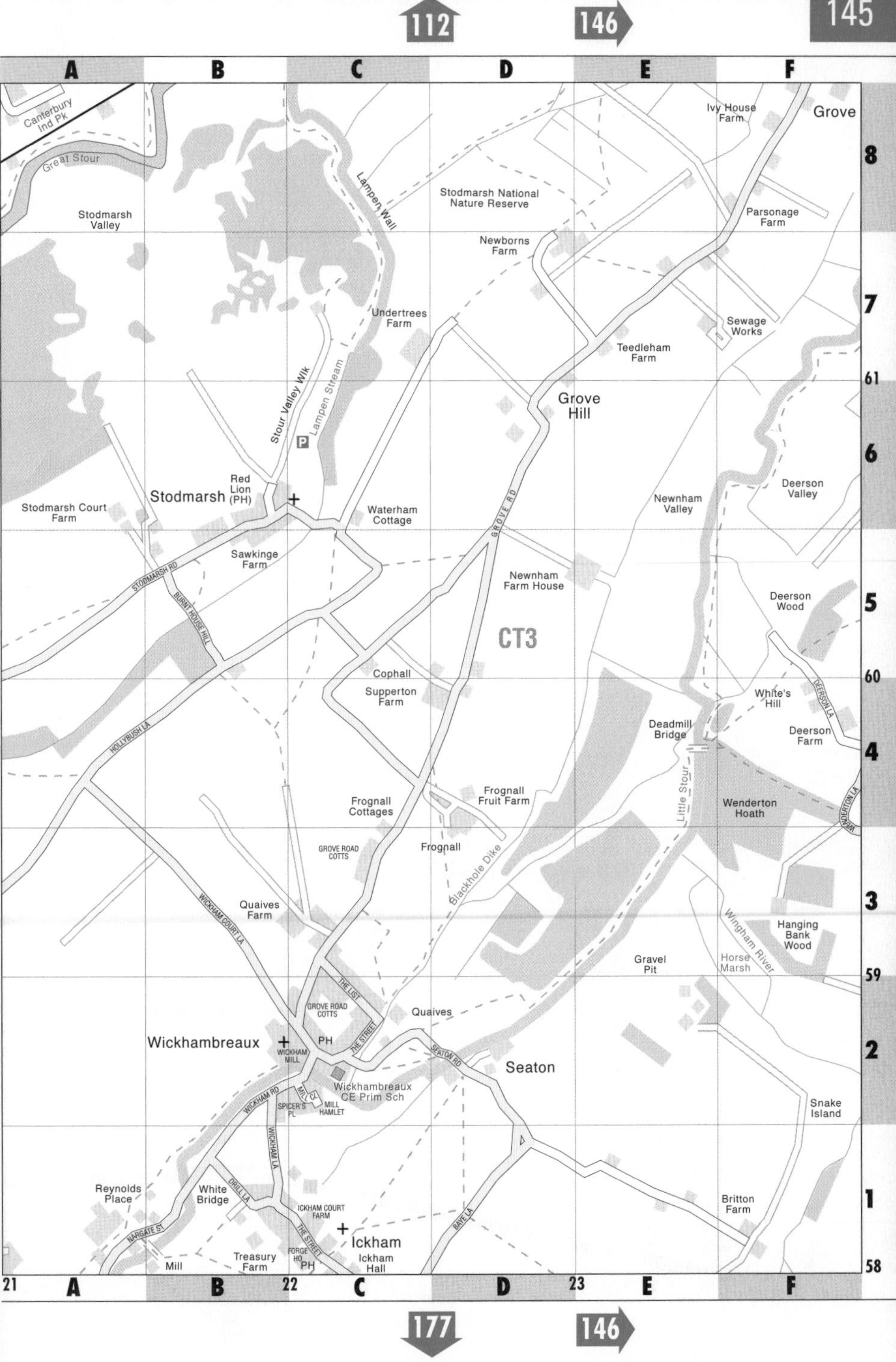
A B C D E F
Canterbury Ind Pk
Great Stour
Stodmarsh Valley
Lampen Wall
Stodmarsh National Nature Reserve
Ivy House Farm
Grove
8
Parsonage Farm
Newborns Farm
Undertrees Farm
Sewage Works
Teedleham Farm
7
61
Grove Hill
Stour Valley Wlk
Lampen Stream
6
Red Lion (PH)
Stodmarsh
Stodmarsh Court Farm
Waterham Cottage
Deerson Valley
Newnham Valley
GROVE RD
Sawkinge Farm
STODMARSH RD
BURNT HOUSE HILL
Newnham Farm House
Deerson Wood
5
CT3
Cophall
Supperton Farm
60
White's Hill
DEERSON LA
Deadmill Bridge
Deerson Farm
HOLLYBUSH LA
4
Little Stour
Frognall Fruit Farm
Frognall Cottages
Wenderton Hoath
WENDERTON LA
GROVE ROAD COTTS
Frognall
Blackhole Dike
WICKHAM COURT LA
Quaives Farm
3
Wingham River
Hanging Bank Wood
Gravel Pit
Horse Marsh
59
THE LIST
GROVE ROAD COTTS
Quaives
Wickhambreaux
WICKHAM MILL
PH
THE STREET
SEATON RD
Seaton
2
Wickhambreaux CE Prim Sch
WICKHAM RD
MILL CL
SPICER'S PL
MILL HAMLET
Snake Island
WICKHAM LA
Reynolds Place
White Bridge
DRILL LA
ICKHAM COURT FARM
Ickham
BAYE LA
Britton Farm
1
MARGATE ST
THE STREET
Mill
Treasury Farm
FORGE HO
PH
Ickham Hall
58
21 A B 22 C D 23 E F

177
146

145
113

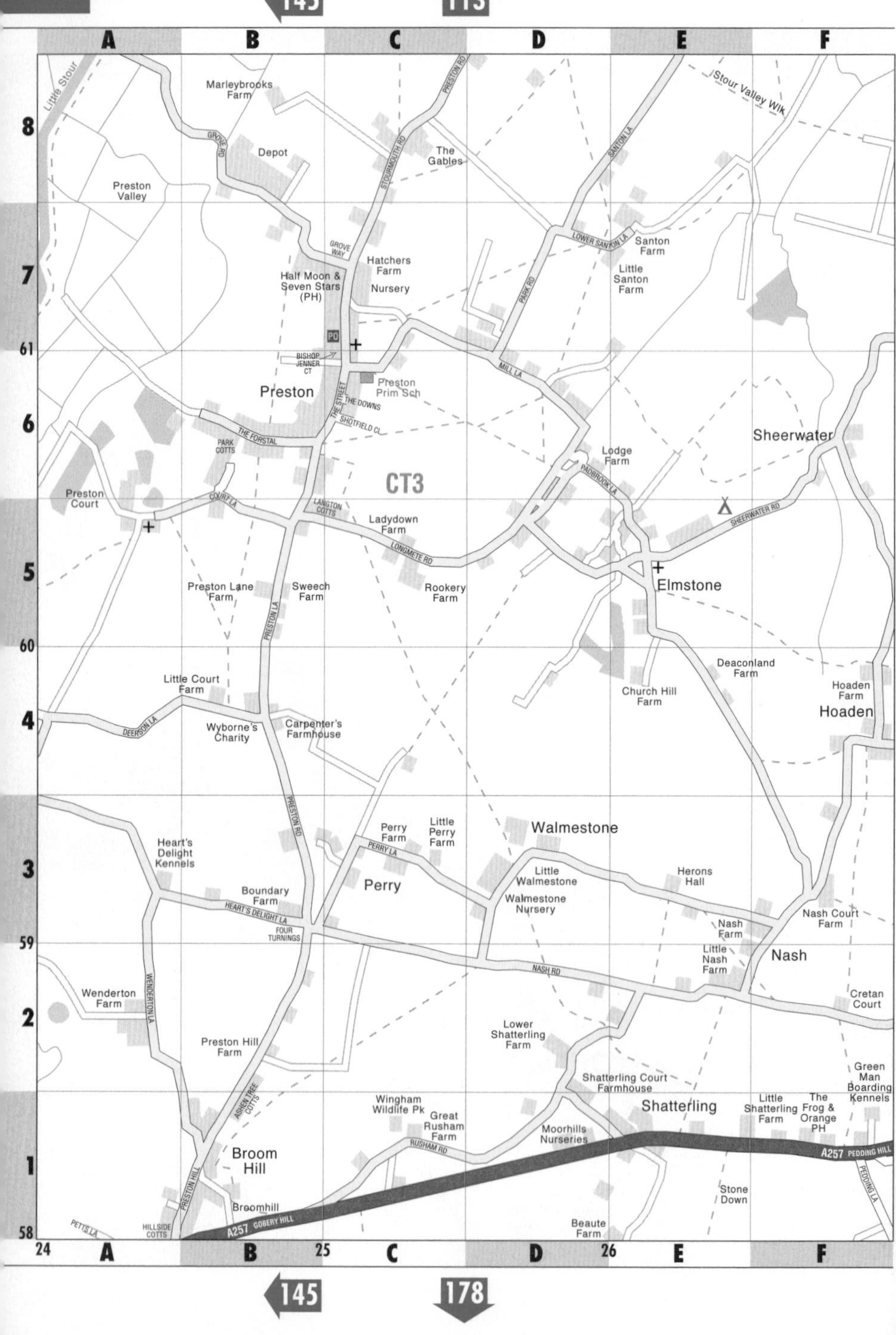
Marleybrooks Farm
Depot
Preston Valley
The Gables
Stour Valley Wlk
Hatchers Farm
Half Moon & Seven Stars (PH)
Nursery
Santon Farm
Little Santon Farm
Preston
Preston Prim Sch
Sheerwater
Lodge Farm
CT3
Preston Court
Ladydown Farm
Elmstone
Preston Lane Farm
Sweech Farm
Rookery Farm
Deaconland Farm
Church Hill Farm
Hoaden Farm
Hoaden
Little Court Farm
Wyborne's Charity
Carpenter's Farmhouse
Walmestone
Perry Farm
Little Perry Farm
Heart's Delight Kennels
Little Walmestone
Herons Hall
Perry
Boundary Farm
Walmestone Nursery
Nash Court Farm
Nash Farm
Little Nash Farm
Nash
Wenderton Farm
Cretan Court
Lower Shatterling Farm
Preston Hill Farm
Green Man Boarding Kennels
Shatterling Court Farmhouse
Shatterling
Wingham Wildlife Pk
Great Rusham Farm
Little Shatterling Farm
The Frog & Orange PH
Moorhills Nurseries
Broom Hill
Broomhill
Stone Down
Beaute Farm
A257 GOBERY HILL
A257 PEDDING HILL
PRESTON RD
STOURMOUTH RD
GROVE RD
SANTON LA
LOWER SANTON LA
PARK RD
MILL LA
THE STREET
THE DOWNS
SHOTFIELD CL
THE FORSTAL
PADBROOK LA
SHEERWATER RD
COURT LA
LONGMETE RD
PRESTON LA
DEERSON LA
PERRY LA
HEART'S DELIGHT LA
FOUR TURNINGS
NASH RD
WENDERTON LA
ASHEN TREE COTTS
RUSHAM RD
PRESTON HILL
HILLSIDE COTTS
PETTS LA
PEDDING LA
GROVE WAY
BISHOP JENNER CT
PARK COTTS
LANGTON COTTS
Little Stour
A B C D E F
8 7 61 6 5 60 4 3 59 2 1 58
24 25 26

145
178

114 146

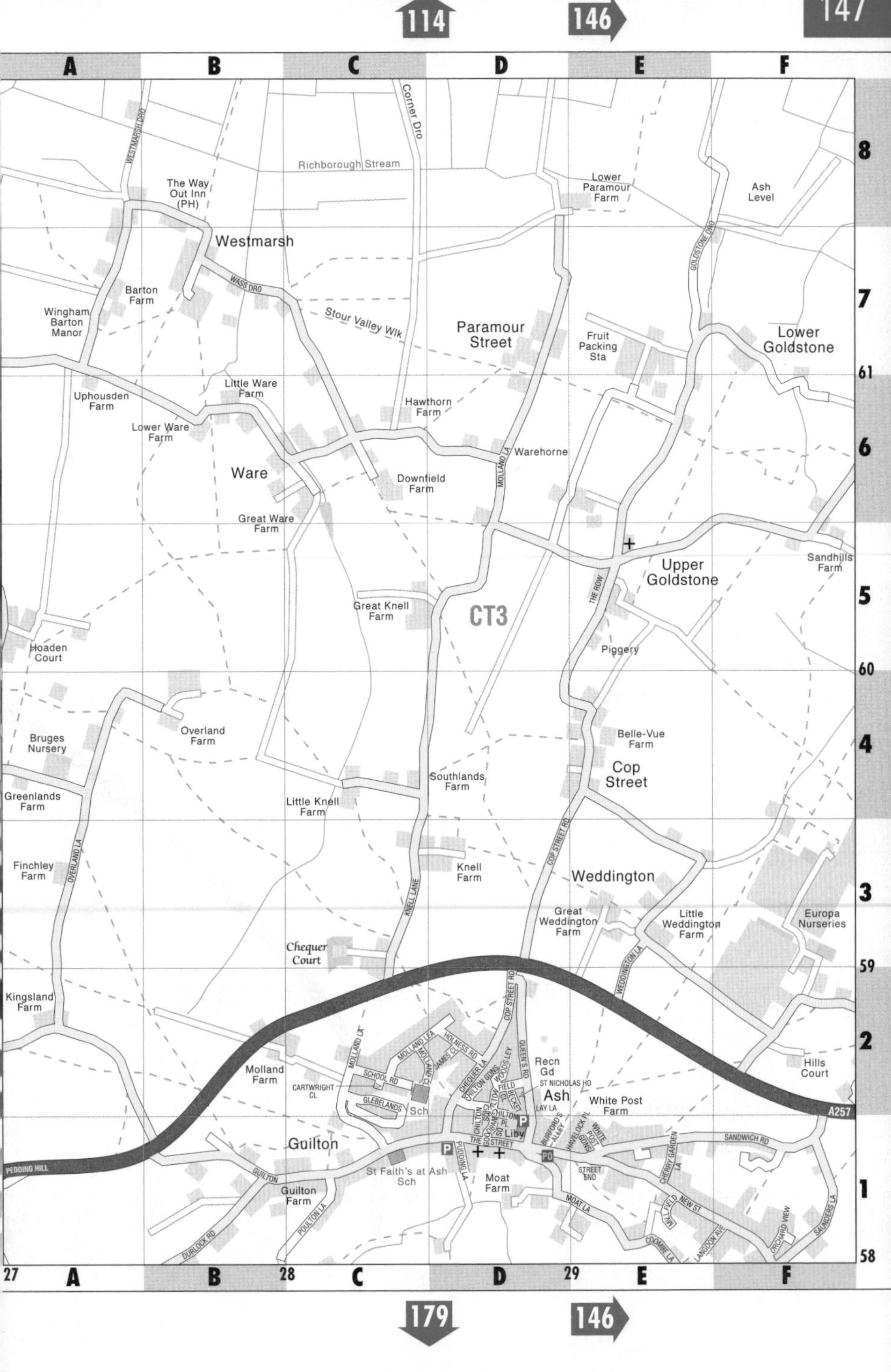

A B C D E F
8 7 61 6 5 60 4 3 59 2 1 58
27 28 29
Corner Dro
Richborough Stream
WESTMARSH DRO
The Way Out Inn (PH)
Westmarsh
WASS DRO
Barton Farm
Wingham Barton Manor
Stour Valley Wlk
Lower Paramour Farm
Ash Level
GOLDSTONE DRO
Paramour Street
Fruit Packing Sta
Lower Goldstone
Uphousden Farm
Little Ware Farm
Hawthorn Farm
Lower Ware Farm
Warehorne
MOLLAND LA
Ware
Downfield Farm
Great Ware Farm
Upper Goldstone
Sandhills Farm
THE ROW
Great Knell Farm
CT3
Hoaden Court
Piggery
Overland Farm
Bruges Nursery
Belle-Vue Farm
Cop Street
Southlands Farm
Greenlands Farm
Little Knell Farm
COP STREET RD
Finchley Farm
OVERLAND LA
Knell Farm
Weddington
KNELL LANE
Great Weddington Farm
Little Weddington Farm
Europa Nurseries
Chequer Court
WEDDINGTON LA
Kingsland Farm
COP STREET RD
MOLLAND LA
MOLLAND LEA
HOLNESS RD
JAMES CL
WOODS LEY
QUEEN'S RD
Recn Gd
Hills Court
Molland Farm
SCHOOL RD
CARTWRIGHT CL
CHEQUER LA
CHILTON GDNS
FIELD CL
BECKET CL
ST NICHOLAS HO
Ash
White Post Farm
A257
GLEBELANDS
Sch
LAY LA
HAVELOCK PL
WHITE POST GDNS
BURFORD'S ALLEY
Liby
THE STREET
SANDWICH RD
Guilton
PUDDING LA
PO
CHERRY GARDEN LA
PEDDING HILL
St Faith's at Ash Sch
STREET END
GUILTON
Guilton Farm
Moat Farm
MOAT LA
NEW ST
MILL FIELD
POULTON LA
DURLOCK RD
COOMBE LA
LANGDON AVE
ORCHARD VIEW
SAUNDERS LA

179 146

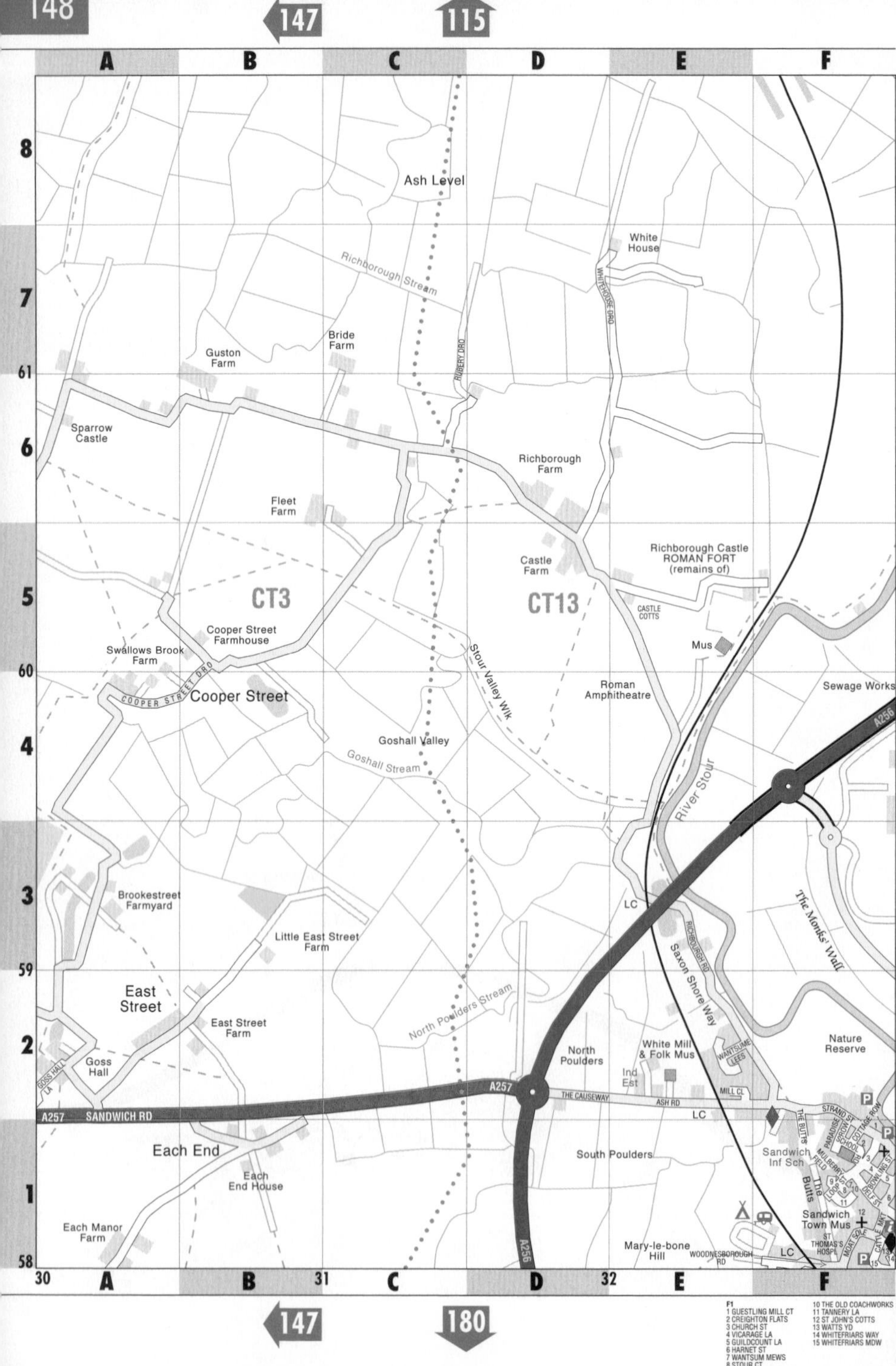

147
115

Ash Level

White House

Richborough Stream

Bride Farm

Guston Farm

Sparrow Castle

Fleet Farm

Richborough Farm

Castle Farm

Richborough Castle ROMAN FORT (remains of)

CASTLE COTTS

CT3

CT13

Cooper Street Farmhouse

Swallows Brook Farm

COOPER STREET DRO

Cooper Street

Goshall Valley

Goshall Stream

Stour Valley Wlk

Mus

Roman Amphitheatre

Sewage Works

A256

River Stour

Brookestreet Farmyard

Little East Street Farm

LC

The Monks' Wall

East Street

East Street Farm

North Poulders Stream

North Poulders

White Mill & Folk Mus

Ind Est

Saxon Shore Way

LC

Nature Reserve

Goss Hall

A257   SANDWICH RD

A257

South Poulders

THE CAUSEWAY

ASH RD

LC

Sandwich Inf Sch

The Butts

Each End

Each End House

Mary-le-bone Hill

WOODNESBOROUGH RD

Sandwich Town Mus

Each Manor Farm

A256

116

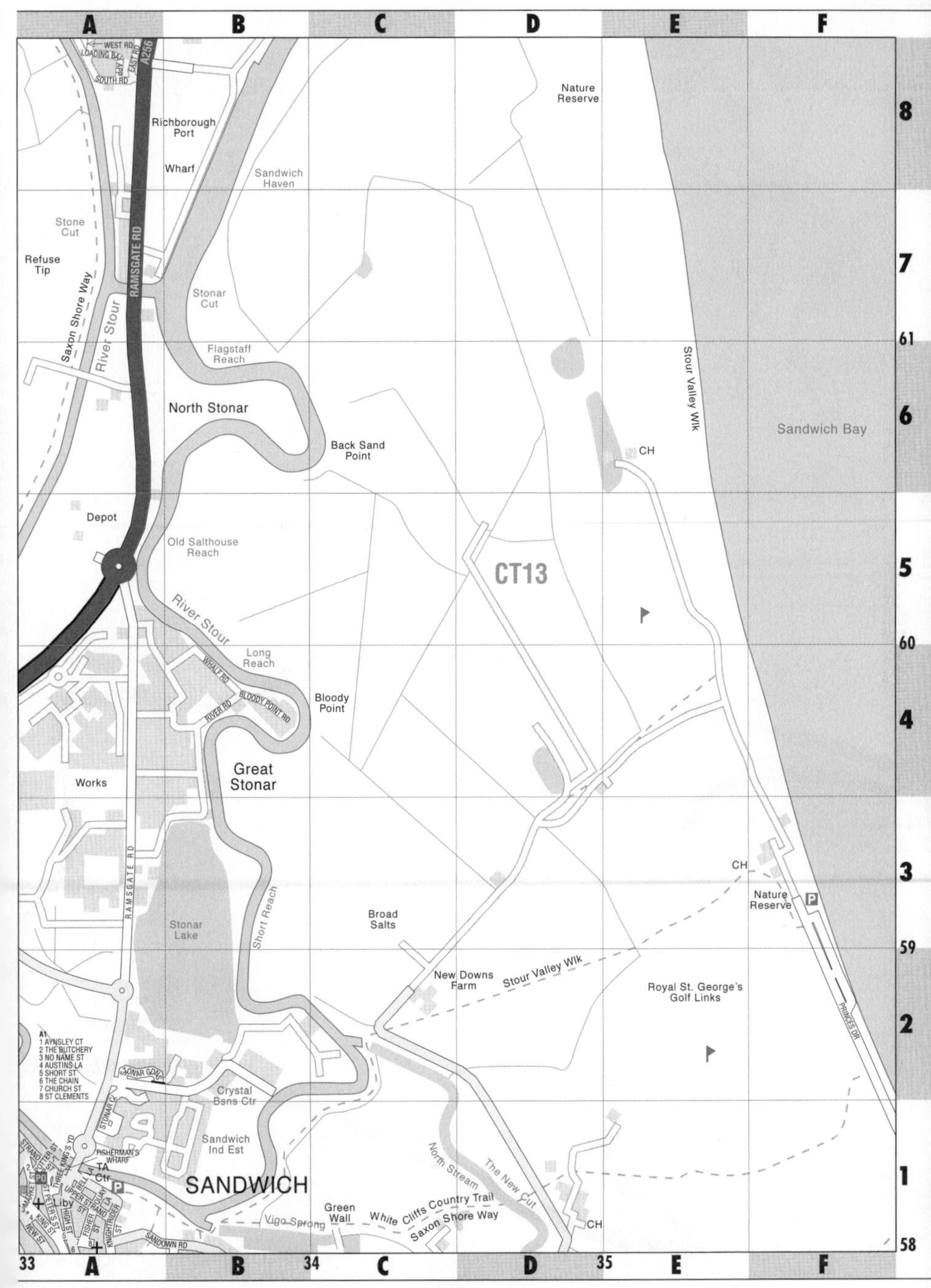

A
B
C
D
E
F
WEST RD
LOADING BAY APP
EAST RD
A256
SOUTH RD
Richborough Port
Wharf
Sandwich Haven
Nature Reserve
8
Stone Cut
Refuse Tip
RAMSGATE RD
7
Saxon Shore Way
River Stour
Stonar Cut
Flagstaff Reach
61
Stour Valley Wlk
North Stonar
6
Sandwich Bay
Back Sand Point
CH
Depot
Old Salthouse Reach
CT13
5
River Stour
60
Long Reach
WHALF RD
BLOODY POINT RD
RIVER RD
Bloody Point
4
Great Stonar
Works
RAMSGATE RD
CH
3
Nature Reserve
Broad Salts
Stonar Lake
Short Reach
59
New Downs Farm
Stour Valley Wlk
Royal St. George's Golf Links
2
PRINCES DR
A1
1 AYNSLEY CT
2 THE BUTCHERY
3 NO NAME ST
4 AUSTINS LA
5 SHORT ST
6 THE CHAIN
7 CHURCH ST
8 ST CLEMENTS
SONAR GDNS
Crystal Bsns Ctr
Sandwich Ind Est
FISHERMAN'S WHARF
TA Ctr
North Stream
The New Cut
1
SANDWICH
Liby
Green Wall
White Cliffs Country Trail
Saxon Shore Way
Vigo Sprong
CH
SANDOWN RD
58
33
34
35

181

118

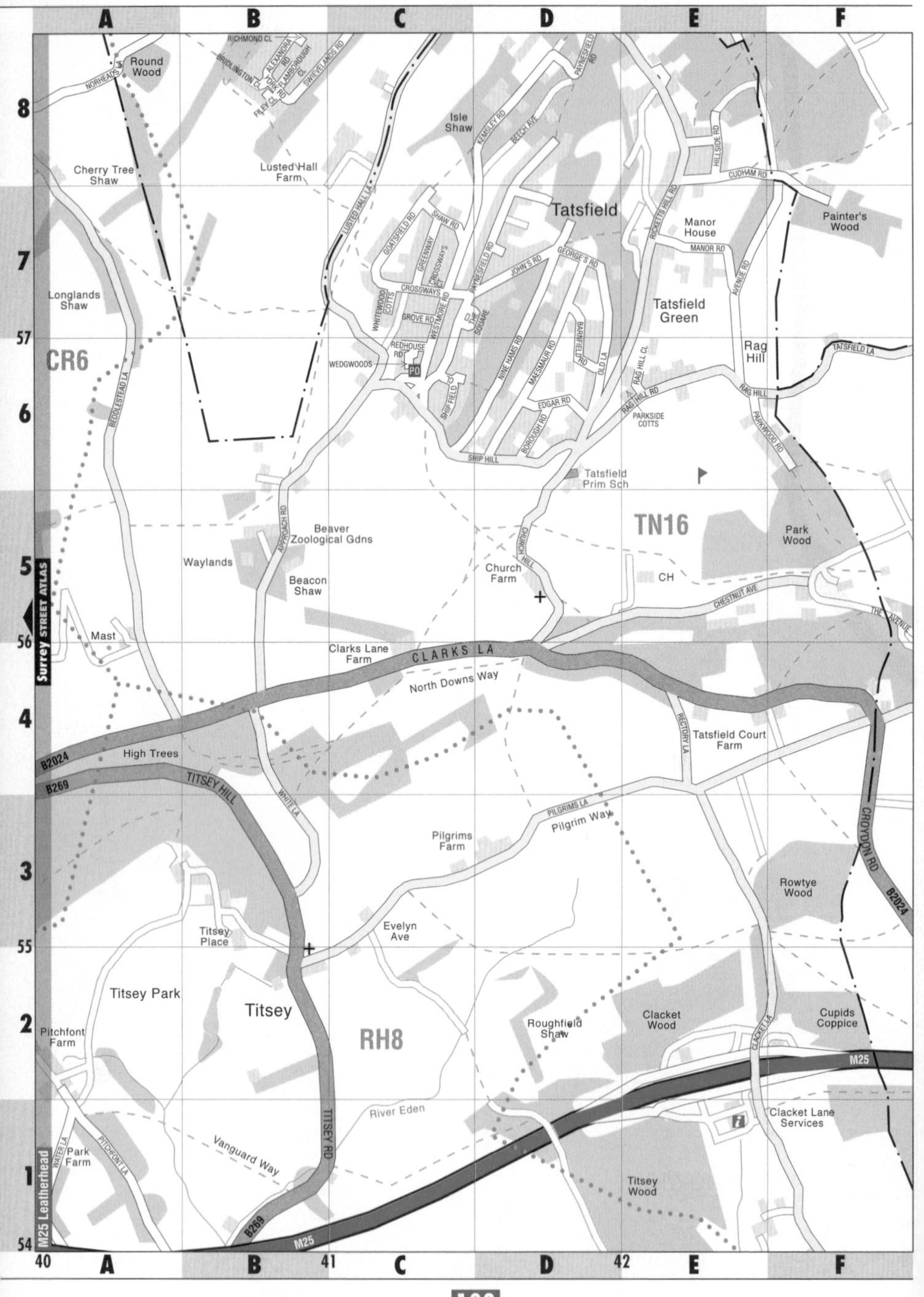

A
B
C
D
E
F
8
7
6
5
4
3
2
1
57
56
55
54
40
41
42
Round Wood
Isle Shaw
Cherry Tree Shaw
Lusted Hall Farm
Tatsfield
Manor House
Painter's Wood
Longlands Shaw
Tatsfield Green
Rag Hill
CR6
WEDGWOODS
PO
Tatsfield Prim Sch
TN16
Beaver Zoological Gdns
Park Wood
Waylands
Church Farm
CH
Beacon Shaw
Mast
Clarks Lane Farm
CLARKS LA
North Downs Way
Tatsfield Court Farm
High Trees
B2024
B269
TITSEY HILL
Pilgrims Farm
Pilgrim Way
PILGRIMS LA
Rowtye Wood
CROYDON RD
Titsey Place
Evelyn Ave
Titsey Park
Titsey
RH8
Roughfield Shaw
Clacket Wood
Cupids Coppice
Pitchfont Farm
M25
River Eden
Clacket Lane Services
Park Farm
Vanguard Way
Titsey Wood
TITSEY RD
Surrey STREET ATLAS
M25 Leatherhead

183

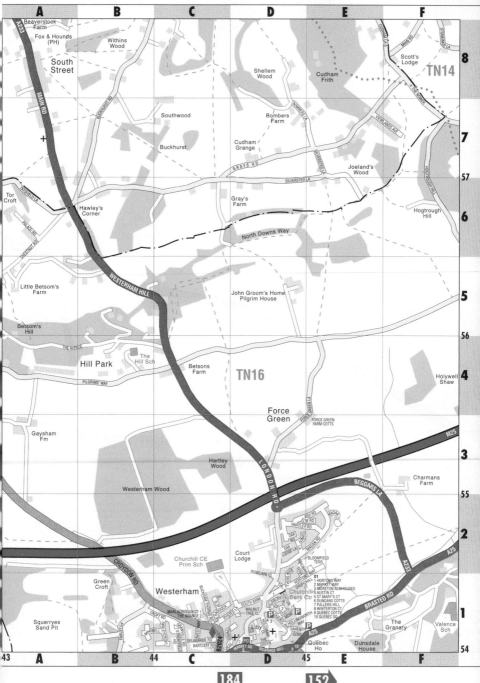
119

152

A
B
C
D
E
F
8
7
57
6
5
56
4
3
55
2
1
54
43
44
45
Beaverstock Farm
Fox & Hounds (PH)
South Street
Withins Wood
Shellem Wood
Cudham Frith
Scott's Lodge
TN14
MAIN RD
A233
BUCKHURST RD
Southwood
Bombers Farm
BOMBERS LA
VIEWLANDS AVE
THE NOWER
CUDHAM LA S
MAIN RD
STONEINGS LA
Buckhurst
Cudham Grange
GRAYS RD
SILVERSTED LA
Joeland's Wood
HOGTROUGH HILL
Tor Croft
TATSFIELD LA
Hawley's Corner
Gray's Farm
Hogtrough Hill
PALACE RD
CHESTNUT AVE
North Downs Way
WESTERHAM HILL
Little Betsom's Farm
John Groom's Home
Pilgrim House
Betsom's Hill
THE AVENUE
The Hill Sch
Hill Park
Betsons Farm
TN16
PILGRIMS' WAY
Holywell Shaw
Force Green
FORCE GREEN LA
FORCE GREEN FARM COTTS
Gaysham Fm
M25
Hartley Wood
LONDON RD
Charmans Farm
BEGGARS LA
Westerham Wood
ASH RD
ELM RD
MADAN CL
HARTLEY RD
OAK RD
SAND LA
MADAN RD
OAK LODGE LA
Court Lodge
Churchill CE Prim Sch
BLOOMFIELD TERR
CROYDON RD
A233
A25
ROSELARE CL
RAILWAY TERR
HORTONS WAY
THE PLYERS WAY
CHURCHILL CT
Churchill Bsns Ctr
D1
1 HORTONS WAY
2 MARKET WAY
3 MORETON ALMHOUSES
4 AUSTIN CT
5 ST MARY'S CT
6 DUNCANS COTTS
7 FULLERS HILL
8 WINTERTON CT
9 QUEBEC COTTS
10 QUEBEC SQ
Green Croft
Westerham
BUCKHAM THORNS RD
THE SLIP
THE PADDOCK
SOUTH BANK
WALNUT TREE CL
RYSTED LA
QUEBEC AVE
COSTELLS MDW
HOLLINGWORTH WAY
BRASTED RD
MARLBOROUGH CT 1
THE GRANGE 2
CROFT RD
Squerryes Sand Pit
FARLEY LA
FARLEYCROFT
MARWELL
GRANVILLE RD
STREATFIELD HO
WESTWAYS
DELAGARDE RD
BARTLETT RD
B2024
Liby
HOLCOMBE CL
THE GREEN
MARKET SQ
VICARAGE HILL
DARENTH GDNS
PO
P
Quebec Ho
Dunsdale House
The Granary
Valence Sch

184

152

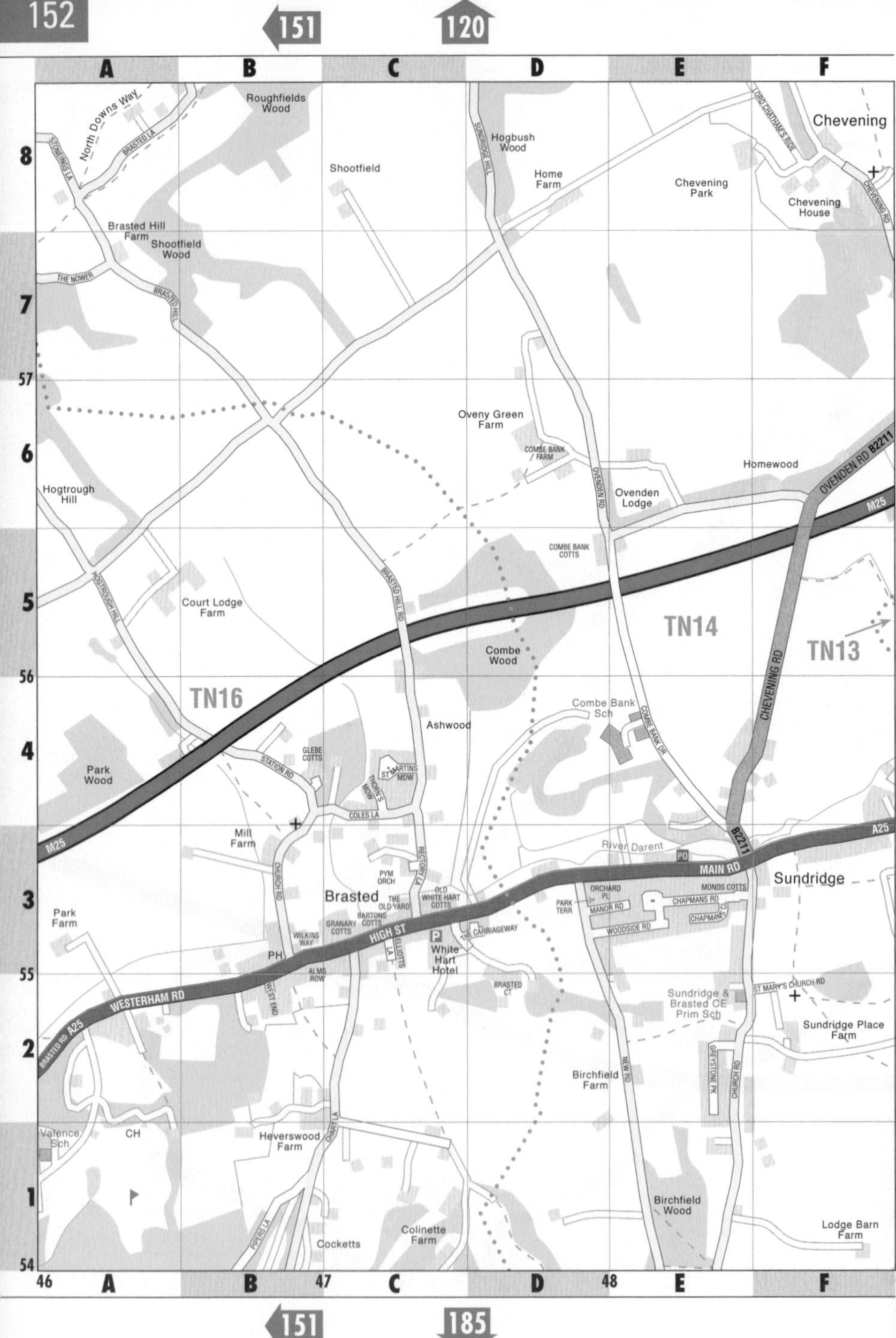

151
120

8

7

57

6

5

56

4

3

55

2

1

54

A   B   C   D   E   F

North Downs Way
Roughfields Wood
STONEHOUSE LA
BRASTED LA

Shootfield

Hogbush Wood
BUNKERS HILL

Chevening

LORD DERMAN'S SIDE

Home Farm

Chevening Park

Chevening House

CHEVENING RD

Brasted Hill Farm
Shootfield Wood

THE HOWER
BRASTED HILL

Oveny Green Farm

COMBE BANK FARM

Homewood

OVENDEN RD B2211

Hogtrough Hill

WOODSIDE HILL

COMBE BANK COTTS

Ovenden Lodge

CHEVENING RD

M25

Court Lodge Farm

BRASTED HILL RD

TN14

TN13

TN16

Combe Wood

Ashwood

Combe Bank Sch

COMBE BANK DR

M25

Park Wood

STATION RD
GLEBE COTTS

ST MARTINS MDW
THE THRIFTS MDW

COLES LA

River Darent

MAIN RD

Sundridge

A25

B2211

Mill Farm

CHURCH RD

PYM ORCH

RECTORY LA

THE OLD WHITE HART COTTS

ORCHARD PL

MANOR RD

CHAPMANS RD

CHAPMAN

PO

Park Farm

Brasted

WILKINS WAY

BARTONS COTTS
GRANARY COTTS

THE OLD YARD

PARK TERR
WOODSIDE RD

MONDS COTTS

HIGH ST

PH

ALMS ROW

WEST END

P

WHITE HART COTTS
THE CARRIAGEWAY

White Hart Hotel

BRASTED CT

Sundridge & Brasted CE Prim Sch

ST MARY'S CHURCH RD

Sundridge Place Farm

GREYSTONE PK
RD HOMEFIELD

WESTERHAM RD

BRASTED RD A25

Birchfield Farm

NEW RD

Valence Sch

CH

Heverswood Farm

CHART LA

Birchfield Wood

Lodge Barn Farm

Cocketts

Colinette Farm

PIPER'S LA

46   A   B   47   C   D   48   E   F   54

151
185

121 154

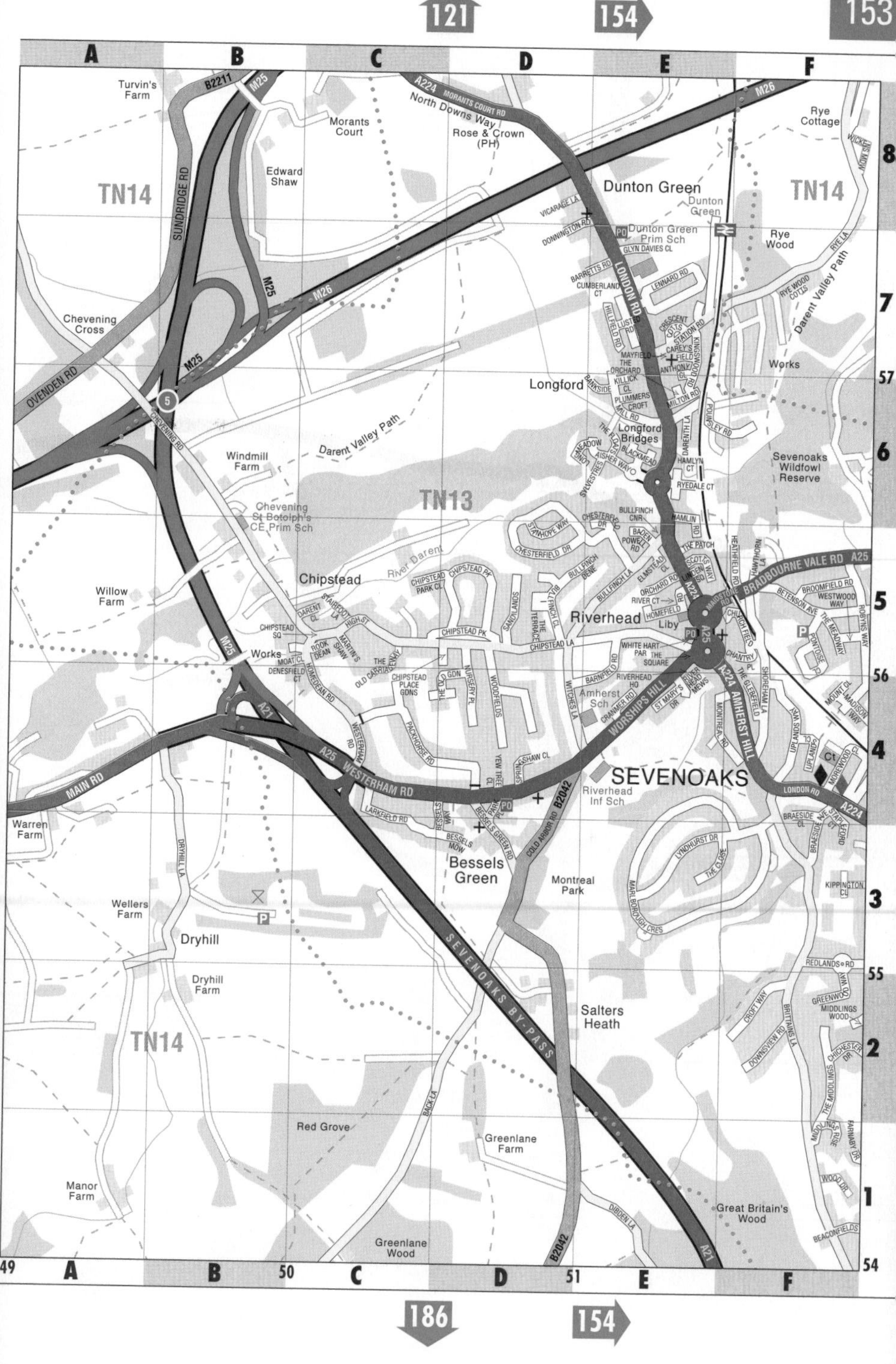
A B C D E F
Turvin's Farm
Morants Court
Edward Shaw
North Downs Way
Rose & Crown (PH)
MORANTS COURT RD
TN14
Dunton Green
Dunton Green Prim Sch
Rye Cottage
Rye Wood
Chevening Cross
OVENDEN RD
SUNDRIDGE RD
LONDON RD
Longford
Longford Bridges
Works
Darent Valley Path
Windmill Farm
TN13
Sevenoaks Wildfowl Reserve
Chevening St Botolph's CE Prim Sch
Chipstead
River Darent
Willow Farm
Riverhead
BRADBOURNE VALE RD
Works
WESTERHAM RD
MAIN RD
SEVENOAKS
Amherst Sch
Riverhead Inf Sch
WORSHIPS HILL
AMHERST HILL
Warren Farm
Bessels Green
Montreal Park
Wellers Farm
Dryhill
Dryhill Farm
SEVENOAKS BY-PASS
Salters Heath
TN14
Red Grove
Greenlane Farm
Manor Farm
Great Britain's Wood
Greenlane Wood
49 50 51 54
55 56 57
1 2 3 4 5 6 7 8

186 154

153 122

A B C D E F

8

7

57

6

56

5

4

55

3

2

1

54

52 A B 53 C D 54 E F

153 187

River Darent
Sevenoaks Wildfowl Reserve
Childsbridge Farm
Vestry Cotts
Jubilee Cotts
Riverside Ret Pk
Ind Est
TN14
OTFORD RD
The Moor Rd
Swanzy Rd
Crampton's Rd
Coombe Ct
Garwick Way
Waterworks Cotts
Bat & Ball Ent Ctr
Sevenoaks Bsns Ctr
Bat & Ball
Great Oaks
The Shellings
Sealcroft Cotts
Seal CE Prim Sch
Zambra Way
Cemy
Greatness
Highlands Pk
SEAL RD
Pinewood Ave
The Wildernesse Sch
HIGH ST
Liby
A25
Camden Terr 1
Johnsons Ct 2
Seal Ho 3
School Cotts 4
Church Rd 5
Zion St 6
Pudding La 7
Bretaneby 8
The Bradbourne Sch
Bradbourne Farm
BRADBOURNE VALE RD
A25
Wealden Ct
Sevenoaks Liby
H
St James's Rd
St John's
Sevenoaks Prim Sch
Walthamstow Hall (Nursery Unit)
Camden Rd
Davis
Westfield
Hillingdon Ave
The Crescent
Dorton House Sch
Dorton House Sch (for The Blind)
1 Park Ho
2 Athill Ct
3 The Glen Dunlop Ho
4 Wood Lodge (Grange)
5 Ferndale
6 St John's Ct
Linden Chase
TN13
Betenson Ave
Cavendish Ave
Hill Crest
Meadow Cl
Lake View Rd
Clock House La
Woodside Rd
The Glade
Charterhouse Dr
Quaker La
ST JOHN'S HILL
Barrack Cnr
Tockwith Rd
St John's CE Prim Sch
Wildernesse
SEAL HOLLOW RD
Woodland Rise
TN15
Serpentine Ct
Hillborough Ave
The Old Timber Top Cotts
The Acorns
The Granville Sch
Kirkcourt Rd
Mount Harry Rd
Hitchen Hatch La
Chestnut Rd
Ashley Rd
Vine Ave
Walthamstow Hall
Hollybush La
The Paddock
Parkfield
Buckhall La
A224
Quarry Cotts
Littlecourt Rd
The Mews
Royal Pde
DARTFORD RD
B2020
Avenue Rd
Vine Lodge
Blackhall
Duchess Plantation
Courtwood Dr
Station Par
Sevenoaks
Granville Ct
TUBS HILL
ST BOTOLPH'S RD
Park View
Plymouth Dr
CH
SEVENOAKS
Yeomans Mdw
Redlands Rd
Middlings Wood
Birch Pl
Claret Ho
Eardley Rd
Oak Lodge
Gordon Rd
Clarendon Rd
Clarendon Ct
Pembroke Rd
Blights
LONDON RD
The Old Court Yd
Lady Boswell's CE Prim Sch
Godden Wood
Kippington
Beacon Rise
Clendon Farm
Grassy La
Oakfields
St Nicholas Ct
Park La
St Thomas RC Prim Sch
Rockdale
HIGH ST
A224
A25
Mus Liby
Buckhurst Ave
Webb's Mdw
Hoopers Yd
Almshouses
Sevenoaks Sch
Sevenoaks Sch Int Ctr
Webb's Alley
Knole Park (Deer Park)
Greensand Way
Knole House
Knole La
1 Oastfield Ct
2 Blights Ho
3 Blights Wlk
4 Brewery La
5 Bank St
6 Black's Yd
7 Dorset St
8 The Shambles
9 Lock's Yd
10 Park Cotts
1 Richmond Ct 3
2 Marlow Ct 4
1 Eton Ct
3 Hanley Ct

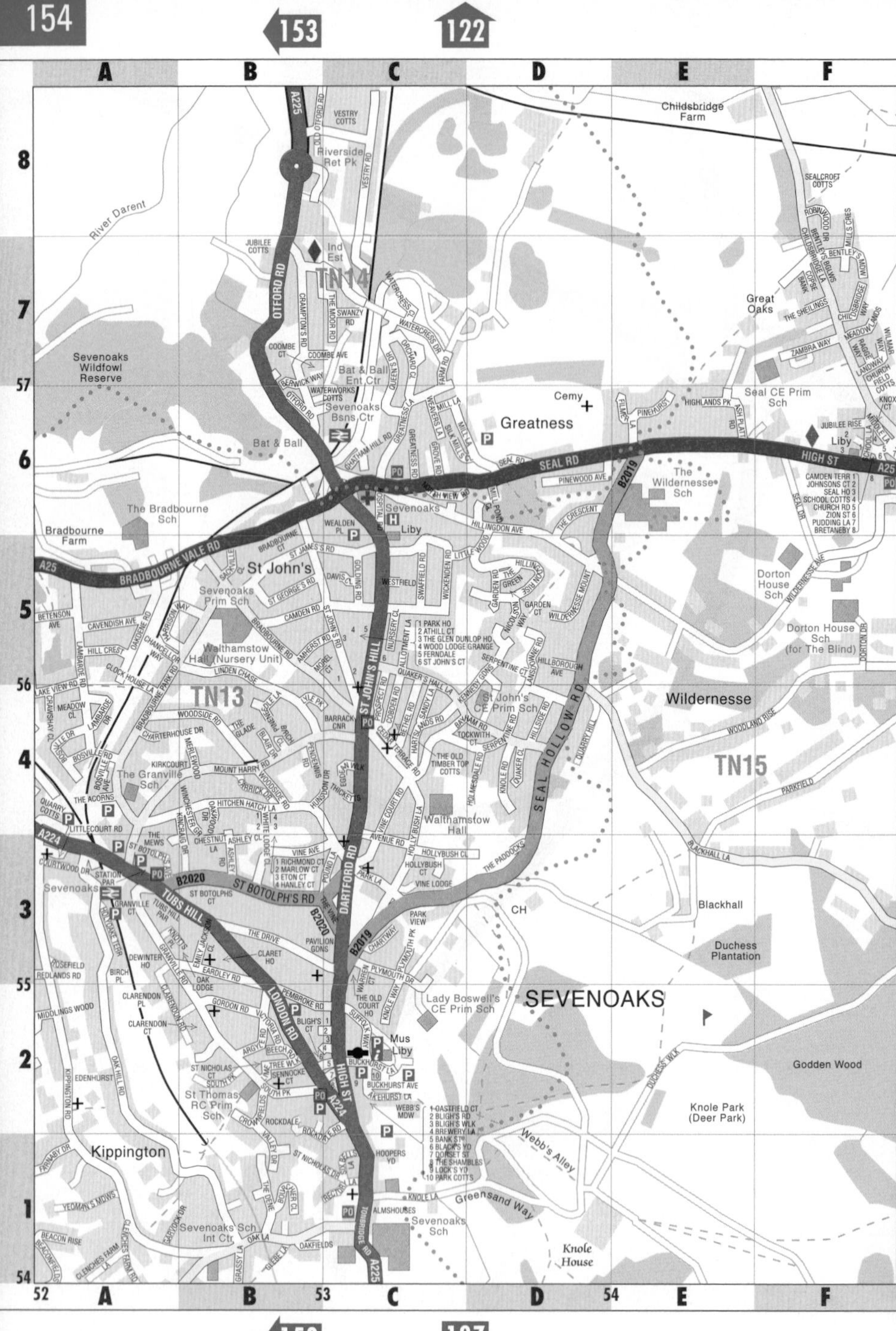

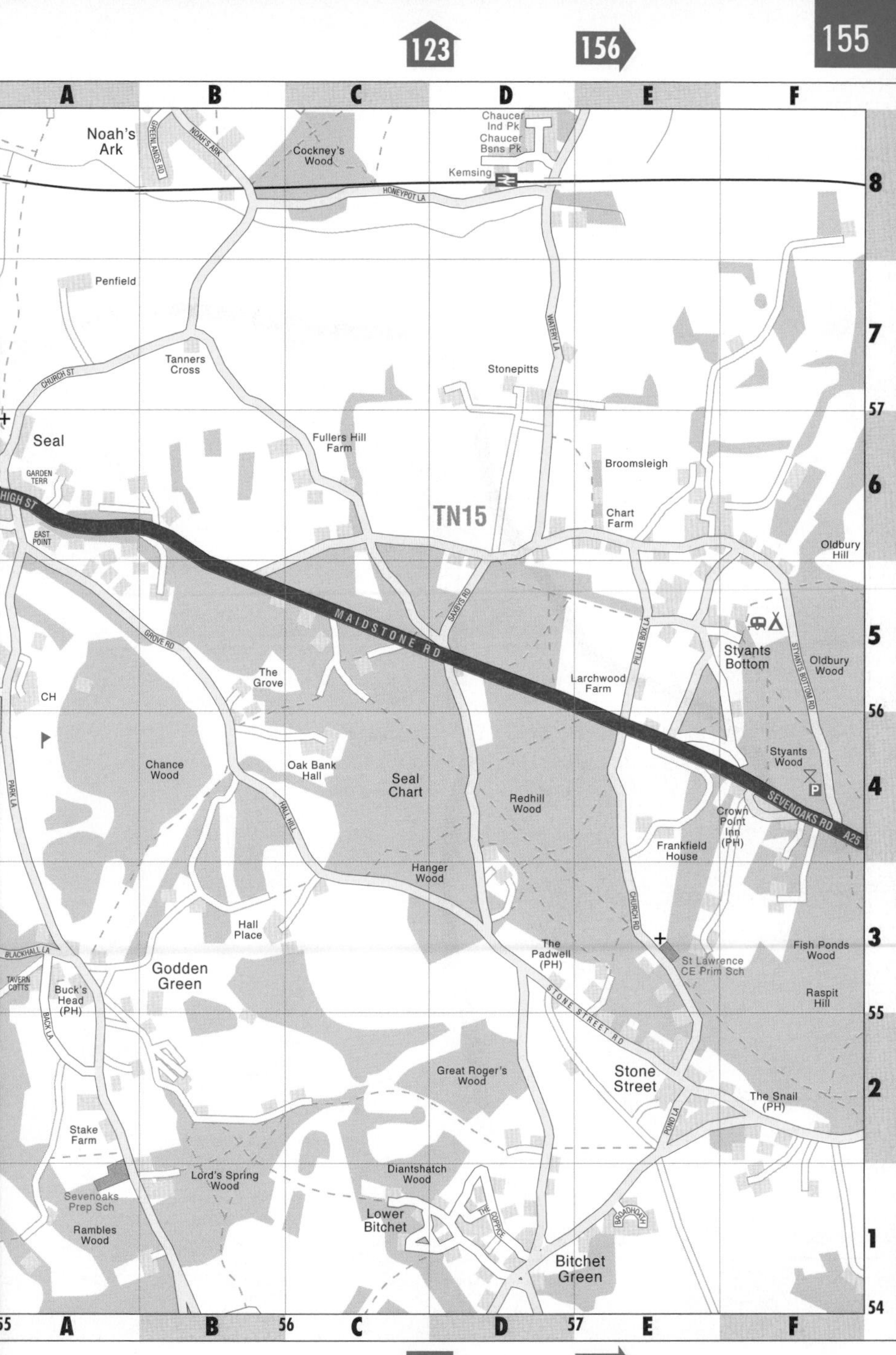

A   B   C   D   E   F

8

Noah's
Ark

Cockney's
Wood

Chaucer
Ind Pk
Chaucer
Bsns Pk

Kemsing

HONEYPOT LA

GREEN HILL RD

NOAH'S ARK

7

Penfield

57

Tanners
Cross

Stonepitts

WATERY LA

CHURCH ST

Seal

Fullers Hill
Farm

TN15

6

GARDEN
TERR

HIGH ST

Broomsleigh

Chart
Farm

Oldbury
Hill

EAST
POINT

MAIDSTONE RD

GROVE RD

The
Grove

Larchwood
Farm

Styants
Bottom

5

PILGRIMS WAY

Oldbury
Wood

CH

56

Chance
Wood

Oak Bank
Hall

Seal
Chart

Redhill
Wood

Styants
Wood

SEVENOAKS RD

A25

4

PARK LA

HALL HILL

Crown
Point
Inn
(PH)

Frankfield
House

STYANTS BOTTOM RD

Hanger
Wood

Hall
Place

The
Padwell
(PH)

St Lawrence
CE Prim Sch

Fish Ponds
Wood

Raspit
Hill

3

BLACKHALL LA

TAVERN
COTTS

Buck's
Head
(PH)

Godden
Green

STONE STREET RD

CHURCH RD

55

BACK LA

Great Roger's
Wood

Stone
Street

The Snail
(PH)

2

Stake
Farm

PONT LA

BRADBOURNE

Sevenoaks
Prep Sch

Lord's Spring
Wood

Diantshatch
Wood

Lower
Bitchet

THE COPSE

Bitchet
Green

Rambles
Wood

1

55   A   B   56   C   D   57   E   F   54

155
124

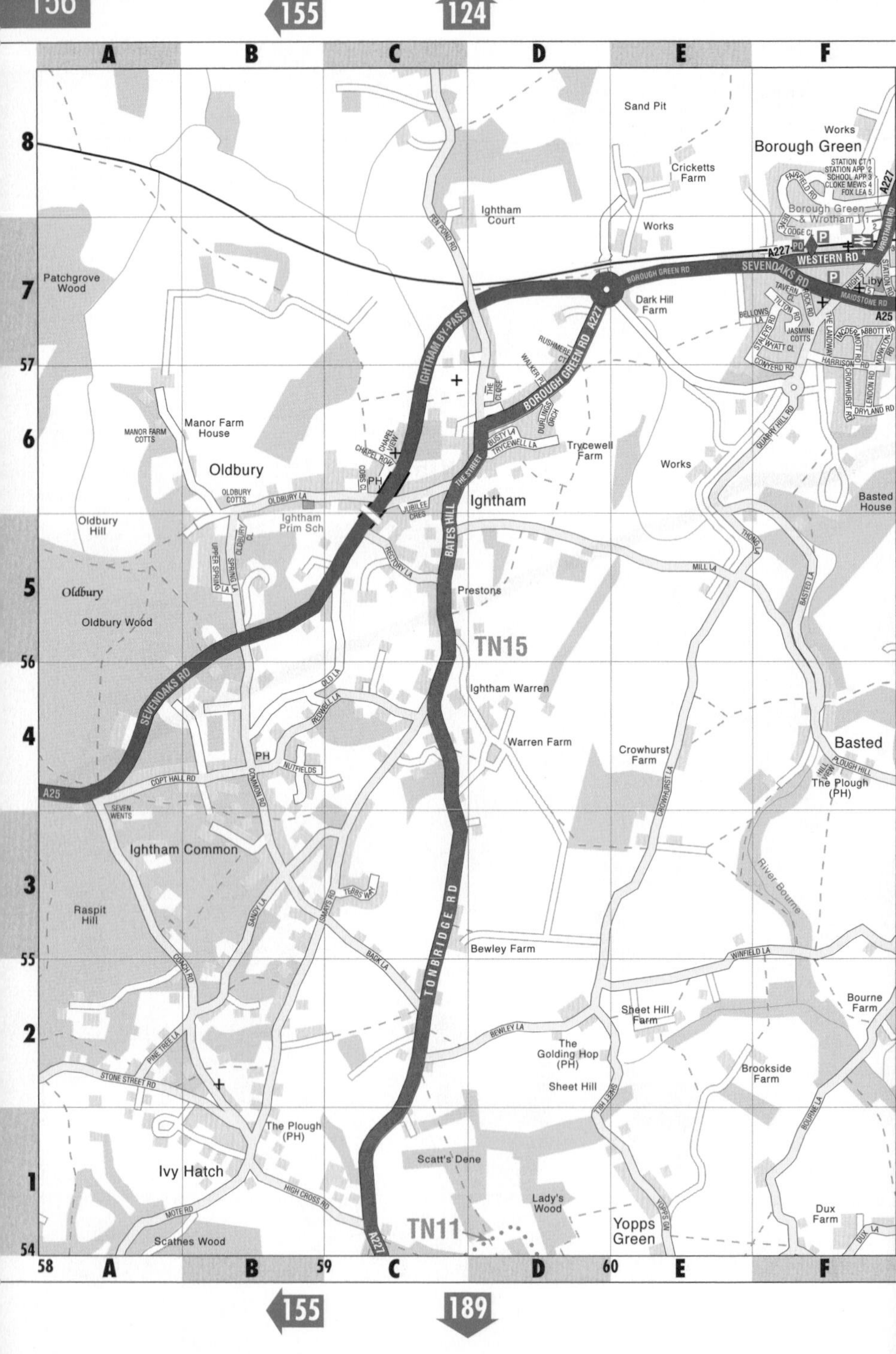
Sand Pit
Works
Borough Green
Cricketts Farm
Ightham Court
Works
Borough Green & Wrotham
Patchgrove Wood
Dark Hill Farm
Manor Farm House
MANOR FARM COTTS
Oldbury
Trycewell Farm
Works
Ightham
Ightham Prim Sch
Oldbury Hill
Basted House
Oldbury
Oldbury Wood
Prestons
TN15
Ightham Warren
Warren Farm
Crowhurst Farm
Basted
The Plough (PH)
Ightham Common
Raspit Hill
Bewley Farm
Sheet Hill Farm
Bourne Farm
The Golding Hop (PH)
Sheet Hill
Brookside Farm
The Plough (PH)
Scatt's Dene
Ivy Hatch
Lady's Wood
Yopps Green
Dux Farm
Scathes Wood
TN11
River Bourne
IGHTHAM BY-PASS
BOROUGH GREEN RD
SEVENOAKS RD
WESTERN RD
MAIDSTONE RD
BATES HILL
TONBRIDGE RD
COPT HALL RD
STONE STREET RD
HIGH CROSS RD
MOTE RD
BEWLEY LA
WINFIELD LA
MILL LA
CROWHURST LA
BASTED LA
BOURNE LA
A25
A227

155
189

125
158

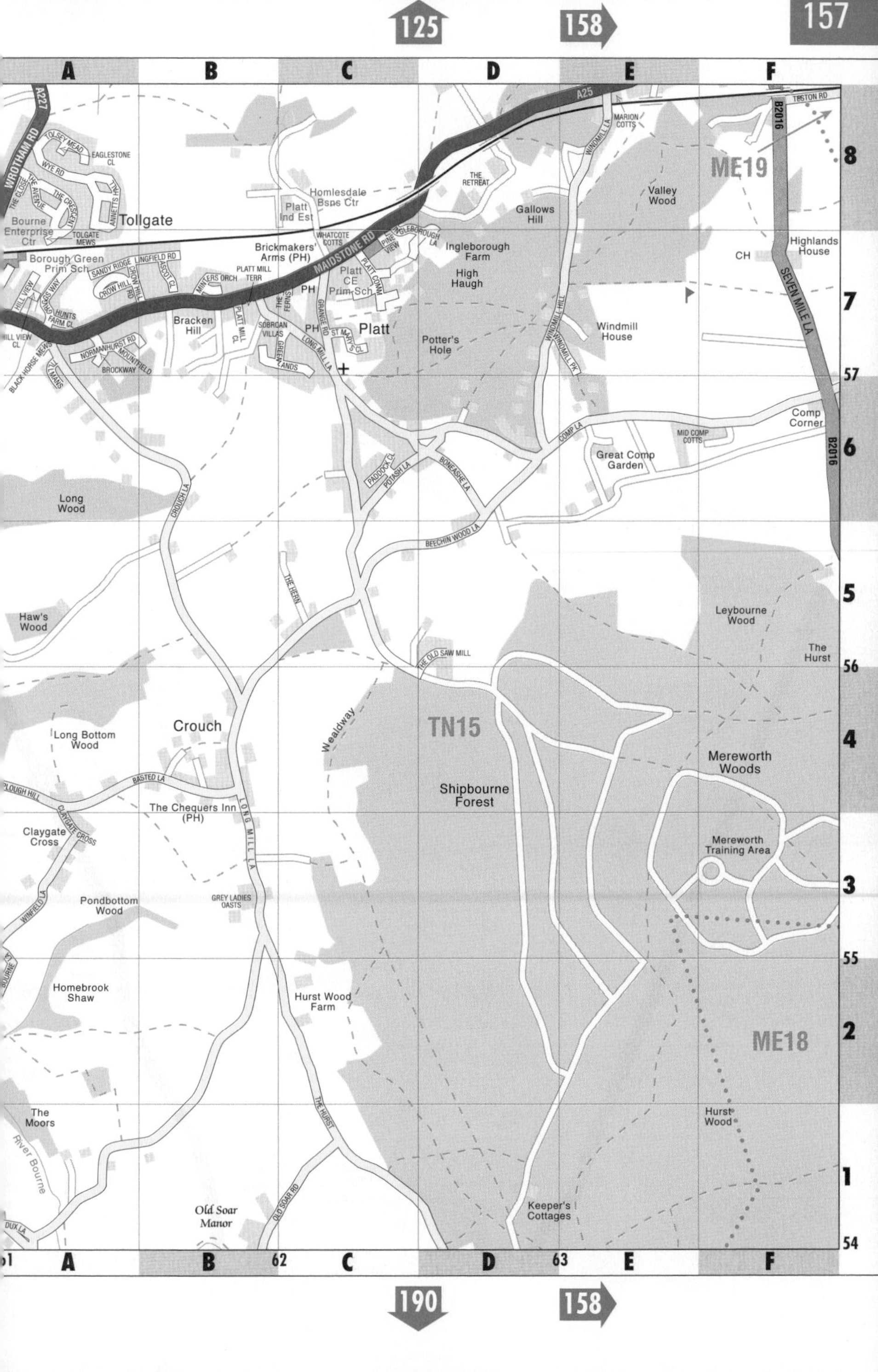

Tollgate
Bourne Enterprise Ctr
Borough Green Prim Sch
Homlesdale Bsns Ctr
Platt Ind Est
Brickmakers' Arms (PH)
Platt CE Prim Sch
Platt
Bracken Hill
Ingleborough Farm
High Haugh
Potter's Hole
Gallows Hill
Valley Wood
Windmill House
Highlands House
ME19
Comp Corner
Great Comp Garden
Long Wood
Haw's Wood
Leybourne Wood
The Hurst
TN15
Shipbourne Forest
Mereworth Woods
Mereworth Training Area
Crouch
Long Bottom Wood
The Chequers Inn (PH)
Claygate Cross
Pondbottom Wood
Homebrook Shaw
Hurst Wood Farm
ME18
Hurst Wood
The Moors
River Bourne
Old Soar Manor
Keeper's Cottages
Wealdway
MAIDSTONE RD
A25
A227
B2016
SEVEN MILE LA
LONG MILL LA
CROUCH LA
BEECHIN WOOD LA
COMP LA
WINDMILL HILL
BASTED LA

190
158

157
126

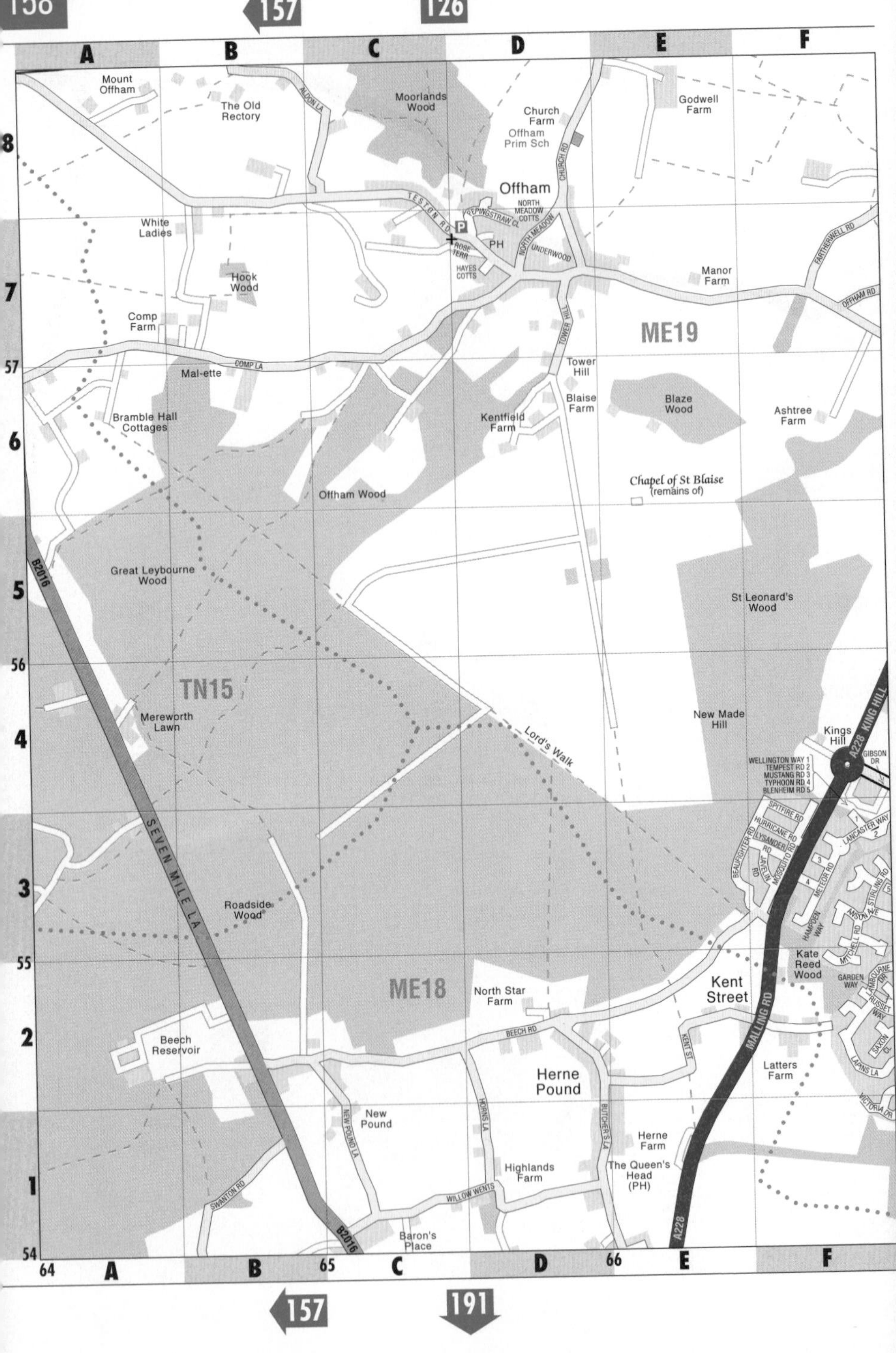
Mount Offham
The Old Rectory
Moorlands Wood
Church Farm
Offham Prim Sch
Godwell Farm
Offham
White Ladies
Hook Wood
Comp Farm
Manor Farm
ME19
COMP LA
Mal-ette
Tower Hill
Blaise Farm
Blaze Wood
Ashtree Farm
Bramble Hall Cottages
Kentfield Farm
Chapel of St Blaise (remains of)
Offham Wood
Great Leybourne Wood
St Leonard's Wood
TN15
Mereworth Lawn
New Made Hill
Kings Hill
Lord's Walk
SEVEN MILE LA
Roadside Wood
ME18
North Star Farm
Kent Street
Kate Reed Wood
Beech Reservoir
Herne Pound
Latters Farm
New Pound
Highlands Farm
Herne Farm
The Queen's Head (PH)
Baron's Place
B2016
A228
MALLING RD
KING HILL
BEECH RD
HORNS LA
NEW POUND LA
BUTCHER'S LA
WILLOW WENTS
SWANTON RD
KENT ST
TESTON RD
CHURCH RD
NORTH MEADOW
UNDERWOOD
TOWER HILL
ALDON LA
FARTHERWELL RD
OFFHAM RD
WELLINGTON WAY 1
TEMPEST RD 2
MUSTANG RD 3
TYPHOON RD 4
BLENHEIM RD 5
SPITFIRE RD
HURRICANE RD
LYSANDER RD
BEAUFIGHTER RD
JAVELIN RD
MOSQUITO RD
METEOR RD
HAMPDEN WAY
ANSON AVE
MITCHELL RD
STIRLING RD
LANCASTER WAY
GARDEN WAY
LAMBOURNE DR
RUSSET WAY
SAXON CL
LAPINS LA
VICTORIA DR
GIBSON DR

157
191

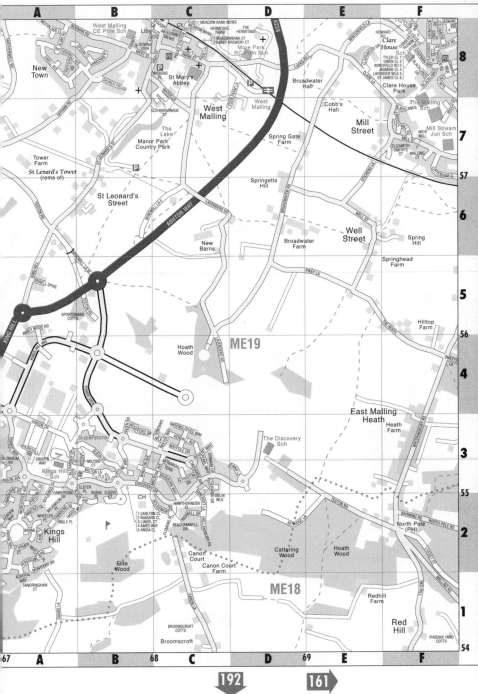

A B C D E F

West Malling CE Prim Sch
Liby
Ct
MEADOW BANK MEWS
MEADOW BANK
HERMITAGE FARM
THE HERMITAGE
1 MEADOWBANK CT
2 ABBEY BREWERY CT
More Park RC Prim Sch
A228
WOODLAND CL
NORMAN RD
ALMA RD
FARTHERWELL RD
FARTHERWELL AVE
EPSOM CL
SANDOWN RD
EWELL AVE
STRATFORD RD
COUNTY GR
DOWNS VIEW
WEST ST
KING ST
HIGH ST
RYARSH LA
ABINGDON MEWS
POLICE STATION RD
SWAN ST
FROG LA
New Town
CHURCH FIELDS
WICKENS PL
St Mary's Abbey
WATER LA
OLD PARSONAGE CT
OFFHAM RD
EDEN FARM LA
West Malling
West Malling
The Lake
Manor Park Country Park
ST LEONARD'S ST
Tower Farm
St Lenard's Tower (rems of)
St Leonard's Street
TESTON RD
WINDMILL LA E
ASHTON WAY
LAVENDERS RD
New Barns
KING HILL
ORWELL SPIKE
WINDMILL LA W
TESTON RD
SPORTSMANS COTTS
ABBEY WOOD RD
KINGS HILL AVE
KING HILL
Hoath Wood
ME19
LAVENDERS RD
TOWER VIEW
WINTERFIELD LA
LUCKS HILL
HOWARD RD
Clare House
CLAREWOOD DR
COBBETT CL
RUSKIN GR
TEMPLE WAY
LISTER CL
TYLER CL 1
OWEN CL 2
BONDFIELD RD 3
JASMINE CL 4
LAVENDER WLK 5
ST JAMES CL 6
CLARE LA
Sch
CHAPMAN WAY
BLACKLANDS DR
LAVENDER CRES
CARNATION RD
COLUMBINE
JASMINE RD
LAVENDER RD
TWISDEN RD
EDWARD WLK
ELM CRES
Broadwater Hall
Clare House Park
Cobb's Hall
The Malling Sch
BLACKLANDS
BEECH RD
Mill Street
MIDDLE MILL RD
WEIR MILL
Mill Stream Jun Sch
MILL ST
ELIZABETH SMITH'S CT
MALLING CT
Spring Gate Farm
STICKENS LA
COTTENHAM CL
Springetts Hill
BROADWATER RD
WELL ST
Well Street
Broadwater Farm
Spring Hill
Springhead Farm
PIKEY LA
THE HEATH
Hilltop Farm
SWEETS LA
East Malling Heath
Heath Farm
WATERINGBURY RD
The Discovery Sch
GIBSON DR
Superstore
HAZEN RD
WOODFORD GR
CARDINAL WLK
GREENSLEEVES WAY
KENDALL AVE
BAXTER WAY
MAYPOLE DR
REGENT WAY
COBHAM DR
PEARL WAY
DAWN LA
FOREST WAY
CHURCHILL SQ
BLENHEIM RD
CRISPIN WAY
ALEXANDER GR
TAXTON
QUEEN ST
MILTON CT
MILTON LA
FORTUNE WAY
WINSTON AVE
MELROSE AVE
MONARCH TERR
BRAEBURN WAY
ALFRISTON GR
BOVARDE AVE
ALDERWICK GR
Kings Hill Sch
ELSTER PL
RUBIN PL
CLEEVE CT
DISCOVERY DR
HAWKRIDGE GR
HAWTHORNDEN CL
BANCROFT LA
OSLIN WLK
CH
ROUGEMONT
REDWELL GR
HOLLANDBURY PK
WORCESTER AVE
CHESTNUT CL
GOLDINGS CL
WILKINSON PL
TOWNSEND SQ
HAYES WLK
CRABTREE CL
WHEELER PL
INGLE PL
1 CARLTON CL
2 NIAGARA CL
3 LINDEL CT
4 AMES WAY
5 ANSIA CL
CLEMENS PL
BEACHAMWELL DR
GARDEN WAY
BRAMLEY WAY
Kings Hill
PIPPIN WAY
STURMER CT
MERCERS PL
PEREGRINE RD
MONTFORT DR
ADMIRAL WAY
SANDRINGHAM CT
Flite Wood
Canon Court
Canon Court Farm
Cattering Wood
KENTWOGE LA
TESTON RD
Hoath Wood
BARMING RD
NORTH POLE RD
North Pole (PH)
LIVESEY ST
MALLING RD
RED HILL
ME18
Redhill Farm
DANNS LA
CANON LA
BROOMSCROFT COTTS
Broomscroft
Red Hill
PHOENIX YARD COTTS

8 7 57 6 5 56 4 3 55 2 1 54

67 A B 68 C D 69 E F

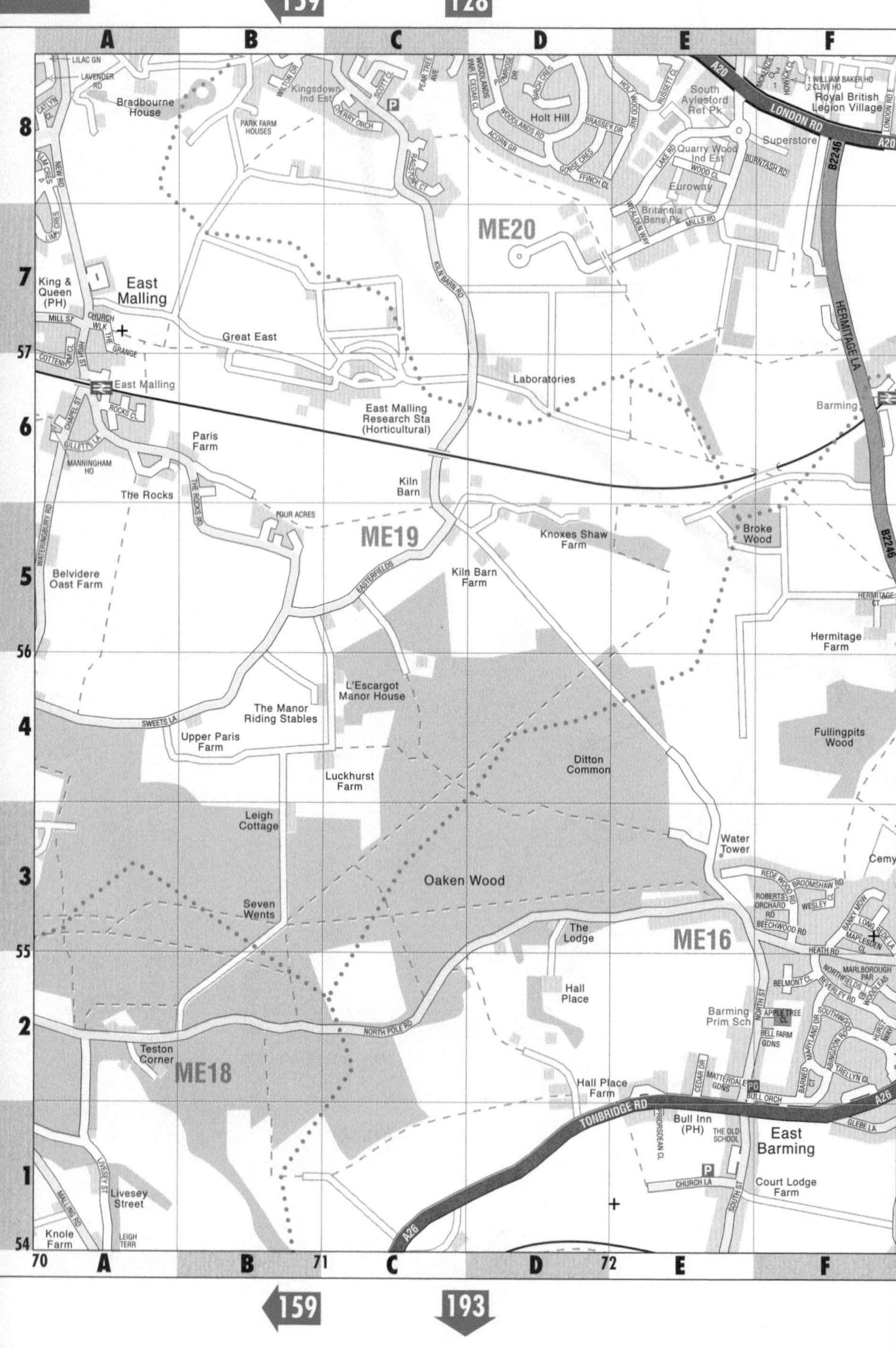

159
128

A   B   C   D   E   F

8

Bradbourne
House

LILAC GN
LAVENDER
RD

Kingsdown
Ind Est

PARK FARM
HOUSES

Holt Hill

South
Aylesford
Ret Pk

1 WILLIAM BAKER HO
2 CLIVE HO
Royal British
Legion Village

LONDON RD
A20

Superstore

Quarry Wood
Ind Est

Euroway

ME20

Britannia
Bens Pk

7

King &
Queen
(PH)

East
Malling

MILL ST

CHURCH
WLK

THE GRANGE

Great East

57

East Malling

Barming

6

Paris
Farm

The Rocks

MANNINGHAM
HO

GILLETTS

FOUR ACRES

East Malling
Research Sta
(Horticultural)

Laboratories

Kiln
Barn

ME19

Knoxes Shaw
Farm

Broke
Wood

B2246

5

Belvidere
Oast Farm

EASTERFIELDS

Kiln Barn
Farm

HERMITAGE
CT

HERMITAGE LA

Hermitage
Farm

56

SWEETS LA

The Manor
Riding Stables

L'Escargot
Manor House

Fullingpits
Wood

4

Upper Paris
Farm

Luckhurst
Farm

Ditton
Common

Leigh
Cottage

Water
Tower

Cemy

3

Oaken Wood

Seven
Wents

The
Lodge

ME16

55

NORTH POLE RD

Hall
Place

Barming
Prim Sch

2

Teston
Corner

ME18

Hall Place
Farm

TONBRIDGE RD

Bull Inn
(PH)

THE OLD
SCHOOL

East
Barming

A26

1

Livesey
Street

LEIGH
TERR

CHURCH LA

Court Lodge
Farm

Knole
Farm

54

70   A   B   71   C   D   72   E   F

159
193

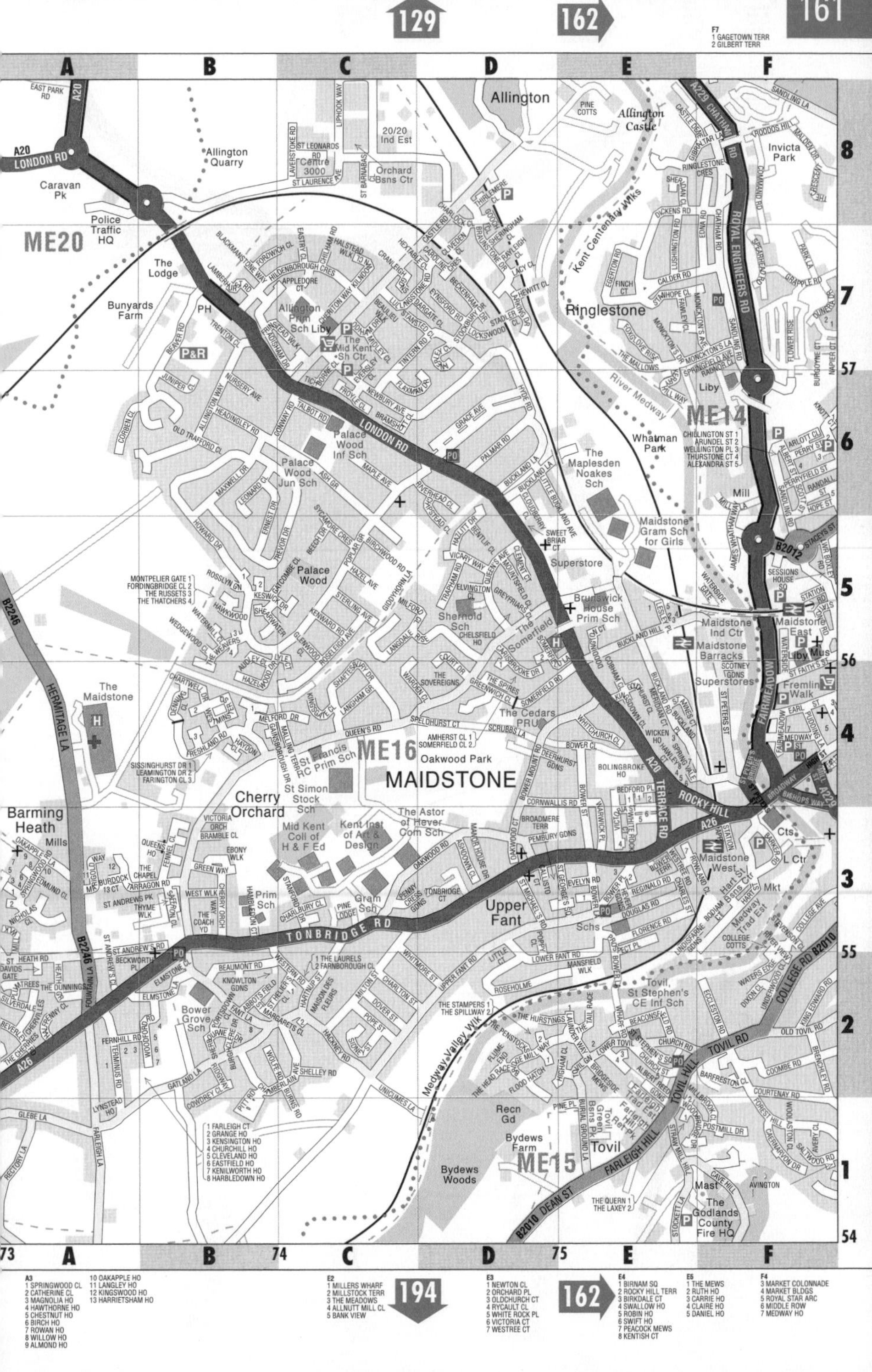

129
162
161
F7
1 GAGETOWN TERR
2 GILBERT TERR
A
B
C
D
E
F
8
7
57
6
5
56
4
3
55
2
1
54
73
74
75
Allington
Allington Castle
Allington Quarry
20/20 Ind Est
Centre 3000
Orchard Bsns Ctr
Caravan Pk
Police Traffic HQ
ME20
The Lodge
Bunyards Farm
Invicta Park
Ringlestone
Kent Centenary Wks
River Medway
Whatman Park
ME14
The Maplesden Noakes Sch
Maidstone Gram Sch for Girls
Superstore
Allington Prim Sch
The Mid Kent Sh Ctr
Palace Wood Inf Sch
Palace Wood Jun Sch
Palace Wood
Sherwold Sch
Brunswick House Prim Sch
The Somerfield
Maidstone Ind Ctr
Maidstone Barracks
Maidstone East
Superstores
Fremlin Walk
The Maidstone
The Cedars PRU
ME16
Oakwood Park
MAIDSTONE
St Francis RC Prim Sch
St Simon Stock Sch
Cherry Orchard
The Astor of Hever Com Sch
Mid Kent Coll of H & F Ed
Kent Inst of Art & Design
Barming Heath
Upper Fant
Maidstone West
Medway Trad Est
Bower Grove Sch
Tovil, St Stephen's CE Inf Sch
Recn Gd
Bydews Farm
Bydews Woods
ME15
Tovil
Medway Valley Wlk
The Godlands County Fire HQ
LONDON RD
TONBRIDGE RD
ROYAL ENGINEERS RD
FAIRMEADOW
ROCKY HILL
TERRACE RD
HERMITAGE LA
TOVIL HILL
FARLEIGH HILL
COLLEGE RD
TOVIL RD
DEAN ST
A20
A26
A229
B2246
B2012
B2010
MONTPELIER GATE 1
FORDINGBRIDGE CL 2
THE RUSSETS 3
THE THATCHERS 4
SISSINGHURST DR 1
LEAMINGTON DR 2
FARINGTON CL 3
AMHERST CL 1
SOMERFIELD CL 2
CHILLINGTON ST 1
ARUNDEL ST 2
WELLINGTON PL 3
THURSTONE CT 4
ALEXANDRA ST 5
1 THE LAURELS
2 FARNBOROUGH CL
THE STAMPERS 1
THE SPILLWAY 2
THE QUERN 1
THE LAXEY 2
1 FARLEIGH CT
2 GRANGE HO
3 KENSINGTON HO
4 CHURCHILL HO
5 CLEVELAND HO
6 EASTFIELD HO
7 KENILWORTH HO
8 HARBLEDOWN HO
A3
1 SPRINGWOOD CL
2 CATHERINE CL
3 MAGNOLIA HO
4 HAWTHORNE HO
5 CHESTNUT HO
6 BIRCH HO
7 ROWAN HO
8 WILLOW HO
9 ALMOND HO
10 OAKAPPLE HO
11 LANGLEY HO
12 KINGSWOOD HO
13 HARRIETSHAM HO
E2
1 MILLERS WHARF
2 MILLSTOCK TERR
3 THE MEADOWS
4 ALLNUTT MILL CL
5 BANK VIEW
194
E3
1 NEWTON CL
2 ORCHARD PL
3 OLDCHURCH CT
4 RYCAULT CL
5 WHITE ROCK PL
6 VICTORIA CT
7 WESTREE CT
162
E4
1 BIRNAM SQ
2 ROCKY HILL TERR
3 BIRKDALE CT
4 SWALLOW HO
5 ROBIN HO
6 SWIFT HO
7 PEACOCK MEWS
8 KENTISH CT
E5
1 THE MEWS
2 RUTH HO
3 CARRIE HO
4 CLAIRE HO
5 DANIEL HO
F4
3 MARKET COLONNADE
4 MARKET BLDGS
5 ROYAL STAR ARC
6 MIDDLE ROW
7 MEDWAY HO

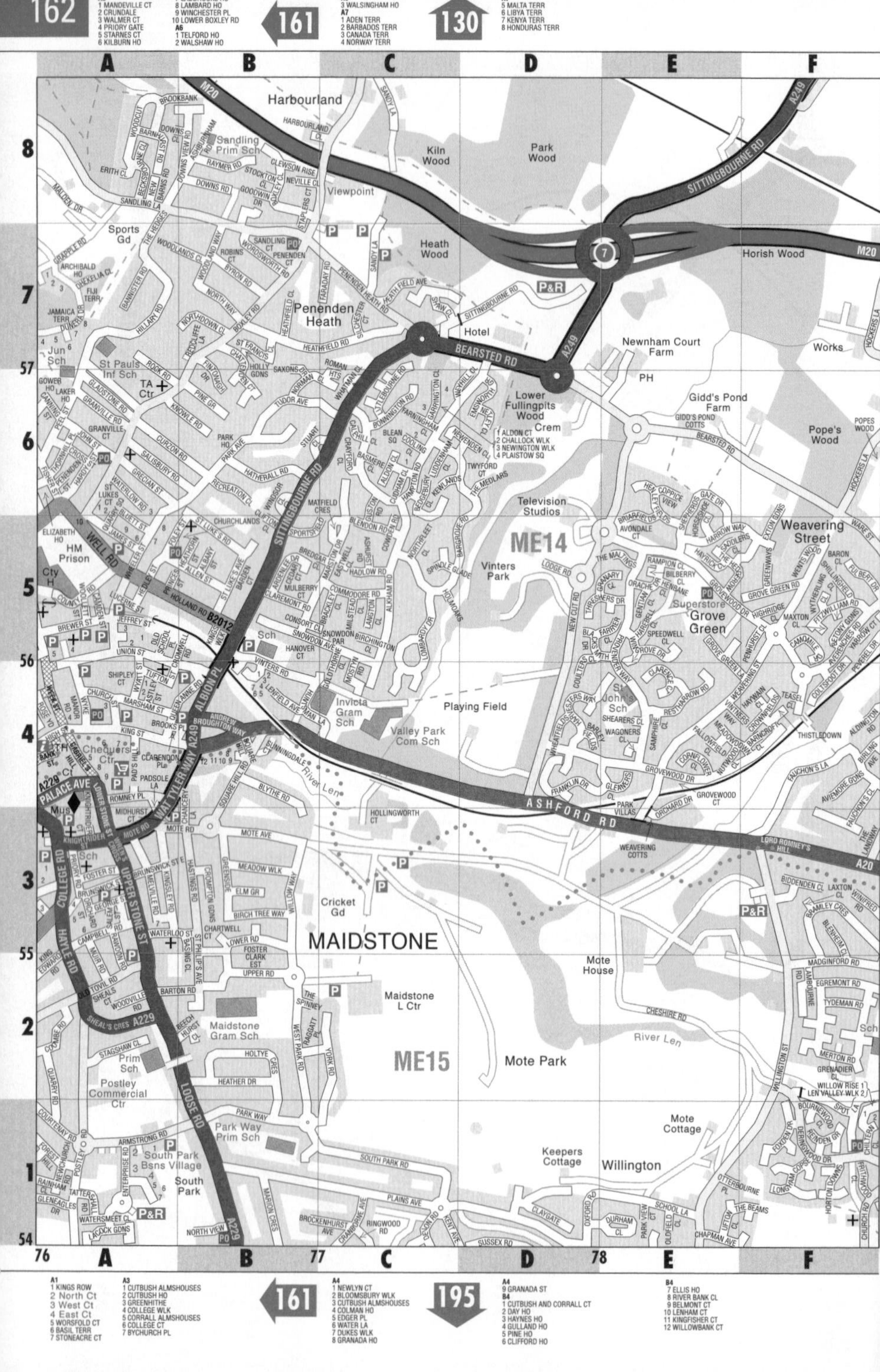
162
A5
1 MANDEVILLE CT
2 CRUNDALE
3 WALMER CT
4 PRIORY GATE
5 STARNES CT
6 KILBURN HO
7 LADBROOKE HO
8 LAMBARD HO
9 WINCHESTER PL
10 LOWER BOXLEY RD
A6
1 TELFORD HO
2 WALSHAW HO
161
A6
3 WALSINGHAM HO
A7
1 ADEN TERR
2 BARBADOS TERR
3 CANADA TERR
4 NORWAY TERR
130
A7
5 MALTA TERR
6 LIBYA TERR
7 KENYA TERR
8 HONDURAS TERR
A
B
C
D
E
F
8
7
57
6
5
56
4
3
55
2
1
54
76
77
78
M20
A249
Harbourland
Sandling Prim Sch
Kiln Wood
Park Wood
SITTINGBOURNE RD
Viewpoint
Sports Gd
Heath Wood
Horish Wood
P&R
Penenden Heath
Hotel
BEARSTED RD
Newnham Court Farm
Works
Jun Sch
St Pauls Inf Sch
TA Ctr
PH
Lower Fullingpits Wood
Crem
Gidd's Pond Farm
Pope's Wood
Television Studios
HM Prison
Cty H
WELL RD
ME14
Vinters Park
Weavering Street
Superstore
Grove Green
B2012
HOLLAND RD
Sch
Playing Field
Invicta Gram Sch
Valley Park Com Sch
Chequers Ctr
A229
PALACE AVE
Mus
WAT TYLER WAY
ASHFORD RD
River Len
A20
Cricket Gd
MAIDSTONE
Mote House
Maidstone L Ctr
Maidstone Gram Sch
River Len
ME15
Mote Park
Prim Sch
Postley Commercial Ctr
LOOSE RD
Park Way Prim Sch
Mote Cottage
Keepers Cottage
Willington
South Park Bsns Village
South Park
A1
1 KINGS ROW
2 North Ct
3 West Ct
4 East Ct
5 WORSFOLD CT
6 BASIL TERR
7 STONEACRE CT
A3
1 CUTBUSH ALMSHOUSES
2 CUTBUSH HO
3 GREENHITHE
4 COLLEGE WLK
5 CORRALL ALMSHOUSES
6 COLLEGE CT
7 BYCHURCH PL
161
A4
1 NEWLYN CT
2 BLOOMSBURY WLK
3 CUTBUSH ALMSHOUSES
4 COLMAN HO
5 EDGER PL
6 WATER LA
7 DUKES WLK
8 GRANADA HO
195
A4
9 GRANADA ST
B4
1 CUTBUSH AND CORRALL CT
2 DAY HO
3 HAYNES HO
4 GULLAND HO
5 PINE HO
6 CLIFFORD HO
B4
7 ELLIS HO
8 RIVER BANK CL
9 BELMONT CT
10 LENHAM CT
11 KINGFISHER CT
12 WILLOWBANK CT

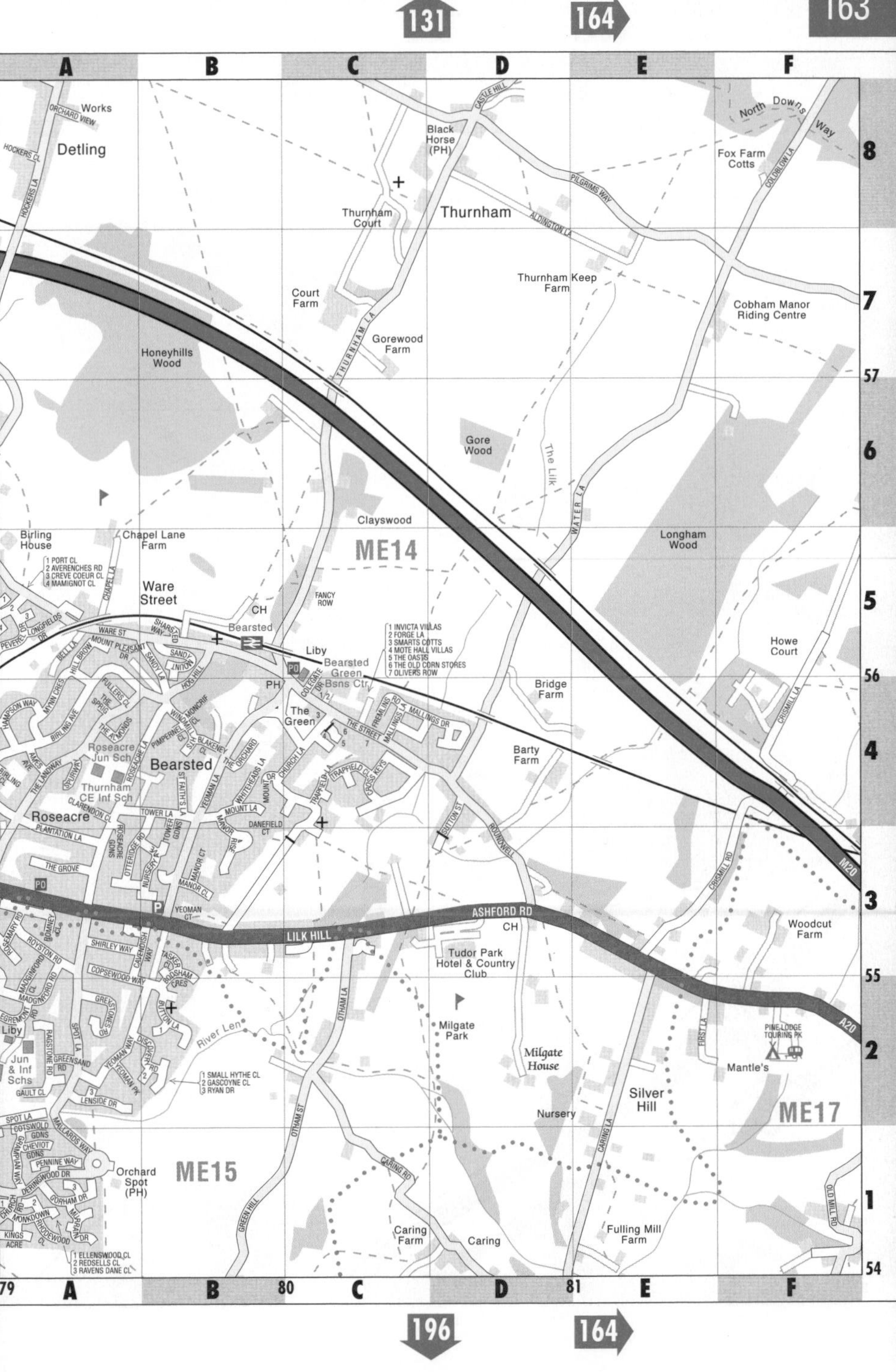
131
164
Detling
Works
Black Horse (PH)
Thurnham Court
Thurnham
Fox Farm Cotts
North Downs Way
Thurnham Keep Farm
Court Farm
Cobham Manor Riding Centre
Gorewood Farm
Honeyhills Wood
Gore Wood
The Lilk
Clayswood
ME14
Longham Wood
Birling House
Chapel Lane Farm
Ware Street
Bearsted
Liby
Bearsted Green Bsns Ctr
Howe Court
The Green
Bridge Farm
Barty Farm
Roseacre Jun Sch
Thurnham CE Inf Sch
Roseacre
Woodcut Farm
Tudor Park Hotel & Country Club
Milgate Park
Milgate House
Mantle's
Silver Hill
Nursery
ME17
Jun & Inf Schs
Orchard Spot (PH)
ME15
Caring Farm
Caring
Fulling Mill Farm
LILK HILL
ASHFORD RD
M20
A20
River Len
1 INVICTA VILLAS
2 FORGE LA
3 SMARTS COTTS
4 MOTE HALL VILLAS
5 THE OASTS
6 THE OLD CORN STORES
7 OLIVERS ROW
1 PORT CL
2 AVERENCHES RD
3 CREVE COEUR CL
4 MAMIGNOT CL
1 SMALL HYTHE CL
2 GASCOYNE CL
3 RYAN DR
1 ELLENSWOOD CL
2 REDSELLS CL
3 RAVENS DANE CL
A B C D E F
8 7 57 6 5 56 4 3 55 2 1 54
79 80 81
196
164

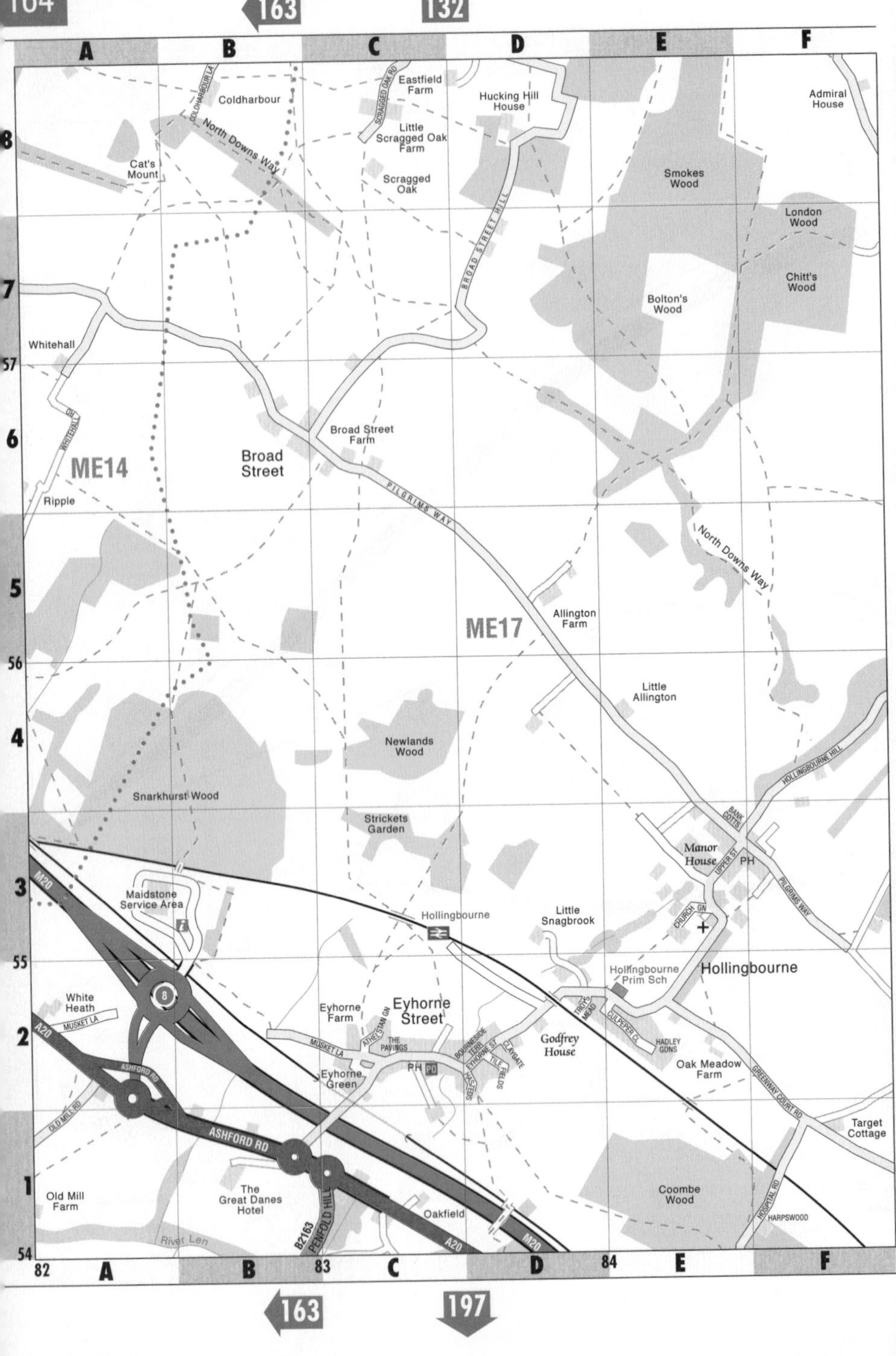
A
B
C
D
E
F
Coldharbour
Eastfield Farm
Hucking Hill House
Admiral House
COLDHARBOUR LA
SCRAGGED OAK RD
North Downs Way
Little Scragged Oak Farm
Cat's Mount
Scragged Oak
Smokes Wood
London Wood
Chitt's Wood
Bolton's Wood
BROAD STREET HILL
Whitehall
WHITEHALL RD
Broad Street Farm
Broad Street
ME14
Ripple
PILGRIMS WAY
North Downs Way
Allington Farm
ME17
Little Allington
Newlands Wood
Snarkhurst Wood
HOLLINGBOURNE HILL
Strickets Garden
BANK COTTS
Manor House
UPPER ST
PH
PILGRIMS WAY
M20
Maidstone Service Area
Hollingbourne
Little Snagbrook
CHURCH GN
Hollingbourne Prim Sch
Hollingbourne
8
White Heath
MUSKET LA
Eyhorne Farm
ATHELSTAN GN
Eyhorne Street
TROYS MEAD
CULPEPER CL
Godfrey House
A20
MUSKET LA
THE PAVINGS
BOURNESIDE TERR
EYHORNE ST
CLAYGATE
TILEFIELDS
HADLEY GDNS
Oak Meadow Farm
ASHFORD RD
Eyhorne Green
PH
PO
HASTED RD
GREENWAY COURT RD
OLD MILL RD
ASHFORD RD
Target Cottage
Old Mill Farm
The Great Danes Hotel
Coombe Wood
PENFOLD HILL
B2163
Oakfield
HOSPITAL RD
HARPSWOOD
River Len
A20
M20
8
7
57
6
5
56
4
3
55
2
1
54
82
83
84
A
B
C
D
E
F

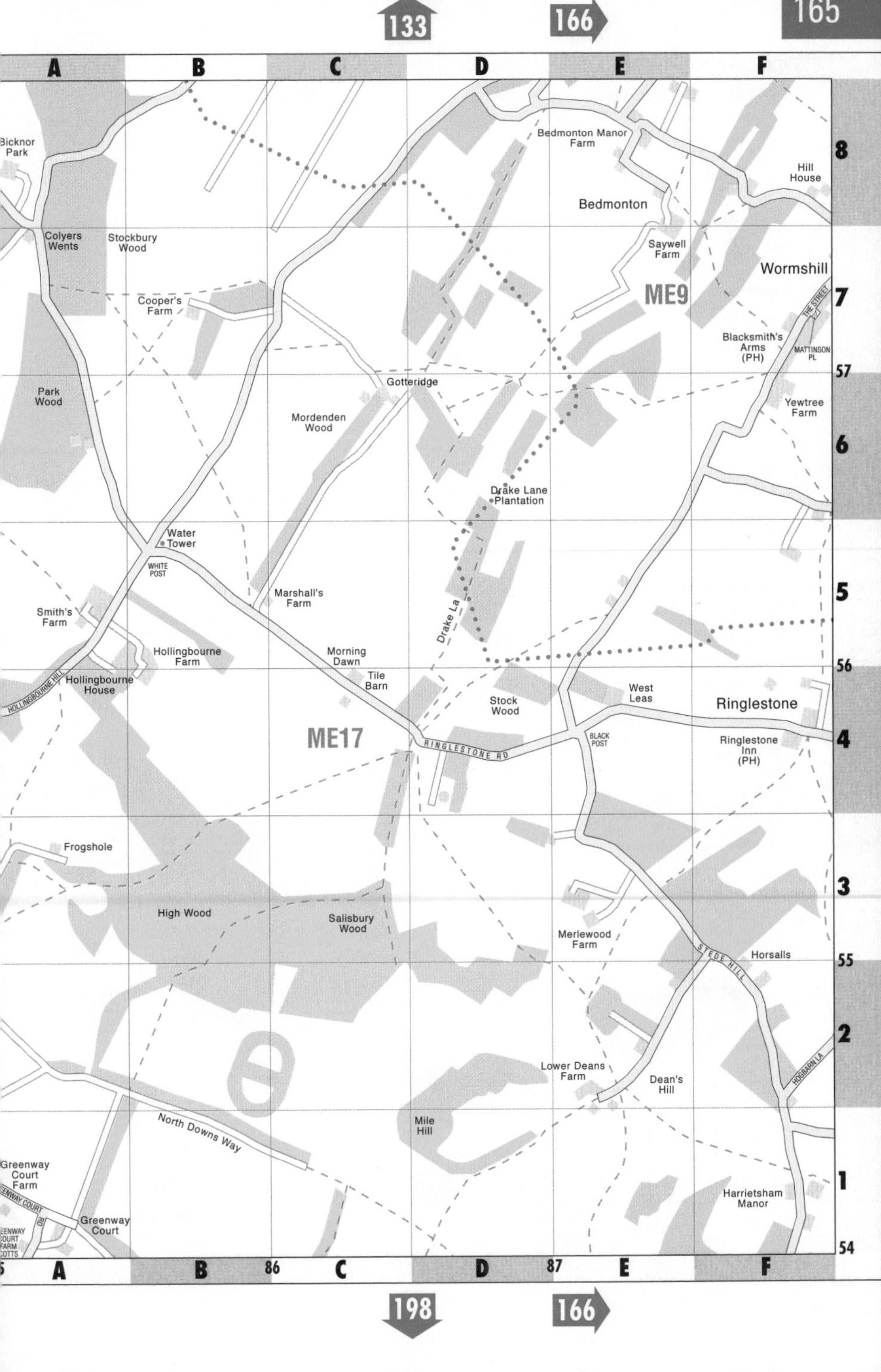
A
B
C
D
E
F
Bicknor Park
Bedmonton Manor Farm
Hill House
Bedmonton
8
Colyers Wents
Stockbury Wood
Saywell Farm
Wormshill
ME9
7
Cooper's Farm
THE STREET
Blacksmith's Arms (PH)
MATTINSON PL
57
Gotteridge
Park Wood
Mordenden Wood
Yewtree Farm
6
Drake Lane Plantation
Water Tower
WHITE POST
5
Marshall's Farm
Smith's Farm
Drake La
Hollingbourne Farm
Morning Dawn
56
HOLLINGBOURNE HILL
Hollingbourne House
Tile Barn
West Leas
Stock Wood
Ringlestone
ME17
BLACK POST
RINGLESTONE RD
Ringlestone Inn (PH)
4
Frogshole
3
High Wood
Salisbury Wood
Merlewood Farm
STEDE HILL
Horsalls
55
2
Lower Deans Farm
Dean's Hill
HOGBARN LA
North Downs Way
Mile Hill
Greenway Court Farm
1
Harrietsham Manor
GREENWAY COURT RD
Greenway Court
GREENWAY COURT FARM COTTS
54
A
B
86
C
D
87
E
F

165
134

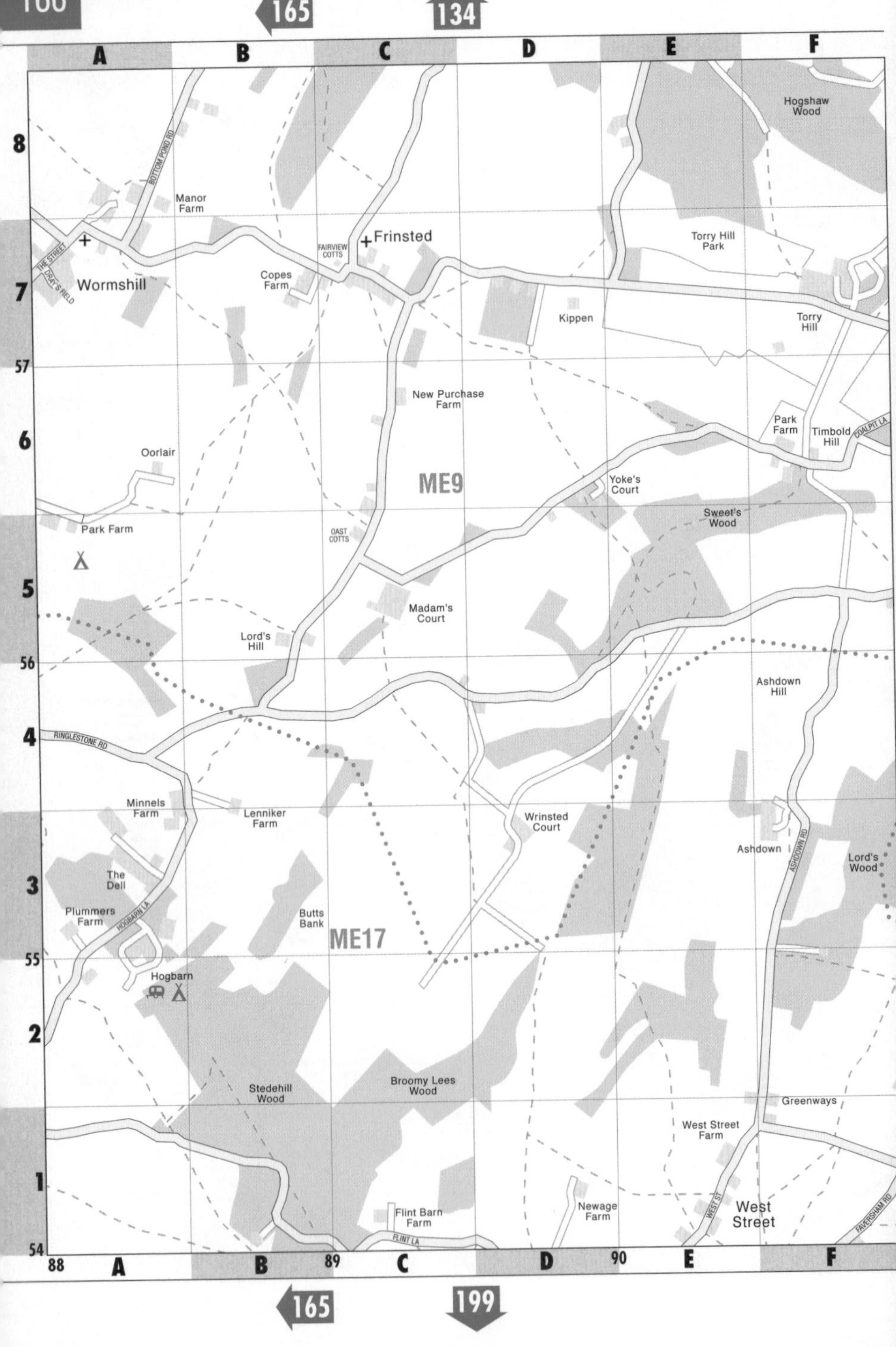
A
B
C
D
E
F
8
7
57
6
5
56
4
3
55
2
1
54
88
89
90
Hogshaw Wood
BOTTOM POND RD
Manor Farm
Frinsted
FAIRVIEW COTTS
Torry Hill Park
THE STREET
DRAY'S FIELD
Wormshill
Copes Farm
Kippen
Torry Hill
New Purchase Farm
Park Farm
Timbold Hill
COALPIT LA
Oorlair
ME9
Yoke's Court
Sweet's Wood
Park Farm
OAST COTTS
Madam's Court
Lord's Hill
Ashdown Hill
RINGLESTONE RD
Minnels Farm
Lenniker Farm
Wrinsted Court
Ashdown
ASHDOWN RD
Lord's Wood
The Dell
Plummers Farm
HOGBARN LA
Butts Bank
ME17
Hogbarn
Stedehill Wood
Broomy Lees Wood
Greenways
West Street Farm
Flint Barn Farm
Newage Farm
WEST ST
West Street
FAVERSHAM RD
FLINT LA

165
199

135
168

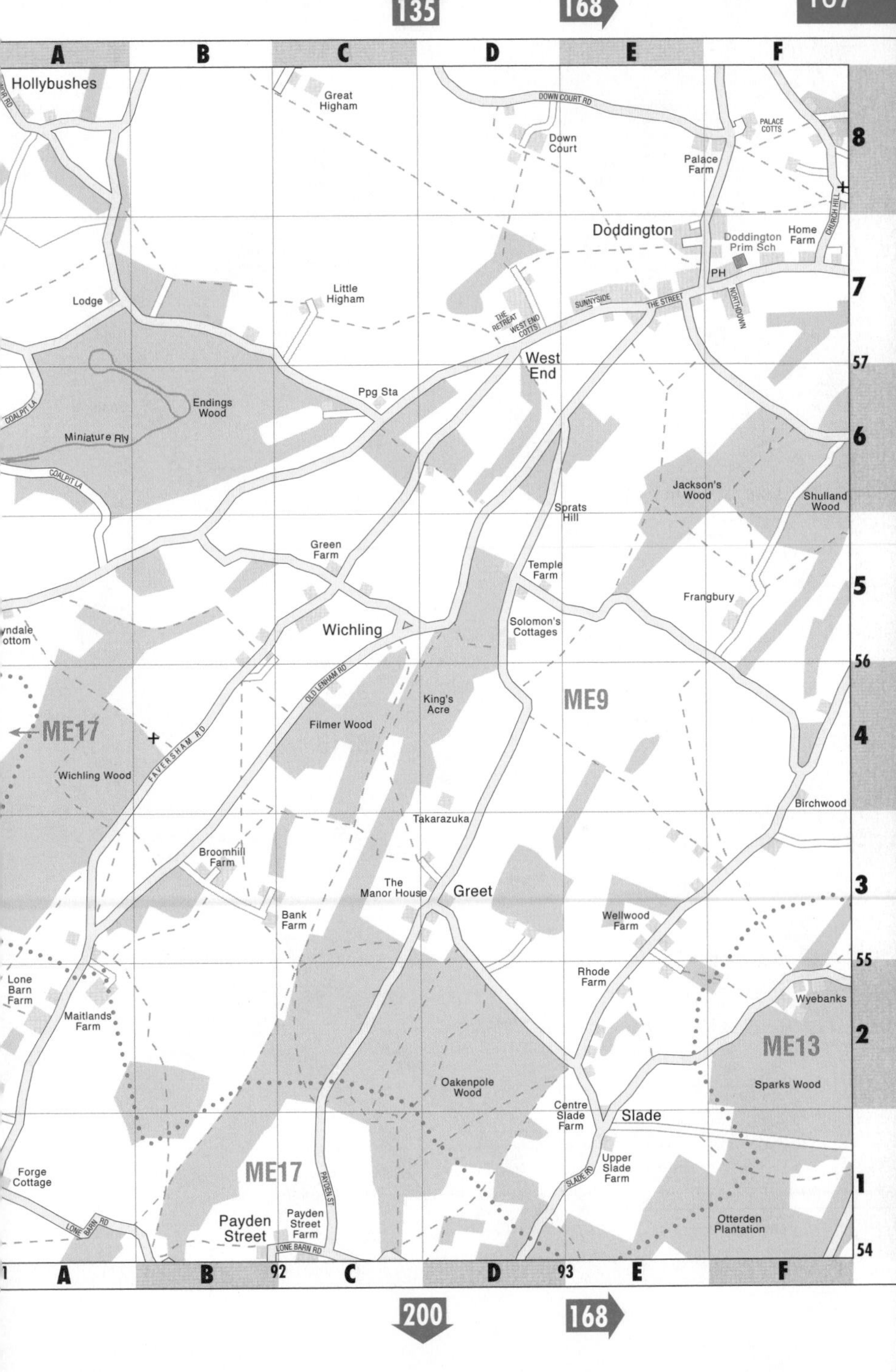
Hollybushes
Great Higham
DOWN COURT RD
Down Court
PALACE COTTS
Palace Farm
Doddington
Doddington Prim Sch
Home Farm
CHURCH HILL
PH
NORTHDOWN
THE STREET
SUNNYSIDE
THE RETREAT
WEST END COTTS
Little Higham
Lodge
West End
Ppg Sta
Endings Wood
COALPIT LA
Miniature Rly
Jackson's Wood
Shulland Wood
Sprats Hill
Green Farm
Temple Farm
Frangbury
Wichling
Solomon's Cottages
OLD LENHAM RD
King's Acre
ME9
ME17
Filmer Wood
FAVERSHAM RD
Wichling Wood
Birchwood
Takarazuka
Broomhill Farm
The Manor House
Greet
Bank Farm
Wellwood Farm
Rhode Farm
Lone Barn Farm
Maitlands Farm
Wyebanks
ME13
Oakenpole Wood
Sparks Wood
Centre Slade Farm
Slade
Upper Slade Farm
SLADE RD
PAYDEN ST
Forge Cottage
ME17
LONE BARN RD
Payden Street
Payden Street Farm
LONE BARN RD
Otterden Plantation
A
B
C
D
E
F
8
7
57
6
5
56
4
3
55
2
1
54
92
93

200
168

167
136

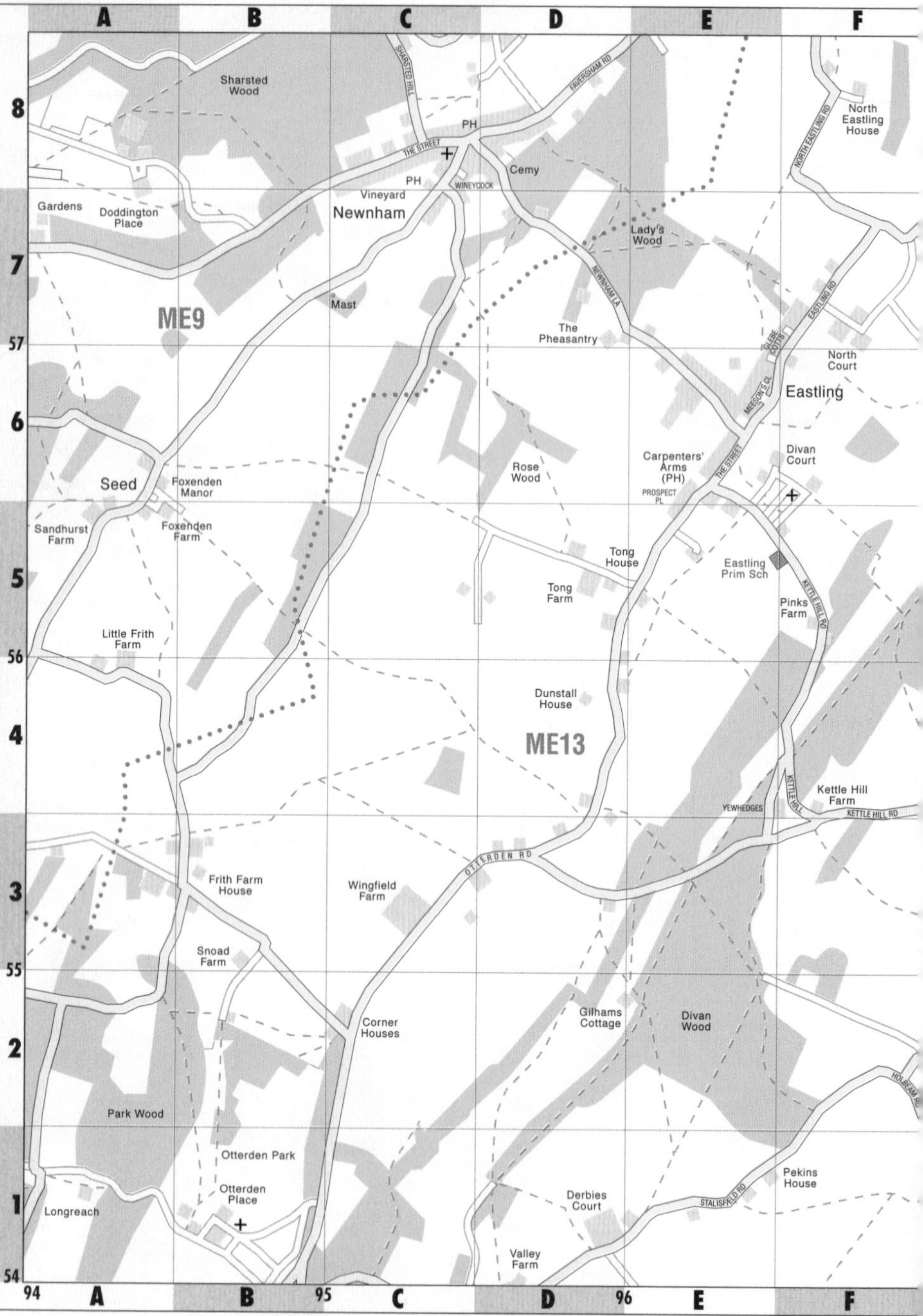

A B C D E F

8

Sharsted Wood

North Eastling House

PH

THE STREET

Cemy

PH

Vineyard

WINEYOCK

Gardens Doddington Place

Newnham

Lady's Wood

7

FAVERSHAM RD

NEWNHAM LA

Mast

57

ME9

The Pheasantry

North Court

Eastling

EASTLING RD

6

Rose Wood

Carpenters' Arms (PH)

Divan Court

Seed

Foxenden Manor

PROSPECT PL

THE STREET

Sandhurst Farm

Foxenden Farm

Tong House

Eastling Prim Sch

5

Tong Farm

Pinks Farm

Little Frith Farm

56

Dunstall House

KETTLE HILL RD

4

ME13

Kettle Hill Farm

YEWHEDGES

KETTLE HILL RD

Frith Farm House

Wingfield Farm

OTTERDEN RD

3

Snoad Farm

55

Gilhams Cottage

Divan Wood

Corner Houses

2

Park Wood

Otterden Park

Pekins House

Otterden Place

Derbies Court

STALISFIELD RD

1

Longreach

Valley Farm

54

94 A B 95 C D 96 E F

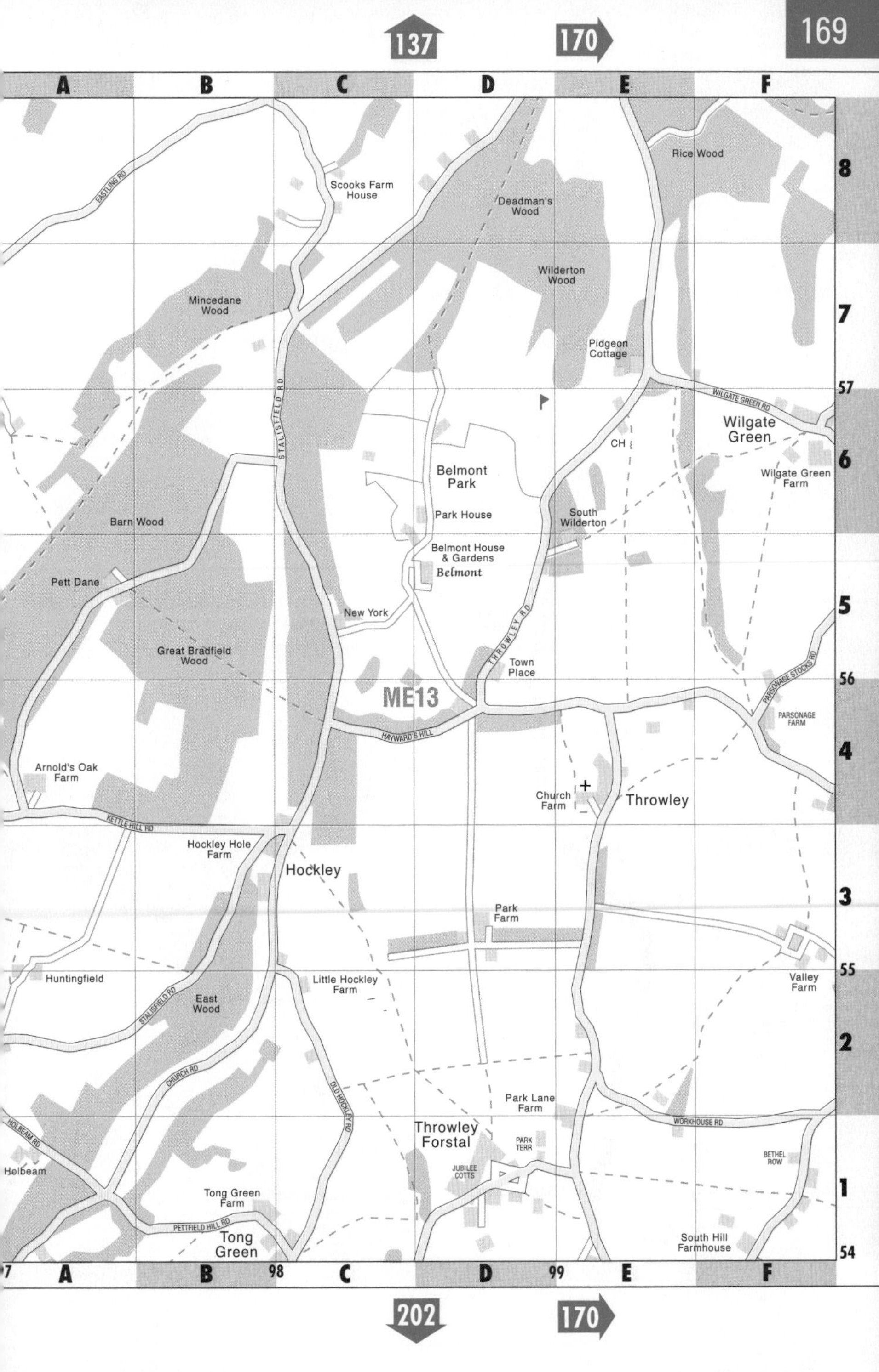
A
B
C
D
E
F
8
7
57
6
5
56
4
3
55
2
1
54
EASTLING RD
Scooks Farm House
Rice Wood
Deadman's Wood
Wilderton Wood
Mincedane Wood
Pidgeon Cottage
STALISFIELD RD
WILGATE GREEN RD
Wilgate Green
CH
Belmont Park
Wilgate Green Farm
Barn Wood
Park House
South Wilderton
Belmont House & Gardens
Belmont
Pett Dane
New York
THROWLEY RD
Great Bradfield Wood
Town Place
PARSONAGE STOCKS RD
ME13
PARSONAGE FARM
HAYWARD'S HILL
Arnold's Oak Farm
Church Farm
Throwley
KETTLE HILL RD
Hockley Hole Farm
Hockley
Park Farm
Huntingfield
Little Hockley Farm
Valley Farm
STALISFIELD RD
East Wood
CHURCH RD
OLD HOCKLEY RD
Park Lane Farm
WORKHOUSE RD
HOLBEAM RD
Throwley Forstal
PARK TERR
BETHEL ROW
Holbeam
JUBILEE COTTS
Tong Green Farm
PETTFIELD HILL RD
Tong Green
South Hill Farmhouse
98
99

169
138

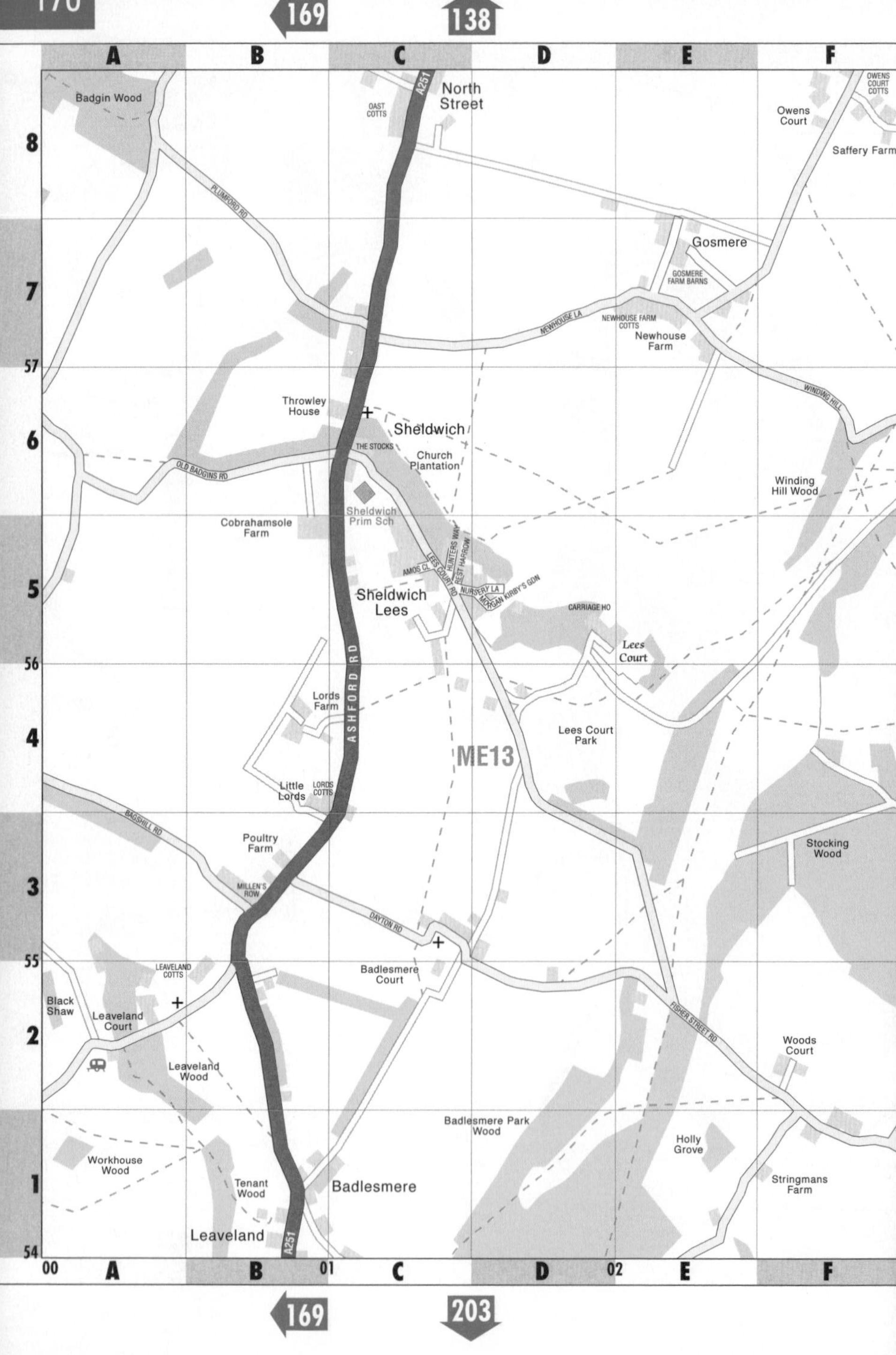
A
B
C
D
E
F
8
7
57
6
5
56
4
3
55
2
1
54
00
01
02
Badgin Wood
North Street
OAST COTTS
A251
OWENS COURT COTTS
Owens Court
Saffery Farm
PLUMFORD RD
Gosmere
GOSMERE FARM BARNS
NEWHOUSE LA
NEWHOUSE FARM COTTS
Newhouse Farm
WINDING HILL
Throwley House
Sheldwich
THE STOCKS
Church Plantation
OLD BADGINS RD
Winding Hill Wood
Sheldwich Prim Sch
Cobrahamsole Farm
AMOS CL
LEES COURT RD
HUNTERS WAY
WEST HARROW
NURSERY LA
MORGAN KIRBY'S GDN
Sheldwich Lees
CARRIAGE HO
Lees Court
ASHFORD RD
Lords Farm
Lees Court Park
ME13
Little Lords
LORDS COTTS
BAGSHILL RD
Poultry Farm
Stocking Wood
MILLEN'S ROW
DAYTON RD
LEAVELAND COTTS
Badlesmere Court
Black Shaw
Leaveland Court
FISHER STREET RD
Woods Court
Leaveland Wood
Badlesmere Park Wood
Holly Grove
Workhouse Wood
Tenant Wood
Badlesmere
Stringmans Farm
Leaveland

169
203

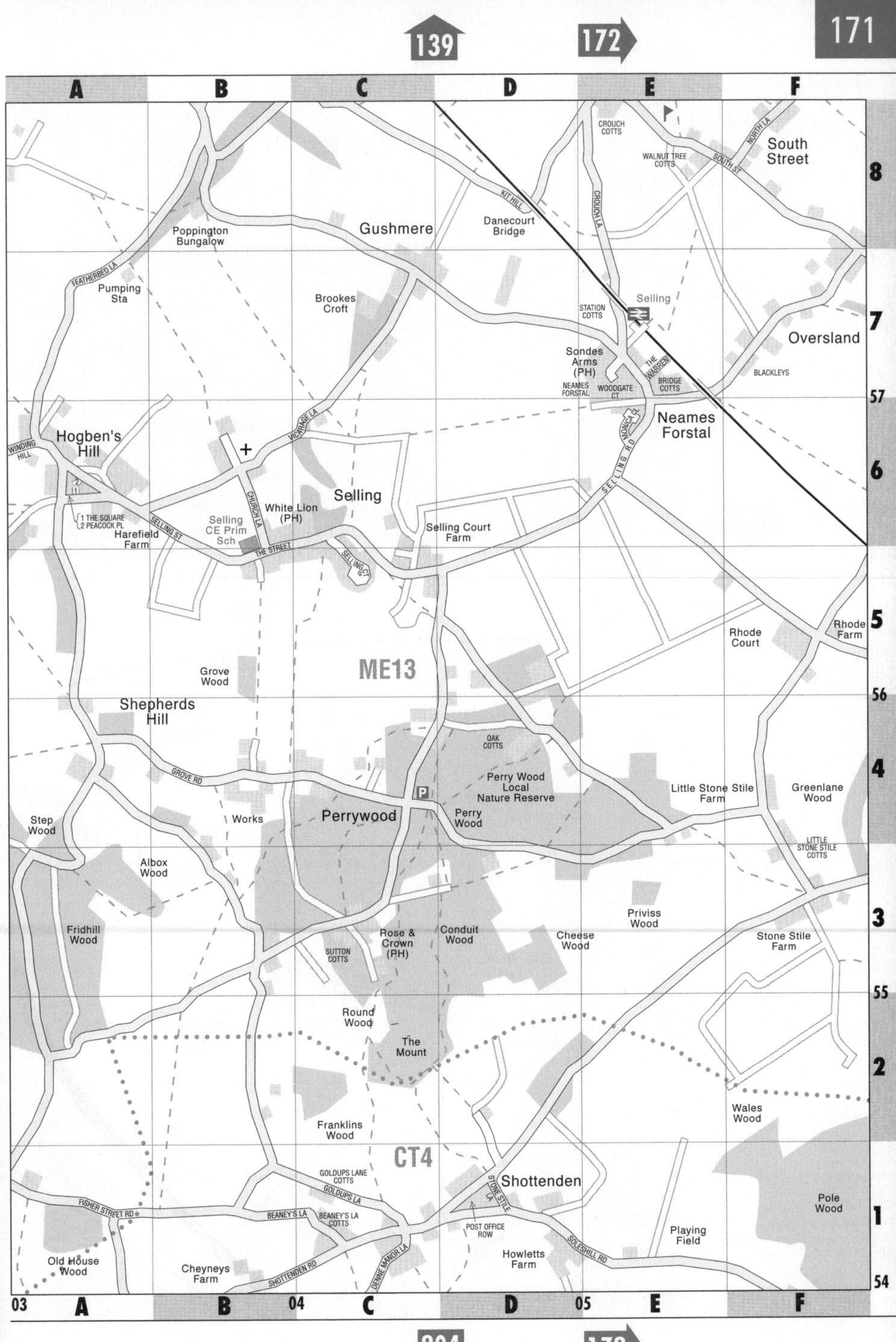

A   B   C   D   E   F

8
7
57
6
5
56
4
3
55
2
1
54

South Street
Crouch Cotts
Walnut Tree Cotts
NORTH LA
SOUTH ST

Gushmere
Danecourt Bridge
KIT HILL
CHURCH LA

Poppington Bungalow
FEATHERBED LA
Pumping Sta

Brookes Croft

Selling
STATION COTTS

Oversland
BLACKLEYS
THE WARREN

Sondes Arms (PH)
NEAMES FORSTAL
WOODGATE CT
BRIDGE COTTS

Neames Forstal
SELLING RD
MONKS LA

Hogben's Hill
WINDING HILL

HORSELEES LA

Selling
White Lion (PH)

Selling CE Prim Sch
SELLING RD
CHURCH LA
THE STREET
SELLING RD

1 THE SQUARE
2 PEACOCK PL
Harefield Farm

Selling Court Farm

Rhode Court

Rhode Farm

Grove Wood

ME13

Shepherds Hill

GROVE RD

Step Wood

Works

Perrywood

P

Perry Wood Local Nature Reserve

Oak Cotts

Perry Wood

Little Stone Stile Farm

Greenlane Wood

LITTLE STONE STILE COTTS

Albox Wood

Fridhill Wood

Priviss Wood

Stone Stile Farm

Rose & Crown (PH)

SUTTON COTTS

Conduit Wood

Cheese Wood

Round Wood

The Mount

Wales Wood

Franklins Wood

CT4

GOLDUPS LANE COTTS
GOLDUPS LA

Shottenden
STONE STILE

Pole Wood

FISHER STREET RD
BEANEY'S LA
BEANEY'S LA COTTS
SHOTTENDEN RD
DENNE MANOR LA

POST OFFICE ROW

BODENHILL RD

Howletts Farm

Playing Field

Old House Wood

Cheyneys Farm

03   04   05

A   B   C   D   E   F

171
140

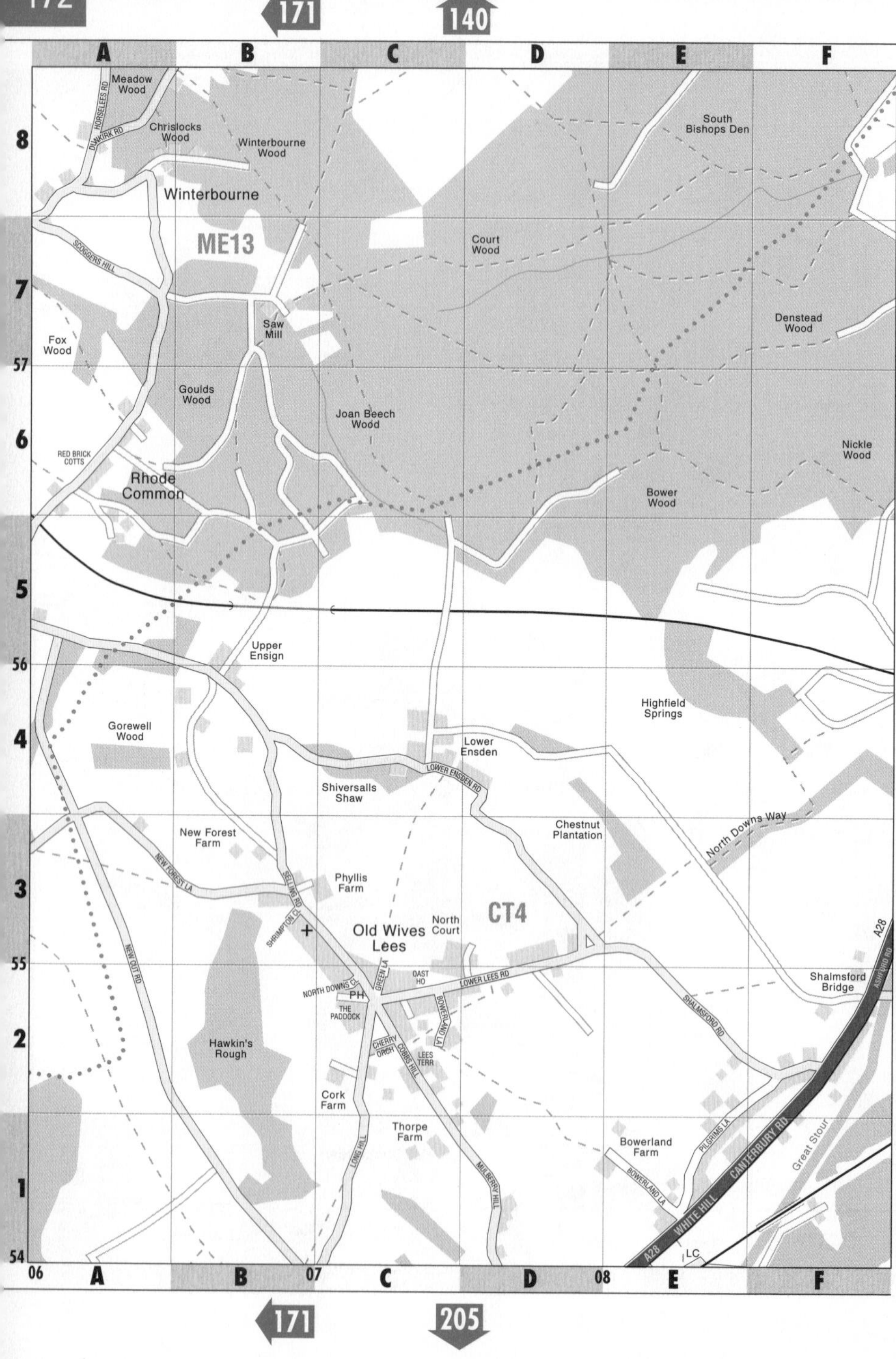
A
B
C
D
E
F
8
7
57
6
5
56
4
3
55
2
1
54
06
07
08
Meadow Wood
HORSELEES RD
DUNKIRK RD
Chrislocks Wood
Winterbourne Wood
South Bishops Den
Winterbourne
ME13
SCOGGERS HILL
Court Wood
Saw Mill
Fox Wood
Denstead Wood
Goulds Wood
Joan Beech Wood
RED BRICK COTTS
Nickle Wood
Rhode Common
Bower Wood
Upper Ensign
Highfield Springs
Gorewell Wood
Lower Ensden
LOWER ENSDEN RD
Shiversalls Shaw
New Forest Farm
Chestnut Plantation
North Downs Way
NEW FOREST LA
SELLING RD
Phyllis Farm
CT4
SHRIMPTON CL
Old Wives Lees
North Court
A28
ASHFORD RD
NEW CUT RD
GREEN LA
OAST HO
LOWER LEES RD
Shalmsford Bridge
NORTH DOWNS CL
PH
THE PADDOCK
BOWERLAND LA
SHALMSFORD RD
CHERRY ORCH
COBBS HILL
LEES TERR
Hawkin's Rough
Cork Farm
Thorpe Farm
LONG HILL
PILGRIMS LA
CANTERBURY RD
Great Stour
Bowerland Farm
BOWERLAND LA
MULBERRY HILL
WHITE HILL
A28
LC

171
205

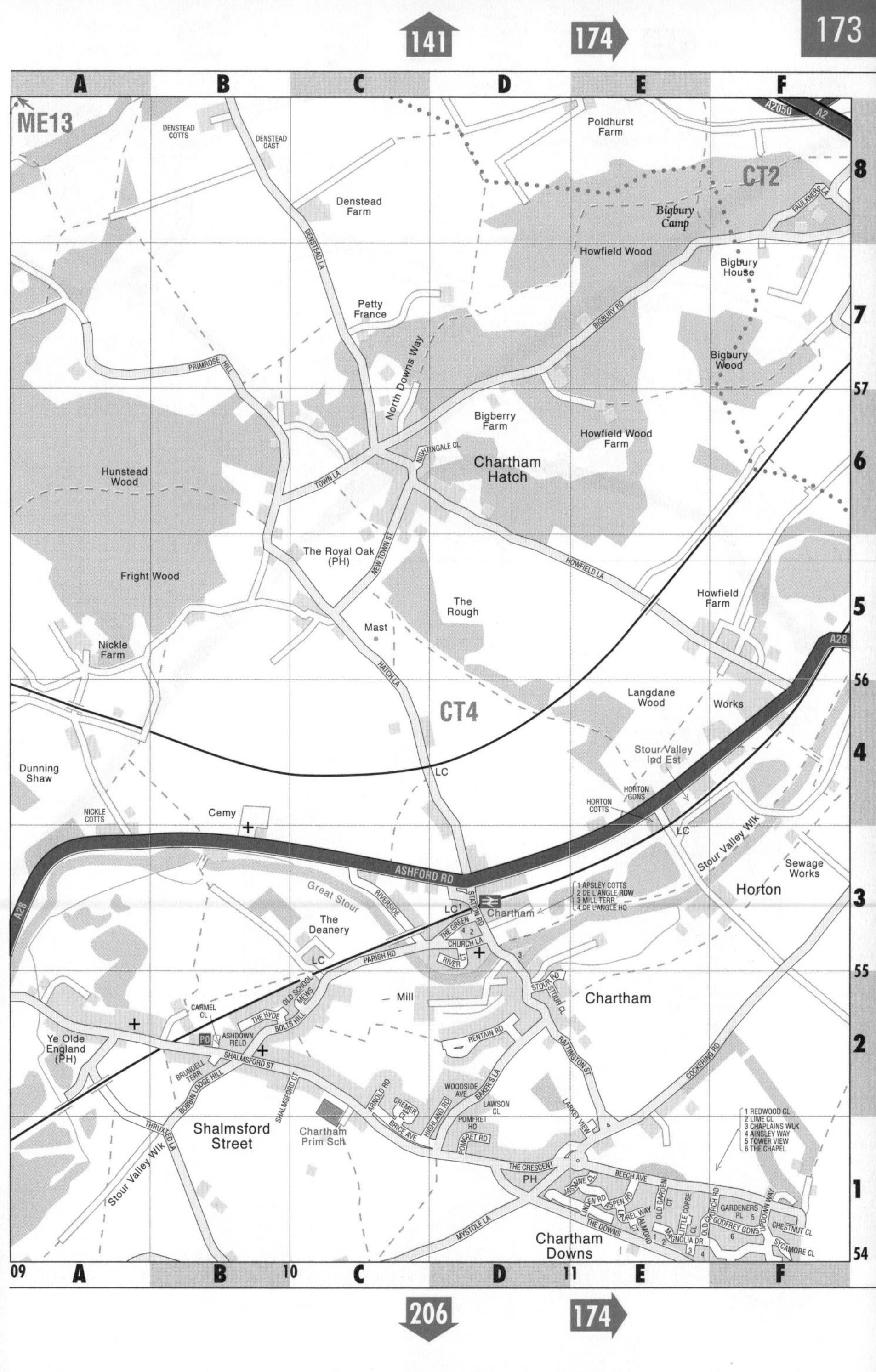
A
B
C
D
E
F
ME13
DENSTEAD COTTS
DENSTEAD OAST
Poldhurst Farm
A2050
A2
CT2
Denstead Farm
DENSTEAD LA
Bigbury Camp
FAULKNERS LA
Howfield Wood
Bigbury House
Petty France
BIGBURY RD
North Downs Way
PRIMROSE HILL
Bigbury Wood
Bigberry Farm
Howfield Wood Farm
NIGHTINGALE CL
Chartham Hatch
TOWN LA
Hunstead Wood
NEW TOWN ST
The Royal Oak (PH)
HOWFIELD LA
Fright Wood
The Rough
Howfield Farm
Mast
Nickle Farm
HATCH LA
A28
Langdane Wood
Works
CT4
Dunning Shaw
Stour Valley Ind Est
LC
HORTON GDNS
HORTON COTTS
NICKLE COTTS
Cemy
Stour Valley Wlk
ASHFORD RD
Sewage Works
RIVERSIDE
Great Stour
STATION RD
1 APSLEY COTTS
2 DE L'ANGLE ROW
3 MILL TERR
4 DE L'ANGLE HO
Horton
The Deanery
Chartham
THE GREEN
CHURCH LA
PARISH RD
RIVER CT
STOUR RD
STOUR CL
OLD SCHOOL MEWS
Mill
Chartham
CARMEL CL
THE HYDE
BOLTS HILL
ASHDOWN FIELD
PO
RENTAIN RD
RATTINGTON ST
Ye Olde England (PH)
BRUNDELL TERR
SHALMSFORD ST
BOBBIN LODGE HILL
COCKERING RD
SHALMSFORD CT
ARNOLD RD
CREMER CL
HIGHLAND RD
WOODSIDE AVE
BAKER'S LA
LAWSON CL
LARKEY VIEW
POMFRET HO
POMFRET RD
BRICE AVE
THRUXTED LA
Shalmsford Street
Chartham Prim Sch
1 REDWOOD CL
2 LIME CL
3 CHAPLAINS WLK
4 AINSLEY WAY
5 TOWER VIEW
6 THE CHAPEL
THE CRESCENT
PH
BEECH AVE
JASMINE CL
LINDEN RD
ASPEN RD
LAUREL WAY
OLD GARDEN CT
LITTLE COPSE CL
OLD CHURCH RD
GARDENERS PL
UPDOWN WAY
GODFREY GDNS
CHESTNUT CL
SYCAMORE CL
ALMOND CT
MAGNOLIA DR
THE DOWNS
MYSTOLE LA
Chartham Downs
8
7
57
6
5
56
4
3
55
2
1
54
09
10
11

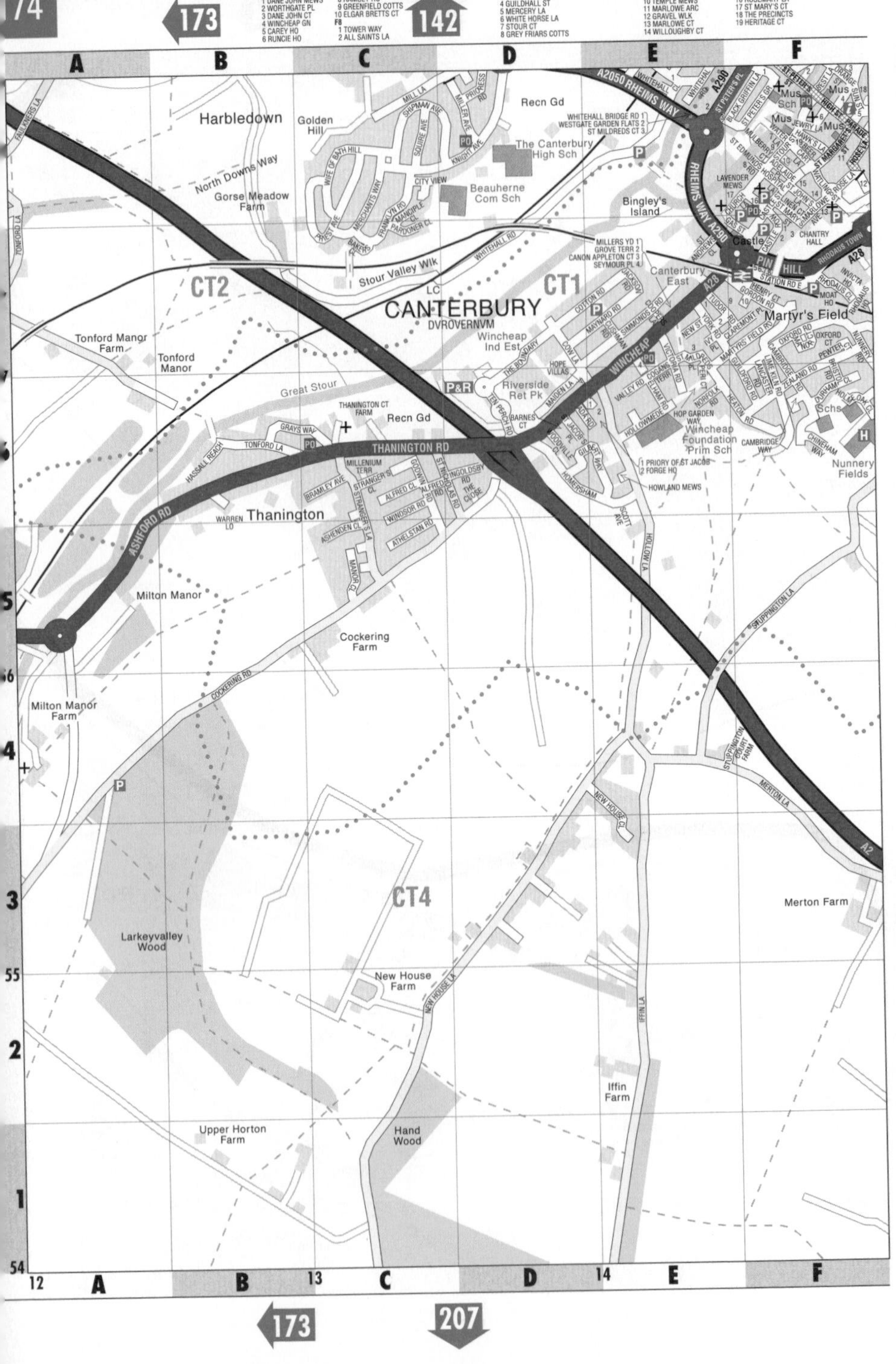

173
142
F7
1 DANE JOHN MEWS
2 WORTHGATE PL
3 DANE JOHN CT
4 WINCHEAP GN
5 CAREY HO
6 RUNCIE HO
7 COGGAN HO
8 RAMSEY HO
9 GREENFIELD COTTS
10 ELGAR BRETTS CT
F8
1 TOWER WAY
2 ALL SAINTS LA
F8
3 TURNAGAIN LA
4 GUILDHALL ST
5 MERCERY LA
6 WHITE HORSE LA
7 STOUR CT
8 GREY FRIARS COTTS
F8
9 STOURVILLE
10 TEMPLE MEWS
11 MARLOWE ARC
12 GRAVEL WLK
13 MARLOWE CT
14 WILLOUGHBY CT
15 LULLINGSTONE CT
16 ROSEMARY LA
17 ST MARY'S CT
18 THE PRECINCTS
19 HERITAGE CT
Harbledown
Golden Hill
Recn Gd
The Canterbury High Sch
Beauherne Com Sch
North Downs Way
Gorse Meadow Farm
Bingley's Island
WHITEHALL BRIDGE RD 1
WESTGATE GARDEN FLATS 2
ST MILDREDS CT 3
MILLERS YD 1
GROVE TERR 2
CANON APPLETON CT 3
SEYMOUR PL 4
Stour Valley Wlk
CT2
CT1
CANTERBURY
DVROVERNVM
Canterbury East
Castle
CHANTRY HALL
Martyr's Field
Tonford Manor Farm
Tonford Manor
Wincheap Ind Est
Riverside Ret Pk
Great Stour
THANINGTON CT FARM
Recn Gd
THANINGTON RD
WINCHEAP
HOP GARDEN WAY
Wincheap Foundation Prim Sch
1 PRIORY OF ST JACOB
2 FORGE HO
HOWLAND MEWS
Schs
Nunnery Fields
Thanington
WARREN LO
ASHFORD RD
Milton Manor
Cockering Farm
COCKERING RD
Milton Manor Farm
STUPPINGTON LA
STUPPINGTON COURT FARM
MERTON LA
CT4
Merton Farm
Larkeyvalley Wood
New House Farm
NEW HOUSE LA
IFFIN LA
Iffin Farm
Upper Horton Farm
Hand Wood
A2050 RHEIMS WAY
A290
A28
A2

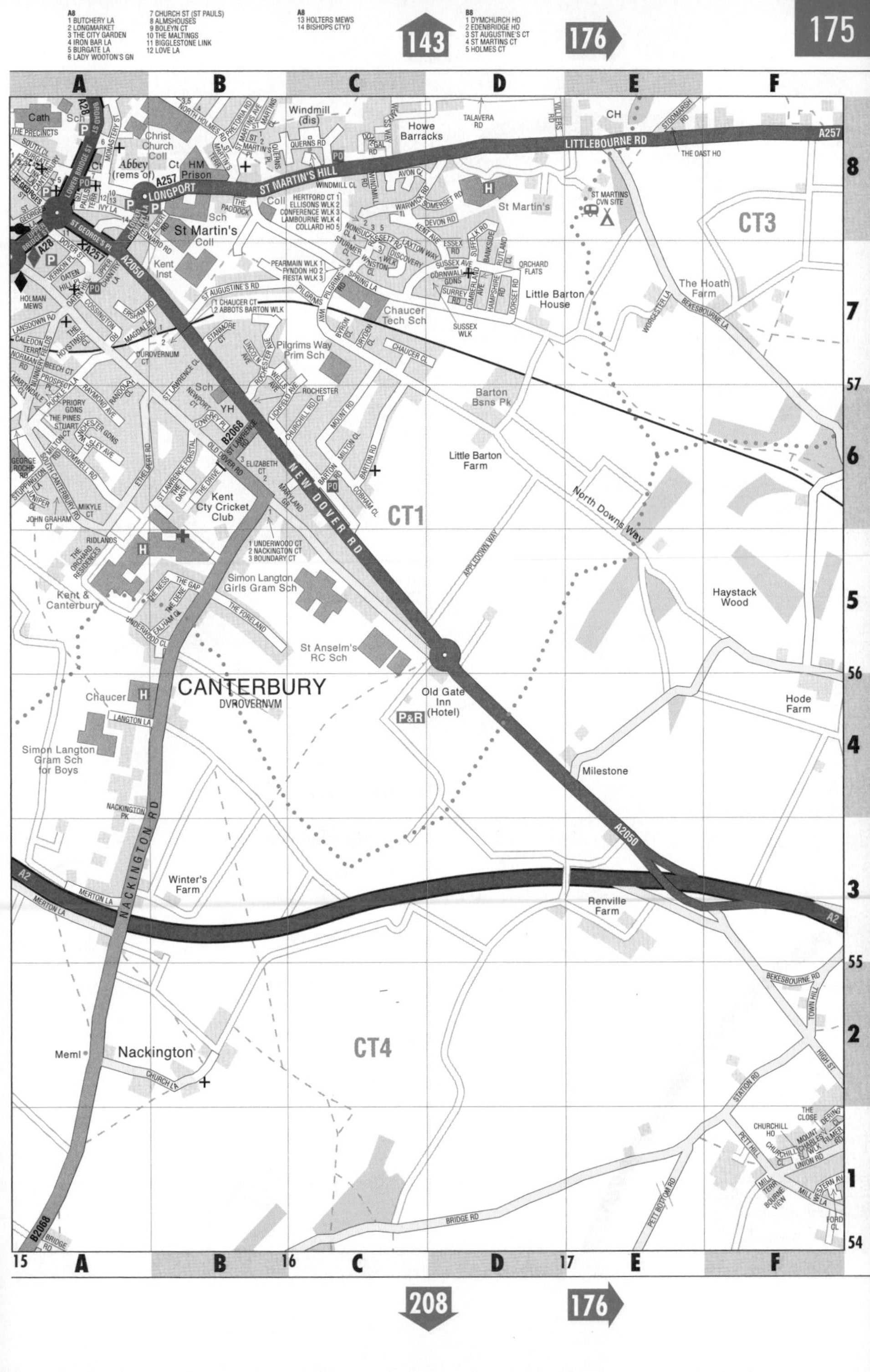
A8
1 BUTCHERY LA
2 LONGMARKET
3 THE CITY GARDEN
4 IRON BAR LA
5 BURGATE LA
6 LADY WOOTON'S GN
7 CHURCH ST (ST PAULS)
8 ALMSHOUSES
9 BOLEYN CT
10 THE MALTINGS
11 BIGGLESTONE LINK
12 LOVE LA
A8
13 HOLTERS MEWS
14 BISHOPS CTYD
143
176
B8
1 DYMCHURCH HO
2 EDENBRIDGE HO
3 ST AUGUSTINE'S CT
4 ST MARTINS CT
5 HOLMES CT
A
B
C
D
E
F
8
7
57
6
5
56
4
3
55
2
1
54
15
16
17
Cath
Christ Church Coll
Abbey (rems of)
HM Prison
LONGPORT
ST MARTIN'S HILL
LITTLEBOURNE RD
A257
A28
A2050
B2068
A2
Windmill (dis)
Howe Barracks
St Martin's
St Martin's Coll
Kent Inst
ST MARTINS CVN SITE
THE OAST HO
CT3
CT1
CT4
The Hoath Farm
Little Barton House
Chaucer Tech Sch
Pilgrims Way Prim Sch
Barton Bsns Pk
Little Barton Farm
North Downs Way
NEW DOVER RD
Kent Cty Cricket Club
Simon Langton Girls Gram Sch
Kent & Canterbury
St Anselm's RC Sch
Haystack Wood
CANTERBURY
DVROVERNVM
Chaucer
Old Gate Inn (Hotel)
P&R
Hode Farm
Simon Langton Gram Sch for Boys
Milestone
NACKINGTON RD
Winter's Farm
Renville Farm
MERTON LA
Nackington
Meml
CHURCH LA
BRIDGE RD
PETT BOTTOM RD
STATION RD
BEKESBOURNE RD
BEKESBOURNE LA
TOWN HILL
HIGH ST
208
176

175
144

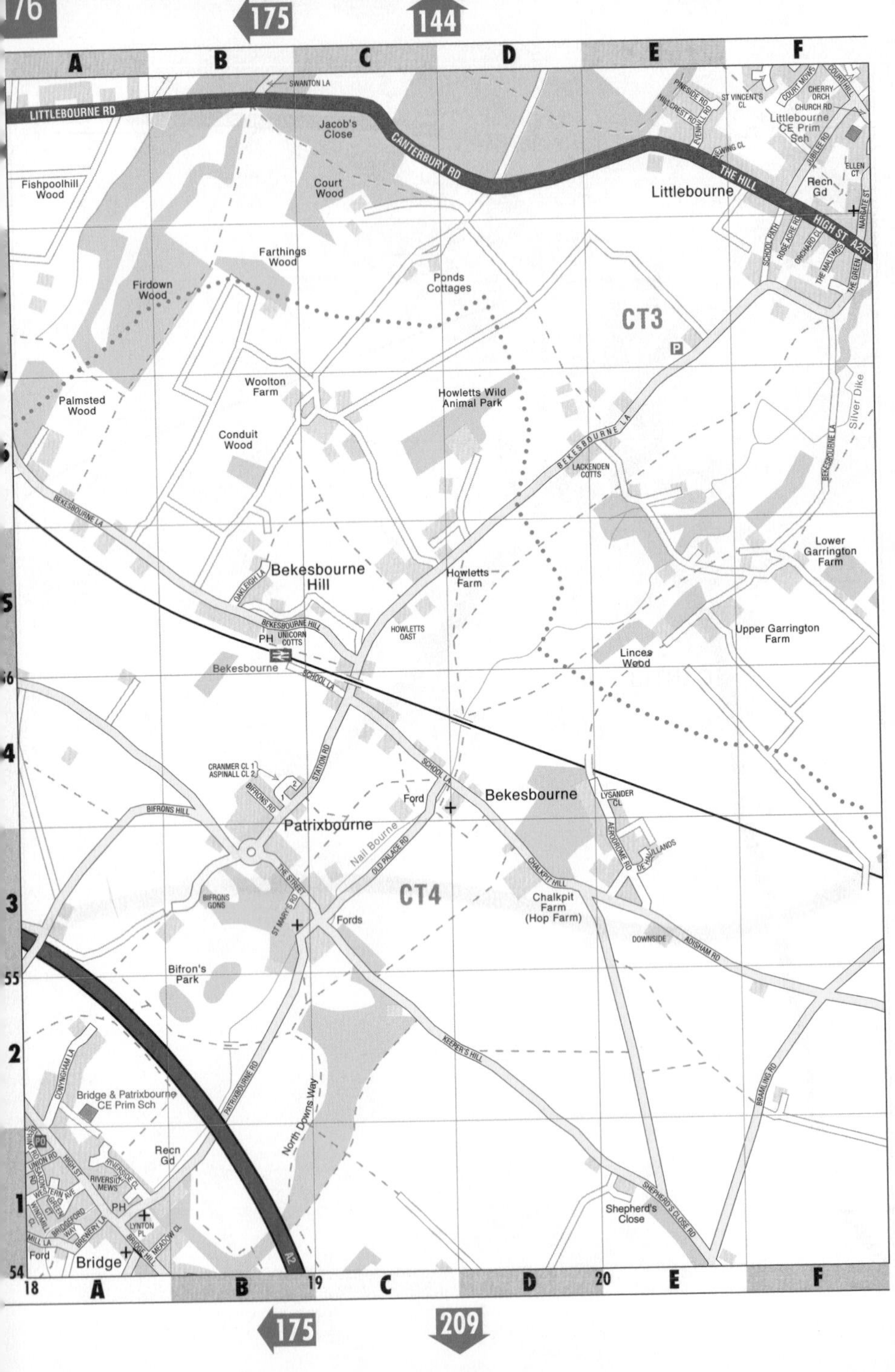
LITTLEBOURNE RD
SWANTON LA
Jacob's Close
CANTERBURY RD
Court Wood
Fishpoolhill Wood
Farthings Wood
Firdown Wood
Ponds Cottages
Palmsted Wood
Woolton Farm
Howletts Wild Animal Park
Conduit Wood
CT3
Littlebourne
THE HILL
HIGH ST. A257
Littlebourne CE Prim Sch
Recn Gd
BEKESBOURNE LA
LACKENDEN COTTS
Lower Garrington Farm
Upper Garrington Farm
Bekesbourne Hill
Howletts Farm
HOWLETTS OAST
Linces Wood
PH
UNICORN COTTS
Bekesbourne
SCHOOL LA
CRANMER CL 1
ASPINALL CL 2
STATION RD
BIFRONS RD
BIFRONS HILL
Patrixbourne
Ford
Bekesbourne
LYSANDER CL
AERODROME RD
DE HAVILLANDS
Nail Bourne
OLD PALACE RD
THE STREET
CT4
CHALKPIT HILL
Chalkpit Farm (Hop Farm)
BIFRONS GDNS
ST MARY'S RD
Fords
DOWNSIDE
ADISHAM RD
Bifron's Park
KEEPER'S HILL
CONYNGHAM LA
Bridge & Patrixbourne CE Prim Sch
PATRIXBOURNE RD
North Downs Way
BRAMLING RD
Recn Gd
RIVERSIDE CL
RIVERSIDE MEWS
HIGH ST
PH
LYNTON PL
BRIDGE HILL
MEADOW CL
BREWERY LA
Ford
Bridge
A2
Shepherd's Close
SHEPHERD'S CLOSE RD
Silver Dike
A B C D E F
18 19 20
54 55 56

175
209

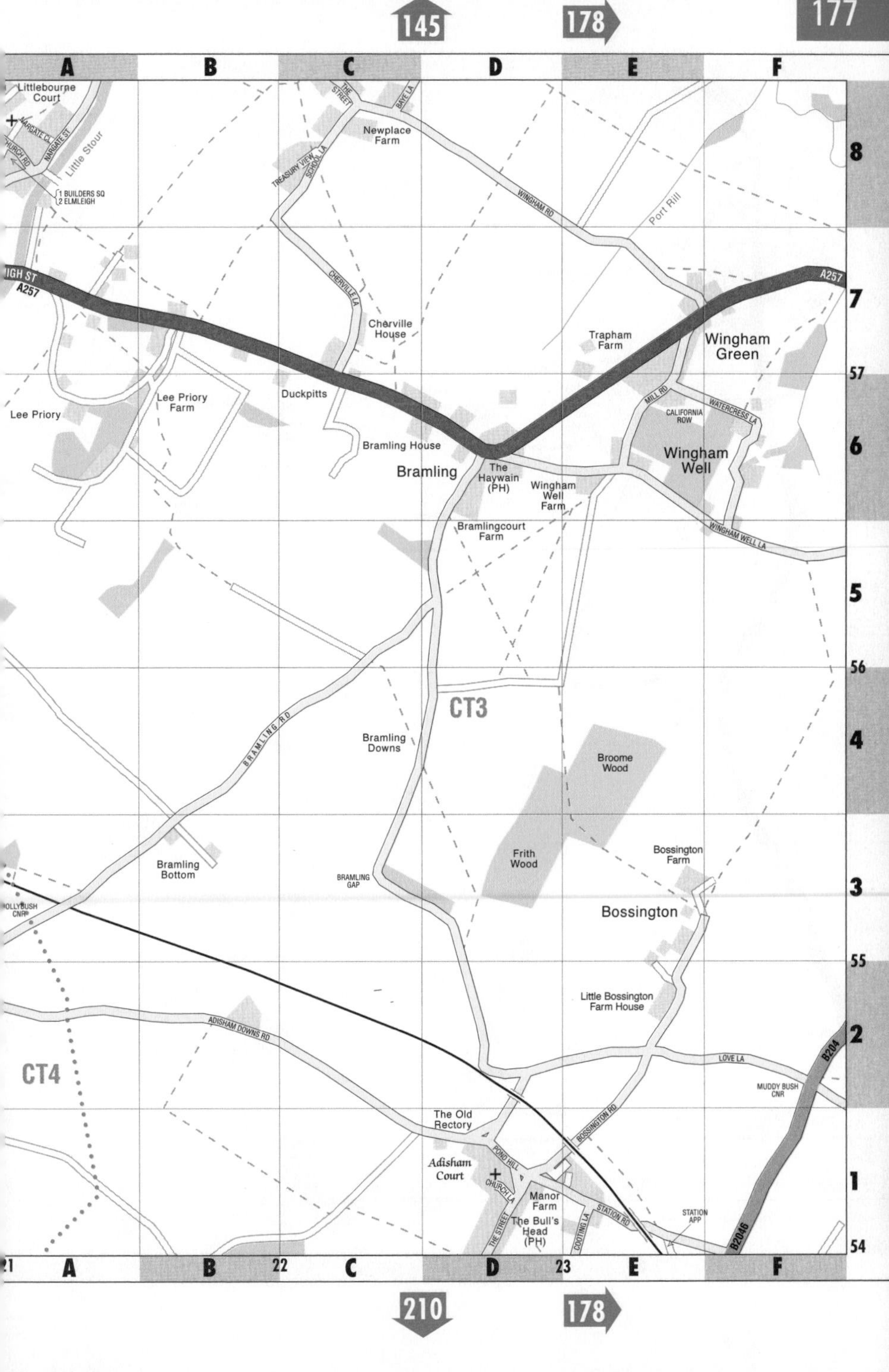
A
B
C
D
E
F
8
7
57
6
5
56
4
3
55
2
1
54
22
23
Littlebourne Court
NARGATE CL
NARGATE ST
CHURCH RD
Little Stour
1 BUILDERS SQ
2 ELMLEIGH
THE STREET
BAYE LA
Newplace Farm
TREASURY VIEW
SCHOOL LA
WINGHAM RD
Port Rill
IGH ST
A257
CHERVILLE LA
Cherville House
Trapham Farm
Wingham Green
Lee Priory Farm
Duckpitts
Lee Priory
MILL RD
CALIFORNIA ROW
WATERCRESS LA
Bramling House
Wingham Well
Bramling
The Haywain (PH)
Wingham Well Farm
Bramlingcourt Farm
WINGHAM WELL LA
CT3
Bramling Downs
BRAMLING RD
Broome Wood
Frith Wood
Bossington Farm
Bramling Bottom
BRAMLING GAP
Bossington
Little Bossington Farm House
ADISHAM DOWNS RD
LOVE LA
B204
MUDDY BUSH CNR
CT4
The Old Rectory
BOSSINGTON RD
POND HILL
Adisham Court
CHURCH LA
Manor Farm
The Bull's Head (PH)
THE STREET
COOTING LA
STATION RD
STATION APP
B2046

177
146

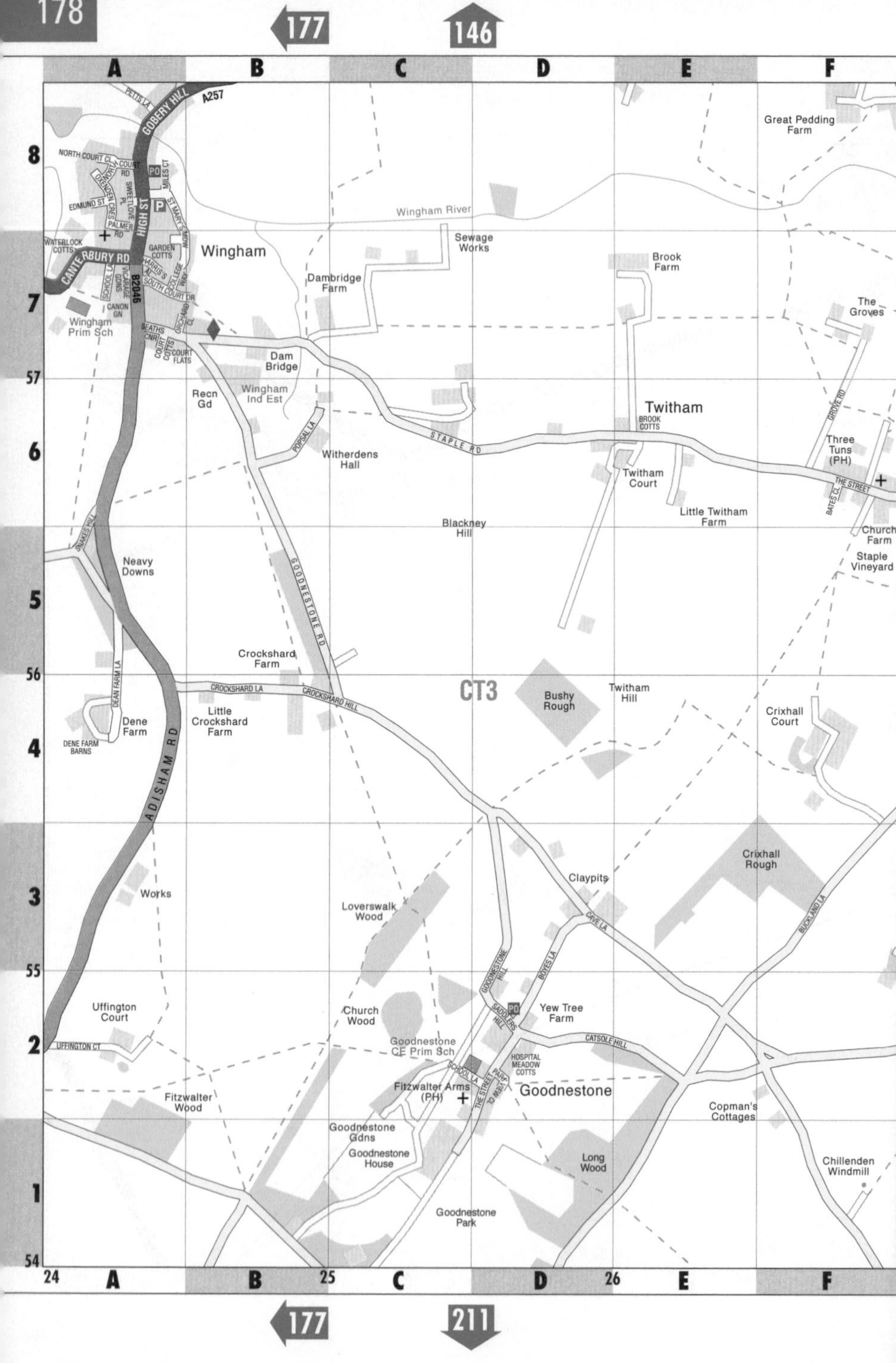
Wingham
Wingham River
Sewage Works
Great Pedding Farm
Brook Farm
Dambridge Farm
The Groves
Wingham Prim Sch
Dam Bridge
Recn Gd
Wingham Ind Est
Twitham
BROOK COTTS
STAPLE RD
Witherdens Hall
Twitham Court
Three Tuns (PH)
THE STREET
Little Twitham Farm
Blackney Hill
Church Farm
Staple Vineyard
Neavy Downs
GOODNESTONE RD
Crockshard Farm
CROCKSHARD LA
CROCKSHARD HILL
CT3
Bushy Rough
Twitham Hill
Crixhall Court
Dene Farm
DENE FARM BARNS
Little Crockshard Farm
ADISHAM RD
Crixhall Rough
Claypits
Works
Loverswalk Wood
CAVE LA
BUCKLAND LA
Uffington Court
UFFINGTON CT
Church Wood
Yew Tree Farm
CATSOLE HILL
Goodnestone CE Prim Sch
HOSPITAL MEADOW COTTS
Fitzwalter Arms (PH)
Goodnestone
Fitzwalter Wood
Copman's Cottages
Goodnestone Gdns
Goodnestone House
Long Wood
Chillenden Windmill
Goodnestone Park
GOBERY HILL
A257
B2046
HIGH ST
CANTERBURY RD
NORTH COURT CL
COURT RD
EDMUND ST
PALMER RD
WATERLOCK COTTS
GARDEN COTTS
SOUTH COURT DR
SCHOOL LA
VICARAGE GDNS
CANON GN
ORCHARD CL
POPSAL LA
GROVE RD
BATES CL
SNAKES HILL
DEAN FARM LA
BOYES LA
GOODNESTONE HILL
SADDLERS HILL
SCHOOL LA
THE STREET
PARK VIEW CL
A B C D E F
8 7 57 6 5 56 4 3 55 2 1 54
24 25 26

177
211

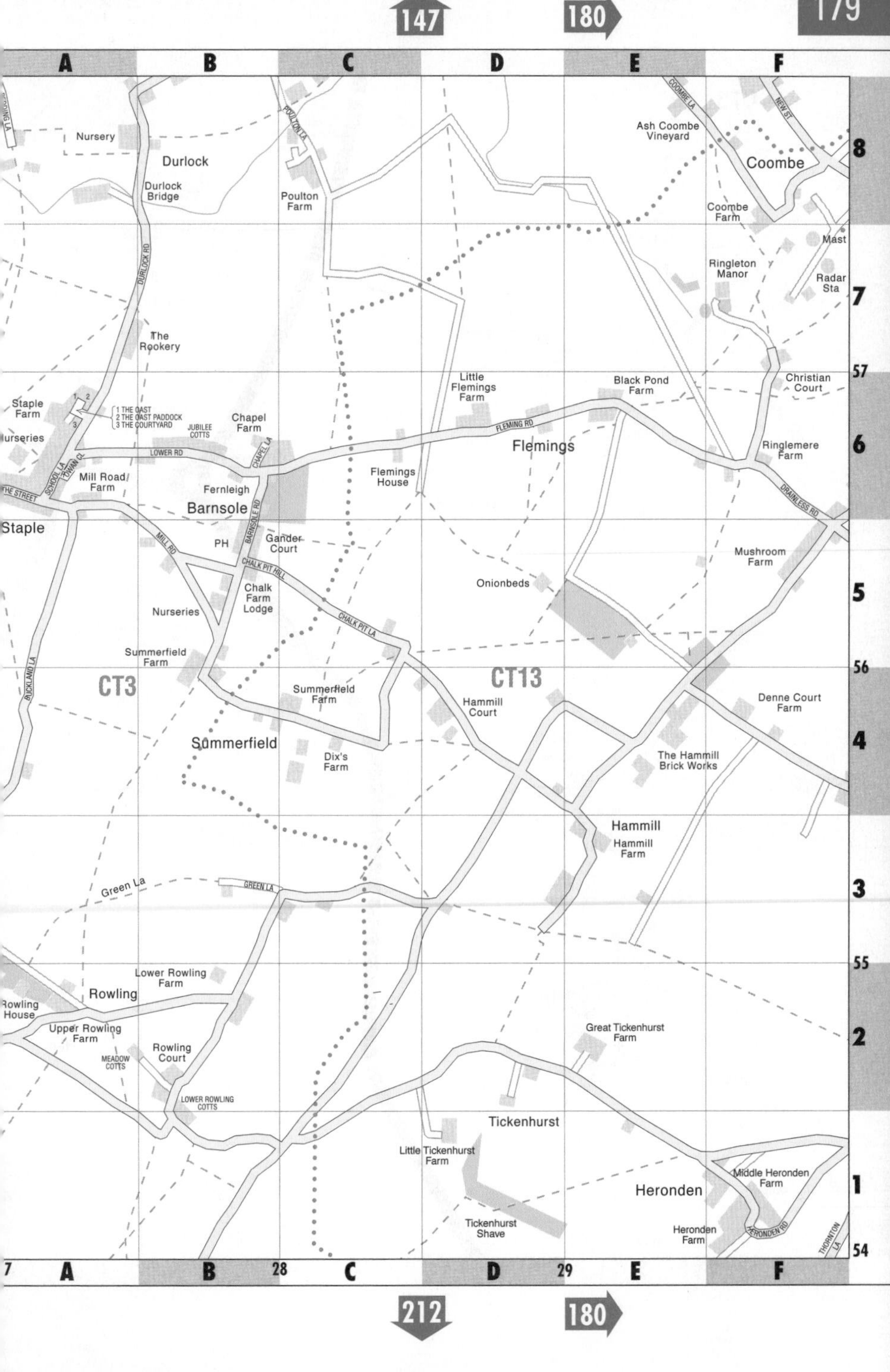
A
B
C
D
E
F
Nursery
Durlock
Durlock Bridge
Poulton Farm
POULTON LA
COOMBE LA
NEW ST
Ash Coombe Vineyard
Coombe
Coombe Farm
Mast
Ringleton Manor
Radar Sta
DURLOCK RD
The Rookery
Little Flemings Farm
Black Pond Farm
Christian Court
Staple Farm
1 THE OAST
2 THE OAST PADDOCK
3 THE COURTYARD
JUBILEE COTTS
Chapel Farm
FLEMING RD
Flemings
Ringlemere Farm
LOWER RD
CHAPEL LA
SCHOOL LA
TOWN CL
Mill Road Farm
Fernleigh
Flemings House
THE STREET
Barnsole
BARNSOLE RD
DRAINLESS RD
Staple
MILL RD
PH
Gander Court
Mushroom Farm
CHALK PIT HILL
Chalk Farm Lodge
Onionbeds
Nurseries
CHALK PIT LA
Summerfield Farm
CT3
CT13
Summerfield Farm
Hammill Court
Denne Court Farm
BUCKLAND LA
Summerfield
Dix's Farm
The Hammill Brick Works
Hammill
Hammill Farm
Green La
GREEN LA
Lower Rowling Farm
Rowling
Rowling House
Upper Rowling Farm
MEADOW COTTS
Rowling Court
LOWER ROWLING COTTS
Great Tickenhurst Farm
Tickenhurst
Little Tickenhurst Farm
Middle Heronden Farm
Heronden
Tickenhurst Shave
Heronden Farm
HERONDEN RD
THORNTON LA
8
7
57
6
5
56
4
3
55
2
1
54
28
29

179
148

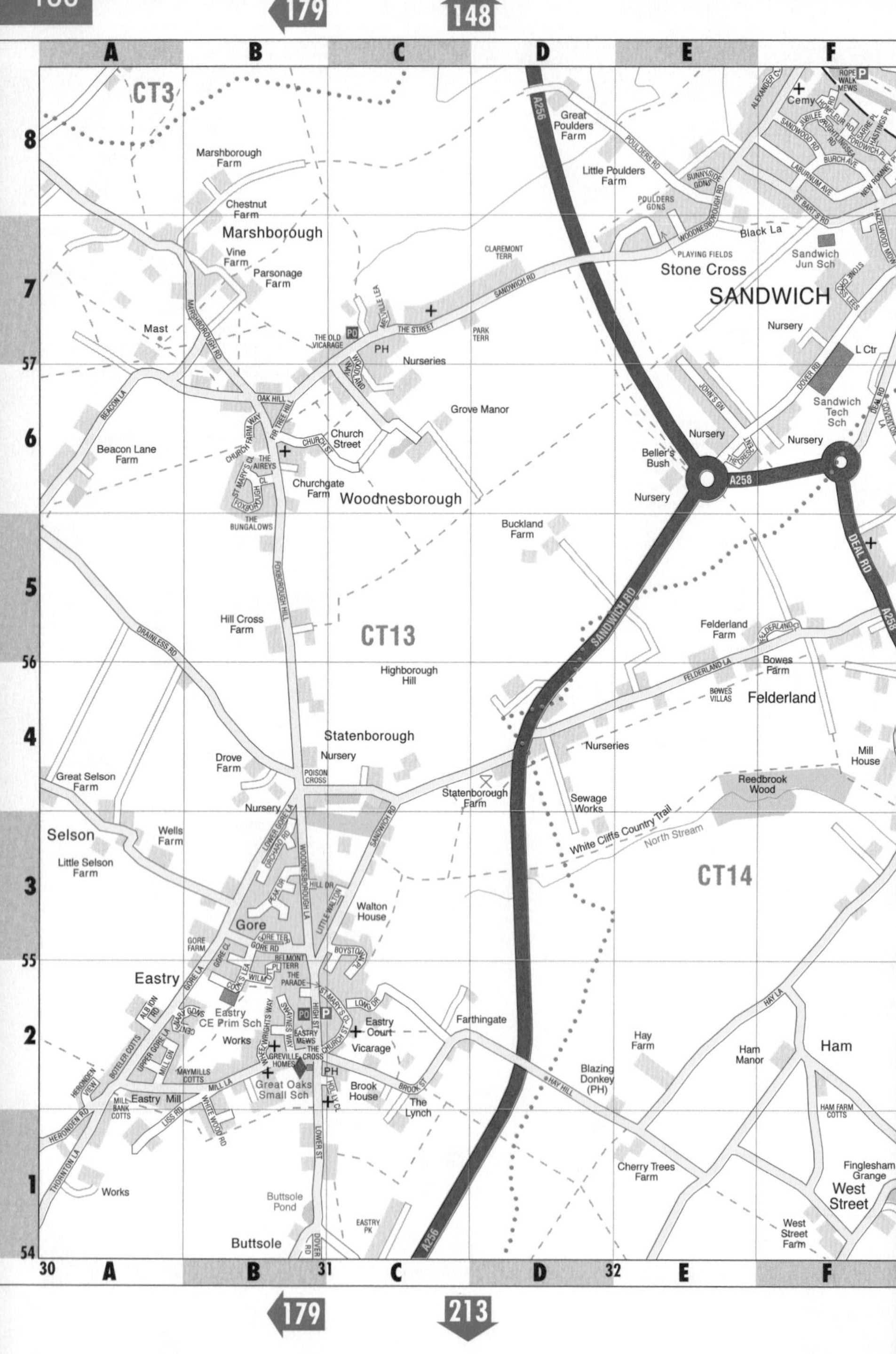
CT3
Marshborough Farm
Chestnut Farm
Marshborough
Vine Farm
Parsonage Farm
Mast
Beacon Lane Farm
Great Poulders Farm
Little Poulders Farm
Stone Cross
SANDWICH
Sandwich Jun Sch
Sandwich Tech Sch
L Ctr
Nursery
Church Street
Churchgate Farm
Woodnesborough
Grove Manor
Nurseries
Beller's Bush
Buckland Farm
Hill Cross Farm
CT13
Highborough Hill
Statenborough
Felderland Farm
Bowes Farm
Felderland
Drove Farm
Great Selson Farm
Selson
Wells Farm
Little Selson Farm
Statenborough Farm
Sewage Works
Reedbrook Wood
Mill House
White Cliffs Country Trail
North Stream
CT14
Gore
Walton House
Eastry
Eastry CE Prim Sch
Works
Eastry Court
Vicarage
Farthingate
Hay Farm
Blazing Donkey (PH)
Ham Manor
Ham
Eastry Mill
Great Oaks Small Sch
Brook House
The Lynch
Works
Buttsole Pond
Buttsole
Cherry Trees Farm
Finglesham Grange
West Street
West Street Farm
A256
A258
SANDWICH RD
DEAL RD
HAY HILL
FELDERLAND LA
DRAINLESS RD
FOXBOROUGH HILL
WOODNESBOROUGH LA
LOWER ST
DOVER RD
30
31
32
54
55
56
57

179
213

149
182

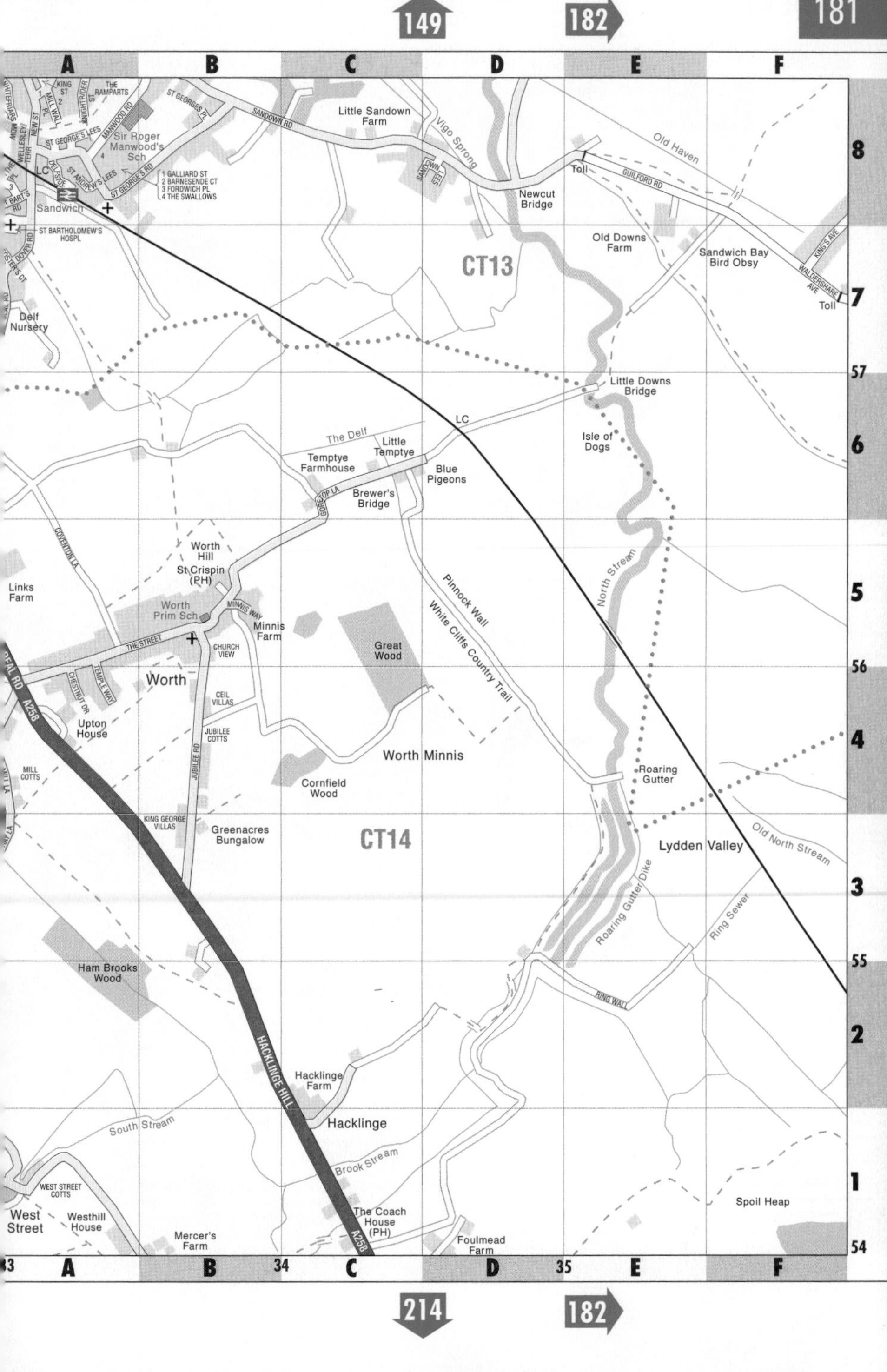
A
B
C
D
E
F
8
7
57
6
5
56
4
3
55
2
1
54
34
35
Little Sandown Farm
Vigo Sprong
SANDOWN RD
ST GEORGES PL
Sir Roger Manwood's Sch
MANWOOD RD
THE RAMPARTS
KING ST
MILL WALL PL
NEW ST
ST GEORGE'S LEES
ST ANDREW'S LEES
ST GEORGE'S RD
DELFSIDE
LC
Sandwich
1 GALLIARD ST
2 BARNESENDE CT
3 FORDWICH PL
4 THE SWALLOWS
ST BARTHOLOMEW'S HOSPL
DOVER RD
Delf Nursery
Old Haven
Toll
GUILFORD RD
Newcut Bridge
Old Downs Farm
Sandwich Bay Bird Obsy
KING'S AVE
WALDERSHARE AVE
Toll
CT13
Little Downs Bridge
LC
The Delf
Little Temptye
Temptye Farmhouse
Blue Pigeons
Brewer's Bridge
GORE OP LA
Isle of Dogs
COVENTON LA
Worth Hill
St Crispin (PH)
Links Farm
Worth Prim Sch
MINNIS WAY
Minnis Farm
Pinnock Wall
White Cliffs Country Trail
North Stream
Great Wood
THE STREET
CHURCH VIEW
Worth
CHESTNUT DR
TEMPLE WAY
CEIL VILLAS
A258
Upton House
JUBILEE COTTS
JUBILEE RD
MILL COTTS
Worth Minnis
Roaring Gutter
Cornfield Wood
KING GEORGE VILLAS
Greenacres Bungalow
CT14
Lydden Valley
Old North Stream
Roaring Gutter Dike
Ring Sewer
Ham Brooks Wood
RING WALL
HACKLINGE HILL
Hacklinge Farm
Hacklinge
South Stream
Brook Stream
WEST STREET COTTS
West Street
Westhill House
Mercer's Farm
The Coach House (PH)
A258
Foulmead Farm
Spoil Heap

214
182

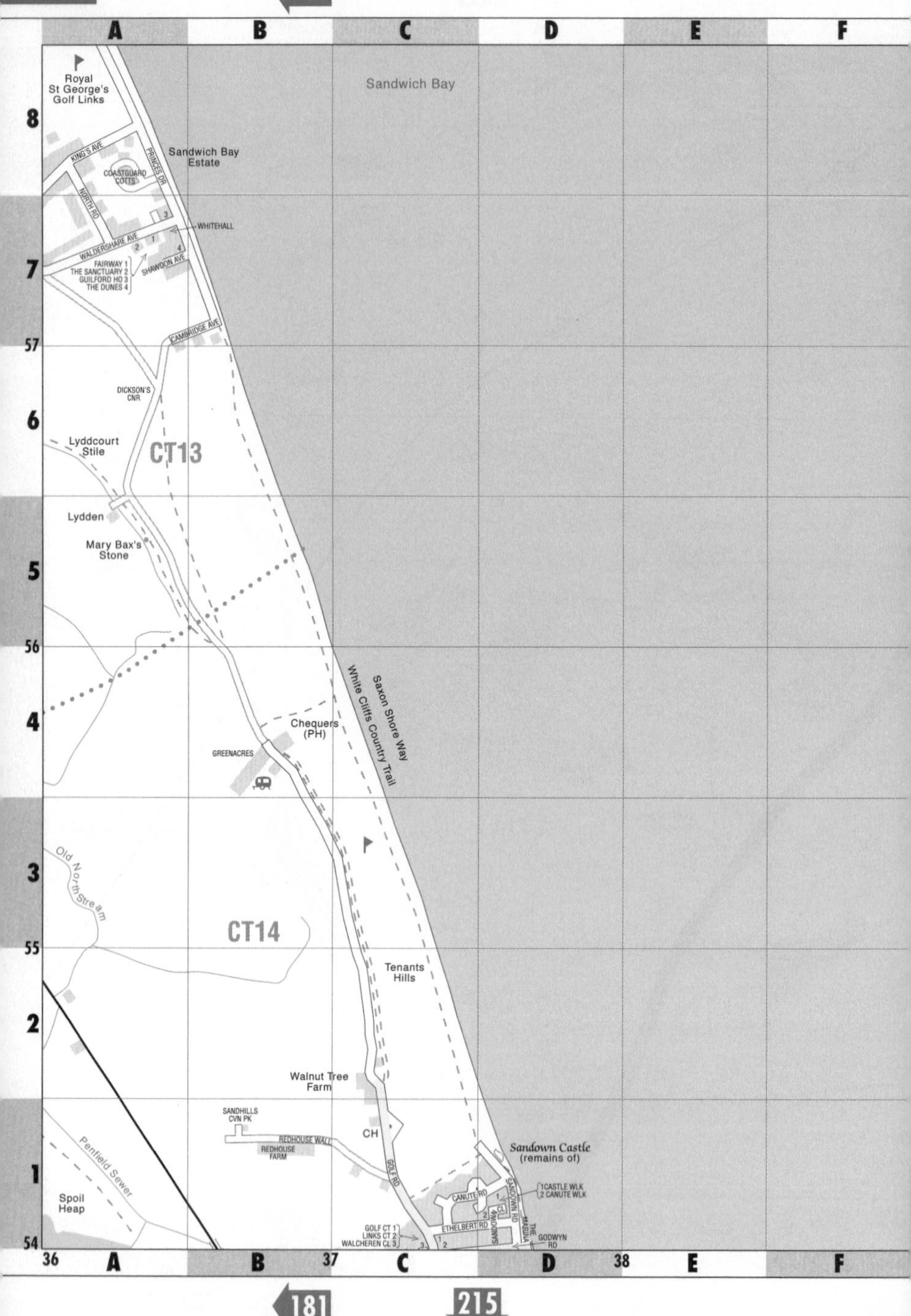

Sandwich Bay

Royal St George's Golf Links

KING'S AVE
PRINCES DR
COASTGUARD COTTS
NORTH RD
Sandwich Bay Estate
WHITEHALL
WALDERSHARE AVE
SHANNON AVE
FAIRWAY 1
THE SANCTUARY 2
GUILFORD HO 3
THE DUNES 4
CAMBRIDGE AVE

DICKSON'S CNR

CT13

Lyddcourt Stile

Lydden

Mary Bax's Stone

White Cliffs Country Trail
Saxon Shore Way

Chequers (PH)

GREENACRES

Old North Stream

CT14

Tenants Hills

Walnut Tree Farm

SANDHILLS CVN PK
REDHOUSE WALL
REDHOUSE FARM
CH

Penfield Sewer

Spoil Heap

Sandown Castle (remains of)
1 CASTLE WLK
2 CANUTE WLK
CANUTE RD
ETHELBERT RD
SANDOWN RD
SANDOWN RD
GODWYN RD
THE QUARTERDECK
GOLF CT 1
LINKS CT 2
WALCHEREN CL 3

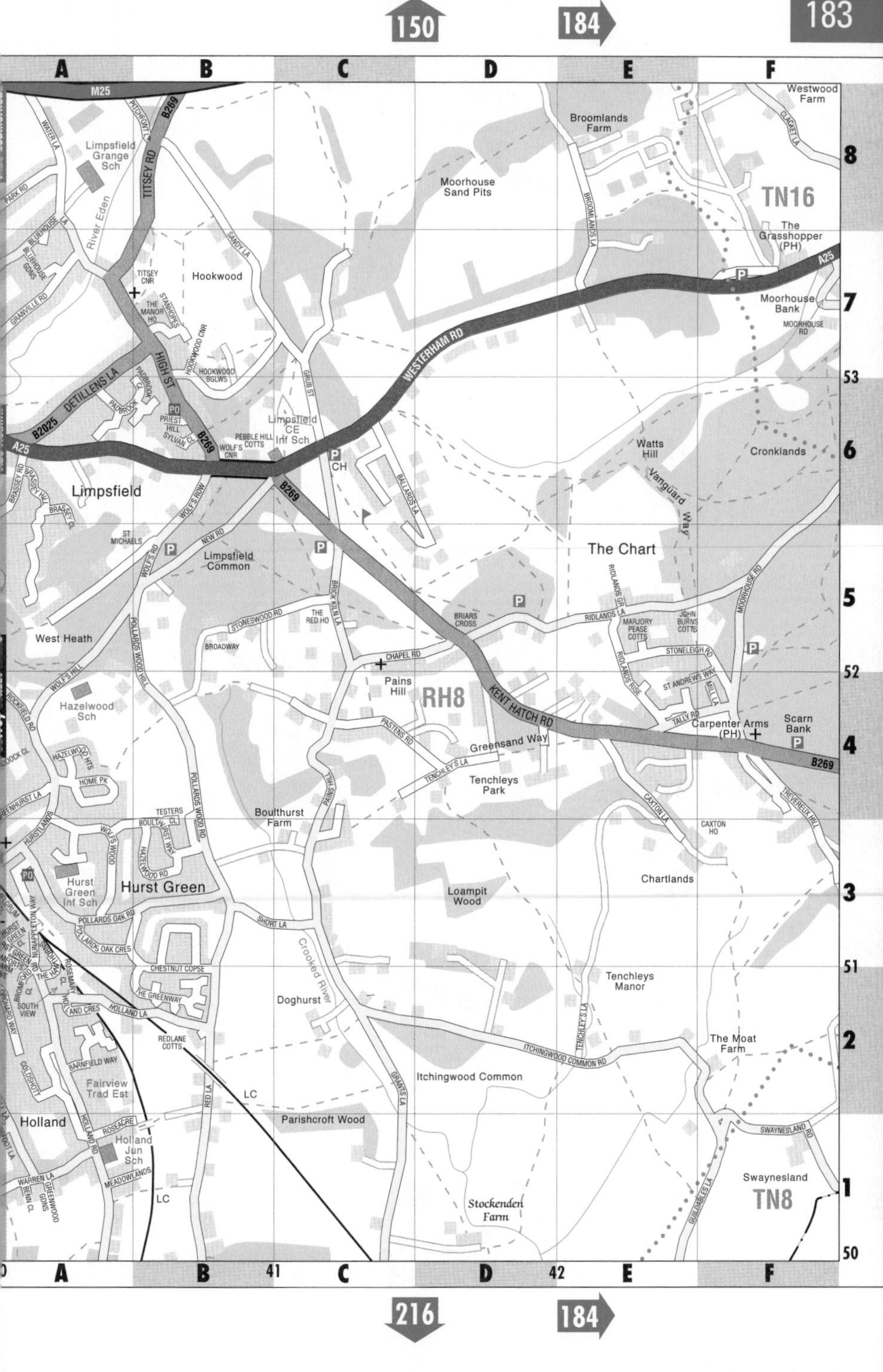
150
184
A
B
C
D
E
F
M25
Westwood Farm
Broomlands Farm
Limpsfield Grange Sch
Moorhouse Sand Pits
TN16
The Grasshopper (PH)
TITSEY RD
B269
River Eden
Hookwood
SANDY LA
BROOMLANDS LA
A25
Moorhouse Bank
MOORHOUSE RD
TITSEY CNR
THE MANOR HO
HOOKWOOD CNR
HOOKWOOD BGLWS
HIGH ST
DETILLENS LA
WESTERHAM RD
GRUB ST
B2025
Limpsfield CE Inf Sch
PEBBLE HILL COTTS
WOLF'S CNR
CH
Watts Hill
Cronklands
Vanguard Way
Limpsfield
BALLARDS LA
BRASSEY RD
BRASSEY HILL
BRASSEY CL
ST MICHAELS
NEW RD
WOLF'S ROW
WOLF'S RD
Limpsfield Common
The Chart
MOORHOUSE RD
RIDLANDS GR
BRICK KILN LA
STONESWOOD RD
THE RED HO
BRIARS CROSS
RIDLANDS LA
MARJORY PEASE COTTS
JOHN BURNS COTTS
West Heath
BROADWAY
POLLARDS WOOD HILL
CHAPEL RD
STONELEIGH RD
Pains Hill
RH8
RIDLANDS RISE
ST ANDREWS WAY
MILL LA
KENT HATCH RD
TALLY RD
Carpenter Arms (PH)
Scarn Bank
Hazelwood Sch
PASTENS RD
Greensand Way
ROCKFIELD RD
WOLF'S HILL
HAZELWOOD HTS
HOME PK
TENCHLEY'S LA
Tenchleys Park
B269
PAINS HILL
TREVEREUX HILL
TESTERS CL
Boulthurst Farm
BOULTHURST WAY
HAZELWOOD RD
CAXTON LA
CAXTON HO
HURSTLANDS
WOLF'S WOOD
POLLARDS WOOD RD
Chartlands
Hurst Green Inf Sch
Hurst Green
Loampit Wood
POLLARDS OAK RD
POLLARDS OAK CRES
SHORT LA
Crooked River
NUNAPPLETON WAY
CHESTNUT COPSE
Tenchleys Manor
THE GREENWAY
HOLLAND CRES
HOLLAND LA
Doghurst
SOUTH VIEW
REDLANE COTTS
ITCHINGWOOD COMMON RD
The Moat Farm
BARNFIELD WAY
GRANTS LA
Itchingwood Common
Fairview Trad Est
LC
RED LA
Holland
ROSEACRE
Parishcroft Wood
SWAYNESLAND RD
HOLLAND RD
Holland Jun Sch
MEADOWLANDS
GUILDABLES LA
Swaynesland
TN8
WARREN LA
BENN CL
GREENWOOD GDNS
Stockenden Farm
8
7
53
6
5
52
4
3
51
2
1
50
41
42
216
184

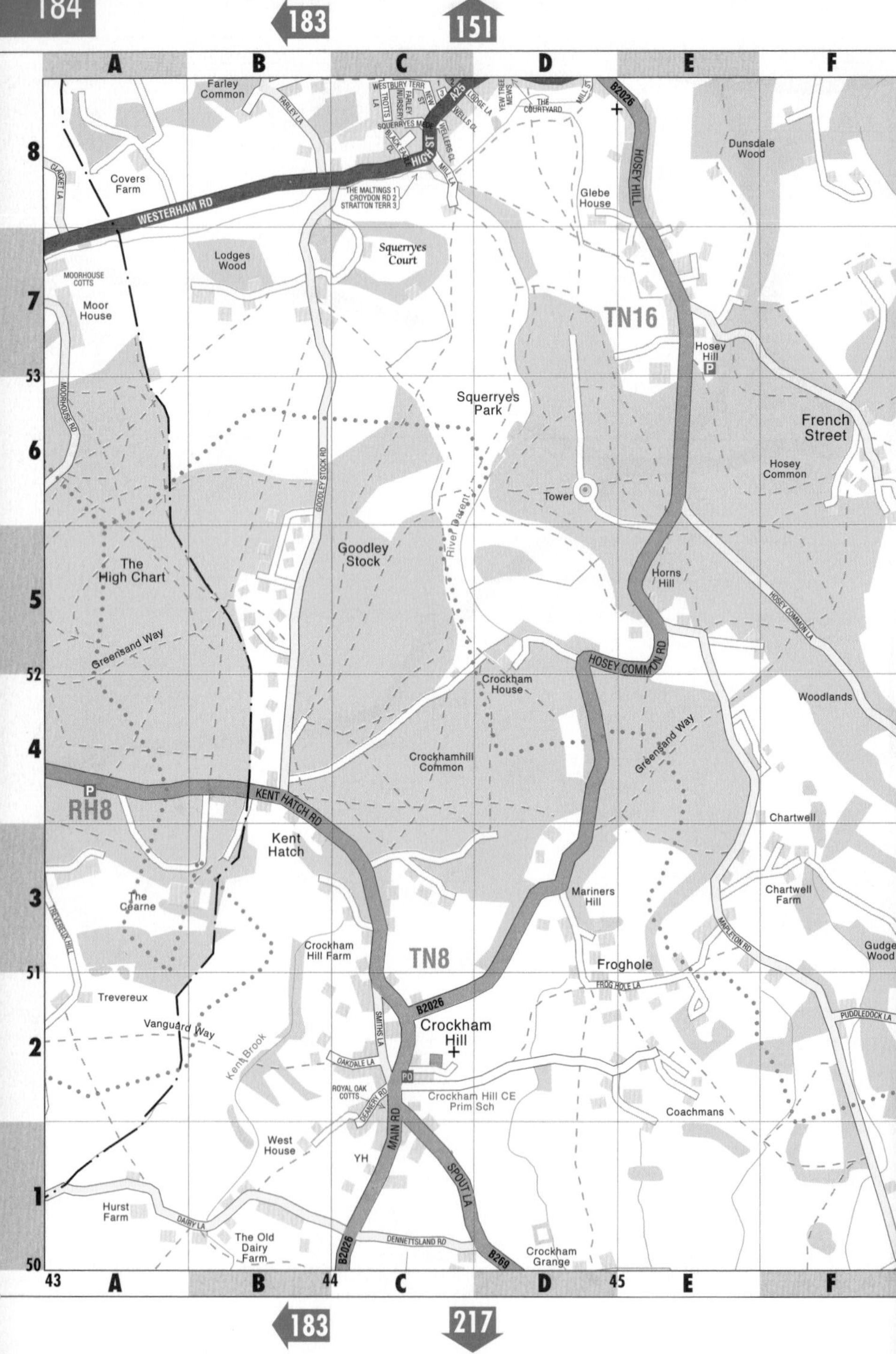

183
151

A B C D E F

8

Farley
Common

Covers
Farm

WESTBURY TERR
FARLEY
TROTTS LA
WELLS CL
HIGH ST
B25
LODGE LA
WELL ST
THE COURTYARD

B2026

Dunsdale
Wood

WESTERHAM RD

THE MALTINGS 1
CROYDON RD 2
STRATTON TERR 3

HOSEY HILL

Glebe
House

7

MOORHOUSE
COTTS

Moor
House

Lodges
Wood

Squerryes
Court

TN16

Hosey
Hill
P

53

MOORHOUSE RD

Squerryes
Park

French
Street

6

Tower

Hosey
Common

Goodley
Stock

GOODLEY STOCK RD

River Darent

HOSEY COMMON LA

5

The
High Chart

Goodley
Stock

Horns
Hill

Greensand Way

52

Crockham
House

HOSEY COMMON RD

Woodlands

4

P

RH8

KENT HATCH RD

Crockhamhill
Common

Greensand Way

Chartwell

Kent
Hatch

3

The
Cearne

Crockham
Hill Farm

Mariners
Hill

Chartwell
Farm

MAPLETON RD

51

Trevereux

TN8

Froghole

Gudge
Wood

FROG HOLE LA

PUDDLEDOCK LA

Vanguard Way

Kent Brook

SMITHS LA

B2026

Crockham
Hill

2

DAKDALE LA

MAIN RD

Crockham Hill CE
Prim Sch

Coachmans

ROYAL OAK
COTTS

BACKSIDE RD

West
House

YH

SPOUT LA

1

Hurst
Farm

DAIRY LA

B2026

The Old
Dairy
Farm

DENNETTSLAND RD

B269

Crockham
Grange

50

43 A B 44 C D 45 E F

152
186

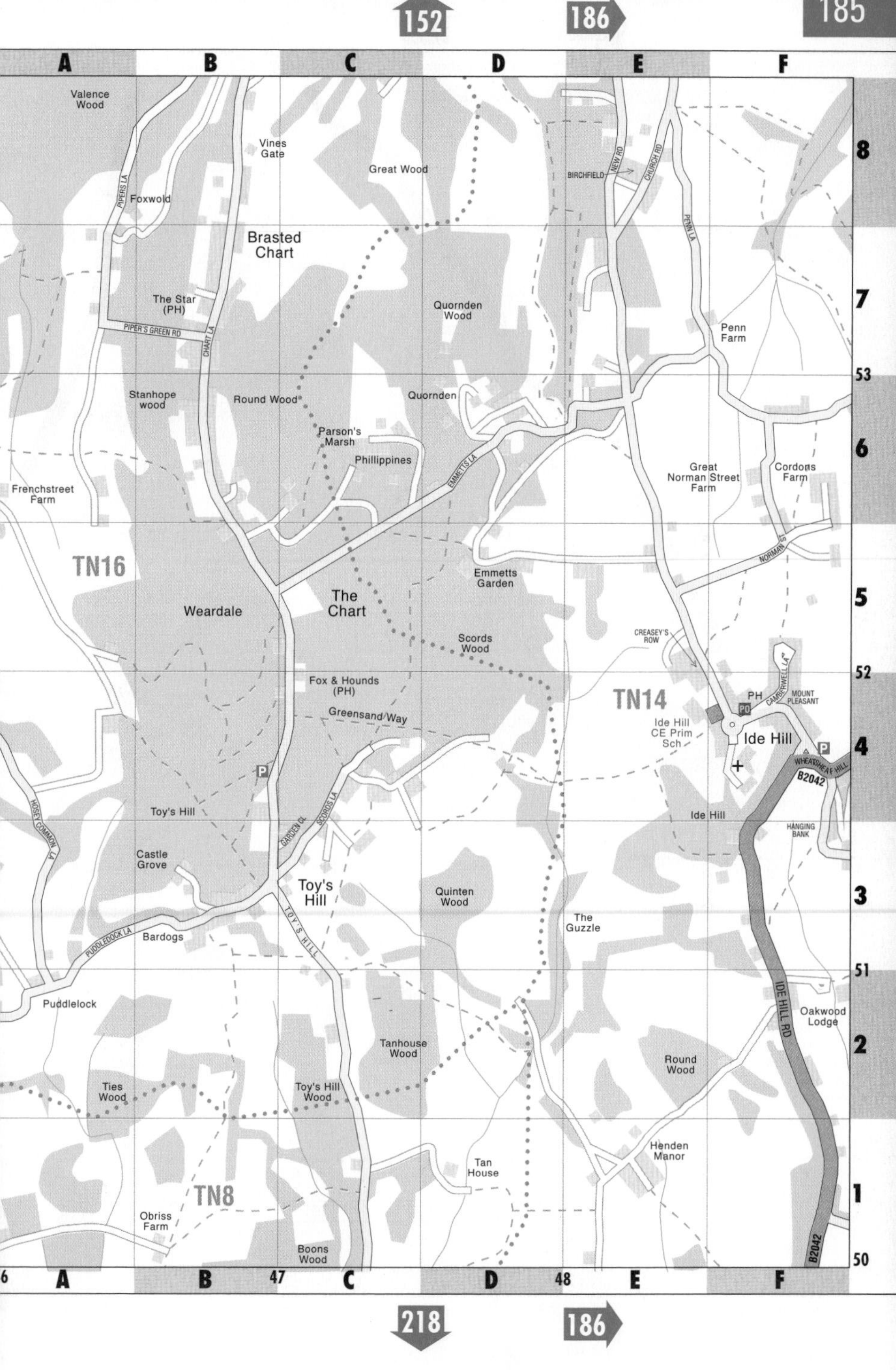
A
B
C
D
E
F
Valence Wood
Vines Gate
Great Wood
BIRCHFIELD
NEW RD
CHURCH RD
PIPERS LA
Foxwold
Brasted Chart
PENN LA
The Star (PH)
PIPER'S GREEN RD
CHART LA
Quornden Wood
Penn Farm
Stanhope wood
Round Wood
Quornden
Parson's Marsh
Phillippines
EMMETTS LA
Great Norman Street Farm
Cordons Farm
Frenchstreet Farm
NORMAN ST
TN16
Emmetts Garden
Weardale
The Chart
Scords Wood
CREASEY'S ROW
Fox & Hounds (PH)
TN14
PH
PO
CAMBERWELL LA
MOUNT PLEASANT
Greensand Way
Ide Hill CE Prim Sch
Ide Hill
P
WHEATSHEAF HILL
B2042
Toy's Hill
HOSEY COMMON LA
GARDEN CL
SCORDS LA
Ide Hill
HANGING BANK
Castle Grove
Toy's Hill
Quinten Wood
The Guzzle
PUDDLEDOCK LA
Bardogs
TOY'S HILL
Puddlelock
IDE HILL RD
Oakwood Lodge
Tanhouse Wood
Round Wood
Ties Wood
Toy's Hill Wood
Henden Manor
Tan House
TN8
Obriss Farm
Boons Wood
B2042
8
7
53
6
5
52
4
3
51
2
1
50
46
47
48

218
186

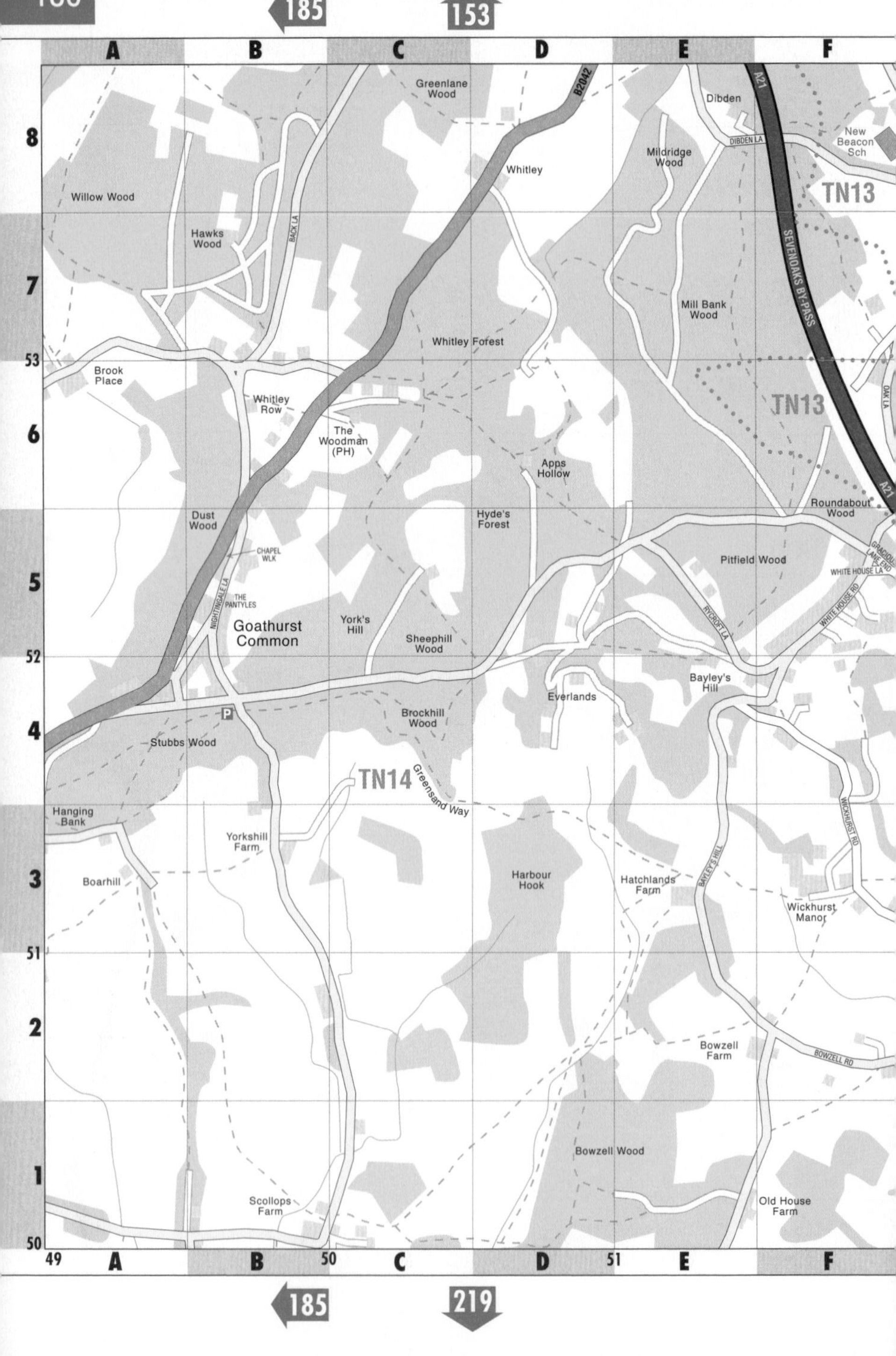

185
153

A **B** **C** **D** **E** **F**

Greenlane Wood

B2042

Dibden

A21

New Beacon Sch

DIBDEN LA

TN13

8

Whitley

Mildridge Wood

Willow Wood

Hawks Wood

BACK LA

Mill Bank Wood

SEVENOAKS BY-PASS

7

OAK LA

53

Whitley Forest

TN13

Brook Place

Whitley Row

The Woodman (PH)

A21

6

Apps Hollow

Roundabout Wood

Dust Wood

CHAPEL WLK

Hyde's Forest

Pitfield Wood

CARDING LA PLOT

WHITE HOUSE LA

WHITE HOUSE RD

5

NIGHTINGALE LA

THE PANTYLES

York's Hill

Sheephill Wood

STONE LA

52

Goathurst Common

Bayley's Hill

Everlands

4

P

Brockhill Wood

TN14

Greensand Way

Stubbs Wood

Hanging Bank

RAYLEY HILL

NICKHURST RD

Yorkshill Farm

3

Boarhill

Harbour Hook

Hatchlands Farm

Wickhurst Manor

51

2

Bowzell Farm

BOWZELL RD

1

Bowzell Wood

Old House Farm

50

Scollops Farm

49 **A** **B** 50 **C** **D** 51 **E** **F**

185
219

154
188

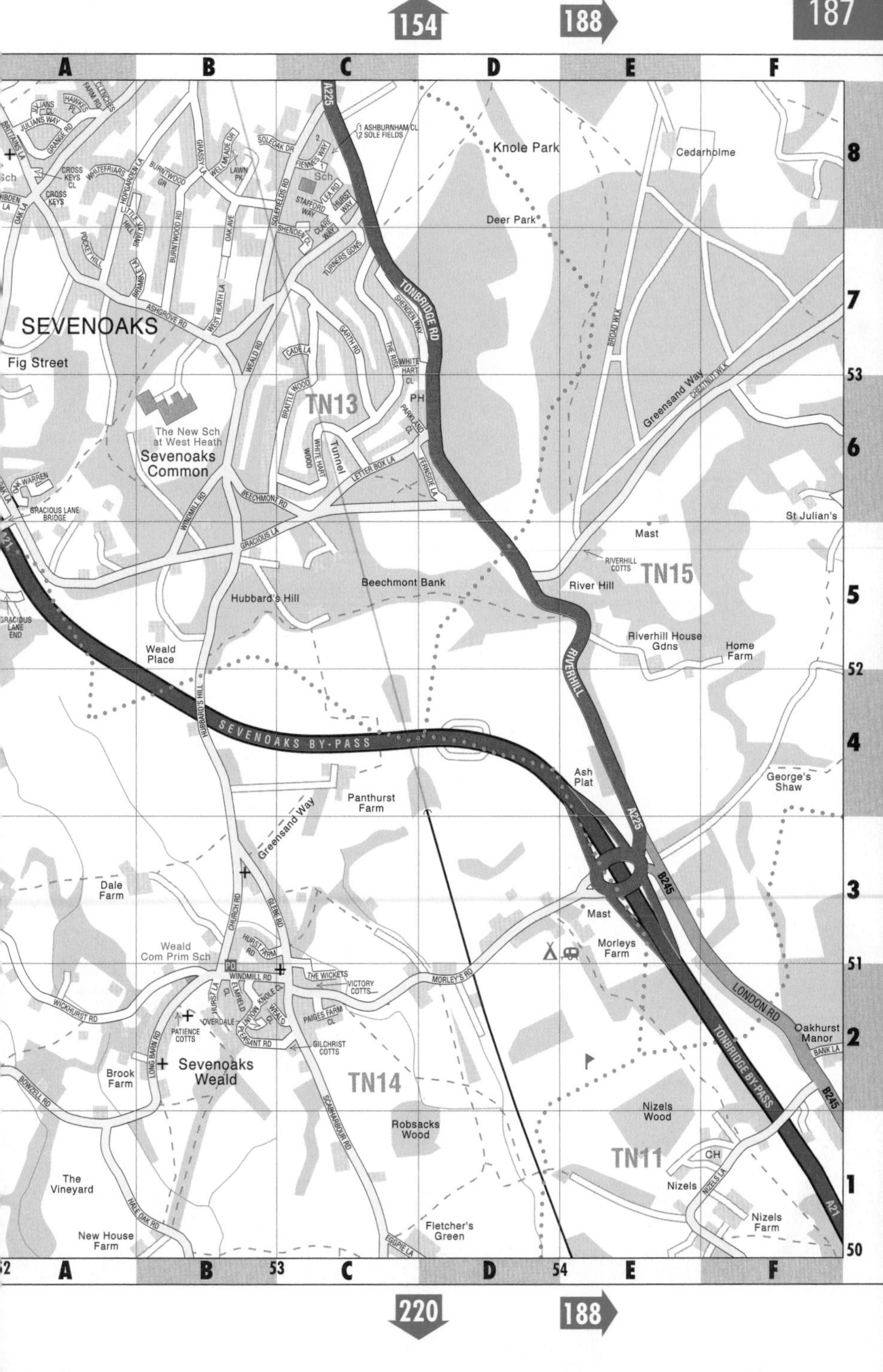
SEVENOAKS
Fig Street
The New Sch at West Heath
Sevenoaks Common
Knole Park
Deer Park
Cedarholme
TN13
TN14
TN15
TN11
Tunnel
Beechmont Bank
Hubbard's Hill
Weald Place
River Hill
Mast
St Julian's
Riverhill House Gdns
Home Farm
SEVENOAKS BY-PASS
TONBRIDGE RD
RIVERHILL
Greensand Way
Ash Plat
George's Shaw
Panthurst Farm
Dale Farm
Weald Com Prim Sch
Morleys Farm
Sevenoaks Weald
Brook Farm
Robsacks Wood
Oakhurst Manor
LONDON RD
TONBRIDGE BY-PASS
Nizels Wood
Nizels
Nizels Farm
The Vineyard
New House Farm
Fletcher's Green
A225
B245
A21
1 ASHBURNHAM CL
2 SOLE FIELDS
GRACIOUS LANE BRIDGE
GRACIOUS LANE END
RIVERHILL COTTS
VICTORY COTTS
PATIENCE COTTS
GILCHRIST COTTS
WICKHURST RD
BOWZELL RD
HALE OAK RD
LONG BARN RD
SCABHARBOUR RD
EGGPIE LA
MORLEY'S RD
WINDMILL RD
CHURCH RD
GLEBE RD
HUBBARD'S HILL
GRACIOUS LA
BEECHMONT RD
LETTER BOX LA
WEALD RD
ASHGROVE RD
CHESTNUT WLK
BROAD WLK
BANK LA
A B C D E F
8 7 6 5 4 3 2 1
53 52 51 50 54

220
188

187
155

A **B** **C** **D** **E** **F**

8

Fawke Farm House

Fawke Common

Bitchet Common

Broadhoath Wood

Starvecrow House

7

Redlands Wood

One Tree Hill

P

Rooks Hill

Shingle Hill

Wilmot Hill

53

Carter's Hill

Greensand Way

Greensand Way

CHESTNUT LA

6

Kettleshill Farm

CARTER'S HILL

TN15

Budd's Dell

5

FORGE VIEW

Absalom's Farm

Ducks Grove

Budd's Green

Cold Blows

Valley Farm

The White Rock Inn (PH)

Underriver House

Underriver

UNDERRIVER HOUSE RD

ROOKS HILL

ROUTE 15

52

+

4

Romshed Farm

Underriver Farm

Budd's Toll

HILDENBOROUGH RD

Barr Wood

Marchurst

3

MILL LA

Thomas's Wood

Tumbling Bay

Fairhill

51

Kentlands

Great Hollanden Farm

Twelve Acre Plantation

TN11

2

Oakhurst Farm

MILL LA

RIDING LA

HILDENBROOK FARM

Hilden Brook

1

Oakhurst Wood

PH

LONDON RD

GROVE WOOD COTTS

B245

Cock Wood

VINES LA

Roughetts Wood

Coldharbour

50

The Vines

Alexander House

55 **A** **B** **56** **C** **D** **57** **E** **F**

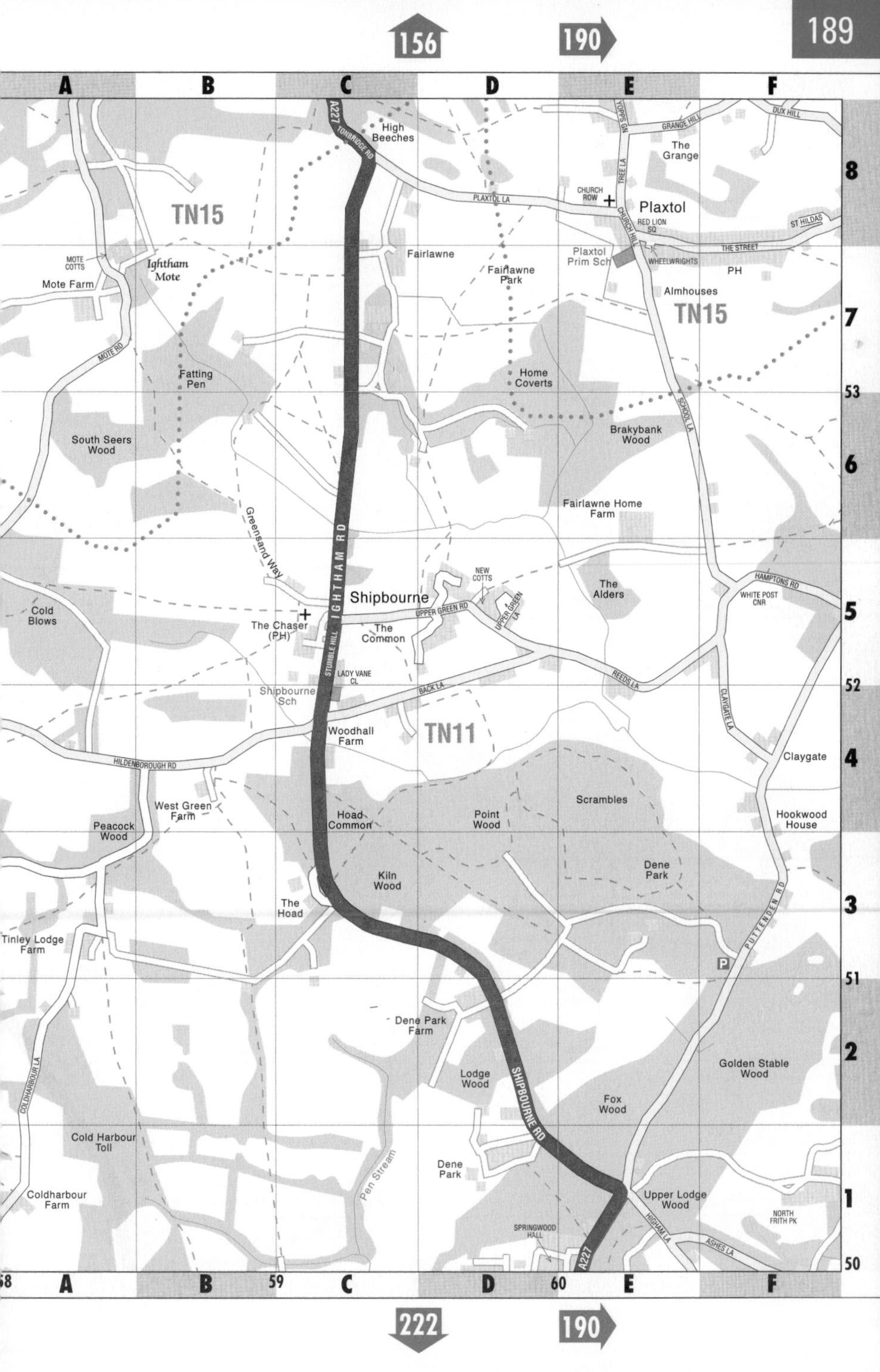

A B C D E F

8

TN15

Mote
Cotts
Mote Farm

Ightham
Mote

High
Beeches

PLAXTOL LA

Fairlawne

Fairlawne
Park

CHURCH
ROW

Plaxtol

RED LION
SQ

Plaxtol
Prim Sch

WHEELWRIGHTS

THE STREET

PH

Almshouses

TN15

TREE LA

CHURCH RD

VOSS DR

GRANGE HILL

DUX HILL

The
Grange

ST HILDAS

7

Fatting
Pen

South Seers
Wood

Home
Coverts

Brakybank
Wood

Fairlawne Home
Farm

53

6

Greensand Way

IGHTHAM RD

TONBRIDGE RD

A227

STUMBLE HILL

Cold
Blows

Shipbourne

The Chaser
(P.H)

The
Common

Shipbourne
Sch

NEW
COTTS

UPPER GREEN RD

UPPER GREEN
LA

LADY VANE
CL

BACK LA

The
Alders

REEDS LA

HAMPTONS RD

WHITE POST
CNR

OLDBURY LA

CLAYGATE LA

5

52

TN11

HILDENBOROUGH RD

West Green
Farm

Peacock
Wood

Woodhall
Farm

Hoad
Common

Point
Wood

Scrambles

Dene
Park

Claygate

Hookwood
House

4

3

COLDHARBOUR LA

Tinley Lodge
Farm

The
Hoad

Kiln
Wood

Cold Harbour
Toll

Coldharbour
Farm

Pen Stream

Dene Park
Farm

Lodge
Wood

Dene
Park

SPRINGWOOD
HALL

SHIPBOURNE RD

Fox
Wood

Golden Stable
Wood

Upper Lodge
Wood

NORTH
FRITH PK

PUTTENDEN RD

HIGHWAY

A227

ASHES LA

P

51

2

1

50

58 A B 59 C D 60 E F

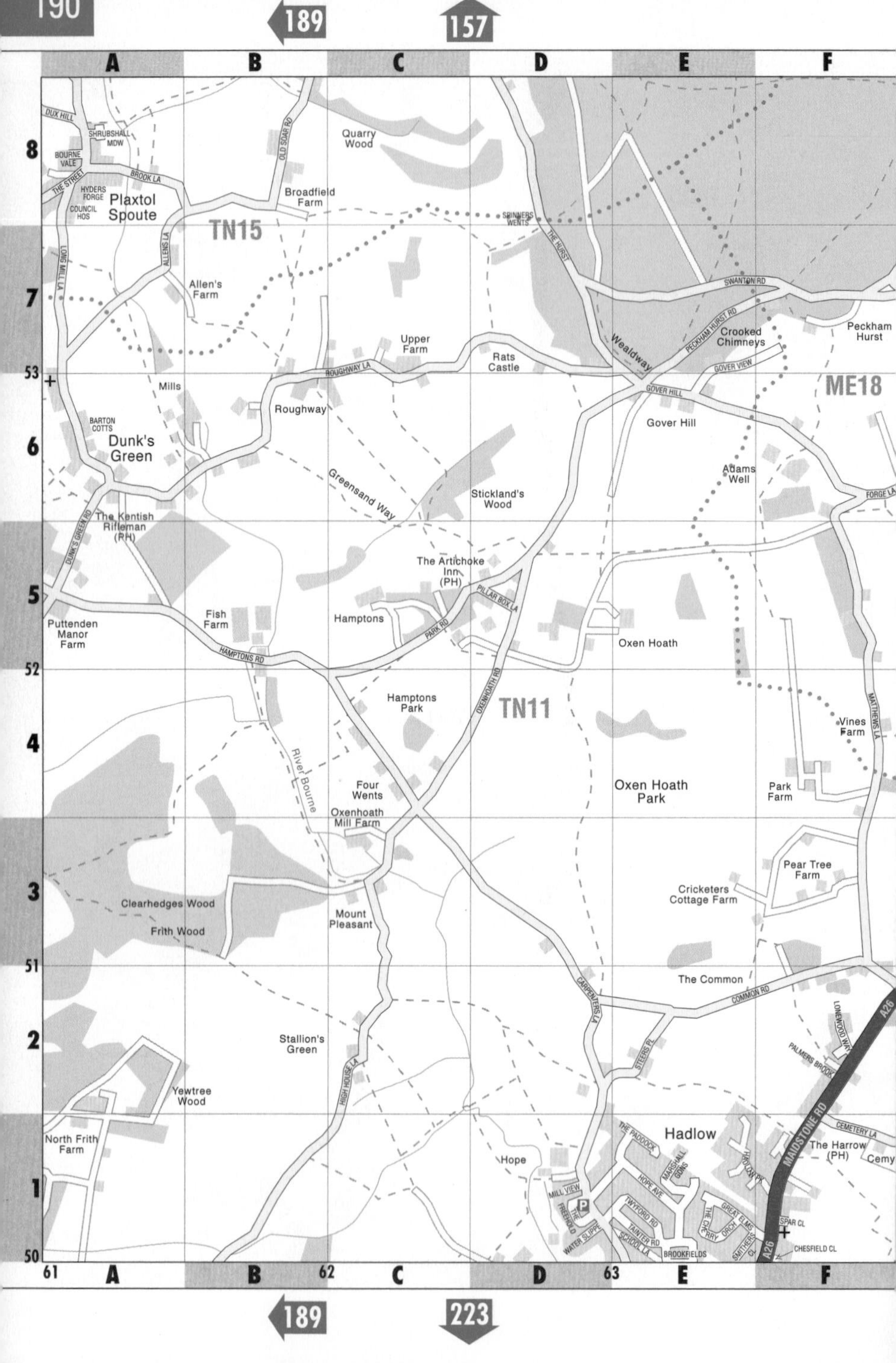

189
157
A
B
C
D
E
F
8
7
53
6
5
52
4
3
51
2
1
50
61
62
63
DUX HILL
SHRUBSHALL MDW
BOURNE VALE
THE STREET
BROOK LA
HYDERS FORGE
COUNCIL HOS
Plaxtol Spoute
OLD SOAR RD
Quarry Wood
Broadfield Farm
TN15
SPINNERS WENTS
THE HURST
LONG MILL LA
ALLENS LA
Allen's Farm
SWANTON RD
PECKHAM HURST RD
Crooked Chimneys
Peckham Hurst
Wealdway
Upper Farm
Rats Castle
ROUGHWAY LA
GOVER VIEW
ME18
Mills
Roughway
GOVER HILL
Gover Hill
BARTON COTTS
Dunk's Green
Greensand Way
Stickland's Wood
Adams Well
FORGE LA
DUNK'S GREEN RD
The Kentish Rifleman (PH)
The Artichoke Inn (PH)
PILLAR BOX LA
Fish Farm
Hamptons
PARK RD
Oxen Hoath
Puttenden Manor Farm
HAMPTONS RD
OXENHOATH RD
Hamptons Park
TN11
MATTHEWS LA
Vines Farm
River Bourne
Four Wents
Oxen Hoath Park
Park Farm
Oxenhoath Mill Farm
Pear Tree Farm
Clearhedges Wood
Mount Pleasant
Cricketers Cottage Farm
Frith Wood
The Common
CARPENTERS LA
COMMON RD
A26
LONEWOOD WAY
PALMERS BROOK
Stallion's Green
STEERS PL
Yewtree Wood
HIGH HOUSE LA
MAIDSTONE RD
CEMETERY LA
Hadlow
THE PADDOCK
North Frith Farm
The Harrow (PH)
Cemy
Hope
HOPE AVE
MARSHALL GDNS
HARLOW PK
MILL VIEW
THE FREEHOLD
TWYFORD RD
THE CHERRY ORCH
GREAT ELMS
SPAR CL
WATER SLIPPE
SCHOOL LA
TAINTER RD
BROOKFIELDS
SMITHERS CL
CHESFIELD CL
189
223

158
192

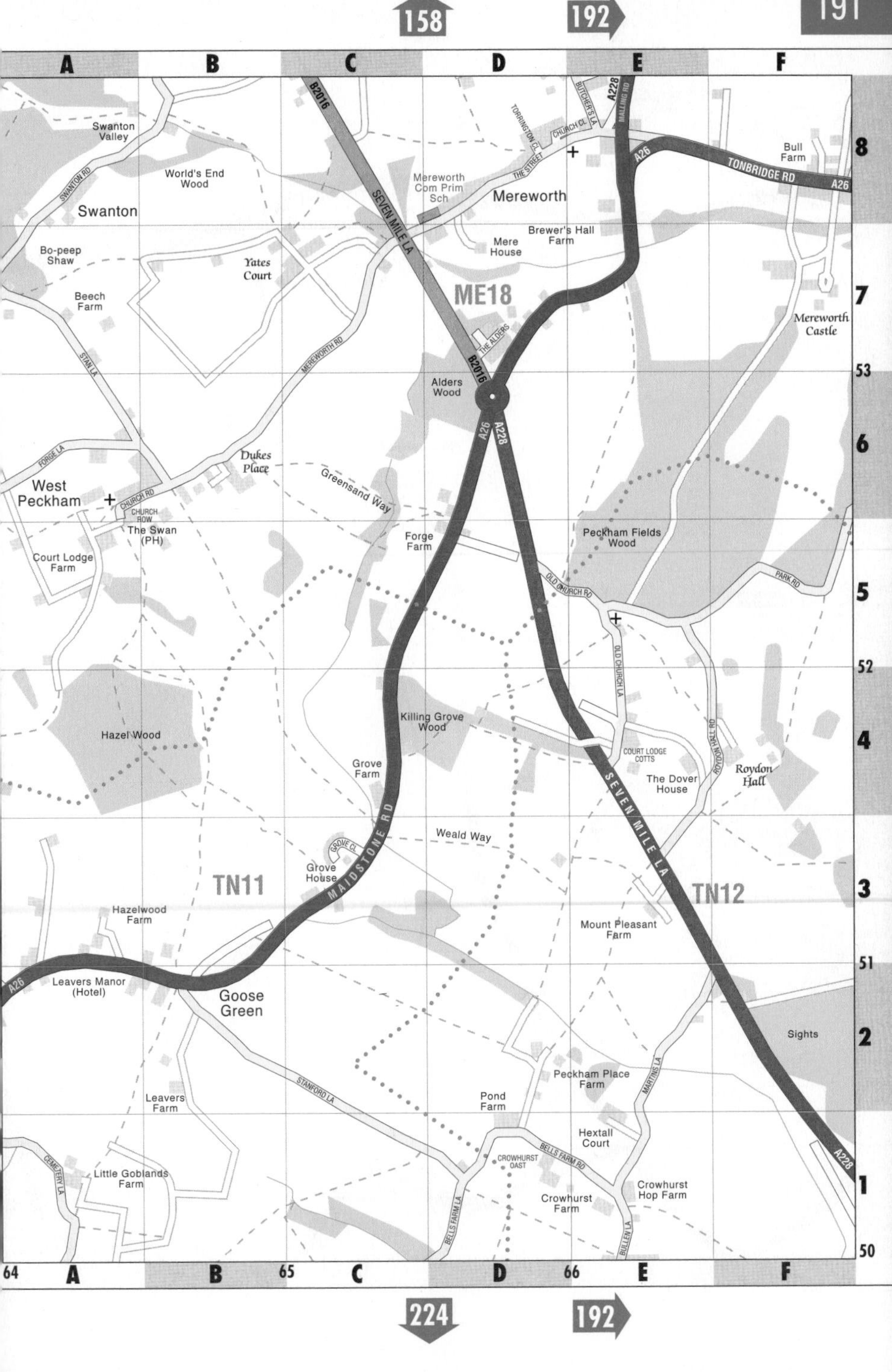
A
B
C
D
E
F
Swanton Valley
World's End Wood
Swanton
Bo-peep Shaw
Beech Farm
Yates Court
Mereworth Com Prim Sch
Mereworth
Brewer's Hall Farm
Mere House
Bull Farm
TONBRIDGE RD
A26
A228
B2016
SEVEN MILE LA
MALLING RD
ME18
THE ALDERS
Mereworth Castle
Alders Wood
MEREWORTH RD
STAN LA
SWANTON RD
FORGE LA
West Peckham
CHURCH RD
CHURCH ROW
The Swan (PH)
Dukes Place
Greensand Way
Court Lodge Farm
Forge Farm
Peckham Fields Wood
OLD CHURCH RD
PARK RD
OLD CHURCH LA
Hazel Wood
Killing Grove Wood
Grove Farm
COURT LODGE COTTS
The Dover House
ROYDON HALL RD
Roydon Hall
Weald Way
GROVE CL
Grove House
MAIDSTONE RD
TN11
TN12
Hazelwood Farm
Mount Pleasant Farm
Leavers Manor (Hotel)
Goose Green
Sights
Leavers Farm
STANFORD LA
Pond Farm
Peckham Place Farm
MARTINS LA
Hextall Court
CROWHURST OAST
BELLS FARM RD
Crowhurst Hop Farm
Crowhurst Farm
CEMETERY LA
Little Goblands Farm
BELLS FARM LA
BULLEN LA
TORRINGTON CL
BUTCHER'S LA
CHURCH CL
THE STREET
8
7
53
6
5
52
4
3
51
2
1
50
64
65
66

224
192

191
159

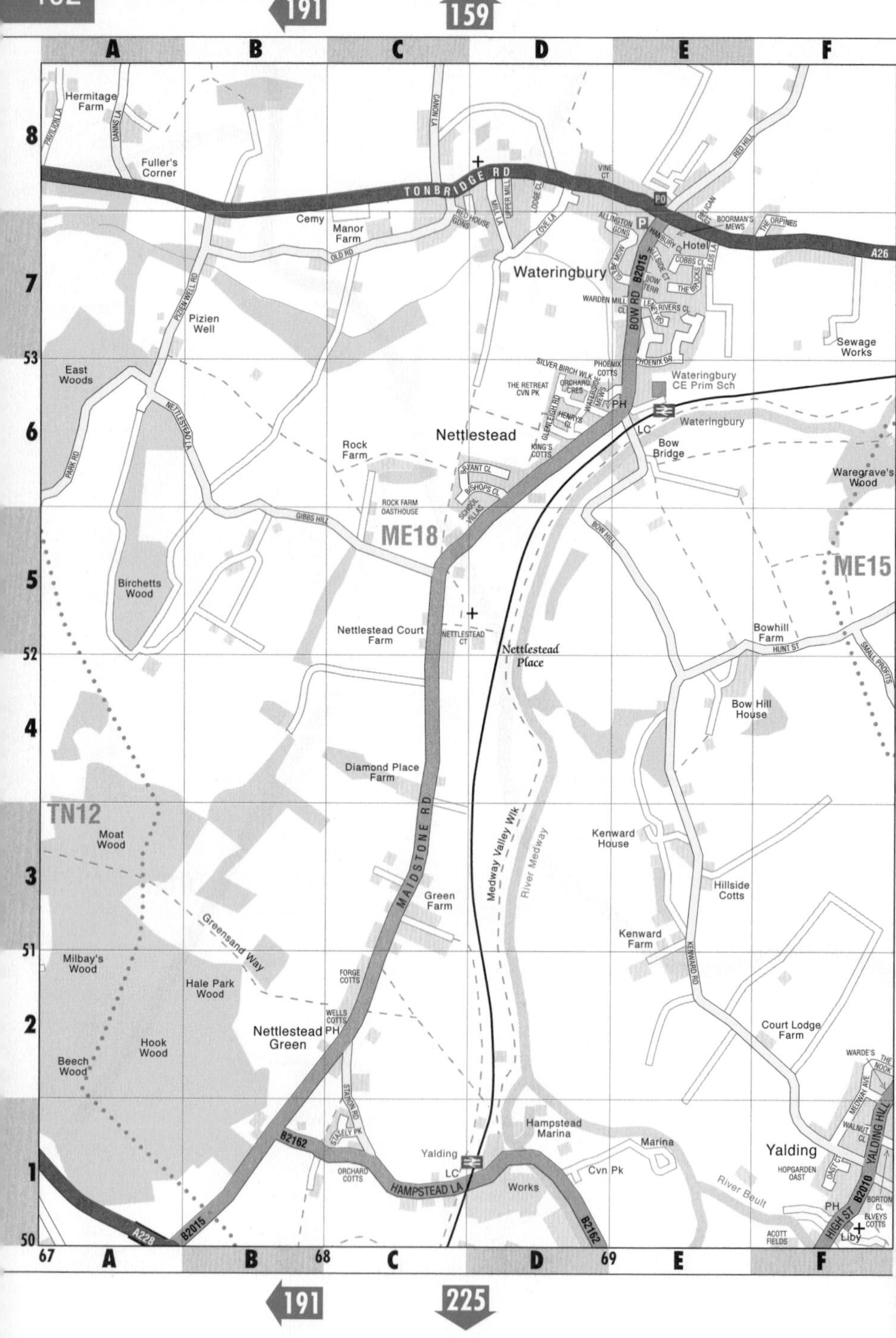
Hermitage Farm
Fuller's Corner
TONBRIDGE RD
Cemy
Manor Farm
Waterinbury
Wateringbury
Pizien Well
East Woods
Nettlestead
Rock Farm
Wateringbury CE Prim Sch
Bow Bridge
Waregrave's Wood
ME18
ME15
Birchetts Wood
Nettlestead Court Farm
Nettlestead Place
Bowhill Farm
Bow Hill House
Diamond Place Farm
TN12
Moat Wood
Kenward House
Green Farm
Hillside Cotts
Medway Valley Wlk
River Medway
Greensand Way
Kenward Farm
Milbay's Wood
Hale Park Wood
Nettlestead Green
Court Lodge Farm
Hook Wood
Beech Wood
Hampstead Marina
Marina
Yalding
Works
Cvn Pk
River Beult
MAIDSTONE RD
HAMPSTEAD LA
A26
A228
B2015
B2162
B2010
Sewage Works

191
225

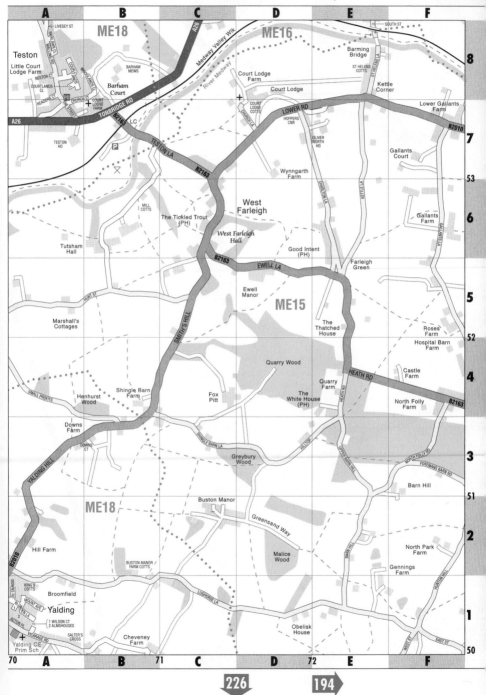

A   B   C   D   E   F

ME18   ME16

8

Teston
Little Court
Lodge Farm

LIVESEY ST

NESTOR CT
COURTLANDS
CL
READERS CL

BARHAM
MEWS

Barham
Court

WOOLLETT ST

COOL PK

CHURCH ST

COURT
LODGE
FARM

TONBRIDGE RD

B2163

LC

A26

P

TESTON LA

TESTON
HO

B2163

Medway Valley Wlk

River Medway

A26

Court Lodge
Farm

Court Lodge

COURT
LODGE
COTTS

LOWER RD

HOPPERS
CNR

Barming
Bridge

ST HELENS
COTTS

SOUTH ST

ST HELENS LA

Kettle
Corner

Lower Gallants
Farm

B2010

7

CHURCH LA

OLIVER
NORTH
HO

KETTLE LA

Gallants
Court

53

Wynngarth
Farm

West
Farleigh

MILL
COTTS

The Tickled Trout
(PH)

West Farleigh
Hall

Good Intent
(PH)

Farleigh
Green

Gallants
Farm

GALLANTS LA

6

B2163

Tutsham
Hall

B2163

EWELL LA

Ewell
Manor

ME15

The
Thatched
House

Roses
Farm

5

52

HUNT ST

Marshall's
Cottages

SMITH'S HILL

Quarry Wood

Quarry
Farm

HEATH RD

Castle
Farm

North Folly
Farm

B2163

4

SMALL PROFITS

Shingle Barn
Farm

Henhurst
Wood

Fox
Pitt

The
White House
(PH)

HEATH RD

3

Downs
Farm

DOWNS
CT

SHINGLE BARN LA

Greybury
Wood

HILLTOP

UPPER BARN HILL

NORTH FOLLY RD

FOREMANS BARN RD

Barn Hill

51

YALDING HILL

ME18

Buston Manor

Greensand Way

North Park
Farm

BARN HILL

2

B2010

Hill Farm

BUSTON MANOR
FARM COTTS

Malice
Wood

Gennings
Farm

HUNTON HILL

KING'S
COTTS

MOUNT AVE

BLADENS LA

Broomfield

Yalding

1 WILSON CT
2 ALMSHOUSES

LUGHORSE LA

WEST ST

EAST ST

1

ORPINES CT

VICARAGE RD

ANTON PL

SALTER'S
CROSS

Yalding CE
Prim Sch

Cheveney
Farm

Obelisk
House

50

70   A   B   71   C   D   72   E   F

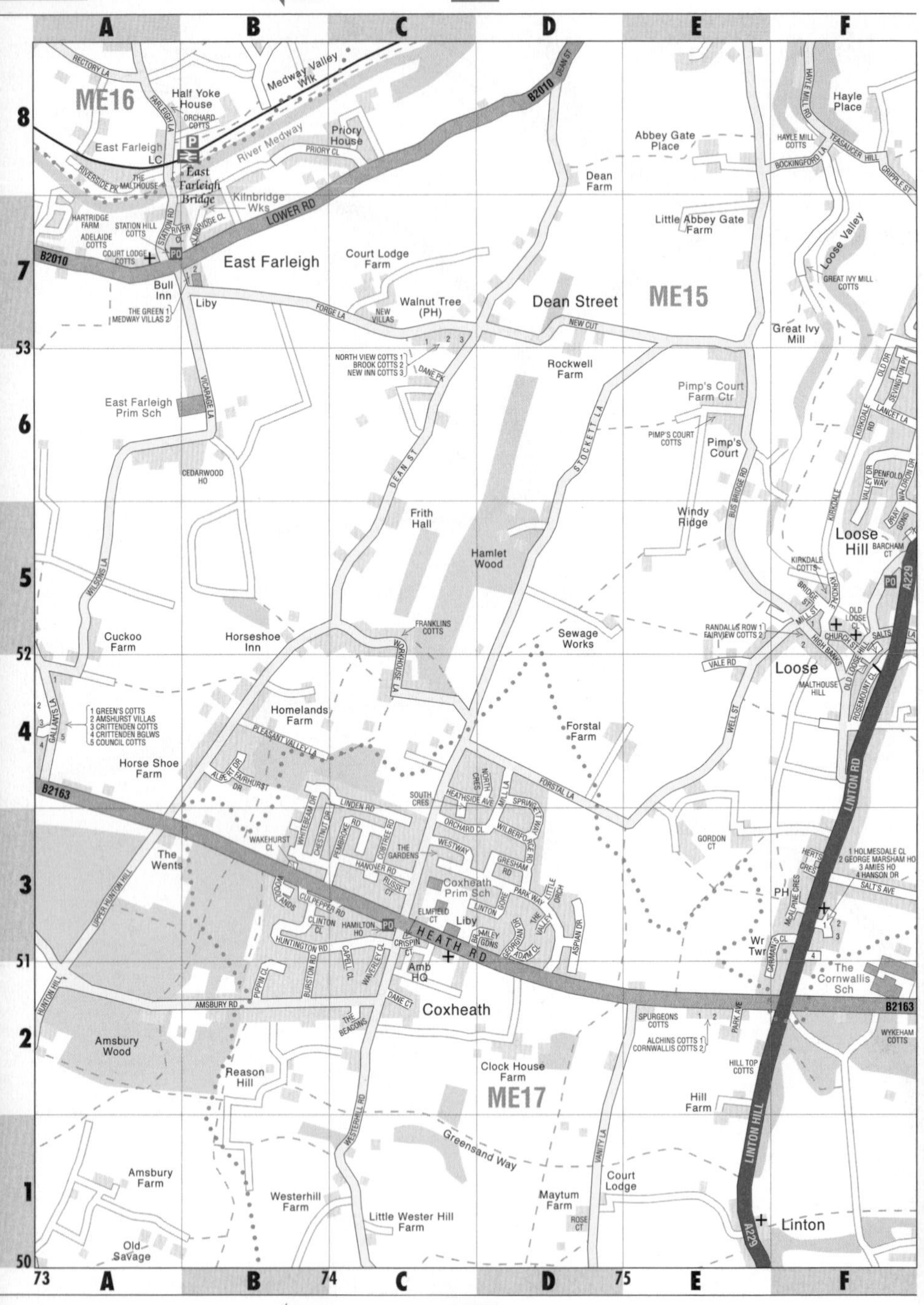

193
161

A   **B**   **C**   **D**   **E**   **F**

8

RECTORY LA
ME16
Half Yoke House
ORCHARD COTTS
Medway Valley Wlk
B2010
Hayle Place
Abbey Gate Place
HAYLE MILL COTTS
HAWLEY ML TI
TEGASTER HILL
GEORGE ST
BOCKINGFORD LA
East Farleigh
Priory House
PRIORY CL
River Medway

P
East Farleigh LC
THE MALTHOUSE
RIVERSIDE PK
Kilmbridge Wks
LOWER RD
Dean Farm
Little Abbey Gate Farm
Loose Valley

7

HARTRIDGE FARM
ADELAIDE COTTS
STATION HILL COTTS
Court Lodge Farm
GREAT IVY MILL COTTS
B2010
East Farleigh Bridge
COURT LODGE COTTS
PO
East Farleigh
Walnut Tree (PH)
Dean Street
ME15
Great Ivy Mill

Bull Inn
THE GREEN 1
MEDWAY VILLAS 2
Liby
FORGE LA
NEW VILLAS
NEW CUT

53

NORTH VIEW COTTS 1
BROOK COTTS 2
NEW INN COTTS 3
DANE LA
Rockwell Farm
Pimp's Court Farm Ctr
LANCET A

6

East Farleigh Prim Sch
VICARAGE LA
DEAN ST
PIMP'S COURT COTTS
Pimp's Court
PIMP'S COURT COTTS
PENFOLDS WAY

CEDARWOOD HO
Frith Hall
Windy Ridge
Loose Hill
BARCHAM CT

5

HELEN'S LA
Hamlet Wood
KIRKDALE COTTS
OLD LODGE CL
PO
A229

52

Cuckoo Farm
Horseshoe Inn
FRANKLINS COTTS
Sewage Works
RANDALLS ROW 1
FAIRVIEW COTTS 2
VALE RD
Loose
MALTHOUSE HILL

4

1 GREEN'S COTTS
2 AMSHURST VILLAS
3 CRITTENDEN COTTS
4 CRITTENDEN BGLWS
5 COUNCIL COTTS
GALLANTS LA
Homelands Farm
PLEASANT VALLEY LA
Forstal Farm
FORSTAL LA
GORDON CT
WELL ST

Horse Shoe Farm
B2163
The Wents
ALBERT DR
FAIRHURST
WAKEHURST CL
LINDEN RD
THE GARDENS
HANMER RD
SOUTH CRES
ORCHARD CL
WILBERG RD
WESTWAY

3

1 HOLMESDALE CL
2 GEORGE MARSHAM HO
3 AMIES HO
4 HANSON DR
SALT'S AVE
MALTINE CRES
PH
The Cornwallis Sch

Coxheath Prim Sch
Liby
ELMFIELD CT
Coxheath
HAMILTON HO
PO
HEATH RD

51

HUNTINGTON RD
COPSELL CL
Amb HQ

2

Amsbury Wood
PIPER CL
THE BEANSING
DANE CT
AMSBURY RD
Coxheath
SPURGEONS COTTS
ALCHINS COTTS 1
CORNWALLIS COTTS 2
PARK DR
HILL TOP COTTS
WYKEHAM COTTS
B2163

Reason Hill
Clock House Farm
ME17
Hill Farm

1

Amsbury Farm
Westerhill Farm
Greensand Way
Maytum Farm
Court Lodge
Hill Farm
Linton
A229

50

Old Savage
Little Wester Hill Farm
ROSE CT

193
227

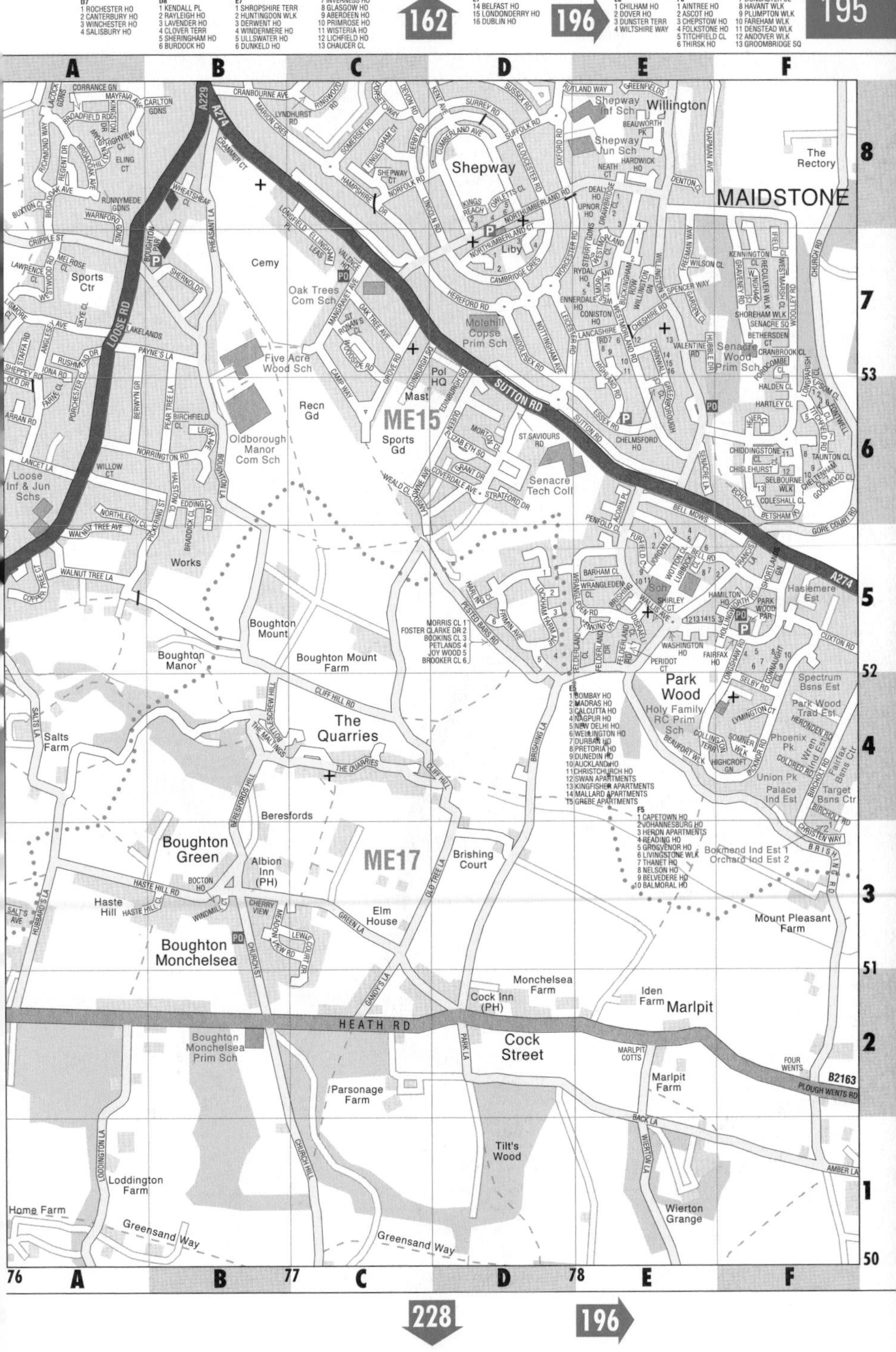
D7
1 ROCHESTER HO
2 CANTERBURY HO
3 WINCHESTER HO
4 SALISBURY HO
D8
1 KENDALL PL
2 RAYLEIGH HO
3 LAVENDER HO
4 CLOVER TERR
5 SHERINGHAM HO
6 BURDOCK HO
E7
1 SHROPSHIRE TERR
2 HUNTINGDON WLK
3 DERWENT HO
4 WINDERMERE HO
5 ULLSWATER HO
6 DUNKELD HO
7 INVERNESS HO
8 GLASGOW HO
9 ABERDEEN HO
10 PRIMROSE HO
11 WISTERIA HO
12 LICHFIELD HO
13 CHAUCER CL
162
E7
14 BELFAST HO
15 LONDONDERRY HO
16 DUBLIN HO
196
E8
1 CHILHAM HO
2 DOVER HO
3 DUNSTER TERR
4 WILTSHIRE WAY
F6
1 AINTREE HO
2 ASCOT HO
3 CHEPSTOW HO
4 FOLKSTONE HO
5 TITCHFIELD CL
6 THIRSK HO
7 DONCASTER CL
8 HAVANT WLK
9 PLUMPTON WLK
10 FAREHAM WLK
11 DENSTEAD WLK
12 ANDOVER WLK
13 GROOMBRIDGE SQ
A
B
C
D
E
F
8
7
53
6
5
52
4
3
51
2
1
50
76
77
78
Shepway Inf Sch
Willington
Shepway Jun Sch
The Rectory
Shepway
MAIDSTONE
Cemy
Sports Ctr
Oak Trees Com Sch
Liby
Molehill Copse Prim Sch
Senacre Wood Prim Sch
Five Acre Wood Sch
Pol HQ
Mast
Recn Gd
ME15
Sports Gd
Oldborough Manor Com Sch
Loose Inf & Jun Schs
Senacre Tech Coll
SUTTON RD
LOOSE RD
A229
A274
Works
Haslemere Est
Boughton Mount
Boughton Manor
Boughton Mount Farm
MORRIS CL 1
FOSTER CLARKE DR 2
BODKINS CL 3
PETLANDS 4
JOY WOOD 5
BROOKER CL 6
Park Wood
Holy Family RC Prim Sch
Spectrum Bsns Est
Park Wood Trad Est
The Quarries
Salts Farm
E5
1 BOMBAY HO
2 MADRAS HO
3 CALCUTTA HO
4 NAGPUR HO
5 NEW DELHI HO
6 WELLINGTON HO
7 DURBAN HO
8 PRETORIA HO
9 DUNEDIN HO
10 AUCKLAND HO
11 CHRISTCHURCH HO
12 SWAN APARTMENTS
13 KINGFISHER APARTMENTS
14 MALLARD APARTMENTS
15 GREBE APARTMENTS
F5
1 CAPETOWN HO
2 JOHANNESBURG HO
3 HERON APARTMENTS
4 READING HO
5 GROSVENOR HO
6 LIVINGSTONE WLK
7 THANET HO
8 NELSON HO
9 BELVEDERE HO
10 BALMORAL HO
Phoenix Pk
Wren Ind Est
Fairfax Bsns Ctr
Union Pk
Palace Ind Est
Target Bsns Ctr
Beresfords
Boughton Green
Albion Inn (PH)
ME17
Brishing Court
Bockmend Ind Est 1
Orchard Ind Est 2
Haste Hill
Elm House
Mount Pleasant Farm
Boughton Monchelsea
Monchelsea Farm
Iden Farm
Marlpit
Cock Inn (PH)
HEATH RD
Boughton Monchelsea Prim Sch
Cock Street
Marlpit Farm
FOUR WENTS
B2163
PLOUGH WENTS RD
Parsonage Farm
Tilt's Wood
Loddington Farm
Home Farm
Wierton Grange
Greensand Way
Greensand Way

228
196

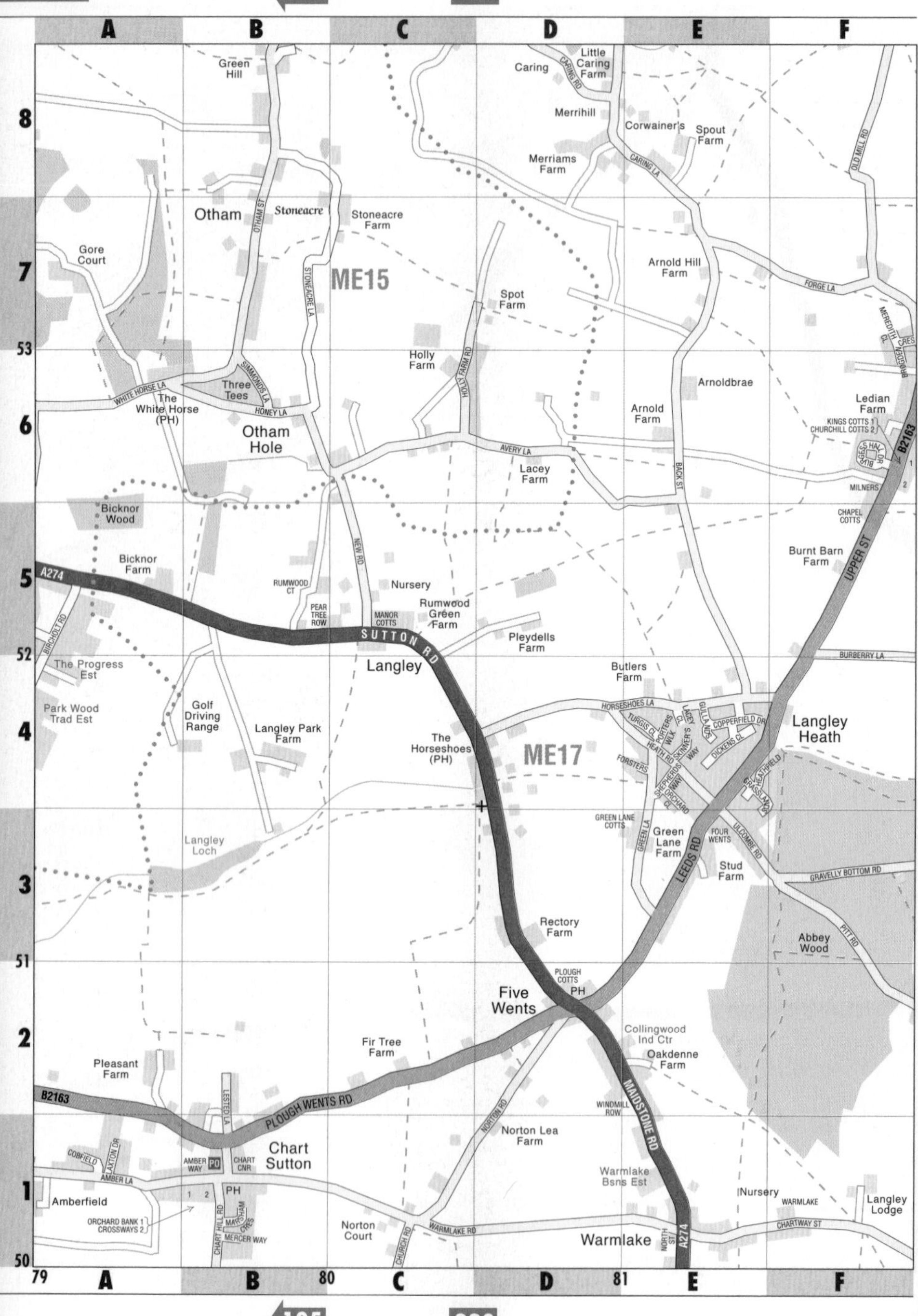

195
163

A   B   C   D   E   F

8

7

53

6

5

52

4

3

51

2

1

50

Green
Hill

Caring

Little
Caring
Farm

Merihill

Merriams
Farm

Corwainer's

Spout
Farm

Otham

Stoneacre

Stoneacre
Farm

Gore
Court

ME15

Arnold Hill
Farm

Spot
Farm

Holly
Farm

Arnoldbrae

Three
Tees

The
White Horse
(PH)

Otham
Hole

Arnold
Farm

Lacey
Farm

Ledian
Farm

KINGS COTTS 1
CHURCHILL COTTS 2

MILNERS

Bicknor
Wood

Bicknor
Farm

A274

Burnt Barn
Farm

CHAPEL
COTTS

RUMWOOD
CT

PEAR
TREE
ROW

MANOR
COTTS

Nursery

Rumwood
Green
Farm

Pleydells
Farm

SUTTON RD

BURBERRY LA

The Progress
Est

Langley

Butlers
Farm

Langley
Heath

Park Wood
Trad Est

Golf
Driving
Range

Langley Park
Farm

The
Horseshoes
(PH)

ME17

Langley
Loch

Green Lane
Cotts

Green
Lane
Farm

Four
Wents

Stud
Farm

GRAVELLY BOTTOM RD

Rectory
Farm

Abbey
Wood

PLOUGH
COTTS
PH

Five
Wents

Pleasant
Farm

B2163

PLOUGH WENTS RD

Fir Tree
Farm

Collingwood
Ind Ctr

Oakdenne
Farm

MAIDSTONE RD

WINDMILL
ROW

Chart
Sutton

PH

Norton Lea
Farm

Warmlake
Bsns Est

Nursery

WARMLAKE

Langley
Lodge

Amberfield

ORCHARD BANK 1
CROSSWAYS 2

MERCER WAY

Norton
Court

WARMLAKE RD

Warmlake

A274

CHARTWAY ST

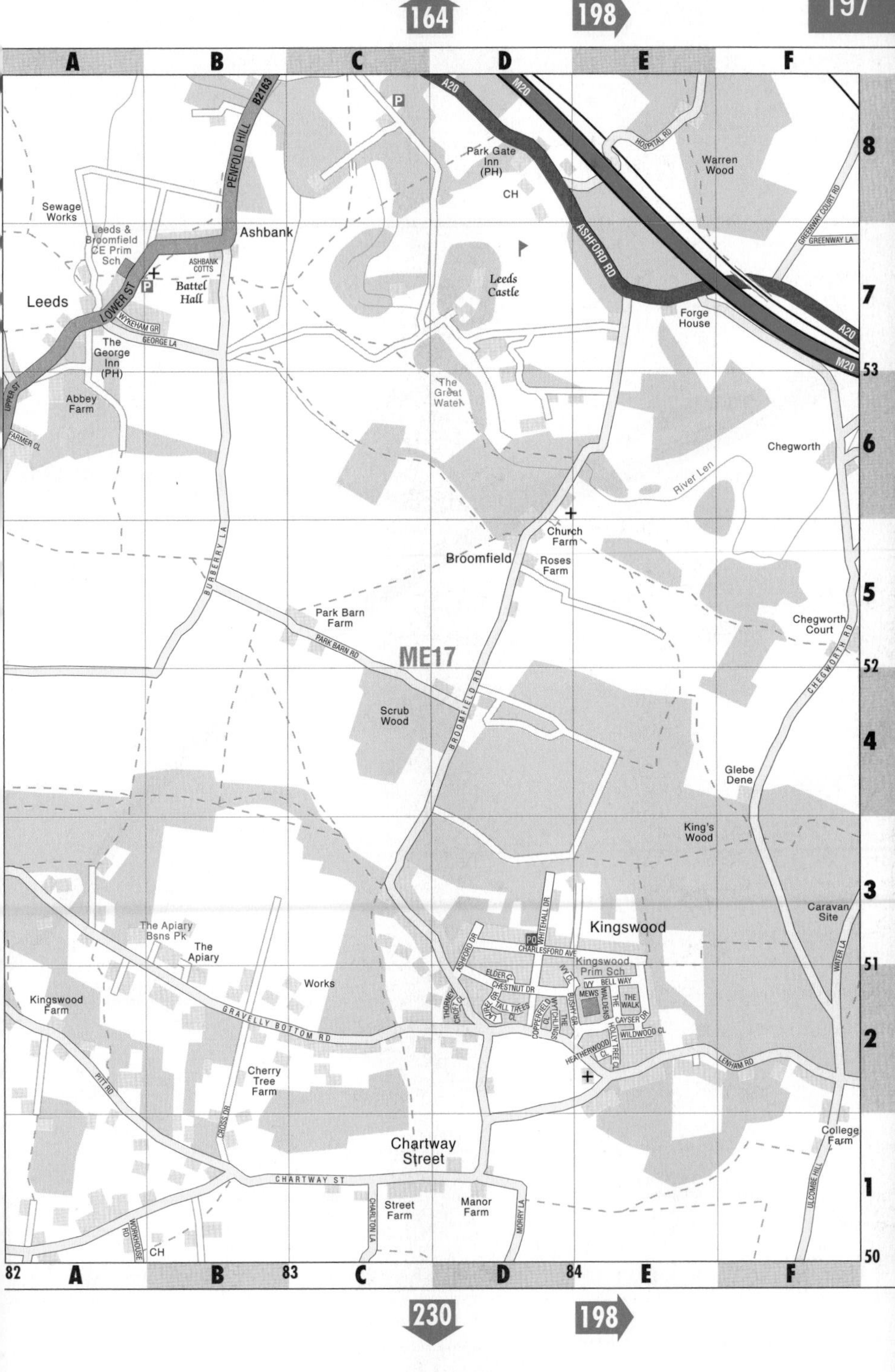

164
198
230
198

A **B** **C** **D** **E** **F**

8

7

53

6

5

52

4

3

51

2

1

50

Sewage Works

Leeds & Broomfield CE Prim Sch

Ashbank

ASHBANK COTTS

Leeds

WYKEHAM GR

LOWER ST

PENFOLD HILL

B2163

Battel Hall

The George Inn (PH)

GEORGE LA

Abbey Farm

FARMER CL

UPPER ST

A20

M20

Park Gate Inn (PH)

CH

HOSPITAL RD

Warren Wood

ASHFORD RD

GREENWAY COMBE RD

GREENWAY LA

Leeds Castle

Forge House

A20

M20

The Great Water

Chegworth

River Len

Church Farm

Broomfield

Roses Farm

Park Barn Farm

TURBERRY LA

PARK BARN RD

BROOMFIELD RD

Chegworth Court

CHEGWORTH RD

ME17

Scrub Wood

Glebe Dene

King's Wood

Caravan Site

WATER LA

The Apiary Bsns Pk

The Apiary

Works

Kingswood

PO

Kingswood Prim Sch

CHARLESFORD AVE

ASHFORD DR

WHITEHALL DR

ELDER CL

CHESTNUT DR

THORNE CL

ALL TREES CL

COPPER FIELD

THE LINKWALL

MEWS

IVY

BELL WAY

THE WALK

CAYSER DR

WILDWOOD CL

HEATHERWOOD

GRAVELLY BOTTOM RD

Kingswood Farm

PITT RD

CROSS DR

Cherry Tree Farm

LENHAM RD

College Farm

ULCOMBE HILL

Chartway Street

CHARTWAY ST

Street Farm

CHARLTON LA

Manor Farm

MORRY LA

CH

WIERTON RD

82 83 84

230
198

197 165

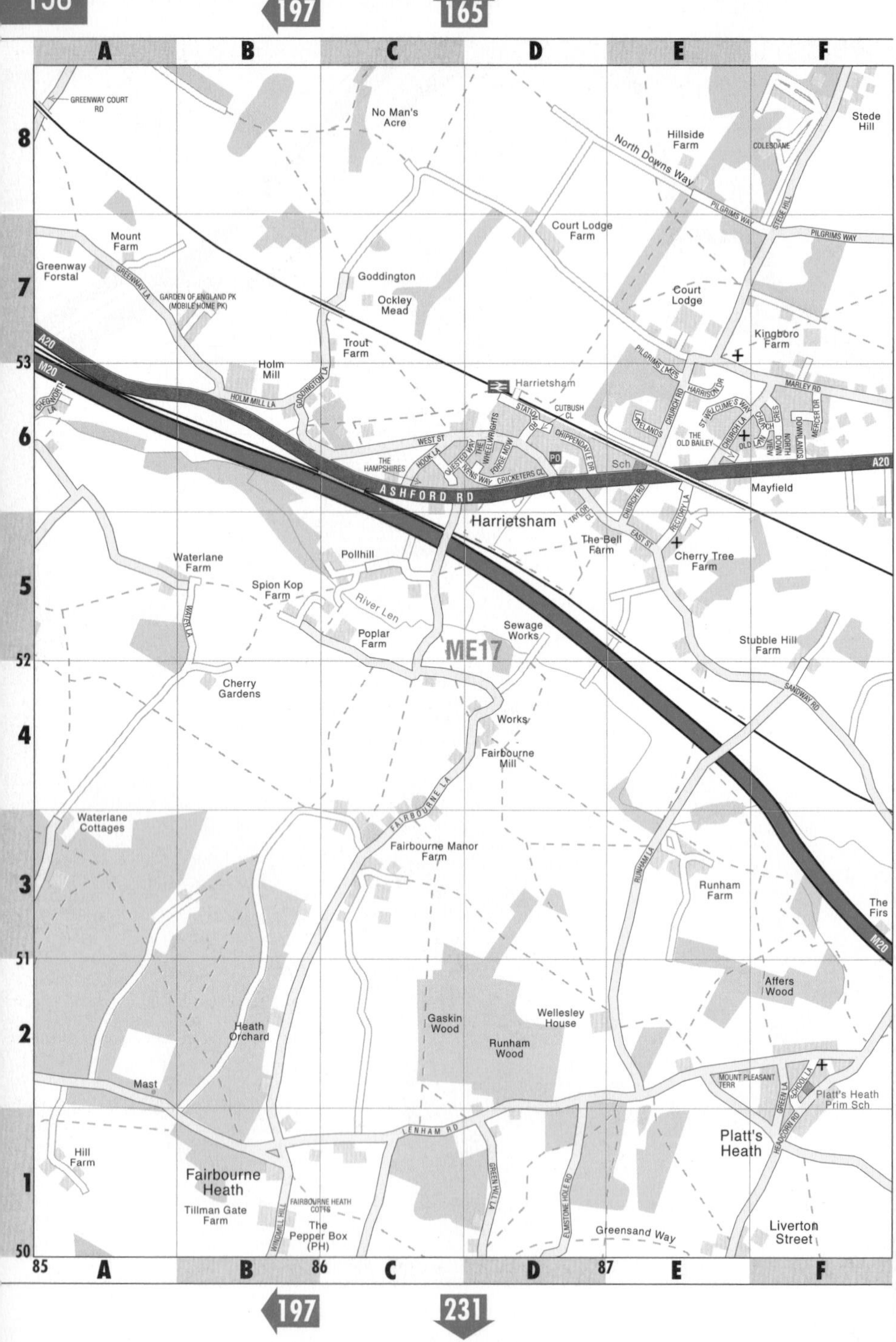
A B C D E F
8 7 6 5 4 3 2 1
53 52 51 50
85 86 87
GREENWAY COURT RD
No Man's Acre
Hillside Farm
North Downs Way
COLESDANE
Stede Hill
PILGRIMS WAY
STEDE HILL
Mount Farm
Greenway Forstal
GREENWAY LA
GARDEN OF ENGLAND PK (MOBILE HOME PK)
Court Lodge Farm
Goddington
Ockley Mead
Court Lodge
Kingboro Farm
Trout Farm
A20
M20
Holm Mill
HOLM MILL LA
GODDINGTON LA
Harrietsham
PILGRIMS LAKES
HARRISON DR
MARLEY RD
MERCER DR
STATION RD
CUTBUSH CL
CHURCH RD
LAKELANDS
ST WELCUME'S WAY
CHURCH LA
OLD LA
CHURCH VIEW
DOWN CRES
NORTH DOWNLANDS
THE OLD BAILEY
WEST ST
HOOK LA
QUESTED WAY
THE WHEELWRIGHTS
FORGE MDW
NENS WAY
CRICKETERS CL
CHIPPENDAYLE DR
PO
Sch
THE HAMPSHIRES
ASHFORD RD
Mayfield
Harrietsham
TAYLOR CL
RECTORY LA
EAST ST
The Bell Farm
Cherry Tree Farm
Waterlane Farm
Pollhill
Spion Kop Farm
River Len
WATER LA
Poplar Farm
ME17
Sewage Works
Stubble Hill Farm
Cherry Gardens
SANDWAY RD
Works
Fairbourne Mill
Waterlane Cottages
FAIRBOURNE LA
Fairbourne Manor Farm
Runham Farm
RUNHAM LA
The Firs
Affers Wood
Gaskin Wood
Wellesley House
Runham Wood
Heath Orchard
Mast
MOUNT PLEASANT TERR
GREEN LA
SCHOOL LA
Platt's Heath Prim Sch
LENHAM RD
Platt's Heath
HEADCORN RD
Hill Farm
Fairbourne Heath
Tillman Gate Farm
WINDMILL HILL
FAIRBOURNE HEATH COTTS
The Pepper Box (PH)
GREEN HILL LA
ELMSTONE HOLE RD
Greensand Way
Liverton Street

197 231

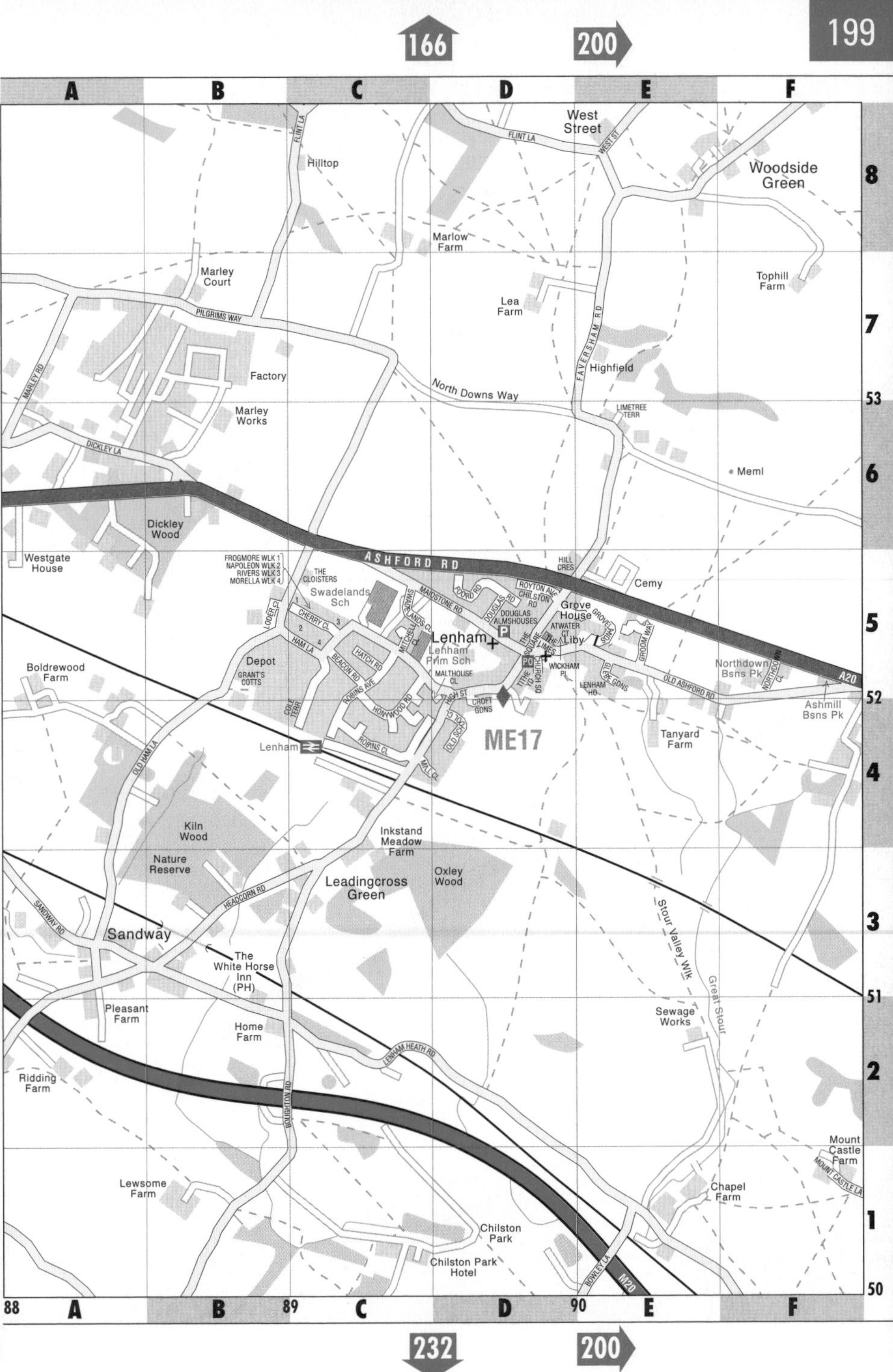
A
B
C
D
E
F
West Street
FLINT LA
WEST ST
Hilltop
Woodside Green
8
Marlow Farm
Marley Court
Lea Farm
Tophill Farm
PILGRIMS WAY
FAVERSHAM RD
7
Factory
Highfield
MARLEY RD
North Downs Way
Marley Works
LIMETREE TERR
53
DICKLEY LA
Meml
6
Dickley Wood
Westgate House
ASHFORD RD
FROGMORE WLK 1
NAPOLEON WLK 2
RIVERS WLK 3
MORELLA WLK 4
THE CLOISTERS
HILL CRES
Cemy
Swadelands Sch
MAIDSTONE RD
ROYTON AVE
CHILSTON RD
DOUGLAS ALMSHOUSES
Grove House
GROOM WAY
LODER CL
CHERRY CL
5
Lenham
Lenham Prim Sch
ATWATER CT
Liby
HAM LA
Depot
HATCH RD
BEACON RD
THE SQUARE
CHURCH SQ
Boldrewood Farm
GRANT'S COTTS
MALTHOUSE CL
WICKHAM PL
OLD ASHFORD RD
Northdown Bsns Pk
A20
ROBINS AVE
HIGH ST
LENHAM HO
52
COLE TERR
CROFT GDNS
Ashmill Bsns Pk
ME17
Tanyard Farm
ROBINS CL
Lenham
OLD HAM LA
MILL CL
4
Kiln Wood
Inkstand Meadow Farm
Nature Reserve
Oxley Wood
Leadingcross Green
HEADCORN RD
SANDWAY RD
Stour Valley Wlk
3
Sandway
The White Horse Inn (PH)
Great Stour
51
Pleasant Farm
Sewage Works
Home Farm
LENHAM HEATH RD
2
Ridding Farm
BOUGHTON RD
Mount Castle Farm
MOUNT CASTLE LA
Lewsome Farm
Chapel Farm
1
Chilston Park
Chilston Park Hotel
BOWLEY LA
M20
50
88
89
90

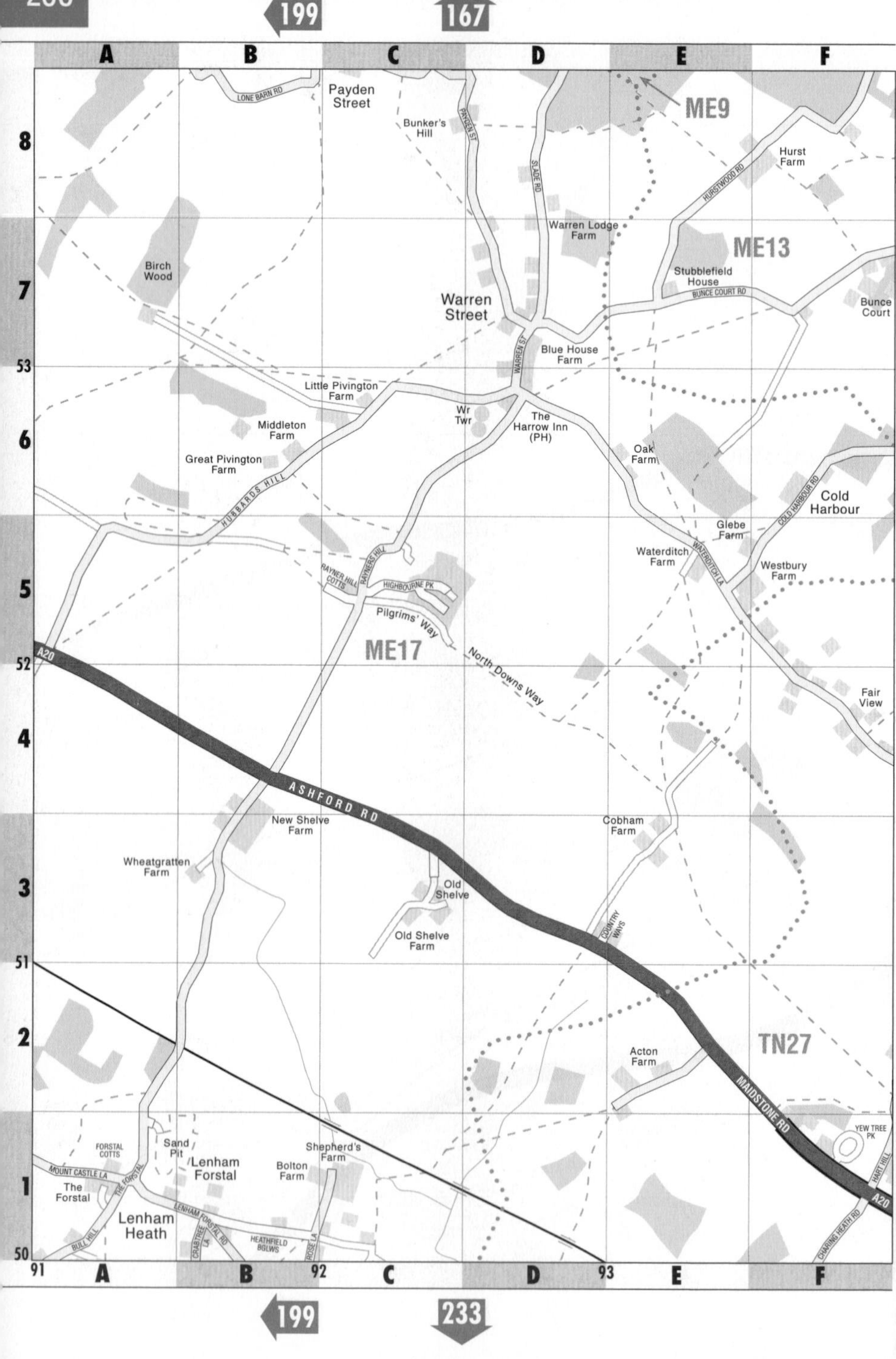

A | B | C | D | E | F

8

Lone Barn Rd
Payden Street
Bunker's Hill

ME9

Hurst Farm

7
Birch Wood
Warren Lodge Farm

ME13
Stubblefield House
BUNCE COURT RD
Bunce Court

53
Warren Street
Little Pivington Farm
Blue House Farm

6
Middleton Farm
Wr Twr
The Harrow Inn (PH)

Great Pivington Farm
Oak Farm
HUBBARDS HILL

Cold Harbour

Glebe Farm
Waterditch Farm
Westbury Farm
COLD HARBOUR RD

5
RAYNER HILL COTTS
HIGHBOURNE PK
Pilgrims' Way

ME17
North Downs Way

Fair View

52
A20

4
ASHFORD RD

New Shelve Farm
Cobham Farm

3
Wheatgratten Farm
Old Shelve
Old Shelve Farm

51

2
COUNTRY WAYS
Acton Farm

TN27
MAIDSTONE RD

Forstal Cotts
Sand Pit
Shepherd's Farm
MOUNT CASTLE LA
THE FORSTAL
Lenham Forstal
Bolton Farm
YEW TREE PK

1
The Forstal
Lenham Heath
HEATHFIELD BOLWS
HART HILL
A20
CHARING HEATH RD

50
91 | A | B | 92 | C | D | 93 | E | F

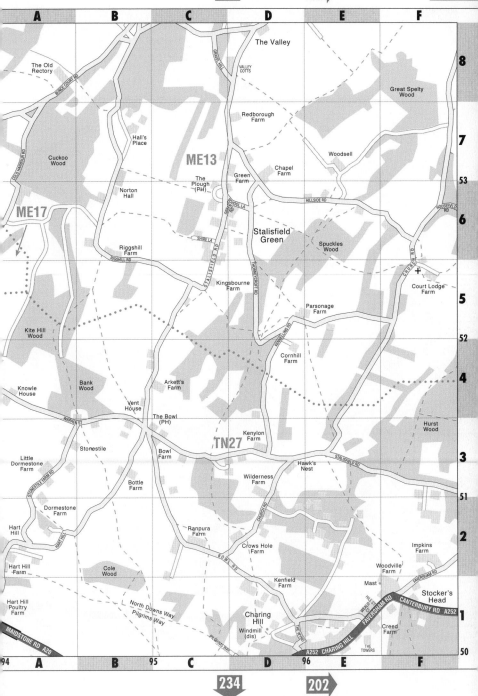

201
169

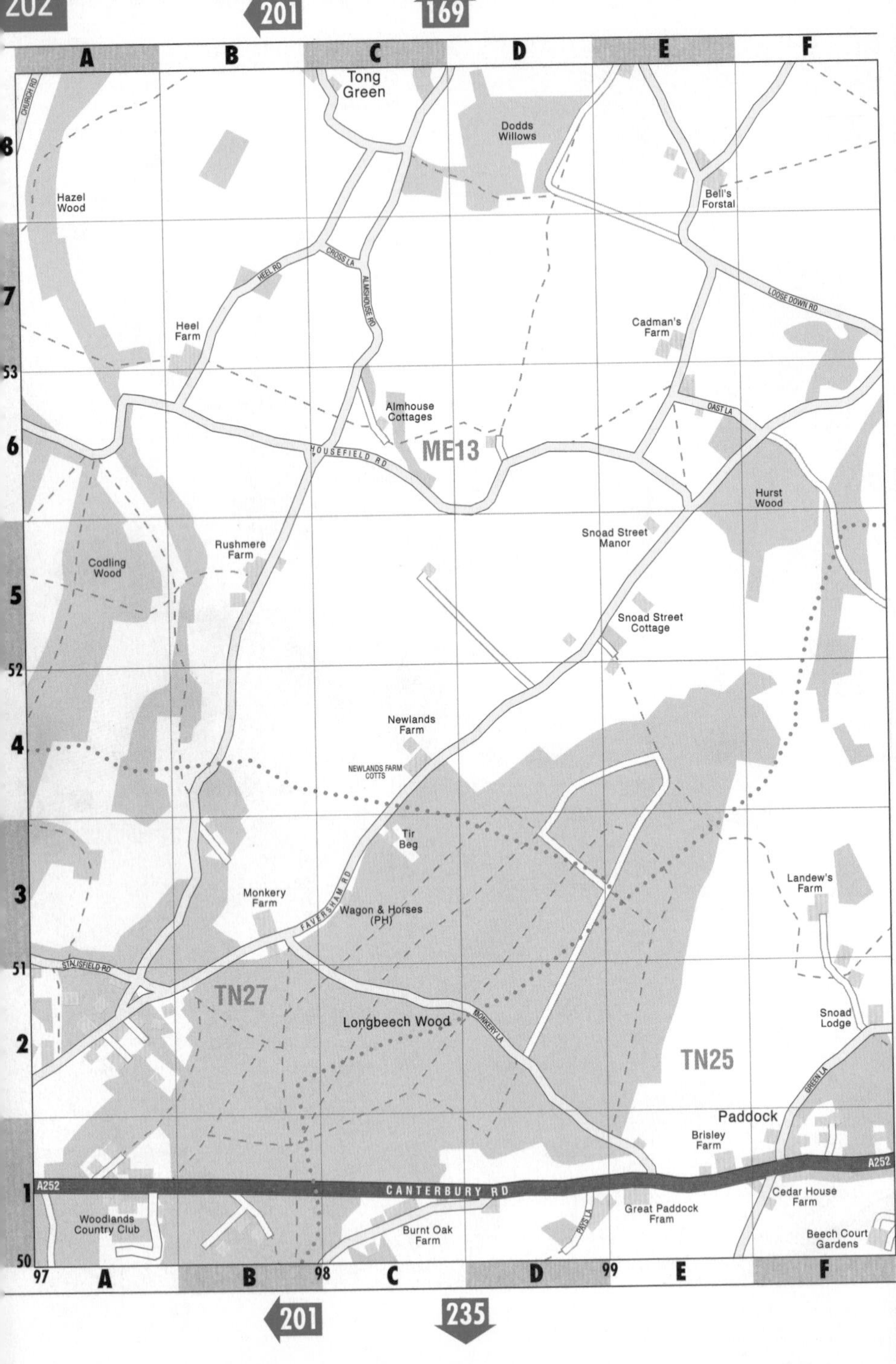
A
B
C
D
E
F
Tong Green
Dodds Willows
Hazel Wood
Bell's Forstal
CHURCH RD
HEEL RD
CROSS LA
ALMSHOUSE RD
Heel Farm
LOOSE DOWN RD
Cadman's Farm
Almhouse Cottages
OAST LA
ME13
HOUSEFIELD RD
Hurst Wood
Snoad Street Manor
Rushmere Farm
Codling Wood
Snoad Street Cottage
Newlands Farm
NEWLANDS FARM COTTS
Tir Beg
Landew's Farm
Monkery Farm
FAVERSHAM RD
Wagon & Horses (PH)
STALISFIELD RD
TN27
Longbeech Wood
MONKERY LA
Snoad Lodge
TN25
GREEN LA
Paddock
Brisley Farm
A252
A252
CANTERBURY RD
Cedar House Farm
Woodlands Country Club
Great Paddock Fram
PAYS LA
Burnt Oak Farm
Beech Court Gardens
8
7
53
6
5
52
4
3
51
2
1
50
97
98
99

201
235

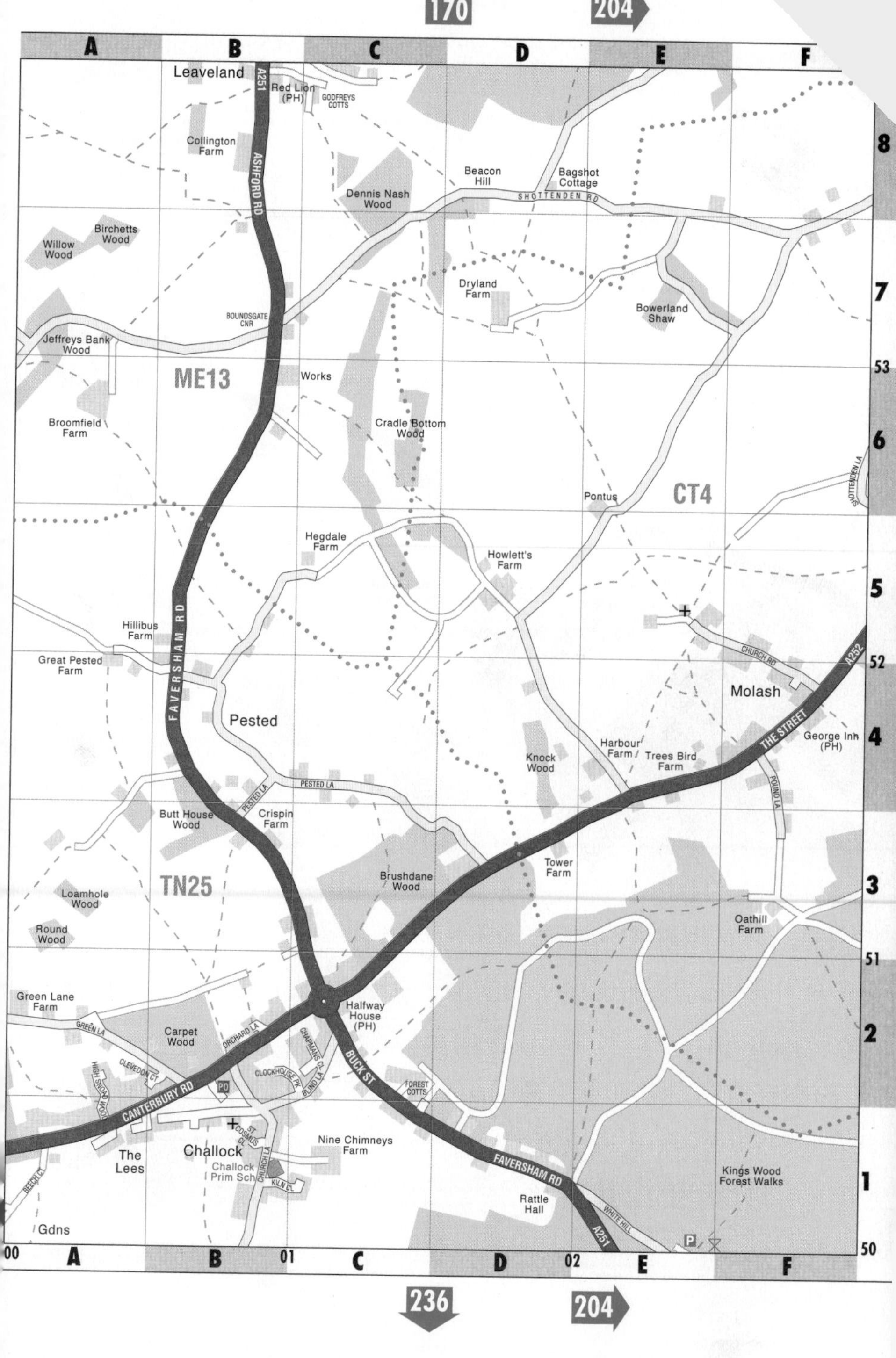

170
204
A
B
C
D
E
F
Leaveland
A251
Red Lion (PH)
GODFREYS COTTS
Collington Farm
ASHFORD RD
Beacon Hill
Bagshot Cottage
SHOTTENDEN RD
Dennis Nash Wood
Birchetts Wood
Willow Wood
Dryland Farm
Bowerland Shaw
BOUNDSGATE CNR
Jeffreys Bank Wood
ME13
Works
Broomfield Farm
Cradle Bottom Wood
Pontus
CT4
SHOTTENDEN LA
Hegdale Farm
Howlett's Farm
Hillibus Farm
Great Pested Farm
FAVERSHAM RD
CHURCH RD
A252
Molash
Pested
Harbour Farm
Trees Bird Farm
Knock Wood
George Inn (PH)
THE STREET
PESTED LA
Butt House Wood
Crispin Farm
POUND LA
Tower Farm
TN25
Brushdane Wood
Loamhole Wood
Round Wood
Oathill Farm
Green Lane Farm
GREEN LA
Carpet Wood
ORCHARD LA
Halfway House (PH)
CHAPMANS CL
BUCK ST
CLEVEDON CT
HIGH SNOAD WOOD
CANTERBURY RD
PO
CLOCKHOUSE PK
BLIND LA
FOREST COTTS
ST COSMUS CL
Nine Chimneys Farm
The Lees
Challock
Challock Prim Sch
CHURCH LA
KILN CL
FAVERSHAM RD
Kings Wood Forest Walks
BEECH CL
Rattle Hall
WHITE HILL
A251
Gdns
P
8
7
53
6
5
52
4
3
51
2
1
50
00
01
02
236
204

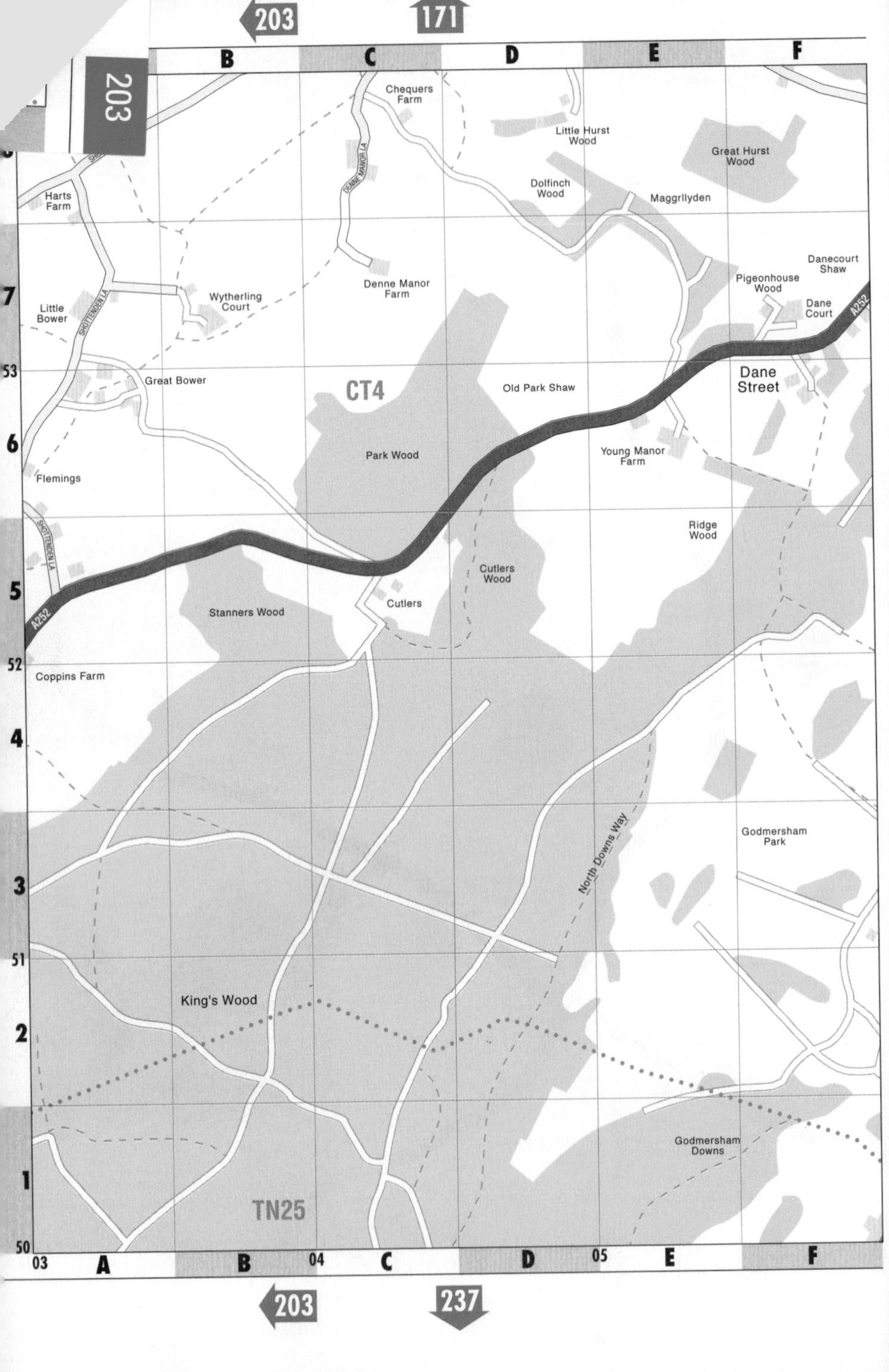

203
171
203
B
C
D
E
F
Chequers Farm
Little Hurst Wood
Great Hurst Wood
DENNE MANOR LA
Harts Farm
Dolfinch Wood
Maggrllyden
Danecourt Shaw
Pigeonhouse Wood
Denne Manor Farm
Dane Court
7
Little Bower
SHOTTENDEN LA
Wytherling Court
A252
53
Great Bower
CT4
Old Park Shaw
Dane Street
6
Park Wood
Young Manor Farm
Flemings
SHOTTENDEN LA
Ridge Wood
Cutlers Wood
5
Cutlers
Stanners Wood
52
Coppins Farm
4
North Downs Way
Godmersham Park
3
51
King's Wood
2
Godmersham Downs
1
TN25
50
03
A
B
04
C
D
05
E
F
203
237

A B C D E F

Badger's Hill Open Farm
SOLESHILL RD
PICKELDEN LA
MEADOW CL
A28
CANTERBURY RD
MULBERRY HILL
CHURCH HILL
FELBOROUGH CL
Woolpack Inn
A252
Chilham
Stile Farm
TAYLORS HILL
THE SQUARE
BAGHAM RD
ARDEN GRANGE
BAGHAM LA
HERONS CL
THE STREET
PO
P
DOVECOTE CT
STABLE CT
Sch
SCHOOL HILL
HAMBROOK CL
HAMBROOK LA
Bagham
LC
MILL LA
Chilham
BRANCH RD
Chilham Castle
Julliberrie's Grave Long Barrow
Long Wood
Sewage Works
Julliberrie Downs
North Downs Way
Chilmans Downs
Church Wood
Chilham Park
MOUNTAIN ST
Mountain Street
Great Stour
Down Wood
East Stour Farm
Stour Valley Wlk
CT4
ASHFORD RD
Hurst Farm
POPE ST
Brooks Wood
Wintergates Wood
Woodsdale Farm
Pope Street Farm
Stump Shave
Forest Farm
Godmersham Park
Coneyearth Wood
Blue Downs
EGGARTON LA
Court Lodge Farm
Godmersham
THE STREET
PURR WOOD
Eggarton Manor
CANTERBURY RD
A28
TN25
Purr Wood

8 7 53 6 5 52 4 3 51 2 1 50

06 A B 07 C D 08 E F

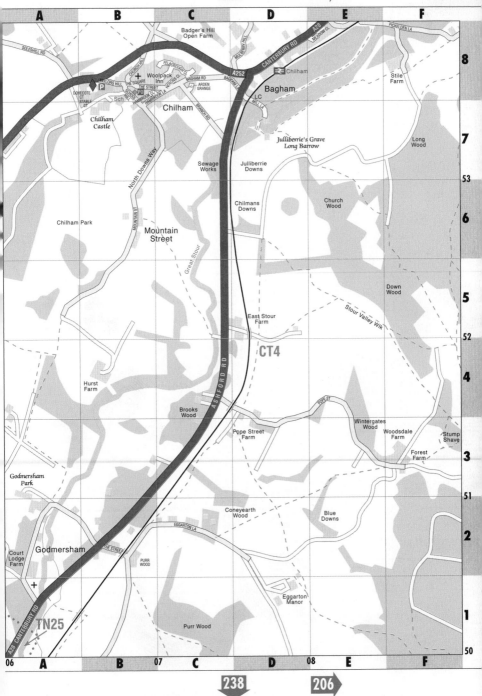

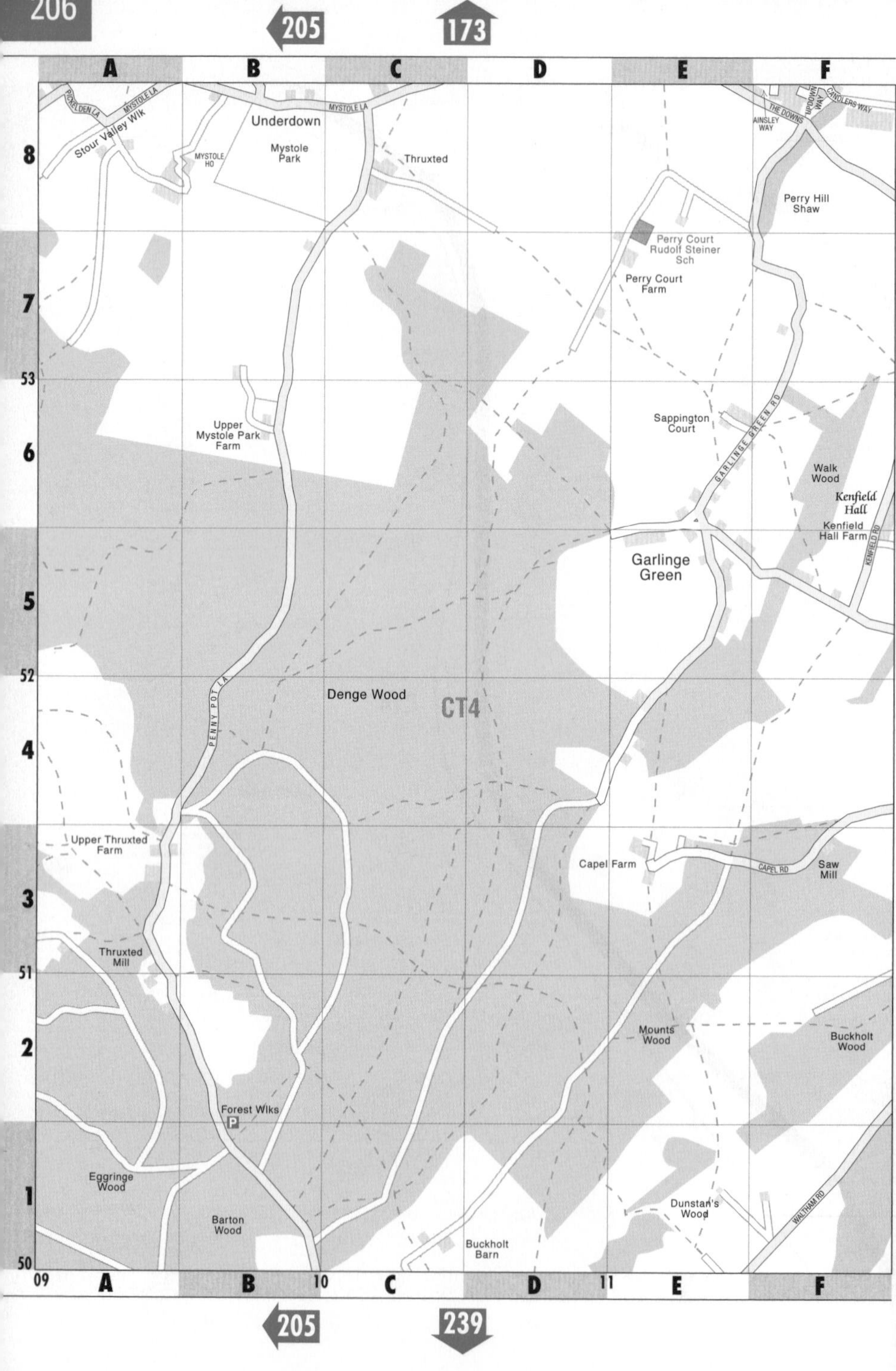

205
173

A **B** **C** **D** **E** **F**

Stour Valley Wlk

POXDEN LA

MYSTOLE LA

MYSTOLE LA

Underdown

MYSTOLE HO

Mystole Park

Thruxted

8

THE DOWNS

CHOLLERS WAY

AINSLEY WAY

Perry Hill Shaw

Perry Court Rudolf Steiner Sch

Perry Court Farm

7

53

Upper Mystole Park Farm

Sappington Court

GARLINGE GREEN RD

Walk Wood

Kenfield Hall

Kenfield Hall Farm

KENFIELD RD

6

Garlinge Green

5

52

PENNY POT LA

Denge Wood

CT4

4

Upper Thruxted Farm

Capel Farm

CAPEL RD

Saw Mill

3

51

Thruxted Mill

Mounts Wood

Buckholt Wood

2

Forest Wlks
P

Eggringe Wood

Dunstan's Wood

WALTHAM RD

1

Barton Wood

Buckholt Barn

50

09 **A** **B** 10 **C** **D** 11 **E** **F**

205
239

174

208

A B C D E F
Oakfield Shaw
Long Shaw
Iffin Wood
Lower Heppington
Red Wood Lees
Rabbit Wood
THE DOWNS
NEW HOUSE LA
IFFIN LA
FAUSSETT HILL
B2068
Little Iffin Wood
The Granville (PH)
CHARTHAM DOWNS RD
Street End
HARDRES COURT RD
Rabbit Bank Wood
Chartham Downs
Street End Place
KENFIELD RD
SWARLING HILL RD
REDHOUSE LA
Swarling Manor Farm
Kenfield Hall Farm
Harmansole Farm
JERSEY LA
Park Wood
WATERY LA
Well Wood
Cobsdane Wood
TOWN RD
Debden Court
Young's Farm
GARLINGE GREEN RD
WOOTTON DR
CT4
EAST WOOTTON COTTS
WOOTTON CL
Shoot Wood
CATT'S WOOD RD
Little Catt's Farm
CAPEL RD
VICARAGE HILL
Petham
THE STREET
CHURCH LA
Cattshill Shaw
Petham Prim Sch
STONE ST
Great Catt's Farm
TILLARD CL
Cattshill Wood
Broadway Green Farm
Petham House
Homeshole Shaw
BROADWAY
CHEQUERS HILL
Bowhill Shaw
BOW HILL
Chequers (PH)
HOGG LA
YEW TREE PK CVN & CAMPING SITE
DUCKPITS RD
Earley Wood
Brockhanger Wood
Dane Farm
Hunt's Wood
B2068
8 7 53 6 5 52 4 3 51 2 1 50
12 13 14

240
208

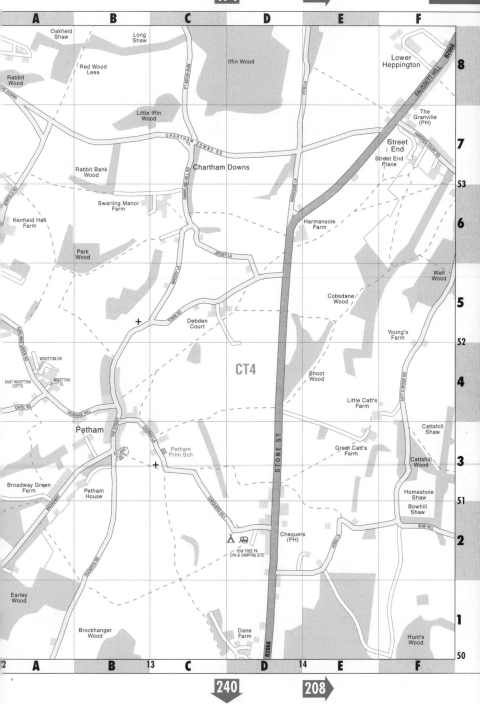

207 175

A B C D E F

8

Whitehill
Wood

Middle
Pett
Farm

North Court
Farm

Warren
Wood

7

Little
Pett
Farm

Redhill
Wood

The
Shave

53

Lower
Hardres

BUTTS CT

Little
Eaton
Farm

Lenhall
Farm

6

BUTTS
MDW
PH

SCHOOL LA

Stockfield
Wood

Avenue
Wood

Pett
Bottom

CT4

5

Cook's
Farm

The
Duck
(PH)

HEALEY'S HILL

PETT BOTTOM RD

52

Gorsley
Wood

4

PILOTS FARM RD

Pilot's
Wood

Broxhall
Farm

HARDRES COURT RD

Broxhall
Wood

SCHOOL RD

St Andrew's
Wood

Equestrian
Centre

Langham
Park
Farm

WOODGATE

PHEASANTS HILL RD

51

Bursted
Manor

BOW HILL

2

Hardres
Court
Farm

BURSTED HILL

Bursted
Wood

Park
Rough

Upper
Hardres
Court

Reed
Farm

1

The
Manor
House

Westwood
Farm

Marley
Wood

50

15 A B 16 C D 17 E F

207 241

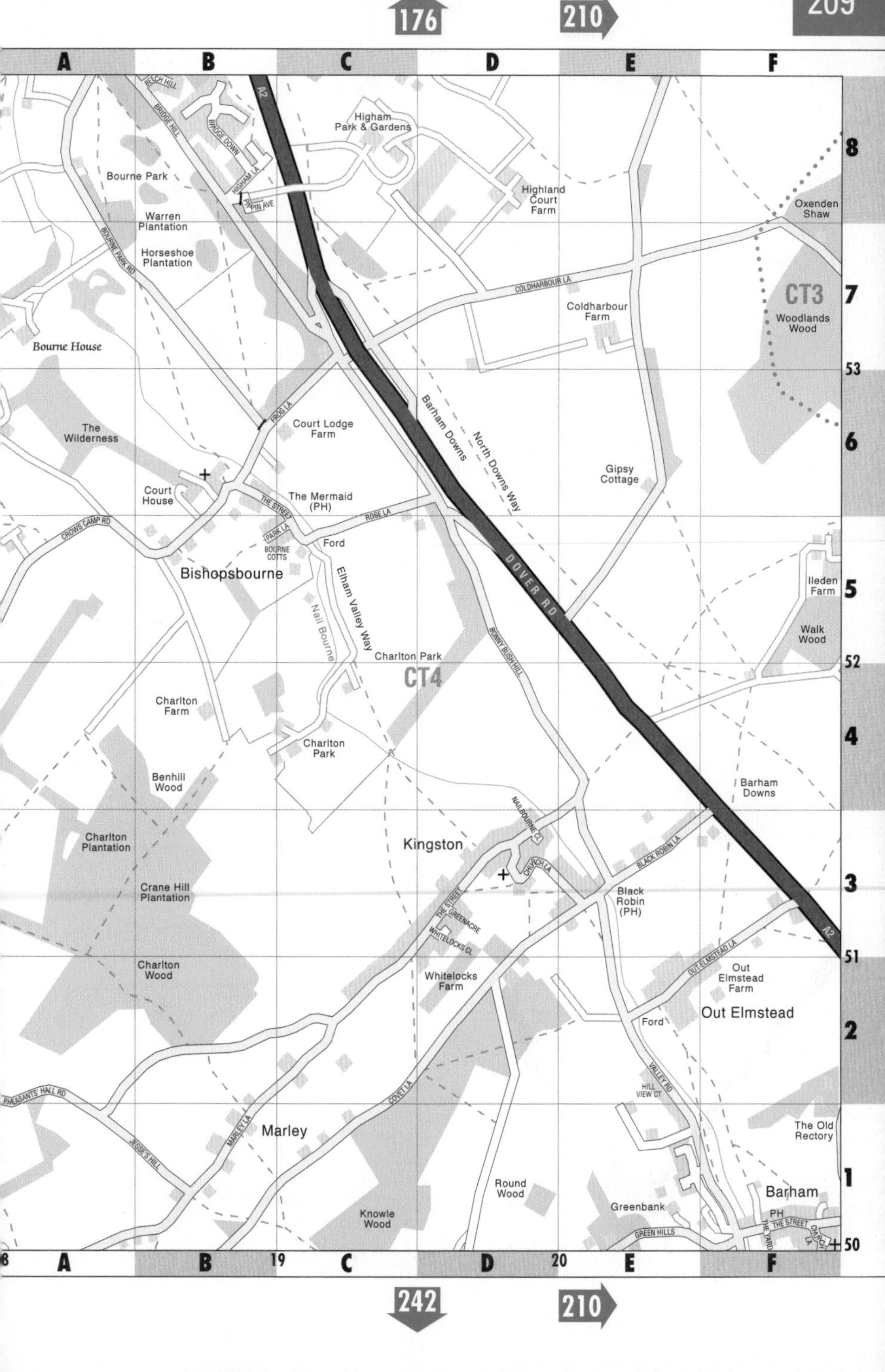
176
210
A
B
C
D
E
F
8
7
53
6
5
52
4
3
51
2
1
50
19
20
242
210
Higham Park & Gardens
Highland Court Farm
Oxenden Shaw
Bourne Park
Warren Plantation
Horseshoe Plantation
Bourne House
COLDHARBOUR LA
Coldharbour Farm
CT3
Woodlands Wood
The Wilderness
Court Lodge Farm
Barham Downs
North Downs Way
Gipsy Cottage
Court House
The Mermaid (PH)
ROSE LA
Ford
Bishopsbourne
Elham Valley Way
Nail Bourne
DOVER RD
Ileden Farm
Walk Wood
Charlton Park
CT4
Charlton Farm
Charlton Park
Benhill Wood
Barham Downs
Charlton Plantation
Kingston
Crane Hill Plantation
Black Robin (PH)
BLACK ROBIN LA
Charlton Wood
Whitelocks Farm
Out Elmstead Farm
OUT ELMSTEAD LA
Out Elmstead
Ford
A2
BEECH HILL
BRIDGE HILL
BRIDGE DOWN
HIGHAM LA
PIN AVE
BOURNE PARK RD
FROG LA
THE STREET
PARK LA
BOURNE COTTS
CROWS CAMP RD
BONNY BUSH HILL
NAILBOURNE CL
CHURCH LA
THE STREET
THE GREENACRE
WHITELOCKS CL
VALLEY RD
HILL VIEW CT
PHEASANTS' HALL RD
JESSE'S HILL
MARLEY LA
COVET LA
Marley
Round Wood
Knowle Wood
Greenbank
GREEN HILLS
The Old Rectory
Barham
PH
THE STREET
THE YARD
CHURCH LA

209
177

A   B   C   D   E   F

CT4

8
Twelve Acre Shaw
Adisham CE Prim Sch
Adisham
Bloodden
Adisham   Hotel
Ratling Court
PO
WOODLANDS RD
THE STREET
DONKEY LA

7
Woodlands Manor
Oxenden Wood
Cooting Farm
COOTING LA

53
Pitt Wood

6
Woodlands Wood
CT3
1 ULLSWATER GDNS
2 ENNERDALE GDNS
TENNYSON
COLERIDGE GDNS
THIRLMERE
BUTTERMERE
WORDSWORTH GDNS
CORNWALLIS AVE
SPINNEY
WINDERMERE GDNS
DORMAN AVE N

5
Well Wood
Aylesham Prim Sch
WOODLAND AVE
Aylesham
Liby
SNOWDOWN
EASTRY CT
HAWTHORN CL
NEWMAN RD
VALE RD
LITTLE
ASH
BOULEVARD COURRIERES
MARKET
QUEENS RD
HYDE PL
SPINNEY LA
CLARENDON RD

52
Cooting Downs

4
Ileden Wood
Aylesham Wood
COVERT RD
SPINNEY LA
Aylesham Ind Est
Ackholt Wood

3
Barham Downs
AYLESHAM CNR
Willow Wood
CT15

51
A2
Upper Digges Farm
ADISHAM RD
NORTH DOWNS WAY
POND LA
Well Wood
Nethersole Farm
Chalk Wood

2
DOVER RD
Cemy
Aylesham Farm
Nethersole Farm
Womenswold
THE STREET
RECTORY LA

1
DOVER RD
B2046
Westmore Ho
Woodpeckers Country Hotel
Snow Down
Woolage Village
THE PLACE
THE GREEN
NETHERSOLE RD

50
OLD DOVER RD
GRAVEL CASTLE RD
A260

21   A   B   22   C   D   23   E   F

CT4

209
243

178
212

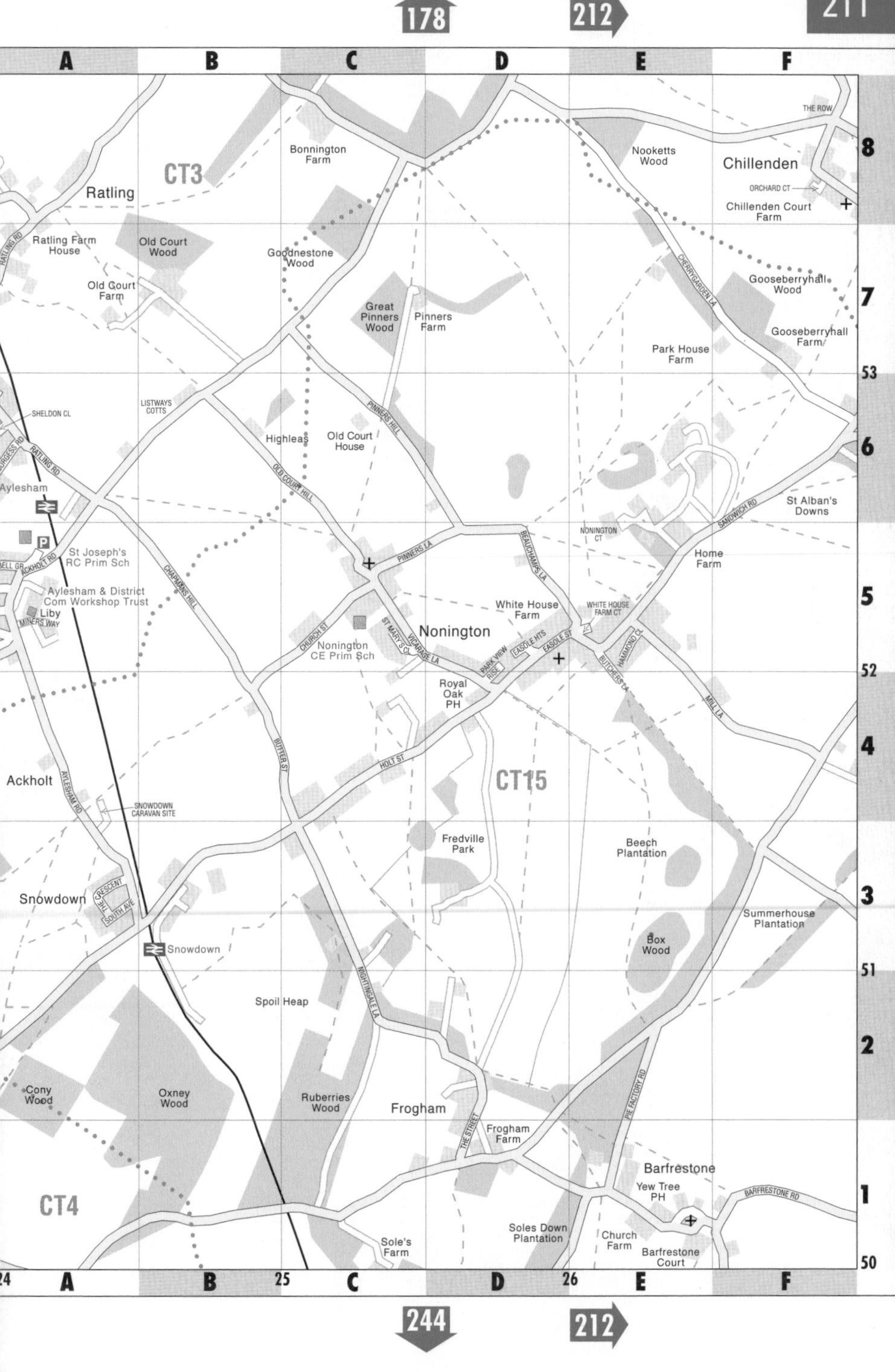
A
B
C
D
E
F
CT3
Ratling
Bonnington Farm
Nooketts Wood
Chillenden
THE ROW
ORCHARD CT
Chillenden Court Farm
RATLING RD
Ratling Farm House
Old Court Wood
Goodnestone Wood
Old Court Farm
Great Pinners Wood
Pinners Farm
CHERRYGARDEN LA
Gooseberryhall Wood
Gooseberryhall Farm
Park House Farm
LISTWAYS COTTS
SHELDON CL
PINNERS HILL
Highleas
Old Court House
BURGESS RD
RATLING RD
Aylesham
OLD COURT HILL
St Alban's Downs
SANDWICH RD
NONINGTON CT
St Joseph's RC Prim Sch
ACKHOLT RD
PINNERS LA
BEAUCHAMPS LA
Home Farm
Aylesham & District Com Workshop Trust
CHAPMANS HILL
White House Farm
WHITE HOUSE FARM CT
Liby
MINERS WAY
CHURCH ST
ST MARY'S CL
Nonington
Nonington CE Prim Sch
VICARAGE LA
PARK VIEW RISE
EASOLE HTS
EASOLE ST
HAMMOND CL
BUTCHERS LA
Royal Oak PH
MILL LA
BUTTER ST
HOLT ST
CT15
Ackholt
AYLESHAM RD
SNOWDOWN CARAVAN SITE
Fredville Park
Beech Plantation
Snowdown
THE CRESCENT
SOUTH AVE
Summerhouse Plantation
Box Wood
Snowdown
NIGHTINGALE LA
Spoil Heap
Cony Wood
Oxney Wood
Ruberries Wood
Frogham
PIE FACTORY RD
THE STREET
Frogham Farm
Barfrestone
Yew Tree PH
BARFRESTONE RD
CT4
Soles Down Plantation
Church Farm
Sole's Farm
Barfrestone Court
8
7
53
6
5
52
4
3
51
2
1
50
24
25
26

244
212

211
179

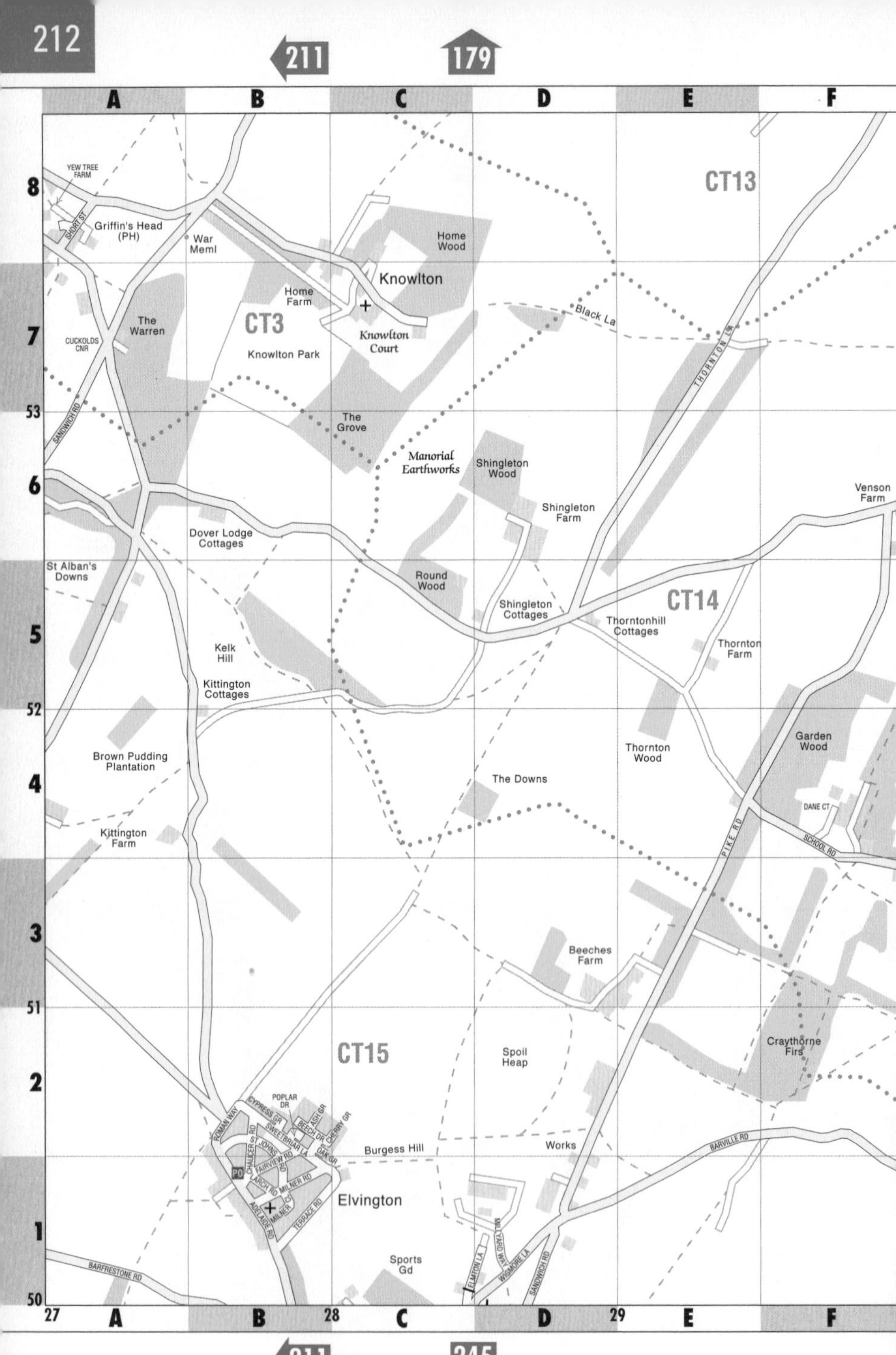
A
B
C
D
E
F
8
7
53
6
5
52
4
3
51
2
1
50
27
28
29
YEW TREE FARM
SHORT ST
Griffin's Head (PH)
War Meml
Home Wood
Knowlton
Home Farm
CT13
CT3
The Warren
Knowlton Court
Knowlton Park
Black La
THORNTON LA
CUCKOLDS CNR
SANDWICH RD
The Grove
Manorial Earthworks
Shingleton Wood
Venson Farm
Shingleton Farm
Dover Lodge Cottages
St Alban's Downs
Round Wood
CT14
Shingleton Cottages
Thorntonhill Cottages
Kelk Hill
Thornton Farm
Kittington Cottages
Garden Wood
Brown Pudding Plantation
Thornton Wood
The Downs
DANE CT
SCHOOL RD
PIKE RD
Kittington Farm
Beeches Farm
CT15
Spoil Heap
Craythorne Firs
POPLAR DR
CYPRESS GR
ROMAN WAY
ASH GR
CHERRY GR
BEECH DR
SWEETBRIAR LA
OAK GR
Burgess Hill
Works
BARVILLE RD
CHAUCER RD
ST JOHNS RD
FAIRVIEW RD
PO
LARCH RD
MILNER RD
MILNER CT
ADELAIDE RD
TERRACE RD
Elvington
MILLYARD WAY
ELMTON LA
WIGMORE LA
SANDWICH RD
BARFRESTONE RD
Sports Gd

211
245

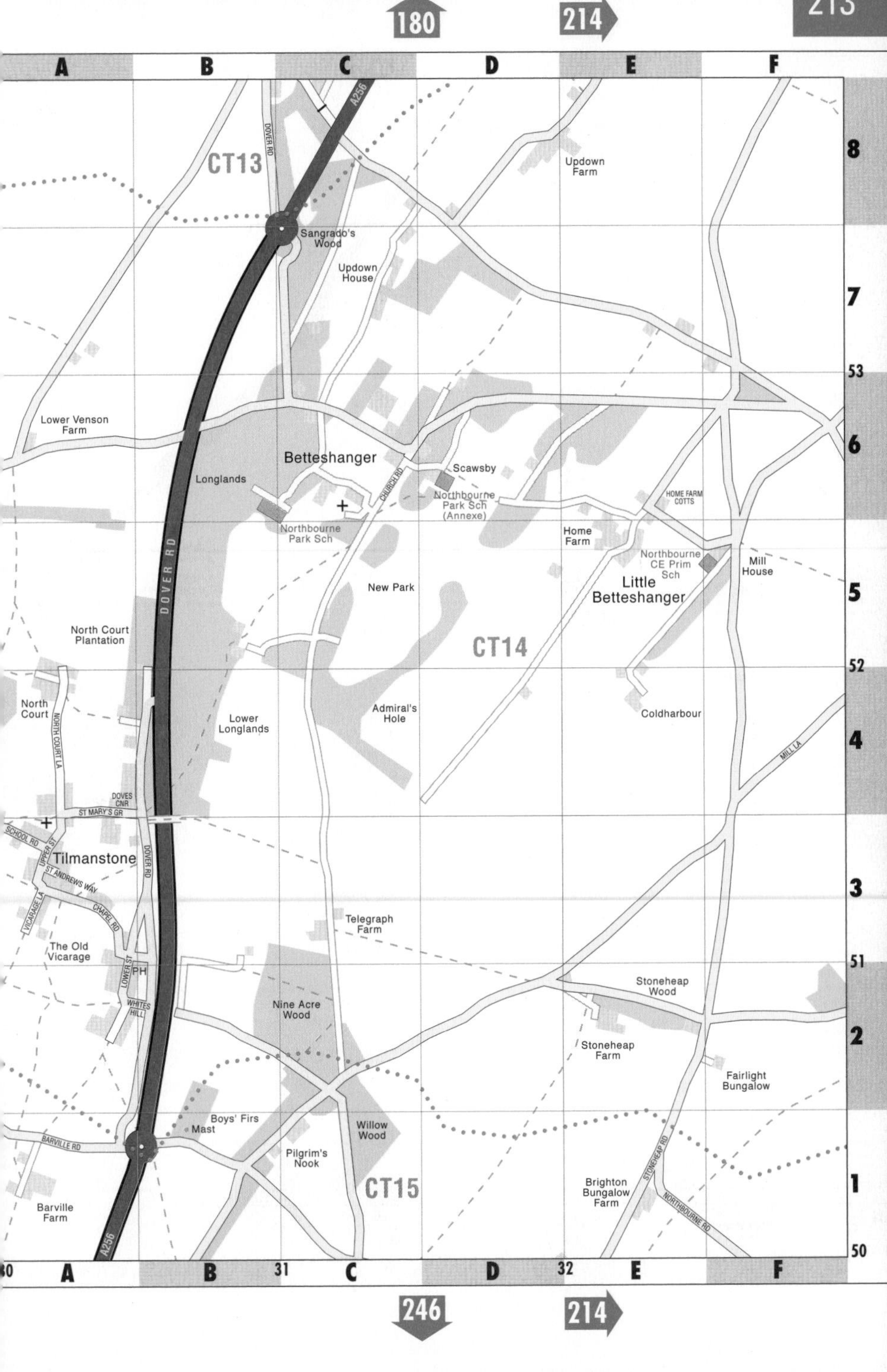
180
214
A
B
C
D
E
F
8
7
53
6
5
52
4
3
51
2
1
50
30
31
32
CT13
A256
DOVER RD
Updown Farm
Sangrado's Wood
Updown House
Lower Venson Farm
Betteshanger
CHURCH RD
Scawsby
Longlands
Northbourne Park Sch (Annexe)
Northbourne Park Sch
HOME FARM COTTS
Home Farm
Northbourne CE Prim Sch
Mill House
Little Betteshanger
New Park
CT14
North Court Plantation
North Court
NORTH COURT LA
Lower Longlands
Admiral's Hole
Coldharbour
MILL LA
DOVES CNR
ST MARY'S GR
SCHOOL RD
UPPER ST
Tilmanstone
ST ANDREWS WAY
CHAPEL RD
VICARAGE LA
Telegraph Farm
The Old Vicarage
LOWER ST
PH
WHITES HILL
Nine Acre Wood
Stoneheap Wood
Stoneheap Farm
Fairlight Bungalow
Boys' Firs
Mast
BARVILLE RD
Willow Wood
Pilgrim's Nook
CT15
Brighton Bungalow Farm
STONEHEAP RD
NORTHBOURNE RD
Barville Farm
246
214

213
181

	A	B	C	D	E	F

8

Finglesham Farm

FINGLESHAM FARM BARNS

Crown Inn

THE STREET

Iggulden

Marley

Finglesham

Lower Farm

Howe Wall Farm

Marley Farm Nurseries

MARLEY LA

7

BROAD LA

Sewage Works

North Stream

Cottington Court Farm

53

NORTH WAY

CIRCULAR RD

Mast

Turnerhouse Nurseries

HULL PL

6

Betteshanger Colliery (Dis)

Broad Dike

White Cliffs County Trail

The Sportsman (PH)

SHOLDEN NEW RD

MARSH LA

Churchfield Farm

Sholden

5

THE DROVE

CHURCH RD

The Park

CT14

Sholden Downs

Sholden Downs Nursery

Sholden CE Prim / Sch

LONDON RD

A258

New Mill (dis)

THE STREET

Northbourne Court Gardens

52

MILL LA

COLD BLOW GR

MILL LANE COTTS

Hare & Hounds (PH)

Northbourne

Works

Mongeham Prim Sch

PHOENIX CL

PATTERSON CL

GOOD HOPE

4

DEAL RD

White Cliffs Country Trail

NORTHBOURNE RD

Sparrow Court

MONGEHAM CHURCH CL

Church Farm

Mongeham Farm

Mongeham View

SHOLDEN BANK

ST NICHOLAS CL

ST AUGUSTINE'S RD

ST EDMUND'S RD

ST FRANCIS CL

HECTOR RD

ST RICHMETE CT

CAVELL SQ

3

WILLOW RD

Beaconhill Cottages

Great Mongeham

Great Mongeham Farm

ASHTON CL

Brewery Cotts

CHURCH PATH

PIXWELL LA

CHERRY LA

ELLEN'S HILL

Hillside Farm

ROWAN CL

LONDON RD

St Mary's RC Prim Sch

51

Manor Farm

Pixhill Cottage

Pixhill Cottage

2

Little Mongeham

Beacon Hill

Pixwell Point

Black Hill

ELLEN'S RD

1

CT15

Sutton Hill

Homeside Farm

Glen Farm

MANTLES HILL

BUNTIS RD

CHURCH LA

Ripple

Church Farm

50

| **33** | A | **34** | B | C | **35** | D | E | F |

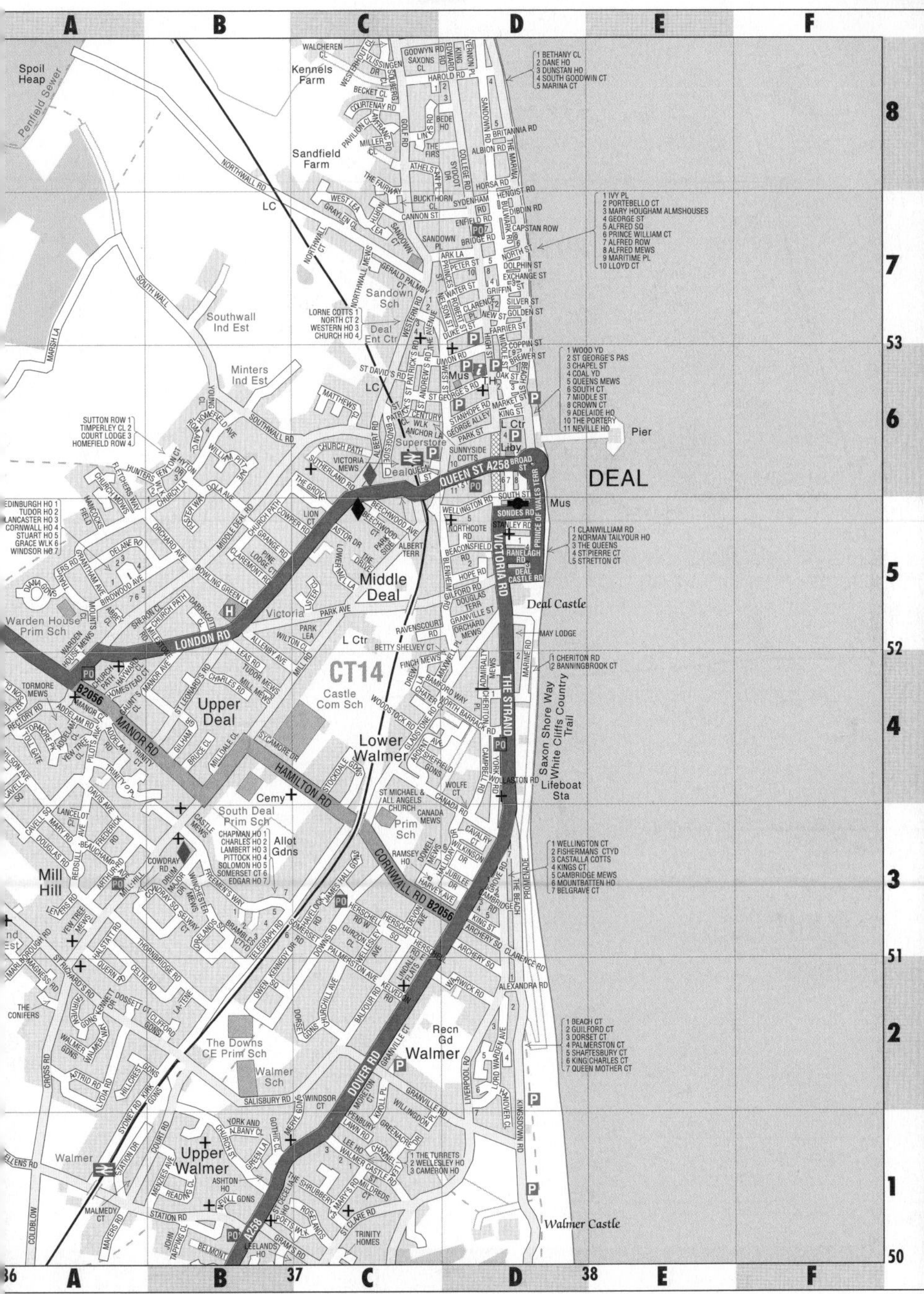

182

8
7
53
6

DEAL

5
52
4
3
51
2
1
50

CT14

Middle
Deal

Upper
Deal

Lower
Walmer

Mill
Hill

Walmer

Upper
Walmer

Deal Castle

Walmer Castle

248

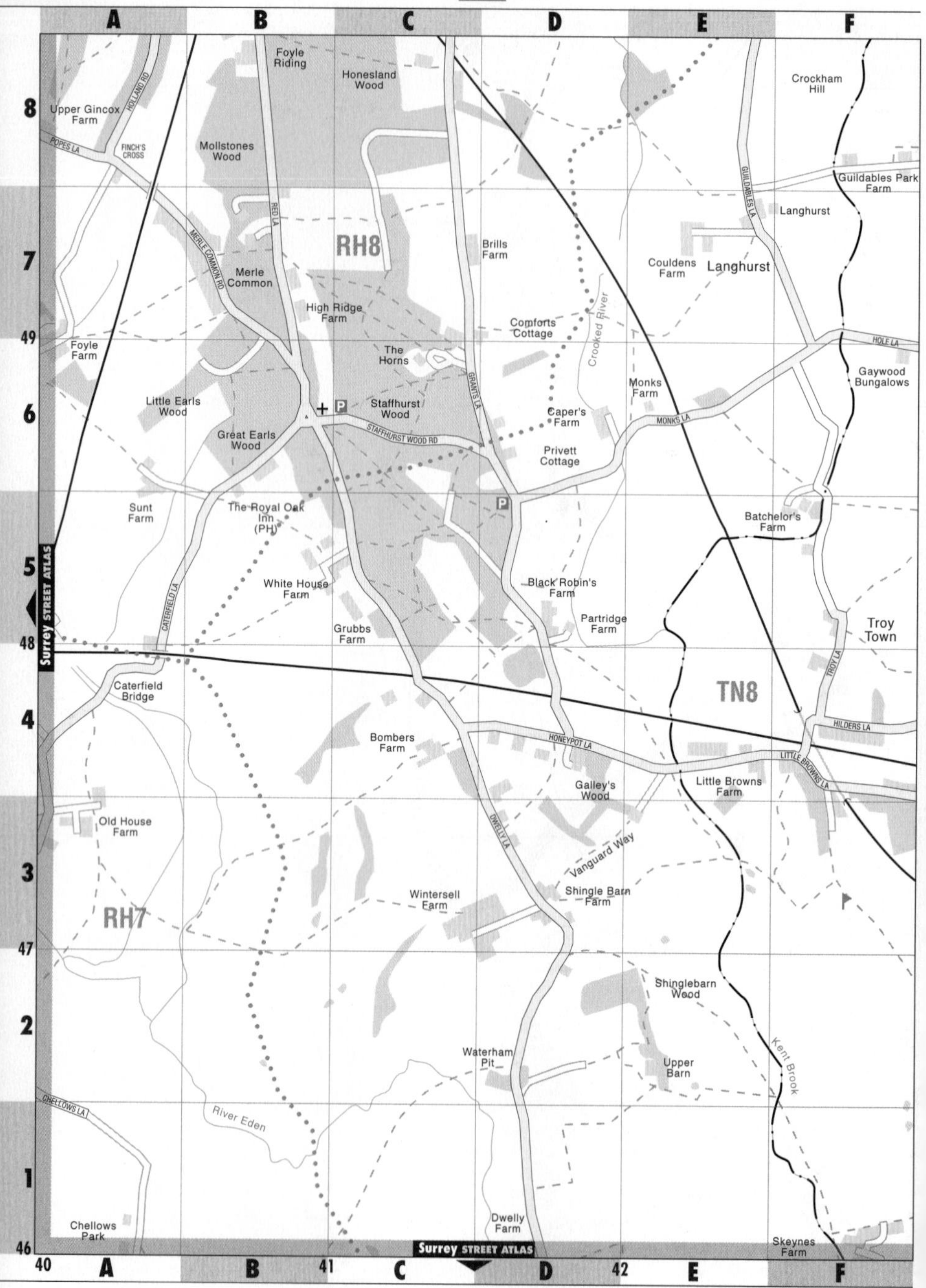

183

A   B   C   D   E   F

8   Upper Gincox
     Farm

     Foyle
     Riding
            Honesland
            Wood
                                                    Crockham
                                                    Hill

     Mollstones
     Wood
            FINCH'S
            CROSS

                    RH8
                                    Brills
                                    Farm
                                                    Couldens
                                                    Farm   Langhurst

7   Langhurst

     Merle
     Common

     High Ridge
     Farm
                        Comforts
                        Cottage

49   Foyle
     Farm
            The
            Horns
                                        Monks
                                        Farm
                                                            Gaywood
                                                            Bungalows

6   Little Earls
     Wood
            Staffhurst
            Wood
                    Caper's
                    Farm
                            MONKS LA

     Great Earls
     Wood
            STAFFHURST WOOD RD
                    Privett
                    Cottage

5   Sunt
     Farm
            The Royal Oak
            Inn
            (PH)
                                                    Batchelor's
                                                    Farm

     White House
     Farm
            Black Robin's
            Farm

48   Partridge
                                    Farm
                                                        Troy
                                                        Town

     Grubbs
     Farm

4   Caterfield
     Bridge
                                                HILDERS LA

            Bombers
            Farm
                    HONEYPOT LA
                            Little Browns
                            Farm   TN8

                        Galley's
                        Wood

     Old House
     Farm
                        Vanguard Way

3   Shingle Barn
                         Farm

     RH7   Wintersell
            Farm

47   Shinglebarn
                        Wood

2   Kent Brook

                Waterham
                Pit
                        Upper
                        Barn

     River Eden

1

     CHELLOWS LA

     Chellows
     Park
                        Dwelly
                        Farm
                                        Skeynes
                                        Farm

46
     40   A   B   41   C   D   42   E   F

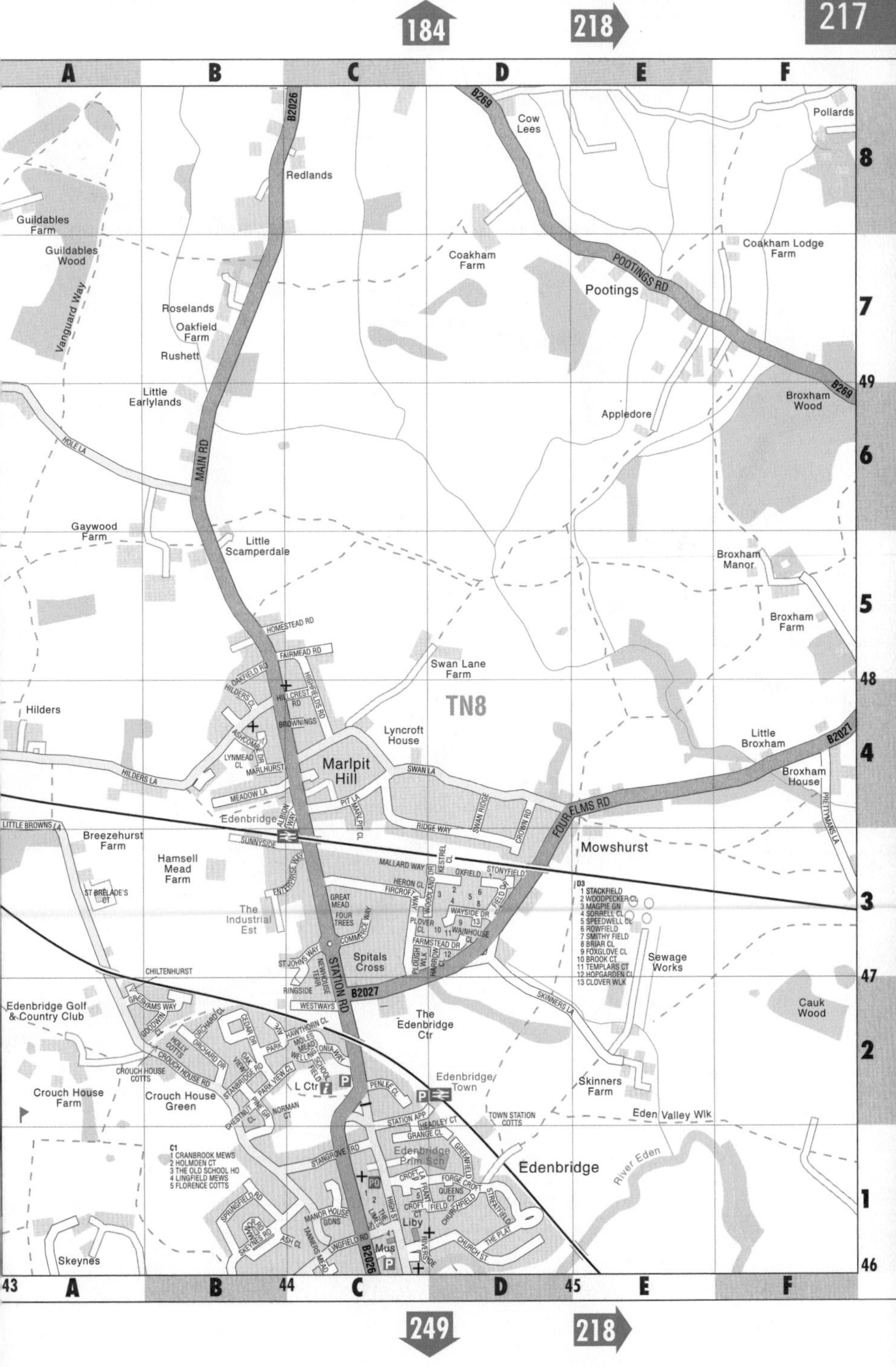
184
218
Guildables Farm
Guildables Wood
Vanguard Way
Redlands
Cow Lees
Pollards
Coakham Farm
Coakham Lodge Farm
Pootings
POOTINGS RD
B269
B2026
Roselands
Oakfield Farm
Rushett
Little Earlylands
Broxham Wood
Appledore
HOLE LA
MAIN RD
Gaywood Farm
Little Scamperdale
Broxham Manor
Broxham Farm
HOMESTEAD RD
FAIRMEAD RD
Swan Lane Farm
TN8
Hilders
Lyncroft House
Little Broxham
B2027
Marlpit Hill
SWAN LA
Broxham House
HILDERS LA
MEADOW LA
FOUR ELMS RD
PRETTYMANS LA
Edenbridge
LITTLE BROWNS LA
Breezehurst Farm
SUNNYSIDE
RIDGE WAY
Mowshurst
Hamsell Mead Farm
MALLARD WAY
ST BRELADE'S CT
The Industrial Est
Spitals Cross
STATION RD
D3
1 STACKFIELD
2 WOODPECKER CL
3 MAGPIE GN
4 SORRELL CL
5 SPEEDWELL CL
6 ROWFIELD
7 SMITHY FIELD
8 BRIAR CL
9 FOXGLOVE CL
10 BROOK CT
11 TEMPLARS CT
12 HOPGARDEN CL
13 CLOVER WLK
Sewage Works
CHILTENHURST
Edenbridge Golf & Country Club
The Edenbridge Ctr
SKINNERS LA
Cauk Wood
CROUCH HOUSE RD
Crouch House Farm
Crouch House Green
L Ctr
Edenbridge Town
Skinners Farm
Eden Valley Wlk
TOWN STATION COTTS
C1
1 CRANBROOK MEWS
2 HOLMDEN CT
3 THE OLD SCHOOL HO
4 LINGFIELD MEWS
5 FLORENCE COTTS
Edenbridge Prim Sch
Edenbridge
River Eden
Liby
Mus
Skeynes
LINGFIELD RD
CHURCH ST
A B C D E F
1 2 3 4 5 6 7 8
43 44 45 46 47 48 49
249
218

217
185

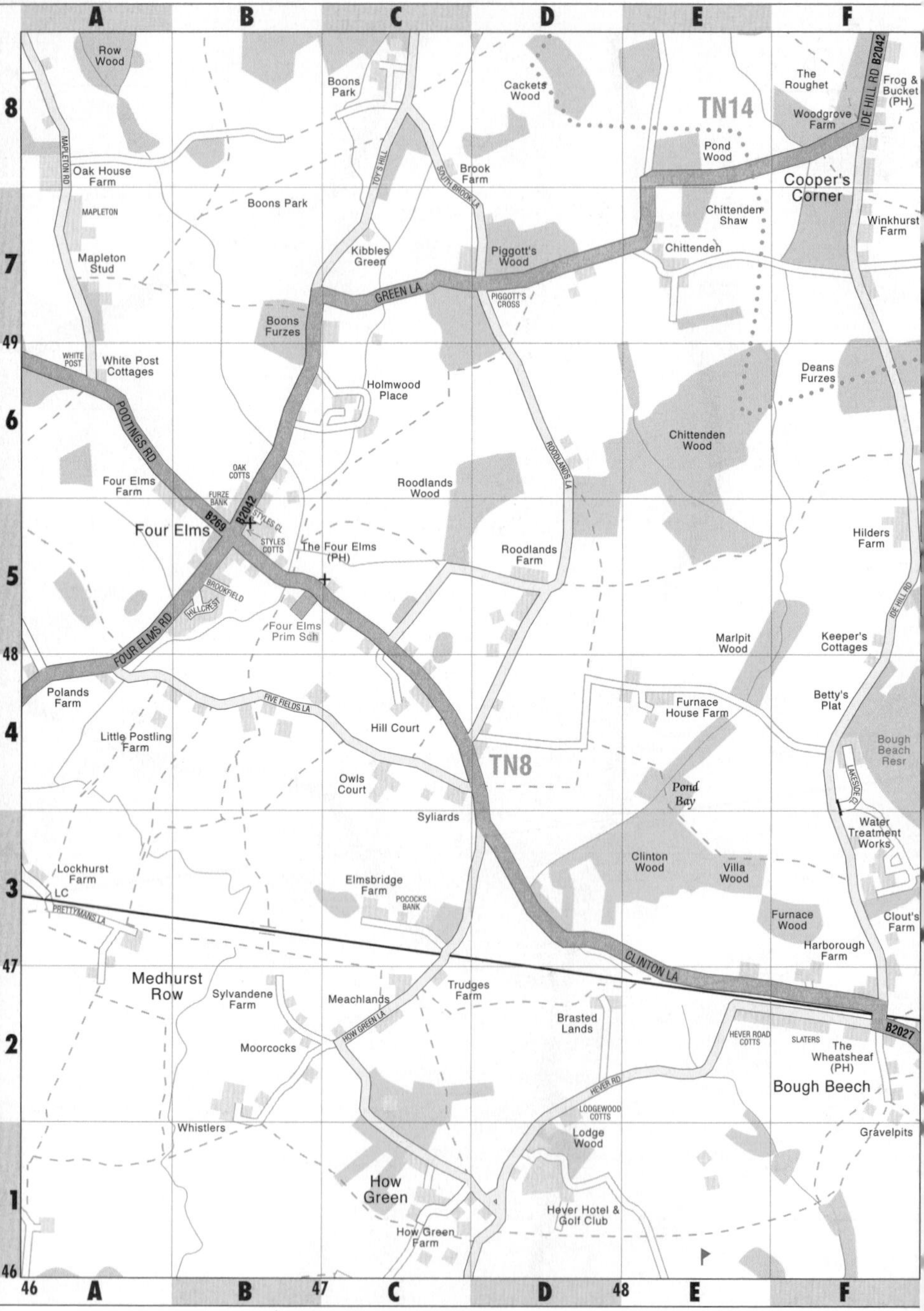

A B C D E F

8
Row Wood
Boons Park
Cackets Wood
The Roughet
Frog & Bucket (PH)
TN14
Woodgrove Farm
Oak House Farm
Brook Farm
Pond Wood
MAPLETON RD
IDE HILL RD B2042
Cooper's Corner

7
MAPLETON
Boons Park
Kibbles Green
Piggott's Wood
Chittenden Shaw
Chittenden
Winkhurst Farm
Mapleton Stud
IVY'S HILL
SOUTH BROOK LA
GREEN LA
PIGGOTT'S CROSS

49
WHITE POST
White Post Cottages
Boons Furzes
Holmwood Place
Deans Furzes

6
POOTINGS RD
Four Elms Farm
OAK COTTS
Roodlands Wood
ROODLANDS LA
Chittenden Wood
Hilders Farm

FURZE BANK
B2042
STYLES PL

5
Four Elms
The Four Elms (PH)
STYLES COTTS
Roodlands Farm
Marlpit Wood
Keeper's Cottages
IDE HILL RD
BROOKFIELD
HILLCREST
Four Elms Prim Sch
Betty's Plat

48
FOUR ELMS RD
Polands Farm
FIVE FIELDS LA
Hill Court
Furnace House Farm
Bough Beech Resr
LAKESIDE

4
Little Postling Farm
Owls Court
Syliards
TN8
Pond Bay
Clinton Wood
Villa Wood
Water Treatment Works

3
Lockhurst Farm
LC
Elmsbridge Farm
POCOCKS BANK
Furnace Wood
Clout's Farm
PRETTYMANS LA
CLINTON LA
Harborough Farm

47
Medhurst Row
Sylvandene Farm
Meachlands
Trudges Farm
Brasted Lands
HEVER ROAD COTTS
SLATERS
The Wheatsheaf (PH)
B2027

2
Moorcocks
HOW GREEN LA
HEVER RD
Bough Beech
LODGEWOOD COTTS
Gravelpits

1
Whistlers
How Green
Lodge Wood
How Green Farm
Hever Hotel & Golf Club

46
A 46 B 47 C D 48 E F

217
250

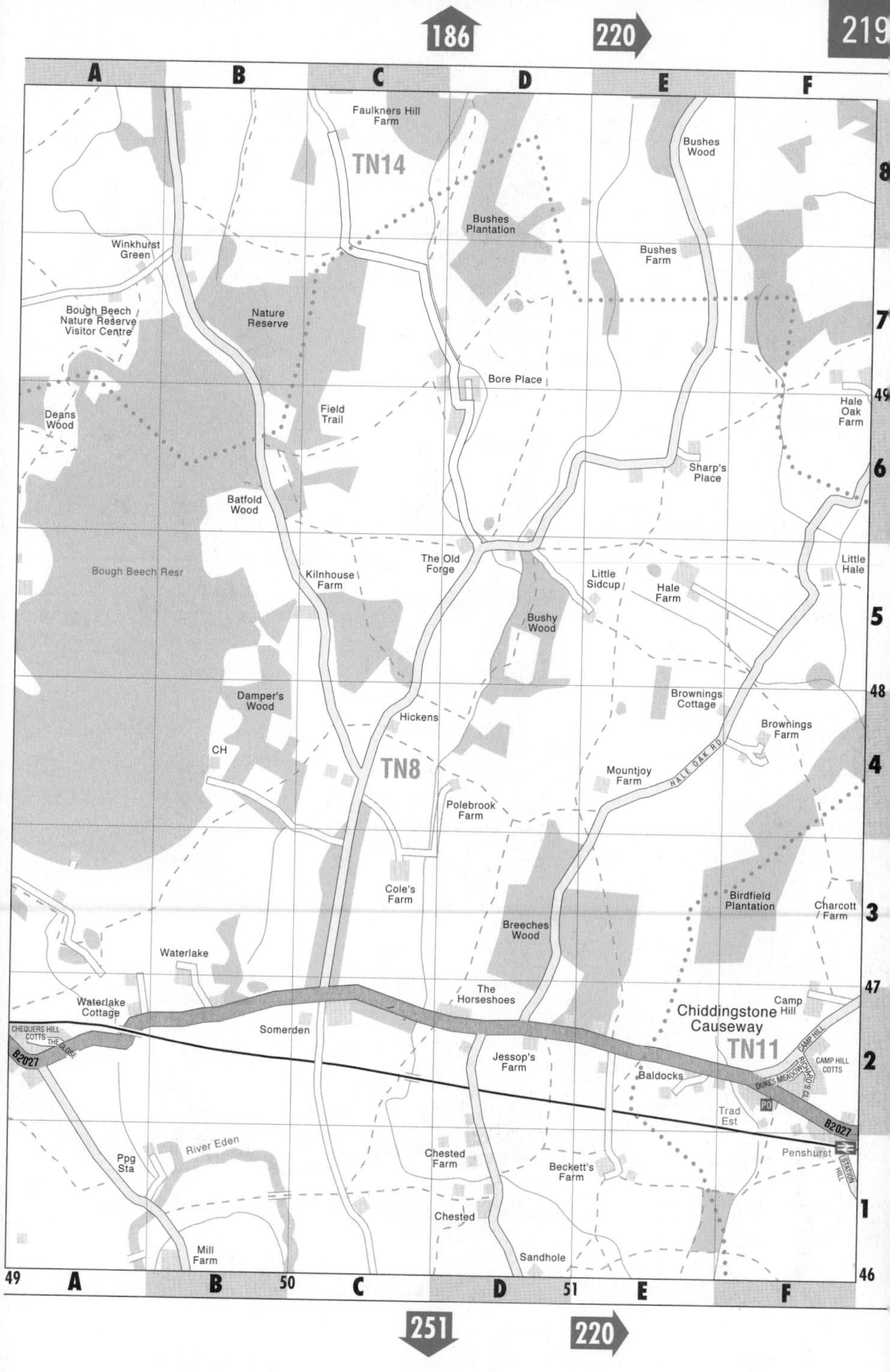
186
220
A
B
C
D
E
F
Faulkners Hill Farm
TN14
Bushes Wood
Bushes Plantation
Winkhurst Green
Bushes Farm
Bough Beech Nature Reserve Visitor Centre
Nature Reserve
Bore Place
Deans Wood
Field Trail
Hale Oak Farm
Sharp's Place
Batfold Wood
The Old Forge
Little Hale
Bough Beech Resr
Kilnhouse Farm
Little Sidcup
Hale Farm
Bushy Wood
Damper's Wood
Brownings Cottage
Hickens
Brownings Farm
CH
TN8
Mountjoy Farm
HALE OAK RD
Polebrook Farm
Cole's Farm
Birdfield Plantation
Charcott Farm
Breeches Wood
Waterlake
The Horseshoes
Waterlake Cottage
Camp Hill
Chiddingstone Causeway
CHEQUERS HILL COTTS
THE CLOSE
Somerden
TN11
CAMP HILL
B2027
Jessop's Farm
CAMP HILL COTTS
Baldocks
DUKES MEADOW
RICHARD'S CL
PO
Trad Est
B2027
Ppg Sta
River Eden
Chested Farm
Penshurst
STATION HILL
Beckett's Farm
Chested
Mill Farm
Sandhole
8
7
49
6
5
48
4
3
47
2
1
46
49
50
51
251
220

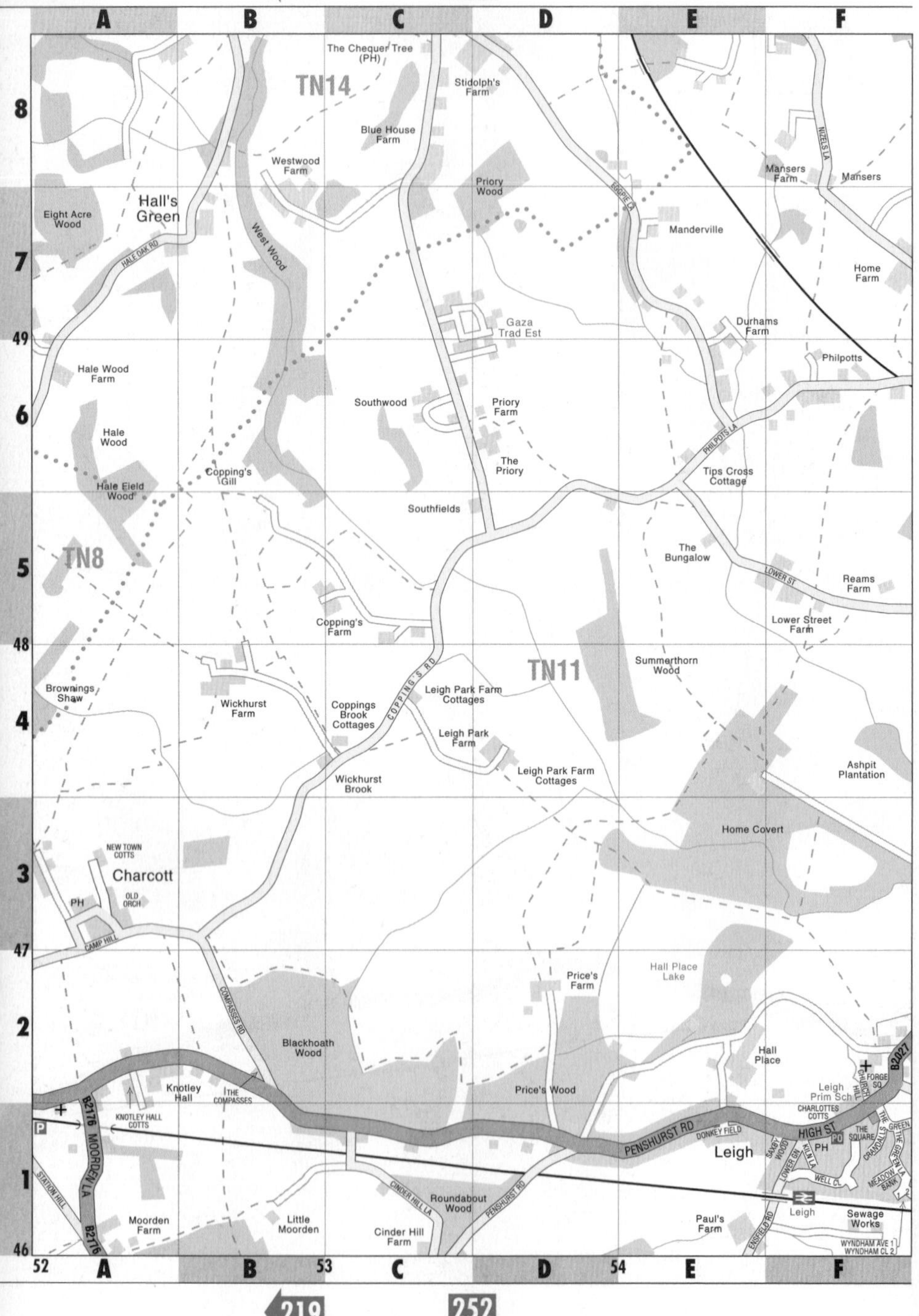

The Chequer Tree (PH)
TN14
Stidolph's Farm
Blue House Farm
Westwood Farm
Priory Wood
Mansers Farm
Mansers
Hall's Green
Eight Acre Wood
West Wood
Manderville
Home Farm
Hale Wood Farm
Gaza Trad Est
Durhams Farm
Philpotts
TN8
Hale Wood
Southwood
Priory Farm
Copping's Gill
Hale Field Wood
The Priory
Tips Cross Cottage
Southfields
The Bungalow
LOWER ST
Reams Farm
Copping's Farm
Lower Street Farm
Brownings Shaw
Wickhurst Farm
Coppings Brook Cottages
Leigh Park Farm Cottages
TN11
Summerthorn Wood
Leigh Park Farm
Wickhurst Brook
Leigh Park Farm Cottages
Ashpit Plantation
NEW TOWN COTTS
Charcott
OLD ORCH
Home Covert
PH
CAMP HILL
Price's Farm
Hall Place Lake
Blackhoath Wood
Hall Place
Knotley Hall
THE COMPASSES
Price's Wood
Leigh Prim Sch
CHARLOTTES COTTS
HIGH ST
Leigh
KNOTLEY HALL COTTS
PENSHURST RD
PH
Moorden Farm
Little Moorden
Cinder Hill Farm
Roundabout Wood
Paul's Farm
Leigh
Sewage Works
WYNDHAM AVE 1
WYNDHAM CL 2

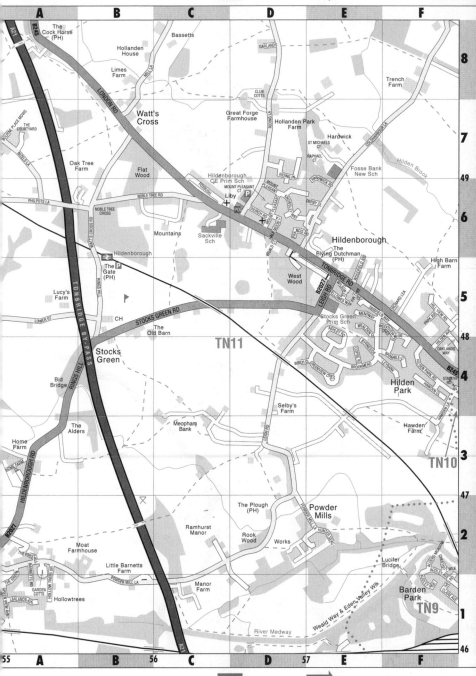

A B C D E F

The Cock Horse (PH)
Bassetts
Hollanden House
Limes Farm
GARLANDS
MILL LA
LONDON RD
CLUB COTTS
Trench Farm
Watt's Cross
Great Forge Farmhouse
Hollanden Park Farm
RIDING LA
Hardwick
BOURNE PLACE MDWS
THE COURTYARD
NIZELS LA
ST MICHAELS CT
RAPHAEL CT
COLDHARBOUR LA
Oak Tree Farm
Flat Wood
Fosse Bank New Sch
Hilden Brook
RIDING PL
Hildenborough CE Prim Sch
FOXBUSH
MOUNT PLEASANT CT
MOUNT PLEASANT
HARDWICK RD
NOBLE TREE RD
PHILPOTS LA
Liby
PO
NOBLE TREE CROSS
CHURCH RD
KNOWSLEY WAY
DERBY CL
MOUNT PLEASANT
HALF MOON
FRANCIS RD
WATTS CROSS RD
Mountains
Sackville Sch
WEALD CT
Hildenborough
The Flying Dutchman (PH)
Hildenborough
The Gate (PH)
High Barn Farm
West Wood
WOODFIELD AVE
TONBRIDGE RD
RINGS HILL
TONBRIDGE BY-PASS
B2027
LEIGH RD
WILSON CL
FIR TREE CL
ORCHARD LEA
Lucy's Farm
FELLOWES WAY
HILL VIEW RD
FAIRFIELD WAY
MEADWAY
PARK AVE
LOWER ST
CH
STOCKS GREEN RD
Stocks Green Prim Sch
WEALDEN CL
WOODVIEW CRES
ELM GR
HILDEN AVE
The Old Barn
ASHLEY RD
TN11
BYRNESIDE
OAKLANDS WAY
Stocks Green
COPSE RD
BRAMBLE CL
HILDEN PARK RD
BIRCH CL
BROOKMEAD
LEYBANK
B245
GREENVIEW CRES
STACEY RD
RINGS HILL
Bid Bridge
Hilden Park
HAWDEN CL
Selby's Farm
HAWDEN LA
The Alders
Meopham Bank
Hawden Farm
LEIGH RD
Home Farm
HOME FARM CL
HILDENBOROUGH RD
TN10
The Plough (PH)
Powder Mills
POWDER MILL LA
Ramhurst Manor
B2021
Moat Farmhouse
Rook Wood
Works
HUNTER SEAL
ALDERS MEADOW
CHESTNUT WLK
THE FORSTAL
Lucifer Bridge
AUDLEY AVE
BARNETTS RD
HOLLOW TREES DR
Little Barnetts Farm
AUDLEY RI
IVES RD
THE GREEN
POWDER MILL LA
CLARE AVE
GARDEN COTTS
Manor Farm
Barden Park
GREEN VIEW AVE
LEALANDS AVE
Hollowtrees
Weald Way & Eden Valley Wlk
TN9
River Medway
A21

8
7
49
6
5
48
4
3
47
2
1
46

55 A B 56 C D 57 E F

253
222

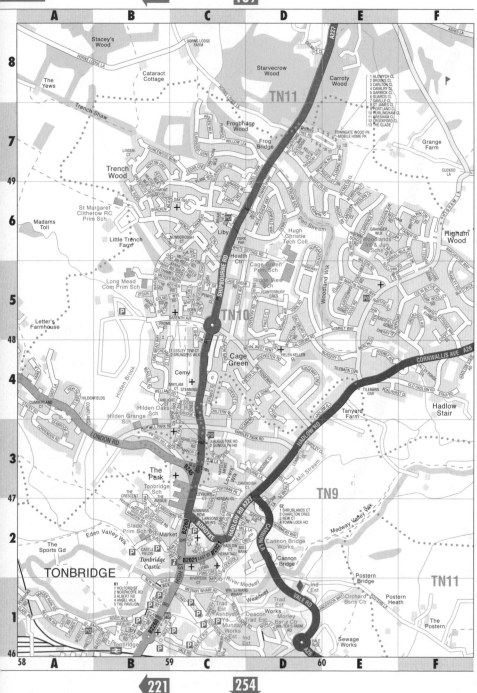

221
189

A B C D E F

8

7

49

6

5

48

4

3

47

2

1

46

58 A B 59 C D 60 E F

TN11

Stacey's Wood
Cataract Cottage
Starvecrow Wood
Carroty Wood

1 ALDWYCH CL
2 BROOKS CL
3 CARLTON CL
4 CAVALRY CL
5 GARRICK CL
6 GUARDS CL
7 SAVILLE CL
8 ST JAMES CL
9 PORTLAND CL
10 PURLINGHAM CL
11 GRESHAM CL
12 CROCKFORD CL
13 THE GLADE

The Yews

HORNS LODGE LA

HORNS LODGE FARM

Trench Shaw

TOWNGATE WOOD PK MOBILE HOME PK

Grange Farm

CUCKOO LA

ASHES LA

A227

LINDEN CT

Frogbridge Wood

Frog Bridge

WILLOW LEA

Trench Wood

Madams Toll

St Margaret Clitherow RC Prim Sch

Little Trench Farm

Long Mead Com Prim Sch

BRACKEN

NEWBOROUGH CT

Liby

York Par

Pan Stream

Hugh Christie Tech Coll

Higham Wood

Woodlands Inf & Jun Schs

GRAINGER WLK

Health Ctr

Cage Green Prim Sch

Ridge View Sch

Letter's Farmhouse

Hilden Brook

Cage Green

CANTERBURY CRES

Woodland Wlk

TN10

Helen Keller Cl

ROMNEY WAY

Cornwallis Ave A26

Cumberland Ct

Hildenfields

LONDON RD

Hilden Grange Sch

Hilden Oaks Sch

Cemy

MAYLAM CT

1 LESLEY YEW CT
2 BRUNGERS WLK

FAIRLIGHT

CHILTERN

YARDLEY PARK RD

Tilebarn Cnr

Tilebarn Cnr

Tanyard Farm

Old Hadlow Rd

Hadlow Stair

1 AUGUSTINE HO
2 DUNDOLI HO

The Park

Tonbridge Sch

THE CRESCENT

THE AVENUE

B245

HADLOW RD A227

Mill Stream

TN9

Slade Prim Sch

Eden Valley Wlk

The Sports Gd

B2260

B2260

Market

TONBRIDGE

Tonbridge Castle

B1
1 HOLFORD ST
2 NORTHCOTE RD
3 ALBERT RD
4 ANGEL WLK
5 THE PAVILION

BURBOKE

HIGH ST

LA CANNON

CANNON LA

C2
1 SHRUBLANDS CT
2 CHARLTON CRES
3 NEW CT
4 TOWN LOCK HO

Cannon Bridge Works

Cannon Bridge

Medway Valley Wlk

Postern Bridge

Postern Heath

TN11

River Medway

WHITEFRIARS WHARF

Ind Est

Orchard Bsns Ctr

Postern

The Postern

Vale Rd

VALE RD

Trad Works

Ashbys

Deacon Trad Est

Munday Works

Yd

Morley Barns Ctr WALTER'S FARM RD

Ind Est

Sewage Works

Tonbridge

VALE RD

A26

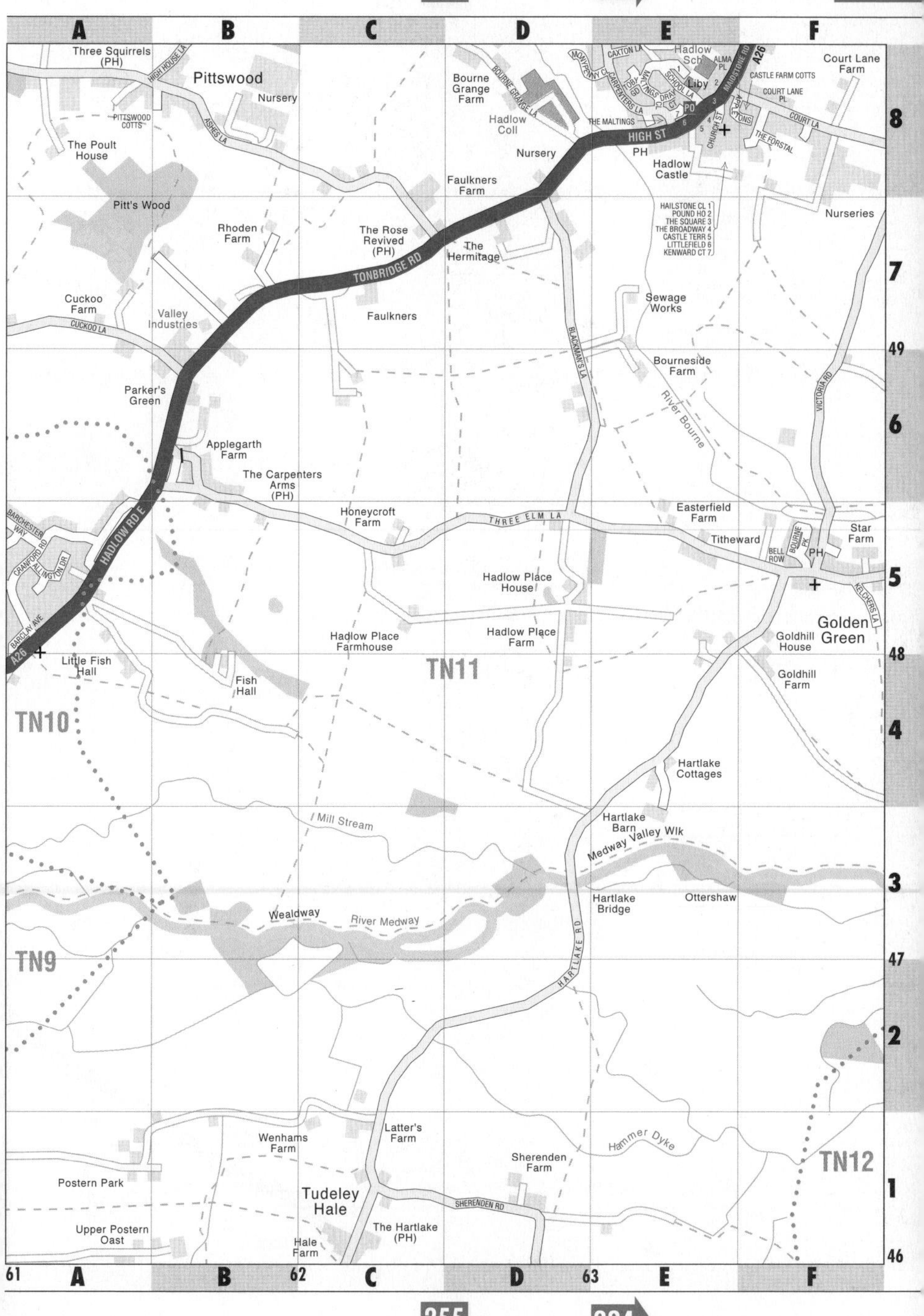

Three Squirrels (PH)
Pittswood
Nursery
PITTSWOOD COTTS
The Poult House
Pitt's Wood
Rhoden Farm
ASHES LA
HIGH HOUSE LA
Bourne Grange Farm
BOURNE GRANGE LA
MORTON LA
CAXTON LA
Hadlow
Hadlow Sch
Liby
Castle Farm Cotts
Court Lane Farm
COURT LANE PL
CARPENTERS LA
PO
The Maltings
HIGH ST
PH
Hadlow Coll
Nursery
Hadlow Castle
CHURCH ST
MAIDSTONE RD
A26
COURT LA
The Forstal
Faulkners Farm
The Rose Revived (PH)
The Hermitage
TONBRIDGE RD
Faulkners
HAILSTONE CL 1
POUND HO 2
THE SQUARE 3
THE BROADWAY 4
CASTLE TERR 5
LITTLEFIELD 6
KENWARD CT 7
Nurseries
Cuckoo Farm
CUCKOO LA
Valley Industries
Sewage Works
Bourneside Farm
River Bourne
VICTORIA RD
Parker's Green
Applegarth Farm
The Carpenters Arms (PH)
Honeycroft Farm
THREE ELM LA
Easterfield Farm
Titheward
BELL ROW
BOURNE LA
(PH)
Star Farm
BLACKMANS LA
HADLOW RD E
BARCHESTER WAY
CRANFORD RD
HOLMESDALE RD
A26
BARDEN RD
Little Fish Hall
Fish Hall
Hadlow Place Farmhouse
Hadlow Place House
Hadlow Place Farm
TN11
Golden Green
Goldhill House
BLOCKERS LA
Goldhill Farm
TN10
Hartlake Cottages
Mill Stream
Hartlake Barn
Medway Valley Wlk
Hartlake Bridge
Ottershaw
Wealdway
River Medway
HARTLAKE RD
TN9
Hammer Dyke
TN12
Postern Park
Wenhams Farm
Latter's Farm
Sherenden Farm
Upper Postern Oast
Tudeley Hale
Hale Farm
The Hartlake (PH)
SHERENDEN RD

223
191

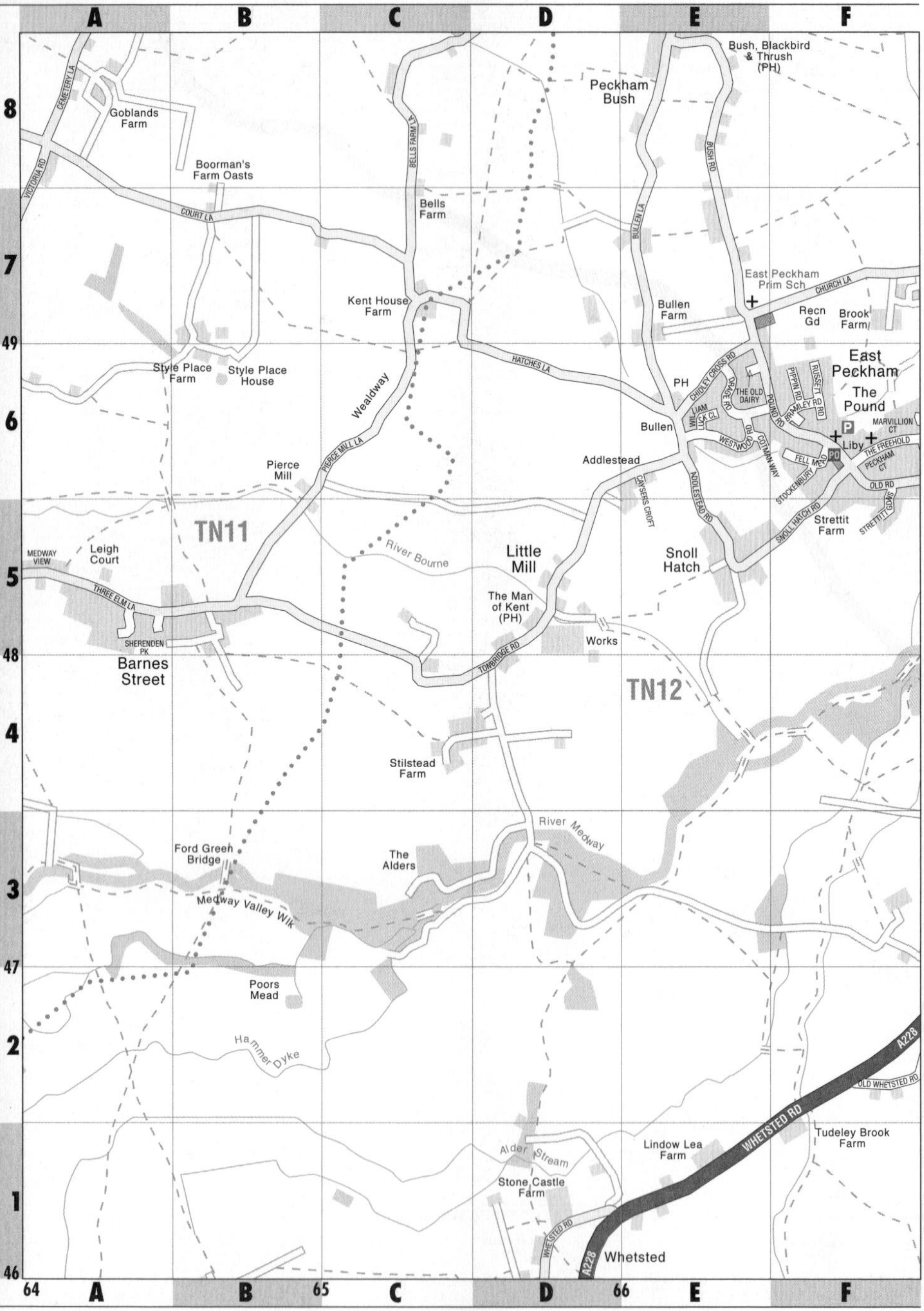

A

Ceneter LA

Goblands
Farm

VICTORIA RD

COURT LA

Boorman's
Farm Oasts

B

Bells
Farm

Kent House
Farm

BELLS FARM LA

Wealdway

PIERCE MILL LA

Style Place
Farm

Style Place
House

Pierce
Mill

TN11

MEDWAY
VIEW

Leigh
Court

THREE ELM LA

SHERENDEN
PK

Barnes
Street

C

HATCHES LA

River Bourne

D

Peckham
Bush

Bush, Blackbird
& Thrush
(PH)

BUSH RD

Addlestead

CARVERS CROFT

Little
Mill

The Man
of Kent (PH)

TONBRIDGE RD

Works

Stilstead
Farm

The
Alders

River Medway

Ford Green
Bridge

Medway Valley Wlk

Poors
Mead

Hammer Dyke

Alder Stream

Stone Castle
Farm

WHETSTED RD

Lindow Lea
Farm

A228

Whetsted

WHETSTED RD

E

East Peckham
Prim Sch

CHURCH LA

Bullen
Farm

Recn
Gd

Brook
Farm

PH

CHIDLEY CROSS RD

BRANCH RD

East
Peckham

The
Pound

Bullen

Bullen

THE OLD
DAIRY

HAM
LA

SCH CT

POUND RD

PIPPIN RD

HURST RD

HALEY RD

MARVILLION
CT

Liby

THE FREEHOLD
PECKHAM
CT

WEST RD

COTMAN WAY

ADDLESTEAD RD

STOCKENBURY

TELL MEAD

OLD RD

Snoll
Hatch

SNOLL HATCH RD

Strettit
Farm

STRETTIT RD

TN12

Tudeley Brook
Farm

OLD WHETSTED RD

F

TN12

Snoll
Hatch

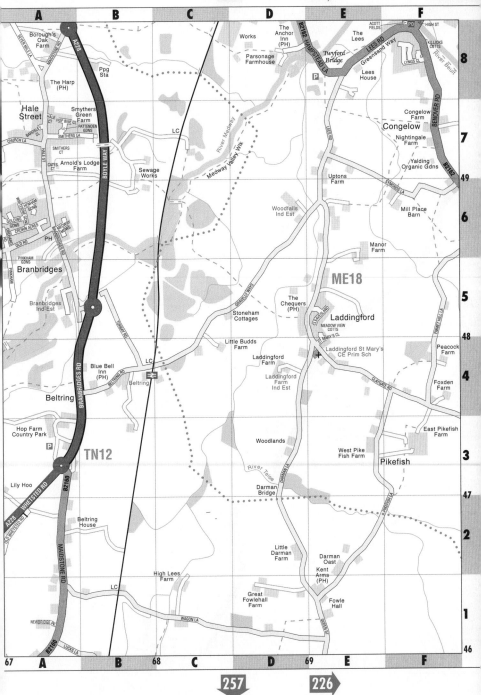

A B C D E F

Borough's Oak Farm
The Harp (PH)
Ppg Sta
Hale Street
Smythers Green Farm
Arnold's Lodge Farm
Sewage Works
Works
The Anchor Inn (PH)
Parsonage Farmhouse
Twyford Bridge
The Lees
Lees House
Congelow Farm
Congelow
Nightingale Farm
Yalding Organic Gdns
Uptons Farm
Mill Place Barn
Woodfalls Ind Est
Manor Farm
Branbridges
Branbridges Ind Est
ME18
The Chequers (PH)
Laddingford
Stoneham Cottages
Little Budds Farm
Laddingford Farm
Laddingford St Mary's CE Prim Sch
Laddingford Farm Ind Est
Peacock Farm
Foxden Farm
Blue Bell Inn (PH)
Beltring
Hop Farm Country Park
TN12
Woodlands
East Pikefish Farm
West Pike Fish Farm
Pikefish
Lily Hoo
Darman Bridge
Beltring House
Little Darman Farm
Darman Oast
Kent Arms (PH)
High Lees Farm
Great Fowlehall Farm
Fowle Hall
River Medway
Medway Valley Wlk
River Teise
River Beult
Greensand Way
A228 BOYLE WAY
BRANBRIDGES RD
B2162 HAMPSTEAD LA
LEES RD
BENOVER RD
SYMONDS LA
GRAVELLY WAYS
CLAYGATE RD
EMMET HILL LA
DARMAN LA
PIKEFISH LA
QUEEN ST
WAGON LA
MAIDSTONE RD
B2160
WHETSTED RD
OLD WHETSTED RD
LUCKS LA
NEWBRIDGE PK
TORBAY RD
BELTRING RD
SEVEN MILE LA
HALE ST
CHURCH LA
OLD RD
PINKHAM
PINKHAM GDNS
ORCHARD RD
CROWN ACRES
GOLDING GDNS
WHITEBINE GDNS
HENHAM GDNS
MEDWAY MDWS
SMITHERS LA
SMITHERS CT
CATES CT
BARDSLEY CL
HOP BINE CL
PATTENDEN GDNS
HALE CT
CLEAVESLAND
MEADOW VIEW COTTS
ST MARY'S CL
ACOTT FIELDS
HIGH ST
KILLICKS COTTS
LYNGS CL
LC

8 7 49 6 5 48 4 3 47 2 1 46

67 A B 68 C D 69 E F

225
193

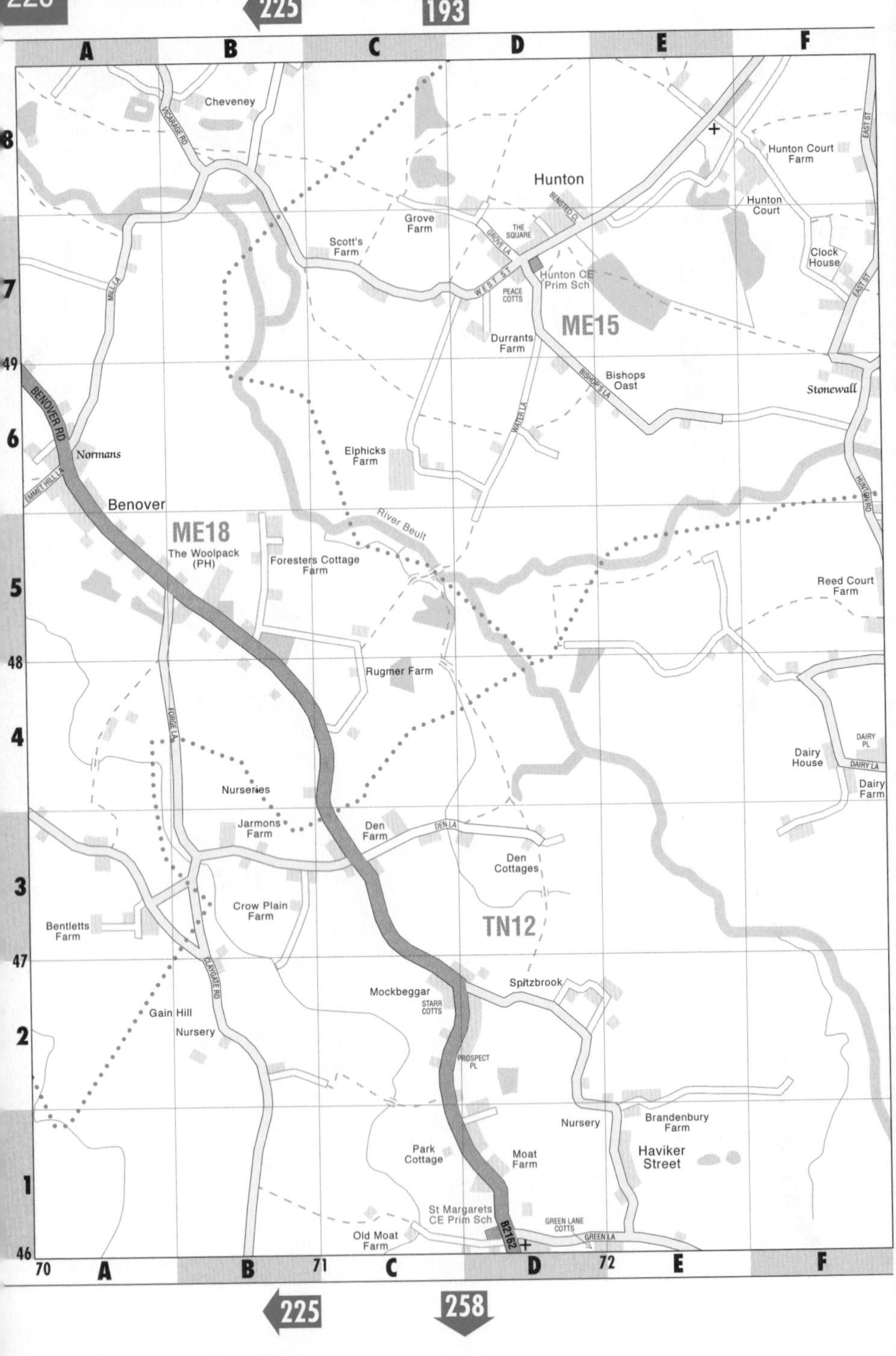
A
B
C
D
E
F
Cheveney
VICARAGE RD
Hunton
Hunton Court Farm
Hunton Court
Clock House
BENSTED CL
THE SQUARE
GROVE LA
Grove Farm
Scott's Farm
WEST ST
Hunton CE Prim Sch
PEACE COTTS
MILL LA
ME15
Durrants Farm
EAST ST
BISHOP'S LA
Bishops Oast
Stonewall
BENOVER RD
WATER LA
Normans
Elphicks Farm
EMMET HILL LA
Benover
HUNTON RD
River Beult
ME18
The Woolpack (PH)
Foresters Cottage Farm
Reed Court Farm
Rugmer Farm
FORGE LA
DAIRY PL
Dairy House
DAIRY LA
Dairy Farm
Nurseries
Jarmons Farm
Den Farm
DEN LA
Den Cottages
Crow Plain Farm
Bentletts Farm
TN12
CLAYGATE RD
Spitzbrook
Mockbeggar
STARR COTTS
Gain Hill
Nursery
PROSPECT PL
Nursery
Brandenbury Farm
Park Cottage
Moat Farm
Haviker Street
St Margarets CE Prim Sch
B2162
GREEN LANE COTTS
GREEN LA
Old Moat Farm
8
7
49
6
5
48
4
3
47
2
1
46
70
71
72

225
258

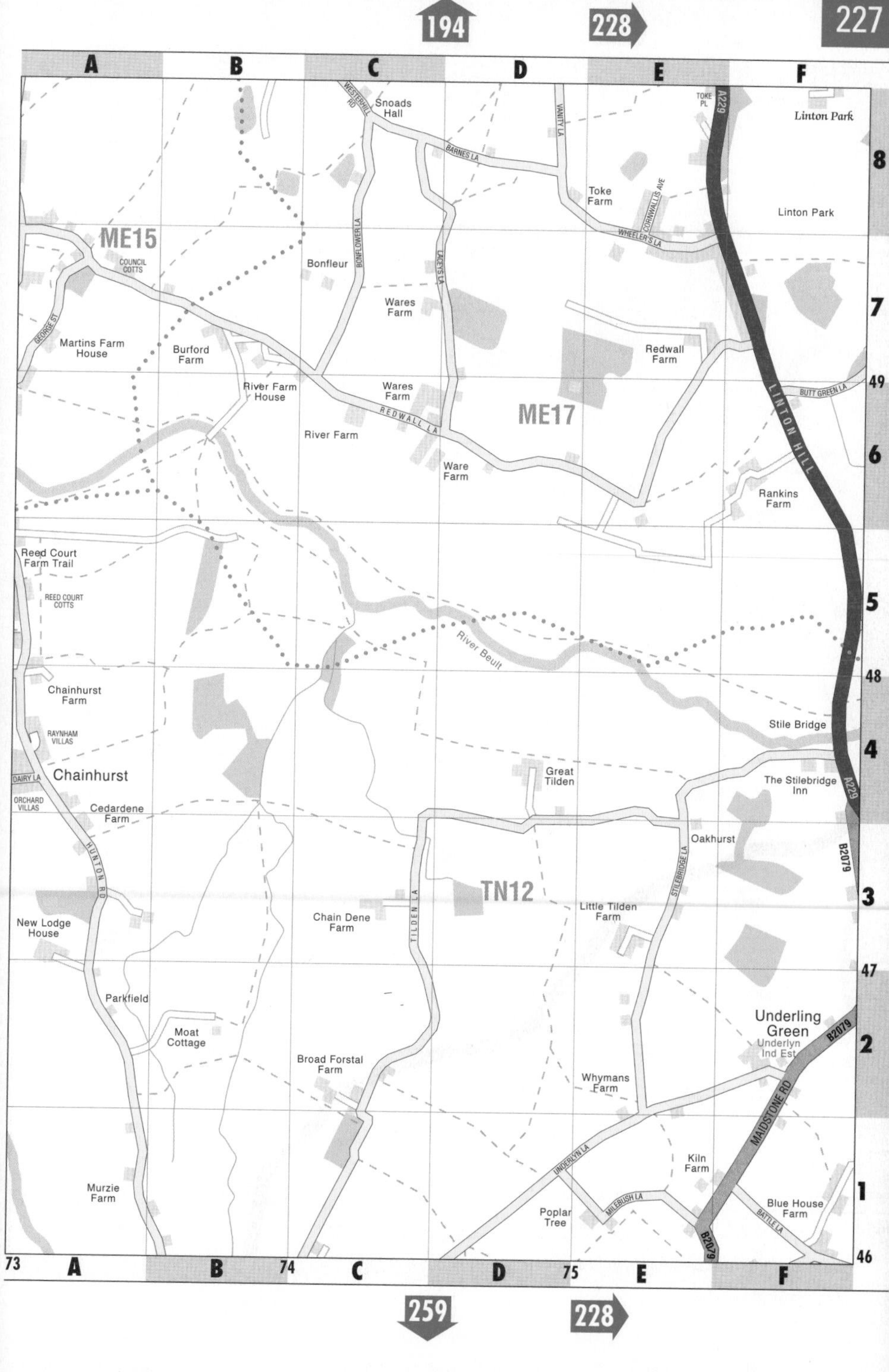
194
228
Snoads Hall
WESTERHILL RD
BARNES LA
VANITY LA
TOKE PL
A229
Linton Park
Toke Farm
CORNWALLIS AVE
WHEELER'S LA
Linton Park
ME15
COUNCIL COTTS
Bonfleur
BONFLOWER LA
LACEYS LA
Wares Farm
GEORGE ST
Martins Farm House
Burford Farm
Redwall Farm
River Farm House
Wares Farm
LINTON HILL
BUTT GREEN LA
ME17
REDWALL LA
River Farm
Ware Farm
Rankins Farm
Reed Court Farm Trail
REED COURT COTTS
River Beult
Chainhurst Farm
RAYNHAM VILLAS
Stile Bridge
Chainhurst
DAIRY LA
ORCHARD VILLAS
Cedardene Farm
Great Tilden
The Stilebridge Inn
Oakhurst
HUNTON RD
B2079
TN12
STILEBRIDGE LA
New Lodge House
Chain Dene Farm
TILDEN LA
Little Tilden Farm
Parkfield
Moat Cottage
Underling Green
Underlyn Ind Est
Broad Forstal Farm
Whymans Farm
MAIDSTONE RD
Kiln Farm
UNDERLYN LA
Murzie Farm
Poplar Tree
MILEBUSH LA
Blue House Farm
BATTLE LA
A
B
C
D
E
F
8
7
49
6
5
48
4
3
47
2
1
46
73
74
75
259
228

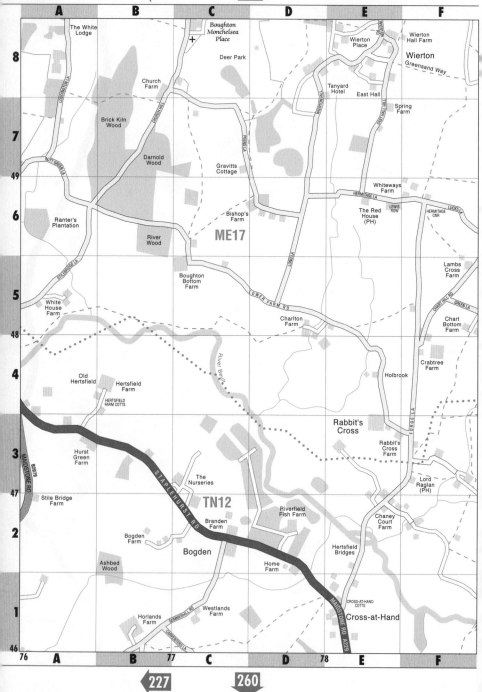

A B C D E F

8

The White Lodge

Boughton Monchelsea Place

Deer Park

Wierton Hall Farm

Wierton Place

Wierton

Greensand Way

Church Farm

Tanyard Hotel

East Hall

Spring Farm

7

Brick Kiln Wood

Darnold Wood

Gravitts Cottage

Whiteways Farm

49

BUTT GREEN LA

PERNS LA

HERMITAGE LA

LEWIS ROW

HERMITAGE CNR

LUCKS LA

6

Ranter's Plantation

River Wood

Bishop's Farm

ME17

The Red House (PH)

Lambs Cross Farm

STILEBRIDGE LA

LOWER RD

CHART HILL RD

GREEN LA

5

White House Farm

Boughton Bottom Farm

LOWER FARM RD

Charlton Farm

Chart Bottom Farm

48

River Beult

Crabtree Farm

4

Old Hertsfield

Hertsfield Farm

HERTSFIELD FARM COTTS

Holbrook

FORGE LA

3

MAIDSTONE RD

B2079

Hurst Green Farm

STAPLEHURST RD

Rabbit's Cross

Rabbit's Cross Farm

Lord Raglan (PH)

47

Stile Bridge Farm

The Nurseries

TN12

Riverfield Fish Farm

Chaney Court Farm

2

Bogden Farm

Branden Farm

Bogden

Hertsfield Bridges

Ashbed Wood

Home Farm

1

SUMMERHILL RD

Horlands Farm

Westlands Farm

MAIDSTONE RD A229

CROSS-AT-HAND COTTS

Cross-at-Hand

46

A B C D E F

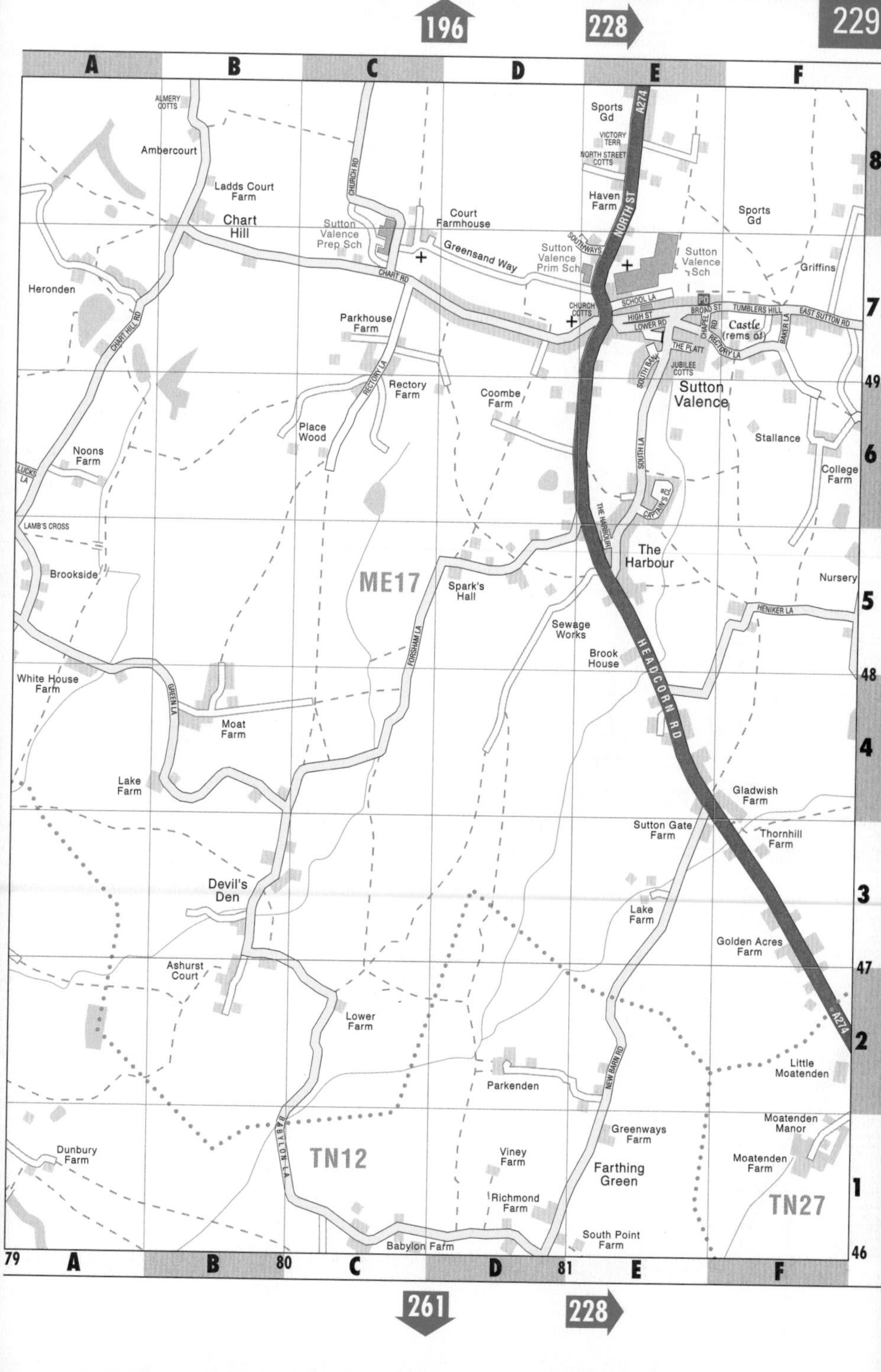
196
228
A
B
C
D
E
F
ALMERY COTTS
Ambercourt
Ladds Court Farm
Chart Hill
CHURCH RD
Sutton Valence Prep Sch
Court Farmhouse
Greensand Way
Sports Gd
VICTORY TERR
NORTH STREET COTTS
Haven Farm
NORTH ST
A274
SOUTHWAYS
Sutton Valence Prim Sch
Sutton Valence Sch
Sports Gd
Griffins
Heronden
CHART HILL RD
CHART RD
Parkhouse Farm
CHURCH COTTS
SCHOOL LA
HIGH ST
LOWER RD
BROAD ST
TUMBLERS HILL
EAST SUTTON RD
CHAPEL RD
BAKER LA
Castle (rems of)
THE PLATT
RECTORY LA
JUBILEE COTTS
SOUTH BANK
Sutton Valence
Rectory Farm
Coombe Farm
Place Wood
Noons Farm
LUCKS LA
Stallance
College Farm
SOUTH LA
CAPTAIN'S CL
THE HARBOUR
The Harbour
LAMB'S CROSS
Brookside
ME17
Spark's Hall
Nursery
HENIKER LA
FORSHAM LA
Sewage Works
Brook House
HEADCORN RD
White House Farm
GREEN LA
Moat Farm
Lake Farm
Gladwish Farm
Sutton Gate Farm
Thornhill Farm
Devil's Den
Lake Farm
Golden Acres Farm
Ashurst Court
Lower Farm
Parkenden
NEW BARN RD
Little Moatenden
Moatenden Manor
Greenways Farm
Dunbury Farm
BABYLON LA
TN12
Viney Farm
Farthing Green
Moatenden Farm
Richmond Farm
TN27
South Point Farm
Babylon Farm
8
7
49
6
5
48
4
3
47
2
1
46
79
80
81
261
228

229
197

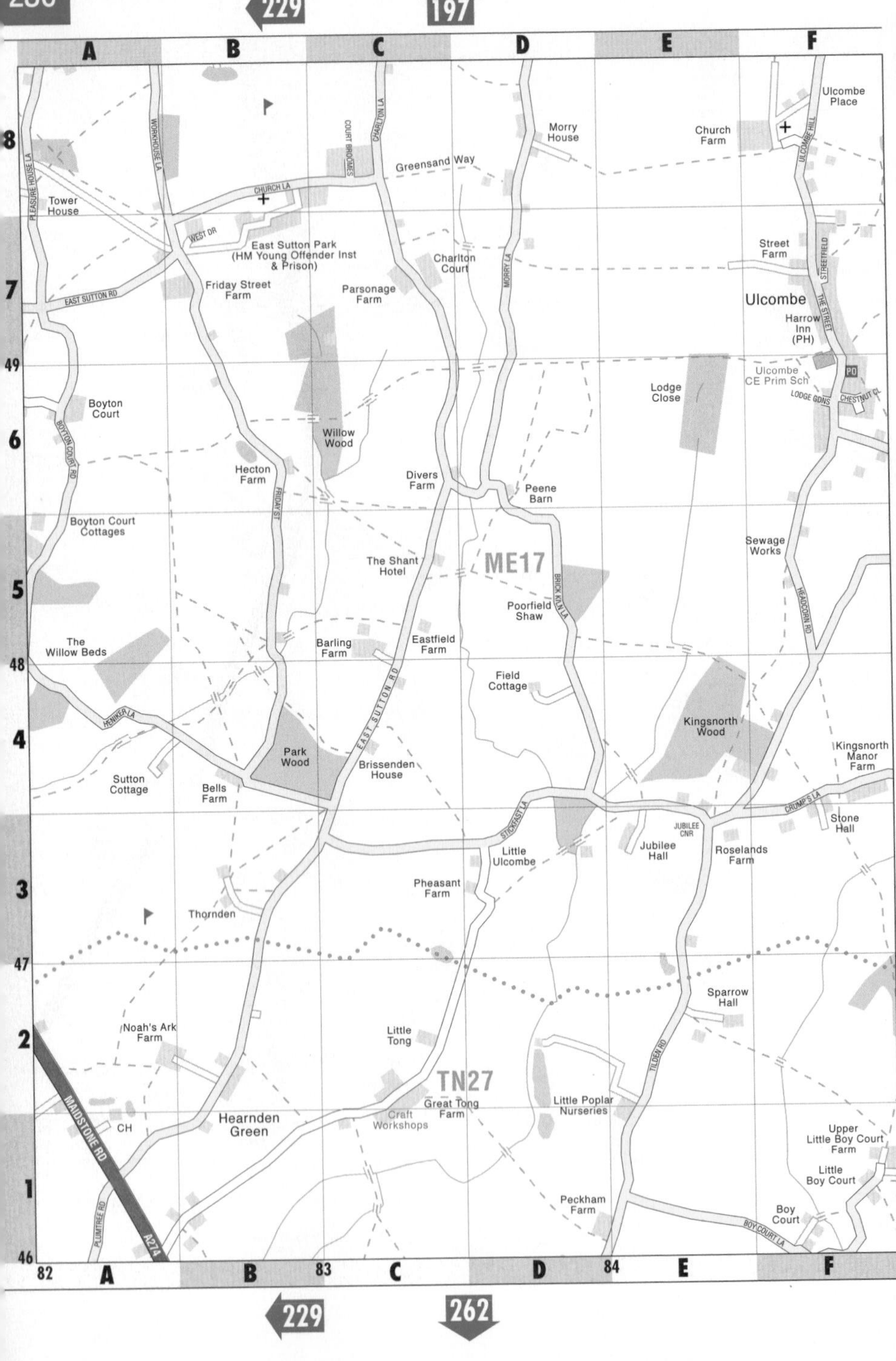
A
B
C
D
E
F
8
7
49
6
5
48
4
3
47
2
1
46
82
83
84
Ulcombe Place
Church Farm
Morry House
Greensand Way
COURT BROOMES
CHARLTON LA
WORKHOUSE LA
PLEASURE HOUSE LA
Tower House
CHURCH LA
WEST DR
East Sutton Park
(HM Young Offender Inst
& Prison)
Charlton Court
Street Farm
STREETFIELD
ULCOMBE HILL
Friday Street Farm
Parsonage Farm
MORRY LA
EAST SUTTON RD
Ulcombe
THE STREET
Harrow Inn (PH)
Ulcombe CE Prim Sch
PO
Lodge Close
LODGE GDNS
CHESTNUT CL
Boyton Court
BOYTON COURT RD
Willow Wood
Hecton Farm
Divers Farm
Peene Barn
FRIDAY ST
Boyton Court Cottages
Sewage Works
The Shant Hotel
ME17
BRICK KILN LA
Poorfield Shaw
HEADCORN RD
The Willow Beds
Barling Farm
Eastfield Farm
Field Cottage
EAST SUTTON RD
Kingsnorth Wood
HENIKER LA
Park Wood
Brissenden House
Kingsnorth Manor Farm
Sutton Cottage
Bells Farm
STICKFAST LA
CRUMP'S LA
JUBILEE CNR
Stone Hall
Little Ulcombe
Jubilee Hall
Roselands Farm
Pheasant Farm
Thornden
Sparrow Hall
Noah's Ark Farm
Little Tong
TILDEN RD
TN27
MAIDSTONE RD
Little Poplar Nurseries
Great Tong Farm
Hearnden Green
CH
Craft Workshops
Upper Little Boy Court Farm
Little Boy Court
Peckham Farm
Boy Court
BOY COURT LA
PLUMTREE RD
A274

229
262

198

232

A
B
C
D
E
F
Elmstone Hole Farm
Elmstone Hole
Greensand Way
GREEN HILL LA
ELMSTONE HOLE RD
Upperhill Farm
Weald View Farm
Green Hill Farm
Dunstall Wood
Ivy House Farm
Jobshole Shaw
Green Hill
Lower Willows
HEADCORN RD
Liverton Hill Farm
WINDMILL HILL
Knowle Hill Farm
Blenberry Farm
Rough Park Shaw
Park Shaw
CHURCH RD
Nursery
Homesby Court
Knowle Hill
Mansion Farm
Grafty Green
PO
King's Head (PH)
Ash Tree Farm
Lower Knowle Hill Farm
ME17
Hopper Farm
Offen Farm
Pye Corner
Rain Farm
Eastwood
The Provender (PH)
Eastwood Farm
Woodcock Farm
WOODCOCK LA
Works
EASTWOOD RD
Telpits Farm
Three Chimney Shaw
Who'd A Thought It (PH)
Birch Wood
Yewtree
Judge House Farm
Kingsnoad Farm
Broadstone
Great Humphries Farm
COLDBRIDGE LA
Nurseries
Blackpit Wood
Kingsnoad
CRUMP'S LA
Mansion House Farm
Orchard Cottage Farm
East Kent Farm
LENHAM RD
Park House
Woodsden Villas
Parsons Wood
TN27
Southpark Wood
BARHAM'S MILL RD
The Black House
Barham's Mill Farm
Woodsden
Thornden
SOUTHERNDEN RD
Thornden Cottage
Thornden Farm
Little Southernden Farm
Newcome Farm
Wallet Court
8
7
49
6
5
48
4
3
47
2
1
46
85
86
87

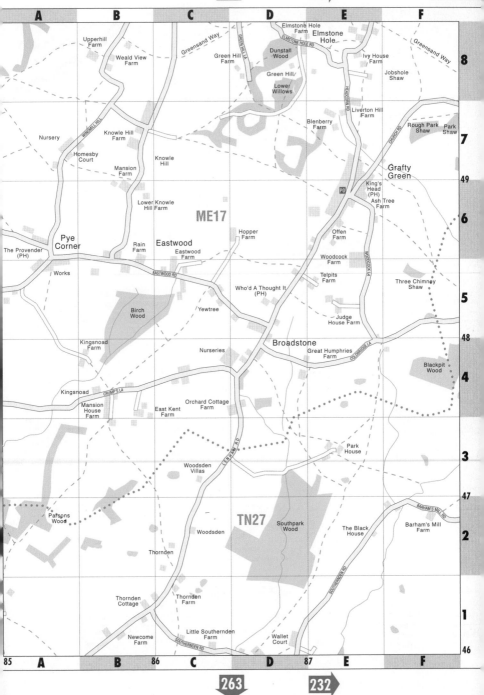

231
199

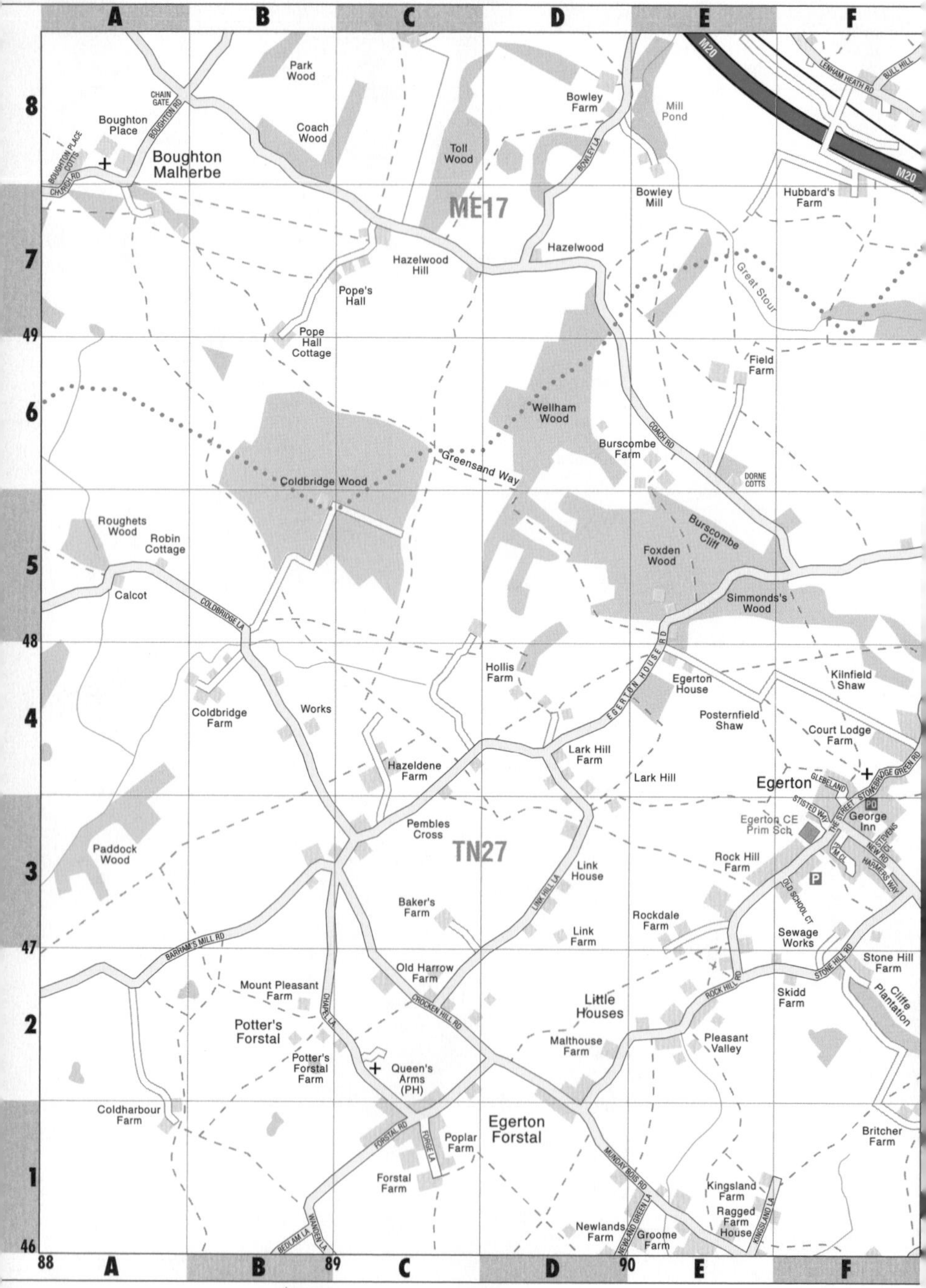

A | **B** | **C** | **D** | **E** | **F**

8

CHAIN GATE
Boughton Place
Park Wood
Coach Wood
Bowley Farm
Mill Pond
LENHAM HEATH RD
BULL HILL
M20

Boughton Malherbe
Toll Wood
Bowley Mill
Hubbard's Farm

ME17

7

Hazelwood Hill
Hazelwood
Pope's Hall

49

Pope Hall Cottage
Field Farm

6

Greensand Way
Wellham Wood
Burscombe Farm
COACH RD
DORNE COTTS

Coldbridge Wood
Roughets Wood
Robin Cottage
Burscombe Cliff
Foxden Wood

5

Calcot
COLDBRIDGE LA
Simmonds's Wood

48

Coldbridge Farm
Works
Hollis Farm
Egerton House
Kilnfield Shaw
EGERTON HOUSE RD
Posternfield Shaw
Court Lodge Farm

4

Hazeldene Farm
Lark Hill Farm
Lark Hill
Egerton
TONBRIDGE OVEN RD
George Inn
STISTED BOWER

Paddock Wood
Pembles Cross
TN27
Egerton CE Prim Sch
OLD SCHOOL CT
NEW RD
HASTED PL

3

Link House
Rock Hill Farm

47

BARHAM'S MILL RD
Baker's Farm
Link Farm
Rockdale Farm
Sewage Works
STONE HILL RD
Stone Hill Farm

Mount Pleasant Farm
Old Harrow Farm
Little Houses
Skidd Farm
Cliffe Plantation

2

Potter's Forstal
CHART LA
CHICKEN HILL RD
Malthouse Farm
Pleasant Valley
ROCK HILL

Potter's Forstal Farm
Queen's Arms (PH)
Coldharbour Farm

1

FORSTAL RD
FORGE LA
Poplar Farm
Egerton Forstal
MUNDAY BOIS RD
Kingsland Farm
Britcher Farm

Forstal Farm
Newlands Farm
Groome Farm
Ragged Farm House
KINGSLAND LA

46

88 | **A** | **B** | **89** | **C** | **D** | **90** | **E** | **F**

231
264

200
234

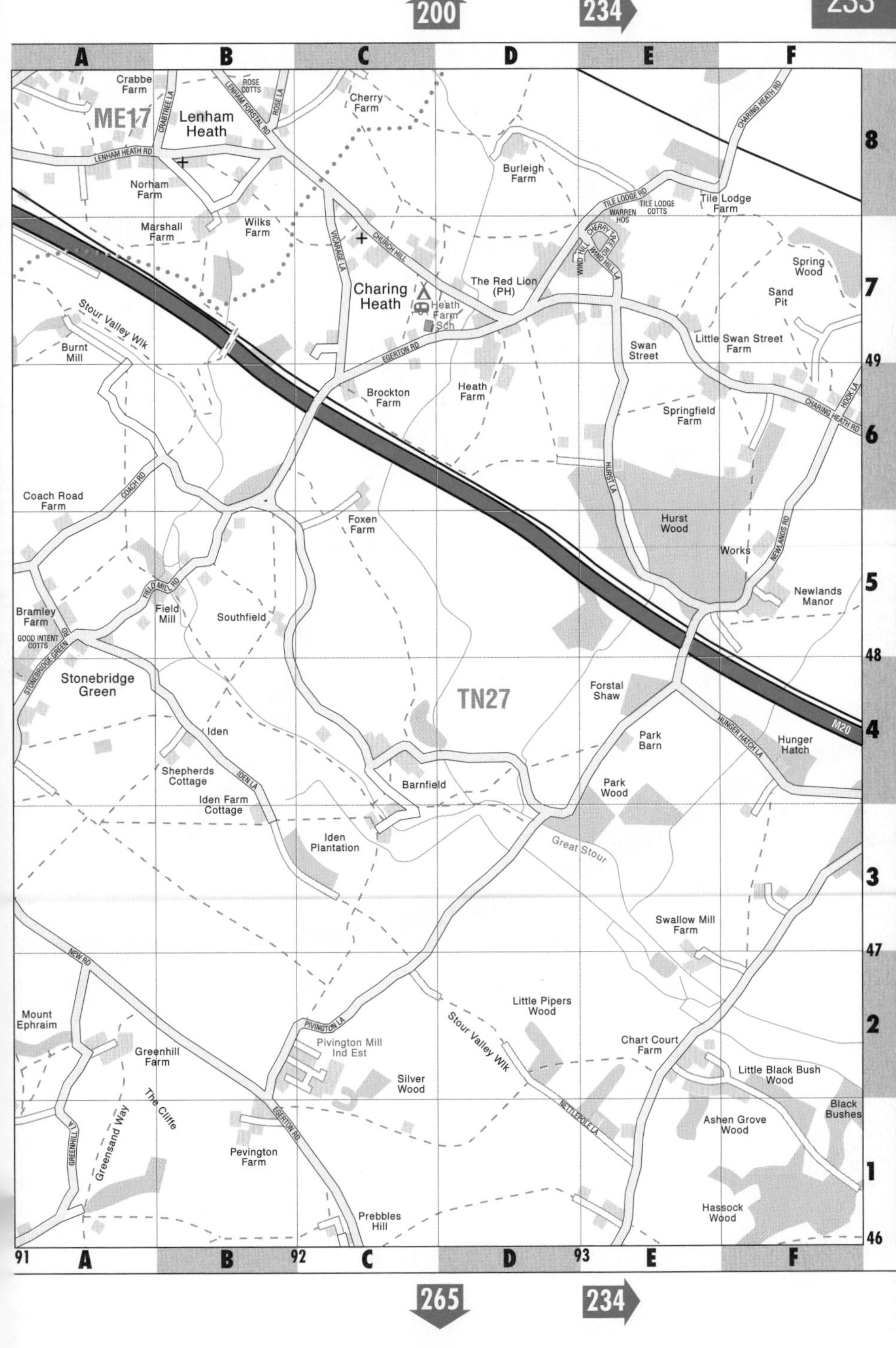
A
B
C
D
E
F
Crabbe Farm
ROSE COTTS
Cherry Farm
ME17
Lenham Heath
LENHAM FORSTAL RD
ROSE LA
CRABTREE LA
CHARING HEATH RD
LENHAM HEATH RD
Burleigh Farm
Norham Farm
TILE LODGE RD
TILE LODGE COTTS
Tile Lodge Farm
WARREN HOS
Marshall Farm
Wilks Farm
CHURCH HILL
VICARAGE LA
CHERRY TREE RD
WIND HILL
WIND HILL LA
Spring Wood
Charing Heath
Heath Farm Sch
The Red Lion (PH)
Sand Pit
Stour Valley Wlk
Burnt Mill
EGERTON RD
Swan Street
Little Swan Street Farm
Brockton Farm
Heath Farm
Springfield Farm
HOOK LA
CHARING HEATH RD
Coach Road Farm
COACH RD
HURST LA
Foxen Farm
Hurst Wood
Works
NEWLANDS RD
FIELD MILL RD
Newlands Manor
Bramley Farm
Field Mill
Southfield
GOOD INTENT COTTS
STONEBRIDGE GREEN RD
Stonebridge Green
TN27
Forstal Shaw
HUNGER HATCH LA
M20
Iden
Park Barn
Hunger Hatch
Shepherds Cottage
IDEN LA
Park Wood
Barnfield
Iden Farm Cottage
Iden Plantation
Great Stour
Swallow Mill Farm
NEW RD
Little Pipers Wood
Mount Ephraim
PIVINGTON LA
Stour Valley Wlk
Chart Court Farm
Greenhill Farm
Pivington Mill Ind Est
Silver Wood
Little Black Bush Wood
The Cliffe
Black Bushes
Greensand Way
EGERTON RD
NETTLEPOLE LA
Ashen Grove Wood
GREENHILL LA
Pevington Farm
Prebbles Hill
Hassock Wood
8
7
49
6
5
48
4
3
47
2
1
46
91
92
93

265
234

233
201

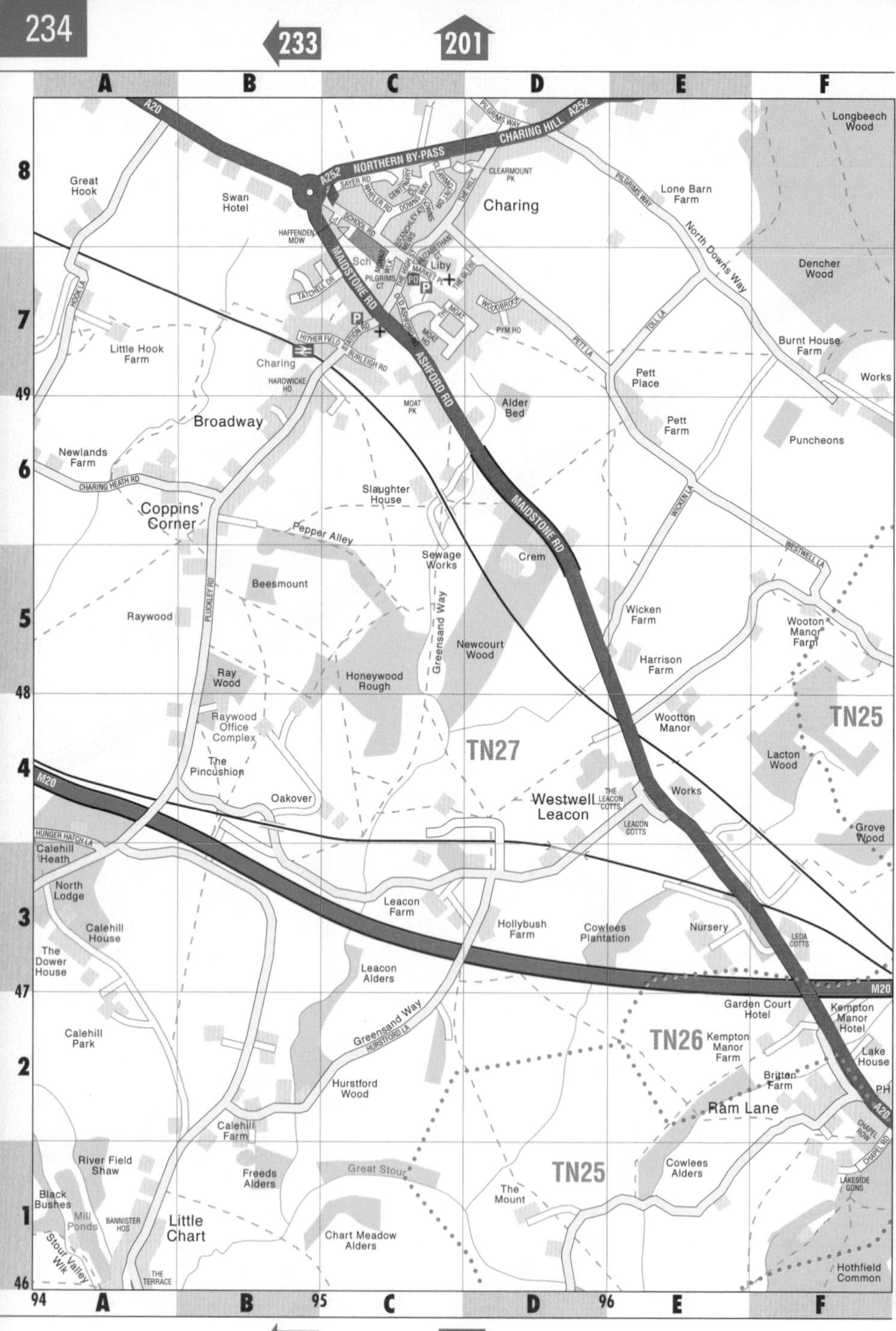
A
B
C
D
E
F
8
7
49
6
5
48
4
3
47
2
1
46
94
95
96
A20
A252
NORTHERN BY-PASS
CHARING HILL
PILGRIMS WAY
Longbeech Wood
Great Hook
Swan Hotel
SAYER RD
SCHOOL RD
CLEARMOUNT PK
Charing
Lone Barn Farm
North Downs Way
HAFFENDEN MDW
MAIDSTONE RD
Sch
Liby
MARKET PL
THE GLEBE
PILGRIMS CT
PO
P
TATCHELL DR
Dencher Wood
HOOK LA
WOODBROOK
THE MOAT
PYM HO
TOLL LA
HITHER FIELD
STATION RD
BURLEIGH RD
OLD ASHFORD RD
MOAT HO
PETT LA
Little Hook Farm
Charing
Burnt House Farm
Works
HARDWICKE HO
ASHFORD RD
Pett Place
MOAT PK
Alder Bed
Broadway
Pett Farm
Puncheons
Newlands Farm
CHARING HEATH RD
Slaughter House
Coppins' Corner
Pepper Alley
Sewage Works
Crem
WICKEN LA
WESTWELL LA
Beesmount
Raywood
PLUCKLEY RD
Greensand Way
Wicken Farm
Wooton Manor Farm
Newcourt Wood
Harrison Farm
Ray Wood
Honeywood Rough
Raywood Office Complex
Wootton Manor
TN25
TN27
Lacton Wood
The Pincushion
M20
Oakover
Westwell Leacon
THE LEACON COTTS
LEACON COTTS
Works
Grove Wood
HUNGER HATCH LA
Calehill Heath
North Lodge
Leacon Farm
Calehill House
Hollybush Farm
Cowlees Plantation
Nursery
LEDA COTTS
The Dower House
Leacon Alders
M20
Garden Court Hotel
Kempton Manor Hotel
Calehill Park
Greensand Way
HURSTFORD LA
TN26
Kempton Manor Farm
Lake House
Britton Farm
Hurstford Wood
PH
Ram Lane
A20
CHAPEL ROW
Calehill Farm
CHAPEL RD
River Field Shaw
Freeds Alders
Great Stour
TN25
Cowlees Alders
LAKESIDE GDNS
Black Bushes
Mill Ponds
BANNISTER HOS
Little Chart
The Mount
Chart Meadow Alders
Stour Valley Wlk
Hothfield Common
THE TERRACE

233
266

202
236

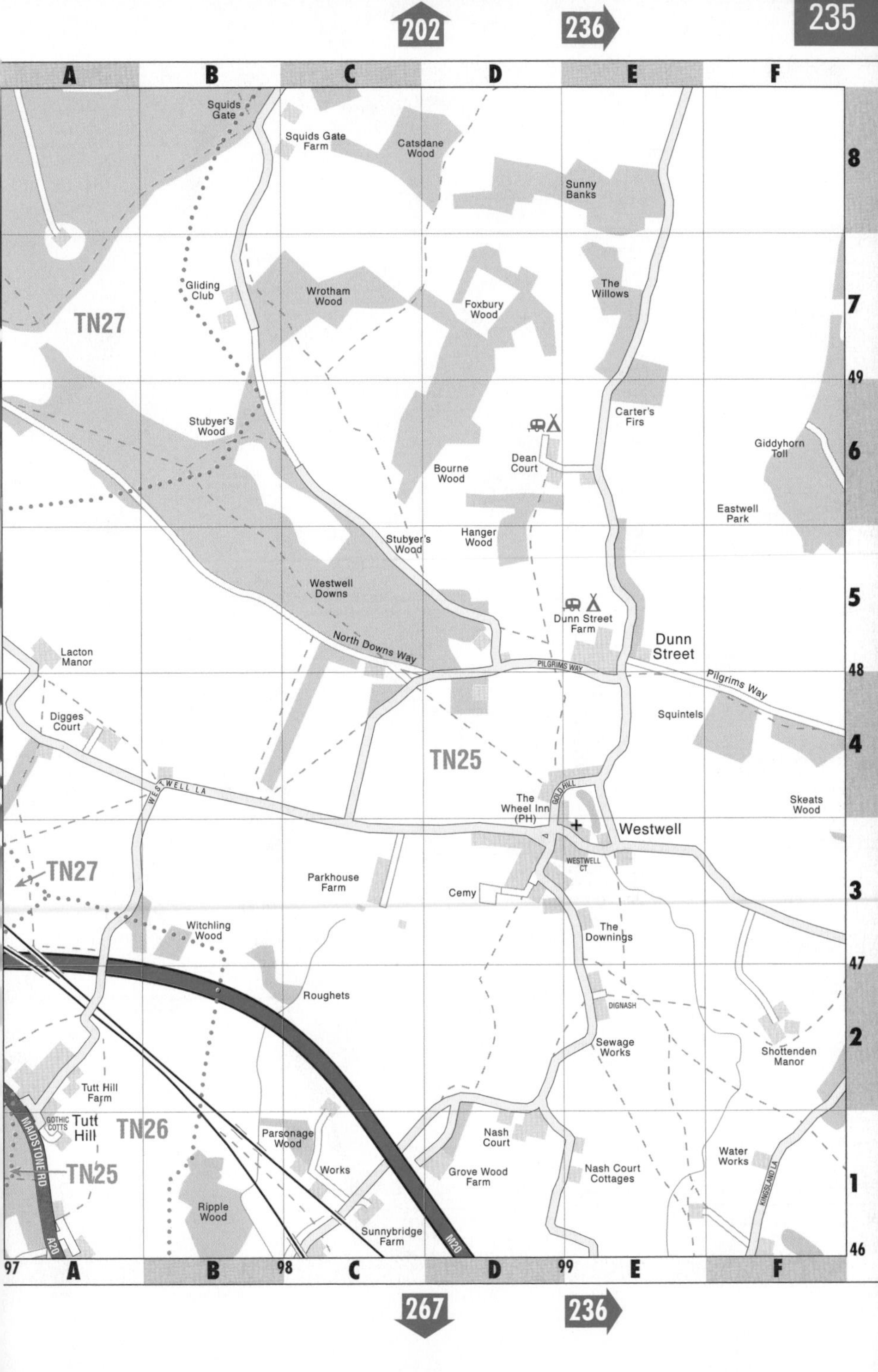
A
B
C
D
E
F
Squids Gate
Squids Gate Farm
Catsdane Wood
Sunny Banks
Gliding Club
Wrotham Wood
Foxbury Wood
The Willows
TN27
Stubyer's Wood
Carter's Firs
Dean Court
Bourne Wood
Giddyhorn Toll
Eastwell Park
Stubyer's Wood
Hanger Wood
Westwell Downs
Dunn Street Farm
North Downs Way
Dunn Street
Lacton Manor
PILGRIMS WAY
Pilgrims Way
Digges Court
Squintels
TN25
WESTWELL LA
GOLD HILL
The Wheel Inn (PH)
Skeats Wood
Westwell
TN27
Parkhouse Farm
Cemy
WESTWELL CT
Witchling Wood
The Downings
Roughets
DIGNASH
Sewage Works
Shottenden Manor
Tutt Hill Farm
GOTHIC COTTS
Tutt Hill
TN26
Parsonage Wood
Nash Court
Water Works
MAIDSTONE RD
TN25
Works
Grove Wood Farm
Nash Court Cottages
KINGSLAND LA
Ripple Wood
Sunnybridge Farm
A20
M20
8
7
49
6
5
48
4
3
47
2
1
46
97
98
99

267
236

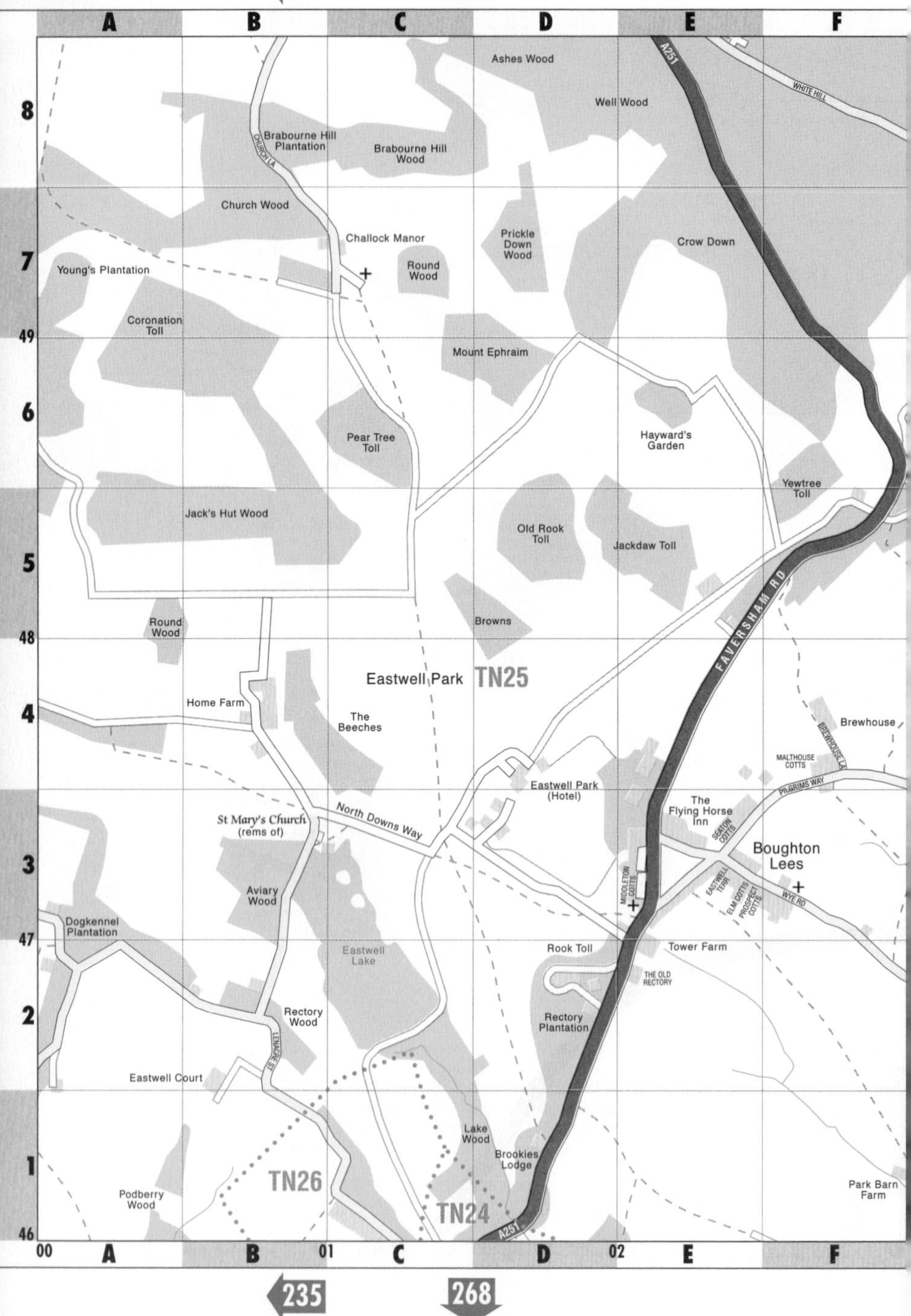

A   **B**   **C**   **D**   **E**   **F**

8

Ashes Wood

Well Wood

A251

WHITE HILL

Brabourne Hill
Plantation

Brabourne Hill
Wood

Church Wood

7

Challock Manor

Round
Wood

Prickle
Down
Wood

Crow Down

Young's Plantation

49

Coronation
Toll

Mount Ephraim

6

Pear Tree
Toll

Hayward's
Garden

Yewtree
Toll

Jack's Hut Wood

Old Rook
Toll

Jackdaw Toll

5

FAVERSHAM RD

Browns

48

Round
Wood

Eastwell Park   **TN25**

4

Home Farm

The
Beeches

Brewhouse

BREWHOUSE CL

MALTHOUSE
COTTS

PILGRIMS WAY

Eastwell Park
(Hotel)

The
Flying Horse
Inn

SEASON
COTTS

St Mary's Church
(rems of)

North Downs Way

Boughton
Lees

3

Aviary
Wood

MIDDLE VIEW
COTTS

EASTWELL
VIEW

ELM DRIFTS
PROSPECT
COTTS

WYE RD

Dogkennel
Plantation

47

Eastwell
Lake

Rook Toll

Tower Farm

THE OLD
RECTORY

2

Rectory
Wood

Rectory
Plantation

Eastwell Court

Lake
Wood

1

TN26

Podberry
Wood

Brookies
Lodge

TN24

A251

Park Barn
Farm

46

00   **A**   **B**   01   **C**   **D**   02   **E**   **F**

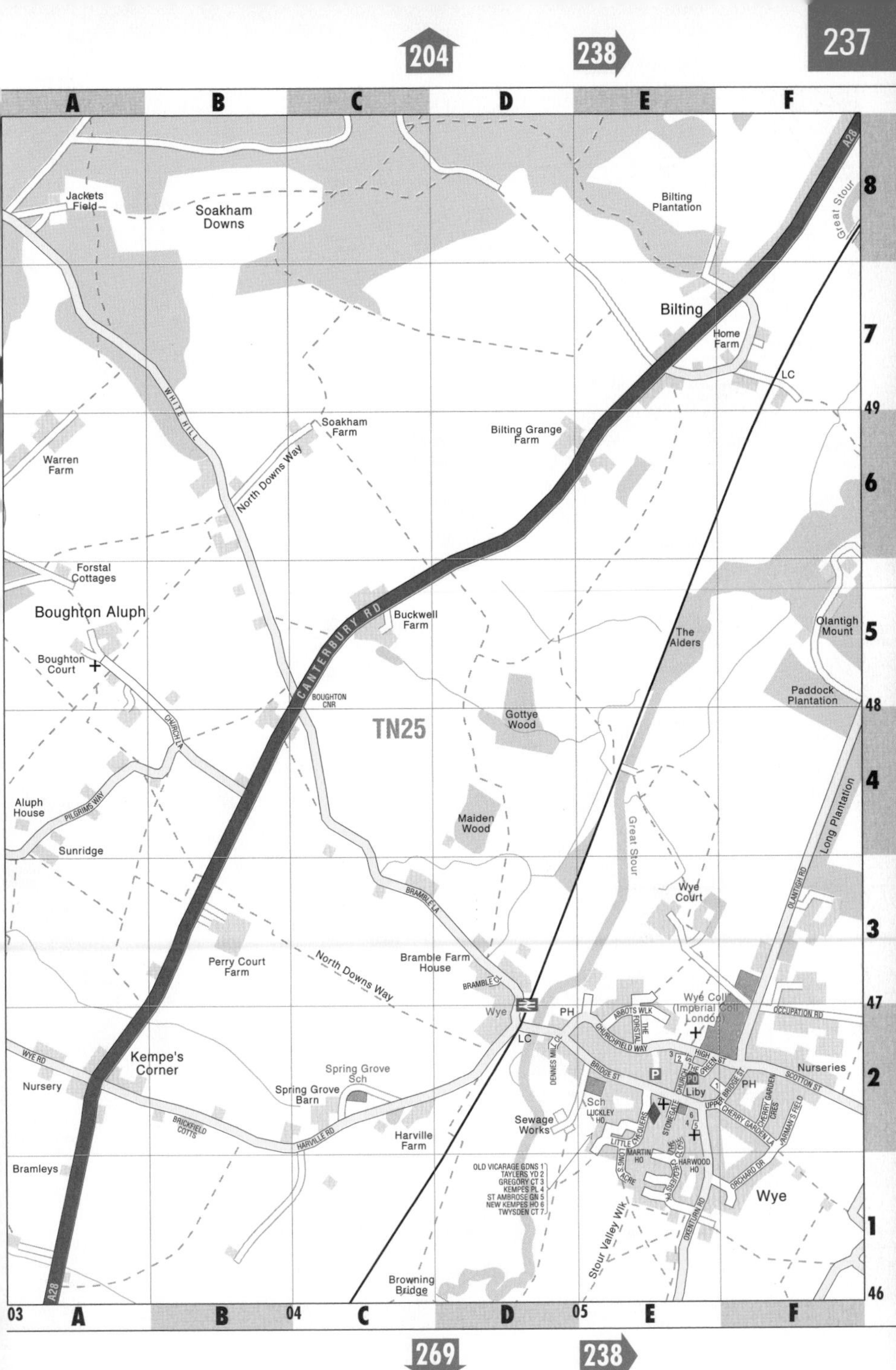

A B C D E F

8
7
49
6
5
48
4
3
47
2
1
46

Jackets Field
Soakham Downs
Bilting Plantation
Bilting
Home Farm
LC
Warren Farm
Soakham Farm
North Downs Way
WHITE HILL
Bilting Grange Farm
Forstal Cottages
Boughton Aluph
Buckwell Farm
CANTERBURY RD
BOUGHTON CNR
Boughton Court
CHURCH
The Alders
Olantigh Mount
TN25
Gottye Wood
Paddock Plantation
Aluph House
PILGRIMS WAY
Sunridge
Maiden Wood
Great Stour
Long Plantation
BRAMBLE LA
Wye Court
OLANTIGH RD
Perry Court Farm
North Downs Way
Bramble Farm House
BRAMBLE CL
Wye
PH
Wye Coll (Imperial Coll London)
OCCUPATION RD
47
SCOTTON ST
Nurseries
LC
DENNES MILL RD
BRIDGE ST
CHURCHFIELD WAY
Kempe's Corner
WYE RD
Nursery
Spring Grove Sch
Spring Grove Barn
P
Liby
PH
Sch
Bramleys
BRICKFIELD COTTS
HARVILLE RD
Harville Farm
Sewage Works
LUCKLEY HO
MARTINS HO
C HARWOOD HO
ORCHARD DR
Wye
OLD VICARAGE GDNS 1
TAYLERS YD 2
GREGORY CT 3
KEMPES PL 4
ST AMBROSE GN 5
NEW KEMPES HO 6
TWYSDEN CT 7
Stour Valley Wlk
Browning Bridge
A28

03 04 05

237
205

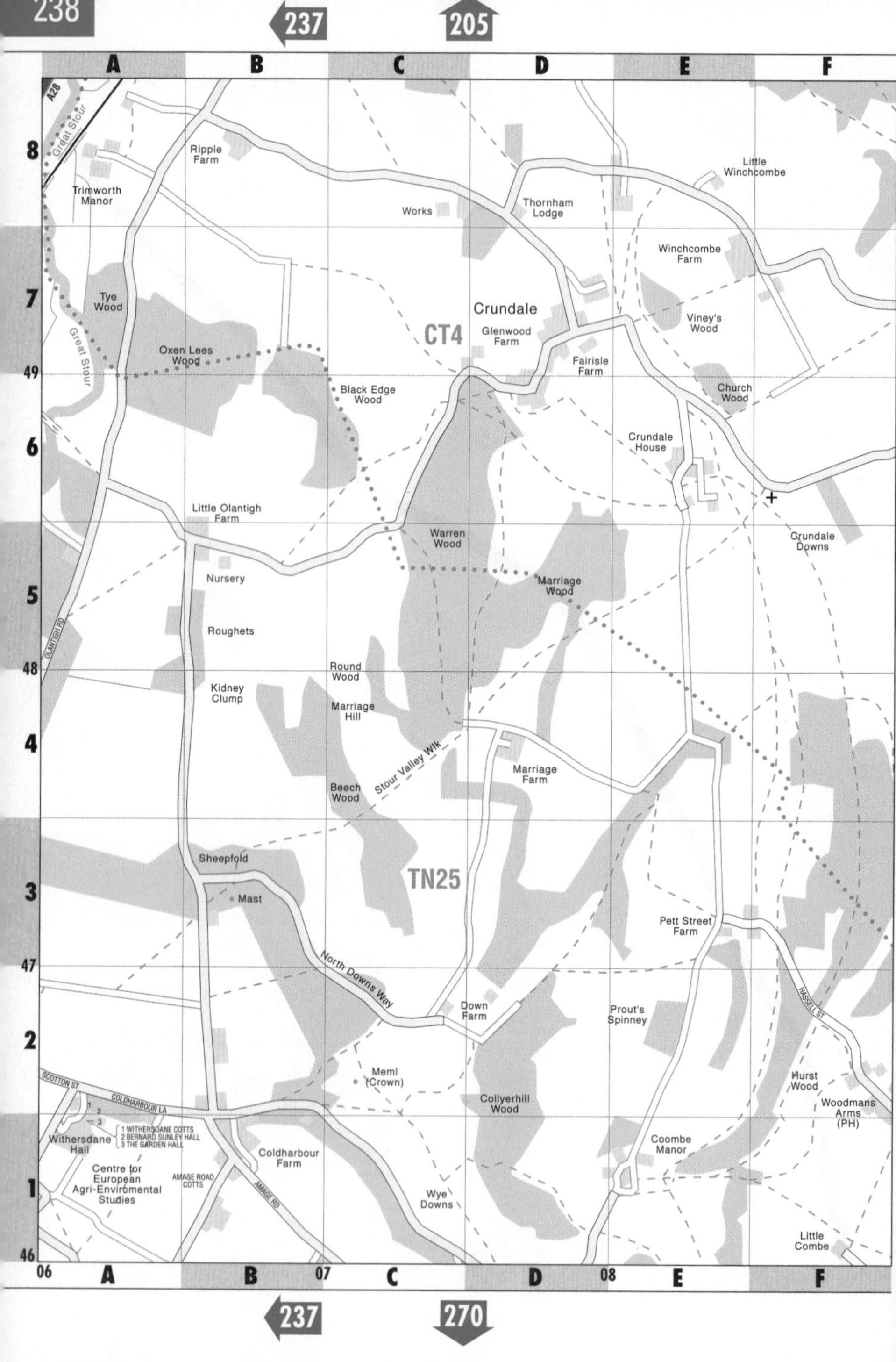
A
B
C
D
E
F
8
7
49
6
5
48
4
3
47
2
1
46
06
07
08
A28
Great Stour
Ripple Farm
Trimworth Manor
Works
Thornham Lodge
Little Winchcombe
Winchcombe Farm
Tye Wood
Crundale
CT4
Glenwood Farm
Viney's Wood
Oxen Lees Wood
Fairisle Farm
Church Wood
Black Edge Wood
Crundale House
Little Olantigh Farm
Warren Wood
Crundale Downs
Nursery
Marriage Wood
OLANTIGH RD
Roughets
Round Wood
Kidney Clump
Marriage Hill
Stour Valley Wlk
Marriage Farm
Beech Wood
Sheepfold
TN25
Mast
Pett Street Farm
North Downs Way
HASSELL ST
Down Farm
Prout's Spinney
Meml (Crown)
SCOTTON ST
COLDHARBOUR LA
Collyerhill Wood
Hurst Wood
Woodmans Arms (PH)
1 WITHERSDANE COTTS
2 BERNARD SUNLEY HALL
3 THE GARDEN HALL
Withersdane Hall
Coldharbour Farm
Coombe Manor
Centre for European Agri-Enviromental Studies
AMAGE ROAD COTTS
AMAGE RD
Wye Downs
Little Combe

237
270

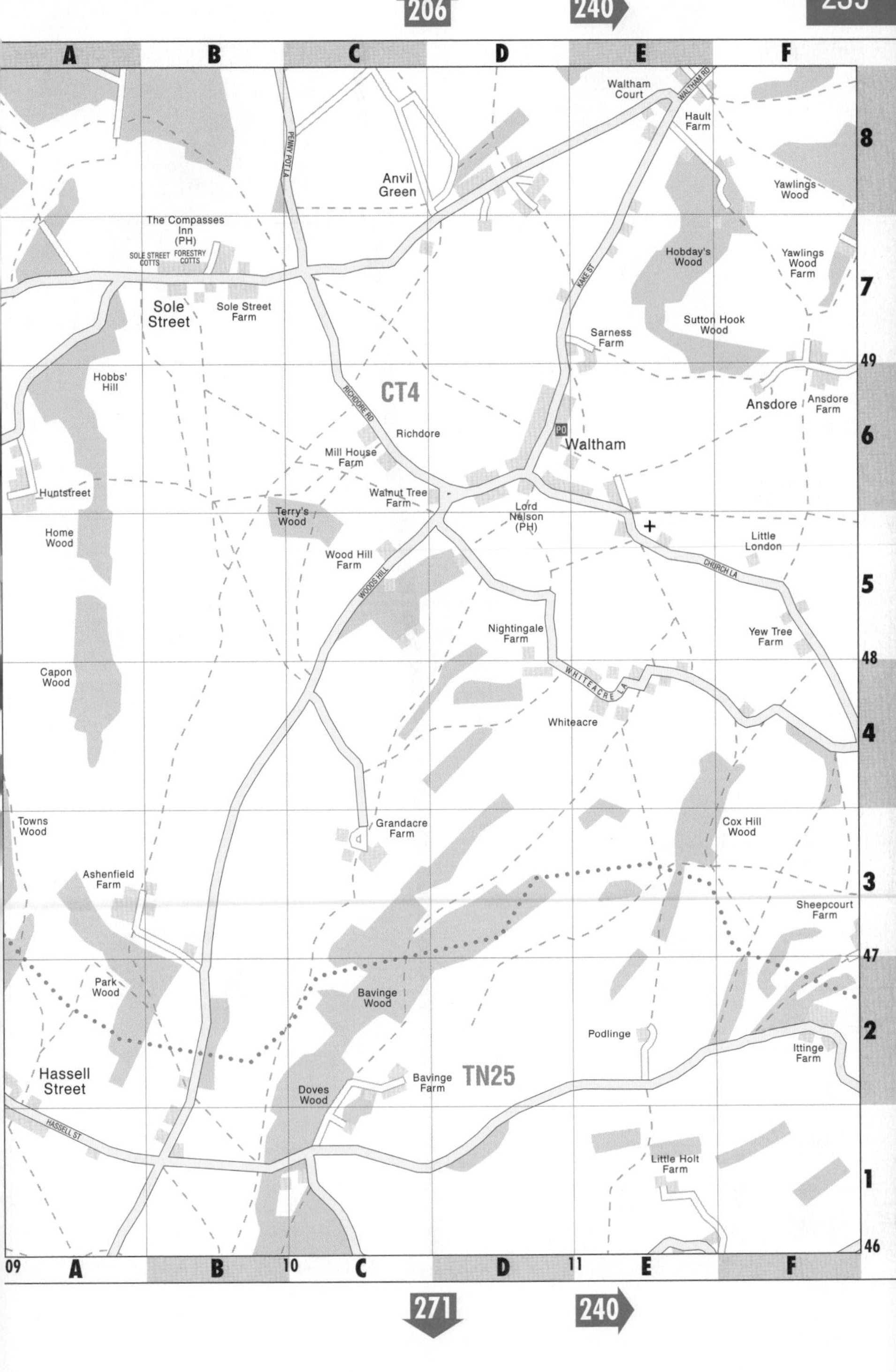

A B C D E F

8

Waltham
Court

Hault
Farm

WALTHAM RD

Anvil
Green

Yawlings
Wood

The Compasses
Inn
(PH)

Hobday's
Wood

Yawlings
Wood
Farm

7

SOLE STREET
COTTS

FORESTRY
COTTS

Sole Street
Farm

AKE ST

Sutton Hook
Wood

Sole
Street

Sarness
Farm

49

Hobbs'
Hill

CT4

Richdore

Ansdore

Ansdore
Farm

6

PO

Waltham

Mill House
Farm

Huntstreet

Walnut Tree
Farm

Terry's
Wood

Lord
Nelson
(PH)

Little
London

Home
Wood

+

CHURCH LA

5

Wood Hill
Farm

WOODS HILL

Nightingale
Farm

Yew Tree
Farm

48

Capon
Wood

WHITEACRE LA

Whiteacre

4

Cox Hill
Wood

Towns
Wood

Grandacre
Farm

d

Sheepcourt
Farm

3

Ashenfield
Farm

47

Park
Wood

Bavinge
Wood

Podlinge

Ittinge
Farm

2

Hassell
Street

Bavinge
Farm

TN25

Doves
Wood

HASSELL ST

Little Holt
Farm

1

46

09 A B 10 C D 11 E F

8

New Barn Farm

Dane Chantry

Homestead Farm

Upper Hardres Wood

Round Wood

7

Waddenhall Wood

Stubb's Wood

Nursery

STONEWAY PK

Little Bossingham Farm

Dunlies Wood

The Hollies

49

Stelling Lodge Farm

HOMESIDE FARM

6

Yockletts Banks

Waddenhall Farm

Little Wadden Hall

Parkmead

Stelling Minnis CE Prim Sch

WADDENHALL BARNS

Wadden Hall Cottages

Doghouse Farm

Church Wood

5

Syngate Wood

Syngate House

48

Cherry Garden Farm

Yockletts Farm

CHURCH LA

4

Nature Reserve

CT4

Common

Holly Tree Farm

Butts Farm

Yewtree Farmhouse

Mead Farm

3

Westcroft Farm

North Leigh

Gaylees Farmhouse

Prim Farm

The Laurels

47

Little Buckett Farm

Malt Farm

Stelling Minnis

Rose & Crown (PH)

CROWN LA

BEAN HILL

THORN LA

DUTTS LA

Chapel Farm

2

Little North Leigh Farm

Thorn Farm

Knowler Farm

1 MINNIS GN
2 MINNIS FIELD

Windmill (dis)

Dean Farm

Scarp's Farm

TN25

1

Great Dowles Farm

Courthope Farm

46

12   **A**   **B**   **13**   **C**   **D**   **14**   **E**   **F**

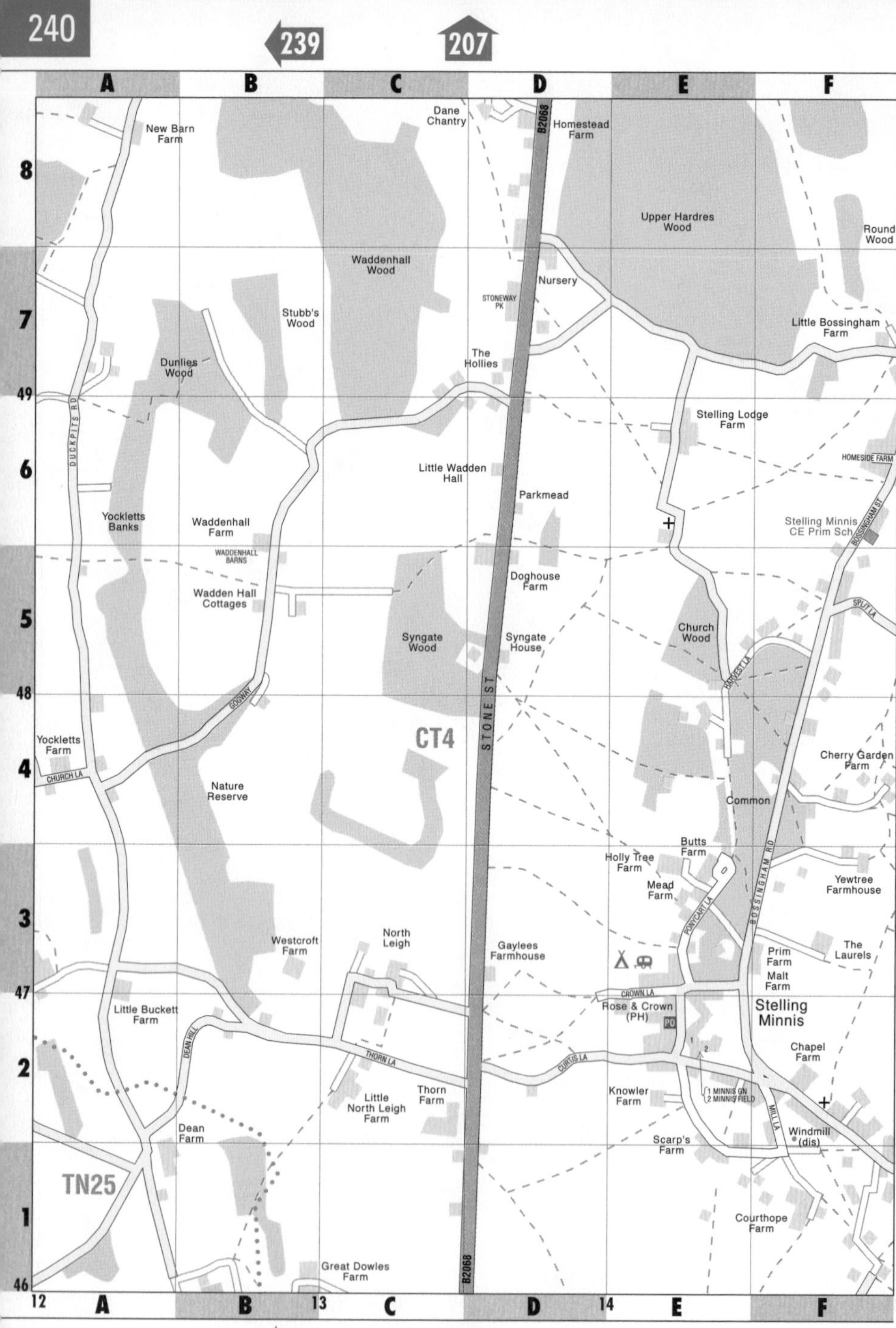

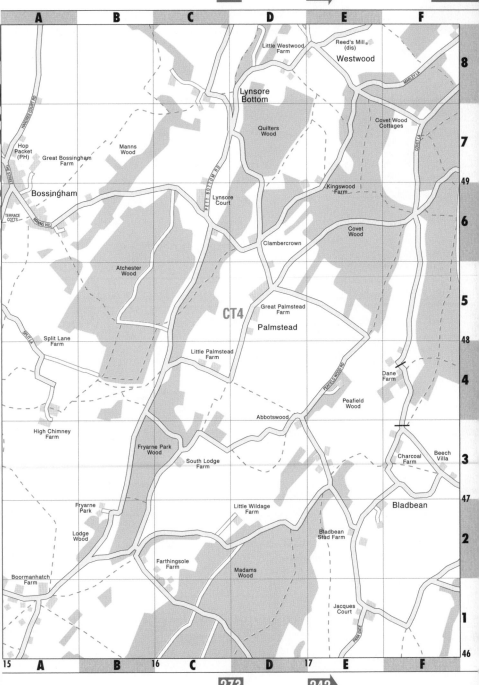

8

Little Westwood Farm

Reed's Mill (dis)

Westwood

Lynsore Bottom

Quilters Wood

Covet Wood Cottages

7

Hop Packet (PH)

Great Bossingham Farm

Manns Wood

49

Kingswood Farm

Bossingham

TERRACE COTTS

Lynsore Court

6

Clambercrown

Covet Wood

Atchester Wood

CT4

Great Palmstead Farm

5

Palmstead

48

Split Lane Farm

Little Palmstead Farm

Dane Farm

4

Peafield Wood

High Chimney Farm

Abbotswood

Fryarne Park Wood

South Lodge Farm

Charcoal Farm

Beech Villa

3

47

Fryarne Park

Little Wildage Farm

Bladbean

Lodge Wood

Bladbean Stad Farm

2

Farthingsole Farm

Madams Wood

Boormanhatch Farm

Jacques Court

1

46

241
209

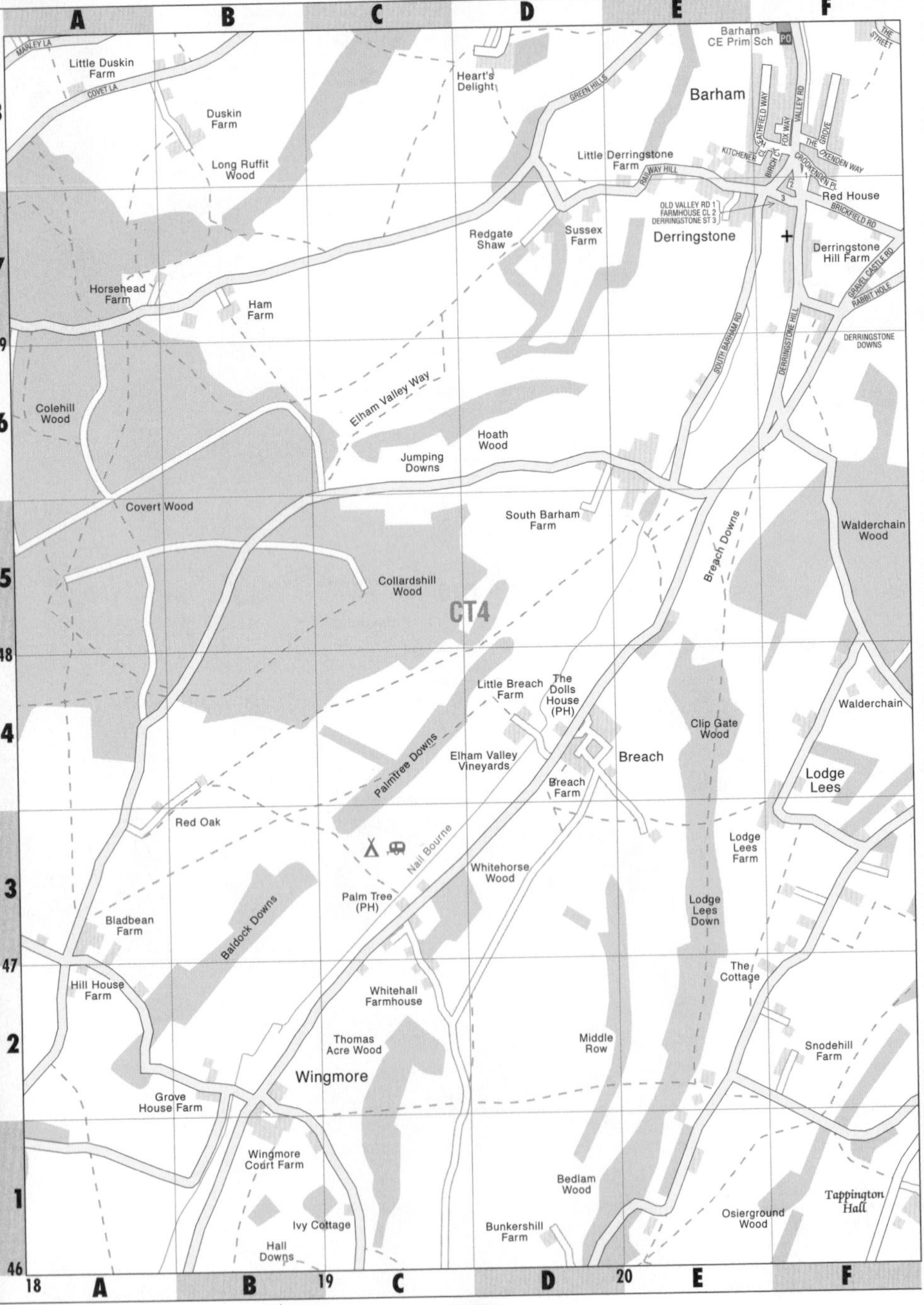

A B C D E F

8

Manley La

Little Duskin Farm

Covet La

Duskin Farm

Heart's Delight

GREEN HILL LA

Barham CE Prim Sch

RD

THE STREET

Barham

Long Ruffit Wood

Little Derringstone Farm

WAY HILL

FAIRFIELD WAY

KITCHENER

BRODGRNENE PL

VALLEY RD

THE GROVE

OXENDEN WAY

7

Redgate Shaw

Sussex Farm

Derringstone

OLD VALLEY RD 1
FARMHOUSE CL 2
DERRINGSTONE ST 3

Red House

BRICKFIELD RD

+

Derringstone Hill Farm

GRAVEL CASTLE RD

RABBIT HOLE

DERRINGSTONE DOWNS

Horsehead Farm

Ham Farm

49

6

Colehill Wood

Elham Valley Way

Hoath Wood

Jumping Downs

SOUTH BARHAM RD

DERRINGSTONE HILL

Covert Wood

South Barham Farm

Breach Downs

Walderchain Wood

5

Collardshill Wood

CT4

48

4

Little Breach Farm

The Dolls House (PH)

Clip Gate Wood

Walderchain

Walderchain

Palmtree Downs

Elham Valley Vineyards

Breach

Lodge Lees

Breach Farm

Red Oak

Nail Bourne

Whitehorse Wood

Lodge Lees Farm

3

Palm Tree (PH)

Lodge Lees Down

Bladbean Farm

Baldock Downs

The Cottage

47

2

Hill House Farm

Whitehall Farmhouse

Thomas Acre Wood

Middle Row

Snodehill Farm

Wingmore

Grove House Farm

1

Wingmore Court Farm

Bedlam Wood

Tappington Hall

Ivy Cottage

Osierground Wood

Hall Downs

Bunkershill Farm

46

18 A B 19 C D 20 E F

210
244

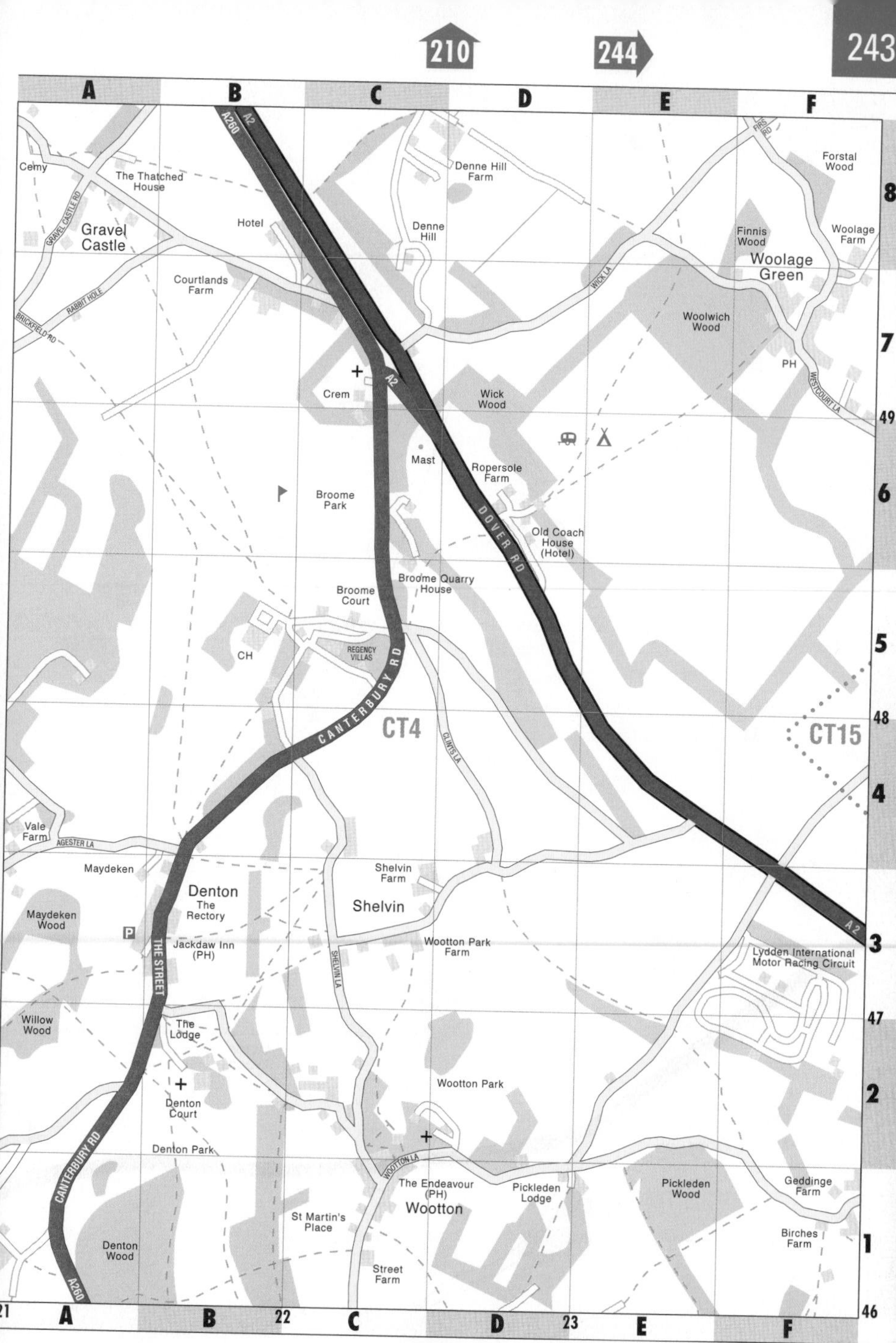
A
B
C
D
E
F
Cemy
The Thatched House
Gravel Castle
GRAVEL CASTLE RD
Hotel
Courtlands Farm
RABBIT HOLE
BRICKFIELD RD
A260
A2
Denne Hill Farm
Denne Hill
FIRS RD
Forstal Wood
Finnis Wood
Woolage Farm
Woolage Green
WICK LA
Woolwich Wood
PH
WESTCOURT LA
Crem
Wick Wood
Mast
Ropersole Farm
Broome Park
DOVER RD
Old Coach House (Hotel)
Broome Quarry House
Broome Court
CH
REGENCY VILLAS
CANTERBURY RD
CT4
CLINTS LA
CT15
Vale Farm
AGESTER LA
Maydeken
Denton
The Rectory
Shelvin Farm
Shelvin
Maydeken Wood
Jackdaw Inn (PH)
THE STREET
Wootton Park Farm
SHELVIN LA
Lydden International Motor Racing Circuit
Willow Wood
The Lodge
Denton Court
Wootton Park
Denton Park
WOOTTON LA
The Endeavour (PH)
Wootton
Pickleden Lodge
Pickleden Wood
Geddinge Farm
St Martin's Place
Denton Wood
Street Farm
Birches Farm
8
7
49
6
5
48
4
3
47
2
1
46
21
22
23

275
244

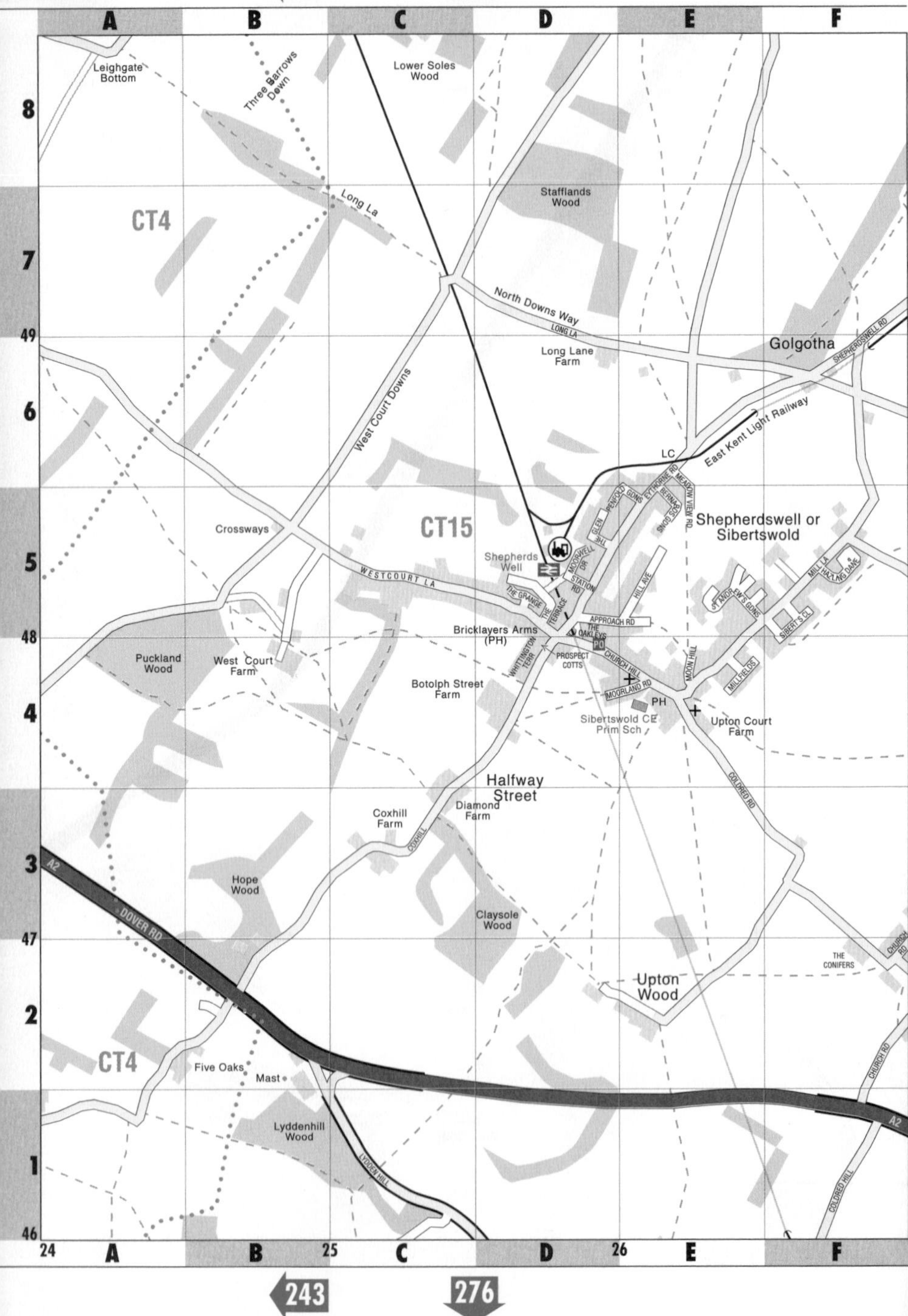

A B C D E F

8

7

49

6

5

48

4

3

47

2

1

46

Leighgate
Bottom

Three Barrows
Down

Lower Soles
Wood

CT4

Long La

Stafflands
Wood

North Downs Way

LONG LA

Golgotha

West Court Downs

Long Lane
Farm

East Kent Light Railway

LC

CT15

Shepherdswell or
Sibertswold

Crossways

WESTCOURT LA

Shepherds
Well

Puckland
Wood

West Court
Farm

Bricklayers Arms
(PH)

APPROACH RD

Botolph Street
Farm

THE GRANGE

PROSPECT
COTTS

CHURCH HILL

MOORLAND RD

PH

Sibertswold CE
Prim Sch

Upton Court
Farm

Halfway
Street

Coxhill
Farm

COXHILL

Diamond
Farm

A2

Hope
Wood

DOVER RD

Claysole
Wood

COLDRED RD

THE
CONIFERS

Upton
Wood

CHURCH

CT4

Five Oaks

Mast

Lyddenhill
Wood

LYDDEN HILL

COLDRED HILL

A2

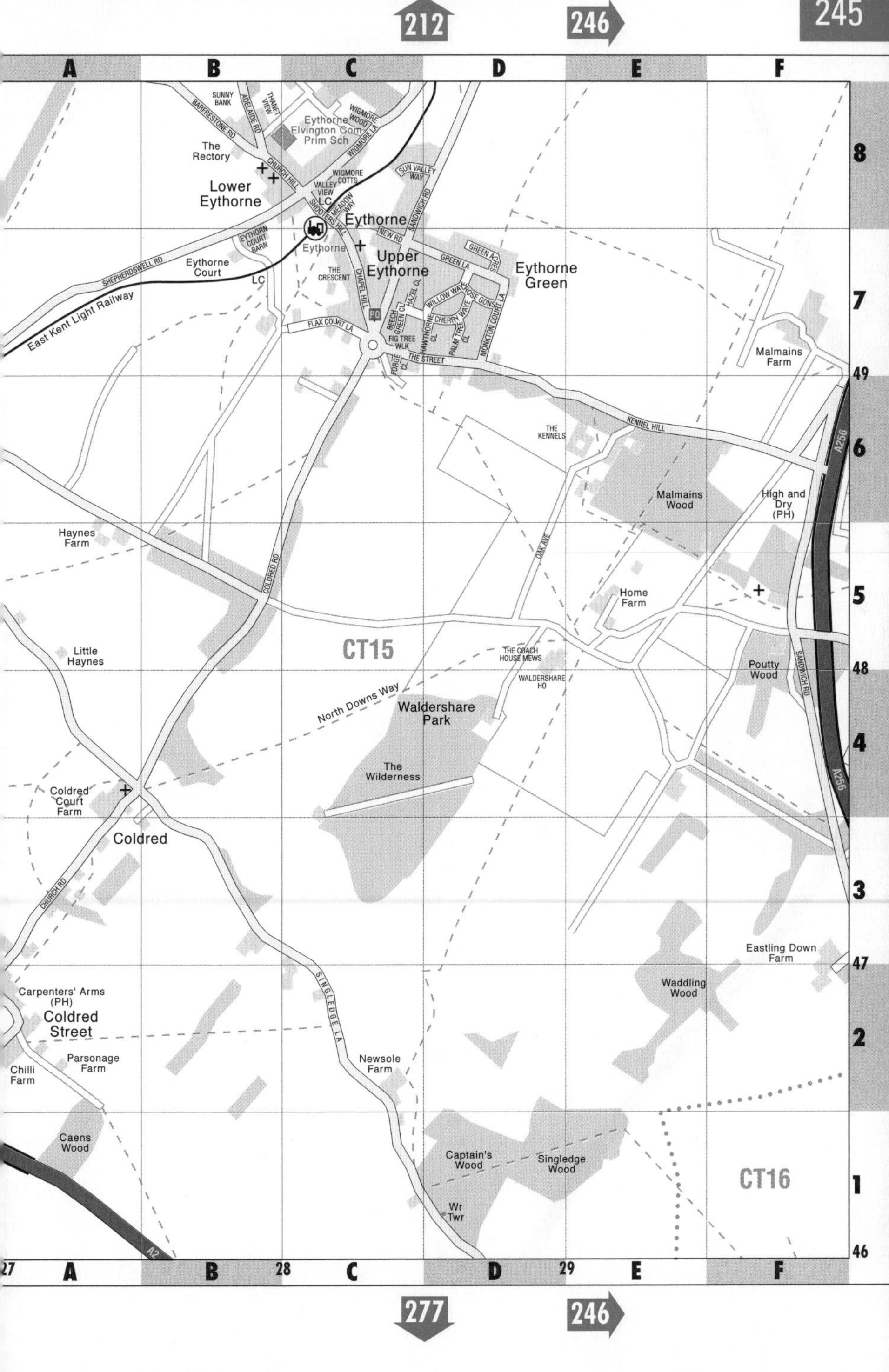

A B C D E F

8

Lower Eythorne

The Rectory

SUNNY BANK
BARRETSTONE RD
ARCADE RD
THANET VIEW
WIGMORE WOOD
Eythorne Elvington Comm Prim Sch
WIGMORE COTTS
CHURCH HILL
VALLEY VIEW
SUN VALLEY WAY
7

Eythorne

Eythorne Court

East Kent Light Railway

SHEPHERDSWELL RD

LC

EYTHORNE COURT BARN

Eythorne

THE CRESCENT

CHAPEL HILL

FLAX COURT LA

Upper Eythorne

NEW RD

GREEN LA

GREEN ACRES

HAZEL LA

WILLOW WALK

BIRCH CL

HAWTHORN CL

CHERRY WALK

FIG TREE WALK

PALM TREE

THE STREET

MONKTON CL

YOKE LA

GORE RD

Eythorne Green

Malmains Farm

49

THE KENNELS

KENNEL HILL

Malmains Wood

High and Dry (PH)

A256

6

Haynes Farm

COLDRED RD

OAK LANE

Home Farm

Poutty Wood

SANDHOLT RD

5

Little Haynes

CT15

THE COACH HOUSE MEWS

WALDERSHARE HO

North Downs Way

Waldershare Park

48

4

Coldred Court Farm

The Wilderness

3

Coldred

CHURCH RD

Eastling Down Farm

47

Carpenters' Arms (PH)

Coldred Street

STREETLEDGE LA

Waddling Wood

2

Parsonage Farm

Chilli Farm

Newsole Farm

Caens Wood

Captain's Wood

Singledge Wood

CT16

1

A2

Wr Twr

46

27 A B 28 C D 29 E F

245
213

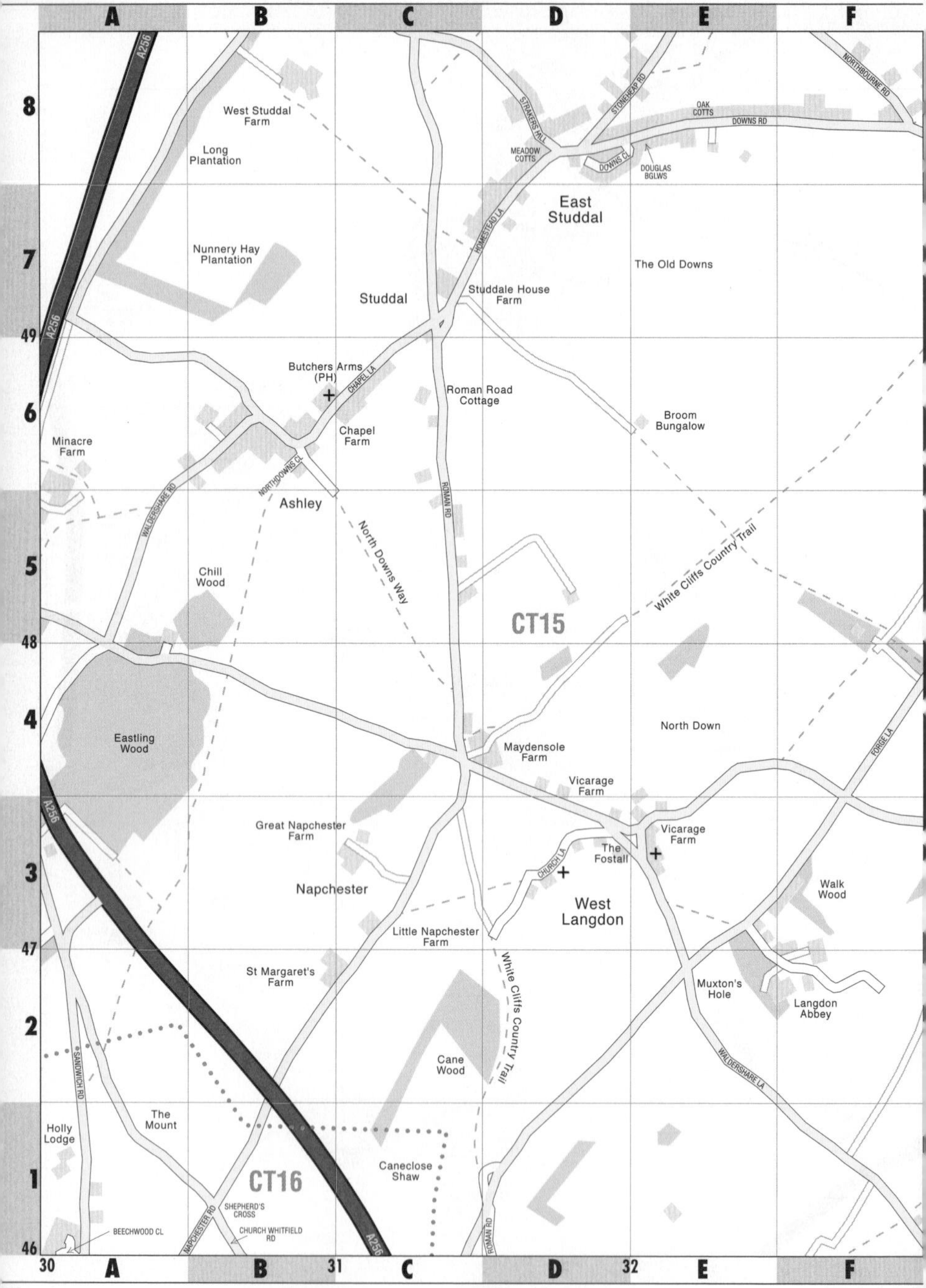

A **B** **C** **D** **E** **F**

8

West Studdal
Farm

Long
Plantation

A256

OAK
COTTS

DOWNS RD

NORTHBOURNE RD

STOCKDALE RD

MEADOW
COTTS

DOWNS CL

DOUGLAS
BGLWS

East
Studdal

7

Nunnery Hay
Plantation

The Old Downs

49

PRICKETTS LA

Studdal

Studdale House
Farm

Butchers Arms
(PH)

Roman Road
Cottage

Broom
Bungalow

6

Minacre
Farm

Chapel
Farm

CHAPEL LA

NORTHGOWER CL

Ashley

White Cliffs Country Trail

5

Chill
Wood

WALDERSHARE RD

ROMAN RD

North Downs Way

CT15

48

Eastling
Wood

North Down

FORGE LA

4

A256

Maydensole
Farm

Vicarage
Farm

Vicarage
Farm

Great Napchester
Farm

CHURCH LA

The
Fostall

Walk
Wood

3

Napchester

West
Langdon

47

Little Napchester
Farm

White Cliffs Country Trail

Muxton's
Hole

Langdon
Abbey

St Margaret's
Farm

WALDERSHARE LA

2

Cane
Wood

SANDWICH RD

Holly
Lodge

The
Mount

CT16

Caneclose
Shaw

OLD WAY RD

1

NAPCHESTER RD

SHEPHERD'S
CROSS

BEECHWOOD CL

CHURCH WHITFIELD
RD

A256

46

30 **A** **B** 31 **C** **D** 32 **E** **F**

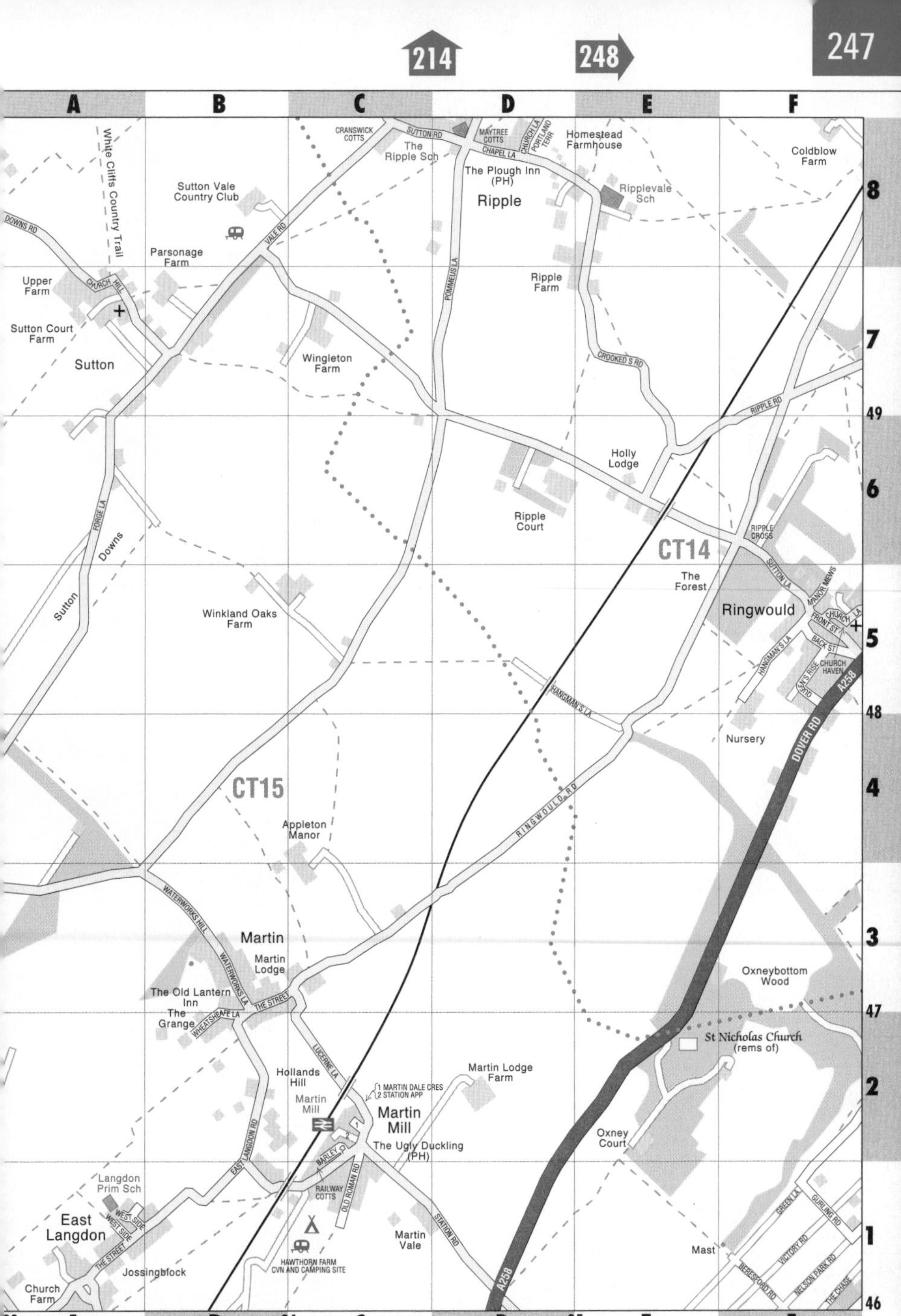

White Cliffs Country Trail

Downs Rd

CRANSWICK COTTS
SUTTON RD
The Ripple Sch
MAYTREE COTTS
CHAPEL LA
CHURCH LA
PORTLAND TERR
Homestead Farmhouse
Coldblow Farm

Sutton Vale Country Club

The Plough Inn (PH)

Ripplevale Sch

Ripple

8

Parsonage Farm

VALE RD

POMANDS LA

Ripple Farm

Upper Farm

CHURCH HILL

7

Sutton Court Farm

49

Sutton

CROOKED S RD

RIPPLE RD

Wingleton Farm

Downs

FORGE LA

Holly Lodge

6

Sutton

Ripple Court

RIPPLE CROSS

CT14

The Forest

SUTTON LA

MANOR HEIGHTS

Ringwould

Winkland Oaks Farm

HANGMAN S LA

HANGMAN S LA

CHURCH ST

HUNT ST

SACK ST

5

CHURCH HAVEN

BAY HILL

CROSS

DOVER RD

48

RINGWOULD RD

Nursery

A258

CT15

4

Appleton Manor

Oxneybottom Wood

3

Martin

WATERWORKS HILL

Martin Lodge

The Old Lantern Inn

WATERWORKS HILL

THE STREET

47

The Grange

WHEATSHEAF LA

St Nicholas Church (rems of)

2

Hollands Hill

EASKONE LA

Martin Lodge Farm

Martin Mill

EAST LANGDON RD

MALET LA

1 MARTIN DALE CRES
2 STATION APP

Oxney Court

Martin Mill

The Ugly Duckling (PH)

RAILWAY COTTS

OLD FENWAY RD

Langdon Prim Sch

WEST HILL

Oxney Court

East Langdon

THE STREET

Martin Vale

FENTON RD

A258

Mast

GREEN LA

BERE RD

VICTORY RD

NELSON PARK RD

1

Church Farm

Jossingbrock

HAWTHORN FARM CVN AND CAMPING SITE

SPEARES RD

THE CHASE

46

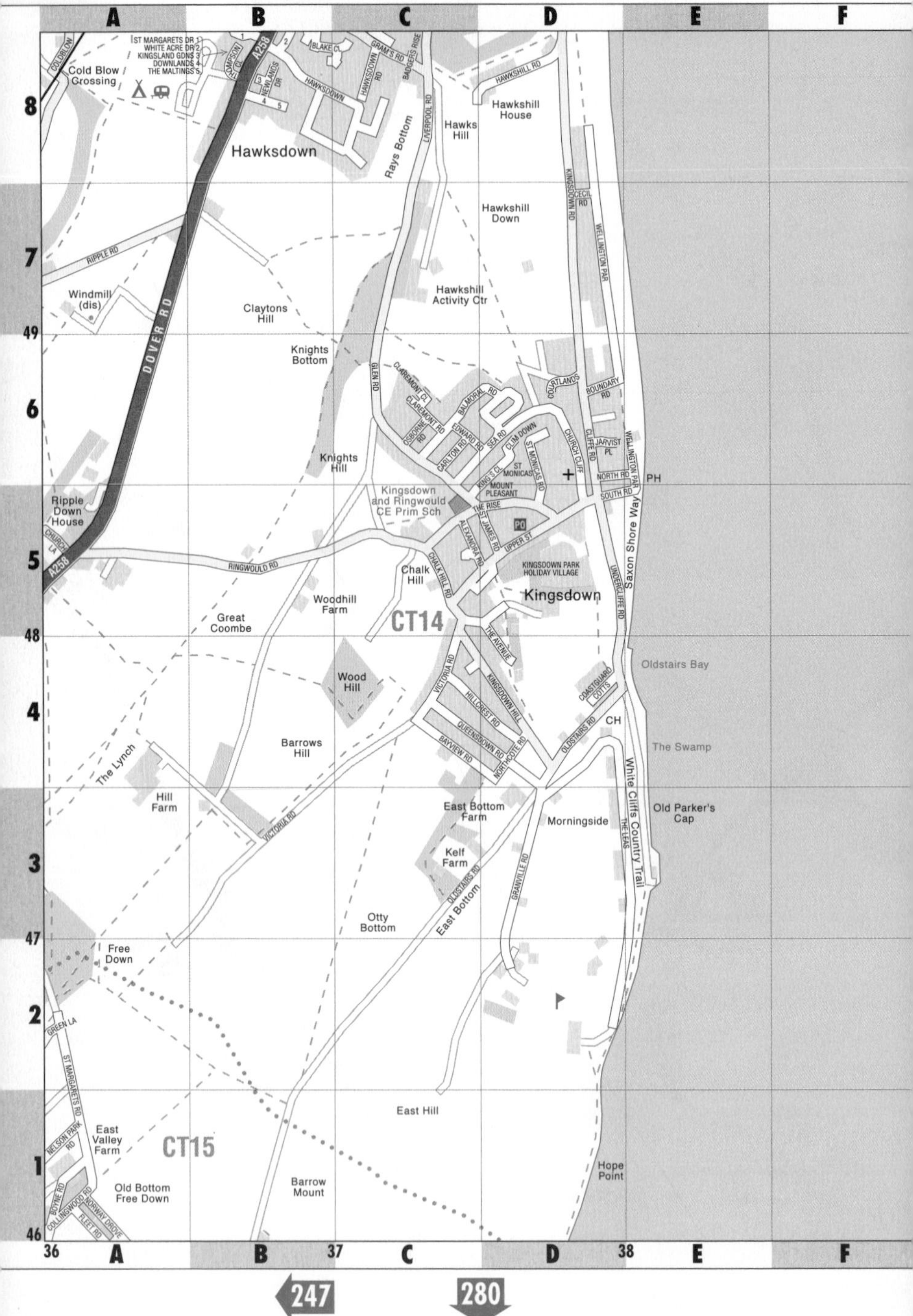

247
215

A **B** **C** **D** **E** **F**

Cold Blow / Crossing

ST MARGARETS DR 1
WHITE ACRE DR 2
KINGSLAND GDNS 3
DOWNLANDS 4
THE MALTINGS 5

BLAKE CL

Hawkshill Rd

Hawkshill House

8

Hawksdown

Rays Bottom

Hawks Hill

Hawkshill Down

7

Windmill (dis)

Claytons Hill

Hawkshill Activity Ctr

49

RIPPLE RD

DOVER RD

Knights Bottom

6

Knights Hill

Kingsdown and Ringwould CE Prim Sch

MOUNT PLEASANT

ST MONICA'S

PH

Ripple Down House

Ringwould Rd

Chalk Hill

5

Woodhill Farm

KINGSDOWN PARK HOLIDAY VILLAGE

Kingsdown

CT14

48

Great Coombe

Wood Hill

Oldstairs Bay

4

The Lynch

Barrows Hill

The Swamp

CH

Hill Farm

East Bottom Farm

Morningside

Old Parker's Cap

VICTORIA RD

Kelf Farm

3

Otty Bottom

East Bottom

White Cliffs Country Trail

47

Free Down

GREEN LA

2

ST MARGARETS RD

East Valley Farm

CT15

East Hill

Hope Point

1

Old Bottom Free Down

Barrow Mount

46

A 36 **B** 37 **C** **D** 38 **E** **F**

247
280

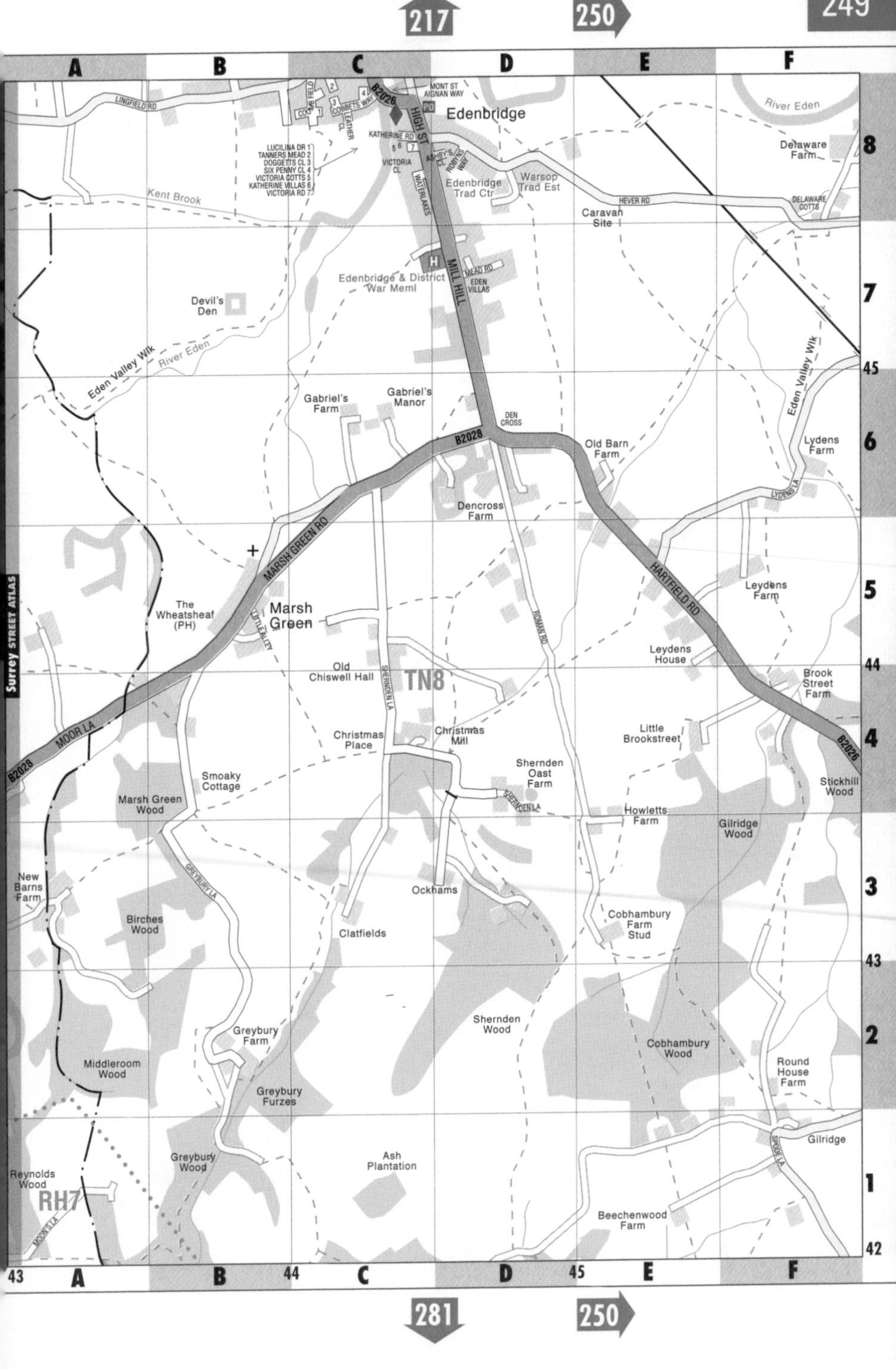
217
250
A
B
C
D
E
F
Edenbridge
LINGFIELD RD
HIGH ST
MONT ST AIGNAN WAY
COBBETS WAY
LEATHER CL
KATHERINE RD
ASHBY'S CL
ROBYNS WAY
VICTORIA CL
WATERLAKES
LUCILINA DR 1
TANNERS MEAD 2
DOGGETTS CL 3
SIX PENNY CL 4
VICTORIA COTTS 5
KATHERINE VILLAS 6
VICTORIA RD 7
Edenbridge Trad Ctr
Warsop Trad Est
HEVER RD
River Eden
Delaware Farm
DELAWARE COTTS
Kent Brook
Caravan Site
MILL HILL
MEAD RD
EDEN VILLAS
Edenbridge & District War Meml
Devil's Den
Eden Valley Wlk
River Eden
Gabriel's Farm
Gabriel's Manor
DEN CROSS
B2028
Old Barn Farm
Lydens Farm
LYDENS LA
Dencross Farm
MARSH GREEN RD
HARTFIELD RD
Leydens Farm
The Wheatsheaf (PH)
Marsh Green
LITTLE ALLEY
ROMAN RD
Leydens House
Old Chiswell Hall
SHERNDEN LA
TN8
Brook Street Farm
MOOR LA
Christmas Place
Christmas Mill
Little Brookstreet
B2026
Shernden Oast Farm
SHERNDEN LA
Smoaky Cottage
Marsh Green Wood
Howletts Farm
Stickhill Wood
Gilridge Wood
GREYBURY LA
New Barns Farm
Ockhams
Birches Wood
Clatfields
Cobhambury Farm Stud
Shernden Wood
Greybury Farm
Cobhambury Wood
Middleroom Wood
Round House Farm
Greybury Furzes
Gilridge
SPODE LA
Greybury Wood
Ash Plantation
Reynolds Wood
RH7
MOON'S LA
Beechenwood Farm
Surrey STREET ATLAS
8
7
45
6
5
44
4
3
43
2
1
42
43
44
45
281
250

249
218

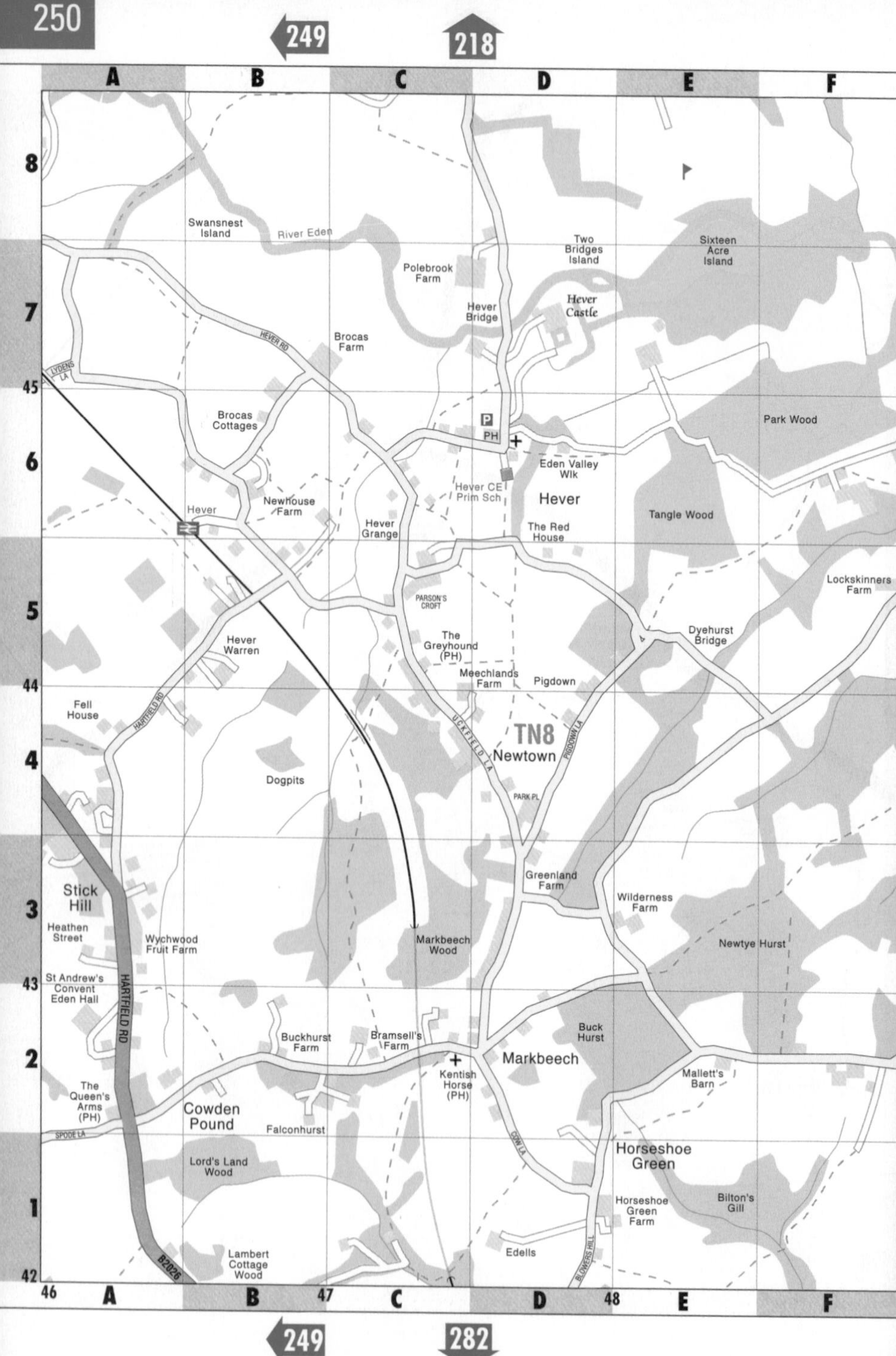
A
B
C
D
E
F
8
7
45
6
5
44
4
3
43
2
1
42
46
47
48
Swansnest Island
River Eden
Polebrook Farm
Two Bridges Island
Sixteen Acre Island
Hever Bridge
Hever Castle
Brocas Farm
HEVER RD
LYDENS LA
Park Wood
Brocas Cottages
PH
Eden Valley Wlk
Hever CE Prim Sch
Hever
Newhouse Farm
Hever
Tangle Wood
Hever Grange
The Red House
Lockskinners Farm
PARSON'S CROFT
Dyehurst Bridge
The Greyhound (PH)
Hever Warren
Meechlands Farm
Pigdown
Fell House
HARTFIELD RD
UCKFIELD LA
PIGDOWN LA
TN8
Newtown
Dogpits
PARK PL
Greenland Farm
Stick Hill
Wilderness Farm
Heathen Street
Wychwood Fruit Farm
Markbeech Wood
Newtye Hurst
St Andrew's Convent Eden Hall
HARTFIELD RD
Buck Hurst
Buckhurst Farm
Bramsell's Farm
Markbeech
Kentish Horse (PH)
Mallett's Barn
The Queen's Arms (PH)
Cowden Pound
SPODE LA
Falconhurst
COW LA
Horseshoe Green
Lord's Land Wood
Bilton's Gill
Horseshoe Green Farm
Edells
BLOWERS HILL
Lambert Cottage Wood
B2026

249
282

219
252

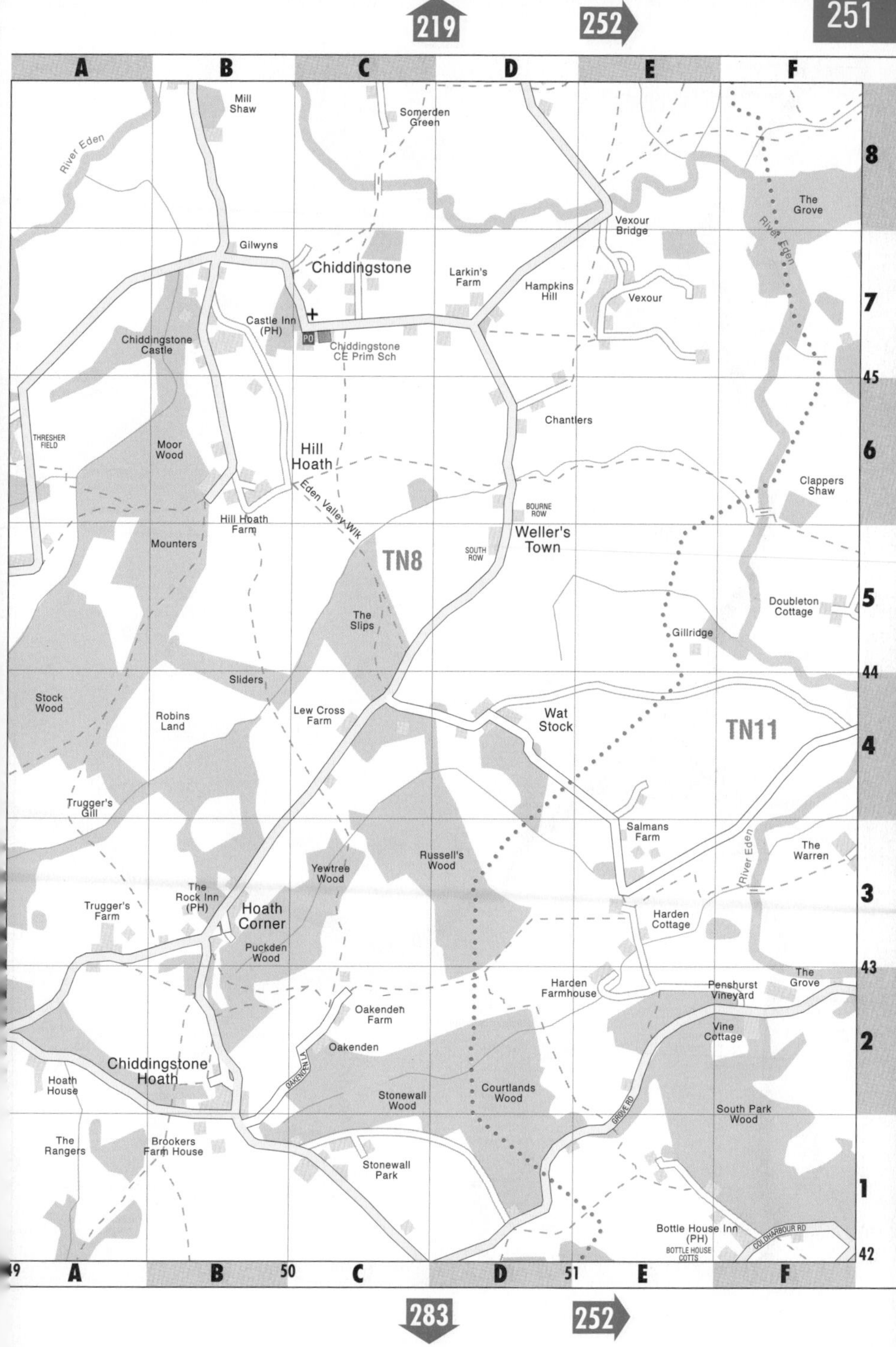
A
B
C
D
E
F
Mill Shaw
Somerden Green
River Eden
The Grove
Vexour Bridge
Gilwyns
Chiddingstone
Larkin's Farm
Hampkins Hill
Vexour
Castle Inn (PH)
PO
Chiddingstone CE Prim Sch
Chiddingstone Castle
Chantlers
THRESHER FIELD
Moor Wood
Hill Hoath
Eden Valley Wlk
Clappers Shaw
BOURNE ROW
Hill Hoath Farm
Weller's Town
Mounters
SOUTH ROW
TN8
Doubleton Cottage
The Slips
Gillridge
Sliders
Stock Wood
Lew Cross Farm
Wat Stock
Robins Land
TN11
Trugger's Gill
Salmans Farm
Russell's Wood
The Warren
Yewtree Wood
The Rock Inn (PH)
Trugger's Farm
Hoath Corner
Harden Cottage
Puckden Wood
Harden Farmhouse
Penshurst Vineyard
The Grove
Oakenden Farm
Vine Cottage
Oakenden
Chiddingstone Hoath
Hoath House
OAKENDEN LA
Stonewall Wood
Courtlands Wood
GROVE RD
South Park Wood
The Rangers
Brookers Farm House
Stonewall Park
Bottle House Inn (PH)
BOTTLE HOUSE COTTS
COLDHARBOUR RD
8
7
45
6
5
44
4
3
43
2
1
42
49
50
51

283
252

251
220

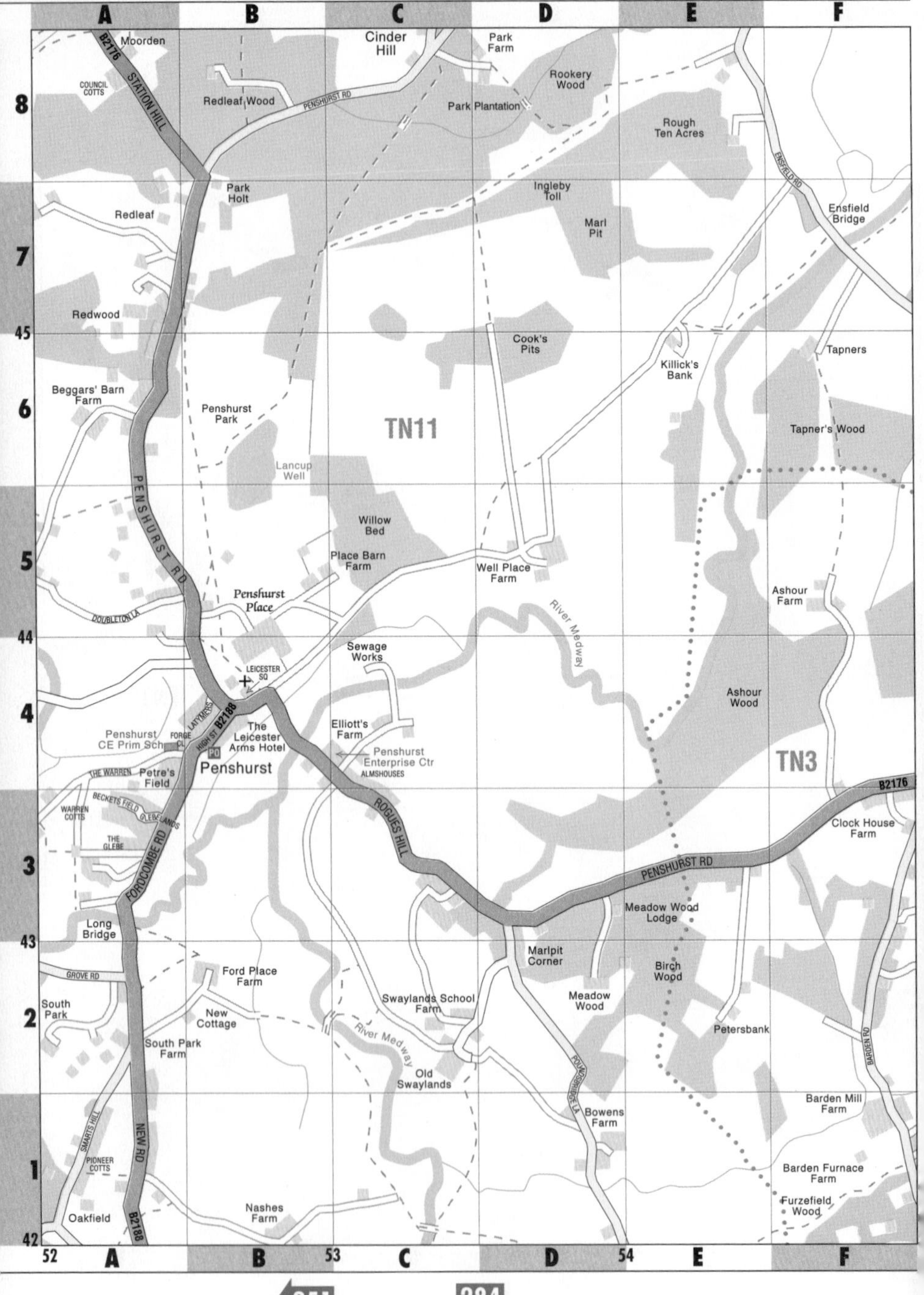
A
B
C
D
E
F
Moorden
Cinder Hill
Park Farm
COUNCIL COTTS
B2176
STATION HILL
Redleaf Wood
PENSHURST RD
Rookery Wood
Park Plantation
Rough Ten Acres
8
Park Holt
Ingleby Toll
ENSFIELD RD
Ensfield Bridge
Redleaf
Marl Pit
7
Redwood
45
Cook's Pits
Tapners
Killick's Bank
Beggars' Barn Farm
6
Penshurst Park
TN11
Tapner's Wood
Lancup Well
PENSHURST RD
Willow Bed
5
Place Barn Farm
Well Place Farm
Penshurst Place
Ashour Farm
DOUBLETON LA
River Medway
44
Sewage Works
LEICESTER SQ
Ashour Wood
4
LATYMERS
B2188
The Leicester Arms Hotel
Elliott's Farm
Penshurst CE Prim Sch
FORGE CL
HIGH ST
PO
Penshurst
Penshurst Enterprise Ctr
ALMSHOUSES
TN3
THE WARREN
Petre's Field
BECKETS FIELD
GLEBELANDS
WARREN COTTS
ROGUES HILL
B2176
Clock House Farm
THE GLEBE
3
FORDCOMBE RD
PENSHURST RD
Meadow Wood Lodge
Long Bridge
43
Marlpit Corner
GROVE RD
Ford Place Farm
Birch Wood
Meadow Wood
South Park
2
New Cottage
Swaylands School Farm
River Medway
Petersbank
South Park Farm
POUNDSBRIDGE LA
BARDEN RD
Old Swaylands
Bowens Farm
Barden Mill Farm
SMARTS HILL
NEW RD
1
PIONEER COTTS
Barden Furnace Farm
Nashes Farm
Furzefield Wood
Oakfield
B2188
42
52
A
B
53
C
D
54
E
F

251
284

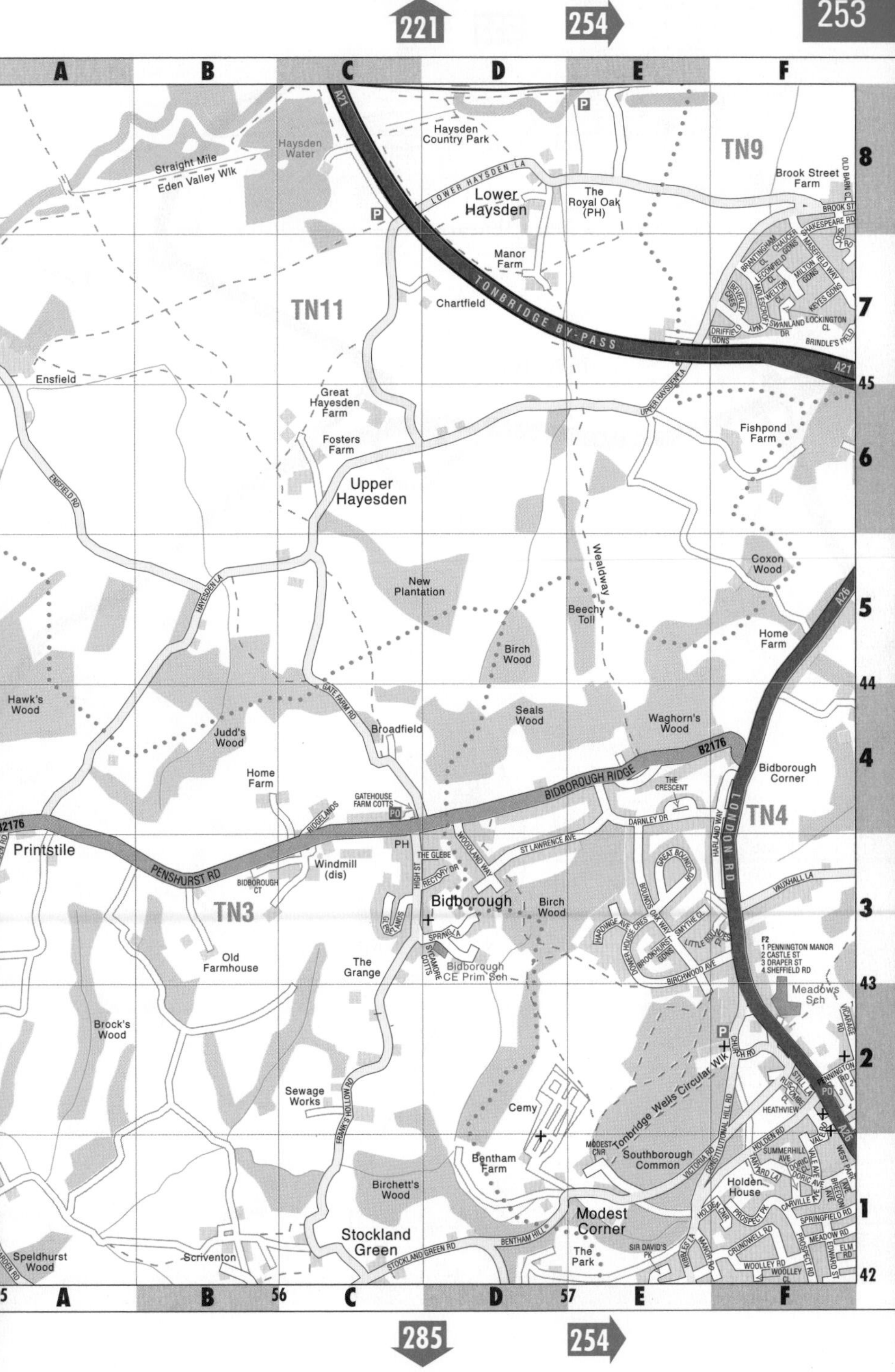

TN9

Brook Street
Farm

Straight Mile
Eden Valley Wlk

Haysden
Water

Haysden
Country Park

Haysden
Lower

Lower
Haysden

The
Royal Oak
(PH)

OLD BARN LA

BROOK ST

SHAKESPEARE RD

MANSFIELD WAY

DRYLANDS RD

BRINDLE'S PATH

Manor
Farm

TN11

Chartfield

TONBRIDGE BY-PASS

8

7

45

Ensfield

ENSFIELD RD

Great
Hayesden
Farm

Fosters
Farm

Upper
Hayesden

Fishpond
Farm

UPPER HAYSDEN LA

Coxon
Wood

New
Plantation

Wealdway

Beechy
Toll

Home
Farm

A26

6

5

44

Hawk's
Wood

HAYSDEN LA

BATTERS RD

Judd's
Wood

Home
Farm

Broadfield

Birch
Wood

Seals
Wood

Waghorn's
Wood

BIDBOROUGH RIDGE

B2176

Bidborough
Corner

TN4

4

B2176
Printstile

PENSHURST RD

RIDGELANDS

GATEHOUSE
FARM COTTS

THE
CRESCENT

Darnley Dr

LONDON RD

3

Windmill
(dis)

BIDBOROUGH
CT

PH

THE GLEBE

ST LAWRENCE AVE

GREAT BOUNDS DR

VAUXHALL LA

TN3

RECTORY DR

Bidborough

Birch
Wood

F2
1 PENNINGTON MANOR
2 CASTLE ST
3 DRAPER ST
4 SHEFFIELD RD

43

Old
Farmhouse

The
Grange

SYCAMORE
COTTS

Bidborough
CE Prim Sch

BIRCHWOOD AVE

Meadows
Sch

Brock's
Wood

Sewage
Works

FRANT HOLLOW RD

Cemy

Tonbridge Wells Circular Wlk

HEATHVIEW

SUMMERHILL

HOLDEN RD

P

2

Bentham
Farm

MODEST
CNR

Southborough
Common

Holden
House

CARVILLE

SPRINGFIELD RD

MEADOW RD

1

Speldhurst
Wood

Scriventon

Birchett's
Wood

Stockland
Green

STOCKLAND GREEN RD

Modest
Corner

BENTHAM HILL

The
Park

SIR DAVID'S

WOOLLEY RD

42

B8
1 ST AUGUSTINE HO
2 BECKET CT
3 QUARRY HILL PAR
4 THE LOWRY
5 BICKLEY RD
6 MONKS WLK
7 DEANS CT
8 MARY MAGDALENE HO
9 MERRYFIELD CT
10 TONBRIDGE CHAMBERS
11 ST GEORGES MEWS
12 GARDYNE MEWS
13 WHITE OAK CL
14 ALMSHOUSES
15 SKINNER'S TERR

253
222

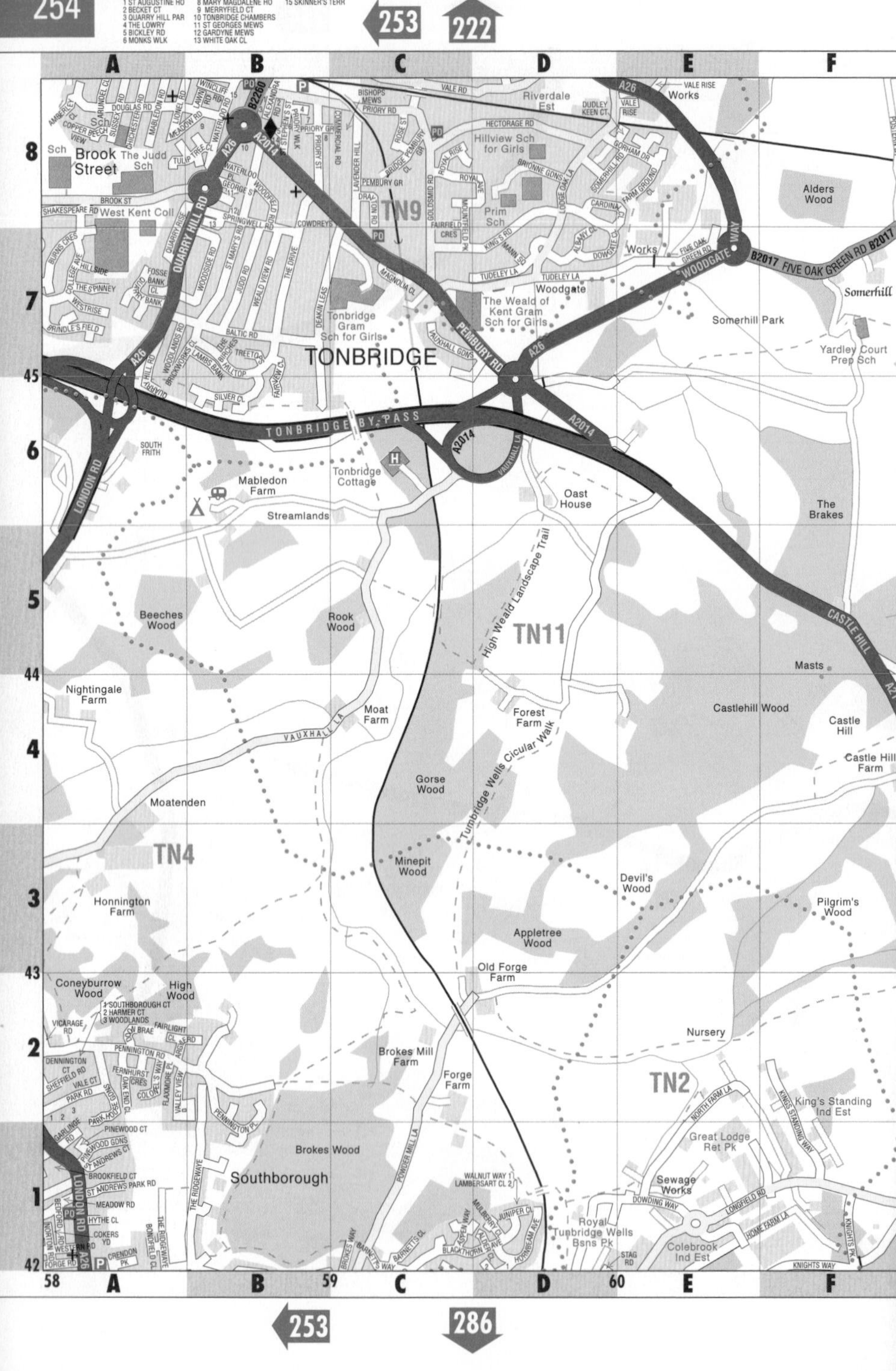

253
286

223
256

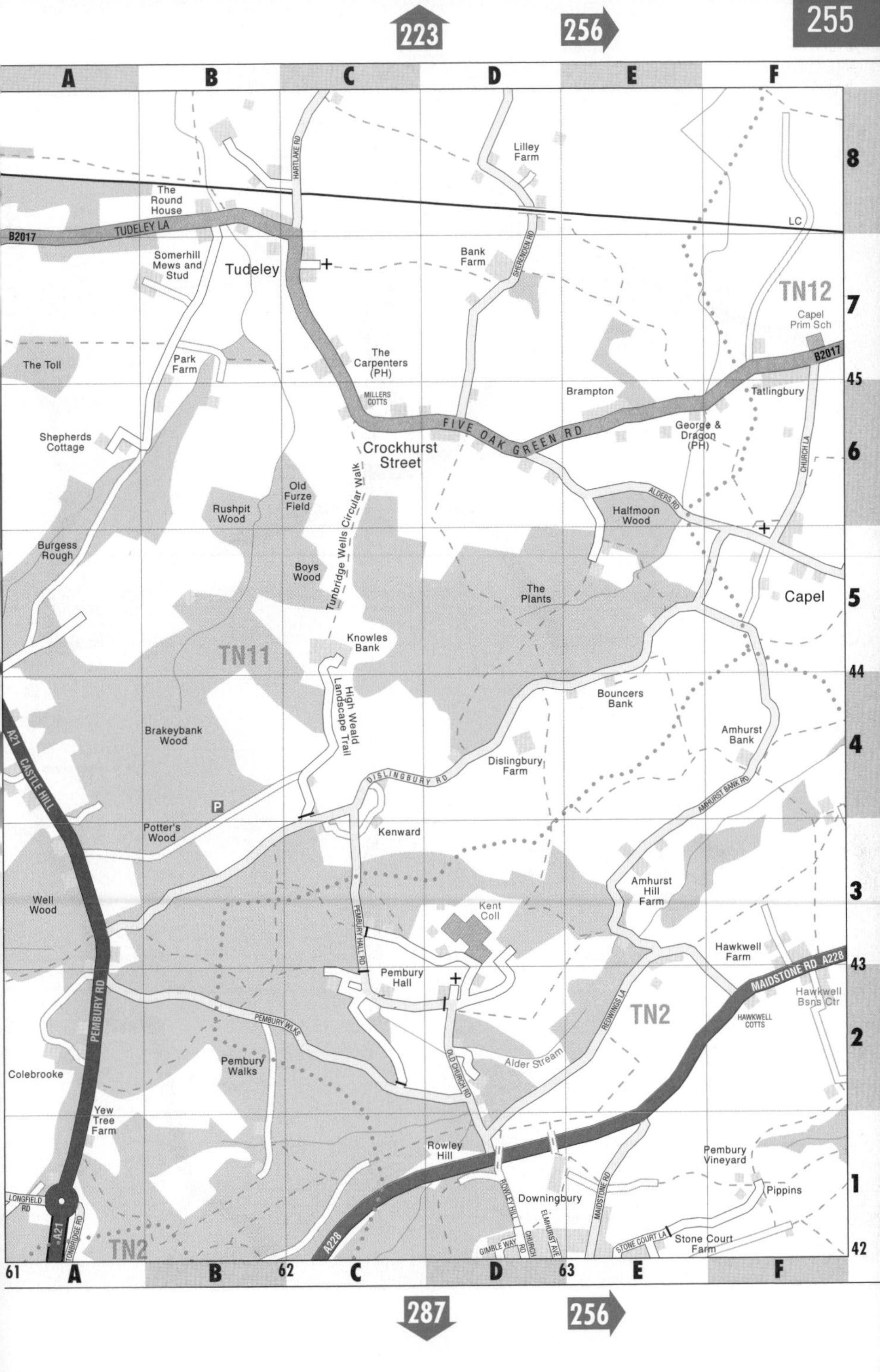
A
B
C
D
E
F
8
7
6
5
4
3
2
1
45
44
43
42
61
62
63
The Round House
TUDELEY LA
B2017
HARTLAKE RD
Lilley Farm
LC
Somerhill Mews and Stud
Tudeley
Bank Farm
SHERENDEN RD
TN12
Capel Prim Sch
The Toll
Park Farm
The Carpenters (PH)
MILLERS COTTS
Brampton
Tatlingbury
Shepherds Cottage
FIVE OAK GREEN RD
George & Dragon (PH)
Crockhurst Street
CHURCH LA
Old Furze Field
Rushpit Wood
ALDERS RD
Halfmoon Wood
Burgess Rough
Boys Wood
Tunbridge Wells Circular Walk
The Plants
Capel
Knowles Bank
TN11
High Weald Landscape Trail
Bouncers Bank
Brakeybank Wood
Amhurst Bank
A21
CASTLE HILL
DISLINGBURY RD
Dislingbury Farm
AMHURST BANK RD
Potter's Wood
Kenward
Well Wood
Amhurst Hill Farm
Kent Coll
PEMBURY HALL RD
Hawkwell Farm
MAIDSTONE RD
A228
Pembury Hall
Hawkwell Bsns Ctr
HAWKWELL COTTS
PEMBURY RD
PEMBURY WLKS
REDWINGS LA
TN2
Alder Stream
Pembury Walks
OLD CHURCH RD
Colebrooke
Yew Tree Farm
Rowley Hill
Pembury Vineyard
ROWLEY HILL
MAIDSTONE RD
Pippins
Downingbury
LONGFIELD RD
TONBRIDGE RD
A228
GIMBLE WAY
RD
CHURCH
ELMHURST AVE
STONE COURT LA
Stone Court Farm
TN2

287
256

← 255
↑ 224

A **B** **C** **D** **E** **F**

8

Moat Farm

Watersmeet Farm

Ploggs Hall

Whetsted Farm

Eastlands

DIAMOND COTTS
THE FORGE

Bridge Bsns Pk

Paddock Wood

7

WILLOW CRES
RIGHTONS WAY
FORGE CL
MOON CL

Recn Gd

Whetsted Wood

Works
ELDON WAY

FIVE OAK GREEN RD

BROOKDENE

PO PH

PALMOUR

P

Capel Grange

RIBSTON GDNS
LAXTON GDNS
BRAMLEY GDNS
NEWTON GDNS
WOODLANDS
LLINGTON RD

Five Oak Green

PEMBLE CL
TOLHURST RD

MOUNT PLEASANT
KEYWORTH CL

45

SYCHEM PL

STYLES CT

6

Lydd Farm

Brook Farm

Capel Grange Farm

Badsell Manor Farm

YEOMAN GDNS
CHALLENGERS CL
WARRINGTON RD
PINEWOOD
ASHCROFT

Putlands

HORNBEAM CL

REDWOOD PK

Alder Stream

BADSELL RD

P

MASCALL'S

5

PH
ALDERS COTTS

COLTS HILL PL

Tudeley Brook

Foal Hurst Wood

Mascalls Farm

MASCALL'S COURT RD

B2017

44

Reeds Farm

Spring Farm

Mascalls Sec Sch

4

MAIDSTONE RD

Mascalls Pound Farm

Colt's Hill

Crittenden

Brick Kiln Wood

CHANTLERS HILL

3

Lord's Wood

Badsell Park Farm

CRITTENDEN RD

Gedge's Wood

GEDGE'S HILL

43

TN2

Gedges Farm

2

Sewage Works

The Nurseries

Crundalls Farm
White Barn Farm

PRALL'S LA

Cinderhill Farm

Horse Pasture

CINDERHILL WOOD

1

Cinderhill Wood

CINDERHILL WOOD CVN SITE

Foxhole Farm

MAIDSTONE RD

STANDINGS CROSS

Brenchley Wood

FOXHOLE LA
MASCOTTS LA
CHESTNUT LA
BIRCH CL

B2160

BRENCHLEY RD

COPPESS LA

42

Albans Farm House

TN12

A **B** **C** **D** **E** **F**

64 65 66

A B C D E F

Swatlands Farm
Orchards Bsns Ctr
Depot
Works
Paddock Wood
Superstore
Cemy
Recn Gd
Sch
Church Farm
Cemy
Little Fowle Hall Farm
New Barns Farm
Rhoden Farm
Little Rhoden Farm
Sewage Works
Queen Street
Upper Fowle Hall Farm
River Teise
Park Farm
Ledger's Farm
Knell's Farm
Elm Tree (PH)
TN12
Great Old Hay
Jason's Farm
Oasthouse Farm
Mascall's Court
Catts Place
Greenfields Farm
Mascalls Sec Sch
Mile Oak
Three Tax Farm
Trenches Farm
Pearson's Green
Biggenden Farmhouse
Biggenden Barn
Longbrooks
Moatlands Park
The Knowle
Latters Toll
Parsonage Wood
Hill Top
The Crook
Great Wood
Castle Hill
Poulhurst
Poulhurst Farm

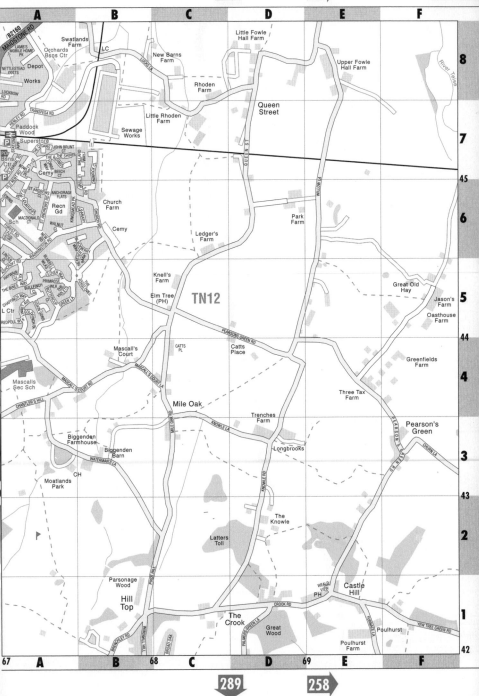

257
226

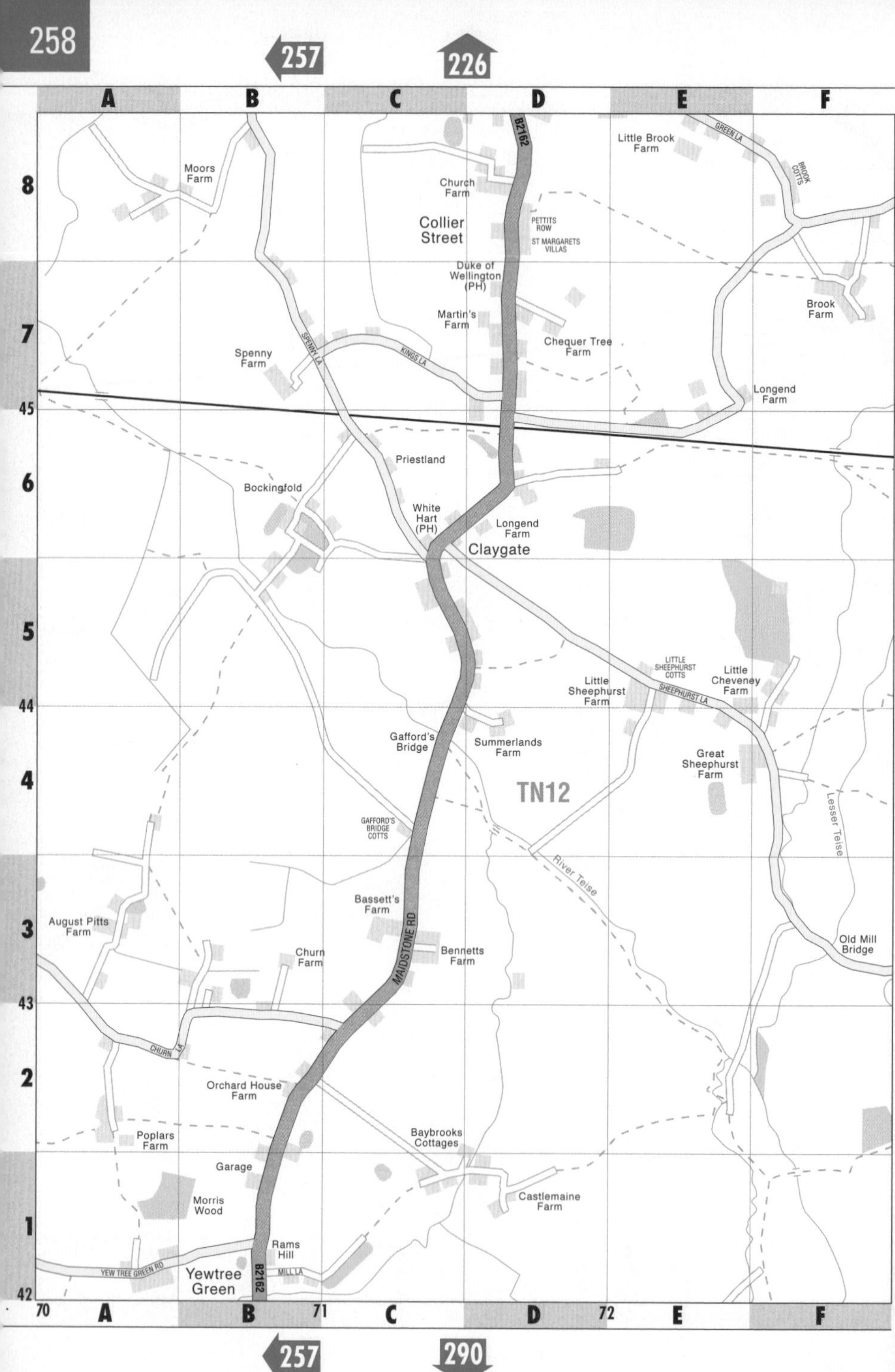
A
B
C
D
E
F
8
7
45
6
5
44
4
3
43
2
1
42
70
71
72
B2162
Moors Farm
Church Farm
Collier Street
PETTITS ROW
ST MARGARETS VILLAS
Duke of Wellington (PH)
Little Brook Farm
GREEN LA
BROOK COTTS
Brook Farm
Martin's Farm
Chequer Tree Farm
Spenny Farm
SPENNY LA
KINGS LA
Longend Farm
Priestland
Bockingfold
White Hart (PH)
Longend Farm
Claygate
LITTLE SHEEPHURST COTTS
Little Sheephurst Farm
Little Cheveney Farm
SHEEPHURST LA
Gafford's Bridge
Summerlands Farm
Great Sheephurst Farm
TN12
Lesser Teise
GAFFORD'S BRIDGE COTTS
River Teise
Bassett's Farm
August Pitts Farm
Churn Farm
Bennetts Farm
MAIDSTONE RD
Old Mill Bridge
CHURN LA
Orchard House Farm
Poplars Farm
Baybrooks Cottages
Garage
Castlemaine Farm
Morris Wood
Rams Hill
YEW TREE GREEN RD
MILL LA
Yewtree Green

257
290

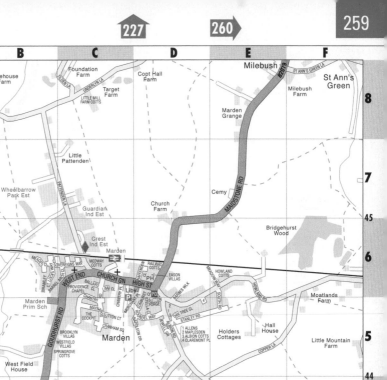

A B C D E F

Milebush
B2079
ST ANN'S GREEN LA
St Ann's Green
Milebush Farm
Spitz Bridge
Gatehouse Farm
Foundation Farm
TILDEN LA
UNDERLYN LA
Copt Hall Farm
Target Farm
LITTLE MILL FARM COTTS
Mill Farm
HUNTON RD
Marden Grange
8
Little Pattenden
PATTENDEN LA
Wheelbarrow Park Est
Cemy
MAIDSTONE RD
7
Guardian Ind Est
Church Farm
45
Crest Ind Est
Bridgehurst Wood
Marden
6
MEADES CL
SOVEREIGNS WAY
MEDWAY COTTS
HAFFENDEN CL
RAILWAY COTTS
PH
EASON VILLAS
MEADOW WAY
HOWLAND COTTS
WEST END
CHURCH GN
HIGH ST
CT LUCKS WAY
BARREL ARCH CL
BRAMLEY
PROVIDENCE CHAPEL
BALLARD CL
LIME CL
CHANTRY PL
Liby
P
PO
SUNBURST CL
STELLA CL
SUTTON FORGE
BARNES WLK
SOUTH RD
HOWLAND RD
Turkey Farmhouse
Moatlands Farm
Marden Prim Sch
CHANTRY RD
MERCHANT PL
MAYNARDS
SUTTON CT
THE COCKPIT
OAK TREE CL
STANLEY RD
ROUNDEL WAY
Hall House
CRANHAM SQ
GOUDHURST RD
NAPOLEON DR
JEWELL GR
ALBION RD
1 ALLENS
2 MAPLESDEN
3 ALBION COTTS
4 CLAREMONT PL
Holders Cottages
BROOKLYN VILLAS
Marden
5
Little Mountain Farm
WESTFIELD VILLAS
SPRINGROVE COTTS
COPPER LA
Gravelpit Farm House
West Field House
44
TN12
Cannon Farm
Roughlands Farm
Poulters Hall
4
PLAIN RD
THORN RD
Longridge Farm
The Plain
3
Thorn Farm
SHEEPHURST LA
Marden Beech
Beech Farm
Marden Thorn
Widehurst
43
Beale Farm
Cornwells Farm
2
Springfield
Susans Farm
Great Cheveney Farm
Widehurst Wood
1
Cockle Wood
Great Cheveney House
Wilden Wood
Tavern Farm
Forstal Farm
B2079
SHERENDEN LA
42

73 A B 74 C D 75 E F

259
228

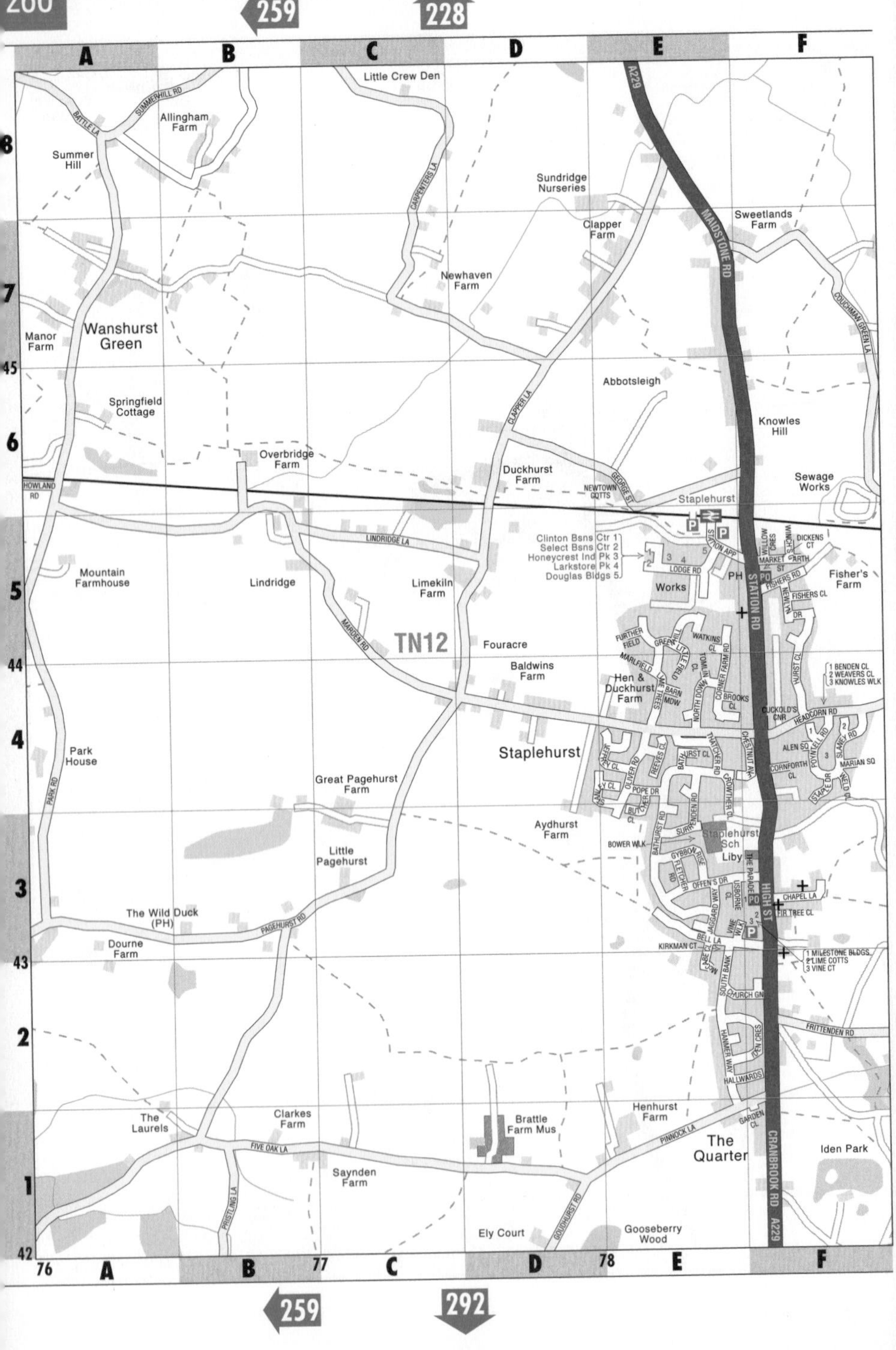
A
B
C
D
E
F
Little Crew Den
A229
SUMMERHILL RD
BATTLE LA
Allingham Farm
Summer Hill
CARPENTERS LA
Sundridge Nurseries
MAIDSTONE RD
Sweetlands Farm
Clapper Farm
Newhaven Farm
COUCHMAN GREEN LA
Wanshurst Green
Manor Farm
45
Abbotsleigh
Springfield Cottage
CLAPPER LA
Knowles Hill
Overbridge Farm
Duckhurst Farm
GEORGE ST
Sewage Works
HOWLAND RD
NEWTOWN COTTS
Staplehurst
LINDRIDGE LA
STATION APP
Clinton Bsns Ctr 1
Select Bsns Ctr 2
Honeycrest Ind Pk 3
Larkstore Pk 4
Douglas Bldgs 5
LODGE RD
WILLOW CRES
WINCH'S GARTH
DICKENS CT
MARKET ST
FISHERS RD
Mountain Farmhouse
Lindridge
Limekiln Farm
Works
PH
STATION RD
FISHERS CL
Fisher's Farm
NEWLYN DR
MARDEN RD
TN12
Fouracre
FURTHER FIELD
GREEN HILL
WATKINS CL
LITTLE FIELD
TOMLIN CL
CORNER FARM RD
44
Baldwins Farm
MARLFIELD
HURST CL
1 BENDEN CL
2 WEAVERS CL
3 KNOWLES WLK
Hen & Duckhurst Farm
LIME TREES
BARN MDW
NORTH DOWN
BROOKS CL
CUCKOLD'S CNR
HEADCORN RD
Park House
Staplehurst
JEFFERY CL
REEVES CL
THATCHER RD
CHESTNUT AV
ALEN SQ
POYNTELL RD
SLANEY RD
OLIVER RD
BATHURST CL
CORNFORTH CL
MARIAN SQ
Great Pagehurst Farm
POPE DR
CROWTHER CL
STAPLE DR
WEALD CL
PARK RD
BUTCHER CL
BATHURST RD
SURRENDEN RD
Aydhurst Farm
BOWER WLK
Staplehurst Sch
Liby
Little Pagehurst
GYBBON RISE
FLETCHER RD
THE PARADE
OFFEN'S DR
USBORNE CL
HIGH ST
CHAPEL LA
PO
FIR TREE CL
The Wild Duck (PH)
JAGGARD WAY
VINE WLK
PAGEHURST RD
Dourne Farm
BELL LA
KIRKMAN CT
1 MILESTONE BLDGS
2 LIME COTTS
3 VINE CT
43
SOUTH BANK
CHURCH GN
FRITTENDEN RD
HAMMER WAY
IDEN CRES
HALLWARDS
Henhurst Farm
GARDEN CL
The Laurels
Clarkes Farm
Brattle Farm Mus
PINNOCK LA
The Quarter
CRANBROOK RD
Iden Park
FIVE OAK LA
Saynden Farm
PRISTLING LA
GOUDHURST RD
Ely Court
Gooseberry Wood
42
76
77
78
8
7
6
5
4
3
2
1

259
292

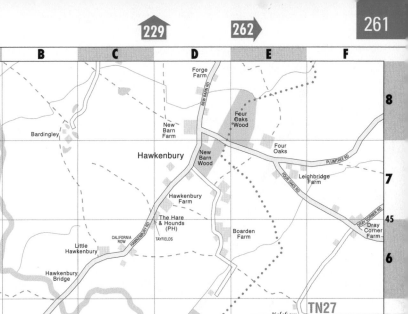

A B C D E F

8
7
45
6
5
44
4
3
43
2
1
42

Forge Farm

Four Oaks Wood

New Barn Farm

Hawkenbury

New Barn Wood

Four Oaks

Bardingley

Sweetlands Couchman Green

Newstead Farm

Hawkenbury Farm

Leighbridge Farm

PLUMTREE RD

DRAY CORNER RD

Dray Corner Farm

The Hare & Hounds (PH)

California Row

Little Hawkenbury

TAYFIELDS

Boarden Farm

HAWKENBURY RD

Hawkenbury Bridge

Turley Farm

Kelsham Farm

TN27

Sewage Farm

THE FLEX

COUCHMAN GREEN LA

SWEETLANDS LA

Slaney Place

River Beult

TN12

Cottons Farm

Spills Hill Farm

Place Farm

Works

RADDON RD

Sunny Mead

Chickenden Farm

CH

Crab Tree Farm

Oak Tree Farm

CHICKENDEN LA

Spilsill Farm

CRADDOCK LA

Spilsill Court

Bailey Farm

Little Craddock

Exhurst Manor

TRITTENDEN RD

Folly Farm

Iden Croft Herbs

Nursery

Staplehurst Manor

Maplehurst Farm

Park Wood

PARK WOOD LA

MILL LA

Broadlake

STAPLEHURST RD

The Twins

TN17

Sinkhurst Green

Pullen Barn

Sandhurst Bridge Farm

Appleton Farm House

Sandhurst Bridge

SANDHURST CROSS

Great Hungerden Farm

79 A B 80 C D 81 E F

261
230

	A	B	C	D	E	F

8

Plumtree Green

Little Peckham Farm

Plumtrees Farm

Pinkhorn Farm

Barradale Farm

Little Tilden

Nursery

Kattlebury Rd

Tattlebury

Tilden

7

Stonestile Bsns Pk

Sunnyside Farm

Rosemead Sons Nursery

Witherden Farm

45

Providence Pl

Sunhill Farm

Four Oaks Rd

Hazelpits Farm

Woodside Farm

6

Summerhill Farm

Hoggs Bridge

The Ringles (Nursery)

Black Mill Farm

Millbank

Headcorn Prim Sch

Thatch Barn Rd

Liby

Vineyard

5

Stephen's Bridge

Moat Rd

White Horse (PH)

Chantry Farm

Sherway

Sewage Works

CHURCH WLK

Kings Arms (PH)

HIGH ST

STATION RD

WHEELER ST

Frank's Bridge

Little East End

44

Kettle Bridge

Pell Bridge

Rushford Cl

THE MEWS
FOREMAN'S WLK
Foreman Ctr

Headcorn

Smarden Rd

Waterlane Farm

Forstal Farm

River Beult

TN27

Headcorn

4

New House Farm

Dairy

New Bridge

Wick Farm

3

Bletchenden

Headcorn Airfield

43

Brook Wood Farm

Hammer Stream

Brook Wood

Waterman Quarter

BIDDENDEN RD

The Hall

2

Stanley House

Vine Farm

TN17

Little Brookwood

Curtis Farm

Tile Barn Farm

1

Little Hungerden Farm

Coldharbour Farm

42

82	A		B	83	C		D	84	E		F

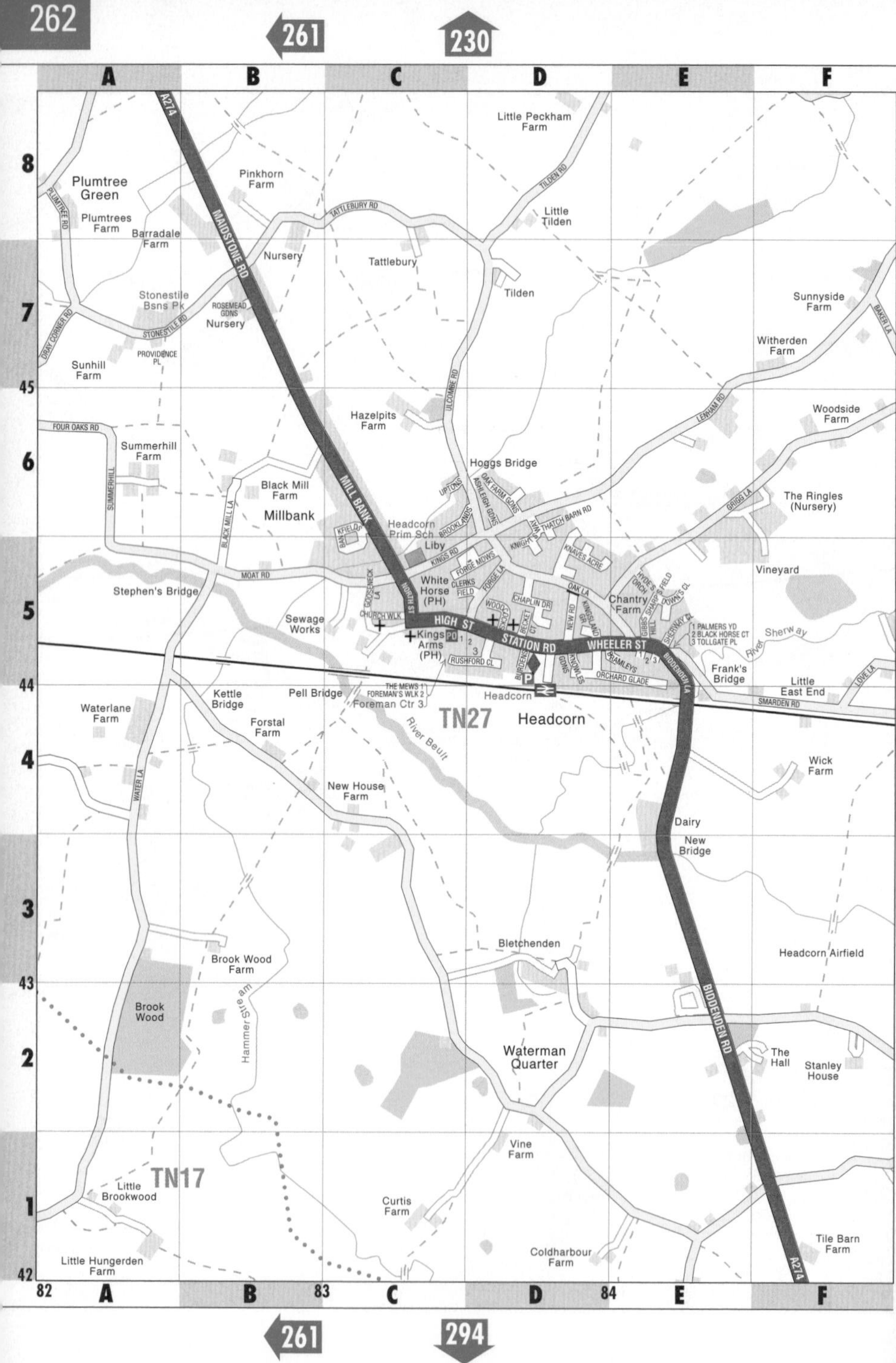

261
294

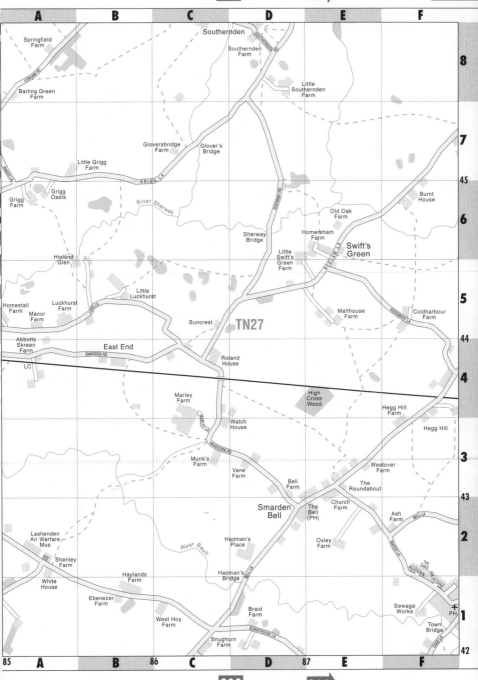
231
264

A B C D E F
Southernden
Springfield Farm
Southernden Farm
SOUTHERNDEN RD
LENHAM RD
Little Southernden Farm
Barling Green Farm
Gloversbridge Farm
Glover's Bridge
Little Grigg Farm
BAKER LA
GRIGG LA
Grigg Oasts
Grigg Farm
River Sherway
SHERWAY RD
Burnt House
Old Oak Farm
Sherway Bridge
Homersham Farm
Swift's Green
BEDLAM LA
Little Swift's Green Farm
Hieland Glen
Little Luckhurst
Homestall Farm
Luckhurst Farm
Manor Farm
LOVE LA
Malthouse Farm
ROSEMARY LA
Coldharbour Farm
Suncrest
TN27
Abbotts Skreen Farm
East End
SMARDEN RD
Roland House
LC
Marley Farm
MARLEY LA
High Cross Wood
Hegg Hill Farm
Hegg Hill
Watch House
HEADCORN RD
Munk's Farm
Vane Farm
Westover Farm
Bell Farm
The Roundabout
Smarden Bell
The Bell (PH)
Church Farm
Ash Farm
MILL LA
Lashenden Air Warfare Mus
Hadman's Place
Oxley Farm
River Beult
WATER LA
Shenley Farm
THE OAKS
ASHENDEN
THE ACORNS
Haylands Farm
Hadman's Bridge
BELL LA
White House
Ebenezer Farm
Sewage Works
PH
Braid Farm
West Hoy Farm
Town Bridge
BURNTHOUSE LA
Snughorn Farm
CAGE LA
8 7 45 6 5 44 4 3 43 2 1 42
85 86 87

263
232

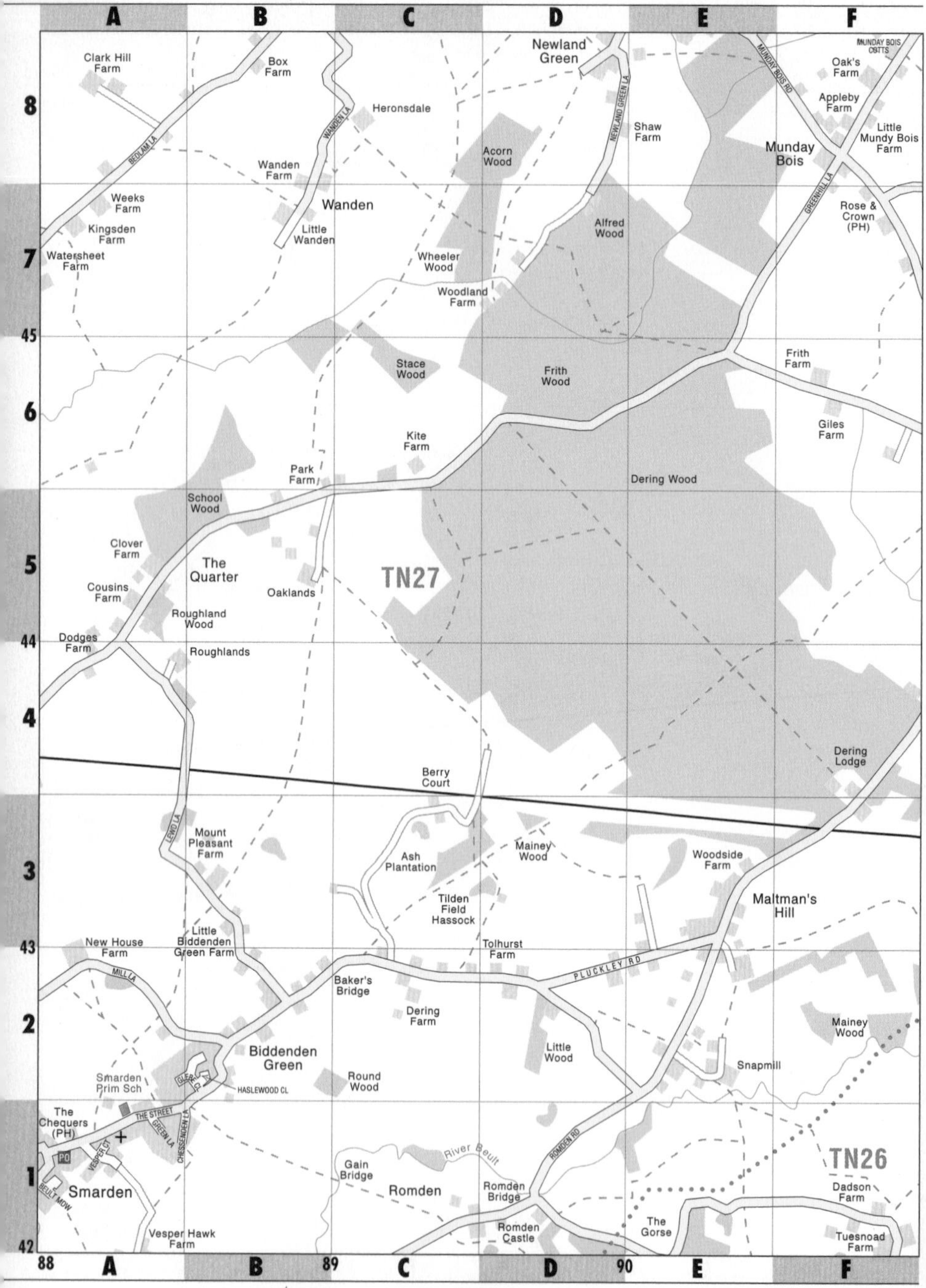

	A	B	C	D	E	F

Clark Hill Farm

Box Farm

Newland Green

MUNDAY BOIS OBITS

Oak's Farm

Appleby Farm

8

Heronsdale

Shaw Farm

Little Mundy Bois Farm

Munday Bois

BEULAH LA

WANDEN LA

NEWLAND GREEN RD

MUNDAY BOIS RD

Wanden Farm

Acorn Wood

Rose & Crown (PH)

Weeks Farm

Wanden

Alfred Wood

GREENHILL LA

Kingsden Farm

Little Wanden

7

Watersheet Farm

Wheeler Wood

Woodland Farm

45

Stace Wood

Frith Wood

Frith Farm

6

Park Farm

Kite Farm

Giles Farm

School Wood

Dering Wood

Clover Farm

5

The Quarter

TN27

Cousins Farm

Oaklands

Roughland Wood

44

Dodges Farm

Roughlands

4

Dering Lodge

Berry Court

LEWIS LA

Mount Pleasant Farm

Ash Plantation

Mainey Wood

Woodside Farm

3

Maltman's Hill

New House Farm

Little Biddenden Green Farm

Tilden Field Hassock

Tolhurst Farm

PLUCKLEY RD

43

MILL LA

Baker's Bridge

Dering Farm

Mainey Wood

2

CRESSENDEN LA

Biddenden Green

Round Wood

Little Wood

Snapmill

Smarden Prim Sch

HASLEWOOD CL

ROMDEN RD

The Chequers (PH)

THE STREET

BELL LA

River Beult

TN26

PD

1

Gain Bridge

Romden

Romden Bridge

The Gorse

Dadson Farm

Smarden

BELL MDW

Vesper Hawk Farm

Romden Castle

Tuesnoad Farm

42

88 | A | B | 89 | C | | D | 90 | E | | F |

263
296

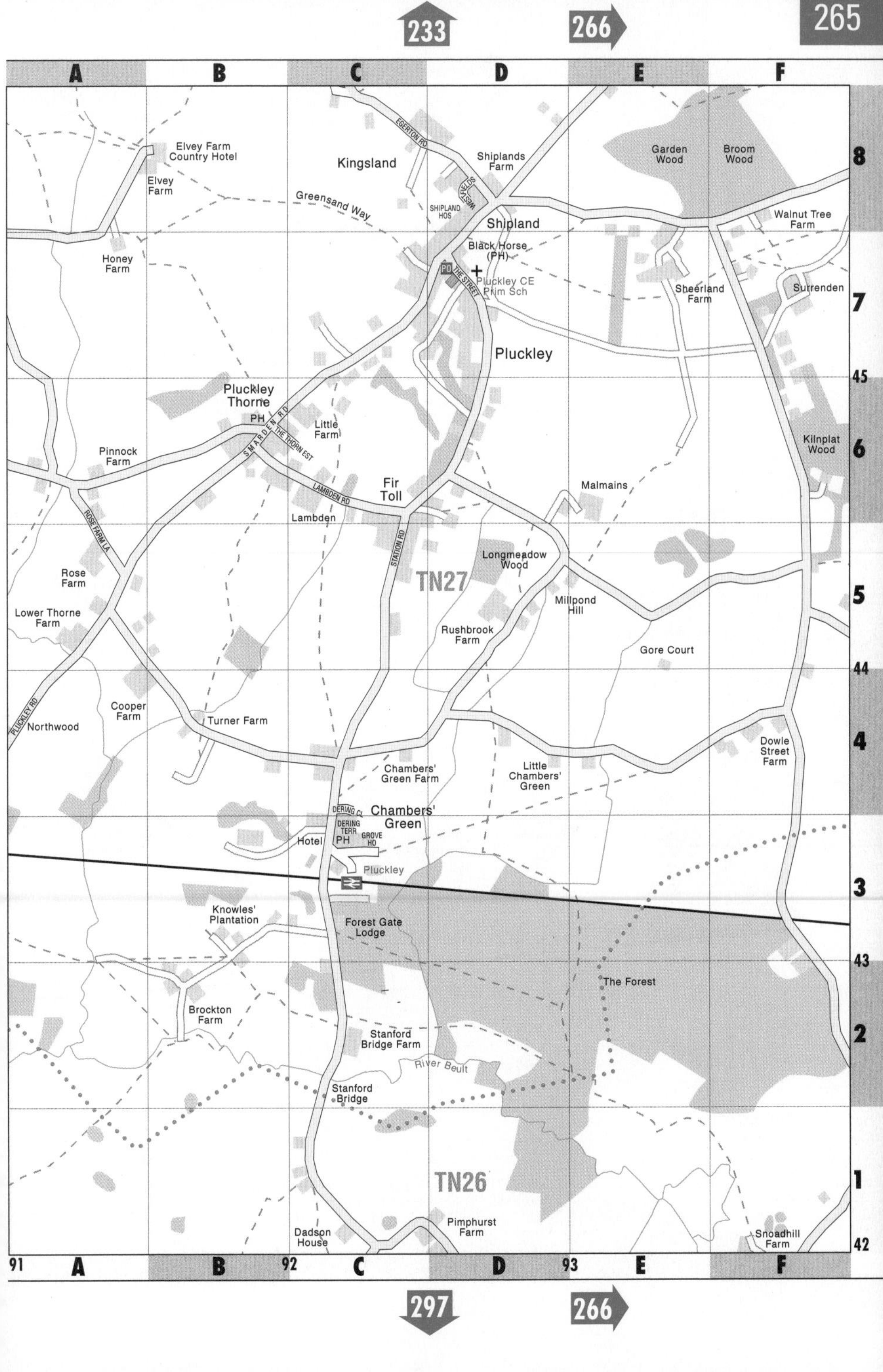

233
266

A   **B**   **C**   **D**   **E**   **F**

Elvey Farm Country Hotel

Kingsland

Shiplands Farm

Garden Wood

Broom Wood

8

Elvey Farm

Greensand Way

SHIPLAND HOS

Walnut Tree Farm

Honey Farm

Shipland

Black Horse (PH)

Pluckley CE Prim Sch

PO

Sheerland Farm

Surrenden

7

Pluckley

45

Pluckley Thorne

PH

THE THORN EST

Little Farm

Kilnplat Wood

6

Pinnock Farm

LAMBDEN RD

Fir Toll

Malmains

Lambden

ROSE FARM LA

STATION RD

TN27

Longmeadow Wood

Rose Farm

Millpond Hill

5

Lower Thorne Farm

Rushbrook Farm

Gore Court

44

Cooper Farm

Turner Farm

Dowle Street Farm

4

Northwood

PLUCKLEY RD

Chambers' Green Farm

Little Chambers' Green

DERING CL

DERING TERR

GROVE RD

Chambers' Green

Hotel

PH

Pluckley

3

Knowles' Plantation

Forest Gate Lodge

43

The Forest

Brockton Farm

Stanford Bridge Farm

River Beult

2

Stanford Bridge

TN26

1

Dadson House

Pimphurst Farm

Snoadhill Farm

42

91   **A**   **B**   92   **C**   **D**   93   **E**   **F**

297
266

265
234

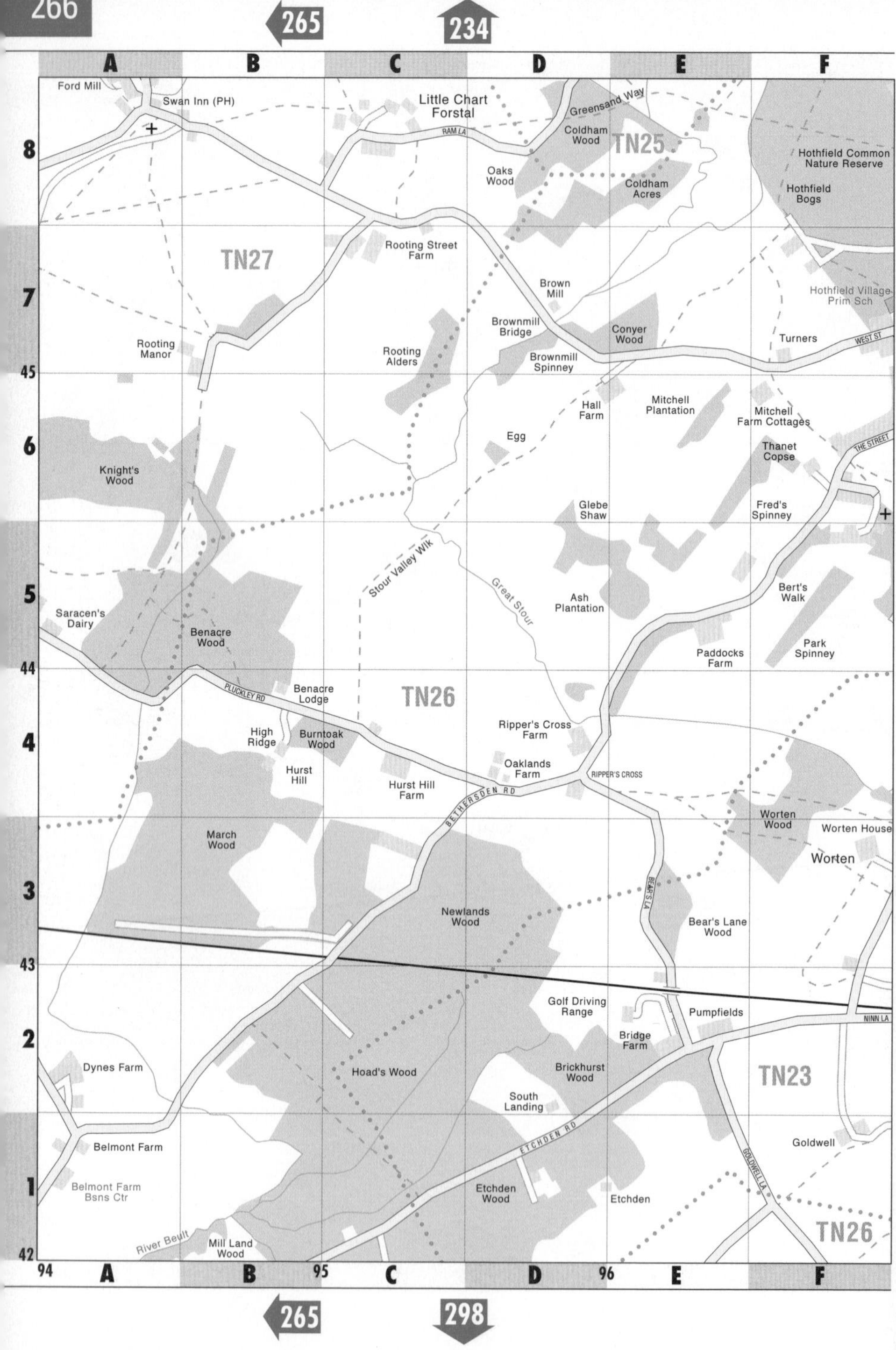
A
B
C
D
E
F
8
7
45
6
5
44
4
3
43
2
1
42
94
95
96
Ford Mill
Swan Inn (PH)
Little Chart
Forstal
RAM LA
Greensand Way
Coldham
Wood
TN25
Hothfield Common
Nature Reserve
Hothfield
Bogs
Oaks
Wood
Coldham
Acres
TN27
Rooting Street
Farm
Brown
Mill
Hothfield Village
Prim Sch
Rooting
Manor
Brownmill
Bridge
Rooting
Alders
Conyer
Wood
Turners
WEST ST
Brownmill
Spinney
Hall
Farm
Mitchell
Plantation
Mitchell
Farm Cottages
Egg
THE STREET
Thanet
Copse
Knight's
Wood
Glebe
Shaw
Fred's
Spinney
Stour Valley Wlk
Great Stour
Saracen's
Dairy
Benacre
Wood
Ash
Plantation
Bert's
Walk
Paddocks
Farm
Park
Spinney
PLUCKLEY RD
Benacre
Lodge
TN26
Ripper's Cross
Farm
High
Ridge
Burntoak
Wood
Hurst
Hill
Oaklands
Farm
RIPPER'S CROSS
Hurst Hill
Farm
BETHERSDEN RD
March
Wood
Worten
Wood
Worten House
Worten
BEAR'S LA
Newlands
Wood
Bear's Lane
Wood
Golf Driving
Range
Pumpfields
NINN LA
Bridge
Farm
Dynes Farm
Hoad's Wood
Brickhurst
Wood
TN23
South
Landing
ETCHDEN RD
Belmont Farm
Goldwell
GOLDWELL LA
Belmont Farm
Bsns Ctr
Etchden
Wood
Etchden
River Beult
Mill Land
Wood
TN26

265
298

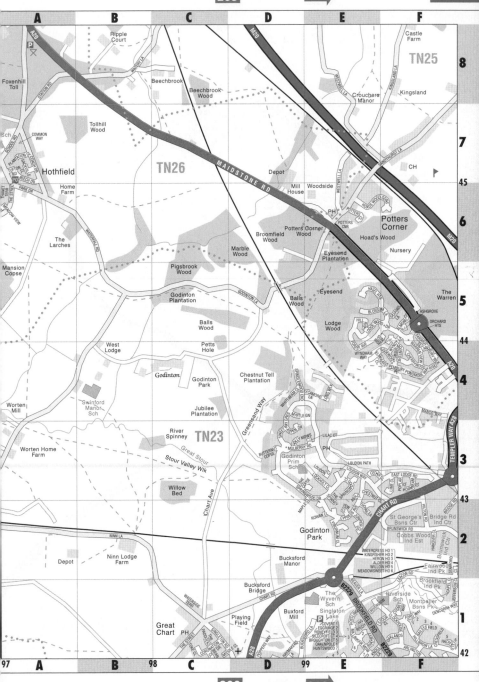

A B C D E F
8 7 45 6 5 44 4 3 43 2 1 42
97 98 99
TN25
TN26
TN23
A20
M20
Ripple Court
Foxenhill Toll
Beechbrook
Beechbrook Wood
Crouchers Manor
Kingsland
Castle Farm
Tollhill Wood
Hothfield
Home Farm
MAIDSTONE RD
Depot
Mill House
Woodside
CH
Potters Corner
Potters Corner Wood
Broomfield Wood
Hoad's Wood
Nursery
The Larches
Marble Wood
Eyesend Plantation
Mansion Copse
Pigsbrook Wood
Godinton Plantation
Eyesend
Balls Wood
Lodge Wood
The Warren
Balls Wood
West Lodge
Petts Hole
Godinton
Godinton Park
Chestnut Tell Plantation
Swinford Manor Sch
Worten Mill
Jubilee Plantation
Greensand Way
River Spinney
Worten Home Farm
Great Stour
Stour Valley Wlk
Willow Bed
Chart Ave
Godinton Prim Sch
Godinton Park
St George's Bsns Ctr
Bridge Rd Ind Ctr
Cobbs Wood Ind Est
Brunswick Ind Ctr
Fairwood Ind Pk
Brookfield Ind Pk
Depot
Ninn Lodge Farm
Bucksford Manor
Bucksford Bridge
The Wyvern Sch
Singleton Lake
Riverside Sch
Montpelier Bsns Pk
Buxford Mill
Playing Field
Great Chart
PH
TEMPLER WAY A28
CHART RD
B2229 BROOKFIELD RD
A28
NINN LA
WATERFALL RD
GODINTON LA
WATERY LA
STATION RD
WESTWELL LA
KINGSLAND LA
SANDYHURST LA
WATERCRESS HO 1
KINGFISHER HO 2
HERON HO 3
ALDER HO 4
WILLOW HO 5
MEADOWSWEET HO 6
COVERT 1
EGGRINGE 2
HONEYFIELD 3
SILECROFT CT 4
BROUGHTON CT 5
OAKENPOLE 6
HUNTSWOOD 7

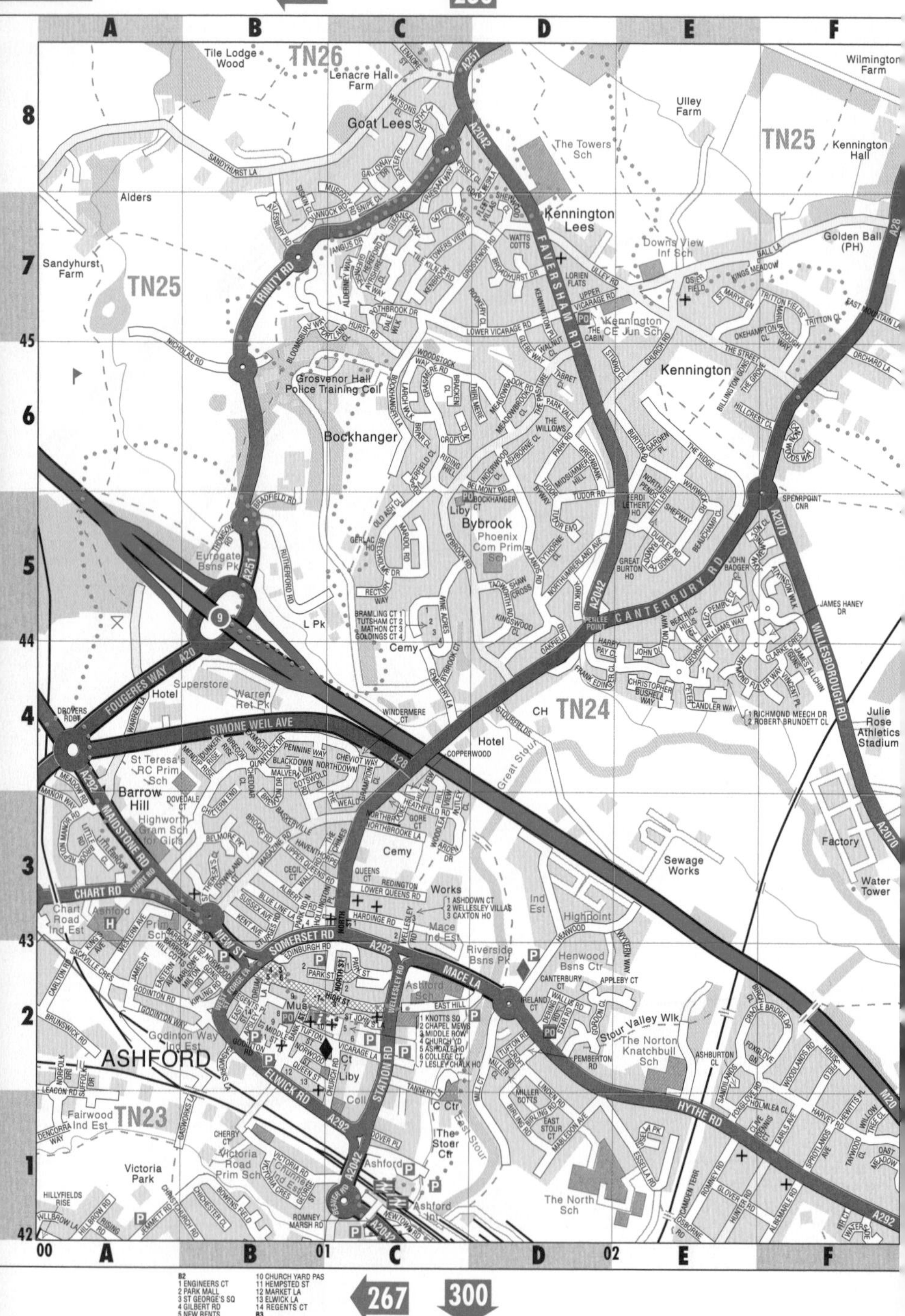

B2
1 ENGINEERS CT
2 PARK MALL
3 ST GEORGE'S SQ
4 GILBERT RD
5 NEW RENTS
6 CASTLE ST
7 KINGS PAR
8 COUNTY SQ
9 TUFTON WLK

10 CHURCH YARD PAS
11 HEMPSTED ST
12 MARKET LA
13 ELWICK LA
14 REGENTS CT
B3
1 BARROW HILL TERR
2 BARROW HILL PL
3 GRAVEL WLK
4 WOLSELEY PL

237
270

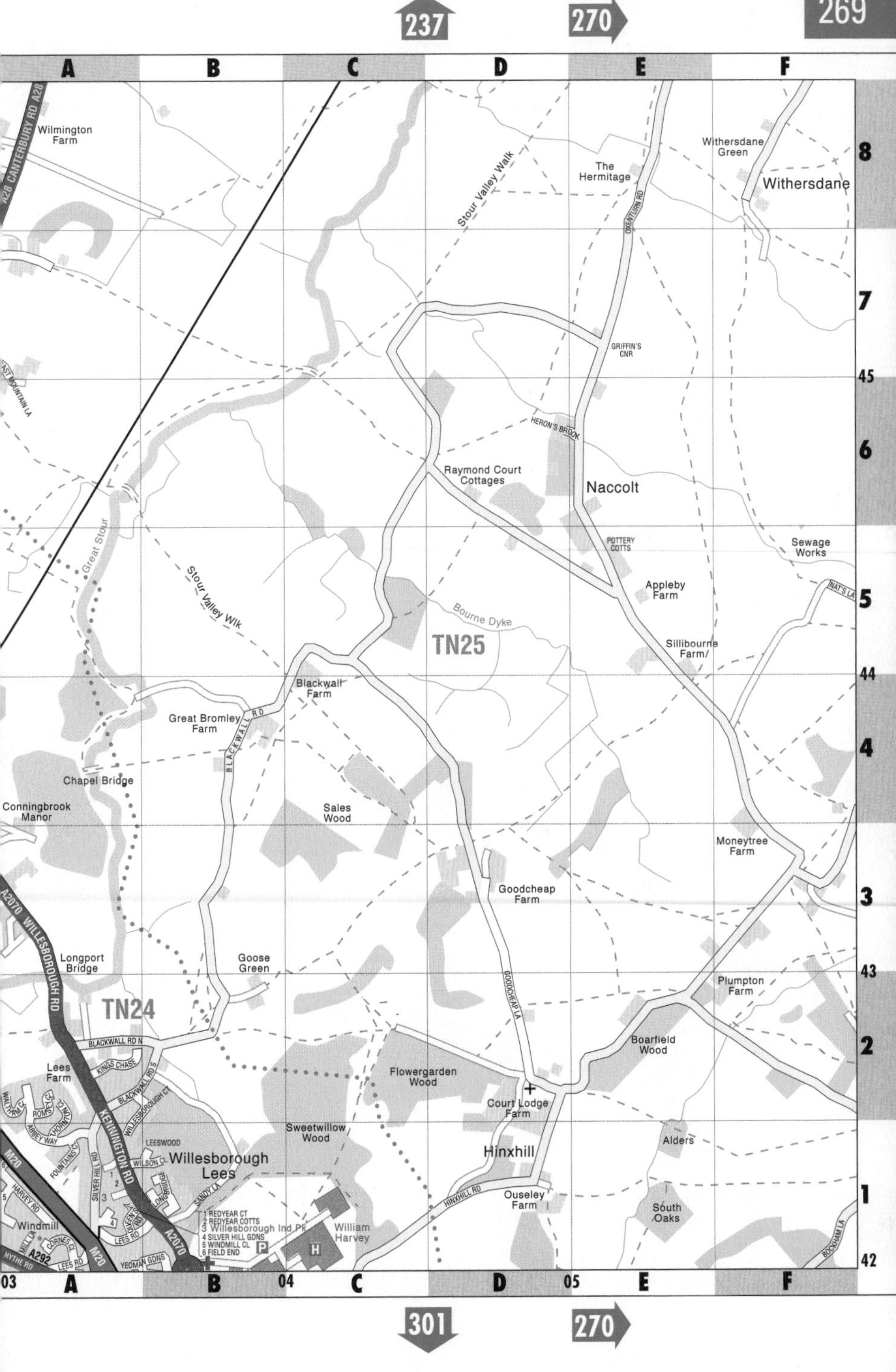
A
B
C
D
E
F
A28 CANTERBURY RD A28
Wilmington Farm
Stour Valley Walk
The Hermitage
OKENTURN RD
Withersdane Green
Withersdane
8
7
GRIFFIN'S CNR
45
EAST MOUNTAIN LA
HERON'S BROOK
6
Raymond Court Cottages
Naccolt
Great Stour
POTTERY COTTS
Sewage Works
Stour Valley Wlk
Appleby Farm
NAT'S LA
5
Bourne Dyke
TN25
Sillibourne Farm
44
Blackwall Farm
Great Bromley Farm
BLACKWALL RD
4
Chapel Bridge
Sales Wood
Conningbrook Manor
Moneytree Farm
Goodcheap Farm
3
A2070 WILLESBOROUGH RD
Longport Bridge
Goose Green
GOODCHEAP LA
43
Plumpton Farm
TN24
BLACKWALL RD N
Boarfield Wood
2
Lees Farm
KINGS CHASE
BLACKWALL RD S
WILLESBOROUGH CT
Flowergarden Wood
Court Lodge Farm
ROMSEY CL
ABBEY WAY
HORNTON CL
KENNINGTON RD
Sweetwillow Wood
Alders
M20
FOUNTAINS CL
LEESWOOD
SILVER HILL RD
WILSON CL
Willesborough Lees
Hinxhill
HARVEY RD
LONGBRIDGE
SANDY LA
HINXHILL RD
Ouseley Farm
1
South Oaks
QUEEN'S RD
LEES RD
1 REDYEAR CT
2 REDYEAR COTTS
3 Willesborough Ind Pk
4 SILVER HILL GDNS
5 WINDMILL CL
6 FIELD END
William Harvey
Windmill
MILL LA
CORNES CL
A2070
A292
HYTHE RD
LEES RD
YEOMAN GDNS
BOCKHAM LA
42
03
04
05

301
270

269
238

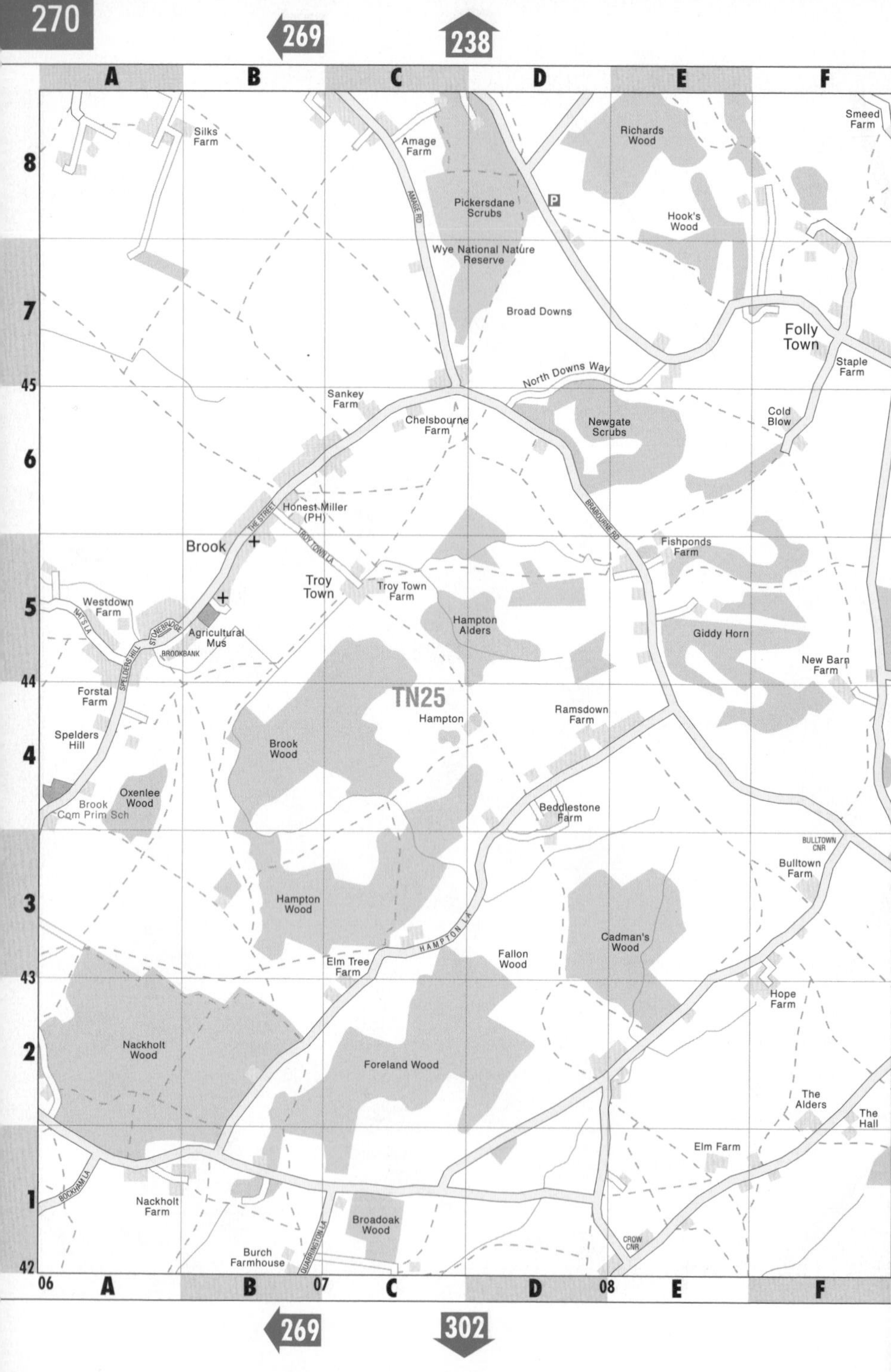
A
B
C
D
E
F
8
7
45
6
5
44
4
3
43
2
1
42
06
07
08
Silks Farm
Amage Farm
AMAGE RD
Richards Wood
Smeed Farm
Pickersdane Scrubs
Hook's Wood
Wye National Nature Reserve
Broad Downs
Folly Town
North Downs Way
Staple Farm
Sankey Farm
Chelsbourne Farm
Newgate Scrubs
Cold Blow
THE STREET
Honest Miller (PH)
TROY TOWN LA
BRABOURNE RD
Brook
Fishponds Farm
Troy Town
Troy Town Farm
Westdown Farm
NATS LA
STOWBRIDGE
Agricultural Mus
Hampton Alders
Giddy Horn
BROOKBANK
SPELDERS HILL
New Barn Farm
Forstal Farm
TN25
Hampton
Ramsdown Farm
Spelders Hill
Brook Wood
Oxenlee Wood
Brook Com Prim Sch
Beddlestone Farm
BULLTOWN CNR
Bulltown Farm
Hampton Wood
Cadman's Wood
HAMPTON LA
Fallon Wood
Elm Tree Farm
Hope Farm
Nackholt Wood
Foreland Wood
The Alders
The Hall
Elm Farm
BOCKHAM LA
Nackholt Farm
Broadoak Wood
QUARRINGTON LA
CROW CNR
Burch Farmhouse
A
B
07
C
D
08
E
F

269
302

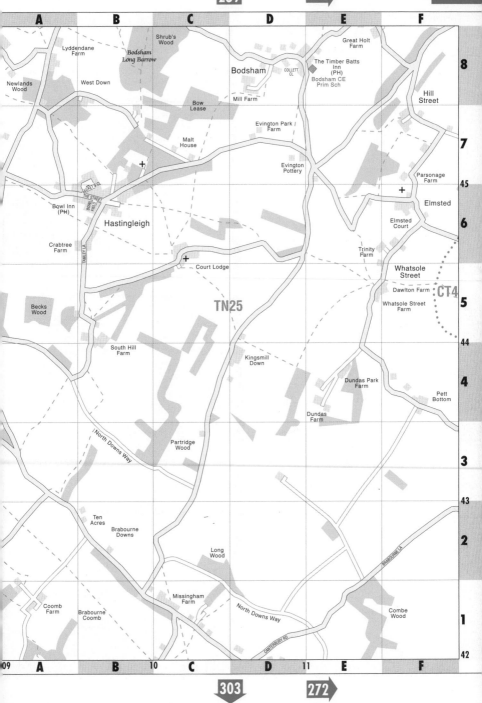

8

7

45

6

5

44

4

43

2

1

42

A B C D E F

Lyddendane Farm

Shrub's Wood

Bodsham Long Barrow

Great Holt Farm

Bodsham

COLLETT CL

The Timber Batts Inn (PH)

Bodsham CE Prim Sch

Hill Street

Newlands Wood

West Down

Bow Lease

Mill Farm

Evington Park Farm

Malt House

Evington Pottery

Parsonage Farm

Elmsted

COLLETT'S CL

THE STREET

BOWL INN LA

Bowl Inn (PH)

Hastingleigh

Elmsted Court

Crabtree Farm

TANBY LA

Court Lodge

Trinity Farm

Whatsole Street

Dawlton Farm

CT4

Becks Wood

TN25

Whatsole Street Farm

South Hill Farm

Kingsmill Down

Dundas Park Farm

Pett Bottom

Dundas Farm

North Downs Way

Partridge Wood

Ten Acres

Brabourne Downs

Long Wood

BRABOURNE LA

Coomb Farm

Brabourne Coomb

Missingham Farm

North Downs Way

Combe Wood

CANTERBURY RD

09 A B 10 C D 11 E F

271
240

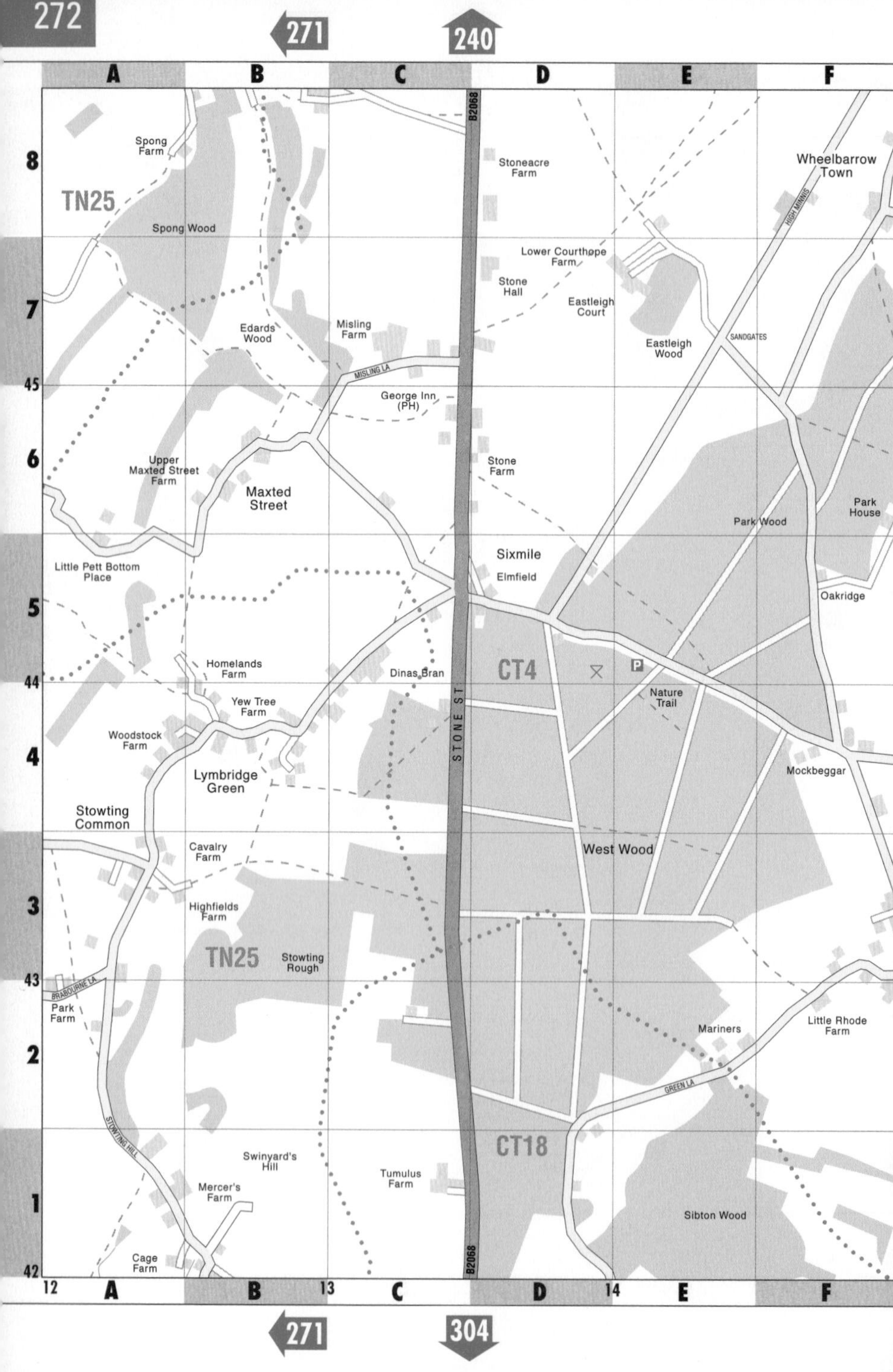
A
B
C
D
E
F
8
7
45
6
5
44
4
3
43
2
1
42
12
13
14
B2068
Spong Farm
TN25
Spong Wood
Stoneacre Farm
Wheelbarrow Town
HIGH MINNIS
Lower Courthope Farm
Stone Hall
Eastleigh Court
Edards Wood
Misling Farm
Eastleigh Wood
SANDGATES
MISLING LA
George Inn (PH)
Upper Maxted Street Farm
Maxted Street
Stone Farm
Park Wood
Park House
Sixmile
Elmfield
Little Pett Bottom Place
Oakridge
Homelands Farm
CT4
Dinas Bran
Nature Trail
Yew Tree Farm
STONE ST
Woodstock Farm
Lymbridge Green
Mockbeggar
Stowting Common
Cavalry Farm
West Wood
Highfields Farm
TN25
Stowting Rough
BRABOURNE LA
Park Farm
Mariners
Little Rhode Farm
GREEN LA
STOWTING HILL
CT18
Swinyard's Hill
Tumulus Farm
Mercer's Farm
Sibton Wood
Cage Farm

271
304

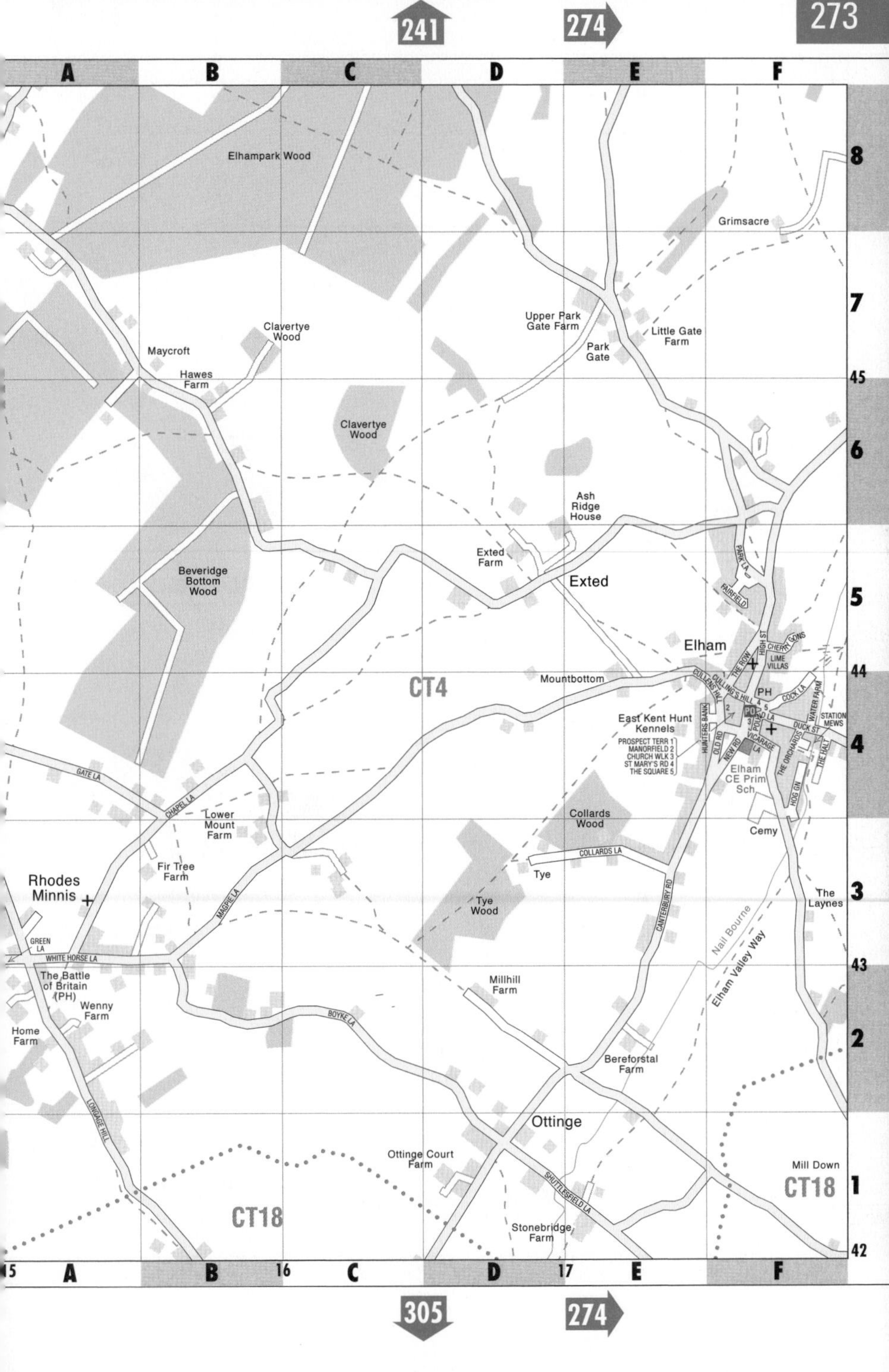

Elhampark Wood

Grimsacre

Clavertye Wood

Maycroft

Hawes Farm

Upper Park Gate Farm

Park Gate

Little Gate Farm

Clavertye Wood

Ash Ridge House

Beveridge Bottom Wood

Exted Farm

Exted

Elham

CT4

Mountbottom

PH

STATION MEWS

East Kent Hunt Kennels

PROSPECT TERR 1 MANORFIELD 2 CHURCH WLK 3 ST MARY'S RD 4 THE SQUARE 5

GATE LA

Collards Wood

Elham CE Prim Sch

Cemy

Lower Mount Farm

Fir Tree Farm

COLLARDS LA

Tye

The Laynes

Rhodes Minnis

Tye Wood

Nail Bourne

Elham Valley Way

GREEN LA WHITE HORSE LA

The Battle of Britain (PH)

Wenny Farm

Home Farm

BOYNE LA

Millhill Farm

Bereforstal Farm

Ottinge

Ottinge Court Farm

SHUTTLESFIELD LA

Mill Down

CT18

CT18

Stonebridge Farm

273
242

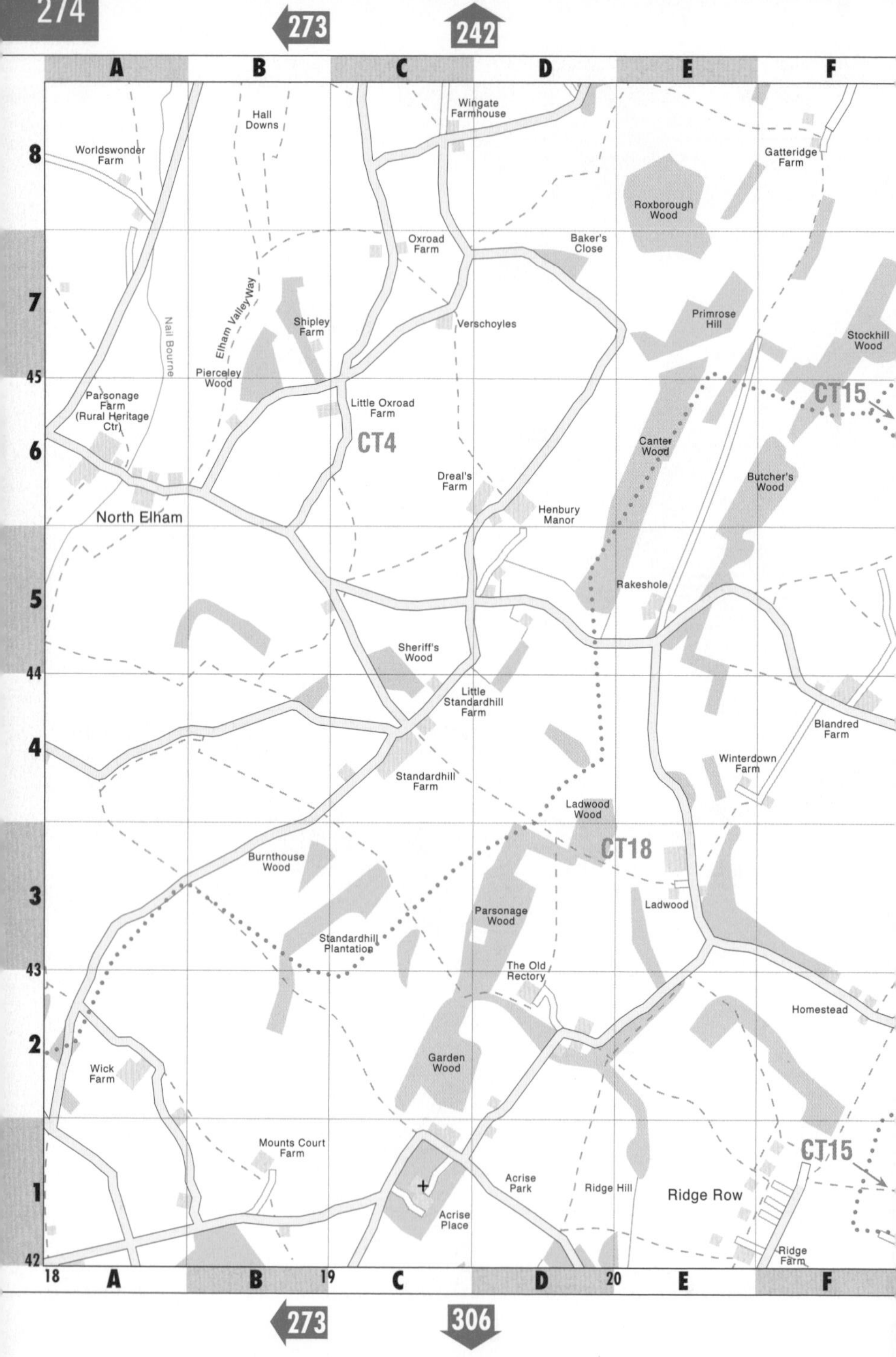
A
B
C
D
E
F
8
7
45
6
5
44
4
3
43
2
1
42
18
19
20
Wingate Farmhouse
Hall Downs
Worldswonder Farm
Gatteridge Farm
Roxborough Wood
Oxroad Farm
Baker's Close
Elham Valley Way
Nail Bourne
Shipley Farm
Verschoyles
Primrose Hill
Stockhill Wood
Pierceley Wood
Parsonage Farm (Rural Heritage Ctr)
Little Oxroad Farm
CT15
CT4
Canter Wood
Butcher's Wood
Dreal's Farm
Henbury Manor
North Elham
Rakeshole
Sheriff's Wood
Little Standardhill Farm
Blandred Farm
Winterdown Farm
Standardhill Farm
Ladwood Wood
CT18
Burnthouse Wood
Ladwood
Parsonage Wood
Standardhill Plantation
The Old Rectory
Homestead
Garden Wood
Wick Farm
Mounts Court Farm
CT15
Acrise Park
Ridge Hill
Ridge Row
Acrise Place
Ridge Farm

273
306

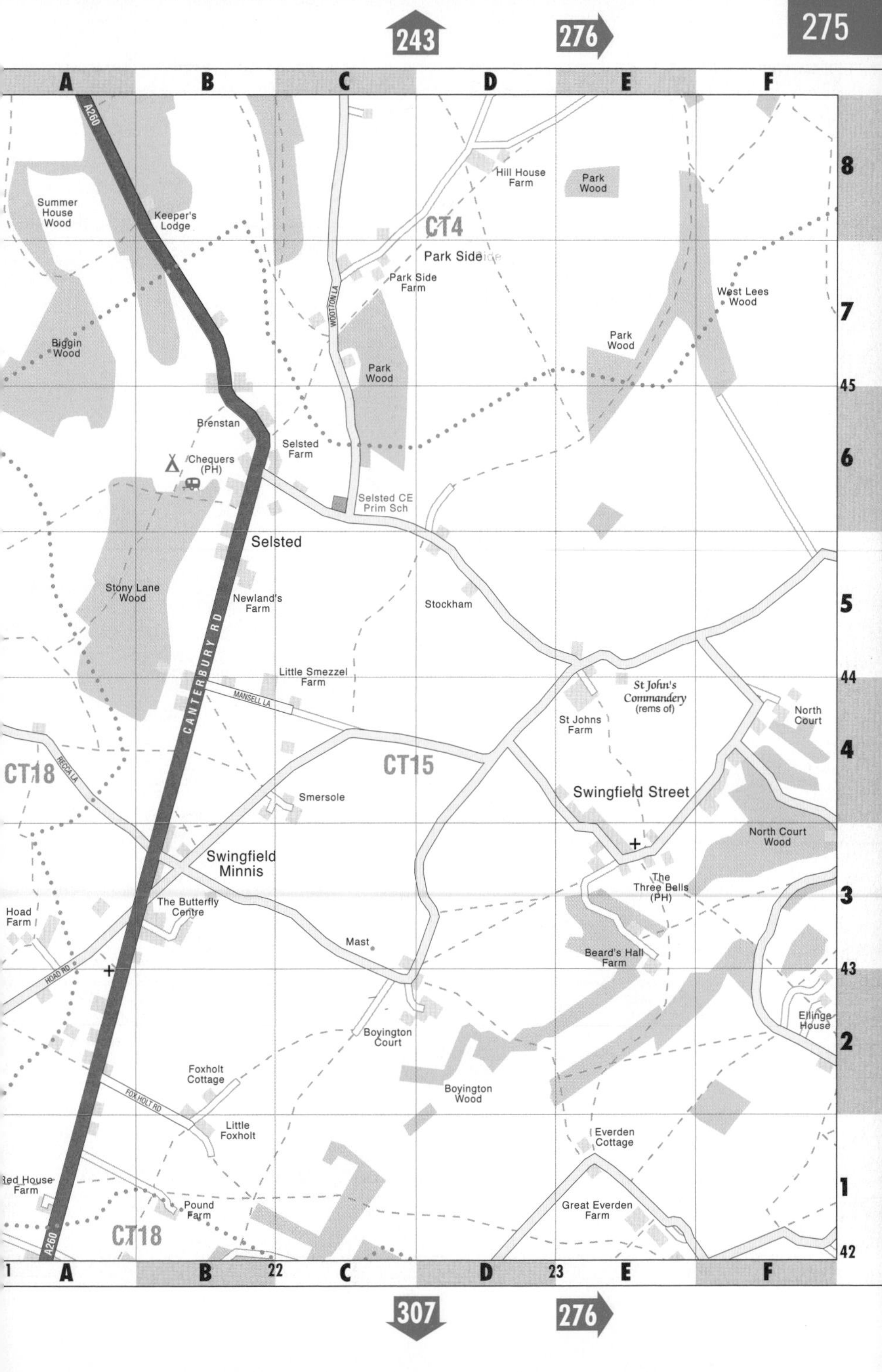

243
276

Summer House Wood
Keeper's Lodge
Biggin Wood

A260

CT4
Hill House Farm
Park Wood
Park Side
Park Side Farm
Park Wood
West Lees Wood
Park Wood

Brenstan
Chequers (PH)
Selsted Farm
Selsted CE Prim Sch
Selsted

CANTERBURY RD

Stony Lane Wood
Newland's Farm
Stockham

Little Smezzel Farm
MANSELL LA
St John's Commandery (rems of)
North Court

CT18
Smersole
CT15
St Johns Farm
Swingfield Street
North Court Wood

BIGGIN LA

Swingfield Minnis
The Butterfly Centre
The Three Bells (PH)

Hoad Farm
HOAD RD
Mast
Beard's Hall Farm

Ellinge House

Boyington Court
Boyington Wood

FOX HOLT RD
Foxholt Cottage
Little Foxholt

Everden Cottage

Red House Farm
A260
Pound Farm
Great Everden Farm
CT18

8
7
45
6
5
44
4
43
2
1
42

A   B   22   C   23   D   E   F

307
276

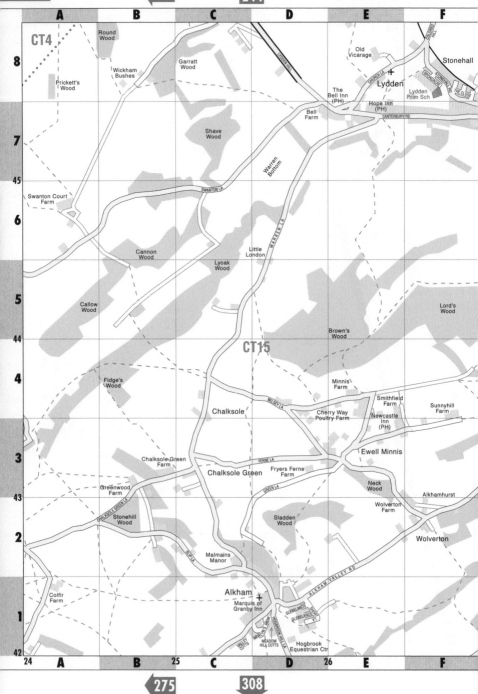

275
244
275
308

CT4

Round Wood

Wickham Bushes

Garratt Wood

Prickett's Wood

Shave Wood

Old Vicarage

Lydden

Stonehall

The Bell Inn (PH)

Hope Inn (PH)

Lydden Prim Sch

Bell Farm

CANTERBURY RD

SWANTON LA

Warren Bottom

Swanton Court Farm

WARREN LA

Cannon Wood

Little London

Lyoak Wood

Callow Wood

Lord's Wood

Brown's Wood

CT15

Fidge's Wood

Minnis Farm

Smithfield Farm

Chalksole

BELSEY LA

Cherry Way Poultry Farm

Newcastle Inn (PH)

Sunnyhill Farm

Ewell Minnis

Chalksole Green Farm

Chalksole Green

FERNE LA

Fryers Ferne Farm

Neck Wood

Alkhamhurst

Greenwood Farm

GREEN LA

Wolverton Farm

CHALKSOLE GREEN LA

Stonehill Wood

Sladden Wood

Wolverton

SLIP LA

Malmains Manor

ALKHAM VALLEY RD

Colfir Farm

Alkham

Marquis of Granby Inn

GLEBELANDS

VALLEY COTTS

MEADOW HILL COTTS

HOGBROOK HILL LA

NEWLAND'S ROW

Hogbrook Equestrian Ctr

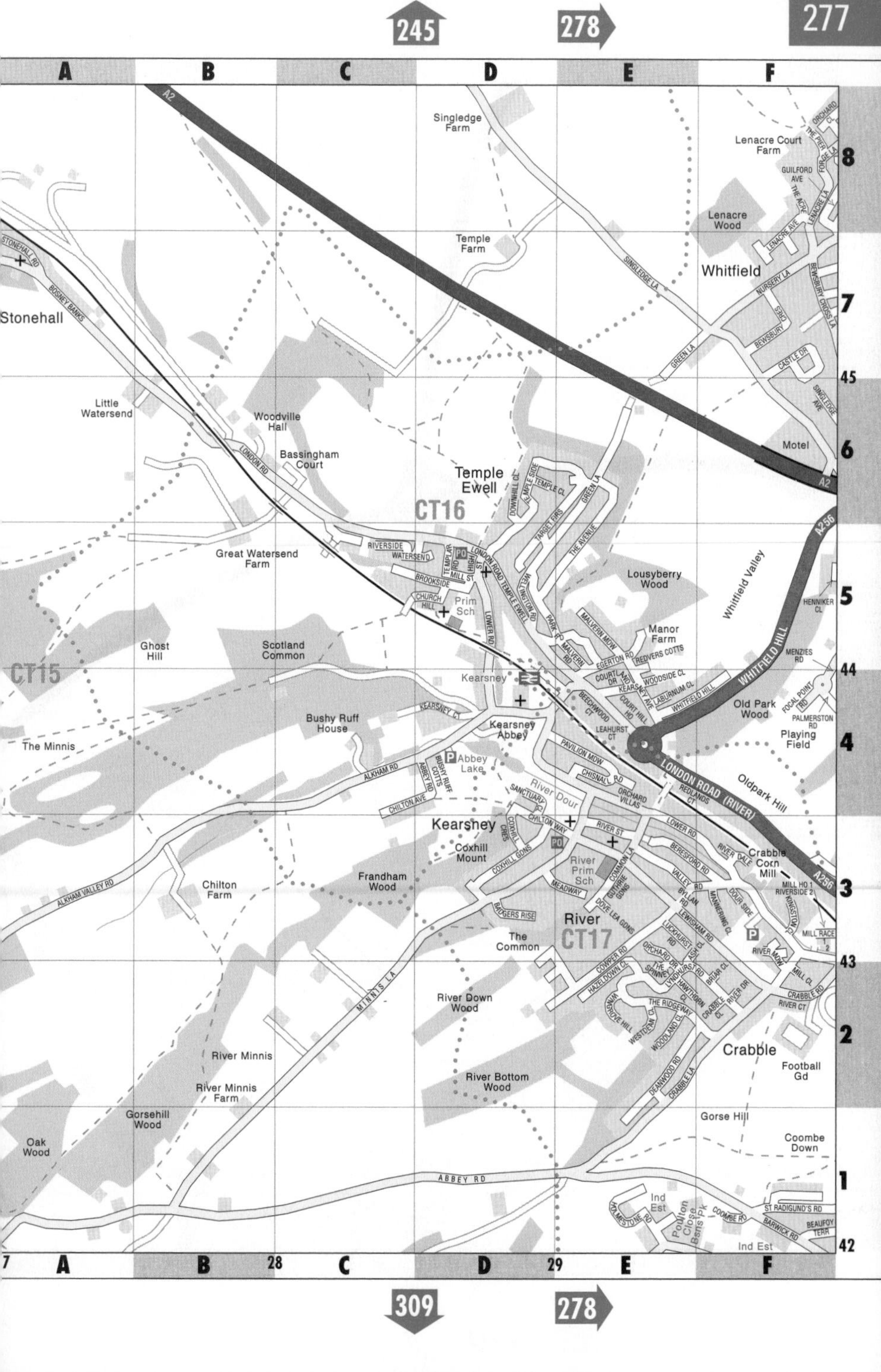
245
278
A
B
C
D
E
F
Singledge Farm
Lenacre Court Farm
Lenacre Wood
Temple Farm
Whitfield
Stonehall
Little Watersend
Woodville Hall
Bassingham Court
Temple Ewell
CT16
Motel
Great Watersend Farm
Lousyberry Wood
Whitfield Valley
Manor Farm
Ghost Hill
Scotland Common
CT15
Kearsney
Bushy Ruff House
Kearsney Abbey
Old Park Wood
The Minnis
Abbey Lake
Playing Field
Oldpark Hill
River Dour
Kearsney
Coxhill Mount
Crabble Corn Mill
Chilton Farm
Frandham Wood
River Prim Sch
River
CT17
The Common
River Down Wood
Crabble
River Minnis
River Minnis Farm
River Bottom Wood
Football Gd
Gorsehill Wood
Gorse Hill
Oak Wood
Coombe Down
Ind Est
Poulton Close Bsns Pk
Ind Est
A2
A256
LONDON ROAD (RIVER)
WHITFIELD HILL
ALKHAM VALLEY RD
ALKHAM RD
MINNIS LA
ABBEY RD
LONDON RD
STONEHALL RD
BOSNEY BANKS
SINGLEDGE LA
GREEN LA
NURSERY LA
LENACRE AVE
BEWSBURY CROSS LA
CASTLE DR
THE AVENUE
WELLINGTON RD
LONDON ROAD TEMPLE EWELL
LOWER RD
KEARSNEY CT
PAVILION MDW
ABBEY RD
CHILTON AVE
HOLMESTONE RD
COOMBE RD
ST RADIGUND'S RD
BARWICK RD
45
44
43
42
28
29
8
7
6
5
4
3
2
1
309
278

	A	B	C	D	E	F

Grid references: 8, 7, 45, 6, 5, 44, 4, 3, 43, 2, 1, 42

Column markers: 30 — A — 31 — B — C — 32 — D — E — F

Place names and features:
WHITFIELD LODGE, CHAPEL HILL, Church Whitfield, Parsonage Farm, Little Pineham Farm, Pineham, Great Pineham Farm, Poison Down, Enifer Down, Limekiln Down, Gifford's Covert, Whitfield, GREEN GATES, WITLEY WLK, Whitfield Sch & Aspen Specl Unit, Light Hill, Gustoncourt Farm, NEW COTTS, Guston, Honeywood, White Cliffs Bsns Pk, White Cliffs Bsns Ctr, BURGOYNE GR, Superstore, HONEYWOOD PARKWAY, Bsns Pk, Mast, Old Park, HENNIKER CL, Archers Court Sch, CT16, CT15, Copthorne, Chance Inn (PH), Buckland Valley, Frith Farm, Playing Field, The Powell Sch, Melbourne Com Prim Sch, Green Lane Hill, HOLY ECKHORN HO, Johannesburg Rd, Mast, Whiting Farm, Shaft, Duke of York's Royal Military Sch, Recn Gd, 1 WINNIPEG CL, 2 PERTH WAY, Long Hill, Guston CE Prim Sch, South Foreland, Mast, PRIORESS WLK, PILGRIMS WAY, KNIGHT'S WAY, HOBART CRES, Mast, The Danes Recn Gd, Cemy, Buckland, CT17, St Radigund's, St Radigund's Com Prim Sch, SPLIT HO, DALMATIA RD, Cemys, DOVER, Connaught Park, St Edmund's RC Sch, St Richard's RC Prim Sch, Fort Burgoyne (Casemated Barracks), Connaught Barracks, Dover Gram Schl for Girls, BEAUFOY TERR, COOMBE VALLEY RD, Buckland, BARTON RD, LONDON RD, FRITH RD, Prim Sch, TA Ctr, Connaught, Edinburgh Hill, Dover Castle, Bleriot Meml, YH, 1 PRIMROSE PL, 2 KNIGHTS CT, 3 CASTLEVIEW CT, 4 CHARLES LISTER CT, 5 KINGSFORD CT, 6 HERBERT ST, 1 CRAFFORD ST, 2 GODWYNE CT, 3 RICHMOND CT, 4 CASTLEMOUNT RD, 5 LONSDALE CT, 6 FERN CT, 7 PARK HO, A2, A256, A258, A2

North Downs Way / White Cliffs County Trail

B2	B3	C1	
1 ST ANNE'S CT	1 FITZWALTER CT	1 ALEXANDRA PL	10 WARDEN CT
2 OSPREY CT	2 WELLINGTON GDNS	2 BARTON VIEW TERR	11 TEMPLAR CT
3 MAYFIELD CT	3 BRUNSWICK GDNS	3 LEIGHTON CT	12 DOUR MEWS
4 MAGPIE LODGE	4 WASHINGTON CL	4 ST ALPHEGE RD	
5 CHAFFINCH LODGE	5 BOSTON CL	5 SHOOTER'S HILL	
6 HERON LODGE	6 TORONTO CL	6 BARTHOLOMEW ST	
	7 HUDSON CL	7 CHURCHILL ST	
	8 MONTREAL CL	8 PAUL'S PL	
		9 MATTHEW'S PL	

247
280

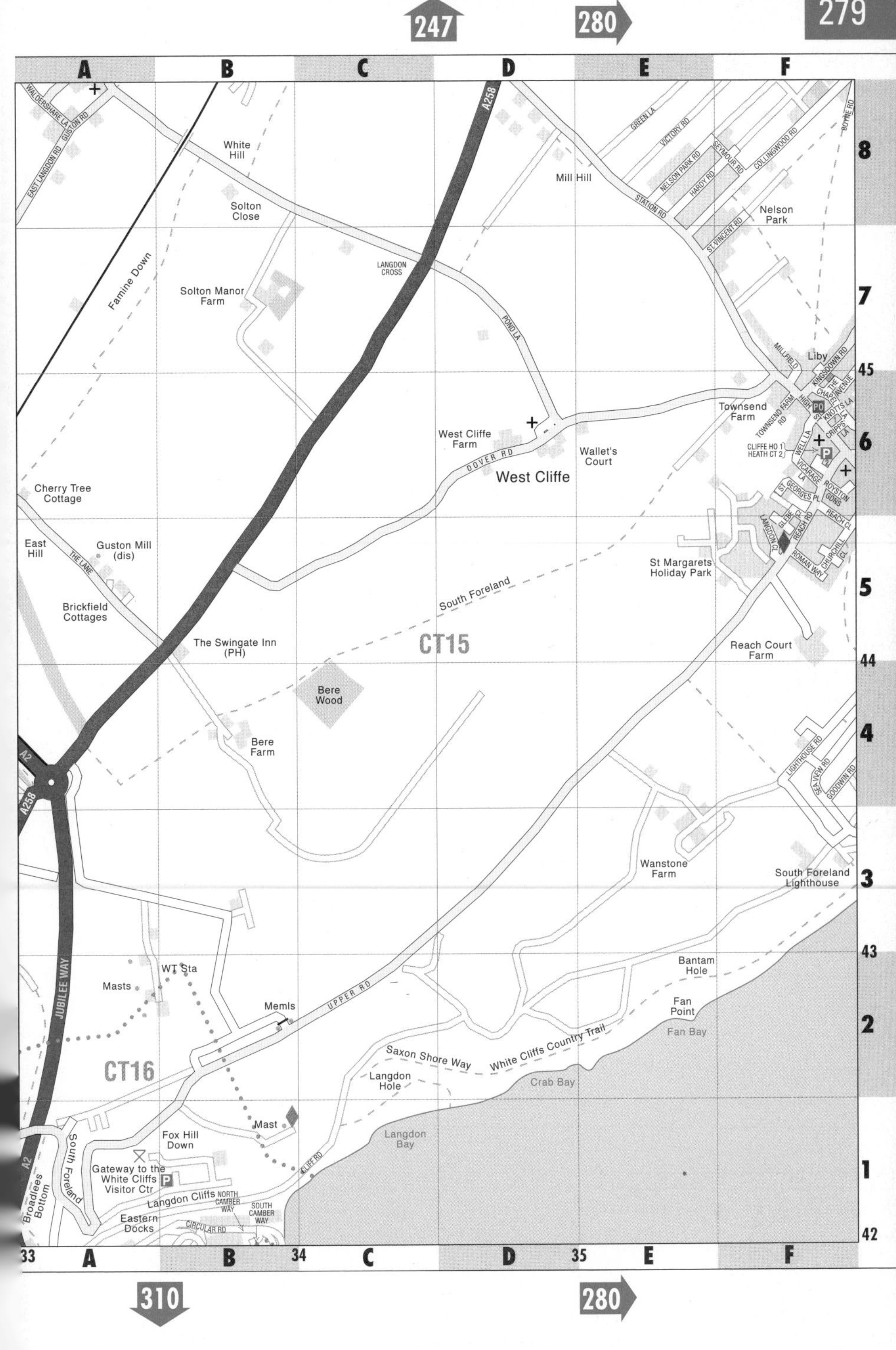
A
B
C
D
E
F
White Hill
Solton Close
Famine Down
Solton Manor Farm
LANGDON CROSS
A258
POND LA
Mill Hill
GREEN LA
VICTORY RD
NELSON PARK RD
SEYMOUR RD
HARDY RD
COLLINGWOOD RD
STATION RD
ST VINCENT RD
BOYNE RD
Nelson Park
Liby
MILLFIELD
KINGSDOWN RD
Townsend Farm
TOWNSEND FARM RD
PO
West Cliffe Farm
DOVER RD
West Cliffe
Wallet's Court
CLIFFE HO 1
HEATH CT 2
Cherry Tree Cottage
East Hill
THE LANE
Guston Mill (dis)
Brickfield Cottages
St Margarets Holiday Park
South Foreland
CT15
The Swingate Inn (PH)
Reach Court Farm
Bere Wood
Bere Farm
A2
LIGHTHOUSE RD
SEA VIEW RD
GOODWIN RD
Wanstone Farm
South Foreland Lighthouse
JUBILEE WAY
WT Sta
Masts
Bantam Hole
Memls
UPPER RD
Fan Point
Fan Bay
Saxon Shore Way
White Cliffs Country Trail
CT16
Langdon Hole
Crab Bay
Mast
Fox Hill Down
Langdon Bay
Gateway to the White Cliffs Visitor Ctr
South Foreland
Broadlees Bottom
Langdon Cliffs
NORTH CAMBER WAY
SOUTH CAMBER WAY
Eastern Docks
CIRCULAR RD
CLIFF RD
WALDERSHARE LA
GUSTON RD
EAST LANGDON RD
8
7
45
6
5
44
4
3
43
2
1
42
33
34
35

310
280

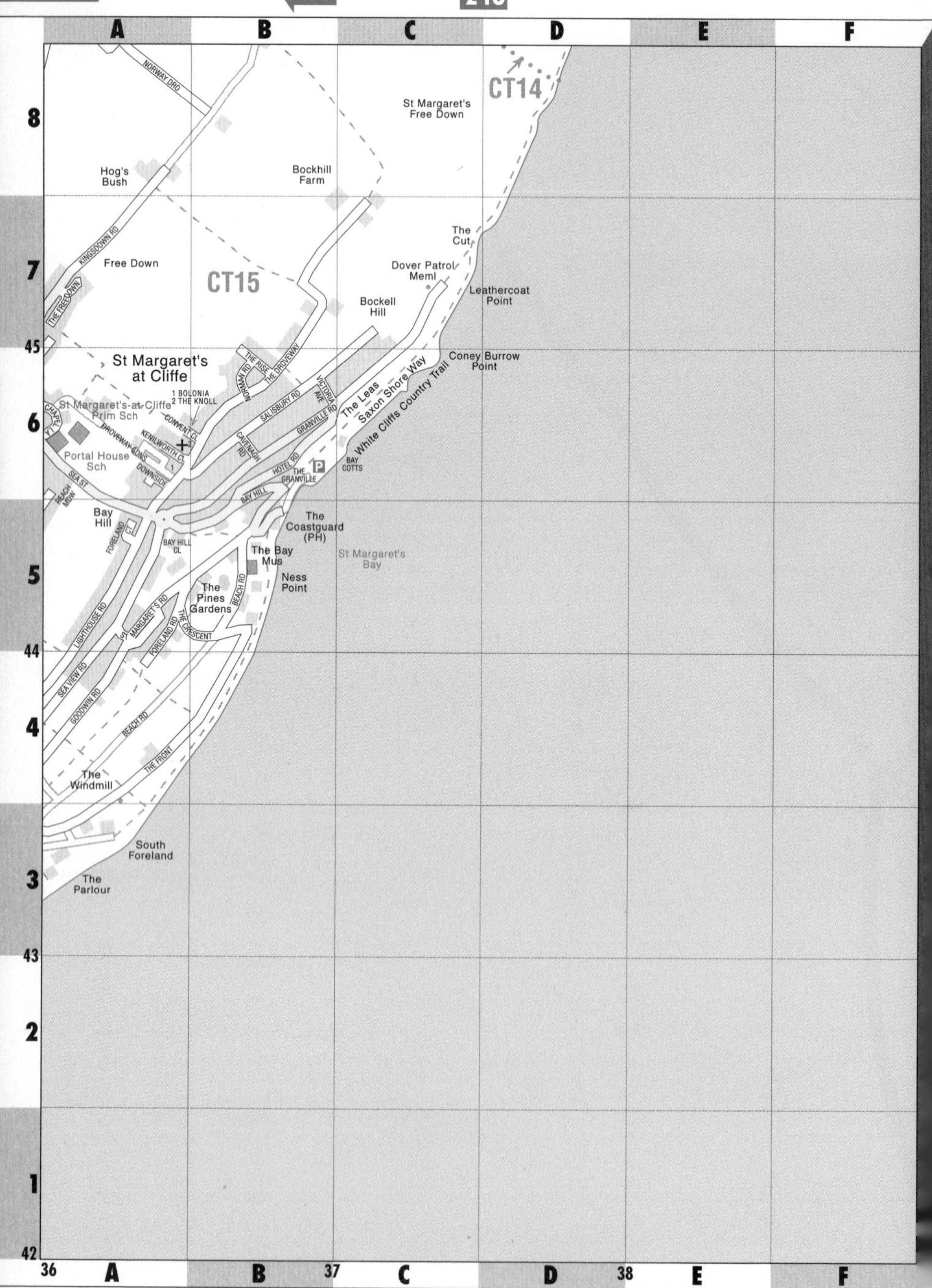

CT14

St Margaret's
Free Down

Hog's
Bush

Bockhill
Farm

The
Cut

Free Down

Dover Patrol
Meml

CT15

Leathercoat
Point

Bockell
Hill

Coney Burrow
Point

St Margaret's
at Cliffe

The Leas

Saxon Shore Way

St Margaret's-at-Cliffe
Prim Sch

1 BOLONIA
2 THE KNOLL

White Cliffs Country Trail

CONVENT RD

Portal House
Sch

SALISBURY RD

GRANVILLE RD

BAY
COTTS

HOTEL RD

THE GRANVILLE

P

Bay
Hill

BAY HILL

The
Coastguard
(PH)

The Bay
Mus

St Margaret's
Bay

BAY HILL
CL

The
Pines
Gardens

Ness
Point

BEACH RD

MARGARET RD

LIGHTHOUSE RD

FORELAND CRESCENT

SEA VIEW RD

GOODWIN RD

BEACH RD

THE FRONT

The
Windmill

South
Foreland

The
Parlour

A B C D E F

RH7
Dry Hill
Jules Wood
Ten Acre Wood
Willow Bed
Minepit Wood
Crippenden Manor
Ludwells Farm
Polefields
Spode La
8

Beeches Farm
Old Furzefield Wood
Goudhurst Gill
Leighton Manor
Liveroxhill Wood
Ravenscroft Farm
7
41

Woodlands Farm
Vanguard Way
Marlpit Shaw
Sussex Border Path
TN8
Clay's Wood
6
Waystrode Manor

West Sussex STREET ATLAS

Lower Stonehurst Farm
Basing & Smithers Farm
Drews Rough
Scarletts
Furnace Farm
Pondtail
5
40

Gatwick Farm Cotts
Shepherdsgrove La
Vanguard Way
Scarletts Lake
Kent Water
Mill Wood
Reading's Wood
Furnace Pond
Cleavers Farm
4
Bank Farm
Roger's Town
Holtye Common

A264 East Grinstead
A264 Holtye Rd
Steadleaze Wood
Cooper's Wood
Countess of Thanet's Almshouses
High Meadows
Home Farm
RH19
Holtye
Hammerwood
A264
3
CH
White Horse (PH)
39

Brooklands Farm
Hammerwood Park
Hammer Wood
Cansiron La
Wet Wood
2
Cansiron Wood

Little Cansiron Farm
Sewage Works
1
The Grove
Dog Cotts
Water Wood
TN7
38

East Sussex STREET ATLAS

43 A B 44 C D 45 E F

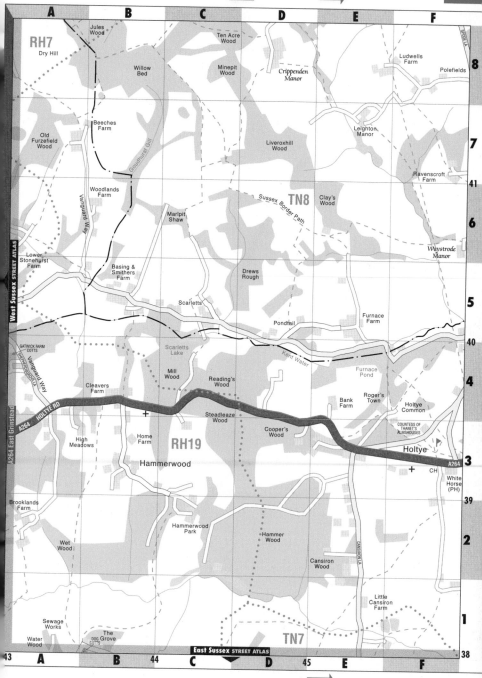

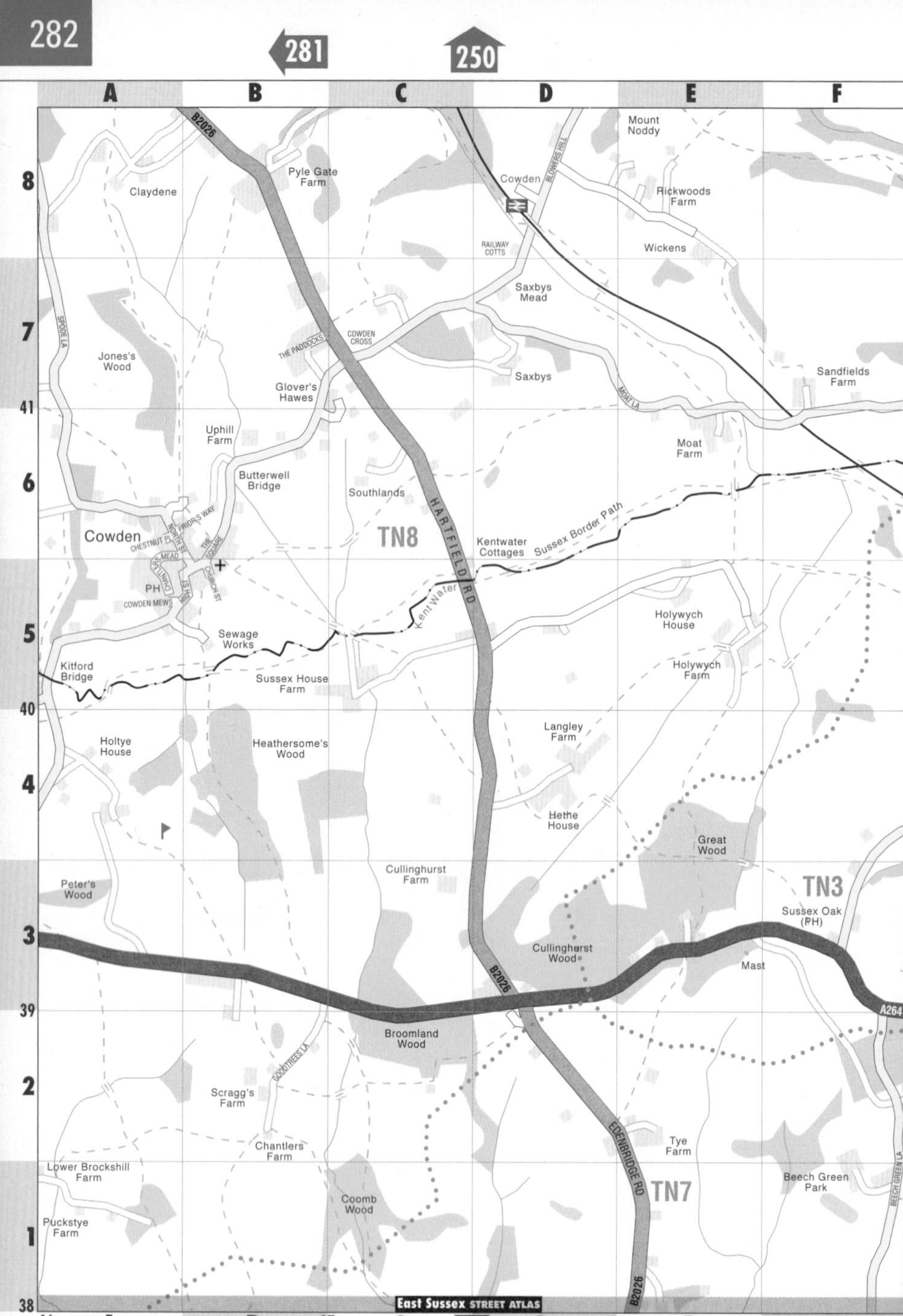

East Sussex STREET ATLAS

281
250
B
C
D
F
8
7
41
6
5
40
4
3
39
2
1
38
46
47
48
B2026
Pyle Gate Farm
Claydene
Mount Noddy
Cowden
BLOWERS HILL
Rickwoods Farm
RAILWAY COTTS
Wickens
Saxbys Mead
SPODE LA
Jones's Wood
THE PADDOCKS
COWDEN CROSS
Saxbys
Sandfields Farm
Glover's Hawes
MOAT LA
Uphill Farm
Moat Farm
Butterwell Bridge
Southlands
PRIOR'S WAY
NORTH ST
THE SQUARE
Cowden
CHESTNUT PL
HARTFIELD RD
TN8
Kentwater Cottages
Sussex Border Path
MEAD
CHURCH ST
PH
COWDEN MEWS
HIGH ST
Kent Water
Sewage Works
Holywych House
Kitford Bridge
Sussex House Farm
Holywych Farm
Holtye House
Heathersome's Wood
Langley Farm
Hethe House
Great Wood
Peter's Wood
Cullinghurst Farm
TN3
Sussex Oak (PH)
Cullinghurst Wood
Mast
A264
Broomland Wood
GOODTREES LA
Scragg's Farm
EDENBRIDGE RD
Tye Farm
Chantlers Farm
Lower Brockshill Farm
Beech Green Park
BEECH GREEN LA
TN7
Coomb Wood
Puckstye Farm

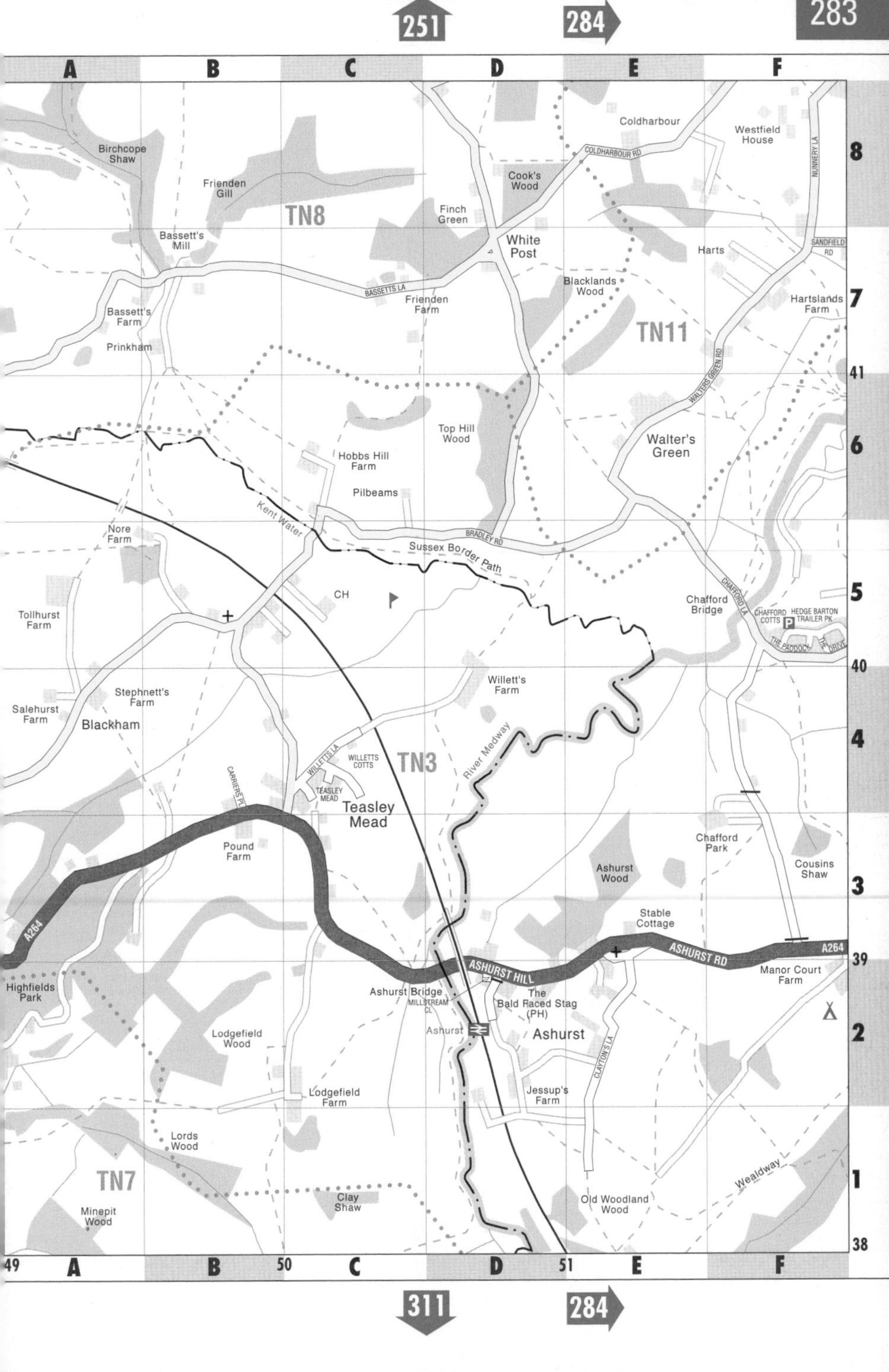
251
284
A
B
C
D
E
F
8
7
41
6
5
40
4
3
39
2
1
38
49
50
51
Birchcope Shaw
Frienden Gill
TN8
Cook's Wood
Coldharbour
COLDHARBOUR RD
Westfield House
NUNNERY LA
Finch Green
White Post
Bassett's Mill
BASSETTS LA
Frienden Farm
Blacklands Wood
Harts
SANDFIELD RD
Hartslands Farm
Bassett's Farm
Prinkham
TN11
WALTERS GREEN RD
Top Hill Wood
Walter's Green
Hobbs Hill Farm
Pilbeams
Kent Water
BRADLEY RD
Sussex Border Path
Nore Farm
CH
Chafford Bridge
CHAFFORD LA
CHAFFORD COTTS
HEDGE BARTON TRAILER PK
THE PADDOCK
THE DRIVE
Tollhurst Farm
Willett's Farm
Stephnett's Farm
Salehurst Farm
Blackham
River Medway
WILLETTS LA
WILLETTS COTTS
TN3
CARRIERS PL
TEASLEY MEAD
Teasley Mead
Pound Farm
Chafford Park
Cousins Shaw
Ashurst Wood
A264
Stable Cottage
ASHURST RD
A264
ASHURST HILL
Manor Court Farm
Highfields Park
Ashurst Bridge
MILLSTREAM CL
The Bald Faced Stag (PH)
Ashurst
Ashurst
Lodgefield Wood
CLAYTON'S LA
Lodgefield Farm
Jessup's Farm
Lords Wood
Wealdway
TN7
Clay Shaw
Old Woodland Wood
Minepit Wood
311
284

283 252

	A	B	C	D	E	F

8

Smart's Hill
PH
SAINTS HILL
B2188 NEW RD
Poundsbridge
Hallborough
Stone Wood
FURZEFIELD AV
TN11

Saint's Hill
SPRING HILL
River Medway
Hamsell Farm
GROOMBRIDGE HILL
POUNDSBRIDGE HILL
PENSHURST RD
BULLINGSTONE COTTS
Cock Pit Wood

7

Colliersland Bridge
Bullingstone
BULLINGSTONE LA

SANDFIELD RD

41

Palmers Farm
Little Hickman's
Hickman's Farm
Avery's Wood
EMFIELD LA

6

Springhill Farm
BROOK LANE FARM CL
Danemore Park
POINT CROSS LA

5

Chafford Farm
PH
Fordcombe CE Prim Sch
PADDOCK
REEVES CT
ST PETERS ROW
STONE ROW
THE LANE
Silcocks Farm
Fordcombe
Danemore Farm
LEGGS LA
PYE HURST RD
WATERFRETS COTTS

40

CHAFFORD LA
Mitre Farm
OLD HOUSE LA
Shirley Hall

4

Fitchetts Farm
BROAD LA
Wealdway
Stubbs Wood
Black Lion House
FORDCOMBE RD
TN3
Priest Wood
Tunbridge Wells Circular Walk
Ashurst Place
Langton Green Prim Sch
LAMPINGTON ROW
WINSTONE SCOTT AVE
P
COURTENWELL
RUSSELL
GIBBETTS
GREAT FOOTPATH

3

Stone Cross Farm
Queens Spinney
The Tunbridge Wells Ind
H
Park Farm
Langton Green
The Hare (PH)
LANGTON RD
A264
HAZELBANK
WIDBURY
UPTON CROSS LA

39

Stone Cross
ASHURST RD
B2188
Wr Twr
HOLMEWOOD RIDGE
BROOM PK
Broomlands

2

Stone Cross Wood
Burrs Wood
Newpark Wood
B2110
CROCKERS HATCH CNR
The Hollonds
The Moltens
Hollonds Wood
Broom Farm
BROOK LA
VY PASSAGE

1

OLD POUNDBRIDGE RD
GROOMBRIDGE HILL
Top Hill Farm
STONE ROW COTTS
Sewage Works
Hollonds Wood
High Weald Landscape Trail

38

B2110
Harness Well Wood

52	A	B	53	C	D	54	E	F

283 312

253
286

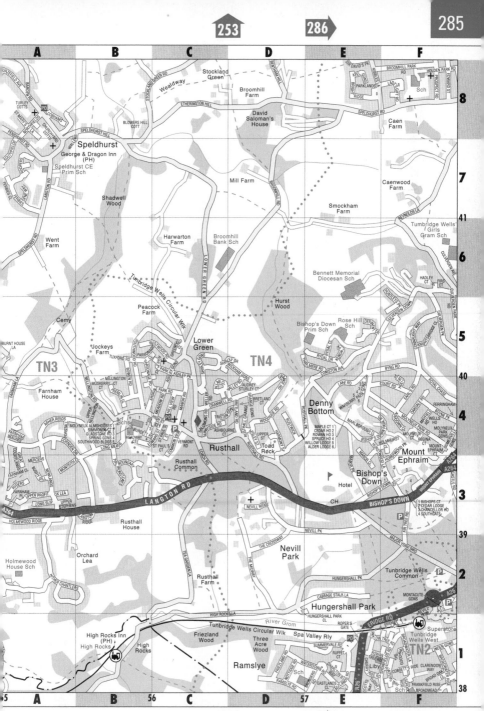
A
B
C
D
E
F
8
7
41
6
5
40
4
3
39
2
1
38
55
56
57
Stockland Green
Wealdway
Broomhill Farm
ETHERINGTON HILL
STOCKLAND GREEN RD
BENTHAM HILL
SIR DAVID'S PK
BROOMHILL PARK RD
HOLDEN PARK RD
KEEL GDNS
PARKLANDS
BRIGHT RIDGE
KIBBLES LA
LADY'S GIFT RD
PROSPECT RD
EDWARD ST
Sch
SPELDHURST RD
Caen Farm
David Saloman's House
FURZEFIELD AVE
BARDEN RD
TURLEY COTTS
PO
COBHAMS
ST MARY'S
NORTHFIELDS
LA
CHURCHYARD COTTS
PENSHURST RD
SOUTHFIELDS
BLOWERS HILL COTT
SPELDHURST HILL
WALLERS
Speldhurst
George & Dragon Inn (PH)
Speldhurst CE Prim Sch
ROOPERS
LANGTON RD
FERBIES CL
FERBIES
DENE WAY
Shadwell Wood
Mill Farm
BROOMHILL RD
Caenwood Farm
Smockham Farm
REYNOLDS LA
Tunbridge Wells' Girls Gram Sch
SPELDHURST RD
Went Farm
Harwarton Farm
Broomhill Bank Sch
LOWER GREEN RD
CULVERDEN AVE
Bennett Memorial Diocesan Sch
HADLEY CT
FIRS CT
Tunbridge Wells Circular Wlk
Peacock Farm
Hurst Wood
HUNTLEYS PK
CULVERDEN DOWN
CULVERDEN PARK RD
Cemy
Bishop's Down Prim Sch
Rose Hill Sch
DERNIER RD
BURNT HOUSE LA
Jockeys Farm
Lower Green
TN3
TN4
RYDAL CL
KENDAL PK
RYDAL DR
THIRLMERE RD
CONISTON AVE
CONNAUGHT WAY
KNIGHTSBRIDGE CL
CULVERDEN PK
TUXFORD RD
SOUTHWOOD RD
PARSONAGE
WESTWOOD RD
GREENFIELD CL
ASHLEY GDNS
ASHLEY PK
ASHLEY PARK CL
SHIRLEY GDNS
SHIRLEY GR
WICKHAM GDNS
BYNG RD
FARNHAM LA
Farnham House
NELLINGTON RD
NELLINGTON CT
MUSKERRY CT
BOWEN RD
PARSONAGE RD
ERSKINE PARK RD
AUDREY STURLEY CT
VALLEY RD
LAKE RD
COURT RD
EARL'S RD
ROYAL CHASE
HILL ST
Denny Bottom
WARBERRY PARK GDNS
OAKDALE RD
FERRINGHAM
UPPER NELLINGTON
MEADOW RD
HILL VIEW RD
MANOR RD
CRANWELL RD
BRETLAND CT
BRETLAND RD
GRANGE GDNS
RUSTHALL GRANGE
WOODSIDE RD
RUSTWICK
RUSTHALL PK
MAYFIELD RD
BOYNE PK
WELLS HO
ASHER REEDS
FORSTALL
MOLYNEUX ALMSHOUSES 1
SIMMONDS CT 2
GLADSTONE RD 3
SPRING GDNS 4
SOUTHWOOD BLDGS 5
Schs
Liby
HIGH ST
BURDETT RD
EDWARD ST
ST PAUL'S ST
PO
P
SALOMONS RD
WELLER RD
TRISTAN GDNS
SUNNYSIDE RD
ASHBOURNE CT
UPPER ST
APSLEY ST
HARMONY ST
MAPLE CT 1
CEDAR HO 2
ROWAN HO 3
SPRUCE HO 4
WILLOW LODGE 5
ALDER LODGE 6
MARLBOROUGH CL
BISHOP'S DOWN PARK RD
MOLYNEUX PARK RD
MOLYNEUX CT
REGINA CT
MOLYNEUX PARK GDNS
MOUNT EPHRAIM CT
SOMERVILLE GDNS
FARNHAM BEECHES
DORNDEN DR
HEADWAY CT
ST PAUL'S CT
COMMON VIEW
VERMONT RD
Toad Rock
RUSTHALL RD
HOLMHURST CL
HURSTWOOD LA
HURSTWOOD PK
Mount Ephraim
MONTEITH CL
LONG MEADS
BOUNDARY
THE IRONS
Rusthall
COACH RD
Rusthall Common
MANOR CL
MAYOR RD
Bishop's Down
A264
COURTLANDS
GREAT
MERCERS
NEWLANDS
BUSHY GILL
FARNHAM CL
RYDERS
FARNHAM PL
UPPER PROFIT
OX LEA
LONG SLIP
UPPER STEPHENS
LANGTON RD
Hotel
BISHOP'S DOWN RD
MOUNT EPHRAIM
CASTLE RD
NEVILL RIDGE
CH
BISHOP'S DOWN
1 BISHOPS CT
2 CEDAR LODGE
3 CHANCELLOR HO
4 SOUTHGATE
HOLMEWOOD RIDGE
LANGTON RIDGE
Rusthall House
NEVILL PK
FIR TREE RD
MAJOR YORK'S RD
THE CROSSWAY
Orchard Lea
TEA GARDEN LA
Nevill Park
THE MIDWAY
Holmewood House Sch
Rusthall Farm
HITHER CHANTLERS
HUNGERSHALL PK
Tunbridge Wells Common
CABBAGE STALK LA
MONTACUTE GDNS
A26
Hungershall Park
HIGH ROCKS LA
HUNGERSHALL PARK CL
NEVILL TERR
ERIDGE RD
River Grom
ROPER'S GATE
High Rocks Inn (PH)
High Rocks
Friezland Wood
Tunbridge Wells Circular Wlk
Spa Valley Rly
Superstore
Tunbridge Wells West
Three Acre Wood
SUMMERVALE RD
RUFFET CT
LOW TREE RD
TN2
LINDEN GDNS
FRIEZLAND RD
NOTTIDGE RD
WATERDOWN RD
CHARLTON'S WAY
ROWAN TREE RD
SHOWFIELDS RD
BROADWATER LA
CLARENDON WAY
BROADWATER RISE
Ramslye
Sch
Liby
CHERRY TREE RD
COBBETT'S RIDE
BROAD OAK CL
RAMSLYE RD
SAUNDERS RD
EASTLANDS CL
EASTLANDS RD
SCOTTS WAY
TUDOR CT
HUNTERS WAY
SCHOOL RISE
FRANKFIELD RISE
BROADMEAD

← 285
254 ↑

ROYAL TUNBRIDGE
WELLS

314
↓ 285

A2
1 CHRIST CHURCH AVE
2 CASTLE ST
3 WHITE BEAR PAS
4 WARWICK RD
5 BELGROVE
6 SPENCER MEWS
7 BERKELEY RD
8 SION WLK
9 EDEN WLK

10 CUMBERLAND GDNS
11 CUMBERLAND YD
12 CUMBERLAND MEWS
13 BEDFORD TERR
14 CHAPEL PL
15 KENTISH MANS
16 MARKET PL
17 MARKET ST
18 COACH & HORSES PAS
19 SUSSEX MEWS

20 THE PANTILES
21 REGENCY HALL
22 UNION SQ
23 CUMBERLAND COTTS

A4
1 SUFFOLK MEWS
2 ALEXANDER CT

B3
1 CALVERLEY PARK CRES
2 MOUNT PLEASANT AVE
3 GREAT HALL ARC
4 MOUNTFIELD CT
5 THE MEWS
6 MEADOW HILL RD
7 GUILDFORD RD

B4
1 ELIZABETH GARLICK CT
2 CAMDEN CT
3 GROVER ST
4 RICHARD BEAU NASH APARTMENTS
5 MONSON WAY
6 CADOGAN GDNS
7 CATHERINE PL
8 LANSDOWNE SQ

9 GARDEN HO
10 SPENCER MEWS

255
288

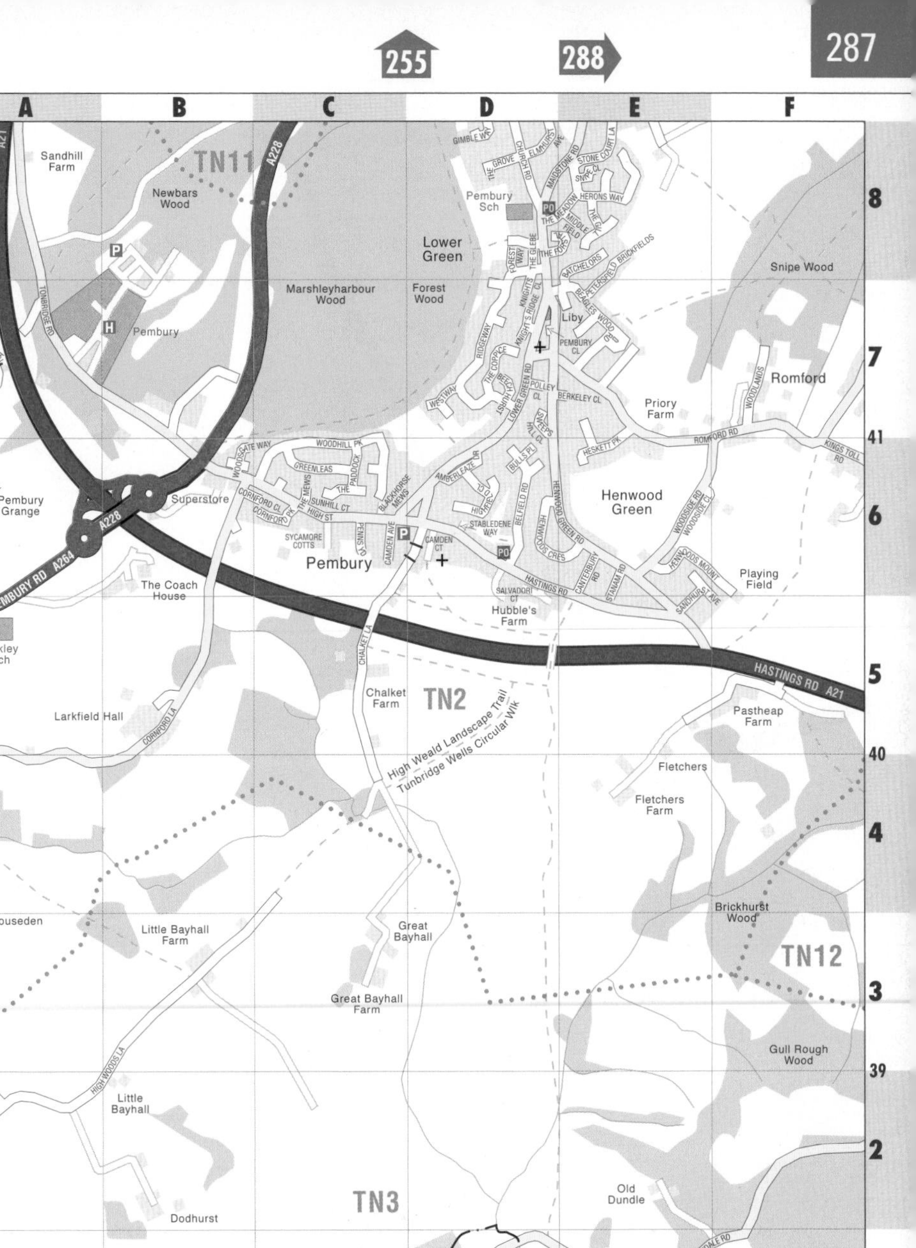
A
B
C
D
E
F
TN11
Sandhill Farm
Newbars Wood
Pembury
Marshleyharbour Wood
Forest Wood
Lower Green
Pembury Sch
Liby
Snipe Wood
Romford
Priory Farm
Henwood Green
Pembury Grange
Superstore
Pembury
Playing Field
The Coach House
Hubble's Farm
Oakley Sch
Chalket Farm
TN2
Larkfield Hall
High Weald Landscape Trail
Tunbridge Wells Circular Wlk
Pastheap Farm
Fletchers
Fletchers Farm
Mouseden
Little Bayhall Farm
Great Bayhall
Great Bayhall Farm
Brickhurst Wood
TN12
Gull Rough Wood
Little Bayhall
Old Dundle
TN3
Dodhurst
Dundale Farm
River Teise
Brown's Lodge
Dundale Wood
A21
A228
A264
PEMBURY RD
HASTINGS RD
TONBRIDGE RD
BLACKHURST LA
SANDOWN PK
PEMBURY GRANGE
WOODSGATE WAY
WOODHILL PK
GREENLEAS
THE PADDOCK
THE MEWS
SUNHILL CT
HIGH ST
CORNFORD CL
CORNFORD PK
BLACKHORSE MEWS
SYCAMORE COTTS
PENNS YD
CAMDEN AVE
CAMDEN CT
STABLEDENE WAY
AMBERLEAZE DR
BELFIELD RD
BULLS PL
HENWOOD GREEN RD
HENWOODS CRES
CANTERBURY RD
STANAM RD
SALVADORI CT
HESKETT PK
WOODSIDE RD
WOODSIDE CL
HENWOODS MOUNT
SANDHURST AVE
ROMFORD RD
KINGS TOLL RD
WOODLANDS
BERKELEY CL
POLLEY CL
LOWER GREEN RD
WESTWAY
RIDGEWAY
THE COPPICE
BEECHHURST
KNIGHT'S RIDGE CL
KNIGHTS
PEMBURY CL
BEAGLES WOOD
PETERSFIELD
BRICKFIELDS
BATCHELORS
THE FORGE
THE GLEBE
FOREST WAY
THE MEADOW
MIDDLE FIELD
THE GILL
HERONS WAY
STONE COURT LA
SNIPE CL
MAIDSTONE RD
ELMHURST AVE
CHURCH RD
THE GROVE
GIMBLE WAY
CHALKET LA
CORNFORD LA
HIGH WOODS LA
DUNDALE RD
8
7
6
5
4
3
2
1
41
40
39
38
61
62
63

315
288

287
256

A **B** **C** **D** **E** **F**

Matfield

Widmore
Farm

Nature
Reserve

BRENCHLEY RD

LL STIL

B2160

8

High Weald Landscape Trail

The Wheelwrights
Arms (PH)

Tutty's
Farmhouse

DAYFIELD RD

Court
Farm House

Goshen
Farm

Three Towns
Farm

ROMFORD RD

Grove Cottage
Farm

The
Hopbine
(PH)

TIBBS COURT LA

7

Hayes View
Farm

Friars
Coach House

Romford
Manor

TN2

Lodge
Farm

BRENCHLEY LA

Porter's
Wood

PORTERS
WOOD

Petteridge

PETTERIDGE LA

41

Wellgrove
Farm

MAIDSTONE RD

HUMPHREYS

TN12

6

KINGS TOLL RD

Egypt
Farm

Matfield
Grange

Kings Toll
Farm

Becketts
Grove

SOPURST LA

Cryals
CT

Cryals
Farm

5

Kingsmead

Becketts
Grove
Farm

SOPURST
WOOD

CRYALS RD

Old
Cryals

Kipping's Cross
Farm

Kingsmead
Farm

B2160

40

HASTINGS RD

Kipping's
Cross

Bassetts
Farm

SANDHOLE
COTTS

4

Blue
Boys
Inn
(PH)

Beech
Wood

BEDGBURY RD

Marlpit
Wood

Hanger
Wood

Elmhurst
Farm

Mast

Key's
Green

BEDDLA

3

Old
Farm

39

Beechers
Lodge

Brookland
Wood

Little Dunks
Farm

2

Great
Sandhurst
Wood

Swan
Farm

TN3

The
Grange

Lindridge
Place
Farm

Little
Sandhurst
Wood

Three
Horseshoe
Farm

PERGOLA

Lamberhurst
Quarter

BEDGBURY LA

1

CAT MILL RD

Little
Grange

Lindridge
Lodge
Farm

A21

38

64 **A** **B** 65 **C** **D** 66 **E** **F**

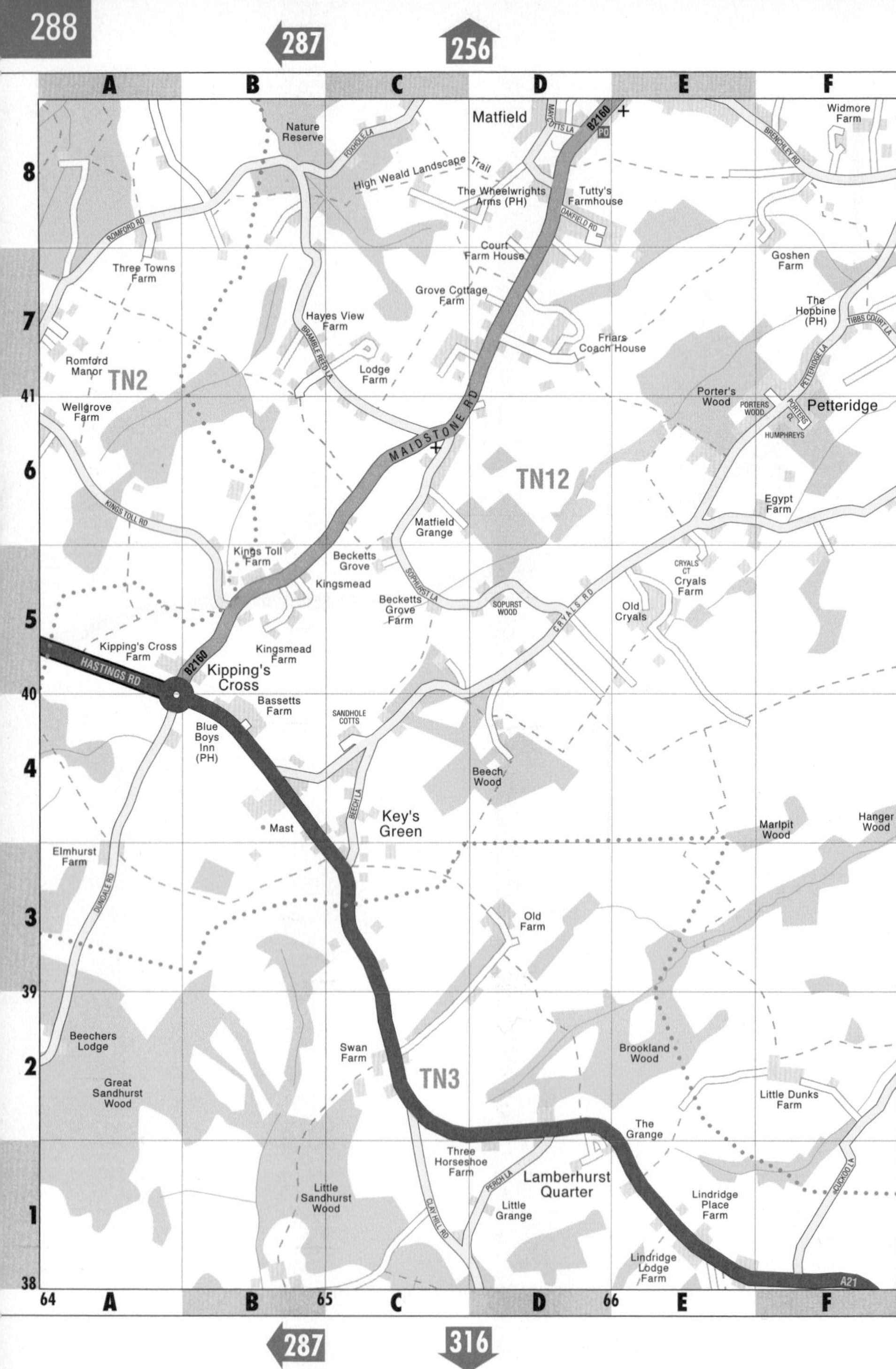

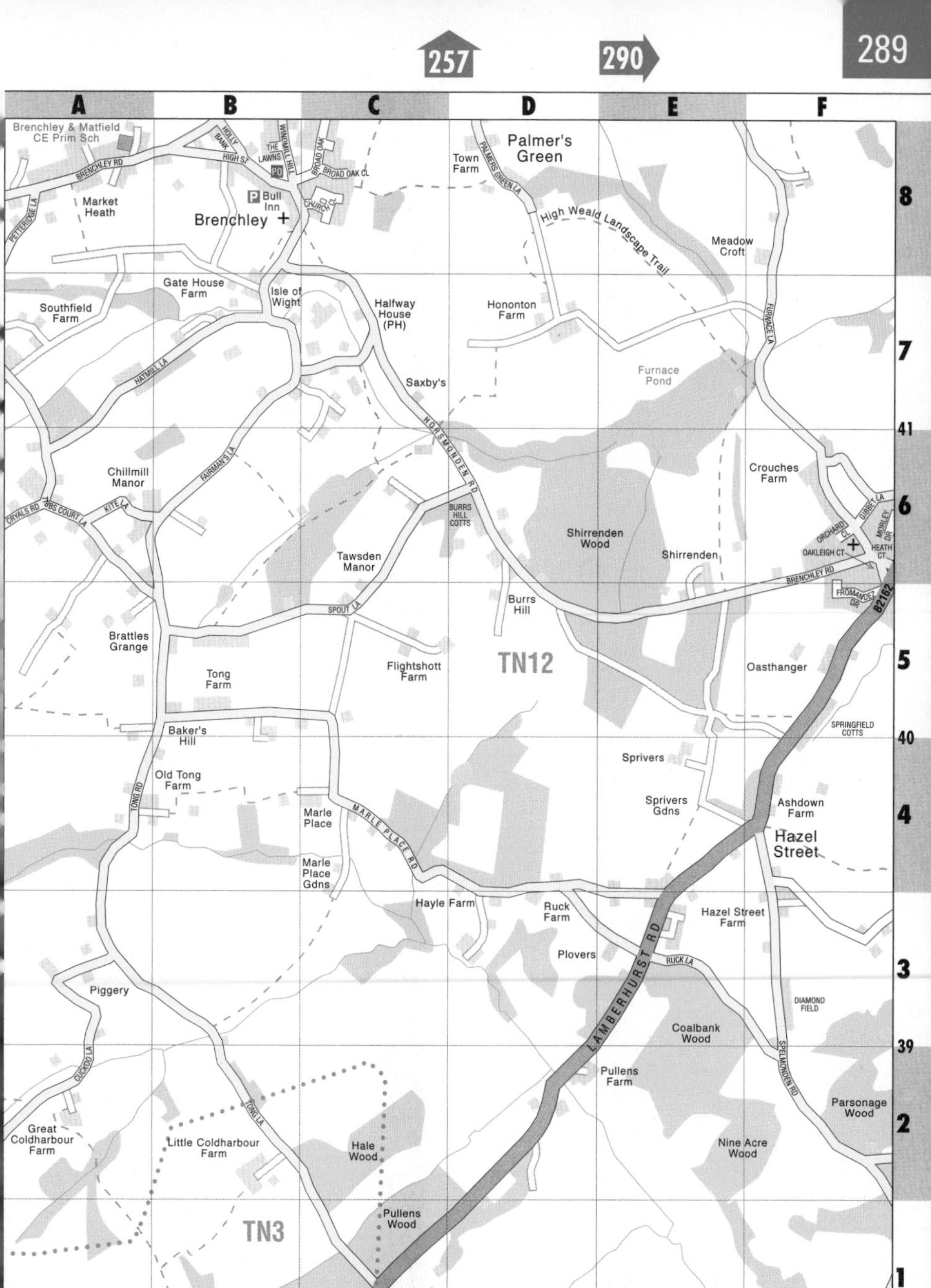
A
B
C
D
E
F
Brenchley & Matfield CE Prim Sch
Palmer's Green
Town Farm
Market Heath
Bull Inn
Brenchley
High Weald Landscape Trail
Meadow Croft
Gate House Farm
Isle of Wight
Southfield Farm
Halfway House (PH)
Hononton Farm
Furnace Pond
Saxby's
Chillmill Manor
Crouches Farm
Shirrenden Wood
Shirrenden
Tawsden Manor
Burrs Hill
Brattles Grange
TN12
Flightshott Farm
Oasthanger
Tong Farm
Baker's Hill
SPRINGFIELD COTTS
Sprivers
Old Tong Farm
Sprivers Gdns
Ashdown Farm
Marle Place
Hazel Street
Marle Place Gdns
Hayle Farm
Ruck Farm
Hazel Street Farm
Plovers
Piggery
DIAMOND FIELD
Coalbank Wood
Pullens Farm
Parsonage Wood
Great Coldharbour Farm
Little Coldharbour Farm
Hale Wood
Nine Acre Wood
Pullens Wood
TN3
BRENCHLEY RD
HIGH ST
HATMILL LA
FAIRMAN'S LA
HORSMONDEN RD
SPOUT LA
MARLE PLACE RD
LAMBERHURST RD
RUCK LA
SPELMONDEN RD
TONG RD
TONG LA
CUCKOO LA
FURNACE LA
B2162
8
7
41
6
5
40
4
3
39
2
1
38
67
68
69

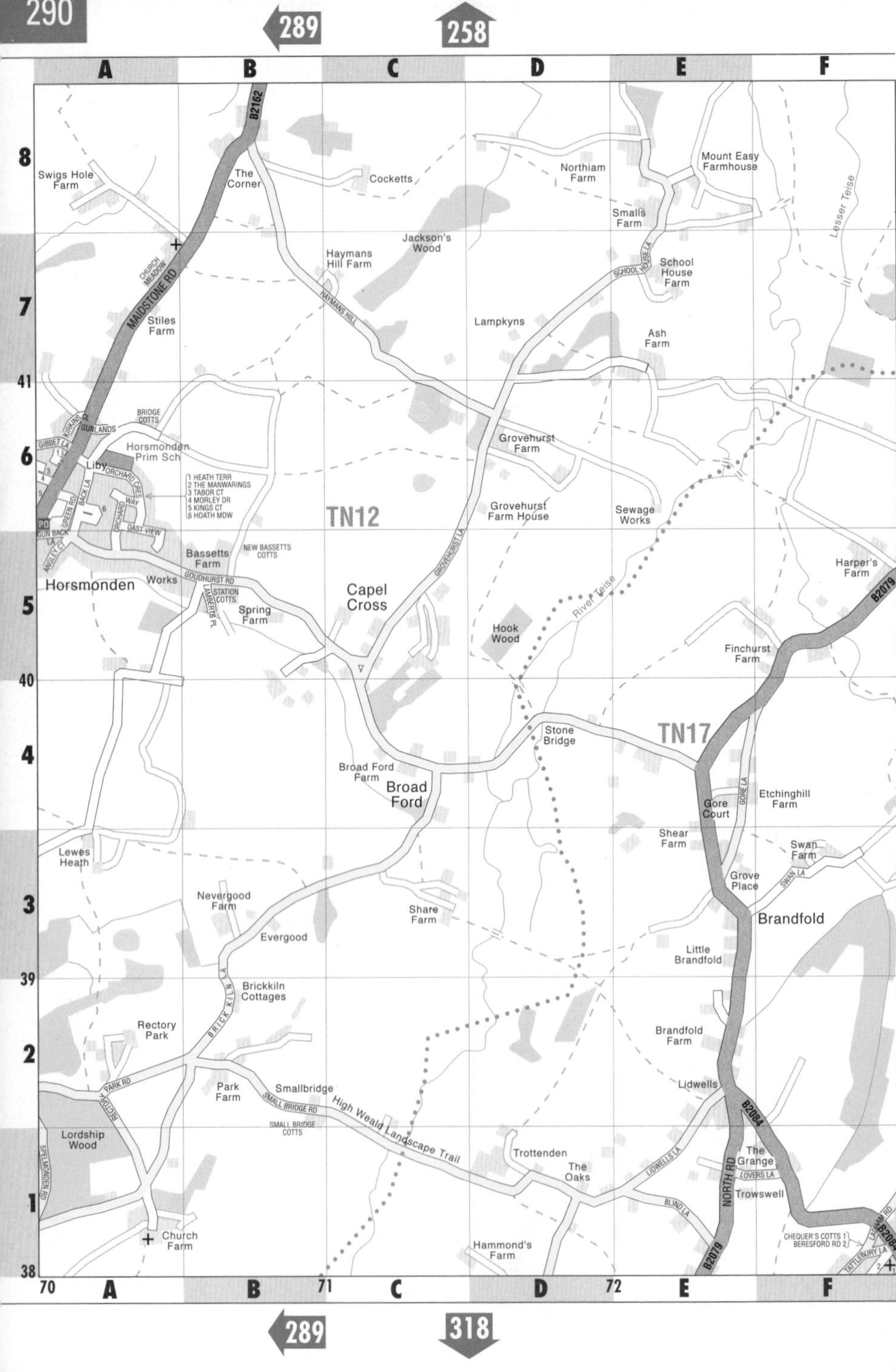

289
258
A
B
C
D
E
F
8
7
41
6
5
40
4
3
39
2
1
38
70
71
72
Swigs Hole Farm
The Corner
Cocketts
Northiam Farm
Mount Easy Farmhouse
Smalls Farm
Lesser Teise
Jackson's Wood
Haymans Hill Farm
School House Farm
CHURCH MEADOW
MAIDSTONE RD
B2162
HAYMANS HILL
SCHOOL HOUSE LA
Stiles Farm
Lampkyns
Ash Farm
BRIDGE COTTS
KIRKINS CL
GUNLANDS
GIBBET LA
Horsmonden Prim Sch
Liby
ORCHARD CRES
BACK LA
GREEN RD
ORCHARD
WAY
OAST VIEW
1 HEATH TERR
2 THE MANWARINGS
3 TABOR CT
4 MORLEY DR
5 KINGS CT
6 HOATH MDW
Grovehurst Farm
Grovehurst Farm House
Sewage Works
TN12
PO
GUN BACK LA
ANGLEY CT
NEW BASSETTS COTTS
Bassetts Farm
Horsmonden
Works
GOUDHURST RD
STATION COTTS
LAMBERTS PL
Spring Farm
Capel Cross
GROVEHURST LA
River Teise
Hook Wood
Harper's Farm
B2079
Finchurst Farm
Stone Bridge
TN17
Broad Ford Farm
Broad Ford
Gore Court
GORE LA
Etchinghill Farm
Shear Farm
Swan Farm
Lewes Heath
Grove Place
SWAN LA
Nevergood Farm
Share Farm
Brandfold
Evergood
Little Brandfold
Brickkiln Cottages
BRICK KILN LA
Rectory Park
Brandfold Farm
PARK RD
Park Farm
Smallbridge
Lidwells
RECTORY
SMALL BRIDGE RD
High Weald Landscape Trail
SMALL BRIDGE COTTS
B2084
Lordship Wood
SPELMONDEN RD
Trottenden
The Oaks
LIDWELLS LA
The Grange
LOVERS LA
NORTH RD
Trowswell
BLIND LA
Church Farm
Hammond's Farm
CHEQUER'S COTTS 1
BERESFORD RD 2
TATTLEBURY LA
B2079
289
318

259
292

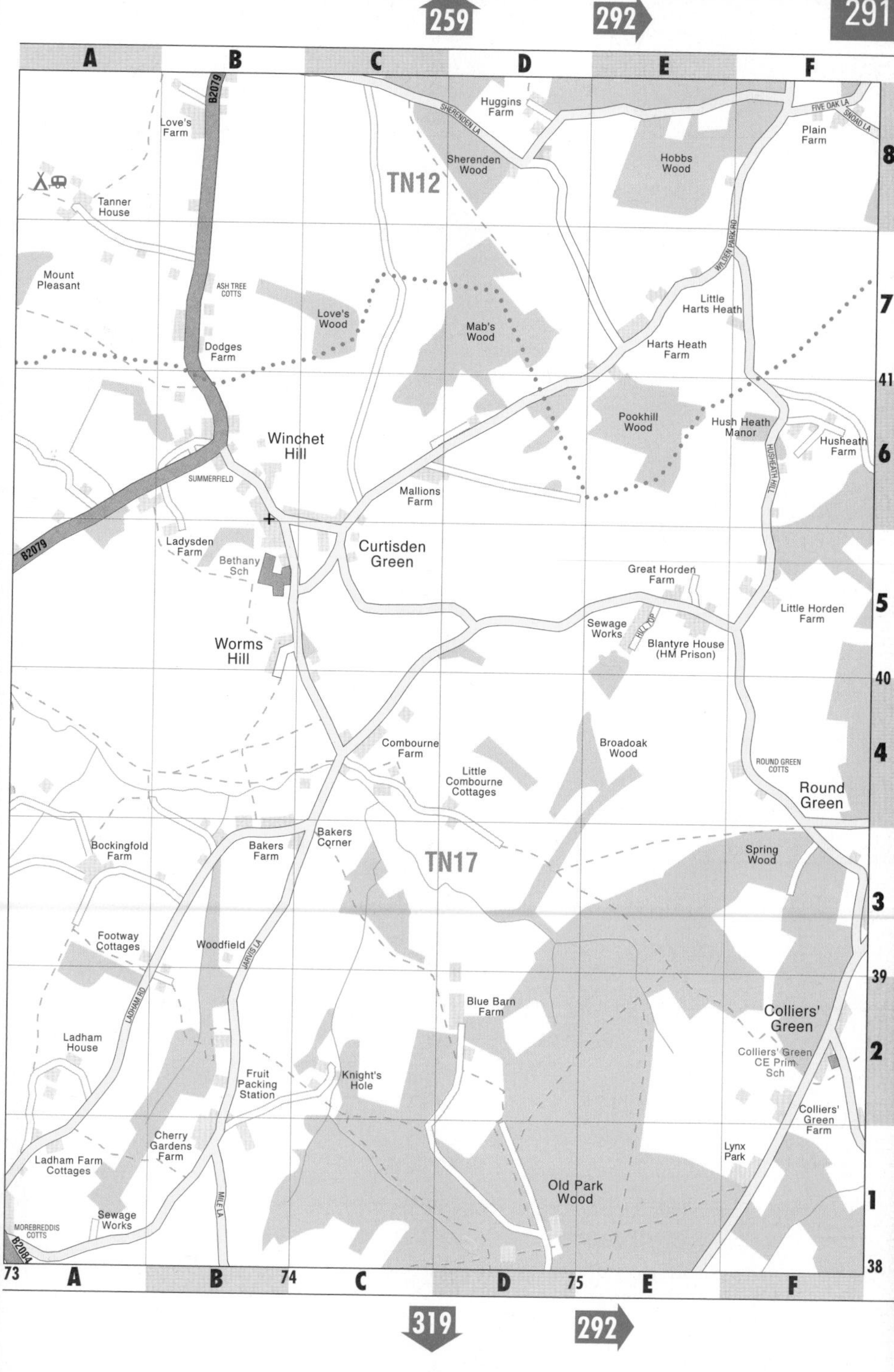
A
B
C
D
E
F
B2079
Love's Farm
Tanner House
Huggins Farm
SHERENDEN LA
Sherenden Wood
TN12
Hobbs Wood
FIVE OAK LA
SNOAD LA
Plain Farm
8
Mount Pleasant
ASH TREE COTTS
Love's Wood
Mab's Wood
WILDEN PARK RD
Little Harts Heath
7
Dodges Farm
Harts Heath Farm
41
Winchet Hill
Pookhill Wood
Hush Heath Manor
HUSHEATH HILL
Husheath Farm
6
SUMMERFIELD
Mallions Farm
Ladysden Farm
Bethany Sch
Curtisden Green
Great Horden Farm
5
Little Horden Farm
Sewage Works
HILL TOP
Blantyre House (HM Prison)
Worms Hill
40
Combourne Farm
Little Combourne Cottages
Broadoak Wood
ROUND GREEN COTTS
4
Round Green
Bockingfold Farm
Bakers Farm
Bakers Corner
TN17
Spring Wood
3
Footway Cottages
Woodfield
JARVIS LA
LADHAM RD
39
Blue Barn Farm
Colliers' Green
Ladham House
2
Colliers' Green CE Prim Sch
Fruit Packing Station
Knight's Hole
Colliers' Green Farm
Cherry Gardens Farm
Ladham Farm Cottages
Lynx Park
Old Park Wood
1
MILE LA
Sewage Works
MOREBREDDIS COTTS
B2084
38
73
74
75

319
292

291
260

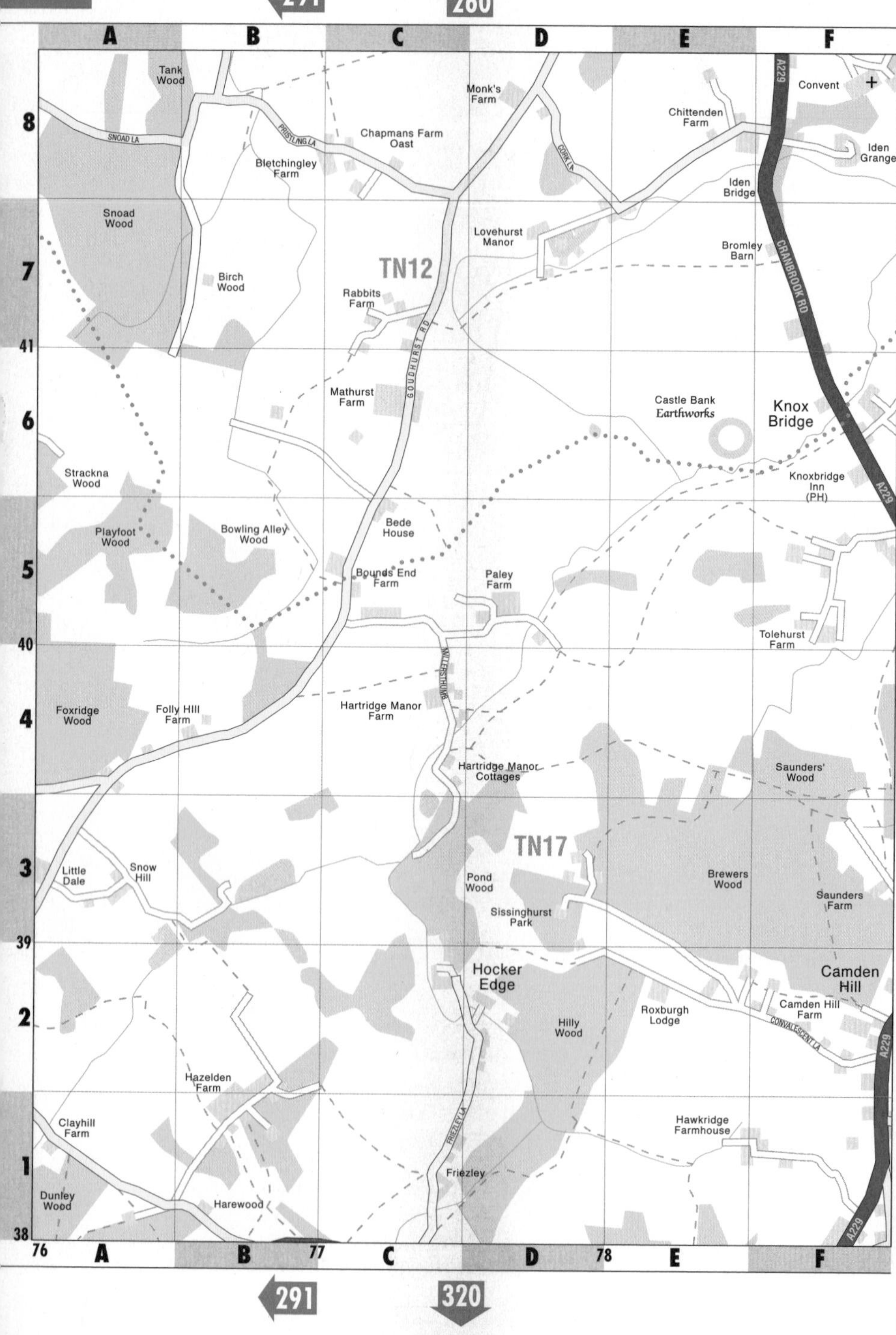
A
B
C
D
E
F
Tank Wood
Monk's Farm
Convent
Chittenden Farm
Iden Grange
SNOAD LA
PRISTLING LA
Chapmans Farm Oast
Bletchingley Farm
CORK LA
Iden Bridge
Snoad Wood
Lovehurst Manor
Bromley Barn
TN12
Birch Wood
Rabbits Farm
CRANBROOK RD
A229
GOUDHURST RD
Mathurst Farm
Castle Bank Earthworks
Knox Bridge
Strackna Wood
Knoxbridge Inn (PH)
Playfoot Wood
Bowling Alley Wood
Bede House
Bounds End Farm
Paley Farm
Tolehurst Farm
MILLERSTHUMB
Foxridge Wood
Folly Hill Farm
Hartridge Manor Farm
Hartridge Manor Cottages
Saunders' Wood
TN17
Little Dale
Snow Hill
Pond Wood
Brewers Wood
Sissinghurst Park
Saunders Farm
Hocker Edge
Camden Hill
Hilly Wood
Roxburgh Lodge
Camden Hill Farm
CONVALESCENT LA
Hazelden Farm
Clayhill Farm
Hawkridge Farmhouse
FRIEZLEY LA
Friezley
Dunley Wood
Harewood
8
7
41
6
5
40
4
3
39
2
1
38
76
77
78

291
320

261
294

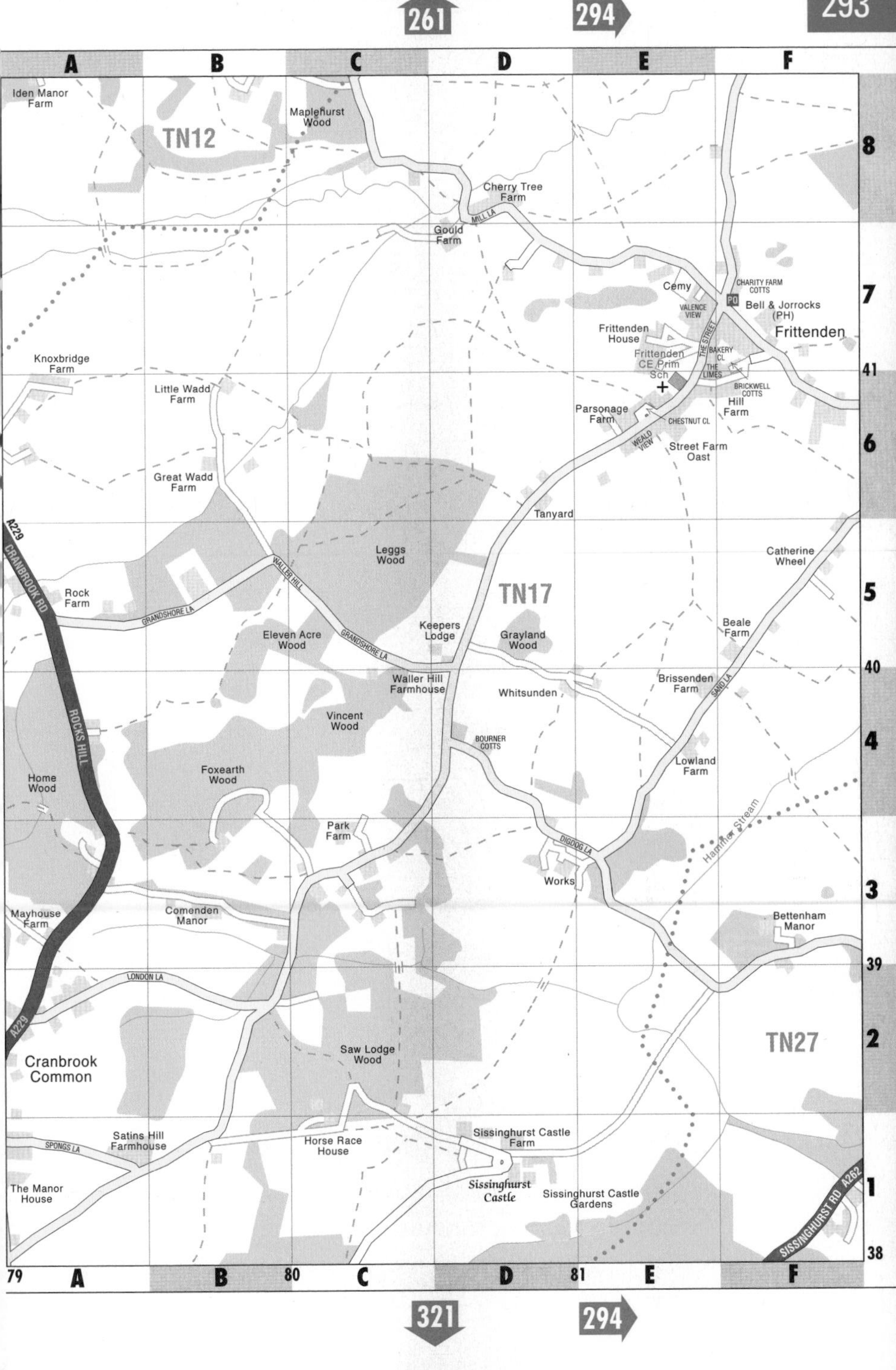
Iden Manor Farm
Maplehurst Wood
TN12
Cherry Tree Farm
MILL LA
Gould Farm
Cemy
CHARITY FARM COTTS
PO
Bell & Jorrocks (PH)
Frittenden
VALENCE VIEW
THE STREET
Frittenden House
Frittenden CE Prim Sch
BAKERY CL
THE LIMES
BRICKWELL COTTS
Hill Farm
Knoxbridge Farm
Little Wadd Farm
Parsonage Farm
CHESTNUT CL
WEALD VIEW
Street Farm Oast
Great Wadd Farm
Tanyard
A229
CRANBROOK RD
Leggs Wood
Catherine Wheel
WALLER HILL
Rock Farm
GRANDSHORE LA
TN17
Keepers Lodge
Grayland Wood
Beale Farm
Eleven Acre Wood
Waller Hill Farmhouse
Whitsunden
Brissenden Farm
SAND LA
Vincent Wood
ROCKS HILL
BOURNER COTTS
Lowland Farm
Home Wood
Foxearth Wood
Park Farm
Hammer Stream
DIGDOG LA
Works
Mayhouse Farm
Comenden Manor
Bettenham Manor
LONDON LA
TN27
Cranbrook Common
Saw Lodge Wood
Satins Hill Farmhouse
SPONGS LA
Horse Race House
Sissinghurst Castle Farm
Sissinghurst Castle
Sissinghurst Castle Gardens
The Manor House
SISSINGHURST RD A262
A B C D E F
8 7 41 6 5 40 4 3 39 2 1 38
79 80 81

321
294

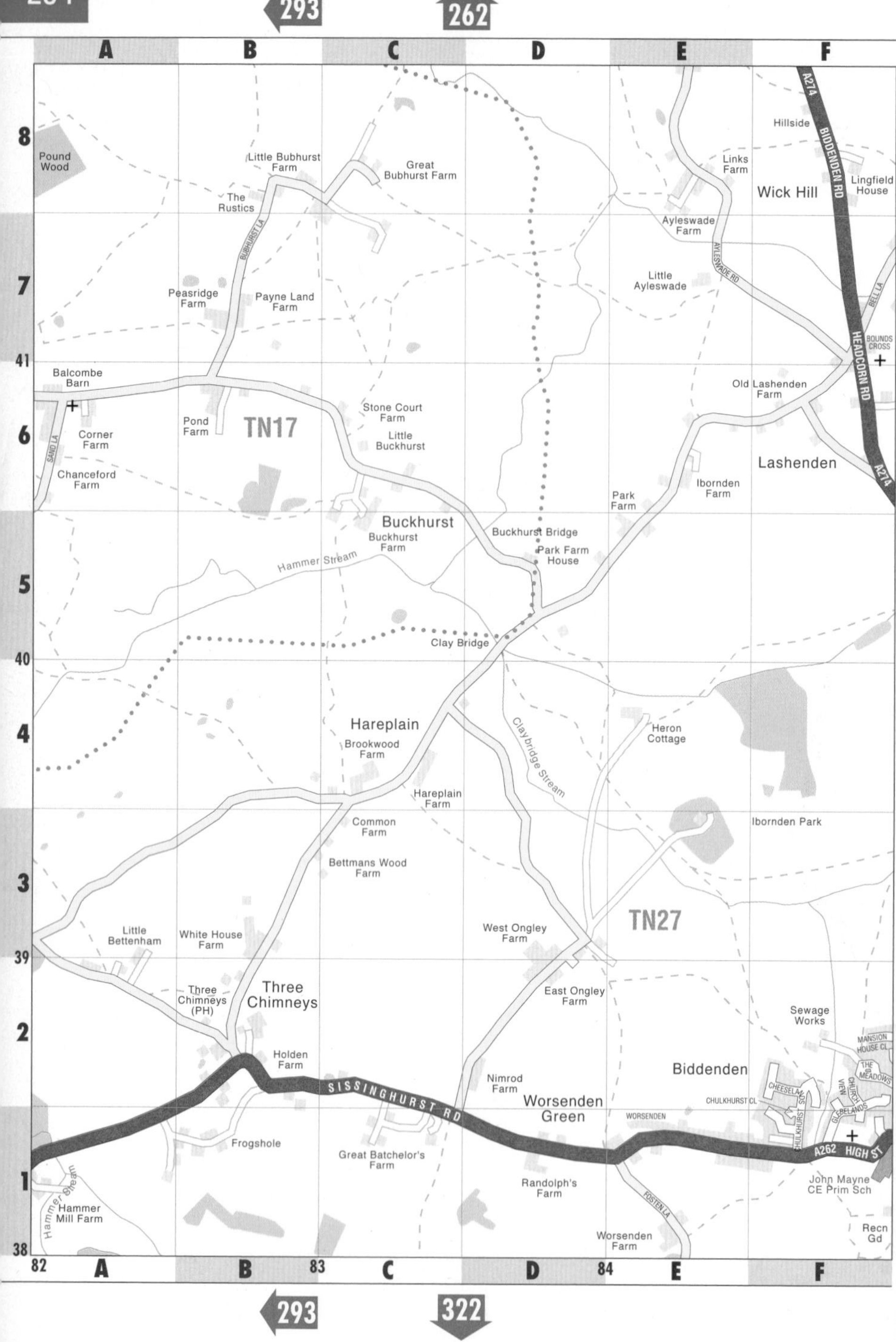

	A	B	C	D	E	F

8

Pound Wood

Little Bubhurst Farm

Great Bubhurst Farm

The Rustics

Hillside

Links Farm

Wick Hill

Lingfield House

A274

BIDDENDEN RD

Ayleswade Farm

7

Peasridge Farm

Payne Land Farm

Little Aing Land Ayleswade

BUBHURST LA

PELE LA

HEADCORN RD

41

BOUNDS CROSS

Balcombe Barn

Stone Court Farm

Old Lashenden Farm

6

Corner Farm

Pond Farm

TN17

Little Buckhurst

Lashenden

A274

SAND LA

Chanceford Farm

Park Farm

Ibornden Farm

Buckhurst Bridge

5

Buckhurst

Buckhurst Farm

Park Farm House

Hammer Stream

40

Clay Bridge

4

Hareplain

Brookwood Farm

Heron Cottage

Clay Bridge Stream

Hareplain Farm

Common Farm

Ibornden Park

3

Bettmans Wood Farm

Little Bettenham

White House Farm

West Ongley Farm

TN27

Sewage Works

MANSION HOUSE CL

39

Three Chimneys (PH)

Three Chimneys

East Ongley Farm

THE MEADOWS

2

Holden Farm

Biddenden

CHEESELANE

CHULKHURST CL

Nimrod Farm

Worsenden Green

SISSINGHURST RD

WORSENDEN

HIGH ST

A262

Frogshole

Great Batchelor's Farm

Randolph's Farm

John Mayne CE Prim Sch

1

Hammer Stream

Hammer Mill Farm

Worsenden Farm

FOSTEN LA

Recn Gd

38

82	A	B	83	C	D	84	E	F

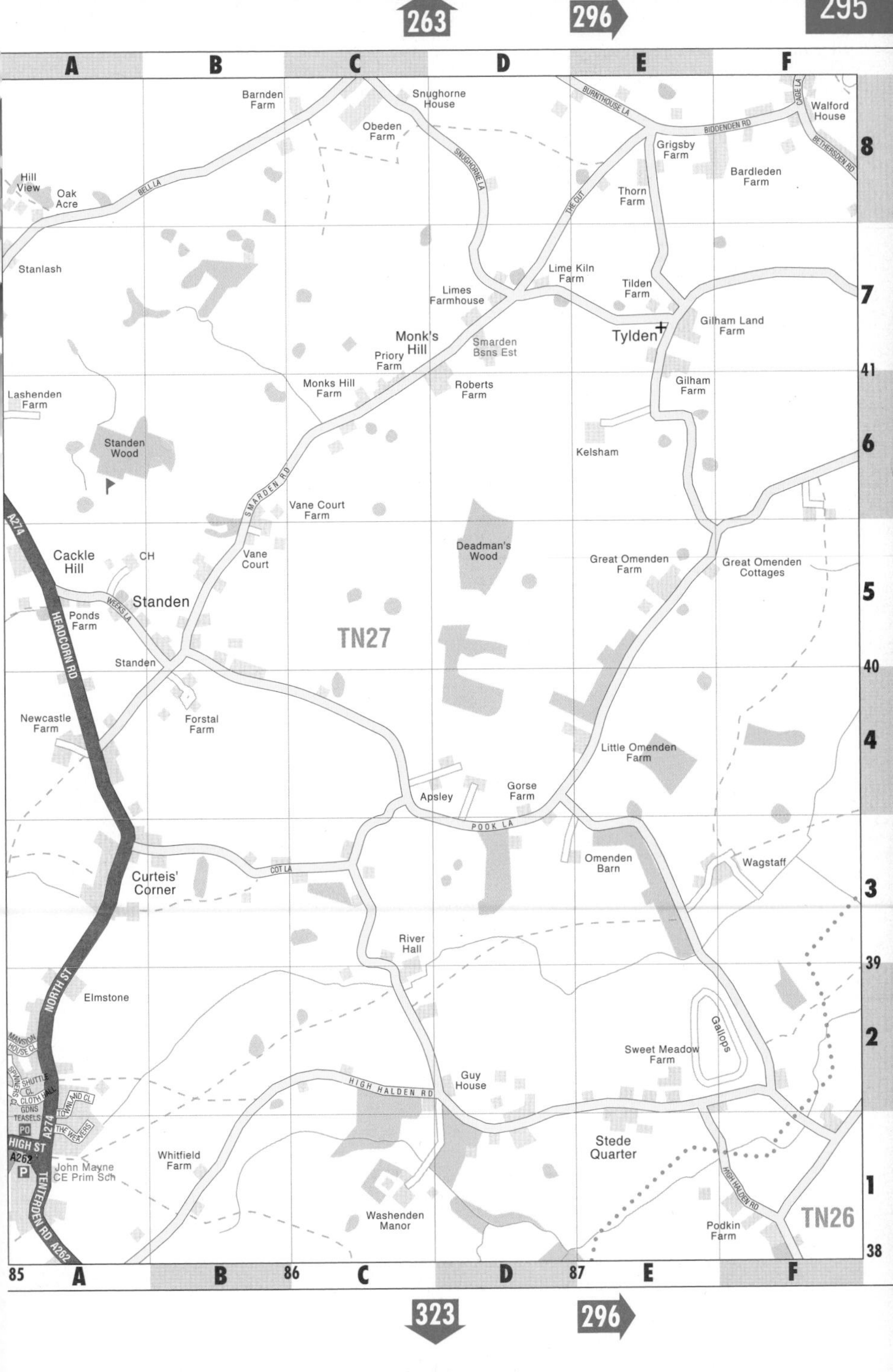

263
296
A
B
C
D
E
F
8
7
41
6
5
40
4
3
39
2
1
38
85
86
87
Barnden Farm
Snughorne House
Obeden Farm
BURNTHOUSE LA
BIDDENDEN RD
CAGE LA
Walford House
BETHERSDEN RD
Grigsby Farm
Bardleden Farm
SNUGHORNE LA
Hill View
Oak Acre
BELL LA
THE CUT
Thorn Farm
Stanlash
Lime Kiln Farm
Tilden Farm
Limes Farmhouse
Gilham Land Farm
Tylden
Monk's Hill
Smarden Bsns Est
Priory Farm
Monks Hill Farm
Roberts Farm
Gilham Farm
Lashenden Farm
Standen Wood
Kelsham
SMARDEN RD
Vane Court Farm
A274
Deadman's Wood
Cackle Hill
CH
Vane Court
Great Omenden Farm
Great Omenden Cottages
Standen
WEEKS LA
Ponds Farm
HEADCORN RD
TN27
Standen
Newcastle Farm
Forstal Farm
Little Omenden Farm
Gorse Farm
Apsley
POOK LA
Omenden Barn
Wagstaff
Curteis' Corner
COT LA
River Hall
NORTH ST
Elmstone
Gallops
MANSION HOUSE CL
SPINNERS CL
SHUTTLE CL
CLOTH HALL GDNS
TEASELS
TOWNLAND CL
THE WEAVERS
Sweet Meadow Farm
Guy House
HIGH HALDEN RD
PO
A274
HIGH ST
A262
P
TENTERDEN RD
A262
Whitfield Farm
John Mayne CE Prim Sch
Stede Quarter
HIGH HALDEN RD
Washenden Manor
Podkin Farm
TN26
323
296

295
264

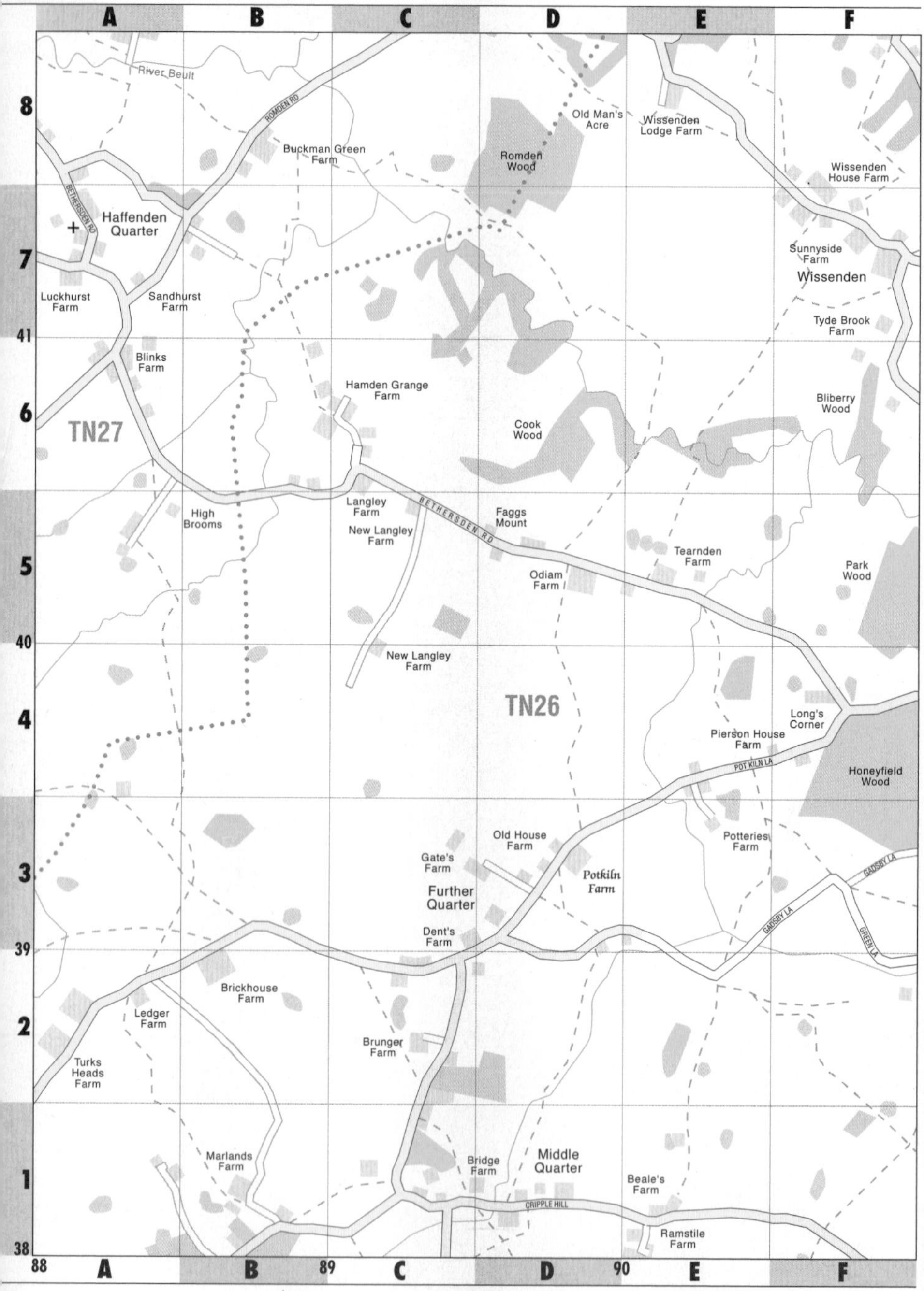

A **B** **C** **D** **E** **F**

8

River Beult

ROMDEN RD

Buckman Green
Farm

Old Man's
Acre

Wissenden
Lodge Farm

Romden
Wood

Wissenden
House Farm

7

Haffenden
Quarter

Sunnyside
Farm

Wissenden

41

Luckhurst
Farm

Sandhurst
Farm

Tyde Brook
Farm

Blinks
Farm

Hamden Grange
Farm

6

TN27

Cook
Wood

Bliberry
Wood

High
Brooms

Langley
Farm

Faggs
Mount

BETHERSDEN RD

New Langley
Farm

5

Tearnden
Farm

Park
Wood

Odiam
Farm

40

New Langley
Farm

TN26

4

Long's
Corner

Pierson House
Farm

POT KILN LA

Honeyfield
Wood

3

Gate's
Farm

Old House
Farm

Potteries
Farm

Potkiln
Farm

GADSBY LA

GREEN LA

Further
Quarter

39

Dent's
Farm

2

Brickhouse
Farm

Ledger
Farm

Brunger
Farm

Turks
Heads
Farm

1

Marlands
Farm

Bridge
Farm

Middle
Quarter

Beale's
Farm

38

CRIPPLE HILL

Ramstile
Farm

88 **A** **B** 89 **C** **D** 90 **E** **F**

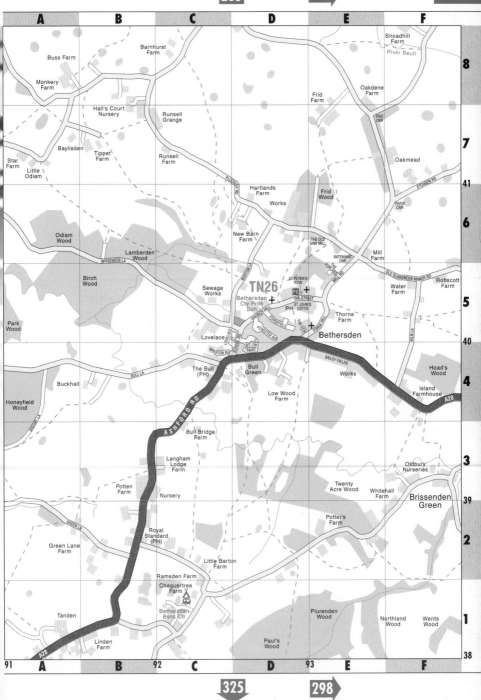

A B C D E F
8 7 41 6 5 40 4 3 39 2 1 38
91 92 93
Snoadhill Farm
River Beult
Barnhurst Farm
Buss Farm
Monkery Farm
Oakdene Farm
Frid Farm
Hall's Court Nursery
Runsell Grange
FRID CNR
Baylisden
Tippet Farm
Runsell Farm
Star Farm
Little Odiam
Oakmead
PLUCKLEY RD
ETCHDEN RD
Hartlands Farm
Frid Wood
Works
PARIS CNR
New Barn Farm
Odiam Wood
THE OLD SAW MILL
Lamberden Wood
WISSENDEN LA
BATEMANS CNR
Mill Farm
THE POPLARS
NORTON LA
MILL RD
OLD SURRENDEN MANOR RD
Birch Wood
ST PETER'S ROW
TN26
Robscott Farm
Water Farm
Sewage Works
PO
Bethersden Cty Prim Sch
THE STREET
ST JOHN'S COTTS
PH
CHURCH HILL
FORGEFIELD
Thorne Farm
Park Wood
THE DENE
FORGE HILL
CHESTER AVE
Bethersden
KILN LA
Lovelace
LOVELACE CT
SCHOOL RD
ORCHARD FIELD
WHISTON AVE
BAILEY FIELDS
The Bull (PH)
Bull Green
Works
Hoad's Wood
BULL LA
Buckhall
Island Farmhouse
Low Wood Farm
A28
Honeyfield Wood
GADSBY LA
ASHFORD RD
Bull Bridge Farm
Langham Lodge Farm
Oldbury Nurseries
Twenty Acre Wood
Potten Farm
Nursery
Whitehall Farm
Brissenden Green
GREEN LA
Potter's Farm
Royal Standard (PH)
Green Lane Farm
Little Barton Farm
Ramsden Farm
Chequertree Farm
Bethersden Bsns Ctr
Plurenden Wood
Tanden
Northland Wood
Wents Wood
Linden Farm
Paul's Wood
A28

297
266

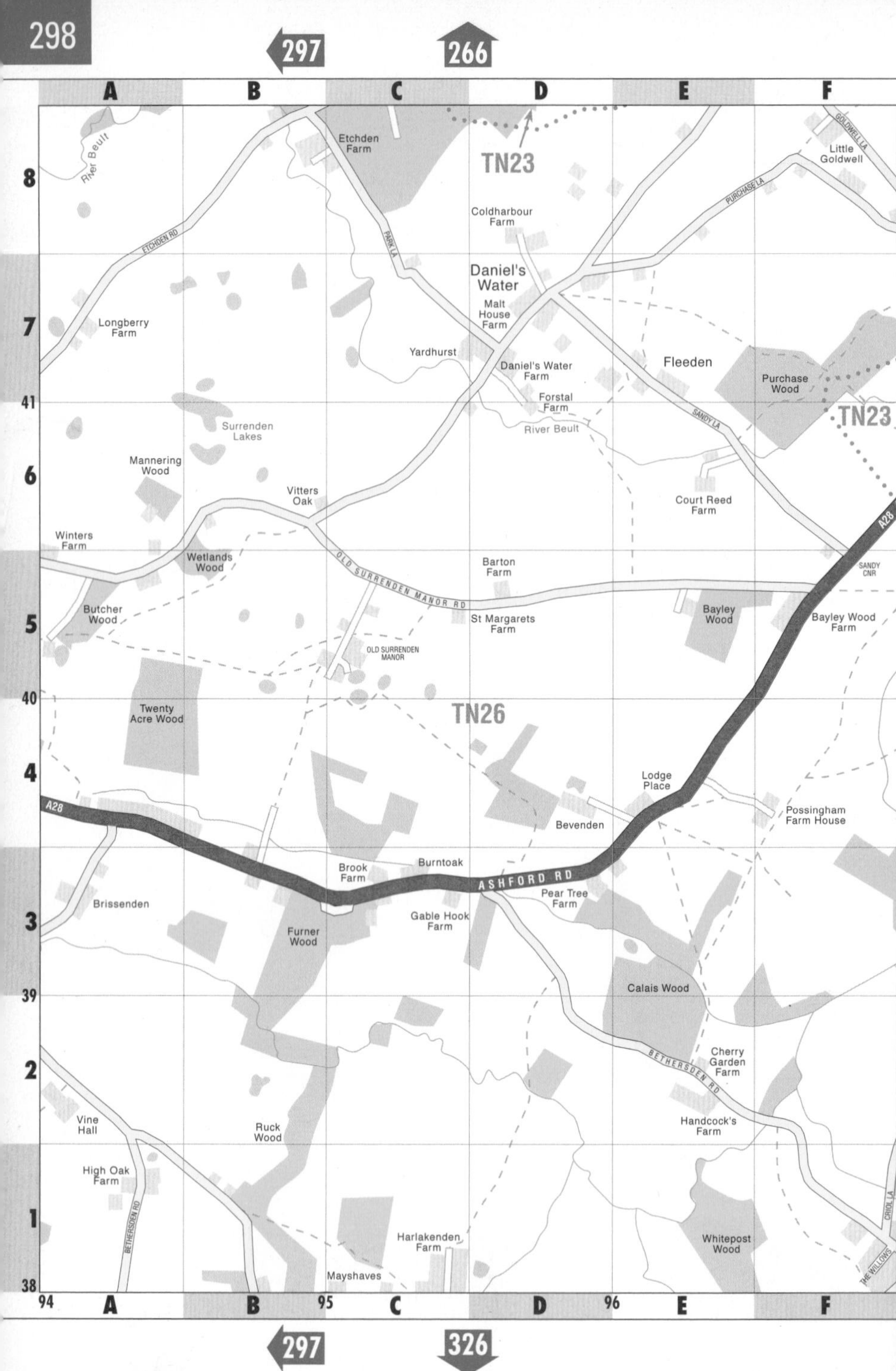
A
B
C
D
E
F
8
7
41
6
5
40
4
3
39
2
1
38
94
95
96
River Beult
Etchden Farm
TN23
Little Goldwell
GOLDWELL LA
PURCHASE LA
ETCHDEN RD
PARK LA
Coldharbour Farm
Daniel's Water
Malt House Farm
Longberry Farm
Yardhurst
Daniel's Water Farm
Fleeden
Purchase Wood
Forstal Farm
River Beult
SANDY LA
TN23
Surrenden Lakes
Mannering Wood
Vitters Oak
Court Reed Farm
Winters Farm
Wetlands Wood
Barton Farm
A28
SANDY CNR
OLD SURRENDEN MANOR RD
Butcher Wood
St Margarets Farm
Bayley Wood
Bayley Wood Farm
OLD SURRENDEN MANOR
Twenty Acre Wood
TN26
Lodge Place
A28
Possingham Farm House
Bevenden
Burntoak
Brook Farm
ASHFORD RD
Pear Tree Farm
Brissenden
Gable Hook Farm
Furner Wood
Calais Wood
Cherry Garden Farm
BETHERSDEN RD
Vine Hall
Ruck Wood
Handcock's Farm
High Oak Farm
CRIOL LA
BETHERSDEN RD
Harlakenden Farm
Whitepost Wood
Mayshaves
THE WILLOWS

297
326

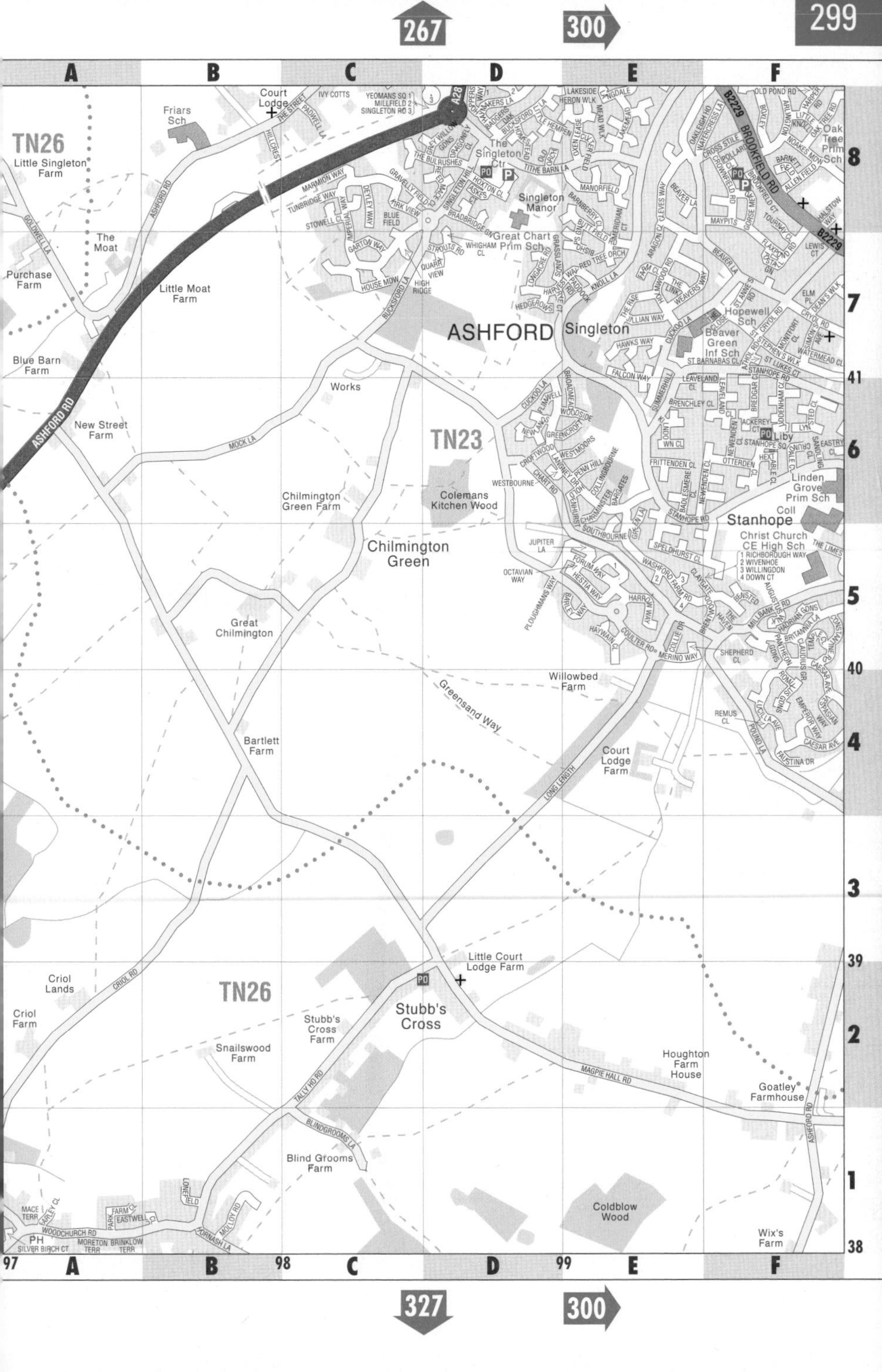
267
300
A
B
C
D
E
F
TN26
Little Singleton Farm
Friars Sch
Court Lodge
ASHFORD RD
The Moat
Purchase Farm
Little Moat Farm
Blue Barn Farm
New Street Farm
MOCK LA
Works
Chilmington Green Farm
TN23
Colemans Kitchen Wood
Chilmington Green
Great Chilmington
Bartlett Farm
Greensand Way
Willowbed Farm
Court Lodge Farm
LONG LENGTH
ASHFORD
Singleton
The Singleton Ctr
Singleton Manor
Great Chart Prim Sch
BLUE FIELD
HIGH RIDGE
BUCKSFORD LA
Hopewell Sch
Beaver Green Inf Sch
Liby
Linden Grove Prim Sch
Coll
Stanhope
Christ Church CE High Sch
1 RICHBOROUGH WAY
2 WIVENHOE
3 WILLINGDON
4 DOWN CT
B2229
BROOKFIELD RD
Oak Tree Prim Sch
Little Court Lodge Farm
Stubb's Cross
Stubb's Cross Farm
Criol Lands
Criol Farm
CRIOL RD
Snailswood Farm
TALLY HO RD
BLINDGROOMS LA
Blind Grooms Farm
MAGPIE HALL RD
Houghton Farm House
Goatley Farmhouse
Coldblow Wood
Wix's Farm
WOODCHURCH RD
PH
8
7
41
6
5
40
4
3
39
2
1
38
97
98
99
327
300

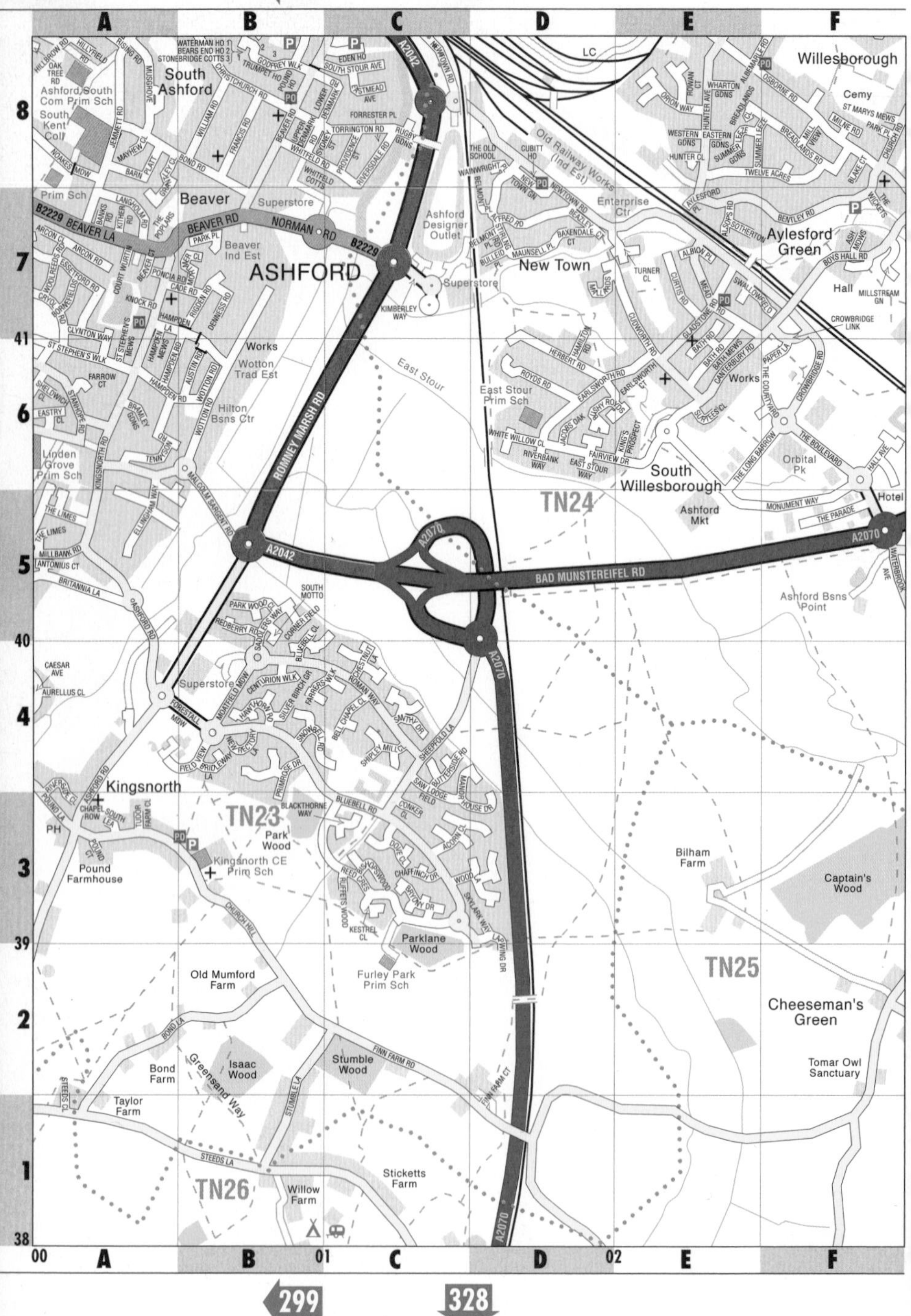

299
268

A   B   C   D   E   F

8

South
Ashford

Ashford South
Com Prim Sch
South
Kent
Coll

Prim Sch

Beaver

Superstore

BEAVER LA

B2229 BEAVER LA

NORMAN RD

B2229

7

ASHFORD

Beaver
Ind Est

Works

Wotton
Trad Est

Hilton
Bsns Ctr

41

ROMNEY MARSH RD

East Stour

Linden
Grove
Prim Sch

6

Ashford
Designer
Outlet

KIMBERLEY
WAY

Superstore

East Stour
Prim Sch

New Town

Enterprise
Ctr

Willesborough

Cemy
St Mary's
Sch

Aylesford
Green

Hall

MILLSTREAM
GN

CROWBRIDGE
LINK

Works

TN24

South
Willesborough

Ashford
Mkt

Orbital
Pk

The Boulevard

Hotel

Ashford Bsns
Point

5

A2042

A2042

A2070

BAD MUNSTEREIFEL RD

A2070

MONUMENT WAY

THE PARADE

40

Superstore

Caesar
Ave
Aurellus Cl

4

Kingsnorth

PH

Pound
Farmhouse

TN23

Blackthorne
Way

Park
Wood

Kingsnorth CE
Prim Sch

BLUEBELL RD

Bilham
Farm

Captain's
Wood

39

Kestrel
Cl

Parklane
Wood

Furley Park
Prim Sch

TN25

Cheeseman's
Green

3

2

Old Mumford
Farm

Bond
Farm

Isaac
Wood

Greensand Way

Stumble
Wood

FINN FARM RD

Tomar Owl
Sanctuary

Taylor
Farm

STUMBLE LA

STEEDS LA

38

1

TN26

Willow
Farm

Sticketts
Farm

A2070

00   A   B   01   C   D   02   E   F

299
328

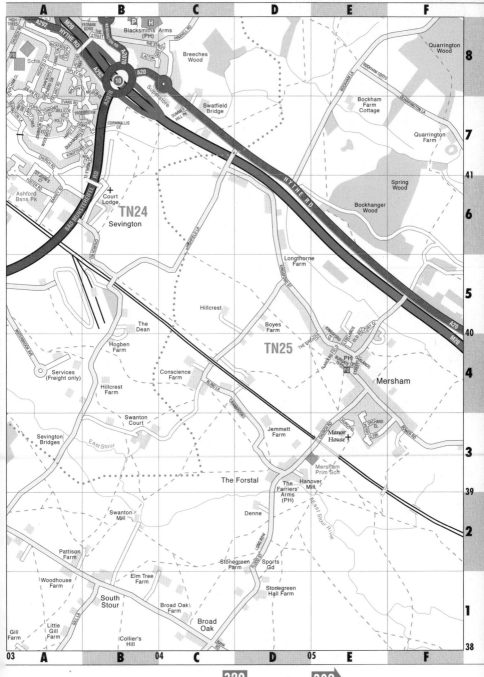

302

A B C D E F

HIGH TREES CL
CHURCH RD
A292
M20
HYTHE RD
YEOMAN GDNS
THE STREET
KENNINGTON RD
Blacksmiths' Arms (PH)
HINXHILL RD
THE STREET
LACTON OAST
A2070
Breeches Wood
PO
Schs
WICKENDEN CRES
CHARLTON CL
HIGHFIELD RD
LACTON WAY
RIPLEY RD
HAYWARD CL
SHEPHERD DR
COLLARD RD
RALEIGH CL
NELSON CL
10
A20
Superstore
JULIEN PL
EVANS RD
LUCKHURST RD
COWDREY CL
JELLICOE CL
TROUBRIDGE CL
FOLEY CL
DRAKE RD
JOHNSON CL
WOOLMER DR
HARDY CL
DUCKWORTH CL
KINGFISHER CL
NIGHTINGALE CL
CORNWALLIS CL
SUMMER HILL PK
Swatfield Bridge
BOCKHAM LA
BOCKHAM COTTS
Bockham Farm Cottage
QUARRINGTON LA
Quarrington Wood
Quarrington Farm
CHURCH RD
ST JOHN'S CT
FOSTER RD
BARREY RD
Ashford Bsns Pk
BAD MUNSTEREIFEL RD
Court Lodge
TN24
Sevington
HIGHFIELD LA
HYTHE RD
Spring Wood
Bockhanger Wood
Longthorne Farm
KINGSFORD ST
Hillcrest
The Dean
Boyes Farm
WATERBROOK AVE
Hogben Farm
TN25
THE ORCHIDS
KINGSFORD CL
GLEBELANDS
OLD RECTORY CL
FLANDERS FIELD
BURGATE TERR
THE STREET
OAKLANDS
PH
PO
A20
M20
Services (Freight only)
Conscience Farm
Mersham
Hillcrest Farm
BLIND LA
CRANBROOKS
Swanton Court
CHURCH RD
CHURCH CL
CHERRY GLEBE
ORCHARD CL
Manor House
BOWER RD
Jemmett Farm
Sevington Bridges
East Stour
Mersham Prim Sch
The Forstal
The Farriers' Arms (PH)
Hanover Mill
East Stour River
Swanton Mill
Denne
LONG ROW
Pattison Farm
Stonegreen Farm
FLOOD ST
Sports Gd
Woodhouse Farm
Elm Tree Farm
Stonegreen Hall Farm
South Stour
Broad Oak Farm
GILL LA
Broad Oak
Gill Farm
Little Gill Farm
Collier's Hill
BANK RD

8 7 41 6 5 40 4 3 39 2 1 38

03 A B 04 C D 05 E F

301
270

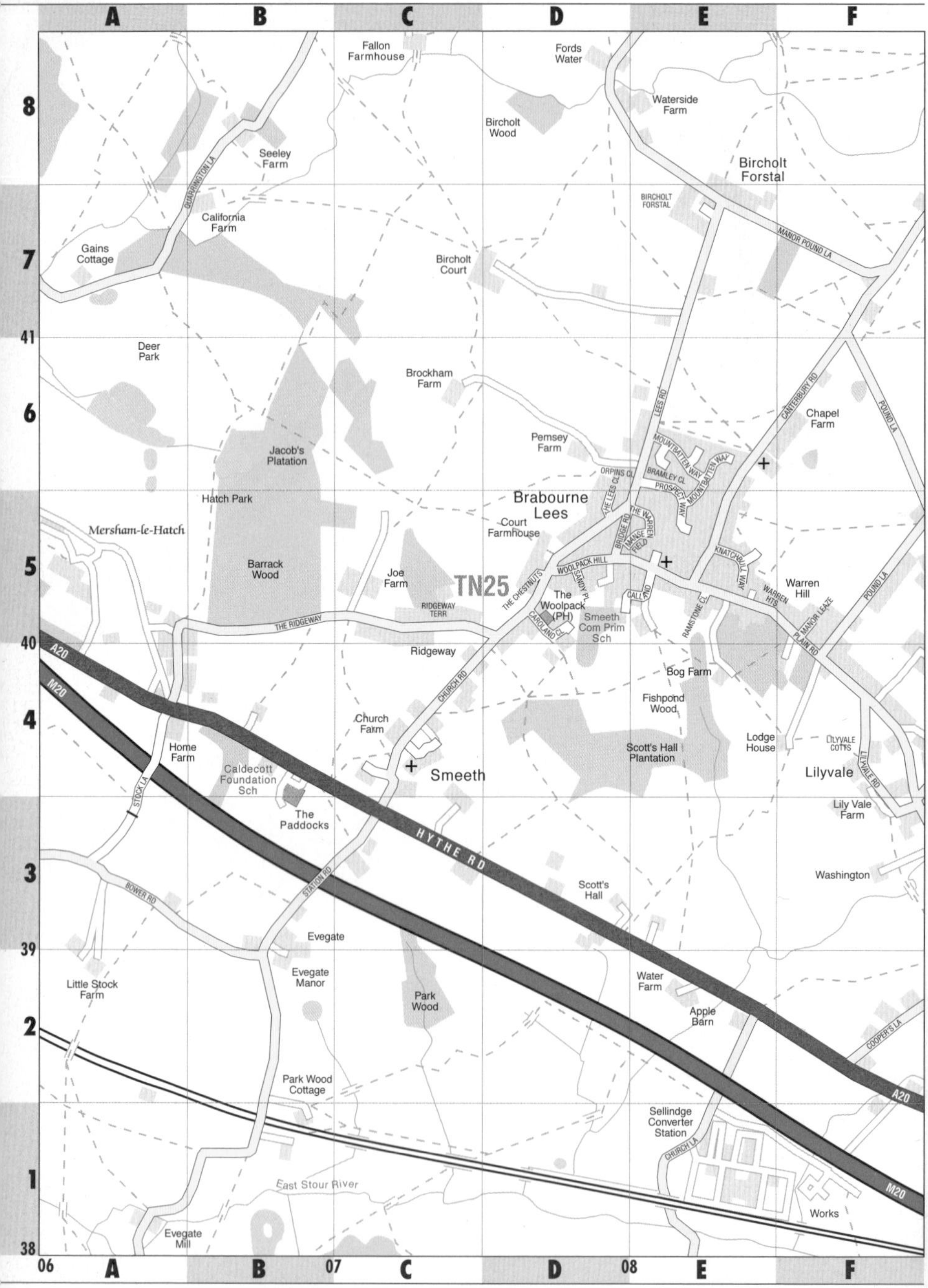

A **B** **C** **D** **E** **F**

8

Fallon
Farmhouse

Fords
Water

Waterside
Farm

Bircholt
Wood

Bircholt
Forstal

Seeley
Farm

BIRCHOLT
FORSTAL

California
Farm

7

Gains
Cottage

Bircholt
Court

41

Deer
Park

Brockham
Farm

6

Chapel
Farm

Jacob's
Platation

Pernsey
Farm

Hatch Park

ORPINS CL

Brabourne
Lees

Mersham-le-Hatch

Court
Farmhouse

5

Barrack
Wood

Joe
Farm

TN25

Warren
Hill

RIDGEWAY
TERR

The
Woolpack
(PH)

WOOLPACK HILL

WARREN
HTS

THE CHESTNUTS

Smeeth
Com Prim
Sch

40

THE RIDGEWAY

Ridgeway

GALL RD

A20

Bog Farm

M20

Fishpond
Wood

LILYVALE
COTTS

4

Home
Farm

Church
Farm

Lodge
House

Lilyvale

STICK LA

Caldecott
Foundation
Sch

Scott's Hall
Plantation

Lily Vale
Farm

CHURCH RD

Smeeth

The
Paddocks

HYTHE RD

Washington

3

BOWER RD

Scott's
Hall

39

Evegate

Water
Farm

Evegate
Manor

Park
Wood

2

Little Stock
Farm

Apple
Barn

A20

Park Wood
Cottage

M20

Sellindge
Converter
Station

CHURCH LA

1

East Stour River

Works

Evegate
Mill

38

06   07   08

A **B** **C** **D** **E** **F**

271
304
30

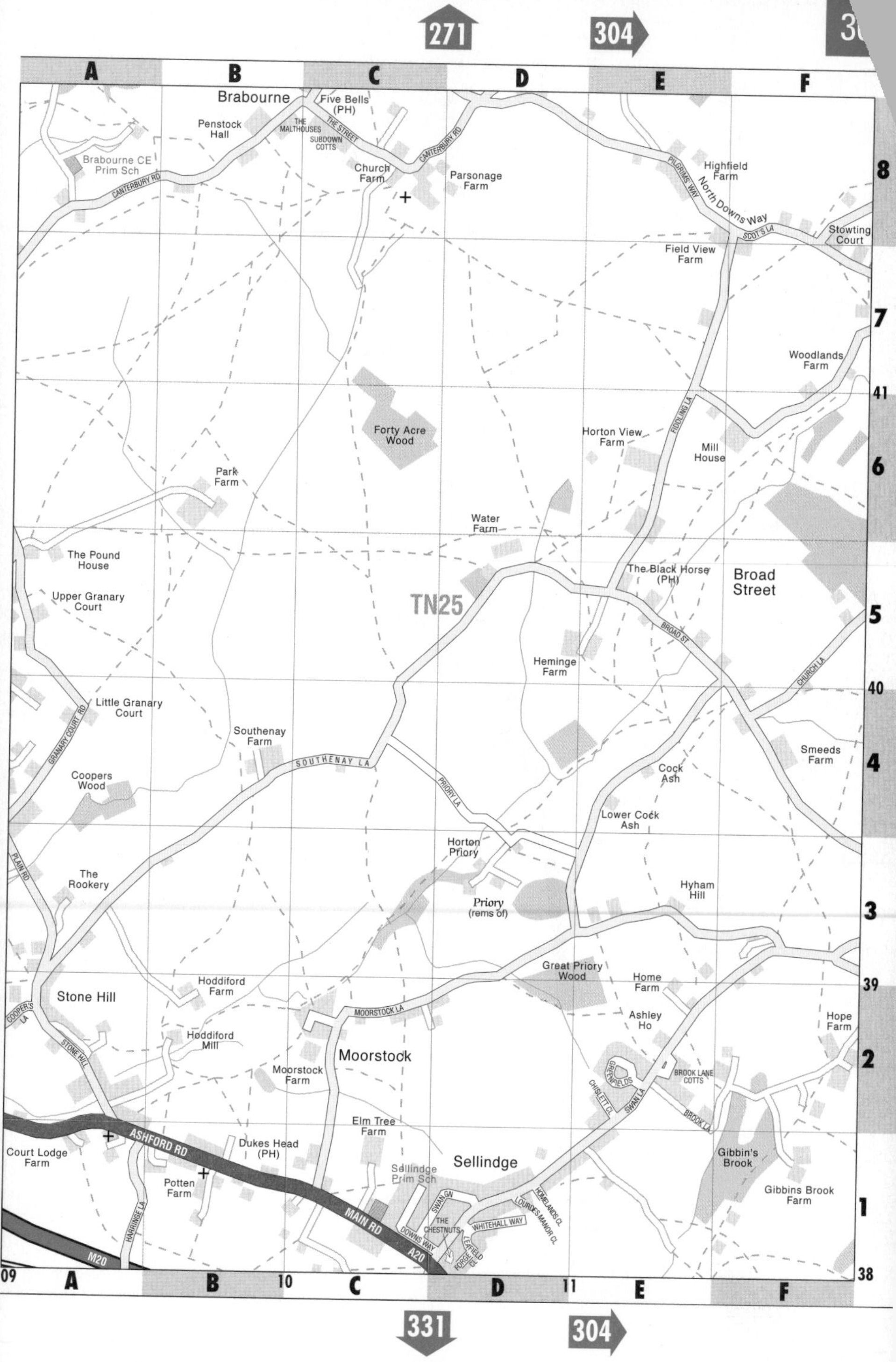
A
B
C
D
E
F
Brabourne
Five Bells (PH)
Penstock Hall
THE MALTHOUSES
THE STREET
SUBDOWN COTTS
CANTERBURY RD
Brabourne CE Prim Sch
Church Farm
Parsonage Farm
Highfield Farm
PILGRIMS WAY
North Downs Way
SCOT'S LA
Stowting Court
Field View Farm
Woodlands Farm
Forty Acre Wood
Horton View Farm
FIDDLING LA
Mill House
Park Farm
Water Farm
The Pound House
Upper Granary Court
The Black Horse (PH)
Broad Street
TN25
BROAD ST
Heminge Farm
CHURCH LA
Little Granary Court
GRANARY COURT RD
Southenay Farm
SOUTHENAY LA
Smeeds Farm
Coopers Wood
PRIORY LA
Cock Ash
Lower Cock Ash
Horton Priory
PLAIN RD
The Rookery
Priory (rems of)
Hyham Hill
Great Priory Wood
Home Farm
Stone Hill
Hoddiford Farm
COOPER'S LA
MOORSTOCK LA
Ashley Ho
Hope Farm
Hoddiford Mill
STONE HILL
Moorstock
Moorstock Farm
GREENFIELDS
BROOK LANE COTTS
CHISLETT CL
SWAN LA
BROOK LA
ASHFORD RD
Elm Tree Farm
Court Lodge Farm
Dukes Head (PH)
Sellindge
Gibbin's Brook
Potten Farm
Sellindge Prim Sch
SWAN GN
HOMELANDS CL
LOURDES MANOR CL
Gibbins Brook Farm
MAIN RD
THE CHESTNUTS
WHITEHALL WAY
HARRINGE LA
DOWNS WAY
LEAFIELD CL
FORGE CL
M20
A20
8
7
41
6
5
40
4
3
39
2
1
38
09
10
11

331
304

303
272

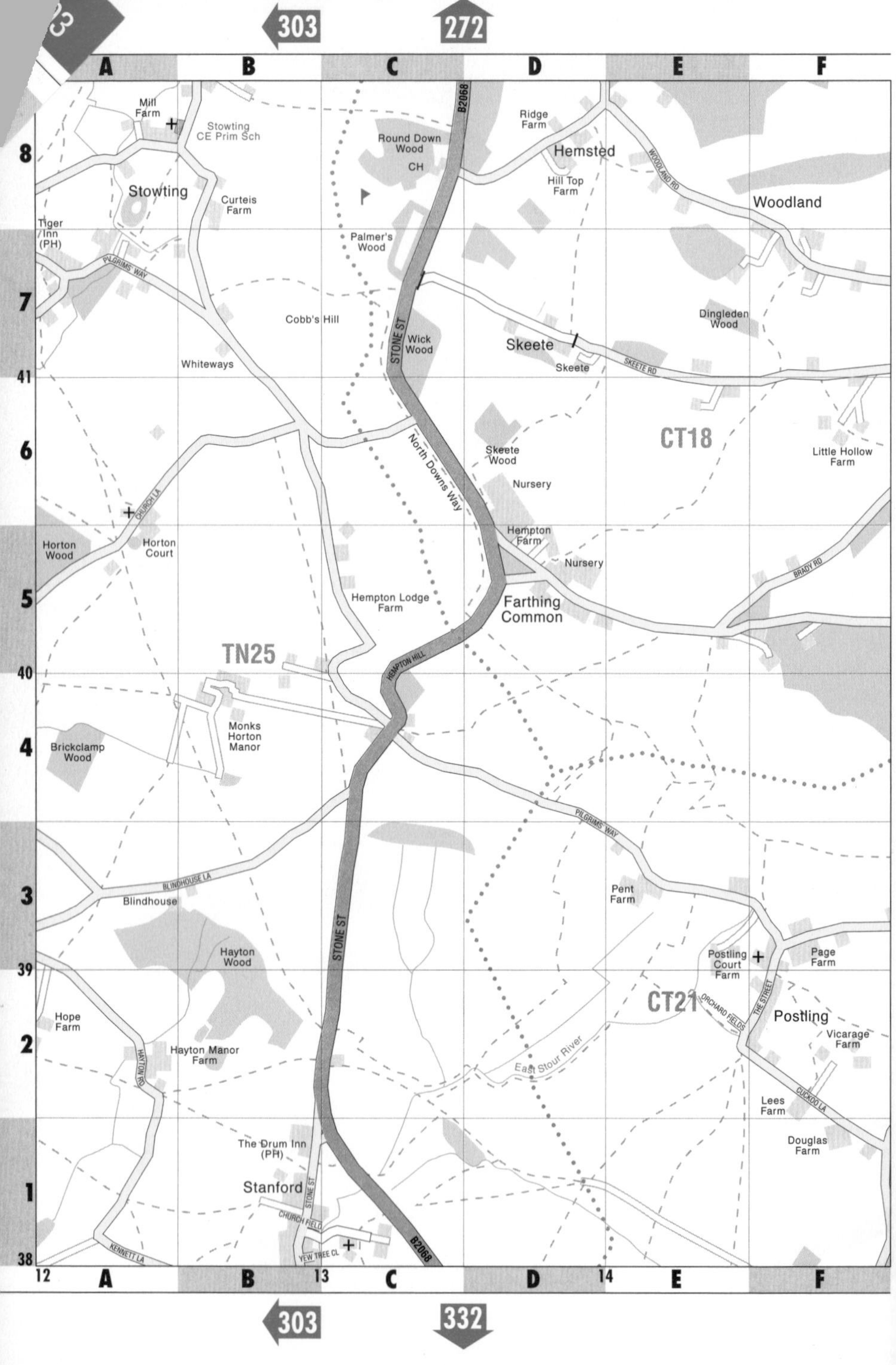
A
B
C
D
E
F
8
7
41
6
5
40
4
3
39
2
1
38
12
13
14
Mill Farm
Stowting CE Prim Sch
Stowting
Curteis Farm
Tiger Inn (PH)
PILGRIMS WAY
Round Down Wood
CH
Palmer's Wood
Cobb's Hill
Whiteways
STONE ST
Wick Wood
B2068
Ridge Farm
Hemsted
Hill Top Farm
WOODLAND RD
Woodland
Dingleden Wood
Skeete
SKEETE RD
CT18
Little Hollow Farm
North Downs Way
Skeete Wood
Nursery
Hempton Farm
Horton Wood
Horton Court
CHURCH LA
Hempton Lodge Farm
Farthing Common
BRADY RD
TN25
HEMPTON HILL
Monks Horton Manor
Brickclamp Wood
PILGRIMS WAY
BLINDHOUSE LA
Blindhouse
Pent Farm
Hayton Wood
Postling Court Farm
Page Farm
CT21
ORCHARD FIELDS
THE STREET
Postling
Vicarage Farm
Hope Farm
Hayton Manor Farm
HAYTON RD
East Stour River
CUCKOO LA
Lees Farm
Douglas Farm
The Drum Inn (PH)
Stanford
CHURCH FIELD
YEW TREE CL
KENNETT LA

303
332

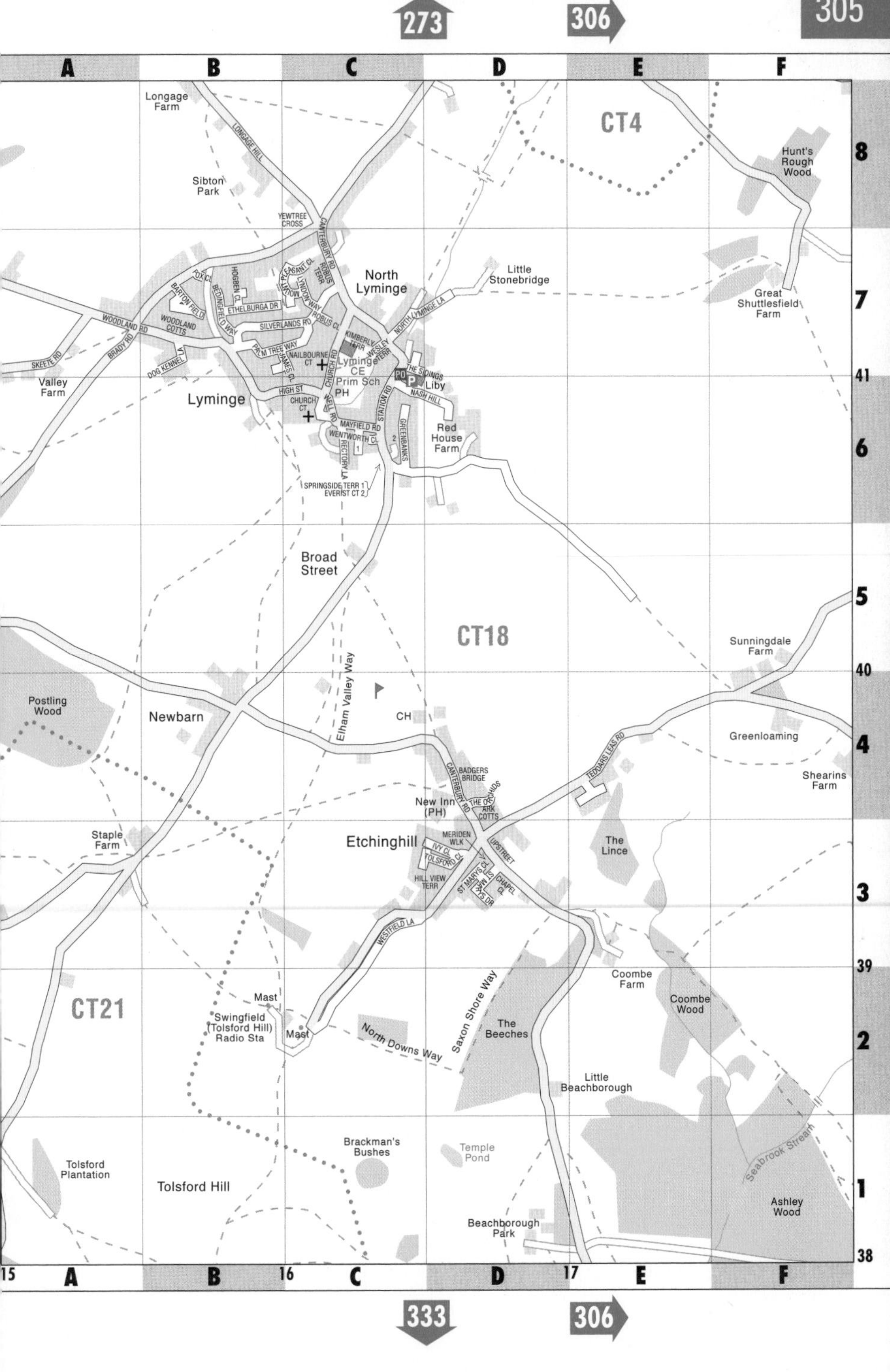

CT4

Hunt's Rough Wood

8

Longage Farm

Sibton Park

YEWTREE CROSS

North Lyminge

Little Stonebridge

Great Shuttlesfield Farm

7

WOODLAND RD

SKEET'S RD

BRADY RD

WOODLAND COTTS

ODO KESNEL

SILVERLANDS RD

M TREE WAY

NAILBOURNE CT

THELBURGA DR

BEECHWOOD

HOBBERS

CAVANT CL

LYNTON GDNS

KIMBERLEY

HOLLIS RD

NORTH LYMINGE LA

NORTH RD

STATION RD

THE SIDINGS

Liby

41

Valley Farm

Lyminge

HIGH ST

CHURCH CT

CHURCH RD

Lyminge CE Prim Sch

PH

P

P

NASH HILL

MAYFIELD RD

RECTORY LA

WENTWORTH CL

GREENBANKS

Red House Farm

6

SPRINGSIDE TERR 1
EVERIST CT 2

Broad Street

CT18

5

Sunningdale Farm

40

Elham Valley Way

CH

Postling Wood

Newbarn

Greenloaming

4

BADGERS BRIDGE

CANTERBURY RD

TEDDARS LEAS RD

Shearins Farm

Staple Farm

New Inn (PH)

THE DIG ARK COTTS

Etchinghill

MERIDEN WLK

IVY CL

TOLSFORD

POSTNET

The Lince

HILL VIEW TERR

ST MARY'S LA

CHAPEL LA

OAK

CL

39

CT21

Coombe Farm

Coombe Wood

Mast

Swingfield (Tolsford Hill) Radio Sta

Mast

North Downs Way

Saxon Shore Way

The Beeches

Little Beachborough

Seabrook Stream

2

Brackman's Bushes

Temple Pond

Tolsford Plantation

Tolsford Hill

Ashley Wood

1

Beachborough Park

38

305
274

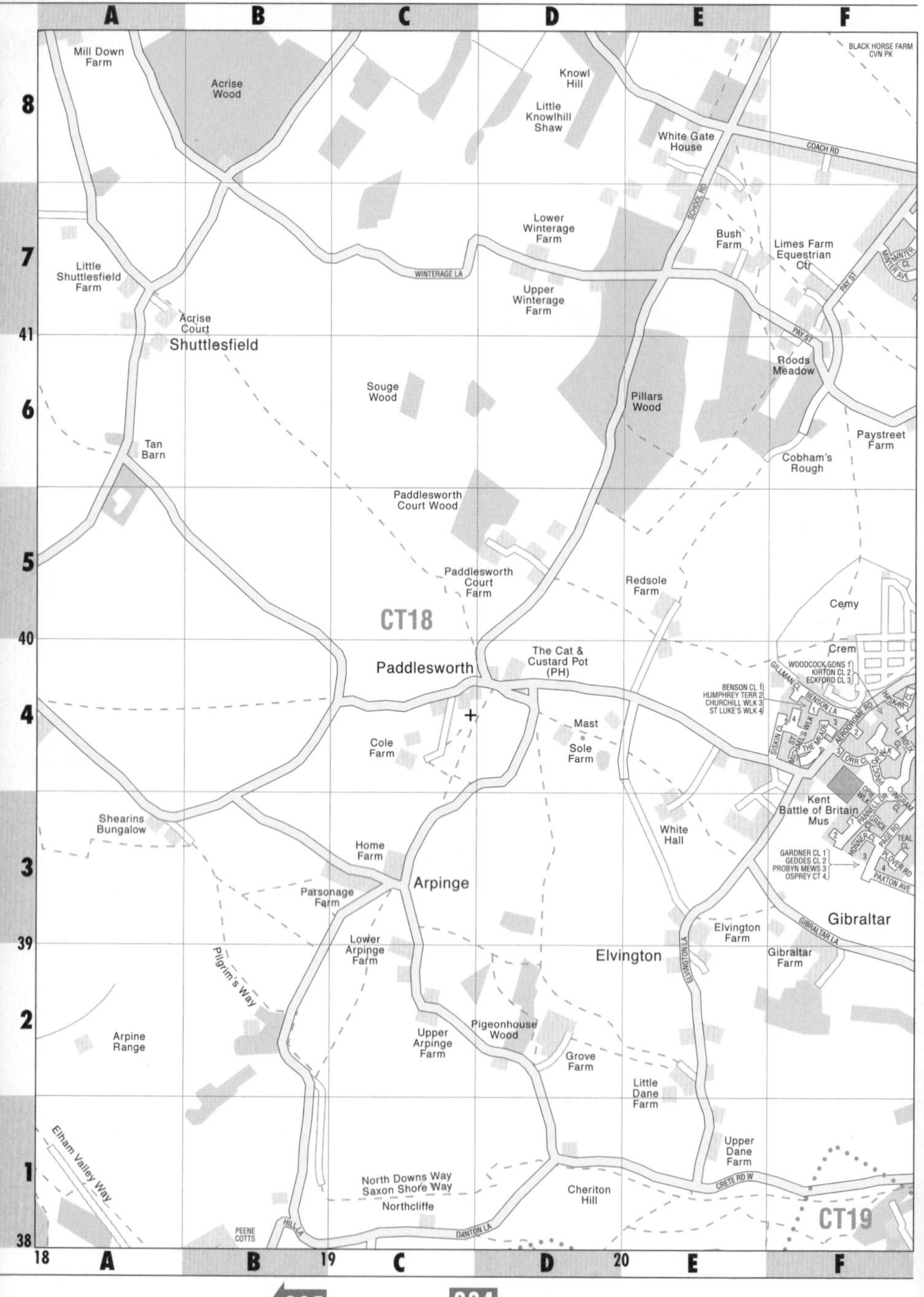
A
B
C
D
E
F
Mill Down Farm
Acrise Wood
Knowl Hill
Little Knowlhill Shaw
BLACK HORSE FARM CVN PK
White Gate House
COACH RD
SCHOOL RD
Lower Winterage Farm
Bush Farm
Limes Farm Equestrian Ctr
Little Shuttlesfield Farm
WINTERAGE LA
Upper Winterage Farm
PAY ST
MINTER AVE
Acrise Court
Shuttlesfield
Roods Meadow
Souge Wood
Pillars Wood
Tan Barn
Paystreet Farm
Cobham's Rough
Paddlesworth Court Wood
Paddlesworth Court Farm
Redsole Farm
Cemy
CT18
Crem
Paddlesworth
The Cat & Custard Pot (PH)
WOODCOCK GDNS 1
KIRTON CL 2
ECKFORD CL 3
BENSON CL 1
HUMPHREY TERR 2
CHURCHILL WLK 3
ST LUKE'S WLK 4
GILLMAN CL
BENSON LA
AERODROME RD
Mast
Cole Farm
Sole Farm
SISKIN CL
ST MICHAEL'S WLK
THE MEADE
ORR CL
Kent Battle of Britain Mus
Shearins Bungalow
White Hall
Home Farm
GARDNER CL 1
GEDDES CL 2
PROBYN MEWS 3
OSPREY CT 4
PAXTON AVE
Arpinge
Parsonage Farm
Gibraltar
Elvington Farm
GIBRALTAR LA
Lower Arpinge Farm
Elvington
Gibraltar Farm
ELVINGTON LA
Pilgrim's Way
Pigeonhouse Wood
Upper Arpinge Farm
Arpine Range
Grove Farm
Little Dane Farm
Elham Valley Way
Upper Dane Farm
North Downs Way
Saxon Shore Way
CRETE RD W
Cheriton Hill
Northcliffe
CT19
HILL LA
PEENE COTTS
DANTON LA
8
7
41
6
5
40
4
3
39
2
1
38
18
19
20

305
334

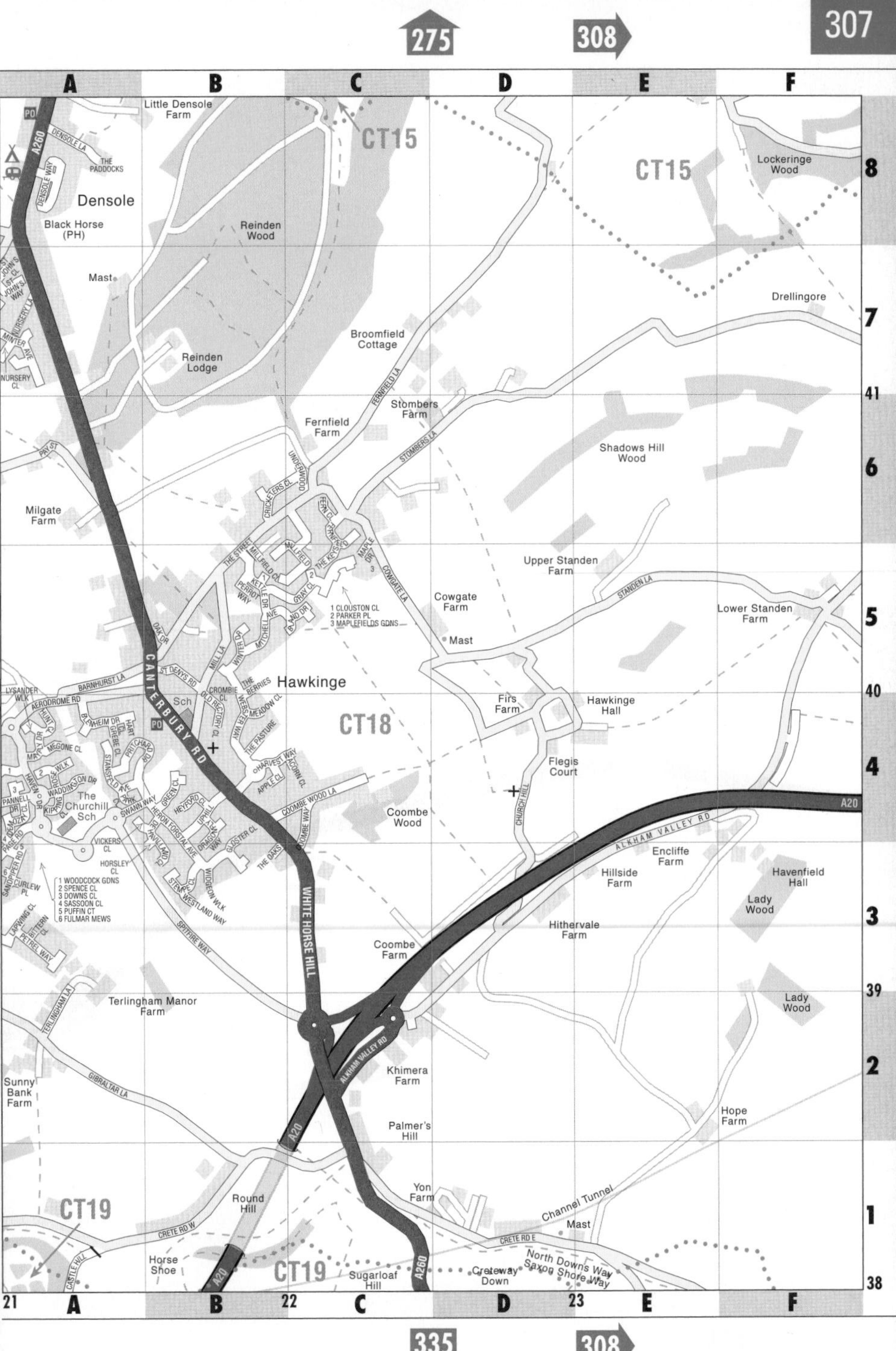
A
B
C
D
E
F
Little Densole Farm
CT15
Lockeringe Wood
Densole
Black Horse (PH)
Reinden Wood
Mast
Drellingore
Broomfield Cottage
Reinden Lodge
Stombers Farm
Fernfield Farm
Shadows Hill Wood
Milgate Farm
Upper Standen Farm
Cowgate Farm
Lower Standen Farm
1 CLOUSTON CL
2 PARKER PL
3 MAPLEFIELDS GDNS
Mast
Hawkinge
Firs Farm
Hawkinge Hall
CT18
Flegis Court
The Churchill Sch
Coombe Wood
Encliffe Farm
Hillside Farm
Havenfield Hall
Lady Wood
1 WOODCOCK GDNS
2 SPENCE CL
3 DOWNS CL
4 SASSOON CL
5 PUFFIN CT
6 FULMAR MEWS
Hithervale Farm
Coombe Farm
Terlingham Manor Farm
Lady Wood
Khimera Farm
Sunny Bank Farm
Palmer's Hill
Hope Farm
Yon Farm
CT19
Round Hill
Channel Tunnel
Mast
Horse Shoe
North Downs Way
Saxon Shore Way
Creteway Down
Sugarloaf Hill
CT19
A260
A20
CANTERBURY RD
WHITE HORSE HILL
ALKHAM VALLEY RD
STANDEN LA
STOMBERS LA
FERNFIELD LA
COWGATE LA
CHURCH HILL
GIBRALTAR LA
CRETE RD W
CRETE RD E
SPITFIRE WAY
8
7
41
6
5
40
4
3
39
2
1
38
21
22
23

307
276

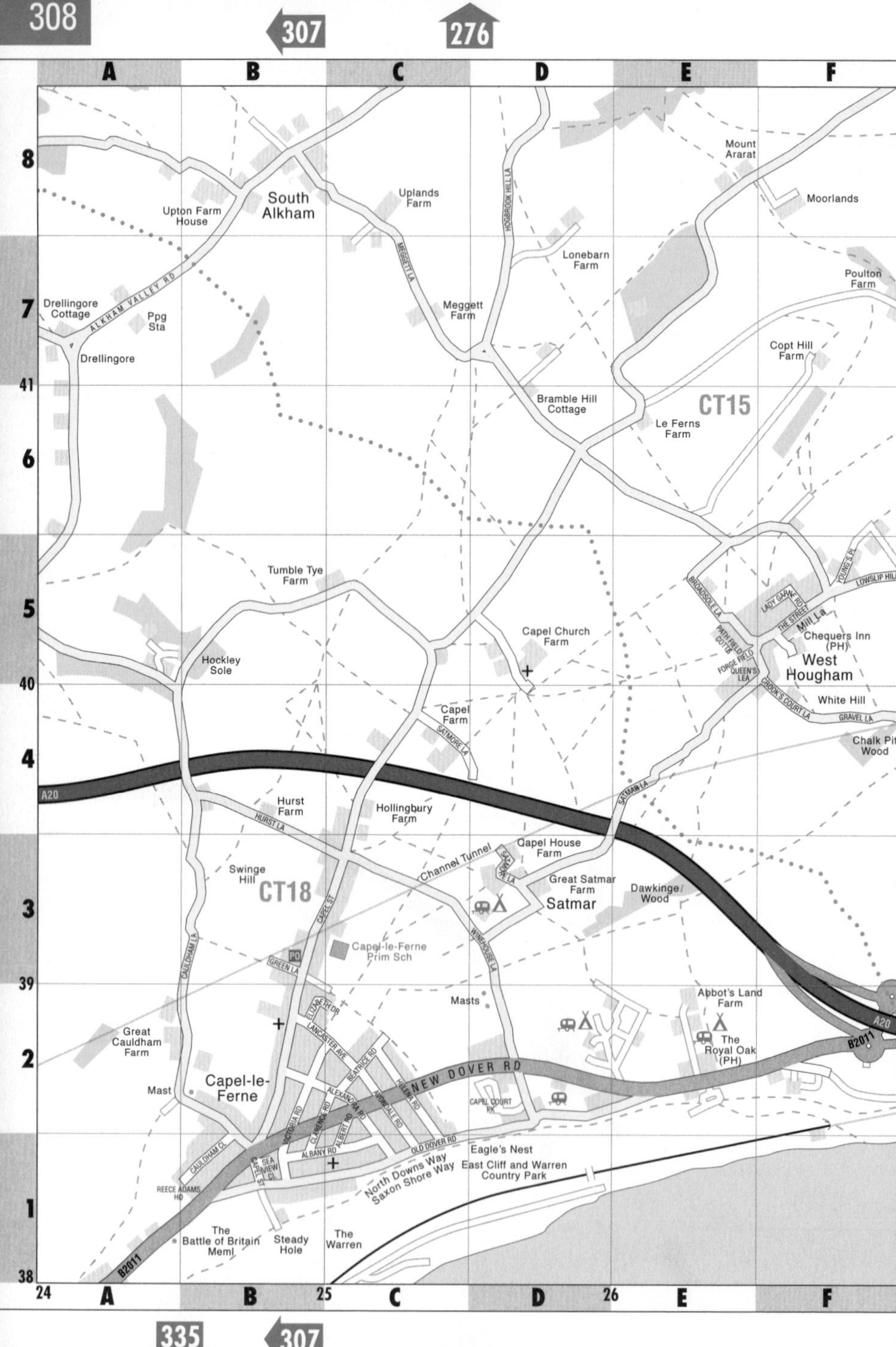
A
B
C
D
E
F
8
7
41
6
5
40
4
3
39
2
1
38
24
25
26
South Alkham
Upton Farm House
Uplands Farm
Mount Ararat
Moorlands
HOGBROOK HILL LA
MEGGETT LA
Lonebarn Farm
Poulton Farm
Drellingore Cottage
ALKHAM VALLEY RD
Ppg Sta
Drellingore
Meggett Farm
Copt Hill Farm
Bramble Hill Cottage
CT15
Le Ferns Farm
Tumble Tye Farm
BROADSOLE LA
YOUNG'S PL
LOWSLIP HILL
LADY GARNE RD
THE STREET
Mill La
PATH FIELD COTTS
Chequers Inn (PH)
Capel Church Farm
Hockley Sole
FORGE FIELD
QUEEN'S LEA
West Hougham
CROOK'S COURT LA
White Hill
GRAVEL LA
Capel Farm
SATMORE LA
Chalk Pit Wood
A20
SATMAR LA
Hurst Farm
Hollingbury Farm
HURST LA
Capel House Farm
Channel Tunnel
Swinge Hill
CT18
Great Satmar Farm
Satmar
Dawkinge Wood
CAPEL ST
PO
Capel-le-Ferne Prim Sch
GREEN LA
CAULDHAM LA
WINEHOUSE LA
Masts
Abbot's Land Farm
Great Cauldham Farm
LANCASTER AVE
The Royal Oak (PH)
B2011
NEW DOVER RD
Mast
Capel-le-Ferne
BEATRICE RD
HELENA RD
ALEXANDRA RD
AVONDALE RD
VICTORIA RD
CLARENCE RD
ALBERT RD
CAPEL COURT PK
CAULDHAM CL
OLD DOVER RD
Eagle's Nest
ALBANY RD
SEA VIEW CL
CAPEL ST
North Downs Way
Saxon Shore Way
East Cliff and Warren Country Park
REECE ADAMS HO
The Battle of Britain Meml
Steady Hole
The Warren

335
307

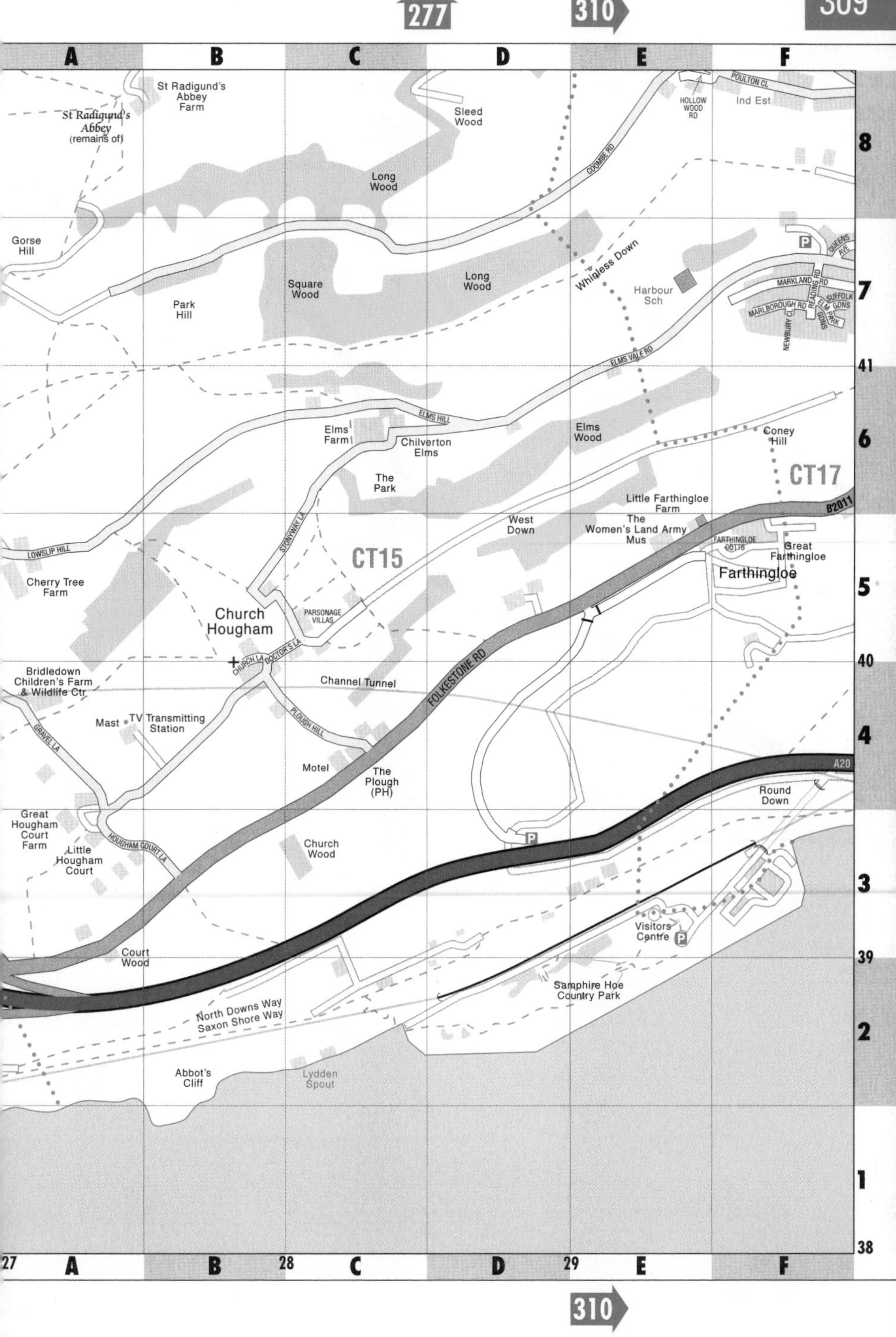
A
B
C
D
E
F
St Radigund's Abbey Farm
St Radigund's Abbey (remains of)
Sleed Wood
POULTON CL
HOLLOW WOOD RD
Ind Est
8
Long Wood
COOMBE RD
Gorse Hill
QUEENS AVE
Whinless Down
Square Wood
Long Wood
Park Hill
Harbour Sch
MARKLAND RD
READING RD
SUFFOLK GDNS
MARLBOROUGH RD
ELM PARK GDNS
NEWBURY CL
7
ELMS VALE RD
41
ELMS HILL
Elms Farm
Chilverton Elms
Elms Wood
Coney Hill
6
The Park
CT17
Little Farthingloe Farm
B2011
West Down
The Women's Land Army Mus
FARTHINGLOE COTTS
Great Farthingloe
STONYWAY LA
LOWSLIP HILL
CT15
Farthingloe
Cherry Tree Farm
5
Church Hougham
PARSONAGE VILLAS
CHURCH LA
DOCTOR'S LA
40
Bridledown Children's Farm & Wildlife Ctr
Channel Tunnel
FOLKESTONE RD
Mast
TV Transmitting Station
GRAVEL LA
PLOUGH HILL
4
A20
Motel
The Plough (PH)
Round Down
Great Hougham Court Farm
HOUGHAM COURT LA
Little Hougham Court
Church Wood
3
Visitors Centre
Court Wood
39
Samphire Hoe Country Park
North Downs Way
Saxon Shore Way
2
Abbot's Cliff
Lydden Spout
1
38
27
28
29

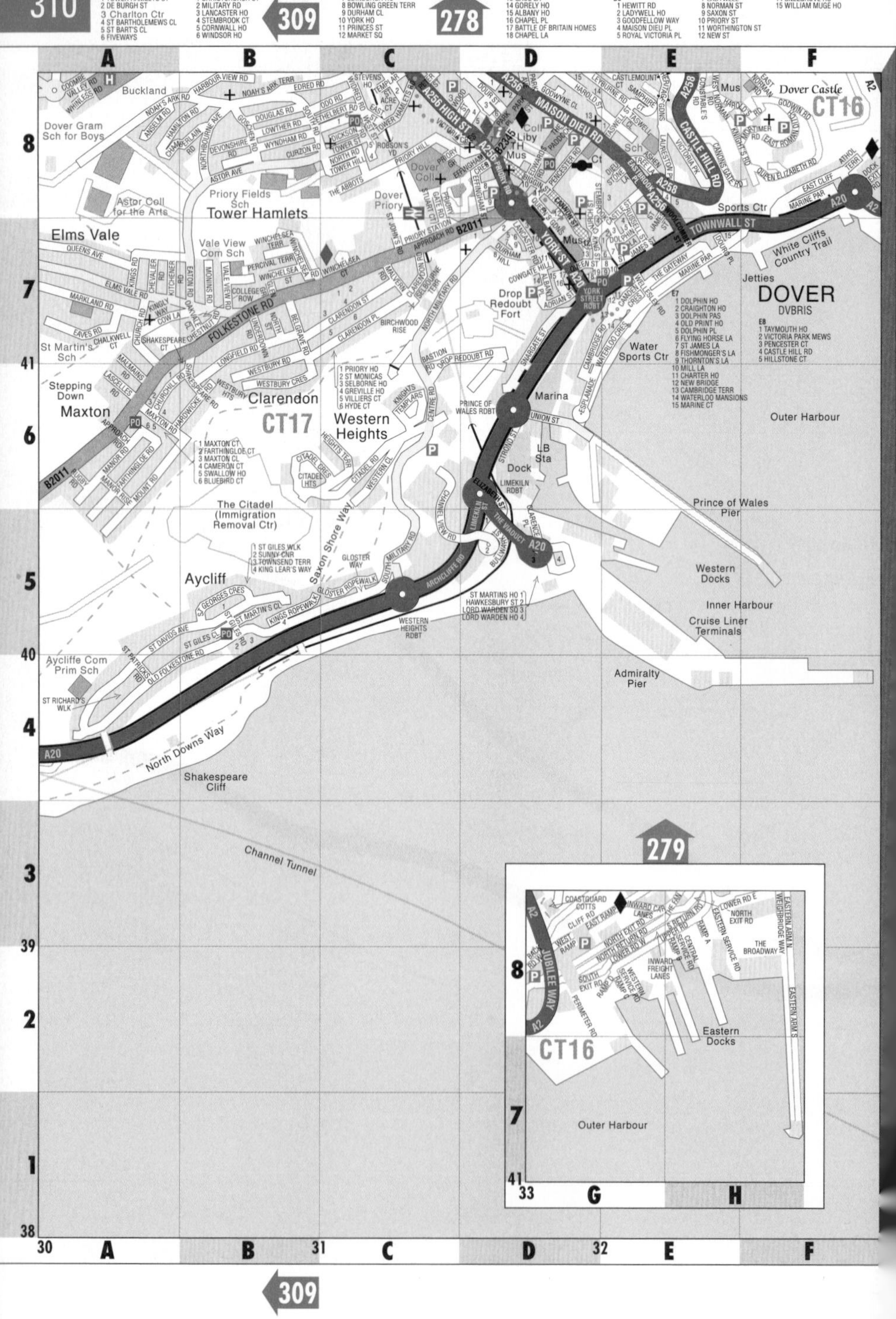

283
312

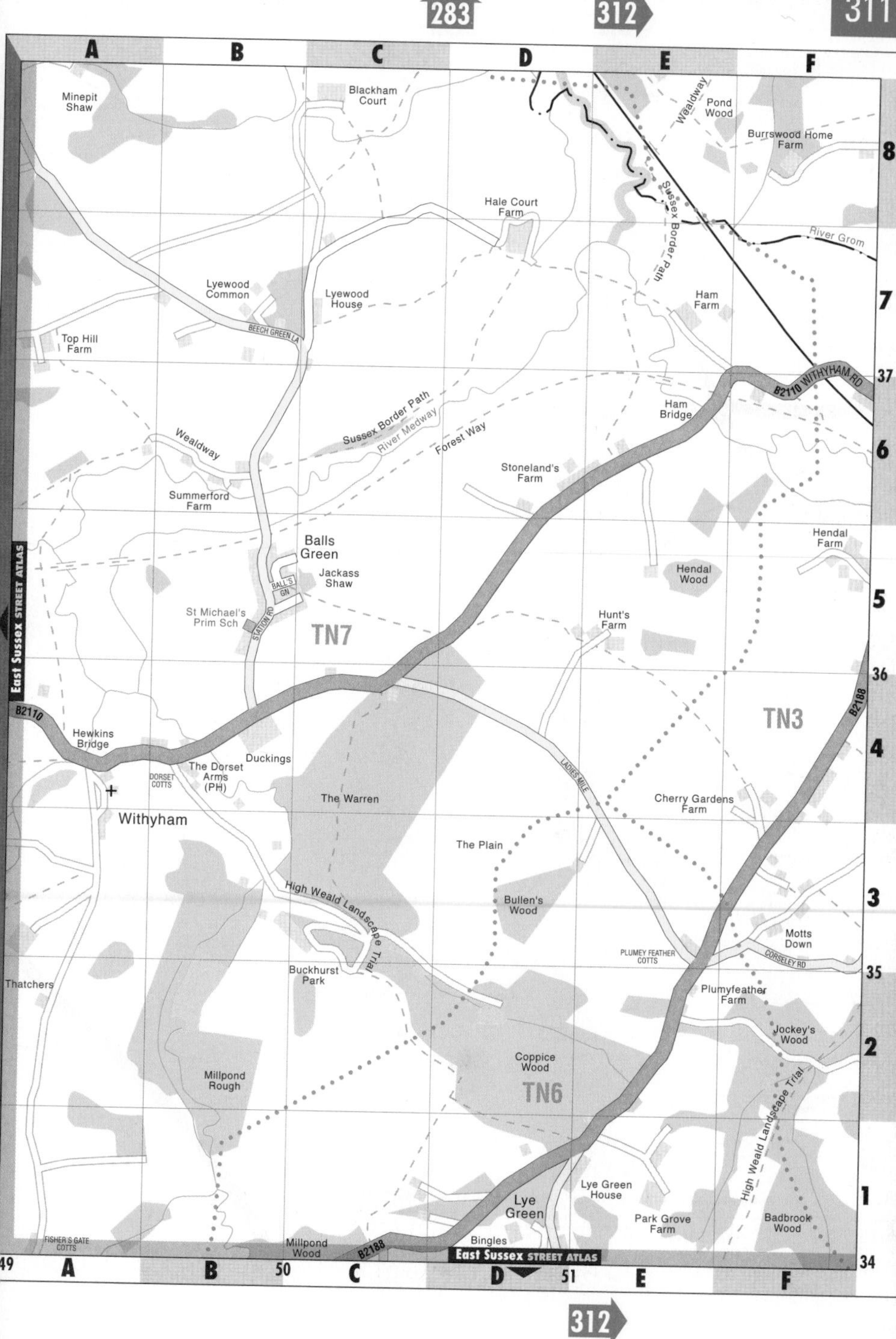
A
B
C
D
E
F
Minepit Shaw
Blackham Court
Pond Wood
Wealdway
Burrswood Home Farm
8
Hale Court Farm
Sussex Border Path
River Grom
Lyewood Common
Lyewood House
Ham Farm
7
Top Hill Farm
BEECH GREEN LA
37
B2110 WITHYHAM RD
Ham Bridge
Sussex Border Path
River Medway
Forest Way
Wealdway
6
Stoneland's Farm
Summerford Farm
Balls Green
Jackass Shaw
Hendal Farm
Hendal Wood
BALL'S GN
5
St Michael's Prim Sch
STATION RD
TN7
Hunt's Farm
36
B2110
TN3
B2188
Hewkins Bridge
4
Duckings
The Dorset Arms (PH)
DORSET COTTS
LADIES MILE
Withyham
The Warren
Cherry Gardens Farm
The Plain
3
High Weald Landscape Trail
Bullen's Wood
Motts Down
Buckhurst Park
PLUMEY FEATHER COTTS
CORSELEY RD
35
Thatchers
Plumyfeather Farm
Jockey's Wood
2
Coppice Wood
Millpond Rough
TN6
High Weald Landscape Trail
1
Lye Green
Lye Green House
Park Grove Farm
Badbrook Wood
Bingles
FISHER'S GATE COTTS
Millpond Wood
B2188
34
49
50
51
East Sussex STREET ATLAS

312

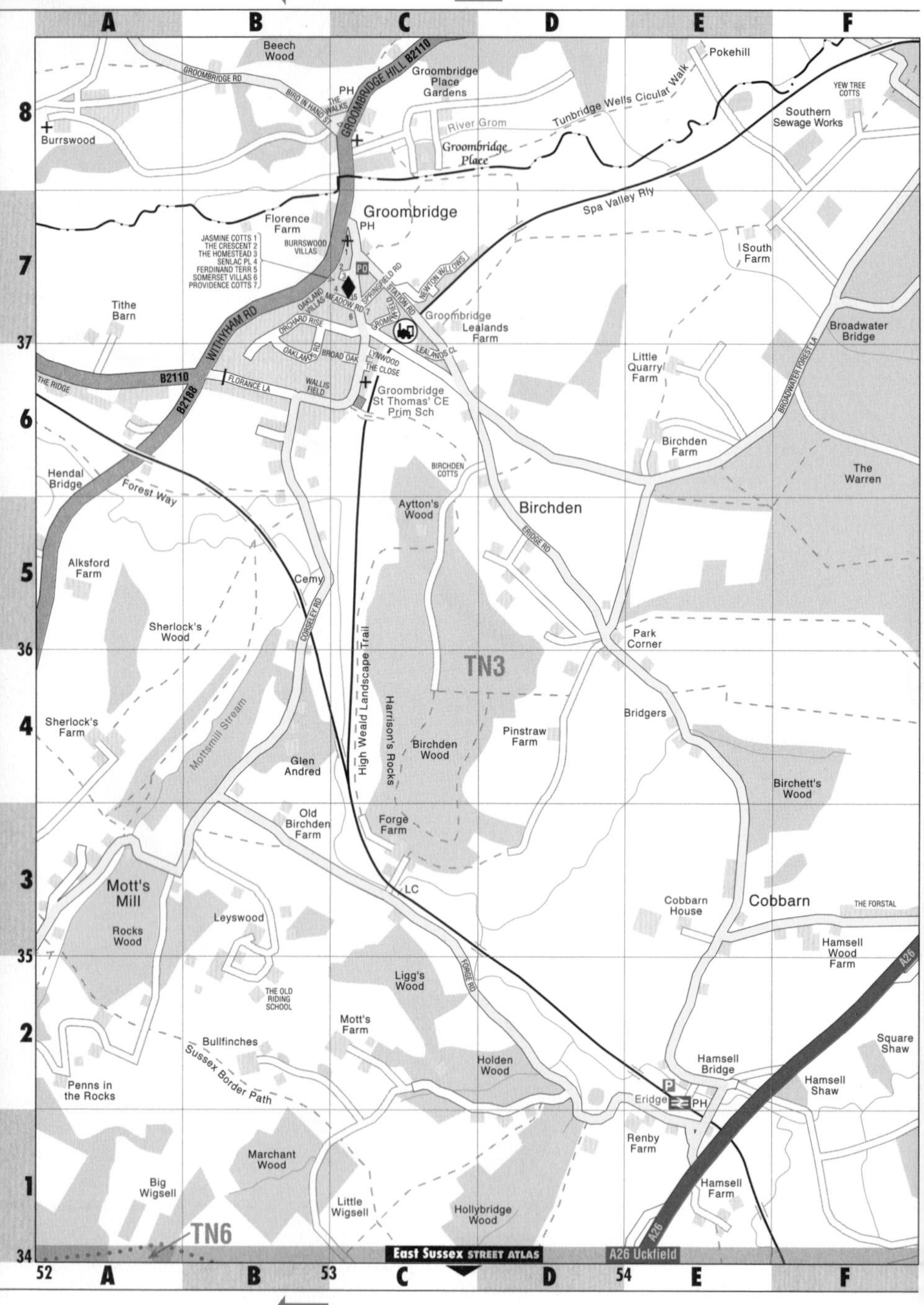

A **B** **C** **D** **E** **F**

8

Burrswood

Beech Wood

PH
THE

GROOMBRIDGE HILL B2110

Groombridge Place Gardens

River Grom

Tunbridge Wells Cicular Walk

Pokehill

YEW TREE COTTS

Southern Sewage Works

GROOMBRIDGE RD

BIRD IN HAND WALKS

Groombridge Place

7

Florence Farm

Groombridge

PH

JASMINE COTTS 1
THE CRESCENT 2
THE HOMESTEAD 3
SENLAC PL 4
FERDINAND TERR 5
SOMERSET VILLAS 6
PROVIDENCE COTTS 7

BURRSWOOD VILLAS

Tithe Barn

37

WITHYHAM RD

OAKLAND VILLAS

ORCHARD RISE

OAKLANDS

MEADOW RD

SPRINGFIELD RD

OAKMEAD

Spa Valley Rly

Groombridge Lealands Farm

South Farm

Broadwater Bridge

Little Quarry Farm

BROADWATER FOOTPATH

6

THE RIDGE

B2110

B2110

FLORANCE LA

BROAD OAK

WALLIS FIELD

LYNWOOD
THE CLOSE

Groombridge St Thomas' CE Prim Sch

LEALANDS CL

BIRCHDEN COTTS

Birchden Farm

The Warren

Hendal Bridge

Forest Way

Aytton's Wood

Birchden

RIDGE RD

5

Alksford Farm

Cemy

Sherlock's Wood

Mottsmill Stream

DENSLEY RD

Park Corner

36

Sherlock's Farm

Glen Andred

High Weald Landscape Trail

Harrison's Rocks

TN3

Birchden Wood

Pinstraw Farm

Bridgers

Birchett's Wood

4

Old Birchden Farm

Forge Farm

FORGE RD

3

Mott's Mill

Leyswood

Rocks Wood

LC

Ligg's Wood

Cobbarn House

Cobbarn

THE FORSTAL

Hamsell Wood Farm

A26

35

T

THE OLD RIDING SCHOOL

Mott's Farm

Holden Wood

Hamsell Bridge

Square Shaw

2

Bullfinches

Sussex Border Path

Penns in the Rocks

Marchant Wood

Hollybridge Wood

Eridge PH

P

Renby Farm

Hamsell Shaw

Hamsell Farm

A26

1

Big Wigsell

Little Wigsell

TN6

34

East Sussex STREET ATLAS

A26 Uckfield

52 **A** **B** 53 **C** **D** 54 **E** **F**

285
314

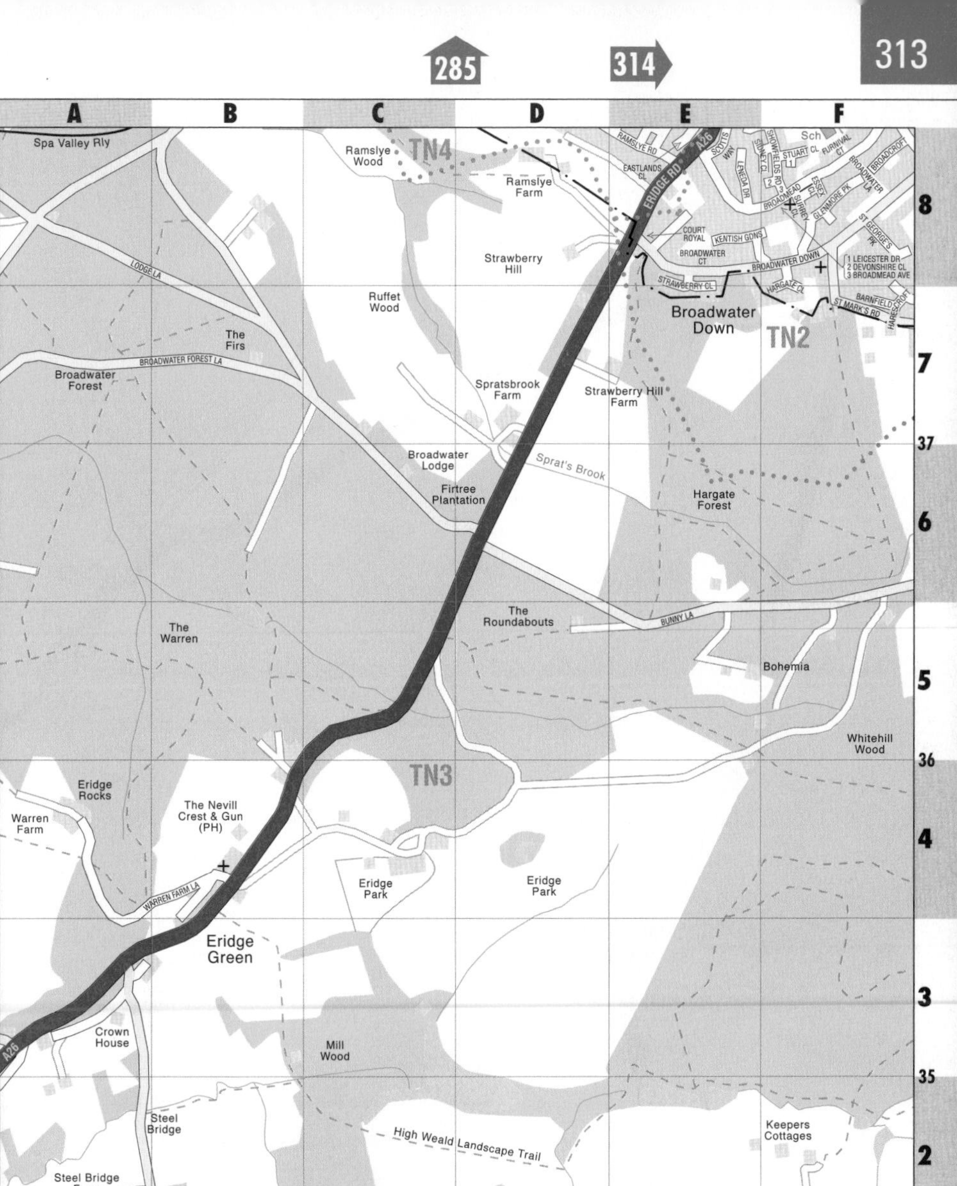
A
B
C
D
E
F
Spa Valley Rly
Ramslye Wood
TN4
Ramslye Farm
RAMSLYE RD
EASTLANDS CL
ERIDGE RD
A26
SCOTTS WAY
LENEDA DR
SIDNEY CL
SHOWFIELDS RD
STUART CL
FURNIVAL CT
Sch
BROADCROFT
BROADWATER LA
BROADMEAD
ESSEX CL
SURREY CL
GLENMORE PK
ST GEORGE'S PK
COURT ROYAL
KENTISH GDNS
BROADWATER CT
BROADWATER DOWN
1 LEICESTER DR
2 DEVONSHIRE CL
3 BROADMEAD AVE
STRAWBERRY CL
HARGATE CL
BARNFIELD
ST MARK'S RD
HARESCROFT
Strawberry Hill
Ruffet Wood
LODGE LA
Broadwater Down
TN2
The Firs
BROADWATER FOREST LA
Broadwater Forest
Spratsbrook Farm
Strawberry Hill Farm
Broadwater Lodge
Sprat's Brook
Firtree Plantation
Hargate Forest
The Roundabouts
BUNNY LA
The Warren
Bohemia
Whitehill Wood
TN3
Eridge Rocks
The Nevill Crest & Gun (PH)
Warren Farm
Eridge Park
Eridge Park
WARREN FARM LA
Eridge Green
Crown House
Mill Wood
Steel Bridge
High Weald Landscape Trail
Keepers Cottages
Steel Bridge Farm
Forge Wood
Eridge Old Park
Bushy Wood
Bushy Shaw
Great Robbins Shaw
8
7
37
6
5
36
4
3
35
2
1
34
55
56
57

314

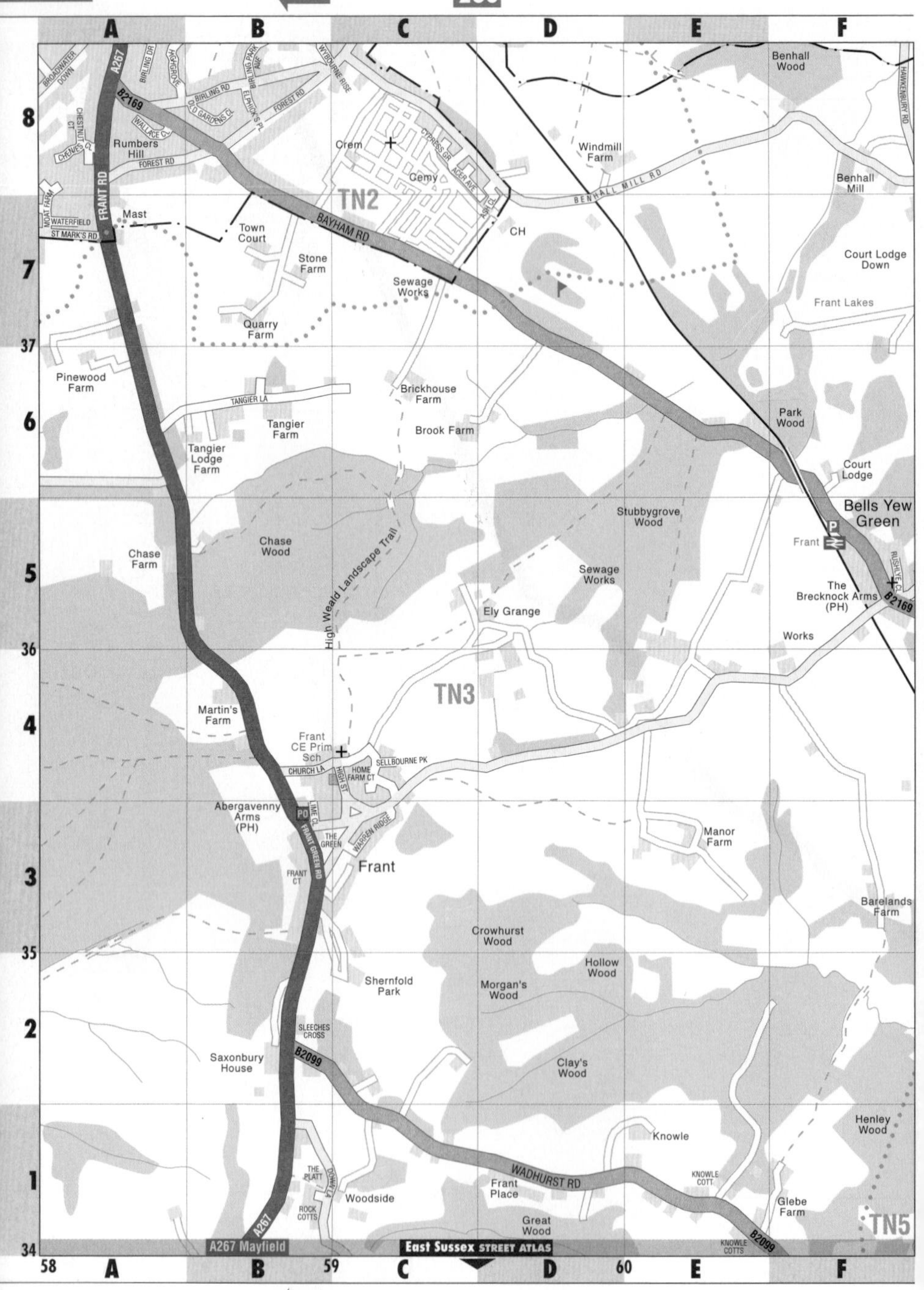

A   B   C   D   E   F

8

7

37

6

5

36

4

35

2

1

34

58   A   B   59   C   D   60   E   F

BROADWATER DOWN
BIRLING DR
HAZELHURST
A267
B2169
NAILE PLACE
DENNY
CHESTNUT CT
FOREST RD
BIRLING RD
OLD GARDENS CT
CLANRICARDE GARDENS
WESTFIELD RISE
FOREST RD
Crem
+
Benhall Wood
Windmill Farm

WATERFIELD
ST MARK'S RD
CHESTNUT CT
Rumbers Hill
FOREST RD
FRANT RD
Mast
TN2
CHARLES ST
Gemy
CH
BENHALL MILL RD
Benhall Mill
Court Lodge Down

Town Court
BAYHAM RD
Stone Farm
Sewage Works
Frant Lakes

Pinewood Farm
Quarry Farm
Brickhouse Farm
Park Wood

TANGIER LA
Tangier Farm
Brook Farm
Court Lodge

Tangier Lodge Farm
Bells Yew Green

Chase Farm
Chase Wood
Stubbygrove Wood
Frant
P
B2169
The Brecknock Arms (PH)

High Weald Landscape Trail
Sewage Works
Works

Ely Grange
Martin's Farm
TN3

Frant CE Prim Sch
+
SELLBOURNE PK
HOME FARM CT
CHURCH LA
Manor Farm

Abergavenny Arms (PH)
PO
HAZDEN RIDGE
THE GREEN
FRANT GREEN RD
Frant
Barelands Farm

FRANT CT
Crowhurst Wood

Shernfold Park
Morgan's Wood
Hollow Wood

SLEECHES CROSS
Saxonbury House
B2099
Clay's Wood

Knowle
Henley Wood

THE PLATT
COLTS LA
Woodside
WADHURST RD
Frant Place
KNOWLE COTT.
Glebe Farm
B2099
TN5

ROCK COTTS
Great Wood
KNOWLE COTTS
A267
A267 Mayfield
East Sussex STREET ATLAS

287
316

Brown's Wood
Coker's Down
Sunninglye Farmhouse
Rushlye Down
Coneyburrow Wood
Furnace Wood
River Teise
Oxpasture Wood
Tollslye
The Bothy
Bayham Lake
Hollow Wood
Jews Wood
Great Coppice Wood
Rushlye Farmhouse
CRICKETERS CL
IVY LA
Highfield
Abbots Down
Diamonds
TN3
MIDDLE RD
B2169
Forest Lodge
Burnt Wood
BAYHAM RD
Upper Sluice Wood
LITTLE BAYHAM COTTS
B2169
Little Bayham
Bartley Mill Wood
BARTLEY MILL LA
Higham Wood
Higham Farm
Verridge Wood
Bartley Mill
Churchfield Wood
Wickhurst Farmhouse
Little Shoesmiths
Bartley House
BARTLEY MILL RD
Sewers Bridge
Brookland Wood
Grigg's Wood
Shoesmith's Wood
Brick Kiln Wood
Camden Wood
Great Shoesmith Farm
Henley Wood
TN5
Hewley Wood
Sussex Border Path
WHITEGATES LA
DEWHURST LA
Sewage Works
A
B
C
D
E
F
8
7
37
6
5
36
4
3
35
2
1
34
61
62
63

336
316

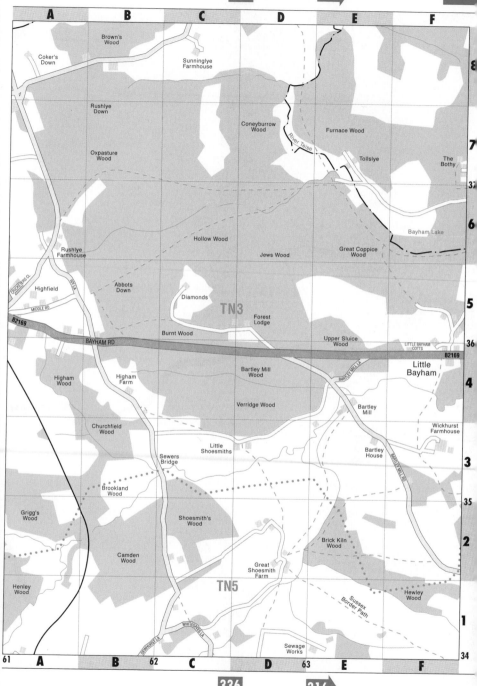

315
288

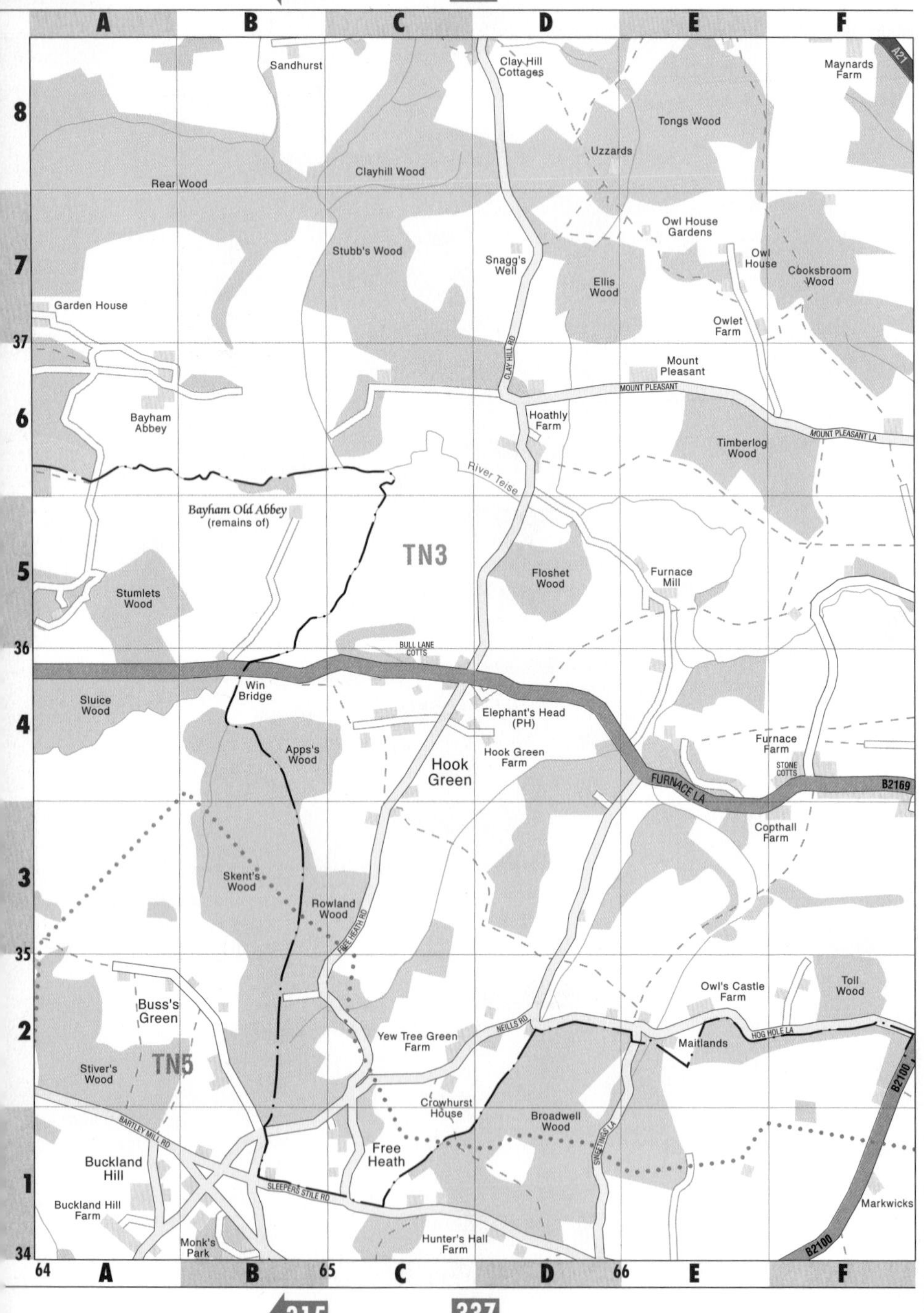
A
B
C
D
E
F
Sandhurst
Clay Hill Cottages
Maynards Farm
A21
8
Tongs Wood
Uzzards
Clayhill Wood
Rear Wood
Owl House Gardens
7
Stubb's Wood
Snagg's Well
Ellis Wood
Owl House
Cooksbroom Wood
Garden House
Owlet Farm
37
CLAY HILL RD
Mount Pleasant
MOUNT PLEASANT
6
Bayham Abbey
Hoathly Farm
MOUNT PLEASANT LA
Timberlog Wood
River Teise
Bayham Old Abbey
(remains of)
TN3
5
Floshet Wood
Furnace Mill
Stumlets Wood
36
BULL LANE COTTS
Win Bridge
Sluice Wood
4
Elephant's Head (PH)
Apps's Wood
Hook Green
Hook Green Farm
Furnace Farm
STONE COTTS
FURNACE LA
B2169
Copthall Farm
3
Skent's Wood
Rowland Wood
FREE HEATH RD
35
Owl's Castle Farm
Toll Wood
Buss's Green
NEILLS RD
2
Yew Tree Green Farm
Maitlands
HOG HOLE LA
Stiver's Wood
TN5
B2100
Crowhurst House
BARTLEY MILL RD
Broadwell Wood
SINGEHINGS LA
Free Heath
Buckland Hill
1
SLEEPERS STILE RD
Buckland Hill Farm
Markwicks
Monk's Park
Hunter's Hall Farm
B2100
34
64
A
B
65
C
D
66
E
F

315
337

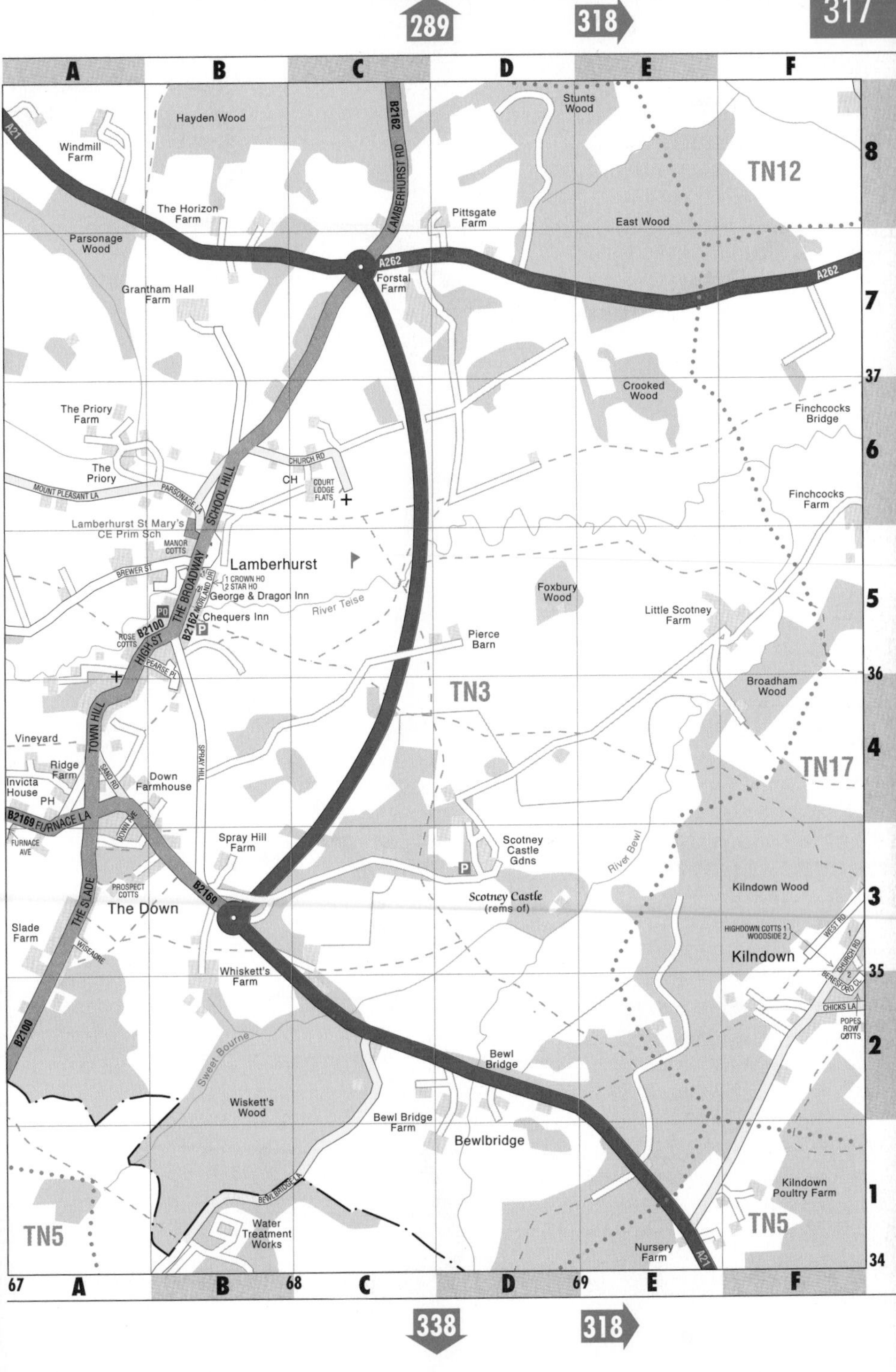
A
B
C
D
E
F
8
7
37
6
5
36
4
3
35
2
1
34
67
68
69
Windmill Farm
Hayden Wood
Stunts Wood
TN12
The Horizon Farm
Pittsgate Farm
East Wood
Parsonage Wood
Grantham Hall Farm
Forstal Farm
A21
A262
B2162
LAMBERHURST RD
Crooked Wood
Finchcocks Bridge
The Priory Farm
The Priory
CH
CHURCH RD
COURT LODGE FLATS
Finchcocks Farm
MOUNT PLEASANT LA
PARSONAGE LA
SCHOOL HILL
THE BROADWAY
Lamberhurst St Mary's CE Prim Sch
MANOR COTTS
Lamberhurst
BREWER ST
1 CROWN HO
2 STAR HO
MORLAND DR
George & Dragon Inn
Foxbury Wood
River Teise
Little Scotney Farm
PO
Chequers Inn
B2100
ROSE COTTS
HIGH ST
Pierce Barn
PEARSE PL
TN3
Broadham Wood
TOWN HILL
Vineyard
Ridge Farm
SPRAY HILL
TN17
Invicta House
PH
SAND RD
Down Farmhouse
B2169
FURNACE LA
FURNACE AVE
DOWN AVE
Spray Hill Farm
Scotney Castle Gdns
River Bewl
PROSPECT COTTS
THE SLADE
Kilndown Wood
Scotney Castle (rems of)
The Down
Slade Farm
WISEACRE
HIGHDOWN COTTS 1
WOODSIDE 2
WEST RD
Kilndown
CHURCH RD
BERESFORD CL
Whiskett's Farm
CHICKS LA
POPES ROW COTTS
Sweet Bourne
Bewl Bridge
Wiskett's Wood
Bewl Bridge Farm
Bewlbridge
Kilndown Poultry Farm
BEWLBRIDGE LA
TN5
Water Treatment Works
Nursery Farm

317
290

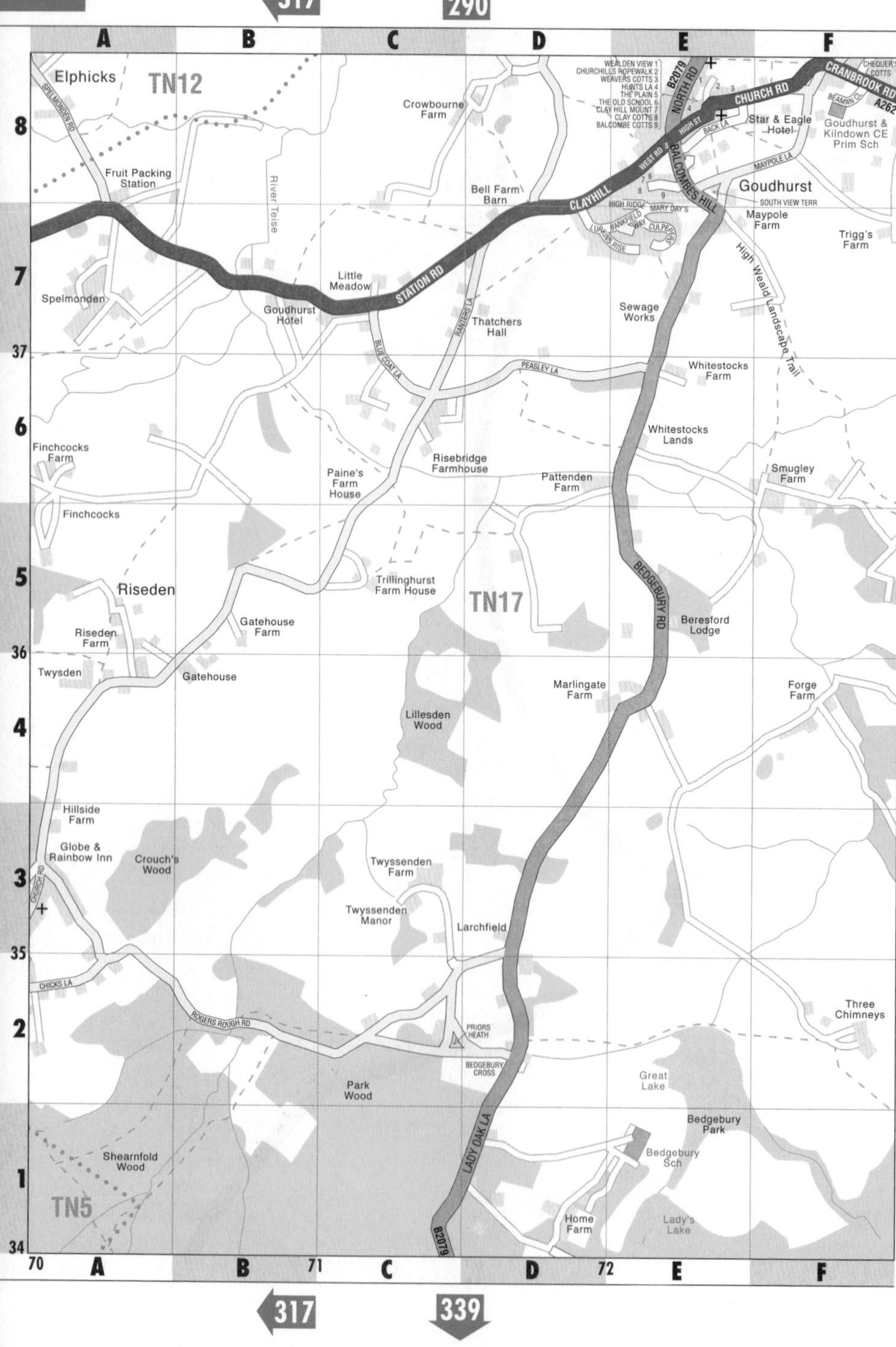
A
B
C
D
E
F
WEALDEN VIEW 1
CHURCHILLS ROPEWALK 2
WEAVERS COTTS 3
HUNTS LA 4
THE PLAIN 5
THE OLD SCHOOL 6
CLAY HILL MOUNT 7
CLAY COTTS 8
BALCOMBE COTTS 9
Elphicks
TN12
SPELMONDEN RD
Crowbourne Farm
B2079
NORTH RD
CHURCH RD
CRANBROOK RD
CHEQUER'S COTTS
A262
Star & Eagle Hotel
Goudhurst & Kilndown CE Prim Sch
8
Fruit Packing Station
River Teise
Bell Farm Barn
CLAYHILL
WEST RD
HIGH ST
BACK LA
BALCOMBES HILL
MAYPOLE LA
Goudhurst
SOUTH VIEW TERR
HIGH RIDGE
MARY DAY'S
BANKFIELD WAY
LURKINS RISE
CULPEPERS
Maypole Farm
Trigg's Farm
7
Spelmonden
Little Meadow
STATION RD
Goudhurst Hotel
RANTERS LA
Thatchers Hall
Sewage Works
High Weald Landscape Trail
37
BLUE COAT LA
PEASLEY LA
Whitestocks Farm
6
Finchcocks Farm
Whitestocks Lands
Risebridge Farmhouse
Paine's Farm House
Pattenden Farm
Smugley Farm
Finchcocks
5
Riseden
Trillinghurst Farm House
TN17
BEDGEBURY RD
Beresford Lodge
Gatehouse Farm
Riseden Farm
36
Twysden
Gatehouse
Marlingate Farm
Forge Farm
4
Lillesden Wood
Hillside Farm
Globe & Rainbow Inn
Crouch's Wood
3
CHURCH RD
Twyssenden Farm
Twyssenden Manor
Larchfield
35
CHICKS LA
2
ROGERS ROUGH RD
PRIORS HEATH
BEDGEBURY CROSS
Three Chimneys
Great Lake
Park Wood
Bedgebury Park
Bedgebury Sch
LADY OAK LA
Shearnfold Wood
1
TN5
Home Farm
Lady's Lake
B2079
34
70
A
B
71
C
D
72
E
F

317
339

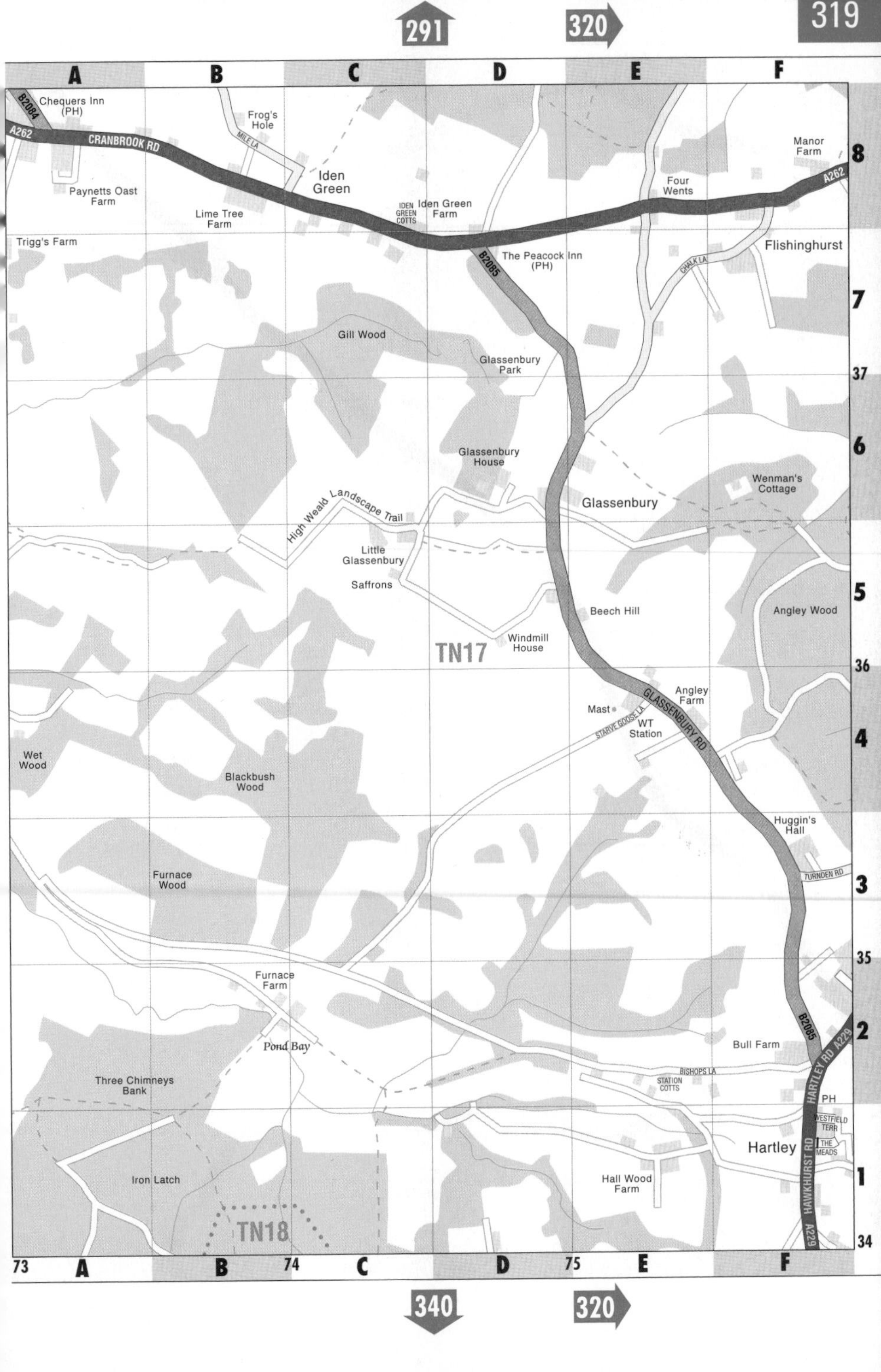

8

Chequers Inn (PH)
B2084
A262
Paynetts Oast Farm
CRANBROOK RD
Frog's Hole
MILE LA
Lime Tree Farm
Iden Green
IDEN GREEN COTTS
Iden Green Farm
Four Wents
Manor Farm
A262

Trigg's Farm
The Peacock Inn (PH)
B2085
Flishinghurst
CHALK LA

7

Gill Wood
Glassenbury Park

37

Glassenbury House
Glassenbury
Wenman's Cottage

6

High Weald Landscape Trail
Little Glassenbury
Saffrons
Beech Hill
Angley Wood

5

TN17
Windmill House
Angley Farm

36

Mast
WT Station
STARVE CROW LA
GLASSENBURY RD
Angley Farm

4

Wet Wood
Blackbush Wood
Huggin's Hall

Furnace Wood
TURNDEN RD

3

Furnace Farm

35

Pond Bay
Bull Farm
B2086
HARTLEY RD A229

2

Three Chimneys Bank
BISHOPS LA
STATION COTTS
PH
WESTFIELD TERR
THE MEADS
Hartley
HAWKHURST RD
A229

Iron Latch
Hall Wood Farm

1

TN18

34

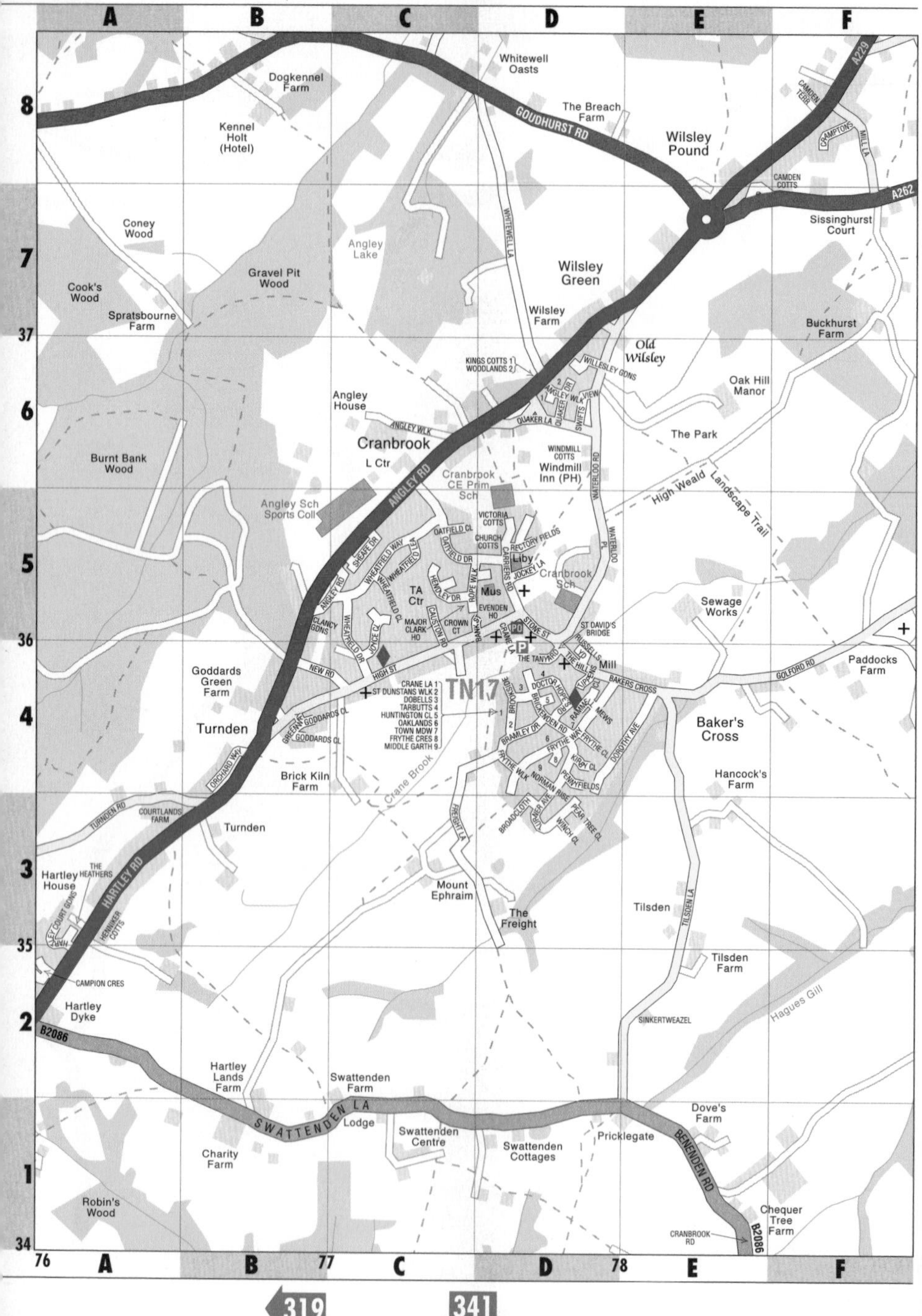

319
292
319
341

A B C D E F

8

7

37

6

5

36

4

3

35

2

1

34

76 77 78

GOUDHURST RD

A229

A262

Whitewell
Oasts

The Breach
Farm

Wilsley
Pound

CAMDEN
TERR

CRAMPTONS

MILE LA

CAMDEN
COTTS

Sissinghurst
Court

Dogkennel
Farm

Kennel
Holt
(Hotel)

Coney
Wood

Cook's
Wood

Spratsbourne
Farm

Gravel Pit
Wood

Angley
Lake

WHITEHILL LA

Wilsley
Green

Wilsley
Farm

Wilsley
Green

Old
Wilsley

Oak Hill
Manor

Buckhurst
Farm

KINGS COTTS 1
WOODLANDS 2

WILLSLEY GDNS

ANGLEY WLK

QUAKER LA

Angley
House

Cranbrook

L Ctr

ANGLEY RD

Burnt Bank
Wood

Angley Sch
Sports Coll

Cranbrook
CE Prim
Sch

WINDMILL
COTTS

Windmill
Inn (PH)

The Park

High Weald Landscape Trail

WATERLOO RD

WHEATFIELD WAY

WHEATFIELD

WHEATFIELD DR

GATFIELD CL

GATFIELD DR

HEADLY DR

VICTORIA
COTTS

CHURCH
COTTS

RECTORY FIELDS

JOCKEY LA

Liby

Mus

Cranbrook
Sch

St DAVID'S
BRIDGE

Sewage
Works

GOLFORD RD

Paddocks
Farm

TA
Ctr

MAJOR
CLARK
HO

CLANCY
GDNS

CROWN
CT

EVENDEN
HO

NEW RD

Goddards
Green
Farm

CRANE LA 1
St DUNSTANS WLK 2
DOBELLS 3
TARBUTTS 4
HUNTINGTON CL 5
OAKLANDS 6
TOWN MDW 7
FRYTHE CRES 8
MIDDLE GARTH 9

TN17

Mill

The TANYARD

P

BAKERS CROSS

Baker's
Cross

Hancock's
Farm

Turnden

GREENE GODDARDS CL

GODDARDS CL

ORCHARD WAY

Brick Kiln
Farm

Crane Brook

BRAMLEY DR

FRYTHE WLK

NURSERY DRIVE

FRYTHE CL

BROADCLOTH

DOCTOR AVE

FRYTHE FIELDS

HIGH CL

PEAR TREE CL

TILSDEN LA

BENENDEN RD

Turnden

TURNDEN RD

COURTLANDS
Farm

HARTLEY RD

Hartley
House

THE
HEATHERS

COLE BOND

HOMER
COTTS

CAMPION CRES

Hartley
Dyke

B2086

Mount
Ephraim

The
Freight

Tilsden

Tilsden
Farm

Hagues Gill

SINKERTWEAZEL

SWATTENDEN LA

Hartley
Lands
Farm

Swattenden
Farm

Lodge

Charity
Farm

Swattenden
Centre

Swattenden
Cottages

Pricklegate

Dove's
Farm

Robin's
Wood

CRANBROOK
RD

Chequer
Tree
Farm

B2086

293
322

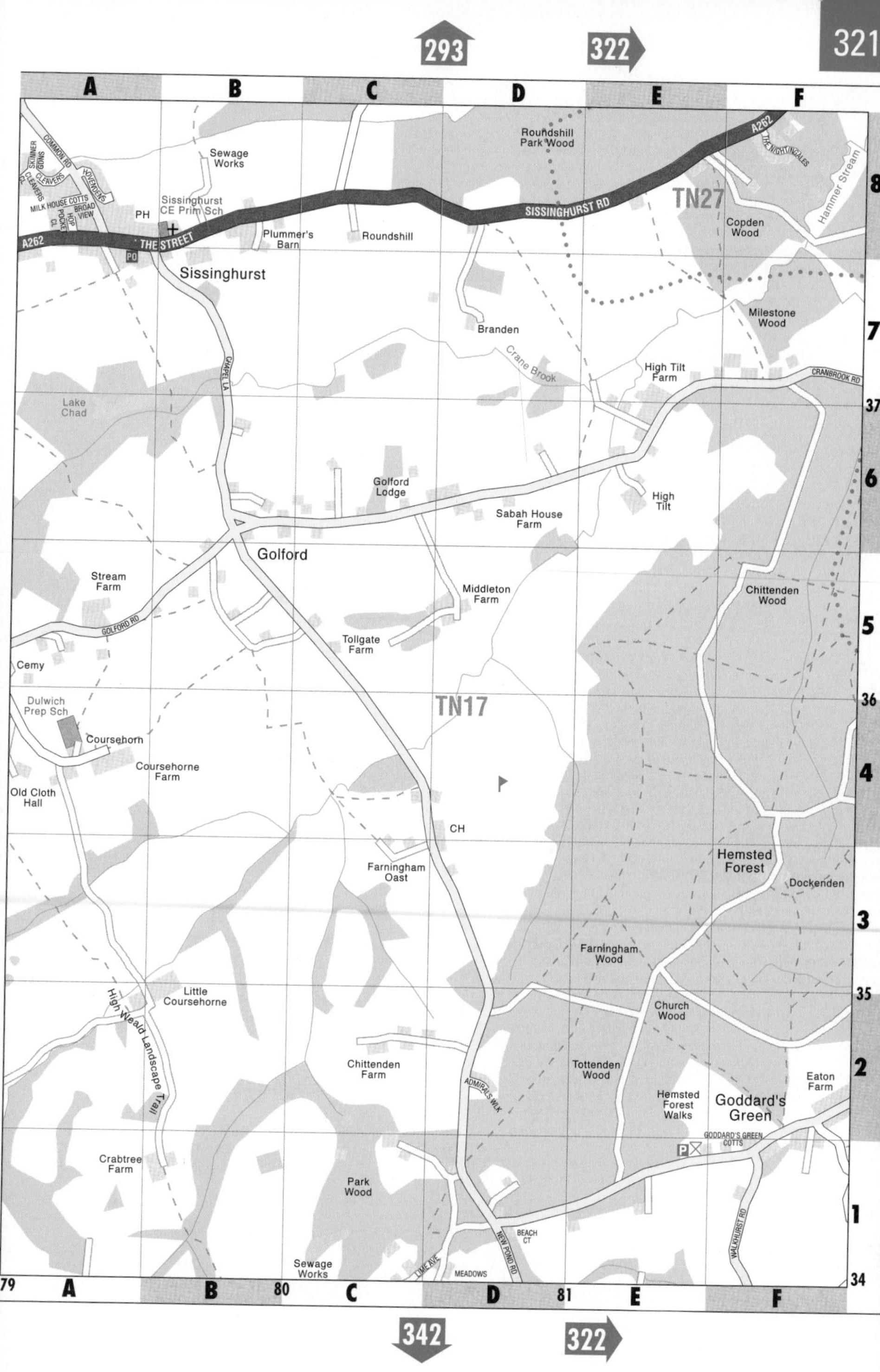
A
B
C
D
E
F
Roundshill
Park Wood
A262
THE NIGHTINGALES
Hammer Stream
Sewage
Works
SKINNER
GDNS
COMMON RD
CLEVERS
CLEVERS
CL
HOVENDENS
MILK HOUSE COTTS
HOP
POCKET
CL
BROAD
VIEW
PH
Sissinghurst
CE Prim Sch
A262
THE STREET
PO
Plummer's
Barn
Roundshill
SISSINGHURST RD
TN27
Copden
Wood
8
Sissinghurst
Milestone
Wood
Branden
7
Crane Brook
High Tilt
Farm
CRANBROOK RD
CHAPEL LA
Lake
Chad
37
Golford
Lodge
High
Tilt
6
Sabah House
Farm
Golford
Stream
Farm
Middleton
Farm
Chittenden
Wood
GOLFORD RD
Tollgate
Farm
5
Cemy
Dulwich
Prep Sch
TN17
36
Coursehorn
Coursehorne
Farm
Old Cloth
Hall
4
CH
Hemsted
Forest
Farningham
Oast
Dockenden
3
Farningham
Wood
Little
Coursehorne
High Weald Landscape Trail
35
Church
Wood
Tottenden
Wood
Chittenden
Farm
2
ADMIRALS WLK
Hemsted
Forest
Walks
Goddard's
Green
Eaton
Farm
GODDARD'S GREEN
COTTS
Crabtree
Farm
Park
Wood
1
WALKHURST RD
BEACH
CT
NEW POND RD
LIME AVE
MEADOWS
Sewage
Works
34
79
A
B
80
C
D
81
E
F

342
322

321
294

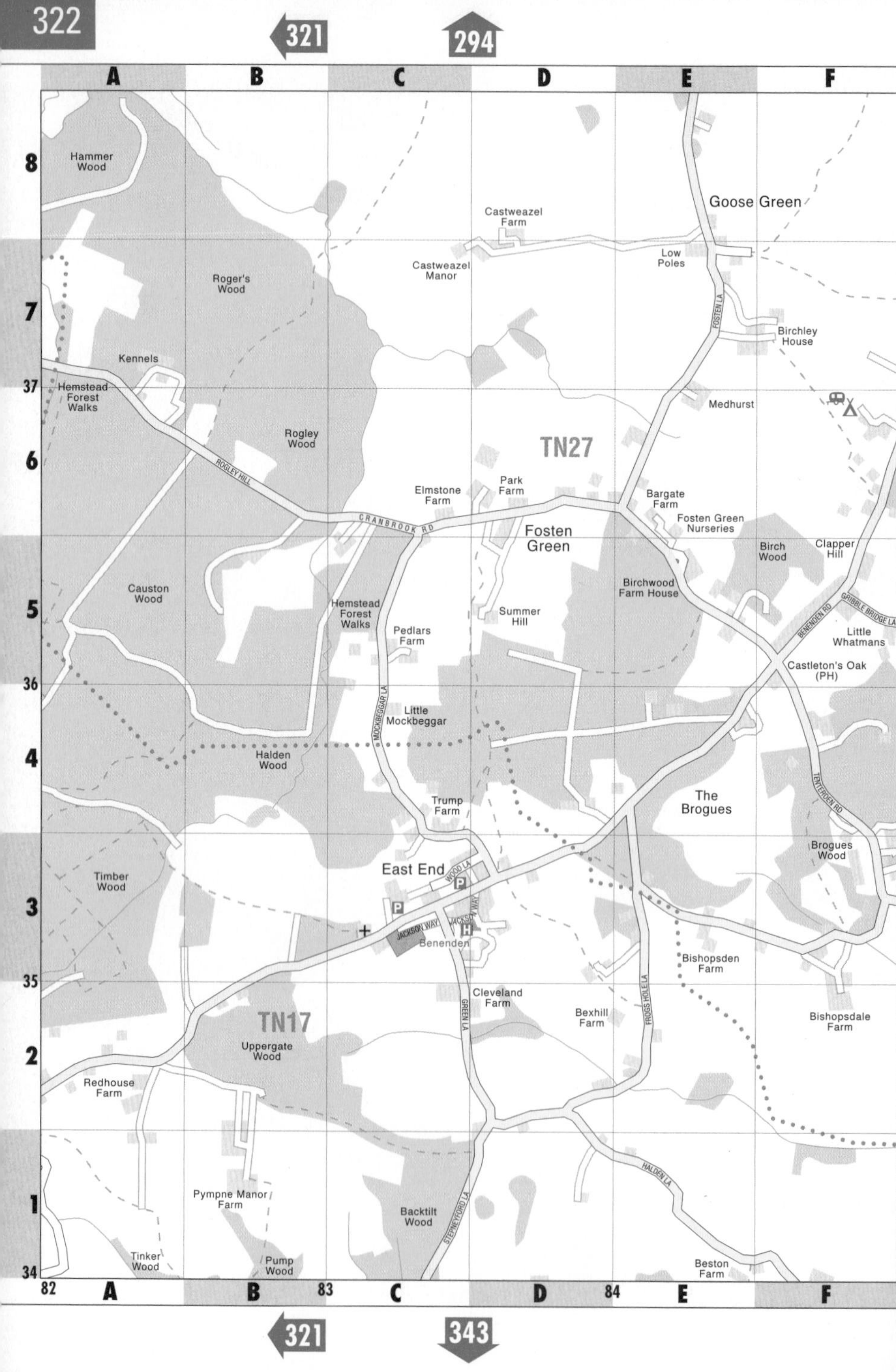
A
B
C
D
E
F
8
7
37
6
5
36
4
3
35
2
1
34
82
83
84
Hammer Wood
Goose Green
Castweazel Farm
Low Poles
Castweazel Manor
Roger's Wood
FOSTEN LA
Birchley House
Kennels
Hemstead Forest Walks
Medhurst
Rogley Wood
TN27
ROGLEY HILL
Park Farm
Elmstone Farm
Bargate Farm
CRANBROOK RD
Fosten Green Nurseries
Fosten Green
Birch Wood
Clapper Hill
Causton Wood
Birchwood Farm House
Hemstead Forest Walks
Summer Hill
BENENDEN RD
GRIBBLE BRIDGE LA
Pedlars Farm
Little Whatmans
Castleton's Oak (PH)
MOCKBEGGAR LA
Little Mockbeggar
Halden Wood
TENTERDEN RD
The Brogues
Trump Farm
Brogues Wood
East End
WOOD LA
Timber Wood
JACKSON WAY
Benenden
Bishopsden Farm
Cleveland Farm
GREEN LA
Bexhill Farm
FROGS HOLE LA
Bishopsdale Farm
TN17
Uppergate Wood
Redhouse Farm
HALDEN LA
Pympne Manor Farm
Backtilt Wood
STEPNEYFORD LA
Tinker Wood
Pump Wood
Beston Farm

321
343

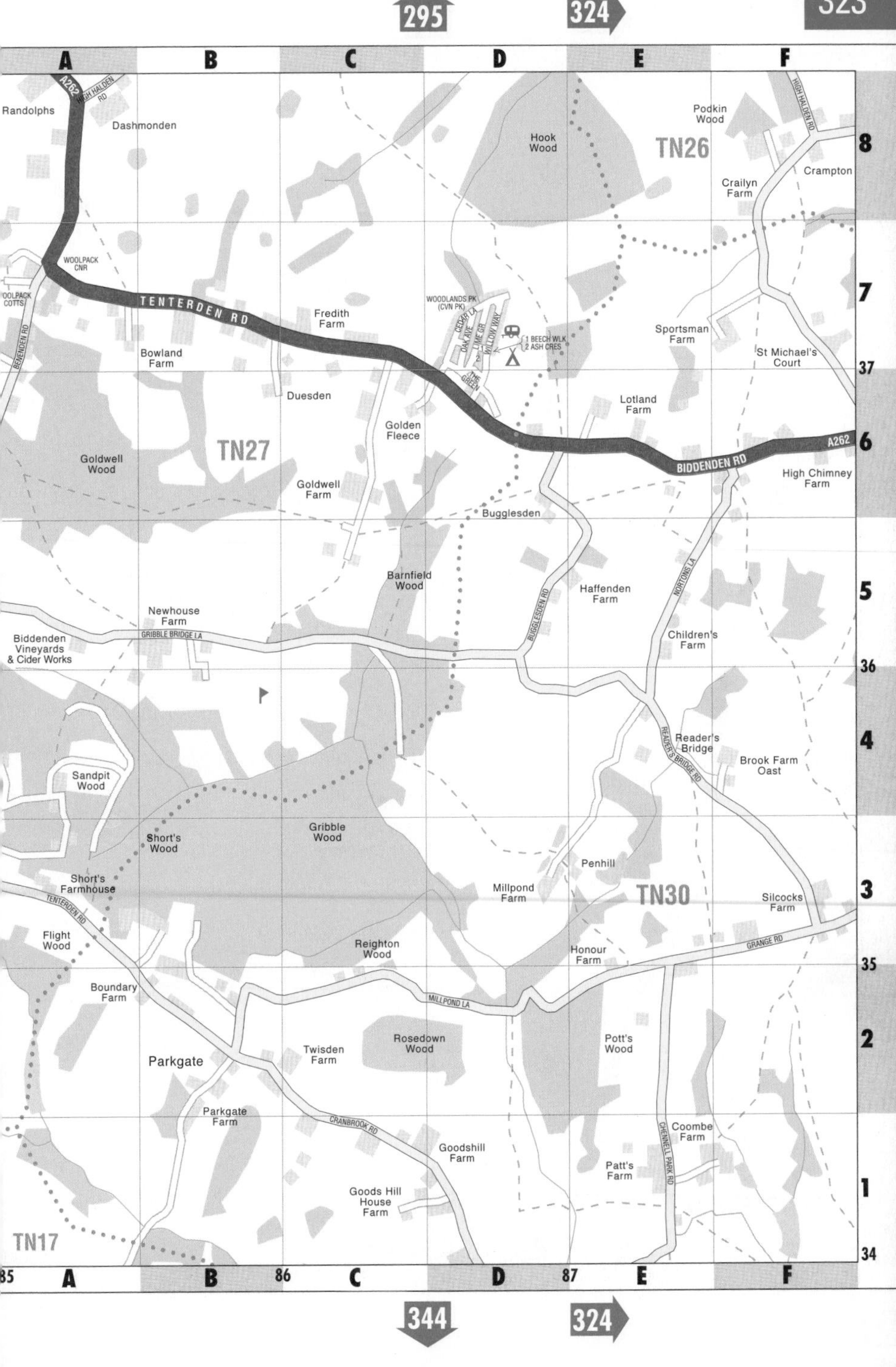
295
324
A
B
C
D
E
F
Randolphs
Dashmonden
A262
HIGH HALDEN RD
Hook Wood
Podkin Wood
TN26
HIGH HALDEN RD
8
Crampton
Crailyn Farm
WOOLPACK CNR
OOLPACK COTTS
TENTERDEN RD
Fredith Farm
WOODLANDS PK (CVN PK)
CEDAR LA
OAK AVE
LIME GR
WILLOW WAY
1 BEECH WLK
2 ASH CRES
THE GREEN
7
Sportsman Farm
St Michael's Court
37
BENENDEN RD
Bowland Farm
Duesden
Lotland Farm
Golden Fleece
TN27
Goldwell Wood
A262
6
BIDDENDEN RD
High Chimney Farm
Goldwell Farm
Bugglesden
Barnfield Wood
Haffenden Farm
NORTONS LA
5
BUGGLESDEN RD
Newhouse Farm
GRIBBLE BRIDGE LA
Biddenden Vineyards & Cider Works
Children's Farm
36
Reader's Bridge
READER'S BRIDGE RD
4
Brook Farm Oast
Sandpit Wood
Gribble Wood
Short's Wood
Penhill
Short's Farmhouse
Millpond Farm
TN30
3
Silcocks Farm
TENTERDEN RD
Flight Wood
Reighton Wood
Honour Farm
GRANGE RD
35
Boundary Farm
MILLPOND LA
Rosedown Wood
Pott's Wood
2
Twisden Farm
Parkgate
Parkgate Farm
CRANBROOK RD
Coombe Farm
Goodshill Farm
CHENNELL PARK RD
Patt's Farm
1
Goods Hill House Farm
TN17
34
85
A
B
86
C
D
87
E
F
344
324

323
296

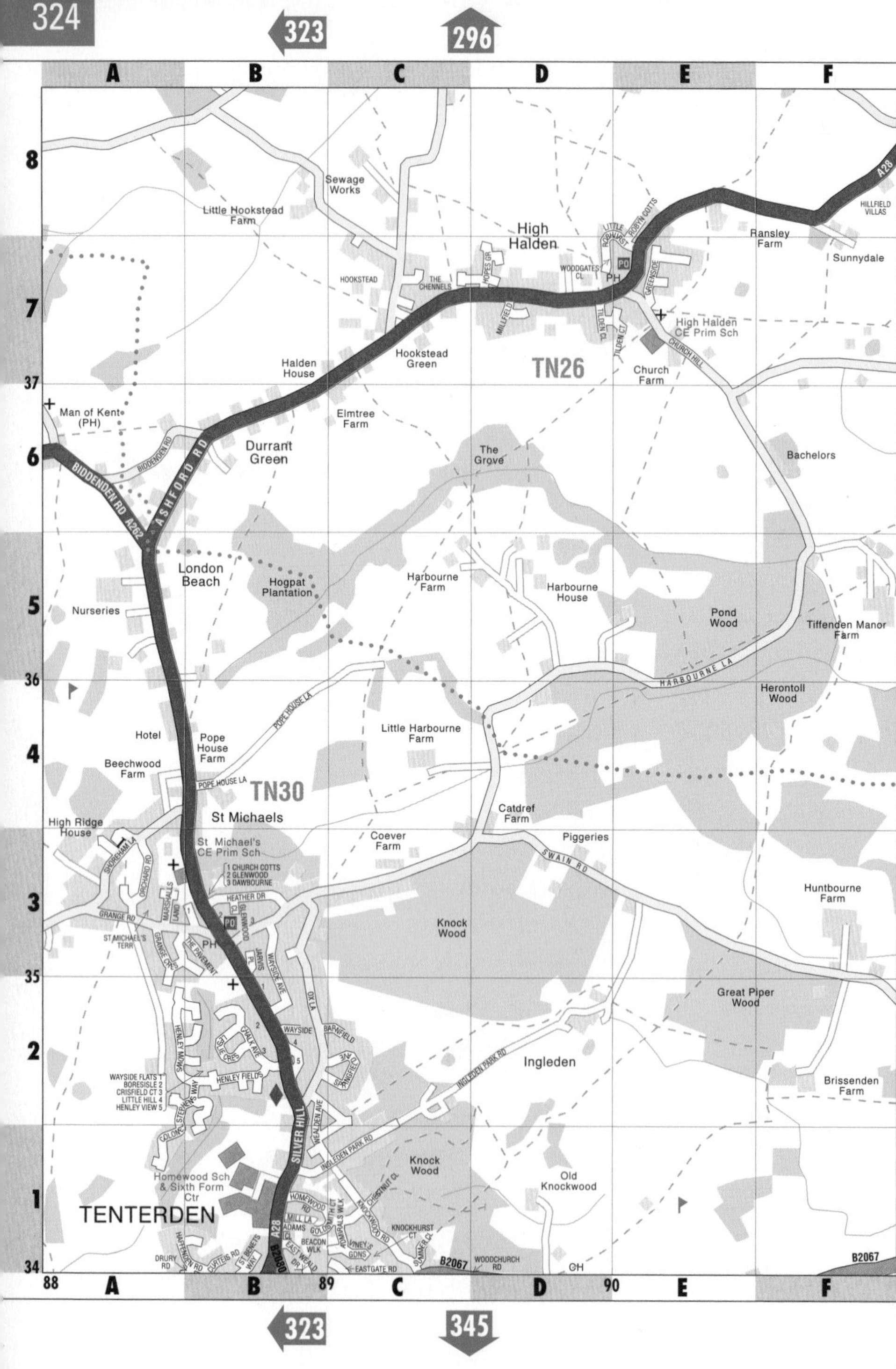
A
B
C
D
E
F
8
7
37
6
5
36
4
3
35
2
1
34
88
89
90
Sewage Works
Little Hookstead Farm
High Halden
HOOKSTEAD
THE CHENNELS
POPES GR
MILLFIELD
WOODGATES CL
LITTLE ROBHURST
ROBYN COTTS
PO
PH
GREENSIDE
TILDEN CL
TILDEN CT
A28
HILLFIELD VILLAS
Ransley Farm
Sunnydale
High Halden CE Prim Sch
CHURCH HILL
Church Farm
TN26
Halden House
Hookstead Green
Man of Kent (PH)
Elmtree Farm
Durrant Green
The Grove
Bachelors
BIDDENDEN RD
ASHFORD RD
BIDDENDEN RD A262
London Beach
Hogpat Plantation
Harbourne Farm
Harbourne House
Pond Wood
Nurseries
Tiffenden Manor Farm
HARBOURNE LA
Herontoll Wood
POPE HOUSE LA
Hotel
Pope House Farm
Little Harbourne Farm
Beechwood Farm
TN30
St Michaels
Catdref Farm
High Ridge House
Coever Farm
Piggeries
St Michael's CE Prim Sch
SWAIN RD
1 CHURCH COTTS
2 GLENWOOD
3 DAWBOURNE
SHOREHAM LA
ORCHARD RD
MARSHALLS LAND
HEATHER DR
Huntbourne Farm
GRANGE RD
ST MICHAEL'S TERR
GRANGE CR
THE PAVEMENT
JARVIS PL
WAYSIDE AVE
Knock Wood
OX LA
Great Piper Wood
HENLEY MWS
LESLIE CRES
CHALK AVE
WAYSIDE
BARNFIELD
SPRINGFIELD
HENLEY FIELDS
INGLEDEN PARK RD
Ingleden
Brissenden Farm
WAYSIDE FLATS 1
BORESISLE 2
CRISFIELD CT 3
LITTLE HILL 4
HENLEY VIEW 5
STEPHENS WAY
SILVER HILL
WEALDEN AVE
Knock Wood
Old Knockwood
CHESTNUT CL
Homewood Sch & Sixth Form Ctr
TENTERDEN
HOMEWOOD RD
MILL LA
ADAMS CL
KNOCKWOOD RD
KNOCKHURST CT
BEACON WLK
ADMIRALS WLK
EAST WEALD DR
VINEY'S GDNS
SUMNER CL
DRURY RD
HAFFENDEN RD
CURTEIS RD
ST BENETS WAY
B2080
EASTGATE RD
B2067
WOODCHURCH RD
CH

323
345

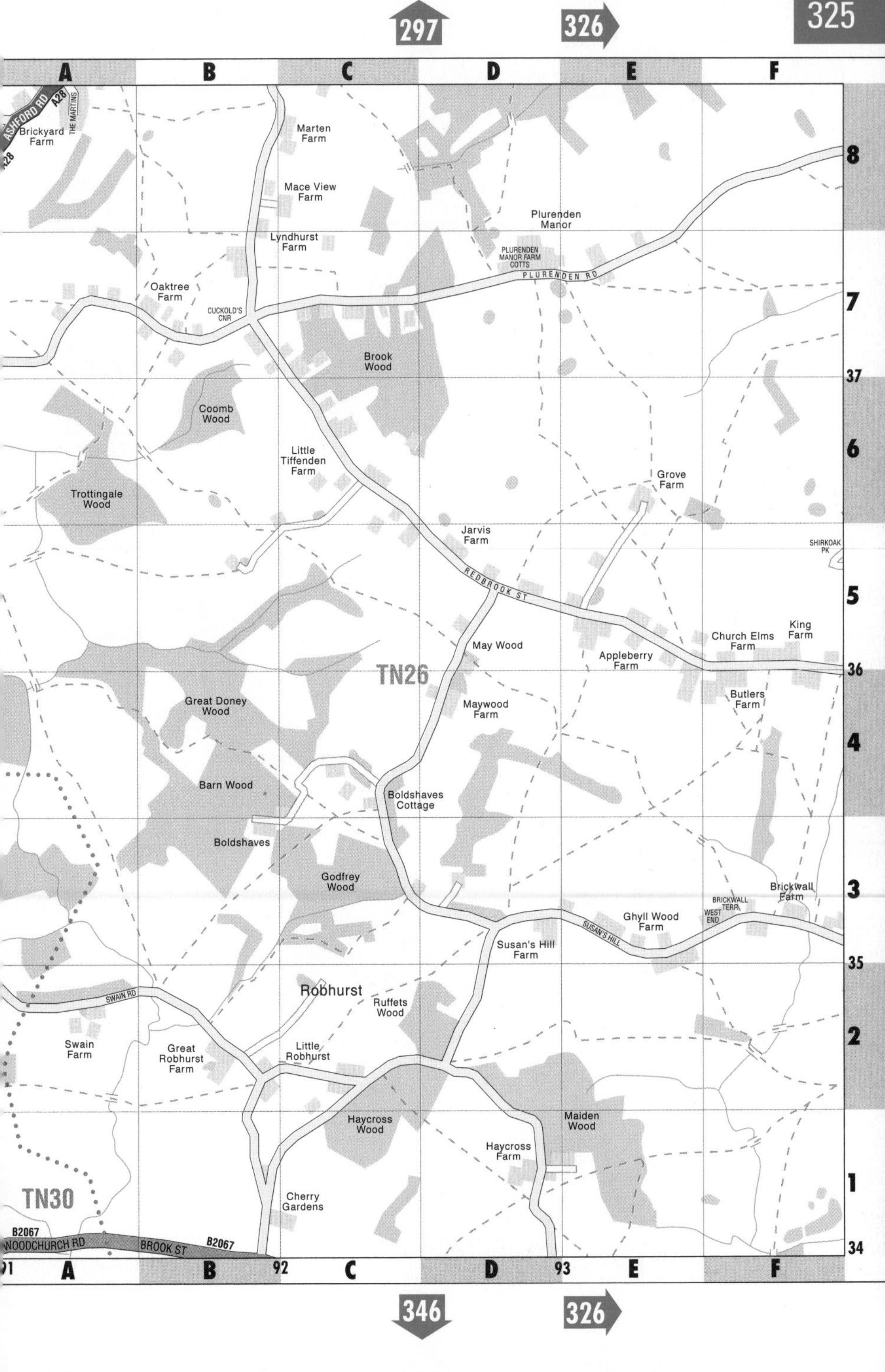

A B C D E F

8

7

37

6

5

36

4

3

35

2

1

34

ASHFORD RD A28
A28
Brickyard Farm
THE MALTING
Marten Farm
Mace View Farm
Lyndhurst Farm
Plurenden Manor
PLURENDEN MANOR FARM COTTS
PLURENDEN RD
Oaktree Farm
CUCKOLD'S CNR
Brook Wood
Coomb Wood
Little Tiffenden Farm
Grove Farm
SHIRKOAK PK
Trottingale Wood
Jarvis Farm
REDBROOK ST
TN26
May Wood
Appleberry Farm
Church Elms Farm
King Farm
Great Doney Wood
Maywood Farm
Butlers Farm
Barn Wood
Boldshaves Cottage
Boldshaves
Godfrey Wood
Ghyll Wood Farm
BRICKWALL TERR
WEST END
Brickwall Farm
Susan's Hill Farm
SUSAN'S HILL
SWAIN RD
Robhurst
Ruffets Wood
Swain Farm
Great Robhurst Farm
Little Robhurst
Haycross Wood
Maiden Wood
Haycross Farm
TN30
Cherry Gardens
B2067
WOODCHURCH RD
BROOK ST
B2067
B2067

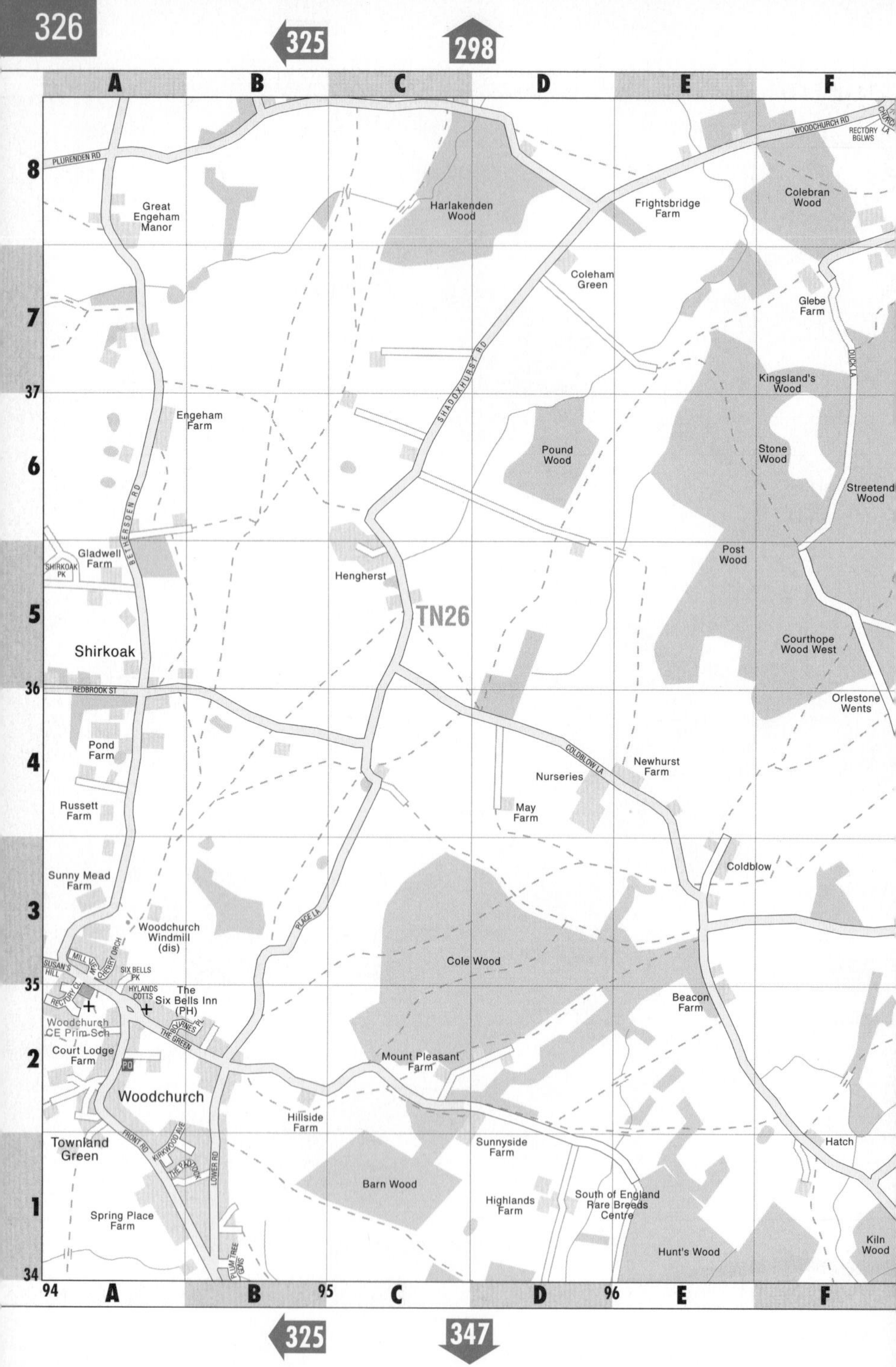

325
298

A B C D E F

8

PLURENDEN RD

Great
Engeham
Manor

WOODCHURCH RD

RECTORY
BGLWS

Colebran
Wood

Harlakenden
Wood

Frightsbridge
Farm

Coleham
Green

7

Glebe
Farm

37

Engeham
Farm

Kingsland's
Wood

6

Pound
Wood

Stone
Wood

Streetend
Wood

Gladwell
Farm

SHIRKOAK
PK

Hengherst

Post
Wood

5

TN26

Courthope
Wood West

Shirkoak

36

REDBROOK ST

Orlestone
Wents

4

Pond
Farm

COLDBLOW LA

Newhurst
Farm

Russett
Farm

Nurseries

May
Farm

Sunny Mead
Farm

Coldblow

3

Woodchurch
Windmill
(dis)

Cole Wood

Beacon
Farm

MILL LA

SIX BELLS
PK

HYLANDS
COTTS

The
Six Bells Inn
(PH)

35

SUSAN'S
HILL

RECTORY

Woodchurch
CE Prim Sch

THE GREEN

2

Court Lodge
Farm

PO

Mount Pleasant
Farm

Woodchurch

Hillside
Farm

Townland
Green

FRONT RD

Sunnyside
Farm

Hatch

THE CHASE

LOWER RD

1

Spring Place
Farm

Barn
Wood

Highlands
Farm

South of England
Rare Breeds
Centre

Hunt's Wood

Kiln
Wood

34

94 A B 95 C D 96 E F

325
347

299
328

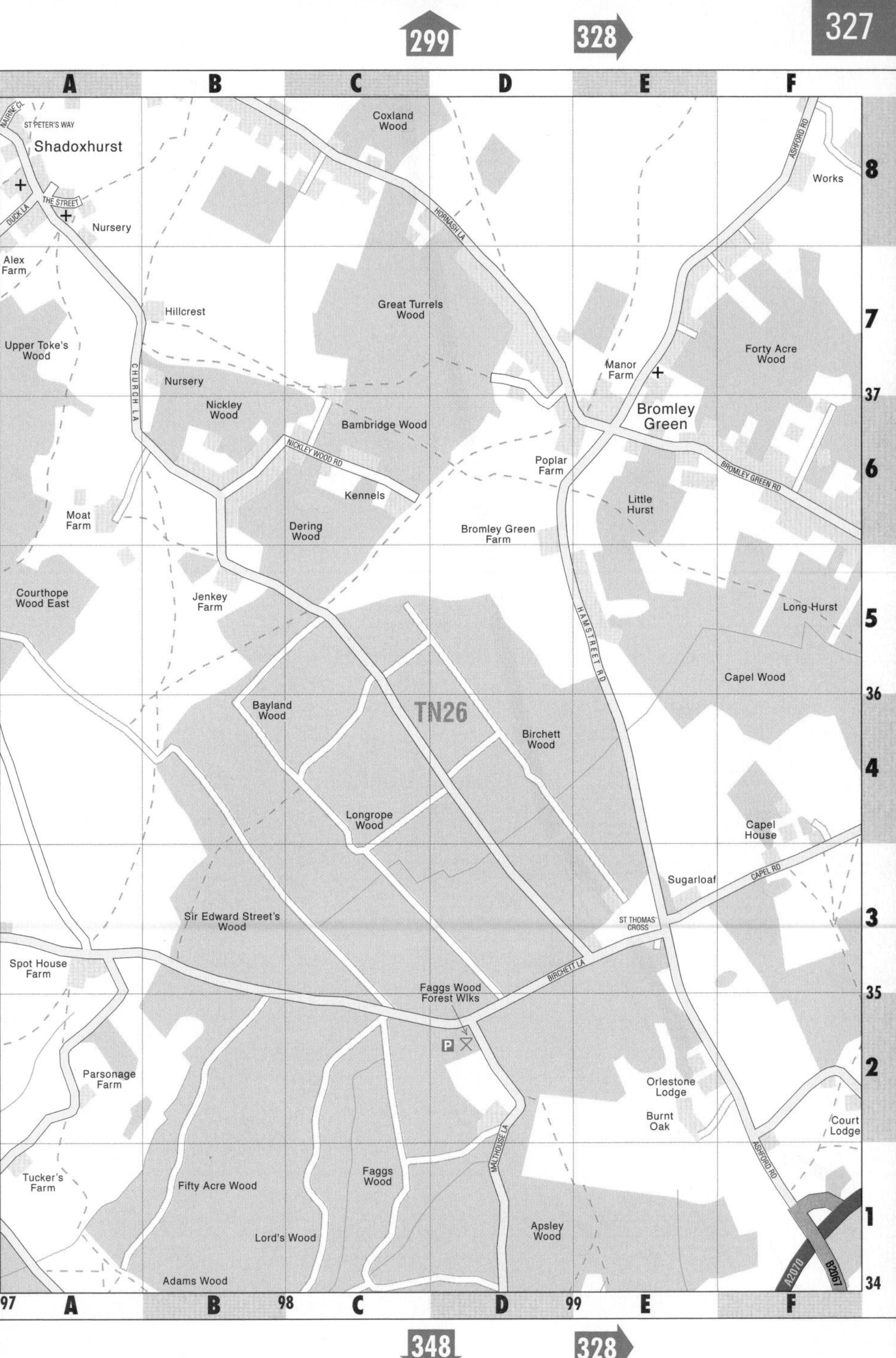
A
B
C
D
E
F
NAIRNE CL
ST PETER'S WAY
Shadoxhurst
THE STREET
DUCK LA
Nursery
Alex Farm
Coxland Wood
HORNASH LA
ASHFORD RD
Works
8
Great Turrels Wood
Hillcrest
7
Upper Toke's Wood
CHURCH LA
Nursery
Forty Acre Wood
Manor Farm
Nickley Wood
Bambridge Wood
37
Bromley Green
NICKLEY WOOD RD
Poplar Farm
BROMLEY GREEN RD
6
Kennels
Little Hurst
Moat Farm
Dering Wood
Bromley Green Farm
Courthope Wood East
Jenkey Farm
Long Hurst
5
HAMSTREET RD
Capel Wood
36
Bayland Wood
TN26
Birchett Wood
4
Longrope Wood
Capel House
Sugarloaf
CAPEL RD
Sir Edward Street's Wood
ST THOMAS' CROSS
3
Spot House Farm
BIRCHETT LA
Faggs Wood Forest Wlks
35
P
Parsonage Farm
2
Orlestone Lodge
Burnt Oak
Court Lodge
MALTHOUSE LA
ASHFORD RD
Tucker's Farm
Faggs Wood
Fifty Acre Wood
1
Apsley Wood
Lord's Wood
A2070
B2067
Adams Wood
34
97
98
99

348
328

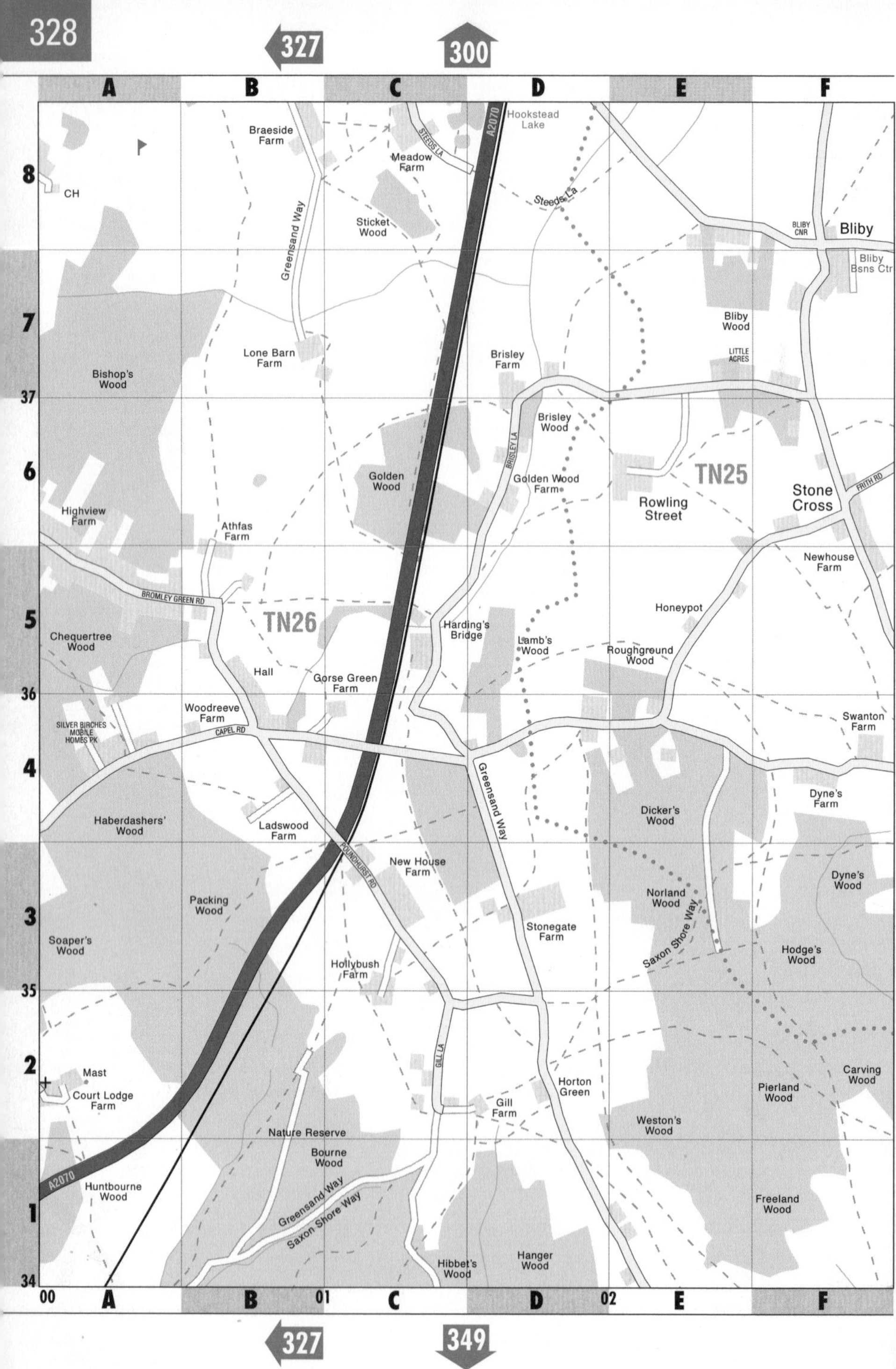

327
300

8

CH

Braeside Farm

Meadow Farm

Greensand Way

Sticket Wood

STEEDS LA

A2070

Hookstead Lake

Steeds La

BLIBY CNR

Bliby

Bliby Bsns Ctr

7

Lone Barn Farm

Brisley Farm

Bliby Wood

LITTLE ACRES

37

Bishop's Wood

Brisley Wood

6

Highview Farm

Athfas Farm

Golden Wood

Golden Wood Farm

Rowling Street

TN25

Stone Cross

Newhouse Farm

FRITH RD

BROMLEY GREEN RD

5

Chequertree Wood

TN26

Harding's Bridge

Llamb's Wood

Honeypot

Roughground Wood

36

Hall

Gorse Green Farm

Swanton Farm

4

SILVER BIRCHES MOBILE HOMES PK

CAPEL RD

Woodreeve Farm

Greensand Way

Dicker's Wood

Dyne's Farm

3

Haberdashers' Wood

Ladswood Farm

ASHFORD INST RD

New House Farm

Norland Wood

Saxon Shore Way

Dyne's Wood

Packing Wood

Stonegate Farm

Hodge's Wood

35

Soaper's Wood

Hollybush Farm

2

Mast

Court Lodge Farm

GILL LA

Gill Farm

Horton Green

Weston's Wood

Pierland Wood

Carving Wood

Nature Reserve

Bourne Wood

Freeland Wood

A2070

1

Huntbourne Wood

Greensand Way

Saxon Shore Way

Hibbet's Wood

Hanger Wood

34

00

01

02

301
330

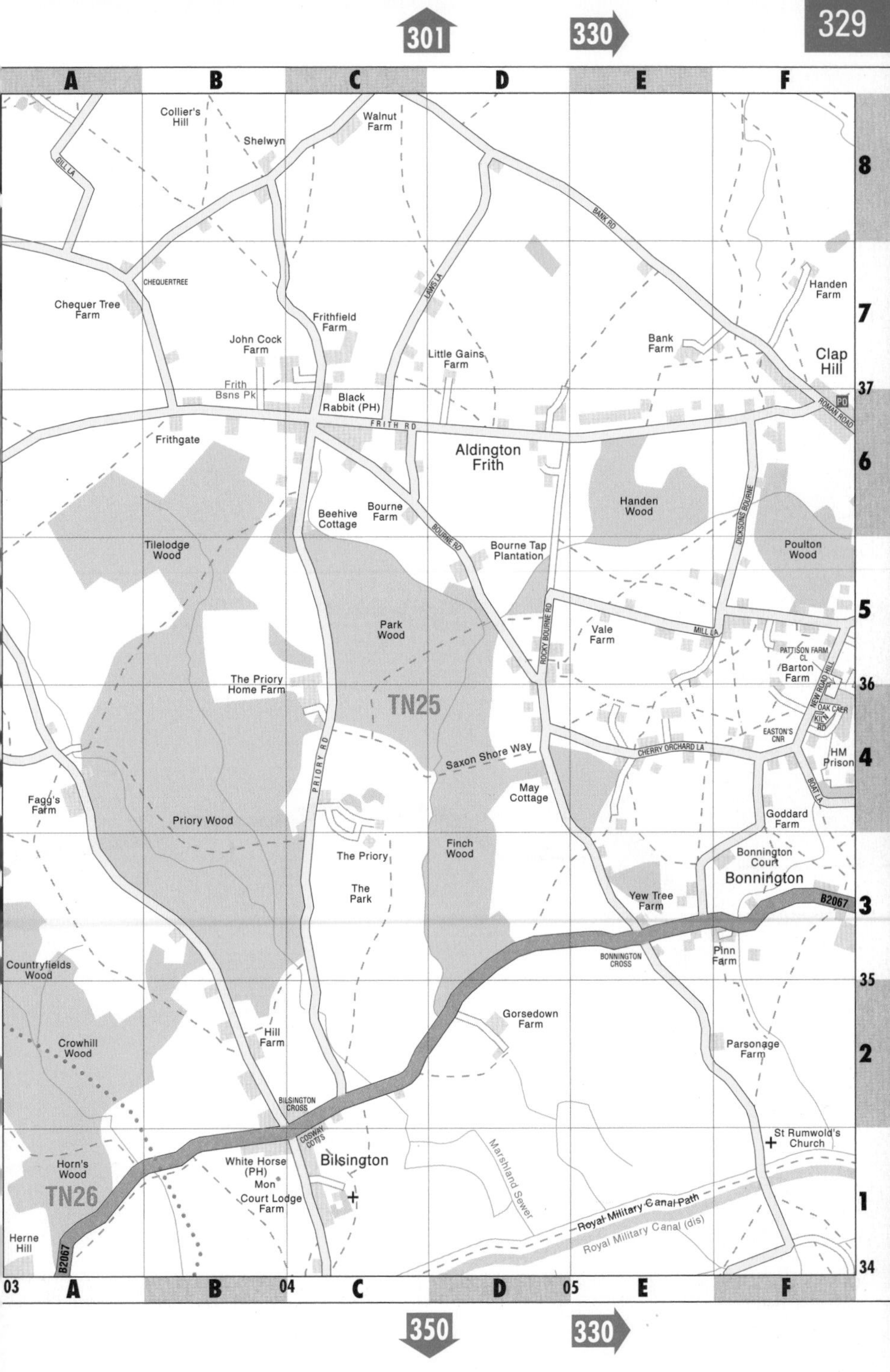
A
B
C
D
E
F
8
7
6
5
4
3
2
1
37
36
35
34
03
04
05
Collier's Hill
Shelwyn
Walnut Farm
GILL LA
BANK RD
CHEQUERTREE
Chequer Tree Farm
LAWS LA
Frithfield Farm
John Cock Farm
Little Gains Farm
Bank Farm
Handen Farm
Clap Hill
Frith Bsns Pk
Black Rabbit (PH)
FRITH RD
ROMAN ROAD
Frithgate
Aldington Frith
Beehive Cottage
Bourne Farm
Handen Wood
DICKSONS BOURNE
BOURNE RD
Tilelodge Wood
Bourne Tap Plantation
Poulton Wood
Park Wood
ROCKY BOURNE RD
Vale Farm
MILL LA
PATTISON FARM CL
Barton Farm
NEW ROAD HILL
The Priory Home Farm
TN25
OAK CAER
KILN RD
EASTON'S CNR
PRIORY RD
Saxon Shore Way
CHERRY ORCHARD LA
HM Prison
Fagg's Farm
May Cottage
BOAT LA
Priory Wood
Goddard Farm
Finch Wood
The Priory
Bonnington Court
Bonnington
The Park
Yew Tree Farm
B2067
BONNINGTON CROSS
Pinn Farm
Countryfields Wood
Gorsedown Farm
Crowhill Wood
Hill Farm
Parsonage Farm
BILSINGTON CROSS
St Rumwold's Church
COSWAY COTTS
Marshland Sewer
Horn's Wood
White Horse (PH)
Bilsington
Mon
Court Lodge Farm
TN26
Royal Military Canal Path
Royal Military Canal (dis)
Herne Hill
B2067

350
330

329
302

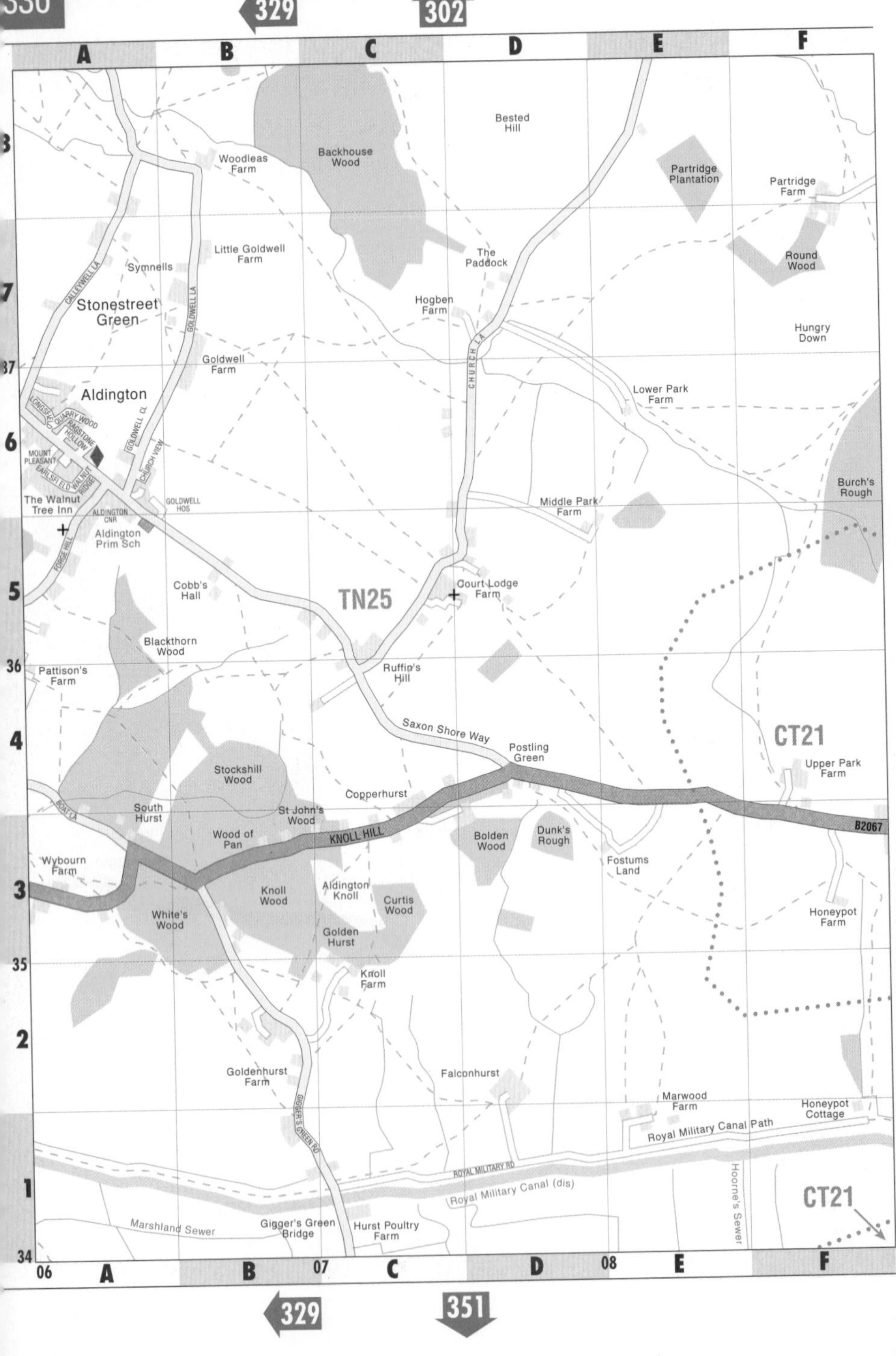
A
B
C
D
E
F
Bested Hill
Backhouse Wood
Woodleas Farm
Partridge Plantation
Partridge Farm
Little Goldwell Farm
Symnells
The Paddock
Round Wood
Stonestreet Green
Hogben Farm
Hungry Down
Goldwell Farm
Aldington
Lower Park Farm
The Walnut Tree Inn
Middle Park Farm
Burch's Rough
Aldington Prim Sch
Cobb's Hall
TN25
Court Lodge Farm
Blackthorn Wood
Pattison's Farm
Ruffin's Hill
Saxon Shore Way
Postling Green
CT21
Stockshill Wood
Upper Park Farm
Copperhurst
South Hurst
St John's Wood
Wood of Pan
KNOLL HILL
Bolden Wood
Dunk's Rough
B2067
Wybourn Farm
Fostums Land
Knoll Wood
Aldington Knoll
Curtis Wood
White's Wood
Honeypot Farm
Golden Hurst
Knoll Farm
Goldenhurst Farm
Falconhurst
Marwood Farm
Honeypot Cottage
Royal Military Canal Path
ROYAL MILITARY RD
Royal Military Canal (dis)
Hoorne's Sewer
CT21
Marshland Sewer
Gigger's Green Bridge
Hurst Poultry Farm
GIGGER'S GREEN RD
CALLEYWELL LA
GOLDWELL LA
GOLDWELL CL
CHURCH VIEW
CHURCH LA
QUARRY WOOD
BAGSTONE HOLLOW
MOUNT PLEASANT
EARLSFIELD
WALNUT RIDGE
ALDINGTON CNR
GOLDWELL HOS
FORGE HILL
BOAT LA
06
07
08
34
35
36
37
1
2
3
4
5
6
7

329
351

303
332

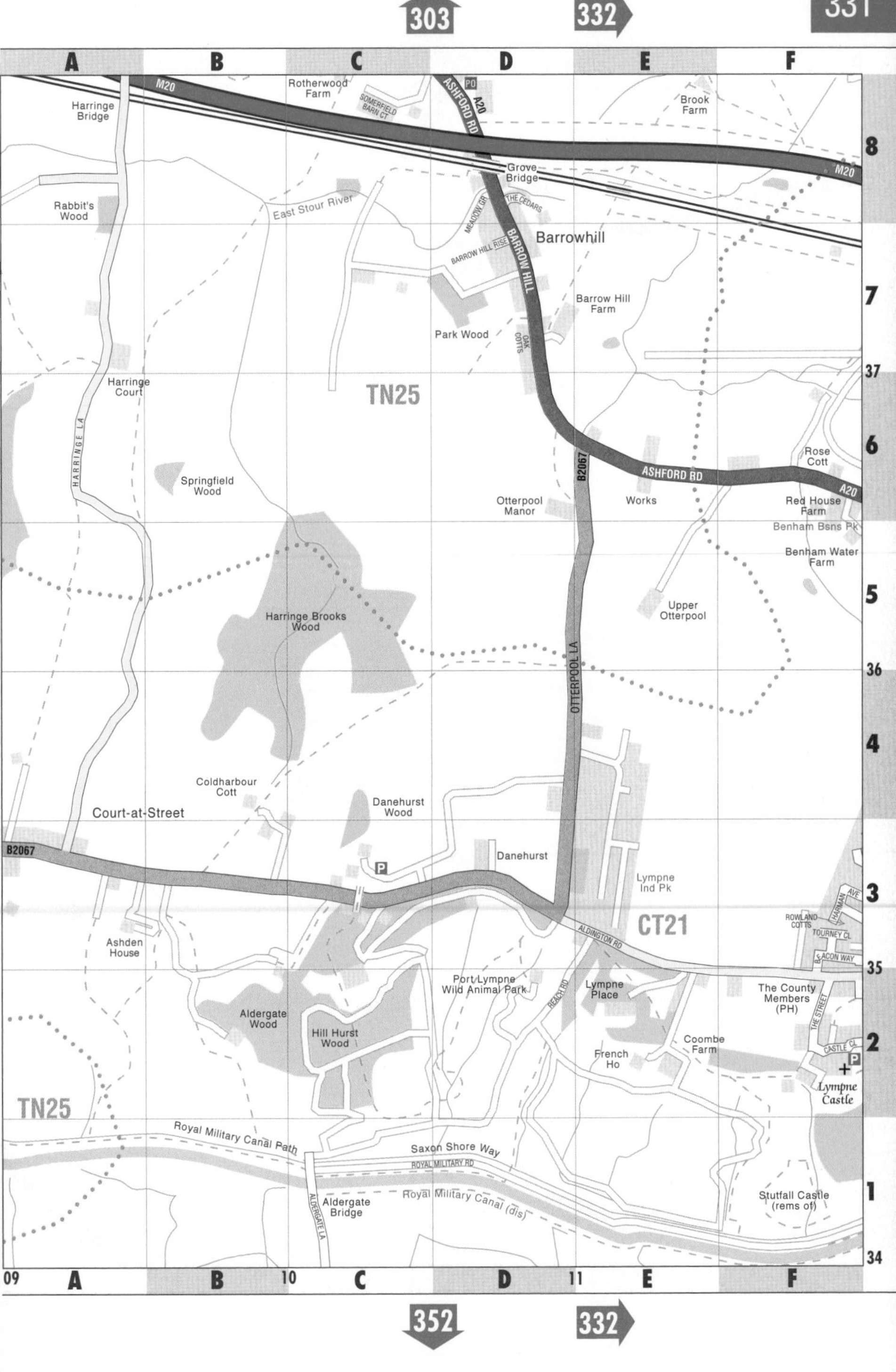
A
B
C
D
E
F
M20
Harringe Bridge
Rotherwood Farm
SOMERFIELD BARN CT
ASHFORD RD
A20
PO
Brook Farm
8
Grove Bridge
Rabbit's Wood
East Stour River
MEADOW GR
THE CEDARS
Barrowhill
BARROW HILL RISE
BARROW HILL
7
Barrow Hill Farm
Park Wood
OAK COTTS
37
Harringe Court
TN25
HARRINGE LA
6
Rose Cott
Springfield Wood
B2067
ASHFORD RD
A20
Otterpool Manor
Works
Red House Farm
Benham Bsns Pk
Benham Water Farm
5
Upper Otterpool
Harringe Brooks Wood
OTTERPOOL LA
36
4
Coldharbour Cott
Court-at-Street
Danehurst Wood
B2067
P
Danehurst
Lympne Ind Pk
3
HARMAN AVE
ROWLAND COTTS
TOURNEY CL
CT21
ALDINGTON RD
BEACON WAY
Ashden House
35
Port Lympne Wild Animal Park
REACH RD
Lympne Place
The County Members (PH)
THE STREET
Aldergate Wood
Hill Hurst Wood
2
Coombe Farm
CASTLE CL
French Ho
P
Lympne Castle
TN25
Royal Military Canal Path
Saxon Shore Way
ROYAL MILITARY RD
1
Royal Military Canal (dis)
Stutfall Castle (rems of)
ALDERGATE LA
Aldergate Bridge
34
09
A
B
10
C
D
11
E
F

352
332

331
304

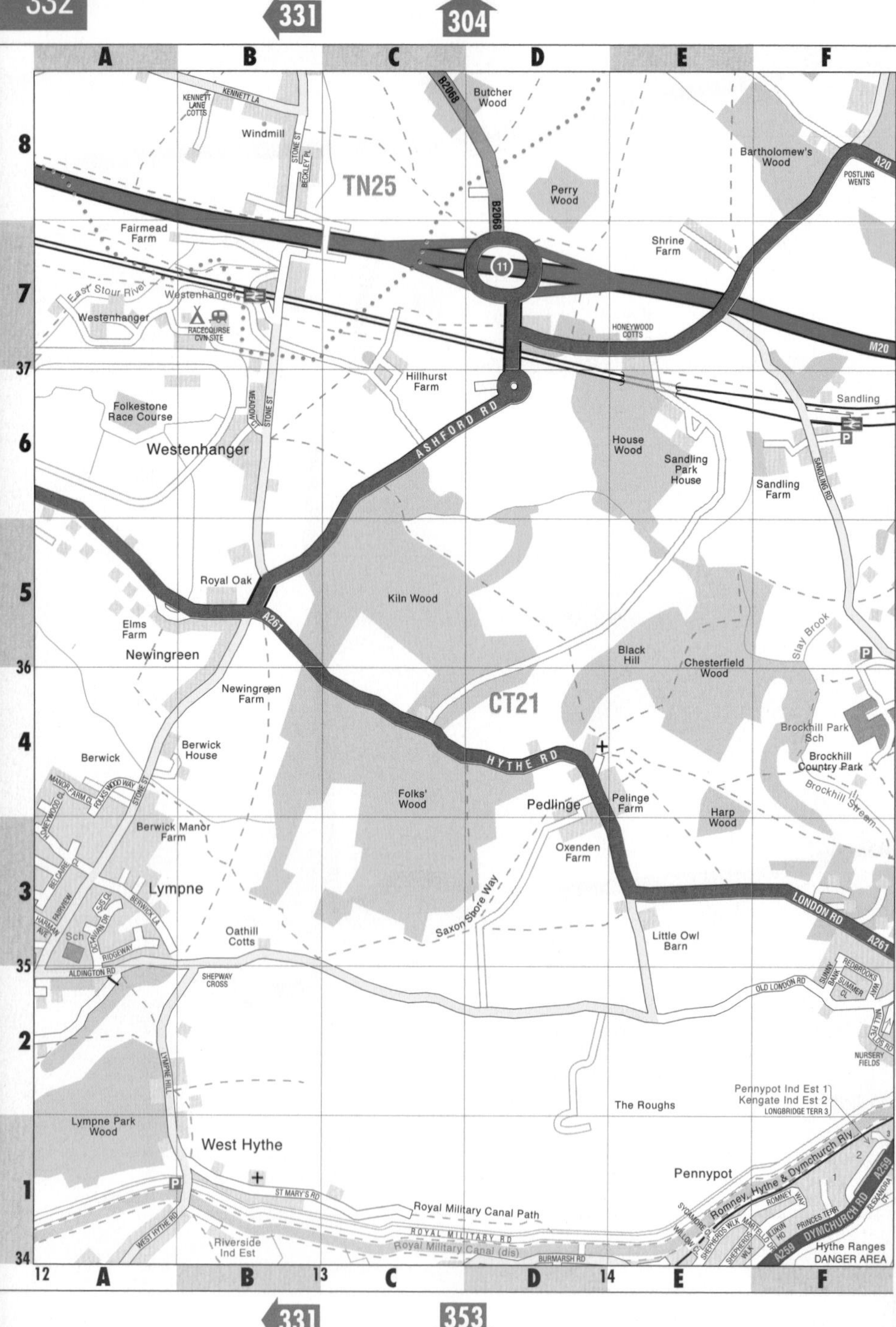
TN25
CT21
Butcher Wood
Windmill
Perry Wood
Bartholomew's Wood
Fairmead Farm
Shrine Farm
Westenhanger
East Stour River
RACECOURSE CVN SITE
HONEYWOOD COTTS
Hillhurst Farm
Folkestone Race Course
Sandling
House Wood
Sandling Park House
Sandling Farm
Royal Oak
Kiln Wood
Elms Farm
Newingreen
Newingreen Farm
Black Hill
Chesterfield Wood
Berwick
Berwick House
Brockhill Park Sch
Brockhill Country Park
Folks' Wood
Pedlinge
Pelinge Farm
Harp Wood
Berwick Manor Farm
Oxenden Farm
Lympne
Oathill Cotts
Little Owl Barn
Saxon Shore Way
SHEPWAY CROSS
The Roughs
Lympne Park Wood
West Hythe
Pennypot
Pennypot Ind Est 1
Kengate Ind Est 2
LONGBRIDGE TERR 3
Romney, Hythe & Dymchurch Rly
Royal Military Canal Path
ROYAL MILITARY RD
Royal Military Canal (dis)
Riverside Ind Est
Hythe Ranges DANGER AREA
ASHFORD RD
HYTHE RD
LONDON RD
STONE ST
A20
M20
B2068
A261
A259
DYMCHURCH RD

331
353

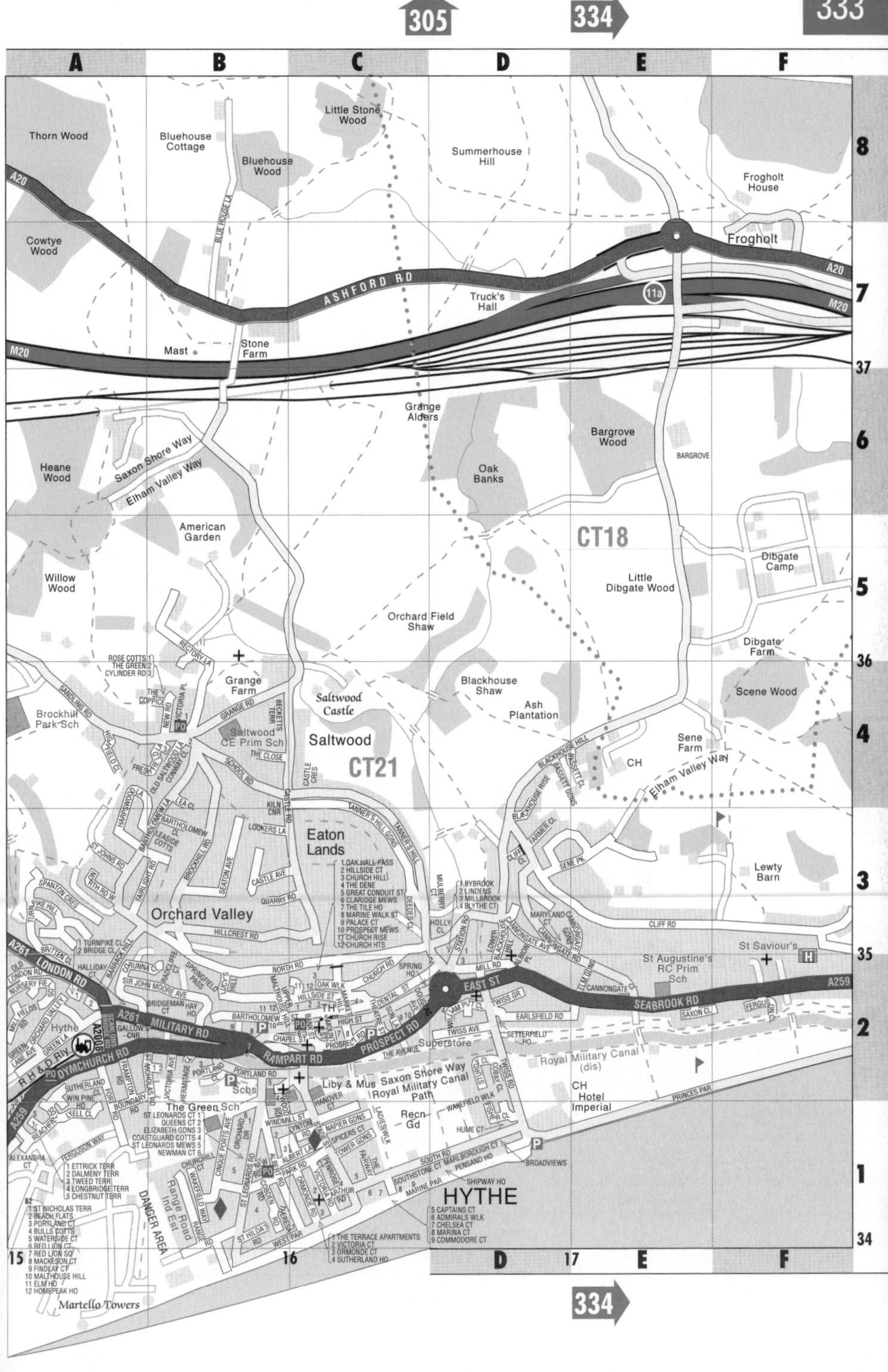

305
334
A
B
C
D
E
F
8
7
37
6
5
36
4
3
35
2
1
34
15
16
17
Thorn Wood
Bluehouse Cottage
Little Stone Wood
Bluehouse Wood
Summerhouse Hill
Frogholt House
Frogholt
Cowtye Wood
BLUE HOUSE LA
ASHFORD RD
A20
M20
11a
Truck's Hall
Mast
Stone Farm
Grange Alders
Bargrove Wood
BARGROVE
Heane Wood
Saxon Shore Way
Elham Valley Way
Oak Banks
CT18
American Garden
Dibgate Camp
Little Dibgate Wood
Willow Wood
Orchard Field Shaw
Dibgate Farm
Grange Farm
Blackhouse Shaw
Scene Wood
Saltwood Castle
Ash Plantation
Brockhill Park Sch
Saltwood CE Prim Sch
Saltwood
Sene Farm
CT21
CH
Eaton Lands
Lewty Barn
Orchard Valley
CLIFF RD
St Saviour's
St Augustine's RC Prim Sch
A261
LONDON RD
A259
SEABROOK RD
EAST ST
Hythe
A261 MILITARY RD
A2008
R H & D Rly
DYMCHURCH RD
RAMPART RD
PROSPECT RD
Superstore
Royal Military Canal (dis)
Liby & Mus
Saxon Shore Way
Royal Military Canal Path
CH
Hotel Imperial
Schs
The Green Sch
Recn Gd
PRINCES PAR
HYTHE
DANGER AREA
Range Road Ind Est
Martello Towers
ROSE COTTS 1
THE GREEN 2
CYLINDER RD 3
1 OAK HALL PASS
2 HILLSIDE CT
3 CHURCH HILL
4 THE DENE
5 GREAT CONDUIT ST
6 CLARIDGE MEWS
7 THE TILE HO
8 MARINE WALK ST
9 PALACE CT
10 PROSPECT MEWS
11 CHURCH RISE
12 CHURCH HTS
1 BYBROOK
2 LINDENS
3 MILLBROOK
4 BLYTHE CT
1 TURNPIKE CL
2 BRIDGE CL
ST LEONARDS CT 1
QUEENS CT 2
ELIZABETH GDNS 3
COASTGUARD COTTS 4
ST LEONARDS MEWS 5
NEWMAN CT 6
1 ETTRICK TERR
2 DALMENY TERR
3 TWEED TERR
4 LONGBRIDGE TERR
5 CHESTNUT TERR
B2
1 ST NICHOLAS TERR
2 BEACH FLATS
3 PORTLAND CT
4 BULLS COTTS
5 WATERSIDE CT
6 RED LION CT
7 RED LION SQ
8 MACKESON CT
9 FINDLAY CT
10 MALTHOUSE HILL
11 ELM HO
12 HOMEPEAK HO
1 THE TERRACE APARTMENTS
2 VICTORIA CT
3 ORMONDE CT
4 SUTHERLAND HO
5 CAPTAINS CT
6 ADMIRALS WLK
7 CHELSEA CT
8 MARINA CT
9 COMMODORE CT

334

333
306

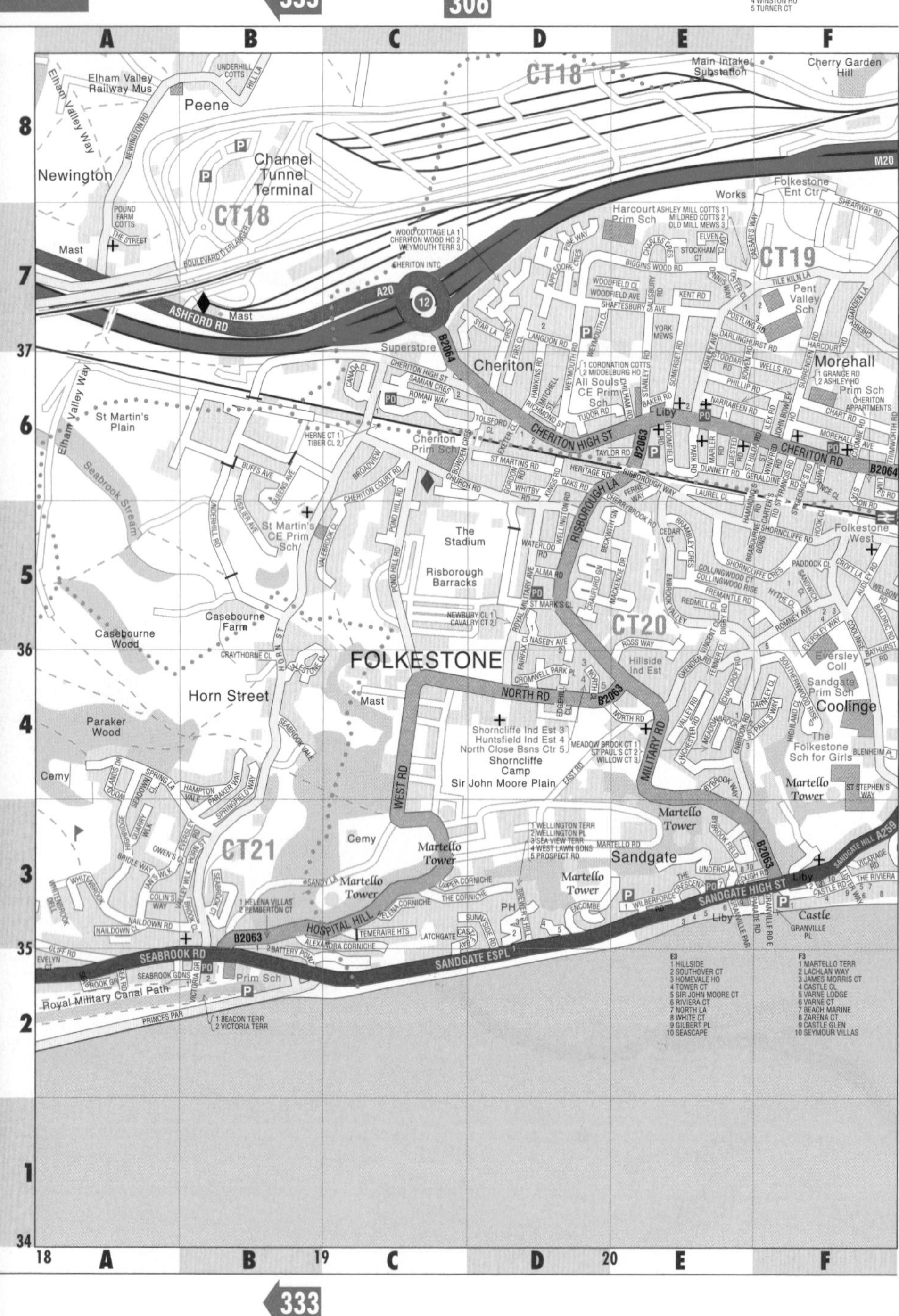
F5
1 WALMER WAY
2 CHURCHILL HO
3 SPENCER HO
4 WINSTON HO
5 TURNER CT
A
B
C
D
E
F
8
7
37
6
5
36
4
3
35
2
1
34
18
19
20
Elham Valley Railway Mus
Elham Valley Way
UNDERHILL COTTS
Peene
NEWINGTON RD
Newington
Channel Tunnel Terminal
CT18
Main Intake Substation
Cherry Garden Hill
M20
POUND FARM COTTS
THE STREET
Mast
BOULEVARD D'ERLANGER
WOOD COTTAGE LA 1
CHERITON WOOD HO 2
WEYMOUTH TERR 3
CHERITON INTC
A20
12
ASHFORD RD
Mast
Works
Folkestone Ent Ctr
SHEARWAY RD
Harcourt Prim Sch
ASHLEY MILL COTTS 1
MILDRED COTTS 2
OLD MILL MEWS 3
CT19
PINE WAY
APPLEDORE CRES
CHARLES CRES
ELVEN CL
STOCKHAM CT
BIGGINS WOOD RD
CAESAR'S WAY
TILE KILN LA
Pent Valley Sch
WOODFIELD CL
WOODFIELD AVE
SHAFTESBURY AVE
KENT RD
DENNIS WAY
FOSTER CL
POSTLING RD
STAR LA
FIRS LA
LANGDON RD
YORK MEWS
DARLINGHURST RD
HARCOURT RD
Superstore
B2064
FIRS CL
HAWKINS RD
MITCHELL ST
WEYMOUTH RD
SALISBURY RD
1 CORONATION COTTS
2 MIDDELBURG HO
STANLEY RD
SOMERSET RD
ASHLEY AVE
STODDART RD
BOWEN RD
WELLS RD
SURRENDEN RD
Morehall
1 GRANGE RD
2 ASHLEY HO
Prim Sch
CHERITON APPARTMENTS
CHERITON HIGH ST
SAMIAN CRES
ROMAN WAY
CANADA CL
Cheriton
All Souls' CE Prim Sch
CHILHAM RD
BAKER RD
Liby
PHILLIP RD
NARRABEEN RD
CHART RD
Elham Valley Way
St Martin's Plain
HERNE CT 1
TIBER CL 2
TOLSFORD CL
RICHMOND ST
TUDOR RD
CHERITON HIGH ST
B2063
BROOMFIELD RD
PARK RD
MARLER RD
QUESTED RD
ST HILDA RD
ST WINIFRED RD
JOHN BOWLEY
ILEX RD
MOREHALL AVE
CHERITON RD
COOMBE RD
TRIMWORTH RD
Seabrook Stream
BUFFS AVE
QUEENS AVE
Cheriton Prim Sch
BOWDEN CRES
ST MARTINS RD
TAYLOR RD
HERITAGE RD
DUNNETT RD
GERALDINE RD
ST FRANCIS RD
B2064
BROADVIEW
CHERITON COURT RD
CHURCH RD
GORDON RD
EXETER CL
WHITBY RD
KINGS RD
OAKS RD
RISBOROUGH LA
FERNE WAY
RISBOROUGH WAY
LAUREL CL
HAMMONDS RD
CARTER'S RD
ST GEORGE'S RD
LAWRENCE CL
FUSILIER AVE
UNDERHILL RD
St Martin's CE Prim Sch
VALEBROOK CL
POND HILL RD
The Stadium
WATERLOO RD
WELLINGTON RD
CHERRYBROOK RD
BECKWITH GN
CEDAR CT
BRAMBLEY CRES
BRABOURNE GDNS
SHORNCLIFFE RD
HOOK CL
Folkestone West
Risborough Barracks
ALMA RD
ROYAL MILITARY AVE
CRAUFURD GN
MACKENZIE DR
EMBROOK VALLEY
COLLINGWOOD CT
COLLINGWOOD RISE
SHORNCLIFFE CRES
PADDOCK CL
CROFT LA
FREMANTLE RD
HYTHE CL
SANDWICH CL
AUDLEY RD
WELSON RD
ST MARK'S CL
NEWBURY CL 1
CAVALRY CT 2
REDMILL CL
DIGBY RD
ROMNEY AVE
BALDRIC RD
CT20
Casebourne Farm
Casebourne Wood
HORN ST
NASEBY AVE
ROSS WAY
EVERSLEY WAY
COOLINGE LA
BATHURST RD
CRAYTHORNE CL
FOLKESTONE
FAIRFAX CL
CROMWELL PARK PL
NORTH CL
Hillside Ind Est
OXENDEN RD
VINCENT CL
FENNER CL
CHALCROFT RD
Eversley Coll
Sandgate Prim Sch
Coolinge
Horn Street
Mast
NORTH RD
B2063
EDGEHILL CL
NORTH RD
SEABROOK VALE
Paraker Wood
Shorncliffe Ind Est 3
Huntsfield Ind Est 4
North Close Bsns Ctr 5
Shorncliffe Camp
Sir John Moore Plain
MEADOW BROOK CT 1
ST PAUL'S CT 2
WILLOW CT 3
MILITARY RD
VALLEY RD
CHICHESTER RD
EMBROOK RD
DARLEY CL
ST PAUL'S WAY
SOUTHERNWOOD RISE
HIGHLAND CL
The Folkestone Sch for Girls
BLENHEIM PL
Cemy
SPRING LA
HAMPTON VALE
PARAKER WAY
SPRINGFIELD WAY
SEADOWN CL
QUARRY WLK
EAST RD
WEST RD
BYBROOK WAY
Martello Tower
Martello Tower
ST STEPHEN'S WAY
CT21
OWEN'S CL
EVERSLEY RD
BRIDLE WAY
VALLEY WLK
HORN ST
Cemy
1 WELLINGTON TERR
2 WELLINGTON PL
3 SEA VIEW TERR
4 WEST LAWN GDNS
5 PROSPECT RD
MARTELLO RD
BYBROOK FIELD
Martello Tower
Martello Tower
Sandgate
Martello Tower
UNDERCLIFF
B2063
A259
SANDGATE HILL
VICARAGE RD
THE RIVIERA
COLIN'S WAY
SEABROOK CT
SANDY LA
UPPER CORNICHE
THE CORNICHE
1 HELENA VILLAS
2 PEMBERTON CT
HELENA CORNICHE
BRENZETT HILL
PH
SANDGATE HIGH ST
Liby
CASTLE RD
LISTER WAY
Castle
GRANVILLE PL
NAILDOWN RD
NAILDOWN CL
WHITEBROOK DELL
HOSPITAL HILL
TEMERAIRE HTS
LATCHGATE
SUNNYSIDE RD
ENCOMBE
WILBERFORCE RD
GRANVILLE PAR
GRANVILLE RD E
OLIFF RD
EVELYN CT
B2063
BATTERY PDE
ALEXANDRA CORNICHE
SEABROOK RD
SEABROOK GDNS
VICTORIA GR
Prim Sch
SANDGATE ESPL
Royal Military Canal Path
PRINCES PAR
1 BEACON TERR
2 VICTORIA TERR
E3
1 HILLSIDE
2 SOUTHOVER CT
3 HOMEVALE HO
4 TOWER CT
5 SIR JOHN MOORE CT
6 RIVIERA CT
7 NORTH LA
8 WHITE CT
9 GILBERT PL
10 SEASCAPE
F3
1 MARTELLO TERR
2 LACHLAN WAY
3 JAMES MORRIS CT
4 CASTLE CL
5 VARNE LODGE
6 VARNE CT
7 BEACH MARINE
8 ZARENA CT
9 CASTLE GLEN
10 SEYMOUR VILLAS

333

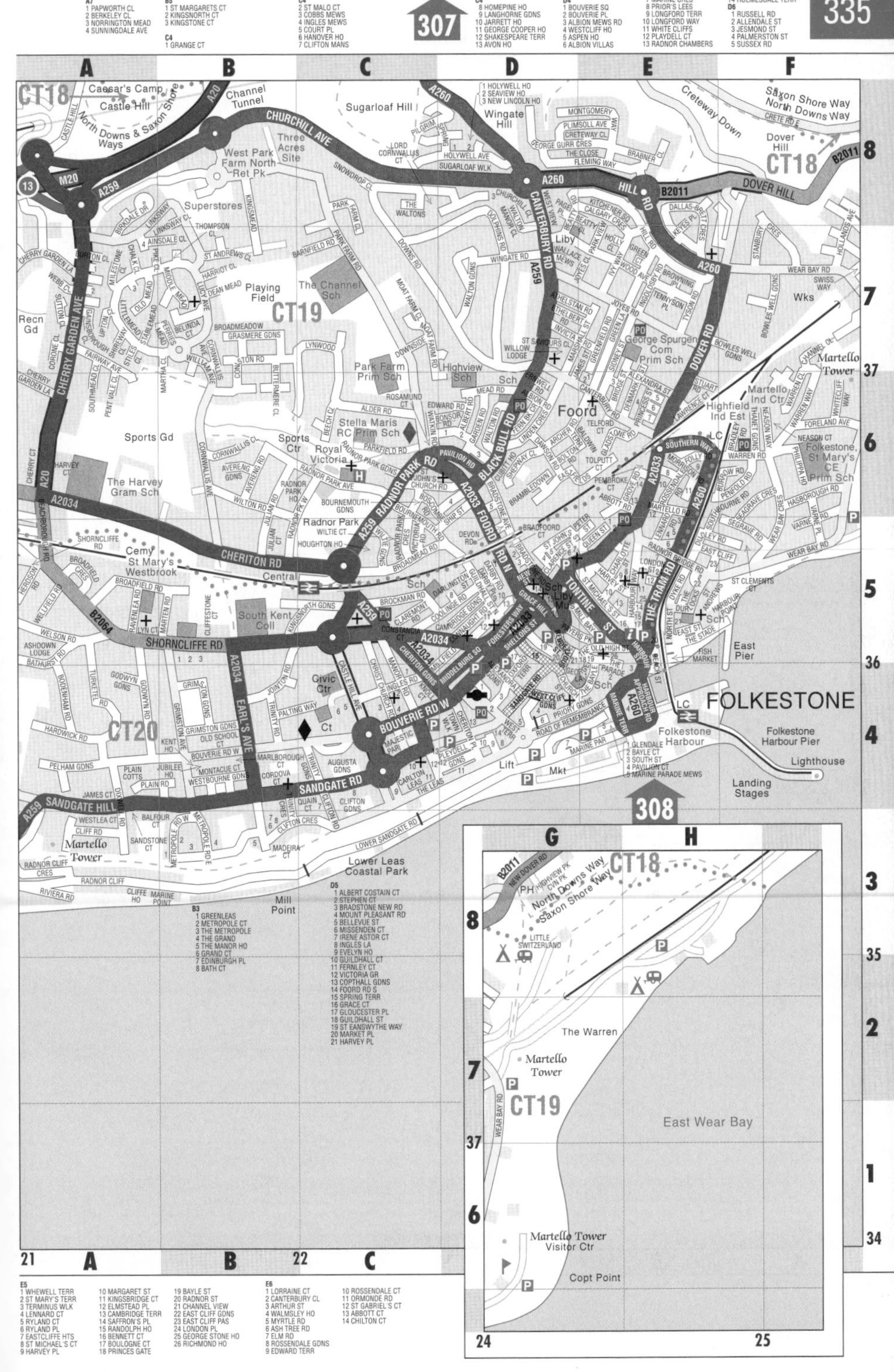
A7
1 PAPWORTH CL
2 BERKELEY CL
3 NORRINGTON MEAD
4 SUNNINGDALE AVE
B5
1 ST MARGARETS CT
2 KINGSNORTH CT
3 KINGSTONE CT
C4
1 GRANGE CT
C4
2 ST MALO CT
3 COBBS MEWS
4 INGLES MEWS
5 COURT PL
6 HANOVER HO
7 CLIFTON MANS
307
C4
8 HOMEPINE HO
9 LANGHORNE GDNS
10 JARRETT HO
11 GEORGE COOPER HO
12 SHAKESPEARE TERR
13 AVON HO
D4
1 BOUVERIE SQ
2 BOUVERIE PL
3 ALBION MEWS RD
4 WESTCLIFF HO
5 ASPEN HO
6 ALBION VILLAS
7 MARINE CRES
8 PRIOR'S LEES
9 LONGFORD TERR
10 LONGFORD WAY
11 WHITE CLIFFS
12 PLAYDELL CT
13 RADNOR CHAMBERS
14 HOLMESDALE TERR
D6
1 RUSSELL RD
2 ALLENDALE ST
3 JESMOND ST
4 PALMERSTON ST
5 SUSSEX RD
A B C D E F
8 7 37 6 5 36 4 3 35 2 1 34
CT18
Caesar's Camp
Castle Hill
North Downs & Saxon Shore Ways
Channel Tunnel
Sugarloaf Hill
Wingate Hill
1 HOLYWELL HO
2 SEAVIEW HO
3 NEW LINCOLN HO
Creteway Down
Saxon Shore Way
North Downs Way
Dover Hill
CHURCHILL AVE
West Park Farm North Ret Pk
Three Acres Site
Superstores
CHERRY GARDEN AVE
CANTERBURY RD
DOVER HILL
DOVER RD
Playing Field
The Channel Sch
CT19
Recn Gd
Park Farm Prim Sch
Highview Sch
George Spurgen Com Prim Sch
Foord
Stella Maris RC Prim Sch
Royal Victoria
Sports Gd
Sports Ctr
The Harvey Gram Sch
Highfield Ind Est
Martello Ind Ctr
Martello Tower
Folkestone, St Mary's CE Prim Sch
Wks
Radnor Park
Cemy
St Mary's Westbrook
CHERITON RD
Central
South Kent Coll
SHORNCLIFFE RD
SANDGATE RD
BOUVERIE RD W
RADNOR PARK RD
BLACK BULL RD
FOORD RD
TONTINE ST
THE TRAM RD
Civic Ctr
CT20
EARL'S AVE
SANDGATE HILL
The Leas
Lift
Mkt
East Pier
FOLKESTONE
Folkestone Harbour
Folkestone Harbour Pier
Lighthouse
Landing Stages
1 GLENDALE
2 BAYLE CT
3 SOUTH ST
4 PAVILION CT
5 MARINE PARADE MEWS
308
Martello Tower
LOWER SANDGATE RD
Lower Leas Coastal Park
Mill Point
B3
1 GREENLEAS
2 METROPOLE CT
3 THE METROPOLE
4 THE GRAND
5 THE MANOR HO
6 GRAND CT
7 EDINBURGH PL
8 BATH CT
D5
1 ALBERT COSTAIN CT
2 STEPHEN CT
3 BRADSTONE NEW RD
4 MOUNT PLEASANT RD
5 BELLEVUE ST
6 MISSENDEN CT
7 IRENE ASTOR CT
8 INGLES LA
9 EVELYN HO
10 GUILDHALL CT
11 FERNLEY CT
12 VICTORIA GR
13 COPTHALL GDNS
14 FOORD RD S
15 SPRING TERR
16 GRACE CT
17 GLOUCESTER PL
18 GUILDHALL ST
19 ST EANSWYTHE WAY
20 MARKET PL
21 HARVEY PL
G H
CT18
North Downs Way
Saxon Shore Way
LITTLE SWITZERLAND
The Warren
Martello Tower
CT19
East Wear Bay
Martello Tower Visitor Ctr
Copt Point
24 25
21 A B 22 C
E5
1 WHEWELL TERR
2 ST MARY'S TERR
3 TERMINUS WLK
4 LENNARD CT
5 RYLAND CT
6 RYLAND PL
7 EASTCLIFFE HTS
8 ST MICHAEL'S CT
9 HARVEY PL
10 MARGARET ST
11 KINGSBRIDGE CT
12 ELMSTEAD PL
13 CAMBRIDGE TERR
14 SAFFRON'S PL
15 RANDOLPH HO
16 BENNETT CT
17 BOULOGNE CT
18 PRINCES GATE
19 BAYLE ST
20 RADNOR ST
21 CHANNEL VIEW
22 EAST CLIFF GDNS
23 EAST CLIFF PAS
24 LONDON PL
25 GEORGE STONE HO
26 RICHMOND HO
E6
1 LORRAINE CT
2 CANTERBURY CL
3 ARTHUR ST
4 WALMSLEY HO
5 MYRTLE RD
6 ASH TREE RD
7 ELM RD
8 ROSSENDALE GDNS
9 EDWARD TERR
10 ROSSENDALE CT
11 ORMONDE RD
12 ST GABRIEL'S CT
13 ABBOTT CT
14 CHILTON CT

315

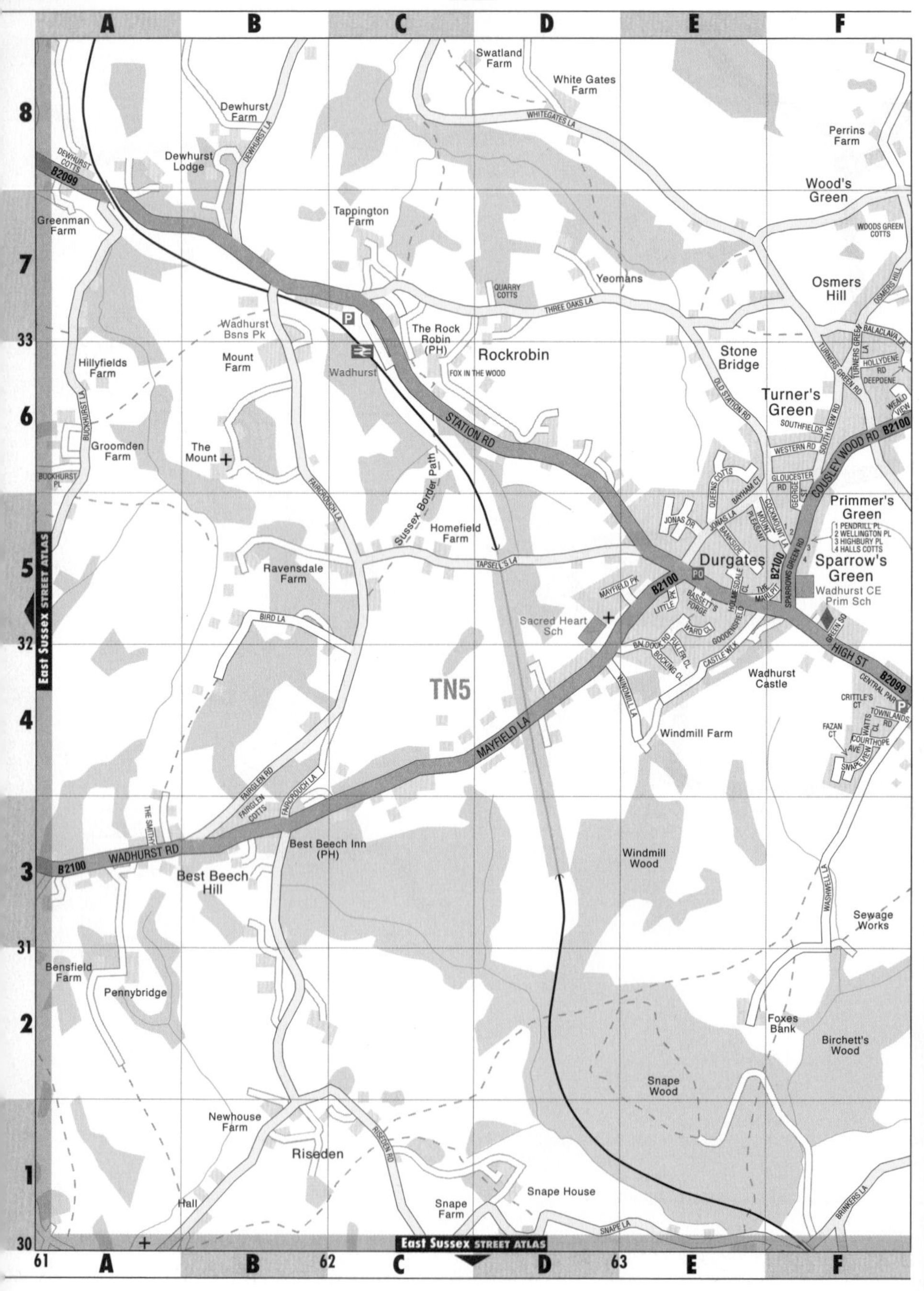

A
B
C
D
E
F
8
7
33
6
5
32
4
3
31
2
1
30
61
62
63
Swatland Farm
White Gates Farm
WHITEGATES LA
Dewhurst Farm
DEWHURST LA
Perrins Farm
Dewhurst Lodge
DEWHURST COTTS
B2099
Wood's Green
WOODS GREEN COTTS
Greenman Farm
Tappington Farm
Yeomans
Osmers Hill
OSMERS HILL
QUARRY COTTS
THREE OAKS LA
BALACLAVA LA
Wadhurst Bsns Pk
The Rock Robin (PH)
Rockrobin
Stone Bridge
HOLLYDENE RD
DEEPDENE
Mount Farm
Hillyfields Farm
Wadhurst
FOX IN THE WOOD
TURNERS GREEN RD
TURNERS GREEN LA
Turner's Green
OLD STATION RD
WEALD VIEW
SOUTH VIEW RD
STATION RD
SOUTHFIELDS
BUCKHURST LA
Groomden Farm
The Mount
WESTERN RD
COUSLEY WOOD RD
B2100
BUCKHURST PL
QUEENS COTTS
BAYHAM CT
GLOUCESTER RD
FAIRCROUCH LA
Sussex Border Path
GEORGE ST
COCKMOUNT LA
MOUNT PLEASANT
Primmer's Green
JONAS DR
JONAS LA
BANKSIDE
1 PENDRILL PL
2 WELLINGTON PL
3 HIGHBURY PL
4 HALLS COTTS
Homefield Farm
Durgates
Sparrow's Green
Ravensdale Farm
TAPSELL'S LA
PO
SPARROWS GREEN RD
Wadhurst CE Prim Sch
MAYFIELD PK
HOLMESDALE CL
THE MARLPIT
LITTLE PK
BASSETT'S FORGE
BIRD LA
Sacred Heart Sch
WARD CL
GOODENSFIELD
GREEN SQ
BALDOCK RD
FULLER CL
BOCKING CL
CASTLE WLK
HIGH ST
Wadhurst Castle
CENTRAL PARADE
TN5
WINDMILL LA
CRITTLE'S CT
TOWNLANDS RD
Windmill Farm
FAZAN CT
WATTS CL
COURTHOPE AVE
SNAPE VIEW
MAYFIELD LA
FAIRGLEN RD
FAIRCROUCH LA
FAIRGLEN COTTS
THE SMITHY
WADHURST RD
Best Beech Inn (PH)
Windmill Wood
Best Beech Hill
WASHWELL LA
Sewage Works
Bensfield Farm
Pennybridge
Foxes Bank
Birchett's Wood
Snape Wood
Newhouse Farm
RISEDEN RD
Riseden
Snape House
Hall
Snape Farm
SNAPE LA
BRINKERS LA
East Sussex STREET ATLAS

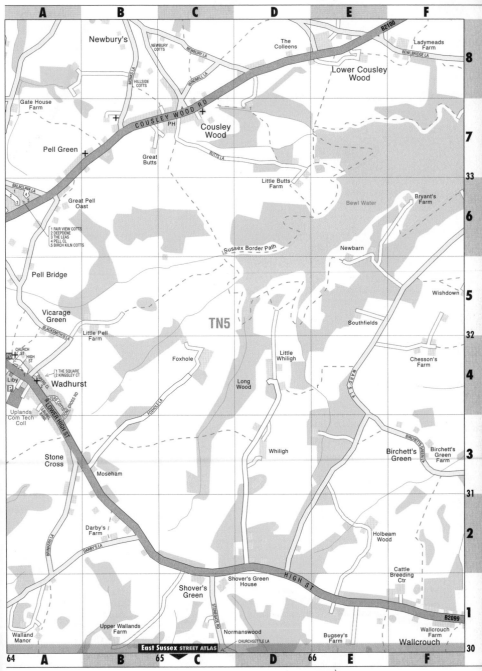

Newbury's

NEWBURY COTTS

NEWBURY LA

WINDMILL LA

MUNGS LA

HILLSIDE COTTS

The Colleens

Lower Cousley Wood

Ladymeads Farm

BEWLBRIDGE LA

Gate House Farm

COUSLEY WOOD RD

PH

Cousley Wood

Pell Green

Great Butts

BUTTS LA

BALACLAVA LA

1 FAIR VIEW COTTS
2 DEEPDENE
3 THE LEAS
4 PELL CL
5 BIRCH KILN COTTS

Great Pell Oast

Little Butts Farm

Bewl Water

Bryant's Farm

Newbarn

Sussex Border Path

Pell Bridge

Wishdown

Vicarage Green

BLACKSMITH'S LA

Little Pell Farm

TN5

Southfields

Foxhole

Little Whiligh

Chesson's Farm

CHURCH ST

HIGH ST

1 THE SQUARE
2 KINGSLEY CT

Liby

P

Wadhurst

Long Wood

WARD'S LA

FOXHOLE LA

LOWER HIGH ST

Uplands Com Tech Coll

Whiligh

BIRCHETTS GREEN LA

Birchett's Green

Birchett's Green Farm

Stone Cross

Moseham

Whiligh

BRINKERS LA

Darby's Farm

DARBY'S LA

Holbeam Wood

HIGH ST

Cattle Breeding Ctr

Shover's Green House

Shover's Green

STONEGATE RD

Walland Manor

Upper Wallands Farm

Normanswood

CHURCHSETTLE LA

Bugsey's Farm

Wallcrouch Farm

B2099

Wallcrouch

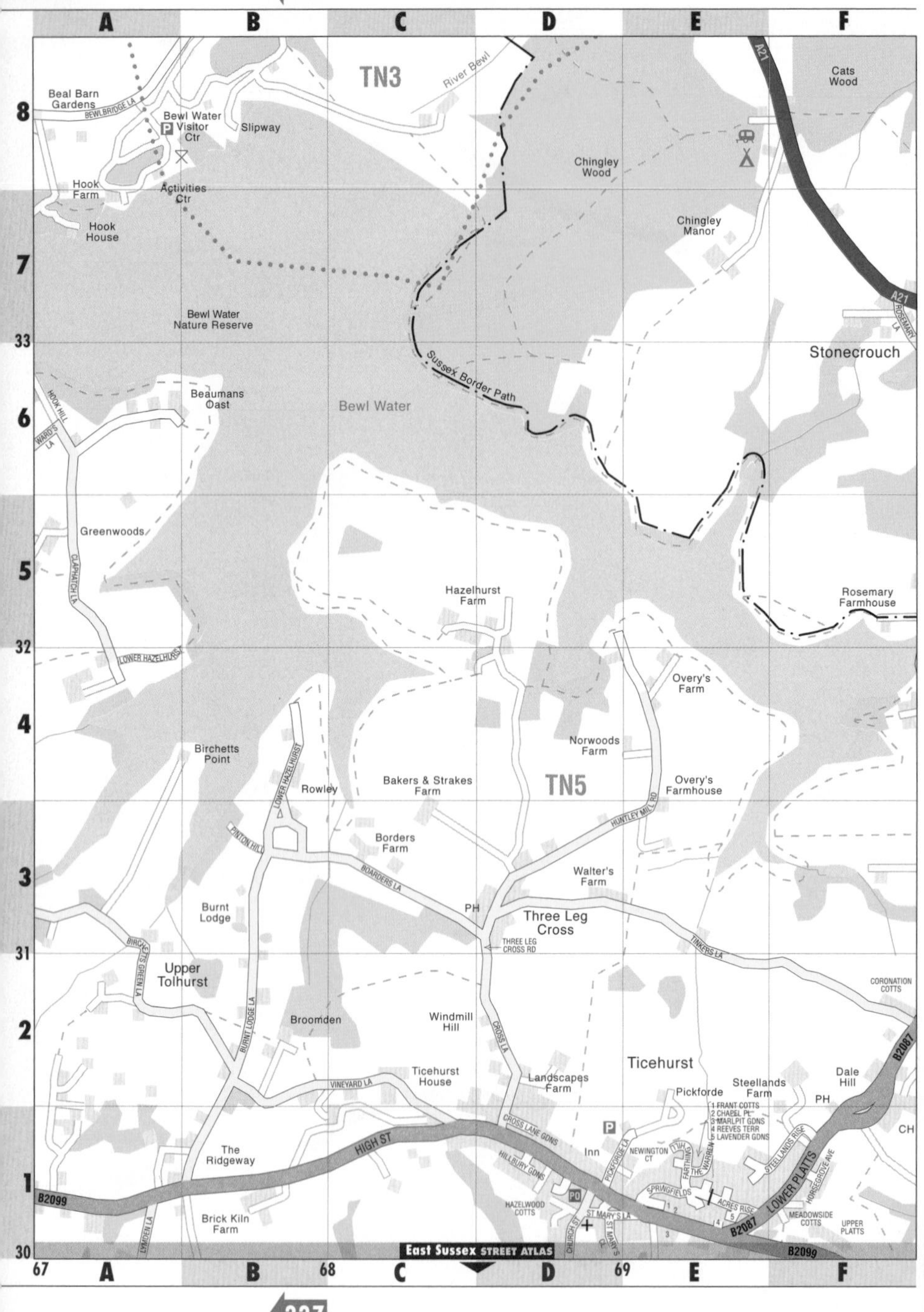

337 317

TN3

River Bewl

Beal Barn Gardens
BEWLBRIDGE LA
Bewl Water Visitor Ctr
Slipway

Hook Farm

Activities Ctr

Hook House

8

Cats Wood

Chingley Wood

Chingley Manor

7

Bewl Water Nature Reserve

33

Stonecrouch

Sussex Border Path

NOOK HILL LA

Beaumans Oast

Bewl Water

6

Greenwoods

CAPHURST LA

5

Hazelhurst Farm

Rosemary Farmhouse

32

LOWER HAZELHURST

Overy's Farm

4

Birchetts Point

LOWER HAZELHURST

Rowley

Bakers & Strakes Farm

TN5

Norwoods Farm

Overy's Farmhouse

Borders Farm

FINTON HILL

Walter's Farm

HUNTLEY MILL LA

3

BORDERS LA

PH

Three Leg Cross

31

BIRCHETTS LA

Burnt Lodge

THREE LEG CROSS RD

FINGLES LA

CORONATION COTTS

Upper Tolhurst

Broomden

BURNT LODGE LA

Windmill Hill

DOSSE LA

Ticehurst

Steellands Farm

Dale Hill

B2087

2

Ticehurst House

Landscapes Farm

Pickforde

PH

CH

VINEYARD LA

The Ridgeway

HIGH ST

CROSS LANE GDNS

HILLBURY GDNS

Inn

NEWINGTON CT

LOWER PLATTS

1 FRANT COTTS
2 CHAPEL PL
3 MARLPIT GDNS
4 REEVES TERR
5 LAVENDER GDNS

1

THEBHILL LA

Brick Kiln Farm

HAZELWOOD COTTS

ST MARY'S LA

SPRINGFIELDS

ACRES RISE

MEADOWSIDE COTTS

UPPER PLATTS

B2099

B2087

B2099

30

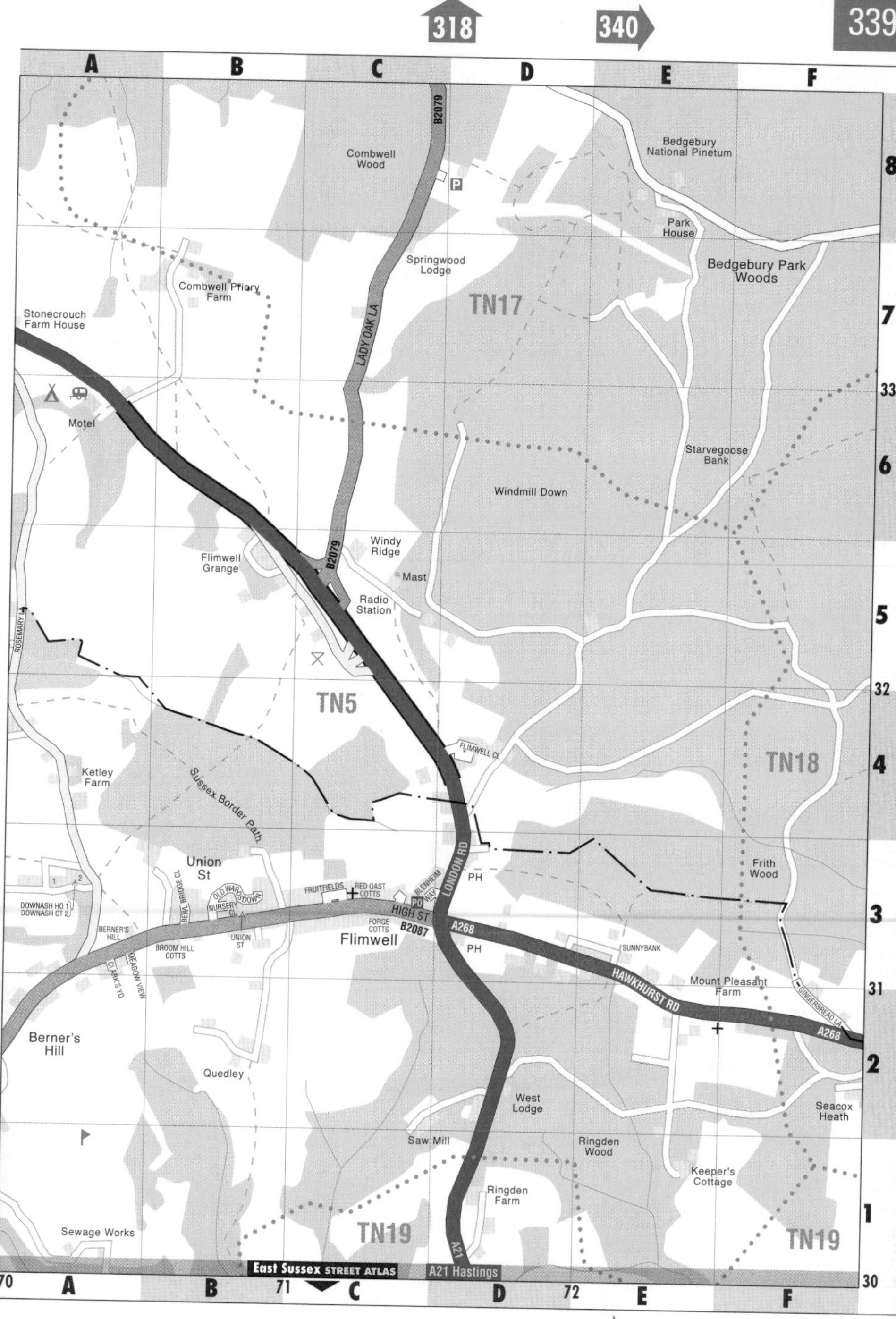

8

Bedgebury
National Pinetum

Combwell
Wood

P

B2079

Park
House

Bedgebury Park
Woods

Springwood
Lodge

Combwell Priory
Farm

Stonecrouch
Farm House

TN17

33

Motel

Starvegoose
Bank

6

Windmill Down

Windy
Ridge

Flimwell
Grange

B2079

Mast

Radio
Station

5

ROSEMARY

32

TN5

Sussex Border Path

TN18

Ketley
Farm

Flimwell Cl

4

Frith
Wood

Union
St

LONDON RD

PH

DOWNASH HO 1
DOWNASH CT 2

OLD WAY

NURSERY CL

FRUITFIELDS

RED GAST
COTTS

BLENHEIM

PO
HIGH ST

PH

3

BERNER'S
HILL

BROOM HILL
COTTS

UNION
ST

FORGE
COTTS

B2087

A268

SUNNYBANK

HAWKHURST RD

Mount Pleasant
Farm

A268

LIMBERSHEAD LA

31

MEADOW VIEW

Flimwell

Berner's
Hill

Quedley

West
Lodge

PH

2

Seacox
Heath

Saw Mill

Ringden
Wood

Keeper's
Cottage

A21

Sewage Works

Ringden
Farm

1

TN19

TN19

30

339
319

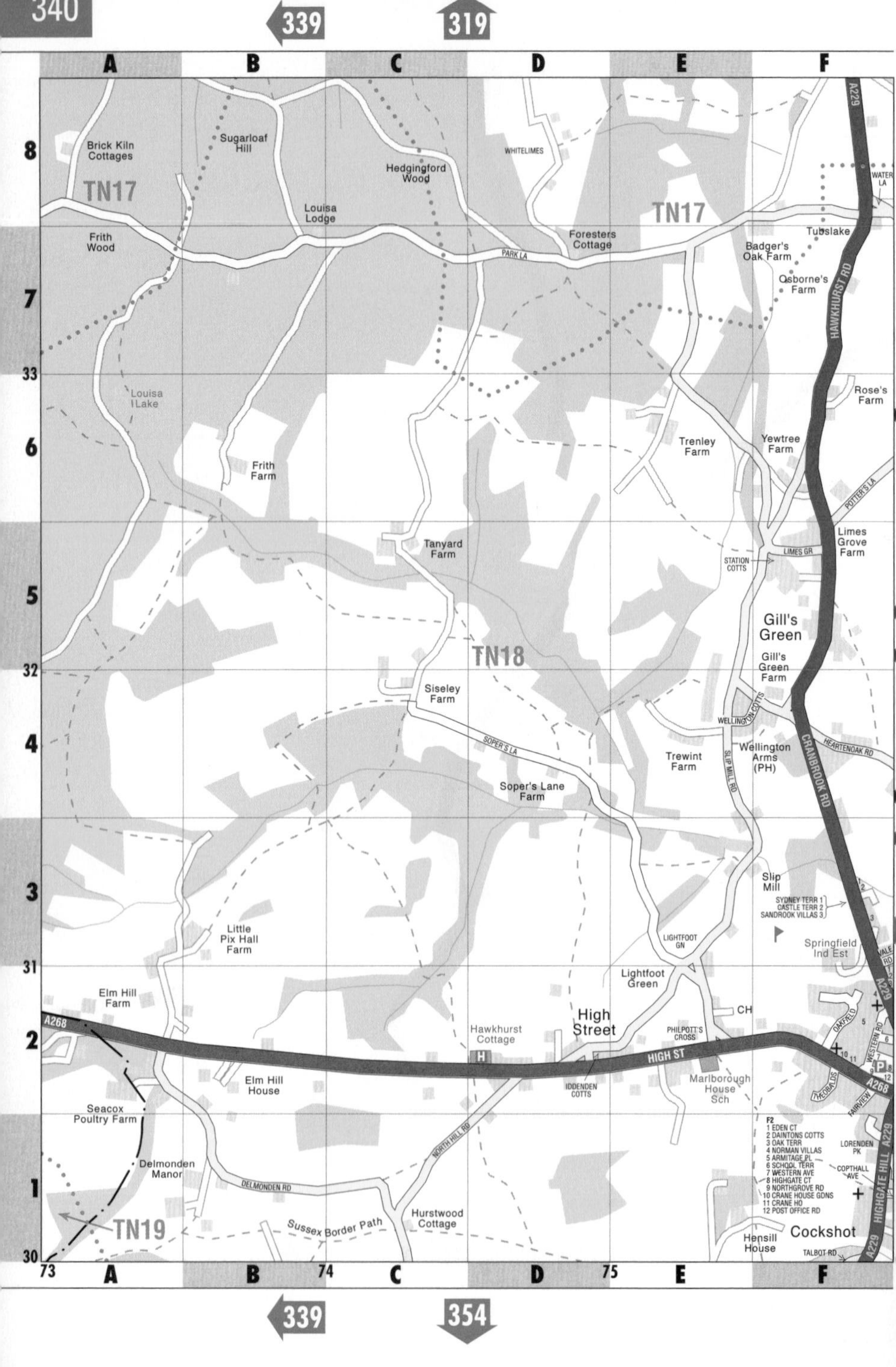
A
B
C
D
E
F
8
7
33
6
5
32
4
3
31
2
1
30
73
74
75
Brick Kiln Cottages
Sugarloaf Hill
Hedgingford Wood
WHITELIMES
TN17
Louisa Lodge
Frith Wood
PARK LA
Foresters Cottage
TN17
Tubslake
Badger's Oak Farm
Osborne's Farm
WATER LA
A229
HAWKHURST RD
Rose's Farm
Louisa Lake
Trenley Farm
Yewtree Farm
Frith Farm
POTTER'S LA
Tanyard Farm
Limes Grove Farm
STATION COTTS
LIMES GR
Gill's Green
TN18
Gill's Green Farm
Siseley Farm
WELLINGTON COTTS
SOPER'S LA
Trewint Farm
Wellington Arms (PH)
HEARTENOAK RD
CRANBROOK RD
SLIP MILL RD
Soper's Lane Farm
Slip Mill
SYDNEY TERR 1
CASTLE TERR 2
SANDROOK VILLAS 3
Little Pix Hall Farm
LIGHTFOOT GN
Springfield Ind Est
Lightfoot Green
Elm Hill Farm
High Street
CH
A268
Hawkhurst Cottage
PHILPOTT'S CROSS
HIGH ST
OAKFIELD
WESTERN RD
Elm Hill House
IDDENDEN COTTS
Marlborough House Sch
THEOBALDS
A268
FAIRVIEW
Seacox Poultry Farm
NORTH HILL RD
F2
1 EDEN CT
2 DAINTONS COTTS
3 OAK TERR
4 NORMAN VILLAS
5 ARMITAGE PL
6 SCHOOL TERR
7 WESTERN AVE
8 HIGHGATE CT
9 NORTHGROVE RD
10 CRANE HOUSE GDNS
11 CRANE HO
12 POST OFFICE RD
LORENDEN PK
Delmonden Manor
COPTHALL AVE
HIGHGATE HILL
DELMONDEN RD
Hurstwood Cottage
TN19
Sussex Border Path
Cockshot
Hensill House
TALBOT RD
A229

339
354

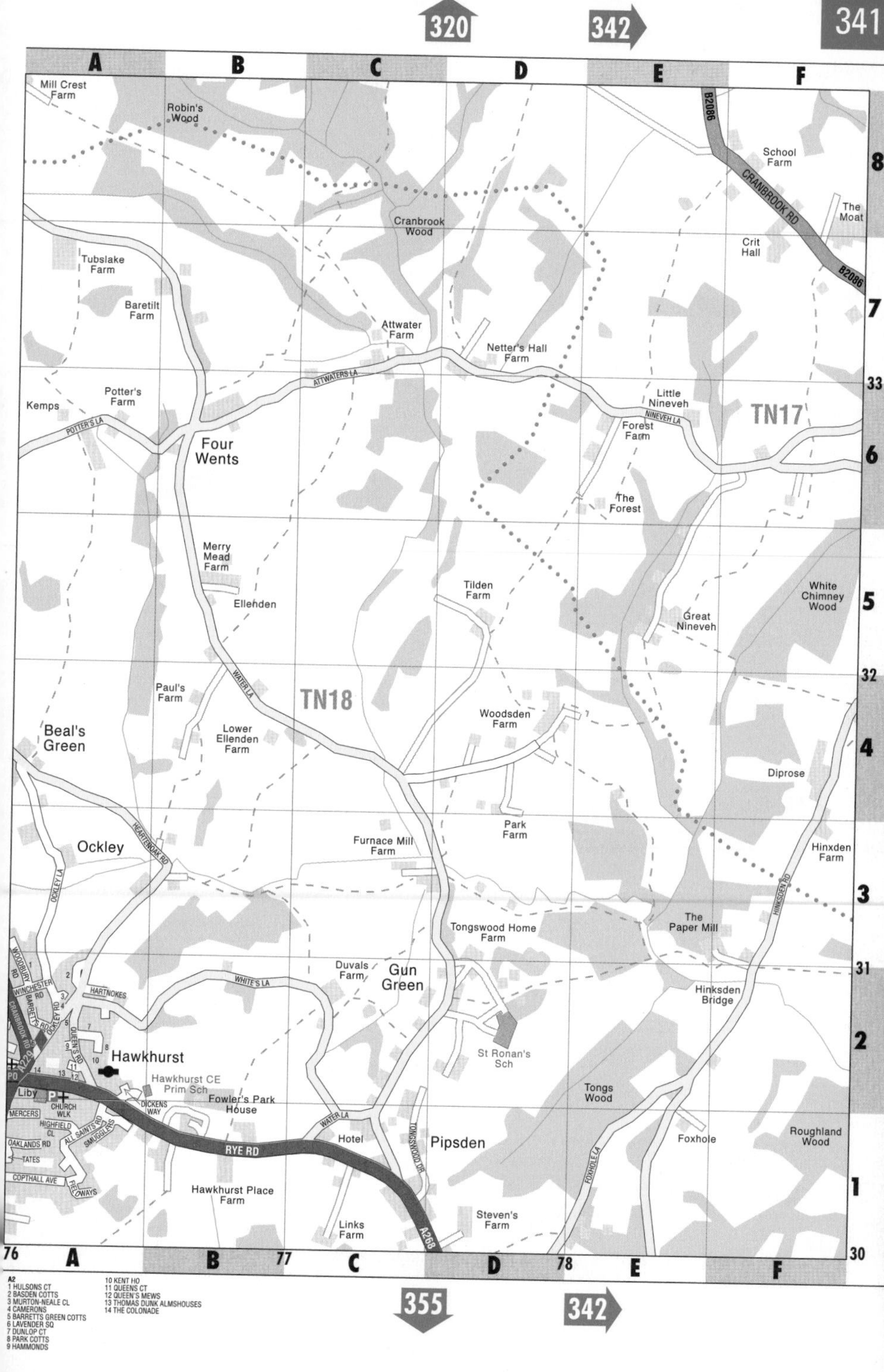

Mill Crest Farm
Robin's Wood
Cranbrook Wood
School Farm
The Moat
Crit Hall
Tubslake Farm
Baretilt Farm
Attwater Farm
Netter's Hall Farm
ATTWATERS LA
Kemps
Potter's Farm
POTTER'S LA
Little Nineveh
NINEVEH LA
Forest Farm
TN17
Four Wents
The Forest
Merry Mead Farm
Tilden Farm
Great Nineveh
White Chimney Wood
Ellenden
WATER LA
Paul's Farm
TN18
Woodsden Farm
Diprose
Beal's Green
Lower Ellenden Farm
Park Farm
Ockley
Furnace Mill Farm
Hinxden Farm
HINXDEN RD
Tongswood Home Farm
The Paper Mill
Duvals Farm
Gun Green
Hinksden Bridge
WHITE'S LA
HARTNOKES
St Ronan's Sch
Hawkhurst
Hawkhurst CE Prim Sch
Fowler's Park House
Tongs Wood
Liby
CHURCH WLK
DICKENS WAY
WATER LA
Pipsden
Foxhole
Roughland Wood
MERCERS
HIGHFIELD RD
OAKLANDS RD
TATES
COPTHALL AVE
Hotel
RYE RD
A268
TONGSWOOD DR
FOXHOLE LA
Hawkhurst Place Farm
Links Farm
Steven's Farm

B2086
CRANBROOK RD
B2086

KEATING RD
OCKLEY LA
WINCHESTER
RUCKS RD

76 A B 77 C D 78 E F 30

A2
1 HULSONS CT
2 BASDEN COTTS
3 MURTON-NEALE CL
4 CAMERONS
5 BARRETTS GREEN COTTS
6 LAVENDER SQ
7 DUNLOP CT
8 PARK COTTS
9 HAMMONDS
10 KENT HO
11 QUEENS CT
12 QUEEN'S MEWS
13 THOMAS DUNK ALMSHOUSES
14 THE COLONADE

8
33
7
6
5
32
4
3
31
2
1

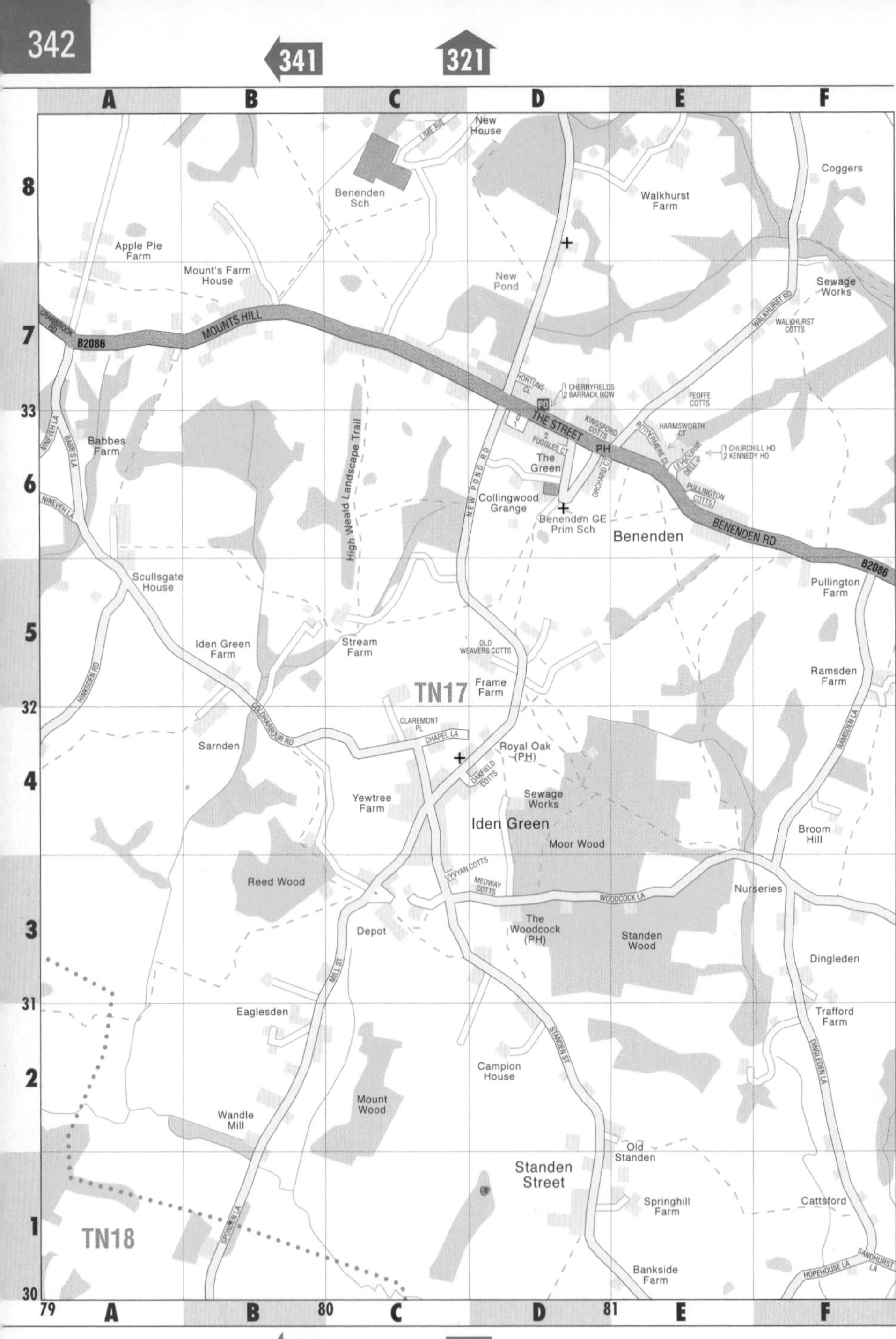

A **B** **C** **D** **E** **F**

8

New House

Benenden Sch

Walkhurst Farm

Coggers

Apple Pie Farm

Mount's Farm House

New Pond

Sewage Works

7

B2086

MOUNTS HILL

WALKHURST RD

WALKHURST COTTS

33

HORTONS CL

PO

1 CHERRYFIELDS
2 BARRACK ROW

PEOFFE COTTS

Babbes Farm

THE STREET

KINGSFORD COTTS

HARMSWORTH CT

1 CHURCHILL HO
2 KENNEDY HO

FUGGLES CT

PH

6

The Green

ORCHARD CL

PULLINGTON COTTS

Collingwood Grange

Benenden CE Prim Sch

Benenden

BENENDEN RD

B2086

Scullsgate House

Pullington Farm

5

Iden Green Farm

Stream Farm

OLD WEAVERS COTTS

Ramsden Farm

32

TN17

Frame Farm

Claremont Pl

CHAPEL LA

Sarnden

ORFIELD COTTS

Royal Oak (PH)

4

Yewtree Farm

Sewage Works

Broom Hill

Iden Green

Moor Wood

Reed Wood

LYCHYN COTTS

MEDWAY COTTS

Nurseries

3

Depot

The Woodcock (PH)

WOODCOCK LA

Standen Wood

Dingleden

31

Eaglesden

Trafford Farm

2

Campion House

Wandle Mill

Mount Wood

Old Standen

Cattsford

1

TN18

Standen Street

Springhill Farm

Bankside Farm

HOPEHOUSE LA

SANDHURST LA

30

79 **A** **B** 80 **C** **D** 81 **E** **F**

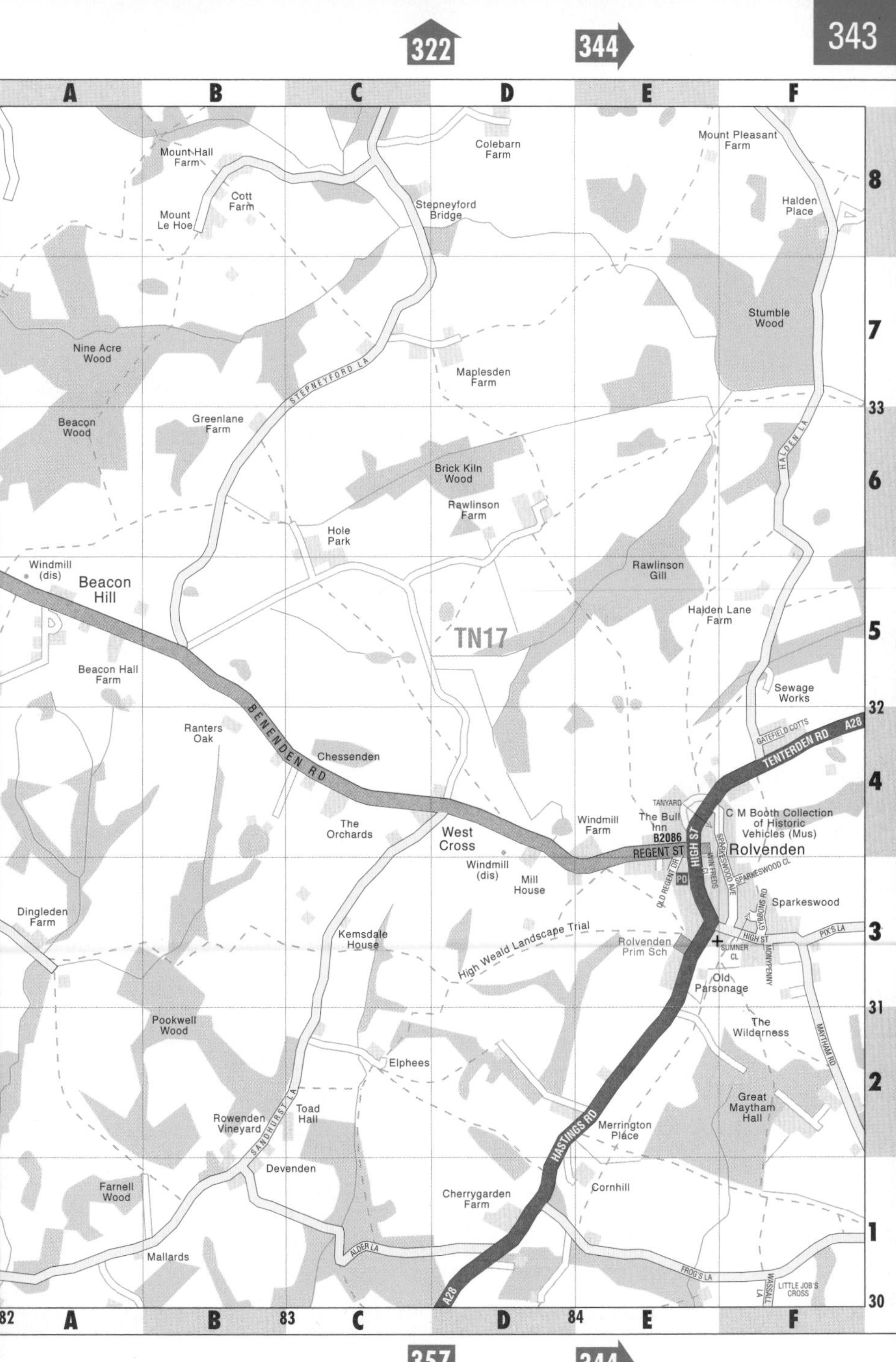

A   B   C   D   E   F

8

Mount-Hall
Farm

Colebarn
Farm

Mount Pleasant
Farm

Cott
Farm

Stepneyford
Bridge

Halden
Place

Mount
Le Hoe

7

Nine Acre
Wood

STEPNEYFORD LA

Maplesden
Farm

Stumble
Wood

HALDEN LA

33

Beacon
Wood

Greenlane
Farm

Brick Kiln
Wood

6

Rawlinson
Farm

Hole
Park

Rawlinson
Gill

Windmill
(dis)

5

Beacon
Hill

Halden Lane
Farm

Beacon Hall
Farm

TN17

Sewage
Works

32

Ranters
Oak

BENENDEN RD

GATEHERD COTTS

TENTERDEN RD   A28

Chessenden

4

The
Orchards

West
Cross

Windmill
Farm

TANYARD

The Bull
Inn

C M Booth Collection
of Historic
Vehicles (Mus)

B2086

REGENT ST

Rolvenden

HIGH ST

Dingleden
Farm

Windmill
(dis)

Mill
House

OLD REGENT DR

SPARKESWOOD AV

SPARKESWOOD CL

Sparkeswood

PIX'S LA

Kemsdale
House

High Weald Landscape Trial

Rolvenden
Prim Sch

SUMNER
CL

3

OLD OLDBURY

MONTPENNY

Old
Parsonage

The
Wilderness

31

Pookwell
Wood

MAYTHAM RD

Elphees

SPARKHURST LA

Rowenden
Vineyard

Toad
Hall

Merrington
Place

Great
Maytham
Hall

2

HASTINGS RD

Devenden

Farnell
Wood

Cornhill

1

Cherrygarden
Farm

ALDER LA

FROG'S LA

Mallards

A28

WITTERSHAM RD

WISSALL LA

Little Job's
Cross

30

82   A   B   83   C   D   84   E   F

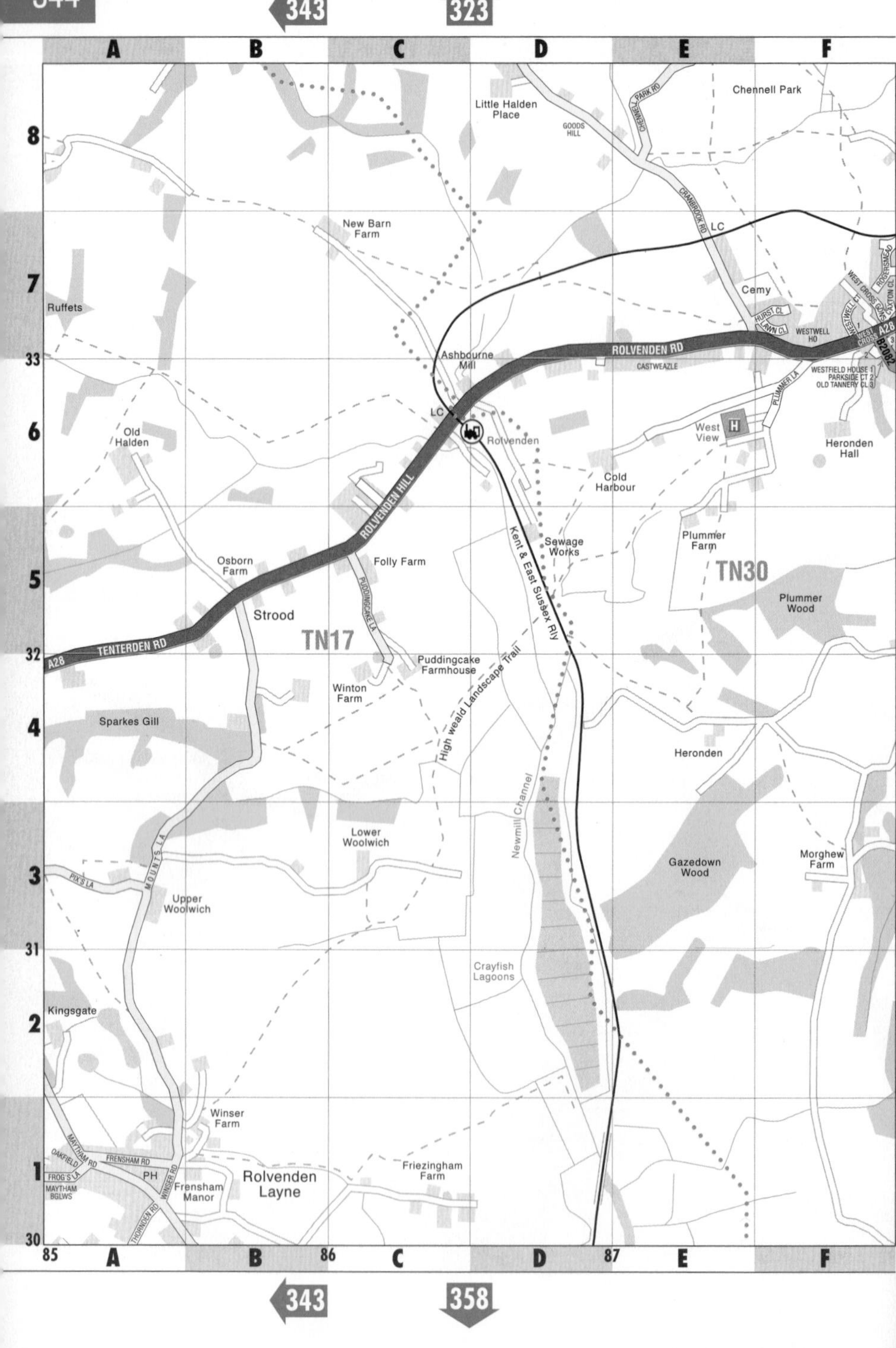

343
323

| | A | B | C | D | E | F |

8

Little Halden
Place

Chennell Park

GOODS
HILL

PARK RD

7

New Barn
Farm

Cemy

OAKBROOK RD

LC

WEST CROSS LANE

Ruffets

33

Ashbourne
Mill

ROLVENDEN RD

WESTWELL
HO

A28
B2082

CASTWEAZLE

WESTFIELD HOUSE 1
PARKSIDE CT 2
OLD TANNERY CL 3

6

Old
Halden

LC

Rolvenden

Cold
Harbour

West
View

H

Heronden
Hall

ROLVENDEN HILL

Sewage
Works

Plummer
Farm

5

Osborn
Farm

Folly Farm

TN30

Plummer
Wood

KENROBERTS LA

Strood

Puddingcake
Farmhouse

TN17

32

A28

TENTERDEN RD

Winton
Farm

Kent & East Sussex Rly

High Weald Landscape Trail

Heronden

4

Sparkes Gill

Lower
Woolwich

Newmill Channel

Gazedown
Wood

Morghew
Farm

MOUNTS LA

3

PIX'S LA

Upper
Woolwich

31

2

Kingsgate

Crayfish
Lagoons

WINSER RD

Winser
Farm

1

MAYTHAM RD

FRENSHAM RD

PH

Rolvenden
Layne

Friezingham
Farm

FROG S LA
OAKFIELD

MAYTHAM
BGLWS

THORNDEN RD

Frensham
Manor

30

| 85 | A | B | 86 | C | D | 87 | E | F |

343
358

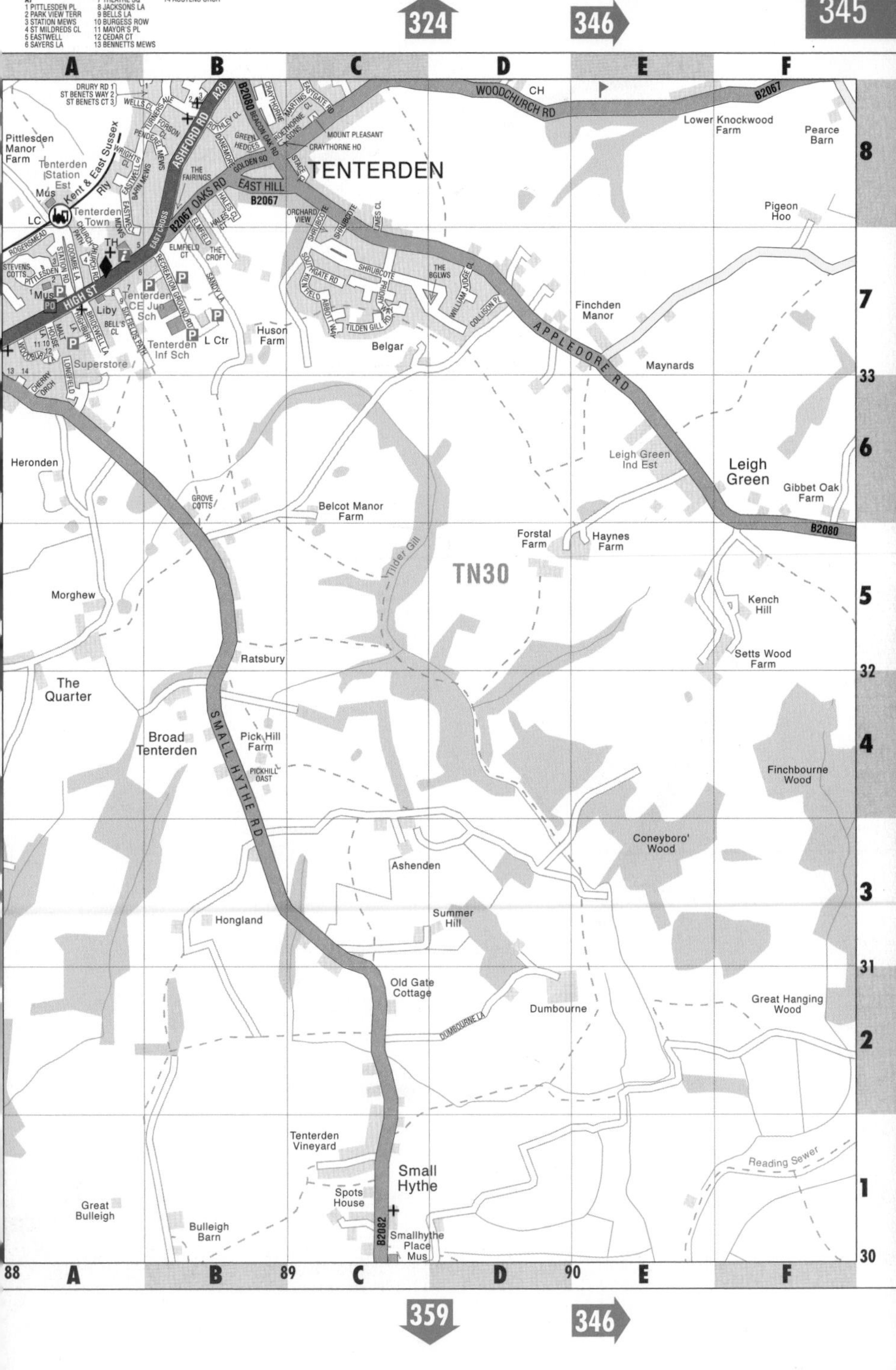

345
325

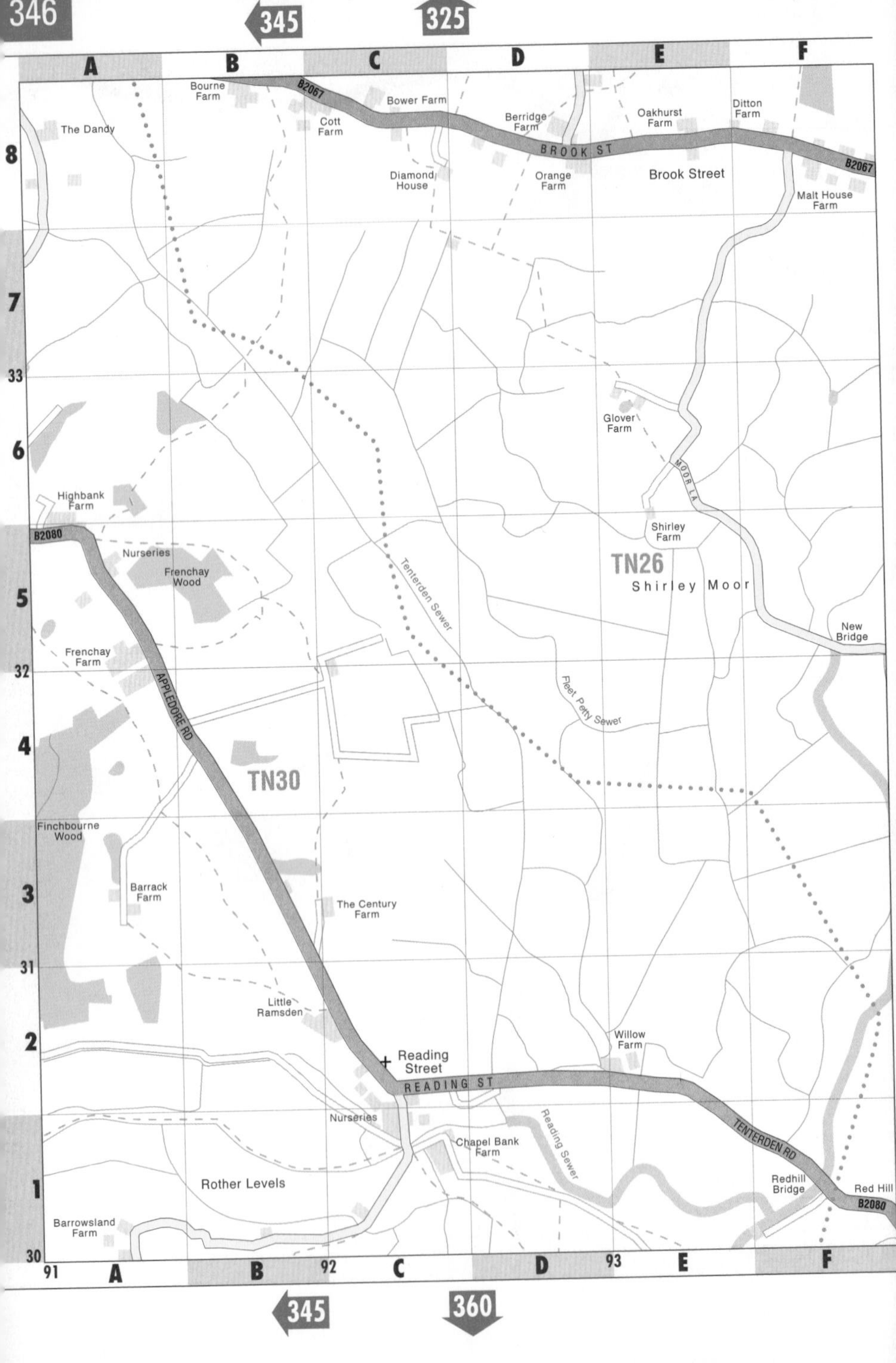
A
B
C
D
E
F
8
7
33
6
5
32
4
3
31
2
1
30
91
92
93
Bourne Farm
B2067
Cott Farm
Bower Farm
Berridge Farm
Oakhurst Farm
Ditton Farm
The Dandy
BROOK ST
Diamond House
Orange Farm
Brook Street
Malt House Farm
Glover Farm
MOOR LA
Highbank Farm
B2080
Nurseries
Frenchay Wood
Shirley Farm
TN26
Shirley Moor
Tenterden Sewer
New Bridge
Frenchay Farm
Fleet Petty Sewer
APPLEDORE RD
TN30
Finchbourne Wood
Barrack Farm
The Century Farm
Little Ramsden
Willow Farm
Reading Street
READING ST
Nurseries
Chapel Bank Farm
Reading Sewer
TENTERDEN RD
Rother Levels
Redhill Bridge
Red Hill
Barrowsland Farm

345
360

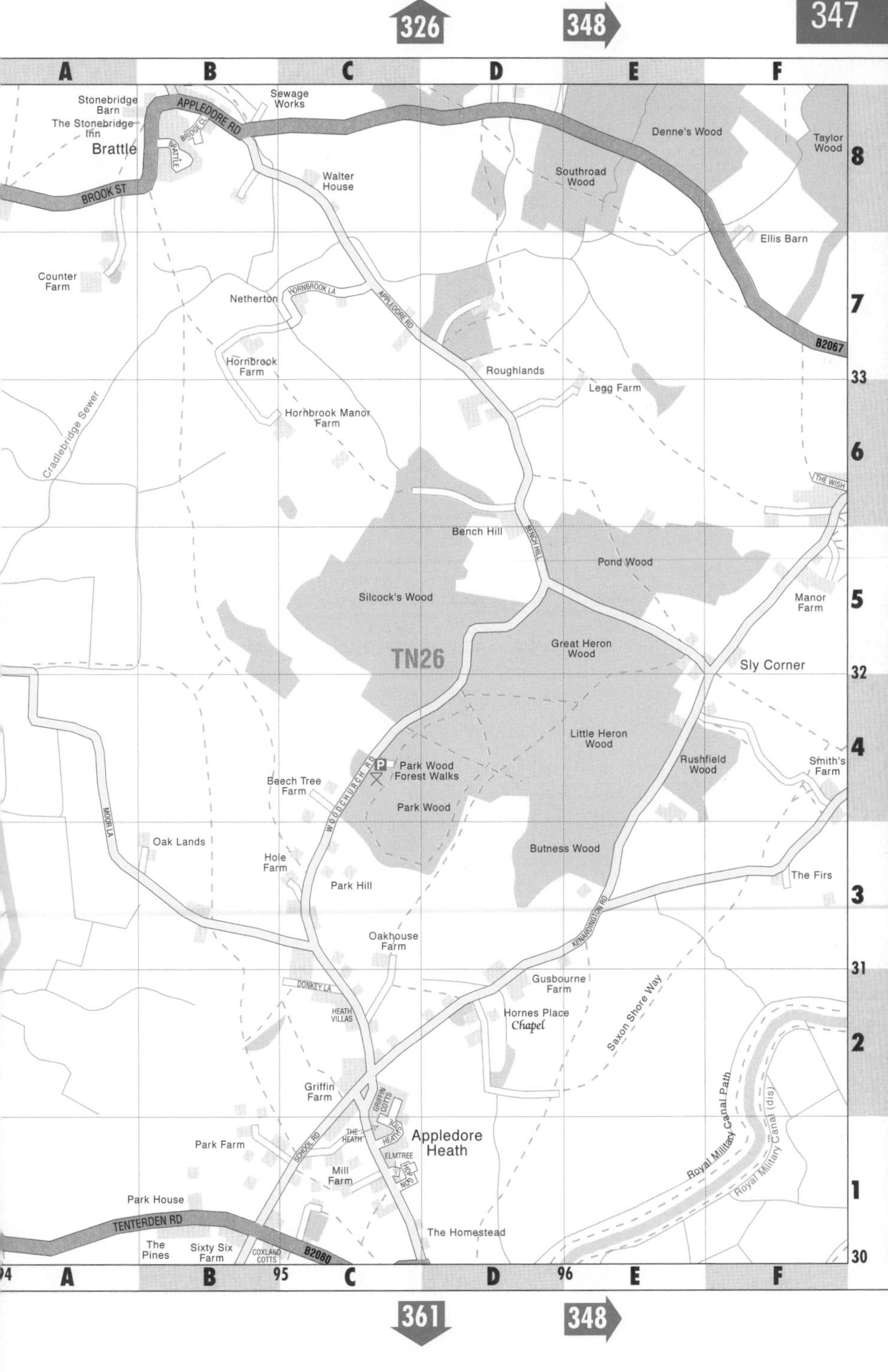
A
B
C
D
E
F
Stonebridge Barn
The Stonebridge Inn
Brattle
Sewage Works
APPLEDORE RD
BRIDGE CL
BRATTLE
BROOK ST
Walter House
Denne's Wood
Southroad Wood
Taylor Wood
Ellis Barn
Counter Farm
Netherton
HORNBROOK LA
APPLEDORE RD
B2067
Hornbrook Farm
Roughlands
Legg Farm
Hornbrook Manor Farm
Cradlebridge Sewer
THE WISH
Bench Hill
BENCH HILL
Pond Wood
Silcock's Wood
Manor Farm
Great Heron Wood
TN26
Sly Corner
Little Heron Wood
Rushfield Wood
Smith's Farm
Park Wood Forest Walks
Beech Tree Farm
WOODCHURCH RD
Park Wood
MOOR LA
Oak Lands
Hole Farm
Butness Wood
The Firs
Park Hill
KENARDINGTON RD
Oakhouse Farm
Gusbourne Farm
DONKEY LA
HEATH VILLAS
Hornes Place
Chapel
Saxon Shore Way
Griffin Farm
GRIFFIN COTTS
THE HEATH
HEATHSIDE
Appledore Heath
SCHOOL RD
Park Farm
ELMTREE
HOP
Mill Farm
Royal Military Canal Path
Royal Military Canal (dis)
Park House
TENTERDEN RD
The Homestead
The Pines
Sixty Six Farm
COXLAND COTTS
B2080
8
7
33
6
5
32
4
3
31
2
1
30
94
95
96

A B C D E F

8

Penfold Wood

High Hockley Farm

Birch Wood

Hockley

Woodlands Farm

MALTHOUSE LA

Hamstreet Prim Sch

A2070

B2061

ASHFORD RD

Sewage Works

7

Leacon Farm

The Leacon

Smallman's Wood

Burr Farm

Elm Farm

PROSPECT PL

VIADUCT TERR

WAREHORNE RD

B2067

33

B2067

POPLARS

The World's Wonder (PH)

Place Farm

High House Farm

Stone Farm

Warehorne

Lofty Lands

Parker Farm

6

Kenardington

HARDEN'S VIEW

The Woolpack (PH)

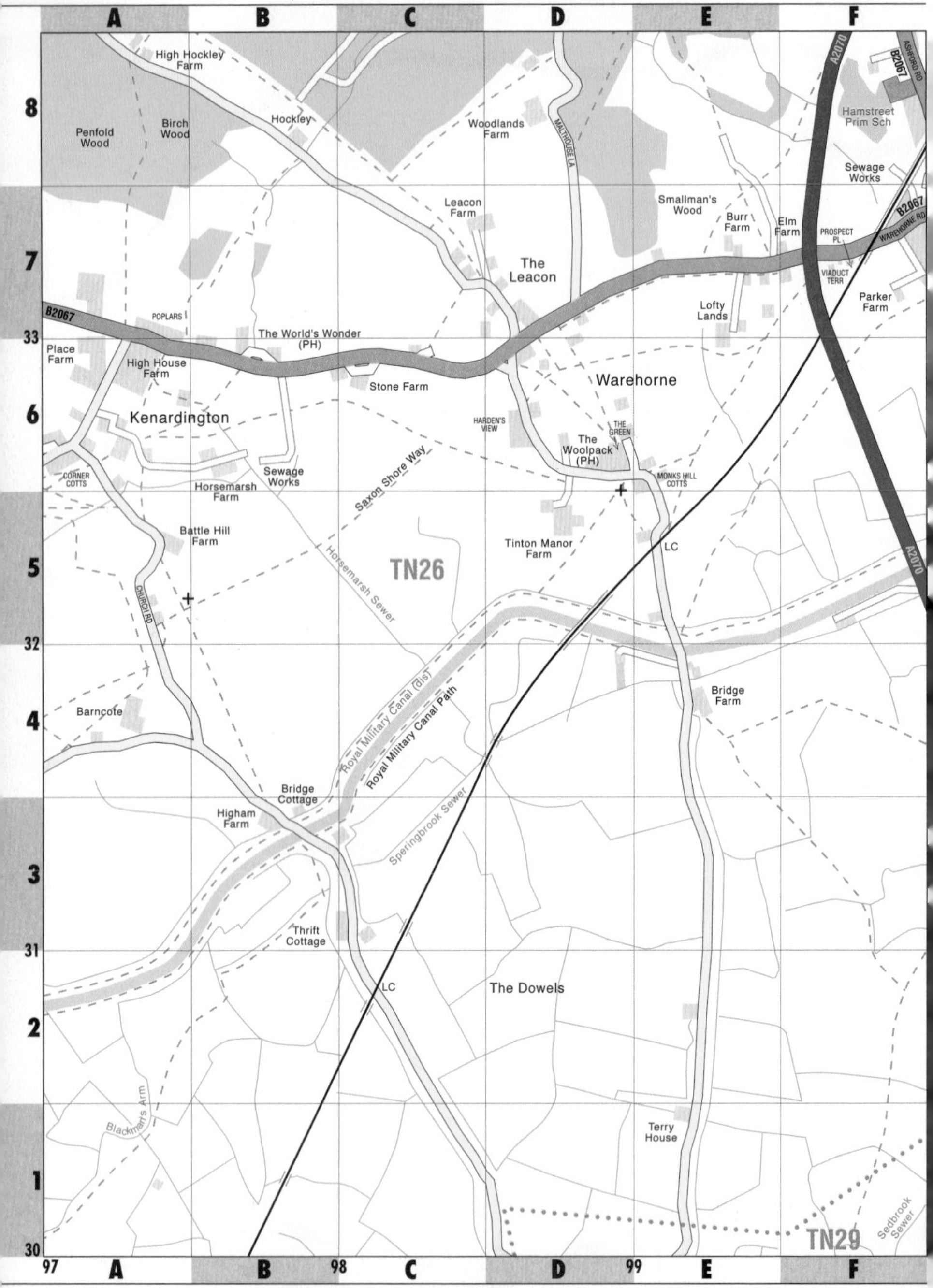

THE GREEN

MONKS HILL COTTS

CORNER COTTS

Horsemarsh Farm

Sewage Works

Saxon Shore Way

5

Battle Hill Farm

Horsemarsh Sewer

TN26

Tinton Manor Farm

LC

CHURCH RD

A2070

32

Royal Military Canal (fis)

Royal Military Canal Path

Bridge Farm

4

Barncote

Springbrook Sewer

3

Bridge Cottage

Higham Farm

31

Thrift Cottage

LC

The Dowels

2

Blackmans Arm

1

Terry House

Sedbrook Sewer

TN29

30

97 **A** 98 **B** **C** 99 **D** **E** **F**

328
350

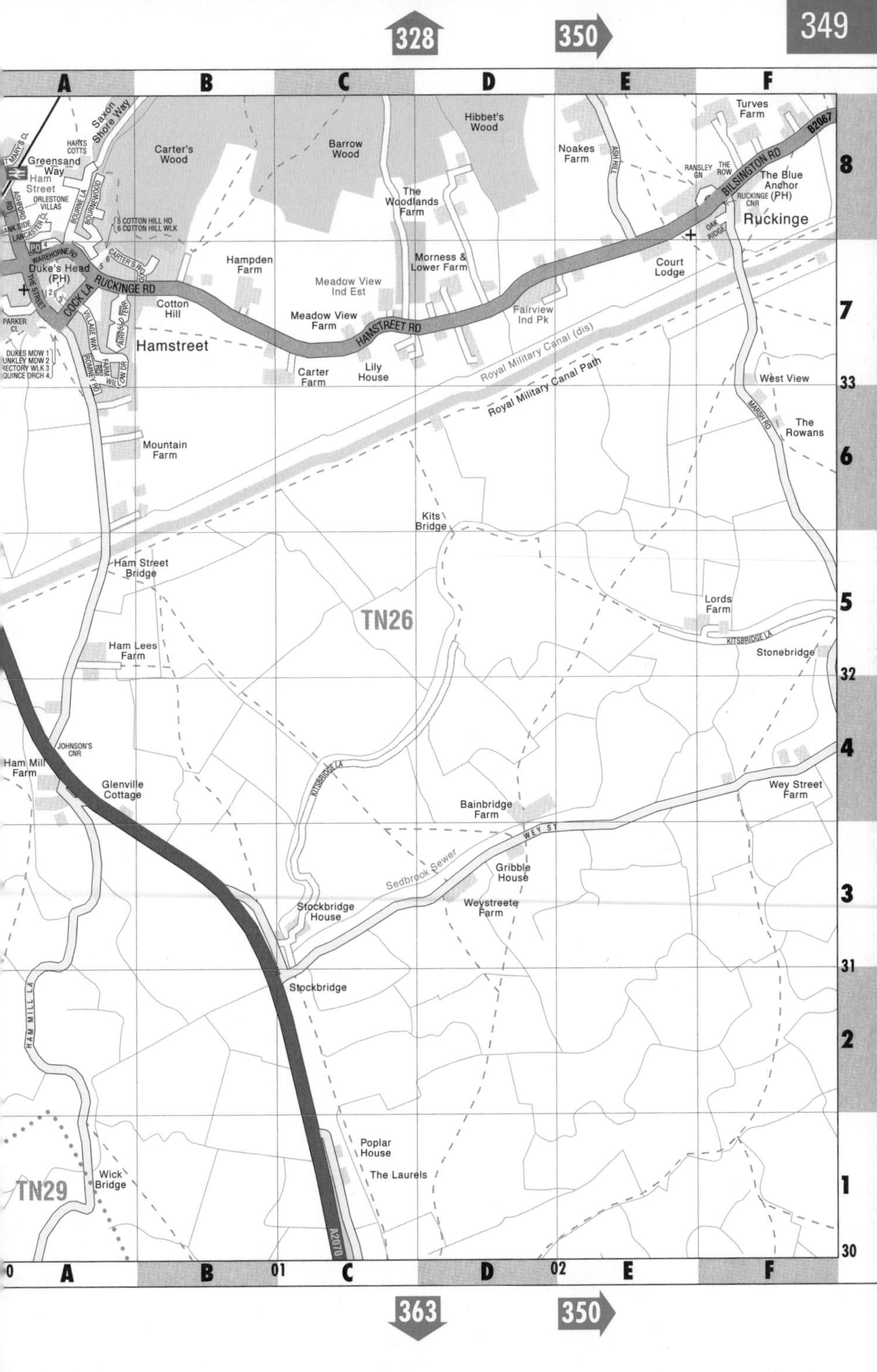
A
B
C
D
E
F
8
7
33
6
5
32
4
3
31
2
1
30
0
01
02
Saxon Shore Way
Carter's Wood
Barrow Wood
Hibbet's Wood
Noakes Farm
Turves Farm
Greensand Way
Ham Street
HARTS COTTS
ORLESTONE VILLAS
BOURNE LA
BOURNEWOOD
5 COTTON HILL HO
6 COTTON HILL WLK
The Woodlands Farm
ASH HILL
RANSLEY GN
THE ROW
BILSINGTON RD
B2067
The Blue Anchor (PH)
RUCKINGE CNR
Ruckinge
OAK RIDGE
WAREHORNE RD
LANCASTER CL
Duke's Head (PH)
THE STREET
CARTER'S WOOD
RUCKINGE RD
COCK LA
Hampden Farm
Morness & Lower Farm
Meadow View Ind Est
Court Lodge
Cotton Hill
Meadow View Farm
HAMSTREET RD
Fairview Ind Pk
PARKER CL
VILLAGE WAY
FAIRFIELD TERR
Hamstreet
DUKES MDW 1
DUNKLEY MDW 2
RECTORY WLK 3
QUINCE ORCH 4
ROMNEY RD
FARM RD
WILLOW DR
Carter Farm
Lily House
Royal Military Canal (dis)
Royal Military Canal Path
West View
MARSH RD
The Rowans
Mountain Farm
Kits Bridge
Ham Street Bridge
TN26
Lords Farm
KITSBRIDGE LA
Stonebridge
Ham Lees Farm
JOHNSON'S CNR
Ham Mill Farm
Glenville Cottage
KITSBRIDGE LA
Bainbridge Farm
Wey Street Farm
WEY ST
Sedbrook Sewer
Gribble House
Stockbridge House
Weystreete Farm
Stockbridge
HAM MILL LA
Poplar House
The Laurels
Wick Bridge
TN29
A2070

363
350

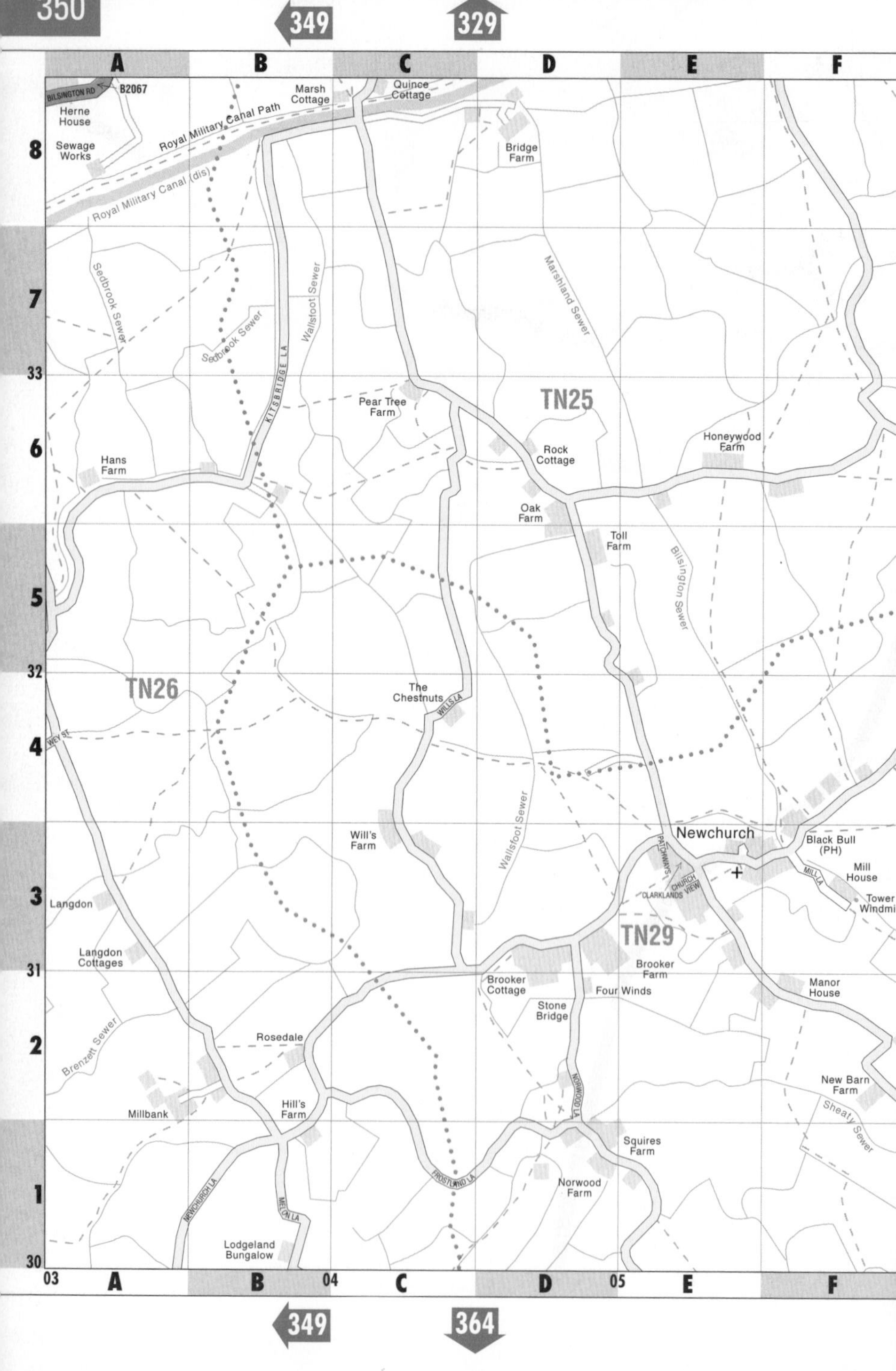

349
329

A B C D E F

BILSINGTON RD
B2067
Herne House
Sewage Works

8

Royal Military Canal Path
Marsh Cottage
Quince Cottage

Royal Military Canal (dis)

Bridge Farm

Sedbrook Sewer

Wallstool Sewer

Sedbrook Sewer

7

33

Pear Tree Farm

TN25

KELSBRIDGE LA

Marshland Sewer

Honeywood Farm

6

Hans Farm

Rock Cottage

Oak Farm

Toll Farm

Bilsington Sewer

5

32

TN26

WEST ST

The Chestnuts

WILLS LA

Wallstool Sewer

Will's Farm

Newchurch

Black Bull (PH)

4

PETT DOWN ST

CHURCH VIEW

CLARKLANDS

Mill House
Tower Windmi

MILL LA

3

Langdon

TN29

Brooker Farm

Langdon Cottages

31

Brenzett Sewer

Rosedale

Brooker Cottage

Stone Bridge

Four Winds

Manor House

2

Millbank

Hill's Farm

NEWCHURCH LA

MELON LA

Squires Farm

Norwood Farm

New Barn Farm

Sheaf Sewer

FRISTLING LA

1

Lodgeland Bungalow

30

03 A B 04 C D 05 E F

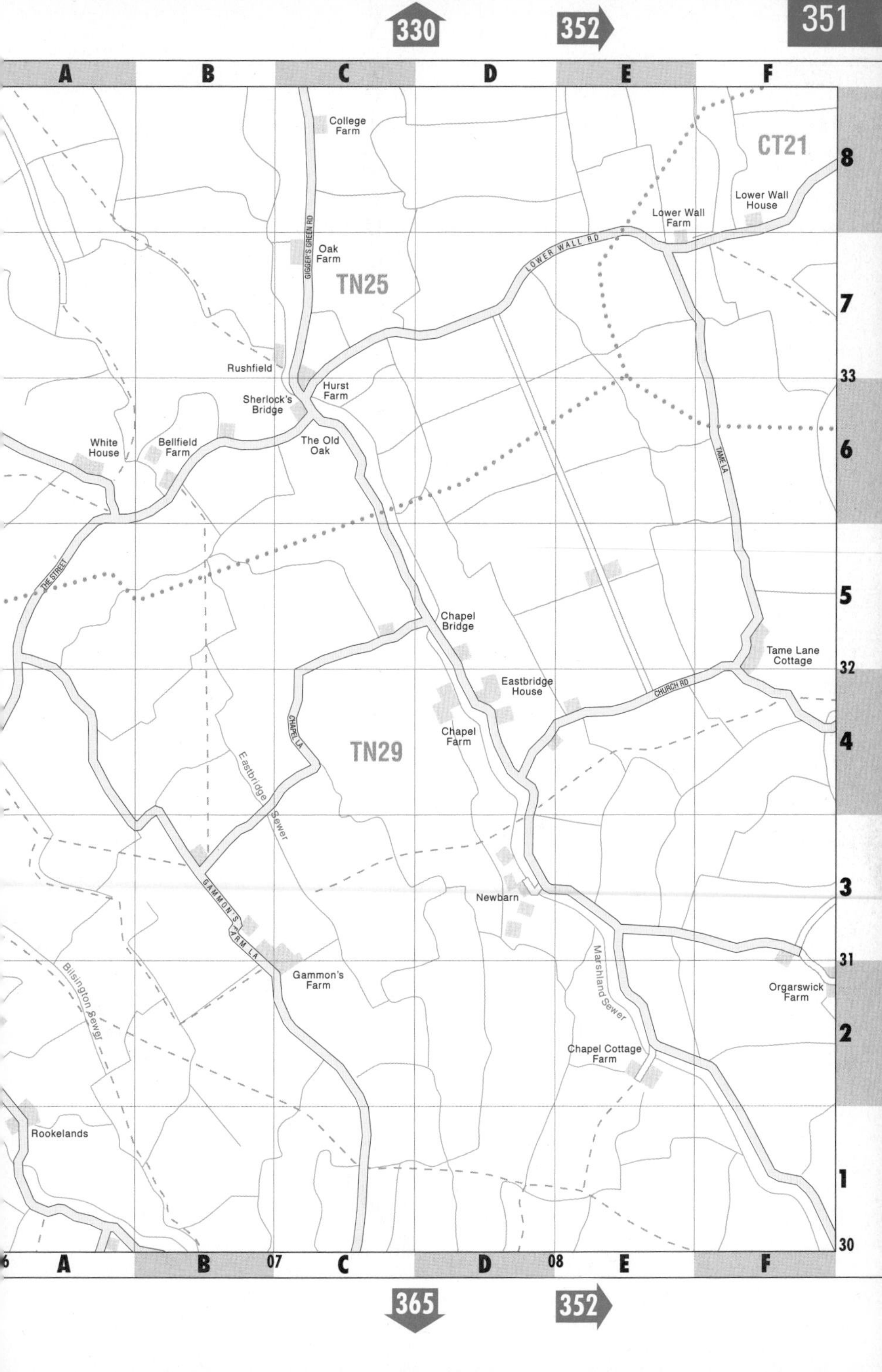

A B C D E F

8

CT21

Lower Wall House

College Farm

Lower Wall Farm

Sudgers Green Rd

Oak Farm

TN25

LOWER WALL RD

7

33

Rushfield

Hurst Farm

Sherlock's Bridge

White House

Bellfield Farm

The Old Oak

6

Tame La

Jhe Street

5

Chapel Bridge

Tame Lane Cottage

32

Eastbridge House

CHURCH RD

Chapel Farm

TN29

4

Chapel La

Eastbridge Sewer

3

Newbarn

Gammon's Farm La

31

Bilsington Sewer

Gammon's Farm

Marshland Sewer

Orgarswick Farm

2

Chapel Cottage Farm

Rookelands

1

30

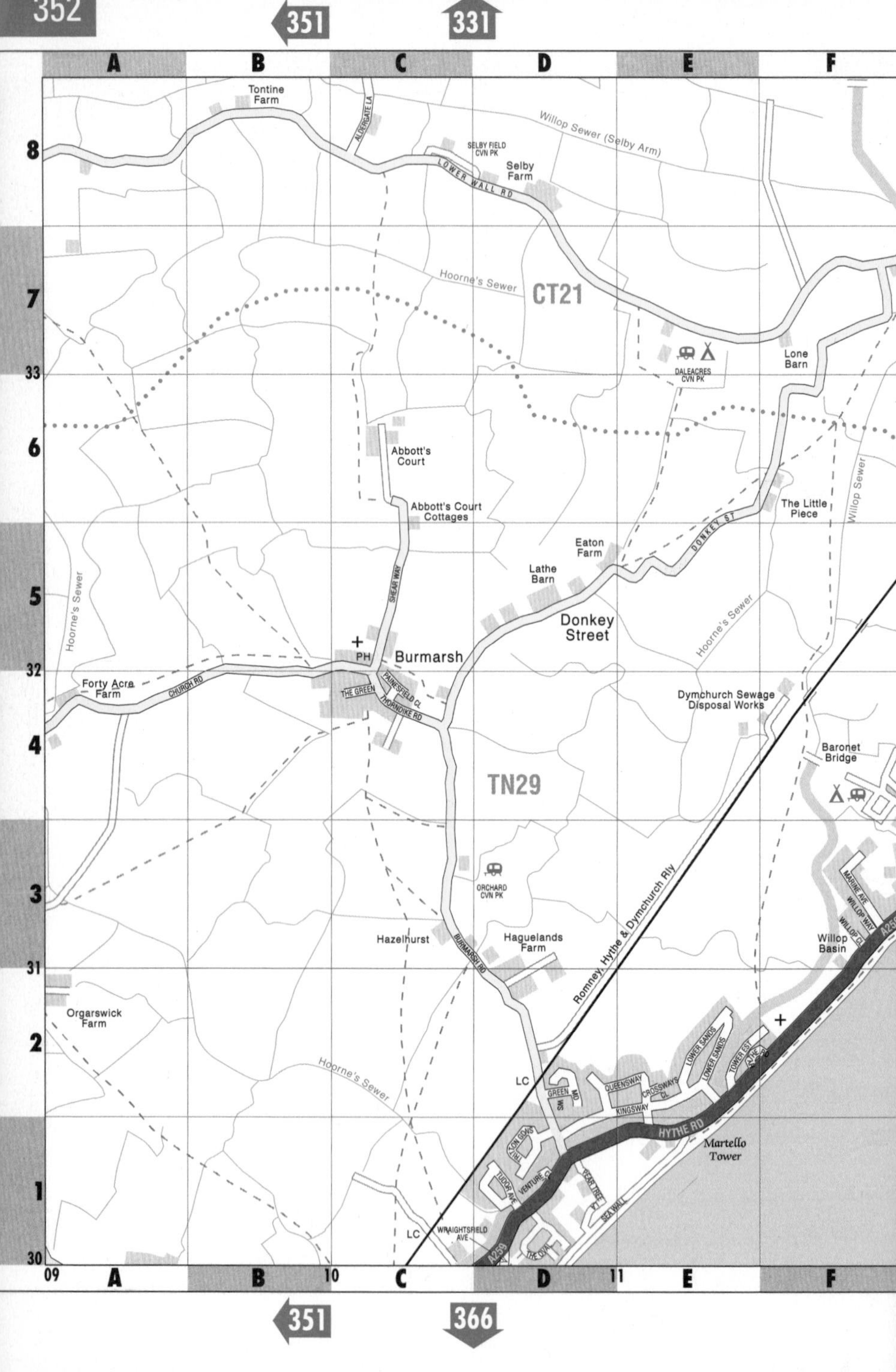
A
B
C
D
E
F
8
7
33
6
5
32
4
3
31
2
1
30
09
10
11
Tontine Farm
ALDERGATE LA
SELBY FIELD CVN PK
Selby Farm
Willop Sewer (Selby Arm)
LOWER WALL RD
Hoorne's Sewer
CT21
DALEACRES CVN PK
Lone Barn
Abbott's Court
Abbott's Court Cottages
The Little Piece
Willop Sewer
DONKEY ST
Eaton Farm
Lathe Barn
SHEAR WAY
Hoorne's Sewer
Donkey Street
Hoorne's Sewer
PH
Burmarsh
Forty Acre Farm
CHURCH RD
THE GREEN
PAINESFIELD CL
THORNDIKE RD
Dymchurch Sewage Disposal Works
Baronet Bridge
TN29
ORCHARD CVN PK
MARINE AVE
WILLOP WAY
WILLOP CL
A259
Willop Basin
Hazelhurst
BURMARSH RD
Haguelands Farm
Romney, Hythe & Dymchurch Rly
Orgarswick Farm
Hoorne's Sewer
LC
GREEN
SW
MD
QUEENSWAY
CROSSWAYS CL
LOWER SANDS
LOWER SANDS
TOWER EST
KINGSWAY
HYTHE RD
Martello Tower
TRITON GDNS
TUDOR AVE
VENTURE CL
PEAR TREE CT
SEA WALL
LC
WRAIGHTSFIELD AVE
THE OVAL
A259

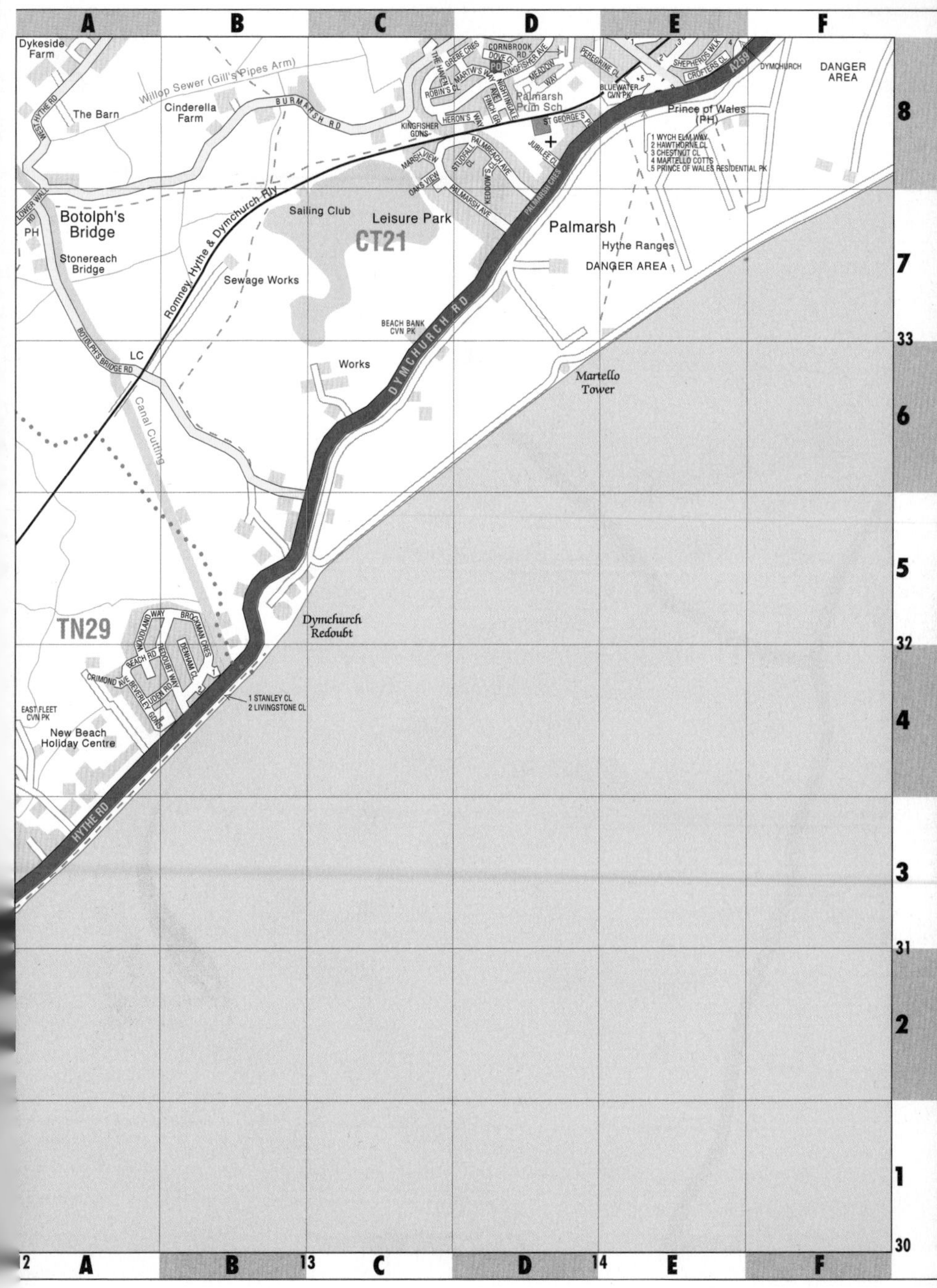

Dykeside
Farm

The Barn

Cinderella
Farm

Willop Sewer (Gill's Pipes Arm)

BURMARSH RD

CORNBROOK
RD
DOVE CL
KINGFISHER AVE
MEADOW
WAY
DYMCHURCH

DANGER
AREA

ROBIN'S CL
HERON'S CL
KINGFISHER
GDNS
MARSH VIEW
OWL VIEW
PALMARSH AVE
STUDELL CL
PALMARSH AVE
MARSDEN AVE
JUBILEE CL
ST GEORGE'S
Palmarsh
Prim Sch
ST GEORGE'S
BLUE WATER
CVN PK

Prince of Wales
(PH)

1 WYCH ELM WAY
2 HAWTHORNE CL
3 CHESTNUT CL
4 MARTELLO COTTS
5 PRINCE OF WALES RESIDENTIAL PK

LOWER WALL RD
OLD HYTHE RD
PH
Botolph's
Bridge

Stonereach
Bridge

ROMNEY, HYTHE & DYMCHURCH RLY

Sailing Club

Leisure Park

CT21

Palmarsh

Hythe Ranges
DANGER AREA

Sewage Works

BOTOLPH'S BRIDGE RD
LC

Canal Cutting

BEACH BANK
CVN PK

Works

DYMCHURCH RD

Martello
Tower

TN29

WOODLAND WAY
BROCKMAN CRES
BEACH RD
COBDEN BDGE
BRYONY CT
BEACH RD
ORMONDE RISE
BEVERLEY CL
Dymchurch
Redoubt

1 STANLEY CL
2 LIVINGSTONE CL

EAST FLEET
CVN PK

New Beach
Holiday Centre

HYTHE RD

340

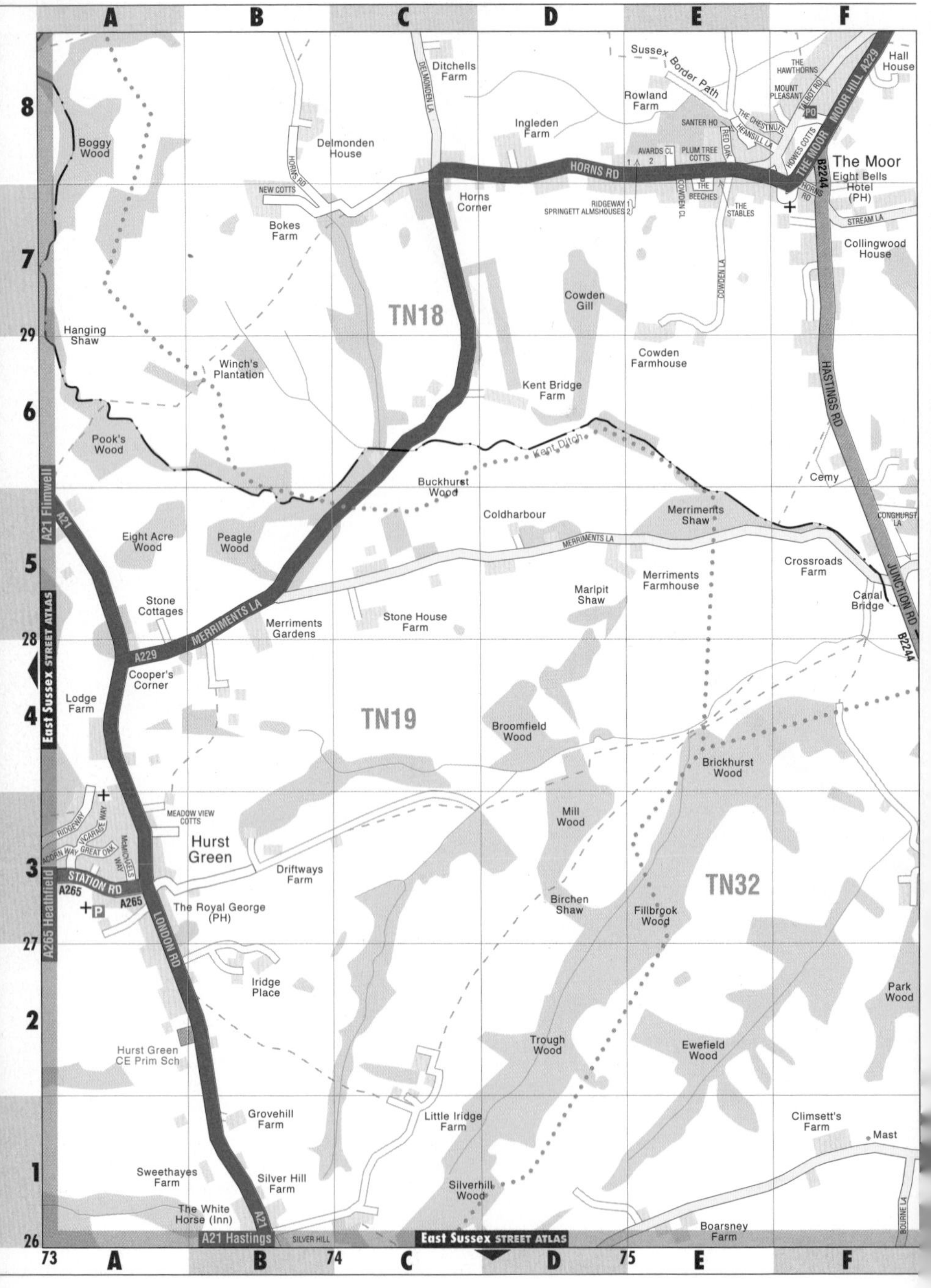

A
B
C
D
E
F
8
7
29
6
5
28
4
3
27
2
1
26
73
74
75
Ditchells Farm
DELMONDEN LA
Sussex Border Path
Rowland Farm
Hall House
THE HAWTHORNS
MOUNT PLEASANT
TALBOT RD
MOOR HILL A229
Ingleden Farm
Delmonden House
Boggy Wood
SANTER HO
THE CHESTNUTS
HEANSILL LA
RED OAK
HOWES COTTS
THE MOOR
The Moor
Eight Bells Hotel (PH)
AVARDS CL
PLUM TREE COTTS
HORNS RD
HORNS RD
NEW COTTS
THE BEECHES
RIDGEWAY
SPRINGETT ALMSHOUSES
COWDEN CL
THE STABLES
B2244
STREAM LA
Horns Corner
Bokes Farm
Collingwood House
COWDEN LA
TN18
Cowden Gill
Hanging Shaw
Winch's Plantation
Cowden Farmhouse
Kent Bridge Farm
HASTINGS RD
Pook's Wood
Kent Ditch
Buckhurst Wood
Cemy
A21 Flimwell
A21
Coldharbour
Merriments Shaw
CONGHURST LA
Eight Acre Wood
Peagle Wood
MERRIMENTS LA
Crossroads Farm
Merriments Farmhouse
Marlpit Shaw
JUNCTION RD
Canal Bridge
Stone Cottages
MERRIMENTS LA
Merriments Gardens
Stone House Farm
A229
B2244
East Sussex STREET ATLAS
Cooper's Corner
Lodge Farm
TN19
Broomfield Wood
Brickhurst Wood
MEADOW VIEW COTTS
Mill Wood
RIDGEWAY
VICARAGE WAY
ACORN WAY
GREAT OAK
MCMICHAELS WAY
Hurst Green
Driftways Farm
TN32
STATION RD
A265
A265
A265 Heathfield
The Royal George (PH)
Birchen Shaw
Fillbrook Wood
LONDON RD
Iridge Place
Park Wood
Hurst Green CE Prim Sch
Trough Wood
Ewefield Wood
Grovehill Farm
Little Iridge Farm
Climsett's Farm
Mast
Sweethayes Farm
Silver Hill Farm
Silverhill Wood
BOURNE LA
The White Horse (Inn)
A21 Hastings
SILVER HILL
East Sussex STREET ATLAS
Boarsney Farm

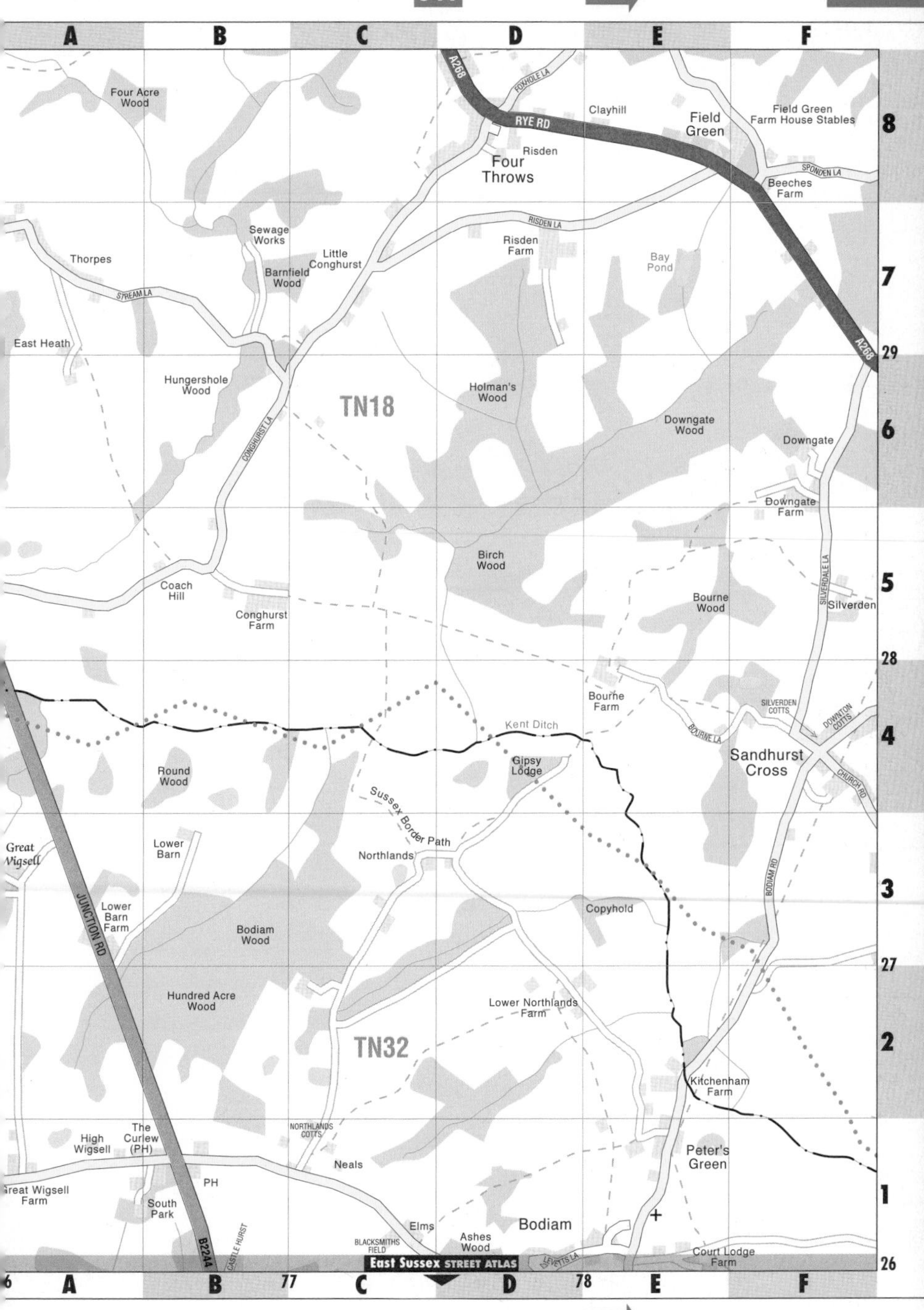

A B C D E F

Four Acre Wood

RYE RD

FOXHOLE LA

Clayhill

Field Green

Field Green Farm House Stables

8

SPONDEN LA

Risden

Four Throws

Beeches Farm

RISDEN LA

Thorpes

Sewage Works

Little Conghurst

Risden Farm

STREAM LA

Barnfield Wood

7

A268

East Heath

29

Hungershole Wood

TN18

Holman's Wood

Downgate Wood

Downgate

6

CONGHURST LA

Downgate Farm

SILVERDEN LA

Coach Hill

Birch Wood

Bourne Wood

Silverden

5

Conghurst Farm

28

Kent Ditch

Bourne Farm

Silverden Cotts

DOWNTON COTTS

4

Round Wood

Gipsy Lodge

BOURNE LA

Sandhurst Cross

CHURCH RD

Great Wigsell

Sussex Border Path

Lower Barn

Northlands

RD BODIAM

3

JUNCTION RD

Lower Barn Farm

Bodiam Wood

Copyhold

27

Hundred Acre Wood

Lower Northlands Farm

TN32

2

High Wigsell

The Curlew (PH)

NORTHLANDS COTTS

Kitchenham Farm

Great Wigsell Farm

PH

Neals

Peter's Green

1

B2244

South Park

CASTLE HURST

Elms

Bodiam

Ashes Wood

SHOPTON LA

Court Lodge Farm

26

BLACKSMITHS FIELD

East Sussex STREET ATLAS

A B 77 C D 78 E F

355
342

	A	B	C	D	E	F

8

Standen Street

TN17

Hope House

SPONDEN LA

Sponden House

Sponden Farmhouse

HOPE REYNOLDS LA

7

Alderden Manor

Reynolds Farm

Hopemill Bridge

29

Orchard Farm

Lords Wood

A268 MEGRIMS HILL

Sewage Works

6

Malthouse Farm

ANGEL TERR BROOKFIELD
ANGEL ROW

Sandhurst

Puxtye

Hoad's Farm

QUEEN ST THE ROPE WLK

PH

Sandhurst Prim Sch

Sandhurst Vineyards

CROUCH LA

STONE PILLA

5

OLD ORCHARD

BACK RD

DALE'S CORNER

Sandhurst Farm

Scurms Farm

Lomas

LOMAS LA

LINKDEN COTTS

RINGLE GN

BURNT HOUSE

Burnt Farm House

28

Brickhouse Farmhouse

BODIAM RD

Boxhurst Farm

PH

Linkhill

Hollowdene

A26

TWYSDEN COTTS

Castlegate Farm

TN18

SANDHURST CL

1
2

1 BETHERINDEN COTTS
2 FORGEFIELD COTTS

4

Glassocks

Boxhurst

ETHAM LA

3

CHURCH RD

Barnfield Shaw

Burnt House Farm

MARSH QUARTER LA

Little Boxhurst

Ethnam Farm Bungalow

Twisden Plantation

Cledge Wood

27

Old Sandhurst Place

Great Ethnam Farm

Ethnam

Old Place Farm

2

Marsh Quarter Farm

River Rother

1

Kent Ditch

Kent & East Sussex Rly

TN32

TN31

Dyneshill Wood

26

79	A		B	80		C		D	81		E		F

355

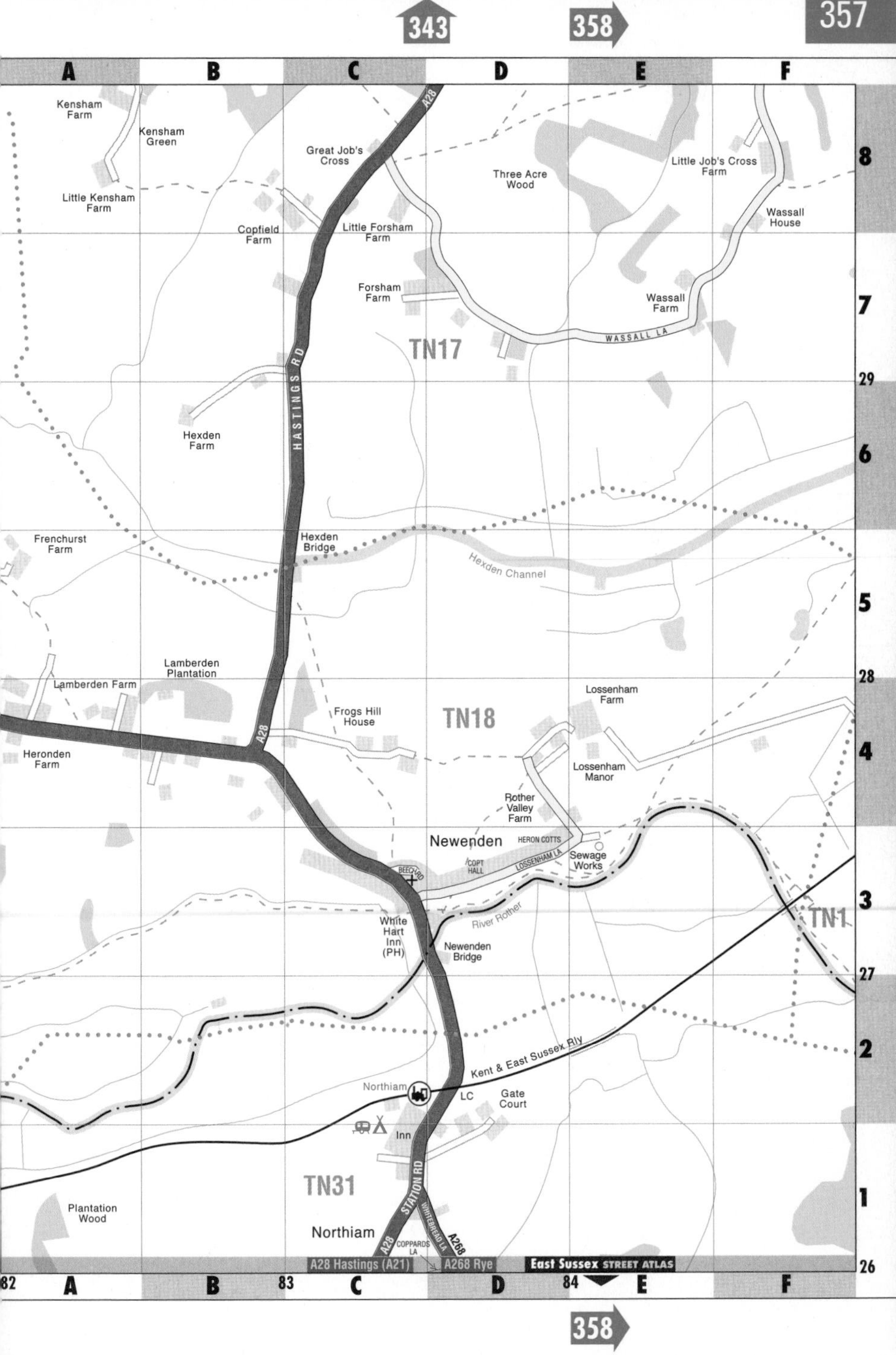
A
B
C
D
E
F
Kensham Farm
Kensham Green
Great Job's Cross
Three Acre Wood
Little Job's Cross Farm
Little Kensham Farm
Wassall House
Copfield Farm
Little Forsham Farm
Forsham Farm
Wassall Farm
WASSALL LA
TN17
HASTINGS RD
A28
Hexden Farm
Frenchurst Farm
Hexden Bridge
Hexden Channel
Lamberden Plantation
Lamberden Farm
Lossenham Farm
Frogs Hill House
TN18
Heronden Farm
Lossenham Manor
Rother Valley Farm
Newenden
HERON COTTS
COPT HALL
LOSSENHAM LA
BEECH RD
Sewage Works
River Rother
White Hart Inn (PH)
Newenden Bridge
TN1
Kent & East Sussex Rly
Northiam
LC
Gate Court
Inn
STATION RD
TN31
Plantation Wood
Northiam
WHITEBREAD LA
A268
COPPARDS LA
A28 Hastings (A21)
A268 Rye
East Sussex STREET ATLAS
8
7
29
6
5
28
4
3
27
2
1
26
82
83
84

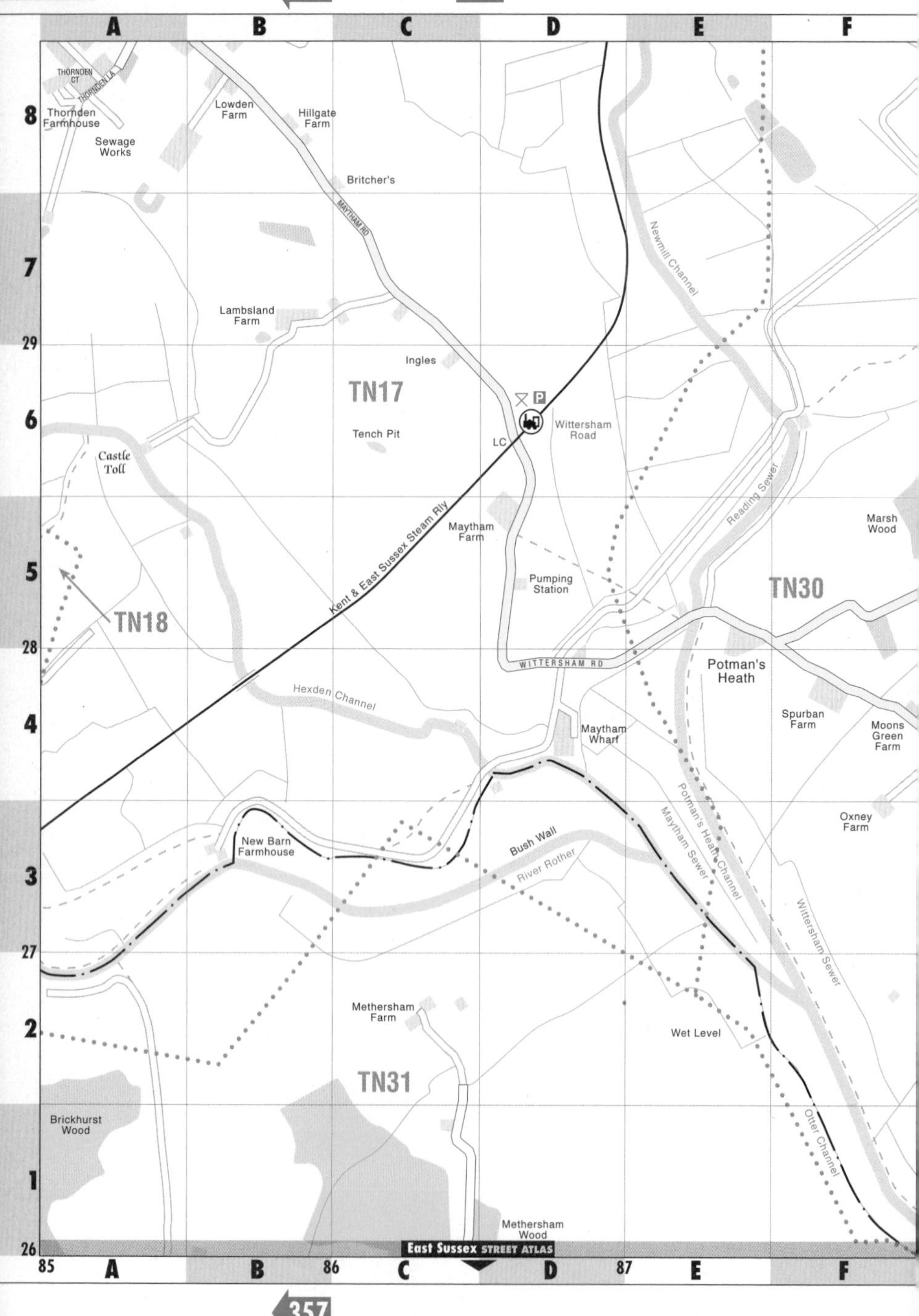

THORNDEN CT

Thornden Farmhouse

Sewage Works

Lowden Farm

Hillgate Farm

Britcher's

MAYTHAM RD

Lambsland Farm

Ingles

TN17

Tench Pit

Wittersham Road

LC

Castle Toll

Kent & East Sussex Steam Rly

Maytham Farm

TN30

Pumping Station

Marsh Wood

TN18

Reading Sewer

Hexden Channel

WITTERSHAM RD

Potman's Heath

Spurban Farm

Moons Green Farm

Maytham Wharf

Oxney Farm

New Barn Farmhouse

Bush Wall

River Rother

Potman's Heath Channel

Maytham Sewer

Wittersham Sewer

Methersham Farm

Wet Level

TN31

Brickhurst Wood

Otter Channel

Methersham Wood

345
360

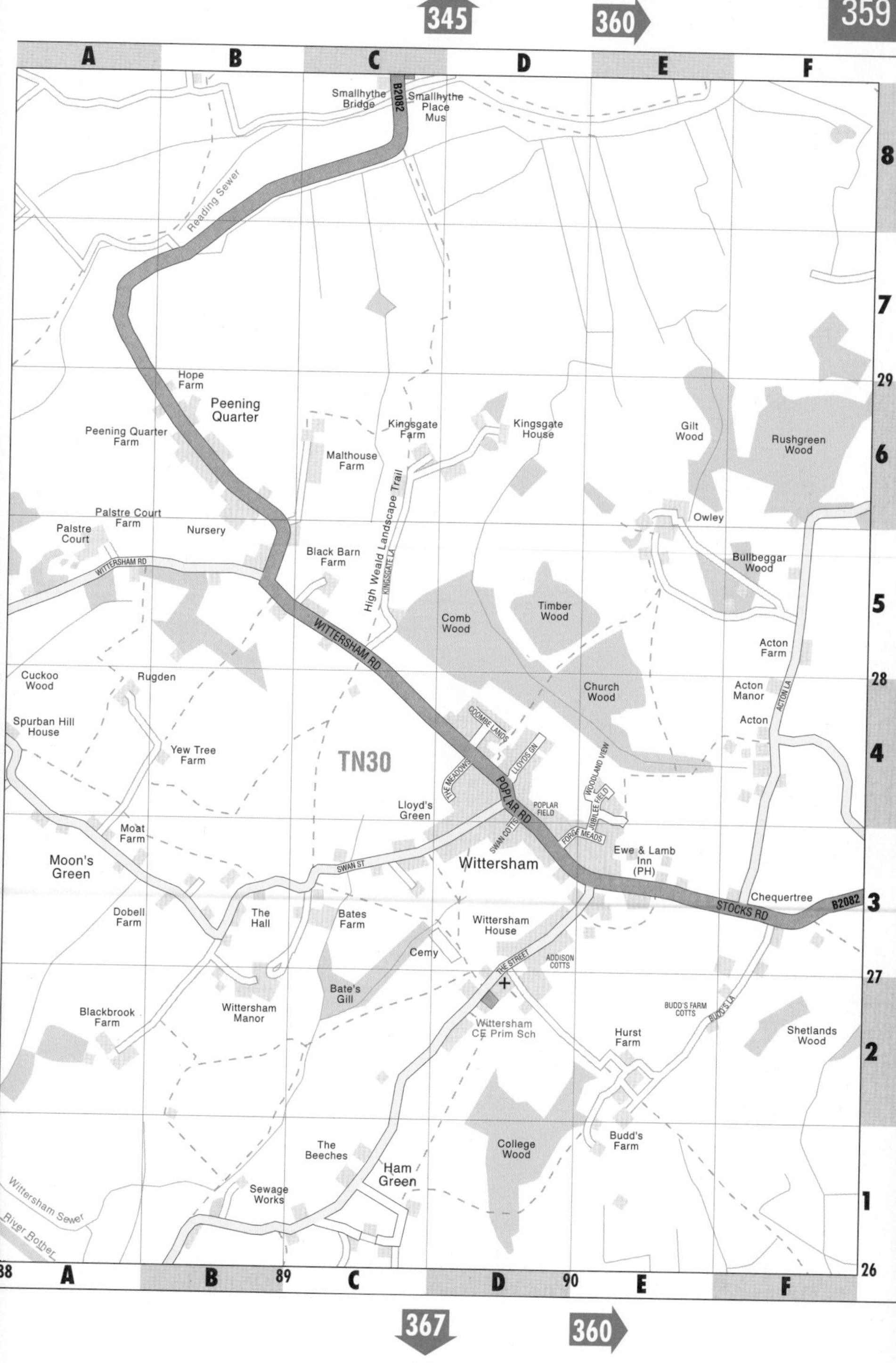
A
B
C
D
E
F
Smallhythe Bridge
B2082
Smallhythe Place Mus
Reading Sewer
Hope Farm
Peening Quarter
Peening Quarter Farm
Kingsgate Farm
Kingsgate House
Gilt Wood
Rushgreen Wood
Malthouse Farm
High Weald Landscape Trail
Palstre Court Farm
Palstre Court
Nursery
Black Barn Farm
Owley
Bullbeggar Wood
WITTERSHAM RD
KINGSGATE LA
Comb Wood
Timber Wood
Acton Farm
Cuckoo Wood
Rugden
Church Wood
Acton Manor
Acton
ACTON LA
Spurban Hill House
Yew Tree Farm
TN30
COOMBE LANDS
LLOYDS GN
THE MEADOWS
WOODLAND VIEW
POPLAR RD
Lloyd's Green
POPLAR FIELD
JUBILEE FIELD
SWAN COTTS
FORGE MEADS
Moat Farm
Ewe & Lamb Inn (PH)
Moon's Green
SWAN ST
Wittersham
Chequertree
STOCKS RD
Dobell Farm
The Hall
Bates Farm
Wittersham House
Cemy
ADDISON COTTS
THE STREET
Bate's Gill
BUDD'S FARM COTTS
BUDD'S LA
Blackbrook Farm
Wittersham Manor
Wittersham CE Prim Sch
Hurst Farm
Shetlands Wood
The Beeches
College Wood
Budd's Farm
Ham Green
Sewage Works
Wittersham Sewer
River Rother
8
7
29
6
5
28
4
3
27
2
1
26
88
89
90

367
360

359
346

	A	B	C	D	E	F

TN26

8 High House Farm

Hayes Farm

Ramsden Farm

7 Chapel Bank

Reading Sewer

29 Stone Corner Farm

STONE CNR

6 HOGPOUND CNR

Whole Farm

Saxon Shore Way

Little Odiam Farm

LOWER RD

5 Stemp's Wood

Rosehill Farmhouse

Odiam Farm

Stone Farm

Luckhurst

28 ROSE HILL

TN30

4 Isle of Oxney

Curteis Wood

Luckhurst Wood

Stone in Oxney

The Crown (PH)

Green Acres

Maynes Farm

Twelve Acre Wood

Catt Farm

STONE GN

The Stocks Wr Twr

Lord's Wood

Scrub's Wood

CATT'S HILL

3 STOCKS RD

Windmill (dis)

Stocks Farm

WITTERSHAM RD

Holman's Farm

QUARRY COTTS

Four Acre Wood

WADDLE CNR

WATTLE CNR

TOP RD

Huggit's Farm

CHURCH HILL

27 Prospect House

Oxenden

Little Prawls Farm

KNOCK HILL

2 Tophill Farm

RYE RD

Rook Wood

Tighe Farm

Saxon Shore Way

Great Prawls Farm

Cliff Farm

Underhill Farmhouse

1 Rother Levels

Stone Cliff

B2082

26

91	A	B	92	C	D	93	E	F

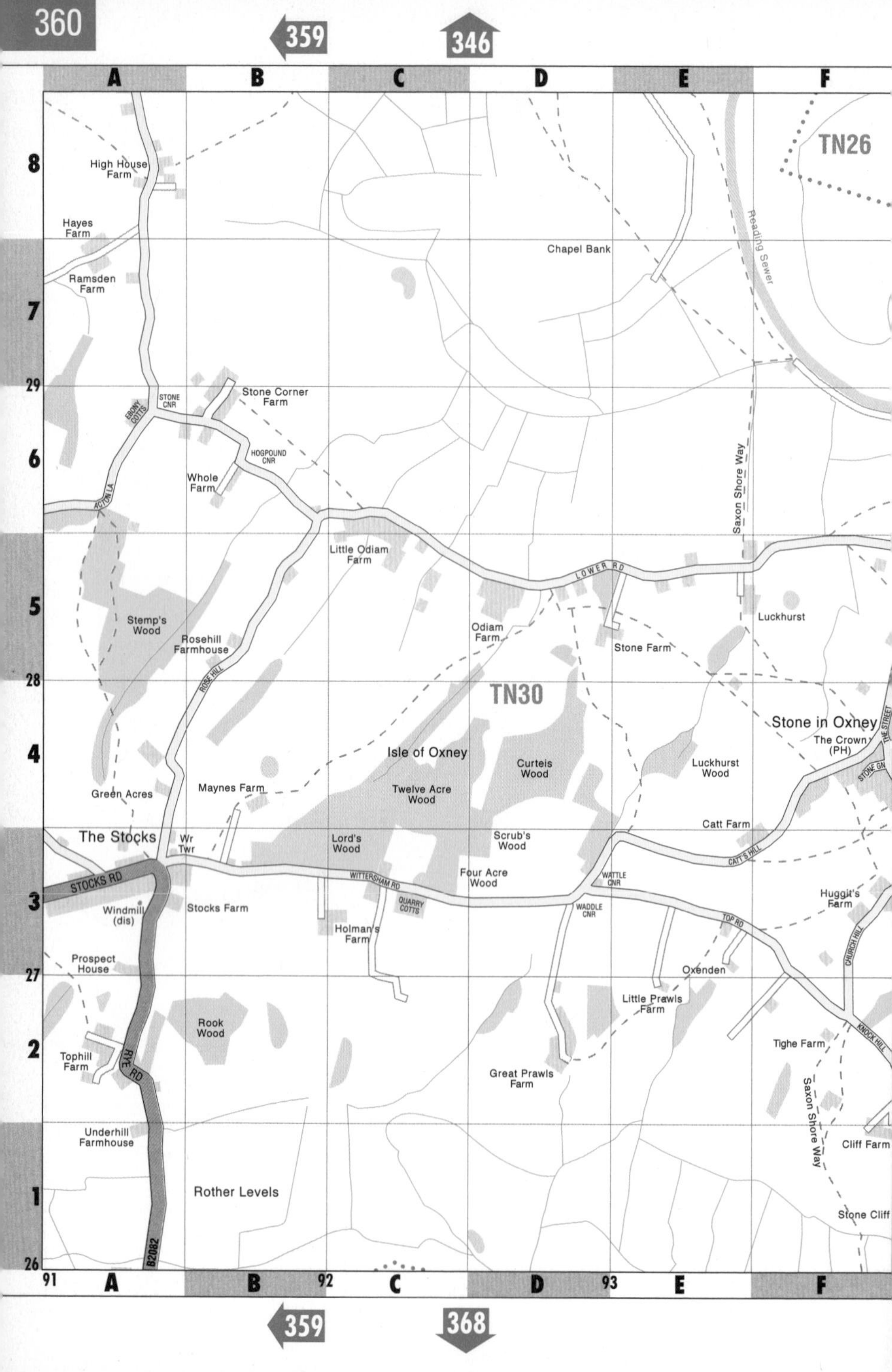

359
368

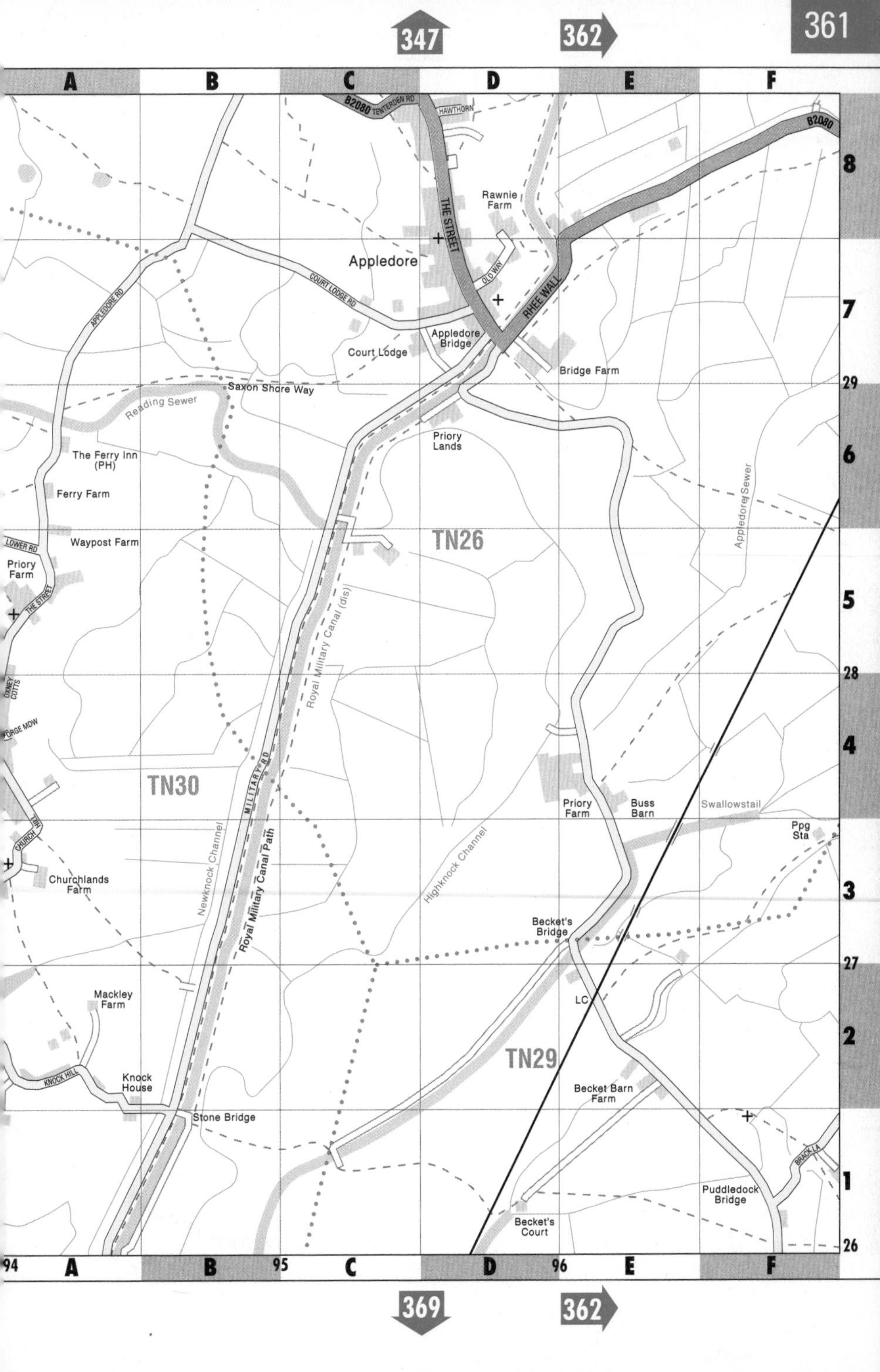
A
B
C
D
E
F
B2080
TENTERDEN RD
HAWTHORN
B2080
8
THE STREET
Rawnie Farm
Appledore
COURT LODGE RD
OLD WAY
RHEE WALL
APPLEDORE RD
7
Appledore Bridge
Court Lodge
Bridge Farm
29
Saxon Shore Way
Reading Sewer
Priory Lands
The Ferry Inn (PH)
6
Ferry Farm
Appledore Sewer
TN26
LOWER RD
Waypost Farm
Priory Farm
THE STREET
5
Royal Military Canal (dis)
OXNEY COTTS
28
FORGE MDW
4
TN30
MILITARY RD
Priory Farm
Buss Barn
Swallowstail
Newknock Channel
CHURCH
Ppg Sta
Churchlands Farm
Highknock Channel
Royal Military Canal Path
3
Becket's Bridge
27
Mackley Farm
LC
2
TN29
KNOCK HILL
Knock House
Becket Barn Farm
Stone Bridge
BRACK LA
1
Puddledock Bridge
Becket's Court
26
94
95
96

361
348

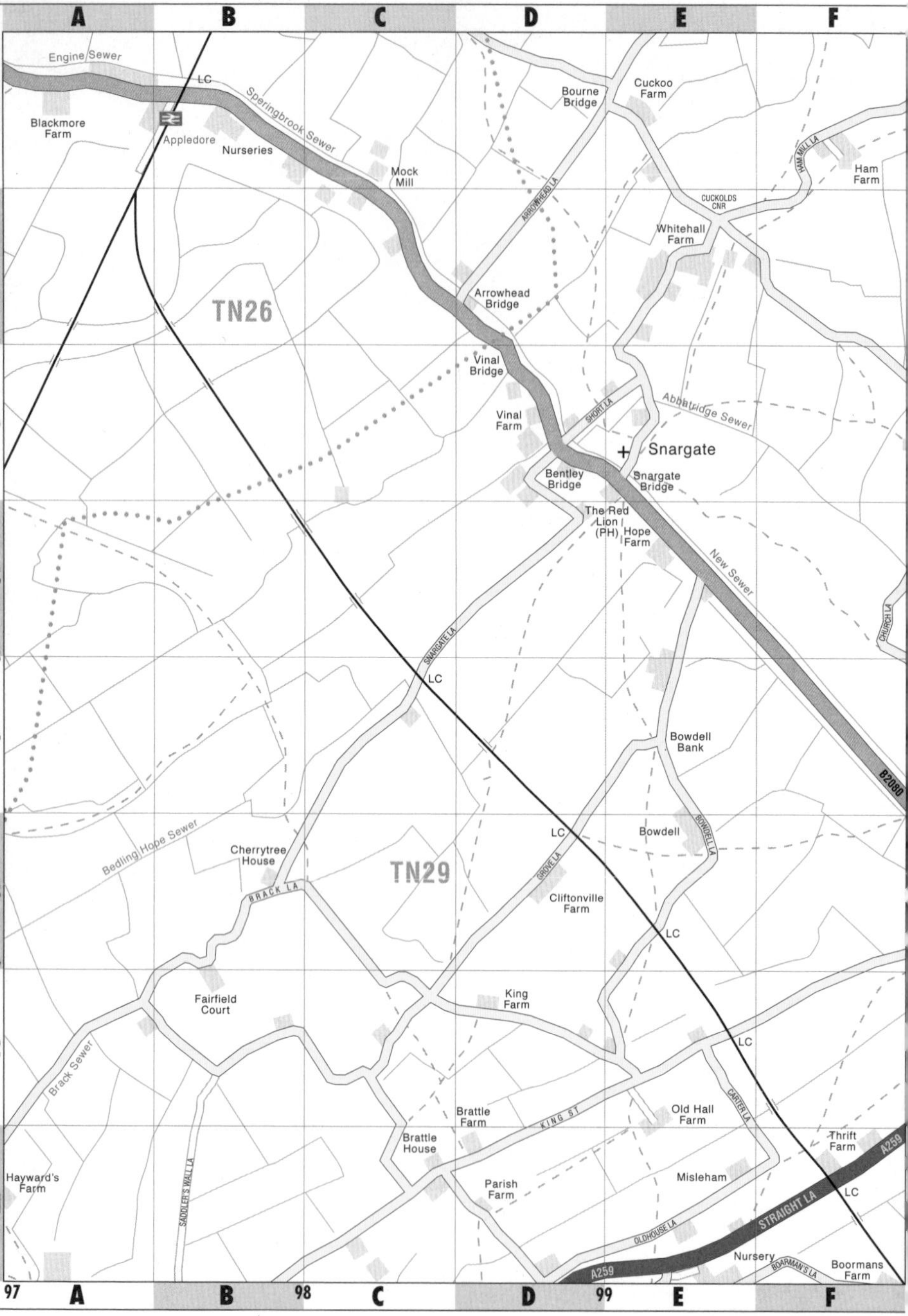

A B C D E F

Engine Sewer

LC

8

Blackmore
Farm

Appledore
Nurseries

Springbrook Sewer

Mock
Mill

Bourne
Bridge

Cuckoo
Farm

Ham
Farm

HAM MILL LA

CUCKOLDS
CNR

Whitehall
Farm

7

TN26

MOCKMILL LA

Arrowhead
Bridge

29

Vinal
Bridge

Abbatbridge Sewer

6

Vinal
Farm

GROVE LA

Snargate

Snargate
Bridge

Bentley
Bridge

The Red
Lion
(PH)

Hope
Farm

New Sewer

5

Bedling Hope Sewer

SNARGATE LA

LC

28

CHURCH LA

B2080

4

Bowdell
Bank

Cherrytree
House

BRACK LA

TN29

LC

Bowdell

BOWDELL LA

3

Cliftonville
Farm

GROVE LA

LC

27

Fairfield
Court

King
Farm

2

Brack Sewer

SADDLER'S WALL LA

Brattle
Farm

KING ST

Old Hall
Farm

CARTER LA

LC

Misleham

Thrift
Farm

A259

1

Hayward's
Farm

Brattle
House

Parish
Farm

STRAIGHT LA

LC

26

OLDHOUSE LA

A259

Nursery

BOORMAN'S LA

Boormans
Farm

97 A B 98 C D 99 E F

361
370

349
364

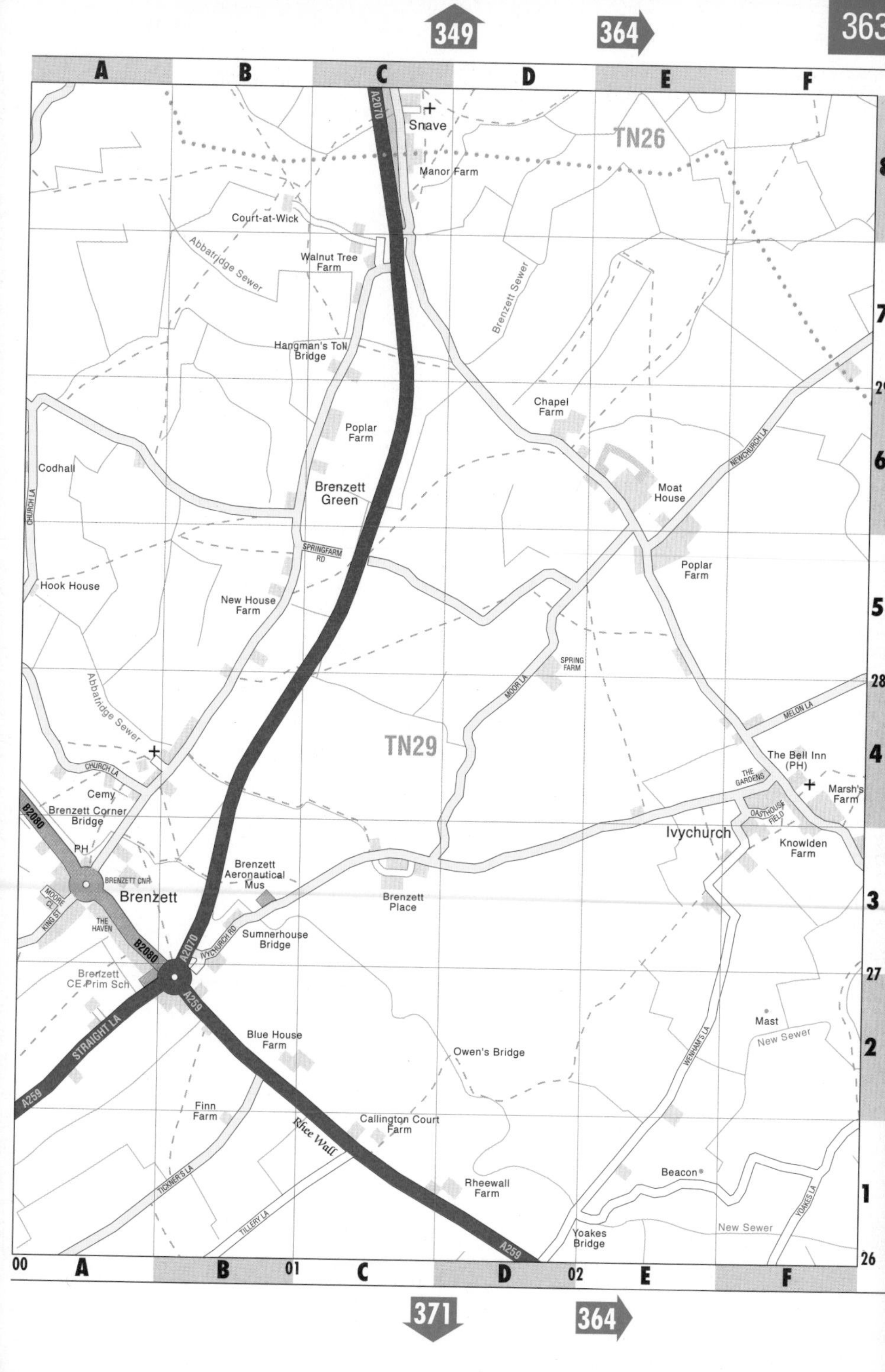
A
B
C
D
E
F
Snave
TN26
Manor Farm
Court-at-Wick
Abbatridge Sewer
Walnut Tree Farm
Brenzett Sewer
Hangman's Toll Bridge
Chapel Farm
Poplar Farm
NEWCHURCH LA
Codhall
CHURCH LA
Brenzett Green
Moat House
SPRINGFARM RD
Poplar Farm
Hook House
New House Farm
SPRING FARM
MOOR LA
Abbatridge Sewer
TN29
MELON LA
The Bell Inn (PH)
CHURCH LA
THE GARDENS
Marsh's Farm
Cemy
Brenzett Corner Bridge
B2080
OASTHOUSE FIELD
Ivychurch
PH
Knowlden Farm
Brenzett Aeronautical Mus
BRENZETT CNR
MOORE CL
Brenzett
KING ST
Brenzett Place
THE HAVEN
Sumnerhouse Bridge
IVYCHURCH RD
B2080
A2070
Brenzett CE Prim Sch
A259
STRAIGHT LA
Mast
Blue House Farm
New Sewer
Owen's Bridge
WENHAM'S LA
A259
Finn Farm
Callington Court Farm
Rhee Wall
Beacon
TICKNER'S LA
Rheewall Farm
YOAKES LA
TILLERY LA
New Sewer
Yoakes Bridge
A259
8
7
29
6
5
28
4
3
27
2
1
26
00
01
02

371
364

363
350

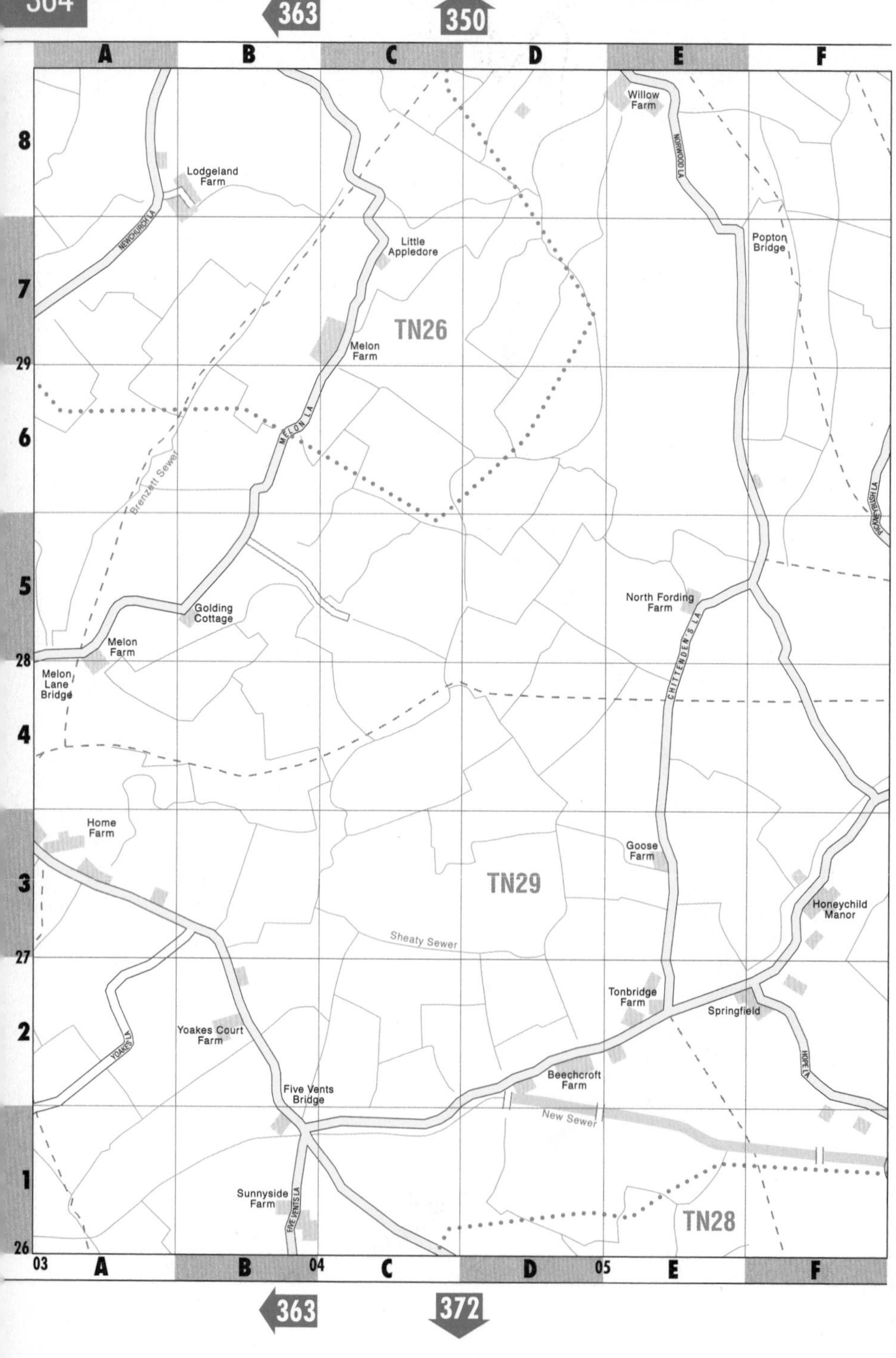
A
B
C
D
E
F
8
7
29
6
5
28
4
3
27
2
1
26
03
04
05
Lodgeland Farm
NEWCHURCH LA
Little Appledore
Willow Farm
NORWOOD LA
Popton Bridge
TN26
Melon Farm
MELON LA
Brenzett Sewer
PICKNEYBUSH LA
North Fording Farm
Golding Cottage
Melon Farm
Melon Lane Bridge
CHITTENDEN'S LA
Home Farm
Goose Farm
TN29
Honeychild Manor
Sheaty Sewer
Tonbridge Farm
Springfield
Yoakes Court Farm
YOAKES LA
HOPE LA
Beechcroft Farm
Five Vents Bridge
New Sewer
Sunnyside Farm
FIVE VENTS LA
TN28

363
372

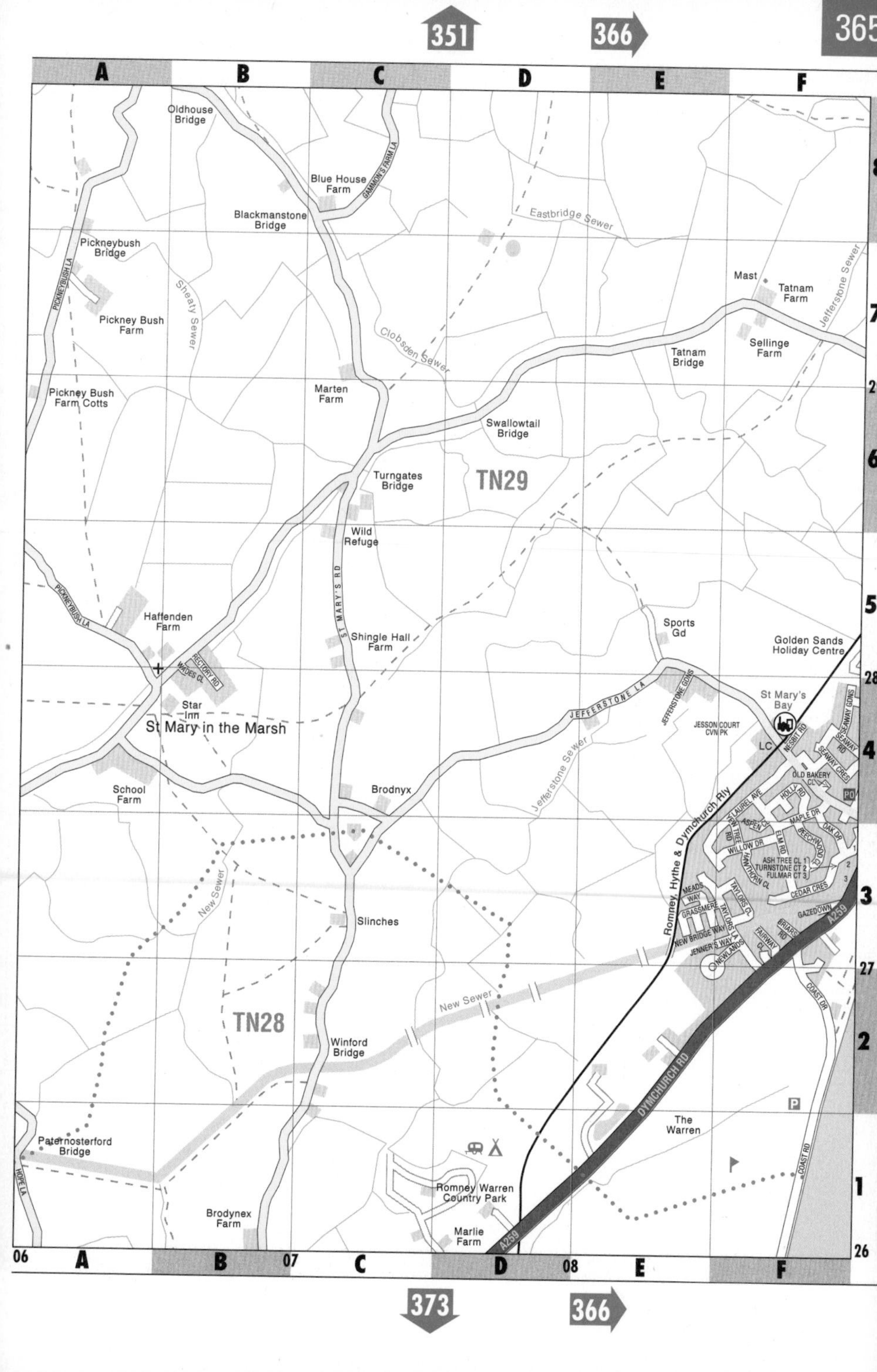
351
366
A
B
C
D
E
F
Oldhouse Bridge
Blue House Farm
GAMMON'S FARM LA
Blackmanstone Bridge
Eastbridge Sewer
Pickneybush Bridge
PICKNEYBUSH LA
Sheaty Sewer
Mast
Tatnam Farm
Jefferstone Sewer
Pickney Bush Farm
Clobsden Sewer
Tatnam Bridge
Sellinge Farm
Pickney Bush Farm Cotts
Marten Farm
Swallowtail Bridge
Turngates Bridge
TN29
Wild Refuge
ST MARY'S RD
Haffenden Farm
Shingle Hall Farm
Sports Gd
Golden Sands Holiday Centre
RECTORY RD
WADES CL
Star Inn
JEFFERSTONE LA
JEFFERSTONE GDNS
St Mary's Bay
St Mary in the Marsh
JESSON COURT CVN PK
LC
NESBIT RD
SEAWAY GDNS
SEAWAY RD
SEAWAY CRES
Jefferstone Sewer
OLD BAKERY CL
School Farm
Brodnyx
Romney, Hythe & Dymchurch Rly
LAUREL AVE
HOLLY RD
PO
ASPEN
YEW TREE RD
MAPLE DR
OAK DR
BEECHWOOD CT
WILLOW DR
ELM RD
ASH TREE CL 1
TURNSTONE CT 2
FULMAR CT 3
HAWTHORN CL
New Sewer
MEADS WAY
TAYLORS CL
CEDAR CRES
GRASSMERE
TAYLORS LA
GAZEDOWN
Slinches
NEW BRIDGE WAY
FAIRWAY CL
BRIARS RD
A259
JENNER'S WAY
NEWLANDS
COAST DR
New Sewer
TN28
Winford Bridge
DYMCHURCH RD
P
The Warren
Paternosterford Bridge
HOPE LA
COAST RD
Romney Warren Country Park
Brodynex Farm
Marlie Farm
A259
7
2
6
5
28
4
3
27
2
1
26
06
07
08
A
B
C
D
E
F
373
366

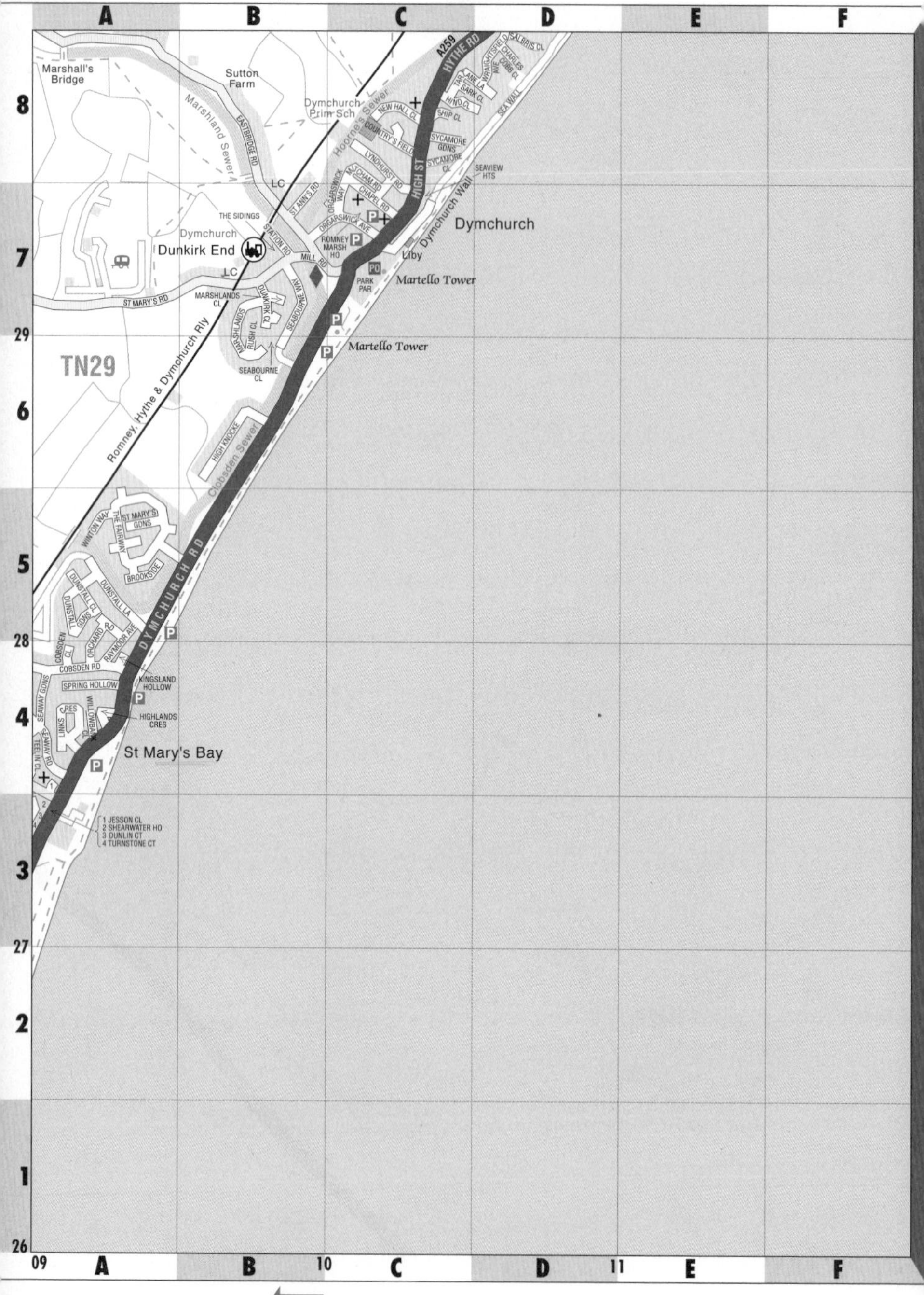

A   B   C   D   E   F

Marshall's
Bridge

Sutton
Farm

Marshland Sewer

ASTBRIDGE RD

Dymchurch
Prim Sch

A259
HYTHE RD

ST ALBANS CL

NEW HALL CL

HIGH ST

SEA WALL

SYCAMORE
GDNS

SYCAMORE
CL

SEAVIEW
HTS

8

THE SIDINGS

LC

Dymchurch
Dunkirk End

Dymchurch Wall

Dymchurch

ST MARY'S RD

MARSHLANDS
CL

MILL RD

ROMNEY
MARSH
HO

P

Liby

PO

Martello Tower

7

29

SEABOURNE
CL

P

Martello Tower

TN29

Romney, Hythe & Dymchurch Rly

Glossden Sewer

HIGH KNOCK

6

ST MARY'S
GDNS

BROOKSIDE

DYMCHURCH RD

P

5

28

COBSDEN RD

SPRING HOLLOW

KINGSLAND
HOLLOW

P

HIGHLANDS
CRES

4

P

St Mary's Bay

1 JESSON CL
2 SHEARWATER HO
3 DUNLIN CT
4 TURNSTONE CT

3

27

2

1

26

09   A   B   10   C   D   11   E   F

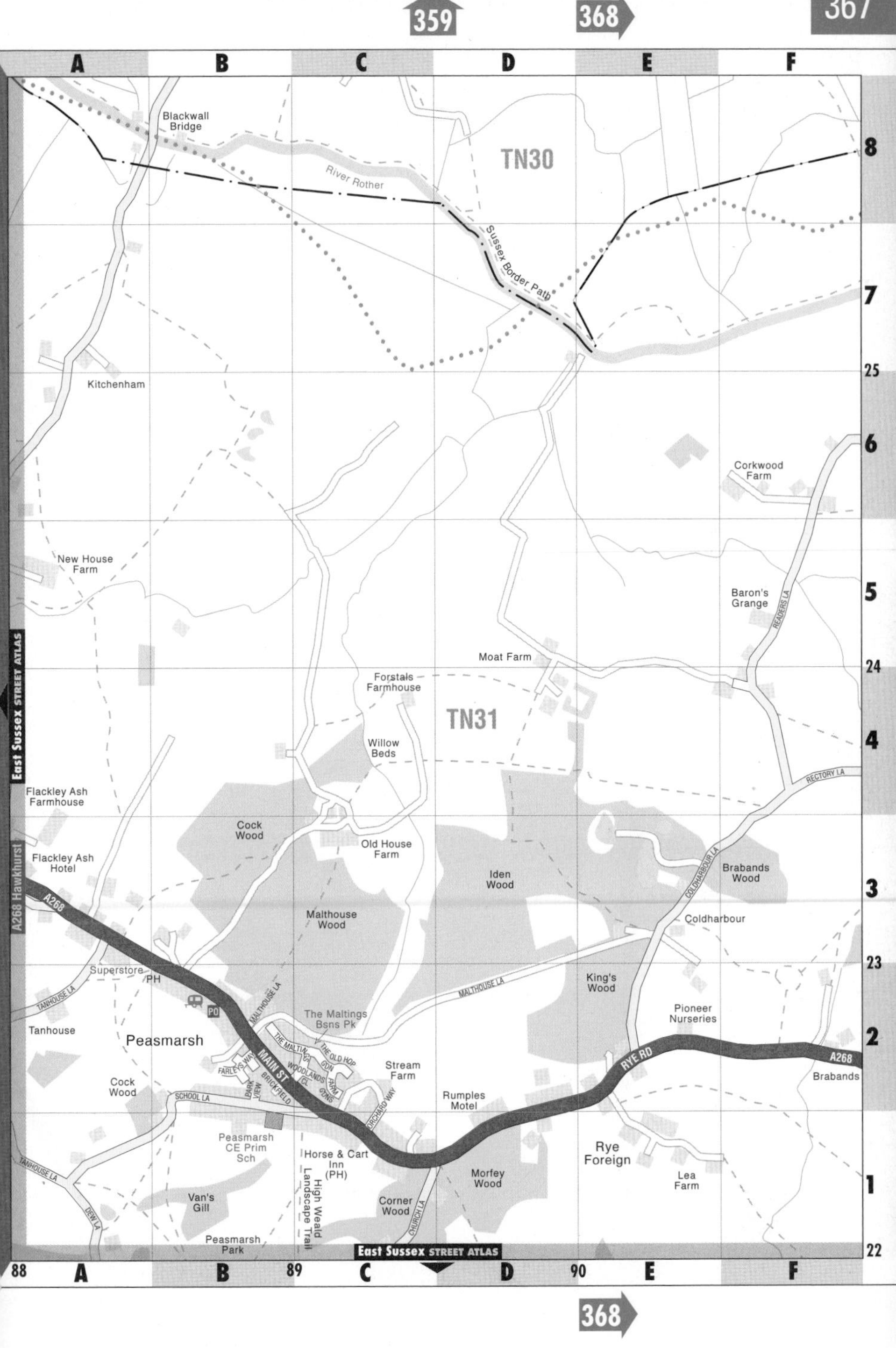

A B C D E F

8

TN30

River Rother

Sussex Border Path

7

25

Blackwall
Bridge

Kitchenham

6

Corkwood
Farm

New House
Farm

5

Baron's
Grange

24

Moat Farm

Forstals
Farmhouse

TN31

4

Willow
Beds

RECTORY LA

Flackley Ash
Farmhouse

Cock
Wood

Old House
Farm

Iden
Wood

Brabands
Wood

Flackley Ash
Hotel

3

Coldharbour

Malthouse
Wood

23

Superstore

PH

MALTHOUSE LA

King's
Wood

Pioneer
Nurseries

The Maltings
Bsns Pk

Tanhouse

Peasmarsh

2

RYE RD

A268

Brabands

Cock
Wood

SCHOOL LA

Stream
Farm

Rumples
Motel

Rye
Foreign

Lea
Farm

Peasmarsh
CE Prim
Sch

Horse & Cart
Inn
(PH)

High Weald
Landscape Trail

Morfey
Wood

1

Van's
Gill

Corner
Wood

Peasmarsh
Park

22

A268 Hawkhurst

A268

TANHOUSE LA

VINE LA

East Sussex STREET ATLAS

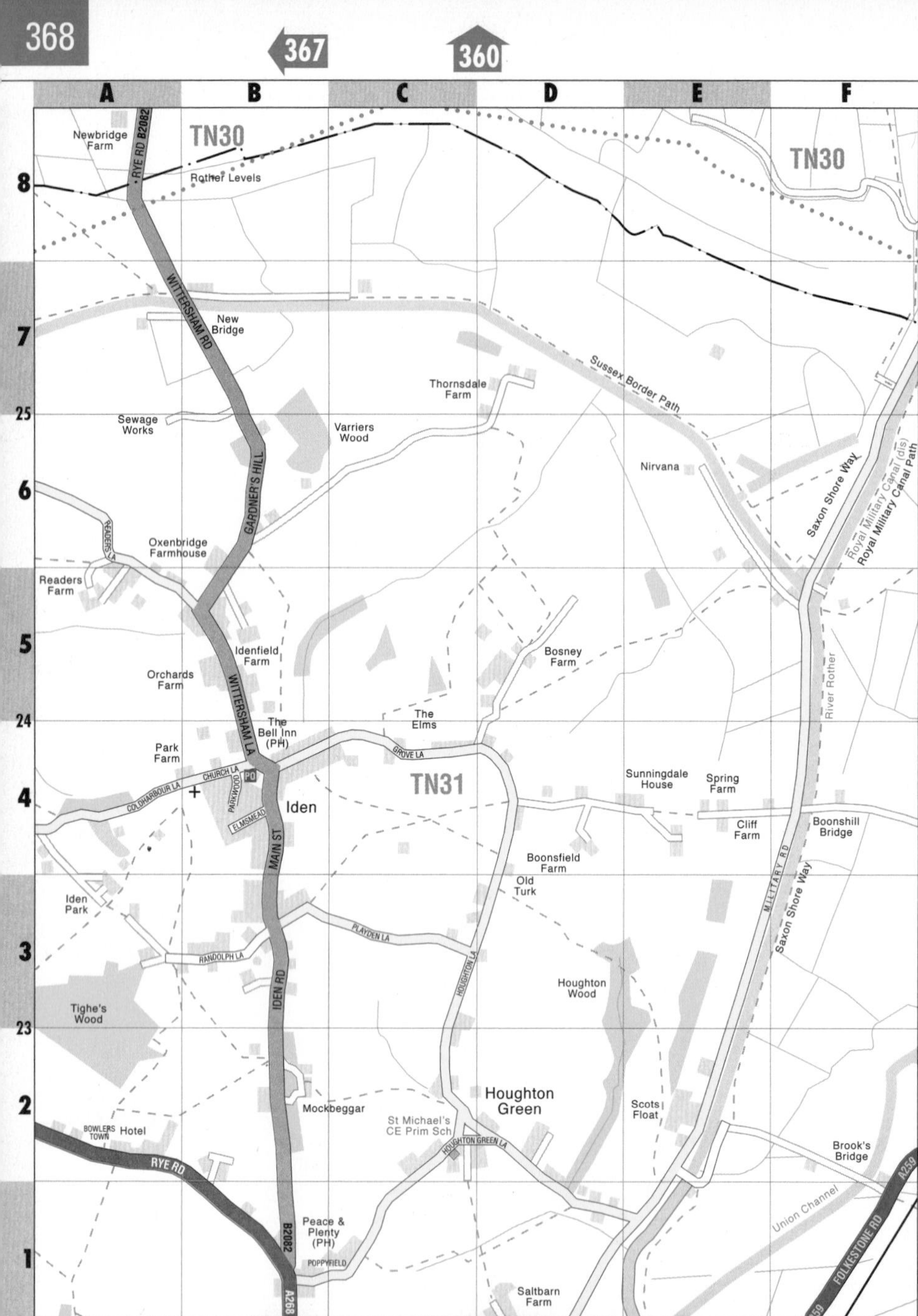

TN30

TN30

A B C D E F

Newbridge
Farm

Rother Levels

RYE RD B2082

New
Bridge

WITTERSHAM RD

Sewage
Works

GARDNER'S HILL

Thornsdale
Farm

Varriers
Wood

Nirvana

Sussex Border Path

Saxon Shore Way

Royal Military Canal (dis)
Royal Military Canal Path

Oxenbridge
Farmhouse

HEAVEN'S LA

Readers
Farm

Idenfield
Farm

Orchards
Farm

WITTERSHAM LA

The Bell Inn
(PH)

Park
Farm

CHURCH LA

COLDHARBOUR LA

ELMSMEAD

DOOR WAY

Iden

The
Elms

GROVE LA

TN31

Bosney
Farm

River Rother

Sunningdale
House

Spring
Farm

Cliff
Farm

Boonshill
Bridge

MAIN ST

IDEN RD

Iden
Park

Boonsfield
Farm

Old
Turk

Saxon Shore Way

MILITARY RD

RANDOLPH LA

PLATNIX LA

Tighe's
Wood

HOUGHTON LA

Houghton
Wood

Mockbeggar

St Michael's
CE Prim Sch

Houghton
Green

Scots
Float

Brook's
Bridge

BOWLERS
TOWN

Hotel

RYE RD

HOUGHTON GREEN LA

A259

FOLKESTONE RD

Peace &
Plenty
(PH)

B2082

POPPYFIELD

Union Channel

Saltbarn
Farm

A268

A268 Rye

East Sussex STREET ATLAS

A259

8

25

6

5

24

4

3

23

2

1

22

91 A B 92 C D 93 E F

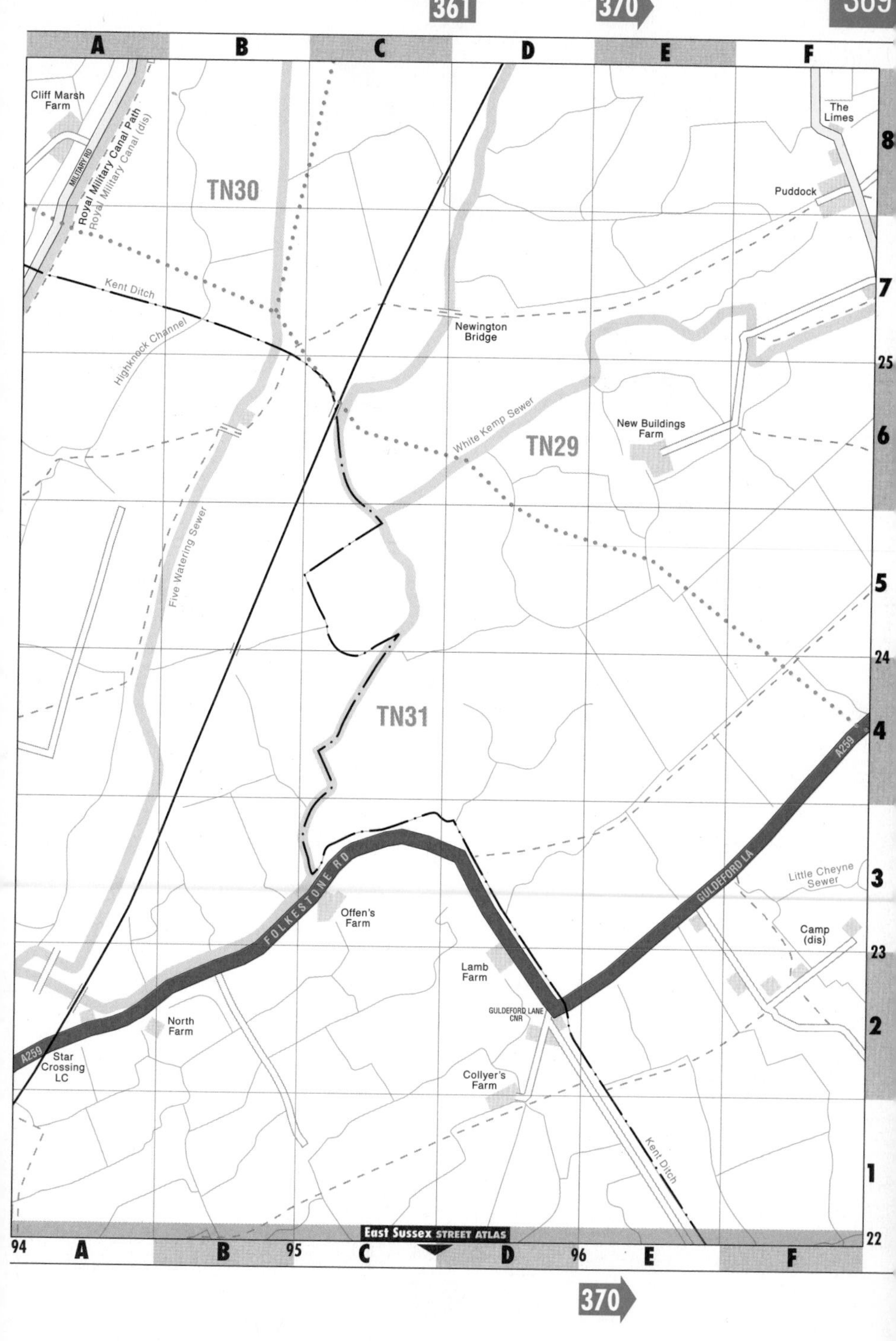
A
B
C
D
E
F
Cliff Marsh Farm
MILITARY RD
Royal Military Canal Path
Royal Military Canal (dis)
TN30
The Limes
Puddock
Kent Ditch
Highknock Channel
Newington Bridge
White Kemp Sewer
New Buildings Farm
TN29
Five Watering Sewer
TN31
A259
FOLKESTONE RD
GULDEFORD LA
Little Cheyne Sewer
Offen's Farm
Camp (dis)
Lamb Farm
GULDEFORD LANE CNR
North Farm
Star Crossing LC
Collyer's Farm
Kent Ditch
8
7
25
6
5
24
4
3
23
2
1
22
94
95
96

369
362

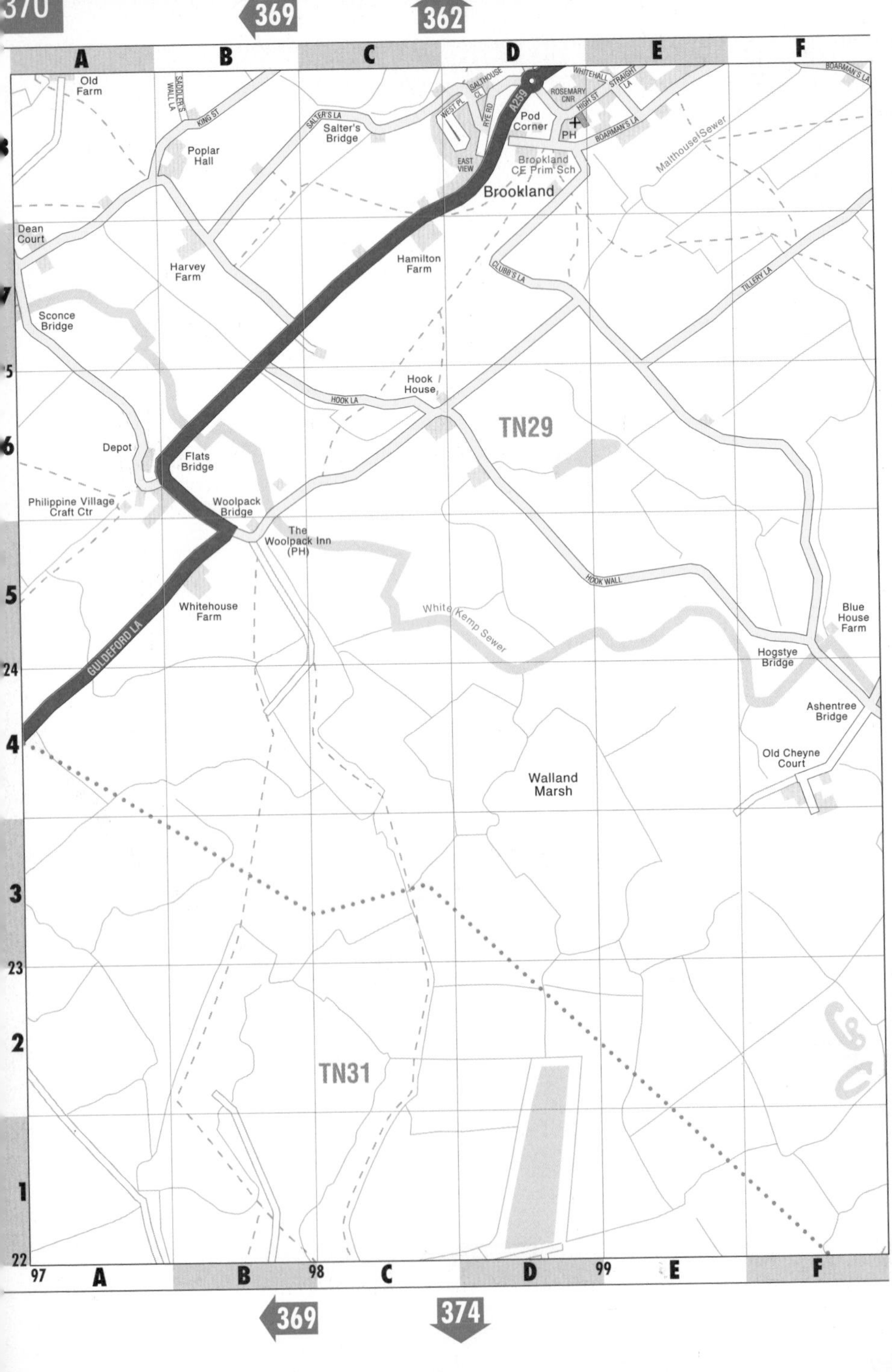
A
B
C
D
E
F
Old Farm
SADDLER'S WALL LA
KING ST
SALTHOUSE CL
WHITEHALL
STRAIGHT LA
BOARMAN'S LA
ROSEMARY CNR
HIGH ST
SALTER'S LA
Salter's Bridge
WEST PL
RYE RD
A259
Pod Corner
PH
Poplar Hall
EAST VIEW
Brookland CE Prim Sch
Malthouse Sewer
Brookland
Dean Court
Harvey Farm
Hamilton Farm
CLUBB'S LA
TILLERY LA
Sconce Bridge
Hook House
HOOK LA
TN29
Depot
Flats Bridge
Philippine Village Craft Ctr
Woolpack Bridge
The Woolpack Inn (PH)
HOOK WALL
Whitehouse Farm
White Kemp Sewer
Blue House Farm
GULDEFORD LA
Hogstye Bridge
Ashentree Bridge
Old Cheyne Court
Walland Marsh
TN31
24
23
22
97
98
99
8
7
6
5
4
3
2
1

369
374

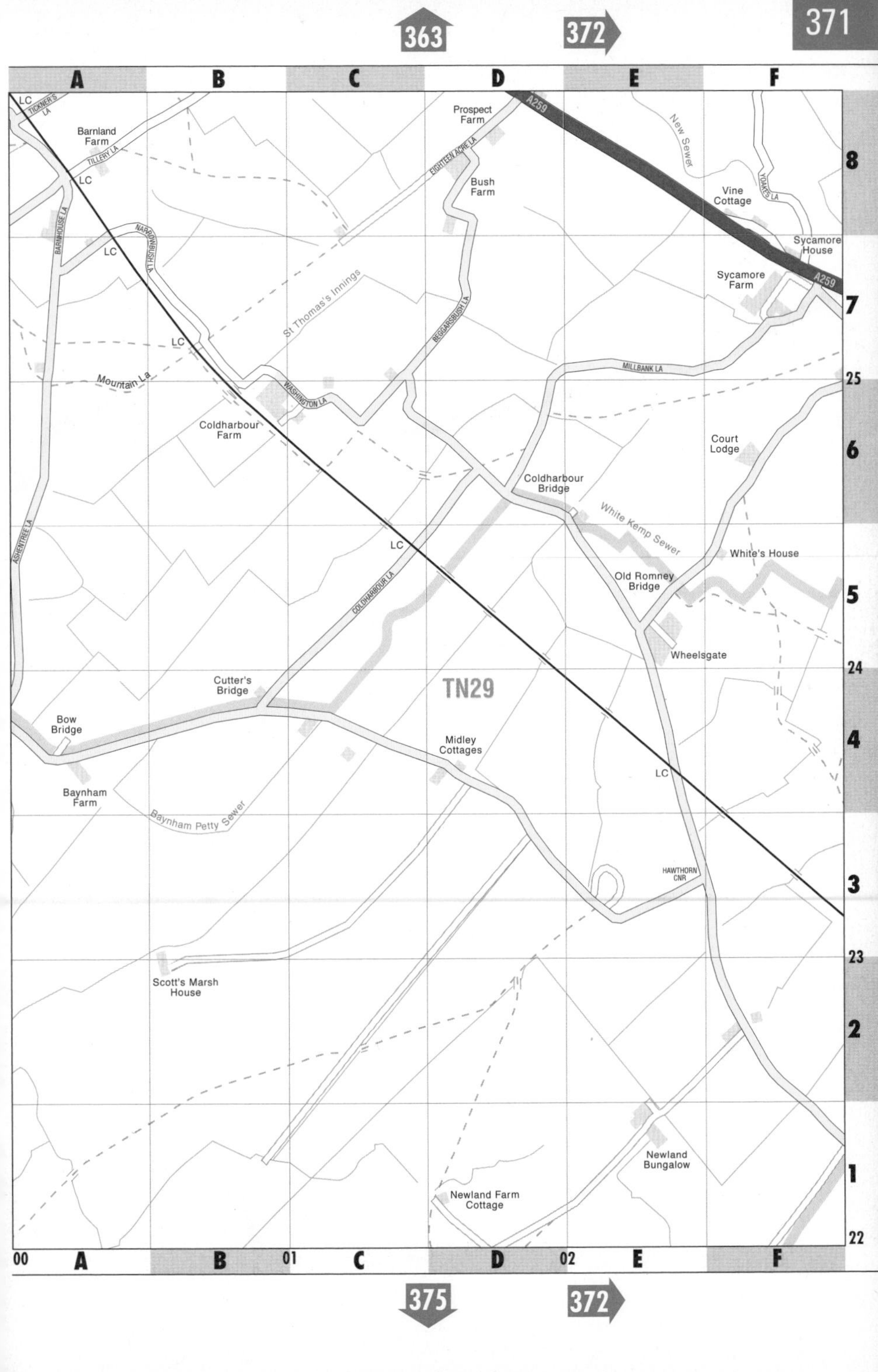

363
372

A **B** **C** **D** **E** **F**

LC
Tigner's LA
Barnland Farm
Tillery LA
LC
Prospect Farm
A259
New Sewer
8
Bawdehouse LA
Nags Head LA
Eighteen Acre LA
Bush Farm
Vine Cottage
Yokes LA
LC
St Thomas's Innings
Begorse LA
Sycamore House
Sycamore Farm
A259
LC
7
Mountain LA
Washington LA
Millbank LA
25
Coldharbour Farm
Court Lodge
6
Coldharbour Bridge
Aspen The LA
White Kemp Sewer
LC
White's House
Coldharbour LA
Old Romney Bridge
5
TN29
Wheelsgate
24
Cutter's Bridge
Bow Bridge
Midley Cottages
LC
4
Baynham Farm
Baynham Petty Sewer
HAWTHORN CNR
3
Scott's Marsh House
23
2
Newland Bungalow
1
Newland Farm Cottage
22

00 **A** **B** 01 **C** **D** 02 **E** **F**

375
372

371
364

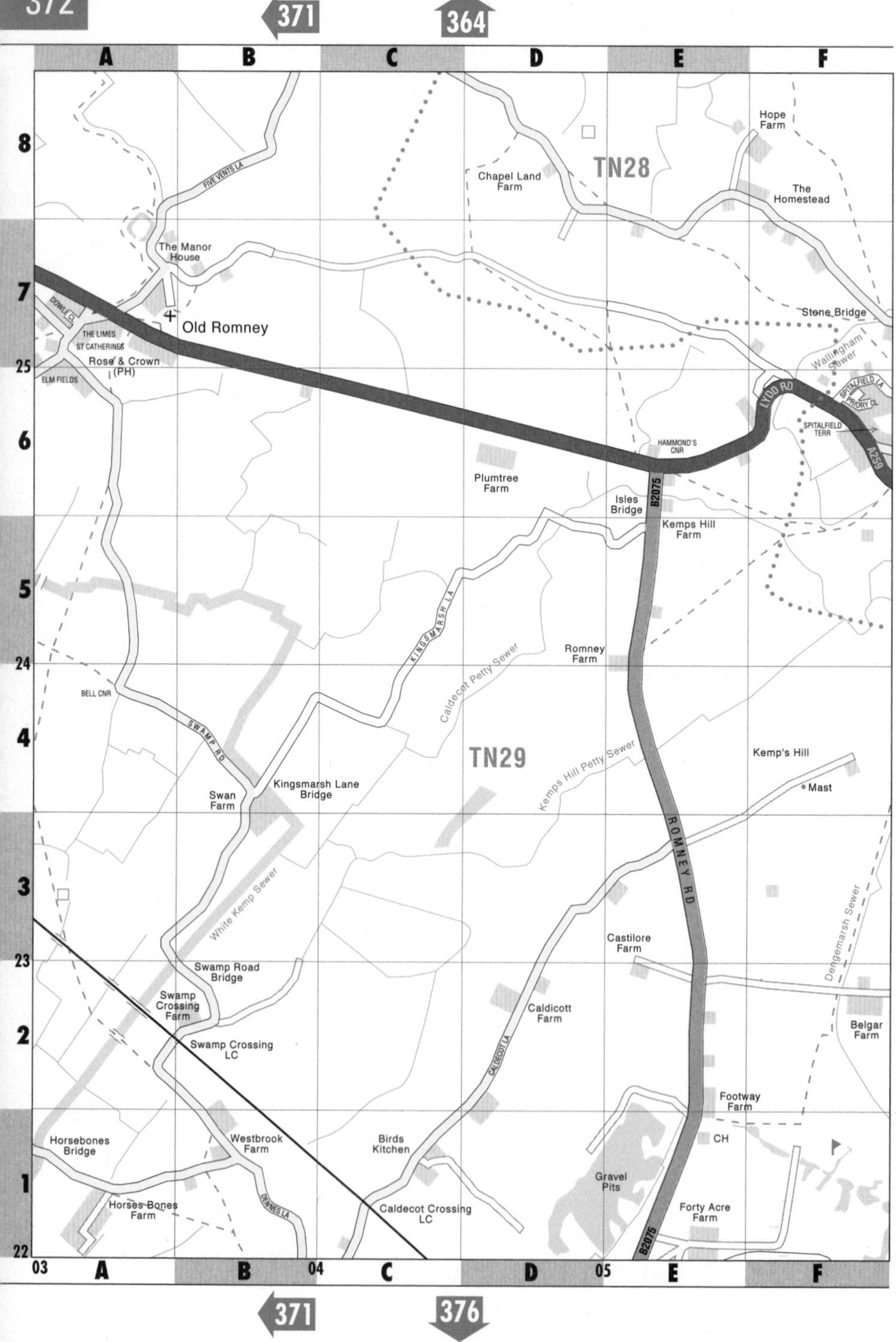
A
B
C
D
E
F
8
7
6
5
4
3
2
1
25
24
23
22
03
04
05
TN28
TN29
Hope Farm
Chapel Land Farm
The Homestead
FIVE VENTS LA
The Manor House
Old Romney
DOWLE CL
THE LIMES
ST CATHERINES
Rose & Crown (PH)
ELM FIELDS
Stone Bridge
Wallingham Sewer
LYDD RD
SPITALFIELD LA
PRIORY CL
SPITALFIELD TERR
A259
HAMMOND'S CNR
Plumtree Farm
Isles Bridge
B2075
Kemps Hill Farm
KINGSMARSH LA
Romney Farm
Caldecot Petty Sewer
BELL CNR
SWAMP RD
Kemp's Hill
Kemps Hill Petty Sewer
Mast
Swan Farm
Kingsmarsh Lane Bridge
ROMNEY RD
White Kemp Sewer
Castilore Farm
Dengemarsh Sewer
Swamp Road Bridge
Swamp Crossing Farm
Caldicott Farm
Belgar Farm
Swamp Crossing LC
CALDECOT LA
Footway Farm
Horsebones Bridge
Westbrook Farm
Birds Kitchen
CH
Gravel Pits
Horses Bones Farm
DENNES LA
Caldecot Crossing LC
Forty Acre Farm

371
376

365

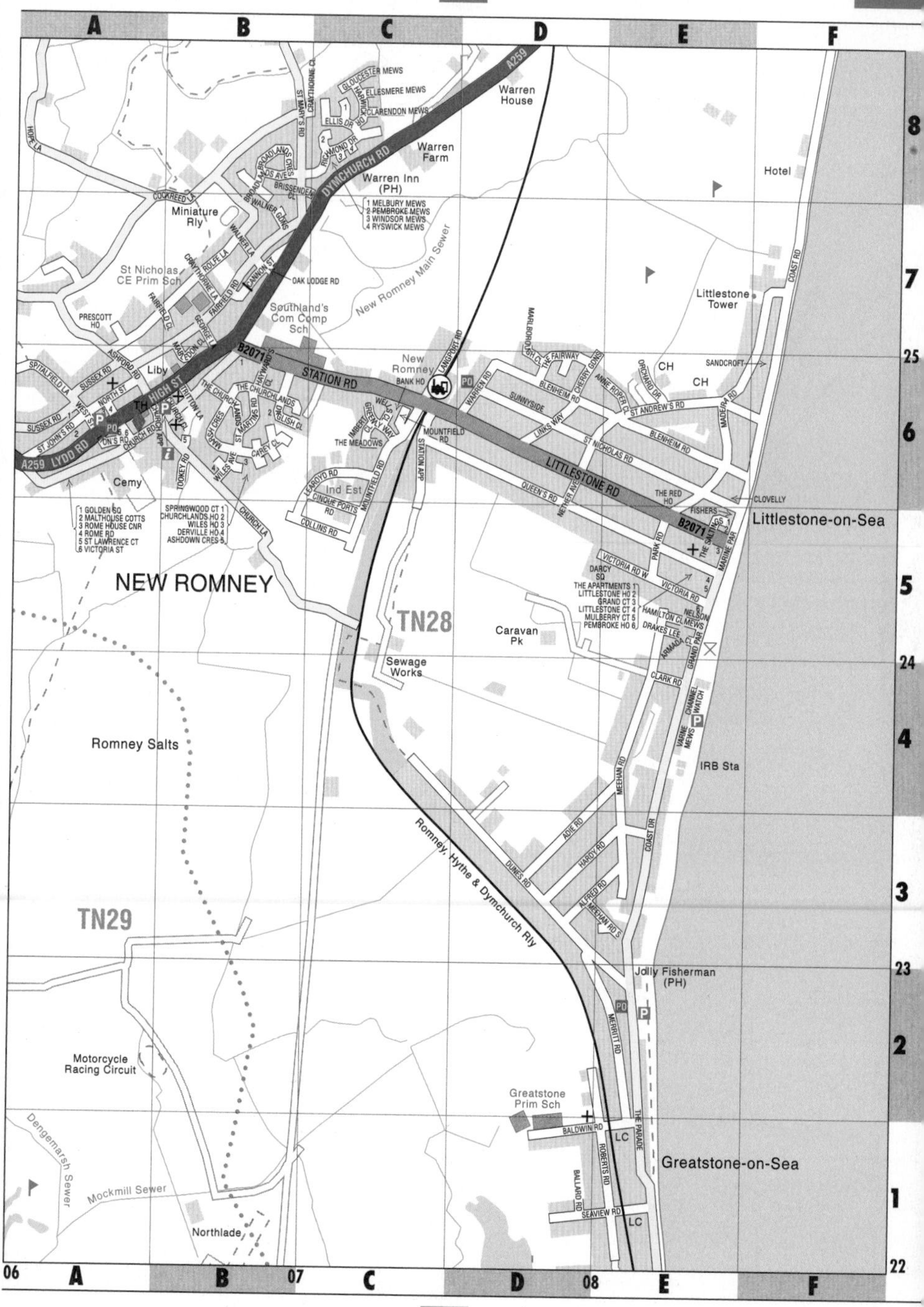

A
B
C
D
E
F
Warren House
Warren Farm
Warren Inn (PH)
1 MELBURY MEWS
2 PEMBROKE MEWS
3 WINDSOR MEWS
4 RYSWICK MEWS
GLOUCESTER MEWS
ELLESMERE MEWS
CLARENDON MEWS
ELLIS DR
RICHMOND DR
DYMCHURCH RD
A259
HOPE LA
COCKREED LA
Miniature Rly
St Nicholas CE Prim Sch
OAK LODGE RD
New Romney Main Sewer
Southland's Com Comp Sch
PRESCOTT HO
Hotel
Littlestone Tower
SANDCROFT
CH
COAST RD
New Romney
LANGPORT RD
BANK HO
STATION RD
B2071
LITTLESTONE RD
HIGH ST
LYDD RD
Liby
TH
Cemy
THE FAIRWAY
BLENHEIM RD
SUNNYSIDE
LINKS WAY
ST ANDREW'S RD
ST NICHOLAS RD
QUEEN'S RD
THE RED HO
CLOVELLY
FISHERS
Littlestone-on-Sea
MOUNTFIELD RD
THE MEADOWS
STATION APP
Ind Est
CINQUE PORTS RD
COLLINS RD
1 GOLDEN SQ
2 MALTHOUSE COTTS
3 ROME HOUSE CNR
4 ROME RD
5 ST LAWRENCE CT
6 VICTORIA ST
SPRINGWOOD CT 1
CHURCHLANDS HO 2
WILES HO 3
DERVILLE HO 4
ASHDOWN CRES 5
NEW ROMNEY
TN28
Caravan Pk
DARCY SQ
THE APARTMENTS 1
LITTLESTONE HO 2
GRAND CT 3
LITTLESTONE CT 4
MULBERRY CT 5
PEMBROKE HO 6
VICTORIA RD
HAMILTON CL
NELSON MEWS
DRAKES LEE
ARMADA CL
GRAND PAR
CLARK RD
CHANNEL WATCH
VARNE MEWS
IRB Sta
Sewage Works
Romney Salts
Romney, Hythe & Dymchurch Rly
DUNES RD
ADIE RD
HARDY RD
ALFRED RD
MEEHAN RD
COAST DR
TN29
Jolly Fisherman (PH)
MERRITT RD
Motorcycle Racing Circuit
Greatstone Prim Sch
BALDWIN RD
ROBERTS RD
BALLARD RD
SEAVIEW RD
THE PARADE
LC
Greatstone-on-Sea
Dengemarsh Sewer
Mockmill Sewer
Northlade
8
7
6
5
4
3
2
1
25
24
23
22
06
07
08

377

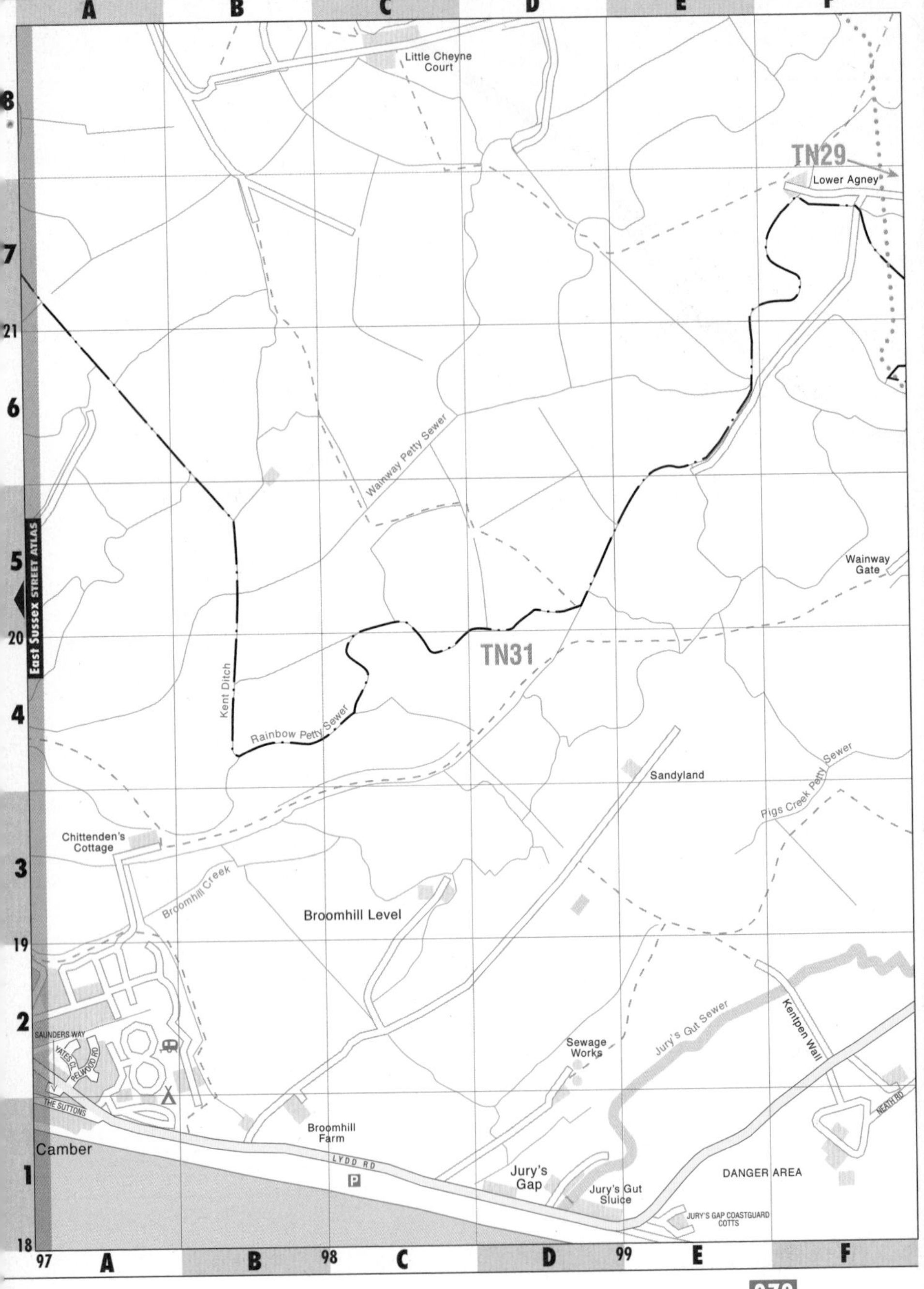

A B C D E F

8

7
21

6

5
20
East Sussex STREET ATLAS

4

3
19

2

1
18
97 A B 98 C D 99 E F

Little Cheyne
Court

TN29
Lower Agney

Wainway
Gate

Warvey Petty Sewer

TN31

Kent Ditch

Rainbow Petty Sewer

Sandyland

Pigs Creek Petty Sewer

Chittenden's
Cottage

Broomhill Creek

Broomhill Level

Jury's Gut Sewer

Kentpen Wall

Saunders Way

The Suttons

Camber

Broomhill
Farm

LYDD RD

Sewage
Works

Jury's
Gap

Jury's Gut
Sluice

DANGER AREA

Jury's Gap Coastguard
Cotts

HEADS RD

371
376

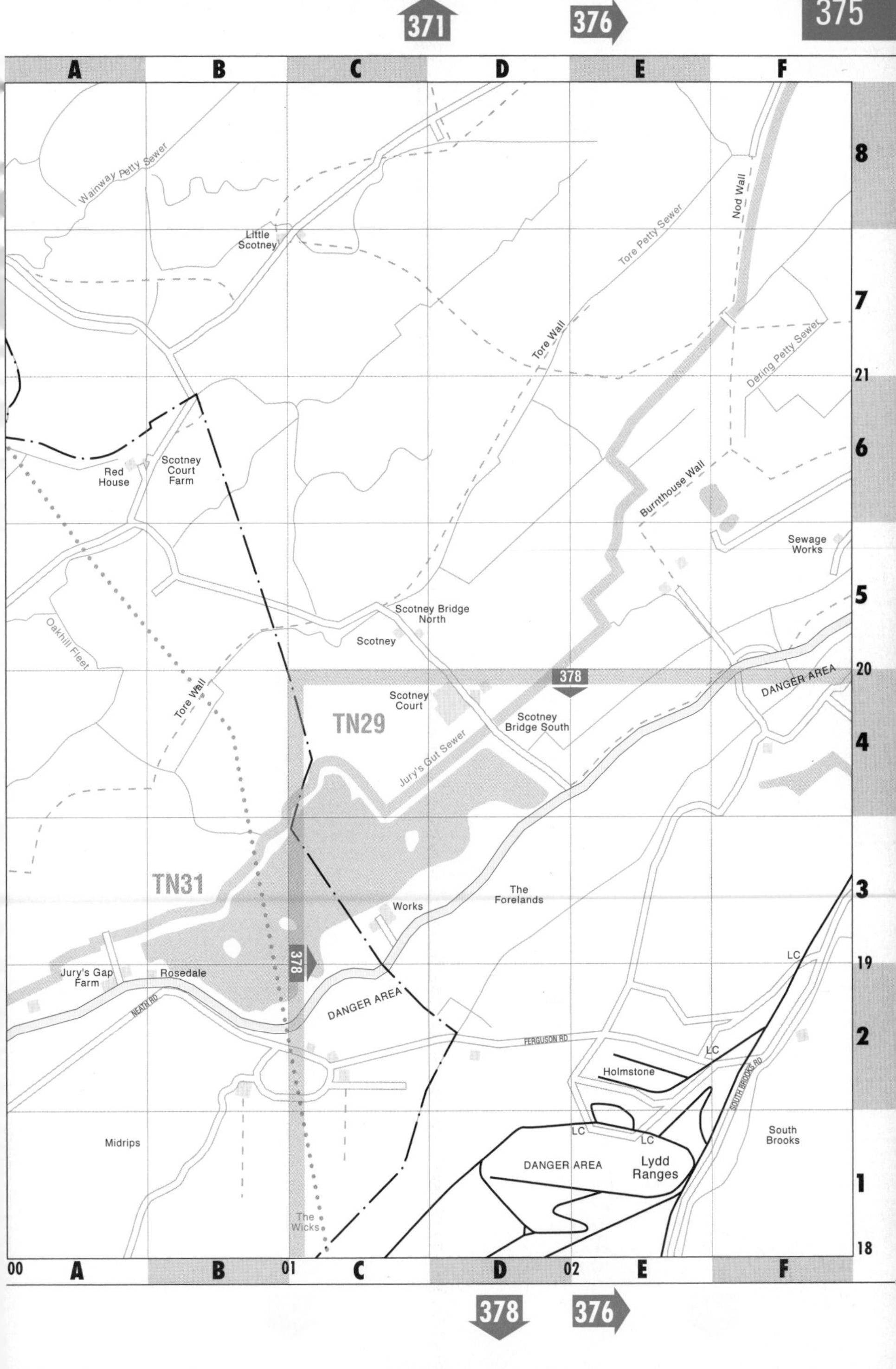
A
B
C
D
E
F
8
7
21
6
5
20
4
3
19
2
1
18
00
01
02
Wainway Petty Sewer
Little Scotney
Tore Petty Sewer
Nod Wall
Tore Wall
Dering Petty Sewer
Red House
Scotney Court Farm
Burnthouse Wall
Sewage Works
Scotney Bridge North
Scotney
Oakhill Fleet
Tore Wall
Scotney Court
TN29
Scotney Bridge South
378
DANGER AREA
Jury's Gut Sewer
TN31
The Forelands
Works
LC
Jury's Gap Farm
Rosedale
NEATH RD
DANGER AREA
FERGUSON RD
LC
Holmstone
SOUTH BROOKS RD
South Brooks
Midrips
LC
LC
DANGER AREA
Lydd Ranges
The Wicks

378
376

375
372

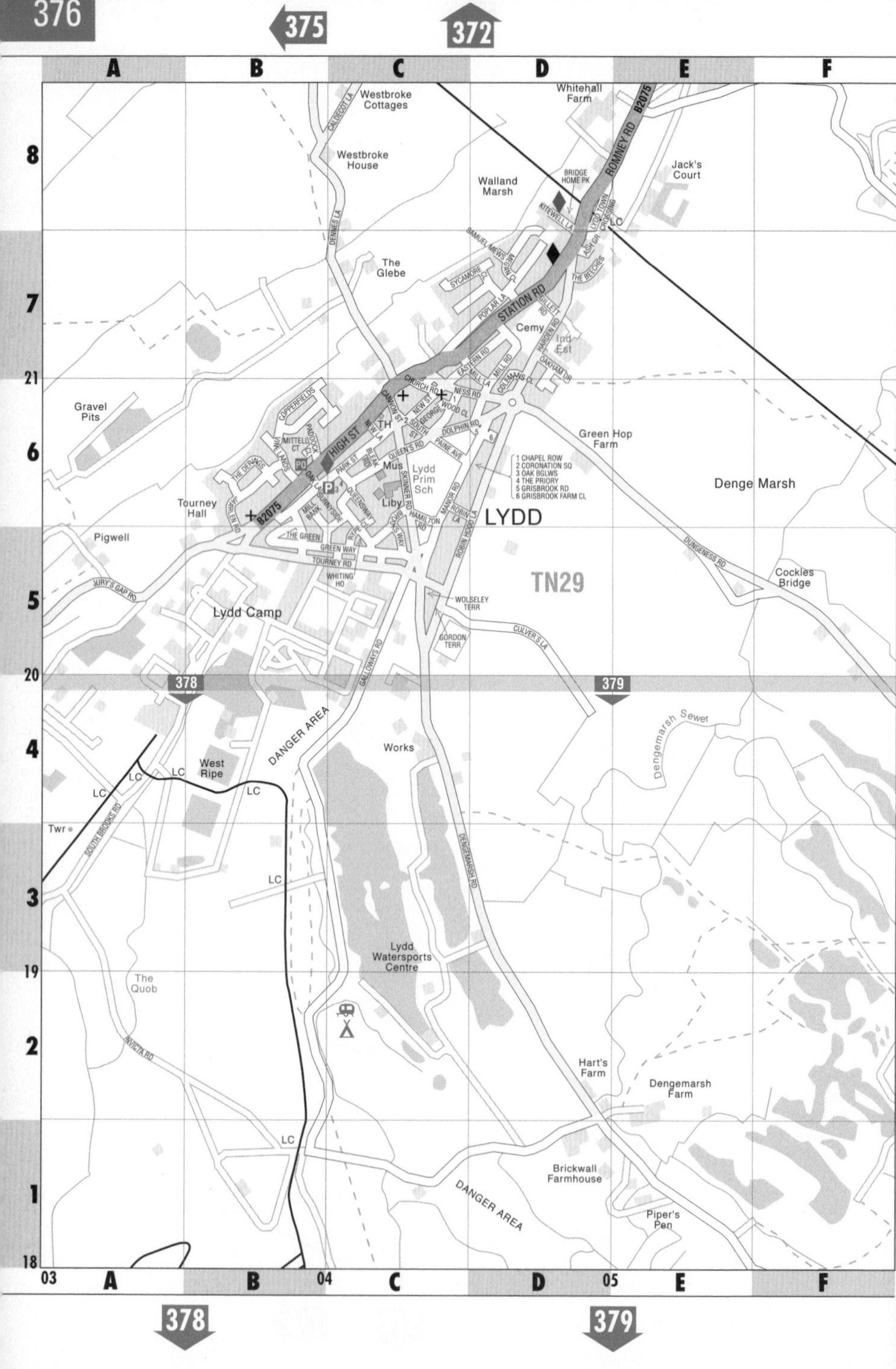
Westbroke Cottages
Westbroke House
Whitehall Farm
Walland Marsh
Jack's Court
BRIDGE HOME PK
ROMNEY RD
B2075
KITEWELL LA
LYDD TOWN CROSSING
The Glebe
STATION RD
Cemy
Ind Est
Gravel Pits
HIGH ST
LYDD
TN29
Green Hop Farm
Denge Marsh
1 CHAPEL ROW
2 CORONATION SQ
3 OAK BGLWS
4 THE PRIORY
5 GRISBROOK RD
6 GRISBROOK FARM CL
Tourney Hall
Pigwell
Mus
Lydd Prim Sch
Liby
Cockles Bridge
DUNGENESS RD
JURY'S GAP RD
Lydd Camp
TOURNEY RD
WHITING HO
WOLSELEY TERR
GORDON TERR
CULVER'S LA
GALLOWAYS RD
DANGER AREA
Works
West Ripe
Dengemarsh Sewer
SOUTH BROOKS RD
Twr
DENGEMARSH RD
Lydd Watersports Centre
The Quob
INVICTA RD
Hart's Farm
Dengemarsh Farm
Brickwall Farmhouse
Piper's Pen

378
379

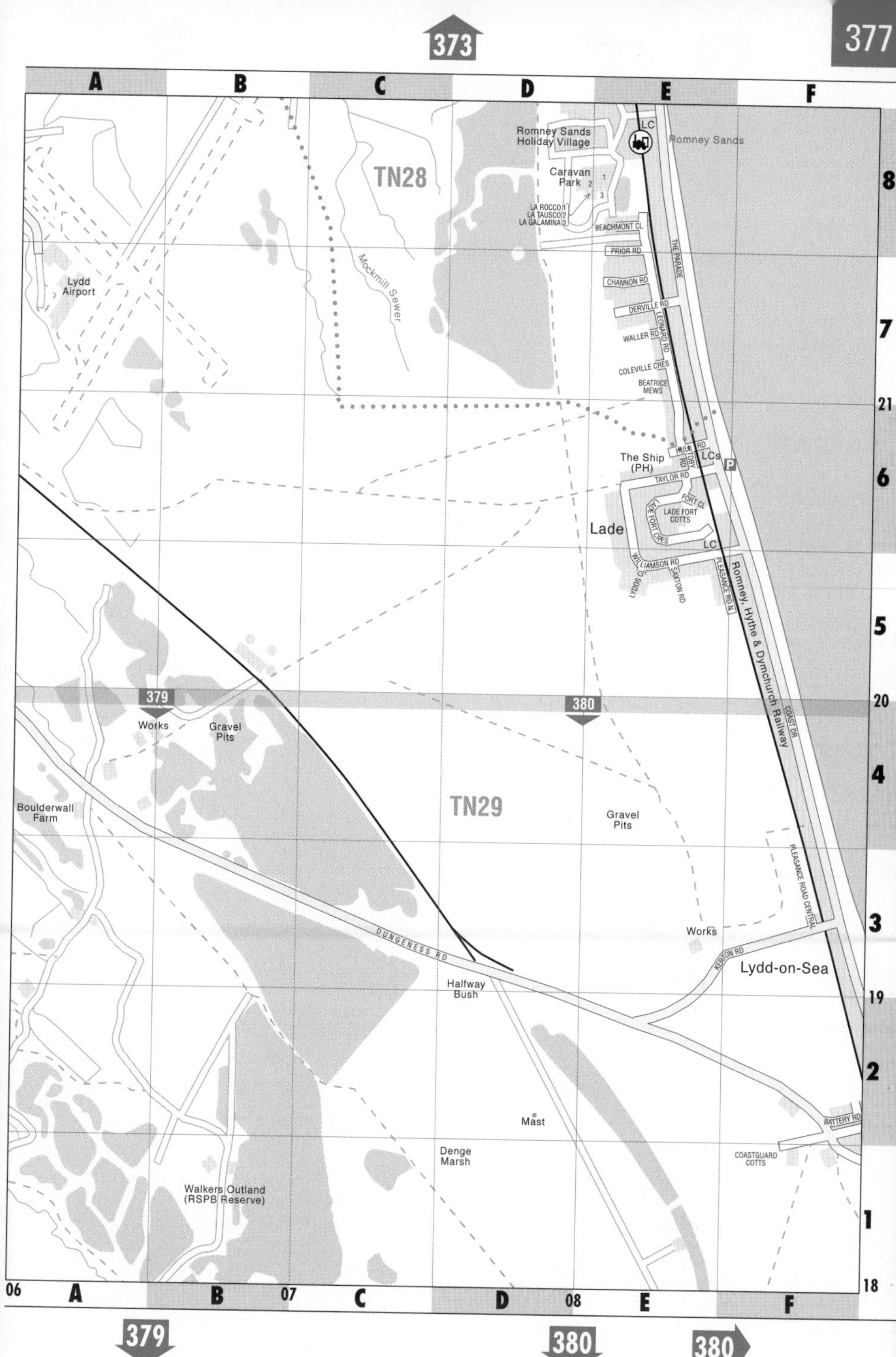

A B C D E F

8

TN28

Romney Sands
Holiday Village

LC

Romney Sands

Caravan
Park

LA ROCCO
LA TAUSCO
LA GALAMINA

BEACHMONT CL

PRIOR RD

Lydd
Airport

CHANNON RD

DERVILLE RD

WALLER RD

COLEVILLE CRES

BEATRICE
MEWS

THE PARADE

7

21

Mockmill Sewer

The Ship
(PH)

LCs

P

6

TAYLOR RD

FORT CL

LADE FORT
COTTS

Lade

FORT CRES

LAMSON RD

SEATON RD

LC

COAST DR

Romney, Hythe & Dymchurch Railway

PLEASANCE ROAD S.

5

20

379

380

Works

Gravel
Pits

TN29

Gravel
Pits

PLEASANCE ROAD CENTRAL

4

Boulderwall
Farm

Works

3

DUNGENESS RD

KERTON RD

Lydd-on-Sea

19

Halfway
Bush

2

Mast

BATTERY RD

Denge
Marsh

COASTGUARD
COTTS

Walkers Outland
(RSPB Reserve)

1

06 **A** **B** 07 **C** **D** 08 **E** **F** 18

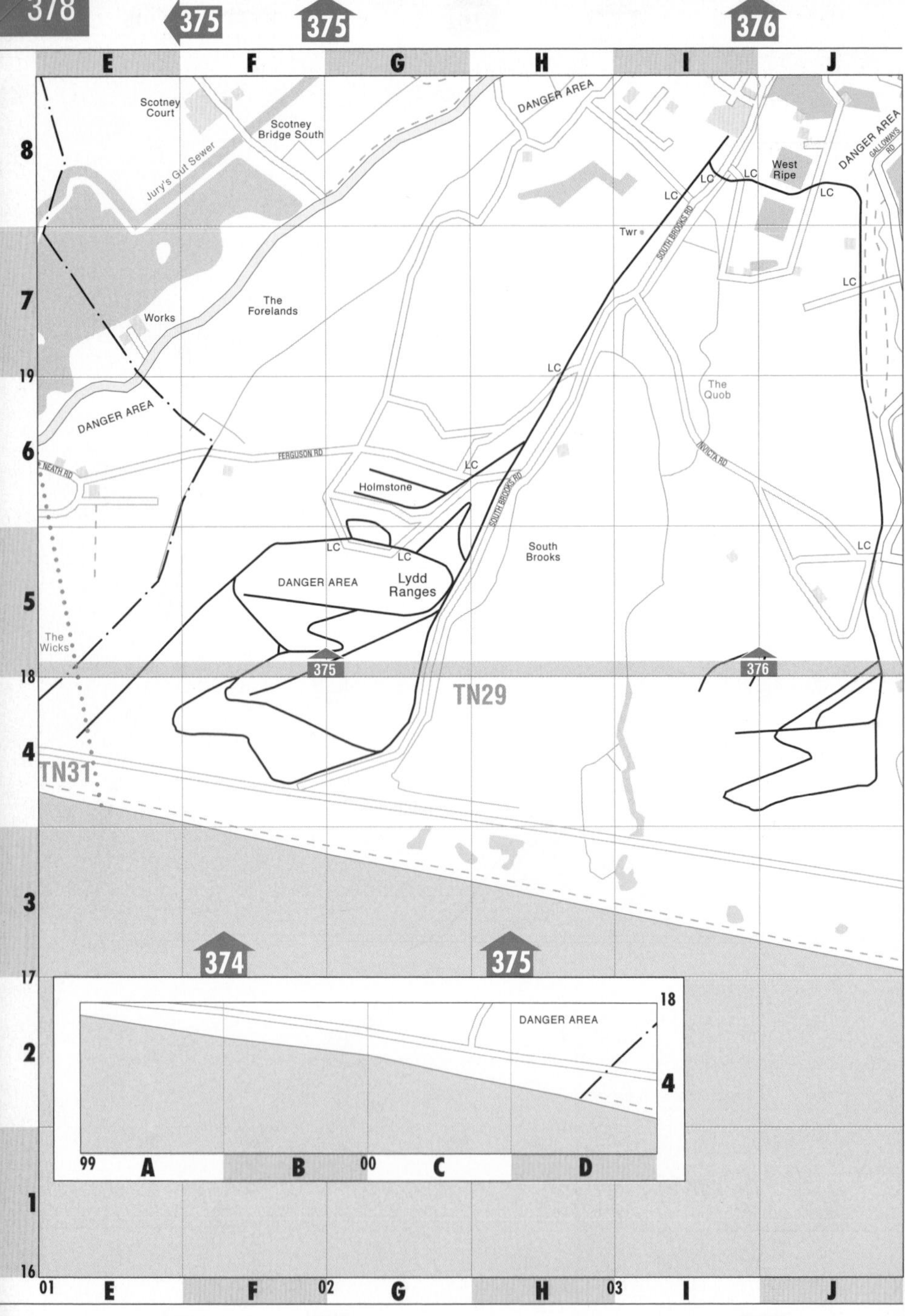
375
375
376
E
F
G
H
I
J
Scotney Court
Scotney Bridge South
DANGER AREA
DANGER AREA
GALLOWAYS RD
Jury's Gut Sewer
West Ripe
LC
Twr
SOUTH BROOKS RD
The Forelands
Works
8
7
19
6
5
18
4
3
17
2
1
16
The Quob
DANGER AREA
FERGUSON RD
NEATH RD
INVICTA RD
Holmstone
South Brooks
DANGER AREA
Lydd Ranges
The Wicks
TN29
TN31
374
375
DANGER AREA
99
A
B
00
C
D
01
02
03

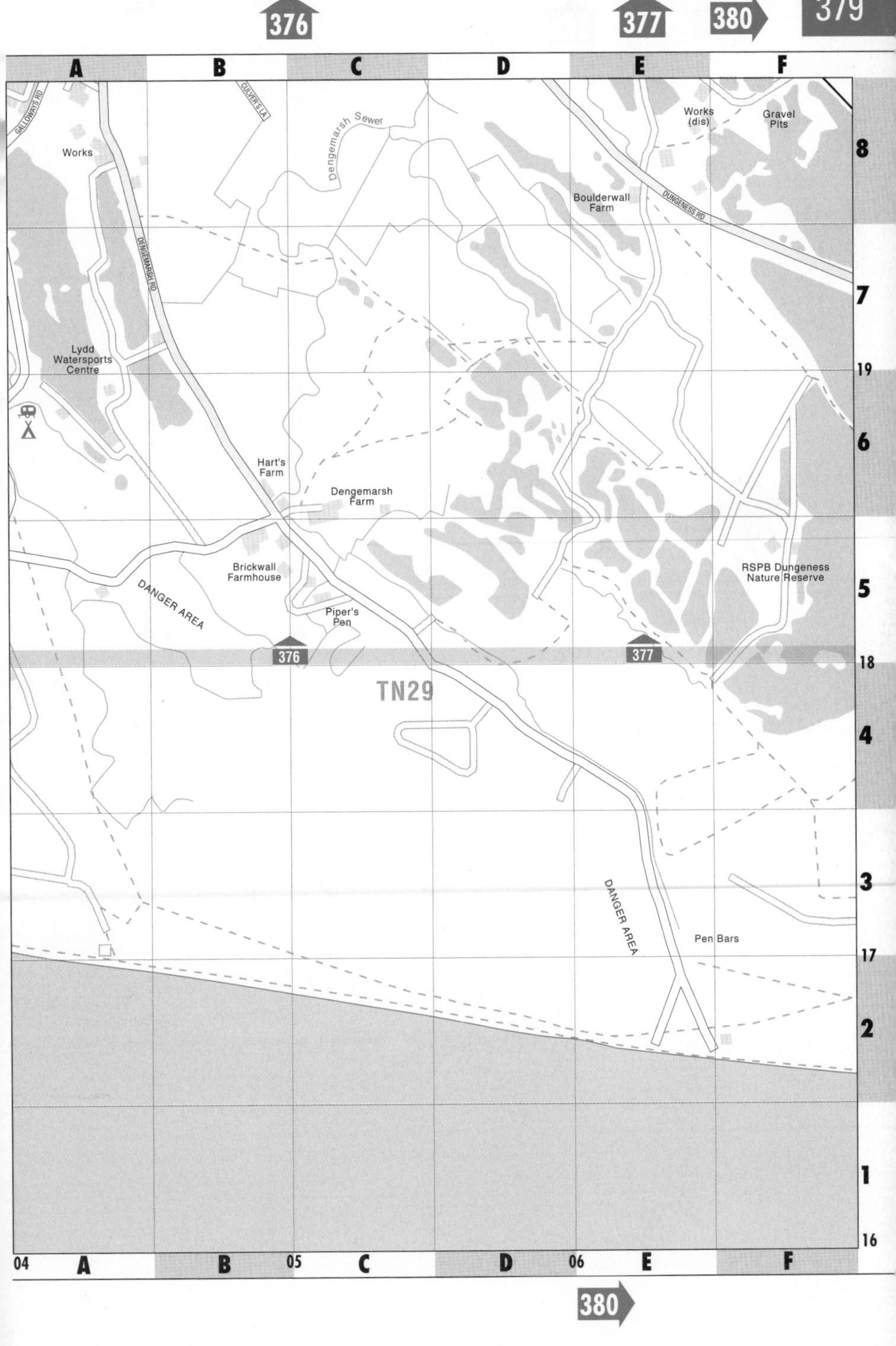

A B C D E F

8
7
19
6
5
18
4
3
17
2
1
16

Works

Dengemarsh Sewer

Works (dis)

Gravel Pits

Boulderwall Farm

DUNGENESS RD

Lydd Watersports Centre

Hart's Farm

Dengemarsh Farm

Brickwall Farmhouse

Piper's Pen

DANGER AREA

376

TN29

377

RSPB Dungeness Nature Reserve

DANGER AREA

Pen Bars

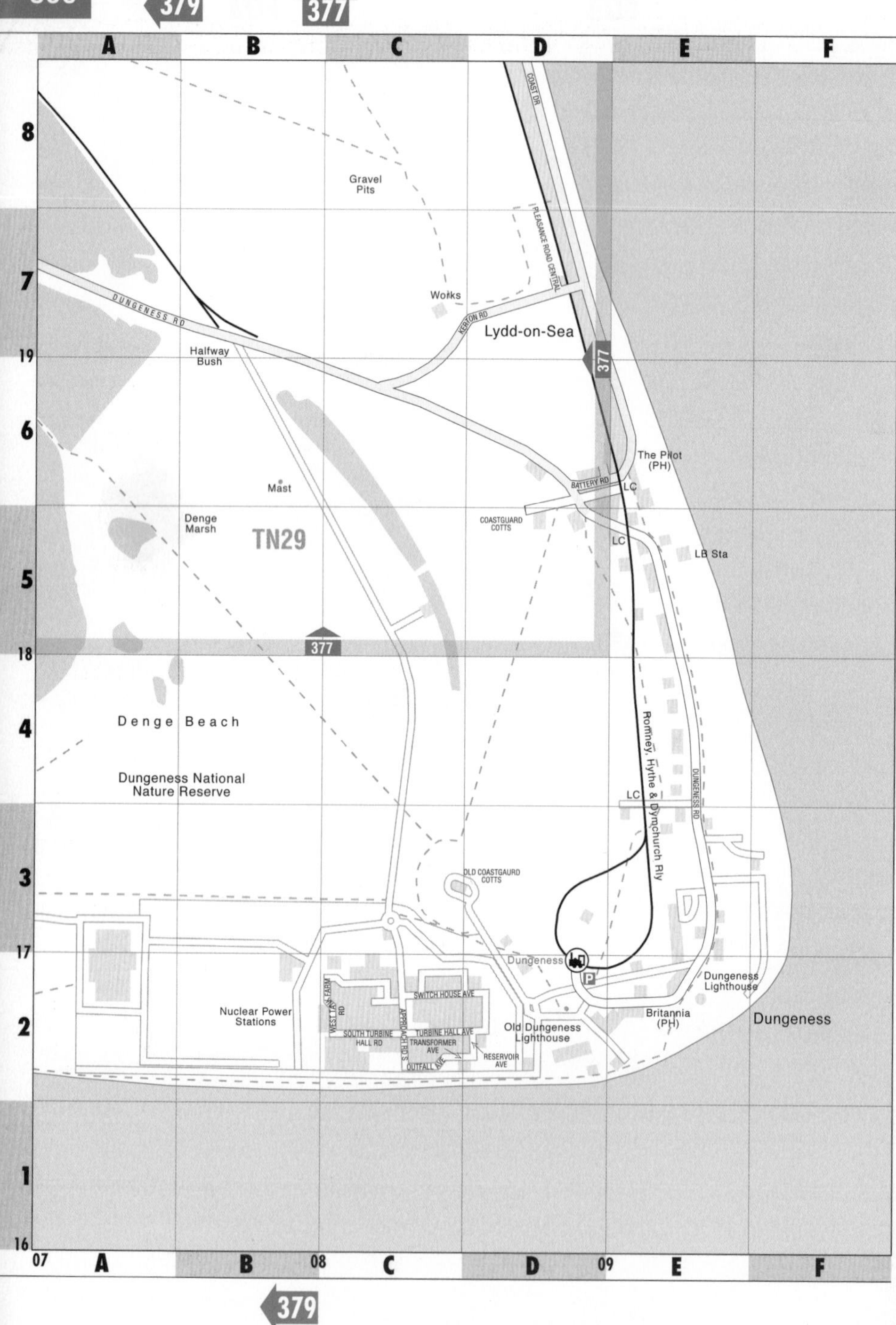

379

377

A B C D E F

8

Gravel
Pits

7

DUNGENESS RD

Works

KERTON RD

PLEASANCE ROAD CENTRAL

COAST DR

Lydd-on-Sea

19

Halfway
Bush

377

6

Mast

The Pilot
(PH)

BATTERY RD

LC

Denge
Marsh

TN29

COASTGUARD
COTTS

LC

LB Sta

5

18

377

4

Denge Beach

Dungeness National
Nature Reserve

Romney, Hythe & Dymchurch Rly

DUNGENESS RD

LC

3

OLD COASTGAURD
COTTS

17

Dungeness

P

Dungeness
Lighthouse

2

Nuclear Power
Stations

WEST LADE FARM
RD

SOUTH TURBINE
HALL RD

S. TER. PUMP RD

SWITCH HOUSE AVE

TURBINE HALL AVE

TRANSFORMER
AVE

OUTFALL

RESERVOIR
AVE

Old Dungeness
Lighthouse

Britannia
(PH)

Dungeness

1

16

379

Church Rd **6** Beckenham BR2..........**53** C6

Place name	Location number	Locality, town or village	Postcode district	Page and grid square
May be abbreviated on the map	Present when a number indicates the place's position in a crowded area of mapping	Shown when more than one place has the same name	District for the indexed place	Page number and grid reference for the standard mapping

Public and commercial buildings are highlighted in magenta. Places of interest are highlighted in blue with a star★

Abbreviations used in the index

Acad	**Academy**	Comm	**Common**	Gd	**Ground**	L	**Leisure**	Prom	**Prom**
App	**Approach**	Cott	**Cottage**	Gdn	**Garden**	La	**Lane**	Rd	**Road**
Arc	**Arcade**	Cres	**Crescent**	Gn	**Green**	Liby	**Library**	Recn	**Recreation**
Ave	**Avenue**	Cswy	**Causeway**	Gr	**Grove**	Mdw	**Meadow**	Ret	**Retail**
Bglw	**Bungalow**	Ct	**Court**	H	**Hall**	Meml	**Memorial**	Sh	**Shopping**
Bldg	**Building**	Ctr	**Centre**	Ho	**House**	Mkt	**Market**	Sq	**Square**
Bsns, Bus	**Business**	Ctry	**Country**	Hospl	**Hospital**	Mus	**Museum**	St	**Street**
Bvd	**Boulevard**	Cty	**County**	HQ	**Headquarters**	Orch	**Orchard**	Sta	**Station**
Cath	**Cathedral**	Dr	**Drive**	Hts	**Heights**	Pal	**Palace**	Terr	**Terrace**
Cir	**Circus**	Dro	**Drove**	Ind	**Industrial**	Par	**Parade**	TH	**Town Hall**
Cl	**Close**	Ed	**Education**	Inst	**Institute**	Pas	**Passage**	Univ	**University**
Cnr	**Corner**	Emb	**Embankment**	Int	**International**	Pk	**Park**	Wk, Wlk	**Walk**
Coll	**College**	Est	**Estate**	Intc	**Interchange**	Pl	**Place**	Wr	**Water**
Com	**Community**	Ex	**Exhibition**	Junc	**Junction**	Prec	**Precinct**	Yd	**Yard**

Index of localities, towns and villages

A

Abbey Wood 3 B3
Ackholt 211 A4
Acol 81 B3
Addington 126 C3
Adisham 210 D8
Aldington 330 A6
Aldington Frith 329 D6
Aldon 126 B1
Alkham 276 C1
Allhallows 9 D1
Allhallows-on-Sea 9 D3
Allington 161 D8
Ansdore 239 F6
Anvil Green 239 C8
Aperfield 118 F2
Appledore 361 C7
Appledore Heath 347 C1
Arpinge 306 C3
Ash New Ash Green 91 E5
Ash Sandwich 147 D2
Ashbank 197 B7
Ashford 268 A2
Ashley 246 B5
Ashurst 283 D2
Avery Hill 12 C1
Aycliff 310 B5
Aylesford 128 E2
Aylesford Green 300 F7
Aylesham 210 F5

B

Badgers Mount 88 B1
Badlesmere 170 C1
Bagham 205 D8
Baker's Cross 320 E4
Balls Green 311 C5
Banner Farm 286 C2
Bapchild 102 E3
Barden Park 221 F1
Barfrestone 211 E1
Barham 209 F1
Barking 3 B8
Barming Heath 161 A3
Barnehurst 14 D4
Barnes Cray 15 B3
Barnes Street 224 A4
Barnsole 179 B6
Barrow Green 103 D3
Barrowhill 331 D7
Barrow Hill 268 A3
asted 156 F4
ay View 49 D2
eacon Hill 343 A5
eal's Green 341 A4
Bean 35 C5
Bearsted 163 B4
Beaver 300 B7
Beckton 2 A8
Bedmonton 165 E8
Bekesbourne 176 D4
Bekesbourne Hill 176 B5
Bells Yew Green 314 F5
Beltinge 77 E4
Beltring 225 A4
Belvedere 4 B2
Benenden 342 E6
Benover 226 A6
Berry's Green 119 B3
Bessels Green 153 D3
Best Beech Hill 336 B3
Bethersden 297 E5
Betsham 35 F4
Betteshanger 213 C6
Bewlbridge 317 D1
Bexley 13 C3
Bexleyheath 13 F4
Bexon 134 B4
Bickley 52 F7
Bicknor 133 C2
Bidborough 253 D3
Biddenden 294 E2
Biddenden Green 264 B2
Biggin Hill 118 E3
Bilsington 329 C1
Bilting 237 E7
Birchden 312 D5
Birchett's Green 337 F3
Birchington 80 E7
Bircholt Forstal 302 E8
Birchwood Corner 55 C8
Birling 127 C6
Bishopsbourne 209 B5
Bishop's Down 285 E3
Bishopstone 77 F5
Bitchet Green 155 D1
Blackfen 13 A1
Blackheath Park 11 A3
Blackhurst 286 F5
Bladbean 241 F2
Blean 142 A6
Bliby 328 F8
Blooden 210 E8
Bluetown 135 B1
Blue Town 28 B2
Bluewater 35 A8
Bobbing 101 A7
Bockhanger 268 C6
Bodiam 355 D1
Bodsham 271 D8
Bogden 228 C2
Bogle 136 B8
Bonnington 329 F3
Borden 101 B3
Borough Green 156 F8
Borstal 63 B2
Bossingham 241 A6
Bossington 177 E3
Botolph's Bridge 353 A7
Bottom Pond 134 D2
Bough Beech 218 F2
Boughton Aluph 237 A5
Boughton Green 195 B3
Boughton Lees 236 E3
Boughton Malherbe 232 A8
Boughton Monchelsea 195 B3
Boughton Street 140 A3
Bow Arrow 16 B1
Bowmans 32 F8
Boxley 130 D2
Boyden Gate 112 C8
Brabourne 303 B8
Brabourne Lees 302 D5
Bramling 177 C6
Branbridges 225 A5
Brandfold 290 F3
Brasted 152 C3
Brasted Chart 185 B7
Brattle 347 A8
Breach 99 F8
Bredgar 134 A6
Bredhurst 98 B1
Brenchley 289 B8
Brenzett 363 A3
Brenzett Green 363 C6
Bridge 176 A1
Brissenden Green 297 F3
Broad Ford 290 C4
Broadoak 134 E5
Broad Oak Ashford 301 C1
Broad Oak Sturry 143 D7
Broadstairs 84 C5
Broadstone 231 D4
Broad Street
Hoo St Werburgh 41 B5
Broad Street Lyminge 305 C5
Broad Street Maidstone 164 B6
Broad Street Sellindge 303 F5
Broad Tenterden 345 B4
Broadwater Down 313 E7
Broadway 234 B6
Bromley 52 B6
Bromley Common 52 E3
Bromley Green 327 E6
Brompton 64 A5
Bromstone 83 E3
Brook 270 B5
Brookland 370 D8
Brooklands 33 F7
Brooks End 80 E4
Brook Street Tenterden 346 E8
Brook Street Tonbridge 254 A8
Broomfield Herne Bay 77 D1
Broomfield Kingswood 197 D5
Broom Hill Ash 146 B1
Broom Hill Orpington 53 F2
Broom Street 106 D2
Buckhurst 294 C5
Buckland 278 C2
Buckland Valley 278 C4
Buck's Cross 87 F5
Bullingstone 284 F7
Bullockstone 110 D8
Burham 95 E1
Burmarsh 352 C5
Buttsole 180 B1
Bybrook 268 D5

C

Cage Green 222 C4
Camber 374 A1
Camden Hill 292 F2
Camden Park 286 C2
Canning Town 1 B8
Canterbury 174 C7
Capel 255 F5
Capel Cross 290 C5
Capel-le-Ferne 308 B2
Capstone 97 E7
Castle Hill 257 E1
Cellarhill 103 C1
Chainhurst 227 A4
Chalk 38 A7
Chalksole 276 C4
Chalkwell 101 D4
Challock 203 B1
Chambers' Green 265 C4
Channel Tunnel
Terminal 334 B8
Charcott 220 A3
Charing 234 D8
Charing Heath 233 C6
Charing Hill 201 D1
Charlton 11 D8
Chartham 173 E2
Chartham Downs 173 D1
Chartham Hatch 173 D6
Chart Hill 229 B8
Chart Sutton 196 B1
Chartway Street 197 C1
Chatham 63 E5
Chattenden 40 F4
Cheeseman's Green 300 F2
Chelsfield 87 E5
Cheriton 334 D6
Cherry Orchard 161 B4
Chesley 100 A3
Chestfield 75 E1
Chestnut Street 100 E4
Chevening 152 F8
Chiddingstone 251 C7
Chiddingstone
Causeway 219 F2
Chiddingstone Hoath 251 A2
Chilham 205 C7
Chillenden 211 F8
Chilmington Green 299 C5
Chipstead 153 C5
Chislehurst 53 B7
Chislehurst West 30 A2
Chislet 112 D5
Chislet Forstal 112 B5
Christian Fields 37 C4
Church Hougham 309 B5
Church Street Higham 21 C1
Church Street Whitstable 74 F1
Church Whitfield 278 B8
Clapham Hill 108 D5
Clap Hill 329 F7
Clarendon 310 B6
Claygate 258 D6
Clement Street 33 D2
Cliffe 22 B5
Cliffe Woods 40 B7
Cliffs End 116 D6
Cliftonville 51 D2
Cobbarn 312 F3
Cobham 60 F6
Cockshot 340 F1
Cock Street 195 D2
Coldblow 32 D7
Coldharbour 188 F1
Cold Harbour Lenham 200 F6
Cold Harbour
Sittingbourne 100 F7
Coldred 245 A3
Coldred Street 245 A2
Colliers' Green 291 F2
Collier Street 258 C8
Colt's Hill 256 B4
Congelow 225 F7
Conyer 103 F5
Cooling 22 F5
Coolinge 334 F4
Cooling Street 22 D2
Coombe 179 F8
Cooper's Corner 218 F8
Cooper Street 148 B4
Coppins' Corner 234 A6
Cop Street 147 E4
Cousley Wood 337 C7
Cowden 282 A6
Cowden Pound 250 B2
Coxheath 194 C2
Crabble 277 F2
Cranbrook 320 C6
Cranbrook Common 293 A2
Crayford 14 D1
Creekmouth 2 F8
Crockenhill 55 D3
Crockham Hill 184 C2
Crockhurst Street 255 C6
Crofton 86 D8
Cross-at-Hand 228 E1
Crossways 16 D3
Crouch 157 B4
Crowdleham 123 D2
Crundale 238 D7
Cudham 119 D4
Culmers 106 E1
Culverstone Green 92 E2
Curteis' Corner 295 A3
Curtisden Green 291 C5
Custom House 1 C7
Cuxton 62 B2
Cyprus 2 B6

D

Danaway 100 C3
Dane Street 204 F6
Daniel's Water 298 D7
Darenth 34 B4
Dargate 140 E7
Darland 97 E8
Dartford 15 E2
David Street 93 B5
Davington 138 A8
Deal 215 E6
Deans Bottom 133 C5
Deans Hill 133 D6
Dean Street 194 D7
Deerton Street 104 A2
Denny Bottom 285 E4
Densole 307 A8
Denstroude 141 C8
Denton Folkestone 243 B3
Denton Gravesend 37 E8
Derringstone 242 E7
Derry Downs 54 D3
Detling 131 B1
Devil's Den 229 B3
Ditton 128 C1
Doddington 167 E7
Donkey Street 352 D5
Dover 310 F7
Downe 119 A8
Dryhill 153 B3
Dumpton 83 E2
Dungate 135 B3
Dungeness 380 F2
Dunkirk 140 D3
Dunkirk End 366 B7
Dunk's Green 190 A6
Dunn Street Gillingham 131 A8
Dunn Street Westwell 235 E5
Dunton Green 153 E8

Durgates 336 E5
Durlock 179 B8
Durrant Green 324 B6
Dymchurch 366 C7

E

Each End 148 B1
East Barming 160 F1
Eastchurch 48 E3
East End Benenden 322 C3
East End Headcorn 263 B4
East Farleigh 194 B7
East Hill 90 B1
East Langdon 247 A1
Eastling 168 F6
East Malling 160 A7
East Malling Heath 159 E4
East Peckham 224 F6
Eastry 180 A2
East Stourmouth 113 E1
East Street Addington 126 E3
East Street Sandwich 148 A2
East Studdal 246 D7
East Tilbury 20 C7
East Wickham 13 A7
Eastwood 231 C6
Eaton Lands 333 C3
Eccles 128 F6
Eddington 76 F3
Edenbridge 217 D1
Egerton 232 F4
Egerton Forstal 232 D1
Elham 273 F5
Elmstead 29 D2
Elmsted 271 F6
Elmstone 146 E5
Elmstone Hole 231 E8
Elms Vale 310 A7
Elphicks 318 A8
Eltham 11 E1
Elvington Eythorne 212 C1
Elvington Hawkinge 306 E2
Eridge Green 313 B3
Erith 4 C1
Erriottwood 135 F3
Etchinghill 305 C3
Ewell Minnis 276 E3
Exted 273 E5
Eyhorne Street 164 C2
Eynsford 89 D7
Eythorne 245 C8
Eythorne Green 245 D7

F

Fairbourne Heath 198 B1
Fairfield 83 E4
Fairseat 125 C7
Falconwood 12 E3
Farnborough 86 D5
Farningham 56 F2
Farthing Common 304 D5
Farthing Green 229 E1
Farthingloe 309 F5
Farthing Street 85 F2
Faversham 138 A5
Fawkham Green 91 B8
Felderland 180 F4
Fenn Street 24 B4
Ferndale 286 D5
Fernleigh 101 C2
Field Green 355 E8
Fig Street 187 A7
Finglesham 214 B8
Fir Toll 265 C6
Fishinghurst 319 F7
Five Oak Green 256 B7
Five Wents 196 D2
Fleet-Downs 34 D7
Flemings 179 D6
Flimwell 339 C3
Folkestone 335 F4
Folly Town 270 F7
Foord 335 D6
Foots Cray 31 B2
Force Green 151 D4
Ford 111 E8
Fordcombe 284 B5
Fordwich 144 A4
Forstal 129 B2
Fostall 140 A7
Fosten Green 322 D6
Four Elms 218 A5
Four Throws 355 D8
Four Wents 341 B6
Foxendown 93 C8
Frant 314 C3
French Street 184 F6
Frindsbury 63 C8
Frinsted 166 C7
Frittenden 293 F7
Frogham 211 C2
Froghole 184 D3
Frogholt 333 F7
Further Quarter 296 C3

G

Garlinge 82 A8
Garlinge Green 206 E5
Gibralter 306 F3
Gillingham 64 D3
Gill's Green 340 F5
Glassenbury 319 E6
Goathurst Common 186 B5
Goat Lees 268 C8
Goddard's Green 321 F2
Godden Green 155 B3
Goddington 87 C7
Godington Park 267 E2
Godmersham 205 A2
Golden Green 223 F5
Gold Street 60 E4
Golford 321 B5
Golgotha 244 F6
Goodnestone Faversham 139 D7
Goodnestone Wingham 178 D2
Goose Green Biddenden 322 E8
Goose Green Hadlow 191 B2
Gore 180 B3
Goudhurst 318 F8
Grafty Green 231 F7
Grain 27 B6
Grange 65 B6
Gravel Castle 243 A8
Graveney 106 E2
Gravesend 19 B2
Grays 18 A7
Great Chart 267 C1
Great Mongeham 214 C3
Greatness 154 D6
Great Stonar 149 B4
Greatstone-on-Sea 373 E1
Greenhill 76 D2
Greenhithe 17 B2
Green Street Green Hartley 35 A2
Green Street Green Orpington 86 E4
Greenwich 1 A3
Greet 167 D3
Groombridge 312 C7
Grove 145 F8
Grove End 134 C7
Grove Green 162 E5
Grove Hill 145 D6
Grove Park 29 B5
Grubb Street 58 B8
Guilton 147 C1
Gun Green 341 C2
Gushmere 171 C8
Guston 278 E6

H

Hacklinge 181 C1
Hadlow 190 E1
Hadlow Stair 222 F4
Haffenden Quarter 296 A7
Haine 82 F2
Hale Birchington 80 B4
Hale Chatham 97 D8
Hales Place 143 A3
Hale Street 225 A7
Halfway Houses 46 E7
Halfway Street 244 D4
Halling 95 B5
Hall's Green 220 A7
Halstead 120 F6
Ham 180 F2
Ham Green Upchurch 66 F6
Ham Green Wittersham 359 C1
Hamlet of Shellness 73 E5
Hammerwood 281 B3
Hammill 179 E3
Hampton 76 B5
Hamstreet 349 B7
Harbledown 174 B8
Harbourland 162 B8
Hareplain 294 C4
Harman's Corner 101 A2
Harrietsham 198 D5
Hartley Cranbrook 319 F1
Hartley New Barn 58 F3
Hartley Green 58 E4
Hartlip 99 E5
Harvel 93 C3
Hassell Street 239 A2
Hastingleigh 271 B6
Haviker Street 226 E1
Hawkenbury Headcorn 261 D7
Hawkenbury Royal Tunbridge Wells 286 D2
Hawkhurst 341 A2
Hawkinge 307 C5
Hawksdown 248 B8
Hawley 33 F3
Hawthorn Corner 78 A3
Hayes 52 A2
Hazel Street Bredgar 133 A3
Hazel Street Horsmonden 289 F4
Hazelwood 119 D8
Headcorn 262 D4
Hearnden Green 230 B1
Hearts Delight 101 B1
Heath Side 32 F5
Heaverham 123 E2
Hempstead 98 A5
Hemsted 304 D8
Henhurst 60 E8
Henley Street 60 F3
Henwood Green 287 E6
Herne 111 B8
Herne Bay 76 E6
Herne Common 110 F6
Herne Pound 158 D2
Hernhill 140 B6
Heronden 179 F1
Hersden 111 F1
Hever 250 D6
Hextable 32 E1
Hickmans Green 140 A2
Hicks Forstal 111 A4
Higham 39 B4
Higham Wood 222 F6
High Brooms 286 C8
High Halden 324 D7
High Halstow 23 F3
Highstead 78 A1
Highsted 134 F7
Highstreet 107 F2
High Street 340 D2
Hildenborough 221 E6
Hilden Park 221 F4
Hillborough 78 A4
Hill Green 99 C1
Hill Hoath 251 C6
Hill Park 151 B4
Hill Street 271 F8
Hill Top 257 B1
Hinxhill 269 D1
Hoaden 146 F4
Hoath 111 F5
Hoath Corner 251 B3
Hockenden 55 B6
Hocker Edge 292 D2
Hockley 169 C3
Hodsoll Street 92 D2
Hogben's Hill 171 A6
Holborough 95 A2
Holland 183 A1
Hollingbourne 164 E2
Hollow Street 112 C4
Hollybushes 167 A8
Holtye 281 F3
Hone Sundridge 152 F3
Honey Hill 141 E8
Hoo 114 F6
Hook Green Lamberhurst 316 C4
Hook Green Meopham Station 60 A3
Hook Green Northfleet 36 A2
Hoo St Werburgh 41 F5
Horns Green 119 E2
Horn Street Folkestone 334 B4
Horn Street Snodland 127 D6
Horselees 140 A2
Horseshoe Green 250 E1
Horsmonden 290 A5
Horton 173 F3
Horton Kirby 57 D5
Hothfield 267 A7
Houghton Green 368 D2
How Green 218 C1
Hucking 132 E1
Hungershall Park 285 E2
Hunters Forstal 77 C1
Hunton 226 D8
Hurst Green Hawkhurst 354 B3
Hurst Green Oxted 183 B3
Hythe 333 D1

I

Ickham 145 C1
Ide Hill 185 F4
Iden 368 B4
Iden Green Goudhurst 319 C8
Iden Green Hawkhurst 342 D4
Ightham 156 D6
Igtham Common 156 A3
Istead Rise 59 E8
Ivychurch 363 E3
Ivy Hatch 156 A1
Iwade 68 D4

J

Joyden's Wood 32 F4
Jury's Gap 374 D1

K

Kearsney 277 D3
Kemsing 123 B2
Kemsley 68 E1
Kemsley Street 98 C2
Kenardington 348 A6
Kennington 268 E6
Kennington Lees 268 D7
Kent Hatch 184 B3
Kent Street 158 E2
Keston 85 D6
Keston Mark 85 D8
Kevingtown 54 E3
Keycol 100 E6
Key's Green 288 C4
Key Street 101 A5
Kidbrooke 11 C5
Kilndown 317 F3
Kingsdown Deal 248 D5
Kingsdown Lynsted 135 E4
Kingsdown Park 74 F3
Kings Farm 37 C5
Kingsgate 51 G1
Kings Hill 159 A2
Kingsland 265 C8
Kingsnorth Ashford 300 A4
Kingsnorth Hoo St Werburgh 42 D5
Kingston 209 D3
Kingswood 197 E3
Kipping's Cross 288 B5
Kippington 154 A1
Kit's Coty 129 C7
Knatts Valley 123 D8
Knaves Ash 111 C5
Knockhall 17 C1
Knockholt 120 B2
Knockholt Pound 120 D4
Knockmill 123 F7
Knowlton 212 C7
Knox Bridge 292 F6

L

Labour-in-vain 124 F5
Laddingford 225 E5
Lade 377 E6
Lamberhurst 317 B5
Lamberhurst Quarter 288 D1
Lane End 34 D3
Langhurst 216 E7
Langley 196 C4
Langley Heath 196 F4
Langton Green 284 E3
Larkfield 128 A2
Lashenden 294 F6
Leadingcross Green 199 C3
Leaveland 203 B8
Leaves Green 118 D8
Leeds 197 A7
Leigh 220 E1
Leigh Green 345 F6
Lenham 199 D5
Lenham Forstal 200 B1
Lenham Heath 233 B8
Lessness Heath 4 B1
Letts Green 119 F3
Lewisham 29 C6
Lewson Street 136 E7
Leybourne 127 D2
Leysdown-on-Sea 49 H2
Lidsing 97 F1
Lilyvale 302 F4
Limpsfield 183 A6
Linkhill 356 E4
Linton 194 F1
Little Bayham 315 F4
Little Betteshanger 213 E5
Littlebourne 176 E8
Little Chart 234 A1
Little Chart Forstal 266 C8
Little Houses 232 D2
Little Mill 224 D5
Little Mongeham 214 A2
Littlestone-on-Sea 373 F5
Liverton Street 198 F1
Locksbottom 86 B7
Lodge Lees 242 F4
London Beach 324 B5
Longfield 58 E7
Longfield Hill 59 D5
Longford 153 D6
Longlands 30 D5
Loose 194 F4
Loose Hill 194 F5
Lords Wood 97 C1
Lower Bitchet 155 C1
Lower Bush 61 F3
Lower Cousley Wood 337 E8
Lower Cox Street 131 D6
Lower Eythorne 245 B8
Lower Goldstone 147 F7
Lower Green Pembury 287 D8
Lower Green Rusthall 285 C5
Lower Halstow 67 C3
Lower Hardres 208 A6
Lower Hartlip 99 E4
Lower Haysden 253 D8
Lower Heppington 207 F8
Lower Herne 76 F1
Lower Higham 39 D6
Lower Island 74 C1
Lower Luddesdown 61 A2
Lower Newlands 104 A2
Lower Rainham 65 F3
Lower Stoke 25 C5
Lower Twydall 65 C5
Lower Upnor 41 A3
Lower Walmer 215 C4
Low Street 19 E8
Luddesdown 60 F1
Lunsford 127 E4
Luton 64 B2
Luxted 119 A5
Lydd 376 D6
Lydd Camp 376 B5
Lydden 276 E8
Lydd-on-Sea 380 D7
Lye Green 311 D1
Lymbridge Green 272 B4
Lyminge 305 B6
Lympne 332 A3
Lynsore Bottom 241 D8
Lynsted 136 A6

M

Macklands 66 A2
Madeira Park 286 B2
Maidstone 162 C3
Maltman's Hill 264 E3
Manston 82 E1
Maplescombe 90 B5
Marden 259 C5
Marden Beech 259 B3
Marden Thorn 259 F3
Margate 50 H2
Marine Town 28 E2
Markbeech 250 D2
Marley Barham 209 B1
Marley Deal 214 A8
Marlpit 195 E2
Marlpit Hill 217 C4
Marshborough 180 B7
Marsh Green 249 B5
Marshside 78 D1
Martin 247 B3
Martin Mill 247 C2
Martyr's Field 174 F7
Matfield 288 D8
Maxted Street 272 B6
Maxton 310 A6
Maypole Dartford 32 E7
Maypole Herne Bay 111 F6
Maypole Orpington 87 F4
Medhurst Row 218 A2
Meopham 93 B8
Meopham Green 93 A7
Meopham Station 60 B4
Meresborough 99 A5
Mereworth 191 D8
Merryman's Hill 47 C8
Mersham 301 E4
Middle Deal 215 C5
Middle Quarter 296 D1
Middle Stoke 25 B4
Milebush 259 E8
Mile Oak 257 C4
Mile Town 28 B1
Millbank Headcorn 262 B6
Millbank Herne Bay 111 F7
Mill Hill 215 A3
Mill Street 159 E7
Milstead 134 E2
Milton 19 D1
Milton Regis 101 C6
Minster Sheppey 47 B7
Minster Thanet 115 A6
Mockbeggar 104 B1
Modest Corner 253 E1
Molash 203 F4
Monk's Hill 295 C7
Monkton 114 D7
Moon's Green 359 A3
Moorstock 303 C2
Moor Street 99 B7
Morehall 334 F6
Mottingham 29 D6
Mott's Hill 312 A3
Mountain Street 205 B6
Mount Ephraim 285 F4
Mount Sion 286 A2
Mowshurst 217 E3
Munday Bois 264 F8
Murston 102 B5

N

Naccolt 269 E6
Nackington 175 A2
Napchester 246 C3
Nash Ash 146 F2
Nash Keston 85 A4
Nash Street 60 A7
Neames Forstal 171 E6
Nethercourt 117 A7
Nettlestead 192 D6
Nettlestead Green 192 B2
New Ash Green 91 F8
Newbarn 305 B4
New Barn 59 A7
Newbury 135 D4
Newbury's 337 B8
New Charlton 1 C2
Newchurch 350 E3
New Eltham 30 C6
Newenden 357 D3
Newham 1 C6
New House 36 F6
New Hythe 128 B4
Newingreen 332 A5
Newington Folkestone 334 A8
Newington Ramsgate 83 B1
Newington Sittingbourne 100 A6
Newland Green 264 D8
Newnham 168 C7
New Romney 373 A5
New Street 92 D5
Newtown 250 D4
New Town Ashford 300 D7
New Town Dartford 16 A1
New Town Halling 95 A6
New Town West Malling 159 A8
Noah's Ark 155 A8
Noke Street 40 B4
Nonington 211 D5
Northbourne 214 A4
North Cray 31 F5
Northdown 51 D1
North Elham 274 A6
North End 14 F6
Northfleet 18 D1
Northfleet Green 36 C3
Northgate 143 A1
North Halling 95 B8
Northiam 357 C1
North Lyminge 305 C7
North Stonar 149 B6
North Street Faversham 138 C1
North Street Hoo St Werburgh 24 E1
Northumberland Heath 14 C7
Northwood 83 C3
North Woolwich 2 B4

O

Oad Street 100 E1
Oare 105 A3
Ockley 341 A3
Offham 158 D8
Old Bexley 32 B8
Oldbury 156 B6
Old Romney 372 B7
Old Wives Lees 172 C3
Orchard Valley 333 B3
Orpington 54 C2
Osmers Hill 336 F7
Ospringe 138 B6
Otford 122 A3
Otham 196 B7
Otham Hole 196 B6
Otterham Quay 66 C3
Ottinge 273 D1
Out Elmstead 209 F2
Oversland 171 F7

P

Paddlesworth 306 C4
Paddock 202 E1
Paddock Wood 256 F8
Painter's Forstal 137 E3
Palmarsh 353 D7
Palmer's Green 289 D8
Palmstead 241 D5
Paramour Street 147 D7
Parkgate 323 B2
Park Wood Gillingham 98 D4
Park Wood Maidstone 195 E4
Parrock Farm 37 D4
Patrixbourne 176 B3
Payden Street 167 B1
Pearson's Green 257 F3
Peasmarsh 367 A2
Peckham Bush 224 E8
Pedlinge 332 D4
Peene 334 B8
Peening Quarter 359 B6
Pegwell 117 B5
Pell Bridge 337 A5
Pell Green 337 A7
Pembury 287 C6
Penenden Heath 162 B7
Pennypot 332 E1
Penshurst 252 B4
Pepper Hill 36 C5
Perry 146 C3
Perry Street 36 F8
Perrywood 171 C4
Pested 203 B4
Petham 207 B3
Pett Bottom 208 B5
Petteridge 288 F6
Pettings 92 B3
Petts Wood 53 D5
Pikefish 225 F3
Pinden 58 C7
Pineham 278 D8
Pipsden 341 D1
Pittswood 223 B8
Plaistow 29 A2
Platt 157 C7
Platt's Heath 198 E1
Plaxtol 189 E8
Plaxtol Spoute 190 A8
Pluckley 265 D7
Pluckley Thorne 265 B6
Plucks Gutter 113 F3
Plumstead 2 E2
Plumtree Green 262 A8
Pootings 217 E7
Postling 304 F2
Potman's Heath 358 E4
Potten Street 79 D3
Potters Corner 267 F6
Potter's Forstal 232 B2
Poundsbridge 284 D8
Poverest 54 A4
Powder Mills 221 E2
Pratling Street 129 C3
Pratt's Bottom 87 D1
Preston Ash 146 B6
Preston Faversham 138 D6
Priestwood 93 B5
Priestwood Green 93 C5
Primmer's Green 336 F5
Princes Park 97 B6
Printstile 253 A3
Puddledock 32 E2
Purfleet 16 A8
Putlands 256 F5
Pye Corner 231 A6

Q

Queenborough 46 A5
Queen Street 257 D7

R

Rabbit's Cross 228 E3
Radfall 109 C5
Radfield 103 A2
Rainham Essex 4 F8
Rainham Kent 65 E8
Ram Lane 234 E2
Ramsden 54 C1
Ramsgate 117 C4
Ramslye 285 D1
Ratling 211 A8
Reading Street Broadstairs 83 F7
Reading Street Tenterden 346 C2
Reculver 78 C7
Red Hill 159 F1
Red Street 36 B2
Rhode Common 172 A6
Rhodes Minnis 273 A3
Ridge Row 274 E1
Ridley 92 B4
Ringlestone Harrietsham 165 F4
Ringlestone Maidstone 161 E7
Ringwould 247 F5
Ripple 247 D8
Riseden Durgates 336 B1
Riseden Kilndown 318 A5
River 277 E1
Riverhead 153 E5

Riverview Park 37 E4
Robhurst 325 C2
Rochester 63 B6
Rockrobin 336 D6
Rodmersham 135 C8
Rodmersham Green 135 B7
Rolvenden 343 F4
Rolvenden Layne 344 B1
Romden 264 C1
Romford 287 F7
Roseacre 163 A4
Rosherville 18 E1
Rough Common 142 B3
Round Green 291 F4
Round Street 60 D5
Rowling 179 A2
Rowling Street 328 E6
Royal Tunbridge Wells 286 D3
Ruckinge 349 F8
Rushenden 45 F3
Rusthall 285 C4
Ruxley 31 E1
Ryarsh 126 F4
Rye Foreign 367 E1

S

St Ann's Green 259 F8
St Dunstan's 142 D1
St John's
Royal Tunbridge Wells 286 A5
St John's Sevenoaks 154 B5
St Lawrence 117 B8
St Leonard's Street 159 B6
St Margarets 34 D1
St Margaret's at Cliffe 280 A6
St Martin's 175 B8
St Mary Cray 54 B4
St Mary Hoo 24 D6
St Mary in the Marsh 365 B4
St Mary's Bay 366 A4
St Mary's Island 41 C1
St Michaels 324 B4
St Nicholas at Wade 79 E1
St Paul's Cray 54 A7
St Peter's 83 E5
St Radigund's 278 A2
Saint's Hill 284 A8
St Stephen's 142 F2
Saltwood 333 C4
Sandgate 334 E3
Sandhurst 356 C6
Sandhurst Cross 355 F4
Sandling 129 F1
Sandway 199 A3
Sandwich 149 B1
Sarre 113 D7
Satmar 308 D3
Seal 155 A6
Seasalter 108 A7
Seaton 145 D2
Seed 168 A6
Sellindge 303 D1
Selling 171 C6
Selson 180 A3
Selsted 275 B5
Sepham Heath 121 B6
Sevenoaks 154 D2
Sevenoaks Weald 187 B2
Sevington 301 B6
Shadoxhurst 327 A8
Shalmsford Street 173 B1
Shatterling 146 E1
Sheerness 28 C3
Sheerwater 146 F6
Sheldwich 170 C6
Sheldwich Lees 170 C5
Shelvin 243 C3
Shepherds Hill 171 A4
Shepherdswell or
Sibertswold 244 E5
Shepway 195 D8
Sherwood 286 E6
Shipbourne 189 C5
Shipland 265 D8
Shirkoak 326 A5
Sholden 214 F5
Shooters Hill 12 C6
Shoreham 121 F8
Shorne 38 E3
Shorne Ridgeway 38 E2
Shottenden 171 D1
Shover's Green 337 C1
Shuttlesfield 306 A6
Sibertswold or
Shepherdswell 244 E5
Sidcup 31 A3
Silver Street 133 F5
Silvertown 1 C4
Single Street 119 B4
Singleton 299 E7
Singlewell 37 D2
Sinkhurst Green 261 E2
Sissinghurst 321 B7
Sittingbourne 101 D8
Sixmile 272 D5
Skeete 304 D7
Slade 167 E1
Slade Green 15 B6
Slutshole 140 A5
Sly Corner 347 F5
Small Hythe 345 C1
Smarden 264 A1
Smarden Bell 263 D2
Smeeth 302 C4
Snargate 362 E6
Snipeshill 102 D4
Snodland 128 B7
Snoll Hatch 224 E5
Snowdown 211 A3
Sole Street Gravesend 60 C4
Sole Street Wye 239 B7
South Alkham 308 B8
South Ashford 300 A8
Southborough Bromley 52 F3
Southborough
Royal Tunbridge Wells 254 B1
South Darenth 57 D8
Southdowns 57 D7
Southernden 263 C8
Southfleet 36 A3
South Green 133 A5
South Stour 301 B1
South Street Biggin Hill 151 A8
South Street Meopham 92 F4
South Street Selling 171 F8
South Street Stockbury 132 C7
South Street Whitstable 109 A7
South Tankerton 75 A1
South Willesborough 300 E6
Sparrow's Green 336 F5
Speed Gate 90 F8
Speldhurst 285 B7
Stalisfield Green 201 D6
Standen 295 B5
Standen Street 342 D1
Stanford 304 B1
Stanhope 299 F6
Stansted 91 F1
Staple 179 A5
Staplehurst 260 D4
Staplestreet 140 A5
Statenborough 180 C4
Stede Quarter 295 E1
Stelling Minnis 240 F2
Stick Hill 250 A3
Stiff Street 133 E7
Stockbury 132 E8
Stocker's Head 201 F1
Stockland Green 253 C1
Stocks Green 221 B4
Stodmarsh 145 B6
Stoke 25 A3
Stone 16 F2
Stone Bridge 336 E6
Stonebridge Green 233 A4
Stone Cross
Aldington Frith 328 F6
Stone Cross
Langton Green 284 A2
Stone Cross Sandwich 180 E7
Stone Cross Wadhurst 337 A3
Stonecrouch 338 F6
Stonehall 276 F8
Stone Hill 303 A2
Stone in Oxney 360 F4
Stone Street 155 E2
Stonestreet Green 330 A7
Stowting 304 A8
Stowting Common 272 A4
Street End 207 F7
Strood Rochester 62 F7
Strood Tenterden 344 B5
Stubb's Cross 299 C2
Studdal 246 C7
Studd Hill 76 A4
Sturry 143 E6
Styants Bottom 155 F5
Summerfield 179 B4
Sundridge 29 C2
Sutton 247 A7
Sutton at Hone 34 A1
Sutton Valence 229 E6
Swalecliffe 75 E3
Swanley 55 E5
Swanley Village 56 B7
Swanscombe 17 D2
Swanton 191 A8
Swift's Green 263 E6
Swingfield Minnis 275 B3
Swingfield Street 275 E4

T

Tankerton 75 A3
Tatsfield 150 D7
Teasley Mead 283 C4
Temple Ewell 277 D6
Temple Hill 16 A3
Tenterden 345 C8
Teston 193 A8
Teynham 103 C3
Teynham Street 103 E4
Thamesmead 3 A5
Thanington 174 B6
The Brents 105 D1
The Chart Limpsfield 183 E5
The Chart Toys Hill 185 C5
The Crook 257 D1
The Down 317 A3
The Forstal 301 D3
The Harbour 229 E5
The Leacon 348 D7
The Lees 203 A1
The Moor 354 F8
The Quarries 195 C4
The Quarter
Headcorn 264 B5
The Quarter
Staplehurst 260 E1
The Quarter
Tenterden 345 A4
The Stocks 360 A3
The Valley 201 D8
Thong 38 A2
Three Chimneys 294 B2
Three Legged Cross 338 D3
Throwley 169 E4
Throwley Forstal 169 D1
Thurnham 163 D8
Thurston Park 74 E1
Ticehurst 338 E2
Tickenhurst 179 D1
Tickham 136 D6
Tilbury 19 B4
Tilmanstone 213 A3
Timberden Bottom 88 D1
Titsey 150 B2
Tollgate 157 A8
Tonbridge 222 A2
Tonge Corner 102 F7
Tong Green 169 B1
Tovil 161 E1
Tower Hamlets 310 B8
Townland Green 326 A1
Toy's Hill 185 C3
Trench Wood 222 B7
Trottiscliffe 126 A5
Troy Town Brook 270 B5
Troy Town Edenbridge 216 F5
Tudeley 255 B7
Tudeley Hale 223 C1
Tunstall 134 D8
Turnden 320 B4
Turner's Green 336 F6
Tutt Hill 235 A1
Twitham 178 E6
Twitton 121 E4
Twydall 65 B2
Tylden 295 E7
Tyler Hill 142 E6

U

Ulcombe 230 F7
Underdown 206 B8
Underling Green 227 F2
Underriver 188 A5
Union Street 339 B3
Upchurch 66 F4
Upper Bush 61 F2
Upper Deal 215 B4
Upper Eythorne 245 C7
Upper Fant 161 D3
Upper Goldstone 147 E5
Upper Halling 94 E5
Upper Harbledown 141 F1
Upper Harvel 93 C3
Upper Hayesden 253 C6
Upper Rodmersham 135 C6
Upper Ruxley 32 A1
Upper Tolhurst 338 A2
Upper Upnor 40 F1
Upper Walmer 215 B1
Upstreet 112 D3
Upton 83 F4
Upton Wood 244 E2

V

Vicarage Green 337 A5
Vigo Village 126 B8

W

Wadhurst 337 A4
Wainscott 40 D3
Walderslade 96 F1
Walderslade Bottom 97 A2
Wallcrouch 337 F1
Walmer 215 C2
Walmestone 146 D3
Walter's Green 283 E6
Waltham 239 E6
Wanden 264 B7
Wanshurst Green 260 A7
Warden 49 D4
Warehorne 348 D6
Ware Street 163 B5
Warmlake 196 D1
Warren Street 200 D7
Waterham 107 C2
Wateringbury 192 D7
Waterman Quarter 262 D2
Watts's Cross 221 B7
Way 115 E7
Wayfield 97 A8
Weardale 185 B5
Weavering Street 162 F5
Weddington 147 E3
Weed's Wood 96 F3
Weller's Town 251 D5
Well Hill 88 B4
Welling 13 B4
Well Street 159 E6
Westbere 144 C7
Westbrook 50 E1
West Cliffe 279 D6
Westcourt 37 E6
West Cross 343 D4
West Dumpton 83 D2
West End Doddington 167 D7
West End Herne Bay 110 B8
Westenhanger 332 B6
Westerham 151 C1
Western Heights 310 C6
West Farleigh 193 D6
Westgate-on-Sea 50 B2
West Heath 13 D8
West Hougham 308 F5
West Hythe 332 B1
West Kingsdown 90 F2
West Langdon 246 D3
West Malling 159 C7
Westmarsh 147 B7
West Minster 46 A7
West Peckham 191 A6
West Stourmouth 113 D2
West Street Eastry 180 F1
West Street Lenham 166 E1
West Thurrock 17 B8
West Tilbury 19 E8
Westwell 235 E3
Westwell Leacon 234 D4
Westwood Barham 241 E8
Westwood Broadstairs 83 B5
Westwood Hartley 35 D1
Wetham Green 66 F5
Whatsole Street 271 F5
Wheelbarrow Town 272 F8
Whetsted 224 E1
Whitehall 83 C1
Whitehill 58 D7
White Oak 55 F7
White Post 283 D7
Whitfield 278 A7
Whitstable 74 C3
Wichling 167 C5
Wickhambreaux 145 B2
Wick Hill 294 F8
Widmore 52 E7
Wierton 228 F8
Wigmore 98 B4
Wilgate Green 169 F6
Willesborough 300 F8
Willesborough Lees 269 B1
Willington 162 E1
Wilmington 33 C4
Wilsley Green 320 D7
Wilsley Pound 320 E8
Winchet Hill 291 B6
Windmill Hill 37 A7
Wingham 178 B7
Wingham Green 177 F7
Wingham Well 177 E6
Wingmore 242 B2
Winterbourne 172 A8
Wissenden 296 F7
Withersdane 269 F8
Withyham 311 A3
Wittersham 359 D3
Wolverton 276 F2
Wombwell Park 36 D6
Womenswold 210 D2
Woodchurch Margate 81 F3
Woodchurch Tenterden 326 A2
Woodland 304 F8
Woodlands 123 C6
Woodnesborough 180 C6
Wood's Green 336 F8
Woodside Green 199 F8
Woodstock 134 E6
Woolage Green 243 F8
Woolage Village 210 F1
Woolwich 2 B3
Wooton 243 C1
Wormshill 166 A7
Worms Hill 291 B5
Worsenden Green 294 D2
Worten 266 F3
Worth 181 B4
Wouldham 95 D5
Wrotham 124 F2
Wrotham Heath 126 A1
Wye 237 F1

Y

Yalding 192 F1
Yelsted 99 A1
Yewtree Green 258 B1
Yopps Green 156 E1
Yorkletts 107 F2

20/20 Ind Est ME16 161 C8

A

Aaron Hill Rd E6 2 A8
Abbess Cl [12] E6 1 E8
Abbeville Ho ME1 63 C4
Abbey Brewery Ct ME19 159 C8
Abbey Cl Deal CT14 215 A5
Minster (Sheppey) ME12 47 D6
Abbey Court Specl Sch ME2 62 E8
Abbey Cres DA17 4 A2
Abbey Ct
Westgate-on-S CT8 81 D7
Whitstable CT5 75 A3
Abbey Dr DA2 32 E6
Abbey Fields Ct ME13 138 E7
Abbey Fields ME13 138 E7
Abbey Gate Cotts ME14 129 F2
Abbey Gate CT11 117 B5
Abbey Gdns
Canterbury CT2 143 A2
Chislehurst BR7 53 A8
Abbey Gr
Minster (Thanet) CT12 115 C5
Ramsgate CT11 117 B5
Woolwich SE2 3 B2
Abbeyhill Rd DA15 31 C6
Abbey Ho SE2 3 D1
Abbey Life Ct E13 1 B8
Abbey Lodge SE12 29 B4
Abbey Mount DA17 3 F1
Abbey Pl Dartford DA1 15 D2
Faversham ME13 138 D8
Abbey Rd
Bexley DA6,DA7 13 E3
Erith DA17 3 E3
Faversham ME13 138 D8
Gillingham ME8 65 A2
Gravesend DA12 37 E7
Kearsney CT16 277 D4
River CT15,CT17 277 D1
Rochester ME2 62 F8
Swanscombe DA9 17 C2
Abbey Sch The
Faversham ME13 138 C5
Westgate-on-S CT8 81 E8
Abbey St ME13 138 D8
Abbey Terr SE2 3 C2
Abbeyview Dr ME12 47 B6
Abbey Way TN24 269 A1
Abbey Wood Golden Jubilee Cvn site SE2 3 C1
Abbey Wood Rd
Kings Hill ME19 159 A5
Woolwich SE2 3 C2
Abbey Wood Sch SE2 3 A3
Abbey Wood Sta SE2 3 C3
Abbots Barton Wlk CT1 175 B7
Abbotsbury Hts CT2 143 B4
Abbots Cl BR5 53 C1
Abbots Court Rd ME3 41 F4
Abbots Field
Gravesend DA12 37 C2
Maidstone ME16 161 B2
Abbots Hill ME13 137 E5
Abbot's Hill CT11 117 E6
Abbots Pl CT1 142 F1
Abbots Rd ME13 138 F7
Abbots The CT17 310 C8
Abbots Wlk TN25 237 E2
Abbotswood Cl [7] DA17 3 E3
Abbott Ct [13] CT20 335 E6
Abbott Rd
Borough Green TN15 156 F7
Folkestone CT20 335 E6
Abbotts Cl
Rochester ME1 63 B3
Swanley BR8 56 A5
Woolwich SE28 3 C6
Abbott's Wlk DA7 13 D7
Abbott Way TN30 345 C7
Aberdeen Cl CT3 112 D3
Aberdeen Ho [9] ME15 195 E7
Aberford Gdns SE18 11 E6
Abergeldie Rd SE12 11 B1
Abery St SE18 2 E2
Abigail Cres ME5 97 A1
Abingdon Gr CT3 112 D3
Abingdon Mews ME19 159 C8
Abingdon Rd ME16 160 F2
Abingdon Way BR6 87 B6
Abinger Cl BR1 52 E6
Abinger Dr ME5 97 D2
Absalom Ct ME8 65 C2
Acacia Cl BR5 53 D4
Acacia Ct DA11 37 A8
Acacia Dr CT3 144 D8
Acacia Rd
Dartford DA1 33 D7
Stone DA9 16 E1
Acacia Terr ME10 101 C4
Acacia Way DA15 30 F7
Acacia Wlk BR8 55 D7
Academy Dr ME7 64 F1
Academy Pl SE18 12 A6
Academy Rd SE18 11 F7
Acer Ave TN2 314 C8
Acer Rd TN16 118 D3
Achilles Rd ME5 97 C2
Ackerey Ct TN23 299 F6
Ackholt Rd CT3 211 A5
Acland Cl SE18 12 D7
Acol Hill CT7 81 B4
Acorn Cl Chislehurst BR7 30 C3
Acorn Cl *continued*
Five Oak Green TN12 256 B7
Hawkinge CT18 307 C4
Kingsnorth TN23 300 C3
Acorn Gr ME20 160 D8
Acorn Ind Pk DA1 15 A2
Acorn Pl ME15 195 E6
Acorn Rd Crayford DA1 14 F2
Gillingham ME7 64 F4
Acorns The
Sevenoaks TN13 154 A4
Smarden TN27 263 F1
Acorn St ME12 28 C1
Acorn Terr ME9 66 E2
Acorn Trad Ctr RM20 17 E8
Acorn Way
Hurst Green TN19 354 A3
Orpington BR6 86 B6
Acorn Wharf Rd ME1 63 C6
Acott Fields ME18 225 F8
Acre Cl ME1 63 E1
Acre Ct CT17 310 C8
Acre Gr ME2 95 A4
Acres Rise TN5 338 E1
Acre The CT16 277 F8
Acton La TN30 359 F4
Acton Pl ME18 193 A1
Acton Rd CT5 74 D2
Acworth Ho [1] SE18 12 B8
Acworth Pl DA1 15 C1
Adam Cl ME17 194 D3
Adam Ct [1] CT9 51 B2
Adams Cl TN30 324 B1
Adamson Rd E16 1 A7
Adams Sq DA6 13 E4
Ada Rd CT1 174 D6
Adbert Dr ME15 194 B4
Adcot Wlk [7] BR6 86 F6
Addelam Cl CT14 215 A4
Addelam Rd CT14 215 A4
Adderley Gdns SE9 30 A4
Addington La ME19 126 B4
Addington Pl CT11 117 E6
Addington Rd
Margate CT9 50 J2
Sittingbourne ME10 101 E3
Addington Sq CT9 50 J2
Addington St
Margate CT9 50 J2
Ramsgate CT11 117 D6
Addiscombe Gdns CT9 50 J1
Addiscombe Rd CT9 51 A1
Addison Cl
Orpington BR5 53 C3
West Malling ME19 127 F1
Addison Cotts TN30 359 D3
Addison Dr SE12 11 B2
Addison Rd BR2 52 D4
Addlestead Rd TN12 224 E6
Adelaide Dr ME10 101 C4
Adelaide Gdns
Halfway Houses ME12 46 E6
[19] Ramsgate CT11 117 E6
Adelaide Ho
Deal CT14 215 D6
Sheerness ME12 28 H1
Adelaide Pl CT1 174 F8
Adelaide Rd
Chislehurst BR7 30 B3
Elvington CT15 212 B1
Gillingham ME7 64 C4
Tilbury RM18 18 F5
Adelaide The ME3 39 C6
Aden Terr [1] ME14 162 A7
Adie Rd TN28 373 D3
Adisham CE Prim Sch CT3 210 D8
Adisham Downs Rd CT3,CT4 177 B2
Adisham Dr ME16 161 B7
Adisham Gn ME10 101 F8
Adisham Rd
Bekesbourne CT4 176 E3
Wingham CT3 178 A4
Womenswold CT4,CT3 210 C2
Adisham Sta CT3 210 E8
Adisham Way CT9 51 C1
Admaston Rd SE18 12 C8
Admers Wood DA13 126 B8
Admiral Cl BR5 54 D5
Admiral Ct ME7 64 D6
Admiral Moore Dr ME20 128 F1
Admirals Ct E6 2 B7
Admiral Seymour Rd SE9 11 F3
Admiral's Wlk ME4 63 F7
Admirals Wlk
Chatham ME5 97 B3
Goddard's Green TN17 321 D2
Halfway Houses ME12 46 E6
Hythe CT21 333 C1
Swanscombe DA9 17 B2
Tenterden TN30 324 C1
Admiralty Cl ME13 138 B8
Admiralty Mews CT14 215 D4
Admiralty Rd ME2 40 F1
Admiralty Terr
[1] Chatham ME7 64 A7
Rochester ME2 40 F1
Admiralty Wlk CT5 108 A7
Admiral Way ME19 159 A1
Adrian Mews CT8 50 D1
Adrian Sq CT8 50 D1
Adrian St CT17 310 D7
Aerodrome Est ME14 131 E4
Aerodrome Rd
Bekesbourne CT4 176 E3
Hawkinge CT18 307 A4
Afghan Rd
Broadstairs CT10 83 F8
Chatham ME4 63 E4
Agate Cl E16 1 D7
Agaton Rd SE9 30 C6
Agester La CT4 243 A4
Agnes Cl E6 2 A6
Agricultural Mus Brook The* TN25 270 B5
Ailsa Mews ME1 62 F2
Ainsdale Cl
Folkestone CT19 335 B7
Orpington BR6 53 D1
Ainsley Way CT4 206 F8
Aintree Cl DA12 37 B5
Aintree Ho [1] ME15 195 F6
Aintree Rd ME5 97 C3
Airedale Cl
Dartford DA2 34 C7
Margate CT9 51 A1
Aireys The CT13 180 B6
Airfield View ME12 71 C8
Airport Ind Est TN16 118 D4
Airport Rdbt E16 1 D5
Aisher Rd SE28 3 C6
Aisher Way TN13 153 E6
Aisne Dr CT1 143 D1
Ajax Rd ME1 96 C8
Akehurst La TN13 154 C2
Alabama St SE18 12 E7
Alamein Ave ME5 96 F7
Alamein Cl CT15 278 F3
Alamein Gdns DA2 34 D8
Alamein Rd DA10 17 D1
Alanbrooke DA12 37 C8
Alan Cl DA1 15 C3
Alan Marre Ho SE7 11 D8
Alanthus Cl SE12 11 A1
Alaseun Terr ME12 47 A5
Alban Cres DA4 57 A1
Albany Cl Sidcup DA5 31 D8
Tonbridge TN9 254 D7
Albany Dr CT6 76 D4
Albany Hill TN2 286 C5
Albany Ho [15] CT17 310 D7
Albany Mews BR1 29 A2
Albany Park Sta DA14 31 D6
Albany Pl CT17 310 D7
Albany Rd Bexley DA17 13 F8
Capel-le-F CT18 308 C1
Chatham ME4 64 B2
Chislehurst BR7 30 B3
Gillingham ME7 64 D4
Rochester ME1 63 C4
Sidcup DA5 31 C8
Sittingbourne ME10 101 E3
Tilbury RM18 19 A6
Albany St ME14 162 B5
Albany Terr
Chatham ME4 63 E4
Gillingham ME7 64 D4
Albatross Ave ME2 62 C6
Albatross Cl E6 1 F8
Albatross St SE18 12 E7
Albemarle Rd
Ashford TN24 268 F1
Chatham ME5 97 C2
Alberta Cl CT16 278 B3
Alberta Rd DA8 14 C6
Albert Costain Ct [1] CT20 335 D5
Albert Cotts TN1 286 B4
Albert Ct
[8] Ramsgate CT12 117 E6
[9] Whitstable CT5 74 D2
Albert Ho SE28 2 C3
Albert La CT21 333 C1
Albert Manor ME7 64 B5
Albert Murray Cl DA12 37 C8
Albert Pl ME2 63 B7
Albert Rd Ashford TN24 268 B3
Broadstairs CT10 83 E8
Bromley,Bromley Common BR2 52 D4
Bromley,Mottingham SE9 29 E5
Canterbury CT1 175 B8
Capel-le-F CT18 308 C2
Chatham ME4 64 A3
Dartford DA2 33 C5
Deal CT14 215 C6
Dover CT16 278 D1
Erith DA17 3 F1
Folkestone CT19 335 D6
Gillingham ME7 64 C4
Hythe CT21 333 B1
Margate CT9 50 H2
Newham E16 1 F5
Orpington BR5 54 B3
Orpington,Green Street Green BR6 87 A5
Ramsgate CT11 117 F7
Rochester ME1 63 C3
Sidcup DA5 32 B8
Swanscombe DA10 17 F1
[3] Tonbridge TN9 222 B1
Albert Reed Gdns ME15 161 E2
Albert Row CT11 117 C5
Albert St
Maidstone ME14 161 F6
Ramsgate CT11 117 E6
Royal Tunbridge Wells TN1 286 B4
Whitstable CT5 74 D2
Albert Terr Deal CT14 215 C5
Margate CT9 50 I2
Minster (Sheppey) ME12 48 A5
Albert Wlk E16 2 B4
Albion Cl CT6 111 A8
Albion Cotts TN12 259 D5
Albion Ct
Ramsgate CT11 117 E6
[2] Woolwich SE18 1 E2
Albion Hill [7] CT11 117 E6
Albion Ho E16 2 B5
Albion La CT6 111 A8
Albion Mews CT11 117 F6
Albion Mews Rd [3] CT20 335 D4
Albion Mews TN1 286 C5
Albion Pl Ashford TN24 300 E7
Canterbury CT1 143 A1
Chattenden ME2 41 A3
Faversham ME13 138 C7
Hythe CT21 333 D2
Maidstone ME14 162 B4
Newington ME9 100 B6
Ramsgate CT11 117 E6
Albion Rd Bexley DA6 14 A3
Birchington CT7 81 A7
Broadstairs CT10 83 F6
Chatham ME5 97 B2
Deal CT14 215 D8
Eastry CT13 180 A2
Folkestone CT19 335 D6
Gravesend DA12 37 C8
Marden TN12 259 D5
Margate CT9 51 B3
Ramsgate CT11 117 F7
Royal Tunbridge Wells TN1 286 C5
Albion St CT10 84 B4
Albion Terr
Gravesend DA12 19 D1
Sittingbourne ME10 101 E6
Albion Villas [6] CT20 335 D4
Albion Way TN8 217 C4
Albright Ind Est RM13 4 F8
Albuhera Sq CT1 143 D1
Albury Ave DA7 13 E5
Albury Cl ME5 97 D2
Albyfield BR1 52 F6
Alchins Cotts ME17 194 E2
Alconbury DA6 14 B2
Aldeburgh Pl SE10 1 A2
Aldeburgh St SE10 1 A1
Alder Cl
Royal Tunbridge Wells TN4 254 D1
West Minst ME12 46 A8
Aldergate La CT21 331 C1
Alder Ho TN23 267 F1
Alder La TN17 343 C1
Alder Lodge TN4 285 E4
Alderman Cl DA1 32 E8
Aldermary Rd BR1 52 A8
Alderney Gdns CT10 83 E5
Alderney Rd DA8 15 A7
Alderney Way TN24 268 C7
Alder Rd
Folkestone CT19 335 C6
Sidcup DA14 30 F5
Alders Cotts TN12 256 A5
Aldersgrove Ave SE9 29 D5
Aldershot Rd ME5 97 A7
Alders Meadow TN9 221 F2
Alders Rd TN11,TN12 255 E6
Alders The ME18 191 D7
Alder Way BR8 55 D7
Alderwick Gr ME18 159 C3
Alderwood Prim Sch SE9 12 E1
Alderwood Rd SE9 12 D1
Aldington Cl ME5 97 B5
Aldington Cnr TN25 330 A6
Aldington La ME14 163 D8
Aldington Prim Sch TN25 330 A5
Aldington Rd
Greenwich SE18 1 D3
Lympne CT21 331 E3
Maidstone ME14 162 F4
Aldon Cl ME14 162 C6
Aldon Ct ME14 162 C6
Aldon La ME19 158 C8
Aldred Rd ME13 138 C6
Aldridge Cl CT6 76 B3
Aldwick Cl SE9 30 D5
Aldwych Cl TN10 222 D7
Alec Pemble Cl TN24 268 E5
Alefe Way ME9 68 D3
Alen Sq TN12 260 F4
Alers Rd DA6 13 D2
Alestan Beck Rd E16 1 D7
Alexander Cl Hayes BR2 52 A1
Sandwich CT13 180 F8
Sidcup DA15 12 E1
Alexander Cotts ME2 39 C6
Alexander Ct
Greenwich SE3 11 B5
[1] Rochester ME2 63 B8
[2] Royal Tunbridge Wells TN1 286 A4
[1] Sittingbourne ME10 101 E5
Alexander Dr ME13 138 B7
Alexander Gr ME18 159 A3
Alexander McLeod Prim Sch SE2 3 B1
Alexander Rd
Bexley DA7 13 D5
Chislehurst BR7 30 B3
Swanscombe DA9 17 C2
Alexandra Ave ME7 64 E4
Alexandra Cl
Sittingbourne ME10 101 E7
Swanley BR8 55 E7
Alexandra Corniche CT20,CT21 334 C3
Alexandra Ct CT21 333 A1
Alexandra Dr CT14 214 F3
Alexandra Gdns CT20 335 D4
Alexandra Glen ME5 97 A1
Alexandra Homes CT9 50 I1
Alexandra Hospl The ME5 130 A8
Alexandra Mews ME12 28 D2
Alexandra Pl [1] CT17 278 C1
Alexandra Rd
Biggin Hill TN16 150 B8
Birchington CT7 81 A5
Alexandra Rd *continued*
Broadstairs CT10 84 B4
Capel-le-F CT18 308 C2
Chatham ME4 64 B2
Deal CT14 215 D2
Erith DA8 14 F8
Gravesend DA12 37 E8
Kingsdown CT14 248 C5
Margate CT9 82 E8
Ramsgate CT11 117 D8
Sheerness ME12 28 D2
Tilbury RM18 18 F5
Tonbridge TN9 254 B8
Whitstable CT5 108 C8
Alexandra St
Folkestone CT19 335 E6
Maidstone ME14 161 F6
Newham E16 1 A8
Alexandra Terr CT9 50 I1
Alexandra Wlk DA4 57 E7
Alexandria Dr CT6 76 C5
Alex Hughes Cl ME6 127 F6
Alfan La DA2 32 D3
Alford Ho [6] SE18 12 B8
Alford Rd DA8 4 C1
Alford Snell Lodge TN2 286 D2
Alfred Cl
Canterbury CT1 174 C6
Chatham ME4 64 B2
Alfred Ho
Gravesend DA11 37 B6
[5] Northfleet DA11 36 F7
Alfred Mews CT14 215 D7
Alfred Pl DA11 36 F7
Alfred Rd
Ashford TN24 300 D7
Birchington CT7 80 D8
Canterbury CT1 174 C6
Dover CT16 278 B2
Erith DA17 3 F1
Gravesend DA11 37 B6
Greatstone-on-Sea TN28 373 D3
Hawley DA2 33 F4
Margate CT9 51 B1
Alfred Row CT14 215 D7
Alfred Sq CT14 215 D7
Alfred St RM17 18 C8
Alfriston Cl DA1 14 E1
Alfriston Gr ME19 159 C3
Alice Thompson Cl SE12 29 C6
Alicia Ave CT9 82 A8
Alicia Ho DA16 13 B6
Alison Cl Birchington CT7 81 B8
Newham E6 2 A7
Whitfield CT16 278 A6
Alison Cres CT16 278 A7
Alkerden La DA9,DA10 17 C1
Alkham Cl CT9 51 F2
Alkham Rd
Maidstone ME14 162 C5
Temple Ewell CT15, CT16 277 C4
Alkham Tower [9] BR5 54 C5
Alkham Valley Rd
Alkham CT15 276 E1
Hawkinge CT18,CT15 307 E4
Allan Cl TN4 285 C4
Allandale Pl BR6 87 D7
Allandale Rd TN2 286 D7
Alland Grange La CT12 81 E2
Allan Rd CT5 107 E6
Allard Cl BR5 54 C2
Allen Ave CT8 81 D7
Allenby Ave CT14 215 B5
Allenby Rd
Biggin Hill TN16 118 E2
Ramsgate CT12 83 C2
Woolwich SE28 2 C3
Allenby Wlk ME10 101 B5
Allen Cl ME5 97 C6
Allen Ct ME12 47 A5
Allendale Cl DA2 34 D7
Allendale St [2] CT19 335 D6
Allen Field TN23 299 F8
Allen Gardiner Ho TN2 286 C3
Allens La TN15,TN11 190 A7
Allens TN12 259 D5
Allen St ME14 162 B5
Allenswood Rd SE9 11 F5
Allhallows-on-Sea Est ME3 9 E4
Allhallows Prim Sch ME3 9 D2
Allhallows Rd
Lower Stoke ME3 25 C5
Newham E6 1 E7
Alliance Rd Newham E13 1 C8
Ramsgate CT11 117 F6
Woolwich SE18 13 A7
Alliance Way TN12 256 F6
Allington Cl DA12 37 F7
Allington Dr
Rochester ME2 62 E8
Tonbridge TN10 223 A5
Allington Gdns ME18 192 E7
Allington Prim Sch ME16 161 C7
Allington Rd
Gillingham ME8 65 A3
Orpington BR6 53 E1
Paddock Wood TN12 256 F7
Allington Way ME16 161 B6
Allison Ave ME7 64 E1
Allnutt Mill Cl [4] ME15 161 E2
Allotment La TN13 154 C5
All Saints' Ave CT9 50 H1
All Saints' CE Prim Sch ME4 64 A3
All Saints CE Prim Sch ME15 162 A
All Saints Cl DA10 17
All Saints' Cl CT5 74
All Saints Ind Est CT9 50
All Saints La [2] CT1 174
All Saints Rd
Allhallows ME3 9 D
Hawkhurst TN18 341
All Saints' Rd DA11 36
All Saints Rd
Royal Tunbridge Wells TN4 286
Sittingbourne ME10 102
All Saints Rise TN4 286 A
All Saints View ME13 106
All Souls' CE Prim Sch CT19 334
Allsworth Cl ME9 100
Alma Pl
[2] Canterbury CT1 143 A
Hadlow TN11 223
Ramsgate CT11 117
Rochester ME2 63 A
Alma Rd Eccles ME20 128
Folkestone CT20 334
Herne Bay CT6 77 C
Margate CT9 50
Orpington BR5 87
Ramsgate CT11 117
Sheerness ME12 28 C
Sidcup DA14 31 A
Swanscombe DA10 17
West Malling ME19 159 A
Almarina CT8 50 C
Alma St CT1 143 A
Alma Street Pas ME12 28 D
Alma St ME12 28 D
Alma The DA12 37 F
Almery Cotts ME17 229 E
Almond Cl
Ashford TN23 267 F
Broadstairs CT10 83 C
Bromley BR2 53 A
Whitstable CT5 75 D
Almond Ct CT4 173 E
Almond Dr BR8 55 D
Almond Gr ME7 98 A
Almond Ho [9] ME16 161 A
Almond Rd DA2 34 C
Almonds The ME14 163 A
Almond Tree Cl ME12 46 A
Almond Way BR2 53 A
Almon Pl ME1 63 D
Almshouse Rd ME13 202 C
Almshouses
[8] Canterbury CT1 175 A
Crockenhill BR8 55 D
Penshurst TN11 252 C
Sevenoaks TN13 154 C
[14] Tonbridge TN9 254 B
Yalding ME18 193 A
Alms Row TN16 152 B
Alnwick Ct [8] DA2 16 B
Alnwick Rd Eltham SE12 29 B
Newham E16 1 C
Alonso Ho [4] DA17 4 A
Alpha Cl ME3 42 D
Alpha Rd
Birchington CT7 81 A
Ramsgate CT11 117 D
Alpine Bsns Ctr E6 2 A
Alpine Copse [2] BR1 53 A
Alpine Way E6 2 A
Alsager Ave ME11 45 F
Alsike Rd DA18 3 E
Alsops Rd TN24 300 E
Alston Cl ME12 47 C
Altash Way SE9 30 A
Altbarn Ind Est ME5 130 C
Alton Ave ME19 159 A
Alton Cl DA5 31 E
Alton Cotts DA4 89 E
Alverstone Gdns SE9 30 C
Alvis Ave CT6 76 A
Alwold Cres SE12 11 C
Amage Rd TN25 270 C
Amage Road Cotts TN25 238 B
Amanda Cl ME5 96 F
Amar Ct SE18 2 F
Amardeep Ct SE18 2 F
Ambassador Gdns E6 1 F
Amber Cl ME9 103 D
Amber Ct ME7 64 D
Amber La ME17 196 A
Amberleaze Dr TN2 287 D
Amberley Cl
[2] Orpington BR6 86 F
Tonbridge TN9 254 A
Amberley Ct
Royal Tunbridge Wells TN4 286 C8
Sidcup DA14 31 C3
Amberley Rd SE2 13 D8
Amber Rise ME10 101 C
Amber Way ME17 196 B
Amblecote Cl SE12 29 B5
Amblecote Mdw SE12 29 B5
Amblecote Rd SE12 29 B5
Ambleside ME13 138 E6
Ambleside Rd DA7 14 A5
Ambleside ME10 102 C
Ambley Gn ME8 98 A8
Ambley Rd ME8 98 B8
Ambley Wood Nature Reserve* ME7,ME8 98 A8
Ambrook Rd DA17 4 A3
Ambrose Cl
Crayford DA1 15 A3
[6] Newham E6 1 F8
Orpington BR6 86 F7
Ambrose Hill ME5 64 C2

Amels Hill ME9 132 F8
Ames Ave ME14 163 A4
Amesbury Rd BR1 52 D6
Ames Rd DA10 17 E1
Ames Way ME18 159 B3
Amethyst Ave ME5 96 E6
Amherst Cl
Maidstone ME16 161 D4
Margate CT9 51 C1
Orpington BR5 54 A5
Amherst Dr BR5 54 A5
Amherst Hill
Chatham ME7 64 A6
Sevenoaks TN13 153 F4
Amherst Prim Sch TN13 153 E4
Amherst Rd
Rochester ME1 63 D3
Royal Tunbridge Wells TN4 286 A5
Sevenoaks TN13 154 B5
Amherst Redoubt ME4 64 A5
Amhurst Bank Rd TN2, TN11,TN12 255 F4
Amhurst Wlk SE28 3 A5
Amies Ho ME15 194 F3
Amos Cl Herne Bay CT6 77 C3
Sheldwich ME13 170 C5
Ampleforth Cl BR6 87 C6
Ampleforth Rd SE2 3 C4
Amsbury Rd ME15, ME17 194 B2
Amshurst Villas ME15 194 A4
Anatase Cl ME10 101 C7
Ancaster St SE18 12 E7
Anchorage Cl ME3 25 C3
Anchorage Flats TN12 257 A6
Anchorage Point Ind Est SE7 1 C3
Anchor Bay Ind Est DA8 15 A8
Anchor Bsns Pk ME10 102 B6
Anchor Bvd DA2 16 D3
Anchor Ct DA7 13 E6
Anchor Hill 4 CT9 50 J2
Anchor Ho E16 1 C7
Anchor & Hope La SE7 1 C2
Anchor Ho ME1 63 B4
Anchor La Deal CT14 215 C6
Sheerness ME12 27 F3
Sheerness ME12 28 A3
Anchor Rd ME1 63 C1
Ancona Rd SE18 2 D1
Ancress Cl CT2 143 A4
Andace Pk BR1 52 C8
Anderson Way DA17 4 B4
Andorra Ct BR1 52 C8
Andover Ave E16 1 D7
Andover Rd BR6 53 E1
Andover Wlk 12 ME15 195 F6
Andrew Broughton Way ME14 162 B4
Andrew Cl DA1 14 D2
Andrewes Gdns E6 1 E7
Andrew Manor ME7 64 C6
Andrew Rd TN4 286 C8
Andrews Cl
Orpington BR5 54 D6
Royal Tunbridge Wells TN2 286 D5
Andrews Pl DA2 32 E6
Andrews Wlk ME10 101 B5
Andrew Wells Ho 8 BR1 29 B1
Andringham Lodge 7 BR1 52 B8
Andwell Cl SE2 3 B4
Anemone Way CT6 110 E7
Anerley Cl ME16 161 D7
Angel Cotts ME8 66 A2
Angelica Dr E6 2 A8
Angel La TN9 222 B1
Angel Row TN18 356 B5
Angel Terr TN18 356 B6
Angel Wlk 4 TN9 222 B1
Angerstein Bsns Pk SE10 1 A2
Angle Rd RM20 17 D8
Anglesea Ave SE18 2 B2
Anglesea Pl 19 DA11 19 B1
Anglesea Rd
Orpington BR5 54 C3
Woolwich SE18 2 B2
Anglesey Ave ME15 195 A7
Anglesey Cl ME5 97 B7
Angley Ct TN12 290 A5
Angley Rd TN17 320 C6
Angley Sch Sports Coll TN17 320 C5
Angley Wlk
Cranbrook TN17 320 C6
Cranbrook TN17 320 D6
Anglia Ctr The RM13 4 E8
Anglian Ind Est IG11 3 A8
Anglo Saxon Ho DA12 37 E8
Angus Dr TN24 268 C7
Ankerdine Cres SE18 12 B6
Annandale Rd DA15 30 F8
Anna Pk CT7 80 F8
Anne Boleyn Cl ME12 48 E3
Anne Cl CT7 81 B7
Anne Green Wlk 8 CT1 143 B2
Anne of Cleves Rd DA1 15 D1
Anne Roper Cl TN28 373 E6
Annesley Rd SE3 11 B6
Anne's Rd CT10 84 C7
Annetts Hall TN15 157 A8
Annex The BR8 56 B6
Annie Rd ME6 127 F6
Ann's Rd CT11 117 E8
Ann Stroud Ct SE12 11 A2
Ann St SE18 2 D2
Annvera Ho 2 ME7 64 C7
Ansell Ave ME4 64 A1
Anselm Cl ME10 101 E4
Anselm Rd CT17 310 A8
Ansia Cl ME18 159 B3
Anson Ave M18,ME19 158 F3
Anson Cl
Broadstairs CT10 83 D3
Chatham ME5 97 C6
Anson Pl SE28 2 D4
Anstee Rd CT17 278 C1
Anstridge Rd SE9 12 D1
Antelope Rd SE18 1 F3
Anthony Cl TN13 153 E7
Anthony Cres CT5 108 B6
Anthony Rd DA16 13 A6
Anthony Roper Prim Sch The DA4 89 E8
Anthonys La BR8 56 A8
Anthonys Way ME2 63 E8
Antolin Way CT10,CT12 83 A3
Antonius Ct TN23 300 A5
Anvil Cl CT7 81 A6
Anvil Terr DA2 32 E6
Anzio Cres CT15 278 E2
Anzio Ho 15 CT1 143 B2
Apartments The TN28 373 E5
Aperfield Rd
Biggin Hill TN16 118 E2
Erith DA8 14 F8
Apiary Bsns Pk The ME17 197 B3
Apollo Ave BR1 52 B8
Apollo Ho ME5 97 A6
Apollo Way
St Mary's Island ME4 41 C2
3 Woolwich SE28 2 D3
Appleby Cl ME1 96 D7
Appleby Ct TN24 268 D2
Appleby Rd E16 1 A7
Apple Cl
Hawkinge CT18 307 B4
Snodland ME6 128 A6
Apple Craft Ctr* ME13 138 E5
Applecross Cl ME1 63 B4
Apple Ct TN12 256 F6
Appledore Ave
Bexley DA7 14 D5
West Minst ME12 46 B8
Appledore Cl
Hayes BR2 52 A4
Margate CT9 51 C1
Appledore Cres
Folkestone CT19 334 D7
Sidcup DA14 30 F5
Appledore Ct ME16 161 C7
Appledore Rd
Appledore TN26,TN30 361 A7
Brattle TN26 347 C7
Gillingham ME8 65 A3
Tenterden TN30 345 E7
Appledore Sta TN26 362 B8
Appledown Way CT1 175 D5
Appleford Dr ME12 46 F7
Applegarth Dr DA1 33 F6
Applegarth Ho DA8 14 F5
Applegarth Pk CT5 108 A6
Applegarth Rd SE28 3 C6
Apple Orch BR8 55 D5
Appleshaw Cl DA11 37 A3
Appleton Cl DA7 14 C5
Appleton Dr DA2 33 B5
Appleton Rd SE9 11 E4
Appletons TN11 223 E8
Apple Tree Cl ME16 160 F2
Appletree Ct 5 ME8 98 F8
Apple Tree La TN2 286 D8
Appold St DA8 14 F8
Approach Rd
Broadstairs CT10 84 A4
Dover CT17 310 A6
Margate CT9 51 A2
Approach Rd S TN29 380 C2
Approach Rd
Shepherdswell CT15 244 D5
Tatsfield CR6,TN16 150 B5
Approach The BR6 86 F8
April Cl BR6 86 F5
April Rise
Birchington CT7 80 D8
Whitstable CT5 108 B7
Apsledene DA12 37 D2
Apsley Cotts CT4 173 D3
Apsley Ct BR5 54 B3
Apsley St Ashford TN23 268 B2
Rusthall TN4 285 D4
Aragon Cl
Ashford TN23 299 E7
Orpington BR2 52 F1
Arborfield DA13 60 A4
Arbroath Rd SE9 11 E4
Arbrook Cl BR5 54 A6
Arbrook Ct BR5 54 A8
Arbury Ho BR1 29 E1
Arbuthnot La DA5 13 E1
Arcade The 2 SE9 12 A1
Arcadian Ave DA5 13 E1
Arcadian Cl DA5 13 E1
Arcadian Rd DA5 13 E1
Arcadia Rd DA13 59 F8
Archbishop's Sch The CT2 142 E3
Archcliffe Rd CT17 310 C5
Archer Ho ME3 40 F6
Archer Rd Chatham ME5 97 B6
Folkestone CT19 335 D6
Orpington BR5 54 A4
Archer's Court Rd CT15,CT16 278 B7
Archers Court Sch CT16 278 B5
Archer Way BR8 56 A7
Archery Cl ME3 40 B7
Archery House Hospl DA2 16 B1
Archery Rd SE9 11 F2
Archery Sq CT14 215 D3
Archibald Ho ME14 162 A7
Archway Ct
Dartford DA1 33 D8
4 Rochester ME2 63 B8
Archway Rd
Ramsgate CT11 117 E6
Sheerness ME12 28 A3
Arcon Cl TN23 300 A7
Arcon Rd TN23 300 A7
Arden Bsns Pk ME2 63 E7
Arden Cl SE28 3 D7
Arden Dr TN24 268 C3
Arden Grange CT4 205 C8
Arden Gr BR6 86 B6
Arden Jun Sch ME7 64 D6
Ardenlee Dr ME14 162 B5
Arden Rd
Faversham ME13 138 E7
Herne Bay CT6 77 C2
Arden St ME7 64 C6
Ardent Ave CT14 215 C4
Arethusa Pl DA9 17 B3
Arethusa Rd ME1 96 C8
Argali Ho 3 DA18 3 E3
Argent Rd ME11 46 A2
Argent St RM17 18 B7
Argent Way ME10 101 C6
Argles Cl 4 DA9 17 A2
Argyle Ave CT9 50 G1
Argyle Cl ME1 96 E8
Argyle Gdns CT9 50 G1
Argyle Rd Newham E16 1 B7
Royal Tunbridge Wells TN4 254 A2
Sevenoaks TN13 154 B2
Whitstable CT5 74 D1
Argyll Dr CT11 83 F1
Argyll Rd SE18 2 C3
Ariel Cl DA12 37 F4
Ariel Ct 5 DA17 4 A1
Ark Cotts CT18 305 D4
Ark La CT14 215 D7
Arkley Rd CT6 76 F4
Arklow Sq 6 CT11 117 F7
Arkwright Rd RM18 19 A5
Arlington TN23 299 F8
Arlington Cl DA15 30 E8
Arlington Gdns CT9 83 C8
Arlington Ho CT9 50 H2
Arlington Sq CT9 50 H2
Arlott Cl ME14 161 F6
Armada Cl TN28 373 E5
Armada Ct ME4 63 E1
Armadale CT10 51 F1
Armada Way
Chatham ME4 63 F3
Newham E6 2 C7
Armitage Pl 5 TN18 340 F2
Armourers Wlk CT16 278 A3
Armoury Dr DA12 37 C8
Armstrong Cl
Badgers Mount TN14 121 B4
Bromley BR1 52 E6
Newham E6 1 F7
Armstrong Rd
Maidstone ME15 162 A1
Woolwich SE18 2 C3
Armstrong Sq CT6 76 A3
Armytage Cl ME3 41 E4
Arne Cl TN10 222 E6
Arne Gr BR6 86 F7
Arnhem Dr ME5 96 F7
Arnold Ave DA13 93 B8
Arnolde Cl ME2 63 F7
Arnold Pl RM18 19 C6
Arnold Rd
Chartham CT4 173 C2
Gravesend DA12 37 D6
5 Margate CT9 50 J1
Arnolds La DA4 34 A2
Arnott Cl SE28 3 C5
Arnsberg Way DA6,DA7 14 A3
Arnside Rd DA7 14 A6
Arolla Rd CT6 77 C4
Arran Cl DA8 14 D8
Arrandene Ho 3 BR5 54 B7
Arran Gn ME2 62 C6
Arran Mews 4 CT1 143 B2
Arran Rd ME15 195 A6
Arras Ho Bexley SE2 13 D8
Erith SE2 3 D1
Arrowhead La TN26, TN29 362 D7
Arsenal Rd SE9 11 F4
Arsenal Way SE18 2 C3
Artemis Cl DA12 37 E8
Arthur Ct 11 RM17 18 C8
Arthur Gr SE18 2 C2
Arthur Kennedy Cl ME13 139 F3
Arthur Rd
Biggin Hill TN16 118 C3
Birchington CT7 80 D8
Deal CT14 215 A3
Gillingham ME8 98 E7
Hythe CT21 333 C1
Margate CT9 51 A3
Rochester ME1 63 D3
Arthur Ruxley Est DA14 31 D2
Arthur St W DA11 37 A8
Arthur Salmon Cl ME13 138 B7
Arthur St Erith DA8 14 F7
3 Folkestone CT19 335 E6
Gravesend DA11 37 A8
Grays RM17 18 C8
Sittingbourne ME10 101 E4
Arthur Toft Ho 6 RM17 18 B8
Artillery Gdns 12 CT1 143 A1
Artillery Ho
13 Canterbury CT1 143 A1
Woolwich SE18 2 A1
Artillery Pl SE18 2 A2
Artillery Rd CT11 117 F7
Artillery Row DA12 37 C8
Artillery St 11 CT1 143 A1
Artington Cl BR6 86 C6
Artisan Cl E6 2 B6
Arun Ct BR5 54 C1
Arundel Ave ME10 101 E1
Arundel Cl Bexley DA5 13 F1
Chatham ME5 97 D1
Tonbridge TN9 254 A8
Arundel Ct 2 DA6 13 E3
Arundel Dr BR6 87 B5
Arundel Ho TN1 286 A3
Arundel Rd
Cliffs End CT12 116 D7
Dartford DA1 15 C3
Margate CT9 51 B2
Royal Tunbridge Wells TN1 286 B2
Arundel DA14 31 A3
Arundel St ME14 161 F6
Ascot Cl
Borough Green TN15 157 B7
Chatham ME5 97 C2
Ascot Ct Bromley BR1 52 E7
Sidcup DA5 31 F8
Ascot Gdns CT8 81 E7
Ascot Ho 2 ME15 195 F6
Ascot Rd
Gravesend DA12 37 B5
Orpington BR5 53 F5
Ashbank Cotts ME17 197 B7
Ashbee Cl ME6 128 A7
Ashbee Gdns CT6 77 C5
Ashborne Cl TN24 268 D6
Ashbourne Ave DA7 13 E7
Ashbourne Ct TN4 285 D4
Ashbourne Rise BR6 86 E6
Ashburn Ct BR1 29 A1
Ashburn Gdns CT6 77 C5
Ashburnham Cl TN13 187 C8
Ashburnham Rd
Erith DA17 4 C2
Maidstone ME14 162 B8
Ramsgate CT11 117 C7
Tonbridge TN10 222 C3
Ashburn Mews ME7 64 E3
Ashburton Cl TN24 268 E2
Ashburton Rd E16 1 A7
Ashby Cl ME2 95 A4
Ashby's Cl TN8 249 D8
Ashbys Yd TN9 222 C1
Ash Cl Ashford TN23 267 E3
Aylesford ME20 128 E1
Broadstairs CT10 83 C4
Chatham ME5 64 C1
Crabble CT17 277 E3
Edenbridge TN8 217 B1
Gillingham ME8 65 B3
Herne Bay CT6 76 F1
Orpington BR5 53 D4
Royal Tunbridge Wells TN2 314 D7
Sidcup DA14 31 B5
Swanley BR8 55 D7
Ashcombe Dr TN8 217 B4
Ash Cres
Biddenden TN27 323 D7
Hersden CT3 111 E1
Higham ME3 39 C3
Ashcroft Ave DA15 13 A1
Ashcroft Cres DA15 13 A1
Ashcroft Ct
Dartford DA1 34 A8
5 Eltham SE9 12 A1
Ash Croft Ct DA3 91 F7
Ashcroft Rd
Paddock Wood TN12 257 A5
Rochester ME2 40 B2
Ash Ct Cliffs End CT12 116 D4
Lewisham SE12 29 A8
Ashdale Ho TN23 268 C2
Ashdale Rd SE12 29 B7
Ashden Wlk TN10 222 C7
Ashdown Cl
Coldblow DA5 32 C8
Herne Bay CT6 77 B2
Maidstone ME16 161 D3
Royal Tunbridge Wells TN4 285 F4
Ashdown Cres TN28 373 B6
Ashdown Ct TN24 268 C3
Ashdown Field CT4 173 B2
Ashdown Lodge CT20 335 A5
Ashdown Rd ME17, ME9 166 F3
Ashenden Cl
Canterbury CT1 174 C5
Rochester ME2 40 C2
Ashendene Gr CT2 144 A6
Ashenden TN27 263 F2
Ashenden Wlk TN2 286 E8
Ashen Dr DA1 15 A1
Ashen Grove Mobile Home Pk TN15 90 B1
Ashen Grove Rd TN15 90 B1
Ashen E6 2 A7
Ashen Tree Cotts CT3 146 B1
Ashen Tree La CT16 310 E8
Ashentree La TN29 371 A5
Asher Reeds TN3 285 A4
Ashes La Plaxtol TN11 189 F1
Tonbridge TN11 223 B8
Ashfield La BR7 30 C1
Ashfield Pl BR7 30 D1
Ashford Borough Mus* TN23 268 B2
Ashford Bsns Pk TN24 301 A6
Ashford Bsns Point TN24 300 F5
Ashford Designer Outlet TN24 300 C7
Ashford Dr ME17 197 D3
Ashford Hospl TN23 268 A3
Ashford Int Sta TN24 268 C1
Ashford Rd
Ashford TN23 299 B8
Bethersden TN26,TN23 297 C4
Charing TN27 234 C7
Chartham CT4,CT1 173 C3
Folkestone CT18,CT19 334 B7
Godmersham CT4 205 C4
Hamstreet TN26 327 F1
Harrietsham ME17 198 C6
Kingsnorth TN23,TN26 300 A4
Maidstone,Grove Green ME14 162 D4
Maidstone ME14 163 D3
New Romney TN28 373 A6
Sellindge TN25 303 B1
Sheldwich ME13 170 C4
Tenterden,High Halden TN26,TN30 324 A6
Tenterden TN30 345 B8
Westenhanger CT21, TN25,CT18 332 C6
Ashford Sch TN23 268 C2
Ashford South Com Prim Sch TN23 300 A8
Ashford Sta TN24 268 C1
Ash Gr Elvington CT15 212 B2
Lydd TN29 376 D7
Maidstone ME16 161 C6
Ashgrove Ashford TN23 267 F5
Lewisham SE12 29 A7
Ashgrove Rd TN13 187 B7
Ash Ho BR5 54 C5
Ashington Cl ME10 101 C5
Ash Keys DA13 126 B8
Ashlar Pl 4 SE18 2 B2
Ash La TN15 91 D2
Ashleigh Cl DA13 92 F1
Ashleigh Commercial Est SE18 1 D3
Ashleigh Gdns TN27 262 D6
Ashley Ave CT19 334 E6
Ashley Cl
Halfway Houses ME12 46 C5
Ramsgate CT12 83 B2
Sevenoaks TN13 154 B3
Ashley Dr CT5 108 A7
Ashley Gdns
Orpington BR6 86 E5
Rusthall TN4 285 C5
Ashley Ho
Folkestone CT19 334 E6
Orpington BR5 54 A7
Ashley Mill Cotts CT19 334 E7
Ashley Park Cl TN4 285 C5
Ashley Pk TN4 285 C5
Ashley Rd
Gillingham ME8 65 C2
Sevenoaks TN13 154 B3
Tonbridge TN11 221 E5
Ashly Ct 22 DA14 31 A5
Ash Mdws TN24 300 F7
Ashmead Cl ME5 97 C3
Ashmead Gate BR1 52 C8
Ashmill Bsns Pk ME17 199 F6
Ashmore Gdns DA11 36 D5
Ashmore Gr DA16 12 E4
Ashmore La BR2 118 C8
Ash Platt Rd TN15 154 E6
Ash Rd Aylesham CT3 210 E5
Dartford DA1 33 D7
Gravesend DA12 37 C4
Hartley DA3 58 F3
Hawley DA2 33 F4
New Ash Green DA3, TN15 91 E7
Orpington BR6 86 F3
Rochester ME2 62 F6
Sandwich CT13 148 E2
Westerham TN16 151 E2
Ashridge Cres SE18 12 C7
Ashridge House DA14 30 F4
Ash Row BR2 53 A3
Ashtead Dr ME9 102 D2
Ashton Cl CT14 214 D4
Ashton Ct 4 CT10 83 E5
Ashton Ho CT14 215 B1
Ashton Mews 21 CT10 84 B4
Ashton Way ME19 159 C6
Ash Tree Cl CT7 81 B7
Ashtree Cl BR6 86 B6
Ash Tree Cl
St Mary's Bay TN29 365 F3
West Kingsdown TN15 90 F2
Ash Tree Cotts TN12 291 B7
Ash Tree Dr TN15 90 F2
Ashtree Ho ME10 102 B3
Ash Tree La ME5 64 D1
Ash Tree Rd 6 CT19 335 E6
Ashtrees CT6 77 B3
Ashurst Ave CT5 108 C6
Ashurst Cl DA1 14 F4
Ashurst Gdns CT9 51 E3
Ashurst Hill TN3 283 D2
Ashurst Rd
Maidstone ME14 162 C5
Stone Cross TN3 284 B2
Ashurst Sta TN3 283 D2
Ashwater Rd SE12 29 A7
Ashwell Cl 9 E6 1 E7
Ashwood Cl ME3 40 C7
Ashwood Pl DA2 35 B5
Askern Cl DA6 13 D3
Askes Ct TN23 299 D8
Askews Farm La RM17, RM20 17 E8
Askham Lodge 10 SE12 29 A8
Aspdin Rd DA11 36 E5
Aspen Cl Orpington BR6 87 A5
St Mary's Bay TN29 365 F3
Swanley BR8 55 D8
Aspen Copse BR1 52 F7
Aspen Ct DA1 16 A2
Aspen Dr TN23 267 D3
Aspen Gn DA18 3 F3
Aspen Ho
5 Folkestone CT20 335 D4
2 Sidcup DA15 31 A5
Aspen Rd
Chartham CT4 173 E1
Herne CT6 110 E7
Aspen Way
2 Chatham ME5 96 E4
Royal Tunbridge Wells TN4 254 C1
Aspian Dr ME17 194 D3
Aspinall Cl CT4 176 B4
Asquith Rd ME8 98 C6
Association Wlk ME1 96 C7
Aster Rd ME3 41 E3
Astley Ave CT16 278 C2
Astley Ct CT16 278 C2
Astley RM17 17 F8
Astley St ME14 162 A4
Aston Cl Chatham ME5 97 A2
Sidcup DA14 31 A5
Aston Pl CT10 83 E6
Astor Ave CT17 310 B8
Astor Coll for the Arts CT17 310 A8
Astor Ct E16 1 C7
Astor Dr CT14 215 C5
Astor of Hever Com Sch The ME16 161 C3
Astor Rd
Broadstairs CT10 83 F8
West Kingsdown TN15 90 E4
Astra Dr DA12 37 F3
Astrid Rd CT14 215 A2
Atcost Rd IG11 3 A8
Athelstan Gn ME17 164 C2
Athelstan Pl CT14 215 C8
Athelstan Rd
Canterbury CT1 174 C5
Chatham ME4 63 F2
Faversham ME13 138 C6
Folkestone CT19 335 D7
Margate CT9 51 A3
Athelstan Way BR5 54 A8
Athena Ct CT9 51 A3
Athill Ct TN13 154 C5
Athol Pl ME13 138 A8
Athol Rd Ashford TN23 299 F7
Erith DA8 4 C1
Whitstable CT5 74 F2
Athol Terr CT16 310 F8
Atkinson Cl BR6 87 A5
Atkinson Rd E16 1 C8
Atkinson Wlk TN24 268 F5
Atlanta Ct ME4 63 D3
Atlantic Cl DA10 17 E2
Atlas Gdns SE7 1 C2
Atlas Rd DA1 15 F4
Atterbury Cl TN16 151 D1
Attlee Ave CT3 210 E5
Attlee Dr DA1 16 A2
Attlee Rd SE28 3 B6
Attlee Way ME10 101 E8
Attwaters La TN18 341 C6
Atwater Ct ME17 199 D5
Aubretia Wlk ME10 102 A3
Auckland Ave CT12 117 A8
Auckland Cl RM18 19 A5
Auckland Cres CT16 278 C3
Auckland Dr ME10 101 C3
Auckland Ho 10 ME15 195 E5
Auckland Rd TN1 286 C5
Auden Rd ME20 128 A3
Audley Ave
Gillingham ME7 64 E1
Margate CT9 50 E1
Tonbridge TN9 221 F2
Audley Cl ME16 161 B5
Audley Dr E16 1 B5
Audley Rd CT20 334 F5
Audley Rise TN9 221 F1
Audley Wlk BR5 54 C3
Audre Lorde Ho E16 1 B8
Audrey Sturley Ct TN4 285 D4
Auger Cl ME9 99 E5
Augusta Cl 1 ME7 64 C7
Augusta Gdns CT20 335 C4
Augusta Pl 14 CT11 117 F7
Augusta Rd CT11 117 F7
Augustine Ho TN10 222 C3
Augustine Rd
Gravesend DA12 37 C8
Minster (Sheppey) ME12 47 B8
Minster (Thanet) CT12 115 B6
Orpington BR5 54 D6
Augustus Wlk TN23 299 F5
Aultmore Ct TN2 286 D3
Aurellus Cl TN23 300 A4
Austell Manor 5 ME7 64 C6
Austen Cl
Swanscombe DA9 17 C1
Tilbury RM18 19 C5
Woolwich SE28 3 B5
Austen Gdns DA1 15 F3
Austen Rd DA8 14 B7
Austens Orch 14 TN30 345 A7

Austen Way ME20 127 F4
Austin Ave Bromley BR2 52 E4
Herne Bay CT6 75 F4
Austin Cl Gillingham ME5 64 E2
Sittingbourne ME10 102 A8
Austin Ct 4 TN16 151 D1
Austin Rd
Ashford TN23 300 B6
Northfleet DA11 36 F7
Orpington BR5 54 A4
Austins La 4 CT13 149 A1
Austral Cl DA15 30 F5
Autumn Glade ME5 130 D8
Avalon Cl BR6 87 D7
Avalon Rd BR5,BR6 87 C8
Avard Gdns BR6 86 C6
Avards Cl TN18 354 E8
Avebury Ave
Ramsgate CT11 117 G8
Tonbridge TN9 222 B1
Avebury Rd BR6 86 D7
Aveley Cl DA8 14 F8
Aveling Cl ME3 41 D6
Aveling Ct 2 ME2 63 B7
Avenons Rd 3 E16 1 A8
Avent Wlk ME9 102 E2
Avenue Gdns CT9 51 C3
Avenue Le Puy TN9 222 C1
Avenue of Remembrance
ME10 101 F3
Avenue Rd
Bexley DA7,DA6 13 E4
Dover CT16 278 C1
Erith DA8 14 D7
Herne Bay CT6 76 E5
Ramsgate CT11 117 F7
Sevenoaks TN13 154 C3
Tatsfield TN16 150 E7
Avenue The
Aylesford ME20 128 E1
Biggin Hill TN16 150 F5
Borough Green TN15 157 A8
Bromley BR1 52 D6
Deal CT14 215 C7
Gravesend DA11 37 A8
Hersden CT3 111 E1
Hill Park TN16 151 A4
Hythe CT21 333 C2
Kingsdown CT14 248 D4
Margate CT9 51 A1
Orpington BR6 86 F8
Orpington,Keston Mark
BR2 85 D7
Orpington,St Paul's Cray
BR5 31 B1
St Margaret's at Cliffe
CT15 279 F6
St Mary's Island ME4 41 C2
Sidcup DA5 31 D8
Swanscombe DA9 17 B2
Temple Ewell CT16 277 E5
Tonbridge TN9 222 B2
Averenches Rd ME14 162 F5
Avereng Gdns CT19 335 B6
Avereng Rd CT19 335 B6
Avery Cl
Allhallows-on-S ME3 9 E3
Maidstone ME15 161 F1
Avery Ct ME3 9 E3
Avery Hill Rd SE9 30 D7
Avery La ME15, ME17 196 D6
Avery Way Allhallows ME3 9 D2
Dartford DA1 33 F6
Aviation Ct ME12 48 E3
Aviemore Gdns ME14 162 F4
Avington Cl ME15 161 F1
Avocet Mews SE28 2 D3
Avocet Wlk ME5 97 D2
Avon Cl Canterbury CT1 175 C8
Gravesend DA12 37 D6
Tonbridge TN10 222 C5
Avon Ct DA14 31 B5
Avondale Cl CT5 109 A8
Avondale Ct ME14 162 E5
Avondale Pl ME3 25 C4
Avondale Rd
Bexley DA16 13 C5
Bromley,Mottingham SE9 29 E6
Bromley,Plaistow BR1 29 A2
Capel-le-F CT18 308 C2
Gillingham ME7 64 D5
Avon Ho 18 CT20 335 C4
Avonmouth Rd DA1 15 D2
Avonstowe Cl BR6 86 C7
Avon St TN1 286 C5
Awliscombe Rd DA16 12 F5
Axford Ct ME8 99 A8
Axminster Cres DA16 13 C6
Axtaine Rd BR5 54 D2
Axtane DA13 35 F1
Axtane Cl DA4 57 C8
Axton Chase Sch DA3 58 F6
Aycliffe Cl BR1 52 F5
Aycliffe Com Prim Sch
CT17 310 A4
Ayelands La DA3 91 E8
Ayelands DA3 91 E8
Ayers Cotts BR8 33 E2
Aylesbury Rd
Ashford TN25 268 B7
Bromley BR2 52 A6
Aylesford Cres ME8 65 B4
Aylesford Pl TN24 300 E7
Aylesford Prim Sch
ME20 128 D1
Aylesford Sch ME20 128 D1
Aylesford Sta ME20 128 D2
Aylesham Cnr CT3 210 D3
Aylesham & District Com
Workshop Trust CT3 211 A5
Aylesham Ind Est CT3 210 E4
Aylesham Prim Sch
CT3 210 E5
Aylesham Rd
Aylesham CT15,CT3 211 A4
Orpington BR6 53 F2
Aylesham Sta CT3 211 A6
Ayleswade Rd TN27 294 E7
Aylewyn Gn ME10 101 F8
Aynscombe Angle BR6 54 A2
Aynsley Ct 1 CT13 149 A1
Ayrshire Cl TN24 268 C7
Ayton Rd CT11 117 C6
Azalea Dr BR8 55 E5

B

Babbacombe Rd BR1 29 B1
Babb's La TN17 342 A6
Babington House Sch
BR7 29 F2
Babs Oak Hill CT2 144 B7
Babylon La ME17,TN12 229 B1
Backfields ME1 63 B4
Back La
6 Faversham ME13 138 D7
Godden Green TN15 155 A2
Goudhurst TN17 318 E8
Horsmonden TN12 290 A6
Ightham TN15 156 C2
Maidstone ME17 195 E1
Minster (Sheppey) ME12 47 D6
Sevenoaks TN13,TN14 153 C1
Shipbourne TN11 189 D4
Sidcup DA5 32 A8
Back Rd
Sandhurst TN18 356 B5
Sidcup DA14 31 A4
Back Rd W CT16 310 G8
Back St Leeds ME17 196 E6
Ringwould CT14 247 F5
Baddlesmere Rd CT5 75 A2
Baden Powell Ho 11
DA17 4 A3
Baden Powell Rd
TN13 153 E5
Baden Rd ME7 64 D7
Bader Cres ME5 97 A7
Bader Wlk DA11 36 F5
Badger's Hill Open Farm*
CT4 205 C8
Badger Rd ME5 97 C1
Badgers Bridge CT18 305 D4
Badgers Cl CT2 142 A7
Badgers Copse BR6 86 F8
Badgers Croft SE9 30 A5
Badgers Holt TN2 286 E5
Badgers Oak TN23 299 D8
Badgers Rd TN14 88 B1
Badgers Rise
Badgers Mount TN14 88 A1
Deal CT14 248 C8
Kearsney CT17 277 D3
Badlesmere Cl TN23 299 E6
Badlow Cl DA8 14 E7
Badminton Mews E16 1 A5
Bad Munstereifel Rd
TN23,TN24 300 D5
Badsell Park Farm
TN12 256 C3
Badsell Rd TN12 256 E5
Baffin Cl ME4 63 F2
Bagham La CT4 205 D8
Bagham Rd CT4 205 C8
Bagshaw Ho 6 BR1 52 A8
Bagshill Rd ME13 170 A3
Bailey Dr ME7 65 A1
Bailey Fields TN26 297 E4
Baileys Field TN23 267 F1
Baird Ho 13 DA17 4 A3
Baird's Hill CT10 83 F6
Bairdsley Cl CT10 83 F6
Bakenham Ho 1 ME1 63 C1
Baker Beall Ct DA7 14 B4
Baker Cl ME9 103 C2
Baker Hill Cl DA11 36 F4
Baker La
Headcorn TN27 262 F7
Sutton Valence ME17 229 F7
Baker Rd
Folkestone CT19 334 E6
Woolwich SE18 11 E7
Bakers Ave TN15 90 E3
Bakers Cl CT2 174 C7
Bakers Cross TN17 320 E4
Bakers Ct CT11 117 E7
Baker's La CT4 173 D2
Bakers Mews 9 BR6 86 F4
Baker St Burham ME1 95 F1
Rochester ME1 63 C3
Baker's Wlk ME1 63 C6
Bakery Cl TN17 293 E7
Bakery Cotts ME14 129 E3
Bakery The ME9 134 A6
Balaclava La TN5 337 A6
Balas Dr ME10 101 C7
Balcaskie Rd SE9 11 F2
Balchen Rd SE3 11 D5
Balcomb Cres CT9 83 C8
Balcombe Cl DA6 13 D3
Balcombe Cotts TN17 318 E8
Balcombes Hill TN17 318 E8
Balder Rise SE12 29 B6
Baldock Rd TN5 336 E4
Baldric Rd CT20 334 F5
Baldwin Rd
Greatstone-on-Sea
TN28 373 D1
Minster (Sheppey) ME12 47 D7
Baldwin Terr CT19 335 D6
Baldwyns Mans DA2 32 D6
Baldwyn's Pk DA5 32 D6
Baldwyn's Rd DA5 32 D6
Balfour Ct CT20 335 B3
Balfour Inf Sch ME1 63 E1
Balfour Jun Sch ME4 63 E2
Balfour Rd Bromley BR2 52 D4
Chatham ME4 63 E2
Deal CT14 215 C2
Dover CT16 278 C1
Balgowan St SE18 2 F2
Baliol Rd CT5 74 E2
Ballamore Rd BR1 29 A5
Ballard Bsns Pk ME2 62 F5
Ballard Cl TN12 259 C6
Ballard Ct 20 DA14 31 A5
Ballard Ind Est ME5 130 C8
Ballard Rd TN28 373 D1
Ballards La RH8 183 C6
Ballard Way TN12 257 B7
Ballens Rd ME5 97 C3
Balliemoor Ct CT11 83 F1
Balliol Rd Bexley DA16 13 B5
Broadstairs CT10 83 F8
Ball La TN24 268 F7
Balls Cotts ME3 40 F4
Ball's Gn TN7 311 B5
Balmer Cl ME8 98 D7
Balmoral Ct SE12 29 B4
Balmoral Gdns DA5 31 F8
Balmoral Ho 10 ME15 195 F5
Balmoral Pl 12 CT11 117 F7
Balmoral Rd
Gillingham ME7 64 D5
Kingsdown CT14 248 C6
4 Margate CT9 82 B8
Sutton at H DA4 34 B1
Balmoral Terr ME10 101 D4
Balmoral Trad Est E6 2 F8
Baltic Ho TN1 286 B5
Baltic Rd TN9 254 B7
Baltic Wharf 1 DA11 19 A1
Baltimore Pl DA16 12 F5
Bamford Way CT14 215 C4
Banbury Villas DA13 35 F1
Banchory Rd SE3 11 B7
Banckside DA3 58 E5
Bancroft Gdns BR6 53 F1
Bancroft La ME18 159 C2
Bancroft Rd TN15 124 F3
Bangor Rd ME2 62 D6
Banister Ho RM20 17 D8
Bank Cotts ME17 164 E3
Bankfields TN27 262 C5
Bankfield Way TN17 318 E7
Bank Ho
New Romney TN28 373 C6
Sheerness ME12 28 C2
Bank Hos DA2 34 A3
Bank Ho TN15 125 A3
Bank La TN11,TN15 188 A3
Bank Rd TN25 329 E8
Bankside
Canterbury CT1 175 D7
Chatham ME5 97 B8
Bankside Cl
Biggin Hill TN16 118 C1
Joyden's Wood DA5 32 D4
Bankside TN5 336 E5
Bank Side TN26 349 A8
Bankside
Northfleet DA11 18 C1
Sevenoaks TN13 153 E6
Banks La DA6 13 F3
Banks Rd Ashford TN23 300 A7
Rochester ME2 63 C8
Bank St Ashford TN23 268 B2
Chatham ME4 64 B3
Cranbrook TN17 320 C5
Faversham ME13 138 C7
Gravesend DA12 19 B1
Banks The CT10 83 F6
Bank St Herne Bay CT6 76 F5
Hythe CT21 333 C2
Maidstone ME14 162 A4
Sevenoaks TN13 154 C2
Tonbridge TN9 222 C1
Bank View 5 ME15 161 E2
Banky Fields Cl ME8 66 B1
Banky Mdw ME16 160 F3
Banner Farm Rd TN2 286 B2
Banner Way ME12 46 E6
Banningbrook Ct
CT14 215 D4
Banning St ME2 63 B8
Bannister Gdns BR5 54 C6
Bannister Hill ME9 101 B2
Bannister Hos TN26 234 A1
Bannister Rd ME14 162 A7
Bannockburn Prim Sch
SE18 2 F2
Bannockburn Rd SE18 2 F2
Banstead Ct 3 BR1 52 E6
Banwell Rd DA5 13 D1
Bapchild Pl 6 BR5 54 C5
Bapchild & Tonge CE Prim
Sch ME9 102 D3
Barbados Terr 2
ME14 162 A7
Barber's Almshouses 11
CT11 117 D6
Barberry Ave ME5 96 E5
Barcham Ct ME15 194 F5
Barchester Way TN10 222 F6
Barclay Ave TN10 223 A5
Barclay Ct CT8 50 C1
Barclay Field TN15 122 E2
Barcombe Cl BR5 54 A6
Bardell Terr ME1 63 D5
Barden Ct ME14 162 B5
Barden Park Rd TN9 222 A1
Barden Rd
Penshurst TN3 252 F2
Speldhurst TN3 285 A8
Tonbridge TN9 222 B1
Barden St SE18 12 E7
Bardsley Cl TN12 225 A7
Barfield Rd BR1,BR7 53 A6
Barfield DA4 57 B8
Barfleur Manor 3 ME7 64 A6
Barfreston Cl ME15 161 F2
Barfrestone Rd CT15 212 A1
Bargate Cl SE18 2 F1
Bargates TN23 299 E6
Bargehouse Rd E16 2 B4
Barges The CT5 74 E3
Bargrove CT18 333 E6
Bargrove Rd ME14 162 C5
Barham CE Prim Sch
CT4 242 F8
Barham Cl
Chislehurst BR7 30 B3
Gravesend DA12 37 F7
Maidstone ME15 195 E5
Orpington BR2 52 E1
Barham Ct BR2 52 E1
Barham Mews ME18 193 B8
Barham Rd
Chislehurst BR7 30 B3
Dartford DA1 34 A8
Barham's Mill Rd
TN27 232 B3
Baring Cl SE12 29 A6
Baring Prim Sch SE12 29 A8
Baring Rd SE12 29 A6
Barker Rd ME16 161 F3
Barkers Ct ME10 101 D4
Bark Hart Rd BR6 54 B1
Barkis Cl ME1 96 D7
Barler Pl ME11 46 A5
Barley Cl Herne Bay CT6 77 D2
Martin Mill CT15 247 C2
Barleycorn Dr ME8 98 E6
Barleycorn ME19 127 E1
Barley Fields ME14 162 D4
Barleymow Cl ME5 97 C7
Barley Way TN23 299 E5
Barling Cl ME5 96 D1
Barlow Cl ME8 98 E5
Barlow Dr SE18 11 E6
Barlow Way RM13 4 E8
Barlow Way S RM13 4 E7
Barming Prim Sch
ME16 160 F2
Barming Rd ME18 159 F2
Barming Sta ME16 160 F6
Barnaby Terr ME1 63 D2
Barnard Cl
Chislehurst BR7 53 D8
Woolwich SE18 2 A3
Barnard Ct
Chatham ME4 64 A2
21 Dartford DA2 16 B1
Barnberry Cl TN23 299 E8
Barn Cl Borden ME9 101 A2
Hoath CT3 111 E5
Yorkletts CT5 108 A3
Barn Cres CT9 50 F1
Barncroft Cl ME14 162 F4
Barncroft Dr ME7 97 F4
Barndale Ct DA12 38 E3
Barned Ct ME16 160 F2
Barnehurst Ave DA7,
DA8 14 C6
Barnehurst Cl DA8 14 C6
Barnehurst Inf Sch
DA8 14 C6
Barnehurst Jun Sch
DA8 14 C6
Barnehurst Rd DA7 14 C5
Barnehurst Sta DA7 14 C5
Barn End Ctr DA2 33 C5
Barn End Dr DA2 33 C5
Barn End La DA2 33 C4
Barnes Ave CT9 50 F1
Barnes Cl ME13 138 B8
Barnes Cray Prim Sch
DA1 15 A3
Barnes Cray Rd DA1 15 A3
Barnes Ct
Canterbury CT1 174 D6
Newham E16 1 C8
Barnesdale Cres BR5 54 A4
Barnesende Ct CT13 181 A8
Barnes La ME17 227 D8
Barnes Wlk TN12 259 D6
Barnet Dr BR2 85 E8
Barnet's La CT2 143 D8
Barnett Cl DA8 14 F5
Barnett Ct
Minster (Thanet) CT12 115 C5
Ramsgate CT12 83 B1
Barnett Field TN23 299 F8
Barnetts Cl TN4 254 C1
Barnetts Rd TN11 221 A2
Barnetts Way TN4 286 C8
Barnet Wood Rd BR2 85 C8
Barney Cl SE7 1 C1
Barnfield ME5 97 A8
Barnfield Cl
Crockenhill BR8 55 C2
New Barn DA3 59 D6
Stone DA9 16 F1
Barnfield Cres TN15 122 E2
Barnfield Gdns SE18 12 B8
Barnfield
Gravesend DA11 37 A6
Herne Bay CT6 76 C2
Barnfield Rd
Bexley DA17 13 F8
Faversham ME13 138 C8
Folkestone CT19 335 C7
Orpington BR5 54 D6
Sevenoaks TN13 153 E4
Tatsfield TN16 150 D6
Woolwich SE18 12 B8
Barnfield
Royal Tunbridge Wells
TN2 313 F7
Tenterden TN30 324 C2
Barnfield Way RH8 183 A2
Barnham Dr SE28 2 F5
Barnhill Ave BR2 52 A4
Barn Hill ME15 193 E2
Barnhouse La TN29 371 A8
Barnhurst La CT18 307 A5
Barnhurst Rd ME14 162 A8
Barn Mdw
Staplehurst TN12 260 E4
Upper Halling ME2 94 E4
Barnock Cl DA1 32 E8
Barn Platt TN23 300 A8
Barnsley Cl ME12 28 E2
Barnsole Inf Sch ME7 64 E4
Barnsole Jun Sch ME7 64 E4
Barnsole Rd
Gillingham ME7 64 E3
Staple CT3 179 B5
Barn The ME9 101 A2
Barn Tye Cl CT15 278 E6
Barnwell Pl ME7 64 C5
Barnwell Rd DA1 15 F4
Barnwood Cl ME1 96 B8
Baron Cl Gillingham ME7 64 E7
Maidstone ME14 162 F5
Barons Ct TN4 286 A5
Barrack Cnr TN13 154 C4
Barrack Hill CT21 333 A2
Barrack Rd ME4 64 B8
Barrack Row
Benenden TN17 342 D6
17 Gravesend DA11 19 B1
Barrel Arch Cl TN12 259 C6
Barretts Green Cotts 5
TN18 341 A2
Barretts Rd
Hawkhurst TN18 341 A2
Sevenoaks TN13 153 E7
Barrey Rd TN24 301 A6
Barrie Dr 7 ME20 127 F4
Barrier Point Rd E16 1 C5
Barrier Rd ME4 63 F5
Barrington Cl ME5 96 F5
Barrington Cres CT7 81 B7
Barrington Prim Sch
DA7 13 D5
Barrington Rd DA7 13 D5
Barrington Villas SE18 12 A6
Barrowfields ME5 97 D1
Barrow Grove Jun Sch
ME10 101 D3
Barrow Gr ME10 101 D3
Barrow Hill
Ashford TN23 268 B2
Barrowhill TN25 331 D7
Barrow Hill Cotts
TN23 268 A2
Barrow Hill Pl 2
TN23 268 B3
Barrow Hill Rise
TN25 331 D7
Barrow Hill Terr 1
TN23 268 B3
Barrow La TN3 284 F2
Barrows Cl CT7 81 A6
Barr Rd DA12 37 F6
Barry Ave DA7 13 E7
Barry Cl BR6 86 E7
Barry Rd E6 1 E7
Barth Mews SE18 2 E2
Bartholomew Cl CT21 333 B3
Bartholomew La CT21 333 B3
Bartholomew St
6 Dover CT16 278 C1
Hythe CT21 333 B2
Bartholomew Way BR8 55 E6
Barth Rd SE18 2 E2
Bartlett Cl ME5 97 C1
Bartlett Dr CT5 75 A1
Bartlett Rd
Gravesend DA11 37 A7
Westerham TN16 151 C1
Bartletts Cl ME12 46 C5
Bartley Mill La TN3 315 E4
Bartley Mill Rd TN3 315 F3
Barton Bsns Pk CT1 175 D6
Barton Cl Bexley DA6 13 E2
2 Newham E6 1 F7
Barton Cotts TN11 190 A6
Barton Court Gram Sch
CT1 175 B8
Barton Ct 4 CT11 117 E7
Barton Field CT18 305 B7
Barton Hill Dr ME12 47 A5
Barton Jun Sch CT16 278 C2
Barton Mill Ct 2 CT2 142 F1
Barton Mill Rd CT1 143 B2
Barton Rd
Canterbury CT1 175 C6
Dover CT16 278 C2
Maidstone ME15 162 A2
Rochester ME2 63 A7
Sidcup DA14 31 E2
Sutton at H DA4 57 B8
Bartons Cotts TN16 152 C3
Barton's Point Coastal Pk*
ME12 28 F2
Barton View Terr 2
CT17 278 C1
Barville Rd CT15 212 E2
Barwick Rd CT17 277 F1
Bascombe Gr DA1 14 E1
Basden Cotts 2 TN18 341 A2
Baseing Cl E6 2 A6
Bashford Barn La
Bredgar ME9 134 A4
Silver Street ME9 133 F4
Basi Cl ME2 40 C1
Basildon Rd SE2 3 A1
Basilon Rd DA7 13 E5
Basil Terr 6 ME15 162 A1
Basing Cl ME15 162 B3
Basing Dr DA5 13 F1
Baskerville TN24 268 B3
Basket Gdns SE9 11 E2
Basmere Cl ME14 162 C6
Bassant Rd SE18 12 F8
Basser Hill ME9 67 E3
Bassett Cl CT21 333 E4
Bassett Gdns CT21 333 D4
Bassett Rd ME10 101 D4
Bassetts Cl BR6 86 B6
Bassett's Forge TN5 336 E5
Bassetts La TN8,TN11 283 C7
Bassetts Way BR6 86 B6
Basted La Basted TN15 156 F5
Crouch TN15 157 B4
Bastion Rd Dover CT17 310 C6
Woolwich SE2 3 A1
Baston Manor BR2 85 B6
Baston Manor Rd BR2,
BR4 85 B6
Baston Rd BR2 85 B7
Baston Sch BR2 85 B8
Bat & Ball Ent Ctr
TN14 154 C7
Bat & Ball Sta TN14 154 C6
Batchelors TN2 287 E8
Batchelor St ME4 64 A4
Batchwood Gn BR5 54 B6
Bateman Cnr TN26 297 E6
Bates Cl
New Hythe ME20 128 A3
Staple CT3 178 F6
Bates Hill TN15 156 C5
Bateson St SE18 2 E2
Bath Ct 8 CT20 335 B3
Bath Hard ME1 63 D5
Bath Mews TN24 300 E6
Bath Pl CT9 50 J2
Bath Rd Ashford TN24 300 E6
Dartford DA1 33 B8
Margate CT9 50 J2
Baths Rd BR2 52 D5
Bath St DA11 19 B1
Bathurst Cl
Ramsgate CT12 83 B1
Staplehurst TN12 260 E4
Bathurst Rd
Folkestone CT20 335 A5
Staplehurst TN12 260 E3
Bathway 13 SE18 2 A2
Batten Cl E6 1 F7
Batteries Cl ME9 136 B8
Batteries Terr ME9 136 B8
Battery Point CT21 334 B2
Battery Rd
Lydd-on-S TN29 380 D6
Woolwich SE28 2 E4
Battlefields TN15 124 F3
Battle La TN12 260 A8
Battle of Britain Homes 17
CT17 310 D7
Battle of Britain Meml
The* CT18 308 A1
Battle Rd DA8,DA17 4 C2
Battlesmere Rd ME3 40 B8
Battle St DA12 60 F6
Batt's Rd DA12 61 A4
Baugh Rd DA14 31 C3
Bawden Cl CT2 143 A4
Baxendale Ct TN24 300 D7
Baxter Rd E16 1 C7
Baxter Way ME18 159 C3
Bayard Ct DA6 14 B3
Bay Banks ME13 137 E2
Bay Cl ME3 41 E3
Bay Cotts CT15 280 C6
Baye La CT3 145 D1
Bayeux Ho 11 SE7 11 C8
Bayfield ME13 137 E2
Bayfield Rd SE9 11 D3
Bayford Rd ME10 102 A4
Bayhall Rd TN2 286 C3
Bayham Ct TN5 336 E6
Bayham Old Abbey*
TN3 316 B5
Bayham Rd
Bells Yew Green TN3 315 B4
Royal Tunbridge Wells
TN2,TN3 314 C7
Sevenoaks TN13 154 D4
Bay Hill Cl CT15 280 A5
Bay Hill CT15 280 B6
Bayle Ct CT20 335 E4
Bayle St 10 CT20 335 E5
Bayle The CT20 335 E4
Bayley's Hill TN14 186 E3
Bayley Wlk SE2 3 E1
Bayliss Ave SE28 3 D6
Bayly Rd DA1 16 A1
Bay Manor La RM20 16 F8
Bay Mus The* CT15 280 B5
Bayne Cl E6 1 F7
Baynham Cl DA5 13 F1
Bays The BR5 54 C6
Bayswater Dr ME8 98 E4
Bay The DA13 126 A8
Baytree Cl Bromley BR1 52 D8
Sidcup DA15 30 F7
Bay View Gdns ME12 49 D2
Bay View Hts CT7 80 D8
Bay View Rd CT10 84 A2
Bayview Rd
Kingsdown CT14 248 C4
Whitstable CT5 108 D7
Baywell ME19 127 E2
Bazes Shaw DA3 91 F8
Beach Alley 15 CT5 74 D2
Beacham Cl SE7 11 D8
Beachamwell Dr
ME18 159 C2

Beach App ME12 49 E3
Beach Ave CT7 80 F8
Beach Bank Cvn Pk
CT21 353 C7
Beachborough Rd
CT19,CT20 335 A5
Beach Ct Deal CT14 215 D2
Eltham SE9 11 E1
Goddard's Green TN17 321 D1
Westgate-on-S CT8 50 D1
Beachfield Lodge
ME12 28 C2
Beach Flats 2 CT21 333 B2
Beach Hos CT9 50 G2
Beach House Mews
CT8 50 D1
Beach Marine 7 CT20 334 F3
Beachmont Cl TN28 377 E8
Beach Rd
Dymchurch TN29 353 A4
St Margaret's at Cliffe
CT15 280 B5
Westgate-on-S CT8 50 D1
Beach Rise CT8 50 D1
Beach St Deal CT14 215 D6
Folkestone CT20 335 E4
Herne Bay CT6 76 F5
Sheerness ME12 28 B2
Beach Terr ME12 28 B2
Beach The CT14 215 D3
Beach Wlk CT5 74 E3
Beacon Ave CT6 77 B5
Beacon Cl ME8 98 D7
Beacon Dr DA2 35 C5
Beaconfields TN13 154 A1
Beacon Hill
Gillingham ME5 64 D2
Herne Bay CT6 77 B5
Beacon Hill La ME3 40 F4
Beacon La CT13 180 A6
Beacon Oak Rd TN30 345 B8
Beacon Rd
Broadstairs CT10 83 F7
Chatham ME5 64 C2
Erith DA8 15 B7
Herne Bay CT6 77 A5
Lenham ME17 199 C5
Beacon Rise TN13 154 A1
Beacons Cl 11 E6 1 E8
Beaconsfield Ave
Dover CT16 278 C1
Gillingham ME7 64 E5
Beaconsfield Cl SE3 11 A8
Beaconsfield Gdns
CT10 83 F5
Beaconsfield Par SE9 29 E4
Beaconsfield Rd
Bromley,Mottingham SE9 29 E4
Bromley,Widmore BR1 52 D6
Canterbury CT2 142 F2
Chatham ME4 63 F3
Deal CT14 215 D5
Dover CT16 278 C1
Greenwich SE3 11 A8
Maidstone ME15 161 E2
Maypole DA5 32 E6
Sittingbourne ME10 102 C4
Beaconsfield CT5 107 F6
Beacons The ME17 194 C2
Beacon Terr CT21 334 B2
Beacon Way CT21 331 F3
Beacon Wlk
Herne Bay CT6 77 A5
Tenterden TN30 324 B1
Beacon Wood Ctry Pk*
DA2 35 B4
Beadon Rd BR2 52 A4
Beagles Cl BR5 87 D8
Beagles Wood Rd
TN2 287 E7
Beal Cl DA16 13 A6
Beaman Cl TN17 318 F8
Beamish Rd BR5 54 C2
Beamont Cl CT12 81 F2
Beams The ME15 162 F1
Bean Cl TN23 267 C1
Beane Croft DA12 37 F7
Beaney's La Cotts
CT4 171 C1
Beaney's La CT4 171 C1
Bean Hill Cotts DA2 35 C4
Bean La DA2 35 B6
Bean Prim Sch DA2 35 C4
Bean Rd Bexley DA6 13 D3
Swanscombe DA9 17 B1
Beanshaw SE9 30 A4
Bears End Ho TN23 300 B8
Bear's La TN23,TN26 266 E3
Bearsted Cl ME8 65 B3
Bearsted Green Bsns Ctr
ME14 163 C4
Bearsted Rd ME14 162 E6
Bearsted Sta ME14 163 B5
Beaton Cl DA9 17 B2
Beatrice Gdns DA11 36 E6
Beatrice Hills Cl TN24 268 E5
Beatrice Mews TN28 377 E7
Beatrice Rd
Capel-le-F CT18 308 C2
Margate CT9 82 E8
Beatty Ave ME7 64 F4
Beatty Cl CT19 335 E8
Beatty Cotts ME3 9 D1
Beatty Rd
Folkestone CT19 335 D8
Rochester ME1 96 D8
Beauchamp Ave CT14 215 A3
Beauchamp Cl TN24 268 E5
Beauchamps La CT15 211 D5
Beaufighter Rd ME19 158 E3
Beaufort Ave CT12 117 B8
Beaufort Ct ME2 63 E6
Beaufort E6 2 A8
Beaufort Rd ME2 62 E8
Beaufort Wlk ME15 195 E4
Beaufoy Rd CT17 278 A1
Beaufoy Terr CT17 277 F1
Beauherne Com Sch
CT2 174 D8
Beaulieu Ave E16 1 B5
Beaulieu Rd TN10 222 B4
Beaulieu Rise ME1 63 D1
Beaulieu Wlk ME16 161 C7
Beaumanor Gdns SE9 30 A4
Beaumanor CT6 77 A3
Beaumont Davy Cl
ME13 138 C5
Beaumont Dr DA11 36 F8
Beaumont Rd
Maidstone ME16 161 B2
Orpington BR5 53 D3
Beaumont St CT6 76 C4
Beaumont Terr ME13 138 D6
Beauvoir Dr ME10 102 A8
Beauworth Pk ME15 195 E8
Beauxfield CT16 278 A7
Beaverbank Rd SE9 30 D7
Beaver Ct TN23 300 A7
Beaver Green Inf Sch
TN23 299 E7
Beaver Ind Est TN23 300 B7
Beaver La
Ashford,Beaver TN23 300 A7
Ashford,Singleton TN23 299 F7
Ashford TN23 267 E1
Beaver Rd
Ashford TN23 300 B8
Maidstone ME16 161 B7
Beavers Lodge DA14 30 F3
Beaverwood Rd BR7 30 E2
Beaverwood Sch for Girls
BR7 30 E2
Beaver Zoological Gdns*
TN16 150 B5
Beazley Ct TN24 300 D7
Bebbington Rd SE18 2 E2
Beblets Cl 4 BR6 86 F5
Beckenham Dr ME16 161 D7
Becket Ave CT2 142 D1
Becket Cl Ash CT3 147 D2
Deal CT14 215 C8
Whitstable CT5 75 B1
Becket Ct
Headcorn TN27 262 D5
2 Tonbridge TN9 254 B8
Becket Mews CT2 142 F1
Becket's Cl TN25 271 B6
Beckets Field TN11 252 A3
Beckett Cl DA17 3 F3
Becketts Cl BR6 86 F7
Becketts Terr CT21 333 B4
Beckett St 4 ME13 138 C7
Becketts Wood CT3 112 E3
Beckford Dr BR5 53 D2
Beckley Cl DA12 38 B6
Beckley Hill Works
ME2 39 B8
Beckley Mews ME5 96 F5
Beckley Pl TN25 332 B8
Beckley Rd ME12 28 E2
Beckman Cl TN14 121 C4
Becksbourne Cl ME14 162 A8
Becks Rd DA14 31 A5
Beckton Park Sta E6 1 F6
Beckton Rd E16 1 A8
Beckton Ret Pk E6 2 A8
Beckton Sta E6 2 A8
Beckwith Gn CT20 334 E5
Beckworth Pl ME16 161 B2
Becton Pl DA8 14 C6
Bedale Wlk DA2 34 B7
Beddalls Farm Ct 7 E6 1 E8
Beddington Gn BR5 53 F8
Beddington Rd BR5 53 F8
Beddlestead La CR6 150 A6
Beddow Way ME20 129 B3
Bede Ho CT14 215 D8
Bedens Rd DA14 31 E3
Bedford Ave ME8 65 D1
Bedford Ct CT10 84 B6
Bedford Pl ME16 161 E4
Bedford Rd
Dartford DA1 34 A8
Northfleet DA11 36 F6
Orpington BR6 54 B1
Royal Tunbridge Wells
TN4 254 A1
Sidcup DA15 30 E5
Bedford Sq
Longfield DA3 58 E6
Ramsgate CT12 83 B2
Bedford Terr 13 TN1 286 A2
Bedford Way CT7 79 F1
Bedgebury Cl
Maidstone ME14 162 C6
Rochester ME1 96 D8
Bedgebury Cross
TN17 318 D2
Bedgebury National
Pinetum* TN17 339 E8
Bedgebury Rd
Eltham SE9 11 D3
Goudhurst TN17 318 E5
Bedgebury Sch TN17 318 E1
Bedingfield Way CT18 305 B7
Bedivere Rd BR1 29 A5
Bedlam Court La
CT12 115 C6
Bedlam La
Egerton Forstal TN27 264 A8
Swift's Green TN27 263 E6
Bedmonton La ME9 134 B2
Bedonwell Inf Sch
DA17 13 E8
Bedonwell Jun Sch
DA17 13 E8
Bedonwell Rd
Bexley,Bexleyheath DA7 13 F6
Bexley,West Heath DA7,
DA17 13 E8
Bedson Wlk ME8 66 B1
Bedwell Rd DA17 4 A1
Bedwin Cl ME1 96 D7
Beeby Rd E16 1 B8
Beecham Rd TN10 222 E6
Beech Ave
Chartham CT4 173 E1
Sidcup DA15 31 A8
Swanley BR8 55 F5
Tatsfield TN16 150 D8
Beech Cl
Faversham ME13 138 B7
Folkestone CT19 335 C6
Beech Copse BR1 52 F7
Beech Court Gdns*
TN25 202 F1
Beechcroft Ave DA7 14 D5
Beechcroft BR7 30 A1
Beechcroft Cl BR6 86 D6
Beechcroft Gdns CT11 117 F8
Beechcroft Rd BR6 86 D6
Beechcroft CT5 75 D1
Beech Ct
Canterbury CT1 175 A7
Dartford DA1 16 A1
Paddock Wood TN12 257 A7
Royal Tunbridge Wells
TN2 286 D4
Beech Dell BR2,BR4 85 F6
Beech Dr
Broadstairs CT10 83 D4
Elvington CT15 212 B2
Hothfield TN26 267 A7
Maidstone ME16 161 C5
Beechen Bank Rd ME5 97 A1
Beechenlea La BR8 56 B6
Beecher Ct SE12 29 B5
Beeches Ct BR1 29 A2
Beeches The
Aylesford ME20 128 E1
Chatham ME5 97 A4
Hextable BR8 32 F1
Lydd TN29 376 D7
New Barn DA3 59 C7
Royal Tunbridge Wells
TN2 286 D5
Sole Street DA13 60 D5
The Moor TN18 354 E7
Tilbury RM18 19 B5
Beechfield Cotts 6
BR1 52 C7
Beechfield Rd
Bromley BR1 52 C7
Erith DA8 14 E7
Beech Gr CT12 116 C5
Beech Green Cl CT15 245 C7
Beech Green La
Cowden TN7 282 F1
Withyham TN7 311 B7
Beech Gr ME3 39 C4
Beech Haven Ct DA1 14 D2
Beech Hill CT4 209 B8
Beechhill Rd SE9 12 A2
Beech Ho 7 DA15 31 A5
Beech Hurst Cl ME15 162 B2
Beech Hurst TN2 287 D7
Beeching Rd ME5 97 B3
Beechings Gn ME8 65 C3
Beechings Way ME8 65 C3
Beechings Way Ind Ctr
ME8 65 B4
Beechin Wood La
TN15 157 D5
Beech La TN12 288 C4
Beechlands Cl DA3 59 A4
Beech Manor TN2 286 D3
Beech Mast DA13 126 B8
Beechmont Rd TN13 187 B6
Beechmont Rise TN10 222 B6
Beechmore Dr ME5 97 A2
Beecholme Dr TN24 268 C5
Beech Rd
Biggin Hill TN16 118 C2
Dartford DA1 33 D7
East Malling ME19 159 F7
Herne Pound ME18 158 D2
Hoo St Werburgh ME3 41 E3
Newenden TN18 357 C3
Orpington BR6 87 A3
Rochester ME2 62 F6
Sevenoaks TN13 154 B2
Beech St TN1 286 B4
Beechway
Meopham Station DA13 60 B2
Sidcup DA5 13 D1
Beech Wlk
Biddenden TN27 323 D7
Crayford DA1 15 A3
Beechwood Ave
Deal CT14 215 C5
Gillingham ME5 64 D2
Orpington BR6 86 E4
Sittingbourne ME10 101 E6
Beechwood Cl
St Mary's Bay TN29 365 F3
Whitfield CT16 246 A1
Beechwood Cres DA7 13 E4
Beechwood Ct
Deal CT14 215 C5
Temple Ewell CT16 277 E4
Beechwood Dr
Culverstone Green DA13 93 A1
Orpington BR2 85 D6
Beechwood Gdns DA13 93 A1
Beechwood Mews
TN2 286 E4
Beechwood Rd ME16 160 F3
Beechwood Rise BR7 30 B4
Beechwood Sacred Heart
Sch TN2 286 E4
Beechy Lees Rd TN14 122 E3
Beecroft Cl CT2 143 A4
Beeken Dene BR6 86 C6
Beer Cart La CT1 174 F8
Beesfield La DA4 57 A1
Beeston Ct 4 DA1 16 B1
Begbie Rd SE3 11 C6
Beggarsbush La TN29 371 D7
Beggars Cnr CT3 113 D1
Beggars La TN16 151 E3
Begonia Ave ME8 65 C2
Beke Rd ME8 98 D4
Bekesbourne Hill CT4 176 B5
Bekesbourne La
Bekesbourne CT3,CT4 176 E6
Canterbury CT3 175 F7
Littlebourne CT3 176 F6
Bekesbourne Rd CT4 175 F2
Bekesbourne Sta CT4 176 B5
Bekesbourne Tower 12
BR5 54 D1
Belcaire Cl CT21 332 A3
Beldam Haw TN14 121 A8
Belfast Ho 14 ME15 195 E7
Belfield Rd TN2 287 D6
Belford Gr SE18 2 A2
Belgrave Cl
5 Orpington BR5 54 C5
Ramsgate CT11 117 D7
Belgrave Ct Deal CT14 215 D3
Greenwich SE7 11 C7
Belgrave Rd
Dover CT17 310 B7
Halfway Houses ME12 46 C5
Margate CT9 50 I2
Royal Tunbridge Wells
TN1 286 B4
Belgrave St ME20 128 F6
Belgrove 5 TN1 286 A2
Belinda Ct CT19 335 B7
Bellarmine Cl SE28 2 F4
Bell Chapel Cl TN23 300 C4
Bell Cl DA9 16 F2
Bell Cnr TN29 372 A4
Bell Cotts ME9 67 B3
Bell Cres ME1 128 F8
Bell-Davies Dr CT12 82 A1
Bellefield Rd BR5 54 B4
Belle Friday Cl ME9 103 C2
Bellegrove Cl DA16 12 F5
Bellegrove Par DA16 12 F4
Bellegrove Rd DA16 12 E5
Bellevue Ave CT11 117 F7
Bellevue Rd DA6 13 F2
Belle Vue Rd
Farthing Street BR6 86 A1
Herne Bay CT6 77 B5
Bellevue Rd
Minster (Sheppey) ME12 47 C6
Ramsgate CT11 117 F7
Whitstable CT5 108 F8
Bellevue St 5 CT20 335 D5
Bell Farm Gdns ME16 160 F2
Bell Farm La ME12 48 A6
Bellfield Cl SE3 11 B7
Bellflower Ave ME12 47 A4
Bellflower Cl 2 E6 1 E8
Bell Gdns BR5 54 C4
Bell Gr CT3 211 A5
Bellgrove Ct ME5 130 A8
Bell Ho Erith SE2 3 D1
Grays RM17 17 F8
Bellingham Way
ME20 128 B3
Bell La Burham ME1 128 F8
Chatham ME14 130 B7
Larkfield ME20 128 B2
Maidstone ME14 163 A5
Newham E16 1 A5
Sandwich CT13 149 A1
Standen TN27 295 B8
Staplehurst TN12 260 E3
Bellman Ave DA12 37 E7
Bell Mdw ME15 195 E6
Bellows La TN15 156 F7
Bell Rd
Maidstone ME15 195 E5
Sittingbourne ME10 101 F3
Bellring Cl DA17 14 A8
Bell Row TN11 223 F5
Bell's Cl TN30 345 A7
Bells Farm La TN11 224 C8
Bells Farm Rd TN11,
TN12 191 D1
Bell Sh Ctr ME10 101 F4
Bell's La ME3 41 E6
Bells La 9 TN30 345 A7
Bell St SE18 11 E6
Bell Water Gate SE18 2 A3
Bell Way ME17 197 E2
Bellwood Ct ME3 24 C3
Bell Wood Prim Sch
ME15 195 E5
Belmont Ave DA16 12 E4
Belmont Cl ME16 160 F2
Belmont Ct
9 Maidstone ME15 162 B4
2 Ramsgate CT11 117 D7
Belmont CT14 215 B1
Belmont Farm Bsns Ctr
TN26 266 A1
Belmont House & Gdns*
ME13 169 D5
Belmont La BR7 30 C3
Belmont Par BR7 30 C3
Belmont Pl TN24 300 D7
Belmont Prim Sch DA8 14 A7
Belmont Rd
Ashford TN24 268 D6
Broadstairs CT10 84 A4
Chislehurst BR7 30 B3
Belmont Rd continued
Erith DA8 14 B6
Faversham ME13 138 C6
Gillingham ME7 64 C4
Grays RM17 17 F8
Halfway Houses ME12 46 E6
Ramsgate CT11 117 D7
Sittingbourne ME10 101 E3
Westgate-on-S CT8 81 F8
Whitstable CT5 74 D1
Belmont St CT11 117 E7
Belmont Terr CT13 180 B3
Belmont Yd 8 CT5 74 D1
Belmore Pk TN24 268 B3
Belnor Ave
Cold Harbour ME9 100 F8
Lower Halstow ME9 67 F1
Belsey La CT15 276 D4
Belson Rd SE18 1 F2
Beltana Dr DA12 37 E4
Belting Dr CT6 77 E5
Beltinge Rd CT6 77 B5
Belton Cl CT5 108 E8
Belton Rd DA14 31 A4
Beltring Rd
Beltring TN12,ME18 225 B4
Royal Tunbridge Wells
TN4 286 A6
Beltring Sta TN12 225 B4
Beltwood Rd DA17 4 C2
Beluncle Villas ME3 42 C7
Belvedere Cl
Faversham ME13 138 D8
Gravesend DA12 37 C7
Belvedere Ct DA17 3 F3
Belvedere Ho 9
ME15 195 F5
Belvedere Ind Est DA17 4 D5
Belvedere Inf Sch DA17 4 B3
Belvedere Jun Sch DA17 4 B3
Belvedere Link Bsns Pk
DA17 4 C3
Belvedere Mews SE3 11 B7
Belvedere Rd
Bexley DA7 13 F5
Biggin Hill TN16 118 F1
Broadstairs CT10 84 B4
Erith SE28 3 D5
Faversham ME13 138 D8
Belvedere Sta DA17 4 B3
Belvoir Cl SE9 29 E5
Benacre Rd CT5 108 D6
Benares Rd SE18 2 F2
Bench Hill TN26 347 D5
Bench St 10 CT16 310 D7
Benden Cl TN12 260 F4
Bendmore Ave SE2 3 A2
Bendon Way ME8 98 D8
Benedict Cl 9 Erith DA17 3 E3
Halling ME2 95 B4
Orpington BR6 86 E7
Benenden CE Prim Sch
TN17 342 D6
Benenden Gn BR2 52 A4
Benenden Hospl
TN17 322 C3
Benenden Manor ME8 65 B3
Benenden Rd
Benenden TN17 343 B4
Cranbrook TN17 320 E1
Fosten Green TN27 322 F5
Rochester ME2 40 C1
Benenden Sch TN17 342 C8
Bengal Rd CT12 83 A1
Benhall Mill Rd TN2,
TN3 314 D8
Benham Bsns Pk
CT21 331 F5
Benjamin Ct 4 DA17 13 F8
Benn Cl RH8 183 A1
Bennells Ave CT5 75 B3
Bennett Cl DA16 13 A5
Bennett Ct 16 CT20 335 E5
Bennett Ho DA11 36 F5
Bennett Memorial Diocesan
Sch TN4 285 E6
Bennetts Ave TN15 124 C7
Bennetts Copse BR7 29 E2
Bennetts Cotts ME7 131 A8
Bennetts Gdns ME13 137 D8
Bennetts Mews 13
TN30 345 A7
Bennett Way DA2 34 D3
Benn Ho SE7 1 C1
Benover Rd ME18 225 F7
Benson Cl CT18 306 F4
Benson La CT18 306 F4
Benson Rd RM17 18 C8
Bensted TN23 299 F5
Bensted Cl ME15 226 D7
Benstede Cl CT6 77 A1
Bensted Gr ME13 138 A7
Bentfield Gdns SE9 29 D5
Bentham Hill TN3,TN4 253 D1
Bentham Rd SE28 3 B5
Bentham Sq ME12 28 A3
Ben Tillet Cl E16 1 F5
Bentley Ave CT6 76 B4
Bentley Cl
Aylesford ME20 128 F1
Chatham ME5 97 D2
New Barn DA3 59 C7
Bentley Rd TN24 300 F7
Bentleys Bglws TN15 154 F7
Bentley's Mdw TN15 154 F7
Bentley St DA12 19 C1
Bentley Street Ind Est
DA12 19 C1
Bentlif Cl ME16 161 D5
Berber Rd ME2 63 B8
Bercta Rd SE9 30 C6
Bere Cl DA9 17 C2
Berengrave La ME8 65 F2
Berengrave Nature
Reserve* ME8 66 A3
Berens Ct DA14 30 F4
Berens Rd BR5 54 D4
Berens Way BR5 53 F6
Beresford Ave ME1 63 E2
Beresford Cl TN17 317 F2
Beresford Ct 7 CT7 80 F8
Beresford Dr BR1 52 E6
Beresford Gap CT7 80 F8
Beresford Gdns CT9 51 C3
Beresford Rd
Gillingham ME7 64 D4
Goudhurst TN17 290 F1
Kit's Coty ME20 129 D7
Northfleet DA11 36 E8
Ramsgate CT11 117 D6
River CT17 277 E3
St Margaret's at Cliffe
CT15 247 F1
Whitstable CT5 74 D1
Beresfords Hill ME17 195 B4
Beresford Square Market
Pl SE18 2 B2
Beresford St SE18 2 B3
Berger Cl BR5 53 E3
Bergland Pk ME2 63 D8
Bering Wlk E16 1 D7
Berkeley Ave DA7 13 D6
Berkeley Cl
Boughton Street ME13 140 B3
2 Folkestone CT19 335 A7
Orpington BR5 53 E2
Pembury TN2 287 E7
Rochester ME1 96 D8
Berkeley Cres DA1 33 F7
Berkeley Ct
Sittingbourne ME10 101 D3
6 Swanley BR8 55 E6
Berkeley Mount 8
ME4 63 F4
Berkeley Rd
Birchington CT7 80 F8
7 Royal Tunbridge Wells
TN1 286 A2
Berkeley Terr RM18 19 A7
Berkhampstead Rd 9
DA17 4 A1
Berkley Cres DA12 19 C1
Berkley Rd DA12 19 B1
Berkshire Cl ME5 97 C8
Bermuda Rd RM18 19 A5
Bernal Cl SE28 3 D6
Bernard Ashley Dr SE7 1 B1
Bernards Ct DA15 30 E7
Bernards Gdns CT15 244 E5
Bernard St 24 DA12 19 B1
Bernard Sunley Hall
TN25 238 A2
Berner's Hill TN5 339 A3
Bernersmede SE3 11 A4
Berridge Rd ME12 28 C2
Berries The CT18 307 B5
Berryfield Cl BR1 52 E7
Berryhill SE9 12 B3
Berryhill Gdns SE9 12 B3
Berrylands Hartley DA3 59 A3
Orpington BR6 87 C7
Berry Rd ME3 41 E3
Berry's Green Rd
TN16 119 B2
Berry's Hill TN16 119 B4
Berry St ME10 101 F4
Bertha Hollamby Ct
DA14 31 C3
Bertha James Ct BR2 52 B5
Bertrand Way SE28 3 C6
Bert Reilly Ho 1 SE18 2 D1
Bertrey Cotts TN16 119 B3
Berwick Cres DA15 12 E1
Berwick Ct 12 DA2 16 B1
Berwick La CT21 332 A3
Berwick Rd Bexley DA16 13 B6
Newham E16 1 C7
Berwick Way TN14 154 B7
Berwyn Gr ME15 195 A6
Beryl Ave E6 1 E8
Beryl Ho 3 SE18 2 F1
Besant Ct 15 SE28 3 B6
Bessels Green Rd
TN13 153 D3
Bessels Meadow
TN13 153 D3
Bessels Way TN13 153 D4
Bessie Lansbury Cl E6 2 A7
Best La CT1 174 F8
Best St ME4 63 F4
Beta Rd ME3 42 D7
Betenson Ave TN13 153 F5
Bethany Cl CT14 215 C8
Bethany Sch TN17 291 B5
Bethel Rd Bexley DA16 13 C4
Sevenoaks TN13 154 C4
Bethel Row ME13 169 F1
Betherinden Cotts
TN18 356 A4
Bethersden Bsns Ctr
TN26 297 C1
Bethersden Ct ME15 195 F7
Bethersden Cty Prim Sch
TN26 297 D5
Bethersden Rd
Hothfield TN26 266 D4
Shadoxhurst TN26 298 E2
Smarden TN27,TN26 296 C5
Woodchurch TN26 326 A6
Beths Gram Sch DA5 14 B1
Betjeman Cl ME20 127 F3
Betony Gdns ME14 162 F5

Betsham Rd
Betsham DA13 35 D3
Erith DA8 14 F7
Maidstone ME15 195 F6
Swanscombe DA10 35 E8
Betterton Dr DA14 31 E6
Bettescombe Rd ME8 98 E7
Betts Rd E16 1 B6
Betty Shelvey Ct CT14 215 D4
Beulah Rd TN1 286 C4
Beult Mdw TN27 264 A1
Beult Rd DA1 15 A3
Bevan Pl BR8 55 F5
Bevan Rd SE2 3 B1
Bevans Cl DA9 17 C1
Bevan Way CT3 210 E5
Bevercote Wlk 1 DA17 13 F8
Beveridge Ct 1 SE28 3 B6
Beverley Ave DA15 30 F8
Beverley Cl ME8 98 F8
Beverley Cres TN9 253 F7
Beverley Ct 8 DA14 31 B4
Beverley Gdns TN29 353 A4
Beverley Ho CT2 142 F2
Beverley Holiday Camp ME12 49 A5
Beverley Rd Bexley DA7 14 C5
Canterbury CT2 142 E2
Maidstone ME16 160 F2
Orpington BR2 85 E8
Beverley Way CT12 83 C1
Beverly Cl CT7 81 B8
Bevile Ho RM17 18 B7
Bevis Cl DA2 34 C8
Bewl Bridge Cl TN5 339 B3
Bewlbridge La
Lamberhurst TN3,TN5 317 B1
Lower Cousley Wood TN5 337 F8
Bewley La TN15 156 D2
Bewl Water Nature Reserve* TN5 338 B7
Bewl Water Visitor Ctr* TN3 338 B8
Bewsbury Cres CT16 277 F7
Bewsbury Cross La CT16 277 F7
Bexhill Dr RM17 17 F8
Bexley Cl DA1 14 E2
Bexley Coll Erith DA17 4 B1
Erith DA17 4 C2
Bexley Coll (St Joseph's Campus) SE2 13 D8
Bexley Cotts DA4 57 C5
Bexley Gram Sch DA16 13 B3
Bexleyheath Sch DA6 13 F4
Bexleyheath Sta DA7 13 E5
Bexley High St DA5 32 B7
Bexley La Crayford DA1 14 E2
Sidcup DA14 31 C5
Bexley Rd Eltham SE9 12 C2
4 Erith DA8 4 E1
Erith DA8 4 F1
Erith,Northumberland Heath DA8 14 C8
Bexley Sta DA5 32 A7
Bexley St CT5 74 D2
Bexon La Bredgar ME9 134 C4
Silver Street ME9 133 F5
Bhutan Rd CT6 77 C4
Bickley Cres BR1 52 E5
Bickley Ct 2 BR1 52 E6
Bickley Park Rd BR1 52 F6
Bickley Park Sch BR1 52 E6
Bickley Prim Sch BR1 52 C7
Bickley Rd Bromley BR1 52 E7
5 Tonbridge TN9 254 B8
Bickley Sta BR1 52 E6
Bickmore Way TN9 222 D3
Bicknor Cl CT2 143 B4
Bicknor Court Cotts ME9 133 C2
Bicknor La ME9 133 D3
Bicknor Rd
Maidstone ME15 195 F4
Orpington BR6 53 F2
Bidborough CE Prim Sch TN3 253 D3
Bidborough Ct TN3 253 B3
Bidborough Ridge TN4 253 E4
Biddenden Cl
Maidstone ME15 162 F3
Margate CT9 51 C1
Biddenden La TN27 262 E5
Biddenden Rd
Headcorn TN27 262 E2
Tenterden TN26,TN26 324 A6
Tenterden TN30 323 E6
Tylden TN27 295 F8
Biddenden Vineyards & Cider Works* TN27 323 A5
Biddenden Way
Eltham SE9 30 A4
Istead Rise DA13 36 E1
Biddulph Ho 17 SE18 1 F2
Bideford Rd DA16 13 B7
Bierce Ct CT7 80 F7
Bierce Ct Cotts CT7 80 F7
Bifrons Gdns CT4 176 B3
Bifrons Hill CT4 176 B4
Bifrons Rd CT4 176 B4
Bigbury Rd CT2,CT4 173 E7
Biggin Hill Airport TN16 118 D5
Biggin Hill Bsns Pk TN16 118 D4
Biggin Hill Jun & Inf Schs TN16 118 E3
Biggin La RM16 19 B8
Biggin St CT16 310 D8
Biggins Wood Rd CT19 334 E7
Bigglestone Link 11 CT1 175 A8
Bignell Rd SE18 2 B1
Bilberry Cl ME14 162 E5
Billet Hill TN15 91 C6
Bill Hamling Cl SE9 29 F6
Billings DA3 58 F3
Billington Gdns TN24 268 E6
Bill Street Rd ME2 40 C1
Bilsby Gr SE9 29 D4
Bilsington Cl ME5 97 B5
Bilsington Cross TN25 329 C2
Bilton Rd DA8 15 A8
Bimbury La ME14,ME9 132 A5
Bindon Blood Rd CT16 278 A5
Bines The TN12 257 A5
Bingham Point 5 SE18 2 B2
Bingham Rd ME2 40 C1
Bingley Cl ME6 127 F8
Bingley Rd Newham E16 1 C7
1 Rochester ME1 63 E4
Binland Gr ME5 96 D5
Binnacle Rd ME1 96 C8
Binney Rd ME3 9 D2
Binnie Cl CT10 83 F2
Binsey Wlk 1 SE2 3 C4
Birbetts Rd SE9 29 F6
Birch Cl Ashford TN24 268 F2
Broadstairs CT10 83 C3
Eynsford DA4 89 D7
Matfield TN12 256 D1
New Barn DA3 59 C7
Royal Tunbridge Wells TN2 286 D7
Sevenoaks TN13 154 B4
Tonbridge TN11 221 D4
Birch Cres ME20 160 D8
Birch Ct Barham CT4 242 F8
Ramsgate CT11 117 D8
Birchden Cotts TN3 312 C6
Birchdene Dr SE28 3 A5
Birch Dr ME5 97 D1
Birches The
Birchington CT7 81 B7
Greenwich SE7 11 B8
Orpington BR6 86 A6
Swanley BR8 55 E7
Tonbridge TN9 254 B7
Birchett TN23 267 E1
Birchett La TN26 327 D3
Birchetts Ave TN3 284 E3
Birchetts Green La TN5 338 A2
Birchfield Cl ME15 195 B6
Birchfield TN14 185 E8
Birchfields ME5 97 A3
Birch Gr Bexley DA16 13 A3
Gillingham ME7 98 A4
Birch Hill Ct CT7 81 B7
Birch Ho
6 Maidstone ME16 161 A3
Sheerness ME12 28 B2
Sittingbourne ME10 102 B3
Birchin Cross Rd TN15 123 A5
Birchington CE Prim Sch CT7 81 A6
Birchington Cl
Bexley DA7 14 B6
Maidstone ME14 162 C5
Orpington BR5 54 C1
Birchington-On-Sea Sta CT7 80 F7
Birch Kiln Cotts TN5 337 A6
Birch Mead BR6 86 A8
Bircholme TN2 286 D7
Bircholt Forstal TN25 302 E7
Bircholt Rd ME15 195 F4
Birch Pl
Sevenoaks TN13 154 A3
Stone DA9 16 E1
Birch Rd
Hoo St Werburgh ME3 41 E3
Paddock Wood TN12 257 A6
Whitstable CT5 109 A8
Birch Row BR2 53 A3
Birch Tree Ho 18 SE7 11 C8
Birch Tree Way ME15 162 B3
Birch Way TN2 286 D7
Birchway TN15 90 F2
Birchwood Ave
Bidborough TN4 253 E3
Sidcup DA14 31 C5
Birchwood Dr DA2 32 E4
Birchwood La TN14 120 F4
Birchwood Par DA2 32 E4
Birchwood Park Ave BR8 55 F6
Birchwood Prim Sch BR8 55 D8
Birchwood Rd
Joyden's Wood DA2,BR8 32 D3
Maidstone ME16 161 C5
Orpington BR5 53 E5
Birchwood Rise CT17 310 C7
Birchwood Terr BR8 55 C8
Birchwood Wlk CT2 142 E2
Birdbrook Rd SE3 11 C4
Birdham Cl BR1 52 E4
Bird House La BR6 119 A5
Bird in Hand La BR1 52 D7
Bird in Hand St TN3 312 B8
Bird La TN5 336 B5
Birds Ave CT9 82 B7
Birdwood Ave CT14 215 A5
Birkbeck Prim Sch DA14 31 B5
Birkbeck Rd DA14 31 A5
Birkdale Cl Erith SE28 3 D7
Orpington BR6 53 D2
Whitstable CT5 109 D8
Birkdale Ct 3 ME16 161 E4
Birkdale Dr CT19 335 A8
Birkdale Gdns CT6 76 D2
Birkdale Rd SE2 3 A2
Birkdale TN1 286 B6
Birken Rd TN2 286 D6
Birkhall Cl ME5 97 A5
Birling Ave
Gillingham ME8 65 E1
Maidstone ME14 163 A4
Birling Cl ME14 163 A4
Birling Dr TN2 286 A1
Birling Hill DA13,ME19, ME6 94 B1
Birling Park Ave TN2 314 B8
Birling Pk ME19 127 C5
Birling Rd
Ashford TN24 268 D1
Bexley DA8 14 E6
Leybourne ME19 127 C3
Royal Tunbridge Wells TN2 314 B8
Ryarsh ME19 127 A5
Snodland ME6 127 F7
Birnam Sq 1 ME16 161 E4
Birtrick Dr DA13 59 F4
Bishopbourne Gn ME8 65 B4
Bishop Butt Cl BR6 86 F7
Bishop Ct
4 Sittingbourne ME10 101 E5
Whitstable CT5 74 F2
Bishopden Ct CT2 142 C4
Bishop Jenner Ct CT3 146 C6
Bishop John Robinson CE Prim Sch SE28 3 C6
Bishop La ME9 66 E3
Bishop's Ave CT10 84 B6
Bishops Ave BR1 52 C6
Bishopsbourne Ho 2 BR1 29 B1
Bishops Cl Eltham SE9 30 C6
Nettlestead ME18 192 D6
Bishops Ct
Royal Tunbridge Wells TN4 285 F3
Stone DA9 16 E2
Bishops Ctyd 14 CT1 175 A8
Bishop's Down Park Rd TN4 285 F4
Bishop's Down Prim Sch TN4 285 E5
Bishop's Down Rd TN4 285 F3
Bishop's Down TN4 285 F3
Bishops Gn
Ashford TN23 299 E7
Bromley BR1 52 C8
Bishops La TN17 319 E2
Bishop's La ME15 226 D6
Bishops Mews TN9 254 C8
Bishops Oak Ride TN10 222 C6
Bishopstone Dr CT6 77 F6
Bishopstone La CT6 77 F5
Bishops Way
Canterbury CT2 142 D1
Maidstone ME15 161 F4
Bishops Wlk
Chislehurst BR7 53 C8
Rochester ME1 63 C5
Bishopswood TN23 300 C3
Bittern Cl CT18 307 A3
Blackberry Field BR5 54 A8
Blackberry Way
Paddock Wood TN12 257 B6
Whitstable CT5 109 B8
Blackbrook La BR1,BR2 53 A5
Black Bull Rd CT19 335 D6
Blackburn Rd CT6 76 B2
Blackdale Farm Cotts DA1 34 B6
Blackdown Dr TN24 268 B4
Black Eagle Cl TN16 184 C8
Blacketts Cotts ME9 103 B7
Blacketts Rd ME9 103 A6
Blackfen Par DA16 13 A1
Blackfen Rd DA15 13 B1
Blackfen Sch for Girls DA15 13 B1
Blackfriars St 16 CT1 142 F1
Black Griffin La CT1 174 F8
Blackhall La TN15 154 E3
Blackheath Bluecoat CE Sec Sch SE3 11 B7
Blackheath High Sch GPDST (Jun Dept) SE3 11 A5
Blackheath High Sch SE3 11 A7
Blackheath Pk SE3 11 A5
Blackheath Prep Sch SE3 11 A6
Black Horse Ct TN27 262 E5
Black Horse Farm Cvn Pk CT18 306 F8
Black Horse Mews TN15 157 A7
Blackhorse Mews TN2 287 C6
Black Horse Rd 14 DA14 31 A4
Blackhouse Hill CT18, CT21 333 D4
Blackhouse Rise CT21 333 D3
Blackhurst La TN2 286 F6
Blacklands Dr ME19 159 F8
Blacklands
East Malling ME19 159 F7
East Malling ME19 159 F8
Blackleys ME13 171 F7
Blackman Cl ME3 41 D7
Blackmans Cl DA1 33 C7
Blackman's La TN11 223 D6
Blackmanstone Way ME16 161 B7
Blackmead TN13 153 E6
Black Mill La TN27 262 B6
Blackness La BR2 85 D2
Black Post ME17 165 E4
Black Robin La CT4 209 E3
Black Rock Gdns ME7 98 B4
Blacksmith Dr ME14 162 D5
Blacksmiths Field TN32 355 C1
Blacksmiths La BR5 54 C4
Blacksmith's La TN5 337 A5
Blacksole La TN15 124 F3
Blacksole Rd TN15 124 F3
Blackstable Ct CT5 108 D8
Black's Yd TN13 154 C2
Blackthorn Ave
Chatham ME5 97 A3
Royal Tunbridge Wells TN4 254 C1
Blackthorn Cl TN15 90 F2
Blackthorn Dr ME20 128 B2
Blackthorne Rd ME8 99 B8
Blackthorne Way TN23 300 C3
Blackthorn Gr DA7 13 E4
Blackthorn Rd
Biggin Hill TN16 118 E3
Hersden CT3 144 D8
Blackwall Rd TN24, TN25 269 B4
Blackwall Rd N TN24 269 A2
Blackwall Rd S TN24 269 A2
Blackwater Cl RM13 4 E8
Bladindon Dr DA5 31 D8
Blainey Ho ME3 40 F6
Blair Cl DA15 12 E2
Blair Dr TN13 154 B4
Blake Cl Bexley DA16 12 E6
Deal CT14 248 C8
Blake Ct Ashford TN24 300 F8
6 Ramsgate CT11 117 D7
Blake Dr 3 ME20 127 F4
Blake Gdns DA1 15 F3
Blakemore Way DA17 3 E3
Blakeney Cl ME14 163 B4
Blaker Ave ME1 63 E1
Blaker Ct SE7 11 C7
Blake Way
Royal Tunbridge Wells TN2 286 D7
Tilbury RM18 19 C5
Blanchard Cl SE9 29 E5
Blanchard Ho BR7 30 C2
Bland Dr CT18 307 C5
Blandford Gdns ME10 101 E1
Bland St SE9 11 D3
Blanmerle Rd SE9 30 B7
Blann Cl SE9 11 D1
Blatcher Cl ME12 47 B6
Blatchford Cl ME19 127 F1
Blatchington Rd TN1 286 B1
Blaxland Cl ME13 138 B8
Bleak Hill La SE18 12 F8
Bleak Ho* CT10 84 B4
Bleak Rd TN29 376 C6
Bleakwood Rd 6 ME5 96 F5
Blean Comm CT2 142 A6
Blean Hill CT2 142 A5
Blean Prim Sch CT2 142 B4
Blean Rd ME8 65 C2
Blean Sq ME14 162 C6
Blean View Rd CT6 76 B2
Blean Woods Nature Reserve* CT2 141 F4
Bledlow Cl SE28 3 C6
Blendon Dr DA5 13 D1
Blendon Rd
Maidstone ME14 162 C5
Sidcup DA5 13 D1
Blendon Terr SE18 12 C8
Blenheim Ave
Canterbury CT1 143 D1
Chatham ME4 63 E2
Faversham ME13 138 E5
Blenheim Cl
Broadstairs CT10 83 D3
Dartford DA1 15 C1
Herne Bay CT6 77 A1
Maidstone ME15 162 F3
Meopham DA13 93 B8
Blenheim Ct
Chatham ME4 63 E3
Sidcup DA15 30 D5
Blenheim Dr
Bexley DA16 12 F6
Dover CT16 278 C3
Hawkinge CT18 307 A4
Blenheim Gr DA12 37 C8
Blenheim Ho
Margate CT9 51 C3
Woolwich SE18 2 C3
Blenheim Pl CT20 334 F4
Blenheim Prim Sch BR6 87 C8
Blenheim Rd
Bromley BR1 52 E5
Dartford DA1 15 C1
Deal CT14 215 D5
Littlestone-on-Sea TN28 373 D6
Orpington BR5,BR6 87 C8
Sidcup DA15 31 C7
Sittingbourne ME10 102 B2
Blenheim Way TN5 339 C3
Bleriot Meml* CT16 278 F1
Bletchington Ct 3 DA17 4 A2
Blewbury Ho 3 SE2 3 C4
Bliby Bsns Ctr TN25 328 F7
Bliby Cnr TN25 328 F8
Bligh Inf Sch ME2 62 C7
Bligh Jun Sch ME2 62 C7
Bligh Rd DA11 19 A1
Bligh's Ct TN13 154 B2
Bligh's Rd TN13 154 B2
Bligh's Wlk TN13 154 C2
Bligh Way ME2 62 D6
Blindgrooms La TN26 299 C1
Blindhouse La TN25 304 B3
Blind La Bredhurst ME7 98 A1
Challock TN25 203 C2
Gillingham ME7 97 F1
Goudhurst TN17 290 E1
Mersham TN25 301 C4
Blind Mary's La ME9 133 E4
Bliss Way TN10 222 E5
Blithdale Rd SE2 3 A2
Blockhouse Rd 7 RM17 18 C8
Blockmakers Ct ME4 64 B1
Bloody Point Rd CT13 149 B4
Bloomfield Rd
Bromley BR2 52 D4
Woolwich SE18 2 B1
Bloomfield Terr TN16 151 E2
Bloomsbury Rd CT11 117 C6
Bloomsbury Way TN24 268 B7
Bloomsbury Wlk 2 ME15 162 A4
Bloors La ME8 65 D1
Bloors Wharf Rd ME7 65 F4
Blossom La TN25 267 E5
Blowers Hil Cott TN3 285 B8
Blowers Hill TN8 282 D8
Blowers Wood Gr ME7 98 B3
Bloxam Gdns SE9 11 E2
Blue Anchor La RM18 19 E8
Bluebell Cl
Gillingham ME7 64 F6
Kingsnorth TN23 300 B4
Orpington BR6 86 C8
Bluebell Rd TN23 300 C3
Bluebell Wlks TN12 257 A5
Bluebell Woods Mobile Home Pk CT2 143 D6
Blueberry La TN14 120 C4
Bluebird Ct CT17 310 A6
Bluebird Way SE28 2 D4
Blue Boar La ME1 63 D5
Blue Chalet Ind Pk TN15 90 D4
Blue Coat La TN17 318 C6
Blue Field TN23 299 C8
Bluefield Mews CT5 108 C6
Bluehouse Gdns RH8 183 A7
Blue House La CT21 333 B8
Bluehouse La RH8 183 A8
Blue Line La TN24 268 B3
Bluett St ME14 162 A5
Bluewater Cvn Pk CT21 353 E8
Bluewater Parkway DA9 34 E8
Bluewater DA9 34 F8
Blunden La ME18 193 A1
Blunts Rd SE9 12 A2
Blythe Cl ME10 102 C5
Blythe Ct Hythe CT21 333 D2
Lewisham SE12 29 A8
Blythe Hill BR5 54 A8
Blythe Rd ME15 162 B4
Blyth Ho 5 DA8 4 E1
Blyth Rd SE28 3 C6
Boakes Mdw TN14 121 F8
Boarders La TN5 338 C3
Boarley Ct ME14 129 F1
Boarley La ME14 129 F2
Boarman's La TN29 370 E8
Boathouse Rd ME12 27 F3
Boat La TN25 330 A4
Bob Amor Cl ME13 138 E7
Bobbing Hill ME9 101 A6
Bobbing Village Sch ME9 101 B7
Bobbin Lodge Hill CT4 173 B2
Bockham Cotts TN25 301 E8
Bockham La
Ashford TN25 270 A1
Mersham TN25 301 E8
Bockhanger Ct TN24 268 D5
Bockhanger La TN24 268 C6
Bocking Cl TN5 336 E4
Bockingford La ME15 194 F8
Bocton Ho ME17 195 B3
Bodenham Rd CT20 335 A4
Bodiam Cl ME8 65 C3
Bodiam Ct ME16 161 F3
Bodiam Rd TN18,TN32 355 F3
Bodkins Cl ME17 195 D5
Bodle Ave DA10 17 E1
Bodmin Cl BR5 54 C1
Bodsham CE Prim Sch TN25 271 E8
Bodsham Cres ME15 163 B3
Boevey Path
2 Bexley DA17 13 F8
Erith DA17 3 F1
Bogarde Dr ME2 40 B2
Bogey La BR6 86 A3
Bogle Rd ME9 136 C7
Bognor Dr CT6 76 D4
Bognor Rd DA16 13 D6
Bogshole La
Herne Bay CT6 77 D3
Whitstable CT5 108 E4
Boley Hill ME1 63 C6
Boleyn Ave CT9 50 E1
Boleyn Ct 9 CT1 175 A8
Boleyn Rd TN15 122 E2
Boleyn Way DA10 35 E8
Bolingbroke Ho ME16 161 E3
Bollon Ct 9 SE12 29 B5
Bolner Cl ME5 96 F2
Bolonia CT15 280 A6
Bolton Rd CT19 335 D6
Bolton St CT11 117 D8
Bolts Hill CT4 173 C2
Bombay Ho 1 ME15 195 E5
Bombers La TN16 151 D7
Bonar Pl BR7 29 E1
Bonaventure Ct DA12 37 F4
Bonchester Cl BR7 30 A1
Bond Cl TN14 120 D4
Bondfield Cl TN4 254 A1
Bondfield Ho SE18 12 A7
Bondfield Rd
East Malling ME19 159 F8
4 Newham E6 1 F8
Bondfield Wlk DA1 15 F4
Bond La TN23 300 A2
Bond Rd Ashford TN23 300 B8
Gillingham ME8 98 E5
Bond St RM17 18 C8
Boneashe La TN15 157 D6
Boneta Rd SE18 1 F3
Bonetta Ct ME12 46 B8
Bonflower La ME17 227 C7
Bonham Dr ME10 102 B5
Bonners Alley 19 CT5 74 D2
Bonney Way BR8 55 E6
Bonnington Cross TN25 329 E3
Bonnington Gn ME8 65 C3
Bonnington Rd ME14 162 C6
Bonnington Twr BR2 52 E3
Bonny Bush Hill CT4 209 D5
Bonsor Rd CT19 335 D6
Boorman's Mews ME18 192 E7
Bootham Cl ME2 62 D5
Booth Cl SE28 3 B6
Booth Pl CT9 50 J3
Booth Rd ME4 63 F2
Borden CE Prim Sch ME9 100 F3
Borden Gram Sch ME10 101 F3
Borden La ME10,ME9 101 C3
Bordyke TN9 222 C2
Boreham Ave E16 1 A7
Boresisle TN30 324 B2
Borgard Ho SE18 11 E6
Borgard Rd SE18 1 F2
Borkwood Ct BR6 86 F6
Borkwood Pk BR6 86 F6
Borkwood Way BR6 86 E6
Borland Cl 5 DA9 17 A2
Bornefields TN23 300 A7
Borough CT1 143 A1
Borough Green Prim Sch TN15 157 A7
Borough Green Rd
Borough Green TN15 156 E7
Ightham TN15 156 D6
Wrotham TN15 125 A1
Borough Green & Wrotham Sta TN15 156 F7
Borough Rd
Gillingham ME7 64 D4
Queenborough ME11 46 B4
Tatsfield TN16 150 D6
Borrowdale Ave CT11 117 A7
Borstal Ave CT5 108 D6
Borstal Hill CT5 108 D7
Borstal HM Prison & Youth Custody Ctr ME1 63 B1
Borstal Manor Com Sch ME1 62 F2
Borstal Mews ME1 63 A2
Borstal Rd ME1 63 B3
Borstal St ME1 63 A2
Borton Cl ME18 192 F1
Boscobel Cl BR1 52 F7
Boscombe Rd CT19 335 C6
Bosney Banks CT15 277 A7
Bossingham Rd CT4 240 F3
Bossingham St CT4 240 F6
Bossington Rd CT3 177 E1
Bostall Hill SE2 3 B1
Bostall La SE2 3 B1
Bostall Manorway SE2 3 B2
Bostall Park Ave DA7 13 E7
Bostall Rd BR5 31 B1
Boston Cl 5 CT16 278 B3
Boston Gdns ME8 65 C1
Boston Rd ME5 97 C2
Bosville Ave TN13 154 A4
Bosville Dr TN13 154 A4
Bosville Rd TN13 154 A4
Boswell Cl BR5 54 C3
Boswell Ho BR2 52 D4
Bosworth Ho 3 DA8 4 E1
Botany Bay La BR7 53 C7
Botany Cl ME12 28 B1
Botany Rd CT10 51 F2
Botany TN9 222 C1
Boteler Cotts CT13 180 A2
Botha Rd E13 1 C8
Bothwell Cl 7 E16 1 A8
Botolph's Bridge Rd CT21 353 A6
Botsom La TN15 90 D4
Bottle House Cotts TN11 251 F1
Bottlescrew Hill ME17 195 B4
Bottles La ME9 135 A6
Bottom Pond Rd ME9 134 D3
Bott Rd DA2 33 F4
Boucher Dr DA11 36 F4
Bough Beech Nature Reserve Visitor Ctr* TN14 219 A7
Boughton Ave CT10 84 A2

Boughton Church Cotts ME13 139 D1
Boughton Cl ME8 65 B3
Boughton Cnr TN25 237 C5
Boughton Field Cotts ME13 139 A5
Boughton Hill ME13 140 C3
Boughton Ho BR1 29 E1
Boughton La ME15 195 B6
Boughton Monchelsea Prim Sch ME17 195 B2
Boughton Par ME15 195 A7
Boughton Place Cotts ME17 232 A8
Boughton Rd
Sandway ME17 199 B2
Woolwich SE28 2 E3
Boughton-Under-Blean Meth Prim Sch ME13 139 F3
Boulevard Courrieres CT3 210 E5
Boulevard D'erlanger CT18 334 B7
Boulevard The
Ashford TN24 300 F6
Swanscombe DA9 17 C3
Boulogne Ct 17 CT20 335 E5
Boulthurst Way RH8 183 B3
Boultwood Rd E6 1 F7
Boundary Chase CT5 109 B8
Boundary Cl ME12 47 E6
Boundary Ct CT1 175 B6
Boundary Ho 4 DA11 36 F7
Boundary Rd
Chatham ME4 63 E3
Deal CT14 248 D6
Hythe CT21 333 A2
Ramsgate CT11 117 E7
Royal Tunbridge Wells TN2 286 D1
Sidcup DA15 12 E2
Boundary St 2 DA8 14 F7
Boundary The
Canterbury CT1 174 D7
Langton Green TN3 285 B3
Bounds Cross TN27 294 F7
Boundsgate Cnr ME13 203 B7
Bounds La ME13 140 A3
Bounds Oak Way TN4 253 E3
Bounds The ME20 128 E1
Bourchier Cl TN13 154 B1
Bourdillon Ct SE9 29 E6
Bournbrook Rd SE3, SE9 11 D4
Bourne Cl TN9 222 D3
Bourne Cotts CT4 209 C5
Bourne Ct ME1 63 D5
Bourne Ent Ctr TN15 157 A7
Bourne Grange La TN11 223 D8
Bourne Gr ME10 101 C5
Bourne Ind Pk DA1 14 E2
Bourne La
Cranbrook TN32 354 F1
Hamstreet TN26 349 A8
Plaxtol TN15 156 F1
Sandhurst Cross TN18 355 E4
Tonbridge TN9 222 D3
Bourne Lodge Cl CT2 142 A7
Bourne Mead DA5 14 D2
Bournemouth Dr CT6 76 D4
Bournemouth Gdns CT19 335 C6
Bournemouth Rd CT19 335 C5
Bourne Park Rd CT4 209 A7
Bourne Par DA5 32 B8
Bourne Pk TN11 223 F5
Bourne Place Mdws TN11 221 A7
Bourner Cotts TN17 293 D4
Bourne Rd
Aldington Frith TN25 329 D5
Bexley DA1,DA5 14 D2
Bromley BR2 52 D5
Gravesend DA12 37 F6
Sidcup DA5 32 B8
Bourne Row TN8 251 D6
Bournes Cl CT2 143 F7
Bourneside Terr ME17 164 D2
Bournes Pl TN26 326 A2
Bourne Vale Hayes BR2 52 A2
Plaxtol Spoute TN15 190 A8
Bourne View CT4 175 F1
Bourne Way Hayes BR2 85 A8
Swanley BR8 55 C6
Bournewood Cl ME15 162 F1
Bournewood TN26 349 A8
Bournewood Rd
Orpington BR5 54 C2
Woolwich SE18,SE2 13 A7
Bournville Ave ME4 63 F1
Bouverie Pl 2 CT20 335 D4
Bouverie Rd W CT20 335 C4
Bouverie Sq 1 CT20 335 D4
Bovarde Ave ME19 159 C3
Bow Arrow La
Dartford DA2 16 A1
Dartford DA2 16 B1
Bowater Pl SE3 11 B7
Bowater Rd SE18 1 D3
Bowdell La TN29 362 E3
Bowden Cres CT20 334 C6
Bowen Ct CT11 117 D7
Bowen Rd
Folkestone CT19 334 E6
Rusthall TN4 285 B4
Bowens Field TN23 268 B1
Bower Cl ME16 161 E4
Bower Gn ME5 97 C1
Bower Grove Sch ME16 161 B2
Bower La Eynsford DA4 89 F6
Maidstone ME16 161 E3
Bowerland La
Chilham CT4 172 E1
Old Wives Lees CT4 172 C2
Bower Mount Rd ME16 161 D4
Bower Pl ME16 161 E3
Bower Rd Hextable BR8 33 A2
Smeeth TN25 302 A3
Bowers Ave DA11 36 F4
Bowers Ho ME7 64 E7
Bowers Rd TN14 121 F8
Bower St ME16 161 E4
Bowers Wlk 1 E6 1 F7
Bower Terr ME16 161 E3
Bower Wlk TN12 260 E3
Bowes Ave CT9 50 E1
Bowes Cl DA15 13 B1
Bowes Ct 24 DA2 16 B1
Bowesden La DA12 38 F1
Bowes La CT6 77 A3
Bowes Rd ME2 63 B8
Bowes Villas CT14 180 E4
Bowes Wood DA3 91 F7
Bowford Ave DA7 13 E6
Bow Hill
Lower Hardres CT4 207 F2
Wateringbury ME18 192 D5
Bowland Cl CT6 77 C2
Bowlers Town TN31 368 A2
Bowles Well Gdns CT19 335 F7
Bowley La ME17 232 D8
Bowl Field TN25 271 B6
Bowling Green La CT14 215 B5
Bowling Green Row 1 SE18 1 F2
Bowling Green Terr 8 CT17 310 D7
Bowling St CT13 148 F1
Bowl Rd TN27 201 D2
Bowls Pl TN12 257 A7
Bowman Ave E16 1 A6
Bowman Cl ME5 97 C5
Bowman Ct CT17 278 A1
Bowmans Rd DA1 32 F8
Bowmead SE9 29 F6
Bown Cl RM18 19 B5
Bowness Rd DA7 14 B5
Bow Rd ME18 192 E7
Bowser Cl CT14 214 F4
Bow Terr ME18 192 E7
Bowyer Cl E6 1 F8
Bowyer Rd CT5 107 F7
Bowzell Rd TN14 187 A2
Boxgrove Prim Sch SE2 3 C3
Boxgrove Rd SE2 3 C3
Box La ME13 137 D1
Boxley TN23 299 F8
Boxley Cl
Maidstone ME14 162 B8
West Minst ME12 46 B7
Boxley Rd Chatham ME5 97 B2
Maidstone ME14 162 B7
Boxley St E16 1 B5
Boxmend Ind Est ME15 195 F3
Boxshall Ho 7 SE18 12 B8
Boxted La ME9 67 A1
Box Tree Wlk 26 BR5 54 D1
Boyard Rd SE18 2 B1
Boyces Hill ME9 100 D6
Boy Court La TN27 230 F1
Boyden Gate Hill CT3 112 B8
Boyes La CT3 178 D3
Boyke La CT4 273 C2
Boyle Ho 12 DA17 4 A3
Boyle Way TN12 225 B7
Boyne Pk TN4 285 F4
Boyne Rd CT15 248 A1
Boys Hall Rd TN24 300 F7
Boystown Pl CT13 180 C3
Boyton Court Rd ME17 230 A6
Brabazon Rd ME12 48 C1
Brabner Cl CT19 335 E8
Brabourne Ave ME8 65 C3
Brabourne CE Prim Sch TN25 303 A8
Brabourne Cl CT2 143 A4
Brabourne Cres DA7 13 F8
Brabourne Gdns CT20 334 E5
Brabourne La TN25 271 F2
Brabourne Rd TN25 270 D6
Bracken Cl
Ashford TN24 268 C6
Newham E6 1 F8
Royal Tunbridge Wells TN2 286 E5
Bracken Ct
3 Broadstairs CT10 83 E5
Sittingbourne ME10 102 C5
Brackendene DA2,DA5 32 E4
Bracken Hill ME5 97 A1
Bracken Lea ME5 64 C1
Bracken Rd TN2 286 E5
Brackens The BR6 87 A5
Bracken Wlk TN10 222 B6
Brack La TN29 362 B3
Brackley Cl ME14 162 C5
Brackwood Cl ME8 98 D5
Bracondale Ave DA13 59 F8
Bracondale Rd SE2 3 A2
Bracton La DA2 32 F6
Bradbery Ct 3 DA11 36 F7
Bradbourne Ct TN13 154 B6
Bradbourne La ME20 128 B1
Bradbourne Park Rd TN13 154 A4
Bradbourne Parkway ME19 128 A1
Bradbourne Rd
Grays RM17 18 B8
Sevenoaks TN13 154 B5
Sidcup DA5 32 A8
Bradbourne Sch The TN13 154 A6
Bradbourne Vale Rd TN13,TN14 154 A5
Bradbridge Gn TN23 299 D8
Bradbury Ct 4 SE3 11 A7
Braddick Cl ME15 195 B6
Bradenham Ave DA16 13 A3
Bradfield Ave ME9 103 D2
Bradfield Rd
Ashford TN24 268 B5
Newham E16 1 B4
Bradfields Ave ME5 96 F5
Bradfields Ave W ME5 96 F5
Bradfields Sch ME5 97 A6
Bradfoord Ct CT20 335 D5
Bradford Cl BR2 52 F1
Bradfords Cl ME4 41 B2
Bradford St TN9 222 B1
Bradley Dr ME10 101 E2
Bradley House ME3 25 C4
Bradley Rd
Ashurst TN3 283 D5
Folkestone CT19 335 F6
Ramsgate CT12 83 C1
Upper Halling ME2 94 E5
Bradley Stone Rd E6 1 F8
Bradshaw Cl ME9 66 E3
Bradstone Ave CT19 335 D6
Bradstone New Rd 3 CT20 335 D5
Bradstone Rd CT20 335 D5
Bradstow Sch CT10 84 A3
Bradstow Way CT10 84 A5
Bradymead E6 2 B7
Brady Rd CT18 305 A7
Braeburn Way ME19 159 C3
Braemar Ave DA7 14 C3
Braemar Gdns DA15 30 D5
Braeside Ave TN13 153 F3
Braeside CT10 84 B3
Braeside Cl TN13 153 F4
Braeside Cres DA7 14 C3
Braes The ME3 39 C3
Braesyde Cl DA17 3 F2
Braggs La CT6 110 E6
Braithwaite Ct ME7 65 A5
Brake Ave ME5 96 E5
Brakefield Rd DA13 36 B1
Brakes Pl TN15 90 E4
Bramber Ct 9 DA2 16 B1
Bramble Ave DA2 35 C5
Bramble Bank DA13 125 F7
Bramblebury Rd SE18 2 C1
Bramble Cl
Maidstone ME16 161 B3
Tonbridge TN11 221 F4
Wye TN25 237 D3
Bramble Croft DA8 4 C2
Brambledown
Chatham ME5 97 B8
Folkestone CT19 335 D6
Hartley DA3 58 F5
Bramblefield Cl DA3 58 E6
Bramblefield La ME10, ME9 68 E1
Bramblefields Cl CT6 77 B2
Bramblehill Rd ME13 138 C8
Bramble La
Sevenoaks TN13 187 B7
Wye TN25 237 C3
Bramble Reed La TN12 288 B7
Brambles Ctyd CT14 215 B3
Brambletree Cotts ME1 62 E2
Brambletree Cres ME1 62 F2
Bramble Wlk TN2 286 D7
Brambley Cres CT20 334 E5
Brambling Rise ME10 101 E6
Bramdean Cres SE12 29 A7
Bramdean Gdns SE12 29 A7
Bramhope Ho 16 SE7 11 C8
Bramhope La SE7 11 B8
Bramis Ho TN16 118 D3
Bramley Ave
Canterbury CT1 174 C6
Faversham ME13 138 E6
Bramley Cl
Brabourne Lees TN25 302 E6
Eastchurch ME12 48 D3
Gillingham ME8 99 B8
Istead Rise DA13 36 F1
Newington ME9 100 A5
Orpington BR6 53 B1
Swanley BR8 55 E5
Bramley Cres ME15 162 F3
Bramley Ct Bexley DA16 13 B6
15 Erith DA17 4 A1
Marden TN12 259 B6
Bramley Dr TN17 320 D4
Bramley Gdns
Ashford TN23 300 A6
Coxheath ME17 194 C3
Herne Bay CT6 77 D2
Paddock Wood TN12 256 E7
Bramley Pk ME12 48 E5
Bramley Pl DA1 15 A3
Bramley Rd
East Peckham TN12 224 F6
Snodland ME6 128 A8
Bramley Rise ME2 62 E8
Bramleys TN27 262 D5
Bramley Way
Eastchurch ME12 48 D3
Kings Hill ME19 159 A2
Bramling Gap CT3 177 C3
Bramling Rd CT3,CT4 177 B4
Brampton Prim Sch DA7 13 D5
Brampton Rd DA7 13 E6
Bramshaw Rd CT2 142 E2
Bramshot Ave SE3,SE7 11 B8
Bramshott Cl ME16 161 C6
Bramston Rd ME12 47 C6
Branbridges Ind Est TN12 225 A5
Branbridges Rd TN12 225 B4
Branchley Mews TN27 234 C8
Branch Rd CT4 205 C7
Branch St CT16 278 C1
Brandon Rd
Dartford DA1 34 A8
Ramsgate CT12 83 A1
Brandon St DA11 37 B8
Brandon Way CT7 81 B6
Brandreth Rd E6 1 F7
Brands Hatch Circuit* DA3 90 E6
Brands Hatch Cotts DA3 91 A6
Brands Hatch Rd DA3 91 A7
Branham Ho 1 SE18 2 B1
Bransell Cl BR8 55 C3
Bransgore Cl ME8 98 D7
Branston Cres BR5 53 D1
Branstone Ct RM19 16 B8
Brantingham Cl TN9 253 F7
Branton Rd DA9 16 F1
Brantwood Ave DA8 14 C7
Brantwood Rd DA7 14 B4
Brantwood Way BR5 54 C6
Brasenose Rd ME7 64 E4
Brasier Ct ME12 47 A5
Brassey Ave CT10 83 F3
Brassey Cl RH8 183 A6
Brassey Dr ME20 160 D8
Brassey Hill RH8 183 A6
Brassey Rd RH8 183 A6
Brasted Cl Bexley DA6 13 D2
Orpington BR6 87 A8
Brasted Ct
Brasted TN16 152 D2
Rochester ME2 40 A1
Brasted Hill TN14 152 A7
Brasted Hill Rd TN16 152 C5
Brasted La TN14 120 A1
Brasted Rd Erith DA8 14 E7
Westerham TN16 151 E1
Brattle Farm Mus* TN12 260 D1
Brattle TN26 347 B8
Brattle Wood TN13 187 C6
Braundton Ave DA15 30 F7
Braunstone Dr ME16 161 D7
Bray Gdns ME15 194 F5
Bray Pas E16 1 A6
Braywood Rd SE9 12 D3
Breach La
Lower Halstow ME9 67 A2
Newington ME9 99 F8
Breach Rd RM20 16 F8
Breadlands Cl TN24 300 E8
Breadlands Rd TN24 300 F8
Breakneck Hill DA9 17 B2
Breakspears Dr BR5 54 A8
Bream Cl ME20 128 A5
Breaside Prep Sch BR1 52 D8
Breckonmead BR1 52 C7
Brecon Chase ME12 47 C7
Brecon Ct 7 SE9 12 A1
Brecon Rise TN24 268 B4
Brecon Sq CT12 83 A1
Bredgar CE Prim Sch ME9 134 A5
Bredgar Cl
Ashford TN23 299 F6
Maidstone ME14 162 C5
Bredgar Ho 1 BR5 54 D1
Bredgar Rd ME8 65 B4
Bredgar & Wormshill Light Rly* ME9 133 E1
Bredhurst CE Prim Sch ME7 98 B1
Bredhurst Cl ME12 46 B7
Bredhurst Rd ME8 98 B4
Bredlands La CT3,CT2 111 C1
Breedon Ave TN4 253 F1
Bremner Cl BR8 56 A5
Brenchley Ave
Deal CT14 214 F4
Gravesend DA11 37 B3
Brenchley Cl
Ashford TN23 299 E6
Chislehurst BR7 53 A8
Rochester ME1 63 D2
Brenchley & Matfield CE Prim Sch TN12 289 A8
Brenchley Rd
Gillingham ME8 65 B2
Horsmonden TN12 289 F6
Maidstone ME15 161 F2
Matfield TN12 288 F8
St Paul's Cray BR5 53 F7
Sittingbourne ME10 101 F2
Brenda Ct 4 DA14 31 A4
Brenda Terr DA10 35 E8
Brendon Ave ME5 97 A3
Brendon Cl Bexley DA8 14 E6
Royal Tunbridge Wells TN2 286 D5
Brendon Dr TN24 268 B3
Brendon Rd SE9 30 D6
Brendon 16 DA14 31 A4
Brenley Cnr ME13 139 B4
Brenley Gdns SE9 11 D3
Brenley La ME13 139 C2
Brennan Ct ME7 64 D6
Brennan Rd RM18 19 B5
Brent Cl Chatham ME5 96 E5
Dartford DA2 16 B1
Brent Cl *continued*
Sidcup DA5 31 E7
Brentfield Rd DA1 34 B8
Brent Hill ME13 138 C8
Brent La DA1 34 A7
Brentlands Dr DA1 34 A7
Brentor Ct TN2 286 D6
Brent Prim Sch The DA2 34 C8
Brent Rd
Faversham ME13 138 C8
Newham E16 1 A8
Woolwich SE18 12 B7
Brents Ind Est ME13 105 D1
Brent The Dartford DA1 34 B8
Tonbridge TN10 222 C6
Brent Way DA2 16 B1
Brentwood TN23 299 F5
Brentwood Cl SE9 30 C7
Brentwood Ho SE18 11 D7
Brenzett Aeronautical Mus* TN29 363 B3
Brenzett CE Prim Sch TN29 363 A2
Brenzett Cl ME5 97 B5
Brenzett Cnr TN29 363 A3
Brenzett Ho 6 BR5 54 C4
Bretaneby TN15 154 F6
Bretland Ct TN4 285 D4
Bretland Rd TN4 285 D4
Breton Rd ME1 63 C2
Brett Wlk ME8 98 D4
Brewer Rd ME3 40 B7
Brewers Field DA2 33 C4
Brewer's Hill CT20 334 D3
Brewers Rd DA12 61 C8
Brewer St Deal CT14 215 D6
Lamberhurst TN3 317 A5
Maidstone ME14 162 A5
Brewery Cotts CT14 214 E4
Brewery La Bridge CT4 176 A1
Sevenoaks TN13 154 C2
Brewery Rd
Orpington BR2 52 E1
Sittingbourne ME10 101 E6
Woolwich SE18 2 D1
Brewery Sq CT3 113 D2
Brewhouse La TN25 236 F4
Brewhouse Rd SE18 1 F2
Brewhouse Yd 15 DA12 19 B1
Brewster Cotts ME9 135 E2
Brian Cres TN4 286 B8
Brian Roberts Ho CT6 76 F5
Briar Cl Ashford TN24 268 C6
Aylesham CT3 210 F5
Crabble CT17 277 F2
Larkfield ME20 128 A2
8 Marlpit Hill TN8 217 D3
Briar Dale ME3 39 B4
Briar Fields ME14 162 E5
Briar Rd DA5 32 D5
Briars Cross RH8 183 D5
Briars Rd TN29 365 F3
Briars The
West Kingsdown TN15 90 D4
Whitstable CT5 108 C6
Briars Way DA3 59 A4
Briars Wlk CT10 83 F3
Briarswood Way BR6 86 F5
Briar Wlk TN10 222 C6
Briary Cl CT9 82 A8
Briary Ct DA14 31 B3
Briary Gdns BR1 29 B3
Briary Prim Sch CT6 76 C2
Brice Ave CT4 173 C1
Brice Rd ME3 39 B3
Brick Ct RM17 18 A8
Brickenden Rd TN17 320 D4
Brickfield Cotts
Bexley SE18 12 F8
Wye TN25 237 B2
Brickfield Farm Gdns BR6 86 C6
Brickfield Farm DA3 59 A6
Brickfield La ME13 139 E2
Brickfield TN31 367 B2
Brickfield Rd CT4 242 F7
Brickfields
Pembury TN2 287 E8
West Malling ME19 127 B1
Brick Field View ME2 40 C1
Brick Kiln La
Horsmonden TN12 290 B2
Limpsfield RH8 183 C5
Ulcombe ME17 230 D5
Brickmakers Ind Est ME10 102 B6
Brickwall Terr TN26 325 F3
Brickwell Cotts TN17 293 F6
Brickworks Cl TN9 254 B7
Bridewell La TN30 345 A7
Bridewell Pk CT5 75 A1
Bridge App The CT5 74 F1
Bridge Bsns Pk TN12 256 C7
Bridge Cl Dartford DA2 16 D4
Hythe CT21 333 A2
Tonbridge TN9 254 C8
Woodchurch TN26 347 B8
Bridge Cotts
Horsmonden TN12 290 A6
Selling ME13 171 E7
Teynham ME9 103 D2
Bridge Ct
28 Dartford DA2 16 B1
Grays RM17 18 B8
Bridge Down CT4 209 B8
Bridgefield Ct CT5 75 B3
Bridgefield Rd CT5 75 B3
Bridgeford Way CT4 176 A1
Bridge Hill Bridge CT4 209 B8
Finglesham CT14 214 C8
Bridge Home Pk TN29 376 D8
Bridge Ho
Ramsgate CT11 117 C7
Rochester ME1 63 B4
Royal Tunbridge Wells TN4 286 B5
Bridgeland Rd E16 1 A6
Bridgeman Ct CT21 333 B2
Bridge Mill Way ME15 161 D2
Bridgen Rd DA5 31 E8
Bridge & Patrixbourne CE Prim Sch CT4 176 A2
Bridge Pl ME20 128 F2
Bridge Rd
Ashford TN23 267 F2
Bexley DA7 13 E5
Brabourne Lees TN25 302 D5
Bridge CT4 175 D1
Deal CT14 215 D7
Erith DA8 14 F6
Faversham ME13 138 D8
Gillingham ME7 64 C7
Grays RM17 18 B8
Bridge Rd Ind Ctr TN23 267 F2
Bridge Rd Margate CT9 50 E1
Orpington BR5 54 B3
Rochester ME1 63 C2
Sheerness ME12 28 B2
Bridges Cl CT7 79 E2
Bridges Dr DA1 16 B2
Bridgeside CT14 215 C6
Bridgeside Mews ME15 161 E2
Bridge St Dover CT16 278 C1
Folkestone CT19 335 E6
Maidstone ME15 194 F5
Wye TN25 237 E2
Bridge View Ind Est
Rushenden ME11 46 A2
West Thurrock RM20 16 F8
Bridge View DA9 17 B3
Bridgewater Cl BR7 53 E6
Bridgewater Pl ME19 127 E2
Bridgewater Rd ME12 46 B8
Bridgeway CT5 74 F2
Bridledown Children's Farm & Wildlife Ctr* CT15 309 A4
Bridleway Gdns CT10 83 E3
Bridle Way
Herne Bay CT6 76 D3
Hythe CT21 334 A3
Bridleway La TN23 300 B4
Bridle Way BR6 86 C6
Bridlington Cl TN16 150 B8
Brielle Way
Queenborough ME11, ME12 46 A6
Sheerness ME12 28 A2
Brier Cl ME5 97 C8
Brier Rd ME10 101 B4
Briganda Wlk CT11 117 E8
Bright Cl DA17 3 D2
Bright Ct 8 SE28 3 C5
Brightlands DA11 36 E4
Brightlingsea Rd CT13 180 F8
Bright Rd 3 ME4 64 B2
Bright Ridge TN4 285 E8
Bright's Pl CT11 117 F7
Brigstock Rd DA17 4 B2
Brimpsfield Cl SE2 3 B3
Brimp The ME3 9 D3
Brimstone Cl BR6 87 C3
Brimstone Hill DA13 93 D8
Brindle Gate DA15 30 E7
Brindle Gr CT11 83 F1
Brindle's Field TN9 254 A7
Brindle Way ME5 97 C1
Brindley Cl DA7 14 B4
Brindley Way BR1 29 A3
Brinkburn Cl SE2 3 A2
Brinkers La TN5 337 A2
Brinklow Cres SE18 12 B7
Brinklow Terr TN26 299 A1
Brionne Gdns TN9 254 D8
Brisbane Ave ME10 101 C4
Brisbane Dr CT12 83 A1
Brisbane Ho RM18 18 F6
Brisbane Rd ME4 64 A3
Briset Rd SE9 11 D3
Brishing Cl ME15 195 E5
Brishing La ME17 195 D4
Brishing Rd ME15, ME17 195 F3
Brisley La TN26 328 D6
Brisley's Row ME1 95 F1
Brissenden Cl
Chattenden ME2 41 A3
New Romney TN28 373 B8
Bristles Cnr CT3 111 E6
Bristol Cl ME2 62 D5
Bristol Pl CT11 117 D7
Bristol Rd
Canterbury CT1 174 F6
Gravesend DA12 37 D5
Bristow Rd DA7 13 E6
Britannia Ave CT5 108 B7
Britannia Bsns Pk ME20 160 E7
Britannia Cl Erith DA8 14 F8
Halling ME2 95 A4
Sittingbourne ME10 101 E7
Britannia Dr DA12 37 F3
Britannia Gate E16 1 A5
Britannia La TN23 299 F5
Britannia Rd
Deal CT14 215 D8
Fenn Street ME3 24 A3

Britannia Village Prim Sch E16 1 B5
Briton Ct ME12 46 B8
Briton Rd ME13 138 C7
Brittain Ct SE9 29 E7
Brittain Ho SE9 29 E7
Brittains La TN13 153 F2
Britten Cl Hythe CT21 333 A3
Tonbridge TN10 222 F6
Brittenden Cl [1] BR6 86 F4
Brittenden Par BR6 86 F4
Britton St ME7 64 B5
Brixham Rd DA16 13 D6
Brixham St E16 2 A5
Broadacre
Lydden CT15 276 F8
Teynham ME9 103 D2
Broadbridge Cl SE3 11 A7
Broadcloth TN17 320 D3
Broadcroft Rd BR5 53 D2
Broadcroft TN2 313 F8
Broad Ditch Rd DA13 36 D1
Broader La ME14 131 B2
Broadfield Cres CT20 335 A5
Broadfield Rd
Folkestone CT20 335 A5
Loose ME15 195 A8
Broadgate Hall [1] CT11 117 F7
Broadgate Rd E16 1 D7
Broad Gr TN2 286 A1
Broadheath Dr BR7 29 F3
Broadhoath TN15 155 E1
Broadhurst Dr TN24 268 D7
Broad La Dartford DA2 33 B4
Finglesham CT14 214 B7
Fordcombe TN3 284 A4
Broadlands Ave TN28 373 B8
Broadlands Cres TN28 373 B8
Broadlands Dr ME5 97 B4
Broadlands Ind Est CT2 142 A7
Broadlands Rd BR1 29 B4
Broadlands CT2 143 F6
Broad Lawn SE9 30 A7
Broadley Ave CT7 80 F5
Broadley Rd CT10,CT9 83 C7
Broadmead TN23 299 E6
Broadmead Ave TN2 313 F8
Broadmead Manor CT10 84 B7
Broadmeadow CT19 335 B7
Broadmead Rd CT19 335 C5
Broadmead TN2 313 F8
Broadmere Terr ME16 161 D3
Broadoak Ave ME15 195 A8
Broad Oak TN12 289 C8
Broad Oak Cl
Brenchley TN12 289 C8
Orpington BR5 54 A7
Royal Tunbridge Wells TN2 285 F1
Broadoak Cl DA4 34 A2
Broadoak Ent Village ME9 134 F6
Broad Oak TN3 312 C6
Broadoak ME19 127 E2
Broad Oak Rd CT2 143 B3
Broadoak Rd Erith DA8 14 D7
Sittingbourne ME9 134 E6
Broad Rd DA10 17 E1
Broadsole La CT15 308 E5
Broadstairs Rd CT10 83 E5
Broadstairs Sta CT10 84 A4
Broad St
Canterbury CT1 143 A1
Deal CT14 215 D6
Margate CT9 50 I3
Ramsgate CT11 117 E7
Broad Street Hill ME17 164 D7
Broad St
Sellindge TN25 303 E5
Sheerness ME12 28 B2
Sutton Valence ME17 229 E7
Broadview Ave ME8 98 E8
Broadview
Folkestone CT20 334 C6
Meopham DA13 92 F6
Broadviews CT21 333 D1
Broad View TN17 321 A8
Broadwater Ct TN2 313 E8
Broadwater Down Prim Sch TN2 285 F1
Broadwater Down TN2 313 F8
Broadwater Forest La TN3 313 B7
Broadwater Gdns BR6 86 C6
Broadwater Ho DA12 19 D1
Broadwater La
Royal Tunbridge Wells TN2 313 F8
Royal Tunbridge Wells TN2,TN4 285 F1
Broadwater Rd
East Malling ME19 159 D6
Woolwich SE28 2 D3
Broadwater Rise TN2 285 F1
Broadway Bexley DA6 13 F3
Bexley DA6 14 A3
Crockenhill BR8 55 C3
Gillingham ME8 65 A3
Grays RM17 18 C8
Limpsfield RH8 183 B5
Maidstone ME14 161 F4
Petham CT4 207 A2
Broadway Sh Ctr [5] DA6 14 A3
Broadway ME12 28 C2
Broadway Square Sh Ctr DA6 14 A3
Broadway The
Broadstairs CT10 84 A4
Dover CT16 310 H8
Hadlow TN11 223 E8
Herne Bay CT6 76 C5
Lamberhurst TN3 317 B5
Minster (Sheppey) ME12 47 B7
Broadway RM18 18 F5
Broad Wlk
Eltham SE3,SE9 11 E5
Orpington BR6 87 D7
Sevenoaks TN15 187 E7
Broadwood DA11 37 B3
Broadwood Rd ME3 41 A4
Brockbank Cl ME5 97 A1
Brockdene Dr BR2 85 D6
Brockenhurst Ave ME15 162 C1
Brockenhurst Cl
Canterbury CT2 142 E2
Gillingham ME8 98 C7
Brockenhurst Rd CT11 117 G8
Brockhill Ctry Pk* CT21 332 F4
Brockhill Park Sch CT21 332 F4
Brockhill Rd CT21 333 B3
Brocklebank Ho [7] E16 2 A5
Brocklebank Rd SE7 1 B2
Brocklebank Rd Ind Est SE7 1 B2
Brockley Rd CT9 51 A2
Brockman Cres TN29 353 B4
Brockman Rd CT20 335 C5
Brockman's Cl CT12 115 B7
Brock Rd E13 1 B8
Brockway TN15 157 A7
Brockwell Cl BR5 53 F4
Brodrick Gr SE2 3 B2
Brogdale Farm Cotts ME13 138 A3
Brogdale Farm* ME13 138 B4
Brogdale Pl ME13 138 B6
Brogdale Rd ME13 138 B5
Brogdale World of Fruit* ME13 138 B4
Brogden Cres ME17 196 F7
Broke Farm Dr BR6 87 C2
Brokes Way TN4 286 B8
Brome Ho SE18 11 E6
Brome Rd SE9 11 F4
Bromford Cl RH8 183 A2
Bromhedge SE9 29 F5
Bromholm Rd SE2 3 B3
Bromley Cl ME5 97 B4
Bromley Coll [9] BR1 52 A8
Bromley Coll of F Ed & H Ed (Old Town Hall) BR1 52 A7
Bromley Coll of F Ed & H Ed (Rookery Lane Campus) BR2 52 D3
Bromley Comm BR2 52 D3
Bromley RM17 17 F8
Bromley Green Rd TN26 328 A5
Bromley High Sch BR1 53 A5
Bromley Ind Ctr BR1 52 D6
Bromley La BR7 30 D1
Bromley Manor Mans [3] BR2 52 A6
Bromley Mus* BR6 54 B2
Bromley North Sta BR1 52 A8
Bromley Rd BR7 53 B8
Bromley South Sta BR1 52 A6
Bromley Valley Gymnastics Ctr BR5 54 A7
Brompton Dr DA8 15 B7
Brompton Farm Rd ME2 40 A2
Brompton Hill ME4 63 F6
Brompton La ME2 63 A8
Brompton Rd ME7 64 B6
Brompton Villas CT15 278 E6
Brompton-Westbrook Prim Sch ME7 64 A5
Bromstone Mews CT10 83 E3
Bromstone Prim Sch CT10 83 D3
Bromstone Rd CT10 83 E3
Bronington Cl ME5 97 A5
Bronte Cl Erith DA8 14 B7
Lunsford ME20 127 F3
Tilbury RM18 19 C5
Bronte Gr DA1 15 F3
Bronte Sch DA11 37 A8
Bronte View DA12 37 C7
Bronze Age Way DA8, DA17 4 C3
Brookbank Brook TN25 270 A5
Maidstone ME14 162 A8
Brook Cl Herne Bay CT6 76 C3
Hythe CT21 334 B3
Brook Com Prim Sch TN25 270 A4
Brook Cotts
Collier Street TN12 258 F8
East Farleigh ME15 194 C7
Staple CT3 178 E6
Teynham ME9 104 A2
Brook Ct
[1] Lewisham SE12 29 C5
[10] Marlpit Hill TN8 217 D3
Brookdale Rd DA5 13 E1
Brookdene TN12 256 B7
Brookdene Rd SE18 2 F2
Brooke Ave CT9 82 B7
Brooke Dr DA12 38 B7
Brookend Rd DA15 30 E7
Brooker Cl ME17 195 D5
Brooke Rd TN24 268 B3
Brookes Pl ME9 100 B6
Brookfield Ave
Dover CT16 278 B2
New Hythe ME20 128 A4
Brookfield Ct
Ashford TN23 299 F8
Royal Tunbridge Wells TN4 254 A1
Brookfield TN8 218 B5
Brookfield Ind Pk TN23 267 F1
Brookfield Inf Sch ME20 128 A2
Brookfield Jun Sch ME20 128 A2
Brookfield TN15 122 E2
Brookfield Pl CT16 278 B2
Brookfield Rd
Ashford TN23 299 F8
Dover CT16 278 A3
Brookfield TN18 356 B5
Brookfields TN11 190 E1
Brook Hill Cl SE18 2 B1
Brookhill Rd SE18 2 B1
Brookhurst Gdns TN4 253 E3
Brook La Bexley DA5 13 D2
Bromley BR1 29 A2
Cliffs End CT12 115 F4
Brook La Cotts TN25 303 E2
Brook La SE3 11 B5
Brookland CE Prim Sch TN29 370 D8
Brooklands Ave DA15 30 D6
Brooklands Cl CT2 143 F4
Brooklands DA1 33 E7
Brooklands Farm Cl TN3 284 A6
Brooklands TN27 262 C6
Brooklands Pk SE3 11 A4
Brooklands Prim Sch SE3 11 A4
Brooklands Rd ME20 128 A4
Brooklands TN2 286 D7
Brook La
Plaxtol Spoute TN15 190 A8
Reculver CT6 78 B5
Sellindge TN25 303 E2
Snodland ME6 128 A6
Tonbridge TN9 222 D2
Brooklyn Paddock ME7 64 D6
Brooklyn Rd BR2 52 D4
Brooklyn Villas TN12 259 C5
Brookmead Ave BR1 52 F4
Brookmead Cl BR5 54 B3
Brookmead Rd ME3 40 B7
Brookmead TN11 221 E4
Brookmead Way BR5 54 B3
Brook Pk DA1 34 A6
Brook Rd
Faversham ME13 105 D1
Lunsford ME20 127 F4
Northfleet DA11 36 E7
Royal Tunbridge Wells TN2 286 D7
Swanley BR8 55 D7
Whitstable CT5 75 C3
Brooks Cl Eltham SE9 30 A6
Staplehurst TN12 260 E4
Tonbridge TN10 222 E7
Brookside
Cranbrook TN17 320 D4
Hoo St Werburgh ME3 41 E5
Orpington BR6 53 F2
Brookside Pk ME12 48 F6
Brookside Rd DA13 36 F1
Brookside
St Mary's Bay TN29 366 A5
Temple Ewell CT16 277 D5
Brooks Pl ME14 162 A4
Brook Sq SE18 11 E6
Brook St Eastry CT13 180 C2
Erith DA8 14 B7
Snodland ME6 128 B8
Tonbridge TN9 254 A8
Woodchurch TN26 346 D8
Brooks Way TN29 376 C5
Brook The ME4 64 A4
Brook Vale DA8 14 B6
Brookvale Workshops DA11 36 C7
Brookway SE3 11 A4
Broom Ave BR5 54 B7
Broom Cl BR2 52 E3
Broomcroft Rd ME8 65 F2
Broomfield Cres CT9 51 F2
Broomfield Gate CT5 109 D5
Broomfield Ho [4] BR5 54 B7
Broomfield Rd
Bexley DA6 14 A2
Faversham ME13 138 C8
Folkestone CT19 334 E6
Herne Bay CT6 77 C2
Kingswood ME17 197 D4
Sevenoaks TN13 153 F5
Swanscombe DA10 17 E2
Broomfields DA3 58 E4
Broomhill Bank Sch TN3 285 C6
Broom Hill Cotts TN5 339 B3
Broomhill Park Rd TN4 285 F8
Broomhill Rd
Dartford DA1 15 B1
Orpington BR6 54 A2
Broom Hill Rd ME2 62 F8
Broomhill Rd TN3 285 D7
Broomhill Rise DA6 14 A2
Broomhills DA13 35 E4
Broom La TN3 284 F1
Broomlands La RH8 183 E8
Broomleigh [3] BR1 52 A8
Broom Mead DA6 14 A2
Broom Pk TN3 284 E3
Broom Rd ME10 102 C5
Broomscroft Cotts ME18 159 C1
Broomshaw Rd ME16 160 F3
Broomsleigh TN16 118 E2
Broomwood Cl DA5 32 D6
Broomwood Rd BR5 54 B7
Brotherhood Cl CT2 142 D4
Brougham Ct [5] DA2 16 B1
Broughton By-Pass ME13 140 C2
Broughton Ct TN23 267 E1
Broughton Rd
Orpington BR6 86 D8
Otford TN14 122 A3
Brow Cl BR5 54 D2
Brow Cres BR5 54 D2
Browndens Rd ME2 94 E4
Brownelow Copse ME5 97 B1
Brownhill Cl ME5 97 A4
Browning Cl
Bexley DA16 12 E6
[6] Lunsford ME20 127 F4
Browning Pl CT19 335 E7
Browning Rd DA1 15 F3
Brownings TN8 217 C4
Brownings Orch ME9 135 A7
Browning Wlk RM18 19 C5
Brown Lo ME12 28 H1
Brown Rd DA12 37 E7
Brownspring Dr SE9 30 B5
Browns Sch BR6 87 F5
Brown St ME8 65 F1
Broxbourne Rd BR6 53 F2
Broxhall Rd CT4 208 B3
Bruce Cl Bexley DA16 13 B6
Deal CT14 215 B4
Bruce Ct DA15 30 F4
Bruce Gr BR6 54 A1
Bruces Wharf Rd RM17 18 A8
Brucks The ME18 192 E7
Bruges Ct ME10 68 F1
Brummel Cl DA7 14 C4
Brundell Terr CT4 173 B2
Brunel Cl RM18 19 B4
Brunel Way ME4 64 A7
Brungers Wlk TN10 222 B5
Brunswick Cl DA6 13 D3
Brunswick Cotts ME9 103 E6
Brunswick Ct [3] CT11 117 E7
Brunswick Field ME9 103 E6
Brunswick Gdns [3] CT16 278 B3
Brunswick House Prim Sch ME16 161 E5
Brunswick Ind Ctr TN23 267 F2
Brunswick Rd
Ashford TN23 267 F2
Bexley DA6 13 E3
Birchington CT7 81 A5
Brunswick St E ME15 162 A3
Brunswick Sq CT6 76 E5
Brunswick St
Maidstone ME15 162 A3
Ramsgate CT11 117 E7
Brunswick Terr TN1 286 A2
Brunswick Wlk [1] DA12 37 D8
Brushwood Lodge [1] DA17 4 A2
Bruton Cl BR7 29 F1
Bryanston Rd RM18 19 C5
Bryant Cl ME18 192 D6
Bryant Rd ME2 63 A7
Bryant St ME4 64 A3
Bryces Alley CT5 74 D2
Brymore Cl CT1 143 B2
Brymore Rd CT1 143 B2
Bryony Dr TN23 300 C3
Bryony Sch ME8 98 F5
Bubblestone Rd TN14 122 B3
Bubhurst La TN17 294 B7
Buckden Cl SE12 11 A1
Buckham Thorns Rd TN16 151 C1
Buckhole Farm Rd ME23 23 C4
Buckhurst Ave TN13 154 C2
Buckhurst Dr CT9 51 F2
Buckhurst La
Rockrobin TN5 336 A6
Sevenoaks TN13 154 C2
Buckhurst Pl TN5 336 A6
Buckhurst Rd TN16 151 B7
Buckingham Ave DA16 12 E3
Buckingham Cl BR5 53 E2
Buckingham Dr BR7 30 C3
Buckingham Rd
[15] Broadstairs CT10 84 B4
Gillingham ME7 64 D5
Margate CT9 50 I1
Northfleet DA11 36 D8
Royal Tunbridge Wells TN1 286 B2
Whitstable CT5 75 B2
Buckingham Row ME15 195 E7
Buckland Ave CT16 278 B2
Buckland Cl ME5 97 A2
Buckland Cotts ME13 137 B8
Buckland Hill ME16 161 E5
Buckland Hospl CT17 278 A1
Buckland La
Maidstone ME16 161 D6
Staple CT3 179 A4
Buckland Pl ME16 161 E4
Buckland Rd
Cliffe Woods ME3 40 A8
Luddesdown DA13 94 A7
Maidstone ME16 161 E4
Orpington BR6 86 E6
Buckler Gdns SE9 29 F5
Bucklers Cl
Royal Tunbridge Wells TN2 286 C3
Warden ME12 49 E4
Buckles Ct DA17 3 D2
Buckley Cl DA1 14 F5
Bucks Cross Rd
Chelsfield BR6 87 E5
Northfleet DA11 36 F5
Bucksford La TN23 299 C7
Buck St TN25 203 C2
Buckthorn Cl CT14 215 C7
Buckthorne Ho ME12 47 A4
Buckthorne Rd ME12 47 A4
Buckthorn House DA15 30 F5
Buckwheat Ct DA18 3 D3
Budd Ho [4] SE7 1 C1
Buddle Dr ME12 46 E7
Budd's Farm Cotts TN30 359 E2
Budd's La TN30 359 F2
Budgin's Hill BR6 120 C8
Budleigh Cres DA16 13 C6
Buenos Ayres CT9 50 H2
Buffs Ave CT20 334 B6
Bugglesden Rd TN27, TN30 323 D5
Bugsby's Way SE10,SE7 1 B2
Builders Sq CT3 177 A8
Bullace La [3] DA1 15 E1
Bull Alley DA16 13 B4
Bullbanks Rd DA17 4 C2
Bulldog Rd ME5 97 B2
Bulleid Pl TN24 300 D7
Bullen La TN12 224 E7
Buller Rd ME4 63 F2
Buller's Ave CT6 76 E4
Bullers Cl DA14 31 E3
Bullers Wood Dr BR7 29 F1
Bullers Wood Sch BR7 52 E8
Bull Fields ME6 128 A8
Bullfinch Cl
Paddock Wood TN12 257 A5
Sevenoaks TN13 153 D5
Bullfinch Cnr TN13 153 E5
Bullfinch Dene TN13 153 D5
Bullfinch La TN13 153 E5
Bull Hill
Horton Kirby DA4 57 C5
Lenham Heath ME17 200 A1
Bullingstone Cotts TN3 284 E7
Bullingstone La TN3 284 F7
Bullion Cl TN12 256 F6
Bullivant Cl [3] DA9 17 A2
Bull La
Bethersden TN26 297 B4
Boughton Street ME13 139 F4
Chislehurst BR7 30 D1
Eccles ME20 128 F5
Lower Higham ME3 39 D7
Bull Lane Cotts
Hook Green TN3 316 C4
Yelsted ME9 99 E1
Bull La Wrotham TN15 125 A3
Yelsted ME9 99 E2
Bullockstone Rd CT6 110 E7
Bull Orch ME16 160 F2
Bull Rd ME19 127 C5
Bulls Cotts [4] CT21 333 B2
Bulls Pl TN2 287 D6
Bulltown Cnr TN25 270 F3
Bullwark St CT17 310 D5
Bull Yd [6] DA11 19 B1
Bulrush Cl ME5 96 F3
Bulrushes The TN23 299 D8
Bulwark Rd CT14 215 D7
Bumbles Cl ME1 96 D7
Bunce Court Rd ME13, ME17 200 E7
Bungalows The
Faversham ME13 138 A4
Tenterden TN30 345 D7
Woodnesborough CT13 180 B5
Bunkers Hill Ave CT17 278 B1
Bunker's Hill
Dover CT17 278 B2
Erith DA17 4 A2
New Ash Green TN15 92 B4
Bunkers Hill Rd CT17 278 A1
Bunkers Hill DA14 31 F5
Bunkley Mdw TN26 349 A7
Bunny La TN3 313 E5
Bunters Hill Rd ME3 40 B4
Bunton St SE18 2 A3
Burberry La ME17 197 B5
Burcharbro Rd SE2 13 D8
Burch Ave CT13 180 F8
Burch Rd DA11 18 F1
Burdens TN27 262 D5
Burdett Ave DA12 38 F4
Burdett Cl DA14 31 E3
Burdett Rd TN4 285 B4
Burdock Ct ME16 161 A3
Burdock Ho [6] ME15 195 D8
Burford's Alley CT3 147 D1
Burford Rd BR1 52 E5
Burgate CT1 175 A8
Burgate Cl DA1 14 F4
Burgate La [5] CT1 175 A8
Burgate Terr TN25 301 E4
Burgess Cl
Minster (Thanet) CT12 115 C7
Whitfield CT16 278 B7
Burgess Gn CT14 214 C8
Burgess Hall Dr ME17 196 F6
Burgess Rd
Aylesham CT3 210 F6
Rochester ME2 63 B7
Burgess Row [10] TN30 345 A7
Burghclere Dr ME16 161 B2
Burghfield Rd DA13 36 F1
Burgoyne Ct ME14 161 F7
Burgoyne Gr CT16 278 A5
Burgoyne Hts CT15 278 E3
Burham CE Prim Sch ME1 128 F8
Burham Rd ME1 95 E8
Burial Ground La ME15 161 E1
Burkeston Cl ME10 102 A8
Burleigh Ave DA15 12 F2
Burleigh Cl ME2 62 E8
Burleigh Dr ME14 129 F1
Burleigh Rd TN27 234 C7
Burley Rd Newham E16 1 C8
Sittingbourne ME10 101 E4
Burlings La TN14 119 F2
Burlington Cl
[6] Newham E6 1 E7
Orpington BR6 86 B8
Burlington Dr CT6 77 D5
Burlington Gdns
Gillingham ME8 98 E4
Margate CT9 82 C8
Burlington Lodge BR7 29 F1
Burma Cres CT1 143 D1
Burman Cl DA2 34 C8
Burmarsh Cl ME5 97 B5
Burmarsh Rd
Burmarsh TN29 352 C3
Hythe CT21 353 C8
Burma Way ME5 96 F6
Burnaby Rd DA11 18 E1
Burnan Ct CT5 75 C2
Burnan Rd CT5 75 C2
Burnell Ave DA16 13 A5
Burnett Rd DA8 15 D8
Burnham Cl ME10 101 E8
Burnham Cres DA1 15 C3
Burnham Rd
Dartford DA1 15 C3
Sidcup DA14 31 E6
Burnham Trad Est DA1 15 D3
Burnham Wlk ME8 98 E3
Burnley Rd RM20 17 A6
Burns Ave DA15 13 B1
Burns Cl Bexley DA16 12 F6
Erith DA8 14 F6
Burns Cres TN9 254 A7
Burns Ho DA16 13 C6
Burns Pl RM18 19 B6
Burn's Rd ME7 64 C7
Burns Rd ME16 161 C2
Burnt Ash Heights BR1 29 B3
Burnt Ash Hill SE12 29 A7
Burnt Ash La BR1,SE12 29 B3
Burnt Ash Prim Sch BR1 29 A3
Burntash Rd ME20 160 F8
Burnt House Cl
Rochester ME2 40 C2
Sandhurst TN18 356 C5
Burnt House Hill CT3 145 B5
Burnt House La
Dartford DA1 33 F5
Hawley DA2 33 F4
Langton Green TN3 285 A5
Burnthouse La TN27 263 D1
Burnt Lodge La TN5 338 B2
Burnt Oak Jun Sch DA15 31 A7
Burnt Oak La DA15 13 A1
Burnt Oak Terr ME7 64 D6
Burnt Oast Rd ME13 140 A3
Burntwick Dr ME9 67 B3
Burntwood Gr TN13 187 B8
Burntwood Rd TN13 187 B7
Burnup Bank ME10 102 C5
Burrage Gr SE18 2 C2
Burrage Pl SE18 2 B1
Burrage Rd SE18 2 C1
Burrard Rd E16 1 B7
Burr Bank Terr DA2 33 C4
Burr Cl DA7 13 F4
Burrfield Dr BR5 54 D4
Burritt Mews ME1 63 C3
Burrow Rd CT19 335 F6
Burrows La ME3 25 C3
Burrs Hill Cotts TN12 289 D6
Burrs The ME10 101 F3
Burrstock Way ME8 66 B2
Burrswood Villas TN3 312 B7
Bursdon Cl DA15 30 F6
Bursill Cres CT12 83 B1
Burslem Rd TN2 286 E7
Bursted Hill CT4 208 B2
Bursted Wood Prim Sch DA7 14 B5
Burston Rd ME17 194 B2
Burton Cl
Folkestone CT19 335 A7
Rochester ME3 40 C3
Burton Fields CT6 77 B4
Burton Rd TN24 268 E6
Burt Rd E16 1 C5
Burts Wharf DA17 4 C5
Burwash Ct BR5 54 C4
Burwash Rd SE18 2 D1
Burwood Ave BR2 85 B8
Burwood Ho TN2 286 E5
Burwood Sch BR6 87 D8
Bus Bridge Rd ME15 194 E6
Busbridge Rd ME6 127 E7
Bush Ave CT12 83 B1
Bush Cl ME9 133 F5
Bushell Way BR7 30 A3
Bushey Ave BR5 53 D2
Bushey Cl ME13 139 F3

Bushey Ct DA8 15 A6
Busheyfields Rd CT6 110 F6
Bushey Ho SE9 29 C5
Bushey Lees DA15 12 F1
Bushfield Wlk DA10 35 E8
Bushmeadow Rd ME8 65 F2
Bushmoor Cres SE18 12 B6
Bush Rd Cuxton ME2 62 B2
East Peckham TN12 224 E8
Bush Row ME20 129 A3
Bushy Gill TN3 285 A3
Bushy Gr ME17 197 D2
Bushy Hill Rd CT2 144 D7
Bushy Royds TN24 300 D6
Bushy Ruff Cotts
CT16 277 D4
Business Acad Bexley Prim
Section The DA18 3 E4
Buston Manor Farm Cotts
ME18 193 B2
Busty La TN15 156 D6
Butcher Cl TN12 260 E3
Butcher's La ME19 158 D1
Butchers La
New Ash Green TN15 91 D8
Nonington CT15 211 E5
Butchers Rd E16 1 A7
Butchers Yd BR6 119 A8
Butcher Wlk DA10 35 E8
Butchery La 1 CT1 175 A8
Butchery The 2 CT13 149 A1
Butler Ho 9 RM17 18 B8
Butler's Cotts DA7 14 A5
Butler's Hill ME13 140 D7
Butler's Pl DA3 91 E7
Buttercup Cl TN12 257 A5
Butterfield Sq 10 E6 1 F7
Butterfly Ave DA1 33 F6
Butterfly Centre The*
CT15 275 B3
Butterfly La SE9 12 B1
Buttermere Cl
Folkestone CT19 335 B6
Gillingham ME7 65 A5
Buttermere ME13 138 E6
Buttermere Gdns CT3 210 F6
Buttermere Rd BR5 54 D5
Butternut Copse
TN23 267 D3
Butterside Rd TN23 300 C4
Butter St CT15 211 C4
Butt Field Rd TN23 299 E7
Butt Green La ME17 228 A7
Butt Haw Cl ME3 41 E5
Buttmarsh Cl SE18 2 B1
Button Dr ME3 25 C5
Button Ho ME3 40 F6
Button La ME15 163 B2
Button St BR8,DA4 56 C5
Butts Ct CT4 208 A6
Butts Hill ME13 139 F5
Butts La TN5 337 C7
Butts Mdw CT4 208 A6
Butts The Otford TN14 122 B2
Sandwich CT13 148 F1
Sittingbourne ME10 101 F4
Buttway La ME3 22 A6
Buxton Cl Chatham ME5 97 D1
Loose ME15 195 A8
Buxton Rd Erith DA8 14 D7
Ramsgate CT12 83 B2
Buzzard Creek Ind Est
IG11 3 A8
Bybrook Ct TN24 268 C4
Bybrook Field CT20 334 E3
Bybrook CT21 333 D3
Bybrook Rd TN24 268 C5
Bybrook Way CT20 334 E4
Bychurch Pl 7 ME15 162 A3
Bycliffe Mews 2 DA11 36 F8
Bycliffe Terr 3 DA11 36 F8
Byland Cl SE2 3 B3
Byllan Rd CT17 277 E3
Byng Rd TN4 285 F5
Bynon Ave DA7 13 F4
Byrneside TN11 221 E4
Byron Ave CT9 50 J1
Byron Cl
Canterbury CT1 175 C7
Woolwich SE28 3 C5
Byron Cres CT16 278 B4
Byron Dr DA8 14 B7
Byron Gdns RM18 19 C6
Byron Prim Sch ME7 64 C3
Byron Rd Dartford DA1 15 B3
Gillingham ME7 64 C3
Maidstone ME14 162 B7
Bysing Wood Cotts
ME13 104 F1
Bysing Wood Prim Sch
ME13 138 A8
Bysing Wood Rd
ME13 138 B8
Bythorne Ct ME8 66 B1
Bywater Ho SE18 1 E3

C

Cabbage Stalk La TN4 285 E2
Cabin The TN24 268 D7
Cables Cl DA8 4 C3
Cacket's La TN14 119 E4
Cade La TN13 187 C7
Cade Rd TN23 300 B7
Cades Orch ME13 137 E3
Cadlocks Hill TN14 87 F1
Cadnam Cl
Canterbury CT2 142 E3
Rochester ME2 62 E8
Cadogan Ave DA2 34 D8
Cadogan Gdns 6 TN1 286 B4
Cadogan Rd SE18 2 C3
Cadwallon Rd SE9 30 C6
Caerleon Cl DA14 31 C3
Caerleon Terr SE2 3 B2
Caernarvon Ct
Erith DA8 14 D7
12 Orpington BR5 54 C6
Caernarvon Dr ME15 161 F1
Caernarvon Gdns CT10 84 B5
Caesar Ave TN23 299 F4
Caesar's Way CT19 334 E7
Cage Green Prim Sch
TN10 222 D5
Cage Green Rd TN10 222 C5
Cage La TN27 263 F1
Cagney Cl ME3 40 C3
Cairns Cl DA1 15 D2
Cairns Mews SE18 11 E6
Caistor Rd TN9 222 A1
Caithness Gdns DA15 12 F1
Calais Cotts DA3 91 A8
Calais Hill CT2 142 E6
Calcott Wlk SE9 29 D4
Calcraft Mews 6 CT1 143 B2
Calcroft Ave DA9 17 C2
Calcutta Ho 3 ME15 195 E5
Calcutta Rd RM18 19 A5
Caldecote Cl ME8 66 B1
Caldecot La TN29 372 D2
Caldecott Foundation Sch
TN25 302 B4
Calder Rd ME14 161 F7
Calderwood DA12 37 E2
Calderwood St SE18 2 A2
Caldew Ave ME8 65 C1
Caldew Gr ME10 102 A3
Caldy Rd DA17 4 B3
Caledonian Ct ME8 98 E8
Caledon Terr CT1 175 A7
Calehill Cl ME14 162 C6
Caley Rd TN2 286 D7
Calfstock La DA4 56 F5
Calgary Cres CT19 335 E8
California Row
Hawkenbury TN12 261 C6
Wingham CT3 177 E6
Caling Croft DA3 58 F1
Caliph Cl DA12 37 F5
Callams Cl ME8 98 D6
Calland TN25 302 E5
Callaways La ME9 100 B6
Calleywell La TN25 330 A7
Callis Court Rd CT10 83 F6
Callis Grange Inf Sch
CT10 83 F7
Callisto Ct ME16 161 D3
Callis Way ME8 98 D5
Calshot Ct 17 DA2 16 B1
Calverden Rd CT12 83 A1
Calverley Ct TN1 286 C3
Calverley Park Cres 1
TN1 286 B3
Calverley Park Gdns
TN1 286 C4
Calverley Pk TN1 286 B3
Calverley Rd
Royal Tunbridge Wells
TN1 286 B3
Royal Tunbridge Wells
TN1 286 B4
Calverley St TN1 286 B4
Calvert Cl Erith DA17 4 B2
Sidcup DA14 31 E2
Calvert Dr DA2 32 D6
Calverton Prim Sch E16 1 D7
Calvin Cl BR5 54 D6
Calydon Rd SE7 1 B1
Cambert Way SE3 11 B3
Camberwell La TN14 185 F4
Camborne Manor 2
ME7 64 C6
Camborne Rd
Bexley DA16 12 F5
Sidcup DA14 31 C5
Cambourne Ave CT8 81 D8
Cambrai Ct CT1 143 D1
Cambray Rd BR6 53 F2
Cambria Ave ME1 62 F2
Cambria Cl DA15 30 E7
Cambria Cres DA12 37 F4
Cambria Ho 2 DA8 14 E7
Cambrian Gr DA11 37 A8
Cambrian Rd TN4 286 C7
Cambridge Ave
Bexley DA16 12 F3
Sandwich CT13 182 B7
Cambridge Barracks Rd 5
SE18 1 F2
Cambridge Cl CT7 81 B7
Cambridge Cres
ME15 195 D7
Cambridge Dr SE12 11 A2
Cambridge Gdns
Folkestone CT20 335 D5
Royal Tunbridge Wells
TN2 286 B2
Cambridge Gn SE9 30 B7
Cambridge Ho 7 SE18 1 F2
Cambridge La ME9 136 C8
Cambridge Mews
CT14 215 D3
Cambridge Rd
Bromley BR1 29 A1
Canterbury CT1 174 F6
Deal CT14 215 D3
Dover CT17 310 D7
Faversham ME13 138 B6
Gillingham ME8 98 C6
Rochester ME2 63 A8
Sidcup DA14 30 E4
Sittingbourne ME10 102 B3
Cambridge Row SE18 2 B1
Cambridge St TN2 286 C3
Cambridge Terr
1 Chatham ME4 63 F4
13 Dover CT16,CT17 310 E7
13 Folkestone CT20 335 E5
Margate CT9 51 B1
Cambridge Way CT1 174 F6
Cambus Rd E16 1 A8
Camdale Rd SE18 12 F7
Camden Ave TN2 287 C6
Camden Cl
Chatham ME5 97 B5
Chislehurst BR7 53 C8
Northfleet DA11 36 C7
Camden Cotts TN17 320 F8
Camden Cres CT16 310 E7
Camden Ct 10 Erith DA17 4 A1
Pembury TN2 287 D6
2 Royal Tunbridge Wells
TN1 286 B4
Camden Gr BR7 30 B2
Camden Hill TN2 286 B3
Camden Park Rd BR7 30 A1
Camden Pk TN2 286 C2
Camden Rd
Broadstairs CT10 83 E7
Gillingham ME7 64 D7
Ramsgate CT11 117 E6
Royal Tunbridge Wells
TN1 286 B4
Sevenoaks TN13 154 B5
Sidcup DA5 31 F8
Camden Sq 10 CT11 117 E7
Camden St ME14 162 A5
Camden Terr
Ashford TN24 268 E1
Seal TN15 154 F6
Sissinghurst TN17 320 F8
Camden Way BR7 30 A1
Camellia Cl
Gillingham ME8 98 D7
2 Margate CT9 82 B8
Camelot Cl
Biggin Hill TN16 118 C3
Woolwich SE28 2 D4
Camel Rd E16 1 E5
Camer Gdns DA13 60 C3
Cameron Cl
Chatham ME5 97 B8
Joyden's Wood DA5 32 E5
Cameron Ct CT17 310 A6
Cameron Ho CT14 215 C1
Cameron Rd BR2 52 A4
Camerons 4 TN18 341 A2
Cameron Terr 10 SE12 29 B5
Camer Park Ctry Pk*
DA13 60 C2
Camer Park Rd DA13 60 C2
Camer Rd DA13 60 C3
Camer St DA13 60 C3
Camomile Dr ME14 162 F5
Campbell Cl
Herne Bay CT6 77 C3
Woolwich SE18 12 A6
Campbell Ho ME3 40 F6
Campbell Rd
Deal CT14 215 D4
Maidstone ME15 162 A3
Northfleet DA11 36 F8
Royal Tunbridge Wells
TN4 286 A6
Camperdown Manor 5
ME7 64 A6
Campfield Rd SE9 29 D8
Camp Hill TN11 220 A3
Camp Hill Cotts TN11 219 F2
Campion Cl
Chatham ME5 96 E3
Newham E6 1 F6
Northfleet DA11 36 E4
Campion Cres TN17 320 A2
Campion Ct 6 RM17 18 D8
Campion Pl SE28 3 B5
Campleshon Rd ME8 98 D5
Camp Site The DA14 32 A1
Campus Way ME8 98 A8
Camp Way ME15 195 C6
Camrose Ave DA8 14 B8
Camrose St SE2 3 A2
Canada Cl CT19 334 C6
Canada Farm Rd DA4 58 A6
Canada Mews CT14 215 C3
Canada Rd Deal CT14 215 D3
Erith DA8 15 B7
Canada Terr 3 ME14 162 A7
Canadian Ave ME7 64 F4
Canal Basin DA12 19 D1
Canal Rd
Gravesend DA12 19 D1
Higham ME3 39 C8
Rochester ME2 63 C7
Canal Road Ind Pk 2
DA12 37 D8
Canberra Gdns ME10 101 C4
Canberra Rd
Bexley DA7 13 D8
Greenwich SE7 11 D8
Canberra Sq RM18 19 A5
Canbury Path BR5 54 A5
Candlers Way CT4 206 F8
Canning St ME14 162 A6
Cannon Bridge Works
TN9 222 D2
Cannonbury Rd CT11 117 D6
Cannongate Ave CT21 333 D3
Cannongate Cl CT21 333 E2
Cannongate Gdns
CT21 333 E3
Cannongate Rd CT21 333 D3
Cannon La TN9 222 D2
Cannon Pl SE7 1 E1
Cannon Rd Bexley DA7 13 F6
Ramsgate CT11 117 D7
Cannon St Deal CT14 215 C7
Cannon St *continued*
Dover CT16 310 D8
Lydd TN29 376 C6
New Romney TN28 373 B7
Canon Appleton Ct
CT1 174 E7
Canon Cl ME1 63 B2
Canon Gn CT3 178 A7
Canon La ME18 159 C1
Canon Rd BR1 52 D6
Canons Gate Rd CT16 310 E8
Canon Woods Way
TN24 268 F6
Cansiron La TN7,TN8 281 E2
Canterbury Ave DA15 31 C6
Canterbury Cathedral*
CT1 175 A8
Canterbury Centre The
(Mus)* CT1 142 F1
Canterbury Christ Church
Univ Coll CT10 83 C4
Canterbury Christ Church
Univ Coll (The Mount)
CT3 143 F1
Canterbury Cl
Broadstairs CT10 83 D5
Dartford DA1 34 A8
2 Folkestone CT19 335 E6
7 Newham E6 1 F7
Canterbury Coll CT1 175 B8
Canterbury Cres
TN10 222 D5
Canterbury Ct
Ashford TN24 268 D2
7 Lewisham SE12 29 B5
Canterbury East Sta
CT1 174 F7
Canterbury High Sch The
CT2 174 D8
Canterbury Hill CT2 142 E5
Canterbury Ho
6 Erith DA8 14 F7
2 Maidstone ME15 195 D7
Canterbury Ind Pk
CT3 145 A8
Canterbury La
Canterbury CT1 175 A8
Gillingham ME8,ME9 66 C1
Canterbury Rd
Ashford,Kennington
TN24 268 E5
Ashford TN24 300 E6
Barham CT4 243 C5
Boughton Aluph TN25 237 C5
Boughton Street ME13 139 D4
Brabourne Lees TN25 302 F6
Brabourne TN25 303 C8
Challock TN25,TN27 202 C1
Chilham CT4 172 F1
Denton CT4 243 A1
Dunkirk ME13 140 C3
Elham CT4 273 E3
Canterbury Rd E CT11,
CT12 117 A6
Canterbury Rd
Etchinghill CT18 305 D4
Faversham ME13 138 E5
Folkestone CT19 335 D7
Folkestone,Foord CT19 335 E6
Gravesend DA12 37 C6
Hawkinge CT18,CT19,
CT15,CT4 307 B4
Herne Bay CT6 77 A3
Herne CT3,CT6 110 E5
Littlebourne CT3 176 C8
Lydden CT15 276 E7
Lyminge CT18 305 C7
Pembury TN2 287 E6
Sarre CT7 113 E7
Sittingbourne ME10 102 B3
Canterbury Rd W
CT12 116 D7
Canterbury Rd
Whitstable CT5 108 D8
Wingham CT3 178 A7
Canterbury Road
Birchington CT7 81 B7
Canterbury Road Margate
CT9 50 G1
Canterbury Road Prim Sch
ME10 102 B3
Canterbury Road Westgate
CT8,CT9 81 E8
Canterbury St ME7 64 C4
Canterbury Tale The*
CT1 174 F8
Canterbury Way DA1,
DA2,RM20 16 D5
Canterbury West Sta
CT2 142 F1
Cantwell Ho SE18 12 B7
Cantwell Rd SE18 12 B7
Canute Rd
Birchington CT7 80 D7
Deal CT14 182 C1
Faversham ME13 138 C6
Canute Wlk CT14 182 D1
Capability Way DA9 17 C3
Capelands DA3 92 A8
Capel Cl Ashford TN23 267 F1
Broadstairs CT10 51 F1
Gillingham ME8 98 D4
Orpington BR2 52 E1
Capel Court Pk CT18 308 D2
Capella Ho 1 SE7 11 B8
Capel Cl ME17 194 C3
Capel-le-Ferne Prim Sch
CT18 308 C3
Capel Pl DA2 33 C4
Capel Prim Sch TN12 255 F7
Capel Rd
Bromley Green TN26 328 B4
Faversham ME13 138 B7
Capel Rd *continued*
Petham CT4 206 F3
Sittingbourne ME10 101 E2
Capel St CT18 308 B3
Capetown Ho 1 ME15 195 F5
Capital Ind Est DA17 4 B3
Capstan Ct DA2 16 C3
Capstan Ctr RM18 18 D7
Capstan Mews 4 DA11 36 E8
Capstan Row CT14 215 D7
Capstone Farm Country
Pk* ME7 97 D5
Capstone Rd
Chatham ME5 64 D1
Gillingham ME7 97 F6
Lewisham BR1 29 A4
Captain's Cl ME17 229 E6
Captains Ct CT21 333 C1
Capulet Mews E16 1 A5
Caraway Cl E13 1 B8
Cardens Rd ME3 40 B8
Cardiff St SE18 12 E7
Cardigan Cl ME23 23 F3
Cardinal Cl
Chislehurst BR7 53 D8
Minster (Sheppey) ME12 47 D7
Tonbridge TN9 254 D8
Cardinal Wlk ME18 159 C3
Cardine Cl ME10 101 E7
Cardwell Prim Sch SE18 1 F2
Carew Ho 18 SE18 1 F2
Carey Cl TN28 373 B6
Carey Ct DA6 14 B2
Carey Ho 5 CT1 174 F7
Carey's Field TN13 153 E7
Caring La ME14,ME17 163 E1
Caring Rd ME15,ME17 163 C1
Carisbrooke Ave DA5 31 D7
Carisbrooke Ct
23 Dartford DA2 16 B1
20 Sidcup DA14 31 A4
Carisbrooke Dr ME16 161 D4
Carisbrooke Rd
Bromley BR2 52 C5
Rochester ME2 39 E1
Carl Ekman Ho DA11 36 D8
Carleton Pl DA4 57 C5
Carleton Rd DA1 34 A8
Carlisle Cl ME2 62 C6
Carlisle Rd DA1 16 A1
Carlsden Cl CT17 278 A3
Carlton Ave
Broadstairs CT10 84 A5
Gillingham ME7 64 E4
Ramsgate CT11 117 D6
Sheerness ME12 28 B1
Stone DA9 16 E1
Carlton Cl
Kings Hill ME18 159 B3
Tonbridge TN10 222 E7
Carlton Cres
Chatham ME5 97 D8
Royal Tunbridge Wells
TN1 286 C4
Carlton Gdns ME15 195 B8
Carlton Gn DA14 30 F4
Carlton Hill CT6 76 C4
Carlton Leas CT20 335 C4
Carlton Mans CT9 51 A3
Carlton Par BR5 54 B2
Carlton Rd
Ashford TN23 268 A2
Bexley DA16 13 B4
Erith DA8 14 C8
Carlton Rd E CT8 81 D8
Carlton Rd
Kingsdown CT14 248 C6
Royal Tunbridge Wells
TN1 286 C4
Sidcup DA14 30 F3
Whitstable CT5 108 D2
Carlton Rd W CT8 81 D8
Carlton Rise CT8 81 C8
Carlyle Ave BR1 52 D6
Carlyle Rd SE28 3 C6
Carman's Cl ME15,
ME17 194 F3
Carmel Ct CT4 173 B2
Carmel Ct 2 CT7 80 F8
Carmelite Way DA3 58 F4
Carnation Cl 1 ME19 128 A1
Carnation Cres ME19 127 F1
Carnation Rd ME2 62 D7
Carnation St SE2 3 B1
Carn Brae CT9 50 J2
Carnbrook Rd SE3 11 D4
Carnecke Gdns SE9 11 E2
Carnet Cl DA1 32 E8
Carnoustie Cl Erith SE28 3 D7
Whitstable CT5 109 E8
Caroland Cl TN25 302 D5
Caroline Cl CT5 108 B6
Caroline Cres
Broadstairs CT10 83 E6
Maidstone ME16 161 D7
Caroline Sq CT9 50 J3
Carolyn Dr BR6 87 A7
Carp Cl ME20 128 A4
Carpeaux Cl ME4 64 A4
Carpenters Cl ME1 63 E2
Carpenters Ct BR1 52 D7
Carpenters La
Hadlow TN11 190 D2
Staplehurst TN12 260 C8
Carpinus Cl ME5 97 B1
Carrack Ho 1 DA8 4 E1
Carr Gr SE18 1 E2
Carr Ho DA1 14 E2
Carriage Ho ME13 170 D5
Carriage Mews CT2 142 F1
Carriageway The
TN16 152 D3
Carrick Dr TN13 154 B4
Carrie Ho 3 ME16 161 E5
Carriers Pl TN3 283 B4
Carriers Rd TN17 320 D5
Carrill Way DA17 3 D3
Carrington Cl ME7 64 F6
Carrington Rd DA1 16 A1
Carrington DA14 31 A3
Carroll Cl ME2 95 A4
Carroll Gdns ME20 127 F3
Carronade Pl SE28 2 D3
Carroway's Pl CT9 50 J2
Carsington Gdns DA1 33 D6
Carson Rd E16 1 A8
Carston Cl SE12 11 A2
Carter La TN29 362 E2
Carter's Hill SE9 29 C7
Carters Hill Cl SE9 29 C7
Carters Hill La DA13 92 F2
Carter's Hill TN15 188 B6
Carter's Rd CT20 334 F5
Carters Row DA11 36 F6
Carter's Wood TN26 349 B7
Cartmel Rd DA7 14 A6
Carton Cl ME1 63 D2
Carton Rd ME3 39 B3
Cartwright Cl CT3 147 C2
Cartwright & Kelsey CE
Prim Sch CT3 147 C2
Carville Ave TN4 253 F1
Carvoran Way ME8 98 C5
Cascade Cl BR5 54 C6
Caslocke St 2 ME13 138 C7
Caspian Way DA10 17 E2
Caspian Wlk E16 1 D7
Cassilda Rd SE2 3 A2
Cassino Ho 16 CT1 143 B2
Cassino Sq CT15 278 E2
Casstine Cl BR8 32 F1
Castalia Ct DA1 15 F4
Castalla Cotts CT14 215 D3
Casterbridge Rd SE3 11 A4
Castfield Cl ME3 22 E1
Castile Rd 12 SE18 2 A2
Castilion Prim Sch SE28 3 C7
Castleacres Ind Pk
ME10 102 B6
Castle Ave
Broadstairs CT10 84 B6
Dover CT16 278 D1
Hythe CT21 333 B3
Rochester ME1 63 C4
Castle Bay CT20 334 D3
Castle Cl
4 Folkestone CT20 334 F3
Lympne CT21 331 F2
Castlecombe Prim Sch
SE9 29 E3
Castlecombe Rd SE9 29 E4
Castle Com Sch CT14 215 C4
Castle Cotts CT13 148 E5
Castle Cres CT21 333 C4
Castle Dene ME14 161 F8
Castle Dr
Kemsing TN15 122 E2
Whitfield CT16 277 F7
Castle Farm Cotts
TN11 223 F8
Castle Farm Rd TN14 89 A3
Castlefields DA13 59 F8
Castle Fields TN9 222 B2
Castleford Ave SE9 30 B7
Castle Glen 9 CT20 334 F3
Castle Hill Ave CT20 335 C4
Castle Hill Ct ME1 63 C6
Castle Hill
Folkestone CT19,CT18 335 A8
Hartley DA3 58 E4
Castle Hill Rd 4 CT16 310 E8
Castle Hill
Rochester ME1 63 C6
Thurnham ME14 131 D1
Tonbridge TN11 254 F5
Castle Ho CT5 74 F3
Castle Hurst TN32 355 B1
Castle La DA12 38 B6
Castlemaine Ave ME7 64 F6
Castle Mayne Ave CT7 81 F3
Castlemere Ave ME11 46 B5
Castle Mews CT14 215 A4
Castlemount Ct CT16 310 E8
Castlemount Rd CT16 278 D1
Castle Rd Chatham ME4 64 B2
Eynsford DA4 89 C5
Folkestone CT20 334 F3
Grays RM17 17 F8
Hythe CT21 333 B4
Maidstone ME16 161 D7
Royal Tunbridge Wells
TN4 286 A3
Sittingbourne ME10 102 B5
Swanscombe DA10 17 F1
Whitstable CT5 74 F2
Castle Road Bsns Prec
ME10 102 B6
Castle Road Tech Ctr
ME10 102 B6
Castle Rough La ME10 68 F1
Castle Row CT1 174 F7
Castle St
6 Ashford TN23 268 B2
Canterbury CT1 174 F8
Dover CT16 310 E8
Queenborough ME11 46 A5
Rochester ME2 40 E1
2 Royal Tunbridge
Wells,Mount Sion TN1 286 A2
2 Royal Tunbridge
Wells,Southborough
TN4 253 F2
Stone DA9 17 A2

Castle St *continued*
Swanscombe DA10 17 F1
Tonbridge TN9 222 C2
Wouldham ME1 95 C4
Castle Terr
Hadlow TN11 223 E8
Hawkhurst TN18 340 F3
Castleton Ave DA7 14 D5
Castleton Rd SE9 29 D4
Castle View Bsns Ctr ME1 63 C6
Castleview Ct CT17 278 B1
Castle View Mews ME1 63 C6
Castle View Rd ME2 63 A7
Castle Way ME19 127 D2
Castle Wlk Deal CT14 182 D1
Durgates TN5 336 E4
Castlewood Day Hospl SE18 12 A6
Castlewood Dr SE9 11 F5
Castweazle TN30 344 E6
Caterfield La RH7,RH8 216 A5
Cates Ct TN12 225 A7
Cathcart Dr BR6 53 E1
Cathedral View CT2 143 A2
Catherine Cl 2 ME16 161 A3
Catherine of Aragon Ct DA15 30 D8
Catherine Pl 7 TN1 286 B4
Catherine St ME1 63 D3
Catherine Way CT10 84 A6
Catkin Cl ME5 96 F1
Catlyn Cl ME19 160 A8
Catsole Hill CT3 178 D2
Catterick Rd ME5 97 D2
Cattistock Rd SE9 29 F3
Cattle Market CT13 148 F1
Catt's Hill TN30 360 E3
Catts Pl TN12 257 C4
Catt's Wood Rd CT4 207 F4
Cauldham Cl CT18 308 B1
Cauldham La CT18 308 B3
Caulkers Ho 7 ME4 64 B2
Causeway The
Canterbury CT1 142 F1
Sandwich CT13 148 D2
Causton Rd TN17 320 C5
Cavalry Cl TN10 222 E7
Cavalry Ct Deal CT14 215 D3
Folkestone CT20 334 D5
Cave Hill ME15 161 F1
Cave La CT3 178 D3
Cavell Cres DA1 16 A3
Cavell Sq CT14 215 A3
Cavell Way ME10 101 D5
Cavenagh Rd CT15 280 B6
Cavendish Ave
Bexley DA16 12 F4
Erith DA8 14 C8
Gillingham ME7 64 E6
Sevenoaks TN13 154 A5
Sidcup DA15 31 A8
Cavendish Cl TN10 222 D7
Cavendish Ct
Herne Bay CT6 77 A5
Tonbridge TN9 222 D3
Cavendish Dr TN2 286 B1
Cavendish Pl 2 CT11 117 E6
Cavendish Rd
Herne Bay CT6 77 A5
Rochester ME1 63 D3
Cavendish Sq DA3 58 D6
Cavendish St CT11 117 E6
Cavendish Way ME15 163 B3
Caversham Cl ME8 65 F1
Caveside Cl BR7 53 A8
Cavour Rd
Faversham ME13 138 C7
Sheerness ME12 28 C2
Caxton Cl Hartley DA3 58 F5
Tenterden TN30 344 F7
Caxton Ho
Ashford TN24 268 C3
The Chart RH8 183 F3
Caxton La
Hadlow TN11 223 E8
The Chart RH8 183 E4
Caxton Rd CT9 82 C8
Cayser Dr ME17 197 E2
Caysers Croft TN12 224 E6
Cazeneuve St ME1 63 C5
Cecil Ave
Gillingham ME8 65 A2
Rochester ME2 63 B8
Sheerness ME12 28 B1
Cecil Burns Lodge TN2 286 D2
Cecil Ct Ashford TN24 268 B3
Herne Bay CT6 77 A4
Cecilia Gr CT10 83 F6
Cecilia Rd CT11 117 E8
Cecil Kidby Ho TN2 286 F6
Cecil Pk CT6 77 A4
Cecil Rd
Kingsdown CT14 248 D7
Northfleet DA11 36 F7
Rochester ME1 63 C3
Cecil Road Prim Sch DA11 36 F7
Cecil Sq CT9 50 I2
Cecil St CT9 50 I2
Cecil Way BR2 52 A1
Cedar Ave
Gravesend DA12 37 C4
Sidcup DA15 31 A8
Cedar Cl Ashford TN24 267 E3
Birchington CT8 81 B7
Broadstairs CT10 83 F7
Ditton ME20 160 D8
Margate CT9 51 B1
Cedar Cl *continued*
Meopham Station DA13 60 A3
Orpington BR2 85 E7
Sittingbourne ME10 102 B2
Swanley BR8 55 C7
Cedar Copse BR1 52 F7
Cedar Cres
Orpington BR2 85 E7
St Mary's Bay TN29 365 F3
Tonbridge TN10 222 C7
Cedar Ct Eltham SE9 11 E1
Folkestone CT20 334 E5
21 Greenwich SE7 11 C8
Maidstone ME14 162 B5
Royal Tunbridge Wells TN4 286 A5
12 Tenterden TN30 345 A7
Cedar Dr
Edenbridge TN8 217 B2
Maidstone ME16 160 E2
Sutton at H DA4 57 B7
Cedar Gdns ME9 132 E8
Cedar Gr Gillingham ME7 98 A5
Sidcup DA5 13 D1
Cedar Ho
Royal Tunbridge Wells TN4 285 E4
Sheerness ME12 28 B2
Cedarhurst Cotts 5 DA5 32 A8
Cedarhurst Dr SE9 11 C2
Cedar La TN27 323 D7
Cedar Lodge TN4 285 F3
Cedarmore Ct BR7 53 C8
Cedar Mount SE9 29 D7
Cedar Pl 3 SE7 1 C1
Cedar Rd Bromley BR1 52 C7
Dartford DA1 33 D7
Erith DA8 15 A6
Hoo St Werburgh ME3 41 E3
Rochester ME2 62 F6
Sturry CT2 144 A6
Cedar Ridge TN2 286 D5
Cedars PRU The ME16 161 D4
Cedars Sch The ME1 63 C4
Cedars The
Barrowhill TN25 331 D8
Paddock Wood TN12 257 A7
Sittingbourne ME10 102 C5
Cedar Terrace Rd TN13 154 C4
Cedar Terr ME13 138 A4
Cedarview CT2 142 C1
Cedarwood Ho ME15 194 B6
Cedric Rd Eltham SE9 30 C5
Westgate-on-S CT8 50 C1
Ceil Villas CT14 181 B4
Celandine Dr SE28 3 B5
Celestine Cl ME5 97 A1
Cellar Hill ME9 136 C8
Celt Cl ME10 101 F8
Celtic Rd CT14 215 A2
Cement Block Cotts 8 RM17 18 C8
Cement Industry Heritage Ctr* DA11 18 B2
Cemetery La
Ashford TN24 268 C4
Hadlow TN11 191 A1
Woolwich SE7 11 E8
Cemetery Rd
Halling ME2 95 A4
Snodland ME6 94 F1
Woolwich SE2 13 B7
Centenary Cl TN27 234 C8
Centenary Ct DA4 57 A2
Centenary Gdns CT13 180 A2
Central Ave
Bexley DA16 13 A5
Chatham ME4 64 B8
Gravesend DA12 37 B5
Herne Bay CT6 76 D4
Sittingbourne ME10 101 F4
Tilbury RM18 19 A6
Central Beach Pk ME12 49 G2
Central Bsns Pk ME2 63 E7
Central Ct 3 SE18 2 B2
Central Lodge TN15 125 E6
Central Par CT6 76 E5
Central Park Gdns ME4 63 E2
Central Par
Rochester ME1 63 D2
Sidcup DA15 31 A5
Central Par Villas BR5 54 C7
Central Par TN5 336 F4
Central Pk CT12 114 D6
Central Rd Dartford DA1 15 E2
New Hythe ME20 128 B4
Ramsgate CT11 117 D8
Rochester ME2 63 A7
Central Service Rd CT16 310 H8
Central Sta CT19 335 C5
Central Terr ME3 40 F6
Central Way SE28 3 B6
Centre 2000
Maidstone ME16 161 C8
8 Sittingbourne ME10 102 A4
Centre Common Rd BR7 30 C1
Centre Ct ME2 63 E7
Centre Rd Dover CT17 310 C6
New Ash Green DA3 91 E7
Centre The Margate CT9 50 I2
Ramsgate CT12 83 A1
Centurian Way DA18 4 A3
Centurion Cl ME8 64 F1
Centurion Wlk TN23 300 B4
Century Ct ME1 63 C5
Century Rd
Faversham ME13 138 E7
Century Rd *continued*
Gillingham ME8 98 D8
Century Wlk CT14 215 C6
Ceres Ct ME10 102 C5
Ceres Rd SE18 2 F2
Cerne Rd DA12 37 E5
Cervia Way DA12 37 F5
Chada Ave ME7 64 E3
Chadd Dr BR1 52 E6
Chadfields RM18 19 A7
Chadwell Hill RM17 19 A8
Chadwick Cl DA11 36 E5
Chadwick Ct
2 Dartford DA1 15 D1
4 Woolwich SE28 3 B5
Chadwick Way SE28 3 D6
Chadwin Rd E13 1 B8
Chaffe's La ME9 66 E3
Chaffes Terr ME9 66 E2
Chaffey Ho 6 SE7 1 C1
Chaffinch Cl ME5 97 A7
Chaffinch Dr TN23 300 C3
Chaffinch Lodge 5 CT16 278 B2
Chaffinch Way TN12 257 A5
Chafford Cotts TN3 283 F5
Chafford La TN3 283 F5
Chafy Cres CT2 143 F5
Chain Gate ME17 232 A8
Chain The 6 CT13 149 A1
Chalcombe Rd SE2 3 B3
Chalcroft Rd CT20 334 E4
Chalet Cl DA5 32 D4
Chalfont Ct 3 DA17 4 A1
Chalfont Dr
Gillingham ME8 98 D6
Herne Bay CT6 77 D2
Chalgrove Mews ME2 95 A5
Chalice Way DA9 16 F2
Chalk Ave TN30 324 B2
Chalk Cl CT19 335 A7
Chalk Ct RM17 18 A8
Chalkenden Ave ME8 65 A2
Chalkers Way ME8 65 B4
Chalket La TN2 287 C5
Chalk Hill CT11,CT12 116 F6
Chalk Hill Rd CT14 248 C5
Chalk La TN17 319 E7
Chalk Pit Ave BR5 54 D6
Chalkpit Hill CT4 176 D3
Chalk Pit Hill
Chatham ME4 64 A3
Staple CT3 179 B5
Chalk Pit La CT13,CT3 179 C5
Chalk Rd Chalk DA12 38 A6
Lower Higham ME3 39 C6
Newham E13 1 C8
Queenborough ME11 46 A5
Chalksole Green La CT15 276 B2
Chalkstone Cl DA16 13 A6
Chalkways TN15 122 F3
Chalkwell Ct CT17 310 A7
Chalkwell Rd ME10 101 D5
Chalky Bank DA11 37 A3
Chalky Bank Rd ME8 65 F2
Chalky Rd ME9 132 C6
Challenge Cl DA12 37 F4
Challenger Cl
Paddock Wood TN12 256 F6
Sittingbourne ME10 101 E7
Challock Cl TN16 118 C3
Challock Ct CT9 51 F2
Challock Ho
3 Erith DA8 14 F7
3 Orpington BR5 54 D1
Challock Prim Sch TN25 203 B1
Challock Wlk ME14 162 C6
Chalmers Way ME8 65 A4
Chamberlain Ave ME16 161 C2
Chamberlain Cl 5 SE28 2 D3
Chamberlain Ct ME8 98 B5
Chamberlain Dr CT6 76 B4
Chamberlain Rd
Chatham ME4 64 B2
Dover CT17 310 B8
Chambers Cl 2 DA9 17 A2
Chancel Cl TN15 90 E3
Chancel Ct CT2 142 D1
Chancellor Ho TN4 285 F3
Chancellor Way TN13 154 A5
Chancelot Rd SE2 3 B2
Chance Mdw CT15 278 E6
Chancery Ct DA1 34 A7
Chancery La ME15 162 B3
Chancery Rd ME3 22 B5
Chanctonbury Chase CT5 108 A6
Chanctonbury Cl SE9 30 B5
Chandler Ave CT16 1 A8
Chandlers Dr DA8 4 E2
Chandler's Hill DA13 93 C5
Chandlers Mews DA9 17 C3
Chandler's Rd DA13 93 C5
Chandlers Wharf ME1 63 B5
Chandos Rd
17 Broadstairs CT10 84 B4
Royal Tunbridge Wells TN1 286 C5
Chandos Sq 18 CT10 84 B4
Chandos Terr CT12 117 E7
Channel Cl CT19 335 F7
Channel Lea CT14 215 C1
Channel Rd CT9 83 A6
Channel Sch The CT19 335 C7
Channel Tunnel Terminal CT18 334 B8
Channel View Ct 19 CT11 117 F7
Channel View 21 CT19 335 E5
Channel View Rd CT17 310 C5
Channel Watch TN28 373 E4
Channon Rd TN28 377 E7
Chantler's Hill TN12 257 A4
Chantlers Mead TN8 282 A5
Chantry Ave DA3 58 E3
Chantry Cl DA14 31 E3
Chantry Ct
15 Canterbury CT1 142 F1
Gravesend DA12 19 C1
Chantry Hall CT1 174 F7
Chantry Her Ctr* DA12 19 C1
Chantry La BR2 52 D4
Chantry Pk CT7 113 D7
Chantry Pl
Marden TN12 259 C6
Sevenoaks TN13 153 F5
Chantry Prim Sch DA12 19 C1
Chantry Rd TN12 259 C5
Chapel Alley Cotts TN14 122 A8
Chapel Cl Crayford DA1 14 E2
Etchinghill CT18 305 D3
Ryarsh ME19 126 F5
West Thurrock RM20 17 B8
Chapel Cotts ME17 196 F5
Chapel Ct DA10 17 E1
Chapel Farm Rd SE9 29 F6
Chapel Field Cotts DA4 57 B8
Chapel Hill Cl CT9 82 F7
Chapel Hill
Crayford DA1 14 E2
Eythorne CT15 245 C7
Margate CT9 83 A6
Chapel Hos ME2 94 E4
Chapel La Blean CT2 142 A7
Broad Oak CT2 143 D7
18 Dover CT16 310 D7
East Studdal CT15 246 C6
Egerton Forstal TN27 232 B2
Gillingham ME7 98 A2
Gillingham ME7 98 A4
Iden Green TN17 342 C4
Maidstone ME14 163 A5
Newchurch TN29 351 C4
Rhodes Minnis CT4 273 B4
Ripple CT14 247 D8
St Margaret's at Cliffe CT15 279 F6
Sissinghurst TN17 321 B7
Staple CT3 179 B6
Staplehurst TN12 260 F3
Sturry CT2 143 F5
Upper Halling ME2 94 C4
Chapel Mews TN23 268 C2
Chapel Place La CT11 117 D7
Chapel Pl
10 Dover CT17 310 D7
Ramsgate CT11 117 D7
14 Royal Tunbridge Wells TN1 286 A2
Ticehurst TN5 338 E1
Chapel Rd Bexley DA7 14 A3
Dymchurch TN29 366 C7
Grain ME3 27 B5
Limpsfield RH8 183 C5
Ram Lane TN26 234 F1
Ramsgate CT11 117 C7
Snodland ME6 128 A8
Sutton Valence ME17 229 E7
Tilmanstone CT14 213 A3
Whitfield CT16 278 A8
Chapel Row Herne CT6 111 A8
Ightham TN15 156 C6
Kingsnorth TN23 300 A3
Lydd TN29 376 C6
Ram Lane TN26 234 F2
Chapelsite Ct 6 DA17 4 A2
Chapel St Deal CT14 215 D6
East Malling ME19 160 A6
Faversham ME13 138 D6
Herne Bay CT6 77 A5
Hythe CT21 333 B2
Minster (Sheppey) ME12 47 D6
Ryarsh ME19 126 F5
Sheerness ME12 28 A2
Chapel The
Chartham CT4 173 F1
Maidstone ME16 161 B3
Chapel View TN15 156 C6
Chapel Wlk
Goathurst Common TN14 186 B5
Maypole DA2 32 E6
Chapel Wood DA3 91 E8
Chapel Wood Rd DA3, TN15 91 E8
Chaplains Wlk CT4 173 E1
Chaplin Cl ME3 40 C3
Chaplin Dr TN27 262 D5
Chapman Ave ME15 195 E8
Chapman Ho CT14 215 B3
Chapman Rd DA17 4 B1
Chapmans Cl
Challock TN25 203 C2
Sundridge TN14 152 E3
Chapmans End BR5 54 E7
Chapmans Hill CT15, CT3 211 B5
Chapman's Hill DA13, TN15 92 E4
Chapman's La
Orpington BR5,BR8 54 D7
Swanley BR8 55 A7
Chapmans Rd TN14 152 E3
Chapman Way
East Malling ME19 159 F8
Royal Tunbridge Wells TN2 286 C8
Chappell Way ME10 101 E6
Chapter Rd ME2 62 F8
Chapter Sch ME2 62 D7
Chardwell Cl E6 1 F7
Charford Rd E16 1 A8
Charing CE Prim Sch TN27 234 C8
Charing Cl
Orpington BR6 86 F6
Ramsgate CT12 117 C8
Charing Cres CT8 81 D7
Charing Heath Rd
Charing Heath TN27 233 F8
Charing TN27 234 A6
Charing Hill TN27 201 E1
Charing Ho 5 DA8 14 F7
Charing Rd ME8 65 B3
Charing Sta TN27 234 B7
Chariot Way ME2 62 F4
Charity Farm Cotts TN17 293 F7
Charlbury Cl ME16 161 C3
Charldane Rd SE9 30 B5
Charlecote Ct ME8 98 D8
Charles Busby Ct ME20 128 F1
Charles Cl Sidcup DA14 31 B4
Snodland ME6 128 A8
Charles Cobb Cl TN29 366 D8
Charles Cres CT19 334 E7
Charles Ct Erith DA8 14 E8
Royal Tunbridge Wells TN2 286 C3
Westgate-on-S CT8 81 F8
Charles Darwin Ho 5 BR1 29 B1
Charles Darwin Sch TN16 118 F3
Charles Dickens Ave ME3 39 C2
Charles Dickens Ctr (Mus)* ME1 63 C5
Charles Dickens Sch The CT10 83 E4
Charles Drayson Ct ME13 138 E7
Charles Dr ME2 62 B2
Charlesfield SE9 29 C5
Charles Flemwell Mews E16 1 A5
Charlesford Ave ME17 197 D3
Charles Garvice Ct SE3 11 D4
Charles Grinling Wlk SE18 2 A2
Charles Ho CT14 215 B3
Charles Lister Ct CT17 278 B1
Charles Rd
Badgers Mount TN14 88 B1
Deal CT14 215 B4
Ramsgate CT11 117 E8
Charles St Chatham ME4 63 E3
Grays RM17 18 C8
Herne Bay CT6 77 A5
Maidstone ME16 161 E3
Newham E16 1 C5
Charles Street Centre PRU The TN4 286 A8
Charles St
Rochester ME2 63 A7
Royal Tunbridge Wells TN4 286 A8
Sheerness ME12 28 A3
Stone DA9 16 F2
Charleston Ct CT10 84 B3
Charles Whincup Rd E16 1 B5
Charlesworth Dr CT7 81 B7
Charlieville Rd DA8 14 C7
Charlock Cl ME16 161 D8
Charlotte Cl Bexley DA6 13 E2
Chatham ME5 97 B6
Charlotte Ct
Chislehurst BR7 30 B2
4 Ramsgate CT11 117 E6
Charlotte Dr ME8 65 C1
Charlotte Park Ave BR1 52 E6
Charlotte Pl
2 Margate CT9 50 J1
West Thurrock RM20 17 B8
Charlottes Cotts TN11 220 F1
Charlotte Sq 8 CT9 50 J2
Charlotte St
13 Broadstairs CT10 84 B4
Folkestone CT20 335 E5
Sittingbourne ME10 101 E5
Charlton Ave CT16 278 C1
Charlton CE Prim Sch CT16 278 C1
Charlton Church La SE7 1 C1
Charlton Cl
Ashford TN24 301 A8
Ramsgate CT12 83 B2
Charlton Cres 2 TN9 222 C2
Charlton Ctr 3 CT17 310 C8
Charlton Dene SE7 11 D7
Charlton Dr TN16 118 D2
Charlton Gate Bsns Pk SE7 1 C2
Charlton Gn CT16 278 C1
Charlton La
Chartway Street ME17 197 C1
Greenwich SE7 1 D1
Sutton Valence ME17 230 C8
West Farleigh ME15 193 E6
Charlton Manor ME7 64 B5
Charlton Manor Prim Sch SE7 11 D7
Charlton Park La SE7 11 E8
Charlton Park Rd SE7 11 D8
Charlton Rd SE3,SE7 11 B8
Charlton Sch SE7 11 E8
Charlton Sta SE7 1 C1
Charlton St RM20 17 D8
Charltons The ME13 139 F4
Charlton St ME16 161 C2
Charlton's Way TN4 285 E1
Charminster TN23 299 E6
Charminster Rd SE9 29 D4
Charmouth Rd DA16 13 C6
Charmwood La BR6 87 B1
Charmwood Villas BR6 87 C1
Charne The TN14 122 A2
Charnock BR8 55 E5
Charnwood Rd CT6 77 B1
Charnwood CT5 75 D1
Charollais Cl CT2 143 A2
Chartam Terr CT11 117 D5
Chart Cl ME13 138 B7
Chart Cnr ME17 196 B1
Charter Dr DA5 31 E8
Charter Ho 11 CT16 310 E7
Charterhouse Dr TN13 154 A4
Charterhouse Rd BR6 87 A2
Charter St Chatham ME4 63 F2
Gillingham ME7 64 C7
Chartham Downs Rd CT4 207 C7
Chartham Prim Sch CT4 173 C2
Chartham Sta CT4 173 D3
Chart Hill Rd
Chart Sutton ME17 196 B1
Sutton Valence ME17 229 A7
Chart Hills Cl SE28 3 E7
Chart La TN16 185 B7
Chart Mill Gun Powder Mills* ME13 138 B7
Charton Cl 5 DA17 13 F8
Chart Pl ME8 98 C3
Chart Rd
Ashford,Godinton Park TN23 267 F2
Ashford,Great Chart TN23 267 D1
Ashford,Stanhope TN23 299 D6
Folkestone CT19 334 F6
Sutton Valence ME17 229 C7
Chart Road Ind Est TN23 268 A3
Chart View TN15 123 B2
Chartway TN13 154 C3
Chartway St ME17 197 C1
Chartwell Ave CT6 77 D4
Chartwell Bsns Ctr BR1 52 D6
Chartwell Cl
Rochester ME2 40 B1
Sidcup SE9 30 D6
Chartwell Ct
Chatham ME4 63 E4
Maidstone ME15 162 B3
Chartwell Dr
Maidstone ME16 161 B4
Orpington BR6 86 D5
Chartwell Gr ME10 101 C3
Chartwell* TN16 184 F4
Chase Sq 14 DA11 19 B1
Chase The Bexley DA7 14 B4
Bromley BR1 52 B6
Chatham ME4 63 D2
Gillingham ME8 65 A2
Kemsing TN15 122 E3
Pratt's Bottom BR6 87 A1
Ramsgate CT11 83 F1
St Margaret's at Cliffe CT15 247 F1
Tonbridge TN10 222 C5
West Thurrock RM20 17 D8
Chastilian Rd DA1 33 A8
Chater Cl CT14 215 C4
Chatfield Way ME19 128 B1
Chatham Ave BR2 52 A2
Chatham Ct CT11 117 D8
Chatham Gram Sch for Boys ME4 96 F8
Chatham Gram Sch for Girls ME5 64 C2
Chatham Gr ME4 63 F1
Chatham Hill ME4 64 B3
Chatham Hill Rd TN14 154 C6
Chatham House Gram Sch for Boys CT11 117 E7
Chatham Ho 16 SE18 1 F2
Chatham Pl CT11 117 E7
Chatham Rd
Kit's Coty ME20 129 D6
Sandling ME14 129 E1
Sandling ME14 129 E4
Chatham Ski Ctr ME7 97 E6
Chatham South Sch ME4 96 F8
Chatham Sta ME4 63 E4
Chatham St CT11 117 E7
Chatsworth Ave
Bromley BR1 29 B4
Sidcup DA15 31 A7
Chatsworth Dr
Rochester ME2 40 B1
Sittingbourne ME10 101 B5
Chatsworth Ho 3 BR2 52 A5
Chatsworth Inf Sch DA15 31 A7
Chatsworth Par BR5 53 C4
Chatsworth Rd
Dartford DA1 15 C3
10 Gillingham ME7 64 C6
Chattenden Barracks Royal Sch of Military Engineering ME3 40 F5
Chattenden Ct ME14 162 B6
Chattenden La ME3 40 F5
Chattenden Prim Sch ME3 40 F4

Chattenden Terr ME3 ..... 40 F4
Chatterton Rd BR2 .... 52 D4
Chatwell Ct ME7 .... 64 C5
Chaucer Ave CT5 .... 75 B1
Chaucer Bsns Pk
TN15 .... 155 D8
Chaucer Cl
Canterbury CT1 .... 175 C7
13 Maidstone ME15 ..... 195 E7
Rochester ME2 .... 63 E8
Tilbury RM18 .... 19 C5
Chaucer Coll CT2 ...... 142 D3
Chaucer Cres CT16 ..... 278 B3
Chaucer Ct CT1 .... 175 B7
Chaucer Gdns TN9 ..... 253 F7
Chaucer Hospl CT4 ..... 175 A4
Chaucer Ind Pk TN15 ... 155 D8
Chaucer Mews CT2 ..... 141 E1
Chaucer Pk DA1 .... 33 F8
Chaucer Rd Bexley DA16 .. 12 F6
Broadstairs CT10 .... 84 A3
Canterbury CT1 .... 143 C1
Elvington CT15 .... 212 B2
Gillingham ME7 .... 64 D3
Northfleet DA11 .... 36 D5
Sidcup DA15 .... 31 C7
Sittingbourne ME10 ..... 101 D3
Chaucer Tech Sch
CT1 .... 175 C7
Chaucer Way
Dartford DA1 .... 16 A3
New Hythe ME20 .... 128 A3
Chaucer Wood Ct CT1 .. 143 B1
Chaundrye Cl SE9 .... 11 F1
Chauntler Cl E16 .... 1 B6
Chave Rd DA2 .... 33 E5
Cheddar Cl TN24 .... 268 B4
Cheeselands TN27 ..... 294 F2
Cheesmans Cl CT12 ... 115 C5
Cheffins Ho ME7 .... 64 E7
Chegwell Dr ME5 .... 97 B4
Chegworth Gdns
ME10 .... 101 E1
Chegworth La ME17 .... 198 A6
Chegworth Rd ME17 ... 197 F5
Cheldoc Rise ME4 .... 41 C2
Chellows La RH7 .... 216 A1
Chelmar Rd ME7 .... 64 B4
Chelmsford Cl E6 .... 1 F7
Chelmsford Ho ME15 ... 195 E6
Chelmsford Rd ME2 ..... 62 D6
Chelsea Ct
6 Bromley BR1 .... 52 E6
Hythe CT21 .... 333 C1
Chelsea Rd CT1 .... 143 C4
Chelsfield Hill BR6 .... 87 C2
Chelsfield Ho ME16 ... 161 D5
Chelsfield La
Badgers Mount BR6,TN14 ... 88 B2
Chelsfield BR5,BR6 .... 87 D7
Orpington BR5 .... 54 D1
Chelsfield Park Hospl
BR6 .... 87 F5
Chelsfield Prim Sch
BR6 .... 87 E5
Chelsfield Rd BR5 .... 54 C3
Chelsfield Sta BR6 .... 87 B5
Chelsiter Ct DA14 .... 30 F4
Chelsworth Dr SE18 ..... 12 D8
Cheltenham Cl
Gravesend DA12 .... 37 C3
Maidstone ME15 .... 195 F6
Cheltenham Rd BR6 ...... 87 A7
Cheney Cl ME8 .... 98 D5
Cheney Hill ME9 .... 135 A5
Cheney Rd ME13 .... 138 F7
Chenies Cl TN2 .... 314 A8
Chenies The
Joyden's Wood DA2 .... 32 E4
Orpington BR6 .... 53 E3
Chennell Park Rd
TN30 .... 323 E1
Chennels The TN26 .... 324 C7
Chepstow Ho 3 ME15 .. 195 F6
Chequer La CT3 .... 147 D2
Chequer's Terr ME12 ..... 48 A5
Chequers Cl
Chatham ME5 .... 130 A8
Istead Rise DA13 .... 59 F7
Orpington BR5 .... 53 F5
Chequer's Cotts TN17 .. 318 F8
Chequers Ctr ME15 ..... 162 A4
Chequers Ct ME2 .... 40 A1
Chequers Hill Cotts
TN8 .... 219 A2
Chequers Hill CT4 ...... 207 C2
Chequers La RM9 .... 3 F8
Chequers Pk TN25 ..... 237 E1
Chequers Rd ME12 .... 47 E6
Chequertree TN25 ...... 329 B7
Cherbourg Cres ME5 ..... 96 F7
Cherbury Cl SE28 .... 3 D7
Cheriton Apartments
CT19 .... 334 F6
Cheriton Ave Hayes BR2 .. 52 A4
Ramsgate CT12 .... 117 B8
Cheriton Court Rd
CT20 .... 334 C6
Cheriton Ct 12 SE12 ...... 29 A8
Cheriton Dr SE18 .... 12 D8
Cheriton Gdns CT20 ... 335 C4
Cheriton High St
CT19 .... 334 D6
Cheriton Intc CT19 ..... 334 C7
Cheriton Pl Deal CT14 .. 215 D4
Folkestone CT20 .... 335 D4
Cheriton Prim Sch
CT20 .... 334 C6
Cheriton Rd Deal CT14 .. 215 D4
Folkestone CT19,CT20 ... 335 B5
Folkestone, Morehall
CT19 .... 334 F6
Gillingham ME8 .... 98 D8
Cheriton Way ME16 .... 161 C7
Cheriton Wood Ho
CT19 .... 334 D7
Cherries The ME16 ..... 161 A2
Cherry Amber Cl ME8 .... 98 F8
Cherry Ave
Canterbury CT2 .... 142 D2
Swanley BR8 .... 55 D5
Cherrybrook Rd CT20 .. 334 D6
Cherry Cl
Lenham ME17 .... 199 C5
Sittingbourne ME10 ..... 101 D6
Cherrycot Hill BR6 .... 86 D6
Cherrycot Rise BR6 ...... 86 C6
Cherry Ct
Ashford TN23 .... 268 B1
Broadstairs CT10 .... 83 E7
Folkestone CT19 .... 335 A6
Sidcup DA14 .... 31 B5
Cherrydown Rd DA14 .... 31 D6
Cherry Dr CT2 .... 142 D2
Cherryfields TN17 ...... 342 D6
Cherry Fields ME10 .... 101 A5
Cherry Garden Ave
CT19 .... 335 A7
Cherry Garden Cres
TN25 .... 237 F2
Cherry Garden La CT3 .. 147 E1
Cherrygarden La
CT15,CT3 .... 211 E7
Cherry Garden La
Folkestone CT19 .... 334 F7
Wye TN25 .... 237 F2
Cherry Garden Rd
CT2 .... 142 D2
Cherry Gdns
Broadstairs CT10 .... 83 C3
Elham CT4 .... 273 F5
Herne Bay CT6 .... 76 F4
Littlestone-on-Sea TN28 .. 373 D6
Teynham ME9 .... 103 C2
Cherry Glebe TN25 ..... 301 E3
Cherry Gr
Elvington CT15 .... 212 B2
Tonbridge TN10 .... 222 E5
Cherry Hill Ct ME9 ..... 100 B6
Cherry La CT14 .... 214 D3
Cherry Orchard Cl BR5 ... 54 C4
Cherry Orchard La
TN25 .... 329 E4
Cherry Orchard Mews
CT3 .... 144 F1
Cherry Orchard Prim Sch
SE7 .... 11 C7
Cherry Orchard Rd
BR2 .... 85 E8
Cherry Orchard Way
ME16 .... 161 B3
Cherry Orch
Ditton ME20 .... 160 C8
Greenwich SE7 .... 11 C8
Littlebourne CT3 .... 144 F1
Old Wives Lees CT4 ..... 172 C2
Tenterden TN30 .... 345 A6
Cherry Orch The
TN11 .... 190 E1
Cherry Orch
Whitstable CT5 .... 109 C8
Woodchurch TN26 ...... 326 A3
Cherry Rd ME3 .... 41 E3
Cherry Tree Ave CT16 .. 278 C1
Cherry Tree Cl
Grays RM17 .... 18 C8
Teynham ME9 .... 103 D2
West Minst ME12 .... 46 A8
Cherry Tree Ct 19 SE7 .... 11 C8
Cherry Tree Dr ME13 ... 104 F3
Cherry Tree Gdns CT12 .. 83 B3
Cherry Tree Gr TN15 ..... 90 B1
Cherry Tree La DA2 ...... 32 F5
Cherry Tree Rd
Charing Heath TN27 .... 233 E7
Gillingham ME8 .... 98 F8
Royal Tunbridge Wells
TN2 .... 285 E1
Tonbridge TN10 .... 222 D7
Cherry Trees DA3 .... 58 F4
Cherry View ME17 ...... 195 B3
Cherry Waye CT15 ..... 245 D7
Cherry Wlk BR2 .... 52 A1
Cherrywood Dr DA11 ..... 36 E5
Cherrywood Rise
TN25 .... 267 F4
Cherville La CT3 .... 177 C7
Chervilles ME16 .... 161 A2
Chervil Mews SE28 .... 3 B5
Cherwell Cl TN10 ...... 222 B4
Chesfield Cl TN11 ...... 190 F1
Chesham Ave BR5 .... 53 B3
Chesham Dr ME8 .... 98 E6
Cheshire Rd
Maidstone ME15 .... 195 E7
Maidstone,Willington
ME15 .... 162 E2
Cheshunt Cl DA13 .... 60 A3
Cheshunt Rd DA17 .... 4 A1
Chesil Ho 1 BR7 .... 53 D8
Chessenden La TN27 ... 264 A1
Chessington Ave DA7 .... 13 E7
Chester Ave
Bethersden TN26 .... 297 D5
Royal Tunbridge Wells
TN2 .... 286 D2
Chester Cl ME2 .... 62 D6
Chesterfield Cl BR5 ..... 54 D5
Chesterfield Dr
Dartford DA1 .... 15 B2
Sevenoaks TN13 .... 153 D5
Chesterford Ho SE18 .... 11 D7
Chester Rd
Gillingham ME7 .... 64 D2
Sidcup DA15 .... 12 E2
Westgate-on-S CT8 .... 81 F8
Chesterton Rd
Cliffe ME3 .... 22 B5
5 Lunsford ME20 .... 127 F4
Chesterton Way RM18 .... 19 C5
Chestfield Cl ME8 .... 65 E2
Chestfield Rd CT5 ...... 109 C7
Chestfield & Swalecliffe
Sta CT5 .... 75 D2
Chestnut Ave
Blean CT2 .... 142 A7
Chatham ME5 .... 96 F3
Hill Park TN16 .... 151 A6
Royal Tunbridge Wells
TN4 .... 286 B8
Staplehurst TN12 .... 260 F4
Stone DA9 .... 34 F8
Tatsfield TN16 .... 150 E5
Chestnut Cl
Ashford TN23 .... 267 E3
Chartham CT4 .... 173 F1
Edenbridge TN8 .... 217 B2
Frittenden TN17 .... 293 E6
Hythe CT21 .... 353 E8
Kings Hill ME19 .... 159 A2
Northfleet DA11 .... 18 F1
Orpington BR6 .... 87 A5
Royal Tunbridge Wells
TN4 .... 286 B8
Sidcup DA15 .... 31 A6
Tenterden TN30 .... 324 C1
Ulcombe ME17 .... 230 F6
Whitfield CT16 .... 278 A8
Chestnut Copse RH8 ... 183 B2
Chestnut Ct
Boughton Street ME13 ... 140 A3
Royal Tunbridge Wells
TN2 .... 314 A8
Chestnut Dr Bexley DA7 .. 13 E4
Broadstairs CT10 .... 83 D4
Coxheath ME17 .... 194 B3
Herne Bay CT6 .... 76 D3
Kingswood ME17 .... 197 D2
Sturry CT2 .... 144 A7
Worth CT14 .... 181 A4
Chestnut Gr DA2 .... 32 E4
Chestnut Ho 5 ME16 ... 161 A3
Chestnut La
Kingsnorth TN23 .... 300 C4
Matfield TN12 .... 256 D1
Sevenoaks TN13 .... 154 B3
Vigo Village DA13 .... 126 B8
Chestnut Pl TN8 .... 282 A6
Chestnut Rd
Dartford DA1 .... 33 D7
Dover CT17 .... 310 B7
Rochester ME2 .... 62 E6
Chestnut Rise SE18 .... 2 E1
Chestnuts Royal BR7 .... 30 D1
Chestnut St ME9 .... 100 E4
Chestnuts The
Addington ME19 .... 126 C3
Brabourne Lees TN25 ... 302 D5
Chislehurst BR7 .... 30 D1
7 Erith DA17 .... 3 F1
Sellindge TN25 .... 303 D1
The Moor TN18 .... 354 F8
Woolwich SE18 .... 12 B6
Chestnut Terr CT21 .... 333 A1
Chestnut Wlk
Larkfield ME20 .... 128 B2
Sevenoaks TN15 .... 187 F6
Tonbridge TN9 .... 221 F2
Chestnut Wood La
ME9 .... 100 E3
Cheswick Cl DA1 .... 14 F3
Chesworth Cl DA8 .... 14 E5
Chetney Cl ME2 .... 62 C7
Chetney View ME9 .... 68 D4
Chetwood Wlk 15 E6 .... 1 E8
Chevalier Rd CT17 ..... 310 A7
Chevender BR7 .... 30 B1
Cheveney Wlk 2 BR2 .... 52 A6
Chevening CE Prim Sch
TN13 .... 153 B5
Chevening Cl ME5 .... 97 A5
Chevening Ct BR6 .... 87 A8
Chevening House BR5 .... 54 A8
Chevening La TN14 .... 120 E3
Chevening Rd
3 Greenwich SE10 .... 1 A1
Sevenoaks TN13,TN14 ... 153 B6
Sundridge TN14 .... 152 F4
Chevenings The DA14 .... 31 C5
Cheviot Cl Bexley DA7 ... 14 E5
Tonbridge TN9 .... 222 C4
Cheviot Ct CT10 .... 84 B5
Cheviot Gdns ME15 .... 163 A1
Cheviot Ho DA11 .... 18 D1
Cheviot Way TN24 ..... 268 C4
Chevron Cl E16 .... 1 A7
Chevron Ho RM17 .... 18 B7
Cheyne Cl
Orpington BR2 .... 85 E7
Sittingbourne ME10 ..... 101 F8
Cheyne Mid Sch The
ME12 .... 28 D2
Cheyne Rd ME12 .... 48 D3
Cheyne Wlk
Longfield DA3 .... 58 D6
Meopham DA13 .... 93 A8
Chicago Ave ME7 .... 64 F5
Chichester Cl
Ashford TN23 .... 268 B1
Gillingham ME8 .... 99 A8
Greenwich SE3 .... 11 C6
Newham E6 .... 1 E7
Chichester Ct 3 DA5 ..... 32 A8
Chichester Dr TN13 .... 153 F2
Chichester Rd
Folkestone CT20 .... 334 E4
Ramsgate CT12 .... 83 B1
Stone DA9 .... 16 F1
Tonbridge TN9 .... 254 A8
Chichester Rise DA12 ... 37 D4
Chichester Wharf 14
DA8 .... 4 E1
Chichester Wlk CT12 ..... 83 B1
Chickenden La NT17 ... 261 C4
Chickfield Gdns 4
ME5 .... 64 C2
Chicks La TN17 .... 317 F2
Chiddingfold Cl ME12 ... 47 D6
Chiddingstone Ave
DA7 .... 13 F7
Chiddingstone Castle*
TN8 .... 251 B7
Chiddingstone CE Prim Sch
TN8 .... 251 C7
Chiddingstone Cl
ME15 .... 195 F6
Chidley Cross Rd
TN12 .... 224 E6
Chieftain Cl ME7 .... 65 B1
Chieveley Dr TN2 ...... 286 D1
Chieveley Par DA7 .... 14 B4
Chieveley Rd DA7 .... 14 B3
Chiffinch Gdns DA11 ..... 36 E5
Childgate Rd CT5 ...... 107 F2
Childsbridge La TN15 .. 154 F7
Childsbridge Way
TN15 .... 154 F7
Childs Cres DA10 .... 17 D1
Childscroft Rd ME8 ...... 65 F2
Childs Way TN15 ...... 124 F3
Chilham Ave CT8 .... 81 D7
Chilham Cl
Chatham ME4 .... 63 E3
Sidcup DA5 .... 31 F8
West Minst ME12 .... 46 B8
Chilham Ho
1 Maidstone ME15 ..... 195 E8
Rochester ME2 .... 40 C1
Chilham Rd Bromley SE9 .. 29 E4
Folkestone CT19 .... 334 E6
Gillingham ME8 .... 65 A3
Maidstone ME16 .... 161 C7
Chilham Sta CT4 .... 205 D8
Chilham Way BR2 .... 52 A2
Chillenden Windmill*
CT3 .... 178 F1
Chillington Cl ME2 .... 94 E4
Chillington St ME14 .... 161 F6
Chilliwack Rd ME3 .... 40 F5
Chilston Cl TN4 .... 286 A5
Chilston Rd
Lenham ME17 .... 199 D5
Royal Tunbridge Wells
TN4 .... 286 A5
Chiltenhurst TN8 .... 217 A2
Chiltern Cl Bexley DA7 ... 14 E6
Maidstone ME15 .... 162 F1
Chiltern Ct 11 SE9 .... 12 A1
Chiltern End TN24 ..... 268 B3
Chiltern Rd DA11 .... 36 E5
Chilterns DA14 .... 31 A3
Chilterns, The BR1 .... 52 B7
Chiltern Way TN9 ...... 222 C4
Chiltern Wlk TN2 ...... 286 D4
Chilton Ave
Sittingbourne ME10 ..... 102 A3
Temple Ewell CT16 ...... 277 C4
Chilton Ct
14 Folkestone CT20 .... 335 E6
Gillingham ME8 .... 65 E1
Chilton Dr ME3 .... 39 B3
Chilton Field CT3 ...... 147 D2
Chilton Gdns CT3 ...... 147 D2
Chilton La CT11 .... 117 A6
Chilton Pl CT3 .... 147 D2
Chilton Prim Sch
CT11 .... 117 A6
Chilton Sq CT3 .... 147 D2
Chilton Way CT17 ..... 277 D3
Chimes The
Ashford TN24 .... 268 C3
Rochester ME1 .... 63 C5
Chinbrook Cres 8
SE12 .... 29 B5
Chinbrook Rd SE12 ...... 29 B5
Chine Farm Pl TN14 ... 120 D3
Chineham Way CT1 .... 174 F6
Chinnery Ct DA13 .... 60 A2
Chippendale Cl ME5 ..... 96 F1
Chippendayle Dr
ME17 .... 198 D6
Chipperfield Rd
Orpington BR5 .... 54 A7
Orpington BR5 .... 54 B5
Chipstead Cl ME16 .... 161 D6
Chipstead La TN13 .... 153 D5
Chipstead Park Cl
TN13 .... 153 C5
Chipstead Pk TN13 .... 153 D5
Chipstead Place Gdns
TN13 .... 153 D5
Chipstead Rd Erith DA8 .. 14 E7
Gillingham ME8 .... 98 D4
Chipstead Sq TN13 .... 153 C5
Chislehurst Caves*
BR7 .... 53 A8
Chislehurst Cl ME15 ... 195 F6
Chislehurst High St
BR7 .... 30 B2
Chislehurst Rd
Bromley BR1,BR2 .... 52 E8
Orpington BR6 .... 54 A2
Orpington,Broom Hill BR6 ... 53 F2
Orpington,Petts Wood
BR5,BR6 .... 53 E4
Sidcup DA14 .... 31 A3
Chislehurst (St Nicholas)
CE Prim Sch BR7 .... 30 C1
Chislehurst & Sidcup Gram
Sch DA15 .... 31 B6
Chislehurst Sta BR7 ...... 53 A7
Chislet CE Prim Sch
CT3 .... 112 C5
Chislet Ct CT6 .... 76 E5
Chislet Park Cotts
CT3 .... 111 F1
Chislet Park Farm Cotts
CT3 .... 111 F2
Chislett Cl TN25 .... 303 E2
Chislet Wlk ME8 .... 98 D5
Chisnall Rd CT17 ...... 277 E4
Chiswell Sq SE3 .... 11 B5
Chittenden's La TN29 .. 364 E5
Chitty La CT3 .... 112 D6
Chorleywood Cres BR5 ... 54 A7
Christchurch Ave DA8 .... 14 E8
Christ Church Ave 1
TN1 .... 286 A2
Christ Church CE High Sch
TN23 .... 299 F5
Christ Church CE Jun Sch
CT11 .... 117 C6
Christ Church CE Sch
SE18 .... 12 A6
Christ Church Coll
CT1 .... 175 B8
Christ Church Cres 2
DA12 .... 37 C8
Christchurch Ct
3 Chatham ME5 .... 64 C2
1 Dover CT17 .... 310 D7
Christ Church Erith CE
Prim Sch DA8 .... 14 D8
Christchurch Ho 11
ME15 .... 195 E5
Christchurch Rd
Ashford TN23 .... 300 B8
Dartford DA1 .... 15 C1
Christ Church Rd
Folkestone CT20 .... 335 C4
3 Gravesend DA12 .... 37 C8
Christchurch Rd
Sidcup DA15 .... 30 F5
Tilbury RM18 .... 19 A6
Christchurch Way
CT16 .... 278 B3
Christen Way ME15,
ME17 .... 195 F3
Christian Ct 3 ME2 ...... 63 C8
Christian Fields Ave
DA12 .... 37 C4
Christie Cl ME5 .... 97 B6
Christie Dr 8 ME20 .... 127 F4
Christie Ho DA6 .... 14 B2
Christies Ave TN14 ...... 88 B1
Christmas La ME23 .... 23 F3
Christmas St ME7 .... 64 E7
Christopher Bushell Way
TN24 .... 268 E4
Christopher Cl DA15 ..... 12 F2
Christopher's Row
ME9 .... 136 A3
Christy Rd TN16 .... 118 C4
Chrysler Ave CT6 .... 76 B4
Chudleigh 7 DA14 .... 31 B4
Chulkhurst TN27 .... 294 F1
Chulkhurst Cl TN27 .... 294 F1
Chunnel Ind Est TN23 .. 268 B1
Church Alley 11 DA11 .... 19 B1
Church App TN28 ...... 373 A6
Church Ave DA14 .... 31 B3
Churchbury Rd SE9 ...... 29 D8
Church Cl
Brenchley TN12 .... 289 C8
Cliffe ME3 .... 22 B6
Church Cliff CT14 ...... 248 D6
Church Cl
Mereworth ME18 .... 191 D8
Mersham TN25 .... 301 E3
New Romney TN28 ..... 373 B6
Church Cotts
Cranbrook TN17 .... 320 D5
Crockenhill BR8 .... 55 D2
Rodmersham ME9 ...... 135 D8
Shoreham TN14 .... 122 A8
Sutton Valence ME17 ... 229 E7
Tenterden TN30 .... 324 B3
Church Court Gr CT10 ... 83 E6
Church Cres ME17 ..... 198 F6
Church Ct Dartford DA2 .. 33 D5
Lyminge CT18 .... 305 C6
Church Farm Cl
Crockenhill BR8 .... 55 D3
Hoo St Werburgh ME3 .... 41 E4
Church Farm Rd ME9 .... 66 E3
Church Farm Way
CT13 .... 180 B6
Churchfield ME19 ...... 126 D3
Church Field Cotts
TN15 .... 154 F7
Church Field DA2 .... 33 D6
Churchfield TN8 .... 217 D1
Churchfield Pl CT9 .... 50 I2
Churchfield Rd DA16 .... 13 A4
Churchfields CT10 .... 83 F7
Churchfield Sch SE2 .... 3 A2
Church Field TN13 ..... 153 F5
Churchfields CT9 .... 50 J1
Church Field
Snodland ME6 .... 95 B1
Stanford TN25 .... 304 B1
Churchfields Terr ME1 ... 63 B4
Church Fields ME19 ... 159 B8
Churchfield Way
TN25 .... 237 E2
Church Gn
Marden TN12 .... 259 C6
Rochester ME2 .... 63 C8
Staplehurst TN12 .... 260 E2
Church Green ME17 ... 164 E3
Church Haven CT14 ... 247 F5
Church Hill
Bethersden TN26 .... 297 D5
Boughton Street ME13 ... 140 A5
Church Hill continued
Canterbury CT2 .... 142 C1
Charing Heath ME17,
TN27 .... 233 C7
Chatham ME5 .... 64 C2
Chilham CT4 .... 205 B8
Crayford DA1 .... 14 E3
Cudham TN14,TN16 ..... 119 C4
Dartford DA2 .... 33 D6
Doddington ME9 .... 167 F8
Eythorne CT15 .... 245 C8
Hawkinge CT18 .... 307 D4
High Halden TN26 ...... 324 E7
Hythe CT21 .... 333 C2
Kingsnorth TN23 .... 300 B3
Leigh TN11 .... 220 F2
Linton ME17 .... 228 B7
Loose ME17 .... 195 C1
Orpington BR6 .... 54 A2
Plaxtol TN15 .... 189 E8
Ramsgate CT11 .... 117 E7
Shepherdswell CT15 .... 244 D4
Stockbury ME9 .... 132 F7
Stone DA9 .... 16 E2
Stone in Oxney TN30 ... 360 F3
Sutton CT15 .... 247 A7
Tatsfield TN16 .... 150 D5
Temple Ewell CT16 ...... 277 D5
Church Hill Wood BR5 ... 53 F4
Church Hill SE18 .... 1 F3
Church Ho CT14 .... 215 C7
Church Hts CT21 .... 333 C2
Church Hyde SE18 .... 12 E8
Churchill Ave
Chatham ME5 .... 97 A7
Deal CT14 .... 215 C2
Folkestone CT19 .... 335 C8
Herne Bay CT6 .... 77 D4
Churchill Bsns Ctr
TN16 .... 151 D1
Churchill CE Prim Sch
TN16 .... 151 C2
Churchill Cl
Bridge CT4 .... 175 F1
Dartford DA1 .... 34 B7
Folkestone CT19 .... 335 D8
St Margaret's at Cliffe
CT15 .... 279 F5
Churchill Cotts ME17 ... 196 F6
Churchill Ct
Hythe CT21 .... 333 B1
4 Orpington BR6 .... 86 C5
1 Ramsgate CT11 ...... 117 D7
Westerham TN16 .... 151 D1
Churchill Ho
Benenden TN17 .... 342 E6
Bridge CT4 .... 175 F1
2 Folkestone CT20 ..... 334 F5
Maidstone ME16 .... 161 B2
Sittingbourne ME10 ..... 102 C4
Teynham ME9 .... 103 C3
1 Woolwich SE18 .... 2 B2
Churchill Pk DA1 .... 16 A2
Churchill Rd
Canterbury CT1 .... 175 C6
Dover CT17 .... 310 A6
Grays RM17 .... 18 D8
Horton Kirby DA4 .... 57 C5
Minster (Sheppey) ME12 .. 47 D6
Newham E16 .... 1 C7
Northfleet DA11 .... 36 F7
Churchill Sch The
CT18 .... 307 A4
Churchill Sq ME19 ..... 159 A3
Churchills Ropewalk
TN17 .... 318 E8
Churchill St 7 CT16 ... 278 C1
Churchill Way
Biggin Hill TN16 .... 118 D4
Bromley BR1 .... 52 A7
Faversham ME13 .... 105 B1
Churchill Wlk CT18 .... 306 F4
Church La
Adisham CT3 .... 177 D1
Aldington TN25 .... 330 D7
Barham CT4 .... 209 F1
Boughton Aluph TN25 ... 237 B4
Boyden Gate CT3 .... 112 C7
Brenzett TN29 .... 362 F5
Canterbury CT1 .... 174 F8
21 Canterbury,Northgate
CT1 .... 143 A1
Capel TN12 .... 255 F6
Chalk DA12 .... 38 C6
Challock TN25 .... 236 B8
Chartham CT4 .... 173 D3
Chatham ME4 .... 63 F6
Chislehurst BR7 .... 53 C8
Church Hougham CT15 ... 309 B5
Deal CT14 .... 215 B6
East Peckham TN12 .... 224 F7
Frant TN3 .... 314 B4
Harrietsham ME17 ...... 198 E6
Iden TN31 .... 368 B4
Kemsing TN15 .... 123 B2
Kingston CT4 .... 209 D3
Lower Hardres CT4 ..... 175 B2
Lydden CT15 .... 276 E8
Maidstone,Bearsted
ME14 .... 163 C4
Maidstone ME16 .... 160 E1
Churchlands Ho TN28 ... 373 B6
Churchlands ME14 ..... 162 B5
Churchlands The
TN28 .... 373 B6
Church La
Newington ME9 .... 100 B6
New Romney TN28 ..... 373 B5
Orpington BR2 .... 52 E1
Peasmarsh TN31 .... 367 C1

Church La *continued*
Petham CT4 ... 207 C3
Ringwould CT14 ... 247 F5
Ripple CT14 ... 214 D1
Selling ME13 ... 171 B6
Shadoxhurst TN26 ... 327 A7
Stockbury ME9 ... 132 E8
Stourmouth CT3 ... 113 C2
Stowting TN25 ... 304 A6
Sturry CT2 ... 143 F5
Sutton Valence ME17 ... 230 B8
Tonbridge TN9 ... 222 C2
Trottiscliffe ME19 ... 126 B5
Waltham CT4 ... 239 F5
Westbere CT2 ... 144 C7
West Farleigh ME15 ... 193 D7
West Langdon CT15 ... 246 D3
Whitstable CT5 ... 108 A6
Womenswold CT4 ... 210 D2
Church Manorway DA8 ... 4 D3
Church Manor Way SE18,SE2 ... 3 A2
Church Marshes Ctry Pk* ME10 ... 102 A7
Church Mdws CT14 ... 215 A6
Church Meadow TN12 ... 290 A7
Church Mews
Gillingham ME8 ... 98 F8
Iwade ME9 ... 68 E4
Church Path
Deal CT14 ... 215 B5
Gillingham ME7 ... 64 E6
Great Mongeham CT14 ... 214 D3
Lower Halstow ME9 ... 67 C3
Northfleet DA11 ... 18 C1
Stone DA9 ... 16 F1
Church Rd
Ashford,Aylesford Green TN24 ... 301 A7
Ashford,Kennington TN24 ... 268 E6
Ashford TN23 ... 268 C2
Ashford,Willesborough TN24 ... 301 A8
Bexley DA7,DA6 ... 13 F4
Bexley,Welling DA16 ... 13 B5
Biggin Hill TN16 ... 118 E2
Bitchet Green TN15 ... 155 E3
Boughton Malherbe ME17 ... 232 A8
Brasted TN16 ... 152 B3
1 Broadstairs CT10 ... 84 B4
Bromley BR1,BR2 ... 52 A7
Burmarsh TN29 ... 351 E4
Charing TN27 ... 201 D2
Chart Sutton ME17 ... 196 C1
Chelsfield BR6 ... 87 D4
Coldred CT15 ... 245 A3
Crockenhill BR8 ... 55 D2
Dover CT17 ... 310 A7
Eastchurch ME12 ... 48 D2
Eastling ME13 ... 169 B2
Erith DA8 ... 4 D1
Faversham ME13 ... 138 D7
Faversham,Oare ME13 ... 105 B3
Faversham,The Brents ME13 ... 138 D8
Folkestone CT20 ... 334 C6
Goudhurst TN17 ... 318 F8
Grafty Green ME17 ... 231 F7
Gravesend DA12,DA13 ... 37 D1
Halstead TN14 ... 120 F7
Harrietsham ME17 ... 198 E6
Hartley DA3 ... 59 A2
Hawley DA4 ... 33 F1
Henhurst DA13 ... 60 C8
Hoath CT3 ... 111 E5
Hucking ME17 ... 132 E1
Hythe CT21 ... 333 C2
Kenardington TN26 ... 348 A5
Kilndown TN17 ... 317 F3
Lamberhurst TN3 ... 317 C6
Littlebourne CT3 ... 177 A8
Lydd TN29 ... 376 C6
Lyminge CT18 ... 305 C7
Maidstone ME15 ... 195 F7
Maidstone,Tovil ME15 ... 161 E2
Margate CT9 ... 50 J1
Mersham TN25 ... 301 E3
Molash CT4 ... 203 F5
New Romney TN28 ... 373 A6
Northbourne,Betteshanger CT14 ... 213 C6
Northbourne CT14 ... 214 A5
Offham ME18 ... 158 D8
Orpington BR6 ... 86 D5
Orpington, Keston BR2 ... 85 D3
Paddock Wood TN12 ... 257 B6
Pembury TN2 ... 255 D1
Pembury TN2 ... 287 D8
Ramsgate CT11 ... 117 E7
Royal Tunbridge Wells,Southborough TN4 ... 253 F2
Royal Tunbridge Wells TN1 ... 286 A3
Ryarsh ME19 ... 127 A3
Sandhurst Cross TN18 ... 355 F4
Seal TN15 ... 154 F6
Sevenoaks Weald TN14 ... 187 B3
Sevington TN24 ... 301 B6
Sidcup DA14 ... 31 A4
Sittingbourne ME9 ... 102 E5
Sittingbourne,Murston ME10 ... 102 B5
Smeeth TN25 ... 302 C4
Stalisfield Green ME13 ... 201 F5
Stone DA9 ... 16 F2
Sundridge TN14 ... 152 E2
Sutton at H DA4 ... 34 A2
Church Rd *continued*
Sutton Valence ME17 ... 229 C8
Swanley Village BR8 ... 56 D8
Swanscombe DA10 ... 17 F1
Tenterden TN30 ... 345 A7
Tilbury RM18 ... 18 F6
Tonbridge TN11 ... 221 D6
West Kingsdown TN15 ... 90 E3
West Peckham ME18 ... 191 A6
West Tilbury RM18 ... 19 E8
Church Rise CT21 ... 333 C2
Church Road Bsns Ctr ME10 ... 102 B6
Church Row BR7 ... 53 C8
Church Row Mews BR7 ... 30 C1
Church Row
Plaxtol TN15 ... 189 E8
Snodland ME6 ... 128 A7
West Peckham ME18 ... 191 B6
Churchsettle La TN5 ... 337 C1
Churchside Cl TN16 ... 118 C2
Churchside DA13 ... 126 A8
Church Sq
2 Broadstairs CT10 ... 84 B4
Lenham ME17 ... 199 D5
Church St
Broadstairs CT10 ... 83 E6
Burham ME1 ... 95 F1
Canterbury CT2 ... 142 E1
Chatham ME4 ... 64 A4
Cliffe ME3 ... 22 B5
Cowden TN8 ... 282 B5
Deal CT14 ... 215 B1
Dover CT16 ... 310 D7
Eastry CT13 ... 180 C2
Edenbridge TN8 ... 217 D1
Faversham ME13 ... 138 D8
Folkestone CT20 ... 335 D4
Gillingham ME7 ... 64 E6
Gravesend DA11 ... 19 B1
Grays RM17 ... 18 C8
Hadlow TN11 ... 223 E8
Hoo St Werburgh ME3 ... 41 E5
Lower Higham ME3 ... 39 D7
Maidstone, Boughton Monchelsea ME17 ... 195 B2
Maidstone,Loose ME15 ... 194 F5
Maidstone ME14 ... 162 A4
Maidstone,Tovil ME15 ... 161 E2
Margate CT9 ... 50 J1
Minster (Thanet) CT12 ... 115 C5
Newham E16 ... 2 B5
Nonington CT15 ... 211 C5
Northfleet DA13 ... 36 A3
Church Street (St Pauls) 7 CT1 ... 175 A8
Church St
Rochester ME1 ... 63 D4
Rodmersham ME9 ... 135 C8
7 Sandwich CT13 ... 149 A1
3 Sandwich,The Butts CT13 ... 148 F1
Seal TN15 ... 155 A7
Shoreham TN14 ... 122 A8
5 Sittingbourne ME10 ... 101 E4
Sittingbourne ME10 ... 101 E5
Teston ME18 ... 193 A8
Ticehurst TN5 ... 338 D1
Tonbridge TN9 ... 222 C2
Wadhurst TN5 ... 337 A4
Whitstable CT5 ... 74 F1
Woodnesborough CT13 ... 180 B6
Wye TN25 ... 237 E2
Church Terr
Chatham ME5 ... 64 C2
Minster (Sheppey) ME12 ... 47 C7
Church Trad Est DA8 ... 15 A7
Church View
Aldington TN25 ... 330 A6
Biddenden TN27 ... 294 F2
4 Dartford DA1 ... 15 E1
Herne Bay CT6 ... 77 C4
Newchurch TN29 ... 350 E3
Swanley BR8 ... 55 D6
Worth CT14 ... 181 B5
Church Way CT5 ... 75 D3
Church Whitfield Rd CT16 ... 278 B8
Church Wlk
Dartford DA2 ... 33 D5
East Malling ME19 ... 160 A7
Elham CT4 ... 273 F4
Eynsford DA4 ... 89 E7
Gravesend DA12 ... 37 D7
Gravesend DA12 ... 37 D8
Hawkhurst TN18 ... 341 A1
Headcorn TN27 ... 262 C5
Church Wood Cl CT2 ... 142 B2
Churchwood Dr CT5 ... 75 D1
Churchyard Cotts TN3 ... 285 A8
Church Yard Pas 10 TN23 ... 268 B2
Church Yd TN23 ... 268 C2
Churn La TN12 ... 258 A2
Chute Cl ME8 ... 98 D4
Chyngton Ct DA15 ... 30 F5
Cimba Wood DA12 ... 37 E4
Cinder Hill La TN11 ... 220 C1
Cinderhill Wood Cvn Site TN12 ... 256 C1
Cinderhill Wood TN12 ... 256 C2
Cinder Path CT10 ... 84 A4
Cinnabar Cl ME5 ... 97 A1
Cinnabar Dr ME10 ... 101 C6
Cinque Ports Ave CT21 ... 333 B1
Cinque Ports Rd TN28 ... 373 C5
Circle The RM18 ... 19 A6
Circuit Rd SE28 ... 3 A4
Circular Rd
Dover CT16 ... 279 B1
Finglesham CT14 ... 214 B7
Circular Way SE18 ... 12 A8
Circus The CT6 ... 76 E4
Cirrus Cres DA12 ... 37 E3
Citadel Cres CT17 ... 310 B6
Citadel Hts CT17 ... 310 B6
Citadel Rd CT17 ... 310 C6
Citadel The (Immigration Removal Ctr) CT17 ... 310 B5
Citroen Cl CT6 ... 76 B4
City Bsns Pk CT1 ... 143 C3
City Garden The 3 CT1 ... 175 A8
City View CT2 ... 174 C8
City Way ME1 ... 63 D2
Civic Sq RM18 ... 19 A5
Civic Way TN1 ... 286 A3
CJ Gallards Almshouses TN4 ... 286 A8
Clacket La
Tatsfield TN16 ... 150 E2
Westerham TN16 ... 184 A8
Clacketts Farm ME19 ... 127 B5
Claire Ct Birchington CT7 ... 80 F7
Broadstairs CT10 ... 84 B5
Claire Ho 4 ME16 ... 161 E5
Clancy Gdns TN17 ... 320 B5
Clandon Ct BR1 ... 29 A2
Clandon Rd ME5 ... 97 D2
Clanricarde Gdns 1 TN1 ... 286 A3
Clanricarde Rd 2 TN1 ... 286 A3
Clanwilliam Rd CT14 ... 215 D5
Clapham Hill CT5 ... 108 D5
Claphatch La TN5 ... 338 A5
Clapper La TN12 ... 260 D6
Clara Pl SE18 ... 2 A2
Clare Ave TN9 ... 221 F1
Clare Cnr SE9 ... 30 B8
Clare Cswy DA9 ... 16 F3
Clare Ct BR7 ... 52 F8
Clare Dr CT6 ... 76 C2
Clare La ME19 ... 159 E8
Claremont Cl
Kingsdown CT14 ... 248 C6
Newham E16 ... 2 A5
Orpington BR6 ... 86 A6
Claremont Cres DA1 ... 14 E3
Claremont Ct 4 TN2 ... 286 C7
Claremont Gdns
Ramsgate CT11 ... 117 C7
Royal Tunbridge Wells TN2 ... 286 B2
Claremont Pl
Canterbury CT1 ... 174 F7
1 Gravesend DA11 ... 37 B8
Iden Green TN17 ... 342 C4
Marden TN12 ... 259 D4
Claremont Prim Sch TN2 ... 286 B2
Claremont Rd
Bromley BR1 ... 52 F5
Deal CT14 ... 215 B5
Folkestone CT20 ... 335 C5
Hextable BR8 ... 32 E1
Kingsdown CT14 ... 248 C6
Maidstone ME14 ... 162 B5
Royal Tunbridge Wells TN1 ... 286 B2
Claremont St
Herne Bay CT6 ... 76 C4
Newham E16 ... 2 A4
Claremont Terr CT13 ... 180 D7
Claremont Way 2 ME4 ... 63 F3
Clarence Ave
Bromley BR1 ... 52 E5
Margate CT9 ... 51 D2
Rochester ME1 ... 63 C4
Clarence Cres DA14 ... 31 B5
Clarence Ct
2 Grays RM17 ... 18 B8
Maidstone ME14 ... 162 E4
Pratt's Bottom BR6 ... 87 C2
Clarence Gdns ME12 ... 49 E3
Clarence Lodge TN1 ... 286 A3
Clarence Pl Deal CT14 ... 215 D7
Dover CT17 ... 310 D5
Gravesend DA12 ... 37 B7
Clarence Rd Bexley DA6 ... 13 E3
Biggin Hill TN16 ... 118 F1
Bromley,Mottingham SE9 ... 29 E6
Bromley,Widmore BR1 ... 52 E6
Capel-le-F CT18 ... 308 B2
Chatham ME4 ... 64 B2
Deal CT14 ... 215 D3
Grays RM17 ... 18 B8
Herne Bay CT6 ... 76 D5
Ramsgate CT11 ... 117 C6
Royal Tunbridge Wells TN1 ... 286 A3
Sidcup DA14 ... 31 B5
Clarence Row
Gravesend DA12 ... 37 B8
Royal Tunbridge Wells TN1 ... 286 A3
Sheerness ME12 ... 28 B2
Clarence St
Folkestone CT20 ... 335 D5
Herne Bay CT6 ... 76 E5
Clarendon Cl
Maidstone ME14 ... 163 A4
Orpington BR5 ... 54 A6
Sittingbourne ME10 ... 101 F1
Clarendon Ct TN13 ... 154 A2
Clarendon Dr ME2 ... 40 A1
Clarendon Gdns
Dartford DA2 ... 34 D8
7 Ramsgate CT11 ... 117 D6
Royal Tunbridge Wells TN2 ... 286 A1
Clarendon Gn BR5 ... 54 A5
Clarendon Gr BR5 ... 54 A5
Clarendon House Gram Sch CT11 ... 117 E6
Clarendon Mews
1 Broadstairs CT10 ... 84 A4
New Romney TN28 ... 373 C8
Sidcup DA5 ... 32 B7
Clarendon Path BR5 ... 54 A6
Clarendon Pl
Dover CT17 ... 310 C7
Joyden's Wood DA2 ... 32 E3
Maidstone ME14 ... 162 A4
Sevenoaks TN13 ... 154 A2
Clarendon Rd
Aylesham CT3 ... 210 F5
Broadstairs CT10 ... 84 A4
Dover CT17 ... 310 C7
Gravesend DA12 ... 19 C1
Margate CT9 ... 51 A2
Sevenoaks TN13 ... 154 A2
Clarendon St
Dover CT17 ... 310 C7
Herne Bay CT6 ... 76 C4
Clarendon Way
Royal Tunbridge Wells TN2 ... 286 A1
St Paul's Cray BR5,BR7 ... 53 F6
Clare Rd CT5 ... 74 E2
Claret Ho TN13 ... 154 B3
Clareville Rd BR5 ... 86 C8
Clare Way Bexley DA7 ... 13 E6
Sevenoaks TN13 ... 187 C8
Clarewood Dr ME19 ... 159 E8
Claridge Ct ME7 ... 97 F4
Claridge Mews CT21 ... 333 C2
Claridge TN1 ... 286 B6
Clarkbourne Dr RM17 ... 18 D8
Clark Cl DA8 ... 15 A6
Clarke Cres TN24 ... 268 F4
Clarke's Cl CT14 ... 214 F4
Clarkes Green Rd TN15 ... 123 B5
Clarklands TN29 ... 350 E3
Clark Mews ME20 ... 128 F1
Clark Rd TN28 ... 373 E4
Clarks La
Halstead TN14 ... 120 F7
Titsey CR6,RH8,TN16 ... 150 C4
Clark's Yd TN5 ... 339 A3
Claston Cl DA1 ... 14 E3
Claudius Gr TN23 ... 299 F5
Clavadal Rd TN12 ... 257 A7
Clavell Cl ME8 ... 98 E4
Claxfield Cotts ME9 ... 103 A2
Claxfield Rd ME9 ... 136 A8
Claybridge Rd SE12 ... 29 C4
Clay Cotts TN17 ... 318 E8
Claydown Mews SE18 ... 2 A1
Clayfarm Rd SE9 ... 30 C6
Claygate TN23 ... 299 F5
Claygate Cross TN15 ... 157 A3
Claygate ME17 ... 164 D2
Claygate La TN11 ... 189 F4
Claygate ME15 ... 162 D1
Claygate Rd TN12 ... 226 B2
Clayhill Cres SE9 ... 29 D4
Clayhill TN17 ... 318 D8
Clay Hill Mount TN17 ... 318 E8
Clay Hill Rd TN3 ... 316 D6
Claymill Ho 2 SE18 ... 2 C1
Clayton Cl 3 E6 ... 1 F7
Clayton Croft Rd DA2 ... 33 A6
Clayton's La TN3 ... 283 E2
Claytonville Terr DA17 ... 4 C4
Clay Wood Cl BR6 ... 53 E2
Claywood La DA2 ... 35 D5
Clayworth Cl DA15 ... 13 B1
Cleanthus Cl SE18 ... 12 B6
Cleanthus Rd SE18 ... 12 B6
Clearmount Dr TN27 ... 234 C8
Clearmount Pk TN27 ... 234 D8
Clearways Bsns Est TN15 ... 90 E3
Clearways Mobile Home Pk TN15 ... 90 D3
Clearway ME19 ... 126 A1
Cleave Ave BR6 ... 86 E4
Cleave Rd ME7 ... 64 E3
Cleaver La CT11 ... 117 E7
Cleavers Cl TN17 ... 321 A8
Cleavers TN17 ... 321 A8
Cleavesland ME18 ... 225 E5
Cleeve Ave TN2 ... 286 D2
Cleeve Ct ME19 ... 159 B3
Cleeve Park Gdns DA14 ... 31 B6
Cleeve Park Sch DA14 ... 31 C5
Clegg Ho SE3 ... 11 B3
Clematis Ave ME8 ... 98 B5
Clemens Pl ME18 ... 159 C2
Clement Cl
Canterbury CT1 ... 143 B1
Sittingbourne ME10 ... 101 E8
Clement Ct ME16 ... 161 D5
Clementine Cl CT6 ... 77 D4
Clements Ave E16 ... 1 A6
Clement's Rd CT12 ... 83 C2
Clement St BR8,DA4 ... 33 E2
Cleminson Ct DA14 ... 31 D2
Clenches Farm La TN13 ... 154 A1
Clenches Farm Rd TN13 ... 154 A1
Clendon Way SE18 ... 2 D2
Clerke Dr ME10 ... 102 A8
Clerks Field TN27 ... 262 D5
Clermont Cl ME7 ... 98 A4
Clevedon Ct TN25 ... 203 B2
Clevedon Ho BR1 ... 29 E1
Cleveland Cl CT16 ... 278 B3
Cleveland Ct CT9 ... 51 A3
Cleveland Ho
Maidstone ME16 ... 161 B2
Northfleet DA11 ... 18 D1
Cleveland Rd
Bexley DA16 ... 12 F5
Gillingham ME7 ... 64 D6
Cleveland TN2 ... 286 D4
Cleveley Lo CT11 ... 83 E2
Clevely Cl SE7 ... 1 D2
Cleven Lodge CT7 ... 113 D6
Cleve Rd DA14 ... 31 D5
Cleves Rd TN15 ... 122 E2
Cleves View 4 DA1 ... 15 D1
Cleves Way TN23 ... 299 E8
Clewer Ho 8 SE2 ... 3 D4
Clewer Lo CT5 ... 74 F2
Clewson Rise ME14 ... 162 B8
Cliff Ave CT6 ... 77 C5
Cliff Cl CT21 ... 333 D3
Cliff Cottage Chalet Pk ME12 ... 48 F6
Cliff Dr Herne Bay CT6 ... 76 C4
Warden ME12 ... 49 E4
Cliffe Ave CT9 ... 50 F1
Cliffe Ct ME3 ... 22 B5
Cliffe Ho
Folkestone CT20 ... 335 A3
St Margaret's at Cliffe CT15 ... 279 F6
Cliffe Pools Nature Reserve* ME3 ... 5 E1
Cliffe Rd Deal CT14 ... 248 D6
Rochester ME2 ... 40 A1
Cliffestone Ct CT20 ... 335 B5
Cliffe Woods Prim Sch ME3 ... 40 C8
Cliff Field CT8 ... 81 C8
Cliff Gdns ME12 ... 47 E7
Cliff Hill ME17 ... 195 D4
Cliff Hill Rd ME17 ... 195 C4
Clifford Ave BR7 ... 29 F2
Clifford Gdns CT14 ... 215 B2
Clifford Ho 6 ME14 ... 162 B4
Clifford Rd CT5 ... 108 F8
Cliff Prom CT10 ... 84 C7
Cliff Rd Birchington CT7 ... 80 F8
Broadstairs CT10 ... 84 B7
Dover CT15,CT16 ... 279 C1
Folkestone CT20 ... 335 A3
Hythe CT21 ... 333 E3
Whitstable CT5 ... 74 F3
Cliff Reach DA9 ... 16 F1
Cliff Sea Gr CT6 ... 76 C4
Cliffs End Gr CT12 ... 116 D5
Cliffs End Rd CT12 ... 116 E5
Cliffside Dr CT10 ... 84 A1
Cliff St CT11 ... 117 E6
Cliff Terr CT9 ... 50 J3
Clifftown Gdns CT6 ... 76 B4
Cliff View Gdns
Leysdown-on-S ME12 ... 49 D1
Warden ME12 ... 49 E4
Cliff View Rd CT12 ... 116 D6
Clifton Cl
Maidstone ME14 ... 162 B5
8 Orpington BR6 ... 86 C5
Rochester ME2 ... 62 F7
Clifton Cotts TN2 ... 286 D8
Clifton Cres CT20 ... 335 B3
Clifton Gdns
Canterbury CT2 ... 142 D2
Folkestone CT20 ... 335 C4
Margate CT9 ... 50 J3
Whitstable CT5 ... 108 D8
Clifton Gr DA11 ... 37 B8
Clifton Lawn CT11 ... 117 D5
Clifton Mans 7 CT20 ... 335 C4
Clifton Marine Par DA11 ... 18 F1
Clifton Pl Margate CT9 ... 51 A3
Royal Tunbridge Wells TN1 ... 286 B2
Clifton Rd Bexley DA16 ... 13 C4
Folkestone CT20 ... 335 C4
Gillingham ME7 ... 64 C7
Gravesend DA11 ... 19 A1
Margate CT9 ... 51 A2
Ramsgate CT11 ... 117 B8
Royal Tunbridge Wells TN2 ... 286 C7
Sidcup DA14 ... 30 E4
Whitstable CT5 ... 74 D1
Clifton St CT9 ... 50 J3
Cliftonville Ave
Margate CT9 ... 51 A2
Ramsgate CT12 ... 83 B1
Cliftonville Ct
Lewisham SE12 ... 29 A7
Margate,Cliftonville CT9 ... 51 B3
Margate CT9 ... 51 A3
Cliftonville Mews CT9 ... 51 A3
Cliftonville Prim Sch CT9 ... 51 C2
Clim Down CT14 ... 248 D6
Clinch Ct 15 E16 ... 1 A8
Clinch St ME3 ... 24 A4
Clinton Ave Bexley DA16 ... 13 A3
Rochester ME2 ... 62 E8
Clinton Bsns Ctr TN12 ... 260 E5
Clinton Cl ME17 ... 194 B3
Clinton La TN8 ... 218 E3
Clints La CT4 ... 243 D4
Clipper Bvd DA9 ... 16 E3
Clipper Bvd W DA2 ... 16 D4
Clipper Cl ME2 ... 63 E7
Clipper Cres DA12 ... 37 F4
Clipper Ct ME2 ... 63 E7
Clive Ave DA1 ... 14 F1
Clive Ct CT9 ... 51 B2
Cliveden Cl ME16 ... 161 D7
Clive Dennis Ct TN24 ... 268 E1
Clive Ho ME20 ... 160 F8
Clive Rd
Cliffs End CT12 ... 116 D6
Erith DA17 ... 4 A2
Gravesend DA11 ... 19 B1
Clive Rd *continued*
Margate CT9 ... 83 A5
Rochester ME1 ... 63 C3
Sittingbourne ME10 ... 101 B5
Clock Ho The DA15 ... 31 A7
Clockhouse TN23 ... 267 F1
Clock House La TN13 ... 154 A4
Clockhouse Pk TN25 ... 203 C2
Clockhouse TN2 ... 286 F6
Clock Tower Mews
Snodland ME6 ... 95 A1
Woolwich SE28 ... 3 B6
Clocktower Par CT2 ... 142 A6
Cloisterham Rd ME1 ... 96 D7
Cloisters Ave BR2 ... 52 F4
Cloisters Ct DA7 ... 14 B4
Cloisters The
18 Canterbury CT1 ... 142 F1
1 Dartford DA1 ... 15 E1
Lenham ME17 ... 199 C5
Ramsgate CT11 ... 117 D5
8 Sittingbourne ME10 ... 101 E4
Whitstable CT5 ... 74 F2
Cloke Mews TN15 ... 156 F7
Cloonmore Ave BR6 ... 86 F6
Clopton Ct ME8 ... 98 D8
Close The
Addington ME19 ... 126 C2
Ashford TN23 ... 299 F7
Birling ME19 ... 127 B5
Borough Green TN15 ... 157 A8
Bough Beech TN8 ... 219 A2
Bridge CT4 ... 175 F1
Canterbury CT1 ... 174 D6
Canterbury,Hales Place CT2 ... 142 F4
Canterbury,St Dunstan's CT2 ... 142 C3
Cudham TN16 ... 119 B3
Dartford DA2 ... 33 D5
Faversham ME13 ... 138 C6
Folkestone CT19 ... 335 E8
Groombridge TN3 ... 312 C6
Hythe CT21 ... 333 B4
Ightham TN15 ... 156 D6
Lydden CT15 ... 276 F8
New Barn DA3 ... 59 B7
Orpington BR5 ... 53 E3
Rochester ME1 ... 63 C4
Royal Tunbridge Wells TN2 ... 286 C8
Sevenoaks TN13 ... 153 E3
Sidcup DA14 ... 31 B3
1 Sidcup,Old Bexley DA5 ... 32 A8
Wye TN25 ... 237 E2
Cloth Hall Gdns TN27 ... 295 A2
Clothier Ho SE7 ... 1 E1
Clothworkers Rd SE18 ... 12 D7
Cloudberry Cl ME16 ... 161 D6
Cloudesley Cl ME1 ... 63 B1
Cloudesley Rd
Bexley DA7 ... 13 F6
Erith DA8 ... 14 F6
Clouston Cl CT18 ... 307 B5
Clovelly Dr ME12 ... 47 B8
Clovelly TN28 ... 373 E6
Clovelly Rd Bexley DA7 ... 13 E8
Whitstable CT5 ... 108 D7
Clovelly Way BR6 ... 53 F3
Clover Bank View ME5 ... 97 B6
Clover Ct
12 Grays RM17 ... 18 D8
Sittingbourne ME10 ... 102 B5
Cloverdale Gdns DA15 ... 12 F1
Clover Lay ME8 ... 66 B2
Cloverlay Ind Pk ME8 ... 66 C1
Clover Rd ME3 ... 41 E3
Clover Rise CT5 ... 75 B1
Clover St 3 ME4 ... 63 F4
Clovers The DA11 ... 36 E4
Clover Terr 4 ME15 ... 195 D8
Clover Way TN12 ... 257 A5
Clover Wlk 13 TN8 ... 217 D3
Clowes Ct CT2 ... 142 C4
Clubb's La TN29 ... 370 D7
Club Cotts TN11 ... 221 D8
Club Gardens Rd BR2 ... 52 A2
Cluny Rd ME13 ... 138 F7
Clyde Rd TN10 ... 222 C6
Clydesdale Ho DA18 ... 3 E4
Clyde St
1 Canterbury CT1 ... 143 A1
Sheerness ME12 ... 28 D2
Clydon Cl DA8 ... 14 E8
Clynton Way TN23 ... 300 A7
C M Booth Collection of Historic Vehicles (Mus)* TN17 ... 343 E4
Coach Dr TN26 ... 267 A7
Coach Dr The DA13 ... 125 E7
Coach & Horses Pas 18 TN2 ... 286 A2
Coach House Mews 8 BR1 ... 52 A6
Coach House Mews The CT15 ... 245 D5
Coach Rd
Charing Heath TN27 ... 233 A6
Densole CT18 ... 306 F8
Egerton ME17,TN27 ... 232 E6
Ightham TN15 ... 156 B2
Rusthall TN4 ... 285 C3
Coach Yd The ME16 ... 161 B3
Coal Ct RM17 ... 18 A8
Coalhouse Fort* RM18 ... 20 E6
Coalpit La ME9 ... 167 A6
Coast Dr
Greatstone-on-Sea TN28 ... 373 E3
Lydd-on-S TN29 ... 380 D8
St Mary's Bay TN29 ... 365 F2

Coa–Cor 395

Coastguard Alley CT5 .... 74 C1
Coastguard Cotts
Birchington CT7 .... 80 D8
Conyer ME9 .... 103 E6
Dover CT16 .... 310 G8
Grain ME3 .... 27 B5
Herne Bay CT6 .... 75 F4
Hythe CT21 .... 333 B1
Kingsdown CT14 .... 248 D4
Leysdown-on-S ME12 .... 73 E4
Lydd-on-S TN29 .... 380 D5
Minster (Sheppey) ME12 .. 48 C5
23 Ramsgate,East Cliff CT11 .... 117 F7
Ramsgate,Pegwell CT11 .. 117 A5
Sandwich CT13 .... 182 A8
Coastguard Cotts The ME12 .... 28 H1
Coastguard Hos ME12 .... 49 C5
Coast Rd TN28 .... 373 F7
Coates Hill Rd BR1 .... 53 A7
Coats Ave ME12 .... 46 A8
Cobay Cl CT21 .... 333 D2
Cobb Cl ME2 .... 62 D8
Cobb Ct CT9 .... 50 I3
Cobbets Way TN8 .... 249 C8
Cobbett Cl ME19 .... 159 F8
Cobbett Rd SE9 .... 11 E4
Cobbett's Ride TN2 .... 285 F1
Cobblers Bridge Rd CT6 .... 76 D3
Cobblestones ME7 .... 97 F5
Cobbs Cl
Paddock Wood TN12 .... 256 F6
Wateringbury ME18 .... 192 E7
Cobbs Hill CT4 .... 172 C2
Cobbs Mews 3 CT20 .... 335 C4
Cobbs Pl CT9 .... 50 I3
Cobbs Wood Ind Est TN23 .... 267 F2
Cobb Wlk ME13 .... 138 B8
Cobden Ct Bromley BR2 .. 52 C5
9 Woolwich SE28 .... 3 C5
Cobden Pl 18 CT1 .... 143 A1
Cobden Rd
4 Chatham ME4 .... 64 B2
Hythe CT21 .... 333 B1
Orpington BR6 .... 86 D6
Sevenoaks TN13 .... 154 C4
Cobdown Cl ME20 .... 128 C2
Cobdown Gr ME8 .... 66 A2
Cob Dr DA12 .... 38 E3
Cobfield ME17 .... 196 A1
Cobham Ave ME10 .... 101 E1
Cobhambury Rd DA12 .... 61 B4
Cobham Chase ME13 .... 138 B8
Cobham Cl Bromley BR2 .. 52 E2
Canterbury CT1 .... 175 C6
Maidstone ME16 .... 161 E4
Rochester ME2 .... 62 E7
2 Sidcup DA15 .... 13 B1
Swanscombe DA9 .... 17 B1
Cobham Dr ME18 .... 159 C3
Cobham Hall Sch DA12 .... 61 C6
Cobham Ho 4 DA8 .... 14 F7
Cobham Pl DA6 .... 13 D2
Cobham Prim Sch DA12 .... 61 A5
Cobham Rise ME7 .... 64 F5
Cobhams TN3 .... 285 A8
Cobham St DA11 .... 37 B8
Cobham Terr DA9 .... 17 B1
Cobland Rd SE12 .... 29 C4
Cobs Cl TN15 .... 156 C6
Cobsden Cl TN29 .... 366 A4
Cobsdene DA12 .... 37 D2
Cobsden Rd TN29 .... 366 A4
Cobtree Cl ME5 .... 97 C8
Cobtree Rd ME17 .... 194 C3
Cobtree Wharf ME20 .... 129 C2
Cobweb Cnr CT2 .... 142 B4
Cockerhurst Rd TN14 .... 88 E2
Cockering Rd
Canterbury CT1,CT4 .... 174 B4
Chartham CT4 .... 173 E2
Cock La Elham CT4 .... 273 F4
Hamstreet TN26 .... 349 A7
Cockmannings La BR5 .... 54 E1
Cockmannings Rd BR5 .. 54 D2
Cockmount La TN5 .... 336 F5
Cockpit The TN12 .... 259 C5
Cockreed La TN28 .... 373 B7
Cocksett Ave BR6 .... 86 E4
Cocksure La DA14 .... 32 A4
Codrington Cres DA12 .. 37 D3
Codrington Gdns DA12 .. 37 D3
Codrington Rd CT11 .... 117 D7
Cogans Terr CT1 .... 174 E6
Cogate Rd TN12 .... 256 E6
Coggan Ho 7 CT1 .... 174 F7
Cokers Yd TN4 .... 254 A1
Colburn Rd CT10 .... 84 A2
Colchester Cl ME5 .... 97 A7
Cold Arbor Rd TN13 .... 153 D3
Cold Blow Cres DA5 .... 32 D7
Coldblow CT14 .... 215 A1
Coldblow La
Hucking ME14 .... 132 A2
Woodchurch TN26 .... 326 D4
Coldbridge La TN27 .... 232 B5
Cold Harbour CT1 .... 143 A2
Coldharbour Crest SE9 .. 30 A5
Coldharbour La
Aylesford ME20 .... 129 A1
Bridge CT4,CT3 .... 209 D7
Hucking ME14,ME9 .... 132 B1
Cold Harbour La ME9 .. 100 F6
Coldharbour La
Old Romney TN29 .... 371 C5
Peasmarsh TN31 .... 367 E3
Rainham RM13 .... 4 F6
Shipbourne TN11 .... 189 A2
Sittingbourne ME10 .... 68 F1
Coldharbour La *continued*
Tonbridge TN11 .... 221 E7
Wye TN25 .... 238 A2
Coldharbour Rd
Ashurst TN8,TN11 .... 283 E8
Gravesend DA11 .... 37 A4
Iden Green TN17 .... 342 B4
Northfleet DA11 .... 36 F5
Cold Harbour Rd ME13 .... 201 A7
Coldharbour Sports Ctr SE9 .... 30 A6
Coldred Hill CT15 .... 244 F1
Coldred Rd
Coldred CT15 .... 245 B5
Maidstone ME15 .... 195 F4
Shepherdswell CT15 .... 244 E3
Coldrum La ME19 .... 126 C6
Coldshott RH8 .... 183 A2
Coldswood Rd CT12 .... 82 F2
Colebrooke Ct DA14 .... 31 B4
Colebrook Ind Est TN2 .... 254 E1
Colebrook Rd TN4 .... 286 C8
Colebrook St 1 DA8 .... 14 F8
Cole Cl SE28 .... 3 B5
Colegate Dr ME14 .... 163 C4
Colegates Cl ME13 .... 105 B2
Colegates Ct ME13 .... 105 B2
Colegates Rd ME13 .... 105 A2
Coleman Cres CT12 .... 83 C1
Coleman Dr ME10 .... 68 F1
Coleman Rd DA17 .... 4 A2
Colemans Cl TN29 .... 376 D7
Colemans Heath SE9 .... 30 B5
Coleman's Stairs Rd CT7 .... 81 A8
Coleman's Yd 3 CT11 .... 117 E6
Colepits Wood Rd SE9 .. 12 D2
Coleraine Rd 1 SE3 .... 11 A8
Cole Rd ME13 .... 138 E7
Coleridge Cl 4 ME20 .... 127 F4
Coleridge Gdns CT3 .... 210 F6
Coleridge Rd
Dartford DA1 .... 16 B3
Tilbury RM18 .... 19 C5
Coleridge Way BR6 .... 54 A3
Coles Ct TN2 .... 286 C3
Colesdane ME17 .... 198 E8
Coleshall Cl ME15 .... 195 F6
Coleshall Cotts ME9 .... 68 D3
Coles La TN16 .... 152 C4
Cole Terr ME17 .... 199 C4
Colets Orch TN14 .... 122 B3
Colette Cl CT10 .... 51 G2
Coleville Cres TN28 .... 377 E7
Colewood Dr ME2 .... 62 B8
Colewood Rd CT5 .... 75 E3
Colfe's Prep Sch SE12 .... 11 B1
Colfe Way ME10 .... 102 A8
Colin Blythe Rd TN10 .. 222 F5
Colin Chapman Way DA3 .... 90 E6
Colin Cl DA2 .... 16 B1
Colin's Way CT21 .... 334 A3
Collard Cl CT6 .... 77 A4
Collard Ho CT1 .... 175 C8
Collard Rd TN24 .... 301 A8
Collards Cl CT12 .... 114 D7
Collards La CT4 .... 273 E3
College Ave
Gillingham ME7 .... 64 B4
Maidstone ME15 .... 161 F3
Tonbridge TN9 .... 254 A7
College Cotts ME16 .... 161 F3
College Ct
Ashford TN23 .... 268 C2
Canterbury CT1 .... 143 B1
6 Maidstone ME15 .... 162 A3
College Dr TN2 .... 286 D4
College Gn 10 BR1 .... 52 A8
College Pl DA9 .... 17 C3
College Rd Bromley BR1 .. 29 A1
Canterbury CT1 .... 143 B1
Chatham ME4 .... 64 A7
Deal CT14 .... 215 D8
Hextable BR8 .... 32 F1
Maidstone ME15 .... 161 F2
Margate CT9 .... 51 A1
New Hythe ME20 .... 128 B3
Northfleet DA11 .... 18 B2
Ramsgate CT11 .... 83 E1
Sittingbourne ME10 .... 101 D3
College Row CT17 .... 310 B7
College Sq 2 CT9 .... 50 J2
College View SE9 .... 29 D7
College Way CT3 .... 178 A7
College Wlk
4 Maidstone ME15 .... 162 A3
3 Margate CT9 .... 50 J2
College Yd ME1 .... 63 C6
Coller Cres DA2 .... 34 E3
Collet Rd TN15 .... 122 E2
Collett Cl TN25 .... 271 D8
Collet Wlk ME8 .... 98 D4
Collie Dr TN23 .... 299 E5
Collier Cl E6 .... 2 B6
Colliers' Green CE Prim Sch TN17 .... 291 F2
Colliers Shaw BR2 .... 85 D5
Collindale Ave
Erith DA8 .... 14 B8
Sidcup DA15 .... 31 A7
Collingbourne TN23 .... 299 E6
Collinge Cl ME19 .... 128 A1
Collings Wlk ME8 .... 98 D4
Collington Cl DA11 .... 36 E8
Collington Ho 3 SE7 .... 11 B8
Collington Terr ME15 .. 195 E4
Collingwood Cl
Broadstairs CT10 .... 83 E4
Westgate-on-S CT8 .... 81 D7
Collingwood Ct
Folkestone CT20 .... 334 E5
7 Ramsgate CT11 .... 117 D7
Collingwood Ho DA9 .... 17 D2
Collingwood Ind Ctr ME17 .... 196 E2
Collingwood Rd
Kit's Coty ME20 .... 129 C7
St Margaret's at Cliffe CT15 .... 279 F8
Whitstable CT5 .... 74 C1
Collingwood Rise CT20 .... 334 E5
Collingwood Wlk ME10 .... 101 B5
Collins Rd
Herne Bay CT6 .... 76 C2
New Romney TN28 .... 373 C5
Collison Pl TN30 .... 345 D7
Collis St ME2 .... 63 A8
Colman Ho 4 ME14 .... 162 A4
Colman Rd E16 .... 1 C8
Colne Rd TN10 .... 222 B5
Colney Rd DA1 .... 15 F1
Colombo Sq CT12 .... 83 A1
Colonade The 14 TN18 .... 341 A2
Colonel's La ME13 .... 140 A3
Colonel Stephens Way TN30 .... 324 B2
Colonel's Way TN4 .... 254 A2
Colorado Cl CT16 .... 278 B3
Colson Dr ME9 .... 68 E3
Coltness Cres SE2 .... 3 B1
Colton Cres CT16 .... 278 B4
Coltsfoot Ct RM17 .... 18 D8
Coltsfoot Dr ME14 .... 162 F4
Coltsfoot Ho E16 .... 1 B8
Coltsfoot La RH8 .... 183 A1
Colts Hill Pl TN12 .... 256 B5
Coltstead DA3 .... 91 E7
Columbia Ave CT5 .... 108 B7
Columbia Wharf Rd RM17 .... 18 A8
Columbine Ave E6 .... 1 E8
Columbine Cl
Rochester ME2 .... 62 E7
West Malling ME19 .... 127 F1
Whitstable CT5 .... 108 C6
Columbine Rd
East Malling ME19 .... 159 F8
Rochester ME2 .... 62 E7
Columbus Ave CT12 .... 81 D1
Columbus Sq DA8 .... 14 F8
Colveiw Ct SE9 .... 29 D7
Colyer Cl SE9 .... 30 B6
Colyer Ho SE2 .... 3 D1
Colyer Rd DA11 .... 36 D6
Colyers Cl DA8 .... 14 D6
Colyers La DA8 .... 14 D6
Colyers Prim Sch DA8 .... 14 D6
Colyers Wlk DA8 .... 14 E6
Colyton Cl DA16 .... 13 D6
Combe Bank Cotts TN14 .... 152 D5
Combe Bank Dr TN14 .. 152 E4
Combe Bank Farm TN14 .... 152 D6
Combe Bank Sch TN14 .... 152 E4
Combedale Rd SE10 .... 1 A1
Combeside SE18 .... 12 F7
Combwell Cres SE2 .... 3 A3
Com Coll Whitstable The CT5 .... 108 F8
Comforts Farm Ave RH8 .... 183 A3
Comfrey Ct RM17 .... 18 D8
Command Rd ME14 .... 161 F8
Commerce Way TN8 .... 217 C3
Commercial Pl DA12 .... 19 C1
Commercial Rd
Paddock Wood TN12 .... 256 F6
Rochester ME2 .... 63 B7
Royal Tunbridge Wells TN1 .... 286 B5
Tonbridge TN9 .... 254 C8
Commissioners Ct ME4 .. 63 F6
Commissioner's Rd ME2 .... 63 C8
Commodore Ct CT21 .... 333 C1
Commodore Rd ME14 .. 162 C5
Common La Cliffe ME3 .. 22 C6
Crabble CT17 .... 277 E3
Dartford DA2 .... 33 B5
Common Rd
Burham ME5 .... 96 B1
Cliffe Woods ME3 .... 40 B5
Hadlow TN11 .... 190 E2
Ightham TN15 .... 156 B4
Sissinghurst TN17 .... 321 A8
Commonside BR2 .... 85 C6
Common The ME1 .... 63 C6
Common View TN4 .... 285 C4
Common Wall ME3 .... 22 D6
Common Way TN26 .... 267 A7
Commonwealth Cl ME10 .... 102 B3
Commonwealth Ho 5 RM18 .... 19 A5
Commonwealth Way SE2 .... 3 C1
Commority Rd DA13 .... 126 B8
Compass Cl ME1 .... 63 C1
Compass Ct DA11 .... 18 E1
Compass Ctr ME4 .... 64 B8
Compasses Rd TN11 .... 220 B2
Compasses The TN11 .... 220 B2
Comp La TN15 .... 157 E6
Compton Cl ME5 .... 97 D2
Compton Pl DA8 .... 14 F8
Concord Ave ME5 .... 96 E5
Concord Cl
Paddock Wood TN12 .... 256 E7
Royal Tunbridge Wells TN2 .... 286 C4
Concorde Bsns Pk TN16 .... 118 D4
Concorde Dr E6 .... 1 F8
Concrete Cotts ME3 .... 21 E4
Condor Cl ME12 .... 49 E3
Condover Cres SE18 .... 12 B7
Condovers Cotts RM18 .. 19 F8
Conduit Ho The* CT1 .... 143 B1
Conduit Rd SE18 .... 2 B1
Conduit St ME13 .... 138 D8
Coneyburrow Rd TN2 .. 286 E5
Coney Mews ME4 .... 64 A1
Conference Rd SE2 .... 3 C2
Conference Wlk CT1 .... 175 C8
Conghurst La TN18 .... 355 B6
Congleton Gr SE18 .... 2 C1
Congo Rd SE18 .... 2 D1
Congress Rd SE2 .... 3 C2
Congreve Rd SE9 .... 11 F4
Congreve Wlk 6 E16 .... 1 D8
Conifer Ave DA3 .... 58 E3
Conifer Cl BR6 .... 86 D6
Conifer Ct CT8 .... 50 D1
Conifer Dr
Chatham ME5 .... 97 D1
Culverstone Green DA13 .. 92 F2
Conifers The
Deal CT14 .... 215 A2
Shepherdswell CT15 .... 244 F2
Conifer Way BR8 .... 55 C8
Conisborough Ct 13 DA2 .... 16 B1
Coniscliffe Cl BR7 .... 53 A8
Coniston Ave
Bexley DA16 .... 12 E4
Purfleet RM19 .... 16 C8
Ramsgate CT11 .... 117 A7
Royal Tunbridge Wells TN4 .... 285 E5
Coniston Cl Bexley DA7 .... 14 C6
Dartford DA1 .... 33 B7
Erith DA8 .... 14 E7
Gillingham ME7 .... 65 A6
Coniston Dr CT3 .... 210 F6
Coniston Ho ME15 .... 195 E7
Coniston Rd Bexley DA7 .. 14 C6
Folkestone CT19 .... 335 B7
Conker Cl TN23 .... 300 C3
Connaught Barracks CT16 .... 278 E1
Connaught Bridge E16 .... 1 D6
Connaught Cl ME15 .... 195 F4
Connaught Gdns 9 CT9 .... 50 J1
Connaught Mews
2 Chatham ME4 .... 64 C2
Woolwich SE18 .... 2 A1
Connaught Rd
Chatham ME4 .... 64 C2
Dover CT16 .... 278 D1
Folkestone CT20 .... 335 D5
Gillingham ME7 .... 64 D5
Margate CT9 .... 50 J1
Newham,Silvertown E16 .... 1 D5
Sittingbourne ME10 .... 101 E3
Woolwich SE18 .... 2 B1
Connaught Way TN4 .... 285 F5
Conquest Ind Est ME2 .... 63 A5
Conrad Ave CT1 .... 143 C3
Conrad Cl ME8 .... 98 D4
Consort Cl ME14 .... 162 B5
Constable Ave E16 .... 1 B5
Constable Rd
Birchington CT7 .... 81 A8
Northfleet DA11 .... 36 E5
Tonbridge TN10 .... 222 E5
Constable's Rd CT16 .... 310 E8
Constance St E16 .... 1 E5
Constancia Ct CT20 .... 335 C5
Constantine Rd TN23 .... 299 F5
Constitutional Hill Rd TN4 .... 253 F1
Constitution Cres DA12 .. 37 B7
Constitution Hill
8 Chatham ME5 .... 64 B3
Gravesend DA12 .... 37 C7
Snodland ME6 .... 128 A8
Constitution Rd ME5 .... 64 B2
Constitution Rise SE18 .. 12 A6
Consul Cl CT6 .... 76 B4
Consul Gdns BR8 .... 33 A1
Contessa Cl BR6 .... 86 E5
Continental App CT9 .... 82 F6
Convalescent La TN17 .. 292 F2
Convent Cl CT15 .... 280 B6
Conventina Ho 3 CT11 .... 117 D7
Convent Rd CT10 .... 51 G1
Convent Wlk CT11 .... 117 B5
Conway Cl
Birchington CT7 .... 80 E7
Hythe CT21 .... 333 B4
Rochester ME2 .... 39 E1
Conway Ct BR5 .... 54 C5
Conway Gdns RM17 .... 18 B7
Conway Hall 10 ME7 .... 64 A6
Conway Mews ME7 .... 64 A6
Conway Prim Sch SE18 .... 2 E2
Conway Rd
Maidstone ME16 .... 161 C6
Woolwich SE18 .... 2 E2
Conyerd Rd TN15 .... 156 F6
Conyer Rd ME9 .... 103 F4
Conyers Wlk ME8 .... 98 D4
Conyngham Cl CT12 .... 83 B2
Conyngham La CT4 .... 176 A2
Conyngham Rd
Herne Bay CT6 .... 77 D5
Conyngham Rd *continued*
Minster (Thanet) CT12 .... 115 C5
Cooden Cl Bromley BR1 .... 29 B1
Gillingham ME8 .... 66 A2
Cook Cl ME5 .... 97 C6
Cookham Dene Cl BR7 .. 53 D8
Cookham Hill ME1 .... 63 A2
Cookham Rd DA14,BR8 .. 55 A8
Cookham Wood Rd ME1 .... 96 B8
Cookhill Rd SE2 .... 3 B3
Cooks La ME10 .... 101 F6
Cook's Lea CT13 .... 180 B2
Cookson Gr DA8 .... 14 B7
Cook Sq DA8 .... 14 F7
Cooks Wharf ME1 .... 63 E4
Coolfin Rd E16 .... 1 B7
Cooling Castle* ME3 .... 22 E4
Cooling Cl ME14 .... 162 C6
Cooling Comm ME3 .... 40 D8
Coolinge La CT20 .... 334 F4
Coolinge Rd CT20 .... 335 D5
Cooling Rd Cliffe ME3 .... 22 C4
High Halstow ME23 .... 23 C4
Rochester ME2 .... 40 B2
Cooling St ME3 .... 22 D1
Coombe Ave TN14 .... 154 B7
Coombe Cl
Chatham ME5 .... 97 B3
Dover CT17 .... 278 A1
Snodland ME6 .... 128 A7
Coombe Ct Dover CT17 .. 278 A1
Sevenoaks TN14 .... 154 B7
Coombe Dr ME10 .... 102 C4
Coombe Farm La ME3 .... 24 E6
Coombe La CT13,CT3 .... 179 E8
Coombe Lands TN30 .... 359 D4
Coombe La TN30 .... 345 A7
Coombe Lea BR1 .... 52 E6
Coombe Lodge SE7 .... 11 C8
Coombe Rd
Crabble CT17 .... 277 F1
Dover CT15,CT17 .... 309 E8
Folkestone CT19 .... 334 F6
Gravesend DA12 .... 37 C6
Hoo St Werburgh ME3 .... 41 E5
Maidstone ME15 .... 161 F2
Otford TN14 .... 122 C4
Coombe Valley Rd CT17 .... 278 A1
Coombe Way CT18 .... 307 C4
Coombe Wlk CT5 .... 108 A2
Coombe Wood La CT18 .... 307 C4
Coombfield Dr DA2 .... 34 D4
Comb Field TN8 .... 249 C8
Cooper Cl DA9 .... 16 F2
Cooper Ct SE18 .... 12 B8
Cooper Rd Chatham ME5 .. 97 B3
Snodland ME6 .... 127 F6
Coopers Cl DA4 .... 57 D8
Coopers Cotts DA2 .... 34 A4
Coopers Dr DA2 .... 32 E6
Cooper Shaw Rd RM18 .. 19 E7
Cooper's Hill CT6 .... 76 F5
Cooper's La TN25 .... 302 F2
Coopers La
Canterbury CT1 .... 174 E7
Lewisham SE12 .... 29 B6
Coopers' Lane Prim Sch SE12 .... 29 B6
Coopers La TN11,TN3 .... 284 C7
Cooper's Rd DA11 .... 36 F7
Coopers Tech Coll BR7 .... 53 C8
Cooper Street Dro CT3 .... 148 B4
Coote Rd DA7 .... 13 F6
Cooting La CT3 .... 210 D8
Cooting Rd CT3 .... 210 E4
Copenhagen Rd ME7 .... 64 C4
Copinger Cl CT2 .... 143 A4
Copland Ave ME12 .... 47 C6
Copley Dene BR1 .... 52 D8
Coppards La TN31 .... 357 D1
Copper Beech Cl
Gravesend DA12 .... 37 D8
7 Orpington BR5 .... 54 C4
Copper Beech View TN9 .... 254 A8
Copperfield Cl
Ashford TN24 .... 268 C6
Chalk DA12 .... 38 A7
Kingswood ME17 .... 197 D2
Copperfield Cres ME3 .... 39 C2
Copperfield Ct
Broadstairs CT10 .... 84 B5
Crayford DA1 .... 14 E2
Copperfield Dr ME17 .... 196 E4
Copperfield ME12 .... 48 F5
Copperfield Ho 6 ME4 .... 63 F4
Copperfield Rd
Erith SE28 .... 3 C7
Rochester ME1 .... 63 C2
Copperfields Cl TN15 .... 122 F2
Copperfields
2 Dartford DA1 .... 15 E1
Kemsing TN15 .... 122 F2
Lydd TN29 .... 376 B6
Copperfields Orch TN15 .... 122 F2
Copperfields The ME1 .... 63 B4
Copperfields Wlk TN15 .... 122 F2
Copperfield Way BR7 .... 30 C2
Coppergate CT2 .... 142 F2
Coppergate Cl BR1 .... 52 B8
Coppergate ME7 .... 97 F5
Copperhouse La ME7 .... 65 B6
Copperhouse Rd ME2 .... 62 C7
Copperhurst Wlk CT9 .... 51 F2
Copper La TN12 .... 259 E5
Copperpenny Dr ME7 .... 98 B3
Coppers Ct TN4 .... 286 A8
Coppers La TN12 .... 256 E1
Copper Tree Ct ME15 .... 195 A5
Copper Tree Wlk ME5 .... 97 C1
Copperwood TN24 .... 268 C4
Coppice Ct ME7 .... 98 B4
Coppice Rd ME5 .... 97 C2
Coppice The
Aylesford ME20 .... 128 E1
Bitchet Green TN15 .... 155 D1
Hythe CT21 .... 333 B4
Joyden's Wood DA5 .... 32 D5
Pembury TN2 .... 287 D7
Sturry CT2 .... 143 F6
Vigo Village DA13 .... 126 B8
Coppice View ME14 .... 162 E6
Copping's Rd TN11 .... 220 C4
Coppins La ME9 .... 101 B2
Coppin St CT14 .... 215 D6
Coppock Cl CT12 .... 83 B1
Copse Bank TN15 .... 154 F7
Copse Cl Greenwich SE7 .... 11 B8
Rochester ME1 .... 63 E1
Copsehill ME19 .... 127 E2
Copse Rd TN11 .... 221 E4
Copse Side DA3 .... 58 E6
Copse The
Ashford TN23 .... 267 D3
Hoo St Werburgh ME3 .... 41 E3
Copsewood Cl DA15 .... 12 E1
Copsewood Way ME15 .... 163 A3
Cop Street Rd CT3 .... 147 D3
Copt Cl CT2 .... 143 F7
Coptefield Dr DA17 .... 3 E3
Copthall Ave TN18 .... 341 A1
Copthall Gdns 13 CT20 .... 335 D5
Copt Hall TN18 .... 357 D3
Copt Hall Rd
Ightham TN15 .... 156 A4
Sole Street DA13 .... 60 B5
Copthorne Ave BR2 .... 85 F8
Coralline Wlk 4 SE2 .... 3 C4
Corben Cl ME16 .... 161 B6
Corbridge Ho SE2 .... 3 C3
Corbylands Rd DA15 .... 30 E7
Cordelia Cres ME1 .... 62 F2
Cordingham Rd CT5 .... 108 A6
Cordova Ct CT20 .... 335 B4
Corelli Rd SE18,SE3 .... 11 E6
Corhaven Ho 3 DA8 .... 14 E7
Corinthian Ct ME3 .... 27 B5
Corinthian Manorway DA8 .... 4 D2
Corinthian Rd DA8 .... 4 D2
Cork Ho BR5 .... 54 B6
Cork La TN12 .... 292 D8
Cork St ME20 .... 128 F6
Corkwell St ME4 .... 63 E3
Cormorant Cl ME2 .... 62 C7
Cormorant Way CT6 .... 77 F4
Cornbrook Rd CT21 .... 353 D8
Cornel Ho 4 DA15 .... 31 A5
Cornelia Pl DA8 .... 14 E8
Cornelis Dr CT12 .... 115 B5
Cornell Cl DA14 .... 31 E2
Corner Cotts TN26 .... 348 A6
Corner Farm Rd TN12 .. 260 E4
Corner Field TN23 .... 300 B5
Corner Gn SE3 .... 11 A5
Cornes Cl TN24 .... 269 A1
Cornfield Way TN10 .... 222 D6
Cornflower Cl ME14 .... 162 E4
Cornford Cl Hayes BR2 .... 52 A4
Pembury TN2 .... 287 B6
Cornford La TN2 .... 287 B5
Cornford Pk TN2 .... 287 C6
Cornford Rd CT7 .... 81 A7
Cornforth Cl TN12 .... 260 F4
Cornhill 15 CT11 .... 117 E6
Corniche The CT20 .... 334 C3
Corn Mill Dr BR6 .... 54 A2
Cornwall Ave
Bexley DA16 .... 12 F4
Ramsgate CT11 .... 117 F8
Cornwall Cl ME15 .... 195 E7
Cornwall Cres ME1 .... 95 D4
Cornwall Dr BR5 .... 31 C1
Cornwall Gdns
Canterbury CT1 .... 175 D7
Margate CT9 .... 51 B3
Cornwall Ho
Deal CT14 .... 215 A5
5 Dover CT17 .... 310 D7
Cornwallis Ave
Aylesham CT3 .... 210 F6
Chatham ME4 .... 63 E1
Folkestone CT19 .... 335 B6
Gillingham ME8 .... 65 A4
Herne Bay CT6 .... 77 C3
Linton ME17 .... 227 E8
Sidcup SE9 .... 30 D6
Tonbridge TN10 .... 222 F4
Cornwallis Circ CT5 .... 74 D1
Cornwallis Cl
Ashford TN24 .... 301 B7
Erith DA8 .... 14 F8
Folkestone CT19 .... 335 B6
Cornwallis Cotts ME17 .... 194 E2
Cornwallis Gdns CT10 .... 84 A6
Cornwallis Rdbt ME8 .... 65 A4
Cornwallis Rd
Maidstone ME16 .... 161 D4
Woolwich SE18 .... 2 B3
Woolwich SE18 .... 2 C3
Cornwallis Sch The ME15 .... 194 F2
Cornwallis Wlk SE9 .... 11 F4

Cornwall Rd
Dartford DA1 15 F4
Deal CT14 215 C3
Gillingham ME7 64 D6
Herne Bay CT6 76 B2
Rochester ME1 63 C3
Cornwell Ave DA12 37 C5
Corona Rd SE12 29 A8
Corona Terr ME6 127 F6
Coronation Cl
Bexley DA5 13 D1
Broadstairs CT10 83 E7
Coronation Cotts
Folkestone CT19 334 D6
Stoke ME3 25 A3
Ticehurst TN5 338 F2
Coronation Cres
Margate CT9 82 B8
Queenborough ME11 45 F5
Coronation Ct DA8 14 D7
Coronation Dr
Ashford TN23 267 C1
Leysdown-on-S ME12 49 D2
Coronation Flats 5
ME4 63 F3
Coronation Rd
Chatham ME5 64 C2
Grain ME3 27 B5
Ramsgate CT11 117 D6
Sheerness ME12 28 D1
Coronation Sq TN29 376 C6
Corone Cl CT19 335 A7
Corporation Rd ME7 64 D7
Corporation St ME1 63 C6
Corral Cl ME5 64 D2
Corral Hts 13 DA8 4 E1
Corrall Almshouses 5
ME15 162 A3
Corrance Gn ME15 195 A8
Correnden Rd TN10 222 A3
Corseley Rd TN3 312 B5
Corsican Wlk CT6 77 C3
Cortanore ME10 101 E2
Cortland Cl
Crayford DA1 14 E1
Sittingbourne ME10 101 E6
Cortland Mews ME10 101 E6
Corunna Cl CT21 333 A2
Corunna Pl CT15 278 E3
Corylus Dr CT5 108 A7
Cory's Rd ME1 63 D6
Cossack St ME1 63 D3
Cossington Rd
Canterbury CT1 175 A7
Chatham ME5 97 B1
Costells Mdw TN16 151 D1
Cosway Cotts TN25 329 C1
Cot La TN27 295 B3
Cotleigh Ave DA5 31 D6
Cotmandene Cres BR5 54 A7
Cotman's Ash La
TN15 123 D4
Cotman Way TN12 224 E6
Coton Rd DA16 13 A4
Cotswold Cl
Ashford TN24 268 B4
Bexley DA7 14 E5
Cotswold Gdns ME15 163 A2
Cotswold Rd DA11 36 E5
Cotswold Rise BR6 53 F3
Cottage Ave BR2 52 E1
Cottage Field Cl DA14 31 C7
Cottage Rd
Chatham ME4 63 F6
Ramsgate CT11 117 E6
Cottage Row CT13 148 F1
Cottall Ave ME4 63 F2
Cottenham Cl ME19 159 F7
Cottington Rd CT12 116 B5
Cotton Hill Ho TN26 349 A7
Cotton Hill Wlk TN26 349 A7
Cotton La DA2,DA9 16 C2
Cotton Rd CT1 174 E7
Couchman Green La
TN12 260 F7
Coulman St ME7 64 D5
Coulson Gr CT14 214 A5
Coulter Ho DA9 17 C2
Coulter Rd
Ashford TN23 299 E5
Herne Bay CT6 76 B2
Coulters Cl ME14 162 D5
Coulton Ave DA11 36 E7
Coultrip Cl ME12 48 B5
Council Ave DA11 18 C1
Council Cotts
Chainhurst ME15 227 A7
Chiddingstone Causeway
TN11 252 A8
Coxheath ME15 194 A4
Council Hos TN15 190 A8
Countess Mountbatten Ct
CT8 81 E8
Countess of Thanet's
Almshouses TN8 281 F3
Country's Field TN29 366 C8
Country Ways ME17 200 D3
County Gate SE9 30 C5
County Gr ME19 159 B8
County Ho SE18 12 A8
County Rd
Maidstone ME14 162 A5
Newham E6 2 B8
County Sq 6 TN23 268 B2
Coupland Pl SE18 2 C1
Courier Rd RM13 4 D8
Course The SE9 30 A5
Courtaulds Cl SE28 3 A5
Court Ave DA17 3 F1
Court Broomes ME17 230 C8
Court Cotts
St Nicholas at Wade CT7 79 E2
Wingham CT3 178 A7
Court Cres BR8 55 E5
Court Dr ME16 161 D4
Courtenay Ho ME13 140 C3
Courtenay Rd
Boughton Street CT2,
ME13 140 E5
Deal CT14 215 C8
Maidstone ME15 161 F2
Courteney Rd ME8 98 B8
Courtenwell TN3 284 F4
Court Farm Rd SE9 29 E5
Courtfield Ave ME5 97 B3
Court Flats CT3 178 A7
Court Hall Mus*
ME10 101 E6
Court Hall ME11 45 F5
Court Hill Ho CT16 277 E4
Court Hill CT3 144 E2
Courthope Ave TN5 336 F4
Courthope TN12 257 A6
Court La Detling ME14 131 C5
Hadlow TN11 224 B7
Courtland Ave CT16 278 A6
Courtland Dr CT16 277 E4
Courtland Gr SE28 3 D6
Courtlands Ave SE12 11 B2
Courtlands BR7 30 B2
Courtlands Cl
Cliffs End CT12 116 E5
Teston ME18 193 A8
Courtlands CT14 248 D6
Courtlands Farm
TN17 320 A3
Courtlands
Herne Bay CT6 77 B3
Teston ME18 193 A8
Tonbridge TN10 222 A3
Courtlands Way CT8 50 D1
Court Lane Pl TN11 223 F8
Court Lea CT3 146 B6
Courtleet Dr DA8 14 B6
Court Lodge Cotts
East Farleigh ME15 194 A7
Horton Kirby DA4 57 C6
Mereworth TN12 191 E4
West Farleigh ME15 193 D7
Court Lodge
Deal CT14 215 B6
Erith DA17 4 A1
Court Lodge Farm
ME18 193 B7
Court Lodge Flats
TN3 317 C6
Court Lodge Rd
Appledore TN26 361 C7
Gillingham ME7 64 F6
Court Lodge DA12 38 E2
Court Mdws CT3 176 F8
Court Mdw TN15 124 F3
Court Meadow ME8 65 B2
Court Mews DA11 18 B1
Court Mount CT7 81 A6
Court Pl 5 CT20 335 C4
Court Rd Burham ME1 128 F8
Dartford DA2 34 E3
Deal CT14 215 B1
Eltham SE9 29 F7
Royal Tunbridge Wells
TN4 285 F4
St Nicholas at Wade CT7 79 E2
Sittingbourne ME10 101 F7
Court Road (Orpington
By-Pass)
Chelsfield BR6,TN14 87 D5
Orpington BR6 54 B2
Court Royal TN2 313 E8
Court St Bromley BR1 52 A7
Faversham ME13 138 D7
Courts The CT9 50 E1
Court Tree Dr ME12 48 B5
Courtwood Dr TN13 154 A3
Court Wurtin TN23 300 A7
Courtyard Gdns TN15 124 F3
Courtyard The
Ashford TN24 300 F6
Gillingham ME8 98 A8
Staple CT3 179 A6
Watt's Cross TN11 221 A7
Westerham TN16 184 D8
Court Yd SE9 11 F1
Cousley Wood Rd
TN5 337 C7
Couthurst Rd SE3 11 B7
Coutts Ave DA12 38 E4
Covelees Wall E6 2 A7
Coventon La CT14 181 A5
Coventry Cl
9 Newham E6 1 F7
Rochester ME2 62 D6
Coventry Gdns CT6 77 E5
Coventry Rd TN10 222 D5
Coverdale Ave ME15 195 D6
Coverdale Cl ME5 97 B7
Covert TN23 267 E1
Covert Rd CT3 210 E4
Covert The
Chatham ME5 97 B1
Orpington BR6 53 E3
Vigo Village DA13 125 E7
Covesfield DA11 36 F8
Covet La CT4 209 C2
Covet Wood Cl BR5 53 F3
Covey Hall Rd ME6 95 A1
Cowan Cl E6 1 E8
Cowbeck Cl ME8 98 D6
Cowden Cl TN18 354 E8
Cowden Cross TN8 282 C7
Cowden La TN18 354 E7
Cowden Mews TN8 282 A5
Cowden Rd
Maidstone ME14 162 C5
Orpington BR6 53 F2
Cowden Sta TN8 282 D8
Cowdray Rd CT14 215 A3
Cowdray Sq CT14 215 A3
Cowdrey Cl
Ashford TN24 301 A7
Maidstone ME16 161 B2
Rochester ME1 63 B2
Cowdrey Ct DA1 33 B8
Cowdrey Pl CT1 175 B6
Cowdreys TN9 254 C8
Cowen Ho 4 SE18 12 B8
Cowgate Hill CT17 310 D7
Cowgate La CT18 307 C5
Cow La Canterbury CT1 174 D7
Dover CT17 310 A7
Horseshoe Green TN8 250 D1
Cow Leaze E6 2 A7
Cowley Ave DA9 17 A2
Cowley Rise CT9 83 C8
Cowper Ave RM18 19 B6
Cowper Cl Bexley DA16 13 A2
Bromley BR2 52 D5
Whitstable CT5 75 D3
Cowper Rd Bromley BR2 52 D5
Crabble CT17 277 E3
Deal CT14 215 C5
Erith DA17 4 A2
Gillingham ME7 64 D3
Margate CT9 50 J1
Sittingbourne ME10 102 B4
Cowstead Rd ME9 99 D2
Coxes Ave CT12 83 B3
Coxes La CT12 83 B3
Coxett Hill ME13 137 D5
Cox Gdns ME8 65 A2
Coxheath Prim Sch
ME17 194 C3
Coxhill Cres CT17 277 D3
Coxhill Gdns CT17 277 D3
Coxhill CT15 244 C3
Coxland Cotts TN26 347 B1
Coxmount Rd SE7 1 D1
Cox's Cl ME6 127 F8
Cox St ME14 131 E6
Coxwell Rd SE18 2 D1
Cozenton Cl ME8 65 E1
Crabble Ave CT17 278 A2
Crabble Cl CT17 277 F2
Crabble Corn Mill*
CT17 277 F3
Crabble Hill CT16,
CT17 278 A2
Crabble La CT17 277 E2
Crabble Mdws CT17 278 A2
Crabble Rd CT17 278 A3
Crabbs Croft Cl 7 BR6 86 C5
Crabtree Cl ME19 159 A2
Crabtree La ME17 233 B8
Crabtree Manorway N
DA17 4 C5
Crabtree Manorway S
DA17 4 C3
Crabtree Rdbt ME14 129 E2
Crabtree Rd ME8 98 D8
Craddock Dr 8 CT1 143 B1
Craddock Ho CT1 143 B1
Craddock Rd CT1 143 B1
Craddock Way ME8 98 D5
Cradducks La TN12 261 B4
Cradle Bridge Dr
TN24 268 F2
Cradles Rd ME9 99 C2
Cradley Rd SE9 30 D7
Crafford St CT16 278 D1
Craft Workshops
TN27 230 C1
Cragie Wlk ME8 98 E4
Craigerne Rd SE3 11 B7
Craig Ho SE3 11 B7
Craigholm SE18 12 A6
Craig Ho ME1 63 E1
Craighton Ho 2 CT16 310 E7
Craigie Ct DA1 34 A8
Craigton Rd SE9 11 F3
Crales Ho SE18 1 E3
Cramonde Pl DA16 13 A5
Crampton Ct CT10 84 A4
Crampton's Rd TN14 154 B7
Cramptons TN17 320 F8
Cranborne Ave ME15 162 C1
Cranborne Wlk CT2 142 E3
Cranbourne Ave ME15 195 B8
Cranbourne Cl CT11 117 F8
Cranbrook CE Prim Sch
TN17 320 D5
Cranbrook Cl
Gillingham ME8 65 C3
Hayes BR2 52 A3
Maidstone ME15 195 F7
Margate CT9 51 E1
Cranbrook Dr ME10 101 D1
Cranbrook Ho 1 DA8 14 F7
Cranbrook Mews 1
TN8 217 C1
Cranbrook Mus*
TN17 320 D5
Cranbrook Rd
Benenden TN17 341 F8
Bexley DA7 13 F6
Fosten Green TN27 322 C6
Goudhurst TN17 319 A8
Hawkhurst TN18 340 F4
Knox Bridge TN12,TN17 292 F7
Parkgate TN30 323 C1
Tenterden TN30 344 E7
Cranbrook Sch TN17 320 D5
Cranbrooks TN25 301 D4
Cranbrook Union Mill*
TN17 320 D4
Crandalls TN11 220 F1
Cranden Wlk DA4 57 E7
Crane Ho 11 TN18 340 F2
Crane House Gdns 10
TN18 340 F2
Crane La TN17 320 D5
Cranford Cl ME8 65 D1
Cranford Ho DA1 15 A2
Cranford Rd
Dartford DA1 33 E7
Tonbridge TN10 223 A5
Cranham Sq TN12 259 C5
Cranleigh Cl
Orpington BR6 87 A7
Sidcup DA5 14 B1
Cranleigh Ct CT5 108 E8
Cranleigh Dr
Swanley BR8 55 E5
Whitfield CT16 278 B7
Cranleigh Gdns
Chatham ME4 63 D3
Maidstone ME16 161 C7
Whitstable CT5 108 E8
Cranley Par SE9 29 E4
Cranley Rd E13 1 B8
Cranmer Cl CT4 176 B4
Cranmer Ct ME15 195 B8
Cranmere Ct ME2 63 C8
Cranmer Ho 6 CT2 142 E1
Cranmer Rd TN13 153 E4
Cranmore Rd BR7 29 F3
Cranstone Ct 12 DA14 31 B4
Cranswick Cotts CT14 247 C8
Cranwell Rd TN4 285 C4
Crates Yd TN4 286 A5
Crathie Rd SE12 11 B1
Craufurd Gn CT20 334 D5
Craven Cl CT9 82 C8
Craven Rd BR6 87 D7
Crawford Ct SE18 13 A8
Crawford Gdns CT9 51 B2
Crawford Rd CT10 83 F5
Crawfords BR8 32 E1
Crawley Ct 1 DA11 19 B1
Crawshay Cl TN13 154 A4
Cray Ave BR5 54 B4
Cray Bldgs DA14 31 C2
Craybrooke Rd DA14 31 B4
Crayburne DA13 35 F4
Craybury End SE9 30 C6
Cray Cl DA1 15 A3
Craydene Rd DA8 14 F6
Crayfields Bsns Pk BR5 54 C8
Crayfields Ind Pk BR5 54 C7
Crayford Cl
Maidstone ME14 162 C6
Newham E6 1 E7
Crayford Commercial Ctr
DA1 14 E1
Crayford High St DA1 14 E2
Crayford Ind Est DA1 14 F2
Crayford Rd DA1 14 F2
Crayford Sta DA1 14 E1
Crayford Way DA1 15 A3
Craylands La DA10 17 D2
Craylands BR5 54 C6
Craylands Sq DA10 17 D2
Crayleigh Terr DA14 31 C2
Craymill Sq DA1 14 F5
Cray Rd Crockenhill BR8 55 C3
Erith DA17 14 A8
Sidcup DA14 31 C2
Crayside Ind Est DA1 15 B3
Crays Par The BR5 54 C7
Craythorne Cl
Hythe CT21 334 B4
New Romney TN28 373 B8
Craythorne Ho TN30 345 B8
Craythorne La TN28 373 B7
Craythorne TN30 345 B8
Cray Valley Rd BR5 54 B4
Creasey's Row TN14 185 E5
Credenhall Dr BR2 52 F1
Crediton Rd E16 1 A7
Credo Way RM20 17 B8
Creek La ME3 25 B2
Creek The DA11 18 B2
Creek Way RM13 4 E8
Creighton Flats 2
CT13 148 F1
Cremer Cl CT4 173 C2
Cremer Pl ME13 138 A8
Cremers Rd ME10 102 B5
Cremorne Rd 1 DA11 36 F8
Crendon Pk TN4 286 A8
Crescent Ave RM17 18 D8
Crescent Cotts TN13 153 E7
Crescent Ct
1 Grays RM17 18 D8
Sidcup DA15 31 A5
Crescent Dr BR5 53 C3
Crescent Gdns BR8 55 C7
Crescent Ho
Margate CT9 51 A2
Ramsgate CT12 117 C7
Rochester ME2 63 C7
Crescent Rd
Birchington CT7 81 A7
Broadstairs CT10 84 C8
Bromley BR1 29 A1
Erith DA8 14 F8
Faversham ME13 138 D7
Margate CT9 50 H2
Ramsgate CT11 117 D7
Royal Tunbridge Wells
TN1 286 B3
Sidcup DA15 30 F5
Woolwich SE18 2 B2
Crescent St 1 ME10 101 F4
Crescent The
Aylesham CT15 211 A3
Bidborough TN4 253 E4
Borough Green TN15 157 A8
Boughton Street ME13 140 A3
Crescent The *continued*
Canterbury CT2 142 F4
Chartham CT4 173 D1
Eythorne CT15 245 C7
Folkestone CT20 334 E3
Groombridge TN3 312 C7
Halfway Houses ME12 46 E6
Longfield DA3 58 E6
Lower Halstow ME9 67 C3
Maidstone ME14 161 F8
Northfleet DA11 36 F6
St Margaret's at Cliffe
CT15 280 A5
St Mary's Island ME4 41 B1
Sandwich CT13 180 E6
Sevenoaks TN13 154 D6
Sheerness ME12 28 C2
Sidcup DA14 30 F4
Sidcup DA5 31 E8
Sittingbourne ME10 69 A1
Swanscombe DA9 17 C2
Teynham ME9 103 D3
Tonbridge TN9 222 B2
Crescent Way
Chatham ME5 96 D5
Orpington BR6 86 E5
Cressey Ct 7 ME4 63 E4
Cressfield TN23 267 F1
Cressingham Ct 1 DA17 4 A3
Cress Way ME13 138 A7
Cresta Cl CT6 75 F4
Crest Ave RM17 18 B7
Crest Cl TN14 121 B8
Crest Ind Est TN12 259 C6
Crest Rd ME1 63 C1
Crest View Dr BR5 53 C4
Crest View DA9 17 A3
Crestway ME5 97 B8
Crete Hall Rd DA11 18 E1
Crete Rd E CT18,CT19 307 D1
Crete Rd W CT18 307 B1
Creteway Cl CT19 335 E8
Creton St SE18 2 A3
Creve Coeur Cl ME14 163 A5
Crevequer Chambers 1
ME8 65 F1
Cricketers Cl
Bells Yew Green TN3 315 A5
Erith DA8 4 E1
Harrietsham ME17 198 D6
Hawkinge CT18 307 B6
Sittingbourne ME10 101 F8
Cricketers Dr DA13 93 A7
Cricket Ground Rd BR7 53 B8
Crimond Ave TN29 353 A4
Criol Rd TN26 299 A2
Cripple Hill TN26 296 D1
Cripple St ME15 195 A7
Cripps Cl CT3 210 E5
Cripps' La CT15 279 F6
Crisfield Ct TN30 324 B2
Crismill La ME14 163 F4
Crismill Rd ME14,ME17 163 F3
Crispe Cl ME8 98 D4
Crispe Park Cl CT7 81 B7
Crispe Rd CT7 81 A3
Crispin Cl ME13 138 D8
Crispin Ct ME17 194 C3
Crispin Rd ME2 62 E8
Crispin Way ME19 159 A3
Crittall's Cnr DA14 31 C1
Crittenden Bglws
ME15 194 A4
Crittenden Cotts
ME15 194 A4
Crittenden Rd TN12 256 D3
Crittle's Ct TN5 336 F4
Crockenhall Way DA13 36 E1
Crockenhill Hill BR5 54 D4
Crockenhill La BR8,DA4 56 C2
Crockenhill Prim Sch
BR8 55 C3
Crocken Hill Rd TN27 232 C2
Crockenhill Rd BR5,BR8 54 E4
Crockers Hatch Cnr
TN3 284 D2
Crockford Cl TN10 222 E7
Crockham Hill CE Prim Sch
TN8 184 C2
Crockham La ME13 140 B6
Crockham Rd ME13 140 C6
Crockham Way SE9 30 A4
Crockshard Hill CT3 178 B4
Crockshard La CT3 178 B4
Croft Cl Bromley BR7 29 F3
Chatham ME5 97 C1
Erith DA17 3 F1
Tonbridge TN10 222 F5
Croft Ct TN8 217 C1
Crofters Cl CT21 353 E8
Crofters The ME8 98 F7
Croft Gdns ME17 199 D4
Croft La
Edenbridge TN8 217 C1
Folkestone CT20 334 F5
Crofton Ave
Orpington BR5,BR6 86 C8
Sidcup DA5 31 D8
Crofton Cl TN24 268 C6
Crofton Inf Sch BR5 53 D2
Crofton Jun Sch BR5 53 D2
Crofton La BR5,BR6 53 D2
Crofton Rd
Orpington BR6 86 B8
Westgate-on-S CT8 81 E7
Croft Rd Ashford TN24 268 D2
Bromley BR1 29 A2
Westerham TN16 151 C1
Croftside DA13 126 A8
Croft's Pl 8 CT10 84 B4
Croft The
Leybourne ME19 127 E2
Swanley BR8 55 C6
Croft The *continued*
Tenterden TN30 345 B7
Croft Way
Sevenoaks TN13 153 F2
Sidcup DA15 30 E5
Croftwood TN23 299 D6
Croidene Ct ME12 47 A6
Cromarty Ct 8 BR1 52 C7
Crombie Cl CT18 307 B5
Crombie Rd DA15 30 D7
Cromer Pl 5 BR6 53 D1
Cromer Rd
Rochester ME2 63 B8
Sittingbourne ME9,
ME10 134 F8
Cromer St TN9 222 A1
Cromford Cl BR6 86 E7
Cromlix Cl BR7 53 B7
Crompton Gdns ME15 162 B3
Crompton Tower Rly Mus*
CT10 84 A4
Cromwell Ave BR2 52 B5
Cromwell Cl BR2 52 B5
Cromwell Mews BR7 53 A8
Cromwell Park Pl
CT20 334 D4
Cromwell Rd
Canterbury CT1 175 A6
Maidstone ME14 162 B5
Royal Tunbridge Wells
TN2 286 C3
West Minst ME11 45 F7
Whitstable CT5 74 E1
Cromwell Terr ME4 64 A3
Cronin Cl 2 ME20 127 F4
Crooked La DA11,DA12 19 B1
Crooked S Rd CT14 247 E7
Crookenden Pl CT4 242 F8
Crook Log DA6 13 D3
Crook Log Prim Sch
DA6 13 D3
Crook Rd TN12 257 D1
Crook's Court La
CT15 308 F4
Crookston Rd SE9 12 A4
Croombs Rd E16 1 C8
Crosby House DA1 15 A1
Crosier Cl SE3 11 E6
Crosier Ct ME9 66 E3
Crosley Rd ME7 64 D3
Cross-at-Hand Cotts
TN12 228 E2
Crossbrook Rd SE3 11 E4
Cross Ct 11 SE28 3 B6
Cross Dr ME17 197 B1
Cross Keys Cl TN13 187 A8
Cross Keys
Maidstone ME14 163 C4
Sevenoaks TN13 187 A8
Cross La 7 ME13 138 D7
Cross Lane E DA12 37 B6
Cross Lane Gdns TN5 338 D1
Cross Lane W DA11 37 B6
Cross La Sidcup DA5 31 F8
Sittingbourne ME10 101 E6
Throwley Forstal ME13 202 C7
Ticehurst TN5 338 D2
Crossley Ave CT6 75 F4
Crossley Cl TN16 118 D4
Crossmead SE9 29 F7
Cross Rd Birchington CT7 81 B8
Dartford DA1 15 C1
Deal CT14 215 A2
Hawley DA2 33 F4
Northfleet DA11 18 F1
Orpington,Keston Mark
BR2 85 E8
Orpington,St Mary Cray
BR5 54 B4
Sidcup DA14 31 B4
Cross St
2 Canterbury CT2 142 E1
Chatham ME4 64 A4
Erith DA8 14 E8
Gillingham ME7 64 C6
27 Gravesend DA12 19 B1
Herne Bay CT6 76 D3
Cross Stile TN23 299 F8
Cross St
Maidstone ME14 162 A6
Rochester ME2 63 B8
Cross The CT13 180 B2
Crossway Chatham ME5 96 E6
Erith SE28 3 D7
Orpington BR5 53 D4
Cross Way ME1 63 C3
Crossways Ave CT9 83 A5
Crossways Bvd DA2,
DA9 16 E3
Crossways
Canterbury CT2 142 F4
Chart Sutton ME17 196 B1
Crossways Cl TN29 352 E2
Crossways Ct TN16 150 C7
Crossways Hextable BR8 32 F1
Sittingbourne ME10 101 F1
Tatsfield TN16 150 C7
Crossway The
Bromley SE9 29 D6
Royal Tunbridge Wells
TN4 285 D2
Crouch Cotts ME13 171 E8
Crouch Croft SE9 30 A5
Crouch Hill Ct ME9 67 C3
Crouch House Cotts
TN8 217 B2
Crouch House Rd TN8 217 B2
Crouch La
Crouch TN15 157 B6
Linkhill TN18 356 B6
Selling ME13 171 E8
Crowbridge Link
TN24 300 F7

Crowbridge Rd TN24 300 F6
Crow Cnr
Brabourne TN25 270 E1
Rochester ME1 63 C5
Crowden Way SE28 3 C6
Crow Dr TN14 121 C4
Crowfoot Cl SE28 2 E5
Crow Hill
Borough Green TN15 157 A7
Broadstairs CT10 84 B5
Crow Hill Rd
Borough Green TN15 157 A7
Margate CT9 82 B8
Crowhurst La
Basted TN15 156 E4
West Kingsdown TN15 91 B4
Crowhurst Oast TN12 191 D1
Crowhurst Rd TN15 156 F6
Crowhurst Way BR5 54 C4
Crow La ME1 63 C5
Crown Acres TN12 225 A6
Crown Cl BR6 87 A6
Crown Ct Bromley BR2 52 E4
Cranbrook TN17 320 C5
Deal CT14 215 D6
Eltham SE12 11 B1
Tilbury RM18 19 A5
Crownfield Rd TN23 299 F8
Crownfields
Maidstone ME14 162 F4
Sevenoaks TN13 154 B2
Crown Gdns CT2 142 E1
Crown Gn DA12 38 E3
Crown Hill Rd CT6 76 C4
Crown Ho
Lamberhurst TN3 317 B5
Rochester ME1 63 B4
Crown La Bromley BR2 52 D4
Chislehurst BR7 53 C8
Crown Lane Spur BR2 52 D3
Crown La Shorne DA12 38 E4
Stelling Minnis CT4 240 E3
Crown Quay La 5
ME10 102 A4
Crown Rd Grays RM17 18 A8
Marlpit Hill TN8 217 D4
Orpington BR6 87 A5
Shoreham TN14 88 F1
Sittingbourne ME10 101 E6
Crown St ME7 64 D6
Crown Woods Sch SE9 12 C2
Crown Woods Way
SE9 12 D2
Crows Camp Rd CT4 209 A5
Crowther Cl TN12 260 E4
Croxley Cl BR5 54 B7
Croxley Gn BR5 54 B8
Croyde Cl DA15 30 D8
Croydon Cl ME5 97 C4
Croydon Rd
Hayes BR2,BR4,BR6 85 C7
Tatsfield TN16 150 F3
Westerham TN16 151 B2
Crozier Ho SE3 11 B4
Cruden Rd DA12 37 F6
Cruise Liner Terminal
CT17 310 E4
Crumpsall St SE2 3 C2
Crump's La ME17 231 B4
Crundale Cl TN23 299 F6
Crundale 2 ME14 162 A5
Crundale Rd ME8 65 C3
Crundale Tower BR5 54 C1
Crundale Way CT9 51 E1
Crundwell Rd TN4 253 F1
Crusader Cl ME8 98 B8
Crusader Ct DA1 15 F3
Crusoe Rd DA8 4 D1
Crutches La ME3,ME2 39 B1
Cryalls Bsns Est ME10 101 C4
Cryalls La ME10,ME9 101 C3
Cryals Ct TN12 288 E5
Cryals Rd TN12 288 D5
Cryol Rd TN23 300 A7
Crystal Bsns Ctr CT13 149 B2
Crystal Ho 2 SE18 2 F1
Ctr for European
Agri-Enviromental
Studies TN25 238 A1
Cubitt Ho CT19 335 D6
Cuckmere Ct 18 BR5 54 D1
Cuckolds Cnr CT3 212 A7
Cuckold's Cnr
High Halden TN26 325 B7
Lower Higham ME3 39 C6
Cuckolds Cnr
New Ash Green DA3 92 B7
Snargate TN29 362 E7
Cuckold's Cnr TN12 260 F4
Cuckolds Green Rd
ME3 25 B5
Cuckoo La
Ashford,Singleton TN23 299 E7
Ashford TN23 299 D6
Lamberhurst TN12 289 A2
Postling CT21 304 F2
Tonbridge TN11 223 A7
Cuckoowood Ave
ME14 129 F1
Cudham CE Prim Sch
TN16 119 A3
Cudham Cl ME14 162 C6
Cudham Gdns CT9 51 E2
Cudham La N TN14 119 D7
Cudham La S TN14 119 D2
Cudham Park Rd TN14 86 E1
Cudham Rd
Downe BR6 119 B7
Tatsfield TN16 150 E8
Cudworth Rd TN24 300 E7
Cuff Cres SE9 11 D1
Cugley Rd DA2 34 C8
Culcroft DA3 58 F6
Cullens Hill CT4 273 F4
Cullet Dr ME11 46 A3
Culling's Hill CT4 273 F4
Culmers Terr ME13 139 E8
Culpeper Cl
Hollingbourne ME17 164 E2
Rochester ME2 63 E6
Culpepers TN17 318 E7
Culpepper Cl CT2 143 A4
Culpepper Rd
Coxheath ME17 194 B3
Gillingham ME8 98 D4
Culter Field TN23 299 E8
Culverden Ave TN4 286 A6
Culverden Down TN4 285 F5
Culverden Park Rd
TN4 285 F5
Culverden Pk TN4 285 F5
Culverden Sq TN4 286 A5
Culverden St TN1 286 A4
Culver's La TN29 376 D5
Culverstone Green Prim
Sch DA13 92 F3
Culverstone Ho BR5 54 B6
Culverton Ct 19 DA14 31 A4
Culvey Cl DA3 58 E4
Cumberland Ave
Bexley DA16 12 F3
Broadstairs CT10 84 A5
Canterbury CT1 175 D7
Gravesend DA12 37 C8
Maidstone ME15 195 D8
Cumberland Cotts 23
TN1 286 A2
Cumberland Ct
Sevenoaks TN13 153 E7
Tonbridge TN10 222 A4
Cumberland Dr
Dartford DA1 33 F8
Erith DA7 13 E7
Lower Halstow ME9 67 C3
Cumberland Gdns 10
TN1 286 A2
Cumberland Ho SE28 2 D4
Cumberland Mews 12
TN1 286 A2
Cumberland Rd
Chatham ME4,ME7 64 B7
Gillingham ME7 64 C7
Margate CT9 51 B3
Newham E13 1 B8
1 Ramsgate CT11 117 D6
Cumberland Sch E16 1 A8
Cumberland Villas 5
DA12 37 C8
Cumberland Wlk TN1 286 A2
Cumberland Yd 11
TN1 286 A2
Cumbrian Ave DA7 14 E5
Cumbrian Cl CT5 108 C8
Cundy Rd E16 1 C7
Cunningham Cl TN4 286 B7
Cunningham Cres
Birchington CT7 80 E7
Chatham ME5 97 A8
Cunningham Ho ME1 63 B4
Cunningham Rd TN4 286 B7
Cupola Cl BR1 29 B3
Curates Wlk DA2 33 D5
Curlew Ave ME9 67 B3
Curlew Cl Erith SE28 3 D6
Herne Bay CT6 77 C2
Curlew Cres ME2 62 C6
Curlew Pl CT18 307 A3
Curlews The DA12 37 D6
Curlinge Ct CT11 117 A6
Curran Ave DA15 12 F2
Currie Rd TN4 286 A5
Curteis Rd TN30 324 B1
Curtis Ct BR6 54 A2
Curtis La CT4 240 D2
Curtismill Cl BR5 54 B6
Curtismill Way BR5 54 B6
Curtis Rd TN24 300 E7
Curtis Way
1 Faversham ME13 138 C7
Rochester ME1 96 D7
7 Woolwich SE28 3 B6
Curtis Wood Park Rd
CT6 111 A7
Curtis Wood Rd CT6 110 F7
Curzon Cl Deal CT14 215 C3
Orpington BR6 86 D6
Curzon Ct SE9 30 C5
Curzon Dr RM17 18 C7
Curzon Ho 5 CT11 117 D6
Curzon Rd Chatham ME4 63 F3
Dover CT17 310 B8
Maidstone ME14 162 A6
Cushings Wlk 18 CT5 74 D2
Cushman Rd CT1 174 E7
Custom House for Excel Sta
E16 1 B6
Cutbush Almshouses
3 Maidstone ME14 162 A4
1 Maidstone ME15 162 A3
Cutbush and Corrall Ct 1
ME14 162 B4
Cutbush Cl ME17 198 D6
Cutbush Ho 2 ME15 162 A3
Cuthbert Rd CT8 81 E8
Cutmore St DA11 37 B8
Cutter Cl ME2 40 F3
Cutter Ho 6 DA8 4 E1
Cutter Ridge Rd DA13 61 A1
Cut The TN27 295 E8
Cuttings The CT12 117 C8
Cutty Sark Ct 6 DA9 17 A2
Cuxton Cl DA6 13 E2
Cuxton Com Inf Sch
ME2 62 B2
Cuxton Com Jun Sch
ME2 62 B2
Cuxton Ind Est ME2 62 C2
Cuxton BR5 53 C4
Cuxton Rd
Maidstone ME15 195 F5
Rochester ME2 62 F5
Cuxton Sta ME2 62 C2
Cyclamen Rd BR8 55 D5
Cygnet Cl ME20 128 A2
Cygnet Gdns DA11 36 F6
Cygnet L Ctr DA11 36 E6
Cygnet Rd ME5 97 C2
Cygnet Way TN23 267 F1
Cylinder Rd CT21 333 B4
Cypress Ave
Ashford TN23 267 E2
Hoo St Werburgh ME3 41 E3
Cypress Cl CT5 108 C7
Cypress Ct ME7 64 F6
Cypress Gr
Elvington CT15 212 B2
Royal Tunbridge Wells
TN2 314 C8
Cypress Rd ME2 40 C1
Cypress Tree Cl DA15 30 F7
Cyprus Ct ME13 138 E7
Cyprus Pl E6 2 A6
Cyprus Rd ME13 138 E7
Cyprus Sta E6 2 A6
Cyril Hall Ct DA11 18 F1
Cyril John Gange Lodge
TN2 286 D2
Cyril Lodge 6 DA14 31 A4
Cyril Rd Bexley DA7 13 E5
Orpington BR6 54 A2

D

D2 Trad Est ME10 102 B6
Dabbling Cl DA8 15 B7
Daerwood Cl BR2 52 F1
Daffodil Rd ME2 62 E7
Daglish Cl TN28 373 B6
Dagmar Rd ME4 64 B2
Dagonet Gdns BR1 29 A5
Dagonet Rd BR1 29 A5
Dahlia Dr BR8 55 F7
Dahlia Rd SE2 3 B2
Daimler Ave CT6 76 B3
Dainton Cl 2 BR1 52 B8
Daintons Cotts 2
TN18 340 F2
Dairsie Ct 4 BR1 52 C7
Dairsie Rd SE9 12 A4
Dairy Cl 3 Bromley BR1 29 B1
Sutton at H DA4 34 B1
Dairy La
Chainhurst TN12 226 F4
Crockham Hill TN8 184 B1
Woolwich SE18 1 F2
Dairy Pl TN12 226 F4
Daisy Munns Ho SE9 30 C7
Dajen Bsns Pk ME4 64 C1
Dalberg Way SE2 3 D3
Dalby Rd CT9 51 A3
Dalby Sq CT9 51 A3
Daleacres Cvn Pk
CT21 352 E7
Dale Cl Crayford DA1 14 F1
Greenwich SE3 11 A4
Dale Ct Bromley BR1 52 D6
Chatham ME5 97 A2
Dale End DA1 14 F1
Dalemain Mews E16 1 A5
Dale Rd Crayford DA1 14 F1
Northfleet DA13 36 A4
Rochester ME1 63 C3
Swanley BR8 55 C6
Daleside Cl BR6 87 A4
Daleside BR6 87 A5
Dale St Chatham ME4 63 E2
Royal Tunbridge Wells
TN1 286 B4
Dale The BR2 85 D6
Dale View DA8 14 F5
Dale Wlk Ashford TN24 268 C7
Dartford DA2 34 C7
Dale Wood Rd BR6 53 E1
Dalewood ME10 102 A2
Dalison Ct ME2 95 B4
Dallas-Brett Cres
CT19 335 E8
Dallinger Rd 1 CT7 80 F8
Dallin Rd Bexley DA6 13 D3
Woolwich SE18 12 B7
Dalmatia Ct CT17 278 A1
Dalmeny Ave CT9 51 D1
Dalmeny Rd DA8 14 B6
Dalmeny Terr CT21 333 A1
Dalton Cl BR6 86 E7
Dalton Ct 7 CT11 117 E7
Daltons Rd BR6,BR8 88 C7
Dalton St ME7 64 C6
Dame Janet Com Inf Sch
CT12 83 B2
Dame Janet Com Jun Sch
CT12 83 B2
Damerham Cl CT2 142 E3
Damiem Cl ME4 64 A2
Damigos Rd DA12 37 F7
Damon Cl DA14 31 B5
Damon Ct DA14 31 B5
Damson Ct BR8 55 D5
Damson Dr ME3 41 E3
Danaway Cotts ME9 100 C3
Dando Cres SE3 11 B4
Dan Dr ME13 138 A8
Dane Cl Chatham ME5 97 C2
Hartlip ME9 99 D6
Orpington BR6 86 D5
Sidcup DA5 32 A8
Danecourt Com Sch
ME8 65 A2
Dane Court Gdns CT10 83 D5
Dane Court Gram Sch
CT10 83 E4
Dane Court Rd CT10 83 C6
Dane Cres CT11 117 E8
Dane Ct
Coxheath ME17 194 C2
Tilmanstone CT14 212 F4
Danedale Ave ME12 47 F6
Dane End Rd CT8 81 D8
Danefield Ct ME14 163 B4
Dane Gdns CT9 83 B8
Dane Hill Gr CT9 50 J2
Dane Hill CT9 50 J3
Dane Hill Row CT9 50 J2
Danehill Wlk DA14 31 A5
Dane Ho CT14 215 D8
Danehurst CT8 50 C1
Dane John Ct 3 CT1 174 F7
Dane John Mews 1
CT1 174 F7
Dane La ME9 99 D6
Danemore TN30 345 B8
Dane Mount CT9 83 C8
Dane Park Rd
Margate CT9 50 J2
Ramsgate CT11 117 E8
Dane Park Villas CT9 51 A2
Dane Pk ME15 194 C6
Dane Rd Birchington CT7 80 D7
Margate CT9 51 A2
Otford TN14 121 F2
Ramsgate CT11 117 E8
Danes Cl DA11 36 C5
Danescombe SE12 29 A7
Danes Ct CT16 278 D2
Danes Dr ME12 49 D2
Danes Hill ME7 65 A6
Danes Mead ME10 68 F1
Danesmead Terr CT9 50 J2
Dane Valley Rd CT10,
CT9 83 C8
Daniel Ho 5 ME16 161 E5
Daniels Ct CT5 74 C1
Danley Mid Sch ME12 46 E7
Danley Rd ME12 46 E7
Danns La ME18,ME19 159 A1
Dansington Rd DA16 13 A3
Danson Cres DA16 13 B4
Danson House* DA6 13 C3
Danson La DA16 13 B3
Danson Mead DA16 13 C4
Danson Prim Sch DA16 13 A3
Danson Rd Bexley DA5 13 D1
Bexley DA5,DA6 13 D2
Danson Underpass
DA5 13 C1
Danson Way ME8 65 D2
Danton La CT18 306 C1
Danvers Rd TN9 222 B1
Darby Gdns ME3 39 B3
Darby Pl CT20 335 D5
Darby Rd CT20 335 D5
Darby's La TN5 337 B2
D'arcy Pl BR2 52 A5
Darcy Sq TN28 373 E5
Darent Cl TN13 153 C5
Darenth Ave TN10 222 C5
Darenth Cl CT6 77 B3
Darenth Cotts TN14 121 F8
Darenth Ct 19 BR5 54 D1
Darenth Dr DA12 38 B7
Darenth Gdns TN16 151 D1
Darenth Hill DA2 34 C3
Darenth La TN13 153 E6
Darenth Park Ave DA2 34 D6
Darenth Prim Sch DA2 34 E2
Darenth Rd Bexley DA16 13 A6
Dartford DA1 33 F7
Darenth Rd S DA2 34 B4
Darenth Rise ME5 97 B3
Darenth Way TN14 122 A8
Darenth Wood Rd DA2 34 E6
Darent Ind Pk DA8 15 D8
Darent Mead DA4 57 B8
Darent Valley Hospl
DA2 34 E7
Dargate Cl ME16 161 D7
Dargate Rd
Dargate CT2,ME13 140 F7
Yorkletts CT5 108 A3
Dargets Rd ME5 97 A3
Dark Hill ME13 138 C8
Darland Ave ME7 64 E1
Darland Ho SE9 12 D1
Darlinghurst Rd CT19 334 E7
Darlington Dr ME12 47 A6
Darlington St CT20 335 D5
Darlton Cl DA1 14 F4
Darman La TN12,ME18 225 D3
Darnets Field TN14 121 F2
Darnley Cl
Broadstairs CT10 83 F3
Folkestone CT20 334 F4
Rochester ME2 62 D6
Darnley Ct DA11 37 A8
Darnley Dr TN4 253 E4
Darnley Rd
Gravesend DA11 37 A8
1 Grays RM17 18 B8
Rochester ME2 62 E6
Darnley St DA11 37 B8
Darns Hill BR8 55 C2
Darracott Cl CT14 215 B5
Darrell Cl CT6 76 C3
Darren Gdns CT10 83 F2
Darrick Wood Ho BR6 86 C7
Darrick Wood Inf & Jun
Schs BR6 86 B6
Darrick Wood Rd BR6 86 D8
Darrick Wood Sch BR6 86 B7
Darrick Wood Sports Ctr
BR6 86 B7
Dart Cl ME2 62 F7
Dartford Borough Mus*
DA1 33 E8
Dartford Gram Sch
DA1 15 C1
Dartford Gram Sch for Girls
DA1 33 C8
Dartford Hospl Specl Sch
DA3 59 A6
Dartford Rd
Coldblow DA5 32 C7
Dartford DA1 15 B1
Farningham DA4 57 A5
Sevenoaks TN13 154 C3
Dartford Sta DA1 15 E1
Dartford Technology Coll
DA1 33 D8
Dartford Trad Pk DA1 33 F6
Dartford West Technology
Coll for Girls DA1 33 C8
Dartmouth Rd BR2 52 A2
Darwin Cl BR6 86 D5
Darwin Coll CT2 142 E5
Darwin Ct Eltham SE9 12 A1
Rochester ME1 63 D5
Darwin Dr TN10 222 D6
Darwin Rd Bexley DA16 12 F4
Birchington CT7 80 F8
Canterbury CT2 142 E5
Tilbury RM18 18 F6
Daryngton Ave CT7 80 C7
Dashmonden Cl ME2 40 C2
Dashwood Cl DA6 14 A2
Dashwood Rd DA11 37 A6
Davall Ho 10 RM17 18 B8
Davema Cl BR7 53 A8
Davenport Ave ME7 64 E7
Davenport Rd DA14 31 E6
Davey Ct ME1 63 C5
David Ave CT9 51 D2
David Coffer Ct DA17 4 B2
David Ho 23 DA14 31 A5
David Ramsey Ho SE18 2 D2
David Saloman's Ho*
TN3 285 D8
Davids Cl CT10 84 B3
Davidson Ho DA9 17 C2
Davidson Rd CT2 142 D1
Davie Cl ME12 46 B8
Davie Ct ME12 46 B8
Davington Hill ME13 138 C8
Davington Prim Sch
ME13 138 C8
Davis Ave Deal CT14 215 A4
Northfleet DA11 36 E7
Davis Cl TN13 154 C5
Davy's Pl DA12 37 E2
Dawbourne TN30 324 B3
Dawell Dr TN16 118 C2
Dawes Cl DA9 16 F2
Dawes Rd CT2,ME13 140 C4
Dawes St ME7 64 C5
Dawn La ME18 159 D3
Dawn Rise ME12 48 F6
Dawson Ave BR5 54 B7
Dawson Cl SE18 2 C2
Dawson Ct 7 ME7 64 A6
Dawson Dr BR8 32 E1
Dawson Rd CT19 335 D6
Dawson's Row ME13 138 A6
Day Ho 2 ME14 162 B4
Days Lane Prim Sch
DA15 12 F1
Days La DA15 30 E8
Daytona Way CT6 76 A4
Dayton Dr DA8 15 D8
Dayton Rd ME13 170 C3
Deacon Cl ME2 62 E8
Deacon Est The ME20 129 A2
Deacons Leas BR6 86 D6
Deacon Trad Ctr ME2 63 A6
Deacon Trad Est TN9 222 D1
Deakin Leas TN9 254 B7
Deakins Terr BR6 54 A2
Deal Castle* CT14 215 D5
Deal Castle Rd CT14 215 D5
Deal Ent Ctr CT14 215 C7
Deal Ho ME15 195 E8
Deal Maritime & Local
History Mus* CT14 215 D6
Deal Parochial CE Prim Sch
CT14 215 C3
Deal Rd
Northbourne CT14 214 A4
Sandwich CT13,CT14 180 F5
Deal Sta CT14 215 C6
Dean & Chapter Cotts
DA13 36 B2
Dean Croft CT6 77 B5
Dean Ct 14 CT1 143 A1
Deane Cl CT5 108 E7
Deane Ct 8 ME7 64 C6
Deanery Rd TN8 184 C2
Dean Hill CT4,TN25 240 B2
Dean La DA13 93 C5
Dean Mead CT19 335 B7
Dean Rd
Luddesdown DA13 93 E8
Rochester ME2 62 F8
Sittingbourne ME10 101 E6
Woolwich SE28 3 A6
Deans Ct 7 TN9 254 B8
Deansfield Prim Sch
SE9 12 A4
Deans Hill Rd ME9 133 D5
Deans Mill Ct CT1 142 F1
Dean St ME15 194 C6
Deansway Ave CT2 143 F7
Dean's Wlk TN23 299 F7
Deanwood Cl ME8 98 D6
Deanwood Dr ME8 98 E4
Deanwood Prim Education
Tech Sch ME8 98 D3
Deanwood Rd CT17 277 E2
Deborah Cl CT5 108 F7
Debrabant Cl DA8 14 D8
De Burgh Hill CT17 278 C1
De Burgh St 2 CT17 310 C8
Decimus Pl TN1 286 B4
Decoy Hill Rd ME23 23 F6
Deedes Cl CT21 333 C3
Deepdene Rd DA16 13 A4
Deepdene TN5 337 A6
Deerhurst Cl DA3 59 C6
Deerhurst Gdns ME16 161 D4
Deering Cl ME4 41 B2
Deerleap La TN14 120 E6
Deerson La CT3 146 A4
Deerton St ME9 104 A2
Defiance Wlk SE18 1 F3
Defiant Cl ME5 97 B6
Defoe Cl Chatham ME5 97 B6
Erith DA8 14 F6
Degema Rd BR7 30 B3
Deham Ho ME10 101 D5
De Havilland Cl CT18 307 B4
De Havillands CT4 176 E3
Deidre Chapman Ho
DA10 17 E1
Delacourt Cl CT12 116 D5
Delacourt Rd SE3 11 B7
Delafield Rd SE7 1 C1
Delagarde Rd TN16 151 C1
Delamark Rd ME12 28 C2
Delamere Gdns 3
ME6 128 A8
Delamere Rd ME6 128 A8
Delane Rd CT14 215 A5
De L'angle Row CT4 173 D3
De Lapre Cl BR5 54 D2
Delarue Cl TN11 222 D8
Delaware Cl CT2 143 F6
Delaware Cotts TN8 249 F8
Delce Jun & Inf Schs
ME1 63 D2
Delce Rd ME1 63 D4
Delfside CT13 181 A8
Delf St CT13 148 F1
Delisle Rd SE28 2 E4
Delius Dr TN10 222 F6
Dell Dr TN2 286 D4
Dell The Maypole DA5 32 E7
Swanscombe DA9 17 B2
Woolwich SE2 3 A1
Delmaney Cl CT10 84 B5
Delmar Cl CT5 75 D3
Delme Cres SE3 11 B5
Delmonden La TN18 354 C8
Delmonden Rd TN18 340 B1
De L'angle Ho CT4 173 D3
De Luci Rd DA8 4 C1
De Lucy Prim Sch SE2 3 B4
De Lucy St SE2 3 B2
Delvan Cl SE18 12 A7
Delves Ave TN2 286 C1
Demelza Cl ME2 62 A2
Demelza House Hospice
ME9 100 F6
De Mere Cl ME8 98 D6
Demozay Cl CT18 307 A4
Denbeigh Dr TN10 222 D6
Denberry Dr DA14 31 B5
Denbigh Ave ME8 65 D1
Denbigh Cl Bromley BR7 29 F2
Sittingbourne ME10 101 E7
Denbigh Rd
Ramsgate CT12 83 A1
Royal Tunbridge Wells
TN4 286 C7
Denbridge Rd BR1 52 F7
Dence Cl CT6 77 B5
Dence Pk CT6 77 B4
Dencorra Way TN23 268 A1
Den Cross TN8 249 D6
Dene Ave DA15 31 B8
Dene Cl DA2 32 E4
Denecourt BR5 54 C1
Dene Dr New Barn DA3 59 B7
Orpington BR6 87 B7
Dene Farm Barns CT3 178 A4
Dene Farm La CT3 178 A4
Dene Holm Rd DA11 36 E5
Dene Lodge Cl TN15 156 F7
Dene Rd DA1 33 F8
Denesfield Ct TN13 153 C4
Denesway DA13 60 B3
Dene The
Bethersden TN26 297 D5
Canterbury CT1 175 B5
Hythe CT21 333 C2
Sevenoaks TN13 154 B1
Dene Way TN3 285 A7
Dene Wlk Longfield DA3 58 E6
Margate CT9 82 F7
Dengemarsh Rd TN29 379 A7
Dengrove Cvn Site
CT2 143 D6
Denham Cl Bexley DA16 13 C4
Dymchurch TN29 353 B4
Denham Rd ME9 100 B7
Denham St 2 SE10 1 A1
Denison Mews ME3 25 C4
Deniston Ave DA5 31 E7
Den La TN12 226 C3
Denmark Ho 10 SE18 1 E2
Denmark Rd
Bromley BR1 52 B8
Ramsgate CT11 117 E8
Denmark St
Folkestone CT19 335 E6
Newham E13 1 B8
Dennard Way BR6 86 A6
Denne Cl CT2 143 F7

398 Den–Dum

Denne Manor La CT4 ... 204 C8
Dennes La TN29 ... 376 C8
Dennes Mill Cl TN25 ... 237 D2
Denness Rd TN23 ... 300 B7
Dennettsland Rd TN8 ... 184 C1
Denning Cl ME16 ... 161 B4
Dennington Ct TN4 ... 254 A2
Dennis Cadman Ho ME20 ... 128 F1
Dennis Rd DA11 ... 37 B5
Dennis Way CT19 ... 334 E7
Dennis Wilcocks Cl ME9 ... 100 B6
Denny Cl 18 E6 ... 1 E8
Denny Ct 2 DA2 ... 16 B1
Densole La CT18 ... 307 A8
Densole Way CT18 ... 307 A8
Denstead Cotts CT4 ... 173 B8
Denstead Ct CT2 ... 142 C4
Denstead La CT4,ME13 ... 173 C7
Denstead Oast CT4 ... 173 B8
Denstead Wlk 11 ME15 ... 195 F6
Denstroude La CT2 ... 141 D8
Dental Cl ME10 ... 101 A5
Dental St CT21 ... 333 C2
Dent-De-Lion Ct CT9 ... 82 A8
Dent-De-Lion Rd
Margate CT9 ... 82 A8
Westgate-on-S CT8 ... 50 C1
Denton Cl ME15 ... 195 E8
Denton Court Rd DA12 ... 37 E8
Denton Ct BR2 ... 53 A2
Denton Gn ME8 ... 65 B4
Denton Rd Bexley DA16 ... 13 C7
Dartford DA1 ... 32 E8
Maypole DA5 ... 32 E7
Denton St DA12 ... 37 E8
Denton Terr DA5 ... 32 E6
Denton Way CT9 ... 51 C1
Denver Cl BR6 ... 53 E3
Denver Ind Est RM13 ... 4 F8
Denver Rd DA1 ... 33 A8
De Quincey Mews E16 ... 1 A5
Derby Cl
Sittingbourne ME10 ... 101 D6
Tonbridge TN11 ... 221 E6
Derby Rd Gillingham ME5 ... 64 E2
Grays RM17 ... 18 B8
Maidstone ME15 ... 195 C8
Derby Road Bridge RM17 ... 18 B8
Derifall Cl E6 ... 1 F8
Dering Cl Bridge CT4 ... 175 F1
Pluckley TN27 ... 265 C4
Dering Rd
Ashford TN24 ... 268 D2
Bridge CT4 ... 176 A1
Herne Bay CT6 ... 76 F4
Derings The TN29 ... 376 B6
Dering Terr TN27 ... 265 C3
Dering Way DA12 ... 37 F7
Deringwood Dr ME15 ... 162 F1
Dernier Rd TN10,TN9 ... 222 C4
Derrick Gdns SE7 ... 1 C3
Derringstone Downs CT4 ... 242 F6
Derringstone Hill CT4 ... 242 F6
Derringstone St CT4 ... 242 F7
Derry Downs BR5 ... 54 C3
Derville Ho TN28 ... 373 B6
Derville Rd TN29 ... 377 E7
Derwent Ave CT11 ... 117 A7
Derwent Cl DA1 ... 33 B7
Derwent Cres DA7 ... 14 A5
Derwent Dr
Orpington BR5 ... 53 D2
Royal Tunbridge Wells TN4 ... 285 E5
Derwent Ho 3 ME15 ... 195 E7
Derwent Rd TN10 ... 222 C5
Derwent Way
Aylesham CT3 ... 210 F6
Gillingham ME8 ... 98 D8
Desmond Cres ME13 ... 139 A5
D'este Rd CT11 ... 117 F7
Detillens La RH8 ... 183 A6
Detling Ave CT10 ... 84 A1
Detling CE Prim Sch ME14 ... 131 A1
Detling Cl
Gillingham ME8 ... 65 C2
West Minst ME12 ... 46 B7
Detling Hill ME14 ... 131 B2
Detling Rd Bromley BR1 ... 29 A3
Erith DA8 ... 14 D7
Northfleet DA11 ... 36 D7
Devalls Cl E6 ... 2 A6
Devenish Rd SE2 ... 3 A4
Devon Ave CT14 ... 215 C3
Devon Cl Chatham ME5 ... 97 C7
Rainham ME8 ... 65 F1
Devon Ct Ramsgate CT12 ... 83 B2
Sutton at H DA4 ... 57 B8
Devon Gdns CT7 ... 80 F7
Devon Rd
Canterbury CT1 ... 175 D8
Folkestone CT19 ... 335 D5
Maidstone ME15 ... 195 C8
Sutton at H DA4 ... 57 C8
Devonshire Ave DA1 ... 15 B1
Devonshire Cl TN2 ... 313 F8
Devonshire Gdns CT9 ... 51 C3
Devonshire Rd
Bexley DA6 ... 13 E3
Bromley SE9 ... 29 E6
Dover CT17 ... 310 B8
Gillingham ME7 ... 64 D7
Gravesend DA12 ... 37 B6
Newham E16 ... 1 B7
Devonshire Rd *continued*
Orpington BR6 ... 54 A2
West Thurrock RM20 ... 17 E8
Devonshire Sq BR2 ... 52 B5
Devonshire Terr CT10 ... 84 B5
De Warren Ho DA11 ... 18 D1
Dewberry Cl ME4 ... 41 B1
Dewberry Gdns E6 ... 1 E8
Dewhurst Cotts TN5 ... 336 A8
Dewhurst La TN5 ... 336 B8
DeWinter Ho TN13 ... 154 A3
Dewlands Ave DA2 ... 34 B8
Dew La TN31 ... 367 A1
Dexter Cl TN25 ... 268 C8
Dexter Ho 2 DA18 ... 3 E3
Deyley Way TN23 ... 299 C8
Dhekelia Cl ME14 ... 162 A7
Dial Cl Gillingham ME7 ... 64 F6
Swanscombe DA9 ... 17 D2
Dial Rd ME7 ... 64 F6
Diameter Rd BR5 ... 53 C3
Diamond Cotts TN12 ... 256 B7
Diamond Ct ME12 ... 28 B1
Diamond Field TN12 ... 289 F3
Diamond Rd CT5 ... 74 E2
Diana Ct DA8 ... 14 E8
Diana Gdns CT14 ... 215 A5
Diana Rd ME4 ... 64 A2
Dianne Ct SE12 ... 29 A7
Dianthus Cl SE2 ... 3 B1
Dibden La TN13,TN14 ... 186 E8
Dibdin Rd CT14 ... 215 D7
Dickens Ave
Canterbury CT1 ... 143 D2
Dartford DA1 ... 16 A3
Tilbury RM18 ... 19 B6
Dickens Cl Erith DA8 ... 14 B7
Hartley DA3 ... 58 F4
Langley Heath ME17 ... 196 E4
Dickens Ct Higham ME3 ... 39 C4
Rochester ME2 ... 63 D8
Staplehurst TN12 ... 260 F5
Dickens Dr
Chislehurst BR7 ... 30 C2
West Malling ME19 ... 127 F1
Dickens Ho 3 DA17 ... 3 F1
Dickens House Mus* CT10 ... 84 B4
Dickensian Cl ME3 ... 25 A2
Dickens Rd
Broadstairs CT10 ... 84 B5
Gravesend DA12 ... 37 E7
Maidstone ME14 ... 161 E8
Rochester ME1 ... 63 C2
Dickens Way TN18 ... 341 A2
Dickens Wlk CT10 ... 84 B4
Dickley La ME17 ... 199 A6
Dickson Ct 7 ME10 ... 102 B4
Dickson Ho SE18 ... 11 E6
Dickson Rd
Dover CT17 ... 310 C8
Eltham SE9 ... 11 E4
Dicksons Bourne TN25 ... 329 F6
Dickson's Cnr CT13 ... 182 A6
Dieu Stone La CT16 ... 310 E8
Digby Rd CT20 ... 334 E5
Digdog La TN12,TN17 ... 293 D3
Diggerland* ME2 ... 62 F4
Dignals Cl ME8 ... 65 F2
Dignash TN25 ... 235 E2
Dilhorne Cl SE12 ... 29 B5
Diligent Dr ME10 ... 101 F7
Dillon Way TN2 ... 286 D7
Dillywood Cotts ME3 ... 39 F2
Dilly Wood Fields ME3 ... 40 A3
Dillywood La ME3 ... 39 F2
Dilnot La CT7 ... 81 B3
Dimmock Cl TN12 ... 257 B7
Dingleden La TN17 ... 342 F2
Diocesan & Payne Smith CE Prim Sch CT1 ... 143 A1
Dippers Cl TN15 ... 122 F2
Discovery Dr ME19 ... 159 B3
Discovery Rd ME15 ... 163 B2
Discovery Sch The ME18 ... 159 D3
Discovery Wlk CT1 ... 175 C7
Dislingbury Rd TN11 ... 255 C4
Disraeli Cl
Maidstone ME15 ... 195 E5
Woolwich SE28 ... 3 C5
Dittisham Rd SE9 ... 29 E4
Ditton CE Jun Sch ME20 ... 128 C1
Ditton Court Cl ME20 ... 128 B1
Ditton Inf Sch ME20 ... 128 C1
Ditton Pl ME20 ... 128 B1
Ditton Rd DA6 ... 13 E2
Dixon Cl
Maidstone ME15 ... 161 F2
4 Newham E6 ... 1 F7
Dixon Ho SE2 ... 3 C1
Dixwell Cl ME8 ... 98 D5
Dixwell Rd CT20 ... 335 A4
Dobbie Cl ME10 ... 101 E6
Dobell Rd SE9 ... 11 F2
Dobells TN17 ... 320 D4
Dobson Rd DA12 ... 37 E3
Dock Approach Rd RM17 ... 18 E8
Dock Exit Rd CT16 ... 310 F8
Dock Head Rd
Chatham ME4 ... 64 A8
St Mary's Island ME4 ... 41 A1
Dockland St E16 ... 2 A5
Dock Rd Chatham ME4 ... 63 F6
Chatham ME4 ... 64 A7
Grays RM17 ... 18 D8
Grays RM17 ... 18 E7
Tilbury RM18 ... 18 E5
Dockside Outlet Ctr ME4 ... 64 A8
Dockside Rd E16 ... 1 D6
Doctor Hope's Rd TN17 ... 320 D4
Doctor's La CT15 ... 309 B5
Doddington Ct ME16 ... 161 E5
Doddington Place Gdns* ME9 ... 168 A7
Doddington Prim Sch ME9 ... 167 F7
Doddington Rd ME8 ... 65 D3
Dodd Rd TN10 ... 222 E5
Dodd's La CT16 ... 278 A3
Doebury Wlk SE18 ... 13 A8
Does Alley 4 ME10 ... 101 F4
Dog Cotts RH19 ... 281 B1
Doggerel Acre CT5 ... 108 F7
Doggetts Cl TN8 ... 249 C8
Doggetts Row ME3 ... 27 B6
Dog Kennel La CT18 ... 305 B7
Dogwood Cl
Chatham ME5 ... 97 D1
Northfleet DA11 ... 36 F4
Dola Ave CT14 ... 215 B6
Dolphin Cl
Broadstairs CT10 ... 51 G3
Erith SE28 ... 3 D7
Dolphin Dr ME8 ... 98 E5
Dolphin Ho
1 Dover CT16 ... 310 E7
Rochester ME1 ... 63 E5
Dolphin La CT16 ... 310 E7
Dolphin Pas 3 CT16 ... 310 E7
Dolphin Pk ME10 ... 102 B5
Dolphin Pl 5 CT16 ... 310 E7
Dolphin Rd Lydd TN29 ... 376 C6
Sittingbourne ME10 ... 102 B5
Dolphins Rd CT19 ... 335 D7
Dolphin St Deal CT14 ... 215 D7
Herne Bay CT6 ... 76 E5
Dolphin Yard Sailing Barge Mus* ME10 ... 102 A5
Dombey Cl Higham ME3 ... 39 C3
Rochester ME1 ... 63 C3
Domneva Rd
Minster (Thanet) CT12 ... 115 B6
Westgate-on-S CT8 ... 81 D8
Domonic Dr SE9 ... 30 B5
Donald Biggs Dr DA12 ... 37 D8
Donald Moor Ave ME9 ... 103 C2
Donaldson Rd SE18 ... 12 A6
Donald Troup Ho ME1 ... 63 C4
Doncaster Cl 7 ME15 ... 195 F6
Donegal Rd CT1 ... 175 C8
Donemowe Dr ME10 ... 101 F8
Donet Cl ME8 ... 98 C5
Dongola Rd ME2 ... 40 B1
Donkey Field TN11 ... 220 E1
Donkey La
Adisham CT3 ... 210 C8
Appledore Heath TN26 ... 347 C2
Maplescombe DA4 ... 90 B8
Donkey St CT21,TN29 ... 352 E5
Donnahay Rd CT12 ... 83 C3
Donnington Ct 1 DA2 ... 16 B1
Donnington Rd TN13 ... 153 D7
Donnithorne Ho CT6 ... 76 E5
Doon Brae TN4 ... 254 A2
Dorado Gdns BR6 ... 87 D7
Doran Gr SE18 ... 12 E7
Dorcas Gdns CT10 ... 84 A6
Dorchester Ave DA5 ... 31 D8
Dorchester Cl
Cliffe Woods ME3 ... 40 B7
Dartford DA1 ... 33 F7
Orpington BR5 ... 31 B1
Dorchester Rd DA12 ... 37 D5
Dorchester TN1 ... 286 B6
Dorcis Ave DA7 ... 13 E5
Doreen Bird Coll (Birbeck Ctr) DA15 ... 31 A5
Doreen Bird Coll (Studio Ho) DA15 ... 31 A5
Doria Dr DA12 ... 37 F5
Doric Ave TN4 ... 253 F1
Doric Cl TN4 ... 253 F1
Doric Ct CT11 ... 117 C5
Dorin Ct TN2 ... 286 C3
Doris Ave DA8 ... 14 C6
Dorking Rd TN1 ... 286 C6
Dorman Ave N CT3 ... 210 E6
Dorman Ave S CT3 ... 210 F5
Dormers Dr DA13 ... 60 B2
Dornberg Cl SE3 ... 11 A7
Dornberg Rd SE3 ... 11 B7
Dornden Dr TN3 ... 285 A4
Dornden Gdns ME5 ... 97 B2
Dorne Cotts TN27 ... 232 E6
Dorney Rise BR5 ... 53 F5
Dorothy Ave TN17 ... 320 E4
Dorothy Dr CT12 ... 83 C2
Dorothy Evans Cl DA7 ... 14 B3
Dorrit Way
Chislehurst BR7 ... 30 C2
Rochester ME1 ... 63 D2
Dorset Ave DA16 ... 12 F3
Dorset Cl CT5 ... 108 B7
Dorset Cotts TN7 ... 311 B4
Dorset Cres DA12 ... 37 E4
Dorset Ct Deal CT14 ... 215 D2
Ramsgate CT12 ... 83 B2
Dorset Gdns
Birchington CT7 ... 80 F7
Deal CT14 ... 215 C2
Dorset Pl ME13 ... 138 C7
Dorset Rd Bromley SE9 ... 29 E6
Canterbury CT1 ... 175 D7
Royal Tunbridge Wells TN2 ... 286 D2
West Minst ME12 ... 46 A8
Dorset Road Inf Sch SE9 ... 29 E6
Dorset Sq ME8 ... 65 D1
Dorset St TN13 ... 154 C2
Dorset Way ME15 ... 195 C8
Dorton Dr TN15 ... 154 F5
Dorton House (Royal London Society Sch for the Blind) TN15 ... 154 F5
Dorton House Sch TN15 ... 154 F5
Dorville Rd SE12 ... 11 A2
Dossett Ct CT14 ... 215 A2
Dothill Rd SE18 ... 12 C7
Dotterel Cl ME5 ... 97 D2
Doubleday Dr ME9 ... 102 E2
Doubleton La TN11 ... 252 A5
Douglas Almshouses ME17 ... 199 D5
Douglas Ave
Hythe CT21 ... 333 C2
Whitstable CT5 ... 74 E1
Douglas Bglws CT15 ... 246 E8
Douglas Bldgs TN12 ... 260 E5
Douglas Cl CT10 ... 83 E5
Douglas Ct TN16 ... 118 E2
Douglas Rd Bexley DA16 ... 13 B6
Deal CT14 ... 215 A3
Dover CT17 ... 310 B8
Herne Bay CT6 ... 77 A4
Lenham ME17 ... 199 D5
Maidstone ME16 ... 161 E3
6 Newham E16 ... 1 A8
Tonbridge TN9 ... 254 A8
Douglas Terr CT14 ... 215 D5
Doug Siddons Ct 12 RM17 ... 18 C8
Dour Ho The 13 CT16 ... 310 D8
Dour Mews 12 CT16 ... 278 C1
Douro Cl CT1 ... 143 D1
Douro Pl CT16 ... 310 E7
Douro Stables TN4 ... 286 A4
Dour Side CT17 ... 277 F3
Dour St CT16 ... 310 D8
Doust Way ME1 ... 63 D5
Dove App E6 ... 1 E8
Dove Cl Chatham ME5 ... 97 B6
Herne CT6 ... 110 E7
Hythe CT21 ... 353 D8
Kingsnorth TN23 ... 300 C3
Whitstable CT5 ... 108 C7
Dovecote Ct CT4 ... 205 B8
Dove Ct 6 CT11 ... 117 E7
Dovedale CT7 ... 81 B7
Dovedale Cl DA16 ... 13 A5
Dovedale Ct
Ashford TN24 ... 268 B4
Birchington CT7 ... 81 B7
Dovedale Rd DA2 ... 34 C7
Dove Lea Gdns CT17 ... 277 E3
Doveney Cl BR5 ... 54 D6
Dover Castle & Princess of Wales Regiment Mus* CT16 ... 310 F8
Dover Coll CT17 ... 310 C8
Dove Rd TN10 ... 222 C6
Dover Gram Sch for Boys CT17 ... 310 A8
Dover Gram Sch for Girls CT16 ... 278 C1
Dover Hill CT19 ... 335 F8
Dover Ho
2 Maidstone ME15 ... 195 E8
Rochester ME2 ... 40 C1
Dover Mus* CT16 ... 310 D7
Dover Patrol SE3 ... 11 B5
Dover Patrol Meml* CT15 ... 280 C7
Dover Pl TN23 ... 268 C1
Dover Priory Sta CT17 ... 310 C8
Dover Rd Barham CT4 ... 210 A1
Bishopsbourne CT4 ... 209 D5
Dover CT15 ... 278 E4
Dover Rd E DA11 ... 36 F7
Dover Rd
Folkestone CT19,CT20 ... 335 E7
Northfleet DA11 ... 36 D8
Ringwould CT14 ... 248 A6
St Margaret's at Cliffe CT15 ... 279 D6
Sandwich CT13 ... 180 F6
Tilmanstone CT13,CT14 ... 213 B5
Woolage Green CT4 ... 243 D6
Woolwich DA16 ... 12 C5
Dover Road Com Prim Sch DA11 ... 36 E7
Dover St
Canterbury CT1 ... 175 A7
Maidstone ME16 ... 161 C2
1 Sittingbourne ME10 ... 101 E4
Doves Cl BR2 ... 85 E8
Doves Cnr CT14 ... 213 A4
Dowding Ho TN12 ... 256 F6
Dowding Rd TN16 ... 118 D4
Dowding Way TN2 ... 254 E1
Dowding Wlk 3 DA11 ... 36 E5
Dowell Mews CT14 ... 215 C3
Dower Ho The DA14 ... 31 F5
Dower House Cres TN4 ... 253 E3
Dowgate Cl TN9 ... 254 D7
Dowle Cl TN29 ... 372 A7
Dowlerville Rd BR6 ... 86 F4
Dowling Cl ME6 ... 127 E7
Dowling Ho DA17 ... 3 F3
Downage The DA11 ... 37 A6
Downash Ct TN5 ... 339 A3
Downash Ho TN5 ... 339 A3
Down Ave TN3 ... 317 A4
Downbank Ave DA7 ... 14 D5
Down Barton Farm Cotts CT7 ... 79 D1
Down Barton Rd CT7 ... 79 E1
Down Court Rd ME9 ... 135 C1
Down Ct TN23 ... 299 E5
Downderry Way ME20 ... 128 B1
Downe Ave TN14 ... 119 D8
Downe Cl DA16 ... 13 C7
Downe Ho 10 SE7 ... 11 C8
Downend SE18 ... 12 B7
Downe Prim Sch BR6 ... 96 E8
Downer Ct ME1 ... 96 E8
Downe Rd
Cudham BR6,TN14 ... 119 C5
Farthing Street BR2 ... 85 E2
Downham Way BR1 ... 29 A4
Downhill Cl CT16 ... 277 D6
Down House Mus* BR6 ... 119 A7
Downings E6 ... 2 A7
Downings The CT6 ... 77 A2
Down La TN3 ... 314 B1
Downland Ct TN24 ... 268 B3
Downlands Deal CT14 ... 248 B8
Harrietsham ME17 ... 198 F6
Downleys Cl SE9 ... 29 F6
Downman Rd SE9 ... 11 E4
Downs Ave Bromley BR7 ... 29 F3
Dartford DA1 ... 34 A8
Whitstable CT5 ... 74 E1
Downs CE Prim Sch The CT14 ... 215 B2
Downs Cl Charing TN27 ... 234 C8
East Studdal CT15 ... 246 D8
Hawkinge CT18 ... 307 A4
Down's Cl TN27 ... 262 E5
Downs Cl
Maidstone ME14 ... 162 B8
Sittingbourne ME10 ... 101 D2
Downs Ct ME18 ... 193 B3
Downside
Bekesbourne CT4 ... 176 E3
Folkestone CT19 ... 335 C7
Downside Rd CT16 ... 278 B7
Downside
Rochester ME2 ... 63 A7
St Margaret's at Cliffe CT15 ... 280 A6
Downsland Ho ME2 ... 62 C2
Downs Pk CT6 ... 77 A5
Downs Rd
Canterbury CT2 ... 142 F4
Deal CT14 ... 215 C3
East Studdal CT15 ... 246 E8
Folkestone CT19 ... 335 C7
Istead Rise DA13 ... 36 D3
Maidstone ME14 ... 162 B8
Ramsgate CT11 ... 117 B6
Yalding ME18 ... 193 A1
Downs The
Chartham CT4 ... 173 E1
Chatham ME5 ... 96 D1
Preston CT3 ... 146 C6
Ramsgate CT11 ... 117 D5
Downs Valley DA3 ... 58 E5
Downs View ME1 ... 95 F1
Downsview ME5 ... 97 C8
Downs View Cl BR6 ... 87 C1
Downsview Cl BR8 ... 55 F6
Downs View Inf Sch TN24 ... 268 E7
Downsview Prim Sch BR8 ... 56 A6
Downs View Rd ME14 ... 162 B8
Downsview Rd TN13 ... 153 F2
Downsview ME19 ... 126 A5
Downs View ME19 ... 159 B8
Downs Way TN27 ... 234 C8
Downsway BR6 ... 86 E5
Downs Way TN25 ... 303 C1
Downs Wood DA13 ... 125 F8
Downton Cotts TN18 ... 355 F4
Doyle Cl DA8 ... 14 E6
Doyle Way RM18 ... 19 C5
Drage Rd TN12 ... 224 E6
Dragonfly Cl TN23 ... 299 D8
Dragonfly Way CT18 ... 307 B4
Dragoon Ho 10 CT1 ... 143 A1
Drainless Rd CT13 ... 180 A5
Drake Ave ME12 ... 47 D5
Drake Cres SE28 ... 3 C7
Drake Ct Orpington BR5 ... 54 B3
3 Ramsgate CT11 ... 117 F8
Drake Hall E16 ... 1 B5
Drake Mews BR2 ... 52 C5
Drake Point 12 DA8 ... 4 E1
Drake Rd TN24 ... 301 B7
Drake's Ave ME2 ... 62 F8
Drakes Cl ME9 ... 66 E2
Drakes Lee TN28 ... 373 E5
Draper Cl DA17 ... 3 F2
Draper Ct BR1 ... 52 E5
Drapers Almshouses CT9 ... 83 A8
Drapers Ave CT9 ... 82 F8
Drapers Cl CT9 ... 83 A8
Drapers Mills Prim Sch CT9 ... 83 A8
Draper St 3 TN4 ... 253 F2
Drapers Windmill* CT9 ... 51 A1
Drawbridge Cl ME15 ... 195 E8
Drawell Cl SE18 ... 2 E1
Dray Corner Rd TN27 ... 261 F7
Dray Ct TN11 ... 223 E8
Drays Cotts DA4 ... 57 B5
Dray's Field ME9 ... 166 A7
Drayton Ave BR6 ... 53 B1
Drayton Cl ME23 ... 23 E4
Drayton Rd TN9 ... 254 C8
Dreadnought Ave ME12 ... 47 A6
Dreamland Family Fun Pk* CT9 ... 50 I2
Dresden Ct CT8 ... 81 D8
Drewery Dr ME8 ... 98 C5
Drew La CT14 ... 215 C4
Drew Prim Sch E16 ... 1 E5
Drew Rd E16 ... 1 E5
Driffield Gdns TN9 ... 253 F7
Drift The BR2 ... 85 D7
Drill La CT3 ... 145 B1
Drive The Ashurst TN3 ... 283 F5
Bexley DA5 ... 31 D8
Broadstairs CT10 ... 83 F6
Canterbury CT1 ... 175 B6
Chislehurst BR7 ... 53 E8
Deal CT14 ... 215 C5
Erith DA8 ... 14 B8
Gravesend DA12 ... 37 E4
New Barn DA3 ... 59 B6
Orpington BR6 ... 86 F8
Royal Tunbridge Wells TN2 ... 286 B1
St Paul's Cray BR7 ... 53 F6
Sevenoaks TN13 ... 154 B3
Sidcup DA14 ... 31 B4
Tonbridge TN9 ... 254 B7
Whitstable CT5 ... 109 D8
Drop Redoubt Fort* CT17 ... 310 D7
Drop Redoubt Rd CT17 ... 310 D7
Drove Rd ME12 ... 46 E7
Drovers Rdbt TN24 ... 268 A4
Drove The
Fordwich CT2 ... 144 A4
Monkton CT12 ... 114 B6
Northbourne CT14 ... 214 A5
Whitfield CT16 ... 278 A8
Whitstable CT5 ... 109 D8
Droveway Gdns CT15 ... 280 A6
Drove Way The DA13 ... 36 E1
Droveway The CT15 ... 280 B6
Drudgeon Way DA2 ... 35 B5
Druidstone Wildlife Pk* CT2 ... 141 F7
Drum La TN23 ... 268 B2
Drum Major Dr CT14 ... 215 B3
Drummond Cl DA8 ... 14 E6
Drury Rd TN30 ... 324 B1
Dry Bank Ct TN10 ... 222 C4
Dry Bank Rd TN10 ... 222 C4
Drybeck Ave CT11 ... 116 F7
Dryden Cl CT1 ... 175 C7
Dryden Ho BR2 ... 52 D4
Dryden Pl RM18 ... 19 B6
Dryden Rd Bexley DA16 ... 12 F6
Dover CT16 ... 278 B3
Dryden Way BR6 ... 54 A1
Dry End Rd ME20 ... 128 C3
Dryhill La TN14 ... 153 B3
Dry Hill Park Cres TN10 ... 222 C3
Dry Hill Park Rd TN10 ... 222 B3
Dryhill Rd DA17 ... 13 F8
Dry Hill Rd TN9 ... 222 B3
Dryland Ave 6 BR6 ... 86 F6
Dryland Rd
Borough Green TN15 ... 156 F6
Snodland ME6 ... 127 F8
Drywall Ind Est ME10 ... 102 B6
Dublin Ho 16 ME15 ... 195 E7
Duchess Cl ME2 ... 62 E8
Duchess of Kent Ct The ME20 ... 128 F1
Duchess Of Kent Dr ME5 ... 97 B3
Duchess' Wlk TN15 ... 154 E2
Ducie Ho 9 SE7 ... 11 C8
Ducketts Rd DA1 ... 14 F2
Duck La
Canterbury CT1 ... 143 A1
Shadoxhurst TN26 ... 326 F7
Duckpits Rd CT4 ... 240 A6
Duck St CT4 ... 273 F4
Duckworth Cl TN24 ... 301 B7
Duddington Cl SE9 ... 29 D4
Dudely Rd DA11 ... 36 E8
Dudley Ave CT8 ... 81 C8
Dudley Keen Ct TN9 ... 254 E8
Dudley Lodge TN2 ... 286 C4
Dudley Rd
Ashford TN24 ... 268 E5
Folkestone CT19 ... 335 E5
Royal Tunbridge Wells TN1 ... 286 A4
Dudsbury Rd
Dartford DA1 ... 15 B2
Sidcup DA14 ... 31 B2
Duggan Dr BR7 ... 29 E2
Duke of Clarence Trad Est The ME12 ... 28 A3
Duke Of Wellington Ave SE18,SE28 ... 2 C3
Duke of York's Royal Military Sch CT15 ... 278 F4
Dukes Mdw TN26 ... 349 A7
Dukes Meadow TN11 ... 219 F2
Dukes Meadow Dr ME7 ... 97 F6
Dukes Orch DA5 ... 32 C7
Dukes Rd TN1 ... 286 C5
Duke St Deal CT14 ... 215 D7
Margate CT9 ... 50 I3
Dukes Wlk 7 ME15 ... 162 A4
Dukeswood CT5 ... 109 D6
Dully Rd Lynsted ME9 ... 135 E6
Sittingbourne ME9 ... 102 E1
Dulverton Prim Sch SE9 ... 30 D6
Dulverton Rd SE9 ... 30 D6
Dulwich Prep Sch TN17 ... 321 A4
Dumbourne La TN30 ... 345 D2
Dumbreck Rd SE9 ... 12 A4
Dumergue Ave ME11 ... 46 B5
Dumpton Gap Rd CT10 ... 84 A2
Dumpton La CT11 ... 83 E1
Dumpton Park Dr CT10, CT11 ... 84 A2

Dumpton Park Rd
CT11 117 E8
Dumpton Park Sta
CT11 83 F1
Dunbar Ct BR2 52 A5
Dunblane Rd SE9 11 E5
Duncan Cl CT5 108 D7
Duncan Dr CT7 80 E8
Duncan Ho 2 SE7 11 B8
Duncan Rd
Gillingham ME7 64 D5
Ramsgate CT11 117 D7
Whitstable CT5 108 D7
Duncans Cotts 6
TN16 151 D1
Duncroft SE18 12 E7
Dundale Rd TN12,TN3 288 A3
Dundonald Cl 7 E6 1 E7
Dundonald Rd
11 Broadstairs CT10 84 B4
Ramsgate CT11 117 C7
Dunedin Cl ME10 101 C3
Dunedin Dr CT16 278 B3
Dunedin Ho
9 Maidstone ME15 195 E5
Newham E16 1 F5
2 Tilbury RM18 19 A5
Dunedin Rd CT12 83 A1
Dunera Dr ME14 162 A7
Dunes Rd TN28 373 D3
Dunes The CT13 182 A7
Dungeness Nature National
Reserve* TN29 380 B4
Dungeness Rd TN29 380 A7
Dungeness Sta*
TN29 380 D2
Dunkeld Ho 6 ME15 195 E7
Dunkery Rd SE9 29 E5
Dunkery Rise TN24 268 B4
Dunkin Rd DA1 16 A3
Dunkirk Cl
Dymchurch TN29 366 B7
Gravesend DA12 37 C3
Dunkirk Dr ME5 96 F6
Dunkirk Rd N ME13 140 B2
Dunkirk Rd S ME13 140 B1
Dunkirk Sq CT15 278 F3
Dunkirk Village Sch
ME13 140 D2
Dunkley Villas TN15 125 F1
Dunk's Green Rd
TN11 190 A5
Dunlin Ct TN29 366 A3
Dunlin Dr ME4 41 C2
Dunlop Ct 7 TN18 341 A2
Dunlop Rd RM18 18 F6
Dunnett Rd CT19 334 E6
Dunning's La ME1 63 C4
Dunnings The ME16 161 A2
Dunn Lodge TN2 286 D2
Dunnock Rd
Ashford TN25 268 B7
Newham E6 1 E7
Dunnose Ct RM19 16 B8
Dunn Street Rd ME7 131 A8
Dunoon Cotts BR6 119 A5
Dunoon Ct CT11 83 F1
Dunorlan Farm Cotts
TN2 286 E4
Dunorlan Farm TN2 286 E4
Dunstable Ct 5 SE3 11 A7
Dunstall Cl TN29 366 A5
Dunstall Gdns TN29 366 A5
Dunstall La TN29 366 A5
Dunstall Welling Est
DA16 13 B5
Dunstan Ave CT8 81 D7
Dunstan Glade BR5 53 D3
Dunstan Gr TN4 286 B6
Dunstan Ho CT14 215 D8
Dunstan Rd TN4 286 B6
Dunster Ct 16 DA2 16 B1
Dunster Terr 3 ME15 195 E8
Dunton Green Prim Sch
TN13 153 E7
Dunton Green Sta
TN13 153 F7
Dunvegan Rd SE9 11 F3
Dunwich Rd DA7 13 F6
Dupree Rd SE7 1 B1
Durant Rd BR8 33 A2
Durban Cl CT12 83 A2
Durban Cres CT16 278 C4
Durban Ho 7 ME15 195 E5
Durban Rd CT9 51 A1
Durham Cl
Canterbury CT1 174 F6
9 Dover CT17 310 D7
Maidstone ME15 162 E1
Durham Hill CT17 310 D7
Durham Rd Bromley BR2 52 A5
Gillingham ME8 98 C7
Sidcup DA14 31 B3
Durham Rise SE18 2 D1
Duriun Way DA8 15 B7
Durley Gdns BR6 87 B7
Durling Ct ME8 66 A1
Durlings Orch TN15 156 D6
Durlock Ave CT11 117 B5
Durlock CT12 115 C5
Durlock Rd CT3 179 B7
Durlocks The CT19 335 E5
Durndale La
Northfleet DA11 36 E4
Northfleet DA11 36 F5
Durnford Cl CT2 142 E2
Durovernum Ct CT1 175 A7
Durrant Way
Orpington BR6 86 D5
Swanscombe DA10 35 E8
Durrell Gdns ME5 64 C1
Dursley Cl SE3 11 C5
Dursley Gdns SE3 11 D6
Dursley Rd SE3 11 C5
Duval Dr ME1 96 E8
Duvard's Pl ME9 100 F1
Duxberry Cl BR2 52 E4
Dux Court Rd ME23 23 D2
Duxford Ho 12 SE2 3 D4
Dux Hill TN15 189 F8
Dux La TN15 156 F1
Dwelly La TN8 216 D3
Dyke Dr BR5 54 C2
Dyke Rd CT19 335 E5
Dykewood Cl DA5 32 E5
Dylan Rd DA17 4 A3
Dymchurch Cl BR6 86 E6
Dymchurch Ho 1
CT1 175 B8
Dymchurch Prim Sch
TN29 366 C8
Dymchurch Rd
Hythe CT21,TN29 353 C6
St Mary's Bay TN29,
TN28 366 A5
Dymchurch Sta*
TN29 366 B7
Dyneley Rd SE12 29 C5
Dynes Rd TN15 122 E2
Dynevor Rd TN4 286 C7
Dyngley Cl ME10 101 E6

E

Eadred Way ME10 69 A1
Eagle Cl ME20 128 A2
Eagle Cotts 8 CT11 117 D7
Eagle Heights Bird of Prey
Ctr* DA4 89 B8
Eagle Hill CT11 117 D7
Eagle Ho RM17 17 F8
Eagles Cl ME10 102 C4
Eagles Dr TN16 118 D1
Eaglesfield Rd SE18 12 B6
Eaglesfield Sch SE18 12 A6
Eagles Rd DA9 17 B2
Eaglestone Cl TN15 157 A8
Eagle Way DA11 18 A2
Ealdham Prim Sch SE9 11 C3
Ealdham Sq SE9 11 C3
Ealham Cl
Ashford TN24 301 A8
Canterbury CT4 175 B5
Ealing Cl ME5 97 C4
Eardemont Cl DA1 14 F3
Eardley Point 2 SE18 2 B2
Eardley Rd Erith DA17 4 A1
Sevenoaks TN13 154 B3
Earl Cl ME5 97 B4
Earl Rd DA11 36 E6
Earl Rise SE18 2 D2
Earls Ave TN24 268 F1
Earl's Ave CT20 335 B4
Earlsfield TN25 330 A6
Earlsfield Rd CT21 333 D2
Earlshall Rd SE9 12 A3
Earlsmead Cres CT12 116 C5
Earl's Rd TN4 285 F4
Earl St ME14 161 F4
Earlsworth Ct TN24 300 E6
Earlsworth Rd TN24 300 D6
Easole Hts CT15 211 D5
Easole St CT15 211 D5
Eason Villas TN12 259 D6
East Beckton District Ctr
E6 1 F8
East Blean Wood (Nature
Reserve)* CT3,CT6 111 B6
East Borough Prim Sch
ME14 162 B5
Eastbridge Rd TN29 366 B8
Eastbrook Pl CT16 310 E8
Eastbrook Rd SE3 11 B6
Eastbury Rd Newham E6 2 A8
Orpington BR5 53 D3
Eastchurch CE Prim Sch
ME12 48 E4
Eastchurch Holiday Camp
ME12 48 F5
Eastchurch Rd
Margate CT9 51 E3
Minster (Sheppey) ME12 48 B5
East Cliff CT16 310 F8
Eastcliffe Hts 7 CT20 335 E5
East Cliff CT19 335 E5
East Cliff Gdns 22
CT19 335 E5
East Cliff Par CT6 77 A5
East Cliff Pas 23 CT19 335 E5
East Cliff Rd TN4 286 A6
East Cliff & Warren Ctry
Pk* CT18 308 D1
Eastcombe Ave SE7 11 B8
Eastcote BR6 53 F1
Eastcote Prim Sch
DA16 12 D4
Eastcote Rd DA16 12 D5
Eastcourt Gn ME8 65 B4
Eastcourt La
Gillingham ME7,ME8 65 B4
Gillingham ME8 65 B3
East Court Sch CT11 117 G7
East Crescent Rd DA12 19 C1
East Cross TN30 345 B7
East Ct 4 ME15 162 A1
East Dr BR5 54 B3
East End Rd ME4,ME7 64 D8
Easterfields ME19 160 C5
Eastern Arm N CT16 310 H8
Eastern Arm S CT16 310 H8
Eastern Ave
Ashford TN23 268 A2
Halfway Houses ME12 46 D6
Queenborough ME11 46 B4
West Thurrock RM20 16 F8
Eastern Espl
Broadstairs CT10 84 B5
Margate CT9 51 B3
Eastern Gdns TN24 300 E8
Eastern Holiday Camp
ME12 49 G2
Eastern Rd
Gillingham ME7 64 F6
Leysdown-on-S ME12 49 G2
Lydd TN29 376 D7
Eastern Service Rd
CT16 310 H8
Eastern View TN16 118 C2
Eastern Way Erith SE28 3 D5
1 Grays RM17 18 A8
East Farleigh Prim Sch
ME15 194 B6
East Farleigh Sta
ME16 194 B8
Eastfield Gdns TN10 222 E5
Eastfield Ho ME16 161 B2
Eastfield Rd 1 CT7 81 A7
Eastfields CT19 335 D6
East Fleet Cvn Pk
TN29 353 A4
Eastgate Cl Erith SE28 3 D7
Herne Bay CT6 77 B3
Eastgate Ct ME1 63 C5
Eastgate Rd TN30 345 C8
Eastgate ME1 63 C5
Eastgate Terr ME1 63 C5
East Gn ME10 69 A1
East Hall Hill ME17 228 E7
East Hall La ME10 102 C5
East Hall Rd BR5 54 F2
East Ham Ind Est E6 1 E8
East Ham Manor Way
E6 2 A7
East Hill Ashford TN24 268 C2
Biggin Hill TN16 118 B1
Dartford DA1 33 F8
East Hill Dr DA1 33 F8
East Hill Farm Cvn Pk
TN15 90 C1
East Hill Farm Pk TN15 90 B1
East Hill Rd TN15 123 B7
East Hill Sutton at H DA4 57 D7
Tenterden TN30 345 B8
East Ho DA1 15 F4
East Holme DA8 14 D6
East Kent Ave DA11 18 C1
East Kent Light Rly*
CT15 245 A7
East Kent Light Rly*
CT15 244 E6
East Kent Ret Pk CT10 83 B4
Eastland Ct 3 BR1 52 C7
Eastlands Cl TN4 313 E8
Eastlands Rd TN4 285 E1
East Langdon Rd
Guston CT15 278 F7
Martin Mill CT15 247 B2
East La Sheerness ME12 28 A2
Sutton at H DA4 57 D7
Eastleigh Rd DA7 14 C4
Eastling Cl ME8 65 D3
Eastling Ho 8 BR5 54 D1
Eastling Prim Sch
ME13 168 F5
Eastling Rd
Eastling ME13 168 F7
Painters Forstal ME13 137 D2
East Lodge Rd TN23 267 F3
East Malling Research Sta
(Horticultural) ME19 160 C6
East Malling Sta
ME19 160 A6
East Mascalls 17 SE7 11 C8
Eastmead Ave TN23 300 C8
Eastmead Cl BR1 52 E7
East Mill DA11 18 F1
East Milton Rd DA12 37 D8
Eastmoor Pl SE7 1 D3
Eastmoor St SE7 1 D3
East Mountain La
TN24 268 F7
East Norman Rd CT16 278 E1
Eastnor Rd SE9 30 C7
East Northdown Cl CT9 51 E1
Easton's Cnr TN25 329 F4
East Park Rd ME20 161 A8
East Peckham Prim Sch
TN12 224 E7
East Point TN15 155 A6
East Ramp CT16 310 G8
East Rd Bexley DA16 13 B5
Chatham ME4 64 A7
Folkestone CT20 334 D4
Sandwich CT13 149 A8
East Rochester Way
Coldblow DA1 32 D8
Sidcup DA5,DA15 13 C1
East Roman Ditch
CT16 310 F8
East Row ME1 63 C5
Eastry CE Prim Sch
CT13 180 B2
Eastry Cl Ashford TN23 300 A6
Maidstone ME16 161 C7
Eastry Ct CT3 210 F5
Eastry Mews CT13 180 B2
Eastry Pk CT13 180 C1
Eastry Rd DA8 14 A7
East St Addington ME19 126 D3
Ashford TN23 268 B2
Bexley DA7 14 A3
Bromley BR1 52 A7
Canterbury CT1 143 C3
Chatham ME4 64 A3
Dover CT17 310 C8
Faversham ME13 138 D7
Folkestone CT19 335 E5
Gillingham ME7 64 D6
East St *continued*
Grays RM20 17 E8
Harrietsham ME17 198 E5
Herne Bay CT6 77 A5
Hunton ME15 226 F7
Hythe CT21 333 D2
East Stour Ct TN24 268 D1
East Stour Prim Sch
TN24 300 D6
East Stour Way TN24 300 D6
East Street N ME19 126 D3
East St
Sittingbourne ME10 102 A4
Snodland ME6 128 B8
Tonbridge TN9 222 C2
East Sutton Park (HM
Young Offender Inst &
Prison) ME17 230 B7
East Sutton Rd
Sutton Valence ME17 230 A7
Sutton Valence ME17,
TN27 230 C4
East Terr
Gravesend DA12 19 C1
Sidcup DA15 30 E7
East Thamesmead Bsns Pk
DA18 3 F4
East Thurrock Rd
RM17 18 C8
Eastview Ave SE18 12 E7
East View
Brookland TN29 370 D8
Hersden CT3 111 F1
Eastway BR2 52 A2
East Weald Dr TN30 324 B1
Eastwell Barn Mews
TN30 345 A8
Eastwell Cl
Maidstone ME14 162 C5
Paddock Wood TN12 256 E6
Shadoxhurst TN26 299 B1
Eastwell Mdws TN30 345 A8
Eastwell 5 TN30 345 A7
Eastwell Terr TN25 236 E3
East Wickham Inf Sch
DA16 12 F6
East Wickham Jun Sch
DA16 13 A6
Eastwood Cotts ME9 103 E6
Eastwood Rd
Eastwood ME17 231 C5
Sittingbourne ME10 101 D5
East Woodside DA5 31 E7
East Wootton Cotts
CT4 207 A4
Eaton Ct BR7 30 C2
Eaton Hill CT9 50 I2
Eaton Rd Dover CT17 310 B7
Margate CT9 50 I1
Sidcup DA14 31 D6
Eaton Sq DA3 58 D6
Eaves Ct ME10 102 B5
Eaves Rd CT17 310 A7
Ebbsfleet Ind Est DA11 18 A2
Ebbsfleet La CT12 116 A3
Ebbsfleet Wlk DA11 18 B1
Ebdon Way SE3 11 B4
Ebony Cotts TN30 360 A6
Ebony Wlk ME16 161 B3
Ebury Cl BR2 85 E7
Eccles Row ME20 128 F6
Eccleston Cl BR6 53 D1
Eccleston Rd ME15 161 F2
Echo Cl ME15 195 F6
Echo Ct DA12 37 C6
Echo Ho ME10 102 B3
Echo Sq DA12 37 C6
Echo Wlk ME12 47 D6
Eckford Cl CT18 306 F4
Eclipse Dr ME10 101 E8
Eclipse Rd E13 1 B8
Edam Ct 11 DA14 31 A5
Eddie Willet Rd CT6 76 B3
Eddington Cl ME15 195 B6
Eddington La CT6 76 F3
Eddington Way CT6 76 E3
Eden Ave ME5 97 A7
Edenbridge Cl BR5 54 D5
Edenbridge & District War
Meml Hospl TN8 249 D7
Edenbridge Dr ME12 46 B8
Edenbridge Ho 2
CT1 175 B8
Edenbridge Prim Sch
TN8 217 D1
Edenbridge Rd TN7 282 E1
Edenbridge Sta TN8 217 C3
Edenbridge Town Sta
TN8 217 D2
Edenbridge Trad Ctr
TN8 249 D8
Eden Cl DA5 32 D4
Eden Ct
1 Hawkhurst TN18 340 F2
17 Orpington BR5 54 D1
Tonbridge TN10 222 C5
Edendale Rd DA7 14 D5
Eden Farm La ME19 159 D8
Edenfield CT7 81 B7
Eden Ho TN23 300 C8
Eden Holiday Camp
ME12 49 A5
Edenhurst TN13 154 A2
Eden Pl DA12 37 B8
Eden Rd
High Halstow ME23 23 E4
Joyden's Wood DA5 32 D4
Royal Tunbridge Wells
TN1 286 A2
Whitstable CT5 108 A7
Edensmuir Ct SE3 11 A7
Eden Valley Mus*
TN8 217 C1
Eden Villas TN8 249 D7
Eden Wlk 9 TN1 286 A2
Edgar Cl Swanley BR8 55 F6
Whitstable CT5 75 D3
Edgar Ho CT14 215 B3
Edgar Rd
Canterbury CT1 143 B1
Dover CT17 278 B1
Kemsing TN15 122 E2
Margate CT9 51 A3
Minster (Thanet) CT12 115 B6
Tatsfield TN16 150 D6
Edgeborough Way BR1 52 D8
Edgebury BR7,SE9 30 B4
Edgebury Prim Sch
BR7 30 C4
Edgebury Wlk BR7 30 C5
Edge End Rd CT10 83 F4
Edgefield Cl DA1 34 B7
Edgehill Cl CT20 334 D4
Edge Hill Ct DA14 30 F4
Edgehill Gdns DA13 59 F8
Edgehill Rd BR7 30 C4
Edge Hill SE18 12 B8
Edgeler Ct ME6 127 F7
Edger Pl 5 ME15 162 A4
Edgeway ME4 41 B2
Edgewood Dr BR6 87 A5
Edgeworth Rd SE9 11 D3
Edgington Way DA14 31 D1
Edinburgh Ct DA8 14 D7
Edinburgh Ho
Deal CT14 215 A5
7 Dover CT17 310 D7
Edinburgh Mews RM18 19 B5
Edinburgh Pl 7 CT20 335 B3
Edinburgh Rd
Ashford TN24 268 B2
Chatham ME4 64 C2
Gillingham ME7 64 D5
Grain ME3 27 B5
Margate CT9 82 B8
Edinburgh Sq ME15 195 C7
Edinburgh Wlk 5 CT9 82 B8
Edington Rd SE2 3 B3
Edisbury Wlk ME8 98 D5
Edison Gr SE18 12 F7
Edison Rd Bexley DA16 12 F6
2 Bromley BR2 52 A7
Edith Cavell Way SE18 11 E6
Edith Ct BR1 52 D6
Edith Pond Ct SE9 30 B6
Edith Rd
Faversham ME13 138 C6
Orpington BR6 87 A5
Ramsgate CT11 117 C6
Westgate-on-S CT8 50 D1
Ediva Rd DA13 60 A4
Edmanson Ave CT9 50 E1
Edmund Cl
Maidstone ME16 161 A3
Meopham Station DA13 60 A4
Edmund Hurst Dr E6 2 B8
Edmund Rd Bexley DA16 13 A4
Orpington BR5 54 C3
Edmunds Ave BR5 54 D6
Edmund St CT3 178 A8
Edna Rd ME14 161 F8
Edred Rd CT17 310 B8
Edward Ct Chatham ME5 64 C1
2 Newham E16 1 A8
Edward Dr CT7 81 B7
Edward Harvey Ct DA17 3 F1
Edward Rd
Biggin Hill TN16 118 E1
Bromley BR1 29 C1
Canterbury CT1 175 A8
Chislehurst BR7 30 B3
Folkestone CT19 335 D6
Kingsdown CT14 248 C6
Queenborough ME11 46 B5
Edwards Cl ME8 98 C5
Edwards Ct DA4 89 E7
Edwards Gdns BR8 55 D5
Edwards Rd
Dover CT16 310 D8
Erith DA17 4 A2
Edward St Chatham ME4 64 A3
Rochester ME2 63 B7
Royal Tunbridge Wells
TN4 285 F8
Rusthall TN4 285 C4
Sheerness ME12 28 A3
Edward Terr 9 CT20 335 E6
Edward Tyler Rd SE12 29 C6
Edward Wlk ME19 159 F8
Edwina Ave ME12 47 A7
Edwin Arnold Ct DA15 30 F4
Edwin Cl DA7 13 F8
Edwin Petty Pl DA2 34 C8
Edwin Rd Dartford DA2 33 C5
Gillingham ME8 98 C8
Edwins Pl ME9 100 C7
Edwin St
Gravesend DA12 37 B8
Newham E16 1 A8
Edyngham Cl ME10 102 A8
Effingham Cres CT17 310 D8
Effingham St
Dover CT17 310 D8
Ramsgate CT11 117 E6
Egbert Rd
Birchington CT7 80 D8
Faversham ME13 138 C6
Minster (Thanet) CT12 115 B6
Westgate-on-S CT8 50 C1
Egdean Wlk TN13 154 C4
Egerton Ave BR8 55 F8
Egerton CE Prim Sch
TN27 232 F3
Egerton Cl DA1 33 B7
Egerton Dr CT9 51 E2
Egerton House Rd
TN27 232 E4
Egerton Rd
Charing Heath TN27 233 C7
Maidstone ME14 161 E7
Pluckley TN27 233 B1
Temple Ewell CT16 277 E5
Eggarton La CT4 205 C2
Eggpie La TN11,TN14 220 E7
Eggringe TN23 267 E1
Egham Rd E13 1 B8
Eglantine La DA4 57 B3
Eglinton Hill SE18 12 B7
Eglinton Prim Sch
SE18 12 A8
Eglinton Rd
Swanscombe DA10 17 F1
Woolwich SE18 12 B8
Egremont Rd ME15 162 F2
Egret Cl ME4 41 B2
Eider Cl CT6 76 D2
Eighteen Acre La
TN29 371 D8
Eileen Ct BR7 30 A3
Eisenhower Dr E6 1 E8
Elaine Ave ME2 62 E7
Elaine Ct ME2 62 E6
Elaine Prim Sch ME2 62 E6
Elbourne Trad Est DA17 4 B3
Elbury Dr E16 1 A7
Elder Cl
Kingswood ME17 197 D2
Sidcup DA15 30 F7
Elder Ct ME8 98 D6
Elderslie Rd SE9 12 A2
Elders The CT3 144 F1
Eldon Pl 4 CT10 84 B4
Eldon St ME4 64 A4
Eldon Way TN12 256 F7
Eldred Dr BR5 87 D8
Eleanor Dr ME10 101 E8
Eleanor Smith Sch E16 1 C8
Eleanor Wlk 10 SE18 1 F2
Elford Cl SE3 11 C3
Elford Rd ME3 22 B5
Elfrida Cl CT9 83 C8
Elgal Cl BR6 86 B5
Elgar Bretts Ct 10 CT1 174 F7
Elgar Cl TN10 222 E6
Elgar Gdns RM18 19 B6
Elgar Pl CT11 117 D7
Elgin Gdns ME2 62 D5
Elham CE Prim Sch
CT4 273 F4
Elham Cl Bromley BR1 29 D1
Gillingham ME8 65 B3
Margate CT9 51 C1
Elham Rd CT1 174 E6
Elham Valley Railway
Mus* CT18 334 A8
Elham Valley Vineyards*
CT4 242 D4
Elham Way CT10 84 A2
Elibank Rd SE9 12 A3
Eling Ct ME15 195 A8
Eliot Coll CT2 142 E4
Eliot Rd DA1 16 B2
Elizabethan Ct TN27 234 C7
Elizabeth Carter Ave
CT14 214 F4
Elizabeth Cl RM18 19 B5
Elizabeth Cotts DA4 89 E8
Elizabeth Ct
Broadstairs CT10 84 B6
Canterbury CT1 175 B6
Chatham ME5 97 A7
Dartford DA2 34 D3
Erith DA8 14 D7
Gillingham ME8 65 C1
6 Gravesend DA11 19 A1
Herne Bay CT6 76 F5
Elizabeth Dr CT18 308 B2
Elizabeth Fry Pl SE18 11 E6
Elizabeth Garlick Ct 1
TN1 286 B4
Elizabeth Garrett Anderson
Ho 9 DA17 4 A3
Elizabeth Gdns CT21 333 B1
Elizabeth Ho
Maidstone ME14 162 A6
Rochester ME1 63 C4
Elizabeth Huggins Cotts
DA11 37 B6
Elizabeth Kemp Ct
CT12 83 C1
Elizabeth Pl DA4 56 E3
Elizabeth Rd CT11 117 F6
Elizabeth Smith's Ct
ME19 159 F7
Elizabeth St
Dover CT17 310 D6
Stone DA9 16 E2
Elizabeth Terr SE9 11 F1
Elizabeth Way
Herne Bay CT6 77 B3
Orpington BR5 54 C4
Eliza Cook Cl DA9 17 B3
Ellard Ct DA16 13 C4
Ellen Ave CT11 83 E2
Ellenborough Rd DA14 31 E3
Ellen Cl BR1 52 D6
Ellen Ct CT3 176 F8
Ellenden Ct CT2 142 C4
Ellen's Hill CT14 214 E3
Ellen's Pl ME9 100 C6
Ellens Rd CT14 214 F2
Ellenswood Cl ME15 163 A1
Ellen Wilkinson Prim Sch
E6 1 E8
Ellerman Rd RM18 18 F5

Ellerslie **5** DA12 ... 37 D8
Ellerslie DA12 ... 37 D8
Ellesmere Ct SE12 ... 29 F3
Ellesmere Mews
TN28 ... 373 C8
Ellingham Leas ME15 ... 395 C3
Ellingham Way TN23 ... 300 A5
Ellington Ave CT9 ... 82 B8
Ellington Inf Sch
CT11 ... 117 C7
Ellington Pl CT11 ... 117 C7
Ellington Rd CT11 ... 117 D7
Ellington Sch for Girls
CT11 ... 117 C7
Elliot Cl CT11 ... 143 C3
Elliot Ct CT16 ... 77 C4
Elliots Pl ME13 ... 138 D7
Elliott Park Sch ME12 ... 47 A7
Elliott Rd BR2 ... 52 D5
Elliotts La TN16 ... 152 C3
Elliott St DA12 ... 37 D8
Ellis Cl Eltham SE9 ... 30 C6
Swanley BR8 ... 65 D5
Elliscombe Mount SE7 ... 11 C8
Elliscombe Rd SE7 ... 11 C8
Ellis Ct DA1 ... 34 87
Ellis Ho **7** ME14 ... 162 B4
Ellison Cl CT5 ... 75 C1
Ellison Ct ME13 ... 138 E6
Ellison Rd DA15 ... 30 D7
Ellisons Wlk CT1 ... 175 C8
Ellison Way ME8 ... 66 A2
Ellis Rd CT5 ... 75 A3
Elliston Ho **8** SE18 ... 2 A2
Ellis Way Dartford DA1 ... 33 F6
Herne Bay CT6 ... 77 C2
Elm Ave Chatham ME4 ... 63 E1
Chattenden ME3 ... 41 A4
Elmbank Dr BR1 ... 52 D7
Elmbourne Dr DA17 ... 4 82
Elmbrook Gdns SE9 ... 11 E3
Elm Cl Dartford DA1 ... 33 C7
Egerton TN27 ... 232 F3
Higham ME3 ... 39 C3
Elm Cotts
Boughton Lees TN25 ... 236 E3
Swanley Village BR8 ... 56 B8
Elm Court Ind Est ME7 ... 97 E3
Elm Cres ME19 ... 159 F8
Elmcroft Ave DA15 ... 13 A1
Elmcroft Rd BR6 ... 54 A2
Elm Ct CT8 ... 81 E8
Elmdene Rd SE18 ... 2 81
Elm Dr BR8 ... 55 D7
Elmfield Cl
Gravesend DA11 ... 37 87
Sevenoaks Weald TN14 ... 187 B2
Elmfield Ct Bexley DA16 ... 13 86
Coxheath ME17 ... 194 C3
Tenterden TN30 ... 345 88
Elmfield ME8 ... 65 A3
Elmfield Pk BR1 ... 52 A6
Elmfield Rd BR1 ... 52 A6
Elm Fields TN29 ... 372 A6
Elmfield TN30 ... 345 88
Elm Gdns CT21 ... 333 E2
Elm Gr Erith DA8 ... 14 D7
Maidstone ME15 ... 162 B3
Manston CT12 ... 82 D1
Orpington BR6 ... 53 F1
Sittingbourne ME10 ... 102 B4
Tonbridge TN11 ... 221 F5
Westgate-on-S CT8 ... 81 E8
Elm Ho **11** CT21 ... 333 B2
Elmhurst Ave TN2 ... 287 D8
Elmhurst DA17 ... 13 E8
Elmhurst CT15 ... 267 F4
Elmhurst Cvn Pk ME12 ... 48 F6
Elmhurst Gdns ME4 ... 63 E3
Elmhurst Rd SE9 ... 29 E5
Elmhurst DA9 ... 17 81
Elmington Cl DA5 ... 14 81
Elm La
Marden (Sheppey) ME12 ... 47 E5
Tonbridge TN10 ... 222 C3
Elmlee Cl BR7 ... 29 F2
Elmleigh Rd CT3 ... 177 A8
Elmley Cl **10** E6 ... 1 E8
Elmley Ind Est ME11 ... 46 A2
Elmley Marshes Nature
Reserve* ME12 ... 70 F4
Elmley Rd ME12 ... 47 D3
Elmley St SE18 ... 2 D2
Elmley Way CT9 ... 82 F6
Elm Park Gdns CT17 ... 309 F7
Elm Par **10** DA14 ... 31 A4
Elm Pl CT21 ... 299 F7
Elm Rd Aylesham CT3 ... 210 E5
Dartford DA1 ... 33 D7
Erith DA8 ... 15 A6
7 Folkestone CT19 ... 335 E6
Gillingham ME7 ... 64 E6
Gravesend DA12 ... 37 C5
Grays RM17 ... 18 C8
Orpington BR6 ... 87 A3
Royal Tunbridge Wells
TN4 ... 253 F1
St Mary's Bay TN29 ... 365 F3
Sidcup DA14 ... 31 A4
Stone DA9 ... 16 E1
Westerham TN16 ... 151 E2
Elms Ave CT11 ... 117 D6
Elms Hill CT15 ... 309 D6
Elmshurst Gdns TN10 ... 222 C7
Elmslie CT14 ... 12 A1
Elmsmead TN31 ... 368 B4
Elmstead Ave BR7 ... 29 F3
Elmstead Cl TN13 ... 153 E5

Elmstead Glade BR7 ... 29 F2
Elmstead La BR7 ... 29 F3
Elmstead Pl **12** CT20 ... 335 E5
Elmstead Rd DA8 ... 14 E8
Elmstead Woods Sta
BR7 ... 29 E2
Elms The Hersden CT3 ... 111 E1
Teynham ME9 ... 104 A2
Elmstone Cl ME16 ... 161 B2
Elmstone Gdns CT9 ... 51 E2
Elmstone Hole Rd
Fairbourne Heath ME17 ... 198 D1
Platt's Heath ME17 ... 231 D8
Elmstone La ME16 ... 161 B2
Elmstone Rd
Gillingham ME8 ... 98 D7
Ramsgate CT11 ... 117 D7
Elmstone Terr **8** BR5 ... 54 C5
Elms Vale Rd CT15,
CT17 ... 309 E7
Elmton Cl CT15 ... 212 C1
Elmton La CT15 ... 347 C1
Elm Tree Ave ME7 ... 64 D2
Elmtree Cotts TN14 ... 120 D4
Elm Tree Cotts ME4 ... 40 F6
Elm Tree **20** SE7 ... 11 C8
Elm Tree Dr ME1 ... 63 A2
Elmway ME12 ... 48 F6
Elm Wlk
Aylesford ME20 ... 128 E1
Orpington BR6 ... 85 F7
Elmwood Ave CT10 ... 84 A8
Elmwood Cl CT10 ... 84 A7
Elm Wood Cl CT5 ... 75 C2
Elmwood Dr DA5 ... 31 E8
Elmwood Rd ME7 ... 33 F6
Elm Wood W CT5 ... 75 C2
Elphick's Pl TN2 ... 314 88
Elrick Cl DA8 ... 14 E8
Elsa Rd DA16 ... 13 C5
Elsinore Ho **8** SE18 ... 1 E2
Elster Pl ME19 ... 159 B3
Elstow Cl Eltham SE9 ... 11 D7
Sittingbourne ME9 ... 12 A2
Elstree Gdns DA17 ... 4 82
Eltham Ave **14** DA14 ... 31 A5
Eltham CE Prim Sch
SE9 ... 11 F2
Eltham Coll SE9 ... 29 D6
Eltham Green Rd SE9 ... 11 C3
Eltham Green Sch SE9 ... 11 C1
Eltham High St SE9 ... 11 F1
Eltham Hill SE9 ... 11 D1
Eltham Hill Tech Coll for
Girls SE9 ... 11 C1
Eltham Palace* SE9 ... 11 E1
Eltham Palace Rd SE9 ... 11 D1
Eltham Park Gdns SE9 ... 12 A3
Eltham Rd SE12,SE9 ... 11 E2
Eltham Sta SE9 ... 11 F2
Elventon Cl CT19 ... 334 E7
Everland La ME1,
ME9 ... 137 82
Elveys Cotts ME18 ... 192 F1
Elvington Cl ME16 ... 161 D5
Elvington La CT18 ... 306 E2
Elwick Cl DA1 ... 15 A3
Elwick La **13** TN13 ... 268 82
Elwick Rd TN23 ... 268 82
Elwill Way DA13 ... 59 F8
Elwin Rd CT21 ... 299 D8
Ely Cl Erith DA8 ... 14 E8
Gillingham ME8 ... 65 E2
Ely Ct TN1 ... 286 84
Elysian Ave BR5 ... 53 F3
Embassy Cl ME7 ... 64 F1
Embassy Ct Bexley DA16 ... 13 84
Sidcup DA14 ... 31 85
Ember Cl BR5 ... 52 A1
Emblin Ct **2** DA14 ... 31 A4
Emelina Way CT5 ... 108 86
Emerald Cl Newham E16 ... 1 E7
Rochester ME1 ... 96 D7
Emerald Cres ME10 ... 101 D6
Emerald View ME12 ... 49 E4
Emersons Ave BR8 ... 32 C1
Emerton Cl DA6 ... 13 E3
Emes Rd DA8 ... 14 C7
Emily Jackson Cl
TN13 ... 154 83
Emily Jackson Ho
TN13 ... 154 83
Emily Rd ME5 ... 97 86
Emmanuel Ho **2** SE18 ... 2 D1
Emmerson Gdns CT5 ... 75 D3
Emmet Mill La ME10 ... 117 87
Emmetts Garden*
TN14 ... 185 D5
Emmetts La TN14,
TN16 ... 185 D6
Emperor Way TN23 ... 299 F4
Empire Terr CT9 ... 51 A3
Empress Dr BR7 ... 30 88
Empress Gdns ME12 ... 49 D4
Empress Rd DA12 ... 37 E8
Emsworth Gr ME14 ... 162 D6
Enbrook Rd CT20 ... 334 E4
Enbrook Valley CT20 ... 334 C3
Encombe CT20 ... 334 D3
Endeavour Foyer The **8**
ME7 ... 64 82
Enderfield Ct BR7 ... 53 A8
Enfield Rd CT14 ... 215 D7
Engineer Cl SE18 ... 2 81
Engineers Ct **1** TN23 ... 268 82
Englefield Cl BR5 ... 54 A5
Englefield Cres
Cliffe Woods ME3 ... 40 87
Orpington BR5 ... 54 A5

Englefield Path BR5 ... 54 A5
English Martyrs' RC Prim
Sch ME2 ... 63 88
Ennerdale ME13 ... 138 E6
Ennerdale Gdns CT3 ... 210 F6
Ennerdale Ho ME15 ... 195 E7
Ennerdale Rd DA7 ... 14 A6
Ennis Rd SE18 ... 12 C8
Ensfield Rd Leigh TN11 ... 220 E1
Tonbridge TN11 ... 253 A6
Ensign Ho RM17 ... 17 F8
Enslin Rd SE9 ... 30 A8
Enterprise Bsns Est
ME2 ... 63 E7
Enterprise Cl ME2 ... 63 D8
Enterprise Ctr TN24 ... 300 E7
Enterprise Ctr The
ME15 ... 162 A1
Enterprise Rd
Maidstone ME15 ... 162 A1
Margate CT9 ... 83 A6
Enterprise Way TN8 ... 217 C3
Enticott Cl CT5 ... 75 A1
Epaul La ME1 ... 63 88
Epping Cl CT6 ... 77 82
Epple Bay Ave CT7 ... 81 88
Epple Bay Rd CT7 ... 81 A8
Epple Rd CT7 ... 81 88
Epps Rd ME10 ... 101 E3
Epsom Cl Bexley DA7 ... 14 84
Maidstone ME15 ... 195 F6
West Malling ME19 ... 159 88
Epstein Rd SE28 ... 3 85
Erebus Dr SE28 ... 2 C4
Erica Ct BR8 ... 55 E5
Eric Rd CT17 ... 278 82
Eridge Ct TN2 ... 285 F1
Eridge Green Ct BR5 ... 54 C1
Eridge Rd
Groombridge TN3 ... 312 D5
Royal Tunbridge Wells
TN2,TN4 ... 285 E1
Eridge Sta TN3 ... 312 E2
Erindale Terr SE18 ... 12 D8
Erindale Terr SE18 ... 12 D8
Erith & District Hospl
DA8 ... 14 D8
Erith High St DA8 ... 4 E1
Erith Mus* DA8 ... 4 E1
Erith Rd Bexley DA7 ... 14 84
Northumberland Heath DA8,
DA7 ... 14 84
Erith Sch DA8 ... 14 D7
Erith Small Bsns Ctr **2**
DA8 ... 14 F8
Erith St CT17 ... 278 81
Ermington Rd SE9 ... 30 C6
Ernest Dr ME16 ... 161 85
Ernest Rd ME4 ... 64 A3
Ernwell Rd CT19 ... 335 D6
Ersham Rd CT1 ... 175 A7
Erskine Ho **8** SE7 ... 11 C8
Erskine Park Rd TN4 ... 285 C4
Erskine Rd DA13 ... 126 88
Erwood Rd SE7 ... 1 E6
Escott Gdns SE9 ... 29 E4
Escreet Gr SE18 ... 2 A2
Eshcol Rd ME3 ... 42 C6
Esher Cl DA5 ... 31 E7
Eskdale Ave CT11 ... 117 A7
Eskdale Cl DA2 ... 34 C7
Eskdale Rd DA7 ... 14 A6
Esmonde Dr CT12 ... 81 F2
Esmonde Ho **15** ME7 ... 64 A6
Esplanade Dover CT17 ... 310 D6
Rochester ME1 ... 63 85
Westgate-on-S CT8 ... 50 C1
Essella Pk TN24 ... 268 E1
Essella Rd TN24 ... 268 E1
Essenden Rd DA17 ... 4 A1
Essetford Rd TN23 ... 300 A7
Essex Ave CT6 ... 76 84
Essex Cl TN2 ... 313 F8
Essex Gdns CT17 ... 80 F6
Essex Rd
Canterbury CT1 ... 175 D7
Dartford DA1 ... 15 D1
Gravesend DA11 ... 37 A7
Halling ME2 ... 95 A6
Longfield DA3 ... 58 D7
Maidstone ME15 ... 195 E6
Westgate-on-S CT8 ... 37 A8
West Thurrock RM20 ... 17 A8
Essex St CT5 ... 108 C8
Estelle Cl ME1 ... 96 D7
Esther Ct ME10 ... 101 E8
Estridge Way TN10 ... 222 F5
Estuary Cotts RM18 ... 20 D7
Estuary Rd ME12 ... 28 88
Estuary Way CT5 ... 75 E3
Etchden Rd TN26 ... 298 A8
Etfield Gr DA14 ... 31 83
Ethelbert Cres CT9 ... 51 A3
Ethelbert Gdns CT9 ... 50 J3
Ethelbert Rd
Birchington CT7 ... 80 D8
Bromley BR1 ... 52 46
Canterbury CT1 ... 175 86
Deal CT14 ... 182 C1
Dover CT16 ... 310 C8
Erith DA8 ... 14 C7
Faversham ME13 ... 138 C6
Folkestone CT19 ... 335 D7
Hawley DA2 ... 33 E3
Margate CT9 ... 50 J3
Orpington BR5 ... 54 D6
Ramsgate CT11 ... 117 D6
Rochester ME1 ... 63 C4
Ethelbert Road Inf Sch
ME13 ... 138 C6
Ethelbert Sq CT8 ... 50 C1

Ethelbert Terr
Margate CT9 ... 51 A3
Westgate-on-S CT8 ... 50 C1
Ethel Brooks Ho SE18 ... 12 88
Ethelburga Dr CT18 ... 305 87
Ethel-Maud Ct ME7 ... 64 D7
Ethel Rd
Broadstairs CT10 ... 83 F5
Newham E16 ... 1 87
Ethelred Ct ME13 ... 138 C6
Ethelred Rd CT8 ... 50 C1
Ethel Terr BR6 ... 87 A2
Etherington Hill TN3 ... 285 C8
Ethnam La TN18 ... 356 E4
Ethronvi Rd DA7 ... 13 E4
Eton Cl ME5 ... 96 F4
Eton Ct TN13 ... 154 84
Eton Rd BR6 ... 87 86
Eton Way DA1 ... 15 C3
Ettrick Terr CT21 ... 333 A2
Eugenie Mews BR7 ... 52 E2
Eurogate Bsns Pk
TN24 ... 268 85
Eurolink Bsns Pk
ME14 ... 102 85
Eurolink Way ME10 ... 101 F4
Europa Pk RM20 ... 17 C8
Europa Trad Est DA8 ... 4 D1
Europe Rd SE18 ... 1 F3
Euroway ME20 ... 160 E8
Eustace Pl **8** SE18 ... 1 F2
Evanlode Ho **5** SE2 ... 3 C4
Evans Cl DA9 ... 17 A3
Evans Ct SE9 ... 29 E6
Evans Rd TN24 ... 301 A7
Eva Rd ME7 ... 64 D3
Evelings Alley **15** CT5 ... 74 D2
Evelyn Cl ME2 ... 63 C8
Evelyn Cres CT21 ... 334 A2
Evelyn Denington Rd E6 ... 1 F8
Evelyn Ho
5 Folkestone CT20 ... 335 D7
6 Rochester ME2 ... 63 C8
Evelyn Rd
Maidstone ME16 ... 161 E3
Newham E16 ... 1 85
Otford TN14 ... 153 B6
Evenden Ho TN17 ... 320 D5
Evenden Rd DA13 ... 60 A2
Evenhill Rd CT3 ... 176 E8
Everard Ave BR2 ... 52 A1
Everard Rd Bexley DA7 ... 13 F5
Everest Cl **18** DA11 ... 36 E5
Everest Ct SE9 ... 29 E6
Everest Dr ME3 ... 41 A1
Everest Mews ME3 ... 41 A1
Everest Pl BR8 ... 55 D5
Everest Rd SE9 ... 11 F2
Everett Wlk DA17 ... 3 F1
Everglade TN16 ... 118 D1
Everglade Cl DA3 ... 58 F5
Everglades The ME7 ... 97 F6
Evergreen Cl
Gillingham ME7 ... 98 A5
Higham ME3 ... 39 83
Iwade ME9 ... 100 D5
Leybourne ME19 ... 127 87
Everist Ct CT18 ... 305 C6
Eversfield Ct SE12 ... 29 86
Eversleigh Rise CT5 ... 108 F7
Eversley Ave DA7,DA8 ... 14 E5
Eversley Cl ME15 ... 161 C6
Eversley Coll CT20 ... 334 C4
Eversley Cross DA7 ... 14 E5
Eversley Rd
Greenwich SE7 ... 11 88
Hythe CT21 ... 334 83
Eversley Way CT20 ... 334 83
Everthorpe Rd DA12 ... 37 D6
Evington Pottery*
TN25 ... 271 D7
Evison Cl CT16 ... 278 82
Evorg Ho **6** ME4 ... 64 82
Evry Rd DA14 ... 31 C2
Ewart Rd ME4 ... 63 E1
Ewehurst La TN3 ... 284 F6
Ewell Ave ME19 ... 159 A8
Ewell La ME15 ... 193 D5
Ewins Cl TN12 ... 257 A6
Excel Waterfront E16 ... 1 86
Exchange St CT14 ... 215 D7
Exchange The CT5 ... 74 F3
Exciroak Dr SE9 ... 12 D2
Exeter Cl
Folkestone CT20 ... 334 D6
Newham E6 ... 1 F7
Tonbridge TN10 ... 222 D4
Exeter Rd Bexley DA16 ... 13 A5
Gravesend DA12 ... 37 D5
Newham E16 ... 1 A8
Exeter Wlk ME1 ... 96 C7
Exford Gdns SE12 ... 29 87
Exford Rd SE12 ... 29 87
Exmoor Rise TN24 ... 268 84
Exmouth Rd
Bexley DA16 ... 13 C5
Gillingham ME7 ... 64 C7
Grays RM17 ... 18 88
Exton Cl ME5 ... 97 C2
Exton Gdns ME14 ... 162 F5
Eye The ME4 ... 63 F6
Eyhorne St ME17 ... 164 D2
Eynsford Castle* DA4 ... 89 87
Eynsford Cl BR5 ... 53 C2
Eynsford Rd
Crockenhill BR8 ... 56 F1
Eynsford DA4 ... 89 C8
Maidstone ME15 ... 161 D7
Swanscombe DA10 ... 17 C2
Eynsford Rise DA4 ... 89 D6

Eynsford Sta DA4 ... 89 D6
Eynsham Dr SE2 ... 3 83
Eynsworth Ct DA4 ... 31 C3
Eythorn Court Barn
CT15 ... 245 87
Eythorne Cl TN24 ... 268 D5
Eythorne Elvington Com
Prim Sch CT15 ... 245 C8
Eythorne Rd CT15 ... 244 E6
Eythorne Sta CT15 ... 245 C8

F

Fackenden La TN14 ... 122 C7
Factory Rd Newham E16 ... 1 E5
Northfleet DA11 ... 18 C1
Faesten Way DA5 ... 32 E5
Faggs Wood Forest Wlks*
TN26 ... 327 D2
Fagus Cl ME5 ... 97 81
Fairacre CT10 ... 83 E4
Fairacre Pl DA3 ... 58 86
Fairacres Cl CT6 ... 77 C4
Fair Acres BR2 ... 52 A4
Fairbairn Way ME5 ... 97 E2
Fairbank Ave BR6 ... 86 88
Fairbourne Heath Cotts
ME17 ... 198 81
Fairbourne La ME17 ... 198 C4
Fairby La DA3 ... 58 E3
Fairby Grange ME19 ... 11 82
Faircrouch La TN5 ... 336 85
Fairfax Bsns Ctr ME15 ... 195 F4
Fairfax Cl
Folkestone CT20 ... 334 D5
Gillingham ME8 ... 98 D5
Fairfax Dr CT6 ... 77 81
Fairfax Gdns SE3 ... 11 C6
Fairfax Ho ME15 ... 195 F5
Fairfax Mews E16 ... 1 85
Fairfax Rd RM18 ... 18 F6
Fairfield Ave TN2 ... 286 C5
Fairfield Cl
Kemsing TN15 ... 123 A1
New Romney TN28 ... 373 87
Sidcup DA15 ... 12 F1
Fairfield Cres TN9 ... 254 C8
Fairfield Deal CT14 ... 214 F6
Elham CT4 ... 273 F5
Fairfield Gr SE7 ... 11 D8
Fairfield Pk CT10 ... 83 F2
Fairfield Rd Bexley DA7 ... 13 F5
Borough Green TN15 ... 156 F8
Broadstairs CT10 ... 83 F2
Bromley BR1 ... 29 A1
Minster (Thanet) CT12 ... 115 87
New Romney TN28 ... 373 87
Orpington BR5 ... 53 D3
Ramsgate CT11 ... 83 E2
Fairfields DA12 ... 37 E3
Fairfield Terr TN24 ... 349 A7
Fairfield Way TN11 ... 221 F5
Fairford Ave DA7 ... 14 D6
Fairglen Cotts TN5 ... 336 83
Fairglen Rd TN5 ... 336 84
Fairings The TN30 ... 345 88
Fairland Ho BR2 ... 52 85
Fairlands Ct **6** SE9 ... 12 A1
Fairlawn Ave DA7 ... 13 D5
Fairlawn Cl ME16 ... 193 A8
Fairlawn Ct SE7 ... 11 C7
Fairlawn SE7 ... 11 C8
Fairlawn Rd CT12 ... 82 83
Fairlead Rd ME1 ... 63 D1
Fairleas ME10 ... 102 82
Fairlight Ave CT12 ... 117 88
Fairlight La TN14 ... 254 A2
Fairlight Cotts **8**
ME13 ... 138 C7
Fairlight Cross DA3 ... 59 C6
Fairlight Ct TN10 ... 222 84
Fairlight Rd TN23 ... 333 A3
Fairman's La TN12 ... 289 86
Fairmead Rd ME1 ... 161 F4
Fairmead Ct BR1 ... 52 F5
Fairmead CT3 ... 161 F4
Fairmead Rd TN8 ... 217 C5
Fairmile Rd ME5 ... 54 A7
Fairmile Rd TN2 ... 286 E5
Fairmont Cl DA17 ... 3 F1
Fairoak Cl BR5 ... 53 82
Fairoak Dr SE9 ... 12 D2
Fairoaks CT5 ... 74 D3
Fairseat La
Fairseat TN15 ... 125 85
Stansted TN15 ... 92 A1
Fairservice Cl ME10 ... 102 C5
Fairstone Ct **4** CT16 ... 331 A3
Fairthorn Rd SE7 ... 1 A1
Fairtrough Rd BR6 ... 88 82
Fairview Ave ME8 ... 98 85
Fairview Cl Margate CT9 ... 51 A2
Royal Tunbridge Wells
TN2 ... 286 C5
Fairview Com Inf Sch
ME8 ... 98 C5
Fair View Com Jun Sch
ME8 ... 98 C5
Fairview Cotts TN15 ... 194 F5
Fair View Cotts TN5 ... 337 A6
Fairview Ct CT9 ... 166 C7
Fairview Dr
Ashford TN24 ... 300 D6
Chatham ME5 ... 96 E4
Higham ME3 ... 39 84
Orpington BR6 ... 86 D6
Shanklin CT21 ... 334 C1
Fairview Gdns
Deal CT14 ... 215 F2
Meopham Station DA13 ... 60 A4
Sturry CT2 ... 144 A6
Fairview TN18 ... 340 F2

Fairview Ind PK
Reanham DA3 ... 4 D8
Ruckinge TN26 ... 349 D7
Fairview Lympne CT21 ... 332 A3
New Ash Green DA3 ... 91 87
Fairview Rd
Elvington CT15 ... 212 81
Istead Rise DA13 ... 36 E1
Sittingbourne ME10 ... 102 A3
Fairview Trad Est
RHB ... 183 A2
Fairwater Ave DA16 ... 13 A3
Fairway Arn CT19 ... 335 A7
Fairway DA6 ... 13 C1
Fairway Cl
Rochester ME3 ... 63 C1
St Mary's Bay TN29 ... 365 F3
Fairway Cres CT5 ... 108 A7
Fairway Ct **15** SE9 ... 12 A1
Fairway Dr Dartford DA2 ... 34 88
Erith SE28 ... 3 F3
Fairway Orpington BR5 ... 53 D4
Sandwich CT13 ... 182 A7
Fairways Cl **11** DA11 ... 37 88
Fairways The
Faversham ME13 ... 138 A6
Royal Tunbridge Wells
TN4 ... 286 A7
Fairway The
Bromley,Southborough
BR1 ... 52 F4
2 Bromley,Sundridge
BR1 ... 29 83
Deal CT14 ... 215 C8
Gravesend DA11 ... 37 86
Herne Bay CT6 ... 76 D2
Hythe CT21 ... 333 C2
Littlestone-on-Sea TN28 ... 373 D6
Rochester ME1 ... 63 C3
St Mary's Bay TN29 ... 366 A5
Sittingbourne ME10 ... 101 E5
Fairwood Ind Est
TN23 ... 268 A3
Falcon Ave Bromley BR1 ... 52 E5
Grays RM17 ... 18 C2
Falcon Cl Dartford DA1 ... 15 F2
Herne CT6 ... 110 F2
Falcon Ct ME10 ... 102 A2
Falcon Gdns ME12 ... 47 D7
Falcon Ho ME12 ... 102 A4
Falcon Mews DA11 ... 36 E2
Falcons Cl TN16 ... 118 D2
Falcon Way TN23 ... 299 E7
Falconwood Ave DA16 ... 12 E1
Falconwood Par DA16 ... 12 F2
Falconwood Sta SE9 ... 12 D2
Falkland Pl ME5 ... 96 E1
Fallowfield Bean DA2 ... 35 85
Chatham ME5 ... 96 F3
Fallowfield Cl ME14 ... 162 84
Fallowfield ME10 ... 102 A1
Falmouth Pl TN12 ... 256 C3
Falstaff Cl DA1 ... 32 E4
Fancett Rd ME5 ... 97 83
Fancy Row ME14 ... 163 C1
Fane Way ME8 ... 98 D4
Fans La ME9 ... 68 D1
Fantail Cl SE28 ... 3 C6
Fan The CT16 ... 310 H6
Fanshaw Gr La ME8 ... 161 89
Faraday Ave DA14 ... 31 81
Faraday Ho Erith DA17 ... 4 A1
Rochester ME1 ... 63 D1
Faraday Lodge TN2 ... 286 E5
Faraday Rd Bexley DA16 ... 13 A6
Maidstone ME14 ... 162 C1
Faraday Way
Greenwich SE18 ... 1 D6
Orpington BR5 ... 54 8
Fareham Wlk **14** ME15 ... 195 F7
Faringdon Ave BR2 ... 53 A1
Farington Cl ME16 ... 161 85
Farjeon Rd SE18,SE3 ... 11 D8
Farleigh Ave BR2 ... 52 A8
Farleigh Ct ME15 ... 161 E2
Farleigh Hill ME15 ... 161 E1
Farleigh Hill Ret Pk
ME15 ... 161 E2
Farleigh La ME16 ... 161 A6
Farleigh Rd CT2 ... 143 A6
Farleigh Trad Est
ME15 ... 161 E2
Farley Cl Chatham ME5 ... 97 D1
Shadoxhurst TN26 ... 299 A4
Farleycroft TN16 ... 151 C2
Farley La TN16 ... 184 88
Farley Nursery TN16 ... 184 C1
Farley Rd
Gravesend DA12 ... 37 F6
Margate CT9 ... 82 F7
Farleys Way TN31 ... 367 89
Farlow Cl DA11 ... 36 E4
Farm Ave BR8 ... 55 C5
Farm Cl TN23 ... 299 C4
Farmcombe Cl TN2 ... 286 86
Farmcombe La TN2 ... 286 C6
Farmcombe Rd TN2 ... 286 C6
Farmcote Rd SE12 ... 29 A6
Farm Cres ME10 ... 102 A4
Farmcroft DA11 ... 37 87
Farmdale Ave SE10 ... 1 A1
Farmdale Rd SE10 ... 1 A1
Farmer Cl Hythe CT21 ... 333 D2
Leeds ME17 ... 197 A4
Farm Gdns TN31 ... 367 E8
Farm Ground Cl TN9 ... 254 88
Farm Hill Ave ME2 ... 63 C4
Farm Holt DA3 ... 91 88
Farmhouse Cl CT4 ... 242 B6
Farm House Cl CT5 ... 108 88

Farm La CT14 214 F6
Farmland Wlk BR7 30 B3
Farm La TN10 222 A4
Farm Pl DA1 15 A3
Farm Rd Chatham ME5 96 E3
Hamstreet TN26 349 A7
Sevenoaks TN14 154 C7
Farmstead Dr TN8 217 D3
Farm Vale DA5 14 B1
Farnaby Dr TN13 154 A1
Farnaby Rd SE9 11 C3
Farnborough Cl ME16 161 C2
Farnborough Comm
BR6 86 A6
Farnborough Ct 2
BR6 86 C5
Farnborough Hill BR6 86 E5
Farnborough Prim Sch
BR6 86 C5
Farnborough Way BR6 86 D5
Farncombe Way CT16 278 B7
Farne Cl ME15 195 A6
Farnham Beeches
TN3 285 A4
Farnham Cl
Gillingham ME8 66 B1
Gillingham ME8 99 A8
Langton Green TN3 285 A3
Farnham La TN3 285 A4
Farnham Pl TN3 285 A3
Farnham Rd DA16 13 C5
Farningham Cl ME14 162 C6
Farningham Hill Rd
DA4 56 D4
Farningham Road Sta
DA4 57 B7
Farningham Wood (Nature Reserve)★ BR8,DA4 56 D5
Farnol Rd DA1 16 A3
Faro Cl BR1 53 A7
Farraday Cl ME1 96 D8
Farrance Ct TN1 286 B4
Farrant Cl BR6 87 A3
Farrants Ct BR1 52 F7
Farrar Rd CT7 81 A6
Farrell Ct DA2 33 C5
Farrers Wlk TN23 300 B4
Farrier Cl
Ashford TN23 267 F5
Bromley BR1 52 D6
Maidstone ME14 162 E5
Farriers Cl DA12 37 F7
Farriers Ct ME8 99 C8
Farrier St CT14 215 D7
Farrington Ave BR5 54 B6
Farrington Pl BR7 30 D1
Farringtons & Stratford Ho Sch BR7 30 D1
Farrow Ct TN23 300 A6
Fartherwell Ave ME19 159 A8
Fartherwell Rd ME19 159 A8
Farthing Cl DA1 15 F3
Farthing Cnr ME9 98 E3
Farthingfield TN15 125 A3
Farthing Hill TN5 338 E1
Farthingloe Cotts
CT15 309 F5
Farthingloe Ct CT17 310 A6
Farthingloe Rd CT17 310 A6
Farthings Cotts ME14 129 F1
Farthings Ct CT2 142 C4
Farthing St BR6 85 F2
Farwell Rd DA14 31 C4
Farwig La BR1 52 A8
Fashoda Rd BR2 52 D5
Fauchon's Cl ME14 162 F3
Fauchon's La ME14 162 F4
Faulkners La CT2 142 A1
Faussett Hill CT4 207 F8
Faustina Dr TN23 299 F4
Faversham Cottage Hospl
ME13 138 C7
Faversham Ind Est
ME13 138 F7
Faversham Miniature Rly★
ME13 138 B4
Faversham Rd
Boughton Lees TN24,
TN25 236 E5
Challock ME13,TN27 202 C3
Charing TN27 201 E1
Lenham ME17 199 E7
Lewson Street ME13,
ME9 137 B5
Pested TN25,ME13 203 B4
Whitstable CT5 107 C6
Wichling ME17,ME9 167 B4
Faversham Reach
ME13 138 D8
Faversham Sta ME13 138 D6
Faversham Stone Chap★
ME13 137 E7
F Ave SE18 2 B3
Favourite Rd CT5 108 B6
Fawkes Ave DA1 33 F6
Fawkham Ave DA3 59 C6
Fawkham CE Prim Sch
DA3 58 B1
Fawkham Green Rd
DA3 91 B7
Fawkham Ho 10 BR5 54 D1
Fawkham Manor Hospl
DA3 58 C1
Fawkham Rd
Longfield DA3 58 D6
West Kingsdown TN15 91 A4
Fawley Cl ME14 161 E7
Fay Cl ME1 63 B3
Faygate Cres DA6 14 A2
Fazan Ct TN5 336 F4
Fearon St SE10 1 A1
Featherbed La
Iwade ME9 68 E2
Featherbed La *continued*
Selling ME13 171 A7
Featherby Cotts ME7 64 F6
Featherby Inf Sch ME8 65 A3
Featherby Jun Sch
ME8 65 A3
Featherby Rd
Gillingham,Grange ME7 65 A5
Gillingham,Twydall ME8 65 A3
Federation Rd SE2 3 C2
Feenan Highway RM18 19 B6
Felborough Cl CT4 205 C8
Felderland Cl
Maidstone ME17 195 E5
Sandwich CT14 180 F5
Felderland Dr ME17 195 E5
Felderland La CT14 180 E4
Felderland Rd ME17 195 E5
Feldspar Cl
Chatham ME5 97 A1
Sittingbourne ME10 101 D6
Felhampton Rd SE9 30 B5
Felix Manor BR7 30 E2
Felixstowe Ct E16 2 B5
Felixstowe Rd SE2 3 B3
Fell Mead TN12 224 F6
Fellowes Way TN11 221 E5
Fellows Cl ME8 98 B6
Felltram Way SE7 1 A1
Felma Ho 12 SE7 11 C8
Felspar Cl SE18 2 F1
Felstead Rd BR6 87 B8
Felsted Rd E16 1 D7
Felton Cl BR5 53 B3
Felton Ho SE3 11 C3
Felton Lea DA14 30 F3
Fendyke Rd DA17 3 D3
Fen Gr DA15 12 F1
Fen Mdw TN15 124 C1
Fenn Cl BR1 29 A2
Fennel Cl ME16 161 B3
Fennell Cl ME1 63 B3
Fennell St SE18 12 A8
Fenner Cl CT20 334 E4
Fenn St ME3 24 B4
Fenoulhet Way CT6 77 A5
Fen Pond Rd TN15 156 C7
Fens Way BR8 33 A2
Fenton Cl BR7 29 F3
Fenton Ct CT14 215 B6
Fenwick Cl 16 SE18 12 A8
Feoffe Cotts TN17 342 E7
Ferbies Cl TN3 285 A7
Ferbies TN3 285 A7
Ferby Ct DA15 30 F4
Ferdi Lethert Ho
TN24 268 E5
Ferdinand Terr TN3 312 C7
Ferguson Ave DA12 37 C4
Ferguson Cl CT21 333 F2
Ferguson Rd TN29 378 F6
Ferguson Way CT21 333 A1
Fernbank Cl ME5 96 F2
Fern Bank Cres CT19 335 D6
Fern Bank DA4 89 E8
Fern Cl Erith DA8 15 B6
Hawkinge CT18 307 C6
Whitstable CT5 75 C1
Fern Ct Bexley DA7 14 A3
Broadstairs CT10 84 B5
Dover CT16 278 D1
Ferndale BR1 52 C7
Ferndale Cl Bexley DA7 13 E6
Halfway Houses ME12 46 D6
Royal Tunbridge Wells
TN2 286 C4
Ferndale Ct CT7 81 A6
Ferndale Point TN2 286 C4
Ferndale Rd
Gillingham ME7 64 E5
Gravesend DA12 37 B6
Ferndale
Royal Tunbridge Wells
TN2 286 D5
Sevenoaks TN13 154 C5
Ferndale St E6 2 B7
Ferndale Way BR6 86 D5
Ferndell Ave DA5 32 D5
Ferndene DA3 59 D6
Ferndown Ave BR6 53 D1
Ferndown CT7 80 D8
Ferndown Cl ME7 98 A5
Ferndown Rd SE9 29 D8
Fern Down DA13 126 B8
Ferne La CT15 276 D3
Ferne Way CT20 334 E6
Fernfield CT18 307 C6
Fernfield La CT18 307 C7
Fernheath Way DA2 32 D3
Fern Hill Pl 3 BR6 86 C5
Fernhill Rd ME16 161 A2
Fernhill St E16 1 F5
Fernholt TN10 222 C7
Fernhurst Cres TN4 254 A2
Fernlea Ave CT6 76 E4
Fernleigh Cl ME13 140 B3
Fernleigh Rise ME20 128 B2
Fernley Ct 11 CT20 335 D5
Fernside La TN13 187 D6
Ferns The
Larkfield ME20 128 B1
Platt TN15 157 C7
Royal Tunbridge Wells
TN1 286 C4
Fern Wlk ME10 102 C5
Fernwood Cl BR1 52 C7
Ferranti Cl SE18 1 D3
Ferrier Cl ME8 98 E4
Ferrier Point 8 E16 1 A8
Ferringham TN4 285 F4
Ferry La Ind Est RM13 4 F8
Ferry La Rainham RM13 4 E7
Wouldham ME1 95 C4
Ferry Pl SE18 2 A3
Ferry Rd Halling ME2 95 B4
Iwade ME9 68 E4
Queenborough ME11,
ME12 46 D1
Tilbury RM18 19 A4
Ferry View ME11 45 F3
Festival Ave DA3 59 D6
Festival Cl Erith DA8 14 F7
Sidcup DA5 31 D7
Festoon Way E16 1 D6
Ffinch Cl ME20 160 D8
Fiddlers Cl DA9 17 B3
Fiddling La TN25 303 E6
Field Ave CT1 143 D3
Field Cl Bromley BR1 52 C7
Chatham ME5 96 E6
Field Dr TN8 217 D3
Field End TN24 269 A1
Field End Pl ME13 140 A3
Fielder Cl ME10 102 C5
Fieldfare Rd SE28 3 C6
Fielding Ave RM18 19 B6
Fielding Dr ME20 128 A3
Fielding St ME13 138 C7
Fieldings The ME10 101 E2
Field Mill Rd TN27 233 B5
Field Rd DA13,TN15 92 E6
Fieldside Cl BR6 86 C6
Fields La ME18 192 E7
Fieldview Cl ME12 46 C6
Field View
Kingsnorth TN23 300 B4
Whitstable CT5 108 B7
Fieldway BR5 53 D3
Fieldways TN18 341 A1
Field Way CT2 143 F5
Fieldworks Rd ME7 64 A7
Fiennes Way TN13 187 C8
Fiesta Dr RM9 4 C8
Fiesta Wlk CT1 175 C7
Fife Rd Herne Bay CT6 76 B3
Newham E16 1 A8
Fifteenpenny Fields
SE9 12 A2
Fifth Ave Margate CT9 51 B3
West Thurrock RM20 17 A8
Fig Tree Rd CT10 83 F7
Fig Tree Wlk CT15 245 C7
Fiji Terr ME14 162 A7
Filborough Way DA12 38 B6
Filer Rd ME12 46 E7
Filey Cl TN16 150 B8
Filmer La TN14 154 E6
Filmer Rd CT4 175 F1
Filston La TN14 121 E5
Filston Rd DA8 4 C1
Finchale Rd SE2 3 A3
Finchcocks★ TN17 318 A5
Finch Ct
Maidstone ME14 161 E7
Sidcup DA14 31 B5
Finches The
St Nicholas at Wade CT7 79 E2
Sittingbourne ME10 101 F3
Finch Gr CT21 353 D8
Finchley Cl DA1 16 A1
Finchley Rd RM17 18 B8
Finch Mews CT14 215 C4
Finch's Cross RH8 216 A8
Findlay Cl ME8 98 D6
Findlay Ct 9 CT21 333 B2
Finglesham Cl BR5 54 D1
Finglesham Ct ME15 195 C8
Finglesham Farm Barns
CT14 214 A8
Finlay Cl ME13 138 B7
Finn Farm Ct TN23 300 D1
Finn Farm Rd TN23 300 C2
Finsbury Ct CT11 117 E8
Finsbury Rd CT11 117 E8
Finsbury Way DA5 13 F1
Fintonagh Dr ME14 162 B6
Finucane Dr BR5 54 C2
Finwell Rd ME8 66 A2
Firbank Cl E16 1 D8
Firbank Gdns CT9 82 D7
Firbanks CT5 108 F8
Fircroft Way TN8 217 C3
Fir Ct TN24 268 F1
Fir Dene BR6 86 A7
Firecrest Cl DA3 59 B6
Firepower (Mus)★ SE18 2 B3
Firethorn Cl ME7 64 E6
Firmin Ave ME17 195 D5
Firmingers Rd BR6 88 C5
Firmin Rd DA1 15 C2
Firs Cl Aylesford ME20 128 E1
Folkestone CT19 334 D7
Firs Ct TN4 285 F6
Firside Gr DA15 30 F7
Firs La CT19 334 D7
Firs Rd CT4 210 F1
First Ave Bexley DA7 13 C7
Broadstairs CT10 51 F2
Chatham ME4 64 C2
Eastchurch ME12 48 E5
Gillingham ME7 64 E3
Margate CT9 51 A3
Northfleet DA11 36 E7
Rushenden ME11 45 F3
Sheerness ME12 28 C1
West Thurrock RM20 17 A8
Firs The Coldblow DA5 32 D7
Deal CT14 215 C8
Hersden CT3 111 E1
Sidcup DA15 30 F5
First La ME17 163 E2
First St TN3 284 F3
Fir Tree Cl Grays RM17 18 D8
5 Orpington BR6 86 F5
Ramsgate CT11 117 C6
Firtree Cl CT2 142 B3
Fir Tree Cl
Staplehurst TN12 260 F3
Tonbridge TN11 221 E5
Fir Tree Gr
Bredhurst ME7 98 B1
Chatham ME5 97 D1
Fir Tree Hill CT13 180 B6
Fir Tree Rd TN4 285 F3
Fisher Cl CT21 333 D1
Fisherman's Wharf
CT13 149 A1
Fishermans Ctyd
CT14 215 D3
Fishermans Wlk SE28 2 E4
Fishermen's Hill DA11 18 B2
Fisher Rd
Canterbury CT2 142 D1
Chatham ME5 97 B7
Fishers Cl TN12 260 F5
Fisher's Gate Cotts
TN7 311 A1
Fishers TN28 373 E5
Fishers Rd TN12 260 F5
Fisher St
Maidstone ME14 162 A6
Newham E16 1 A8
Fisher Street Rd
ME13 170 E2
Fisher St CT13 149 A1
Fisher's Way DA17 4 C5
Fishguard Way E16 2 B5
Fish Market CT19 335 E5
Fishmonger's La 8
CT16 310 E7
Fishponds Rd BR2 85 D5
Fitzgerald Ave CT6 76 C4
Fitzmary Ave CT9 50 E1
Fitzroy Ave
Broadstairs CT10 51 G2
Margate CT9 51 B1
Ramsgate CT12 83 B2
Fitzroy Ct DA1 34 B7
Fitzroy Rd CT5 74 F2
Fitzthorold Ho ME7 64 F7
Fitzwalter Ct 1 CT16 278 B3
Fitzwilliam Mews E16 1 A5
Fitzwilliam Rd ME14 162 F5
Five Acre Wood Sch
ME15 195 B7
Five Arches Bsns Est
DA14 31 D3
Fiveash Rd DA11 36 F8
Five Bells La 5 ME1 63 D4
Five Elms Rd BR2 85 C7
Five Fields La TN8 218 B4
Five Oak Green Rd
Capel TN11,TN12 255 D6
Tonbridge TN11 254 F7
Five Oak La TN12 260 B1
Five Oaks Mews BR1 29 A5
Five Vents La TN29 372 B8
Five Ways Ct ME4 64 A4
Fiveways 6 CT17 310 C8
Fiveways L Ctr ME4 64 A4
Fiveways Rise CT14 214 F5
Five Ways TN1 286 B4
Five Wents BR8 56 A7
Flack Gdns ME3 41 E5
Flamborough Cl TN16 150 B8
Flamingo Cl ME5 97 A7
Flamingo Dr CT6 76 E3
Flamsteed Rd SE7 1 E1
Flanders Cl ME10 68 F1
Flanders Field TN25 301 E4
Flats The
Gravesend DA12 37 E8
Swanscombe DA9 17 C2
Flax Court La CT15 245 C7
Flaxman Ct 13 ME7 64 A6
Flaxman Ct DA17 4 A1
Flaxman Dr ME16 161 C6
Flaxmore Ct DA7 14 B4
Flaxmore Pl TN4 254 A2
Flaxpond Rd TN23 299 F7
Flaxton Rd SE18 12 E7
Fleet Ave Dartford DA2 34 C7
Sheerness ME12 28 B1
Fleet Dale Par DA2 34 C7
Fleetdown Inf Sch DA2 34 C6
Fleetdown Jun Sch
DA2 34 C6
Fleet Ho DA13 36 B2
Fleet Rd Dartford DA2 34 C7
Northfleet DA11 36 C6
Rochester ME1 63 D1
St Margaret's at Cliffe
CT15 248 A1
Fleets La CT2 142 D7
Fleet Terr DA11 36 D7
Fleet Villas TN24 268 D7
Fleetwood Ave CT6 76 D4
Fleetwood Cl
Minster (Sheppey) ME12 47 B6
Newham E16 1 D8
Fleetwood Ct
1 Newham E6 1 F8
Orpington BR6 86 A6
Fleming Gdns RM18 19 C6
Fleming Ho SE2 3 C1
Fleming Rd CT13,CT3 179 D6
Fleming Way Erith SE28 3 D6
Folkestone CT19 335 E8
Tonbridge TN10 222 E7
Fletcher Battery Camp Site
ME12 49 A6
Fletcher Cl E6 2 B6
Fletcher Rd
Staplehurst TN12 260 E3
Whitstable CT5 75 B1
Fletchers Cl BR2 52 B5
Fletchers Way CT14 215 A5
Fletching Rd SE7 11 D8
Flete Rd CT9 82 D5
Fleur de Lis Heritage Ctr★
ME13 138 D7
Flimwell TN23 299 D6
Flimwell Cl TN5 339 D4
Flint Cl 8 Orpington BR6 86 F4
Sittingbourne ME10 101 E8
Flint Cotts CT7 80 F6
Flint Down Cl BR5 54 A8
Flint Gn ME5 97 C3
Flint Gr CT10 83 E5
Flint Ho CT9 50 J3
Flint La ME17 166 C1
Flintmill Cres SE3,SE9 11 E5
Flint St RM20 17 B8
Floathaven Cl SE28 3 A5
Floats The TN13 153 E6
Flodden Rd CT14 214 F3
Flood Hatch ME15 161 D2
Flood La ME13 138 C8
Flood St TN25 301 D2
Florance La TN3 312 B6
Flora Rd CT11 117 E8
Flora St DA17 3 F1
Florence Ave CT5 108 B7
Florence Cl RM17,RM20 17 E8
Florence Cotts
5 Edenbridge TN8 217 C1
Ramsgate CT11 117 D6
Florence Ct CT9 51 B3
Florence Farm Mobile Home Pk TN15 90 D4
Florence Ho SE18 11 F6
Florence Rd
4 Bromley BR1 52 A8
Erith DA17,SE2 3 C2
Maidstone ME16 161 E3
3 Ramsgate CT11 117 D6
Florence St 3 ME2 63 B8
Florida Cl CT16 278 B3
Florin Dr ME1 63 B4
Flowerfield TN14 121 F2
Flowerhill Way DA13 36 E1
Flower Rise ME14 161 F7
Floyd Cl TN4 286 A7
Floyd Rd SE7 1 C1
Flume End ME15 161 D2
Flyers Way The TN16 151 D1
Flying Horse La 6
CT16 310 E7
Foads Hill CT12 116 D6
Foads La CT12 116 D5
Foalhurst Cl TN10 222 E4
Focal Point Rd CT16 277 F4
Fodbury Ct CT8 50 C1
Foley Cl TN24 301 A7
Foley Ct DA1 34 B7
Foley Rd TN16 118 D1
Foley St ME14 162 A5
Folkestone, Christ Church CE Prim Sch CT20 335 C5
Folkestone Ent Ctr
CT19 334 F8
Folkestone Harbour Sta
CT20 335 E4
Folkestone Mus★
CT20 335 D5
Folkestone Race Course
CT21 332 A6
Folkestone Rd
Brookland TN31 369 B3
Church Hougham CT15 309 D4
Dover CT17,CT15 310 B7
Folkestone, St Mary's CE Prim Sch CT19 335 F6
Folkestone, St Peter's CE Prim Sch CT19 335 E5
Folkestone Sch for Girls The CT20 334 F4
Folkestone West Sta
CT18 334 F5
Folkstone Ho 4 ME15 195 F6
Folkstone, St Martin's CE Prim Sch CT18 334 B5
Folks Wood Way
CT21 332 A4
Folly Rd CT20 335 E6
Fonblanque Rd ME12 28 C2
Fontwell Cl ME15 195 F6
Fontwell Dr BR2 53 A4
Foord Almshouses
ME1 63 B3
Foord Cl DA2 34 E6
Foord Rd ME17 199 D5
Foord Rd N CT19,CT20 335 D5
Foord Rd S 14 CT20 335 D5
Foord St ME1 63 D4
Footbury Hill Rd BR6 54 A2
Foots Cray High St
DA14 31 D2
Foots Cray La DA14 31 C7
Footscray Rd SE9 30 C7
Forbes Rd ME13 138 C6
Force Green Farm Cotts
TN16 151 E3
Force Green La TN16 151 E4
Ford Cl Bridge CT4 175 F1
Herne Bay CT6 76 A4
Fordcombe CE Prim Sch
TN3 284 B5
Fordcombe Cl ME15 195 F7
Fordcombe Rd
Fordcombe TN3 284 C4
Penshurst TN11 252 A3
Fordcroft Rd BR5 54 B4
Forde Ave BR1 52 C6
Fordgate Bsns Pk DA17 4 C4
Ford Hill CT3,CT6 111 E8
Ford Ho 2 SE18 2 B1
Fordingbridge Cl
ME16 161 B5
Ford La
Trottiscliffe ME19 126 A4
Ford La *continued*
Wrotham Heath TN15,
ME19 125 F2
Fordoun Rd CT10 83 F5
Ford Rd DA11 18 B2
Fords Park Rd E16 1 A7
Ford Way TN23 267 F1
Fordwich Cl
Maidstone ME16 161 B7
Orpington BR6 53 F2
Fordwich Dr ME2 40 A2
Fordwich Gn ME8 65 C3
Fordwich Gr CT10 83 E7
Fordwich Pl CT13 180 F8
Fordwich Rd CT2 143 F4
Fordwich TH★ CT2 144 A4
Ford Wlk CT5 108 A3
Foreland Ave
Folkestone CT19 335 F6
Margate CT9 51 D1
Foreland Ct
Birchington CT7 80 D8
Ramsgate CT11 117 D5
St Margaret's at Cliffe
CT15 280 A5
Foreland Hts CT10 84 B7
Foreland Park Ho CT10 84 B7
Foreland Rd CT15 280 A4
Foreland Sch The CT10 84 A6
Forelands Sq CT14 215 B3
Foreland St SE18 2 D2
Foreland The CT1 175 B5
Foreman Ctr TN27 262 D5
Foremans Barn Rd
ME15 193 F3
Foreman's Wlk TN27 262 D5
Foreness Cl CT10 51 G3
Forestall Mdw TN23 300 B4
Forest Ave TN25 267 E4
Forest Cl BR7 53 A8
Forest Cotts TN25 203 C2
Forestdale Rd ME5 130 A8
Forest Dene TN2 286 C1
Forest Dr Chatham ME5 96 F2
Orpington BR2 85 E6
Foresters Cl ME5 96 F2
Foresters Cres DA7 14 B3
Foresters Homes The
DA7 14 B3
Foresters Way CT20 335 D5
Forest Gr TN10 222 C5
Forest Hill ME15 161 F1
Forest Lawns BR1 52 C8
Forest Rd Erith DA8 15 A6
Paddock Wood TN12 257 A6
Royal Tunbridge Wells
TN2 286 C1
Forest Ridge BR2 85 F6
Forestry Cotts CT4 239 B7
Forest Way
Eltham DA15 30 D8
Kings Hill ME19 159 A3
Orpington BR5 53 F4
Pembury TN2 287 D8
Royal Tunbridge Wells
TN2 286 D1
Forge Cl Eythorne CT15 245 C7
Five Oak Green TN12 256 B7
Hayes BR2 52 A1
Penshurst TN11 252 B4
Sellindge TN25 303 D1
Sturry CT2 143 F5
Forge Cotts
Boyden Gate CT3 112 C8
Broadstairs CT10 84 B5
Faversham ME13 139 D8
Flimwell TN5 339 C3
Nettlestead Green
ME18 192 C2
Wrotham Heath TN15 125 E1
Forge Croft TN8 217 D1
Forgefield
Bethersden TN26 297 D5
Biggin Hill TN16 118 D3
Forgefield Cotts TN18 356 A4
Forgefield Ct BR5 54 C4
Forgefields CT6 111 B8
Forge Field CT15 308 E5
Forge Hill
Aldington TN25 330 A5
Bethersden TN26 297 E5
Forge Ho
Canterbury CT1 174 E6
Ickham CT3 145 C1
Forge La Ashford TN23 268 B2
Benover ME18 226 B4
Boxley ME14 130 C2
Boyden Gate CT3 112 C8
Bredhurst ME7 98 A1
East Farleigh ME15 194 C7
Egerton Forstal TN27 232 C1
Gillingham ME7 64 E7
Gravesend DA12 37 F6
Headcorn TN27 262 D5
Higham ME3 39 C3
High Halstow ME3 23 E3
Horton Kirby DA4 57 C5
Leeds ME17 196 F7
Maidstone ME14 163 C4
Rabbit's Cross ME17,
TN12 228 F3
Ramsgate CT11 117 C7
Shorne DA12 38 E3
Sutton CT15 247 A6
Upchurch ME9 66 F3
West Kingsdown TN15 91 A1
West Peckham ME18 191 A6
Whitfield CT16 278 A8
Whitstable CT5 108 D8

Forge Mdw
Harrietsham ME17 198 D6
Stone in Oxney TN30 361 A4
Forge Meadows TN27 262 D5
Forge Meads TN30 359 E3
Forge Path CT16 278 A8
Forge Pl DA12 37 F7
Forge Rd Cobbarn TN3 312 C2
Royal Tunbridge Wells TN4 254 A1
Sittingbourne ME10 101 E6
Forge Sq TN11 220 F2
Forge The TN12 256 B7
Forge View TN15 188 B5
Forge Way
Paddock Wood TN12 257 A7
Shoreham TN14 121 F8
Formation The E16 2 B4
Formby Rd ME2 95 A7
Formby Terr ME2 95 A6
Forrens The 15 CT1 143 A1
Forrester Cl CT1 143 C2
Forsham La ME17 229 C5
Forson Cl TN30 345 B8
Forstal Cl BR2 52 A6
Forstal Cotts
Forstal ME20 129 B2
Lenham Heath ME17 200 A1
Forstal La ME17 194 D4
Forstall TN3 285 A4
Forstall The TN11 221 A2
Forstal Rd
Egerton Forstal TN27 232 C1
Forstal ME20 129 C2
Woolage Village CT4 210 E1
Forstal The
Cobbarn TN3 312 F3
Hadlow TN11 223 F8
Lenham Heath ME17 200 A1
Pembury TN2 287 E8
Preston CT3 146 B6
Wye TN25 237 E2
Forsters ME17 196 E4
Forsyth Cl ME19 128 A1
Forsyth Ct 7 ME7 64 C7
Fort Amherst Heritage Pk & Caverns* ME4 63 F5
Fort Burgoyne (Casemated Barracks) CT15 278 E2
Fort Burgoyne Rd CT16 278 E1
Fort Cl TN29 377 E6
Fort Cotts CT10 84 B4
Fort Cres CT9 50 J3
Fort Hill CT9 50 I3
Fortis Cl E16 1 C7
Fort Lower Prom CT9 50 J3
Fort Luton (Mus)* ME4 64 A1
Fort Paragon CT9 50 J3
Fort Pitt Gram Sch ME4 63 E4
Fort Pitt Hill ME1,ME4 63 E4
Fort Pitt St ME4 63 E3
Fort Prom CT9 50 J3
Fort Rd
Badgers Mount TN14 121 C4
Broadstairs CT10 84 B4
Hythe CT21 333 A2
Margate CT9 50 I3
Tilbury RM18 19 C5
Fortrye Cl DA11 36 E6
Fort St Newham E16 1 B5
Rochester ME1 63 D4
Fortuna Cl DA3 58 F5
Fortuna Ct CT11 117 D7
Fortune Way ME18 159 B3
Fortune Wlk 7 SE28 2 D3
Forty Acre La E16 1 A8
Forty Acres Hill ME12 47 C4
Forty Acres Rd CT2 142 E2
Forum The 2 ME10 101 F4
Forum Way TN23 299 E5
Forward Way ME1 96 C6
Fossdene Prim Sch SE7 1 B1
Fossdene Rd SE7 1 B1
Fosse Bank Cl TN9 254 A7
Fosse Bank New Sch TN11 221 E7
Fosse Rd TN9 222 B2
Fossett Lodge DA7 14 C6
Fossington Rd DA17 3 D2
Fostall Gn TN23 299 F7
Fostall Rd ME13 105 C1
Fosten La TN27 322 E7
Foster Clarke Dr ME17 195 D5
Foster Clark Est ME15 162 B2
Foster Cl CT19 334 E7
Foster Rd TN24 301 A6
Foster's Ave CT10 83 E7
Fosters Cl BR7 29 F3
Foster's Ct CT13 181 A7
Fosters Mews DA3 58 E7
Fosters Old School DA16 13 B5
Fosters Prim Sch DA16 13 C4
Foster St ME15 162 A3
Foster Way CT14 215 B5
Fostington Way ME5 96 F1
Fougeres Way TN24 268 A4
Foulds Cl ME8 98 B5
Founder Cl E6 2 B7
Foundry Wharf ME1 63 E4
Fountain Ct
Eynsford DA4 89 E8
Sidcup DA15 13 B1
Fountain Inn Ct CT9 50 I3
Fountain La
Maidstone ME16 161 A2
Fountain La *continued*
Sheerness ME12 28 A2
Fountain Rd ME2 39 E1
Fountains Cl TN24 269 A1
Fountain St
2 Sittingbourne ME10 101 E4
3 Whitstable CT5 74 D2
Fountain Wlk DA11 18 F1
Fouracre Cotts ME9 99 E6
Four Acres ME19 160 B5
Four Elms Hill ME3 40 E4
Four Elms Prim Sch TN8 218 B5
Four Elms Rdbt ME3 40 E3
Four Elms Rd TN8 217 D4
Four Horseshoes Pk ME13 106 D1
Four Oaks ME13 137 E8
Four Oaks Rd TN12, TN27 261 E7
Fourth Ave
Eastchurch ME12 48 F5
Gillingham ME7 64 E4
West Thurrock RM20 17 A8
Four Trees TN8 217 C3
Four Turnings CT3 146 B3
Four Wents
Langley Heath ME17 196 E3
Maidstone ME17 195 F2
Fourwents Rd ME3 41 D7
Fowey Cl ME5 97 C5
Fowler Cl
Gillingham ME8 98 C3
Sidcup DA14 31 E3
Foxborough Cl CT13 180 B6
Foxborough Hill CT13 180 B5
Foxborough La CT12 115 C6
Foxburrow Cl ME8 98 D5
Foxbury Ave BR7 30 D2
Foxbury Cl Bromley BR1 29 B2
Orpington BR6 87 A5
Foxbury Dr BR6 87 A4
Foxbury DA3 91 E7
Foxbury Rd BR1 29 B2
Foxbury Wlk DA11 36 D4
Foxbush TN11 221 C6
Fox Cl Lyminge CT18 305 B7
Newham E16 1 A8
Orpington BR6 87 A5
Foxcroft Rd SE18 12 B6
Foxden Dr ME15 162 F1
Foxdene Cl CT5 107 F6
Foxdene Rd CT5 107 F6
Foxdown Cl CT2 142 E2
Foxearth Cl TN16 118 E1
Foxendown La DA13 60 B1
Foxes Dale SE3 11 A4
Foxfield Prim Sch SE18 2 C1
Foxfield Rd BR6 86 D8
Foxglove Cl
9 Marlpit Hill TN8 217 D3
Sidcup DA15 13 A1
Foxglove Cres ME5 96 E4
Foxglove Gn TN24 268 F2
Foxglove Rd TN24 268 E1
Foxglove Rise ME14 161 E7
Foxgloves The TN12 257 B5
Foxgrove Path SE28 2 E5
Foxgrove Rd CT5 75 A1
Foxgrove ME10 101 E7
Fox Hill Keston BR2 85 C5
Sittingbourne ME10, ME9 102 D3
Foxhole La
Four Throws TN18 355 D8
Hawkhurst TN18 341 E1
Matfield TN12 288 C8
Wadhurst TN5 337 B4
Foxhole Rd SE9 11 E2
Fox Hollow Cl 2 SE18 2 E1
Fox Hollow Dr DA7 13 D4
Fox Holt Rd CT15 275 B2
Foxhome Cl BR7 30 A2
Fox House Rd DA17 4 B1
Foxhunter Pk The CT12 114 D6
Fox in the Wood TN5 336 C6
Fox La BR2 85 C5
Fox Lea TN15 156 F7
Foxley Rd ME11 46 A5
Fox Manor Way RM20 17 B8
Fox's Cross Hill CT5 108 A3
Fox's Cross Rd CT5 108 C3
Fox's Cross CT5 108 B4
Fox St ME7 64 C6
Foxtail Cl ME4 41 B2
Foxton Ho E16 2 A4
Foxton Rd RM20 17 D8
Fox Way CT4 242 F8
Foxwood Gr
Northfleet DA11 36 E7
Pratt's Bottom BR6 87 C1
Foxwood Rd DA2 35 B5
Foxwood Way DA3 59 D7
Framley Rd TN10 222 F5
Framlingham Cres SE9 29 F4
Frampton Rd CT21 333 A2
France Rd CT16 278 A5
Frances Gdns CT11 117 F8
Frances St SE18 1 F2
Francis Ave DA7 14 A5
Francis Cl CT12 116 D5
Francis Ct 7 DA8 4 E1
Francis Dr ME5 97 A2
Francis La ME15 195 F5
Francis Rd
Ashford TN23 300 B8
Broadstairs CT10 84 B7
Dartford DA1 15 D2
Orpington BR5 54 D6
Tonbridge TN11 221 D6
Frankapps Cl ME9 100 B6
Frank Burton Cl 5 SE7 1 B1
Frank Edinger Cl TN24 268 D4
Frankfield Rise TN2 286 A1
Frank Godley Ct DA14 31 B3
Franklin Dr ME14 162 D4
Franklin Pas SE9 11 E4
Franklin Rd Bexley DA7 13 E6
Gillingham ME7 64 D5
Gravesend DA12 37 D3
Maypole DA2 32 E6
Franklins Cotts ME15 194 C5
Franklyn Ho CT2 143 F5
Franklyn Rd CT2 174 C8
Franks Ct ME8 65 B2
Frank's Hollow Rd TN3 253 C2
Franks La DA4 57 B4
Frankswood Ave BR5 53 C4
Frank Walters Bsns Pk The CT10 83 D3
Frank Woolley Rd TN10 222 F5
Frant CE Prim Sch TN3 314 B4
Frant Cotts TN5 338 E1
Frant Ct TN3 314 B3
Frant Field TN8 217 C1
Frant Green Rd TN3 314 B3
Frant Rd TN2,TN3 314 A7
Frant Sta TN3 314 F5
Fraser Cl Coldblow DA5 32 C7
4 Newham E6 1 E7
Fraser Ho 3 SE18 2 A2
Fraser Rd DA8 4 D1
Freathy La TN25 268 C8
Freda Cl CT10 83 F1
Frederick Andrews Ct RM17 18 D8
Frederick Ho 4 SE18 1 E3
Frederick Pl SE18 2 B1
Frederick Rd
Deal CT14 215 A3
Gillingham ME7 64 C4
Frederick St ME10 101 E4
Freedown The CT15 280 A7
Free Heath Rd TN3, TN5 316 C3
Freehold The
East Peckham TN12 224 F6
Hadlow TN11 190 D1
Freeland Ct 24 DA14 31 A5
Freelands Gr BR1 52 B8
Freelands Rd
Bromley BR1 52 B8
Snodland ME6 127 F8
Freeland Way DA8 15 A6
Freeman Ct 3 ME10 101 E4
Freeman Gdns ME4 63 F2
Freeman Rd DA12 37 E5
Freeman's Cl CT5 108 A6
Freeman's Rd CT12 115 B6
Freeman Way ME15 195 E7
Freemasons Rd E16 1 B7
Freemen's Way CT14 215 B3
Freesia Cl
Gillingham ME7 64 F6
Orpington BR6 86 F5
Freight La TN17 320 C3
Fremantle Ho RM18 18 F6
Fremantle Rd Erith DA17 4 A2
Folkestone CT20 334 E5
Fremlin Cl TN4 285 B4
Fremlins Rd ME14 163 C4
Frencham Cl CT2 143 A4
French's Row ME9 103 D2
Frensham Cl ME10 102 B4
Frensham Rd
Rolvenden TN17 344 A1
Sidcup SE9 30 D6
Frensham Wlk ME5 96 F1
Freshfield La CT21 333 B4
Freshland Rd ME16 161 B4
Freshlands CT6 77 E5
Freshwater Cl CT6 76 B3
Freshwater Rd ME5 97 B7
Freta Rd DA6 13 F2
Frewing Cl BR7 30 A3
Friar Rd BR5 54 A4
Friars Ave ME5 96 F2
Friars Cl CT5 75 A1
Friars Mews SE9 12 A2
Friars Pk ME20 128 E2
Friars Sch TN23 299 B8
Friars The* ME20 128 E2
Canterbury CT1 142 F1
Friars Way Dover CT16 278 A3
Royal Tunbridge Wells TN2 286 D6
Friars Wlk SE2 3 D1
Friary Pl 3 ME2 63 B7
Friary Prec ME2 63 B7
Friary Way CT2 142 D2
Friday Rd DA8 4 D1
Friday St ME17 230 B6
Frid Cnr TN26 297 E7
Friendly Cl CT9 51 D1
Friends Ave CT9 83 D8
Friesian Way TN24 268 C8
Friezland Rd TN4 285 D1
Friezley La TN17 292 C1
Frimley Ct DA14 31 C3
Frindsbury Hill ME2 40 C1
Frindsbury Rd ME2 63 B8
Frinstead Gr BR5 54 D5
Frinstead Wlk ME16 161 B7
Frinsted Cl ME8 65 C3
Frinsted Rd Erith DA8 14 D7
Milstead ME9 134 E2
Frinton Rd DA14 31 E6
Friston Way ME1 96 D8
Friswell Pl 1 DA6 14 A3
Frith Bsns Pk TN25 329 B6
Frith Rd
Aldington Frith TN25 329 C6
Dover CT16 278 C1
Frithwood Cl ME15 162 F1
Frittenden CE Prim Sch TN17 293 E6
Frittenden Cl TN23 299 E6
Frittenden Rd
Rochester ME2 40 D2
Staplehurst TN12 261 B2
Frobisher Cl ME10 101 E7
Frobisher Ct
3 Dartford DA1 15 D1
2 Ramsgate CT11 117 F8
Frobisher Gdns ME1 63 C2
Frobisher Rd Erith DA8 15 A7
Newham E6 2 A7
Frobisher Way
Gravesend DA12 37 E3
Swanscombe DA9 17 B3
Frog Farm Cotts ME9 67 A4
Frog Hole La TN8, TN16 184 D2
Frog La
Bishopsbourne CT4 209 C6
Rainham RM13 4 D8
Royal Tunbridge Wells TN1 286 A2
West Malling ME19 159 C8
Frogmore Wlk ME17 199 C5
Frognal Ave DA14 31 A2
Frognal Cl ME9 103 B2
Frognal Cnr BR7 30 F2
Frognal Gdns ME9 103 C2
Frognal La ME9 103 B2
Frognal Pl DA14 31 A3
Frogs Hole La TN17, TN27 322 E3
Frog's La TN17 343 E1
Froissart Rd SE9 11 E2
Fromandez Dr TN12 289 F5
Frome Ct TN10 222 B5
Front Brents ME13 138 D8
Front Rd TN26 326 A1
Front St CT14 247 F5
Front The CT15 280 A4
Frost Cres ME5 97 A7
Frostland La TN26, TN29 350 C1
Froyle Cl ME16 161 C6
Fruiterer's Cl ME9 135 B7
Fruitfields TN5 339 C3
Fry Cl ME3 27 A6
Fry's Cotts ME3 25 C4
Frythe Cl TN17 320 D4
Frythe Cres TN17 320 D4
Frythe Way TN17 320 D4
Frythe Wlk TN17 320 D4
Fuchsia St SE2 3 B1
Fuggles Cl TN12 256 E6
Fuggles Ct TN17 342 D6
Fulbert Dr ME14 162 F5
Fulbert Rd CT16 278 B5
Fulham Ave CT9 82 C7
Fuller Cl Durgates TN5 336 E5
Orpington BR6 86 F5
Fullers Cl ME14 163 A4
Fullers Hill 7 TN16 151 D1
Fullers Yd CT9 50 J2
Fulmar Ct TN29 365 F3
Fulmar Mews CT18 307 A3
Fulmar Rd ME2 62 D6
Fulmar Way CT6 77 F4
Fulmer Rd E16 1 D8
Fulsam Pl CT9 50 H1
Fulston Manor Sch ME10 101 F2
Fulston Pl ME10 102 A3
Fulthorp Rd SE3 11 A5
Fulwich Rd DA1 15 F1
Furfield Cl ME17 195 E5
Furley Park Prim Sch TN23 300 C2
Furnace Ave TN3 317 A3
Furnace La
Hook Green TN3 316 E4
Horsmonden TN12 289 F7
Furner Cl DA1 14 F4
Furness Sch BR8 32 F2
Furnival Ct TN2 313 F8
Furrell's Rd ME1 63 D5
Further Field TN12 260 E5
Furze Bank TN8 218 B5
Furzefield Ave TN3 285 A8
Furzefield Cl BR7 30 B2
Furzefield Rd SE3 11 B7
Furze Hill Cres ME12 46 E6
Furzehill Sq BR5 54 B5
Fusilier Ave CT20 334 B5
Fyfe Way BR1 52 A7
Fyndon Ho CT1 175 C7

G

Gable Cl DA1 15 A2
Gables Cl SE12 29 A7
Gables The
11 Bromley BR1 29 B1
New Barn DA3 59 C6
Gabriel Gdns DA12 37 E3
Gabriel's Hill ME15 162 A4
Gabrielspring Rd DA3 90 B8
Gabriel Spring Road (East) DA3 90 F8
Gadby Rd ME10 101 C5
Gadsby La TN26 297 A3
Gads Hill ME7 64 F6
Gads Hill Sch ME3 39 C2
Gadwall Cl E16 1 B7
Gadwall Way SE28 2 D4
Gafford's Bridge Cotts TN12 258 C4
Gagetown Terr 1 ME14 161 F7
Gainsboro Rd 4 CT7 80 F8
Gainsborough Ave
Dartford DA1 15 C2
Margate CT9 83 C8
Tilbury RM18 19 B6
Gainsborough Cl
Folkestone CT19 335 A7
Gillingham ME8 98 D6
Sittingbourne ME10 101 B5
Gainsborough Ct 3 BR2 52 C5
Gainsborough Dr
Herne Bay CT6 77 E5
Maidstone ME16 161 B4
Northfleet DA11 36 D5
Gainsborough Gdns TN10 222 E5
Gainsborough Ho ME1 63 D5
Gainsborough Sq DA7 13 D4
Gaitskell Rd SE9 30 C7
Galahad Ave ME2 62 E6
Galahad Rd BR1 29 A4
Galena Cl Chatham ME5 97 A1
Sittingbourne ME10 101 C6
Galena Ho 4 SE18 2 F1
Gallants La
Coxheath ME15 194 A2
East Farleigh ME15 193 F6
Galleon Bvd DA2 16 D3
Galleon Cl Erith DA8 4 D2
Rochester ME1 96 C8
Galleon Mews 3 DA11 36 E8
Galleon Way ME2 40 F3
Galley Hill Rd DA11, DA10 17 F2
Galley Hill Trad Est DA10 17 E2
Galliard St CT13 181 A8
Gallions Mount Prim Sch SE18 2 F1
Gallions Prim Sch E6 2 B7
Gallions Rd SE7 1 B2
Gallions Reach Sh Pk E6 2 C8
Gallions Reach Sta E6 2 B6
Gallions View Rd SE28 2 E4
Gallon Cl SE7 1 C2
Gallops The DA13 125 F7
Gallosson Rd SE18 2 E2
Galloway Dr
Ashford TN25 268 C8
Dartford DA1 32 E8
Galloways Rd TN29 376 C5
Gallow's Cnr CT21 333 A2
Gallows Wood DA3 91 A6
Gallus Sq SE3 11 B4
Gallwey Ave CT7 80 E7
Galsworthy Cl SE28 3 B5
Galsworthy Cres SE3 11 C6
Galsworthy Rd RM18 19 C6
Galton Ho SE18 11 F6
Galway Rd ME12 28 C1
Games Ho 7 SE7 11 C8
Gamma Rd ME3 42 D7
Gammon's Farm La TN29 351 B3
Gammons Yd 6 CT2 142 F1
Gandy's La ME17 195 C2
Gange Mews 3 ME13 138 D7
Gann Rd CT5 74 F2
Gaol La 13 CT16 310 D7
Gap House Sch CT10 84 B2
Gap The Blean CT2 142 A7
Canterbury CT1 175 B5
Garden Ave DA7 14 A4
Garden Cl
Lewisham SE12 29 B5
Maidstone ME15 195 E7
Rough Common CT2 142 A2
Staplehurst TN12 260 F1
Toy's Hill TN16 185 C3
Garden Cotts
Leigh TN11 221 A2
Orpington BR5 54 C7
Wingham CT3 178 A7
Garden Ct
10 Eltham SE9 12 A1
Sevenoaks TN13 154 D5
Wouldham ME1 95 C5
Gardeners Cl SE9 29 E5
Gardeners Pl CT4 173 F1
Garden Hall The TN25 238 A1
Garden Ho 9 TN1 286 B4
Gardenia Cl ME2 40 B2
Garden La BR1 29 B2
Garden of England Pk (Mobile Home Pk) ME17 198 B7
Garden Pl
Ashford TN24 268 E6
Dartford DA2 33 D5
Garden Rd Bromley BR1 29 B2
Folkestone CT19 335 D6
Royal Tunbridge Wells TN1 286 B4
Sevenoaks TN13 154 D5
Tonbridge TN9 222 D2
Garden Row DA11 36 F5
Garden St ME7 64 A6
Gardens The
Coxheath ME17 194 C3
Ivychurch TN29 363 F4
Garden St TN1 286 B4
Garden Terr TN15 155 A6
Garden Way ME19 158 F2
Gardiner Cl BR5 54 C7
Gardiner Ho SE18 11 E7
Gardiner's Hill TN31 368 B6
Gardiner St ME7 64 C6
Gardner Cl CT18 306 F3
Gardyne Mews 12 TN9 254 B8
Gareth Gr BR1 29 A4
Garfield Pl 4 ME13 138 D7
Garfield Rd
Gillingham ME7 64 D6
Margate CT9 50 H2
Garganey Wlk SE28 3 D6
Gargery Cl DA12 37 F7
Garibaldi St SE18 2 E2
Garland Rd SE18 12 D7
Garlands TN11 221 D8
Garlinge Green Rd CT4 206 E6
Garlinge Inf Sch CT9 82 C8
Garlinge Jun Sch CT9 82 B8
Garlinge Rd TN4 254 A1
Garner Ct RM18 18 F5
Garner Dr ME19 128 A1
Garnett Cl SE9 11 F4
Garnet Wlk 9 E6 1 E8
Garrard Ave CT9 82 B8
Garrard Cl Bexley DA7 14 A4
Chislehurst BR7 30 B3
Garrick Cl TN10 222 E7
Garrick Dr SE28 2 D3
Garrick St 18 DA11 19 B1
Garrington Cl ME14 162 C6
Garrison Cl SE18 12 A7
Garrison Rd ME12 28 A3
Garrolds Cl BR8 55 D7
Garrow DA3 59 B6
Garside Cl SE28 2 D3
Garth Rd TN13 187 C7
Gartly Cotts DA1 15 C1
Garton Way TN23 299 C7
Garvary Rd E16 1 B7
Garvock Dr TN13 154 A1
Gascoyne Cl ME15 163 B2
Gascoyne Dr DA1 14 F4
Gas House Rd ME1 63 C6
Gas La ME13 139 F3
Gasoline Alley TN15 125 D2
Gas Rd
Sittingbourne ME10 101 F5
Sittingbourne,Murston ME10 102 B6
Gasson Rd DA10 17 E1
Gassons Rd ME6 127 E8
Gas St CT1 174 F7
Gasworks La TN23 268 B2
Gatcombe Cl
Chatham ME5 97 A5
Maidstone ME16 161 B5
Gatcombe Rd E16 1 A5
Gateacre Ct 14 DA14 31 B4
Gateacre Rd CT5 108 A6
Gate Farm Rd TN3, TN11 253 C4
Gatefield Cotts TN17 343 F4
Gatefield La 9 ME13 138 D7
Gate House Cotts SE12 29 B6
Gatehouse Farm Cotts TN3 253 C4
Gatekeeper Chase ME8 98 F8
Gate La CT4 273 A4
Gate Quays CT9 50 I2
Gates Green Rd BR2, BR4 85 A6
Gateway Ct 21 CT11 117 F7
Gateway Par DA12 37 F4
Gateway Prim Sch The DA2 16 B1
Gateway The CT16 310 E7
Gatland La ME16 161 B2
Gatling Rd SE2 3 A1
Gattons Way DA14 31 F4
Gatwick Farm Cotts RH19 281 A4
Gatwick Rd DA12 37 B6
Gault Cl ME15 163 A2
Gaunt's Cl CT14 215 A4
Gautrey Sq 5 E6 1 F7
Gavestone Cres SE12 29 B8
Gavestone Rd SE12 29 B8
Gavestone Terr SE12 29 B8
Gavin Ho SE18 2 E2
Gayhurst Cl ME8 98 D6
Gayhurst Dr ME10 101 C5
Gaylor Rd RM18 18 F6
Gayton Rd SE2 3 C3
Gaza Trad Est TN11 220 D7
Gazedown TN29 365 F3
Gaze Hill Ave ME10 102 A3
Gazelle Glade DA12 37 F3
Gean Cl ME5 130 A8
Geddes Cl CT18 306 F3
Geddes Pl 3 DA6 14 A3
Gedge's Hill TN12 256 F3
Geffery's Ct SE9 29 E5
General Gordon Pl 2 SE18 2 B2
Genesta Ave CT5 108 B7
Genesta Cl ME10 101 E7
Genesta Glade DA12 38 A3
Genesta Rd SE18 12 C8
Geneva Ave ME8 65 A2
Gentian Cl
4 Chatham ME5 96 E4
Maidstone ME14 162 E5
Geoffrey Ct CT7 81 A7
George Akass Ho 3 SE18 2 C1
George Alley CT14 215 D6
George Cooper Ho 11 CT20 335 C4
George Crooks Ho 7 RM17 18 B8
George Gurr Cres CT19 335 D8
George Hill Rd CT10, CT9 51 E1

George La
Boughton Street ME13 139 F3
Folkestone CT20 335 D4
Hayes BR2 52 B1
Leeds ME17 197 B7
New Romney TN28 373 B7
Rochester ME1 63 C6
George Marsham Ho ME15 194 F3
George Parris Ct ME12 47 C6
George Pk CT9 50 F1
George Roche Rd CT1 175 A6
George's Ave CT5 108 A7
Georges Cl BR5 54 C6
George Spurgen Com Prim Sch CT19 335 E7
George's Rd TN16 150 D7
George St
Ashford TN23 268 B1
Chainhurst ME15 227 A7
Deal CT14 215 D7
Dover CT17 278 C1
Grays RM17 18 A8
Maidstone ME15 162 A3
George Stone Ho 25 CT20 335 E5
George St
Ramsgate CT11 117 E7
Royal Tunbridge Wells TN2 286 C3
Sittingbourne ME10 102 B4
Sparrow's Green TN5 336 F5
Staplehurst TN12 260 E6
Tonbridge TN9 254 B8
George Summers Cl ME2 63 E8
George V Ave CT9 82 C8
George Warren Ct 1 CT9 50 J1
George Williams Way TN24 268 E5
George Wood Cl TN29 376 C6
Georgian Cl Hayes BR2 52 B1
Rushenden ME11 46 A3
Georgian Dr ME17 194 D3
Georgian Way ME8 98 C4
Georgia Pl TN2 286 C4
Geraint Rd BR1 29 A4
Gerald Ave ME4 63 F2
Geraldine Rd CT19 334 F6
Gerald Palmby Ct CT14 215 C7
Gerald Rd DA12 37 E8
Gerda Rd SE9 30 C6
Gerdview Dr DA2 33 C4
Gerlac Ho TN24 268 C5
Gerrard Ave ME1 96 E8
Gerrard Ho 4 BR2 52 C5
Gerrards Dr ME10 101 F2
Gertrude Rd DA17 4 A2
Gibbet La TN12 289 F6
Gibbetts TN3 284 F3
Gibbons Rd ME10 101 B5
Gibbs Hill
Headcorn TN27 262 E5
Nettlestead ME18 192 B5
Gibraltar Ave ME7 64 B7
Gibraltar Hill ME4 63 F4
Gibraltar La
Hawkinge CT18 307 A2
Maidstone ME14 161 F8
Gibraltar Sq CT15 278 E3
Gibson Cl DA11 36 F5
Gibson Dr ME19 158 F4
Gibson Ho ME3 40 F6
Gibson St ME10 101 E4
Gidd's Pond Cotts ME14 162 E6
Giddyhorn La ME16 161 C5
Gideon Cl DA17 4 B2
Gifford Cl ME8 65 C3
Gigger's Green Rd TN25 351 C7
Giggs Hill BR5 54 A8
Gighill Rd ME20 127 F4
Gilbert Cl
Gillingham ME7 98 A5
Swanscombe DA10 17 D1
Woolwich SE18 11 F6
Gilbert Pl 9 CT20 334 E3
Gilbert Rd
4 Ashford TN24 268 B2
Bromley BR1 29 A1
Erith DA17 4 A3
Ramsgate CT11 117 D8
Gilbert Terr 2 ME14 161 F7
Gilbert Way CT1 174 E6
Gilbourne Rd SE18 12 F8
Gilchrist Ave CT6 76 C2
Gilchrist Cotts TN14 187 C2
Gildenhill Rd BR8 33 C1
Gildersome St SE18 12 A8
Giles Field DA12 37 F7
Giles Gdns CT9 82 F8
Giles La CT2 142 D4
Giles-Young Ct 7 ME10 101 E5
Gilford Rd CT14 215 D5
Gilham Gr CT14 215 B4
Gillan Ct 1 SE12 29 B5
Gill Ave Newham E16 1 A7
Rochester ME2 40 D2
Gill Cres DA11 36 F5
Gill Ct SE18 2 C2
Gillett Rd TN29 376 D7
Gilletts La ME19 160 A6
Gillies Ct DA14 30 E4
Gillies Rd TN15 90 E5
Gillingham Coll The ME7 64 F4
Gillingham Gate ME7 64 C8
Gillingham Gate Rd ME7 64 C8
Gillingham Gn ME7 64 E6
Gillingham Rd ME7 64 D5
Gillingham Sta ME7 64 D5
Gill La
Aldington Frith TN25 329 A8
Ruckinge TN26 328 C2
Gillman Cl CT18 306 F4
Gillmans Rd BR5 54 B1
Gillon Mews 9 CT1 143 B2
Gill's Rd
Green Street Green DA2 35 B1
Sutton at H DA4 57 F8
Gills Terr ME8 66 C3
Gill The TN2 287 E8
Gilroy Way BR5 54 B2
Gimble Way TN2 255 D1
Gingerbread La TN18 339 F2
Ginsbury Cl ME2 63 E6
Gipps Cross La TN3 284 F3
Gipsy La RM17 18 C8
Gipsy Rd DA16 13 D5
Giralda Cl E16 1 D8
Giraud Dr ME13 138 B8
Glack Rd CT14 214 F4
Glade Bsns Ctr The RM20 16 F8
Glades Sh Ctr The BR1 52 A7
Glades The DA12 37 D2
Gladeswood Rd DA17 4 B2
Glade The Bromley BR1 52 D7
Chatham ME5 97 A2
Deal CT14 214 F6
Greenwich SE7 11 C7
Sevenoaks TN13 154 B4
Tonbridge TN10 222 E7
Gladstone Ct CT10 83 F4
Gladstone Dr ME10 102 C4
Gladstone Rd
Ashford TN24 300 E7
Broadstairs CT10 83 F4
Chatham ME4 63 E2
Dartford DA1 15 F1
Deal CT14 215 C4
Folkestone CT19 335 E6
Maidstone ME14 162 A6
Margate CT9 50 I1
Orpington BR6 86 C5
Rusthall TN4 285 B4
Tonbridge TN9 222 B1
Whitstable CT5 74 D2
Gladwell Rd BR1 29 A2
Gladwyn Cl ME8 98 D4
Glamford Rd ME2 62 D5
Glamis Cl ME5 97 A5
Glanfield Ct TN1 286 C5
Glanville Rd
Bromley BR2 52 B6
Gillingham ME7 64 D5
Rochester ME2 63 A8
Glasbrook Rd SE9 29 D8
Glasgow Ho 8 ME15 195 E7
Glassenbury Rd TN17 319 E4
Glassmill La BR2 52 A7
Glass Yd SE18 2 A3
Glastonbury Cl BR5 54 C1
Gleaming Wood Dr ME5 130 D8
Gleaners Cl ME14 162 E4
Gleanings Mews ME1 63 C5
Glebe Cl
St Margaret's at Cliffe CT15 279 F6
Smarden TN27 264 B2
Glebe Cotts
Brasted TN16 152 B4
Eastling ME13 168 E7
Glebe Ct CT12 115 B5
Glebefield The TN13 153 F4
Glebe Gdns
Lenham ME17 199 E5
6 Margate CT9 82 B8
Glebe House Dr BR2 52 B1
Glebe Ho 7 SE18 2 A2
Glebe La ME16 161 A1
Glebeland TN27 232 F4
Glebelands
Alkham CT15 276 D1
Ash CT3 147 C2
Bidborough TN3 253 C3
Biddenden TN27 294 F1
Crayford DA1 14 F3
Mersham TN25 301 E4
Penshurst TN11 252 A3
Glebe La
Sevenoaks TN13 154 B1
Sittingbourne ME10 102 B2
Glebe Mdw ME18 192 E7
Glebe Pl DA4 57 C5
Glebe Rd Bromley BR1 52 A8
Gillingham ME7 64 E3
Margate CT9 82 B8
Northfleet DA11 36 F7
Sevenoaks Weald TN14 187 B3
Glebe The
Bidborough TN3 253 D3
Charing TN27 234 D7
Chislehurst BR7 53 C8
Cuxton ME2 62 C2
Pembury TN2 287 D8
Penshurst TN11 252 A3
Glebe Way
Ashford TN24 268 D6
Erith DA8 14 E8
Whitstable CT5 108 D8
Gleeson Dr BR6 86 F6
Glemsford Cotts CT2 141 E1
Glenalvon Way 7 SE18 1 E2
Glen Ave CT6 77 C5
Glenavon Ho CT10 84 B7
Glenbarr Cl SE9 12 B4
Glenbervie Dr CT6 77 E5
Glenbrook Cl CT6 77 D5
Glenbrook Gr ME10 101 E7
Glencairne Cl E16 1 D8
Glencoe Jun Sch ME4 64 A2
Glencoe Rd
Chatham ME4 64 A2
Margate CT9 51 A1
Glen Ct Lewisham SE12 29 A8
Sidcup DA14 31 A4
Glendale Cl SE9 12 A4
Glendale Ct TN2 286 D6
Glendale CT20 335 E4
Glendale Rd Erith DA8 4 C2
Minster (Sheppey) ME12 47 B7
Northfleet DA11 36 E5
Glendale ME8 55 F4
Glendale Way SE28 3 C6
Glendower Cres BR6 54 A3
Glendown Rd SE2 3 A1
Glen Dunlop Ho The TN13 154 C5
Gleneagles Cl BR6 53 D1
Gleneagles Ct ME5 96 F2
Gleneagles Dr ME15 162 A1
Gleneagles Gn 1 BR6 53 D1
Glenesk Rd SE9 12 B3
Glenfield Rd CT16 278 B3
Glengall Rd DA7 13 E4
Glen Gr CT17 310 B7
Glenhead Cl SE9 12 B4
Glen Ho 6 E16 2 A5
Glenhouse Rd SE9 12 A2
Glenhurst Ave DA5 31 F7
Glen Iris Ave CT2 142 C2
Glen Iris Cl CT2 142 C2
Glenister St E16 2 A4
Glenlea Rd SE9 12 A3
Glenleigh Rd ME18 192 D6
Glenluce Rd SE3 11 A8
Glenlyon Rd SE9 12 A2
Glenmore Pk TN2 313 F8
Glenmore Rd DA16 12 F6
Glenmount Path 1 SE18 2 C1
Glen Rd CT14 248 C6
Glenrose Ct DA14 31 B3
Glenshiel Rd SE9 12 A2
Glenside Ave CT1 143 B2
Glenside CT5 109 A8
Glen The
Minster (Sheppey) ME12 47 B7
Orpington BR6 86 A7
Shepherdswell CT15 244 D5
Upstreet CT3 112 D3
Glentrammon Ave BR6 86 F4
Glentrammon Cl BR6 86 F5
Glentrammon Gdns BR6 86 F4
Glentrammon Rd
Orpington BR6 86 F4
Orpington BR6 87 A4
Glenure Rd SE9 12 A2
Glenview SE2 13 D8
Glen View DA12 37 C7
Glen View Rd BR1 52 D7
Glen Wlk CT5 108 A3
Glenwood Cl
Chatham ME5 64 C1
Gillingham ME7 98 A7
Maidstone ME16 161 C5
Tenterden TN30 324 B3
Glenwood Ct 18 DA14 31 A4
Glenwood Dr ME12 47 C6
Glenwood TN30 324 B3
Glimpsing Gn DA18 3 E3
Glistening Glade ME8 98 E6
Gload Cres BR5 87 D8
Globe Ct SE18 12 C8
Globe La ME4 63 F5
Globe Yd 15 DA11 19 B1
Gloster Cl CT18 307 B3
Gloster Ropewalk CT17 310 C5
Gloster Way CT17 310 C5
Gloucester Ave
Bexley DA16 12 F3
Broadstairs CT10 83 F3
Margate CT9 51 D2
Sidcup DA15 30 E6
Gloucester Cl ME8 99 A8
Gloucester Ct RM18 18 F5
Gloucester Mews TN28 373 C8
Gloucester Par DA15 13 A2
Gloucester Pl 17 CT20 335 D5
Gloucester Rd
Dartford DA1 33 B8
Erith DA17 3 F1
Gravesend DA12 37 C4
Maidstone ME15 195 D8
Turner's Green TN5 336 F6
Whitstable CT5 74 F2
Glover Cl
Sittingbourne ME10 68 F1
Woolwich SE2 3 C2
Glover Rd TN24 268 E1
Glovers Cl TN16 118 B3
Glovers Cres ME10 101 F3
Glovers Mill ME4 63 D3
Gloxinia Rd DA13 36 B2
Glyn Davies Cl TN13 153 E7
Glyndebourne Pk BR6 86 B8
Glynde Rd DA7 13 E4
Glyndon Rd SE18 2 D2
Glyn Dr DA14 31 B4
Glynne Cl ME8 98 D6
Goad Ave ME5 97 B3
Goat Lees La TN25 268 D8
Goatsfield Rd TN16 150 C7
Gobery Hill CT3 146 B1
Goddards Cl TN17 320 B4
Goddard's Green Cotts TN17 321 F1
Godden Rd
Canterbury CT2 143 A4
Snodland ME6 127 F8
Godden Way ME8 65 A4
Goddings Dr ME1 63 A3
Goddington Chase BR6 87 B6
Goddington Ho BR6 87 C7
Goddington La
Harrietsham ME17 198 B6
Orpington BR6 87 A7
Goddington Rd ME2 63 B8
Godfrey Cl ME2 39 F1
Godfrey Evans Cl TN10 222 F5
Godfrey Gdns CT4 173 F1
Godfrey Hill SE18 1 E2
Godfrey Ho CT5 108 E8
Godfrey's Grave ME13 140 B7
Godfrey Rd SE18 1 F2
Godfreys Cotts ME13 203 C8
Godfrey Wlk TN23 300 B8
Godinton* TN23 267 C4
Godinton La TN23, TN26 267 D5
Godinton Prim Sch TN23 267 D3
Godinton Rd TN23 268 A2
Godinton Way TN23 268 A2
Godinton Way Ind Est TN23 268 B2
Godstow Rd SE2 3 C4
Godwin Bglws CT9 51 B3
Godwin Cl ME10 68 F1
Godwin Cotts CT9 51 A3
Godwin Ho SE18 11 F6
Godwin Rd Bromley BR2 52 C6
Canterbury CT1 174 C6
Dover CT16 310 F8
Margate CT9 51 A3
Godwyne Cl CT16 310 D8
Godwyne Ct CT16 278 D1
Godwyne Rd CT16 278 D1
Godwyn Gdns CT20 335 A4
Godwyn Rd Deal CT14 215 C8
Folkestone CT20 335 A4
Gogway CT4 240 B4
Goldace RM17 17 F8
Goldcrest Cl
Newham E16 1 D8
Woolwich SE28 3 C6
Goldcrest Dr ME4 41 C2
Goldcrest Wlk CT5 108 B6
Golden Acre La CT8 81 D7
Golden Cl CT8 81 D7
Golden Hill CT5 108 F6
Golden Plover Cl E16 1 A7
Golden Sq
New Romney TN28 373 A6
Tenterden TN30 345 B8
Golden St CT14 215 D7
Golden Wood Cl ME5 130 D8
Goldfinch Cl
Faversham ME13 105 C1
Herne Bay CT6 77 C2
Larkfield ME20 128 A2
Orpington BR6 87 A5
Paddock Wood TN12 257 A5
Goldfinch Rd SE28 2 D3
Gold Hill TN25 235 D4
Goldie Leigh Hospl SE2 13 C8
Golding Cl Ditton ME20 128 C1
Rochester ME1 63 E1
Golding Gdns TN12 225 A6
Golding Rd TN13 154 C5
Goldings Cl ME19 159 A3
Goldings TN12 256 E5
Goldings The ME8 98 C8
Goldmark Ho SE3 11 B4
Goldsel Rd BR8 55 E5
Goldsmid Rd TN9 254 C8
Goldsmid St 3 SE18 2 E1
Goldsmith Ct TN30 324 B1
Goldsmith RM17 17 F8
Goldsmith Rd ME8 98 E5
Goldstone Dro CT3 147 E7
Goldstone Wlk ME5 97 A1
Gold St DA12,DA13 60 E4
Goldsworth Dr ME2 40 A1
Goldthorne Cl ME14 162 C5
Goldups Lane Cotts CT4 171 C1
Goldups La CT4 171 C1
Goldwell Cl TN25 330 A6
Goldwell Hos TN25 330 A6
Goldwell La
Aldington TN25 330 B7
Great Chart TN23,TN26 298 F8
Goldwing Cl E16 1 A7
Golf Ct CT14 182 C1
Golf Links Ave DA11 37 B3
Golford Rd TN17 320 F4
Golf Rd Bromley BR1 53 A6
Deal CT14 215 C8
Golf Road Pl CT14 215 C8
Gollogly Terr 8 SE7 1 C1
Gooch Cl ME16 161 D8
Goodall Cl ME8 98 E5
Goodban Sq CT3 147 D1
Goodbury Rd TN15 123 B6
Goodcheap La TN25 269 D2
Goodensfield TN5 336 E5
Goodfellow Way 3 CT16 310 D8
Good Hope CT14 214 F4
Gooding Ho SE7 1 C1
Good Intent Cotts TN27 233 A5
Goodley Stock Rd TN8,TN16 184 B6
Goodmead Rd BR6 54 A2
Goodnestone CE Prim Sch CT3 178 C2
Goodnestone Gdns* CT3 178 C1
Goodnestone Hill CT3 178 D2
Goodnestone Rd
Sittingbourne ME10 102 B4
Wingham CT3 178 B5
Goods Hill TN30 344 D8
Goods Station Rd TN1 286 B4
Goodtrees La TN8 282 B2
Goodwin Ave CT5 75 E2
Goodwin Cl TN8 217 B2
Goodwin Ct CT9 51 D3
Goodwin Dr
Maidstone ME14 162 B8
Sidcup DA14 31 D6
Goodwin Pk CT9 83 A5
Goodwin Rd
Cliffe Woods ME3 40 B7
Ramsgate CT11 117 B5
St Margaret's at Cliffe CT15 280 A4
Goodwins The TN2 285 F1
Goodwood Cl
High Halstow ME23 23 E4
Maidstone ME15 195 F6
Goodwood Cres DA12 37 C2
Goodworth Rd TN15 124 F3
Goosander Way SE28 2 D3
Goose Cl ME5 97 A7
Goose Farm CT2 143 D7
Goosefields ME13 106 E1
Goose Green Cl BR5 54 A7
Gooseneck La TN27 262 C5
Goose Sq 8 E6 1 F7
Gordon Ave ME11 46 A4
Gordon Cl
Ashford TN24 268 D2
East Tilbury RM18 20 D7
Sittingbourne ME10 102 C4
Gordon Cotts ME9 134 B6
Gordon Ct ME17 194 E3
Gordon Gr CT8 50 C1
Gordon Ho SE12 29 A8
Gordon Inf Sch ME2 63 A8
Gordon Jun Sch ME2 63 A8
Gordon Pl DA12 19 C1
Gordon Prim Sch SE9 11 F3
Gordon Promenade E DA12 19 D1
Gordon Rd
Canterbury CT1 174 F7
Chatham,Luton ME4 64 B2
Chatham ME4 64 A7
Dartford DA1 33 D8
Dover CT16 278 A5
Erith DA17 4 C2
Faversham ME13 138 E8
Folkestone CT20 334 D6
Gillingham ME7 64 E5
Herne Bay CT6 76 F4
Hoo St Werburgh ME3 41 D5
Margate CT9 51 A3
Margate, Westwood CT9 83 A5
Northfleet DA11 36 E8
Ramsgate CT11 117 D8
Rochester ME2 63 A8
Royal Tunbridge Wells TN4 286 C7
Sevenoaks TN13 154 B2
Sidcup DA15 12 E2
Whitstable CT5 108 D8
Gordon Sq
Birchington CT7 80 F7
Faversham ME13 138 E7
Gordon Terr
Lydd TN29 376 C5
Rochester ME1 63 C4
Gordon Way BR1 52 A8
Gore Cl CT13 180 B3
Gore Cotts Dartford DA2 34 C4
Upchurch ME9 66 E1
Gore Court Rd
Maidstone ME15 195 F5
Sittingbourne ME10 101 E2
Gore Ct TN24 268 C3
Gore End Cl CT7 80 F7
Gore Farm Cotts DA2 34 C5
Gore Farm CT13 180 B3
Gore Farm Trails* ME9 66 D1
Gore Green Rd ME3 39 E7
Gore La Brandfold TN17 290 E4
Eastry CT13 180 B2
Gorely Ho 14 CT17 310 D7
Gore Mews 3 CT1 143 B2
Gore Rd Dartford DA2 34 C6
Eastry CT13 180 B3
Silver Street ME9 133 F5
Gore Street Farm Cotts CT12 114 A7
Gore Terr CT13 180 B3
Goretop La CT14 181 C6
Gorham Cl ME6 127 F7
Gorham Dr
Maidstone ME15 163 A1
Tonbridge TN9 254 E8
Gorman Rd SE18 1 F2
Gorrell Rd CT5 74 E1
Gorringe Ave DA4 57 D7
Gorse Ave ME5 96 F5
Gorse Cl E16 1 A7
Gorse Cres ME20 160 D8
Gorse La CT6 77 C2
Gorse Mead TN23 299 F8
Gorse Rd Orpington BR5 88 A8
Rochester ME2 62 F8
Royal Tunbridge Wells TN2 286 E5
Sittingbourne ME10 102 C5
Gorse Way DA3 59 A4
Gorse Wood Rd
Hartley DA3 59 A5
New Barn DA3 59 A6
Gorst St ME7 64 C5
Goschen Rd CT17 310 B8
Gosfield Rd CT6 77 A4
Goshawk Ho 1 ME10 102 A4
Gosmere Farm Barns
Doddington ME13 167 E7
Sheldwich ME13 170 E7
Gossage Rd SE18 2 D1
Gosselin St CT5 108 E8
Goss Hall La CT3 148 A2
Goss Hill BR8,DA2 33 C2
Gosshill Rd BR7 53 A7
Gossington Cl BR7 30 B4
Goteley Mere TN24 268 C7
Gothic Cl Dartford DA1 33 D5
Deal CT14 215 B1
Gothic Cotts TN26 235 A1
Goudhurst Cl
Canterbury CT2 143 A4
Maidstone ME16 161 E4
Goudhurst & Kilndown CE Prim Sch TN17 318 F8
Goudhurst Rd
Cranbrook TN17 320 D8
Gillingham ME8 65 B3
Horsmonden TN12 290 B5
Knox Bridge TN12,TN17 292 C6
Marden TN12 259 B5
Gouge Ave DA11 36 E7
Gough Rd CT20 334 E3
Gould Rd ME5 97 B3
Gourock Rd SE9 12 A2
Gover Hill TN11,ME18 190 E6
Gover View TN11 190 E7
Gower Ho ME14 162 A6
Grace Ave Bexley DA7 13 F5
Maidstone ME16 161 D6
Grace Cl SE9 29 D5
Grace Ct 16 CT20 335 D5
Grace Hill CT20 335 D5
Grace Mdw CT16 278 A7
Grace Rd ME12 28 A1
Grace Sch CT20 335 D5
Grace Wlk CT14 215 A5
Gracious Lane Bridge TN13 187 A6
Gracious Lane End TN14 186 F5
Gracious La TN13 187 B5
Grafton Ave ME1 96 E8
Grafton Rd
Broadstairs CT10 83 F8
Sittingbourne ME10 101 F4
Grafton Rise CT6 76 C4
Graham Cl ME4 63 F6
Graham Ct 12 BR1 29 B1
Graham Ho SE18 12 B7
Graham Rd DA7 14 A3
Grainey Field ME9 99 E4
Grainger Wlk TN10 222 E6
Grain Rd Gillingham ME8 98 C3
Grain ME3 26 D3
Grampian Cl
Orpington BR6 53 F3
Royal Tunbridge Wells TN2 286 D5
Grampian Way ME15 163 A1
Grampion Cl TN24 268 C4
Gram Sch for Girls Wilmington The DA2 33 B5
Gram's Rd CT14 248 C8
Granada Ho 8 ME15 162 A4
Granada St 9 ME15 162 A4
Granary Cl
Maidstone ME14 162 E5
Rainham ME8 65 F1
Granary Cotts TN16 152 C3
Granary Court Rd TN25 303 A4
Granary TN12 257 B6
Granary Pl CT5 108 D8
Granby Ho 8 SE18 1 F2
Granby Rd Eltham SE9 11 F4
Northfleet DA11 18 D1
Woolwich SE18 2 B3
Grand Ct
6 Folkestone CT20 335 B3
7 Gillingham ME7 64 C6
Littlestone-on-Sea TN28 373 E5
Grand Depot Rd SE18 2 A1
Grand Dr CT6 76 C4
Grand Mans CT10 84 B3
Grand Par TN28 373 E5
Grand Pavilion CT5 74 F3
Grandshore La TN17 293 B5
Grandsire Gdns ME3 41 E6
Grand The 4 CT20 335 B3
Grand View Ave TN16 118 C3
Grange Cl
Edenbridge TN8 217 C1
Leybourne ME19 127 C2
Sidcup DA15 31 A5
Westerham TN16 151 C1
Grange Cres
6 Dartford DA2 16 B1
Erith SE28 3 C7
Tenterden TN30 324 A3
Grange Ct
1 Folkestone CT20 335 C4
9 Ramsgate CT11 117 C6
Grange Dr Bromley BR7 29 F2
Pratt's Bottom BR6 87 C2
Grange Gdns TN4 285 D4
Grange Hill
Chatham ME5 64 B3
Plaxtol TN15 189 E8
Grangehill Pl SE9 11 F4

Grangehill Rd SE9 11 F3
Grange Ho Erith DA8 15 A5
Gravesend DA11 37 A8
Maidstone ME16 161 A2
Grange La
Boxley ME14 130 A1
Hartley DA3 59 B2
Grange Park Sch
ME19 127 B3
Grange Rd CT10 83 F6
Grange Rdbt ME7 65 A6
Grange Rd Deal CT14 215 B5
Folkestone CT19 334 E6
Gillingham ME7 65 A6
Gravesend DA11 37 A8
Grays RM17 18 B8
Herne Bay CT6 77 C4
Hythe CT21 333 B4
Orpington BR6 86 C8
Platt TN15 157 C7
Ramsgate CT11 117 C6
Rochester ME2 63 B7
Rusthall TN4 285 D4
Sevenoaks TN13 187 A8
Tenterden TN30 323 F3
Tenterden TN30 324 A3
Grange The
East Malling ME19 160 A7
Shepherdswell CT15 244 D5
Sutton at H DA4 57 D8
Westerham TN16 151 C1
West Kingsdown TN15 90 F2
Whitstable CT5 108 A6
Grange Way
Broadstairs CT10 83 F2
Erith DA8 15 B7
Hartley DA3 58 F3
Rochester ME1 63 C3
Grangeways Cl DA11 36 F4
Grangewood DA5 31 F7
Granite St SE18 2 F1
Grant Cl
Broadstairs CT10 83 E6
Rainham ME7 65 B1
Grant Dr ME15 195 D6
Grantham Ave CT14 215 A5
Grantley Cl TN23 300 A8
Granton Rd DA14 31 C2
Grant's Cotts ME17 199 B5
Grant Rd ME3 40 C3
Grants La TN8,RH8 216 C6
Granville Ave
Broadstairs CT10 84 B3
Ramsgate CT12 83 B1
Granville Cl ME13 138 C7
Granville Ct Deal CT14 215 C2
Erith SE2 3 D1
Maidstone ME14 162 A6
Sevenoaks TN13 154 A3
Granville Dr CT6 76 B2
Granville Farm Mews [24]
CT11 117 F7
Granville Ho [18] CT11 117 F7
Granville Marina [20]
CT11 117 F7
Granville Mews DA14 31 A4
Granville Par CT20 334 E3
Granville Pl
Folkestone CT20 334 F3
Sheerness ME12 28 C2
Granville Rd
Bexley DA16 13 C4
Broadstairs CT10 84 B3
Deal CT14 215 C2
Granville Rd E CT20 334 F3
Granville Rd
Gillingham ME7 64 E5
Kingsdown CT14 248 D3
Limpsfield RH8 183 A7
Maidstone ME14 162 A6
Northfleet DA11 36 F7
Royal Tunbridge Wells
TN1 286 C5
St Margaret's at Cliffe
CT15 280 B6
Sevenoaks TN13 154 A3
Sheerness ME12 28 C2
Sidcup DA14 31 B4
Westerham TN16 151 C1
Granville Sch The
TN13 154 A4
Granville St Deal CT14 215 D5
Dover CT16 278 C1
Granville The CT15 280 B6
Grapple Rd ME14 162 A7
Grasdene Rd SE18 13 A7
Grasmere Ave
Orpington BR6 86 B7
Ramsgate CT11 117 A7
Grasmere Gdns
Folkestone CT19 335 B7
Orpington BR6 86 B7
Grasmere Gr ME2 40 C2
Grasmere Pk CT5 109 B8
Grasmere Rd
Ashford TN24 268 C6
Bexley DA7 14 C5
Orpington BR6 86 B7
Whitstable CT5 109 B8
Grasmere Way CT3 210 F6
Grasshaven Way SE28 2 F5
Grassington Rd [11]
DA14 31 A4
Grasslands
Ashford TN23 299 D7
Langley Heath ME17 196 E4
Grassmere
Leybourne ME19 127 F2
St Mary's Bay TN29 365 E3
Grassy Glade ME7 98 B6
Grassy La TN13 187 B8
Gravel Castle Rd CT4 243 A8
Gravel Hill DA6 14 B2
Gravel Hill Cl DA6 14 B1
Gravel Hill Prim Sch
DA6 14 B3
Gravel Hill ME13 201 C8
Gravel La CT15 309 A4
Gravelly Bottom Rd
ME17 197 B2
Gravelly Field TN23 299 C8
Gravelly Ways TN12 225 D5
Gravel Pit Way BR6 54 A1
Gravel Rd Orpington BR2 85 E8
Sutton at H DA4 34 B1
Gravel Wlk
[3] Ashford TN23 268 B3
[12] Canterbury CT1 174 F8
Rochester ME1 63 D5
Gravelwood Cl BR7 30 C5
Graveney Cl ME3 40 C7
Graveney Prim Sch
ME13 106 E1
Graveney Rd
Faversham ME13 138 F7
Maidstone ME15 195 F7
Gravesend Gram Sch for
Girls DA11 37 A7
Gravesend Gram Sch
DA12 37 D8
Gravesend & North Kent
Hospl DA11 19 A1
Gravesend Rd
Higham ME2,ME3,DA12 39 C2
Rochester ME2 62 F8
Shorne DA12 38 D5
Vigo Village TN15 125 D6
Gravesend Sta DA11 19 B1
Graves Est DA16 13 B5
Gravesham Ct [8] DA12 37 B8
Gravesham Mus*
DA11 19 B1
Gray Cl CT18 307 C5
Gray Ho SE2 3 D1
Grayland Cl BR1 52 D8
Graylands RM17 17 E8
Graylen Cl CT14 215 C7
Graylings Ct ME10 101 C2
Graylings The ME1 63 B3
Grayne Ave ME3 27 B5
Grays Farm Prim Sch
BR5 54 B8
Grays Farm Production
Village BR5 54 B8
Grays Farm Rd BR5 54 B8
Grayshott Cl ME10 101 F3
Grays Rd TN16 151 D7
Grays Sh Ctr RM17 18 A8
Grays Sta RM17 18 A8
Graystone Rd CT5 75 A2
Grays Way CT1 174 B6
Grazeley Cl DA6 14 C2
Great Ash BR7 30 A1
Great Basin Rd ME12 27 F2
Great Bounds Dr TN4 253 E3
Great Brooms Rd TN4 286 C8
Great Burton Ho TN24 268 E5
Great Chart Prim Sch
TN23 299 D8
Great Conduit St
CT21 333 C2
Great Courtlands TN3 285 A3
Great Elms TN11 190 E1
Great Elms Rd BR2 52 C5
Great Footway TN3 284 F3
Great Hall Arc [3] TN1 286 B3
Great Harry Dr SE9 30 A5
Great Ivy Mill Cotts
ME15 194 F7
Great Lines ME7 64 B5
Great Lodge Ret Pk
TN2 254 E1
Great Maytham Hall*
TN17 343 F2
Great Mead TN8 217 C3
Greatness La TN14 154 C6
Greatness Rd TN14 154 C6
Great Oak
Hurst Green TN19 354 A3
Royal Tunbridge Wells
TN2 286 D6
Great Oaks Small Sch
CT13 180 B2
Great Queen St DA1 15 F1
Great South Ave ME4 64 A1
Greatstone Prim Sch
TN28 373 D2
Great Stour Pl [3] CT2 142 F1
Great Thrift BR5 53 C5
Great Till Cl TN14 121 E3
Greatwood BR7 30 A1
Grebe Apartments [15]
ME15 195 E5
Grebe Cl
Hawkinge CT18 307 A4
Lower Stoke ME3 25 C4
Grebe Cres CT21 353 C8
Grebe Ct ME20 127 F1
Grecian Rd TN1 286 B2
Grecian St ME14 162 A6
Greenacre Cl
Chatham ME5 97 A5
Swanley BR8 55 E5
Greenacre DA1 33 D6
Greenacre Dr CT14 215 C1
Greenacre CT4 209 D3
Greenacre Sch ME5 96 F5
Green Acres Cl CT6 77 B3
Greenacres Cl BR6 86 C6
Greenacres Deal CT14 182 B4
Eltham SE9 12 A1
Green Acres CT15 245 D7
Greenacres Prim Sch &
Language Impairment
Unit SE9 30 A6
Green Acres DA14 30 F4
Greenbank
Ashford TN24 268 D6
Chatham ME5 97 B8
Green Bank Cl ME7 98 A5
Greenbank Lodge [2]
BR7 53 A8
Greenbanks
Dartford DA1 33 E6
Lyminge CT18 305 C6
Greenbay Rd SE7 11 D7
Greenborough Cl
ME15 195 E6
Green Cl CT18 307 B4
Green Cloth Mews [2]
CT1 143 B2
Green Cl ME1 63 D2
Green Court Rd BR8 55 D3
Greencourt Rd BR5 53 E4
Greencroft TN23 299 E6
Greencroft Cl E6 1 D8
Green Ct Bridge CT4 176 A1
Folkestone CT19 335 E7
Greendale Wlk [4]
DA11 36 E5
Green Dell CT2 142 F4
Green Farm Cl BR6 86 F5
Green Farm La DA12 38 E5
Greenfield Cl
Eccles ME20 129 A6
Rusthall TN4 285 C5
Greenfield Cotts
Boxley ME14 130 C3
[9] Canterbury CT1 174 F7
Greenfield Ct SE9 29 E5
Greenfield Dr BR1 52 C7
Greenfield TN8 217 D1
Greenfield Gdns BR5 53 D2
Greenfield Rd
Folkestone CT19 335 E7
Gillingham ME7 64 D6
Joyden's Wood DA2 32 D3
Ramsgate CT12 83 C2
Greenfields Cl ME3 40 D3
Greenfields
Maidstone ME15 195 E8
Sellindge TN25 303 E2
Greenfinches
Gillingham ME7 97 F6
New Barn DA3 59 B6
Greenfrith Dr TN10 222 B6
Green Gates CT16 278 A8
Green Gdns BR6 86 C5
Greenhaven Dr SE28 3 B7
Green Hedges TN30 345 B8
Green Hill BR6 118 F7
Greenhill Bridge Rd
CT6 76 D3
Greenhill Cl CT12 115 B7
Greenhill Cts SE18 1 F1
Greenhill Gdns
Herne Bay CT6 76 D3
Minster (Thanet) CT12 115 B7
Green Hill La ME17 198 D1
Greenhill La TN27 264 F7
Green Hill ME15 163 B1
Greenhill Rd
Herne Bay CT6 76 C2
Northfleet DA11 36 F6
Otford TN14 122 C5
Green Hills CT4 242 D8
Greenhill TN12 260 E5
Greenhill Terr SE18 1 F1
Green Hill SE18 1 F1
Greenhithe Cl DA15 30 E8
Greenhithe for Bluewater
Sta DA9 17 A2
Greenhithe [3] ME15 162 A3
Greenholm Rd SE9 12 B2
Greenhouse La CT2 142 E2
Greenhurst La
Limpsfield RH8 183 A4
Oxted RH8 183 A3
Greening St SE2 3 C2
Green La Alkham CT15 276 D3
Ashford TN23 299 E5
Bethersden TN26 297 A2
Broadstairs CT10 83 E5
Capel-le-F CT18 308 B3
Challock TN25 203 A2
Cliffe ME3 22 B6
Collier Street TN12 258 E8
Deal CT14 215 B1
Dover CT16 278 B3
East End TN17 322 C2
Eltham BR7,SE9 30 B5
Eythorne CT15 245 D7
Folkestone CT19 335 E7
Four Elms TN8 218 C7
Goodnestone CT3 179 B3
Grain ME3 27 B5
Hythe CT21 333 A2
Langley Heath ME17 196 E3
Maidstone ME17 195 C3
Margate CT9 83 E8
Meopham Station DA13 60 B2
Greenlands TN15 157 C7
Greenlands Rd TN15 155 B8
Greenlands DA12 60 D4
Green Lane Ave CT21 333 A2
Green Lane Bsns Pk
SE9 30 A6
Green Lane Cotts
Collier Street TN12 226 D1
Langley Heath ME17 196 E3
Green La
Old Wives Lees CT4 172 C2
Paddock Wood TN12 257 A5
Platt's Heath ME17 198 F2
Green La *continued*
Rhodes Minnis CT4,
CT18 272 E2
Rodmersham ME9 135 B7
St Margaret's at Cliffe
CT15 247 F1
Smarden TN27 264 A1
Sutton Valence ME17 229 B4
Temple Ewell CT16 277 E6
Green La The TN11 220 F1
Green La
Trottiscliffe ME19 126 A5
Whitfield CT16 277 E7
Whitstable CT5 108 D8
Green Lawns [10] SE18 2 B2
Greenlaw St SE18 2 A3
Green La ME9 99 F1
Greenleas
[1] Folkestone CT20 335 B3
Pembury TN2 287 C6
Green Leas CT5 75 D1
Greenlees Cl ME10 101 B5
Green Lees ME13 137 E2
Greenleigh Ave BR5 54 B5
Greenly Way TN28 373 C6
Green Mdws TN29 352 D2
Greenoak Rise TN16 118 C1
Green Pl DA1 14 E2
Green Porch Cl ME10 101 F7
Green Rd
Birchington CT7 80 F8
Horsmonden TN12 290 A6
Stalisfield Green ME13 201 C6
Greensand Rd ME15 163 A2
Green Sands ME5 130 C8
Green's Cotts ME15 194 A4
Greens End SE18 2 B2
Greenshields Ind Est
E16 1 A4
Greenside TN26 324 E7
Greenside Ho CT9 50 F1
Greenside
Maidstone ME15 162 B3
Sidcup DA5 31 E7
Swanley BR8 55 D7
Greenside Wlk TN16 118 B1
Greenslade Prim Sch
SE18 12 D8
Greensleeves Way
ME18 159 C3
Greensole La CT12 82 E1
Green Sq TN5 336 F5
Green St ME7 64 C5
Green Street Green Prim
Sch BR6 86 F4
Green Street Green Rd
DA1,DA2 34 D4
Green The
Bexley,Bexleyheath DA7 14 A6
Bexley,Falconwood DA16 12 E3
Biddenden TN27 323 D6
Blean CT2 142 A6
Burmarsh TN29 352 C4
Chartham CT4 173 D3
Dartford DA2 34 D6
East Farleigh ME15 194 B7
Frant TN3 314 B3
Harbledown CT2 141 E1
Hayes BR2 52 A2
Hythe CT21 333 B4
Langton Green TN3 284 E3
Leigh TN11 220 F1
Lewisham BR1 29 A5
Littlebourne CT3 176 F7
Lower Halstow ME9 67 B3
Lydd TN29 376 B5
Manston CT12 82 D1
Orpington BR5 31 B1
Sevenoaks TN13 154 D5
Sheerness ME12 28 H1
Sidcup DA14 31 A4
Warehorne TN26 348 D6
Westerham TN16 151 D1
West Tilbury RM18 19 E8
Woodchurch TN26 326 A2
Woolage Village CT4 210 E1
Wye TN25 237 E2
Greentrees Ave TN10 222 F5
Green Vale DA6 13 D2
Greenvale Gdns ME8 65 B2
Greenvale Inf Sch ME4 64 A2
Greenvale Rd SE9 12 A3
Green View Ave TN11 221 A1
Greenview Cres TN11 221 E4
Greenview Wlk ME8 65 A4
Green Way BR2 52 E3
Greenway Chatham ME5 96 D6
Chislehurst BR7 30 B3
Greenway Court Farm Cotts
ME17 165 A1
Greenway Court Rd
ME17 165 A1
Greenway TN17 320 B4
Green Way SE9 11 D2
Greenway ME13 138 B8
Green Way DA3 58 E4
Greenway La ME17 198 A7
Green Way Lydd TN29 376 C5
Maidstone ME16 161 B3
Royal Tunbridge Wells
TN2 286 E8
Greenways
Addington ME19 126 E2
Lower Halstow ME9 67 B3
Maidstone ME14 162 F5
New Barn DA3 59 D6
Sittingbourne ME10 102 B3
Greenways The TN12 256 F5
Greenway TN16 150 C7
Greenway The
Orpington BR5 54 B3
Oxted RH8 183 B2
Greenwich Cl
Chatham ME5 97 B4
Maidstone ME16 161 D4
Greenwich Com Coll
SE18 2 C2
Greenwich Cres E6 1 E8
Greenwich Hts SE18 11 E7
Greenwich Sh Pk SE7 1 B2
Green Wlk DA1 14 F3
Greenwood Cl
Orpington BR5 53 E3
Sidcup DA15 31 A6
Greenwood Gdns RH8 183 A1
Greenwood Ho [8]
RM17 18 B8
Greenwood Pl TN15 125 A2
Greenwood Rd DA5 32 D4
Greenwood Way TN13 153 F2
Greggs Wood Rd TN2 286 E7
Gregor Mews SE3 11 A7
Gregory Cl
Gillingham ME8 98 E4
Sittingbourne ME10 102 A8
Gregory Cres SE9 29 D8
Gregory Ct TN25 237 E2
Gregory Ho SE3 11 B5
Grenada Rd SE7 11 C7
Grenadier Cl
Gillingham ME8 66 B2
Maidstone ME15 162 F2
Grenadier St E16 2 A5
Grenfell Cl TN16 118 C7
Grenham Bay Ave CT7 80 E8
Grenham Rd CT7 80 F8
Grenville Cl DA13 93 A8
Grenville Gdns CT7 80 E8
Grenville Way CT10 83 E4
Gresham Ave
Hartley DA3 58 F4
Margate CT9 50 E1
Gresham Cl
[3] Rainham ME8 65 F1
Sidcup DA5 13 F1
Tonbridge TN10 222 E7
Gresham Rd
Coxheath ME17 194 D3
Newham E16 1 B7
Greshams Way TN8 217 A2
Greswell Cl DA14 31 A5
Greville Ho CT17 310 C7
Greville Homes CT13 180 B2
Greybury La TN8 249 B3
Greyfriars Cl ME16 161 D5
Grey Friars Cotts [8]
CT1 174 F8
Greyfriars Ct CT10 51 F1
Greyhound Way DA1 14 E1
Grey Ladies Oasts
TN15 157 B3
Greys Park Cl BR2 85 D5
Greystone Pk TN14 152 E2
Greystones Cl TN15 122 E2
Greystones Rd
Cliffs End CT12 116 D5
Maidstone ME15 163 A2
Grey Wethers ME14 129 E4
Grey Willow Gdns
TN23 299 D8
Gribble Bridge La
TN27 323 B5
Grice Ave TN16 118 C6
Grice Cl CT18 306 F3
Grieveson Ho ME4 64 A4
Grieves Rd DA11 36 F5
Griffin Cotts TN26 347 C2
Griffin Manor Way SE28 2 D3
Griffin Rd SE18 2 D2
Griffin's Cnr TN25 269 E7
Griffin St CT14 215 D7
Griffin Way SE28 2 E3
Griffin Wlk DA9 16 F2
Griffiths Ho [2] SE18 12 B8
Grigg La TN27 263 C7
Grigg's Cross BR5 54 D3
Griggs Way TN15 157 A7
Grimsby Gr E16 2 B4
Grimshill Ct CT2 142 C4
Grimshill Rd CT5 108 E8
Grimston Ave CT20 335 B4
Grimston Gdns CT20 335 B4
Grimthorpe Ave CT5 108 C7
Grinling Ho [6] SE18 2 A2
Grinsell Hill CT12 115 E6
Grisbrook Farm Cl
TN29 376 D6
Grisbrook Rd TN29 376 D6
Grizedale Cl ME1 96 D8
Gromenfield TN3 312 C7
Groombridge Cl DA16 13 A2
Groombridge Hill
TN3 284 D1
Groombridge Place Gdns*
TN3 312 C8
Groombridge Place*
TN3 312 C8
Groombridge Rd TN3 284 A1
Groombridge St Thomas'
CE Prim Sch TN3 312 C6
Groombridge Sq [13]
ME15 195 F6
Groombridge Station*
TN3 312 C7
Groom Cl BR2 52 B5
Groom Way ME17 199 E6
Grosmont Rd SE18 2 F1
Grosvenor Ave ME4 63 E3
Grosvenor Bridge
TN1 286 B5
Grosvenor Cotts CT7 81 B3
Grosvenor Cres DA1 15 D2
Grosvenor Gdns CT9 50 I1
Grosvenor Hill CT9 50 I2
Grosvenor Ho [5]
ME15 195 F5
Grosvenor Manor DA5 32 D6
Grosvenor Pk TN1 286 A4
Grosvenor Pl CT9 50 I2
Grosvenor Rd
Ashford TN24 268 D7
Bexley DA6 13 E2
Broadstairs CT10 84 A4
Erith DA17 14 A8
Gillingham ME7 65 A1
Orpington BR5 53 E3
Ramsgate CT11 117 C7
Royal Tunbridge Wells
TN1 286 A4
Whitstable CT5 108 D7
Grosvenor Sq DA3 58 E6
Grosvenor Wlk TN1 286 A4
Grotto Gdns [6] CT9 50 J2
Grotto Hill CT9 50 J2
Grotto Rd [5] CT9 50 J2
Grove Ave
Leysdown-on-S ME12 49 G2
Royal Tunbridge Wells
TN1 286 A2
Grovebury Cl DA8 14 D8
Grovebury Ct DA6 14 B2
Grovebury Rd SE2 3 B4
Grove Cl
Faversham ME13 138 A6
Goose Green TN11 191 C3
Hayes BR2 85 A8
Grove Cotts TN30 345 B6
Grove Court Farm
ME13 140 A3
Grove Ct Greenwich SE3 11 A6
[4] Rochester ME2 63 B7
Grove Dairy Farm
ME9 101 A6
Grove Ferry Hill CT3 112 E3
Grove Ferry Rd CT3 113 A2
Grove Gdns [6] CT9 50 G1
Grove Green La ME14 162 E5
Grove Green Rd ME14 162 F5
Groveherst Rd DA1 15 F4
Grove Hill Gdns TN1 286 B2
Grove Hill Ho TN1 286 B3
Grove Hill Rd TN1 286 B3
Grove Ho TN27 265 C3
Grovehurst Ave ME10 68 F1
Grovehurst La TN12 290 C5
Grovehurst Rd ME10,
ME9 68 E2
Grove La
Brookland TN29 362 D3
Hunton ME15 226 D7
Iden TN31 368 C4
Grovelands ME17 199 E5
Grovelands Rd BR5 31 A1
Grovelands Way RM17 17 F8
Grove Market Pl SE9 11 F1
Grove Park Ave ME10 101 B5
Grove Park Prim Sch
ME10 101 B6
Grove Park Rd SE9 29 D6
Grove Park Sta SE12 29 B5
Grove Pl ME13 138 A6
Grove Rd
Bexley,Bexleyheath DA7 14 C3
[8] Bexley,West Heath
DA17 13 F8
Chatham ME4 64 B2
Deal CT14 215 D3
Folkestone CT20 335 E6
Gillingham ME7 65 A6
Grays RM17 18 C8
Maidstone ME15 195 C7
Northfleet DA11 18 B2
Penshurst TN11,TN8 251 E2
Preston CT3 146 B8
Ramsgate CT11 117 D6
Rochester ME2 63 B8
Seal TN15 155 B5
Selling ME13 171 B4
Sevenoaks TN14 154 C6
Staple CT3 178 F6
Tatsfield TN16 150 C7
Upper Halling ME2 94 E5
Wickhambreaux CT3 145 D6
Grove Road Cotts
Wickhambreaux CT3 145 C2
Wickhambreaux,Frognall
CT3 145 C3
Grover St [3] TN1 286 B4
Groves The ME6 127 F7
Grove Terr CT1 174 E7
Grove The
Ashford TN24 268 E6
Barham CT4 242 F8
Bexley DA6 13 D3
Biggin Hill TN16 118 E1
Deal CT14 215 C6
Dover CT16 278 C1
Fawkham Green DA3 58 A2
Gravesend DA12 37 B8
Herne Bay CT6 76 C2
Maidstone ME14 163 A3
Pembury TN2 287 D8
Sidcup DA14 31 E4
Swanley BR8 55 F6
Swanscombe DA10 17 F2
Westgate-on-S CT8 81 F8
West Kingsdown TN15 90 F1
Grove Vale BR7 30 A2
Groveway ME12 49 F2
Grove Way CT3 146 C7
Grove Wood Cotts
TN11 188 A1
Grovewood Ct ME14 162 E4
Grovewood Dr ME14 162 E4
Grub St RH8 183 C6
Grummock Ave CT11 117 B7
Grundy's Hill [13] CT11 117 E6

Guardian Ct ME8 ... 65 C1
Guardian Ind Est TN12 ... 259 C7
Guards Cl TN10 ... 222 E7
Guernsey Way TN24 ... 268 C7
Guestling Mill Ct 1 CT13 ... 148 F1
Guestwick TN10 ... 222 F5
Guibal Rd SE12 ... 29 B7
Guildables La RH8, TN8 ... 216 E7
Guildcount La 5 CT13 ... 148 F1
Guildford Ave CT8 ... 81 E8
Guildford Gdns ME2 ... 62 C6
Guildford Lawn 1 CT11 ... 117 E6
Guildford Rd
Canterbury CT1 ... 174 F6
Newham E6 ... 1 F7
7 Royal Tunbridge Wells TN1 ... 286 B3
Guildhall Ct 10 CT20 ... 335 D5
Guildhall Mus* ME11 ... 45 F5
Guildhall Mus The* ME1 ... 63 C6
Guildhall St N CT19, CT20 ... 335 D5
Guildhall St
4 Canterbury CT1 ... 174 F8
18 Folkestone CT20 ... 335 D5
Guild Rd Erith DA8 ... 14 F7
Greenwich SE7 ... 11 D8
Guilford Ave CT16 ... 278 A8
Guilford Ct CT14 ... 215 D2
Guilford Ho CT13 ... 182 A7
Guilford Rd CT13 ... 181 E8
Guilton CT3 ... 147 B1
Guiness Dr ME2 ... 40 B2
Guldeford La TN29, TN31 ... 369 F3
Guldeford Lane Cnr TN31 ... 369 D2
Gulland Ho 4 ME14 ... 162 B4
Gullands ME17 ... 196 E4
Gulliver Rd DA15 ... 30 E6
Gumley Rd RM20 ... 17 E8
Gumping Rd BR5,BR6 ... 86 C8
Gun Back La TN12 ... 290 A5
Gundulph Ho TN10 ... 222 C3
Gundulph Rd
Bromley BR2 ... 52 C6
Rochester ME1 ... 63 E4
Gundulph Sq ME1 ... 63 C6
Gunfleet Cl DA12 ... 37 E8
Gun Hill RM18 ... 19 D8
Gunlands TN12 ... 290 A6
Gun La ME2 ... 63 B7
Gunner La SE18 ... 2 A1
Gunnery Terr SE18 ... 2 C3
Gunning St SE18 ... 2 E2
Gunnis Cl ME8 ... 98 D4
Gunn Rd DA10 ... 17 E1
Gun Tower Mews ME1 ... 63 B4
Gurdon Rd SE7 ... 1 B1
Gurling Rd CT15 ... 247 F1
Guston CE Prim Sch CT15 ... 278 E3
Guston Rd
East Langdon CT15 ... 279 A8
Maidstone ME14 ... 162 C6
Guthrie Gdns CT17 ... 277 E3
Guy Barnett Gr SE3 ... 11 A4
Guy Cl CT10 ... 84 A7
Gwillim Cl DA15 ... 13 A2
Gwynn Rd DA11 ... 36 C6
Gwyn Rd CT12 ... 83 C2
Gybbon Rise TN12 ... 260 E3
Gybbons Rd TN17 ... 343 F3
Gypsy Cnr CT5 ... 109 D3
Gypsy Way ME23 ... 23 E3

H

Hackfield TN23 ... 267 F1
Hackington Cl CT2 ... 142 E4
Hackington Pl CT2 ... 142 F2
Hackington Rd CT2 ... 142 F7
Hackington Terr CT2 ... 142 F2
Hackling Hill CT14 ... 181 B2
Hackney Rd ME16 ... 161 C2
Hadden Rd SE28 ... 2 E3
Haddon Dene Sch CT10 ... 83 F4
Haddon Gr DA15 ... 31 A8
Haddon Rd BR5 ... 54 C4
Hadleigh Ct ME7 ... 98 A3
Hadleigh Gdns CT6 ... 77 B5
Hadleigh Wlk 1 E6 ... 1 E7
Hadley Cl DA13 ... 93 B8
Hadley Ct TN4 ... 285 F6
Hadley Gdns ME17 ... 164 E2
Hadley House BR5 ... 53 F7
Hadley Rd DA17 ... 3 F2
Hadlow Coll
Canterbury CT1 ... 175 B8
Hadlow TN11 ... 223 D8
Hadlow Coll Mottingham Ctr SE12 ... 29 C7
Hadlow Coll Nature Reserve* SE12 ... 29 C7
Hadlow Ct TN9 ... 222 C2
Hadlow Dr CT9 ... 51 E2
Hadlow Pk TN11 ... 190 E1
Hadlow Rd DA16 ... 13 C7
Hadlow Rd E TN10, TN11 ... 223 A5
Hadlow Rd
Maidstone ME14 ... 162 C5
Sidcup DA14 ... 31 A4
Tonbridge TN9 ... 222 D3
Hadlow Sch TN11 ... 223 E8
Hadlow Stair Rd TN10 ... 222 F4
Hadlow Way DA13 ... 36 E1
Hadrian Gdns TN23 ... 299 F5
Haffenden Cl TN12 ... 259 D6
Haffenden Mdw TN27 ... 234 C8
Haffenden Rd TN30 ... 324 B1
Ha-Ha Rd SE18 ... 11 F8
Haig Ave Chatham ME1 ... 63 D1
Chatham ME4 ... 64 A2
Gillingham ME7 ... 64 E4
Haig Ct BR7 ... 30 B3
Haig Gdns DA12 ... 37 C8
Haig Rd TN16 ... 118 E2
Haig Villas ME3 ... 41 A5
Haileybury Rd BR6 ... 87 A6
Hailey Rd Bsns Pk DA18 ... 4 A4
Hailey Rd DA18 ... 4 A4
Hailing Mews BR2 ... 52 B6
Hailstone Cl TN11 ... 223 E8
Haimo Prim Sch SE9 ... 11 D2
Haimo Rd SE9 ... 11 D2
Hainault St SE9 ... 30 B7
Haine Ind Est CT12 ... 82 F1
Haine Rd CT12,CT10 ... 82 F2
Halcot Ave DA6 ... 14 C2
Haldane Gdns DA11 ... 36 C7
Haldane Rd SE28 ... 3 D6
Halden Cl ME15 ... 195 F6
Halden La TN17 ... 343 F6
Hale Cl BR6 ... 86 C6
Hale Cotts DA9 ... 17 C2
Hale Ct TN12 ... 225 A7
Hale La TN14 ... 121 F2
Hale Oak Rd
Hall's Green TN8,TN14 ... 219 E4
Sevenoaks Weald TN14 ... 187 B1
Hale Rd ME3 ... 40 C7
Hales Cl TN30 ... 345 B8
Hales Ct TN30 ... 345 B8
Hales Dr CT2 ... 142 F3
Hales Rd ME10 ... 101 D1
Hale St TN12 ... 225 A7
Haleys Pl ME1 ... 129 A8
Halfmile Ride CT9 ... 82 E6
Half Moon La TN11 ... 221 D6
Half Moon Way ME23 ... 23 E3
Halford Cl CT6 ... 77 B2
Halfpence La DA12 ... 61 B7
Halfpenny Cl ME16 ... 161 A2
Halfway Houses Prim Sch ME12 ... 46 D6
Halfway Rd ME12 ... 46 D8
Halfway St DA15 ... 30 E7
Halifax Cl ME5 ... 97 B6
Halifield Dr DA17 ... 3 E3
Hallam Cl BR7 ... 29 F3
Hall Ave TN24 ... 300 F6
Hall By The Sea Rd CT9 ... 50 H2
Hall Cl ME10 ... 101 E6
Hall Cres CT14 ... 214 F5
Hallcroft Ct CT11 ... 117 C7
Hallett Wlk 10 CT1 ... 143 B2
Hallford Way DA1 ... 15 C2
Hallgate SE3 ... 11 A4
Hall Hill TN15 ... 155 C4
Halliday Ct CT21 ... 333 A2
Halliday Dr CT14 ... 215 D3
Halling Prim Sch ME2 ... 95 B3
Halling Sta ME2 ... 95 A5
Hall Place* DA5 ... 14 C1
Hall Place Cres DA1, DA5 ... 14 D2
Hall Rd Aylesford ME20 ... 128 F1
Chatham ME5 ... 97 C3
Dartford DA1 ... 15 F3
High Halstow ME3 ... 24 C6
Northfleet,Pepper Hill DA11 ... 36 C5
Northfleet,Wombwell Park DA11 ... 36 D6
Wouldham ME1 ... 95 C3
Halls Cotts TN5 ... 336 F5
Hallsfield Rd ME5 ... 96 D2
Hall's Hole Rd TN2 ... 286 E4
Hallsville Prim Sch E16 ... 1 A7
Hall The SE3 ... 11 A4
Hall View SE9 ... 29 D6
Hallwards TN12 ... 260 E2
Hallwood Cl ME8 ... 98 D5
Hallwood Ho ME5 ... 97 C2
Hallywell Cres E6 ... 1 F8
Halons Rd SE9 ... 30 A8
Halsbrook Rd SE3 ... 11 D4
Halstatt Rd CT14 ... 215 A3
Halstead Cl CT2 ... 143 B4
Halstead Com Prim Sch TN14 ... 120 F7
Halstead Gdns CT9 ... 51 F3
Halstead La TN14 ... 120 E5
Halstead Rd DA8 ... 14 E6
Halstead Wlk ME16 ... 161 C7
Halstow Cl ME15 ... 195 B6
Halstow Prim Sch SE10 ... 1 A1
Halstow Rd SE10,SE3 ... 1 A1
Halstow Way TN23 ... 299 F8
Halt Cvn Pk The TN15 ... 90 E1
Halt Robin La DA17 ... 4 B2
Halt Robin Rd DA17 ... 4 B2
Halt The Elham CT4 ... 273 F4
Whitstable CT5 ... 109 A7
Hambledon Ct ME16 ... 161 B3
Hambledown Rd DA15 ... 30 E8
Hamble Rd TN10 ... 222 B5
Hambro Ave BR2 ... 52 A1
Hambrook Cl CT4 ... 205 B8
Hambrook La CT4 ... 205 C8
Hambrook Wlk ME10 ... 101 F8
Hamele The CT2 ... 143 F5
Hamelin Rd ME7 ... 97 F8
Hamerton Rd DA11 ... 18 B2
Ham Farm Cotts CT14 ... 180 F2
Hamill Terr CT1 ... 143 B2
Hamilton Cl
Littlestone-on-Sea TN28 ... 373 E5
Ramsgate CT12 ... 83 B1
Hamilton Cres ME10 ... 101 C3
Hamilton Ct
Chatham ME5 ... 64 C1
Rochester ME1 ... 63 B4
Royal Tunbridge Wells TN4 ... 286 A5
Hamilton Ho
Coxheath ME17 ... 194 C3
Maidstone ME15 ... 195 F5
Royal Tunbridge Wells TN4 ... 286 A5
Hamilton Rd
Ashford TN24 ... 300 D6
Bexley DA7 ... 13 E5
Deal CT14 ... 215 C4
Dover CT17 ... 310 B8
Gillingham ME7 ... 64 D7
Lydd TN29 ... 376 C6
Sidcup DA15 ... 31 A4
Whitstable CT5 ... 74 D1
Hamilton Wlk DA8 ... 14 F7
Ham La Gillingham ME7 ... 97 E3
Lenham ME17 ... 199 C5
Hamlea Cl SE12 ... 11 A2
Hamlet Est DA8 ... 4 D1
Hamlet Ho Eltham SE9 ... 12 A2
5 Erith DA8 ... 14 E7
Hamlin Rd TN13 ... 153 E6
Hamlyn Ct TN13 ... 153 E6
Hammelton Rd 2 BR1 ... 52 A8
Hammerwood Pk* RH19 ... 281 C2
Ham Mill La TN26, TN29 ... 349 A2
Hammond Cl CT15 ... 211 E5
Hammond's Cnr TN29 ... 372 E6
Hammonds 9 TN18 ... 341 A2
Hammond's Rd CT20 ... 334 E5
Hammonds Sq ME6 ... 128 A8
Hammond Way 2 SE28 ... 3 B6
Hamond Hill 6 ME4 ... 63 E4
Hampden La TN23 ... 300 A7
Hampden Mews TN23 ... 300 A7
Hampden Rd TN23 ... 300 A6
Hampden Way ME19 ... 158 F3
Hampshire Cl ME5 ... 97 C7
Hampshire Dr ME15 ... 195 C8
Hampshire Rd CT1 ... 175 D7
Hampshires The ME17 ... 198 C6
Hampson Way ME14 ... 163 A4
Hampstead Cl SE28 ... 3 B5
Hampstead La ME18 ... 192 C1
Hampton Cl
Chatham ME5 ... 97 A5
Herne Bay CT6 ... 76 A3
Hampton Cotts TN14 ... 120 F4
Hampton Cres DA12 ... 37 E6
Hampton Ct DA8 ... 14 D7
Hampton Gdns CT6 ... 76 A3
Hampton Ho DA7 ... 14 B5
Hampton La TN25 ... 270 C3
Hampton Pier Ave CT6 ... 76 B4
Hampton Prim Sch CT6 ... 76 C4
Hampton Rd ME14 ... 162 C6
Hamptons Rd TN11 ... 190 B5
Hampton Vale CT21 ... 334 B4
Ham Rd ME13 ... 105 C1
Ham River Hill ME3 ... 40 A6
Ham Shades Cl 1 DA15 ... 31 A5
Ham Shades La CT5 ... 75 A1
Hamstreet Prim Sch TN26 ... 348 F8
Hamstreet Rd
Bromley Green TN26 ... 327 E5
Hamstreet TN26 ... 349 C7
Ham Street Sta TN26 ... 349 A8
Hamwick Gn ME5 ... 97 C1
Hanameel St E16 ... 1 B5
Hanbury Cl ME18 ... 192 E7
Hanbury Dr TN16 ... 118 B6
Hanbury Wlk DA5 ... 32 E5
Hancock Cl ME3 ... 40 B1
Hancocks Field CT14 ... 215 A5
Handel Cres RM18 ... 19 A7
Handel Wlk TN10 ... 222 E6
Hands Wlk E16 ... 1 A7
Hanes Dene ME2 ... 94 F5
Hang Grove Hill BR6 ... 119 B6
Hanging Bank TN14 ... 185 F3
Hangmans Cnr BR7 ... 53 B8
Hangman's La CT14 ... 247 F5
Hanley Ct TN13 ... 154 B4
Hanmer Way TN12 ... 260 E2
Hanover Ave E16 ... 1 A5
Hanover Cl
Ashford TN23 ... 267 F2
Deal CT14 ... 215 D2
Margate CT9 ... 51 E2
Sittingbourne ME10 ... 101 E2
Hanover Ct
Broadstairs CT10 ... 83 F4
10 Bromley BR2 ... 52 A6
Faversham ME13 ... 138 B8
Hythe CT21 ... 333 C1
Maidstone ME14 ... 162 B5
Hanover Dr
Chislehurst BR7 ... 30 C4
Gillingham ME8 ... 98 C4
Hanover Gn ME20 ... 127 F3
Hanover Ho 6 CT20 ... 335 C4
Hanover Pl
Canterbury CT2 ... 142 F2
New Ash Green DA3 ... 91 F8
Hanover Rd
Coxheath ME17 ... 194 C3
Royal Tunbridge Wells TN1 ... 286 A4
Hanover Sq CT6 ... 76 F5
Hanover St CT6 ... 76 F5
Hanover Way DA7 ... 13 D4
Hanscomb Ho CT2 ... 142 E2
Hanslett's La ME13 ... 137 D3
Hansol Rd DA6 ... 13 E2
Hanson Terr 1 BR1 ... 52 B8
Hanson Dr ME15 ... 194 F3
Hanway ME8 ... 65 A2
Happy Valley Holiday Camp ME12 ... 49 E2
Harbex Cl DA5 ... 32 B8
Harbledown Gdns CT9 ... 51 E3
Harbledown Ho ME16 ... 161 B2
Harbledown Manor ME8 ... 65 B3
Harbledown Pk CT2 ... 142 C1
Harbledown Pl 7 BR5 ... 54 C5
Harborough Ave DA15 ... 30 F8
Harbour Approach Rd CT20 ... 335 E4
Harbourland Cl ME14 ... 162 B8
Harbourne La TN26, TN30 ... 324 E5
Harbour Par CT11 ... 117 E6
Harbour Point CT19 ... 335 F5
Harbour Sch CT15 ... 309 E7
Harbour St
Broadstairs CT10 ... 84 B4
Folkestone CT20 ... 335 E5
Ramsgate CT11 ... 117 E6
Whitstable CT5 ... 74 D2
Harbour The ME17 ... 229 E5
Harbour Twrs 16 CT11 ... 117 E6
Harbour View Rd CT17 ... 310 B8
Harbour Way CT20 ... 335 E5
Harcourt Ave DA15 ... 31 C8
Harcourt Dr
Canterbury CT2 ... 142 D2
Herne Bay CT6 ... 76 B5
Harcourt Gdns ME8 ... 98 E4
Harcourt Prim Sch CT19 ... 334 E7
Harcourt Rd Bexley DA6 ... 13 E3
Folkestone CT19 ... 334 F7
Harden Ct 1 SE18 ... 1 E2
Harden's View TN26 ... 348 D6
Harden Rd Lydd TN29 ... 376 D7
Northfleet DA11 ... 36 F6
Hardie Cl ME19 ... 127 F1
Hardinge Ave TN4 ... 253 E3
Hardinge Cl ME8 ... 98 D4
Hardinge Cres SE18 ... 2 C3
Hardinge Rd TN24 ... 268 C3
Hardinge St SE18 ... 2 B3
Harding Ho 9 SE18 ... 1 F2
Harding Rd DA7 ... 13 F5
Hardman Rd SE7 ... 1 B1
Hardres Court Rd CT4 ... 208 A3
Hardres Rd CT11 ... 117 E8
Hardres St CT11 ... 117 E7
Hardres Terr BR5 ... 87 D8
Hards Town ME4 ... 64 A4
Hardwick Cres 2 DA2 ... 16 B1
Hardwick Ct DA8 ... 14 D8
Hardwicke Ho TN27 ... 234 B7
Hardwicke Rd CT17 ... 310 B6
Hardwick Ho ME15 ... 195 E8
Hardwick Rd
Folkestone CT20 ... 335 A4
Tonbridge TN11 ... 221 E6
Hardy Ave Newham E16 ... 1 A5
Northfleet DA11 ... 36 E6
Hardy Cl Ashford TN24 ... 301 A7
Canterbury CT2 ... 142 C1
Chatham ME5 ... 97 B6
Hardy Gr DA1 ... 16 A3
Hardy Lodge ME1 ... 63 B4
Hardy Rd
Greatstone-on-Sea TN28 ... 373 D3
2 Greenwich SE3 ... 11 A8
St Margaret's at Cliffe CT15 ... 279 E8
Hardy St ME14 ... 162 A6
Harebell Cl
3 Chatham ME5 ... 96 F4
Maidstone ME14 ... 162 E5
Minster (Sheppey) ME12 ... 47 A4
Harebell Dr E6 ... 2 A8
Harebrook CT11 ... 83 F1
Haredale Cl ME1 ... 96 D7
Harefield Rd DA14 ... 31 D5
Harenc Sch DA14 ... 31 C3
Harescroft TN2 ... 313 F7
Hare St 2 Chatham ME4 ... 64 B3
Woolwich SE18 ... 2 A3
Harewood Lincoln Ho DA11 ... 18 D1
Harfst Way BR8 ... 55 C8
Hargate Cl TN2 ... 313 F8
Hargood Rd SE3 ... 11 C6
Harkness Ct 6 ME10 ... 102 B4
Harkness Dr CT2 ... 142 E2
Harland Ave DA15 ... 30 E6
Harland Rd SE12 ... 29 A7
Harlands Gr BR6 ... 86 B6
Harland Way TN4 ... 253 F4
Harlech Cl ME2 ... 39 F1
Harlequin Ho 1 DA18 ... 3 E3
Harley 5 BR7 ... 53 D8
Harleyford BR1 ... 52 C8
Harley Gdns BR6 ... 86 E6
Harling Cl ME17 ... 195 D5
Harlinger St SE18 ... 1 E3
Harlington Rd DA7 ... 13 E4
Harman Ave
Gravesend DA11 ... 37 B3
Lympne CT21 ... 331 F3
Harman Ct ME5 ... 97 B3
Harman Dr DA15 ... 12 F1
Harmer Ct
Royal Tunbridge Wells TN4 ... 254 A2
Swanscombe DA10 ... 17 F1
Harmer Rd DA10 ... 17 F1
Harmer St DA12 ... 19 C1
Harmers Way TN27 ... 232 F3
Harmony St TN4 ... 285 D4
Harmony Way 1 BR1, BR2 ... 52 A7
Harmsworth Ct TN17 ... 342 E6
Harmsworth Gdns CT10 ... 84 A5
Harness Rd SE28 ... 3 A4
Harnet St 6 CT13 ... 148 F1
Harnetts Cl BR8 ... 55 D2
Harold Ave Erith DA17 ... 3 F1
Gillingham ME7 ... 64 E4
Westgate-on-S CT8 ... 81 E8
Harold Campbell Ct DA1 ... 33 D8
Harold Ct ME13 ... 138 C6
Harold Gibbons Ct SE7 ... 11 C8
Harold Ho 2 TN2 ... 286 C7
Harold Rd
Birchington CT7 ... 80 E8
Cuxton ME2 ... 62 C3
Deal CT14 ... 215 D8
Hawley DA2 ... 33 F4
Margate CT9 ... 51 B3
Sittingbourne ME10 ... 102 B4
Harold's Rd CT16 ... 310 E8
Harold St Dover CT16 ... 310 D8
Queenborough ME11 ... 46 A4
Harper Rd
Ashford TN23 ... 299 F8
Newham E6 ... 1 F7
Harp Farm Rd ME14 ... 130 C6
Harple La ME14 ... 130 F1
Harps Ave ME12 ... 47 C6
Harpswood ME17 ... 164 F1
Harpswood La CT21 ... 333 A4
Harptree Dr ME5 ... 96 F5
Harraden Rd SE3 ... 11 C6
Harrier Dr ME10 ... 102 A2
Harrier Mews SE28 ... 2 D4
Harrier Way E6 ... 1 F8
Harries Rd TN2 ... 286 E7
Harriestsham Sta ME17 ... 198 D6
Harriet Dr ME1 ... 63 B3
Harriets Cnr CT5 ... 108 B5
Harrietsham Ho 13 ME16 ... 161 A3
Harrietsham Prim Sch ME17 ... 198 E6
Harringe La CT21, TN25 ... 331 A6
Harrington Ho 7 BR1 ... 52 A8
Harrington Way SE18 ... 1 D3
Harriot Cl CT19 ... 335 B7
Harris Cl DA11 ... 36 F5
Harris Gdns ME10 ... 102 C5
Harris Ho ME2 ... 95 B4
Harrison Ct 4 ME8 ... 65 F1
Harrison Dr
Harrietsham ME17 ... 198 E6
High Halstow ME23 ... 23 E4
Harrison Rd
Borough Green TN15 ... 156 F7
4 Ramsgate CT11 ... 117 D6
Harrison Terr ME13 ... 105 A2
Harrison Way TN13 ... 154 A5
Harris Rd Bexley DA7 ... 13 F6
Sheerness ME12 ... 28 C2
Harris's Alley CT3 ... 178 A7
Harrogate Ct 6 SE12 ... 29 A8
Harrowby Gdns DA11 ... 36 E6
Harrow Cl TN8 ... 217 D3
Harrow Ct Chatham ME5 ... 97 C4
Stockbury ME9 ... 132 D8
Harrow Dene CT10 ... 83 E6
Harrow Gdns BR6 ... 87 B6
Harrow Manor Way SE2 ... 3 C3
Harrow Rd
Gillingham ME7 ... 97 F6
Halstead TN14 ... 120 E4
Harrow Way
Ashford TN23 ... 299 E5
Maidstone ME14 ... 162 E5
Harry Pay Cl TN24 ... 268 D4
Harrys Rd ME9 ... 103 D3
Harry Wells Rd CT6 ... 76 B3
Hart Cl CT18 ... 307 A4
Hart Dyke Cres BR8 ... 55 D6
Hart Dyke Rd
Orpington BR5 ... 54 C1
Swanley BR8 ... 55 D6
Hartfield Cl TN10 ... 222 E5
Hartfield Cres BR4 ... 85 A7
Hartfield Pl DA11 ... 36 D8
Hartfield Rd
Cowden TN8 ... 282 C6
Hayes BR4 ... 85 A6
Hever TN8 ... 250 A4
Hartford Rd DA5 ... 14 A1
Hartford Wlk 13 DA17 ... 4 A1
Hart Hill TN27 ... 201 A2
Hart Ho BR6 ... 54 A2
Harting Rd SE9 ... 29 E5
Hartington Cl BR6 ... 86 C5
Hartington Rd E16 ... 1 B7
Hartington St ME4 ... 64 A3
Hartlake Rd TN11 ... 223 D3
Hartlands Cl DA5 ... 13 F1
Hartlepool Ct E16 ... 2 B4
Hartley Bottom Rd DA3 ... 59 C2
Hartley Cl Bromley BR1 ... 52 F7
Maidstone ME15 ... 195 F6
Hartley Court Gdns TN17 ... 320 A3
Hartley Hill DA3 ... 59 A1
Hartley Mews ME8 ... 65 B3
Hartley Prim Sch DA3 ... 58 E3
Hartley Rd Bexley DA16 ... 13 C7
Hartley TN17 ... 320 A3
Longfield DA3 ... 58 E7
Westerham TN16 ... 151 D2
Hartlip CE Prim Sch ME9 ... 99 D5
Hartlip Cl ME12 ... 46 B7
Hartlip Hill ME9 ... 99 F7
Hartmann Rd E16 ... 1 E5
Hartnokes TN18 ... 341 A2
Hartnup St ME16 ... 161 C2
Harton Cl BR1 ... 52 D8
Hartpiece Cl ME8 ... 65 F2
Hartridge Farm ME15 ... 194 A7
Harts Cotts TN26 ... 349 A8
Hartsdown Rd CT9 ... 82 D8
Hartsdown Tech Coll CT9 ... 82 D8
Hart Shaw DA3 ... 59 B7
Hartshill Rd DA11 ... 36 F6
Harts Holiday Camp ME12 ... 49 G1
Hartslands Rd TN13 ... 154 C4
Harts La 6 CT5 ... 74 D2
Hartslock Dr DA18,SE2 ... 3 D4
Hartsmead Rd SE9 ... 29 F6
Hart St ME16 ... 161 F3
Hart Street Bsns Ctr ME16 ... 161 F3
Hartville Rd SE18 ... 2 E2
Hartwell Ho 2 SE7 ... 1 B1
Harty Ave ME8 ... 98 B3
Harty Ferry Cotts ME13 ... 105 C5
Harty Ferry Rd ME12 ... 72 E4
Harty Ferry View CT5 ... 108 C6
Harty Terr ME12 ... 48 A5
Harvard Ct 9 SE9 ... 12 A1
Harvel Ave ME2 ... 62 F7
Harvel Cl BR5,BR7 ... 54 A6
Harvel Cres SE2 ... 3 D1
Harvel La DA13 ... 93 B2
Harvel Rd DA13 ... 126 A8
Harvel St DA13 ... 93 C3
Harvest Bank Rd BR4 ... 85 A7
Harvesters Cl ME8 ... 98 E7
Harvesters Way ME14 ... 162 D4
Harvest La CT4 ... 240 E5
Harvest Rd TN10 ... 222 D6
Harvest Ridge ME19 ... 127 D2
Harvest Way
Ashford TN23 ... 299 D7
Crockenhill BR8 ... 55 D2
Hawkinge CT18 ... 307 B4
Harvey Ave CT14 ... 215 C3
Harvey Ct CT19 ... 335 A6
Harvey Dr
Sittingbourne ME10 ... 102 A2
Whitstable CT5 ... 75 B1
Harvey Gdns SE7 ... 1 C1
Harvey Gram Sch The CT19 ... 335 A6
Harvey Pl
21 Folkestone CT20 ... 335 D5
9 Folkestone CT20 ... 335 E5
Harvey Point 9 E16 ... 1 A8
Harvey Rd
Ashford TN24 ... 268 F1
Gillingham ME8 ... 98 E8
Harvey St CT20 ... 335 E5
Harville Rd TN25 ... 237 C2
Harvill Rd DA14 ... 31 E3
Harwich St CT5 ... 108 D8
Harwick Dr TN28 ... 373 C8
Harwood Ave BR1 ... 52 B7
Harwood Ct 3 RM17 ... 18 C8
Harwood Ho TN25 ... 237 E1
Harwood Rd ME8 ... 66 B1
Hasborough Rd CT19 ... 335 F6
Haskard Cl CT18 ... 306 F4
Haslemere Est ME15 ... 195 F5
Haslemere Rd DA7 ... 14 A5
Hasler Cl SE28 ... 3 C6
Hasletts Cl TN1 ... 286 B6
Haslewood Cl TN27 ... 264 B2
Hassall Reach CT1 ... 174 B6
Hassell St TN25 ... 238 F2
Hassendean Rd SE3 ... 11 B7
Hassock Wood BR2 ... 85 E6
Hassop Wlk SE9 ... 29 E4
Hasted Cl DA9 ... 17 C1
Hasted Rd Greenwich SE7 ... 1 D1
Newington ME9 ... 100 B7
Hasteds ME17 ... 164 D2
Haste Hill Cl ME17 ... 195 B3
Haste Hill Rd ME17 ... 195 B3
Hast Hill Ho BR2 ... 85 B6
Hastings Ave CT9 ... 51 A1
Hastings Cl RM17 ... 17 E8
Hastings Ho SE18 ... 1 F2
Hastings Pl CT13 ... 180 F8
Hastings Rd
Maidstone ME15 ... 162 B3
Newenden TN17,TN18 ... 357 C6
Orpington BR2 ... 85 E8
Pembury,Kipping's Cross TN2 ... 287 F5
Pembury TN2 ... 287 D6
The Moor TN18 ... 354 F6
Hastings St SE18 ... 2 C3
Hatches La TN11,TN12 ... 224 D6
Hatch La CT4 ... 173 C5
Hatch Rd ME17 ... 199 C5
Hatch St 3 ME13 ... 138 C7
Hatfield Ct SE3 ... 11 A7
Hatfield Rd
Margate CT9 ... 50 G2
Ramsgate CT11 ... 117 D7

Hatfield Rd *continued*
Rochester ME2 ... 63 A8
Hatham Green La TN15 ... 91 D1
Hathaway Cl BR2 ... 52 F1
Hathaway Ct
Gillingham ME8 ... 98 D8
Rochester ME1 ... 63 B5
Hatherall Rd ME14 ... 162 B6
Hatherley Cres DA14 ... 31 A6
Hatherley Ct CT9 ... 51 A3
Hatherley Rd DA14 ... 31 A5
Hathern Gdns SE9 ... 30 A4
Hatmill La TN12 ... 289 A7
Hattersfield Cl DA17 ... 3 F2
Hatton Cl
Northfleet DA11 ... 36 E5
Woolwich SE18 ... 12 D7
Hatton Ct BR7 ... 29 F1
Hatton Rd ME5 ... 97 C3
Havant Wlk 8 ME15 ... 195 F6
Havelock Pl CT3 ... 147 E1
Havelock Rd
Bromley BR2 ... 52 C5
Dartford DA1 ... 15 B1
Deal CT14 ... 215 C3
Erith DA17 ... 3 F2
Northfleet DA11 ... 36 F7
Tonbridge TN9 ... 222 B2
Havelock St CT1 ... 143 A1
Haven Cl
Eltham SE9 ... 29 F5
Istead Rise DA13 ... 59 F8
Rochester ME1 ... 63 C2
Sidcup DA14 ... 31 C2
Swanley BR8 ... 55 F7
Haven Dr
Hawkinge CT18 ... 307 A4
Herne Bay CT6 ... 77 F6
Havengore Ave DA12 ... 37 E8
Haven Hill TN15 ... 92 A3
Haven Lodge 9 SE18 ... 2 B2
Haven St ME3 ... 40 C5
Haven The
Ashford TN23 ... 299 F5
Brenzett TN29 ... 363 A3
Hythe CT21 ... 353 C8
Haventhorpe TN24 ... 268 C3
Haven Way ME4 ... 41 B1
Havering Cl TN2 ... 286 F6
Haverstock Ct 2 BR5 ... 54 B7
Haverthwaite Rd BR6 ... 86 D7
Havisham Cl ME1 ... 63 D2
Havisham Rd DA12 ... 38 A7
Hawbeck Rd ME8 ... 98 C3
Hawden Cl TN11 ... 221 F4
Hawden La TN11 ... 221 F4
Hawden Rd TN9 ... 222 B2
Hawe Cl CT2 ... 143 A4
Hawe Farm Way CT6 ... 77 B2
Hawe La CT2 ... 144 A7
Hawes Ave CT11 ... 117 B7
Hawes Rd BR1 ... 52 B8
Hawfield Bank BR6 ... 87 D7
Hawk Cl CT5 ... 108 C7
Hawkenbury Cl TN2 ... 286 D2
Hawkenbury Mead
TN2 ... 286 D1
Hawkenbury Rd
Hawkenbury TN12 ... 261 C6
Royal Tunbridge Wells
TN2, TN3 ... 286 E1
Hawkenbury Rise ME2 ... 40 B2
Hawkesbury St CT17 ... 310 D5
Hawkes Cl RM17 ... 18 B8
Hawkes Pl TN13 ... 187 A8
Hawkes Rd ME20 ... 128 F5
Hawkhurst CE Prim Sch
TN18 ... 341 B2
Hawkhurst Cl CT7 ... 81 B8
Hawkhurst Cottage Hospl
TN18 ... 340 D2
Hawkhurst Rd
Flimwell TN5,TN18 ... 339 E2
Gillingham ME8 ... 65 B3
Gill's Green TN17,TN18 ... 340 F7
Hawkhurst Way CT10 ... 84 A2
Hawkinge Prim Sch
CT18 ... 307 B4
Hawkinge Wlk BR5 ... 54 B6
Hawkins Ave DA12 ... 37 C4
Hawkins Cl
Chatham ME7 ... 64 A6
Sittingbourne ME10 ... 101 E7
Hawkins Rd CT19 ... 334 D6
Hawkridge Gr ME18 ... 159 A3
Hawksdown CT14 ... 248 B8
Hawksdown Rd CT14 ... 248 C8
Hawks Hill La ME9 ... 134 C4
Hawkshill Rd CT14 ... 248 D8
Hawk's La CT1 ... 174 F8
Hawksmoor Cl
3 Newham E6 ... 1 E7
Woolwich SE18 ... 2 E1
Hawksmoor Sch SE28 ... 3 B6
Hawks Rd CT6 ... 76 B2
Hawks Way TN23 ... 299 E7
Hawkwell Bsns Ctr
TN2 ... 255 F2
Hawkwell Cotts TN2 ... 255 F2
Hawkwood Cl ME1 ... 63 D5
Hawkwood La BR7 ... 53 C8
Hawkwood ME16 ... 161 B5
Hawley Ct ME16 ... 161 E4
Hawley Rd DA1,DA2,DA4 ... 34 A4
Hawley Sq CT9 ... 50 J2
Hawley St CT9 ... 50 I2
Hawley Terr DA2 ... 34 A4
Hawley Vale DA2 ... 34 A4
Hawser Rd ME1 ... 63 C1
Hawstead La BR6 ... 87 F5
Hawthorn TN26 ... 361 D8
Hawthorn Ave
Canterbury CT2 ... 143 A2
West Minst ME12 ... 46 A8
Hawthorn Cl
Aylesham CT3 ... 210 E4
Crabble CT17 ... 277 E2
Edenbridge TN8 ... 217 C2
Gravesend DA12 ... 37 C4
Hythe CT21 ... 353 E8
Orpington BR5 ... 53 D3
Ramsgate CT11 ... 83 E1
St Mary's Bay TN29 ... 365 F3
Hawthorn Cnr
Herne Bay CT6 ... 78 A3
Old Romney TN29 ... 371 E3
Hawthorn Cotts 6
DA16 ... 13 A4
Hawthornden Cl
ME18 ... 159 C3
Hawthorndene Cl BR2 ... 85 A8
Hawthorndene Rd BR2 ... 85 A8
Hawthorne Ave
Biggin Hill TN16 ... 118 D4
Gillingham ME8 ... 65 C2
Hawthorne Cl
Bromley BR1 ... 52 F6
Eythorne CT15 ... 245 D7
Hawthorne Ho 4
ME16 ... 161 A3
Hawthorne Rd BR1 ... 52 F6
Hawthorn Farm Cvn &
Camping Site CT15 ... 247 C1
Hawthorn Ho
5 Chatham ME5 ... 96 F5
10 Sittingbourne ME10 ... 101 E4
Hawthorn La TN13 ... 153 F5
Hawthorn Pl DA8 ... 4 C1
Hawthorn Rd
Bexley DA6 ... 13 F3
Dartford DA1 ... 33 D7
Kingsnorth TN23 ... 300 B4
Rochester ME2 ... 62 E6
Sittingbourne ME10 ... 101 E4
Hawthorns
Chatham ME5 ... 96 F1
Hartley DA3 ... 58 F5
Hawthorns The
Aylesford ME20 ... 128 E1
Broadstairs CT10 ... 83 C4
Chatham ME5 ... 96 F6
Oxted RH8 ... 183 A2
The Moor TN18 ... 354 F8
Hawthorn Terr DA15 ... 12 F2
Hawthorn Wlk
Royal Tunbridge Wells
TN2 ... 286 E8
Tonbridge TN10 ... 222 C7
Haxted Rd BR1 ... 52 B8
Hayday Rd E16 ... 1 A8
Haydens Cl BR5 ... 54 C3
Haydens Mews TN9 ... 222 C3
Haydens The TN9 ... 222 C3
Haydon Cl ME16 ... 161 B4
Hayes Alley 17 CT5 ... 74 D2
Hayesbrook Sch TN9 ... 254 A8
Hayes Cl Hayes BR2 ... 85 A8
Higham ME3 ... 39 C3
West Thurrock RM20 ... 17 C8
Hayes Cotts ME19 ... 158 D7
Hayesden La TN11,TN3 ... 253 B5
Hayesford Park Dr BR2 ... 52 A4
Hayes Gdn BR2 ... 52 A1
Hayes La Hayes BR2 ... 52 A4
Stockbury ME9 ... 132 F6
Hayes Prim Sch BR2 ... 52 B1
Hayes Rd Bromley BR2 ... 52 A5
Stone DA9 ... 34 E8
Hayes Sch BR2 ... 85 B8
Hayes Sta BR2 ... 52 A1
Hayes St BR2 ... 52 B1
Hayes Terr DA12 ... 38 E3
Hayes Wlk ME19 ... 159 A2
Hayes Wood Ave BR2 ... 52 B1
Hayfield ME19 ... 127 E2
Hayfield Rd BR5 ... 54 A4
Hayfields ME5 ... 97 D2
Haygate Ho ME1 ... 63 C4
Hay Hill CT13,CT14 ... 180 D2
Hay Ho CT21 ... 333 B2
Hay La CT14 ... 180 F2
Hayle Mill Cotts ME15 ... 194 F8
Hayle Mill Rd ME15 ... 194 F8
Hayle Rd ME15 ... 162 A3
Hayley Cl ME2 ... 62 C2
Hayley Ho DA17 ... 14 A8
Haymakers La TN23 ... 299 D8
Haymans Hill TN12 ... 290 C7
Hayman Wlk ME20 ... 128 F6
Haymen St ME4 ... 63 E3
Haynes Ho 3 ME14 ... 162 B4
Haynes Rd
Gravesend DA11 ... 37 A6
Northfleet DA11 ... 36 F5
Hayrick Cl ME14 ... 162 E5
Haysden Ctry Pk*
TN11 ... 253 D8
Haysel ME10 ... 102 A2
Hay's Mead DA13 ... 60 F3
Hays Rd ME6 ... 127 F6
Hayton Rd TN25 ... 304 A2
Haywain Cl
Ashford TN23 ... 299 E5
Maidstone ME14 ... 162 F4
Paddock Wood TN12 ... 257 A5
Hayward Ave ME2 ... 63 B8
Hayward Cl
Ashford TN24 ... 301 A8
Crayford DA1 ... 14 D2
Deal CT14 ... 215 A4
Hayward Dr DA1 ... 33 F6
Hayward's Cl TN28 ... 373 B6
Hayward's Hill ME13 ... 169 C4
Hayward's Ho ME1 ... 63 C6
Haywood Rd BR2 ... 52 D5
Haywood Rise BR6 ... 86 E5
Hazard Ho 4 DA11 ... 19 A1
Hazebrouck Rd ME13 ... 138 A7
Hazel Ave
Hoo St Werburgh ME3 ... 41 E3
Maidstone ME16 ... 161 C5
Hazelbank TN3 ... 284 F3
Hazel Cl CT15 ... 245 C7
Hazel Cotts TN14 ... 121 A6
Hazel Ct Birchington CT7 ... 80 D8
Hersden CT3 ... 144 D8
Hazelden Cl TN15 ... 91 A2
Hazelden Cotts ME2 ... 39 C6
Hazeldene Chalet Pk
ME12 ... 48 F5
Hazeldene Rd DA16 ... 13 C5
Hazeldown Cl CT17 ... 277 E2
Hazel Dr DA8 ... 15 B6
Hazel End BR8 ... 55 E4
Hazel Gr Chatham ME5 ... 97 B8
Orpington BR6 ... 86 B8
Sheerness ME12 ... 28 G1
Hazel Hts TN25 ... 267 E5
Hazelmere Rd BR5 ... 53 D5
Hazelmere 8 DA14 ... 31 A4
Hazelmere Way BR2 ... 52 A3
Hazel Rd Dartford DA1 ... 33 D6
Erith DA8 ... 15 A6
Hazel Shaw TN10 ... 222 D7
Hazels The ME8 ... 98 B5
Hazel Street Rd ME9 ... 133 A4
Hazelview ME19 ... 126 E3
Hazel Wlk
Broadstairs CT10 ... 83 C4
Bromley BR2 ... 53 A3
Hazelwood Cl TN2 ... 286 D8
Hazelwood Cotts TN5 ... 338 D1
Hazelwood Dr ME16 ... 161 B4
Hazelwood Hts RH8 ... 183 A4
Hazelwood Mdw CT13 ... 180 F7
Hazelwood Rd
Downe TN14 ... 119 D8
Oxted RH8 ... 183 B3
Hazelwood Sch RH8 ... 183 A4
Hazen Rd ME18 ... 159 B3
Hazlemere Dr
Gillingham ME7 ... 65 A5
Herne Bay CT6 ... 77 D5
Hazlemere Rd CT5 ... 108 A7
Hazling Dane CT15 ... 244 F5
Hazlitt Ct 4 SE28 ... 3 C5
Hazlitt Dr ME16 ... 161 D5
Headcorn Dr CT2 ... 143 B4
Headcorn Gdns CT9 ... 51 E2
Headcorn Prim Sch
TN27 ... 262 C5
Headcorn Rd
Bromley BR1 ... 29 A3
Gillingham ME8 ... 65 B4
Lashenden TN27 ... 295 A5
Platt's Heath ME17 ... 198 F1
Smarden Bell TN27 ... 263 C3
Staplehurst TN12 ... 261 B4
Sutton Valence ME17 ... 229 E4
Ulcombe ME17 ... 230 F5
Headcorn Sta TN27 ... 262 D4
Head Hill ME13 ... 139 D7
Head Hill Rd ME13 ... 139 D8
Headingley Rd ME16 ... 161 B6
Headley Ct TN8 ... 217 C2
Headley Ho 5 BR5 ... 54 B7
Head Race The ME15 ... 161 D2
Heagam Ct TN4 ... 285 B4
Healy Dr 1 BR6 ... 86 F6
Heansill La TN18 ... 354 E8
Heard Way ME10 ... 102 B5
Hearne Cl ME10 ... 102 B5
Hearns Rd BR5 ... 54 C5
Heartenoak Rd TN18 ... 341 B3
Heart In Hand Cnr CT3 ... 77 F2
Heart In Hand Rd CT6 ... 77 F2
Heart's Delight La
CT3 ... 146 B3
Hearts Delight ME9 ... 101 B1
Hearts Delight Rd
ME9 ... 101 B1
Heath Ave DA7 ... 13 D8
Heath Cl BR5 ... 54 C3
Heathclose Ave DA1 ... 33 B8
Heathclose Rd DA1 ... 33 B7
Heath Cl Sturry CT2 ... 143 F7
Swanley BR8 ... 55 E7
Heathcote Cl ME20 ... 128 F2
Heath Ct
Horsmonden TN12 ... 289 F6
St Margaret's at Cliffe
CT15 ... 279 F6
Heathdene Dr DA17 ... 4 B2
Heathend Rd DA5 ... 32 E7
Heatherbank BR7 ... 53 A7
Heatherbank Cl DA1 ... 14 E1
Heatherbank SE9 ... 11 F5
Heather Bank TN12 ... 257 B6
Heather Cl Chatham ME5 ... 96 F4
Margate CT9 ... 82 C8
Newham E6 ... 2 A7
Sittingbourne ME10 ... 102 A3
Heather Dr
Dartford DA1 ... 33 A8
Maidstone ME15 ... 162 B2
Tenterden TN30 ... 324 B3
Heather End BR8 ... 55 D5
Heather Rd SE12 ... 29 A7
Heatherside Rd DA14 ... 31 C5
Heathers The TN17 ... 320 A3
Heather Wlk TN10 ... 222 B6
Heatherwood Cl ME17 ... 197 E2
Heath Farm Sch TN27 ... 233 C7
Heathfield Ave
Dover CT16 ... 278 B2
Maidstone ME14 ... 162 C7
Heathfield Bglws
ME17 ... 200 B1
Heathfield BR7 ... 30 C2
Heathfield Cl
Chatham ME5 ... 97 B7
Maidstone ME14 ... 162 B7
Newham E16 ... 1 D8
Orpington BR2 ... 85 C5
Heathfield Ct DA14 ... 31 B3
Heathfield La BR7 ... 30 C2
Heathfield ME17 ... 196 E4
Heathfield Rd
Ashford TN24 ... 268 C3
Bexley DA6 ... 13 F3
Maidstone ME14 ... 162 C7
Orpington BR2 ... 85 D5
Sevenoaks TN13 ... 153 F5
Heathfields TN2 ... 286 D4
Heathfield Terr
Bexley SE18 ... 12 F8
Swanley BR8 ... 55 D7
Heathfield Way CT4 ... 242 F8
Heath Gdns DA1 ... 33 C7
Heath Gr ME16 ... 161 A2
Heath Ho CT3 ... 111 E5
Heath House DA15 ... 30 F4
Heath La Dartford DA1 ... 33 C7
Dartford DA1,DA2 ... 33 B7
Heathlands Rise DA1 ... 15 B1
Heathlee Rd DA1 ... 14 E1
Heathley End BR7 ... 30 C2
Heathorn St ME14 ... 162 B5
Heath Park Dr BR1 ... 52 E6
Heath Rd Coldblow DA5 ... 32 C7
Coxheath ME17 ... 194 C3
Crayford DA1 ... 14 F1
East Farleigh ME15 ... 193 E4
Langley Heath ME17 ... 196 E4
Maidstone,Cock Street
ME17 ... 195 C2
Maidstone,East Barming
ME16 ... 160 F3
Heath Rise BR2 ... 52 A3
Heathside TN26 ... 347 C1
Heathside Ave
Bexley DA7 ... 13 E5
Coxheath ME17 ... 194 C4
Heath Side BR5 ... 53 C2
Heath St DA1 ... 33 D8
Heath Terr TN12 ... 290 A6
Heath The
Appledore Heath TN26 ... 347 C1
Well Street ME19 ... 159 F5
Whitstable CT5 ... 75 B1
Heathview Ave DA1 ... 14 E1
Heathview Cres DA1 ... 33 B7
Heath View Dr SE2 ... 13 D8
Heathview TN4 ... 253 F2
Heath Villas
Appledore Heath TN26 ... 347 C2
Woolwich SE18 ... 2 F1
Heath Way DA7,DA8 ... 14 D6
Heathway SE3 ... 11 A7
Heathwood Dr CT11 ... 83 E1
Heathwood Gdns
Swanley BR8 ... 55 C7
Woolwich SE7 ... 1 E1
Heathwood Wlk DA5 ... 32 E7
Heaton Rd CT1 ... 174 F6
Heaverham Rd TN15 ... 123 C2
Heavitree Cl 3 SE18 ... 2 D1
Heavitree Rd SE18 ... 2 D1
Hectorage Rd TN9 ... 254 D8
Hector St SE18 ... 2 E2
Hedge Barton Trailer Pk
TN3 ... 283 F5
Hedgend Ind Est CT7 ... 79 F3
Hedge Place Rd DA9 ... 17 A1
Hedgerows TN23 ... 299 D7
Hedgerows The DA11 ... 36 E6
Hedgerow The ME14 ... 162 E5
Hedges The ME14 ... 162 A7
Hedley Ave RM20 ... 17 C8
Hedley St ME14 ... 162 A5
Heel La CT2 ... 143 C8
Heel Rd ME13 ... 202 B7
Heights Terr CT17 ... 310 C6
Heights The
Greenwich SE7 ... 1 C1
Whitstable CT5 ... 108 C6
Helding Cl CT6 ... 77 B2
Helegan Cl BR6 ... 86 F6
Helena Ave CT9 ... 82 E8
Helena Corniche
CT20 ... 334 C3
Helen Allison Sch
DA13 ... 60 A2
Helena Rd CT18 ... 308 C2
Helena Villas CT21 ... 334 B3
Helen Cl DA1 ... 33 B8
Helen Ct 9 DA14 ... 31 B4
Helen Keller Cl TN10 ... 222 D4
Helen St SE18 ... 2 B2
Helen Thompson Cl
ME9 ... 68 E4
Hellyar Ct ME1 ... 63 C4
Helmdon Cl CT12 ... 83 C2
Helvellyn Ave CT11 ... 117 B7
Hemmings Cl DA14 ... 31 B6
Hempstead Inf Sch
ME7 ... 98 A5
Hempstead Jun Sch
ME7 ... 98 A5
Hempstead La ME9 ... 102 E3
Hempstead Rd
Gillingham ME7 ... 98 A5
Gillingham ME7,ME8 ... 98 B6
Hempstead Valley Dr
ME7 ... 98 A4
Hempstead Valley Sh Ctr
ME7 ... 98 A3
Hempsted St 11 TN23 ... 268 B2
Hempton Hill TN25 ... 304 C5
Hemstead Forest Walks*
TN27 ... 322 A7
Hemstead Forest Walks*
TN27 ... 322 C5
Hemsted Forest Walks*
TN17 ... 321 E2
Hemsted Rd DA8 ... 14 E7
Henbane Cl ME14 ... 162 E5
Henderson Dr DA1 ... 16 A3
Henderson Rd TN16 ... 118 C7
Hendley Dr TN17 ... 320 C5
Hendry Ho ME3 ... 40 F6
Hendy Rd ME6 ... 128 B8
Henfield Cl DA5 ... 14 A1
Hengist Ave CT9 ... 51 B1
Hengist Rd
Birchington CT7 ... 80 C7
Deal CT14 ... 215 D7
Eltham SE12 ... 29 B8
Erith DA8 ... 14 C7
Westgate-on-S CT8 ... 81 D8
Westgate-on-S CT8 ... 81 E8
Hengrove Ct DA5 ... 31 E7
Henham Gdns TN12 ... 225 A6
Henhurst Hill DA12 ... 60 D8
Henhurst Rd
Gravesend DA13 ... 37 E1
Henhurst DA12 ... 60 E8
Heniker La ME17 ... 230 A4
Henley Bsns Pk ME2 ... 63 D7
Henley Cl Chatham ME5 ... 97 A6
Gillingham ME8 ... 98 D8
Royal Tunbridge Wells
TN2 ... 286 C4
Henley Ct DA5 ... 31 F8
Henley Deane DA11 ... 36 E4
Henley Fields
Maidstone ME14 ... 162 E6
Tenterden TN30 ... 324 B2
Henley Mdws TN30 ... 324 A2
Henley Rd Newham E16 ... 1 F4
Paddock Wood TN12 ... 257 A7
Henley St DA13 ... 60 F3
Henley View TN30 ... 324 B2
Henniker Cl CT16 ... 278 A5
Henniker Cotts TN17 ... 320 A3
Henry Addlington Cl E6 ... 2 B8
Henry Cooper Way SE9 ... 29 D4
Henry Ct CT1 ... 174 F7
Henrys Cl ME18 ... 192 D6
Henry St Bromley BR1 ... 52 B8
Chatham ME4 ... 64 B3
Gillingham ME8 ... 66 A1
14 Grays RM17 ... 18 C8
Henson Cl BR6 ... 86 B8
Henville Rd BR1 ... 52 B8
Henwick Prim Sch SE9 ... 11 E4
Henwick Rd SE9 ... 11 E4
Henwood TN24 ... 268 D3
Henwood Bsns Ctr
TN24 ... 268 D2
Henwood Green Rd
TN2 ... 287 E6
Henwoods Cres TN2 ... 287 D6
Henwoods Mount
TN2 ... 287 E6
Herald Wlk DA1 ... 15 F2
Herbert Dane Ct 10
ME13 ... 138 D7
Herbert Pl SE18 ... 12 B8
Herbert Rd
Ashford TN24 ... 300 D6
Bexley DA7 ... 13 E5
Bromley BR2 ... 52 E4
Chatham ME4 ... 64 A3
Gillingham ME8 ... 98 E8
Hextable BR8 ... 33 B2
Ramsgate CT11 ... 117 C6
Swanscombe DA10 ... 17 F1
Woolwich SE18 ... 12 B8
Herbert St CT17 ... 278 B1
Herdsdown ME3 ... 41 D5
Herdson Rd CT20 ... 335 A5
Hereford Cl
Ashford TN24 ... 268 C7
Gillingham ME8 ... 65 D2
Hereford Gdns CT7 ... 80 F6
Hereford Rd ME15 ... 195 D7
Hereson Rd CT11 ... 117 F8
Hereson Sch The CT10 ... 84 A3
Hereward Ave CT7 ... 80 E8
Heritage Cl CT5 ... 108 A6
Heritage Ct 19 CT1 ... 174 F8
Heritage Dr ME7 ... 64 F1
Heritage Gdns CT16 ... 310 E8
Heritage Hill BR2 ... 85 C5
Heritage Quay DA12 ... 19 C1
Heritage Rd
Chatham ME5 ... 97 A6
Folkestone CT20 ... 334 D6
Heritage The BR6 ... 54 A2
Herman Terr ME4 ... 64 A3
Hermitage Cl
Hythe CT21 ... 333 B2
Woolwich SE2 ... 3 C3
Hermitage Cnr ME17 ... 228 F6
Hermitage Ct
Maidstone ME16 ... 160 F5
Tonbridge TN9 ... 222 C2
Hermitage Farm
ME19 ... 159 C8
Hermitage La
Detling ME14 ... 131 B4
Maidstone ME16,ME20 ... 160 F6
Rabbit's Cross ME17 ... 228 E6
Hermitage Rd ME3 ... 39 E4
Hermitage The ME19 ... 159 D8
Herne Ave CT6 ... 77 A4
Herne Bay High Sch
CT6 ... 76 D3
Herne Bay Inf Sch CT6 ... 76 F4
Herne Bay Jun Sch
CT6 ... 76 F4
Herne Bay Mus* CT6 ... 76 F5
Herne Bay Rd
Sturry CT3 ... 110 E2
Whitstable CT5 ... 75 C3
Herne Bay Sta CT6 ... 76 E3
Herne Bay West Ind Est
CT6 ... 76 C3
Herne CE Inf Sch CT6 ... 111 B8
Herne CE Jun Sch
CT6 ... 111 A8
Herne Ct CT19 ... 334 C6
Herne Dr CT6 ... 76 C2
Herne Rd ME8 ... 65 C2
Herne St CT6 ... 111 A8
Herneville Gdns CT6 ... 77 B4
Herne Windmill* CT6 ... 77 B2
Hernhill CE Prim Sch
ME13 ... 140 B7
Hern The TN15 ... 157 C5
Hero Ho ME12 ... 28 B2
Heron Apartments 3
ME15 ... 195 F5
Heron Cl
Lower Halstow ME9 ... 67 B3
Marlpit Hill TN8 ... 217 C3
Heron Cotts TN18 ... 357 D3
Heron Cres DA14 ... 30 E4
Heron Ct BR2 ... 52 C5
Heronden Rd
Eastry CT13 ... 179 F1
Maidstone ME15 ... 195 F4
Heronden View CT13 ... 180 A2
Heron Dr ME12 ... 47 B5
Heron Forestall Ave
CT18 ... 307 B4
Herongate Rd BR8 ... 32 E2
Heron Hill DA17 ... 3 F2
Heron Hill La DA13 ... 93 A4
Heron Ho Ashford TN23 ... 267 F1
Sidcup DA14 ... 31 B5
Heron Lodge 6 CT16 ... 278 B2
Heron Rd ME20 ... 127 F1
Heron's Brook TN25 ... 269 E6
Herons Cl CT4 ... 205 C8
Heronsgate Prim Sch
SE28 ... 2 D3
Heron's Way CT21 ... 353 D8
Herons Way TN2 ... 287 E8
Heron Way
Chatham ME5 ... 97 B7
Lower Stoke ME3 ... 25 C4
Heron Wlk TN23 ... 299 E8
Hero Wlk ME1 ... 96 C7
Herringham Rd SE7 ... 1 C3
Herschell Rd CT7 ... 80 F8
Herschell Rd E CT14 ... 215 C3
Herschell Rd W CT14 ... 215 C3
Herschell Sq CT14 ... 215 C3
Hersden Com Prim Sch
CT3 ... 111 E1
Hertford Ct CT1 ... 175 C8
Hertford Ho
Herne Bay CT6 ... 77 A5
17 Ramsgate CT11 ... 117 E6
Hertford Pl CT11 ... 117 E6
Hertford Rd CT9 ... 83 C8
Hertford St CT11 ... 117 E6
Herts Cres ME15 ... 194 F3
Hertsfield Ave ME2 ... 40 A2
Hertsfield Farm Cotts
TN12 ... 228 B4
Hervey Rd SE3 ... 11 B6
Herying Cl ME2 ... 95 B4
Hesketh Ave DA2 ... 34 B7
Heskett Pk TN2 ... 287 E6
Hestia Way TN23 ... 299 E5
Hever Ave TN15 ... 90 E4
Hever Castle* TN8 ... 250 D7
Hever CE Prim Sch
TN8 ... 250 D6
Hever Cl ME15 ... 195 F6
Hever Court Rd DA12 ... 37 D2
Hever Croft Eltham SE9 ... 30 A4
Rochester ME2 ... 62 F5
Hever Gdns
Bromley BR1 ... 53 A7
Maidstone ME16 ... 161 E3
Heverham Rd SE18 ... 2 E2
Hever Ho ME2 ... 40 C1
Hever Pl
Canterbury CT2 ... 143 A3
Sittingbourne ME10 ... 101 D3
Hever Rd
Bough Beech TN8 ... 218 D2
Hever TN8 ... 250 B7
West Kingsdown TN15 ... 90 E4
Hever Road Cotts TN8 ... 218 E2
Heversham Rd DA7 ... 14 A6
Hever Sta TN8 ... 250 B6
Heverswood TN14 ... 88 A2
Hever Wood Rd TN15 ... 90 E4
Hewett Ho 7 SE18 ... 2 B1
Hewett Pl BR8 ... 55 D5
Hewitt Cl Gillingham ME7 ... 64 F6
Maidstone ME16 ... 161 D7
Hewitt Rd 1 CT16 ... 310 D8
Hewitts Pl TN24 ... 268 F1
Hewitts Rd BR6,TN14 ... 87 F3
Hextable Cl
Ashford TN23 ... 299 F6
Maidstone ME16 ... 161 D7
Hextable Inf Sch BR8 ... 32 F2
Hextable Jun Sch BR8 ... 32 F2
Hextable Sch BR8 ... 55 F8
Heyford Cl CT18 ... 307 B4
Hibbs Cl BR8 ... 55 D7
Hibernia Dr DA12 ... 37 F5
Hibernia Point 11 SE2 ... 3 D4
Hibernia St 6 CT11 ... 117 E6
Hickin Cl SE7 ... 1 D2
Hickman Cl E16 ... 1 D8
Hickory Dell ME7 ... 98 A5
Hicks Forstal Rd CT3 ... 111 B5

Hide E6 2 A7
Higgins' La ME4 63 F5
Higham Cl ME15 161 E2
Higham Gdns TN10 222 F5
Higham La Bridge CT4 209 B8
Tonbridge TN10,TN11 222 F6
Higham Park & Gdns* CT4 209 C8
Higham Prim Sch ME3 39 C5
Higham Rd Cliffe ME3 22 A4
Rochester ME3 40 C3
Higham School Rd TN10 222 E6
Higham Sta ME3 39 D6
Higham View ME14 129 E4
High Bank ME1 63 D2
Highbanks Cl DA16 13 B7
High Banks ME15 194 F5
High Beeches
Orpington BR6 87 A4
Royal Tunbridge Wells TN2 286 D6
Sidcup DA14 31 E3
Highberry ME19 127 E2
Highbrook Rd SE3 11 D4
High Brooms Ind Pk TN2 286 C8
High Brooms Rd TN4 286 C7
High Brooms Sta TN4 286 C7
Highbury Gdns CT12 83 B3
Highbury La TN30 345 A7
Highbury Pl TN5 336 F5
Highbury Wlk CT12 83 B2
Highcombe Cl SE9 29 E7
Highcombe SE7 11 B8
High Croft Cotts BR8 56 A5
Highcroft Gn ME15 195 F4
Highcroft Hall BR8 55 D1
Highcross Rd DA13 35 D2
High Cross Rd TN15 156 B1
High Dewar Rd ME8 99 A8
Highdown Cotts TN17 317 F3
High Elms Ctry Pk* BR6 86 D3
High Elms ME8 65 E1
High Elms Rd BR6 86 C2
Highfield Ave Erith DA8 14 B8
Orpington BR6 86 F5
Highfield Cl
Gillingham ME8 98 D7
Hawkhurst TN18 341 A1
Hythe CT21 333 A4
Pembury TN2 287 D6
Ramsgate CT12 83 B3
Rough Common CT2 142 B3
Highfield Cotts DA2 33 B2
Highfield Ct
Dartford DA1 33 D8
Herne Bay CT6 76 E4
5 Margate CT9 51 B2
Ramsgate CT12 83 B2
Highfield Gdns CT9 50 H1
Highfield Ind Est CT19 335 F6
Highfield La TN24, TN25 301 C6
Highfield Rd
Ashford TN24 301 A8
Bexley DA6 13 F2
Biggin Hill TN16 118 C3
Bromley BR1 52 F5
Dartford DA1 33 D8
Gillingham ME8 98 D7
Halfway Houses ME12 46 E6
Kemsing TN15 122 F3
Highfield Rd N DA1 15 D1
Highfield Rd
Ramsgate CT12 83 B3
Royal Tunbridge Wells TN4 286 C7
St Paul's Cray BR7 53 F6
Highfield Rd S DA1 33 D7
Highfields Ave CT6 77 D4
Highfields Rd TN8 217 C4
Highfields View CT6 77 C4
High Firs Prim Sch BR8 55 F5
High Firs BR8 55 E5
Highgate Ct 8 TN18 340 F2
Highgate Hill TN18 340 F1
Highgate Rd CT5 75 B1
High Gr BR1 52 D8
Highgrove Cl BR7 52 E8
Highgrove Rd ME5 97 A5
Highgrove TN2 314 A8
High Gr SE18 12 D6
High Halden CE Prim Sch TN26 324 E7
High Halden Rd TN26, TN27 295 C2
High Halstow Prim Sch ME23 23 E3
High Hilden Cl TN10 222 A4
High House La TN11 190 C2
High Knocke TN29 366 B6
Highland Cl CT20 334 F4
Highland Rd
Badgers Mount TN14 121 B8
Bexley DA6 14 A3
Chartham CT4 173 D1
Maidstone ME15 195 E6
Highlands Cl ME2 62 D5
Highlands Cres TN29 366 A4
Highlands DA1 33 C8
Highlands Glade CT12 82 E1
Highlands Hill BR8 56 A8
Highlands Pk TN15 154 E6
Highlands Rd BR5 54 C2
Highlands TN2 286 D7
High Mdw CT17 278 C1
Highmead SE18 12 F7
High Meads Rd E16 1 D7
High Minnis CT4 272 F8
High Oak Hill ME9 100 D8
Highpoint TN24 268 D3
High Point SE9 30 B5
High Rd DA2 33 C5
High Ridge TN23 299 C7
Highridge Cl ME14 162 F5
Highridge ME7 64 F1
High Ridge TN17 318 E8
Highridge CT21 334 A3
High Rocks La TN3, TN4 285 C1
High Rocks* TN3 285 B1
High Rocks Sta* TN3 285 B1
High St The TN27 234 C7
High Snoad Wood TN25 203 A1
High St Ashford TN23 268 C2
Aylesford ME20 128 F3
Bean DA2 35 B5
Bidborough TN3 253 C3
Biddenden TN27 294 F1
Borough Green TN15 156 F7
Brasted TN14,TN16 152 C3
Brenchley TN12 289 B8
Bridge CT4 176 A1
Broadstairs CT10 83 E5
Broadstairs,St Peter's CT10 84 A4
Bromley BR1 52 A6
Bromley BR1 52 A7
Brookland TN29 370 E8
Canterbury CT1 174 F8
8 Canterbury,Northgate CT1 143 A1
Chatham ME4 64 A4
Chatham ME7 64 A6
Cowden TN8 282 B5
Cranbrook TN17 320 C4
Dartford DA1 15 E1
Deal CT14 215 D6
Dover CT16 310 C8
Downe BR6 119 A8
Dymchurch TN29 366 C8
Highstead Cres DA8 14 E7
High St Eastchurch ME12 48 D3
East Malling ME19 160 A6
Eastry CT13 180 B2
Edenbridge TN8 217 C1
Highsted Gram Sch ME10 101 F2
Highsted Rd ME9, ME10 101 F1
High St Elham CT4 273 F5
Eynsford DA4 89 E8
Farningham DA4 56 F2
Flimwell TN5 339 C3
Fordwich CT2 144 A4
Frant TN3 314 C4
Gillingham ME7 64 C5
Gillingham,Rainham ME8 98 F8
Goudhurst TN17 318 E8
Grain ME3 27 B6
Gravesend DA11 19 B1
2 Grays RM17 18 A8
Hadlow TN11 223 E8
Halling ME2 95 A4
Hawkhurst TN18 340 E2
Headcorn TN27 262 C5
Herne Bay CT6 76 F5
Hythe CT21 333 C2
Kemsing TN15 123 B2
Lamberhurst TN3 317 B5
Leigh TN11 220 F1
Lenham ME17 199 D5
Limpsfield RH8 183 B7
Littlebourne CT3 176 F7
Lower Stoke ME3 25 C4
Lydd TN29 376 C6
Lyminge CT18 305 C6
Maidstone ME14 161 F4
Manston CT12 116 D8
Marden TN12 259 D6
Margate CT9 50 I2
Margate,Garlinge CT9 82 B7
Minster (Sheppey) ME12 47 D6
Minster (Thanet) CT12 115 C6
Newington ME9 100 C6
New Romney TN28 373 B6
Northfleet DA11 18 C1
Orpington,Broom Hill BR6 54 A1
Orpington,Farnborough BR6 86 C5
Orpington,Green Street Green BR6 86 F4
Orpington,St Mary Cray BR5 54 C4
Otford TN14 122 A3
Pembury TN2 287 C6
Penshurst TN11 252 B4
Queenborough ME11 45 F5
Ramsgate CT11 117 E7
Highstreet Rd
Waterham ME13 107 D2
Yorkletts CT5,ME13 107 E2
High Street St Lawrence CT11 117 B7
High St Rochester ME1 63 C6
Rochester,Strood ME2 63 B7
Rochester,Upper Upnor ME2 40 F1
Rolvenden TN17 343 E4
Royal Tunbridge Wells TN1 286 A2
Rusthall TN4 285 C4
St Margaret's at Cliffe CT15 279 F6
Sandwich CT13 149 A1
Seal TN15 154 F6
Sevenoaks,Chipstead TN13 153 C5
Sevenoaks TN13 154 C2
Sheerness,Blue Town ME12 28 A3
High St *continued*
Sheerness ME12 28 C2
Shoreham TN14 88 F1
Sidcup DA14 31 A4
Sittingbourne ME10 101 F4
Sittingbourne,Milton Regis ME10 101 E6
Snodland ME6 128 A8
Staplehurst TN12 260 F3
Sturry CT2 143 F5
Sutton Valence ME17 229 E7
Swanley BR8 55 F5
Swanscombe DA10 17 F2
Swanscombe,Greenhithe DA9 17 B3
Temple Ewell CT16 277 D5
Tenterden TN30 345 A7
Ticehurst TN5 338 C1
Tonbridge TN9 222 C2
Wadhurst TN5 336 F4
Westerham TN16 184 C8
West Malling ME19 159 C8
Whitstable CT5 74 D2
Wingham CT3 178 A8
Wouldham ME1 95 C5
Wrotham TN15 125 A3
Wye TN25 237 E2
Yalding ME18 192 F1
High Tor Cl BR1 29 B1
High Tor View SE28 2 E5
High Trees Cl TN24 301 A8
High Trees DA2 16 B1
High View Ave CT6 76 B5
Highview Cl
Boughton Street ME13 140 B3
Loose ME15 195 A8
Highview Dr ME5 96 D5
High View ME3 39 C4
Highview Pk Cvn Pk CT18 335 G8
Highview Rd
Minster (Sheppey) ME12 47 C7
Sidcup DA14 31 B4
Highview Sch CT19 335 D6
Highview
Vigo Village DA13 126 B8
Woolwich SE18 12 B7
Highway Prim Sch The BR6 87 C5
Highway The BR6 87 C5
Highwood Cl BR6 86 C8
Highwood Dr BR6 86 C8
Highwoods Cl ME3 39 C4
High Woods La TN3 287 B3
Highworth Gram Sch for Girls TN24 268 A3
Hilary Cl Bexley DA8 14 C6
Herne Bay CT6 77 C4
Hilary Gdns ME1 62 F1
Hilbert Cl TN2 286 C5
Hilbert Rd TN2 286 C5
Hilborough Way BR6 86 D5
Hilda May Ave BR8 55 E7
Hilda Rd Chatham ME4 64 A3
Halfway Houses ME12 46 D6
Hilda Vale Cl BR6 86 A6
Hilda Vale Rd BR6 86 B6
Hilden Ave TN11 221 F4
Hildenborough CE Prim Sch TN11 221 D6
Hildenborough Cres ME16 161 C7
Hildenborough Rd
Leigh TN11 221 A3
Shipbourne TN11,TN15 188 E4
Hildenborough Sta TN11 221 B6
Hildenbrook Farm TN11 188 E2
Hilden Dr DA8 15 B7
Hildenfields TN10 222 A4
Hilden Grange Sch TN10 222 B3
Hilden Oaks Sch TN10 222 B3
Hilden Park Rd TN11 221 F4
Hilders Cl TN8 217 B4
Hildersham Cl CT10 83 E5
Hilders La TN8 217 A4
Hillary Ave DA11 36 E5
Hillary Ct SE9 29 E6
Hillary Rd ME14 162 A7
Hill Ave CT15 244 E5
Hillborough Ave TN13 154 D5
Hillborough Bsns Pk CT6 77 F4
Hillborough Dr CT6 77 F5
Hillborough Gr ME5 97 A5
Hillborough Rd CT6 77 B5
Hillbrow Ave
Herne Bay CT6 77 B2
Sturry CT2 143 F7
Hill Brow BR1 52 D8
Hillbrow Cl DA5 32 D4
Hill Brow DA1 14 F1
Hillbrow La TN23 267 F1
Hill Brow ME14 163 A5
Hillbrow Rd
Ashford TN23 268 A1
Ramsgate CT11 117 D8
Hill Brow ME10 101 D2
Hillbury Gdns TN5 338 D1
Hill Chase ME5 96 E3
Hill Cl Chislehurst BR7 30 B3
Istead Rise DA13 36 E1
Hill Cres Aylesham CT3 210 E5
Coldblow DA5 32 C7
Lenham ME17 199 D5
Hillcrest TN23 299 B8
Hillcrest Ave RM20 17 A8
Hillcrest Cl TN24 268 E6
Hillcrest Dr Cuxton ME2 62 C2
Royal Tunbridge Wells TN2 286 D7
Hillcrest Dr *continued*
Stone DA9 17 A2
Hillcrest TN8 218 B5
Hillcrest Gdns
Deal CT14 215 A2
Ramsgate CT11 117 B6
Hillcrest Rd
Biggin Hill TN16 118 D3
Bromley BR1 29 A4
Chatham ME4 63 F2
Dartford DA1 32 F8
Hythe CT21 333 B3
Kingsdown CT14 248 D4
Littlebourne CT3 176 E8
Marlpit Hill TN8 217 C4
Orpington BR6 87 A8
Hill Crest
Royal Tunbridge Wells TN4 286 B8
Sevenoaks TN13 154 A5
Sidcup DA15 31 B8
Hillcroft DA4 89 D7
Hillcroft Rd
Herne Bay CT6 77 B3
Newham E6 2 B8
Hill Ct Charing TN27 201 E1
Chattenden ME3 40 F4
Hillden Shaw ME15 195 A8
Hilldown Lodge BR6 87 B8
Hill Dr CT13 180 B3
Hilldrop Rd BR1 29 B2
Hill End Orpington BR6 86 F8
Woolwich SE18 12 A6
Hiller Cl CT10 84 A6
Hill Farm Cl ME23 23 E3
Hillfield Rd TN13 153 E7
Hillfield Villas TN26 324 F8
Hillgarth TN4 286 A8
Hill Green Rd ME9 132 D8
Hill House Dr CT12 115 C7
Hill House Rd DA2 34 C8
Hillingdale TN16 118 B1
Hillingdon Ave TN13 154 D6
Hillingdon Rd
Bexley DA7 14 C4
Gravesend DA11 37 B6
Hillingdon Rise TN13 154 D5
Hill La CT18 306 B1
Hillman Ave CT6 76 A4
Hill Rd Dartford DA2 33 E6
Folkestone CT19 335 E8
Folkestone,Foord CT19 335 F7
Rochester ME1 63 A2
Wouldham ME1 95 F5
Hillreach SE18 1 F1
Hill Rise Ashford TN25 267 E5
Dartford DA2 34 E3
Hill Sch The TN16 151 B4
Hillsgrove Cl DA16 13 C7
Hillsgrove Prim Sch DA16 13 C7
Hillshaw Cres ME2 62 D5
Hill Shaw DA3 58 F3
Hillside Ave
Canterbury CT2 142 C2
Gravesend DA12 37 D6
Rochester ME2 63 B8
Rushenden ME11 45 F3
Hillside Cotts
Newbury's TN5 337 B8
Wingham CT3 146 A1
Hillside Ct Hythe CT21 333 C2
2 Rochester ME2 63 A7
Swanley BR8 56 A5
Wateringbury ME18 192 E7
Hillside DA2 34 E3
Hillside Dr DA12 37 D6
Hillside Erith DA17 4 C2
Farningham DA4 56 F2
1 Folkestone CT20 334 E3
Hillside Ind Est CT20 334 E4
Hillside La BR2 85 A8
Hillside Prim Sch BR5 54 C2
Hillside Rd
Chatham ME4 64 A4
Dartford DA1 15 A1
Dover CT17 278 A2
Kemsing TN15 122 F2
Minster (Sheppey) ME12 47 B7
Sevenoaks TN13 154 D4
Stalisfield Green ME13 201 E6
Tatsfield TN16 150 E8
Whitstable CT5 75 A1
Hillside ME1 63 A2
Hillside St CT21 333 C2
Hillside Terr DA12 37 B7
Hillside The BR6 87 B2
Hillside TN9 254 A7
Hills La TN15 123 C7
Hillsley Ct 13 DA14 31 A4
Hill's Terr ME4 63 F3
Hillstone Ct 5 CT16 310 E8
Hill St TN1 286 B5
Hill The Charing TN27 234 D8
Cranbrook TN17 320 D4
Littlebourne CT3 176 F8
Northfleet DA11 18 C1
Hill Top Cotts ME17 194 E2
Hilltop Gdns
Dartford DA1 15 F2
Orpington BR6 86 E8
Hilltop Ho CT2 142 C3
Hill Top TN17 291 E5
Hilltop Prim Sch ME2 40 C1
Hill Top Rd CT6 77 B5
Hilltop Rd
Minster (Sheppey) ME12 47 A5
Rochester ME2 40 C1
West Thurrock RM20 17 B8
Hilltop Tonbridge TN9 254 B7
West Farleigh ME15 193 D3
Whitstable CT5 108 D7
Hill View Ashford TN24 268 C3
Hill View *continued*
Basted TN15 156 F4
Borough Green TN15 157 A7
Hill View Cl TN15 157 A7
Hillview Cres BR6 53 F1
Hill View Ct CT4 209 E2
Hill View Dr
Bexley DA16 12 E5
Woolwich SE28 2 E5
Hillview Ho DA12 37 C7
Hill View CT9 82 D7
Hillview Rd
Canterbury CT2 142 C2
Eltham BR7 30 A4
Hill View Rd
New Barn DA3 59 B6
Orpington BR6 86 F8
Rusthall TN4 285 C4
Tonbridge TN11 221 F5
Hillview Rd CT5 108 D8
Hillview Sch for Girls TN9 254 D8
Hill View Terr CT18 305 D3
Hill View Way ME5 96 E5
Hillydeal Rd TN14 122 C4
Hillyfield Cl ME2 39 F1
Hillyfield Rd TN23 300 A8
Hillyfields Rise TN23 268 A1
Hilton Bsns Ctr TN23 300 B6
Hilton Cl ME13 138 D6
Hilton Dr ME10 101 B6
Hilton Rd Ashford TN23 267 F2
Cliffe Woods ME3 40 B7
Hinchliffe Way CT9 83 D8
Hind Cl TN29 366 C8
Hind Cres DA8 14 D7
Hinde Cl ME10 101 F7
Hinde Ho ME10 101 E6
Hines Terr ME5 64 C1
Hinksden Rd TN17, TN18 341 F3
Hinksey Path SE2 3 D3
Hinstock Rd SE18 12 C7
Hinton Cl SE9 29 E7
Hinton Cres ME7 98 A6
Hinxhill Rd TN24,TN25 269 D1
Hirst Cl CT16 278 B4
Historic Dockyard The* ME4 64 A8
Hitchen Hatch La TN13 154 B4
Hither Chantlers TN3 285 A2
Hither Farm Rd SE3 11 C4
Hither Field TN27 234 C7
Hive La DA11 18 B2
Hive The DA11 18 B1
Hoades Wood Rd CT2 144 A7
Hoad Rd CT15,CT18 275 A2
Hoads Wood Gdns TN25 267 E6
Hoath Cl ME8 98 B7
Hoath Farm The CT3 175 F7
Hoath La ME8 98 B7
Hoath Mdw TN12 290 A6
Hoath Prim Sch CT3 111 E5
Hoath Rd CT3 111 C3
Hoath Way ME7,ME8 98 B5
Hobart Cres CT16 278 C3
Hobart Gdns ME10 101 C4
Hobart Rd
Ramsgate CT12 83 A1
Tilbury RM18 19 A6
Hoblands End BR7 30 E2
Hockenden La BR8 55 B7
Hockeredge Gdns CT8 81 F8
Hockers Cl ME14 163 A8
Hockers La ME14 163 A8
Hoddesdon Rd DA17 4 A1
Hodge's Gap CT9 51 C3
Hodgkins Cl SE28 3 D6
Hodgson Cres ME6 95 A1
Hodgson Rd CT5 107 F7
Hodsoll Ct BR5 54 D4
Hodsoll St TN15 92 D1
Hodson Cres BR5 54 D3
Hogarth Cl
Herne Bay CT6 77 E5
Newham E16 1 D8
Hogarth Ho ME11 45 F5
Hogbarn La ME17 165 F2
Hogben Cl CT18 305 B7
Hogben's Hill ME13 171 A6
Hogbrook Hill La CT15 308 D8
Hogg La CT4 207 E2
Hog Gn CT4 273 F4
Hog Hill ME14 163 B5
Hog Hole La TN3 316 F2
Hog La DA11 36 D5
Hognore La TN15 125 D6
Hogpound Cnr TN30 360 B6
Hogs Orch BR8 56 B8
Hogtrough Hill TN16 152 A5
Holbeach Gdns DA15 12 F1
Holbeam Rd ME13 169 A1
Holborn La ME4 63 F5
Holborn Rd E13 1 B8
Holborough Rd ME6 95 A1
Holbourn Cl CT6 111 B8
Holbrook Dr CT12 83 B1
Holbrook Ho BR7 53 D8
Holbrook La BR7 30 D1
Holbrook Way BR2 52 F4
Holburne Cl SE3 11 C6
Holburne Gdns SE3 11 D6
Holburne Rd SE3 11 D6
Holcombe Cl TN16 151 D1
Holcombe Rd
Chatham ME4 63 F2
Rochester ME1 63 C3
Holcote Cl DA17 3 E3
Holden Cnr TN4 253 F1
Holdenhurst TN23 299 E6
Holden Park Rd TN4 286 A8
Holden Rd TN4 253 F1
Holder Cl ME5 97 C6
Holding St ME8 65 F1
Hole La TN8 217 A6
Holford St 1 TN9 222 B1
Holgate St SE7 1 D3
Hollandbury Pk ME18 159 C2
Holland Cl
Broadstairs CT10 51 G2
Sheerness ME12 28 B1
Holland Cres RH8 183 A2
Holland Ho ME1 63 D5
Holland Jun Sch RH8 183 A1
Holland La RH8 183 A2
Holland Rd
Chatham ME5 96 E4
Maidstone ME14 162 B5
Oxted RH8 183 A1
Hollands Ave CT19 335 F7
Hollands Cl DA12 38 E3
Hollicondane Rd CT11 117 E8
Hollies Ave DA15 30 F7
Hollies The
Gravesend DA12 37 D2
New Barn DA3 59 C6
Sidcup DA15 31 A8
Holligrave Rd BR1 52 A8
Hollin Cl TN4 285 F4
Hollingbourne Ave DA7 13 F6
Hollingbourne Hill ME17 164 F4
Hollingbourne Prim Sch ME17 164 E2
Hollingbourne Rd ME8 65 C2
Hollingbourne Sta ME17 164 C3
Hollingbourne Tower 4 BR5 54 D1
Hollington Ct BR7 30 B2
Hollington Pl TN24 268 B3
Hollingworth Ct ME14 162 C3
Hollingworth Rd
Maidstone ME15 195 F5
Orpington BR2,BR5 53 B2
Hollingworth Way TN16 151 D1
Hollow La
Canterbury CT1 174 E5
Hartlip ME9 99 E5
Snodland ME6 127 F6
Hollowmede CT1 174 E6
Hollow Rd CT3 112 B6
Hollow St CT3 112 C5
Hollow Trees Dr TN11 221 A1
Hollow Wood Rd CT17 309 E8
Holly Bank TN12 289 B8
Hollybank Hill ME10 101 D4
Hollybrake Cl BR7 30 D1
Hollybush Cl TN13 154 C3
Hollybush Cnr CT4 177 A3
Hollybush Ct TN13 154 C3
Hollybush La BR6 88 A4
Holly Bush La TN13 154 C3
Hollybush La CT3 145 A4
Hollybush Rd DA12 37 C6
Holly Cl
Broadstairs CT10 83 C4
Chatham ME5 97 C8
Eastry CT13 180 B2
Folkestone CT19 335 E7
Gillingham ME7 64 E6
Hythe CT21 333 D3
Holly Cotts TN8 217 B2
Hollycroft ME2 62 C2
Holly Ct 1 DA14 31 B4
Hollydale Dr BR2 85 F7
Hollydene Rd TN5 336 F6
Holly Farm Rd ME15 196 C6
Holly Gdns Bexley DA7 14 C3
Maidstone ME14 162 B7
Margate CT9 51 C2
Holly Hill DA13 93 F3
Holly Hill Rd
Erith DA8,DA17 4 B1
Hernhill ME13 140 D5
Holly La CT9 51 C2
Holly Mdws TN23 267 D3
Holly Rd Dartford DA1 33 D7
Orpington BR6 87 A3
Ramsgate CT11 117 E8
Rochester ME2 40 D2
Rochester,Strood ME2 62 E5
St Mary's Bay TN29 365 F4
Hollyshaw Cl TN2 286 C2
Hollyshaw TN2 286 C2
Hollytree Ave BR8 55 E7
Holly Tree Cl ME17 197 E2
Hollytree Dr ME3 39 B3
Hollytree Par DA14 31 C2
Hollywood La
Knockmill TN15 123 F8
Rochester ME2 40 C2
Hollywood Way DA8 15 B6
Holman Mews CT1 175 A7
Holmbury Manor 21 DA14 31 A4
Holmbury Pk BR7 29 E1
Holmcroft Way BR2 52 F4
Holm Ct 5 SE12 29 B5
Holmdale Rd BR7 30 C3
Holmden Ct 2 TN8 217 C1
Holmdene Ct 5 BR1 52 E6
Holme Oak Cl CT1 174 F6
Holmes Cl ME23 23 E3
Holmes Ct
5 Canterbury CT1 175 B8
Ryarsh ME19 126 F4

Holmesdale Cl
Durgates TN5 ... 336 E5
Maidstone ME15 ... 194 F3
Holmesdale Hill DA4 ... 57 D8
Holmesdale Rd
Bexley DA7 ... 13 D5
Sevenoaks TN13 ... 154 D4
Sutton at H DA4 ... 57 C8
Holmesdale Tech Coll ME6 ... 127 F7
Holmesdale Terr 14 CT20 ... 335 D4
Holmestone Rd CT17 ... 277 E1
Holmes Way CT12 ... 83 A3
Holmewood House Sch TN3 ... 285 A2
Holmewood Rd TN4 ... 286 C7
Holmewood Ridge TN3 ... 284 F3
Holmhurst Cl TN4 ... 285 F4
Holmhurst Rd DA17 ... 4 B1
Holmlea Cl TN24 ... 268 E1
Holmleigh Ave DA1 ... 15 C2
Holm Mill La ME17 ... 198 B6
Holm Oak Gdns CT10 ... 83 F4
Holmoaks
Gillingham ME8 ... 65 E2
Maidstone ME14 ... 162 C5
Holmscroft Rd CT6 ... 77 D5
Holmsdale Gr DA1,DA7 ... 14 E4
Holmside Ave ME12 ... 46 D6
Holmside ME7 ... 64 E3
Holm Wlk SE3 ... 11 A5
Holmwood Cotts BR6 ... 87 C1
Holmwood Ct DA14 ... 30 F3
Holmwood Rd TN23 ... 299 E7
Holness Rd CT3 ... 147 D2
Holstein Way 6 DA18 ... 3 E3
Holt Cl SE28 ... 3 C6
Holters Mews 13 CT1 ... 175 A8
Holters Mill CT2 ... 142 F2
Holton Cl CT7 ... 81 A6
Holt Rd E16 ... 1 E5
Holt St CT15 ... 211 C4
Holt Wood Ave ME20 ... 160 E8
Holtwood Cl ME8 ... 98 D6
Holtye Cres ME15 ... 162 B2
Holtye Rd RH19 ... 281 A4
Holwood Park Ave BR2, BR4 ... 85 F6
Holy Family RC Prim Sch
Eltham SE3 ... 11 C3
Maidstone ME15 ... 195 F4
Holyhead Cl 3 E6 ... 1 F8
Holy Innocents RC Prim Sch BR6 ... 86 F7
Holyoake Terr TN13 ... 154 A3
Holyrood Dr ME12 ... 47 A5
Holyrood Mews E16 ... 1 A5
Holy Trinity CE Prim Sch
Broadstairs CT10 ... 84 A1
Dartford DA1 ... 15 C2
Gravesend DA12 ... 37 C8
Holy Trinity Coll Prep Sch BR1 ... 52 C8
Holy Trinity Lamorbey CE Prim Sch DA15 ... 31 A7
Holy Trinity & St John's CE Prim Sch CT9 ... 50 J2
Holywell Ave CT19 ... 335 D8
Holywell Cl
Greenwich SE3 ... 11 A8
Orpington BR6 ... 87 A6
Holywell Ho CT19 ... 335 D8
Holywell La ME9 ... 66 F2
Holywell Prim Sch ME9 ... 66 F3
Homebirch Ho 6 CT7 ... 80 F8
Homedean Rd TN13 ... 153 C4
Home Farm BR6 ... 88 A5
Home Farm Cl TN11 ... 221 A3
Home Farm Cotts
East Studdal CT14 ... 213 E6
Orpington BR5 ... 54 D8
Home Farm Ct TN3 ... 314 C4
Homefarm Est ME20 ... 128 F1
Home Farm La TN2 ... 286 E8
Homefern Ho CT9 ... 50 I3
Homefield Ave CT14 ... 215 B6
Homefield Cl
Orpington BR5 ... 54 B5
Swanley BR8 ... 55 F6
Homefield Dr ME8 ... 66 B2
Homefield Rd
Bromley BR1 ... 52 C8
Sevenoaks TN13 ... 153 E5
Homefield Rise BR6 ... 54 A1
Homefield Row CT14 ... 215 B6
Homefleet Ho 13 CT11 ... 117 F7
Home Gdns DA1 ... 15 E1
Home Hill BR8 ... 32 F1
Homelands Cl TN25 ... 303 D1
Home Lea BR6 ... 86 F5
Homeleigh Rd CT12 ... 83 B3
Home Mead Cl 6 DA12 ... 37 B8
Homemead 7 DA12 ... 37 B8
Homemead Rd BR2 ... 52 F4
Homemead DA9 ... 17 B1
Homepeak Ho 12 CT21 ... 333 B2
Homepine Ho 8 CT20 ... 335 C4
Home Pk RH8 ... 183 A4
Homer Cl DA7 ... 14 C6
Homersham CT1 ... 174 D6
Homesdale Bsns Ctr BR1 ... 52 D6
Homesdale Rd
Bromley BR1,BR2 ... 52 C6
Orpington BR5 ... 53 E2
Homeside Farm CT4 ... 240 F6
Homespire Ho 10 CT1 ... 143 A1
Homestall Ct CT2 ... 142 C4
Homestall La ME13 ... 139 B5
Homestall Rd ME9 ... 136 D3
Homestead TN23 ... 299 D8
Homestead Cl 7 CT9 ... 50 J1
Homestead Ct CT14 ... 215 A4
Homestead La CT15 ... 246 C7
Homestead Rd
Marlpit Hill TN8 ... 217 B5
Orpington BR6 ... 87 B4
Homestead The
Crayford DA1 ... 14 E2
Dartford DA1 ... 15 C1
Groombridge TN3 ... 312 C7
Homestead View ME9 ... 101 B2
Homestead Village CT11 ... 117 C5
Homevale Cotts TN14 ... 120 E4
Homevale Ho 8 CT20 ... 334 E3
Homeview 3 ME10 ... 102 B4
Homeview Terr 2 ME10 ... 102 B4
Homewards Rd ME3 ... 9 B2
Homewood Ave ME10 ... 101 D3
Homewood Cotts DA12 ... 38 E1
Homewood Cres BR7 ... 30 E2
Homewood Inf Sch ME10 ... 101 D4
Homewood Rd
Langton Green TN3 ... 284 F3
Sturry CT2 ... 144 A6
Tenterden TN30 ... 324 B1
Homewood Sch & Sixth Form Ctr TN30 ... 324 B1
Homlesdale Bsns Ctr TN15 ... 157 C8
Homoepathic Hospl TN1 ... 286 A3
Honduras Terr 8 ME14 ... 162 A7
Hone St ME2 ... 63 B8
Honeyball Wlk ME9 ... 103 C2
Honey Bee Glade ME8 ... 98 E6
Honeybourne Way BR5 ... 53 D1
Honey Cl ME7 ... 98 A5
Honeycombe Lodge DA11 ... 18 D1
Honeycrest Ind Pk TN12 ... 260 E5
Honeycrock Hill ME9 ... 132 F8
Honeyden Rd DA14 ... 31 E2
Honeyfield TN23 ... 267 E1
Honey Hill CT2,CT5 ... 141 F8
Honey La ME15 ... 196 B6
Honeypot Cl ME2 ... 63 B8
Honeypot La
Hodsoll Street TN15 ... 92 D2
Kemsing TN15 ... 155 C8
Limpsfield TN8 ... 216 D4
Honeysuckle Cl
3 Chatham ME5 ... 96 E4
Gillingham ME7 ... 97 F4
Margate CT9 ... 82 C8
Honeysuckle Ct
4 Lewisham SE12 ... 29 A8
Sittingbourne ME10 ... 102 B5
Honeysuckle Rd CT11 ... 117 F8
Honeysuckle Way CT6 ... 77 D2
Honeywood Cl
Canterbury CT1 ... 143 B2
Dover CT16 ... 278 A6
Lympne CT21 ... 332 A4
Honeywood Ho CT16 ... 278 A6
Honeywood Parkway CT16 ... 278 B5
Honeywood Rd CT16 ... 278 A6
Honfleur Rd CT13 ... 180 F8
Honiton House Sch CT9 ... 51 A3
Honiton Rd DA16 ... 12 F5
Honner Cl CT18 ... 306 F3
Honywood Rd ME17 ... 199 C4
Hoo Comm ME3 ... 41 A4
Hood Ave BR5 ... 54 B4
Hoo Farm CT12 ... 114 F6
Hook Cl Chatham ME5 ... 96 E5
Folkestone CT20 ... 334 F5
Hook Farm Rd BR2 ... 52 D4
Hookfields DA11 ... 36 E5
Hook Green Ct DA13 ... 60 A4
Hook Green La DA2 ... 32 F5
Hook Green Rd DA13 ... 35 F1
Hook Hill TN5 ... 338 A6
Hook La Bexley DA16 ... 13 A4
Brookland TN29 ... 370 C6
Charing TN27 ... 234 A7
Harrietsham ME17 ... 198 C6
Hook Lane Prim Sch DA16 ... 13 A4
Hook Place Cotts DA13 ... 36 A2
Hook Rd ME6 ... 127 F8
Hookstead TN26 ... 324 C7
Hook Wall TN29 ... 370 E5
Hookwood Bglws RH8 ... 183 B7
Hookwood Cnr RH8 ... 183 B7
Hookwood Cotts TN14 ... 120 C8
Hookwood Rd BR6, TN14 ... 120 C7
Hooper Rd E16 ... 1 A7
Hoopers La
Herne Bay CT6 ... 77 D3
St Mary Hoo ME3 ... 24 F5
Hooper's Pl ME1 ... 63 C4
Hooper's Rd ME1 ... 63 C4
Hoopers Yd TN13 ... 154 C1
Hoo Rd ME2,ME3 ... 40 D3
Hoo St Werburgh Prim Sch ME3 ... 41 D5
Hop Bine Cl TN12 ... 225 A7
Hope Ave TN11 ... 190 E1
Hope Cl SE12 ... 29 B5
Hope Cotts DA2 ... 35 B6
Hopedale Rd SE7 ... 11 B8
Hopehouse La TN17, TN18 ... 356 E7
Hope La
New Romney TN28 ... 373 A8
St Mary in the Marsh TN29 ... 364 F2
Hope Rd Deal CT14 ... 215 D5
Swanscombe DA10 ... 17 F1
Hopes Gr TN26 ... 324 D7
Hope's La CT12 ... 83 C3
Hope St Chatham ME4 ... 64 A3
Maidstone ME14 ... 161 F6
Sheerness ME12 ... 28 B2
Hope Terr ME3 ... 39 D7
Hope Villas CT1 ... 174 D6
Hopeville Ave CT10 ... 83 E6
Hopewell Bsns Ctr ME5 ... 97 C8
Hopewell Dr
Chatham ME5 ... 97 C8
Gravesend DA12 ... 37 F3
Hopewell Sch TN23 ... 299 E7
Hop Farm Country Pk* TN12 ... 225 A3
Hopgarden Cl 12 TN8 ... 217 D3
Hopgarden La TN13 ... 187 A8
Hopgarden Oast ME18 ... 192 F1
Hopgarden Rd TN10 ... 222 D6
Hop Garden Way CT1 ... 174 E6
Hop Gdn TN26 ... 347 C1
Hoppers Cnr ME15 ... 193 D7
Hoppers Way TN23 ... 299 D8
Hop Pocket Cl TN17 ... 321 A8
Hop Pocket La TN12 ... 256 F7
Hopsons Pl ME12 ... 47 C5
Hopton Ct BR2 ... 52 A1
Hopton Rd SE18 ... 2 B3
Hopwood Gdns TN4 ... 286 A6
Horatio Pl ME1 ... 63 B4
Horizon Cl TN4 ... 286 B8
Horley Cl DA6 ... 14 A2
Horley Rd SE9 ... 29 E4
Hornash La TN26 ... 327 D8
Hornbeam Ave
Chatham ME5 ... 97 B2
Royal Tunbridge Wells TN4 ... 254 D1
Hornbeam Cl
Ashford TN23 ... 267 F3
Larkfield ME20 ... 128 B2
Paddock Wood TN12 ... 256 F5
Hornbeam Ho 6 DA15 ... 31 A5
Hornbeam La DA7 ... 14 C5
Hornbeams DA13 ... 126 B8
Hornbeam Way BR2 ... 53 A3
Hornbrook La TN26 ... 347 C7
Horncastle Cl SE12 ... 29 A8
Horncastle Rd SE12 ... 29 A8
Horne Ho SE18 ... 11 E6
Hornes Place Chapel* TN26 ... 347 D2
Hornet Cl CT10 ... 83 D3
Hornfair Rd SE7 ... 11 D7
Hornfield Cotts DA13 ... 93 C3
Horn Hill ME9 ... 134 E2
Horning Cl SE9 ... 29 E4
Horn La SE10 ... 1 A2
Horn Link Way SE10 ... 1 A2
Horn Park Cl SE12 ... 11 B2
Horn Park La SE12 ... 11 B1
Horn Park Prim Sch SE12 ... 29 B8
Horns La ME18 ... 158 D1
Horns Lodge Farm TN11 ... 222 C8
Horns Lodge La TN11 ... 222 A8
Horn's Oak Rd DA13 ... 93 B6
Horns Rd
The Moor TN18 ... 354 B8
The Moor TN18 ... 354 D8
The Moor TN18 ... 354 F7
Horn St CT19,CT20, CT21 ... 334 B4
Horn Yd 7 DA11 ... 19 B1
Horsa Rd
Birchington CT7 ... 80 D7
Deal CT14 ... 215 D8
Eltham SE12 ... 29 C8
Erith DA8 ... 14 C7
Horsebridge Rd CT5 ... 74 D2
Horsecroft Cl BR6 ... 54 B1
Horsegrove Ave TN5 ... 338 F1
Horse Leaze E6 ... 2 A7
Horselees Rd ME13 ... 140 A2
Horsell Rd BR5 ... 54 B8
Horseshoe Cl
Gillingham ME7 ... 97 F5
Maidstone ME14 ... 162 E5
Horseshoes La ME17 ... 196 E4
Horse Wash La ME1 ... 63 C6
Horsfeld Gdns SE9 ... 11 E2
Horsfeld Rd SE9 ... 11 D2
Horsfield Cl DA2 ... 34 C8
Horsford Wlk ME13 ... 138 A8
Horsham Hill ME9 ... 66 E4
Horsham La ME8,ME9 ... 66 D3
Horsham Rd DA6 ... 14 A2
Horshams The CT6 ... 77 D5
Horsley Cl CT18 ... 307 B4
Horsley Ho SE18 ... 12 A7
Horsley Rd Bromley BR1 ... 52 B8
Rochester ME1 ... 63 B4
Horsmonden Cl BR6 ... 53 F2
Horsmonden Prim Sch TN12 ... 290 A6
Horsmonden Rd TN12 ... 289 D6
Horsted Ave ME4 ... 63 E1
Horsted Inf Sch ME4 ... 96 D5
Horsted Jun Sch ME5 ... 96 D5
Horsted Ret Pk ME5 ... 96 D5
Horsted Way ME1 ... 96 D7
Horton Cotts CT4 ... 173 E4
Horton Downs ME15 ... 162 F1
Horton Gdns CT4 ... 173 E4
Horton Kirby CE Prim Sch DA4 ... 57 C6
Horton Pl TN16 ... 151 D1
Horton Rd DA4 ... 57 C6
Hortons Cl TN17 ... 342 D7
Hortons Way 1 TN16 ... 151 D1
Horton Tower 2 BR5 ... 54 C5
Horton Way DA4 ... 56 F2
Horwood Cl ME1 ... 96 B8
Hoselands View DA3 ... 58 E5
Hoser Ave SE12 ... 29 A6
Hoser Gdns CT7 ... 81 A7
Hosey Common La TN16 ... 184 F5
Hosey Common Rd TN8,TN16 ... 184 D5
Hosey Hill TN16 ... 184 E8
Hoskin's Cl E16 ... 1 C7
Hospital Hill CT20, CT21 ... 334 C3
Hospital La
Canterbury CT1 ... 174 F8
3 Chatham ME1 ... 63 E4
Hospital Meadow Cotts CT3 ... 178 D2
Hospital of Thomas the Martyr Eastbridge The* CT1 ... 174 F8
Hospital Rd
Hollingbourne ME17 ... 197 E8
Sevenoaks TN13 ... 154 C6
Hostier Cl ME2 ... 95 B4
Hotel Rd Gillingham ME8 ... 65 A2
St Margaret's at Cliffe CT15 ... 280 B6
Hotham Cl
Sutton at H DA4 ... 34 B1
Swanley Village BR8 ... 56 B8
Hothfield Common Nature Reserve* TN26 ... 266 F8
Hothfield Rd ME8 ... 65 F1
Hothfield Village Prim Sch TN26 ... 266 F7
Hottsfield DA3 ... 58 E6
Hougham Court La CT15 ... 309 A3
Hougham Ho 11 BR5 ... 54 D1
Houghton Ave ME7 ... 98 B3
Houghton Green La TN31 ... 368 C2
Houghton Ho CT19 ... 335 C5
Houghton La TN31 ... 368 C3
Housefield TN24 ... 268 F2
Housefield Rd ME13 ... 202 C6
Houselands Rd TN9 ... 222 B2
House Mdw TN23 ... 299 C7
Hove Cl RM17 ... 18 A8
Hovenden Cl CT2 ... 143 A4
Hovendens TN17 ... 321 A8
Hoveton Rd SE28 ... 3 C7
Howard Ave
Rochester ME1 ... 63 D3
Sidcup DA5 ... 31 C8
Sittingbourne ME10 ... 101 D6
Howard Cl ME12 ... 47 C7
Howard Dr ME16 ... 161 B5
Howard Gdns TN2 ... 286 A1
Howard Rd
Broadstairs CT10 ... 84 A3
Bromley BR1 ... 29 A1
Dartford DA1 ... 16 A1
East Malling ME19 ... 159 F8
Howard Sch The ME8 ... 98 D8
Howarth Rd SE2 ... 3 A2
Howbury Ctr PRU The DA8 ... 15 A7
Howbury La DA8 ... 15 A5
Howbury Wlk ME8 ... 98 D4
Howden Cl SE28 ... 3 D6
Howells Cl TN15 ... 90 E4
Howerd Way SE18 ... 11 E6
Howes Cotts TN18 ... 354 F8
Howfield La CT4 ... 173 E5
How Green La TN8 ... 218 C2
Howick Cl ME20 ... 160 F8
Howick Mans SE18 ... 1 E3
Howland Cotts TN12 ... 259 E6
Howland Mews CT1 ... 174 E6
Howland Rd TN12 ... 259 E6
Howlands Ct TN15 ... 124 F4
Howlands TN15 ... 124 F4
Howletts Oast CT4 ... 176 C5
Howletts Wild Animal Pk* CT4 ... 176 D6
Howlsmere Cl ME2 ... 95 B3
Hoxton Cl TN23 ... 299 D8
Hoystings Cl The CT1 ... 175 A7
Hubbards Cotts ME8 ... 66 C2
Hubbard's Hill TN13, TN14 ... 187 B4
Hubbards Hill ME17 ... 200 B6
Hubbard's La ME15 ... 195 A3
Hubble Dr ME15 ... 195 E7
Hubert Way CT10 ... 83 E6
Huckleberry Cl ME5 ... 97 B3
Hudson Cl
7 Dover CT16 ... 278 B3
Rainham ME8 ... 65 C1
Sturry CT2 ... 143 F6
Hudson Ho DA4 ... 57 D7
Hudson Pl SE18 ... 2 C1
Hudson Rd Bexley DA7 ... 13 F6
Canterbury CT1 ... 143 B2
Huggen's College Almshouses DA11 ... 18 B2
Hugh Christie Tech Coll TN10 ... 222 D6
Hughes Dr ME2 ... 40 D2
Hugh Pl 5 ME13 ... 138 D7
Hugh Price Cl ME10 ... 102 C5
Hugin Ave CT10 ... 83 E7
Hulberry Farm DA4 ... 89 B8
Hulkes La ME1 ... 63 E4
Hull Pl Deal CT14 ... 214 F6
Newham E16 ... 2 C5
Hull Rd TN29 ... 377 E6
Hulsewood Cl DA2 ... 33 B5
Hulsons Ct 1 TN18 ... 341 A2
Humber Ave CT6 ... 75 F4
Humber Cres ME2 ... 62 F7
Humber Rd
Dartford DA1 ... 15 D2
Greenwich SE3 ... 11 A8
Humboldt Ct TN2 ... 286 D5
Hume Ave RM18 ... 19 B5
Hume Cl RM18 ... 19 A4
Hume Ct CT21 ... 333 D1
Hume Terr E16 ... 1 B7
Humphreys TN12 ... 288 F6
Humphrey Terr CT18 ... 306 F4
Hundred of Hoo Comp Sch The ME3 ... 41 C5
Hundreds Cl CT8 ... 81 D7
Hunger Hatch La TN27 ... 233 F4
Hungershall Park Cl TN4 ... 285 E1
Hungershall Pk TN4 ... 285 E2
Hunsdon Dr TN13 ... 154 B4
Hunstanton Cl ME8 ... 98 E3
Hunt Cl CT18 ... 307 A4
Hunter Ave TN24 ... 300 E8
Hunter Cl TN24 ... 300 E8
Hunter Rd TN24 ... 268 E1
Hunters Bank CT4 ... 273 F4
Hunters Chase
Herne Bay CT6 ... 77 C2
Whitstable CT5 ... 108 E7
Hunters Cl DA5 ... 32 E5
Hunters Ct 5 ME7 ... 64 C7
Hunter Seal TN11 ... 221 E2
Huntersfield Cl ME5 ... 97 C1
Hunters Forstal Rd CT6 ... 77 C2
Hunter's Gr BR6 ... 86 C6
Hunters Lodge 10 DA15 ... 31 A5
Hunters Way
Gillingham ME7 ... 64 E1
Royal Tunbridge Wells TN2 ... 285 F1
Sheldwich ME13 ... 170 C5
Hunters Way W ME5 ... 64 E1
Hunters Wlk
Deal CT14 ... 215 B6
Knockholt TN14 ... 120 E5
Huntingdon Wlk 2 ME15 ... 195 E7
Huntingfield Rd DA13 ... 60 A2
Hunting Gate CT7 ... 80 F8
Huntington Cl TN17 ... 320 D4
Huntington Rd ME17 ... 194 B3
Huntley Ave DA11 ... 18 C1
Huntley Mill Rd TN5 ... 338 E3
Huntleys Pk TN4 ... 285 F5
Hunton CE Prim Sch ME15 ... 226 D7
Hunton Gdns CT2 ... 143 A4
Hunton Hill
Coxheath ME15 ... 194 A2
Hunton ME15 ... 193 F1
Hunton Ho 4 BR5 ... 54 C4
Hunton Rd TN12 ... 227 A3
Hunt Rd Northfleet DA11 ... 36 F5
Tonbridge TN10 ... 222 E6
Hunts Farm Cl TN15 ... 157 A7
Huntsfield Ind Est CT20 ... 334 D4
Hunts La TN17 ... 318 E8
Huntsman Ho 2 DA11 ... 36 F8
Huntsman La
Maidstone ME14 ... 162 B4
Wrotham Heath TN15 ... 125 E1
Huntsmans Cl ME1 ... 63 E1
Huntsman's Cnr ME4 ... 96 E8
Hunts Mede Cl BR7 ... 29 F1
Huntsmoor House BR5 ... 54 B5
Hunt St
Nettlestead ME15,ME18 ... 192 F5
West Farleigh ME15 ... 193 B5
Huntswood TN23 ... 267 E1
Hurlfield DA2 ... 33 C5
Hurlingham Cl TN10 ... 222 E7
Hurlingham Rd DA7 ... 13 F7
Huron Cl 5 BR6 ... 86 F4
Hurricane Rd ME19 ... 158 F3
Hurstbourne Cotts DA5 ... 32 B8
Hurst Cl Chatham ME5 ... 96 E6
Staplehurst TN12 ... 260 F4
Tenterden TN30 ... 344 F7
Hurst Ct Newham E6 ... 1 D8
Sidcup DA15 ... 31 A6
Hurst Farm Rd TN14 ... 187 B3
Hurstfield BR2 ... 52 A4
Hurstford La TN26, TN27 ... 234 C2
Hurst Green CE Prim Sch TN19 ... 354 A2
Hurst Green Cl RH8 ... 183 A3
Hurst Green Inf Sch RH8 ... 183 A3
Hurst Green Rd RH8 ... 183 A3
Hurst Gr CT12 ... 83 C1
Hurst Hill ME5 ... 96 E2
Hurst Ho SE2 ... 3 D1
Hurstings The ME15 ... 161 D2
Hurst La
Capel-le-F CT18 ... 308 B4
Charing Heath TN27 ... 233 E6
Erith SE2 ... 3 D1
Hurstlands RH8 ... 183 A3
Hurst La
Sevenoaks Weald TN14 ... 187 B2
Sittingbourne ME10 ... 68 F1
Hurstmere Foundation Sch for Boys DA15 ... 31 C7
Hurst Pl Gillingham ME8 ... 98 F8
Woolwich SE2 ... 3 C1
Hurst Prim Sch DA5 ... 31 D7
Hurst Rd Ashford TN24 ... 268 C7
Erith DA8 ... 14 C7
Sidcup DA5 ... 31 D7
Hurst Springs DA5 ... 31 E7
Hurst The Crouch TN11 ... 190 D7
Plaxtol Spoute TN15 ... 157 C1
Royal Tunbridge Wells TN2 ... 286 E7
Hurst Way
Maidstone ME16 ... 160 F2
Sevenoaks TN13 ... 187 C8
Hurstwood Ave
Bexley DA7,DA8 ... 14 E6
Sidcup DA5 ... 31 E7
Hurstwood ME5 ... 96 E4
Hurstwood Dr BR1 ... 52 F6
Hurstwood La TN4 ... 285 F3
Hurstwood Pk TN4 ... 285 F3
Hurstwood Rd
Bredhurst,Bredhurst Hurst ME14 ... 131 B7
Bredhurst ME7 ... 98 B1
Warren Street ME13 ... 200 E8
Husheath Hill TN17 ... 291 F6
Hussar Ho ME1 ... 63 C3
Husseywell Cres BR2 ... 52 A1
Hustlings Dr ME12 ... 48 B5
Hutchings Cl ME10 ... 102 C5
Hutchins Rd SE28 ... 3 A5
Hutsford Cl ME8 ... 98 D5
Hutson Terr RM19 ... 16 D8
Huxley Ct 3 ME1 ... 63 D4
Huxley Ho SE2 ... 3 D1
Huxley Rd DA16 ... 12 F4
Hyacinth Rd ME2 ... 62 E6
Hybrid Cl ME1 ... 63 D1
Hyde Ct CT17 ... 310 C7
Hyde Dr BR5 ... 54 B5
Hyde Pl CT3 ... 210 F5
Hyde Rd Bexley DA7 ... 13 F5
Maidstone ME16 ... 161 D6
Hyders Forge TN15 ... 190 A8
Hyde's Orch TN27 ... 262 E5
Hyde The CT4 ... 173 B2
Hylands Cotts TN26 ... 326 A2
Hylton St SE18 ... 2 F2
Hyndford Cres DA9 ... 17 C2
Hyperion Dr ME2 ... 39 F1
Hythe Ave DA7 ... 13 F7
Hythe Cl
Folkestone CT20 ... 334 F5
Orpington BR5 ... 54 C5
Royal Tunbridge Wells TN4 ... 254 A1
Hythe Com Sch CT21 ... 333 B1
Hythe Pl CT13 ... 181 A8
Hythe Rd Ashford TN24 ... 268 E1
Dymchurch TN29 ... 352 E1
Lympne CT21 ... 332 D4
Sittingbourne ME10 ... 101 D5
Smeeth TN25,TN24 ... 302 C3
Hythe, St Leonard's CE Jun Sch CT21 ... 333 B2
Hythe Sta* CT21 ... 333 A2
Hythe St Dartford DA1 ... 15 E1
Dartford DA1 ... 15 E2
Hyton Dr CT14 ... 215 B6

I

Ian's Wlk CT21 ... 334 A3
Ibis Cl CT5 ... 108 B6
Ice Bowl The* ME8 ... 65 A1
Ickham Court Farm CT3 ... 145 C1
Ickleton Rd SE9 ... 29 E4
Icough Ct SE3 ... 11 B7
Iddenden Cotts TN18 ... 340 D2
Ide Hill CE Prim Sch TN14 ... 185 F4
Ide Hill Rd
Bough Beech TN8,TN14 ... 218 F5
Ide Hill TN14 ... 185 F2
Iden Cres TN12 ... 260 F2
Iden Croft Herbs* TN12 ... 261 A1
Iden Green Cotts TN17 ... 319 C8
Iden La TN27 ... 233 B4
Iden Rd Iden TN31 ... 368 B3
Rochester ME2 ... 40 C1
Idenwood Cl ME8 ... 98 D6
Idleigh Court Rd DA3, DA13 ... 92 C8
Iffin La CT4 ... 174 E2
Ifield Cl ME15 ... 195 F7
Ifield Sch The DA12 ... 37 C3
Ifield Way DA12 ... 37 D2
Ightham By-Pass TN15 ... 156 C7
Ightham Cotts DA2 ... 35 B6
Ightham Mote* TN15 ... 189 A7
Ightham Prim Sch TN15 ... 156 B6
Ightham Rd Bexley DA8 ... 14 A7
Shipbourne TN11,TN15 ... 189 C5
Ilex Rd CT19 ... 334 F6
Ilkley Rd E16 ... 1 C8
Illustrious Cl ME5 ... 97 A6
Imber Ct 4 SE9 ... 12 A1
Imbert Cl TN28 ... 373 C6
Impala Gdns TN4 ... 286 B6
Imperial Ave ME12 ... 47 D7
Imperial Bsns Pk DA11 ... 18 F1

Imperial Ct BR7 30 B2
Imperial Dr
Gravesend DA12 37 F3
Warden ME12 49 E4
Imperial Pl BR7 53 A8
Imperial Rd ME7 64 C3
Imperial Ret Pk DA11 19 A1
Imperial Way
Ashford TN23 299 C8
Chislehurst BR7 30 C5
Impton La ME5 97 A1
Inca Dr SE9 30 B8
Ince Rd CT2 143 F7
Indus Rd SE7 11 C7
Industrial Est The
TN8 217 B3
Ingleborough La
TN15 157 C8
Ingleby Way BR7 30 A3
Ingle Cl CT7 81 B7
Ingleden Cl ME10 101 F8
Ingleden Park Rd
TN30 324 C1
Ingledew Rd SE18 2 D1
Ingle Pl ME18 159 A2
Ingle Rd ME4 63 F2
Ingleside Gr 3 SE3 11 A8
Ingles La 8 CT20 335 D5
Ingles Mews 4 CT20 335 C4
Ingles Rd CT20 335 C4
Ingleton Ave DA16 13 A2
Inglewood BR7 30 D2
Inglewood Copse BR1 52 F7
Inglewood Rd DA7 14 D3
Inglewood BR8 55 E7
Ingoldsby Rd
Birchington CT7 80 E7
Canterbury CT1 174 D6
Folkestone CT19 335 E7
Gravesend DA12 37 F7
Ingram Cl CT18 306 F3
Ingram Rd Dartford DA1 33 E7
Gillingham ME7 64 E6
Ingress Gdns DA9 17 D2
Ingress Park Ave DA9 17 C3
Ingress Terr DA13 35 E4
Inigo Jones Rd SE7 11 E7
Inner Lines ME7 64 A6
Institute Rd
Chatham ME4 64 A4
Faversham ME13 138 D7
Instone Rd DA1 33 D8
Inverary Ct CT11 83 E1
Inverary Pl SE18 12 D8
Inverine Rd SE7 1 B1
Invermore Pl SE18 2 C2
Inverness Ho 7 ME15 195 E7
Inverness Mews E16 2 C5
Inverness Terr CT10 84 A3
Invicta Bsns Pk TN15 125 C2
Invicta Cl BR7 30 A3
Invicta Ct ME10 101 F7
Invicta Gram Sch
ME14 162 C4
Invicta Ho
Canterbury CT1 174 F7
Margate CT9 51 C1
Invicta Par 3 DA14 31 B4
Invicta Prim Sch SE3 11 A7
Invicta Rd Dartford DA2 16 B1
Folkestone CT19 335 D7
Greenwich SE3 11 A8
Lydd TN29 378 I6
Margate CT9 83 B8
Sheerness ME12 28 C2
Whitstable CT5 108 F8
Invicta Villas ME14 163 C4
Inward Car Lanes
CT16 310 G8
Inward Freight Lanes
CT16 310 G8
Io Ctr SE18 2 C3
Iona Cl ME5 97 D1
Iona Rd ME15 195 A7
Ionia Wlk DA12 37 F5
Irchester St 11 CT11 117 F7
Ireland Cl E6 1 F8
Ireland Ct TN24 268 D2
Irene Astor Ct 7
CT20 335 D5
Irene Rd BR6 53 F2
Iris Ave DA5 13 E1
Iris Cl ME5 130 A8
Iris Cres DA7 13 F8
Iron Bar La 4 CT1 175 A8
Iron Mill La DA1 14 F3
Iron Mill Pl DA1 14 F3
Ironside Cl ME5 97 A8
Ironstones TN3 285 B3
Irvine Dr CT9 83 C8
Irvine Rd ME3 39 B3
Irvine Way BR6 53 F2
Irving Ho TN1 286 B5
Irving Way BR8 55 D7
Irving Wlk DA10 35 E8
Irwin Ave SE18 12 E7
Isabella Dr BR6 86 C6
Isis Cl CT21 332 A3
Island Rd
Upstreet CT3,CT7 112 D2
Westbere CT2,CT3 144 C7
Island Wall CT5 74 C1
Island Way E ME4 41 C1
Island Way W ME4 41 B2
Isla Rd SE18 12 C8
Islehurst Cl BR7 53 A8
Isle of Sheppey Holiday
Village ME12 49 F2
Islingham Farm Rd
ME3 40 D4
Ismays Rd TN15 156 C3
Istead Rise DA13 36 F1
Istead Rise Prim Sch
DA13 59 E8
Itchingwood Common Rd
RH8 183 E2
Ito Way ME8 65 A3
Ivanhoe Rd
Herne Bay CT6 77 A4
Westgate-on-S CT8 50 C1
Ivedon Rd DA16 13 C5
Ivens Way ME17 198 D6
Iverhurst Cl DA6 13 D2
Iversgate Cl ME8 65 F2
Ives Holiday Camp
ME12 49 G1
Ives Rd TN9 221 F1
Ivor Gr SE9 30 B7
Ivor Ho DA14 31 C3
Ivory Cl ME13 105 A1
Ivorydown BR1 29 A4
Ivy Bower Cl DA9 17 B2
Ivybridge Ct 1 BR7 53 A8
Ivychurch Gdns CT9 51 E2
Ivychurch Rd TN29 363 B3
Ivy Cl Dartford DA1 34 A8
Etchinghill CT18 305 D3
Gravesend DA12 37 D5
Kingswood ME17 197 D2
Ivy Cottage Hill CT12 115 E7
Ivy Cotts TN23 299 C8
Ivy Ct CT2 142 E6
Ivy House La TN13,
TN14 121 E2
Ivy House Rd CT5 74 F1
Ivy La
Bells Yew Green TN3 315 A5
Canterbury CT1 175 A8
Knockholt TN14 120 E3
Ramsgate CT11 117 D6
Ivy Mews ME17 197 E2
Ivy Pl Canterbury CT1 174 E7
Deal CT14 215 D7
Rochester ME1 63 A2
Ivy Rd E16 1 A7
Ivyside CT8 50 C1
Ivy St ME8 98 F8
Ivy Villas DA9 17 A2
Ivy Way CT19 335 E7
Iwade Com Prim Sch
ME9 68 D4
Izane Rd DA6 13 F3

J

Jaarlen Rd TN29 376 B6
Jacinth Dr ME10 101 C6
Jackass La BR2 85 C4
Jacklin Cl ME5 96 F2
Jackson Ave ME1 96 E8
Jackson Cl
Rainham ME8 65 C1
1 Stone DA9 17 A2
Jackson Ho 4 SE7 11 B8
Jackson Rd
Canterbury CT1 174 E7
Orpington BR2 85 F8
Jackson's Cnr ME3 24 A3
Jacksons La 8 TN30 345 A7
Jacksons Stables CT8 50 D1
Jackson St SE18 12 A8
Jackson Way TN17 322 C3
Jacob Cl CT9 82 E7
Jacob Ho 5 DA18 3 D4
Jacobs Ho ME12 28 C2
Jacob's La ME3 42 B6
Jacobs Oak TN24 300 D6
Jacob Yd 8 ME13 138 D7
Jade Cl Newham E16 1 D7
Sittingbourne ME10 101 C7
Jade Hill ME2 95 A6
Jaffa Ct CT5 108 D8
Jaffray Rd BR2 52 D5
Jaggard Way TN12 260 E3
Jagger Cl DA2 34 C8
Jago Cl SE18 12 C8
Jail La Biggin Hill TN16 118 E3
Cudham TN16 119 A3
Jamaica Terr ME14 162 A7
James Allchin Gdns
TN24 268 F4
James Cl Ash CT3 147 D2
Lyminge CT18 305 C7
James Ct
Folkestone CT20 335 A4
2 Margate CT9 51 B2
James Hall Gdns
CT14 215 C3
James Haney Dr TN24 268 F5
James Morris Ct 3
CT20 334 F3
James Newman Ct SE9 30 A5
James Rd Cuxton ME2 62 C2
Dartford DA1 15 A1
James St Ashford TN23 268 A2
5 Chatham ME4 63 F4
Folkestone CT19 335 D6
Gillingham ME7 64 C6
Maidstone ME14 162 A5
8 Ramsgate CT11 117 D6
Rochester ME1 63 C4
Sheerness ME12 28 D2
James Watt Way DA8 14 F8
James Whath an Way
ME14 161 F5
Jane Seymour Ct DA15 30 D8
Janet Ct 4 DA7 14 A3
Janson Ct 11 DA14 31 B4
Japonica Cl ME5 97 C2
Jaquets Ct DA5 32 A6
Jarman's Field TN25 237 F2
Jarrah Cotts RM19 16 D8
Jarrett Ave ME2 40 C2
Jarrett Ho 10 CT20 335 C4
Jarrett's Ct 1 ME10 102 B4
Jarvis Dr TN24 301 A7
Jarvis La TN17 291 B3
Jarvis Pl TN30 324 B3
Jarvist Pl CT14 248 D6
Jasmine Cl
Chartham CT4 173 E1
2 Chatham ME5 96 F4
East Malling ME19 159 F8
Orpington BR6 86 B8
Jasmine Cotts
Borough Green TN15 156 F7
Groombridge TN3 312 C7
Jasmine Ct SE12 11 A1
Jasmine Rd ME19 159 F8
Jason Wlk SE9 30 A4
Jasper Ave ME1 63 D2
Jasper Rd E16 1 D7
Javelin Rd ME19 158 F3
Jay Gdns BR7 29 F4
Jayne Wlk CT5 108 B6
Jefferson Cl TN23 267 F1
Jefferson Dr ME8 65 C1
Jefferson Rd ME12 28 D2
Jefferson Wlk 13 SE18 12 A8
Jefferstone Gdns
TN29 365 E4
Jefferstone La TN29 365 E4
Jeffery St ME7 64 C6
Jeffrey Cl TN12 260 E4
Jeffrey Ct DA8 14 C7
Jeffrey Row SE12 11 B2
Jeffrey St ME14 162 A5
Jeken Rd SE9 11 C3
Jellicoe Ave DA12 37 C5
Jellicoe Ave W DA12 37 C5
Jellicoe Cl TN24 301 A7
Jemmett Rd TN23 300 A8
Jenkins' Dale ME4 63 F3
Jenkins Dr ME15 195 E5
Jenner Cl DA14 31 A4
Jenner Ho 4 DA17 4 A3
Jenner Rd ME1 63 C4
Jenner's Way TN29 365 F3
Jenner Way ME20 128 F6
Jennifer Ct ME3 41 F5
Jennifer Gdns CT9 83 C8
Jenningtree Rd DA8 15 B7
Jenningtree Way DA17 4 C4
Jenton Ave DA7 13 E5
Jerome Rd ME20 127 F4
Jersey Cl TN24 268 C8
Jersey Dr BR5 53 D3
Jersey La CT4 207 C6
Jersey Rd Newham E16 1 C8
Rochester ME2 63 A8
Jeskyns Rd DA12 60 E6
Jesmond St 3 CT19 335 D6
Jessamine Pl DA2 34 C8
Jessamine Terr BR8 55 C8
Jesse's Hill CT4 209 B1
Jessett Cl DA8 4 D2
Jessica Mews
2 Canterbury CT1 143 B1
Sittingbourne ME10 101 E7
Jesson Cl TN29 366 A4
Jesson Court Cvn Pk
TN29 365 F4
Jessup Cl SE18 2 C2
Jesuit Cl CT2 143 A4
Jesus Hospl CT1 143 A1
Jetty Rd Kingsnorth ME3 42 D7
Sheerness ME12 28 A3
Warden ME12 49 E4
Jetty Wlk 3 RM17 18 A8
Jevington Way SE12 29 B7
Jewell Gr TN12 259 D5
Jewels Hill TN16 118 A6
Jewry La CT1 174 F8
Jeyes Rd ME7 64 C4
Jezreels Rd ME7 64 D3
Jillian Way TN23 299 E7
Jim Bradley Cl 10 SE18 2 A2
Jiniwin Rd ME1 96 D7
Joan Cres SE9 29 D8
Jo-Ann's Ct 5 CT10 84 A4
Jockey La TN17 320 D5
Johannesburg Ho 2
ME15 195 F5
Johannesburg Rd
CT16 278 C4
John Anderson Ct 11
ME13 138 D7
John Badger Cl TN24 268 E5
John Bowley Ho CT19 334 F6
John Brunt Ct TN12 257 A7
John Burns Cotts RH8 183 E5
John Coopper Ho ME3 25 C5
John Dutton Way
TN24 268 E4
John Graham Ct CT1 175 A6
John Hall Cl ME13 105 B2
John Hunt Ct SE9 29 E6
John Mayne CE Prim Sch
TN27 294 F1
John Nash Cl ME9 136 B8
John Newington Cl
TN24 268 F5
John Newton Ct DA16 13 B4
Johns Cl DA3 58 F4
John's Gn CT13 180 E6
Johnson Ave ME7 64 C7
Johnson Cl
Ashford TN24 301 A7
Northfleet DA11 36 D5
Johnson Ct ME13 105 B1
Johnson Ho ME10 101 D4
Johnson's Cnr TN26 349 A4
Johnson Rd
Bromley BR2 52 D4
Sittingbourne ME10 101 D4
Johnsons Ave TN14 88 B1
Johnsons Ct TN15 154 F6
Johnsons Way DA9 17 C1
Johnson Way ME12 47 A7
John Spare Ct TN4 286 A6
Johns Rd TN16 119 B3
John's Rd
Meopham Station DA13 59 F4
Tatsfield TN16 150 D7
John St Broadstairs CT10 84 B4
Grays RM17 18 C8
Maidstone ME14 162 A6
Rochester ME1 63 C4
Royal Tunbridge Wells
TN4 286 A5
John Tapping Cl CT14 215 B1
John Wesley Ct SE9 12 A3
John Wilson Bsns Pk
CT5 75 B1
John Wilson St SE18 2 A2
Joiners Ct ME4 64 B2
Jointon Rd CT20 335 B4
Jonas Dr TN5 336 E5
Jonas La TN5 336 E5
Jordan Cl ME15 195 E5
Joseph Conrad Ho
CT2 142 D1
Joseph Wilson Ind Est
CT5 109 A7
Josling Cl RM17 17 F8
Joss Gap Rd CT10 51 H1
Joyce Cl TN17 320 C5
Joyce Dawson Way
SE28 3 A6
Joyce Green Ho DA1 15 F4
Joyce Green Hspl DA1 15 E4
Joyce Green La
Dartford DA1 15 E6
Dartford,Temple Hill DA1 15 F4
Joyce Green Wlk DA1 15 F3
Joyce Page Cl SE7 11 D8
Joydens Wood Inf Sch
DA5 32 E4
Joydens Wood Jun Sch
DA2 32 E4
Joyden's Wood Rd DA5 32 E5
Joyes Cl
Folkestone CT19 335 E7
Whitfield CT16 278 B7
Joyes Rd
Folkestone CT19 335 E7
Whitfield CT16 278 B7
Joy Lane Inf Sch CT5 108 C7
Joy Lane Jun Sch
CT5 108 C7
Joy La CT5 108 B8
Joy Rd DA12 37 C7
Joy Wood ME17 195 D5
Jubilee Cl Hythe CT21 353 D8
Swanscombe DA9 17 C1
Jubilee Cnr ME17 230 E3
Jubilee Cotts
Sevenoaks TN14 154 B7
Staple CT3 179 B6
Sutton Valence ME17 229 E7
Throwley ME13 169 D1
Worth CT14 181 B4
Jubilee Cres
Gravesend DA12 37 E6
Ightham TN15 156 C6
Queenborough ME11 45 F5
Jubilee Ct
19 Broadstairs CT10 84 B4
Dartford DA1 33 D8
17 Ramsgate CT11 117 F7
Whitstable CT5 75 A3
Jubilee Dr CT14 215 D3
Jubilee Fields ME8 66 D2
Jubilee Field TN30 359 E4
Jubilee Ho CT20 335 B4
Jubilee Park Ctry Pk*
BR1,BR5 53 B5
Jubilee Prim Sch SE28 3 C6
Jubilee Rd
Chelsfield BR6 88 A4
Littlebourne CT3 176 F8
Sandwich CT13 180 F8
West Thurrock RM20 17 B8
Worth CT14 181 B4
Jubilee Rise TN15 154 F6
Jubilee St ME10 101 E5
Jubilee Terr
Gillingham ME7 64 C6
Knockholt TN14 120 E4
Jubilee Way
Dover CT15,CT16 279 A2
Sidcup DA14 31 A6
Judd Rd
Faversham ME13 138 A7
Tonbridge TN9 254 B7
Judd Sch The TN9 254 A8
Judeth Gdns DA12 37 E3
Judkins Cl ME5 97 C6
Juglans Rd BR6 54 A1
Julia Garfield Mews E16 1 B5
Julian Ct
Folkestone CT19 335 B5
3 Sidcup DA14 31 A4
Julian Rd
Folkestone CT19 335 B6
Orpington BR6 87 A4
Julians Cl TN13 187 A8
Julians Way TN13 187 A8
Julie Cl CT10 84 A7
Julien Pl TN24 301 A8
Junction Rd
Bodiam TN18,TN32 355 A3
Dartford DA1 15 D1
Gillingham ME7 64 D4
Herne Bay CT6 76 C2
Junior King's Sch
CT2 143 E5
Juniper Cl
Ashford TN23 267 E2
Biggin Hill TN16 118 E2
Juniper Cl *continued*
Canterbury CT1 175 A6
Chatham ME5 97 A4
Maidstone ME16 161 B6
Royal Tunbridge Wells
TN4 254 D1
Whitstable CT5 74 F1
Juniper La E6 1 E8
Juniper Wlk BR8 55 D7
Jupiter La TN23 299 E5
Jury's Gap Coastguard
Cotts TN31 374 E1
Jury's Gap Rd TN29 376 A5
Jury St 12 DA11 19 B1
Jutland Cl ME3 9 D1
Jutland Ho SE18 1 E2

K

K9 Est RM13 4 E7
Kain Ct CT12 83 B1
Kake St CT4 239 E7
Kale Rd DA18 3 E4
Karloff Way ME2 40 B2
Kashgar Rd SE18 2 F2
Kashmir Rd SE7 11 D7
Katherine Ct ME5 97 B2
Katherine Gdns SE9 11 D3
Katherine Rd TN8 249 C8
Katherine Villas TN8 249 C8
Kay St DA16 13 B6
Kearsney Abbey*
CT16 277 D4
Kearsney Ave CT16 277 E4
Kearsney Ct CT16 277 D4
Kearsney Sta CT16 277 D4
Keary Rd DA10 35 F8
Keat Farm Cl CT6 77 F5
Keating Cl ME1 63 A3
Keats Ave E16 1 B5
Keats Gdns RM18 19 B5
Keats Ho DA1 14 E2
Keats Rd Bexley DA16 12 F6
Erith DA17 4 C3
Lunsford ME20 127 F3
Kechill Gdns BR2 52 A2
Keddow's Cl CT21 353 D8
Kedleston Dr BR5 53 F4
Kedleston Rd CT16 278 C5
Keeble Cl SE18 12 B8
Keedonwood Rd BR1 29 A3
Keefe Cl ME5 96 D1
Keeley Mews ME7 64 E3
Keel Gdns TN4 285 E8
Keeling Rd SE9 11 D2
Keemor Cl SE18 12 A7
Keeper's Hill CT4 176 D2
Keep The SE3 11 A5
Keightley Dr SE9 30 C7
Keir Hardie Prim Sch
E16 1 A8
Keir Hardy Ho 7 DA17 4 A3
Keith Ave
Ramsgate CT12 117 A8
Sutton at H DA4 34 B2
Keith Park Cres TN16 118 C7
Keith Sutton House
SE9 30 C6
Kelbrook Rd SE3 11 E4
Kelchers La TN11 223 F5
Kelham Ho 10 SE18 12 B8
Kellaway Rd
Chatham ME5 97 A2
Greenwich SE3 11 D5
Kellner Rd SE28 2 F3
Kelly Dr ME7 64 C7
Kelly Ho
15 Greenwich SE7 11 C8
Rochester ME1 96 C7
Kelsall Cl SE3 11 B5
Kelsey Rd BR5 54 B7
Kelso Dr DA12 37 F4
Kelvedon Rd CT14 215 C2
Kelvin Cl TN10 222 D7
Kelvin Ho 3 DA17 4 A3
Kelvin Par BR6 53 E1
Kelvin Rd Bexley DA16 13 A4
Tilbury RM18 19 A5
Kemble Cl TN2 286 E7
Kemble Dr BR2 85 E7
Kembleside Rd TN16 118 C1
Kemnal Rd BR7 30 D3
Kemnal Tech Coll BR5 31 B1
Kemnal Warren BR7 30 D2
Kemp Alley 2 CT5 74 D1
Kemp Cl ME5 96 E4
Kempes Pl TN25 237 E2
Kempley Ct 2 RM17 18 D8
Kemp Rd CT5 75 C2
Kempton Cl
Chatham ME5 97 C2
Erith DA8 14 C8
Kempt St SE18 12 A8
Kemsdale Rd ME13 139 F6
Kemsing Cl DA5 31 E8
Kemsing Gdns CT2 143 B4
Kemsing Prim Sch
TN15 123 A2
Kemsing Rd
Greenwich SE10 1 A1
Wrotham TN15 124 C3
Kemsing Sta TN15 155 D8
Kemsley Cl
Northfleet DA11 36 F4
Swanscombe DA9 17 B1
Kemsley Ct BR5 54 B8
Kemsley Down Sta
ME10 69 C1
Kemsley Mill Railway
Mus* ME10 69 C1
Kemsley Rd TN16 150 D8
Kemsley Sta ME10 68 E1
Kemsley Street Rd
ME7 98 C1
Kenardington Rd
TN26 347 E3
Kenbrook TN24 268 C7
Kencot Cl DA18 3 F4
Kendal Cl
Ramsgate CT11 117 B6
Tonbridge TN9 222 C2
Kendal Dr TN9 222 C2
Kendall Ave ME18 159 C3
Kendall Ct DA15 31 A5
Kendall Gdns DA11 36 F8
Kendall Lodge 9 BR1 52 B8
Kendall Pl 1 ME15 195 D8
Kendall Rd SE18 11 E6
Kendal Mdw CT5 75 E1
Kendal Pk TN4 285 E5
Kendal Rise CT10 84 A5
Kendal Way ME8 98 D8
Kendon Bsns Pk ME2 63 D8
Kenfield Rd CT4 207 A6
Kengate Ind Est CT21 332 F1
Kenia Wlk DA12 37 F5
Kenilworth Cl CT15 280 A6
Kenilworth Ct
10 Dartford DA2 16 B1
Sittingbourne ME10 101 C5
Kenilworth Dr ME8 98 D6
Kenilworth Gdns
Gillingham ME8 98 D7
Woolwich SE18 12 B5
Kenilworth Ho ME16 161 B2
Kenilworth Rd BR5 53 C3
Kenley Cl
St Paul's Cray BR7 53 E6
Sidcup DA5 32 A8
Kenley Ho 6 BR5 54 B7
Kenmere Rd DA16 13 C5
Kennacraig Cl E16 1 A5
Kennard Cl ME1 62 F2
Kennard St E16 1 F5
Kennedy Cl
Faversham ME13 138 D8
Orpington BR5 53 D1
Kennedy Dr CT14 215 B2
Kennedy Gdns TN13 154 D5
Kennedy Ho
Benenden TN17 342 E6
Northfleet DA11 36 D5
8 Ramsgate CT11 117 F7
Kennel Barn Rd ME9 133 C5
Kennel Hill CT15 245 E6
Kennelling Rd ME13,
TN27 201 D5
Kennels The CT15 245 E6
Kennet Ct 2 BR8 55 E6
Kennet Rd Crayford DA1 15 A4
Tonbridge TN10 222 C5
Kennett Ct 16 BR5 54 D1
Kennett Dr CT14 215 A2
Kennett Lane Cotts
TN25 332 B8
Kennett La TN25 332 B8
Kennington CE Jun Sch
TN24 268 E7
Kennington Cl
Gillingham ME8 65 B4
Maidstone ME15 195 F7
Kennington Pl TN24 268 D7
Kennington Rd TN24 269 A1
Kensington Ct 5 RM17 18 C8
Kensington Ho ME16 161 A2
Kensington Rd CT1 143 C4
Kent Ave Ashford TN24 268 B3
Bexley DA16 12 F2
Canterbury CT1 175 D8
Maidstone ME15 162 C1
Minster (Sheppey) ME12 47 B6
Sittingbourne ME10 101 D3
Kent Battle of Britain
Mus* CT18 306 F4
Kent & Canterbury Hospl
CT1 175 A5
Kent Cl Orpington BR6 86 E4
Paddock Wood TN12 257 A6
Rochester ME1 96 C8
Kent Coll CT2 142 C3
Kent Coll Inf & Jun Sch
CT2 142 A1
Kent Coll TN2 255 D3
Kent County Optholmic &
Aural Hospl ME14 162 A4
Kent County Show Gd
ME14 131 C3
Kent & East Sussex Rly
Mus* TN30 345 A8
Kent & East Sussex Rly*
TN17 344 D5
Kent & East Sussex Steam
Rly* TN17 358 C5
Kent Gdns CT7 80 F7
Kent Hatch Rd
Crockham Hill RH8,TN8 184 B4
The Chart RH8,TN8 183 D4
Kent Ho
4 Broadstairs CT10 84 A4
Folkestone CT20 335 B4
10 Hawkhurst TN18 341 A2
Royal Tunbridge Wells
TN1 286 C6
Sutton at H DA4 57 D7
Kent Inst of Art & Design
Canterbury CT1 175 B7
Maidstone ME16 161 C3
Rochester ME1 63 E4
Kent International Airport
CT12 82 B1
Kentish Ct 8 ME16 161 E4
Kentish Gdns TN2 313 E8

Kentish Mans 15 TN1 286 A2
Kentish Rd DA17 4 A2
Kentish Way BR1,BR2 52 B6
Kent Kraft Ind Est DA11 17 F2
Kentlea Rd SE28 2 E4
Kentmere Ave CT11 116 F7
Kentmere Rd SE18 2 E2
Kent Music Sch CT1 142 F1
Kenton Gdns CT12 115 B6
Kent Pl CT11 117 F6
Kent Rd Dartford DA1 15 E1
Folkestone CT19 334 E7
Gravesend DA11 37 A7
4 Grays RM17 18 C8
Halling ME2 95 A6
Longfield DA3 58 D7
Margate CT9 83 B8
Orpington BR5 54 B3
Royal Tunbridge Wells TN4 286 A6
Sheerness ME12 28 B1
Snodland ME6 128 A6
Kent Science Pk ME9 134 D6
Kent St ME18 158 E2
Kentstone Ct ME4 64 A4
Kent St CT5 108 D8
Kent & Sussex Hospl TN4 286 A4
Kent Terr
Gillingham ME8 66 C2
Lower Higham ME3 39 D7
Meopham DA13 93 A7
Ramsgate CT11 117 F6
Kent View Dr ME12 48 D1
Kenward Ct TN11 223 E8
Kenward Rd Eltham SE9 11 D2
Maidstone ME16 161 C5
Yalding ME18 192 E2
Kenwood Ave
Chatham ME5 97 A4
New Barn DA3 59 C6
Kenwyn Rd DA1 15 D2
Kenya Rd SE7 11 D7
Kenya Terr 7 ME14 162 A7
Kenyon Wlk ME8 98 B3
Kerry Cl E16 1 B7
Kerry Hill Way ME14 161 E6
Kersey Gdns SE9 29 E4
Kerton Rd TN29 380 D7
Kesteven Cl ME2 95 B5
Kestlake Rd DA5 13 C1
Keston Ave BR2 85 C5
Keston CE Prim Sch BR2 85 D5
Keston Cl DA16 13 C7
Keston Ct
Gillingham ME8 65 A2
Sidcup DA5 31 E8
Keston Gdns BR2 85 C6
Keston Park Cl BR2 85 F7
Kestrel Ave E6 1 E8
Kestrel Cl
Kingsnorth TN23 300 C3
Marlpit Hill TN8 217 D3
Sittingbourne ME10 102 A2
Kestrel Ct
4 Sittingbourne ME10 102 A4
Whitstable CT5 75 A3
Kestrel Ho ME7 64 B6
Kestrel Rd ME5 97 C2
Keswick Ave ME10 102 C3
Keswick Cl TN9 222 C2
Keswick Ct ME7 65 A5
Keswick Dr ME16 161 B5
Keswick Gdns RM19 16 C8
Keswick Rd Bexley DA7 14 A6
Orpington BR6 54 A2
Ketridge La ME18 159 D2
Kettle Dr CT18 307 B5
Kettle Hill ME13 168 F4
Kettle Hill Rd
Eastling ME13 168 F5
Throwley ME13 169 A4
Kettle La ME15 193 E6
Kettlewell Ct BR8 55 F7
Kevin Dr CT11 117 B6
Kevington Cl BR5 53 F5
Kevington Dr BR7 53 F5
Kewlands ME14 162 C6
Keycol Hill ME9 100 F5
Keyes Ave ME4 63 F2
Keyes Gdns TN9 253 F7
Keyes Pl CT19 335 E7
Keyes Rd DA1 16 A3
Keymer Cl TN16 118 D3
Keynes Coll CT2 142 D4
Keynes Ct 9 SE28 3 B6
Keynsham Gdns SE9 11 E2
Keynsham Rd SE9 11 E2
Keys The CT18 307 C5
Key St ME10 101 A5
Keyworth Cl TN12 256 F6
Keyworth Mews 7 CT1 143 B2
Khalsa Ave DA12 37 C8
Khartoum Pl DA12 19 C1
Khartoum Rd ME4 63 F6
Khartoum Sq CT16 278 A6
Khyber Rd ME4,ME7 64 B7
Kibbles La TN4 285 E8
Kidbrooke Gdns SE3 11 A6
Kidbrooke Gr SE3 11 B6
Kidbrooke La SE9 11 E3
Kidbrooke Park Cl SE3 11 B6
Kidbrooke Park Prim Sch SE3 11 C6
Kidbrooke Park Rd SE12,SE3 11 B4
Kidbrooke Sch SE3 11 D5
Kidbrooke Sta SE3 11 B4
Kidbrooke Way SE3 11 B5
Kiddens BR8 55 B7
Kidd Pl SE7 1 E1
Kidds Cotts BR8 55 D3
Kierbeck Bsns Complex E16 1 B4
Kilbride Ct CT11 83 F1
Kilburn Ho 6 ME14 162 A5
Kildare Rd E16 1 A8
Killewarren Way BR5 54 C3
Killick Cl TN13 153 E6
Killick Rd ME3 41 D5
Killicks Cotts ME18 225 F8
Killigarth Ct 22 DA14 31 A4
Kilnbank TN2 286 C7
Kiln Barn Rd ME19,ME20 160 C7
Kilnbridge Cl ME15 194 B7
Kilnbridge Wks ME15 194 B7
Kiln Cl Challock TN25 203 B1
Sittingbourne ME10 102 A3
Kiln Cnr CT21 333 B4
Kilndown Cl
Ashford TN23 299 E6
Maidstone ME16 161 C7
Kilndown Gdns
Canterbury CT2 143 A4
Margate CT9 51 E2
Kilndown DA12 37 D2
Kilnfields BR6 88 A4
Kiln Field TN30 345 C7
Kiln La
Bethersden TN26 297 F5
Leigh TN11 220 F1
Kiln Rd TN25 329 F4
Kiln Way TN12 257 A5
Kilnwood TN14 120 F6
Kimbell Pl SE3 11 C3
Kimber Ho 11 SE18 12 B8
Kimberley Cl CT16 278 C3
Kimberley Cnr CT10 83 F8
Kimberley Ct CT8 50 C1
Kimberley Dr DA14 31 D6
Kimberley Gr CT5 107 F6
Kimberley Rd
Gillingham ME7 64 D3
Ramsgate CT12 83 A1
Kimberley Way TN24 300 C7
Kimberly Ct DA17 3 F2
Kimberly Terr CT18 305 C7
Kimmeridge Gdns SE9 29 E4
Kimmeridge Rd SE9 29 E4
Kincraig BR7 53 A8
Kincraig Dr TN13 154 B4
Kinder Cl SE28 3 D6
King and Queen Cl SE9 29 E4
King Arthur Ct ME10 101 E3
King Arthur Rd CT12 116 D7
King Arthur's Dr ME2 40 A1
King Charles Ct CT14 215 D2
King Edward Ave
Broadstairs CT10 84 A4
Dartford DA1 15 D1
Herne Bay CT6 77 B4
King Edward Ct CT6 77 B4
King Edward Rd
Birchington CT7 81 A5
Chatham ME4 63 F2
Deal CT14 215 D8
Gillingham ME7 64 F6
Maidstone ME15 161 F2
1 Ramsgate CT11 117 C6
Rochester ME1 63 C5
Stone DA9 17 A2
King Edward St CT5 74 D1
King Ethelbert Sch CT7 81 C7
Kingfisher Apartments 13 ME15 195 E5
Kingfisher Ave CT21 353 D8
Kingfisher Cl
Ashford TN24 301 A7
Erith SE28 3 C6
Iwade ME9 68 E4
Margate CT9 82 B8
Orpington BR5 54 D5
Whitstable CT5 108 C7
Kingfisher Com Prim Sch ME5 97 B7
Kingfisher Ct
Herne Bay CT6 76 D3
11 Maidstone ME15 162 B4
West Kingsdown TN15 90 E3
Kingfisher Dr
Chatham ME5 97 C7
Swanscombe DA9 17 A1
Kingfisher Gdns CT21 353 C8
Kingfisher Ho
Ashford TN23 267 F1
Orpington BR5 54 C8
Kingfisher Pl DA4 57 C7
Kingfisher Rd ME20 128 A2
Kingfisher St E6 1 E8
Kingfisher Wlk CT10 83 F5
King George Ave E16 1 D7
King George Rd ME5 96 E4
King George V Hill TN1 286 C5
King George VI Ave TN16 118 D3
King George Villas CT14 181 B3
King George V Memorial Houses ME8 65 C2
King Harolds Way DA7 13 E7
King Henry Mews 2 BR6 86 F5
King Hill ME19 159 A5
King John's Wlk SE9 11 E1
King Lear's Way CT17 310 B5
Kingly Way CT17 310 A7
King's Prospect TN24 300 E6
Kings Acre ME15 163 A1
Kingsand Rd SE12 29 A6
King's Ave
Ashford TN23 268 A2
Birchington CT7 80 D7
Broadstairs CT10 84 B6
Kings Ave BR1 29 A2
King's Ave
Ramsgate CT12 83 B1
Rochester ME1 63 C3
Sandwich CT13 182 A8
Whitstable CT5 74 E1
King's Bastion ME7 64 A5
Kingsbridge Ct 11 CT20 335 E5
Kings Chase TN24 269 A2
Kings Cl DA1 14 E3
King's Cl CT14 248 D6
Kings Cotts
Cranbrook TN17 320 D6
Leeds ME17 196 F6
King's Cotts
Wateringbury ME18 192 D6
Yalding ME18 193 A1
Kings Ct Deal CT14 215 D3
Horsmonden TN12 290 A6
21 Sidcup DA14 31 A5
Kingsdale Ct
Chatham ME5 64 C1
Swanscombe DA10 17 E1
Kingsdale Rd SE18 12 F8
Kingsdown Cl
Gillingham ME7 98 B4
Gravesend DA12 37 F7
Maidstone ME16 161 E4
Kingsdown Cotts ME9 135 E4
Kingsdown Hill CT14 248 D4
Kingsdown Ind Est ME20 160 B8
Kingsdown Park Holiday Village CT14 248 D5
Kingsdown Pk CT5 74 F2
Kingsdown Rd
Kingsdown CT14 248 D7
Lynsted ME9 135 D4
St Margaret's at Cliffe CT15 280 A7
Kingsdown & Ringwould CE Prim Sch CT14 248 C5
Kingsdown Way BR2 52 A3
Kings Dr DA12 37 B5
Kings Farm Prim Sch DA11 37 C3
Kingsfield Ho SE9 29 D5
Kingsfield Rd CT6 77 B2
Kingsford Cl TN25 301 E4
Kingsford Com Sch E6 1 F7
Kingsford Cotts TN17 342 D6
Kingsford Ct CT17 278 B1
Kingsford St TN25 301 D5
Kingsford Way E6 1 F8
Kingsgate Ave CT10 51 F1
Kingsgate Bay Rd CT10 51 H2
Kingsgate Castle CT10 51 H2
Kingsgate Cl Bexley DA7 13 E6
Maidstone ME16 161 C4
Orpington BR5 54 C6
Kingsgate Coll CT10 84 A8
Kingsgate La TN30 359 C5
Kingsground SE9 11 E1
King's Head Alley ME12 28 A3
King's Highway SE18, SE2 12 F8
Kings Hill Ave ME19 159 A4
Kingshill Dr ME3 41 D6
Kings Hill Sch ME19 159 A3
Kingsholm Gdns SE9 11 E3
Kingshurst Rd SE12 29 A8
Kingsingfield Cl TN15 90 E3
Kingsingfield Rd TN15 90 E2
Kings La TN12 258 C7
Kingsland Gdns CT14 248 B8
Kingsland Gr TN27 262 D5
Kingsland Hollow TN29 366 A4
Kingsland La
Egerton Forstal TN27 232 E1
Westwell TN25 235 F1
Kingsley Ave DA1 16 A2
Kingsley Ct Bexley DA6 14 A3
Wadhurst TN5 337 A4
1 Woolwich SE28 3 C5
Kingsley Mews BR7 30 B2
Kingsley Rd
Maidstone ME15 162 A3
Orpington BR6 86 F3
Whitstable CT5 108 E8
Kingsley Wood Dr SE9 29 F5
Kingsman Par SE18 1 F3
Kingsman St SE18 1 F2
Kingsmarsh La TN29 372 C5
Kings Mdw TN24 268 E7
Kingsmead TN16 118 D3
Kingsmead Cl DA15 31 A6
Kingsmead Cotts BR2 52 E1
Kingsmead CT19 335 B8
Kingsmead Pk
Allhallows-on-S ME3 9 E3
Paddock Wood TN12 257 A6
Kingsmead Prim Sch CT1 143 A1
Kingsmead Rd CT1, CT2 143 A2
Kingsmead CT8 50 C1
Kingsmere BR7 52 E8
Kings Mews 7 CT1 143 A1
Kings Mill Cl ME10 101 E5
Kingsnorth CE Prim Sch TN23 300 B3
Kingsnorth Cl ME3 41 E6
Kingsnorth Ct
Crockenhill BR8 55 C3
Kingsnorth Ct *continued*
2 Folkestone CT20 335 B5
Kingsnorth Gdns CT20 335 C5
Kingsnorth Ind Est ME3 42 D7
Kingsnorth Rd
Ashford TN23 300 A6
Faversham ME13 138 C6
Gillingham ME8 65 C4
Kings Oak Mews ME5 96 F4
King's Orch Eltham SE9 11 E1
Rochester ME1 63 C5
Kings Par 7 TN24 268 B2
King's Pk CT1 143 B1
Kings Pk TN2 286 D3
King's Pl 5 CT11 117 E6
Kings Rd Aylesham CT3 210 F6
Biggin Hill TN16 118 C2
King's Rd
Birchington CT7 81 A6
Chatham ME5 64 D1
Kings Rd CT17 310 A7
King's Rd ME13 138 C7
Kings Rd
Folkestone CT20 334 D6
Headcorn TN27 262 C5
King's Rd CT6 76 F5
Kings Rd
Minster (Sheppey) ME12 47 D7
Orpington BR6 86 F6
King's Rd
Ramsgate CT11 117 D8
Tonbridge TN9 254 D7
Kings Reach ME15 195 D8
Kingsridge Gdns DA1 15 D1
Kings Ropewalk CT17 310 B5
Kings Row
1 Maidstone ME15 162 A1
Rochester ME1 63 B4
King's Sch Canterbury The CT1 143 A1
King's Sch ME1 63 C5
King's Sch The CT1 175 A8
King's Standing Ind Est TN2 254 F2
Kings Standing Way TN2 254 F1
King St Brookland TN29 362 D2
Canterbury CT1 142 F1
Chatham ME4 64 A4
Deal CT14 215 D6
Deal, Walmer CT14 215 D3
Dover CT16 310 D7
Fordwich CT2 144 A4
Gillingham ME7 64 C6
Gravesend DA12 19 B1
Maidstone ME14 162 A4
Margate CT9 50 J3
Kings Toll Rd TN2 288 A6
Kingston Ave CT9 82 C7
Kingston Cl
Crabble CT17 277 F3
Herne Bay CT6 77 F5
Ramsgate CT12 83 B2
Kingston Cres ME5 97 C4
Kingston Ct DA11 18 B1
Kingston Dr ME15 195 A8
Kingstone Ct 3 CT20 335 B5
King St Ramsgate CT11 117 E7
Rochester ME1 63 C4
Sandwich CT13 149 A1
Sheerness ME12 28 A2
Sittingbourne ME10 101 E5
West Malling ME19 159 C8
Kingsway Chatham ME5 64 D1
Dymchurch TN29 352 E2
Gillingham ME7 64 E1
Orpington BR5 53 D4
Kingswear Gdns ME2 63 C8
Kings Wlk Grays RM17 18 A8
Maidstone ME14 162 B5
Kingswood Ave
Chatham ME4 63 F2
Erith DA17 3 F2
Swanley BR8 55 F6
Kingswood Cl
Ashford TN24 268 D5
Dartford DA1 15 C1
Orpington BR6 53 D2
Royal Tunbridge Wells TN2 286 C3
Kings Wood Forest Wlks* TN25 203 F1
Kingswood Ho
12 Maidstone ME16 161 A3
16 Sidcup DA14 31 B4
Kingswood Prim Sch ME17 197 E2
Kingswood Rd
Gillingham ME7 64 D6
Kit's Coty ME20 129 D8
Royal Tunbridge Wells TN2 286 C3
Sevenoaks TN13 153 E7
Kingswood Villas CT17 278 A2
King William Rd 6 ME7 64 C7
Kinlet Rd SE18 12 C6
Kinnell Ct 13 DA14 31 B4
Kinnings Row TN9 222 C2
Kinross Cl ME5 97 B7
Kinveachy Gdns SE7 1 E1
Kipling Ave RM18 19 C6
Kipling Dr ME20 127 F4
Kipling Rd
Ashford TN23 268 B2
Bexley DA7 13 E6
Dartford DA1 16 B2
Kipping Cl CT18 307 A4
Kippington Cl TN13 153 F3
Kippington Dr SE9 29 D7
Kippington Rd TN13 154 A2
Kirby Cl TN17 320 D4
Kirby's Hts 8 CT2 142 F1
Kirby Rd Chattenden ME3 40 F5
Dartford DA2 34 D8
Kirby's La CT2 142 F1
Kirkcourt TN13 154 A4
Kirkdale Cl ME5 97 D1
Kirkdale Cotts ME15 194 F5
Kirkdale ME15 194 F5
Kirkdale Rd
Maidstone ME15 194 F6
Royal Tunbridge Wells TN1 286 B4
Kirk Gdns CT14 215 B2
Kirkham Rd E6 1 E7
Kirkham St SE18 12 E8
Kirkins Cl TN12 290 A6
Kirkland Cl DA15 12 E1
Kirk La SE18 12 C8
Kirkman Ct TN12 260 E3
Kirkside Rd SE3 11 A8
Kirkstone Ave CT11 116 F7
Kirk View TN23 299 C8
Kirkwood Ave TN26 326 A1
Kirton Cl CT18 306 F4
Kitchener Ave
Chatham ME4 64 A1
Gravesend DA12 37 C5
Kitchener Cl CT4 242 F8
Kitchener Cotts ME3 25 C4
Kitchener Rd
Chattenden ME3 40 F4
Dover CT17 310 A7
Rochester ME2 63 A8
Kitchener Sq CT19 335 E8
Kite Farm CT5 75 D3
Kite La TN12 289 A6
Kitewell La TN29 376 D8
Kither Rd TN23 300 A7
Kit Hill Ave ME5 96 E3
Kit Hill ME13 171 D8
Kitsbridge La
Hamstreet TN26 349 C4
Ruckinge TN25,TN26 350 B6
Kit's Coty House* ME20 129 C6
Kittiwake Cl CT6 77 F5
Klondyke Ind Est ME11 45 F4
Knatchbull Way TN25 302 E5
Knatts La TN15 123 E8
Knatts Valley Rd TN15 90 D2
Knavesacre Ct ME8 98 D5
Knaves Acre TN27 262 D5
Knave Wood Rd TN15 122 E2
Knee Hill Cres SE2 3 C2
Knee Hill SE2 3 C1
Knell La CT3 147 C3
Knight Ave
Canterbury CT2 174 D8
Gillingham ME7 64 D7
Knighton Rd TN14 121 F2
Knight Rd
Rochester ME2 63 A6
Tonbridge TN10 222 E6
Knightrider Ct ME15 162 A3
Knightrider St
Maidstone ME15 162 A3
Sandwich CT13 149 A1
Knights Alley 20 CT5 74 D2
Knight's Ave CT10 84 B6
Knightsbridge Cl TN4 285 F5
Knightsbridge Ct TN1 286 B6
Knightsbridge Mews BR7 29 F1
Knights Cl
Hoo St Werburgh ME3 41 E5
Pembury TN2 287 D7
Knights Croft DA3 91 F7
Knights Ct CT17 278 B1
Knight's Ct 7 DA8 14 F7
Knights Ct ME10 101 E3
Knights Field DA4 89 E7
Knightsfield Rd ME10 101 D7
Knights Manor Way DA1 15 F1
Knights Pk
Rochester ME2 63 A6
Royal Tunbridge Wells TN11 254 F1
Knight's Rd CT16 310 E8
Knights Rd
Hoo St Werburgh ME3 41 D5
Newham E16 1 A4
Knights Ridge BR6 87 B5
Knight's Ridge TN2 287 D7
Knights Templars CT17 310 C6
Knights Way CT16 278 A3
Knight's Way TN27 262 D6
Knights Way TN2,TN11 254 F1
Knockhall Chase DA9 17 C2
Knockhall Com Prim Sch DA9 17 C2
Knockhall Rd DA9 17 C2
Knock Hill TN30 361 A2
Knockholt Rd
Eltham SE9 11 D2
Halstead TN14 120 F6
Margate CT9 51 F3
Knockholt Sta TN14 87 E2
Knockhurst Ct TN30 324 C1
Knock Mill La TN15 124 A5
Knock Rd TN23 300 A7
Knockwood Rd TN30 324 C1
Knold Pk CT9 82 E8
Knole Cl TN14 187 B2
Knole Gate DA15 30 E5
Knole House* TN15 154 D1
Knole La TN13,TN15 154 C1
Knole Rd Chatham ME5 97 C3
Dartford DA1 33 B8
Sevenoaks TN13 154 D4
Knole The Eltham SE9 30 A
Faversham ME13 138 B
Istead Rise DA13 36 E
Knole Way TN13 154 C
Knoll Ct
Folkestone CT20 335 C
Orpington BR6 86 F
Knoll Hill TN25 330 C
Knoll La TN23 299 E
Knoll Pl CT14 215 C
Knoll Rd Sidcup DA14 31 B
Sidcup,Old Bexley DA5 14 A
Knoll Rise BR6 53 F
Knoll The Hayes BR2 52 A
St Margaret's at Cliffe CT15 280 A
Knoll Way ME12 49 D
Knotley Hall Cotts TN11 220 A
Knott Cres TN24 301 A
Knott Ct ME14 161 F
Knott's La 20 CT1 143 A
Knotts La CT15 279 F
Knotts Pl TN13 154 A
Knotts Sq TN23 268 C
Knowle Ave DA7 13 F
Knowle Cl TN3 284 F
Knowle Cott TN3 314 E
Knowle Cotts TN3 314 E
Knowle La TN12 257 C
Knowle Lodge BR7 29 F
Knowle Rd
Maidstone ME14 162 B
Orpington BR2 85 E
Paddock Wood TN12 257 D
Wouldham ME1 95 D
Knowler Way CT6 77 C
Knowles Gdns TN27 262 D
Knowles Wlk TN12 260 F
Knowlton Gdns ME16 161 B
Knowlton Gn BR2 52 A
Knowlton Wlk 1 CT1 143 B
Knowsley Way TN11 221 D
Knox Ct TN15 154 F
Kohima Pl CT15 278 F
Koonowla Cl TN16 118 D
Kydbrook Cl BR5 53 C
Kyetop Wlk ME8 98 D
Kynaston Rd
Bromley BR1 29 A
Orpington BR5 54 B

L

La Belle Alliance Sq 9 CT11 117 E
Labour-in-vain Rd TN15 124 E
Laburnham Pl SE9 12 A
Laburnum Ave
Dartford DA1 33 D
Sandwich CT13 180 F
Swanley BR8 55 D
Laburnum Cl CT16 277 E
Laburnum Ct TN2 286 C
Laburnum Dr ME20 128 A
Laburnum Gr
Northfleet DA11 36 D
Sheerness ME12 28 H
Laburnum Ho ME12 28 B
Laburnum La CT2 144 B
Laburnum Pl ME10 101 E
Laburnum Rd ME2 62 E
Laburnum Way BR2 53 B
Labworth Cl ME12 46 E
Lacebark Cl DA15 30 F
Lacey Cl ME17 196 E
Laceys La ME17 227 C
Lachlan Way 2 CT20 334 F
Lackenden Cotts CT3 176 D
Lacknut Cotts DA13 92 E
Lacock Gdns
Loose ME15 195 A
Maidstone ME15 162 A
Lacton Oast TN24 301 B
Lacton Way TN24 301 A
Lacy Cl ME16 161 D
Ladbrooke Cres DA14 31 D
Ladbrooke Ho 7 ME14 162 A
Laddingford Farm Ind Est ME18 225 D
Laddingford St Mary's CE Prim Sch ME18 225 E
Ladds Cnr ME7 65 B
Ladds La ME6 95 A
Ladds Way BR8 55 D
Lade Fort Cotts TN29 377 E
Lade Fort Cres TN29 377 E
Ladham Rd TN17 291 A
Ladies Mile TN6,TN7 311 D
Ladies Wlk CT21 333 C
Lady Boswell's CE Prim Sch TN13 154 C
Ladyclose Ave ME3 40 A
Ladycroft Gdns 6 BR6 86 C
Ladycroft Way BR6 86 C
Ladyfern Ct TN2 286 C
Ladyfields ME5 97 D
Ladyfields Cl ME9 100 F
Ladyfields
Herne Bay CT6 77 D
Northfleet DA11 36 F
Lady Garne Rd CT15 308 F
Lady Joanna Thornhill Endowed Prim Sch TN25 237 E
Lady Oak La TN5,TN17 339 C
Lady's Gift Rd TN4 285 F
Ladysmith Gr CT5 107 F
Ladysmith Rd
Eltham SE9 12 A

Ladysmith Rd *continued*
Whitstable CT5 108 C5
Lady Vane Cl TN11 189 C5
Ladywell 7 CT16 310 D8
Ladywell Ho
2 Dover CT16 310 D8
7 Orpington BR5 54 B7
Ladywood Ave BR5 53 E4
Ladywood Rd
Cuxton ME2 62 B2
Dartford DA2 34 E3
Sturry CT2 143 F7
Lady Wootton's Gn 6 CT1 175 A8
La Galamina TN28 377 E8
Lagonda Way DA1 15 C3
Lagoon Rd BR5 54 B4
Lagos Ave CT12 83 A1
Lake Ave BR1 29 A2
Lakedale Rd SE18 2 E1
Lake Dr ME3 39 C6
Lakelands
Harrietsham ME17 198 E6
Loose ME15 195 A7
Lakeman Way TN4 286 B7
Lakemead TN23 299 E8
Lake Rd Ditton ME20 160 E8
Royal Tunbridge Wells TN4 285 E4
Laker Ho ME14 162 A6
Laker Rd ME1 96 C6
Lakeside TN23 299 E8
Lakeside Ave SE28 3 A5
Lakeside Cl
Bexley DA5,DA15 13 C2
Bough Beech TN8 218 F4
Lakeside Dr BR2 85 E7
Lakeside Gdns TN26 234 F1
Lakeside Pk ME2 63 E7
Lakeside
Royal Tunbridge Wells TN2 286 E6
Snodland ME6 127 F6
Lakes Rd BR2 85 C5
Lakes The ME20 128 A4
Lakesview International Bsns Pk CT3 112 A1
Lakeswood Rd BR5 53 C3
Lakeview Cl ME6 128 A6
Lakeview Rd DA16 13 B3
Lake View Rd TN13 154 A4
Lake Wlk ME20 128 A5
Lakewood Dr ME8 98 C6
Laking Ave CT10 84 B7
Laleham Gdns CT9 51 B2
Laleham Rd CT9 51 B1
Laleham Sch CT9 51 B1
Laleham Wlk CT9 51 B1
Lambarde Ave SE9 30 A4
Lambarde Cl ME2 95 A4
Lambarde Dr TN13 154 A4
Lambarde Rd TN13 154 A5
Lambardes Cl TN14 120 C8
Lambardes DA3 91 F7
Lambard Ho 8 ME14 162 A5
Lamb Cl RM18 19 C5
Lambden Rd TN27 265 C6
Lamberhurst Cl 14 BR5 54 D1
Lamberhurst Farm ME13 107 F1
Lamberhurst Gn ME8 65 B3
Lamberhurst Rd
Horsmonden TN12,TN3 289 E3
Lamberhurst TN3,TN12 317 C8
Maidstone ME16 161 B7
Lamberhurst St Mary's CE Prim Sch TN3 317 B6
Lamberhurst Vineyard* TN3 317 A4
Lamberhurst Way CT9 51 F3
Lambersart Cl TN4 254 D1
Lambert Cl TN16 118 D3
Lambert Ct DA8 14 C8
Lambert Ho CT14 215 B3
Lambert Mews 4 ME6 128 A8
Lambert Rd E16 1 B7
Lamberts Pl TN12 290 B5
Lamberts Rd TN2 286 D8
Lambert's Yd TN9 222 B1
Lambes Ct ME8 98 D5
Lambeth Cl ME5 97 B4
Lambeth Rd CT1 143 C4
Lambourn Dr ME19 159 A2
Lambourne Pl
Gillingham ME8 66 A2
Greenwich SE3 11 B6
Lambourne Rd ME15 162 F2
Lambourne Wlk CT1 175 C8
Lambourn Ho BR1 29 E1
Lambourn Way
Chatham ME5 97 C2
Royal Tunbridge Wells TN2 286 D1
Lambs Bank TN9 254 B7
Lambscroft Ave SE9 29 D5
Lamb's Cross ME17 229 A5
Lambsfrith Gr ME7 98 B3
Lamb's Mobile Home Pk TN12 257 A7
Lamb's Wlk CT5 108 C6
Lambton Rd CT17 278 A1
Laming Rd CT7 81 B6
Lammas Dr ME10 101 E6
Lammas Gate ME13 138 D8
Lamorbey Cl DA15 30 F6
Lamorna Ave DA12 37 D6
Lamorna Cl BR6 54 A2
Lampington Row TN3 284 E3
Lamplighters Cl
2 Dartford DA1 15 F1
Gillingham ME7 97 F5
Lamport Cl SE18 1 F2
Lamson Rd RM13 4 F8
Lancashire Rd ME15 195 E7
Lancaster Ave CT18 308 C2
Lancaster Cl
Hamstreet TN26 349 A8
Ramsgate CT12 83 B1
Lancaster Ct
Gillingham ME8 98 C7
Gravesend DA12 37 C5
Lancaster Gdns
Birchington CT7 80 F6
Bromley BR1 52 E4
Herne Bay CT6 77 D5
Lancaster Ho
Deal CT14 215 A5
3 Dover CT17 310 D7
Lancaster Rd
Canterbury CT1 174 F6
Dover CT17 310 D7
Lancaster The CT10 84 B3
Lancaster Way ME19 158 F3
Lance Cl ME10 101 F8
Lance Croft DA3 91 F8
Lancelot Ave ME2 62 E7
Lancelot Cl Deal CT14 215 A3
Rochester ME2 62 E6
Lancelot Ct BR6 87 B8
Lancelot Rd DA16 13 A4
Lancer Ho ME1 63 C3
Lances Cl DA13 60 A2
Lancet La ME15 195 A6
Lancey Cl SE7 1 E2
Lanchester Cl CT6 76 A3
Lancing Rd BR6 87 B8
Landale Gdns DA1 33 C8
Landbury Wlk TN23 267 F4
Landon Rd CT6 77 C4
Landor Ct ME7 98 A3
Landrail Rd ME9 67 B3
Landseer Ave DA11 36 D5
Landseer Cl TN10 222 E6
Landstead Rd SE18 12 D7
Land Way ME3 39 D5
Landway TN15 154 F7
Landway The
Borough Green TN15 156 F7
Kemsing TN15 123 A2
Maidstone ME14 163 A4
Orpington BR5 54 C6
Lane Ave DA9 17 C1
Lane End Bexley DA7 14 B4
Herne Bay CT6 76 D5
Lanes Ave DA11 37 A5
Laneside BR7 30 C3
Lanes The CT12 115 D6
Lane's Wlk CT5 74 E2
Lane The
Fordcombe TN3 284 C5
Greenwich SE3 11 A4
Guston CT15 278 F6
Lanfranc Gdns CT2 142 C1
Lanfranc Ho 5 CT1 143 A1
Lanfranc Rd CT14 215 C8
Langafel CE Prim Sch DA3 59 A6
Langafel Cl DA3 58 E7
Langbrook Rd SE3 11 D5
Lang Ct CT5 75 C3
Langdale TN23 299 E8
Langdale Ave CT11 117 A7
Langdale Cl
Gillingham ME8 65 D1
Orpington BR6 86 B7
Langdale Cres DA7 14 A6
Langdale Rise ME16 161 C5
Langdale Wlk 5 DA11 36 E5
Langdon Ave CT3 147 F1
Langdon Cl CT15 279 F5
Langdon Cross CT15 279 C7
Langdon Prim Sch CT15 247 A1
Langdon Rd
Bromley BR2 52 B6
Folkestone CT19 334 D7
Rochester ME1 63 C4
Langdon Shaw DA14 30 F3
Langford Pl DA14 31 A5
Langham Cl CT9 50 F1
Langham Gr ME16 161 C4
Langholm Rd
Ashford TN23 300 A7
Langton Green TN3 284 F3
Langhorne Gdns 9 CT20 335 C4
Langhorne Ho 6 SE7 11 C8
Langlands Dr DA2 34 E3
Langley Ct 13 SE9 12 A1
Langley Gdns
2 Bromley BR2 52 C5
Margate CT9 51 E3
Orpington BR5 53 B3
Langley Ho
6 Bromley BR1 29 B1
11 Maidstone ME16 161 A3
Langley Rd Bexley DA16 13 C8
Sittingbourne ME10 101 F7
Langmore Ct DA7 13 D4
Langney Dr TN23 299 E6
Langport Rd TN28 373 C6
Langton Cl ME14 162 C5
Langton Cotts CT3 146 B5
Langton Green Prim Sch TN3 284 E4
Langton La CT4 175 A4
Langton Rd
Rusthall TN3,TN4 285 C3
Speldhurst TN3 285 A7
Langton Ridge TN3 285 B3
Langton Way SE3 11 B7
Langworth Cl DA2 33 D5
Lankester Parker Rd ME1 96 C6
Lannoy Rd SE9 30 C7
Lanridge Rd SE2 3 D3
Lansbury Cres DA1 16 A2
Lansbury Ct 4 SE28 3 B6
Lansbury Gdns RM18 19 A6
Lansbury Ho 5 DA17 3 F1
Lansdowne Ave
Bexley DA7 13 D7
Maidstone ME15 195 C6
Orpington BR6 53 B1
Lansdowne Ct 9 ME4 63 F4
Lansdowne La SE7 1 D1
Lansdowne Mews SE7 1 D1
Lansdowne Prim Sch
Sittingbourne ME10 102 C3
Tilbury RM18 18 F5
Lansdowne Rd
Bromley BR1 29 B1
Chatham ME4 63 E2
Royal Tunbridge Wells TN1 286 B4
Sevenoaks TN13 154 D5
Tonbridge TN9 222 B2
Lansdowne Sq
Northfleet DA11 18 F1
8 Royal Tunbridge Wells TN1 286 B4
Lansdown Pl DA11 36 F7
Lansdown Rd
Canterbury CT1 175 A7
Sidcup DA14 31 B5
Sittingbourne ME10 102 C4
Tilbury RM18 18 F5
Lantern Ho SE18 2 A1
Lanthorne Mews
Royal Tunbridge Wells,Calverley Park TN1 286 B3
Royal Tunbridge Wells TN1 286 B5
Lanthorne Rd CT10 84 A6
Lapins La ME19 158 F2
Lapis Cl DA12 38 B7
La Providence ME1 63 C5
Lapwing Cl Erith DA8 15 B7
Hawkinge CT18 307 A3
Minster (Sheppey) ME12 47 B5
Lapwing Dr
Ashford TN23 300 D3
Lower Halstow ME9 67 B3
Lapwing Rd ME3 27 B5
Lapwings DA3 59 B6
Lapwings The DA12 37 D6
Lapworth Cl BR6 87 C8
Larch Cl
Broadstairs CT10 83 D4
Larkfield ME20 128 B2
Larch Cres
Hoo St Werburgh ME3 41 E3
Tonbridge TN10 222 C6
Larchcroft ME5 97 A4
Larch Dene BR6 86 A8
Larches The
Faversham ME13 138 A8
Higham ME3 39 C3
Whitstable CT5 108 C8
Larch Gr
Paddock Wood TN12 256 F6
Sidcup DA15 30 F7
Larch Rd Dartford DA1 33 D7
Elvington CT15 212 B1
Larch Terr ME12 46 A8
Larch Way BR2 53 A2
Larch Wlk
Ashford TN24 268 C6
Swanley BR8 55 D7
Larch Wood Cl ME5 97 D1
Larchwood Rd SE9 30 B6
Largo Wlk DA8 14 E6
Larkey View CT4 173 E1
Larkfield Ave
Gillingham ME7 64 E4
Sittingbourne ME10 101 E6
Larkfield Cl Hayes BR2 85 A8
Larkfield ME20 128 A1
Larkfield TN12 256 A7
Larkfield Rd
Larkfield ME20 128 B1
Sevenoaks TN13 153 C4
Sidcup DA14 30 F5
Larkfields DA11 36 E5
Larkfield Trad Est ME20 128 B5
Larkin Cl ME2 40 B2
Larking Dr ME16 161 D7
Larkscliff Ct CT7 80 D8
Larks Field DA3 58 F5
Larksfield Rd ME13 105 C1
Larkspur Cl
2 East Malling ME19 128 A1
4 Newham E6 1 E8
Orpington BR6 87 C7
Larkspur Lodge DA14 31 B5
Larkspur Rd
Chatham ME5 96 E4
West Malling ME19 127 F1
Larkstore Pk TN12 260 E5
Larkswood Cl DA8 15 A6
Larkwell La DA3 58 F5
Larner Rd DA8 14 E7
La Rocco TN28 377 E8
Lascelles Rd CT17 310 A6
Laser Quay ME2 63 D6
Lashenden Air Warfare Mus* TN27 263 A2
Lassa Rd SE9 11 F2
La Tausco TN28 377 D8
Latchgate CT20 334 C3
La-Tene CT14 215 B2
Latham Cl
Biggin Hill TN16 118 C3
Dartford DA2 34 E6
Newham E6 1 E7
Latham Rd DA6 14 A2
Lathe Barn* TN29 352 D5
Latimer Cl CT6 76 B2
Latimer Pl 4 ME7 64 C7
Latona Dr DA12 37 F3
La Tourne Gdns BR6 86 C7
Latymers TN11 252 B4
Launcelot Prim Sch BR1 29 A4
Launcelot Rd BR1 29 A4
Launder Way ME15 161 E2
Laundry Rd CT12 115 D7
Launton Dr DA6 13 D3
Laura Dr BR8 33 A1
Laura Pl ME1 63 A2
Laura Villas CT6 76 E5
Laureate Cl CT9 51 B2
Laurel Ave
Gravesend DA12 37 C6
St Mary's Bay TN29 365 F4
Laurel Bank
Royal Tunbridge Wells TN4 286 B8
Wadhurst TN5 337 A4
Laurel Cl Dartford DA1 33 C7
Folkestone CT20 334 E6
Sidcup DA14 31 A5
Laurel Gdns BR1 52 E5
Laurel Gr ME17 197 D2
Laurel Ho
Greenwich SE7 11 C8
Sheerness ME12 28 B2
Laurel Rd
Gillingham ME7 64 C7
Royal Tunbridge Wells TN2 286 D7
Laurels The
12 Bromley BR1 52 B8
Bromley BR2 52 A5
Dartford DA2 33 C5
18 Erith DA17 4 A1
Maidstone ME16 161 C2
New Barn DA3 59 D6
Laurel Way
Chartham CT4 173 E1
Royal Tunbridge Wells TN2 286 D7
Laurel Wlk ME8 98 E6
Laurensfield CT12 115 C7
Laureston Pl CT16 310 E8
Laurice Ct 6 CT11 117 C6
Laurie Gray Ave ME5 96 D1
Lauriston Cl CT11 117 A5
Lauriston Mount CT10 84 A5
Lausanne Rd CT9 50 J2
Lausanne Terr 11 CT9 50 J2
Lavenda Cl ME7 98 A4
Lavender Cl
Bromley BR2 52 E3
1 Chatham ME5 96 E4
East Malling ME19 159 F8
Margate CT9 82 C8
Whitstable CT5 75 C2
Lavender Ct ME10 102 A3
Lavender Gdns TN5 338 E1
Lavender Hill
Swanley BR8 55 D6
Tonbridge TN9 254 C8
Lavender Ho 3 ME15 195 D8
Lavender La CT12 116 C5
Lavender Mews CT1 174 F8
Lavender Rd ME19 159 F8
Lavender Sq 6 TN18 341 A2
Lavenders Rd ME19 159 C6
Lavender Wlk ME19 159 F8
Lavernock Rd DA7 14 A5
Laverstoke Rd ME16 161 C8
Lavidge Rd SE9 29 F6
Lavinia Rd 1 DA1 15 F1
Lavisham Ho BR1 29 B3
Lawford Gdns DA1 15 C2
Lawley Cl CT12 83 C1
Lawn Cl Bromley BR1 29 B1
Chatham ME4 64 B2
Swanley BR8 55 C7
Tenterden TN30 344 F7
Lawn Pk TN13 187 B8
Lawn Prim Sch DA11 18 C1
Lawn Rd
Broadstairs CT10 84 A4
Deal CT14 215 C1
Northfleet DA11 18 C1
Tonbridge TN9 254 B8
Lawns Cres RM17 18 D8
Lawns The
Brenchley TN12 289 B8
15 Ramsgate CT11 117 F7
Sidcup DA14 31 B4
Lawn Villas CT11 117 E6
Lawrance Sq DA11 36 F5
Lawrence Cl
Folkestone CT19 334 F6
Loose ME15 195 A7
Lawrence Ct CT19 335 E6
Lawrence Dr DA12 61 A5
Lawrence Gdns
Herne Bay CT6 77 C4
Tilbury RM18 19 B7
Lawrence Hill Gdns DA1 15 C1
Lawrence Hill Rd DA1 15 C1
Lawrence Rd Erith DA8 14 B7
Hayes BR4 85 A6
Tonbridge TN10 222 E6
Lawrence St ME7 64 C5
Laws La TN25 329 D7
Lawson Cl
Chartham CT4 173 D2
Newham E16 1 C8
Lawson Gdns DA1 15 D3
Lawson Ho 1 SE18 12 A8
Lawson Rd DA1 15 D3
Lawsons Mews TN9 222 C2
Laxey Rd BR6 86 F4
Laxey The ME15 161 E1
Laxton Cl ME15 162 F3
Laxton Dr ME17 196 A1
Laxton Gdns TN12 256 E7
Laxton Way
Canterbury CT1 175 C7
Faversham ME13 138 E5
Sittingbourne ME10 101 D6
Whitstable CT5 75 C1
Laxton Wlk ME18 159 B3
Layfield Cotts ME9 68 D1
Layfield Ho 4 SE10 1 A1
Layfield Rd ME7 64 F7
Layhams Rd BR2 85 A3
Lay La CT3 147 D2
Laylam Cl CT10 83 D5
Laymarsh Cl DA17 3 F3
Layzell Wlk SE9 29 D7
Lazarus Hart Havens of Rest The 4 CT11 117 F8
Leach Ho ME13 140 A3
Lea Cl CT21 333 B4
Leacon Cotts The TN27 234 E4
Leacon Cotts TN27 234 E4
Leacon Rd TN23 267 F2
Lea Ct ME4 63 E1
Leafield La DA14 31 F5
Leafield TN25 303 D1
Leafy Glade ME8 98 B6
Leafy Gr BR2 85 C5
Leafy La DA13 93 A3
Leafy Oak Rd SE12 29 C5
Leahurst Ct CT16 277 E4
Leake Ho 2 ME1 63 C1
Lealands Ave TN11 221 A1
Lealands Cl TN3 312 C6
Leaman Cl ME23 23 E4
Leamington Ave
Bromley BR1 29 C3
Orpington BR6 86 E6
Leamington Cl BR1 29 C3
Leamington Dr ME16 161 B4
Leamouth Rd E6 1 E8
Leander Dr DA12 37 F4
Leander Rd ME1 96 C7
Lea Rd TN13 187 C8
Learoyd Gdns E6 2 A6
Learoyd Rd TN28 373 C6
Leas Dale SE9 30 A5
Leas Gn
Broadstairs CT10 83 D4
Chislehurst BR7 30 F2
Leaside Cotts CT21 333 B3
Leas Rd CT14 215 B4
Leas The
Faversham ME13 138 B8
Folkestone CT20 335 C4
Kingsdown CT14 248 D3
Minster (Sheppey) ME12 47 C8
Sheerness ME12 28 H1
Turner's Green TN5 337 A6
Whitstable CT5 75 D1
Woolwich SE18 12 B6
Leatherbottle Gn DA18 3 F3
Leather Cl TN8 249 C8
Leatt Cl CT10 83 F4
Lea Vale DA1 14 D3
Leaveland Cl TN23 299 F6
Leaveland Cotts ME13 170 B2
Leaves Gn BR2 118 D8
Leaves Green Cres BR2 118 C8
Leaves Green Rd
Biggin Hill BR2 118 D8
Keston BR2 85 D1
Lebanon Gdns TN16 118 D2
Lebrun Sq SE3 11 B4
Leckwith Ave DA7 13 E8
Leclair Ho SE3 11 B4
Leconfield Cl TN9 253 F7
Leda Cotts TN25 234 F3
Leda Rd SE18 1 F3
Leechcroft Ave
Sidcup DA15 12 F2
Swanley BR8 55 F6
Leech Ct ME1 63 D5
Leeds & Broomfield CE Prim Sch ME17 197 A7
Leeds Castle* ME17 197 D7
Leeds Cl BR6 87 D8
Leeds Ho ME2 40 C1
Leeds Rd ME17 196 E3
Leeds Sq ME8 65 B3
Lee Gn BR5 54 A4
Lee Green Rd ME3 40 B6
Lee Ho CT14 215 C1
Leelands Ho CT14 215 B1
Lee Rd ME6 128 A8
Lees Cl The TN25 302 D5
Lees Court Rd ME13 170 C5
Leesons Hill BR5,BR7 54 A6
Leesons Prim Sch BR5 54 B6
Leesons Way BR5 53 F7
Lees Rd Ashford TN24 269 A1
Brabourne Lees TN25 302 E6
Congelow ME18 225 E7
Lee Sta SE12 11 A1
Lees Terr CT4 172 C2
Lees The CT6 77 C5
Leeswood TN24 269 B1
Leet Cl Gillingham ME7 64 E6
Minster (Sheppey) ME12 48 B5
Leeward Rd ME1 63 C1
Leewood Cl SE12 11 A1
Leewood Pl BR8 55 D5
Legatt Rd SE9 11 D2
Legge La ME19 127 D6
Leggett's La 10 CT5 74 D2
Leggs' La TN3 284 E5
Leghorn Rd SE18 2 D1
Leicester Ave CT9 51 C2
Leicester Ct CT9 51 D3
Leicester Dr TN2 313 F8
Leicester Gdns ME12 49 E3
Leicester Rd
Maidstone ME15 195 D7
Tilbury RM18 18 F6
Leicester Sq TN11 252 B4
Leigh Ave ME15 195 B6
Leigh City Tech Coll The DA1 34 A7
Leigh Ct ME12 46 F5
Leigh Green Ind Est TN30 345 E6
Leigh Halt TN11 220 F1
Leigh Pl DA16 13 A5
Leigh Prim Sch TN11 220 F1
Leigh Rd
Gravesend DA11 37 B6
Ramsgate CT12 82 F1
Rochester ME3 40 C3
Tonbridge TN11 221 D3
Leigh Terr
2 Orpington BR5 54 B6
Teston ME18 160 A1
Leighton Cl TN4 286 A7
Leighton Ct 3 CT16 278 C1
Leighton Gdns RM18 19 A7
Leighton Rd CT16 278 C1
Leighville Dr CT6 76 D4
Leila Parnell Pl 22 SE7 11 C8
Leitch Row ME7 64 A7
Leith Hill Gn BR5 54 A8
Leith Hill BR5 54 A8
Leith Park Rd DA12 37 B7
Leivers Rd CT14 215 A3
Le May Ave SE12 29 B5
Lemonwell Ct SE9 12 C2
Lemonwell Dr SE9 12 C2
Lenacre Ave CT16 277 F7
Lenacre La CT16 277 F8
Lenacre St TN25,TN26 236 B2
Len Clifton Ho 6 SE18 1 F2
Lenderyou Ct DA1 33 E8
Lendon Rd TN15 156 F6
Lendrim Cl 11 ME7 64 A6
Leneda Dr TN2 313 E8
Leney Rd ME18 192 E7
Lenfield Ave ME14 162 B4
Length The CT7 79 F2
Lenham Cl CT10 84 A2
Lenham Ct 10 ME15 162 B4
Lenham Forstal Rd ME17 233 B8
Lenham Gdns CT9 82 B8
Lenham Heath Rd ME17 199 C2
Lenham Ho
Lenham ME17 199 E5
13 Orpington BR5 54 D1
Lenham Prim Sch ME17 199 C5
Lenham Rd Bexley DA7 13 F8
Broadstone TN27,ME17 231 D3
Fairbourne Heath ME17 198 C1
Headcorn TN27 262 E6
Lenham Sta ME17 199 C4
Lenham Way ME8 65 A3
Lennard Ct 4 CT20 335 E5
Lennard Rd
Folkestone CT20 335 E5
Orpington BR2 52 F1
Sevenoaks TN13 153 E7
Lennox Ave DA11 19 A1
Lennox Ho 6 DA17 4 A3
Lennox Rd E DA11 37 A8
Lennox Rd
Gravesend DA11 37 A8
Northfleet DA11 36 F8
Lenor Cl DA6 13 E3
Lensbury Way SE2 3 D3
Lenside Dr ME15 163 A2
Lenton St SE18 2 D2
Len Valley Wlk ME15 162 F1
Leona Ct 8 CT9 51 B2
Leonard Ave
Otford TN14 122 B3
Swanscombe DA10 35 E8
Leonard Cl ME16 161 B6
Leonard Ct DA14 31 B5
Leonard Judge Ho DA2 34 E3
Leonard Pl BR2 85 E7
Leonard Rd
7 Chatham ME4 64 B3
Greatstone-on-S TN28 377 E7
Leonard Robbins Path 3 SE28 3 B6
Leonard's Ave CT11 83 E1
Leonard St E16 1 E5
Leonie Ct CT6 76 D4
Leopold Rd
2 Chatham ME4 64 A3
Ramsgate CT11 117 E8
Leopold St CT11 117 E6
Le Roux Cl CT18 306 F4
Lerryn Gdns CT10 83 F8
Lesley Ave CT1 175 A6
Lesley Chalk Ho TN23 268 C2
Lesley Cl
Istead Rise DA13 59 F8
Sidcup DA5 32 B8
Swanley BR8 55 D6
Lesley Pl ME16 161 E5
Lesley Tew Ct TN10 222 C5
Leslie Ave CT9 82 B8
Leslie Cres TN30 324 B2
Leslie Rd
Birchington CT7 81 A8
Gillingham ME7 64 D7
Newham E16 1 B7
Leslie Smith Dr ME13 138 C7

Leslie Smith Sq 7 SE18 12 A8
Lesnes Abbey (remains of)* SE2 3 D2
Lesney Park Rd DA8 14 D8
Lesney Pk DA8 14 D8
Lessness Ave DA7 13 D7
Lessness Heath Prim Sch DA17 4 A1
Lessness Pk DA17 4 A1
Lessness Rd 12 DA17 4 A1
Les Spickett Cl ME13 138 E6
Lested La ME17 196 B1
Lester Rd ME4 64 A3
Lestock Ho SE3 11 D6
Letchworth Ave ME4 63 F1
Letchworth Cl BR2 52 A4
Letchworth Dr BR2 52 A4
Le Temple Rd TN12 257 B6
Letter Box La TN13 187 C6
Leverholme Gdns SE9 30 A4
Levett Cl ME3 27 B6
Levetts La TN32 355 D1
Leviathan Way ME4 41 A1
Lewd La TN27 264 A3
Lewes Cl RM17 18 A8
Lewes Rd BR1 52 D7
Lewin Ct SE18 2 E2
Lewing Cl BR6 53 E1
Lewin Rd DA6 13 E3
Lewis Ave ME8 65 B2
Lewis Cl ME13 138 A7
Lewis Court Dr ME17 195 C3
Lewis Cres CT9 51 B3
Lewis Ct Ashford TN23 299 F7
Northfleet DA11 36 F6
Lewisham Rd CT17 277 E3
Lewis King Ho 7 BR1 29 B1
Lewis Mews ME6 127 F6
Lewis Rd Bexley DA16 13 C4
Istead Rise DA13 59 F8
Sidcup DA14 31 C5
Swanscombe DA10 17 E1
Lewis Row ME17 228 E6
Lewson Street Rd ME9 136 E8
Leybank TN11 221 F4
Leybourne Cl
Chatham ME5 97 A2
Hayes BR2 52 A3
Leybourne Dell TN17 342 E6
Leybourne Dr CT9 82 B8
Leybourne Rd ME2 62 F8
Leybourne, St Peter & St Paul CE Prim Sch ME19 127 E2
Leybourne Way ME20 127 F4
Leybourn Rd CT10 84 B2
Leybridge Ct SE12 11 A2
Leyburn Ct TN9 222 C3
Leyburne Rd CT16 310 D8
Leyburn Ho SE18 11 E7
Leycroft Cl CT2 142 E3
Leycroft Gdns DA8 15 B6
Leydenhatch La BR8 55 D8
Leyes Rd E16 1 D7
Leyhill Cl BR8 55 E4
Leyland Rd SE12 11 A2
Leysdown Ave DA7 14 C3
Leysdown Rd
Eastchurch ME12 48 E3
Eltham SE9 29 F6
Leysdown-on-S ME12 49 C1
Leysdown View CT5 108 C6
Leys The CT12 82 D1
Leyton Ave ME7 64 E1
Leyton Cross DA2 33 A6
Leyton Cross Rd DA2 32 F5
Leywood Rd DA13 93 D3
Lezayre Rd BR6 86 F4
Liberty Mews BR6 86 F8
Library Rd CT2 142 D4
Libya Terr 6 ME14 162 A7
Lichdale Cl 8 BR6 86 F6
Lichfield Ave CT1 175 B6
Lichfield Cl ME8 65 D2
Lichfield Ho 12 ME15 195 E7
Liddon Rd BR1 52 D6
Lidsing Rd ME14 130 E6
Lidwells La TN17 290 E1
Liege Cl ME10 68 F1
Lieth Park Rd DA12 37 C7
Liffler Rd SE18 2 E1
Lighterman's Mews 2 DA11 36 E8
Lightermans Way DA9 17 C3
Lightfoot Gn TN18 340 E3
Lighthouse Rd CT15 280 A5
Lilac Cres ME2 62 E6
Lilac Ct TN23 267 E3
Lilac Gdns BR8 55 D6
Lilac Gn 4 ME19 128 A1
Lilac Pl DA13 60 B2
Lilac Rd ME2 62 E5
Lila Pl BR8 55 E5
Lilburne Gdns SE9 11 E2
Lilburne Rd SE9 11 E2
Lilian Barker Cl SE12 11 A2
Lilk Hill ME14 163 C3
Lillechurch Rd ME3 39 F7
Lillian Rd CT11 117 F8
Lillieburn ME19 127 D2
Lillie Rd TN16 118 D1
Lily Nichols Ho E16 1 E5
Lilyvale Cotts TN25 302 F4
Lilyvale Rd TN25 302 F4
Limavady Ho SE18 2 A2
Lime Ave
Benenden TN17 342 C8
Northfleet DA11 36 D8
Lime Cl Ashford TN23 267 F3
Bromley BR1 52 E5
Chartham CT4 173 E1
Frant TN3 314 B3
Marden TN12 259 C6
Lime Cotts TN12 260 F3
Lime Cres ME19 160 A7
Lime Ct Eltham SE9 30 B6
Gillingham ME8 98 C3
Lime Gr
Biddenden TN27 323 D7
Halfway Houses ME12 46 D5
Orpington BR6 86 B8
Sidcup DA15 12 F1
Sittingbourne ME10 102 A4
Lime Hill Rd TN1 286 A4
Lime Kiln Dr SE7 11 B8
Limekiln Rdbt CT17 310 D6
Lime Kiln Rd CT1 174 F6
Limekiln St CT17 310 D5
Lime Kiln Wharf ME11 46 A5
Lime Pit La TN13,TN14 121 C2
Limepits Cross ME9 100 F3
Lime Rd BR8 55 D6
Lime Row DA18 3 F3
Limes Cl TN30 345 C8
Limes Gr TN18 340 F5
Limes Pl 15 ME13 138 D7
Limes Rd Dover CT16 278 C1
Folkestone CT19 334 F6
Limes Row BR6 86 B5
Limes The
Ashford TN23 300 A5
Edenbridge TN8 217 C1
Frittenden TN17 293 E6
Lenham ME17 199 D5
Old Romney TN29 372 A7
Orpington BR2 85 E8
Lime Tree Ave DA9 35 A7
Limetree Cl ME5 97 B8
Lime Tree Cl TN9 222 C2
Lime Trees TN12 260 E4
Limetree Terr
5 Bexley DA16 13 A4
Lenham ME17 199 E6
Lime Tree Wlk TN13 154 B2
Lime Villas CT4 273 F5
Limewood Rd DA8 14 C7
Limpsfield CE Inf Sch RH8 183 C6
Limpsfield Grange Sch RH8 183 A8
Linces The CT16 278 B4
Linchmere Rd 7 SE12 29 A8
Lincoln Ave CT1 175 B7
Lincoln Cl Erith DA8 14 F5
Rochester ME2 62 D6
Whitstable CT5 75 D3
Lincoln Ct 3 SE12 29 C5
Lincoln Gdns CT7 80 F7
Lincoln Green Rd BR5 53 F4
Lincoln Rd DA8 14 F5
Lincol n Rd ME7 64 D7
Lincoln Rd
Maidstone ME15 195 D8
Sidcup DA14 31 B3
Lincolnshire Terr DA2 34 D4
Lincolnshott DA13 36 B3
Lindale Flats CT14 215 C2
Lindel Ct ME18 159 B3
Linden Ave
Broadstairs CT10 84 B5
Dartford DA1 33 C7
Herne Bay CT6 76 E4
Whitstable CT5 74 F1
Linden Chase
Canterbury CT2 142 E1
Sevenoaks TN13 154 B5
Linden Cl Orpington BR6 87 A5
Paddock Wood TN12 257 A6
Purfleet RM19 16 C8
Royal Tunbridge Wells TN4 286 A2
Sittingbourne ME10 101 D3
Westgate-on-S CT8 81 E7
Linden Cres CT19 335 D6
Linden Ct Sidcup DA14 30 E4
Tonbridge TN10 222 B7
Linden Dr ME12 46 A7
Lindenfield BR7 53 B7
Linden Gdns TN2 285 F1
Linden Gr CT2 142 E1
Linden Grove Prim Sch TN23 299 F6
Linden Ho
4 Bromley BR1 29 B1
5 Chatham ME5 96 F4
Linden Park Rd TN2 286 A2
Linden Rd
Ashford TN24 268 D1
Chartham CT4 173 E1
Coxheath ME17 194 C4
Gillingham ME7 64 E5
Westgate-on-S CT8 81 F8
Lindens CT21 333 D2
Linden Sq TN13 153 E5
Lindens The ME20 128 E1
Lindenthorpe Rd CT10 84 A6
Lindfield Cotts ME13 138 A6
Lindisfarne Cl DA12 37 E6
Lindisfarne Gdns ME16 161 E3
Lindridge Cl CT6 111 A8
Lindridge La TN12 260 C5
Lindsay Ho 2 SE18 2 A2
Lindsey Cl BR1 52 E6
Lindwood Cl 8 E6 1 F8
Lineacre Cl ME8 98 D6
Linen Ct CT1 174 F8
Lines Terr ME4 64 A4
Lingey Cl DA15 30 F6
Lingfield Ave DA2 34 B8
Lingfield Cres SE9 12 D3
Lingfield Mews 4 TN8 217 C1
Lingfield Rd
Borough Green TN15 157 B7
Edenbridge TN8 249 A8
Gravesend DA12 37 B6
Lingley Dr ME2 40 C2
Ling Rd Erith DA8 14 C8
Newham E16 1 A8
Lingwood DA7 14 B5
Linington Rd CT7 81 A6
LINK 20 Bsns Pk ME20 128 B3
Linkden Cotts TN18 356 E5
Link Field BR2 52 A3
Link Hill La TN27 232 D3
Link La CT1 175 A8
Link Rd Broadstairs CT10 83 F7
Tyler Hill CT2 142 E6
Links Cl CT6 77 A3
Links Cres TN29 366 A4
Links Ct Deal CT14 182 C1
Eltham SE9 30 B7
Linksfield Ct CT8 81 D7
Linksfield Rd CT8 81 D7
Links Rd CT14 215 C8
Links The
Addington ME19 126 E2
Chatham ME5 97 B8
Links View Dartford DA1 33 C7
Woolwich SE18 12 B6
Linksway Cl CT19 335 B8
Linksway CT19 335 B8
Links Way TN28 373 D6
Link The Ashford TN23 299 E7
Eltham SE9 30 A5
New Ash Green DA3 91 F8
Link Way BR2 52 E2
Linkway Ditton ME20 128 C1
Iwade ME9 68 D4
Link Way TN2 286 E8
Linley Cl RM18 20 D7
Linley Rd CT10 83 E7
Linnet Ave
Paddock Wood TN12 257 A5
Whitstable CT5 108 B6
Linnet Cl SE28 3 C6
Linslade Rd BR6 87 A4
Linsted Ct SE9 12 E1
Linton Cl Bexley DA16 13 B6
2 Greenwich SE7 1 C1
Linton Dann Cl ME3 41 D6
Linton Gdns E6 1 E7
Linton Gore ME17 194 D3
Linton Hill TN12 227 F6
Linton Mead Prim Sch SE28 3 B6
Linton Rd ME15 194 F4
Lintorn Symonds Rd ME3 40 F5
Linwood Ave ME2 62 E8
Lionard Ho 3 CT2 142 E1
Lion Ct CT14 215 C5
Lionel Gdns SE9 11 D2
Lionel Oxley Ho 5 RM17 18 B8
Lionel Rd Eltham SE9 11 D2
Tonbridge TN9 254 A8
Lion Field ME13 138 B7
Lion Rd Bexley DA6 13 F3
Newham E6 1 F8
Lions Cl SE9 29 D5
Lion's Rd TN28 373 A6
Lion Yd
Faversham ME13 138 A6
3 Sittingbourne ME10 101 F4
Liphook Way ME16 161 C8
Lipscombe Rd TN2 286 D6
Lipton Cl SE28 3 C6
Liptraps La TN2 286 D7
Lipwell Hill ME23 23 B4
Lisa Ct CT5 75 A2
Liskeard Cl BR7 30 C2
Liskeard Gdns SE3 11 A6
Lisle Cl DA12 38 B6
Lismore Cl ME15 195 A7
Lismore Rd
Herne Bay CT6 77 D5
Whitstable CT5 109 B8
Liss Rd CT13 180 A1
Lister Cl Deal CT14 215 C5
Dover CT17 278 B1
East Malling ME19 159 F8
Lister Ho Erith SE2 3 D1
Margate CT9 83 A8
Lister Rd Margate CT9 83 A8
Tilbury RM18 19 A5
Lister Way CT20 334 F3
Lister Wlk SE28 3 D6
Listmas Rd ME4 64 B3
List The CT3 145 C2
Listways Cotts CT3 211 B6
Little Acres TN25 328 E7
Little Alley TN8 249 B5
Little Ave CT14 214 F3
Little Bayham Cotts TN3 315 F4
Little Birches DA15 30 E6
Little Boundes Cl TN4 253 F3
Littlebourne Ave ME8 65 B4
Littlebourne CE Prim Sch CT3 176 F8
Littlebourne Rd
Canterbury CT1,CT3 175 E8
Maidstone ME14 162 C6
Littlebrook Cl TN23 268 A3
Little Brook Hospl DA2 16 C1
Littlebrook Manor Way DA1 16 A2
Little Brook Rd TN23 268 A3
Little Browns La TN8 216 F4
Little Buckland Ave ME16 161 D6
Little Charles St CT6 76 F5
Little Chequers TN25 237 E2
Littlecombe SE7 11 B8
Little Copse Cl CT4 173 E1
Littlecourt Rd TN13 154 A3
Littlecroft Eltham SE9 12 A4
Istead Rise DA13 36 E1
Little Ct ME16 161 D2
Littledale Dartford DA2 34 C5
Woolwich SE2 13 A8
Littlefield TN11 223 E8
Littlefield Rd ME8 66 B2
Little Field TN12 260 E5
Little Footway TN3 284 F3
Little Glovers ME10 101 F3
Little Groves Cvn & Chalet Pk ME12 49 F2
Little Groves Holiday Camp ME12 49 F2
Little Heath Rd DA7 13 F7
Little Heath SE7 1 E1
Little Hempen TN23 299 D8
Little Hill TN30 324 B2
Little Job's Cross TN17 343 F1
Little John Ave ME5 96 F2
Littlejohn Rd BR5 54 B4
Little Julians Hill TN13 187 A8
Little Kit's Coty House* ME20 129 C5
Little Knoll TN23 299 F8
Little Mallett TN3 284 F3
Little Market Row ME19 127 E2
Little Mdw CT2 141 E1
Littlemead CT19 335 A7
Littlemede SE9 29 F5
Little Mill Farm Cotts TN12 259 C8
Littlemore Rd SE2 3 A4
Little Mount Sion TN1 286 A2
Little Oakham Ct ME3 25 C4
Little Orch ME17 194 D3
Little Oxley ME19 127 E2
Little Paddocks CT5 109 D7
Little Pk TN5 336 E5
Little Queen St DA1 33 F8
Little Redlands BR1 52 E7
Little Robhurst TN26 324 D8
Little Sheephurst Cotts TN12 258 E5
Littlestone Ct TN28 373 E5
Littlestone Ho TN28 373 E5
Littlestone Rd TN28 373 D6
Little Stone Stile Cotts ME13 171 F4
Little Switzerland CT19 335 G8
Little Thrift BR5 53 C5
Little Walton CT13 180 C3
Little Wood Cl BR5 54 A8
Little Wood TN13 154 D5
Little York Mdws ME7 65 C4
Liverpool Lawn 18 CT11 117 E6
Liverpool Rd CT14 215 D2
Liveryman Wlk DA9 17 C3
Livesey Cl SE28 2 C3
Livesey St ME18 160 A1
Livingstone Bldgs ME7 64 D5
Livingstone Circ ME7 64 D5
Livingstone Cl TN29 353 B4
Livingstone Gdns DA12 37 D3
Livingstone Hospl DA1 33 F8
Livingstone Rd
Broadstairs CT10 83 E6
Gillingham ME7 64 E5
Gravesend DA12 37 D3
Livingstone Wlk 6 ME15 195 F5
Lizban St SE3 11 B7
Llanover Rd SE18 12 A7
Lloyd Ct CT14 215 D7
Lloyd Ho BR1 29 B3
Lloyd Rd CT10 84 A5
Lloyds Gn TN30 359 D4
Loading Bay App CT13 149 A8
Loaland Bsns Ctr ME2 63 D8
Loam Ct DA1 33 E7
Loampits Cl TN9 222 D3
Lobelia Cl
Gillingham ME7 64 E6
5 Newham E6 1 E8
Locarno Ave ME8 65 A2
Lochat Rd ME3 40 E6
Lochmere Cl DA8 14 B8
Lockesley Dr BR5 54 A3
Lockham Farm Ave ME17 195 D5
Lockholt Cl TN23 267 E3
Lockington Cl TN9 253 F7
Lockington Gr ME1 63 C5
Lock La ME14 129 D1
Lockside TN9 222 C2
Locksley Cl ME5 96 E2
Lock St ME7 64 C5
Lockswood ME16 161 D7
Lock's Yd TN13 154 C2
Lockyer Rd RM19 16 C8
Lockyers Hill DA13 93 F5
Lodden Ct 15 BR5 54 D1
Loddington La
Linton ME17 228 A8
Maidstone,Boughton Monchelsea ME17 195 A1
Loder Cl ME17 199 B5
Lodge Ave DA1 15 C1
Lodge Cl Orpington BR6 54 B1
Wateringbury ME18 192 D8
Lodge Cres BR6 54 B1
Lodge Farmhouse ME20 128 E3
Lodge Field Rd CT5 75 D1
Lodge Gdns ME17 230 F6
Lodge Hill DA16 13 B7
Lodge Hill La ME3 40 F7
Lodge La Cobham DA12 61 B5
Royal Tunbridge Wells TN3 313 A8
Sidcup DA5 13 D1
Westerham TN16 184 C8
Lodge Oak La TN9 254 D8
Lodge Rd Bromley BR1 29 C1
Maidstone ME14 162 D5
Staplehurst TN12 260 E5
Tonbridge TN9 222 B2
Lodgewood Cotts TN8 218 D2
Lodge Wood Dr TN25 267 E5
Logs Hill BR1,BR2 52 E8
Logs Hill Cl BR7 52 E8
Lolland Ho 9 SE18 1 E2
Lomaria Ct TN2 286 C4
Lomas La TN18 356 F5
Lomas Rd ME10,ME9 102 D4
Lombard St
Horton Kirby DA4 57 C5
Margate CT9 50 I3
Lombard Trad Est SE7 1 B2
Lombard Wall SE7 1 B2
Lombardy Cl ME7 98 A6
Lombardy Dr ME14 162 C5
Lomer Farm DA13 93 A8
London City Airport E16 1 E5
Londonderry Ho 15 ME15 195 E7
Londonderry Par DA8 14 D7
London Ind Pk E6 2 B8
London La Bromley BR1 29 A1
Sissinghurst TN17 293 A2
London Pl 24 CT20 335 E5
London Rd
Addington ME19 126 D2
Badgers Mount TN14 121 C6
Bidborough TN4 253 F3
Bromley BR1 52 A8
Canterbury CT2 142 D1
Chelsfield TN14 87 F2
Crayford DA1 14 D2
Deal CT14 215 B5
Ditton ME20 128 C1
Dover CT16,CT17 278 B1
Dunkirk ME13 140 E2
London Rd E ME20 160 F8
London Rd
Farningham BR8,DA4 56 D3
Faversham ME13 138 B6
Flimwell TN5 339 D3
Gillingham ME8 65 C1
Grays RM17,RM20 17 E8
Hartlip ME8,ME9 99 D7
Hildenborough TN11, TN13,TN15 221 B7
Hurst Green TN19 354 A3
Hythe CT21 332 F3
Maidstone ME16 161 C6
Newington ME9 100 A6
Northfleet DA11 18 E1
Otford TN13 121 D1
Ramsgate CT11 117 B6
Rochester ME2 63 A7
Royal Tunbridge Wells,Mount Sion TN1 286 A3
Royal Tunbridge Wells TN4 286 A8
Sevenoaks,Dunton Green TN13 153 E7
Sevenoaks TN13 154 B2
Sittingbourne ME10 101 C4
Stone DA2,DA9 16 E1
Swanley BR8 55 D7
Swanley BR8 55 E6
Swanscombe DA9 17 C2
Temple Ewell CT15, CT16 277 B6
Teynham ME9 103 C1
Tilbury RM18 19 B5
Tonbridge TN10,TN11 222 B3
West Kingsdown TN15 91 A1
Wrotham Heath TN15, ME19 125 F1
Wrotham TN15 125 B3
London Road Purfleet RM19 16 C8
London Road (River) CT16,CT17 277 F4
London Road Temple Ewell CT16 277 D5
London Road Trad Est ME10 101 D4
London Road West Thurrock RM20 17 A8
London St CT20 335 E5
Lone Barn Rd ME17 200 B8
Lonefield TN26 299 B1
Lonewood Way TN11 190 F2
Long Acre Cl CT2 142 E2
Long Acre BR6 87 D8
Longacre Rd TN23 299 D7
Longacre CT5 75 D1
Longage Hill CT18,CT4 273 A1
Long Barn Rd TN14 187 B2
Long Barrow The TN24 300 E6
Long Beech TN23 267 E1
Longbridge TN24 269 B1
Longbridge Terr CT21 332 F1
Longbury Cl BR5 54 B6
Longbury Dr BR5 54 B7
Long Catlis Rd ME8 98 D4
Longcroft SE9 30 A5
Longdon Wood BR2 85 E6
Longdown Ho ME5 96 F6
Long Dr CT13 180 C2
Longfellow Rd ME7 64 C3
Longfield Ave
High Halstow ME23 23 E4
New Barn DA3,DA13 59 D7
Longfield Cl CT5 75 D2
Longfield Ct CT5 75 D2
Longfield Pl ME15 195 C8
Longfield Rd
Dover CT17 310 B7
Meopham Station DA3, DA13 59 E3
Royal Tunbridge Wells TN1,TN2,TN11 254 E1
Longfields Dr ME14 163 A5
Longfield Sta DA3 58 E6
Longfield TN30 345 A6
Longford Cl ME8 99 A8
Longford Ct ME8 99 A8
Longford Terr 9 CT20 335 D4
Longford Way 10 CT20 335 D4
Longham Copse ME15 162 F1
Longhill Ave ME5 64 B3
Long Hill CT4 172 C1
Longhurst Dr ME5 96 F2
Long La DA7 13 E6
Longlands Ct DA15 30 F5
Longlands Park Cres DA15 30 E6
Longlands Prim Sch DA15 30 E5
Longlands Rd DA15 30 F5
Long La
Rabbit's Cross ME17 228 D5
Shepherdswell CT15 244 D7
Longleat Ct 3 DA6 13 E3
Longleigh La SE2,DA7 13 C8
Long Length TN23 299 D4
Longley Rd
Rainham ME8 65 F1
Rochester ME1 63 C4
Longmarket 2 CT1 175 A8
Long Mark Rd 5 E16 1 D8
Longmarsh La SE28 2 E5
Longmarsh View DA4 57 B8
Long Mdw CT12 114 D6
Longmead BR7 53 A7
Longmead Cl CT6 76 C3
Long Mead Com Prim Sch TN10 222 B5
Longmead Dr DA14 31 D6
Longmeade DA12 37 F7
Longmeadow Rd DA15 30 E7
Longmeadow TN13 153 D6
Long Meadow Way CT2 143 A4
Long Meads TN3 285 B4
Long Mead Way TN10 222 B4
Longmete Rd CT3 146 C5
Long Mill La
Crouch TN15 157 B3
Platt TN15 157 C7
Longmore Dr ME12 48 C1
Longparish Cl ME15 195 F6
Longport CT1 175 B8
Long Reach Cl CT5 108 C6
Longreach Rd DA8 15 B7
Long Rede La ME16 160 F3
Longridge ME10 102 B2
Long Rock CT5 75 D3
Long Row TN25 301 D2
Long's Acre TN25 237 E1
Longsfield TN25 330 A6
Longshaw Rd ME15 195 F5
Long Slip TN3 285 A3
Longtail Rise CT6 76 E2
Longten's Cotts DA12 38 E6
Longtown Ct 19 DA2 16 B1
Longtye Dr CT5 109 C7
Longview Way TN2 286 D7
Longwalk DA13 59 E8
Long Wlk Ashford TN23 267 E4
Woolwich SE18 12 B8
Longwood ME5 97 B1
Longworth Cl SE28 3 D7
Lonsdale Ave CT9 51 C3
Lonsdale Cl SE9 29 D5
Lonsdale Cres DA2 34 C7
Lonsdale Ct CT16 278 D1
Lonsdale Dr
Gillingham ME8 98 E7
Herne Bay CT6 76 B5
Sittingbourne ME10 101 C5
Lonsdale Gdns TN1 286 A3
Lonsdale Rd DA7 13 F5
Lookers La CT21 333 B3
Loop Court Mews 9 CT13 148 F1
Loop Rd BR7 30 C2
Loop St CT13 148 F1
Loose Down Rd ME13 202 F7
Loose Inf & Jun Schs ME15 195 A6
Loose Rd ME15 195 A7
Loraine Ct BR7 30 B3
Lord Chatham's Ride TN14 120 D2
Lord Cornwallis Ct CT19 335 C8
Lord Roberts Terr SE18 2 A1
Lord Romney's Hill ME14 162 F3
Lords Cl ME9 102 E2
Lords Cotts ME13 170 C4
Lord St Gravesend DA12 37 B8
Newham E16 1 E5
Lords Wood Cl ME5 97 B2
Lordswood Cl DA2 34 E4
Lordswood Ind Est ME5 130 C8

Lordswood Inf & Jun Sch
ME5 .... 97 B3
Lords Wood La ME5 ...... 97 B3
Lord Warden Ave
CT14 .... 215 D2
Lord Warden Ho
CT17 .... 310 D5
Lord Warden Sq CT17 .. 310 D5
Lord Warwick St SE18 ..... 1 F3
Lorenden Park Nature
Reserve* ME13 .... 137 F3
Lorenden Pk TN18 ..... 340 F1
Lorenden Prep Sch
ME13 .... 137 E3
Lorien Flats TN24 ...... 268 D7
Lorimar Bsns Ctr RM13 .... 4 E8
Lorimar Ct ME10 .... 101 C7
Lorina Rd CT12 .... 117 C8
Lorne Cotts CT14 .... 215 C7
Lorne Rd
Dover CT16,CT17 .... 278 B2
Ramsgate CT11 .... 117 C6
Lorraine Ct
1 Folkestone CT19 ..... 335 E6
Swanscombe DA9 .... 17 B1
Lorton Cl DA12 .... 37 E6
Lossenham La TN18 .... 357 D3
Lotus Rd TN16 .... 118 F1
Loudon Ct TN23 .... 267 E3
Loudon Path TN23 ..... 267 E3
Loudon Way TN23 ...... 267 E3
Loughborough Ct 2
CT11 .... 117 E7
Louise Ct 8 DA6 .... 13 E3
Louis Gdns BR7 .... 29 F4
Louisville Ave ME7 ...... 64 D4
Lourdes Manor Cl
TN25 .... 303 D1
Louvain Rd DA9 .... 34 E8
Lovage App E6 .... 1 E8
Love La Adisham CT3 ..... 177 F2
12 Canterbury CT1 .... 175 A8
Lovelace Ave BR2 .... 53 A3
Lovelace Cl
Gillingham ME8 .... 98 D4
West Kingsdown TN15 ..... 90 E4
Lovelace Ct TN26 .... 297 C5
Lovelace Gn SE9 .... 11 F4
Love La
East Tilbury RM18 .... 20 C8
Faversham ME13 .... 138 F6
Margate CT9 .... 50 I3
Minster (Sheppey) ME12 .. 47 D7
Rochester ME1 .... 63 C5
Sidcup DA5 .... 14 A1
Swift's Green TN27 ...... 263 B5
Lovel Ave DA16 .... 13 A5
Love La
Wateringbury ME18 ..... 192 D7
Woolwich SE18 .... 2 B2
Lovell Rd
Minster (Sheppey) ME12 ... 47 A5
Rough Common CT2 ..... 142 B3
Lovers La TN17 .... 290 F1
Lover's La DA9,DA10 ..... 17 D3
Loves Holiday Camp
ME12 .... 49 F3
Love Street Cl CT6 .... 76 C2
Lovibonds Ave BR6 .... 86 B7
Low Cl DA9 .... 17 A2
Lowe Ave E16 .... 1 A8
Lower Bannister Cotts
ME9 .... 101 B2
Lower Bell La ME20 .... 128 B2
Lower Blackhouse Hill
CT21 .... 333 D3
Lower Bloors La ME8 ..... 65 E3
Lower Boxley Rd 10
ME14 .... 162 A5
Lower Bridge St CT1 ... 175 A8
Lower Camden BR7 .... 52 F8
Lower Chantry La
CT1 .... 175 A8
Lower Church Hill DA9 ... 16 E2
Lower Croft BR8 .... 55 F5
Lower Denmark Rd
TN23 .... 300 C8
Lower Ensden Rd CT4 .. 172 D4
Lower Fant Rd ME16 ... 161 D2
Lower Farm Rd ME17 .. 228 D5
Lower Gn TN11 .... 220 F1
Lower Gore La CT13 .... 180 B3
Lower Gravel Rd BR2 ..... 52 F1
Lower Green Rd
Pembury TN2 .... 287 D7
Rusthall TN3,TN4 .... 285 C6
Lower Halstow Prim Sch
ME9 .... 67 B2
Lower Hartlip Rd ME9 .... 99 E5
Lower Haysden La
TN11,TN9 .... 253 D8
Lower Hazelhurst
Ticehurst TN5 .... 338 A4
Ticehurst TN5 .... 338 B4
Lower Herne Rd CT6 ... 110 E8
Lower Higham Rd
DA12 .... 38 B7
Lower High St TN5 ..... 337 A4
Lower Lees Rd CT4 ..... 172 D2
Lower Mill La CT14 ..... 215 C5
Lower Northdown Ave
CT9 .... 51 B2
Lower Norton La ME9 .. 104 A1
Lower Park Rd DA17 ...... 4 A2
Lower Platts TN5 ...... 338 F1
Lower Queens Rd
TN24 .... 268 C3
Lower Rainham Rd
Gillingham,Lower Rainham
ME8 .... 66 A3
Gillingham ME7 .... 65 D5
Lower Range Rd DA12 .... 37 E8
Lower Rd
Eastchurch ME12 .... 48 B3
East Farleigh ME15 ..... 194 B7
Lower Rd E CT16 .... 310 H8
Lower Rd Erith DA17 .... 4 B3
Erith DA8 .... 4 D2
Faversham ME13 .... 137 C8
Hextable BR8 .... 33 B1
Higham DA12,ME3 .... 39 B6
Maidstone ME15 .... 162 B3
Minster (Sheppey) ME12 .. 46 E4
Northfleet DA11 .... 18 A3
Orpington BR5 .... 54 B3
River CT17 .... 277 E3
Shorne DA12 .... 38 E6
Staple CT3 .... 179 B6
Stone in Oxney TN30 .... 360 D5
Sutton Valence ME17 ... 229 E7
Temple Ewell CT16 ...... 277 D5
Teynham,Lower Newlands
ME9,ME13 .... 103 E2
Teynham ME9 .... 103 B3
Lower Rd W CT16 ...... 310 G8
Lower Rd
West Farleigh ME15 ..... 193 D7
Woodchurch TN26 ...... 326 B1
Lower Rochester Rd
ME3 .... 39 E6
Lower Rowling Cotts
CT3 .... 179 B2
Lower Sandgate Rd
CT20 .... 335 C3
Lower Sands TN29 ..... 352 E2
Lower Santon La CT3 .. 146 D7
Lower Station Rd DA1 .... 14 E1
Lower St Eastry CT13 .... 180 B1
Leeds ME17 .... 197 A7
Lower Stone St ME15 .. 162 A3
Lower St
Tilmanstone CT14 .... 213 A2
Tonbridge TN11 .... 220 F5
Lower Tovil ME15 .... 161 E2
Lower Twydall La ME7,
ME8 .... 65 C4
Lower Vicarage Rd
TN24 .... 268 D7
Lower Wall Rd
Burmarsh CT21 .... 352 D8
Dymchurch CT21 .... 353 A7
Lower Warren Rd
ME20 .... 129 E6
Lower Woodlands Rd
ME7 .... 65 A6
Lowestoft Mews E16 ...... 2 B4
Lowfield Rd ME12 .... 46 E6
Lowfield St DA1 .... 33 E8
Low Meadow ME2 .... 95 B5
Lownds Ct BR1 .... 52 A7
Lowry Cl DA8 .... 4 D2
Lowry The 4 TN9 .... 254 B8
Lowslip Hill CT15 ...... 309 A5
Low Street La RM18 ...... 19 F8
Lowther Rd CT17 .... 310 B8
Loxwood Cl
Orpington BR5,BR6 .... 87 D8
Whitfield CT16 .... 278 B7
Lubbock Cl ME15 .... 195 E5
Lubbock Ct BR7 .... 29 F1
Lubbock Ho BR6 .... 86 E8
Lubbock Rd BR7 .... 29 F1
Lubbock Wlk ME8 .... 98 D5
Lucas Cres DA9 .... 17 C3
Lucas Rd ME6 .... 127 E7
Lucerne Ct 5 Erith DA18 ... 3 E3
Whitstable CT5 .... 107 F6
Lucerne Dr CT5 .... 107 F6
Lucerne La CT15 .... 247 C2
Lucerne Rd BR6 .... 53 F1
Lucerne St ME14 .... 162 A5
Lucilina Dr TN8 .... 249 C8
Lucilla Ave TN23 .... 299 F4
Luckhurst Gdns CT9 ...... 51 E3
Luckhurst Rd
Ashford TN24 .... 301 A7
Crabble CT17 .... 277 E3
Luckley Ho TN25 .... 237 E2
Lucknow Cl CT15 .... 278 F3
Lucknow Rd TN12 ...... 257 A8
Lucknow St SE18 .... 12 E7
Lucks Hill ME19 .... 159 D8
Lucks La
Paddock Wood TN12 ..... 257 B8
Rabbit's Cross ME17 .... 228 F6
Lucks Way TN12 .... 259 B6
Lucy Ave CT19 .... 335 B7
Lucy's Hill CT21 .... 333 B2
Luddenham Cl
Ashford TN23 .... 299 F6
Maidstone ME14 .... 162 C6
Luddenham Sch ME13 .. 104 E1
Luddesdon Rd DA8 .... 14 A7
Luddesdown Ho 5
BR5 .... 54 C4
Luddesdown Rd DA13 .... 61 A2
Ludgate Rd ME9 .... 135 F5
Ludham Cl SE28 .... 3 C7
Ludlow Cl BR2 .... 52 A6
Luffield Rd SE2 .... 3 B3
Luffman Rd SE12 .... 29 B5
Lughorse La ME15,
ME18 .... 193 C1
Lukes Cl CT17 .... 278 B1
Lukin Ho CT21 .... 332 F1
Lullarook Cl TN16 ..... 118 C3
Lullingstone Ave BR8 ..... 55 F6
Lullingstone Castle*
DA4 .... 89 B5
Lullingstone Cl
Gillingham ME7 .... 98 B3
Orpington BR5 .... 31 B1
Lullingstone Cres BR5 ..... 31 B1
Lullingstone Ct 15
CT1 .... 174 F8
Lullingstone La DA4 ...... 89 C8
Lullingstone Pk* DA4 .... 88 F6
Lullingstone Pk Visitor
Ctr* DA4 .... 89 B4
Lullingstone Rd
3 Bexley DA17 .... 13 F8
Maidstone ME16 .... 161 C7
Lullingstone Roman Villa
(rems of)* DA4 .... 89 B7
Lulworth Rd
Bexley DA16 .... 12 F5
Bromley SE9 .... 29 E6
Lumley Cl DA17 .... 4 A1
Lumsden Terr 8 ME4 ..... 63 E4
Lunar Cl TN16 .... 118 D3
Lunedale Rd DA2 .... 34 C7
Lunsford District Ctr
ME20 .... 128 A4
Lunsford La ME20 ...... 127 F2
Lunsford Prim Sch
ME20 .... 128 A2
Lupton Cl SE12 .... 29 B4
Lurkins Rise TN17 ...... 318 D7
Lushington Rd ME14 ... 161 E7
Lusted Hall La TN16 ... 150 C7
Lusted Rd TN13 .... 153 E7
Luton Ave CT10 .... 83 F3
Luton Ct CT10 .... 83 F3
Luton High St ME5 .... 64 C2
Luton Inf Sch ME5 .... 64 C2
Luton Jun Sch ME4 .... 64 C2
Luton Rd
Chatham ME4,ME5 .... 64 B2
Faversham ME13 .... 138 E7
Sidcup DA14 .... 31 C5
Luxfield Rd SE9 .... 29 E7
Luxon Rd DA13 .... 93 E4
Luxted Rd BR6 .... 119 A6
Lyall Way ME8 .... 98 E4
Lychfield Dr ME2 .... 63 A8
Lych Gate Rd BR6 .... 54 A1
Lydbrook Cl ME10 ...... 101 D4
Lydd Airport TN29 ..... 377 A7
Lydd Cl DA14 .... 30 E5
Lydden Ct SE9 .... 12 E1
Lydden Hill CT15 ...... 244 C1
Lydden International Motor
Racing Circuit CT4 ...... 243 F3
Lydden Prim Sch
CT15 .... 276 F8
Lydd Prim Sch TN29 ... 376 C6
Lydd Rd Bexley DA7 ...... 13 F7
Chatham ME5 .... 97 B5
New Romney TN28,
TN29 .... 372 F6
Lydd Town Crossing
TN29 .... 376 D8
Lydd Town Mus*
TN29 .... 376 C6
Lydens La TN8 .... 249 F6
Lydford Ct 18 DA2 .... 16 B1
Lydia Cotts 2 DA11 ...... 37 B8
Lydia Rd Deal CT14 ..... 215 A2
Erith DA8 .... 14 F8
Lydos Cl TN29 .... 377 E5
Lydstep Rd BR7 .... 30 A4
Lyeat Ct CT2 .... 142 C4
Lyell Cl CT21 .... 333 A1
Lyell Ct 5 CT7 .... 80 F8
Lyell Rd CT7 .... 80 F8
Lyford St SE18 .... 1 E2
Lyle Cl ME2 .... 63 B8
Lyle Ct ME16 .... 161 C5
Lyle Pk TN13 .... 154 B4
Lyme Farm Rd SE12 ...... 11 B3
Lyme Rd DA16 .... 13 B6
Lyminge CE Prim Sch
CT18 .... 305 C7
Lyminge Cl
Gillingham ME8 .... 65 C2
Sidcup DA14 .... 30 F4
Lyminge Way CT9 .... 51 C1
Lymington Cl 2 E6 .... 1 F8
Lymington Ct ME15 .... 195 F4
Lymington Rd CT8 .... 81 E7
Lympne Castle*
CT21 .... 331 F2
Lympne CE Prim Sch
CT21 .... 332 A3
Lympne Hill CT21 ...... 332 A2
Lympne Ind Pk CT21 ... 331 E3
Lynacre CT2 .... 142 C1
Lyn Ct CT20 .... 335 A5
Lyndale Est RM20 .... 17 B8
Lyndean Ind Est SE2 ...... 3 C3
Lynden Way BR8 .... 55 D6
Lyndhurst Ave
Gillingham ME8 .... 98 C7
Margate CT9 .... 51 B2
Lyndhurst BR7 .... 30 B2
Lyndhurst Cl Bexley DA7 ... 14 B4
Canterbury CT2 .... 142 E3
Orpington BR6 .... 86 B6
Lyndhurst Dr TN13 ..... 153 E3
Lyndhurst Gr ME10 .... 101 E2
Lyndhurst Rd
Bexley DA7 .... 14 B4
Broadstairs CT10 .... 84 A6
Crabble CT17 .... 277 E2
Dymchurch TN29 .... 366 C8
Maidstone ME15 .... 195 C8
Ramsgate CT11 .... 117 F7
Lyndhurst Way DA13 ..... 59 F8
Lyndon Ave DA15 .... 12 F2
Lyndon Rd DA17 .... 4 A2
Lyndon Way CT18 ..... 305 C7
Lynette Ave ME2 .... 40 A1
Lyngate Ct CT9 .... 51 D2
Lyngs Cl ME18 .... 225 F8
Lynmead Cl TN8 .... 217 B4
Lynmere Rd DA16 .... 13 B5
Lynmouth Dr ME12 .... 47 C7
Lynmouth Rise BR5 ...... 54 B5
Lynne Cl 7 BR6 .... 86 F4
Lynors Ave ME2 .... 40 A1
Lynstead Cl BR1 .... 52 C7
Lynstead Ho ME16 ..... 161 A1
Lynsted Cl
Ashford TN23 .... 299 F6
Bexley DA6 .... 14 B2
Lynsted Gdns SE9 .... 11 D4
Lynsted La ME9 .... 136 B7
Lynsted & Norton Prim Sch
ME9 .... 136 A7
Lynsted Rd
Gillingham ME8 .... 65 B3
Halfway Houses ME12 ..... 46 E7
Lynton Ave BR5 .... 54 B5
Lynton Court Mans
CT9 .... 51 B3
Lynton Dr ME5 .... 97 B3
Lynton Pl CT4 .... 176 A1
Lynton Rd
Gravesend DA11 .... 37 A7
Hythe CT21 .... 333 C1
Lynton Rd S DA11 .... 37 A7
Lynwood
Folkestone CT19 .... 335 C7
Groombridge TN3 ...... 312 C6
Lynwood Gr BR6 .... 53 E1
Lynx Way E16 .... 1 D6
Lyons Cres TN9 .... 222 C2
Lyons The TN9 .... 222 C2
Lyoth Rd BR5 .... 86 C8
Lysander Cl
Broadstairs CT10 .... 83 C3
Littlebourne CT4 .... 176 E4
Lysander Rd ME19 ..... 158 F3
Lysander Way BR6 .... 86 C7
Lysander Wlk CT18 .... 307 A4
Lytchet Rd BR1 .... 29 B1
Lytham Ave CT6 .... 76 D1
Lytham Cl SE28 .... 3 E7
Lytton Strachey Path 8
SE28 .... 3 B6
Lyveden Rd SE3 .... 11 B7

M

Mabbett Ho 2 SE18 .... 12 A8
Mabel Cotts DA3 .... 59 A6
Mabel Rd BR8 .... 33 A2
Mabledon Ave TN24 .... 268 D1
Mabledon Cl TN28 ...... 373 B6
Mabledon Rd TN9 ...... 254 A8
Macallister Ho 8 SE18 ... 12 B8
Macaulay Cl ME20 ...... 128 A4
Macaulay Way 2 SE28 ..... 3 B5
Macbean St SE18 .... 2 B3
Macdonald Ct TN12 .... 257 A6
Macdonald Par CT5 .... 108 A6
Macdonald Rd
Dover CT17 .... 278 A1
Gillingham ME7 .... 64 D6
Mace Ct RM17 .... 18 E8
Mace Farm Cotts
TN14 .... 119 E6
Mace Ind Est TN24 ..... 268 C3
Mace La Ashford TN24 ... 268 C2
Downe TN14 .... 119 D6
Mace Terr TN26 .... 299 A1
Macgregor Rd E16 .... 1 C8
Mackenders Cl ME20 ... 129 A6
Mackenders Gn ME20 .. 129 A6
Mackenders La ME20 ... 129 A6
Mackenzie Dr CT20 .... 334 E5
Mackenzie Way DA12 ..... 37 D2
Mackeson Ct 8 CT21 ... 333 B2
Mackintosh Cl ME23 ...... 23 F3
Macklands Ho ME8 ...... 66 A2
Macklands Way ME8 ..... 66 A2
Macleod Ho SE18 .... 11 E6
Macmillan Gdns 2
DA1 .... 16 A3
Macoma Rd SE18 .... 12 D8
Macoma Terr SE18 .... 12 D8
Madan Cl TN16 .... 151 E2
Madan Rd TN16 .... 151 E2
Mada Rd BR6 .... 86 B7
Madden Ave ME5 .... 96 E5
Madden Cl DA10 .... 17 E1
Maddocks Cl DA14 .... 31 E3
Madeira Ct CT20 .... 335 B3
Madeira Pk TN2 .... 286 B2
Madeira Rd
Littlestone-on-Sea TN28 .. 373 E6
Margate CT9 .... 51 A2
Madeira Wlk CT11 ..... 117 E6
Madginford Cl ME15 ... 163 A2
Madginford Park Inf Sch
ME15 .... 163 A2
Madginford Park Jun Sch
ME15 .... 163 A2
Madginford Rd ME15 .. 162 F2
Madison Cres DA7 .... 13 C7
Madison Gdns DA7 ...... 13 C7
Madison Way TN13 .... 153 F4
Madras Ho 2 ME15 .... 195 E5
Maesmaur Rd TN16 .... 150 D6
Mafeking Rd ME5 .... 96 F3
Magazine Rd TN24 .... 268 B3
Magdala Rd
Broadstairs CT10 .... 83 E6
Dover CT17 .... 278 B1
Magdalen Cl ME7 .... 98 A4
Magdalen Ct
Broadstairs CT10 .... 84 A6
Canterbury CT1 .... 175 B7
Magdelan Gr BR6 .... 87 B6
Magness Rd CT14 ..... 215 A2
Magnet Rd RM20 .... 17 C8
Magnolia Ave
Gillingham ME8 .... 98 B5
Margate CT9 .... 51 D2
Magnolia Cl TN9 .... 254 C7
Magnolia Dr
Biggin Hill TN16 .... 118 E3
Chartham CT4 .... 173 E1
Magnolia Ho 3 ME16 ... 161 A3
Magnolia Rise CT6 ...... 77 D2
Magpie Bottom TN15 ... 122 E6
Magpie Cl ME20 .... 128 A1
Magpie Ct ME12 .... 47 A6
Magpie Gn 3 TN8 ...... 217 D3
Magpie Hall Cl BR2 ...... 52 E3
Magpie Hall La BR2 ...... 52 F3
Magpie Hall Rd
Chatham ME4 .... 64 A2
Stubb's Cross TN26 ..... 299 E2
Magpie La
Rhodes Minnis CT4 ..... 273 B3
Yelsted ME9,ME14 .... 98 F1
Magpie Lodge 4
CT16 .... 278 B2
Magwitch Cl ME1 .... 63 B4
Maida Rd Chatham ME4 ... 64 B4
Erith DA17 .... 4 A3
Maida Vale Rd DA1 ...... 15 A2
Maiden Erlegh Ave
DA5 .... 31 E7
Maiden La
Canterbury CT1 .... 174 D6
Crayford DA1 .... 15 A3
Maidstone Barracks Sta
ME16 .... 161 E5
Maidstone East Sta
ME14 .... 161 F5
Maidstone Gram Sch for
Girls ME16 .... 161 E5
Maidstone Gram Sch
ME15 .... 162 B2
Maidstone Hospl The
ME16 .... 161 A4
Maidstone Ind Ctr
ME14 .... 161 F5
Maidstone L Ctr ME15 .. 162 C2
Maidstone Mus & Bentlif
Art Gallery* ME14 ..... 161 F5
Maidstone Rd
Bredhurst ME7,ME8 ...... 98 B2
Charing TN25,TN26,
TN27 .... 234 D6
Chatham ME4 .... 63 F2
Chatham ME5 .... 96 D4
Colt's Hill TN12,TN2 .... 256 B4
Danaway ME9 .... 100 D4
Five Wents ME17 .... 196 E2
Gillingham ME8 .... 98 C6
Goose Green ME18,
TN11 .... 191 C3
Grays RM17 .... 18 A8
Headcorn TN27 .... 262 B7
Horsmonden,Claygate
TN12 .... 258 C3
Horsmonden TN12 ...... 290 A7
Lenham ME17 .... 199 D5
Matfield TN12 .... 288 C6
Nettlestead Green
ME18 .... 192 C3
Pembury TN2 .... 255 E1
Platt TN15 .... 157 C7
Potters Corner TN25,
TN26 .... 267 D7
Rochester ME1 .... 63 C3
Seal TN15 .... 155 C5
Sevenoaks TN13 .... 153 E5
Sidcup DA14 .... 31 F1
Staplehurst TN12 ...... 260 E7
Swanley DA14,BR8 .... 55 B8
Underling Green TN12 ... 227 F2
Maidstone St Michaels CE
Jun Sch ME16 .... 161 E3
Maidstone West Sta
ME16 .... 161 F3
Mailyns The ME8 .... 98 D7
Maine Cl CT16 .... 278 B3
Main Gate Rd ME4 .... 63 F7
Main Rd
Biggin Hill TN16 .... 118 C5
Chattenden ME3 .... 40 F4
Cooling ME3 .... 22 F4
Crockenhill BR8 .... 55 D3
Crockham Hill TN8 ..... 184 C1
Cudham TN16 .... 151 A7
Farningham DA4 .... 56 F3
Halstead TN14 .... 120 C3
Hoo St Werburgh ME3 ..... 41 C5
Kingsnorth ME3 .... 42 D7
Longfield DA3 .... 58 E7
Marlpit Hill TN8 .... 217 B6
Orpington BR5 .... 54 C7
Queenborough ME11,
ME12 .... 46 B5
Sellindge TN25 .... 303 C1
Sheerness ME12 .... 28 A3
Sidcup DA14,DA15 .... 30 E5
Sundridge TN14 .... 152 E3
Sutton at H DA4 .... 34 B1
Swanley BR8 .... 55 F8
Mainridge Rd BR7 .... 30 A4
Main Road Gorse Hill
DA4 .... 90 D7
Main St Iden TN31 ...... 368 B4
Peasmarsh TN31 .... 367 B2
St Mary's Island ME4 ..... 41 B2
Maison Des Fleurs
ME16 .... 161 C2
Maison Dieu* ME13 .... 138 A6
Maison Dieu Pl 4
CT16 .... 310 D8
Maison Dieu Rd CT16 .. 310 D8
Maitland Ct ME13 ..... 105 B1
Majendie Rd SE18 .... 2 D1
Majestic Par CT20 ..... 335 C4
Major Clark Ho TN17 .. 320 C5
Major Cl CT5 .... 108 B6
Major York's Rd TN4 ... 285 F3
Makenade Ave ME13 ... 138 E6
Malan Cl TN16 .... 118 E2
Malcolm Sargent Rd
TN23 .... 300 B5
Malden Dr ME14 ...... 162 A8
Malham Dr CT9 .... 51 A1
Mallard Apartments 14
ME15 .... 195 E5
Mallard Cl Dartford DA1 ... 15 F2
Herne Bay CT6 .... 76 E2
Mallard Cres ME9 .... 68 D4
Mallard Ct ME12 .... 47 A6
Mallard Path 6 SE28 ...... 2 D3
Mallards TN24 .... 300 D7
Mallards Way ME15 ... 163 A1
Mallard Way
Lower Stoke ME3 .... 25 C4
Marlpit Hill TN8 .... 217 C3
Mallard Wlk
Larkfield ME20 .... 127 F2
Sidcup DA14 .... 31 C2
Malling Ct ME19 .... 159 F7
Mallingdene Cl ME3 ...... 40 B8
Malling Rd
Kings Hill M18,ME19 .... 158 F2
Lunsford ME6,ME20 ..... 127 F5
Snodland ME6 .... 128 A7
Teston ME18 .... 160 A1
Malling Sch The ME19 .. 159 F7
Mallings Dr ME14 ..... 163 C4
Mallings La ME14 ..... 163 C4
Malling Terr ME16 .... 161 C4
Mallory Cl CT12 .... 83 C2
Mallow Cl DA11 .... 36 E4
Mallow Ct RM17 .... 18 D8
Mallows The ME14 .... 161 E7
Mallow Way 1 ME5 ...... 96 F4
Mall The 6 Bexley DA6 .... 14 A3
4 Bromley BR1 .... 52 A6
Faversham ME13 .... 138 C6
Mallys Pl DA4 .... 57 C8
Malmains Rd CT17 .... 310 A6
Malmaynes Hall Rd
ME3 .... 24 D3
Malmedy Ct CT14 ..... 215 A1
Malory Sch BR1 .... 29 A4
Malta Ave ME5 .... 97 A7
Malta Ho 17 CT1 ...... 143 B2
Malta Rd RM18 .... 18 F5
Malta Terr 5 ME14 .... 162 A7
Maltby Cl BR6 .... 54 A1
Malthouse Cl ME17 ... 199 D5
Malthouse Cotts
Boughton Lees TN25 .... 236 F4
New Romney TN28 ..... 373 A6
Malthouse Hill
10 Hythe CT21 .... 333 B2
Maidstone ME15 .... 194 F4
Malthouse La
Hamstreet TN26 .... 327 D1
Peasmarsh TN31 .... 367 D2
Shorne DA12 .... 38 E3
Malt House La TN30 ... 345 A7
Malthouse Rd
Canterbury CT2 .... 142 F2
Stansted TN15 .... 91 F2
Malthouses The
Birchington CT7 .... 80 F7
Brabourne TN25 .... 303 B8
Malthouse The ME16 ... 194 A8
Malthus Path 7 SE28 ..... 3 C5
Maltings Bsns Pk The
TN31 .... 367 C2
Maltings Cl TN11 ..... 223 E8
Maltings Ent Ctr The
DA12 .... 37 F7
Maltings Hall The
CT11 .... 117 D7
Maltings The
7 Canterbury,St Dunstan's
CT2 .... 142 E1
10 Canterbury,St Martin's
CT1 .... 175 A8
Deal CT14 .... 248 B8
Faversham ME13 .... 138 D8
Gillingham ME8 .... 99 A8
3 Gravesend DA11 .... 19 A1
Hadlow TN11 .... 223 E8
Littlebourne CT3 ...... 176 F7
Loose ME17 .... 195 B4
Maidstone, Grove Green
ME14 .... 162 E5
Orpington BR6 .... 53 F1
Peasmarsh TN31 .... 367 C2
Westerham TN16 .... 184 C8
Malt Mews ME1 .... 63 C5
Malton Mews SE18 ...... 12 E8
Malton St SE18 .... 12 E8
Malton Way TN2 ...... 286 F7
Malt Shovel Cotts DA4 .. 89 D7
Malus Cl ME5 .... 97 B1
Malvern Ave DA7 .... 13 E7
Malvern Ho DA11 .... 18 D1
Malvern Mdw CT16 .... 277 E5
Malvern Pk CT6 .... 77 D4
Malvern Rd
Ashford TN24 .... 268 B4
Dover CT17 .... 310 C7
Gillingham ME7 .... 64 E3
Orpington BR6 .... 87 B6
Temple Ewell CT16 ..... 277 E5
Malvina Ave DA12 .... 37 C6
Malyons Rd BR8 .... 32 F1
Mamignot Cl ME14 .... 163 A5
Manchester Cl ME5 ...... 97 C6
Manchester Ct E16 .... 1 B7
Manciple Cl CT2 ...... 174 C8
Mandarin La CT6 .... 76 E2
Mandela Ho SE18 .... 12 D8
Mandela Rd E16 .... 1 A7
Mandeville Cl 1 SE3 ..... 11 A7

Mandeville Ct 1 ME14 162 A5
Mandeville Rd CT2 142 E2
Manford Ind Est DA8 15 B8
Mangers La CT16 278 A2
Mangers Pl CT16 278 A3
Mangold Way 4 DA18 3 E3
Mangravet Ave ME15 195 C7
Manister Rd SE2 3 A3
Manitoba Gdns 6 BR6 86 F4
Manktelow Ct CT10 83 F2
Manley Cl CT16 278 A7
Manley Ho CT16 278 A7
Mannering Cl CT17 277 F3
Manning Ct 3 SE28 3 B5
Manningham Ho ME19 160 A6
Manning Rd BR5 54 D4
Mannock Ho 6 CT1 143 B1
Mannock Rd DA1 15 F4
Manns Hill CT4 241 A6
Mann Sq TN9 254 D7
Manor Ave CT14 215 B4
Manorbrook SE3 11 A3
Manor Cl
Canterbury CT1 174 C5
Chalk DA12 38 B6
Crayford DA1 14 E3
Dartford DA2 33 A5
Deal CT14 215 A4
Erith SE28 3 C7
Herne Bay CT6 77 F6
Maidstone ME14 163 B3
Royal Tunbridge Wells TN4 285 E3
Rushenden ME11 46 A3
Manor Cotts
Hernhill ME13 140 B6
Lamberhurst TN3 317 B5
Langley ME17 196 C5
Manor Ct
Canterbury CT1 174 F7
Gillingham ME7 65 C4
Maidstone ME14 163 B3
Sole Street DA13 60 D4
Manordene Rd SE28 3 D7
Manor Dr
Birchington CT7 80 F6
Hartley DA3 59 A3
Manor Farm Cl CT21 332 A4
Manor Farm Cotts TN15 156 A6
Manorfield
Ashford TN23 299 E8
Elham CT4 273 F4
Manorfields Cl BR7 53 F6
Manor Field DA12 38 E3
Manor Forstal DA3 91 F7
Manor Gdns
Chatham ME5 96 F4
Whitfield CT16 278 A8
Manor Gr
Sittingbourne ME10 101 D3
Tonbridge TN10 222 C3
Manor Ho
14 Chatham ME7 64 A6
Chislehurst BR7 53 D8
Manor Ho The
Canterbury CT2 142 F2
5 Folkestone CT20 335 B3
Limpsfield RH8 183 B7
Sarre CT7 113 D6
Sidcup DA15 31 A7
Sidcup,Old Bexley DA5 32 B7
Manor House Dr
Ashford TN23 300 D3
Maidstone ME16 161 D3
Manor House Gdns TN8 217 C1
Manor La
Fawkham Green DA3 58 C2
Hartley DA3 59 A3
Rochester ME1 62 F3
Manor Lea Rd CT7 79 F1
Manor Leaze TN25 302 F5
Manor Mews CT14 247 F5
Manor Oak Prim Sch BR5 54 D4
Manor Park Ctry Pk* ME19 159 B7
Manor Park Rd BR7 53 D8
Manor Pk
Chislehurst BR7 53 D8
Erith DA8 15 A8
Royal Tunbridge Wells TN4 285 E3
Manor Pl Bromley BR1 52 E8
Chislehurst BR7 53 D7
Manor Pound La TN25 302 F7
Manor Rd
3 Broadstairs CT10 84 A4
Chatham ME4 63 F4
Crayford DA1 14 E3
Deal CT14 215 A4
Dover CT17 310 A6
Edenbridge TN8 217 B1
Erith DA8 15 B8
Folkestone CT20 335 C4
22 Gravesend DA12 19 B1
Grays RM17 18 C8
Herne Bay CT6 77 F6
Knockmill TN15 123 F8
Lydd TN29 376 C6
Milstead ME9 134 F2
New Barn DA3 59 C4
Royal Tunbridge Wells TN4 253 E1
Rushenden ME11 46 A3
Rusthall TN4 285 C4
St Nicholas at Wade CT7 79 F1
Manor Rd *continued*
Sidcup DA15 31 A5
Sidcup,Old Bexley DA5 32 B7
Sole Street DA13 60 D4
Sundridge TN14 152 D3
Swanscombe DA10 35 E8
Tatsfield TN16 150 E7
Tilbury RM18 19 A5
West Thurrock RM20 17 C8
Whitstable CT5 75 A2
Manor Rise
Dover CT17 310 A6
Maidstone ME14 163 B3
Manorside Cl SE2 3 D2
Manor St ME7 64 A6
Manor The TN2 286 E5
Manor Way
Ashford TN23 267 F4
Bexley DA7 14 D4
Bromley BR2 52 E3
Manor Way Bsns Ctr RM13 4 D8
Manor Way Eltham SE3 11 A3
Grays RM17 18 B7
Grays RM17 18 D7
Leysdown-on-S ME12 49 H2
Northfleet DA11 18 A3
Orpington BR5 53 C5
Sidcup DA5 32 A7
Swanscombe DA10 17 E3
Warden ME12 49 D6
Manse Ct DA14 31 C3
Manse Field TN25 302 E5
Mansel Dr ME1 63 A2
Mansell La CT15 275 B4
Manse Par BR8 56 A5
Mansergh Cl SE18 11 E7
Manse Way BR8 56 A5
Mansfield Cl BR5 54 D2
Mansfield Dr ME9 68 D3
Mansfield Rd BR8 32 F2
Mansfield Wlk ME16 161 E2
Mansion Gdns CT16 278 A4
Mansion House Cl TN27 295 A2
Mansion Row ME7 64 A6
Mansions The CT10 83 E4
Mansion St CT9 50 I3
Manston Court Cotts CT12 82 C2
Manston Court Rd CT12,CT9 82 D3
Manston Pk CT12 81 D2
Manston Rd
Acol CT12,CT7 81 D4
Margate CT12,CT9 82 C4
Ramsgate CT11,CT12 117 A8
Mansum Ct CT7 79 F2
Manthorpe Rd SE18 2 C1
Mantles Hill CT14 214 D1
Manton Rd SE2 3 A2
Manwarings The TN12 290 A6
Manwood Almshouse CT2 142 F3
Manwood Ave CT2 142 F3
Manwood Cl ME10 101 F2
Manwood Rd CT13 181 A8
Manwood St E16 1 F5
Maple Ave
Gillingham ME7 64 E6
Maidstone ME16 161 C6
Maple Cl Ashford TN23 267 E3
Broadstairs CT10 51 E1
Larkfield ME20 128 A2
Orpington BR5 53 D4
Rough Common CT2 142 B3
Royal Tunbridge Wells TN2 286 A1
Swanley BR8 55 E7
Maple Cres DA15 13 A1
Maplecroft Cl E6 1 E7
Maple Ct Erith DA8 14 F7
Hersden CT3 144 E8
Newham E6 2 A8
Royal Tunbridge Wells TN4 285 E4
Sidcup DA14 31 B3
Stone DA9 34 E8
Mapledene BR7 30 C3
Maple Dr
Hawkinge CT18 307 C5
St Mary's Bay TN29 365 F4
Maplefields Gdns CT18 307 C5
Maple Gdns CT3 144 E8
Maplehurst Cl DA2 32 E6
Maple Leaf Cl TN16 118 D3
Maple Leaf Dr DA15 30 F7
Maple Rd Dartford DA1 33 C7
Gravesend DA12 37 C4
Grays RM17 18 C8
Hoo St Werburgh ME3 41 E3
Rochester ME2 62 F6
Maplescombe Farm Cotts DA4 90 B5
Maplescombe La DA4 90 B6
Maplesden Cl ME16 160 F3
Maplesden TN12 259 D5
Maplesden Noakes Sch The ME16 161 E6
Maples The
Broadstairs CT10 83 D4
Minster (Sheppey) ME12 47 B6
New Barn DA3 59 B6
Maple St ME12 28 C1
Mapleton Cl BR2 52 A3
Mapleton TN8 218 A7
Mapleton Rd
Four Elms TN8 218 A8
Westerham TN8,TN16 184 E3
Maple Tree Pl SE3 11 E6
Maplin Ho 9 SE2 3 D4
Maplin Rd E16 1 B7
Maplins Cl 5 ME8 65 F1
Mara Ct ME4 63 F1
Maran Way DA18 3 D3
Marathon Paddock ME7 64 D4
Marathon Way SE28 2 F4
Marble Ho 1 SE18 2 F1
Marbrook Ct SE12 29 C5
Marc Brunel Way ME4 64 A7
Marcellina Way BR6 86 F7
Marcet Rd DA1 15 C2
Marconi Ho SE2 3 C1
Marconi Rd DA11 36 D5
Marconi Way ME1 96 D7
Marcroft CT10 84 B7
Marcus Rd DA1 33 A8
Mardale Cl ME8 66 A1
Marden Ave Hayes BR2 52 A3
Ramsgate CT12 117 B8
Marden Cres DA5 14 C2
Marden Prim Sch TN12 259 B5
Marden Rd
Rochester ME2 40 C1
Staplehurst TN12 260 C5
Marden Sta TN12 259 C6
Mardol Rd TN24 268 C5
Marechal Niel Ave DA15 30 D5
Marechal Niel Par DA15 30 D5
Maresfield Cl CT16 278 B2
Margaret Barr Row DA10 35 E8
Margaret Ct CT6 76 F4
Margaret Gardner Dr SE9 29 F6
Margaret Rd DA5 13 D1
Margaret St 10 CT20 335 E5
Margate Caves* CT9 50 J3
Margate Cl ME7 64 E6
Margate Hill CT7 81 C4
Margate Rd
Herne Bay,Broomfield CT6 77 D2
Herne Bay CT6 77 C3
Ramsgate CT10,CT12, CT11 83 B3
Margate Sta CT9 50 H2
Margetts La ME1 95 D1
Margetts Pl ME2 41 A3
Mar Ho 5 SE7 11 C8
Marian Ave ME12 47 A7
Marian Sq TN12 260 F4
Marigold Way ME16 161 A3
Marilyn Cres CT7 81 B7
Marina Cl 1 BR2 52 A6
Marina Ct Deal CT14 215 D8
Hythe CT21 333 C1
Marina Dr Bexley DA16 12 E5
Dartford DA1 34 A7
Minster (Sheppey) ME12 47 A7
Northfleet DA11 18 F1
Marina Espl CT11 117 F7
Marina Rd CT11 117 F7
Marina The CT14 215 D8
Marine Ave TN29 352 F3
Marine Cres
7 Folkestone CT20 335 D4
Whitstable CT5 75 B3
Marine Ct
18 Dover CT16 310 E7
Whitstable CT5 74 F3
Marine Dr
Broadstairs CT10 51 G3
Hoo St Werburgh ME3 41 E3
Margate CT9 50 I2
Woolwich SE18 1 F2
Marine Gap CT5 74 C1
Marine Gdns CT9 50 I2
Marine Ho CT5 74 F3
Marine Hts CT8 50 D1
Marine Parade Mews CT20 335 E4
Marine Par Dover CT16 310 E7
Folkestone CT20 335 E4
Hythe CT21 333 C1
Littlestone-on-Sea TN28 373 E5
Sheerness ME12 28 E2
Whitstable CT5 75 A3
Marine Point CT20 335 A3
Marine Rd CT14 215 D4
Mariners Ct
Swanscombe DA9 17 B3
Whitstable CT5 108 D8
Mariners Lea CT10 83 D4
Mariners Lee CT5 74 E3
Mariners The ME1 63 B4
Mariners View ME7 64 F7
Mariners Way 5 DA11 36 E8
Mariners Wlk DA8 14 F8
Marine Terr
Folkestone CT20 335 E4
Margate CT9 50 H2
Whitstable CT5 74 C1
Marine View ME4 41 B1
Marine Walk St CT21 333 C2
Marion Cl ME5 97 A2
Marion Cotts TN15 157 E8
Marion Cres
Maidstone ME15 195 B8
Orpington BR5 54 B4
Maritime Ave CT6 77 C4
Maritime Cl
Rochester ME2 63 D8
Swanscombe DA9 17 B2
Maritime Est ME2 63 D8
Maritime Gate DA11 36 E8
Maritime Ind Est SE7 1 B2
Maritime Pl CT14 215 D7
Maritime Way ME4 64 A8
Marjan Cl CT17 278 A1
Marjorie McClure Sch BR7 53 C8
Marjory Pease Cotts RH8 183 E5
Mark Ave CT11 117 B5
Mark Cl Bexley DA7 13 E6
Orpington BR2 85 E6
Markers Lodge DA12 37 E8
Market Alley 9 DA11 19 B1
Market Bldgs 4 ME14 161 F4
Market Colonnade 3 ME14 161 F4
Market Hill CT21 333 C2
Market La 12 TN23 268 B2
Market Mdw BR5 54 C5
Market Par
Bromley BR1 52 A8
5 Sidcup DA14 31 B4
Market Pl
Aylesham CT3 210 F5
2 Bexley DA6 14 A3
Charing TN27 234 C7
Dartford DA1 33 E8
1 Faversham ME13 138 D7
20 Folkestone CT20 335 D5
Margate CT9 50 I3
16 Royal Tunbridge Wells TN2 286 A2
1 Tilbury RM18 19 A5
Market Sq Bromley BR1 52 A7
12 Dover CT16,CT17 310 D7
Royal Tunbridge Wells TN1 286 B4
Westerham TN16 151 D1
Market St Dartford DA1 33 E8
Deal CT14 215 D6
Faversham ME13 138 D7
Herne Bay CT6 76 F5
Margate CT9 50 I3
17 Royal Tunbridge Wells TN2 286 A2
Sandwich CT13 149 A1
Staplehurst TN12 260 F5
Woolwich SE18 2 A2
Market View CT3 210 F5
Market Way
Canterbury CT2 143 A2
2 Westerham TN16 151 D1
Mark La DA12 19 E1
Markland Rd CT17 309 F7
Marks Sq DA11 36 F4
Mark St ME4 64 A2
Mark Way BR8 56 A4
Marlborough Cl
Broadstairs CT10 83 E3
Littlestone-on-Sea TN28 373 D6
Orpington BR6 53 F3
Royal Tunbridge Wells TN4 285 E4
Marlborough Cres TN13 153 E3
Marlborough Ct
Folkestone CT20 335 B4
Hythe CT21 333 D1
Westerham TN16 151 C1
Marlborough Ho
4 Gillingham ME8 98 F8
Margate CT9 51 C3
Marlborough House Sch TN18 340 E2
Marlborough La SE7 11 C7
Marlborough Park Ave DA15 31 A7
Marlborough Par ME16 160 F2
Marlborough Rd
Bexley DA7 13 D4
Bromley BR2 52 C5
Dartford DA1 15 C1
Deal CT14 215 A2
Dover CT17 309 F7
Gillingham ME7 64 B5
Margate CT9 50 I1
6 Ramsgate CT11 117 D6
Whitstable CT5 108 D5
Woolwich SE18 2 C3
Marlborough Road Ind Est CT14 215 A3
Marlborough Sch DA15 31 A8
Marlborough Way TN24 268 F7
Marle Place Gdns* TN12 289 C4
Marle Place Rd TN12 289 C4
Marler Ho DA8 14 F5
Marley Rd CT19 334 E6
Marley Ave DA7 13 D8
Marley Ct CT2 142 C4
Marley La Chislet CT3 112 A5
Finglesham CT14 214 A8
Kingston CT4 209 B1
Smarden Bell TN27 263 C3
Marley Rd
Harrietsham ME17 198 F6
Hoo St Werburgh ME3 41 D6
Marley Way ME1 63 C2
Marlfield TN12 260 E4
Marlhurst TN8 217 B4
Marlin Ct 12 DA14 31 A4
Marling Cross DA12 37 E1
Marlings Cl BR7 53 E5
Marlings Park Ave BR7 53 E6
Marling Way DA12 37 E3
Marlow Cl CT5 75 B1
Marlow Copse ME5 96 F1
Marlow Ct TN13 154 B4
Marlowe Arc 11 CT1 174 F8
Marlowe Ave CT1 174 F8
Marlowe Cl BR7 30 D2
Marlowe Ct 13 CT1 174 F8
Marlowe Gdns SE9 12 A1
Marlowe Rd
Ashford TN23 268 B2
Marlowe Rd *continued*
Dover CT16 278 B3
Margate CT9 83 C8
New Hythe ME20 128 A3
Marlowes The DA1 14 D3
Marlow Ho CT7 81 B7
Marlow Mdws CT2 143 F5
Marlpit Cl TN8 217 C4
Marlpit Cotts ME17 195 E2
Marlpit Gdns TN5 338 E1
Marlpit The TN5 336 E5
Marlwood Cl DA15 30 E6
Marmadon Rd SE18 2 F2
Marmion Way TN23 299 C8
Marne Ave DA16 13 A4
Marquis Dr ME7 98 B3
Marrabon Cl DA15 31 A7
Marram Ct RM17 18 E8
Marr Cl ME12 46 F7
Marrians View 1 ME5 64 C2
Marriott Rd DA1 34 A8
Marriotts Wharf 2 DA11 19 B1
Marrose Ave CT12 83 B3
Marrowbone Hill ME12 48 B5
Marsden Way 2 BR6 86 F6
Marshall Cres
Broadstairs CT10 83 E4
Rushenden ME11 45 F3
Marshall Gdns TN11 190 E1
Marshall Path 10 SE28 3 B6
Marshall Rd ME8 98 C8
Marshalls Gr SE18 1 E2
Marshalls Land TN30 324 A3
Marshall St CT19 335 E7
Marsham Cl BR7 30 B3
Marsham Cres ME17 196 B1
Marsham St ME14 162 A4
Marsham Way ME2 95 A5
Marshborough Rd CT13 180 B7
Marshbrook Cl SE3 11 D4
Marsh Cres
High Halstow ME23 23 E4
New Romney TN28 373 B6
Marsh Farm Rd CT12 115 B4
Marsh Green Rd TN8 249 C5
Marsh La Cliffe ME3 22 B6
Deal CT14 215 A7
Marshlands Cl TN29 366 B7
Marshlands TN29 366 B7
Marshland View ME3 25 C5
Marsh La ME9 104 A4
Marsh Quarter La TN18 356 C3
Marsh Rd Halling ME2 95 B5
Ruckinge TN26 349 F6
Marsh Rise ME10 69 A1
Marsh St Dartford DA1 16 A3
Dartford DA1 16 A5
Rochester ME2 63 B7
Marsh View
Gravesend DA12 37 F7
Hythe CT21 353 C8
Marsh Way
New Hythe ME20 128 A4
Rainham RM13 4 D8
Marshwood Cl CT1 143 C3
Marstan Cl ME9 66 E2
Marston Cl ME5 96 E3
Marston Ct DA14 30 F4
Marston Dr ME14 162 C5
Marston Ho RM17 18 A8
Marston Wlk ME5 96 E3
Martello Cotts CT21 353 E8
Martello Dr CT21 332 F1
Martello Ind Ctr CT19 335 F6
Martello Rd
Folkestone CT20 335 E6
Folkestone, Sandgate CT20 334 E3
Martello Terr 1 CT20 334 F3
Martello Tower Mus TN29 366 C7
Martello Tower Visitor Ctr* CT19 335 A6
Martello Twr* TN29 366 C7
Marten Rd CT20 335 B5
Martens Ave DA7 14 C3
Martens Cl DA7 14 C3
Martha Cl CT19 335 B7
Martham Cl SE28 3 D6
Martin Bowes Rd SE9 11 F4
Martin Ct ME7 98 A3
Martindale Ave
Newham E16 1 A6
Orpington BR6 87 A5
Martindale Cl CT1 175 A7
Martin Dale Cres CT15 247 C2
Martin Dene DA6 13 F2
Martindown Rd CT5 108 C7
Martin Dr DA2 16 C1
Martin Hardie Way TN10 222 E5
Martin Ho Dartford DA2 34 C8
Gravesend DA11 37 A5
Martin House DA11 36 F6
Martin Ho TN25 237 E2
Martin Mill Sta CT15 247 C2
Martin Rd Dartford DA2 33 C5
Rochester ME2 63 B8
Martin Rise DA6 13 F2
Martins Cl
Lower Higham ME3 39 D6
Orpington BR5 54 D6
Martin's Cl CT12 83 C2
Martins Cl TN30 345 C8
Martins La TN12 191 E2
Martins Pl SE28 2 E5
Martin Sq ME20 128 A2
Martin's Shaw TN13 153 C5
Martins The TN26 325 A8
Martin St SE28 2 E5
Martin's Way CT21 353 D8
Martins Wlk SE28 2 E5
Martyn Ho SE2 13 D8
Martyrs' Field Rd CT1 174 F7
Marvels Cl SE12 29 B6
Marvels La SE12 29 C5
Marvels Lane Prim Sch SE12 29 C4
Marvillion Ct TN12 224 F6
Marvin Ho 9 SE18 12 B8
Marwell TN16 151 B1
Marwood Cl DA16 13 B4
Marybank SE18 1 F2
Mary Burrows Gdns TN15 123 B2
Mary Ct ME4 64 A2
Mary Day's TN17 318 E7
Maryfield Cl DA5 32 E5
Mary Green Wlk 5 CT1 143 B2
Mary Hougham Almshouses CT14 215 D7
Maryland Ct
Gillingham ME8 98 E5
Hythe CT21 333 D3
Maryland Dr ME16 160 F2
Maryland Gr CT1 175 C6
Maryland Rd TN2 286 D1
Mary Last Cl ME6 127 E7
Mary Lawrenson Pl 2 SE3 11 A7
Mary Macarthur Ho 5 DA17 4 A3
Mary Magdalene Ho 8 TN9 254 B8
Maryon Ct BR5 54 B5
Maryon Gr SE7 1 E2
Maryon Rd SE7,SE18 1 E2
Mary Rd CT14 215 A3
Mary Rose Mall E6 1 F8
Mary Slessor Ho 14 DA17 4 A3
Maryville DA16 12 F5
Mascall's Court La TN12 257 B4
Mascall's Court Rd TN12 257 A4
Mascalls Ct 23 SE7 11 C8
Mascalls Pk TN12 256 F5
Mascalls Rd SE7 11 C8
Mascalls Sec Sch TN12 257 A4
Masefield Cl DA8 14 F6
Masefield Dr ME3 40 B8
Masefield Rd
Dartford DA1 16 B2
Lunsford ME20 127 F4
Northfleet DA11 36 D5
Masefield View BR6 86 C7
Masefield Way TN9 253 F7
Masham Ho 6 DA18 3 D4
Mason Cl Bexley DA7 14 B4
Newham E16 1 A6
Masons Hill
Bromley BR2 52 B5
Woolwich SE18 2 B2
Masons Rd CT17 278 B1
Mason's Rise CT10 84 A5
Mason Way ME2 40 B2
Master Gunner Pl SE18 11 E6
Masters La ME19 127 B5
Masterson Ho DA4 57 D7
Masthead Cl DA2 16 C3
Matchless Dr SE18 12 A7
Matfield Cl BR2 52 A4
Matfield Cres ME14 162 C5
Matfield Rd DA17 14 A8
Matilda Cl ME8 98 B8
Matrix Bsns Ctr DA1 15 E2
Matterdale Gdns ME16 160 E2
Matthews Cl CT14 215 C6
Matthews Ho 13 SE7 11 C8
Matthews La TN11, ME18 190 F4
Matthew's Pl 9 CT16 278 C1
Matthews Rd CT6 76 C2
Mattinson Pl ME9 165 F7
Matts Hill Rd ME9 98 E2
Maud Cashmore Way SE18 1 F3
Maude Rd BR8 33 A2
Maudslay Rd SE9 11 F4
Maugham Ct CT5 108 D8
Maundene Sch ME5 97 B5
Maunders Cl ME5 97 C8
Maunsell Pl TN24 300 D7
Maurice Ct CT9 51 B3
Mavelstone Cl BR1 52 E8
Mavelstone Rd BR1 52 E8
Mavis Wlk 10 E6 1 E8
Maxey Rd SE18 2 C2
Maximfeldt Rd DA8 4 E1
Maximilian Dr ME2 95 B4
Maxim Rd Crayford DA1 14 E2
Erith DA8 4 E2
Maxine Gdns CT10 83 F5
Maxted Ct CT6 77 C4
Maxton Cl Dover CT17 310 A6
Maidstone ME14 162 F5
Maxton Ct CT17 310 A6
Maxton Rd CT17 310 A6
Maxwell Dr ME16 161 B6
Maxwell Gdns BR6 86 F7
Maxwell House BR7 30 B1
Maxwell Ho 12 SE18 12 B8
Maxwell Pl CT14 215 C4
Maxwell Rd Bexley DA16 13 A4
Chatham ME7 64 A6
May Ave DA11 36 F7
May Avenue Est 1 DA11 36 F7

May Ave BR5 54 B4
Maybrook Ind Est
CT1 143 D4
Maybury Ave DA2 34 C7
Maybury Cl BR5 53 B4
Maycotts La TN12 256 D1
May Ct RM17 18 E8
Mayday Gdns SE3 11 E5
Maydowns Rd CT5 75 D2
Mayerne Rd SE9 11 D2
Mayers Rd CT14 215 A1
Mayes Cl BR8 56 A5
Mayeswood Rd SE12 29 C4
Mayfair Ave Bexley DA7 13 D6
Loose ME15 195 A8
Mayfair Rd DA1 15 D2
Mayfair 2 ME2 63 C8
Mayfield Ave
Dover CT16 278 C2
Orpington BR6 53 F2
Mayfield DA7 13 F4
Mayfield Cl
Chatham ME5 97 A1
Gillingham ME8 65 E2
Mayfield Ct
3 Dover CT16 278 B2
Sidcup DA14 31 B3
Mayfield Gdns CT16 278 C2
Mayfield La TN5 336 D4
Mayfield Pk TN5 336 E5
Mayfield Rd
Bromley BR1 52 E4
Erith DA17 4 C2
Herne Bay CT6 77 A3
Lyminge CT18 305 C6
Northfleet DA11 36 F8
Royal Tunbridge Wells
TN4 285 F4
Whitfield CT16 278 A7
Mayfield
Sevenoaks TN13 153 E7
Swanscombe DA10 17 E1
Mayfield Villas DA14 31 C2
Mayflower Ho ME1 63 B4
Mayfly Cl BR5 54 D5
Mayfly Dr CT18 307 A4
Mayford Rd ME5 97 D2
Mayforth Gdns CT11 117 B6
Mayhew Cl TN23 300 A8
Mayhill Rd SE7 11 B8
Maylam Ct TN10 222 C4
Maylam Gdns ME10 101 B4
Maylands Dr DA14 31 D5
May Lodge CT14 215 D5
Maymills Cotts CT13 180 B2
Maynard Ave CT9 82 B8
Maynard Cl DA8 14 F7
Maynard & Cotton's Spital
9 CT1 174 F8
Maynard Ho SE18 2 C2
Maynard Pl ME5 64 D2
Maynard Rd CT1 174 E7
Maynards TN12 259 C5
Mayor's La DA2 33 C3
Mayor's Pl 11 TN30 345 A7
Maypits TN23 299 F8
Mayplace Ave DA1 15 A3
Mayplace Cl DA7 14 B4
Mayplace La
Woolwich SE18 12 B7
Woolwich SE18 12 B8
Mayplace Prim Sch
DA7 14 D3
Mayplace Rd E DA7 14 C4
Mayplace Rd W DA7 14 A3
May Pl DA12 60 D4
Maypole Cotts BR6 88 A4
Maypole Cres DA8 15 D8
Maypole Dr ME18 159 C3
Maypole La
Goudhurst TN17 318 F8
Hoath CT3 111 E6
Maypole Prim Sch DA5 32 E5
Maypole Rd
Chelsfield BR6 87 F4
Gravesend DA12 37 F7
Hoath CT3 111 E6
May Rd Gillingham ME7 64 C4
Hawley DA2 33 F4
Rochester ME1 63 C3
Mays Rd 3 CT11 117 C6
May St Cuxton ME2 62 B2
Herne Bay CT6 77 F4
Mayston Mews 6 SE10 1 A1
Maystreet Cross CT6 77 F3
May St ME6 128 B8
May Terr 2 ME7 64 A7
Maytham Bglws TN17 344 A1
Maytham Rd TN17 358 C7
Mayton La CT2 110 C1
Maytree Cotts CT14 247 D8
Mayview DA1 33 E7
Mayville Rd CT10 83 E6
Mayweed Ave ME5 96 E4
May Wynne Ho E16 1 B7
McAlpine Cres ME15 194 F3
McAuley Cl SE9 12 A2
McCabe Cl TN12 260 E2
McCall Cres SE7 1 E1
McCarthy Ave CT2 143 F7
McClean Wlk ME12 71 C8
McCudden Rd DA1 15 F4
McCudden Row 8
ME7 64 A6
McDermott Rd TN15 156 F7
McDowall Cl 11 E16 1 A8
McIntyre Ct 6 SE18 1 E2
McKenzie Cl ME20 160 F8
McKenzie Rd ME5 97 A3
McKillop Way DA14 31 C1
McKinlay Ct
Bexley DA16 13 C4
Birchington CT7 80 D8
McLeod Rd SE2 3 B2
McMichaels Way
TN19 354 A3
McMillan Cl DA12 37 C4
Mead Cl BR8 56 A4
Mead Cres DA1 33 D7
Meades Cl TN12 259 B6
Meade The CT18 306 F4
Meadfield Rd DA13 93 A8
Mead Gn ME5 97 C3
Mead Ho TN16 118 D3
Meadow Bank Cl TN15 90 F2
Meadowbank Ct
ME19 159 C8
Meadow Bank TN11 220 F1
Meadow Bank Mews
ME19 159 C8
Meadow Bank ME13 137 F2
Meadowbank Rd ME4 64 A4
Meadow Bank ME19 159 C8
Meadowbrook Cl
TN24 268 D6
Meadow Brook Ct
CT20 334 E4
Meadowbrook CT20 334 E4
Meadowbrook Rd
TN24 268 D6
Meadow Cl Bexley DA6 13 F2
Bridge CT4 176 A1
Chatham ME5 96 F5
Chilham CT4 205 E8
Chislehurst BR7 30 B3
Hawkinge CT18 307 B4
Herne Bay CT6 77 C4
Iwade ME9 68 D4
Sevenoaks TN13 154 A4
Upper Halling ME2 94 E4
Meadow Cotts
East Studdal CT15 246 D8
Goodnestone CT3 179 A2
Meadow Cres ME2 94 E4
Meadow Croft BR1 52 F6
Meadow Ct Margate CT9 83 B8
Westenhanger CT21 332 B6
Meadowdown Cl ME7 98 A4
Meadowdown ME14 162 E4
Meadow Dr CT5 109 D8
Meadowford Cl SE28 3 A6
Meadow Gr TN25 331 D8
Meadow Hill Cotts
CT15 276 D1
Meadow Hill Rd 6
TN1 286 B3
Meadow Ho ME9 101 B2
Meadow La
Culverstone Green DA13 93 A1
Lewisham SE12 29 B5
Marlpit Hill TN8 217 B4
Meadowlands
Oxted RH8 183 A1
Seal TN15 154 F7
Meadow Rd
Ashford TN23 268 A4
Canterbury CT2 142 C2
Gravesend DA11 37 A6
Groombridge TN3 312 C7
Margate CT9 50 F1
Northfleet DA11 36 C7
Royal Tunbridge
Wells,Southborough
TN4 253 F1
Royal Tunbridge Wells
TN1 286 A4
Rusthall TN4 285 C4
Sturry CT2 143 F6
Tonbridge TN9 254 B8
Meadow Rise ME9 68 D4
Meadows Ct DA14 31 B2
Meadows TN17 321 D1
Meadowside Cotts
TN5 338 F1
Meadowside
Dartford DA1 33 E7
Eltham SE3,SE9 11 C3
Meadows Sch TN4 253 F2
Meadows The
Biddenden TN27 294 F2
Halstead TN14 120 F6
Herne Bay CT6 77 D2
3 Maidstone ME15 161 E2
New Romney TN28 373 C6
Orpington BR6 87 C4
Sittingbourne ME10 101 F2
Wittersham TN30 359 D4
Meadowsweet Cl 3 E16 1 D8
Meadowsweet Ho
TN23 267 F1
Meadowsweet View
ME4 41 B2
Meadow The
Chislehurst BR7 30 C2
Pembury TN2 287 E8
Meadow View Cotts
Hurst Green TN19 354 A3
Laddingford ME18 225 E5
Meadow View
Flimwell TN5 339 A3
Hothfield TN26 267 A6
Meadow View Ind Est
TN26 349 C7
Meadow View CT12 114 D6
Meadowview BR5 54 C6
Meadow View Rd
Maidstone ME17 195 B3
Shepherdswell CT15 244 E5
Meadowview Rd DA5 13 F1
Meadow View DA15 31 B8
Meadow Way
Dartford DA2 34 C8
Eythorne CT15 245 C8
Hythe CT21 353 D8
Marden TN12 259 E6
Orpington BR6 86 A7
Meadow Way *continued*
Wouldham ME1 95 C5
Meadow Wlk
Dartford DA2 33 C4
Maidstone ME15 162 B3
Snodland ME6 127 F7
Whitstable CT5 108 C6
Mead Rd Ashford TN24 300 E7
Chislehurst BR7 30 C2
Dartford DA1 33 D7
Edenbridge TN8 249 D7
Folkestone CT19 335 D6
Gravesend DA11 37 B6
Mead Road Inf Sch
BR7 30 C2
Meads Ave The ME10 101 D7
Mead Sch The TN2 286 A1
Meadside Wlk ME5 96 F6
Meads The
Hartley TN17 319 F1
Royal Tunbridge Wells
TN2 286 C2
Meads Way TN29 365 E3
Mead The
Leybourne ME19 127 E2
New Ash Green DA3 91 E8
Mead Wall ME3 5 F2
Mead Way CT2 142 E1
Meadway TN14 120 F6
Mead Way BR2 52 A3
Meadway CT17 277 E3
Meadway The
Orpington BR6 87 B4
Sevenoaks TN13 153 F5
Meadway TN11 221 E5
Mead Wlk TN23 299 E8
Meath Cl BR5 54 B4
Medbury Rd DA12 37 F7
Medebourne Cl SE3 11 A4
Mede Ho BR1 29 B3
Medhurst Cres DA12 37 F6
Medhurst Gdns DA12 37 F5
Medick Ct RM17 18 E8
Medina Ave CT5 108 B7
Medina Ho 6 DA8 14 E7
Medina Rd
Ditton ME20 128 C1
Tonbridge TN10 222 C6
Medlar Cl ME9 134 A6
Medlar Gr ME7 98 A4
Medlar Ho 3 DA15 31 A5
Medlar Rd RM17 18 E8
Medlars The
Maidstone ME14 162 D6
Meopham Station DA13 60 A3
Medway Ave
High Halstow ME23 23 E4
Yalding ME18 192 F1
Medway City Est ME2 63 D7
Medway Cl ME10 101 D4
Medway Com Coll ME4 64 A1
Medway Cotts
Iden Green TN17 342 D3
Marden TN12 259 C6
Medway Ct
Aylesford ME20 128 F2
20 Orpington BR5 54 D1
Medway Ent Ctr ME2 63 D8
Medway Gdns ME4 63 F7
Medway Heights 5
ME4 63 E4
Medway Heritage Ctr*
ME4 63 F5
Medway Ho 7 ME14 161 F4
Medway Maritime Hospl
ME7 64 B4
Medway Mdws TN12 225 A6
Medway Rd
Crayford DA1 15 A4
Gillingham ME7 64 C7
Royal Tunbridge Wells
TN1 286 B5
Sheerness ME12 28 B1
Medway St
Chatham ME4 63 F5
Maidstone ME14 161 F4
Medway Trad Est
ME16 161 F3
Medway View
Barnes Street TN11 224 A5
Middle Stoke ME3 25 C3
Medway Villas ME15 194 B7
Medway Wharf Rd
TN9 222 C1
Meehan Rd TN28 373 E4
Meehan Rd S TN28 373 E3
Meerbrook Rd SE3 11 C4
Meeres Court La
ME10 102 C5
Meeson's Cl ME13 168 E6
Meeson's La RM17 17 F8
Meeting Ct CT9 50 I3
Meeting House La 2
ME4 63 F4
Meeting St CT11 117 E7
Megan Cl TN29 376 D7
Megby Cl ME8 98 D6
Meggett La CT15 308 C7
Megone Cl CT18 307 A4
Megrims Hill TN18 356 A6
Meirs Court Rd ME8 98 E6
Melanda Cl BR7 29 F3
Melanie Cl DA7 13 E6
Melba Gdns RM18 19 A7
Melbourne Ave
Dover CT16 278 C4
Ramsgate CT12 83 B1
Melbourne Cl BR6 53 E2
Melbourne Com Prim Sch
CT16 278 C4
Melbourne Ct RM18 18 E6
Melbourne Quay 4
DA11 19 B1
Melbourne Rd
Chatham ME4 64 A3
Tilbury RM18 18 E6
Melbury Cl BR7 29 F2
Melbury Grange BR1 52 E8
Melbury Mews TN28 373 C8
Meldrum Cl
Orpington BR5 54 C3
Oxted RH8 183 A3
Melford Dr ME16 161 C4
Mellanby Cl CT7 81 A6
Melliker La DA13 60 A3
Melling St SE18 12 E8
Mellish Ind Est SE18 1 D3
Mellor Row ME10 68 F1
Mells Cres SE9 29 F4
Melody Cl
Gillingham ME8 98 C4
Warden ME12 49 E4
Melody Rd TN16 118 C1
Melon La TN26,TN29 364 B6
Melrose Ave
Dartford DA1 32 E8
Kings Hill ME19 159 C3
Melrose Cl
Lewisham SE12 29 B7
Loose ME15 195 A7
Melrose Cres BR6 86 D5
Melrose Rd TN16 118 C3
Melsetter Cl CT7 81 B7
Melthorpe Gdns SE3 11 E6
Melville Ct ME4 63 F6
Melville Lea CT13 180 C7
Melville Rd
Maidstone ME15 162 A3
Sidcup DA14 31 C6
Memess Path 4 SE18 12 A8
Memorial (General) Hospl
ME10 101 F3
Memorial Hospl SE18 12 A5
Mendfield St 5 ME13 138 C7
Mendip Ho DA11 18 D1
Mendip Rd DA7 14 E6
Mendip Rise TN24 268 B4
Mendip Wlk TN2 286 D5
Menin Rd ME10 68 F1
Mennie Ho SE18 11 F6
Mentmore Ho CT12 83 C3
Mentmore Rd CT12 83 C3
Menzies Ave CT14 215 B1
Menzies Ct ME12 47 A5
Menzies Rd CT16 278 A5
Meon Ct 21 BR5 54 D1
Meopham Com Prim Sch
Meopham DA13 93 A8
Meopham Station DA13 60 A2
Meopham Sta DA13 60 A4
Mera Dr DA7 14 A3
Merbury Rd SE28 2 E4
Mercer Cl ME20 128 B4
Mercer Dr ME17 198 F6
Mercers Cl TN12 256 E6
Mercers
Hawkhurst TN18 341 A1
Langton Green TN3 285 A3
Mercers Pl ME19 159 A2
Mercer St TN1 286 B5
Mercer Way ME17 196 B1
Mercery La 5 CT1 174 F8
Merchant Pl TN12 259 C5
Merchant Store The 7
CT2 142 F1
Merchants Way CT2 174 C8
Merchland Rd SE9 30 C7
Mercury Cl ME1 63 A3
Mere Cl BR6 86 B8
Meredale Sch ME8 66 A1
Meredith Cl ME17 196 F7
Mere Gate CT9 50 I1
Meresborough Cotts
ME8 98 F5
Meresborough La ME8,
ME9 99 B5
Meresborough Rd ME8 99 A7
Mereside BR6 86 A8
Merevale Ho 3 TN1 286 A3
Merewood Cl 1 BR1 53 A7
Merewood Rd DA7 14 C5
Mereworth Cl ME8 65 A3
Mereworth Com Prim Sch
ME18 191 D8
Mereworth Dr SE18 12 C7
Mereworth Ho ME2 40 C1
Mereworth Rd
Royal Tunbridge Wells
TN4 286 A6
West Peckham ME18 191 C7
Merganser Gdns SE28 2 D3
Meriden Cl BR1 29 D1
Meriden Wlk CT18 305 D3
Meridian Ct
Ashford TN23 299 E7
Maidstone ME16 161 E4
Meridian Pk ME2 63 E6
Meridian Rd SE7 11 D7
Meridian Trad Est SE7 1 B2
Meriel Wk DA9 17 B3
Merifield Rd SE9 11 C3
Merileys Cl DA3 59 C6
Merino Pl DA15 13 A2
Merino Way TN23 299 E5
Merivale Gr ME5 97 B4
Merleburgh Dr ME10 101 F8
Merle Common Rd
RH8 216 B7
Merlewood Dr BR7 52 F8
Merlewood TN13 154 B4
Merlin Ave ME20 127 F2
Merlin Cl
Sittingbourne ME10 102 A3
Tonbridge TN10 222 E4
Merlin Gdns BR1 29 A5
Merlin Ho Chatham ME4 64 B8
Merlin Ho *continued*
2 Sittingbourne ME10 102 A4
Merlin Prim Sch BR1 29 A5
Merlin Rd DA16 13 A3
Merlin Rd N DA16 13 A3
Mermaid Cl
Chatham ME5 97 A6
Northfleet DA11 36 D8
Mermerus Gdns DA12 37 F4
Merrals Wood Rd ME2 62 D5
Merrilees Rd DA15 30 E8
Merriman Ho ME3 40 F6
Merriman Rd SE3 11 C6
Merriments Gdns*
TN19 354 B5
Merriments La
Hurst Green TN18,
TN19 354 D5
Hurst Green TN19 354 B5
Merrion Cl TN4 286 B7
Merrion Way TN4 286 B7
Merritt Rd TN28 373 E2
Merrivale Hts CT10 84 A2
Merry Boys Rd ME3 40 B8
Merrydown Way BR7 52 F8
Merryfield Ct 9 TN9 254 B8
Merryfield SE3 11 A5
Merryfield Ho 4 SE9 29 C5
Merryfields Cl DA3 58 F5
Merryfields ME2 40 A1
Merryhills Cl TN16 118 D3
Merryweather Cl DA1 15 F1
Merrywood Gr CT6 77 D2
Mersey Rd TN10 222 B5
Mersham Prim Sch
TN25 301 E3
Merston Ct ME3 39 C4
Merton Ave DA3 58 F5
Merton Cl ME5 97 C5
Merton Court Sch
DA14 31 C4
Merton Ct DA16 13 B5
Merton Gdns BR5 53 B4
Merton La CT4 174 F4
Merton Rd ME15 162 F2
Mervyn Ave SE9 30 C6
Mervyn Stockwood House
SE9 30 C6
Meryl Gdns CT14 215 C1
Mesne Way TN14 121 F7
Messent Rd SE9 11 D2
Messeter Pl SE9 12 A1
Metcalfe Mews 1
CT1 143 B2
Meteor Ave CT5 108 B7
Meteor Cl ME10 101 E8
Meteor Rd ME19 158 F3
Methuen Rd Bexley DA6 13 F3
Erith DA17 4 B2
Metro Ctr The BR5 54 B3
Metropole Ct 2 CT20 335 B3
Metropole Rd E CT20 335 B3
Metropole Rd W CT20 335 B3
Metropole The 3
CT20 335 B3
Meverall Ave CT12 116 E5
Mewsend TN16 118 D1
Mews The
Headcorn TN27 262 C5
Longfield DA3 58 E6
1 Maidstone ME16 161 E5
Pembury TN2 287 C6
Rochester ME2 62 F7
5 Royal Tunbridge Wells
TN1 286 B3
Sevenoaks TN13 154 A3
7 Sidcup DA14 31 A4
Sittingbourne ME10 101 F2
Meyer Rd DA8 14 D8
Meyrick Rd ME12 28 C2
Micawber Cl ME5 97 A1
Michael Ave CT11 117 G8
Michael Gdns DA12 37 E3
Michael Marshall House
SE9 30 C6
Michaels La DA3,TN15 91 C8
Michele Cotts ME3 39 C6
Michele Gdns CT9 82 A8
Micketts Gdns ME10 101 B4
Mickleburgh Ave CT6 77 B4
Mickleburgh Hill CT6 77 B4
Mickleham Cl BR5 54 A7
Mickleham Rd BR5 54 A7
Mid Comp Cotts TN15 157 E6
Middelburg Ho CT19 334 D6
Middelburg Sq CT20 335 D4
Middle Cl TN23 267 C1
Middle Deal Rd CT14 215 B5
Middle Field TN2 287 E8
Middlefields ME8 99 A8
Middle Garth TN17 320 D4
Middleham Ct 26 DA2 16 B1
Middle La TN15 154 F6
Middle Mead CT19 335 B7
Middle Mill Rd ME19 159 F7
Middle Park Ave SE9 29 E8
Middle Park Prim Sch
SE9 29 D8
Middle Rd TN3 315 A5
Middle Row
Ashford TN23 268 C2
2 Faversham ME13 138 D7
6 Maidstone ME14 161 F4
Middlesex Rd ME15 195 D7
Middle St
Ashford TN23 268 B2
4 Chatham ME7 64 A6
Deal CT14 215 D6
Middleton Ave DA14 31 C3
Middleton Cl ME8 98 E4
Middleton Cotts TN25 236 E3
Middleton Ct
13 Bromley BR1 29 B1
Middleton Ct *continued*
9 Sittingbourne ME10 101 E4
Middletune Ave ME10 101 E7
Middle Wall CT5 74 D2
Middle Way ME10 102 B3
Middle Wlk TN2 286 E8
Middlings Rise TN13 153 F1
Middlings The TN13 153 F2
Middlings Wood
TN13 154 A2
Midfield Ave
Bexley DA7 14 C4
Hextable BR8 33 B2
Midfield Prim Sch BR5 31 A1
Midfield Way BR5 54 B8
Midhurst Ct ME15 162 A3
Midhurst Hill DA6 14 A2
Mid Kent Bsns Pk
ME6 128 B7
Mid Kent Coll (City Way
Ctr) ME1 63 D4
Mid Kent Coll of H & F Ed
ME16 161 C3
Mid Kent Coll of Higher & F
Ed ME5 96 E6
Mid Kent Sh Ctr The
ME16 161 C7
Midley Cl ME16 161 C7
Midsummer Ct SE12 11 A3
Midsummer Hill TN24 268 D6
Midsummer Rd ME6 127 E8
Midway The TN4 285 D2
Midwinter Cl 3 DA16 13 A4
Mierscourt Cl ME8 99 A8
Miers Court Prim Sch
ME8 98 F7
Mierscourt Rd ME8 99 E6
Mike Spring Ct DA12 37 D4
Mikyle Ct CT1 175 A6
Milbourne Gr ME10 101 E7
Milburn Rd ME7 64 C7
Mildmay Pl TN14 121 F8
Mildred Cl DA1 16 A1
Mildred Cotts CT19 334 F7
Mildred Rd DA8 4 E1
Milebush La TN12 227 E1
Mile End Green Cotts
DA3 58 D7
Mile La TN17 319 B8
Mile Oak Rd TN12 257 C3
Mile Rd CT12 113 F6
Miles Ct CT3 178 A8
Miles Dr SE28 2 E5
Miles Pl ME1 63 D3
Milestone Bldgs TN12 260 F3
Milestone Cl CT19 335 A7
Mile Stone Rd DA2 16 B1
Milestone Rd CT14 215 B5
Miles Way CT7 80 F7
Milford Cl Bexley SE2 13 E8
Maidstone ME16 161 D5
Military Rd
Canterbury CT1 143 A1
Chatham ME4 63 F5
2 Dover CT17 310 D7
Folkestone CT20 334 E4
Houghton Green TN31 368 E3
Hythe CT21 333 B2
Ramsgate CT11 117 E6
Stone in Oxney TN26,
TN30 361 B4
Milk House Cotts
TN17 321 A8
Milking La
Biggin Hill,Downe BR6 118 E7
Biggin Hill,Leaves Green
BR2 118 D8
Milk St Bromley BR1 29 B2
Newham E16 2 B5
Millais Pl RM18 19 A7
Millais Rd CT16 278 C1
Millars Mdw SE12 11 A3
Mill Bank Cotts CT13 180 A2
Mill Bank TN27 262 C6
Millbank La TN29 371 E7
Mill Bank TN29 376 B6
Millbank Rd TN23 299 F5
Mill Bank TN9 222 C2
Millbank Way SE12 11 A2
Mill Bay CT20 335 E5
Millbrook Ave DA16 12 D3
Millbrook Cl ME15 161 F1
Millbrook Hythe CT21 333 D2
Leybourne ME19 127 D1
Millbrook Mdw TN23 267 E1
Mill Brook Rd BR5 54 C5
Millbro BR8 56 A8
Mill Cl Crabble CT17 277 F2
Lenham ME17 199 C4
Rochester ME2 40 B1
Sandwich CT13 148 E2
Wickhambreaux CT3 145 C2
Mill Cotts
Queenborough ME11 46 A5
Ramsgate CT11 117 D6
West Farleigh ME15 193 B6
Worth CT14 181 A4
Mill Court Cl CT6 77 B2
Mill Cres TN9 222 C2
Millcroft Rd ME3 22 B4
Mill Ct Ashford TN24 268 D2
Sittingbourne ME10 102 A3
Sutton at H DA4 57 C7
14 Woolwich SE28 3 B6
Milldale Cl CT14 215 B4
Millen Ct DA4 57 C5
Millenium Terr CT1 174 C6
Millenium Cl E16 1 B7
Millennium Way
Broadstairs CT10 83 C4

Millennium Way *continued*
Sheerness ME12 .... 28 B2
Millen Rd ME10 .... 101 E5
Millen's Row ME13 .... 170 B3
Miller Ave CT2 .... 174 D8
Miller Cl Ashford TN24 .... 268 D2
Bromley BR1 .... 29 B3
Deal CT14 .... 215 C8
Sittingbourne ME10 .... 102 A8
Miller Cotts TN24 .... 268 D2
Miller Ct Bexley DA7 .... 14 B4
Minster (Sheppey) ME12 .... 47 A5
Miller Rd DA12 .... 38 A6
Millers Cotts TN11 .... 255 C6
Millers Ct
Ramsgate CT12 .... 83 B1
Whitstable CT5 .... 108 D7
Millers La CT12 .... 114 C7
Millersthumb TN17 .... 292 C4
Millers Wharf 1
ME15 .... 161 E2
Millers Wlk DA13 .... 93 A7
Millers Yd CT1 .... 174 E7
Miller Way ME2 .... 40 D2
Mill Field CT3 .... 147 E1
Millfield TN23 .... 299 D8
Mill Field CT10 .... 83 F5
Millfield Cl CT18 .... 307 B5
Millfield Dr DA11 .... 36 E6
Millfield
Folkestone CT20 .... 335 D5
Hawkinge CT18 .... 307 C5
High Halden TN26 .... 324 D7
Millfield La DA3 .... 91 E8
Millfield Manor CT5 .... 74 E1
Millfield DA3 .... 91 E8
Millfield Rd
Faversham ME13 .... 138 E7
Ramsgate CT12 .... 83 B3
West Kingsdown TN15 .... 90 D4
Millfield CT15 .... 279 F7
Millfields ME5 .... 97 D2
Millfields Cl BR5 .... 54 B5
Millfields Cotts BR5 .... 54 B5
Millfield ME10 .... 102 A3
Mill Fields Rd CT21 .... 332 F2
Millfields CT15 .... 244 E4
Millfordhope Rd ME2 .... 62 C7
Mill Gn CT13 .... 180 A2
Millhall ME20 .... 128 E2
Mill Hall Bsns Est The
ME20 .... 128 D2
Mill Hall Rd ME20 .... 128 C3
Mill Hamlet CT3 .... 145 C2
Mill Hill Deal CT14 .... 215 A3
Edenbridge TN8 .... 249 D7
Mill Hill La DA12 .... 38 D3
Mill Ho CT17 .... 277 F3
Mill House Cl DA4 .... 56 E1
Millhouse La ME19 .... 126 D3
Mill La Ashford TN24 .... 269 A1
Benover ME18 .... 226 A7
Birchington CT7 .... 80 F6
Bonnington TN25 .... 329 E5
Bridge CT4 .... 175 F1
Canterbury CT1 .... 142 F1
Canterbury,Harbledown
CT2 .... 174 C8
Chatham,Bluebell Hill
ME5 .... 96 D1
Chatham,Luton ME5 .... 64 C1
Chilham CT4 .... 205 D7
Coxheath ME17 .... 194 D4
10 Dover CT16 .... 310 E7
Eastry CT13 .... 180 B2
Eynsford DA4 .... 56 E1
Farthing Street BR6 .... 86 B1
Frittenden TN17 .... 293 D8
Hartlip ME9 .... 99 E6
Hawkinge CT18 .... 307 B5
Herne Bay CT6 .... 77 B2
Hildenborough TN11,
TN15 .... 188 C2
Horsmonden TN12 .... 258 B1
Ightham TN15 .... 156 E5
Lydd TN29 .... 376 D7
Lynsted ME9 .... 136 C5
Maidstone ME14 .... 161 F6
Margate CT9 .... 50 I2
Mill Lane Cotts CT14 .... 214 A4
Mill La Newchurch TN29 .... 350 F3
Nonington CT15 .... 211 F4
Northbourne CT14 .... 213 F4
Oxted RH8 .... 183 A1
Preston CT3 .... 146 D6
Sevenoaks TN14 .... 154 D6
Shepherdswell CT15 .... 244 F5
Shoreham TN14 .... 88 F1
Sissinghurst TN17 .... 320 F8
Smarden TN27 .... 264 A2
Snodland ME6 .... 128 B8
Stelling Minnis CT4 .... 240 F2
Tenterden TN30 .... 324 B1
The Chart RH8 .... 183 F4
Tonbridge TN9 .... 222 C2
Wateringbury ME18 .... 192 D7
Westerham TN16 .... 184 C8
West Thurrock RM20 .... 17 D8
Whitfield CT16 .... 278 A8
Woolwich SE18 .... 2 A1
Worth CT14 .... 181 A4
Millman Ct SE3 .... 11 B7
Millmead Ave CT9 .... 51 D1
Millmead Gdns CT9 .... 51 D1
Millmead Rd CT9 .... 51 C1
Mill Mews CT14 .... 215 B4
Mill Pl Chislehurst BR7 .... 53 B8
Crayford DA1 .... 15 A3
Faversham ME13 .... 138 D8
Millpond Cl ME2 .... 63 B8
Mill Pond Cl TN14 .... 154 D6
Millpond La TN30 .... 323 D2
Mill Pond Rd DA1 .... 15 E1
Mill Race CT17 .... 277 F3
Mill Rd
Bethersden TN26 .... 297 E5
Bramling CT3 .... 177 E6
Deal CT14 .... 215 C4
Dymchurch TN29 .... 366 B7
Erith DA8 .... 14 C7
Gillingham ME7 .... 64 C6
Hawley DA2 .... 33 F4
Hoath CT3 .... 111 F5
Hythe CT21 .... 333 D2
Lydd TN29 .... 376 D7
Newham E16 .... 1 B5
Northfleet DA11 .... 36 E8
Rochester ME2 .... 63 B8
Sevenoaks TN13 .... 153 E6
Staple CT3 .... 179 B5
Sturry CT2 .... 143 F5
Mill Row Birchington CT7 .... 80 F6
Sidcup DA5 .... 32 B8
Mills Cl ME12 .... 46 F6
Mills Cres TN15 .... 154 F8
Millside Ind Est DA1 .... 15 D3
Mills Rd ME20 .... 160 E7
Mill St ME19 .... 159 F7
Mills Terr ME4 .... 64 A3
Mill St
Iden Green TN17,TN18 .... 342 C3
Maidstone,Loose ME15 .... 194 F5
Maidstone ME15 .... 161 F4
Millstock Terr 2
ME15 .... 161 E2
Mill Stone Cl DA4 .... 57 C7
Millstone Mews DA4 .... 57 C8
Millstream Cl
Ashurst TN3 .... 283 D2
Faversham ME13 .... 138 C7
Whitstable CT5 .... 74 E1
Millstream Cotts CT5 .... 108 E8
Millstream Gn TN24 .... 300 F7
Mill Stream Jun Sch
ME19 .... 159 F7
Mill Stream Pl TN9 .... 222 D3
Millstrood Rd CT5 .... 108 E8
Mill St
Sittingbourne ME10 .... 101 E5
Snodland ME6 .... 128 B8
Temple Ewell CT16 .... 277 D5
Westerham TN16 .... 184 D8
Mill Terr Bridge CT4 .... 175 F1
Chartham CT4 .... 173 D3
Mill Vale BR2 .... 52 A7
Mill View Ashford TN24 .... 300 F8
Hadlow TN11 .... 190 D1
Mill View Rd CT6 .... 77 A1
Mill View TN26 .... 326 A3
Mill Wall Pl CT13 .... 181 A8
Mill Way ME10 .... 101 F6
Mill Wlk ME16 .... 161 A3
Millwood Ct 4 ME4 .... 63 F4
Millwood Ho 1 SE28 .... 2 D3
Millwood Rd BR5 .... 54 C6
Millyard Way CT15 .... 212 D1
Milne Gdns SE9 .... 11 E2
Milne Ho 11 SE18 .... 1 F2
Milner Cl CT15 .... 212 B1
Milner Cres CT3 .... 210 E5
Milne Rd TN24 .... 300 F8
Milner La CT2 .... 143 F5
Milner Rd
Elvington CT15 .... 212 B1
Gillingham ME7 .... 64 D7
Whitstable CT5 .... 108 A6
Milners ME17 .... 196 F6
Milner Wlk SE9 .... 30 D7
Milroy Ave DA11 .... 36 E6
Milstead Cl
Maidstone ME14 .... 162 C5
West Minst ME12 .... 46 B7
Milstead & Frinstead CE
Prim Sch ME9 .... 134 E1
Milsted Rd ME8 .... 65 C3
Milton Ave
Badgers Mount TN14 .... 88 B1
Cliffe Woods ME3 .... 40 B8
Gravesend DA12 .... 37 C7
Margate CT9 .... 50 J1
Milton Cl
Canterbury CT1 .... 175 C6
Dover CT16 .... 278 B4
Milton Court Prim Sch
ME10 .... 101 E6
Milton Ct
Gravesend DA12 .... 37 C6
Kings Hill ME18 .... 159 A3
Milton Dr TN2 .... 286 D7
Milton Gdns
Tilbury RM18 .... 19 B6
Tonbridge TN9 .... 253 F7
Milton Hall Rd DA12 .... 37 D7
Milton Ho DA1 .... 14 E2
Milton La ME18 .... 159 B3
Milton Lodge 9 DA14 .... 31 A4
Milton Pl DA12 .... 19 C1
Milton Rd
Ashford TN23 .... 268 B2
Bexley DA16 .... 12 F6
Milton Rd Bsns Pk 4
DA12 .... 37 C8
Milton Rd
Canterbury CT1 .... 175 A6
Dover CT16 .... 278 B4
Erith DA17 .... 4 A2
Gillingham ME7 .... 64 C3
Gravesend DA12 .... 37 C8
Sevenoaks TN13 .... 153 E6
Sittingbourne ME10 .... 101 E4
Swanscombe DA10 .... 17 E1
Milton Regis Halt
ME10 .... 102 A6
Milton Sq 4 CT9 .... 50 J1
Milton St
Maidstone ME16 .... 161 C2
Swanscombe DA10 .... 17 D1
Milverton Way SE9 .... 30 A4
Milward Wlk 14 SE18 .... 12 A8
Mimosa Cl BR6 .... 87 C8
Mincers Cl ME5 .... 97 C2
Mineral St SE18 .... 2 E2
Miners Way CT3 .... 211 A5
Minerva Ave CT16 .... 278 C2
Minerva Cl DA14 .... 30 E4
Minerva Ho 4 CT11 .... 117 D7
Minerva Rd ME2 .... 63 A8
Ministry Way SE9 .... 29 F6
Minnis Field CT4 .... 240 E2
Minnis Gn CT4 .... 240 E2
Minnis La CT15,CT17 .... 277 C2
Minnis Rd CT7 .... 80 E7
Minnis Terr CT17 .... 278 A2
Minnis Way CT14 .... 181 B5
Minshaw Ct DA14 .... 30 F4
Minster Abbey* ME12 .... 47 D6
Minster Abbey*
CT12 .... 115 C5
Minster Agriculture & Rural
Life Mus* CT12 .... 115 C5
Minster CE Prim Sch
CT12 .... 115 B5
Minster Cl CT10 .... 84 A2
Minster Coll ME12 .... 46 F6
Minster Dr
Herne Bay CT6 .... 76 D4
Minster (Sheppey) ME12 .... 47 B8
Minster Gatehouse Mus*
ME12 .... 47 D6
Minster-in-Sheppey Prim
Sch ME12 .... 47 C7
Minster Lodge 4
CT11 .... 117 C6
Minster Rd
Acol CT12,CT7 .... 81 C2
Bromley BR1 .... 29 B1
Faversham ME13 .... 138 E7
Gillingham ME8 .... 65 C3
Minster (Sheppey) ME12 .... 47 B6
Ramsgate CT11 .... 117 B5
Westgate-on-S CT8 .... 81 F7
Minster Sta CT12 .... 115 C5
Mint Bsns Pk E16 .... 1 A8
Mintching Wood La
ME9 .... 134 F2
Minter Ave CT18 .... 306 F7
Minter Cl CT18 .... 306 F7
Minterne Ave ME10 .... 101 D2
Minterne Com Jun Sch
ME10 .... 101 D2
Minters Ind Est CT14 .... 215 B6
Minters Orch TN15 .... 157 B7
Mint The CT2 .... 142 C1
Miranda Ct ME12 .... 28 B1
Miranda Ho 6 DA17 .... 4 A1
Mirfield St SE7 .... 1 D3
Miriam Ct DA14 .... 31 B4
Miriam Rd SE18 .... 2 E1
Mirror Path SE9 .... 29 C5
Miskin Cotts ME3 .... 22 B6
Miskin Rd Dartford DA1 .... 33 D8
Hoo St Werburgh ME3 .... 41 E5
Miskin Way DA12 .... 37 D2
Misling La CT4 .... 272 C7
Missenden Ct 6 CT20 .... 335 D5
Mitcham Rd TN29 .... 366 C8
Mitchell Ave
Chatham ME4 .... 63 F2
Hawkinge CT18 .... 307 B5
Northfleet DA11 .... 36 D6
Mitchell Cl Dartford DA1 .... 33 E6
Erith DA17 .... 4 C3
Lenham ME17 .... 199 C5
Woolwich SE2 .... 3 C2
Mitchell Rd
Kings Hill ME19 .... 158 F2
Orpington BR6 .... 86 F6
Mitchell St CT19 .... 334 D6
Mitchell Way 5 BR1 .... 52 A8
Mitchell Wlk Newham E6 .... 1 F8
Swanscombe DA10 .... 35 E8
Mitchem Cl TN15 .... 90 E3
Mitre Ct 5 Erith DA17 .... 4 A2
Tonbridge TN9 .... 222 C2
Mitre Rd ME1 .... 63 B4
Mittell Ct TN29 .... 376 B6
Moatbridge Sch SE9 .... 11 D1
Moat Cl Orpington BR6 .... 86 F4
Sevenoaks TN13 .... 153 D5
Moat Croft DA16 .... 13 C4
Moat Ct Eltham SE9 .... 11 F1
Sidcup DA15 .... 30 F5
Moat Farm Cl CT19 .... 335 C7
Moat Farm Rd
Folkestone CT19 .... 335 C7
St Mary Hoo ME3 .... 24 D6
Moat Farm TN2 .... 314 A7
Moatfield Mdw TN23 .... 300 B4
Moat Ho
Canterbury CT1 .... 174 F7
Charing TN27 .... 234 C7
Moat La Ash CT3 .... 147 E1
Cowden TN8 .... 282 E7
Erith DA8 .... 15 A6
Fordwich CT2 .... 144 A3
Rough Common CT2 .... 142 B4
Moat Pk TN27 .... 234 C6
Moat Rd TN27 .... 262 B5
Moat Sole CT13 .... 148 F1
Moat The TN27 .... 234 C7
Moat Way ME11 .... 46 A5
Mockbeggar La TN17,
TN27 .... 322 C4
Mockett Ct 4 ME10 .... 101 E4
Mockett Dr CT10 .... 83 F7
Mock La TN23 .... 299 B6
Model Farm Cl SE9 .... 29 E5
Modest Cnr TN4 .... 253 E1
Moira Rd SE9 .... 11 F3
Molash Rd BR5 .... 54 D5
Molehill Cnr CT5 .... 109 D8
Molehill Copse Prim Sch
ME15 .... 195 D7
Molehill Rd
Herne Bay CT6 .... 76 A1
Whitstable CT5,CT6 .... 109 E8
Molescroft SE9 .... 30 C5
Molescroft Way TN9 .... 253 F7
Moles Mead TN8 .... 217 C2
Molineux Rd CT12 .... 115 B6
Molland Cl CT3 .... 147 C2
Molland La
Ash,Guilton CT3 .... 147 C2
Ash,Paramour Street
CT3 .... 147 D6
Molland Lea CT3 .... 147 C2
Mollison Rise DA12 .... 37 E3
Molloy Rd TN26 .... 299 B1
Molyneux Almshouses
TN4 .... 285 B4
Molyneux Ct TN4 .... 285 F4
Molyneux Park Gdns
TN4 .... 285 F4
Molyneux Park Rd
TN4 .... 285 F4
Monarch Cl
Chatham ME5 .... 97 A6
Tilbury RM18 .... 19 B5
Monarch Dr E16 .... 1 D8
Monarch Rd 8 DA17 .... 4 A3
Monarch Terr ME18 .... 159 C3
Monastery Ave CT16 .... 278 E1
Monastery St CT1 .... 175 A8
Monckton's Ave ME14 .... 161 F7
Monckton's Dr ME14 .... 161 E7
Monckton's La ME14 .... 161 F7
Moncrieff Cl 5 E6 .... 1 E7
Moncrif Cl ME14 .... 163 B4
Monds Cotts TN14 .... 152 E3
Mongeham Church Cl
CT14 .... 214 D3
Mongeham Prim Sch
CT14 .... 214 F4
Mongeham Rd CT14 .... 214 E3
Mongeham View
CT14 .... 214 E4
Monica Cl ME13 .... 171 E6
Monica James Ho 12
DA14 .... 31 A5
Monins Rd Dover CT17 .... 310 B7
Iwade ME9 .... 68 D3
Monkdown ME15 .... 163 A1
Monk Dr E16 .... 1 A6
Monkery La TN25,
TN27 .... 202 D2
Monkreed Villas DA3 .... 59 D4
Monks Cl
Canterbury CT2 .... 143 A2
Erith SE2 .... 3 D2
Faversham ME13 .... 138 B8
Monks Hill Cotts
TN26 .... 348 E6
Monkshill Rd ME13 .... 107 B2
Monks La
Limpsfield TN8 .... 216 E6
Newbury's TN5 .... 337 B8
Monks Orch DA1 .... 33 D6
Monk St SE18 .... 2 A2
Monks Way
Dover CT16 .... 278 A3
Orpington BR5 .... 53 D1
Monk's Well DA9 .... 17 C3
Monks Wlk
Charing TN27 .... 234 C7
Northfleet DA13 .... 36 A2
6 Tonbridge TN9 .... 254 B8
Monkton CE Prim Sch
CT12 .... 114 D7
Monkton Court La
CT15 .... 245 D7
Monkton Gdns CT9 .... 51 E3
Monkton Manor CT12 .... 114 C7
Monkton Pl CT11 .... 117 D7
Monkton Rd
Bexley DA16 .... 12 F5
Borough Green TN15 .... 156 F7
Monkton Rdbt CT12 .... 114 D8
Monkton Rd CT12 .... 115 A6
Monkton St CT12 .... 114 D7
Monkwood Cl ME1 .... 96 B8
Monmouth Cl
Bexley DA16 .... 13 A3
Gillingham ME8 .... 65 D2
Mons Ct ME10 .... 68 F1
Monson Rd TN1 .... 286 B4
Monson Way 5 TN1 .... 286 B4
Mons Way BR2 .... 52 E3
Montacue Ct CT20 .... 335 B4
Montacute Gdns TN2 .... 285 F2
Montacute Rd TN2 .... 286 A1
Montague Ct
Sheerness ME12 .... 28 B1
15 Sidcup DA15 .... 31 A5
Montague Pl BR8 .... 55 F5
Montague Rd CT11 .... 117 E8
Montague St CT6 .... 76 D5
Montague Terr 1 BR2 .... 52 A5
Montbelle Prim Sch
SE9 .... 30 B5
Montbelle Rd SE9 .... 30 B5
Montbretia Cl BR5 .... 54 C5
Montcalm Cl BR2 .... 52 A3
Montcalm Rd SE7 .... 11 D7
Montefiore Ave
Broadstairs CT10 .... 84 A1
Ramsgate CT11 .... 83 F1
Montefiore Cotts
CT11 .... 117 F8
Monteith Cl TN3 .... 285 A3
Monterey Cl DA5 .... 32 C6
Montfort Cl
Ashford TN23 .... 299 F7
Canterbury CT2 .... 143 A4
Montfort Dr ME19 .... 159 A2
Montfort Rd
Chatham ME5 .... 96 F2
Kemsing TN15 .... 122 E2
Rochester ME2 .... 63 A8
Montgomery Ave ME5 .... 97 A7
Montgomery Cl DA15 .... 12 F1
Montgomery Rd
Gillingham ME7 .... 64 C3
Royal Tunbridge Wells
TN4 .... 286 B7
Sutton at H DA4 .... 57 D8
Montgomery Sch CT2 .... 144 C8
Montgomery Way
CT19 .... 335 E8
Montpelier Ave
Sidcup DA5 .... 31 D8
Whitstable CT5 .... 108 D6
Montpelier Bsns Pk
TN23 .... 267 F1
Montpelier Gate
ME16 .... 161 B5
Montreal Cl 8 CT16 .... 278 B3
Montreal Rd
Sevenoaks TN13 .... 153 E4
Tilbury RM18 .... 19 A5
Montrose Ave
Bexley DA16 .... 12 E4
Gillingham ME5 .... 64 E2
Sidcup DA15 .... 31 A8
Montrose Cl DA16 .... 12 F4
Mont St Aignan Way
TN8 .... 249 C8
Monument Way TN24 .... 300 F5
Monypenny Cl TN11 .... 223 D8
Monypenny TN17 .... 343 F3
Moon Ct SE12 .... 11 A3
Moonfleet Cl ME10 .... 69 A1
Moon Hill CT15 .... 244 E4
Moon's La RH7 .... 249 A1
Moonstone Dr ME5 .... 97 B2
Moonstone Sq ME10 .... 101 D6
Moorcroft Gdns BR2 .... 52 E4
Moorden La TN11 .... 220 A1
Moordown SE18 .... 12 B6
Moore Ave Grays RM20 .... 17 E8
Tilbury RM18 .... 19 B5
Moore Cl
Brenzett TN29 .... 363 A3
Dartford DA2 .... 34 D6
Mooreland Rd 1 BR1 .... 52 A8
Moore Rd DA10 .... 17 E1
Moore St ME2 .... 63 A8
Moorfield CT2 .... 142 F4
Moorfield Rd BR6 .... 54 A2
Moorhead Way SE3 .... 11 B4
Moorhen Cl DA8 .... 15 B7
Moor Hill TN18 .... 354 F8
Moorhouse Cotts
TN16 .... 184 A7
Moorhouse Rd RH8,
TN16 .... 184 A6
Mooring Rd ME1 .... 63 D1
Moorings The
Conyer ME9 .... 103 E6
Newham E16 .... 1 C8
Moor La
Edenbridge TN8 .... 249 A4
Ivychurch TN29 .... 363 D4
Moorland Rd CT15 .... 244 E4
Moorlands BR7 .... 30 B1
Moor La TN26 .... 346 E6
Moor Park Cl ME8 .... 99 A8
Moor Rd The TN14 .... 154 C7
Moorside Rd BR1 .... 29 A4
Moor St ME8 .... 99 B8
Moorstock La TN25 .... 303 C2
Moor The TN18 .... 354 F8
Moorwell Dr CT15 .... 244 D5
Morants Court Cross
TN14 .... 121 C1
Morants Court Rd
TN13 .... 153 C8
Moray Ave CT7 .... 80 F8
Mordaunt Ave CT8 .... 81 E8
Morden Rd SE3 .... 11 A5
Morden Road Mews
SE3 .... 11 A5
Morden St ME1 .... 63 C4
Morebreddis Cotts
TN17 .... 291 A1
Morehall Ave CT19 .... 334 F6
Morehall Prim Sch
CT19 .... 334 F6
Morel Ct TN13 .... 154 B5
Morella Wlk ME17 .... 199 C5
Morello Cl Swanley BR8 .... 55 D5
Teynham ME9 .... 103 C2
Morement Rd ME3 .... 41 D6
More Park RC Prim Sch
ME19 .... 159 D8
Moreton Almshouses 3
TN16 .... 151 D1
Moreton Ct
Crayford DA1 .... 14 E4
Deal CT14 .... 215 C2
Moreton Ind Est BR8 .... 56 A4
Moreton DA14 .... 31 A3
Moreton Terr TN26 .... 299 A1
Morewood Cl TN13 .... 153 F4
Morgan Dr DA9 .... 34 E8
Morgan Kirby's Gdn
ME13 .... 170 D5
Morgan Rd Bromley BR1 .... 29 A1
Rochester ME2 .... 63 A8
Morgan St E16 .... 1 A8
Morhen Cl ME6 .... 127 E7
Morland Ave DA1 .... 15 B2
Morland Dr
Lamberhurst TN3 .... 317 B5
Rochester ME2 .... 40 A1
Morland Ho 4 BR7 .... 53 A8
Morley Bsns Ctr TN9 .... 222 D1
Morley Cl BR6 .... 86 B8
Morley Dr TN12 .... 290 A6
Morley Rd
Chislehurst BR7 .... 53 C8
Tonbridge TN9 .... 222 D1
Morley's Rd TN14 .... 187 D2
Morne Cotts TN14 .... 121 F8
Morning Cross Cotts
ME3 .... 22 B4
Mornington Ave BR1 .... 52 C6
Mornington Cl TN16 .... 118 D2
Mornington Ct DA5 .... 32 D7
Morris Ave CT6 .... 75 F4
Morris Cl
Maidstone ME17 .... 195 D5
Orpington BR6 .... 86 E7
West Malling ME19 .... 127 F1
Morris Court Cl ME9 .... 102 D2
Morris Gdns DA1 .... 16 A2
Morrison Rd CT20 .... 335 E6
Morry La
Chartway Street ME17 .... 197 D1
Ulcombe ME17 .... 230 D7
Morston Gdns SE9 .... 29 F4
Mortgramit Sq SE18 .... 2 A3
Mortimer Cl TN23 .... 300 B7
Mortimer Rd
Biggin Hill TN16 .... 118 C7
Dover CT16 .... 310 F8
Erith DA8 .... 14 D8
Orpington BR6 .... 54 A1
Mortimers Ave ME3 .... 40 A8
Mortimer St CT6 .... 76 F5
Mortlake Rd E16 .... 1 B7
Mortley Cl TN9 .... 222 C2
Morton Cl
Maidstone ME15 .... 195 D6
Swanley BR8 .... 55 E7
Morvale Cl DA17 .... 3 F2
Moselle Rd TN16 .... 118 F1
Mosquito Rd ME19 .... 158 F3
Mossbank ME5 .... 97 A3
Mossdown Cl DA17 .... 4 A2
Moss End Mews CT11 .... 83 E2
Mosslea Rd
Bromley BR2 .... 52 D4
Orpington BR6 .... 86 C7
Moss Way DA2 .... 34 D4
Mossy Glade ME8 .... 98 E6
Mostyn Rd ME14 .... 162 C4
Mosul Way BR2 .... 52 E3
Mosyer Dr BR5 .... 87 D8
Mote Ave ME15 .... 162 B3
Mote Cotts TN15 .... 189 A7
Mote Hall Villas ME14 .... 163 C4
Mote Pk ME15 .... 162 D2
Mote Rd
Maidstone ME15 .... 162 A3
Shipbourne TN15,TN11 .... 189 A7
Mote The DA3 .... 91 F8
Motherwell Way RM20 .... 17 A8
Motney Hill Rd ME8 .... 66 A4
Mottingham Ct SE9 .... 29 F7
Mottingham Gdns SE9 .... 29 D7
Mottingham La
Bromley SE12,SE9 .... 29 C7
Eltham SE12 .... 29 C8
Mottingham Prim Sch
SE9 .... 29 F5
Mottingham Rd SE9 .... 29 F5
Mottingham Sta SE9 .... 29 F7
Mottisfont Rd SE2 .... 3 B2
Mouchotte Cl TN16 .... 118 C7
Moultain Hill BR8 .... 56 A5
Mound The SE9 .... 30 A5
Mountain Cl TN15 .... 124 F3
Mountain St CT4 .... 205 B6
Mount Ave ME18 .... 193 A1
Mountbatten Ave
Chatham ME5 .... 97 A7
Higham ME3 .... 39 C4
Mountbatten Cl SE18 .... 12 E8
Mountbatten Ho CT14 .... 215 D3
Mountbatten Way
TN25 .... 302 E6
Mount Castle La ME17 .... 199 F1
Mount Charles Wlk
CT4 .... 175 F1
Mount Cl Bromley BR1 .... 52 E8
Sevenoaks TN13 .... 153 F4
Mount Culver Ave
DA14 .... 31 D2
Mount Dr Bexley DA6 .... 13 E2
Maidstone ME14 .... 163 B4
Mount Edgcumbe Rd
TN4 .... 286 A3
Mount Ephraim*
ME13 .... 140 A4
Mount Ephraim Ct
TN4 .... 285 F4
Mount Ephraim Rd
TN1 .... 286 A4
Mount Ephraim TN4 .... 286 A4
Mountfield TN15 .... 157 A7
Mountfield Cl DA13 .... 92 F2
Mountfield Ct 4 TN1 .... 286 B3
Mount Field ME13 .... 138 B6
Mountfield Gdns TN1 .... 286 B3
Mountfield Pk TN9 .... 254 C8
Mount Field ME11 .... 46 A5
Mountfield Rd
New Romney TN28 .... 373 C6
Royal Tunbridge Wells
TN1 .... 286 B3
Mountfield Way
1 Orpington BR5 .... 54 C5
Westgate-on-S CT8 .... 81 D6

Mount Green Ave CT12 116 D5
Mount Harry Rd TN13 154 B4
Mounthurst Rd BR2 52 A2
Mountjoy Cl SE2 3 B4
Mount La Hartlip ME9 99 D4
Maidstone ME14 163 B4
Mount Lodge ME1 63 B2
Mount Pleasant TN25 330 A6
Mount Pleasant Ave 2 TN1 286 B3
Mount Pleasant
Aylesford ME20 129 A3
Biggin Hill TN16 118 D2
Blean CT2 142 A6
Chatham ME5 64 B3
Mount Pleasant Cl CT18 305 C7
Mount Pleasant Ct TN11 221 D6
Mount Pleasant Dr ME14 163 A5
Mount Pleasant
Durgates TN5 336 E5
Faversham ME13 105 B2
Ide Hill TN14 185 F4
Kingsdown CT14 248 D5
Mount Pleasant La TN3 317 A6
Mount Pleasant
Lamberhurst TN3 316 E6
Minster (Thanet) CT12 115 C8
Paddock Wood TN12 256 F7
Mount Pleasant Pl SE18 2 D2
Mount Pleasant Rd
Dartford DA1 15 F1
4 Folkestone CT20 335 D5
Royal Tunbridge Wells TN1 286 A3
Sevenoaks Weald TN14 187 B2
Mount Pleasant TN30 345 C8
Mount Pleasant Terr ME17 198 E2
Mount Pleasant
The Moor TN18 354 F8
Tonbridge TN11 221 D6
Mount Pleasant Wlk DA5 14 C2
Mount Rd Bexley DA6 13 E2
Canterbury CT1 175 C6
Chatham ME4 63 F3
Crayford DA1 14 F1
Dover CT17 310 A6
Rochester ME1 63 B2
Mounts Cl CT14 215 A5
Mountsfield Cl ME16 161 D5
Mounts Hill TN17 342 B7
Mount Sion TN1 286 A2
Mounts La TN17 344 A3
Mounts Rd DA9 17 B1
Mount St CT21 333 C2
Mounts View TN23 267 F4
Mount The Bexley DA6 14 B2
3 Chislehurst BR7 53 A8
Mountview ME9 101 B2
Mount View Ct 3 ME4 63 F3
Mount View ME13 138 A5
Mount View Rd CT6 77 A2
Mountview Rd BR6 54 A2
Moyes Cl CT12 116 D5
Moyle Cl ME8 98 D4
Mozart Ct ME4 63 E3
Muddy Bush Cnr CT3 177 F2
Muddy La ME10 102 B2
Muir Rd
Maidstone ME15 162 A2
Ramsgate CT11 117 F8
Muir St E16 1 E5
Mulbarton Ct BR7 30 D2
Mulberry Cl
Gillingham ME7 98 A4
Greenwich SE7 11 D8
Meopham Station DA13 60 B3
Ramsgate CT11 117 F8
Royal Tunbridge Wells TN4 254 D1
Mulberry Ct
Bexley DA16 12 F5
Canterbury CT1 174 F8
Hythe CT21 333 D3
Littlestone-on-Sea TN28 373 E5
Maidstone ME14 162 B5
Mulberry Field CT13 148 F1
Mulberry Hill CT4 172 D1
Mulberry Rd
Ashford TN23 267 D3
Northfleet DA11 36 E4
Mulberry Way DA17 4 C4
Mulgrave Ho 13 SE18 1 F2
Mulgrave Prim Sch SE18 2 B3
Mulgrave Rd SE18 2 A2
Mullein Ct 7 RM17 18 D8
Mullender Ct DA12 38 A7
Muller Ho SE18 2 A1
Multon Rd TN15 90 E4
Mummery Ct ME13 137 E2
Munday Bois Cotts TN27 264 F8
Munday Bois Rd TN27 232 E1
Munday Rd E16 1 A7
Munday Works Est TN9 222 C1
Mundella Prim Sch CT19 335 D6
Munford Dr DA10 35 E8
Mungeam Ho ME1 63 C4
Mungo Park Rd DA12 37 D3
Mungo Park Way BR5 54 D2
Munnery Way BR6 86 B8
Munnings Ho E16 1 B5
Munn's La ME9 99 E6
Munsgore La ME9 100 E3
Murchison Ave DA5 31 E7
Murrain Dr ME15 163 A1
Murray Ave BR1 52 B7
Murray Bsns Ctr BR5 54 B6
Murray Ho 16 SE18 1 F2
Murray Lodge TN2 286 D2
Murray Rd
Orpington BR5 54 B6
Rochester ME2 63 C8
Murray Sq E16 1 B6
Murston Inf Sch ME10 102 B4
Murston Jun Sch ME10 102 B5
Murston Rd ME10 102 B4
Murthwaite Ct ME12 47 A5
Murton-Neale Cl 3 TN18 341 A2
Murton Pl ME13 106 E1
Muscovy Ho DA18 3 E4
Muscovy Rd TN25 268 C7
Muscovy Way CT6 76 E3
Museum of Canterbury* CT1 174 F8
Museum of Kent Rural Life* ME14 129 D1
Musgrave Cl CT12 81 F2
Musgrave Rd ME10 101 F6
Musgrove TN23 300 A8
Muskerry Ct TN4 285 B4
Musket La
Eyhorne Street ME17 164 C2
Leeds ME17 164 A2
Mus of Artillery in the Rotunda* SE18 1 F1
Mussenden La DA3,DA4 57 E3
Mustang Rd ME19 158 F3
Mustards Rd ME12 49 D2
Mutrix Gdns CT9 50 E1
Mutrix Rd CT9 82 B8
Mutton La ME13 138 A6
Mycenae Rd SE3 11 A8
Mymms Cl CT5 109 C8
Mynn Cres ME14 163 A4
Myra St SE2 3 A2
Myrtle Alley SE18 2 A3
Myrtle Cl DA8 14 E6
Myrtle Cres ME5 96 F5
Myrtledene Rd SE2 3 A1
Myrtle Gn TN23 267 D4
Myrtle Pl DA2 34 D8
Myrtle Rd
Dartford DA1 33 D6
5 Folkestone CT19 335 E6
Mystole Ho CT4 206 B8
Mystole La CT4 206 C8

N

Nacholt Cl CT5 75 A2
Nackington Ct CT1 175 B6
Nackington Pk CT4 175 A4
Nackington Rd CT1, CT4 175 A3
Nadine St SE7 1 C1
Nagpur Ho 4 ME15 195 E5
Nag's Head La
Bexley DA16 13 B4
Rochester ME1 63 D4
Nailbourne Cl CT4 209 D3
Nailbourne Ct CT18 305 C7
Naildown Cl CT21 334 A3
Naildown Rd CT21 334 A3
Nairn Ct RM18 18 F5
Nairne Cl TN26 327 A8
Naldera CT10 84 C7
Namur Pl CT15 278 F3
Nansen Rd DA12 37 D4
Napchester Rd CT16 278 A8
Napier Cl ME10 101 C4
Napier Com Sch ME7 64 D4
Napier Ct
2 Lewisham SE12 29 B5
Maidstone ME14 161 F7
Napier Gdns CT21 333 C1
Napier Rd
Broadstairs CT10 83 E6
Bromley BR2 52 B5
Dover CT16 278 B2
Erith DA17 3 F2
Gillingham ME7 64 D4
Northfleet DA11 36 F7
Royal Tunbridge Wells TN2 286 D2
Napleton Ct 7 CT11 117 C6
Napleton Rd
Faversham ME13 138 C7
Ramsgate CT11 117 C6
Napoleon Dr TN12 259 D5
Napoleon Wlk ME17 199 C5
Napwood Cl ME8 98 D6
Nares Rd ME8 98 D4
Nargate Cl CT3 177 A8
Nargate St CT3 177 A8
Narrabeen Rd CT19 334 E6
Narrow Boat Cl SE28 2 D4
Narrowbush La TN29 371 B7
Narrow Way BR2 52 E3
Naseby Ave CT20 334 D5
Naseby Ct DA14 30 F4
Nash Bank DA13 59 F7
Nash Cl ME5 97 C2
Nash Cotts 16 DA14 31 A5
Nash Court Farming World* ME13 139 D4
Nash Court Gdns CT9 82 F8
Nash Court Rd CT9 82 F8
Nash Croft DA11 36 E4
Nashenden Farm La ME1 96 A8
Nashenden La ME1 62 F1
Nash Gdns CT10 84 B4
Nash Gn BR1 29 A2
Nash Hill CT18 305 D6
Nash La Margate CT9 82 F7
Nash BR2 85 A4
Nash Rd
Margate CT9,CT10 82 F7
Wingham CT3 146 D2
Nash St DA13 60 A7
Nasmyth Rd CT7 81 A8
Nassau Path 6 SE28 3 C5
Natal Rd Chatham ME4 64 A3
Dover CT16 278 C4
Nathan Way SE28,SE18 2 E3
Nativity Cl ME10 101 E4
Nat's La TN25 270 A5
Nautilus Cl ME12 47 A6
Nautilus Dr ME12 47 A6
Naval Terr ME12 28 A3
Naylands CT9 50 H1
Naylor's Cotts ME7 98 B1
Neale St ME4 63 F2
Neal Rd TN15 90 E5
Neal's Place Rd CT2 142 C3
Neame Rd CT7 81 A7
Neames Forstal ME13 171 E7
Neason Ct CT19 335 F6
Neason Way CT19 335 F6
Neath Rd TN29 375 A2
Neatscourt Cotts ME12 46 C4
Neatscourt Rd E6 1 D8
Neills Rd TN3 316 D2
Nellington Ct TN4 285 B4
Nellington Rd TN3, TN4 285 B4
Nelson Ave
Minster (Sheppey) ME12 47 D5
Tonbridge TN9 222 A1
Nelson Cl
Ashford TN24 301 B8
Biggin Hill TN16 118 E2
West Minst ME12 46 A8
Nelson Cres CT11 117 E6
Nelson Ct
Birchington CT7 80 E8
Chatham ME5 64 C1
Nelson Gdns ME13 138 C6
Nelson Ho
8 Maidstone ME15 195 F5
Swanscombe DA9 17 D2
Nelson Mandela Rd SE3 11 C4
Nelson Mews TN28 373 E5
Nelson Park Rd CT15 279 E8
Nelson Pl CT10 84 B5
Nelson Rd Bromley BR2 52 C5
Dartford DA1 15 C1
Erith DA17 3 F1
Gillingham ME7 64 D4
Northfleet DA11 36 F6
Royal Tunbridge Wells TN2 286 D2
Sidcup DA14 31 A4
Whitstable CT5 74 D1
Wouldham ME1 95 C5
Nelson St Deal CT14 215 D7
Faversham ME13 138 C6
Nelson Terr ME5 64 C1
Nelson Wlk ME10 101 B5
Nepicar Farm* TN15 125 D1
Nepicar La TN15 125 D3
Neptune Bsns Pk ME2 63 E7
Neptune Cl ME2 63 E7
Neptune Terr ME12 28 D2
Neptune Way ME2 63 E6
Neptune Wlk DA8 4 D2
Nesbit Rd Eltham SE9 11 D3
St Mary's Bay TN29 365 F4
Nesbitt Ho DA6 14 B2
Ness Rd Erith DA8 15 D8
Lydd TN29 376 C6
Ness The CT1 175 B5
Nestor Ct ME18 193 A8
Nether Ave TN28 373 D6
Nethercombe Ho 4 SE3 11 A8
Nethercourt Cir CT12 117 A6
Nethercourt Farm Rd CT11 117 B7
Nethercourt Gdns CT11 117 B6
Nethercourt Hill CT11 117 B6
Nethergong Hill CT3 112 D3
Netherhale Farm Rd CT7 80 B3
Nethersole Cl CT2 143 A4
Nethersole Rd CT4 210 F1
Nethewode Ct DA17 4 B3
Netley Cl ME14 162 D6
Nettlefield TN24 268 E5
Nettlepole La TN27 233 D1
Nettlestead Cotts TN12 257 A7
Nettlestead Ct ME18 192 C5
Nettlestead La ME18 192 A6
Nevill Ct ME19 127 C1
Neville Cl
Maidstone ME14 162 B8
Sidcup DA15 30 F4
Neville Ho CT14 215 D6
Neville Rd ME4 63 E2
Nevill Gate TN2 286 B1
Nevill Gdns CT14 215 B1
Nevill Lodge TN2 286 C4
Nevill Pk TN4 285 E3
Nevill Pl ME6 128 A7
Nevill Rd ME6 128 A7
Nevill Ridge TN4 285 D3
Nevill St TN2 286 A2
Nevill Terr TN2 285 F2
New Acres Rd SE28 2 E4
Newark Ct 1 ME2 63 B7
Newark Knok E6 2 A7
Newark Yd ME2 63 B7
New Ash Green Prim Sch DA3 91 F8
Newbarn La TN14, TN16 119 C2
New Barn Pk BR8 55 E8
New Barn Rd
Northfleet DA13 36 C3
Sutton Valence ME17, TN12 229 E2
Swanley BR8 55 F8
New Barns Rd ME14 162 A8
New Barn St E13 1 B8
New Bassetts Cotts TN12 290 B5
New Beach Holiday Centre TN29 353 A4
New Beacon Sch TN14 186 F8
Newbery Rd DA8 14 F6
New Beverley Ho CT2 142 F2
Newborough Ct TN10 222 C6
Newbridge Ave ME10 101 E7
New Bridge 12 CT16 310 E7
Newbridge Pk TN12 225 A1
New Bridge Way TN29 365 E3
Newbury Ave ME16 161 C6
Newbury Cl
Birchington CT7 81 B6
Cliffe Woods ME3 40 B8
Dartford DA1 34 B8
Dover CT17 309 F7
Folkestone CT20 334 D5
Newbury Cotts TN5 337 B8
Newbury Ct DA14 30 F4
Newbury La TN5 337 C8
Newbury Rd BR2 52 A6
Newcastle Hill 8 CT11 117 E7
Newchurch La TN26 364 A7
Newchurch Rd ME15 162 A1
New College of Cobham DA12 61 A5
Newcomen Rd
Royal Tunbridge Wells TN4 286 A5
Sheerness ME12 28 C2
New Cotts Bean DA2 35 B5
Guston CT15 278 E6
Harbledown CT2 141 E1
Shipbourne TN11 189 D5
Teynham ME9 103 A4
The Moor TN18 354 B7
Tilbury RM16 19 B8
New Covenant Pl 4 ME1 63 D4
New Cross St CT9 50 I2
New Ct 3 TN9 222 C2
New Cut Chatham ME4 63 F4
East Farleigh ME15 194 D7
New Cut Rd
Chilham CT4,ME13 172 A3
Harbledown ME13 141 A1
Maidstone ME14 162 D5
New Delhi Ho 5 ME15 195 E5
New Dover Rd
Canterbury CT1,CT4 175 C6
Capel-le-F CT18 308 C2
New Eltham Sta SE9 30 C7
Newenden Cl
Ashford TN23 299 F6
Maidstone ME14 162 D6
Newenden Rd ME2 40 C2
New England Rd TN4 286 A7
New Farm Ave BR2 52 A5
New Ferry App SE18 2 A3
New Forest La CT4 172 B3
New Gardens Rd ME9 103 C2
Newgate Gap CT9 51 A3
Newgate Lower Prom CT9 51 A3
Newgate Prom CT9 51 A3
New Haine Rd CT12 83 A3
New Hall Cl TN29 366 C8
New Hall Farm La ME3 25 B6
Newham Coll of FE (Royal Docks Campus) E16 2 C5
Newham Way E13 1 B8
Newhaven Gdns SE9 11 D3
Newhaven La 4 E16 1 A8
New House Cl CT1 174 E4
Newhouse Cnr CT3 113 D1
Newhouse Farm Cotts ME13 170 E7
New House La
Canterbury CT4 174 C2
Gravesend DA11 37 A6
Newhouse La ME13 170 D7
Newhouse Terr TN8 217 C3
New Hythe La ME20 128 B3
New Hythe Sta ME20 128 C4
Newick Cl DA5 14 B1
Newing Cl CT3 176 E8
Newing Gn BR1 29 D1
Newington CE Prim Sch ME9 100 B7
Newington Ct
Ramsgate CT12 83 B1
Ticehurst TN5 338 E1
Newington Ent Ctr ME9 100 C8
Newington Ho 9 BR5 54 D1
Newington Ind Est ME9 99 F6
Newington Inf Sch CT12 117 B8
Newington Jun Foundation Sch CT12 117 A8
Newington Rd
Peene CT18 334 A8
Ramsgate CT12,CT11 83 B1
Newington Sta ME9 100 B6
Newington Wlk ME14 162 C6
New Inn Cotts ME15 194 C7
Newitt Rd ME3 41 E5
New Kempes Ho TN25 237 E2
New La TN29 376 C6
Newland Green La TN27 264 D8
Newland Rd ME12 45 F7
Newlands TN23 299 D6
Newlands Ave ME10 101 B5
Newlands Ct 8 SE9 12 A1
Newlands Dr CT14 248 B8
Newlands Farm Cotts ME13 202 C4
Newlands Farm Rd ME3 24 B4
Newlands Ho CT11 83 E2
Newlands La DA13 92 F1
Newlands TN3 285 A3
Newlands La CT12 83 D2
Newlands Lodge DA8 14 D8
Newlands Prim Sch CT11 83 E1
Newlands Rd
Charing TN27 233 F5
Ramsgate CT12 83 D1
Royal Tunbridge Wells TN4 286 B7
Newlands Rise TN4 286 A6
Newlands TN29 365 F3
Newland St E16 1 F5
Newlands Way TN4 286 B7
Newlands CT16 278 B6
New Lincoln Ho CT19 335 D8
Newling Cl E6 1 F7
New Lydenburg Commercial Est SE7 1 C3
New Lydenburg St SE7 1 C3
Newlyn Cl BR6 87 A6
Newlyn Ct 1 ME14 162 A4
Newlyn Dr TN12 260 F5
Newlyn Rd DA16 12 F5
Newlyn's Mdw CT15 276 D1
Newman Ct
11 Bromley BR1 52 A8
Hythe CT21 333 B1
Newman Dr ME10 102 A8
Newman Ho SE18 12 A7
Newman Rd
Aylesham CT3 210 E5
Bromley BR1 52 A8
Newmans Cl CT10 84 A6
Newman's Rd DA11 36 F6
Newmarket Gn SE9 29 D8
Newmarsh Rd SE28 2 F5
New Mill Rd BR5 54 C8
Newnham Cl ME8 65 C2
Newnham La ME9, ME13 168 D7
Newnham Lodge DA17 4 A1
Newnhams Cl BR1 52 F6
Newnham St ME4 64 B3
New Pond Rd TN17 342 D6
Newport Ct CT1 175 B6
Newports BR8 55 D2
New Pound La ME18 158 C1
New Rd Bexley DA16 13 B5
Burham ME1 95 F1
Chatham ME4 63 F4
Cliffe ME3 22 A4
Cranbrook TN17 320 B4
Ditton ME20 128 C1
East Malling ME19 160 A8
Egerton TN27 233 A2
Elham CT4 273 F4
Erith SE2 3 D1
Eythorne CT15 245 C7
Fordcombe TN11 252 A1
Gravesend DA11 19 B1
Grays RM17 18 B8
Harbledown CT2 141 D3
Headcorn TN27 262 D5
Herne CT2,CT6 110 C4
Hextable BR8 32 F1
Hythe CT21 333 B1
Hythe, Saltwood CT21 333 B4
Langley ME17 196 C5
Limpsfield RH8 183 B5
Meopham Station DA13 59 F4
Minster (Sheppey) ME12 47 C6
Orpington BR6 54 A2
Paddock Wood TN12 257 A6
Rochester ME1 63 D4
Rough Common CT2 142 B3
Sheerness ME12 28 A1
Sundridge TN14 152 E2
Sutton at H DA4 57 D7
Swanley BR8 55 F6
New Rectory La TN23 300 B4
New Rents 5 TN23 268 B2
New Road Ave ME4 63 E4
New Road Cotts CT6 110 E5
New Road Hill
Bonnington TN25 329 F4
Farthing Street BR2,BR4 85 F2
New Road Ind Est ME12 28 A1
New Road Sch ME4 64 A3
New Romney Pl CT13 180 F8
New Romney Sta TN28 373 C6
New Ruttington La CT1 143 A1
New Sch at West Heath The TN13 187 B6
New Stairs ME4 63 F6
New St Ash CT3 147 E1
Ashford TN24 268 B2
Canterbury CT1 174 E7
Canterbury,St Dunstan's CT2 142 E1
Chatham ME4 63 E3
Deal CT14 215 D7
12 Dover CT16,CT17 310 D8
Newstead Ave BR6 86 E8
Newstead Wood Sch for Girls BR6 86 D7
New St
Folkestone CT20 335 D5
Herne Bay CT6 76 F5
Lydd TN29 376 C6
Margate CT9 50 I2
New Street TN15 92 D4
New Street Hill BR1 29 C3
New Street Rd DA13, TN15 92 C6
New St Sandwich CT13 181 A8
Sheerness ME12 28 B1
Westerham TN16 184 C8
2 Whitstable CT5 74 D2
New Swan Yd 8 DA12 19 B1
New Tavern Fort* DA12 19 C1
Newton Abbot Rd DA11 36 F6
Newton Ave TN10 222 E7
Newton Cl Chatham ME5 97 C2
1 Maidstone ME16 161 E3
Newton Ct 4 BR1 52 E6
Newton Gdns TN12 256 F7
Newton Ho
Swanscombe DA9 17 D2
Woolwich SE2 3 C1
Newton Rd Bexley DA16 13 A4
Faversham ME13 138 D7
Royal Tunbridge Wells TN1 286 B4
Tilbury RM18 19 A5
Whitstable CT5 75 B2
Newton's Ct DA9 16 D3
Newton Terr BR2 52 D3
Newton Willows TN3 312 C7
New Town Cotts TN11 220 A3
Newtown Cotts TN12 260 E6
New Town Gn TN24 300 D8
Newtown Rd TN23, TN24 300 D7
New Town St
Canterbury CT1 143 B2
Chartham CT4 173 C5
New Villas ME15 194 C7
New Wharf Rd TN9 222 B1
New Wlk TN15 124 F3
New Years La BR6, TN14 120 A5
Niagara Cl ME18 159 B3
Nicholas Cl ME16 161 A3
Nicholas Ct SE12 29 A7
Nicholas Dr CT12 116 D5
Nicholas Rd TN24 268 B6
Nicholas Stacey Ho 4 SE7 1 B1
Nichol La BR1 29 A1
Nicholls Ave CT10 83 F2
Nicholson Ho SE18 11 E7
Nickelby Cl SE28 3 C7
Nicklaus Dr ME5 96 F3
Nickleby Cl ME1 63 C2
Nickleby Rd DA12 38 A7
Nickle Cotts CT4 173 A4
Nickley Wood Rd TN26 327 C6
Nicola Terr DA7 13 E6
Nicolson Rd BR5 54 D2
Nicolson Way TN13 154 D5
Nigeria Rd SE7 11 D7
Nightingale Ave
Hythe CT21 353 D8
Whitstable CT5 108 B6
Nightingale Cl
Ashford TN24 301 B7
Biggin Hill TN16 118 C4
Chartham CT4 173 C6
Gillingham ME8 98 E6
Larkfield ME20 127 F2
Northfleet DA11 36 E4
Nightingale Cnr BR5 54 D5
Nightingale Ct ME2 62 C6
Nightingale Gr 3 DA1 16 A3
Nightingale Ho SE18 2 A1
Nightingale La
Bromley BR1 52 D7
Goathurst Common TN14 186 B5
Nonington CT15 211 C2
Nightingale Pl
Margate CT9 51 A2
Woolwich SE18 12 B8
Nightingale Prim Sch SE18 2 B1
Nightingale Rd
Dover CT16 278 C2
Faversham ME13 138 C7
Herne CT6 110 F7
Kemsing TN15 122 E2
Orpington BR5 53 C3
Nightingales The
Royal Tunbridge Wells TN4 286 A5
Sissinghurst TN27 321 F8
Nightingale Vale SE18 12 A8
Nightingale Way
Newham E6 1 E8
Swanley BR8 55 E6
Nile Path 6 SE18 12 A8
Nile Rd ME7 64 C4
Nimrod Ho E16 1 B8
Nine Acres TN24 268 C5
Nine Acres Rd ME2 62 B3
Nine Ash La ME13 139 D3
Nine Elms Gr DA11 37 A8
Nine Hams Rd TN16 150 D6
Nineveh La TN17,TN18 341 E6
Ninhams Wood BR6 86 A6
Ninn La TN23 267 B2

Nita Ct SE12 29 A7
Nithdale Rd SE18 12 C7
Niven Cl ME3 40 C3
Nixon Ave CT12 83 C1
Nizels La TN11 220 F8
No 1 St SE18 2 B3
Noah's Ark TN15 123 B1
Noah's Ark Rd CT17 310 A8
Noah's Ark Terr CT17 310 B8
Noakes Mdw TN23 300 A8
Nobel Cl ME9 103 C2
Nobel Ct ME13 138 C7
Noble Ct CT9 82 A8
Noble Gdns CT9 82 A8
Noble Tree Cross TN11 221 B6
Noble Tree Rd TN11 221 B6
Noel Terr 15 DA14 31 B4
No Name St 3 CT13 149 A1
Nonington CE Prim Sch CT15 211 C5
Nonington Ct CT15 211 E5
Nonsuch Cl CT1 175 C8
Nook The ME18 192 F2
Norah La ME3 39 B3
Nordenfeldt Rd DA8 4 D1
Nore Cl Gillingham ME7 64 E1
Sheerness ME12 28 C1
Noreen Ave ME12 47 A6
Norfield Rd DA2 32 D3
Norfolk Cl Chatham ME5 97 C3
Dartford DA1 16 A2
Gillingham ME8 65 D2
Norfolk Cres DA15 30 E8
Norfolk Dr TN23 268 A2
Norfolk Gdns DA7 13 F6
Norfolk Pl DA16 13 A5
Norfolk Rd
Canterbury CT1 174 E6
Gravesend DA12 37 D8
Maidstone ME15 195 C8
Margate CT9 51 B3
Margate,Lydden CT9 82 D5
Royal Tunbridge Wells TN1 286 B2
Tonbridge TN9 222 A1
Norfolk Sq CT12 83 B2
Norfolk St CT5 108 D8
Norham Ct 23 DA2 16 B1
Norheads La TN16 118 B2
Norlands Cres BR7 53 B8
Norman Castle* CT1 174 F7
Norman Cl
Gillingham ME8 98 B5
Kemsing TN15 122 D2
Maidstone ME14 162 B6
Orpington BR6 86 C7
Rochester ME2 62 F4
Norman Ct TN8 217 B2
Normandy Prim Sch DA7 14 D6
Normandy Terr E16 1 B7
Normandy Way DA8 14 E6
Normanhurst Ave DA7, DA16 13 D6
Normanhurst Rd
Borough Green TN15 157 A7
Orpington BR5 54 B7
Norman Par DA14 31 D6
Norman Rd
Ashford TN23,TN24 300 B7
Broadstairs CT10 83 F6
Canterbury CT1 175 A7
Dartford DA1 33 E7
Erith DA17 4 B3
Erith DA17 4 B5
Faversham ME13 138 C7
Ramsgate CT11 117 B6
Royal Tunbridge Wells TN1 286 B5
St Margaret's at Cliffe CT15 280 B6
Snodland ME6 128 A6
Warden ME12 49 A6
Westgate-on-S CT8 50 D1
West Malling ME19 159 B8
Whitstable CT5 108 E8
Norman Rise TN17 320 D4
Normans Cl DA11 37 A8
Norman St
8 Dover CT17 310 D8
Ide Hill TN14 185 F5
Norman Tailyour Ho CT14 215 D5
Norman Villas 4 TN18 340 F2
Norreys Rd ME8 98 E7
Norrie Rd CT7 81 A6
Norrington Mead 3 CT19 335 A7
Norrington Rd ME15 195 B6
Norris Ho 14 SE7 11 C8
Norris Way DA1 14 F4
Norstead Gdns TN4 286 B8
Norsted La BR6 120 B8
Northall Rd DA7 14 C5
North Ash Rd DA3 91 F7
North Ave CT11 117 D6
North Bank Cl ME2 62 F5
North Barrack Rd CT14 215 D4
North Beckton Prim Sch E6 1 F8
North Borough Jun Sch ME14 162 A6
Northbourne Ave CT17 310 B8
Northbourne CE Prim Sch CT14 213 F5
Northbourne Court Gdns* CT14 214 B5
Northbourne BR2 52 A2
Northbourne Park Sch (Annexe) CT14 213 D6
Northbourne Park Sch CT14 213 C6
Northbourne Rd
East Studdal CT15 213 E1
Gillingham ME8 65 B4
Great Mongeham CT14 214 C4
Northbourne Way CT9 51 E2
Northbrooke TN24 268 C3
Northbrooke La TN24 268 C3
North Camber Way CT16 279 B1
North Cl Bexley DA6 13 D3
Folkestone CT20 334 D4
Northcliffe Gdns CT10 84 A7
North Close Bsns Ctr CT20 334 D4
Northcote Rd
Deal CT14 215 D5
Kingsdown CT14 248 D4
Northfleet DA11 36 F7
Rochester ME2 63 A7
Sidcup DA14 30 E4
2 Tonbridge TN9 222 B1
North Court Cl CT3 178 A8
North Court La CT14 213 A4
Northcourt Prim Sch DA12 37 E7
North Court Rd CT3 178 A8
North Cray Rd DA14 31 E4
North Cres ME17 194 D4
North Ct 4 Bromley BR1 52 B8
Deal CT14 215 C7
2 Maidstone ME15 162 A1
Ramsgate CT12 83 B2
North Dane Way ME5 97 C4
Northdown TN24 268 C4
Northdown Ave CT9 51 B2
Northdown Bsns Pk ME17 199 F6
Northdown Cl
Lenham ME17 199 F6
Maidstone ME14 162 B7
Paddock Wood TN12 256 F6
Northdown ME9 167 F7
Northdown Hill CT10, CT9 83 D7
Northdown Park Rd CT9 51 C1
Northdown Prim Sch CT9 51 C1
Northdown Rd
Bexley DA16 13 C5
Broadstairs CT10 83 E6
Kemsing TN15 122 E2
Longfield DA3 58 E7
Margate CT9 51 B2
North Downs Bsns Pk TN13 121 C3
Northdowns Cl CT15 246 B6
North Downs Cl CT4 172 C2
North Down TN12 260 E4
North Downs Terr ME19 126 A5
Northdown ME9 132 D8
North Down View ME17 198 F6
Northdown Way CT9 51 C1
North Dr BR6 86 E6
North Eastling Rd ME13 168 F8
North End Farm DA13 35 F4
North End La BR6 86 B2
Northend Prim Sch DA8 14 F6
Northend Rd DA8 14 F6
North End Trad Est DA8 14 E6
Northern By-Pass TN27 234 C8
North Exit Rd CT16 310 H8
North Farm La TN2 254 E2
North Farm Rd TN2 286 C8
Northfield Ave BR5 54 C3
Northfield Cl BR1 52 E8
Northfield DA3 58 F6
Northfields
Maidstone ME16 160 F2
Speldhurst TN3 285 A8
Northfleet Cl ME14 162 C5
Northfleet Ind Est DA11 17 F3
Northfleet Sch for Girls DA11 36 D6
Northfleet Sta DA11 18 B1
Northfleet Tech Coll DA11 36 D7
North Folly Rd ME15 193 F3
North Foreland Ave CT10 84 B7
North Foreland Hill CT10 84 B8
North Foreland Rd CT10 84 B7
North Frith Pk TN11 189 F1
Northgate
Canterbury CT1 143 A1
Rochester ME1 63 C6
North Glade The DA5 31 F7
Northgrove Rd 9 TN18 340 F2
North Hill Rd TN18 340 C1
North Holmes Rd CT1 175 B8
Northiam Sta* TN31 357 C2
North Kent Ave DA11 18 C1
North La
Canterbury CT2 142 F1
Faversham ME13 138 C8
7 Folkestone CT20 334 E3
Northlands Ave BR6 86 E6
Northlands 6 BR1 52 C7
Northlands Cotts TN32 355 C1
North La ME13 171 F8
North Lea CT14 215 C7
Northleigh Cl ME15 195 A6
North Lockside Rd ME4 64 D8
North Lyminge La CT18 305 C7
North Meadow Cotts ME19 158 D7
North Meadow ME19 158 D7
North Military Rd CT17 310 C7
Northolme Rise BR6 86 E8
Northover BR1 29 A4
North Pends TN24 268 E5
North Pk SE9 12 A1
Northpoint 12 BR1 52 A8
Northpoint Bsns Est ME2 63 D8
North Pole La BR2 85 A4
North Pole Rd ME16, ME18 160 C2
North Pondside Rd ME4 64 A8
North Quay
Conyer ME9 103 E6
Faversham ME13 105 D1
North Rd Bromley BR1 52 B8
Chatham ME4 64 B8
Chatham ME4,ME7 64 A7
Cliffe ME3 22 B6
Cliffs End CT13 116 A1
Dartford DA1 15 A1
Deal CT14 248 D6
Dover CT17 310 C8
Erith DA17 4 B4
Folkestone CT20 334 D4
Goudhurst TN17 290 E1
Hythe CT21 333 B2
Queenborough ME11 45 F5
Sandwich CT13 182 A7
North Rd W CT21 333 A3
North Rd SE18 2 E2
North Return Rd CT16 310 G8
Northridge Rd DA12 37 C5
North Riding DA3 59 D6
North Sch The TN24 268 D1
Northside Rd BR1 52 A8
North Side Three Rd ME4 64 C8
North St Ashford TN23 268 C2
Bexley DA7 14 A3
Biddenden TN27 295 A2
Bromley BR1 52 A8
Cowden TN8 282 A6
Dartford DA1 33 D8
Deal CT14 215 D7
Dover CT17 310 B7
Folkestone CT19 335 E5
Gravesend DA12 37 B8
Headcorn TN27 262 C5
Herne Bay CT6 77 A5
Maidstone ME16 160 F2
New Romney TN28 373 A6
North Street Cotts ME17 229 E8
North St Rochester ME2 63 B7
Royal Tunbridge Wells TN2 286 C3
Sheldwich ME13 170 C8
Sittingbourne ME10 101 F7
Sutton Valence ME17 229 E8
Warmlake ME17 196 E1
North Terr ME3 40 F6
Northumberland Ave
Ashford TN24 268 D5
Bexley DA16 12 E4
Gillingham ME8 65 E1
Margate CT9 51 C2
Northumberland Cl DA8 14 C7
Northumberland Ct
Bexley DA8 14 C6
Maidstone ME15 195 D7
Margate CT9 51 C3
Northumberland Gdns BR1 53 A5
Northumberland Heath Prim Sch DA8 14 B7
Northumberland Pk DA8 14 C7
Northumberland Rd
Istead Rise DA13 36 F1
Maidstone ME15 195 D8
Newham E6 1 E7
Northumberland Way DA8 14 D6
Northview Ave RM18 19 A6
North View Cotts ME15 194 C7
North View
Hersden CT3 111 F1
Maidstone ME15 162 B1
North View Rd TN13, TN14 154 C6
Northview BR8 55 E7
Northwall Ct CT14 215 C7
Northwall Mews CT14 215 C7
Northwall Rd CT14 215 B8
Northward Hill Nature Reserve* ME23 23 E5
North Way
Finglesham CT14 214 A7
Maidstone ME14 162 B7
North West Kent College (Dartford Campus) DA1 33 C6
North West Kent Coll DA12 37 F7
Northwood Ave ME23 23 E4
Northwood Dr ME10 101 F1
Northwood Pl DA18 3 F3
Northwood Prim Sch DA18 3 F3
Northwood Rd
Broadstairs, Ramsgate CT10,CT12 83 C3
Tonbridge TN10 222 C6
Whitstable CT5 74 F2
North Woolwich Old Sta Mus* E16 2 A4
North Woolwich Rdbt E16 1 D5
North Woolwich Rd E16 1 A5
North Woolwich Sta E16 2 A4
Norton Ave CT6 111 A8
Norton Cres TN10 222 B7
Norton Dr CT12 115 B6
Norton Gr ME5 96 E3
Norton Knatchbull Sch The TN24 268 E2
Norton La TN26 297 D5
Norton Rd
Five Wents ME17 196 D1
Lewson Street ME13, ME9 136 E5
Royal Tunbridge Wells TN4 254 A1
Nortons La TN30 323 E5
Nortons Way TN12 256 B7
Norvic Ho DA8 14 F7
Norview Rd CT5 108 B7
Norway Dro CT15 280 A8
Norway Terr 4 ME14 162 A7
Norwich Ave TN10 222 D5
Norwich Cl ME2 62 D6
Norwich Pl 7 DA6 14 A3
Norwood Cl ME3 22 B4
Norwood Ct 5 DA1 16 A3
Norwood Gdns TN23 268 B2
Norwood La
Meopham Station DA13 60 B3
St Mary in the Marsh TN29 364 E8
Norwood Rise ME12 47 C7
Norwood St TN23 268 B2
Norwood Wlk E ME10 101 C5
Norwood Wlk W ME10 101 B5
Notley St CT1 143 A1
Notley Terr 3 CT1 143 A1
Notre Dame RC Prim Sch SE18 12 B8
Nottidge Rd TN4 285 D1
Nottingham Ave
Maidstone ME15 195 D7
Newham E16 1 C7
Nottingham Rd CT7 80 F5
Nottingham Wlk ME2 62 D6
Nouds La ME9 136 D6
Nouds Rd ME9 136 D7
Novar Cl BR6 53 F2
Novar Rd SE9 30 C7
Nower The TN14,TN16 151 F8
Nuffield Hospl TN2 286 C3
Nuffield Rd BR8 33 A2
Nugent Ind Pk BR5 54 C5
Nunappleton Way RH8 183 A3
Nunnery Fields CT1 175 A7
Nunnery Fields Hospl CT1 174 F6
Nunnery La TN11 283 F8
Nunnery Rd CT1 174 F7
Nunnington Cl SE9 29 E5
Nursery Ave Bexley DA7 13 F4
Maidstone,Bearsted ME14 163 B3
Maidstone ME16 161 B6
Nursery Cl Dartford DA2 34 C8
Densole CT18 307 A7
Flimwell TN5 339 B3
Orpington BR6 54 A2
Ramsgate CT11 117 C7
Sevenoaks TN13 154 C5
Sheerness ME12 28 D1
Swanley BR8 55 C7
Tonbridge TN10 222 E4
Whitstable CT5 75 A1
Nursery Fields Acol CT7 81 B3
Hythe CT21 333 A2
Nursery Gdns
Broadstairs CT10 51 E1
Chislehurst BR7 30 B2
Hoo St Werburgh ME3 41 E5
Nursery Ho DA4 57 C5
Nursery La CT18 307 A7
Nurserylands CT6 76 F3
Nursery La
Sheldwich ME13 170 D5
Whitfield CT16 277 F7
Nursery Pl TN13 153 D4
Nursery Rd
Ditton ME20 128 C1
Gillingham ME8 98 D8
Meopham Station DA13 60 A4
Paddock Wood TN12 256 F8
Royal Tunbridge Wells TN4 286 B8
Nursery The DA8 14 F7
Nursery Wlk CT2 142 E2
Nurstead Ave DA3 59 D6
Nurstead Church La DA13 60 A5
Nurstead La DA3,DA13 59 D5
Nurstead Rd DA8 14 A7
Nutberry Cl ME9 103 D2
Nutfield Cl ME5 97 B8
Nutfield Ct 7 BR1 52 A6
Nutfields
Ightham TN15 156 B4
Sittingbourne ME10 102 B3
Nutfield Way BR6 86 B8
Nuthatch Gdns SE28 2 D4
Nuthatch DA3 59 B7
Nutley Cl Ashford TN24 268 C3
Swanley BR8 55 F8
Nutmead Cl DA5 32 C7
Nuttall Ct BR5 54 B6
Nut Tree Cl BR6 87 D7
Nutts Ave ME12 49 G2
Nutts Cvn Site ME12 49 H1
Nutwood Cl ME14 162 E4
Nuxley Rd DA17 4 A1
Nyanza St SE18 12 D8

O

Oak Apple Ct SE12 29 A7
Oakapple Ho 10 ME16 161 A3
Oakapple La ME16 161 A3
Oak Ave
Biddenden TN27 323 D7
Eythorne CT15 245 D5
Gillingham ME7 64 E6
Minster (Sheppey) ME12 47 F6
Sevenoaks TN13 187 B7
Oak Bglws TN29 376 C6
Oakbrook Cl BR1 29 B4
Oak Caer TN25 329 F4
Oak Cl Crayford DA1 14 F3
Hoo St Werburgh ME3 41 E3
Oak Cotts
Barrowhill TN25 331 D7
East Studdal CT15 246 E8
Four Elms TN8 218 B6
Selling ME13 171 D4
Oakcroft 3 SE12 29 B5
Oak Ct BR1 52 F7
Oakdale La TN8 184 C2
Oakdale Rd
Herne Bay CT6 77 A4
Royal Tunbridge Wells TN4 285 F4
Oakdene Ave
Chislehurst BR7 30 A3
Erith DA8 14 C8
Oakdene Rd
Orpington BR5 54 A3
Ramsgate CT12 83 C1
Sevenoaks TN13 154 A5
Oak Dr
Boughton Street ME13 140 A3
Hawkinge CT18 307 B5
Higham ME3 39 B4
Larkfield ME20 128 B2
St Mary's Bay TN29 365 F3
Oak End Cl TN4 254 A2
Oakenden La TN8 251 C2
Oakenden Rd DA13 60 E1
Oakenholt Ho 1 SE2 3 D4
Oakenpole TN23 267 E1
Oakes Cl E6 1 F7
Oak Farm Gdns TN27 262 D6
Oak Farm La TN15 92 E1
Oakfield Cotts TN17 342 D4
Oakfield Court Rd TN2 286 C3
Oakfield Ct CT12 117 B8
Oakfield TN18 340 F2
Oakfield Inf Sch DA1 33 D6
Oakfield Jun Sch DA1 33 D6
Oakfield La
Dartford DA1,DA2 33 B6
Orpington BR2 85 D6
Oakfield Park Rd DA1 33 D6
Oakfield Pl DA1 33 D6
Oakfield Rd
Ashford TN24 268 D5
Marlpit Hill TN8 217 B5
Matfield TN12 288 D8
Oakfield TN17 344 A1
Oakfields
Sevenoaks TN13 154 B1
Sittingbourne ME10 101 C3
Oak Gr CT15 212 B2
Oak Hall Pass CT21 333 C2
Oakham Dr Bromley BR2 52 A5
Lydd TN29 376 D7
Oakhill House BR5 54 A8
Oakhill Rd BR6 86 F8
Oak Hill Rd TN13 154 A2
Oak Hill CT13 180 B6
Oak Ho 6 Chatham ME5 96 F4
3 Royal Tunbridge Wells TN2 286 C7
13 Sidcup DA15 31 A5
Oakhouse Rd DA6 14 A2
Oakhurst Ave DA7 13 E7
Oakhurst Cl
Bromley BR7 52 F8
Chatham ME5 96 F3
Oakhurst Gdns DA7 13 E7
Oak La Gillingham ME8 99 D8
Headcorn TN27 262 D5
Lydd TN29 376 B6
Minster (Sheppey) ME12 47 F7
Oakland Cl ME5 96 F3
Oakland Ct
Cliffs End CT12 116 C5
Herne Bay CT6 76 E5
Oaklands TN23 267 F1
Oaklands Ave
Broadstairs CT10 83 E5
Sidcup DA15 30 F8
Oaklands BR7 30 D2
Oaklands Cl Bexley DA6 13 F2
Orpington BR5 53 E3
West Kingsdown TN15 90 E4
Oaklands TN17 320 D4
Oaklands Ct BR6 86 C8
Oaklands Inf & Jun Sch ME5 96 F4
Oaklands Inf Sch TN16 118 C3
Oaklands Jun Sch TN16 118 C3
Oaklands La TN16 118 C5
Oaklands TN25 301 E4
Oaklands Rd Bexley DA6 13 F2
Dartford DA2 34 C7
Groombridge TN3 312 B6
Hawkhurst TN18 341 A1
Northfleet DA11 36 F4
Oaklands CT2 144 B7
Oaklands Way
Sturry CT2 144 B7
Tonbridge TN11 221 F4
Oakland Villas TN3 312 B7
Oak La Sevenoaks TN13 187 A8
Upchurch ME9 66 D2
Oaklea Rd TN12 256 F6
Oakleigh Cl
Chatham ME5 96 E2
Swanley BR8 55 E6
Oakleigh Ct TN12 289 F6
Oakleigh Gdns BR6 86 E6
Oakleigh Ho TN23 299 E8
Oakleigh La CT4 176 B5
Oakleigh Park Ave BR7 53 A8
Oakley Cl 8 Newham E6 1 E7
West Thurrock RM20 17 C8
Oakley Ct DA1 34 B7
Oakley Dr Orpington BR2 85 E7
Sidcup SE9 30 D7
Oakley Lodge SE12 29 A8
Oakley Pk DA5 31 C8
Oakley Rd BR2 85 E8
Oakleys The CT15 244 D5
Oak Lodge La TN16 151 D2
Oak Lodge Rd TN28 373 B7
Oak Lodge
Royal Tunbridge Wells TN2 286 D2
Sevenoaks TN13 154 A3
Oakmead Ave BR2 52 A3
Oakmead
Meopham DA13 93 A8
Tonbridge TN10 222 C6
Oakmere Rd SE2 13 A8
Oakmont Pl 6 BR6 53 D1
Oak Rd Erith DA8 15 A5
Erith,Northumberland Heath DA8 14 C7
Five Oak Green TN12 256 B7
Gravesend DA12 37 C4
Grays RM17 18 C8
Hoo St Werburgh ME3 41 E3
Orpington BR6 87 A3
Rochester ME2 62 E6
Royal Tunbridge Wells TN2 286 D7
Sittingbourne ME10 102 C5
Stone DA9 16 E1
Westerham TN16 151 D2
Oakridge CT10 51 G1
Oak Ridge TN26 349 F8
Oaks Ave CT6 76 D2
Oaks Bsns Village The ME5 97 C1
Oaks Com Inf Sch The ME10 101 D2
Oaks Dene ME5 96 F1
Oaks Forstal TN18 356 C5
Oakside Rd CT3 210 E5
Oaks Pk CT2 142 B3
Oaks Rd
Folkestone CT20 334 D6
Tenterden TN30 345 B8
Oak St CT14 215 D6
Oaks The
Aylesford ME20 128 E1
Broadstairs CT10 83 F7
Dartford DA2 16 B1
Hawkinge CT18 307 B3
Hersden CT3 111 F1
St Nicholas at Wade CT7 79 F2
Smarden TN27 263 F2
Swanley BR8 55 E7
Whitstable CT5 108 B6
Woolwich SE18 2 C1
Oaks View CT21 353 C8
Oak Terr 3 TN18 340 F2
Oak Tree Ave
Maidstone ME15 195 C7
Stone DA9 34 F8
Oak Tree Cl
Marden TN12 259 D5
Royal Tunbridge Wells TN2 286 A1
Oak Tree Gdns BR1 29 B3
Oak Tree Gr CT9 82 A8
Oaktree Ho ME10 102 B3
Oak Tree Prim Sch TN23 299 F8
Oak Tree Rd TN23 299 F8
Oak Trees Com Sch ME15 195 C7
Oakum Ct ME4 64 B2
Oakvale Cl CT17 310 B7
Oak View TN8 217 B2
Oak Warren TN13 187 A6
Oakway Cl DA5 13 E1
Oakways SE9 12 B1
Oak Wlk CT21 333 C2
Oakwood Ave BR2 52 B6
Oakwood Cl
Chislehurst BR7 30 A2
Dartford DA1 34 B7
Oakwood Ct
Maidstone ME16 161 D3
Swanley BR8 55 C7
Oakwood Dr Bexley DA7 14 C3
Sevenoaks TN13 154 B4

Oakwood Dr *continued*
Whitstable CT5 75 A1
Oakwood Gdns BR6 86 C8
Oakwood Ind Est
Broadstairs CT10 83 E6
Northfleet DA11 18 A2
Oakwood CT9 83 C8
Oakwood Park Gram Sch
ME16 161 C3
Oakwood Rd
Maidstone ME16 161 D3
Orpington BR6 86 C8
Sturry CT2 144 A7
Oakwood Rise
Longfield DA3 58 E6
Royal Tunbridge Wells
TN2 286 E7
Oakwood Sch DA7 14 D3
Oakwood Terr ME10 102 C4
Oakwood Villas CT11 83 E1
Oare Marshes Nature
Reserve* ME13 105 B6
Oare Marshes Nr & Watch
Tower Info Ctr*
ME13 105 C6
Oare Rd ME13 105 C1
Oasis The 7 BR1 52 C7
Oast Cl TN2 286 D7
Oast Cotts
Dargate ME13 140 D8
Sheldwich ME13 170 C8
Wormshill ME9 166 C5
Oast Ct Margate CT9 82 F8
Sittingbourne ME10 101 E2
Yalding ME18 192 F1
Oastfield Ct TN15 154 C2
Oast Ho CT4 172 C2
Oast Ho The
Canterbury CT3 175 F8
3 Gillingham ME8 98 F8
Oasthouse Field TN29 363 F4
Oast House Way BR5 54 B5
Oast La
Throwley Forstal ME13 202 E6
Tonbridge TN10 222 A4
Oast Mdw TN24 268 F1
Oast Paddock The
CT3 179 A6
Oasts The ME14 163 C4
Oast The
Canterbury CT1 175 B6
Staple CT3 179 A6
Oastview ME8 99 A8
Oast View TN12 290 A6
Oast Way DA3 58 E3
Oaten Hill CT1 175 A7
Oaten Hill Pl CT1 175 A7
Oatfield Cl TN17 320 C5
Oatfield Dr TN17 320 C5
Oatfield Rd BR6 53 F1
Oaze The CT5 108 C6
Occupation La SE18 12 B6
Occupation Rd TN25 237 F2
Ocean Cl CT7 81 B8
Ocean View
Broadstairs CT10 84 A1
Herne Bay CT6 77 F6
Ocelot Ct 6 ME4 64 B3
Ockham Dr BR5 31 A1
Ockley Ct DA14 30 E5
Ockley La TN18 341 A3
Ockley Rd TN18 341 A2
Octavia Ct ME5 97 B3
Octavian Dr CT21 332 A3
Octavian Way TN23 299 E5
Octavia Way 12 SE28 3 B6
Odeon Ct 1 E16 1 A8
Odeon Par SE9 11 E3
Odiham Dr ME16 161 C7
Odo Rd CT17 310 C8
Offenham Rd SE9 29 F4
Offen's Dr TN12 260 E3
Offham Prim Sch
ME19 158 D8
Offham Rd ME19 159 A7
Officers' Rd ME4 64 B8
Officers Terr ME4 63 F7
Offley Cl CT9 51 C1
Ogilby St SE18 1 F2
Ogilvy Ct CT10 83 E7
Okehampton Cl TN24 268 F7
Okehampton Cres
DA16 13 C6
Okemore Gdns BR5 54 C5
Olantigh Ct CT7 81 A7
Olantigh Rd TN25 237 F3
Olave Rd CT9 51 B1
Old Ash Cl TN24 268 C5
Old Ashford Rd
Charing TN27 234 C7
Lenham ME17 199 E5
Old Badgins Rd ME13 170 B6
Old Bailey The ME17 198 E6
Old Bakery Cl TN29 365 F4
Old Bakery Mews
ME13 139 F4
Old Bakery The ME12 46 F5
Old Barn Cl
Gillingham ME7 97 F6
Kemsing TN15 123 A2
Tonbridge TN9 253 F8
Old Barn Rd ME19 127 E2
Old Barn Way DA7 14 D4
Old Bexley Bsns Pk
DA5 32 B8
Old Bexley CE Prim Sch
DA5 31 F7
Old Bexley La DA5 32 E6
Old Billet La ME12 48 C6
Oldborough Manor Com
Sch ME15 195 B6
Old Boundary Rd CT8 50 D1
Old Bridge Rd CT5 74 E1
Oldbury Cl
Oldbury TN15 156 B5
Orpington BR5 54 D5
Oldbury Cotts TN15 156 B6
Oldbury La TN15 156 B6
Old Carriageway The
Gillingham ME7 97 F4
Sevenoaks TN13 153 C5
Old Castle Wlk ME8 98 D4
Old Chapel Rd BR8 55 C2
Old Charlton Rd CT16 278 D2
Old Chatham Rd
Kit's Coty ME20 129 D6
Sandling ME14 129 F1
Oldchurch Ct 3 ME16 161 E3
Old Church La TN12 191 E4
Old Church Rd
Burham ME1 95 C1
Chartham CT4 173 E1
Mereworth ME18,TN12 191 D5
Pembury TN2 255 D2
Old Clem Sq 12 SE18 12 A8
Old Coach Rd TN15 124 E5
Old Coachworks The 10
CT13 148 F1
Old Coal Yd The 7
CT5 74 D1
Old Coastguard Cotts
TN29 380 D3
Old Corn Stores The
ME14 163 C4
Old Court Hill CT15,
CT3 211 C6
Old Court Ho The
TN13 154 C3
Old Crossing Rd 1
CT9 82 B8
Old Ctyd The BR1 52 B8
Old Dairy Cl 4 CT11 117 F7
Old Dairy The TN12 224 E6
Old Dairy Yd CT12 117 C7
Old Dartford Rd DA4 56 F3
Old Dover Rd
Barham CT4 210 B1
Canterbury CT1 175 B6
Capel-le-F CT18 308 C1
Greenwich SE3 11 B7
Old Downs DA3 58 E4
Old Downs The DA3 58 E4
Old Dr ME15 194 F6
Old Dungeness
Lighthouse* TN29 380 D2
Old Farm Ave DA15 30 E6
Old Farm Cl CT5 108 C6
Old Farm Gdns BR8 55 F6
Old Farmhouse The
BR8 32 E1
Old Farm Rd CT7 80 D7
Old Farm Rd E DA15 31 A6
Old Farm Rd W DA15 30 F6
Old Ferry Rd ME9 68 E7
Oldfield Cl Bromley BR1 52 F5
Gillingham ME8 98 D8
Maidstone ME15 162 E1
Oldfield Dr ME1 95 C5
Oldfield Rd Bexley DA7 13 E5
Bromley BR1 52 F5
Old Fire Sta The SE18 12 B7
Old Flour Mill The
CT17 278 B2
Old Fold CT5 109 C8
Old Folkestone Rd
CT17 310 A4
Old Forge La ME9 132 F3
Old Forge Way DA14 31 B4
Old Garden Ct CT4 173 E1
Old Gardens Cl TN2 314 B8
Old Gate Rd ME13 138 B8
Old Gdn The TN13 153 D4
Old George Ct ME3 40 F4
Old Green Rd
Broadstairs CT10 83 F7
Margate CT9 51 C1
Old Hadlow Rd TN10 222 F4
Old Hall Dr CT12 116 C5
Old Halls The 8 CT5 74 D2
Old Ham La ME17 199 A4
Oldhawe Hill CT3,CT6 111 D7
Old High St The CT20 335 E5
Old Hill Chislehurst BR7 53 A8
Orpington BR6 86 E4
Old Hockley Rd ME13 169 C2
Old Homesdale Rd BR2 52 C5
Old Hook Rd ME12 47 F2
Old Hop Gdn The
TN31 367 C2
Old Ho The BR7 53 D8
Oldhouse La TN29 362 E1
Old House La
Hartlip ME9 99 E4
Langton Green TN3 284 D4
Old Kent Rd TN12 257 A6
Old Kingsdown Cl CT10 83 E3
Old La TN15 156 C4
Old Lain ME17 198 F6
Old La TN16 150 D6
Old Lenham Rd ME9 167 C4
Old London Rd
Badgers Mount TN14 88 A1
Halstead TN14 120 E4
Hythe CT21 332 F2
Tonbridge TN10 222 C3
Wrotham TN15 124 F4
Old Loose Cl ME15 194 F5
Old Loose Hill ME15 194 F4
Old Maidstone Rd
Keycol ME9 100 F5
Sidcup DA14 31 F1
Oldman Ct SE12 29 B6
Old Manor Dr DA12 37 C7
Old Manor Way
Bexley DA7 14 D5
Bromley BR7 29 F3
Old Mead CT19 335 A7
Old Mill Cl DA4 56 E1
Old Mill La ME20 129 C3
Old Mill Mews CT19 334 F7
Old Mill Rd
Maidstone ME17 163 F1
Woolwich SE18 12 D8
Old Oast Bsns Ctr The
ME20 129 A1
Old Orchard La ME19 127 D1
Old Orchard TN18 356 B5
Old Orch Ashford TN23 299 D8
Charcott TN11 220 A3
Old Orch The ME8 99 A8
Old Otford Rd TN14 122 B1
Old Palace Rd CT4 176 C3
Old Park Ave
Canterbury CT1 143 C2
Dover CT16 278 A3
Old Park Cl CT16 278 A4
Old Park Ct CT1 143 C2
Old Park Hill CT16 278 B4
Old Park Rd
Dover CT16 278 B2
Woolwich SE2 3 A1
Old Parsonage Ct
ME19 159 C7
Old Pattens La ME4 63 D2
Old Perry St
Chislehurst BR7 30 E1
Northfleet DA11 36 E6
Old Polhill TN14 121 D4
Old Police Sta The 4
CT5 74 D2
Old Pond Rd TN23 299 F8
Old Post Office La SE3 11 B4
Old Print Ho 4 CT16 310 E7
Old Priory Sch The
CT11 117 D6
Old Railway Works (Ind
Est) TN24 300 D8
Old Rd Chatham ME4 63 F4
Crayford DA1,DA7 14 D3
East Peckham TN12 225 A6
Old Rd E DA12 37 D7
Old Rd Elham CT4 273 F4
Sarre CT7 113 C6
Wateringbury ME18 192 C7
Old Rd W DA11 37 A7
Old Rectory Cl
Hawkinge CT18 307 B4
Mersham TN25 301 E5
Old Rectory The TN25 236 E2
Old Regent Dr TN17 343 E3
Old Riding School The
TN3 312 B2
Old Roman Rd CT15 247 C1
Old Ruttington La
CT1 143 A1
Old Saltwood La CT21 333 B4
Old Saw Mill The
Bethersden TN26 297 E6
Platt TN15 157 D5
Old School Cl
Lenham ME17 199 D4
Sturry CT2 143 F6
Old School Ct
Chattenden ME3 40 F4
Egerton TN27 232 F3
Folkestone CT20 335 B4
Swanley BR8 55 E7
Old School Gdns CT9 51 A1
Old School Ho The 3
TN8 217 C1
Old School La ME19 126 F4
Old School Mews CT4 173 C2
Old School Pl ME14 162 A5
Old School The
Ashford TN24 300 D8
Goudhurst TN17 318 E8
Maidstone ME16 160 E1
Old School Yd
2 Broadstairs CT10 83 E5
Gravesend DA12 37 E8
Old Sch The BR6 86 B5
Old Soar Manor*
TN15 157 B1
Old Soar Rd TN15 157 C1
Old Stables The CT11 117 C5
Oldstairs Rd CT14 248 D4
Old Station Rd TN5 336 E6
Old Surrenden Manor
TN26 298 C5
Old Surrenden Manor Rd
TN26 298 C5
Old Tannery Cl TN30 344 F7
Old Terry's Lodge Rd
TN15 124 A4
Old Timber Top Cotts The
TN13 154 C4
Old Timber Yard Ind Est
CT11 117 A7
Old Tovil Rd ME15 162 A2
Old Town Gaol Mus*
CT17 310 D8
Old Town Hall Mus*
CT9 50 I3
Old Trafford Cl ME16 161 B6
Old Tramyard SE18 2 E2
Old Tree La ME17 195 D3
Old Tree Rd CT3 112 B7
Old Tye Ave TN16 118 E3
Old Valley Rd CT4 242 F7
Old Vicarage Gdn CT2 143 F6
Old Vicarage Gdns
TN25 237 E2
Old Vicarage The
Meopham DA13 60 A1
Woodnesborough CT13 180 C7
Old Wardsdown TN5 339 B3
Old Watling St
Gravesend DA11 37 A3
Rochester ME2 62 B8
Old Way TN26 361 D7
Old Weavers Cotts
TN17 342 D5
Old Whetsted Rd
TN12 225 A2
Old White Hart Cotts
TN16 152 C3
Old Wlk The TN14 122 C2
Old Yard The TN16 152 C3
Old Yews The DA3 59 B6
Oleander Cl BR6 86 D5
Olive Gr 2 CT11 117 F7
Oliver Cl Chatham ME4 64 B2
West Thurrock RM20 16 F7
Oliver Cres DA4 56 F2
Oliver Ct SE18 2 C2
Olive Rd DA1 33 D7
Oliver Gdns E6 1 E8
Oliver North Ho ME15 193 E7
Oliver Rd
Staplehurst TN12 260 E4
Swanley BR8 55 D6
West Thurrock RM20 16 F7
West Thurrock RM20 17 A7
Olivers Mill DA3 91 E8
Olivers Row ME14 163 C4
Oliver Twist Cl ME1 63 B4
Olivier Dr ME2 40 B2
Olivine Cl
Chatham ME5 130 A8
Sittingbourne ME10 101 C7
Olliffe Cl ME5 96 F2
Olron Cres DA6 13 E2
Olven Rd SE18 12 C8
Olyffe Ave DA16 13 A5
Omer Ave CT9 51 C2
O'Neill Path 11 SE18 12 A8
Onslow Cres BR7 53 B8
Onslow Dr DA14 31 D6
Onslow Rd ME1 63 D3
Ontario Way CT16 278 B3
Opal Cl E16 1 D7
Opal Gn ME5 97 B2
Openshaw Rd SE2 3 B2
Opie Wlk CT18 306 F3
Orache Dr ME14 162 E5
Orange Court La BR6 86 A2
Orangery La SE9 11 F2
Orange St CT1 174 F8
Orange Terr ME1 63 D5
Orbital One DA1 34 B6
Orbital Pk TN24 300 F6
Orbit Cl ME5 130 A8
Orchard Ave
Aylesford ME20 128 E1
Bexley DA17 13 F8
Dartford DA1 33 B7
Deal CT14 215 B5
Gravesend DA11 37 B3
Rochester ME2 39 F1
Orchard Bank ME17 196 B1
Orchard Bsns Ctr
Maidstone ME16 161 C8
Paddock Wood TN12 257 A8
Royal Tunbridge Wells
TN2 286 D8
Tonbridge TN9 222 E1
Orchard Cl Bexley DA7 13 E6
Canterbury CT2 142 F4
Coxheath ME17 194 C3
Edenbridge TN8 217 B2
Horsmonden TN12 289 F6
Langley Heath ME17 196 E4
Littlebourne CT3 176 F7
Mersham TN25 301 E3
Minster (Thanet) CT12 115 B7
New Barn DA3 59 B7
Ramsgate CT12 83 B3
Royal Tunbridge Wells
TN2 286 D6
Sevenoaks TN14 154 C7
Whitfield CT16 277 F8
Whitstable CT5 74 F3
Wingham CT3 178 A7
Orchard Cotts
Chislehurst BR7 30 E2
East Farleigh ME16 194 A8
Nettlestead Green
ME18 192 C1
Orchard Cres
Horsmonden TN12 290 A6
Wateringbury ME18 192 D6
Orchard Ct
Benenden TN17 342 D6
Chillenden CT3 211 F8
Herne Bay CT6 76 F1
Sidcup DA15 12 F2
Orchard Cvn Pk TN29 352 D3
Orchard Dr
Crabble CT17 277 E3
Edenbridge TN8 217 B2
Hythe CT21 333 B1
Littlestone-on-Sea TN28 373 E6
Maidstone ME14 162 E4
Meopham Station DA13 59 F4
Newington ME9 100 A5
Tonbridge TN10 222 E5
Wye TN25 237 F1
Orchard End CT11 117 A5
Orchard Field TN26 297 D4
Orchard Fields CT21 304 E2
Orchard Flats CT1 175 D7
Orchard Gdns CT9 82 A8
Orchard Glade TN27 262 E5
Orchard Gn
Bromley BR1 52 C8
Orpington BR6 86 E8
Orchard Gr
Larkfield ME20 128 B2
Minster (Sheppey) ME12 47 C6
Orpington BR6 53 F1
Royal Tunbridge Wells
TN1 286 B5
Orchard Hill DA1 14 E2
Orchard Ho Erith DA8 14 F6
9 Faversham ME13 138 C7
Orchard Hts TN23 267 F5
Orchard Ind Est ME15 195 F3
Orchard La
Ashford TN24 268 F6
Challock TN25 203 B2
Monkton CT7,CT12 114 A8
St Nicholas at Wade CT7 79 F1
Orchardlea DA13 35 F3
Orchard Lea TN11 221 F5
Orchard Mews CT14 215 D5
Orchard Pk CT6 77 D4
Orchard Pl
Faversham ME13 138 D7
Keston BR2 85 D2
2 Maidstone ME16 161 E3
Orpington BR5 54 C6
Sittingbourne ME10 102 A3
Sundridge TN14 152 D3
Orchard Prim Sch
DA14 31 B3
Orchard Rd Bexley DA16 13 B4
Bromley BR1 52 C8
East Peckham TN12 225 A6
Eastry CT13 180 B3
Erith DA17 4 A2
Herne Bay CT6 76 F3
Margate CT9 82 A8
Northfleet DA11 36 C6
Orpington BR6 86 B5
Otford TN14 121 F3
Pratt's Bottom BR6 87 C1
St Mary's Bay TN29 366 A5
Sevenoaks TN13 153 E5
Sidcup DA14 30 E4
Swanscombe DA10 17 E2
Tenterden TN30 324 A3
Orchard Residences The
CT1 175 A5
Orchard Rise E DA15 12 F2
Orchard Rise TN3 312 B7
Orchard Rise W DA15 12 E2
Orchard Row CT6 77 A1
Orchard Sch The CT1 174 F6
Orchards Sh Ctr The
DA1 15 E1
Orchard St
Canterbury CT2 142 E1
Dartford DA1 15 E1
Gillingham ME8 98 E8
Orchards The CT4 273 F4
Orchard St ME15 162 A3
Orchard Terr DA9 16 E2
Orchard The
Maidstone ME14 163 B4
Monkton CT12 114 D6
Sevenoaks TN13 153 E6
Swanley BR8 55 D7
Orchard Valley CT21 333 A2
Orchard View Ash CT3 147 F1
Detling ME14 163 A8
Tenterden TN30 345 C8
Teynham ME9 103 C3
Orchard Villas
Chainhurst TN12 227 A4
1 Chatham ME4 63 F3
Chislehurst BR7 30 E2
Kearsney CT17 277 E4
Sidcup DA14 31 C2
Orchard Way
Cranbrook TN17 320 B4
Dartford DA2 33 D5
Eastchurch ME12 48 D1
Horsmonden TN12 290 A6
Kemsing TN15 123 A2
Oxted RH8 183 A2
Peasmarsh TN31 367 C1
Snodland ME6 127 F7
Orchid Cl
Minster (Sheppey) ME12 47 A4
1 Newham E6 1 E8
Rochester ME2 62 C6
Orchidhurst TN2 286 D7
Orchids The
Etchinghill CT18 305 D4
Mersham TN25 301 E4
Ordnance Rd
Gravesend DA12 19 C1
Woolwich SE18 12 A8
Ordnance St ME4 63 E3
Ordnance Terr 9 ME4 63 E4
Oregon Sq BR6 53 D1
Orford Ct 7 DA2 16 B1
Orgarswick Ave TN29 366 C7
Orgarswick Way TN29 366 C7
Oriental Rd E16 1 D5
Orient Pl CT2 142 F1
Oriole Way
Larkfield ME20 127 F2
Woolwich SE28 3 B6
Orion Rd ME1 96 C7
Orion Way TN24 300 E8
Orissa Rd SE18 2 E1
Orlestone Gdns BR6 87 E5
Orlestone Villas TN26 349 A8
Orlick Rd DA12 38 B7
Ormesby Cl SE28 3 D6
Ormiston Rd SE10 1 A1
Ormonde Ave BR6 86 C8
Ormonde Ct CT21 333 C1
Ormonde Rd
11 Folkestone CT20 335 E6
Hythe CT21 333 C1
Ormsby Gn ME8 98 E3
Ormsby Point 8 SE18 2 B2
Orpines The ME18 192 F7
Orpington By-Pass
TN14 88 A2
Orpington Coll of Further
Education BR6 54 A1
Orpington Hospl BR6 86 F6
Orpington Rd BR7 53 E6
Orpington Sta BR6 86 E8
Orpington Trad Est 10
BR5 54 C5
Orpins Cl TN25 302 D6
Orr Cl CT18 306 F4
Orwell Cl
Lunsford ME20 127 F3
Rainham RM13 4 D8
Orwell Spike ME19 159 A5
Osberton Rd SE12 11 A2
Osborne Gdns CT6 77 D4
Osborne Rd
Ashford TN24 300 F8
Bexley DA17 13 F8
Gillingham ME7 64 C5
Kingsdown CT14 248 C6
Osborne Terr CT9 50 J1
Osbourn Ave CT8 81 E8
Osbourne Rd
Broadstairs CT10 83 F4
Dartford DA2 16 B1
Oscar Rd CT10 84 B4
Osgood Ave BR6 86 F5
Osgood Gdns 1 BR6 86 F5
Osier Field TN24 268 E7
Osier Rd ME9 103 E3
Oslin Wlk ME18 159 C2
Osmers Hill TN5 336 F7
Osmunda Ct TN2 286 C4
Osney Ho 4 SE2 3 D4
Osney Way DA12 37 F6
Osprey Ave ME5 64 E2
Osprey Cl Newham E6 1 E8
Whitstable CT5 108 C7
Osprey Ct
2 Dover CT16 278 B2
Hawkinge CT18 306 F3
Sittingbourne ME10 102 A3
Osprey Wlk ME20 127 F1
Ospringe CE Prim Sch
ME13 138 A6
Ospringe Ct SE9 12 D1
Ospringe Pl
Faversham ME13 138 B6
Royal Tunbridge Wells
TN2 286 F6
Ospringe Rd ME13 138 B7
Ospringe St ME13 138 A6
Ostend Ct ME10 68 F1
Osterberg Rd DA1 15 F3
Osterley Cl BR5 54 A8
Ostlers Ct 2 ME6 128 A8
Ostlers La CT7 113 D6
Oswald Pl CT17 278 B2
Oswald Rd CT17 278 B2
Otford Cl Bromley BR1 53 A6
Sidcup DA5 14 B1
Otford Court (St Michael's
Sch) TN14 122 E4
Otford La TN14 121 B6
Otford Prim Sch TN14 122 B3
Otford Rd TN14 154 B7
Otford Sta TN14 122 C3
Otham Cl CT2 143 A4
Otham La ME15 163 C2
Otham St
Maidstone ME15 163 C2
Otham ME15 196 B7
Otley Rd E16 1 C7
Otlinge Rd BR5 54 D5
Ottawa Cres CT16 278 C3
Ottawa Rd RM18 19 A5
Ottawa Way CT16 278 B3
Otterbourne Pl ME15 162 E1
Otterden Cl
Ashford TN23 299 F6
Orpington BR6 86 E6
Otterden Rd ME13 168 D3
Otterham Quay La
Gillingham ME8 66 B2
Gillingham ME8 99 B8
Otteridge Rd ME14 163 A3
Otterpool La CT21,
TN25 331 D4
Otters Cl BR5 54 D5
Ottershaw Ho BR5 54 B8
Otway St Chatham ME4 64 A3
Gillingham ME7 64 D6
Otway Terr 1 ME4 64 A3
Oulton Cl SE28 3 C7
Our Lady of Grace RC Prim
Sch SE7 11 B8
Our Lady of Hartley RC
Prim Sch DA3 58 F4
Our Lady of the Rosary RC
Prim Sch DA15 12 E1
Our Lady's RC Prim Sch
DA1 15 D1
Out Elmstead La CT4 209 F2
Outfall Ave TN29 380 C2
Oval The
Dymchurch TN29 352 D1
New Barn DA3 59 C6
Sidcup DA15 31 A8
Ovenden Rd
Sevenoaks TN14 152 F6
Sundridge TN14 152 D6
Overcliffe DA11 19 A1
Overcourt Cl DA15 13 B1
Overdale TN14 187 B2
Overland La CT3 147 A3
Overmead Eltham DA15 30 D8
Swanley BR8 55 E4
Over Minnis DA3 91 F7
Overton Ho ME12 28 C2
Overton Rd SE2 3 D3
Overy Liberty DA1 33 E8
Overy St DA1 15 E1

Owen Cl
East Malling ME19 159 F8
Woolwich SE28 3 C5
Owenite St SE2 3 B2
Owen's Cl CT21 334 B3
Owens Court Cotts ME13 170 F8
Owen Sq CT14 215 B2
Owens Way ME7 65 A6
Owletts Cl ME15 195 D8
Owletts* DA12 60 F6
Owl House Gdns* TN3 316 E7
Owl's Hatch Rd CT6 76 C1
Oxenden Cnr CT3 77 F1
Oxenden Cres CT3 178 A8
Oxenden Park Dr CT6 76 E4
Oxenden Rd CT20 334 E4
Oxenden St CT6 76 E5
Oxenden Way CT4 242 F8
Oxenden Wood Rd BR6 87 C4
Oxenhill Rd TN15 122 E2
Oxenhoath Rd TN11 190 D4
Oxen Lease TN23 299 E8
Oxenturn Rd TN25 269 E8
Oxfield TN8 217 D3
Oxford Cl
Gravesend DA12 37 F6
[5] Whitstable CT5 74 D1
Oxford Ct
Canterbury CT1 174 F7
Sidcup DA14 30 F4
Oxford Mans [6] CT5 74 D1
Oxford Mews DA5 32 A8
Oxford Rd
Canterbury CT1 174 F7
Gillingham ME7 64 D3
Maidstone ME15 195 D8
Sidcup DA14 31 B3
Oxford St
[6] Margate CT9 50 J1
Snodland ME6 128 A8
Whitstable CT5 74 D1
Oxford Terr CT20 335 D4
Oxhawth Cres BR2 53 B3
Ox La TN30 324 B2
Ox Lea TN3 285 A3
Oxleas Cl DA16 12 D5
Oxleas E6 2 B7
Oxleas Wood Nature Reserve* SE18 12 C4
Oxley Shaw La ME19 127 E2
Oxney Cl CT7 80 F7
Oxney Cotts TN30 361 A4
Oyster Catchers Cl E16 1 B7
Oyster Cl Herne Bay CT6 76 B3
Sittingbourne ME10 101 E6
Oyster Mews [4] CT5 74 D1
Ozolins Way E16 1 A7

P

Pacific Cl DA10 17 E2
Pacific Rd E16 1 A7
Packer Pl ME5 97 A8
Packer's La [5] CT11 117 E7
Packham Cl BR6 87 C7
Packham Rd DA11 36 F5
Packhorse Rd TN13 153 C4
Packmores Rd SE9 12 E2
Padbrook Cl RH8 183 B6
Padbrook La CT3 146 D6
Padbrook RH8 183 A6
Paddlesworth Rd ME6 94 D1
Paddock Cl Deal CT14 214 F5
Folkestone CT20 334 F5
Fordcombe TN3 284 B5
Greenwich SE3 11 A5
Limpsfield RH8 183 A4
Lydd TN29 376 B6
Orpington BR6 86 B6
Platt TN15 157 C6
Sutton at H DA4 57 C8
Paddock Rd
Ashford TN23 299 E7
Bexley DA6 13 E3
[2] Birchington CT7 81 A7
Paddocks Cl BR5 87 D8
Paddocks The
Ashford TN23 267 C1
Broadstairs CT10 83 F7
Cowden TN8 282 B7
Densole CT18 307 A8
Gillingham ME7 98 A5
Herne Bay CT6 77 F5
Margate CT9 51 C1
Sevenoaks TN13 154 D3
Paddock The
Ashurst TN3 283 F5
Canterbury CT1 175 B8
Chatham ME4 63 F4
Dartford DA2 34 E6
Dover CT16 310 D8
Farthing Street BR2 85 E2
Hadlow TN11 190 E1
Old Wives Lees CT4 172 C2
Pembury TN2 287 C6
Vigo Village DA13 125 F7
Westerham TN16 151 C1
Woodchurch TN26 326 A1
Paddock View CT5 108 E7
Paddock Way BR7 30 D1
Paddock Wood Bsns Ctr TN12 257 A7
Paddock Wood Prim Sch TN12 257 A6
Paddock Wood Sta TN12 257 A7
Pad's Hill ME15 162 A4
Padsole La ME15 162 A4
Padstow Cl [3] BR6 86 F6
Padstow Manor [1] ME7 64 C6
Padwell La TN23 299 C8
Paffard Cl CT2 143 F6
Paffard Ct CT2 143 F6
Pageant Cl RM18 19 C6
Page Cl DA2 35 C5
Page Cres DA8 14 F7
Page Heath La BR1 52 D6
Page Heath Villas BR1 52 D6
Pagehurst Rd TN12 260 B3
Page Pl CT19 335 D8
Page Rd CT18 306 F3
Paget Gdns BR7 53 B8
Paget Rise SE18 12 A7
Paget Row ME7 64 C5
Paget St ME7 64 C5
Paget Terr SE18 12 B8
Pagitt St ME4 63 E3
Paiges Farm Cl TN14 187 C2
Paine Ave TN29 376 C6
Painesfield Cl TN29 352 C4
Pains Hill RH8 183 C4
Painters Ash La DA11 36 D5
Painters Ash Prim Sch DA11 36 D5
Painters Farm Camping & Cvn Site ME13 137 E3
Painter's Forstal Rd ME13 137 E3
Palace Ave ME15 162 A4
Palace Cl CT5 75 B2
Palace Cotts ME9 167 F8
Palace Ct
[5] Bromley BR1 52 B8
Eltham SE9 11 F1
Gillingham ME5 64 D2
Hythe CT21 333 C2
Palace Gr BR1 52 B8
Palace Ind Est ME15 195 F4
Palace Rd Bromley BR1 52 B8
Hill Park TN16 151 A6
Palace St [17] CT1 143 A1
Palace View
Bromley BR1 52 B6
Lewisham SE12 29 A6
Palace Wood Inf Sch ME16 161 C6
Palace Wood Jun Sch ME16 161 C6
Palewell Cl BR5 54 B7
Pallant Way BR6 86 A7
Pallet Way SE18 11 E6
Palmar Cres DA7 14 A5
Palmar Rd Bexley DA7 14 A5
Maidstone ME16 161 D6
Palmars Cross Hill CT2 142 A1
Palmarsh Ave CT21 353 D7
Palmarsh Cres CT21 353 D7
Palmarsh Prim Sch CT21 353 D8
Palmarsh Rd BR5 54 D5
Palm Ave DA14 31 D2
Palm Bay Ave CT9 51 D3
Palm Bay Gdns CT9 51 C3
Palm Bay Prim Sch CT9 51 D3
Palmbeach Ave CT21 353 D8
Palm Ct CT8 50 C1
Palmeira Rd DA7 13 D4
Palmer Ave DA12 37 D4
Palmer Cl CT6 111 B8
Palmer Cres CT9 83 C8
Palmer Rd CT3 178 A8
Palmers Brook TN11 190 F2
Palmers Green La TN12 257 D1
Palmers Orch TN14 121 F8
Palmerston Ave
Broadstairs CT10 84 B3
Deal CT14 215 C2
Palmerston Cres SE18 12 C8
Palmerston Ct CT14 215 D2
Palmerston Rd
Chatham ME4 63 F1
Dover CT16 277 F4
Grays RM20 17 D8
Orpington BR6 86 C5
Palmerston St [4] CT19 335 D6
Palmerston Wlk ME10 102 C4
Palmers Yd TN27 262 E5
Palm Tree Cl CT15 245 D7
Palm Tree Way CT18 305 B7
Palting Way CT20 335 B4
Pamela Ct ME7 64 D5
Panbro Ho SE18 11 F6
Panfield Rd SE2 3 A3
Pankhurst Ave E16 1 B5
Pankhurst Ho SE18 12 A7
Pankhurst Rd ME3 41 D6
Pannell Dr CT18 306 F4
Pannell Rd ME3 27 A6
Panteny La ME9 102 E2
Panter's BR8 32 F1
Pantheon Gdns TN23 299 F5
Pantiles The Bexley DA7 13 F7
Bromley BR1 52 E6
[20] Royal Tunbridge Wells TN2 286 A2
Panton Cl ME5 97 C4
Pantyles The TN14 186 B5
Paper La TN24 300 F6
Papillons Wlk SE3 11 A4
Papion Gr ME5 96 E2
Papworth Cl [1] CT19 335 A7
Parade CT1 174 F8
Parade Rd CT20 334 F3
Parade The
Ashford TN24 300 F5
Parade The *continued*
Birchington CT7 80 D8
Crayford DA1 14 F2
Eastry CT13 180 B2
Folkestone CT20 335 E5
Gravesend DA12 37 D6
Greatstone-on-S TN28, TN29 377 E7
Kemsing TN15 122 E2
Margate CT9 50 I3
Meopham Station DA13 60 A2
Rochester ME2 62 E8
Sittingbourne ME10 101 F2
Staplehurst TN12 260 F3
Swanscombe DA10 17 F2
Paradise Cotts ME9 99 E5
Paradise Path SE28 3 A5
Paradise Pl [14] SE18 1 E2
Paradise CT11 117 D7
Paradise Row CT13 148 F1
Paragon Cl E16 1 A7
Paragon CT11 117 E5
Paragon St CT11 117 D5
Paragon The SE3 11 A5
Paraker Way CT21 334 B4
Parbrook Rd ME3 24 B2
Pardoner Cl CT2 174 C7
Pardoners Way CT16 278 A3
Parfitt Way CT16 278 B2
Parham Cl CT1 143 B2
Parham Ct CT1 143 B2
Parham Rd
Canterbury CT1 143 B2
Chatham ME4 63 F2
Paris Cnr TN26 297 F6
Parish CE Prim Sch BR1 29 A1
Parish Gate Dr DA15 12 E1
Parish Rd
Chartham CT4 173 C3
Minster (Sheppey) ME12 47 A5
Parish Wharf [5] SE18 1 E2
Park App DA16 13 B3
Park Ave
Birchington CT7 81 A6
Broadstairs CT10 83 E2
Bromley BR1 29 A2
Deal CT14 215 C5
Dover CT16 278 D1
Edenbridge TN8 217 B2
Gillingham ME7 64 D3
Gravesend DA12 37 C7
Leysdown-on-S ME12 49 G1
Maidstone ME17 194 E2
Maidstone, Penenden Heath ME14 162 B6
Northfleet DA11 36 E7
Park Avenue Holiday Village ME12 49 G1
Park Ave Orpington BR6 86 A8
Orpington BR6 87 B7
Queenborough ME11 46 B4
Sittingbourne ME10 101 E1
Tonbridge TN11 221 F5
West Thurrock RM20 17 B8
Whitstable CT5 74 F3
Park Barn Rd ME17 197 C5
Park Chase CT10 83 E2
Park Cl CT18 307 A4
Park Cliff Rd DA9 17 C3
Park Cl CT9 51 D1
Park Corner Rd DA13 35 F4
Park Cotts
[8] Hawkhurst TN18 341 A2
Preston CT3 146 B6
Ramsgate CT11 83 E2
Sevenoaks TN13 154 C2
Park Crescent Rd
Erith DA8 14 D8
Margate CT9 51 A1
Park Cres Chatham ME4 96 F8
Erith DA8 14 D8
Park Ct ME13 138 E7
Parkdale Rd SE18 2 E1
Park Dr Hothfield TN26 267 A6
Longfield DA3 58 E6
Sittingbourne ME10 101 D1
Woolwich SE7 11 E8
Parker Ave RM18 19 C6
Parker Cl
Gillingham ME8 98 E5
Hamstreet TN26 349 A7
Newham E16 1 E5
Parker Ho [4] SE18 2 B1
Parker Ind Ctr DA1 34 C7
Parker Pl CT18 307 C5
Parker Rd RM17 17 F8
Parker's Cnr ME3 9 C2
Parker St E16 1 E5
Park Farm Cl
Folkestone CT19 335 C8
Shadoxhurst TN26 299 A1
Tyler Hill CT2 142 E6
Park Farm Houses ME20 160 B8
Park Farm Prim Sch CT19 335 C6
Park Farm Rd
Bromley BR1 52 D8
Folkestone CT19 335 C7
Ryarsh ME19 126 F6
Parkfield DA3 58 E5
Parkfield Rd
Folkestone CT19 335 C6
Rainham ME8 65 F1
Parkfield TN15 154 F4
Parkfields ME2 62 C7
Parkfield Way BR2 52 F4
Park Gate CT10 83 F2
Parkgate Cotts BR6 88 C6
Parkgate Rd BR6 88 C6
Park Gdns DA8 4 D2
Park Gr Bexley DA7 14 C3
Park Gr *continued*
Bromley BR1 52 B8
Park Hill Bromley BR1 52 F5
Meopham Station DA13 59 F5
Park Hill Rd TN14 122 E2
Parkhill Rd Sidcup DA15 30 E5
Sidcup, Old Bexley DA5 31 F8
Park Ho Dover CT16 278 D1
Maidstone ME14 162 B6
Sevenoaks TN13 154 C5
Sidcup DA14 31 A3
Park House Cotts DA4 89 F5
Park House Gdns TN4 254 A2
Parkhurst Gdns [2] DA5 32 A8
Parkhurst Rd DA5 32 A8
Park La
Bethersden TN26 298 C8
Birchington CT7 81 A6
Bishopsbourne CT4 209 C5
Elham CT4 273 F5
Gill's Green TN17,TN18 340 D7
Godden Green TN15 155 A4
Kemsing TN15 123 A1
Maidstone, Cock Stone ME17 195 D2
Maidstone, Ringlestone ME14 161 F7
Margate CT9 51 A2
Parkland Cl TN13 187 D6
Parkland Ct CT10 83 F6
Parklands TN4 285 E8
Park La
Sevenoaks TN13 154 C3
Swanley Village BR8 56 C7
Park Lea CT14 215 C5
Park Mall [2] TN24 268 B2
Park Manor ME7 64 B5
Park Mead DA15 13 B1
Park Mews
Chislehurst BR7 30 B2
[6] Dover CT16 310 D8
Parkmore BR7 30 B1
Park Par TN29 366 C7
Park Place [8] BR1 52 B8
Park Pl
Ashford,Beaver TN23 300 B7
Ashford,Willesborough TN24 300 F8
Dover CT16 310 D8
Gravesend DA12 37 C8
Herne CT6 111 A8
Hever TN8 250 D4
Margate CT9 50 I1
Sevenoaks TN13 153 D4
Park Rd
Addington ME19 126 C3
Ashford TN24 268 D6
Broadstairs CT10 84 B6
Bromley BR1 52 B8
Chislehurst BR7 30 B2
Dartford DA1 34 A8
Dover CT16 278 B2
Dunk's Green TN11 190 C5
Faversham ME13 138 D7
Folkestone CT19 334 E6
Gravesend DA11 37 B7
Herne Bay CT6 76 F4
Hythe CT21 333 B1
Leybourne ME19 127 D3
Limpsfield RH8 183 A8
Littlestone-on-Sea TN28 373 E5
Marden Thorn TN12 260 A4
Margate CT9 51 A2
Mereworth TN12 191 F5
Park Rd N TN24 268 B3
Park Rd Orpington BR5 54 C4
Preston CT3 146 D7
Queenborough ME11 45 F5
Ramsgate CT11 117 C7
Royal Tunbridge Wells,Southborough TN4 254 A2
Royal Tunbridge Wells TN4 286 B5
Sheerness ME12 28 D1
Sittingbourne ME10 101 E3
Swanley BR8 55 F5
Swanscombe DA10 17 E1
Temple Ewell CT16 277 D5
Westgate-on-S CT7 81 D6
Park Road Ind Est BR8 55 F6
Parkside Ave
Bexley DA1,DA7 14 E5
Bromley BR1 52 E5
Tilbury RM18 19 B5
Parkside ME3 40 B7
Parkside Com Prim Sch CT1 143 D2
Parkside Cotts TN16 150 E6
Parkside Cross DA7 14 E5
Parkside Ct
Herne Bay CT6 76 F5
Ramsgate CT11 117 D7
Tenterden TN30 344 F7
Park Side CT14 215 C5
Parkside TN14 120 F6
Parkside Lodge DA17 4 C1
Parkside Par DA1 14 F5
Parkside Pl CT1 143 D3
Parkside Rd DA17 4 C2
Parkside DA14 31 B6
Park St Ashford TN24 268 C2
Deal CT14 215 D6
Dover CT16 310 D8
Lydd TN29 376 C6
Royal Tunbridge Wells TN2 286 C3
Park Terr
Sundridge TN14 152 D3
Swanscombe DA9 17 B2
Throwley ME13 169 D1
Woodnesborough CT13 180 D7
Park The DA14 31 A3
Park Vale TN24 268 D6
Park View Cl
Edenbridge TN8 217 B2
Goodnestone CT3 178 D2
Parkview Ct DA11 37 A6
Park View Ct
[2] Lewisham SE12 29 C5
Maidstone ME15 162 E1
Park View
Folkestone CT19 335 E7
Hodsoll Street TN15 92 C2
Margate CT9 51 A2
Peasmarsh TN31 367 B2
Park View Rd DA16 13 C4
Parkview Rd SE9 30 B6
Park View Rise CT15 211 D4
Parkview TN2 286 D4
Park View
Sevenoaks TN13 154 C3
Sturry CT2 143 F6
Park View Terr [2] TN30 345 A7
Park Villas ME14 162 E4
Park Way ME17 194 D3
Parkway DA18 3 E3
Park Way
Joyden's Wood DA5 32 E5
Maidstone ME15 162 B1
Parkway Prim Sch DA18 3 E3
Park Way Prim Sch ME15 162 B1
Parkway The CT7 81 B7
Parkway TN10 222 D5
Parkwood Cl CT10 83 F2
Park Wood Cl TN23 300 B5
Parkwood Cl TN2 286 C6
Park Wood Forest Wlks* TN26 347 C4
Park Wood Gn ME8 98 D5
Parkwood Hall Sch BR8 56 B6
Parkwood TN31 368 B4
Parkwood Inf Sch ME8 98 E5
Parkwood Jun Sch ME8 98 E5
Park Wood La TN12 261 C1
Park Wood Par ME15 195 F5
Parkwood Rd TN16 150 F6
Park Wood Rd CT2 142 C4
Parkwood Rd DA5 31 F8
Park Wood Trad Est
Maidstone ME15 195 F4
Otham ME15 196 A4
Paroma Rd DA17 4 A3
Parr Ave ME7 64 D6
Parr Ct DA10 35 E8
Parrock Ave DA12 37 C7
Parrock Rd DA12 37 C7
Parrock St DA12 37 B8
Parrock The DA12 37 C7
Parrs Head Mews ME1 63 C6
Parry Ave E6 1 F7
Parry Pl SE18 2 B2
Parsonage Chase ME12 46 F5
Parsonage Cl TN4 285 B5
Parsonage Cotts ME9 134 A5
Parsonage Farm (Rural Heritage Ctr)* CT4 274 A6
Parsonage Farm ME13 169 F4
Parsonage Fields CT12 114 C7
Parsonage La
Cold Harbour ME9 100 F8
Lamberhurst TN3 317 B6
Rochester ME2 63 C8
Sidcup DA14 31 F4
Sittingbourne ME9 101 A8
Sutton at H DA4 34 B2
Parsonage Manorway DA17 14 A8
Parsonage Oast CT12 114 C7
Parsonage Rd
Herne Bay CT6 77 A3
Rusthall TN4 285 B5
West Thurrock RM20 17 C8
Parsonage Stocks Rd ME13 169 F5
Parsonage Villas CT15 309 C5
Parson's Croft TN8 250 C5
Parsons La Dartford DA2 33 B5
Stansted TN15 91 E1
Partridge Ave ME20 127 F3
Partridge Cl
Herne Bay CT6 77 C3
[1] Newham E16 1 D8
Partridge Dr
Orpington BR6 86 C7
St Mary's Island ME4 41 B1
Partridge Gn SE9 30 A5
Partridge La ME13 138 D7
Partridge Rd DA14 30 E4
Partridge Sq [3] E6 1 E8
Pasadena Cvn Pk TN15 90 B1
Pasley Rd ME4,ME7 64 A7
Pasley Rd E ME7 64 B7
Pasley Rd N ME4 64 B7
Pasley Rd W ME7 64 A7
Passey Pl SE9 11 F1
Passfield Ho SE18 2 D2
Passfield Path [13] SE28 3 B6
Pastens Rd RH8 183 C4
Pastime Cl ME10 101 E8
Paston Cres SE12 29 B8
Pasture The
Ashford TN24 268 D6
Hawkinge CT18 307 B4
Patagonia Ho TN2 286 C3
Pat Bassant Row DA10 35 E8
Patch The TN13 153 E5
Patchways TN29 350 E3
Pat Drew Ho BR1 52 C8
Path Field Cotts CT15 308 E5
Patience Cotts TN14 187 B2
Patricia Ct Bexley SE2 13 B7
Chislehurst BR7 53 D8
Patricia Way CT10 83 D3
Patrixbourne Ave ME8 65 C2
Patrixbourne Rd CT4 176 B2
Pattenden Gdns TN12 225 A7
Pattenden La TN12 259 C7
Pattens Gdns ME1 63 E2
Pattens La ME1,ME4 63 E1
Pattens Pl ME1 63 D2
Patterdale Rd DA2 34 D7
Patterson Cl CT14 215 A4
Patterson Ct DA1 16 A2
Pattinson Point [14] E16 1 A8
Pattison Farm Cl TN25 329 F4
Pattison Wlk SE18 2 C1
Paulinus Cl BR5 54 C6
Paul's Pl [8] CT16 278 C1
Pavement The TN30 324 B3
Pavilion Cl CT14 215 C8
Pavilion Ct CT20 335 E4
Pavilion Dr ME10 68 F1
Pavilion Gdns TN13 154 C3
Pavilion La ME18 192 A8
Pavilion Mdw CT17 277 E4
Pavilion Rd CT19 335 D6
Pavilion The [5] TN9 222 B1
Pavings The ME17 164 C2
Paxton Ave CT18 306 F3
Paxton Ct [5] SE12 29 C5
Paxton Rd BR1 29 A1
Payden St ME17 200 D8
Payers Pk CT20 335 D5
Paynes Cotts TN13 121 D1
Paynesfield Rd
Tatsfield TN16 150 D7
Tatsfield TN16 150 D8
Payne's La ME15 195 B7
Pays La TN25 202 D1
Pay St CT18 306 F7
Payton Cl CT9 83 A7
Payton Mews [4] CT1 143 B1
Peace Cotts ME15 226 D7
Peace St SE18 12 A8
Peach Croft DA11 36 E4
Peach Hall TN10 222 C6
Peacock Mews [7] ME16 161 E4
Peacock Pl ME13 171 A6
Peacock Rise ME5 97 A4
Peacock St DA12 37 C8
Peacock Wlk E16 1 B7
Peafield Wood Rd CT4 241 E4
Peak Dr CT13 180 B3
Peal Cl ME3 41 E5
Pean Court Rd CT5 108 D3
Pean Hill CT5 108 D2
Peareswood Rd DA8 14 F6
Pearl Cl E6 2 A7
Pearl Way ME18 159 C3
Pearmain Wlk CT1 175 C7
Pearman Cl ME8 66 A1
Pearse Pl TN3 317 B5
Pearson's Green Rd
Paddock Wood,Mile Oak TN12 257 D5
Paddock Wood,Pearson's Green TN12 257 F3
Pearson's Way CT10 83 E7
Pearson Way DA1 33 F6
Pear Tree Alley [2] ME10 101 E5
Pear Tree Ave ME20 128 C1
Peartree Cl DA8 14 D6
Pear Tree Cl
Broadstairs CT10 83 C4
Cranbrook TN17 320 D3
Swanley BR8 55 D7
Peartree Cotts ME8 99 B8
Pear Tree La
Dymchurch TN29 352 D1
Gillingham ME7 97 E7
Peartree La DA12 39 A2
Pear Tree La ME15 195 B6
Pear Tree Pl ME3 39 B3
Peartree Rd CT6 77 C3
Pear Tree Row ME17 196 B5
Peartree Way SE10 1 A2
Pear Tree Wlk ME9 100 A5
Pease Hill TN15 91 F4
Peasley La TN17 318 D6
Peasmarsh CE Prim Sch TN31 367 B1
Peatfield Cl DA15 30 E5
Peat Way ME3 10 D1
Pebble Hill Cotts RH8 183 B6
Peckham Cl ME2 63 C8
Peckham Ct TN12 224 F6
Peckham Ho [6] BR5 54 D1
Peckham Hurst Rd TN11 190 E7
Pedding Hill CT3 147 A1
Pedding La CT3 179 A8
Pedham Place Est BR8 56 A4
Peel Dr ME10 102 C4
Peelers Ct CT2 142 F1
Peel Rd BR6 86 C5
Peel St ME14 162 A6
Peel Yates Ho [12] SE18 1 E2
Peene Cotts CT18 306 B1
Peens La ME17 228 C7
Pegasus Ct DA12 37 C5
Peggoty Cl ME3 39 B3
Pegley Gdns SE12 29 A6
Pegwell Ave CT11 117 A5
Pegwell Bay Ctry Pk* CT12 116 C2
Pegwell Bay Nature Reserve* CT12 116 C3

Pegwell Cl CT11 117 A5
Pegwell Ct CT11 117 B5
Pegwell Rd CT11 117 B5
Pegwell St SE18 12 E7
Pelham Cotts DA5 32 B7
Pelham Ct 19 DA14 31 A5
Pelham Gdns CT20 335 A4
Pelham Prim Sch DA7 14 A4
Pelham Rd Bexley DA7 14 A4
Gravesend DA11 37 A8
Pelham Rd S DA11 36 F7
Pelham Terr 4 DA11 36 F8
Pelican Cl ME2 62 C6
Pelican Ct ME18 192 E7
Pell Cl TN5 337 A6
Pellipar Gdns SE18 1 F1
Pellipar Rd SE18 1 F1
Pells La TN15 124 A7
Pelwood Rd TN31 374 A2
Pemberton Ct CT21 334 B3
Pemberton Gdns BR8 55 E7
Pemberton Rd TN24 268 D2
Pemberton Sq 4 ME2 63 C8
Pemble Cl TN12 256 A7
Pembroke Ave CT9 50 F1
Pembroke ME4 64 B8
Pembroke Cl DA8 4 D2
Pembroke Ct
Chatham ME4 64 A4
Folkestone CT19 335 E6
1 Ramsgate CT11 117 E7
Pembroke Gdns ME8 98 E4
Pembroke Ho TN28 373 E5
Pembroke Lodge Mus & Art Gall CT7 80 F7
Pembroke Mews TN28 373 C8
Pembroke Par DA8 4 C1
Pembroke Pl DA4 57 B8
Pembroke Rd
Bromley BR1 52 D7
Coxheath ME17 194 C3
Erith DA8 4 D2
Newham E6 1 F8
Sevenoaks TN13 154 B2
Tonbridge TN9 222 A1
Pembroke Rise ME4 64 A7
Pembury Cl TN2 287 D7
Pembury Cres DA14 31 E6
Pembury Ct 6 ME10 101 E4
Pembury Gdns ME16 161 D3
Pembury Grange TN2 287 A6
Pembury Gr TN9 254 C8
Pembury Hall Rd TN11,TN2 255 C3
Pembury Hospl TN2 287 B7
Pembury Pl TN25 267 F4
Pembury Rd Bexley DA7 13 E8
Pembury TN11 255 A2
Royal Tunbridge Wells TN2 286 E4
Tonbridge TN11,TN9 254 D7
Pembury Sch TN2 287 D8
Pembury St ME10 101 E4
Pembury Vineyard* TN2 255 F1
Pembury Way ME8 65 E2
Pembury Wlks TN11, TN2 255 C2
Penbury CT14 215 C1
Pencester Ct 3 CT16 310 E8
Pencester Rd CT16 310 D8
Pencroft Dr DA1 33 C8
Pendant Ct BR6 87 A5
Penda Rd DA8 14 B7
Pendennis Rd
Orpington BR6 87 C8
Sevenoaks TN13 154 B4
Penderel Mews TN30 345 B8
Pendlebury Gn SE18 11 E6
Pendragon Rd BR1, SE12 29 A5
Pendragon Sch BR1 29 A5
Pendrell St SE18 12 D8
Pendrill Pl TN5 336 F5
Penenden Ct ME14 162 B7
Penenden Heath Rd ME14 162 C7
Penenden DA3 91 F8
Penenden St ME14 162 A6
Penfield La ME9 135 A4
Penfold Cl Chatham ME5 97 B7
Maidstone ME15 195 E5
Penfold Gdns CT15 244 E5
Penfold Hill ME17 197 B8
Penfold Ho 14 SE18 12 B8
Penfold La DA5 31 D7
Penfold Rd CT19 335 F6
Penfolds Cl TN10 222 C5
Penfold Way ME15 194 F6
Penford Gdns SE9 11 D4
Pengarth Rd DA5 13 D1
Pengelly Pl CT2 142 F2
Penguin Cl ME2 62 D6
Penhale Cl BR6 87 A6
Penhall Rd SE7 1 D2
Penhill Rd DA5 31 C8
Penhurst Cl ME14 162 F5
Peninsular Park Rd SE7 1 A2
Penlee Cl TN8 217 C2
Penlee Point TN24 268 D5
Penmon Rd SE2 3 A3
Pennant Rd ME1 96 C7
Penn Cl ME10 102 B2
Penney Cl DA1 33 D8
Penn Gdns BR7 53 B7
Penn Hill TN23 299 E6
Pennine Way
Ashford TN24 268 B4
Bexley DA7 14 E6
Maidstone ME15 163 A1
Northfleet DA11 36 E5
Pennine Wlk TN2 286 D5
Pennington Cl CT2 144 C7
Pennington Manor 1 TN4 253 F2
Pennington Pl TN4 254 B1
Pennington Rd TN4 254 A2
Pennington Way SE12 29 B6
Penn La Bexley DA5 13 D1
Ide Hill TN14 185 E8
Penns Yd TN2 287 C6
Penny Cress Gdns ME16 161 C3
Penny Cress Rd ME12 47 A4
Penn Yd TN2 287 C6
Pennyfields TN17 320 D4
Pennypot Ind Est CT21 332 F1
Penny Pot La CT4 206 B4
Pennyroyal Ave E6 2 A7
Penny Spring Farm (Cvn Pk) ME14 131 B2
Penpool La DA16 13 B4
Penrith Ct ME7 65 A5
Penrose Ct CT21 333 C1
Penryn Manor 4 ME7 64 C6
Pensand Ho CT21 333 D1
Penshurst Ave DA15 13 A1
Penshurst CE Prim Sch TN11 252 A4
Penshurst Cl
Canterbury CT2 143 A3
Gillingham ME8 65 E2
New Barn DA3 59 D7
West Kingsdown TN15 90 E4
Penshurst Enterprise Ctr TN11 252 C4
Penshurst Gdns CT9 51 F2
Penshurst Place* TN11 252 B4
Penshurst Rd
Bexley DA7 13 F6
Penshurst TN3,TN11 252 A5
Poundsbridge TN11,TN3 284 E8
Ramsgate CT11 117 F7
Penshurst Rise ME13 138 B8
Penshurst Sta TN11 219 F1
Penshurst Vineyard* TN11 251 F2
Penshurst Way BR5 54 C5
Penstocks The ME15 161 D2
Pentagon Sh Ctr ME4 63 F4
Penton Ho 3 SE2 3 D4
Pentstemon Dr DA10 17 E2
Pent Vale Cl CT19 335 A6
Pent Valley Sch CT19 334 F7
Penventon Ct 3 RM18 19 A5
Pen Way TN10 222 E5
Pepingstraw Cl ME19 158 D7
Pepper Cl E6 1 F8
Pepperhill La DA11 36 C5
Pepper Hill DA11 36 C5
Pepys Ave ME12 28 B2
Pepys Cl
4 Dartford DA1 16 A3
Northfleet DA11 36 D5
Tilbury RM18 19 C6
Pepys Cres E16 1 A5
Pepys Rise BR6 53 F1
Pepy's Way ME2 62 F8
Perch La TN3 288 D1
Percival Rd BR6 86 B8
Percival Terr CT17 310 B7
Percy Ave CT10 51 F2
Percy Rd Bexley DA7 13 E5
Broadstairs CT10 83 F5
Margate CT9 51 A3
Ramsgate CT11 117 D8
Percy St 13 RM17 18 C8
Percy Terr TN4 286 A6
Peregrine Cl CT21 353 D8
Peregrine Ct DA16 12 F6
Peregrine Dr ME10 102 A2
Peregrine Rd ME19 159 A2
Peri Ct CT1 174 F6
Peridot Ct ME15 195 E5
Peridot St E6 1 E8
Perie Row 9 ME7 64 A6
Perimeter Rd
Dover CT16 310 G8
New Hythe ME20 128 C3
Periton Rd SE9 11 D3
Periwinkle Cl ME10 101 E5
Periwinkle Ct 3 ME10 101 E5
Perkins Ave CT9 82 F8
Perkins Cl DA9 16 F2
Perpins Rd SE9 12 E1
Perran Cl DA3 58 F5
Perries Mead CT19 335 B7
Perrot Way CT18 307 B5
Perry Court Rudolf Steiner Sch CT4 206 E7
Perryfield St ME14 161 F6
Perry Gr DA1 16 A3
Perry Hall Cl BR6 54 A2
Perry Hall Prim Sch BR6 53 F3
Perry Hall Rd BR6 54 A2
Perry Hill ME3 22 C1
Perry Ho DA14 31 A3
Perry La CT3 146 C3
Perrys La BR6,TN14 120 C6
Perry St Chatham ME4 63 E3
Chislehurst BR7 30 E2
Crayford DA1 14 E4
Maidstone ME14 161 F6
Northfleet DA11 36 F7
Perry Street Gdns BR7 30 E2
Perry Wood Local Nature Reserve* ME13 171 D4
Perth Gdns ME10 101 C4
Perth Ho 4 RM18 19 A5
Perth Way CT16 278 C3
Pescot Ave DA3 59 B6
Pested Bars Rd ME17 195 D5
Pested La TN25 203 C4
Petchart Cl ME2 62 C3
Petchell Mews 11 CT1 143 B2
Peterborough Gdns ME2 62 C6
Peter Candler Way TN24 268 E4
Peters Cl DA16 12 E5
Petersfield Dr DA13 92 F1
Petersfield TN2 287 E7
Petersham Dr BR5 54 A6
Petersham Gdns BR5 53 F7
Peter St Deal CT14 215 D7
Dover CT16 310 C8
Folkestone CT20 335 E5
5 Gravesend DA12 37 B8
Peterstone Rd SE2 3 B4
Petfield Cl ME12 47 C6
Petham Court Cotts BR8 55 F4
Petham Gn ME8 65 C2
Petham Prim Sch CT4 207 C3
Petlands ME17 195 D5
Petrel Cl CT6 77 F4
Petrel Way CT18 307 A3
Petrie Ho 3 SE18 12 A8
Pett Bottom Rd CT4 208 C5
Petten Cl BR5 54 D1
Petten Gr BR5 54 D1
Petteridge La TN12 288 F7
Pettfield Hill Rd ME13 169 B1
Pett Hill CT4 175 F1
Pettits Row TN12 258 D8
Pett La TN27 234 D7
Pett Lane ME9 133 B7
Pettman Cl CT6 76 F3
Pettman Cres SE28,SE18 2 D3
Pettman Ct 5 CT10 83 E5
Pettmans Mews CT5 74 C2
Pett's Cres CT12 115 B5
Petts La CT3 178 A8
Pett St SE18 1 E2
Petts Wood Rd BR5 53 D4
Petts Wood Sta BR5 53 C4
Petworth Rd DA6 14 A2
Peverel Dr ME14 163 A5
Peverel Gn ME8 98 D4
Peverell Rd CT16 278 B4
Peverel E6 2 A7
Peveril Ct 15 DA2 16 B1
Pewter Ct CT1 174 F7
Phalarope Way ME4 41 C2
Pharos Dr CT16 278 E1
Pheasant Cl E16 1 B7
Pheasant La ME15 195 B8
Pheasant Rd ME4 64 C2
Pheasants' Hall Rd CT4 208 F2
Phelps Cl TN15 90 E4
Philimore Cl SE18 2 E1
Philip Ave BR8 55 D5
Philip Corby Cl CT9 51 B2
Philipine Craft Ctr* TN29 370 A6
Philipot Almshouse SE9 11 F1
Philipot Path SE9 11 F1
Philippa Gdns SE9 11 D2
Philippa Ho CT19 335 F6
Phillippa Ct ME10 101 E8
Phillip Rd CT19 334 E6
Phillips Cl DA1 15 B1
Phillips Ct ME8 65 B2
Phillips Rd CT7 81 A6
Philpots La TN11 220 E6
Philpott's Cross TN18 340 E2
Phineas Pett Rd SE9 11 E4
Phipps Ho 1 SE7 1 B1
Phoenix Com Prim Sch TN24 268 D5
Phoenix Cotts ME18 192 D6
Phoenix Ct 11 ME7 64 C6
Phoenix Dr
Orpington BR2 85 D7
Wateringbury ME18 192 E7
Phoenix Ind Est ME2 63 D7
Phoenix Pk ME15 195 F4
Phoenix Pl DA1 33 D8
Phoenix Rd ME5 97 B2
Phoenix Yard Cotts ME18 159 F1
Picardy Manorway DA17 4 B3
Picardy Rd DA17 4 A2
Picardy St DA17 4 A3
Piccadilly Apartments 4 ME5 64 B3
Pickelden La CT4 205 F8
Pickering Ct 20 DA2 16 B1
Pickering Ho 4 SE18 2 A2
Pickering St ME15 195 B6
Pickford Cl DA7 13 E5
Pickforde La TN5 338 D1
Pickford La DA7 13 E5
Pickford Rd DA7 13 E4
Pickhill Oast TN30 345 B4
Pickhurst La BR2 52 A1
Pickle's Way ME3 22 A6
Pickmoss La TN14 122 A3
Pickneybush La TN29 365 A7
Pickwick Cres ME1 63 C3
Pickwick Ct SE9 29 F7
Pickwick Gdns DA11 36 D5
Pickwick House DA11 36 D5
Pickwick Way BR7 30 C2
Picton Rd CT11 117 C7
Piedmont Rd SE18 2 D1
Pie Factory Rd CT15 211 E2
Pier Approach Rd ME7 64 D7
Pier Ave Herne Bay CT6 76 E4
Whitstable CT5 75 A2
Pierce Mill La TN11 224 C6
Piermont Pl BR1 52 E7
Pier Par 3 E16 2 A5
Pier Pl ME2 41 A3
Pierpoint Rd CT5 108 D7
Pier Rd Erith DA8 14 F8
Gillingham ME7 64 E7
Pier Rd Ind Est ME7 64 D7
Pier Rd Newham E16 2 A4
Northfleet DA11 18 F1
Swanscombe DA9 17 B3
Pierremont Ave CT10 84 A4
Pier The CT16 277 F8
Pier Way SE28 2 D3
Pigdown La TN8 250 D4
Pigeon La CT6 77 A2
Piggott's Cross TN8 218 D7
Pigsdean Rd DA13 61 B2
Pigtail Cnr ME12 47 E6
Pike Cl Bromley BR1 29 B3
Folkestone CT19 335 A7
New Hythe ME20 128 A4
Pikefields ME8 65 C2
Pikefish La TN12,ME18 225 F2
Pike Rd CT14,CT15 212 E4
Pikey La ME19 159 E5
Pilar Ct CT8 50 D1
Pilckem Cl CT1 143 D1
Pile La TN12 261 A5
Pilgrims Ct
Charing TN27 234 C7
Dartford DA1 16 A2
Greenwich SE3 11 A6
Pilgrims La CT4 172 E1
Pilgrims Lakes ME17 198 E6
Pilgrims La Titsey RH8 150 D3
Whitstable CT5 108 B4
Pilgrim Spring CT19 335 D8
Pilgrims Rd CT1 175 C7
Pilgrims' Rd DA10 17 E3
Pilgrims Rd
Upper Halling ME2 94 F6
Wouldham ME1 95 E5
Pilgrims View
Sandling ME14 129 E3
Swanscombe DA9 17 C1
Pilgrims Way
Boughton Aluph TN25 237 A4
Boxley ME14 130 E3
Pilgrims' Way TN25 303 E8
Pilgrims Way
Broad Street ME14, ME17 164 C6
Canterbury CT1 175 C7
Charing TN27 234 E8
Pilgrim's Way Cotts TN15 123 A2
Pilgrims Way
Cuxton ME2 62 C3
Dartford DA1 34 B8
Detling ME14 131 B1
Dover CT16 278 A3
Eccles ME20 129 B6
Pilgrims Way E TN14 122 D3
Pilgrims' Way TN16 151 B4
Pilgrims Way ME17 164 F3
Pilgrims' Way TN14, TN15 123 C3
Pilgrims Way ME17 199 B7
Pilgrims Way Prim Sch CT1 175 C7
Pilgrims Way
Thurnham ME14 163 E8
Upper Halling ME2,ME6, ME19 94 D3
Vigo Village ME19 126 B7
Westwell TN25 235 D5
Pilgrims Way W TN14 121 E3
Pilgrims Way
Wrotham TN15 125 A3
Wrotham TN15 125 C4
Pilkington Rd BR6 86 C8
Pillar Box La
Crouch TN11 190 D5
Oldbury TN15 155 E5
Pilot Rd ME1 96 C8
Pilots Ave CT14 215 A4
Pilot's Farm Rd CT4 208 A4
Pilots Pl DA12 19 C1
Pimpernel Cl ME14 163 B4
Pimpernel Way ME5 96 E4
Pimp's Court Cotts ME15 194 E6
Pimp's Court Farm Ctr ME15 194 E6
Pinchbeck Rd BR6 86 F4
Pincott Rd DA6 14 A3
Pincroft Wood DA3 59 C6
Pincus Ho ME10 101 D5
Pine Ave DA12 37 D7
Pine Cl Larkfield ME20 128 A2
Swanley BR8 55 F5
Pine Cotts ME14 161 E8
Pinecrest Gdns BR6 86 B6
Pinecroft DA16 13 A7
Pine Glade BR6 85 F6
Pine Gr Edenbridge TN8 217 B2
Gillingham ME7 98 A5
Maidstone ME14 162 B6
Pineham Rd CT15 278 D6
Pine Ho
3 Chatham ME5 96 F5
5 Maidstone ME14 162 B4
Pinehurst
Chislehurst BR7 30 B2
Sevenoaks TN14 154 E6
Pinehurst Wlk 4 BR6 53 D1
Pine Lodge Ct CT14 215 B5
Pine Lodge ME16 161 C3
Pine Lodge Touring Pk ME17 163 F2
Pineneedle La TN13 154 B4
Pine Pl ME15 161 E1
Pine Rd ME2 62 F6
Pine Ridge TN10 222 B6
Pine Rise DA13 60 A3
Pinesfield La ME19 126 B6
Pines Gardens The* CT15 280 B5
Pineside Rd CT3 176 E8
Pines Rd BR1 52 E7
Pines The
Broadstairs CT10 83 D4
Canterbury CT1 175 A6
Pine Tree Ave CT2 142 E2
Pine Tree Cl CT7 81 B7
Pinetree Cl CT5 74 F3
Pine Tree La TN15 156 A2
Pine View TN15 157 C7
Pine Way CT19 334 D7
Pine Wlk CT6 77 E5
Pinewood Ave
Sevenoaks TN13 154 D6
Sidcup DA15 30 E7
Pinewood BR7 30 A2
Pinewood Cl
Orpington BR6 53 D1
Paddock Wood TN12 256 F6
Ramsgate CT12 83 C1
Pinewood Ct TN4 254 A1
Pinewood Dr
Chatham ME5 130 D8
Orpington BR6 86 E5
Pinewood Gdns TN4 254 A1
Pinewood Pl DA2 32 E6
Pinewood Rd
Bexley SE2 13 D8
Bromley BR2 52 A5
Royal Tunbridge Wells TN2 286 D5
Pin Hill CT1 174 F7
Pinkham TN12 225 A5
Pinkham Gdns TN12 225 A6
Pinks Cnr CT12 115 D6
Pinks Hill BR8 55 E4
Pinnacle Hill DA7 14 B3
Pinnacle Hill N DA7 14 B3
Pinnacles The ME4 41 C1
Pinnell Rd SE9 11 D3
Pinners Hill CT15,CT3 211 C6
Pinners La CT15 211 C5
Pinnock La TN12 260 E1
Pinnock's Ave DA11 37 B7
Pintail Cl Grain ME3 27 B6
Newham E6 1 E8
Pintail Dr ME9 68 E3
Pintails The ME4 41 B1
Pintail Way CT6 77 C2
Pinton Hill TN5 338 B3
Pinto Way SE3 11 B3
Pioneer Bsns Pk CT11 117 C8
Pioneer Cotts TN11 252 A1
Pioneer Ct 5 DA11 19 A1
Pioneer Rd CT16 278 A3
Pioneer Way BR8 55 E6
Pipers Cl TN5 337 A4
Piper's Green Rd TN16 185 B7
Pipers La TN16 185 A8
Pippenhall SE9 12 B1
Pippin Ave CT4 209 B8
Pippin Cl
Coxheath ME17 194 B2
Sittingbourne ME10 101 D6
Pippin Croft ME7 98 A6
Pippin Rd TN12 224 F6
Pippins The DA13 60 A3
Pippin Way ME19 159 A2
Pip's View ME3 22 F5
Pirbright Cl ME5 97 D2
Pirie St E16 1 B5
Pirrip Cl DA12 37 F6
Pitchfont La RH8 183 B8
Pitfield Cres SE28 3 A5
Pitfield Dr DA13 92 F7
Pitfield DA3 58 F5
Pitfold Cl SE12 11 B1
Pitfold Rd SE12 11 A1
Pit La TN8 217 C4
Pitstock Rd ME9 135 B5
Pittlesden Pl 1 TN30 345 A7
Pittlesden TN30 345 A7
Pittock Ho CT14 215 B3
Pitt Rd
Chartway Street ME17 197 A2
Maidstone ME16 161 B1
Orpington BR6 86 C6
Pittsmead Ave BR2 52 A2
Pittswood Cotts TN11 223 A8
Pivington La TN27 233 C2
Pivington Mill Ind Est TN27 233 C2
Pixot Hill TN12 257 B2
Pix's La TN17 344 A3
Pixwell La CT14 214 D3
Pizien Well Rd ME18 192 B7
Place Farm Ave BR6 53 D1
Place La Hartlip ME9 99 D4
Woodchurch TN26 326 B3
Place The CT4 210 F1
Plain Cotts CT20 335 A4
Plain Rd
Brabourne Lees TN25 302 F5
Folkestone CT20 335 B4
Marden TN12 259 C4
Plains Ave ME15 162 C1
Plains of Waterloo CT11 117 F7
Plain The TN17 318 E8
Plaistow Gr BR1 29 B1
Plaistow La BR1 52 C8
Plaistow Sq ME14 162 C6
Plane Ave DA11 36 D8
Plane Tree Ho SE7 1 D1
Plane Wlk TN10 222 C7
Plantagenet Ho SE18 1 F3
Plantation Cl
Hothfield TN26 267 A7
Plantation Cl *continued*
Stone DA9 16 F1
Plantation Dr BR5 54 D1
Plantation La ME14 163 A3
Plantation Rd Erith DA8 15 A6
Faversham ME13 138 C7
Gillingham ME7 65 A6
Hextable BR8 33 A2
Whitstable CT5 75 D2
Plantation The SE3 11 A5
Platt CE Prim Sch TN15 157 C7
Platt Comm TN15 157 C7
Platters The ME8 98 C7
Plat The TN8 217 D1
Platt House La TN15 125 C6
Platt Ind Est TN15 157 C8
Platt Mill Cl TN15 157 B7
Platt Mill Terr TN15 157 B7
Platt's Heath Prim Sch ME17 198 F2
Platt The Frant TN3 314 B1
Sutton Valence ME17 229 E7
Plaxdale Green Rd TN15 124 D7
Plaxtol Cl BR1 52 C8
Plaxtol La TN15,TN11 189 D8
Plaxtol Prim Sch TN15 189 E7
Plaxtol Rd DA8 14 A7
Playdell Ct 12 CT20 335 D4
Playden La TN31 368 C3
Playing Fields CT13 180 E7
Playstool Cl ME9 100 B6
Playstool Rd ME9 100 A6
Plaza Ct 7 ME10 102 A4
Pleasance Rd N TN29 377 E5
Pleasance Rd BR5 54 B6
Pleasance Road Central TN29 380 D7
Pleasant Row 10 ME7 64 A6
Pleasant Valley La ME15 194 B4
Pleasant View
15 Erith DA8 4 E1
Orpington BR6 86 C5
Pleasaunce Ct SE9 11 F3
Pleasent Pl ME12 46 E6
Pleasure House La ME17 230 A8
Plenty Brook Dr CT6 76 F3
Plewis Ho ME7 64 E7
Pleydell Cres CT2 143 F7
Pleydell Gdns CT20 335 D4
Plimsoll Ave CT19 335 E8
Plomley Cl ME8 98 D4
Plough Cotts ME17 196 D2
Plough Ct CT6 77 D2
Plough Hill
Basted TN15 156 F4
Church Hougham CT15 309 C4
Plough La CT5 75 D3
Ploughmans Way
Ashford TN23 299 D5
Chatham ME5 97 A1
Gillingham ME8 98 E6
Plough Rd ME12 48 C5
Plough Wents Rd ME17 196 B2
Plough Wlk TN8 217 C3
Plover Cl Chatham ME5 97 D1
Herne Bay CT6 77 F5
Marlpit Hill TN8 217 C3
Plover Rd
Hawkinge CT18 306 F3
Larkfield ME20 127 F2
Minster (Sheppey) ME12 47 A5
Plowenders Cl ME19 126 D2
Pluckley CE Prim Sch TN27 265 D7
Pluckley Cl ME8 65 C3
Pluckley Gdns CT9 51 E2
Pluckley Rd
Bethersden TN26 297 D7
Charing TN27 234 B5
Hothfield TN26,TN27 266 B4
Smarden TN27 264 D2
Pluckley Sta TN27 265 C3
Plug La DA13 93 D5
Plumcroft Prim Sch SE18 12 C8
Plumey Feather Cotts TN6 311 E3
Plumford Rd ME13 138 A2
Plum La SE18 12 C7
Plummer La TN30 344 F6
Plummers Croft TN13 153 E6
Plumpton Wlk
5 Canterbury CT1 143 B1
9 Maidstone ME15 195 F6
Plumpudding La ME13 107 E1
Plumstead Common Rd SE18 12 C8
Plumstead High St SE18, SE2 2 E2
Plumstead Manor Sch SE18 12 D8
Plumstead Rd SE18 2 C2
Plumstead Sta SE18 2 D2
Plumstone Rd CT7 80 F1
Plum Tree Cotts TN18 354 E8
Plum Tree Gdns TN26 326 B1
Plumtree Gr ME7 98 A4
Plum Tree La ME9 132 B8
Plumtree Rd TN27 261 F7
Plumtrees ME16 161 A2
Plurenden Manor Farm Cotts TN26 325 D7
Plurenden Rd TN26 325 E7

Plymouth Dr TN13 154 C3
Plymouth Pk TN13 154 C3
Plymouth Rd
Bromley BR1 52 B8
Newham E16 1 A8
Plympton Cl 8 DA17 3 E3
Plymstock Rd DA16 13 C7
Poachers Cl ME5 97 C5
Pochard Cl ME4 41 B1
Pochard Cres CT6 76 E3
Pocket Hill TN13 187 A7
Pococks Bank TN8 218 C3
Podkin Wood ME5 129 F8
Poets Cnr CT9 50 J1
Poets Wlk CT14 215 C1
Pointer Cl SE28 3 D7
Pointer Sch The SE3 11 A7
Poison Cross CT13 180 B4
Poldark Ct 22 CT11 117 F7
Polebrook Rd SE3 11 C4
Polegate Cotts RM17 17 E8
Polesden Rd TN2 286 D2
Polesteeple Hill TN16 118 D2
Poles The ME9 66 E4
Polhill TN13,TN14 121 C4
Polhill Dr ME5 96 F2
Police Station Rd
ME19 159 C8
Pollard Cl
Ashford TN23 299 F8
Newham E16 1 A6
Pollard Ct ME7 64 C5
Pollard Pl CT5 108 C6
Pollards Oak Cres
RH8 183 A3
Pollards Oak Rd RH8 183 A3
Pollards Wood Hill
RH8 183 B5
Pollards Wood Rd
RH8 183 B4
Pollard Wlk DA14 31 C2
Polley Cl TN2 287 D7
Pollyhaugh DA4 89 E7
Polo Way CT5 75 D1
Polperro Cl BR6 53 F3
Polthorne Gr SE18 2 D2
Polytechnic St 14 SE18 2 A2
Pomfret Ho CT4 173 D1
Pomfret Rd CT4 173 D1
Pommeus La CT14 247 D7
Poncia Rd TN23 300 A7
Pond Cl SE3 11 A5
Pond Cotts
Herne Bay CT6 77 D2
Sittingbourne ME10 134 D8
Pond Dr ME10 102 A2
Pond Farm Rd
Hucking ME17 132 D1
Oad Street ME9 100 F1
Pondfield La DA12 38 E1
Pondfield Rd BR6 86 B7
Pond Hill Adisham CT3 177 D1
Cliffe ME3 22 B6
Pond Hill Rd CT20 334 C5
Pond La
St Margaret's at Cliffe
CT15 279 D7
Stone Street TN15 155 E2
Womenswold CT4,CT3 210 D3
Pondmore Way TN25 267 F4
Pond Path BR7 30 B2
Pondwood Rise BR6 53 E2
Pontefract Rd BR1 29 A3
Pontoise Cl TN13 153 F5
Ponycart La CT4 240 E3
Pook La TN27 295 D3
Poona Rd TN1 286 B2
Poorhole La CT10 83 B5
Pootings Rd TN8 217 E7
Poot La ME9 66 E5
Pope Dr TN12 260 E4
Pope House La TN30 324 B4
Pope Rd BR2 52 D4
Popes La
Limpsfield RH8 216 A8
Sturry CT2 143 F7
Popes Row Cotts
TN17 317 F2
Pope St
Godmersham CT4 205 E4
Maidstone ME16 161 C2
Pope Street Ct SE9 29 F7
Popes Wood ME14 162 F6
Poplar Ave
Gravesend DA12 37 C4
Orpington BR6 86 B8
Poplar Cl Ashford TN23 267 F3
Hoo St Werburgh ME3 41 E3
Rochester ME2 62 F5
Poplar Dr
Elvington CT15 212 B2
Herne Bay CT6 76 D2
Poplar Field TN30 359 D4
Poplar Gr ME16 161 C5
Poplar La TN29 376 D7
Poplar Mount DA17 4 C2
Poplar Pl SE28 3 C6
Poplar Rd
Broadstairs CT10 83 E6
Ramsgate CT11 117 D7
Rochester ME2 62 E5
Wittersham TN30 359 D4
Poplars Cl DA3 59 C6
Poplars TN26 348 A7
Poplars The
Ashford TN23 300 A7
Bethersden TN26 297 E5
Gravesend DA12 37 E8
Hersden CT3 111 F1
Poplar View ME13 139 E3
Poplar Wlk DA13 60 B3
Poplicans Rd ME2 62 B3
Poppy Cl Erith DA17 4 B4
Gillingham ME7 64 E5
Maidstone ME16 161 D3
Poppyfield TN31 368 C1
Popsal La CT3 178 B6
Porchester Cl
Hartley DA3 58 F5
Loose ME15 195 A6
Porchfield Cl DA12 37 C6
Porcupine Cl SE9 29 E6
Porrington Cl BR7 53 A8
Portal House Sch
CT15 280 A6
Port Ave DA9 17 B1
Port Cl Chatham ME5 97 B3
Maidstone ME14 163 A5
Portebello Ct CT14 215 D7
Porter Cl
Minster (Sheppey) ME12 47 A6
West Thurrock RM20 17 C8
Porter Rd E6 1 F7
Porters Cl TN12 288 F6
Porter's La ME13 138 B2
Porters Wlk ME17 196 E4
Porters Wood TN12 288 E6
Portery The CT14 215 D6
Porteus Ct DA1 33 D6
Port Hill BR6 120 B7
Porthkerry Ave DA16 13 A3
Portland Ave
Gravesend DA12 37 B6
Sidcup DA15 13 A1
Sittingbourne ME10 102 C4
Portland Cl
Ashford TN24 268 C7
Hythe CT21 333 B2
Tonbridge TN10 222 D7
Portland Cres SE9 29 E6
Portland Ct
3 Hythe CT21 333 B2
Ramsgate CT11 117 E7
Portland Pl 1 ME6 128 A8
Portland Rd
Bromley,Mottingham SE9 29 E6
Bromley,Sundridge BR1 29 C3
Gillingham ME7 64 E6
Gravesend DA12 37 B7
Hythe CT21 333 B2
Northfleet DA11 18 D1
Wouldham ME1 95 C4
Portland St 1 ME4 64 B2
Portland Terr
Ripple CT14 247 D8
Sheerness ME12 28 C2
Portland Villas DA12 37 B7
Portlight Pl CT5 108 A6
Port Lympne Wild Animal
Pk* CT21 331 D2
Portman Cl Bexley DA7 13 E4
Maypole DA5 32 E7
Portman Pk TN9 222 C3
Portmeadow Wlk SE2 3 D4
Portobello Par TN15 91 A2
Portree Mews ME7 64 E3
Port Rise ME4 63 F3
Portsdown Cl ME16 161 B2
Portsea Rd RM18 19 C6
Portsmouth Cl ME2 62 D6
Portsmouth Mews E16 1 B5
Port Victoria Rd ME3 27 C4
Portway Gdns SE18 11 D7
Portway Rd ME3 40 B7
Portway CT5 108 C8
Post Barn Rd ME4 63 F2
Postern La TN9,TN11 222 E1
Postley Commercial Ctr
ME15 162 A2
Postley Rd ME15 162 A1
Postling TN23 267 E1
Postling Rd CT19 334 E7
Postling Wents CT21 332 F8
Postmill Dr ME15 161 F1
Post Office Rd 12
TN18 340 F2
Post Office Row CT4 171 D1
Post Office Sq TN1 286 A3
Potash La TN15 157 C6
Pot Kiln La TN26 296 E4
Potten Street Rd CT7 79 E3
Potteries The ME9 66 E3
Potters Cl TN24 267 E6
Potters Cnr TN24 267 E6
Potter's La TN18 341 A6
Potter St CT13 149 A1
Pottery Cotts TN25 269 E5
Pottery Rd
Coldblow DA5 32 C6
Hoo St Werburgh ME3 41 D5
Potyn Ho ME1 63 C4
Pouces Cotts CT12 81 F1
Poulders Gdns CT13 180 E8
Poulders Rd CT13 180 E8
Poulsen Ct 8 ME10 102 B4
Poulters Wood BR2 85 D5
Poulton Cl CT17 309 F8
Poulton Close Bsns Pk
CT17 277 E1
Poulton La CT3 179 C8
Pound Bank Cl TN15 90 F2
Pound Cl BR6 86 D8
Pound Court Dr BR6 86 D8
Pound Ct TN23 300 A3
Pound Farm Cotts
CT18 334 A7
Poundfield Rd TN18 356 B5
Pound Green Ct 4
DA5 32 A8
Pound Ho
Ashford TN23 300 B8
Hadlow TN11 223 E8
Poundhurst Rd TN26 328 C3
Pound La Ashford TN23 299 F4
Brabourne Lees TN25 302 F5
Canterbury CT1 142 F1
Elham CT4 273 F4
Halstead TN14 120 D4
Molash CT4 203 F4
Sevenoaks TN13 154 C3
Pound Park Rd SE7 1 D2
Pound Pl SE9 12 A1
Pound Rd TN12 224 F6
Poundsbridge Hill
TN11,TN3 284 D7
Poundsbridge La
TN11 252 D2
Pounsley Rd TN13 153 E6
Pout Rd ME6 127 F7
Poverest Prim Sch BR5 54 A4
Poverest Rd BR5 54 A4
Povey Ave ME2 40 C2
Powdermill Cl TN4 286 C8
Powder Mill La
Dartford DA1 33 F6
Leigh TN11 221 B1
Royal Tunbridge Wells
TN4 286 B8
Tonbridge TN11 221 E2
Powell Ave DA2 34 E6
Powell Cl ME20 129 A3
Powell Cotton Dr CT7 81 B6
Powell-cotton Mus*
CT7 81 B5
Powell Sch The CT16 278 B4
Power Ind Est DA8 15 A6
Powerscroft Rd DA14 31 C2
Power Station Rd
Grain ME3 27 B4
Halfway Houses ME12 46 E7
Powis St SE18 2 A3
Powlett Rd ME2 40 C1
Powster Rd BR1 29 B3
Powys Cl DA7 13 D8
Poynder Rd RM18 19 B6
Poynings Cl BR6 87 C8
Poyntell Cres BR7 53 D8
Poyntell Rd TN12 260 F4
Pragnell Rd SE12 29 B6
Prall's La TN12 256 E2
Pratling St ME20 129 C4
Pratts Bottom Prim Sch
TN14 120 C8
Precincts The CT1 175 A8
Premier Bsns Ctr ME4 64 C1
Premier Par ME20 128 E1
Prentis Cl ME10 101 C5
Prentis Quay ME10 101 F5
Prentiss Ct SE7 1 D2
Prescott Ave BR5 53 B3
Prescott Cl CT15 278 E6
Prescott Ho TN28 373 A7
Presentation Ho 9
DA12 37 B8
Prestbury Sq SE9 29 F4
Prestedge Ave CT11 83 E2
Preston Ave
Faversham ME13 138 E6
Gillingham ME7 64 E1
Preston Ct
Faversham ME13 138 D6
Sidcup DA14 30 F4
Preston Dr DA7 13 D6
Preston Gr ME13 138 D6
Preston Hall Gdns
ME12 49 E4
Preston Hall Hospl
ME20 128 F1
Preston Hill CT3 146 B1
Preston Ho
Sutton at H DA4 57 D7
1 Woolwich SE18 2 A2
Preston La
Faversham ME13 138 D6
Preston CT3 146 B5
Preston Malt Ho
ME13 138 D6
Preston Par CT5 107 F7
Preston Pk ME13 138 D6
Preston Prim Sch
CT3 146 C6
Preston Rd
Manston CT12 82 E2
Northfleet DA11 36 E7
Stourmouth CT3 113 D1
Tonbridge TN9 222 A1
Wingham CT3 146 B3
Prestons Rd BR2 85 A8
Preston St ME13 138 D7
Preston Way ME8 65 B2
Prestwood Cl SE18 13 A8
Pretoria Ho
4 Erith DA8 14 E7
8 Maidstone ME15 195 E5
Pretoria Rd
Canterbury CT1 175 B8
Chatham ME4 63 F2
Gillingham ME7 64 D3
Prettymans La TN8 217 F4
Price's Ave Margate CT9 51 B2
Ramsgate CT11 117 C6
Prices Ct 5 ME10 102 B4
Pridmore Rd ME6 127 F8
Priest Ave CT2 174 C7
Priestdale Ct ME4 63 E3
Priestfield Rd ME7 64 E5
Priest Fields CT6 77 F5
Priestfields ME1 63 B3
Priestfield Stad
(Gillingham FC) ME7 64 E5
Priest Hill RH8 183 B6
Priestlands Park Rd
DA15 30 F5
Priestley Dr
Lunsford ME20 127 F4
Tonbridge TN10 222 E7
Priest & Sow Cnr CT5 75 B3
Priest's Wlk DA12 38 A6
Priest Wlk CT5 75 C3
Priestwood Rd DA13 93 C5
Primmett Cl TN15 90 E4
Primrose Ave ME8 98 B5
Primrose Cl ME4 96 E7
Primrose Dr
Aylesford ME20 128 D1
Kingsnorth TN23 300 B4
Primrose Gr ME9 134 A6
Primrose Hill CT4 173 B7
Primrose Ho 10 ME15 195 E7
Primrose La ME9 134 A6
Primrose Pl CT17 278 B1
Primrose Rd
Dover CT17 278 A1
Upper Halling ME2 94 E5
Primrose Terr DA12 37 C7
Primrose Way
Cliffs End CT12 116 C5
Whitstable CT5 75 C1
Primrose Wlk TN12 257 A5
Prince Andrew Rd
CT10 83 E7
Prince Arthur Rd ME7 64 B6
Prince Charles Ave
Chatham ME5 97 B4
Minster (Sheppey) ME12 47 C6
Sittingbourne ME10 102 C3
Sutton at H DA4 57 D7
Prince Charles Rd
CT10 83 E7
Prince Consort Dr BR7 53 D8
Prince Henry Rd SE7 11 D7
Prince Imperial Rd
Chislehurst BR7 30 B1
Woolwich SE18 11 F6
Prince John Rd SE9 11 E2
Prince Michael of Kent Ct
DA1 15 A5
Prince of Wales Rdbt
CT17 310 D6
Prince Of Wales Rd
SE3 11 A6
Prince Of Wales
Residential Pk CT21 353 E8
Prince Of Wales Terr
CT14 215 D5
Prince Phillip Lodge The
ME20 128 F1
Prince Regent La E16 1 C7
Prince Regent Sta E16 1 C6
Prince Rupert Rd SE9 11 F3
Princes Ave
Chatham ME5 97 B5
Dartford DA2 34 B7
Minster (Sheppey) ME12 47 D7
Orpington BR5 53 E4
Prince's Ave CT12 83 B1
Princes Cl
Birchington CT7 80 D7
Sidcup DA14 31 D5
Princes Cres 10 CT9 50 J2
Princes Dr CT13 182 A8
Princes Gate 18 CT20 335 E5
Prince's Gdns CT9 51 C2
Princes Par CT21 333 E2
Prince's Plain BR2 52 E1
Princes Plain Prim Sch
BR2 52 E2
Princes Rd Dartford DA1 33 D7
Dartford,Fleet-Downs
DA1 34 C7
Gravesend DA12 37 C5
Hextable BR8 33 A2
Prince's Rd CT11 117 D8
Princess Alice Way
SE28 2 D4
Princess Anne Rd CT10 83 E7
Princess Cl Erith SE28 3 D7
Whitstable CT5 75 C3
Princess Margaret Ave
Margate CT9 51 E2
Ramsgate CT12 83 A1
Princess Margaret Rd
RM18 20 D7
Princess Mary Ave
ME4 64 B7
Princess Par BR6 86 A7
Princess Rd CT5 75 C3
Princess Royal University
Hospl BR6 86 A6
Princess St Bexley DA7 13 F4
Folkestone CT19 335 E6
Princes St Deal CT14 215 D7
11 Dover CT16 310 D7
Gravesend DA11 19 B1
Maidstone ME14 162 A5
Prince's St Margate CT9 50 J2
9 Ramsgate CT11 117 E6
Rochester ME1 63 C4
Royal Tunbridge Wells
TN2 286 C3
Princes Terr CT21 332 F1
Princes View DA1 34 A7
Princes Way
Canterbury CT2 142 E1
Detling ME14 131 A1
Prince's Wlk CT9 51 D3
Prince William Ct
CT14 215 D7
Prinys Dr ME8 98 C4
Priolo Rd SE7 1 C1
Prioress Cres DA9 17 C3
Prioress Rd CT2 174 D8
Prioress Wlk CT16 278 A3
Prior Rd TN28 377 E8
Priorsdean Cl ME16 160 E1
Priorsford Ave BR5 54 B5
Priors Heath TN17 318 C2
Prior's Lees 8 CT20 335 D4
Prior's Way TN8 282 A6
Priory Ave BR5 53 D3
Priory Cl
Broadstairs CT10 83 F3
Bromley BR7 52 F8
Dartford DA1 15 D2
East Farleigh ME15 194 B8
New Romney TN28 372 F6
Priory Ct
5 Dartford DA1 15 D1
Gillingham ME8 65 A2
Leysdown-on-S ME12 49 G1
Rochester ME1 63 D5
Priory Ctr The DA1 33 E8
Priory Dr SE2 3 D1
Priory Fields DA4 89 F8
Priory Fields Sch
CT17 310 B8
Priory Gate 4 ME14 162 A5
Priory Gate Rd CT17 310 C8
Priory Gdns
Canterbury CT1 175 A6
Dartford DA1 15 D2
Folkestone CT20 335 D4
Priory Gdns* BR6 54 B2
Priory Gr
Aylesford ME20 128 D1
Dover CT17 310 C8
Tonbridge TN9 254 B8
Priory Hill Camp ME12 49 H1
Priory Hill Dartford DA1 15 D1
Dover CT17 310 C8
Priory Ho Dover CT17 310 C7
4 Greenwich SE7 11 C8
Priory Hospl Hayes Grove
The BR2 85 A8
Priory Inf Sch CT11 117 D7
Priory La Eynsford DA4 56 F1
Herne Bay CT6 77 A3
Sellindge TN25 303 D4
Priory Leas SE9 29 E7
Priory Mews DA2 34 C8
Priory of St Jacob
CT1 174 E6
Priory Pl Dartford DA1 15 D1
Faversham ME13 105 C1
Priory Rd
Aldington Frith TN25 329 C4
Dartford DA1 15 D1
Dartford DA1 15 D2
Dover CT16,CT17 310 D8
Faversham ME13 138 C8
Gillingham ME8 65 A2
Maidstone ME15 162 A3
Ramsgate CT11 117 D6
Rochester ME2 63 A6
Tonbridge TN9 254 C8
Priory Retail Pk DA1 15 D2
Priory Row ME13 138 C8
Priory Sch The BR5 54 C1
Priory Station Approach Rd
CT17 310 C7
Priory St
10 Dover CT16 310 D8
Tonbridge TN9 254 B8
Priory The TN29 376 C6
Priory Way TN30 345 C7
Priory Wlk TN9 254 B8
Pristling La TN12 292 B8
Pritchard Ct ME7 64 C3
Pritchard Dr CT18 307 A4
Probyn Mews CT18 306 F3
Proctor Wlk CT18 306 F4
Progress Est The
ME15 196 A4
Promenade
Birchington CT7 80 F8
Deal CT14 215 D3
Promenade The ME12 49 G2
Prospect Ave ME2 63 B8
Prospect Cl Erith DA17 4 A2
Westgate-on-S CT8 81 E7
Prospect Cotts
Boughton Lees TN25 236 E3
Harbledown CT2 141 E1
Lamberhurst TN3 317 A3
Pratt's Bottom BR6 87 C2
Shepherdswell CT15 244 D4
Prospect Ct 20 CT11 117 E6
Prospect Gdns CT12 115 B7
Prospect Gr DA12 37 D8
Prospect Hill CT6 77 A5
Prospect Mews CT21 333 C2
Prospect Pk TN4 253 F1
Prospect Pl
7 Broadstairs CT10 84 B4
Bromley BR2 52 B6
Canterbury CT1 175 A7
Collier Street TN12 226 C2
Dartford DA1 15 F1
Dover CT17 278 B1
Eastling ME13 168 E6
Gravesend DA12 37 D8
Grays RM17 18 B8
Hamstreet TN26 348 F7
Maidstone ME16 161 E3
St Nicholas at Wade CT7 79 E1
Prospect Rd
Birchington CT7 80 F7
Broadstairs CT10 84 B4
Folkestone CT20 334 D3
Hythe CT21 333 C2
Minster (Thanet) CT12 115 B6
Royal Tunbridge
Wells,Camden Park TN2 286 C3
Royal Tunbridge Wells
TN4 285 F8
Sevenoaks TN13 154 C4
Prospect Row
Chatham ME4 64 A3
Chatham ME7 64 A6
Prospect Terr
Elham CT4 273 F4
21 Ramsgate CT11 117 E6
Prospect Vale SE18 1 E2
Prospect Way TN25 302 E5
Prospero Ho 7 DA17 4 A1
Provender La ME13,
ME9 137 A6
Provender Way ME14 162 E5
Providence Chapel
TN12 259 C6
Providence Cotts
Groombridge TN3 312 C7
Higham ME3 39 B2
Providence Pl TN27 262 A7
Providence St
Ashford TN23 300 C8
Stone DA9 17 A2
Prudhoe Ct 27 DA2 16 B1
Puckle La CT1 175 A6
Pucknells Cl BR8 55 C8
Puddingcake La TN17 344 C5
Pudding La Ash CT3 147 D1
Maidstone ME14 161 F4
Seal TN15 154 F6
Pudding Rd ME8 98 F8
Puddledock La
Hextable BR8,DA2 32 F2
Toy's Hill TN16 185 A3
Puffin Ct CT18 307 A3
Puffin Rd Grain ME3 27 B5
Herne Bay CT6 77 F4
Pullington Cotts TN17 342 E6
Pullman Cl CT12 117 C8
Pullman Mews SE12 29 B5
Pullman Pl SE9 11 E2
Pump Cl ME19 127 D1
Pump La Chelsfield BR6 88 B5
Gillingham ME7,ME8 65 D3
1 Margate CT9 50 J2
Pump Terr TN1 286 B4
Punch Croft DA3 91 E7
Purbeck Rd ME4 63 E2
Purcell Ave TN10 222 F6
Purchas Ct CT2 142 C4
Purchase La TN26 298 E8
Purfleet By-Pass RM19 16 D8
Purland Rd SE28 2 F4
Purneys Rd SE9 11 D3
Purrett Rd SE18 2 F1
Purr Wood CT4 205 B2
Purser Way ME7 64 C7
Pursey Cl TN15 90 E4
Puttenden Rd TN11 189 F3
Puttney Dr ME10 102 A8
Pye Alley La CT5 108 C3
Pym Ho TN27 234 D7
Pym Orch TN16 152 C3
Pynham Cl SE2 3 B3
Pynson's Ind Est CT10 83 D4
Pyott Mews 3 CT1 143 B1
Pyrus Cl ME5 130 A8
Pyson's Rd CT10,CT12 83 D3
Pyson's Road Ind Est
CT10 83 D3

Q

Quadrant The DA7 13 D7
Quaggy Wlk SE3 11 A3
Quain Ct CT20 335 C4
Quaker Cl TN13 154 D4
Quaker Dr TN17 320 D6
Quaker La TN17 320 D6
Quakers Cl DA3 58 E6
Quaker's Hall La
TN13 154 C5
Quantock Cl TN2 286 D5
Quantock Dr TN24 268 B4
Quantock Gdns CT12 83 B3
Quantock Rd DA1 14 E5
Quarries The ME17 195 C4
Quarrington La TN25 302 B8
Quarry Bank TN9 254 A7
Quarry Cotts
Rockrobin TN5 336 D7
Sevenoaks TN13 154 A4
Stone in Oxney TN30 360 C3
Quarry Hill Par 3
TN9 254 B8
Quarry Hill Rd
Borough Green TN15 156 F6
Tonbridge TN9 254 B8
Quarry Hill TN15 154 D4
Quarry Rd Hythe CT21 333 B3
Maidstone ME15 162 A2
Royal Tunbridge Wells
TN1 286 B5
Quarry Rise TN9 254 A7
Quarry Sq ME14 162 A5
Quarry View TN23 299 D7
Quarry Wlk CT21 334 A3
Quarry Wood TN25 330 A6
Quarry Wood Ind Est
ME20 160 E8
Quay Cotts ME9 103 E6
Quay Ct CT5 74 E2
Quay La
Faversham ME13 138 D8
Sandwich CT13 149 A1
Swanscombe DA9 17 B3
Quayside ME4 64 B8
Quay The ME9 103 E6
Quebec Ave TN16 151 D1
Quebec Cotts 9
TN16 151 D1
Quebec Ho* TN16 151 D1
Quebec Rd RM18 19 A5
Quebec Sq TN16 151 D1
Queen Anne Ave BR2 52 A6
Queen Anne Gate DA7 13 D4
Queen Anne Rd ME14 162 B4
Queen Bertha Rd
CT11 117 C6

- Queen Bertha's Ave CT7 81 C8
- Queenborough Dr ME12 47 B7
- Queenborough Fst Sch ME11 46 B5
- Queen Borough Gdns BR7 30 D2
- Queenborough Rd
  - Halfway Houses ME12 46 C6
  - Queenborough ME12 46 C4
- Queenborough Sta ME11 46 A5
- Queenbridge Ind Pk RM20 17 A8
- Queendown Ave ME8 98 D5
- Queendown Rd CT7 82 A3
- Queen Elizabeth Ave CT9 51 D1
- Queen Elizabeth Military Hospl The SE18 11 E7
- Queen Elizabeth Rd CT16 310 F8
- Queen Elizabeth's Gram Sch ME13 138 D8
- Queen Elizabeth Sq ME15 195 D6
- Queen Elizabeth the Queen Mother Hospl CT9 82 F8
- Queen Mary's Hospl DA14 31 A2
- Queen Mother Ct CT14 215 D2
- Queen Mother Ct The ME1 63 B4
- Queen's Ct CT6 77 A4
- Queen's Lea CT15 308 E5
- Queen's Ave
  - Birchington CT7 80 D7
  - Broadstairs CT10 84 B6
- Queens Ave
  - Canterbury CT2 142 E1
  - Dover CT17 310 A7
  - Folkestone CT20 334 B6
  - Herne Bay CT6 77 D5
- Queen's Ave
  - Maidstone ME16 161 D5
  - Margate CT9 50 I1
  - Ramsgate CT12 83 B1
  - Snodland ME6 128 A8
- Queensbridge Dr CT6 76 C4
- Queens Cotts TN5 336 E6
- Queenscroft Rd SE9 11 D1
- Queens Ct
  - Ashford TN24 268 C3
  - Edenbridge TN8 217 D1
  - Gillingham ME8 99 A8
  - 11 Hawkhurst TN18 341 A2
  - Hythe CT21 333 B1
  - Margate CT9 51 A3
  - 1 Sidcup DA14 31 A4
- Queensdown Rd CT14 248 D4
- Queen's Dr TN14 154 C7
- Queen's Farm Rd DA12 38 E7
- Queens Gate Gdns BR7 53 D8
- Queen's Gate Rd CT11 117 C8
- Queens Gdns
  - Broadstairs CT10 84 B3
  - Dartford DA2 34 B7
- Queen's Gdns CT16, CT17 310 D8
- Queens Gdns CT6 76 F5
- Queen's Gdns TN4 286 B6
- Queens Ho ME16 161 B3
- Queensland Ct RM18 18 F5
- Queensland Ho 2 E16 2 A5
- Queens Lodge CT9 51 B3
- Queens Mews CT14 215 D6
- Queen's Mews 12 TN18 341 A2
- Queens Par
  - 12 Faversham ME13 138 D7
  - Margate CT9 51 A3
- Queen's Pas BR7 30 B2
- Queen's Prom CT9 51 B3
- Queen's Rd Ash CT3 147 D2
  - Ashford TN24 269 A1
- Queens Rd CT3 210 F5
- Queen's Rd Bexley DA16 13 B5
  - Broadstairs CT10 84 B4
  - Bromley BR1 52 A7
  - Chatham ME5 64 D1
  - Chislehurst BR7 30 B2
- Queens Rd DA8 14 E8
- Queen's Rd
  - Faversham ME13 138 B7
  - Gillingham ME7 64 C4
- Queens Rd DA12 37 C5
- Queen's Rd
  - Hawkhurst TN18 341 A2
  - Littlestone-on-Sea TN28 373 D6
  - Lydd TN29 376 C6
  - Maidstone ME16 161 C4
- Queens Rd ME12 47 D7
- Queen's Rd
  - Ramsgate CT11 117 F7
  - Royal Tunbridge Wells TN4 286 B6
  - Snodland ME6 128 A8
  - Westgate-on-S CT8 81 F8
- Queens Rd CT5 75 A2
- Queen's Rise CT14 247 F5
- Queen St Ashford TN23 268 B2
  - Bexley DA7 13 F4
  - Chatham ME4 64 A4
  - Deal CT14 215 D6
  - Dover CT16,CT17 310 D7
  - Erith DA8 14 E8
  - Folkestone CT20 335 E5
  - Gravesend DA12 19 B1
- Queens The CT14 215 D5
- Queen St Herne Bay CT6 76 F5
- Queen St *continued*
  - Kings Hill ME18 159 B3
  - Margate CT9 50 I2
  - Paddock Wood TN12 257 D7
  - Ramsgate CT11 117 E6
  - Rochester ME1 63 C4
  - Sandhurst TN18 356 B5
- Queensway ME3 9 D3
- Queens Way ME14 131 A1
- Queensway
  - Dymchurch TN29 352 E2
  - Hayes BR2,BR4 85 A6
  - Lydd TN29 376 C6
  - Orpington BR5 53 C3
- Queen's Way ME12 46 A8
- Queenswood Rd
  - Kit's Coty ME20 129 D7
  - Sidcup DA15 12 F1
- Queen Victoria Meml Hospl CT6 77 B4
- Quentins Rd TN16 119 B3
- Quernmore Cl BR1 29 A2
- Quernmore Rd BR1 29 A2
- Quern Rd CT14 215 A2
- Querns Pl CT1 175 B8
- Querns Rd CT1 175 C8
- Quern The ME15 161 E1
- Quested Rd CT19 334 E6
- Quested Way ME17 198 C6
- Questor DA1 33 F6
- Quetta Rd CT12 82 F1
- Quex Ct CT7 81 B6
- Quex House & Gdns* CT7 81 B5
- Quex Rd CT8 81 F8
- Quex View Rd CT7 81 A5
- Quickrells Ave ME3 22 B5
- Quickstep Cl ME10 101 F8
- Quickthorn Cres ME5 96 E5
- Quiet Nook BR2 85 D7
- Quilter Rd BR5 54 D1
- Quilter St SE18 2 F1
- Quince Orch TN26 349 A7
- Quincewood Gdns TN10 222 B7
- Quinion Cl ME5 130 A8
- Quinnell St ME8 65 E1
- Quinton Rd ME10 101 C7
- Quixote Cres ME2 40 B1

R

- Rabbit Hole CT4 243 A7
- Rabbits Rd DA4 57 E7
- Rablus Pl DA4 56 F3
- Racecourse Cvn Site CT21 332 B7
- Racefield Cl DA12 38 E1
- Rackham Cl DA16 13 B5
- Radburn Pl DA10 17 E2
- Radcliffe Ct CT21 333 B2
- Radfall Cnr CT5 109 C6
- Radfall Gate CT5 109 C6
- Radfall Hill CT5 109 D5
- Radfall Rd CT5 109 D4
- Radfall Ride CT5 109 C5
- Radfield Way DA15 30 D8
- Radland Rd E16 1 A7
- Radleigh Gdns ME1 63 E1
- Radley Cl CT10 84 A6
- Radley Ho 13 SE2 3 D4
- Radnor Ave DA16 13 B2
- Radnor Bridge Rd CT19,CT20 335 E5
- Radnor Chambers 13 CT20 335 D4
- Radnor Cl
  - Chislehurst BR7 30 E2
  - Herne Bay CT6 77 B1
- Radnor Cliff Cres CT20 335 A3
- Radnor Cliff CT20 335 A3
- Radnor Cl ME14 161 E7
- Radnor Cres SE18 13 A7
- Radnor Park Ave CT19 335 C6
- Radnor Park Cres CT19 335 C5
- Radnor Park Gdns CT19 335 C6
- Radnor Park Ho CT19 335 C6
- Radnor Park Rd CT19 335 C6
- Radnor Pk W CT19 335 B6
- Radnor St 20 CT19 335 E5
- Radzan Cl DA2 32 E6
- Raeburn Ave DA1 15 B2
- Raeburn Cl TN10 222 E6
- Raeburn Rd DA15 12 E1
- Rafford Way BR1 52 B6
- Raggatt Pl ME15 162 B2
- Ragge Way TN15 154 F7
- Raggleswood BR7 53 A8
- Rag Hill Cl TN16 150 E6
- Rag Hill Rd TN16 150 E6
- Rag Hill TN16 150 E6
- Raglan Ct SE12 11 A2
- Raglan Pl 10 CT10 84 B4
- Raglan Prim Sch BR2 52 D5
- Raglan Rd Bromley BR2 52 C5
  - Erith DA17 3 F2
  - Woolwich SE18 2 C1
- Ragstone Ct ME20 160 C8
- Ragstone Hollow TN25 330 A6
- Ragstone Rd ME15 163 A2
- Railway Ave CT5 74 E1
- Railway Cotts
  - Cowden TN8 282 D8
  - Marden TN12 259 D6
  - Teynham ME9 103 D3
- Railway Hill CT4 242 E8
- Railway Pl Erith DA17 4 A3
- Railway Pl *continued*
  - 21 Gravesend DA12 19 B1
- Railway Rd ME12 28 B2
- Railway St Ind Pk ME7 64 D6
- Railway Sidings The DA13 60 A4
- Railway St Chatham ME4 63 F4
  - Gillingham ME7 64 D6
  - Northfleet DA11 18 A2
- Railway Terr
  - Margate CT9 50 H1
  - Queenborough ME11 46 A5
  - Westerham TN16 151 D1
- Rainham Cl
  - Maidstone ME15 162 A1
  - Sidcup SE9 12 E1
- Rainham Mark Gram Sch ME8 65 D2
- Rainham Rd ME5 64 C3
- Rainham Sch for Girls ME8 98 C8
- Rainham Sh Ctr 2 ME8 65 F1
- Rainham Sta ME8 65 F1
- Rainton Rd SE7 1 A1
- Raleigh Cl
  - Ashford TN24 301 A8
  - Chatham ME5 97 A6
  - Erith DA8 14 F8
- Raleigh Ct 1 CT11 117 F8
- Raleigh Mews 6 BR6 86 F5
- Raleigh Way ME12 46 E6
- Ramac Ind Est SE7 1 B1
- Ramac Way SE7 1 B1
- Ramillies Cl ME5 97 A6
- Ramillies Rd DA15 13 B1
- Ram La TN25,TN27 266 C8
- Rammell Mews TN17 320 D4
- Ramp A CT16 310 H8
- Rampart Rd CT21 333 B2
- Ramparts The CT13 181 A8
- Ramp B CT16 310 H8
- Ramp C CT16 310 G8
- Ramp D CT16 310 G8
- Rampion Cl ME14 162 E5
- Ramsden Cl BR5 54 C1
- Ramsden La TN17 342 F4
- Ramsden Rd Erith DA8 14 D7
  - Orpington BR5 54 B1
- Ramsey Cl CT2 142 E1
- Ramsey Ho
  - 8 Canterbury CT1 174 F7
  - Deal CT14 215 C3
- Ramsgate Cl E16 1 B5
- Ramsgate Maritime Mus* CT12 117 E6
- Ramsgate Model Village* CT11 117 D5
- Ramsgate Motor Mus* CT11 117 D5
- Ramsgate Rd
  - Broadstairs CT10 84 B4
  - Broadstairs,Dumpton CT10,CT11 83 F2
  - Margate CT10,CT9 83 A6
  - Sandwich CT13 149 A7
- Ramsgate Sch The CT12 83 A2
- Ramsgate Sta CT12 117 C8
- Ramslye Rd TN4 313 E8
- Ramstone Cl TN25 302 E5
- Ramus Wood Ave BR6 86 E5
- Rance Ho 11 SE18 1 E2
- Rancliffe Gdns SE9 11 E3
- Rancorn Rd CT9 50 G1
- Randall Cl DA8 14 C8
- Randall Hill Rd TN15 124 F3
- Randall Rd ME4 63 E1
- Randalls Row ME15 194 F5
- Randall St ME14 161 F6
- Randle's La TN14 120 D5
- Randle Way ME9 102 E2
- Randolph App E16 1 C7
- Randolph Cl Bexley DA7 14 C4
  - Canterbury CT1 175 A7
- Randolph Cotts ME2 40 B1
- Randolph Ct CT8 50 C1
- Randolph Gdns TN24 268 E5
- Randolph Ho
  - 15 Folkestone CT20 335 E5
  - Gillingham ME7 64 C5
- Randolph La TN31 368 B3
- Randolph Rd
  - Dover CT17 278 B1
  - Gillingham ME7 64 C5
  - Orpington BR2 52 F1
- Randolph Sq CT9 50 J3
- Ranelagh Gdns
  - 1 Broadstairs CT10 83 E5
  - Northfleet DA11 36 F8
- Ranelagh Gr CT10 83 E5
- Ranelagh Rd
  - Deal CT14 215 D5
  - Sheerness ME12 28 C2
- Rangefield Rd BR1 29 A3
- Range Rd
  - Eastchurch ME12 48 D1
  - Gravesend DA12 37 E8
  - Hythe CT21 333 B1
- Range Road Ind Est CT21 333 B1
- Rangeworth Pl DA15 30 F5
- Rankine Rd TN2 286 D7
- Ranleigh Gdns DA7 13 F7
- Ranmore Path BR5 54 A5
- Ranscombe Cl ME2 62 D5
- Ranscombe Farm Cotts ME2 62 C4
- Ransley Gn TN26 349 F8
- Ransome Way CT7 80 F6
- Ransom Rd 1 SE7 1 C1
- Ranters La TN17 318 C7
- Ranworth Cl DA7,DA8 14 E5
- Raphael Ave RM18 19 B7
- Raphael Ct TN11 221 E7
- Raphael Rd DA12 37 D8
- Rashleigh Way DA4 57 C5
- Raspberry Hill La ME9 68 D6
- Ratcliffe Cl SE12 29 A8
- Ratcliffe Highway
  - High Halstow ME3 24 D5
  - Hoo St Werburgh ME3 41 C6
- Rathmore Rd
  - Gravesend DA11 37 B8
  - Greenwich SE7 1 B1
- Ratling Rd CT3 210 F7
- Rattington St CT4 173 E2
- Ravelin Ho ME12 28 C2
- Raven Cl ME20 128 A1
- Ravenlea Rd CT20 335 A5
- Ravensbourne Ave CT6 77 B3
- Ravensbourne Coll of Design & Communication BR7 29 F3
- Ravensbourne Ct 23 BR5 54 D1
- Ravensbourne Rd
  - Bromley BR1 52 A6
  - Crayford DA1 15 A4
- Ravensbourne Sch The BR2 52 B5
- Ravensbury Rd BR5 54 A5
- Ravenscourt Rd
  - Deal CT14 215 C5
  - Orpington BR5 54 B7
  - Rough Common CT2 142 B3
- Ravenscroft Cl 5 E16 1 A8
- Ravenscroft Cres SE9 29 F5
- Ravenscroft Rd E16 1 A8
- Ravens Dane Cl ME15 163 A1
- Ravenshill BR7 53 B8
- Raven's Hoe DA14 31 A3
- Ravens Knowle ME1 95 D4
- Ravensleigh Gdns BR1 29 B3
- Ravensquay Bsns Ctr BR5 54 B4
- Ravens Way SE12 11 A2
- Ravenswood Ave
  - Rochester ME2 40 B1
  - Royal Tunbridge Wells TN2 286 D6
- Ravens Wood Sch for Boys BR2 85 D7
- Ravenswood DA5 31 E7
- Ravensworth Rd SE9 29 F4
- Ravine Gr SE18 12 E8
- Rawdon Rd
  - Maidstone ME15 162 A3
  - Ramsgate CT11 117 C6
- Rawlings Cl 3 BR6 86 F5
- Rawling St ME9 134 F3
- Rawsthorne Cl E16 1 F5
- Rayfield Cl BR2 52 E3
- Rayfield Ct ME6 95 B1
- Rayford Cl DA1 15 C2
- Rayham Rd CT5 109 A8
- Ray Lamb Way DA8 15 B7
- Rayleas Cl SE18 12 B6
- Rayleigh Cl ME16 161 D7
- Rayleigh Ho 2 ME15 195 D8
- Rayleigh Rd E16 1 B5
- Raymere Gdns SE18 12 E7
- Raymer Rd ME14 162 B8
- Raymond Ave CT1 175 A6
- Raymond Fuller Way TN24 268 E4
- Raymond Postgate Ct 5 SE28 3 B6
- Raymoor Ave TN29 366 A4
- Raynehurst Jun & Inf Sch DA12 37 F5
- Rayner Hill Cotts ME17 200 C5
- Rayners Ct DA11 18 B1
- Rayners Hill ME17 200 C5
- Raynham Villas TN12 227 A4
- Rays Hill DA4 57 C4
- Raywood Office Complex TN27 234 B4
- Reach Cl CT15 279 F5
- Reachfields CT21 333 A1
- Reach Mdw CT15 280 A6
- Reach Rd Lympne CT21 331 D2
  - St Margaret's at Cliffe CT15 279 F5
- Reader's Bridge Rd TN30 323 E4
- Readers Ct ME18 193 A8
- Readers La TN31 367 F5
- Reading Cl CT14 215 B1
- Reading Ho 4 ME15 195 F5
- Reading Rd CT17 309 F7
- Reading St CT10 83 F8
- Reading Street Rd CT10,CT9 83 E8
- Reading St TN30 346 C2
- Readscroft Rd ME8 98 D5
- Read Way DA12 37 E3
- Rebecca Ct
  - 6 Margate CT9 51 B2
  - Sidcup DA14 31 B4
- Recca La CT15,CT18 275 A4
- Recreation Ave ME6 128 A8
- Recreation Cl ME14 162 B6
- Recreation Ground Rd TN30 345 B7
- Recreation Way ME10 69 A1
- Rectory Bglws TN26 326 F8
- Rectory Bsns Ctr 2 DA14 31 B4
- Rectory Cl Crayford DA1 14 E3
  - Sidcup DA14 31 B4
  - Snodland ME6 128 A8
  - Woodchurch TN26 326 A2
  - Wouldham ME1 95 C5
- Rectory Ct 3 RM17 18 D8
- Rectory Dr TN3 253 D3
- Rectory Field Cres SE7 11 C7
- Rectory Fields TN17 320 D5
- Rectory Gdns CT5 75 D2
- Rectory Grange ME1 63 C2
- Rectory La
  - Barham CT4 210 A2
  - Brasted TN16 152 C3
  - Harrietsham ME17 198 E5
  - Hythe CT21 333 B5
  - Ightham TN15 156 C5
  - Lyminge CT18 305 C6
  - Maidstone ME16 161 A1
- Rectory La N ME19 127 E2
- Rectory La
  - Sevenoaks TN13 154 C1
  - Sidcup DA14 31 C4
- Rectory La S ME19 127 E1
- Rectory La
  - Sutton Valence ME17 229 C6
  - Sutton Valence ME17 229 F7
  - Titsey TN16 150 E4
- Rectory Mdw DA13 36 A2
- Rectory Paddock Sch BR5 54 C7
- Rectory Park Rd TN12 290 A2
- Rectory Pl SE18 2 A2
- Rectory Rd
  - Broadstairs CT10 84 B5
  - Cliffe ME3 22 A3
  - Deal CT14 214 F4
  - 4 Grays RM17 18 D8
  - New Ash Green TN15 92 C5
  - Orpington BR2 85 D3
  - St Mary in the Marsh TN29 365 B4
  - Sittingbourne ME10 102 B3
  - Swanscombe DA10 35 E8
  - West Tilbury RM18 19 D8
- Rectory Way TN24 268 C5
- Rectory Wlk TN26 349 A7
- Reculver Ave CT7 80 E8
- Reculver CE Prim Sch CT6 78 A4
- Reculver Cl CT6 77 F5
- Reculver Ctry Pk* CT6 78 B6
- Reculver Dr CT6 77 E5
- Reculver La CT6 78 B6
- Reculver Rd CT6 77 D5
- Reculvers Rd CT8 81 F7
- Reculver Wlk ME15 195 F7
- Redan Pl ME12 28 D2
- Redbank ME19 127 E2
- Red Barracks Rd 4 SE18 1 F2
- Redberry Rd TN23 300 B5
- Redbourne Dr SE28 3 D7
- Red Brick Cotts ME13 172 A6
- Redbridge Cl ME5 97 C4
- Redbrook St TN26 325 D5
- Redbrooks Way CT21 332 F2
- Red Cedars Rd BR6 53 E2
- Redcliffe La ME14 162 B7
- Redcot La CT2 144 B7
- Redding Cl DA2 34 E6
- Redding Ho SE18 1 E3
- Reddy Rd DA8 14 F8
- Rede Court Rd ME2 62 E8
- Rede Wood Rd ME16 160 F3
- Redfern Ave ME7 64 E5
- Redfern Ho ME2 94 F5
- Redgate Dr BR2 85 B8
- Red Hill BR7 30 B3
- Red Hill Prim Sch BR7 30 B3
- Redhill Rd
  - New Ash Green DA3 91 F6
  - Westgate-on-S CT8 81 E8
- Red Hill ME18 159 F1
- Redhill Wood DA3 92 A7
- Red Ho The
  - Limpsfield RH8 183 C5
  - Littlestone-on-Sea TN28 373 E6
- Red House* DA6 13 E3
- Redhouse Farm CT14 182 B1
- Red House Gdns ME18 192 C7
- Red House La DA6 13 E3
- Redhouse La CT4 207 D6
- Redhouse Rd TN16 150 C6
- Redhouse Wall CT14 182 B1
- Redington TN24 268 C3
- Red La RH8 216 B7
- Redlands Ct CT17 277 E4
- Redland Shaw ME4 63 E1
- Redlands Rd TN13 153 F3
- Redlane Cotts RH8 183 B2
- Red La RH8 183 B2
- Redleaf Cl Erith DA17 14 A8
  - Royal Tunbridge Wells TN2 286 D6
- Red Lion Cl BR5 54 C3
- Red Lion Ct 6 CT21 333 B2
- Red Lion La
  - 11 Whitstable CT5 74 D2
  - Woolwich SE18 12 A6
- Red Lion Pl SE18 12 A6
- Red Lion Sq
  - 7 Hythe CT21 333 B2
  - Plaxtol TN15 189 E8
- Red Lodge Cres DA5 32 E5
- Red Lodge Rd DA5 32 D5
- Redmans Ind Est RM18 20 A8
- Redmans La BR6,TN14 88 E4
- Redmill Cl CT20 334 E5
- Red Oak Cl BR6 86 B8
- Red Oak TN18 354 E8
- Red Oast Cotts TN5 339 C3
- Redoubt Way TN29 353 B4
- Redpoll Way DA18 3 D3
- Redpoll Wlk TN12 257 A5
- Red Rd CT2 140 D5
- Red Robin Cotts ME9 100 B6
- Redruth Manor 3 ME7 64 C6
- Redsells Cl ME15 163 A1
- Redshank Rd ME4 41 B1
- Redstart Cl E6 1 E8
- Red St DA13 36 B2
- Redsull Ave CT14 215 A3
- Red Tree Orch TN23 299 E7
- Redvers Cotts CT16 277 E5
- Redvers Rd ME4 64 A2
- Redwall La ME15,ME17 227 C6
- Redwell Gr ME18 159 C2
- Redwell La TN15 156 B4
- Redwing Cl ME20 128 A2
- Redwing Path SE28 2 D4
- Redwing Rd ME5 97 B7
- Redwings La TN2 255 E2
- Redwood Cl
  - Canterbury CT2 142 E2
  - Chartham CT4 173 E1
  - Chatham ME5 97 B2
  - Sidcup DA15 31 A7
- Redwood Ct DA1 16 A1
- Redwood Pk TN12 256 A5
- Redyear Cotts TN24 269 A1
- Redyear Ct TN24 269 A1
- Reece Adams Ho CT18 308 B1
- Reed Ave
  - Canterbury CT1 143 D3
  - Orpington BR6 86 E7
- Reed Cl Eltham SE12 11 A2
  - Newham E16 1 A8
  - New Hythe ME20 128 A5
- Reed Court Cotts TN12 227 A5
- Reed Court Farm Trail* TN12 227 A5
- Reed Cres TN23 300 C3
- Reedham Cres ME3 40 C7
- Reedland Cres ME13 138 C8
- Reedmace Cl TN23 299 D8
- Reeds Cl CT6 77 C4
- Reeds La TN11 189 E5
- Reed St ME3 22 B6
- Reeves Alley 1 CT5 74 D1
- Reeves Cl TN12 260 E4
- Reeves Cres BR8 55 D6
- Reeves Ct Ditton ME19 128 A1
  - Fordcombe TN3 284 B5
- Reeves Pas 7 ME13 138 C7
- Reeves Rd SE18 12 B8
- Reeves Terr TN5 338 E1
- Reeves Way CT5 75 C2
- Reeves Yd CT5 74 D2
- Reflection The E16 2 B4
- Reform Rd ME4 64 B2
- Regency Cl
  - Gillingham ME8 98 C3
  - Sheerness ME12 28 A3
  - West Kingsdown TN15 90 E4
  - Whitstable CT5 108 F7
- Regency Ct ME10 101 D4
- Regency Hall 21 TN2 286 A2
- Regency Ho TN2 286 B2
- Regency Pl CT1 143 B2
- Regency Villas CT4 243 C5
- Regency Way DA6 13 E4
- Regent Dr ME15 195 A8
- Regent Pl TN2 286 D3
- Regent Rd ME7 64 C4
- Regents Ct
  - 14 Ashford TN23 268 B2
  - 3 Gravesend DA11 19 B1
- Regents Dr BR2 85 D5
- Regents Pl TN23 268 B2
- Regent's Pl SE3 11 A5
- Regent Sq DA17 4 B2
- Regent St
  - Rolvenden TN17 343 E4
  - Whitstable CT5 74 D2
- Regents Wlk CT6 77 D5
- Regent Way ME18 159 C3
- Regina Ct TN4 285 F4
- Reginald Ave ME2 62 C3
- Reginald Rd ME16 161 E3
- Regis Bsns Pk ME12 28 A1
- Regis Cres ME10 101 F7
- Regis Manor Com Prim Sch ME10 101 E7
- Regvlbivm Roman Fort & Reculver Twrs* CT6 78 D7
- Reidhaven Rd SE18 2 E2
- Reigate Rd BR1,SE12 29 A5
- Reinckendorf Ave SE9 12 D1
- Reinden Gr ME15 162 F1
- Rembrandt Cl TN10 222 E6
- Rembrandt Dr DA11 36 E5
- Remington Rd E6 1 E7
- Remston Mews 12 CT1 143 B2
- Remus Cl TN23 299 F4
- Renault Cl CT6 76 A4
- Rendezvous St CT20 335 D5
- Rendezvous The CT9 50 I3
- Rendlebury Ho 12 SE18 1 F2
- Renfrew Cl E6 2 A6
- Rennets Cl SE9 12 E2
- Rennets Wood Ho SE9 12 D2
- Rennets Wood Rd SE9 12 D2
- Renovation The E16 2 B4
- Renown Rd ME5 97 C2
- Renshaw Cl 7 DA17 13 F8
- Rentain Rd CT4 173 D2
- Renton Dr BR5 54 D2
- Repository Rd SE18 1 F1
- Repton Cl CT10 83 F6
- Repton Manor Rd TN23 268 A3
- Repton Rd BR6 87 A6
- Repton Way ME5 96 F4
- Reservoir Ave TN29 380 D2

Reservoir Cl DA9 17 C1
Reservoir Rd CT5 74 E2
Resolution Cl ME5 97 A6
Resolution Wlk SE18 1 F3
Restavon Cvn Pk
TN16 119 B3
Restharrow Rd ME14 162 E4
Rest Harrow ME13 170 C5
Restharrow Way ME4 41 C1
Restmore Cl ME3 22 A4
Restons Cres SE9 12 E1
Retreat Cvn Pk The
ME18 192 D6
Retreat The
Birchington CT7 81 B8
Doddington ME9 167 D7
Grays RM17 18 B8
Orpington BR6 87 B4
Platt TN15 157 D8
Ramsgate CT12 117 B8
Rettendon Dr ME10 101 F8
Revell Rise SE18 12 F8
Revenge Rd ME5 130 C8
Reventlow Rd SE9 30 C7
Reynard Cl BR1 53 A6
Reynolah Gdns 3 SE7 1 B1
Reynolds Cl
Herne Bay CT6 77 B4
Tonbridge TN10 222 E6
Reynolds Fields ME3 39 C6
Reynolds La
Herne Bay CT3 78 D3
Royal Tunbridge Wells
TN4 285 F7
Reynolds Pl SE3 11 B7
Rhee Wall TN26 361 D7
Rheims Ct CT2 142 D1
Rheims Way CT1,CT2 174 E8
Rhodaus Cl CT1 174 F7
Rhodaus Ho CT1 174 F7
Rhodaus Town CT1 174 F7
Rhodes Gdns CT10 84 A6
Rhodes Ho 6 ME5 64 C2
Rhode St ME4 64 A4
Rhodewood Cl ME15 163 A1
Rhododendron Ave
DA13 93 A2
Ribblesdale Rd DA2 34 C7
Ribston Cl BR2 52 F1
Ribston Gdns TN12 256 F7
Ricardo Path 5 SE28 3 C5
Rice Par BR5 53 D4
Richard Beau Nash
Apartments 4 TN1 286 B4
Richard Cl SE18 1 E2
Richard Ct 7 CT9 51 B2
Richard House Dr E16 1 E7
Richard Neve Ho SE18 2 E2
Richard's Cl TN11 219 F2
Richardson Cl 7 DA9 17 A2
Richardson Rd TN4 286 A5
Richardson Way CT12 116 D5
Richard St Chatham ME4 63 F4
Rochester ME1 63 C3
Richborough Castle &
Mus* CT13 148 E5
Richborough Cl BR5 54 D5
Richborough Drive
ME2 40 A1
Richborough Rd CT8 81 F7
Richborough Way
TN23 299 E5
Richbourgh Rd CT13 148 E3
Richdore Rd CT4 239 C6
Richings House BR5 54 A8
Richmer Rd DA8 15 A7
Richmond Ave CT9 51 B1
Richmond Cl
Biggin Hill TN16 150 B8
Chatham ME5 97 B4
Rochester ME2 40 F1
Richmond Ct
Bromley BR1 29 B1
Dover CT16 278 D1
Sevenoaks TN13 154 B4
Richmond Dr
Gravesend DA12 37 E6
Herne Bay CT6 77 E5
New Romney TN28 373 C8
Sittingbourne ME10 101 E7
Richmond First Sch
ME12 28 D2
Richmond Gdns CT2 142 C2
Richmond Ho 26 CT20 335 E5
Richmond Inf Sch ME7 64 C6
Richmond Meech Dr
TN24 268 E4
Richmond Pl
Royal Tunbridge Wells
TN2 286 B1
Woolwich SE18 2 C2
Richmond Rd
Gillingham ME7 64 C7
1 Grays RM17 18 C8
Ramsgate CT11 117 D6
Whitstable CT5 75 B1
Richmond St
Folkestone CT19 334 D6
Herne Bay CT6 76 F5
Sheerness ME12 28 D2
Richmond Way ME15 195 A8
Richmount Gdns SE3 11 A4
Ricketts Hill Rd TN16 150 E7
Rickyard Path SE9 11 E3
Riddlesdale Ave TN4 286 A6
Riddles Rd ME10,ME9 101 C3
Riddons Rd SE12 29 C4
Rideout St SE18 1 F2
Rider Cl DA15 12 E1
Ridge Ave DA1 14 F1
Ridgebrook Rd SE3 11 D4
Ridge Cl SE28 2 D4
Ridgecroft Cl DA5 32 C7
Ridge La DA13 93 A2
Ridgelands TN3 253 C4
Ridge Meadow Prim Sch
ME5 96 F6
Ridge The
Ashford TN24 268 E6
Groombridge TN3 312 A6
Orpington BR6 86 D8
Sidcup DA5 31 F8
Ridge View Sch TN10 222 D5
Ridgeway Ave DA12 37 B5
Ridgeway Bglws DA12 38 F1
Ridgeway Cliff CT6 76 C5
Ridge Way DA1 14 F1
Ridgeway Crescent Gdns
BR6 86 E7
Ridgeway Cres
Orpington BR6 86 E7
Tonbridge TN10 222 D4
Ridgeway DA2 34 E3
Ridgeway Dr BR1 29 B4
Ridgeway E DA15 12 F2
Ridgewaye The TN4 254 B1
Ridgeway Hayes BR2 85 A8
Hurst Green TN19 354 A3
Lympne CT21 332 A3
Ridge Way TN8 217 D4
Ridgeway TN2 287 D7
Ridgeway Rd CT6 111 A7
Ridgeway Terr TN25 302 C5
Ridgeway The
Boughton Street ME13 140 A3
Broadstairs CT10 83 F3
Chatham ME4 96 E7
Crabble CT17 277 E2
Gillingham ME7 64 C7
Margate CT9 51 B1
Ridgeway TN18 354 E8
Ridgeway The
Shorne DA12 38 E1
Smeeth TN25 302 B5
Tonbridge TN10 222 D4
Ridgeway CT5 75 C1
Ridgeway Wlk CT6 111 A7
Ridgeway W DA15 12 E2
Ridgewood DA3 59 C7
Ridgway ME16 161 B2
Ridgwell Rd E16 1 C8
Ridgy Field Cl TN15 125 A2
Ridham Ave ME10 69 A1
Ridham Dock ME9 69 B6
Riding Hill TN24 268 C6
Riding La TN11 188 D2
Riding Pk TN11 221 D7
Ridings The
Biggin Hill TN16 118 E2
7 Canterbury CT1 143 B1
Margate CT9 51 F3
Paddock Wood TN12 257 A7
Royal Tunbridge Wells
TN2 286 F6
Whitstable CT5 75 D1
Ridlands CT1 175 A5
Ridlands Gr RH8 183 E5
Ridlands La RH8 183 E5
Ridlands Rise RH8 183 E4
Ridley Cl CT6 111 A8
Ridley Ct BR6 86 C6
Ridley Rd Bexley DA16 13 B6
Bromley BR2 52 A6
Rochester ME1 63 B4
Riefield Rd SE9 12 C2
Rigden Rd TN23 300 B7
Rigden's Ct 6 ME10 101 E5
Riggall Ct ME2 62 A3
Riggs Way TN15 124 F3
Rigshill Rd ME13 201 B6
Riley Ave CT6 75 F4
Rimpton Ct CT10 83 F7
Ring Cl BR1 29 B1
Ringden Ave TN12 256 F6
Ringer's Ct 5 BR1 52 A6
Ringer's Rd BR1 52 A6
Ringle Gn TN18 356 C5
Ringlestone Cres
ME14 161 F8
Ringlestone Rd ME17 165 D4
Ringlet Cl E16 1 B8
Ringlet Rd ME4 41 B2
Ringmer Way BR1 52 F4
Ringold Ave CT12 117 A8
Ringshall Rd BR5 54 A6
Rings Hill TN11 221 B4
Ringside TN8 217 C2
Ringsloe Ct CT7 80 D8
Ring Wall CT14 181 E2
Ringwood Ave BR6 87 C1
Ringwood Cl
Canterbury CT2 142 E3
Gillingham ME8 98 D8
Ringwood Rd ME15 195 C8
Ringwould Rd
Kingsdown CT14 248 B5
Ringwould CT14,CT15 247 D4
Ripley Cl BR1 52 F4
Ripley Rd
Ashford TN24 301 A8
Erith DA17 4 A2
Newham E16 1 C7
Ripleys Market DA1 33 E8
Ripon Cl ME8 65 D3
Ripon Rd SE18 12 B8
Ripper's Cross TN26 266 D4
Rippersley Rd DA16 13 A6
Ripple Cross CT14 247 F6
Ripple Rd CT14 247 F7
Ripple Sch The CT14 247 D8
Ripplevale Sch CT14 247 E8
Rippolson Rd SE18 2 F1
Risborough La CT19,
CT20 334 D5
Risborough Way CT20 334 E6
Risden La TN18 355 D7
Risdon Cl CT2 143 F6
Risedale Rd DA7 14 C4
Riseden Rd TN5 336 C1
Rise The Ashford TN23 299 E7
Borden ME9 101 B2
Chatham ME4 64 A7
Crayford DA1 14 F3
Gillingham ME7 98 A3
Gravesend DA12 37 E4
Halfway Houses ME12 46 C5
Kingsdown CT14 248 D5
Rochester ME1 63 D3
St Margaret's at Cliffe
CT15 280 B6
Sevenoaks TN13 187 C7
Sidcup DA5 31 C8
Rising Rd TN23 268 A1
Ritch Rd ME6 127 E8
Ritter St SE18 12 A8
Ritz Blgs TN1 286 A3
Rivendell Cl ME3 27 B5
River Bank Cl 8
ME15 162 B4
Riverbank Rd BR1 29 A5
Riverbank Way TN24 300 D6
Riverbourne Ct 6
ME10 101 F4
River Cl ME15 194 A7
River Cotts BR5 54 C7
River Ct Chartham CT4 173 D3
Crabble CT17 277 F2
Sevenoaks TN13 153 E5
River Dale CT17 277 F3
Riverdale Est TN9 254 D8
Riverdale Rd
Canterbury CT1 143 B2
Erith DA8 4 C1
Sidcup DA5 13 F1
Woolwich SE18 2 F1
River Dr Crabble CT17 277 F2
Rochester ME2 62 E7
Riverhead Cl
Maidstone ME16 161 D6
Margate CT9 51 B1
Sittingbourne ME10 101 C3
Riverhead Ho TN13 153 E5
Riverhead Inf Sch
TN13 153 E4
Riverhead Mews
TN13 153 E4
Riverhill Cotts TN15 187 E5
Riverhill House Gdns*
TN15 187 E5
Riverhill TN15 187 E4
Riverhope Mans SE18 1 E3
River Lawn Rd TN9 222 B1
River Mdw CT17 277 F3
Rivermead ME4 41 C2
Rivermead Sch ME7 64 E6
River Park View BR6 54 B2
River Prim Sch CT17 277 E3
River Rd Barking IG11 3 A8
Sandwich CT13 149 B4
Rivers Cl ME18 192 E7
Riversdale DA11 36 E5
Riversdale Rd
Ashford TN23 300 C8
Ramsgate CT12 83 B1
Riverside Bsns Pk
TN24 268 D2
Riverside CT4 173 C3
Riverside Cl
Bridge CT4 176 A1
Kingsnorth TN23 300 A4
Orpington BR5 54 C7
Riverside Cotts TN14 88 F1
Riverside CT17 277 F3
Riverside Ct
11 Canterbury CT2 142 F1
2 Orpington BR5 54 C4
Riverside Ctry Pk & Visitor
Ctr* ME7 65 D5
Riverside Ct TN9 222 C1
Riverside East Rd ME4 41 C1
Riverside
Edenbridge TN8 217 C1
Eynsford DA4 89 D8
Greenwich SE7 1 B3
Riverside Ind Est
Dartford DA1 15 E2
West Hythe CT21 332 B1
Riverside Mews CT4 176 A1
Riverside Pk ME16 194 A8
Riverside Prim Sch
ME8 66 A1
Riverside Rd
Cliffs End CT13 116 A1
Sidcup DA14 31 E6
Riverside Ret Pk
Canterbury CT1 174 D6
Sevenoaks TN14 154 C8
Riverside Sch TN23 267 F1
Riverside CT16 277 C5
Riverside Way DA1 15 E2
Rivers Rd ME9 103 D2
River St 6 ME7 64 A6
Riverston Sch SE12 11 A2
River St CT17 277 E3
Rivers Wlk ME17 199 C5
Riverview TN23 267 E1
River View Cl 6 ME4 63 F3
Riverview Ct
10 Erith DA17 4 A1
Stone DA9 16 F1
Riverview 6 DA1 16 A3
River View
Gillingham ME8 65 D3
Greenwich SE7 1 C3
Riverview Hts SE18 12 B7
Riverview Inf Sch DA12 37 E4
Riverview Jun Sch
DA12 37 E4
River View ME15 161 F2
Riverview Rd DA9 17 A2
River View
Rushenden ME11 45 F3
Sturry CT2 143 F7
River Way ME20 128 B4
River Wlk TN9 222 B1
Riverwood La BR7 53 D8
Riviera Ct 6 CT20 334 E3
Riviera Rd CT20 335 A3
Riviera The CT20 334 F3
Rixon Ho SE18 12 B8
Roach St ME2 63 A7
Road of Remembrance
CT20 335 D4
Roan Ct ME2 62 F8
Robert Brundett Cl
TN24 268 E5
Robert Napier Sch The
ME7 64 E3
Roberton Dr BR1 52 C8
Roberts Cl Eltham SE9 30 D7
8 Orpington BR5 54 C4
Sittingbourne ME10 101 D7
Roberts Ho SE18 11 E6
Roberts Mews BR6 54 A1
Robertson Ho SE18 11 F6
Roberts Orchard Rd
ME16 160 F3
Roberts Rd Erith DA17 4 A1
Gillingham ME8 98 E8
Greatstone-on-Sea
TN28 373 E1
Snodland ME6 127 F8
Whitstable CT5 107 F6
Robert St Deal CT14 215 D7
Newham E16 2 B5
Woolwich SE18 2 D2
Robeshaw ME9 134 E2
Robina Cl DA6 13 D3
Robina Ct Margate CT9 51 D3
Swanley BR8 56 A5
Robin Cres E6 1 D8
Robin Ct
6 Rochester ME1 63 D4
Whitstable CT5 75 A3
Robin Hill Dr BR7 29 E2
Robin Ho 5 ME16 161 E4
Robin Hood Gn BR5 54 A4
Robin Hood La
Bexley DA6 13 E2
Chatham ME5 96 D1
Lydd TN29 376 C5
Robin Hood Lane (Lower)
ME5 96 F2
Robin Hood Lane (Upper)
ME5 96 E1
Robinia Ave DA11 36 D8
Robin La TN29 376 C6
Robins Ave ME17 199 C5
Robin's Cl CT21 353 C8
Robins Cl ME17 199 C4
Robins Ct
Lewisham SE12 29 C5
Maidstone ME14 162 B7
Robins Gr BR4 85 A7
Robin Way BR5 54 B6
Robinwood Dr TN15 154 F8
Robson Cl E6 1 E7
Robson Dr
Aylesford ME20 128 D2
Hoo St Werburgh ME3 41 D6
Robson Ho SE18 12 A7
Robson's Yd CT17 310 C8
Robus Cl CT18 305 C7
Robus Terr CT18 305 C7
Robyn Cotts TN26 324 E8
Robyns Croft 6 DA11 36 E5
Robyns Way
Edenbridge TN8 249 D8
Sevenoaks TN13 153 F5
Rocfort Rd ME6 128 A8
Rochdale Ho TN1 286 C5
Rochdale Rd
Royal Tunbridge Wells
TN1 286 C6
Woolwich SE2 3 B2
Rochester Airport Ind Est
ME1 96 C5
Rochester Airport ME1,
ME5 96 C6
Rochester Ave
Bromley BR1 52 B7
Canterbury CT1 175 B7
Rochester ME1 63 C4
Rochester Castle*
ME1 63 C6
Rochester Cath* ME1 63 C6
Rochester Cl 1 DA15 13 B1
Rochester Cres ME3 41 D6
Rochester Ct
Canterbury CT1 175 B6
Rochester ME2 63 E8
Rochester Dr DA5 14 A1
Rochester Gate ME1 63 D5
Rochester Gram Sch for
Girls The ME1 63 C2
Rochester Ho 1
ME15 195 D7
Rochester Ind Coll
ME1 63 D4
Rochester Rd
Burham ME1 95 E2
Chalk DA12 38 B6
Chatham ME1,ME5 96 C4
Dartford DA1 34 A8
Pratling Street ME20 129 B4
Rochester ME2 62 D4
Tonbridge TN10 222 D4
Rochester Sta ME1 63 D5
Rochester St ME4 63 E3
Rochester Way
Dartford DA1 32 F8
Eltham,Kidbrooke SE3,
SE9 11 D4
Eltham SE9 12 B4
Rock Ave ME7 64 C3
Rock Cotts TN3 314 B1
Rockdale Rd TN13 154 C2
Rockdale TN13 154 B2
Rock Farm Oasthouse
ME18 192 C6
Rock Hill BR6 88 B4
Rock Hill Rd TN27 232 E2
Rockingham Pl CT6 77 B2
Rockliffe Manor Prim Sch
SE18 12 F8
Rockmount Rd SE18 2 F1
Rock Rd
Borough Green TN15 156 F7
Maidstone ME14 162 A6
Sittingbourne ME10 101 E4
Rocks Cl ME19 160 A6
Rocks Hill TN17 293 A4
Rocks Rd The ME19 160 B6
Rockstone Way CT12 83 A1
Rock Villa Rd TN1 286 A4
Rocky Bourne Rd
TN25 329 D5
Rocky Hill ME16 161 E4
Rocky Hill Terr 2
ME16 161 E4
Rodeo Cl DA8 15 B6
Roding Rd E6 2 B8
Rodmell Rd TN2 286 A2
Rodmer Cl ME12 47 C8
Rodmersham Gn ME9 135 B7
Rodmersham Sch
ME9 135 B7
Rodney Ave TN10 222 E4
Rodney Gdns BR4 85 A6
Rodney St CT11 117 D6
Rodway Rd BR1 52 B8
Roebourne Way E16 2 A5
Roebuck Ho ME1 63 E5
Roebuck Rd
Faversham ME13 138 A7
Rochester ME1 63 C5
Roedean Cl BR6 87 B6
Roedean Rd TN2 286 A1
Roehampton Cl DA12 37 E8
Roehampton Dr BR7 30 C2
Roentgen Ho ME10 101 D5
Roethorne Gdns TN30 345 B8
Roffen Rd ME1 63 C2
Rogers Ct BR8 56 A5
Rogersmead TN30 345 A7
Rogers Rough Rd
TN17 318 B2
Rogers Wood La DA3 91 B6
Rogley Hill TN27 322 B6
Rogues Hill TN11 252 C3
Rokesby Cl DA16 12 D5
Rokesley Rd CT16 278 B5
Rolfe La TN28 373 B7
Rolinsden Way BR2 85 D6
Rollesby Way SE28 3 C7
Rolleston Ave BR5 53 B3
Rolleston Cl BR5 53 B2
Rollo Rd BR8 32 F1
Roll's Ave ME12 48 C1
Rolvenden Ave ME8 65 C3
Rolvenden Dr ME10 101 B5
Rolvenden Gdns BR1 29 D1
Rolvenden Hill TN17 344 C5
Rolvenden Prim Sch
TN17 343 E3
Rolvenden Rd
Rochester ME2 40 C2
Tenterden TN30 344 E7
Rolvenden Sta*
TN17 344 D6
Roly Eckhoff Ho CT16 278 B3
Roman Amphitheatre*
CT13 148 E4
Roman Cl Chatham ME5 96 D1
Deal CT14 215 B6
Roman Hts ME14 162 C6
Roman Rd
East Studdal CT15 246 C5
Edenbridge TN8 249 D5
Faversham ME13 138 C7
Northfleet DA11 36 C5
Ramsgate CT12 83 C2
Snodland ME6 127 F8
Whitfield CT15 278 D8
Roman Sq
Sittingbourne ME10 101 F3
Woolwich SE28 3 A5
Roman Villa Rd DA2,
DA4 34 C2
Roman Way
Crayford DA1 14 E2
Elvington CT15 212 B2
Folkestone CT19 334 C6
Kingsnorth TN23 300 C4
Rochester ME2 62 F4
St Margaret's at Cliffe
CT15 279 F5
Romany Ct ME5 64 D1
Romany Rd ME8 65 C2
Romany Rise BR5 53 C1
Romden Rd TN27 296 B8
Rome House Cnr
TN28 373 A6
Rome Rd TN28 373 A6
Romero Sq SE3 11 C3
Rome Terr ME4 63 F4
Romford Rd TN2 287 F7
Romilly Gdns CT12 83 C2
Romney Ave CT20 334 F5
Romney Cl
4 Birchington CT7 81 A7
Romney Cl *continued*
Maidstone ME14 163 A3
Romney Ct ME10 101 E5
Romney Dr BR1 29 D1
Romney Gdns DA7 13 F6
Romney, Hythe &
Dymchurch Rly*
CT21 333 A2
Romney Marsh Ho
TN29 366 C7
Romney Marsh Rd
TN23,TN24 300 B6
Romney Pl ME15 162 A4
Romney Rd
Ashford TN24 268 E1
Chatham ME5 97 B5
Hamstreet TN26 349 A7
New Romney TN29 372 E3
Northfleet DA11 36 E5
Woolwich SE18 2 C3
Romney Sands Holiday
Village TN28 377 D8
Romney Sands Sta
TN28 377 E8
Romney St TN15 123 A7
Romney Street Cvn Pk
TN15 123 A7
Romney Warren Ctry Pk*
TN28 365 D1
Romney Way
Hythe CT21 332 F1
Tonbridge TN10 222 E5
Romsey Cl
Ashford TN24 269 A2
Orpington BR6 86 C6
Rochester ME2 62 E8
Romulus Gdns TN23 299 F4
Ronald Ho SE3 11 C3
Ronalds Ct 6 ME10 102 A4
Ronalds Rd BR1 52 A8
Ronaldstone Rd DA15 12 E1
Ronfearn Ave BR5 54 D4
Ron Green Ct DA8 14 D8
Ronver Rd SE12 29 A7
Roodlands La TN8 218 D6
Rookdean TN13 153 C5
Rookery Cl
Ashford TN24 268 D7
Bredgar ME9 134 A6
Rookery Cres ME3 22 B6
Rookery Ct RM20 17 A8
Rookery Dr BR7 53 A8
Rookery Gdns BR5 54 C4
Rookery Hill ME6 127 F8
Rookery La BR2 52 D3
Rookery Lodge ME3 22 C5
Rookery Rd BR6 86 A1
Rookery The RM20 17 A8
Rookery View RM17 18 D8
Rookesley Rd BR5 54 D2
Rook La ME9 100 F6
Rookley Cl TN2 286 D2
Rooks Hill TN15 188 D6
Rookston Cnr CT3 113 D1
Rook Wlk 2 E6 1 E7
Roonagh Ct ME10 101 E2
Roopers TN3 285 A7
Roosevelt Ave ME5 97 A8
Roosevelt Rd CT16 278 B3
Ropemakers Ct ME4 64 A1
Roper Cl
Canterbury CT2 142 E1
Gillingham ME8 98 C3
Roper Rd
Canterbury CT2 142 E1
Teynham ME9 103 D3
Roper's Gate TN2 285 E1
Roper's Green La ME3 24 B2
Roper's La ME3 41 F8
Roper St 1 SE9 12 A1
Ropery Bsns Pk SE7 1 C2
Rope Walk Mews
CT13 180 F8
Rope Wlk Chatham ME4 63 F5
Cranbrook TN17 320 C5
Rope Wlk The TN18 356 B5
Rope Yard Rails SE18 2 B3
Rosamund Ct CT19 335 C6
Roseacre Cl CT2 142 E1
Roseacre Ct CT9 51 E2
Roseacre Gdns ME14 163 A3
Roseacre Jun Sch
ME14 163 A4
Roseacre La ME14 163 A4
Roseacre RH8 183 A1
Roseacre Rd DA16 13 B4
Rose Acre Rd CT3 176 F7
Rose Ave DA12 37 E7
Rosebank Gdns DA11 36 E7
Rosebank Wlk 13 SE18 1 E2
Roseberry Gdns
Dartford DA1 33 C8
Orpington BR6 86 E7
Rosebery Ave
Herne Bay CT6 77 E5
Ramsgate CT11 83 F1
Sidcup DA15 30 E8
Rosebery Cl ME10 102 D4
Rosebery Ct DA11 36 F7
Rosebery Rd
Chatham ME4 63 E2
Gillingham ME7 64 D7
Grays RM17 17 E8
Rose Bruford Coll
DA15 31 B7
Rose Cotts Hythe CT21 333 B4
Lamberhurst TN3 317 A5
Lenham Heath ME17 233 B8
Ramsgate CT12 82 F2
Rochester ME2 62 B8
St Mary Hoo ME3 24 E6
Rosecroft Cl
Biggin Hill TN16 118 F1

Rosecroft Cl *continued*
Orpington BR5 54 C3
Rose Ct ME17 194 D1
Rosedale Cl
Dartford DA2 34 B8
Woolwich SE2 3 B3
Rosedale Cnr BR7 52 F8
Rose Dale BR6 86 B8
Rosedale Rd CT9 51 A1
Rosedene Cl DA1 33 C8
Rose Farm La TN27 265 A5
Rosefield
Sevenoaks TN13 154 A3
15 Sidcup DA14 31 A4
Rosegarth DA13 59 E8
Rose Gdns
Birchington CT7 80 F6
Eythorne CT15 245 D7
Herne Bay CT6 77 C4
Minster (Thanet) CT12 115 B6
Rose Hill 11 CT11 117 E6
Rosehill Rd TN16 118 C2
Rose Hill Sch TN4 285 E5
Rose Hill TN30 360 B5
Rosehill Wlk TN1 286 A3
Roseholme ME16 161 D2
Rose La
Bishopsbourne CT4 209 C6
Canterbury CT1 174 F8
Lenham Heath ME17 233 B8
Roselands CT14 215 C1
Roselands Gdns CT2 142 D2
Roselare Cl TN16 151 D1
Roselawn Gdns 3 CT9 82 B8
Roselea Ave CT6 76 F3
Roseleigh Ave ME16 161 C5
Roseleigh Rd ME10 101 D2
Rosemary Ave
Broadstairs CT10 84 A3
Halfway Houses ME12 46 D6
Rosemary Cl
4 Chatham ME5 96 F4
Oxted RH8 183 A2
Rosemary Cnr TN29 370 D8
Rosemary Ct 1 ME1 63 D4
Rosemary Gdns
Broadstairs CT10 83 F2
Whitstable CT5 109 A8
Rosemary La
16 Canterbury CT1 174 F8
Flimwell TN5 339 A5
Hodsoll Street TN15 92 D3
Swift's Green TN27 263 F5
Rosemary Rd
Bexley DA16 12 F6
Maidstone ME15 163 A3
West Malling ME19 127 F1
Rosemead Gdns TN27 262 B7
Rosemount Cl ME15 194 F4
Rosemount Ct ME2 40 A1
Rosemount Dr BR1 52 F5
Rosenheath Cl BR6 87 C3
Rose St DA11 18 B1
Rose Street Prim Sch
ME12 28 B2
Rose St Rochester ME1 63 D3
Sheerness ME12 28 B2
Tonbridge TN9 254 C8
Rose Terr
Faversham ME13 138 D5
Offham ME19 158 D7
Rosetower Ct CT10 83 F8
Rosetta Prim Sch E16 1 B8
Roseveare Rd SE12 29 C4
Rose Way SE12 11 A2
Rose Wlk CT18 307 A4
Rosewood Cl DA14 31 C5
Rosewood Ct BR1 52 D8
Rosewood Dr TN25 267 F4
Rosewood DA2 32 E4
Rosewood Way CT7 81 B7
Rose Yd ME14 162 A4
Rosher Ho DA11 18 F1
Rosherville CE Prim Sch
DA11 18 E1
Rosherville Way DA11 18 E1
Rosiers Ct 1 CT2 142 E1
Roslin Way BR1 29 A3
Ross Ct BR7 29 F1
Rossdale TN2 286 D5
Rosse Mews SE3 11 B6
Rossendale Ct 10
CT20 335 E6
Rossendale Gdns 8
CT20 335 E6
Rossendale Rd CT20 335 E6
Rossetti Ct CT7 80 F7
Rossetti Rd CT7 80 F8
Ross Gdns CT2 142 B3
Ross House SE18 11 E6
Rossland Cl DA6 14 B2
Rossland Rd CT12 117 A8
Rosslyn Gn ME16 161 B5
Rossmore DA14 31 A3
Ross Rd DA1 15 A1
Ross St ME1 63 D4
Ross Way Eltham SE9 11 E4
Folkestone CT20 334 E5
Rothbrook Dr TN24 268 C7
Rother Ct 24 BR5 54 D1
Rothermere Cl TN17 342 E6
Rother Rd TN10 222 C5
Rother Vale ME5 97 C3
Rothesay Ct 6 SE12 29 B5
Rothley Cl TN30 345 B8
Rothsay Ct CT11 83 F1
Rouge La DA12 37 B7
Rougemont ME18 159 C2
Rough Common Rd
CT2 142 B3
Roughetts Rd ME19 126 F3
Roughway La TN11 190 C7
Round Ash Way DA3 58 E3
Roundel Cl ME9 103 D2
Roundel The ME10 101 F2
Roundel Way TN12 259 D5
Round Green Cotts
TN17 291 F4
Roundhay ME19 127 E1
Roundhill Rd TN2 286 D1
Roundlyn Gdns BR5 54 B5
Round St DA12,DA13 60 D5
Roundtable Rd BR1 29 A5
Roundway TN16 118 D4
Roundwell ME14 163 D3
Roundwood BR7 53 B7
Round Wood Cl ME5 97 A1
Routh St E6 1 F8
Rover Rd ME5 97 B2
Rowan Cl Ashford TN23 267 E2
Aylesford ME20 128 E1
Meopham Station DA13 60 B3
Paddock Wood TN12 256 F5
Staple CT3 179 A6
Sturry CT2 143 F6
Rowan Cres DA1 33 C7
Rowan Ct
Ashford TN24 300 E8
Broadstairs CT10 84 A5
2 Lewisham SE12 29 A8
Rowan Ho
4 Chatham ME5 96 F5
7 Maidstone ME16 161 A3
Royal Tunbridge Wells
TN4 285 E4
Rowan House DA14 30 F5
Rowan Lea ME5 64 B1
Rowan Rd Bexley DA7 13 E4
Swanley BR8 55 D6
Rowans Cl DA3 58 D7
Rowan Shaw TN10 222 D6
Rowans The ME12 47 B7
Rowan Tree Pk CT5 108 B6
Rowan Tree Rd TN2 285 E1
Rowan Wlk
Chatham ME4 63 E3
Orpington BR2 85 F7
Rowanwood Ave DA15 31 A7
Rowbrocke Cl ME8 98 D3
Rowdow La TN14,TN15 122 E5
Rowe Cl CT9 82 F7
Rowena Rd CT8 50 C1
Rowenden Vineyard*
TN17 343 B2
Rowe Pl ME20 128 F6
Rowetts Way ME12 48 D3
Rowfield 6 TN8 217 D3
Rowhill Cotts DA2 32 E2
Rowhill Rd DA2 33 A3
Rowhill Sch DA2 33 C4
Rowland Ave ME7 64 E2
Rowland Cl
Gillingham ME7 64 E1
Maidstone ME16 161 E3
Rowland Cotts CT21 331 F3
Rowland Cres CT6 77 E5
Rowland Dr CT6 76 C2
Rowlands Manor BR5 54 C3
Rowlatt Cl DA2 33 C4
Rowlatt Rd DA2 33 C5
Rowley Ave DA15 31 B8
Rowley Hill TN2 255 D1
Rowmarsh Cl DA11 36 D4
Rowntree Path 1 SE28 3 B5
Row The Ash CT3 147 E5
Chillenden CT3 211 F8
Elham CT4 273 F5
New Ash Green DA3 91 F8
Ruckinge TN26 349 F8
Rowton Rd SE18 12 C7
Rowzill Rd BR8 32 F2
Roxburgh Rd CT8 50 D1
Royal Albert Sta E16 1 E6
Royal Albert Way
Newham,Cyprus E6 2 A6
Newham E16 1 E6
Royal Ave
Tonbridge TN9 254 D8
Whitstable CT5 108 C5
Royal Chase TN4 285 F4
Royal Cl
Broadstairs CT10 83 F4
Orpington BR6 86 B6
Royal Connaught
Apartments E16 1 D5
Royal Cres Margate CT9 50 H2
Ramsgate CT11 117 D5
Royal Ct Eltham SE9 29 F7
Whitstable CT5 75 A3
Royal Docks Com Sch The
E16 1 C7
Royal Docks Rd E6 2 B7
Royal Eagle Cl ME2 63 E7
Royal Engineers Mus*
ME7 64 B6
Royal Engineers' Rd
ME14 161 F7
Royal Espl Margate CT9 50 F1
Ramsgate CT11 117 C5
Royal Fountain Mews
ME12 28 A2
Royal Harbour App
CT11 117 C5
Royal Mews 16 CT11 117 F7
Royal Military Ave
CT20 334 D5
Royal Military Rd
Aldington TN25 330 D1
Hythe CT21 332 D1
Royal Mus & art Gallery
with Buffs Regimental
Mus* CT1 174 F8
Royal Oak Cotts TN8 184 C2
Royal Oak Rd DA6 13 F3
Royal Oak Terr DA12 37 C7
Royal Parade Mews
BR7 30 C1
Royal Par BR7 30 C1
Royal Park Prim Sch
DA14 31 E5
Royal Par CT11 117 E6
Royal Pier Rd DA12 19 C1
Royal Rd Newham E16 1 D7
Ramsgate CT11 117 D6
Sheerness ME12 28 C2
Sidcup DA14 31 D5
Sutton at H DA2 34 A3
Royal Rise TN9 254 C8
Royal St George's Golf
Links* CT13 149 E2
Royal Sch of Military
Engineering ME3 40 C4
Royal School for Deaf
Children CT9 50 J2
Royal Sovereign Ave
ME4 64 B7
Royal Star Arc 5
ME14 161 F4
Royal Tunbridge Wells
Bsns Pk TN2 254 D1
Royal Victoria Hospl
CT19 335 C6
Royal Victoria Pl
5 Dover CT16 310 D8
Newham E16 1 B5
Royal Tunbridge Wells
TN1 286 B4
Royal Victoria Sq E16 1 B6
Royal Victoria Sta E16 1 A6
Royal West Kent Ave
TN10 222 D4
Roydene Rd SE18 2 E1
Roydon Hall* TN12 191 F4
Roydon Hall Rd TN12 191 F4
Royds Rd TN24 300 D6
Royston Gdns CT15 279 F6
Royston Rd
Crayford DA1 14 F1
Maidstone ME15 163 A3
Roystons Cl ME8 65 F2
Royton Ave ME17 199 D5
RSPB Dungeness Nature
Reserve* TN29 379 F5
Rubery Dro CT3 148 C7
Rubin Pl ME19 159 B3
Ruckinge Cnr TN26 349 F8
Ruckinge Rd TN26 349 A7
Ruckinge Way ME8 65 C3
Ruck La TN12 289 E3
Ruddstreet Cl SE18 2 C2
Rudge Cl ME5 97 D2
Rudland Rd DA7 14 B4
Ruegg Ho 5 SE18 12 A8
Ruffet Ct TN2 285 E1
Ruffets Wood
Gravesend DA12 37 C2
Kingsnorth TN23 300 C3
Rugby Cl
Broadstairs CT10 83 F5
Chatham ME5 96 F4
Rugby Gdns TN23 300 C8
Rugby Rd CT17 310 A6
Rugless Cl ME23 23 E3
Ruins Barn Rd ME10,
ME9 134 D6
Rule Ct ME12 46 B8
Rumania Wlk DA12 37 F5
Rumfields Rd CT10 83 D4
Rumstead La ME17,
ME9 132 D4
Rumstead Rd ME9 132 E4
Rumwood Ct ME17 196 B5
Runcie Ho 6 CT1 174 F7
Runcie Pl CT2 142 D1
Runciman Cl BR6 87 C1
Runham La ME17 198 E3
Running Horse Rdbt The
ME14 129 E1
Runnymede Ct DA2 34 C7
Runnymede Gdns
ME15 195 A8
Runnymede Mews
ME13 138 C7
Rural Vale DA11 36 E8
Ruscombe Cl TN4 253 F2
Rusham Rd CT3 146 C1
Rushbrook Rd SE9 30 C6
Rush Cl Chatham ME5 97 A3
Dymchurch TN29 366 B6
Rushdean Rd ME2 62 D5
Rushdene SE2 3 D3
Rushdene Wlk TN16 118 D2
Rushenden Ct ME11 45 F3
Rushenden Rd ME11 46 A4
Rushes The ME20 128 B4
Rushet Rd BR5 54 A7
Rushetts TN3 284 F4
Rushetts Rd TN15 90 E3
Rusheymead Ho 5 SE18 2 F1
Rushford Cl TN27 262 D5
Rushgrove St SE18 1 F2
Rushley Cl BR2 85 E6
Rushlye Cl TN3 314 F5
Rushmead Cl CT2 142 D2
Rushmead Dr ME15 195 A7
Rushmere Ct TN15 156 D7
Rushmore Cl BR1 52 E6
Rushmore Hill BR6,
TN14 120 D6
Rushymead TN15 123 A1
Ruskin Ave DA16 13 A5
Ruskin Cl ME19 159 F8
Ruskin Ct SE9 11 F1
Ruskin Dr Bexley DA16 13 A4
Orpington BR6 86 E7
Ruskin Gr Bexley DA16 13 A5
Dartford DA1 16 A2
Ruskin Rd DA17 4 A2
Ruskins View CT6 77 A1
Ruskin Wlk BR2 52 F3
Rusland Ave BR6 86 D7
Russell Cl Bexley DA7 14 A3
Crayford DA1 15 A3
Greenwich SE7 11 C7
Sittingbourne ME10 101 C3
Russell Ct ME4 64 B3
Russell Dr CT5 75 D3
Russell House Sch
TN14 122 C3
Russell Pl
Faversham ME13 105 B3
Sutton at H DA4 57 A8
Russell Quay 2 DA11 19 A1
Russell Rd
1 Folkestone CT19 335 D6
Gravesend DA12 19 D1
Kit's Coty ME20 129 D7
Newham E16 1 B7
Tilbury RM18 18 F5
Tilbury RM18 18 F6
Russells Ave ME8 99 A8
Russell Sq DA3 58 D6
Russell St Dover CT16 310 E7
Sheerness ME12 28 B2
Russells Yd TN17 320 D4
Russell Terr DA4 57 C5
Russet Ave ME13 138 E5
Russet Cl ME2 62 E8
Russet Ct
Coxheath ME17 194 C3
17 Erith DA17 4 A1
Russet Ho RM17 18 C7
Russets The
Maidstone ME16 161 B5
Meopham Station DA13 60 A3
Whitstable CT5 75 D1
Russett Cl Ditton ME20 160 E8
Orpington BR6 87 B5
Russett Rd
Canterbury CT1 175 C8
East Peckham TN12 224 F6
Russett Way BR8 55 D8
Russet Way ME19 158 F2
Rusthall Grange TN4 285 D4
Rusthall Pk TN4 285 D4
Rusthall Rd TN4 285 D4
Rustic Wlk E16 1 B7
Ruston Rd SE18 1 E3
Rustwick TN4 285 D4
Rutherford Coll CT2 142 E4
Rutherford Rd TN24 268 B5
Rutherford Way TN10 222 D7
Rutherglen Rd SE2 13 A8
Ruth Ho 2 ME16 161 E5
Ruthin Rd SE3 11 A8
Ruth St ME4 64 A2
Rutland Ave
Margate CT9 51 C2
Sidcup DA15 31 A8
Rutland Cl
Canterbury CT1 175 D7
Dartford DA1 33 D8
Sidcup DA5 31 D7
Rutland Ct
Chislehurst BR7 53 A8
Sidcup SE9 30 C6
Rutland Gate DA17 4 B1
Rutland Gdns
Birchington CT7 80 F7
Margate CT9 51 C2
Rutland Ho
3 Margate CT9 51 B2
10 Woolwich SE18 1 F2
Rutland Pl ME8 98 C3
Rutland Rd CT16 278 B3
Rutland Way
Maidstone ME15 195 E8
Orpington BR5 54 C3
Ruxley Cl DA14 31 E2
Ruxley Cnr DA14 31 E2
Ruxley Corner Ind Est
DA14 31 D2
Ruxley Ct 1 BR1 52 C7
Ruxton Cl BR8 55 E6
Ruxton Ct 5 BR8 55 E6
Ryan Cl SE3 11 C3
Ryan Dr ME15 163 A2
Ryarsh Cres BR6 86 E6
Ryarsh La ME19 127 B1
Ryarsh Pk ME19 126 F4
Ryarsh Prim Sch
ME19 127 A4
Ryarsh Rd ME19 127 B5
Rycault Cl 4 ME16 161 E3
Rycaut Cl ME8 98 D3
Rycroft La TN14 186 E5
Rydal Ave CT11 117 B7
Rydal Cl TN4 285 E5
Rydal Dr Bexley DA7 14 A6
Royal Tunbridge Wells
TN4 285 E5
Rydal Ho ME15 195 E7
Ryde Cl ME5 97 B8
Rydens Ho SE9 29 C5
Ryder Cl BR1 29 B3
Ryder's Ave CT8 81 D8
Ryders TN3 285 A3
Ryde St CT2 142 E1
Rydons Cl SE9 11 E4
Rye Cl DA5 14 B1
Rye Cres BR5 54 D1
Ryecroft
Gravesend DA12 37 E3
New Barn DA3 59 D5
Ryecroft Rd
Orpington BR5 53 D3
Otford TN14 122 A2
Rye Ct TN23 299 D7
Ryedale Ct TN13 153 E6
Rye Field 25 BR5 54 D1
Ryegrass Cl ME5 97 C6
Ryelands Cres SE12 11 C1
Rye La Otford TN14 122 A2
Sevenoaks TN13,TN14 153 F7
Rye Rd Brookland TN29 370 D8
Four Throws TN18 355 D8
Hawkhurst TN18 341 B1
Peasmarsh TN31 367 E2
Wittersham TN30 360 A2
Rye Wlk CT6 77 C2
Rye Wood Cotts TN14 153 F7
Ryland Ct 8 CT20 335 E5
Ryland Pl 6 CT20 335 E5
Rylands Rd TN24 268 D5
Rymers Cl TN2 286 D7
Rymill St E16 2 A5
Rype Cl TN29 376 C5
Rysted La TN16 151 D1
Ryswick Mews TN28 373 C8

S

Sabre Ct ME7 65 A1
Sackett's Gap CT9 51 C3
Sacketts Hill CT10 83 C6
Sackville Ave BR2 52 A1
Sackville Cl
Hothfield TN26 267 A7
Sevenoaks TN13 154 B5
Sackville Cres TN23 268 A2
Sackville Rd DA2 33 E6
Sackville Sch TN11 221 C6
Sacred Heart Sch
TN5 336 D5
Saddington St DA12 37 C8
Saddlebrook Pk ME12 49 E2
Saddlers Cl ME14 162 E5
Saddlers Hill CT3 178 D2
Saddlers Mews CT5 75 D1
Saddler's Pk DA4 89 D7
Saddler's Wall La
TN29 362 B1
Saddlers Way TN23 300 B5
Saddleton Gr CT5 108 D8
Saddleton Rd CT5 108 D8
Sadlers Cl ME5 96 D2
Saffron Cl ME16 161 B3
Saffron's Pl 14 CT20 335 E5
Saffron Way
1 Chatham ME5 96 F5
Sittingbourne ME10 101 F7
Sage Cl 7 E6 1 F8
Sage Rd ME1 63 B3
Saigasso Cl E16 1 D7
Sailfield Ct ME4 63 F7
Sailmakers Ct 5 ME4 64 B2
St Agnes Gdns ME12 28 C1
St Aidan's Way DA12 37 E5
St Albans Cl ME7 64 E7
St Alban's Cl DA12 37 D5
St Alban's Gdns DA12 37 D5
St Alban's Rd
Dartford DA1 15 F1
Hersden CT3 111 E1
St Alban's Rd Inf Sch
DA1 15 F1
St Albans Rd ME2 62 D6
St Alfege Rd SE7 11 D8
St Alphege CE Prim Sch
CT5 74 D1
St Alphege Cl CT5 108 B7
St Alphege La 17 CT1 142 F1
St Alphege Rd 4
CT16 278 C1
St Ambrose Gn TN25 237 E2
St Andrews Cl
Canterbury CT1 174 E7
Erith SE28 3 D7
Folkestone CT19 335 B7
Herne Bay CT6 77 A4
St Andrew's Cl ME16 161 A2
St Andrews Cl
Margate CT9 82 F7
Paddock Wood TN12 257 A6
St Andrew's Cl CT5 108 E7
St Andrews Ct
26 Gravesend DA12 19 B1
Royal Tunbridge Wells
TN4 254 A1
St Andrew's Ct 4 BR8 55 E6
St Andrews Dr BR5 54 B2
St Andrews CT19 335 E5
St Andrews Gdns
CT17 278 B2
St Andrew's Gdns
CT15 244 E5
St Andrews Ho BR1 29 B2
St Andrews Lees
CT13 181 A8
St Andrews Mews SE3 11 A7
St Andrews Park Rd
TN4 254 A1
St Andrews Pk ME16 161 A3
St Andrew's Rd CT14 215 C6
St Andrews Rd ME7 64 D7
St Andrews Rd
10 Gravesend DA12 37 B8
Littlestone-on-Sea TN28 373 E6
Maidstone ME16 161 A3
St Andrews Rd TN12 257 A6
St Andrew's Rd CT11 117 F8
St Andrews Rd DA14 31 D5
St Andrew's Rd RM18 18 E5
St Andrews Sch ME1 63 C4
St Andrews Way
The Chart RH8 183 F4
Tilmanstone CT14 213 A3
St Andrew's Wlk ME3 9 D2
St Andrew Terr CT17 278 A2
St Angela's Sch CT8 81 D7
St Anne's Ct
1 Dover CT16 278 B2
Herne Bay CT6 76 E5
St Annes Ct ME16 161 E4
St Anne's Dr CT6 76 D4
St Anne's Gdns CT9 82 F8
St Anne's Rd
Ashford TN23 299 F7
Whitstable CT5 74 F2
St Ann's Green La
TN12 259 F8
St Ann's Rd
Dymchurch TN29 366 B7
Faversham ME13 138 B7
St Anns Way TN16 119 B3
St Anselm's RC Prim Sch
DA1 16 A2
St Anselm's RC Sch
CT1 175 C5
St Anthony's Ct BR6 86 B8
St Anthony's Sch CT9 51 C1
St Anthony's Way CT9 51 C1
St Aubyns Cl BR6 86 F7
St Aubyns Gdns BR6 86 F8
St Audrey Ave DA7 14 A5
St Augustine Ho 1
TN9 254 B8
St Augustine of Canterbury
RC Prim Sch ME8 98 D3
St Augustine's Abbey
CT11 117 D5
St Augustine's Abbey (rems
of)* CT1 175 A8
St Augustine's Ave
Bromley BR2 52 E4
Margate CT9 82 F8
St Augustines Bsns Pk
CT5 75 E3
St Augustine's Cres
CT5 75 D3
St Augustine's Ct 3
CT1 175 B8
St Augustines Ct CT6 76 F2
St Augustine's of
Canterbury CE Prim Sch
DA17 3 F2
St Augustine's Pk
CT11 117 C6
St Augustine's RC Prim Sch
Hythe CT21 333 E2
Royal Tunbridge Wells
TN4 286 A7
St Augustine's Rd
Canterbury CT1 175 B7
Deal CT14 214 F4
Erith DA17 3 F2
Ramsgate CT11 117 D5
St Barnabas CE Prim Sch
TN1 286 B5
St Barnabas Cl
Ashford TN23 299 F7
Gillingham ME7 64 D3
Maidstone ME16 161 C8
St Barnabas' Cl TN1 286 B5
St Bartholemews Cl 4
CT17 310 C8
St Bartholomew's Hospl
Rochester ME1 63 E4
Sandwich CT13 181 A7
St Bartholomew's La 4
ME1 63 E4
St Bartholomews RC Prim
Sch BR8 55 E6
St Bartholomew's Terr 2
ME1 63 E4
St Bart's Cl 5 CT17 310 C8
St Bart's Rd CT13 180 F8
St Benedict Rd ME6 127 E8
St Benedict's Ave DA12 37 E6
St Benedict's Lawn
CT11 117 D5
St Benedicts RC Prim Sch
ME5 97 C2
St Benets Ct TN30 345 B8
St Benet's Rd CT8 81 E7
St Benets Way TN30 345 B8
St Benjamins Dr BR6 87 C2
St Bernards Rd TN10 222 C6
St Blaise Ave BR1 52 B7
St Boltophs Ct TN13 154 B3
St Botolph Rd DA11 36 D5
St Botolph's Ave
TN13 154 A3
St Botolph's CE Prim Sch
DA11 36 D8
St Botolph's Rd TN13 154 B3
St Brelade's Ct TN8 217 A3
St Brides Cl DA18 3 D4
St Catherines Ct
Ramsgate CT11 83 F1
Rochester ME1 63 D5
St Catherine's Dr
ME13 138 D6
St Catherine's Gr CT12 82 D1
St Catherine's Hospl
ME1 63 D4
St Catherines TN29 372 A7
St Catherine's RC Sch for
Girls DA6 14 B2
St Cecelia Ho CT14 215 B1
St Chad's Dr DA12 37 E5
St Chad's Rd RM18 19 A7
St Chad's Sch RM18 19 A6
St Christopher Cl CT9 83 D8
St Christophers Gn
CT10 83 F5
St Christopher's Sch
CT1 175 B6
St Clare Rd CT14 215 C1
St Clement's Ave RM20 17 B8
St Clements Cl
Leysdown-on-S ME12 49 D2
Northfleet DA11 36 F5

St Clements Ct
Broadstairs CT10 ....83 E6
Folkestone CT20 ....335 F5
Grays RM17 ....17 F8
St Clement's Ct CT6 ....77 A3
St Clements Ct CT11 ...117 D7
St Clement's Ho ME1 ....63 D5
St Clements Rd ME12 ....49 E3
St Clement's Rd
Westgate-on-S CT8 ....50 C1
West Thurrock RM20 ....17 C7
St Clements 8 CT13 ...149 A1
St Clement's Way
RM20 ....16 F8
St Clere Hill Rd TN15 ...123 F7
St Columba's Cl DA12 ....37 E5
St Columba's RC Boys Sch
DA6 ....14 B2
St Cosmus Cl TN25 ....203 B1
St Crispin's Com Prim Inf
Sch CT8 ....81 E7
St Crispin's Rd CT8 ....81 E7
St Cuby CT10 ....84 C7
St Davids Ave CT17 ....310 A5
St David's Bridge
TN17 ....320 D4
St David's Cl
Birchington CT7 ....81 B8
Whitstable CT5 ....108 E8
St David's Cres DA12 ....37 D4
St Davids Gate ME16 ...161 A2
St David's Rd
Allhallows ME3 ....9 D2
Deal CT14 ....215 C6
Hextable BR8 ....32 F1
Ramsgate CT11 ....83 F1
Royal Tunbridge Wells
TN4 ....286 B6
St Denys Rd CT18 ....307 B5
St Domingo Ho SE18 ....1 F3
St Dunstan's Cl CT2 ....142 E1
St Dunstans Ct 4 CT2 ...142 E1
St Dunstan's Dr DA12 ....37 E5
St Dunstan's Rd CT9 ....51 A2
St Dunstan's St CT2 ....142 E1
St Dunstan's Terr CT2 ...142 E1
St Dunstans Wlk
TN17 ....320 D4
St Eanswythe's CE Prim
Sch CT20 ....335 D4
St Eanswythe Way 19
CT20 ....335 D5
St Edith's Rd TN15 ....123 A2
St Edmund Ho SE2 ....13 D8
St Edmunds Cl DA18 ....3 D4
St Edmund's Cotts
TN15 ....91 A2
St Edmund's Ct TN15 ....91 A2
St Edmund's RC Sch
CT16 ....278 D2
St Edmunds Rd
Canterbury CT1 ....174 F8
Dartford DA1 ....16 A3
St Edmund's Rd CT14 ...214 E4
St Edmund's Sch CT2 ...142 C3
St Edmunds Way ME8 ....66 B1
St Edward's RC Prim Sch
ME12 ....28 B2
St Elisabeth Ho CT1 ....143 A1
St Ethelbert's RC Prim Sch
CT11 ....117 F8
St Faith's at Ash Sch
CT3 ....147 C1
St Faith's La ME14 ....163 B4
St Faith's St ME14 ....161 F4
St Fidelis RC Prim Sch
DA8 ....14 C8
St Fidelis' Rd DA8 ....4 D1
St Francis Ave DA12 ....37 E4
St Francis Cl
Deal CT14 ....214 F4
Maidstone ME14 ....162 B7
Margate CT9 ....83 D8
Orpington BR6 ....53 E3
Rochester ME2 ....62 E6
St Francis RC Prim Sch
ME15 ....161 C4
St Francis' Rd DA8 ....4 D2
St Francis Rd
Folkestone CT19 ....334 F6
Harvel DA13 ....93 B3
St Gabriel's Ct 12
CT20 ....335 E6
St Georges Ave ME12 ....48 D2
St George's Ave
Herne Bay CT6 ....76 D4
Sheerness ME12 ....28 B1
St George's Bickley CE
Prim Sch BR1 ....52 D7
St George's Bsns Ctr
TN23 ....267 F2
St Georges Bsns Pk
ME10 ....102 B4
St George's CE Foundation
Sch CT10 ....83 C5
St George's CE Mid Sch
ME12 ....47 E6
St George's CE Prim Sch
TN15 ....124 F3
St George's CE Sch
DA11 ....37 A6
St Georges Cl SE28 ....3 D7
St George's Cl CT5 ....108 E7
St Georges Cres CT17 ...310 B5
St George's Cres DA12 ...37 D4
St Georges Ct CT17 ....278 A2
St George's Ctr DA11 ....19 B1
St Georges Ct TN4 ....286 A5
St George's Ct
West Minst ME12 ....46 B8
St George's Ct *continued*
Wrotham TN15 ....124 F3
St Georges La CT1 ....175 A8
St George's Lees
CT13 ....181 A8
St Georges Mews 11
TN9 ....254 B8
St George's Pas CT14 ...215 D6
St George's Pk TN2 ....313 F8
St George's Pl
Canterbury CT1 ....175 A8
Hythe CT21 ....353 D8
St Georges Pl
St Margaret's at Cliffe
CT15 ....279 F6
Sandwich CT13 ....181 B8
St George's Rd CT10 ....84 A4
St Georges Rd BR1 ....52 F6
St George's Rd
Deal CT14 ....215 D6
Folkestone CT19 ....334 F6
Gillingham ME7 ....64 C6
St Georges Rd BR5 ....53 D3
St George's Rd
Ramsgate CT11 ....117 F8
Sandwich CT13 ....181 A8
Sevenoaks TN13 ....154 B5
Sidcup DA14 ....31 D2
St Georges Rd BR8 ....55 F5
St Georges Rd W BR1 ....52 E7
St George's Sq 3
TN24 ....268 B2
St Georges Sq DA3 ....58 E6
St George's Sq ME16 ....161 E3
St Georges St CT1 ....175 A8
St George's Terr CT6 ....76 E5
St George's Wlk ME3 ....9 D2
St German's Pl SE3 ....11 A6
St Giles Cl Dover CT17 ...310 B5
Orpington BR6 ....86 D5
St Giles Rd CT17 ....310 B5
St Giles Wlk CT17 ....310 B5
St Gregory's Ct CT1 ....143 B1
St Gregory's 9 CT1 ....143 A1
St Gregory's Cl CT14 ...214 F4
St Gregory's Cres DA12 ...37 E6
St Gregory's Ct DA12 ....37 E6
St Gregory's RC Comp Sch
TN4 ....286 A7
St Gregory's RC Prim Sch
CT9 ....82 E8
St Gregory's Rd CT1 ....143 B1
St Helens CE Prim Sch
ME3 ....22 B5
St Helens Cotts ME15 ...193 E8
St Helens La ME15 ....193 E8
St Helens Rd Cliffe ME3 ...22 B5
7 Erith DA18 ....3 D4
St Helen's Rd ME12 ....28 D1
St Helens DA14 ....31 B5
St Helier's Cl ME16 ....161 B2
St Hilary Ho SE2 ....13 D8
St Hilda Rd CT19 ....334 E6
St Hildas TN15 ....189 F8
St Hilda's Rd CT21 ....333 B1
St Hilda's Way DA12 ....37 E5
St Jacob's Pl CT1 ....174 D6
St James' Ave
Broadstairs CT10 ....83 E5
Ramsgate CT12 ....83 B1
St James' CE Inf Sch
TN2 ....286 C4
St James' CE Jun Sch
TN2 ....286 C4
St James' CE Prim Sch
ME3 ....27 B6
St James Cl
East Malling ME19 ....159 F8
Grain ME3 ....27 B6
Tonbridge TN10 ....222 D7
Warden ME12 ....49 E4
St James Ct
3 Bromley BR2 ....52 A7
Greenwich SE3 ....11 B6
Stone DA9 ....16 F1
St James' Gdns CT5 ....108 D8
St James' Inf Sch
ME19 ....159 F8
St James La 7 CT16 ....310 E7
St James' La DA9 ....34 E8
St James Oaks DA11 ....37 A8
St James' Park Rd CT9 ...82 A8
St James' Pk TN1 ....286 C5
St James Pl DA1 ....15 D1
St James RC Prim Sch
BR5 ....53 B4
St James Rd Grain ME3 ...27 B5
Kingsdown CT14 ....248 D5
St James' Rd TN1 ....286 C5
St James's Ave DA11 ....37 A8
St James's Cl SE18 ....2 C1
St James's Ct TN1 ....286 B4
St James Sq DA3 ....58 E6
St James's Rd
Gravesend DA11 ....19 A1
Sevenoaks TN13 ....154 B5
St James's St DA11 ....19 A1
St James St CT16 ....310 E7
St James's Terr CT7 ....81 B8
St James Way DA14 ....31 E3
St Jean's Rd CT8 ....81 E7
St Joachim's RC Prim Sch
E16 ....1 C7
St John Bsns Ctr The 10
CT9 ....50 J1
St John Fisher RC Comp
(Lower) Sch ME4 ....63 F2
St John Fisher RC Comp
Sch ME4 ....63 E3
St John Fisher RC Prim Sch
DA18 ....3 E3
St John's Cotts
Bethersden TN26 ....297 D5
St John's Cotts *continued*
12 Sandwich CT13 ....148 F1
St John's Ave
Ramsgate CT12 ....83 A1
Sittingbourne ME10 ....102 B3
St John's CE Inf Sch
ME4 ....63 E3
St John's CE Prim Sch
Maidstone ME14 ....162 E4
Royal Tunbridge Wells
TN4 ....286 B7
Sevenoaks TN13 ....154 D4
St John's Church Rd
CT19 ....335 C6
St John's Cl
Densole CT18 ....307 A7
Higham ME3 ....39 C4
St John's Commandery
(rems of)* CT15 ....275 E4
St Johns Cres CT2 ....142 D6
St John's Ct TN24 ....301 A6
St Johns Ct DA8 ....4 D1
St John's Ct TN13 ....154 C5
St John's Hill TN13,
TN14 ....154 C5
St John's Hospl 6
CT1 ....143 A1
St John's Jerusalem*
DA4 ....34 B1
St John's La
Ashford TN23,TN24 ....268 C2
Canterbury CT1 ....174 F8
Hartley DA3 ....58 F3
St John's Par 4 DA14 ....31 B4
St John's Pk
Greenwich SE3 ....11 A7
Royal Tunbridge Wells
TN4 ....286 A8
St John's Pl CT1 ....143 A1
St John's RC Comp Sch
DA12 ....37 D7
St John's RC Prim Sch
DA12 ....37 E7
St John's Rd
Bexley DA16 ....13 B4
Dartford DA2 ....34 C8
Dover CT17 ....310 C7
St Johns Rd CT15 ....212 B2
St John's Rd Erith DA8 ....4 D1
Faversham ME13 ....138 D7
Gillingham ME7 ....64 C3
Gravesend DA12 ....37 D8
Higham ME3 ....39 C4
St Johns Rd
Hoo St Werburgh ME3 ....41 E6
Hythe CT21 ....333 A3
St John's Rd
Margate CT9 ....50 J2
Newham E16 ....1 A7
New Romney TN28 ....373 A6
Orpington BR5 ....53 E3
Royal Tunbridge Wells
TN4 ....286 A6
Sevenoaks TN13 ....154 C5
Sidcup DA14 ....31 B4
Whitstable CT5 ....75 D3
St John's St
Folkestone CT20 ....335 D5
7 Margate CT9 ....50 J2
St John's Terr SE18 ....12 D8
St John's Way CT18 ....307 A7
St Johns Way
Edenbridge TN8 ....217 C3
Rochester ME1 ....63 A2
St Josephs Cl BR6 ....86 F6
St Josephs Ct 4 SE12 ....29 B5
St Josephs Prep Sch
DA12 ....37 C6
St Joseph's RC Prim Sch
Aylesham CT3 ....211 A5
Broadstairs CT10 ....83 F5
Bromley BR1 ....29 B1
Crayford DA1 ....14 E3
Northfleet DA11 ....36 D8
St Julien Ave CT1 ....143 D1
St Justin Cl BR5 ....54 D6
St Katharine's Knockholt
CE Prim Sch TN14 ....120 B2
St Katherine Rd ME12 ....46 E7
St Katherines Cotts
DA12 ....38 E4
St Katherine's La ME6 ...127 F7
St Katherines Rd DA18 ....3 D4
St Katherine's Sch
ME6 ....127 F7
St Keverne Rd SE9 ....29 E4
St Kilda Rd BR6 ....53 F1
St Laurence Ave
ME16 ....161 C8
St Laurence Cl
Orpington BR5 ....54 D6
Sittingbourne ME9 ....102 D2
St Laurence Ct CT11 ...117 C7
St Laurence In Thanet CE
Jun Sch CT11 ....117 B8
St Lawrence Ave
Bidborough TN4 ....253 D3
Ramsgate CT11 ....117 B5
St Lawrence CE Prim Sch
TN15 ....155 E3
St Lawrence Cl CT1 ....175 B6
St Lawrence Coll Jun Sch
CT11 ....117 E8
St Lawrence Coll
CT11 ....117 D8
St Lawrence Ct TN28 ....373 A6
St Lawrence Forstal
CT1 ....175 B6
St Lawrence Gd (Kent Cty
Cricket Club) CT1 ....175 B6
St Lawrence Ind Est
CT11 ....117 B7
St Lawrence Rd CT1 ....175 B6
St Lenard's Tower*
ME19 ....159 A7
St Leonards Ave ME4 ....63 F2
St Leonards Cl
4 Bexley DA16 ....13 A4
Grays RM17 ....17 F8
St Leonards Ct CT21 ....333 B1
St Leonards Mews
CT21 ....333 B1
St Leonard's Rd CT14 ...215 B4
St Leonards Rd
Hythe CT21 ....333 B1
Maidstone ME16 ....161 C8
St Leonards Rise BR6 ....86 E6
St Leonard's St ME19 ....159 B7
St Louis Gr CT6 ....76 C4
St Luke's Wlk CT18 ....306 F4
St Luke's Ave
Maidstone ME14 ....162 B5
Ramsgate CT11 ....117 E8
St Luke's CE Inf Sch
TN4 ....286 C7
St Lukes Cl
Dartford DA2 ....34 E3
Swanley BR8 ....55 D7
St Luke's Cl CT8 ....81 E8
St Lukes Cl CT5 ....108 E7
St Lukes Cotts BR8 ....55 D7
St Lukes Ct
Ashford TN23 ....299 F7
Maidstone ME14 ....162 A6
St Luke's Rd
Maidstone ME14 ....162 B5
Ramsgate CT11 ....117 E8
Royal Tunbridge Wells
TN4 ....286 B6
St Luke's Way ME3 ....9 D2
St Magnus Cl CT7 ....81 A8
St Magnus Ct CT7 ....81 A8
St Malo Ct 2 CT20 ....335 C4
St Margaret Clitherow RC
Prim Sch
Tonbridge TN10 ....222 B6
Woolwich SE28 ....3 B5
St Margaret's-at-Cliffe
Prim Sch CT15 ....280 A6
St Margaret's at Troy Town
CE Prim Sch ME1 ....63 C4
St Margarets Ave DA15 ...30 D5
St Margaret's Banks
ME1 ....63 D5
St Margaret's CE Jun Sch
ME8 ....98 E8
St Margarets CE Prim Sch
TN12 ....226 D1
St Margaret's CE Prim Sch
SE18 ....2 C1
St Margaret's Cl DA2 ....34 D6
St Margarets Cl
Maidstone ME16 ....161 B2
Orpington BR6 ....87 B6
St Margaret's Cl CT5 ....108 A6
St Margaret's Cres
DA12 ....37 E5
St Margarets Ct 1
CT20 ....335 B5
St Margaret's Ct
6 Gillingham ME8 ....98 F8
High Halstow ME23 ....23 E3
St Margarets Dr
Deal CT14 ....248 B8
Gillingham ME8 ....98 C5
St Margaret's Gr SE18 ....12 C8
St Margaret's Inf Sch
ME8 ....98 E8
St Margaret's Mews
ME1 ....63 C5
St Margaret's Rd
Dartford DA2,DA4 ....34 E2
Northfleet DA11 ....36 E7
St Margarets Rd CT15 ...248 A1
St Margaret's Rd
CT15 ....280 A5
St Margarets Rd CT7 ....81 F3
St Margaret's Rd CT8 ....81 E7
St Margaret's St
Canterbury CT1 ....174 F8
Rochester ME1 ....63 C5
St Margaret's Terr SE18 ...2 C1
St Margarets Villas
TN12 ....258 D8
St Mark's Ave DA11 ....36 F8
St Mark's CE Prim Sch
BR2 ....52 A6
St Marks CE Prim Sch
ME20 ....128 F6
St Mark's CE Prim Sch
TN4 ....285 D1
St Mark's Cl CT20 ....334 D5
St Marks Cl CT5 ....108 E8
St Marks Ct ME20 ....128 F6
St Marks Ho ME7 ....64 C5
St Marks Ind Est E16 ....1 D5
St Mark's Rd
Bromley BR2 ....52 B6
Royal Tunbridge Wells
TN2 ....313 F7
St Martins Ave CT1 ....175 B8
St Martins Cl CT1 ....175 B8
St Martin's Cl
Detling ME14 ....131 A1
Dover CT17 ....310 B5
St Martins Cl Erith DA18 ...3 D4
Newington ME9 ....100 C7
St Martins Ct 4 CT1 ....175 B8
St Martins Cvn Site
CT3 ....175 E8
St Martin's Dr DA4 ....89 D7
St Martin's Hill CT1 ....175 C8
St Martins Ho CT17 ....310 D5
St Martin's Hospl CT1 ...175 D8
St Martins Mdw TN16 ....152 C4
St Martin's Pl CT1 ....175 B8
St Martin's Rd
Canterbury CT1 ....143 B1
Dartford DA1 ....15 F1
Deal CT14 ....214 F4
Dover CT15 ....278 E4
St Martins Rd
Folkestone CT20 ....334 D6
New Romney TN28 ....373 B6
St Martin's Sch CT17 ....310 A7
St Martin's Terr CT1 ....175 B8
St Martin's View CT6 ....111 A8
St Mary Cray Prim Sch
BR5 ....54 C3
St Mary Cray Sta BR5 ....54 B5
Saint Mary Magdalene CE
Prim Sch SE18 ....2 A2
St Mary of Charity CE Prim
Sch ME13 ....138 D7
St Mary's Ct CT6 ....76 E4
St Mary's Abbey
ME19 ....159 C8
St Mary & St Joseph's RC
Sch DA14 ....31 A3
St Mary's Ave
Margate CT9 ....51 D1
Margate CT9 ....83 D8
St Mary's Bay Sta
TN29 ....365 F4
St Mary's CE Prim Sch
Ashford TN23 ....268 A3
Chilham CT4 ....205 B8
Dover CT16 ....310 E8
Swanley BR8 ....55 E5
St Mary's Church Rd
TN14 ....152 F2
St Mary's Church*
CT6 ....78 C7
St Mary's Cl CT13 ....180 C2
St Marys Cl CT18 ....305 D3
St Mary's Cl
Gravesend DA12 ....37 C6
Grays RM17 ....18 D8
Hamstreet TN26 ....349 A8
Laddingford ME18 ....225 E4
Nonington CT15 ....211 C5
Orpington BR5 ....54 C7
Platt TN15 ....157 C7
Ticehurst TN5 ....338 D1
Woodnesborough CT13 ....180 B6
St Mary's Ct
17 Canterbury CT1 ....174 F8
Erith DA17 ....3 D2
5 Westerham TN16 ....151 D1
St Marys Ct SE7 ....11 D7
St Marys Dr CT18 ....305 D3
St Mary's Dr TN13 ....153 E4
St Mary's Gdns
Chatham ME4 ....64 B7
St Mary's Bay TN29 ....366 A5
Upstreet CT3 ....112 E3
St Marys Gn TN24 ....268 E7
St Mary's Gn TN16 ....118 C1
St Mary's Gr
Biggin Hill TN16 ....118 C1
Tilmanstone CT14 ....213 A4
Whitstable CT5 ....107 F7
St Mary's Island CE Prim
Sch ME4 ....41 B2
St Mary's La
Speldhurst TN3 ....285 A8
Ticehurst TN5 ....338 D1
St Mary's Mdw CT3 ....178 A8
St Marys Mews TN24 ....300 F8
St Mary's Pl Eltham SE9 ...12 A1
Newington ME9 ....100 C7
St Mary's Prim Sch
ME2 ....63 B7
St Mary's RC Prim Sch
Deal CT14 ....214 F3
Eltham SE9 ....12 A2
Gillingham ME7 ....64 D6
Tilbury RM18 ....18 F5
Whitstable CT5 ....74 F2
St Mary's Rd
5 Broadstairs CT10 ....84 B4
Coldblow DA5 ....32 C7
Deal CT14 ....215 C1
Elham CT4 ....273 F4
Faversham ME13 ....138 D7
Gillingham ME7 ....64 C6
Minster (Thanet) CT12 ....115 B6
Patrixbourne CT4 ....176 B3
Rochester ME2 ....63 B7
St Mary in the Marsh
TN28,TN29 ....365 C5
Stone DA9 ....16 E2
Swanley BR8 ....55 E5
Tonbridge TN9 ....254 B7
West Hythe CT21 ....332 B1
Wrotham TN15 ....125 A2
St Mary's Row ME12 ....47 A6
St Mary's ME3 ....24 D5
St Mary's St CT1 ....174 F8
St Mary's Terr 2
CT20 ....335 E5
St Mary St SE18 ....2 A2
St Mary's View ME9 ....100 C7
St Marys Way DA3 ....58 E6
St Mary's Westbrook
CT20 ....335 A5
St Mary's Wlk ME1 ....95 F1
St Matthew's CE Inf Sch
ME1 ....63 A2
St Matthew's Cl ME9 ....100 C7
St Matthews Dr
Bromley BR1 ....52 F6
Rochester ME1 ....63 A2
St Matthew's High Brooms
CE Prim Sch TN4 ....286 B8
St Matthew's Way ME3 ....9 D2
St Mawes CT8 ....50 C1
St Mellion Cl SE28 ....3 D7
St Merryn Cl SE18 ....12 D7
St Michael & All Angels
Church CT14 ....215 C4
St Michael's CE Prim Sch
TN31 ....368 C2
St Michael's Wlk
CT18 ....306 F4
St Michael's Alley 14
CT11 ....117 E6
St Michaels Ave CT9 ....83 D8
St Michael's CE Inf Sch
ME16 ....161 E3
St Michael's CE Prim Sch
TN30 ....324 A3
St Michaels Cl
Bromley BR1 ....52 E6
Canterbury CT2 ....142 A1
St Michael's Cl
Chatham ME4 ....63 F3
Erith DA18 ....3 D4
St Michaels Cl
4 Newham E16 ....1 D8
Pratling Street ME20 ....129 C3
St Michael's Cl 5
ME10 ....101 F4
St Michael's Ct
8 Folkestone CT20 ....335 E5
6 Rochester ME2 ....63 B8
St Michaels Ct TN11 ....221 E7
St Michaels Dr TN14 ....122 E3
St Michael's East Wickham
CE Prim Sch DA16 ....13 C6
St Michaels RH8 ....183 A5
St Michael's Pl CT2 ....142 E2
St Michael's Prim Sch
TN7 ....311 B5
St Michael's RC Prim Sch
ME4 ....63 F3
St Michael's Rd
Bexley DA16 ....13 B4
Canterbury CT2 ....142 E2
Maidstone ME16 ....161 D3
Royal Tunbridge Wells
TN4 ....286 B7
Sittingbourne ME10 ....101 F4
St Michael's Rise DA16 ...13 B6
St Michael's St CT20 ....335 E5
St Michael's Terr
TN30 ....324 A3
St Mildred's Ave
Birchington CT7 ....80 E8
Broadstairs CT10 ....84 A4
Ramsgate CT11 ....117 B5
St Mildred's Cl 4
TN30 ....345 A7
St Mildreds Ct
Canterbury CT1 ....174 E8
Deal CT14 ....215 C1
Westgate-on-S CT8 ....50 D1
St Mildred's Gdns CT8 ...50 D1
St Mildreds Pl CT1 ....174 E7
St Mildred's Prim Inf Sch
CT10 ....84 A4
St Mildreds Rd 5 SE12 ...29 A8
St Mildred's Rd
Margate CT9 ....51 A2
Minster (Thanet) CT12 ....115 B5
Ramsgate CT11 ....117 C6
Westgate-on-S CT8 ....50 C1
St Monicas Deal CT14 ....248 D6
Dover CT17 ....310 C7
St Monicas Rd CT14 ....248 D6
St Nicholas at Wade CE
Prim Sch CT7 ....79 E2
St Nicholas CE Inf Sch
ME2 ....63 A7
St Nicholas CE Prim Sch
TN28 ....373 B7
St Nicholas Cl
Deal CT14 ....214 F4
Sturry CT2 ....143 F7
St Nicholas Cnr CT7 ....79 F1
St Nicholas Ct TN13 ....154 B2
St Nicholas Dr TN13 ....154 C1
St Nicholas Gdns ME2 ....62 F7
St Nicholas Ho CT3 ....147 D2
St Nicholas Hospl
CT2 ....142 C1
St Nicholas Rdbt CT7 ....80 B2
St Nicholas Rd
Canterbury CT1 ....174 D6
Faversham ME13 ....138 A7
Hythe CT21 ....333 A2
Littlestone-on-Sea TN28 ....373 E6
Woolwich SE18 ....2 F2
St Nicholas Sch CT1 ....174 F6
St Nicholas Terr 1
CT21 ....333 B2
St Nicolas La BR7 ....52 E8
St Olaves Prep Sch
SE9 ....30 B6
St Olave's & St Saviour's
Gram Sch BR6 ....87 B7
St Patrick's Row ME9 ...135 B7
St Patrick's Cl
Deal CT14 ....215 C6
Whitstable CT5 ....108 E7
St Patrick's Gdns DA12 ...37 D5
St Patrick's RC Prim Sch
SE18 ....2 D2
St Patrick's Rd CT14 ....215 C6
St Patricks Rd CT17 ....310 A4
St Patrick's Rd CT11 ....117 F8
St Paulinus' CE Prim Sch
DA1 ....14 E3
St Paulinus Ct DA1 ....14 E3
St Paul's Ave ME13 ....138 A7
St Pauls CE Inf Sch
TN4 ....285 B4
St Pauls CE Jun Sch
TN4 ....285 B4
St Paul's CE Prim Sch
BR8 ....56 B8

St Paul's Cl
Greenwich SE7 1 D1
Rochester ME2 62 D5
Swanscombe DA10 35 E8
St Pauls Cl TN10 222 D5
St Paul's Cray CE Prim Sch BR5 54 D6
St Paul's Cray Rd BR5, BR7 53 D8
St Pauls Cres ME13 140 A3
St Paul's Ct
Folkestone CT20 334 E4
Rusthall TN4 285 C4
St Pauls Inf Sch ME14 162 A7
St Paul's RC Sch SE2 13 A8
St Pauls Rd ME13 140 A3
St Paul's Rd Erith DA8 14 C7
Margate CT9 51 A3
St Paul's Sq BR2 52 A7
St Paul's St
Rusthall TN4 285 C4
Sittingbourne ME10 101 E5
St Pauls Terr CT1 175 A8
St Paul's Way CT20 334 F4
St Paul's Wood Hill BR5 53 F7
St Peter Ave TN16 119 B3
St Peter Chanel RC Prim Sch DA14 31 C3
St Peter-in-Thanet CE Jun Sch CT10 83 F7
St Peter's Row TN26 297 D5
St Peter's Way TN26 327 A8
St Peter & St Paul RC Prim Sch BR5 53 E7
St Peter's Bridge ME14 161 F4
St Peter's CE Prim Sch
Aylesford ME20 129 A3
Royal Tunbridge Wells TN2 286 C3
St Peters Cl
Chislehurst BR7 30 D1
Ditton ME20 128 B1
St Peter's Cl
Halfway Houses ME12 46 D6
Swanscombe DA10 35 F8
St Peters Cotts [5] CT5 74 D2
St Peter's Ct
Broadstairs CT10 83 F5
Ditton ME20 128 C1
Faversham ME13 138 A7
St Peter's Footpath
Margate CT9 50 J1
Margate,Drapers Mill CT9 83 A8
St Peter's Gr CT1 174 F8
St Peter's Inf Sch ME1 63 C3
St Peter's La CT1 142 F1
St Peters La BR5 54 A7
St Peter's Meth Prim Sch CT1 174 F8
St Peter's Park Rd CT10 83 F5
St Peter's Path ME1 63 D5
St Peter's Pl CT1,CT2 174 F8
St Peters Pl
Eccles ME20 128 F6
Lynsted ME9 136 A6
St Peter's RC Prim Sch
Sittingbourne ME10 101 D2
Woolwich SE18 2 B2
St Peter's Rd
Boughton Street ME13 140 A3
Broadstairs CT10 83 F5
St Peters Rd ME20 128 B1
St Peter's Rd
Margate CT10,CT9 83 A7
Whitstable CT5 74 D2
St Peters Row TN3 284 B5
St Peter's St CT1,CT2 174 F8
St Peters St ME16 161 F4
St Peter's St
Royal Tunbridge Wells TN2 286 C3
Sandwich CT13 149 A1
St Peter St ME1 63 D4
St Philip Howard RC Prim Sch CT6 76 E5
St Philip's Ave ME15 162 B2
St Philips Ct TN2 286 D6
St Philomena's RC Prim Sch BR5 54 C2
St Pierre Ct CT14 215 D5
St Quentin Rd DA16 12 F4
St Radigund's Ct CT17 278 A1
St Radigund's Com Prim Sch CT17 278 A1
St Radigund's Pl CT1 143 A1
St Radigund's Rd CT17 278 A1
St Radigunds St CT1 142 F1
St Richard's RC Prim Sch CT16 278 D1
St Richard's Rd CT14 214 F3
St Richard's Wlk CT17 310 A4
St Ronan's Cl ME15 195 C7
St Ronan's Sch TN18 341 D2
St Saviours CE Jun Sch CT8 81 E8
St Saviour's Cl ME13 138 E7
St Saviours Cl CT19 335 D7
St Saviours Ct CT8 81 E8
St Saviour's Hospl CT21 333 F2
St Saviours Rd ME15 195 D6
Saints Hill TN11 284 A8
St Simon of England RC Prim Sch TN23 300 A8
St Simon Stock Sch ME16 161 C4
St Stephen's Manor CT10 84 B7
St Stephen's Mews TN23 300 A6
St Stephen's Cl
Canterbury CT2 142 F2
Newington ME9 100 C7
St Stephen's Cotts TN1 286 B5
St Stephen's Ct
Canterbury CT2 142 F2
Royal Tunbridge Wells TN1 286 B5
St Stephens Fields [5] CT2 142 F1
St Stephen's Gn CT2 142 F3
St Stephen's Hill CT2 142 E4
St Stephens Ho [1] CT2 142 F1
St Stephen's Inf Sch CT2 142 F3
St Stephen's Jun Sch CT2 142 F3
St Stephen's Lodge CT2 142 F2
St Stephens Mews ME1 96 E8
St Stephens Pathway [4] CT2 142 F1
St Stephen's Prim Sch TN9 254 D8
St Stephen's RC Prim Sch DA16 13 A5
St Stephen's Rd CT2 142 F2
St Stephen's Sq ME15 161 E2
St Stephen's St TN9 254 B8
St Stephen's Way CT20 334 F4
St Stephen's Wlk TN23 299 F7
St Swithin's Rd CT5 75 B3
St Teresa's RC Prim Sch TN24 268 B4
St Theresa's Cl TN24 268 B3
St Thomas-a-Becket RC Prim Sch SE2 3 A3
St Thomas' Cross TN26 327 E3
St Thomas Ct DA5 32 A8
St Thomas' Dr BR5 53 C1
St Thomas Hill CT2 142 D3
St Thomas More RC Prim Sch
Bexley DA7 13 F5
Eltham SE9 11 E4
St Thomas More RC Sec Sch SE9 12 A1
St Thomas More Roman Catholic Prim Sch ME5 97 A5
St Thomas of Canterbury RC Prim Sch ME8 65 B2
St Thomas' RC Prim Sch
Canterbury CT1 143 A1
Grays RM17 18 C8
St Thomas RC Prim Sch TN13 154 B2
St Thomas Rd Erith DA17 4 C4
Newham E16 1 A7
Northfleet DA11 36 E6
St Thomas's Almshouses DA11 37 B7
St Thomas's Ave DA11 37 B7
St Thomas's Hospl CT13 148 F1
St Thomas's Pl [15] RM17 18 C8
St Timothy's Mews [3] BR1 52 B8
St Vincent Rd CT15 279 F7
St Vincents Ave DA1 16 A2
St Vincent's Cl
Littlebourne CT3 144 F1
Whitstable CT5 108 E7
St Vincents La ME19 126 A2
St Vincents RC Prim Sch SE9 29 E4
St Vincents Rd DA1 16 A1
St Welcume's Way ME17 198 E6
St Werburgh Cres ME3 41 D5
St Werburgh Ct ME3 41 D5
St William of Perth RC Prim Sch ME1 63 B2
St William's Way ME1 63 D2
St Winifred Rd CT19 334 F6
St Winifred's Rd TN16 118 F1
Sala Ho SE3 11 B3
Salamons Way RM13 4 E7
Salbris Cl TN29 366 D8
Salcote Rd DA12 37 E3
Salem Pl DA11 36 D8
Salem St ME15 162 A3
Salhouse Cl SE28 3 C7
Salisbury Ave
Broadstairs CT10 83 F2
Gillingham ME8 98 D8
Ramsgate CT11 117 F8
Swanley BR8 56 A5
Salisbury Cl
Sittingbourne ME10 102 C4
Tonbridge TN10 222 D5
Salisbury Ho
Canterbury CT2 142 D2
[4] Maidstone ME15 195 D7
Salisbury Mews BR2 52 E4
Salisbury Rd
Bromley BR2 52 E4
Canterbury CT2 142 E2
Chatham ME4 64 A3
Dartford DA2 34 C7
Deal CT14 215 B2
Dover CT16 278 D1
Folkestone CT19 334 E7
Salisbury Rd *continued*
[2] Grays RM17 18 C8
Herne Bay CT6 77 C5
Kit's Coty ME20 129 D7
Langton Green TN3 284 F3
Maidstone ME14 162 A6
Northfleet DA11 36 F7
Royal Tunbridge Wells TN4 286 C8
St Margaret's at Cliffe CT15 280 B6
Sidcup DA5 32 A7
Tonbridge TN10 222 D4
Whitstable CT5 108 D8
Salix Rd RM17 18 D8
Sallow Cl ME4 41 C1
Sallows Shaw DA13 60 C4
Sally Port ME7 64 A6
Sally Port Gdns ME7 64 B6
Salmestone Grange* CT9 82 E8
Salmestone Prim Sch CT9 82 E8
Salmestone Rd CT9 82 F8
Salmestone Rise CT9 82 E8
Salmon Cres ME12 46 F6
Salmon Rd Dartford DA1 15 F4
Erith DA17 4 A1
Salomons Rd
Newham E13 1 C8
Rusthall TN4 285 C4
Saltash Rd DA16 13 C6
Saltbox Hill TN16 118 B6
Saltcote Cl DA1 14 E1
Salter's Cross ME18 193 A1
Salter's La TN29 370 C8
Salters La ME13 138 D4
Saltford Cl [2] DA8 4 E1
Salthouse Cl TN29 370 D8
Saltings Rd ME6 128 A7
Saltings The
Littlestone-on-Sea TN28 373 E5
[16] Whitstable CT5 74 D2
Saltley Cl E6 1 E7
Salt Marsh La [21] CT5 74 D2
Salt's Ave ME15 194 F3
Salts Cl CT5 74 D1
Salt's Dr CT10 83 E5
Salts La ME15 195 A4
Saltwood CE Prim Sch CT21 333 B4
Saltwood Cl BR6 87 C6
Saltwood Gdns CT9 51 E2
Saltwood Rd ME15 161 F1
Salvadori Ct TN2 287 D6
Samara Cl ME5 97 A1
Sam Bartram Cl SE7 1 C1
Samian Cres CT19 334 C6
Samphire Cl ME14 162 E4
Samphire Ct
Dover CT16 310 E8
Grays RM17 18 E8
Samphire Hoe Ctry Pk* CT15 309 E2
Samphire Way ME4 41 A2
Sampson Cl DA17 3 D3
Samson Ho SE18 2 C2
Samuel Cl SE18 1 E2
Samuel Ct CT9 51 A3
Samuel Mews TN29 376 D7
Samuel Palmer Ct BR6 54 A2
Samuel St SE18 1 F2
Sancroft Ave CT2 142 C1
Sanctuary Cl
Broadstairs CT10 83 F2
Dartford DA1 15 D1
Kearsney CT17 277 D4
Sanctuary Rd ME8 65 A3
Sanctuary The
Sandwich CT13 182 A7
Sidcup DA5 13 D1
Sandalwood Dr CT7 79 F1
Sandalwood House DA15 30 F5
Sandbach Ho CT9 51 B3
Sandbach Pl SE18 2 C1
Sandbanks Hill DA2 35 B2
Sandbanks Rd ME13 106 C2
Sandbourne Dr ME14 129 F1
Sandby Gn SE9 11 E4
Sandcliff Rd DA8 4 D1
Sandcroft TN28 373 F7
Sand Ct ME12 49 G2
Sand End CT5 108 C6
Sanderling Ct SE28 3 C6
Sanderling Rd CT6 77 F5
Sanderling Way
Iwade ME9 68 D5
Swanscombe DA9 17 A1
Sanders Ct ME12 47 A5
Sandersons Ave TN14 88 B1
Sanderson Way TN9 222 E1
Sanderstead Rd BR5 54 B3
Sandfield Rd TN11 284 A7
Sandford Rd
Bexley DA7,DA6 13 E4
Bromley BR2 52 A5
Sittingbourne ME10 101 B5
Sandgate Ct ME8 98 F4
Sandgate Espl CT20, CT21 334 D2
Sandgate High St CT20 334 E3
Sandgate Hill CT20 335 A4
Sandgate Prim Sch CT20 334 F4
Sandgate Rd
Bexley DA16 13 C7
Folkestone CT20 335 C4
Sandgates CT4 272 E7
Sandham Point SE18 2 B2
Sandhill La ME3 39 D6
Sandhills Cvn Pk CT14 182 B1
Sandhole Cotts TN12 288 C4
Sandhurst Ave TN2 287 E5
Sandhurst Cl
Canterbury CT2 143 A4
Gillingham ME8 65 C3
Royal Tunbridge Wells TN2 286 C6
Sandhurst Cross TN18 356 A4
Sandhurst Cross TN12 261 F1
Sandhurst Ho TN2 286 D5
Sandhurst La TN17 343 B2
Sandhurst Pk TN2 286 C6
Sandhurst Prim Sch TN18 356 C5
Sandhurst Rd
Bexley DA5 13 D2
Margate CT9 51 F2
Orpington BR6 87 A6
Royal Tunbridge Wells TN2 286 D6
Sidcup DA15 31 A5
Tilbury RM18 19 C5
Sandhurst Vineyards* TN18 356 E5
Sandilands
Ashford TN24 268 E2
Sevenoaks TN13 153 D5
Sand La TN17 293 F4
Sandle's Rd CT7 80 F7
Sandling Cl TN23 299 F6
Sandling Ct ME14 162 B7
Sandling La ME14 162 A8
Sandling Prim Sch ME14 162 B8
Sandling Rd
Hythe CT21 332 F6
Maidstone ME14 161 F6
Maidstone,Ringlestone ME14 161 F7
Sandling Rise SE9 30 A5
Sandling Sta CT21 332 F6
Sandling Way ME4 41 B1
Sandown Cl Deal CT14 182 D1
Royal Tunbridge Wells TN2 286 F6
Sandown Cotts
Margate CT9 51 A3
Teynham ME9 103 E1
Sandown Ct CT14 215 C7
Sandown Dr
Gillingham ME8 98 D7
Herne Bay CT6 76 D4
Sandown Gr TN2 286 F6
Sandown Lees CT13 181 D8
Sandown Pk TN2 286 F6
Sandown Pl CT14 215 C7
Sandown Rd
Deal CT14 215 D8
Gravesend DA12 37 C2
Sandwich CT13 181 B8
West Malling ME19 159 B8
Sandown Sch CT14 215 C7
Sandpiper Cl DA9 17 A1
Sandpiper Ct
[3] Birchington CT7 80 F8
Margate CT9 50 I3
Sandpiper Dr DA8 15 B7
Sandpiper Rd
Chatham ME5 97 D2
Hawkinge CT18 307 A3
Whitstable CT5 108 B7
Sandpipers The DA12 37 D6
Sandpiper Way BR5 54 D6
Sandpit Hill CT3 112 C4
Sandpit Pl SE7 1 E1
Sandpit Rd DA1 15 C3
Sandra Ct [5] ME2 63 B8
Sand Rd TN3 317 A4
Sandringham Ct ME19 159 A1
Sandringham Dr
Bexley DA16 12 E5
Maypole DA2 32 E6
Sandringham Ho ME1 63 B4
Sandringham Mews TN4 286 A5
Sandringham Rd
Bromley BR1 29 A3
Gillingham ME8 98 E3
Sandrock Ho TN2 286 D4
Sandrock Rd TN2 286 C4
Sandrook Villas TN18 340 F3
Sandshaw Ct DA3 58 E4
Sandstone Ct CT20 335 A3
Sandstone Dr ME10 101 E8
Sandstone La E16 1 B6
Sandstone Rd SE12 29 B6
Sandstone Rise ME5 130 C8
Sandtoft Rd SE7 11 B8
Sandway Path [6] BR5 54 C5
Sandway Rd
Harrietsham ME17 198 F4
Orpington BR5 54 C5
Sandwich Bay Bird Obsy* CT13 181 E7
Sandwich Cl CT20 334 F5
Sandwich Ind Est CT13 149 B1
Sandwich Inf Sch CT13 148 F1
Sandwich Jun Sch CT13 180 F7
Sandwich Rd Ash CT3 147 F1
Cliffs End CT12 116 D4
Eastry CT13 180 C3
Eythorne CT15 245 C8
Nonington CT15,CT3 211 F6
Sandwich CT13,CT14 180 D5
Whitfield CT15,CT16 278 A7
Woodnesborough CT13 180 D7
Sandwich Sta CT13 181 A8
Sandwich Tech Sch CT13 180 F6
Sandwich Town Mus* CT13 148 F1
Sandwood Rd
Ramsgate CT10 83 F1
Sandwich CT13 180 F8
Sandy Bank Rd DA12 37 B7
Sandy Bury BR6 86 D7
Sandy Cnr TN26 298 F5
Sandycroft Rd ME2 39 F1
Sandycroft SE2 13 A8
Sandy Dell ME7 98 A3
Sandy Hill Ave SE18 2 B1
Sandy Hill La SE18 2 B2
Sandy Hill Rd SE18 2 B1
Sandyhurst La TN25 268 B8
Sandy La Ashford TN24 269 B1
Bean DA13,DA2 35 D5
Daniel's Water TN26 298 E6
Hythe CT20,CT21 334 B3
Ightham TN15 156 B3
Limpsfield RH8 183 B7
Maidstone,Harbourland ME14 162 C8
Maidstone,Penenden Heath ME14 162 C7
Maidstone,Ware Street ME14 163 B5
New Town ME19 127 A1
Orpington BR6 54 A2
Ruxley BR5 54 D8
Sevenoaks TN13 154 C4
Snodland ME6,ME19 127 E6
Tenterden TN30 345 B7
Tilbury RM16 19 B8
Westerham TN16 151 D2
West Thurrock RM20 17 B8
Wrotham Heath TN15, ME19 125 F1
Sandy Mount ME14 163 B5
Sandy Pl TN25 302 D5
Sandy Ridge
Borough Green TN15 157 A7
Chislehurst BR7 30 A2
Sanger Cl CT9 50 I1
Sangro Pl CT1 143 D1
San Remo CT8 50 C1
Sanspareil Ave ME12 47 A6
Santana Ho SE18 12 B7
Santer Ho TN18 354 E8
Santon La CT3 146 E8
Sapho Pk DA12 37 F4
Saphora Cl BR6 86 D5
Sappers Wlk ME7 64 C5
Sapphire Cl Newham E6 2 A7
Sittingbourne ME10 101 C7
Saracen Cl ME7 65 A1
Saracen Fields ME5 130 C8
Sara Cres DA9 17 B3
Sarafand Ho ME1 63 B4
Sarah Ct [7] DA6 13 E3
Sarah Gdns CT9 83 D8
Sara Ho [1] DA8 14 E7
Sara Pk DA12 37 E4
Sara Turnbull Ho [3] SE18 1 F2
Sark Cl TN29 366 C8
Sark Wlk E16 1 B7
Sarre Ct CT7 113 D6
Sarre Mill* CT7 113 D7
Sarre Pl CT13 180 F8
Sarsen Hts ME5 96 F1
Sarsens Cl DA12 60 F6
Sassoon Cl
Hawkinge CT18 307 A4
New Hythe ME20 128 A4
Satanita Cl E16 1 D7
Satis Ave ME10 101 E7
Satmar La CT15,CT18 308 E4
Satmore La CT18 308 C4
Saunders Cl DA11 36 E6
Saunder's Cross TN14 88 B2
Saunders La CT3 147 F1
Saunders Rd
Royal Tunbridge Wells TN4 285 E1
Woolwich SE18 2 F1
Saunders St
[7] Chatham ME4 63 F3
Gillingham ME7 64 C6
Saunders Way
Camber TN31 374 A2
Dartford DA1 33 F6
Woolwich SE28 3 B6
Savage Gdns E6 1 F7
Savage Rd ME5 97 B3
Savernake Dr CT6 77 B2
Saville Cl TN10 222 D7
Saville Ho E16 2 B5
Saville Rd E16 1 E5
Savoy Rd DA1 15 D2
Savoy The [8] CT11 117 C6
Saw Lodge Field TN23 300 C4
Sawpit Rd ME9 135 B2
Sawyers Ct ME4 64 B2
Saxbys Rd TN15 155 D5
Saxby Wood TN11 220 F1
Saxon Ave ME12 47 B6
Saxon Cl Hythe CT21 333 E2
Kings Hill ME19 158 F2
Northfleet DA11 36 C5
Otford TN14 121 F2
Rochester ME2 39 F1
Saxon Pl
Horton Kirby DA4 57 C4
Rochester ME2 62 F5
Saxon Rd Bridge CT4 176 A1
Bromley BR1 29 A1
Faversham ME13 138 C7
Hawley DA2 33 E4
Ramsgate CT11 117 B6
Saxon Rd *continued*
Westgate-on-S CT8 50 D1
Saxons Cl CT14 215 C8
Saxons Dr ME14 162 B7
Saxon Shore
Sittingbourne ME10 69 A1
Whitstable CT5 108 C8
Saxon St [9] CT17 310 D8
Saxon Way Prim Sch ME7 64 E6
Saxon Wlk Iwade ME9 68 D4
Sidcup DA14 31 C2
Saxton Rd TN29 377 E5
Saxton St ME7 64 C5
Saxville Rd BR5 54 B6
Sayer Cl DA9 17 A2
Sayer Rd TN27 234 C8
Sayers La [6] TN30 345 A7
Sayes Court Rd BR5 54 B5
Scabharbour Rd TN14 187 C1
Scadbury Gdns BR5 54 A7
Scadbury Park Nature Reserve* BR7 30 F2
Scads Hill Cl BR6 53 F3
Scanlons Bridge Rd CT21 333 A2
Scarborough Cl TN16 118 C1
Scarborough Dr ME12 47 C8
Scarborough La ME1 95 D2
Scarlet Cl BR5 54 B5
Scarlett Cl ME5 97 C5
Scarsbrook Rd SE3 11 D4
Sceales Dr CT12 116 D6
Sceptre Way CT5 108 B7
Schofield Wlk SE3 11 A7
Scholars Rise ME2 62 D7
Scholey Cl ME2 95 B4
School App TN15 156 F7
School Ave ME7 64 E4
School Cl DA13 60 A2
School Cl The CT8 50 C1
School Cotts
Bromley BR1 29 A1
Crockenhill BR8 55 D2
Seal TN15 154 F6
Sidcup DA14 31 C3
School Cres DA1 14 F3
School Field TN8 217 C2
Schoolfield Rd RM20 17 A8
School Hill
Chilham CT4 205 B8
Lamberhurst TN3 317 B6
School Ho ME10 101 E3
School House La TN12 290 E7
School La Bean DA2 35 C5
Bekesbourne CT4 176 C4
Bexley DA16 13 B4
Blean CT2 142 A6
Boughton Street ME13 139 F3
Chestnut Street ME9 100 F4
Culverstone Green DA13 93 A2
Fordwich CT2 144 A4
Goodnestone CT3 178 D2
Hadlow TN11 223 E8
Herne Bay CT6 77 B1
Hextable BR8 33 B1
Higham ME3 39 C5
Hoath CT3 111 E6
Horton Kirby DA3,DA4 57 E4
Ickham CT3 177 C8
Iwade ME9 68 C4
Knockmill TN15 123 F8
Lower Halstow ME9 67 B2
Lower Hardres CT4 208 B6
Maidstone ME15 162 E1
Newington ME9 100 B7
Peasmarsh TN31 367 B2
Platt's Heath ME17 198 F2
Plaxtol TN11,TN15 189 E6
Ramsgate CT11 117 E7
Seal TN15 154 F6
Sittingbourne ME9 102 D2
Stalisfield Green ME13 201 D6
Staple CT3 179 A6
Stourmouth CT3 113 E2
Sutton Valence ME17 229 E7
Trottiscliffe ME19 126 A5
Wingham CT3 178 A7
Wouldham ME1 95 D5
School Path CT3 176 F7
School Rd
Appledore Heath TN26 347 C1
Ash CT3 147 C2
Bethersden TN26 297 D4
Charing TN27 234 C8
Chislehurst BR7 30 C1
Densole CT18 306 E7
Faversham ME13 138 C6
Gravesend DA12 37 C5
Hothfield TN26 267 A7
Hythe CT21 333 B4
Sandwich CT13 148 F1
Sittingbourne ME10 102 B3
Tilmanstone CT14 212 F4
School Rise TN2 285 F1
School Terr [6] TN18 340 F2
School View ME9 134 C8
School Villas ME18 192 D5
Schooner Ct DA2 16 C3
Schooner Ho [11] DA8 4 E1
Schooner Wlk ME2 40 F3
Schrieber Mews ME7 64 D5
Scilla Ct [11] RM17 18 D8
Scimitar Cl ME7 65 A1
Scocles Cotts ME12 47 C5
Scocles Rd ME12 47 C5
Scoggers Hill ME13 172 A7
Scoones Cl ME9 102 E2
Scords La TN16 185 C4

Scotby Ave ME5 97 B4
Scotchmen Cl ME12 46 E7
Scotland La DA12 60 F6
Scotney Castle Gdns* TN3 317 D3
Scotney Castle* TN3 317 D3
Scotney Cl BR6 86 A6
Scotney Ho ME2 40 C1
Scotsdale Cl BR5 53 E5
Scotsdale Rd SE12 11 B2
Scot's La TN25 303 F8
Scott Ave
Canterbury CT1 174 E6
Gillingham ME8 66 A1
Gillingham ME8 99 A8
Scott Cl ME20 160 C8
Scott Cres DA8 14 F6
Scotteswood Ave ME4 63 F2
Scott Ho 4 DA17 3 F1
Scotton St TN25 237 F2
Scott Rd
Gravesend DA12 37 D3
Tonbridge TN9 253 F7
Scotts Ho DA16 13 C6
Scotts Park Prim Sch BR1 52 C8
Scotts Passage 11 SE18 2 B2
Scotts Rd BR1 29 A1
Scotts Terr SE9 29 E6
Scott's Terr ME4 63 F3
Scott St ME14 161 F6
Scotts Way
Royal Tunbridge Wells TN2 313 E8
Sevenoaks TN13 153 E5
Scott Wilkie Prim Sch E16 1 C7
Scoulding Rd E16 1 A7
Scragged Oak Cvn Pk ME14 131 B2
Scragged Oak Rd
Detling ME14 131 C5
Hucking ME17 132 C1
Scrapsgate Rd ME12 47 A7
Scraps Hill ME9 102 F4
Scratchers La DA3 90 E7
Scratton Fields DA12 60 D4
Scrubbs La ME16 161 D4
Scudders Hill DA3 58 C3
Sea App ME12 49 E4
Seabourne Cl TN29 366 B6
Seabourne Way TN29 366 B7
Seabrook CE Prim Sch CT21 334 B2
Seabrook Ct CT21 334 B3
Seabrooke Rise RM17 18 B8
Seabrook Gdns CT21 334 B2
Seabrook Gr CT21 334 A2
Seabrook Rd
Hythe CT21 333 E2
Tonbridge TN10 222 A3
Seabrook Vale CT21 334 B4
Seacourt Rd SE2 3 D4
Seacroft Rd CT10 84 A1
Seadown Cl CT21 334 A4
Seafield Rd
Broadstairs CT10 84 A4
Ramsgate CT11 117 C6
Whitstable CT5 75 B3
Seaford Ct ME1 63 B5
Seagar Rd ME13 105 B1
Seager Rd ME12 28 E2
Seagrave Cres CT19 335 F6
Seagull La E16 1 A6
Seagull Rd ME2 62 D6
Sealand Ct ME1 63 B5
Seal CE Prim Sch TN15 154 F7
Sealcroft Cotts TN15 154 F8
Seal Dr TN15 154 F6
Seal Hollow Rd TN13 154 D4
Seal Ho TN15 154 F6
Seal Rd TN13,TN14, TN15 154 D6
Seamark Cl CT12 114 D7
Seamark Rd CT12,CT7 80 E2
Seamew Ct ME2 62 C7
Seapoint Rd CT10 84 B3
Sea Rd Deal CT14 248 D6
Hythe CT21 334 A2
Westgate-on-S CT8 50 C1
Searles Dr E6 2 B8
Seasalter Beach CT5 108 A7
Seasalter Cl ME12 49 E4
Seasalter Cross CT5 108 A6
Seasalter La CT5 108 A5
Seasalter Rd ME13 106 E3
Seascape 10 CT20 334 E3
Seaside Ave ME12 47 C8
Sea St Herne Bay CT6 76 C3
St Margaret's at Cliffe CT15 280 A6
Whitstable CT5 74 D2
Seathorpe Ave ME12 47 C8
Seaths Cnr CT3 178 A7
Seaton Ave CT21 333 B3
Seaton Cotts TN25 236 E3
Seaton Rd Bexley DA16 13 C7
Dartford DA1 33 A8
Gillingham ME7 64 E3
Wickhambreaux CT3 145 D2
Sea View Ave CT7 80 E8
Seaview Ave ME12 49 H1
Sea View Cl CT18 308 B1
Seaview Cotts 6 CT10 84 B4
Sea View Cotts ME9 67 B3
Seaview Ct CT10 84 B3
Seaview Cvn & Chalet Pk CT5 75 E4
Sea View Gdns ME12 49 E3
Seaview ME3 27 B5
Seaview Ho CT19 335 D8
Seaview Holiday Camp ME12 49 E3
Sea View Hts CT7 80 D8
Seaview Hts TN29 366 C7
Sea View Rd
Birchington CT7 80 E8
Broadstairs CT10 84 A6
Cliffs End CT12 116 D6
Seaview Rd
Gillingham ME7 64 C4
Greatstone-on-Sea TN28 373 E1
Sea View Rd
Herne Bay CT6 77 C5
St Margaret's at Cliffe CT15 279 F4
Sea View Sq CT6 76 F5
Sea View Terr
Folkestone CT20 334 D3
Margate CT9 50 G2
Minster (Sheppey) ME12 48 A5
Seaville Dr CT6 77 E5
Sea Wall
Dymchurch TN29 366 D8
Whitstable CT5 74 D2
Seaway Cotts CT5 74 C1
Seaway Cres TN29 365 F4
Seaway Gdns TN29 365 F4
Seaway Rd TN29 366 A4
Second Ave
Broadstairs CT10 51 G2
Chatham ME4 64 C1
Eastchurch ME12 48 F5
Gillingham ME7 64 E3
Margate CT9 51 B3
Rushenden ME11 45 F3
Sheerness ME12 28 B1
West Thurrock RM20 17 A8
Secretan Rd ME1 63 B1
Sedcombe Cl DA14 31 C4
Sedgebrook Rd SE3 11 D4
Sedge Cres ME5 96 E4
Sedge Ct RM17 18 E7
Sedgemere Rd SE2 3 C3
Sedgemoor Ho ME1 63 E5
Sedley Cl
Aylesford ME20 128 F2
Cliffe Woods ME3 40 C7
Gillingham ME8 98 C3
Sedley DA13 36 A2
Sedley's CE Prim Sch DA13 36 A3
Seeshill Cl CT5 108 E8
Sefton Cl BR5 53 F5
Sefton Rd BR5 53 F5
Segrave Rd CT19 335 F5
Sejant Ho 4 RM17 18 B8
Selah Dr BR8 55 C8
Selbey Cl CT6 77 C4
Selborne Ave DA5 31 E7
Selborne Ho CT17 310 C7
Selborne Rd
Margate CT9 83 B8
Sidcup DA14 31 B4
Selbourne Cl DA3 59 D6
Selbourne Rd ME7 64 D7
Selbourne Terr CT17 310 C7
Selbourne Wlk ME15 195 F6
Selby Cl Chislehurst BR7 30 A2
14 Newham E6 1 E8
Selby Field Cvn Pk CT21 352 D8
Selby Rd
Maidstone ME15 195 F4
Newham E13 1 B8
Select Bsns Ctr TN12 260 E5
Selkirk Dr DA8 14 E6
Selkirk Rd CT16 278 B3
Sellbourne Pk TN3 314 C4
Sellindge Prim Sch TN25 303 C1
Selling CE Prim Sch ME13 171 B6
Selling Ct ME13 171 C5
Sellinge Gn ME8 65 C3
Selling Rd Chilham CT4 172 B3
Faversham ME13 138 F3
Selling ME13 171 E6
Selling Sta ME13 171 E7
Selling St ME13 171 B6
Sellwood Ct DA1 34 B7
Selsea Ave CT6 76 D4
Selsey Cres DA16 13 D6
Selstead Cl ME8 65 C2
Selsted CE Prim Sch CT15 275 C6
Selway Ct CT14 215 B3
Selwood Cl ME12 46 E6
Selwood Ho BR7 30 C2
Selwyn Cres DA16 13 B3
Selwyn Ct CT10 83 F5
Selwyn Dr CT10 83 F5
Selwyn Pl 1 BR5 54 B6
Selwyn Rd RM18 18 F5
Semaphore Rd CT7 80 F8
Semple Cl CT12 115 C7
Semple Gdns ME4 63 E3
Senacre La ME15 195 E6
Senacre Sq ME15 195 F7
Senacre Tech Coll ME15 195 D6
Senacre Wood Prim Sch ME15 195 F7
Senator Wlk 4 SE28 2 D3
Sencler Ho Bexley SE2 13 D8
Erith SE2 3 D1
Sene Pk CT21 333 D3
Senlac Cl CT11 117 B6
Senlac Pl TN3 312 C7
Senlac Rd SE12 29 B7
Sennen Wlk SE9 29 E5
Sennocke Ct TN13 154 B2
Sequoia Gdns BR6 53 F2
Serene Ct 12 CT10 84 B4
Serene Pl 9 CT10 84 B4
Sermon Dr BR8 55 C6
Serpentine Ct TN13 154 D5
Serpentine Rd TN13 154 D4
Serviden Dr BR1 52 D8
Sessions House Sq ME14 161 F5
Setford Rd ME5 97 C6
Setterfield Ho CT21 333 D2
Setterfield Rd CT9 50 J1
Settington Ave ME5 64 C1
Sevastopol Pl CT1 143 D1
Sevenacre Rd ME13 138 C8
Seven Acres
Crockenhill BR8 55 D3
New Ash Green DA3 91 E7
Seven Mile La
Kings Hill TN15,ME18 158 A3
Mereworth TN11,TN12 191 E3
Wrotham Heath TN15 157 F7
Sevenoaks Bsns Ctr TN14 154 C6
Sevenoaks By-Pass TN13,TN14 186 F7
Sevenoaks Cl DA7 14 B3
Sevenoaks Hospl TN13 154 C6
Sevenoaks Mus & Gallery* TN13 154 C2
Sevenoaks Prep Sch TN15 155 A1
Sevenoaks Prim Sch TN13 154 B5
Sevenoaks Rd
Borough Green TN15 156 F7
Ightham TN15 156 A4
Orpington BR6 86 F6
Otford TN14 122 B3
Pratt's Bottom BR6,TN14 87 C2
Sevenoaks Sch Int Ctr TN13 154 B1
Sevenoaks Sch TN13 154 C1
Sevenoaks Sta TN13 154 A3
Sevenoaks Way Ind Est 1 BR5 54 C6
Sevenoaks Way BR5 54 C7
Sevenoaks Wildfowl Reserve* TN14 154 A7
Sevenscore CT12 116 A5
Sevenscore Farm Cotts CT12 116 A5
Seven Stones Dr CT10 84 A1
Seven Wents TN15 156 A4
Severn Cl TN10 222 C5
Severn Rd ME5 97 C5
Sevington La TN24 301 A7
Sevington Pk ME15 194 F6
Sewell Cl CT7 81 A6
Sewell Rd SE2 3 B4
Sexburga Dr ME12 47 B8
Sextant Pk ME2 63 E6
Sexton Rd RM18 18 F6
Seymour Ave
Westgate-on-S CT9 50 D1
Whitstable CT5 74 E1
Seymour Cl CT6 77 B1
Seymour Dr BR2 52 F1
Seymour Pl CT1 174 E7
Seymour Rd
1 Chatham ME5 64 B3
Gillingham ME8 66 C1
Gillingham ME8 99 C8
Northfleet DA11 36 F6
St Margaret's at Cliffe CT15 279 F8
Tilbury RM18 18 F6
Seymour St SE18 2 C3
Seymour Villas 10 CT20 334 F3
Seymour Wlk DA10 35 E8
Shacklands Rd TN14 88 D1
Shackleton Cl ME5 97 B6
Shades The ME2 62 C7
Shadoxhurst Rd TN26 326 C7
Shaftesbury Ave CT19 334 E7
Shaftesbury Cl ME19 127 F1
Shaftesbury Ct
Deal CT14 215 D2
Erith DA8 14 F6
3 Woolwich SE28 3 C5
Shaftesbury Dr ME16 161 C4
Shaftesbury La DA1 16 B3
Shaftesbury Rd
Canterbury CT2 142 F3
Hersden CT3 111 E1
Royal Tunbridge Wells TN4 286 A5
Whitstable CT5 74 D1
Shaftsbury Ct E6 2 A7
Shaftsbury St CT11 117 F7
Shah Pl CT11 117 D7
Shakespeare Ave RM18 19 B6
Shakespeare Ct CT17 310 B7
Shakespeare Farm Rd ME3 24 F7
Shakespeare Ho 1 DA17 3 F1
Shakespeare Pas CT9 50 H2
Shakespeare Rd
Bexley DA7 13 E6
Birchington CT7 81 A8
Dartford DA1 16 A3
Dover CT17 310 B6
Gillingham ME7 64 C3
Margate CT9 50 J1
Sittingbourne ME10 102 A4
Tonbridge TN9 253 F8
Shakespeare Terr 12 CT20 335 C4
Shalder Ho ME7 64 D7
Shalfleet Cl 1 ME5 97 A7
Shalford Cl BR6 86 C6
Shalloak Rd CT2 143 D6
Shallons Rd SE9 30 B4
Shallows Rd CT10 83 D6
Shalmsford Ct CT4 173 C2
Shalmsford Rd CT4 172 E2
Shalmsford St CT4 173 B2
Shambles The TN13 154 C2
Shamel Bsns Ctr ME2 63 C7
Shamley Rd ME5 97 D2
Shamrock Ave CT5 108 B7
Shamrock Rd DA12 37 F8
Shandon Cl TN2 286 C4
Shanklin Cl ME5 97 C8
Shannon Ct BR6 54 A2
Shapland Cl CT6 77 C3
Share & Coulter Rd CT5 75 D1
Sharfleet Cres ME9 68 D4
Sharfleet Dr ME2 62 B7
Sharland Rd DA12 37 C6
Sharman Ct DA14 31 A4
Sharnal La ME6 128 A7
Sharnal St ME3 24 A2
Sharnbrooke Cl DA16 13 C4
Sharon Cres ME5 96 F4
Sharon Ct 10 DA14 31 B4
Sharp's Field TN27 262 E5
Sharps Gn ME8 65 D5
Sharp Way DA1 15 F4
Sharsted Hill ME9 168 C8
Sharsted Way
Gillingham ME7 98 A3
Maidstone ME14 163 B5
Shawbrooke Rd SE9 11 D3
Shaw Cl
Cliffe Woods ME3 40 B8
Maidstone ME14 162 C7
Woolwich SE28 3 B5
Shaw Cres RM18 19 B6
Shaw Cross TN24 268 D5
Shawdon Ave CT13 182 A7
Shawfield Pk BR1 52 D7
Shawhill Ho ME19 126 B1
Shaw Ho 6 Erith DA17 3 F1
5 Newham E16 2 A5
Shaw Rd TN16 150 C7
Shawstead Rd ME7,ME7 97 D5
Shaws Way ME1 63 C3
Shaw The TN2 286 C2
Sheafe Dr TN17 320 C5
Sheal's Cres ME15 162 A2
Sheals Ct ME15 162 A2
Shearers Cl ME14 162 E4
Shears Cl DA2 33 C6
Shears Green Ct DA11 37 A6
Shears Green Inf Sch DA11 36 F5
Shears Green Jun Sch DA11 36 F5
Shearwater Ave CT5 108 C7
Shearwater Cl ME2 62 C7
Shearwater Ct ME12 46 B8
Shearwater Ho TN29 366 A3
Shearwater
Maidstone ME16 161 B5
New Barn DA3 59 B6
Shear Way TN29 352 C5
Shearway Rd CT19 334 F7
Shearwood Cres DA1 15 A4
Sheen Ct CT9 50 I2
Sheen Rd BR5 53 F5
Sheepbarn La TN16 118 A7
Sheepcote La BR5,BR8 54 F4
Sheepfold La TN23 300 C4
Sheephurst La TN12 258 E5
Sheerness Harbour Est
Sheerness ME12 27 F3
Sheerness ME12 28 A3
Sheerness Heritage Ctr (Mus)* ME12 28 C2
Sheerness Mews E16 2 B4
Sheerness-on-Sea Sta ME12 28 B2
Sheerstone ME9 68 D4
Sheerwater Rd
Newham E16 1 D8
Preston CT3 146 F5
Sheerways ME13 138 A6
Sheet Glass Rd ME11 46 A3
Sheet Hill TN15 156 D2
Sheffield Gdns CT14 215 C4
Sheffield Rd 4 TN4 253 F2
Sheilings The TN15 154 F7
Shelbury Cl DA14 31 A5
Shelden Dr ME8 98 F8
Sheldon Bsns Ctr ME2 63 D8
Sheldon Cl
Aylesham CT3 211 A6
Eltham SE12 11 B2
Sheldon Rd DA7 13 F6
Sheldon Way ME20 128 B3
Sheldrake Cl E16 1 F5
Sheldwich Cl TN23 300 A6
Sheldwich Prim Sch ME13 170 C6
Sheldwich Terr BR2 52 E3
Shellbank La DA2 35 B4
Shellbeach ME12 73 D6
Shell Cl BR2 52 E3
Shelldrake Cl ME3 27 B5
Shelley Ave CT1 143 C2
Shelley Cl BR6 86 E7
Shelley Dr DA16 12 E6
Shelley Ho DA1 14 E2
Shelley Pl RM18 19 B6
Shelley Rd ME16 161 C2
Shelley Rise ME1 63 A3
Shelleys La TN14 120 A3
Shell Grotto* CT9 50 J2
Shell Ness Nature Reserve* ME12 73 E4
Shellness Rd ME12 73 D7
Shellons St CT20 335 D5
Shelton Cl TN10 222 C5
Shelvin La CT4 243 C3
Shenden Cl TN13 187 C7
Shenden Way TN13 187 C7
Shenfield Ho SE18 11 D7
Shenley Gr ME14 129 F2
Shenley Rd DA1 34 A8
Shenstone Cl DA1 14 D3
Shenstone Sch DA1 14 D3
Shepherd Cl TN23 299 E5
Shepherd Dr TN24 301 A8
Shepherds Cl BR6 86 F7
Shepherd's Close Rd CT4 176 E1
Shepherd's Cross CT15 246 B1
Shepherdsgate CT2 142 F1
Shepherdsgate Dr CT6 111 A8
Shepherds Gate Dr ME14 162 E6
Shepherds Gate ME7 97 F5
Shepherds Gn BR7 30 D1
Shepherdsgrove La RH19 281 A4
Shepherds La
Dartford DA1 33 B8
Woolwich SE28 2 E5
Shepherds Leas SE9 12 D3
Shepherd St DA11 36 D8
Shepherds Way
Langley Heath ME17 196 E4
Lower Stoke ME3 25 C4
Whitstable CT5 109 C8
Shepherdswell Rd CT15 245 A7
Shepherds Well Sta CT15 244 D5
Shepherds Wlk
Hythe CT21 332 E1
Royal Tunbridge Wells TN2 286 D4
Whitstable CT5 109 C8
Sheppards Coll 8 BR1 52 A8
Shepperton Cl ME5 97 C4
Shepperton Rd BR5 53 C3
Sheppey Beach Villas ME12 49 H2
Sheppey Cl
3 Birchington CT7 81 A7
Erith DA8 15 B7
Sheppey Coll ME12 28 B3
Sheppey Com Hospl ME12 47 C7
Sheppey Community Hospl ME12 47 A5
Sheppey Cotts ME12 28 D2
Sheppey Rd ME15 195 A7
Sheppey St ME12 28 A2
Sheppey Terr ME12 47 F5
Sheppey View CT5 108 C6
Sheppey Way
Iwade ME9 68 F6
Queenborough ME12, ME9 46 D2
Sittingbourne ME9 101 B7
Sheppy Ho 1 BR1 29 B1
Sheppy Pl DA12 37 B8
Shepway TN24 268 E5
Shepway Cl CT19 335 D6
Shepway Cross CT21 332 B3
Shepway Ct ME15 195 C8
Shepway Inf Sch ME15 195 E8
Shepway Jun Sch ME15 195 E8
Sherard Mans SE9 11 F2
Sherard Rd SE9 11 E2
Sheraton Ct ME5 96 F1
Sherborne Gr TN15 123 A2
Sherborne Rd BR5 53 F4
Sherbourne Cl
Royal Tunbridge Wells TN2 286 D2
West Kingsdown TN15 90 E4
Sherbourne Dr
Maidstone ME16 161 B2
Rochester ME2 40 A1
Sherbrooke Cl DA7 14 A3
Sherenden La TN12 291 D8
Sherenden Pk TN11 224 A5
Sherenden Rd TN11 255 D7
Sherfield Rd RM17 18 B8
Sheridale Bsns Ctr ME2 63 A6
Sheridan Cl
Chatham ME5 97 C7
Maidstone ME14 161 E8
Swanley BR8 55 F6
Sheridan Cres BR7 53 B7
Sheridan Ct
Dartford DA1 16 A3
Rochester ME1 63 A2
Sheridan Lodge 1 BR2 52 C5
Sheridan Rd Bexley DA7 13 E4
Dover CT16 278 B3
Erith DA17 4 A2
Sheriff Dr ME5 97 A2
Sheringham Cl ME16 161 D7
Sheringham Ho 5 ME15 195 D8
Sherington Prim Sch SE7 11 B8
Sherington Rd SE7 11 B8
Sherlies Ave BR6 86 E8
Sherman Cl ME7 65 B1
Sherman Rd BR1 52 A8
Shernden La TN8 249 C4
Shernold Sch ME16 161 D5
Shernolds ME15 195 B7
Sheron Cl CT14 215 A5
Sherriffs Court La CT12 114 E6
Sherway Cl TN27 262 E5
Sherway Rd TN27 263 D6
Sherwin Knight Inf Sch ME2 62 E5
Sherwin Knight Jun Sch ME2 62 E5
Sherwood Ave ME5 97 A2
Sherwood Cl
Ashford TN24 268 D7
Faversham ME13 105 B1
Herne Bay CT6 77 C2
Sidcup DA5 13 C1
Whitstable CT5 108 C6
Sherwood Ct CT8 50 C1
Sherwood Dr CT5 108 C6
Sherwood Gdns CT11 83 E1
Sherwood Ho
Chatham ME5 97 A3
Erith DA8 14 E8
Sherwood Park Ave DA15 13 B1
Sherwood Park Com Prim Sch TN2 286 D6
Sherwood Park Prim Sch DA15 13 B1
Sherwood Pl TN3 284 E3
Sherwood Rd
Bexley DA16 12 E4
Birchington CT7 80 F5
Royal Tunbridge Wells TN2 286 E5
Sherwood Way TN2 286 D6
Shieldhall St SE2 3 C2
Shillingheld Cl ME14 162 F5
Shinecroft TN14 122 A3
Shingle Barn La ME15 193 C3
Shinglewell Rd DA8 14 A7
Shipbourne Rd
Shipbourne TN11 189 D2
Tonbridge TN10 222 C5
Shipbourne Sch TN11 189 C4
Ship Cl TN29 366 C8
Ship Field Cl TN16 150 C6
Ship Hill TN16 150 D6
Shipland Hos TN27 265 D8
Ship La Rochester ME1 63 E4
Sutton at H BR8,DA4 56 E8
Shipley Ct ME14 162 A4
Shipley Hills Rd DA13 59 E1
Shipley Mill CL TN23 300 C4
Shipman Ave CT2 174 C8
Shipman Rd E16 1 C7
Shipmans Way CT16 278 A3
Ship St CT19 335 D6
Shipway Ho CT21 333 D1
Shipwrights Ave ME4 64 B2
Shipwrights Lee CT5 74 C2
Shipyard Area ME13 105 D1
Shirebrook Rd SE3 11 D4
Shire Ct DA18 3 D3
Shirehall Rd DA2 33 E4
Shire La
Farthing Street BR6 86 C3
Orpington BR6 86 E5
Stalisfield Green ME13 201 C6
Shires The TN12 257 A7
Shireway Cl CT19 335 A7
Shirkoak Pk TN26 326 A5
Shirley Ave
Chatham ME5 96 D5
Ramsgate CT11 83 E1
Sidcup DA5 31 D7
Shirley Cl Chalk DA12 38 B6
Dartford DA1 15 C3
Shirley Ct ME15 195 E5
Shirley Gdns TN4 285 C5
Shirley Gr TN4 285 C5
Shirley House Dr SE7 11 C7
Shirley Hts 5 DA6 13 E3
Shirley Rd DA15 30 E5
Shirley Way ME15 163 A3
Shoebury Terr ME12 48 A5
Sholden Bank CT14 214 E4
Sholden CE Prim Sch CT14 214 F5
Sholden Gdns BR5 54 C4
Sholden New Rd CT14 214 F6
Sholden Rd ME2 40 C1
Shooter's Hill 5 CT17 278 C1
Shooters Hill CT15 245 C8
Shooters Hill Rd SE18, SE3 11 D6
Shooters Hill SE18 12 A6
Shore Cl Birchington CT7 80 D8
Herne Bay CT6 76 B3
Shorefields ME8 66 B2
Shoregate La ME9 66 F6
Shoreham Aircraft Mus* TN14 121 F8
Shoreham Cl DA5 31 D7
Shoreham Ho TN14 122 A8
Shoreham La
Badgers Mount TN14 121 A7
Chelsfield BR6 88 A3
Sevenoaks TN13 153 F4
Tenterden TN30 324 A3
Shoreham Pl TN14 122 A7
Shoreham Rd
Orpington BR5 54 B7
Otford TN14 122 B5
Shoreham Sta TN14 122 B8
Shoreham Village Sch TN14 121 F8
Shoreham Way BR2 52 A3
Shoreham Wlk ME15 195 F7
Shorehill Ct TN15 122 F2
Shorehill La TN15 122 F4
Shore The
Northfleet DA11 18 C2

Shore The *continued*
Northfleet,Rosherville DA11 18 F1
Shorland Ct ME1 63 B5
Shorncliffe Cres CT20 334 E5
Shorncliffe Ind Est CT20 334 D4
Shorncliffe Rd CT20 334 F5
Shorne CE Prim Sch DA12 38 E3
Shorne Cl
Orpington BR5 54 D5
3 Sidcup DA15 13 B1
Shornefield Cl BR1 53 A6
Shorne Ifield Rd DA12 38 C2
Shornells Way SE2 3 C1
Shorne Wood Ctry Pk* DA12 38 C1
Short La Alkham CT15 276 D1
Limpsfield RH8 183 B3
Shortlands Cl DA17 3 F3
Shortlands Gn ME15 195 F5
Shortlands Rd ME10 102 B4
Short La TN29 362 D6
Short Path SE18 12 B8
Short's Prospect ME12 71 C8
Short St
3 Chatham ME4 64 B3
Chillenden CT3 212 A8
5 Sandwich CT13 149 A1
Sheerness ME12 28 B2
Shorts Way ME1 63 A3
Shortway SE9 11 E4
Shotfield Cl CT3 146 C6
Shottendane Rd CT9, CT8 82 C7
Shottenden La CT4 204 A7
Shottenden Rd
Gillingham ME7 64 D7
Shottenden CT4,ME13 203 D8
Shottery Cl SE9 29 E5
Showfields Rd TN2 285 F1
Shrapnel Cl SE18 11 E7
Shrapnel Rd SE9 11 F4
Shrewsbury La SE18 12 B6
Shrimpton Cl CT4 172 B3
Shroffold Rd BR1 29 A5
Shropshire Terr 1 ME15 195 E7
Shrubbery Rd
Gravesend DA12 37 C7
Sutton at H DA4 57 D8
Shrubbery The CT14 215 C1
Shrubcote TN30 345 C7
Shrub Hill Rd CT5 109 D7
Shrublands Ct
Royal Tunbridge Wells TN2 286 C4
1 Tonbridge TN9 222 C2
Shrubsall Cl SE9 29 E7
Shrubshall Mdw TN15 190 A8
Shrubsole Ave ME12 28 C1
Shrubsole Dr ME14 129 F3
Shuart La CT7 79 F4
Shurland Ave
Leysdown-on-S ME12 49 H1
Minster (Sheppey) ME12 47 B6
Sittingbourne ME10 101 F1
Shurland Pk ME12 48 E5
Shurlock Ave BR8 55 D7
Shurlock Dr BR6 86 C6
Shuttle Cl
Biddenden TN27 295 A2
Sidcup DA15 30 F8
Shuttlemead DA5 31 F8
Shuttle Rd
Broadstairs CT10 84 B5
Crayford DA1 15 A4
Shuttlesfield La CT4 273 D1
Sibert's Cl CT15 244 F5
Sibertswold CE Prim Sch CT15 244 E4
Sibley Cl DA6 13 E2
Sibthorpe Rd SE12 29 C8
Sidcup By Pass Rd
Orpington BR5,BR7,DA14 31 B1
Sidcup DA14 30 E4
Sidcup Hill Gdns DA14 31 C3
Sidcup Hill DA14 31 B3
Sidcup Pl DA14 31 A3
Sidcup Rd SE12,SE9 29 D7
Sidcup Sta DA15 31 A6
Sidcup Tech Ctr DA14 31 D2
Sidewood Rd SE9 30 D7
Sidings The
Dymchurch TN29 366 B7
Lyminge CT18 305 C7
Whitstable CT5 74 E2
Sidmouth Ct DA1 34 B7
Sidmouth Rd
Bexley DA16 13 C7
Orpington BR5 54 B5
Sidney Cl TN2 313 F8
Sidney Gdns TN14 122 C2
Sidney Ho SE18 11 F6
Sidney Rd
Gillingham ME7 64 C7
Rochester ME1 63 A2
Sidney St
Folkestone CT19 335 E7
Maidstone ME16 161 C2
Siebert Rd SE3 11 A8
Siedle Ho 9 SE18 12 A8
Siemens Rd SE18 1 D3
Signal Ct 6 ME8 65 F1
Silchester Ct ME14 162 C7
Silecroft Ct TN23 267 E1
Silecroft Rd DA7 14 A6
Silk Cl SE12 11 A1
Silk Mills Cl TN13 154 C6
Silvanus Ho 5 CT11 117 D7
Silver Ave CT7 81 B6
Silver Bank ME5 97 A6
Silver Birch Ave DA13 92 F1
Silver Birch Cl
Joyden's Wood DA2 32 E4
Woolwich SE28 3 A5
Silver Birch Ct TN26 299 A1
Silver Birches ME5 97 A3
Silver Birches Mobile Homes Pk TN26 328 A4
Silver Birches ME12 28 G1
Silver Birch Gr TN23 300 B4
Silver Birch Wlk ME18 192 D6
Silver Cl TN9 254 B6
Silverdale Ave ME12 47 A6
Silverdale Dr
Bromley SE9 29 E6
Gillingham ME8 98 F7
Herne Bay CT6 77 D2
Silverdale Gr ME10 101 D3
Silverdale DA3 58 F5
Silverdale La
Royal Tunbridge Wells TN4 286 B6
Sandhurst Cross TN18 355 F5
Silverdale ME16 161 A2
Silverdale Rd
Bexley DA7 14 B5
Orpington,Petts Wood BR5 53 C5
Orpington,St Paul's Cray BR5 54 A6
Ramsgate CT11 117 A5
Royal Tunbridge Wells TN4 286 B6
Silverden Cotts TN18 355 F4
Silver Hill ME4 63 F3
Silver Hill Gdns
Ashford TN24 269 A1
4 Chatham ME4 63 F3
Silver Hill TN19 354 B1
Silver Hill Rd TN24 269 A1
Silver Hill
Rochester ME1 62 F2
Tenterden TN30 324 B1
Silverhurst Dr TN10 222 C7
Silverlands Rd CT18 305 C7
Silverland St E16 1 F5
Silverlocke Rd RM17 18 D8
Silver Rd DA12 37 E6
Silverspot Cl ME8 98 F7
Silver Spring Cl DA8 14 B8
Silver St CT14 215 D7
Silversted La TN16 151 D6
Silvers The CT10 83 C4
Silverstone Ct 10 BR1 52 C7
Silver St ME9 133 F5
Silvertown Sta E16 1 E5
Silvertown Way E16 1 A5
Silver Tree ME5 97 B1
Silverweed Rd ME5 96 F4
Silwood Cl TN2 286 E7
Simmonds Ct TN4 285 B4
Simmonds Dr DA3 59 A4
Simmonds La ME15 196 B6
Simmonds Rd CT1 174 E7
Simmons Rd SE18 2 B1
Simnel Rd SE12 29 B8
Simon Ave CT9 51 D2
Simon Ct 5 SE28 3 B5
Simone Cl BR1 52 D8
Simone Weil Ave TN24 268 B4
Simon Langton Girls Gram Sch CT1 175 C5
Simon Langton Gram Sch for Boys CT4 175 A4
Simon's Ave TN23 299 F7
Simpson Rd
Sittingbourne ME10 101 C5
Snodland ME6 128 A6
Simpson's Cotts BR2 85 C7
Simpsons Pl 6 BR1 52 A6
Simpson's Rd BR1,BR2 52 A6
Sinclair Cl ME8 98 E5
Sinclair Way DA2 34 D4
Sindal Shaw Ho ME5 96 E4
Singapore Dr ME7 64 B5
Singer Ave CT6 76 B4
Singledge Ave CT16 277 F6
Singledge La CT15 245 C2
Single's Cross TN14 120 D4
Single's Cross La TN14 120 C5
Single St TN16 119 B4
Singleton Cl CT12 115 B6
Singleton Ctr The TN23 299 D8
Singleton Hill TN23 299 D8
Singleton Rd TN23 267 C1
Singlewell Prim Sch DA12 37 D2
Singlewell Rd DA11 37 B4
Sinkertweazel TN17 320 E2
Sion Hill CT11 117 E6
Sion Pass 12 CT11 117 E6
Sion Wlk 8 TN1 286 A2
Sirdar Strand DA12 37 F3
Sir David's Pk TN4 253 E1
Sir Evelyn Rd ME1 63 B1
Sir John Hawkins Hospl ME4 63 E4
Sir John Hawkins Way ME4 63 F4
Sir John Moore Ave CT21 333 B2
Sir John Moore Ct 5 CT20 334 E3
Sir Joseph Williamson's Mathematical Sch ME1 63 C1
Sir Martin Bowes Ho 11 SE18 2 A2
Sir Roger Manwood's Sch CT13 181 B8
Sir Thomas Longley Rd ME2 63 E6
Siscup Rd SE9 30 B6
Siskin Cl Ashford TN25 268 B7
Hawkinge CT18 306 F4
Siskin Gdns TN12 257 A5
Siskin Wlk ME20 127 F2
Sissinghurst Castle Gdns* TN17 293 D1
Sissinghurst CE Prim Sch TN17 321 B8
Sissinghurst Dr ME16 161 B4
Sissinghurst Rd
Biddenden TN27 294 C2
Sissinghurst TN17,TN27 321 D8
Sittingbourne Com Coll ME10 102 C2
Sittingbourne Ind Pk ME10 101 F5
Sittingbourne & Kemsley Light Rly* ME10 102 A7
Sittingbourne Rd
Maidstone,Detling ME14 162 E8
Maidstone,Penenden Heath ME14 162 B6
Sittingbourne Retail Pk ME10 101 F5
Sittingbourne Sta ME10 101 F4
Siward Rd BR2 52 C6
Six Bells La TN13 154 C1
Six Bells Pk TN26 326 A3
Six Fields Path TN30 345 A7
Six Penny Cl TN8 249 C8
Sixth Ave ME12 49 A5
Skeete Rd CT18 304 E7
Skeet Hill La BR5,BR6 87 E8
Skeffington St SE18 2 C3
Skene Cl ME8 66 A1
Skeynes Rd TN8 217 B1
Skibbs La BR5,BR6 87 E7
Skinner Gdns TN17 321 A8
Skinner Rd TN29 376 C6
Skinner's Alley 3 CT5 74 D1
Skinners Cl ME20 129 A6
Skinners La TN8 217 D2
Skinners' Sch The TN4 286 A6
Skinner St ME4 63 F3
Skinner's Terr 15 TN9 254 B8
Skinner St ME7 64 C5
Skinner Street Prim Sch ME7 64 C6
Skinner's Way ME17 196 E4
Skinney La DA4 57 D6
Skippers Cl DA9 17 B2
Skua Ct ME2 62 C7
Skye Cl ME15 195 A7
Skylark Way TN23 300 D3
Sky Studios E16 2 A4
Sladebrook Rd SE3 11 D4
Slade Cl ME5 97 B2
Sladedale Rd SE18 2 E1
Slade Gdns DA8 14 F6
Slade Green Inf Sch DA8 15 A7
Slade Green Jun Sch DA8 15 A7
Slade Green Rd DA8 15 B7
Slade Green Sta DA8 15 A6
Slade Prim Sch TN9 222 B2
Slade Rd ME17 200 D8
Slades Cl CT5 109 C8
Slades Dr BR7 30 C4
Slade The
Lamberhurst TN3 317 A3
Tonbridge TN9 222 B2
Woolwich SE18 12 E8
Slaney Rd TN12 260 F4
Slater Cl 9 SE18 2 A2
Slaters TN8 218 F2
Slatin Rd ME2 63 B8
Sleeches Cross TN3 314 B2
Sleepers Stile Rd TN5 316 B1
Sleigh Rd CT2 143 F6
Slicketts Hill ME4 64 A4
Slip La CT15 276 C2
Slip Mill Rd TN18 340 E4
Slip The TN16 151 C1
Slipway Rd ME12 27 F3
Sloane Gdns BR6 86 C7
Sloane Sq DA3 58 E6
Slocum Cl SE28 3 C6
Sloe La CT10,CT9 83 B6
Slough Rd ME9 135 A3
Small Bridge Cotts TN17 290 B2
Small Bridge Rd TN12, TN17 290 B2
Small Grains DA3 91 B7
Small Hythe Cl ME15 163 B2
Smallhythe Place (Mus)* TN30 359 C8
Smallhythe Place* TN30 345 C1
Small Hythe Rd TN30 345 B4
Small Profits ME15, ME18 193 A4
Smarden Bsns Est TN27 295 D7
Smarden Cl 8 DA17 4 A1
Smarden Gr SE9 29 F4
Smarden Prim Sch TN27 264 A1
Smarden Rd
Pluckley TN27 265 B6
Standen TN27 295 B6
Swift's Green TN27 263 B4
Smarden Wlk ME8 66 B1
Smarts Cotts ME14 163 C4
Smarts Hill TN11 252 A1
Smarts Rd DA12 37 C6
Smeed Cl 4 ME10 102 B4
Smeed-Dean Ctr The ME10 102 A4
Smeeth Com Prim Sch TN25 302 D5
Smetham Gdns ME2 40 B1
Smithers Cl TN11 190 E1
Smithers Ct TN12 225 A7
Smithers La TN12 225 A7
Smithfield Rd ME3 27 C5
Smithies Rd SE2 3 B2
Smith Rd ME5 97 B3
Smith's Hill ME15 193 C5
Smiths La TN8 184 C2
Smiths Orch ME9 133 F5
Smith St ME2 63 A6
Smithy Dr TN23 300 C4
Smithy Field 7 TN8 217 D3
Smithy The TN5 336 A3
Smugglers TN18 341 A1
Smugglers Leap Cvn Pk CT12 115 C8
Smuggler's Way CT7 81 A8
Smugglers Wlk DA9 17 B2
Smythe Cl TN4 253 E3
Smythe Rd DA4 57 A8
Snag La TN14 119 D7
Snakes Hill CT3 178 A5
Snape La TN5 336 D1
Snape View TN5 336 F4
Snargate La TN29 362 C5
Snargate St CT17 310 D7
Snelgrove Ho 14 CT16 310 D8
Snell Gdns CT6 76 B2
Snelling Ave DA11 36 F6
Snipe Cl Ashford TN25 268 C7
Erith DA8 15 B7
Pembury TN2 287 E8
Snipe Ct ME2 62 C7
Snoad La TN12 292 A8
Snodhurst Ave ME5 96 E5
Snodhurst Ho 2 ME5 97 A7
Snodland CE Prim Sch ME6 127 F8
Snodland Rd ME19 127 D7
Snodlands Cl BR6 86 A1
Snodland Sta ME6 128 B8
Snoll Hatch Rd TN12 224 F5
Snowbell Rd TN23 300 B4
Snowdon Ave ME14 162 B5
Snowdon Cl ME5 97 B7
Snowdon Par ME14 162 C5
Snowdown Caravan Site CT15 211 A4
Snowdown Ct CT3 210 F5
Snowdown Sta CT15 211 B3
Snowdrop Cl CT19 335 C8
Snow Ho ME7 64 E7
Snughorne La TN27 295 D8
Sobraon Villas TN15 157 C7
Sobraon Way CT1 143 D1
Solar Ct CT12 117 C7
Solefield Prep Sch TN13 187 C8
Solefields Rd TN13 187 C8
Sole Fields TN13 187 C8
Solent Gdns ME5 97 B8
Soleoak Dr TN13 187 B8
Soleshill Rd CT4 171 E1
Sole Street Cotts CT4 239 B7
Sole Street Farm ME3 40 B3
Sole Street Sta DA13 60 D4
Sole St DA12,DA13 60 D4
Solomon Ho CT14 215 B3
Solomon Rd
Gillingham ME8 66 A1
Gillingham ME8 99 A8
Rainham ME8 65 F1
Solomons La ME13 138 D7
Solomons Rd ME4 63 F4
Somerden Rd BR5 54 D2
Somerfield Barn Ct TN25 331 C8
Somerfield Cl ME16 161 D5
Somerfield Hospl The ME16 161 E5
Somerfield La ME16 161 D4
Somerfield Rd ME16 161 D4
Somerhill Ave DA15 31 B8
Somerhill Rd
Bexley DA16 13 B5
Tonbridge TN9 254 D8
Somerset Ave DA16 12 F3
Somerset Cl
Chatham ME5 97 C8
Sittingbourne ME10 101 C4
Whitstable CT5 108 B7
Somerset Ct
2 Broadstairs CT10 84 A4
Deal CT14 215 B3
Ramsgate CT12 83 B2
Somerset Rd
Ashford TN24 268 B3
Canterbury CT1 175 D8
Dartford DA1 33 B8
Deal CT14 215 C3
Folkestone CT19 334 E6
Maidstone ME15 195 C8
Orpington BR6 54 A2
Royal Tunbridge Wells TN4 286 A6
Somerset Villas TN3 312 C7
Somersham Rd DA7 13 E5
Somertrees Ave SE12 29 B6
Somerville Gdns TN4 285 F4
Somerville Rd DA1 15 F1
Somme Ct CT1 143 D1
Sommerville Cl ME13 138 E7
Somner Cl CT2 142 D1
Somner Wlk ME15 195 F4
Sondes Cl CT6 77 A2
Sondes Rd CT14 215 D5
Sonnet Wlk TN16 118 C1
Sonora Way ME10 101 C7
Soper's La TN18 340 D4
Sophia Rd E16 1 B7
Sophurst La TN12 288 C5
Sopurst Wood TN12 288 D5
Sopwith Cl TN16 118 D3
Sorrel Cl SE28 3 A5
Sorrel Ct 8 RM17 18 D8
Sorrel Gdns E6 1 E8
Sorrell Cl 4 TN8 217 D3
Sorrell Rd ME5 96 F4
Sorrell Way DA11 36 E4
Sortmill Rd ME6 128 B7
Sotherton TN24 300 E7
Souberg Cl CT14 215 C8
Sounds Lodge BR8 55 C3
Southall Cl CT12 115 C7
Southampton Mews E16 1 B5
South Ash Rd TN15 91 E4
South Ave
Aylesham CT15 211 A3
Gillingham ME8 65 B2
South Avenue Jun & Inf Schs ME10 102 A3
South Ave ME10 102 A3
South Aylesford Ret Pk ME20 160 E8
South Bank Cliffe ME3 22 B2
Staplehurst TN12 260 E2
Sutton Valence ME17 229 E7
Westerham TN16 151 D1
South Barham Rd CT4 242 E6
Southborough CE Prim Sch & Tunbridge Wells Language Unit TN4 285 F8
Southborough Ct TN4 254 A2
Southborough La BR2 52 F4
Southborough Prim Sch BR2 53 A4
South Borough Prim Sch ME15 162 A2
Southborough Rd BR1 52 E5
Southbourne TN23 299 E5
Southbourne Gdns SE12 11 B2
Southbourne Gr ME5 97 A4
Southbourne BR2 52 A2
Southbourne Rd CT19 335 E5
South Brook La TN8 218 C7
South Brooks Rd TN29 378 H6
South Bush La ME8 99 B6
South Camber Way CT16 279 B1
South Canterbury Rd CT1 175 A6
South Cl Bexley DA6 13 D3
Canterbury CT1 175 A8
South Cliff Par CT10 84 B1
South Court Dr CT3 178 A7
South Cres ME17 194 C4
Southcroft Ave DA16 12 E4
Southcroft Rd BR6 86 E7
South Ct Deal CT14 215 D6
Ramsgate CT12 83 B2
Royal Tunbridge Wells TN4 286 A6
South Deal Prim Sch CT14 215 B4
Southdene TN14 120 F6
Southdown Rd ME12 46 E6
South Dr BR6 86 E5
South Eastern Rd
Ramsgate CT11 117 D7
Rochester ME2 63 C7
Southenay La TN25 303 C4
Southend Cl SE9 12 B1
Southend Cres SE9 12 B1
Southernden Rd TN27 231 E1
Southern Pl BR8 55 D5
Southern Way CT19 335 E6
Southernwood Rise CT20 334 F4
South Exit Rd CT16 310 G8
Southey Mews E16 1 A5
Southey Way 1 ME20 127 F4
Southey Wlk RM18 19 B6
Southfield Ct DA1 15 F4
Southfield Rd
Orpington BR7 54 A6
Royal Tunbridge Wells TN4 286 A6
Southfield Shaw DA13 93 B1
Southfields BR8 32 F1
Southfields Rd TN15 90 F2
Southfields ME1 63 C3
Southfields Sch DA11 37 C3
Southfields
Speldhurst TN3 285 A7
Turner's Green TN5 336 F6
Southfields Way TN4 286 B8
Southfleet Ave DA3 59 B7
Southfleet Rd Bean DA2 35 C4
8 Northfleet DA11 36 F7
Orpington BR6 86 E6
Swanscombe DA10 36 A7
South Frith TN4 254 A6
Southgate Rd TN30 345 C7
Southgate TN4 285 F3
South Gipsy Rd DA16 13 D4
South Glade The DA5 31 F7
South Goodwin Ct CT14 215 D8
South Green La ME9 132 F6
South Gr TN1 286 A2
South Hall Cl DA4 56 F2
South Hill BR7 29 F2
South Hill Rd DA12 37 C7
Southill Rd Bromley BR7 29 F1
Chatham ME4 63 F3
South Kent Ave DA11 18 C1
South Kent Coll
Dover CT16 310 D8
Folkestone CT20 335 B5
South Kent Coll Jemmett Campus TN23 300 A8
South Kent Coll of Tech TN23 268 C1
South Kent Coll South Ashford Campus TN23 299 F6
Southland's Com Comp Sch TN28 373 B7
Southland Rd SE18 12 F7
Southlands Ave BR6 86 E5
Southlands Ct BR2 52 D5
Southlands Gr BR1 52 E6
Southlands Rd BR1,BR2 52 D5
South La ME17 229 E6
South Lea TN23 300 A3
Southlees La ME9 132 F3
South Lodge Cl CT5 74 E3
South Lodge CT5 74 E3
Southmead Cl CT19 335 A6
South Military Rd CT17 310 C5
South Molton Rd E16 1 A7
South Motto TN23 300 B5
South of England Rare Breeds Ctr* TN26 326 D1
Southold Rise SE9 29 F5
Southover BR1 29 A3
Southover Ct 2 CT20 334 E3
South Park Bsns Village ME15 162 A1
South Park Rd ME15 162 C1
South Pk TN13 154 B2
South Pondside Rd ME4 64 A8
Southport Rd SE18 2 D2
South Quay ME13 105 D1
South Rd Chatham ME4 64 B7
Chatham ME4,ME7 64 A7
Dover CT17 310 B8
Erith DA8 14 F7
Faversham ME13 138 C7
Herne Bay CT6 77 A5
Hythe CT21 333 D1
Kingsdown CT14 248 D5
Marden TN12 259 E5
Sandwich CT13 149 A8
South Ridge BR2 52 C5
South Rise Prim Sch SE18 2 D1
South Rise Way SE18 2 D2
South Row
Greenwich SE3 11 A5
Penshurst TN8 251 D5
Southsea Ave ME12 47 C8
Southsea Dr CT6 76 D4
South Side Three Rd ME4 64 C8
Southspring DA15 30 D8
South St Bromley BR1 52 A7
Canterbury CT1 143 C2
Deal CT14 215 D6
Folkestone CT20 335 E4
Gravesend DA12 37 B8
Lydd TN29 376 C6
Maidstone ME16 160 E1
Southstone Ct CT21 333 C1
South Stour Ave TN23 300 C8
South St ME11 45 F5
Southstreet Crossing CT5 109 A7
South Street Rd ME9 132 C7
South St Selling ME13 171 F8
Whitstable CT5 109 A7
South Swale Nature Reserve* ME13 106 A6
South Terr
Chattenden ME3 40 F6
Farningham DA4 56 F2
South Turbine Hall Rd TN29 380 C2
Southview Ave RM18 19 A6
South View BR1 52 C7
South View Cl DA5 13 F1
Southview Cl BR8 56 A5
South View Ct 11 BR1 52 C7
South View Gdns ME12 28 C1
South View CT3 111 F1
Southview Hts RM20 17 C8
South View RH8 183 A2
South View Rd
Dartford DA2 33 D5
Royal Tunbridge Wells TN4 286 B8
Turner's Green TN5 336 F6
West Thurrock RM20 17 C8
Whitstable CT5 108 D6
South View Terr TN17 318 E8
South Wall CT14 215 B7
Southwall Ind Est CT14 215 B7
Southwall Rd CT14 215 B6
Southwark Pl BR1 52 F6
Southwark Rd ME2 62 D6
Southway BR2 52 A2
Southways ME17 229 E7
Southwell Rd ME2 62 D6
Southwold Pl CT8 81 E7
Southwold Rd DA5 14 B1
Southwood Ave TN4 286 A6
Southwood Bldgs TN4 285 B4
Southwood Cl BR1 52 F5
Southwood Gdns CT11 117 B6
Southwood Ho SE9 30 B6
Southwood Hts CT11 117 C6

Southwood ME16 160 F2
Southwood Rd
Eltham SE9 30 B6
Ramsgate CT11 117 C6
Rusthall TN4 285 B5
Whitstable CT5 75 B2
Woolwich SE28 3 B5
Sovereign Bvd ME7,
ME8 65 A2
Sovereign Ct
Bromley BR2 52 F3
Sutton at H DA4 57 B8
Sovereign Ho SE18 1 F3
Sovereigns The ME16 161 D4
Sovereigns Way TN12 259 C6
Sovereign Way TN9 222 C1
Soverign Ho BR7 30 D1
Sowell St CT10 83 F5
Sowerby Cl SE9 11 F2
Spade La ME9 99 C6
Spa Ind Pk TN2 286 E8
Spanton Cres CT21 333 A3
Spar Cl TN11 190 F1
Sparepenny La DA4 56 E1
Sparkes Cl BR2 52 B5
Sparkeswood Ave
TN17 343 F3
Sparkeswood Cl TN17 343 F3
Sparrow Castle [3] CT9 50 J1
Sparrow Dr BR5 53 D1
Sparrow's Farm L Ctr
SE9 30 C8
Sparrows Green Rd
TN5 336 F5
Sparrows La SE9 30 C7
Spa Valley Rly* TN3 312 D7
Speakman Ct [5] CT11 117 C6
Spearhead Rd ME14 161 F7
Spearman St [5] SE18 12 A8
Spearpoint Cnr TN24 268 F5
Spectrum Bsns Ctr
ME2 63 E8
Spectrum Bsns Est
ME15 195 F4
Speedgate Farm DA3 90 F8
Speedgate Hill DA3 91 A8
Speedwell Ave ME5 96 F4
Speedwell Cl
Gillingham ME7 64 E5
Maidstone ME14 162 E5
[5] Marlpit Hill TN8 217 D3
Speedwell Ct RM17 18 E7
Speedwell Rd CT5 108 B6
Spekehill SE9 29 F5
Speke Rd CT10 83 E6
Spekes Rd ME7 98 B6
Spelders Hill TN25 270 A5
Speldhurst CE Prim Sch
TN3 285 A7
Speldhurst Cl TN23 299 E5
Speldhurst Ct ME16 161 D4
Speldhurst Gdns CT9 51 F3
Speldhurst Hill TN3 285 B8
Speldhurst Rd
Langton Green TN3 284 F5
Royal Tunbridge Wells
TN3,TN4 285 E8
Spelmonden Rd TN12 289 F2
Spembley Ct ME4 63 E4
Spence Cl CT18 307 A4
Spencer Cl
Chatham ME5 97 A5
Orpington BR6 86 F8
Spencer Ct [5] BR6 86 C5
Spencer Flats ME5 97 B8
Spencer Gdns SE9 11 F2
Spencer Ho [3] CT20 334 F5
Spencer Mews
[6] Royal Tunbridge
Wells,Mount Sion TN1 286 A2
[10] Royal Tunbridge Wells
TN1 286 B4
Spencer Rd CT7 81 A8
Spencer Sq CT11 117 D6
Spencer St
Gravesend DA11 37 A8
[9] Ramsgate CT11 117 D6
Spencer Way ME15 195 E7
Spencer Wlk RM18 19 B5
Spenlow Dr ME5 130 A8
Spenny La TN12 258 B7
Spenser Rd CT6 76 F4
Speranza St SE18 2 F1
Speyside TN10 222 B5
Spicer Homes ME10 101 F2
Spicers Ct CT21 333 C1
Spicers Field CT6 77 D2
Spicer's Pl CT3 145 C2
Spielman Rd DA1 15 F3
Spiers The ME7 65 C5
Spillett Cl ME13 138 B6
Spillway The ME15 161 D2
Spindle Cl SE18 1 E3
Spindle Glade ME14 162 C5
Spindle Ho [5] DA15 31 A5
Spindles RM18 19 A7
Spindlewood Cl ME5 97 B3
Spindlewood End
TN23 267 D4
Spinel Cl SE18 2 F1
Spinnaker Ct [4] ME1 63 C1
Spinnens Acre Com Jun
Sch ME5 97 C1
Spinners Cl TN27 295 A2
Spinners Wents TN11 190 D8
Spinney La CT3 210 E4
Spinney Oak BR1 52 E7
Spinneys The BR1 52 F7
Spinney The
Ashford TN23 267 E3
Spinney The *continued*
Chatham ME5 97 B1
Crabble CT17 277 E2
Maidstone ME15 162 B2
Margate CT9 51 E1
Sidcup DA14 31 E3
Swanley BR8 55 E7
Tonbridge TN9 254 A7
Spinney Way TN14 119 D8
Spire Ave CT5 109 A8
Spire Cl DA12 37 B7
Spires The
Canterbury CT2 142 F2
Dartford DA1 33 D6
Maidstone ME16 161 D4
Rochester ME2 62 D5
Spitalfield La TN28 372 F6
Spitalfield Terr TN28 372 F6
Spital St DA1 15 D1
Spitfire Cl ME5 97 B6
Spitfire & Hurricane Memls
Mus* CT12 82 A2
Spitfire Rd ME19 158 F3
Spitfire Way CT18 307 B3
Split Ho CT17 278 A1
Split La CT4 241 A5
Spode La TN8 282 A7
Sponden La TN18 356 A7
Spongs La TN17 293 A1
Sportsfield ME14 162 B5
Sportsmans Cotts
ME19 159 B5
Spot La ME15 163 A2
Spout La
Brenchley TN12 289 C5
Crockham Hill TN8 184 C1
Spratling La CT12 82 F1
Spratling St CT12 82 E1
Spray Hill TN3 317 B4
Spray St SE18 2 B2
Sprig The ME14 163 A4
Spring Cott DA1 33 D8
Springcroft DA3 59 A4
Spring Cross DA3 92 A7
Spring Ct [17] DA15 31 A5
Springdale Cotts ME3 40 A3
Springett Almshouses
TN18 354 E8
Springett Cl ME20 128 F6
Springett Way ME17 194 D3
Spring Farm TN29 363 D5
Springfarm Rd TN29 363 C5
Springfield Ave
Maidstone ME14 161 F7
Swanley BR8 55 F5
Tenterden TN30 324 C2
Springfield Cl CT11 83 E2
Springfield Cotts
TN12 289 F5
Springfield Gdns BR1 52 F5
Springfield Gr SE7 11 C8
Springfield Ind Est
TN18 340 F3
Springfield Pass CT21 333 B2
Springfield Rd
Bexley,Bexleyheath DA7 14 B3
Bexley,Welling DA16 13 B4
Bromley BR1 52 F5
Dover CT16 278 B2
Edenbridge TN8 217 B1
Gillingham ME7 64 E6
Groombridge TN3 312 C7
Lunsford ME20 127 F4
Margate CT9 51 E3
Royal Tunbridge Wells
TN4 253 F1
Sittingbourne ME10 101 D5
Springfields TN5 338 E1
Springfield Terr [7]
ME4 63 F4
Springfield Way CT21 334 B3
Springfield Wlk [3] BR6 53 D1
Spring Gdns
Biggin Hill TN16 118 C1
Orpington BR6 87 B4
Rusthall TN4 285 B4
Spring Gr DA12 37 B7
Spring Grove Sch
TN25 237 C2
Springhead Ent Pk
DA11 36 C7
Springhead Rd
Erith DA8 14 F8
Faversham ME13 105 D1
Spring Head Rd TN15 122 F2
Springhead Rd DA11 36 C7
Springhead TN2 286 D5
Spring Hill TN11,TN3 284 A7
Spring Ho CT21 333 C2
Spring Hollow TN29 366 A4
Springholm Cl TN16 118 C1
Spring La
Bidborough TN3 253 D3
Canterbury CT1 175 C7
Fordwich CT2 144 A4
Hythe CT21 334 A4
Oldbury TN15 156 B5
Spring Lodge [3] BR5 54 C4
Springrove Cotts
TN12 259 B5
Springshaw Cl TN13 153 D4
Spring Shaw Rd BR5 54 A8
Springside Terr CT18 305 C6
Spring Terr [15] CT20 335 D5
Spring Vale DA7 14 B3
Spring Vale Cl BR8 55 F8
Springvale Ct
Eltham SE12 11 A3
Northfleet DA11 36 C6
Spring Vale DA1 33 D8
Springvale
Gillingham ME8 98 C6
Iwade ME9 68 D4
Spring Vale ME16 161 E4
Spring Vale N DA1 33 D8
Springvale Ret Pk [2]
BR5 54 C6
Spring Vale S DA1 33 D8
Spring Vale DA9 17 C1
Springvale Way BR5 54 C6
Springview Apartments
TN2 286 D6
Springwater Cl SE18 12 A6
Springwell Rd TN9 254 B8
Spring Wlk CT5 108 C7
Springwood Cl
Ashford TN23 267 E3
[1] Maidstone ME16 161 A3
Springwood Ct TN28 373 B6
Springwood Dr TN23 267 E3
Springwood Hall
TN11 189 D1
Springwood Rd ME16 161 A3
Sprivers Gdns* TN12 289 E4
Sprotlands Ave TN24 268 F1
Sprotshill Cl ME10 101 E6
Spruce Cl ME20 128 B2
Sprucedale Cl BR8 55 E7
Spruce Ho TN4 285 E4
Spruce Rd TN16 118 D3
Spurgeon Cl RM17 18 C8
Spurgeons Cotts
ME17 194 E2
Spur Rd BR6 87 A8
Spurrell Ave DA5 32 D4
Spurway ME14 163 A4
Square Hill ME15 162 B4
Square Hill Rd ME15 162 B4
Square The
Birchington CT7 81 A7
Chilham CT4 205 B8
Cowden TN8 282 B6
Elham CT4 273 F4
Hadlow TN11 223 E8
Hunton ME15 226 D7
Leigh TN11 220 F1
Lenham ME17 199 D5
Selling ME13 171 A6
Sevenoaks TN13 153 E5
Sittingbourne ME10 68 F1
Swanley BR8 55 D6
Tatsfield TN16 150 C7
Wadhurst TN5 337 A4
Squeeze Gut Alley [14]
CT5 74 D2
Squerryes Court*
TN16 184 C7
Squerryes Mede TN16 184 C8
Squire Ave CT2 174 C8
Squires Cl ME2 62 B7
Squires Ct ME12 48 E3
Squires Field BR8 55 F8
Squires Ho [3] SE18 12 B8
Squires Way
Dover CT16 278 A3
Joyden's Wood DA2 32 D4
Squires Wood Dr BR7 29 F1
Squirrel La TN25 267 F5
Squirrel Way TN2 286 E5
Stable Cl ME5 97 C5
Stable Ct Chilham CT4 205 B7
Faversham ME13 138 D6
Stabledene Way TN2 287 D6
Stablemead CT19 335 A7
Stables End BR6 86 C7
Stables The TN18 354 E8
Stace Cl TN30 345 C8
Stacey Cl DA12 37 E3
Stacey Rd TN10 222 A4
Staceys St ME14 161 F5
Stackfield [1] TN8 217 D3
Stack La DA3 58 F4
Stacklands Cl TN15 90 E4
Stack Rd DA4 57 D5
Stade St CT21 333 C1
Stade The CT19 335 E5
Stadium Rd SE18 11 F8
Stadium Way
Crayford DA1 14 E2
Sittingbourne ME10 102 C6
Stadler Cl ME16 161 D7
Staffa Rd ME15 195 A7
Staffhurst Wood Rd
TN8,RH8 216 C6
Stafford Cl
Ashford TN23 267 F2
Stone DA9 16 F2
Stafford Rd
Royal Tunbridge Wells
TN2 286 E4
Sidcup DA14 30 E4
Tonbridge TN9 222 B2
Staffordshire St [11]
CT11 117 E7
Stafford St ME7 64 C5
Stafford Way TN13 187 C8
Stag Rd Chatham ME5 97 B5
Royal Tunbridge Wells
TN2 286 D8
Stagshaw Cl ME15 162 A2
Stainer House SE3 11 C3
Stainer Rd TN10 222 F6
Staines Hill CT2 144 B7
Staines Pl CT10 84 B5
Staines Wlk DA14 31 C2
Stainmore Cl BR7 53 D8
Stairfoot La TN13 153 C5
Stair Rd TN10 222 F4
Stake La ME2 95 A6
Staleys Rd TN15 156 F7
Stalham Ct ME7 98 B4
Stalin Ave ME5 97 B8
Stalisfield Pl BR6 86 A1
Stalisfield Rd
Charing TN27 201 E3
Stalisfield Rd *continued*
Stalisfield Green ME13,
TN27 201 C5
Throwley ME13 169 C6
Stamford Villas ME12 48 C2
Stampers The ME15 161 D2
Stanam Rd TN2 287 E6
Stanbridge Rd TN8 217 B2
Stanbrook Rd
Northfleet DA11 36 F8
Woolwich SE2 3 B4
Stanbury Cres CT19 335 F7
Stancomb Ave CT11 117 C5
Standard Ave CT6 76 A4
Standard Ind Est E16 1 F4
Standard Rd Bexley DA6 13 E3
Erith DA17 4 A1
Farthing Street BR6 86 A4
Standen Cl ME8 98 E4
Standen La CT18 307 E5
Standen St
Benenden TN17,TN18 342 D2
Royal Tunbridge Wells
TN4 286 A5
Standen Street TN17 356 E8
Standings Cross TN12 256 E1
Standish Ho SE3 11 B3
Staner Ct CT12 117 A8
Staner Hill CT12 116 F8
Stane Way SE18 11 E7
Stanford Dr ME16 161 C3
Stanford La TN11 191 C2
Stanford Way ME2 62 C2
Stangate Dr ME9 68 D4
Stangate Rd
Birling ME19 127 B8
Rochester ME2 62 C7
Stangrove Rd TN8 217 C1
Stanham Pl DA1 15 A3
Stanham Rd DA1 15 C2
Stanhill Cotts DA2 32 D2
Stanhope Ave
Hayes BR2 52 A1
Sittingbourne ME10 102 A3
Stanhope Cl ME14 161 E7
Stanhope Rd
Ashford TN23 299 E6
Bexley DA7 13 E5
Deal CT14 215 D6
Dover CT16 278 C2
Rochester ME2 63 A7
Royal Tunbridge Wells
TN1 286 C5
Sidcup DA15 31 A4
Swanscombe DA10 17 F1
Stanhopes RH8 183 B7
Stanhope Sq TN23 299 F6
Stanhope Way TN13 153 D5
Stan La ME18 191 A7
Stanley Ave
Minster (Sheppey) ME12 47 D7
Queenborough ME11 46 A4
Stanley Cl
Dymchurch TN29 353 B4
Staplehurst TN12 260 E4
Stone DA9 16 E2
Stanley Cotts DA2 34 E3
Stanley Cres DA12 37 D3
Stanley Gdns CT6 76 F3
Stanley Glyn Ct BR7 30 A3
Stanley Holloway Ct E16 1 A7
Stanley Pl
Broadstairs CT10 84 A4
Ramsgate CT11 117 E7
Stanley Rd
Broadstairs CT10 84 A6
Bromley BR2 52 C5
Chatham ME5 97 C6
Deal CT14 215 D5
Folkestone CT19 334 E6
Gillingham ME7 64 C6
Grays RM17 18 B8
Herne Bay CT6 76 F4
Marden TN12 259 D5
Margate CT9 51 A3
Northfleet DA11 36 E7
Orpington BR6 53 F1
Ramsgate CT11 117 D8
Royal Tunbridge Wells
TN1 286 B5
Sidcup DA14 31 A5
Swanscombe DA10 17 F1
Whitstable CT5 108 D7
Stanley Way BR5 54 B4
Stanmore Ct CT1 175 B7
Stanmore Ho SE12 29 B7
Stanmore Rd DA17 4 C2
Stansfeld Ave CT18 307 A4
Stansfeld Rd E16 1 D7
Stansted CE Prim Sch
TN15 91 F1
Stansted Cl ME16 161 D7
Stansted Cres DA5 31 D7
Stansted Hill TN15 92 A1
Stansted La TN15 91 C1
Stanton Cl BR5 54 C2
Stanton Ct
[2] Bromley BR1 52 C7
[5] Sidcup DA15 31 A5
Staple Cl
Joyden's Wood DA5 32 D5
Sittingbourne ME10 101 E5
Staple Dr TN12 260 F4
Stapleford Ct TN13 153 F4
Staplehurst Ave CT10 84 A2
Staplehurst Gdns CT9 51 E2
Staplehurst Ho BR5 54 C4
Staplehurst Lodge Ind Est
ME10 101 D5
Staplehurst Rd
Bogden TN12 228 C2
Frittenden TN12,TN17 261 D1
Gillingham ME8 65 B3
Staplehurst Rd *continued*
Sittingbourne ME10 101 D5
Staplehurst Sch TN12 260 E3
Staplehurst Sta TN12 260 E5
Staple Rd CT3 178 C6
Staplers Ct ME14 162 B8
Staples Ho E6 2 A7
Staple St ME13 139 F5
Staples The BR8 56 B8
Staplestreet Rd ME13 140 A4
Stapleton Rd
Bexley DA7 13 F8
Orpington BR6 86 F7
Staple Vineyard*
CT3 178 F5
Stapley Rd DA17 4 A1
Starboard Ave DA9 17 B1
Star Bsns Ctr RM13 4 D8
Star Hill DA1 14 E2
Star Hill Rd TN14 121 A2
Star Hill ME1 63 D5
Star Ho TN3 317 B5
Star La
Folkestone CT19 334 D7
Gillingham ME7 98 A7
Margate CT9 83 A5
Orpington BR5,BR8 54 E5
Starle Cl CT1 143 B1
Starling Cl DA3 59 B6
Star Mill Ct ME5 64 D2
Star Mill La ME5 64 D2
Starnes Ct [5] ME14 162 A5
Starr Cotts TN12 226 C2
Star Rd TN24 268 D2
Starts Cl BR6 86 A7
Starts Hill Ave BR6 86 B6
Starts Hill Rd BR6 86 B6
Starvation Cnr [1] CT5 74 D2
Starveacre La ME9 101 B1
Starve Goose La TN17 319 E4
State Farm Ave BR6 86 C6
Stately Pk ME18 192 C1
Station App
Adisham CT3 210 E8
Bexley,Barnehurst DA7 14 C5
Bexley,Bexleyheath DA7 13 E5
Bexley,Welling DA16 13 A5
Birchington CT7 80 F7
Borough Green TN15 156 F7
Bromley BR7 29 E2
Chelsfield BR6 87 B5
Chislehurst BR7 53 A7
Dartford DA1 15 E1
Edenbridge TN8 217 C2
Grays RM17 18 A8
Greenwich SE3 11 B4
Halling ME2 95 A5
Hayes BR2 52 A1
Maidstone ME16 161 F3
Martin Mill CT15 247 C2
Minster (Thanet) CT12 115 C5
New Romney TN28 373 C6
Orpington BR6 86 F8
Orpington,St Mary Cray
BR5 54 B5
Otford TN14 122 C3
Paddock Wood TN12 257 A7
Station Approach Rd
CT11 117 D8
Station App
Staplehurst TN12 260 E5
Swanley BR8 55 E5
Station Cotts
Gill's Green TN18 340 F5
Hartley TN17 319 E2
Horsmonden TN12 290 B5
Selling ME13 171 E7
Station Cres SE3 1 A1
Station Ct TN15 156 F7
Station Dr CT14 215 A1
Station Hill TN11 252 A8
Station Hill Cotts
ME15 194 A7
Station Hill BR2 85 A8
Station Mews
Elham CT4 273 F4
[3] Tenterden TN30 345 A7
Station Par
Sevenoaks TN13 154 A3
Sidcup DA15 31 A6
Station Rd
Adisham CT3 177 E1
Ashford TN23 268 C2
Aylesford ME20 128 E2
Bekesbourne CT4 176 C4
Betsham DA13 36 A4
Bexley DA7 13 E4
Birchington CT7 81 A7
Borough Green TN15 156 F7
Brasted TN16 152 B4
Bridge CT4 175 F2
Bromley BR1 52 A8
Charing TN27 234 C7
Chartham CT4 173 D3
Cliffe ME3 22 B3
Crayford DA1 14 F1
Cuxton ME2 62 C2
Deal CT14 215 B1
Dymchurch TN29 366 B7
East Farleigh ME15 194 A7
East Tilbury RM18 20 B7
Station Rd E CT1 174 F7
Station Rd
Edenbridge TN8 217 C2
Erith DA17 4 A3
Eynsford DA4 89 D7
Faversham ME13 138 D6
Folkestone CT19 334 F5
Gillingham ME8 66 A2
Goudhurst TN17 318 C7
Groombridge TN3 312 C7
Halstead TN14 120 F8
Harrietsham ME17 198 D6
Station Rd *continued*
Headcorn TN27 262 D5
Herne Bay CT6 76 E4
Hurst Green TN19 354 A3
Hythe CT21 333 D3
Longfield DA3 58 E6
Lydd TN29 376 D7
Lyminge CT18 305 C6
Maidstone ME14 161 F5
Margate CT9 50 H2
Martin Mill CT15 247 D1
Meopham Station DA13 60 A4
Minster (Thanet) CT12 115 C5
Station Rd N DA17 4 B3
Station Rd
Nettlestead Green
ME18 192 C1
Newington ME9 100 B6
New Romney TN28 373 C6
Northfleet DA11 18 B1
Northiam TN31 357 C1
Orpington BR6 86 F8
Orpington,St Mary Cray
BR5 54 C5
Otford TN14 122 C3
Paddock Wood TN12 256 F7
Pluckley TN27 265 C5
Rainham ME8 65 F1
Rochester ME2 63 C7
Rockrobin TN5 336 C6
St Margaret's at Cliffe
CT15 279 E8
Sevenoaks TN13 153 E7
Shepherdswell CT15 244 D5
Shoreham TN14 122 A7
Sidcup DA14,DA15 31 A5
Smeeth TN25 302 B3
Staplehurst TN12 260 F5
Stone DA9 17 A2
Sutton at H DA4 57 B7
Swanley BR8 55 E5
Tenterden TN30 345 A7
Teynham ME9 103 D2
Station Rd W CT2 142 F1
Station Rd
Westgate-on-S CT8 50 D1
Whitstable CT5 74 E2
Withyham TN7 311 B5
Station Row ME9 103 D3
Station Sq BR5 53 C4
Station St Newham E16 2 B5
Sittingbourne ME10 101 F4
Station Terr TN28 373 C6
Steadman Cl ME3 39 C6
Stede Hill ME17 165 F3
Stedley [17] DA14 31 A4
Stedman Cl DA5 32 E5
Steed Cl CT6 111 B8
Steeds Cl TN23 300 A1
Steeds La TN23,TN26 300 B1
Steele Ave DA9 17 A2
Steele's La DA13 93 A6
Steele St ME2 63 A8
Steele Wlk DA8 14 B7
Steellands Rise TN5 338 F1
Steep Cl BR6 86 F4
Steephill Sch DA3 58 D5
Steeple Heights Dr
TN16 118 D2
Steerforth Cl ME1 63 C2
Steers Pl TN11 190 E2
Stella Cl TN12 259 D5
Stella Maris RC Prim Sch
CT19 335 C6
Stelling Minnis CE Prim
Sch CT4 240 F6
Stelling Rd DA8 14 D7
Stembrook Ct [4]
CT16 310 D7
Stembrook CT16 310 D8
Stempe Cl CT18 307 B3
Stenning Ct TN10 222 C4
Stephen Cl
Broadstairs CT10 84 A4
Orpington BR6 86 F7
Stephen Ct [2] CT20 335 D5
Stephen Rd DA7 14 C4
Stephens Cl ME13 138 B8
Stephen's Cl CT9 82 B7
Stephens Cl CT11 117 C8
Stephenson Ave RM18 19 A6
Stephenson Ho SE2 3 D1
Stephenson Rd CT2 142 F3
Stephen's Rd TN4 286 B6
Stepneyford La TN17 343 C7
Steps Hill Rd ME9 132 D6
Step Style ME10 102 B2
Sterling Ave ME16 161 C5
Sterling Cl CT10 83 E5
Sterling Ct [12] CT1 142 F1
Sterling Ho SE3 11 B3
Sterling Rd
Queenborough ME11 46 A5
Sittingbourne ME10 101 D1
Sterndale Rd DA1 33 F8
Sterry Gdns ME15 195 E7
Stevanne Ct [1] DA17 4 A1
Stevedale Rd DA16 13 C5
Steven Cl ME4 64 A3
Stevens Cl Dartford DA2 34 E3
Egerton TN27 232 F3
Joyden's Wood DA5 32 D4
Snodland ME6 128 A8
Stevens Cotts TN30 345 A7
Stevens Ho CT17 310 C8
Stevenson Cl Erith DA8 15 B7
Maidstone ME15 161 F3
Stevenson Way ME20 127 F4
Stevens Rd ME20 128 F6
Stewart Cl BR7 30 B4
Stewart Ho ME3 40 F6
Stewart Rd TN4 286 C7
Steyning Gr SE9 29 F4

Steynton Ave DA5 ... 31 D6
Stickens La ME19 ... 159 E7
Stickfast La
Sittingbourne ME9 ... 68 A1
Ulcombe ME17 ... 230 D3
Stickland Rd 2 DA17 ... 4 A2
Stilebridge La
Underling Green ME17 ... 228 A5
Underling Green TN12 ... 227 E3
Stiles Cl Bromley BR2 ... 52 F3
Erith DA8 ... 4 B1
Folkestone CT19 ... 335 A7
Minster (Sheppey) ME12 ... 47 A6
Still La TN4 ... 253 F2
Stillwater Mews ME4 ... 41 B2
Stirling Cl
Gillingham ME8 ... 98 E4
Rochester ME1 ... 63 A3
Sidcup DA14 ... 30 F4
Stirling Dr BR6 ... 87 B5
Stirling Ho 5 SE18 ... 2 B1
Stirling Rd ME19 ... 158 F3
Stirling Way CT12 ... 83 A2
Stirlng Rd TN24 ... 300 D7
Stisted Way TN27 ... 232 F3
Stockbury Dr ME16 ... 161 D7
Stockbury Gdns CT9 ... 51 E2
Stockbury Ho 7 BR5 ... 54 D1
Stockdale Gdns CT14 ... 215 C4
Stockenbury TN12 ... 224 F6
Stockers Brow ME9 ... 135 A7
Stocker's Hill ME13 ... 139 E4
Stockers Hill ME9 ... 135 A7
Stockett La ME15 ... 194 D6
Stockham Ct CT19 ... 334 E7
Stock Hill TN16 ... 118 D2
Stock La DA2 ... 33 C4
Stockland Green Rd
TN3 ... 285 B8
Stock La TN25 ... 302 A4
Stocks Green Prim Sch
TN11 ... 221 E5
Stocks Green Rd
TN11 ... 221 C5
Stocks Rd TN30 ... 359 F3
Stocks The ME13 ... 170 C6
Stockton Cl ME14 ... 162 B8
Stockwell Cl BR1 ... 52 B7
Stockwood Chase
CT2 ... 142 A2
Stoddart Rd CT19 ... 334 E6
Stodmarsh National Nature
Reserve* CT3 ... 145 D8
Stodmarsh Rd CT3 ... 144 C3
Stofield Gdns SE9 ... 29 D5
Stoke Com Sch ME3 ... 25 C5
Stoke Rd Allhallows ME3 ... 9 C1
Hoo St Werburgh ME3 ... 41 F6
Kingsnorth ME3 ... 42 C8
Lower Stoke ME3 ... 24 E1
Stokesay Ct 14 DA2 ... 16 B1
Stombers La CT18 ... 307 C6
Stonar Cl
Ramsgate CT11 ... 83 E1
Sandwich CT13 ... 149 A1
Stonar Gdns CT13 ... 149 A2
Stoneacre Cl ME8 ... 98 D5
Stoneacre Ct 7 ME15 ... 162 A1
Stoneacre La ME15 ... 196 B7
Stoneacre* ME15 ... 196 B7
Stone Barn Ave CT7 ... 81 A6
Stone Bay Sch CT10 ... 84 B6
Stonebridge TN25 ... 270 A5
Stonebridge Cotts
TN23 ... 300 B8
Stonebridge Green Rd
TN27 ... 233 A4
Stonebridge Rd DA11 ... 18 B2
Stonebridge Way
ME13 ... 138 B7
Stonechat Sq 6 E6 ... 1 E8
Stone Cnr TN30 ... 360 A6
Stone Cotts TN3 ... 316 F4
Stone Court La TN2 ... 287 E8
Stonecroft Rd DA8 ... 14 C7
Stonecroft DA13 ... 126 A8
Stonecrop Cl ME4 ... 41 C1
Stone Crossing Halt
DA9 ... 16 E2
Stonecross Lea ME5 ... 64 C1
Stone Cross Lees
CT13 ... 180 F7
Stone Cross Rd TN5 ... 337 A4
Stone Ct DA8 ... 4 F1
Stonedane Ct ME13 ... 138 C8
Stonefield Cl DA7 ... 14 A4
Stonefield Way SE7 ... 11 D7
Stonegate Cl BR5 ... 54 C6
Stonegate Rd TN5 ... 337 C1
Stonegate TN25 ... 237 E2
Stone Gdns CT10 ... 84 B5
Stone Gn TN30 ... 360 F4
Stonehall Rd CT15 ... 276 F8
Stoneheap Rd CT14,
CT15 ... 213 E1
Stone Hill Rd TN27 ... 232 F2
Stone Hill TN25 ... 303 A2
Stonehill Woods Pk
DA14 ... 32 B2
Stone Ho CT10 ... 84 B7
Stonehorse Ct ME3 ... 40 A3
Stonehorse La ME2 ... 40 A2
Stonehouse Cnr RM19 ... 16 E8
Stone House Hospl
DA2 ... 16 C1
Stonehouse La
Halstead TN14 ... 120 E8
Pratt's Bottom TN14 ... 87 E1
Purfleet RM19 ... 16 E8
Stone House Mews
CT10 ... 84 B7
Stonehouse Rd BR6,
TN14 ... 87 D1
Stoneings La TN14 ... 151 F8
Stone Lake Ind Pk SE7 ... 1 C2
Stone Lake Ret Pk SE7 ... 1 C2
Stoneleigh Rd RH8 ... 183 E5
Stone Lodge Farm Park*
DA2 ... 16 D1
Stoneness Rd RM20 ... 17 C7
Stone Pit La TN18 ... 356 E5
Stone Place Rd DA9 ... 16 E2
Stone Rd
Broadstairs CT10 ... 84 B5
Bromley BR2 ... 52 A5
Stone Row Cotts TN3 ... 284 D1
Stone Row TN3 ... 284 B5
Stone, St Mary's CE Prim
Sch DA9 ... 34 E8
Stones Cross Rd BR8 ... 55 C4
Stones Rdbt ME4 ... 41 B1
Stone St
Cranbrook TN17 ... 320 D5
Faversham ME13 ... 138 C7
Gravesend DA11 ... 19 B1
Stonestile Bsns Pk
TN27 ... 262 A7
Stonestile Farm Rd
TN27 ... 201 A3
Stone Stile La CT4 ... 171 D1
Stonestile Rd TN27 ... 262 A7
Stone St CT21 ... 332 A4
Stone Street Rd TN15 ... 155 E2
Stone St
Royal Tunbridge Wells
TN1 ... 286 B4
Stanford TN25 ... 304 C3
Stelling Minnis CT4 ... 240 D4
Westenhanger TN25,
CT21 ... 332 B6
Stoneswood Rd RH8 ... 183 B5
Stonewall E6 ... 2 A8
Stonewall Park Rd
TN3 ... 284 F3
Stoneway Pk CT4 ... 240 D7
Stone Wood DA2 ... 35 C5
Stonewood Cl TN4 ... 286 A8
Stonewood Rd DA8 ... 4 E1
Stoney Alley SE18 ... 12 A5
Stoney Bank ME7 ... 64 F1
Stoney Rd ME13 ... 140 B3
Stony Cnr DA13 ... 59 E6
Stonyfield TN8 ... 217 D3
Stony La ME1 ... 96 C5
Stonyway La CT15 ... 309 C5
Stopford Rd ME7 ... 64 D4
Storehouse Wharf
ME12 ... 27 F3
Store Rd E16 ... 2 A4
Storey St E16 ... 2 A4
Stornaway Strand
DA12 ... 37 F4
Stotfold BR1 ... 52 E8
Stour Cl Ashford TN23 ... 267 E1
Chartham CT4 ... 173 D2
Orpington BR2 ... 85 C6
Rochester ME2 ... 62 F7
Tonbridge TN10 ... 222 B5
Stour Cres CT1 ... 143 D3
Stour Ct
7 Canterbury CT1 ... 174 F8
22 Orpington BR5 ... 54 D1
8 Sandwich CT13 ... 148 F1
Stourfields TN24 ... 268 D4
Stourmouth Rd CT3 ... 146 C8
Stour Rd Chartham CT4 ... 173 D2
Crayford DA1 ... 15 A4
Stourside Studios 13
CT1 ... 142 F1
Stour St CT1 ... 174 F8
Stour Valley Cl CT3 ... 112 D3
Stour Valley Ind Est
CT4 ... 173 E4
Stourville 9 CT1 ... 174 F8
Stow Ct DA2 ... 34 C8
Stowell Cl TN23 ... 299 C8
Stowe Rd BR6 ... 87 B6
Stowting CE Prim Sch
TN25 ... 304 B8
Stowting Hill TN25 ... 272 A1
Stowting Rd BR6 ... 86 E6
Straight La TN29 ... 362 F1
Strait Rd E6 ... 1 F6
Strakers Hill CT15 ... 246 D8
Strand Approach Rd
ME7 ... 64 E7
Strand Cl DA13 ... 60 A3
Strand Ct SE18 ... 2 E1
Strandfield Cl SE18 ... 2 E1
Strand Rdbt The ME7 ... 64 E7
Strand St CT13 ... 148 F1
Strand The CT14 ... 215 D4
Stranger's Cl CT1 ... 174 C6
Stranger's La CT1 ... 174 C6
Strangford Pl CT6 ... 77 B2
Strangford Rd CT5 ... 74 F2
Strasbourg St CT9 ... 83 A6
Stratfield Ho SE12 ... 29 A6
Stratford Ave ME8 ... 98 D8
Stratford Dr ME15 ... 195 D6
Stratford House Ave
BR1 ... 52 E6
Stratford La 2 ME8 ... 98 F8
Stratford Rd ME19 ... 159 A8
Stratford St TN1 ... 286 C5
Strathaven Rd SE12 ... 11 B1
Stratheden Par SE3 ... 11 A7
Stratheden Rd SE3 ... 11 A7
Stratton Cl DA7 ... 13 E4
Stratton Rd DA7 ... 13 E4
Stratton Terr TN16 ... 184 C8
Strawberry Cl TN2 ... 313 E7
Strawberry Fields BR8 ... 55 E7
Strawberry Vale TN9 ... 222 C1
Straw Mill Hill ME15 ... 161 E1
Streamdale SE2 ... 13 B8
Stream La TN18 ... 355 A7
Stream Pit La TN18 ... 356 B5
Streamside Cl BR2 ... 52 A5
Streamside ME20 ... 128 B1
Stream Side TN10 ... 222 D6
Stream The ME20 ... 128 C1
Stream Way DA17 ... 14 A8
Stream Wlk CT5 ... 74 D2
Streatfield TN8 ... 217 D1
Streatfield Ho TN16 ... 151 C1
Streete Court Rd CT8 ... 81 F8
Streete Ct CT8 ... 81 F8
Street End CT3 ... 147 E1
Street End Rd ME5 ... 64 B1
Street Farm Cotts ME3 ... 41 F6
Streetfield CT6 ... 111 B8
Streetfield Mews SE3 ... 11 A4
Streetfield Rd ME8 ... 65 F1
Streetfield ME17 ... 230 F7
Street The Acol CT7 ... 81 B3
Adisham CT3 ... 210 C8
Appledore TN26 ... 361 D8
Ash CT3 ... 147 D1
Ashford,Great Chart
TN23 ... 267 C1
Ashford,Kennington
TN24 ... 268 E6
Ashford,Willesborough Lees
TN24 ... 301 B8
Ash TN15 ... 91 E5
Barham CT4 ... 209 F1
Benenden TN17 ... 342 D6
Bethersden TN26 ... 297 D5
Bishopsbourne CT4 ... 209 C6
Borden ME9 ... 101 B2
Bossingham CT4 ... 241 A7
Boughton Street ME13 ... 140 A3
Boxley ME14 ... 130 C3
Brabourne TN25 ... 303 C8
Bredgar ME9 ... 134 A5
Bredhurst ME7 ... 98 B1
Brook TN25 ... 270 B6
Chilham CT4 ... 205 B8
Cobham DA12 ... 60 F6
Deal CT14 ... 214 F6
Denton CT4 ... 243 B3
Detling ME14 ... 131 A1
Doddington ME9 ... 167 E7
East Langdon CT15 ... 247 A1
Eastling ME13 ... 168 E6
Egerton TN27 ... 232 F3
Eythorne CT15 ... 245 D7
Faversham ME13 ... 105 B2
Finglesham CT14 ... 214 B8
Frittenden TN17 ... 293 E7
Godmersham CT4 ... 205 B2
Goodnestone CT3 ... 178 D2
Guston CT15 ... 278 E6
Hamstreet TN26 ... 349 A7
Hartlip ME9 ... 99 D5
Hastingleigh TN25 ... 271 B6
Hawkinge CT18 ... 307 B5
High Halstow ME23 ... 23 E3
Horton Kirby DA4 ... 57 C5
Hothfield TN26 ... 267 A6
Ickham CT3 ... 145 C1
Ightham TN15 ... 156 D6
Iwade ME9 ... 68 E4
Kingston CT4 ... 209 D3
Lower Halstow ME9 ... 67 B3
Lympne CT21 ... 331 F2
Lynsted ME9 ... 136 A6
Maidstone ME14 ... 163 C4
Martin Mill CT15 ... 247 B3
Meopham DA13 ... 60 A1
Mereworth ME18 ... 191 D8
Mersham TN25 ... 301 E4
Molash CT4 ... 203 F4
Newnham ME9 ... 168 C8
Nonington CT15 ... 211 D1
Northbourne CT14 ... 214 A5
Patrixbourne CT4 ... 176 B3
Peene CT18 ... 334 A7
Petham CT4 ... 207 B3
Plaxtol TN15 ... 189 F7
Pluckley TN27 ... 265 D7
Postling CT21 ... 304 F2
Preston CT3 ... 146 C6
Ryarsh ME19 ... 126 F4
St Nicholas at Wade CT7 ... 79 F2
Selling ME13 ... 171 B6
Shadoxhurst TN26 ... 327 A8
Shorne DA12 ... 38 E3
Silver Street ME9 ... 133 F5
Sissinghurst TN17 ... 321 B8
Sittingbourne ME9 ... 102 E3
Smarden TN27 ... 264 A1
Staple CT3 ... 178 F6
Stockbury ME9 ... 132 E8
Stone in Oxney TN30 ... 361 A5
Stourmouth CT3 ... 113 E1
Teston ME18 ... 193 A7
Trottiscliffe ME19 ... 126 A5
Ulcombe ME17 ... 230 F7
Upchurch ME9 ... 66 F4
Upper Halling ME2 ... 94 E5
West Hougham CT15 ... 308 F5
Wickhambreaux CT3 ... 145 C2
Wittersham TN30 ... 359 D3
Womenswold CT4 ... 210 D2
Woodnesborough CT13 ... 180 C7
Wormshill ME9 ... 166 A7
Worth CT14 ... 181 B5
Strettitt Gdns TN12 ... 224 F5
Stretton Ct CT14 ... 215 D5
Strickland Ave DA1 ... 15 F4
Strickland Way 5 BR6 ... 86 F6
Stringer Dr CT7 ... 81 A6
Strode Cres ME12 ... 28 C2
Strode Park Rd CT6 ... 77 A2
Strond St CT17 ... 310 D6
Strongbow Cres SE9 ... 11 F2
Strongbow Rd SE9 ... 11 F2
Strood Ret Pk ME2 ... 63 B7
Strood Sta ME2 ... 63 C7
Strouts Rd TN23 ... 299 D7
Strover St ME7 ... 64 C7
Struttons Ave DA11 ... 36 F6
Stuart Ave BR2 ... 52 A1
Stuart Cl Hextable BR8 ... 33 A1
Maidstone ME14 ... 162 C6
Royal Tunbridge Wells
TN2 ... 313 F8
Stuart Ct
Canterbury CT1 ... 175 A6
Dover CT17 ... 310 C8
Stuart Evans Cl DA16 ... 13 C4
Stuart Ho CT14 ... 215 A5
Stuart Mantle Way DA8 ... 14 E7
Stuart Rd Bexley DA16 ... 13 B6
Folkestone CT19 ... 335 E6
Gillingham ME7 ... 64 D3
Gravesend DA11 ... 19 A1
Stubbs Hill BR6,TN14 ... 120 C6
Studds Cotts CT6 ... 76 A3
Studfall Cl CT21 ... 353 D8
Studio Cl TN24 ... 268 E6
Studios The DA3 ... 91 F8
Studland Cl DA15 ... 30 F5
Studley Cres DA3 ... 59 C7
Studley Ct DA14 ... 31 B3
Stumble Hill TN11 ... 189 C5
Stumble La TN23 ... 300 B1
Stuppington Court Farm
CT1 ... 174 E4
Stuppington La CT1 ... 174 F5
Sturdee Ave ME7 ... 64 E4
Sturdee Cotts ME3 ... 42 A6
Sturdy Cl CT21 ... 333 D2
Sturges Field BR7 ... 30 D2
Sturges Rd TN24 ... 268 B3
Sturla Rd ME4 ... 64 A3
Sturmer Cl CT1 ... 175 C7
Sturmer Ct ME19 ... 159 A2
Sturry CE Prim Sch
CT2 ... 144 A7
Sturry Court Mews
CT2 ... 143 F5
Sturry Hill CT2 ... 143 F6
Sturry Rd CT1,CT2 ... 143 C3
Sturry Sta CT2 ... 143 F5
Sturry Way ME8 ... 65 C2
Styants Bottom Rd
TN15 ... 155 F5
Style Cl ME8 ... 98 E4
Styles Cl TN8 ... 218 B5
Styles Cotts TN8 ... 218 B5
Styles Ct TN12 ... 256 F7
Styles La ME14 ... 130 C3
Subdown Cotts TN25 ... 303 C8
Sudbury Cres BR1 ... 29 A3
Sudbury E6 ... 2 A7
Sudbury Pl CT8 ... 81 E7
Suffolk Ave
Rainham ME8 ... 65 F1
Westgate-on-S CT8 ... 81 D7
Suffolk Ct 7 ME8 ... 65 F1
Suffolk Dr TN23 ... 268 A2
Suffolk Gdns CT17 ... 309 F7
Suffolk Mews 1 TN1 ... 286 A4
Suffolk Rd
Canterbury CT1 ... 175 D8
Dartford DA1 ... 15 E1
Gravesend DA12 ... 19 D1
Maidstone ME15 ... 195 D8
Sidcup DA14 ... 31 C2
Suffolk St CT5 ... 108 D8
Suffolk Way TN13 ... 154 C2
Sugarloaf Wlk CT19 ... 335 D8
Sullivan Ave E16 ... 1 D8
Sullivan Cl DA1 ... 33 C8
Sullivan Rd
Tilbury RM18 ... 19 A6
Tonbridge TN10 ... 222 E5
Sultan Mews ME5 ... 97 C2
Sultan Rd ME5 ... 97 C2
Summer Cl Hythe CT21 ... 332 F2
Tenterden TN30 ... 324 C1
Summer Ct
Canterbury CT2 ... 142 C1
Whitstable CT5 ... 75 C2
Summerfield Ave CT5 ... 74 F1
Summerfield
6 Bromley BR1 ... 52 B8
Marden TN17 ... 291 B6
Summerfield Rd CT9 ... 51 E2
Summerfield St 9
SE12 ... 29 A8
Summerhill TN23 ... 299 E6
Summerhill Ave TN4 ... 253 F1
Summer Hill
Canterbury CT2 ... 142 C1
Chislehurst BR7 ... 53 A7
Summerhill Cl BR6 ... 86 E7
Summerhill TN27 ... 262 A6
Summer Hill Pk TN24 ... 301 C7
Summerhill Rd
Bogden TN12 ... 228 C1
Dartford DA1 ... 33 D8
Summerhill Villas BR7 ... 53 B8
Summerhouse Dr DA2,
DA5 ... 32 D4
Summerlands Lodge
BR6 ... 86 A6
Summer La CT2 ... 142 E6
Summer Leeze TN24 ... 300 E8
Summer Leeze Gdns
TN24 ... 300 E8
Summer Rd CT7 ... 79 E1
Summerton Way SE28 ... 3 D7
Summervale Rd TN4 ... 285 E1
Summerville Ave ME12 ... 47 A5
Sumner Cl
Orpington BR6 ... 86 C6
Rolvenden TN17 ... 343 F3
Sumpter Way ME13 ... 137 F7
Sunbeam Ave CT6 ... 75 F4
Sunburst Cl TN12 ... 259 D5
Sunbury St SE18 ... 1 F3
Sun Ct DA8 ... 14 F5
Sunderland Cl ME1 ... 63 A3
Sunderland Dr ME8 ... 99 A8
Sunderland Ho 3 ME7 ... 64 C7
Sunderland Point E16 ... 2 C5
Sundew Ct 9 RM17 ... 18 D8
Sundew Gr CT11 ... 117 E8
Sundorne Rd SE7 ... 1 C1
Sundridge Ave
Bexley DA16 ... 12 D4
Bromley BR1 ... 52 D8
Sundridge & Brasted CE
Prim Sch TN14 ... 152 E2
Sundridge Cl
Canterbury CT2 ... 143 A4
Dartford DA1 ... 16 A1
Sundridge Ct 10 BR1 ... 29 B1
Sundridge Dr ME5 ... 97 A4
Sundridge Hill
Cuxton ME2 ... 62 C3
Halstead TN14 ... 120 C1
Sundridge Ho BR1 ... 29 B3
Sundridge La TN14 ... 120 C2
Sundridge Park Sta
BR1 ... 29 B1
Sundridge Rd TN14 ... 153 B8
Sunfields Pl SE3 ... 11 B7
Sunhill Ct TN2 ... 287 C6
Sun Hill DA3 ... 91 A8
Sun La Gravesend DA12 ... 37 C6
Greenwich SE3 ... 11 B7
Hythe CT21 ... 333 C2
Sunland Ave DA6 ... 13 E3
Sun La CT7 ... 79 F2
Sunningdale Ave 4
CT19 ... 335 A7
Sunningdale Cl
Erith SE28 ... 3 E7
Gillingham ME8 ... 98 D6
Sunningdale Ct ME15 ... 162 B4
Sunningdale Dr ME8 ... 98 D6
Sunningdale Rd BR1 ... 52 E4
Sunningdale Wlk CT6 ... 76 D1
Sunninghill DA11 ... 36 E6
Sunningvale Ave
TN16 ... 118 D3
Sunningvale Cl TN16 ... 118 D3
Sunny Bank CT15 ... 245 B8
Sunnybank TN5 ... 339 E3
Sunny Bank
Hythe CT21 ... 332 F2
Sittingbourne ME10 ... 102 B5
Sunny Cnr CT17 ... 310 B5
Sunnydale BR6 ... 86 A8
Sunnydale Rd SE12 ... 11 B2
Sunnyfield Rd BR7 ... 54 A6
Sunnyfields Cl ME8 ... 98 E8
Sunnyfields Dr ME12 ... 46 C6
Sunnyhill Rd CT6 ... 76 C4
Sunnymead Ave ME7 ... 64 E5
Sunnymead Camp
ME12 ... 48 E5
Sunnymead Cvn Pk
ME12 ... 48 F5
Sunnymead CT2 ... 142 D7
Sunnyside Ave ME12 ... 47 A6
Sunnyside Chalet Pk
ME12 ... 48 E5
Sunnyside Cl CT14 ... 214 D1
Sunnyside Cotts CT14 ... 215 C6
Sunnyside Cvn Pk
ME12 ... 48 E5
Sunnyside ME9 ... 167 E7
Sunnyside Gdns CT13 ... 180 E8
Sunnyside
Littlestone-on-Sea TN28 ... 373 D6
Lydd TN29 ... 376 B6
Marlpit Hill TN8 ... 217 B3
Sunnyside Rd
Folkestone CT20 ... 334 D3
Rusthall TN4 ... 285 C4
Sunray Ave Bromley BR2 ... 52 F3
Whitstable CT5 ... 108 B7
Sun Rd DA10 ... 17 F1
Sun Rise TN25 ... 267 F5
Sunset Cl
Eastchurch ME12 ... 48 F6
Erith DA8 ... 15 B7
Whitstable CT5 ... 108 C6
Sunset Rd SE28 ... 3 A5
Sunshine Ct 1 ME8 ... 98 F8
Sun St CT1 ... 174 F8
Sunstone Dr ME10 ... 101 C7
Sun Terr ME5 ... 97 B4
Sun Valley Way CT15 ... 245 C8
Superabbey Est ME20 ... 129 B2
Superior Dr 4 BR6 ... 86 F4
Surf Cres ME12 ... 48 F6
Surlingham Cl SE28 ... 3 D6
Surrenden Rd
Folkestone CT19 ... 334 F6
Staplehurst TN12 ... 260 E3
Surrey Cl
Ramsgate CT12 ... 83 B1
Royal Tunbridge Wells
TN2 ... 313 F8
Surrey Gdns CT7 ... 80 F7
Surrey Rd
Canterbury CT1 ... 175 D7
Maidstone ME15 ... 195 D8
Margate CT9 ... 51 B3
Surtees Cl TN24 ... 300 E6
Susan Rd SE3 ... 11 B5
Susan's Hill TN26 ... 325 E3
Susan Wood BR7 ... 53 A8
Sussex Ave
Ashford TN24 ... 268 B3
Canterbury CT1 ... 175 D7
Margate CT9 ... 50 J1
Sussex Cl Herne Bay CT6 ... 76 B4
Sussex Cl *continued*
Royal Tunbridge Wells
TN2 ... 286 C1
Sussex Dr ME5 ... 97 A4
Sussex Gdns
Birchington CT7 ... 80 F7
Herne Bay CT6 ... 76 B4
Westgate-on-S CT8 ... 50 D1
Sussex Mans CT8 ... 50 D1
Sussex Mews 19 TN2 ... 286 A2
Sussex Rd Dartford DA1 ... 34 A8
Erith DA8 ... 14 B7
5 Folkestone CT19 ... 335 D6
Maidstone ME15 ... 195 D8
New Romney TN28 ... 373 A6
Orpington BR5 ... 54 C3
Sidcup DA14 ... 31 B3
Tonbridge TN9 ... 254 A8
Sussex Road Prim Sch
TN9 ... 254 A8
Sussex St CT11 ... 117 E7
Sussex Wlk CT1 ... 175 D7
Sutcliffe Rd
Bexley DA16 ... 13 C5
Woolwich SE18 ... 12 E8
Sutherland Ave
Bexley DA16 ... 12 E3
Biggin Hill TN16 ... 118 E1
Orpington BR5 ... 53 F4
Sutherland Cl
Chalk DA12 ... 38 B6
Hythe CT21 ... 333 A2
Stone DA9 ... 16 F2
Sutherland Dr CT7 ... 81 B6
Sutherland Gdns ME8 ... 98 E6
Sutherland Ho
Hythe CT21 ... 333 C1
Woolwich SE18 ... 11 F6
Sutherland Rd
Deal CT14 ... 215 C6
Erith DA17 ... 4 A3
Royal Tunbridge Wells
TN1 ... 286 B3
Sutlej Rd SE7 ... 11 C7
Sutton at Hone CE Prim
Sch DA4 ... 34 A1
Sutton Baron Rd ME9 ... 134 A8
Sutton Cl
Folkestone CT19 ... 335 A7
Gillingham ME8 ... 99 A8
Sutton Cotts ME13 ... 171 C3
Sutton Ct TN12 ... 259 C5
Sutton Forge TN12 ... 259 D5
Sutton La CT14 ... 247 F5
Sutton Rd Hersden CT3 ... 111 E1
Langley ME17 ... 196 C5
Maidstone ME15 ... 195 D6
Ripple CT14 ... 247 C8
Sutton Row CT14 ... 215 B5
Suttons The TN31 ... 374 A1
Sutton St ME14 ... 163 D4
Sutton Valence Castle*
ME17 ... 229 F7
Sutton Valence Prep Sch
ME17 ... 229 C7
Sutton Valence Prim Sch
ME17 ... 229 E7
Sutton Valence Sch
ME17 ... 229 E7
Swadelands Cl ME17 ... 199 C5
Swadelands Sch
ME17 ... 199 C5
Swaffield Rd TN13 ... 154 C5
Swain Cl ME2 ... 62 F8
Swain Rd
Gillingham ME8 ... 98 B6
Tenterden TN30 ... 324 D3
Swaisland Rd DA1 ... 15 B1
Swaislands Dr DA1 ... 14 F2
Swakeley Wlk CT5 ... 75 D3
Swale Ave
Rushenden ME11 ... 45 F3
Sheerness ME12 ... 28 B1
Swale Cl CT6 ... 77 A3
Swalecliffe Ave CT6 ... 76 B4
Swalecliffe Com Prim Sch
CT5 ... 75 B2
Swalecliffe Court Dr
CT5 ... 75 D3
Swalecliffe Rd CT5 ... 75 B2
Swaledale Rd DA2 ... 34 C7
Swale Ho ME11 ... 45 F5
Swale Rd Crayford DA1 ... 15 A3
Rochester ME2 ... 62 C7
Swale Sta ME9 ... 69 A7
Swale View ME13 ... 140 B6
Swallow Ave CT5 ... 108 B6
Swallow Cl Bexley DA8 ... 14 E6
Margate CT9 ... 82 C8
Stone DA9 ... 16 F2
Swallow Ct Herne CT6 ... 110 F7
3 Lewisham SE12 ... 29 A8
Swallow Dr TN2 ... 286 F6
Swallowfield TN24 ... 300 E7
Swallowfield Rd SE7 ... 1 B1
Swallowfields 2 DA11 ... 36 E5
Swallow Ho
Dover CT17 ... 310 A6
4 Maidstone ME16 ... 161 E4
Swallow Rd ME20 ... 127 F2
Swallow Rise ME5 ... 97 A5
Swallows The CT13 ... 181 A8
Swallow St E6 ... 1 E8
Swallowtail Cl BR5 ... 54 D5
Swamp Rd TN29 ... 372 B4
Swan Apartments 12
ME15 ... 195 E5
Swan App E6 ... 1 E8
Swanbridge Rd DA7 ... 14 B6
Swan Bsns Pk DA1 ... 15 C3

Swan Cl Orpington BR5 54 A6
Sittingbourne ME10 102 B4
Swan Cotts TN30 359 D3
Swanfield Rd CT5 108 D8
Swan Gn TN25 303 D1
Swan La
Brandfold TN17 290 F3
Dartford DA1 32 F8
Marlpit Hill TN8 217 C4
Swanland Dr TN9 253 F7
Swan La TN25 303 E2
Swanley Ctr BR8 55 E6
Swanley La BR8 55 F6
Swanley New Barn Railway* BR8 55 E8
Swanley Rd DA16 13 C6
Swanley Sch BR8 55 E6
Swanley Sta BR8 55 D5
Swanley Village Rd BR8 56 B8
Swanmead Way TN9 222 D2
Swann Way CT18 307 A4
Swan Rd SE18 1 D3
Swan Ridge TN8 217 D4
Swanscombe Bsns Ctr DA10 17 E2
Swanscombe Ho 1 BR5 54 B7
Swanscombe Inf Sch DA10 35 F8
Swanscombe Sta DA10 17 F2
Swanscombe St DA10 17 F1
Swansea Ct E16 2 B4
Swanstree Ave ME10 102 B2
Swan St
West Malling ME19 159 C8
Wittersham TN30 359 C3
Swanton La
Littlebourne CT3 144 D2
Lydden CT15 276 C6
Swanton Mill* TN25 301 B2
Swanton Rd Erith DA8 14 B7
Mereworth ME18 191 A8
Swan Valley Com Sch DA10 35 F8
Swanzy Rd TN14 154 C7
Sward Rd BR5 54 A3
Swarling Hill Rd CT4 207 C7
Swattenden La TN17 320 B1
Swaylands Rd DA17 14 A8
Swaynesland Rd RH8 183 F1
Swaynes Way CT13 180 B2
Sweechbridge Rd CT6 77 F3
Sweechgate CT2 143 E7
Sweeps Hill Cl TN2 287 D7
Sweeps La BR5 54 D5
Sweet Bay Cres TN23 267 D3
Sweet Briar Ct ME16 161 D5
Sweetbriar La CT15 212 B2
Sweetings La TN3,TN5 316 D1
Sweetlands La TN12 261 A5
Sweetlove Pl CT3 178 A8
Sweets La ME19 160 A4
Swetenham Wlk SE18 2 C1
Sweyne Jun Sch The DA10 35 F8
Sweyne Rd DA10 17 E1
Sweyn Pl SE3 11 A5
Sweyn Rd CT9 51 A3
Swievelands Rd TN16 118 C1
Swift Cl Larkfield ME20 128 A2
Woolwich SE28 3 B6
Swift Cres ME5 97 C6
Swift Ho 6 ME16 161 E4
Swifts View TN17 320 D6
Swiller's La DA12 38 E3
Swinburne Ave CT10 84 A3
Swinburne Gdns RM18 19 B5
Swinford Gdns CT9 83 C8
Swinford Manor Sch TN23 267 B4
Swingate Ave ME3 22 B6
Swingate Cl ME5 97 B2
Swingate Inf Sch ME5 97 C1
Swingate La SE18 12 E7
Swingfield Ct BR2 52 D4
Swinton Ave ME3 40 F5
Swires Shaw BR2 85 D6
Swiss Way CT19 335 F7
Switch House Ave TN29 380 C2
Swithland Gdns SE9 30 A4
Syamore Mews DA8 4 D1
Sycamore Ave
Aylesham CT3 210 E5
Sidcup DA15 12 F1
Sycamore Cl
Broadstairs CT10 83 C4
Chartham CT4 173 F1
Dymchurch TN29 366 C8
Eltham SE9 29 E6
Gravesend DA12 37 D8
Herne Bay CT6 77 C5
Hythe CT21 332 E1
Lydd TN29 376 D7
Margate CT9 82 E7
Tilbury RM18 19 A5
Sycamore Cotts
Bidborough TN3 253 D3
Pembury TN2 287 C6
Sycamore Cres ME16 161 C5
Sycamore Ct Erith DA8 4 D1
Stone DA9 34 E8
Sycamore Dr
Aylesford ME20 128 E1
Deal CT14 215 B4
Swanley BR8 55 E7
Sycamore Gdns
Dymchurch TN29 366 C8
Paddock Wood TN12 256 F5
Sycamore Grange CT11 83 F1
Sycamore La TN23 267 E4
Sycamore Lodge BR6 86 F8
Sycamore Rd
Dartford DA1 33 D7
Rochester ME2 62 E5
Sycamores The CT3 144 E8
Sychem La TN12 256 A6
Sychem Pl TN12 256 A7
Sydcot Dr CT14 215 D8
Sydenham Cotts SE12 29 C6
Sydenham Rd CT14 215 D7
Sydenham St CT5 74 D2
Sydney Ave ME10 101 C4
Sydney Cooper Cl CT2 142 B2
Sydney Cotts 11 BR5 54 C6
Sydney Rd Bexley DA6 13 D3
Chatham ME4 64 A3
Deal CT14 215 A1
Erith SE2 3 D3
Ramsgate CT11 117 F8
Sidcup DA14 30 E4
Tilbury RM18 19 A5
Whitstable CT5 108 E8
Sydney St TN23 300 C8
Sydney Terr TN18 340 F3
Sylewood Cl ME1 96 B8
Sylvan Cl RH8 183 B6
Sylvan Glade ME5 130 A8
Sylvan Mews DA9 17 B3
Sylvan Rd ME8 98 C8
Sylvan Wlk BR1 52 F6
Sylvester Ave BR7 29 F2
Sylvester Cl ME2 95 A4
Sylvestres TN13 153 E6
Symmonds Dr ME10 102 A6
Symonds Cl TN15 90 E5
Symonds La ME18 225 F6
Symonds Rd ME3 22 A4
Symons Ave ME4 64 A2
Syndale Pl 5 CT11 117 F7
Syndale Valley Vineyard* ME9 168 C7
Syon Lodge 11 SE12 29 A8
Syringa Ct 10 RM17 18 D8

T

Tabor Ct TN12 290 A6
Tabret Cl TN24 268 D6
Tadburn Gn ME5 97 B4
Taddington Wood La ME5 96 E2
Taddy Gdns CT9 83 C8
Tadley Ct
Gillingham ME7 64 F6
Rochester ME1 96 C8
Tadworth Rd TN24 268 D5
Taillour Cl ME10 101 F7
Tail Race The ME15 161 E2
Tainter Rd TN11 190 E1
Talavera Rd CT1 175 D8
Talbot Ave CT6 76 B3
Talbot Pk TN2 286 D5
Talbot Rd
Maidstone ME16 161 C6
Margate CT9 51 B2
The Moor TN18 354 F8
Tallents Cl DA4 34 B1
Tallis Cl E16 1 B7
Tallis Gr SE7 11 B8
Tall Trees Cl ME17 197 D2
Tally Ho Rd TN26 299 C2
Tally Rd RH8 183 E4
Tamar Dr ME2 62 F7
Tamarind Cl ME7 98 A4
Tamarisk ME12 73 E5
Tamar Rd TN10 222 B5
Tamar St SE7 1 E2
Tame La CT21,TN29 351 F6
Tamesis Strand DA12 37 E3
Tamley La TN25 271 B6
Tams Gdns ME12 47 D6
Tandridge Dr BR6 53 D1
Tandridge Pl 2 BR6 53 D1
Tangier Cl CT15 278 E3
Tangier La TN3 314 B6
Tangleberry Cl BR1 52 F5
Tanglewood Cl ME8 98 C6
Tanglewood Ct BR5 54 C6
Tangmere Cl ME7 64 F5
Tanhouse La TN31 367 A2
Tanhurst Wlk SE2 3 D3
Tanker Hill ME8 98 D6
Tankerton Cir CT5 74 F3
Tankerton Ct CT5 75 B3
Tankerton Hts CT5 74 E3
Tankerton Mews CT5 74 E3
Tankerton Rd CT5 74 F3
Tanner's Hill Gdns CT21 333 C3
Tanner's Hill CT21 333 C3
Tanners Mead TN8 217 C1
Tanners St ME13 138 C7
Tannery Ct 5 ME10 101 E5
Tannery La
Ashford TN23 268 C2
11 Sandwich CT13 148 F1
Tannery Rd TN9 222 C1
Tansy Cl E6 2 A7
Tanyard Cotts DA12 38 E1
Tanyard Hill DA12 38 E2
Tanyard La TN4 253 F1
Tan Yard La DA5 32 A8
Tanyard
Rolvenden TN17 343 E4
Sandhurst TN18 356 B5
Tanyard The TN17 320 D4
Tapleys Hill CT4 208 B5
Taplin Ct 5 CT7 81 A7
Tappan Dr ME4 41 B2
Tapsell's La TN5 336 D5
Tarbutts TN17 320 D4
Target Bsns Ctr ME15 195 F4
Target Firs CT16 277 D5
Tariff Reform Cotts ME13 138 D5
Tarland Ho TN2 286 D3
Tarling Cl DA14 31 B5
Tarnwood Pk SE9 29 F7
Tarragon Rd ME16 161 B3
Tartane La TN29 366 C8
Taryes Ho 2 CT11 117 C6
Tasker Cl ME15 163 B3
Tasmania Ho RM18 19 A6
Tasman Wlk E16 1 D7
Tassell Cl ME19 128 A1
Tassell's Wlk CT5 75 D3
Taswell Cl CT16 310 E8
Taswell Rd ME8 66 A1
Taswell St CT16 310 E8
Tatchell Dr TN27 234 C7
Tate Rd E16 1 F5
Tates TN18 341 A1
Tates Orch DA3 58 F3
Tatler Cl ME5 97 D2
Tatsfield Cl ME8 65 A2
Tatsfield La
Biggin Hill TN16 150 F6
Hill Park TN16 151 A6
Tatsfield Prim Sch TN16 150 D6
Tattersall Cl SE9 11 E2
Tattershall Ct 22 DA2 16 B1
Tattershall Rd ME15 162 A1
Tattlebury La TN17 290 F1
Tattlebury Rd TN27 262 C8
Taunton Cl Bexley DA7 14 D5
Maidstone ME15 195 F6
Taunton Rd DA11 18 A2
Taunton Vale DA12 37 D5
Tavern Cl TN15 156 F7
Tavern Cotts TN15 155 A3
Taverners Rd ME8 98 E7
Tavistock Cl
Chatham ME5 96 F1
Gillingham ME8 98 E7
Sittingbourne ME10 101 D4
Tavistock Rd
Bexley DA16 13 C6
2 Bromley BR2 52 A5
Ramsgate CT11 83 E1
Tavy Bridge SE2 3 C4
Tawney Rd SE28 3 B6
Tay Cl ME5 97 B5
Tayfields TN12 261 C6
Taylers Yd TN25 237 E2
Taylor Cl
Harrietsham ME17 198 D6
4 Orpington BR6 86 F6
Taylor Ct 1 TN2 286 C7
Taylor Rd
Folkestone CT19 334 E6
Lydd-on-S TN29 377 E6
Minster (Thanet) CT12 115 B6
Snodland ME6 127 F8
Taylor Row DA2 33 C5
Taylor's Bldgs SE18 2 B2
Taylors Cl
St Mary's Bay TN29 365 F3
Sidcup DA14 30 F4
Taylors Hill CT4 205 B8
Taylor's La Higham ME3 39 B5
Rochester ME2 63 B7
Taylors La
St Mary's Bay TN29 365 F3
Vigo Village ME19 125 F6
Taylors Pl ME19 125 E5
Taylor St TN4 286 A8
Taymouth Ho 1 CT16 310 E8
Taywood Cl TN24 268 F1
Tea Garden La TN3 285 C2
Teakcroft Ctr RM13 4 D7
Teal Ave BR5 54 D5
Teal Cl Grain ME3 27 B5
Hawkinge CT18 306 F3
Newham E16 1 D8
Teal Dr CT6 76 E2
Teal Way ME9 68 E3
Teapot La ME20 128 E1
Teardrop Ctr BR8 56 C4
Teasaucer Hill ME15 194 F8
Teasel Cl ME14 162 F4
Teasel Cres SE28 2 E5
Teasel Rd ME5 96 F4
Teasels TN27 295 A1
Teasley Mead TN3 283 C4
Tebbs Way TN15 156 C3
Teddars Leas Rd CT18 305 E4
Tedder Ave ME5 97 A7
Tedder Rd TN4 286 B7
Teddington Cl CT1 143 B2
Teelin Cl TN29 366 A4
Teesdale Rd DA2 34 C7
Teeswater Ct DA18 3 D3
Teign Mews SE9 29 E6
Teignmouth Rd DA16 13 C5
Teise Cl TN2 286 D2
Telegraph Hill ME3 39 C3
Telegraph Hill Ind Pk CT12 115 D7
Telegraph Rd CT14 215 B3
Telemann Sq SE3 11 B4
Telescope Alley ME12 28 D2
Telford Ct
Folkestone CT19 335 E6
Herne Bay CT6 76 C2
Telford Ho 2 Erith DA17 4 A3
1 Maidstone ME14 162 A6
Telford Rd SE9 30 D6
Telford St CT6 76 E5
Telham Ave CT12 117 B8
Tellson Ave SE18 11 E6
Telscombe Cl BR6 86 E8
Telston La TN14 121 F2
Temeraire Hts CT20 334 C3
Temeraire Manor 2 ME7 64 A6
Tempest Rd ME19 158 F3
Templar Ct
8 Canterbury CT2 142 F1
11 Dover CT17 278 C1
Templar Dr Erith SE28 3 D7
Gravesend DA11 37 A3
Templar Rd CT16 277 D5
Templars Ct 11 TN8 217 D3
Templar St CT17 310 C8
Temple Cl
Ashford TN23 299 F5
Temple Ewell CT16 277 D6
Woolwich SE28 2 C3
Temple Ct CT2 142 D1
Temple Ewell CE Prim Sch CT16 277 D5
Temple Gdns
Rochester ME2 63 A6
Sittingbourne ME10 102 B3
Temple Hill Com Prim Sch DA1 16 A2
Temple Hill DA1 15 F2
Temple Hill Sq DA1 15 F2
Templeman Liby CT2 142 E4
Temple Manor* ME2 63 A6
Temple Mews 10 CT1 174 F8
Temple Mill Prim Sch ME2 40 B1
Templemore DA14 31 B3
Temple Rd
Biggin Hill TN16 118 D2
Canterbury CT2 142 D1
Temple Sch ME2 40 B2
Temple Side CT16 277 D6
Temple Way
West Malling ME19 127 F1
Worth CT14 181 A4
Ten Acre Way ME8 66 B1
Tenby Rd DA16 13 D6
Tenchley's La
Limpsfield RH8 183 D4
The Chart RH8 183 E2
Tenney Ho RM17 18 B7
Tennyson Ave
Canterbury CT1 143 D3
Cliffe Woods ME3 40 B7
Tennyson Cl DA16 12 F6
Tennyson Gdns CT3 210 F6
Tennyson Ho
Canterbury CT1 143 D3
2 Erith DA17 3 F1
Tennyson Pl
Canterbury CT1 143 D3
Folkestone CT19 335 E7
Tennyson Rd
Ashford TN23 300 A6
Dartford DA1 16 A2
Gillingham ME7 64 C3
Tennyson Wlk
Northfleet DA11 36 D5
Tilbury RM18 19 B5
Ten Perch Rd CT1 174 D6
Tensing Ave DA11 36 E5
Tenterden CE Jun Sch TN30 345 B7
Tenterden Cl SE9 29 F4
Tenterden & District Mus* TN30 345 A7
Tenterden Dr CT2 143 A4
Tenterden Inf Sch TN30 345 B7
Tenterden Rd
Appledore Heath TN26 347 B1
Biddenden TN27 323 B7
Chatham ME5 97 B5
Fosten Green TN27 322 F4
Rolvenden TN17 344 A5
Tenterden Station Est TN30 345 A8
Tenterden Town Sta* TN30 345 A8
Tenterden Vineyard* TN30 345 C1
Tenterden Way CT9 51 C1
Tent Peg La BR5 53 C4
Tenzing Ct SE9 29 E6
Terance Butler Ave ME2 63 E8
Terence Cl
Chatham ME4 64 A2
Gravesend DA12 37 F6
Terence Ct 6 DA17 13 F8
Terlingham La CT18 307 A2
Terminus Dr CT6 77 D5
Terminus Rd ME16 161 A2
Terminus Wlk 3 CT20 335 E5
Tern Cres ME2 62 C6
Terrace Apartments The CT21 333 C1
Terrace Cotts CT4 241 A6
Terrace Rd
Elvington CT15 212 B1
Maidstone ME16 161 E3
Sittingbourne ME10 102 B3
Terrace St DA12 19 B1
Terraces The DA2 34 C8
Terrace The
Canterbury CT2 142 F3
Faversham ME13 138 A7
25 Gravesend DA12 19 B1
Pluckley TN26 234 A1
Rochester ME1 63 C5
Sevenoaks TN13 153 D5
Shepherdswell CT15 244 D5
Terry's La CT5 74 D2
Terry's Lodge Rd TN15 124 C6
Terry Wlk ME19 127 E2
Testers Cl RH8 183 B3
Teston Ho ME18 193 A7
Teston La ME15,ME18 193 C7
Teston Rd
Kings Hill ME19 159 B5
Offham ME19 158 C7
Red Hill ME18 159 E2
West Malling ME19 159 A6
Tetty Way BR1,BR2 52 A7
Teviot Cl DA16 13 B6
Tewson Rd SE18 2 E1
Teynham Cl CT9 51 F2
Teynham Dr CT5 74 F2
Teynham Gn
Gillingham ME8 65 A4
Hayes BR2 52 A4
Teynham Ho SE9 12 D1
Teynham Parochial CE Prim Sch ME9 103 C2
Teynham Rd
Dartford DA2 34 C8
Whitstable CT5 74 F2
Teynham Sta ME9 103 D3
Teynham St ME9 103 F4
Thackeray Ave RM18 19 B6
Thackeray Rd ME20 127 F3
Thames Ave
Gillingham ME8 98 E8
High Halstow ME23 23 E4
Sheerness ME12 28 B1
Thamesbank Pl SE28 3 C7
Thames Barrier Visitor Ctr* SE18 1 D3
Thames Ct ME12 49 G2
Thames Gate DA1 16 A3
Thamesgate Sh Ctr 20 DA11 19 B1
Thameside Ind Est E16 1 D4
Thameside Inf & Jun Schs RM17 18 C8
Thamesmead Sh Ctr SE28 3 A6
Thamesmere Dr SE28 3 A6
Thames Rd
Crayford DA1 15 A4
Grays RM17 18 B7
Newham E16 1 D5
Tonbridge TN10 222 C5
Thames Road Ind Est E16 1 D4
Thames Terr ME3 22 B6
Thames View ME3 40 C7
Thames View Cotts ME3 39 D3
Thames View Inf Sch ME8 65 D2
Thames View Jun Sch ME8 65 D2
Thamesview Sch DA12 37 F5
Thamesview DA9 17 C2
Thames Way
Gravesend DA11 19 A1
Northfleet DA11 36 E7
Thanet Cl CT10 84 B5
Thanet Coll
Broadstairs CT10 84 A3
Margate CT9 50 I2
Thanet Dr BR2 85 D7
Thanet Ent Ctr CT10 83 D7
Thanet Gdns CT19 335 F6
Thanet Ho
7 Maidstone ME15 195 F5
7 Northfleet DA11 36 F7
Thanet Place Gdns CT10 84 B6
Thanet Rd
Broadstairs CT10 84 B4
Erith DA8 14 E7
Margate CT9 50 J2
Ramsgate CT11 117 F7
Sidcup DA5 32 A8
Westgate-on-S CT8 81 D8
Thanet Reach Bsns Pk CT10 83 C4
Thanet Terr TN26 267 A6
Thanet View
Eythorne CT15 245 B8
St Nicholas at Wade CT7 79 F2
Thanet Way
Boughton Street ME13 139 D6
Herne Bay CT6 77 C3
Whitstable CT5 75 C2
Yorkletts CT5,ME13 107 E2
Thanington Ct Farm CT1 174 C6
Thanington Ct SE9 12 E1
Thanington Rd CT1 174 C6
Thatch Barn Rd TN27 262 D6
Thatcher Ct DA1 33 D8
Thatcher Rd TN12 260 E4
Thatchers La ME3 22 B5
Thatchers The ME16 161 B5
Thaxted Rd SE9 30 C6
Theaker Ho DA4 57 D7
Theatre Sq 7 TN30 345 A7
Theatre St CT21 333 C2
Thelma Cl DA12 37 F3
Thelma Gdns SE3 11 E6
Theobalds Cl TN15 123 A1
Theobalds TN18 340 F2
Theodore Cl TN2 286 E7
Theodore Pl ME7 64 C5
Theresa Rd CT21 333 B1
Thicketts TN13 154 C4
Third Ave Chatham ME5 64 C1
Eastchurch ME12 48 F6
Gillingham ME7 64 F4
Margate CT9 51 B3
West Thurrock RM20 17 A8
Third St TN3 284 F3
Thirlemere Cl ME16 161 D8
Thirlmere TN24 268 D6
Thirlmere Ave CT11 117 A7
Thirlmere Cl
Gillingham ME7 65 A5
Rochester ME2 40 C1
Thirlmere Gdns CT3 210 F6
Thirlmere Rd
Bexley DA7 14 C6
Royal Tunbridge Wells TN4 285 E5
Thirsk Ho 6 ME15 195 F6
Thirza Rd DA1 15 F1
Thistlebank ME5 97 A3
Thistlebrook Ind Est SE2 3 C4
Thistlebrook SE2 3 C4
Thistle Ct DA1 34 B7
Thistledown Cl ME7 98 A4
Thistledown
Gravesend DA12 37 D2
Maidstone ME14 162 F4
Thistle Dr CT5 108 B6
Thistlefield Cl DA5 31 D7
Thistle Hill Way
Minster (Sheppey) ME12 47 A4
Minster (Sheppey) ME12 47 C5
Thistlemead BR7 53 B7
Thistle Rd DA12 37 E8
Thistle Wlk ME10 102 B5
Thomas Aveling Sch The ME1 96 C8
Thomas Cotts DA13 36 B1
Thomas Cribb Mews E6 2 A7
Thomas Ct 9 ME10 102 B4
Thomas Dinwiddy Rd SE12 29 B6
Thomas Dr DA12 37 D6
Thomas Dunk Almshouses 13 TN18 341 A2
Thomas Rd
Faversham ME13 138 D7
Sittingbourne ME10 102 B4
Thomas Seth Bsns Pk ME11 46 A3
Thomas Shearley Ct DA5 32 B8
Thomas St
Rochester ME1 63 C3
Royal Tunbridge Wells TN4 286 A5
Woolwich SE18 2 B2
Thomas Tallis Sch SE3 11 B4
Thomas Wyatt Way TN15 124 F3
Thompson Cl
Deal CT14 248 B8
Folkestone CT19 335 B7
Gillingham ME8 99 A8
Thomson Cl ME6 95 A1
Thomson Rd TN25 268 B5
Thong La Basted TN15 156 F5
Gravesend DA12 38 A2
Thornbridge Rd CT14 215 B2
Thorn Cl Bromley BR2 53 A3
Chatham ME5 96 D1
Thorndale BR7 29 F1
Thorndale Cl ME5 96 D4
Thornden Cl CT6 76 B2
Thornden Ct
Canterbury CT2 142 C4
Rolvenden Layne TN17 358 A8
Thornden La
Rolvenden Layne TN17 358 A8
Rolvenden TN17 344 A1
Thornden Wood Rd
Herne Bay CT6 76 B1
Whitstable CT6 109 E4
Thorndike Cl ME4 96 F8
Thorndike Ho ME4 96 F8
Thorndike Rd TN29 352 C4
Thorndon Cl BR5 53 F7
Thorndon Rd BR5 53 F7
Thorndyke Way TN15 124 F3
Thorne Cl Erith DA8 14 B8
Newham E16 1 A7
Thorne Hill CT12 116 A6
Thorne Rd CT12 115 B6
Thorn Est The TN27 265 B6
Thornet Wood Rd BR1 53 A6
Thorney Croft Cl ME17 197 D2
Thorneycroft Rd ME13 201 D5
Thornfield Gdns TN2 286 F5
Thorn Gdns CT11 83 E1
Thornham Rd ME8 65 C3
Thornhill Ave SE18 12 E7
Thornhill Pl ME14 162 A6
Thorn Hill Rd ME12 49 D4
Thornhurst CT6 77 D4
Thorn La CT4 240 C2
Thornlea TN23 267 E2
Thorn Rd TN12 259 E4
Thorn's Mdw TN16 152 C4
Thornton Cl TN24 269 A1
Thornton Dene DA14 31 A3
Thornton La CT13, CT14 212 E7
Thornton Rd
Bromley BR1 29 A3
Erith DA17 4 B2
Thornton's La 9 CT16 310 E7
Thorntree Prim Sch SE7 1 D1
Thorntree Rd SE7 1 D1
Thorn Wlk ME10 102 C5
Thorold Rd ME5 64 B3
Thorpe Ave TN10 222 C5
Thorpe Cl BR6 86 E8
Thorpe Wlk ME8 98 D3
Thrale Way ME8 98 E4
Thread La ME13 140 B4
Three Acres Site CT19 335 B8
Three Corners DA7 14 B5

Three Elm La TN11 ..... 223 D5
Three Gates Rd DA3 ......58 A2
Three King's Yd CT13 ... 149 A1
Three Leg Cross Rd
TN5 .... 338 D3
Three Oaks La TN5 ..... 336 D7
Thresher Field TN8 .... 251 A6
Threshers Dr ME14 ..... 162 E5
Thrift The DA2 ....35 C5
Throckmorten Rd E16 ..... 1 B7
Throwley Cl SE2 ....3 C3
Throwley Dr CT6 ....76 C4
Throwley Rd ME13 ..... 169 D5
Thrupp Paddock CT10 ... 51 G1
Thrush Cl ME5 ....97 B7
Thruxted La CT4 .... 173 B1
Thunderer Rd RM9 ....3 F8
Thundersland Rd CT6 .....77 B4
Thurlow Ave CT6 ....77 C5
Thurnham CE Inf Sch
ME14 .... 163 A4
Thurnham Ho 5 BR5 .... 54 D1
Thurnham La ME14 ..... 163 C7
Thurrock Bsns Ctr
RM20 ....16 F8
Thurrock Ent Ctr RM18 ...18 A8
Thurrock Park Way
RM17 .... 18 D7
Thursland Rd DA14 ....31 E3
Thursley Rd SE9 ....29 F5
Thurston Dr ME2 .... 62 D7
Thurstone Ct ME14 ..... 161 F6
Thurston Pk CT5 ....74 E1
Thwaite Cl DA8 ....14 C8
Thyer Cl BR6 ....86 C6
Thyme Cl SE3 ....11 C4
Thyme Wlk ME16 .... 161 B3
Tibbs Court La TN12 .... 289 A6
Tiber Cl CT19 .... 334 C6
Ticehurst Cl BR5 ....31 A1
Tichborne Cl ME16 ..... 161 C6
Tickford Cl SE2 ....3 C4
Tickham La ME9 .... 136 C5
Tickner's La TN29 ...... 363 B1
Tidal Basin Rd E16 ....1 A6
Tidebrook Ct 4 BR5 .....54 C5
Tidelock Ho SE28 ....2 D4
Tideside Ct SE18 ....1 E3
Tideway The ME1 ....96 C8
Tidford Rd DA16 ....12 F5
Tiger La BR2 ....52 B5
Tilbrook Rd SE3 .... 11 D4
Tilbury Cl BR5 ....54 B7
Tilbury Fort* RM18 ......19 C3
Tilbury Manor Inf Sch
RM18 ....19 B7
Tilbury Manor Jun Sch
RM18 ....19 B7
Tilbury PRU RM18 ....18 F6
Tilbury Rd ME8 ....66 A2
Tilbury Town Sta RM18 ...18 F5
Tilden Cl TN26 .... 324 D7
Tilden Ct TN26 .... 324 E7
Tilden Gill Rd TN30 .... 345 C7
Tilden La TN12 .... 227 C3
Tilden Rd ME17,TN27 .... 230 E2
Tilebarn Cnr TN10 ..... 222 E4
Tile Farm Rd BR6 .... 86 D7
Tile Fields ME17 .... 164 D2
Tile Ho The CT21 .... 333 C2
Tilehurst Point 2 SE2 .....3 C4
Tile Kiln Hill CT2 ..... 142 B5
Tile Kiln La
Coldblow DA5 ....32 C6
Dartford DA2,DA5 ....32 F5
Folkestone CT19 .... 334 F7
Tile Kiln Rd TN24 ...... 268 C7
Tile Lodge Cotts TN27 .. 233 E8
Tile Lodge Rd TN27 ..... 233 E8
Tilghman Way ME6 ....95 B1
Tillard Cl CT4 .... 207 B3
Till Ave DA4 ....56 F2
Tillery La TN29 .... 371 A8
Tilley Cl ME3 .... 41 D5
Tillingbourne Gn BR5 ....54 A5
Tillmans TN15 .... 157 A7
Tilmans Mead DA4 ....57 A2
Tilsden La TN17 .... 320 E3
Tilton Rd TN15 .... 156 F7
Tilt Yard App SE9 ....11 F1
Timberbank ME5 ....97 A6
Timber Bank DA13 ...... 125 F8
Timber Cl BR7 ....53 A7
Timbercroft La SE18 .....12 E7
Timbercroft Prim Sch
SE18 ....12 E7
Timber Ct RM17 ....18 A8
Timbertop Rd TN16 ..... 118 C1
Timber Tops ME5 .... 130 D8
Timeball Tower Mus*
CT14 .... 215 D5
Timothy Cl DA6 ....13 E3
Timothy Ho DA18 ....3 E4
Timperley Cl CT14 ..... 215 B6
Tina Gdns CT10 ....84 A6
Tinbridge Pk ME13 ..... 139 A5
Tinker Pot La TN15 .... 123 D6
Tinkerpot Rise TN15 ... 123 C5
Tinker's Alley ME4 ....63 F7
Tinkers La TN5 .... 338 E3
Tintagel Gdns ME2 ....62 F7
Tintagel Manor 6 ME7 ...64 C6
Tintagel Rd BR5 ....54 C1
Tintern Rd ME16 .... 161 D7
Tippens Cl TN17 .... 320 D4
Titan Rd RM17 ....18 B8
Titchfield Cl 5 ME15 ... 195 F6
Titchfield Rd ME15 ..... 195 F6
Tithe Barn La TN23 ..... 299 D8
Tithe Yd ME17 .... 199 D5
Titmuss Ave SE28 ....3 B6
Titsey Cnr RH8 .... 183 B7
Titsey Hill CR6,RH8 .... 150 B4
Titsey Place* RH8 ..... 150 B3
Titsey Rd
Limpsfield RH8 .... 183 B8
Titsey RH8 .... 150 B1
Tiverton Dr SE9 ....30 C7
Tivoli Brooks CT9 ....50 I1
Tivoli Gdns
Gravesend DA12 ....37 B7
Woolwich SE18 ....1 E2
Tivoli Park Ave CT9 .... 50 H1
Tivoli Rd CT9 ....82 E8
Tobruk Way ME5 ....96 F6
Toby Gdns TN11 .... 223 E8
Toby Rd TN29 .... 377 E6
Tockwith Ct TN13 ...... 154 D4
Todd Cres ME10 .... 102 A8
Toddington Cres ME5 ... 96 D1
Toke Cl TN23 .... 267 C1
Toke Pl ME17 .... 227 E8
Tolcairn Ct 2 DA17 ....4 A1
Tolgate La ME2 ....63 B7
Tolgate Way ME14 ...... 129 E4
Tolhurst Rd TN12 ...... 256 A7
Tollemache Cl CT12 ....81 F2
Tollgate Cl CT5 .... 108 C8
Toll Gate CT14 .... 215 A4
Tollgate Mews TN15 .... 157 A8
Tollgate Pl TN27 .... 262 E5
Tollgate Rd
Dartford DA2 .... 34 D8
Newham E6 ....1 E8
Toll La TN27 .... 234 E7
Tolputt Ct CT19 .... 335 E6
Tolsey Mead TN15 ...... 157 A8
Tolsford Cl
Etchinghill CT18 ...... 305 D3
Folkestone CT19 .... 334 D6
Tomar Owl Sanctuary*
TN25 .... 300 F2
Tomay Cotts CT6 ....78 A3
Tom Coombs Cl SE9 ......11 E3
Tom Cribb Rd SE28 ....2 D3
Tom Jenkinson Rd E16 .....1 A5
Tom Joyce Cl ME6 ...... 127 F7
Tomlin Cl
Snodland ME6 .... 128 A8
Staplehurst TN12 ...... 260 E4
Tomlin Dr CT9 ....83 C8
Tonbridge By-Pass
Tonbridge,Stocks Green
TN11,TN9,TN4,TN14,
TN15 .... 221 B5
Tonbridge TN4,TN9,
TN11 .... 254 C6
Tonbridge Castle*
TN9 .... 222 B2
Tonbridge Chambers 10
TN9 .... 254 B8
Tonbridge Cottage Hospl
TN11 .... 254 C6
Tonbridge Ct ME16 ..... 161 D3
Tonbridge Gram Sch for
Girls TN9 .... 254 C7
Tonbridge Ho ME2 ....40 C1
Tonbridge Rd
Hadlow TN11 .... 223 C7
Ightham TN15 .... 156 C3
Little Mill TN11,TN12 .... 224 D4
Maidstone,East Barming
ME16 .... 160 E1
Maidstone,Upper Fant
ME16 .... 161 C3
Pembury TN2 .... 287 A7
Sevenoaks TN13,TN15 ... 187 D7
Tonbridge TN11 .... 221 E5
Wateringbury ME18 ..... 192 C8
Tonbridge Sch TN10 .... 222 C3
Tonbridge Sta TN9 ..... 222 B1
Tonford La
Canterbury CT1 .... 174 B6
Harbledown CT2 .... 174 A7
Tonge Rd ME10 .... 102 C4
Tong La TN12 .... 289 B2
Tong Rd TN12,TN3 ...... 289 A4
Tongswood Dr TN18 .... 341 C1
Tontine St CT20 .... 335 E5
Tony Law Ho SE12 ....11 A2
Tookey Rd TN28 .... 373 B6
Tooley St DA11 .... 36 D8
Topaz Dr ME10 .... 101 C6
Topcliffe Dr BR6 .... 86 D6
Top Dartford Rd BR8,
DA2 ....33 A2
Topley Dr ME23 ....23 E3
Topley St SE9 .... 11 D3
Top Rd TN30 .... 360 E3
Torbay Rd TN12 .... 225 B5
Torbrook Cl DA5 ....13 E1
Tor Gr SE28 ....2 E5
Tormore Mews CT14 ... 215 A4
Tormore Pk CT14 .... 215 A4
Tormount Rd SE18 ....12 E8
Toronto Cl 6 CT16 ..... 278 B3
Toronto Rd
Gillingham ME7 ....64 E4
Tilbury RM18 ....19 A5
Tor Rd DA16 ....13 C6
Torrens Wlk DA12 ....37 E3
Torrington Cl ME18 .... 191 D8
Torrington Cotts
CT12 .... 115 D7
Torrington Rd TN23 .... 300 C8
Torver Way BR6 .... 86 D7
Tothill St CT12 .... 115 C7
Totnes Rd DA16 ....13 C7
Tourmaline Dr ME10 ... 101 C6
Tournay Cl TN23 .... 299 F8
Tourney Cl CT21 .... 331 F3
Tourney Rd TN29 .... 376 C5
Tourtel Rd CT1 .... 143 A1
Tovil Gn ME15 .... 161 E2
Tovil Green Bsns Pk
ME15 .... 161 E1
Tovil Hill ME15 .... 161 E2
Tovil Rd ME15 .... 161 F2
Tovil, St Stephen's CE Inf
Sch ME15 .... 161 E2
Tower Bglws CT7 ....81 A8
Tower Cl
Gravesend DA12 ....37 E3
Orpington BR6 ....86 F7
Tower Croft DA4 ....89 E8
Tower Ct 4 CT20 .... 334 E3
Tower Est TN29 .... 352 E2
Towerfields BR2 ....85 E6
Tower Gdns
Hythe CT21 .... 333 C1
Maidstone ME14 .... 163 B4
Tower Hamlets Rd
CT17 .... 310 C8
Tower Hamlets St 1
CT17 .... 310 C8
Tower Hill Dover CT17 ... 310 C8
Offham ME19 .... 158 D7
Whitstable CT5 ....74 E3
Tower Ind Est TN15 .... 124 D5
Tower La ME14 .... 163 B4
Tower Park Rd DA1 ......14 F2
Tower Par CT5 ....74 E3
Tower Rd Bexley DA7 .....14 A3
Dartford DA1 ....15 C1
Erith DA17 ....4 C2
Orpington BR6 ....86 F7
Whitstable CT5 ....74 E2
Tower Ret Pk DA1 ....14 F2
Towers Point ME1 ....63 B4
Towers Sch The TN24 ... 268 D8
Tower St CT17 .... 310 C8
Towers The TN27 ...... 201 E1
Towers View TN24 ..... 268 C7
Towers Wood DA4 .... 57 D8
Tower View
Chartham CT4 .... 173 F1
Kings Hill ME19 .... 159 B3
Tower Way 1 CT1 ...... 174 F8
Tom Acres TN10 .... 222 C4
Towncourt Cres BR5 ..... 53 D5
Towncourt La BR5 .... 53 D2
Townfield Cnr DA12 ..... 37 D7
Towngate Wood Pk Mobile
Home Pk TN10 .... 222 E7
Town Hill CT4 .... 175 F2
Town Hill Cl ME19 ..... 127 C1
Town Hill
Lamberhurst TN3 ...... 317 A4
West Malling ME19 ..... 127 C1
Town La CT4 .... 173 C6
Townland Cl TN27 ...... 295 A2
Townlands Rd TN5 ..... 336 F4
Townley Gram Sch for Girls
DA6 ....13 F2
Townley Rd DA6 ....13 F2
Townley St CT11 .... 117 D6
Town Lock Ho 4 TN9 .. 222 C2
Town Mdw TN17 .... 320 D4
Town Pier Sq 5 DA11 ....19 B1
Town Rd
Cliffe Woods ME3 ....40 A6
Petham CT4 .... 207 C5
Townsend Farm Rd
CT15 .... 279 F6
Townsend Rd ME6 ...... 127 F8
Townsend Sq ME19 ..... 159 A2
Townsend Terr CT17 ... 310 B5
Townshend Cl DA14 ......31 C2
Townshend Ho 14 SE18 ....1 F2
Townshend Rd BR7 ......30 B3
Town Sq DA8 ....14 E8
Town Square Cres DA9 ...34 F8
Town Station Cotts
TN8 .... 217 D1
Townwall St CT16 ...... 310 E7
Town Wlk CT20 .... 335 D4
Toy Mus* CT5 ....74 E3
Toynbec Cl BR7 ....30 B4
Toy's Hill TN16,TN8 .... 185 C3
Tracies The ME9 .... 100 C6
Trader Rd E6 ....2 B7
Tradescant Dr DA13 ......60 B3
Tradewinds CT5 .... 108 B6
Trafalgar Par ME12 ......47 B6
Trafalgar Rd
Dartford DA1 ....33 E6
Gravesend DA11 ....37 A8
Westgate-on-S CT7 ....81 F3
Wouldham ME1 ....95 C5
Trafalgar St ME7 ....64 C5
Tram Rd The CT20 ..... 335 E5
Tramways ME5 ....64 C2
Tranquil Rise DA8 ....4 E1
Transfesa Rd TN12 ..... 257 A7
Transformer Ave
TN29 .... 380 C2
Transmere Cl BR5 ....53 C3
Transmere Rd BR5 ....53 C3
Transom Ho 3 ME1 ......63 C1
Trapfield Cl ME14 ..... 163 C4
Trapfield La ME14 ..... 163 C4
Trapham Rd ME16 ...... 161 D5
Trasa Ct 10 RM17 ....18 C8
Travers Gdns ME9 ..... 133 F5
Travers Rd CT14 .... 215 A5
Travertine Rd ME5 ....97 B1
Treasury View CT3 .... 177 C8
Trebble Rd DA10 ....17 E1
Trebilco Cl TN2 .... 286 D7
Tredegar Rd DA2 ....33 A5
Tredwell Cl BR1 ....52 E5
Treebourne Rd TN16 ... 118 C1
Tree La TN15 .... 189 E8
Tree Rd E16 ....1 C7
Treetops Cl SE2 ....3 E1
Treetops
Gravesend DA12 ....37 B4
Kemsing TN15 .... 123 A2
Tonbridge TN9 .... 254 B7
Treewall Gdns BR1 ......29 B4
Trefoil Ho Erith DA18 .....3 E4
Grays RM17 ....18 B7
Trefoil The ME9,ME13 ... 136 E6
Trefor Jones Ct CT16 ... 278 B2
Tregony Rd BR6 ....86 F6
Trelawn Cres ME5 ....97 B2
Trellyn Cl ME16 .... 160 F2
Trench Rd TN10 .... 222 C6
Trenear Cl BR6 ....87 A6
Trenley Dr CT3 .... 143 F1
Trentham Dr BR5 ....54 A5
Trenton Cl ME16 ...... 161 B7
Trent Rd ME5 ....97 B5
Trevale Rd ME1 ....63 B1
Trevelyan Cl DA1 ....15 F3
Trevereux Hill RH8 .... 183 F4
Trevino Dr ME5 ....96 F2
Trevithick Dr DA1 ....15 F3
Trevor Cl BR2 ....52 A2
Trevor Dr ME16 .... 161 C5
Trewin Cl ME20 .... 128 D2
Trewsbury Ho 2 SE2 .....3 D4
Triangle Ct E16 ....1 C8
Triangle The DA15 ....31 A8
Tribune Ct ME12 ....46 B8
Tribune Dr ME10 ...... 101 F6
Tricorn Ho SE28 ....2 D5
Trident Cl ME2 ....63 E7
Triggs Cotts ME9 ..... 103 D2
Trigg's Row ME9 ...... 103 D2
Trilby Way CT5 .... 108 B6
Trimworth Rd CT19 .... 334 F6
Trinity Cl Orpington BR2 ...52 E1
Royal Tunbridge Wells
TN2 .... 286 D4
Trinity Cres CT20 ..... 335 B4
Trinity Ct
Aylesford ME20 .... 129 A3
Dartford DA1 ....34 B7
Deal CT14 .... 215 A4
Eltham SE9 ....12 B1
Margate CT9 ....50 J3
Trinity Gdns
Dartford DA1 .... 15 D1
Folkestone CT20 ...... 335 C4
Trinity Hill CT9 ....50 J3
Trinity Homes CT14 ... 215 C1
Trinity Mews SE9 .... 12 D1
Trinity Pl Bexley DA6 ....13 F3
Deal CT14 .... 215 A4
Ramsgate CT11 .... 117 F7
Trinity Rd
Ashford TN24 .... 268 B7
Folkestone CT20 ...... 335 B4
Gillingham ME7 ....64 C6
Gravesend DA12 ....37 C8
Sheerness ME12 ....28 C2
Sittingbourne ME10 .... 101 F7
Trinity Sch, Belvedere
DA17 ....4 C2
Trinity Sch ME1 .... 63 D4
Trinity Sq
Broadstairs CT10 ....83 F7
Margate CT9 ....50 J3
Trinity St 12 E16 ....1 A8
Trinity Trad Est ME10 ... 101 F6
Tristan Gdns TN4 ..... 285 D4
Triton Lodge 9 DA8 ....4 E1
Tritton Cl TN24 .... 268 F7
Tritton Fields TN24 ... 268 F7
Tritton Gdns TN29 .... 352 D1
Tritton La TN28 .... 373 B6
Triumph Rd E6 ....1 F7
Trivett Cl DA9 ....17 A2
Trolling Down Hill DA2 ...34 C6
Troodos Hill ME14 .... 161 F8
Troon Cl SE28 ....3 D7
Trosley Ave DA11 ....37 B6
Trosley Ctry Pk*
ME19,DA13 .... 126 A7
Trosley Ctry Pk Visitor
Ctr* DA13 .... 125 E7
Trosley Rd DA17 ....14 A8
Trottiscliffe CE Prim Sch
ME19 .... 126 A5
Trottiscliffe Rd ME19 ... 126 D3
Trotts Hall Gdns ME10 .. 101 D3
Trotts La TN16 .... 184 C8
Trotwood Cl ME5 ...... 130 A8
Trotwood Pl 14 CT10 ....84 B4
Troubridge Cl TN24 ... 301 B7
Troughton Mews CT9 .... 50 H1
Troughton Rd SE7 ....1 B1
Troutbeck Ho ME20 ... 128 C1
Trove Ct 7 CT11 ...... 117 F7
Troy Ct 6 SE18 ....2 B2
Troy La TN8 .... 216 F4
Troy Mews ME1 ....63 C4
Troys Mead ME17 ..... 164 D2
Troy Town La TN25 ... 270 B5
Trubridge Rd ME3 ....41 E5
Trueman Cl CT2 ...... 142 A7
Trumpet Ho TN23 ..... 300 B8
Truro Cl ME8 .... 65 D3
Truro Rd
Gravesend DA12 .... 37 D5
Ramsgate CT11 .... 117 F7
Truro Wlk TN10 .... 222 D5
Trusedale Rd E6 ....1 F7
Trycewell La TN15 ... 156 D6
Tuam Rd SE18 .... 12 D8
Tubbenden Cl BR6 ....86 E7
Tubbenden Dr BR6 ..... 86 D6
Tubbenden Inf & Jun Sch
BR6 .... 86 D6
Tubbenden La BR6 ....86 E7
Tubbenden La S BR6 .... 86 D5
Tubs Hill Par TN13 ... 154 A3
Tubs Hill TN13 .... 154 B3
Tudeley La
Tonbridge TN9 .... 254 D7
Tudeley La *continued*
Tonbridge, Tudeley
TN11,TN9 .... 255 B8
Tudor Ave
Dymchurch TN29 ...... 352 D1
Maidstone ME14 ...... 162 B6
Tudor Byway TN24 .... 268 D6
Tudor Cl Birchington CT7 ...81 B8
Bromley BR7 ....52 F8
Dartford DA1 ....15 B1
Northfleet DA11 ....36 E7
Tudor Cres TN14 ...... 122 D3
Tudor Ct
Biggin Hill TN16 ...... 118 E2
Canterbury CT2 .... 142 C4
Crockenhill BR8 ....55 C2
Royal Tunbridge Wells
TN2 .... 285 E1
Sidcup DA14 ....31 A5
Whitstable CT5 ....75 A3
Tudor Dr TN14 .... 122 C3
Tudor End TN24 ...... 268 D5
Tudor Farm Cl TN23 ... 300 A3
Tudor Gr
Chattenden ME3 ....40 F4
Gillingham ME8 ....98 F8
Tudor Ho Deal CT14 .... 215 A5
Tudor Ho* CT9 ....50 J3
Tudor Mews CT14 ..... 215 B4
Tudor Par SE9 ....11 E3
Tudor Rd Ashford TN24 .. 268 D5
Canterbury CT1 .... 174 E7
Folkestone CT19 ..... 334 D6
Tudor Way BR5 .... 53 D3
Tudor Wlk DA5 ....13 E1
Tudway Rd SE3 ....11 C3
Tufa Cl ME5 ....97 B1
Tuffs Cotts ME3 ....25 C3
Tufnail Rd DA1 ....15 F1
Tufton Rd
Ashford TN24 .... 268 D2
Hothfield TN26 .... 267 A7
Rainham ME8 ....65 F1
Tufton St Ashford TN23 .. 268 B2
Maidstone ME14 ...... 162 A4
Tufton Wlk 9 TN23 .... 268 B2
Tugboat St SE28 ....2 E4
Tugmutton Cl BR6 ....86 B6
Tulip Cl 5 E6 ....1 F8
Tulip Tree Cl TN9 ..... 254 B8
Tumblefield Est TN15 .. 124 F8
Tumblefield Rd TN15 .. 124 E7
Tumblers Hill ME17 ... 229 F7
Tunbridge Way TN23 ... 299 C8
Tunbridge Wells Girls'
Gram Sch TN4 .... 286 A6
Tunbridge Wells Gram Sch
for Boys TN4 .... 286 A7
Tunbridge Wells High Sch
TN2 .... 286 F5
Tunbridge Wells Ind Hospl
The TN3 .... 284 B3
Tunbridge Wells Mus &
Gall* TN1 .... 286 B4
Tunbridge Wells Sta
TN1 .... 286 A3
Tunbridge Wells Trad Pk
TN2 .... 286 D8
Tunbridge Wells West
Sta* TN2 .... 285 F1
Tunbury Ave ME5 ....96 F1
Tunbury Ave S ME5 .....96 F1
Tunbury Prim Sch ME5 ...96 F1
Tunis Ct CT1 .... 143 D1
Tunis Row CT10 ....84 B5
Tunnan Leys E6 ....2 A7
Tunnel Ave 1 SE10 ....1 A1
Tunnel Cotts RM20 ......17 A8
Tunnel Est RM20 ....16 F8
Tunnel Rd TN1 .... 286 B4
Tunstall CE Prim Sch
ME9 .... 134 C8
Tunstall Cl BR6 ....86 E6
Tunstall Rd
Canterbury CT2 ...... 143 A4
Sittingbourne ME10,
ME9 .... 134 D8
Tunstock Way DA17 ......3 E3
Tupman Cl ME1 ....63 B4
Tuppy St SE28 ....2 C3
Turbine Hall Ave
TN29 .... 380 C2
Turgis Cl ME17 .... 196 E4
Turketel Rd CT20 ..... 335 A4
Turks Hall Pl ME2 ......94 E5
Turley Cotts TN3 ..... 285 A8
Turmine Ct ME12 ....47 A5
Turnagain La 3 CT1 ... 174 F8
Turnberry Way BR6 .... 53 D1
Turnbull Cl DA9 ....34 E8
Turnbury Cl SE28 ....3 D7
Turnden Gdns CT9 ....51 E2
Turnden Rd TN17 ..... 320 A3
Turner Ave TN17 ...... 320 D3
Turner Cl Ashford TN24 .. 300 E7
Biggin Hill TN16 ..... 118 C7
Sittingbourne ME10 ... 102 A7
Turner Ct Dartford DA1 ....15 C2
5 Folkestone CT20 .... 334 F5
Margate CT9 ....51 A2
Turner Ho
Gravesend DA12 ....37 C6
5 Greenwich SE7 ....11 B8
Turner Rd Bean DA2 .....35 B5
Tonbridge TN10 ...... 222 E5
Turners Ave TN30 .... 345 B8
Turners Cl ME12 ....28 C1
Turners Gdns TN13 ... 187 C7
Turners Green La TN5 .. 336 F6
Turners Green Rd
TN5 .... 336 F6
Turner's Oak DA3 ....91 E7
Turners Pl DA4 ....57 C8
Turner St Cliffe ME3 ....22 B5
Ramsgate CT11 .... 117 E7
Turnpike Cl CT21 ..... 333 A2
Turnpike Ct DA6 .... 13 D3
Turnpike Dr BR6 .... 87 D2
Turnpike Hill CT21 .... 333 A3
Turnpike La RM18 .... 19 D8
Turnstone Cl ME9 ....68 E4
Turnstone Ct TN29 .... 365 F3
Turnstone DA3 ....59 A7
Turnstone Rd ME5 ......97 C1
Turnstones The DA12 ... 37 D6
Turpington Cl BR2 ......52 E2
Turpington La BR2 .....52 E3
Turpin La DA8 ....15 A8
Turrets The Deal CT14 ... 215 C1
9 Sittingbourne ME10 ... 102 A4
Turton Ho 5 SE18 ....12 B8
Tuscan Dr ME5 ....97 C1
Tuscan Rd SE18 ....2 D1
Tutsham Way TN12 .... 256 F6
Tuxford Rd TN4 .... 285 B5
Tweed Rd TN10 .... 222 C5
Tweed Terr CT21 ..... 333 A1
Tweedy Rd BR1 ....52 A8
Twelve Acres TN24 .... 300 F8
Twigg Cl DA8 ....14 E7
Twin Tumps Way SE28 .....3 A6
Twisden Rd ME19 ..... 159 F8
Twiss Ave CT21 ...... 333 D2
Twiss Gr CT21 .... 333 D2
Twiss Ho 6 SE18 ....2 B1
Twiss Rd CT21 .... 333 D2
Twistleton Ct DA1 ..... 15 D1
Twitton La TN14 ..... 121 E3
Twitton Mdws TN14 .... 121 E3
Two Gates Hill ME3 .....39 F5
Twydall Ent Ctr ME8 ....65 C4
Twydall Gn ME8 ....65 B3
Twydall Inf Sch ME8 ....65 B2
Twydall Jun Sch ME8 ....65 B2
Twydall La ME8 ....65 B2
Twyford Cl ME8 ....66 A2
Twyford Ct ME14 ..... 162 D6
Twyford Rd TN11 ..... 190 E1
Twymans Mill ME13 ... 138 C7
Twyne Cl CT2 .... 144 A6
Twysden Cotts TN18 ... 356 A4
Twysden Ct TN25 ..... 237 E2
Tydeman Rd ME15 .... 162 F2
Tydeman's Ave CT5 .....75 C1
Tye La BR6 ....86 C5
Tyeshurst Cl SE2 ....3 E1
Tyland Barn Wildlife
Conservation Ctr*
ME14 .... 129 E3
Tyland La ME14 ...... 129 F3
Tyler Cl Canterbury CT2 .. 142 F3
East Malling ME19 .... 159 F8
Erith DA8 ....14 B7
Tyler Dr ME8 ....98 E4
Tyler Gr DA1 ....15 F3
Tyler Hill Rd CT2 .... 142 C6
Tylers Green Rd BR8 .....55 C2
Tyler Way CT5 ....75 E3
Tylney Rd BR1 .... 52 D7
Tyndale Pk CT6 ....77 B5
Tyndall Rd DA16 ....12 F4
Tyne Cl ME5 ....97 C5
Tynedale Cl DA2 .... 34 D7
Tynemouth Cl E6 ....2 B7
Tynemouth Rd SE18 ......2 E1
Tyne Rd TN10 .... 222 B5
Typhoon Rd ME19 ..... 158 F3
Tyron Way DA14 ....30 F3
Tyrrell Ave DA16 ....13 B2
Tyrrells Hall Cl 5
RM17 .... 18 D8
Tyrwhitt-Drake Mus of
Carriages* ME15 ..... 162 A3
Tysoe Ct ME12 ....47 A5
Tyson Ave CT9 ....50 E1
Tyson Rd CT19 .... 335 E7

U

Uckfield La TN8 .... 250 D4
Udall Cotts DA15 ....30 E5
Uden Rd TN29 .... 353 B4
Uffington Ct CT3 ..... 178 A2
Ufton Cl ME15 .... 162 E1
Ufton La ME10 .... 101 E3
Ulcombe CE Prim Sch
ME17 .... 230 F6
Ulcombe Gdns CT2 .... 143 A3
Ulcombe Hill ME17 ... 197 F1
Ulcombe Rd
Headcorn TN27 .... 262 C6
Langley Heath ME17 .. 196 E3
Ulley Rd TN24 .... 268 D7
Ullswater Gdns CT3 ... 210 F6
Ullswater Ho 5 ME15 .. 195 E7
Ulster Rd CT9 ....82 F8
Undercliffe Rd CT14 ... 248 D5
Undercliff CT20 ...... 334 E3
Underdown Ave ME4 .....63 F1
Underdown La CT6 ......76 F2
Underdown Rd
Dover CT17 .... 310 B7
Herne Bay CT6 ....76 F5
Underhill Cotts CT18 ... 334 B8
Underhill Rd CT20 .... 334 B5
Underlyn Ind Est
TN12 .... 227 F2
Underlyn La TN12 .... 227 D1
Underriver House Rd
TN15 .... 188 D5
Underwood Cl
Ashford TN24 .... 268 D6

Underwood Cl *continued*
Canterbury CT4 175 B5
Maidstone ME15 161 F2
Underwood Ct CT1 175 B6
Underwood
Hawkinge CT18 307 C6
Offham ME19 158 D7
Underwood The SE9 29 F6
Unicorn Cotts CT4 176 B5
Unicorn Wlk DA9 16 F2
Unicumes La ME16 161 C2
Union Cres CT9 50 J2
Union Pk ME15 195 F4
Union Pl
4 Canterbury CT1 143 A1
Chatham ME4 64 A4
Union Rd Bridge CT4 175 F1
Bromley BR2 52 D4
Deal CT14 215 D6
Minster (Sheppey) ME12 47 C7
Ramsgate CT11 117 F8
Union Row CT9 50 J2
Union Sq
3 Broadstairs CT10 84 B4
22 Royal Tunbridge Wells TN2 286 A2
Union St
Canterbury CT1 143 A1
Chatham ME4 64 A3
Dover CT17 310 D6
Faversham ME13 138 C7
Flimwell TN5 339 B3
Maidstone ME14 162 A5
12 Ramsgate CT11 117 E7
Rochester ME1 63 C5
Sheerness ME12 28 A2
Unity Pl 3 CT11 117 F7
Unity St Sheerness ME12 28 D2
Sittingbourne ME10 101 E3
Unity Way SE18 1 D3
University Gdns DA5 31 F8
University Pl DA8 14 C7
University Rd CT2 142 D3
University Way
Dartford DA1 15 E4
Woolwich E16 2 B6
Univ of East London E16 2 A6
Univ of Greenwich Avery Hill Campus (Mansion Site) SE9 12 C1
Univ of Greenwich Avery Hill Campus (Southwood Site) SE9 12 D1
Univ of Greenwich Avery Hill Campus Southwood Site SE9 30 D8
Univ of Greenwich ME4 64 B8
Univ of Kent at Canterbury CT2 142 D4
Unwin Cl ME20 129 A3
Upbury Arts Coll ME7 64 B4
Upbury Way ME4 64 A4
Upchat Rd ME2,ME3 40 F3
Upchurch Wlk CT9 51 E2
Updale Rd DA14 30 F4
Updown Way CT4 173 F1
Uphill CT18 307 B4
Upland Prim Sch DA7 13 F4
Upland Rd DA7 13 F4
Uplands CT2 142 F4
Uplands Cl
Rochester ME2 62 D6
Sevenoaks TN13 153 F4
Uplands Com Tech Coll TN5 337 A4
Uplands Rd BR6 54 B1
Uplands Way
Halfway Houses ME12 46 C5
Sevenoaks TN13 153 F4
Uplands SE18 2 B1
Uplees Cotts ME13 104 F5
Uplees Rd ME13 105 A3
Upnor Castle* ME2 40 F2
Upnor Ho ME15 195 E8
Upnor Rd ME2 40 E2
Upper Abbey Rd DA17 4 A2
Upper Approach Rd CT10 84 A3
Upper Austin Lodge Farm Cotts DA4 89 E3
Upper Austin Lodge Rd DA4 89 D4
Upper Ave DA13 59 E8
Upper Barn Hill ME15 193 E3
Upper Brents ME13 138 D8
Upper Bridge St
Canterbury CT1 175 A8
Wye TN25 237 F2
Upper Britton Pl ME7 64 B5
Upper Bush Rd ME2 61 F2
Upper Chantry La CT1 175 A7
Upper Church Hill DA9 16 E2
Upper Corniche CT20 334 C3
Upper Cumberland Wlk TN1 286 B1
Upper Dane Ct CT9 51 B1
Upper Dane Rd CT9 51 B1
Upper Denmark Rd TN23 300 B8
Upper Dr TN16 118 C1
Upper Dumpton Park Rd CT11 117 E8
Upper Dunstan Rd TN4 286 B6
Upper East Rd ME4 64 B8
Upper Fans La ME9 68 C4
Upper Fant Rd ME16 161 D2
Upper Field Rd ME10 102 B5
Upper Free Down CT6 77 B2
Upper Gore La CT13 180 A2
Upper Green La TN11 189 D5
Upper Green Rd TN11 189 D5
Upper Gr CT9 50 J2
Upper Grosvenor Rd TN1,TN4 286 B6
Upper Grove Rd DA17 13 F8
Upper Haysden La TN11,TN9 253 E6
Upper Holly Hill Rd DA17 4 B1
Upper Hunton Hill ME15 194 A3
Upper Luton Rd ME5 64 C2
Upper Malthouse Hill CT21 333 B2
Upper Maltings Pl CT7 80 F7
Upper Mill ME18 192 D8
Upper Nellington TN3 285 B4
Upper Park Rd
Bromley BR1 52 C8
Erith DA17 4 B2
Upper Platts TN5 338 F1
Upper Profit TN3 285 A3
Upper Queens Rd TN24 268 B3
Upper Rd
Dover CT15,CT16 279 C2
Dover,Eastern Docks CT16 310 G8
Maidstone ME15 162 B2
Upper Ruxley Cotts DA14 32 A1
Upper St Ann's Rd ME13 138 B6
Upper Sheridan Rd DA17 4 A2
Upper Spring La TN15 156 B5
Upper Stephens TN3 285 A3
Upper St
Hollingbourne ME17 164 E3
Kingsdown CT14 248 D5
Leeds ME17 196 F5
Upper Stone St ME15 162 A3
Upper Strand St CT13 149 A1
Upper Street N DA3 91 F8
Upper Street S DA3 91 F8
Upper St Rusthall TN4 285 D4
Tilmanstone CT14 213 A3
Upper Tickham Cotts ME9 136 D6
Upperton Rd DA14 30 F3
Upper Vicarage Rd TN24 268 D7
Upper Wickham La DA16 13 B6
Upstreet CT18 305 D3
Upton Cl Bexley DA5 13 F1
Folkestone CT19 335 A7
Upton Day Hospl DA6 13 E3
Upton Jun Sch CT10 83 F4
Upton Prim Sch DA6 13 F2
Upton Quarry TN3 284 F3
Upton Rd
Bexley DA5,DA6 13 E2
Broadstairs CT10 83 F5
Upton Rd S DA5 13 F1
Upton Rd SE18 12 C8
Uptons TN27 262 C6
Upton Villas 4 DA6 13 E3
Upwood Rd SE12 11 A1
Uridge Cres TN10 222 C4
Uridge Rd TN10 222 C4
Urquhart Cl ME5 97 A5
Ursula Lodges DA14 31 B3
Ursuline Dr CT8 81 D7
Usborne Cl TN12 260 E3

V

Vaizeys Wharf SE7 1 B3
Vale Ave
Royal Tunbridge Wells,Mount Sion TN1 286 A3
Royal Tunbridge Wells,Southborough TN4 253 F1
Valebrook Cl CT20 334 C5
Vale Cl BR6 86 A6
Vale Cotts ME9 133 A8
Vale Ct
10 Ramsgate CT11 117 D6
Royal Tunbridge Wells TN4 254 A2
Vale Dr ME5 96 E6
Valence Ho ME15 195 C7
Valence Rd DA8 14 D7
Valence Sch TN16 151 F1
Valence View TN17 293 E7
Valenciennes Ho ME4 64 A4
Valenciennes Rd ME10 101 E3
Valentine Ave DA5 31 E7
Valentine Cl ME7 65 A1
Valentine Dr ME23 23 E4
Valentine Rd ME15 195 E7
Vale Pl CT11 117 D6
Vale Rd Broadstairs CT10 83 F4
Bromley BR1 53 A7
Dartford DA1 33 B7
Hawkhurst TN18 340 F3
Maidstone ME15 194 E4
Northfleet DA11 36 E7
Ramsgate CT11 117 D6
Ripple CT14,CT15 247 B8
Royal Tunbridge Wells,Mount Sion TN1 286 A3
Royal Tunbridge Wells,Southborough TN4 253 F1
Tonbridge TN9 222 C1
Vale Rd *continued*
Whitstable CT5 108 D8
Valerian Cl ME5 96 E4
Vale Rise TN9 254 E8
Vale Sq CT11 117 D6
Valestone Cl CT21 334 B4
Vale The CT10 84 A4
Valetta Way ME1 63 B4
Vale View Com Sch CT17 310 B7
Vale View Rd
Aylesham CT3 210 E5
Dover CT17 310 B7
Valiant Ho 5 SE7 1 C1
Valiant Rd ME5 97 C2
Valiant Way E6 1 F8
Valkyrie Ave CT5 108 C7
Vallance The ME9 136 A6
Valley (Charlton Athletic FC) The SE7 1 C1
Valley Cl DA1 14 F1
Valley Cotts
Alkham CT15 276 C1
Stalisfield Green ME13 201 D8
Valley Dr
Gravesend,Riverview Park DA12 37 D4
Gravesend,Singlewell DA12 37 E1
Maidstone ME15 194 F6
Sevenoaks TN13 154 B1
Valley Forge Cl TN10 222 F4
Valley Gdns DA9 17 B1
Valley Gr SE7 1 C1
Valley Hts DA1 15 F3
Valley Industries TN11 223 B7
Valley La DA13 93 B2
Valley L Ctr SE9 30 C8
Valley Mushroom Farm TN16 118 D1
Valley Park Com Sch ME14 162 C4
Valley Rd Barham CT4 209 E2
Canterbury CT1 174 E6
Crabble CT17 277 E3
Crayford DA1 14 F1
Erith DA8 4 D2
Fawkham Green DA3 58 C2
Folkestone CT20 334 E4
Gillingham ME7 64 E4
Margate CT9 82 E4
Orpington BR5 54 B8
Rusthall TN4 285 D4
Valley Rise ME5 96 F1
Valleyside SE7 1 D1
Valley The ME17 194 D3
Valley View
Biggin Hill TN16 118 D1
Eythorne CT15 245 C8
Valley View Rd ME1 63 B1
Valley View
Royal Tunbridge Wells TN4 254 A2
Swanscombe DA9 17 B1
Valley View Terr DA4 56 F1
Valley Wlk CT21 334 B3
Valliers Wood Rd DA15 30 E7
Vambery Rd SE18 12 C8
Vanbrugh Cl 2 E16 1 D8
Vanbrugh Pk SE3 11 A7
Vanburgh Cl BR6 53 E1
Vancouver Cl BR6 87 A6
Vancouver Dr ME8 65 C1
Vancouver Rd CT16 278 C3
Vandome Cl E16 1 B7
Vandyke Cross SE9 11 E2
Vanessa Cl DA17 4 A1
Vanessa Way DA5 32 D5
Vanessa Wlk DA12 37 F3
Vange Cottage Mews ME1 63 B4
Vanguard Cl E16 1 A8
Vanguard Way ME2 63 E8
Vanity Holiday Village ME12 49 G2
Vanity La ME17 194 D1
Vanity Rd ME12 49 F2
Vanoc Gdns BR1 29 A4
Vanquisher Wlk DA12 37 F5
Varley Rd E16 1 B7
Varne Ct 6 CT20 334 F3
Varne Lodge 5 CT20 334 F3
Varne Mews TN28 373 E4
Varne Pl CT19 335 F5
Varne Rd CT19 335 F5
Varnes St ME20 128 F6
Vaughan Ave TN10 222 E6
Vaughan Dr ME10 101 F8
Vaughan Rd DA16 12 F5
Vauxhall Ave
Canterbury CT1 143 C3
Herne Bay CT6 76 A3
Vauxhall Cl DA11 36 F8
Vauxhall Cres
Canterbury CT1 143 C3
Snodland ME6 128 A6
Vauxhall Gdns TN9 254 C7
Vauxhall Industrial Rd CT1 143 D4
Vauxhall La
Bidborough TN11,TN4 254 B4
Tonbridge TN11 254 D6
Vauxhall Pl DA1 33 E8
Vauxhall Rd CT1,CT2 143 C4
Vectis Dr ME10 101 F8
Veitchil Barn BR8 55 F8
Veles Rd ME6 127 F8
Venmead Ct 4 DA17 4 A2
Venners Cl DA7 14 E5
Ventnor Cl ME5 97 C8
Ventnor La 12 CT9 50 J2
Venture Cl
Dymchurch TN29 352 D1
Sidcup DA5 31 E8
Venture Ct SE12 29 A8
Venus Rd SE18 1 F3
Verdun Rd SE18,SE2 13 A8
Vere Rd CT10 84 A4
Vereth Rd 2 CT11 117 D6
Verity Farm Holiday Camp ME12 49 F1
Vermont Rd TN4 285 C4
Vernham Rd SE18 12 C8
Vernon Cl Orpington BR5 54 B6
West Kingsdown TN15 90 F2
Vernon Pl
Canterbury CT1 175 A7
Deal CT14 215 D8
Vernon Rd
Royal Tunbridge Wells TN1 286 C6
Swanscombe DA10 17 F1
Veroan Rd DA7 13 E5
Verona Gdns DA12 37 E4
Verona Ho DA8 14 F7
Vert Ho RM17 18 C7
Verwood Cl CT2 142 E2
Veryan Cl BR5 54 C5
Vespasian Way TN23 299 F4
Vesper Ct TN27 264 A1
Vestey Ct CT8 50 C1
Vestry Cotts
New Barn DA3 59 C5
Sevenoaks TN14 154 C8
Vestry Rd TN14 154 C8
Viaduct Cl CT12 117 C8
Viaduct Terr
Hamstreet TN26 348 F7
Sutton at H DA4 57 C7
Viaduct The CT17 310 D5
Via Romana DA12 38 B7
Viburnum Cl TN23 267 E2
Vicarage Ave SE3 11 A7
Vicarage Cl
Aylesford ME20 128 F3
Erith DA8 14 C8
Halling ME2 95 A5
Stoke ME3 25 A3
Vicarage Cotts ME9 67 C3
Vicarage Cres 8 CT9 50 J1
Vicarage Ct Chalk DA12 38 A7
Newington ME9 100 B7
Vicarage Dr DA11 18 C1
Vicarage Gdn CT12 114 C7
Vicarage Gdns CT3 178 A7
Vicarage Hill
Petham CT4 207 B4
Westerham TN16 151 D1
Vicarage La
Ashford TN23 268 C2
Blean CT2 142 A6
Chalk DA12 38 A6
Charing Heath TN27 233 C7
Deal CT14 214 F5
East Farleigh ME15 194 B6
Elham CT4 273 F4
Faversham ME13 138 A4
Hoo St Werburgh ME3 41 E4
Lower Halstow ME9 67 C3
Nonington CT15 211 C5
St Margaret's at Cliffe CT15 279 F6
4 Sandwich CT13 148 F1
Selling ME13 171 C6
Sevenoaks TN13 153 D8
Tilmanstone CT14 213 A3
Vicarage Pk SE18 2 C1
Vicarage Pl CT9 50 J1
Vicarage Rd
Coldblow DA5 32 B7
Folkestone CT20 334 F3
Gillingham ME7 64 C5
Halling ME2 94 F5
Minster (Sheppey) ME12 47 D7
Rochester ME2 63 B8
Royal Tunbridge Wells TN4 253 F2
Sittingbourne ME10 101 E6
Woolwich SE18 2 C1
Yalding ME18 193 A1
Vicarage Row ME3 39 C4
Vicarage Sq RM17 18 A8
Vicarage St
Broadstairs CT10 83 E5
Faversham ME13 138 D8
Vicarage Way TN19 354 A3
Vicary Way ME16 161 D5
Vickers Cl CT18 307 A4
Vickers Rd DA8 4 D1
Victor Ave CT9 51 D2
Victoria Ave
Broadstairs CT10 83 E8
3 Gravesend DA12 37 B8
Hythe CT21 333 B2
Margate CT9 51 B1
St Margaret's at Cliffe CT15 280 B6
Westgate-on-S CT8 81 F8
Victoria Bglws DA14 31 F1
Victoria Bsns Ctr DA16 13 B5
Victoria Cl
Chatham ME5 96 D2
Edenbridge TN8 249 C8
Victoria Cotts
Cranbrook TN17 320 D5
Edenbridge TN8 249 C8
Victoria Cres
Ashford TN23 268 B1
Dover CT16 310 D8
Victoria Ct Hythe CT21 333 C1
6 Maidstone ME16 161 E3
Victoria Dock Rd E16 1 B6
Victoria Dr CT6 76 C5
Victoria Dr ME19 158 F1
Victoria Dr DA4 57 D7
Victoria Gdns TN16 118 C4
Victoria Gr
12 Folkestone CT20 335 D5
Hythe CT21 334 B2
Victoria Hill Rd BR8 56 A8
Victoria Hospl CT14 215 B5
Victoria Ho 7 CT5 74 D2
Victoria Ind Pk DA1 15 E2
Victoria Mews
Deal CT14 215 C6
Westgate-on-S CT8 50 D1
Victoria Orch ME16 161 B3
Victoria Par CT10 84 B4
Victoria Park Mews 2 CT16 310 E8
Victoria Par CT11 117 F7
Victoria Pk Dover CT16 310 E8
Herne Bay CT6 77 A5
Victoria Pl
Faversham ME13 138 C7
Hythe CT21 333 B4
Victoria Rd
Ashford TN23 268 B1
Bexley DA6 14 A3
Broadstairs CT10 83 E6
Bromley BR2 52 D4
Canterbury CT1 174 E7
Capel-le-F CT18 308 B2
Chatham,Luton ME4 64 B2
Chatham,Walderslade ME5 96 E3
Chislehurst BR7 30 A3
Dartford DA1 15 E2
Deal CT14 215 D5
Edenbridge TN8 249 C8
Erith DA8 14 E8
Folkestone CT19 335 C5
Golden Green TN11 223 F6
Hythe CT21 333 C1
Kingsdown CT14 248 C4
Littlestone-on-Sea TN28 373 E5
Margate CT9 50 J2
Margate,Lydden CT9 82 D4
Northfleet DA11 36 F7
Ramsgate CT11 117 F7
Royal Tunbridge Wells,Southborough TN4 253 E1
Royal Tunbridge Wells TN1 286 B4
Sevenoaks TN13 154 B2
Sidcup DA15 31 A5
Sittingbourne ME10 101 D4
Victoria Rd W TN28 373 E5
Victoria Road Prim Sch TN23 268 B1
Victoria Row
Canterbury CT1 143 A1
Ramsgate CT11 117 C5
Victoria Scott Ct DA1 14 F4
Victoria St Dover CT17 278 B1
Eccles ME20 128 F6
Erith DA17 3 F1
Gillingham ME7 64 D6
Maidstone ME16 161 E3
New Romney TN28 373 A6
Rochester ME1 63 D5
Rochester,Strood ME2 63 B7
Sheerness ME12 28 C1
Whitstable CT5 74 D2
Victoria Terr
Hythe CT21 334 B2
Minster (Sheppey) ME12 48 A5
Rochester ME1 63 A2
Sittingbourne ME10 101 D4
Victoria Way SE7 1 B1
Victoria Wharf DA1 15 E2
Victoria Yd 22 CT1 143 A1
Victor Mills Cotts DA14 32 A1
Victory Cotts TN14 187 C2
Victory Lodge 10 DA8 4 E1
Victory Manor 1 ME7 64 A6
Victory Pk ME2 63 E7
Victory Rd CT15 247 F1
Victory St ME12 28 B2
Victory Terr ME17 229 E8
Victory Way DA2 16 C3
Vidal Manor ME7 64 C5
Vidgeon Ave ME3 41 D6
View Cl TN16 118 C3
Viewfield Rd DA5 31 C7
Viewland Rd SE18 2 F1
Viewlands Ave TN16 151 F7
Viewlands ME5 64 C3
Viewpoint Ct DA3 58 F5
Viewpoint ME14 162 C8
View Rd ME3 40 B7
View The SE2 3 E1
Vigilant Way DA12 37 F3
Vigo Hill ME19,TN15 125 E6
Vigo Rd TN15 125 C7
Vigo Terr ME9 103 C1
Vigo Village Sch DA13 126 A8
Viking Cl
Birchington CT7 80 D8
Rochester ME2 62 F4
Viking Ct
Broadstairs CT10 84 B3
Canterbury CT2 142 F2
Margate CT9 51 A2
Viking Ho 3 SE18 1 E2
Viking Rd DA11 36 C5
Viking Ship* CT12 116 E5
Viking Way Erith DA8 4 C3
West Kingsdown TN15 90 E5
Villa Cl DA12 38 B6
Villacourt Rd SE18,SE2 13 A8
Villa Ct DA1 33 E6
Village Green Ave TN16 118 E2
Village Green Rd DA1 15 A3
Village Green Way TN16 118 E2
Village The SE7 11 D8
Village View ME5 64 C2
Village Way TN26 349 A7
Villa Rd ME3 39 B3
Villas Rd SE18 2 C2
Villas The CT3 112 A1
Villiers Ct CT17 310 C7
Villiers Ho CT10 84 B7
Villiers Rd CT1 143 D1
Vincent Cl
Broadstairs CT10 83 C3
Bromley BR2 52 B5
Folkestone CT20 334 E5
Sidcup DA15 30 E
Vincent Ct ME12 28 C
Vincent Gdns ME12 28 C
Vincent Pl TN24 268 F
Vincent Rd
Kit's Coty ME20 129 C
Margate CT9 82 C
Sittingbourne ME10 102 C
Woolwich SE18 2 B
Vincent Sq TN16 118 C
Vincent St 13 E16 1 A
Vine Ave TN13 154 B
Vine Cl CT11 83 E
Vine Court Rd TN13 154 C
Vine Ct
16 Gravesend DA11 19 B
Staplehurst TN12 260
Wateringbury ME18 192 D
Vine End CT11 83 E
Vine Lands TN29 376
Vine Lodge TN13 154
Vine Lo CT11 83
Vine Rd BR6 86
Vineries The ME7 64
Viners Cl ME10 101
Vines La
Hildenborough TN11 188
Rochester ME1 63
Vine The TN13 154
Vine Wlk TN12 260
Vineyard Cres ME8 66
Vineyard La TN5 338
Viney's Gdns TN30 324
Vinson Cl
Culmers ME13 106
Orpington BR6 54
Vinson Ct DA15 31
Vinten Cl CT6 111
Vinters Rd ME14 162
Vintners Way ME14 162
Viola Ave SE2 3
Violet Ave CT12 83
Violet Cl ME5 130
Violets The TN12 257
VIP Trad Est SE7 1
Virginia Rd
Gillingham ME7 64
Whitstable CT5 109
Virginia Wlk DA12 37
Viscount Dr E6 1
Vista The Eltham SE9 29
Sidcup DA14 30
Vixen Cl ME5 97
Vlissingen Dr CT14 215
Voce Rd SE18 12
Vogue Ct 11 BR1 52
Volante Dr ME10 101
Voyagers Cl SE28 3
Vulcan Cl Chatham ME5 97
Newham E6 2
Whitstable CT5 108
Vyne The DA7 1
Vyvyan Cotts TN17 34
Vyvyan Ho SE18 1

W

Wacher Cl CT2 14
Wadard Terr BR8 5
Waddenhall Barns CT4 2
Waddington Dr CT18 3
Waddle Cnr TN30 3
Wade Ave BR5 5
Wades Cl TN29 3
Wadeville Cl DA17
Wadham Pl ME10 1
Wadhurst Bsns Pk TN5 3
Wadhurst CE Prim Sch TN5 3
Wadhurst Rd TN3 3
Wadhurst Sta TN5 3
Wadlands Rd ME3
Waghorn Rd ME6 1
Waghorn St ME4
Wagoners Cl ME14 1
Wagon La TN12 2
Wagtail Way BR5
Waid Cl DA1
Wain Ct ME12
Wainhouse Cl TN8 2
Wainscott Prim Sch ME2
Wainscott Rd ME2
Wainscott Wlk ME2
Wainwright Ct CT10
Wainwright Pl TN24 3
Waite Davies Rd 8 SE12
Wakefield Cl ME2
Wakefield Rd DA9
Wakefield Way CT21
Wakefield Wlk CT21
Wakehurst Cl ME17
Wakeley Rd ME8
Wakeleys Cotts ME8

Wakely Cl TN16 118 C1
Wake Rd ME1 96 C8
Wakerley Cl 6 E6 1 F7
Walcheren Cl CT14 215 C8
Walcot Pl CT6 77 B3
Waldair Ct E16 2 B4
Waldeck Rd DA1 16 A1
Waldegrave Rd BR1 52 F5
Walden Ave BR7 29 F4
Walden Cl DA17 3 F1
Waldenhurst Rd BR5 54 D2
Walden Par BR7 29 F2
Walden Rd BR7 29 F2
Waldens Cl BR5 54 D2
Waldens Rd BR5 54 E3
Waldens The ME17 197 E2
Waldershare Ave
CT13 182 A7
Waldershare Ho CT15 245 D5
Waldershare La CT15 246 E2
Waldershare Rd CT15 246 A5
Walderslade Ctr ME5 97 A3
Walderslade Girls Sch
ME5 96 F5
Walderslade Prim Sch
ME5 97 A3
Walderslade Rd ME5 96 F6
Walderslade Woods
ME5 96 E2
Waldo Ind Est BR1 52 D6
Waldo Rd BR1 52 D6
Waldrist Way DA18 3 F4
Waldron Dr ME15 194 F6
Waldron Rd CT10 84 B2
Waldstock Rd SE28 3 A6
Walkden Rd BR7 30 A3
Walker Cl Crayford DA1 14 F4
Woolwich SE18 2 C2
Walker La CT7 80 D8
Walker Pl TN15 156 D6
Walkhurst Cotts TN17 342 F7
Walkhurst Rd TN17 342 F7
Walkley Rd DA1 15 B2
Walks The TN3 312 C8
Walk The ME17 197 E2
Wallace Cl Erith SE28 3 D6
Royal Tunbridge Wells
TN2 314 A8
Wallace Gdns DA10 17 E1
Wallace Mews CT19 335 D7
Wallace Rd ME1 96 E8
Wallace Terr TN15 91 E4
Wallace Way CT10 83 E4
Wallbridge La ME8 66 D3
Wall Cl ME3 41 D7
Waller Hill TN17 293 E5
Waller Rd TN28 377 E7
Wallers Rd ME13 138 A7
Wallers TN3 285 A8
Wallhouse Rd DA8 15 C7
Wallis Ave ME15 195 E5
Wallis Cl DA2 32 F5
Wallis Field TN3 312 B6
Wallis Pk DA11 18 B2
Wallis Rd TN24 268 D2
Wall Rd TN24 268 B3
Wall The ME10 101 E5
Wallwood Rd CT11 117 F8
Walmer Castle*
CT14 215 D1
Walmer Castle Rd
CT14 215 C1
Walmer Cl BR6 86 D6
Walmer Ct 3 ME14 162 A5
Walmer Gdns
Cliffs End CT12 116 D5
Deal CT14 215 A2
Sittingbourne ME10 101 D5
Walmer Ho ME2 40 C1
Walmer Rd CT5 108 E8
Walmers Ave ME3 39 A4
Walmer Sch CT14 215 B2
Walmer Sta CT14 215 A1
Walmer Terr SE18 2 D2
Walmer Way
Deal CT14 215 A2
1 Folkestone CT20 334 F5
Walmsley Ho 4 CT19 335 E6
Walmsley Rd CT10 83 F5
Walner Gdns TN28 373 B7
Walner La TN28 373 B7
Walnut Cl
Ashford TN24 268 D6
Broadstairs CT10 83 F2
Chatham ME5 97 B8
Eynsford DA4 89 D7
Paddock Wood TN12 257 A6
Yalding ME18 192 F1
Walnut Hill Rd DA13 59 E6
Walnut Ridge TN25 330 A6
Walnuts Rd BR6 54 B1
Walnuts The BR6 54 A1
Walnut Tree Ave
Dartford DA1 33 E6
Loose ME15 195 A5
Walnut Tree Cl
6 Birchington CT7 81 A7
Chislehurst BR7 53 C8
Westerham TN16 151 D1
Walnut Tree Cotts
ME13 171 E8
Walnut Tree Ct ME20 128 B1
Walnut Tree Dr ME10 101 D4
Walnut Tree La
Loose ME15 195 A5
Westbere CT2 144 D7
Walnut Tree Rd DA8 4 E1
Walnut Tree Way DA13 60 B3
Walnut Way
Royal Tunbridge Wells
TN4 286 D8
Swanley BR8 55 D7
Walpole Cl ME19 127 F1
Walpole Ho 4 BR7 53 D8
Walpole Pl SE18 2 B2
Walpole Rd
Bromley BR2 52 D4
Margate CT9 50 J3
Walsby Dr ME10 102 A8
Walsham Cl SE28 3 D6
Walsham Rd ME5 96 F1
Walshaw Ho 2 ME14 162 A6
Walsingham Cl ME8 98 D3
Walsingham Ho 3
ME14 162 A6
Walsingham Pk BR7 53 D7
Walsingham Rd BR5 54 B8
Walsingham Wlk DA17 14 A8
Walter Burke Ave ME1 95 C5
Walter's Farm Rd
TN9 222 C1
Walters Green Rd
TN11 283 F6
Walters Ho SE18 12 A7
Walters Rd ME3 41 E6
Walterstown Ct DA1 33 D8
Walters Yd BR1 52 A7
Waltham Cl
Ashford TN24 269 A2
Dartford DA1 15 A1
Margate CT9 51 E2
27 Orpington BR5 54 D1
Waltham Rd
Gillingham ME8 65 C3
Waltham CT4 206 F1
Walthamstow Hall (Nursery
Unit) TN13 154 B5
Walthamstow Hall
TN13 154 C4
Walton Gdns CT19 335 D7
Walton Manor Cl
CT19 335 D7
Walton Rd
Folkestone CT19 335 D6
Sidcup DA14 31 C5
Tonbridge TN10 222 F6
Waltons The CT19 335 C8
Walwyn Ave BR1 52 D6
Wanden La TN27 264 C8
Wansbury Way BR8 56 A5
Wanstall Ct CT7 81 A7
Wanstead Cl BR1 52 C7
Wanstead Rd BR1 52 C7
Wansunt Rd DA5 32 C7
Wantsum Cl CT6 77 F5
Wantsume Lees CT13 148 E2
Wantsum Mews 7
CT13 148 F1
Wantsum Way CT7 79 E3
Warberry Park Gdns
TN4 285 E4
Warblers Cl 3 ME2 63 A7
Ward Cl Durgates TN5 336 E5
Erith DA8 14 D8
Warden Bay Pk ME12 49 E3
Warden Bay Rd ME12 49 E3
Warden Cl ME16 161 C4
Warden Ct 10 CT17 278 C1
Warden House Mews
CT14 215 A4
Warden House Prim Sch
CT14 215 A5
Warden Mill Cl ME18 192 E7
Warden Point Way
CT5 108 C6
Warden Rd
Rochester ME1 63 C2
Warden ME12 49 B5
Wardens Field Cl 2
BR6 86 F4
Warden Spring Cvn Pk
ME12 49 D5
Warden Terr ME12 48 A6
Warden View Gdns
ME12 49 D1
Warden Way ME12 49 B5
Warde's ME18 192 F2
Wardona Ct DA10 17 F1
Wardour Cl CT10 84 B4
Wardour Ct 11 DA2 16 B1
Wards Hill Rd ME12 47 C8
Ward's La TN5 337 E4
Wards Wharf App E16 1 D4
Wardwell La
Lower Halstow ME9 67 C1
Newington ME9 100 C8
Warehorne Rd TN26 349 A7
Warepoint Dr SE28 2 D4
Ware St ME14 163 A5
Warham Rd TN14 122 B3
Waring Cl BR6 87 A4
Waring Dr BR6 87 A4
Waring Rd DA14 31 C2
Warland Rd
West Kingsdown TN15 90 F2
Woolwich SE18 12 E7
Warlingham Cl ME8 66 A1
Warmlake Bsns Est
ME17 196 E1
Warmlake Rd ME17 196 C1
Warmlake ME17 196 F1
Warne Pl 4 DA15 13 B1
Warner St ME4 63 F3
Warnett Ct ME6 95 A1
Warnford Gdns ME15 195 A8
Warnford Rd BR6 86 F5
Warre Ave CT11 117 C5
Warren Ave BR6 86 F5
Warren Cl Bexley DA6 14 A2
Folkestone CT19 335 F6
Sittingbourne ME10 102 B2
Warren Cotts TN11 252 A3
Warren Ct TN15 154 C3
Warren Dr
Broadstairs CT10 83 E5
Orpington BR6 87 B5
Warren Dr The CT8 81 D7
Warren Farm La TN3 313 B4
Warren Gdns BR6 87 A5
Warren Hastings Ct
DA11 18 F1
Warren Hos TN27 233 E8
Warren Hts TN25 302 E5
Warren La
Ashford TN24 268 A4
Lydden CT15 276 D6
Oxted RH8 183 A1
Woolwich SE18 2 B3
Yelsted ME9 99 C3
Warren Lo CT1 174 B6
Warren Rd Bexley DA6 14 A2
Dartford DA1 33 E5
Folkestone CT19 335 F6
Hayes BR2 85 A8
Kit's Coty ME5 129 D7
Littlestone-on-Sea TN28 373 D6
Luddesdown ME2 61 D3
Northfleet DA13 36 B3
Orpington BR6 87 C5
Sidcup DA14 31 C5
Warren Ret Pk TN24 268 B4
Warren Ridge TN3 314 C3
Warren Road Prim Sch
BR6 86 F6
Warrens The DA3 58 F3
Warren St
Stalisfield Green TN27 201 A3
Warren Street ME17 200 D7
Warren The
Brabourne Lees TN25 302 E5
Gravesend DA12 37 D4
2 Greenwich SE7 11 C8
Penshurst TN11 252 A4
Selling ME13 171 E7
Ticehurst TN5 338 E1
Whitstable CT5 108 C6
Warren View
Ashford TN23 267 F4
Shorne DA12 38 E2
Warren Way CT19 335 F6
Warren Wlk 1 SE7 11 C8
Warren Wood Cl BR2 85 A8
Warren Wood Com Prim
Sch & Language Unit
ME1 96 C8
Warren Wood Rd ME1 96 C7
Warrington Rd TN12 257 A6
Warrior Ave DA12 37 C4
Warsop Trad Est TN8 249 D8
Warspite Rd SE18 1 E3
Warten Rd CT11 83 F1
Warwall E6 2 B7
Warwick Cl
Orpington BR6 87 A7
Sidcup DA5 31 F8
Warwick Cres
Rochester ME1 62 F2
Sittingbourne ME10 101 C5
Warwick Ct 8 DA8 14 F7
Warwick Dr CT11 117 B5
Warwick Gdns DA13 93 A8
Warwick Pk TN2 286 B1
Warwick Pl
Maidstone ME16 161 E3
Northfleet DA11 18 B2
Warwick Rd
Ashford TN24 268 E5
Bexley DA16 13 C4
Canterbury CT1 175 C8
Deal CT14 215 D2
Margate CT9 51 B2
4 Royal Tunbridge Wells
TN1 286 A2
Sidcup DA14 31 B3
Whitstable CT5 74 D2
Warwick Terr SE18 12 D8
Warwick Way DA1 33 E6
Washford Farm Rd
TN23 299 E5
Washington Cl 4
CT16 278 B3
Washington Ho ME15 195 E5
Washington La TN29 371 C6
Washneys Rd BR6 120 B6
Washwell La TN5 336 F3
Wassall La TN17 357 E7
Wass Dro CT3 147 B7
Watchester Ave CT11 117 C5
Watchester La CT12 115 B5
Watchgate DA2 34 E3
Watchmans Terr 6
ME5 64 C2
Waterbrook Ave TN24 301 A4
Watercress Cl TN14 154 C7
Watercress Dr TN14 154 C7
Watercress Ho TN23 267 F1
Watercress La
Ashford TN23 299 F8
Wingham CT3 177 F6
Watercroft Rd TN14 87 F1
Waterdale Rd SE2 13 A8
Waterdales DA11 36 D7
Waterditch La ME17,
TN27 200 E5
Waterdown Rd TN4 285 E1
Waterfall Rd TN26 267 B6
Water Farm CT4 273 F4
Waterfield Cl Erith DA17 4 A3
Woolwich SE28 3 B5
Waterfield TN2 314 A7
Waterfrets Cotts TN3 284 F5
Waterfront Studios Bsns
Ctr E16 1 A5
Watergate Ho 5 SE18 2 A2
Waterglade Ind Pk
RM20 16 F8
Waterham Rd ME13 107 C1
Waterhead Cl DA8 14 E7
Waterhouse Cl E16 1 D8
Wateringbury CE Prim Sch
ME18 192 E6
Wateringbury Cl BR5 54 B7
Wateringbury Rd
ME19 159 F3
Wateringbury Sta
ME18 192 E6
Water La
Canterbury CT1 174 F8
6 Faversham ME13 138 C7
Harrietsham ME17 198 B5
Hawkhurst TN18 341 B4
Headcorn TN17,TN27 262 A4
Hunton ME15 226 D6
Waterlakes TN8 249 C8
Water La
Kingswood ME17 197 F3
Limpsfield RH8 183 A8
Maidstone,Bearsted
ME14 163 E6
6 Maidstone ME15 162 A4
Painters Forstal ME13 137 F4
Shoreham TN14 121 F6
Sidcup DA14 31 F6
Smarden TN27 263 F2
Sturry CT2 143 F5
West Malling ME19 159 C8
Waterlock Cotts CT3 178 A7
Waterloo Cres CT16,
CT17 310 E7
Waterloo Hill ME12 47 D6
Waterloo Mans 14
CT16,CT17 310 E7
Waterloo Pl
Cranbrook TN17 320 D5
10 Ramsgate CT11 117 F7
Tonbridge TN9 254 B8
Waterloo Rd
Cranbrook TN17 320 D6
Folkestone CT20 334 D5
Gillingham ME7 64 C4
Sittingbourne ME10 101 D5
Tonbridge TN9 254 B8
Whitstable CT5 74 D2
Waterloo St
1 Gravesend DA12 37 C8
Maidstone ME15 162 A3
Waterloo Terr ME12 48 A5
Waterlow Rd
Maidstone ME14 162 A6
Vigo Village DA13 125 F7
Waterman Ho TN23 300 B8
Waterman's La TN12 257 B3
Watermans Way DA9 17 B3
Water Mdws CT2 143 F4
Watermead Cl TN23 299 F7
Watermeadow Cl
Erith DA8 15 B6
Gillingham ME7 97 F6
Watermill Cl
Maidstone ME16 161 B5
Rochester ME2 63 C8
Water Mill Way DA4 57 B7
Watermint Cl BR5 54 D5
Waters Cotts TN5 337 A4
Waters Edge Ct DA8 4 F1
Waters Edge ME15 161 F2
Watersend CT16 277 D5
Waterside TN24 268 F1
Waterside Cl ME13 105 D1
Waterside DA1 14 F2
Waterside Ct
5 Hythe CT21 333 B2
Leybourne ME19 127 E2
Rochester ME2 63 E6
Waterside Dr CT8 50 D1
Waterside Gate ME16 161 F5
Waterside La ME7 64 F7
Waterside ME14 161 F5
Waterside Mews
ME18 192 D6
Waterside Sch SE18 2 D1
Waterside Terr TN23 267 C1
Waterside View ME12 49 E4
Water Slippe TN11 190 D1
Watersmeet Cl ME15 162 A1
Watersmeet Way SE28 3 D7
Waters Pl ME7 98 A6
Water St CT14 215 D7
Waterstone Pl ME13 138 A6
Waterton Ave DA12 37 E8
Waterton BR8 55 D5
Waterworks Cotts
TN14 154 B6
Waterworks Hill CT15 247 B3
Waterworks La CT15 247 B3
Watery La
Heaverham TN15 155 D7
Petham CT4 207 C5
Sidcup BR5,DA14 31 B2
Watford Rd E16 1 A8
Watkin Rd CT19 335 C6
Watkins Cl TN12 260 E5
Watling Ave ME5 64 D2
Watling Ho 10 SE18 12 A8
Watling Pl ME10 102 A3
Watling St
Bexley DA6,DA7 14 C3
Canterbury CT1 174 F8
Dartford DA1,DA2 34 C8
Gillingham ME5 64 D2
Gravesend DA11,DA12 37 C2
Northfleet DA11,DA13 36 C5
Rochester ME2 62 D7
Watson Ave ME5 96 D5
Watson Cl RM20 17 A6
Watsons Cl TN25 268 C8
Watsons Hill ME10 101 E5
Watt Ho SE2 3 C1
Wattle Cnr TN30 360 D3
Watts' Ave ME1 63 C4
Watts Cl Snodland ME6 128 B8
Wadhurst TN5 336 F4
Watts Cotts TN24 268 D7
Watt's Cross Rd TN11 221 B6
Watt's La BR7 53 C8
Watts' St ME4 63 E3
Watts Yd 13 CT13 148 F1
Wat Tyler Way ME15 162 A4
Wauchope Rd CT5 107 F6
Wave Crest CT5 74 C1
Wavell Dr DA15 12 E1
Waveney Rd TN10 222 B5
Waverley Ave ME12 47 B7
Waverley Cl
Bromley BR2 52 D4
Chatham ME5 97 D2
Coxheath ME17 194 C3
Waverley Cres
Woolwich SE18 12 D8
Woolwich SE18 2 D1
Waverley Dr TN2 286 F6
Waverley Gdns E6 1 E8
Waverley Rd
Margate CT9 82 C8
Woolwich SE18 2 D1
Wayborough Hill
CT12 115 D7
Way Farm Cotts CT12 115 E7
Wayfield Com Prim Sch
ME5 97 A7
Wayfield Link SE9 12 D1
Wayfield Rd ME5 97 A7
Way Hill CT12 115 E7
Waylands Cl TN14 120 E4
Waylands BR8 55 F5
Wayne Cl
Broadstairs CT10 83 E5
Orpington BR6 86 F7
Wayne Ct ME2 40 D2
Wayside Ave TN30 324 B3
Wayside 3 BR7 53 D8
Wayside Dr TN8 217 D3
Wayside Flats TN30 324 B2
Wayside Gr SE9 29 F4
Wayside TN30 324 B2
Wayville Rd DA1 34 B8
Way Volante DA12 37 E4
Weald Cl
Istead Rise DA13 36 E1
Maidstone ME15 195 C6
Orpington BR2 85 E8
Sevenoaks Weald TN14 187 C2
Weald Com Prim Sch
TN14 187 B2
Weald Ct Charing TN27 201 E1
Sittingbourne ME10 101 D2
Tonbridge TN11 221 D6
Wealden Ave TN30 324 B1
Wealden Cl TN11 221 E5
Wealden Ct 5 ME5 64 B3
Wealden Pl TN13 154 D6
Wealden View TN17 318 E8
Wealden Way ME20 160 E7
Wealdhurst Pk CT10 83 D5
Weald of Kent Gram Sch
for Girls The TN9 254 C7
Weald Rd TN13 187 B7
Weald The
Ashford TN24 268 C3
Bromley BR7 29 F2
Weald View
Frittenden TN17 293 E6
Paddock Wood TN12 257 E1
Weald View Rd TN9 254 B7
Weald View TN5 336 F6
Wear Bay Cres CT19 335 F6
Wear Bay Rd CT19 335 F5
Weardale Ave DA2 34 C7
Weare Rd TN4 286 C8
Weatherall Cl ME13 140 B2
Weatherly Cl ME1 63 C4
Weatherly Dr CT10 83 F2
Weathersfield Ct SE9 11 F1
Weaver Cl E6 2 B6
Weavering Cl ME2 40 B2
Weavering Cotts
ME14 162 E3
Weavering St ME14 162 F4
Weavers Cl
Gravesend DA11 37 A7
Staplehurst TN12 260 F4
Weavers Cotts TN17 318 E8
Weavers La TN14 154 C6
Weaver's Orch DA13 36 A2
Weavers The
Biddenden TN27 295 A1
Maidstone ME16 161 B5
Weavers Way
Ashford TN23 299 E7
Dover CT16 278 A3
Webb Cl
Folkestone CT19 335 A7
Hoo St Werburgh ME3 41 D6
Webb Ct 6 SE28 3 B6
Webber Cl DA8 15 B7
Webb's Mdw TN15 154 C2
Webster Rd ME8 65 F1
Webster Way CT18 307 B4
Weddington La CT3 147 E2
Wedgewood Cl ME16 161 B5
Wedgewood Ct DA5 31 F8
Wedgewood Dr ME5 97 A7
Wedgwoods TN16 150 C6
Weeds Wood Rd ME5 96 F4
Weekes Ct ME11 46 A5
Weeks La TN27 295 A5
Week St ME14 162 A4
Weigall Pl CT11 117 C7
Weigall Rd SE12,SE3 11 A3
Weighbridge Way
CT16 310 H8
Weird Wood DA3 59 C6
Weir Mill ME19 159 F7
Weir Rd DA5 32 B8
Welbeck Ave
Bromley BR1 29 A4
Royal Tunbridge Wells
TN4 286 C8
Sidcup DA15 31 A7
Welcombe Ct ME8 98 D8
Weld Cl TN12 260 F4
Weldstock Ho 2 SE28 2 D3
Wellan Cl DA16 13 B2
Welland Rd TN10 222 B4
Wellands Cl BR1 52 F7
Wellbrook Rd BR6 86 A6
Well Cl Leigh TN11 220 F1
Sturry CT2 144 A6
Wellcome Ave DA1 15 E3
Weller Ave ME1 63 D2
Weller Pl BR6 119 A8
Weller Rd TN4 285 C4
Wellers Cl TN16 184 C8
Wellesley Ave CT14 215 C3
Wellesley Cl
Broadstairs CT10 83 E3
7 Greenwich SE7 1 C1
Westgate-on-S CT8 81 E7
Wellesley Ho CT14 215 C1
Wellesley Rd
Ashford TN23 268 C2
Dover CT16 310 E7
Margate CT9 51 B1
Sheerness ME12 28 D2
Westgate-on-S CT8 81 E7
Wellesley Terr CT13 181 A8
Wellesley Villas TN24 268 C3
Well Field DA3 58 F5
Wellfield Rd CT20 335 A5
Well Hall* SE9 11 E3
Well Hall Par SE9 11 F3
Well Hall Rd SE18,SE9 11 F5
Well Hill BR6 88 B5
Well Hill La BR6 88 B4
Well Hill Nursery BR6 88 C4
Wellingfield Ct 1
DA16 13 A4
Welling High St DA16 13 B4
Welling Sch DA16 13 B6
Welling Sta DA16 13 A5
Wellington Ave
Sidcup DA15 13 A1
Woolwich SE18 2 B3
Wellington Cl CT8 50 C1
Wellington Cotts
Gill's Green TN18 340 E4
Meopham DA13 93 A7
Wellington Cres CT11 117 F6
Wellington Ct CT14 215 D3
Wellington Gdns
2 Dover CT16 278 B3
Greenwich SE7 1 C1
Margate CT9 50 J3
Wellington Ho
6 Maidstone ME15 195 E5
Margate CT9 51 C3
Wellingtonia Way
TN8 217 C2
Wellington Mews SE7 11 C8
Wellington Par
Bexley DA15 13 A2
Deal CT14 248 D7
Kingsdown CT14 248 E6
Wellington Pl
Folkestone CT20 334 D3
Maidstone ME14 161 F6
Sparrow's Green TN5 336 F5
Wellington Rd
Bexley DA5 13 D2
Bromley BR2 52 C5
Dartford DA1 15 C1
Deal CT14 215 D5
Erith DA17 3 F1
Folkestone CT20 334 D5
Gillingham ME7 64 C4
Margate CT9 82 D4
Orpington BR5 54 C3
Sittingbourne ME10 101 B6
Temple Ewell CT16 277 D5
Tilbury RM18 19 A5
Westgate-on-S CT8 81 E7
Wellington St
Gravesend DA12 37 C8
Woolwich SE18 2 A2
Yorkletts CT5 108 D5
Wellington Terr CT20 334 D3
Wellington Way ME19 158 F3
Welling Way DA16 12 D4
Wellis Gdns CT9 50 G1
Well La
Fordwich CT2,CT3 144 A3
Painters Forstal ME13 137 B3
St Margaret's at Cliffe
CT15 279 F6
Wellmeade Dr TN13 187 B8
Well Penn Rd ME3 22 C3
Well Rd Lyminge CT18 305 C6
Maidstone ME14 162 A5
Otford TN14 122 C3
Queenborough ME11 46 A5
Rushenden ME11 45 F3
Wells Ave CT1 175 B7
Wells Cl
New Romney TN28 373 C6
Royal Tunbridge Wells
TN1 286 A3
Tenterden TN30 345 B8
Tonbridge TN10 222 D4
Westerham TN16 184 C8
Wells Cotts ME18 192 C2
Wells Ct ME2 62 D5
Wells Ho Bromley BR1 29 B3
Royal Tunbridge Wells
TN4 285 F4

Whitfield Hill
Dover CT16 277 F4
Temple Ewell CT16 277 E4
Whitfield Lodge CT16 278 A8
Whitfield Rd DA7 13 F7
Whitfield Rdbt CT16 278 A6
Whitfield Sch & Aspen Specl Unit CT16 278 A7
Whitgift Ct CT2 142 D1
Whiting Cres ME13 138 A8
Whiting Ho TN29 376 C5
Whitings Way E6 2 A8
Whitmore St ME16 161 D2
Whitney Wlk DA14 31 E2
Whitstable Jun Sch CT5 74 D1
Whitstable Mus & Art Gallery* CT5 74 D1
Whitstable Rd
Canterbury CT2 142 D2
Faversham, Goodnestone ME13 139 B6
Faversham ME13 138 E7
Herne Bay CT5,CT6 76 B3
Rough Common CT2 142 B4
Whitstable & Seasalter CE Jun Sch CT5 74 D1
Whitstable & Tankerton Hospl CT5 75 A2
Whitstable & Tankerton Sta CT5 74 E1
Whittaker St ME4 64 A4
Whittington Terr CT15 244 D4
Whitworth Rd SE18 12 A7
Whybornes Chase ME12 47 C7
Whybourne Crest TN2 286 D1
Whyman Ave ME4 64 A1
Whytecliffs CT10 84 A2
Wichling Cl
Canterbury CT2 143 A3
Orpington BR5 54 D1
Wickenden Cres TN24 301 A8
Wickenden Rd TN13 154 C5
Wicken Ho ME16 161 E4
Wicken La TN25,TN27 234 E6
Wickens Pl ME19 159 C8
Wickets The
Ashford TN24 300 F7
Sevenoaks Weald TN14 187 C2
Wickham Ave CT11 117 G8
Wickhambreaux CE Prim Sch CT3 145 C2
Wickham Cl ME9 100 B6
Wickham Common Prim Sch BR4 85 A6
Wickham Court La CT3 145 B3
Wickham Ct DA16 12 E5
Wickham Field TN14 121 F3
Wickham Gdns TN4 285 D5
Wickham La
Ickham CT3 145 B1
Woolwich SE2,SE18 13 A8
Wickham Mill CT3 145 C2
Wickham Pl ME17 199 D5
Wickham Rd CT3 145 B2
Wickham St
Bexley DA16 13 A6
Rochester ME1 63 D3
Wickhams Way DA3 58 F4
Wickham Terr ME11 45 F5
Wickhurst Rd TN14 186 F3
Wick La CT4 243 E7
Wicks Cl SE9 29 D4
Wicksteed Cl DA5 32 D5
Widbury TN3 284 F3
Widecombe Rd SE9 29 E5
Widgeon Cl E16 1 B7
Widgeon Path SE28 2 D3
Widgeon Rd Erith DA8 15 B7
Rochester ME2 62 D6
Widgeon Wlk CT18 307 B3
Widmore Lodge Rd BR1 52 D7
Widmore Rd BR1 52 C7
Widred Rd CT17 310 C8
Wierton Hill ME17 228 D7
Wierton La ME17 195 E1
Wierton Rd ME17 228 E8
Wife Of Bath Hill CT2 174 C8
Wigmore Cotts CT15 245 C8
Wigmore La CT15 245 C8
Wigmore Rd ME8 98 B4
Wigmore Wood CT15 245 C8
Wigwam Paddocks CT7 81 A8
Wihtred Rd ME9 102 D2
Wilberforce Ct 2 SE28 3 C5
Wilberforce Rd
Coxheath ME17 194 D3
Folkestone CT20 334 E3
Wilberforce Way DA12 37 D3
Wilbrough Rd CT7 81 A7
Wilcox Cl CT3 210 D5
Wild Air CT7 80 F8
Wilde Cl RM18 19 C5
Wilden Park Rd TN12 291 E7
Wilde Rd DA8 14 B7
Wilderness Ave TN15 154 F5
Wilderness Mount TN13 154 D5
Wilderness Sch The TN13 154 E6
Wilderness Hill CT9 51 A2
Wilderness Rd BR7 30 B1
Wildfell Cl ME5 130 C8
Wildish Rd ME13 138 A8
Wildman Cl ME8 98 D3
Wildwood Cl
Kingswood ME17 197 E2
1 Lewisham SE12 29 A8
Wildwood Glade ME7 98 B4
Wildwood Rd CT2 143 F6
Wildwood Wealden Forest Pk* CT2,CT6 110 D4
Wiles Ave TN28 373 B6
Wiles Ho TN28 373 B6
Wilford Ho 3 SE18 2 B1
Wilfred Rd CT11 117 C8
Wilfred St 23 DA12 19 B1
Wilgate Green Rd ME13 169 F6
Wilkes Rd CT10 83 E4
Wilkie Rd CT7 81 A8
Wilkinson Cl 1 DA1 16 A3
Wilkinson Dr CT14 215 D3
Wilkinson Pl ME18 159 A2
Wilkinson Rd E16 1 C7
Wilkins Way TN16 152 B3
Wilks Ave DA1 33 F6
Wilks Cl ME8 66 B2
Will Adams Ct 9 ME7 64 C6
Will Adams Rdbt ME8 64 F2
Will Adams Way ME8 64 F1
Will Crooks Gdns SE9 11 D3
Willement Rd ME13 138 B7
Willenhall Rd SE18 2 B1
Willersley Ave
Orpington BR6 86 D7
Sidcup DA15 30 F7
Willersley Cl DA15 30 F7
Willesborough Ct TN24 269 A2
Willesborough Ind Pk TN24 269 A1
Willesborough Inf & Jun Schs TN24 301 A8
Willesborough Rd TN24 268 F4
Willesborough Windmill* TN24 269 A1
Willesley Gdns TN17 320 D6
Willett Cl BR5 53 E3
Willetts Cotts TN3 283 C4
Willetts Hill CT12 114 D7
Willetts La TN3 283 C4
Willett Way BR5,BR6 53 E3
William Ave
Folkestone CT19 335 B7
Margate CT9 83 C8
William Baker Ho ME20 160 F8
William Barefoot Dr SE9 30 A5
William Gibbs Ct 14 ME13 138 D7
William Harvey Hospl TN24 269 C1
William Ho 4 DA12 37 B8
William Judge Cl TN30 345 D7
William Luck Cl TN12 224 E6
William Muge Ho 15 CT16 310 D8
William Pitt Ave CT14 215 B6
William Pitt Cl CT21 333 D2
William Rd
Ashford TN23 300 B8
Cuxton ME2 62 C2
William Rigby Dr ME12 46 E7
William Smith Ho 10 DA17 4 A3
Williamson Rd TN29 377 E5
William St
Faversham ME13 138 D7
Gillingham ME8 66 A1
Gravesend DA12 37 B8
Grays RM17 18 C8
Herne Bay CT6 76 F5
Royal Tunbridge Wells TN4 286 A5
Sittingbourne ME10 101 E4
Whitstable CT5 74 D2
Williams Way DA2 32 D6
Willicombe Ho TN2 286 D4
Willicombe Pk TN2 286 D4
Willingdon TN23 299 E5
Willingdon Pl CT14 215 C1
Willingdon Rd CT16 278 A5
Willington Gn ME15 195 E7
Willington St ME15 162 F2
Willis Ct ME12 46 F5
Willis Ho ME1 63 C4
Willis Rd DA8 4 D2
Willop Cl TN29 352 F3
Willop Way TN29 352 F3
Willoughby Ct 14 CT1 174 F8
Willoughby Way SE7 1 B2
Willow Ave
Broadstairs CT10 83 D4
Faversham ME13 138 A7
Hoo St Werburgh ME3 41 E3
Sidcup DA15 13 A1
Swanley BR8 55 F5
Willowbank Cl TN29 366 A4
Willowbank Ct 12 ME15 162 B4
Willowbank Dr ME23 23 E4
Willow Bank Ind Est ME9 68 E6
Willowby Gdns ME8 98 E4
Willow Cl Bromley BR2 52 F4
Canterbury CT2 143 A2
Hythe CT21 332 E1
Margate CT9 51 C2
Orpington BR5 54 B2
Sidcup DA5 13 F1
Willow Cres
Five Oak Green TN12 256 B7
Staplehurst TN12 260 F5
Willow Ct
Broadstairs CT10 84 A5
Dartford DA1 33 C7
Folkestone CT20 334 E4
Loose ME15 195 A6
Willow Dene Sch SE18 12 E6
Willow Dr
Hamstreet TN26 349 A7
St Mary's Bay TN29 365 F3
Willow Farm Way CT6 77 C2
Willowfields Cl 1 SE18 2 E1
Willow Grange DA14 31 B5
Willow Gr BR7 30 B2
Willowherb Cl ME4 41 C1
Willow Ho
Ashford TN23 267 F1
2 Chatham ME5 96 F5
8 Maidstone ME16 161 A3
Sheerness ME12 28 B2
Sittingbourne ME10 102 B3
Willow La
Paddock Wood TN12 257 E6
Woolwich SE18 2 A2
Willow Lea TN10 222 C7
Willow Lodge
Folkestone CT19 335 D7
Royal Tunbridge Wells TN4 285 E4
Willowmead ME19 127 E2
Willow Pk TN14 121 F2
Willow Rd Dartford DA1 33 C7
Erith DA8 15 A6
Great Mongeham CT14 214 C3
Larkfield ME20 127 F3
Rochester ME2 62 E6
Whitstable CT5 108 C5
Willow Rise ME15 162 F1
Willows Ct CT2 142 C4
Willowside ME6 95 A1
Willows The
Ashford TN24 268 D6
Gillingham ME8 65 E2
Grays RM17 18 D8
Newington ME9 100 B6
Sheerness ME12 28 H1
Sittingbourne ME10 68 F1
Willow Terr DA4 89 E8
Willow Tree Cl
Ashford TN24 268 F1
Herne Bay CT6 77 D5
Willow Tree Ct DA14 30 F3
Willow Tree Rd TN2 285 F1
Willow Tree Wlk BR1 52 B8
Willow Vale BR7 30 B2
Willow Way TN27 323 D7
Willow Waye CT15 245 D7
Willow Way
Maidstone ME15 162 B3
Margate CT9 82 C8
Whitstable CT5 109 C8
Willow Wents ME18 158 D1
Willow Wlk
Culverstone Green DA13 92 F3
Orpington BR6 86 B7
Royal Tunbridge Wells TN2 286 E8
Willow Wood Rd DA13 92 F2
Willrose Cres SE2 3 B1
Wills La TN29 350 C4
Willson's Rd CT11 117 D6
Will Thorne Pav The E16 1 E7
Wilman Rd TN4 286 B7
Wilmar Way TN15 154 F7
Wilmecote Ct ME8 98 D8
Wilmington Ave BR6 87 C8
Wilmington Court Rd DA2 33 A6
Wilmington Gram Sch for Boys DA2 33 B5
Wilmington Hall Sch DA2 33 B5
Wilmington Ho DA2 33 D6
Wilmington Prim Sch DA2 33 B5
Wilmington Way ME8 65 B2
Wilmot Rd DA1 15 B2
Wilmott Pl CT13 180 B2
Wilmount St SE18 2 B2
Wilson Ave Deal CT14 214 F4
Rochester ME1 96 E7
Wilson Cl
Ashford TN24 269 A1
Maidstone ME15 195 E7
Tonbridge TN11 221 E5
Wilson Ct ME18 193 A1
Wilson Ho 3 SE7 11 C8
Wilson La DA4 57 F7
Wilson Rd TN10 222 E5
Wilsons La ME15 194 A5
Wilsons Way DA13 92 F3
Wiltie Ct CT19 335 C5
Wiltie Gdns CT19 335 C5
Wilton Cl CT14 215 C5
Wilton Dr ME20 160 B8
Wilton Ho 2 BR7 53 D8
Wilton Rd
Folkestone CT19 335 B6
Ramsgate CT12 82 F1
Woolwich SE2 3 C2
Wilton Terr ME10 101 B5
Wiltshire Cl
Chatham ME5 97 C8
Dartford DA2 34 D8
Wiltshire Rd BR6 54 A2
Wiltshire Way
4 Maidstone ME15 195 E8
Royal Tunbridge Wells TN2 286 D7
Wimborne Ave BR7 53 F6
Wimborne Ho DA12 37 D5
Wimborne Pl CT12 117 B8
Wimborne 6 DA14 31 B4
Wimbourne Dr ME8 98 D6
Wimpole Cl BR2 52 C5
Winant Way CT16 278 B3
Winch Cl TN17 320 D3
Winchcomb Gdns SE9 11 D4
Wincheap CT1 174 E7
Wincheap Foundation Prim Sch CT1 174 E6
Wincheap Gn 4 CT1 174 F7
Wincheap Ind Est CT1 174 D7
Winchelsea Ave DA7 13 F7
Winchelsea Ct CT17 310 C7
Winchelsea Rd
Chatham ME5 97 B5
Dover CT17 310 B7
Winchelsea St CT17 310 B7
Winchelsea Terr CT17 310 B7
Winchester Ave ME5 96 F4
Winchester Cl 11 E6 1 F7
Winchester Cres DA12 37 D5
Winchester Ct 14 DA17 4 A1
Winchester Gdns CT1 175 A6
Winchester Gr TN13 154 B4
Winchester Ho
3 Maidstone ME15 195 D7
Woolwich SE18 11 D7
Winchester Mews CT14 215 B3
Winchester Pl 9 ME14 162 A5
Winchester Rd
Bexley DA7 13 D5
Hawkhurst TN18 341 A2
Orpington BR6 87 C6
Tonbridge TN10 222 D5
Winchester Way ME8 99 A8
Winch's Garth TN12 260 F5
Wincliff Rd TN9 254 B8
Wincrofts Dr SE9 12 D3
Windermere Ave CT11 117 A7
Windermere Cl
Dartford DA1 33 B7
Orpington BR6 86 B7
Windermere Ct TN24 268 C4
Windermere Dr ME8 98 D7
Windermere ME13 138 E6
Windermere Gdns CT3 210 F6
Windermere Gr ME10 101 D3
Windermere Ho 4 ME15 195 E7
Windermere Rd DA7 14 C5
Wind Hill TN27 233 E7
Wind Hill La TN27 233 E7
Windhover Way DA12 37 E4
Winding Hill ME13 170 F6
Windmill Ave CT12 83 B3
Windmill Cl
Ashford TN24 269 A1
Bridge CT4 176 A1
Canterbury CT1 175 C8
Herne Bay CT6 77 A2
Rochester ME2 40 B1
Windmill Cotts
Cranbrook TN17 320 D6
Lower Stoke ME3 25 C5
Windmill Ct
Maidstone ME17 195 B3
Royal Tunbridge Wells TN2 286 C3
Whitstable CT5 108 C7
Windmill Dr BR2 85 C6
Windmill Grange TN15 90 F3
Windmill Hill
Brenchley TN12 257 B1
Fairbourne Heath ME17 198 B1
Platt TN15 157 D7
Pye Corner ME17 231 B7
Windmill Hts ME14 163 B4
Windmill La
Cousley Wood TN5 337 C8
Durgates TN5 336 E4
Windmill La E ME19 159 C6
Windmill La
Faversham ME13 105 B1
Wrotham Heath TN15 157 E8
Windmill La W ME19 159 A6
Windmill Manor ME7 64 C4
Windmill Par CT11 117 C6
Windmill Pk TN15 157 E7
Windmill Quay Rd ME12 47 E2
Windmill Rd
Canterbury CT1 175 C8
Gillingham ME7 64 C4
Herne Bay CT6 77 A2
Sevenoaks TN13 187 B6
Sevenoaks Weald TN14 187 B2
Sittingbourne ME10 101 D6
Whitstable CT5 108 D7
Windmill Rise ME12 47 E6
Windmill Row ME17 196 D2
Windmill St
Gravesend DA12 37 B7
Hythe CT21 333 B1
Rochester ME2 40 B1
Royal Tunbridge Wells TN2 286 C3
Windmill View CT9 83 A8
Windmill Wlk CT12 83 B1
Windrush Ct 8 DA8 4 E1
Windrush Prim Sch SE28 3 B5
Windsor Ave
Chatham ME4 63 F2
Margate CT9 51 B1
Windsor Cl
Broadstairs CT10 83 E5
Chislehurst BR7 30 B3
Maidstone ME14 162 B6
Windsor Ct
1 Bromley BR1 52 E6
Deal CT14 215 C2
Gillingham ME7 64 D5
Margate CT9 51 B1
18 Sidcup DA14 31 A5
Windsor Dr
Dartford DA1 15 A1
Orpington BR6 87 A4
Sittingbourne ME10 101 D2
Windsor Gdns
Herne Bay CT6 76 B3
Warden ME12 49 D4
Windsor Hall E16 1 B5
Windsor Ho Deal CT14 215 A5
6 Dover CT17 310 D7
Whitstable CT5 74 D1
Windsor Mews
9 Margate CT9 50 J2
New Romney TN28 373 C8
Windsor Rd Bexley DA6 13 E3
Canterbury CT1 174 C6
Cliffs End CT12 116 D7
Gillingham ME7 64 D5
Gravesend DA12 37 B4
Windward Rd ME1 63 C1
Windy Ridge BR1 52 E8
Windyridge ME7 64 E1
Winehouse La CT18 308 D3
Wineycock ME9 168 C8
Winfield La TN15 156 E3
Winford Mews ME1 63 A2
Win'freds Cl TN17 343 E3
Wingate Ct 7 ME10 101 E4
Wingate Rd
Folkestone CT19 335 D7
Sidcup DA14 31 C2
Wingfield Ct DA15 30 F7
Wingfield Prim Sch SE3 11 B4
Wingfield Rd DA12 37 B8
Wingham Cl
Gillingham ME8 65 C3
Maidstone ME15 195 F7
Wingham Ind Est CT3 178 B6
Wingham Prim Sch CT3 178 A7
Wingham Rd CT3 177 D8
Wingham Well La CT3 177 F5
Wingham Wildlife Pk* CT3 146 C1
Wing Ho ME12 49 H1
Wing Rd ME12 49 H1
Wingrove Dr
Maidstone ME14 162 E5
Rochester ME2 63 C7
Wingrove Hill CT17 277 E2
Wings Cl CT10 84 B5
Winifred Ave CT12 83 C2
Winifred Rd
Dartford DA1 15 B2
Erith DA8 4 E1
Maidstone ME15 162 F3
Winifred St E16 1 F5
Winkle Cl CT6 76 B3
Winn Common Rd SE18 12 E8
Winnipeg Cl CT16 278 C3
Winnipeg Dr 3 BR6 86 F4
Winn Rd SE12,SE9 29 B7
Win Pine Ho CT21 333 A1
Winser Rd TN17 344 A1
Winsor Prim Sch E6 2 A7
Winsor Terr E6 2 A8
Winstanley Cres CT11 117 D8
Winstanley Rd ME12 28 C2
Winston Ave ME18 159 B3
Winston Cl
Canterbury CT1 175 C7
Stone DA9 16 F1
Winston Ct
Birchington CT7 81 A8
10 Bromley BR1 52 B8
Winston Dr ME2 40 D2
Winstone Scott Ave TN3 284 E4
Winston Gdns CT6 77 D4
Winston Ho 4 CT20 334 F5
Winston Rd ME2 62 D5
Winterage La CT18 306 C7
Winterborne Ave BR6 86 D7
Winter Dr CT18 307 B5
Winterfield La ME19 159 E8
Wintergarden Cres DA9 35 A8
Wintergreen Cl
8 Newham E16 1 E8
St Mary's Island ME4 41 C1
Winters Croft DA12 37 D2
Winterstoke Cres CT11 117 G8
Winterstoke Way CT11 117 F8
Winterton Ct 8 TN16 151 D1
Winton Ct BR8 55 E5
Winton Rd BR6 86 B6
Winton Way TN29 366 A5
Wireless Rd TN16 118 D4
Wirrals The ME5 97 A4
Wirral Wood Cl BR7 30 A2
Wiseacre TN3 317 A3
Wise Ho SE18 12 A7
Wises La ME10,ME9 101 A4
Wise's La TN15 91 E2
Wishart Rd SE3 11 D5
Wish The TN26 347 F6
Wisley Rd BR5 31 B1
Wissenden La TN26 297 B6
Wistaria Cl BR6 86 B8
Wisteria Gdns BR8 55 D7
Wisteria Ho 11 ME15 195 E7
Witches La TN13 153 D4
Witham Way ME2 62 F7
Withens Cl BR5 54 C5
Withersdane Cotts TN25 238 A2
Witherston Way SE9 30 A5
Withyham Rd TN3 312 B7
Witley Wlk CT16 278 B7
Wittersham CE Prim Sch TN30 359 D2
Wittersham Cl ME5 97 B5
Wittersham Ho 2 BR5 54 D1
Wittersham La TN31 368 B5
Wittersham Rd
Iden TN31 368 B7
Stone in Oxney TN30 360 C3
Wittersham,Potman's Heath TN17,TN30 358 D4
Wittersham TN30 359 C5
Wittersham Road Sta* TN17 358 D6
Wivenhoe TN23 299 E5
Wivenhoe Cl ME8 66 A2
Wixom Ho SE3 11 C3
Woburn Cl SE28 3 D7
Woburn Ct 1 DA6 13 E3
Wodehouse Cl ME20 127 F4
Wodehouse Rd DA1 16 A3
Wold Cvn Pk The ME12 48 F6
Woldham Pl BR2 52 C5
Woldham Rd BR2 52 C5
Wolds Dr BR6 86 A6
Wolfe Cl BR2 52 A3
Wolfe Cres SE7 1 D1
Wolfe Ct CT14 215 D3
Wolfe Rd ME16 161 B2
Wolf Ho ME4 64 B8
Wolf's Cnr RH8 183 B6
Wolf's Hill RH8 183 A4
Wolf's Rd RH8 183 B5
Wolf's Row RH8 183 B6
Wolfs Wood RH8 183 A3
Wollaston Cl ME8 98 D3
Wollaston Rd CT14 215 D4
Wolseley Ave CT6 76 A4
Wolseley Pl 4 TN24 268 B3
Wolseley Rd TN4 286 C7
Wolseley Terr TN29 376 C5
Wolsey Ct SE9 11 F1
Wolsey Mews BR6 86 F5
Wolsley Cl DA1 14 E2
Wolsley Ho DA1 14 E2
Wolvercote Rd SE2 3 D4
Wombwell Gdns DA11 36 E6
Women's Land Army Mus The* CT15 309 E5
Wood Ave CT19 335 E7
Woodberry Dr ME10 102 C3
Woodberry Flats CT10 84 A3
Woodberry Gr DA5 32 D5
Woodbine Cotts ME2 94 E5
Woodbine Rd DA15 30 E7
Woodbridge Dr ME15 161 F1
Woodbrook TN27 234 D7
Woodbrook Rd SE2 13 B8
Woodbury Cl
Biggin Hill TN16 118 F1
Royal Tunbridge Wells TN4 286 A5
Woodbury Gdns SE12 29 B4
Woodbury La TN30 345 A7
Woodbury Park Gdns TN4 286 B5
Woodbury Park Rd TN4 286 B5
Woodbury Rd
Chatham ME5 96 F1
Hawkhurst TN18 341 A2
Woodchurch CE Prim Sch TN26 326 A2
Woodchurch Cl
Chatham ME5 97 B5
Sidcup DA14 30 D5
Woodchurch Cotts CT7 81 F4
Woodchurch Cres ME8 65 C2
Woodchurch Ct 1 BR5 54 C4
Woodchurch Dr BR1 29 D1
Woodchurch House ME8 65 C2
Woodchurch Rd
Appledore Heath TN26 347 C4
Margate CT7,CT9 82 A5
Shadoxhurst TN26 299 A1
Tenterden TN30 345 D8
Westgate-on-S CT7 81 F3
Woodchurch Windmill (dis)* TN26 326 A3
Wood Cl Ditton ME20 160 E8
Joyden's Wood DA5 32 E5
Woodclyffe Dr BR7 53 A7
Woodcock Gdns CT18 307 A4
Woodcock La
Grafty Green ME17 231 E5
Iden Green TN17 342 E3
Woodcocks
Headcorn TN27 262 D5
Newham E16 1 D8
Woodcote Dr BR6 53 D2
Woodcote CT5 75 D1
Wood Cottage La CT19 334 D7
Woodcourt Cl ME10 101 E2
Woodcroft SE9 29 F5
Woodcut ME14 162 A8
Wood Dr Bromley BR7 29 E2
Sevenoaks TN13 153 F1
Wood End BR8 55 C5
Woodfall Dr DA1 14 F3
Woodfalls Ind Est ME18 225 D6
Woodfield Ave
Folkestone CT19 334 E7

Woodfield Ave *continued*
Gravesend DA11 .... 37 B6
Tonbridge TN11 .... 221 E5
Woodfield Cl CT19 ..... 334 E7
Woodfield Rd TN9 ...... 254 B8
Woodfields TN13 .... 153 D4
Woodfield Way ME3 ...... 40 E4
Woodford Ave CT11, CT12 .... 83 D1
Woodford Ct CT7 .... 81 A7
Woodford Gr ME18 ..... 159 B3
Woodford Ho 13 SE18 .... 12 B8
Woodford Rd ME16 ..... 161 B2
Woodgate CT4 .... 208 E3
Woodgate Cl ME13 ..... 138 C8
Woodgate Ct ME13 ..... 171 E7
Woodgate La ME9 ...... 100 C2
Woodgate Rd ME19 .... 126 D4
Woodgates Cl TN26 .... 324 D7
Woodgate Way TN9, TN11 .... 254 E7
Woodgers Gr BR8 .... 55 F7
Woodget Cl E6 .... 1 E7
Woodhall Terr ME11 ...... 46 A5
Woodhatch Cl E6 .... 1 E8
Woodhayes BR7 .... 30 B2
Woodhead Dr BR6 .... 86 E8
Woodhill Pk TN2 ...... 287 C6
Woodhill Prim Sch SE18 ... 1 E2
Wood Hill CT2 .... 142 E6
Woodhill SE18 .... 1 E2
Woodhurst Ave BR5 ...... 53 C3
Woodhurst ME5 .... 96 D4
Woodhurst Cl ME2 .... 62 B2
Woodhurst Rd SE2 .... 3 A2
Woodington Cl SE9 ...... 12 A1
Woodknoll Dr BR7 .... 52 F8
Wood La Dartford DA2 ..... 34 F4
East End TN17 .... 322 C3
Kingsnorth TN23 .... 300 D3
Woodland Ave
Aylesham CT3 .... 210 E5
Birchington CT7 .... 81 B6
Hartley DA3 .... 58 F5
Woodland Cl
Crabble CT17 .... 277 E2
New Barn DA3 .... 59 C6
Royal Tunbridge Wells TN4 .... 286 C7
West Malling ME19 ...... 159 A8
Woodland Cotts CT18 .. 305 B7
Woodland Dr
Marlpit Hill TN8 .... 217 D3
Minster (Sheppey) ME12 ... 47 B7
Woodland Rd
Herne Bay CT6 .... 76 B2
Lyminge CT18 .... 304 E8
Royal Tunbridge Wells TN4 .... 286 C7
Woodland Rise TN15 ... 154 E4
Woodlands Ave
Sidcup DA15 .... 30 E7
Snodland ME6 .... 127 F8
Woodlands Bexley DA6 .... 14 B2
Blean CT2 .... 141 F7
Chatham ME5 .... 97 A2
Woodlands Cl
Bromley BR1 .... 52 F7
Maidstone ME14 .... 162 B7
Peasmarsh TN31 .... 367 C2
Swanley BR8 .... 55 F7
Teston ME18 .... 193 B8
Woodlands
Coxheath ME17 .... 194 B3
Cranbrook TN17 .... 320 D6
Woodlands Ct ME5 .... 96 F3
Woodlands Dr CT21 .... 334 A4
Woodlands Farm DA16 ... 12 C5
Woodlands ME13 .... 140 C7
Woodlands Inf & Jun Schs TN10 .... 222 E6
Woodlands La DA12 ...... 38 E1
Woodlands TN12 .... 256 F7
Woodlands Par ME20 ... 160 D8
Woodlands TN2 .... 287 F7
Woodlands Pk (Cvn Pk) TN27 .... 323 D7
Woodlands Pk DA5 ...... 32 D4
Woodlands Prim Sch ME7 .... 64 F4
Woodlands Rd
Adisham CT3 .... 210 C8
Ashford TN24 .... 268 F2
Bexley DA7 .... 13 E4
Bromley BR1 .... 52 F7
Ditton ME20 .... 160 D8
Gillingham ME7 .... 64 F4
Orpington BR6 .... 87 A4
Sittingbourne ME10 ..... 102 B3
Tonbridge TN9 .... 254 A7
Woodlands Rise BR8 ..... 55 F7
Woodlands TN4 .... 254 A2
Woodlands Terr
Crockenhill BR8 .... 55 B3
Gillingham ME7 .... 64 F3
Woodlands The BR6 ...... 87 B4
Woodlands View TN14 .... 88 A1
Woodland Terr SE7 .... 1 E2
Woodland View TN30 ... 359 E4
Woodland Way
Bidborough TN4 .... 253 D3
Broadstairs CT10 .... 51 G1
Canterbury CT2 .... 142 D4
Dymchurch TN29 .... 353 A5
Erith SE2 .... 3 D2
Maidstone ME14 .... 162 B7
Orpington BR5 .... 53 C4
Swanscombe DA9 .... 17 A3
Woodnesborough CT13 ... 180 C6
Woodlark Rd ME4 .... 41 B1
Woodlawn St CT5 .... 74 D2
Woodlea Ashford TN24 .. 268 C3
Leybourne ME19 .... 127 F2
New Barn DA3 .... 59 C6
Woodleas ME16 .... 160 F2
Woodley Rd BR6 .... 87 C8
Wood Lodge Gdns BR1 ... 29 E1
Wood Lodge Grange TN13 .... 154 C5
Woodman Ave CT5 .... 75 E3
Woodman Par 4 E16 ..... 2 A5
Woodman St E16 .... 2 A5
Woodmere SE9 .... 29 F7
Woodmount BR8 .... 55 D2
Woodnesborough La CT13 .... 180 B3
Woodnesborough Rd CT13 .... 180 E7
Woodpecker Cl 2 TN8 .... 217 D3
Woodpecker Dr ME9 ..... 68 E4
Woodpecker Glade ME8 .... 98 D6
Woodpecker Rd
Larkfield ME20 .... 127 F1
Woolwich SE28 .... 3 C6
Wood Pl DA14 .... 31 A3
Wood Point 10 E16 .... 1 A8
Wood Rd
Biggin Hill TN16 .... 118 C1
Hythe CT21 .... 333 B1
Wood Retreat SE18 ...... 12 D7
Wood Ride BR5 .... 53 E5
Woodrow Chase CT6 ..... 77 A1
Woodrow SE18 .... 1 F2
Woodruff Cl ME8 .... 66 D4
Woodrush Pl ME4 .... 41 B1
Woodsgate Way TN2 .... 287 B6
Woods Green Cotts TN5 .... 336 F7
Woods Hill CT4 .... 239 C5
Woodshole Cotts ME9 .... 68 D1
Woodside TN23 .... 299 E6
Woodside Ave
Chartham CT4 .... 173 D2
Chislehurst BR7 .... 30 C3
Woodside ME13 .... 140 B2
Woodside Cl
Crayford DA7 .... 14 D3
Pembury TN2 .... 287 E6
Temple Ewell CT16 ...... 277 E4
Woodside Cotts ME13 .. 140 B2
Woodside Cres DA15 ..... 30 E5
Woodside Dr DA2 .... 32 E4
Woodside Gdns ME10 .. 101 D2
Woodside ME8 .... 98 C6
Woodside Gn ME3 .... 40 B7
Woodside TN17 .... 317 F2
Woodside La DA5 .... 13 D1
Woodside BR6 .... 87 B5
Woodside Par DA15 ...... 30 E5
Woodside Rd
Bromley BR1 .... 52 E4
Crayford DA7 .... 14 D3
Maidstone ME15 .... 195 C7
Pembury TN2 .... 287 E6
Rusthall TN4 .... 285 D4
Sevenoaks TN13 .... 154 B4
Sidcup DA15 .... 30 E5
Sturry CT2 .... 143 F7
Sundridge TN14 .... 152 E3
Tonbridge TN9 .... 254 B7
Woodside Sch DA17 .... 4 B2
Woodside DA13 .... 125 F8
Woods Ley CT3 .... 147 D2
Wood's Pl CT17 .... 278 B2
Wood St Chatham ME7 .... 64 A6
Cuxton ME2 .... 62 B2
Dover CT16 .... 310 D8
9 Grays RM17 .... 18 C8
Lynsted ME9 .... 135 F8
Woodstock Cl DA5 .... 31 F7
Woodstock Ct SE12 ...... 11 A1
Woodstock Rd
Deal CT14 .... 215 C4
Rochester ME2 .... 63 A7
Sittingbourne ME10 ..... 101 E1
Woodstock Way TN24 .. 268 C6
Wood St
Royal Tunbridge Wells TN1 .... 286 B4
Sheerness ME12 .... 28 C2
Swanley Village BR8 ...... 56 D8
Woodvale Ave CT5 ..... 109 C8
Woodvale Ct BR1 .... 52 B8
Woodview Cl BR6 .... 86 C8
Wood View Cl TN15 ...... 90 E3
Woodview Cres TN11 ... 221 F5
Wood View CT3 .... 111 E5
Woodview Rd BR8 .... 55 D7
Woodview Rise ME2 ...... 39 F1
Woodville Cl
Canterbury CT1 .... 174 D6
Eltham SE12 .... 11 A2
Woodville Gr 2 DA16 .... 13 A4
Woodville SE3 .... 11 B6
Woodville Pl DA12 .... 37 B8
Woodville Rd
Maidstone ME15 .... 162 A2
Ramsgate CT12 .... 83 C1
Woodville St 13 SE18 ...... 1 E2
Woodward Terr DA9 ..... 16 E1
Wood Way BR6 .... 86 A8
Woodyates Rd
Eltham SE12 .... 29 B8
Lewisham SE12 .... 11 A1
Wood Yd CT14 .... 215 D6
Woolacombe Rd SE3 ..... 11 C5
Woolaston Cl ME15 ..... 161 F1
Woolbrook Cl ME8 .... 66 B2
Woolbrook Rd DA1 ...... 14 E1
Woolcomber St CT16 ... 310 E7
Wooldeys Rd ME8 .... 65 F2
Woolett Rd ME10 .... 101 C5
Woolf Cl SE28 .... 3 B5
Woolf Wlk RM18 .... 19 C5
Woollets Cl CT6 .... 76 C3
Woollett Cl DA1 .... 15 A3
Woollett St ME14 ...... 162 A5
Woolley Cl TN4 .... 253 F1
Woolley Rd
Maidstone ME15 .... 195 F7
Royal Tunbridge Wells TN4 .... 253 F1
Woolmer Dr TN24 ...... 301 A7
Woolpack Cnr TN27 .... 323 A7
Woolpack Cotts TN27 .. 323 A7
Woolpack Hill TN25 .... 302 D5
Woolreeds Rd TN23 .... 300 A7
Woolwich Arsenal Sta SE18 .... 2 B2
Woolwich Church St SE18 .... 1 E3
Woolwich Cl ME5 .... 97 A7
Woolwich Comm SE18 ... 12 A8
Woolwich Dockyard Ind Est SE18 .... 1 E3
Woolwich Dockyard Sta SE18 .... 1 F2
Woolwich High St SE18 ... 2 A3
Woolwich Manor Way E6 .... 2 A7
Woolwich Manorway E16 .... 2 B4
Woolwich New Rd SE18 ... 2 B2
Woolwich Polytechnic Sch for Boys SE28 .... 3 A5
Woolwich Rd
Bexley DA7 .... 14 A4
Erith SE2 .... 3 E1
Greenwich SE10,SE7 .... 1 C2
Wootton Cl CT4 .... 207 A4
Wootton Dr CT4 .... 207 A4
Wootton Gn ME8 .... 65 D3
Wootton Ho SE9 .... 12 D1
Wootton La CT15,CT4 ... 275 C7
Wopsle Cl ME1 .... 96 D7
Worcester Ave ME19 ... 159 A2
Worcester Cl
Faversham ME13 .... 138 E6
Istead Rise DA13 .... 36 F1
Minster (Sheppey) ME12 ... 47 C6
Rochester ME2 .... 62 E8
Swanscombe DA9 .... 17 B3
Worcester Dr ME10 ..... 101 D6
Worcester Gr CT10 .... 83 F6
Worcester La CT3 ...... 175 E7
Worcester Rd ME15 .... 195 D7
Wordsworth Cl
Chatham ME5 .... 97 C7
Tilbury RM18 .... 19 C5
Wordsworth Gdns CT3 .... 210 F6
Wordsworth Ho 18 SE18 .... 12 A8
Wordsworth Rd
Bexley DA16 .... 12 E6
Maidstone ME14 .... 162 B7
Wordsworth Way
Dartford DA1 .... 16 A3
New Hythe ME20 .... 128 A4
Workhouse La
Coxheath ME15 .... 194 C4
Sutton Valence ME17 .... 230 A8
Workhouse Rd
Chartway Street ME17 ... 197 A1
Ryarsh ME19 .... 126 F4
Throwley ME13 .... 169 F1
World of Silk* DA1 .... 14 E2
Worlds End La BR6 .... 87 B3
World's End ME9 .... 136 E7
Wormdale Hill ME9 .... 100 B3
Wormdale Rd ME9 ...... 100 B4
Worsenden TN27 .... 294 E1
Worsfold Ct 5 ME15 ... 162 A1
Worships Hill TN13 .... 153 E4
Worth Cl BR6 .... 86 E6
Worthgate Pl 2 CT1 .... 174 F7
Worthing Cl RM17 .... 17 E8
Worthington St 11 CT16,CT17 .... 310 D8
Worth La CT20 .... 334 E3
Worth Prim Sch CT14 ... 181 B5
Wotton Cl ME15 .... 195 E5
Wotton Gn BR5 .... 54 D5
Wotton Rd TN23 .... 300 B6
Wotton Trad Est TN23 ... 300 B6
Wouldham All Saints CE Prim Sch ME1 .... 95 C5
Wouldham Rd
Grays RM17,RM20 .... 17 E8
Rochester ME1 .... 62 E1
Wouldham Terr 3 BR5 ... 54 B6
Wraightsfield Ave TN29 .... 366 D8
Wraik Hill CT5 .... 108 C5
Wrangleden Cl ME15 .. 195 E5
Wrangleden Rd ME15 .. 195 E5
Wrangling La DA13 ...... 93 F3
Wreight Ct ME13 .... 105 B1
Wrekin Rd SE18 .... 12 C7
Wren Cl Larkfield ME20 .. 127 F1
Orpington BR5 .... 54 D6
Wren Ind Est ME15 ...... 195 F4
Wren Path SE28 .... 2 D4
Wren Rd DA14 .... 31 C5
Wrens Croft DA11 .... 36 E4
Wren's Cross ME15 ..... 162 A3
Wrens Ct ME9 .... 134 A8
Wrens Rd
Silver Street ME9 .... 133 F6
Sittingbourne ME9 ...... 134 A7
Wrentham Ave CT6 .... 76 B2
Wren Way ME5 .... 97 B6
Wren Wlk RM18 .... 19 B7
Wricklemarsh Rd
Greenwich SE3 .... 11 B6
Greenwich SE3 .... 11 D6
Wright Cl
Gillingham ME8 .... 65 C2
Swanscombe DA10 .... 17 D1
Wrights Cl TN30 .... 345 A8
Wright's Way ME12 ...... 71 C8
Wrotham Ave 20 CT10 .... 84 B4
Wrotham Hill Rd TN15 .... 125 A6
Wrotham Rd
Bexley DA16 .... 13 C6
Borough Green TN15 .... 157 A8
Broadstairs CT10 .... 84 B4
Culverstone Green DA13 ... 92 F4
Gravesend DA11,DA13 ..... 37 A4
Meopham Station DA13 .... 60 A3
Wrotham Road Prim Sch DA11 .... 37 B8
Wrotham Sch TN15 ...... 125 A1
Wrotham Water La ME19,TN15 .... 125 E5
Wrotham Water Rd TN15,ME19 .... 125 E4
Wrottesley Rd SE18 ...... 12 C8
Wrott & Hill Ct DA4 ...... 57 B8
Wroxham Rd SE28 .... 3 D6
Wulfred Way TN15 ..... 123 B1
Wyatt Cl TN15 .... 156 F7
Wyatt Ho 1 ME2 .... 63 A7
Wyatt Pl ME2 .... 63 A7
Wyatt Rd DA1 .... 14 F4
Wyatt St ME14 .... 162 A4
Wyborne Prim Sch SE9 ... 30 B7
Wybourne Rise TN2 .... 314 B8
Wybournes La ME23 ...... 23 C3
Wych Elm Way CT21 .... 353 E8
Wycherley Cres CT16 ... 278 B4
Wycliffe Cl DA16 .... 12 F6
Wycliffe Ho 6 DA11 ...... 36 F7
Wycliffe Row DA11 .... 36 F7
Wycombe Ct SE3 .... 11 A7
Wydeville Manor Rd SE12 .... 29 B4
Wye Cl BR6 .... 53 F2
Wye Coll (Imperial Coll London) TN25 .... 237 F2
Wye Gdns CT9 .... 51 F2
Wye National Nature Reserve* TN25 .... 270 D7
Wye Rd
Borough Green TN15 .... 157 A8
Boughton Lees TN25 .... 236 F3
Gravesend DA12 .... 37 D6
Tonbridge TN10 .... 222 C5
Wye Sta TN25 .... 237 D2
Wyfold Ho 10 SE2 .... 3 D4
Wykeham Cl
Gravesend DA12 .... 37 E2
Rushenden ME11 .... 45 F3
Wykeham Cotts ME17 .. 194 F2
Wykeham Ct BR7 .... 30 E2
Wykeham Gr ME17 ..... 197 A7
Wykeham Rd ME10 ..... 102 B4
Wykeham St ME2 .... 63 B8
Wyke Manor Rd ME14 .. 162 A4
Wyles Rd ME4 .... 63 E2
Wyles St ME7 .... 64 C7
Wylie Ho ME3 .... 40 F6
Wylie Rd ME3 .... 41 D6
Wyllie Ct ME10 .... 101 E7
Wyncham Ave DA15 ...... 30 E7
Wyncroft Cl BR1 .... 52 F6
Wyndcliff Rd SE3,SE7 ..... 11 B8
Wyndham Ave
Leigh TN11 .... 220 F1
Margate CT9 .... 51 B2
Wyndham Cl
Leigh TN11 .... 220 F1
Orpington BR6 .... 53 C1
Wyndham Rd
Chatham ME4 .... 63 E2
Dover CT17 .... 310 B8
Wynd The TN27 .... 201 D1
Wyndy La TN25 .... 267 F4
Wynford Gr BR5 .... 54 B6
Wynford Pl DA17 .... 14 A8
Wynford Way SE9 .... 29 F5
Wynn Ellis Ho CT5 .... 74 E3
Wynn Rd CT5 .... 75 A2
Wynn's Ave DA15 .... 13 A2
Wytchlings The ME17 ... 197 D2
Wythens Wlk SE9 .... 12 B1
Wytherling Cl ME14 .... 162 F5
Wythes Cl BR1 .... 52 F7
Wythes Rd E16 .... 1 E5
Wythfield Rd SE9 .... 11 F1
Wyvern Cl Dartford DA1 ... 33 C8
Orpington BR6 .... 87 B7
Sittingbourne ME10 ..... 101 E7
Snodland ME6 .... 128 A7
Wyvern Ho 3 RM17 ...... 18 B8
Wyvern Sch The TN23 .. 267 E1
Wyvern Way TN24 ...... 268 E3
Wyvill Cl ME8 .... 98 E5

Y

Yalding Cl ME2 .... 40 B1
Yalding Gr BR5 .... 54 D5
Yalding Hill ME18 ...... 193 A3
Yalding Organic Gdns* ME18 .... 225 F7
Yalding St Peter & St Paul CE Prim Sch ME18 .... 193 A1
Yalding Sta ME18 .... 192 D1
Yantlet Dr ME2 .... 62 C7
Yardhurst Gdns CT9 ...... 51 F3
Yardley Cl TN9 .... 222 D3
Yardley Court Prep Sch TN11 .... 254 F7
Yardley Ho CT10 .... 84 B7
Yardley Park Rd TN9 ... 222 D3
Yard The Barham CT4 .... 209 F1
Chatham ME5 .... 97 B3
Yarnton Way SE2,DA18 ..... 3 E4
Yarrow Cl CT10 .... 84 A3
Yarrow Cres E6 .... 1 E8
Yarrow Ct ME14 .... 162 F5
Yarrow Rd ME5 .... 96 F4
Yateley St SE18 .... 1 D3
Yates Cl TN31 .... 374 A2
Yaugher La ME9 .... 99 C3
Yeates Dr ME10 .... 102 A8
Yellow Sands ME12 .... 73 E5
Yelsted La
Chatham ME14 .... 130 D7
Yelsted ME9 .... 99 A1
Yelsted Rd ME9 .... 132 A7
Ye Olde Tudor Ct BR7 .... 30 B3
Yeoman Cl E6 .... 2 B6
Yeoman Ct ME14 .... 163 B3
Yeoman Dr ME7 .... 64 F1
Yeoman Gdns
Ashford TN24 .... 301 B8
Paddock Wood TN12 .... 256 F6
Yeoman Ho ME1 .... 63 D4
Yeoman La ME14 .... 163 B4
Yeoman Pk ME15 .... 163 A2
Yeoman's Mdws TN13 .. 154 A1
Yeomans Sq TN23 ...... 299 D8
Yeoman Way ME15 ..... 163 A2
Yeovil Cl BR6 .... 86 E8
Yester Dr BR7 .... 29 E1
Yester Pk BR7 .... 29 F2
Yester Rd BR7 .... 29 F1
Yevele Cl ME11 .... 46 A5
Yew Cl TN23 .... 267 E2
Yewhedges ME13 .... 168 E4
Yew Rd ME3 .... 41 E3
Yews The DA12 .... 37 D7
Yew Tree Cl
Aylesford ME20 .... 128 E1
Bexley DA16 .... 13 A6
Broadstairs CT10 .... 83 D4
Chatham ME5 .... 97 D1
Deal CT14 .... 215 A4
New Barn DA3 .... 59 D7
Sevenoaks TN13 .... 153 D4
Stanford TN25 .... 304 B1
Yew Tree Cotts
Groombridge TN3 .... 312 F8
Halstead TN14 .... 120 F7
Sandling ME14 .... 129 F1
Yewtree Cross CT18 .... 305 C8
Yew Tree Farm CT3 ..... 212 A8
Yew Tree Gdns
Birchington CT7 .... 81 A7
Fordwich CT2 .... 144 A4
Yew Tree Green Rd TN12 .... 258 A1
Yewtree Ho 2 ME1 ...... 63 D4
Yewtree Ind Est ME20 .. 128 D2
Yew Tree Mews
Deal CT14 .... 215 A3
Westerham TN16 .... 184 D8
Yew Tree Pk ME17 ...... 200 F1
Yew Tree Pk Cvn & Camping Site CT4 .... 207 D2
Yew Tree Pl ME7 .... 98 B1
Yew Tree Rd
Royal Tunbridge Wells TN4 .... 286 B8
St Mary's Bay TN29 ...... 365 F3
Yoakes La TN29 .... 363 F1
Yoakley Sq CT9 .... 82 F8
Yoke Cl ME2 .... 63 B8
Yokosuka Way ME7, ME8 .... 65 A7
Yolande Gdns SE9 .... 11 E2
Yopps Gn TN15 .... 156 E1
York & Albany Cl CT14 .... 215 B1
York Ave
18 Broadstairs CT10 ...... 84 B4
Chatham ME5 .... 96 F3
Gillingham ME7 .... 64 C4
Sidcup DA15 .... 30 F6
York Cl Herne Bay CT6 .... 76 D4
Newham E6 .... 1 F7
York Hill ME5 .... 64 C2
York Ho 10 CT17 .... 310 D7
Yorkland Ave DA16 .... 12 F3
York Mews CT19 .... 334 E7
York Par TN10 .... 222 C6
York Pl RM17 .... 18 A8
York Rd Ashford TN24 ... 268 D5
Biggin Hill TN16 .... 150 B8
Canterbury CT1 .... 174 E7
Dartford DA1 .... 33 F8
Deal CT14 .... 215 D4
Gravesend DA12 .... 37 C5
Herne Bay CT6 .... 76 D5
Maidstone ME15 .... 162 C2
Northfleet DA11 .... 36 D8
Rochester ME1 .... 63 C3
Royal Tunbridge Wells TN1 .... 286 A4
Tonbridge TN10 .... 222 D5
York Rise BR6 .... 86 E8
York Road Jun Sch DA1 .... 33 F8
York St Broadstairs CT10 ... 84 B4
Dover CT16,CT17 .... 310 D7
Ramsgate CT11 .... 117 E6
York Street Rdbt CT16,CT17 .... 310 D7
York Terr Bexley DA8 ...... 14 C6
Birchington CT7 .... 81 B7
Youens Pl ME3 .... 39 B3
Young Cl CT14 .... 215 B6
Young Rd E16 .... 1 C7
Young's Pl CT15 .... 308 F5
Ypres Ct CT1 .... 143 D1
Ypres Dr ME10 .... 68 F1

Z

Zambra Way TN15 ...... 154 F7
Zangwill Rd SE18,SE3 .... 11 D6
Zarena Ct 8 CT20 ...... 334 F3
Zealand Ho SE18 .... 1 E2
Zealand Rd CT1 .... 174 F6
Zelah Rd BR5 .... 54 C2
Zetland Ave ME7 .... 64 E2
Zillah Gdns ME8 .... 98 C6
Zion Pl Gravesend DA12 ... 37 B8
Margate CT9 .... 50 J3
Zion St TN15 .... 154 F6